EGC
Cellnet Guide 1995

MW01503099

Hotels &
Restaurants

3000 establishments in Great Britain and Ireland including comprehensive London section

Hartwell House - Aylesbury

Egon Ronay's Cellnet Guide 1995:
Hotels & Restaurants of Great Britain and Ireland.

For information, address St. Martin's Press,
175 Fifth Avenue, New York, N.Y. 10010.

ISBN 0-312-11781-7

First published in Great Britain by Pan Macmillan Ltd.

First U.S. Edition

Contents

continued overleaf

cellnet

The 1995 edition of Egon Ronay's Cellnet Guide to Hotels and Restaurants is the first choice for the discerning.

A look through its pages will show why many

people return to the Guide year after year. It offers authoritative information and advice on establishments throughout the UK, allowing informed choices to be made with total confidence for business and leisure alike.

Cellnet also aims to provide value and service, and is at the forefront of new developments giving higher levels of quality and even more choice. Chief of these is Cellnet's new Primetime Plus digital service, now giving business customers access to European mobile phone coverage. In the UK, nearly one and a half million people enjoy the coverage and service offered by Cellnet.

Taken together, Egon Ronay's Cellnet Guide to Hotels and Restaurants and a mobile phone on the Big network are a winning combination.

I hope you make the most of them both.

Stephen Brewer
Sales and Marketing Director

BIG
cove

on
rage.

To make the most of your mobile phone, you need Cellnet, the network that offers truly national UK coverage – and links to the world beyond. After all, if you can't use your mobile wherever life takes you – why have one at all?

For further information call
0800 214000

Serving 98% of the UK population.

Monitoring the Cellnet network. Cellnet's sophisticated mobile communications system is controlled from the Network Management Centre.

From here, Cellnet engineers keep a watchful eye over the entire network ensuring that potential problems are identified and rectified long before they can affect our service to customers.

Cellnet is part of BT – the most advanced company in the telecommunications industry.

Since 1985, over £700 million has been spent in developing our original analogue (TACS) service, and by 1995, a further £300 million will have been invested in our digital service.

Today, Cellnet is one of the largest networks of its kind in the world, covering more than 98% of the UK population.

For further information call
0800 214000

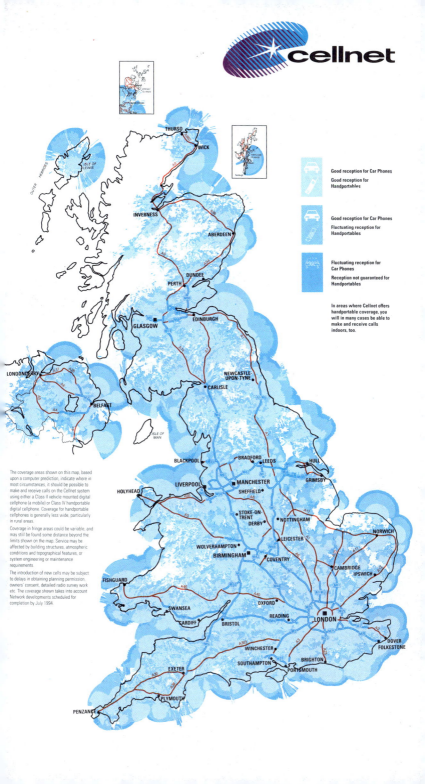

cellnet

Good reception for Car Phones
Good reception for Handportables

Good reception for Car Phones
Fluctuating reception for Handportables

Fluctuating reception for Car Phones
Reception not guaranteed for Handportables

In areas where Cellnet offers handportable coverage, you will in many cases be able to make and receive calls indoors, too.

The coverage areas shown on this map, based upon a computer prediction, indicate where in most circumstances, it should be possible to make and receive calls on the Cellnet system using either a Class II vehicle mounted digital cellphone (a mobile) or Class IV handportable digital cellphone. Coverage for handportable cellphones is generally less wide, particularly in rural areas.

Coverage in fringe areas could be variable, and may still be found some distance beyond the limits shown on the map. Service may be affected by building structures, atmospheric conditions and topographical features, or system engineering or maintenance requirements.

The introduction of new cells may be subject to delays in obtaining planning permission, owners' consent, detailed radio survey work etc. The coverage shown takes into account Network developments scheduled for completion by July 1994.

THURSO
WICK
OUTER HEBRIDES
ISLE OF LEWIS
INVERNESS
ABERDEEN
DUNDEE
PERTH
GLASGOW
EDINBURGH
LONDONDERRY
BELFAST
NEWCASTLE-UPON-TYNE
CARLISLE
ISLE OF MAN
BLACKPOOL
BRADFORD
LEEDS
HULL
LIVERPOOL
MANCHESTER
GRIMSBY
HOLYHEAD
SHEFFIELD
STOKE-ON-TRENT
NOTTINGHAM
DERBY
LEICESTER
NORWICH
WOLVERHAMPTON
BIRMINGHAM
COVENTRY
CAMBRIDGE
IPSWICH
FISHGUARD
SWANSEA
OXFORD
READING
LONDON
CARDIFF
BRISTOL
DOVER
FOLKESTONE
WINCHESTER
BRIGHTON
EXETER
SOUTHAMPTON
PORTSMOUTH
PLYMOUTH
PENZANCE

BIG
on choice.

Choosing the right tariff is important if you're to get the best value from your mobile phone.

Cellnet offers a wide tariff choice so you can choose the best combination of affordability and network features.

What's more, we make it easy to identify the tariff that is ideal for your needs.

**For further information call
0800 214000**

If you need...

- National network coverage
- Lower call costs – business hours
- Advanced call handling services
- Business information lines
- Large choice of handsets

...you need

primetime ™

Cellnet's premier TACS business service..Ideal for the business user needing to make more than 2 calls a day during working hours.

If you need...

- Special call rates within M25
- Access to national network
- All services supported by Cellnet Primetime
- Large choice of handsets

...you need

citytime ™

Ideal for frequent business users who make most of their calls from in and around London, but who still need to be able to make and receive calls from anywhere in the country.

If you need...

- Low cost off-peak calls
- National network coverage
- Callback intelligent messaging

...you need

lifetime ™

Ideal for less frequent users (1 or 2 calls per day) – personal or business – who are likely to receive more calls than they make.

cellnet

Introduction by Managing Editor Andrew Eliel

Making waves

We had hoped to experience the Channel Tunnel crossing and to have compared it with this year's special investigation (see page 97) on short ferry crossings of the Channel. But, as we all know, the opening (for passenger traffic) has been considerably delayed. As I write (late July), the tunnel is scheduled to open in October, more or less at the same time as this Guide is published. We've seen the platforms at Waterloo – remember to make sure your luggage has wheels for there are some long walks – but, sadly, no actual trains, though Eurostar is anticipating a journey time of just three hours from London to Paris with only 25 minutes spent under the sea. This service will obviously appeal to those living and working in the vicinity of London and the South East, but travellers from other parts of the country may well still opt for the more traditional ferry crossing, giving them the opportunity to unwind and relax after a long drive. In fact, some people actually feel that their holidays start on the ferry, but if you're hungry, don't confuse terminal or ferry food with the real thing on offer in either Calais or Boulogne, both of which boast several good restaurants. The message is: pack a few sandwiches, or save your appetite for France.

Glad tidings

It has been a better year for the industry – optimism abounds, with busier restaurants and hotel occupancies up. We may never again witness the heady days of the 80s, but all the signs indicate that recovery is well under way. There have been perceptible changes, with the emphasis on value for money, stable prices and fun (in restaurants). There are bargains to be had and the customer really does rule – ok! With several important new openings (some that have happened, others that are about to), now is clearly the time to be putting down roots. Jarvis Hotels, for instance, snapped up Resort Hotels earlier in the year, making it the 5th largest hotel group in the country. In his hotels, Chairman and Chief Executive John Jarvis has applied sound business sense with good management practice, providing consistent and reliable quality – and not necessarily at the top end of the market. Ken McCulloch, proprietor of *One Devonshire Gardens*, Glasgow, our 1994 Hotel of the Year, has also applied these principles with his new *Malmaisons* in Edinburgh and Glasgow, as will Robin Hutson and Gerard Basset with their *Hotel du Vin & Bistro* in Winchester (see Stop Press p. 1376). Exciting happenings have included the restaurant openings of London's *Aubergine, Butler's Wharf Chop-house, Bengal Clipper, Fulham Road* and *Restaurant Marco Pierre White*. Outside London, it's good to see that Bath's *Hole in the Wall* has been revived and that serious new restaurants as far afield as *The Dining Room* in Reigate, *The Puppet Theatre* in Glasgow and *The Rectory* in Glandore (Ireland) have opened their doors. On a sadder note we record the passing of Kevin Kennedy's *Boulestin* in London, *Pool Court* which moves to *42 The Calls*, Leeds and the departure of Shaun Hill from *Gidleigh Park* (see Stop Press). And on a negative note, our inspectors (and you the readers judging by the number of letters we've received) have experienced inconsistent standards at some hotels in the Queens Moat Houses portfolio.

Food fashions

Even with the advent of *cuisine mondiale* (our term), enabling one to sample different fresh foods from virtually all parts of the world, the most oft recurring items on menus this year have come from nearer home: sea bass, seared scallops, salmon (rarely wild), fish cakes, lamb shanks, confit de canard, pigeons and guinea fowl. Ubiquitous also are wild mushrooms (from where?), rocket leaves, Caesar salads (rarely the real McCoy!), Puy lentils and mash (olive oil, walnut oil, pesto and sage flavours being a few examples). On the pudding and dessert front, there has been a baking and traditional revival (pleasing for Homepride Flour, our new dessert sponsors) with sticky toffee pudding leading the way, closely followed by crème brulée, lemon tart and chocolate desserts. Incidentally, you'll get a mint garnish with almost everything.

By the way, does anyone know why chicken is comparatively unusual on Scottish menus?

Women in hotels/restaurants

With more and more women accounting for an important part of a hotel or restaurant's business, are their needs really being catered for, or are they being fobbed off with an extra cotton bud here and a skirt press there? For most women the primary concern seems to be security – well-lit hotel corridors and walkways from car park to hotel, peep-holes in doors. Nightmare tales abound of bedroom intruders, both in hotels with traditional or credit-card keys. Equally important is an unpatronising manner from staff, especially in restaurants – a decent table when eating alone, an up-to-date attitude when eating in the company of a man. Good staff should be able to ascertain who's entertaining whom. However, women can help smooth the path by making it clear to staff from the outset who is the host and who is the guest, thus preventing later embarrassment. There is no place for nudge, nudge, wink, wink – let common sense prevail.

Perennials

Most years we have something to say on the vexed question of the service charge. Until there is government legislation on whether it must be included in a listed price, the onus is still on you, the customer, not to get ripped off. It's not right, but it's the way of the world. Always double-check whether a service charge has been added to your bill, and don't be fooled into filling out an incomplete credit card slip, soliciting a further service charge/tip. There are still some unscrupulous hoteliers and restaurateurs out to fleece you (sometimes twice!). Hotel telephone charges are another bone of contention: again, make sure you know the costs involved when phoning from your bedroom – is it a fixed price per unit, does the cost go down the more units you use, is there a minimum charge, will you have to pay for reversing the charges etc? Remember, there are alternatives, such as pay phones, charge cards or your own (Cellnet) portable phone!

Best of British
Michael Caine & Richard Shepherd

You'll not find two more enthusiastic supporters of GB Ltd than Michael – his only supporting act in the last 30 years? – and Richard, who have been in tandem at Langan's ("the legend") Brasserie for many years. Their subsequent involvement in other restaurants and therefore their contribution (in London particularly) to the industry is immense. Their busy and popular restaurants of quality attract customers by the barrow-load and include many tourists, who in turn pass the message on to the next round of visitors. Michael, of course, wears two ambassadorial hats, the other being his involvement in the (British) film industry, while Richard, President of the British branch of the *Académie Culinaire de France*, tirelessly gives much of his time to all aspects of the catering industry (especially the colleges) as well as lining the pockets of golf club secretaries around the world!

Readers' recommendations/complaints

We always invite you to complete the forms at the back of the Guide, telling us your good (and bad) experiences. The lifeblood of a Guide is the new recommendations we receive, enabling our inspectors to assess them on merit. This year we're asking for more: we want to hear about your favourite leisure and tourist attractions for the Cellnet Best of British Hospitality Awards 1996. We also want to hear about your best and worst breakfasts: "to eat well in England, you should breakfast three times a day", Somerset Maugham wrote. We are concerned that the great British breakfast may be on the decline (though clearly not in the case of Edinburgh's 'Caley', winner of our Breakfast of the Year award). Do you agree or disagree? Also at the back of this Guide (p. 1373) is a very Special Offer to buy our 1995 *Pubs & Inns* Guide and receive a copy of our 1996 *Hotels & Restaurants* absolutely free of charge!

New

Back (by popular demand) is a selection of photographs of some of the best hotels – no longer alongside their entries, but in their own section. This year we also include county summaries of where to eat as well as where to stay; if sports facilities influence your choice of hotel then you will doubtless enjoy using our new layout of these. I also urge you to enter our Gourmet Crossword competiton on page 93, for which prizes include a Motorola GSM pocket phone and a fabulous trip to Cognac (courtesy of Martell).

Support

Cellnet remains the Guide's overall sponsor, while Ilchester Cheese and American Express continue to represent their segments of the industry. This year we are delighted to welcome on board an international drinks company in Seagram, who have helped judge and select our Cellar and New World Cellar of the Year; the Meat & Livestock Commission, with whom we have joined forces to determine our British Meat Chef of the Year; and National Britannia who are on the look-out for the best kitchens in the UK. We are very grateful for all their support.

Traditional Sunday Lunch Recommendations

Prices quoted are generally for a set-price, three-course Sunday Lunch with a traditional roast as a featured main course; two-course options are occasionally offered. Some may be carvery-style, others may be with full service. £9.95+ indicates the price of the main roast course only. A few of the places listed normally offer a traditional roast, "but not every Sunday". Many places offer reductions for children; negotiate when booking! Booking some way in advance is advised at most places.

England
Avon, Freshford **Homewood Park** (£17.50)
Bedfordshire, Woburn **Paris House** (£25)
Berkshire, Streatley-on-Thames **Swan Diplomat** (£17.50)
Buckinghamshire, Marlow **Compleat Angler** (£28.50)
Cambridgeshire, Keyston **Pheasant** (£9.95+)
Cheshire, Nantwich **Churche's Mansion** (£14)
Cornwall, Veryan **Nare Hotel** (£13.50)
Cumbria, Bowness-on-Windermere **Linthwaite House** (£10.95)
Derbyshire, Hayfield **Bridge End** (£13)
Devon, Lympstone **River House** (from £16)
Dorset, Poole **Haven Hotel** (£14.50)
Durham, Romaldkirk **Rose & Crown** (£10.95)
Essex, Great Dunmow **The Starr** (£9.95+)
Gloucestershire, Chipping Campden **Cotswold House** (£15)
Greater Manchester, Ramsbottom **Village Restaurant** (£14.95)
Hampshire, Eversley **New Mill** (£12.50)
Hereford & Worcester, Harvington **The Mill** (£13.45)
Hertfordshire, Melbourn **Pink Geranium** (£18.95)
Kent, Sissinghurst **Rankin's** (£15.95)
Lancashire, Langho **Northcote Manor** (£16.50)
Leicestershire, Uppingham **The Lake Isle** (£13.50)
Lincolnshire, Beckingham **Black Swan**
London, W8 **Launceston Place** (£16.50)
Middlesex, Twickenham **Hamilton's** (£14.95)
Norfolk, Grimston **Congham Hall** (£15)
Oxfordshire, Old Minster Lovell **Lovells at Windrush Farm** (£16.50)
Shropshire, Worfield **Old Vicarage** (£12.50)
Somerset, Taunton **Castle Hotel** (£16.50)
Staffordshire, Stretton **Dovecliffe Hall** (£13.95)
Suffolk, Ixworth **Theobald's** (£15.95)
Surrey, Dorking **Partners West Street** (£14.95)
East Sussex, Jevington **Hungry Monk** (£20.90)
West Sussex, Midhurst **Angel Hotel** (£14.95)
Warwickshire, Billesley **Billesley Manor** (£17)
Wiltshire, Colerne **Lucknam Park** (£22)
North Yorkshire, Hetton **Angel Inn** (£16)

Scotland
Borders, Peebles **Cringletie House** (£14)
Central, Dunblane **Cromlix House** (£23)
Fife, Markinch **Balbirnie House** (£13.75)
Grampian, Inverurie **Thainstone House** (£14.50)
Lothian, Edinburgh **Caledonian Hotel, Carriages** (£15.50)
Strathclyde, Glasgow **Puppet Theatre** (£15.95)
Tayside, Blairgowrie **Kinloch House** (£13.75)

Wales
Clwyd, Llandrillo **Tyddyn Llan** (£14.75)
Mid Glamorgan, Coychurch **Coed-y-Mwstwr Hotel** (£15.95)
West Glamorgan, Reynoldston **Fairyhill** (£17.50)
Gwent, Clydach **The Drum & Monkey** (£10.95)
Gwynedd, Portmeirion **Hotel Portmeirion** (£16)
Powys, Llangammarch Wells **Lake Country House** (£15.50)

Channel Islands
Guernsey, Castel **La Grande Mare** (£13.95)
Jersey, St Saviour **Longueville Manor** (£17.50)

Look for the ⚓ symbol throughout the gazetteer for other places serving a traditional Sunday lunch

How to Use this Guide

As well as our recommended establishments this Guide includes many interesting features and useful quick reference lists and tables designed to help you select the hotel or restaurant that best suits your requirements. Lists of hotels and restaurants by county, with key statistics and prices, will allow you to see at a glance what is available in the area where you intend to stay. Places of interest are listed after the London gazetteer and under the nearest relevant location throughout the Guide.

Order of Entries & Map References

London appears first, in alphabetical order by **establishment name**. Listings outside London are in alphabetical order by **location** within divisions of England, Scotland, Wales, Channel Islands, Isle of Man, Northern Ireland and the Republic of Ireland. Map references alongside each hotel or restaurant entry are to the map section at the back of the Guide.

Hotels

Hotel entries are identified by the letter '**H**'. The percentage shown on a hotel entry is an individual rating arrived at after careful testing, inspection and calculation according to our unique grading system. Hotels that achieve a grading of 80%+ are classified as De Luxe and listed separately on page 23.

We assess hotels on 23 factors that include the quality of service and the public rooms – their cleanliness, comfort, state of repair and general impression. Bedrooms are looked at for size, comfort, cleanliness and decor. The exterior of the building, efficiency of reception, conduct and appearance of the staff, room service and leisure facilities are among other factors. The percentage is arrived at by comparing the total marks given for the 23 factors with the maximum the hotel could have achieved.

The size of a hotel and the prices charged are not considered in the grading, but the food is, and *if we recommend meals in a hotel a separate entry is made for its restaurant*. Only hotels where we recommend the restaurant food are categorised as '**HR**'. There is thus a very important distinction between '**H**' and '**HR**' entries.

The category of chain hotels offering cheap, practical accommodation and not much else is denoted by the letter '**L**'. Because these lodges are generally built and run to a formula we have included some in the main four groups (Travelodge, Travel Inn, Granada and Campanile) which were not open as we went to press. These will be inspected in due course.

Certain other hotels are ungraded. These may be private house hotels ('**PH**') which are often de luxe 'bed and breakfast' hotels offering comfortable, often luxurious accommodation and personal service, but do not have a public restaurant or public rooms – although some have a drawing room. Also ungraded are modest London hotels, others undergoing major refurbishment programmes and those which opened too late for the fullest inspection.

Inns, identified by the letter '**I**', are ungraded, being distinguished from hotels proper by their more modest nature, usually with respect to the day rooms. For our purposes, an inn is normally either a pub with hotel-style accommodation or a small hotel with a bar and the atmosphere of a pub.

The major characteristics of the leading hotel groups are covered in a special section at the back of the Guide. A new photographic reference section is also included.

Prices

These are based on current high-season rates at the time of going to press and include VAT (also service if applicable), for a *double room for two occupants with private bath and cooked breakfast.*

Bargain breaks. Almost all hotels now offer bargain breaks of some kind. Specific details regarding the availability and price of such breaks should be checked with individual establishments.

Wheelchair access. Lists of hotels providing facilities for guests in wheelchairs are included. See Contents page for details.

Restaurants

Restaurants are identified by the letter '**R**'. We award one to three stars (★ ★★ ★★★) for excellence of cooking. One star represents cooking much above average, two outstanding cooking, and three the best in the land.

↑ beside stars indicates a restaurant at the top of its star range.

↑ by itself indicates a restaurant approaching star status.

The symbol '**RR**' denotes a restaurant with rooms. Food is the main attraction, but accommodation is also available. Details may be found within the Restaurant Round-Up at the back of the Guide.

We include restaurants only if the cooking comes up to our minimum standards, however attractive the place may be in other respects. We take into account how well the restaurant achieves what it sets out to do as reflected in the menu, decor, prices, publicity, atmosphere – factors that add up to some sort of expectation.

Symbols

Crowns are awarded to restaurants offering a degree of traditional luxury ⬬ or some striking modern features ⬛. They have nothing to do with the quality of the cooking.

- ⌀ Represents a wine list that is outstanding (sponsored by Perrier-Jouët).
- ⌀ Signifies a wine list featuring good-quality New World wines (sponsored by Montana Wines).
- ⌀ Signifies a restaurant serving a selection of good-quality wines by the glass.
- ⌀ Signifies a restaurant serving notable desserts (sponsored by Homepride Flour).
- ⌀ Signifies a restaurant serving good British cheeses (sponsored by the Ilchester Cheese Company Ltd).
- ⌀ Signifies that traditional Sunday lunch is offered in a recommended restaurant (see list on page 17).
- 🐄 Member of the Scotch Beef Club.
- ⬛ Member of the Martell Cordon Bleu Association.

Restaurant prices, correct at the time of going to press, are for a *three-course meal for two including one of the least expensive bottles of wine, coffee, service and VAT.* The total is generally rounded up to the nearest £5.

Set-price menus. Prices quoted will often not include service and usually exclude wine. They are not necessarily of three courses. Where two prices are given thus – £14.50/£17.75 – it indicates that there is a 2 or 3-course option; prices given thus – £17.95 & £24.95 – indicates that there are two different set-price menus. A great number of restaurants around the country now *only* offer a set-price menu (although this will usually include a choice).

Starred Restaurants

London ★★★

Chez Nico at Ninety Park Lane **W1**
Le Gavroche **W1**
Restaurant Marco Pierre White **SW1**
Les Saveurs **W1**
La Tante Claire **SW3**

England ★★★

Bray-on-Thames Waterside Inn
Great Milton Le Manoir aux
Quat'Saisons
Shinfield L'Ortolan

Scotland ★★★

Ullapool Altnaharrie Inn

London ★★

Inter-Continental Hotel, Le Soufflé **W1** ↑

Alastair Little **W1**
The Capital **SW3**
The Connaught, Restaurant & Grill
Room **W1**
The Dorchester, The Terrace **W1**
Le Meridien, The Oak Room **W1**
Mirabelle **W1**
Pied à Terre **W1**

England ★★

Baslow Fischer's Baslow Hall
Cheltenham Epicurean
Dartmouth Carved Angel
Hambleton Hambleton Hall
Longridge Paul Heathcote's Restaurant
Ridgeway Old Vicarage

London ★

Aubergine **SW10** ↑
Hilaire **SW7** ↑
Nico Central **W1** ↑
The Square **SW1** ↑

Al San Vincenzo **W2**
The Berkeley **SW1**
Bibendum **SW3**
Blakes Hotel **SW7**
Bombay Brasserie **SW7**
Café Royal Grill Room **W1**
The Canteen **SW10**
Chinon **W14**
Clarke's **W8**
Four Seasons Hotel **W1**

London ★ continued

Fung Shing **WC2**
The Halcyon **W11**
The Halkin **SW1**
The Ivy **WC2**
Kensington Place **W8**
The Lanesborough **SW1**
Ming **W1**
Museum Street Café **WC1**
Neal Street Restaurant **WC2**
Panda Si Chuen **W1**
The Savoy Grill Room **WC2**
The Savoy River Room **WC2**
Simply Nico **SW1**
Le Suquet **SW3**
Tatsuso **EC2**
Turner's **SW3**

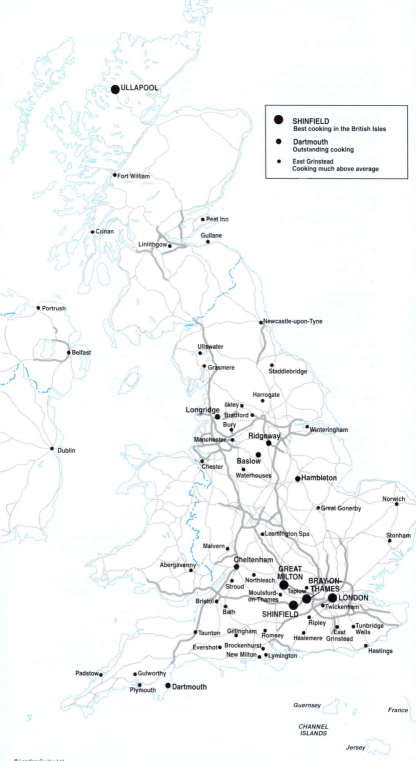

ULLAPOOL

SHINFIELD
Best cooking in the British Isles

Dartmouth
Outstanding cooking

East Grinstead
Cooking much above average

Fort William

Peat Inn
Crinan
Gullane
Linlithgow

Portrush
Newcastle-upon-Tyne
Belfast
Ullswater
Grasmere
Staddlebridge
Harrogate
Ilkley
Longridge
Bradford
Bury
Winteringham
Dublin
Manchester
Ridgeway
Chester
Baslow
Waterhouses
Hambleton
Norwich
Great Gonerby
Stonham
Leamington Spa
Malvern
Cheltenham
Abergavenny
GREAT
MILTON
BRAY-ON-
THAMES
Northleach
Stroud
Taplow
LONDON
Moulsford-
on-Thames
Twickenham
Bristol
SHINFIELD
Bath
Ripley
East
Tunbridge
Wells
Taunton
Gillingham
Romsey
Haslemere
Grinstead
Evershot
Brockenhurst
Hastings
New Milton
Lymington
Padstow
Gulworthy
Plymouth
Dartmouth

Guernsey
France

CHANNEL
ISLANDS

Jersey

© Leading Guides Ltd.

England ★

Bath Royal Crescent Hotel ↑
Gillingham Stock Hill House ↑
Grasmere Michael's Nook ↑
Newcastle-upon-Tyne 21 Queen Street ↑
Padstow Seafood Restaurant ↑
Staddlebridge McCoy's ↑
Stroud Oakes ↑
Taunton Castle Hotel ↑
Waterhouses Old Beams ↑

Bradford Restaurant 19
Bristol Restaurant Lettonie
Brockenhurst Le Poussin
Bury Normandie Hotel & Restaurant
Cheltenham Le Champignon Sauvage
Chester Chester Grosvenor, Arkle
East Grinstead Gravetye Manor
Evershot Summer Lodge
Great Gonerby Harry's Place
Gulworthy The Horn of Plenty
Harrogate Miller's, The Bistro
Haslemere Morel's
Hastings Roser's
Ilkley Box Tree
Leamington Spa Mallory Court
Lymington Gordleton Mill
Malvern Croque-en-Bouche
Manchester Yang Sing
Moulsford-on-Thames Beetle & Wedge, Dining Room
New Milton Chewton Glen
Northleach Old Woolhouse
Norwich Adlard's
Plymouth Chez Nous
Ripley Michels'
Romsey Old Manor House
Stonham Mr Underhill's
Taplow Cliveden, Waldo's Restaurant
Tunbridge Wells Thackeray's House
Twickenham McClements Restaurant
Ullswater Sharrow Bay
Winteringham Winteringham Fields

Scotland ★

Peat Inn The Peat Inn ↑

Crinan Crinan Hotel, Lock 16
Fort William Inverlochy Castle
Gullane La Potinière
Linlithgow Champany Inn

Wales ★

Abergavenny Walnut Tree Inn

Northern Ireland ★

Belfast Roscoff
Portrush Ramore

Republic of Ireland ★

Dublin Patrick Guilbaud ↑
Ahakista Shiro
Boyle Cromleach Lodge
Cork Arbutus Lodge
Cork Clifford's
Dublin Le Coq Hardi
Dublin Le Mistral
Kanturk Assolas Country House
Kenmare Sheen Falls Lodge
Kenmare Park Hotel Kenmare
Moycullen Drimcong House Restaurant
Shanagarry Ballymaloe House

London ↑

L'Accento Italiano **W2**
Albero & Grana **SW3**
Bistrot 190 **SW7**
Le Caprice **SW1**
Chez Max **SW10**
Chutney Mary **SW10**
Del Buongustaio **SW15**
dell'Ugo **W1**
The Dorchester, Oriental Room **W1**
Downstairs at 190 **SW7**
The Eagle **EC1**
L'Escargot **W1**
Fulham Road **SW3**
Greenhouse **W1**
Hyatt Carlton Tower, Chelsea Room **SW1**
Jimmy Beez **W10**
Langan's Brasserie **W1**
Launceston Place **W8**
Mijanou **SW1**
Mr Ke **NW3**
192 **W11**
Le Pont de la Tour **SE1**
Le Quai St Pierre **W8**
Ritz Hotel Restaurant **W1**
Shampan **E1**
Soho Soho **W1**

England ↑

Aston Clinton Bell Inn
Bath Bath Spa Hotel
Bath Hole in the Wall
Brimfield Poppies Restaurant
Goring-on-Thames The Leatherne Bottel
Keyston Pheasant Inn
Langho Northcote Manor
Leeds Brasserie Forty Four
Lower Slaughter Lower Slaughter Manor
Melbourn Pink Geranium
Moulsford-on-Thames Beetle & Wedge, Boathouse Brasserie
New Barnet Mims Restaurant
Nottingham Sonny's
Old Minster Lovell Lovells at Windrush Farm
Oxford Restaurant Elizabeth
Ston Easton Ston Easton Park
Torquay Table Restaurant

Starred Restaurants continued

Scotland ↑

Aberfoyle Braeval Old Mill
Edinburgh The Atrium
Edinburgh The Balmoral
Glasgow Puppet Theatre

Channel Islands ↑

Gorey Jersey Pottery Garden

Northern Ireland ↑

Helen's Bay Deanes on the Square
Londonderry Beech Hill House Hotel

Republic of Ireland ↑

Adare Adare Manor
Adare Mustard Seed
Blackrock Clarets
Cong Ashford Castle, Connaught Room
Dublin Cooke's Café
Dublin Roly's Bistro
Dublin Zen
Killarney Aghadoe Heights Hotel
Kinsale Chez Jean-Marc
Mallow Longueville House
Newmarket-on-Fergus Dromoland Castle

De Luxe Hotels

London

91%	The Connaught **W1**
	The Dorchester **W1**
	The Savoy **WC2**
89%	The Berkeley **SW1**
	Four Seasons Hotel **W1**
	The Lanesborough **SW1**
88%	Claridge's **W1**
87%	Hyatt Carlton Tower **SW1**
	The Regent London **NW1**
86%	Hotel Conrad **SW10**
	47 Park Street **W1**
	The Halkin **SW1**
	The Ritz **W1**
84%	Churchill Inter-Continental Hotel **W1**
	Hotel Inter-Continental London **W1**
	Le Meridien **W1**
83%	The Capital **SW3**
	Grosvenor House **W1**
	The Waldorf **WC2**
82%	Blakes Hotel **SW7**
	Hyde Park Hotel **SW1**
81%	Howard Hotel **WC2**
	May Fair Inter-Continental **W1**

England

92%	**Taplow** Cliveden
89%	**New Milton** Chewton Glen
88%	**Ston Easton** Ston Easton Park
87%	**Bath** Bath Spa Hotel
86%	**Aylesbury** Hartwell House
	Great Milton Le Manoir aux Quat'Saisons
	Stapleford Stapleford Park
85%	**Thundridge** Hanbury Manor
84%	**Bath** Royal Crescent Hotel
	Chester Chester Grosvenor
	East Grinstead Gravetye Manor
	Oakham Hambleton Hall
83%	**Colerne** Lucknam Park
	Torquay Imperial Hotel
82%	**Chagford** Gidleigh Park
	Hintlesham Hintlesham Hall
	Ullswater Sharrow Bay
81%	**Amberley** Amberley Castle
	Woolton Hill Hollington House
80%	**Broadway** Lygon Arms
	Buckland Buckland Manor
	Cheltenham The Greenway
	Thornbury Thornbury Castle
	Leamington Spa Mallory Court
	Lower Slaughter Lower Slaughter Manor

Scotland

90%	**Fort William** Inverlochy Castle
86%	**Auchterarder** Gleneagles Hotel
84%	**Turnberry** Turnberry Hotel
83%	**Edinburgh** The Balmoral
82%	**Dunblane** Cromlix House
	Glasgow One Devonshire Gardens
	St Andrews St Andrews Old Course Hotel
81%	**Alexandria** Cameron House

Wales

81%	**Llyswen** Llangoed Hall

Channel Islands

80%	**St Saviour** Longueville Manor

Republic of Ireland

88%	**Cong** Ashford Castle
87%	**Kenmare** Park Hotel Kenmare
	Kenmare Sheen Falls Lodge
	Straffan Kildare Hotel
84%	**Thomastown** Mount Juliet Hotel
81%	**Adare** Adare Manor
	Gorey Marlfield House

The BIG network congratulates the Egon Ronay's Guides Hotel of the Year 1995.

Hotel of the Year

The Halkin
London

Ambitiously designed by Christina Ong in a distinct Milanese style, this Belgravia hotel is small by London standards. Behind the neo-Georgian facade there's a stunning atrium lobby, a marble mosaic floor (copied from Michelangelo's Piazza del Campidoglio in Rome) and contemporary furniture and fittings complementing the natural theme. Conventional hotel corridors have been replaced by curved ones with black beechwood walls and concealed doors, creating a more intimate feel, while the hi-tech bedrooms, with spacious marble bathrooms, have electronic touch panels controlling most of the gizmos that include CD player, VCR, fax machine, no-hands telephones and personal room safe linked to the central computer. Armani-clad staff, superbly directed by General Manager Nicholas Rettie, are a credit to their profession – this is indeed a magnificent hotel, with a restaurant that does it full credit.

Previous Winners

1994	**One Devonshire Gardens** Glasgow		1989	**The Savoy** London
1993	**The Chester Grosvenor** Chester		1988	**Park Hotel** Kenmare
1992	**The Dorchester** London		1987	**Homewood Park** Freshford
1991	**Longueville Manor** St Saviour			
1990	**Gidleigh Park** Chagford			

cellnet

The BIG network congratulates the Egon Ronay's Guides Restaurant of the Year 1995.

For further information on the BIG network call

0800 214000

Restaurant of the Year

Fischer's Baslow Hall
Baslow, Derbyshire

When the Fischers' previous Bakewell restaurant first appeared in our Guide several years ago, we described chef Max as having "exceptional culinary skills, his cooking and presentation showing great attention to detail, with fine flavour combinations and beautifully made sauces". Nothing we said then has changed, though the restaurant (with rooms) has moved into a lovely house up the road, so the quality of the cooking now has the setting it deserves. Max and Susan have persevered through thick and thin, and their smashing restaurant deserves to be highlighted to the widest possible audience.

Previous Winners

1994	**Le Soufflé, Inter-Continental Hotel** London		1989	**L`Arlequin** London
1993	**The Carved Angel** Dartmouth		1988	**Morels** Haslemere
1992	**Bibendum** London		1987	**Walnut Tree Inn** Abergavenny
1991	**L'Ortolan** Shinfield			
1990	**Waterside Inn** Bray-on-Thames			

The RECIPE FOR SUCCESS

The Meat and Livestock Commission is pleased to be sponsoring the Egon Ronay's Guides British Meat Chef of the Year competition 1995.

Experience any of the delicious British meat meals created with such passion by our top chefs, and you'll understand why British Meat is the 'Recipe for Love'.

British Meat is a firm favourite in all top hotels and restaurants because of its quality, flavour and versatility.

More than ever, British beef, pork and lamb are being used on quality menus throughout the country, satisfying the most discerning of palates and meeting the changing needs of consumers.

Chefs are continually creating new British Meat dishes and menu ideas, some of which you will see in our national TV campaign. Sample these in your favourite restaurant, or cook at home to create your own 'Recipe for Love'.

D Andrews

Derek Andrews
Catering Development and Promotions Manager.

E·G·O·N RONAY'S GUIDES *and* **BRITISH MEAT**

1·9·9·5

CHEF *of the* YEAR
COMPETITION

Following rigorous inspection by the guide's team, Britain's top chefs were assembled in London, to determine the

Egon Ronay's Guides British Meat Chef of the Year 1995.

The selected finalists were:

Scotland:	*David Wilson, Peat Inn, Fife*
North:	*Nigel Haworth, Northcote Manor, Blackburn, Lancashire*
Wales:	*Peter Jackson, Maes-y-Neaudd, Talsarnau, Gwynedd*
London:	*Jean-Christophe Novelli, Four Seasons Hotel, London W1*
South:	*Gerald Röser, Röser's, nr Hastings, East Sussex*
South West:	*Steven Blake, Royal Crescent Hotel, Bath, Avon*

Each finalist submitted three main course menus based on British beef, pork and lamb with a starter and dessert to accompany.

Lots were drawn to decide which chef cooked which meat. The chefs had three hours to prepare their menus, which were judged on balance, creativity, technical ability, quality ingredients and inspired combinations of flavour, texture and taste.

Rob Andrew presenting Nigel with his car

After a tense three hours judging by: Paul Heathcote, Chef of the Year 1994 Catey Hillier, Editor of 'Chef' Magazine Derek Andrews, British Meat's Catering Development & Promotions Manager and Andrew Eliel, Managing Editor, Egon Ronay's Guides, the result was incredibly close. Nigel Haworth was heralded as the winner and presented with his prize, a brand new Ford Mondeo, by English rugby star Rob Andrew. Novelli was second by a whisker and Blake a strong third.

The following menus prove the quality of cooking in Britain compares favourably with the best in the world.

BRITISH MEAT

The Recipe FOR Pork

1·9·95 CHEF of the YEAR COMPETITION

NIGEL HAWORTH

Northcote Manor, Blackburn, Lancashire

Nigel Haworth undertook his early training at Accrington and Rossendale College after which he worked at the Grosvenor Hotel in London and Royal Berkshire in Ascot.

In 1978 he began working in Switzerland in the kitchens of several leading hotels where he perfected his pâtisserie skills. After gaining this valuable international experience he returned to the UK and worked at Gleneagles Hotel.

In 1983 he returned to his native Lancashire and a year later became head chef at Northcote Manor. In 1989, Nigel jointly bought Northcote Manor and during his time there has trained many young chefs who have now progressed to famous restaurants such as Le Gavroche, Tante Claire and The Canteen.

Rob Andrew proclaims Nigel the winner

BRITISH PORK MENU

*Soufflé of lobster wrapped in
spinach infused with tarragon.*

*Braised shin of British pork with broad beans and
plum tomatoes cream'd polenta.*

*Minted nectarine and
raspberry jelly honey sabayon.*

GERALD RÖSER

Röser's, Hastings, East Sussex

Gerald Röser is proprietor of the highly successful restaurant, Röser's, in Hastings, East Sussex, which he opened in 1984.

Prior to owning his own restaurant, Gerald spent two years at Ockenden Manor in West Sussex as head chef with previous stints in Hastings and London.

Gerald began his career with a three year chef's apprenticeship in Germany followed by two years working in leading Swiss establishments.

BRITISH PORK MENU

Pike Soufflé
A light soufflé served with a smoked salmon and dill sauce.

British Pork Fillet with Wild Mushrooms
Free-range British pork fillets served with wild mushrooms and chive pasta.

Caramelised Apple Mille Feuille
Lightly poached apple layered with calvados-flavoured creme patisserie and served with a butterscotch sauce.

The *Recipe* FOR *Beef*

By popular demand British beef retains a central role at the heart of the menu. At its best, it is moist, succulent and delicious to taste.

STEVEN BLAKE
Royal Crescent Hotel, Bath, Avon

Steven Blake began his career at the Russell Hotel in London as an apprentice, later to become the sous chef at restaurant Ninety Park Lane at the Grosvenor Hotel in London.

1·9·9·5
CHEF *of the* YEAR
COMPETITION

In 1985 he moved to open Le Meridien, Piccadilly, London, alongside David Chambers, as executive chef.

Steven's first head chef position was taken at La Talbooth near Colchester in 1987 and after 4 years he moved to The Royal Crescent Hotel as executive head chef.

Steven Blake, a worthy competitor

BRITISH BEEF MENU

Sauté of baby lobster flavoured with a hint of garlic and ginger on a warmed shellfish dressing.

British beef fillet trimmed with backfat, resting on a rosti potato, creamed celeriac and spinach, accompanied by stuffed morilles and red wine shallots.

Assiette of passion fruit and mango.

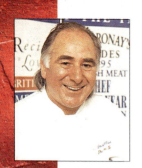

DAVID WILSON
The Peat Inn, Fife, Scotland

David Wilson's interest in cooking stemmed from a love of good food which led him to give up a career in Industrial Marketing to become the 'oldest commis chef in Britain' working at The Pheasant Inn in Keyston.

In 1972 he moved to the Peat Inn near St Andrew's and his training continued with working holidays in France.

David soon earned recognition from all the major food guides including stars from Egon Ronay's Guides. He is a member of Master Chefs of Great Britain.

1·9·9·5
CHEF *of the* YEAR
COMPETITION

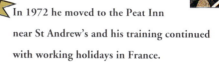

BRITISH BEEF MENU

Scallop and monkfish with spiced British pork in a warm vinaigrette.

Roast rib eye of British beef with shallots.

Trio of caramel desserts.

BRITISH MEAT

The Recipe FOR Lamb

With its delicate flavour British lamb has earned its position as one of the popular favourites of chefs in Britain and on the continent.

1·9·9·5
CHEF of the YEAR
COMPETITION

JEAN-CHRISTOPHE NOVELLI
Four Seasons Hotel, London

Jean-Christophe Novelli moved to the UK from France in 1985 having been a private chef for the Rothschild family for three years.

Originally trained as a baker, he has held positions at Chewton Glen Hotel, Hampshire, Geddes restaurant, Southampton and at Keith Floyd's establishment in Devon.

Prior to joining the Four Seasons, Jean-Christophe was the chef at Provence restaurant in Hampshire where he gained accolade from all the leading guides.

Novelli, a very close second place.

BRITISH LAMB MENU

Tartare de saumon mariné, et blanc de tourteaux, croque verte, son oeuf de caille poché ponte de caviar.

Cured, marinated salmon in crab meat with poached quail eggs topped with caviar and gaspacho sauce.

Cotelettes d'agneau soufflés au roquefort, lentilles du pays.

British Lamb cutlets souffléd with roquefort cheese mousse. Roast potatoes, lentil and jus of tarragon.

Tarte fine croustillante aux pommes, sa glace vanille bourbon.

Warm thin caramelised apple tart with vanilla ice cream.

BRITISH MEAT

1·9 · 9·5
CHEF *of the* YEAR
COMPETITION

Peter Jackson began his career at Nethybridge Hotel and after stints at a number of hotels became 1st commis chef at Gleneagles.

Moving from there to the Station Hotel in Inverness, he then took the position of head chef at Bodysgallen Hall, Llandudno. Having gained further experience at Eastwell Manor in Kent, the Colonial Restaurant in Glasgow and hotels in Clwyd and Isle of Man, Peter took the role of head chef at Hotel Maes-y-Neaudd near Harlech.

Peter has won many awards for his cooking, most recently a Silver Medal at the 1994 World of Hospitality where he was Captain of the Welsh Culinary Team.

BRITISH LAMB MENU

Lobster and scallop pasta with an olive oil fondue.

Smoked British lamb sausage with Sweetbreads, mashed potato and a rich gravy.

Rhubarb and ginger clafoutis served with a blood orange mousse and nougatine.

The Recipe FOR LOVE

For further British Meat information,
contact our consumer hotline on:

0908 23 25 22

BRITISH
MEAT

Distinctive and delicious...
definitively Ilchester

Great British Cheeses

ILCHESTER CHEESE CO LTD
Ilchester, Somerset BA22 8LJ
Telephone: 0935 840531 Telex: 46639 Fax: 0935 841223

British Cheeseboard of the Year

Poppies Restaurant
The Roebuck, Brimfield nr Ludlow Hereford & Worcester

Poppies is a bright, cheerful restaurant, in direct contrast to the dark, beamed and oak-panelled bar just across the corridor of this country pub *par excellence*. Chef/proprietor Carole Evans's constant search for prime ingredients and tireless efforts in the kitchen help to produce wonderful dishes that can be sampled in both bar and restaurant. Her attention to detail carries right through to the extensive choice of British farmhouse cheeses, made from both pasteurised and unpasteurised milk. Merlin, a mild goat's cheese is made with vegetarian rennet; Ty'n Grug is a nutty, organic Cheddar-type cheese made in Lampeter; and there's a choice of some five blue cheeses: from Blue Stilton made in Long Clawson (near Melton Mowbray) to Shropshire Blue with its distinctive orange curd. The 15 or so cheeses on the descriptive list might also include such evocative names as Llanboidy (made from the milk of organically farmed Red Poll cattle), Llangloffan (akin to an old-style Cheshire), Tornegus, Pencarreg, Hereford Hop (like a single Gloucester) and Golden Saye (a washed-rind soft cheese made with milk from the Duke of Wellington's pedigree herd of Golden Guernsey cows). Carole's home-made bread and pickles are the perfect complement to such an array of natural flavours.

Previous Winners

1994   **The Lygon Arms**
Broadway

1993   **Old Vicarage**
Witherslack

British Cheeseboard of the Year Regional Winners

London
Leith's W11

The famous dessert trolley may have disappeared from the dining room but you'll still find a fine trolley of British cheeses wheeled around the tables. The display includes a wicker tray with vine leaves, a selection of fruits, Scottish oatmeal biscuits and home-made breads and brioches to complement the seven or eight carefully chosen cheeses from around the country; Ticklemore hard goat's cheese from Totnes in Devon, St David from Wales, Bonchester from Scotland, creamy Shropshire Blue, and Cumberland from the Lake District often feature (as might an occasional "Stinking Bishop" - not for the faint-hearted!).

Home Counties
Dundas Arms Kintbury

The trend to serve cheeses as a plated course is becoming more and more common throughout the restaurant business. If this saves wastage and allows a greater turnover of fresh cheeses then surely it must be a good thing. At the Dundas Arms you will be offered a selection from around ten or so all-British cheeses such as Cotherstone, Capricorn, Yarg, Colston Bassett Stilton, mature Cheddar, and ash-coated goat's cheese, served with good bread from a local baker.

South of England
Tylney Hall Rotherwick

Keen's Cheddar matured for 10 months, Tornegus (unpasteurised Caerphilly), Wigmore, Harbourne Blue (blue-vein goat's cheese from South Devon), Flower Marie (unpasteurised, mould-ripened ewe's milk cheese from Sussex), Colston Bassett Stilton, River Eden (smoked cow's milk), Bonchester (Camembert-style from Scotland), and Isle of Avalon all appeared on a recent cheese menu - an unexpectedly wide selection of all-British cheeses that shows real interest in the subject. Tylney Hall's new sister hotel, Ashdown Park in Wych Cross, East Sussex, offers a similar range of good British cheeses.

West Country
Table Restaurant Torquay

A 7-year association with the Ticklemore Cheese Shop in Totnes has resulted in a continuous supply of tip-top British cheeses at The Table Restaurant. Served as an optional course on the fixed-price menu, around six or seven mainly local cheeses are offered; these might include Ticklemore ash-covered goat's cheese, the ever-popular Tornegus, Sharpham (a Brie-style cheese made with Jersey milk), Devon Oke (a mature, traditional Curworthy from Rachel Stevens in Okehampton), charcoal-dusted Golden Cross from East Sussex, Colston Bassett Stilton, and Beenleigh Blue made from sheep's milk. A plated selection is presented with celery, grapes, oatcakes and home-made mixed-seed bread.

East of England
The Pheasant Keyston

With regular supplies from Neal's Yard Dairy in London, The Pheasant always offers a small, carefully chosen range of around six cheeses: typically, Colston Bassett Stilton, Appleby's Cheshire (from Shropshire, of course, and more salmon pink than 'red'!), Waterloo from Berkshire, and a soft goat's cheese might be included in the selection. Four different varieties of home-made cheese biscuits are offered, along with walnut bread, grapes, apple and celery.

Midlands/Heart of England
Poppies Restaurant Brimfield

see British Cheeseboard of the Year Winner

North of England
Winteringham Fields Winteringham

Annie and Germain Schwab have made the cheese course "quite an event" and the majority of their customers now take cheese as well as dessert. It's not surprising, really, as there are up to 35 different cheeses on the trolley at any one time; admittedly, they are not *all* British, but the selection is superb and unrivalled in the north-east of England. On any one evening you might find Fountains Gold (a creamy cheese from North Yorkshire with an unusual toasted wheat rind), Swaledale (also from North Yorkshire, a lemony fresh, Wensleydale but softer and more moist) or Curworthy (a sweet, buttery, semi-hard cheese from Stockbeare Farm in Okehampton, Devon) alongside the better-known French names. All are served with dried fruits, celery, grapes and bread or biscuits.

Scotland
Ard-na-Coille Newtonmore

A five-course set meal here always includes a fourth course of cheese; the trolley is wheeled around the dining room with up to ten all-Scottish cheeses such as Dunsyre and Lanark Blue, Bonchester, Teviotdale, Ettrick, St Andrews, Pentland Brie and a choice of goat's cheeses (crottin-style or a hard, matured variety). Wastage is reduced to a minimum, thereby enabling the cheeses to be served in prime condition, and all diners are given the chance to sample a handful of Scotland's finest cheeses complemented by traditional oatcakes.

Wales
Plas Bodegroes Pwllheli

Cheese is also an integral part of the five-course dinner at Chris and Gunna Chown's delightful restaurant with rooms on the Lleyn Peninsula: a choice of Stilton with biscuits, goat's cheese salad (occasionally a cheese strudel) or a plated selection of six or so all-Welsh cheeses. The latter are served with home-made walnut bread and the selection might include Llanboidy, Pencarreg, Llangloffan (made from the milk of Jersey cows grazing on organically managed pastures at Castle Morris near Haverfordwest), Ty'n Grug (a hard Cheddar-like cheese), Caerphilly and St David.

Homepride®

Fred and the
Homepride Flour Graders
would like to say
Congratulations to
the winner of
'Dessert of the Year'
Award but ...

... they <u>never</u> speak
with their mouths full

Homepride Foods – sponsors of the 'Dessert of the Year' Award 1995.

Dessert of the Year

The Castle
Taunton, Somerset

Baked egg custard tart with nutmeg ice cream

Raspberry savarin with
vanilla crème fraiche

Hot chocolate pudding
with bitter chocolate sauce

The Castle has been at the forefront of British cooking for many years, and chef Phil Vickery continues the tradition; there's no greater baking exponent, and his desserts end a meal here in fine style. Whether you choose a tart (baked egg custard, chocolate, glazed passion fruit, apple and candied lemon) or pudding (steamed chocolate, bread-and-butter, Spotted Dick), you will sit back satisfied, and with no thought of counting the calories.

Previous Winners

1994 **John Burton-Race**
L'Ortolan, Shinfield

1993 **Jean-Christophe Novelli**
Le Provence at Gordleton Mill

1992 **Roger Pizey**
Harveys, London

Homepride

Dessert of the Year Regional Winners

In the interests of promoting appreciation of good desserts and puddings, Homepride Flour is sponsoring this special award. A symbol (see How To Use pp18/19) appears against selected restaurants throughout the gazetteer, signifying the availability of outstanding desserts at these establishments. The winner of the Dessert of the Year award is highlighted on page 45. Particularly good desserts were enjoyed by our inspectors during the last year at the following establishments:

London
Oak Room Le Meridien Hotel W1

Very French and very rich, but very, very good! Pancakes filled with pears and raisins laced with 'Poire William' on a caramel sauce, traditional apple crumble served with quince ice cream, or rich (their own description!) chocolate biscuit served with vanilla and caramelised pecan ice cream on a coffee sauce.

Home Counties
Cliveden Taplow

Whether you dine in *Waldo's* or in the dining room, the settings are as undeniably grand as the desserts: sharp lemon tart with mascarpone ice cream, hot apple and ginger pudding, warm chocolate tart, or the intriguing sounding hot puff pastry pillow that comes with mirabelle plums, crème fraiche and an orange marmalade ice cream.

South of England
Amberley Castle Amberley

New pastry chef Clare Jackson offers one of her traditional British desserts daily: lemon tart with caramelised oranges, spicy fruit crumble with vanilla sauce, warm treacle tart, or jam roly poly with jam sauce being typical examples. Our inspector described his chocolate and cinnamon tart as "particularly moreish" - say no more!

West Country
The Castle Taunton
see Dessert of the Year Winner

East of England
Adlard's Norwich

Enjoy the likes of mocha parfait with almond tuile and mint anglaise, caramelised pears and mascarpone cheesecake or dark and white chocolate mousse with a citrus syrup in Norfolk's consistently best and only starred restaurant.

Midlands/Heart of England
Marsh Goose Moreton-in-Marsh

Exciting desserts here created by Sonia Kidney, say, warm mincemeat and frangipane tart, a slice of rich chocolate cake, sticky toffee pudding, or pear and nectarines with ginger shortbread and coconut ice cream.

North of England
Sharrow Bay Ullswater

Francis Coulson (acknowledged as the creator of the sticky toffee pudding) and head patissier Chris Bond provide a veritable array of delightful desserts that include lemon tart with vanilla ice cream, hazelnut shortcake layered with raspberries, traditional bread-and-butter marmalade pudding with apricot sauce and another speciality, Francis's almond puff pastry.

Scotland
Arisaig House Arisaig

Always four desserts on the fixed-price table d'hote menu here, ranging from strawberry tartlet or sticky toffee pudding to caramelised apple tart or warm almond pudding with vanilla ice cream. Both the iced Scotch whisky parfait and yoghurt and passion fruit mousse make frequent appearances too.

Wales
Old Rectory Llansanfraid Glan Conwy

Self-taught Wendy Vaughan concocts some scrumptious puddings, as in a warm and almondy apricot tart with ginger ice cream, choux pastry swans with lemon mousse and raspberries, pear and almond tart or a parcel of strudel pastry with sesame and poppy seeds. Since dining is usually around one large communal table, you can discuss the merits of these fine desserts with a complete stranger!

Northern Ireland
Antica Roma Belfast

Splendid *dolci* include a pastry cornet filled with sorbet and served with fresh fruit, walnut pie served with butterscotch sauce, and a wicked rich almond cake made of layers of mocha butter cream, praline butter cream and chocolate filling, served with vanilla ice cream

Republic of Ireland
Roly's Bistro Dublin

One of Dublin's most exciting and busiest restaurants, where chef Colin O'Daly offers a galaxy of desserts, ranging from banana and raspberry torte and glazed apple flan to ginger shortbread layered with caramelised oranges on a mango sauce and warm pear tart Bourdalou with chocolate sauce.

Turned out nice again

Everything turns out perfectly when you use
Homepride flour – because we've graded every grain
to give you the lightest, finest flour imaginable.
So, whether you use Homepride Plain or Self Raising
flour you can be sure that all your home baking will turn
out for the best.

GRADED GRAINS MAKE FINER FLOUR

Raise your
champagne flutes with

Perrier~Jouët

to salute the
Wine Cellar of the Year.

Since the golden days of the decadent
Belle Epoque, Perrier-Jouët Champagne
has been enjoyed for its delicate
Chardonnay character and exquisite
quality. Perrier-Jouet is famed for its
prestigious Grand Brut and Belle Epoque
champagnes. Today, a hundred years later,
capture some Belle Epoque "joie de vivre"
and celebrate with Perrier-Jouët champagne,
the epitome of that exciting, opulent age.

Cellar of the Year

The Manor
Chadlington, Oxfordshire

For the wine enthusiast, this is the place to come for bargain basement prices, since the wine list offers sensational buying opportunities among the vintage Bordeaux classics. The list, accompanied by 30 pages of handwritten notes, makes no pretence at being comprehensive (France apart, only Germany's Rhine and a strong showing of vintage ports are represented), but contains more excitement than many that extend to volumes. In reaching their unanimous decision, the judges considered The Manor's admittedly somewhat specialist list purely on its merits, with the new award of *New World Cellar of the Year* (see p.55) making the absence of other wines of less importance than in previous years. Owner of The Manor David Grant – who, incidentally, is studying for his Master of Wine – has included a wide range of half bottles on his most unusual wine list and the prices are exceptionally keen. The more expensive (a relative term here!) wines are kept at cellar temperature and need to be ordered 2-3 hours in advance – our choice would be a 1966 *Chateau Latour* at £95!

Previous Winners

1994	**Gravetye Manor** East Grinstead	1990	**La Potinière** Gullane
1993	**Croque-en-Bouche** Malvern	1989	**Old Bridge Hotel** Huntingdon
1992	**The Cross** Kingussie	1988	**Champany Inn** Linlithgow
1991	**White Horse Inn** Chilgrove		

Judging Panel:
Ken Wilkins Operations Director De Ville & Co (Perrier-Jouèt)
Robin Young The Times
Andrew Eliel Egon Ronay's Guides

. CHAMPAGNE .
PERRIER-JOUÈT

See page 1292/3 for Regional Winners

the Champagne with "Joie de vivre"

The champagne house of Perrier-Jouët was founded in 1811 by Pierre Nicolas-Marie Perrier, who added his wife's maiden name to create the elegant name of Perrier-Jouët. Success throughout the 19th century has continued into the twentieth with the prestigious name epitomising fine quality champagne.

The Grand Brut, the house's non-vintage wine, created in the mid-19th century and enjoyed by Queen Victoria and Edward VII, is the basis of Perrier-Jouët's high reputation for excellence. Made by blending the best grapes from the finest vineyards on Montagne de Reims, in the Marne Valley and on the Côte des Blancs the wine is reputed to be one of the best non-vintage champagnes available. Its consistent high quality epitomises Perrier-Jouët.

A delicate Chardonnay character is one of the hallmarks of Perrier-Jouët champagne. A high proportion of top quality Chardonnay grapes is used in blending the champagnes to create a stylish finesse and elegance.

Perrier-Jouët's famous Belle Epoque champagne, epitomising the giddy pleasures of that festive era, is one of the world's best-known prestige cuvées. The distinctive bottle, with its white, gold and green anemones, was designed in 1902 by Emile Gallé, a famous Art Nouveau artist. The attractive design was rediscovered in 1969 and a fine single vintage champagne was created to complement the elegant bottle. Launched at Maxim's restaurant in Paris in

1969 the Cuvée Belle Epoque was a stylish and lasting success.

The 18th century Perrier-Jouët family house in Epernay, known as Maison Belle Epoque is an Art Nouveau showcase. Filled with furniture and works of art by Art Nouveau masters such as Majorelle, Guimard and Lalique the house provides a glimpse into the opulent world of the Belle Epoque, just as the Belle Epoque champagne evokes the flavour of those golden days.

·CHAMPAGNE·
PERRIER-JOUËT

MONTANA WINES LIMITED
New Zealand's Leading Winemaker

The New World Wine Cellar of the Year

"Adventurous", "imaginative", "well-informed" and "discerning" are just a few of the adjectives to describe this selection of wines from the New World.

There is no better way to embark on a discovery of the pleasures of New World Wines than through the vibrant flavours of the still and sparkling wines from Montana, New Zealand's leading winemaker.

Congratulations

New World Cellar of the Year

Hollington House
Woolton Hill, nr Newbury, Berkshire

Quite simply, the list is staggering, with Australian wines by the bucketful, a comprehensive selection from California, and a decent showing from New Zealand and South Africa as well. From Australia, there are lots of half bottles and magnums, bin ends and fortified wines, muscats and dessert wines - all in all a bewildering choice. It will come as no surprise to learn that owners John and Penny Guy used to have a hotel just outside Melbourne, from where, no doubt, many of these fine wines emanate. Plenty of bottles around the £20 mark, some - Penfolds Bin 95 Grange Hermitage, acknowledged as Australia's best red - ten times that price.

MONTANA WINES LIMITED
New Zealand's Leading Winemaker

MONTANA WINES LIMITED

New Zealand's Leading Winemaker

Montana is New Zealand's leading wine producer and exporter to over 20 countries, internationally renowned for its consistent commitment to quality.

Over twenty years ago Montana planted Sauvignon Blanc grapes in Marlborough, a far-reaching decision that has put New Zealand firmly on today's world winemaking map.

New Zealand winemakers enjoy a naturally favourable climate and soil which produce intensely-flavoured grapes, bursting with fruity flavours and aromas.

Montana takes additional advantage of the country's micro-climates to grow a broad range of grapes and has wineries in each of New Zealand's principle winegrowing areas. Marlborough's Riverlands Winery at Blenheim on the South Island produces its famous Sauvignon Blanc, fine sparkling wines, Chardonnay and Cabernet Sauvignons. On the North Island the

historic McDonald Winery in the Hawkes Bay area, specialises in Chardonnay and Cabernet Sauvignon while Gisborne's state-of-the-art winery makes high-quality whites.

Combining traditional winemaking skills with modern technology Montana produces classic varietals such as the award-winning Marlborouh Sauvignon Blanc, rich peachy Chardonnay, full-bodied Cabernet Sauvignon and quality sparkling wines which include Lindauer and Deutz Marlborough Cuvée, marrying venerable Deutz champagne-making traditions with flavourful Marlborough grapes.

Discover the New World of New Zealand wine by sampling Montana's exciting premium wines.

Keeping a skilled eye on the development of Montana's exceptional sparkling wines.

Congratulations

Martell Cognac is delighted to

salute the Host of the Year.

Santé!

Cognac remains the fine golden spirit which French writer Victor Hugo called *"the Liquor of the Gods"*. Since **Martell** was founded in 1715, generous hosts such as Winston Churchill and the Tsar of Russia have offered **Martell** Cognac to their guests.

Celebrate in style and impress new generations of connoisseurs with rich golden **Martell**, the perfect symbol of true hospitality.

Hosts of the Year

Richard and Kate Smith
Beetle & Wedge
Moulsford-on-Thames, Oxfordshire

A certain degree of harmony between kitchen and front-of-house can give obvious benefits to the customer, but when these departments are too close to home and controlled by a husband-and-wife team, there could be problems. Not so here, where Richard and Kate Smith are a winning combination, two dedicated professionals, whose obvious enjoyment of their work and infectious enthusiasm are transmitted to guests and staff alike. Richard, in the kitchen, consistently produces dishes of quality, while Kate oversees the hotel dining room and Boathouse Brasserie, as well as adding her own stylish touches to the picturesque bedrooms. A previous tenant of the establishment was Jerome K Jerome, who would surely have approved of this happy couple. With sheer hard work and dedication they have succeeded in transforming what was merely a pleasant hotel into one of inspiration.

Previous Winners

1994 **Sharrow Bay**
Ullswater

1993 **Stock Hill House**
Gillingham

1992 **Woodhayes**
Whimple

The Story Of

The Founding Of Martell

In 1715 a young man named Jean Martell arrived in the small town of Cognac in the Charente region of France and set up a business trading in *eaux-de-vie*.

Since that time, eight generations of the **Martell** family have perfected the art of producing exceptional quality cognacs, maintaining the company's prestigious name over the centuries.

The Art Of Viniculture

Martell own around 500 hectares of fine vineyards in the officially designated Cognac region, noted for its temperate climate and chalky soil. The accumulated knowledge of vine growing within **Martell** is much of the reason behind the company's high and consistent standards.

THE ART OF DISTILLATION

The delicate process of charentais distillation begins once the wine has fermented and the fires lit under the pot stills. The fine liquid called *brouillis* produced from the condensed vapours is then collected and heated a second time in small batches to create a spirit of the highest quality. The **Martell** distillers, drawing upon their excellent tasting skills and inherent knowledge of Cognac remove the slightly impure substances which are produced at the beginning and end of the distillation. Then patiently and carefully they draw the heart or *bonne chauffe* from this second distillation. The clear, fiery *eau-de-vie*, or water of life, produced by this process is then aged to become golden, mellow Cognac.

THE ART OF AGEING

The ageing process which transforms these *eaux-de-vie* into Cognac is a long one. Skilled coopers make the oak casks by hand, without using nails or glue. The spirit stored in these casks is transformed by oxidation through the pores in the wood, taking colour and flavours from the oak. The spirit lost through evaporation is known poetically as *"le part des anges"* or *"the angels' share"*. As it ages the spirit gradually develops its aromatic bouquet and characteristic golden colour.

THE ART OF BLENDING

Once the *eau-de-vie* has reached its peak it is blended with others from different regions and of varied vintages to create a smooth Cognac. The skill lies in recreating the distinctive nutty **Martell** taste each time. This vital task rests with the Head Taster, who draws on the skills of generations to create the unique **Martell** style.

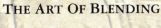

CONGRATULATIONS TO CLIVEDEN WINNER OF KITCHEN OF THE YEAR 1995

0800 373287

NATIONAL BRITANNIA

Environmental Hygiene
Specialists

Kitchen of the Year

Cliveden
Taplow, nr Maidenhead, Berkshire

Just outside *Waldo's* restaurant there are rows of servants' bells that in the old days would have rung to indicate which room in this great house required service. Those servants could not fail to be impressed by the magnificently refurbished kitchens that now serve the hotel; supplied and installed by Falcon Grill (and something of a showcase for the company and blueprint for the future), they have self-contained areas for fish and meat preparation, plus a separate patisserie/bakery section; all have their own fridges and freezers, thereby negating any chance of cross-contamination. *Waldo's* itself has its own kitchen where only the best three chefs from Ron Maxfield's 22-strong brigade are allowed to work here (on a rotational basis), giving all chefs an incentive to perform to their maximum potential. Needless to say, the kitchens are kept sparkling clean.

Are you concerned about

Recent years have seen dramatic changes to legislation relating to food businesses, especially The Food Safety Act 1990. In addition, current and forthcoming European legislation has created additional pressures on establishments. Environmental Health Officers have far reaching powers to protect the consumer. Unlimited fines and even imprisonment are penalties facing proprietors. In their defence, proprietors can plead 'due diligence', but this means taking 'all reasonable precautions' to ensure compliance with the law. Proprietors and managers cannot always be expected to keep up with ever increasing and changing legislation. Advice and assistance is often needed.

The Britannia Food Safety Service

The Britannia Food Safety Service provides this advice and expert help. It provides peace of mind and reassurance that everything is being done to comply with and exceed the demands of the law.

The service offers clients the following:

- **Food Safety & Hygiene Inspections**
  by National Britannia's Environmental Health Officers

- **Full Written Reports**
  detailing findings, observations and recommendations

- **'Due Diligence' Procedures & Records Manuals**
  personalised and easy to follow management procedures which help ensure legislative requirements are met.

- **Emergency Telephone Advice Line**
  Support and advice from your own Expert at all times

- **Food Safety Legislation Update Service**
  Regular written updates of new developments in UK and European legislation.

This cost-effective service is tailored to suit the need of each individual establishment.

For more information about the Britannia Food Safety Service and the Award Scheme call free on 0800 373287

Egon Ronay makes the first Award Presentation to Ricci Obertelli, General Manager of the Dorchester Hotel, Park Lane, London

Food Safety, Hygiene Training Pest Prevention, Fly Control, Health & Safety, Bird Control, Tank Maintenance.

food safety and hygiene?

The Britannia Food Safety & Hygiene Award

In addition, establishments demonstrating the required standard will be rewarded with the Britannia Food Safety & Hygiene Award. Valid for one year it demonstrates and acknowledges the high standards achieved (The award certificate may be removed should standards fall below the level required).

1994 Britannia Food Safety & Hygiene Award Holders include:

British Shoe Corporation, Sunningdale Road, Leicester
Claygate Tandoori, The Parade, Claygate, Surrey
Cliveden, Taplow, Berkshire
Corkers Restaurant & Cafe Bar, 1 High Street, Poole, Dorset
Derwentwater Hotel, Portinscale, Keswick, Cumbria
Don Pepe Restaurant, 99 Frampton Street, London NW8 8NA
The Dorchester Hotel, Park Lane, London, W1A 2HJ
The Edgemoor Hotel, Bovey Tracey, Devon
Fairwater Head Hotel, Hawkeschurch, Nr Axminster, Devon
The Gonville Hotel, Gonville Place, Cambridge
The Knife & Cleaver, The Grove, Houghton Conquest, Bedford

Mr John Hanna, Of Cliveden receives the Award at the House of Commons

Mr Kuet Chinese Takeaway, 3 Fairmead Road, Saltash, Cornwall
La Capannina, 24 Romilly Street W1
Lloyd's of London, Lime Street, London, EC3M
Lucullus Seafood Restaurant, 48 Knightsbridge, London, SW1
Oatlands Park Hotel, Oatlands Drive, Weybridge
The Old Watch House, 1 The Square, St Mawes, Cornwall
The Nobody Inn, Doddiscombsleigh, Nr Exeter, Devon
Poissonnerie de l'Avenue, 82 Sloane Avenue, London, SW3
Porthvean Hotel, Church Town, St Agnes, Cornwall
Saqui Tandoori, 317 Richmond Road, Kingston, Surrey
Serena Restaurant, 12 St Peter's Street, Huddersfield
Sergio's Restaurant, 442c Cowbridge Road East, Cardiff
Splinters, 12 Church Street, Christchurch, Dorset
The Tontine Hotel, 6 Ardgowan Square, Greenock
Torbay Hotel, Station Road, Sidmouth, Devon
Whatley Manor Hotel, Easton Grey, Malmesbury, Wiltshire

National Britannia Ltd Caerphilly Business Park Caerphilly Mid Glamorgan CF8 3ED. Telephone 01222 852000 Facsimile 01222 867738

NATIONAL BRITANNIA

Recommended by

EGON RONAY'S GUIDES

1995

Hotels & Restaurants	Pubs & Inns
Europe	Just a Bite
Family Hotels & Restaurants	Paris
Oriental Restaurants	Ireland
New Zealand & South Pacific	Australia

Egon Ronay's Guides are available from all good bookshops or can be ordered from Leading Guides, 35 Tadema Road, London SW10 0PZ
Tel: 071-352 2485 / 352 0019   Fax: 071-376 5071

Breakfast of the Year

Caledonian Hotel
Edinburgh

Enjoy a fine Scottish breakfast at *Carriages Restaurant* which will take you through the full repertoire, including Caledonian porridge made with double cream, the 'Caley' grill (Ayrshire bacon, grilled tomato, sausage, fried egg, potato scones), potato and salmon fishcake, Stornoway black pudding with sautéed apples, grilled Loch Fyne kipper or poached Finnan haddock. Fine range of teas, excellent coffee.

An easy guide to mobile phones

You can't open a paper or turn on the television today without coming across another article or advertisement for mobile phones. There are so many new systems being launched, different call charges on offer and special deals available that it's confusing.

Ford Motor Company Limited has a separate division, Ford Cellular Systems, which specialises in mobile communications.

If you need advice, it's just a phone call away. Dial **0800 52 66 57** and one of Ford Cellular's knowledgeable operators will answer your questions and help you decide on the best phone and the best call tariff to suit your needs. Or call into your local Ford dealer and ask for the Ford phone specialist.

Two basic decisions

In the end it boils down to two decisions, just like buying a phone for home:

1) Which phone do you want?

2) Which tariff should you choose?

1) Your choice of phone depends on what you plan to use it for. Is it for heavy duty use on a building site or do you want something you can slip into a pocket or handbag? Will you use it solely in the car or do you want to carry it around with you as well?

2) Which tariff should you choose, is a much harder question. A tariff is a combination of the monthly rental for the line and the cost of individual calls. If you only want to use your phone in an emergency, then the lowest monthly rental with higher call charges is best for you; if you make all your calls in

London, there are special tariffs designed for use inside the M25.

To help you choose the right tariff, we'll need to know how often you'll make calls, where you're most likely to be when you make them and whether they're more likely to be during the day, at night or weekends.

Ford Cellular can connect you to either of the major companies in the market, Cellnet or Vodafone, so our advice is impartial.

GSM digital or ETACS analogue? - what does it mean?

Most of the mobile phones in Britain today use analogue technology. GSM (Global System for Mobile Communications) is an alternative system which uses digital technology. It has been adopted as an international standard and will replace analogue eventually.

You can already make and receive calls in several European countries on the GSM network. So, if you want the latest technology, with total security, and the ability ultimately to use the same phone almost anywhere in the world, then you should consider GSM.

Currently analogue phones tend to be lighter and less expensive than GSM, and new products and new tariffs continue to make them attractive.

For help, advice and good quality phones at value for money prices, see your local Ford Dealer or phone Ford Cellular Systems on **0800 52 66 57.**

Business Hotel of the Year

The Churchill Inter-Continental
London

In addition to the business centre, there's a designated Club Inter-Continental floor (the group's first Executive floor concept in the UK) with a Club receptionist/concierge on duty from 6.30am to 11pm. You can have your own fax machine installed in bedrooms and suites on this, the 8th floor, while the centre can organise translators/translations, has a WP for guests' use, as well as a photocopier, fax, telex, an electronic typewriter, and a full-time secretary (conversant with shorthand). Handiest of all, you can rent a handheld mobile phone.

CELLULAR SYSTEMS

HEINEKEN EXPORT.

AS *Recommended* BY YOUR SMOOTH TALKING BAR STEWARD.

MARTELL
CORDON BLEU
ASSOCIATION

Martell Cognac founded the **Cordon Bleu Association** in 1985 in order to support and promote Great Britain's outstanding regional chefs. The Association gathers together over sixty of the country's best privately owned restaurants into an elite band drawn together by their emphasis on quality.

Since its founding in 1715 **Martell** has been noted for the excellence and distinction of its fine cognacs, with knowledge passed down through eight generations of the **Martell** family. It is fitting, therefore, that **Martell** should seek to support high standards of food and wine in some of Great Britain's most prestigious restaurants. What could be more natural after all than a marriage between delicious food and fine cognac?

Patrick Martell
President, Martell Cordon Bleu Association.

ADARE MANOR *Adare*

ADLARDS *Norwich*

AIRDS HOTEL *Port Appin*

ALTNAHARRIE INN *Ullapool*

AMBERLEY CASTLE *Amberley*

BALLYMALOE HOUSE *Shanagarry*

BRAEVAL OLD MILL *Braeval*

THE CASTLE HOTEL *Taunton*

CHEWTON GLEN HOTEL *New Milton*

CHEZ NOUS *Plymouth*

THE COMMONS RESTAURANT *Dublin*

CONGHAM HALL *King's Lynn*

CROMLEACH LODGE *Castle Baldwin*

CROMLIX HOUSE *Kinbuck Dunblane*

CROOKEDWOOD HOUSE *Mullingar*

CROQUE-EN-BOUCHE *Malvern Wells*

THE CROSS *Kingussie*

DRIMCONG HOUSE *Moycullen*

FISCHER'S *Baslow*

GALGORM MANOR *Ballymena*

GIDLEIGH PARK *Chagford*

GRAVETYE MANOR *Nr East Grinstead*

THE GREENWAY *Cheltenham*

HOPE END *Ledbury*

HOWARD'S HOUSE HOTEL *Salisbury*

INVERLOCHY CASTLE *Fort William*

KINGSWOOD COUNTRY HOUSE
& RESTAURANT *Dublin*

KINNAIRD *Kinnaird Estate by Dunkeld*

KNOCKINAAM LODGE *Portpatrick*

LACKEN HOUSE *Kilkenny*

MALLORY COURT *Leamington Spa*

MANLEY'S *Storrington*

LE MANOIR *Great Milton*

THE MARCLIFFE AT PITFODELS *Pitfodels*

McCOY'S *Staddlebridge*

MIDSUMMER HOUSE *Cambridge*

MILLER HOWE *Windermere*

MORELS *Haslemere*

ONE DEVONSHIRE GARDENS *Glasgow*

THE OLD BEAMS *Waterhouses*

L'ORTOLAN *Shinfield*

THE PAINSWICK HOTEL *Painswick*

THE PARK *Kenmare*

THE PEAT INN *Peat Inn*

POOL COURT AT 42 THE CALLS *Leeds*

LA POTINIERE *Gullane*

LE POUSSIN *Brockenhurst*

READ'S *Faversham*

RESTAURANT ELIZABETH *Oxford*

RESTAURANT NINETEEN *Bradford*

RESTAURANT PATRICK
GUILBAUD *Dublin*

ROSCOFFS RESTAURANT *Belfast*

THE SEAFOOD RESTAURANT *Padstow*

SEAVIEW HOTEL *Ballylickey*

SHARROW BAY *Penrith*

STAPLEFORD PARK *Melton Mowbray*

THE STARR *Great Dunmow*

SUMMER ISLES *Achiltibuie*

LE TALBOOTH *Dedham*

TINAKILLY HOUSE *Rathnew*

THE WALNUT TREE *Abergavenny*

WHITECHAPEL MANOR *South Molton*

*For more information on the
Cordon Bleu Association contact:-*

Martell Cordon Bleu Association
PO Box 271.
20-22 Stukeley Street
London WC2B 5LS.

Telephone: 071-430 2276.
Fax: 071 831-7663.

Go your

You've never seen a Ford like it; you've never driven a Ford like it.

The new Probe from Ford is the real thing – a genuine sports coupe. A coupe that has been designed to set your heart racing the way no souped-up, cut down saloon car ever could.

With the Probe you get the choice of two engines – a sporty, 16-valve, 2.0 litre

double-overhead camshaft four cylinder unit, or a silky-smooth, 2.5 litre, 24 valve, four cam V6.

The 5 speed close ratio gearbox is sweet and neat. The ride is right. The engine-sensitive power steering is precise at every speed.

The all disc braking system with ABS fitted as standard, is confidently

own way.

reassuring.

Driver and passenger can relax in the supportive sports seats with the knowledge that airbags are standard for both.

And everything is protected by the electronic engine immobiliser.

The new Probe from Ford – to drive it is to want it.

To discover where you can slip behind the wheel call **0800 111 222** for the address of your nearest Ford Dealer.

The Probe. New from Ford.

Everything we do is driven by you.

BIM
An Bord Iascaigh Mhara
Irish Sea Fisheries Board
is responsible for
developing and expanding
markets at home
and abroad
for Irish Seafood

For information contact:

Market Development Division,
BIM/Irish Sea Fisheries Board/
An Bord Iascaigh Mhara,
Crofton Road,
Dun Laoghaire,
Co.Dublin,
Ireland.

Tel: 353 1 2841544
Fax: 353 1 2841123

IRISH SEAFOOD
...Nature's Best

CORDON BLEU
Old
Classic Cognac

Cordon Bleu was created in 1912 by Edouard Martell, uncle of the company's current President. It is made by blending together different *eaux-de-vie* from the best Cognac regions. The keystone *eau-de-vie* comes from the small Borderies district, where the flinty, clay-rich soil gives the spirit a hallmark nutty taste and roundness of flavour. To this are added complementary Grande and Petite Champagnes and rare old Fins Bois.

The result of this skillful blending is a distinctive tasting Cognac, legendary since it was first created. Enjoyed at the court of the Tsars of Russia and at Winston Churchill's table, **Cordon Bleu** remains a prestigious and much-appreciated Cognac to this very day.

Today **Cordon Bleu** is discreetly but stylishly packaged in a harmonious combination of blue and white with touches of silver and grey. The elegant dark blue gift-box rounds off the presentation and while reminding us of the Cognac's distinguished pedigree, gives it an elegantly fashionable air.

V.S.O.P
Old
Fine Cognac

To lovers of fine Cognac the *"appellation contrôlée"* **V.S.O.P** which means Very Superior Old Pale, is synonymous with superior quality.

In 1874 the **House of Martell** decided to create the **Martell Medaillon V.S.O.P** Cognac. By drawing on ancestral knowledge and skills, and by blending together varied but complementary *eaux-de-vie* from the Cognac region, the **Martell Medaillon V.S.O.P** was born. Vigorous *eaux-de-vie* from the Grande and Petite Champagnes are combined with rounded Borderies and Fins Bois to create a harmonious Cognac with a full-bodied flavour.

Martell Medaillon V.S.O.P is distinguished with a gleaming symbol, a medallion with the image of Louis XIV. This commemorates the year 1715, the last year in the reign of the *"Sun King"* and the year when the **House of Martell** was founded. Splendidly packaged in regal red and gold, **Martell Medaillon V.S.O.P** fully merits the appellation Old Fine Cognac and is indeed a cognac worthy of kings.

Safe
Journey Home.

**Ford want every journey to be a safe
one, that's why we fit a driver's airbag
as standard on every new car.**

Everything we do is driven by you.

The old *smoothie*

(AND PETER BOWLES)

JAMESON

Triple distilled for exceptional smoothness.

THE BIGGER, NEW BOTTLE

With the new,
bigger Britvic bottles, you
now get better value with nearly
60% more juice. And it's even tastier.
So fill your glasses and sink a
few more ice cubes.
Cheers!

NOW LASTS THE ROUND

From
God's own

EARTH

comes
the purity
of
crystal clear

WATER

taken
from source
in the
mythic Celtic
lands of

EIRE

BALLYGOWAN
IRISH SPRING
WATER

Special Old Irish Whiskey

Premium blended whiskey from the oldest licenced distillery in the world.

Go your own way.

For further information call:
0800 111 222

Everything we do is driven by you.

"Specification correct at time of going to press"

Using your mobile overseas.

In addition to superb voice quality, and enhanced call security, Cellnet's digital service enables Primetime Plus subscribers to keep in touch, not only throughout the UK, but also while travelling overseas.

primetime™
plus

One of the key benefits offered by Cellnet's digital network is the facility to make and receive calls while travelling abroad.

This important feature is made available through reciprocal agreements with individual network operators in each country.

At the time of publication – October '94 – mobile coverage embraces virtually all Western Europe and many major trading areas further afield, including: Australia, Hong Kong, South Africa and the United Arab Emirates. During 1995 it is expected that worldwide coverage will be extended considerably.

Ideal for everyone whose work takes them abroad. International Roaming enables users to keep in touch with contacts in the countries they're visiting, as well as Head Office and their families back at home.

cellnet

At the time of publication, October '94, reciprocal agreements have been signed with the following countries. It is expected that this list will be expanded considerably during the next twelve months.

Australia
Austria
Belgium
Denmark
Estonia
Finland
France
Germany
Greece
Hong Kong
Ireland
Italy
Luxembourg
Netherlands
Norway
Portugal
South Africa
Sweden
Switzerland
United Arab Emirates

For further information call
0800 214000

GOURMET CROSSWORD COMPETITION

Over £2,500-worth of Cellnet and Martell Prizes to be won!

The winner will receive:

The Motorola International Micro Tac 7200 GSM
pocket Phone, worth around £400, will be connected free
to Cellnet's Primetime Plus service. The prize also
includes a year's free rental on Primetime Plus, and
£250-worth of free calls

Plus

An all-expenses-paid two-night trip for two to
the Chateau de Chanteloup, including a tour of
the production facilities and a cognac tasting

Enter our *Egon Ronay's Cellnet Guide 1995 Hotels & Restaurants* Crossword Competition and you could win a Motorola International Micro Tac 7200 GSM pocket phone, worth about £400, connected free to Cellnet's Primetime Plus service, for use in the UK, Europe and other countries. Cellnet will also provide a year's free rental on Primetime Plus (worth £300) as well as £250-worth of free calls.

Primetime Plus is Cellnet's digital service, ideal for international business users who need to keep in touch – and be contactable – in the UK and abroad.

The first-prize winner also wins an amazing, all-expenses-paid two-night trip for two, staying at the Chateau de Chanteloup, home of Martell Cognac, and enjoying a tour of the Martell production facilities with a special cognac tasting.

Five runners-up will receive a stylish presentation pack of Martell V.S.O.P. Cognac.

To enter, simply complete our challenging cryptic food and wine-related crossword (opposite) and send the tear-out page, including your name and address, to the address on page 96.

Entries should arrive no later than 31st March 1995 and the draw from all the correct entries will take place on 30th April 1995. Winners will be notified by post shortly afterwards.

COMPETITION RULES

1. Only one entry per person is allowed.
2. Entrants must be living in the UK and be aged 18 years or over.
3. All entries must be on the official entry form – photocopies will not be accepted.
4. All Egon Ronay's Guides, Cellnet, Pan Macmillan and Seagram staff and their relatives, contributors and those associated with the Guides are not eligible.
5. The prizes are as stated. There are no cash alternatives.
6. All entries should arrive no later than 31st March 1995.
7. The winning entries will be drawn from correctly completed crosswords on 30th April 1995, and the winners will be notified shortly afterwards.
8. Details of the competition winners and crossword answers will be published in the 1996 edition of the Guide.
9. The Editor's decision is final.
10. No correspondence can be entered into.
11. No purchase required.
12. The winners will be required to participate in any post-event publicity.

The British Ports

Dover

Approached from either the M2 or preferably the newer M20 via Folkestone, the Hovercraft departs from the Western Docks, a poor cousin of the extensive Eastern Docks complex: departure point for the ferries. Vast though the latter may appear, all is very clearly signposted. A small but neat airline-style terminal is provided for those needing to pick up tickets or with time to spare. The hall houses check-in desks for the two operators with four assistants on the Stena Sealink desk and five on the P&O. The latter also have a smart ticket office in the town centre on the main approach route to the docks, with ample parking provided. The terminal also has a branch of National Westminster Bank, a newsagent, RAC and AA centres as well as a video games room and a refreshment bar serving simple snacks, the filled baguettes being the most substantial offerings when we visited. Boarding procedures are the same with Stena Sealink and P&O, though the latter do place a large black and white computer-readable sticker on your windscreen – supposedly for speedy, efficient loading, though in this respect we found no difference between the two rivals.

Folkestone

A circuitous route, rather poorly signposted, leads you through the winding streets to the harbour, dominated by the white ship-like outline of one of the seafront hotels. The terminal is due for some cosmetic changes (as is the Hovercraft terminal at Western Docks, Dover). Catering facilities are limited to a Café Select selling freshly made good-quality espresso coffee plus a few sweet and savoury snacks. *Pain au chocolat* had too little chocolate, ham and cheese-filled croissants hadn't yet arrived, being 'on a lorry somewhere' at 10.30am. The only savoury choice was a croissant filled with grated cheese and raw mushrooms. With only a microwave to warm it up, it ended up a soggy mess. There is also a retail outlet selling maps and magazines as well as a chilled cabinet selling a few wrapped, filled sandwiches and chilled soft drinks.

The French Ports

Boulogne

Only Hoverspeed's Sea Cat operates between Folkestone and Boulogne. On the French side the vessel docks in the town centre, using one of the quays formerly used by the ferry ships. The route is well signposted through the town and the same food operation exists here as in Hoverspeed's Dover and Folkestone terminals. A recent addition is Dixie's Donuts, which serves all manner of cold doughnuts (to warm, they are microwaved) as well as hot dogs and things called dawn dogs – a breakfast hot dog wrapped in bacon. Excellent duty-free selection.

Calais

The motorway link road (A26) is a fast and direct connection to the port facilities, which are dominated by a large futuristic terminal building. The whole area immediately around the terminal looks as if it's in a state of change with building work and uneven surfaces with parking rather disorganised. Stena Sealink and P&O have Portakabin-type check-in for car drivers with advance tickets. After passport control the facilities for motorists are reduced to a further Portakabin with a severely limited range of snacks including an automatic coin-operated chip machine serving really yukky chips. The main terminal is really best avoided unless you have a query or other essential function to attend to. The ground floor has a hall with ticket and information desks. On the evening we called in there were people sleeping in the stair wells. There's a lift or stairs to the restaurant on the top floor and in between toilets which were dirty with hand-driers that didn't work. The food in the restaurant at 8pm on a Thursday evening can only be described as an absolute disgrace with a counter displaying very dried-up meats, lumps of fish with the sauce dried-up on them, a tray of carrots that had almost become mashed, very wrinkled, hard, desiccated peas, a tray of rice into which a number of chips had been dropped. Sweets, too, were appalling, all appearing to have been on display for too long. Good views though over the docks.

Loading of the vehicles wasn't as well organised as at Dover, with drivers jumping the queue only to find themselves in another, summarily putting paid to their impetuousness.

Calais Hoverport

A simple building facing out to sea with hard plastic seats and a non-slip floor. The duty-free shop is superb, with a great selection of spirits and liqueurs. The food is poor, with little choice – toasted sandwiches were the only hot item available for the 22.30 crossing. Watching the Hovercraft approach is a splendid sight as it emerges from a surrounding sea spray and hovers up the beach.

On Board

Hovercraft

There are no facilities other than toilets: basically, you stay in your seat throughout the crossing. Cabin staff come round and take your order for drinks and duty-free. There is little or no storage space, seating is very cramped and the view from the interior depends on sea conditions. Crossings, always noisy, can also be very bumpy when it's rough; only those passengers with the sturdiest of sea-legs can survive being tossed about on the waves without at least thinking about those handy little paper bags tucked into each seat pocket.

Sea Cat

On board are similar airline-type seats to the Hovercraft but they are better arranged with a wide centre section and a lower level of window seats on either side. A hostess service brought round a trolley with hot drinks serving awful, expensive coffee and tea. There's also plenty of room to walk around, and you can even climb stairs to see what's happening on the bridge. The bar at the rear has a limited range of snacks and the duty-free shop has a meagre selection compared to those available at the terminals. A small rear open deck provides a strong, bracing breeze and good misty spray of Eau de Channel. A film on safety procedures is shown at the start of each crossing. The late arrival of trains from London can result in departure delays which can have a knock-on effect on the Boulogne–Folkestone crossing too. Ours left half an hour late and the crossing took 65 minutes. Beware of the exorbitant exchange rate 9.50FF to the £1. It is advisable to pay for all on-board purchases in the currency quoted on price lists.

Stena Sealink

They currently offer the slowest, most leisurely crossings with sailings hourly day and night. They operate five ships, three British and two French.

Stena Invicta (1,750 passengers, 400 cars)

An actual journey from Dover on the *Stena Invicta*, one of the British ships, involved fast, trouble-free loading with a pleasant stroll around the ship exploring its facilities, which are arranged on two upper decks (there are nine decks in all). The *Invicta* has the most on-board facilities, of any of Stena Sealink's cross-Channel ferries and includes the only à la carte restaurant on this route. The restaurant, with views over the bows, is bright and airy. Called The Grill, on the 11.30am crossing it offered only a £7.50 set-price brunch comprising overcooked, tough minute steak, greasy eggs, sausage of the type mass-produced by a factory conveyor-belt and tasting beautifully of all manner of additives. Masses of chips, hot but pale and not well cooked, accompanied. The regular menu which operates later in the day is a short, standard à la carte selection including fried Dover sole with almonds, medallions of pork with mushrooms and apple rings in an inappropriate red wine sauce and an insipid Belgian chocolate mousse with a raspberry sauce. The alternative is Le Jardin, where the choice is an £8.95 three-course buffet with roast beef or roast of the day with a choice of desserts, tea or coffee. The self-service restaurant offered a reasonable if rather watery soup of the day – watercress and sweetcorn – as well as a special of three not very meaty meatballs tasting mostly of sage and onion stuffing and accompanied by greasy chips and dried-up peas. The Hamburger Café had no customers when we called – no wonder, the hamburgers had been cooked long before and kept warm. The result was a cloud of steam when you opened the carton and an extremely soggy bun, slimy pickles and wilted lettuce. The meat was devoid of taste too. The *Stena Fantasia* has installed a McDonald's on board. In high season children's entertainment is provided by the Great Geffini in his magic lair as well as a modern clown going walkabout around the lounges – a fun touch. Duty-free shopping is good, even if prices are a fraction more than those of the competitors.

Fiesta (1,800 passengers, 600 cars)

One of the two French ships. It was 20 minutes late leaving Calais, and no explanation being offered for the delay. There was a long queue for the self-service restaurant – the only catering facility on board. The choice included rock-hard bread rolls, a prawn cocktail with rotting, yellowed, bruised frisée lettuce, a few prawns and a topping of mayonnaise that was drying up on the outside. Salmon was severely overcooked and came with watery processed peas, carrots and new potatoes. The rest of the food was no better and was dished out by uncomprehending staff. They've got a truly captive market here with no alternative – you eat badly, or you go hungry. There are plenty of bars and areas to lounge and drink (there is even a disco on board) though the Galaxy panoramic bar was closed for some reason. The duty-free shop was truly chaotic, with queues to enter, a hot heaving throng inside and long queues for the tills. They also insisted that for credit-card transactions passports be produced (charges were made in French Francs with a higher than usual exchange rate: 8.50F to the £1, compared to 8.13F at the bank on the same day).

P&O

Pride of Burgundy (1,400 passengers, 600 cars)

A splendid vessel in shipshape order. Once all the passengers were on board, good clear safety instructions were provided over the loudspeakers. There are two passenger decks with ample, comfortable lounge seating and, for children, a video lounge showing cartoons. The restaurant began serving lunch at 11am offering a selection of indifferent food in smart surroundings (though the view out of the window was of lifeboats). Lentil and bacon soup had good flavour though the bacon was fatty. No Dover sole was available so salmon was suggested as an alternative – it came overcooked, with a hot caper sauce and a selection of soggy vegetables. Good bars and duty-free shopping. The exchange rate was 8.84F to the £1. This was a faster crossing, though loading and unloading were the same as for Stena Sealink. It subsequently took 30 minutes to clear customs because two ships unloaded at the same time.

Pride of Dover (2,250 passengers, 650 cars)

Sister ship to the *Pride of Calais*, it left Calais five minutes early. On board are ample lounges including clearly marked no-smoking lounges and there is good provision of wide airline-type seating throughout the passenger decks, and a video screen for children's entertainment. Duty-free shopping was relaxed, with no queues on this 21.45 sailing. From the self-service restaurant we chose chicken satay with Chinese noodles and a sweet and sour sauce, resulting in two small sticks of minced chicken drowned in a sea of sauce; this came with very pasty, tasteless noodles. A vegetarian moussaka had to be ordered. It arrived having been microwaved and was like baby-food purée – very little flavour and only the minutest of what looked like aubergine – perhaps it wasn't but there was so little it was hard to tell. The main, à la carte, restaurant suffered from a forgetful waitress and fried Dover sole meunière with exhausted, not just tired, vegetables. Coffee was very poor.

Duty-Free

Prices were very similar (within 75p per bottle of each other) on the five proprietary brands we checked. Only a 1 litre bottle of Glenfiddich differed widely: £15 on Hoverspeed, £16.75 on Stena Sealink. Remember, if paying by credit card you are likely to pay 5% more, due to exchange rates. Our advice is to pay in cash in the currency marked on the goods.

Conclusion

With speed comes a certain amount of discomfort depending on the weather. Hovercraft flights are quite often cancelled in winter owing to adverse conditions in the Channel. The Sea Cat, too, can be quite bumpy in poor weather. It is, however, the best way across the Channel, offering speed and convenience – Folkestone is, after all, closer to the M20 than Dover. Of the ferry lines, P&O has the more comfortable ships. For all the crossings it is best to avoid the food both at the terminals and on board.

Eating in Town

This Side

Folkestone has two recommendable restaurants, *Paul's* and *La Tavernetta*. There are no recommended restaurants in Dover, but you can eat well at *Wallett's Court* in nearby St Margaret's (see entries).

The Other Side

The situation in Calais and Boulogne is quite the reverse with an abundance of really quite good restaurants and cafés suiting all pockets. Being ports, fish tends to dominate restaurant menus and its cooking is invariably excellent.

In Calais' rue Royale you can snack well at *La Maison Douce* – a tea room at No. 4, open all day every day, where delicious, buttery pastries are an alternative to good, simple savoury dishes like tagliatelle with a creamy mushroom and vegetable sauce or piping hot cheese and ham bake. The hot chocolate is outstanding – very, very rich and very satisfying. Further up the same street is the Café de Paris at No. 72, again open all day, every day. In fine weather the front opens up and here you can enjoy *Flamekueches*, an Alsatian speciality which resembles a pizza – grated cheese, ham and mushrooms on a wonderfully light and crispy, almost biscuit-like base and served on a large wooden platter.

For a more formal meal try *La Courginoise* 2 place de Suède (Tel 21 97 50 00), open lunch and dinner but closed Wednesdays and Sunday evening. It is located a short distance from place d'Armes en route through the town to the car ferries. A charming little restaurant, decorated with brilliant white walls and pale blue upholstery, the cooking is by Sandra Houbion (the owner). Set menus begin at 88F and typical food includes a speciality of little pancake parcels of crab (*aumonières*) with a delicate and delicious garlic cream as well as a mixture of market fish fried in a sorrel sauce. Meat dishes could be a peppered fillet of beef, duck breast with peaches or veal sweetbreads with a juniper sauce. Delicious, simple sweets complete a delightful experience.

Overlooking the town's harbour is *Le Grand Bleu* 8 rue Jean-Pierre Avron (Tel 21 97 97 98), open lunch and dinner with booking advisable. In fine weather, pavement tables take advantage of the setting sun and the port's coming and goings. The food is exclusively fish (one meat dish only). Menus begin at 120F and the specialities are the *plateau de fruits de mer* 150F per person, a *marmite calaisienne*, wonderful fish stew with tender mussels, sea bass, salmon and monkfish – the fish changing according to daily availability. Other typical dishes from a largely classical menu are poached turbot with a hollandaise sauce, grilled lobster or sole meunière. *L'Aquar'aile* rue Jean Moulin (Tel 21 34 00 00), located just behind the sea front, enjoys superb views from its 4th-floor position. The menu is sophisticated and prices quite reasonable for its fine setting.

In Boulogne the choice of where to eat is even greater. High up in the old town a wonderful spot for open-air eating is an enclosed tree-filled courtyard at *Le Restaurant de la Haute-Ville* (Tel 21 80 54 10). Open for lunch and dinner daily, it is excellent for the likes of moules marinière and has kind prices. Down in the town *La Liégeoise* 10 rue de Monsigny (Tel 21 31 61 15), open daily except Sunday evening and all Monday, is right next to the town theatre. Cooking is superb and the setting very smart and classy. *Les Pecheurs d'Etaples* at 31 Grand Rue combines a well-stocked wet fish counter at the front and a spacious, airy restaurant at the rear, serving carefully prepared ultra-fresh seafood. Off place Dalton, down a cobbled lane, is the very charming *Le Doyen* 11 rue Doyen (Tel 21 30 13 08), closed Wednesday evening and Sunday; located on two floors, with a decor that is extremely homely and cosy. Menus begin at 90F and there's a good mix of fish and meat dishes, all superbly prepared and attractively presented. Scallops meunière or with a saffron sauce, monkfish with a delicate garlic sauce or beautifully pink rack of lamb with mushrooms and duck breast with a honey glaze are all typical. The dessert speciality is a super chocolate tart, served warm, with extra-fine pastry and a layer of dark chocolate topped with a soft baked custard.

Five kilometres north of Boulogne, following the easy coastal route, you arrive at the village of Wimereux. On the main street through the village is *L'Epicure*, 1 rue Gare (Tel 21 83 21 83) closed Sunday and Wednesday, a beautiful restaurant decorated in peach and deep blue. Menus begin at 140F and include well prepared modern dishes whose flavours are extraordinarily good. Typical dishes are a delicious salt pork terrine with leeks and an aubergine purée blended with walnut-flavoured vinegar, langoustines sautéed gently in butter served with roast potatoes and deep-fried sage and sea-bream with artichokes and a hint of aniseed. Instead of a cheese course they serve an excellent creamy fromage blanc sorbet and sweets include warm rhubarb with a honey and lemon sauce or a chocolate parfait with cinnamon syrup and candied orange peel.

London

N16   01 Adana   £30

Tel 071-704 6404   **R**

91 Green Lanes Newington Green N16 9BX   **Map 16 D2**

01 is the car registration number for the south-western Turkish city
of Adana. An odd name, indeed, but the style of cooking offered here
originates from the area. Good, well-cooked Turkish classics begin with
lahmacun, a starter of Turkish-style pizza topped with tender minced lamb
and followed by a kebab of boned lamb fillet or an Adana kebab (spicy,
minced lamb) served with a thick, rich and creamy yoghurt. Staff are
friendly and genuinely try their best to be helpful. *Seats 50. Parties 20.
Meals 12-12.* AMERICAN EXPRESS *Access, Diners, Visa.*

W2   Abbey Court   £148

Tel 071-221 7518   Fax 071-792 0858   **PH**

20 Pembridge Gardens W2 4DU   **Map 18 A3**

Efficient staff, good-quality furniture and eye-catching flower arrangements
are the hallmarks of good hotel-keeping in this friendly establishment – a
classic townhouse hotel. It's a five-storey Victorian building in a quiet street
only a few minutes from Notting Hill Gate. Public rooms are limited
to a smart reception area and a conservatory where cooked breakfast
is served and there's an honesty bar. The individually styled and decorated
bedrooms have antiques, Italian marble, whirlpool baths and towelling
robes. Top of the range are the four-poster rooms. 24hr room service.
No children under 12. *Rooms 22.* AMERICAN EXPRESS *Access, Diners, Visa.*

W2   L'Accento Italiano   ↑   £55

Tel 071-243 2201   **R**

16 Garway Road W2 4NH   **Map 18 A3**

Just off Westbourne Grove, the restaurant is particularly noisy when busy
(which is most of the time), mainly because the walls are bare and front
is all glass. Though the decor can be described as minimalist, the food
is anything but – satisfying and decent-size portions of modern rustic
North Italian cooking, commencing with a variety of breads served with
superior virgin olive oil and starters such as bread tart with aubergine,
mozzarella cheese and tomato sauce, ravioli triangles stuffed with pumpkin,
sage butter and Parmesan, or basil taglioni with lobster, tomato and fresh
herbs. For an additional £1.50 starters can be served as main courses – in
their own right. These include fillet of sea bass baked in a foil parcel, osso
buco with saffron risotto, and pan-fried duck breast with apple sauce.
There's also a two-course set menu with three choices in each section
(timballo of polenta with mushrooms, bacon and tomato sauce, followed
by grilled baby chicken with mixed herbs). Desserts might feature an apple
tart, tiramisu or chilled ricotta pudding with white and dark chocolate.
Splendid coffee as you would expect, an inexpensive wine list, and laid-
back service which is cheerfully efficient; when all this is added to the
excellent cooking, you have a premier division restaurant. New rear
conservatory area features a sliding roof for alfresco eating. *Seats 70.
Parties 30. Private Room 30. L 12.30-2.30 D 6.30-11.30 (Sun to 10.30).
Closed Bank Holidays. Set meals £10.50. Access, Visa.*

W12   Adam's Café   £30

Tel 081-743 0572   **R**

77 Askew Road W12   **Map 17 A4**

Frances and Abdel Boukraa have a recipe for success here – English café
by day, Tunisian restaurant by night. Popular starters are the filo pastry
brik filled with an egg, plus tuna, vegetables or seafood. Speciality main
courses are of course couscous, with either lamb, or vegetables, or both
together plus beef meatballs. There are also grilled mullet, king prawns,

and spicy merguez and, to finish, pastries, sorbets or a hot lemon pancake. Wines from Tunisia and Morocco accompany the robust food. *Seats 60. Parties 36. Private Room 24. D only 7-11. Closed Sun, Bank Holidays. No credit cards.*

SW7	**Adelphi Hotel**	**62%**	£112
Tel 071-373 7177 Fax 071-373 7720			**H**
127 Cromwell Road SW7 4DT			Map 19 A5

Smart white-painted period-style hotel on a busy corner of Cromwell Road, with its main entrance in Courtfield Gardens. Accommodation includes Executive rooms and suites. Three conference suites hold up to 70. *Rooms 68.* AMERICAN EXPRESS *Access, Diners, Visa.*

WC2	**Ajimura**	£60
Tel 071-240 0178		**R**
51 Shelton Street WC2H 9HE		Map 21 B1

Sushi and sashimi are the specialities at a popular Japanese restaurant which sticks mainly to familiar dishes with a healthy slant. Chef Susumu Okada founded Ajimura in 1972, and its 23 years make it the longest established Japanese restaurant in Britain. Pre-theatre dinner served Mon-Fri, 6-7.30. The sake served here is specially imported from Mr Okada's home town of Takamatsu. *Seats 58. Private Room 20. L 12-3 D 6-11. Closed L Sat, all Sun, Bank Holidays. Set L from £8 Set D from £13 (6-7.30).* AMERICAN EXPRESS *Access, Diners, Visa.*

W8	**Al Basha**	£70
Tel 071-938 1794 Fax 071-937 3405		**R**
Troy Court 222 Kensington High Street W8 5RG		Map 19 A4

Lebanese restaurant with the accent on comfort and good service. The outdoor seating area has now been covered with a glass conservatory extension. Meze is a house speciality. 15% service is added to all bills. *Seats 140. Private Room 65. Meals 12-12.* AMERICAN EXPRESS *Access, Diners, Visa.*

SW1	**Al Bustan**	£60
Tel 071-235 8277		**R**
27 Motcomb Street Belgravia SW1X 8JU		Map 19 C4

One of the prettiest and best of London's Lebanese restaurants. A generous plateful of salad items is as crisp and fresh as the summery decor. A robust selection of hot and cold hors d'oeuvre accounts for more than half the menu: tabouleh, fish roe with olive oil and garlic, fried or blended baked aubergines, samosas, mini-sausages, grilled chicken wings, grilled quails, lamb's brains, lamb's kidneys. Main courses mostly come from the charcoal grill, though there are four options using raw lamb. Sweet Lebanese pastries, seasonal fresh fruits and *oum ali* – a Middle Eastern version of bread-and-butter pudding. *Seats 70. Meals noon-11pm (Sun to 10pm). Closed 25 & 26 Dec.* AMERICAN EXPRESS *Access, Diners, Visa.*

W1	**Al Hamra**	£55
Tel 071-493 1954		**R**
31 Shepherd Market W1Y 7RJ		Map 18 C3

In the heart of Shepherd Market, this is one of London's best-known and most popular Lebanese restaurants, with close-set tables and outside eating for 20 in fine weather. Munch on crunchy salad, olives and bread while awaiting your meal – typically a selection of hot and cold hors d'oeuvre, something from the charcoal grill and, if you're still not replete, a honey-sticky sweet or two. *Seats 65. Meals 12-12. Closed 25 Dec & 1 Jan.* AMERICAN EXPRESS *Access, Diners, Visa.*

W2   Al San Vincenzo   ★   £70
Tel 071-262 9623   R
30 Connaught Street W2 2AF   **Map 18 B2**

A modest, almost stark, seven-table restaurant close to Marble Arch, with
red and orange candy-striped loose-covered chairs providing almost the
only decorative colour – it's Vincenzo Borgonzolo's food that takes centre
stage, along with service from Elaine and Angela. Vincenzo, born
in Naples, works almost singlehandedly in the downstairs kitchen,
producing Italian dishes with a difference. Traditional bourgeois dishes are
subtly modernised using top-quality ingredients, although this is not
a restaurant to follow the latest fads and trends. Interesting pasta might
include *le vere penne all'arrabbiata* (with pecorino and Parmesan, basil,
peperoncino and pancetta) or "hand-made spaghetti from Puglia" with
fresh clams. Pumpkin, rice, courgettes, peas and Parmesan are transmuted
into a glorious *minestra*, alongside other starters like braised artichoke hearts
with black olives, tuna *carpaccio*, slices of roast chicken with Cremona
mustard, luganega sausage with cannellini beans, and octopus casseroled
with parsley and white wine. Half a dozen or so main courses might
include a salt cod and potato stew, roasted English grey-legged partridge
with grapes and chestnuts, thin slices of beef slowly cooked in a traditional
pizzaiola sauce, *zampone, cotechino e lenticchie* (pig's trotters, pork sausage
and lentils), and a daily fresh fish dish such as pan-fried fillets of red mullet
spread with a thin layer of smooth basil pesto and surrounded by pine
kernels cooked in olive oil with the carefully pounded livers – a brilliant
touch. Vincenzo's innovative and original hand extends to the desserts,
which include his unmissably delicious panettone bread pudding – slices
of panettone dribbled with Cinzano bianco, before being baked with
a sauce of mascarpone, eggs, vin Santo, cinnamon and orange juice – the
result is a rich, moist, creamy creation; hot compote of dried fruits with
spices, semifreddo of chocolate with a sauce of wild berries, panforte and
cantuccini with vin Santo, mango and dolcelatte. Superb organic Italian
farmhouse cheeses – a glass of sweet *aleatico di Puglia* is recommended
to complement it. The carefully chosen wines are exclusively Italian – one
can commence a meal with a glass of *prosecco* (with cassis, peach, pear
or apricot for the house aperitif), moving on through either a dozen or so
reasonably priced wines or a handful of superior reds. **Seats** *22. Parties 4.
L 12.30-2 D 7-10.15. Closed L Sat, all Sun, 2 weeks Christmas. Access, Visa.*

W1   Alastair Little   ★ ★   £85
Tel 071-734 5183   R
49 Frith Street Soho W1V 5TE   **Map 21 A2**

Alastair Little's Soho restaurant is a haven of modern gastronomy. The
stark monochrome fittings are offset only by the modern artwork on the
walls and the whole operation has an air of informality and lack
of pretension that is anathema to some (considering the final bill) but mecca
to others. The intrinsic simplicity of the concept gives no indication as to
the experience, involvement and dedication of the retiring Alastair and his
team of chefs headed by Jeremy Lee. None of the usual two-star pleasantries
like canapés, amuse-gueule or petits fours are to be found here, just a basket
of superb Neal's Yard breads including excellent poppy, sesame and linseed
bread left on the table. As well as the extensive à la carte handwritten
in tight script there's a no-choice 3-course lunch upstairs (crostini of herbed
tomatoes and chicken livers, fillet of Irish sea trout with grilled vegetables
and a butter sauce, panettone bread-and-butter pudding or cheeses) and a 2-
course £10 menu (with a choice: perhaps *pasta fagioli* or charcuterie
followed by braised lamb or Italian sausage with polenta) in the bar
downstairs. The main carte changes daily, offering at least a dozen choices
from which to start dinner: fish soup with mussels and clams, marinated
goat's cheese salad with spicy breadcrumbs, potato pancake with black
pudding, apples and red cabbage, pressed skate terrine with French bean
and red onion salad, or bruschetta with new season's butter beans,

rocket and Parmesan. Follow with magret of duck with parmentier potatoes, rosemary and shallot sauce; pan-fried scallops with stir-fried vegetables, coriander and chili; supreme of brill with 'aromates' and a cream sauce; fillet of red mullet with parsley, grilled artichokes and tomato salad; or medallions of beef with polenta and green sauce. Pacific oysters with shallot relish and spicy sausages – Thai-inspired balls of lightly pan-fried pork, chili, lemon grass, ginger, garlic, lime leaves and fish sauce – and Bresse pigeon with braised cabbage and zampone are considered specialities. Flavours and textures are cleverly balanced, and a sure hand is clearly at work when risotto is cooked to a creamy perfection and sea bass is roasted until its skin is crisp yet the flesh remains moist and succulent; the dish may then be served on a flat-leaf parsley salad with a riot of Mediterranean ingredients and flavours: sun-dried tomatoes, black olives and extra-fine capers with Parmesan, parsley and olive crumbs. To finish, either Spanish or British cheeses or simple classics such as crème brulée, tiramisu, cherry and almond and quince tart with crème fraiche or chocolate brownie with fudge sauce and ice cream. Excluding champagnes, there are only half a dozen wines over £30 and only four half bottles on the short, but otherwise fairly-priced, wine list. *Seats 55. Parties 10. L 12-3 D 6-11.30. Closed L Sat, all Sun, Christmas & Bank Holidays. Set L £10 (basement only) & £25.* AMERICAN EXPRESS *Access, Visa.*

EC1 Alba £60

Tel 071-588 1798 **R**
107 Whitecross Street EC1Y 8JD **Map 16 D3**

Northern Italian is the cooking style at this friendly place close to the Barbican centre. The menu starts at *insalata di campo* ('a green salad of wild and interesting lettuces') and runs through pasta and a couple of fish dishes to breast of chicken in a balsamic vinegar and rosemary sauce, braised rabbit with polenta and grilled lamb cutlets served with mixed mushrooms. Desserts from the trolley, Italian cheeses served with pears. Coffee served with Cantucci biscuits. *Seats 40. L 12-3 D 6-11. Closed Sat, Sun, Bank Holidays, 1 week Christmas.* AMERICAN EXPRESS *Access, Diners, Visa.*

SW3 Albero & Grana ↑ £70

Tel 071-225 1048 Fax 071-581 3259 **R**
Chelsea Cloisters 89 Sloane Avenue SW3 3DX **Map 19 B5**

Spanish food gets a welcome update in this stylish and fashionable restaurant designed by Jose Antonio Garcia. An undulating back wall has the Seville sand colour of the bullring, another wall is of glass bricks and the ceiling is tented with striped cotton ticking. The short evening menu (in Spanish and English) proposes beautifully prepared dishes such as salmon and endive salad, lasagne of black pudding with a green pepper sauce and cold escabeche of duck liver among the starters (entradas) and main courses like scallops served with ratatouille, gilthead baked in sea salt, pork fillet with roast stuffed apples and (a speciality) veal kidney and liver on a black olive sauce. Don't miss the super desserts – perhaps nougat ice cream on a chocolate sauce or caramelised pastry horn filled with honey ice cream and fruits. A loud and busy bar at the front serves traditional tapas lunchtime and evening (from 6pm). The wine list sticks to Spanish wines and sherries, both groups expertly annotated. *Seats 120. L (tapas) 12.30-3 D 7.30 (tapas from 6)-11.30. Closed L Sun, some Bank Holidays.* AMERICAN EXPRESS *Access, Diners, Visa.*

SW7 Alexander Hotel 64% £117

Tel 071-581 1591 Fax 071-581 0824 **H**
9 Sumner Place South Kensington SW7 3EE **Map 19 B5**

Well located in the centre of South Kensington, the Alexander offers quiet accommodation behind an elegant 19th-century town house frontage. Bedroom prices start at £90 (single) and end with £212 for the suite.

A large patio makes an attractive, cool retreat in summer days. Bar and breakfast room are in the basement. No restaurant. No dogs. *Rooms 36.* AMERICAN EXPRESS *Access, Diners, Visa.*

W1   alistair Greig's Grill   £90
Tel 071-629 5613   Fax 071-495 0411   **R**
26 Bruton Place Mayfair W1X 7AA   **Map 18 C3**

Prime Scotch steaks and grills have been the speciality here for 30 years; all are simply grilled with a traditional accompaniment of grilled tomato, button mushrooms and watercress. Behind the red door there's red plush and old-fashioned civility. The set lunch includes a glass of wine. Half bottles are in short supply on the quite pricey wine list. *Seats 60. Parties 30. L 12.30-2.30 D 6.30-11. Closed L Sat, all Sun, 25 & 26 Dec, 1 Jan. Set L £19.50.* AMERICAN EXPRESS *Access, Diners, Visa.*

W11   L'Altro   £60
Tel 071-792 1066   **R**
210 Kensington Park Road W11   **Map 16 B3**

A glass front encloses a stylish recreation of a very Italianate courtyard complete with authentic wall lamps and trompe l'oeil stone walls and classical statues. A sister to *Cibo* (qv), *L'Altro* specialises in seafood prepared simply in the modern Italian manner. The evening menu, which changes daily, could include red mullet wrapped in Parma ham and rosemary, baked sea bream with fennel, and lobster, prawns, langoustines and scallops grilled with pine kernels and basil. Lunch is in the same style, and there is now an antipasto bar. *Seats 43. Parties 20. L 12-2.30 (Sat to 3.30) D 7-11 (Fri & Sat to 11.30). Closed D Sun, Bank Holidays, Christmas, Easter.* AMERICAN EXPRESS *Access, Diners, Visa.*

N1   Anna's Place   £45
Tel 071-249 9379   **R**
90 Mildmay Park Newington Green N1 4PR   **Map 16 D2**

Anna Hegarty's cheerful, informal restaurant is as popular now as when she opened it nearly 20 years ago. The chief reason is the enjoyable, unpretentious food, which includes specialities from Anna's native Sweden. Among these are marinated herrings, gravad lax (a favourite here long before it became ubiquitous), biff Strindberg (diced fillet of beef marinated in Swedish mustard and served with cucumber salad) and waffles with blueberry compote and cream. Other choices always include a vegetarian and a fish dish of the day, and game in season. The menu states that 'all our meat is conservation grade'. *Seats 40. Parties 12. L 12.15-2.15 D 7.15-10.45. Closed Sun, Mon, 1 week Christmas, 2 weeks Easter, Aug. No credit cards.*

W8   Apollo Hotel   £68
Tel 071-835 1133   Fax 071-370 4853   **H**
18-22 Lexham Gardens Kensington W8 5JE   **Map 19 A5**

Long-established bed and breakfast hotel off Cromwell Road (the main road heading west from London) offering decent accommodation with few frills. All rooms have private facilities, TVs and dial-out phones. One child up to 12 can stay free in parents' room. *Rooms 50. Closed Christmas/New Year.* AMERICAN EXPRESS *Access, Diners, Visa.*

W8   Arcadia   NEW   £65
Tel 071-937 4292   Fax 071-937 4393   **R**
Kensington Court 35 Kensington High Street W8 5EB   **Map 19 A4**

Et in Arcadia ego – and very pleasant it is, too. All links with the restaurant previously on the site have been severed, in terms of both decor and cooking. It now looks quite cool and elegant in cream and green, with

smart lightwood for floor and furnishings and a constellation of tiny ceiling
lights. The basement area is in similar style, and in summer the tables
outside are popular. The new co-owner and chef is Nicky Barraclough,
whose multi-cultural cooking background accounts for a menu of more
than usual interest, definable as modern British. Among the dishes available
on early visits were baked ricotta with a salad of Parmesan and pine nuts,
roasted tomato soup with pesto, grilled sole béarnaise, corn-fed guinea fowl
roasted with lemon and served with lentils, cod and smoked haddock
fishcakes with green herb mayonnaise and lamb braised with ginger and
cinnamon, onions and tomatoes, served with basmati rice. The list
of desserts, which included strawberry shortcake, elderflower sorbet and
pear and brown ginger butter tart, was supplemented by a daily special –
rice pudding with cherry compote – which provided an instant trip at least
halfway back to nursery. Salads are interestingly varied (tiny chive flowers
and diced shallots among the leaves), and punchily dressed, fried items spot-
on, sauces and mayonnaises smoothly rich. Most of the starters are also
available as main courses. Launched by dedicated new owners and
professional management, Arcadia looks all set for success. *Seats 80.*
Private Room 16. L 12-2.30 D 6.30-11.15. Set L £13.50/£16.
Closed L Sat & Sun, 2 days Easter, 25 & 26 Dec. AMERICAN EXPRESS *Access, Visa.*

SW3	**The Argyll**	£50
Tel 071-352 0025		**R**
316 Kings Road Chelsea SW3 5UH		Map 19 B6

A change of chef and a change of target has simplified the menu and
brought down the prices at a restaurant which has become a trendy Chelsea
favourite. And that's the way it will probably stay with its new, highly
approachable selection of fashionable dishes: bright, intensely flavoured
roast tomato and red pepper soup served chilled, onion French toast with
wild mushrooms, roast foie gras with cucumber and onion bhaji, tagliatelle
with clams (available as starter or main course), baked lemon sole with
garlic and parsley, chargrilled brill with olive mash and pesto, baby
chicken with spinach and balsamico. Apricot compote with mascarpone ice
cream and white chocolate marquise with dark chocolate sauce are more-
than-appealing desserts. The room is pale (and cool in summer, when the
doors are thrown back), with white linen, plain glass, slim cutlery and soup
plates for most of the meals. The downstairs basement Po-Na-Na-Souk bar
is even trendier than the Argyll itself. *Seats 55. L 12-2.30 D 7-11.15*
(Fri & Sat 6.30-12). Closed L Mon, all Sun, Bank Holidays.
Set L £12.50/£15. AMERICAN EXPRESS *Access, Diners, Visa.*

W1	**Arirang Korean Restaurant**	£50
Tel 071-437 6633		**R**
31 Poland Street W1V 3DB		Map 18 D2

Pleasant service accompanies the fiery flavours of Korean cuisine on the
fringes of Soho. Bulgogi – thinly sliced marinated beef – is the national
dish, while among the more intriguing items are bracken stalks, a pizza
made of ground green peas and wings of skate in a hot chili sauce.
Seats 100. Private Room 30. L 12-3 D 6-11. Closed L Bank Holidays, all Sun,
25 & 26 Dec, 1 & 2 Jan. Set meals from £19.50. AMERICAN EXPRESS *Access,*
Diners, Visa.

W1	**Arisugawa**	£60
Tel 071-636 8913 Fax 071-323 4237		**R**
27 Percy Street W1P 9FF		Map 18 D2

The first choice of many Japanese diners, this smart modern restaurant
in a basement has a menu of more than usual interest. The à la carte
selection contains many unfamiliar dishes (fried sliced burdock roots, boiled
black seaweed, grilled ox tongue), while the set menus are a better bet for
the less adventurous. Teppan cuisine is offered in the ground-floor room,

traditional Japanese in the basement. *Seats 100. Private Room 20. L 12.30-2.30 D 6-10 (Sat to 9.30). Closed L Sat, all Sun, Bank Holidays, Christmas/New Year. Set L from £4.50 Set D from £20.* *Access, Diners, Visa.*

W8   The Ark   £45
Tel 071-229 4024   **R**
122 Palace Gardens Terrace Notting Hill Gate W8 4RT   Map 18 A3

Wood-built neighbourhood restaurant at Notting Hill Gate. The menu retains many of its original (70s) dishes by popular demand – fish pie, liver with sage and bacon, rack of lamb, steak and kidney pie – but also manages to move with the times with the likes of smoked haddock quenelles, or chick pea fritters with aubergines. Chocolate pot and crème brulée are the favourite desserts. Go early in the evening, or book. *Seats 75. Private Room 27. L 12-3 D 6.30-11.15. Closed D Sun, L Bank Holidays, 4 days Christmas. Set L £7.50/£9.75 Set Sun L £10.50.* *Access, Diners, Visa.*

N8   Les Associés   £60
Tel 081-348 8944   **R**
172 Park Road Crouch End N8 8GT   Map 16 C1

Small, cosy and run by three partners, *les associés*, the restaurant serves enjoyably prepared, marginally modernised bourgeois French cooking from a short menu supplemented by a list of the day's specials. Duck confit with grenadine sauce, monkfish with orange and roast shoulder of kid with sage are typical. *Seats 38. Parties 15. L 12.30-2 D 7.30-10. Closed L Tues & Sat, D Mon, all Sun, 1 week Christmas, 1 week Easter, all Aug. Set L £15.95. Access, Visa.*

SW7   Aster House   £91
Tel 071-581 5888   Fax 071-584 4925   **H**
3 Sumner Place South Kensington SW7 3EE   Map 19 B5

A home-from-home at the end of an early-Victorian terrace, run since 1982 by Mr and Mrs Carapiet. Bed and breakfast is offered, with rooms ranging from small singles to a four-poster studio suite, all with private bath/shower, TVs, dial-out phones, fridges and mini-safes. A health-conscious buffet breakfast is served in a delightful, sometimes sunny first-floor conservatory. No smoking. Unlicensed. No children under 12 except babies in cots. No dogs. Minimum booking for two nights, with (most unusually) full payment expected in advance in order to "discourage insincere reservations". *Rooms 12. Garden. Access, Visa.*

Note that all telephone numbers with area codes starting with 0 will start 01 from 16 April 1995.

NW1   Asuka   £70
Tel 071-486 5026   **R**
209a Baker Street NW1 6AB   Map 18 C2

In an arcade at the northern end of Baker Street, Asuka is also the name of a traditional Japanese feast of soup, seven dishes and fruit. That's at the top of the price range, but there's plenty more to choose from, notably the speciality 'saucepan dishes' prepared at the table. These include home-made wheat noodles with seafood, meat or duck and vegetables in a thick broth. *Seats 60. L 12-2.30 D 6-10.30. Closed L Sat, all Sun, Bank Holidays, Christmas, New Year. Set L from £13.50 Set D from £23.90.* *Access, Diners, Visa.*

W1   The Athenaeum £200

Tel 071-499 3464   Fax 071-493 1860   **H**

116 Piccadilly W1V 0BJ   Map 18 C3

Overlooking Green Park a few paces from Hyde Park Corner, the hotel has been undergoing major refurbishment with completion due after we go to press. Public areas will have been completely remodelled with a new clubby restaurant and lounge. In the basement is a brand new leisure complex with a gym, spa pool, sauna, steam room and beauty treatment for hotel residents. The accommodation, which includes 33 fully serviced one-bedroom apartments, is also being given a major facelift. The hotel was graded at 78% in our 1994 guide. *Rooms 156.* AMERICAN EXPRESS *Access, Diners, Visa.*

W8   Atlas Hotel £68

Tel 071-835 1155   Fax 071-370 4853   **H**

24-30 Lexham Gardens Kensington W8 5JE   Map 19 A5

Neighbour of the Apollo Hotel (see p. 110), in the same ownership, with the same facilities. *Rooms 50. Closed Christmas/New Year.* AMERICAN EXPRESS *Access, Diners, Visa.*

NW8   Au Bois St Jean £70

Tel 071-722 0400   Fax 071-586 0410   **R**

122 St John's Wood High Street NW8 7SG   Map 18 B1

Down below a wine bar-cum-bistro is a rustic little restaurant. Intimate, and abounding with dark timber, the impression is of being in a wood – one that is forever autumn. Huge bunches of dried flowers and twigs hang from the beams and pillars while small oil lamps glitter on the tables. In contrast, the menu has the summer flavour of the Mediterranean. Starters include a garlicky Sétois fish soup, lasagne filled with salmon and spinach with a vermouth sauce and aubergine and courgette terrine with a leek sauce. There are fish dishes such as succulent salmon fillet baked in pastry with a dill sauce or grilled red mullet with ratatouille and a red pepper sauce, while meat dishes feature roast rack of lamb with Provençal herbs and garlic butter or a finely flavoured guinea fowl supreme stuffed with vegetables and served with a creamy saffron sauce. Prices are for the number of courses taken. A pianist tinkles away in the evenings and staff are amiable and on the ball. *Seats 60. Parties 25. Private Room 60. D only 7-11.30. Closed 3 days Christmas, 2 days Easter. Set D £18.50/£23.50.* AMERICAN EXPRESS *Access, Diners, Visa.*

W1   Au Jardin des Gourmets £75

Tel 071-437 1816   Fax 071-437 0043   **R**

5 Greek Street Soho W1V 5LA   Map 21 A2

Positioned amidst Soho's culinary revival, this long-established restaurant now operates as two distinct dining rooms. At street level, the *salle à manger*: dark red walls, big Chinese-style mirrors and close-set tables fill the room. Brasserie-style dishes predominate here – hot tomato and olive tart (barely warm when we tried it), Toulouse sausage with Puy lentils, or perhaps confit of duck. The set menu offers particularly good value, with three choices at each course. Upstairs, a comfortable and more formal setting, with a more elaborate and expansive menu. Cassolette of snails with *marchand de vin* sauce, a steamed selection of fish with spring onions and ginger, or a trio of game with three sauces (oddly, perhaps, still available at the end of May) are typical choices. A few dishes must be ordered between two, such as ribs of beef with béarnaise sauce. Unobtrusive service, but can be stretched at lunchtime, particularly downstairs. Exceptional selection of clarets on a super wine list that is predominantly French, though the rest of Europe and the New World are making modest inroads.

See over

Seats 150. Parties 12. Private Rooms 50. L 12.15-2.30 D 6-11.15.
Closed L Sat, all Sun, D Bank Holidays. Set meals £13.50/£17.50/£21.50.
AMERICAN EXPRESS *Access, Diners, Visa.*

| SW10 | Aubergine | ★ ↑ | NEW | £85 |

Tel 071-352 3449   Fax 071-351 1770   **R**

11 Park Walk SW10 0AJ   **Map 19 B5**

With Marco Pierre White a very public backer and chef/patron Gordon
Ramsay a very public protégé of Marco, Aubergine was never going
to lack publicity, and Ramsay's cooking has done the rest. He trained most
informatively with Marco but has also had stints with Roux restaurants,
in Paris with Savoy and Robuchon and finally a short spell with Pierre
Koffmann. The place is booked for dinner quite a way ahead, and as yet
front of house does not run as smoothly as the kitchen. Ramsay's dishes are
extremely well conceived and superbly, often brilliantly, executed:
ballotine of foie gras is an elegant disc with a port jelly perimeter, the foie
gras rich but not heart-stoppingly so, the jelly assertive but not bullying;
cappuccino of haricot blanc with truffle oil is at once subtle and
voluptuous; tortellini of lobster (a speciality) combines soft, delicate pasta
with a shellfish filling just strong enough in flavour and a warm, entirely
apt *vinaigrette crustacés*. Soup of watercress with poached oysters, salad
of roasted wood pigeon with wild mushrooms, millefeuille of tuna with
a confit of tomatoes, vinaigrette of vegetables 'pressé' and tian of scallops
and leeks with sauce champagne completed the choice of eight starters
on a typical one-price-only, three-course menu. To follow, a red mullet dish
comprises a little 'castle' of small fillets built up on a foundation
of aubergine caviar and topped with tiny braised leeks and little beignets
of sage; the castle is surrounded by a punchy Mediterranean moat of olive
oil, chopped olives, anchovies and tomatoes that would get the better
of many fish but proves an excellent mate for the full-flavoured mullet.
Completing the main-course picture might be a pavé of brill with duxelles
of girolles, steamed fillet of sea bass with braised fennel hearts and
a tarragon jus, pigeon 'poché grillé with purée of swede, wild mushroom
ravioli and a tarragon jus, ribeye of Scotch beef, roast rump of lamb niçoise
with millefeuille of aubergine (at last!), guinea fowl 'en cocotte' with
tagliatelle of leeks and caramelised calf's sweetbreads with a *navet* (turnip)
confit. Tarte tatin of pears makes a sensational ending to a great meal; other
dessert choices might include orange tart, crème brulée with 'jus Granny
Smith', millefeuille of vanilla with red fruit, *pavé chocolat* or French cheeses;
assiette de l'Aubergine (for two diners) is a little of everything for the
indulgent or the indecisive! Petits fours served with coffee. Quite
reasonable prices on the modest wine list; room for greater depth
to accompany cooking of this standard. Already one of London's hottest
tickets, Aubergine is destined to join the greats when the service catches
up with the cooking. **Seats** 40. *Parties 10. L 12-2.30 D 7-11. Closed L Sat,
all Sun. Set L £18 Set D £26.* **AMERICAN EXPRESS** *Access, Visa.*

> ⌇ is our symbol for an outstanding wine list.

| NW8 | L'Aventure | | £65 |

Tel 071-624 6232   **R**

3 Blenheim Terrace NW8 0EH   **Map 16 B3**

Owner Catherine Parisot's personality is stamped all over this delightful
little French restaurant with a terrace for summer eating. In a friendly,
intimate atmosphere a short, appealing daily-changing menu offers classical
French cooking such as *parfait de champignons, turbot roti à l'huile de homard,
coquilles St Jacques florentine, canard roti au miel et au thym*, with puddings
like *tarte fine au citron* and *parfait à la nougatine*. **Seats** 45. *L 12.30-2.30
D 7.30-10.30 (Sun to 10). Closed L Sat, 1 week Christmas, 4 days Easter.
Set L £18.50 Set D £25.* **AMERICAN EXPRESS** *Access, Diners, Visa.*

W11   Avenue West Eleven   NEW   £60

Tel 071-221 8144   **R**

157 Notting Hill Gate W11 3LF   Map 18 A3

This sibling to *Brasserie du Marché aux Puces* (qv) has interesting, though minimalist decoration. Mark Hill's vaguely nautical wood and lead structures punctuate the bare walls and berber carpets cover tables whose top cloths are of brown paper. An inventive and eclectic menu might begin with coconut Thai fry with sesame seeds and teriyaki, roast red onion with beetroot and red cabbage salad with hot black pudding, or delicious Dorset crab set in a Chinese-style pancake with shiitake mushrooms and bean curd. Perhaps rabbit and wild mushroom open raviolo with a champagne and mustard sauce, parrot-fish with a dill and lemon gin sauce or the unlikely combination of marinated venison noisette with passion fruit and chocolate tagliatelle to follow. Desserts such as chocolate truffle cake and apple tart are supplemented by devils on horseback or Welsh rarebit on excellent brioche. Always interesting offerings for vegetarians. *Seats 56. L 12-3.15 D 6.30-11.15. Closed Bank Holidays, 4 days Christmas.* AMERICAN EXPRESS® *Access, Visa.*

W1   Bahn Thai   £60

Tel 071-437 8504   **R**

21a Frith Street Soho W1V 5TS   Map 21 A2

Kensington was the original (1981) location of Bahn Thai, and in its Soho premises the aim is unchanged – to prepare and present authentic Thai cooking. The menu has plenty of guidance notes on ordering a Thai meal, making this a useful place to go for those new to the cuisine. For those already familiar with the genre, though, there are equally enticing choices, some not often found on Thai menus, like wild boar, venison, calf's liver and frogs' legs, as well as the less surprising chicken, prawns, scallops and beef. The set meals are excellent for larger groups. *Seats 120. Private Room 50. L 12-2.45 (Sun 12.30-2.30) D 6-11.15 (Sun 6.30-10.30). Closed all Bank Holidays.* AMERICAN EXPRESS® *Diners, Access, Visa.*

W12   Balzac Bistro Restaurant   £50

Tel 081-743 5370   **R**

4 Wood Lane Shepherds Bush W12 7DT   Map 17 B4

Old-fashioned bistro dishes continue to please the regulars at a long-popular restaurant just up from Shepherds Bush Green. French onion soup, grilled mushrooms, asparagus hollandaise, lamb cutlets with garlic, rabbit chasseur and lemon sole dugléré show the style. Main courses are accompanied by copious vegetables, perhaps sauté potatoes, red cabbage and battered courgettes. The decor includes many French knick-knacks, café parasols at some of the tables and signed photographs of visiting stars (the BBC studios are just up the road). *Seats 80. Parties 16. Private Room 60. L 12-2.30 D 7-11. Closed L Sat, all Sun, some Bank Holidays, 10 days after Christmas. Set L & D £9.50/£13.90.* AMERICAN EXPRESS® *Access, Diners, Visa.*

SW7   Bangkok   £40

Tel 071-584 8529   Fax 071-823 7883   **R**

9 Bute Street South Kensington SW7 3EY   Map 19 B5

A long-established Thai restaurant, the Bangkok is sparsely appointed and has been run by the same family since its opening in 1967. The short menu includes beef and pork satay, minced beef omelette, fried prawns, spare ribs, beef and chicken curry and Thai rice-noodles. *Seats 56. Parties 20. L 12.15-2.15 D 7-11.15. Closed Sun, Bank Holidays, Chrsitmas. Set L from £12.50. Access, Visa.*

SW13　Bangkok Garden　NEW

Tel 081-392 9158

R

£35

8 Rocks Lane Barnes SW13 0DB

Map 17 A5

50-seater Thai restaurant in shades of brown and tan behind a huge plate-glass window. The menu, printed on strips of bamboo, offers a fair cross-section of Thai cuisine plus guidance notes on eating Thai food. *Seats 50. L 12-3 D 6-11. Set D £14.95 (min 2).* AMERICAN EXPRESS *Access, Diners, Visa.*

SW15　Bangkok Symphonie　NEW

Tel 081-789 4304

R

£35

141 Upper Richmond Road Putney SW15 2RF

Map 17 B5

Spot the red and gold exterior of a delightful Thai restaurant where the South Circular meets Putney High Street. Inside, charming staff serve a good selection of their native cuisine to the gentle accompaniment of classical music. The menu is full of musical references, with the customer designated as the conductor. *Seats 40. L 12-3 D 6-11.15.* AMERICAN EXPRESS *Access, Diners, Visa.*

SE3　Bardon Lodge　56%

Tel 081-853 4051　Fax 081-858 7387

H

£74

15 Stratheden Road Blackheath SE3 7TH

Map 17 D5

Just off the A2 and conveniently close to the A102(M), the hotel, which has easy access on to Blackheath Common, also offers cosy, homely comforts. Rooms are neatly maintained and all are double-glazed. All but four with showers have baths. There's also a quite separate annexe across on another road; here there's only limited service and guests have to return to the main building for meals. *Rooms 60. Garden.* AMERICAN EXPRESS *Access, Diners, Visa.*

SW3　Basil Street Hotel　71%

Tel 071-581 3311　Fax 071-581 3693

H

£187

Basil Street Knightsbridge SW3 1AH

Map 19 C4

An Edwardian English atmosphere pervades a privately-owned hotel 'just 191 steps' from Harrods (and almost the same from Harvey Nichols!). Public areas have a country house feel, from the antique-lined corridor leading to the dining room to the spacious lounge in sunny yellow with rug-covered polished parquet floor. Well-kept bedrooms are of a good size, usually with a sitting area, traditionally furnished and decorated with understated good taste; most have equally roomy private bathrooms. Family accommodation can cater for up to two adults and three children in two rooms, sharing one bathroom; alternatively, children under 16 may share their parents' room free. Old-fashioned standards of courteous and obliging service include shoe cleaning, servicing of rooms in the evenings and 24hr room service. The Parrot Club is a unique ladies-only retreat, ideal for lunch or tea. 24hr NCP car park within 100 yds. *Rooms 93. Coffee shop (12-3).* AMERICAN EXPRESS *Access, Diners, Visa.*

SW3　The Beaufort

Tel 071-584 5252　Fax 071-589 2834

PH

£140

33 Beaufort Gardens Knightsbridge SW3 1PP

Map 19 C4

In a quiet, tree-lined cul-de-sac 200 yards from Harrods, the Beaufort offers personal service, almost rural peace and a refreshingly different attitude to hotel-keeping that extends to fair (15p per unit) telephone charges. Guests are given front door keys and terms are all-inclusive (including use of videos from their extensive library and even champagne from the 24hr drawing room bar!); Continental breakfast is served only in the bedrooms; membership of a local health club is also included. Air-conditioned, pastel-decorated bedrooms – full of extras large and small – range from a single with shower/WC only to a junior suite. A wonderful collection of over 400 English floral watercolours graces the walls. One night's non-refundable deposit is required for all first-time reservations. No tipping expected (or dogs). **Rooms** 28. Closed 23-28 Dec. AMERICAN EXPRESS Access, Diners, Visa.

NW1   Belgo   £40

Tel 071-267 0718   **R**

72 Chalk Farm Road NW1 8AN   **Map 16 C3**

A remarkable example of post-modern design, with a flat concrete frontage, a high-tech wheel and pulley design for the stairs, an environment-friendly heating and air system using huge chrome pipes, and a restaurant area conceived as a brewery eating hall. Its walls are also concrete, with a frieze inlaid with Rabelais-inspired names of obscure fish. Tables are refectory-style, topped with ash, chairs are minimalist, with wooden axe handle seats which deliver more comfort and support than looks likely. Waiters are dressed in monks' habits, a practical garb for serving the hefty portions of mussels (choose from 10 ways) that are the most popular order – usually with an order of chips. These and other marginally more refined Belgian dishes – mash with smoked wild boar sausage, *witloof au gratin, waterzooi à la gantoise* – are washed down with Belgian beer (they stock 32 varieties), some of it monastery-brewed, some fruit-fermented, one sour and lemony, one as strong as wine! A real one-off and a big hit from the moment it opened, Belgo is a place for tucking into simple, sustaining food, for drinking beer and talking – but definitely not in a whisper. Bookings may be made up to two weeks in advance; tables are allocated for two hours maximum. **Seats** 130. Parties 8. Closed 25 & 26 Dec, 1 Jan. L 12-3 D 6-11.30 (Sat 12-11.30, Sun 12-10.30). Set L from £5 (Mon-Fri, main dish & lager) Set D £8.95/£10. AMERICAN EXPRESS Access, Diners, Visa.

SE1   Bengal Clipper   NEW   £65

Tel 071-357 9001   Fax 071-357 9002   **R**

Cardamom Building Shad Thames Butler's Wharf SE1   **Map 17 D4**

A stone's throw from Conran's Gastrodrome complex and Tower Bridge, this sophisticated Indian dining room on the ground floor of an old spice warehouse is cleverly designed to mimic an old tea clipper – though the atmosphere and service are more in keeping with a modern cruise ship and a dinner-jacketed pianist plays romantic standards. A long menu, particularly strong on fish dishes, includes old favourites such as rogan josh and chicken tikka massala but has been based mainly on dishes from Goa and Bengal. Begin with *kakrar chop* (Goan crab fishcakes), salmon samosas or perhaps *shageor maachher soup* – made with lentils, herbs and fresh mussels. To follow, giant tandoori prawns in a red masala sauce, *xacuti chicken* (hot and flavoured with coconut) or delicious fillets of Bengal catfish with cassia and cumin. Equal care is taken with rice and side dishes, *phool kopee chichinga* (spicy cauliflower in Kerala style) being particularly successful. Service, from crisply dressed 'stewards', is friendly and helpful. **Seats** 75. L 12-3 D 6-11. Set L 18.95. AMERICAN EXPRESS Access, Diners, Visa.

NW3   Benihana   £75

Tel 071-586 9508   **R**

100 Avenue Road Swiss Cottage NW3 3HF   **Map 16 B3**

Part of a world-wide group with branches from Beverly Hills to Tokyo, London's first Benihana is a typically lively establishment in a bright basement ambience next to the Hampstead Theatre. Teppanyaki griddle cooking is the speciality, and the chefs working at their hibachi tables are great entertainment. Steak and lobster are the main attractions, and the entrées, served with multifarious accompaniments, include Rocky's choice (chicken teriyaki, hibachi steak with mushrooms), a lobster feast (steamed whole lobster with caviar sauce) and tuna steak with ginger. Great-value weekday lunches and a Sunday lunch with children's entertainment. Short wine list, but a vast choice of cocktails. *Seats 112. Parties 14. Private Room 8. L 12.30-3 D 6.30-12. Closed L Mon. Set L from £8 (Sun £15).* AMERICAN EXPRESS *Access, Diners, Visa.*

SW3	Benihana	NEW	£75

Tel 071-376 7799 **R**

77 Kings Road Chelsea SW3 4NX   **Map 19 C5**

A plate glass door simply inscribed with the restaurant's name is all that is visible from the exterior while inside a wide staircase rounds a corner presenting a stunningly original and very striking ultra-modern decor. A long gallery leads to a sweeping bifurcated staircase, one side leading down to the spacious tent-ceilinged bar, the other to a sea of white pebbles crossed by 'stepping stones' of black iron to reach the dining area of gleaming hibachi tables. These accommodate up to eight diners, who are treated to the dexterity of the chef preparing the food on the teppanyaki grill. The menu comprises a selection of 21 set meals ranging from simple steaks, chicken and fish to much more elaborate offerings. Each is accompanied by a host of side dishes and accompaniments with extra dishes such as sashimi, sushi, yakitori and various tempura also available. Service is very charming and accommodating in true Japanese fashion. *Seats 140. Parties 8. Private Room 12. L 12.30-3 D 6.30-11. Set L £8.90.* AMERICAN EXPRESS *Access, Diners, Visa.*

W1	Bentinck House Hotel	£73

Tel 071-935 9141   Fax 071-224 5903 **H**

20 Bentinck Street W1M 5RL   **Map 18 C2**

Large, comfortable bedrooms (three family rooms, 9 rooms en suite) in a small hotel behind Oxford Street. *Rooms 20.* AMERICAN EXPRESS *Access, Diners, Visa.*

W1	Bentley's	£80

Tel 071-287 5025   Fax 071-734 4756 **R·**

11 Swallow Street W1R 7HD   **Map 18 D3**

This club-like first-floor dining room has been specialising in fish since its inception in 1916. While keeping abreast of fashion, it has resisted the temptation to cook multi-coloured tropical breeds, and remained faithful to native products – sometimes presented with modern disguises. To begin, oysters, either *au naturel* or glazed with Beluga caviar, risotto of lobster, tarragon and cepes, or potted prawns and shrimps with pickled pear in mustard oil; these might be followed by salmon and crab fishcakes, scallops with celeriac dauphinoise, steamed brill with herbs, new crop vegetables and a tomato and olive butter sauce, or roast lobster on lemon couscous. Chocolate tart with grilled apricots is a good pud. The comfortable atmosphere attracts an expense account clientele, and the fat cigars that match the wallets can spoil some of the kitchen's best efforts. On the ground floor the Oyster Bar offers a shorter, more traditional seafood menu. *Seats 95. Private Room 14. L 12-2.30 D 6-10.30. Closed L Sat, all Sun, Bank Holidays, 1 week Christmas. Set L & D £16.50/£19.50.* AMERICAN EXPRESS *Access, Diners, Visa.*

SW1	The Berkeley	89%	£291

Tel 071-235 6000   Fax 071-235 4330 **HR**

Wilton Place Knightsbridge SW1X 7RL   **Map 19 C4**

Having attained 21 years in 1993 the hotel, which is located in a relatively quiet residential part of Knightsbridge, has some bedrooms commanding impressive views over Hyde Park while a few others have balconies.

Moved from its original site in Piccadilly but still bearing the hallmarks of a hotel 'de grand luxe', it retains such features as panelling by Lutyens and a collection of glittering chandeliers. Outstanding flower arrangements and highly polished marbles of different hues create an impressive entrance. The split-level, relatively dark intimacy of the Perroquet Bar offers an alternative meeting-place to the more formal and traditional lounge with its splendid olive-green leather winged armchairs and others in a fashionable dark bamboo style. The design of each new refurbishment of the bedrooms, usually in small groups, is undertaken by a top designer and this is very evident from the classical, sumptuous decor that breathes style and good taste. There are three presidential suites, one with its own conservatory, and 21 further spacious suites. Even the standard bedrooms are beautifully appointed, differing only from superior rooms in being marginally smaller. Most rooms have a separate dressing room adjacent to the immaculate Italianate marble bathrooms, which feature a wealth of pampering extras including complimentary towelling slippers. Modern comforts like extensive satellite television coverage, video recorders and fax points are common to all as are wall safes. There are valet buttons by beds and baths which are answered promptly all typifying standards of service that are of an exemplary very high standard. On the top floor is a superb leisure complex with a swimming pool that in summer can slide its roof back. **Rooms** *160. Indoor swimming pool, gym, sauna, solarium, beauty & hair salon, valeting, cinema, coffee shop (7am-11.30pm Mon-Sat).* AMERICAN EXPRESS *Access, Diners, Visa.*

Restaurant ★ £105

A collection of framed medieval line portraits set in antiqued mirror surrounds (themselves forming part of ornately carved limed-oak panelling) creates, together with beautifully appointed, well-spaced tables and elaborate flower arrangements, an air of elegant sophistication that is reflected in John William's classical menus. Subtle innovation, introducing modern, carefully thought-out concepts, results in dishes that are at once familiar yet exciting both for presentation and taste. A salad of lobster delicately spiced is accompanied by a coriander-flavoured yoghurt and puréed mango and seared scallops share a plate with a wonderfully creamy saffron risotto. There is no shortage of choice and fish dishes include a baked fillet of wild salmon with Dublin bay prawns and asparagus, roast turbot with a lemon butter sauce and slightly more unusual offerings such as pot-roast saddle of monkfish with basil, tapénade and tomato sauce. Meat and game include excellent grills and roasts as well as the likes of duck breast with Savoy cabbage and Toulouse sausage and veal mignons with creamed celeriac, Stilton and walnuts or quail breasts with goose liver, grapes and sherry vinegar. Well-made desserts from the trolley vie with such delights as a stunning soufflé flavoured with Poire William liqueur and a warm prune and armagnac tart with caramel ice cream. Good balance on a fine wine list that has many classics and a decent showing from the New World. **Seats** *70. Parties 12. Private Room 34. L 12.30-2.30 (Sun to 2.15) D 6.30-10.45 (Sun 7-10). Closed Sat. Set L £19.50 Set D £21.*

W1	**Berkshire Hotel**	**72%**	£231

Tel 071-629 7474   Fax 071-629 8156   **H**

350 Oxford Street W1N 0BY   Map 18 C2

Occupying its own small triangular block on the north side of Oxford Street, almost facing the top of New Bond Street, the Berkshire possesses comfortable though not extensive public rooms, with a chintzy, panelled drawing room and the intimate Ascot Bar. Bedrooms, including approximately 40 designated non-smoking, are attractively appointed, much use being made of rich, colourful fabrics and darkwood furniture. Executive rooms are bigger and have more accessories; suites have whirlpool baths. Children up to 8 stay free in parents' room. 24hr room service. Owners Edwardian Hotels aim for a country-house welcome and an Edwardian feel here. NCP Welbeck Street. *Rooms 147.* AMERICAN EXPRESS® *Access, Diners, Visa.*

W1 **Berners Park Plaza** **72%**	**£130**
Tel 071-636 1629 Fax 071-580 3972	**H**
10 Berners Street W1A 3BE	**Map 18 D2**

Turn-of-the-century splendour survives in the marble columns and intricate moulded ceilings of a hotel a few steps north of Oxford Street. The traditional atmosphere extends to afternoon tea and the cocktail hour. Bedrooms are of a good size, well laid-out, smartly furnished and double-glazed. Tiled bathrooms all have showers as well as tubs. Children up to 12 stay free in parents' room. Half the rooms are designated non-smoking. Four purpose-built function suites can handle up to 180 delegates. *Rooms 229. Coffee shop (7am-11pm).* AMERICAN EXPRESS® *Access, Diners, Visa.*

WC2 **Bertorelli's**	**£60**
Tel 071-836 3969 Fax 081-836 1868	**R**
44a Floral Street Covent Garden WC2E 9DA	**Map 21 B2**

Modern Italian cooking by Maddalena Bonino at a famous address opposite the stage door of the Royal Opera House. There's a very fashionable ring and an excellent taste to dishes such as ricotta and aubergine terrine served with roasted pepper salsa and bruschetta, griddled scallops on fennel couscous with a saffron dressing or grilled calf's liver with a roast onion, pancetta and spinach compote. Pasta dishes may be ordered as starter or main course. There's an associated café/wine bar in the basement. Free parking in the Drury Lane NCP for customers dining in the restaurant after 6pm. *Seats 100. Parties 30. L 12-3 D 5.30-11.30. Closed Sun, 26 Dec.* AMERICAN EXPRESS® *Access, Diners, Visa.*

N16 **Beyoglu Ocakbasi**	**£30**
Tel 071-275 7745	**R**
4 Stoke Newington Road N16 7XN	**Map 16 D2**

Candle-light creates a relaxed mood for enjoying some good Turkish food, which you can see the chef preparing on his ocakbasi, or charcoal grill. The grill provides most of the main courses (lamb, chicken, swordfish), while others including lamb, chicken, prawns and mussels are sautéed and served with a tomato sauce. There's a long list of starters, plus two soups – lentil and lamb. *Seats 36. Meals 12-11.30. Closed 25 Dec, 1 Jan. Set L £7/£10 Set D £10/£12. No credit cards.*

CLOSED

WC2 **Bhatti**	**£50**
Tel 071-831 0817 Fax 071-831 4249	**R**
37 Great Queen Street WC2B 5AA	**Map 21 B2**

Popular, long-established and civilised Indian restaurant in a 17th-century building just off Drury Lane. A fairly familiar range of chicken, lamb and prawn dishes is joined by quail and pomfret fish – both cooked in the clay oven. Murgh makhani, chicken tikka masala, and lamb pasanda are among the 'chef's recommendations'. *Seats 90. Private Room 45. L 11.45-2.45 (Sun to 2) D 5.45-11.45 (Sun to 10.30). Closed 25 & 26 Dec.*

SW3 **Bibendum** ★	**£120**
Tel 071-581 5817 Fax 071-823 7925	**R**
81 Fulham Road SW3 6RD	**Map 19 B5**

Sir Terence Conran's first restaurant venture and still one of the most fashionable eateries in town – making booking pretty much essential. It is located on the first floor of the famous Michelin building, so Bibendum (the Michelin tyre man) himself is naturally the leitmotiv of the decor,

appearing on the plates, sitting on the ashtrays and featuring in a couple
of huge stained-glass windows; even the wine decanters and flower vases
reflect his rotundity. Chairs have loose linen covers with a different colour
used for each season – pale green in spring, mustard yellow in summer etc.
The menu (à la carte at night; fixed-price at lunchtime) is a mixture
of classic French – *tete de veau sauce ravigote, escargots de Bourgogne, entrecote
béarnaise,* coffee bavarois – and Mediterranean-influenced dishes – grilled
squid with aged red wine vinegar, olive oil and gremolata; tomato tart and
buffalo mozzarella, vitello tonnato – plus the likes of Baltic herrings à la
crème, gravad lax and deep-fried fillet of plaice with chips and tartare
sauce. A mascarpone and lemon tart with red fruit compote was
a particular hit on a recent visit although the ficelle bread, the only sort
offered, was rather overbaked. The magnificent wine list, though seriously
French and seriously priced, also features choice bottles from around the
world. Look carefully for real value and remember a further 15% service
is whacked on top, so house champagne exceeds £40. **Seats** *72. Parties 8.
L 12.30-2.30 (Sat & Sun to 3) D 7-11.30 (Sun to 10.30). Closed 4 days
Christmas, Easter Monday. Set L from £25.* AMERICAN EXPRESS *Access, Visa.*

SW3	**Bibendum Oyster Bar**	**£70**
Tel 071-581 5817 Fax 071-823 7925		**R**
Michelin House 81 Fulham Road SW3 6RD		Map 19 B5

At the front and on the ground floor (below its big sister) of the
wonderfully quirky Michelin building, the Oyster Bar serves an all-day
menu, but be warned that tea and coffee are served only with food: despite
the Brompton Cross location, no shop-till-you-drop-coffee-stop this!
Seriously good seafood (as you'd expect from Simon Hopkinson) and a few
other tastes thrown in for good measure – crisp pork belly with pickled
cucumber and chili dip? But the spanking fresh oysters are the thing here,
the best from around northern Europe. Or go with a good friend, tie
on a bib and tuck into the plateau de fruits de mer – it's only served for
two or more. Whites and champagnes dominate the wine list. No children
under 18. **Seats** *44. Parties 18. Meals 12-10.30pm (Sun to 10pm).*
AMERICAN EXPRESS *Access, Visa.*

If we recommend meals in a hotel or inn a separate entry is made for its
restaurant.

NW1	**Big Night Out**	**NEW**	**£55**
Tel 071-586 5768 Fax 071-482 4176			**R**
148 Regents Park Road NW1 8XN			Map 16 C3

Up the spiral staircase is a small, dark, cosy dining room while on the
ground floor the available area is larger and brighter, its walls hung with
huge multiple canvases of modern art inspired by Michelangelo. The menu
is in two parts with a two- or three-course set price option as well
as a short, varied à la carte. The cooking style is up-to-date, with well-
thought-out, innovative combinations. Typical starters are a gougère soufflé
on a bed of rocket with a red pepper oil, lobster chowder with scallops and
watercress or a brill and crab tartlet with a thyme and truffle dressing.
Main dishes include pan-fried sea bass with a parsnip purée and a mussel
and lemon balm dressing, roast rack of lamb in a sage crust with rösti and
wild mushrooms or breast of Norfolk duckling with a gratin of turnips and
swede. Steak, Guinness and oyster pudding with buttered cabbage and
chives is a sample of one or two more traditional offerings. Sunday brunch
price includes an alcoholic drink. Friendly, chatty service. Booking
essential. **Seats** *70. Parties 8. Private Room 30. L 12-3 D 7-11. Closed L Mon,
D Sun, 25 Dec, 1 Jan. Set L £5.50 (Sun £10).* AMERICAN EXPRESS *Access, Visa.*

W1   Bistrot Bruno

Tel 071-734 4545   Fax 071-287 1027

63 Frith Street Soho W1V 5TA

£70

R

Map 21 A2

Pierre Condou and Bruno Loubet's stylishly modish restaurant has a very
laid-back ambience, with coloured walls in dark geometric patterns at the
rear, white at the front. A few, tiny multicoloured enamel fish embedded
here and there – as if in a sea – contribute to a minimalist style of decor.
Tables in deep-blue laminate line the walls of the long, narrow room and
are small and set close together. The menu is short but exceptionally varied
and highly imaginative. Dishes are uncomplicated, relying chiefly on the
quality of the ingredients. To start, a 'cold fish consommé topped with
chervil soup' comprises a light, set fish jelly with a smooth, creamy chervil
purée on top – the latter's delicate fragrance offsetting the fishy flavours
from below. A home-made *boudin blanc* comes on a ragout of shelled broad
beans and spring onions. Main dishes range from a whole steamed young
sea bass served with a soy, black bean and garlic sauce, to grilled quails
with a tarragon jus, stuffed rabbit leg with lime-pickled new potatoes
or duck confit on a corn pancake with grape chutney and a green salad.
The odd classic makes an appearance, too, as in daube of beef niçoise-style
and offal dishes such as calf's brain fritters with tartare sauce or an *assiette
d'agneau* – literally a dish of lamb comprising the pan-fried neck, stuffed
trotter and a baked potato filled with tripe. Sweets include the likes
of poached strawberries with green peppercorn ice cream and chocolate
tartelette with coffee cream. **Seats** 42. Parties 12. L 12.15-2.30
D 6.15-11.30. Closed L Sat & Bank Holidays, all Sun, 5 days Christmas.
AMERICAN EXPRESS *Access, Diners, Visa.*

SW7   Bistrot 190   ↑

Tel 071-581 5666   Fax 071-581 8172

190 Queen's Gate SW7 5EU

£50

R

Map 19 B4

On the one hand one could compare the redoubtable Antony Worrall
Thompson to a juggler who manages to keep more plates up in the air
in London than any other first-division restaurateur, while on the other
hand one could compare him to an alchemist who cleverly transmutes
standard culinary ingredients into 'gold'. Whichever way one looks at it,
AWT has a golden touch and his influences are spreading across the land,
with many restaurateurs quietly copying the odd dish here and there, if not
his complete style; if any menu can be called eclectic then surely Bistrot
190's can. The lofty front room of *The Gore Hotel* (qv) is the setting for the
restaurant and no bookings are taken; it's frequently crowded by 7pm,
so arrive early or late for the likelihood of a table. Good food is served
at reasonable prices through long hours, starting early with breakfast – of
which there's a vast choice, from a Scottish version with haggis and black
pudding to the more cholesterol-conscious Health and Power version with
home-made muesli and egg-white omelette alongside hippy teas, kedgeree
and raw apple muffins – surely London's most diverse breakfast menu.
As the day progresses the menu becomes more modern Mediterranean
in style – on a long list of starters cassoulet of fishes with chili toast and
pan-fried herrring roes with garlic, parsley and olive toast sit happily
alongside steamed mussels with Sicilian tomato sauce and purple basil,
Mediterranean vegetable chowder with pesto crostini, and warm onion tart
with cucumber pickle. The exoticism continues with the main courses:
'aged' rump steak with grilled pesto tomato and chips; salmon fish cakes
with wilted spinach, chips and herb sauce; broccoli, saffron and Parmesan
risotto; roast cod with chorizo, caramelised chicory and grilled mango –
unusual combinations that generally work, some better than others.
Chocolate nut fudge cake, lemon tart with crème fraiche, vanilla croissant
pudding with bay custard and country cheeses with rocket and muscat pear
to finish. Both a Sunday brunch and a fixed-price menu (with a traditional
roast) are offered. All the wines on the shortish, frequently changing wine
list are available by bottle or two-glass *pichets*; over a dozen unusual

bottled beers (see also Downstairs at 190). *Seats 55. Parties 10. Meals 7am-12.30am (Sun to 11.30pm). Set Sun L £12.50. Closed 3 days Christmas.* AMERICAN EXPRESS *Access, Diners, Visa.*

SW3	**Blair House Hotel**	**£102**
Tel 071-581 2323 Fax 071-823 7752		**H**
34 Draycott Place SW3 2SA		Map 19 C5

Well-equipped bed and breakfast hotel conveniently located near Sloane Square with quiet bedrooms at the back. *Rooms 16.* AMERICAN EXPRESS *Access, Diners, Visa.*

SW7	**Blakes Hotel** **82%**	**£183**
Tel 071-370 6701 Fax 071-373 0442		**HR**
33 Roland Gardens SW7 3PF		Map 19 B5

In converting a row of Victorian town houses over the last ten or so years, designer Anouska Hempel has created a small luxury hotel unlike any other; its a dramatic, almost fantastic exercise in personalised opulence and elegance using the finest craftsmen and the choicest raw materials. The small foyer/lounge area is papered black yet warmed by the browns of wood and leather seating piled high with plumped-up cushions. The overall effect is Oriental, a theme carried through to the Chinese Room that leads off the smart basement restaurant where an intimate bar is also to be found. Bedrooms vary widely in decor – from the extravagance of one containing the Empress Josephine's day bed to the clever simplicity of an all-white room with white-painted floorboards and trompe l'oeil wall paintings. The more expensive rooms are singular in design with masses of heavily swagged drapes in unusual fabrics and polished wood floors; furnished with antiques, objets d'art and a profusion of framed prints along with delicate Venetian glassware. Mostly beautiful bathrooms with marble surrounds, though standard rooms have small modern white-tiled ones. In the oldest part, the rooms, some on the small side, have clothed walls, carpets, bedding, draped curtains, upholstery, even the woodwork all in an absolutely identical shade of flannel grey. On the lower floors there are lighter rooms with a monochrome decor, black and white tartans against plain white backgrounds. The newest of all the bedrooms has a stunning Middle Eastern influence. Breakfasts can be English, Continental or Kyoto Country. Room service can provide sandwiches, salads, pastries and refreshments round the clock. The room rate quoted is for one of the smaller doubles. Large doubles and suites range upwards from £267. An unusual and exotic hotel with friendly and helpful staff. *Rooms 52.* AMERICAN EXPRESS *Access, Diners, Visa.*

Blakes Restaurant   ★   £150

The restaurant is every bit as original as the rest of the hotel, with elegant black-and-white furniture and framed Thai costumes and jewellery. Plate-glass screens divide some of the tables in what is a small, discreet and elegantly contemporary room. In this unique setting Peter Thornley presents a range of dishes for which the word 'eclectic' could have been invented, a cuisine which unites East and West in eye-catching harmony. From the Orient come *sashimi,* Szechuan duck with roasted salt and pepper, and *gyuniku teriyaki* (fillet of beef marinated in teriyaki sauce and served with wasabi, wild rice and sake); from nearer home come tortellini with foie gras and wild mushroom risotto. Chicken and crab Fabergé is a Hempel-inspired creation of chicken and crab moulded into the shape of a large egg, tied with a ribbon of nori seaweed to look like a Fabergé egg and served with lime ginger sauce. Short list of expensive wines, all but two French. Drinks and coffee may be served in the Chinese Room or bar. *Seats 40. Parties 16. Private Room 22. L 12.30-2.30 D 7.30-11.30. Set L £26/£32.*

E1 Bloom's £40

Tel 071-247 6001 **R**

90 Whitechapel High Street E1 7RA **Map 16 D3**

Morris Bloom set the ball rolling in 1920, opening a small restaurant
in Brick Lane and quickly establishing a reputation for serving fine kosher
food. The Whitechapel premises opened in 1952 and operate under the
same strict kosher rules – a rabbi and a religious supervisor on the premises
every day. Salt beef is the star of the show, best enjoyed with latkes and
pickled cucumber, but chopped liver, egg and onions, bloomburgers, fried
fish and roast chicken all have a strong following. Finish with lockshen
pudding or halva, drink lemon tea or Israeli wine. Quick service from
wise-cracking, long-serving staff. The restaurant has its own parking.
Seats 150. Meals 11.30-9.30 (Fri to 3am). Closed D Fri, all Sat, Jewish
Holidays, Christmas. AMERICAN EXPRESS *Access, Diners, Visa.*
Also at:
NW11 130 Golders Green Road NW11 8HB Tel 081-455 1338 **Map 16 B1**
Open till 2am Sun-Thur. Closed D Fri, L Sat, Jewish Holidays.

SW6 Blue Elephant £70

Tel 071-385 6595 Fax 071-386 7665 **R**

4-6 Fulham Broadway SW6 1AA **Map 19 A6**

Verdant decor incorporating a waterfall, a bridge over a stream and
a veritable jungle of greenery – an exotic setting in which to enjoy
luxurious, MSG-free Thai cooking. The 17-dish Royal Thai banquet menu
(from £25) is still one of the most popular ways of dining – it includes
at least six starters and six main courses, so everyone gets plenty of taste
sensations. Hot dishes are indicated by little red elephants (up to three)
on the menu. Separate vegetarian set menu at £18.50. The buffet lunch
is now only available on Sundays at £14.50 (special price for children).
Seats 250. Private Room 100. L 12-2.30 D 7-12.30 (Sun to 10.30).
Closed L Sat, 24-27 Dec, 1 Jan. AMERICAN EXPRESS *Access, Diners, Visa.*

SE1 Blue Print Café £60

Tel 071-378 7031 Fax 071-378 6540 **R**

Design Museum Shad Thames Butlers Wharf SE1 2YD **Map 17 D4**

Flashes of red, yellow and blue add colour to a bright, stylish restaurant
on the first floor of the Design Museum with views overlooking the
Thames. Chef Lucy Crabb changes her menu daily, providing dishes in the
modern fashion with influences from far and wide. Spinach and ricotta
gnocchi; steamed salmon with cucumber and smoked salmon sauce; calf's
liver with caramelised onions; grilled tuna with salsa and guacamole; and
roast duck breast *au poivre* show her style. Summer eating on the outside
balcony tables has the added benefit of wonderful views of Tower Bridge.
Seats 85. L 12-3 (Sun to 3.30) D 7-11. Closed D Sun, Christmas.
AMERICAN EXPRESS *Access, Diners, Visa.*

SW7 Bombay Brasserie ★ £70

Tel 071-370 4040 **R**

Courtfield Close Courtfield Road SW7 4UH **Map 19 B5**

The most glamorous Indian restaurant in town, and a hit since opening its
doors in 1982. The handsome room, with its Raj pictures and paddle fans,
is from a time past, evoking a grand hotel of a century ago. Entrance is to
a roomy bar area where mango Bellini is a popular cocktail. One part
of the restaurant proper is a large and flowery conservatory, which despite
its lack of views manages to convey a garden feel. The kitchen garners its
recipes from all parts of the sub-continent and numbers seafood, 'coastal',
tandoori and vegetarian among its specialities. Some of the best dishes are
Bombay roadside and seaside snacks (*ragara pattice* and *sev batata puri*),

pomfret coated with mint chutney steamed in a banana leaf, Goan fish
curry, chicken biryani and lobster *peri peri* (*very very* spicy). Meat and
vegetarian thali provide tasting portions of many dishes. Lunchtime buffet.
Evening pianist. *Seats 175. Parties 20. Private Room 100. L 12.30-3
D 7.30-12 (Sun to 11.30). Closed 25 & 26 Dec. Set buffet from £14.95.
Access, Diners, Visa.*

SW2   Bon Ton Roulet   £40
Tel 081-678 0880   **R**
43 Tulse Hill SW2 2TJ   Map 17 C6

The name is French for 'let the good times roll', which accurately sums
up the friendly, relaxed atmosphere here. The cooking is English/French
plus occasional exotic touches, with produce supplied by the family farm
whenever practical. Favourites include tempura vegetables, paté, stuffed
aubergines, game pie and the day's fish special. Sherry trifle and fruit
crumble are typical puddings. They stock a red or white house wine,
or you can take your own (corkage £1.50 per bottle). *Seats 40. Parties 16.
L Sun in winter only 12.30-2.30 D 6.30-10.30 (Sat to 11). Closed all Mon,
1 week Christmas. Set Sun L £8.50. No credit cards.*

WC1   Bonnington Hotel   61%   £95
Tel 071-242 2828   Fax 071-831 9170   **H**
92 Southampton Row Bloomsbury WC1B 4BH   Map 16 C3

In the same family ownership for 80 years, the Bonnington is just south
of Russell Square – close to the British Museum and within easy walking
distance of the Oxford Street shops. Extensive public areas include a lounge
bar, breakfast room and many conference/banqueting rooms for 130/250
delegates. Bedrooms with all the usual accessories include 40% designated
non-smoking; under-14s share parents' room free. Four rooms are equipped
for disabled guests. Rooms on Southampton Row are double-glazed.
Reduced tariff at weekends. *Rooms 215.* AMERICAN EXPRESS *Diners, Visa.*

SW7   La Bouchée   £35
Tel 071-589 1929   Fax 071-584 8625   **R**
56 Old Brompton Road South Kensington SW7 3DY   Map 19 B5

The simple bistro-style fare served in simple bistro-style surroundings varies
from average to good but always offers decent value for money, so La
Bouchée is usually crowded, particulary in the evenings. Moules marinière,
paté de campagne, steamed salmon with garlic hollandaise, coq au vin, petit
salé and steak frites show the style. *Seats 85. Parties 40. Meals 9.30am-11pm.
Set L £4.95 & £6.95 Set D (early) £6.95. Closed 25 & 26 Dec, 1 Jan.
Access, Visa.*

W8   Boyd's   £70
Tel 071-727 5452   Fax 071-221 0615   **R**
135 Kensington Church Street W8 7LP   Map 18 A3

A very decent neighbourhood restaurant with a pleasant conservatory,
varnished wooden floor, rattan chairs, green-stained table tops, plenty
of greenery, ceiling fans and blinds on the glass dome. It's a bright, pretty
setting, matching the careful presentation of chef/proprietor Boyd
Gilmour's carefully prepared dishes. Charred scallops with mangetout and
red pepper and chive butter sauce is considered a speciality as a starter,
alongside others like chargrilled vegetables with goat's cheese and basil
or home-smoked duck with Puy lentils and red onion confit; main courses
are typified by daily fresh fish dishes, saddle of venison with wild
mushroom sauce, best end of lamb with tapénade and ratatouille, and
langoustine and fennel risotto. Quintet of lemon desserts, tarte tatin with
butterscotch sauce, trio of chocolate with coffee bean sauce or English and
Irish cheeses to finish. The three-course lunch menu provides excellent

value for money: perhaps onion soup or tagliatelle with wild garlic and Parmesan followed by salt beef with red cabbage or smoked salmon with herb butter sauce, then walnut parfait with chocolate sauce or French apple tart with ice cream. *Seats 40. L 12.30-2.30 D 7-11. Closed Sun, 2 weeks Christmas, Easter Bank Holiday. Set L £14.* AMERICAN EXPRESS *Access, Diners, Visa.*

W6   The Brackenbury   £45
Tel 081-748 0107   R
129-131 Brackenbury Road W6 0BQ   Map 17 A4

The Brackenbury is not only one of West London's best patronised neighbourhood restaurants, but from the day it opened in 1991 it has made many ripples extending far beyond its expected hinterland. The reason is clear – a winning mix of good, easy-to-enjoy food, very reasonable prices and a friendly, bustling atmosphere helped along by cheerful, hardworking staff. Moreover, almost all the wines on the broadly based list are available by the glass (more than 20). The place used to be a wine bar, and a bar area still remains; the eating areas are utilitarian yet welcoming, with salmon pink and green paintwork and some pew seating. Adam Robinson cooks a short menu that changes at each session and demonstrates the quality and accessibility of modern British cooking. The plate of savouries which heads the menu offers generous nibbles (often of what is to be found down the list) to accompany drinks and not necessarily to replace starters such as seafood chowder, sushi, fritters of lamb's brains and sweetbreads (a great favourite) or pappardelle with broad beans, bacon and mustard. Main courses are typified by steamed fillet of brill with spinach and hollandaise sauce, confit of duck with fried potatoes and salad, calf's liver with semolina gnocchi and sage, and roast saddle of lamb with haricot beans and mint. Good cheeses, and some tempting desserts – Bramley crumble and custard, orange and almond pudding with poached fruits. *Seats 55. Parties 8. L 12.30-2.45 D 7-10.45. Closed L Mon & Sat, D Sun, Bank Holidays, 1 week Christmas.* AMERICAN EXPRESS *Access, Diners, Visa.*

SW14   Le Braconnier   £60
Tel 081-878 2853   R
467 Upper Richmond Road West East Sheen SW14 7PU   Map 17 A5

A splendid little restaurant offering a fixed-price-only menu of French regional dishes. Start, perhaps, with an individual asparagus tart with a confit of onions, grilled wild boar sausage on an apple and mustard purée or *potage Saint-Germain* (pea soup with sorrel and gammon), following with *cassoulet de Toulouse* (considered a speciality), *carré d'agneau*, *la bourride* (monkfish, sole and salmon in a garlic-flavoured broth) or guinea fowl with spring vegetables and creamy Roquefort sauce. Half a dozen half-bottles on the wine list which features a bargain house champagne (specially imported). *Seats 30. L Sun only Oct-end Mar D 7-11. Closed D Sun, all Mon, 1 week Easter, 2 weeks August, 25-28 Dec. Set D £15.50/£18.* AMERICAN EXPRESS *Access, Visa.*

SW3   La Brasserie   £55
Tel 071-581 3089   R
272 Brompton Road SW3 2AW   Map 19 B5

Go casual or smart, for a quick bite or a slap-up meal, a leisurely breakfast with the newspapers or an evening with friends – this long-popular French brasserie is one the most versatile eating places in town. Breakfast can be anything from a croissant to kippers, French toast to bacon and eggs. *Le petit menu* proposes two dozen dishes, from onion soup and croque monsieur to salads, steaks and pasta. The main menu of brasserie classics is supplemented by blackboard specials such as skate with black butter or an excellent couscous. With a new number 1 and number 2 in the kitchen, the cooking here is as good as it's ever been, and with the easy-going atmosphere and the reasonable prices, it is rightly at the top of many people's list of London favourites. *Seats 130. Parties 20. Meals 8am-midnight (Sun 10am-11.30pm). Closed 25 Dec.* AMERICAN EXPRESS *Access, Diners, Visa.*

W10   Brasserie du Marché aux Puces   £50

Tel 081-968 5828   **R**

349 Portobello Road W10 5SA   Map 16 B3

A bright, informal brasserie with large windows, plain wooden tables and a mahogany bar with a wire fruit basket, a plateau of cheeses and a huge flower display on the counter. The shortish menu, which changes every few weeks, presents an interesting representation of modern European cuisine, some of whose produce comes from local speciality markets. Poached egg with truffles and beurre blanc, crostini with rocket and walnut pesto and smoked salmon mousse, calf's liver with kumquats and roast shallots and spatchcock chicken with hazelnut, onion and dolcelatte confit show the style and range. Few modern restaurants seem to be without sticky toffee pudding, and this one comes with a pecan sauce. *Seats 35. Parties 14. Private Room 35. Meals noon-11pm (Sun 11-4). Closed D Sun, all Bank Holidays. No credit cards (though they have plans to take them).*

SW10   Brasserie Koko   NEW   £40

Tel 071-351 0935   **R**

430 Kings Road Chelsea SW10 0LJ   Map 19 B6

A tiny, spotless Japanese brasserie located in a basement squeezed between charity and designer shops at World's End. Decor is typically minimalist – pale grey and charcoal with a couple of monochrome wall hangings. The menu is short but high in quality with effort also put into presentation. There are simple set lunches (which include an appetiser, soup, rice and fruit) and more elaborate dinners. Tempura soba is a bowl of buckwheat noodles in soup topped with deep-fried prawns and vegetables. Shu-ka-do is a series of three small lacquered boxes each containing a delicious arrangement of food – sashimi of tuna, salmon, sea bass with an oba leaf in one, another with egg roll, grilled salmon, lobster dumpling and sliced prawn tempura while a third has deep-fried bean curd with lobster in a soup with carrot and burdock root. Sliced fresh fruit with sweet red bean dumpling and Japanese green tea make a fitting end. *Seats 32. Parties 6. D only 6-10.30. Closed all Sun, Bank Holidays, 1 week Christmas.*

> Changes in data sometimes occur in establishments after the Guide goes to press. Prices should be taken as indications rather than firm quotes.

SW3   Brasserie St Quentin   £55

Tel 071-581 5131   Fax 071-584 6064   **R**

243 Brompton Road Knightsbridge SW3 2EP   Map 19 B4

Right on Brompton Road, but effectively soundproofed by two doors. It still has the elegance and civilised feel of Brompton Grill days, a Belle Epoque-inspired decor with mirrors and pillars, wall chandeliers, brass, banquettes and flower arrangements. A bar runs down one side, propped up by smartly attired diners awaiting their tables. French staff are kitted out in formal black and white and perform their tasks with youthful gravity and reasonable efficiency. Chef Nigel Davis, previously at *The Ivy*, has also worked in south-west France, and cassoulet, based on a recipe from Toulouse, is one of his specialities. Others are *moules à la crème, terrine de foie gras, confit de canard* and *crème brulée. Seats 80. Private Room 25. L 12-3 D 7-11.30. Set L £8/£11.90.* AMERICAN EXPRESS *Access, Diners, Visa.*

W1   Britannia Intercontinental Hotel   77%   £200

Tel 071-629 9400   Fax 071-629 7736   **H**

Grosvenor Square W1A 3AN   **Map 18 C3**

Behind the grand, colonnaded frontage of three Georgian houses overlooking the Mayfair square is an appropriately elegant interior. The luxurious, chandeliered lobby sets the civilised tone, which the cocktail lounge and bar follow. The latter has live piano music every evening. The Waterloo Despatch bar is in pub style serving traditional ales and snacks. The Best of Both Worlds is open for breakfast, lunch and supper. The main eating outlet is the Adam Restaurant, while the Japanese *Shogun* (see separate entry) is also on the premises. Air-conditioned bedrooms range from standards (decent size, with reproduction furniture) to de luxe, with desks, seating areas and bars, and the top-of-the-range suites, which offer many extras and luxury touches. One floor of rooms (60) is designated non-smoking. A new business centre supports the conference facilities (max 100 delegates) and a health club was planned as we went to press. No dogs. *Rooms 318. Valeting, shopping arcade.* AMERICAN EXPRESS *Access, Diners, Visa.*

E14   Britannia International Hotel   68%   £95

Tel 071-712 0100   Fax 071-712 0102   **H**

Marsh Wall E14 9SJ   **Map 17 D4**

Blending in with the surrounding modern architecture the tall International stands just off West Ferry Road almost in the shadow of the Canary Wharf Tower which faces it across part of the former West India and Millwall Docks. Public rooms make full and good use of the waterside location and the views become panoramic from the bedrooms. There are three restaurants, four bars and no fewer than 15 conference and banqueting rooms. The hotel is colourfully decorated throughout and features numerous large Chinese artefacts. There's limited underground parking. *Rooms 442. Indoor swimming pool, gym, sauna, steam room, solarium, beauty & hair salon.* AMERICAN EXPRESS *Access, Diners, Visa.*

Note that all telephone numbers with area codes starting with 0 will start 01 from 16 April 1995.

WC2   Brixtonian Backayard   £50

Tel 071-240 2769   Fax 071-737 5521   **R**

4 Neal's Yard Covent Garden WC2H 9DP   **Map 21 B1**

Virtually hidden in a corner of Neal's Yard, the Brixtonian has a colourful ground-floor American-style bar featuring a collection of 200 rums and a range of some 20 exotic and potent cocktails of which the most famous is the Brixton Riot – similar to a Pina Colada, but jazzed-up. The restaurant is on the first floor and is dainty, with white broderie anglaise-bordered fabric everywhere. The menu makes a monthly tour of the Caribbean islands with a May menu featuring the influence of St Kitts. In one of the very best West Indian restaurants in the country the menu includes the likes of Creole peanut soup, saltfish with wonderful baked johnny cakes and grilled quail with paw paw sauce among the starters. Main dishes could be a deliciously spicy chicken breast with grilled banana, pork chop with mango creole sauce, red snapper with ginger sauce or green banana pie. Flavours are superb and the cooking first class. Sweets too are excellent including a delicious crème de Kahlua mousse or orange and Christophene cake. No smoking. Fridays reserved for women only. *Seats 36. Parties 20. D only 7-11. Closed Sat & Sun, all Bank Holidays.* AMERICAN EXPRESS *Access, Visa.*
Also at:
SW9 11 Dorrell Street Brixton SW9 8EG Tel 071-978 8870   **Map 17 C5**
Similar decor and menu; prices slightly lower.

W1   Brown's Hotel   76%   £250

Tel 071-493 6020   Fax 071-493 9381   **HR**

Albermarle Street (& Dover Street) W1A 4SW   Map 18 D3

Famously stylish with a rich history going back to Victorian times,
Brown's is an institution and one of London's more genteel hotels. In the
public areas you'll find marvellous panelling, original moulded ceilings and
elaborate cornices, stained-glass windows, a quiet writing room, a chintzy
lounge (where legendary afternoon teas are served – gentlemen must wear
a jacket and tie!), and even a centenary *Times* clock in the reception area.
The air-conditioned bedrooms, with some of the most elegant doors
in town, have recently been refurbished to a high standard with high-
quality fabrics and good antique furniture. Mini-bars, satellite TV and
a host of personal extras are standard. Single rooms are particularly large,
each with a double bed and two easy chairs. Super marble bathrooms
include a bidet and bathrobe, as well as quality toiletries. Service
is impeccably correct throughout. Excellent facilities for small functions
and meetings. No dogs. Forte Exclusive Hotels. *Rooms 118.*
Access, Diners, Visa.

Restaurant   £85

New chef Aidan McCormack has brought a lighter and more modern
touch to dishes served here, in contrast to the polished and rather quaint
service. Alongside the à la carte menu, there's a frequently-changing table
d'hote offered both at lunch and dinner – typical examples being a smooth
chicken and goose liver parfait with a toasted brioche and dribble of oil,
poached red snapper on a bed of cabbage leaves with saffron sauce, carrots
and baby new potatoes, and a warm bread-and-butter pudding from the
dessert trolley, which also features amaretto cake, mango délice and
chocolate mousse cake. Traditional dishes, such as consommé (wild
mushrooms), Dover sole and daube of beef also appear on the menu –
hurrah! Unusually (these days), only filter coffee is served. *Seats 35.
Parties 14. L 12.15-3 (Sun 12.30-2.30) D 6-10 (Sun 6.30-9.30). Set L &
D £22.50.*

EC1   Bubb's   £75

Tel 071-236 2435   **R**

329 Central Markets EC1A 9NB   Map 20 B1

A little corner of France at the junction of Snow Hill and Farringdon
Street. Though it's more or less part of Smithfield market, Bubb's is an
excellent place for fish as well as meat. The fish choice changes according
to what's best on the day, so you might find grilled sardines, poached
salmon or halibut with *sauce dieppoise*. On the meat front come escalope
of veal with lime, duck à l'orange, lamb cutlets with herbs and beef fillet
with mushrooms and béarnaise sauce. *Seats 75. Parties 16. Private Room 25.
L only 12-2.30. Closed Sat, Sun & all Bank Holidays.* AMERICAN EXPRESS *Access,
Diners, Visa.*

SW11   Buchan's   £45

Tel 071-228 0888   Fax 071-924 1718   **R**

62 Battersea Bridge Road SW11 3AG   Map 19 B6

200 yards south of Battersea Bridge, Buchan's announces itself with a bright
blue double-shop frontage. Inside, the area is divided between front bar and
restaurant behind. The style is French/Scottish, with a good choice of bar
snacks (from steak sandwich to wild boar sausages with apple and mashed
tatties) complementing the fortnightly-changing restaurant menu. The
latter might feature deep-fried oysters with garlic on basil croutons, roast
duck salad with pickled cherries, prawn and cod terrine, braised pig's
trotter with wild mushrooms and spicy stuffed vegetable brioche with
a pear salsa alongside haggis with neeps and tatties and good Scottish steaks.

Soufflés are something of a speciality. Spotted Dick with custard and pear and poire William flambé among the puddings, unless Scottish cheeses or Gaelic coffee take your fancy. Sunday lunches offer good value. A few tables are set outside on the pavement in good weather. *Seats* 70. *Parties* 50. *Private Room* 50. L 12-2.45 D 6-10.45 (Sun 7-10.30). Closed 25 & 26 Dec. Set L (Sun) £8.50/£10.50. AMERICAN EXPRESS *Access, Diners, Visa.*

SE1   Butlers Wharf Chop-house   NEW   £75

Tel 071-403 3403   Fax 071-403 3414   **R**

Butlers Wharf Building 36E Shad Thames SE1 2YE   Map 17 D4

Part of Sir Terence Conran's string of restaurants, all of which benefit from a superb riverside location close to Tower Bridge. The bar offers a range of light snacks (Dublin Bay prawns, Scottish smoked salmon, fish and chips, mixed grill, British cheeses, trifle) while the restaurant with its oak banquette seating and tables provides a short selection of well-thought-out modern British dishes. At lunchtimes, a particularly busy period, there is a three-course, fixed-price menu that includes a daily roast and is supplemented by a blackboard of daily specials. Excellent breads precede starters such as a warm kipper and potato salad, a super poached cod salad with baby spinach, asparagus and lemon mayonnaise or spiced beef with piccalilli. Main courses include a few grills like succulent veal chop with anchovy butter or rib steak with bone marrow and a red wine sauce as well as the likes of salmon in pastry, steamed brill with asparagus, tomato and parsley or steak, kidney and oyster pudding (for two evening diners only, oysters optional). Lincolnshire chine with mustard leeks, veal and ham pie with pickles, roast duck breast with peas, bacon and lettuce, and beef stew with orange, celery and walnuts, along with over a dozen good puddings (from seasonal rhubarb fool or banana fritters with caramel to raspberry meringue, sticky toffee pudding and Cambridge burnt cream), complete the evening picture. The weekend brunch menu served in the bar includes a drink – try a pint of Theakston's best bitter or a Greyhound cocktail, a mix of Brut de Chardonnay, Cointreau and grapefruit juice; more traditional offerings (including kedgeree and roast beef and Yorkshire pudding) in the restaurant. Splendidly efficient service comes with a smile even at the busiest times. As in all of Conran's restaurants, a fine and balanced wine list; some good-value clarets are served by the jug, several wines by the glass; only French wines available in half bottles. *Seats* 115 (rest) 40 (bar). *Parties* 12. L 12-3 (Sat & Sun bar from 11.30) D 6-11 Jun-Sept 12-11. Set L £19.50 (weekends: bar brunch £12.50/£14.50). Closed L Sat (Rest), D Sun (all), 4 days Christmas. AMERICAN EXPRESS *Access, Diners, Visa.*

W8   Byblos   £50

Tel 071-603 4422   **R**

262 Kensington High Street W8 6ND   Map 19 A4

A dark, intimate restaurant filled with Middle Eastern artefacts. The Lebanese food is simple yet authentic: hot and cold hors d'oeuvre, charcoal-grilled kebabs, daily specials such as bamia, fassoulia and kebbeh. *Seats* 48. Meals 11.45am-11.45pm. Closed 25 & 26 Dec. Set L £6.85 Set D £9.85. AMERICAN EXPRESS *Access, Diners, Visa.*

SW1   Cadogan Hotel   74%   £153

Tel 071-235 7141   Fax 071-245 0994   **H**

75 Sloane Street SW1X 9SG   Map 19 C4

Lillie Langtry lived here in the 1890s in a house which later became part of the hotel, and it was in the hotel that Oscar Wilde was arrested and taken to Reading Gaol. Management pay great attention to offering a personal welcome and service and panelled drawing room and elegant restaurant are part of its traditional old-fashioned charm. Double bedrooms are large and attractively arranged, and amenities include colour TV, trouser press, mini-bar, hairdryer and safe. Bathrooms are beautifully done out with blue Portuguese tiles. Enquire about the hotel's special rates during the summer, at weekends and during major London shows. Banqueting/conference facilities for 32/40. No dogs. **Rooms** 64. *Garden, tennis. Closed 24-30 Dec.* AMERICAN EXPRESS® *Access, Diners, Visa.*

NW1	Café Delancey	£40

Tel 071-387 1985 Fax 071-383 5314	**R**
3 Delancey Street Camden NW1 7NN	Map 16 C3

Every item on the menu is available throughout the long opening hours at this large and popular Continental-style café just off Camden High Street. This could be anything from a croissant with coffee to a full English breakfast, mushroom feuilleté, sandwiches, omelettes, sausages with onions and rösti, rack of lamb and chargrilled steak. Tables outside in summer. **Seats** 200. *Parties 20. Meals 8am-midnight. Closed 25 & 26 Dec, 1 Jan. Access, Visa.*

SE1	Café dell'Ugo **NEW**	£60

Tel 071-407 6001 Fax 071-357 8806	**R**
56 Tooley Street SE1 2SZ	Map 20 C3

Underneath London Bridge station (occupying one of the vast arches), a few yards from the London Dungeon, this easternmost outpost of the Anthony Worrall Thompson portfolio features a spacious bar on the ground floor serving extensive bar meals while the restaurant above is reached via a wide, central staircase. Under the vaulted brick ceiling, painted in a ragged-effect wine and cream, tables are partly lit by thick round candles which help create a cellar-like ambience. The food is quite simply put together but flavours and textures have been very carefully worked out, producing dishes that are full of sparkle. Seared goat's cheese layered with red onion as a terrine is accompanied by a superb, refreshingly acidic apple chutney and counterpoised by a salad of fresh mixed herbs; spicy sardines come on rösti with harissa and yoghurt and marinated beef carpaccio has a wild watercress salad and polenta crisps. Main dishes follow in the same innovative mould – a rolled soufflé with wilted greens, leeks and cheeses, red pepper sauce and curry oil, a hotchpotch of fishes in a tomato and fennel bisque with cold lime butter or roast cardamom chicken with marinated mushrooms and couscous. Sweets, too, are outstandingly good, ranging from marinated red fruits with mascarpone cream and walnut honey pie to chargrilled bananas and toffee sauce; the top-of-the-form rhubarb, orange and pistachio trifle contains no alcohol, but when it's this good who cares? **Seats** 75. *Parties 18. L 12-3 D 7-11. Closed L Sat, all Sun, Bank Holidays.* AMERICAN EXPRESS® *Access, Diners, Visa.*

See the Restaurant Round-up for easy, quick-reference comparisons.

EC1	Café du Marché	£55

Tel 071-608 1609	**R**
22 Charterhouse Square Charterhouse Mews EC1M 6AH	Map 16 D3

Tucked away in a mews between Smithfield Market and the Barbican, this former meat warehouse has the feel of a converted country barn. The appealing set menus offer French regional cooking made with fresh products and commendable care to detail. The set menu ranges from the traditional (fish soup, *rillons de porc, bavette aux échalotes, choucroute*) to the contemporary (*risotto d'artichaut, tartufo, oeuf poché; salade de pousse, pissenlit et parmesan*). There's also a no-choice menu at £11.50. Le Grenier on the first floor specialises in grills. Booking is advised at lunchtime. **Seats** 60 + 45. *Parties 10. Private Room 66. L 12-2.30 D 6-10. Closed L Sat, all Sun, Bank Holidays, Easter, Christmas/New Year. Set L £11.50 & £19.75 Set D £19.75. Access, Visa.*

SW1   Café Fish   £55

Tel 071-930 3999   Fax 071-839 4880   **R**

39 Panton Street off Haymarket SW1Y 4EA   Map 21 A3

Part of the Chez Gérard group, an informal café-restaurant just off
Haymarket. The menu is more or less all fish from oysters, mussels and
squid to bouillabaisse, roast monkfish, fish cakes and Chinese-style sautéed
scallops. There's also a small section of vegetarian dishes. The cover charge
includes a fish paté starter with French bread. Downstairs is a wine bar
open from 11.30am to 11pm Mon-Sat (closed Sun) and serving a simpler
selection plus steak and club sandwiches. Convenient for Haymarket
theatres and Leicester Square. *Seats 90. Parties 30. L 12-3 D 5.45-11.30.
Closed L Sat, all Sun, 25 & 26 Dec, 1 Jan.* AMERICAN EXPRESS® *Access,
Diners, Visa.*

SW7   Café Lazeez   £60

Tel 071-581 9993   **R**

93 Old Brompton Road South Kensington SW7 3LD Map 19 B5

A minimalist brasserie/restaurant on two floors next to Christie's South
Kensington auction rooms. The cooking of Indian-inspired dishes is as
unlikely as the starkly modern setting. Separate brasserie and restaurant
menus offer a mix of traditional and 'evolved' dishes – from lentil soup and
Indian Welsh rarebit with garlic salami to spiced haddock fillet, tandoori
quail, tuna salad, vegetarian platters and frontier burger as well as more
familiar curries (although the word doesn't appear anywhere on the menus
– it's that different). Sunday brings a fixed-price buffet menu (£8.95).
Omar Kayyam Indian champagne (the 'house bubbly') is also sold by the
glass. No-smoking room. *Seats 130. Private Room 60. Meals 11am-12.30am
(Sun 10.30am-10.30pm). Closed 25 Dec.* AMERICAN EXPRESS® *Access, Diners, Visa.*

Our inspectors *never* book in the name of Egon Ronay's Guides. They
disclose their identity only if they are considering an establishment for
inclusion in the next edition of the Guide.

W1   Café Royal Grill Room   ★   £120

Tel 071-439 9090   **R**

68 Regent Street W1R 6EL   Map 18 D3

The Café Royal, part of London's culinary history, has undergone a sea
change in recent years. As well as refurbishment, Herbert Berger was
brought in to revitalise the kitchens. The jewel in the crown of this
restaurant complex is the Grill Room, splendidly decorated in grand
baroque style, with ornate mirrors, murals and ceiling paintings. The
names are misleading: this is certainly not a café and only a few token grills
(steak, lobster etc.) are offered; the raison d'etre here is the classical French
menu. Ingredients are rich, and customers should be similarly endowed:
to begin, terrine of langoustines with tarragon butter and Sevruga caviar
with blinis set the style. Calf's sweetbreads with foie gras, beef with truffles
or roasted fillet of sea bass with fennel, much enjoyed, might follow.
Desserts are no anti-climax, chocolate millefeuille with orange and Grand
Marnier sabayon, or perhaps a scrumptious almond and apple pithiviers
with blackberry coulis. Service is formal, and well orchestrated by maitre
d' David Arcusi. Definitely a place for the special occasion. Jackets and ties
are required for gentlemen. In the ground-floor, also rather grand,
Brasserie, an all-day menu offers simpler fare à la carte or fixed-price.
*Seats 45. Parties 14. Private Room 50. L 12.30-2.45 D 6-10.15. Closed L Sat,
all Sun, Bank Holidays, 3 days Christmas. Set L £22.50 Set D £36 Brasserie
£14.75/£17.75.* AMERICAN EXPRESS® *Access, Diners, Visa.*

NW3   Caffè Graffiti   £60

Tel 071-431 7579   **R**

71 Hampstead High Street NW3 1QP   Map 16 B2

A former coffee shop transformed into a charming little restaurant with
pavement tables for summer dining. The food is Mediterranean in style
beginning with delicious country bread served with a garlic and herb-
flavoured Tuscan oil or an excellent black and green olive tapénade.
A blackboard lists a selection of daily specials that supplement the short,
imaginative carte. Typical dishes are warm goat's cheese salad with
raspberry vinaigrette, fresh mussels with pesto and garlic croutons to begin
and, to follow, breast of chicken stuffed with mozzarella, basil and sun-
dried tomatoes with olive fettucine or confit of duck on a bed of green
lentils and coriander garnished with deep-fried celeriac. There are good
vegetarian options too and enjoyable sweets such as honey and *fromage frais*
tart or mixed fruit zabaglione. Overall, a simple, friendly local restaurant
where the food's not brilliant but is certainly very acceptable. *Seats 45.*
Parties 20. L 12-3 D 6.30-11 (Sun to 10.30). Closed 25 Dec.
Access, Diners, Visa.

NW1   Camden Brasserie   £55

Tel 071-482 2114   **R**

216 Camden High Street NW1 8QR   Map 16 C3

Busy brasserie with a short menu based around charcoal-grilled meats (all
served with terrific little chips) and fresh pasta. Spicy chicken wings and
gravad lax with dill mustard sauce are among the starters and there are
some excellent salads (spinach and goat's cheese, eel with chorizo and aged
vinegar). From the grill come corn-fed chicken, calf's liver, salmon,
Toulouse sausages, fillets of lamb and steaks. The sister restaurant *The
Underground Café* (see entry) is in the basement. *Seats 105. Parties 18.
L 12-3 (Sun 12.30-3.30) D 6-11.30 (Sun 5-10.30). Closed all 24-26 &
D 31 Dec. Access, Visa.*

W10   Canal Brasserie   £40

Tel 081-960 2732   **R**

Canalot Studios 222 Kensal Road W10 5BN   Map 16 B3

A canalside setting, with tables outside in summer, for enjoying a short
selection of dishes with a contemporary ring: *focaccia* of roast vegetables,
herbs and goat's cheese; white fish cakes; baked breast of chicken with
sweet vegetable salsa and fried rice; penne with broccoli, smoked bacon,
marjoram, mushrooms and crème fraiche. Open for lunch Mon-Fri, and
on certain evenings for theme and special events (phone for details).
Seats 67. L 12-3. Closed Sat, Sun & Bank Holidays. Access, Visa.

SW19   Cannizaro House   76%   £160

Tel 081-879 1464   Fax 081-879 7338   **H**

West Side Wimbledon Common SW19 4UF   Map 17 B6

On the edge of Wimbledon Common, a Georgian mansion where the tone
is set by stately lawned gardens and the bay-windowed drawing room,
which boasts giant flower arrangements, antique furniture, oil paintings
and sumptuous seating. Similar elegance is to be found in the restaurant and
Queen Elizabeth room, with cream, pale green and pink colour scheme,
crystal chandelier, draped curtains and ornate gilt mirror. The bedrooms,
each with its own character, are superbly appointed, with top-quality
reproduction furniture and bathrooms featuring marble fittings, radio/TV
speakers, phones and bathrobes. New-wing rooms are smaller, their views
inferior. Reduced rates at weekends; higher rates during the All England
Lawn Tennis Championships at the end of June. No children under 8 but

8-16s stay free in parents' room. Conference/banqueting facilities for 45/80.
Mount Charlotte Thistle. *Rooms 46. Garden.* AMERICAN EXPRESS *Access,
Diners, Visa.*

SW10   The Canteen   ★   £60

Tel 071-351 7330   Fax 071-351 6189   R

Harbour Yard Chelsea Harbour SW10 0XD   Map 19 B6

It has been very much to Chelsea Harbour's benefit that the triumvirate
of Marco Pierre White, Michael Caine and Claudio Pulze decided to open
The Canteen a couple of years ago. Though he doesn't personally do the
cooking – this is masterminded by Tim Paine and Peter Raffael – Marco's
undeniable flair has created a stimulating and entertaining restaurant with
agreeably accessible prices (by making all the dishes at each stage one-price,
the pricing effectively offers a two-course £19 fixed-price menu). In a light
and airy atmosphere, with the bonus of marina views from much-prized
conservatory window tables, the interior offers plenty of interest as well
as a good buzz. Drinks may be taken in the foyer/bar area where there are
just a few tables and seats at the high bar counter; the distinctive playing
card decor links this area with the main restaurant. In the large, L-shaped
dining room on two levels, begin, perhaps, with a velouté of celery with
poached egg and chervil, gazpacho with crab, saffron or squid ink risotto,
Savoy cabbage alsacienne, artichokes barigoule (stuffed with duxelles)
or parfait of foie gras and chicken livers with toast poilane; papillote
of smoked salmon 'Albert Roux' is served with toasted brioche and roast
sea scallops with sauce vièrge attract a small supplement. Fish is a favourite
ingredient among the main courses with seven or so dishes offered, ranging
from smoked haddock with poached egg and new potatoes to red mullet
with ratatouille provençale, beignets of sage and a tapénade sauce; tuna,
turbot, brill, cod and salmon also featured on a recent menu. Carnivores
may relish roast rump of lamb niçoise, pot-roast pork with spices and
ginger or honey-roast roast duck leg with pommes fondant and
a bittersweet sauce. The choice is diverse, the same menu (changed
seasonally) offered for lunch and dinner, desserts delightful and service on-
the-ball (if sometimes a little dour). Wines are sensibly priced with over 20
bottles under £20; a list of fine wines is also available on request. Easy
parking in the Harbour complex's underground car park, from where lifts
can take you direct to the restaurant area. *Seats 135. Parties 12. L 12-3
(12.30-3.30 Sun) D 6.30-12 (7-11 Sun).* AMERICAN EXPRESS *Access, Visa.*

SE1   Cantina del Ponte   £60

Tel 071-403 5403   Fax 071-403 0267   R

Butlers Wharf Building 36C Shad Thames SE1 2YE   Map 17 D4

The opportunity for fine weather alfresco dining on a terrace overlooking
the Thames is a major feature in this light, airy restaurant's favour. Inside,
rough terracotta-tiled floors, simple square maple tables and rush-seated
chairs create a sunny Mediterranean ambience. The food, too, follows
in being simple, rustic and fashionable – and definitely Mediterranean in its
inspiration. Risotto of mixed mushrooms, warm salad of chargrilled
calamari, sautéed calf's liver with sweet and sour onions and *panna cotta*
with seasonal fruits show the style. Next to *Pont de la Tour* in Sir Terence
Conran's Gastrodrome. *Seats 95. Parties 20. L 12-3 D 6-11. Closed D Sun,
3 days Christmas.* AMERICAN EXPRESS *Access, Diners, Visa.*

SW3   The Capital   83%   £245

Tel 071-589 5171   Fax 071-225 0011   HR

Basil Street SW3 1AT   Map 19 C4

Handily situated just a stone's throw from Harrods, Margaret and David
Levin's splendid little hotel is grand in every other sense. From the moment
you enter the foyer, you cannot help but feel the warmth of welcome,
observe the elegance, charm and quality of the surroundings and marvel

at the sheer professionalism of all the staff. The public areas might be small, but the handsome furnishings more than compensate – even the lift has style! When built in the early 70s the hotel had 60 bedrooms, but the smaller rooms were integrated with the larger ones alongside, thus creating intimate suites with not only a luxurious bathroom, but also a separate cloakroom. Interior designer Nina Campbell was responsible for much of the stylish redecoration in the delightful bedrooms, which are individually appointed with custom-built furniture, quite bold but restful fabrics, good pictures and discreet lighting with bedside controls. Each is equipped with adjustable air-conditioning, mini-bar and satellite TV, and de luxe rooms also have a safe and a guest umbrella hidden inside the wardrobe. Fresh fruit (usually one variety in tip-top condition) is changed daily. As for the fabulous bathrooms – there's no need to bring anything, from exquisite toiletries to bathrobes, bathmats to spare toothbrushes, everything is there. Housekeeping is exemplary, including the turn-down of beds (note the excellent bed linen) in the evening. The first floor provides two elegant dining/meeting rooms for up to 24 guests. Limited own parking. *Rooms 48.* AMERICAN EXPRESS *Access, Diners, Visa.*

Restaurant ★★ £120

Chef Philip Britten will shortly have a 'new' and more spacious restaurant in which to display his skills, and though we may have been slightly critical last year, we are not this year. The restaurant (which will close for several weeks early in 1995) is to be restyled, with a new facade, bay windows, wooden shutters made by David Linley, and etched glass similar to that in the bar area. The various menus (a set-price fish dinner menu at £40, two at lunch, and à la carte) are pleasingly and sensibly written in English, though the style of cooking is not necessarily just British – there's modern French and Mediterranean as well. Presenting two set-price 3-course lunch menus side by side, with three choices in each section, is intriguing, the more so since there's only a £3 price difference between them and no perceptible dissimilarity in the quality of ingredients. Why not just offer one menu at £23.50 with an equally wide choice of courses? No matter, we recently sampled both and the dishes emanating from the kitchen were faultless: a strongly (but correctly) seasoned chicken liver risotto of the right texture with toasted pine nuts and basil, sole gratin with firm asparagus and beautifully browned Muscadet sabayon, tender baked Blackleg chicken with root vegetables and cep sauce, a perfect warm apricot soufflé with an apricot compote, and a crisp millefeuille of strawberries. On the fish menu you'll encounter the likes of ragout of scallops and courgettes with crème fraiche, braised sea bass in champagne and shallots on a coulis(?) of scallops and fricassee of lobster and ginger with spinach pasta and beurre blanc, while à la carte meat dishes include pot-roasted squab pigeon on a bed of roots and cinnamon or best end of lamb wrapped in a purée of artichoke with a rosemary sauce. Cooking is precise, flavours intense and fresh-tasting, presentation inviting, all coming together to create dishes of real merit, and this is matched by unobtrusive service from a younger brigade than previously. All the important extras are in evidence as well: smart table settings and pretty floral decorations, decent bread rolls and good butter, cheeses in tip-top condition, excellent coffee and petits fours, and a fine winelist featuring French classics at not too outrageous prices and many half bottles. *Seats 45. Parties 8. Private Room 25. L 12-2.30 Set D 7-11.15. Set L £22 & £25 D £40.*

SW1   Le Caprice   ↑   £70

Tel 071-629 2239   Fax 071-493 9040   **R**

Arlington House Arlington Street SW1A 1RT   **Map 18 D3**

A cool, fashionable restaurant in black and white, with David Bailey's
classic photographs on the walls. The menu mixes trendy and traditional,
with Thai-spiced shrimp broth, grilled yellow fin tuna and risotto
of butternut squash sharing the list with Caesar salad, eggs Benedict, salmon
fishcakes and steak au poivre. Sunday brunch is launched with pitchers
of Bucks Fizz or Bloody Mary. *Seats 80. Parties 10. L 12-3 (Sun to 3.30)
D 6-12. Closed Christmas-New Year.* AMERICAN EXPRESS *Access, Diners, Visa.*

W1   Caravan Serai   £45

Tel 071-935 1208   Fax 071-431 4969   **R**

50 Paddington Street W1M 3RQ   **Map 18 C2**

Caravan Serai is a cheerful, relaxed place with bright Afghan decor and
artefacts and authentic Afghan cooking that puts the emphasis more
on subtle spices than fiery chili, reminiscent of both Arab and Indian
cuisine. Among the house recommendations are the national dish *ashak* –
pasta filled with leeks served with minced lamb and yoghurt (there's also
a vegetarian version); *poorshuda* – stuffed poussin; and *shahi korma* – king
prawns cooked in delicate spices. Sister restaurant *Buzkash* in Putney has
changed hands. *Seats 55. Private Room 18. L 11-3 D 6-11.30 (Sun to 10.30).
Closed 25 & 26 Dec. Set L £9.95 Set D £19.95.* AMERICAN EXPRESS *Access,
Diners, Visa.*

SE6   Casa Cominetti   £50

Tel 081-697 2314   **R**

129 Rushey Green Catford SE6 4AA   **Map 17 D6**

Italian restaurant with exceptional staying power (it dates back to 1916!).
The menu rarely departs from standard dishes, but cooking is consistently
enjoyable. The chef lists sea bass Mareschal and fillet of beef olives among
his specialities. *Seats 40. L 12-2.30 D 6.30-11. Closed L Sat, all Sun, 25 &
26 Dec. Set L £12.95/£13.95 Set D £13.95.* AMERICAN EXPRESS *Access,
Diners, Visa.*

> If we recommend meals in a hotel or inn a separate entry is made for its
> restaurant.

N1   Casale Franco   £60

Tel 071-226 8994   Fax 071-359 5569   **R**

134 Upper Street Islington N1 1PQ   **Map 16 C3**

The illuminated chevron sign of a Citroën garage locates the alleyway
on Upper Street which opens out into a courtyard with outside tables
(seating for 25). The restaurant has a truly authentic rustic decor with
rough redbrick walls and a concrete floor. The fact that it looks like
an outbuilding is part of its charm. No bookings are taken in the evening
so it's best to arrive before 8pm if queues outside are to be avoided, such
is the continuing popularity of the place. The food is fairly classic Italian,
the staple being pasta with grilled meats, fish and particularly good pizzas.
The latter are not available at lunchtimes or as a single-course meal after
8pm. Flavours are generally true and dishes like mushroom-stuffed smoked
mozzarella, pecorino cheese with pears and walnuts, mixed grill of fish, and
crab (a speciality) are enjoyable. *Seats 130. Parties 50. Private Room 50.
L Fri-Sun 12.30-2.30 D 6.30-11.30 (Sun to 11pm). Closed L Tue-Thu, all
Mon, 1 week end Aug, 1 week Christmas. Access, Visa.*

SW16   Caterino's   £45

Tel 081-764 6022   **R**

1540 London Road Norbury SW16 4EU   **Map 17 C6**

Very much a Caterino family affair, with daughter Mina and Maurizio, the
manager, helping Giovanni at front of house and Maria-Grazia in the
kitchen of this smart Italian restaurant on the A23 Brighton road, near
Norbury BR station. The menu is extensive, with seafood and shellfish
(skate, halibut, trout, prawns, Dover sole) a particular speciality on the
carte. Daily specials such as stuffed aubergine, fresh mussels, and quails –
either with bacon, mushrooms and shallots or oven-baked with polenta and
chick peas – extend the range and there are simpler but equally well-
executed dishes on a choice of economical fixed-price menus. Ample
parking space at the rear. *Uno Plus* is an integral wine bar next door
serving a wide selection of simpler fare – from Mediterranean tapas
to pasta, pizzas and burgers. Open occasional Sunday lunches (eg Mothering
Sunday). *Seats 70. L 12-3 D 6-11.30. Closed L Sat & Bank Holidays, all Sun.
Set meals £10.50 & £12.50.* AMERICANEXPRESS *Access, Diners, Visa.*

SW10   Chapter 11   £50

Tel 071-351 1683   **R**

47 Hollywood Road Fulham SW10   **Map 19 B5**

Just off Fulham Road, opposite the Chelsea & Westminster Hospital, John
Brinkley's informal, busy brasserie serves a menu that mixes traditional and
modern elements: soupe au pistou, bang bang chicken, crab salad with lime
and coriander, Thai prawn curry, rack of lamb with garlic flageolet beans
and parsnip fries, and grilled calf's liver served with bacon, mashed swede
and Lyonnaise potatoes. The price of a main course includes a pudding.
In summer tables (seating 24) are set out in the back garden. *Seats 60.
Parties 12. Private Room 40. D only 7-11.30. Closed Sun, 4 days Easter, 25 &
26 Dec, Bank Holidays.* AMERICANEXPRESS *Access, Visa.*

NW3   Charles Bernard Hotel   60%   £65

Tel 071-794 0101   Fax 071-794 0100   **H**

5 Frognal Hampstead NW3 6AL   **Map 16 B2**

In a quiet suburban setting just off Finchley Road and well connected
by public transport to the West End, this is a 70s' hotel with open-plan day
rooms and practical overnight accommodation. No dogs. *Rooms 57.*
AMERICANEXPRESS *Access, Diners, Visa.*

W5   Charlotte's Place   £50

Tel 081-567 7541   **R**

16 St Matthew's Road Ealing W5 3JT   **Map 17 A4**

Intimate little bistro/restaurant on the edge of Ealing Common (easy
parking) serving unpretentious, mainly English fare from haddock smokie
pie and chicken liver paté to rainbow trout stuffed with cream cheese and
chives, lamb cutlets and a salad of warm duck breast. Specialities include
salmon mousse wrapped in smoked salmon and individual beef Wellington
(served very rare). *Seats 40. Private Room 20. L 12.30-2 D 7.30-10.
Closed L Sat, all Sun, check other closures when booking.
Set L £12.50/£14.50.* AMERICANEXPRESS *Access, Diners, Visa.*

SW1   The Chelsea   63%   £189

Tel 071-235 4377   Fax 071-235 3705   **H**

17-25 Sloane Street Knightsbridge SW1X 9NU   **Map 19 C4**

A modern Sarova Group hotel close to Knightsbridge underground station,
Harrods, fashion shops and Hyde Park. Chief feature of the public areas
is a glass-roofed atrium with a polished steel spiral staircase; this runs up to

a restaurant and bar whose dominant black decor gives a rather stark look. Bedrooms are generally not very roomy, but the expected modern accessories are provided and there's 24hr room service and porterage. One floor of rooms (38) is designated non-smoking. Children up to 14 stay free in parents' room. NCP parking. **Rooms** 225. *Hairdressing, lounge (8am–midnight).* AMERICAN EXPRESS *Access, Diners, Visa.*

NW1	Cheng-Du	£60
Tel 071-485 8058		**R**
9 Parkway Camden Town NW1 7PG		**Map 16 C3**

Friendly Szechuan restaurant next to the Jazz Café at the lower end of Parkway. Among the specialities are braised duck in plum sauce, hot and sour pork and shredded veal with bamboo shoots, carrots and peppers. *Seats* 70. L 12-2.30 D 6.30-11.30. Set D £17.20. Closed 25-27 Dec. AMERICAN EXPRESS *Access, Visa.*

W1	Chesterfield Hotel	70%	£170
Tel 071-491 2622 Fax 071-491 4793			**H**
35 Charles Street W1X 8LX			**Map 18 C3**

Named after the third Earl of Chesterfield, a renowned Mayfairite of the 18th century, this charming hotel has a very English feel. A splendid old chandelier, a huge leather chesterfield and leather buttonback chairs set the tone in the foyer and a pianist enlivens the evenings in the dark-coloured, English club-style bar. By contrast, the Terrace is a light, cheerful, modern room full of plants, where you can take a late breakfast, a snack or a full meal. The bedrooms are comfortably appointed in traditional style, using bold fabrics and darkwood furniture; Executive Club members get extra service such as shoe cleaning, secretarial facilities and complimentary newspaper; there are also several suites. No dogs. **Rooms** 110. AMERICAN EXPRESS *Access, Diners, Visa.*

N4	Chez Liline	£45
Tel 071-263 6550		**R**
101 Stroud Green Road Finsbury Park N4 3PX		**Map 16 C2**

Sister to *La Gaulette*, this Mauritian restaurant offers a long, exclusively fishy menu that could include parrot fish braised with aubergines, sea bass with red wine and oyster mushrooms, Trinidadian prawns with ginger and spring onions, and bourgeois with aïoli. Assiette Créole is a selection of tropical fish with tomatoes, herbs and chili. Lobsters and prawns are other specialities. A family business with a happy atmosphere. *Seats* 44. *Set L & D* £10/£11.75. L 12.30-2.30 D 6.30-10.30. Closed Sun & Bank Holidays. AMERICAN EXPRESS *Access, Visa.*

SW10	Chez Max	↑	NEW	£65
Tel 071-835 0874				**R**
168 Ifield Road SW10 9AF				**Map 19 A5**

The inimitable Renzland brothers, Marc and Max, have given birth to a sibling to join *Le Petit Max* in Hampton Wick (qv). It occupies the former premises of *La Croisette*. A tight spiral staircase brings one to the basement dining room, unusually blessed with natural light. Bare wooden tables, a parquet floor, assorted chairs and vivid green walls hung with framed menus from famous restaurants set the scene. The short table d'hote menu follows the style so successful at Hampton Wick. Indeed, favourites are carried over – salad of duck breasts, imam bayildi and chargrilled guinea fowl with Provence herbs, here served with excellent spiced red cabbage and delicious mash. Other dishes might include escabeche of red mullet with tapénade crostini, or line-caught halibut with hollandaise. All this is accompanied by plump black olives and excellent bread flavoured with *fleur de sel*. To finish, either the cheese of the day, ensuring peak condition and satisfying the new cheese-keeping regulations, or desserts such as almond tart, crème brulée or a tarte tatin of pears are offered. Guests are encouraged to bring their own wine for a corkage charge (£3.50 a bottle, £7 a magnum); but unlike its sister restaurant a small, but carefully chosen, wine list is available. Service, led by Max, is welcoming and attentive. *Seats 50. Parties 8. L 12-2.30 D 7-11. Closed L Mon & Sat, all Sun, Bank Holidays (except Good Friday). Set L £15.50 Set D £23.50.*

W11   Chez Moi   £70

Tel 071-603 8267   **R**

1 Addison Avenue Holland Park W11 4QS   Map 17 B4

Owner-chef Richard Walton continues to keep old friends and win new at his comfortable, discreet little restaurant. He does this with a happy marriage of cooking styles, taking in both traditional and contemporary dishes. In the former category come scampi provençale, omelette Arnold Bennett and poule-au-pot, while flying a more fashionable flag are Thai- and Chinese-style salads, and grilled tuna with a light and creamy pepper sauce. Many of the desserts are on the naughty side, notably chocolate truffle cake with brandy and Benedictine. The set lunch menu offers excellent value for money. Decent wine list with fair prices and plenty of half bottles. *Seats 45. Parties 16. L 12.30-2 D 7-11. Closed L Sat, all Sun, Bank Holidays. Set L £14.* AMERICAN EXPRESS *Access, Diners, Visa.*

W1   Chez Nico at Ninety Park Lane   ★★★   £135

Tel 071-409 1290   Fax 071-355 4877   **R**

90 Park Lane London W1A 3AA   Map 18 C3

Nico's quest for perfection continues apace at Forte's *Grosvenor House.* The opulent dining room is elegantly appointed with honey-coloured panelling brightened by mirrors and discreet lighting and Jean-Luc Giguel leads front-of-house with aplomb, setting exemplary standards of service. Menus are written in refreshingly straightforward English and the choice is long, with over 10 dishes at each stage. Sensational signature dishes remain, as in a salad of foie gras on toasted brioche with caramelised orange – a glorious combination of flavour and texture – and deserve to stay on the menu until the next century! There is no hyperbole, no flowery dish descriptions, and no flowing French. Nico's highly individual style of creativity evolves these days rather than explodes, and the pace is certainly less hectic than previously. Dishes are reworked, often simplifying but also subtly redefining and refining them; invention never takes a back seat, but we will see if the advertisement holds true: will a sun-dried tomato ever make it through the hallowed portals of King Nico's kitchen? Such delights as noisettes of pig's trotter stuffed with morels and sweetbreads and served with leeks, 'lasagne' of Dover sole fillets, or pressed foie gras and duck fillets with cherries, green peppercorns and toasted brioche are among the starters. The choice of fish main courses might include grilled red mullet or John Dory with celeriac chips, brill or steamed sea bass with fennel and basil purée, while eight meat and offal dishes range from veal sweetbreads with Parma ham and morel mushrooms to braised shin of veal in Madeira, and "confied" (confit-ed?) maize-fed chicken with grapes and foie gras pancakes. Diners wishing to push the boat out can indulge on warm lobster with artichoke, avocado and mango followed by fillet of Scotch beef with truffles and foie gras for small supplements to the fixed-price-only menu. Sauces are simply sensational – glossy veal reductions that simply burst with flavour; there are no corners cut in these kitchens. A magnificent climax to a truly unforgettable meal is the grand plate of assorted mini-desserts (£6 supplement) – a tasting of many of the desserts including a slice of chocolate tart with orange-flavoured custard, honey ice cream with gratinated grapefruit, lemon tart with lemon sorbet and raspberry sauce and iced nougat with caramelised nuts. It may be a cliché, but the thin apple tart with caramel sauce and vanilla ice cream is worth the advertised 20-minute wait – after all, a meal here is not one to be hurried.

Cheeses, served from a trolley, are all French and accompanied by grapes –
simple, straightforward, but, as throughout the restaurant, only the best,
tip-top quality ingredients are used. Although many dishes on the lunch
menu are simpler in construction and lighter in design, Nico's lunch
is surely one of London's great bargains – can you resist the idea
of marinated salmon with sweet pickled ginger and corn pancake, then
quail pie with smoked bacon, foie gras and grapes, finishing with poached
pears with crispy almond and chocolate sauce? Consistency is of supreme
importance in a restaurant that heads the Premier Division (London) and
Nico's watchful eye ensures that all is just as it should be. Mostly sky-high
prices (though they are inclusive of VAT and service) on an excellent wine
list that has a fair sprinkling of half bottles. No children under 5. *Seats* 70.
*Parties 10. Private Room 20. L 12-2 D 7-11. Closed L Sat, all Sun, 4 days
Easter, L Bank Holiday Mondays, 11 days Christmas/New Year. Set L £25
Set D £46 (2 courses)/£54.* AMERICAN EXPRESS *Access, Diners, Visa.*

W1	**Chiang Mai**	£40

Tel 071-437 7444 · **R**

48 Frith Street Soho W1V 5TE · **Map 21 A2**

Vatcharin Bhumichitr, author of *The Taste of Thailand* and *Thai Vegetarian
Cooking*, runs this Thai restaurant just by Ronnie Scott's jazz club. The
menu runs from satay, tempura and soups to hot and sour salads flavoured
with lemon and chili and good-value, one-dish rice and noodle dishes.
Vegetarians are well catered for. *Seats 60. Private Room 25. L 12-3 D 6-11.
Closed Bank Holidays. Set meals from £18.* AMERICAN EXPRESS *Access, Visa.*

WC2	**China City** **NEW**	£55

Tel 071-734 3388   Fax 071-734 3833 · **R**

White Bear Yard 25a Lisle Street WC2H 7BA · **Map 21 A2**

This surprisingly spacious and comfortable restaurant in the heart
of Chinatown offers a lengthy carte, with a bemusing selection of carefully
prepared, though fairly standard, Chinese fare. As well as traditional
favourites like pancake rolls, Peking duck and lemon chicken, an unusual
salad of crispy chicken with jelly fish and stir-fried beef in satay sauce (both
coconut and chili featured here) provide a refreshing change. A strong
seafood selection includes lobster, crab, squid and abalone, all on offer for
fair prices and each cooked in several different ways. Numerous set meals
are available, for a minimum of two (from £8 per head). Service is helpful
and friendly. *Seats 450. Meals 12-11.45. Closed Christmas Day.*
AMERICAN EXPRESS *Access, Diners, Visa.*

NW1	**China Jazz**	£70

Tel 071-482 3940 · **R**

29-31 Parkway Camden Town NW1 7PN · **Map 16 C3**

Jazz (live every evening, late at weekends) accompanies fairly expensive
Chinese food cooked without additives, preservatives or artificial colouring.
*Seats 90. Parties 90. L 12.30-3 (Sun 1-3) D 6.30-11.30 (Fri & Sat 7-12am
Sun 6.30-10.30). Closed L Sat.* AMERICAN EXPRESS *Access, Visa.*

W14	**Chinon** ★	£65

Tel 071-602 5968 · **R**

25 Richmond Way Shepherds Bush W14 0AS · **Map 17 B4**

A mainly local clientele frequents this Shepherds Bush restaurant, in which
Jonathan Hayes' cooking goes from strength to strength. The repertoire has
not changed much over the years, but has been carefully honed, while the
list of first-class suppliers has been expanded. The best salad leaves and
unusual vegetables come from Kent, game from Hampshire. Choice
is difficult: tender squid stuffed with pesto and tapénade, served with the
thinnest pasta (flavoured with squid ink) provides three delicious

contrasting textures. This might compete with gateau of fresh crab with avocado and fresh tomato and coriander sauce, or steamed mussels with garlic and ginger. For mains, perfectly cooked saddle of rabbit with Provence herbs and smoked sausage, or breasts of pigeon with spiced pear in filo, or perhaps delicious black pudding set the style. All come beautifully presented with small piles of vegetables and the house trademark – a Chinese cabbage parcel. This generally contains mashed potato; other surprises are not unknown, but they are always relevant to the principle ingredients. As much care is given to the six or so desserts offered, such as the warm pear tart with vanilla ice cream, decorated with spun sugar and strawberry julienne, though some may miss the erstwhile assiette gourmande. No children under 10. *Seats 50. Private Room 34. L 12.30-2, D 6.30-10.30. Closed L Sat, all Sun, most Bank Holidays, last week Aug, 1st week Sep, 1 week Christmas.* AMERICAN EXPRESS® *Access, Visa.*

W4	**Christian's**	**£60**
Tel 081-995 0382		**R**
Station Parade Burlington Lane Chiswick W4 3HD		**Map 17 A5**

A smart striped awning on the outside and an equally elegant interior with Regency striped sage green walls hung with a collection of contemporary art is Christian Gustin's domain. He surveys all from a pristine, white-tiled, raised, open-plan kitchen at the rear. Menus change daily and consist of a short but varied selection of modernised bourgeois classics prepared with considered regard to flavours and textures. Soufflés are a speciality and can appear beautifully risen, moist and featherlight, flavoured with a subtle blend of English cheeses to begin or as a hot chocolate soufflé for dessert. Other choices could be a bowl of creamy broccoli and walnut soup; pressed rabbit terrine with apricot preserve; sautéed corn-fed chicken with apples and calvados; roast cod with capers and parsley or marinated chargrilled lamb with rosemary and a deliciously caramelised onion compote. The plate of desserts is a very tempting finale which, on a visit midweek, produced a syrupy poached plum with home-made vanilla ice cream, a piece of superb apple flan and a slice of rich, ultra-smooth chocolate truffle cake. Service is relaxed and friendly. Annual and public holiday closures are when Christian "feels like it". No children under 10 "unless well behaved". *Seats 42. L (Tue-Fri) 12-2.30 D 7.30-10.30. Closed L Sat, all Sun & Mon.* AMERICAN EXPRESS® *Access, Diners, Visa.*

Set menu prices may not always include service or wine.

WC2	**Christopher's American Grill**	**£80**
Tel 071-240 4222 Fax 071-240 3357		**R**
18 Wellington Street Covent Garden WC2E 7DD		**Map 20 A2**

A grand Victorian building which in 1863 became the first licensed casino in London. Today, a sweeping stone staircase leads past reception (reservations are a must) up to a lofty, tall-windowed dining room resplendent in its stylishly ultra-modern interpretation of neo-classical decor. This is one of London's foremost centres of American food, with steaks (imported from the USA) and 3lb Maine lobsters among the specialities. America and the Med meet throughout the menu with the likes of clam chowder, Caesar salad, burgers and New York strip steak listed by prosciutto with pears, stuffed leg of chicken with roasted vegetables and lentils, and swordfish with pesto and peppers. A pre-theatre menu is available between 6 and 7 (three courses £15). The bar has become a bar-café with a separate menu that includes salads and sandwiches as well as many of the Grill's dishes. Sunday brunch is served in the café between 12 and 3. New World wines (California especially) share the spotlight with France and Italy. Good range under £20. *Seats 100. Private Room 32. L 12-2 D 6-11.30. Closed D Sun, Bank Holidays, 1 week Christmas.* AMERICAN EXPRESS® *Access, Diners, Visa.*

W1   Chuen Cheng Ku   £35

Tel 071-734 3281   **R**

17 Wardour Street W1V 3HD   **Map 21 A2**

Vast Chinese restaurant on several floors serving a long selection
of Cantonese dishes. The popular daytime choice is dim sum, served until
6 from little wagons which ply between the kitchen and the tables.
"Specialities of the House" include fried mussels with black bean sauce,
chicken baked in salt, black mushrooms stuffed with prawns and crabmeat
sauce, Peking and crispy aromatic duck, fillet steak with black pepper,
quail's eggs with vegetables and fried scallops with cashew nuts. *Seats 400.
Private Room 160. Meals 11.30am-11.30pm (Sun to 11). Closed 25 Dec. Set
meals from £18 for 2.* AMERICAN EXPRESS *Access, Diners, Visa.*

W1   Churchill Inter-Continental   84%   £262

Tel 071-486 5800   Fax 071-486 1255   **HR**

30 Portman Square W1A 4ZX   **Map 18 C2**

Improvements and refurbishment have continued apace since the Inter-
Continental group took over last year. The public areas are very grand
indeed with plenty of shiny marble, columns, chandeliers and particularly
comfortable seating in the Terrace Lounge (a favourite spot for afternoon
tea that includes fruit cake made to an authentic recipe from a member
of Winston Churchill's household!). The bar, on the other hand, has a more
club-like atmosphere, a theme repeated on the eighth floor which
is designated the 'Club' floor: 55 bedrooms, own check-in, secretary,
lounge, complimentary continental breakfast, valet service, free use
of boardroom etc – well worth the additional charge of £25. In fact,
business people are really well catered for here – there's a fully-staffed
business centre that includes the hire of mobile phones; the 39 suites, with
a walk-in shower as well as tub in the bathrooms, have a fax machine,
a music centre and VCR (all rooms are equipped with fax/modem points
and hi-tech TVs that allow you not only to receive incoming messages but
also to read your up-to-date bill). The good-sized, air-conditioned and
immaculately kept bedrooms are splendidly furnished in country-house
style with a variety of overseas touches, and the super bathrooms reflect the
exemplary standards of housekeeping and service found throughout the
hotel, under the direction of new General Manager Christopher Cowdray.
Comprehensive 24hr room service (plus mini-bars in all rooms) and all-day
snacks served in the lounge area. Fine banqueting (240) and conference
(250) facilities in a number of meeting rooms. Children up to the age of 14
free in their parents' room. Underground NCP parking. No dogs.
***Rooms** 448. Garden (Portman Square with tennis), business centre, beauty &
hair salons, theatre desk, news kiosk, shop, coffee shop.* AMERICAN EXPRESS *Access,
Diners, Visa.*

Clementine's   £80

A cavernous dining room housing an extensive collection of the best
in contemporary British art, with a marble floor, inlaid in parts with
herring-bone oak, mirrored columns, shuttered windows, pretty dried
flower arrangements, and a long, panelled bar down one side of the room
(its focus being the Cruvinet machine offering generous 6oz measures
of fine wines by the glass). The menu has a distinct Mediterranean slant and
chef Idris Caldora (previously at the *Birmingham Swallow*) cooks with
a sure and lightish touch, his dishes having strong and aromatic flavours.
Supplementing the seasonally-changing à la carte are daily-changing market
specialities, perhaps cream of parsnip soup, breast of chicken on a bed
of leeks with stuffed morels or roulade of salmon with spaghetti, cucumber
and tomato sauce. There are several vegetarian options (open ravioli with
roasted marinated vegetables and herb butter sauce or creamy spinach soup
with crostini) among the starters, some having two prices, the second
as a main-course options. Much enjoyed recently was a ragout of seafood
with lobster, salmon, squid, turbot and monkfish, served with fettuccine

and lobster jus (in reality, more of a sauce). For dessert, look no further than a chocolate marquise with a coffee bean sauce or a cold apricot soufflé with its own coulis. Staff, dressed in boldly striped waistcoats, go about their business efficiently. Bread rolls could be improved, coffee is very strong. Clever wine list with some French country wines priced as low as £8, as well as fairly-priced classics. Sunday brunch is good value at £19.50, children under 12 pay £13. **Seats** 90. *Parties 12. L 12-3 D 6-11. Closed L Sat.*

SW10	Chutney Mary ↑	£60
Tel 071-351 3113 Fax 071-351 7694		**R**
535 Kings Road SW10 0SZ		**Map 19 B6**

Almost on the corner of Kings Road and Lots Road, Chutney Mary has made a niche for itself as 'the world's first Anglo-Indian restaurant'. Behind a nondescript modern facade, it's a roomy, attractive place with Raj pictures on pale walls, mirrored alcoves and a jungly glazed conservatory. The menu is like no other, with dishes from all over India based on recipes of the Memsahibs: stir-fried calamari with Goan spices, crispy salmon samosas from Bombay, noodles Mandalay, a salad of cashew-encrusted goat's cheese, pomfret stuffed with curried prawns, bhuna tandoori lamb chops. Two of the most popular specialities are Country Captain – chicken breast braised with red chilis, almonds, raisins and spices, served with lemon rice; and lamb narangi featuring an orange-flavoured curry sauce. There's plenty of choice for vegetarians, a selection of desserts and regular food festivals. Sunday sees a grand buffet (£13.95) for both lunch and dinner. The colonial-style Verandah Bar at street level serves drinks, snacks and light meals, plus the restaurant menu in the evening. **Seats** 130. *Parties 20. L 12.30-2.30 (Sun to 3) D 7-11.30 (Sun to 10). Closed 26 Dec. Set L from £10 Set D (after 10) £10/£12.95.* AMERICAN EXPRESS Access, Diners, Visa.

W14	Cibo	£70
Tel 071-371 6271 Fax 071-602 1371		**R**
3 Russell Gardens W14 8EZ		**Map 17 B4**

Popular neighbourhood restaurant. Bold pictures line the walls and the regional Italian carte offers a profusion of contemporary dishes, with a strong emphasis on fish. Daily-changing menus might offer sautéed scallops with porcini, marinated aubergine with peperoni and mozzarella or gnocchi in a tomato sauce; followed perhaps by spaghetti with lobster, sea bass and fresh herbs, or rack of lamb with broad beans. A tendency for over-kill with wild mushrooms and cheese dishes was observed on one visit. An antipasti bar is a welcome addition for Sunday lunch. Apart from champagne, the wine list is exclusively Italian. Friendly service in comfortable and vivacious surroundings. **Seats** 62. *Parties 18. L 12-2.30 D 7-11. Closed L Sat, D Sun, Bank Holidays, 4 days Christmas. Set L £12.50 Set D £14.95/£17.95.* AMERICAN EXPRESS Access, Diners, Visa.

W1	Claridge's 88%	£316
Tel 071-629 8860 Fax 071-499 2210		**HR**
Brook Street Mayfair W1A 2JQ		**Map 18 C3**

"We strive for excellence" is Claridge's motto, and a heraldic escutcheon surmounted by a crown is the emblem of this, one of the world's great hotels, and one that is much favoured by foreign royalty and heads of states. Established almost 100 years ago, the hotel is synonymous with classic elegance, grace and dignity which characterise every aspect. From the imposing front entrance to its numerous magnificent suites, to the lilting strains of a Hungarian quartet that plays in the foyer at lunchtime and in the evening, to the handsomely liveried, discreet and attentive staff, Claridge's marries the calm and tranquillity of the past with modern comforts. The Front Hall with a wide, sweeping staircase and black and white marble floor, polished to a mirror-like shine, has been refurbished to its original art deco splendour. There is no bar proper but footmen in scarlet breeches, white hose and gold-braided tail coats are constantly on hand. The Reading Room, a softly-lit lounge, is dominated by a portrait of Mrs William Claridge, the hotel's founder, under whose watchful eye sedate afternoon teas are served. A significant part of the hotel was added in 1932 to include the ballroom and many of the bedrooms. These are all furnished and decorated in a distinctive art deco style, each retaining irreplaceable original furnishings and fittings. The remaining bedrooms contrast in being more traditional in character and ambience featuring fine plaster mouldings and beautiful period furniture; eight rooms are reserved for non-smokers. Modern influences include satellite TVs, dual telephone lines and fax sockets, but thankfully little else has changed over the years. Bathrooms throughout are magnificent, marble-clad and boasting probably the best showers in London with sunflower-size shower heads, many also with additional shoulder showers. Standards of service are exemplary with room buttons to summon maid, valet or floor waiter. For room service breakfast there is no menu but a waiter will discuss and comply with all individual requirements. Gentlemen have the use of the Bath and Racquets Club adjoining the hotel while ladies can visit the Berkeley Hotel's Health Club roof-top swimming pool and gymnasium. Guests with a recognised golf handicap (20 for gentlemen, 30 for Ladies) may play unlimited complimentary golf at Wentworth golf club in Berkshire; similarly, tennis facilities are provided for guests at the Vanderbilt Club in west London. Function rooms are luxurious – from the elegant Orangery and Drawing Room right up to the Ballroom Suite catering for up to 220 seated guests. No dogs. *Rooms 190. Valeting, ladies & gents hairdressers, travel & theatre desk.* ▨▨▨▨▨▨® *Access, Diners, Visa.*

Restaurant   £130

The opulent and magnificent art deco room was originally designed by Basil Ionides in 1926 and now features a fabulous mirrored mural by Christopher Ironside as well as a terrace, off which is the Orangery private dining room accommodating up to 14 guests. In such elegant and very formal surroundings *maitre chef des cuisines* Marjan Lesnik offers a suitably classical, enjoyable French menu with an emphasis on more modern interpretation and presentation. The three-course set menus represent good value with dishes like fillet of red mullet with rosemary risotto, magret of duck with peppered fruit compote and a choice of desserts from a trolley. From the à la carte come dishes such as foie gras terrine with truffles and Sauternes jelly, glazed poached egg with spinach and smoked haddock, roast aubergine, tomato and rosemary, ballotine of duck and cabbage with wild mushroom croquette, simpler grills and fillet of lamb with minted vegetables and celery sauce, the latter considered a speciality. Vegetables are straightforward and simple. Sweets, from a beautifully presented trolley, are enjoyable. The classical wine list is of a sensible length, contains the top growers, and what you see is what you pay, since prices are inclusive of both VAT and service. Service, under Daniel Azoulai, runs as smoothly as the trolley. Dinner dances are now held on Friday and Saturday nights until 1am. *Seats 140. Parties 20. Private Room 220. L 12.30-3 D 7-11.15. Closed L Sat. Set L £21/£26 (Sun £26) Set D £32 (£35 dinner dance).*

The Causerie   £85

The fixed-price (including a drink) lunchtime smörgåsbord is the main attraction here. Simple pre-and post-theatre suppers are served from 5.30-7.30pm and 10.15-11pm. An à la carte is also offered at both lunch and dinner; this might cover a range from Cajun risotto with prawns and lobster bisque to roast game in season, Claridge's hot chicken pie, and rack of lamb with aromatic vegetable crust. *Seats 40. Parties 8. L 12-2.30 D 5.30-11. Closed D Sat, all Sun. Set L £16-£18.50 Set D from £12.*

Consult page 20 for a full list of starred restaurants

W8   Clarke's   ★   £90

Tel 071-221 9225   Fax 071-229 4564   **R**
124 Kensington Church Street W8 4BH   Map 18 A3

Sally Clarke and Elizabeth Payne continue to fill their civilised and stylish
restaurant with cooking that puts the emphasis on tip-top produce and
generally uncomplicated, accessible and highly skilled handling of that
produce. Almost uniquely in London there is no choice on the four-course
evening menu (though the menu changes daily and never repeats itself).
The Mediterranean and California are among the influences, and the
chargrill produces most of the main courses. In the course of a typical week
these could include boned leg of lamb with herbed beans, roasted fennel
and lettuce heart; turbot with light black truffle cream sauce served over
steamed spinach and deep-fried leek; and breast of corn-fed chicken with
a fritter of green beans, baby leeks and red onion. Sea kale salad with thinly
sliced prosciutto, chives, watercress and olive oil is a typical perky, fresh
starter; cheeses with oatmeal biscuits and pear or celery or quince paste
constitute the third course, and desserts are an ever-changing but always
delicious combination of fruits and cream and pastry. Lunch is in similar
style but offers a choice of three dishes per course. Californian wines,
of course, feature prominently on the carefully selected list, but not to the
total exclusion of France and Italy. Fair prices (especially for London!). The
ground-floor room is non-smoking. *Seats 90. Parties 12. L 12.30-2 D 7-10.
Closed Sat & Sun, 4 days Easter, 2 weeks summer, 10 days Christmas.
Set L £22/£26 Set D £37. Access, Visa.*

We publish annually, so make sure you use the current edition.
It's worth it!

W1   The Clifton-Ford   73%   £196

Tel 071-486 6600   Fax 071-486 7492   **H**
47 Welbeck Street W1M 8DN   Map 18 C2

60s-built hotel with conference facilities (max 120) and a handy location
for the shops of Oxford Street. Day rooms are particularly good, especially
the lounge, which has almost a country house atmosphere. The bar feels
more masculine and clubby. Bedrooms, each floor with its own colour
scheme, include some roomy studio suites. Some rooms have fax and
PC points – yellow rooms have ironing boards. One room is specially
adapted for guests in wheelchairs. Covered parking available for 20 cars.
Rooms 212. AMERICAN EXPRESS *Access, Diners, Visa.*

NW3   Clive Hotel   64%   £70

Tel 071-586 2233   Fax 071-586 1659   **H**
Primrose Hill Road NW3 3NA   Map 16 C3

Refurbishment during 1994 of the main function room and public areas
at this modern Hilton-owned hotel on the fringes of Hampstead. Children
up to 12 free in parents' room. Free car park. Conference facilities for
up to 350. *Rooms 96.* AMERICAN EXPRESS *Access, Diners, Visa.*

SW1   Collin House   £56

Tel & Fax 071-730 8031   **H**
104 Ebury Street SW1W 9QD   Map 19 C5

Dafydd and Beryl Thomas, here since 1982, own and manage a welcoming
bed and breakfast hotel in a mid-Victorian town house just minutes from
Victoria railway and coach stations. Most rooms have their own shower
and WC. Good cooked breakfasts. No dogs. *Rooms 13. Closed 2 weeks
Christmas. No credit cards.*

W9   Colonnade Hotel   63%   £80

Tel 071-286 1052   Fax 071-286 1057   **H**

2 Warrington Crescent Maida Vale W9 1ER   Map 18 A2

In the heart of residential Little Venice, the Victorian Grade-II listed building stands across from Warwick Avenue underground station. Owned and personally run for the past 37 years by the Richards family, the hotel is constantly being improved, maintaining an attractive, homely and friendly environment. First-floor rooms are the biggest, but all are of quite good size and are kept in good decorative order. Top of the range are suites and rooms with four-posters. Many of the rooms now feature improved bathrooms. *Rooms 49.* AMERICAN EXPRESS *Access, Visa.*

W2   Columbia Hotel   £58

Tel 071-402 0021   Fax 071-706 4691   **H**

95 Lancaster Gate W2 3NS   Map 18 B3

Returning guests provide much of the business at a privately-owned hotel facing Hyde Park, 400 yards west of Lancaster Gate underground station. Reasonably priced bedrooms (many with park views, all with individual safes), roomy lounge and cocktail bar. Several function rooms, maximum capacity 200 for theatre-style conferences. *Rooms 102. Garden.* AMERICAN EXPRESS *Access, Visa.*

SW5   Concord Hotel   £57

Tel 071-370 4151   Fax 071-244 9091   **H**

155 Cromwell Road SW5 0TQ   Map 19 A5

Bed and breakfast hotel with some family-size bedrooms. Situated on the main road west to the airport, handy for Earls Court, Olympia and the South Kensington museums. Unlicensed. Only 15 of the bedrooms have en-suite facilities. *Rooms 40.* AMERICAN EXPRESS *Access, Visa.*

W1   Concorde Hotel   £84

Tel 071-402 6169   Fax 071-724 1184   **H**

50 Great Cumberland Place Marble Arch W1H 8DD   Map 18 C2

Next door to the *Bryanston Court Hotel* and under the same ownership, it offers cheaper accommodation with colour TV, tea/coffee facilities, hairdryer, new bathrooms and a friendly welcome from the Theodore family, here since 1966. £15 for an extra bed in a room. Furnished apartments also available. *Rooms 28. Closed 1 week Christmas.* AMERICAN EXPRESS *Access, Diners, Visa.*

W1   The Connaught   91%   £POA

Tel 071-499 7070   Fax 071-495 3262   **HR**

Carlos Place W1Y 6AL   Map 18 C3

Built in 1897, the Connaught was opened as a London home for the landed gentry; today's guests may be more cosmopolitan but the gentlemanly atmosphere remains. Impervious to glamour and fashion, it offers unrivalled standards of comfort, service and traditional hospitality with a formal touch. Day rooms, from which business meetings are banned in the interests of tranquillity, are grand in looks but not in scale, with a clubby, oak-panelled, leather-seated bar and elegant lounges. Quiet luxury is the watchword in the bedrooms, which are individually decorated in an English country style with some antiques and a variety of fine fabrics from floral chintzes to restrained damasks. Rooms are not cluttered with such things as fax machines or mini-bars (although each of the 24 suites' sitting rooms has an antique chinoiserie cocktail cabinet), but these, and anything else within reason, are available on request and the next time you stay here you will find that they will have remembered such requirements and any other personal preferences. Only 30 or so rooms have air-conditioning and consommé is the only hot food on the overnight room service menu; but major pluses are the luxurious bathrobes, fine linen bedding and exemplary service throughout. A fine, grand hotel with commendable old-fashioned values. **Rooms** 90. *Access, Diners, Visa.*

Restaurant & Grill Room ★★ £160

Not one restaurant, but two, sharing identical menus of classic French and traditional English cuisine. Highly polished panelling features in the formal restaurant, while the sage-green Grill Room is warmer and more intimate. The whole operation is overseen by *maitre cuisiner de France* Michel Bourdin, whose genius is the way he interprets the dishes with lighter, more refined sauces without changing their essential, unashamedly old-fashioned character. The French dishes are not translated but all sound rather special, which indeed they are: *fonds d'artichauts 'Jeanette'; galette Connaught aux 'diamants noirs'; salade Aphrodite; barquette aux perles blanches et noires; médallions de cailles "Belle Epoque"*. The regular luncheon dishes are, on the other hand, self-explanatory: Monday is steak, kidney and mushroom pie day, Thursday brings boiled silverside, Friday has oxtail and salmon coulibiac. Finish with one of the savouries (Welsh rarebit, devilled sardines, Scotch Woodcock) or choose from the list of classic French and homely British desserts. Service is very traditional with a myriad of waiters organised in an elaborate hierarchy but tempered by an innate and entirely appropriate friendliness. The way fresh tablecloths are put on the tables after the main course, without causing so much as a ripple in the conversation around the table, is a minor miracle, performed nightly. This is an *ancien régime* par excellence, an experience not to be missed. There is nothing from the New World on the classic wine list that only has French, Italian and German wines; prices do not include the additional 15% service charge. Guests are asked to try to refrain from smoking. No children under 6. **Seats** *Restaurant 75. Grill Room 35. Parties 10. Private Room 22. L 12.30-2.30 D 6.30 (Grill from 6)-10.30. Set L £25 (£30 Sun) Set D (Grill only) £35. Grill Room closed weekends Jan-Apr & Public Holidays.*

SW10	Hotel Conrad	86%	£229

Tel 071-823 3000 Fax 071-351 6525 **HR**

Chelsea Harbour SW10 0XG Map 19 B6

Though it might not have a central London location, the hotel has many advantages, not least its quiet waterside setting overlooking the marina (summer outdoor barbecues on the terrace), its superb supervised leisure complex, comprehensive room service, and the benefit of one of London's (and for that matter the UK's) best hotel managers in Doreen Boulding. A further advantage is that there's no traffic noise, in fact all the air-conditioned suites (there are no ordinary bedrooms), some with balconies, have a lobby insulating them from the corridor and this makes them even more peaceful. Designed by David Hicks, the tastefully furnished rooms offer every modern comfort: twin wardrobes, three telephones with two lines, multi-channel TV with video, mini-bar and many extras, such as fresh fruit, flowers, books and magazines, suit-carriers and even an umbrella. In the luxurious marble bathrooms you'll find a walk-in shower as well as a large tub, twin washbasins, bidet, separate loo (some suites also have a guest loo), bathrobes and quality toiletries. There's a cool and relaxing feel in the spacious marble-floored public areas, where uniformed and smartly-dressed staff are always on hand to offer a high standard of service, including valet parking. In addition, there's a free Jaguar limo service to Knightsbridge. Conference/banqueting facilities for up to 200. Start the day with a variety of breakfast suggestions in the brasserie. River cruising and go-karting on the doorstep. **Rooms** *160. Terrace, indoor swimming pool, sauna, solarium, steam room, gym, beauty & hair salon shop.* *Access, Diners, Visa.*

See over

Brasserie   £60

The one thing the restaurant is not is a brasserie – it's an elegant hotel
dining room with smart table settings and polished service. It certainly
doesn't feel like a brasserie, which is not a reflection on Peter Brennan's
cooking. The à la carte menu is supplemented by set menus both
at lunchtime (2/3 courses) and in the evenings (3/4 courses) – typical
dishes: terrine of duck and duck breast with an orange dressing, medallions
of venison with broad beans, and layered apple tart with cinnamon ice
cream. From the grill you could choose Dover sole or rack of lamb, off the
à la carte wild mushroom and Parmesan risotto, tournedo of monkfish
with a smoked butter sauce, guinea fowl with lentils and ceps, and a classic
tarte au citron to finish. Good cheeses and coffee; the wine list feels longer
than it really is, with several decent bottles under £20. *Seats* 45 (*+40 on
terrace*). *Parties 16. L 12.30-3 D 7-10.30. Set L £13.50/16.50 (Sun
champagne brunch £28.50) Set D £22.50/26.50.*

W8   Copthorne Tara   69%   £141
Tel 071-937 7211   Fax 071-937 7100   **H**
Scarsdale Place Kensington W8 5SR   Map 19 A4

A modern 12-storey hotel close enough to Kensington High Street to be
convenient for the shops but far enough away to be free of the bustle and
the traffic. Thoughtfully furnished rooms, ranging from 'Classic' singles
to suites, include non-smoking rooms and facilities for disabled guests, all
with efficient air-conditioning and electronic controls on lighting and other
facilities. There's a purpose-built conference and banqueting centre catering
for up to 500. *Rooms 825. Café.* AMERICAN EXPRESS *Access, Diners, Visa.*

> We endeavour to be as up-to-the-minute as possible, but inevitably
> some changes to key personnel may occur at restaurants and hotels
> after the Guide goes to press.

EC2   Corney & Barrow   £75
Tel 071-638 9308   Fax 071-382 9373   **R**
109 Old Broad Street EC2N 1AP   Map 20 D1

Corney & Barrow have been in Old Broad Street for more than 200 years,
starting as a shop selling port, old sack and claret. Wine is still an important
part of the business but food is also taken seriously in this comfortable,
club-like room, whose green-clad walls are hung with cartoons of notable
regulars. Manager-chef Lorcan Cribbin satisfies traditional and more
contemporary palates with a menu that includes calf's liver with fried
onions and bacon, sirloin steak Café de Paris, brandade of aubergine served
on a bed of spaghetti cucumber and steamed fillets of sole and scallops
served with a coriander and lime jus. Fresh fruit parfait, sorbets, tiramisu,
farmhouse cheeses. *Seats 30. Parties 10. L 11.30-3 D for private parties only.
Closed Sat & Sun, Bank Holidays. Set L £18.95/£21.95.* AMERICAN EXPRESS
Access, Diners, Visa.

W8   Costa's Grill   £25
Tel 071-229 3794   **R**
12-14 Hillgate Street Notting Hill Gate W8 7SR   Map 18 A3

Remember when Greek holidays really were cheap? Relive those memories
at Costa's, where hefty portions of grills and baked dishes are still served
at rock bottom prices. Only fresh fish from the charcoal grill is likely
to make a dent in your drachmae – again, just like over there. Now, what
can we do about the English weather? Keep hoping – there are a few
outside tables on the rear patio in summer. Almost next door is Costa's fish
and chip shop. *Seats 70. Private Room 25. L 12.30-2.30 D 5-10.30.
Closed Sun, Bank Holidays, Sep. No credit cards.*

W2   Craven Gardens Hotel   £66

Tel 071-262 3167   Fax 071-262 2083   **H**

16 Leinster Terrace W2 3ES   **Map 18 B3**

Comfortable, well-kept bed and breakfast hotel just off Bayswater Road, handy for Hyde Park, British Rail Paddington, London Underground stations and the cosmopolitan appeal of Queensway. Children under 7 can stay free in parents' room. No dogs. *Rooms 43.* AMERICAN EXPRESS® *Access, Diners, Visa.*

SW14   Crowthers   £65

Tel 081-876 6372   **R**

481 Upper Richmond Road West Sheen SW14 7PU   **Map 17 A5**

Philip and Shirley Crowther have been at their cosy little neighbourhood restaurant for over 12 years now, serving well-balanced, fixed-price menus of good British produce in French style (matched by the traditional French country decor). You could perhaps start with a parfait of chicken livers served with toasted brioche and port and blackcurrant sauce, or smoked mackerel and spring onion fishcakes with hollandaise; and move on to roast guinea fowl with a sauce of marjoram and Madeira, or grilled monkfish with mixed peppers and herbs. Finish with grilled fruit gratin and calvados sabayon. *Seats 32. L 12-2 D 7-10.30. Closed L Sat, all Sun & Mon, Bank Holidays, 2 weeks Aug, 1 week Christmas. Set L £14.75/£17.50 Set D £15.85/£20.50. Access, Visa.*

W1   Cumberland Hotel   69%   £140

Tel 071-262 1234   Fax 071-724 4621   **H**

Marble Arch W1A 4RF   **Map 18 C3**

London's second largest hotel is at the Marble Arch end of Oxford Street, overlooking Speaker's corner. An impressive octagonal central lobby has bright red columns, white marble and a large floral display as its focal point from where three restaurants and a café (including a carvery – where children under 5 eat free) and *Mon* Japanese restaurant (see separate entry) radiate. Three bars and a shopping arcade add an international air to the public areas. Bedrooms are spacious, well-maintained and attractive, with a good range of amenities. A variety of conference and banqueting suites caters for 475/560. Children under 16 free in their parents' room. *Rooms 890. News kiosk, coffee shop (6.30am-midnight).* AMERICAN EXPRESS® *Access, Diners, Visa.*

SW15   Dan Dan   £50

Tel 081-780 1953   **R**

333 Putney Bridge Road SW15   **Map 17 B5**

Just off the bridge end of Putney High Street, an unpretentious Japanese restaurant offering good-value lunches based around one main dish (plus miso soup, appetiser and fresh fruit) and a wider choice of Japanese classics in the evening. Good fresh sushi and kaiseki dinners with hors d'oeuvre chosen from a trolley. *Seats 60. Parties 40. Private Room 24. L 12-2.30 D 6.30-10. Closed Mon, 1 week Aug, 25 & 26 Dec. Set L from £5.80 Set D from £19. Access, Visa.*

SW3   Dan's   £60

Tel 071-352 2718   Fax 071-352 3265   **R**

119 Sydney Street Chelsea SW3 6NR   **Map 19 B5**

A bright, informal restaurant whose large garden could be said to be its main attraction; the interior has recently been revamped with a new floor laid and the bar moved to the window end. The short menu offers dishes like confit of duck with caramelised shallots, grilled salmon with cepes and watercress salad, herb-crusted roast rack of lamb with thyme sauce, French beans and gratin dauphinois, apple tart with caramel sauce. *Seats 50. Private Rooms 12 & 35. L 12.30-2.30 D 7.30-10.45 (Sat to 10.30). Closed L Sat, D Sun, Bank Holidays, 1 week Christmas. Set L £14/£16.50.* AMERICAN EXPRESS® *Access, Visa.*

NW1   Daphne   £45

Tel 071-267 7322   **R**

83 Bayham Street Camden Town NW1   Map 16 C3

In a part of town where Greek restaurants abound, Daphne has the edge over most of them. Its menu of traditional favourites is given a boost by numerous daily specials with an emphasis on fish: the 'fish combination' includes chargrilled skewers of monkfish, swordfish, baby cuttlefish, scallop and prawn; also gilt-head bream, octopus and red mullet in season. The fish meze is also popular. Choice is also generous for meat-eaters and vegetarians. The restaurant extends over two floors, with a fair-weather roof terrace seating 25. *Seats 85. Parties 30. Private Room 30. L 12-2.30 D 6-11.30. Closed Sun, 25 & 26 Dec. Meze (min 2) £8.25. Access, Visa.*

SW3   Daphne's   £85

Tel 071-589 4257   Fax 071-581 2232   **R**

112 Draycott Avenue SW3 3AE   Map 19 B5

Daphne – a pretty evergreen (such as laurel) with shiny leaves. Daphne – the nymph who was saved from the amorous attentions of Apollo by being changed into a laurel tree. Daphne's – the fashionable Chelsea restaurant that doesn't rest on its laurels – it's far too busy and popular for that! Regulars eat their favourite tables, others go to be seen in glitzy company. Cooking is modern and healthy with northern Italian influences and the menu changes to reflect the seasons. A typical menu might include hot foie gras with polenta, lentils and balsamic blackberry sauce, tortelloni with crab and aubergine, tagliata of duck breast with balsamic plum sauce and parsnip purée, and calf's liver with steamed spinach. Pasta and risotto can be fitted in to the meal where you wish – as starter, main course or in between. Luscious desserts complete the meal. Booking recommended. *Seats 120. L 12-3 (Sun to 4) D 7-11.30. Closed 24 & 25 Dec, 1 Jan.* AMERICAN EXPRESS® *Access, Diners, Visa.*

SW6   De Cecco   £40

Tel 071-736 1145   **R**

189 New Kings Road Parsons Green London SW6 4SW   Map 17 B5

Booking is advisable at this bright, bubbly place, which has a loyal following. The range of pizza and pasta includes several surprises (pizza with smoked salmon and pineapple, fettuccine with lamb's kidneys and spinach), and main courses are typified by osso buco, squid with garlic, lemon, white wine and tomato, and beef in a calvados and wine sauce served on a bed of pappardelle. No young children after 7pm on Saturdays. *Seats 68. Parties 12. L 12.30-2.45 D 7-11. Closed Sun & Bank Holidays. Access, Visa.*

W1   Defune   £80

Tel 071-935 8311   Fax 071-487 3762   **R**

61 Blandford Street W1H 3AJ   Map 18 C2

Book to be sure of a table, as this is a popular (and very small) Japanese restaurant. Otherwise you can sit at the counter and see your sushi and sashimi being prepared. The à la carte spans a fairly familiar Japanese range, from soups and noodle dishes to barbecued beef, pork and fish, and specialities such as *shabu-shabu* and *yosenabe*. *Seats 30. Parties 15. L 12-2.30 D 6-10.30. Closed Sun, Bank Holidays, 1 week Christmas. Set L from £12.* AMERICAN EXPRESS® *Access, Diners, Visa.*

SW15   Del Buongustaio   ↑   £60

Tel 081-780 9361   **R**

283 Putney Bridge Road London SW15 2PT   **Map 17 B5**

Simple but imaginative decor in soft shades of sand and terracotta with
colourful Faenza ceramics sets the tone for a relaxing meal in chef Aurelio
Spagnuolo's and Rochelle Porteous's cheerful country Italian restaurant
('osteria con cucina'). The emphasis is on a slightly updated version of classic
Northern Italian cooking. *Piatto pizzicarello* is an interesting, plated
assortment of savouries to commence a meal, which could follow with
sardelle in sâor (a Venetian dish of fried sardines, onion, pine nuts and
sultanas), roast vegetable salad with olives, salted ricotta and borlotti beans,
or risotto with calamari, artichokes and saffron. half a dozen main courses
might range from casseroled fresh tuna to cuttlefish with potato, onion,
chilis and garlic or herb-marinated, oven-baked lamb loin served with fresh
asparagus and peppers. Co-chef Antonio Strillozzi recommends a five-
course, well-balanced selection on the menu – enough to satisfy the most
ravenous trencherman with a Latin hunger. The unusual mix of Italian and
Australian wines includes ten or so wonderful 'stickies' (*gli ultimi peccati* –
'the final sins') to go with the *golisita* (puds). Fresh cheeses are imported
directly from Naples. Two-course lunches offer excellent value and
a choice of just three dishes at each stage. Sundays see a *degustazione* menu
(three to five courses). **Seats** 45. *Parties 8. L 12-3 (Sun 12.30-3.30)
D 6.30-11.30. Closed L Sat, D Sun, 10 days Christmas/New Year.
Set L £9.50 (Sun £14.50/£17/£19.50) Set D £19.50.* AMERICAN EXPRESS
Access, Visa.

W1   dell'Ugo   ↑   £40

Tel 071-734 8300   Fax 071-734 8784   **R**

56 Frith Street Soho W1V 5TA   **Map 21 A2**

Antony Worrall Thompson continues to set a frightening pace at his
immensely popular and inspirational multi-storey feeding station in the
heart of Soho. dell'Ugo provides something for everyone on a menu which,
after the AWT style, is full of clever ideas, most of which work well. The
Mediterranean influence is strong, covering a wide range, from bruschetta,
crostini 'with fishes' (mussels, smoked salmon, chargrilled squid, marinated
mackerel and salt cod), bresaola, plum tomato and basil tart, and spaghetti
with gorgonzola, cream, spinach and artichoke crisps to seared scallops with
a pancetta and Jersey potato salad and oven-roast ratatouille, and lamb
shank with flageolet beans, rosemary and garlic – the list is endlessly
enticing. Other dishes are homespun favourites with comtemporary tuning
– even the potatoes are cleverly offered as a side order of garlic potatoes,
mash, chips *or* frites! Although essentially fairly simple in concept and
preparation, the emphasis on strong, fresh flavours wins through in dishes
that draw inspiration from around the globe – deep-fried monkfish tails
with chips and mushy peas, chargrilled marinated squid with a fresh bean
and truffle oil salad with parsley and brandade crostini, ginger brulée tart
with maple and banana compote – who could ever imagine more worldly
food? 'Ten Quid Cuisine' (try saying that after a drink or two) in the
ground-floor café/bar is also a major attraction, with a choice of three dishes
at each stage – perhaps courgette blinis with goat's cheese, grilled radicchio
and pepper salsa followed by maize-fed chicken with sesame seeds and
watercress and an orange and peanut dressing, with pecan pie and maple ice
cream or cheeses to finish – superb value, up-to-date combinations.
A constantly-changing wine list is laid out by price and offers affordable
prices, with over a dozen wines by the glass. Finish with Italian coffees
or 'hippy teas'. The first-floor bistro opens from 7pm and continues
to 12.30am, whereas the second-floor restaurant opens from 5.30pm and
closes at 11pm; no bookings are taken in the café. AWT's dell'Ugo must
surely be the epicentre of the movement that we have dubbed *cuisine
mondiale*, a cooking style for which London is now gaining international
recognition. **Seats** 180. *Parties 60. Private Room 14. L 12-3 (not Sat),*

*D 5.30-12.30 (ground-floor café 11am-12.30am inc Sat). Closed all Sun.
Set meals (café) £7.50/£10.* AMERICAN EXPRESS *Access, Diners, Visa.*

W1   The Doghouse   £45

Tel 071-434 2118   R
187 Wardour Street Soho W1V 2RB   Map 18 D2

At the Oxford Street end of Wardour Street, in the heart of London's film
land, the restaurant occupies a basement decorated in an original and
unusual manner. Walls and floors are a multitude of contrasting hues with
the odd scallop shell and giant numeral adding to its outré style. The bar
area is large and painted bright red with a more subdued dining area to the
side. Under-pavement alcoves provide areas for more private drinking and
dining. The menu, which changes daily, might be short in choice but scores
big on imagination. Starters include a salad of tender squid strips in a black
bean dressing and pork satay with a peanut sauce. These could perhaps
be followed by red onion and Parmesan risotto or chargrilled breast
of citrus-marinated chicken with a deliciously spicy Poblano chili couscous.
To accompany are some of the biggest chips anywhere and to finish either
a slice of rich choc chip cheesecake or poached fruits with mascarpone.
Very relaxed, friendly service. ***Seats** 30. Parties 22. L 12.30-3 D 6-11.30.
Closed L Sat, all Sun, Bank Holidays, 1 week Christmas.* AMERICAN EXPRESS *Visa.*

NW8   Don Pepe   £50

Tel 071-262 3834   R
99 Frampton Street St John's Wood NW8 8NA   Map 18 B2

London's first tapas bar when it opened 20 years ago, Don Pepe has
survived and thrived. Besides the tapas there's a full restaurant menu
including Spanish classics such as *gazpacho*, Asturian-style bean stew, *lubina
a la sal* (sea bass cooked in salt) *merluza a la gallega, zarzuela* and *paella*.
***Seats** 50. Private Room 20. L 12-3 D 7-1. Closed D Sun, 24 & 25 Dec.
Set L from £10.50 Set D from £12.95.* AMERICAN EXPRESS *Access, Diners, Visa.*

W1   The Dorchester   91%   £298

Tel 071-629 8888   Fax 071-409 0114   HR
Park Lane W1A 2HJ   Map 18 C3

Since opening its doors in 1931, the Dorchester has been among the
world's top hotels, renowned for its enviable standards of service, comfort
and food. The grand oval foyer, with its rug-strewn black-and-white
marble floor, bustles with the comings and goings of smartly attired
porters, page boys and guests. The splendid, long Promenade, complete
with enormous floral display at one end and rows of faux-marble columns
with ornate gilt capitals, is very much the heart of the hotel and
a wonderful place to take traditional English afternoon tea. Another focal
point is the bar, where an Italian menu is served daily at lunch and supper
time. Bedrooms have an essentially English style with fine fabrics varying
from striking floral prints and delicate damasks to heavy tapestries; the bed
linen is, of course, real linen. All rooms are triple-glazed and have white
Italian marble bathrooms with bidets and hand showers in addition
to powerful showers over the bathtubs; many even have separate shower
cubicles and twin washbasins, while most have natural light (a real luxury
in a hotel bathroom). Four superb roof garden suites, all restored to their
original splendour, put the icing on the cake. Standards of service
throughout the public areas are superlative and are matched on the
bedroom floors following the implementation of the call button system for
valet, maid and waiter room service (the hotel boasts an amazing ratio
of three staff to each room). Breakfasts, as one can expect from a hotel with
such an outstanding culinary history, are first-rate, covering English
(a superior fry-up, poached haddock, grilled kippers, coddled egg with
smoked salmon or chives), Continental (excellent baking includes croissants
and apple scones) or low-fat and low-cholesterol options; served from 7am

(7.30am Sun) in the Grill Room. Among the many elegant public rooms, opulent banqueting and conference facilities (for up to 550) feature over 1500 square metres of gold leaf gilding and are among London's finest. The Dorchester Spa offers thermal therapy as well as the more usual relaxations. **Rooms** *247. Gym, sauna, spa bath, steam room, solarium, beauty & hair salon, shopping gallery.* AMERICAN EXPRESS® *Access, Diners, Visa.*

Terrace Restaurant   ★★   £120

It is currently only possible to take a stroll down the magnificent Promenade and turn left into the opulent splendour of the Terrace on a Friday and Saturday night. Booking is essential to ensure a table in a room that is decorated with great style: there are mirrored columns, Chinese-inspired painted wall panels, a central gazebo where four couples can dine in relative seclusion, and a band which strikes up from mid-evening till late (around 1am), the singer inviting diners to face the music and dance. The menu now offers a fixed-price meal of either three or four courses. Though reduced in extent and content from previous years there has been no let up in quality, the dishes available demonstrating Willi Elsener's superb talents to the full. The choice is still of imaginative, modern, sophisticated dishes. There is also a very extensive vegetarian menu, its dishes a very creditable and worthwhile alternative, and a result of increased demand. From this menu are starters such as tart of caramelised shallots and curd cheese served with a bitter leaf salad, feuilleté of asparagus with a light butter sauce and mixed peppers with, to follow, home-made egg noodles with pesto, a gateau of roasted red peppers, mozzarella, tomato and olives with a garlic and chili sauce or filo pastry filled with spinach, cheese and pine kernels served on stir-fried mixed vegetables. The orthodox menu begins with a super appetiser of, say, a slice of delicate salmon mousse wrapped in smoked salmon and continues with superb pan-fried red mullet served with a perfectly balanced Sauternes wine sauce and a purée of potato and celery or white and green lasagne leaves filled with a melting piece of pan-fried foie gras and accompanied by a deliciously creamy wild mushroom sauce. A granité of, say, dry white wine, follows and for a main dish the choice could be a beautifully fresh fillet of halibut with mussels and vegetables cooked in their own juices, tender and succulent roast duck breast with petits pois or baked rack of lamb, superbly trimmed and accompanied by goat's cheese wrapped in a crispy filo pastry. Examples of the desserts are brought to the table, rendering them irresistible. Typical are a wonderful three chocolate mousse, each layer flavoured with a different liqueur, and pears poached in red wine and spices served with a caramel granité. Service is superbly professional. The wine list is, naturally, grand and offers some of the best growers from both Europe and the New World. Prices are on the high side, but not too unreasonable, and there's plenty of good drinking around £25. No children under 12. **Seats** *81. Parties 14. D only 7-11.30. Closed Sun-Thurs, Aug. Set D £38/£42.*

Grill Room   £130

Largely unchanged since the hotel first opened in 1931; although the decor is grand Spanish, the menu is firmly and splendidly English. Tables are widely spaced, which is just as well given the numerous trolleys that bring not just the traditional roast rib of beef and Yorkshire pudding and the side of smoked salmon – to be sliced at the table – but also the dish of the day (Monday's boiled silverside and caraway dumplings, Friday's fish pie) the wide range of breads, 'bespoke' salads, good desserts and the notably wide selection of British cheeses. The à la carte extends to just about every corner of the British Isles from Jersey potatoes, dressed crab from Cornwall and Morecambe Bay potted shrimps to Dublin Bay prawns (with cardamom, herb and pepper butter), air-dried Cumberland ham, Angus beef, and Dover sole. **Seats** *81. Parties 12. L 12.30-2.30 D 6-11 (Sun & Bank Holidays 7-10.30). Set L £23.50 Set D £28.*

See over

Oriental Room   ↑   £120

London's most exclusive Chinese restaurant and almost certainly the most
expensive, too. Some dishes work better than others on a mainly Cantonese
menu with many luxurious items. Specialities include deep-fried crispy
pigeon with pickled vegetables and steamed fresh eel with black bean sauce.
Staff are smart, charming and knowledgable under a suave and
accomplished manager. No children under 12. Lovely private rooms
(Indian-themed, Chinese, Thai). *Seats 79. Parties 30. Private Rooms 6/10/12.
L 12-2.30 D 7-11. Closed L Sat, all Sun, Aug. Set L £20 (dim sum) & £25
Set D £28.*

Dorchester Bar   £70

Beautiful, Delft-tiled panels alternating with mirrors in a carved, light-oak
framework take the eye in this brightly lit, split-level bar. A baby grand
piano covered in mirror mosaics, crisply-clothed tables, comfortable
banquettes and light tan leather chairs complete a most elegant setting
in which to enjoy excellent modern Italian cooking. A selection of antipasti
(available only at lunchtime) is spread out next to the entrance. This
includes a colourful vegetable terrine, proscuitto with ripe melon,
chargrilled vegetables, fish terrine and stuffed tomatoes. Other choices
could be tagliolini with scampi and a spicy tomato sauce, black noodles
served with baked Scottish lobster or guinea fowl breast with Vin Santo
sauce and white grapes or the speciality of the day, which could be baked
sea bass on a bed of vegetables with saffron potatoes. Simple sweets such
as a deliciously creamy spumone al caffè or tiramisu end off an expensive
but enjoyable experience. Service is first-class. Booking is advisable.
Seats 59. Parties 8. Meals 12-11.45 (Sun 12-2.30 7-10).

Any person using our name to obtain free hospitality is a fraud.
Proprietors, please inform the police and us.

W4   La Dordogne   £50
Tel 081-747 1836   Fax 081-994 9144   **R**
5 Devonshire Road Chiswick W4 2EU   **Map 17 A4**

"A corner of France in west London" whose menu mixes traditional and
more contemporary dishes: foie gras (a glass of sweet Jurançon wine
is recommended to accompany this), vegetable terrine with tomato coulis,
salad of cured and cooked duck breast, fish soup, turbot in champagne
sauce, chicken with tarragon, lamb with honey and mint, fillet of beef and
potato pancake with a Quercy wine or a green peppercorn sauce. Separate
menus for oysters/lobsters and classic desserts. *Seats 80. Private Room 30/20.
L 12-2.30 D 7-11. Closed L Sat & Sun, Bank Holidays.* AMERICAN EXPRESS®
Access, Diners, Visa.

NW1   Dorset Square Hotel   74%   £142
Tel 071-723 7874   Fax 071-724 3328   **H**
39 Dorset Square Marylebone NW1 6QN   **Map 18 C2**

An elegant house amid the white Georgian facade of a garden square just
north of Marylebone Road, with Regent's Park a short walk away. Within,
there's an attractive combination of hand-painted woodwork, gilt-framed
paintings, tapestry cushions and antique furniture giving a warm, refined
atmosphere to the public rooms on the ground floor. The guest lounge
is furnished with colourful armchairs, a 19th-century rolltop desk and
an antique cabinet which holds an honesty bar. Each bedroom has its own
personality, artistically blending patterns and materials. Most rooms are air-
conditioned, and all have satellite TV, books and magazines. Marble and
mahogany bathrooms enjoy natural daylight. Careful thinking has gone
into every detail, making it very much an individual home-from-home.
A chauffeur-driven Bentley Continental is available by prior arrangement.
Rooms 37. Garden. AMERICAN EXPRESS® *Access, Visa.*

SW7   Downstairs at 190   ↑   £60

Tel 071-581 5666   Fax 071-581 8172   **R**

190 Queen's Gate SW7 5EU   Map 19 B4

Underneath *Bistrot 190* (qv), a busy brasserie-style restaurant under the watchful eye of roving chef Antony Worrall Thompson. Seafood dominates the menu, with only a few concessions – chargrilled chicken with roasted garlic, duck confit, steak or calf's liver – to carnivores. Traditional fish and chips are deep-fried in beer batter and served with chunky chips, mushy peas and tartare sauce, while fish cakes get the AWT touch: choose from Thai-style with spicy cucumber salad, salmon with spinach and sorrel sauce, salt cod and rösti with sour cream and salmon caviar or corn and crab with wilted greens, poached eggs and hollandaise. Mussels and/or clams are steamed in five different ways (try them with chili, coconut cream, lemon grass and lime leaves), and the chargrill is put to good use for the daily-changing selection of market-fresh fish and shellfish; a variety of accompaniments is offered, from lemon confit with roast garlic and couscous to soft herring roes and anchovy cream. Non-fish-eating vegetarians might be offered a croustade of wild mushrooms with roast Jerusalem artichokes and beetroot or a 'tarte tatin' of chicory with red chicory salad. A short list of 'snacking food' (crostini, tempura, whitebait, squid) is also offered, along with a handful of puddings: perhaps lemon and lime tart, chocolate délice with Drambuie ice cream or blackberry and pear tart with bay custard. Hobson's choice for tyrophagists is Cashel Irish Blue with fruit compote and soda bread. The splendid (and very comprehensive) wine list has been assembled with great care, enthusiasm and skill; the idea of pricing non-vintage marque champagnes the same (£35) is an excellent one. The balance of between Europe and the New World is even, with Italy, Australia and USA particularly well represented; plenty of half bottles, fair prices. London Regional Cellar of the Year winner (see introduction pages). *Seats 70. Private Room 28. D only 7-12. Closed Sun, Bank Holidays, 1 week Christmas.* AMERICAN EXPRESS *Access, Diners, Visa.*

W1   Dragon Inn   £30

Tel 071-494 0870   **R**

12 Gerrard Street Soho W1   Map 21 A2

Set on three floors, an unsophisticated Cantonese restaurant with a staggeringly long menu covering everything from chicken with cashew nuts to spiced belly pork with yam served in a clay pot. Daytime dim sum are always popular. *Seats 120. Parties 12. Meals 12-11.45 (dim sum 12-4.45). Closed 25-26 Dec & from 8pm 24 Dec. Set meals from £9.* AMERICAN EXPRESS *Access, Visa.*

> Note that all telephone numbers with area codes starting with 0 will start 01 from 16 April 1995.

W1   Dragon's Nest   £45

Tel 071-437 3119   **R**

58 Shaftesbury Avenue W1V 7DE   Map 21 A2

There is a comfortable, old-fashioned air here, much as a Chinese hotel dining room might have been in the 1930s. Favourites, such as sweet and sour prawns, Szechuan crispy duck and beef with oyster sauce vie with the more unusual, perhaps fried eel with yellow bean sauce – all cooked with above average care. A word of warning – the dried red peppers described with some dishes are chilis, not the sweet variety, and definitely to be approached with caution! Useful for pre-and post-theatre dining. *Seats 130. Parties 40. Private Room 60. L 12-3 D 5-11.30 Closed 25 & 26 Dec. Set meals from £10.50.* AMERICAN EXPRESS *Access, Diners, Visa.*

SW3   The Draycott   £150

Tel 071-730 6466   Fax 071-730 0236   **PH**

24-26 Cadogan Gardens SW3 2RP   **Map 19 C4**

Formed from a pair of redbrick Victorian town houses, the Draycott
is announced by a discreet little brass plate. Admission is to a yellow drag-
painted entrance hall beyond which is an appealing drawing room where
Victorian paintings, objets d'art, fresh flowers and a mix of sofas and
armchairs creates a certain old-fashioned elegance enhanced by views
of (and access to) Cadogan Gardens, one of London's most peaceful garden
squares. Bedrooms vary considerably in size and all are individually
decorated in a non-hotel town-house style with antiques, porcelain
ornaments and paintings of rural scenes as well as satellite TVs, video
players and mini-bars. Good bathrooms with Penhaligon toiletries. The
Draycott offers a charming and romantic alternative to more conventional
hotels. 24hr room service makes up for the lack of a restaurant and there
are concierge, fax, limousine and nanny services available. Children stay
free in parents' room. Guests have free use of the nearby Synergy Centre
Health Centre and the Vanderbilt tennis club. No dogs. *Rooms 25.*
AMERICAN EXPRESS *Access, Diners, Visa.*

SW1   Dukes Hotel   79%   £238

Tel 071-491 4840   Fax 071-493 1264   **H**

35 St James's Place SW1A 1NY   **Map 18 D3**

In a quiet cul-de-sac off St James's Street, a charming and secluded hotel
in a tranquil courtyard setting near Green Park. The elegant Edwardian
building is conservatively and tastefully furnished like a private club, with
a cosy sitting room where morning coffee and afternoon tea are served and
a splendid cocktail bar; public rooms reflect the traditional qualities aimed
for by the management and the smartly uniformed staff. Bedrooms have
fine antiques and period furniture complemented by chintzy floral fabrics.
While there is no air-conditioning, there are ceiling fans for sultry days.
Bathrooms are not large but have smart marble tiling and a range
of luxurious toiletries. 26 of the rooms are suites with homely sitting
rooms; some have small kitchens. Four-poster rooms are available. Top
of the range is the Penthouse Suite whose dining room opens on to
a private terrace. New owners took over in April 1994 and the first major
change is that the restaurant is no longer open to non-residents. No dogs.
Rooms 64. AMERICAN EXPRESS *Access, Diners, Visa.*

SW1   Durley House   74%   £240

Tel 071-235 5537   Fax 071-259 6977   **H**

115 Sloane Street SW1X 9PJ   **Map 19 C5**

A finely furnished residence comprising eleven self-contained one-and two-
bedroom suites, Durley House commends itself to clients seeking the quiet
life in central London, a civilised antidote to the bustle of a large hotel.
Indeed, its Sloane Street location is handy as a pied-à-terre for
Knightsbridge stores, yet guests can step literally across the road for a game
of tennis in Cadogan Park. Each of its spacious apartments is individually
designed and furnished with antiques and original oil paintings. Some fine
architectural features, carved wooden mantels and curved panelling are
embellished with flamboyant drapes; king-size beds have crown canopies
and matching covers in bold colours. The lounges include polished
mahogany dining tables and, in some cases, grand pianos. There's a level
of service to match: a full 24hr room service includes breakfast, which
arrives by way of a traditional service lift (there's no restaurant). Under the
same ownership as *Dorset Square* and *Pelham* hotels. *Rooms 11. Garden,
tennis.* AMERICAN EXPRESS *Access, Visa.*

W1   Durrants Hotel   65%   £106
Tel 071-935 8131   Fax 071-487 3510   H
George Street W1H 6BJ   Map 18 C2

In the heart of the West End, opposite the Wallace Collection, Durrants comprises four houses dating back 200 years. Its appeal is traditional and club-like with wood panelling in the foyer, an intimate bar, authentic smoking room and cosy, but not large, bedrooms. Marble bathrooms have quality fittings. Ten rooms are not en suite. No dogs. Hospitality is the keynote here. *Rooms 96.* AMERICAN EXPRESS *Access, Visa.*

EC1   The Eagle   ↑   £40
Tel 071-837 1353   R
159 Farringdon Road EC1R 3AL   Map 16 C3

Sounds like a pub, feels like a pub, tastes sensational! No bookings taken but persevere, share a table, order your food at the top of your voice and enjoy the robust Mediterranean dishes, cooked by David Eyre in an open plan kitchen. Options are marked up on a blackboard, at least nine, changing at least daily. There's always a cheese plate (Spanish Manchego with *dulce de membrillo*, or soft Italian with focaccia and rocket) and a simple dessert. One stalwart: the marinated rump-steak sandwich, *bifeana*, is a permanent fixture. Other recent hits have included prosciutto with grilled asparagus and shaved Parmesan, pappardelle with chicken livers and sage, *bacabada* (Lisbon-style salt cod and potatoes), *fabada* (Spanish butter beans with chorizo, pork, ham and black pudding), and a light lunch of aubergine purée with chopped coriander and Turkish olive bread. Great food, good prices, excellent range of wines by the glass. *Seats 50. L 12.30-2.30 D 6.30-10.30. Closed Sat & Sun, Bank Holidays, 2/3 weeks Christmas. No credit cards.*

SW6   Earls Court Park Inn International   69%   £108
Tel 071-385 1255   Fax 071-381 4450   H
47 Lillie Road Fulham SW6 1UQ   Map 19 A5

Just by the side entrance to Earls Court Exhibition Centre, so it's not surprising that tour parties and conferences are big business (up to 1750 delegates). Children up to 16 free in parents' room. No dogs. *Rooms 501. Business centre, coffee shop (6.30am-midnight).* AMERICAN EXPRESS *Access, Diners, Visa.*

SW1   Ebury Wine Bar   £40
Tel 071-730 5447   R
139 Ebury Street Victoria SW1   Map 19 C4

The Ebury is one of London's original wine bars, having been established in 1959, and it enjoys a strong regular customer base. The food is modern British, and grills are a speciality. Naturally, there's an excellent range of wines by the glass. *Seats 80. Parties 16. L 12-2.45 (Sun to 2.30) D 6-10.30 (Sun to 10). Closed 25 Dec. Set D £18.*

W1   Efes Kebab House   £40
Tel 071-636 1953   Fax 071-323 5082   R
80 Great Titchfield Street W1N 5FD   Map 18 D2

Brothers Khazim and Ibrahim opened their Turkish restaurant in 1974 and it's remained popular ever since. Lamb and chicken kebabs are the principal attraction, preceded by a wide selection of hors d'oeuvre including stuffed vine leaves, *imam bayildi* (aubergines stuffed with onions, tomatoes, parsley and garlic), deep-fried lamb's liver, cream cheese salad and green peppers filled with nuts, raisins and rice. Turkish sweets from a trolley (try *sutlu borek* – cream custard and almonds in pastry). No-smoking room. *Seats 50. Meals 12-11.30. Closed Sun, Christmas, 1 Jan, Good Friday. Set meals from £15.* AMERICAN EXPRESS *Access, Diners, Visa.*

SW3   Egerton House   £184

Tel 071-589 2412   Fax 071-584 6540   **PH**

17-19 Egerton Terrace Knightsbridge SW3 2BX   **Map 19 B4**

In a quiet location overlooking garden squares, this handsome redbrick
Victorian town house is just a short stroll from Harrods. Bedrooms (on
four floors, all served by a lift) are individually decorated with traditional
fabrics, antiques and oil paintings and there's a luxurious look and feel
to the marble bathrooms. Some rooms have four-posters, the majority
overlook gardens and all are air-conditioned. Excellent breakfasts are served
in the rooms or in the bright, basement breakfast room. Extensive room
service, concierge, valet, drinks tray in the smoking room. No dogs.
Rooms 30. AMERICAN EXPRESS *Access, Diners, Visa.*

SW6   El Metro   £45

Tel 071-384 1264   Fax 071-736 5292   **R**

10-12 Effie Road Fulham Broadway SW6 1AA   **Map 19 A6**

Recently expanded bar/café/brasserie in a side street opposite Fulham
Broadway underground station. Breakfasts, burgers, sandwiches, pasta,
steaks, tapas, paella. *Seats 90. Parties 30. Meals 9am-midnight (Sun till 11pm).
Closed 3 days Christmas.* AMERICAN EXPRESS *Access, Diners, Visa.*

SW1   Elizabeth Hotel   £70

Tel 071-828 6812   **H**

37 Eccleston Square SW1V 1PB   **Map 19 D5**

Friendly privately-owned bed and breakfast hotel in a garden square near
Victoria station. Bedrooms range from singles to family-size; en-suite
facilities extend to 28 rooms. No dogs. *Rooms 40. No credit cards.*

SW7   Embassy House Hotel   59%   £105

Tel 071-584 7222   Fax 071-589 8193   **H**

31 Queen's Gate SW7 5JA   **Map 19 B4**

Modern comfort in a late-Victorian building near Hyde Park, the Royal
Albert Hall and the Kensington Museums. Children under 16 can stay free
in their parents' room; in their own room they pay 50% of the adult rate.
15 bedrooms are reserved for non-smokers. Jarvis. *Rooms 69.*
AMERICAN EXPRESS *Access, Diners, Visa.*

WC2   Emerald Garden   NEW   £45

Tel 071-437 5042   **R**

8 Little Newport Street Soho WC2H 7JJ   **Map 21 A2**

A recent addition to the ranks of Chinese restaurants in London's
Chinatown, the Emerald has a tiny and cosy, mirrored ground floor. There
are, however, two other floors, both larger. Decor throughout is bright and
cheerful with pale green and white the main theme. The menu
is Cantonese but with a few other regional specialities such as Szechuan
squid with chili in a salt crust, the squid deliciously dry and almost crispy,
with fresh baked garlic flakes and spring onion adding extra pungency.
The selection of seafood is extensive and familiar favourites such as king
prawns in a black bean sauce or beef in oyster sauce are prepared with good
attention to detail. *Seats 68. Parties 12. Private Room 30. Meals 12-12 (Fri &
Sat to 1am). Closed 25 & 26 Dec. Set L £3.20/£5.50. Set D from £6.50 (min
2 persons).* AMERICAN EXPRESS *Access, Visa.*

SW3   English Garden

£65

Tel 071-584 7272   Fax 071-581 2848

R

10 Lincoln Street off Draycott Avenue SW3 2TS

Map 19 C5

English cooking in a stylishly converted Chelsea town house with a Gothic conservatory. Dishes are mainly traditional or classic, including grilled Cumberland sausage with bubble and squeak, grilled sirloin of beef with Yorkshire pudding and rhubarb crumble with orange custard. More esoteric offerings are typified by salad of chargrilled onions and artichoke hearts tossed with a lemon and anchovy vinaigrette, or liquorice ice cream. *Seats 70. Private Room 24. L 12.30-2.30 (Sun & Bank Holidays till 2) D 7.30-11.30 (Sun & Bank Holidays 7-10). Closed 25 & 26 Dec. Set L £14.75.* AMERICAN EXPRESS *Access, Diners, Visa.*

SW3   English House

£85

Tel 071-584 3002   Fax 071-581 2848

R

3 Milner Street Chelsea SW3 2QA

Map 19 C5

English cooking in a homely Victorian setting just off Kings Road. Salmon and asparagus terrine, wild mushroom tart and duck and goose liver paté with spiced plum chutney are typical starters (on a spring menu – the choice changes seasonally), followed by calf's liver with red onion gravy, rack of lamb with mint pesto, or poached monkfish served with a cider and basil cream sauce. *Seats 45. Parties 28. Private Room 2. L 12.30-2.30 (Sun & Bank Holidays till 2) D 7.30-11.30 (Sun & Bank Holidays 7-10). Closed D 25 Dec, all 26 Dec. Set L £14.75.* AMERICAN EXPRESS *Access, Diners, Visa.*

SW15   Enoteca

£45

Tel 081-785 4449

R

28 Putney High Street SW15 1SQ

Map 17 B5

On a corner site just south of Putney Bridge, Enoteca offers modern Italian cooking at very reasonable prices in a friendly, relaxed atmosphere. The short, interesting menu is strong on pasta (black tagliolini with langoustines, clams and mussels, pappardelle with oyster mushrooms, garlic and parsley) and main courses could include salmon with fennel and saffron, roast guinea fowl with salsify fritters and calf's liver with braised onions. Fixed-price lunches Mon-Fri. Suitable wines are helpfully noted against each dish. Good strong coffee served with amaretti biscuits. *Seats 35. Private Room 45. L 12.30-3 D 7-11.30. Closed L Sat, all Sun, 1 week Christmas. Set L £6.50/£9.50.* AMERICAN EXPRESS *Access, Diners, Visa.*

> Many establishments are currently on the market, so ownership could change after we go to press.

SW3   The Enterprise

£55

Tel 071-584 3148   Fax 071-584 1060

R

35 Walton Street SW3

Map 19 C4

A charming converted pub, tastefully refurbished, with a restaurant and American bar. It's a pleasant retreat for lunch, dinner or a drink. The modern menu offers the likes of smoked trout with fresh horseradish, baby new potato skins with caviar and sour cream, warm crab tart with hollandaise, smoked duck with bacon and croutons, Lincolnshire sausages with mashed potatoes, fried onions and honey mustard gravy, and blackboard specials. Cooking is unpretentious and plates are put together with care. 25 seats outside in good weather. Cheques not accepted. *Seats 35. Parties 15. L 12.30-2.30 D 7-10. Closed 24-28 Dec.* AMERICAN EXPRESS *Access, Visa.*

W1   L'Escargot   ↑   £100

Tel 071-437 6828   Fax 071-437 0790   **R**

48 Greek Street Soho W1V 5LR   Map 21 A2

This long-established Soho stalwart has been revamped to provide
a bustling ground-floor brasserie. Red banquettes, parquet floors and
abstract paintings lend the room a new and stylish accent. The mostly
French menu offers many a traditional favourite such as brandade de morue
with green bean salad, marinated goat's cheese and terrine of foie gras,
followed by entrecote of beef with béarnaise sauce, saddle of hare, skate
with black butter, moules marinière or bourride. Plateau de fruits de mer
and pot au feu must be ordered for two. Provençal soup is served
traditionally, with rouille and Gruyère, but cassoulet isn't everything
it could be. Desserts, however, make up for any disappointment in the main
courses – try the crème brulée, chocolate tart with orange sorbet or passion
fruit tart. Service in the brasserie is friendly and efficient. Above the
bustling brasserie, owner Jimmy Lahoud has cleverly achieved an almost
dinner-party feel with table lamps and comfortably upholstered chairs
in the more intimate, air-conditioned restaurant. The welcome
by classically clad staff is charming, the carte short, intelligent and long
on quality and skill. An amuse-gueule of filo-wrapped snail with nuts and
anchovies set on mash and surrounded by veal jus is not only witty but
tasty, too; moist terrine of chicken and sweetbreads is accompanied by tiny
potato dice and fine olive oil; roast quail with ricotta ravioli or scallop and
artichoke might be other starters. To follow, perhaps a magnificent dish
of best end of lamb Reform served with a beetroot jus flecked with truffle,
plus millefeuille of ox tongue, beetroot and ham topped with two
translucent ravioli filled with chopped ox tongue and gherkins (a slice
of truffle was the crowning glory), or red mullet en papillote – both dishes
equally successful. Finish with farmhouse cheeses served in fine condition,
passion fruit soufflé or ginger parfait with mango coulis, minute apple balls,
cognac sorbet and a crisp tuile (a triumph of taste and texture). A five-
course, no-choice gastronomic menu is offered for a minimum of two
diners. If you choose wines by price, the excellent and comprehensive wine
list is easy to follow, albeit with no tasting notes; it contains top wines
from top growers, including a good cross-section from the New World.
Restaurant service is informed, unintrusive and altogether exemplary. Part
of the Soho scene since 1927, L'Escargot thoroughly deserves its niche
in London's culinary history. **Seats** 80 (*Brasserie*) 38 (*Restaurant*). *Parties 20.
Private Rooms 34 & 50. L 12.15-2.30 D 6-11.30 (Restaurant from 7).
Set L £25 Set D £39.50 (each, for two minimum). Closed L Sat, all Sun,
Easter, Christmas, 1 Jan.* AMERICAN EXPRESS *Access, Diners, Visa.*

We welcome bona fide complaints and recommendations on the tear-out
pages at the back of the book for readers' comments. They are followed
up by our professional team.

W8   L'Escargot Doré   £85

Tel 071-937 8508   **R**

2 Thackeray Street Kensington W8 5ET   Map 19 A4

A cool basement retreat on hot summer days and suitable for intimate
candle-lit dinners. The menu covers a range from crab bisque with mussel
and saffron ravioli to garlic snails, pan-fried scallops with Pernod and
chervil cream sauce and confit of duck with plum sauce. Lighter snacks are
available in *La Petite Brasserie*, a small bar-brasserie area at street level.
Seats 50. *Parties 30. Private Room 25. L 12-2.30 D 7-11.30. Closed L Sat, all
Sun, Bank Holidays, last 2 weeks Aug. Set L & D £14.90.* AMERICAN EXPRESS
Access, Diners, Visa.

W1   Est   £40

Tel 071-437 0666   **R**

54 Frith Street Soho W1V 5TE   **Map 21 A2**

A Soho media restaurant with large windows looking on to Frith Street.
The menu, cooked by Paul Jensen (formerly at *Daphne's*), is very much
in the modern Mediterranean mode, with simple, straightforward dishes.
Very popular with the younger set. *Seats 40. Parties 26. L 12-3 D 6-11
(Fri & Sat to 11.30). Closed L Sat, all Sun, Bank Holidays.* AMERICAN EXPRESS
Access, Diners, Visa.

WC2   L'Estaminet   £60

Tel 071-379 1432   **R**

14 Garrick Street WC2E 9BJ   **Map 21 B2**

An attractive French brasserie on the fringe of Covent Garden (off Floral
Street). The short menu runs from onion or fish soup, moules marinière
and garlic snails to seafood pancakes, king prawn brochettes, *coquelet grand-
mère* and speciality steaks. *Seats 60. Private Room 20. L 12-2.30
D 5.45-11.15. Closed Sun, Bank Holidays. Set D (to 7.45) £9.99.*
AMERICAN EXPRESS *Access, Visa.*

W1   L'Etoile   £80

Tel 071-636 7189   Fax 071-580 0109   **R**

30 Charlotte Street W1P 1HJ   **Map 18 D2**

One of the bastions of traditional French cooking, with salade niçoise, frogs'
legs, fish or onion soup, goujons of sole, veal escalope, Zingara duck
à l'orange and tournedos béarnaise among the favourites. *Seats 60.
Private Room 30. L 12.30-2.30 D 6-11. Closed L Sat, all Sun, Bank Holidays.
Set L & D £14.50.* AMERICAN EXPRESS *Access, Diners, Visa.*

~~NEW CHEF~~

WC1   Euro & George Hotels   £46

Tel 071-387 6789   Fax 071-383 5044   **H**

53 Cartwright Gardens WC1H 9EL   **Map 18 D1**

In a crescent near the British Museum, the George and its neighbour the
Euro offer very reasonably priced accommodation, with children up to 13
staying free in parents' room at winter weekends, and at reduced rates
at other times. Unlicensed. No dogs. Euro is specifically geared towards
business and holiday travellers; George *can* take groups. *Rooms 75.
Access, Visa.*

> If we recommend meals in a hotel or inn a separate entry is made for its
> restaurant.

WC1   Euston Plaza Hotel   66%   £110

Tel 071-383 4105   Fax 071-383 4106   **H**

17 Upper Woburn Place WC1H 0HT   **Map 18 D1**

A stone's throw from the main line station, the hotel posesses a smart,
modern decor inherited from its former Scandinavian owners. The lobby
has polished cream marble floors which continue into the cool, spacious
bar. A lofty Victorian-style plant-filled conservatory is now a wine bar
complete with dripping candles on the white marble tables. Fully air-
conditioned bedrooms have smart lightwood furniture and a good range
of amenities. Children up to 12 stay free in parents' room. The health club
is a major new feature, with gym equipment ranged around a raised jacuzzi
in the centre of an airy room. *Rooms 150. Gym, sauna, spa bath, solarium.*
AMERICAN EXPRESS *Access, Diners, Visa.*

NW1 Fanari £30

Tel 071-586 1969 **R**

40 Chalcot Road NW1 Map 16 C3

Off Regents Park Road, Fanari is a very friendly and unpretentious Greek restaurant where a meal is like a family supper. Portions are generous, flavours robust, prices very reasonable. Dinner ends with a plateful of fresh fruit. *Seats 95. Private Room 40. D only 6-12. Closed Sun. Access, Visa.*

E8 Faulkners £25

Tel 071-254 6152 **R**

424 Kingsland Road E8 4AA Map 16 D2

Busy fish'n'chip restaurant with an even busier takeaway section. Groundnut oil is used to fry generous portions of fish purchased daily from Billingsgate, from cod cutlet or fillet and rock salmon to halibut and Dover sole. Special value children's menu (£2.95). *Seats 60. L 12-2 D 5-10 (Sat 11.30-10, Sun 12-9). Closed Sun, Bank Holidays, 2 weeks Christmas. No credit cards.*

SW3 The Fenja £154

Tel 071-589 7333 Fax 071-581 4958 **PH**

69 Cadogan Gardens SW3 2RB Map 19 C5

A handsome private residence turned into a home-from-home hotel of town house character with bedrooms each named after a notable writer or painter who lived nearby (Turner, Swinburne, Rossetti). Antiques, fresh flowers, marble busts and English prints and paintings of the 18th and 19th centuries are features, and both towels and bedding are of high quality. Breakfast (cooked to order until 2pm for late risers!) and light meals from room service (no restaurant); drinks on a tray in the room or in the cosy drawing room with an open fire. Guests have access to Cadogan Gardens. No dogs. *Rooms 12. Garden.* AMERICAN EXPRESS *Access, Visa.*

SW1 Fifth Floor at Harvey Nichols £80

Tel 071-235 5250 Fax 071-235 5020 **R**

Knightsbridge SW1 Map 19 C4

When the store is closed the fifth-floor restaurant, café and bar are reached by an express lift from either Sloane Street or Seville Street. The restaurant menus (fixed price at lunchtime, fixed and à la carte in the evening) are as fashionable as any in town: Henry's black bean soup, salad of marinated grilled leeks and flat mushrooms with tapénade croutons, salt cod fillets with aubergine caviar, oysters with spicy sausages, baked sea bass with aromats, pan-fried calf's liver, lentils and wild mushrooms, Bury black pudding and pease pudding with parsley and mustard sauce. Separate vegetarian menu. Plenty of desserts – each with a dessert wine suggestion. Sensational is the word that comes to mind when perusing the wine list here. It's a lengthy and brilliantly compiled tome, but well worth studying, and though there are no tasting notes, just seek guidance from *sommelier par excellence* Thierry Dumont. Even the prices are fair – terrific! *Seats 110. Parties 8. L 12-3 (Sat to 3.30) D 6.30-11.30. Set L & D £17.50/£21.50. Closed Sun, 25 & 26 Dec.* AMERICAN EXPRESS *Access, Diners, Visa.*

N8 Florians £50

Tel 081-348 8348 **R**

4 Topsfield Parade Middle Lane Crouch End N8 8RP Map 16 C1

Busy and loud premises with a wine bar at the front. Simple, unfussy Italian food is prepared in the modern, lighter manner, exemplified by potato and beetroot gnocchi with thyme butter, braised duck with prunes and lentils, and chargrilled swordfish served with baby spinach salad. There's also a bar menu. *Seats 67. Parties 12. Private Room 24. L 12-3 D 7-11 (Sun to 10.30). Closed Christmas holidays. Set L & D £5.95 (bar). Access, Visa.*

SW10	Formula Veneta	£50
Tel 071-352 7612 Fax 081-295 1503		**R**
14 Hollywood Road SW10		Map 19 B6

As its name suggest, Gianni Pauro's Formula Veneta offers northern Italian specialities in a setting that manages to look bright and summery (especially in the rear garden) despite its busy West London location. Cooking is mostly in the modern style and you might choose wind-dried venison served with ricotta, or carpaccio of beef or salmon to start. Pasta in a variety of shapes could be served with fresh crab and shrimps, or with spiced beef in rosemary and chili butter. There's a whole page of meat and fish dishes, such as liver and onions Venetian style, or cuttlefish with peas and polenta. For pudding try *panna cotta* with blackcurrants or a concoction of lemon vodka, lemon sorbet and wild fruit. *Seats 60. Parties 30. Private Room 30. L 12.30-2.30 D 7-11.15. Set L £9.95 (Sun £12.95). Closed D Sun, Bank Holidays.* AMERICAN EXPRESS *Access, Diners, Visa.*

WC1	Forte Crest Bloomsbury 65%	£121
Tel 071-837 1200 Fax 071-837 5374		**H**
Coram Street WC1N 1HT		Map 18 D1

A large, modern, purpose-built hotel located in a largely residential part of Bloomsbury. Designed and equipped with the business person very much in mind, there are conference and banqueting facilities for 1200/600 and the normal Crest conveniences. Bright, marble bathrooms and five Lady Crest rooms. 40 family rooms with both a double and single bed; 10 minutes' walk from the British Museum. Special rates in the NCP car park below the hotel. No dogs. *Rooms 284. Brasserie (7am-11pm).* AMERICAN EXPRESS *Access, Diners, Visa.*

SW1	Forte Crest Cavendish 68%	£140
Tel 071-930 2111 Fax 071-839 2125		**H**
81 Jermyn Street SW1Y 6JF		Map 18 D3

The former Forte Crest St James's (and previously the Cavendish), built in 1966, stands directly behind Fortnum & Mason, just a short walk from Piccadilly Circus and Green Park. Marble floors and modern wood panelling set the tone in the foyer and there's a clubby bar. Bedrooms are to the usual Crest standard and all benefit from recent refurbishment. The Executive 15th-floor rooms have a lounge area and jacuzzi baths. 80-space basement car park. Conference and banqueting facilities for 100/80. 24hr room and valet services. *Rooms 256.* AMERICAN EXPRESS *Access, Diners, Visa.*

> See the Hotels by County listings for easy comparison of conference and banqueting facilities.

W1	Forte Crest Regents Park 64%	£99
Tel 071-388 2300 Fax 071-387 2806		**H**
Carburton Street W1P 8EE		Map 18 D2

Several categories of accommodation are available in this large early-70s hotel, including suites and Lady Rooms. Children up to 16 stay free in parents' room. It's a popular base for overseas visitors and also has extensive conference facilities (up to 650 theatre-style). Covered parking for 80 cars. No dogs. Between Great Portland Street and Cleveland Street. *Rooms 318. Coffee shop (6.30am-11pm, from 7am Sun)* AMERICAN EXPRESS *Access, Diners, Visa.*

NW3   Forte Posthouse   65%   £68

Tel 071-794 8121   Fax 071-435 5586   **H**

215 Haverstock Hill NW3 4RB   Map 16 B2

Close to Belsize Park underground station and a short walk from Hampstead Heath. Top-floor bedrooms offer splendid views; 30 Executive rooms are equipped with various extras, including mini-bars and stereo in the bathrooms. Half the bedrooms are designated non-smoking. Children up to 14 stay free in parents' room. Ample free parking. Brasserie with outdoor seating. *Rooms 140.* AMERICAN EXPRESS *Access, Diners, Visa.*

W1   47 Park Street   86%   £326

Tel 071-491 7282   Fax 071-491 7281   **H**

47 Park Street Mayfair W1Y 4EB   Map 18 C3

Even the youngest budding gourmets can relax at 47 Park Street as the suites at this gracious Edwardian town house are spacious, can be equipped with extra beds or cots if need be and can provide a baby sitting service on request. Perhaps this is a reflection of the French attitude towards children and taking them to good restaurants and hotels, ie it's perfectly normal and even to be encouraged. For this most English of establishments is French owned, and French designed (by Monique Roux, wife of Albert, whose *Le Gavroche* (qv) is downstairs and provides the ultimate in 24hr room service). Superlatives flow thick and fast – sumptuous, elegant, tasteful – in describing the suites of rooms themselves (generously proportioned, perfectly equipped) or the standards of maintenance (impeccable). There's a concierge round the clock, a business centre (during normal office hours), leisure facilities adjacent, and the epitome of banqueting/conference facilities for 20/30. It's very probably one of the most expensive places to stay in London, but it's certainly one of the very very best. *Rooms 52. Hotel limousine, valeting (8am-5pm), baby-sitting, hairdressing, shopping service.* AMERICAN EXPRESS *Access, Diners, Visa.*

SW7   Forum Hotel   62%   £157

Tel 071-370 5757   Fax 071-373 1448   **H**

97 Cromwell Road SW7 4DN   Map 19 B5

The exterior of the Forum had a complete clean this year, reflecting its location on a busy main road. The bonus aspect of this setting is that it's ideally located for those coming in from Heathrow with easy connections to the Airbus and tube. This Inter-Continental hotel doesn't offer the same standards as its sister hotels in London but certainly provides the basics. Bedrooms are small and contain all the expected amenities, including satellite TV and a mini-bar; 60 rooms are now non-smoking. Families are well catered for: children up to 15 are free in parents' room. Two bedrooms are equipped for the disabled. Room service is now available 24hrs a day and a new fitness suite has been added. Underground car park for 80. *Rooms 910. Keep-fit equipment.* AMERICAN EXPRESS *Access, Diners, Visa.*

W2   Four Seasons   £50

Tel 071-229 4320   **R**

84 Queensway W2 3RL   Map 18 A3

In an area thronged with Chinese restaurants, this is one of the most up-market in terms of both decor and price. Service is friendly and attentive, and the predominantly Cantonese menu runs the gamut of familiar dishes. Chef's specialities include shredded beef with crispy rice noodles, stuffed bean curd in a hotpot and fried prawn cake with vegetables. Sizzling dishes are also popular. *Seats 70. Parties 12. Meals 12-11.15. Closed 25 & 26 Dec. Set D from £10.50.* AMERICAN EXPRESS *Access, Visa.*

W1   **Four Seasons Hotel**   89%   £315

Tel 071-499 0888   Fax 071-493 1895   **HR**

Hamilton Place Park Lane Mayfair W1A 1AZ   Map 19 C4

Although several storeys high the hotel, fronted by a small garden with
maturing sycamore trees, is somewhat overlooked by its neighbours. Inside,
the modernity of the exterior gives way to a stylish elegance firmly rooted
in classic good taste. The lobby walls are clad in rich mahogany with
a huge Venetian chandelier suspended from the ceiling, while underfoot
is a floor of polished light brown and other matching coloured marbles.
The lounge, as well as being a place to meet and relax, is also where all-day
light meals and superb afternoon teas are served in gracious, supremely
civilised surroundings with colourful, springy carpets and, as elsewhere
in the public areas, vases of exquisite flowers in grandiose arrangements.
Equally grand is the exceptionally wide bifurcated staircase which leads
to the bars, restaurants and banqueting rooms. Among the finest of the
already splendid bedrooms are the 11 Conservatory rooms which are
especially bright and airy. There are 26 suites, including five grand
apartment suites. All these have CD players but all rooms have stereo
televisions, video players and satellite broadcasts in six languages as well
as a Reuters and an in-house channel, the latter showing first releases
on video. There's a library of 200 feature films available for guests' use. Not
only are the rooms beautifully decorated in soft hues with fine furniture
(some with marble tops), spacious and well-equipped but the beds too are
extremely comfortable – queen-size in single rooms and king-size or twin
in double. Bathrooms in fine cream marble live up to expectations with
every facility provided including bidets (not in single rooms), fine toiletries
and ample thick towels. The Conservatory fitness club on the second floor
is for the exclusive use of residents and is an up-to-date, light room with
a comprehensive selection of the latest exercise equipment each with
individual TV monitors and headphones. The hotel has fine banqueting
suites including the magnificent Pine Room with its ornate 18th-century
panelling. Breakfasts are, as one would expect, superb, not only for choice –
a lenghty à la carte is supplemented by four set-price breakfasts including
Japanese and healthy options – but also for quality. Staff are on the whole
excellent, providing efficient, discreet and smiling service. Underground
garage and valet parking. ***Rooms*** *227. Garden, gym, valeting, coffee shop*
(9am-1am). *Access, Diners, Visa.*

Four Seasons Restaurant   ★   £120

A room with a view (out to the small garden), hiding the hideous traffic
of Park Lane during the summer months, is the sophisticated setting for
Jean-Christophe Novelli's always exciting and innovative cooking. The
room, florally decorated in shades of charcoal and pink, has a discreet
elegance which is surpassed by the artistry of what emanates from the
kitchens. Service too doesn't really do the food justice, being old-school and
rather matter-of-fact. None of this deters Novelli, whose aspirations,
a medley of carefully worked-out flavours and textures presented in his
own inimitably flamboyant style, now more restrained than previously,
lead ever upward. Over-elaboration and extensive manipulation of the
dishes has now succumbed to a more classical representation though still
with the occasional, and very effective, flourish. This is more probably due
to imposed restrictions as in the case of a starter – a rather uninspired
carpaccio of duck with a salad of green beans and Parmesan shavings.
Steamed scallop kebab wrapped in lettuce with a reduction of mixed
peppers with olive oil or a warm sausage of poached lobster accompanied
by a couscous with peppers, ginger and cardamom and a marbled terrine
of foie gras and lentils wrapped in smoked salmon are very much more
in his style. A magnificent ragout of lobster, scallops, squid, langoustine and
mussels flavoured with vanilla with broad beans and black noodles
is typical of the main dishes he offers. Other choices are equally exciting,
and from a selection strong in fish, could come a fillet of turbot poached
in coconut milk with bazelle leaves and honey and light almond purée,

pan-fried duck breast with a light carrot juice and mustard seeds served
with chick pea chips, or a wonderful offal platter of veal trotter,
sweetbreads and tail with poached ox tongue and oxtail accompanied
by a potato and celeriac purée. Desserts such as a light rice pudding with
star anise and cardamom with a poached pear in Sangria, a strawberry
mousse with strawberry toffee and white peppercorn sauce or a hot bitter
chocolate cake which when cut oozes rich dark chocolate and
is accompanied by a white chocolate ice cream are just three of a superb
selection that complete a marvellous three courses. Happily, not all the
wines on the list are out of reach of normal pockets, in fact some are quite
fairly priced; it is indeed a fine list, with many great names, lots of half
bottles and several wines available by the glass. *Seats 55. L 12.30-3
D 7-10.30. Set L £25 (Sun £28) Set D £45.*

Lanes Restaurant £80

One of London's most stylish restaurants; although windowless, the room
has a light and contemporary decor and features a central buffet with
wonderful displays throughout the day. Executive chef Eric Deblonde
offers a choice of fixed-price three-course lunch menus all including wine.
Dinner menus are well laid out and simply priced: your pick of the buffet
as first or main course, ditto for pasta, grills, or other main courses like
braised lamb shank or roast salmon in a potato cake. Lanes' Alternative
Cuisine offers light and vegetarian options. Superb breakfasts cover every
option from healthy to self-indulgent, from British to Japanese. The wine
list attracts the same prices as in the main restaurant, but there's a shorter
list; house wines have tasting notes. One half of the restaurant is reserved
for non-smokers. *Seats 75. Parties 10. L 12-3 D 6-12 (Sun 6.30-11).
Set L from £22.75.*

SW3 Foxtrot Oscar £50

Tel 071-352 7179 R

79 Royal Hospital Road Chelsea SW3 4HN Map 19 C5

Long-fashionable neighbourhood Chelsea restaurant serving a large variety
of familiar dishes from an international repertoire: eggs Benedict, herring
roes, burgers, chops, grills, salads. The cocktail list runs to more than two
dozen. A fun place – be sure to book. *Seats 55. Private Room 35.
L 12.30-2.30 (Sat & Sun to 3.30) D 7.30-11.30. Closed 25-28 Dec.*
AMERICAN EXPRESS *Access, Visa.*

> Our inspectors are full-time employees; they are professionally
> trained by us.

SW3 Franklin Hotel £184

Tel 071-584 5533 Fax 071-584 5449 PH

28 Egerton Gardens London SW3 2DB Map 19 B4

Opened in September 1992, the hotel is under the same ownership and
offers similar high standards of accommodation as *Egerton House* (qv), a few
hundred yards away in the next street. A smart and welcoming reception
area sets the tone for beautifully appointed public rooms and bedrooms.
The drawing room and nicest bedrooms overlook the peace and
tranquillity of Egerton Gardens with its trees and well-trimmed lawn. The
bar, decked out in elegant dark red, operates on an honesty principle. There
are nine very spacious garden rooms but all rooms are of good size and are
impressively equipped including air-conditioning. Bathrooms are marble-
lined, some have bidets, all have both hand-held and overhead showers
as well as a selection of Floris toiletries. Good standards of service include
an evening turn-down service as well as a selection of recommended
restaurants vetted by the staff. *Rooms 36. Garden.* AMERICAN EXPRESS *Access,
Diners, Visa.*

N1   Frederick's   £65
Tel 071-359 2888   Fax 071-359 5173   **R**
Camden Passage Islington N1 8EG   Map 16 D3

Smart conservatory restaurant, established in 1969, offering mostly safe,
classical French food on a fortnightly-changing menu. Note early evening
opening times for pre-theatre dinner. The garden patio opens for outdoor
eating in summer, seating 36. Some keen prices on the decent wine list.
Special children's Saturday lunch (£5.95). All prices now include service.
No-smoking area. *Seats 140. Private Room 20. Private Room 30. L 12-2.30
D 6-11.30. Closed Sun, Bank Holidays. Set meals £16.50.* AMERICAN EXPRESS
Access, Diners, Visa.

W1   French House Dining Room   £45
Tel 071-437 2477   **R**
49 Dean Street Soho W1V 5HL   Map 21 A2

On the first floor of an old-fashioned Soho pub, the dining room offers
an interesting menu of essentially English dishes typified by chick pea and
tomato soup, smoked haddock pie, tripe and onions, and roast pickled pork
belly. A couple of good British cheeses, Welsh rarebit, gingerbread
pudding. *Seats 30. Parties 8. L 12.30-3 D 6.30-11.30 Closed Bank Holidays.*
AMERICAN EXPRESS *Access, Diners, Visa.*

W1   Fuji   £70
Tel 071-734 0957   Fax 071-409 3259   **R**
36 Brewer Street W1R 3HD   Map 18 D3

Well-prepared selection of Japanese standards (yakitori, sushi, sashimi and
tempura) served by charming waitresses. You cook some dishes at your
table (after instruction!): these include *shabu-shabu* (beef simmered
in a boiling broth) and *sukiyaki*. There's a separate noodle menu. Prices
on the menu include service charge but not VAT. Japanese tea is served
free with all meals. *Seats 54. L 12-2.30 D 6-10.45. Closed L Sun. Set L from
£10 Set D from £14.* AMERICAN EXPRESS *Access, Diners, Visa.*

SW3   Fulham Road   NEW   ↑   £80
Tel 071-351 7823   **R**
257 Fulham Road SW3 6HY   Map 19 B5

The elephant motifs on the banquettes are amusing, and the studded
leather-look dado rail probably protects the beige-checked walls from
being marked by the backs of the (admittedly comfortable) chairs, but the
overall impression of the Irish-designed (David Collins) restaurant is not
half as striking as Irish chef Richard Corrigan's cooking. Service – under
the charming direction of Marian Scrutton – is pleasant (but quite slow
in between courses in the evenings, which could be more the fault of the
longish menu than the staff), and the accompaniments, such as nibbles,
a variety of freshly-baked breads and petits fours, are first class. Meat,
especially offal, is the thing here, typified by a gutsy sauté of veal kidney
with sweetbreads, crubeens and a super cabbage and bacon tart, robust
navarin of lamb with creamed pasta and lots of jus, but even in the fish
dishes intense and big flavours are the order of the day, roast turbot with
artichokes and a shellfish nage or fillet of brill simmered in bacon broth
with white bean cassoulet. Starters could hardly be called dainty – witness
a broad bean mousse served with Serrano ham, salad leaves and dobs
of gazpacho cream; tartare of veal (rather an offputting appellation) – a rich
dish of chopped meat, lemon and garlic – or the lobster bisque with
tarragon cream (certainly tasty if rather unattractively presented). Fine
vegetables include really good tempura, colcannon, and shredded courgettes
with basil and cream, while the desserts have almost an English air about
them: pear and chestnut rice pudding, drunken brioche-and-butter

pudding, and iced banana parfait with hot fudge sauce. Decent British farmhouse cheese platter too. Fair prices on a sensible wine list that offers a good mix of European and New World wines; half a dozen are served in 50cl jugs, many by the glass – a commendable practice that more restaurants should follow. *Seats 85. L 12.30-2.15 (Sun to 2.30) D 7-11 (Sun to 10). Set L £14.50/£17.50 (Sun £17.50).* AMERICAN EXPRESS® *Access, Visa.*

WC2   Fung Shing   ★   £52

Tel 071-437 1539   **R**

15 Lisle Street Soho WC2 7BE   Map 21 A2

One of London's very best Chinese restaurants, in a street of them. Dishes on the long Cantonese-themed menu read fairly similarly to their Chinatown neighbours, but what arrives on the plate is, quite simply, better – probably because the chef has been here since 1985 when it opened. Deep-fried oysters in batter, soft-shell crab with chili and salt, seafood roll (with what tastes like salad cream in the filling!), superb roasted crispy chicken, shredded beef with spicy sauce, roast duck stuffed with yam, and many other dishes using crab, eel, abalone, carp, prawns are among a selection which includes both familiar favourites and dishes to tempt the adventurous (chicken with preserved clam sauce, crispy fried intestine, double-boiled fluffy supreme shark's fin). Booking is almost essential. *Seats 85. Private Room 30. Meals 12-11.30. Closed 24-26 Dec. Set meals from £11.* AMERICAN EXPRESS® *Access, Diners, Visa.*

W1   La Gaulette   £70

Tel 071-580 7608   **R**

53 Cleveland Street W1P 5PQ   Map 18 D2

The refreshing decor in blue tones, with a tiled floor, soft lights and Mauritian background music, sets the mood for an exclusively fish menu with vegetarian dishes on request. *Soupe de poissons* and half a lobster with garlic and brandy mingle with moules mauricienne or red snapper à la creole. The unusual selection of fish includes bourgeois and parrot fish. The downstairs bistro has the same opening hours and offers a fixed-price menu. *Seats 30. Parties 12. Private Room 50. L 12-2.30 D 6.30-11. Closed L Sat, all Sun, Bank Holidays, 25 & 26 Dec. Set L £17.95 Set L & D £24.* AMERICAN EXPRESS® *Access, Diners, Visa.*

W1   Le Gavroche   ★★★   £160

Tel 071-408 0881   Fax 071-409 0939   **R**

43 Upper Brook Street Mayfair W1Y 1PF   Map 18 C3

To encounter perfection in a restaurant is indeed rare and yet, on the last two occasions that we've been to this bastion of French correctness, it has been achieved. Albert Roux passed on the mantle of head chef to his son Michel Jr a few years ago and any changes have been imperceptible: the menu is more or less the same with the restaurant's classic dishes firmly in place; the staff, under the guiding hand of manager Silvano Giraldin, are so smoothly professional and unobtrusive that you hardly notice them, though at every turn they are there – in force! The setting offers understated elegance, with the street-level reception lounge calmly welcoming, and the plush, basement, club-like dining room cleverly designed – a combination of intimate booths, cosy corners and 'serious' tables for important business discussions. With such surroundings and quality, prices are inevitably stiff, and the archaic practice of presenting only the host with priced menus is almost endearing. On the other hand, the £36 per person lunch menu is a steal, especially when you consider that this price is inclusive of half a bottle of decent wine (*Chablis St Martin "Cuvée Albert Roux" 1993, Domaine Laroche* or the sublimely smooth *Chateau Clerc-Milon 1983 Pauillac*) free Evian, service and VAT. Moreover, there's a choice of three dishes at each stage, including the wondrous trolley of French cheeses, always in tip-top condition, and the ice-cream/sorbet trolley (pink grapefruit, raspberry and apricot on the last visit). A typical lunchtime menu might feature a starter of *roulade de saumon fumé au crabe et sauce verte,* followed by *cuisse de poulet de Bresse sautée à la vigneronne,* with *peche pochée au champagne et mousse à la framboise* to finish. A similar 3-course dinner menu (without wine) will cost you half as much again (£48): *petite gelée de rouget à la tapénade, entrecote poelée canaille (a tarragon sauce), oeufs à la neige au lait d'amande,* again highlighting the tremendous value at lunchtime. In the context of à la carte prices, the *menu exceptionnel* (6 courses, minimum two diners) is also good value, even though it has leapt from last year's £59 to a not inconsiderable £75. However, you can always expect to find two or three classic dishes from the Roux repertoire on this menu, maybe a *petit ragout de homard parfumé au gingembre, bouillon de légumes au foie gras et feuilles vertes,* and signature desserts such as a sablé (depending on the season, raspberry, red fruits or pears and chocolate) or a soufflé. Speaking of puddings, *l'assiette du chef* – a tasting of various desserts – is certainly worth a punt. Still riding high in the à la carte charts are the *soufflé suissesse, mousseline de homard au champagne,* and *daube de boeuf à la bourgeoise,* the latter showing that *cuisine bourgeoise* can go hand in hand with haute cuisine. Before the meal you will be offered a little tray of stunning canapés, and with the coffees or teas a stand of exquisite petits fours that are almost a dessert in themselves for those greedy and wise enough to consume the lot! The wine list is exceptional though expensive, but to be fair, prices have not increased over the last couple of years. From the New World, only the best of California get a look in. And we repeat, no charge for mineral water – other restaurants please note! Minimum evening charge £50. ***Seats*** *60. Parties 20. Private Room 20. L 12-2 D 7-11. Closed Sat & Sun, Bank Holidays, 23 Dec-3 Jan. Set L £36 Set D £48 & £75.* AMERICAN EXPRESS *Access, Diners, Visa.* 🐂

W1	**Gay Hussar**	£60
Tel 071-437 0973		**R**
2 Greek Street Soho W1V 6NB		Map 21 A2

A Soho institution offering hearty portions of traditional Hungarian food. Try the chilled wild cherry soup, roast duck, smoked goose with scholet, veal goulash, chicken paprikash or Transylvanian stuffed cabbage. Desserts include sweet cheese pancakes, poppy-seed strudel and a rum, cream and walnut delicacy. ***Seats*** *70. Parties 12. Private Room 12. L 12.30-2.30 D 5.30-10.45. Closed Sun, Bank Holidays.* AMERICAN EXPRESS *Access, Diners, Visa.*

Many hotels offer reduced rates for weekend or out-of-season bookings. Always ask about special deals.

W8	**Geale's**	£30
Tel 071-727 7969		**R**
2 Farmer Street W8 7SN		Map 18 A3

Tucked away behind Notting Hill's Gate cinema, Geale's has been dispensing fish and chips in the best London tradition for over 50 years, and there are still Geale family members very much in command. Their formula remians the same: the fish cooked in beef dripping, the chips in vegetable fat. English favourites – from cod to halibut – are joined by more unusual offerings like deep-fried clams and parrot fish. Nearly always busy, and no bookings, but you can wait upstairs with a drink for a table. Pavement tables in summer. ***Seats*** *100. Private Room 25. L 12-3 D 6-11. Closed Sun & Mon, Tues after Bank Hol Mons, 2 weeks Christmas, 5 days Easter, 2 weeks Aug. Access, Visa.*

SW7   Gilbert's   £55

Tel 071-589 8947   **R**

2 Exhibition Road SW7 2HF   **Map 19 B5**

A warm red ochre decor and formally set tables set the mood for a quiet
meal. Ann Wregg, one of the original owners, has now retired, but her
partner Julia Chalkley continues as chef-proprietor, with Gina Mahsoudi,
her assistant for three years, sharing the cooking; together they produce
everything including bread, ice cream and fudge. 'Accelerated Cuisine'
is Julia's name for a *prix fixe* lunch offering dishes like sorrel and potato
soup, green bean and hazelnut salad, wild boar terrine with spiced onion
compote, Provençal fish stew with aïoli, egg pasta with spring greens and
walnut sauce or sauté of lamb's kidneys Turbigo (some dishes carry
a supplement). The same dishes appear on the evening menu, with some
splendid English puds like Mrs Beeton's lemon tart or chocolate tipsy cake.
There's also a selection of fine British cheese. Wine is taken seriously here
(ask for details of the Fine Wines & Food Club) and the list presented
mostly by grape style with accompanying tasting notes, changes every two
months. Julia Chalkley selects the wines – don't ignore the suggestions
on the *prix fixe* menu – which are a super mix between Europe and the
New World. Lots of half bottles, fair prices. Opening/closing times are
liable to change during the season of Promenade Concerts at nearby Royal
Albert Hall. **Seats** *32. L 12-2 D 6-10. Closed Sat, Sun, Bank Holidays,
1 week Feb, 1 week Jun. Set L from £9.50 Set D £14.50.* AMERICAN EXPRESS
Access, Diners, Visa.

EC1   Ginnan   £50

Tel 071-278 0008   **R**

1/2 Rosebery Court Rosebery Avenue EC1R 5HP   **Map 16 C3**

Opposite Mount Pleasant, this is a well-run modern Japanese restaurant
where the emphasis is on fresh produce throughout an extensive menu.
Besides the more familiar choice there are many unusual dishes: most parts
of the chicken appear among the *kushiyaki* (charcoal-grilled on a skewer),
there's oxtail boiled with garlic, salmon dipped in sea salt and grilled, and
rice and bitter melon wrapped in seaweed. **Seats** *72. Parties 14. L 12-2.30 D
6-10.30 (Sat 5-10). Closed L Sat, all Sun, Bank Holidays, 11 days
at Christmas/New Year, 1 week Aug.* AMERICAN EXPRESS *Access, Diners, Visa.*

WC2   Giovanni's   £65

Tel 071-240 2877   **R**

10 Goodwin's Court 55 St Martin's Lane WC2AN 4LL **Map 21 B2**

Theatregoers and business people are among those attracted to Giovanni
Colla's long-established Italian restaurant in a little passage off St Martin's
Lane. The menu is familiar Italian, with variations on pasta, meat, poultry
and fish dishes. **Seats** *38. Parties 10. L 12-3, D 6-11.30. Closed L Sat, all Sun,
25 Dec, 1 Jan.* AMERICAN EXPRESS *Access, Diners, Visa.*

SW10   Glaister's Garden Bistro   £40

Tel 071-352 0352   Fax 071-376 7341   **R**

4 Hollywood Road Fulham SW10 9HW   **Map 19 B6**

A summery restaurant and café/bar in a road opposite the new Chelsea &
Westminster Hospital. The blackboard menu in bistro style offers
a generally familiar range, from deep-fried Camembert, gravad lax and
Caesar salad to burgers with fries, sausages and mash, salmon fishcakes, rack
of lamb, steaks and breast of chicken stuffed with wild mushrooms and
spinach on a grain mustard sauce. **Seats** *80. Private Room 40. L 12.30-3
(Sat & Sun to 4) D 7.30-11.30 (Sun to 10.30). Closed Bank Holidays, 2 weeks
Christmas. Set L £5.95.* AMERICAN EXPRESS *Access, Diners, Visa.*

SW7   The Gloucester   75%   £160

Tel 071-373 6030   Fax 071-373 0409   **HR**
4 Harrington Gardens South Kensington SW7 4LH   Map 19 B5

One of the largest hotels and, for its size, probably the best in the area, now newly refurbished throughout with a splendid, very spacious marble-floored foyer lined with beautiful modern wood-panelling. Large jazzy carpets with ample, comfortable seating, equally colourful in turquoise, gold and beige, occupy the centre. Humphreys, an elegant and sophisticated location for a drink, has voluptuous drapes in old gold with exciting splashes of colour provided by the vibrant, watered turquoise upholstery on a few of the chairs. Bedrooms include two club floors on the 6th and 8th. They share an exclusive and comfortable lounge on the 6th where complimentary cocktails are served in the evening together with Continental breakfast and further pampering extras. The bedrooms are all bright and spacious, club rooms having fine yew furniture, fax terminals and two incoming phone lines as well as safes and two relaxing armchairs. A new decor is gradually being introduced, a mixture of influences brought together to create a new style of cool modernity with a great diversity of colours and patterns. In all rooms double beds are king-size while single beds are 4ft wide. Bathrooms are splendid, fitted with brown marble and having excellent shower heads. As part of the changes brought about by the new owners a new café, Boogie Street, opened in September, serving food with a South-East Asian influence. *Rooms 548. News kiosk, coffee shop (6.30am-11.30pm).* AMERICAN EXPRESS® *Access, Diners, Visa.*

South West 7   £60

Opened just before we went to press, South West 7 is a spacious, comfortable, well-appointed room with plenty of staff and an automatic grand piano that knows everything in the repertoire of light standards. The initial menus combined plain grills and classics such as veal saltimbocca with some more elaborate dishes of contemporary influence. Decent cooking, attractive presentation, affable service. *Seats 154. Parties 75. L 12-2.30 D 6-10.45.*

WC1   Gonbei   £45

Tel 071-278 0619   **R**
151 Kings Cross Road WC1X 9BN   Map 16 C3

Popular Japanese restaurant which extended recently into next-door premises. There's a shortish à la carte offering excellent sashimi and deep-fried dishes (prawn, pork, chicken, vegetables, bean curd), plus several set dinner menus. *Seats 40. Private Room 20. D only 6-10.30. Closed Sun, Bank Holidays. Set D from £15. Access, Diners, Visa.*

SW3   Good Earth   £55

Tel 071-584 3658   Fax 071-823 8769   **R**
233 Brompton Road SW3 2EP   Map 19 B4

Comfortable, elegant, smartly staffed, with consistently capable cooking: the usual attributes of a superior non-Soho Chinese restaurant. This one (and its stablemates in Mill Hill and Esher) has two floors of main dining space, plus a large bar with stools. The menu, while not of epic Chinatown proportions, nonetheless offers a more-than-generous variety of dishes from the general repertoire of Chinese favourites. The kitchen is very reliable, and among the chef's specialities are Szechuan prawns, lemon chicken, crispy lamb and an extensive vegetarian choice. *Seats 160. Private Room 32. Meals 12-11.15. Closed 24-28 Dec. Set L & D from £9.95.* AMERICAN EXPRESS® *Access, Diners, Visa.*
Also at:
NW7 143 The Broadway Mill Hill NW7 Tel 081-959 7011.   Map 16 A1
Seats 90. Private Room 30.Open 12-2.30 (Sun to 3) & 6-11.15.

W1   Gopal's of Soho   £40

Tel 071-434 0840   **R**

12 Bateman Street W1V 5TD   **Map 21 A2**

Head chef and co-owner N P Pittal, known to his friends as Gopal, runs one of the capital's best Indian restaurants. Little is likely to disappoint on a menu which includes some very enticing specialities: Mangalorean crab with coconut and spices, potato patties stuffed with lentils, chilis, onions and coriander and served with a sour sauce, *malai* prawns, Goan chicken and *methi* fish with fenugreek. The house thali, meat or vegetarian, gets you little tasters of many dishes. A new branch has recently opened in Great Eastern Street, EC2. *Seats 50. Private Room 30. L 12-2.45 D 6-11.30 (Sun to 11). Closed 25 & 26 Dec. Set meals from £9.75.* AMERICAN EXPRESS *Access, Visa.*

SW7   The Gore   65%   £140

Tel 071-584 6601   Fax 071-589 8127   **H**

189 Queen's Gate SW7 5EX   **Map 19 B4**

Near the Royal Albert Hall and Hyde Park, the Gore is a hotel of pleasantly mellow character, established a little more than 100 years ago. The striking bar-lounge has dark green walls and comfortably arranged sofas. Best bedrooms are elegant and well appointed, with small sitting areas; among them is the fine Tudor room, dark and atmospheric. The hotel houses the successful *Bistrot 190* and *Downstairs at 190*, both masterminded by Antony Worrall Thompson. *Rooms 54.* AMERICAN EXPRESS *Access, Diners, Visa.*

SW1   The Goring   79%   £198

Tel 071-396 9000   Fax 071-834 4393   **HR**

17 Beeston Place Grosvenor Gardens Victoria SW1W 0JW   **Map 19 D4**

There are not that many quality private hotels in London, but this is certainly one of them. Owned since 1961 by George Goring, the hotel (built in 1910 by his grandfather) is meticulously run, in tandem with General Manager and Associate Director William Cowpe, who himself has been in situ for 25 years. Together, they ensure that the customer's needs always come first, exemplified by the high standards of service from all the staff. For this is a very personal and friendly hotel, small enough (by London standards) for guests to be greeted and treated as individuals. As a family-run company, profits (if there are any!) are directed back into the business, and refurbishment is constant, noticeable in the splendid air-conditioned bedrooms (all watched over by a wooden duck and some with balconies overlooking the garden) which are traditionally decorated in restful colours with smart fabrics, handsome furniture and comfortable armchairs/settees. Bathrooms too are up to date with the latest fittings and offer fine toiletries and decent-sized towels. Housekeeping throughout is immaculate, and there's an evening turn-down service, as well as 24hr room service. Public areas and day rooms are most elegant – note the polished marble floor and chandeliers in the entrance hall, the re-upholstered seating in both the garden lounge and bar, and a sheep reclining in front of the open fireplace. Private dining/boardrooms cater for up to 70. Attention to detail is what makes this stylish hotel, close to Victoria Station and Buckingham Palace, so outstanding. Children up to 12 stay free in parents' room. *Rooms 79. Valeting.* AMERICAN EXPRESS *Access, Diners, Visa.*

Restaurant   £90

New screens have divided up the dining room, making it a much more intimate setting in which to enjoy Tony Elliott's almost classical cooking, much of it traditionally English, with a nod to modernity in some dishes (warm goat's cheese with sun-dried tomatoes, salmon fishcakes with a sorrel cream sauce and braised oxtail wrapped in savoy cabbage). Daily-changing luncheon and dinner table d'hote menus, with several choices in each course, sit alongside a sensible à la carte menu, which features favourites such as lobster bisque, roast breast of Gressingham duck with lentils, fillets of Dover sole with button onions and mushrooms and desserts from the trolley. Super and fairly-priced wine list with George Goring's knowledgeable and personal comments – there are always two recommended wines to complement the day's menus and a good selection of wines by the glass. *Seats 75. Parties 20. Private Room 50. L 12.30-2.30 D 6-10. Closed L Sat. Set L £16.50/£19.50 Set D £25.*

SW4	**Grafton Français**	**£65**

Tel 071-627 1048 **R**

45 Old Town Clapham Common SW4 0JL   Map 17 C5

Traditional French cooking in Clapham's oldest building, dating from the 17th century. Typical dishes on the menu include creamy soups (perhaps mussel or celeriac), terrine of duck and fish, herb-marinated skate with bacon and spinach, breast of duck with fruity Calvados, William pear with creamy pear mousse, Grand Marnier soufflé and French cheese. A dozen or so interesting clarets and burgundies on the wine list, which is arranged by grape variety. *Seats 64. Private Rooms 22/28. L 12.30-2.30 D 7.30-11.30. Closed L Sat, all Sun, last 3 weeks Aug, 1 week Christmas. Set L £12.50 Set D £14.95 & £25.* AMERICAN EXPRESS® *Access, Diners, Visa.*

W1	**Grafton Hotel** **63%**	**£160**

Tel 071-388 4131   Fax 071-387 7394 **H**

130 Tottenham Court Road W1P 9HP   Map 18 D1

Edwardian Hotels own the Grafton, whose own Edwardian origins are still in evidence though the bedrooms are modern. There are six family rooms (children under 12 stay free in parents' room). The hotel's location at the northern end of Tottenham Court Road makes it convenient for the British Museum and Regent's Park. *Rooms 324.* AMERICAN EXPRESS® *Access, Diners, Visa.*

W1	**Grahame's Seafare**	**£40**

Tel 071-437 3788   Fax 081-294 1808 **R**

38 Poland Street W1V 3DA   Map 18 D2

Kosher fish, deep-fried, grilled or steamed in simple spick-and-span premises near Oxford Circus underground station. Gefilte fish, chopped herring, egg and onion, potato latkes, new green cucumbers also on the menu. Poland Street car park is 150m away; special rates after 6.30pm. *Seats 84. L 12-2.45 D 5.30-9 (Fri & Sat to 8). Closed Sun, Bank Holidays, Jewish New Year, 2 weeks Christmas.* AMERICAN EXPRESS® *Access, Diners, Visa.*

N1	**Granita**	**£50**

Tel 071-226 3222 **R**

127 Upper Street Islington N1 1QP   Map 16 C3

Granita is in the running as one of London's most minimalist eating places in terms of both decor and menu. Behind a stark concrete frontage, the room is light, bright and airy, with noisy wooden floors, the simplest of tables and chairs, a zinc bar and very little in the way of decor. The chef has a fairly easy time, one supposes, with a menu of four starters, a pasta and four mains, one cheese and five desserts. The style is new Med with a nod to California: lots of salads, beans, olive oil, healthy vegetables and no sauces. Lunch is of two or three courses with a choice of perhaps a soup, a salad and a lentil-based dish followed by salmon or chicken (both chargrilled) then a couple of desserts (cinnamon ice cream with cookies is a favourite). There's plenty of variety on the plate, though portions are not vast: a salad of seared fresh tuna includes little gems, green beans, new potatoes, black olives and plum tomatoes, while roasted guinea fowl comes with mash, sweet garlic, carrots and savoy cabbage. *Seats 62. L 12.30-2.30 (Wed-Sun) D 6.30-10.30 (Tue-Sun). Closed L Tue, all Mon, Bank Holidays, 10 days Christmas, 5 days Easter, 2 weeks August. Set L £11.50/£13.50. Access, Visa.*

NW1   Great Nepalese   £30
Tel 071-388 6737   **R**

48 Eversholt Street NW1 1DA   **Map 18 D1**

Pork and duck are added to a large variety of more familiar Indian dishes in a durable restaurant near Euston station. Specialities include *masco-bara* (black lentil pancakes with a curry sauce or with meat), *haku choyala* (barbecued diced mutton with hot spices, garlic and ginger), *mamocha* (steamed meat or vegetarian pastries) and Nepalese mixed grill of chicken, mutton and prawns. *Seats 48. Parties 30. L 12-2.45 D 6-11.30. Closed 25 & 26 Dec. Set L (business) £5.50 Set D £10.50.* AMERICAN EXPRESS ® *Access, Diners, Visa.*

Note that all telephone numbers with area codes starting with 0 will start 01 from 16 April 1995.

N1   Great Northern Hotel   60%   £78
Tel 071-837 5454   Fax 071-278 5270   **H**

King's Cross N1 9AN   **Map 16 C3**

The Great Northern, opened in 1854 as London's first purpose-built hotel, is a convenient pausing point for travellers and meeting point for businessmen; it's right next to St Pancras British Rail station, one minute from King's Cross and five from Euston. Accommodation is comfortable rather than stylish and includes family rooms, all but a few with en-suite facilities; under-14s share parents' room free. Function facilities for 100 in 11 meeting rooms. Private parking limited to 12 spaces. No dogs. *Rooms 89. Closed 25 & 26 Dec.* AMERICAN EXPRESS ® *Access, Diners, Visa.*

NW8   Greek Valley   £40
Tel 071-624 3217   **R**

130 Boundary Road NW8 0RH   **Map 16 B3**

Effie Bosnic creates something of a party atmosphere in her popular Greek restaurant, while husband Peter satisfies the inner man with some very good cooking. Familiar dishes like taramasalata, kleftiko and moussaka share the menu with some less universal choices such as grilled mushrooms, stuffed cabbage (seasonal and delicious) or prawns baked in tomato sauce with feta cheese. Home-made sausages are particularly good, and special traditional dishes are served at Easter (Greek Easter is not necessarily at the same time as British). Note that Greek Valley is open only in the evening; the lunchtime business is handled by their Café along the road. *Seats 62. Private Room 30. D 6-midnight. Set D £7.95. Access, Visa.*

NW3   Green Cottage   £40
Tel 071-722 5305   **R**

9 New College Parade Finchley Road NW3 5EP   **Map 16 B2**

A Cantonese restaurant that is seemingly the most popular Chinese restaurant of the half dozen in the area. Old favourites like roasted duck and pork, barbecued spare ribs, steamed fish and stir-fried everything are all on offer, while the adventurous should try soyed mixed meats (liver, gizzard, squid and duck wings). Unusual vegetarian Zhai duckling is formed from layers of deep-fried soy bean sheets. *Seats 100. Meals 12-11.30. Closed 25-26 Dec. Set D from £11.50 (min 2).* AMERICAN EXPRESS ® *Access, Visa.*

W1   **Green Park Hotel**   **70%**   **£143**

Tel 071-629 7522   Fax 071-491 8971   **H**

Half Moon Street Mayfair W1Y 8BP   Map 18 C3

A terrace of Georgian town houses has been converted into a comfortable
hotel (in the Sarova Group), whose location just off Piccadilly and opposite
Green Park is a major asset. There are several meeting rooms,
a conservatory and a cocktail bar (the Half Moon) with intimate alcoves.
Grey-wood fitted units furnish the bedrooms, their marble-floored
bathrooms traditionally resplendent with white suites, some including
bidets and spa baths. Children up to 12 stay free in parents' room. No dogs.
Rooms 161. AMERICAN EXPRESS *Access, Diners, Visa.*

SW11   **The Green Room**   **£50**

Tel 071-223 4618   **R**

62 Lavender Hill SW11 5RQ   Map 17 C5

At the Queenstown Road end of Lavender Hill, an organically and
ecologically sound restaurant that's comfortable and unpretentious. The
menu reflects the influences of many cuisines, with Chinese something
of a speciality. Vegetarians are particularly well catered for, with a dozen
starters and nearly as many main courses: cream of asparagus soup, endive
salad, Parmesan garlic toast, baked stuffed peppers, Cantonese stir-fried
vegetables, fried rice with diced peppers, carrots, spring onion and optional
egg. Non-vegetarian choices run from garlic snails and West Indian spicy
fish cake to sesame salmon, aubergine chicken and peppered steak. Also
main-course pasta and salads, with sorbets, pancakes and vegan fruit slice
to finish. *Seats 40. D only 7-11.30.* AMERICAN EXPRESS *Access, Diners, Visa.*

SW1   **Green's Restaurant & Oyster Bar**   **£75**

Tel 071-930 4566   Fax 071-930 1383   **R**

36 Duke Street St James's SW1Y 6DF   Map 18 D3

Reassuringly, Green's goes on and on and happily the standards are
maintained. Booking is advisable to get a table in one of the small dining
rooms but there are also seats around the bar. The best of British produce
is used to good effect, especially the seafood such as scallop and monkfish
risotto; langoustine, prawn and asparagus salad, native oysters (of course),
grilled sea bass with braised fennel and tarragon butter. Meat-eaters are also
well catered for, and pudding enthusiasts will love Scottish clootie
dumpling served with whisky cream, or a lighter port and claret jelly with
red grapes and vanilla cream. Cheeses from Paxton and Whitfield.
*Seats 75. Parties 24. Private Room 26. L 11.30-3 (Sun 12-2.30) D 5.30-11.
Closed D Sun, 25 & 26 Dec. Set Sun L £16.* *Access,
Diners, Visa.*

W1   **Greenhouse**   ↑   **£80**

Tel 071-499 3331   **R**

27a Hays Mews Mayfair W1X 7RJ   Map 18 C3

The Mayfair branch of David Levin's empire (including *L'Hotel* and
Capital Hotel) has a comfortable niche, knows its customer base and has,
in Gary ("just look at that!") Rhodes, the ideal chef to serve it. His cooking
is robust and straightforward, taking the best of traditional British fare and
revamping it for the self-aware '90s. So you can eat grilled calf's liver with
crispy bacon, creamed potatoes and onion gravy followed by steamed
rhubarb sponge with lemon curd ice-cream and be ready for another meal
after the normal digestive gap. More international in origin are dishes like
griddled scallop and crispy aubergine salad, grilled herring fillets
on noodles with a saffron, tomato and caper sauce, and crème brulée; then
it's back to Blighty for smoked eel on toast with a warm poached egg and
horseradish dressing, braised oxtails, and bread-and-butter pudding.

See over

Whatever you choose you can be sure of Gary's inimitable style, served
up with plenty of motherly advice from the friendly staff. There's a concise
list of about 20 wines. Sunday lunch (£18.50 for 3 courses) is a high spot –
note the slight change in times this year. Booking essential. *Seats 90.
Parties 14. L 12-2.30 (Sun 12.30 to 3) D 7-11 (Sun 6.30-10). Closed L Sat,
all Bank Holidays. Set Sun L £18.50.* AMERICAN EXPRESS *Access, Diners, Visa.*

W1 Greig's Grill – see under alistair Greig's Grill page 110.

SW1	The Grenadier	£65

Tel 071-235 3074	R
18 Wilton Row Belgravia SW1 7NR	Map 19 C4

Secreted down a quiet mews near Belgrave Square, a small, but striking
and very typical London pub whose dark, candle-lit restaurant offers good
traditional English fare; eggs Benedict, smoked haddock, smoked salmon,
beef Wellington (a speciality) and lamb noisettes with garlic and sage crust
show the style. *Seats 28. Parties 8. L 12-2.30 D 6-10 (Sun from 7). Closed
D 24 & 31 Dec, all 25 & 26 Dec & 1 Jan.* AMERICAN EXPRESS *Access, Visa.*

SW3	Grill St Quentin	£55

Tel 071-581 8377 Fax 071-584 6064	R
2 Yeoman's Row Knightsbridge SW3 2AL	Map 19 B4

Steps lead from a neon-lit entrance just off Brompton Road to a cool,
stylish basement restaurant with the look and feel of a Parisian brasserie.
French staff of youth and charm provide semi-formal service, and the
whole place invites relaxation over a leisurely meal. Charcoal-grilled steaks,
cutlets and fish served with splendid little chips are the mainstay of the
menu, supported by *plats cuisinés* such as *brandade de morue*, devilled poussin
and sausages with lentils. Also plenty of salads, moules marinière, fish soup,
langoustines, oysters and excellent patisserie from Spécialités St Quentin.
*Seats 140. Parties 25. L 12-3 D 6.30-11.30 (Sun to 10.30).
Set L £8/£11.90.* AMERICAN EXPRESS *Access, Diners, Visa.*

W1	Grosvenor House	83%	£256

Tel 071-499 6363 Fax 071-493 3341	H
90 Park Lane W1A 3AA	Map 18 C3

Overlooking Hyde Park and busy Park Lane, though a haven of peace and
gentility within, Grosvenor House was built on the original site of the Earl
of Grosvenor's 18th-century home. The facade, designed by Sir Edward
Lutyens, has been a famous London landmark since its completion in 1929.
More recently, Forte completed a major modernisation programme,
bringing the building bang up-to-date as their flagship, with superb
overnight accommodation for guests attending some of London's most
popular function rooms. The splendid, unpillared Great Room banqueting
hall (originally an ice rink in the days of society galas) has a capacity
of 1500 and is where the annual Antiques Fair is held each June; the
Ballroom features a sprung dance floor and art deco designs, and can hold
over 500; various smaller private dining and conference suites (from 4-
100+) at 86 Park Lane mean that the hotel is always busy with functions
of every kind. The lavish interior includes a vast lounge and a contrastingly
intimate Japanese-themed bar; there are three restaurants, of which only
Chez Nico at 90 Park Lane – arguably London's finest top-flight restaurant
– is recommended. A wood-panelled Library is an ideal spot to while away
an hour or two. All of the bedrooms are large, light and airy with
a separate lobby and air-conditioning; even 'single' rooms have double
beds. Solid furniture and soft colours please the eye and the bathrooms are
splendid, with marble floors and excellent toiletries; many enjoy natural
light. The fifth floor is the Crown Club, with separate express check-in and
a small lounge and boardroom for Executive guests only; rates include
breakfast, mini-bar, room service dinner and valet pressing. Sovereign

Suites are top of the range with private bars, hi-fi, video and compact disc libraries, private telephone and fax lines, and limousine service to and from the airport. 140 luxury service apartments, with a separate entrance, also offer spacious accommodation and use of the extensive facilities in the Health Club, where a 65ft swimming pool takes centre stage. Round-the-clock room service. Private, charged garaging nearby, with valet parking. No dogs. Forte Exclusive. *Rooms 454. Indoor swimming pool, gym, sauna, solarium, beauty & hair salon, valeting, coffee shop (7am-2am), shops (china, jewellers, perfumery).* AMERICAN EXPRESS *Access, Diners, Visa.*

SW1	**Grosvenor Thistle Hotel**	**64%**	**£138**
Tel 071-834 9494 Fax 071-630 1978			**H**
101 Buckingham Palace Road SW1W 0SJ			Map 19 D4

Built in the 1850s, the Grosvenor Thistle still boasts some handsome Victorian touches, notably in the splendid foyer with pillars and fine tile work. Bedrooms are spacious, with a sitting area and desk space, and bathrooms, too, are more than adequate in size. Useful location for tourists and business travellers: direct access from Victoria railway station. Banqueting/conference facilities for 120/200. Children up to 12 stay free in parents' room. 98 rooms reserved for non-smokers. 24hr lounge and room service. NCP car park nearby. No dogs. *Rooms 366. Coffee shop 6.30am-2am.* AMERICAN EXPRESS *Access, Diners, Visa.*

NW6	**Gung-Ho**		**£50**
Tel 071-794 1444			**R**
330-332 West End Lane Finchley NW6 1LN			Map 16 B2

Stylish Chinese restaurant located on the northern extremity of West End Lane. The decor is a fashionable mix of ochre red and dark blue with direct spotlights on the table centre to highlight the food. The menu offers the usual Szechuan dishes plus "special selections" such as spare ribs with star anise and rock sugar, sautéed calf's liver with onions and soya-mustard sauce, and steamed chicken with red dates, black fungi and golden lilies. Specialities include crispy Mongolian lamb with iceberg lettuce. *Seats 70. L 12-2.30 D 6.30-11.30. Closed 25 & 26 Dec. Set D from £17.20. Access, Visa.*

W11	**The Halcyon**	**79%**	**£235**
Tel 071-727 7288 Fax 071-229 8516			**HR**
81 Holland Park W11 3RZ			Map 17 B4

A splendid, large town house occupying a corner site on Holland Park Avenue. The hotel benefits from spacious and elegant, well-proportioned rooms that retain much of their original Victorian architectural character and include a welcoming reception area-cum-lounge furnished in a fashionable period style with additional homeliness and warmth promoted by an open fireplace and grandfather clock. The bar is below stairs and has an air of intimacy and a collection of outstanding fruit vodkas. Bedrooms are magnificent, including light, airy suites, one with its own tropical-style conservatory. Quality furniture and fabrics, together with fine antiques, feature throughout, with even the more modest single bedrooms possessing charm and character. Bathrooms, in marble, are kept in pristine order and feature spa baths and bidets as well as fine toiletries and ample thick towels. All the usual amenities such as satellite TV and full room service are offered and guests have temporary membership of the exclusive (and expensive) Vanderbilt tennis club nearby. Full 24hr room service, room safes, 1hr valet pressing service, plus a 24hr chauffeur limousine service. No dogs. *Rooms 43.* AMERICAN EXPRESS *Access, Diners, Visa.*

The Room at the Halcyon   ★   **£90**

With its own entrance on Holland Park Avenue, the restaurant is situated on the hotel's lower ground floor, and offers the opportunity in fine

 over

weather for alfresco dining at eight tables under smart canvas parasols
on a patio. The shades of cream and the studiedly arranged contemporary
artwork and mirrors on the walls provide an unpretentiously elegant
setting for chef Martin Hadden's talents. Experience with Nico Ladenis
at *Chez Nico* has resulted in exciting, mouthwatering dishes that are
essentially simple but carefully constructed with flavours achieving a very
desirable level of symmetry. Scallops, softly pan-fried in butter, retain their
fresh sweetness with marinated cucumber and a hint of wasabi (strong
green Japanese horseradish) providing a clever sharper contrast of taste and
texture, the latter also provided by a 'straw hat' of deep-fried, finely
shredded leek. Freshly salted cod is served with an onion cream purée and
a garlic, lentil and tarragon jus; a rich dish of squab pigeon comes with
duck confit and root vegetables, while wonderfully pink, succulent lamb
is roasted under a fragrant coating of herbed breadcrumbs.
Accompaniments are a garlic and rosemary olive oil, very creamy gratin
dauphinois, crunchy mangetout and carrots. Interesting vegetarian options.
There are superb desserts, too, like a banana pancake with butterscotch
sauce, caramelised lemon tart with raspberry sauce and a wonderful
miniature hot chocolate pudding with a crème anglaise delicately flavoured
with Grand Marnier. The captivating Jasmin Pellman oversees very good
standards of service. Two-course business lunch offers a small choice;
Sunday brunch menu includes traditional roast beef. Shortish wine list,
with quite a few bottles under £20. No smoking. The restaurant has
a separate telephone number: 071-221 5411. ***Seats** 50. Parties 20.
Set L £12.95 Set D £17. L 12-2.30 (Sun to 4pm) D 7-10.30 (Fri/Sat to 11,
Sun to 10). Closed L Sat, all Bank Holiday Mondays, 26 Dec.*

W2 **Halepi**	**£50**
Tel 071-262 1070 Fax 071-229 1343	**R**
18 Leinster Terrace Bayswater W2 3ET	Map 18 B3

Greek favourites, including dips, salads, charcoal grills, afelia and moussaka,
are served throughout the day in one of London's most cheerful and
bustling tavernas. More upmarket dishes, too, like milk-fed baby lamb
or sea bass. Meze at £16 a head is a popular choice that should satisfy the
hungriest customer. The owners plan to open a huge sister restaurant in St
Johns Wood by the summer of 1995. *Seats 68. Meals noon-1am.
Closed 25 & 26 Dec.* AMERICAN EXPRESS *Access, Diners, Visa.*

SW1 **The Halkin** **86%**	**£250**
Tel 071-333 1000 Fax 071-333 1100	**HR**
5 Halkin Street Belgravia SW1X 7DJ	Map 19 C4

Secreted away down a quiet street close to Hyde Park Corner, the Halkin
possesses all the style and elegance expected of a top-class up-to-date hotel.
The advanced Italian design that manifests itself throughout is a model
of cool sophistication. The bright, spacious lobby features highly polished
granite and marble floors with a few richly coloured leather armchairs
creating an informal lounge area to one side. A screen separates the rear
of this lounge from a small, intimate bar. Bedrooms are furnished to an
exactingly high standard, each with its own sitting area. Decor
is uncluttered and ultra-modern with mahogany, cherry or rosewood much
in evidence together with thick plate glass and gleaming mirrors.
Individual heating and air-conditioning controls as well as two line phones,
fax machines, wall-safes and mini-bars are standard. All lights are
on dimmer switches and the eleven suites have a VCR and CD player.
Comfortable beds, either king-or queen-size, are fitted with Egyptian
cotton sheets and goosedown pillows and complement the really splendid
all-marble bathrooms, all except eight of which have separate walk-in
showers; costly toiletries, slippers and ample thick towels are some of the
cosseting touches provided. For the inveterate businessman there's an FT
room on the second floor and it is appropriately equipped with a pink
phone and numerous current financial journals. Staff are superb –
professional, discreet and unfailingly helpful, everything you would wish
from a hotel of this class, the worthy recipient of our 1995 Hotel of the
Year award. ***Rooms** 41.* AMERICAN EXPRESS *Access, Diners, Visa.*

Restaurant ★ £100

A strikingly modern restaurant with arched windows overlooking
a floodlit garden. The arches are mirrored on the opposite wall by semi-
circular paintings in a 17th-century style of well-known Italian wine
producing estates. Decor is simple and classical with a highly polished
granite and marble floor, pink marble dado and tables with crisp white
linen and gleaming silverware. At night white candles flicker in double
glass candlesticks adding, together with fresh flowers, a soft romantic touch.
Stefano Cavallini's menu retains some of the influences of Gualtiero
Marchesi. His style is very modish though Marchesi's flamboyance and
some of his extravagance have been suitably toned down. The menu
structure is typically Italian – four courses, here preceded
by a complimentary appetiser of, say, an oyster sitting atop a twist
of spaghetti dressed with a fine dice of peppers. Starters could include
marinated eel stuffed with trout; foie gras terrine with shiitake mushrooms
on a rocket and spinach salad with paper-thin slices of raw beef, asparagus
and truffle. Pasta dishes to follow could be noodles with rabbit and wild
mushrooms, courgette and scallop risotto or a delicious and unusual version
of a Romagnan classic – passatelli, here made with fish and simmered
in a delicate champagne flavoured stock with spinach-wrapped oysters. Fish
and meat dishes offer equally exciting eating, for instance, monkfish stuffed
with mushrooms and walnuts; sea bass in a bread and salt crust; noisettes
of venison with blueberries, polenta and broccoli or veal medallions topped
with Parma ham and Parmesan slices. To round off, a hot poppy seed
soufflé with kirsch cream, iced chocolate truffle and mango tart with
coconut ice cream could precede superb coffee and delicious petits fours.
Service is very civilised, charming, efficient and informed. *Seats 45.*
Private Room 26. L 12.30-2.30 D 7.30-10.30 (Sun 7-10).
Closed L Sat & Sun. Set L £19.50/£26.

WC2   Hampshire Hotel   78% £247
Tel 071-839 9399   Fax 071-930 8122 **HR**
31 Leicester Square WC2 7LH Map 21 A3

A Radisson Edwardian hotel in the very heart of London, with instant
access to theatres, shops and major tourist sights. Low-ceilinged public
rooms have an elaborate decor with a strong Oriental theme through hand-
woven Thai carpets and Chinese furnishings. Although not to scale with
the 124 bedrooms, the small lounge with cosy sofas and fireplace, the
wood-panelled bar and elegant restaurant have the comforting feel
of a private club. A new Hampshire Terrace (50 covers) and a coffee bar
were under construction as we went to press. Bedrooms vary in size, the
most agreeable ones being the suites with large tinted picture windows
overlooking Leicester Square. Decor is rather busy with chintzy flowery
fabrics done in shades of pink or blue. Bathrooms, all in Italian marble and
mahogany finish, are well appointed. The Penthouse suite, which can
accommodate up to 80, has a beautiful view over Trafalgar Square and
Westminster. ***Rooms*** *124.* AMERICAN EXPRESS *Access, Diners, Visa.*

Restaurant £75

Intimate dining room with comfortable seating and an elaborate elegant
decor. Cooking is of English and international influence: grilled meats,
lamb with okra and basmati almond rice, casserole of duck with garbanzos,
chorizo and Mahon cheese. Vegetarian main courses available. Less formal
eating in Oscar's Wine bar. *Seats 55. Parties 50. L 12-3 D 6-10.45.*
Set L £15/£19.50 Set D £27.50.

W1   Harbour City   £40

Tel 071-439 7859   **R**

46 Gerrard Street Soho W1   **Map 21 A2**

From the profusion of Chinese restaurants on Gerrard Street here is one
that stands out. Set on three floors, the restaurant is extremely busy with
an almost exclusively Chinese clientele. Unlike most of its competitors
in the street, staff take good care of their customers, advising on the menu
or recommending dishes. Dim sum (served until 5pm) are selected from
an extensive menu (of nearly 90 items) rather than from a trolley and are
among the best in London, most being prepared to order. The choice
includes all the familiar varieties plus many more 'exotic', such as scallop
dumplings, minced prawn with mango in flaky batter, baked miniature
roast pork pie and spicy soya bean monk's style. The choice is also
extensive elsewhere on the list, which encompasses sections for sizzling hot-
platter dishes, Cantonese hot pots and a dozen chef's specials: baked chicken
in spicy salt garnished with shredded ginger and spring onion, stir-fried
fillet of Dover sole with fresh asparagus in wine sauce set on a deep-fried
crispy fish-bone in batter. *Seats 160. Private Room 60. Meals noon-11.15.
Closed 24 & 25 Dec. Set meals from £10.50.* AMERICAN EXPRESS *Access,
Diners, Visa.*

W1   Hardy's   £50

Tel 071-935 5929   **R**

53 Dorset Street off Baker Street W1   **Map 18 C2**

Lively bistro with tables on the pavement in fine weather. The short,
straightforward menu changes every couple of months or so and
is augmented by daily blackboard specials. Typical dishes might include
gravad lax, steamed mussels, canneloni with spinach and ricotta and
a tomato and chili sauce, liver and bacon with mash, steak and frites,
burger and chips, and lemon sole. *Seats 80. Parties 20. L 12.30-3
D 5.30-10.30. Closed Sat, Sun & Bank Holidays.* AMERICAN EXPRESS *Access, Visa.*

SW7   Harrington Hall   72%   £120

Tel 071-396 9696   Fax 071-396 9090   **H**

5-25 Harrington Gardens South Kensington SW7 4JW   **Map 19 A5**

Now two years old, the impressive, refurbished building on Harrington
Gardens is privately owned. The open-plan public rooms are airy and
comfortable. Meals and afternoon teas are served to the sound
of a mechanical baby grand piano. Large bedrooms offer extensive
amenities: discreet door bells, spy-eyes, message telephone as well as the
usual mini-bar, trouser press and tea/coffee facilities. Bathrooms are more
basic. There is a small fitness centre and sauna. Stylish conference facilities
(for up to 300) and a business centre. *Rooms 200. Gym, sauna.*
AMERICAN EXPRESS *Access, Diners, Visa.*

SW10   Harveys Café   £50

Tel 071-352 0625   **R**

The Black Bull 358 Fulham Road SW10 9UU   **Map 19 A6**

A bright restaurant above the the *Black Bull* pub with huge modern
paintings on the walls and simple decor in Mediterranean blue and pine.
A blue chair (one is suspended outside) is the logo. Owner/chef Harvey
Sambrook prepares a regularly changing menu of modern dishes with
Mediterranean and Californian influences: a good fish soup with all the
usual trimmings plus garlic cloves for rubbing the croutes, roast peppers
with feta cheese, spiced chicken raita. Recent experience suggests that the
cassoulet is not the best dish. *Seats 60. Parties 35. L 12-3 D 7.30-11.
Closed D Sun, all Mon, Set L £5 Tue-Fri. No credit cards.*

NW7   Hee's   £50
Tel 081-959 7109   **R**
27 The Broadway Mill Hill NW7 3DA   Map 16 A1

Enormous Chinese characters are simple but effective wall decorations in a popular restaurant serving well-prepared dishes originating in Peking and Szechuan. The selection is a conservative one with no strong leanings. Starters such as bang bang chicken are big on flavour as are steamed scallops with garlic and spring onion. Main dishes include good deep-fried shredded beef with chili, though there is little fieriness to it and king prawns, quite carefully deveined, come sizzling in a black bean sauce or with sweet and sour sacue. Red bean paste pancakes make a fitting end to an enjoyable meal served by pleasant, courteous staff. *Seats 100. Parties 20. Private Room 40. L 12-2 D 6.15-11.15. Closed 25 & 26 Dec.* AMERICAN EXPRESS *Access, Diners, Visa.*

NW1   Hellas   £30
Tel 071-267 8110   **R**
158 Royal College Street Camden NW1 0TA   Map 16 C3

Good Greek food at very reasonable prices, with a larger-than-usual menu. Chef's specialities include kioftedes (minced lamb grilled or skewered) and chicken grill. *Seats 60. L 12-3 D 6-12. Closed L Sat, all Sun, Bank Holidays.* AMERICAN EXPRESS *Access, Diners, Visa.*

NW4   Hendon Hall   63%   £90
Tel 081-203 3341   Fax 081-203 9709   **H**
Ashley Lane NW4 1HE   Map 16 B1

Once the home of actor/manager David Garrick, this Georgian building with a handsome portico is now a comfortably modernised hotel catering for private guests, banquets and conferences up to 350. The Pavilion Bar is open from 11am to 10pm. Children up to 15 stay free in parents' room. Near A1 and M1, but the setting is peaceful. No dogs. Mount Charlotte Thistle. *Rooms 52. Garden.* AMERICAN EXPRESS *Access, Diners, Visa.*

If we recommend meals in a hotel or inn a separate entry is made for its restaurant.

SW7   Hilaire   ★↑   £85
Tel 071-584 8993   **R**
68 Old Brompton Road South Kensington SW7 3LQ   Map 19 B5

After five years, Bryan Webb is now firmly established in his stylish South Kensington restaurant and the time has come around for him to use the restaurant trade's traditional August closure for some major refurbishment. By the time he re-opens (and this Guide is published) he hopes to have added some extra covers on the ground floor, upgraded the air-conditioning and heating systems, redecorated and replaced carpets and curtains, and redesigned the downstairs bar area. Whatever the end product, it's sure to be a fitting backdrop for Bryan's highly personal, confident cooking. He uses the best possible British produce, his menus changing daily to reflect seasonal availability. Typical spring dishes might be asparagus and tarragon soup, griddled scallops with vegetable relish and rocket, navarin of new season lamb, and orange caramel cream with blood orange sorbet. Prefaced by an inexpensive house selection, the wine list is presented by style of wine, with choices from all around the world; there are a few tasting notes, plus lots of half bottles. *Seats 50. Parties 30. Private Room 30. L 12.30-2.30 D 7-11.30. Closed L Sat, all Sun, Bank Holidays. Set L £12.50 Set D £16/£25.50.* AMERICAN EXPRESS *Access, Diners, Visa.*

W11   Hilton International Kensington   67%   £180

Tel 071-603 3355 Fax 071-602 9397   **HR**
179 Holland Park Avenue W11 4UL   Map 17 B4

Large, busy, modern hotel next to Shepherds Bush roundabout. The
Executive Floor has superior bedrooms and business facilities. 30 rooms
reserved for non-smokers (on 5th and 6th floors). The coffee shop is open
24 hours every day of the week. Breakfast is served from the amazingly
early hour of 5.45am. Banqueting and conference amenities for up to 300.
Children up to 12 free in parents' room. *Rooms 603. Hair & beauty salon,
car hire desk, news kiosk.* AMERICAN EXPRESS *Access, Diners, Visa.*

Hiroko Restaurant   £80

High standards of cooking and service in a Japanese restaurant reached
either from the street or through the hotel. The menu spans a wide range,
including the familiar teriyaki, sushi, sukiyaki, yakitori and tempura. Part
of the Ninjin group of Japanese restaurants and shop. *Seats 72. Parties 30.
L 12-2.30 D 6-10.30. Closed Mon. Set L £15/£18 Set D £30/£32.*

NW8   Hilton International Regent's Park   73%   £149

Tel 071-722 7722   Fax 071-483 2408   **HR**
18 Lodge Road St John's Wood NW8 7JT   Map 18 B1

Close to London Zoo and Lord's cricket ground, this Hilton International
numbers free parking (for 70) and 24hr room service (offering Japanese
and Arabic specialities) among its facilities. There are three restaurants (one
Japanese, one modelled on a New York deli, and the Pavilion bar and
grill), a lounge bar, a well-equipped business centre and several conference
suites, named after cricketers or their paraphernalia and catering for up to
150 delegates. Bedrooms, some with balconies, include Executive rooms
and three-bedded rooms for family occupation. High-pressure showers are
a good feature. There's even Japanese satellite TV. No dogs. *Rooms 377.
Hair salon, coffee shop (7am-2am).* AMERICAN EXPRESS *Access, Diners, Visa.*

Kashinoki Restaurant   £70

Sister restaurant to *Hiroko* (at the *Hilton International Kensington*), offering
classic Japanese food, from a long sushi list (turbot, octopus, ark shell,
yellow tail, flying fish roe...) to yakitori and tempura. Unusual red bean
or green tea ice creams. Choice of à la carte and interesting set menus.
*Seats 42. Parties 10. L 11-2.15 D 5.30-10. Closed Mon, 25 & 26 Dec, 1-3
Jan. Set L from £11 Set D from £30.*

N1   Hodja Nasreddin   £25

Tel 071-226 7757   **R**
53 Newington Green Road N1   Map 16D2

Turkish eating in friendly, homely surroundings. Highlights include
houmus, mixed meze (5 dishes, minimum 2 people), spicy sausages and
succulent kebabs. House specialities are *sote* (lamb in small pieces with
herbs, mushrooms, tomatoes and onions) and Hodja's Special of shish kebab,
shish kofte, doner, izgara kofte, lamb kidney, lamb chops with yoghurt,
tarama, rice and salad. *Seats 48. Parties 20. Private Room 35. Meals
noon-3am. Closed 25 Dec. Access, Visa.*

SW5   Hogarth Hotel   62%   £90

Tel 071-370 6831   Fax 071-373 6179   **H**
Hogarth Road Earls Court SW5 0QQ   Map 19 A5

Modern hotel located in the quiet part of Hogarth Road (off Earls Court
Road) and convenient for Earls Court exhibitions. Bedrooms have
an attractive emerald green decor. Amenities include satellite TV, trouser
press, hairdryer, tea and coffee facilities and a small safe; 18 rooms are

reserved for non-smokers. Bathrooms were due to be refurbished at the end of last year. Children under 12 stay free in their parents' room. Secure underground parking (£10 per night). Limited 24hr room service is available. Marston Hotels. ***Rooms 86.*** AMERICAN EXPRESS *Access, Diners, Visa.*

NW2   Holiday Inn Garden Court   NEW   60%   £82

Tel 081-455 4777   Fax 081-455 4660   **H**

Tilling Road Brent Cross NW2 3DS   **Map 16 A2**

A tall, modern purpose-built hotel just off the roundabout at the foot of the M1. Bedrooms are bright and smart but no room service is offered and breakfast is from a hot and cold buffet. ***Rooms 153.*** AMERICAN EXPRESS *Access, Diners, Visa.*

W1   Holiday Inn Garden Court   NEW   56%   £148

Tel 071-935 4442   Fax 071-487 3782   **H**

57 Welbeck Street W1M 8HJ   **Map 18 C2**

A modernised hotel in a quiet location, just north of the Oxford Street big stores. There is no room service and breakfast is from a hot and cold buffet. Formerly *The Londoner*. ***Rooms 138.*** AMERICAN EXPRESS *Access, Diners, Visa.*

SW7   Holiday Inn Kensington   68%   £160

Tel 071-373 2222   Fax 071-373 0559   **H**

100 Cromwell Road SW7 4ER   **Map 19 B5**

Right on Cromwell Road, opposite Gloucester Road underground station, a stylishly modern hotel behind an Edwardian facade with double or triple glazing for all bedrooms. There's one floor each of Executive and non-smoking rooms, plus 19 Duplex suites; some rooms are adapted for disabled guests. Meeting facilities for up to 125. A £25 supplement gets you membership of the Executive Club and a range of extras, from bathrobe and slippers to superior tea, coffee and cookies. ***Rooms 162.*** *Garden, keep-fit equipment, sauna, spa bath, steam room, lounge bar (9am-1am).* AMERICAN EXPRESS *Access, Diners, Visa.*

WC1   Holiday Inn Kings Cross/Bloomsbury   69%   £145

Tel 071-833 3900   Fax 071-917 6163   **H**

1 Kings Cross Road WC1X 9HX   **Map 16 C3**

Usefully located just a few minutes from Kings Cross, St Pancras and Euston stations. A large floral display takes pride of place in the cool, marble-floored lobby and the lounge, decorated in autumnal shades, is roomy and restful. Bedrooms have all the Holiday Inn hallmarks: large beds (even single rooms get double beds), open clothes-hanging space and powerful showers over short tubs in the bathrooms. Extensive room service (24hr) can run to a choice of hot dishes around the clock. Conference-room facilities for up to 220. Children under 19 stay free in parents' room. The whole hotel is air-conditioned. Good leisure facilities. Very limited parking. ***Rooms 405.*** *Indoor swimming pool, gym, squash, sauna, spa bath, steam room, solarium, beauty & hair salon.* AMERICAN EXPRESS *Access, Diners, Visa.*

W1   Holiday Inn Mayfair   72%   £152

Tel 071-493 8282   Fax 071-629 2827   **H**

3 Berkeley Street W1X 6NE   **Map 18 D3**

A splendid central location just a few steps from Bond Street, Green Park and the Royal Academy. The bar, lounge and restaurant merge one into the other and gain an elegant air from the moulded ceiling and glittering chandeliers. Good-size bedrooms (24hr room service) offer luxuriously large beds and all the expected accessories including air-conditioning and mini-bars. Executive rooms are even more generously proportioned and have fax machines, spa baths and bathrobes. Children up to 19 stay free in parents' room. Conference/banqueting for 70/50. No dogs. *Rooms 185. Coffee lounge (11am-11pm).* AMERICAN EXPRESS *Access, Diners, Visa.*

WC2   Hong Kong   £40
Tel 071-287 0324   **R**
6 Lisle Street Leicester Square WC2   **Map 21 A2**

A cavernous setting serving a daytime selection of dim sum popular with snackers and a Cantonese menu of proverbial favourites like sculptured squid and prawn balls, fried noodles with roast pork, sizzling platters and hotpots (including exceptional braised lamb with dried bean curd). The more adventurous might choose crispy pig's intestines, fried fillet of eel, fried oyster with scrambled egg or even stir-fried carp with superior soup. Finish with a fruit fritter or tapioca cream. *Seats 180. Parties 14. Meals 12-11.30. Closed 25 & 26 Dec. Set L from £10 Set D from £11.* AMERICAN EXPRESS *Access, Visa.*

EC1   The Hope & Sir Loin   £40
Tel 071-253 8525   **R**
94 Cowcross Street Smithfield EC1M 6BH   **Map 16 D3**

Vast breakfasts start the day in the dining room above a traditional Smithfield pub, the largest involving egg, bacon, sausage, black pudding, kidneys, liver, baked beans, tomatoes, mushrooms and toast. Grills and roasts are the lunchtime specialities, plus the likes of deep-fried scampi, veal in cream and mushrooms and steak & kidney pie. *Seats 32. Parties 16. Private Room 20. Meals 7.15am-9.30am & noon-2pm. Closed Sat, Sun, Bank Holidays, 25 Dec-5 Jan.* AMERICAN EXPRESS *Access, Visa.*

W2   Hospitality Inn Bayswater   60%   £103
Tel 071-262 4461   Fax 071-706 4560   **H**
104 Bayswater Road W2 3HL   **Map 18 A3**

Practical and modern, with plenty of free parking in their own underground car park. Immediately opposite Hyde Park (Kensington Gardens) and a short walk from Notting Hill Gate. Children up to 13 stay free in parents' room. *Rooms 175.* AMERICAN EXPRESS *Access, Diners, Visa.*

W1   Hospitality Inn Piccadilly   64%   £143
Tel 071-930 4033   Fax 071-925 2586   **H**
39 Coventry Street W1V 8EL   **Map 21 A3**

A grand Victorian facade, concealing a high level of peace and comfort, given the very central location. Corner rooms look out towards Leicester Square. *Rooms 92.* AMERICAN EXPRESS *Access, Diners, Visa.*

EC3   The Hospitality Suite   NEW   £75
Tel 071-617 5000 ext 5043   **R**
London Underwriting Centre Building 3 Minster Court Mincing Lane EC3R 7DD   **Map 20 D2**

Advance booking is a prerequisite at this smart new colony in the Roux empire – security measures at the impressive Minster Court complex demand an irritating check-in at the reception desk. This is all worthwhile, however, as you will be lunching in a room with one of the best views in London. The Tower of London and its bridge, together with a sizeable stretch of the river, can all be surveyed at leisure through the vast picture windows by almost boardroom-sized tables. The short table d'hote menu changes daily, and, as is the rule with Roux operations, is classically French. Start with celeriac soup flavoured with white truffle oil, a light *salade niçoise* or perhaps perfectly cooked lamb's kidneys with a mustard sauce on a bed of fresh noodles. Grilled lamb with bubble and squeak, fillet of beef with horseradish crust or roast guinea fowl with fresh tarragon sauce might follow. All the dishes are beautifully presented, and cooked with great care. Equal attention is given to the desserts: fresh strawberry tart or maybe honey ice cream (built into a millefeuille with brandy snaps). Cheeses may not maintain the high standard – perhaps too many are on offer for the size of the operation? Service is professional and formal. The short wine list is restrained in its mark-ups for a restaurant of this standard: Georges Duboeuf house wine is £8.60, for example. *Seats 30. L only 12-2.30. Closed Sat, Sun, Bank Holidays, 1 week Christmas. Set L £29.50.* AMERICAN EXPRESS *Access, Diners, Visa.*

SW3   L'Hotel   £125

Tel 071-589 6286   Fax 071-225 0011   **HR**

28 Basil Street Knightsbridge SW3 1AT   Map 19 C4

Just yards from Harrods, accommodation at this *pension* (under the same ownership as *The Capital* hotel next door) comprises 11 individually designed twin-bedded rooms and one suite decorated in French country style. Continental breakfast is served in *Le Metro*. No dogs. *Rooms 12.* AMERICAN EXPRESS *Access, Diners, Visa.*

Le Metro   £40

An ultra modern basement wine bar/brasserie beneath the hotel, where Philip Britten's team produces a lively menu at reasonable prices. Both a light terrine of sole, leeks and mint, and a salad of roasted red peppers with limes, rocket and ricotta were enjoyed recently – these two starters, accompanied by the delicious home-made bread on offer, would happily suffice as a light lunch. Main courses might include calf's liver with bacon and tomatoes, grilled red mullet with olives and rosemary or a fine duck confit with a claret sauce and baby turnips. For dessert, perhaps a fresh and light raspberry yoghurt mousse. Breakfast (both Continental and English) and afternoon teas are also available. Booking advisable. A Cruover machine allows fine wines to be served by the glass; bottles are also fairly priced. *Seats 49. Parties 12. Meals Noon-10.30. Closed Sun, 25 & 26 Dec.*

E1   The Hothouse   NEW   £50

Tel 071-488 4797   Fax 071-488 9500   **R**

78 Wapping Lane E1 9NF   Map 17 D4

Heavy wooden beams and bare brick walls with American Indian decorations are features of this 200-year-old former spice warehouse constructed on two floors. On the ground floor there's a short modern menu ranging from pea and bean soup to parfait of chicken livers and foie gras and tender pan-fried scallops served with a chilled leek mousse. To follow, salt cod fish cakes, roast smoked haddock or a well-cooked breast and leg of pot-roasted guinea fowl with button mushrooms, onions and bacon. Vegetables are priced separately. Sweets include passion fruit tart, pot au chocolat and a passable tarte tatin. There's live jazz on Wednesday and Friday evenings. *Seats 78. Parties 18. Private Room 45. L 12-4 D 6-11 (Sun to 10). Closed some Bank Holidays.* AMERICAN EXPRESS *Access, Visa.*

WC2   The Howard   81%   £254

Tel 071-836 3555   Fax 071-379 4547   **HR**

Temple Place Strand WC2R 2PR   Map 20 A2

Handily sited off the Strand, "where the City of London meets the West End", the Howard is a hotel in the grand tradition. Reception staff and porterage are first-rate, well able to handle the demands of visitors from all over the world. Public areas are dominated by the fine decorations, Adam-style friezes, chandeliers and Italian marble pillars of the foyer-lounge, which typifies the ornate tone throughout. The Temple Bar has views over the tiered garden and leads through into the Quai d'Or restaurant; both are pretty in pink with ruched window drapes, plush green chairs and intricate ceilings. Bedrooms are mainly twin-bedded and classically furnished with

French marquetry pieces and have modern comforts such as air-conditioning, individual heating control and multiple phones, plus superb marbled bathrooms. Best rooms have small terraces with panoramic views over the river Thames – from St Paul's to Westminster. 24hr 'à la carte' room service is offered, and a special Japanese breakfast (among others) with Japanese omelette, seaweed, soya bean soup, pickles, rice and Japanese tea is served either in the restaurant or in your room. Function rooms cater for up to 120. No dogs. *Rooms 137. 24hr lobby service, valeting.* AMERICAN EXPRESS *Access, Diners, Visa.*

Le Quai d'Or   £100

The domed ceiling and renaissance decor make a splendid setting for French cuisine in the classic mould. Feuilleté of seafood Nantua, haddock mousse with a quail's egg or duck terrine with goose foie gras could precede a plain roast, a grill or something a little more elaborate like fillets of sole 'Ile de France' (cooked in Pernod with mushroom and cream, lobster and lobster sauce) or lamb's kidneys with a Roquefort sauce. At lunchtime a silver trolley carries the dish of the day – rib of beef on Wednesday, stuffed salmon on Friday, coq au vin on Saturday. Classic desserts and savouries. *Seats 95. Parties 25. L 12.30-3 D 6.30-11 (Sun till 10.30). Set L £25.*

W2	Hsing	£50
Tel 071-402 0904		**R**
451 Edgware Road W2 1TH		Map 18 B1

Metal, wood, water, fire and earth: Hsing represents the five elements on which the restaurant decor and philosophy are based. The interesting menu puts an emphasis on fish: special crispy fish with vegetables or sweet and sour sauce or Hsing special feast of braised shark fin or abalone. Meat dishes include a delicious, crispy, fragrant and aromatic lamb and vegetarians are not forgotten. *Seats 60. Parties 12. L 12-3 D 6-11.30. Closed Sun, 3 days Christmas.* AMERICAN EXPRESS *Access, Diners, Visa.*

NW1	Hudson's	**NEW**	£65
Tel 071-935 3130			**R**
221b Baker Street NW1 6XE			Map 18 C1

Next door to the Sherlock Holmes museum and owned by it, Hudson's is a successful attempt to recreate the atmosphere of a select Victorian dining room. The room is decorated with heavy red drapes, Victorian furniture, ornaments and pictures, and even the delightful waitresses look the part in their long black dresses and white aprons. Changing with the seasons, the menu is a reworking of Victorian and other old English dishes, made lighter and healthier in keeping with present-day requirements. Traditional cooking methods are used and good-quality raw materials ensure very enjoyable food. Starters include bubble and squeak with wild mushrooms, a tartlet of creamed kidneys and salamagundy – a Victorian salad of pickled vegetables and fruit. Main dishes range from home-made venison sausages and fish pie to fillet of Scotch beef stuffed with red Leicester and wrapped in bacon; sweets are delicious – some, such as marbled bitter chocolate terrine, are liberally drenched in liqueur, Columba in this case. Also open for morning coffee (10-noon) and afternoon tea (3-6pm). *Seats 45. Parties 25. L 12-2.30 (Sun to 3) D 6-10.30 (Sun 7-10). Closed D Bank Holidays, all 25 Dec. Set L £11/£13.50 Set Sun L £13.50/£16.50.* AMERICAN EXPRESS *Access, Diners, Visa.*

SW1	Hunan	£50
Tel 071-730 5712		**· R**
51 Pimlico Road Belgravia SW1W 8NE		Map 19 C5

Small Chinese restaurant where the chef-owner prepares Hunan specialities. The atmosphere is quiet and homely with classical music in the background and very attentive service. Many customers, including regulars, opt for the special 'leave-it-to-us feast', which can be adapted to individual preferences. There's also a good à la carte selection. **Seats** 48. *L 12.30-3 D 6.30-11.30 (Sun 7-11). Closed L Sun, 25 & 26 Dec, 1 Jan.* AMERICAN EXPRESS *Access, Visa.*

SW1	Hyatt Carlton Tower	87%	£240
Tel 071-235 1234 Fax 071-245 6570			HR
2 Cadogan Place Knightsbridge SW1X 9PY			Map 19 C4

Towering high above Cadogan Gardens, this most opulent of London's smart hotels features the fashionable Chinoiserie (all-day snacks and afternoon tea served 3-5.30pm) on the ground floor where enormous flower arrangements burst out of colourful Chinese glazed pots creating an air of elegance which is continued throughout the hotel. The most sought-after bedrooms are those with balconies overlooking the verdant splendour of the square below. There are also balconies on those bedrooms looking out west over Sloane Street and Knightsbridge. The 16 bedroom floors include 62 enormous suites and an 18th-floor (the top) Presidential suite which enjoys both splendid views and high levels of security. Standard rooms are both spacious and well-appointed. King-size beds are a feature of the majority. Decor throughout is a timeless pale cream and beige with elegant furniture to match. The style is typified by the brass carriage clock placed on every desk, and the comfortable armchairs. All rooms have full air-conditioning and there are wall safes for valuables and umbrellas in the wardrobes for rainy days. Bathrooms in marble have fine toiletries as well as thick towels, bathrobes and scales. Excellent standards of housekeeping include a twice-daily maid service with evening turn down but general maintenance in the bedrooms could be improved. The recently renovated Peak Health Club (Mon-Fri 7am-10pm, Sat & Sun 8am-9pm) is a bright, spacious and airy, state-of-the-art 9th-floor rendezvous for fitness fanatics; there's a Club Room (11am-9.30pm) for post-exertion wind-down and a separate work-out studio with sprung floor; the tennis court is in Cadogan Square. Banqueting/conference facilities for 270/150. One child up to 18 may stay free in his/her parents' room. No dogs. **Rooms** 224. *Garden, gym, work-out studio, sauna, steam room, solarium, beauty & hair salon, valeting, Chinoiserie (7am-11pm), news kiosk.* AMERICAN EXPRESS *Access, Diners, Visa.*

Chelsea Room   ↑   £115

Overlooking Cadogan Gardens, under a curving glass conservatory roof, the Chelsea Room is a sumptuous restaurant. There's a bright and open feel to the whole of the dining room, which is elegantly decorated with pickled wood panelling. In the evening, soft lights and piano music complete the picture. Long-serving chef Bernard Gaume's menu offers a suitably standard menu of French classics with a modern touch. Start, perhaps, with *dariole de foie gras chaude aux morilles* or a fresh crabmeat salad with mango and avocado and a saffron mayonnaise, following with straightforward grills, a choice of three vegetarian options or the likes of sautéed scallops with shredded celeriac and mustard, celeriac and lobster lasagne, fillets of duck with citrus fruit segments and green peppercorns, or whole sole baked with a saffron and almond crust, served on a tomato coulis. Salad of langoustines, *foie gras aux raisins* and *petits filets de boeuf* are considered specialities along with a hot passion fruit soufflé and the light *assiette de dessert* (six varieties served with a Grand Marnier sauce) from Robert Mey. The classic wine list includes a short selection of New World wines, but there is little under £20. **Seats** 63. *Parties 30. Private Room 35. L 12.30-2.45 D 7.30-11 (Sun to 10.30). Set L £22.50 Set D £29.50.*

Rib Room   £110

An elegantly appointed, split-level room with rich mahogany panelling and a discreet, clubby ambience. A very traditional and classic carte offers simple, well-prepared dishes, the speciality being the roast ribs of Aberdeen Angus beef served with crisp Yorkshire puddings and jacket potato with sour cream. Lunchtime daily specials might include poached salmon

on Mondays and shepherd's pie on Thursdays. Service is very, very
civilised. Private boardroom-style dining room for 17. *Seats 63. L 12.30-3
D 6.30-11.30 (Sun 7-10.30). Set L £22.50 Set D £29.50.* 🐂

SW1	Hyde Park Hotel	82%	£293

Tel 071-235 2000   Fax 071-235 4552 | **H**

66 Knightsbridge SW1Y 7LA | **Map 19 C4**

Behind the handsome and confident Edwardian facade guests will find
a hotel rich in tradition, a luxurious haven from the busy world outside.
The reception foyer and ornate central lobby are particularly impressive,
with marble walls and floors of eight different colours, pilasters with
Corinthian capitals picked out in gold, ornate ceilings and glittering
chandeliers. The Park Room restaurant, overlooking Hyde Park and
Rotten Row, is elegant and comfortable, and next to it the Ferrari Bar and
Lounge serves as residents' lounge and cocktail bar. Bedrooms are
individually and charmingly decorated, with quality matching fabrics,
traditional polished wood furniture and good armchairs and settees;
bathrooms have loudspeaker extensions, telephones and bidets. Service
is good, with numerous smart and attentive staff. 19 elegant suites all
overlook the park. Up to 250 can be accommodated theatre-style in five
splendid function suites. The most notable feather in the Forte cap
is teaming up here with Marco Pierre White in his 'Restaurant' (see separate
entry under M). Forte Exclusive. *Rooms 185. Gym, hair salon, valeting.*
AMERICAN EXPRESS *Access, Diners, Visa.*

W1	Ikeda		£110

Tel 071-629 2730   Fax 071-628 6982 | **R**

30 Brook Street Mayfair W1Y 1AG | **Map 18 C3**

Traditional Japanese cooking by Mr Ikeda in a quiet, civilised little West
End restaurant, just off New Bond Street and a few steps from Claridge's.
A place at the bar gets you a ringside seat to the sushi show, while the
tables are all close enough to the kitchen to make you feel part of the
action. The daily-changing chef's specials are the choice of many, or you
can venture round an à la carte selection. Specialities are the afore-
mentioned sushi and sashimi ("the finest fresh fish sliced rapidly with
a dangerously sharp knife"). Lunchtime bills are generally much lower than
those for dinner. *Seats 30. Private Room 8. L 12.30-2.30 D 6.30-10.30.
Closed L Sat, all Sun, Bank Holidays. Set L from £14 Set D from £33.*
AMERICAN EXPRESS *Access, Diners, Visa.*

W1	Ikkyu		£50

Tel 071-436 6169 | **R**

67a Tottenham Court Road W1 | **Map 18 D2**

Busy basement Japanese restaurant by Goodge Street underground station
offering fine home-style cooking (*robatayaki*) on a long and varied menu
with short, to-the-point descriptions: sliced onions, fried crab, grilled duck
in brown sauce. Good-value lunchtime menus (from £6) include grilled
fish set, sushi set and ramen noodles. Finish off with fresh fruit. *Seats 65.
Parties 30. L 12.30-2.30 D 6-10.30(Sun 6.30-10), Closed L Sun, D Bank
Holiday Mon, all Sat, 10 days Christmas.* AMERICAN EXPRESS *Access, Diners, Visa.*

EC3	Imperial City		£55

Tel 071-626 3437   Fax 071-338 0125 | **R**

Royal Exchange Cornhill EC3V 3LL | **Map 20 C2**

A busy and popular Chinese restaurant in the brick-lined vaults beneath the
Royal Exchange. The menu, compiled with the help of Ken Hom, is short
and succinct, featuring a mix of regional Chinese dishes with fairly
conservative spicing. Steamed salmon with black bean sauce, Cantonese
pressed duck, 'Lion Head' meatball casserole, crispy lacquered quail and

firecracker sweet wontons are typical dishes. Decor is bright and colourful, service friendly and quick if required. **Seats** *180. Private Room 16. Meals 11.30am-8.30pm. Closed Sat, Sun, Bank Holidays & 24-26 Dec. Set L £13.90 Set D £18.90/£24.80.* AMERICAN EXPRESS *Access, Diners, Visa.*

SW1   L'Incontro   £100

Tel 071-730 3663 Fax 071-730 5062	**R**

87 Pimlico Road SW1W 8PH   Map 19 C5

A stylishly modern, up-market Italian restaurant whose exterior is adorned by flowers in huge terracotta pots. A one-dish lunch (£12-£15.50) has been added to the existing two-or three-course menu, while in the evening the choice is à la carte. Specialities in young Venetian chef Nicola Celmanti's repertoire include baccalà with polenta, cuttlefish in a sauce with its ink, grilled baby chicken in a hot sauce and poached sea bass in a balsamic vinegar sauce. The Piano Bar is a popular venue for private parties. **Seats** *55. Parties 20. Private Room 35. L 12.30-2.30 (Sat to 3) D 7-11.30. Closed 25 & 26 Dec. Set L £13.50/£16.80.* AMERICAN EXPRESS *Access, Diners, Visa.*

W1   Hotel Inter-Continental London   84%   £277

Tel 071-409 3131 Fax 071-409 7460	**HR**

1 Hamilton Place Hyde Park Corner W1V 1QY   Map 19 C4

Always popular with Americans both on business and on holiday, the hotel, located at Hyde Park Corner, has a vast, elegant foyer leading to a stylish lounge well provided with supremely comfortable seating. It's also a fine conference and banqueting venue (1000/850 max) and the fully equipped business centre has four private meeting rooms. There's also a purpose-built Video Conferencing Suite. Bedrooms are sleek and airy with seating areas, air-conditioning, double-glazing and mini-bars; bathrooms provide quality towelling and good toiletries. Rooms extend over eight floors, and those at the top enjoy fine views. The hotel offers a luxury airport service – the chauffeur will telephone ahead to advise reception of your arrival ensuring minimum delay when checking-in. There's underground parking for 100 cars. **Rooms** *469. Plunge pool, gym, sauna, spa bath, solarium, beauty salon, coffee shop (7am-11pm).* AMERICAN EXPRESS *Access, Diners, Visa.*

Le Soufflé Restaurant   ★★↑   £150

In January 1994 Peter Kromberg was named chef-patron at this very elegant, softly lit restaurant, 19 years after arriving and just after Le Soufflé was named Restaurant of the Year in our 1994 edition. He and his brilliant team continue in tip-top form, and that form is nowhere better shown than in the stunning eight-course *choix du chef*, a daily-changing display of artistry and balance. *Terrine de lapereau, crème d'avocat; poelé de Saint Jacques au fumé et lys de bois; sorbet de Bordeaux et framboises; pot au feu de saumon d'Ecosse; cabecou de Périgueux grillé; flan brulée à la crème fraiche;* and *palet aux deux chocolats glacé à la belle sandrine* made up a recent *choix,* producing a meal of total satisfaction without repletion (you can, nonetheless, order your choice of four courses from this menu). Soufflés, the speciality, do not appear on the *choix,* but are available on the splendid Sunday lunch menu and, of course, on the carte. The latter offers two savoury varieties, perhaps lobster with *sauce américaine* and tarragon, and spinach with Tete de Moine cheese, a softly boiled quail's egg in the middle, served with a vinaigrette of black olives and anchovies. There may be four for dessert, including poire William with its ice cream and wild cranberries, or marbled bitter chocolate and orange flavoured with Grand Marnier. Several of the starters and main courses carry the healthy heart symbol, denoting a dish low in fat, calories and carbohydrates and high in fibre. The sommelier's suggestions on the predominantly French wine list represent good value, otherwise it's quite pricey. Two pages of other European and New World wines; worth drinking are some decent wines by the glass. A less formal menu, highlighted by a serve-yourself buffet, is available in the Coffee House, open long hours every day. *Seats 70. Parties 20. L 12.30-3 D 7-10.30. Closed L Sat, D Sun, all Mon, August, 1 week Christmas, 2 weeks Jan. Set L £27.50 (Sun £26) Set D £37.50/£43.*

SW1	Isohama	£60

Tel 071-834 2145 Fax 071-233 7743	**R**
312 Vauxhall Bridge Road Victoria SW1V 1AA	**Map 19 D4**

Whitewashed walls, bare darkwood tables and purple velvet chairs add up to a simply decorated little restaurant just a few steps from Victoria station. Japanese dishes both familiar and less so make up an interesting menu which staff will happily explain to you. Good cooking, unfussy presentation, simpler fare at lunchtime, when there's a good-value set meal. *Seats 30. L 12-2.30 D 6-10.30. Set L from £6.50 Set D from £25.* AMERICAN EXPRESS *Access, Diners, Visa.*

N16	Istanbul Iskembecisi	£30

Tel 071-254 7291 Fax 071-881 3741	**R**
9 Stoke Newington Road N16 8BH	**Map 16 D2**

The smartest Turkish restaurant in the area. Pale pink walls, chandeliers and ornate gilt framed pictures contrast with the taped Turkish music playing in the background. The menu of authentic, simple fare includes tripe soup, boiled sheep's head soup, whole roast lamb's head (boneless) and skewered intestines – dishes popular with a clientele of largely Turkish émigrés. The rest of the menu is rather more familiar, with kebabs and grills as the centrepiece, a wide choice of mezze to start, and sweets such as pastry with mixed nuts and syrup, or dried mixed fruit pudding. Staff are helpful and friendly. *Seats 80. Parties 40. Meals 5pm-4.30am (Sun from 2).* AMERICAN EXPRESS *Access, Visa.*

WC2	The Ivy ★	£70

Tel 071-836 4751 Fax 071-497 3644	**R**
1 West Street WC2H 9NE	**Map 21 B2**

The design-conscious Ivy has mirrored wood panelling, stained-glass diamond lattice windows and art all around. Cooking is modern British with international influences. Some dishes on the neatly laid-out menu are long-time favourites (potted shrimps, eggs Benedict, kedgeree, steak frites, tripe and onions), while others have a more individual stamp (butternut pumpkin salad, griddled chicken salad with piquillos and guacamole, citrus fruits with a kumquat sorbet). Good choice of coffees, teas and tisanes, plenty of reasonably priced drinking on a no-nonsense wine list. The old Ivy was a great favourite with actors and theatre-goers, and this one, in the same ownership as *Le Caprice*, attracts a similar crowd. Two sittings for dinner (during and post-theatre). *Seats 110. Parties 10. Private Room 60. L 12-3 (Sun to 3.30) D 6-12. Closed Bank Holiday lunches. Set L Sat £14 Sun £12.50.* AMERICAN EXPRESS *Access, Diners, Visa.*

N5	Iznik	£45

Tel 071-354 5697	**R**
19 Highbury Park N5 1OJ	**Map 16 D2**

Located midway between Highbury Grove and Blackstock Road, Iznik has immediate appeal. The ceiling sparkles with numerous tiny candle lamps and midnight-blue shaded spot lamps. Walls are of white-painted bricks and also have little candle wall lights as well as a host of Turkish artefacts. The tables, with their richly coloured cotton coverings and brass-encased lights, add to the genuine homely, informal and friendly atmosphere. Here there's a genuine attempt to produce some of the finest Turkish food in North London. The range is extensive and includes a good selection of vegetarian dishes. There are some unusual offerings too, among them exceptional courgette and feta cheese fritters accompanied by *kisir*, a complimentary relish of cracked wheat, parsley, spring onion, lemon juice, tomato and chili. *Hünkâr begendi* is a dish of very tender lamb cubes served in a creamy aubergine sauce with delicious nutty rice. Sweets too are not run-of-the-mill: bramble mousse, perhaps not one of Turkey's better known dishes, is a creamy confection of blackberries and black cherries. *Seats 54. Parties 20. L 10-4 (from 9 weekends) D 6.30-11 (Sun 7-12). Closed 4 days Christmas. No credit cards.*

W1	**Jade Garden**	**£35**
Tel 071-437 5065		**R**
15 Wardour Street Soho W1V 3HA		Map 21 A2

The dim sum are among the best in town and they serve them until 5pm – Sunday lunchtime is particularly popular. Elsewhere on the long menu are sections for prawns, eel, oysters, abalone, a dozen ways with pork, sizzling dishes and noodles (fried or in soup). The cooking is mainly Cantonese, but one of the set menus features Peking cuisine. *Seats 144. Parties 10. Meals 12-11.30. Closed 25 & 26 Dec. Set meals from £9.50.* AMERICAN EXPRESS® *Access, Visa.*

SW10	**Jake's**	**£45**
Tel 071-352 8692		**R**
2 Hollywood Road SW10 9HY		Map 19 B6

On a corner site, Jake's is a bright, summery restaurant with a little open courtyard (seating 20) at the back. The straightforward menu of English and international origin features dishes such as steak, kidney and mushroom pie, salmon fish cakes on a bed of spinach, eggs Benedict, a variety of salads, beef Wellington, calf's liver and bacon with mashed potato – many perennial favourites. *Seats 70. Parties 20. Private Room 45. L 12.30-3 D 7.30-11.45. Closed D Sun, 25-28 Dec. Set L £7.95.* AMERICAN EXPRESS® *Access, Diners, Visa.*

W10	**Jimmy Beez** ↑ **NEW**	**£50**
Tel 081-964 9100		**R**
303 Portobello Road W10 5TD		Map 16 B3

Virtually under the A40(M) flyover, Jimmy Beez has quickly established itself. Very much in the off-beat style of the other restaurants on this road, it is the domain of a mixed crowd with dreadlocks, combats and biker jackets vying with a more chic, radical set. A tiny split-level ground-floor area is supplemented by a windowless basement. The food is outstandingly good with a short lunchtime menu of snacky items and a similar Saturday and Sunday brunch menu which also includes a short list of cocktails. The dinner menu begins with the likes of grilled fresh figs wrapped in prosciutto with rocket and mascarpone, salmon and halibut paté with nori and a basil mayonnaise or crisp tempura king scallops wrapped in red basil leaves and Parmesan. Slightly more substantial are the likes of a superb crispy Peking duck salad with a tangerine and orange sauce or wild mushroom and asparagus risotto. Main dishes are futher examples of the kitchen's innovative approach as in basil tagliatelle with spinach, pine nuts, quail's eggs and Parmesan, chargrilled salmon with crème fraiche and sun-dried tomatoes, magret duck breast with chestnuts, sugared onions and bacon lardons or grilled tuna with a pineapple, mint and chili salsa. Sweet Jamaican potatoes with garlic butter and deep-fried crispy spinach are superb vegetables and sweets are no less delicious. White and dark chocolate slice served with a creamy chocolate sauce, sticky toffee pudding, and cranberry and raspberry tart with a macaroon topping are pure heaven. Service is very laid-back and very friendly. Booking is essential. *Seats 50. Parties 6. Private Room 35. Meals 12-11 (Sat 11-11, Sun 11-10.30). Closed 2 weeks Christmas.* AMERICAN EXPRESS® *Access, Visa.*

NW3   Jinkichi   £60

Tel 071-794 6158   **R**

73 Heath Street Hampstead NW3 6UG   Map 16 B2

A Japanese restaurant which can get noisy and crowded, particularly towards the weekends and at peak meal times. Very much a local place with a simple, unfussy decor and ambience. Bar stools surround a central counter, off the right of which a chef cooks selections of the thirty different yakitori dishes available – from crispy salmon skin and chicken morsels to gigantic prawns – all carefully prepared. Other familiar choices include sushi, tempura and shabu-shabu. Quite pleasant service, though at times it can be off-hand. *Seats 46. Parties 20. L (Sat & Sun only) 12-2.30 D (Wed-Mon only) 6-11.30 (Sun to 10.30). Closed 4 days Christmas, 3 days Easter.* AMERICAN EXPRESS *Access, Diners, Visa.*

WC2   Joe Allen   £40

Tel 071-836 0651   Fax 071-497 2148   **R**

13 Exeter Street WC2E 7DT   Map 20 A2

Still trendy and relatively inexpensive, not much changes at this basement American restaurant, which hardly advertises itself – only a small plaque on a redbrick wall marks its entrance. Staff can sometimes be rather nonchalant, but there are no complaints about the food – Caesar salad, Maryland crab cakes with tartare sauce, baby artichokes with honey and balsamic vinegar, grilled Italian sausages with a chunky ginger, beetroot and apple relish, and vegetable chili with rice. Tables are usually turned over twice in the evenings, the second sitting after theatres turn out. *Seats 180. Parties 8. Meals Noon-12.45am (Sun to 11.45pm). Closed 24 & 25 Dec. No credit cards.*

> Changes in data sometimes occur in establishments after the Guide goes to press. Prices should be taken as indications rather than firm quotes.

SW3   Joe's Cafe   £70

Tel 071-225 2217   **R**

126 Draycott Avenue SW3 3AH   Map 19 B5

Stylish, split-level brasserie-restaurant with an oyster and black decor offering a simple, fashionable menu for its fashion-conscious patrons. Dishes reflect a wide range of cuisines, from sashimi of sea bass, tuna and salmon to Caesar salad, corned beef hash and fried egg, grilled striploin steak, sticky toffee pudding and Stilton with celery. The café theme includes eggs, bacon and chips and 'traditional English tea' on the menu, but fashion man Joseph Ettedgui's cool hangout could hardly be less like a café (note the price for two). Sunday brunch menu. *Seats 80. L 12-4 (Sun 11-5) D 6-11.15 (Sat from 7). Closed D Sun, 25 & 26 Dec.* AMERICAN EXPRESS *Access, Diners, Visa.*

WC2   Joy King Lau   £50

Tel 071-437 1132   Fax 071-437 2629   **R**

3 Leicester Street WC2   Map 21 A2

The decor is modern, done in claret and blue tones with an intimate atmosphere. The menu offers well-executed familiar dishes like Peking duck or beef in black bean sauce, along with more unusual duck webs with sea cucumber, fried pig intestine and braised fish lips. There is a large selection of fish and shellfish on the extensive menu. Dim sum, served until 5pm, are among the best in London. *Seats 240. Parties 12. Private Room 60. Meals noon-11.30pm (Sun 11-10.30). Closed 25 & 26 Dec. Set meals from £8.* AMERICAN EXPRESS *Access, Diners, Visa.*

W11   Julie's   £70
Tel 071-229 8331   Fax 071-229 4050   **R**
135 Portland Road Holland Park W11 4LW   Map 17 B4

A Holland Park institution, popular for its wine bar and Sunday lunches. The succession of dining rooms each has a unique atmosphere, from the flowery champagne bar to a Gothic alcove or even a smart white theme conservatory. The menu takes its influences from near and far: duck and chicken liver paté with onion and raisin pickle, watercress mousse with mint tea jelly and a red pepper coulis, chicken with king prawns and lobster sauce, rack of lamb with wild mushroom crust, steak au poivre. A good selection of English cheeses can be enjoyed with a glass of wine or port from the well-priced list. *Seats 100. Parties 24. Private Room 45. L 12.30-2.45 (Sun 12.30-3) D 7.30-11 (Sun to 10.30). Closed Aug Bank Holidays, 3 days Christmas. Set L & D from £12.95.* AMERICAN EXPRESS *Access, Diners, Visa.*

SW7   Jurys Kensington Hotel   **NEW**   64%   £102
Tel 071-589 6300   Fax 071-581 1492   **H**
109 Queen's Gate SW7 5LR   Map 19 B5

Sited at the corner of Old Brompton Road and Queen's Gate, the hotel has an impressive welcoming lobby decorated in a traditional theme with light oak panelling, richly coloured swags and tents at the windows. It also encompasses a large area and bar. Some corridors may be narrow but bedrooms are mostly spacious, and brightly decorated. Staff are multilingual and helpful. No dogs. *Rooms 171.* AMERICAN EXPRESS *Access, Diners, Visa.*

NW4   Kaifeng   £65
Tel 081-203 7888   Fax 081-203 8263   **R**
51 Church Road Hendon NW4 4DU   Map 16 A1

A smart and expensive restaurant serving an unlikely sounding match of food – Kosher Chinese. The quality of the cooking matches the plush, elegant surroundings in that dishes are carefully cooked and attractively presented, but the menu content is somewhat lacklustre. Some dishes traditionally associated with pork are here made with lamb and the result of this replacement is not always successful. Service is quite formal and rather serious. *Seats 75. L 12.30-2 D 6.30-11. Closed Fri (& Sat April-Sept), all Jewish religious holidays. Set L £9.25/£11.25 (Sun buffet £12) Set D £18.50/£22.50.* AMERICAN EXPRESS *Access, Visa.*

W2   Kalamaras   £40
Tel 071-727·9122   **R**
76-78 Inverness Mews Bayswater W2 3JQ   Map 18 A3

Owner-manager-head chef Stelios Platonos has been at the helm for almost 30 years at one of the best and busiest of London's Greek restaurants. The menu ranges far beyond the usual choice, and the more unfamiliar items include *tsirosalata* (small fillets of dried fish served with wine vinegar), *varkoula* (baked courgettes topped with fresh salmon and béchamel sauce) and *bouyatsa* (a speciality sweet made with eggs, semolina and cinnamon served hot). Fish specials (they vary with the market) are always worth trying, so too the spinach and spring onion filo triangles (*spanakotyropites*) and the casseroled lamb (*arnaki lemonato me spanaki*). There's a list of 20 Greek wines. The restaurant is located at the end of a mews running parallel to Queensway. *Kalamaras Micro*, an unlicensed sibling, is at no. 66 (Tel 071-727 5082). *Seats 88. Private Room 30. D only 6-12. Closed Sun, Bank Holidays. Set D £15.50.* AMERICAN EXPRESS *Access, Diners, Visa.*

W1 Kaspia

£70

Tel 071-493 2612   Fax 071-408 1627

R

18/18a Bruton Place Mayfair W1X 7AH

Map 18 C3

The London offshoot of the renowned Paris caviar shop and restaurant is tucked away discreetly off Berkeley Square. It's a comfortable, well-appointed place, with lightwood panelling, sea-blue tablecloths, Russian pictures and plates on display and Russian bassi profundi gently exercising their tonsils on the sound system. If the order is for caviar all round the bill here will naturally be hefty, but elsewhere on the menu prices are reasonable, particularly for the splendid smoked fish salad – a very generous plateful of smoked salmon, trout, eel, sturgeon and cod roe. Other specialities include oysters, gull's eggs, paté de foie gras, fish cake with lobster sauce, steak tartare and gravad lax. *Seats 60. Private Room 16. L 12-3 D 7-11.30. Set L & D from £27. Closed Sun, also Sat in Aug, Bank Holidays, 24 Dec-4 Jan.* AMERICAN EXPRESS *Access, Diners, Visa.*

W1 Kaya

£70

Tel 071-437 6630

R

22 Dean Street Soho W1V 5AL

Map 21 A2

Korean food, not as varied as Chinese nor as "pretty" as Japanese, finds a friendly home in Soho. Some items, including squid, pork fillet, venison and marinated steak for the national dish *bulgogi*, are prepared at the table. 15% service charge. *Seats 70. Private Room 40. L 12-3 D 6-11. Closed L Sun, also L Bank Holidays & 25 Dec. Set D £38 & £43.* AMERICAN EXPRESS *Access, Diners, Visa.*

SW1 Ken Lo's Memories of China

£75

Tel 071-730 7734   Fax 071-730 2992

R

67 Ebury Street SW1W 0NZ

Map 19 C4

Ken Lo's interests may be divided between here and Chelsea Harbour, but his Pimlico chef of 14 years' standing, Kam-Po But, still cooks in an unchanged style. The large, airy dining room is painted white and decorated with subtle displays of Chinese lettering, almost reminiscent of graffiti. The tables are cleverly separated by Chinese wooden screens, giving the semblance of privacy. Flavours tend to be muted, perhaps to appeal to the largely expense-account clientièle? The carte is well planned, and not overlong by Chinese standards. Bang bang chicken, five-spice spare ribs or *siu mai* (meat-stuffed dumplings) could be followed by steamed sea bass, crispy soft-shell crab, or perhaps one of the many iron-plate sizzlers. New Zealand mussels combine well with black bean and chili sauce, which cleverly exaggerates the flavour of the sea. Peking quick-fried lamb with garlic and spring onions is another success. Specialities are marked on the menu with an asterisk, and make choosing easier. The set menus take you on a gastronomic tour of China, and offer the best choice for two or more people. Don't leave your order too late if you'd like a hot dessert, as the kitchen can close early, leaving you with ice cream or nothing. Cheaper eating is available at the Chelsea branch (qv). *Seats 150. Private Room 20. L 12-2.45 D 7-11.30. Closed L Sun, Bank Holidays, few days at Christmas. Set meals from £15.* AMERICAN EXPRESS *Access, Diners, Visa.*

SW10 Ken Lo's Memories of China

£60

Tel 071-352 4953   Fax 071-351 2096

R

Harbour Yard Chelsea Harbour SW10 0QJ

Map 19 B6

The Chelsea Harbour branch of Ken Lo's Ebury Street original caters for all pockets and purses by offering various à la carte and set menus. Best value is undoubtedly provided by the bar snack menu (12-2.30 Mon-Fri) with main courses priced under £3. The favourite way to start is with a selection of excellent crispy dim sum. The main menu ranges far and wide, with Cantonese lobster and steamed sea bass at the luxury end. Popular main courses include quick-fried beef in oyster sauce with mangetout, spiced pork with shredded vegetables and Peking egg-battered garlic and ginger sliced chicken. Snacks available between full sessions on Sundays. *Seats* 175. Private Room 60. L 12.30-2.30 D 7-10.45 (*Sun to 10*). Closed 25 & 26 Dec, 1 Jan. Set L £13.50/£15.30 Set D £26/£29.60. AMERICAN EXPRESS *Access, Diners, Visa.*

WC1	**Kenilworth Hotel**	**63%**	**£180**

Tel 071-637 3477   Fax 071-631 3133

97 Great Russell Street WC1B 3LB	**Map 21 B1**

A handsome redbrick building near the British Museum. The foyer gives a good impression, decorated in warm colours, with plenty of seating. There are seven conference rooms, with a capacity of 120 in the largest. Bedrooms are quite pretty in floral pinks and green, and some top-floor rooms have four-posters. All are double-glazed, with two armchairs and a desk. In the bedrooms are plenty of shelves and good towels and toiletries. Bedrooms and conference rooms have recently been refurbished. No dogs. Edwardian Hotels. *Rooms* 192. AMERICAN EXPRESS *Access, Diners, Visa.*

NW1	**Kennedy Hotel**	**63%**	**£102**

Tel 071-387 4400   Fax 071-387 5122

Cardington Street Euston NW1 2LP	**Map 18 D1**

Conveniently situated near to the west side of Euston station, a modern hotel with simply decorated rooms. Close to Drummond Street, where there's a fine choice of Indian restaurants. Conference facilities for up to 140, banqueting for 60. Children under 5 share parents' room free. Mount Charlotte Thistle. *Rooms* 360. News kiosk, shop. AMERICAN EXPRESS *Access, Diners, Visa.*

W8	**Kensington Close Hotel**	**59%**	**£109**

Tel 071-937 8170   Fax 071-937 8289

Wrights Lane Kensington W8 5SP	**Map 19 A4**

A minute's walk from the shops of High Street Kensington, the hotel boasts fine leisure/keep-fit facilities and its own underground car park. Bedrooms fall into three categories – standard, refurbished and Executive. There are many function and meeting rooms, and a staffed business centre. Children up to 16 share parents' room free. No dogs. Forte. *Rooms* 530. *Garden, gym, squash, sauna, solarium, beauty salon, news kiosk.* AMERICAN EXPRESS *Access, Diners, Visa.*

SW5	**Kensington Court Hotel**	**£59**

Tel 071-370 5151   Fax 071-370 3499

33 Nevern Place Earls Court SW5 9NP	**Map 19 A5**

A modern block in the heart of Earls Court. All bedrooms are double or triple bedded and have simple en-suite facilities. *Rooms* 35. AMERICAN EXPRESS *Access, Diners, Visa.*

SW7	**Kensington Manor**	**£94**

Tel 071-370 7516   Fax 071-373 3163

8 Emperor's Gate South Kensington SW7 4HH	**Map 19 A4**

Small bed and breakfast hotel just moments from Gloucester Road underground station (cross Cromwell Road into Grenville Place which leads to Emperor's Gate) and handy for the South Kensington museums. 24hr private bar. Extensive buffet breakfast. Children up to 12 share parents' room free of charge. Now under new ownership. Prices are often quoted without VAT. *Rooms* 14. AMERICAN EXPRESS *Access, Diners, Visa.*

W8 Kensington Palace Thistle   67%   £110

Tel 071-937 8121   Fax 071-937 2816   **H**

De Vere Gardens Kensington W8 5AF   **Map 19 A4**

Well-equipped bedrooms, two bars, popular conference rooms (for up to
180) and an all-day restaurant serving dishes from around the world. Just
across the road from Kensington Gardens (by the top of Gloucester Road),
it's convenient for Kensington High Street and the Albert Hall. 113 rooms
reserved for non-smokers. Breakfast is buffet-style only. No dogs.
Rooms 299. *News kiosk, coffee shop (7am-11pm).* AMERICAN EXPRESS *Access,
Diners, Visa.*

W8 Kensington Park Thistle Hotel   67%   £150

Tel 071-937 8080   Fax 071-937 7616   **H**

16-32 De Vere Gardens W8 5AG   **Map 19 A4**

Quiet, comfortable and fairly roomy hotel (100 of the bedrooms
designated non-smoking) opposite Kensington Gardens. Though lacking
the facilities of many big hotels, it has an all-day eating outlet called
Moniques Brasserie. No dogs. *Rooms 332.* AMERICAN EXPRESS *Access,
Diners, Visa.*

W8 Kensington Place   ★   £70

Tel 071-727 3184   Fax 071-229 2025   **R**

205 Kensington Church Street W8 7LX   **Map 18 A3**

Rowley Leigh has been slaving away unseen in the kitchens at the slavishly
trendy KP since its inception in 1987; thousands of customers have posed
and dined behind the tall, windowed frontage, happy to be seen in one
of the capital's culinary hot spots. Since day one, Nick Smallwood's and
Simon Slater's restaurant has created waves across the capital, first for its
famously uncomfortable, angular modern chairs, secondly for its sustained
popularity and thirdly for its uncompromisingly modern menu written
in straightforward English. Others may have tried in vain to copy their
style, but Kensington Place's attractions are endearing and enduring because
the culinarily content is consistently appealing. The cooking is as frill-free
as the table settings and, these days, smoked eel salad with bacon or pigeon
crostini with truffle paste and rocket sit happily on the menu alongside
squid and aubergine or featherblade (a cut from the shoulder of beef) and
oyster stew, red mullet with cumin and lentils, and roast haunch of venison
with chocolate sauce. Griddled foie gras with sweetcorn pancake
is a memorable, luxury starter. For simpler tastes, omelette *fines herbes*, cod
with parsley sauce and fried mozzarella with tomato sauce are likely
to please; sprouts and spring greens with garlic appear among the vegetable
side orders. Noisy, buzzing with lively conversation, KP grants no great
concessions to comfort or ornamentation; at the entrance is a small, glitzy
bar, at the other end of the now-extended long room a vast mural
depicting an alfresco eating scene in gay pastel shades. Wines from around
the world and several dessert wines by the glass to accompany anything
from tiramisu to rhubarb fool, steamed chocolate pudding with custard
or chestnut gratin with chocolate sauce. *Seats 140. Parties 26. L 12-3 (Sat &
Sun to 3.30) D 6.30-11.45 (Sun to 10.15). Closed 24-26 Dec & 1 Jan.
Set L £13.50. Access, Visa.*

SW7 Khan's of Kensington   £50

Tel 071-581 2900   Fax 071-581 5980   **R**

3 Harrington Road South Kensington SW7 3ES   **Map 19 B5**

Just a few steps from South Kensington Station. Light green is the main
colour of the stylish modern decor, and the greens and pinks of the chairs
are taken up in the waiters' waistcoats. Tiny lights are hung from tramline
wires, and a silk banana plant stands in one corner. Downstairs is a colonial-

style lounge bar. The menu includes familiar items from the lexicon
of Indian cuisine and some less usual choices such as *gujrati patra* (lotus
leaves rolled with herbs and sesame seeds), fish *coliwada* (fried pomfret fish
from Bombay), tandoori salmon (marinated in yoghurt, dill and spices) and
simla mirchi (capsicum stuffed with cheese and fresh herbs). Besides the à la
carte there are meat and vegetarian set menus for one, a set lunch (Mon-
Fri) and a Sunday lunchtime buffet (till 5.30). High standards of cooking
and service. *Seats* 60. *Private Room* 25. *L* 12-2.30 *D* 5.30-11.30 (*Sun open
all day*). *Closed 25 & 26 Dec. Set L from £7.50 Set D from £12.50
(vegetarian) & £14.50.* AMERICAN EXPRESS *Access, Diners, Visa.*

SW3   Khun Akorn   £65

Tel 071-225 2688   Fax 071-225 2680   **R**
136 Brompton Road Knightsbridge SW3 1HY   Map 19 B4

Owned by the Imperial Hotel in Bangkok, with a sister branch in Paris,
an up-market Thai restaurant spread across three split levels. Decor features
traditional carvings and plants abound; a snake-shaped bar curves its way
through the centre of the restaurant. The menu lists well-known Thai
specialities ('weeping tiger' steak with chili sauce) and doesn't venture much
into originality. Cooking is reliable and prices substantial, except for
a bargain lunch menu. *Seats* 70. *L* 12-3 *D* 6.30-11. *Closed 25 & 26 Dec,
1 Jan. Set L £12.50 Set D £17.50.* AMERICAN EXPRESS *Access, Diners, Visa.*

SW7   Khyber Pass   £30

Tel 071-589 7311   **R**
21 Bute Street South Kensington SW7 3EY   Map 19 B5

Popular little Indian restaurant established well over 20 years ago and still
attracting a loyal local following with its reliable run-of-the-mill cooking.
Curries climb all the way up to the blistering Bangalore phal. *Seats* 36.
L 12-2.45 *D* 6-11.45. *Closed 25 & 26 Dec.* AMERICAN EXPRESS *Access,
Diners, Visa.*

SW10   Kingdom   £50

Tel 071-352 0206   **R**
457 Fulham Road SW10 9UZ   Map 19 B6

A quiet, civilised restaurant with very polite and obliging staff. Greenery
running up to a skylight is a central feature of the back room, whose walls
are lined with prints of Chinese emperors. The menu is pan-Chinese,
interesting without being outré, and cooking is of a good standard. Best
dishes include prawn-stuffed squid with Szechuan peppercorn salt, grilled
chicken with garlic and sizzling dishes in which you choose your own
sauce from five offered. A hot buffet of 10 dishes is served lunch and
evening. 200 yards west of the new Royal Chelsea & Westminster hospital.
Seats 80. *Private Room* 25. *L* 12-2.30 *D* 6-11.30. *Closed 24-26 Dec.
Set L £5.50 Set D from £8.50 (min 2).* AMERICAN EXPRESS *Access, Diners, Visa.*

SW1   Knightsbridge Green Hotel   ···   £117

Tel 071-584 6274   Fax 071-225 1635   **PH**
159 Knightsbridge SW1X 7PD   Map 19 C4

A family-run private hotel in the very heart of Knightsbridge offering
comfortable, spotlessly-kept accommodation with double-glazing and the
usual conveniences – except, that is, for a restaurant or bar as the hotel
is unlicensed; however, this is hardly an inconvenience given the superb
location. Breakfast (English or Continental) is served in the bedrooms from
7.30am (8am Sun and Bank Hols) and tea/coffee and cakes are available all
day long in the Club Room. No dogs. *Rooms* 24. *Closed 4 days Christmas.*
AMERICAN EXPRESS *Access, Visa.*

SW5   Krungtap   £25

Tel 071-259 2314   **R**

227 Old Brompton Road Earls Court SW5 0EA   Map 19 A5

Acceptable cooking at more than acceptable prices in a particularly jolly
little Thai restaurant at the busy junction of Old Brompton Road and Earls
Court Road. Best are soups, salads, one-plate noodle and rice dishes, and
specials which range from fish cakes, mussels and herring roes to frogs' legs,
rabbit and venison. Weekend lunchtime openings tend to come and go –
phone to enquire. *Seats 30. L (Sat & Sun) 12-2.30 D 5.30-10.30.
Closed 24-26 Dec. Access, Visa.*

SW1   Kundan   £55

Tel 071-834 3434   Fax 071-834 3211   **R**

3 Horseferry Road Westminster SW1P 2AN   Map 19 D5

Politician-spotting comes as a free side order with a meal in this
comfortable and roomy basement restaurant on the division bell circuit.
All parties are agreed on the quality of the rich North Indian cooking and
the chef (Aziz Khan, here for almost 20 years) numbers tandoori prawns
and chicken among his specialities. Another is Karahi kebab Sarhadi – a
dish from the Khyber Pass of diced chicken grilled with spices, chopped
tomatoes and green peppers. Note too the vegetable kebabs and the dal
of the day. *Seats 130. Private Room 20. L 12-3 D 7-11.30. Closed Sun, Bank
Holidays. Set L £15/£20 Set D £12.50/£15.50.* AMERICAN EXPRESS *Access,
Diners, Visa.*

SW1   Kura   £90

Tel 071-581 1820   Fax 081-458 4601   **R**

304 Park Close SW1X 7PQ   Map 19 C4

Tucked away between Knightsbridge and Hyde Park, this delightful little
Japanese restaurant is sure to please. Bare wooden tables are separated
by Japanese screens, there's ethnic piped music and plenty of Japanese
families enjoying the atmosphere. Lunchtime offers the better bargains
here, with a good selection of one-course meals. Dinner is more elaborate,
including several set meals consisting of many courses. One such meal
includes delicious *miso shiru* (clear soup thickened with bean paste), chicken
teriyaki and mixed tempura (which includes king prawns). Assorted
sashimi (sliced raw fish), and other Japanese delicacies are always available,
but prices can mount quickly when choosing from the carte. Short wine
list, but sake seems the favoured beverage. Friendly, helpful service.
Advisable to book, as space is at a premium. *Seats 25. L 12-2.30 D 6-10.30.
Closed L Sun, all Sat, Bank Holidays, 1 week Aug, 1 week Christmas.
Set L from £9.50 Set D from £25.60.* AMERICAN EXPRESS *Access, Diners, Visa.*

W1   Lal Qila   £40

Tel 071-387 4570   **R**

117 Tottenham Court Road W1P 9HN   Map 18 D2

Lal Qila, meaning red fort, is a long-standing restaurant, once a seminal
influence of North Indian cuisine in Britain. Those that followed have
largely caught up, and to some extent found new flavours and textures –
though not necessarily retaining the same authenticity. The traditional food
produced here, *shami kebab, roghan josh, murg makhani* and the like, are all
as they should be. A few Indian desserts follow, for the sweet tooth – *ras
malai, gulab jamun* (fried balls of flour and yoghurt, soaked in syrup),
or perhaps the cooling effect of kulfi. *Seats 64. L 12-3 D 6-11.30.
Closed 25 & 26 Dec.* AMERICAN EXPRESS *Access, Diners, Visa.*

SW1   The Lanesborough   89%   £302

Tel 071-259 5599   Fax 071-259 5606   **HR**

1 Lanesborough Place Hyde Park Corner SW1X 7TA   Map 19 C4

Originally Lanesborough House, a private residence demolished in the 1820s and replaced by St George's Hospital, the Lanesborough enjoys a fine central location on Hyde Park Corner. When the hospital was gutted in 1987 its Regency facade was kept intact and great care was taken faithfully to restore some of the original Regency-era designs and furnishings. Enormous and exotic flower arrangements abound, complementing the polished marble floors and the colourful and stylish neo-Georgian furniture and furnishings. The hotel's bar – The Library – has rich mahogany panelling inset with bookshelves which, along with leather-upholstered seating, creates a deeply civilised effect. Next door is The Withdrawing Room, a sumptuously elegant room with a striking old-gold colour scheme. Public rooms have many quiet corners and a general level of intimacy is to be found here that one might more usually associate with country house hotels in rural England. Very effective triple soundproofed glazing throughout the hotel ensures that outside noises appear as no more than a distant murmur. On arrival, guests are issued with their own personalised stationery and business cards, while each of the 95 bedrooms (which include 46 suites) has two direct-access telephone lines as well as a fax line (their system allows for 1000 numbers with 200 reserved permanently for repeat guests). Security, too, is given a very high priority with 35 surveillance cameras, window sensors and alarms that include a sophisticated door-key system; briefcase-sized safes are also provided. Upon being shown to their rooms, guests are introduced to a butler who, in terms of service and information, is their only point of contact; all the butlers have been trained in the traditional manner and will unpack, pack, iron, and even run baths as required. Bedrooms are equipped to a high-tech standard as well as having exquisite decor, with comfort being paramount. Each has a VCR, CD and tape decks – all fully remote and secreted in attractive pieces of furniture, together with the TVs. Bathrooms are lined with white marble and have every conceivable amenity including, in most, steam showers and spa baths. Exercise equipment can be placed in the rooms at no extra charge and there's free membership of a local health club. Valet parking for the basement car park. *Rooms* 95. *Car hire desk, coffee shop (7am-midnight).* AMERICAN EXPRESS *Access, Diners, Visa.*

The Conservatory   ★   £90

The elegantly flamboyant decor of the restaurant contains ornate Victorian Gothic-style cloisters with beautiful and exotic chinoiserie all under a lofty glass canopy. Paul Gayler now focuses his culinary talents here, the Dining Room currently being used only for private functions. The menu offers a multitude of choices combining elements of lightness, sophistication and price. His innovative skills are demonstrated in such appetisers as pressed foie gras and white chicory terrine with toasted brioche, cured pancetta with a roasted artichoke salad and black pepper and grilled Cornish scallops arranged with asparagus spears and surrounded by a light pesto and delicate orange-flavoured oil. Main dishes too are outstanding with Creole glazed rack of lamb with roast vegetables, poached breast of chicken with lemon coriander broth and roast confit of duck on a white bean brandade and Provençal fricassé being typical. He continues to espouse vegetarianism with a short but imaginative selection and desserts finish off the meal on a suitably high note, his cappucino brulée bring a perfect example of his ability and art. A fine wine list boasts some great names, though with hardly a bargain in sight why not introduce a house selection? *Seats* 106. *Parties 14. L 12.30-2.30 (Sun brunch 11-3) D 7-12. Set L £22.50 (Sun brunch £23 children under 12 £16) Set D £28.50.*

Set menu prices may not always include service or wine.

W1   Langan's Bistro   £65

Tel 071-935 4531   **R**

26 Devonshire Street W1N 1RJ   Map 18 C2

A popular bistro next to its big brother *Odin's* just off Marylebone High
Street. The short menu offers interesting starters like poached egg
on a prawn and sweetcorn fritter or bacon, beetroot and chicory salad,
followed by the likes of spicy lamb couscous, chargrilled breast of chicken
with roasted peppers and Mrs Langan's chocolate pudding. *Seats 38.*
Parties 8. L 12.30-2.30 D 7-11.30. Set L & D £13.95/£15.95. Closed L Sat,
all Sun, Bank Holidays. AMERICAN EXPRESS *Access, Diners, Visa.*

W1   Langan's Brasserie   ↑   £85

Tel 071-491 8822   **R**

Stratton Street W1X 5FD   Map 18 D3

Just off Piccadilly, Richard Shepherd's and Michael Caine's enormous
brasserie is on two floors and its walls are covered in modern art. Langan's
is legendary, not only for its ability to pack in diners by the score but also
for its ability to keep them all satisfied. The long, long menu features
around 80 dishes, from snails, mussels or baked egg, cabbage and bacon
hash to start, followed by Langan's renowned cod and chips, black pudding
with kidneys and bacon, braised knuckle of gammon with butter beans and
roast duck with sage and onion stuffing and appple sauce. The mix covers
both traditional English and French – spinach soufflé served with
an anchovy sauce is the speciality on the ground floor, *carré d'agneau roti*
aux herbes de Provence upstairs. Among the 25 or so desserts you might find
elderflower sorbet, walnut ice cream with caramel sauce and *crepes des*
Alpes. Nursery food addicts could be well pleased with a meal of bangers
and mash with white onion sauce followed by rice pudding, washed down,
of course, with a favourite champagne. The ground floor is always bustling
with busy diners, while upstairs the Venetian room has its own quieter
charm. *Seats 220. Parties 12. L 12.30-3 D 7-11.45 (Sat 8-12.45).*
Closed L Sat, all Sun, Bank Holidays. AMERICAN EXPRESS *Access, Diners, Visa.*

W1   The Langham Hilton   75%   £212

Tel 071-636 1000   Fax 071-436 1346   **H**

Portland Place W1N 3AA   Map 18 D2

The epitome of Victorian high style when built in 1865, the Langham
retained its fashionable status until 1940, when war damage caused its
closure. Fifty years later it was lavishly restored to its original splendour.
It stands across the road from a temple of the 30s – the BBC's Broadcasting
House. Smart doormen in Tsarist uniforms set the tone for the stylish
interior which has been transformed into a sophisticated modern hotel
retaining many of the original features. The Grand Entrance Hall with
polished marble, Oriental rug-strewn floors and thick Portland stone pillars
leads to a light yet fairly intimate Palm Court, where afternoon tea
is served (to the accompaniment of a pianist) and food is available all day
and all night. The Chukha Bar is very much in the gentleman's club
tradition with polo memorabilia decorating the walls. Bedrooms, furnished
in solid, traditional style have all the expected extras but the suites,
of which there are 50, also have video recorders and hi-fi units. Two
rooms offer facilities for disabled guests. Bathrooms throughout are
in white marble and, while all have good showers, only some have bidets.
There are conference rooms for up to 320, banqueting to 300, and a well-
equipped Health Club. The main eating outlets at the Langham are
Memories of the Empire ('modern French with an Eastern flavour') and
Tsar's Restaurant whose offerings include caviar and several ways with
salmon. *Rooms 411. Gym, steam room, sauna.* AMERICAN EXPRESS *Access,*
Diners, Visa.

W8   Launceston Place   ↑   £65

Tel 071-937 6912   Fax 071-938 2412   **R**

1a Launceston Place Kensington W8 5RL   **Map 19 A4**

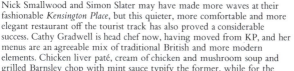

Nick Smallwood and Simon Slater may have made more waves at their fashionable *Kensington Place*, but this quieter, more comfortable and more elegant restaurant off the tourist track has also proved a considerable success. Cathy Gradwell is head chef now, having moved from KP, and her menus are an agreeable mix of traditional British and more modern elements. Chicken liver paté, cream of chicken and mushroom soup and grilled Barnsley chop with mint sauce typify the former, while for the slightly more adventurous palate she produces roasted red onions with peppers, almonds and Parmesan or chicken ramen with coriander, lemon grass and egg noodles. Puddings could include blood orange sorbet or an excellent steamed ginger pudding with butterscotch sauce. Sunday lunch is a particularly jolly occasion here, and the menu offers late-risers the appealing opportunity to catch up on breakfast with a starter such as kippers with lemon and herb butter and move straight on to a roast, sautéed calf's liver or grilled brill and scallops. A late supper menu has recently been introduced (10pm-11.30pm), comprising a dozen dishes (avocado salad with red peppers and grilled courgettes, prawn won tons with chili dip, grilled minute steak with chips) in the price range £3.50-£8.50 with no mimimum charge. Really sensible and easy to use wine list with half the bins under £20 a bottle; mostly French, some New World. *Seats 80. Private Room 30. L 12.30-2.30 (Sun to 3) D 7-11.30. Closed L Sat, D Sun, Bank Holidays. Set L & Set D (7pm-8pm) £13.50/£16.50.* AMERICAN EXPRESS® *Access, Visa.*

NW2   Laurent   £40

Tel 071-794 3603   **R**

428 Finchley Road NW2 2HY   **Map 16 B2**

In surroundings as simple as the menu Laurent Farrugia has run his couscous restaurant since 1983. This excellent North African dish of steamed semolina grain comes in various forms: *vegetarian* with basic vegetables, *complet* with added lamb and merguez, *royal* boosted to festive proportions by lamb chop and brochette; chicken and fish (halibut steak). The only starter is *brique à l'oeuf,* a deep-fried thin pastry parcel with a soft egg inside – fun but tricky to eat. North African wines stand up well to the hearty food. *Seats 36. L 12-2 D 6-11. Closed Sun, 3 weeks Aug.* AMERICAN EXPRESS® *Access, Visa.*

W11   Leith's   £115

Tel 071-229 4481   **R**

92 Kensington Park Road W11 2PN   **Map 18 A3**

The 25th anniversary of Prue Leith's civilised restaurant was marked by major refurbishment to give it a younger, brighter image. It's actually only two years younger than Alex Floyd, who continues attracting discerning diners with cooking that puts an innovative modern slant on classic British dishes. The hors d'oeuvre selection still arrives on a trolley and makes a splendid beginning to a meal that features careful cooking with due thought shown in the flavour combinations. A fixed-price menu, which changes weekly, runs alongside the seasonal à la carte, and there's a separate vegetarian menu. Leith's duckling (for two) remains a great favourite, along with grilled rib of beef with béarnaise, while typifying the more exciting aspect are the likes of ravioli of duck livers and Jerusalem artichokes with vegetable and tarragon broth, mousseline of fish wrapped in sole with a pea and clam sauce, or breast of guinea fowl filled with saffron risotto baked in puff pastry and served with a leek and champagne sauce. Note the splendid cheese trolley, fully deserving of our British Cheeseboard of the Year (London region) award. The dessert menu (rhubarb soufflé with vanilla ice cream, white chocolate truffle torte, apple and caramel millefeuille with apple and ginger sorbet) contains suggestions for dessert wines by bottle, half bottle or glass. Nick Tarayan's splendid and knowledgeably compiled wine list is everything that a list should be; it is not overpriced and wines are well chosen, with a good house selection, monthly specials and helpful tasting notes. No children under 7. *Seats 75. Parties 24. Private Room 40. D only 7.30-11.30. Closed 2 days Aug Bank Holiday, 4 days Christmas. Set D £30-£40.* AMERICAN EXPRESS *Access, Diners, Visa.*

NW1 Lemonia	£30
Tel 071-586 7454 Fax 071-483 2630	**R**
89 Regent's Park Road NW1 8UY	Map 16 B3

Roomy though this splendid Greek restaurant certainly is, it's still full to bursting at peak evening times. Outside and in there's a Mediterranean air, with lots of light and masses of hanging flower baskets. Table settings are very simple, so too the main menu, but Lemonia scores through reliability and the lovely relaxed atmosphere. Specialities are octopus, chicken shashlik, kleftiko and the meze selection at £9.50, which should satisfy even the biggest appetite. Look, too, for the special three-course lunch (Mon-Fri) and daily specials that supplement the regular menu. An offshoot, *Limanaki,* has opened opposite at no.154 (Lemonia's former premises). *Seats 140. Parties 18. Private Room 40. L 12-3 D 6-11.30. Set L £7.95. Closed L Sat, D Sun, 25 & 26 Dec. Access, Visa.*

SW11 Lena's	£40
Tel 071-228 3735	**R**
196 Lavender Hill SW11 1JA	Map 17 C5

Good neighbourhood Thai restaurant in comfortable surroundings. Comprehensive menu, strong on fish dishes. *Pla jian* (steamed fish, with ginger and spring onions), is a successful example of east-meets-west cuisine – the fish being salmon and the wrapping lollo rosso. Curries are a challenge – stick to the green, unless brave! *Seats 50. L 12.30-2.30 D 6.30-11 (Sun from 7). Closed L Sat, all Sun, Christmas, Easter, 1 Jan. Set L £12 Set D £15. Access, Visa.*

W8 Lexham Hotel	£56
Tel 071-373 6471 Fax 071-244 7827	**H**
32 Lexham Gardens W8 5JU	Map 19 A4

In a surprisingly peaceful garden square just off Cromwell Road and within walking distance of Kensington's shops and museums, the Lexham has been in the same family ownership since 1956 and provides good-value bed and breakfast accommodation. Cheapest rooms are without private facilities. There are several large 3- or 4-bedded rooms that are ideal for families. No dogs. *Rooms 66. Garden. Closed 22 Dec – 2 Jan.* AMERICAN EXPRESS *Access, Visa.*

W1 The Lexington	£65
Tel 071-434 3401	**R**
45 Lexington Street W1R 3LG	Map 18 D2

The dining room has a stark modern feel – bare wooden tables, turquoise walls and contemporary artwork – and serves a short carte with a fashionable Mediterranean flavour. Maybe merguez sausage with couscous or mussels in white wine to start; saffron risotto, roast hake with tomato and olive oil dressing or delicious chicken with morels to follow. A short list of rather standard desserts includes home-made ices. Good-value set menu, offering two courses and coffee for £10, is available in the evening. *Seats 42. Private Room 25. L 12-3 D 5-11. Closed L Sat, all Sun, Bank Holidays, 1 week Christmas. Set D £10.* AMERICAN EXPRESS *Access, Diners, Visa.*

W1   Lido   £40
Tel 071-437 4431   **R**
41 Gerrard Street Soho W1V 7LP   **Map 21 A2**

A maze of sparsely decorated rooms behind darkened glass in the middle
of Chinatown's main street. Even longer hours now attract night owls,
who flock here to eat from a wide-ranging menu that's particularly strong
on seafood, with sections for crab and lobster, scallops and squid, prawns,
eel and abalone. For parties on Fridays and Saturdays there's a minimum
charge of £20 a head. *Seats 140. Parties 50. Meals 11am-5am.*
Closed 25 Dec. Set D £10.50. AMERICAN EXPRESS *Access, Diners, Visa.*

W1   Lindsay House   £80
Tel 071-439 0450   Fax 071-581 2848   **R**
21 Romilly Street Soho W1V 5TG   **Map 21 A2**

A touch of country-house elegance in a Soho town house, where guests ring
the bell to gain admittance and take a drink in the comfortable lounge. The
menus, starting with the quick-service 2-course lunch, are staunchly British
and traditional, with the likes of game pie and Cumberland sauce, grilled
Dover sole and roast beef with Yorkshire pudding among the favourites.
Bread-and-butter pudding heads the dessert list, with Stilton and Welsh
rarebit as savoury alternatives. *Seats 36. Private Room 20. L 12.30-2.30*
(Sun & Bank Holidays till 2) D 6-12 (Sun & Bank Holidays 7-10).
Closed 25 & 26 Dec. Set L £10/£14.75. AMERICAN EXPRESS *Access, Diners, Visa.*

W1   Little Akropolis   £30
Tel 071-636 8198   **R**
10 Charlotte Street W1P 1HE   **Map 18 D2**

Long-established Greek restaurant in a street of restaurants. Meze for
variety, klefticon, moussaka (meat or vegetarian), kebabs and the other
Greek classics. Outside tables in summer. *Seats 30. L 12-2.30 D 6-10.30.*
Closed L Sat, all Sun, Bank Holidays, 2 weeks Aug. AMERICAN EXPRESS *Access,*
Diners, Visa.

W1   Lok Ho Fook   £35
Tel 071-437 2001   **R**
4 Gerrard Street Soho W1V 7LP   **Map 21 A2**

The menu at this simply appointed Chinatown restaurant covers
Cantonese, Peking and Szechuan dishes – from a choice of 16 soups to sea-
spice braised egg plant, fried squid cake with minced meat, belly pork and
yam hot pot, to braised carp with ginger and spring onion, and all the
usual favourites. There's also a pictorially descriptive dim sum menu for
daytime eaters (noon until 6pm). *Seats 100. Private Room 40. Meals*
12-11.45 (Sun 11.30-11.15). Closed 25 Dec. Set meals from £8 (min.
5 people). AMERICAN EXPRESS *Access, Diners, Visa.*

W1   London Chinatown   £50
Tel 071-437 3186   Fax 071-437 0336   **R**
27 Gerrard Street Soho W1V 7LP   **Map 21 A2**

At the Wardour Street end of Gerrard Street in the teeming heart
of London's Chinatown, this aptly named restaurant is one of the friendliest
in the area. 'Locals' and visitors interdine on a fine selection of Cantonese
and Peking-style food; aromatic crispy duck with pancakes is a favourite
here, as in many similar establishments, and the dim sum, served until early
evening, are particularly good. *Seats 150. Private Room 70. Meals 12-11.30.*
Closed 25 & 26 Dec. Set D from £7. AMERICAN EXPRESS *Access, Visa.*

W2   London Embassy   68%   £125

Tel 071-229 1212   Fax 071-229 2623   **H**

150 Bayswater Road W2 4RT   Map 18 A3

Modern accommodation overlooking Kensington Gardens, appealing to both business and tourist visitors. Children up to 16 stay free in parents' room. 36 of the rooms are designated non-smoking. There are several conference rooms, the largest of which can accommodate 120. Own car park (48 covered spaces). Jarvis Hotels. *Rooms 193.* AMERICAN EXPRESS *Access, Diners, Visa.*

We do not accept free meals or hospitality – our inspectors pay their own bills.

W1   London Hilton on Park Lane   75%   £282

Tel 071-493 8000   Fax 071-493 4957   **H**

22 Park Lane W1Y 4BE   Map 18 C3

London's first skyscraper hotel, now more than 30 years old, enjoys panoramic views of London from its prime Park Lane location. A few easy chairs and settees on a carpeted island, amidst a sea of marble in the spacious lobby, are the only lounge seating although the Victorian-themed St George's Bar offers comfortable leather tub chairs. Other public areas include an all-day brasserie, Trader Vic's Polynesian-styled restaurant in the basement and the Windows Roof restaurant and cocktail bar on the 28th floor. The views from the restaurant are undoubtedly magnificent, but on recent visits food has been disappointing. The Grand Ballroom can accommodate up to 1250 delegates/banqueters, and there are a dozen smaller rooms for functions/meetings. Standardised bedrooms are of a reasonable size, without feeling spacious, and have polished mahogany furniture, which neatly hides the multi-channel TV, and the convenience of telephones at both desk and bedside in addition to an extension in the marble bathroom. De luxe and Executive rooms are the same size as the others, though bathrooms are larger, but have newer lightwood furniture and more stylish soft furnishings. The latter also enjoy the privilege of a special Club Lounge with complimentary Continental breakfast, drinks, use of small meeting room, free local phone calls (from the lounge) and separate check-in and out. There are over 50 full suites, some luxurious, others in similar style to the standard rooms. Beds are turned down on request and there is an extensive 24hr room service menu. *Rooms 448. Keep-fit equipment, sauna, beauty & hair salon, brasserie (7am-12.45am Fri & Sat to 1.45am).* AMERICAN EXPRESS *Access, Diners, Visa.*

W1   London Marriott   77%   £228

Tel 071-493 1232   Fax 071-491 3201   **H**

Grosvenor Square W1A 4AW   Map 18 C3

A redbrick Georgian facade heralds the prime Mayfair location of this modern hotel (entrance in Duke Street). Public areas include a small foyer with sofas set in mirrored alcoves, a lounge and a panelled bar. Bedrooms are big, well designed and comfortable, with large double beds, armchairs and plenty of modern desk furniture. Greens and pinks predominate among the fairly sober soft furnishings. Each bedroom has its own air-conditioning. Superior Executive rooms and suites enjoy their own lounge and complimentary happy hour cocktails and Continental breakfast. Bathrooms are on the small side, but are comprehensively kitted out. Children up to 12 stay free in parents' room. No dogs. Conference/banqueting facilities for 1000/550. Considerable tariff reductions are sometimes available with advance booking. *Rooms 223. Keep-fit equipment, valeting, flower shop, lounge service (10.30am-1am).* AMERICAN EXPRESS *Access, Diners, Visa.*

W2   London Metropole Hotel   69%   £155

Tel 071-402 4141   Fax 071-724 8866   **H**
Edgware Road W2 1JU   Map 18 B2

The newest part hosts impressive conference facilities (up to 1300
delegates), an open-plan marble lobby and lounge, a well-fitted leisure
centre, two restaurants and the most recent bedrooms. There are 547
Executive rooms, 175 Crown rooms and 20 suites. Crown bedrooms and
suites are attractively shaped and furnished: seating areas, mini-bars and
complimentary newspapers are features, and most bathrooms have separate
showers. 200 rooms are designated non-smoking. *Rooms 742. Indoor
swimming pool, keep-fit equipment, sauna, spa bath, solarium, kiosk, coffee shop
(6.30am-11pm).* AMERICAN EXPRESS *Access, Diners, Visa.*

W1   London Mews Hilton on Park Lane   68%   £179

Tel 071-493 7222   Fax 071-629 9423   **H**
2 Stanhope Row Park Lane W1Y 7HE   Map 18 C3

Close to Park Lane, tucked away behind the London Hilton this is a small
(for the area) hotel with the look of a club or town house. 24hr room
service. Most recent improvements are a new air-conditioning system and
double-glazing in all bedrooms. *Rooms 72.* AMERICAN EXPRESS *Access,
Diners, Visa.*

W14   London Olympia Hilton   66%   £125

Tel 071-603 3333   Fax 071-603 4846   **H**
380 Kensington High Street W14 8NL   Map 17 B4

The closest hotel to the Olympia exhibition halls, a busy conference and
tour group hotel with a choice of standard or superior Plaza rooms. State-
of-the-art TVs and video systems. Refurbishment of bedrooms continues.
Children up to 14 stay free in parents' room. NCP parking available
beneath the hotel. *Rooms 405. Brasserie (6.30am-10.30pm).* AMERICAN EXPRESS
Access, Diners, Visa.

W6   Los Molinos   £35

Tel 071-603 2229   **R**
127 Shepherds Bush Road W6 7LP   Map 17 B4

A popular pine-furnished restaurant by Brook Green, serving a wide
variety of tapas, almost all available in two sizes. Marinated anchovies,
seafood pancakes, battered squid, crab-stuffed mushrooms and garlic prawns
are just a few from the fish section, while on the meat side of the menu are
pork fillet stuffed with Gruyère, cured mountain ham, kidneys in sherry,
coriander lamb croquettes and rabbit Canary Islands-style. There's also
an excellent vegetarian choice. *Seats 80. Parties 12. Private Room 42. L 12-3
D 6-11.30 (Sat from 7). Closed L Sat, all Sun, Bank Holidays, 2 weeks
Christmas.*

SW5   Lou Pescadou   £50

Tel 071-370 1057   **R**
241 Old Brompton Road Earls Court SW5 9HP   Map 19 A5

The nautical decor points to the main attraction, which runs from oysters,
mussels (marinière and stuffed) or fish soup to daily specials such as red
mullet, skate or an excellent *brandade de morue*. The *plateau Pescadou*
(oysters, clams, langoustines) is a popular dish, and others are omelettes,
pasta, pizza and pissaladière; steaks for the red-blooded. Lou Pescadou is just
by the junction with Earls Court Road. Waiters are at their best operating
in their native French. *Seats 55. Private Room 40. L 12-3 D 7-12.
Closed Summer Sun (phone to check) & 10 days Christmas. Set L £8.*
AMERICAN EXPRESS *Access, Diners, Visa.*

SW1   The Lowndes Hyatt Hotel   76%   £233

Tel 071-823 1234   Fax 071-235 1154   **H**

Lowndes Street Belgravia SW1X 9ES   Map 19 C4

The Lowndes Hyatt is the smaller, more intimate sister hotel to the *Hyatt Carlton Tower* in the neighbouring square (where guests may use the Peak Health Club and charge restaurant meals to their room here). Public rooms are limited to a small limed-oak panelled lounge area partly open to the lobby and Brasserie 21, open for breakfast, lunch and dinner, and also operating as a bar for cocktails or pre-dinner drinks, with pavement tables in summer. Bedrooms are appealing with good-quality darkwood furniture, chintzy floral curtains and more masculine check-patterned bedcovers over duvets. All are air-conditioned, but controllably so (and the windows open), and have smart, marble bathrooms with good towelling. There are five splendidly-appointed suites. Beds are turned down in the evening, but room service ends at midnight. 32 of the rooms are designated non-smoking. The wood-panelled Library meeting room overlooks a garden/terrace and holds up to 25 people in theatre-style or 14 round a boardroom table. No dogs. *Rooms 78. Brasserie (7am-11.15pm), tennis.* AMERICAN EXPRESS *Access, Diners, Visa.*

EC3   Luc's Restaurant & Brasserie   £50

Tel 071-621 0666   Fax 071-336 7315   **R**

17-22 Leadenhall Market EC3V 1LR   Map 20 D2

Well located in the very centre of Leadenhall Market, this busy French brasserie is open Monday to Friday for lunch (dinner by arrangement for large parties only). Food is well prepared and deftly served, from fish soup with rouille and croutons, goat's cheese salad and quail stuffed with foie gras to grilled prawns, monkfish in a lettuce leaf with vermouth sauce, and grilled steaks served with béarnaise sauce. Classic desserts include profiteroles and crepes Suzette. *Seats 150. L only 11.30-3. Closed Sat, Sun, Bank Holidays, 5 days Christmas.* AMERICAN EXPRESS *Access, Diners, Visa.*

SE19   Luigi's   £65

Tel 081-670 1843   **R**

129 Gipsy Hill SE19 1QS   Map 17 D6

The standard of cooking here remains reliable and consistent. The long-standing menu offers daily specials to supplement the choice of Italian classics. There are fairly few pasta dishes (linguine with clam sauce "Southern style" and home-made cannelloni are favourites available as either starter or main course) but a decent choice of antipasti, fish, meat and poultry in generally familiar preparations. Between Tooting and Eltham. *Seats 65. Private Room 25. L 12-3 D 6-10.30. Closed L Sat, all Sun, Bank Holidays.* AMERICAN EXPRESS *Access, Diners, Visa.*

WC2   Magno's Brasserie   £70

Tel 071-836 6077   Fax 071-379 6184   **R**

65a Long Acre Covent Garden WC2E 9JH   Map 21 B2

Bustling, Parisian-style brasserie offering good food served by jovial French waiters in relaxing surroundings. Moules marinière, Roquefort in puff pastry or smoked salmon to start, followed perhaps by calf's liver and bacon, coq au vin (here made with free-range chicken) and fillet steak with béarnaise sauce. Sweets could include strawberry tart and crème brulée. Good-value set menus and blackboard specials. A useful place for a pre- or post-theatre meal. *Seats 55. L 12-2.30 D 5.30-11.30. Closed L Sat, all Sun, Bank Holidays, 4 days Christmas. Set L & D £13.50/£16.50.* AMERICAN EXPRESS *Access, Diners, Visa.*

SW7   Majlis   £35
Tel 071-584 3476   **R**
32 Gloucester Road SW7 4RB   Map 19 B4

Same ownership as *Memories of India* a few doors away, with a similar
menu based around lamb, chicken and prawns (plus a fair vegetarian
choice). A la carte, or set menus for one upwards. ***Seats*** *32. L 12-2.30 D
6-12. Closed 25 & 26 Dec. Set meals from £14.15.* **AMERICAN EXPRESS** *Access,
Diners, Visa.*

W8   Malabar   £40
Tel 071-727 8800   **R**
27 Uxbridge Street Notting Hill W8 7TQ   Map 18 A3

Indian restaurant behind the Coronet cinema, with a look and style all its
own. The look is Mediterranean (an Italian restaurant was on the site
previously) but the home-style cooking features not only familiar dishes
but some rarely seen elsewhere. Among the latter are devilled *kaleja*
(charcoal-grilled marinated chicken livers), *hiran* (slices of venison
marinated in tamarind), *long* chicken (cooked with cloves and ginger), and
kaddu (pumpkin fried in butter and fresh herbs). Sunday buffet lunch
£6.95. Menu prices all include service. ***Seats*** *56. Parties 15.
Private Room 20. L 12-2.45 (Sun from 12.30) D 6-11.15. Closed 4 days Xmas,
1 week Aug. Set meals from £11.75. Access, Visa.*

SW6   Mamta   £30
Tel 071-736 5914   **R**
692 Fulham Road London SW6 5SA   Map 17 B5

At the Parsons Green end of Fulham Road, a small restaurant with
something of a spartan air created by quarry-tiled floor and mushroom-
coloured walls hung with earthy-coloured Indian art. "Pure Indian food",
from a partnership of chefs previously at *Mandeer*, has an ethereal quality –
the cooking of vegetables and exotic spices creating a myriad of stunning
flavours and textures completely obviating the need for meat. The selection
of dishes is long and, considering only vegetables are used, surprisingly
varied. Traditional Indian set meals represent excellent value. All the food
is served on and eaten off polished stainless-steel platters with helpful and
amiable service making the experience a highly enjoyable one. ***Seats*** *42.
Parties 20. L 12.30-2.15 D 6-10.15. Closed 25 & 26 Dec, 31 Jan (?).*
AMERICAN EXPRESS *Access, Diners, Visa.*

We endeavour to be as up-to-the-minute as possible, but inevitably
some changes to key personnel may occur at restaurants and hotels
after the Guide goes to press.   •

W2   Mandarin Kitchen   £50
Tel 071-727 9012   **R**
14 Queensway W2 3RX   Map 18 A3

A spacious restaurant with twin arched Artex ceilings, plastic plants and
quaint 70s' mauve vinyl seating. The speciality is seafood with lobsters
heading the list and crabs and king prawns also prominent. The menu
additionally runs through the gamut of familiar dishes, everything being
competently and very enjoyably prepared with good use of fresh spicing.
Quiet at lunchtimes but booking advisable in the evenings, when it's at its
best. ***Seats*** *110. Parties 20. Meals 12-11.30. Closed 25 & 26 Dec. Set meals
from £8.90.* **AMERICAN EXPRESS** *Access, Diners, Visa.*

W1	Mandeville Hotel	62%	£130

Tel 071-935 5599   Fax 071-935 9588

H

Mandeville Place W1M 6BE

Map 18 C2

Just north of Oxford Street, a practical hotel with an all-day coffee shop, two bars and a late night bar-lounge. Children up to 12 stay free in parents' room. *Rooms 165. Coffee shop (12-10.30).* AMERICAN EXPRESS *Access, Diners, Visa.*

EC1	Mange-2	NEW	£70

Tel 071-250 0035

R

2-3 Cowcross Street EC1M 6DR

Map 16 D3

A stone's throw from Smithfield market, this restaurant, having arisen from the embers of an old sausage factory, is a designer's paradise. As well as Dominique Theval's excellent cooking there are plenty of strange metal sculptures and other artworks to keep you amused between courses. Terrine of bouillabaisse with saffron dressing, spinach salad with avocado, mozzarella and crispy bacon and warm lamb's sweetbreads with char-grilled aubergine set the tone. Follow with breast of Barbary duck roasted with apple and spices, fillet of seabass with ratatouille or fried calf's liver with a delicious sauce based on raspberry vinegar. Simple desserts – our crème brulée with thyme seemed to be lacking its herbal flavouring, but was otherwise perfect. A short brasserie-type menu is available throughout the day. A pianist plays from 5 o'clock every day. Short, but thoughtful, wine list. *Seats 65. Private Room 25. L 12-2.30 D 6.30-10.30. Closed L Sat, all Sun, Bank Holidays, 1 week Christmas. Set D £12.50.* AMERICAN EXPRESS *Access, Diners, Visa.*

W11	Manzara		£25

Tel 071-727 3062

R

24 Pembridge Road Notting Hill Gate London W11 3HL

Map 18 A3

In the window is a mouthwatering array of home-baked pastries, beyond it a smart modern restaurant serving Turkish dishes. The house speciality is a selection of hot and cold hors d'oeuvre. Main courses – cooked in foil, casseroled or charcoal grilled – are served with pommes noisettes or Basmati rice. *Seats 40. Meals 8am-midnight (Sun from 10).* AMERICAN EXPRESS *Access, Diners, Visa.*

WC2	Manzi's		£70

Tel 071-734 0224   Fax 071-437 4864

R

1 Leicester Street WC2H 7BL

Map 21 A2

The Manzi family came here in 1928 and down the years this has become one of London's best known and best loved seafood restaurants. The ground-floor room and the quieter upstairs Cabin Room have similar menus, mainly traditional in their range, from oysters, whitebait, jellied or stewed eels and calamares to moules marinière, scallops, trout and sole. The last are a speciality, served grilled, meunière or Colbert on the bone, or filleted with a variety of sauces. The restaurant has 15 basic letting bedrooms (rates start at £63 for a double). *Seats 200. Parties 20. L 12.30-3 D 5.30-11.30 Closed Sun, Christmas.* AMERICAN EXPRESS *Access, Diners, Visa.*

W1	Marble Arch Marriott	68%	£189

Tel 071-723 1277   Fax 071-402 0666

H

134 George Street W1H 6DN

Map 18 C2

Major pluses at the Marble Arch Marriott include a free underground car park (70 cars), health and leisure facilities and a location handy for West End shopping and some of the major tourist sights. Darkwood clubby decor gives an elegant feel throughout. The Executive bedrooms are the most comfortable, with three telephones (one in the bathroom), mini-bar and quality tea/coffee-making facilities. The Executive lounge provides free soft drinks and Continental breakfasts. Rooms in general are of a good size, and many are ideal for families. *Rooms 239. Indoor swimming pool, keep-fit equipment, sauna, spa bath, solarium, whirlpool bath, beauty salon, gift shop, coffee shop(7am-10pm).* AMERICAN EXPRESS *Access, Diners, Visa.*

SW1   Restaurant Marco Pierre White   ★★★   NEW   £175

Tel 071-259 5380   Fax 071-235 4552   **R**

66 Knightsbridge London SW1Y 7LA   Map 19 C4

Heralded by a large dark blue canopy which extends American-style over the pavement boldly bearing in large gold letters the simple inscriptions Marco Pierre White and The Restaurant. Occupying part of the Hyde Park Hotel at street level, the restaurant has succeeded in making this the culinary high spot of Knightsbridge and London. Marco, once known as the enfant terrible of British cooking, is now reaching far greater heights and has begun to surround himself with the trappings of great style and luxury. The interior of his restaurant has soft cream-coloured walls hung with some exceptionally fine works of art. These are set off by discreet lighting and grandly extravagant arrangements of exotic blooms. His erstwhile irascible temperament has bated, though he still isn't one to suffer fools gladly. Salvador Dali is quoted on the menu: 'at 6 I wanted to be a chef, at 7, Napoleon, and my ambitions have been growing ever since'. Marco is a man of growing stature with an immense, almost unbounded energy. He is constantly striving for change with new and exciting concepts forever at his fingertips; a showman, certainly, but not one given to gimmickry or unnecessary accoutrements. Instead, he brings together ingredients in simple, supremely subtle fusions of flavour and texture. His menu offers a stunning selection of starters followed by an almost bewildering choice of main dishes and to finish a plate of wonderful French cheeses and/or exquisite desserts. Starters include an ultra-refreshing tian of crab layered with tomato and avocado served with a vinaigrette of tomato; soft grilled scallops sprinkled with best-quality sea salt and surrounded by a pool of intense squid ink sauce, or a fricassee of crayfish and chanterelles in a supremely light frothed-up creamy extract of the mushrooms. Fish is superbly handled, as in escalope of brill viennoise, the fish layered with spinach and with a crunchy crumb topping, buttered noodles and a sabayon of grain mustard. Offal is beautifully executed, caramelised calf's sweetbreads with almonds, fricassee of wild mushrooms and courgettes with a sherry vinegar sauce being typical. His roast fillet of lamb, cooked to almost melting tenderness, is surrounded by a mix of Provençal vegetables with roast garlic and a superb lamb jus; the most delicious Bresse pigeon with garlic confit, buttered cabbage with bacon and a thyme jus is another example of his affinity with taste and composition. Desserts such as the chocolate leaf 'box' filled with chocolate mousse and brandied cherries, hot raspberry soufflé or caramelised apple tart topped with vanilla ice cream and a dribbling of caramel are yet further demonstrations of his artistry. Serious wine list and mostly serious prices, though there are a few value-for-money bottles to be had. Small selection of really well chosen New World wines; half bottles a little thin on the ground; customers would benefit from a recommended house list. *Seats 50. Parties 12. L 12-2.30 D 7-11.30. Closed L Sat, all Sun, first 2 weeks in Aug, Bank Holidays. Set L £25 Set D £65. Access, Visa.*

WC1   The Marlborough   69%   £167

Tel 071-636 5601   Fax 071-636 0532   **H**

9-14 Bloomsbury Street WC1B 3QD   Map 21 B1

In the heart of Bloomsbury, just off New Oxford Street and close to the British Museum, the restored Edwardian-style facade gives a good impression of the mix of modern amenity and old-fashioned comfort within. Liveried porters, fresh flowers and green leather settees greet guests in the lobby, beyond which there is a mix of both quiet and busy public rooms. Porcelain and polished brass lamps add a touch of elegance to the bedrooms, two floors of which are designated non-smoking. Four rooms have been adapted for disabled guests. Conference/banqueting facilities for 180/260. No dogs. Edwardian Hotels. **Rooms 169.** AMERICAN EXPRESS *Access, Diners, Visa.*

W2	Maroush	£70
Tel 071-723 0773		**R**
21 Edgware Road W2		Map 18 C3

One of London's most luxurious Lebanese restaurants, serving a standard range of above-average hot and cold starters and mainly charcoal-grilled main courses of lamb and chicken. Houmus, quail and stuffed lamb are among the specialities. Cover charge £1.50 lunchtime, £3 in the evening. Minimum charge £38 after 10pm. No cheques. *Seats 95. Parties 95. Meals 12 noon-2am.* AMERICAN EXPRESS *Access, Diners, Visa.*
Also at:
Maroush II 38 Beauchamp Place SW3. Tel 071-581 5434.   Map 18 C3
Open till 5am.
Maroush III 62 Seymour Street W1. Tel 071-724 5024.   Map 19 C4
Open till 1am.

W1	Masako	£100
Tel 071-935 1579		**R**
6 St Christopher's Place W1M 5HB		Map 18 C2

Just off Oxford Street (almost opposite the top of South Molton Street, by Bond Street tube station), a delightful Japanese restaurant with friendly, attentive staff and traditional decor of black lacquered tables, open screens and red plush chairs. A fine selection of set meals provides good value, using quality ingredients and showing delicacy in preparation. The set lunch menus include an appetiser, soy bean soup, something grilled or boiled, a main course, rice, pickles and dessert. *Seats 80. Parties 18. Private Room 35. L 12-2.30 D 6-10. Closed Sun, Bank Holidays. Set L from £20 Set D from £35.* AMERICAN EXPRESS *Access, Diners, Visa.*

W1	May Fair Inter-Continental	81%	£270
Tel 071-629 7777 Fax 071-629 1459			**HR**
Stratton Street W1A 2AN			Map 18 C3

Since her arrival three years ago, General Manager Dagmar Woodward (without doubt one of London's best) has subtly improved this surprisingly intimate hotel, despite the large number of bedrooms it has, 50 of which are suites, including the refurbished May Fair, Maharajah and Penthouse, the latter with a small roof garden and private lift from the street. There's a tranquil atmosphere in the public areas, especially in the lounge, where a harpist plays each afternoon while tea is served. The clubby May Fair bar, with its red leather seating, is a popular rendezvous for people to enjoy English pub fayre, while the smaller Chateau cocktail bar (open to 2am with live piano music) which adjoins the restaurant has a whole wall displaying signed photos of showbiz personalities who have either stayed at the hotel or performed at the theatre (recently refurbished and seating almost 300 for conferences) next door. The spacious bedrooms, many with seating areas, are decorated in two different styles, English or French; the former with green leather armchairs and traditional darkwood furniture, the latter with softer and more contemporary decor. Splendid bathrooms, some with separate walk-in shower as well as bath tub, offer the usual luxury toiletries, generous-sized towels and bathrobes. Extensive round-the-clock room service can provide hot meals at all hours. The business centre is fully staffed during the day, even renting out mobile phones, and the hotel benefits greatly from its luxurious basement health club with swimming pool – a rarity in the West End. Children up to 14 stay free in parents' room (several adjoining). Several meeting rooms, with the Crystal Ballroom accommodating 300. No dogs. *Rooms 287. Indoor swimming pool, sauna, solarium, keep-fit equipment, beauty salon, news kiosk, valeting, café (7-11).* AMERICAN EXPRESS® *Access, Diners, Visa.*

The Chateau £80

Reflecting the slant towards English cooking, 'Le' has become 'The' in the restaurant's name! In an almost Italianate setting, albeit a particularly smart one, executive chef Michael Coaker's cooking pleases, though with just a little more care (additional shellfish on the lunchtime buffet perhaps and attention to the sweet trolley towards the end of service) it could really hit the high spots. A one-page carte includes the chef's daily-changing fixed-price lunch and dinner menus (open seafood ravioli with crab sauce, poached loin of lamb with courgette couscous, vanilla parfait with a strawberry sorbet and a summer fruit coulis) and some dozen choices of first and main courses, such as casserole of seafood with pasta shells, tomato and basil; fish cakes with Pommery mustard sauce; perfectly cooked risotto with grilled peppers and mushrooms; and rosettes of beef with polenta mash and parsley purée. Good cheeses from the trolley and desserts much enjoyed recently were a cassis mousse on a dark chocolate base, and vanilla parfait with strawberry sorbet and summer fruit coulis. Decent coffee, petits fours, and an excellent, sensible wine list with some fair prices and quality wines by the glass. Richard Briggs leads from the front, so service is notably slick. There's a 'special' menu at £25 which includes house wine, and the Sunday jazz brunch buffet includes either a Bucks Fizz or a Bloody Mary. *Seats 65. L 12.30-2.30 D 6.30-10.30 (7-10 Sun). Closed L Sat. Set L £22.50 (from £19 Sun) Set D £29.50.*

SW7	**Memories of India**	£40
Tel 071-589 6450		**R**
18 Gloucester Road SW7 4RB		Map 19 B4

The shiny menu complete with illustrations shows you exactly what to expect at this neighbourhood Indian restaurant and reality at this neighbourhood restaurant, with ceiling fans and rattan chairs, lives up to the expectations. There is the usual range of tandoori and karahi dishes plus set meals (thalis). Sister restaurant to *Majlis*, a few doors away. *Seats 75. Private Room 30. L 12-2.30 D 5.30-11.30. Closed 25 Dec. Set L from £6.95 Set D £14.50.* AMERICAN EXPRESS® *Access, Diners, Visa.*

W1	**Le Meridien**	**84%**	£271
Tel 071-734 8000 Fax 071-437 3574			**HR**
Piccadilly W1V 0BH			Map 18 D3

One of the most centrally located London hotels, and without doubt one of the very best, and a haven of peace and style in the bustle of Piccadilly. A harpist plays under the chandeliers in the grand Lounge during afternoon tea, while a pianist tinkles away in the Burlington bar (open to 1am except Sundays) which evokes the aura of a gentleman's club with its baize-green decor. Bedroom decor is tasteful, with style and quality in equal evidence: pink and turquoise are dominant colours, with flowery quilted bedspreads and reproduction pieces featuring; the marbled bathrooms are nothing short of immaculate; bathrobes are, of course, provided. 4th-floor rooms are reserved for non-smokers. Under-12s stay free in parents' room. Afternoon tea is served in the elegant Tea Lounge (3-6pm). Impeccable service. Membership of Champneys health-club downstairs is free to guests – the fun-dungeon is a real plus point. Conference and banqueting facilities for 250. *Rooms 263. Indoor swimming pool, plunge pools, Turkish baths & sauna, spa bath, solarium, gym & dance studio, squash, snooker, beauty & hair salons, news kiosk & gift shop, coffee shop (7am-11.30pm).* AMERICAN EXPRESS® *Access, Diners, Visa.*

See over

Oak Room Restaurant   ★★   £135

A grand restaurant of majestic proportion and among London's most elegant, with walls panelled in limed oak inlaid with enormous mirrors and surmounted by festoons of classically-inspired gilt mouldings. From the ornate plaster ceiling hang six huge identical crystal chandeliers, with added decoration provided by large Chinese vases bursting with exceptional flower arrangements. Alain Marechal is now the chef: previously at *L'Habit Blanc*, the restaurant at *Le Meridien* in Nice, he joins consultant chef Michel Lorain of *La Cote St Jacques* at Joigny. Lorain comes over three or four times yearly to implement changes to his menus. Now, this formidable twosome offer some of the most exciting cooking in the capital. While current menus are Lorain's, Marechal will gradually introduce a few more Mediterranean dishes of his own as the seasons change. A carte of superb sophistication is supplemented by a truly stunning *menu gourmand* of seven perfectly balanced and remarkably light courses, each very ably demonstrating the kitchen's immense skills and artistry. Our latest dinner was preceded by a tiny appetiser of the most marvellous and intensely flavoured lobster mousse. Next came a terrine of milk-fed lamb set with a fine dice of Provençal vegetables in a light jelly. To follow, a magical combination of fresh white crabmeat steamed in a tender Savoy cabbage leaf was served with a white wine and crab sauce. The fish course was a melting fillet of steamed sea bass set on black noodles and garnished with baby clams in a sauce delicately infused with coriander. Braised knuckle of veal as a main course came with a garnish of caviar and bone marrow as well as with tiny pieces of bacon and vegetables; the combination of the caviar and the veal was a surprising but perfect one. After a selection of prime French cheeses came two desserts, the first so good as almost to defy description, but here goes: paper-thin slices of apple baked to brittle crispness are set in a soft, not too acidic pineapple sorbet and served with a syrup flavoured with vanilla and, an inspired touch, lemon grass. Finally a passion fruit soufflé of flawless consistency, beautifully risen and served with a hot passion fruit sauce was a fitting climax to a meal of tremendous enjoyment; service is by a skilled team headed by the affable maitre d', Jean Quero – good to see him back in London. One wouldn't expect a French-owned hotel to offer a particularly extensive selection of New World wines, but, California apart, surely they could do better than they do? Undeniably good, but mostly expensive French wines, with a short house (called 'business') selection. *Seats 50. L 12-2 D 7-10.30. Closed L Sat, all Sun, 4 weeks Aug. Set L £24.50 Set D £28/£46.*

Terrace Garden Restaurant   £65

Two floors up, overlooking busy Piccadilly, is the lovely, leafy, split-levelconservatory-style restaurant, the front, lower section of which is reserved for non-smokers. Served from breakfast until dinner, dishes range from smoked salmon, shellfish bisque, club sandwich, burger and asparagus omelette to grills, calamari with noodles and calf's liver with artichokes, button onions and bacon in a Sauternes jus. Sunday brunch starts with Kir royal or non-alcoholic fruit punch and proceeds via the buffet and an entrée to dessert and coffee. Fine wines by the glass from a Cruvinet machine. *Seats 130. Parties 30. Meals 7am-11.30pm (Sun 11.30am-2.30pm). Set meals from £18.50 Sun brunch £23 (under-12s half-price). Closed Bank Holidays.*

W1   Merryfield House   £48

Tel 071-935 8326	
42 York Street W1H 1FN	Map 18 C2

Run by the same family since 1958 and ideally located for the West End, just off Gloucester Place and five minutes walk from Baker Street underground station. Full English breakfast is served in the small but comfortable and clean bedrooms, all of which have smart bathrooms en suite. Unlicensed. *Rooms 7. Closed 2 weeks Feb. No credit cards.*

EC1   Le Mesurier   £65

Tel 071-251 8117   Fax 071-608 3504   **R**

113 Old Street EC1V 9JR   Map 16 D3

Competent cooking in a small, intimate and individualistic restaurant.
Lunchtime brings three choices per course, typified by herb brioche filled
with chicken livers and bacon, halibut escalopes with courgettes and cheese
sauce, a classic entrecote bordelaise and pancakes with honey and hazelnuts.
*Seats 25. L only 12-3 (Open in the evening by arrangement for party bookings).
Closed Sat & Sun, Bank Holidays, 10 days Christmas.* AMERICAN EXPRESS *Access,
Diners, Visa.*

SW1   Mijanou   ↑   £95

Tel 071-730 4099   Fax 071-823 6402   **R**

143 Ebury Street SW1W 9QN   Map 19 C5

Sonia and Neville Blech have run their intimate little restaurant since
1980, with Sonia in the kitchen and Neville at front of house organising
the service and indulging his passion for wine. Sonia's style is classically
based, French-inspired and quite distinctive. All of the five dishes at each
course are priced the same (starter £9, main £16, dessert £5). Start,
perhaps, with terrine of oxtail and foie gras on a muscat and passion fruit
jelly served with apple and onion relish, carpaccio of duck with a light pear
and celeriac yoghurt mousse or roulade of sole, tiger prawns and leeks with
a saffron and seafood sauce. Lamb, quail, beef fillet and veal entrecote
might offer a good choice for the main course. Montelimar (honey,
pistachio nuts and almond bavarois), Caribbean pancakes and home-made
sorbets among the desserts. Good-value 2/3-course lunch might offer spicy
mussels or mousseline of asparagus in puff pastry with tomato sauce to start,
followed by lamb cutlets with flageolet beans and pesto or lasagne
basquaise, finishing with iced bavarois of coffee with Tia Maria and pecan
nuts or passion fruit tart. Not so much a wine list, more a wine company,
since you can buy most wines enjoyed in the restaurant by the case. Neville
Blech has cleverly matched dishes on the menu with a suitable wine (or
three!), listed by style. It's a super and comprehensive list, one of the best
around, with helpful notes and quite fair prices. The ground-floor room
is non-smoking. Later evening last orders if booked. *Seats 28.
Private Room 24. L 12-2 D 7-10. Closed Sat & Sun, Bank Holidays, last
3 weeks Aug, 2 weeks Christmas, 10 days Easter. Set L £13.50/£16.50
Set D £21 or £25/£30 & £35.* AMERICAN EXPRESS *Access, Diners, Visa.*

Note that all telephone numbers with area codes starting with 0
will start 01 from 16 April 1995.

W8   The Milestone   78%   £210

Tel 071-917 1000   Fax 071-917 1010   **H**

1-2 Kensington Court W8 5DL   Map 19 A4

A Victorian mansion opposite Kensington Gardens, totally transformed
a few years ago into a hotel of considerable style and class. Original
fireplaces, ornate windows and carved wood panelling have been carefully
restored and bedrooms, individually decorated to high standards, most with
antiques and four-poster beds, offer modern comforts of air-conditioning,
two telephone lines, private fax machines, satellite TV and VCR. Suites
have been cleverly designed, creating mezzanine levels in the 24-foot-high
rooms which overlook the Park. 24hr room service includes a creative
menu for breakfast. Nothing here is left to chance, from the
complimentary basket of fruit on arrival to valet parking (charged at meter
rate) or the house doctor. *Rooms 57. Gym, sauna, spa bath, solarium, coffee
shop (24hrs).* AMERICAN EXPRESS *Access, Diners, Visa.*

SW1   Mimmo d'Ischia   £90

Tel 071-730 5406   Fax 071-730 9439   **R**

61 Elizabeth Street Eaton Square SW1   **Map 19 C5**

Sound, straightforward Italian cooking – but at a serious price – in
a durable and fashionable restaurant whose walls are adorned with signed
photographs of celebrity visitors. Stracciatella, calzone, gnocchi,
an unusually good selection of fish, osso buco, and sweets from a trolley;
spare ribs a speciality! *Seats 90. Private Room 30. L 12-2.30 D 7-11.30.
Closed Sun, Bank Holidays.* AMERICAN EXPRESS *Access, Diners, Visa.*

W1   Ming   ★   £55

Tel 071-734 2721   **R**

35 Greek Street Soho W1V 5LN   **Map 21 A2**

On the corner of Greek Street and Old Compton Street, Ming is thus
slightly adrift from the throb of Chinatown. Its menus are particularly
interesting, based on Northern Chinese cuisine and specialising in prawns,
duck and lamb. Fish is also a popular choice, mainly plaice, lemon sole and
cod. Ming specials include fresh fennel with fish slices or squid, steamed
white fish with salted turnip julienne and duck with aubergine braised
in a hot pot. From the à la carte selection come beef with coriander and
onion pancakes, lettuce-wrapped Mongolian lamb and shredded pork with
raw chili and preserved Szechuan vegetables. The Ming bowl menu offers
dishes which are complete meals in themselves: among these are hot and
sour noodles, Empress beef on rice and steamed or grilled mantou (bread)
with chopped pork or shredded duck with winter green. Friendly staff are
another plus at one of London's best Chinese restaurants. Tables are set
on the pavement in very good weather. A carefully chosen wine list
includes a good choice of champagnes and New World wines
recommended for certain dishes. *Seats 70. Meals 12-11.45 (Bank Holidays
from 5pm). Closed Sun (open Chinese New Year), 25 & 26 Dec.*
AMERICAN EXPRESS *Access, Diners, Visa.*

W1   Mirabelle   ★★   £110

Tel 071-499 4636   Fax 071-499 5449   **R**

56 Curzon Street Mayfair W1Y 8DL   **Map 18 C3**

Re-opened in 1992 under Japanese ownership, setting high standards
of cooking, the Mirabelle continues in top form. The basement setting
is unusual, uniting traditional English (dressed Cornish crab, hot or cold
asparagus, calf's liver and bacon, poached salmon with parsley potatoes),
French and Japanese dining under the same roof (there's even a Japanese tea
room). As you walk towards the dining room, crossing the bar down the
long carpeted corridors, you catch the appetising whiffs from the two
separate teppanyaki rooms. Surprisingly, it is not the basement dining room
that one expects when descending the staircase from the Curzon Street
entrance; it opens on to a terrace and is bathed with light from the glass-
panelled roof. Dinners are not served outside, just drinks. The classic decor
of warm pink tones, velvet bergères and subdued evening lighting sets the
mood for French haute cuisine. The starting point is a traditional menu
from which chef Michael Croft works up a perfect mix of flavours and
textures. The delicate balance of soft and crisp takes an important place
in his cooking with dishes like *galette de pommes de terre et foie gras aux
champignons sauvages et échalotes*, or *chausson de céléri-rave aux morilles
et truffes fraiches* (a crisp parcel of morels and truffles in a Madeira sauce).
Most impressive is his fantastic technique of poaching, cooking salmon
to perfection (keeping the centre raw and warm, an amazing combination
of tastes with its cooked envelope) or giving a new dimension to a fillet
of beef by poaching it in a delectable mushroom broth. A dish of great
luxury and refinement is foie gras 'Mirabelle' – a trio of goose livers
marinated with sea salt, chilled *en terrine* and pan-fried. Separate vegetarian

menu with dishes such as feuilleté of asparagus with leeks and chervil butter or cannelloni with mushrooms. The fixed-price *menu du jour* offers three or so dishes at each course and includes half a bottle of wine per person; *menu surprise* (£45) offers a six-course, daily-changing menu for whole table parties. There's a very grand though not really informative selection of French wines. Since the red bordeaux are listed by vintage (an 1874 magnum of Ch. Lafite Rothschild is a snip at £3500 – plus service ?!), it falls upon the sommelier to advise on which are the best years. *Seats 100. Parties 12. Private Room 30. L 12-2 D 6.30-10.30. Closed L Sat, all Sun, Bank Holidays, 2 weeks Aug, 1 week Christmas. Set L £15/£18 Set D from £28.* AMERICAN EXPRESS *Access, Diners, Visa.*

NW3	**Mr Ke** ↑	**£42**

Tel 071-722 8474   **R**

7 New College Parade Finchley Road NW3 5EP   **Map 16 B3**

Unassuming and simply decorated premises with some of the most genial waitresses of any Chinese restaurants anywhere. The quite lengthy menu specialises in the cooking of Peking, Szechuan and Hunan but no matter which region the characteristics are true, with careful seasoning and fresh ingredients producing dishes of very noteworthy flavours and textures. Sea bass soup – a wonderful light soup with a few small pieces of soft sea bass – has a delicate fragrance imparted by judicious use of fresh coriander and makes a classic accompaniment to a full Chinese meal which could also include carefully de-veined Szechuan prawns with cashew nuts, Peking duck and stir-fried shredded beef. Appetisers include superb fried Peking pork dumplings and Szechuan dumplings in a hot red pepper sauce. *Seats 60. Parties 20. L 12-2.30 D 6-11.30. Closed L Mon-Thur, 25 & 26 Dec. Set meals from £14 (minimum two).* AMERICAN EXPRESS *Access, Diners, Visa.*

SW5	**Mr Wing**	**£65**

Tel 071-370 4450   **R**

242-244 Old Brompton Road Earls Court SW5 0DE   **Map 19 A5**

Many restaurants use flowers and plants in their decor, but beside Mr Wing they have the look of a desert, or at best arid scrubland. Ground floor and basement are almost a jungle of tropical greenery, virtually obliterating other decorative features like the fish tank and the paintings. Prices are high, but the food is acceptable and it's quite fun to be there. Highlights of recent meals have included aromatic crispy lamb (lettuce wrap cuts some of the blatant richness!), sole with pepper and vinegar soup, the dumplings (grilled or steamed), and the sizzling dishes. The restaurant is near the junction of Old Brompton Road and Earls Court Road. *Seats 120. Private Room 10. Meals 1-12. Closed 25 & 26 Dec. Set D £25.* AMERICAN EXPRESS *Access, Diners, Visa.*

> If we recommend meals in a hotel or inn a separate entry is made for its restaurant.

W6	**Mr Wong Wonderful House**	**£40**

Tel 081-748 6887   **R**

313 King Street Hammersmith W6   **Map 17 A4**

One of the friendliest Chinese restaurants in London, decorated in gentle eau-de-nil with Mr Wong leading a team of helpful staff. The food, based on Peking and Singapore cuisine, includes a good selection of daytime dim sum (note, no cheung fun on Mondays). Plenty of sizzling dishes, and bean curd for vegetarians. *Seats 200. Parties 12. Private Room 80. L 12-3 D 6-midnight (Sat & Sun noon-midnight). Closed 25 & 26 Dec. Set meals from £12.50.* AMERICAN EXPRESS *Access, Diners, Visa.*

SW1   Mitsukoshi   £100

Tel 071-839 6714   **R**

Dorland House 14-20 Regent Street SW1 4PH   **Map 18 D3**

In the basement of a Japanese department store, this is a roomy, comfortable restaurant making stylish use of frosted glass panelling. You can choose from the à la carte selection or plump for one of the many set meals. These range from a fairly simple *hana* – appetiser, tempura, grilled fish, rice, miso soup and pickles – through *shabushabu* (beef slices and vegetables boiled and served with lemon-soya and sesame-soya sauces, prepared at table) to sushi, sukiyaki and the ten-course *kaiseki* feasts served in the private rooms. *Seats 140. Parties 22. Private Room 24. L 12-2.30 D 6-10.30. Closed Sun, Bank Holidays. Set L from £20 Set D from £30.* AMERICAN EXPRESS *Access, Diners, Visa.*

EC4   Miyama   £80

Tel 071-489 1937   Fax 071-236 0325   **R**

17 Godliman Street EC4V 5BD   **Map 20 B2**

A stylish operation offering immaculately produced Japanese food in crisp, business-like surroundings: a sushi bar upstairs and tables downstairs. The main menu covers the usual range, from grilled skewered chicken and cold bean curd with bonito to sashimi, soups, tempura and teriyaki. Also interesting set menus both lunchtime and evening. 15% service charge. The entrance is in Knightrider Street. *Seats 85. L 12-2.30 (Sat from 11.30) D 6-10. Closed D Sat, all Sun, Bank Holidays. Set L from £17 Set D from £30.* AMERICAN EXPRESS *Access, Diners, Visa.*

W1   Miyama   £75

Tel 071-499 2443   **R**

38 Clarges Street W1Y 7PJ   **Map 18 C3**

The West End version of the City branch, stylish and modern, with opaque screens for privacy. Cooking is of a high standard, flavours delicate and refined. Set lunches offer the best value (raw fish, grilled fish, tempura, beef or chicken teriyaki, pork ginger or pork deep-fried). The rest of the menu spans the expected range, from *zen-sai* (hors d'oeuvre) to rice and noodle dishes, *nabemono* specialities and teppan yaki meals prepared at the table. Excellent service (for which 15% is added). Between Piccadilly and Curzon Street. *Seats 67. Parties 28. Private Room 17. L 12-2.30 D 6-10.30. Closed L Sat & Sun, all Bank Holidays, Christmas/New Year. Set L £12-£18 Set D £32-£40.* AMERICAN EXPRESS *Access, Diners, Visa.*

WC2   Moat House   65%   £135

Tel 071-836 6666   Fax 071-831 1548   **H**

10 Drury Lane Covent Garden WC2B 5RE   **Map 21 B1**

High-rise hotel handy for Covent Garden and many West End theatres. Maudie's Bar is a good spot to unwind with a drink and smile at the Osbert Lancaster cartoons. Children up to 12 stay free in parents' room: family-sized rooms available. Conference and banqueting facilities for up to 100. Covered parking. *Rooms 153.* AMERICAN EXPRESS *Access, Diners, Visa.*

N1   Mojees   £45

Tel 071-226 0307   **R**

87 Noel Road Islington N1 8HD   **Map 16 D3**

Open only at weekends (apart from party bookings at other times), Mojees is located down a quiet Islington road above the Island Queen pub. Owners Tommy Takacs and his wife Amanda have in 6 years created a concept that has evolved into a remarkable little restaurant. Booking is very essential for one of the paper-covered tables, each of which has a green candle and vase of flowers. The room itself is lofty, painted plain white, with a few leafy plants and discreet ceiling spot lamps creating a charmingly informal ambience. Diners are presented with a menu of just the main courses, with an explanation that they help themselves to a buffet of hot and cold starters in the lobby just outside the dining room. Typical of a delicious selection are plump, very tender mussels marinière; a smooth tomato and roast fennel soup; mousse of carrot, ginger and fresh coriander; mousse of smoked haddock with garlic creamed potato; bulgur wheat salad with capers, gherkins, cumin and red onion; and a few salads including a green leaf one with asparagus dressing. Main dishes range from lamb's liver with roast shallots and a grain mustard sauce to salmon and prawn risotto, leg steak of lamb with a mint crust and green peppercorn sauce and a highly enjoyable baked chicken breast stuffed with blue cheese and sitting on a bed of creamed leaf spinach. Vegetarian options too. Sweets are excellent – plum pudding with chestnut crème anglaise or toasted coconut ice cream with hot chocolate sauce. There is no restriction whatsoever on the amount you can eat – every dish on the menu is included for the £14.95 charge, if you have the appetite. *Seats 45. Parties 30. L Sun only from 1pm D Fri & Sat only 7.30-9.30. Closed all Mon-Thur, D Sun, Bank Holiday weekends, all Aug, 2 weeks Christmas. Set D £14.95.* AMERICAN EXPRESS *Access, Visa.*

W5   Momo   £50
Tel 081-997 0206   R
14 Queens Parade North Ealing W5 3HU   **Map 17 A4**

Cosy Japanese restaurant behind a smoked-glass frontage just off Hanger Lane (by North Ealing underground). One-dish lunches served with rice, miso soup, pickles and a piece of fresh fruit offer particularly good value, as does a fine *shokado bento* box with tempura and sashimi; the extensive menu in the evenings includes the likes of grilled eel, soft-shell crab and pork grilled with ginger sauce. *Seats 24. L 12-2.30 D 6-10. Closed Sun, Bank Holidays, 1 week Christmas. Set L from £7. Set D from £23.50.* AMERICAN EXPRESS *Access, Diners, Visa.*

WC2   Mon Plaisir   £50
Tel 071-836 7243   Fax 071-379 0121   R
21 Monmouth Street WC2H 9DD   **Map 21 B2**

There are daily specials according to market availability but otherwise it's a reassuring case of *plus ça change* at Mon Plaisir, the original of Alain Lhermitte's small group of restaurants. Regulars go back for *rillettes, aiguillettes, poelé de St Jacques, entrecote,* and *blanc de volaille.* Set menus at lunch and pre-theatre times (6-7.15pm). *Seats 95. Parties 25. Private Room 25. L 12-2.15 D 6-11.15. Closed L Sat, all Sun, Bank Holidays. Set L and early D £13.95.* AMERICAN EXPRESS *Access, Diners, Visa.*

W1   Mon   £70
Tel 071-262 6528   Fax 071-706 2531   R
Cumberland Hotel Marble Arch London W1A 3RF   **Map 18 C3**

On the ground floor of the Cumberland Hotel, Mon has all the usual trappings of a smart modern Japanese restaurant. The dining area is divided by low wooden screens with private rooms also available. The menu offers a wide selection of very carefully prepared traditional Japanese dishes with lunchtime offering the best bargains. Set lunches begin at £11.50, the price for grilled fish fillet preceded by a seaweed appetiser, salad, miso soup, rice, dessert and green tea. Evening set menus begin from £35 per person. Service is friendly and helpful. *Seats 95. Parties 8. Private Room 35. L 12-2 D 6-10. Closed 1 week Christmas.* AMERICAN EXPRESS *Access, Diners, Visa.*

SW3   Monkeys   £80

Tel 071-352 4711   **R**

1 Cale Street Chelsea Green SW3 3QT   **Map 19 B5**

A neighbourhood restaurant, in the true sense, where customers are
welcomed as friends into the wood-panelled dining room. There is a feeling
of a private party amid the profusion of fresh flowers and blue linen.
Spinach salad with hot salmon and tarragon, foie gras in two ways (hot
in a salad, cold in a terrine), various mousses and terrines – brill, salmon
and scallop or veal sweetbreads with wild mushrooms, all perfectly judged,
were included in a summer menu. To follow, maybe sautéed veal kidney
with Madeira sauce, roast Bresse pigeon or sea bass (again stuffed with
a superb mousse) and a red pepper sauce. Game is strongly featured when
in season, grouse with red cabbage being a particular favourite. Excellent
French cheeses, carefully kept. Good-value weekday set lunches. Efficient,
friendly service, orchestrated by Brigitte Benham. *Seats 40. Parties 20.
Private Room 10. L 12.30-2.30 D 7.30-11. Closed Sat & Sun, Bank Holidays.
Set L £12.50 D £17.50/£35. Access, Visa.*

WC1   Montague Park Hotel   64%   £150

Tel 071-637 1001   Fax 071-637 2506   **H**

12-20 Montague Street Bloomsbury WC1B 5BJ   **Map 18 D2**

Nine Georgian town houses make up the Montague Park, which stands
in the heart of Bloomsbury right by the British Museum. Public rooms are
spacious and comfortable: the bar has a small terrace looking out on to
private gardens and the basement breakfast room has a bright conservatory
roof. Bedrooms are small but well equipped with satellite TV, trouser
press, hairdryer and tea/coffee facilities. Sparkling clean bathrooms are well
appointed. There are four conference suites. Children up to 12 stay free
in parents' room. *Rooms 109.* AMERICAN EXPRESS *Access, Diners, Visa.*

W1   The Montcalm   76%   £230

Tel 071-402 4288   Fax 071-724 9180   **H R**

Great Cumberland Place W1A 2LF   **Map 18 C2**

The hotel is named after the 18th-century general, the Marquis
de Montcalm, who was apparently known for his dignity and style –
qualities that can be attributed to this elegant town house behind a listed
Georgian facade. As a hotel, it is one of London's better kept secrets, situated
in a residential crescent a stone's throw from Marble Arch and Oxford
Street. The smart new entrance and foyer set the tone for the public areas
which are more akin to a private club than a hotel; this is best illustrated
in the cosy bar which has deep green walls, distinctive wood panelling,
an open fire, a mahogany bookcase and a collection of comfortable leather
chairs and upholstered sofas. Though several of the air-conditioned
bedrooms are on the small side, they are finely decorated and furnished;
four spacious new suites (including the honeymoon suite with half-tester,
heated waterbed – is it the only one in a London hotel? – and bathroom
jacuzzi) have joined the two penthouse suites (with sauna) and twelve
unusual duplex suites with entrances on two floors and a spiral staircase
in between. In the bathrooms there are bathrobes, a bidet and good
toiletries, as well as a telephone extension, while the bedrooms have
minibars and safes in addition to the usual facilites. A nice touch is the
subdued lighting underneath the bedside table, so you don't have to switch
on a light in the middle of the night if you need to get out of bed
in darkness. Under the direction of General Manager Gerhard Schaller
service is first-class, as is the invigorating Japanese breakfast, an unusual
option served from 7am-10am (£17.50 per person), which apart from
being exquisitely served is healthy, nutritious and satisfying. For business,
there are private rooms and an air-conditioned suite which can

accommodate up to 80 for meetings. Children up to 12 stay free in parents' room. 24hr room service. No dogs. *Rooms 115.* AMERICAN EXPRESS *Access, Diners, Visa.*

Crescent Restaurant   £80

Completely redecorated by interior designer Jane Few Brown, the air-conditioned room is dominated by a large mural of a country landscape and garden painted by Lincoln Seligman. Chef Gary Robinson's style leans towards modern British cooking with the set lunches (one, two or three courses) including unlimited house wine or mineral water. The fixed-price dinner menu also includes a half bottle of house wine, but if you prefer to choose from the wine list a £5 reduction per person is made off the price (£19.50 becomes £14.50). Typical dishes might feature starters such as duck consommé with beetroot, wild mushrooms with garlic, and grilled tiger prawns on a tomato salsa, with main courses of fanned breast of duck with black pudding and cabbage on a red wine jus, grilled red mullet with chervil butter sauce, and roast best end of lamb with an apricot raisin chutney and minted gravy. Desserts can be selected from the trolley. Decent cheeses and coffee, service impeccable. *Seats 60. Parties 10. Private Room 16. L 12.30-2.30 D 6-10. Closed L Sat, all Sun, Bank Holidays. Set L £14.50-£19.50 D £19.50.*

W2	Mornington Hotel	63%	£89

Tel 071-262 7361   Fax 071-706 1028   **H**

12 Lancaster Gate W2 3LG   Map 18 B3

In a residential area just north of Hyde Park, the Swedish-owned Mornington (spot the Swedish flag over the entrance) scores on housekeeping and efficiency. There's a fresh, bright look to the place, both in the day rooms (panelled foyer-lounge, library bar) and in the bedrooms. Rates include a Swedish buffet breakfast. Children up to 12 stay free in parents' room. *Rooms 68. Sauna.* AMERICAN EXPRESS *Access, Diners, Visa.*

W1	Mostyn Hotel	62%	£124

Tel 071-935 2361   Fax 071-487 2759   **H**

Bryanston Street W1H 0DE   Map 18 C2

Tucked away quietly behind Marble Arch, the 18th-century building was originally the home of Lady Black, a lady-in-waiting to the Court of George II. Inside, period detail blends with up-to-date amenities, but the most impressive features – a Georgian staircase, Adam carved ceilings and fire surrounds – are in the conference areas, where various rooms cater for up to 130 for banquets and 60 for conferences. Public rooms include the colonial-style Tea Planter restaurant (where breakfast is served) with its own street entrance. Bedrooms come in various sizes. *Rooms 122. Coffee shop (7am-11pm).* AMERICAN EXPRESS *Access, Diners, Visa.*

SW1	Motcomb's		£60

Tel 071-235 9170   Fax 071-245 6351   **R**

26 Motcomb Street Belgravia SW1X 8JU   Map 19 C4

Old-established basement restaurant beneath a wine bar. The menu takes its inspiration from near and far; "Motcomb's Classics" include smoked trout and salmon mousse with marinated cucumber, lentil soup, crab and shrimp cakes with a mild curry sauce and roasted whole sea bass with fennel. Rack of lamb, grilled steaks and seasonal game are among the meaty options. No children under 7 in the evening. *Seats 70. Private Room 22. L 12-3 D 7-11.45. Closed D Sun, all Bank Holiday Mon. Set L from £11.75/£14.75.* AMERICAN EXPRESS *Access, Diners, Visa.*

WC2   Mountbatten Hotel   70%

£207

Tel 071-836 4300   Fax 071-240 3540

H

20 Monmouth Street Covent Garden WC2H 9HD

Map 21 B2

By Seven Dials in Covent Garden, the hotel is themed around the late Lord Louis, with a glass case of memorabilia in the lobby and photographs and cartoons in both the smart, wood-panelled Broadlands drawing room (named after his family home in Hampshire) and the small Polo Bar. The marble-floored reception is elegant, as is the tip-top Lord Mountbatten suite (one of seven). Larry's Bar is open noon till 11 Mon-Fri for food and drink. Decent bedrooms (children up to 14 stay free with parents) have darkwood furniture, mini-bars and remote-control TVs; bathrooms are marble-tiled and luxuriously large bathrobes are provided. Edwardian Hotels.
Rooms 127. AMERICAN EXPRESS *Access, Diners, Visa.*

W1   Le Muscadet

£60

Tel 071-935 2883

R

25 Paddington Street W1M 3RF

Map 18 C2

Classic French bistro dishes are listed on the handwritten menu at this popular little spot. Escalope of fresh foie gras with Madeira is a speciality, while asparagus with hollandaise sauce, sole dugléré, chicken breast with thyme and pepper steak are other favourites. *Seats 35. L 12.30-2.30 D 7.30-10.45 (Sat to 10). Closed L Sat, all Sun, Bank Holidays, 3 weeks Aug. Set L £17. Access, Visa.*

WC1   Museum Street Café   ★

£55

Tel 071-405 3211

R

47 Museum Street Bloomsbury WC1A 1LY

Map 21 B1

Perhaps a café by name but the acquisition of a property directly to the rear and the subsequent expansion to create more space means that now the atmosphere, albeit informal with its bright white walls and simple, dark furniture, is much more that of a restaurant. The granting of a licence means a short selection of very well chosen wines is at long last a reality too, as are printed menus, as opposed to the former blackboard. The choice is still a short one but is as imaginative and eclectic as ever with inspiration for dishes depending on the availability of the fine ingredients that are essential to this simple, unfussy style of cooking. Much use is made of the chargrill and this is Mark Nathan's domain while Gail Koerber's task is preparing the breads, starters and desserts. What comes from the kitchen continues to captivate the palate with its delicacy and subtlety. The food also looks good – witness a fish and coconut soup, simple enough in concept but with a fresh spring-like appearance created by the pale yellow of turmeric and fresh green of the floating coriander leaves. Main dishes often have a mixed leaf salad and roast baby new potatoes. Chargrilled guinea fowl has a delicious vinaigrette dressing of coarsely chopped toasted hazelnuts and parsley and salmon fishcakes come with a sherry and cayenne mayonnaise. Sweets, equally simple, are nevertheless absolutely outstanding as in a lemon ice cream with fresh pineapple, mint and heavenly lemon clove biscuits. *Seats 34. L 12.30-2.30 D 6.30-9.30. Closed Sat & Sun, Bank Holidays. Set L £12/£15 Set D £17/£21. Access, Visa.*

SE1   Mutiara

£25

Tel 071-277 0425

R

14 Walworth Road Elephant & Castle SE1 1HY

Map 17 D4

Indonesian/Malaysian restaurant whose decor is highlighted by large paintings and an enormous vase of exotic leaves. Try classics like satay, prawn fritters, sesame chicken and beef slices with five spices, served by charming, helpful staff. Plenty for vegetarians. *Seats 70. Parties 30. L 12.30-2.30 D 6-11. Closed L Sat, all Sun, Bank Holidays, 1 week Easter, 2 weeks Christmas. Access, Visa.*

W1	**Nakamura**	**£50**
Tel 071-935 2931		**R**
31 Marylebone Lane W1M 5FH		**Map 18 C2**

A sushi bar is at street level, and a narrow stairway spirals down to the sparsely appointed main restaurant. Food takes centre stage with preparation and presentation both receiving detailed attention; specialities include sushi, sashimi, tempura and – prepared at table – sukiyaki and kamo nabe (duck and vegetables in steaming hot broth). Well-priced set lunches (£6-£12.50) comprise a main dish plus appetiser, pickles, soup and fresh fruits. *Seats 35. Parties 25. Private Room 8. L 12-2.30 D 6-10.30 (Sun to 10). Closed L Sun, all Sat. Set L from £6 Set D from £10.90.* AMERICAN EXPRESS® *Access, Diners, Visa.*

N1	**Nam Bistro** **NEW**	**£45**
Tel 071-354 0851		**R**
326 Upper Street Islington N1 2XQ		**Map 16 D3**

An agreeable family-run restaurant with a simple, clean modern line in decor. Occupying the ground floor and basement, space is nevertheless at a premium, so booking is very advisable. The Vietnamese dishes on offer are of the homely variety, simple, straightforward and highly enjoyable, and worth the wait. Fresh herbs and clear spicing ensure that the food is very flavoursome, though, without some of the fieriness associated with food from its close neighbour, Thailand. There are many Chinese influences, too, and the choice runs to 95 dishes with a number of set meals as further options. For those unfamiliar with cooking from this country, advice is willingly given. *Seats 50. Parties 8. Private Room 30. L 12-3 D 6-11. Closed Mon, 25 & 26 Dec.* AMERICAN EXPRESS® *Access, Diners, Visa.*

E1	**Namaste**	**£35**
Tel 071-488 9242 Fax 071-488 9339		**R**
30 Alie Street E1 8DA		**Map 20 D1**

In a neat, simple decor of green walls with framed Indian prints, classical and regional Indian dishes are listed on a special menu which changes every week. Many of the dishes are out of the ordinary, and the menu offers comprehensive and alluring descriptions. Turkey *belliram* is prepared with onion, tomato, coriander and garlic; Goan fish curry is flavoured with *cokum* – a red cherry-like berry "known since Vedic times for its medicinal properties"; mange tout are prepared with red and white kidney beans in a spiced coconut-based curry; Madras Blazers are hot pancakes stuffed with curried veal. *Seats 72. Private Room 40. L 12-3 D 6-11.30 (Sat 7-11). Closed L Sat, all Sun, Bank Holidays.* AMERICAN EXPRESS® *Access, Diners, Visa.*

W6	**Nanking**	**£60**
Tel 081-748 7604		**R**
332 King Street Hammersmith W6		**Map 17 A4**

In a street bursting with ethnic restaurants Nanking is one of the smartest, and quite intimate in atmosphere. Decor is cool, staff admirably helpful and friendly. The menu is strong on Szechuan dishes and a warning fire symbol is much in evidence. "Special selections" include crispy chili squid with onions and peppers, double-sautéed string beans with pork mince and a particularly good sizzle-grilled sesame steak with teriyaki sauce. Mongolian lamb is another speciality. *Seats 95. Private Room 60. L 12-2.30 D 6.30-11.30. Set meals from £17.20.* AMERICAN EXPRESS® *Access, Visa.*

WC2   Neal Street Restaurant   ★   £100
Tel 071-836 8368   Fax 071-497 1361   **R**
26 Neal Street Covent Garden WC2H 9PS   Map 21 B2

Renowned for his love affair with the mushroom, Antonio Carluccio
is now also well espoused to the media. Several books on cooking and
numerous television appearances ensure a growing number of devotees. His
restaurant has never been busier, particularly at lunchtime when the man
himself is on hand to ensure that all is well. New chef Nick Melmoth-
Coombs, an Englishman with a strong affinity for Italian cuisine, produces
dishes that are head and shoulders above the competition. While there are
a few nods to modernity the overall emphasis of the menu is classic
regional Italian cooking. Here are flavours that evoke memories of warmer
climes and azure skies. Starters range from wild mushroom soup, stuffed
calamari on rucola or a salad of home-smoked shellfish and eel
to a delicately fragrant wild garlic consommé served with plump chicken
dumplings. Of the pasta dishes, the fresh tagliolini with creamy truffle sauce
(the Parmesan is already included) is stunning, while other choices could
be black angel hair with scallops and bottarga or pappardelle with funghi.
Fish dishes are executed with precision – a slice of lightly pan-fried turbot,
for example, comes with tiny, succulent honey fungus and the brilliantly
contrasting texture of the almost gelatinous Judas Ears. Piemontese bollito
misto is a great favourite and is carved at the table; other meat dishes could
include roast breast of duck with a port and red wine sauce, a ragu
of sweetbreads and morels or an equally good baked schiaccata (paper-thin
slices of beef with truffle cheese). Sweets include a marvellous Barolo-
poached pear with creamy, golden vanilla ice cream or the definitive
Sicilian cassatina. Remembering that a 15% service charge is automatically
added to all bills, the cheapest *marque* champagne on the well-chosen wine
list is almost £50 – somehwat steep! However, there are some good-value
and unusual wines, especially in the Italian section. Skilful, friendly service.
"Well-behaved" children only. *Seats 60. Parties 12. Private Room 24.
L 12.30-2.30 D 7.30-11. Closed Sun, Bank Holidays, 1 week Christmas/New
Year.* AMERICAN EXPRESS *Access, Diners, Visa.*

See the Restaurant Round-up for easy, quick-reference comparisons.

W1   New Fook Lam Moon   £40
Tel 071-734 7615   **R**
10 Gerrard Street Soho W1   Map 21 A2

A simply furnished restaurant in Soho's Chinatown where meats hang
invitingly in the window. Fast service from a long list of sound Cantonese
cooking. Good choice of one-pot, porridge and noodles in soup dishes –
stewed spare ribs with pig's liver, duck with yam and Mandarin minced
meat with noodles are typical. Order barbecue suckling pig in advance.
*Seats 80. Meals 12-11.30 (Sun to 10.30). Closed 25 & 26 Dec. Set meals from
£9.40.* AMERICAN EXPRESS *Access, Diners, Visa.*

W2   New Kam Tong   £35
Tel 071-229 6065   **R**
59 Queensway W2 4QH   Map 18 A3

Other Queensway restaurants come and go, but New Kam Tong has been
around longer than most. The menu is predominantly Cantonese, with
a huge choice, from deep-fried stuffed crab claws and 17 soups to dozens
of ways with chicken, beef, prawns and pork, plus oodles of noodles and
braised, roast or aromatic crispy duck. Daytime dim sum. Almost next
to Bayswater underground station *Seats 120. Meals 12-11.15. Set meals
from £9.80.* AMERICAN EXPRESS.

W1   New Loon Fung   £60

Tel 071-437 6232   **R**

42 Gerrard Street Soho W1V 7LP   **Map 21 A2**

A fairly steep, wide, mirror-lined staircase makes an impressive entrance
into a first-floor, split-level restaurant located above a Chinese supermarket.
The menu must rank as one of the longest in Chinatown, with 252 dishes
on offer. While a long menu often means the quality of the cooking suffers,
such is not the case here. This is not a restaurant to come for a quick,
inexpensive meal but one where good ingredients are combined to produce
beautifully cooked dishes that are full of flavour and interest. The mainly
Cantonese menu has some Peking and Szechuan dishes, too. Set dinners are
available in either Szechuan or Cantonese style, the former being much
spicier. Steamed scallops come with a separate chili and spring onion
dressing, crispy shredded lamb and Peking duck are offered as starters while
Szechuan spicy prawns and sliced fish in crisp batter with a sweetcorn sauce
are typical of an extensive seafood selection. To finish there are simple
sweets and orange segments to cleanse the palate. *Seats 400. Parties 10.
Private Room 30. Meals 11.30-11.30 (to midnight Fri & Sat). Closed 2-3 days
Christmas.* AMERICAN EXPRESS® *Access, Diners, Visa.*

W1   New World   £35

Tel 071-434 2508   **R**

1 Gerrard Place Soho W1V 7LL   **Map 21 A2**

Join several hundred others and enjoy a meal in one of Soho's most typical
and traditional Chinese restaurants. The menu is suitably vast, starting from
daytime dim sum and ranging through seafood and vegetarian specials,
popular provincial dishes and chef's specialities. *Seats 600.
Private Room 250. Meals 11am-11.45pm (Fri & Sat to 12.15am, Sun 11-11).
Closed 25 & 26 Dec. Set meals from £7.20.* AMERICAN EXPRESS® *Access,
Diners, Visa.*

SW4   Newton's   £55

Tel 081-673 0977   **R**

33 Abbeville Road Clapham Common South Side SW4 9LA **Map 17 C6**

A popular neighbourhood brasserie in two separate rooms, one of which
is non-smoking. The menu is worldly with an eclectic mix of dishes that
ranges from Caesar salad and warm chorizo and pigeon breast salad among
the starters to Thai green chicken curry with pasta noodles and hamburger
and chips, plus a long list of tempting desserts. The Sunday brunch menu
includes a traditional roast and papers on the bar. Good-value, two-course
tables d'hotes include coffee. No-smoking section. Children get a good deal
on Saturdays (12.30-5.30) with a clown, balloons and high-chairs all laid
on along with a special menu of kids' favourites. Outside eating on an
enclosed roadside terrace in good weather. *Seats 70. Parties 36.
L 12.30-2.30 D 7-11.30 (Sat & Sun 12.30-11.30). Closed 25-27 Dec, 3 days
Easter. Set L £6.95 (Sun £9.95) Set D £11.95.* AMERICAN EXPRESS®
Access, Visa.

W1   Nico Central   ★ ↑   £60

Tel 071-436 8846   Fax 071-355 4877   **R**

35 Great Portland Street W1N 5DD   **Map 18 D2**

A single star in Nico Ladenis's firmament, Nico Central stands on the site
previously occupied by *Chez Nico*. It's a smart, brightly-lit, up-market
brasserie nowadays, though, with beautiful modern artwork by Juan Gris
and Picasso on walls which have retained the distinctive mirrored dado
strip. In the ceiling a central stained-glass art deco illuminated skylight
is reflected in a large mirror with ornately engraved edges, while the bar
counter alongside has a polished granite top and two-toned mirrored front;

a stripped-pine floor completes the picture. Lunch and dinner are both à la
carte, but the latter is a fixed-price affair (with only the wonderful dish
of pan-fried foie gras on toasted brioche with caramelised orange attracting
a hefty supplement of £6). The choice is long and varied: from chicken
and foie gras boudin blanc with an apple galette or mushroom tartlet with
poached egg and béarnaise sauce to risotto of cep mushrooms and Parmesan
to start, followed by the likes of baked brill with croutons and Provençal
vegetables (dangerously close to sun-dried tomato-land), griddled salmon
steak with sweet pepper oil, ginger and spring onions, or griddled breast
of duck with plum sauce. Lamb's liver and kidney, grilled rib-eye
of Scottish beef, honey-roasted quail, confit of maize-fed chicken with
sweetcorn pancake – an extensive range aimed to please. Don't be misled
by the seeming simplicty of it all – the art of Nico is to take the familiar
and rework it by returning to its classical origins and embellishing it with
a subtle but telling touch of inspiration. Thus, a crispy leg of duck
is a tender, melting confit served on a bed of plump borlotti beans dressed
in olive oil, the whole surrounded by a mayonnaise tinged with grain
mustard. Vegetables are uncomplicated – served as a plated mixture, and
potatoes that include wonderful crisp chips or purée with olive oil, equally
irresistible. Classic sweets such as chocolate marquise with orange crème
anglaise, lemon tart, tarte tatin and nougat glacé; hot ginger and walnut
sponge with whisky ice cream or honey ice cream with ruby grapefruit
and brandy snap are simply irresistible, particularly when included in the
three-course dinner menu. No children under 5. *Seats 55. Private Room 10.
L 12-2 D 7-11. Closed L Sat and Bank Holidays, all Sun, 10 days Christmas.
Set D £22.* [AMERICAN EXPRESS] *Access, Diners, Visa.*

SW10	Nikita's		£70
Tel 071-352 6326 Fax 081-993 3680			**R**
65 Ifield Road Fulham SW10 9AU			Map 19 A6

For more than 20 years diners have come to this snug red-and-gold
basement restaurant to dive into the fast-flowing waters of the River
Vodka and tuck into hearty Russian food. Speciality dishes include blinis,
smoked fish, shashlik and golupsy (parcels of cabbage filled with spiced
meats, herbs and dried fruits, braised in a rich sauce). *Seats 35.
Private Room 12. D only 7.30-11.30. Closed Sun, Bank Holidays, 2 weeks
Aug. Set D from £18.50.* [AMERICAN EXPRESS] *Access, Visa.*

W1	Ninjin		£60
Tel 071-388 4657			**R**
244 Great Portland St W1N 5HF			Map 18 C2

A modestly appointed Japanese restaurant beneath its own food shop,
Ninjin is in the same group as *Ginnan, Masako, Hiroko* and *Kashinoki.* Set
lunches (£10-£14) include appetiser, miso soup, rice, pickles and fresh
fruit plus one of a dozen main dishes, from fried bean curd and deep-fried
oysters to Scotch salmon, raw fish fillets and beef grilled with teriyaki
sauce. Also *sukiyaki, shabu shabu* and *bento* lunches. Dinner brings more
elaborate set meals plus an à la carte menu featuring *kushiyaki* (skewered
dishes) as a speciality. *Seats 54. Parties 20. L 12-2.30 D 6-10.30. Closed Sun,
some Bank Holidays. Set L from £5.70.* [AMERICAN EXPRESS] *Access, Diners, Visa.*

NW1	Nontas		£30
Tel 071-387 4579 Fax 071-383 0355			**R**
14 Camden High Street London NW1 0JH			Map 16 C3

A bustling, neighbourhood Greek Cypriot restaurant which also offers
overnight accommodation. The menu covers a familiar range, including
the ever-popular meze for two or more (£8.75 per person) and charcoal-
grilled lamb, rump steak, quails and lamb cutlets. The separate Ouzerie area

serves snacks, teas and coffee from 8.30am-11.30pm. *Seats 50. Parties 25.
L 12-2.45 D 6-11.30. Closed Sun, Bank Holidays. Set meals from £8.75.*
AMERICAN EXPRESS *Access, Diners, Visa.*

SW5   Noor Jahan   £40
| Tel 071-373 6522 | R |
| 2a Bina Gardens off Old Brompton Road SW5 | Map 19 B5 |

Popular and durable Indian restaurant with a straight-down-the-line menu:
various styles and heat levels of lamb, chicken and prawn dishes. Swift,
friendly service. *Seats 60. Parties 25. L 12-2.30 D 6-11.45.
Closed 24-26 Dec.* AMERICAN EXPRESS *Access, Diners, Visa.*

SW7   Norfolk Hotel   69%   £145
| Tel 071-589 8191   Fax 071-581 1874 | H |
| 2 Harrington Road South Kensington SW7 3ER | Map 19 B5 |

Close to major museums and the 'French quarter' of South Kensington,
as reflected in the Lycée conference suite (boardroom-style meetings for
up to 24) on the first floor. Built in 1888, the Norfolk retains a certain
Victorian air, although the amenities are up to date. Standard rooms are
in soft pastel shades, with attractive limed wood furniture. Children up to
12 stay free in parents' room. Day rooms include a brasserie, a basement
wine bar (11am-11pm) and a traditionally-styled English pub. Queens
Moat Houses. *Rooms 96. Gym, sauna, spa bath.* AMERICAN EXPRESS *Access,
Diners, Visa.*

SW6   Nosh Brothers   £65
| Tel & Fax 071-736 7311 | R |
| 773 Fulham Road SW6 5HA | Map 17 B5 |

Good neighbourhood ground-floor and basement restaurant serving a daily
changing menu of well-cooked, brasserie-style food. An intentionally passé
atmosphere attracts the "beautiful" people of Fulham. Decor is on the
designer-scruffy side, and the lights get dimmer as the place comes to life
after about 9.30. Vichyssoise or ceviche of monkfish might be followed
by skate with samphire or steak and chips. Carefully chosen ingredients.
Short, but well-balanced wine list which travels the world. Laid-back,
friendly and occasionally quirky service. Booking advisable. *Seats 85.
Private Room 40. D only 7-11.30. Closed Sun & Mon, 24-26 Dec.*
AMERICAN EXPRESS *Access, Diners, Visa.*

W6   Novotel   65%   £89
| Tel 081-741 1555   Fax 081-741 2120 | H |
| 1 Shortlands Hammersmith W6 8DR | Map 17 B4 |

Very large modern hotel alongside (but not accessible from) Hammersmith
flyover. It's popular for banquets and conferences (up to 900 delegates). The
restaurant is open from 6am to midnight. Refurbishment of facade and
bedrooms was due for completion by the end of 1994. *Rooms 635.*
AMERICAN EXPRESS *Access, Diners, Visa.*

WC2   Now & Zen   £75
| Tel 071-497 0376   Fax 071-497 0378 | R |
| Orion House 4a Upper St Martin's Lane WC2H 9EA | Map 21 B2 |

High on interior design (by Rick Mather) and handy for theatreland, this
spectacular, ultra-modern restaurant (now under new ownership) is on
three levels with minimalist decor behind a sleek glass frontage. The menu
is a mix of modern and classic Chinese cooking – from dim sum and snacks
(40 varieties) to some very unusual choices like cold marbled pig's ears,
deep-fried chicken garnished with Yunan ham and nuts, and shin of beef
with coconut flavour served in a clay pot. Plenty of more familiar

favourites, too, such as hot and sour soup, crispy seaweed and Peking duck. *Seats 180. Parties 30. L 12-3 D 6-11.30 (Sun to 11). Closed 25 & 26 Dec.* **AMERICAN EXPRESS** *Access, Diners, Visa.*

SW7   Number Sixteen   £120

Tel 071-589 5232 Fax 071-584 8615	**PH**
16 Sumner Place South Kensington SW7 3EG	**Map 19 B5**

In a terrace of white-painted early-Victorian houses, Number Sixteen offers style, elegance and seclusion. There's a comfortable informality about the drawing room, and the conservatory opens on to a walled garden. Drinks are taken from an honour bar in the library or from mini-bars in the bedrooms, which are smartly furnished with a combination of antiques and traditional pieces. A tea and coffee service is available throughout the day. Room rate includes Continental breakfast. No children under 12. No dogs. *Rooms 36.* **AMERICAN EXPRESS** *Access, Diners, Visa.*

W1   Nusa Dua   £35

Tel & Fax 071-437 3559	**R**
11-12 Dean Street Soho W1V 5AH	**Map 18 D2**

Indonesian food is a delightful mixture of tastes and aromas involving sweet, pungent, hot and spicy. Otto, the manager, who dispenses charm and information in equal measure, comes from Java, where they like their food sweet, but his menu spans the whole range. Set meals provide good value, or you can explore the carte. Chicken, beef, prawn and beancurd satays, whole fish cooked in banana leaves, lamb chops with chili and sweet soya sauce, and mixed vegetables cooked in tamarind soup are just a few of the 70+ dishes on offer. The restaurant, now open seven days a week, is on two levels, lighter at street level, more intimate below. Set meals provide good value, ranging from low-priced lunches to a rijsstafel (rice table) banquet. *Seats 60. Parties 40. Private Room 12. L 12-2.30 D 6-11.30. Closed 25 & 26 Dec. Set L from £4.95 Set D £30 for 2 includes wine & coffee.* **AMERICAN EXPRESS** *Access, Visa.*

W1   O'Keefe's   £45

Tel 071-495 0878 Fax 071-629 7082	**R**
19 Dering Street W1R 9AA	**Map 18 C2**

Minimalist design at this modern restaurant, just away from the rush of Oxford Street. Beth Coventry produces a frequently changing Mediterranean-style menu from her open-plan kitchen. So *bourride* (a fish soup flavoured with aïoli) or roasted peppers with anchovies and focaccia might be followed by chargrilled swordfish with lemon grass vinaigrette or roasted vegetable couscous with goat's cheese and harissa; and to round off, bread-and-butter pudding or pear and raspberry crumble (too many pips to be an unqualified success). Good attention to detail, with excellent bread, sea salt and mignonette pepper on the tables. Candle-lit in the evenings. *Seats 37. Meals 8am-10pm (10-5 Sat). Closed Sun, Bank Holidays, 2 days Christmas. No credit cards.*

NW1   Odette's   £65

Tel 071-586 5486	**R**
130 Regents Park Road Primrose Hill NW1 8XL	**Map 16 C3**

Close to Primrose Hill, amid the bustle of Regents Park Road. The small main dining room is attractively decorated in green with gilded mirrors of all sizes covering the walls. At the back, a charming balcony room overlooks a conservatory. The handwritten menu, which changes daily, offers a mix of English and voguish Mediterranean dishes: carpaccio of pigeon with olive paté crostini and confit of duck with vanilla butter beans and roasted Jerusalem artichokes sit alongside smoked haddock mash,

toasted scallops with grilled black pudding and radicchio, Cornish crab and
potato salad with roasted peppers. The mix and match technique even
extends to ceviche of sardines with a blood orange dressing and Chinese
leaf coleslaw. Desserts are generally more traditional. Strong attention
is paid to wines, with over a dozen served by the glass and a list laid out
by wine style; there's a wine bar in the basement where simpler dishes and
a set lunch are also offered. *Seats* 60. *Parties* 30. *Private Room* 8.
L 12.30-2.30 D 7-11. Closed L Sat, D Sun, 1 week Christmas. Set L £10.
AMERICAN EXPRESS *Access, Diners, Visa.*

W1   Odin's Restaurant   £65

Tel 071-935 7296   R

27 Devonshire Street W1N 1RJ   Map 18 C2

Traditionally appointed, almost club-like premises with a wealth
of artwork on the walls, some of it (along with the menu) depicting
founder Peter Langan. Dishes are, on the whole, staunchly British, from
tomato and tarragon soup, smoked trout with horseradish and wild boar
and orange terrine with Cumberland sauce, to grilled halibut with parsley
butter, rack of lamb and roast duck with sage and onion stuffing and apple
sauce. English farmhouse cheeses, Mrs Langan's chocolate pudding, sorbets,
ice cream. Concise, well-chosen wine list. *Seats* 60. *Parties* 10. *L 12.30-2.30*
D 7-11.30. Closed Sat, Sun, Bank Holidays. Set L & D £17.95/£19.95.
AMERICAN EXPRESS *Access, Diners, Visa.*

SW7   Ognisko Polskie   £55

Tel 071-589 4635   Fax 071-581 8416   R

55 Exhibition Road SW7 2PG   Map 19 B4

Gold is the dominant colour in the slightly faded grandeur of a hotel-style
dining room in the Polish Hearth Club. Staff and most of the guests are
Polish, and the walls are hung with portraits of notable Poles past and
present. The menu is Polish plus Continental, portions more than robust,
flavours bold but certainly not without subtlety. Beetroot soup – a
sparkling, brilliantly fresh-tasting consommé, comes with a herby veal
sausage roll; buckwheat blinis are topped with smoked salmon, cream and
Sevruga caviar; ham knuckle, falling off the bone and beautifully succulent,
is teamed with a splendid mustard sauce; cheesecake is a traditional baked
version with sultanas. The main-course set lunch and dinner menu offers
remarkable value. *Seats* 70. *Private Room* 150. *L 12.30-3 D 6.30-11. Closed*
Bank Holidays, 2/3 days Easter, 4 days Christmas. Set L & D from £7.50.
AMERICAN EXPRESS *Access, Diners, Visa.*

SW17   Oh'Boy   £40

Tel 081-947 9760   R

843 Garratt Lane Tooting SW17 0PG   Map 17 B6

A garish purple neon sign announces a neighbourhood Thai restaurant
whose menu delivers authentic tastes and good-value Royal Thai set meals.
Among the most popular dishes are seafood soup (for 2), fish cakes, Thai
beef salad, roast duck curry and Emerald chicken (fried spicy chicken with
onion, chili and fresh basil leaves). *Seats* 45. *Parties* 25. *Private Room.*
L 12.30-3 D 7-11. Closed Sun. Set D £9.50/£15.50. AMERICAN EXPRESS *Access,*
Diners, Visa.

W14   Oliver's   £35

Tel 071-603 7645   R

10 Russell Gardens Olympia W14 8EZ   Map 17 B4

A friendly little restaurant between Kensington and Shepherds Bush. From
a choice of twenty starters and even more main courses, you might choose
crab soup, salmon mayonnaise or chicken livers and toast to start, then
braised wood pigeon, osso buco, garlic king prawns or one of the popular

CLOSED

steaks to follow. Main-course salads also available, and a traditional roast Sunday lunch. *Seats 75. Meals noon-11.30. Closed 25 & 26 Dec. Set L £9 (Sun £13). Access, Visa.*

SW1   Olivo   £55
Tel 071-730 2505   **R**
21 Eccleston Street SW1W 9LX   Map 19 C5

Modern Italian cooking with an emphasis on Sardinian dishes is offered at this friendly and casual restaurant in the heart of Victoria. There are shorter menus at lunchtime, a longer *carta* in the evening, though some dishes are common to both. Try chargrilled baby squid with plum tomatoes, artichoke risotto, fresh tortelloni stuffed with prawns and spinach, or chargrilled tuna with rucola. Finish with *affogato al caffe* or soft cheese with pears. *Seats 45. Parties 6. L 12-2.30 D 7-11. Closed L Sat, all Sun, Bank Holidays, 3 weeks Aug. Set L £13.50/£15.50.* AMERICAN EXPRESS *Access, Visa.*

W11   192   ↑   £75
Tel 071-229 0482   **R**
192 Kensington Park Road W11 2JF   Map 16 B3

Having spread into adjacent premises this is now a more mainstream restaurant, with an up-to-the-minute modern decor, a clever mix of bold imaginative colours that complement an ambience much favoured by a largely young and arty crowd. A section behind the bar area is popular with a lively local set while the new addition houses comfortable well-spaced tables. The menu, created by the dynamic Albert Clark, is of well-structured dishes which show a distinctly modish Mediterranean influence and his cooking displays a true appreciation for the balance and compatability of flavours. Artichoke with French bean salad and shaved Parmesan, pan-fried lamb sweetbreads with a tomato and basil mayonnaise, sauté of red mullet with couscous salad or an extremely good grilled ceviche of salmon and scallops with a wonderfully little tortilla and exceptional guacamole are typical starters. The main dishes are fine examples of carefully thought-out amalgams of flavour as in calf's liver with onion and roast artichoke, grilled veal chop with citrus and marjoram, saddle of roast lamb with new season garlic and spinach and a fillet of baked sea bass with a well-balanced tomato and tarragon butter. Even the vegetables are above average: crunchy pan-fried courgettes and a terrific salad of new potatoes and spring onions. The selection of desserts may be only four in number but they are outstanding, as shown in a light chocolate and roasted pecan nut brownie simply but effectively served with crème fraiche. Charming, patient service. *Seats 110. Parties 12. Private Room 26. L 12.30-3 (Sun to 3.30) D 7-11.30 (Sun to 11). Closed Aug Bank Holiday, 25 & 26 Dec.* AMERICAN EXPRESS *Access, Diners, Visa.*

SW5   Hotel 167   £68
Tel 071-373 0672   Fax 071-373 3360   **H**
167 Old Brompton Road SW5 0AN   Map 19 B5

Frank Cheevers has transformed a Victorian private house into a most delightful little hotel. Each room has its own character, with inspiration ranging from pine to art deco. Central heating and double-glazing keep things warm and peaceful. Room price includes a buffet Continental breakfast. Unlicensed. No dogs. The hotel is located on the corner of Cresswell Gardens. *Rooms 19.* AMERICAN EXPRESS *Access, Diners, Visa.*

W11   Orsino   NEW   £60

Tel 071-221 3299   **R**
119 Portland Road London W11 4LN   Map 17 B4

A popular West London off-shoot of the Covent Garden *Orso*, with
a menu formatted very similarly. The cooking here too is firmly modern,
middle-class Italian. The place differs in being smaller and instead of being
in a basement it occupies the ground and first floor of an unusual wedge-
shaped building. Black and white prints of old Italian scenes are hung
on the rough pink walls while tables and chairs are in a multitude
of Mediterranean hues. Starters include several light salad options as well
as chargrilled cuttlefish with grilled radicchio and white beans or small
pizzas. In the Italian style a small pasta dish precedes the main dish. This
could be tagliatelle with wild mushrooms, tomato and herbs or superb leek
and ricotta ravioli simply served with fresh sage and butter. Main dishes
rely on the chargrill to a large extent with a typical offering being grilled
swordfish with roasted peppers, grilled lamb fillet with tomato, black
olives and rosemary or veal escalope with artichokes and mozzarella.
To finish there is pecorino cheese and pear, peach and strawberry mousse
or the superb Tuscan speciality, Vin Santo with dried almond biscuits.
Booking is essential. *Seats 106. Parties 8. Private Room 30. Meals 12-10.45
(Sun to 9.45). Closed 25 Dec. Set L £11.50/£13.50. No credit cards.*

WC2   Orso   £65

Tel 071-240 5269   Fax 071-497 2148   **R**
27 Wellington Street Covent Garden WC2E 7DA   Map 20 A2

A fashionable basement restaurant in Covent Garden whose walls are hung
with arty black and white photographs. The menu is of Italian inspiration,
with a contemporary slant. Chicken, white bean and spinach soup, grilled
asparagus with salami and gorgonzola, super little pizzas with anchovies,
black olives, onion and mozzarella, thin pasta with crab, courgettes and
chopped tomato and risotto with Fontina and escarole show the style.
Chocolate cake with coffee zabaglione tempts among the desserts. Waiters
serve and pose with style. Easy-to-use list of good Italian wines. *Seats 100.
Parties 8. Meals 12-12. Closed 24 & 25 Dec. No credit cards.*

SW11   Osteria Antica Bologna   £45

Tel 071-978 4771   **R**
23 Northcote Road SW11 1NG   Map 17 C6

Parking is easier in the side streets off 'strada Northcote' these days, now
that restrictions have largely been lifted. Italian cooking – as different from
a local trattoria as one can imagine – at kind prices in friendly,
unpretentious surroundings that feature wood-covered walls and matching
pottery jugs and vases. That's the Osteria formula, and it works extremely
well. The menu is long and enticing, offering a range from all parts
of Italy: *assaggi dell'osteria* (Bolognese tasting portions – the Italian version
of tapas) are a fun way to start a meal, or can be combined into an excellent
light meal. The choice of a dozen or so runs from marinated olives
to baked fresh sardines and *matusi* (beans, sausage, cabbage, pancetta bacon,
potato and cornmeal). Other sections on the menu cover salads, soft polenta
dishes, a wide choice of unusual pasta combinations – try pugliese pasta
with turnip tops, sun-dried tomatoes, garlic and chilis) – meat and fish
courses (*capretto alla mandorle*: goat cooked with rice, tomato and almond
pesto is a speciality) and traditional puddings, now all home-made in the
kitchen. Bargain two-course lunch with a choice of three dishes at each
stage. The Italian wine list has fair prices and is worth investigating – ask
for advice. *Seats 75. Parties 30. L 12-3 D 6-11 (Fri to 11.30, meals Sat
12-11.30pm, Sun 12.30-10.30). Closed 10 days Christmas/New Year.*
AMERICAN EXPRESS® *Access, Visa.*

NW1   Otafuku   NEW   £60

Tel 071-482 2036   **R**

75 Parkway Camden Town NW1   Map 16 C3

Decor is simple and completely unpretentious with polished wooden tables and bentwood and rattan chairs. The menu is a comprehensive selection of familiar Japanese dishes with the emphasis on sashimi and sushi – there's a 30% discount on the latter on Tuesdays, Thursdays and Saturdays. Otafuku is the name of a celebrated Japanese lady. *Seats 36. D only 6.30-10. Closed Sun, Bank Holidays.* AMERICAN EXPRESS *Access, Diners, Visa.*

SW1   Overtons at St James's   £80

Tel 071-839 3774   Fax 071-584 8082   **R**

St James Street SW1A 1EF   Map 18 D3

This long-established fish restaurant has recently steamed into the nineties with the arrival of chef Nigel Davies. Diners enters a club-like atmosphere, with pine panelling, framed prints and a long bar which has its own menu of lighter dishes. The main dining room beyond is arranged under a huge skylight. Blue and gold are the featured colours, incorporated in the carpet, chair seats and pictures. Shellfish motifs are cleverly woven into the carpet and cut into the glass panels which divide traditional and modern. The menu now includes some contemporary trends: we much enjoyed seared scallops with a smoked bacon risotto, and chargrilled tuna with caramelised onions. Other tempting modern dishes might include fillets of red mullet with Thai-spiced lentils or John Dory provençale. These dishes rub fins with old favourites such as Dover sole, turbot and sirloin steak from the grill. The menu includes a list of daily lunch specials, very fairly priced at £10.50; these are set for each day of the week: Friday's mussel, cod and coriander pie is delicious. Comforting nursery puddings (such as steamed chocolate sponge or crème brulée), with one or two interesting ices, round off the carte. The wine list, naturally strong on whites, includes many illustrious names at reasonable prices. Professional and friendly service is orchestrated by Andrew Baker. *Seats 75. Parties 8. Private Room 20. L 12.30-2.45 D 6.30-10.45. Closed L Sat, all Sun.* AMERICAN EXPRESS *Access, Diners, Visa.*

SW18   Le P'tit Normand   £50

Tel 081-871 0233   **R**

185 Merton Road Southfields SW18 5EF   Map 17 B6

Cheerful *restaurant du quartier* with mock-rustic decor and good honest cooking. The choice is quite simple and straightforward, with some dishes reflecting owner Philippe Herrard's Normandy origins: *gambas au Calvados, boudin noir aux pommes, magret de canard Vallée d'Auge, cote de veau normande. Seats 35. Private Room 40. L 12-1.30 D 7-10.30. Closed L Sat. Set L from £9.95 (Sun £11.95).* AMERICAN EXPRESS *Access, Diners, Visa.*

Consult page 20 for a full list of starred restaurants

W8   La Paesana   £40

Tel 071-229 4332   **R**

30 Uxbridge Street Notting Hill W8 7TA   Map 18 A3

Standard Italian fare in a lively Notting Hill restaurant behind the Coronet cinema. All the antipasti and pastas are available as either starters or main courses. Chef's specialities include taglioline Cenerentola and medallions of veal Nerone. *Seats 90. L 12-2.45 D 6.30-11.45. Closed Sun, Christmas, Easter. Set L £9.95.* AMERICAN EXPRESS *Access, Diners, Visa.*

WC2 Le Palais du Jardin £50

Tel 071-379 5353

R

136 Long Acre London WC2E 9AD

Map 21 B2

Changes have been afoot at Le Palais, almost doubling the number of covers by adding 120 in the gallery area, and adding an extra oyster bar and drinks bar, allowing even more lunchers, dinners and snackers to enjoy Winston Matthews' menu of modern European dishes. Try perhaps the delicious spiced crabmeat with a sweet pea guacamole and deep-fried crab claws, pasta with pleurottes, medallions of venison with braised red cabbage and a redcurrant cream, and a lotus leaf of exotic fruits with passion fruit sorbet to finish. There seems to be something here for most tastes, and it's deservedly popular. *Seats 220. Parties 35. Private Room 22. Meals 12-12 (Sun to 10.50). Closed 25 & 26 Dec.* AMERICAN EXPRESS *Access, Diners, Visa.*

W1 Panda Si Chuen ★ £50

Tel 071-437 2069

R

56 Old Compton Street W1V 5PA

Map 21 A2

Just outside the traditional heart of Chinatown, Panda Si Chuen beacons as a bright Northern star in the firmament of London's Chinese restaurants. Decor is discreetly elegant with a few small ornate gilt carvings on the walls. However it is the food that is the magnet here. The cooking of Szechuan province is renowned for its generally spicy nature. Here it has reached an exalted level which produces dishes of often exquisite flavour. Grilled dumplings to begin burst with succulent meats and juices while Szechuan tea-smoked duck is imbued with a distinct and delicious flavour reminiscent of Lapsong Souchong. Deep-fried oysters are large with a moist, plump inside and crisp outside, kung-po chicken has the fieriness of chili and the sweet crunchiness of cashew nuts. The menu is not overlong but does include some of the more familiar dishes from the south such as sweet and sour pork. Staff are helpful, polite and friendly. *Seats 63. Parties 18. Private Room 13. Meals 12-11.30. Closed Sun, Bank Holidays.* AMERICAN EXPRESS *Access, Diners, Visa.*

W1 The Park Lane Hotel 77% £232

Tel 071-499 6321   Fax 071-499 1965

HR

Piccadilly W1Y 8BX

Map 18 C3

Built in 1927, the hotel retains some of its distinctive art deco features, although the feel throughout the public rooms and bedrooms is very traditional. The Palm Court Lounge, where afternoon teas and 24hr snacks are served, is brightened by a magnificent vaulted ceiling with arched art deco stained glass. Bracewells Bar and the Brasserie (see below) are more modern in style. Standard bedrooms are of a good size but tend to look out on the dark inside courtyard. All rooms have double-glazing, multi-channel TV, mini-bars and bathrobes. The best rooms are 54 suites: all air-conditioned, they look out on to the central court or Green Park and benefit from private sitting rooms and more luxurious bathrooms. 24hr room service. Large-scale banqueting suites (including an art deco ballroom) for up to 600; conference facilities for up to 500. Private parking for 180 cars is provided in a covered garage opposite the main entrance. *Rooms 308. Gym, sun beds, beauty & hair salons, brasserie noon-11.30pm, business centre, news kiosk, shop, garage.* AMERICAN EXPRESS *Access, Diners, Visa.*

Bracewells £70

The restaurant atmosphere is traditional. The decor is of dark carved wood, light flowery panels, mirrors and silver trolleys; jacket and tie are a must. John Tindall plays comfortably with English and French classics adding his own individual touches: salmon and sole sausage topped with fresh crab meat on an avocado sauce, spinach and walnut soufflé, sole meunière, plain

grills, pot-roasted chicken served on a potato cake with braised vegetables.
Pancakes Belmonte, flamed at the table, are the speciality dessert. The wine
list is well constructed and the three-course luncheon menu offers good
value. Good snacking (but little atmosphere) in the rather upmarket
Brasserie on the Park. **Seats** *60. Parties 30. L 12.30-2.30 D 7-10.30
Brasserie 12-3 & 6-11 (12-11 weekends & Bank Holidays). Set L £19.50
Set D £24.50. Bracewells closed L Sat, all Sun, August. Brasserie closed 25 &
26 Dec.*

W2   Parkwood Hotel   £65

Tel 071-402 2241   Fax 071-402 1574   **H**

4 Stanhope Place W2 2HB   **Map 18 C3**

Bed and breakfast town house hotel close to Marble Arch and Oxford
Street shops. 12 of the bedrooms have en-suite facilities. Children under 13
sharing parents' room are charged at £11.50 Mon-Fri, but can stay free
at weekends. Unlicensed. No dogs. **Rooms** *18. Access, Visa.*

SW1   Pearl of Knightsbridge   £80

Tel 071-225 3888   **R**

22 Brompton Road Knightsbridge Green SW1X 7QN   **Map 19 C4**

Comfortable Chinese restaurant on Knightsbridge Green, close to Harrods,
seeming to attract the Knightsbridge affluent. Good-value set lunches, but
prices rise steeply in the evening (there's a £2 evening cover charge and
£15 minimum charge after 6pm). Mainly Cantonese menu with a few
dishes, such as Peking ravioli in chili sauce and Szechuan sliced pork, from
other regions. Strong on seafood dishes: sea bass, Dover sole, abalone and
lobster are all on offer, at a price. Dim sum at weekend lunches. Ask for
a wall table when booking to avoid the bustling service from stoically
unsmiling staff. **Seats** *120. Private Room 40. L 12-3 D 6-11.30.
Closed 3 days Christmas. Set L £8.50/£12.50 Set D from £25.*
AMERICAN EXPRESS® *Access, Diners, Visa.*

EC1   The Peasant   NEW   £45

Tel 071-336 7726   **R**

240 St John Street EC1V 4PH   **Map 16 D3**

Built in 1890, the former George & Dragon, a substantial Victorian gin
palace, has been transformed into a food-orientated pub. The original
mosaic floor, albeit with patched-up sections, has been uncovered after
years of being buried under a layer of concrete. The place now has a bright,
lively ambience during the day and pleasingly subdued lighting in the
evenings. Scrubbed-wood tables and plain wooden seating add a suitably
spartan touch that's reflected in Carla Tomasi's simple peasant-style fare.
Based on new-wave Italian cooking, the rather brief menu, which changes
weekly, includes the likes of mushroom, sage and garlic soup
or a deliciously creamy risotto with lentils and heaps of freshly grated
Parmesan. Starters come with wonderful rustic bread and extra virgin
olive oil. Main dishes are served in outsize china bowls. *Cianfotta* – a
potato, celery and saffron stew with basil – is typical, as is poached lamb
with ginger, lemon grass and Chinese greens or squid with white wine,
olive oil, parsley and capers. Excellent sweets could include lemon tart
or nut torte with coffee cream and English goat's cheese with spiced
poached pear and coriander and semolina bread. Interesting, carefully
selected 'new' wines as well as a first-rate selection of beers (including good
British real ales, Bavarian wheat and Belgian cherry beers). Booking
advisable. **Seats** *80. Parties 30. Private Room 40. L 12.30-2.30 D 6.30-11.
Closed L Sat, D Sun, all Bank Holidays, 24 Dec-3 Jan. Set L Sun
£11.50/£14. Access, Visa.*

SW7   Pelham Hotel   76%   £185

Tel 071-589 8288   Fax 071-584 8444   **HR**

15 Cromwell Place South Kensington SW7 2LA   **Map 19 B5**

Friendly, helpful staff combine with the flair of owners Kit and Tim Kemp to create a charmingly intimate hotel with a country-house feel in the heart of South Kensington, just south of the museums on Cromwell Road and a short walk from Knightsbridge. Day rooms, like the bar with its 18th-century pine panelling and the cosy Victorian snuggery, are most appealing with deeply comfortable armchairs and a profusion of fresh flowers. Paintings and antique furniture have all been carefully chosen throughout. Bedrooms vary from small and cosy to grand and high-ceilinged (on the first floor) but all feature fine fabrics varying from traditional floral prints to bold black and white stripes. Practicalities are not forgotten, either, with all rooms having a useful second telephone by the desk and full air-conditioning. Rooms facing South Kensington tube and the traffic are obviously noisier than those at the rear. Excellent bathrooms. Under the same ownership as *Durley House* and *Dorset Square* hotels (see entries). Valet service and 24hr room service. Guests have free use of the garden and outdoor swimming pool of the hotel's administrative building opposite. ***Rooms*** *37.* AMERICAN EXPRESS® *Access, Visa.*

Kemps   NEW   £50

Pleasant basement restaurant and bar, almost club-like with a library corner, wooden floor, panelling, yellow and blue square motif fabrics, and lots of decent pictures. The food is tasty and simple, being both contemporary and good value, with wines equally fairly priced. Starters feature a fish soup served with garlic croutons and a rouille, grilled polenta with wild mushrooms and rosemary, and a reasonably authentic Caesar salad. Follow with a well-cooked braised lamb shank served with haricots blancs and anchovy, roasted salmon with root vegetables and horseradish, or Toulouse sausages with creamed potatoes and onion gravy. Lovely lemon tart and ginger crème brulée; excellent coffee accompanied by baby Lindt chocolates to finish. Fresh baguette bread, sliced on arrival, is served with unsalted butter. Sunday brunch. Service pleasant, if a little nervous. ***Seats*** *30. Parties 15. Meals 7am-10pm.*

W2   Pembridge Court Hotel   65%   £120

Tel 071-229 9977   Fax 071-727 4982   **H**

34 Pembridge Gardens Notting Hill W2 4DX   **Map 18 A3**

Very close to Portobello Road antiques market, Pembridge Court has personality, warmth and charm thanks to a delightful, long-serving manager (Valerie Gilliat) and well-motivated staff. There's an inviting feeling to the town house as soon as you cross the threshold into the lobby with its exposed brickwork, a style continued in the downstairs bar and Caps restaurant. Bedrooms range from small singles with shower to the very spacious and luxurious air-conditioned Holland Park Room. Most have stylishly co-ordinated fabrics and furnishings and Victorian prints on the wall. Many of the bathrooms have chic Italian tiles. Children up to 10 stay free in parents' room. Good breakfasts. ***Rooms*** *20.* AMERICAN EXPRESS® *Access, Diners, Visa.*

SW7   Periquito Queen's Gate   £62

Tel 071-370 6111   Fax 071-370 0932   **H**

68-69 Queen's Gate SW7 5JT   **Map 19 B5**

Standing on the corner of Cromwell Road and Queen's Gate the hotel is characterised by a bright and colourful decor. Some bedrooms can be very small but all are attractively decorated. First-floor rooms are non-smoking. ***Rooms*** *65.* AMERICAN EXPRESS® *Access, Diners, Visa.*

NW6 Peter's £55

Tel 071-624 5804 **R**

65 Fairfax Road Swiss Cottage NW6 4EE Map 16 B3

Live piano music is still scheduled daily at Peter's, where the 20s' French decor provides a suitable backdrop for chef-partner Jean Charles' fairly traditional style of cooking. There's now a table d'hote menu at £9.95 for two courses or £11.95 for three as well as the carte though some dishes appear on both, such as breast of duck with calvados and ginger. Calf's liver and steaks are given the classical treatment. Sunday lunch is popular – for children under eight it's only £6.95. The wine list is mostly French and reasonably priced. *Seats 60. L 12-3 D 6.30-11.30. Closed L Sat, D Sun, 26 Dec, 1 Jan. Set L & D £9.95/£11.95 Sun L £9.95.* AMERICAN EXPRESS® *Access, Diners, Visa.*

NW5 Le Petit Prince £30

Tel 071-267 0752 **R**

5 Holmes Road Kentish Town NW5 3AA Map 16 C2

Decor is inspired by St Exupéry's *Le Petit Prince* and the atmosphere is often fittingly exuberant. Couscous is the main offering, along with salady starters, spicy fried plantain and a few daily specials. Chocolate mousse is the speciality dessert. Drink Algerian red wine or Normandy cider. *Seats 60. Private Room 30. L 12-3 D 7-12. Closed L Sun, 1 week Christmas. No credit cards.*

W8 Phoenicia £50

Tel 071-937 0120   Fax 071-937 7668 **R**

11-13 Abingdon Road Kensington W8 6AH Map 19 A4

A relaxed and civilised, family-run Lebanese restaurant just off Kensington High Street. Hot and cold hors d'oeuvre, from aubergine, stuffed vine leaves and home-made cream cheese to grilled quails and spicy sausage, precede charcoal-grilled main courses, with delicious sweets to finish. Besides the à la carte there are several set menus, including vegetarian options, and a good-value lunchtime buffet (30 dishes, eat as much as you like). Twenty seats are in a conservatory. *Seats 100. Private Room 50. Meals 12-11.45 (Buffet L 12.15-2.30). Closed 24 & 25 Dec. Set L £9.95 Set D £15.30.* AMERICAN EXPRESS® *Access, Diners, Visa.*

Our inspectors *never* book in the name of Egon Ronay's Guides. They disclose their identity only if they are considering an establishment for inclusion in the next edition of the Guide.

SW11 Phuket £60

Tel 071-223 5924 **R**

246 Battersea Park Road SW11 3BP Map 17 C5

A local Thai restaurant which has established itself as a favourite with the residents of Battersea and Clapham. Clever use of mirrors opens up a rather long and narrow room. The Eastern feel is preserved with tall tropical plants and slow-spinning ceiling fans. Start with prawns in a blanket, a house speciality, or one of the many tom yum soups. Follow with crispy pomfret with mild chilis or a mushroom sauce), a yum salad, – *som tam* with sliced papaya, tomatoes and lime juice, is delicious. Various red and green curries are offered – and their heats can be adjusted on request. The difficult task of balancing strong Thai flavours is achieved with precision and care. *Seats 60. D only 6-11.30. Closed 4 days Christmas. Set D £12.50.* AMERICAN EXPRESS® *Access, Visa.*

W1   Pied à Terre   ★★   £110

Tel 071-636 1178   o   **R**

34 Charlotte Street W1P 1HJ   Map 18 D2

The decor has changed subtly and for the better. The stark white walls,
once hung with artworks by Richard Hamilton, Lichtenstein and Warhol,
are now smooth, with discreet spot-lights focused on the tables, which have
bright apricot tablecloths and colourful rustic hand-painted plates as part
of the place settings. The bar now has a partition partly dividing it from
the restaurant, creating a useful place for pre-or post-dinner drinks. Richard
Neat's background is exemplary, including periods with Joël Robuchon
at *Jamin*, Raymond Blanc at *Le Manoir aux Quat' Saisons* and Marco Pierre
White at *Harveys*. His dishes are of complex construction and he is not
averse to unusual combinations, but they do work, and very successfully,
as in his renowned John Dory with peas and foie gras sauce. He clearly has
a penchant for offal too – a soup of lamb offal with broad bean purée,
roasted veal kidney with turnip purée and lamb fillet with potato purée,
deep-fried tongue and beetroot being typical of his highly imaginative style
where precise, clean-cut and well-judged flavours merge into one another
to create dishes of extraordinary refinement. For a starter, snails are
wrapped in a thin moist casing of chicken mousse, the tiny teaspoon-sized
balls are rolled in ground morello and served with chanterelles, asparagus
spears and a delicate garlic purée. As a main course sea bass is roasted and set
on a bed of finely cooked Provençal vegetables, diced courgettes, peppers
and aubergines and surrounded by a rich creamy bouillabaisse juice which
in turn is bordered by a wonderful purée of fresh sardines cooked in olive
oil to which a little balsamic vinegar is added. Pigeon breast, tender and
pink, sits on a bed of confited paté – the paté being a slice of pigeon leg
meat mixed with duck heart, liver and gizzard and slowly cooked in duck
fat. Here it is served as a thin slice with the sweetness of diced fondant
celeriac adding a perfect balance of flavours. To finish there are outstanding
desserts such as a smoothly luscious pistachio ice cream filled with a soft
chocolate fondant and accompanied by a creamy vanilla sauce.
At lunchtime there's a half-price two-course selection with slightly simpler
dishes than the full menu ending with a choice of excellent cheeses or a slice
of dark, rich chocolate tart with the thinnest of crisp pastry crusts. Service
by partner David Moore and a team of young staff is very knowledgeable
and stylishly executed. *Seats 40. Parties 10. Private Room 10. L 12.15-1.30 D
7.15-9.30. Closed L Sat, all Sun, Bank Holidays. Set L £16.50 Set D £33.*
AMERICAN EXPRESS *Access, Diners, Visa.*

We welcome bona fide complaints and recommendations on the tear-out
pages at the back of the book for readers' comments. They are followed
up by our professional team.

SW3   Poissonnerie de l'Avenue   £95

Tel 071-589 2457   Fax 071-581 3360   **R**

82 Sloane Avenue SW3 3DZ   Map 19 B5

This wood-panelled restaurant has now been feeding the fish-eaters
of South Kensington for 30 years. Traditional but expert handling of good
ingredients, without much pandering to modern fashions. Fish soup with
rouille, crab in pastry on a bed of spinach or seafood risotto to start, perhaps
followed by salmon fish cakes, bouillabaisse or turbot with a delicious
white wine sauce. Daily specials are often offered in addition to the carte,
but check prices before ordering, as mark-ups can be ambitious. Friendly
attentive service. *Seats 90. Parties 14. Private Room 24. L 12.30-3 D 7-11.45.
Closed Sun, Bank Holidays, 10 days Christmas.* AMERICAN EXPRESS *Access,
Diners, Visa.*

SW1   Pomegranates   £80

Tel 071-828 6560   **R**

94 Grosvenor Road Pimlico SW1V 3LE   Map 19 D5

Patrick Gwynn-Jones, for 20 years the amiable chef-patron of this popular basement restaurant by Dolphin Square and the Thames, presents menus of literally world-wide inspiration. Gravad lax, Welsh salt duck, Cantonese roast duck, Mauritian chili prawns and wild mushrooms and escargot pie are among the specialities, and many diners don't even try to resist the home-made honey and cognac ice cream. *Seats 50. Private Room 12. L 12.30-2.15 D 7-11.15. Closed L Sat, all Sun, Bank Holidays. Set L £9.95/£12.95 Set D £13.95/£16.95.* AMERICAN EXPRESS® *Access, Diners, Visa.*

SE1   Le Pont de la Tour   ↑   £95

Tel 071-403 8403   **H**

Butlers Wharf Building 36D Shad Thames Butlers Wharf SE1   Map 17 D4

A beautiful setting on the south bank of the Thames right by Tower Bridge and overlooking St Katharine's Dock across the water. In fine weather the large canopied terrace allows for alfresco dining with a very Continental air. Lunch is a fixed-price affair, the menu offering half a dozen or so starters and main dishes. In the evening a slightly more extensive à la carte applies. Dishes are, as befits the cool, stylish elegance of the setting, very fashionable, with strong Mediterranean influences. Tomato, mozzarella and pesto tart, red mullet escabeche and rillettes of pork with rhubarb and ginger pickle or a delicate warm sole mousse topped with a soft, lightly poached oyster and accompanied by a well-balanced butter sauce make superb starters. These could precede chargrilled veal escalopes with a creamy saffron risotto and zesty gremolata, pot-roast chump of lamb with cannellini beans and rosemary for lunch while in the evening roast duck with a foie gras croute and port sauce, fillet and crépinette of venison with a potato and parsnip rösti or a sauté of scallops with vermouth, leeks and caviar are typical of the more elaborate style. Vegetables and potatoes are priced separately. Desserts are superb – passion fruit tart, white chocolate truffle cake or a stunning blueberry and vanilla millefeuille. Excellent espresso and chocolate coffee beans round off a splendid meal served in exemplary style by on-the-ball staff. You may have difficulty choosing a wine from the exceptional list here, so great is the choice. However, there's a marvellously comprehensive house selection with tasting notes alongside that might help you make up your mind. Note all the best names are represented. In addition to the main restaurant there is a less formal bar and grill open noon to midnight every day. *Seats 105. Parties 12. Private Room 22. L 12-3 D 6-12 (Sun to 11). Closed some Bank Holidays. Set L £25.* AMERICAN EXPRESS® *Access, Diners, Visa.*

Note that all telephone numbers with area codes starting with 0 will start 01 from 16 April 1995.

W2   Poons   £55

Tel 071-792 2884   **R**

Unit 205 Whiteleys Queensway W2 4YN   Map 18 A3

Located in the food court on the third floor and now fully licensed, with a cool, black and white decor. A large range of dim sum, including steamed buns, pot rice and soft rice pasta sheets, is served between noon and 4pm. There's a long and varied main menu. *Seats 120. Meals 12-11 (Sun to 10.30). Closed 25 & 26 Dec. Set meals from £12.* AMERICAN EXPRESS® *Access, Diners, Visa.*

WC1   Poons   £50

Tel 071-580 1188   **R**

50 Woburn Place Russell Square WC1H 0JZ   Map 18 D1

Another outlet in this Chinese chain, but with more than a few out-of-the-
ordinary dishes: quail's eggs and minced prawns on toast, dumplings in red
pepper sauce, deep-fried cod fillets in crab and asparagus sauce, chicken
with dried tiger lilies and fungi, lamb curry enriched with coconut milk.
Specialities include fresh crab and lobster, prepared with either ginger and
sping onion or green pepper and black beans. *Seats 100. Parties 50. L 12-3
D 5.30-11.30. Closed 4 days Christmas. Set meals from £9.* AMERICAN EXPRESS®
Access, Diners, Visa.

WC2   Poons   £30

Tel 071-437 1528   Fax 081-458 0967   **R**

4 Leicester Street WC2H 7BL   Map 21 A2

Unsophisticated, yet wholesome, mainly Cantonese food served swiftly
in simple surroundings (now spread over three floors so a little less
cramped). Wind-dried meats and steamed chicken with Chinese sausage are
specialities here. Original rice hot pot and noodle soup dishes make for
inexpensive eating out. *Seats 130. Parties 55. Meals 12-12.
Closed 3 days Christmas. Set meals from £7. No credit cards.*

WC2   Poons   £30

Tel 071-437 4549   **R**

27 Lisle Street WC2H 7BA   Map 21 A2

William Poon's original Cantonese café has extended to another floor and
is now licensed. The decor plays third fiddle to the food and the rock-
bottom prices. Barbecued and wind-dried food is the speciality, covering
duck, pork, sausages and bacon, and there's a big choice of composite rice
and noodle dishes. *Seats 50. Parties 20. Private Room 30. Meals 12-11.30.
Closed 4 days Christmas. No credit cards.*

EC3   Poons in the City   £50

Tel 071-626 0126   Fax 071-626 0526   **R**

Minster Pavement 2 Minster Court Mincing Lane EC3R 7PP   Map 20 D2

An excellent Chinese restaurant in the Poons group, located below the
stunning Minster Court, and offering classic Cantonese cooking in spacious,
elegant surroundings. Crispy squid, scallops or soft-shell crab, chicken, beef
or lamb satay and Poons' renowned wind-dried bacon are among the
starters, while main courses include some notable duck dishes – Cantonese
roast, fillet in plum sauce, tropical (with ginger and pineapple), Kung Po in
a hot, spicy sauce, crispy aromatic and the three-course Kam Ling special
(crispy skin with hot cakes, soup, stir-fried meat). Also plenty of bean curd
and vegetable dishes, plus dim sum and *plats du jour* from the quick menu.
*Seats 200. Private Room 40. Meals 11.30-11.30pm. Closed Sat, Sun & Bank
Holidays. Set L £11.80 Set D £25.* AMERICAN EXPRESS® *Access, Diners, Visa.*

W11   Portobello Hotel   60%   £120

Tel 071-727 2777   Fax 071-792 9641   **H**

22 Stanley Gardens Notting Hill W11 2NG   Map 18 A3

Two six-floor houses in an 1850 terrace near Portobello antiques market
converted into a unique hotel decorated in an eclectic mix of styles. There
are singles, doubles, twins and suites, plus some compact cabins. The 24hr
bar/restaurant in the basement caters admirably for those guests with
nocturnal life styles. Guests have membership of a nearby health club (daily
fee). *Rooms 25. Closed 2 weeks Christmas.* AMERICAN EXPRESS® *Access,
Diners, Visa.*

SW1   La Poule au Pot   £55

Tel 071-730 7763   Fax 071-259 9651   **R**

231 Ebury Street Victoria SW1W 8UT   **Map 19 C5**

Khaki walls, bare stripped floorboards, lacy tablecloths with cream paper
covers, heaps of straw and wicker baskets filled with dried flowers and
twigs and huge red clay pots with luxuriant weeping figs all combine
to create a suitably rustic ambience for simple homely cuisine *grandmère*.
The choice includes perennial favourites like snails, Gruyère quiche, *assiette
de crudités*, patés, onion or fish soup, *lapin à la moutarde, carré d'agneau,
poussin grillé, caneton roti à l'orange*. To finish, *crème brulée, mousse au chocolat*
or *tarte tatin*. Friendly, young French waiters complete the Gallic picture.
Seats *72. Parties 12. L 12.30-2.30 D 7-11.15 (Sun to 10.30).*
Closed 24-26 Dec. Set L £12.75. AMERICAN EXPRESS *Access, Diners, Visa.*

WC1   President Hotel   £66

Tel 071-837 8844   Fax 071-837 4653   **H**

Russell Square Bloomsbury WC1N 1DB   **Map 18 D2**

Large bed and breakfast hotel opened in 1962, on the corner of Guilford
Street and Russell Square, and close to the British Museum. It caters mainly
for tour parties and exhibition delegates from surrounding sister hotels.
Five of the six floors of bedrooms have recently been refurbished. The
President adjoins the Imperial Hotel in the same ownership. Underground
(pay) car park. ***Rooms*** *447. Coffee shop (10am-2am).* AMERICAN EXPRESS *Access,
Diners, Visa.* •

SW7   Pun   £50

Tel 071-225 1609   **R**

53 Old Brompton Road South Kensington SW7 3JS   **Map 19 B5**

More comfortable, more Westernised and more expensive than its Soho
compatriots, Danny Pun's restaurant is also a much friendlier place than
some of those. The food's pretty good, too, and from a reasonably wide-
ranging menu you could choose Peking ravioli in hot red pepper sauce,
stuffed crab claws, sea bass soup with coriander, prawns done one
of a dozen ways, lemon chicken or baked pork ribs with Szechuan
peppercorn salt. Seasonal specialities, too. ***Seats*** *70. Private Room 30.
L 12-2.30 D 6-11.30 Meals Sat & Sun 12-11.30. Closed 25 & 26 Dec.
Set L £13.80 Set D £18.* AMERICAN EXPRESS *Access, Diners, Visa.*

NW3   Qinggis   £55

Tel 071-586 4251   **R**

30 Englands Lane Belsize Park NW3 4UE   **Map 16 C2**

Of the two floors that comprise this Chinese restaurant, the basement is the
larger and busier, with views up to street level for tables at the front. The
menu is a round-up of familiar Chinese regional dishes and a feature is the
selection of seafood ranging from baked crabs and lobsters to various ways
with Dover sole. ***Seats*** *75. Parties 20. Private Room 15. L 12-2.30 D 6-11.
Closed 24-27 Dec. Set meals from £17.* AMERICAN EXPRESS *Access, Visa.*

SW1   Quaglino's   £70

Tel 071-930 6767   Fax 071-836 2866   **R**

16 Bury Street St James's SW1Y 6AL   **Map 18 D3**

Not quite a "theatre for glamour and excitement" in gastronomic terms,
but certainly London's most fashionable destination over the last year. Now
that owner/designer Sir Terence Conran's publicity machine has subsided
to a quiet roar, the restaurant has settled down to meet its not
inconsiderable task of feeding over 300 demanding diners at a time (many
more, obviously, per session); this challenge has been met with considerable

enthusiasm and, while not without the odd hiccup, both kitchen and staff generally cope admirably. One should not say that in an operation of this size one should *expect* some small mistakes to occur, but one does make the odd allowance for the service that comes under severe pressure at peak times. When Quaglino's opened in recessionary times it was heralded not only as an enormous risk but also as a recipe for disaster – trying to serve what was obviously intended to be modern, quite adventurous food to too many diners at a time; for the team of Conran, Joel Kissin and chef Martin Webb to have succeeded so well (let alone survived) they deserve due praise. After entering through a distinctive glass frontage on Bury Street (just south of Jermyn Street), one descends down a curving stone staircase to a gallery level where there's an informal antipasti bar area (no bookings, live music Fri & Sat nights) serving snacks all day and a private room to one side. This private dining room overlooks the cavernous dining area one floor below, whose ceiling is cleverly lit by a computer-controlled mock skylighting system three floors above. With such an enormous dining area, the volume of diners' incessant chatter often rises to an ear-tiring level – the only serious criticism that one can level at the place (but the owners can hardly be held responsible for the decibel level!). High columns within the dining area are individually painted and the central dividing structure always features a glorious floral display. In contrast, at the other end of the room, is an equally sensational display of shellfish on a mirrored crustacean altar – considered a speciality of the house (try the dressed crab with mirin and soy). A prix-fixe menu at lunch and pre-theatre (5.30-6.30) might offer noodles with ginger, coriander and chili followed by shoulder of pork with crackling and apple sauce or poached egg, lardons, capers and parsley followed by grilled skate with sauce gribiche. A recent à la carte encompassed pigeon salad with pancetta and beans, caviar with crème fraiche and melba toast, grilled bream with spinach and lemon grass, carpaccio of beef, spiced lamb with roast onions, peppered rib of beef with horseradish, and red plum parfait, crème brulée, cherry clafoutis or chocolate tart with Jersey cream to finish. Non-fish specialities include roast rabbit with prosciutto and herbs, and Sauternes custard with Armagnac prunes. Quite a short wine list (nothing wrong with that) with plenty of good drinking under £20; the supplementary fine wine list enables you to push the boat out. Quaglino's now-famous take-away ashtray remains a firm favourite on the menu, but do they add their also famous 15% service to its price as well as to that of your meal? *Seats 338, Bar 90. Parties 12. Private Room 40. L 12-3 D 5.30-12 (Fri, Sat to 1am, Sun to 11). Set 2-course L & pre-theatre D £12.95.* AMERICAN EXPRESS® *Access, Diners, Visa.*

If we recommend meals in a hotel or inn a separate entry is made for its restaurant.

W8	**Le Quai St Pierre**	↑	**£70**
Tel 071-937 6388 Fax 071-938 3435			**R**
7 Stratford Road Kensington W8 3JS			**Map 19 A4**

Decor, menu and staff all evoke the south of France in this well-liked seafood restaurant between upper Earls Court Road and Marloes Road. Lobster, kept live in a tank, heads the list, with langoustines, coquilles St Jacques, clams and mussels available in various preparations. White fish specials change with the market, and other popular choices include feuilletés, salads and steaks. A reliable local with a real flavour of the sea, where the consistent standard of cooking really is akin to that so often found on the other side of the Channel. *Seats 58. L 12-2.30 D 7-11.30. Closed L Mon, all Sun.* AMERICAN EXPRESS® *Access, Diners, Visa.*

EC1   Quality Chop House   £40

Tel 071-837 5093

94 Farringdon Road EC1R 3EA   **R**   Map 16 C3

Chef-proprietor Charles Fontaine reopened a Victorian chop house in 1990 with the aim of providing straightforward, no-nonsense food in friendly, informal surroundings. Much of the original atmosphere survives, and period features include the high-backed mahogany booths and the embossed wallpaper. Value for money is a watchword throughout the menu, which combines traditional English café food with the occasional French or exotic element (confit of duck, bang bang chicken). Popular demand keeps many dishes on the menu, including egg, bacon and chips, corned beef hash, liver and bacon, lamb chops and salmon fishcakes with sorrel sauce. A number of dishes are available as starter or main course. *Seats 40. Parties 8. L 12-3 D 6.30-12 (Sun 7-11.30). Closed L Sat, L Bank Holidays, 25 Dec-2 Jan. No credit cards.*

NW2   Quincy's   £60

Tel 071-794 8499

675 Finchley Road NW2 2JP   **R**   Map 16 B2

The best sort of local restaurant – friendly front-of-house, good quality fresh food, reasonable prices. David Philpott's menu, of British, French and Mediterranean inspiration, is short but varied (it changes monthly) with dishes such as tortellini of Jerusalem artichokes with a herb bouillon, pancake of corn-fed chicken, calf's kidneys in puff pastry with onion confit and Madeira sauce, and fillet steak with mushrooms and beef jus. The fish main course is according to the market. Desserts could be traditional – bread-and-butter pudding, treacle tart – or more modern like poached figs with elderberries and fromage frais sorbet. The meal price includes coffee and petits fours. *Seats 30. Private Room 16. D only 7-11. Closed Sun & Mon, 1 week Christmas. Set D £22.* AMERICAN EXPRESS *Access, Visa.*

W1   Ragam   £35

Tel 071-636 9098

57 Cleveland Street Fitzrovia W1P 5PQ   **R**   Map 18 D2

Popular little South Indian restaurant specialising in Kerala vegetarian cooking making good use of rice and lentil flour, green chilis, semolina, yoghurt, coconut, curry leaves and tamarind juice. It's not exclusively vegetarian by any means, and besides speciality dishes such as *adai* (mixed lentil pancake), *avial* (mixed vegetables cooked with coconut and yoghurt) and *rasam* (hot pepper soup with tomato and tamarind juice) there are plenty of chicken, meat and seafood dishes. *Seats 36. Private Room 20. L 12-3 D 6-11.15 Closed 25 & 26 Dec.* AMERICAN EXPRESS *Access, Diners, Visa.*

Note that all telephone numbers with area codes starting with 0 will start 01 from 16 April 1995.

W12   Rajput   £25

Tel 081-740 9036

144 Goldhawk Road Shepherds Bush W12 8HH   **R**   Map 17 A4

Friendly North Indian restaurant, celebrating 10 years with the same owners. A straightforward menu includes as specialities chicken tikka masala, king prawn patia, and a selection of muglai dishes. The Sunday buffet is very reasonably priced at £5.95. *Seats 50. Parties 20. L 12-2.30 D 6-12. Closed 25 Dec.* AMERICAN EXPRESS *Access, Diners, Visa.*

N3   Rani   £40

Tel & Fax 081-349 4386   **R**

7 Long Lane Finchley Central N3 2PR   Map 16 B1

Five minutes walk from Finchley Central station, Rani is one of London's top Gujerati restaurants – a clean and sparkling family-run diner with a wide frontage and a fine repertoire of vegetarian food. Full use is made of grain flours and various dal combined with fresh, exotic vegetables and delicate spicing and no eggs, fish, meat or animal fats are allowed on the premises. The range is impressive, and the full menu is available Tues-Sun evenings; a buffet operates Mon evening and Tues-Fri and Sun lunch. Among the many specialities are banana methi (ripe bananas, fenugreek leaves and tomato curry), stuffed aubergine and potato curry, home-made cottage cheese with vegetable balls, black lentil fritters and terrific chutneys (coriander, date, coconut, green chili pickle, mango, pineapple). Prices are extremely reasonable and service is by professional, young and motivated staff who operate a 'no tipping' policy. All no-smoking on Mondays and Saturdays. *Seats* 90. L 12.15-3 (*Sun to 4*) D 6-10.30. Closed L Mon & Sat, 25 Dec. Set meals £6-£19. Access, Visa.

SW11   Ransome's Dock   £65

Tel 071-223 1611   Fax 071-924 2614   **R**

35 Parkgate Road Battersea SW11 4NP   Map 19 B6

Martin Lam changes the menu monthly at his comfortable waterside restaurant. The surrounding area still looks rather shabby, as the dock development remains incomplete. The restaurant terrace, however, still provides a quiet haven for alfresco eating. The short menu is Mediterranean in flavour, and always supplemented by daily specials. Asparagus with wood-grilled piquillo peppers and shaved Parmesan and rocket; mushroom and Madeira soup, or a plate of Spanish charcuterie; followed by spiced chicken with Bombay potatoes, sea trout with Provençal vegetables or chargrilled quail with couscous, are typical summer offerings. Ingredients are painstakingly chosen, even down to the delicious vine tomatoes used for salads and coulis. Extended opening hours this year, but cooking standards can slip when Mr Lam is not at the stoves. The comfortable and interesting wine list is very keenly priced and shows no preference to any particular country. Many unusual wines at bargain rates – it's worth experimenting here. Friendly and informed service can sometimes seem laid-back. *Seats* 65. *Parties* 20. Meals 11.30-11 (*Sat to 12*). Closed D Sun, Bank Holidays. Set L £11.50. AMERICAN EXPRESS® Access, Diners, Visa.

See the Restaurant Round-up for easy, quick-reference comparisons.

N16   Rasa   **NEW**   £40

Tel 071-249 0344   **R**

55 Stoke Newington Church Street N16 OAR   Map 16 D2

The former manager of the now defunct Spices restaurant has opened his own establishment very close by. Shiny brass chandeliers combined with an attractive cinnamon and cream decor create a welcoming ambience for a short menu of well-prepared vegetarian dishes, most of which originate from the South Indian states of Kerala, Tamil Nadu and Southern Andra Pradesh, and which are characterised by subtle spicing and deliciously creamy sauces. Examples include steamed rice pancakes *appamo* served with a white potato curry cooked in coconut milk and a delicious *moru kachiathu*, a Travancore yoghurt curry with green beans and mangoes. Friendly service. *Seats* 42. *Parties* 12. *Private Room* 25. L 12-2.30 D 6-11. Closed 25 & 26 Dec. Access, Visa.

W1   Rasa Sayang   £40

Tel 071-734 8720   Fax 071-734 0933
10 Frith Street Soho W1V 5TZ   **R**   Map 21 A2

Singaporean/Malaysian and South-East Asian food (prepared without using MSG) served in congenial surroundings. Set meals provide a good introduction to an interesting cuisine that includes traditional dishes like *sambal udant, kari ayam* and *rendang* (cutlets of beef in coconut gravy). Serve-yourself lunchtime buffet (£5.90) *Seats* 180. L noon-2.45pm D 6-11.30 (Sun 1-10pm). Closed 25 & 26 Dec. AMERICAN EXPRESS *Access, Diners, Visa.*
Also at:
38 Queensway Bayswater W2 Tel 071-229 8417 Fax 071-229 9900   **Map 18 A3**
60 seats. Open Noon-11.15pm.

W1   Rathbone Hotel   69%   £157

Tel 071-636 2001   Fax 071-636 3882
30 Rathbone Street W1P 1AJ   **H**   Map 18 D2

An intimate hotel notable for its location (minutes from Oxford Street) and personal air. Crystal chandeliers, Italian marble and objets d'art adorn the limited public areas. The stylishness is matched in carefully modelled bedrooms (all fully air-conditioned), where smoked-glass mirrors add depth and boldly patterned curtains enrich the colour. Brightly lit, marbled bathrooms all have powerful showers. Executive rooms and suites feature whirlpool baths. Half the bedrooms are designated non-smoking. Not a hotel for children. No dogs. The *Royal Terrace Hotel* in Edinburgh is a sister establishment. **Rooms** 72. AMERICAN EXPRESS *Access, Diners, Visa.*

NW1   Ravi Shankar   £25

Tel 071-388 6458   Fax 071-388 2494
133-135 Drummond Street Euston NW1 2HL   **R**   Map 16 D3

South Indian vegetarian cooking at basement prices in a friendly restaurant which has recently been totally redesigned and refurbished: wooden flooring, hand-painted murals, air-conditioning. The house speciality is Shankar Thali, a complete set meal, while individual orders include wholewheat breads, dosas from Madras and snacks from Bombay. *Seats* 68. *Private Room 25. Meals 12-10.45. Set meals from £2.95. Access, Visa.*
Also at:
422 St John Street EC1 Tel 071-833 5849   **Map 20 C1**
L 12-2.30 D 6-11 (Fri & Sat till 11.30).

W1   La Reash   £35

Tel 071-439 1063
23 Greek Street Soho W1V 5LG   **R**   Map 21 A2

In the heart of Soho, at the junction of Old Compton Street and Greek Street, La Reash specialises in Lebanese and Moroccan cuisine. Meat or vegetarian Mazah (a selection of hot and cold starters) represents the former, couscous and tagines the latter. There's a cheap set-lunch menu which changes every week. Tapas bar beneath the main restaurant. *Seats* 70. Meals 12-12. Closed 25 Dec. AMERICAN EXPRESS *Access, Diners, Visa.*

W1   Red Fort   £70

Tel 071-437 2115   Fax 071-434 0721
77 Dean Street Soho W1V 5HA   **R**   Map 21 A2

Opened in 1983 by Amin Ali, the stylish Red Fort takes its name from the red sandstone fort built by Emperor Shah Jahan on the banks of the river Jamuna in Delhi. Tandoori food is a popular choice (lamb, chicken, prawns, salmon, pomfret) and other specialities include *murgh akbari* (chicken breast stuffed with dried fruits and cumin served with an almond sauce) and Hyderabadi *biryani* (based on lamb slow-cooked with mace and saffron). The restaurant is on two floors: street-level fronted by a bar area with seats, and a more intimate, low-lit basement. **Seats** *120. Private Room 60.* L 12-2.45 D 6-11.30. Buffet L £14.95. AMERICAN EXPRESS *Access, Diners, Visa.*

SW7	**Regency Hotel**	**68%**	**£135**
Tel 071-370 4595 Fax 071-370 5555			**H**
100 Queen's Gate SW7 5AG			Map 19 B5

Privately owned hotel at the junction with Old Brompton Road, near the South Kensington museums and Knightsbridge shopping. Beyond the marble foyer the Terrace (more marble, and natural light) is open day and night, and there's a cocktail bar, a health spa and several conference rooms (maximum capacity 100). Children up to the age of six stay free in parents' room. Full 24hr room service (including a night chef) and an on-site health spa are among the bonuses. No dogs. **Rooms** *198. Gym, sauna, spa bath, steam room, sun beds, beauty salon.* AMERICAN EXPRESS *Access, Diners, Visa.*

NW1	**The Regent London**	**87%**	**£233**
Tel 071-631 8000 Fax 071-631 8080			**HR**
222 Marylebone Road NW1 6JQ			Map 18 B2

Opened two years ago after three and a half years of renovation, returning this impressive piece of Grade II-listed Victorian Gothic architecture to its former glory, the Regent is now a luxurious hotel with a relaxed and informal atmosphere. A glass-canopied entrance leads into a spacious lobby with a polished, pale cream stone floor from which a series of steps leads up to the Winter Garden (informal snacks all day), in an impressive eight-floor-high, glass-covered atrium. On a mezzanine gallery there's a Gazebo with additional, quieter lounge space overlooking the floor below; 60ft coconut palms rise to the occasion. The strains of a pianist and voices sound hushed amid the cathedral-like acoustics. The hotel has six floors of smart bedrooms, all large and well appointed. Junior suites have beautiful black marble-topped executive desks and an armoir that houses the room bar and satellite TV. There are three phone lines to each room plus a data line for PCs and fax. Bathrooms are as splendid as the bedrooms; lined with white marble, most have separate shower cubicles, but only the top suites have bidets. Thick towelling bathrobes, scales, wall safes and even umbrellas are among a host of thoughtful touches provided to pamper guests. Top of the range of the bedrooms are the sixth-floor Penthouse suite and the fifth-floor Presidential suite, the latter featuring two bedrooms, a private dining room and even a grand piano. Families are extremely well catered for (as one would hope for at this level); almost every family accoutrement can be provided; children up to 14 may share their parents' room at no charge. The basement health club features a 15m swimming pool and is open from 6am, when a complimentary healthy breakfast buffet is offered. Breakfast, also available in the dining room, extends to a Japanese version (£18), Finnan haddock, carrot bran muffins and banana pancakes – one of the best breakfast choices to be found in London. Light meals and afternoon tea (3-6pm) are served all day in the Winter Garden. Lunches and evening snacks are also available in the Cellars, an elegant, wood-panelled club-like wine bar with its own entrance (closed all Sun and Bank Holidays) and rich-toned coloured leather seating. Service from young, enthusiastic staff can be one of the hotel's biggest assets – from 24hr room service, picnic baskets in summer and 4-hour rush dry cleaning service to an evening turn-down and an overnight shoe shine (with footwear returned wrapped in tissue). Impressive function rooms hold up to 350; the Tower Suite on the fifth floor is next to the Penthouse suite and has a lovely double-storey-high glass ceiling plus facilities for up to 20 boardroom-style. Limited underground car parking. Business centre with Reuters information. **Rooms** *309. Indoor swimming pool, spa bath, gym, sauna, steam room, beauty & hair salon, shop.* AMERICAN EXPRESS *Access, Diners, Visa.*

See over

Dining Room   £95

Three enormous and magnificent crystal and silver chandeliers dominate
the very elegant and beautifully proportioned room, although the lighting
level is little higher than a romantic level at dinner. The menu encompasses
a mix of mostly modern Italian dishes together with simple French classics,
but the sweet trolley only offers a rather lacklustre selection. Standards
overall are just about acceptable. Italian wines are prominent on a list
presented by style. Many bottles priced under £20. *Seats* 100. *Parties* 14.
L 12-2.30 (Sun from 12.30) D 7-11. Set L £19.50 Set D £25.

NW3   Regent's Park Marriott   73%   £169

Tel 071-722 7711   Fax 071-586 5822   **H**
128 King Henry's Road Swiss Cottage NW3 3ST   Map 16 B3

A modern hotel with a lot to offer: good-sized rooms with large beds,
desks, breakfast tables and easy chairs; 100 free car spaces; facilities for
up to 400 conference delegates; a large indoor swimming pool. The foyer
features marble flooring, pale-wood panelling (also in the bar lounge) and
an enormous vase of flowers. Two children (max age 18) can stay free
in parents' room. Five minutes' walk from Swiss Cottage underground.
*Rooms 303. Garden, indoor swimming pool, sauna, solarium, beauty and hair
salon, gift shop.* AMERICAN EXPRESS *Access, Diners, Visa.*

SW7   Rembrandt Hotel   70%   £144

Tel 071-589 8100   Fax 071-225 3363   **H**
11 Thurloe Place South Kensington SW7 2RS   Map 19 B4

One of the better hotels in the small Sarova group and benefiting from
some recent refurbishment. The location is excellent, being close to the
heart of Knightsbridge as well as directly opposite the Victoria and Albert
museum. Public rooms include a spacious lobby with glittering crystal
pendant lighting. Double doors lead into a quiet, traditional oak dado-
panelled lounge with classical columns and an open fireplace. Bedrooms are
light, decorated in soft pastels and are spacious. Executive rooms are larger
and also have settees, air-conditioning and push-button controls for lights.
Also the majority of their bathrooms have spa baths with bidets and
beautiful polished granite floors. All rooms have a trouser press and hair
dryer (Executive rooms also have an iron and board). Standard bathrooms
can be compact but all have good shower roses. Aquilla is the hotel's
splendid health complex in the basement. *Rooms 195. Indoor swimming pool,
gym, sauna, spa bath, solarium, beauty salon, shop.* AMERICAN EXPRESS *Access,
Diners, Visa.*

SW6   La Réserve   62%   £90

Tel 071-385 8561   Fax 071-385 7662   **H**
422-428 Fulham Road Fulham Broadway SW6 1DU   Map 19 A6

Contemporary small hotel favoured by overseas visitors and people in the
television and music business. Bar and lounge have comfortable modern
leather sofas. Bedrooms (some small road-facing singles; rear rooms look
on to Chelsea football ground) feature modern art and modern technology.
24hr room service (light snacks only after 11pm). *Rooms 40.*
AMERICAN EXPRESS *Access, Diners, Visa.*

W1   The Ritz   86%   £249

Tel 071-493 8181 Fax 071-493 2687   **H R**
150 Piccadilly W1V 9DG   Map 18 D3

Now part of the Mandarin Oriental group, The Ritz was opened in 1906
by César Ritz, whose intention was to create "the most fashionable hotel
in the most fashionable city in the world". With a prime position

in Piccadilly next to Green Park, the Ritz is certainly one of London's most famous landmarks, and continues to maintain its position in the capital's top hotel league. Standards of comfort and housekeeping are enviably high and service is generally everything one might expect from "one of London's smaller hotels" – of the 130 bedrooms, 14 are suites. The "Belle Epoque" feel to the generously proportioned bedrooms is enhanced by delicate pastels and gold leaf, marble fireplaces, Louis XVI furnishings and lavishly equipped marble bathrooms, all with bath and shower; almost incongruously, but welcomed by guests from all around the world, satellite TV is offered. Suites feature elegant lounges, a hallway, personal bar and writing desk; some are air-conditioned. Afternoon tea at the Ritz is part of our heritage and the Palm Court is one of London's most elegant teatime settings. The rest of the hotel is equally grand: the Long Gallery, the sumptuously beautiful restaurant and the private salons. Children up to 14 stay free in parents' room. Conference/banqueting for up to 60. Own, charged parking. No dogs. *Rooms 130. Garden, valeting, dinner dance (Fri & Sat).* AMERICAN EXPRESS *Access, Diners, Visa.*

Louis XVI Restaurant ® ↑ £120

A grandiose dining room of perfect proportions, elegantly furnished in pink, harmoniously matching the marble decor. A giant trompe l'oeil ceiling, from which hangs a carousel of gilded chandeliers, highlights the room. The Italian garden and terrace for alfresco dining are no less sumptuous. Never too stiff, the service is helpful and attentive, giving tempting descriptions of chef David Nicholls' menus which mix ancient and modern dishes (some refreshingly revised). Lunchtime daily specials see a daily roast on the trolley (except on Fridays when there's salmon in puff pastry with champagne sauce) and other British specialities – from steak and kidney pie (Wed) to mixed grill (Sat). Table d'hote menus are offered at both lunch and dinner, alongside the à la cartes. Crab Antoinette, warm oysters, sole Ritz and sea bass are considered specialities, while crown of asparagus with lobster and truffles, Dover sole and Peach Ritz are also popular. Pre-and post-theatre menus (6-6.45 & 10.30-11.15: £30) and also Friday (high season) and Saturday dinner-dances (in the Palm Court from 10pm to 1am). Perhaps surprisingly, children are welcome for Sunday lunch, when high-chairs are available and special consideration accorded – they can choose from a special children's menu (even including potato 'casings' and pizza!) or join their parents in roast Scottish prime rib of beef served with Yorkshire pudding. *Seats 100. Parties 26. Private Room 48. L 12.30-2.30 D 6.30-11.15. Set L £26 Set D from £39.50.*

We publish annually, so make sure you use the current edition.
It's worth it!

SW13   Riva   £65

Tel 081-748 0434   **R**

169 Church Road Barnes SW13 9HR   Map 17 A5

A trip to Barnes and Andrea Riva's sparsely decorated modern restaurant is rewarded by food notable for honest, robust flavours, and many of chef Francesco Zanchetta's regularly changing dishes are seldom seen elsewhere: smoked goose breast on chicory, with oranges, nuts and scallion oil; pan-roasted cod fillet on a bed of Swiss chard 'au gratin'; toasted bread with gorgonzola and chestnut honey. Some are more in the current mainstream, such as grilled vegetables, or wild salmon steak with lentils, while others are updated classics – calf's liver with sage, breaded veal cutlet with matchstick potatoes. The menu, then, is nothing if not interesting, and the Italian wine list is equally appealing and there's a splendid selection of grappa plus good strong espresso. Riva keeps its place in the front rank of modern Italian restaurants. *Seats 45. L 12-2.30 D 7-11. Closed L Sat, Christmas, Easter, 2 weeks Aug. Access, Visa.*

W6   River Café   £80

Tel 071-381 8824   Fax 071-381 6217   **R**

Thames Wharf Studios Rainville Road Hammersmith W6 9HA   Map 17 B5

Major refurbishment was under way as we went to press, (due for
completion during 1994), extending the seating area from 75 to 100 plus
another 40 outside on the terrace, British weather permitting. It remains
to be seen whether the extra space will make it any easier to book a table:
this restaurant seems to have been full since day one with customers
wanting to feel part of the stylish ambience and minimalistic decor. It's
fairly sure that the menu will evolve rather than change, for the rustic
Italian style established by Ruth Rogers and Rose Gray was right on the
pulse when they began in 1987, and the tempo has quickened if anything.
Chargrilling is the favoured form of cooking, be it for meat, fish or the
wide array of vegetables on offer. Menus change twice daily but could
include fresh anchovies marinated in sun-dried chili, lemon and parsley,
or soup of sorrel, lentils, chicken stock and crème fraiche; followed
by grilled and baked sea bass (served deliberately at room temperature)
with a salad of sun-dried plum and vine tomatoes, pine nuts and basil with
salsa verde, or chargrilled calf's liver with blue lentils, peas, mint and broad
beans. To finish there might be River Café caramel ice cream or, for the
brave, chocolate nemesis. Local restrictions insist that diners must leave the
premises by 11pm sharp. *Seats 100. Parties 10. L 12.30-2.30 D 7.30-10.
Closed D Sun, 10 days Christmas, 4 days Easter, Bank Holidays. Access, Visa.*

W2   Romantica Taverna   £40

Tel 071-727 7112   **R**

10 Moscow Road Bayswater W2 4BT   Map 18 A3

Enjoyable, straightforward Greek fare in a long-established restaurant just
off Queensway. Meze for two is the speciality of the house, along with
classic dolmades, afelia, kleftiko and moussaka. Some good fish dishes, too.
Seats 120. Private Room 70. Meals 12-11.30. Closed Bank Holidays.
AMERICAN EXPRESS *Access, Diners, Visa.*

W12   The Rotisserie   £40

Tel 081-743 3028   Fax 081-743 6627   **R**

56 Uxbridge Road Shepherds Bush W12 8LP   Map 17 B4

Friendly and informal eating place next to Shepherds Bush Central Line
underground station. Pride of place in the large room (bright and smart
after recent refurbishment) goes to the charcoal grill/rotisserie, where the
main courses are prepared: corn-fed chicken, paper-wrapped salmon,
Toulouse sausages, Barbary duck, calf's liver, rack of lamb, and the very
popular Aberdeen Angus steaks. It's in the same ownership as the *Camden
Brasserie*, and the little chips are just as good. *Seats 90. Parties 40. L 12-3
D 7-11. Closed L Sat & Sun.* AMERICAN EXPRESS *Access, Visa.*

SW15   Royal China   £60

Tel 081-788 0907   **R**

3 Chelverton Road Putney SW15 1RN   Map 17 B5

Entering the heavy wooden doors, the impression is of being inside a black
lacquer box, with flights of golden birds decorating the walls. This
is a smart restaurant, with almost a nightclub atmosphere. The few steps
separating the smoking and non-smoking areas are edged with tiny disco
lights. Yellow linen on the tables, fresh flowers in wicker baskets and
polished, helpful service add to the elegant feel. The menu is large; both
physically and in terms of choice, with 12 types of fish alone. Peking duck
is available without giving prior notice, unusual outside Soho, and comes
as two separate courses. A la carte prices can be steep. The set dinners
provide the best value, and offer either four or five generous courses,

though the choices may be conservative. A recent meal began with delicious Mandarin spare ribs, included in a mixed hors d'oeuvre, and was followed by crispy Szechuan duck, tiger prawns in a chili sauce and traditional Chinese seasonal vegetables. For those with a strong constitution there follows a choice of desserts. Like most Chinese restaurants, however, the set dinners are not available to lone diners, which is a failing that needs addressing. Good house wine, and an interesting, short wine list. *Seats 65.* L 12-4 D 6.30-11.30. Set L & D £20/£26. AMERICAN EXPRESS® *Access, Diners, Visa.*

W2   Royal China   £50

Tel 071-221 2535   **R**

13 Queensway Bayswater W2 4QJ   Map 18 A3

A high-class Chinese restaurant (sister to the Putney outlet – see below) with striking decor of black lacquered walls, gold and silver inlaid murals and spotlights. The style is Cantonese, with seafood and dim sum among the specialities, the latter (a particularly long and interesting selection) served until 5pm. Favourites include seafood hot pot, stewed pork belly with assorted vegetables and sautéed beef steak with lemon grass. Fresh lobster is prepared in six different ways (hot and spicy salts, mandarin sauce, steamed naturally, ginger and spring onion, yellow bean sauce, black bean sauce) and other items at the luxury end include poached king clams and steamed or pan-fried sea bass and Dover sole. *Seats 100.* Private Room 15. Meals 12-11.15. Set D from £20. AMERICAN EXPRESS® *Access, Diners, Visa.*

SW1   Royal Court Hotel   68%   £164

Tel 071-730 9191   Fax 071-824 8381   **H**

Sloane Square Chelsea SW1W 8EG   Map 19 C5

The reception area, with its panelling and chandeliers, sets an elegant tone for the Royal Court, which stands on a prime site immediately next to Sloane Square tube station. The Tavern is a traditional English pub serving meals at lunchtime, while Courts is an intimate wine bar. Bedrooms feature limed oak period-style furniture and soft pastel colour schemes. Children up to 15 stay free in parents' room. Three exclusive parking spaces (£20 overnight). Conference/banqueting facilities for 48/40. 24hr room service. Queens Moat Houses. *Rooms 102. Closed 25 & 26 Dec.* AMERICAN EXPRESS® *Access, Diners, Visa.*

W8   Royal Garden Hotel

Tel 071-937 8000   Fax 071-938 4532   **H**

Kensington High Street W8 4PT   Map 19 A4

As we went to press, the Royal Garden was closed for a lengthy refit. Reopening date is September 1995.

SW1   Royal Horseguards Thistle   71%   £131

Tel 071-839 3400   Fax 071-925 2263   **H**

2 Whitehall Court SW1A 2EJ   Map 18 D3

A spacious foyer with beautiful Wedgwood-style, moulded ceilings sets the tone of elegant public rooms in a comfortable hotel close to the Thames Embankment. A charming lounge area in cool, pastel lemon shades boasts chandeliers, oil paintings and a country-house style of furniture. The main restaurant is in the style of a gentlemen's club, and the Terrace Coffee Shop is open all day for snacks and light meals. Bedrooms range widely from a single overlooking Whitehall Court to the Tower Suite on two floors with a view of the City. The best are grand, spacious rooms with attractive limed oak furniture, elegant mirrors and colourful chintzy fabrics. Superb marble bathrooms are a stunning feature of some rooms. Children up to the age of 12 are accommodated free in parents' room. *Rooms 376. Coffee shop (7am-11.15pm).* AMERICAN EXPRESS *Access, Diners, Visa.*

W2 Royal Lancaster Hotel 75% £169
Tel 071-262 6737 Fax 071-724 3191 H
Lancaster Terrace Lancaster Gate W2 2TY Map 18 B3

Acquired by new owners in early 1994 the hotel, a landmark on the skyline north of Hyde Park, is undergoing a programme of major refurbishment costing some £5.7 million. The first phase involves three floors of bedrooms and this is scheduled for completion by the winter of 1994. The 81 rooms involved will have a smart modern decor and new marble bathrooms. Contemporaneous with these works will be a new Thai restaurant which will replace the present Mediterranean café. Public areas including a new lobby and reception will follow. *Rooms 418. Hairdressing, news kiosk, car hire desk, garage.* AMERICAN EXPRESS *Access, Diners, Visa.*

WC2 Royal Trafalgar Thistle 65% £141
Tel 071-930 4477 Fax 071-925 2149 H
Whitcomb Street WC2 7HG Map 21 A3

Hidden away south of Leicester Square this hotel has some very small bedrooms and even tinier bathrooms. The 4th floor is a non-smoking floor. All rooms have the standard range of amenities – remote-control TV, trouser press, hairdryer and in-house movies. It's very quiet, considering the central location! *Rooms 108. Hamiltons Brasserie (7am-11.30pm), Battle of Trafalgar pub (11am-11pm).* AMERICAN EXPRESS *Access, Diners, Visa.*

SW1 Royal Westminster Thistle 71% £151
Tel 071-834 1821 Fax 071-828 8933 H
Buckingham Palace Road Victoria SW1W 0QT Map 19 D4

Polished marble and carved wood grace the foyer, where smartly turned-out staff provide a warm and efficient welcome. The Royal Lounge is a stylish venue for afternoon tea, while the Parisian-style Café St Germain provides a relaxed, casual ambience for a drink or snack. Individually air-conditioned bedrooms, including a number of studio rooms and suites, have pickled-pine furnishings and a wide range of accessories. Children up to the age of 16 are accommodated free in parents' room. 24hr room service. The hotel is handily placed for Victoria Station and Buckingham Palace. *Rooms 134. Café (10am-11pm).* AMERICAN EXPRESS *Access, Diners, Visa.*

SE1 RSJ £65
Tel 071-928 4554 R
13a Coin Street Waterloo SE1 8YQ Map 20 B3

Within easy reach of the South Bank complex, thus a handy spot for pre- and post-theatre dinners. Modern British cooking with French influences in a very friendly and relaxing restaurant (upstairs) and brasserie (downstairs). Both areas offer the same, fixed-price 2- or 3-course menu that might offer risotto of preserved tomato, rocket and Parmesan followed by roast rump of lamb with basil mash potato, ending with hazelnut and chocolate layered pie with crème fraiche, coffee and mints. A la carte might include boudin blanc with potted cabbage, terrine of rabbit confit with pulses and a tomato dressing, pot-roasted belly of pork with choucroute and a sage jus, and red mullet on saffron risotto, tomato confit and tapénade. Apple tarte tatin with fresh cream, nougat glacé with raspberry coulis and hot, glazed rice pudding with nutmeg and plum jam typify desserts. For the most part the wine list is dedicated to the Loire Valley; there's nothing wrong with that, especially at such keen prices and with such a diverse choice. The accompanying notes are informative and

make you want to drink. *Seats 95. Parties 10. Private Room 20. L 12-2
D 6-11. Closed L Sat, all Sun, Bank Holidays. Set meals £13.95/£15.95.*
AMERICAN EXPRESS *Access, Visa.*

SW1   Rubens Hotel   66%   £141

Tel 071-834 6600   Fax 071-828 5401   **H**

Buckingham Palace Road SW1W 0PS   Map 19 D4

Opened at the turn of the century, the Rubens stands in a prime position
facing the Royal Mews behind Buckingham Palace; it's also conveniently
close to Victoria Station (2 minutes walk) and Westminster. Comfortable
day rooms in country house style include a library lounge and a cocktail
bar with resident pianist. Well-appointed bedrooms (just one suite) offer
the usual extras. The King's Suite has a four-poster bed. Children up to 12
stay free in parents' room. Five conference suites cater for up to 75
delegates. No dogs. Sarova Hotels. *Rooms 189.* AMERICAN EXPRESS *Access,
Diners, Visa.*

WC2   Rules   £60

Tel 071-836 5314   Fax 071-497 1081   **R**

35 Maiden Lane Covent Garden WC2E 7LB   Map 21 B2

Tradition rules in one of London's oldest eating places (but your order gets
keyed into pocket computers). Oysters, game both furred and feathered,
fish, pies and puddings are the specialities, though the cooking doesn't
always hit the mark. *Seats 140. Parties 9. Private Room 48. Meals 12-11.45.
Set L £15.95 (Sat, Sun served till 4) Set D £12.95 (pre-theatre served 3-6).
Closed 5 days Christmas.* AMERICAN EXPRESS *Access, Visa.*

WC1   Hotel Russell   68%   £141

Tel 071-837 6470   Fax 071-837 2857   **H**

Russell Square WC1B 5BE   Map 18 D2

An imposing late-Victorian hotel, handy for both the City and the West
End, with a hugely impressive marble foyer complete with grand staircase,
crystal chandeliers and ornate plasterwork; public areas include a clubby
panelled bar (snacks at lunchtime, afternoon tea – evening meals are served
in Virginia Woolf's and the Victorian Carving Room). Bedrooms are up-
to-date, with a variety of attractive fabrics and well-maintained bathrooms.
The Executive floor of 24 rooms has its own lounge. Banqueting facilities
for 350, conferences for up to 450. No dogs. Forte Grand. *Rooms 328.*
AMERICAN EXPRESS *Access, Diners, Visa.*

SW3   S & P Thai   £40

Tel 071-351 5692   **R**

181 Fulham Road SW3   Map 19 B5

Thai restaurant on the corner of Sydney Street and Fulham Road. The
menu has all the usual piquant Thai dishes which are currently so popular,
including specialities *tom yum goong* (spicy prawn soup with lemon grass)
and *gang kiew wan gai* (coconut chicken curry with sweet basil). Well-
priced set lunch and Executive set lunch menus. *Seats 60. Private Room 20.
L 12-2.30 D 6.30-11. Set L £7.95 & £9.95 Set D £18. Closed L Sun, 25 &
26 Dec, 1 Jan.* AMERICAN EXPRESS *Access, Diners, Visa.*

NW10   Sabras   £25

Tel 081-459 0340   **R**

263 High Road Willesden NW10 2RX   Map 16 A2

Opened in 1973, Sabras maintains its reputation for excellent vegetarian
cooking from Bombay, Gujarat and South India. Many of the ingredients
are not seen in many London establishments – violet Indian yam, cluster

beans, split pigeon peas, unripe bananas. Value for money is exceptional. *Seats 32. D 6-10. Closed L, all Mon. No credit cards.*

W1	**Saga**	£85
Tel 071-408 2236		**R**
43 South Molton Street W1Y 1HB		Map 18 C3

High-class Japanese cooking in both the main eating area and the sushi bar. The sushi choice is particularly good, so too the table-prepared specialities *sukiyaki*, *shabu-shabu* and *udonsuki* (Japanese noodles, chicken, fish and vegetables cooked in broth and served with mooli and spring onion). 15% service charge in the evening. *Seats 100. Parties 25. Private Room 12. L 12.30-2.30 D 6.30-10. Set L from £6.50 Set D from £37.* AMERICAN EXPRESS *Access, Diners, Visa.*

W1	**St George's Hotel**	65%	£150
Tel 071-580 0111 Fax 071-436 7997			**H**
Langham Place W1N 8QS			Map 18 D2

Modern accommodation in the heart of the West End, with good views of London's rooftop lights. Banqueting/conferences for 25/35. No dogs, no parking. 11 bedrooms are reserved for non-smokers. *Rooms 86. Coffee shop (7am-11pm).* AMERICAN EXPRESS *Access, Diners, Visa.*

WC1	**St Giles Hotel**	£110
Tel 071-636 8616 Fax 071-436 4009		**H**
Bedford Avenue Bloomsbury WC1B 3AS		Map 21 A1

Angular tower block offering neat, practical accommodation (half the rooms non-smoking) among the bright lights of the West End. In the basement are excellent leisure facilities (separately managed but free access to hotel guests). No room service. No dogs. *Rooms 600. Indoor swimming pool, gym, squash, sauna, solarium, beauty salon, badminton.* AMERICAN EXPRESS *Access, Diners, Visa.*

SW1	**St James Court**	73%	£180
Tel 071-834 6655 Fax 071-630 7587			**HR**
41 Buckingham Gate Victoria SW1E 6AF			Map 19 D4

Within walking distance of the magnificent Queen Elizabeth II conference centre opposite Westminster Abbey, and also very close to Buckingham Palace. A grand-scale Edwardian redbrick building has been converted into an almost palatial hotel, at the heart of which is a self-contained business centre offering an extensive range of rooms and services for up to 250 delegates. In the middle of the hotel is a fine open-air courtyard with ornamental trees and a period fountain – an ideal setting for alfresco receptions. Bedrooms are furnished and equipped to a high standard, with smart reproduction furniture and luxurious bathrooms. 75 apartments and 19 suites are also available. Children under 12 may share their parents' room free of charge. The Olympian health club includes a health bar and an aerobic dance studio. The choice of restaurants includes the French, Szechuan-orientated Chinese and the all-day Café Mediterranée serving brasserie-style meals. Daytime valet parking (free after 6.30pm Friday). No dogs. European flagship of Taj International Hotels. *Rooms 391. Gym, sauna, steam room, spa bath, solarium, squash, beauty therapist, business centre, brasserie (7am-11pm).* AMERICAN EXPRESS *Access, Diners, Visa.*

Auberge de Provence	£90

The restaurant is closely linked to *L'Oustau de Baumanière*, in the beautiful village of Les Beaux de Provence. Chef Bernard Briqué is in charge of the kitchen over here, offering a fixed-price lunch (with a good choice) and two interesting evening menus: a three-course *menu provençal* with

a substantial selection, and a *menu surprise*, conceived according
to individual tastes. Salad of artichoke hearts, green beans and pine nuts;
gratin of ratatouille and sea bream with a rosemary sabayon; fillet of red
mullet on a bed of diced tomato, basil and olive oil; duck leg with
courgettes and tomatoes flavoured with tarragon; and sirloin steak with
a rich red wine sauce show the sunny style. *Crepes soufflées, parfait glacé* and
quenelles de chocolat ivoire sauce cacao are typical desserts. The well-designed
wine list includes a selection from Baumanière. Excellent formal service.
Reservations on 071-821 1899. *Seats 65. L 12.30-2.30 D 7.30-11.*
Set L £23.50 Set D £30. Closed L Sat, all Sun, 2 weeks Aug, 26-30 Dec,
1-7 Jan.

W1	**St Moritz**	**£55**
Tel 071-734 3324		**R**
161 Wardour Street Soho W1V 3TA		Map 18 D2

A small, charming Swiss establishment on two floors whose extensive
menu offers meat and cheese fondues for two or more as well as other
Swiss specialities including air-cured beef, rösti potatoes, spatzle noodles and
veal zurichoise. Venison appears in season, notably in the classic Grand
Veneur – saddle with wild mushrooms, spatzle, brussels sprouts, red
cabbage, cherries, chestnuts, pears and apples. *Seats 48. Parties 28. L 12-3*
D 6-11.30. Closed L Sat, all Sun, Bank Holidays. AMERICAN EXPRESS *Access,*
Diners, Visa.

W5	**Sala Thai**	**£35**
Tel 081-560 7407		**R**
182 South Ealing Road W5 4RJ		Map 17 A4

Choosing from the 100 plus dishes on the menu of this friendly Thai
restaurant is a pleasant task with which the staff will gladly assist. Thai dim
sum, fried bean curd skin with crab meat and minced pork, chicken
or pork in a pepper and garlic mixture, dried sweet beef with coriander
seeds, king prawns in oyster sauce with broccoli, piquant salads and Thai
curry with mixed vegetables and prawns or cod show the flavour of what's
on offer. More esoteric are grey mullet (grilled, fried or in soup), Thai
anchovies in coconut and three ways with frogs' legs. *Seats 60. Parties 20.*
L 12-2.30 D 6-11. Closed Sun, 1 week Christmas. AMERICAN EXPRESS *Access,*
Diners, Visa.

SW1	**Sale e Pepe**	**£70**
Tel 071-235 0098		**R**
13 Pavilion Road Knightsbridge SW1		Map 19 C4

The complete Italian job, with singing waiters, a permanent party
atmosphere and a menu of well-prepared dishes from the standard
repertoire. *Seats 75. Parties 12. L 12-2.30 D 7-11.30. Closed Sun, Bank*
Holidays. AMERICAN EXPRESS *Access, Diners, Visa.*

SW1	**Salloos**	**£70**
Tel 071-235 4444		**R**
62-64 Kinnerton Street Knightsbridge SW1X 8ER		Map 19 C4

Established in Lahore in 1966, Salloos has been in London since 1977.
Tandoori grills – fat-free, long marinated and with no added colour – have
a great reputation here, especially the little lamb chops, and other special
dishes include chicken in cheese, *haleem akbari* (shredded lamb cooked
in whole wheat germ, lentils and spices), lamb's kidneys and king prawn
karachi. *Halwa gajar* is a hot sweet prepared from shredded carrots, milk,
almonds and pistachios, topped with edible silver leaf. *Seats 65. L 12-2.30*
D 7-11.15. Closed Sun. Set L from £18.40 Set D from £28.75.
AMERICAN EXPRESS *Access, Diners, Visa.*

SW3   Sambuca   £70

Tel 071-730 6571   **R**

6 Symons Street Chelsea SW3   **Map 19 C5**

Straightforward Italian cooking in a popular, bustling restaurant by Sloane Square (opposite the rear door of *Peter Jones*). The menu sticks mainly to established favourites, with pasta for starters or mains and oven-braised lamb a speciality for two. Long list of Italian wines. *Seats 70. Parties 30. L 12.30-2.30 D 7-11.30. Closed Sun, Bank Holidays.* AMERICAN EXPRESS *Access, Diners, Visa.*

SW6   Samurai   £65

Tel 071-386 7728   Fax 071-365 8582   **R**

539-599 Fulham Road Fulham Broadway SW6   **Map 19 A6**

Comfortable Japanese teppanyaki restaurant below *Bonjour Vietnam* and sharing the same entrance. Good selection of sushi, sashimi and tempura dishes are available as well as the teppanyaki 'griddle' dishes – lobster, scallops, chicken and beef carefully cooked, as you watch. Comprehensive set menus for 2 or more people. *Seats 60. Parties 12. L 11.30-3 D 6-11.30. Closed 25 & 26 Dec. Set meals from £15.* AMERICAN EXPRESS *Access, Diners, Visa.*

SW3   San Frediano   £55

Tel 071-584 8375   Fax 071-589 8860   **R**

62 Fulham Road SW3 6HH   **Map 19 B5**

Buzzing with atmosphere and old-fashioned Italian charm, San Fred is one of the real survivors among London's trattorias. Honest cooking, decent wine, ungreedy prices and slick service have provided nearly 30 years of customer satisfaction and a long list of daily dishes always adds interest to a menu whose specialities include veal and pasta: marinated herrings with beans, crab salad, guinea fowl with wine and grapes, chicken escalopes with cheese and asparagus tips. *Seats 100. Parties 30. L 12-2.45 D 7-11.30. Closed Sun (except Mothering Sunday), some Bank Holidays.* AMERICAN EXPRESS *Access, Diners, Visa.*

SW3   San Lorenzo   £100

Tel 071-584 1074   Fax 071-584 1142   **R**

22 Beauchamp Place Knightsbridge SW3 1NL   **Map 19 C4**

High prices are no deterrent to the smart set who keep this Beauchamp Place hot spot permanently hot. Cooking is capable throughout a fairly standard Italian menu. Almost a club, not always easy to get a booking, and a huge success down the years. *Seats 120. Parties 12. L 12.30-3 D 7.30-11.30. Closed Sun, Bank Holidays, 4 days Easter, 1 week Christmas. No credit cards.*

SW3   San Martino   £60

Tel 071-589 3833   **R**

103 Walton Street SW3 2HP   **Map 19 B5**

One of London's busiest and friendliest Italian restaurants, where Costanzo Martinucci and his family are completely involved. The owner himself grows herbs, vegetables and ingredients for the splendid made-to-order salads and in the summer their land produces up to 500 courgette flowers for the kitchen. Other ingredients are specially imported, including barley from Costanzo's native Lucca to make the splendid barley soup (*zuppa di farro*). The ever-changing menu provides great variety and three of the most renowned dishes are fish soup, tagliatelle with hazelnuts, tarragon and wild mushroom sauce, and spaghetti cooked with seafood in a paper bag. Seasonal game plus chef's recommendations such as wild boar sausages or carpaccio of swordfish add to the choice. *Seats 130. Private Room 40. L 12-3 D 6.30-11.30. Closed 25 & 26 Dec, Easter Monday.* AMERICAN EXPRESS *Access, Diners, Visa.*

SW3   Sandrini   £65

Tel 071-584 1724   **R**

260 Brompton Road SW3 2AS   Map 19 B5

High marks for comfort and smart modern decor. Above-average marks for Italian cooking throughout a menu which mixes the traditional (*mozzarella in carrozza, penne arrabbiata,* liver and onions Venetian style) with the occasional out-of-the-ordinary (wind-dried venison with ricotta cheese). Tables outside in appropriate weather. *Seats 75. L 12-3 D 7-11.30. Set L (Mon-Fri, 1 course, wine, coffee) £10.* AMERICAN EXPRESS *Access, Diners, Visa.*

SW1   Santini   £100

Tel 071-730 4094   Fax 071-730 0544   **R**

29 Ebury Street Victoria SW1W 0NZ   Map 19 C4

Venetian cuisine – top-quality produce cooked in a simple, honest way – is the keyword here, though the watchword is that it's not cheap! Best value is the Mon-Fri business lunch at £16.50 for 2 courses and coffee, though cover and service charges will be added. From the full carte you might choose baked artichoke or succulent carpaccio, tagliatelle with aubergine, pimento and olive, sea bass with herb sauce, roast quails with wine and herbs served with polenta, ices, sorbets, fresh fruit, *panna cotta* or cheeses. The mostly Italian wine list is priced to match the food. Sister to *L'Incontro* in Pimlico Road. *Seats 55. Parties 25. L 12.30-2.30 D 7-11.30 (Sun to 10.30). Closed L Sat & Sun, all Bank Holidays. Set L £16.50.* AMERICAN EXPRESS *Access, Diners, Visa.*

🍾 is our symbol for an outstanding wine list.

W1   SAS Portman Hotel   77%   £195

Tel 071-486 5844   Fax 071-935 0537   **H**

22 Portman Square W1H 9FL   Map 18 C2

The 70s-built Portman is one block from Marble Arch and caters very well for the businessman in a hurry with an in-room check-out via the TV, SAS flight check-in for full-fare passengers, a 3-hour express laundry service and a complimentary buffet for early birds. The traditional hotel comfort and atmosphere remains the same, however, with uniformed, efficient reception staff in the spacious lobby (where afternoon tea is served and there's a news kiosk and gift shop). Bedrooms offer quiet, controllable air-conditioned accommodation with stereo remote-controlled TV and mini-bar; a telephone extension is provided in the marble bathrooms; Superior double bedrooms with sofa beds are ideal for families; Royal Club rooms include further extras like a trouser press, safe, bathrobes, slippers and a wider range of toiletries. Check-out time is set late at 3pm, even later (8pm) on Sundays. Children up to 15 can stay free in their parents' room. The buffet-style Bakery coffee shop also serves a Sunday brunch. Service throughout is on the ball, and the major refurbishment programme (150 bedrooms, a new lobby bar and lounge, enhanced function facilities) due for completion as we went to press will no doubt add further to the hotel's appeal. The 150 bedrooms will have been remodelled into three distinct styles – Oriental, Scandinavian and British. Charged parking in the NCP car park beneath the hotel. *Rooms 272. Coffee shop (11am-11pm).* AMERICAN EXPRESS *Access, Diners, Visa.*

N1   Satay Hut   £30

Tel 071-359 4090   Fax 071-482 4513   **R**

287 Upper Street Islington N1 2TZ   **Map 16 D3**

Larger and more comfortable than the name would suggest, Satay Hut has
a menu that runs through Singapore, Malaysia and Thailand. Satay is the
unsurprising speciality (lamb, beef, chicken, prawns or vegetarian).
Seats *90. D only 6-12 (Sat & Sun 12-12). Closed 25 & 26 Dec.*
AMERICAN EXPRESS *Access, Diners, Visa.*

W1   Les Saveurs   ★★★   £120

Tel 071-491 8919   **R**

37a Curzon Street Mayfair W1Y 8EY   **Map 18 C3**

Our bold move last year to elevate this restaurant into London's top
echelon has, we believe, been vindicated by not only us – and results on the
plate have continued to please our inspectors – but also many readers who
have written to tell us of their findings. In restaurant manager Emmanuel
Menjuzan and sommelier Yves Sauboua, both ultimate professionals, Les
Saveurs has front-of-house staff fully worthy of the food. The restaurant
itself, an elegant and formal basement dining room, is reached down a fine
staircase from the smart reception area. Decorated in soft creamy tones
with subdued lighting, maple-panelled walls, modern flower paintings and
antique mirrors, there's an air of sophistication, further enhanced
by wonderful floral arrangements and exquisite place settings. And, what
of the cooking? Well, chef Joël Antunès firstly has an impeccable track
record with stints in the best restaurants in France, as well as a spell in one
of the world's great hotels, Thailand's Bangkok Oriental, from where many
of his innovative and creative touches, not to mention the stunning
presentation, come. Applying these techniques to a sound classical training,
he is able to infuse every dish with perfectly balanced flavours, retain the
textures of the raw materials to their optimum, and season with the lightest
of touches. All the trappings of luxury eating are demonstrated
by an appetiser before the first course, a pre-dessert *with* petits fours *and* a
post-dessert platter of more petits fours and tuiles of every description, each
a bit part to the main attraction. A variety of menus, all at exceptionally
kind prices for such a high standard of cooking, is offered: a fixed price for
either two or three courses, with the alternative of a fixed-price three-
course lunch (four choices at each stage) or a no-choice five-course dinner
menu. A spring version of the latter had oysters in aspic with horseradish
cream to start, followed by a brochette of Dublin Bay prawns and
mackerel with artichoke; a main course of risotto of pigeon with duck foie
gras (risottos are something of a speciality here: the version with lobster,
ceps and thyme butter has been on the menu since the outset, or mackerel
with pistou); a selection of French cheeses in tip-top condition and a
croustillant of nougatine with vanilla. Such an interesting menu is typical
of the care and understanding that goes into producing the seasonally
changing 'set' menu; dishes are well balanced and impeccably chosen.
Alternatively, the inexpensive lunch – a steal at £21 – has reasonably-
priced wine suggestions to accompany, say, fricassee of baby squid served à
la niçoise, fillet of lamb flavoured with thyme, ending with a feuilleté of
apples served with caramel. On the à la carte menu look out for specialities
such as terrine of foie gras with aubergines, rabbit salad à la niçoise, fillet of
red mullet served with potatoes and a sauce salmis (fish and liver), a pastilla
(sort of crispy envelope) of pigeon served with semolina and cardamom
butter, and sensational desserts such as hot chocolate madeleine served with
almond cream or bitter chocolate sorbet surrounded by a tea syrup. Apart
from the aforesaid wine suggestions, there are few bargains on the
predominantly French wine list, that has many classics and some lesser-
known wines from the South-West. ***Seats*** *55. Parties 16. Private Room 10.
L 12-2.30 D 7-10.30. Closed all Sat & Sun, 2 weeks Aug, two weeks
Christmas/New Year. Set L £21 Set D £34.* AMERICAN EXPRESS *Access,
Diners, Visa.*

WC2 The Savoy 91% £260

Tel 071-836 4343 Fax 071-240 6040 **HR**

The Strand WC2R 0EU Map 20 A2

One of the world's finest hotels, with tip-top standards of service under the direction of General Manager Herbert Striessnig. There's an international feel to the public areas – contrast the genteel Englishness of the peaceful drawing room with the brashness of the American Bar, or the grandeur of the ornate and marble-pillared Thames Foyer (afternoon tea and light snacks) with the 'Upstairs' (see below). Bedrooms, many in the original art deco style, include the much sought-after river suites, and boast such luxuries as real linen bedding, huge cosseting bath sheets, a nightly turn-down of beds and personal maid, valet and waiter bell service. There are banqueting and conference facilities for up to 500, plus a variety of stylish private rooms. The beautifully designed Fitness Gallery, which benefits from natural daylight and fresh air, was added during the rebuilding of the Savoy Theatre over the last couple of years. The leisure centre's facilities are complimentary for guests and include a rooftop swimming pool (the pool atrium), his and hers saunas and steam rooms, warm-up and workout rooms, and a massage room. Guests also have temporary membership of the Wentworth Club, the renowned golf and country club a short drive from London, which has tennis courts and an outdoor pool in addition to several golf courses (proof of handicap required). No dogs in the hotel. *Rooms 200. Indoor swimming pool, gym, sauna, steam room, beauty & hair salon, news kiosk, flower shop, valeting.* AMERICAN EXPRESS *Access, Diners, Visa*

River Restaurant ★ £130

Busier and animated at lunchtime, in contrast to more sedate evenings when there's dancing to a live band (playing old chestnuts) and twinkling lights across the river providing further attraction. Tables located by the picture windows, where the Thames is in the background, are much sought after, but it's such a grand room (except for the ceiling) that you are well placed wherever you're seated. Service under maitre d'hotel Luigi Zambon, here since 1982 (the same length of time as *maitre chef des cuisines* Anton Edelmann), is charming and smooth. Staff glide around almost unnoticeably, whether in charge of the smoked salmon and dessert trolleys, or the silver-domed 'roast of the day' chariot. The daily-changing seasonal dinner menu (five courses, £47) includes wines selected by sommelier Werner Wissmann to complement each course. Alongside this menu are an interesting list of à la carte dishes (lobster and apple salad with light curry dressing, fillet of lamb on aubergine purée, peach mousseline with pistachio tuiles) and a less expensive *diner au choix*, which is similar to the lunchtime *déjeuner au choix* – a recent menu offered haricot bean stew with langoustines, pastry-wrapped breast of duck and crepes Suzette among the choice of six or so dishes at each stage. *Régime naturel* options offer carefully-conceived dishes for health-conscious diets. Naturally, there's a grand and international wine list for such a grand hotel, but there are a few bottles within the reach of mere mortals! A variety of menus is offered in the private dining rooms. Menu prices vary considerably. *Seats 140. Parties 50. Private Rooms for up to 80. L 12.30-2.30 D 6-11.15. Set L from £26.25 (Sun £23.50) Set D £37 & £47.*

Grill Room ★ £120

Booking is essential both lunchtime and evening in the Savoy Grill, which many politicians and leaders of industry regard almost as their dining club. *Maitre chef de cuisine* David Sharland's classic favourites are the main attraction; from asparagus in season and dressed crab to pea, pear and watercress soup, Caesar salad, fishcakes, calf's liver with sage, lamb's kidneys with bacon and straightforward grills. A daily lunchtime *plat du jour* might be sausages with creamed potatoes and onions on Monday, roast rib of beef with Yorkshire pudding on Thursday, or Cornish fish pie on Friday; dinner dishes are more involved: beef Wellington, duck with cherries or *poularde de Bresse grand-mère*. In addition, roast saddle of lamb appears

See over

every day. Sweets from the trolley include the likes of summer pudding, crème brulée and an unusual chocolate pecan pie. The evening theatre menu (6-7pm) allows you to have your first and main courses before the show, returning for coffee and pastries in the Thames Foyer afterwards. Service, under maitre d'hotel Angelo Maresca, is executed with style and panache and shines as brightly as the beautiful polished yew panelling of this mellow-toned, very grand hotel dining room. *Seats 85. Parties 12. L 12.30-2.30 D 6-11. Closed all Sun, Aug. Set D (6-7.30pm) £26.75/£29.75*

Upstairs at the Savoy   £50

An ideal venue for an informal meal, overlooking the comings and goings and hustle and bustle of The Savoy Courtyard – it's a champagne, Chablis and oyster bar specialising in seafood dishes (salmon kedgeree, fricassee of monkfish with wild rice, grilled cod with a white bean stew) and fine wines by the glass. Mainly tables for two, and seats at the long marble counter. *Seats 28. 12.30-midnight (Sat 5-midnight) Closed Sun.*

If we recommend meals in a hotel or inn a separate entry is made for its restaurant.

SW3   Scalini   £70
Tel 071-225 2301   **R**
1 Walton Street SW3 2JD   **Map 19 C5**

The need to move the entrance to Scalini led to doubling the number of covers, so a greater number of visitors can now enjoy the experience of eating traditional Italian food in a smart interior. Freshly made risotti (with seafood, vegetables or chicken) are a speciality, and the pasta is all home-made. Some ingredients get slightly unusual treatments, such as chopped veal kidneys and mushrooms in a cream, mustard seed and brandy sauce, or trout cooked in butter with pine nuts and fresh grapes. *Seats 110. Parties 20. L 12.30-3 D 7-11.30. Closed Bank Holidays.* AMERICAN EXPRESS *Access, Diners, Visa.*

SE16   Scandic Crown Nelson Dock   69%   £124
Tel 071-231 1001   Fax 071-231 0599   **H**
265 Rotherhithe Street SE16 1EJ   **Map 17 D4**

Impressive modern hotel which brings some life to the new development project of Nelson Docks. The stylish building offers two restaurants, a bar, a pub, a small leisure centre and comprehensive conference facilities (for up to 350). Efficiency is the symbol here as in all Scandic Crown hotels. Rooms are spacious but some tend to be darker than others. They are all well equipped, with desk, seating area, mini-bar, trouser press, tea and coffee facilities, satellite TV and in-house movies. Club bedrooms are larger with a view of the Thames, fax point and bathrobes. *Rooms 390. River terrace, indoor swimming pool, gym, sauna, spa bath, solarium, tennis, games room, snooker.* AMERICAN EXPRESS *Access, Diners, Visa.*

SW1   Scandic Crown Victoria   67%   £135
Tel 071-834 8123   Fax 071-828 1099   **H**
2 Bridge Place Victoria SW1V 1QA   **Map 19 D5**

A centrally located hotel which combines Scandinavian practicality and efficiency with agreeably appointed surroundings. Air-conditioned bedrooms are comfortable, with sturdy Scandinavian furniture, duvets and even Scandinavian beers in the mini-bar. Children free up to the age of 14 in parents' room. 24hr room service. Buffet breakfast served 6.30-10.30. Extensive conference and function facilities. No dogs. *Rooms 210. Indoor swimming pool, gym, sauna, spa bath, sun beds, beauty salon, coffee shop (11am-10.30pm).* AMERICAN EXPRESS *Access, Diners, Visa.*

W1   The Selfridge   75%   £171
Tel 071-408 2080   Fax 071-409 2295   H
Orchard Street Marble Arch W1H 0JS   Map 18 C2

A covered porte-cochère with brass lanterns and greenery makes a good
first impression at this modern hotel adjacent to the famous department
store. Warm cedar panelling lends a traditional English feel to the foyer
and a smart first-floor lounge with leather wing armchairs. In complete
contrast, Stoves Bar is olde-worlde rustic with wheelback chairs and
genuine old beams and timbers recovered from a medieval barn. Bedrooms
(96 designated non-smoking) vary in size and are more comfortable than
luxurious, with darkwood units and TV remote controls wired to the
bedside; all have air-conditioning and telephones by the bed, at the desk
and in the modestly-sized bathrooms that also offer good towelling and
marble vanitory units. Children up to 14 stay free in parents' room. Valet
parking. Conferences and banqueting for up to 300. Mount Charlotte
Thistle. **Rooms** 295. *News kiosk, coffee shop (7am-11pm).* AMERICAN EXPRESS
Access, Diners, Visa.

SE22   Sema Thai   £50
Tel 081-693 3213   R
57 Lordship Lane SE22   Map 17 D6

Small, friendly Thai restaurant, offering helpful service, and careful
cooking. Flavours are often enhanced by the use of the charcoal grill.
Particularly recommended are "golden sema" (a selection of deep-fried hors
d'oeuvre), grilled chicken wings stuffed with spinach and *pad thai* noodles
used to good effect as the stuffing for a wafer thin omelette (something
of a house speciality). The strength of the curries can be obligingly adjusted
to suit the individual. **Seats** 70. *Private Room 20. L 12-3 D 6-11.30.
Closed L Mon-Fri, 2 days Christmas. Set meals £17/£19.* AMERICAN EXPRESS
Access, Diners, Visa.

EC3   Seoul   £30
Tel 071-480 5770   R
89a Aldgate High Street EC3   Map 20 D1

A tiny, one-room café/restaurant with the plainest of decor and offering
an enjoyable selection of traditional, simple Korean dishes. Starters include
spring onion pancakes with seafood or dumpling soup, followed, perhaps,
by marinated sirloin steak, Korean pickled cabbage (*kimchi*) fried with pork
fillet, fish and vegetables in hot spicy soup or fried thick noodles with
vegetables and beef. Spicing can be quite strong. **Seats** 30. *L 12-3 D 6-10.
Closed Sat, Sun & Bank Holidays. Access, Visa.*

> Set menu prices may not always include service or wine.

E1   Shampan   ↑   £40
Tel 071-375 0475   R
79 Brick Lane E1 6QL   Map 16 D3

One of the smarter restaurants on Brick Lane, with bright neon signs
outside and plush seating, attractive pink napery and helpful staff within.
The extensive menu covers a wide range of tandoori, biryani, dhansak and
balti dishes. Fish (rarely found in most Indian restaurants) is well
represented here. Two Bangladeshi freshwater fish, *Arr* and *Rhui*, are fine
examples. *Shatkora*, a sour citrus-like fruit, is another unusual item and this
is used to good effect with lamb, chicken and lentils. Dishes are carefully
spiced, with the use of fresh herbs another notable feature. **Seats** 60.
*Parties 25. Private Room 15. L 12-3 D 6-12. Closed 26 Dec. Set L £6.95
Set D £9.10.* AMERICAN EXPRESS *Access, Diners, Visa.*

W1   Shampers

£50

R

Tel 071-437 1692   Fax 071-437 1217

4 Kingly Street W1R 5LF

Map 18 D3

Between Regent Street and Carnaby Street, this is one of the West End's favourite drinking spots and has a thriving food side, too. The menu runs from oysters, gravad lax and salads to grilled noisettes of lamb, calf's liver and a fresh fish of the day. Ham and cheese pie, the day's casserole and steak sandwich are other popular choices. A fun but serious wine list offers quality at ridiculously low prices. *Seats 80. Private Room 45. Restaurant Mon-Fri 12-3, Wine bar 11-11 (Sat 11-3). Closed D Sat (all Sat in Aug), all Sun, Easter, Christmas.* AMERICAN EXPRESS *Access, Diners, Visa.*

W8   Shanghai

£60

R

Tel 071-938 2501

38c Kensington Church Street W8 4BX

Map 19 A4

Stylish Chinese restaurant on two floors, ground and basement, offering well-cooked food in relaxing surroundings. As well as hot and sour soup, lemon chicken, crispy Szechuan duck and other standard dishes, the menu is strong on seafood: crab with black beans and ginger, braised lobster, 'sea-spiced' scallops and sumptuous eel with a salt and pepper crust. Peking dumplings are a house speciality (griddled, boiled or steamed). Friendly service from smart and efficient staff. A pianist plays every night in the comfortable, but window-less basement. On the bend of Kensington Church Street, at the Kensington High Street end. *Seats 65. L 12-2.30 D 6.30-11.30. Closed L Sat, all Sun, 4 days Christmas. Set D £17.50.* AMERICAN EXPRESS *Access, Diners, Visa.*

SW7   Shaw's   **NEW**

£70

R

Tel 071-373 7774

119 Old Brompton Road South Kensington SW7 3RN

Map 19 B5

On the site of the old *Chanterelle*, Shaw's offers the citizens of South Kensington serious cooking and friendly service in civilised, quietly formal surroundings. Decor is elegantly modern, with large feature mirrors (the work of one of the six new owners), and tables are correctly and prettily laid. Two other partners run the place, Gerald (Bill) Atkins conducting front of house operations and his wife Frances in the kitchen. Her dishes strike a happy balance between safe and fashionable, with some very nice ideas but nothing to startle the worthy clientele which is the restaurant's target. Menus – à la carte at lunchtime, fixed-price in the evening – are basically in the modern mode, typified by warm spinach and wood pigeon salad with lentils; crab and potato cake with crisp bacon, cabbage and a shellfish sauce; peppered duck breast with cinnamon apples and green beans; ragout of veal sweetbreads with wild mushrooms, Roquefort and rice; and Angus steak béarnaise. There's always at least one vegetarian main course, and a dessert choice which could include pineapple gratin or hot vanilla soufflé with Grand Marnier sauce. Excellent petits fours served with coffee. Cooking is precise, presentation attractive, flavours true, but not too intense. Thoughtful wine list with quite friendly prices, and tasting notes for each wine; few half bottles. *Seats 44. Parties 12. L 12-2 D 7-10. Closed Sun, 2 weeks Christmas, last 2 weeks Aug.* AMERICAN EXPRESS *Access, Diners, Visa.*

WC2   Sheekey's

£65

R

Tel 071-240 2565   Fax 071-379 1417

28-32 St Martins Court Leicester Square WC2N 4AL

Map 21 B2

Fish restaurant, established in 1896, in the heart of theatre-land. Chef Jonothon Twinam has arrived, from the *Connaught*, to add some zip to the mainly traditional menu. Skate with sweet and sour sauce, scallops with truffles in Madeira and other modern combinations now accompany fishcakes, rock oysters and grilled Dover sole. The restaurant and its accompanying Josef's Brasserie (sharing the same kitchen and entrance), are now open throughout the day – the brasserie with a slightly restricted menu. *Seats 90. Meals 12-11.15 (Sat 6-11.15). Closed L Sat, all Sun, 24 Dec-2 Jan. Set meals £15.95/£18.75.* AMERICAN EXPRESS *Access, Visa.*

SW1   Shepherd's   £55

Tel 071-834 9552   **R**

Marsham Court Marsham Street Westminster SW1P 4LA   Map **19 D5**

The portraits of Richard Shepherd, Michael Caine and their inspirer, Peter Langan, loom large from the menu at what was once Green's. The division bell still features, as does the essentially British fixed-price-only menu of calf's tongue with caper and tarragon vinaigrette, haddock and mussel stew, asparagus, seafood salad, haunch of venison with chestnuts, gamekeeper's pie, Cumberland sausages and mash and lobster or crab salad. Roast Scotch rib of beef with Yorkshire pudding is served from a trolley. Burnt Cambridge cream, baked banana cheesecake and sticky toffee pudding with custard to finish. The setting is as traditional as the menu's ingredients, with darkwood mid-height partitions and almond-green velvet wall seats. For those in a hurry, a selection of cold dishes is available for 14 diners at the horseshoe-shaped, marble-topped bar. *Seats 70. Private Room 32. L 12.30-2.45 D 6.30-11.30 (Bar 5.30-8). Set L & D £16.95/£18.95. Closed Sat, Sun, Bank Holidays.* AMERICAN EXPRESS *Access, Diners, Visa.*

SW1   Sheraton Belgravia   75%   £245

Tel 071-235 6040   Fax 071-259 6243   **HR**

20 Chesham Place Belgravia SW1X 8HQ   Map **19 C4**

Personal service is high on the list of priorities at this luxurious modern hotel and its relatively small size allows it to be achieved. That service starts with valet parking in the NCP (at discounted rates) and a glass of champagne or orange juice at the reception desk in the panelled lobby. Day rooms, including a split-level lounge and library bar, offer abundant comfort, and bedrooms sport freestanding yew furniture; two floors are designated non-smoking. Guests can enjoy the facilities of two nearby health clubs. Children up to 12 stay free in parents' room. Unmanned business centre. No dogs. *Rooms 89.* AMERICAN EXPRESS *Access, Diners, Visa.*

Chesham's   £70

Modern international is the style of cooking in an attractive restaurant designed in sections – one of them with a palm tree, glass-domed roof and wall mirrors. The back section is designated non-smoking. Typical dishes include French onion soup, seared scallop and foie gras salad (a speciality), fish cake with lobster beurre blanc, lamb cutlets with ratatouille and grilled calf's liver with cassis sauce and red cabbage. Best value is provided by "Chesham's choice" – 2 courses + half a bottle of wine. *Seats 45. Parties 16. Private Room 22. L 12.30-2.30 D 6.30-10.30. Closed L Sat & Sun & Bank Holidays. Set L £19.95 Set D £15 incl wine.*

SW1   Sheraton Park Tower   79%   £270

Tel 071-235 8050   Fax 071-235 8231   **H**

101 Knightsbridge SW1X 7RN   Map **19 C4**

One of the most distinctive of London's hotels, a circular high-rise tower within a stone's throw of Harrods. Bedrooms, apart from the 31 luxury suites, are identical in size and feature rather pleasing burr walnut-veneered furniture. Thick quilted bedcovers, turned down at night, match the curtains; TVs and mini-bars are discreetly hidden away. There are telephones by the bed, on the desk and in the bathrooms, which have marble-tiled walls, good shelf space, towels and toiletries. Extra services

on Executive floors include valet unpacking, two-hour laundering, a special
check-out service and extra toiletries. Meeting facilities can handle up to 70
people-theatre style. Children up to 12 stay free in parents' room.
Rooms 295. Beauty & hair salon, coffee shop (7am-7pm). AMERICAN EXPRESS
Access, Diners, Visa.

W1   **Sherlock Holmes Hotel   61%**   **£132**

Tel 071-486 6161   Fax 071-486 0884   **H**

108 Baker Street W1M 1LB   **Map 18 C2**

Conveniently located close to Marylebone Road, a Hilton-owned hotel
with average size but well-equipped bedrooms. Given its name, where else
could it be but Baker Street? Public rooms include Dr Watson's Bar and
221b Baker Street. Children up to 10 free if sharing parents' room.
Banqueting/conferencing for up to 60/80. NCP car parking in Chiltern
Street at the rear of the hotel. *Rooms 125.* AMERICAN EXPRESS *Access,
Diners, Visa.*

SW7   **Shezan**   **£70**

Tel 071-584 9316   **R**

16-22 Cheval Place Knightsbridge SW7 1ES   **Map 19 B4**

Shezan is one of London's most stylish and comfortable Indian restaurants.
A stairway runs down from street level to a bar area and a room of quiet
elegance. There's nothing much to get excited about on the menu, but
cooking is competent throughout a familiar range, and there are plenty
of friendly, attentive staff. *Seats 100. L 12-3 D 7-12. Closed 25 Dec.*
AMERICAN EXPRESS *Access, Diners, Visa.*

W1   **Shogun**   **£90**

Tel 071-493 1877   **R**

Britannia Inter-Continental Hotel Adams Row W1A 3AN   **Map 18 C3**

A stone stairway descends to this basement restaurant at the rear
of a modern hotel. The vaulted room is transformed by samurai weapons,
pictures of ancient warriors and traditionally clad staff into a passable
replica of a medieval Japanese dungeon. In keeping with Japanese custom,
the menu is fish based with a few nods in favour of the carnivorous.
Japanese standards, various teriyakis and sushis are supplemented by six set
dinners – tempura, sashimi, salmon, chicken, duck or beef – and provide
an excellent initiation, all taking dishes from the carte. Our beautifully
presented sashimi included five types of the freshest fish. There
is a shushi/sashimi bar which provides a fascinating insight into the
preparation of these intricate dishes as the chefs work 'on view'. *Seats 65.
Parties 12. D only 6-11. Closed all Mon, Bank Holidays, 1 week Christmas.
Set D £31/£32.*

W13   **Sigiri**   **£30**

Tel 081-579 8000   **R**

161 Northfield Avenue Ealing W13 9QT   **Map 17 A4**

Sri Lankan restaurant decorated with drawings inspired by those found
on the rocks around the ancient island fortress from which Sigiri takes its
name. Among the Sinhalese offerings are unusual rice-flour hoppers, deep-
fried green banana slices, coconut-based curries and sizzling dishes
(yoghurt-marinated chicken with cashew nuts). Help-yourself buffet
Sundays. *Seats 62. Parties 24. L Mon-Sat by arrangement for parties of 12 or
more only (Sun 12-3) D 6.30-11 (Sun 6.30-9.30). Closed L Tues-Sat, all
Mon, 25 & 26 Dec, Bank Holidays. Access, Visa.*

SW1	**Signor Sassi**	**£60**
Tel 071-584 2277		**R**
14 Knightsbridge Green SW1X 7QL		Map 19 C4

Italian restaurant close to Harrods, with a straightforward menu of classic dishes – bresaola with mango and rucola salad, chicken broth with tortellini, calf's liver with butter and sage, ham-stuffed veal escalope and the like. Specialities include sea bass, lobster and lamb with mint. *Seats 70. Parties 40. L 12-2.30 D 7-11.30. Closed Sun, Bank Holidays.* AMERICAN EXPRESS ® *Access, Diners, Visa.*

SE5	**Silver Lake**	**£40**
Tel 071-701 9961 Fax 071-708 5718		**R**
59 Camberwell Church Street SE5 8TR		Map 17 D5

A busy and homely Chinese restaurant offering a mix of Peking, Cantonese and Szechuan cooking of a mostly familiar bent but with some more unusual touches. Try for instance hot mustard sesame chicken, lettuce basket wrap, mussels in black bean sauce or deep-fried shredded beef with chili in bird's nest. *Seats 40. L 12-1.45 D 5.30-11.45 (Fri & Sat to 12.30, Sun & Bank Holidays from 6). Closed Mon. Set L from £5 Set D from £12.* AMERICAN EXPRESS ® *Access, Diners, Visa.*

SW1	**Simply Nico** ★	**£65**
Tel 071-630 8061 Fax 071-355 4877		**R**
48a Rochester Row Westminster SW1P 1JU		Map 19 D4

Nico and Dinah-Jane Ladenis's smaller restaurant lives up to its name, offering delightful, straightforward menus and wine lists (all include VAT and service) without compromising quality in any way. Andrew Barber has been cooking to Nico principles since 1992, and has been joined this year at front of house by Julian Robinson. Menus might include duck terrine with pistachios and cherries, mushroom and artichoke hollandaise in pastry, or fresh pasta with truffle oil, Parmesan, tomato and chives as starters; fillet of cod in a potato crust with tomato sauce, brochette of calf's liver with fried onions and bacon, or fillet of lamb with 'confied' garlic as main courses. Tempting desserts such as armagnac parfait with chestnuts or lemon tart round off a meal: the only extra is £1.50 for coffee. *Seats 45. L 12-2 D 7-11. Closed L Sat, all Sun & Bank Holidays, 11 days Christmas, 4 days Easter. Set L £20/£23.50 Set D £25.* AMERICAN EXPRESS ® *Access, Diners, Visa.*

WC2	**Simpson's-in-the-Strand**	**£75**
Tel 071-836 9112 Fax 071-836 1381		**R**
100 The Strand WC2R 0EW		Map 20 A2

Even in a restaurant as staunchly traditional as Simpson's 'Grand Divan Tavern' some changes occur, the latest here being that it's now open for breakfast (7am-noon Mon-Fri). But it's the roast joints that are still the bedrock of its fame, wheeled around on silver trolleys as they have been since 1848. The same farm in the north of Scotland has supplied the beef for 70 years, and Simpson's gets through 25 loins each day (80% of customers order it). Roast lamb (23 saddles) and roast Aylesbury duck (36 birds) are other favourites, along with steak, kidney and mushroom pie, Cumberland sausage with mashed potatoes and onion gravy, and grilled lamb cutlets. Good-value lunch and pre-theatre menus; fish and vegetarian dishes are also served. Fine British cheeses, comforting puds, old-fashioned savouries. *Seats 450. Parties 120. Private Room 150. L 12-2.30 D 6-11. Closed 25 & 26 Dec, Good Friday. Set L & D £10 (Sun L £17.50).* AMERICAN EXPRESS ® *Access, Diners, Visa.*

W4 Singapore £35

Tel 081-995 7991 **R**

94 Chiswick High Road W4 2EF **Map 17 A4**

Neat, cool and smart little restaurant whose cuisine is Singaporean and Malaysian. The popular curries feature a creamy, spicy coconut sauce. *Seats 60. Private Room 16. L 12.30-2.30 D 6-11.15. Closed L Sat, all Mon, 25 & 26 Dec. Set D from £17.50.* AMERICAN EXPRESS *Access, Diners, Visa.*

NW6 Singapore Garden £45

Tel 071-328 5314 Fax 071-624 0656 **R**

83 Fairfax Road Swiss Cottage NW6 4DY **Map 16 B3**

A long Singaporean, Malaysian and Chinese menu with fresh seasonal choices such as soya bean fish, soft-shell crab and lobster with ginger, chili or black pepper and butter. Sizzling dishes are good, so too beef rendang and the other curries. Steamboat (£31.50 per head) is a traditional Chinese fondue. Daily specials recently have included okra in a spicy prawn paste sauce, pan-fried mackerel and skate served on a banana leaf and deep-fried crispy anchovies served with peanuts. *Seats 100. Private Room 60. L 12-2.45 D 6-10.45 (Fri & Sat to 11.15). Closed 5 days Christmas. Set L & D from £16.* AMERICAN EXPRESS *Access, Diners, Visa.*
Also at:
154 Gloucester Place NW1 6DT Tel 071-723 8233 **Map 18 C2**

W6 Snows on the Green £70

Tel 071-603 2142 **R**

166 Shepherds Bush Road Brook Green W6 7PB **Map 17 B4**

Huge pictures of lavender and sunflower fields and bunches of lavender on the half-tiled tables combine to provide an almost Provençal feel to this corner of Hammersmith whose Mediterranean menu makes marvellous reading and includes some intriguing combinations. A soup of plum tomatoes, bread and mascarpone; baked capsicums with brandade and pine kernels or perhaps millefeuille of snails and celeriac bordelaise (rather light on snails on our visit) to begin, followed by perhaps fillet of mackerel with apples and green peppercorns, lasagne of wild salmon and sorrel, or stuffed pig's trotter with black pudding and white beans. The technique does not always match the promise of the menu. Simple desserts include some fine home-made ices. *Seats 60. Private Room 24. L 12-3 D 7-11. Closed L Sat, D Sun, Bank Holiday Mondays, 1 week Christmas. Set L £11.50/£13.50 (Sun £13.50/£16.50).*

W1 Soho Soho ↑ £70

Tel 071-494 3491 Fax 071-437 3091 **R**

11-13 Frith Street Soho W1 **Map 21 A2**

The Rotisserie and all-day Wine Bar on the ground floor provide a raucously noisy, lively and crowded environment that continues to draw in the young and the fashionable. Upstairs, the Restaurant is equally popular but more select, with bookings and punctuality essential. Decor is Provençal – rustic in the Rotisserie, with its scrubbed, sky-blue-washed furniture and terracotta-tiled floors. Upstairs, chairs are upholstered in the sunburnt colours of the Med – yellow ochre, terracotta and deep azure. Walls in both have gigantic Picasso-esque drawings. In the Rotisserie (no reservations) the menu leans towards the informal with omelettes, pasta, grills and a few more elaborate dishes. The restaurant offers a range of more complex dishes. Both are very much of a classic Provençal inspiration. Soupe de poisson à la marseillaise, gateau de risotto forestière and carpaccio of beef with pecorino are typical starters, while fish dishes might include bouillabaisse with saffron and grilled red mullet fillets in vine leaves. Meat dishes could be corn-fed chicken with olives and capers or a particularly delicious dish of wild boar in red wine and chestnuts served with noodles. Desserts are a fitting finale to a meal of exemplary standards and quality. A bitter chocolate and almond délice is moist and very, very rich and comes with a refreshing and original glass of home-made orange wine. Other choices could be a raspberry clafoutis enhanced with Tahitian vanilla or a yellow plum puff pastry tart with crème fraiche. Classy service. Ask about the free local NCP parking offer for restaurant diners (only) after 6.30pm. *Seats* 65 (*Ground-floor Rotisserie* 70). *Parties* 8. *Private Room* 60. *L* 12-2.45 *D* 6-11.45 (*rotisserie Mon-Sat Noon-1am*). *Closed L Sat, all Sun, 25 & 26 Dec. Set D (pre-theatre)* £14.95 (*post-theatre*) £17.50. AMERICAN EXPRESS *Access, Diners, Visa.*

N16	**Le Soir**	**£35**
Tel 071-275 8781		**R**
226 Stoke Newington High Street N16 7HU		Map 16 D2

Popular neighbourhood restaurant run by a husband-and-wife team. A varied menu could include moules marinière, fried Camembert with apple and calvados jelly, poussin dijonnaise, duck en croute with Grand Marnier sauce and pork escalope with mashed potato and tarragon sauce. Also fish of the day, salads, a vegetarian dish and simple desserts like chocolate mousse. *Seats 46. Parties 10. D only 6-midnight. Closed Sun, 25-30 Dec. Access, Visa.*

N1	**Sonargaon**	**£50**
Tel 071-226 6499		**R**
46 Upper Street Islington N1 OPN		Map 16 C3

A discreetly-lit intimate setting for some carefully spiced classic Indian dishes. The not overlong menu includes a few non-standard items such as ginger chicken, where fresh ginger is used to excellent effect with tender cubes of chicken. Saucing is subtle with the judicious use of spices as a notable feature. Butter chicken or lamb pasanda cooked with fresh cream, nuts and sultanas is as tempting as king prawns cooked with a delicious sweet and sour masala sauce. *Seats 60. Parties 30. L 12-3 D 6-12. Closed 25 Dec.* AMERICAN EXPRESS *Access, Diners, Visa.*

Note that all telephone numbers with area codes starting with 0 will start 01 from 16 April 1995.

SW13	**Sonny's**	**£65**
Tel 081-748 0393		**R**
94 Church Road Barnes SW13 0DQ		Map 17 A5

A café at the front and a split-level restaurant at the rear with a few tables overlooking what must be one of the tiniest patio gardens anywhere. Decor is as modern as the food (now in the capable hands of Redmond Hayward), which has fashionable Mediterranean and Pacific Rim influences. Thus penne come with chorizo, chicken livers and rosemary; goat's cheese crostini with a walnut salad; and soft cheesy polenta is topped with warmed buffalo mozzarella, roast peppers and basil. Main dishes follow in the same vein, for example carefully chargrilled monkfish with chargrilled spring onions and a delicious oriental dressing of olive oil, garlic, ginger and Thai fish sauce or blackened cod with guacamole and tomato salsa, and calf's liver with smoked bacon and Puy lentils. Enjoyable sweets could include an apricot and marsala trifle, pear tarte tatin or iced hazelnut praline with a raspberry sauce. *Seats 100. Parties 10. Private Room 20. L 12.30-2.30 D 7.30-11. Closed D Sun, Bank Holidays. Set L & D* £12.95 (*2-course*), *Sun L* £16.50 (*3-course*). AMERICAN EXPRESS *Access, Visa.*

SW1   The Square   ★ ↑   £80

Tel 071-839 8787   **R**
32 King Street St James's SW1 6RJ   Map 18 D3

A minimally decorated modern restaurant just off St James's Square, its shop-like frontage adorned by large brass mobiles. Deep blue, orange and ochre fabrics are used in the seat upholstery to add a useful splash of colour to an otherwise creamy, well-lit room. Philip Howard's daily-changing menus are firmly in the best modern British style, showing a genuine flair for very well-judged combinations and a keen eye for detail – the results on the plate can be wonderful. Dishes are light and uncomplicated yet may comprise an amazingly wide variety of ingredients – assembled to complement one another, utilising every flavour and texture to the fullest and usually with many more facets than are indicated by the terse menu descriptions: seared tuna, tartare of vegetables, soy wilted greens; roast quail, *tarte fine* of wild mushrooms; sauté of John Dory, ragout of leeks and mussels; rump of lamb with aubergines and olive oil; praline parfait, poached pear, honey madeleines. Splendid cooking and splendid wines – though the list is hardly user-friendly, except the house selection and fine wines (incidentally, what constitutes a fine wine?). The rest are presented by grape style in price order. Service, under new restaurant manager John Davey (previously at *Girardet* in Switzerland, *Guy Savoy* in Paris and *Mosimann's*) is impeccable. *Seats 75. Parties 8. Private Room 30. L 12-2 D 6-11.45. Closed L Sat, most Bank Holidays. Access, Visa.*

SW17   Sree Krishna   £25

Tel 081-672 4250   **R**
192-194 Tooting High Street SW17   Map 17C6

Sound South Indian cooking making good use of freshly ground spices and herbs and sparing use of oil and fat. Vegetarian dishes are the real speciality but there's also a long choice of meat, chicken and prawn preparations. *Seats 120. Parties 50. Private Room 60. L 12-3 D 6-11 (Sat to midnight). Closed 25 & 26 Dec.* AMERICAN EXPRESS *Access, Diners, Visa.*

W1   Sri Siam   £55

Tel 071-434 3544   **R**
14 Old Compton Street Soho W1V 5PE   Map 21 A2

Traditional Thai food cooked to order in a lively Soho atmosphere. Good range of dishes on à la carte and set menus, and a separate vegetarian list. Among the specialities are *homok kai* (chicken cooked in spicy coconut gravy flavoured with lemon grass and presented in banana baskets), *sia rong hai* (sliced grilled sirloin of beef with mint, coriander and green salad) and *kaeng kurry koong* (a yellow curry of king prawns). *Seats 80. L 12-3 D 6-11.15 (Sun to 10.30). Closed L Sun, 24-26 Dec, 1 Jan. Set L £9.50 Set D from £14.95.* AMERICAN EXPRESS *Access, Diners, Visa.*

EC2   Sri Siam City   £55

Tel 071-628 5772   **R**
85 London Wall EC2M 7AD   Map 20 C1

Stylish Thai basement restaurant and bar that's a good alternative to City wine bars. The main menu, supplemented by various set meals, includes classics like tom yum soup, stuffed chicken wings and curries of various hues and some less standard items such as *pla pao numpla wan* – marinated fish grilled in a banana leaf and served with two sauces. Separate vegetarian menu. *Seats 140. Meals 11.30am-8pm. Closed Sat, Sun & Bank Holidays. Set meals from £13.90.* AMERICAN EXPRESS *Access, Diners, Visa.*

SW1   The Stafford   74%   £225

Tel 071-493 0111   Fax 071-493 7121   **H**

16 St James's Place SW1A 1NJ   Map 18 D3

In keeping with its clubland address the Stafford exudes civilised discretion, an impression enhanced by long-serving staff putting the emphasis on personal service. Paintings line the foyer walls and leather chesterfields create a scene of cultured calm. Deeper in, the drawing room, made elegant with antiques and fresh with cut flowers, offers refreshments throughout the day, and the American Bar features a collection of American club and university ties, caps and badges. Outisde the bar is a terrace in a cobbled mews. Accommodation ranges from singles with queen-size beds through doubles and junior suites in the Carriage House to the Terrace Garden suite complete with terrace and fountain. Decor is individual, with fabrics and furniture of a high standard. Part of the Cunard group. No dogs. *Rooms 74.* **AMERICAN EXPRESS** *Access, Diners, Visa.*

W2   Stakis London Coburg   £122

Tel 071-221 2217   Fax 071-229 0557   **H**

129 Bayswater Road W2 4RJ   Map 18 A3

Purchased by Stakis in the spring of 1994 the hotel was, at the time of going to press, about to undergo a much-needed refurbishment programme. The restaurant is due to be completely changed early in the New Year. The hotel was graded at 60% in our 1994 Guide. *Rooms 132.* **AMERICAN EXPRESS** *Access, Diners, Visa.*

SW1   Stakis St Ermin's   71%   £142

Tel 071-222 7888   Fax 071-222 6914   **H**

Caxton Street Victoria SW1H OQW   Map 19 D4

The Stakis St Ermin's is a peaceful haven in an area highly populated by tourists, giving it the double appeal of plenty of activity and the perfect retreat from it all. Extensive conference facilities (for up to 200 delegates theatre-style) also make it a primary choice for functions and banquets. Behind an opulent Edwardian facade day rooms are equally sumptuous: luxurious furnishings follow a green theme and the elegant furniture, much of it antique, finds an ideal setting among marble and ornate plasterwork. A splendid Baroque staircase leads to the five floors of bedrooms, which offer every modern comfort and are well appointed and furnished with taste. 54 rooms are designated non-smoking. Children up to 16 stay free in parents' room. *Rooms 291. Coffee shop (24hrs).* **AMERICAN EXPRESS** *Access, Diners, Visa.*

W2   Standard   £40

Tel 071-727 4818   **R**

21 Westbourne Grove W2 4UA   Map 18 A3

One of the best-known establishments on a street of predominantly ethnic restaurants. Consistently enjoyable food has been produced here for the past 25 years, the menu featuring such classic standards as rogan josh (their most popular lamb dish), chicken biryani and kulfi (Indian ice cream). *Seats 130. Parties 12. Private Room 50. L 12-3 D 6-11.45. Closed 25 Dec.* **AMERICAN EXPRESS** *Access, Diners, Visa.*

W1   Stephen Bull   £80

Tel 071-486 9696   **R**

5-7 Blandford Street W1H 3AA   Map 18 C2

Stephen Bull's eponym has all the trappings, or rather lack of them, of an ultra-modern restaurant. The stark minimalism of the monochromatic decor is emphasised by the wall-to-wall, floor-to-ceiling plate glass frontage.

The style of cuisine is modern British with European influences, and the menus, which change daily, are imaginative, even innovative and adventurous, but never outlandish. Twice-cooked goat's cheese soufflé remains one of the most popular starters, among which you might also find smoked chicken, salsify and bacon soup; home-cured salmon with warm oysters, fennel and curry; or grilled breast of lamb with lemon, coriander, chick peas, cumin and olive oil. Main courses are typified by fried salt cod with almonds and anchovy sauce; roast pheasant with Bayonne ham, turnips and armagnac; and fillet of beef with grilled polenta and salsa verde. Choose an individual dessert (perhaps spiced orange and grapefruit tart or prune and armagnac parfait) or push the boat out with the 'grand selection' or 'variations on a theme of chocolate'. Laid-back, informal ambience and service. **Seats** 55. *L 12.15-2.15 D 6.30-10.45. Closed L Sat, all Sun, Bank Holidays, 10 days Christmas/New Year. Access, Visa.*

EC1	Stephen Bull's Bistro & Bar	£60
Tel 071-490 1750		**R**
71 St John Street EC1 4AN		**Map 16 D3**

Characterised by a similar (but simpler) starkly modern decor to that of its Blandford Street sister restaurant (see entry above), the bistro features plain white walls and black tables and chairs with the odd (and very cleverly arranged) illuminated splash of bright colour. A slight change in the menu means that now there is a weekly-changing selection of imaginative, well-prepared dishes supplemented by a short, daily list of specials. The latter could include a mousseline of salmon with lobster sauce and a pork chop with Thai-curried split peas and an utterly delicious (but very rich) mocha and pear tart with Jack Daniels sauce as one of the sweets. Otherwise, the choice ranges from the likes of black pudding with caramelised onions and soubise sauce to a creamy cabbage, bacon and savoury risotto followed by tender sliced roast chicken breast with a prune and armagnac sauce and polenta 'nero' (with added buckwheat for a variation in taste and texture) or fillet of salt cod with a pistachio crust, mash and parsley sauce. To finish, the ubiquitous but excellent sticky toffee pudding with treacle toffee sauce or an equally irresistible rhubarb and crème fraiche tart with gingerbread ice cream. Splendid service from friendly staff. **Seats** 95. *Parties 20. Private Room 35. L 12-2.30 D 6-10.30 (Sat from 7). Closed L Sat, all Sun, Bank Holidays, 10 days Christmas.* AMERICAN EXPRESS® *Access, Visa.*

W6	Sumos	£35
Tel 081-741 7916		**R**
169 King Street Hammersmith W6 9JT		**Map 17 A4**

An unassuming Japanese snack restaurant on Hammersmith's main shopping street. Besides sushi and sashimi there's tempura (evenings), miso soup, griddle-fried dumplings, beef with ginger, chicken yakitori and sushi. **Seats** 40. *Parties 10. L 12-3 D 6-11. Closed L Sat, all Sun, Bank Holidays, 10 days Christmas-New Year. Set L from £4 Set D from £11. No credit cards.*

SW1	Suntory	£120
Tel 071-409 0201 Fax 071-499 7993		**R**
72 St James's Street SW1A 1PH		**Map 18 D3**

One of London's longest-established Japanese restaurants, with more of a Western style than Oriental; the cooking is of a high standard and staff have an exemplary attitude towards politeness, patience and understanding. The main dining area is on the ground floor, but there are also teppanyaki tables on the lower ground. The complete teppanyaki experience includes appetisers, dobin-mushi soup, sashimi, foie gras, mixed seafood, fillet steak, mixed salad, rice, miso soup, pickled vegetables, dessert and coffee or green tea. Alternatives include turbot, lobster, salmon and chateaubriand with prawns. The traditional side of the menu is also long in choice and ranges from sushi and tempura to one-pot dishes such as shabu-shabu and yosenabe cooked at your table. Prices at lunchtime are considerably less than in the evening. Suitably stylish for expense-account dining. *Seats 120. Private Room 8. L 12-2 D 7-10. Closed Sun, Bank Holidays, Christmas-New Year. Set L from £15 Set D from £49.80.* AMERICAN EXPRESS *Access, Diners, Visa.*

W9	**Supan**	**£35**
Tel 081-969 9387		**R**
4 Fernhead Road W9 3ET		**Map 18 A1**

Just around the corner from Harrow Road, Supan is a really delightful Thai restaurant with charming staff and well-prepared food. Stuffed chicken wings, Thai beef salad, tod mun (fish cakes) and crabmeat-and-cream-cheese pastry parcels to start, then a soup with or without coconut milk and on to a main-course curry or a stir-fry. Plenty of choice for vegetarians. As we went to press, plans were under way to extend into next-door premises, more than doubling the capacity. *Seats 30. Parties 15. L 12-2.30 D 6.30-11.30. Closed L Mon-Fri, all Sun. Access, Visa.*

SW3	**Le Suquet**	★	**£70**
Tel 071-581 1785			**R**
104 Draycott Avenue SW3 3AE			**Map 19 B5**

In surroundings inspired by the seafront at Cannes, fresh fish and shellfish get traditional treatment on a menu whose only changing element is the *plats du jour*. These often include sea bass (sold by weight), sole grilled or meunière and seafood pot au feu. Otherwise it's shellfish almost all the way, and the langoustines, coquilles St Jacques, mussels and clams may be ordered in either full or half-portions. For a major treat the mighty *plateau de fruits de mer* (£16) is a must. Steaks are always available for meat-eaters. Good salads and feuilletés. *Seats 70. Private Room 18. L 12-2.30 D 7-12.30.* AMERICAN EXPRESS *Access, Diners, Visa.*

N1	**Suruchi**	**£30**
Tel 071-241 5213		**R**
82 Mildmay Park Newington Green N1 4TR		**Map 16 D2**

Classical music and pastel prints provide the background to Indian cooking notable for judicious use of fresh herbs and spices. Nearly half the menu is vegetarian. Thalis (set meals) provide particularly good value for money. A conservatory was planned as we went to press. *Seats 34. L 12-2.30 D 6-11.30. Closed 25 Dec. Access, Diners, Visa.*

Our inspectors are full-time employees; they are professionally trained by us.

SW6	**Sushi Gen**	**NEW**	**£50**
Tel 071-610 2120			**R**
585 Fulham Road SW6 5UA			**Map 19 A6**

A split-level restaurant right on the bend of Fulham Broadway. Walls are of old stock bricks and you walk and eat on blond wood. The menu comprises a wide selection of various sushi and makizushi (seaweed rolls) – all meticulously prepared and simply presented. Additionally, there are a few grilled and deep-fried dishes such as breadcrumbed fillet of pork with miso sauce and the familiar tempura. Service is variable but well intentioned. No smoking. *Seats 50. Parties 15. L 12-2.30 D 6-11. Closed 1 week Christmas.* AMERICAN EXPRESS *Access, Visa.*
Also at:

NW6 243 West End Lane Tel 071-431 4031   **Map 16 B2**

SW5   Swallow International Hotel   64%   £134

Tel 071-973 1000   Fax 071-244 8194   H

Cromwell Road SW5 0TH   Map 19 A5

Large, well-maintained hotel on busy Cromwell Road (the main route
to Heathrow and points west), close to Gloucester Road underground
station. Several conference rooms and suites (for up to 230), a leisure club
and practical accommodation that includes 12 top-of-the-range suites. On-
site car park. Children up to 12 stay free in parents' room. *Rooms 415.
Indoor swimming pool, gym, sauna, spa bath, steam room, solarium, hair salon,
news kiosk, coffee shop (7am-midnight).* AMERICAN EXPRESS *Access, Diners, Visa.*

EC4   Sweetings   £60

Tel 071-248 3062   R

39 Queen Victoria Street EC4N 4SA   Map 20 C2

Arrive early to guarantee a seat at this busy and very traditional lunchtime
fish restaurant, as no reservations are taken. Most diners sit on stools at the
various bars, each supervised by its own waiter, although a few long tables
are available at the rear of the dining room. Prawn and crab cocktail
(both overflowing with fish), or perhaps smoked eel or oysters (in winter
months) to start. Dover sole, halibut and maybe a special from the
blackboard to follow. It's worth noting that 'fried' here always means
in breadcrumbs. Fresh fish is the strength of this establishment, not their
accompanying vegetables. School desserts, including excellent steamed
syrup pudding. Very short, but high quality, wine list; black velvet and
Pimms are also popular with city 'suits'. Delicious sandwiches, and a take-
away service available. *Seats 70. L only 11.30-3. Closed Sat, Sun, Bank
Holidays, 1 week Christmas. No credit cards.*

NW3   Swiss Cottage Hotel   62%   £85

Tel 071-722 2281   Fax 071-483 4588   H

4 Adamson Road Swiss Cottage NW3 3HP   Map 16 B3

An unusually individual hotel converted from terraced houses in a quiet
residential street a few minutes from Swiss Cottage underground station.
The bedrooms have plenty of character, with some Victorian/Edwardian
pieces of furniture, plush settees and nice old pictures. Some rooms are not
all that large, and they're linked by warrens of corridors and stairs. The
price quoted is for a standard double/twin. Superior and Executive rooms
are priced considerably higher. Children up to 8 stay free in their parents'
room. The lounge is very appealing: ornate gold wallpaper under
a moulded ceiling, sofas and button-back chairs on bright Oriental rugs,
carved antique furniture and oil paintings. The hotel also has self-catered
studio, one-and two-bedroom serviced apartments nearby, let by the week.
No dogs. *Rooms 81. Garden.* AMERICAN EXPRESS *Access, Diners, Visa.*

SW6   Tandoori Lane   £35

Tel 071-371 0440   R

131a Munster Road Fulham SW6 6DD   Map 17 B5

East Indian and Bangladeshi cooking in a congenial local restaurant. House
specialities include chicken tikka roshoni and king prawn delight. *Seats 58.
Parties 18. L 12-2.30 D 6-11.15. Closed 25 & 26 Dec. Access, Visa.*

SW3   La Tante Claire   ★★★   £140

Tel 071-352 6045   Fax 071-352 3257   R

68 Royal Hospital Road SW3 4HP   Map 19 C5

Quite simply, Pierre Koffmann is in top gear. Over the years, superlatives
about the cooking have been directed towards him by the bucketload,
so you could perhaps excuse the odd bout of complacency. There is none.

The meals we have eaten this year have not disappointed, and even the change in front-of-house, with the arrival of new restaurant Manager Bruno Bellemère, has occurred almost unnoticeably. You enter the restaurant via a narrow corridor, separated from the dining room by etched glass screens; those who do not wish to go straight to their tables can have aperitifs in the comfortable reception area; the dining room itself is smallish, yet tables are not too close together, allowing intimate conversation. Decorated in pale wood and soft pastel colours with several fine modern paintings, it's an airy room. There's a distinct difference in the ambience at lunch and dinner: the former is more lively and animated with a real buzz, almost certainly due to the fact that customers cannot believe their good fortune in eating *déjeuner* of such a high standard at such a ridiculous giveaway price of only £25 for an *amuse-gueule* (perhaps an avocado mousse on a bed of finely chopped beetroot), three courses, coffee and delectable petits fours, not to mention a variety of excellent rolls. Dinner, on the other hand, is usually taken in reverent hushed, tones, as befits the minimum charge of £45 per person. What of the food? Pierre's signature dishes (*galette de foie gras au Sauternes et échalotes roties; coquilles St Jacques à la planche, sauce encre; pied de cochon aux morilles; filet de chevreuil au chocolat amer et vinaigre de framboise*) can always be enjoyed, but recent dishes that live in the memory were a ravioli of langoustines generously flavoured with truffles, the pasta probably coloured by the use of lobster eggs; a slice of marbled terrine of *bouillabaisse en gelée* with a colourful, artistic and quite fiery sauce rouille. Main courses included a perfectly cooked piece of halibut on a bed of lentils with baby onions and lardons, and a stuffed leg of tender young rabbit with wild mushrooms served with light, creamy mashed potato. Among notable desserts have been a tart of cherries topped with crumble and served with a sabayon and vanilla ice cream, and crisp caramelised pastry layers interspersed with fresh strawberries and cream on a fruit coulis. Excellent coffee, splendid French cheeses in tip-top condition, and a comprehensive French-only wine list (including many half bottles) with some quite fair prices. Sadly, most of the bin ends have been snapped up. Service purrs along efficiently and unobtrusively. **Seats** *42. Parties 9. L 12.30-2 D 7-11. Closed Sat & Sun, Bank Holidays, 1 week Christmas, 3 weeks August. Set L £25.* AMERICAN EXPRESS *Access, Diners, Visa.*

SW1	**Tate Gallery Restaurant**	**£55**
Tel 071-887 8877 Fax 071-887 8902		**R**
Millbank SW1P 4RG		Map 19 D5

A basement, lunchtime-only setting useful for more than Gallery visitors: it is a destination restaurant rather than a Gallery snack stop (the separate self-service Gallery coffee shop is open daily 10.30-5.30). The restaurant menus are straightforward, mostly English (with occasional nods overseas) and change monthly (some stalwarts are available year-round). You might try a densely-flavoured roast pepper and tomato soup, or crab mousse with brioche toast; followed by beef in Guinness with root vegetables and rice, or turbot, spinach and prawn parcels with white wine hollandaise; and finish with spiced sherry trifle with ratafia biscuits or bramble and kirsch syllabub. Puddings (at £4.55) come with a complimentary glass of champagne. There's a good selection of British Farmhouse cheeses. There are usually one or two imaginative choices for vegetarians. Extensive wine list that includes a good selection of half bottles. **Seats** *100. Parties 36. L only 12-3. Closed Sun, most Bank Holidays. Access, Visa.*

EC2	**Tatsuso** ★	**£80**
Tel 071-638 5863 Fax 071-638 5864		**R**
32 Broadgate Circle EC2M 2QS		Map 20 D1

A split-level restaurant on one of the lower levels at Broadgate Circle. Immediately next to the entrance lobby is a smart, spacious teppanyaki bar. Also from the lobby a wide staircase leads down to an elegant, formal

Japanese restaurant. Ash is used to create the tables and chairs as well as the low screens that divide them, the blond wood strikingly modern, contrasting with the traditional look of kimono-clad waitresses. An extensive à la carte offers exquisitely prepared sushi and sashimi with authentic garnishes such as imported Japanese oba leaves – these leaves also turn up deep-fried in batter in some tempura dishes adding a refreshing and delicate taste. This is a serious restaurant with no compromise made on quality and the finest raw materials are assembled with infinite precision. Appetisers on the à la carte menu include squid served in sea-urchin paste; raw tuna with grated yam; sea tangle between herring roe wafers; and deep-fried turbot fins. All the dishes that comprise each of the many set dinners are balanced in perfect harmony, the small portions carefully worked out to allow the diner maximum enjoyment and nutritional benefit from the chefs' labours. *Seats 120. Private Room 10. L 11.30-2.30 D 6-9.45. Closed Sat, Sun & Bank Holidays. Set L from £20 Set D from £29.* AMERICAN EXPRESS *Access, Diners, Visa.* 🐂

Changes in data sometimes occur in establishments after the Guide goes to press. Prices should be taken as indications rather than firm quotes.

W2 **Tawana Thai**	**£40**
Tel 071-229 3785	**R**
3 Westbourne Grove W2 4UA	**Map 18 A3**

On the corner of Westbourne Grove and the bottom of Queensway, a pleasant little Thai restaurant offering the likes of spicy prawn and mushroom soup with lemon grass and lime, mousseline-style fish curry with basil steamed in a banana leaf, green vegetable curry ('spicy' is an understatement!), fried rice with taro root, and fresh Thai mango. *Seats 40. Parties 10. L 12-3 D 6-11.15. Closed 1 week Christmas.* AMERICAN EXPRESS *Access, Diners, Visa.*

SW5 **Terstan Hotel**	**£50**
Tel 071-835 1900 Fax 071-373 9268	**H**
29 Nevern Square Earls Court SW5 9PE	**Map 19 A5**

Family-owned and run since 1956, the Terstan bed and breakfast hotel stands in a garden square just south of the A4 Cromwell Road (approach via Earls Court Road), a couple of minutes from Earls Court underground station and Exhibition Centre. Most bedrooms have private facilities, the exception being some budget singles. All have telephone, colour TV, radio, and real coffee-making facilities. An even warmer welcome is now ensured thanks to a thorough overhaul and upgrade of the central heating system, and even speedier access to your upper-floor room by a revitalised lift. Simple, comfortable accommodation at a very reasonable price. *Rooms 48. Closed 3 days Christmas. Access, Visa.*

W2 **Thai Kitchen**	**£50**
Tel 071-221 9984	**R**
108 Chepstow Road W2 5QS	**Map 18 A2**

The decor, kept simple, is full of refined touches like carved wood artwork set off by simply painted walls, an orchid on each table and interesting crafted crockery. The cooking, prepared with authentic Thai ingredients, emphasises freshness and true flavours. Original dishes include fried marinated chicken in pandanus leaves, spare ribs in red wine and fried shrimps with young coconut leaves. Vegetarians are well catered for. Light desserts like pumpkin or coconut custard are freshly made daily. *Seats 40. D only 6.30-11. Closed Sun, 25 Dec.* AMERICAN EXPRESS *Access, Diners, Visa.*

SE14	**Thailand Restaurant**	£35
Tel 081-691 4040		**R**
15 Lewisham Way SE14 6PP		Map 17 D6

North-East Thailand pinpoints the MSG-free cooking of Mrs Kamkhong Cambungoet in this unpretentious little place. Lao dishes are a speciality, among them hot and sour green papaya with lime, garlic, chili and fish sauce; chicken marinated in black peppercorns and garlic and charcoal grilled; and minced chicken, pork or beef with spiced rice balls, to be eaten wrapped in lettuce. Advance notice is required for Scotch salmon prepared with bamboo shoots and Thai herbs and spices and steamed in banana leaf. *Seats 25. D only 6-10.30. Closed Sun & Mon, 10 Apr-10 May.* AMERICAN EXPRESS® *Access, Visa.*

SW3	**Thierry's**	£60
Tel 071-352 3365		**R**
342 Kings Road Chelsea SW3 5UR		Map 19 B6

Cosy and romantic French bistro with window booths and red check tablecloths. *Confit de canard, cassoulet de Toulouse* and *boeuf bourguignon* are main-course specialities, which could follow soup, roasted vegetables on couscous or garlic snails and be followed by ices, Paris-Brest or a plate of French cheeses. Besides the carte there's a *menu rapide* at lunchtime, an evening menu and party menu and an afternoon *casse croute* served from 2.30 (3 on Sunday)-5.30. *Seats 70. Private Room 34. L 12-2.30 (Sun to 3) D 7.30-11 (Sun 7-10.30). Closed Bank Holidays. Set L £9.90 Set D from £14.50.* AMERICAN EXPRESS® *Access, Diners, Visa.*

SE22	**Thistells**	£45
Tel 081-299 1921		**R**
65 Lordship Lane Dulwich SE22 8EP		Map 17 D6

Sami Youssef has firmly established himself as owner and chef at his ornately tiled former grocer's shop which he runs with his wife Anne. It's an unusual and atmospheric place serving good food at reasonable prices and you can have a full meal or a light snack, as you please, from a menu that is a charming mixture of French and Egyptian. Try moules marinière or falafel with tahini; entrecote of beef with Roquefort cheese sauce or *horura*, a main-course soup of pulses, coriander and bread; chocolate mousse with crème de menthe or home-made ices. *Seats 40. L 12-4 D 7-10.30. Closed L Mon, D Sun. Set Sun L £12. Access, Visa.*

SW6	**Tien Phat**	£30
Tel 071-385 7147		**R**
1 The Arcade Fulham Broadway Station SW6		Map 19 A6

Vietnamese and Chinese food in café surroundings. Choose à la carte or house special set dinners (minimum two people). *Seats 40. L 12-3 D 5.30-11.30. Set L £5 Set D £10/£13. Closed 25 Dec.* AMERICAN EXPRESS® *Access, Visa.*

NW11	**Tiger under the Table**	£40
Tel 081-458 9273		**R**
634 Finchley Road Golders Green NW11 7RR		Map 16 B2

The menu suggests that if you have four tiger beers you'll receive a free gift – let's hope that means one beer each at a table of four so that diners can appreciate the fragrant Singapore specialities at this stylish, shiny restaurant at Golders Green. Dishes are sometimes fiery, sometimes subtle: crispy squid, peppered crab, baked chicken in spices, cloud mushroom and scallop soup. The Sunday buffet is very popular with both adults (£10.95) and

children (£6.50). **Seats** 70. *Parties 25. L 12-3 D 6-11.15.*
Closed 25 & 26 Dec. Set L £5.95 Set D from £13.90. AMERICAN EXPRESS *Access,*
Diners, Visa.

| SW1 | **Tophams Ebury Court** | 60% | £115 |

Tel 071-730 8147   Fax 071-823 5966
28 Ebury Street Victoria SW1W 0LU

HR
Map 19 C4

Old-fashioned courtesy and charm in five adjoining houses three minutes
walk from Victoria station (300yds down Lower Belgrave Street).
Accommodation ranges from singles without en-suite facilities to luxury
four-poster/triple rooms with bath. All are equipped with hair-dryers and
satellite TVs. There are plans to provide more Executive singles. **Rooms** 40.
Closed 23 Dec-4 Jan. AMERICAN EXPRESS *Access, Diners, Visa.*

Tophams   £50

Three elegantly appointed rooms, their walls adorned with paintings by the
owners' ancestors, are the setting for meals that combine traditional and
modern elements. Tagliatelle with an olive and mushroom cream sauce
dressed with anchovy, salmon fish cakes with tarragon sauce, honey-glazed
poussin and steak béarnaise are typical items from the carte, while the two-
course lunch (price includes a glass of house wine) offers simple delights
like Welsh rarebit, paté, steak and kidney pie, chicken chasseur and goujons
of fish in a herb batter. Good value for both food and wine. **Seats** 30.
Parties 12. Private Room 24. L 12-2.30 D 6-10. Closed L Sat, all Sun.

| W1 | **Topkapi** | | £35 |

Tel 071-486 1872   Fax 071-480 2063
25 Marylebone High Street W1M 3PE

R
Map 18 C2

Turkish cuisine in an all-day restaurant named after the ancient Ottoman
palace in Istanbul. Hot and cold hors d'oeuvre (stuffed vine leaves, meat
balls, aubergines, yoghurt, peppers); main-course kebab grills. Quick
lunches, relaxed dinners. **Seats** 50. *Meals 12-11. Closed 25 & 26 Dec. Set
meals from £12.50.* AMERICAN EXPRESS *Access, Diners, Visa.*

| E1 | **Tower Thistle** | 66% | £157 |

Tel 071-481 2575   Fax 071-488 4106
St Katharine's Way Tower Bridge E1 9LD

H
Map 20 D3

The enormous Tower Thistle hotel enjoys one of the finest settings in the
capital, next to Tower Bridge and the Tower of London, with views of the
Thames and St Katharine's Dock. Behind a strikingly original modern shell
there's style inside, too, notably in the airy, high-ceilinged marbled foyer.
The Tower Suite can accommodate up to 250 function delegates theatre-
style. All bedrooms are air-conditioned and with the business visitor
in mind the City Club has been developed, with a dedicated check-in desk
and full 24hr room service. A full secretarial service is available in the
Business Services Centre, where guests can hire portable fax machines and
personal computers. Secure parking (mainly covered) for 116 cars.
Children up to 14 stay free in parents' room. No dogs. **Rooms** 808. *News
kiosk, coffee shop (7.30am-10pm), covered garage.* AMERICAN EXPRESS *Access,
Diners, Visa.*

| NW1 | **Trattoria Lucca** | | £45 |

Tel 071-485 6864
63 Parkway Camden Town NW1 7PP

R
Map 16 C3

Popular Italian restaurant whose standard trattoria menu is supplemented
by daily specials which usually include some very good stuffed vegetables.
Pasta, fish and chicken each have their own menu section, and grills are

a speciality, as are some of the steak dishes and *fegato alla veneziana*.
*Seats 65. Parties 40. Private Room 40. L 12-3 D 6-10.45. Closed Sun, Bank
Holidays.* AMERICAN EXPRESS *Access, Diners, Visa.*

SW7   Tui   £45

Tel 071-584 8359

19 Exhibition Road South Kensington SW7 2HE   **R**   **Map 19 B5**

Tom yum, a traditional clear spicy soup scented with lemon grass, lime
leaves and fresh chilis and served in a fire pot, is an almost essential element
in a meal at this civilised Thai restaurant in South Kensington. It comes
in three versions – with chicken, prawns or mixed seafood. *Pud prig* (stir-
fry with chili and basil) is another speciality, along with *mee grorb* (crisp-
fried rice noodles tossed in a tamarind-based sauce of pork and shrimps),
an excellent green curry and spicy cod rissoles. *Seats 52. Parties 12.
L 12-2.30 (Sun 12.30 to 3) D 6.30-11 (Sun 7-10.30). Closed Bank Holidays.*
AMERICAN EXPRESS *Access, Diners, Visa.*

N1   Tuk Tuk   £30

Tel 071-226 0837

330 Upper Street Islington N1 2XQ   **R**   **Map 16 D3**

Named after the rickshaw-style taxis that ply the streets of Bangkok, this
small, stylish and informal Thai restaurant offers satay, chicken wings, fish
patties, hot and sour soup with prawns and rice, a mild or chili-hot curry,
garlicky fried beef and noodles with mixed seafood. *Seats 40.
Private Room 40. L 12-3.30 D 6-10.30. Closed L Sat, all Sun, Bank Holidays.*
AMERICAN EXPRESS *Access, Visa.*

See the hotel by county listings for easy comparison of conference
and banqueting facilities.

SW3   Turner's   ★   £100

Tel 071 -584 6711   Fax 071-584 4441

87/89 Walton Street SW3 2HP   **R**   **Map 19 B5**

An elegant restaurant, close to the fashionable dining enclave of Brompton
Cross, run for many years by Yorkshireman Brian Turner. The dining
room is restfully decorated in pale blue, with gathered blue and yellow
curtains, well-chosen pictures and smart napery. The menu veers towards
the classical rather than trying to keep pace with today's (gone tomorrow!)
food fashions. The main fixed-price menu (£32 – including service – for
two courses) offers several choices written in French with English
translations, beginning perhaps with a confit of duck terrine with rocket
salad and a truffle juice dressing or a consommé of langoustines, followed
by a light stew of monkfish and mussels with morel mushrooms, roast calf's
kidney with a green peppercorn sauce, and roast rack of English lamb
in a herb crust. Incidentally, the roast beef is the centrepiece of Sunday
lunch, which represents particularly good value. Don't miss the excellent
desserts, which include a pear tarte tatin, and bricks of white and dark
chocolate with a mint sauce. Slightly simpler *menus du jour* (two choices
at lunchtime, none in the evening) could offer salmon salad with a pepper
dressing, fillet of cod with a butter sauce, and apple crumble. Lunch is also
a real bargain – two courses for under a tenner! The wine list is carefully
chosen, and has considerably widened its scope outside France during the
last year. A few bin ends at keen prices are listed at the front. Prices are
inclusive of service and VAT – what you see is what you pay! *Seats 50.
L 12.30-2.30 D 7.30-11.15. Closed L Sat, Bank Holidays, 1 week Christmas.
Set L £9.95/£13.50 (Sun £19.50/£23.50) Set D from £23.50.*
AMERICAN EXPRESS *Access, Diners, Visa.*

SW9　　Twenty Trinity Gardens　　£45

Tel 071-733 8838　　**R**

20 Trinity Gardens Brixton SW9 8DP　　Map 17 C5

This popular neighbourhood restaurant is a stone's throw away from Acre Lane – by car, approach from Brighton Terrace. The walls are crammed with a mixture of original artistic photographs (some erotic) and woven tapestries. A plant-filled conservatory makes an ideal setting for Sunday lunch, as well as for a romantic dinner. New chef Paul Churchill changed the slant of the menu from one with Caribbean and Cajun influences to a modern European style. Warm goat's cheese with caramelised apples, carpaccio of fresh tuna and tuna and carrot and coriander soup typify the starters. Main dishes might typically include rump steak marinated in garlic and olive oil and confit of duck (here made with Aylesbury, rather than the more fashionable Lunesdale) with a honey and coriander sauce. Tuesday is bargain night, with a 2-course table d'hote menu for £10, including a carafe of wine. Vegetarians are well catered for. Charming, informal service. **Seats** 54. *Parties 20. Private Room 20. L (Sun only) 12-4 D 7-10.30. Closed Bank Holidays & 4 days Christmas. Set Sun L £9.95/£13.50 Set D from £14.25. Access, Visa.*

SW1　　22 Jermyn Street　　£192

Tel 071-734 2353　Fax 071-734 0750　　**PH**

22 Jermyn Street SW1Y 6HL　　Map 18 D3

50 yards from Piccadilly, 22 Jermyn Street was established as 'residential chambers' by Anthony Glyka in 1915. The fine Edwardian property has been converted with panache by his grandson, Henry Togna, to a small, luxurious and very private hotel. 13 self-contained suites and 5 studios retain their period furniture and objets d'art and are brightened daily with fresh flowers. Business facilities include fax points and a 'speed-dial' phone directory; housekeeping, 24hr room services (including medical and dental support) and Continental breakfast are similarly comprehensive and guests can avail themselves of a personal shopping service. King-size beds, make-up mirrors, bespoke toiletries and monogrammed bathsheets and robes set the tone. Exercise equipment available in suites. **Rooms** 18. AMERICAN EXPRESS *Access, Diners, Visa.*

Many hotels offer reduced rates for weekend or out-of-season bookings. Always ask about special deals.

NW1　　Underground Café　　£55

Tel 071-482 0010　　**R**

214 Camden High Street NW1　　Map 16 C3

In a basement immediately next to the *Camden Brasserie* (in the same ownership too), this restaurant throbs nightly with the bustle of bon viveurs on a budget. Decor is simple but stylish, with plain white walls hung with contemporary art and dripping candle mirrors. The brief menu, augmented by the day's specials, is of Mediterranean origins, consisting of uncomplicated dishes which because of the good-quality ingredients and their careful handling result in very satisfying meals. Typical is a creamy black risotto with baby squid and tender prawns, or bruschetta with a generous amount of tapénade and delicious chopped marinated tomatoes among the starters and grilled tuna steaks with red peppers, braised shank of lamb or spicy Italian sausages with braised red cabbage and garlic potato mash as main dishes. Sweets include an ultra-rich but unmissable chocolate torte with crumbled amaretti and cream. Good espresso coffee and attentive, amiable staff. **Seats** 85. *Parties 20. Private Room 24. D only 6-11. Closed Sun, 1 week Christmas. Access, Visa.*

SW7   The Vanderbilt   62%

£139

Tel 071-589 2424   Fax 071-225 2293   **H**

68-86 Cromwell Road London SW7 5BT   Map 19 B5

This Grade II listed building comprising ten linked town houses on busy Cromwell Road now houses Radisson Edwardian's Vanderbilt, with its classical early Victorian frontage. Inside, the period atmosphere is retained with frescoed ceilings and heavy floral drapes. Rooms include some Executive singles. No dogs. *Rooms 223.* AMERICAN EXPRESS® *Access, Diners, Visa.*

W2   Veronica's

£65

Tel 071-229 5079   **R**

3 Hereford Road Bayswater W2 4AB   Map 18 A3

Veronica Shaw's cosy restaurant, tucked away behind Queensway and facing leafy Leinster Square, is now in its eleventh year. A great deal of thought has gone into the menu, which includes British dishes going back to Tudor times. Dishes are well described, not just with their ingredients and history but also showing if they're low in fat, or suitable for vegetarians or vegans. A typical summer menu included savoury tomato pudding and grilled Wiltshire goat's cheese with elderflower syrup as starters, followed by twice-roasted duck with either horseradish or orange sauce and grilled calf's liver with Victorian Benton sauce. Fish dishes hold equal surprises: 19th-century spiced fish and Tudor pye of salmon and mushroom being just two on offer. As well as a good vegetarian choice, the restaurant prides itself on its selection of British cheese. Outdoor tables in good weather. *Seats 60. Private Room 40. L 12-3 D 7-12. Closed L Sat, all Sun, Bank Holidays.* AMERICAN EXPRESS® *Access, Diners, Visa.*

NW6   Vijay

£25

Tel 071-328 1087   **R**

49 Willesden Lane NW6 7RF   Map 16 B3

Popular preparations of lamb, chicken and prawns supplement vegetarian specialities at this unpretentious establishment, opened more than 30 years ago and among the oldest South Indian restaurants in England. Adai is a pancake made from rice and three varieties of lentils; iddly (a speciality) is a steamed cake made of rice and garam flour; avial mixes several vegetables cooked with ground coconut, yoghurt, butter and curry leaves. *Seats 78. Parties 25. L 12-2.45 D 6-10.45 (Fri & Sat till 11.45). Closed 25 & 26 Dec.* AMERICAN EXPRESS® *Access, Diners, Visa.*

W1   Villandry Dining Room

£45

Tel 071-224 3799   **R**

89 Marylebone High Street W1M 3DE   Map 18 C2

By day, an up-market delicatessen with a small restaurant at the rear offering superior snacks both sweet and savoury plus a few more substantial dishes. However one evening, once a month the whole place transforms into a restaurant. Bookings have to be made well in advance and confirmed a few days beforehand. For this you sit at small bare wood tables surrounded by shelves stacked with the likes of fine olive oils, teas and mustards. Caroline Symmonds' menu is short but varied; her execution is skilled, the presentation simple and the results extremely enjoyable. Lunch sees the likes of a plate of charcuterie, marinated aubergine salad with pimento and lemon, grilled goat's cheese on a tapénade crouton to start, following with roast quail with haricots verts and new potatoes, French ham with Parmesan mashed potatoes, roast new season garlic and Kentish leaves, or pan-fried halibut with a light lemon and butter sauce. Dinner is along the same lines, with a wonderful lack of pretension to the whole proceedings. Excellent breads and fine cheeses – mostly French, but also some superb British examples. Sweets might include strawberry semifreddo, blueberry buttermilk pancake with fresh cream or a good tart. No smoking. *Seats 56. Parties 30. L 12.30-2.30 (D once a month). Closed Sun, Bank Holidays, 10 days Christmas-New Year.* AMERICAN EXPRESS® *Access, Visa*

WC1   Wagamama   £25

Tel 071-323 9223   Fax 071-323 9224   **R**
4 Streatham Street off Bloomsbury Street WC1 1JB   Map 21 B1

No reservations are taken at this ever-busy, trend-setting Japanese noodle restaurant, set in a basement just off New Oxford Street and Bloomsbury Street. 'Positive eating, positive living' is the message, noodles (*ramen*) the medium. Expect to queue at peak times, but not for long as customers are happy with the fast serve, fast out concept. Parties should expect food to arrive as and when it is ready. A successful, self-styled 'non-destination food station'. Raw energy juices and salads, gyoza dumplings, rice dishes and sake complete the picture. *Seats 104. L 12-2.30 (Sat to 3.30) D 6-11. Closed Sun, Bank Holidays (exc Good Friday). No credit cards.*

NW3   Wakaba   £70

Tel 071-586 7960   **R**
122a Finchley Road NW3 5HT   Map 16 B2

Behind curved glass frosted from busy Finchley Road the decor is designer-zero, canteen-style, basically plain white. The menu provides an interesting span of Japanese dishes with a particularly extensive choice from the sushi bar. Sushi is priced either à la carte (more than 30 choices) or by 5, 7 or 9 pieces. Some dishes, including *sukiyaki*, *shabushabu* and *yosenabe* (Japanese-style bouillabaisse) are prepared at the table. *Seats 55. D only 6.30-11. Closed Sun, 4 days Easter, 4 days Christmas. Set D from £23.60.* AMERICAN EXPRESS® *Access, Diners, Visa.*

WC2   The Waldorf   83%   £195

Tel 071-836 2400   Fax 071-836 7244   **H R**
Aldwych WC2B 4DD   Map 20 A2

Opened in 1908 (and in 1958 the first hotel to be acquired by Charles Forte – the company now has over 800), the Waldorf celebrated its 85th anniversary with a multi-million pound refit a couple of years ago. Public areas remain unchanged in style, including the Club Bar with its polished wood panelling, leather chesterfields and marble fireplaces, the pubby Footlights Bar and traditional Aldwych Brasserie. At the heart of the hotel the truly grand Palm Court Lounge is where Saturday and Sunday tea dances (£19.50) are a veritable institution, with their origins in the Waldorf's famous Tango Teas of the 1920s and 30s. Bedrooms were totally transformed in the refurbishment and all now have air-conditioning, secondary sockets for fax or modems and even 110-volt outlets for the convenience of transatlantic guests. Every bedroom has its own entrance lobby, new traditionally-styled polished darkwood furniture and one of nine bold decorative schemes. Elaborately draped curtains and chandeliers hark back to the opulence of the hotel's Edwardian origins, as do the period-style washstands in marble-trimmed bathrooms that all have both fixed and hand-held showers over the tubs; bathrobes, speaker extensions and good toiletries also provided. Children up to 16 share parents' room free. Well-turned-out staff provide a proper turn-down service in the evenings and valet parking, but overnight room service is limited to sandwiches and snacks. Banqueting/conference facilities for up to 420. *Rooms 292.* AMERICAN EXPRESS® *Access, Diners, Visa.*

Restaurant   £90

A grand, high-ceilinged room with Corinthian columns and French doors
opening on to the Palm Court. The menu is strong on grills and fairly
traditional dishes: cock-a-leekie soup, escalope of veal Holstein, steak Diane,
crepes Suzette. The sweet trolley holds no surprises, but the intendedly
formal service might! *Seats 60. Parties 10. L 12.30-2.30 D 6-11 (Sun 7-10).
Set L & D £21/£25. Closed L Sun.*

W1   Walsh's   £60

Tel 071-637 0222   Fax 071-637 0224   **R**

5 Charlotte Street W1P 1HD   Map 18 D2

A smart glittering oyster bar with tall bar stools occupies the front while
elsewhere highly-polished wood tables are arranged in a series of brightly-
lit dining rooms. Efficient staff serve a largely traditional range of well-
prepared seafood dishes, from St Jacques salad and gratin of Arbroath
smokies to lobster (poached, grilled, pan-fried with wild mushrooms,
Thermidor), plaice, sea bass, grilled tuna steak with green and black olives
and half-a-dozen ways with sole. *Seats 70. Parties 25. Private Room 25.
L 12-2.30 D 6-10.30. Closed L Sat, all Sun, Bank Holidays.* AMERICAN EXPRESS
Access, Diners, Visa.

SW3   Waltons of Walton Street   £100

Tel 071-584 0204   Fax 071-581 2848   **R**

121 Walton Street South Kensington SW3 2PH   Map 19 B5

Polished service matches the luxuriously comfortable surroundings and
in the kitchen Paul Hodgson shows his considerable skills in the highly
enjoyable dishes that have made Waltons such a favourite. The à la carte
menu mixes the traditionally English with the modern and international.
It's the former that provide specialities such as saddle of lamb roasted
and served with wild mushroms and a thyme and rosemary sauce,
or medallions of Scottish beef served on a potato cake with roasted shallots
and a rich red wine sauce. Other choices run from Stilton and leek parcels
and seafood sausage to corn-fed guinea fowl with Savoy cabbage, steamed
salmon stuffed with crab mousse and breast of duck with lingonberries and
an armagnac sauce. Well-priced 'Simply Waltons' lunch menu, traditional
three-course Sunday lunch, two-course after-theatre supper menu. *Seats 65.
Parties 20. L 12.30-2.30 (Sun & Bank Holidays till 2) D 7.30-11.30 (Sun &
Bank Holidays 7-10). Closed D 25 & all 26 Dec. Set L £14.75 (Sun £16.50)
Set D £21.* AMERICAN EXPRESS *Access, Diners, Visa.*

Note that all telephone numbers with area codes starting with 0
will start 01 from 16 April 1995.

W1   Washington Hotel   70%   £178

Tel 071-499 7000   Fax 071-495 6172   **H**

5 Curzon Street Mayfair W1Y 8DT   Map 18 C3

Between Berkeley Square and Park Lane, in the heart of Mayfair, a smart
hotel with elegant public areas – from the marble-floored reception
to Madison's lounge-bar with Oriental carpets, comfortable seating,
elaborately draped curtains and bird's-eye maple panelling. Bedrooms vary
in size and shape but have a distinctive 30s' feel, with striking burred oak
furniture in Art Deco style matched by agreeable abstract-patterned fabrics.
Bathrooms have particularly good shower heads over the tubs, plus
convenient phone and loudspeaker extensions. Long beds and a breakfast
table, room safes and a computer-coded locking system are standard
throughout. Over 30 rooms are state rooms or suites. Children up to 16
stay free in parents' room. Bright, modern meeting rooms for up to 100.
24hr room service. Buffet breakfast. No dogs. Sarova Hotels. *Rooms 173.*
AMERICAN EXPRESS *Access, Diners, Visa.*

W1   The Westbury   75%

£191

Tel 071-629 7755   Fax 071-495 1163

H

Conduit Street W1A 4UH

Map 18 D3

The main entrance is on Conduit Street, but the hotel is literally just off New Bond Street. It was opened in 1955 as sister hotel to the *Westbury* in New York and comparisons hold up well, with sparkling chandeliers and smartly liveried porters creating a formal impression on first entering the marble-floored lobby. The pine-panelled Polo Lounge (open 24 hours for refreshments) and dark green Polo Bar boast polo murals and memorabilia, inspired by the original owners who had a passion for the sport – the hotels are actually named after the Long Island polo ground. Bedrooms vary in size from smallish singles through mini-suites to 13 full suites and a penthouse; all share the same traditional-style darkwood furniture with pleasing floral fabrics and many extras like mini-bars. Conference facilities for up to 120. Forte Grand. **Rooms** *244.* AMERICAN EXPRESS *Access, Diners, Visa.*

NW1   White House   71%

£132

Tel 071-387 1200   Fax 071-388 0091

H

Albany Street NW1 3UP

Map 18 D1

Just off Euston Road, close to Regent's Park and opposite Great Portland Street underground station. Built as a block of flats in the 1930s, hence the numerous pillars to be found in the public rooms. There is no separate lounge in the smart marble-floored reception/foyer, but it does offer some seating and the sophisticated bar has plenty of lounge-style armchairs. There's a cocktail lounge, a restaurant, a long-hours garden café and the Wine Press wine bar. Bedrooms vary in size from compact to suites; most have decent lightwood units, soft colour schemes and matching fabrics. All have double-glazed windows and American electric sockets as well as British ones plus mini-bars, security chains and spyholes. One floor, called the Reserve Floor, has separate check-in and lounge plus lots of extras. 24hr room service. No dogs. Conference and banqueting facilities for 120/100. Recent change of ownership. **Rooms** *575. Gym, sauna, coffee shop (7am-11pm), news kiosk & gift shop.* AMERICAN EXPRESS *Access, Diners, Visa.*

W1   White Tower

£70

Tel 071-636 8141

R

1 Percy Street off Tottenham Court Road W1P 0ET

Map 18 D2

George Metaxas and Mary Dunne maintain consistent standards at this comfortable, genteel restaurant specialising mainly in Greek cuisine. The walls are lined with pictures and paintings of Asian Minors and Greek and Middle-Eastern dishes form the bulk of a wordy menu. Two of the most famous dishes are a rich, satisfying beef-based moussaka and Aylesbury duckling *farci à la cypriote* – weighty chaps stuffed with bourgourie, chopped almonds and livers, and roasted to a crisp dark brown. Each provides a festal dish for two (though a single helping may be ordered). Start with mixed patés or mezedes, finish with fresh fruit salad. Some of the staff have seen more than 40 years service in this most traditional of addresses. **Seats** *75. Private Room 18. L 12.30-2.30 D 6.30-10.30. Closed L Sat, all Sun & 3 weeks Aug.* AMERICAN EXPRESS *Access, Diners, Visa.*

W2   Whites Hotel   77%

£191

Tel 071-262 2711   Fax 071-262 2147

H

90 Lancaster Gate Bayswater W2 3NR

Map 18 B3

Originally part of a terrace of private houses, it was built in 1866 in the style then known as French Renaissance. A cobbled forecourt leads through glass-topped canopies into a Victorian mansion with a colonnaded facade. There's a feeling of quiet opulence in day rooms like the graceful reception with a marble fireplace and a rug-covered marble floor, a bar with tub chairs and a partly-panelled writing room. Bedrooms have panel-effect walls, good-quality limed furniture, easy chairs, swagged silk drapes and luxurious Italian marble bathrooms. All are air-conditioned, with satellite TV. There are two suites, one in Louis XV style, the other with an Oriental inspiration. No dogs. Private off-road parking for 25 cars. Valet service. **Rooms 54.** AMERICAN EXPRESS *Access, Diners, Visa.*

EC4	Whittington's	£70

Tel 071-248 5855 | **R**

21 College Hill EC4 2RP | Map 20 C2

Off Upper Thames Street, just north of Southwark Bridge, these 14th-century wine cellars were once owned by Dick Whittington. These days, it's a restaurant/wine bar whose short menu changes every three weeks or so and is supplemented by a daily specials board. Typically, the choice runs from chilled crab soufflé with yoghurt and dill sauce or filo pastry parcel of smoked bacon and goat's cheese to steamed halibut on spinach noodles with a sweet tomato sauce, grilled rump of beef with straw potatoes and pink peppercorn sauce, and calf's liver with bubble and squeak. *Seats 55. Parties 15. L only 11.45-2.15. Closed Sat & Sun, Bank Holidays.* AMERICAN EXPRESS *Access, Diners, Visa.*

SW1	Wilbraham Hotel	55%	£83

Tel 071-730 8296   Fax 071-730 6815 | **H**

Wilbraham Place Sloane Street SW1X 9AE | Map 19 C5

Modest Belgravia hotel formed from three Victorian town houses. Bedrooms and bathrooms are generally quite small and spartan, though there are two large suites on the ground floor. 24hr room service. **Rooms 52.** *No credit cards.*

SW1	Willett Hotel	£91

Tel 071-824 8415   Fax 071-730 4830 | **H**

32 Sloane Gardens SW1W 8DJ | Map 19 C5

All the bedrooms have recently been refurbished at this converted Victorian town house in the heart of Chelsea, now a peaceful hotel offering bed and breakfast accommodation, but limited public rooms. There are all the usual electrical gadgets, and a buffet-style English breakfast. Friendly staff. **Rooms 18.** AMERICAN EXPRESS *Access, Diners, Visa.*

SW1	Wilton's	£110

Tel 071-629 9955   Fax 071-495 6233 | **R**

55 Jermyn Street SW1Y 6LX | Map 18 D3

Oysters, fish and game are the specialities in one of London's best-known restaurants, which has been in business for 250 years. The classic à la carte menu offers a mainstream choice that includes a cold buffet plus cold consommé, potted shrimps, salmon, whitebait, omelettes, sole and lobster and grilled meats. Daily special might offer gull's eggs, smoked turkey breast and brandy peach, together with a good selection of fresh fish. Savouries, British cheeses and traditional puds complete the picture. Service is of the old school, in keeping with and enhancing the club-like atmosphere. As we went to press it was their intention to open on Sundays for both lunch and dinner. **Seats 90. Parties 25. Private Room 18.** *L 12.30-2.30 D 6.30-10.30. Closed L Sat, 24-26 Dec, Bank Holidays.* AMERICAN EXPRESS *Access, Diners, Visa.*

W5   Wine & Mousaka   £40
Tel 081-998 4373   **R**

30 & 33 Haven Green Ealing W5 2NX   **Map 17 A4**

Two separate Greek restaurants – no 30 is considerably smaller (and lighter at lunchtime) – but both are candle-lit by night. Traditional Greek favourites and a few, newer lighter dishes recently introduced. Kebabs and spit-roast meats cooked at open-to-view charcoal grills. Set menus, including grand meze, offer the best value. Sister restaurant in Kew (see entry). *Seats 92 (34 at no 30). L 12-2.30 D 6-11.30. Closed Sun, Bank Holidays. Set L & D £7.95 (not Sat eve) & £11.95.* AMERICAN EXPRESS *Access, Diners, Visa.*

W8   Wodka   £45
Tel 071-937 6513   **R**

12 St Alban's Grove Kensington W8 5PN   **Map 19 A4**

A popular, recently extended drinking and eating spot away from the general Kensington bustle, south of Kensington Square. The menu is Polish by main inspiration, with favourite dishes including veal and wild mushrooms pierogi, blinis with toppings of herring, smoked salmon, aubergine mousse or caviar, excellent chunky fishcakes with dill sauce, veal goulash, pork shank roasted in beer. A dozen vodkas are available by glass or carafe. *Seats 60. Parties 15. Private Room 30. L 12.30-2.30 D 7-11. Closed L Sat & Sun, Bank Holidays.* AMERICAN EXPRESS *Access, Diners, Visa.*

SE9   Yardley Court   £46
Tel 081-850 1850   Fax 081 850 8319   **H**

18 Court Yard Eltham SE9 5PZ   **Map 17 D5**

A neat Victorian house, surrounded by attractive gardens, offering very good value bed and breakfast accommodation. Cots are added free, extra beds for just £5. *Rooms 9. Access, Visa.*

W5   Young's Rendezvous   £40
Tel 081-840 3060   Fax 081-566 3121   **R**

13 Bond Street Ealing W5   **Map 17 A4**

Small, smart, air-conditioned Chinese restaurant one street down from the Broadway centre, with smooth service from waiters and waitresses in tunics. Good sizzling dishes, seafood and Szechuan dishes; particularly fine lobster feast set menu. Try the chef's specials, which now feature up-to-date Hong Kong dishes. Short list of dim sum served every day from 12.15 to 2.45pm; choice of business lunches. Children are very welcome, and Ada Young builds up a good rapport with her customers. *Seats 150. Private Room 30. L 12.15-2.45 D 6.15-11.45 (Fri & Sat to 12). Closed 25 & 26 Dec. Set L £7.50 & £9.50 Set D from £13.50.* AMERICAN EXPRESS *Access, Diners, Visa.*

N16   Yum Yum   £45
Tel 071-254 6751   Fax 071-241 3857   **R**

26 Stoke Newington Church Street N16 0LU   **Map 16 D2**

A friendly, colourful restaurant (now incorporating the next-door *Spices*) run by Moi, owner Atique Choudary's Thai wife. The menu covers a wide range of Thai dishes, making excellent use of fresh herbs and often either steamed or cooked quickly in a wok to retain all the freshness and colour. *Seats 100. Parties 40. L 12-2.30 D 6-11. Closed 1 week Christmas.* AMERICAN EXPRESS *Access, Diners, Visa.*

W1   Yumi   £80

Tel 071-935 8320   **R**

110 George Street W1H 6DJ   Map 18 C2

Decor is simplicity itself, and the menu is scarcely more complicated; set meals offer better value for money and à la carte choices run the gamut of familiar Japanese dishes prepared with skill, from steamed abalone and crab dumplings to fillet of Scoth beef grilled and flavoured with soy sauce. Some of the appetisers are more unusual and are worth trying, such as *chawan mushi* (egg custard gently steamed with morsels of seafood and vegetables), *hotate isobe-yaki* (grilled scallops sandwiched with *nori* seaweed), or *kani shumai* (home-made crab dumplings). Owner Yumi Fujii is always on hand with a smile, a bow and advice. Upstairs and in the private rooms you sit cross-legged at very low tables, and it's only downstairs or in the bar that you can adopt a more conventionally Occidental seat. The private room is only for a set meal of 8 dishes at £65 per head. No children under 10. *Seats* 76. *Parties* 30. *Private Room* 14. *L* 12.30-2.30 *D* 5.30-10.30. *Closed L Sat, all Sun, 2 weeks Christmas. Set L from £20 Set D from £26.* AMERICAN EXPRESS *Access, Diners, Visa.*

W1   Zen Central   £95

Tel 071-629 8089   Fax 071-437 0641   **R**

20 Queen Street Mayfair W1X 7PJ   Map 18 C3

Diners are enticed to 'understand something of the heights to which Chinese cooking can soar' at this smart, Rick Mather-designed restaurant. Certainly, the bill can soar to stratospheric heights but that is unlikely to worry the well-heeled Mayfair clientele who pack the restaurant to the gills. The 'culinary art form' encompasses popular specialities such as crispy duck, baked lobster and steamed sea bass as well as more unusual dishes. *Seats* 100. *L* 12.15-2.30 *D* 6.30-11.30. *Set L £20/£28 Set D £20-£50. Closed 3 days Christmas.* AMERICAN EXPRESS *Diners, Access, Visa.*

SW3   Zen Chelsea   £80

Tel 071-589 1781   Fax 071-584 0596   **R**

Chelsea Cloisters 86 Sloane Avenue SW3   Map 19 B5

The first of the Zen chain has a restrained decor with a pink hue, low ceilings, Chinese zodiac on the windows and a small waterfall near the entrance. The extensive menu covers everything from fried crispy veal sticks, deep-fried crispy oysters, frogs' legs Szechuan-style and lettuce-wrapped minced duck to sea bass soup with chopped spinach, roasted suckling pig (24hrs' notice required), Dover sole fillet in black bean sauce and barbecued eel fillet marinated with honey. Exotica include minced octopus cake with water chestnuts, abalone, jelly fish, spicy duck's tongue and shark's fin soup. Iced almond bean curd, sweetened sago cream with coconut and red bean paste pancakes to finish. Unusual options, long set menus, fancy wine prices, smart surroundings – all at a price. *Seats* 120. *Parties* 20. *Private Room* 22. *L* 12-3 *D* 6-11.30 (*Sun to* 11). *Closed 25 & 26 Dec.* AMERICAN EXPRESS *Access, Diners, Visa.*

NW3   ZeNW3   £45

Tel 071-794 7863   **R**

83 Hampstead High Street NW3 1RE   Map 16 B2

A health-conscious MSG-free zone. The menu is shorter than the usual Chinese, with the emphasis on steaming and quick-frying. Among the more esoteric dishes are cuttlefish cakes wrapped in lettuce with herbs, prawns steamed with fennel seeds, chicken fillet with spring onions cooked in a paper bag and quick-fried diced veal with pine kernels. *Seats* 140. *Parties* 100. *Private Room* 24. *Meals* 12-11.30. *Set L £10.50 Set D £26. Closed Christmas.* AMERICAN EXPRESS *Access, Diners, Visa.*

SW3   Ziani   £65

Tel 071-352 5297   Fax 071-244 8387   **R**
45/47 Radnor Walk SW3 4BT   **Map 19 C5**

A brightly decorated Italian restaurant named after an ancient Venetian
family. Seafood is quite a strength, deep-fried mixed seafood and baby squid
in a spicy tomato sauce being among the specialities. Others are marinated
chargrilled vegetables, bean soup with pasta, chicken stuffed with
mushrooms, mozzarella and salami in brandy sauce and mixed fried
kidneys, liver, brains and sweetbreads. Daily specials are always worth
a try. Decent Italian wine list. **Seats** *57. L 12-2.45 (Sun to 3.15) D 7-11.30
(Sun to 10.30). Closed Bank Holidays.* AMERICAN EXPRESS *Access, Diners, Visa.*

W1   Zoe   £65

Tel 071-224 1122   Fax 071-935 5444   **R**
St Christopher's Place W1M 5HH   **Map 18 C2**

An all-day café on the ground floor with tables spilling out on to the
Barrett Street pavement gives this popular restaurant a smart Continental
air. On a lower level the restaurant, decorated in a multitude of earthy,
sunbaked colours, offers modern Mediterranean cooking and a choice
of two lengthy menus (one meat and poultry-based, the other fishy). The
choice extends from peppered rabbit ballotine and artichoke salad
or melted taleggio on potatoes and leeks with Serrano ham to pan-fried
guinea fowl breast with a chick pea tagine and harissa sauce, herb-crusted
best end of lamb with ratatouille and basil jus and corn crab cakes with
poached eggs, a smoky hollandaise and wilted greens. Decent food, pleasant
service. Booking advisable. **Seats** *150. Parties 25. L 11.30-2.30
D 6.30-11.30. Closed D Sun, Bank Holidays.* AMERICAN EXPRESS *Access,
Diners, Visa.*

If we recommend meals in a hotel or inn a separate entry is made for its
restaurant.

Places of interest

London   Tourist Information

Transport Tel 071-222 1234.
Tourist Board Tel 071-971 0026/7
Railway Termini
Euston & St Pancras 071-387 7070
Kings Cross 071-278 2477
Paddington & Marylebone 071-262 6767
Victoria, Waterloo, Charing Cross & Liverpool Street 071-928 5100

London   Theatres

Adelphi Strand WC2 Tel 071-836 7611.
Albery St. Martins's Lane WC2 Tel 071-867 1115.
Aldwych Aldwych WC2 Tel 071-836 6404.
Ambassadors West Street, Cambridge Circus WC2 Tel 071-836 6111.
Apollo Shaftesbury Avenue W1 Tel 071-437 2663.
Apollo Victoria Wilton Road SW1 Tel 071-630 6262.
Arts 6-7 Gt Newport Street WC2 Tel 071-836 2132.
Astoria Charing Cross Road WC2 Tel 071-434 0403.
Bloomsbury Gordon Street WC1 Tel 071-387 9629.
Comedy Panton Street, Haymarket SW1 Tel 071-867 1045.
Criterion Piccadilly Circus W1 Tel 071-839 4488.
Drury Lane Theatre Royal WC2 Tel 071-836 8108.
Duchess Catherine Street WC2 Tel 071-836 8243.
Duke of York's St. Martin's Lane WC2 Tel 071-836 5122.
Fortune Russell Street WC2 Tel 071-836 2238.
Garrick Charing Cross Road WC2 Tel 071-379 6107.
Globe Shaftesbury Avenue W1 Tel 071-437 3667.
Greenwich Theatre Crooms Hill SE10 Tel 081-858 7755.
Haymarket Theatre Royal SW1 Tel 071-930 9832.
Her Majesty's Haymarket SW1 Tel 071-839 2244.
Lyric King Steeet, Hammersmith W6 Tel 081-741 2311.
Lyric Shaftesbury Avenue W1 Tel 071-437 3686.
Mayfair Stratton Street W1 Tel 071-629 3036.
Mermaid Puddle Dock Blackfriars EC4 Tel 071-410 0000.
National Upper Ground South Bank SE1 Tel 071-928 2252.
New London Parker Street WC2 Tel 071-405 0072.
Old Vic Waterloo Road SE1 Tel 071-928 7616.
Palace Shaftesbury Avenue W1 Tel 071-434 0909.
Palladium Argyll Street W1 Tel 071-437 7373.
Phoenix Charing Cross Road WC2 Tel 071-867 1044.
Piccadilly Denman Street W1 Tel 071-867 1118.
Players Theatre Villiers Street WC2 Tel 071-839 1134.
Prince Edward Old Compton Street W1 Tel 071-734 8951.
Prince of Wales Coventry Street W1 Tel 071-839 5972.
Queens Shaftesbury Avenue W1 Tel 071-494 5040.
Regents Park (Open Air) Regent's Park NW1 Tel 071-486 2431.
Royal Court Sloane Square SW1 Tel 071-730 1745.
St. Martins West Street WC2 Tel 071-836 1443.
Savoy Strand WC2 Tel 071-836 8888.
Shaftesbury Shaftesbury Avenue WC2 Tel 071-379 5399.
Shaw Euston Road NW1 Tel 071-388 1394.
Strand Aldwych WC2 Tel 071-240 0300.
Vaudeville Strand WC2 Tel 071-836 9987.
Victoria Palace Victoria Street SW1 Tel 071-834 1317.
Westminster Palace Street SW1 Tel 071-834 0283.
Whitehall Whitehall SW1 Tel 071-867 1119.
Wyndham's Charing Cross Road WC2 Tel 071-836 3028.
Young Vic 66 The Cut Waterloo SE1 Tel 071-928 6363.

London   Fringe Theatres

Almeida Almeida Street N1 Tel 071-359 4404.
Hackney Empire Mare Street E8 Tel 081-985 2424.

Hampstead Avenue Road NW3 Tel 071-722 9301.
King's Head Upper Street N1 Tel 071-226 1916.
Old Bull Arts Centre High Street, Barnet Tel 081-449 0048.
Riverside Studios Crisp Road W6 Tel 081-748 3354.

London   Concert Halls

Royal Opera House Covent Garden WC2 Tel 071-240 1066/240 1911.
English National Opera – The London Coliseum St Martin's Lane WC2
   Tel 071-836 3161.
Barbican Centre Silk Street EC2 Tel 071-638 4141.
Purcell Room South Bank SE1 Tel 071-928 3002.
Queen Elizabeth Hall South Bank SE1 Tel 071-928 8800.
Royal Albert Hall Kensington Gore SW7 Tel 071-589 8212.
Royal Festival Hall South Bank SE1 Tel 071-928 8800.
St. John's Smith Square Smith Square SW1 Tel 071-222 1061.
Sadlers Wells Rosebery Avenue EC1 Tel 071-278 8916.
Wigmore Hall Wigmore Street W1 Tel 071-935 2141.

London   London Night Life

Hippodrome Charing Cross Road WC2 Tel 071-437 4311.
Limelight Shaftesbury Avenue WC2 Tel 071-434 0572.
Madame Jo-Jo's Brewer Street W1 Tel 071-734 2473.
Ronnie Scott's Frith Street W1 Tel 071-439 0747.
Stringfellows Upper St. Martin's Lane WC2 Tel 071-240 5534.
Stork Club Swallow Street W1 Tel 071-734 3686.
Xenon Piccadilly W1 Tel 071-734 9344.

London   Historic Houses, Castles and Gardens

Wellington Museum Apsley House, Hyde Park Corner W1 Tel 071-499
   5676.
Banqueting House Whitehall SW1 Tel 081-930 4179.
Chelsea Physic Garden Royal Hospital Road SW3 Tel 071-352 5646.
Chiswick House Burlington Lane W4 Tel 081-995 0508.
Ham House (NT) Ham, Richmond Tel 081-940 1950.
Hampton Court Palace East Molesey Tel 081-977 8441.
Hogarth's House Chiswick Tel 081-994 6757.
Keats House Wentworth Place, Keats Grove, Hampstead Tel 071-435 2062.
Kensington Palace W8 Tel 071-937 9561.
Kenwood House Hampstead Tel 081-348 1286.
Marble Hill House Richmond Road, Twickenham Tel 081-892 5115.
Osterley Park (NT) Isleworth, Middlesex TW7 4RB Tel 081-560 3918.
The Queen's House Greenwich SE10 Tel 081-858 4422.
Royal Botanic Gardens (Kew Gardens) Kew Tel 081-940 3321.
Syon House and Park Gardens Brentford Tel 081-560 0881/3.
Tower of London Tower Hill EC3 Tel 071-709 0765.

London   Museums and Art Galleries

Barbican Art Gallery Level 8, Barbican Centre EC2 Tel 071-638 4141 Ext
   306.
Bethnal Green Museum of Childhood Cambridge Heath Road E2 Tel 081-
   980 3204.
Boxing Museum Thomas à Becket Pub, Old Kent Road SE1 Tel 071-703
   2644.
British Museum & British Library Great Russell Street WC1 Tel 071-636
   1555.
Buckingham Palace The Queen's Gallery, Buckingham Palace Road SW1
   Tel 071-799 2331.
Cabinet War Rooms Clive Steps, King Charles Street SW1 Tel 071-930
   6961.
Cutty Sark Clipper Ship King William Walk, Greenwich SE10 Tel 081-858
   3445.
The Design Museum at Butlers Wharf Shad Thames SE1 Tel 071-403
   6933.
Anthony d'Offay Gallery 9/21 & 23 Dering Street, off New Bond Street W1
   Tel 071-499 4100.
Dickens House Museum Doughty Street WC1 Tel 071-405 2127.

Dulwich Picture Gallery College Road SE21 Tel 081-693 5254.
Florence Nightingale Museum Lambeth Palace Road SE1 Tel 071-620 0374.
Freud Museum 20 Maresfield Gardens, Hampstead NW3.
Geffrye Museum Kingsland Road E2 Tel 071-739 8368.
Guinness World of Records The Trocadero, Coventry Street W1 Tel 071-439 7331.
Hayward Gallery South Bank Centre Belvedere Rd SE1 Tel 071-928 3144 *Recorded information 071-261 0127.*
HMS Belfast Morgan's Lane, Tooley Street SE1 Tel 071-407 6434
Horniman Museum London Road, Forest Hill SE23 Tel 081-699 1872/2339/4911.
ICA Carlton House Terrace, The Mall SW1 Tel 071-930 0493 *Recorded Information on 071-930 6393.*
Imperial War Museum Lambeth Road SE1 Tel 071-735 8922.
Keats House (Wentworth Place) Keats Grove, Hampstead NW3 Tel 071-435 2062.
Kenwood House (EH) Hampstead Lane NW3 Tel 081-348 1286/1287.
Leighton House Museum Holland Park W11 Tel 071-602 3316.
London Dungeon Tooley Street SE1 Tel 071-403 0606.
London Planetarium Baker Street NW1 Tel 071-486 1121.
London Transport Museum Covent Garden WC2 Tel 071-379 6344.
Madame Tussaud's Waxworks Museum Baker Street W1 Tel 071-935 6861.
Mall Galleries Carlton House Terrace, The Mall SW1 Tel 071-930 6844.
Museum of Garden History (The Tradescant Trust) St Mary-at-Lambeth, Lambeth Palace Road SE1 Tel 071-261 1891.
Museum of London London Wall EC2 Tel 071-600 3699.
Museum of Mankind Burlington Gardens W1 Tel 071-636 1555.
Museum of the Moving Image (MOMI) South Bank, Waterloo SE1 Tel 071-401 2636.
National Army Museum Royal Hospital Road SW3 Tel 071-730 0717.
The National Gallery Trafalgar Square WC2 Tel 071-839 3321 *Recorded information on 071-839 3526.*
National Maritime Museum Romney Road, Greenwich SE10 Tel 081-858 4422.
National Portrait Gallery St. Martin's Place, Trafalgar Square WC2 Tel 071-306 0055.
Natural History Museum Cromwell Road, South Kensington SW7 Tel 071-938 9123.
Operating Theatre Museum and Herb Garret St. Thomas Street SE1 Tel 071-955 4791.
R.A.F. Museum Hendon NW9 Tel 081-205 2266.
Royal Academy of Arts Piccadilly W1 Tel 071-439 7438.
Science Museum Exhibition Road, South Kensington SW7 Tel 071-938 8000.
Serpentine Gallery Kensington Gardens W2 Tel 071-402 6075.
Sir John Soane's Museum Lincoln's Inn Fields WC2 Tel 071-430 0175.
Tate Gallery Millbank SW1 Tel 071- 821 1313 *Recorded information on 071-821 7128.*
Thames Barrier Visitors' Centre Unity Way, Woolwich SE18 Tel 081-854 1373.
Tower Bridge SE1 Tel 071-403 3761.
Tower of London Tower Hill EC3 Tel 071-709 0765.
Victoria and Albert Museum Cromwell Road, South Kensington SW7 Tel 071-938 8500.
Wallace Collection Hertford House, Manchester Square W1 Tel 071-935 0687.
Whitechapel Art Gallery Whitechapel High Street E1 Tel 071-377 0107.

London   Exhibition Halls

Wembley Arena, Conference and Exhibition Centre Tel 081-900 1234.
Olympia Kensington W14 Tel 071-603 3344.
Earl's Court Warwick Road SW5 Tel 071-385 1200.
Business Design Centre Upper Street N1 Tel 071-359 3535.

London   Cathedrals

St. George's R.C. Cathedral Lambeth Road SE1 Tel 071-928 5256.

St. Paul's Cathedral EC4 Tel 071-248 4619.
Southwark Cathedral Borough High Street SE1 Tel 071-407 2939.
Westminster Abbey Broad Sanctuary SW1 Tel 071-222 5152.
Westminster R.C. Cathedral Ashley Place SW1 Tel 071-834 7452.

London   Swimming Pools and Sports Centres

Chelsea Sports Centre Manor Street, Chelsea Tel 071-352 6985.
Crystal Palace Sports Centre Ledrington Road, Norwood Tel 081-778 0131.
Dolphin Sports Centre Pimlico. Tel 071-798 8686.
Finsbury Leisure Complex 1-11 Ironmongers Row, Finsbury Tel 071-253 4011.
Ken Barrington Centre Fosters Oval, Kennington SE11 Tel 071-582 9495.
Kensington Sports Centre Tel 071- 727 9747.
Marshall Street Leisure Centre Tel 071-798 2007.
Porchester Baths Queensway Tel 071-229 9950.
Queen Mother Sports Centre Vauxhall Bridge Road Tel 071-798 2125.
Richmond Baths Old Deer Park, Richmond Tel 081-940 8461.
Seymour Leisure Centre Bryanston Place, Marylebone Tel 071-298 1421.
White City Pool Bloemfontein Road, White City Tel 081-734 3401.

London   Cricket & Tennis Grounds

Lords St. John's Wood NW8 Tel 071-289 1300
Lords Gestetner Tour Tel 071-266 3825.
The Foster's Oval Kennington SE11 Tel 071-582 6660.
Queen's Club W14 Tel 071-385 3421.
Wimbledon (All England Lawn Tennis & Croquet Club) SW19 Tel 081-946 2244.

London   Football and Rugby Grounds

Arsenal Highbury N5 Tel 071-226 0304.
Charlton Athletic Upton Park E13 Tel 081-293 4567.
Chelsea Stamford Bridge, Fulham SW5 Tel 071-385 5545.
Crystal Palace Selhurst Park SE25 Tel 081-771 8841.
Millwall The Den, Bermondsey SE16 Tel 071-232 1222.
Queens Park Rangers South Africa Road W12 Tel 081-743 0262.
Rugby Football Union Twickenham General Enquiries Tel 081-892 8161.
Tottenham Hotspur High Road, Tottenham N17 Tel 081-808 8080.
Wembley Stadium Tel 081-900 1234.
West Ham United Upton Park E13 Tel 081-472 2740.
Wimbledon Selhurst Park SE25 Tel 081-771 8841.

London   Ice Rinks

Alexandra Palace Wood Green N22 Tel 081-365 2121.
Broadgate Arena Broadgate EC2 Tel 071-588 6565.
Lea Valley Leyton E10 Tel 081-533 3156.
Queens Bayswater W2 Tel 071-229 0172.
Streatham Streatham High Road SW16 Tel 081-769 7771.

London   Dry Ski Slopes

Alexandra Palace Ski Slope Tel 081-888 2284.
Beckton Alps Alpine Way E6 Tel 081-511 0351.
Crystal Palace National Sports Centre Tel 081-778 0131.
Hillingdon Sports Centre Uxbridge Tel 0895 55181.
Woolwich Ski Slope Repository Road SE18 Tel 081-317 1726.

London   Zoos and Wildlife Parks

London Zoo Regent's Park Tel 071-722 3333.
Brent Lodge Park Animal Centre Uxbridge Road Tel 081-579 2424.
Battersea Park Children's Zoo SW11 Tel 081-7530.

London   Other attractions

Battersea Dog's Home Battersea Park Road SW8 Tel 071-622 3626.
Pirate Ships Tobacco Dock E1 Tel 071-702 9681.
Highgate Cemetery Swain's Lane N6 Tel 081-340 1834.

HOTELS LISTED BY COUNTY

LONDON

Swimming pool refers to indoor swimming pools only. See the How to Use This Guide section for explanation of our percentage rating system, room pricing and categories.
Key: QMH (Queens Moat Houses), MtCT (Mount Charlotte Thistle), Whitbread (Country Club Hotels)

Location	Hotel	Group	%	Room Price	Cat	Tel	Rooms	Conf	Banq	Leisure Centre	Swim Pool	Golf
E1	Tower Thistle	MtCT	66%	£157	H	071-481 2575	808	250	225			
E14	Britannia International		68%	£95	H	071-515 1551	442	800	600	yes	yes	
N1	Great Northern Hotel		60%	£78	H	071-837 5454	89	100	90			
NW1	Dorset Square Hotel		74%	£142	H	071-723 7874	37	8	45			
NW1	Kennedy Hotel	MtCT	63%	£102	H	071-387 4400	360	140	60			
NW1	The Regent London		87%	£233	HR	071-631 8000	309	350	360	yes	yes	
NW1	White House		71%	£132	H	071-387 1200	575	120	100			
NW2	Holiday Inn Garden Court		60%	£82	H	081-455 4777	153	55				
NW3	Charles Bernard Hotel		60%	£65	H	071-794 0101	57		52			
NW3	Clive Hotel	Hilton	64%	£70	H	071-586 2233	96	350	100			
NW3	Forte Posthouse	Forte	65%	£68	H	071-794 8121	140	30	25			
NW3	Regent's Park Marriott	Marriott	73%	£169	H	071-722 7711	303	400	300	yes	yes	
NW3	Swiss Cottage Hotel		62%	£85	H	071-722 2281	81	50	70			
NW4	Hendon Hall	MtCT	63%	£90	H	081-203 3341	52	350	240			
NW8	Hilton Internat Regent's Park	Hilton	73%	£149	HR	071-722 7722	377	150	150			
SE3	Bardon Lodge			£74	H	081-853 4051	60	50	55			
SE9	Yardley Court		56%	£46	H	081-850 1850	9					
SE16	Scandic Crown Nelson Dock	Scandic	69%	£124	H	071-231 1001	390	350	300	yes	yes	
SW1	The Berkeley	Savoy Group	89%	£291	HR	071-235 6000	160	220	200	yes	yes	
SW1	Cadogan Hotel	Historic House	74%	£153	H	071-235 7141	64	40	32			

Location	Hotel	Group	%	Room Price	Cat	Tel	Rooms	Conf	Banq	Leisure Centre	Swim Pool	Golf
SW1	Chelsea Hotel		63%	£189	H	071-235 4377	225	120	100			
SW1	Collin House			£56	H	071-730 8031	13					
SW1	Dukes Hotel		79%	£238	H	071-491 4840	66	55	70			
SW1	Durley House		74%	£240	H	071-235 5537	11	30	20			
SW1	Elizabeth Hotel			£70	H	071-828 6812	40	25	15			
SW1	Forte Crest Cavendish	Forte	68%	£140	H	071-930 2111	256	100	80			
SW1	The Goring		79%	£198	HR	071-396 9000	79	50	50			
SW1	Grosvenor Thistle Hotel	MtCT	64%	£138	H	071-834 9494	366	200	120			
SW1	The Halkin		86%	£250	HR	071-333 1000	41	40	26			
SW1	Hyatt Carlton Tower		87%	£240	HR	071-235 5411	224	150	270			
SW1	Hyde Park Hotel	Forte	82%	£293	H	071-235 2000	185	250	275			
SW1	Knightsbridge Green Hotel			£117	PH	071-584 6274	24					
SW1	The Lanesborough		89%	£302	HR	071-259 5599	95	90	90			
SW1	The Lowndes Hyatt Hotel		76%	£233	H	071-823 1234	78	25	20			
SW1	Royal Westminster Thistle	MtCT	71%	£151	H	071-834 1821	134	200	130			
SW1	Royal Horseguards Thistle	MtCT	71%	£131	H	071-839 3400	376	70	700			
SW1	Royal Court Hotel	QMH	68%	£164	H	071-730 9191	102	48	40			
SW1	Rubens Hotel		66%	£141	H	071-834 6600	189	75	25			
SW1	St James Court		73%	£180	HR	071-834 6655	391	250	200			
SW1	Scandic Crown Victoria	Scandic	67%	£135	H	071-834 8123	210	180	180	yes		
SW1	Sheraton Belgravia	Sheraton	75%	£245	HR	071-235 6040	89	30	22			
SW1	Sheraton Park Tower	Sheraton	79%	£270	H	071-235 8050	295	60	150		yes	yes
SW1	The Stafford		74%	£225	H	071-493 0111	74	30	42			
SW1	Stakis St Ermin's	Stakis	71%	£142	H	071-222 7888	291	250	200			
SW1	Tophams Ebury Court		60%	£115	HR	071-730 8147	40	30	24			
SW1	22 Jermyn Street			£192	PH	071-734 2353	18	12				
SW1	Wilbraham Hotel		55%	£83	H	071-730 8296	52					
SW1	Willett Hotel			£91	H	071-824 8415	18					
SW3	Basil Street Hotel		71%	£187	H	071-581 3311	93	75	55			
SW3	The Beaufort			£140	PH	071-584 5252	28					

Area	Hotel	Group	%	Price	Type	Phone	Rooms			
SW3	Blair House Hotel			£90	H	071-581 2323	16			
SW3	The Capital		83%	£245	HR	071-589 5171	48	20	24	
SW3	The Draycott			£150	PH	071-730 6466	25			
SW3	Egerton House			£184	PH	071-589 2412	30	20	20	
SW3	The Fenja			£154	PH	071-589 7333	12	10		
SW3	Franklin Hotel			£184	PH	071-584 5533	36			
SW3	L'Hotel			£125	HR	071-589 6286	12			
SW5	Concord Hotel			£57	H	071-370 4151	40			
SW5	Hogarth Hotel		62%	£90	H	071-370 6831	86	50	30	
SW5	Kensington Court Hotel			£59	H	071-370 5151	35			
SW5	Hotel 167			£68	H	071-373 0672	19			
SW5	Swallow International	Swallow	64%	£134	H	071-973 1000	415	230	230	yes
SW5	Terstan Hotel			£50	H	071-835 1900	48	1750	1450	
SW6	Earls Court Park Inn		69%	£108	H	071-385 1255	501	10	70	
SW6	La Reserve		62%	£90	H	071-385 8561	40	70	60	
SW7	Adelphi Hotel		62%	£112	H	071-373 7177	68			
SW7	Alexander Hotel		64%	£117	H	071-581 1591	36			
SW7	Aster House			£91	H	071-581 5888	12			
SW7	Blakes Hotel		82%	£183	HR	071-370 6701	52	20		
SW7	Embassy House Hotel	Jarvis	59%	£105	H	071-584 7222	69	45	36	
SW7	Forum Hotel	Inter-Continental	62%	£157	H	071-370 5757	910	400	330	
SW7	The Gloucester		75%	£160	HR	071-373 6030	548			
SW7	The Gore		65%	£140	H	071-584 6601	55	14		
SW7	Harrington Hall		72%	£120	H	071-396 9696	200	300	200	
SW7	Holiday Inn Kensington	Holiday Inns	68%	£120	H	071-373 2222	162	126	200	
SW7	Jurys Kensington Hotel		64%	£102	H	071-589 6300	171	80	65	
SW7	Kensington Manor			£94	PH	071-370 7516	14			
SW7	Norfolk Hotel	QMH	69%	£145	H	071-589 8191	96	60	60	
SW7	Number Sixteen			£120	PH	071-589 5232	36			
SW7	Pelham Hotel		74%	£160	HR	071-589 8288	37			
SW7	Periquito Queen's Gate			£62	H	071-370 6111	65			
SW7	Regency Hotel		68%	£135	H	071-370 4595	198	100	185	
SW7	Rembrandt Hotel	Edwardian	70%	£144	H	071-589 8100	195	250	150	yes
SW7	Vanderbilt Hotel		62%	£139	H	071-589 2424	223	120	100	

Location	Hotel	Group	%	Room Price	Cat	Tel	Rooms	Conf	Banq	Leisure Centre	Swim Pool	Golf
SW10	Hotel Conrad		86%	£229	HR	071-823 3000	160	200	200	yes	yes	yes
SW19	Camizaro House	MtCT	76%	£160	H	081-879 1464	46	45	80			
W1	The Athenaeum			£200	HR	071-499 3464	156	55	40			
W1	Bentinck House Hotel			£73	H	071-935 9141	20					
W1	Berkshire Hotel	Edwardian	72%	£231	H	071-629 7474	147	45	25			
W1	Berners Park Plaza		72%	£130	H	071-636 1629	229	180	160			
W1	Britannia Inter-Continental	Inter-Continental	77%	£200	H	071-629 9400	318	100	80			
W1	Brown's Hotel	Forte	76%	£250	HR	071-493 6020	118	35	70			
W1	Chesterfield Hotel		70%	£170	H	071-491 2622	110	100	100			
W1	Churchill Inter-Continental	Inter-Continental	84%	£262	HR	071-486 5800	448	250	240			
W1	Claridge's	Savoy Group	88%	£316	HR	071-629 8860	190	250	220			
W1	The Clifton-Ford	Doyle	73%	£196	H	071-486 6600	193	150	128			
W1	Concorde Hotel			£84	H	071-402 6169	28		22			
W1	The Connaught	Savoy Group	91%	£270	HR	071-499 7070	90					
W1	Cumberland Hotel	Forte	69%	£142	H	071-262 1234	890	475	560	yes		
W1	The Dorchester		91%	£298	HR	071-629 8888	247	550	550		yes	
W1	Durrants Hotel		65%	£106	H	071-935 8131	96	60	55			
W1	Forte Crest Regent's Park	Forte	64%	£99	H	071-388 2300	318	650	550			
W1	47 Park Street		86%	£326	H	071-499 7282	52	30	20			
W1	Four Seasons Hotel		89%	£315	HR	071-499 0888	227	500	400			
W1	Grafton Hotel	Edwardian	63%	£160	H	071-388 4131	324		110			
W1	Green Park Hotel		70%	£143	H	071-629 7522	161	70	80			
W1	Grosvenor House	Forte	83%	£256	H	071-499 6363	454	1,500	1,500	yes	yes	
W1	Holiday Inn Mayfair	Holiday Inns	72%	£152	H	071-493 8282	185	70	50			
W1	Holiday Inn Garden Court		56%	£148	H	071-935 4442	138	30	100			
W1	Hospitality Inn Piccadilly	MtCT	64%	£143	H	071-930 4033	92		16			
W1	Hotel Inter-Continental	Inter-Continental	84%	£277	HR	071-409 3131	469	1,000	850			
W1	The Langham Hilton	Hilton	75%	£212	H	071-636 1000	379	320	300			
W1	London Mews Hilton on Park	Hilton	68%	£179	H	071-493 7222	72					
W1	London Hilton on Park Lane	Hilton	75%	£282	H	071-493 8000	446	1,250	1,250			

	Hotel	Group	%	Price		Telephone					
W1	London Marriott Hotel	Marriott	77%	£228	H	071-493 1232	223	1,000	500		
W1	Mandeville Hotel		62%	£130	H	071-935 5599	165	150	150		yes
W1	Marble Arch Marriott	Marriott	68%	£189	HR	071-723 1277	239	150	300	yes	yes
W1	May Fair Inter-Continental	Inter-Continental	81%	£270	HR	071-629 7777	287	292	250	yes	yes
W1	Le Meridien		84%	£271	H	071-734 8000	263	250	250		yes
W1	Merryfield House			£48	H	071-935 8326	7				
W1	Montcalm Hotel		76%	£230	HR	071-402 4288	115	80	80		
W1	Mostyn Hotel		62%	£124	H	071-935 2361	122	150	130		
W1	The Park Lane Hotel		77%	£232	HR	071-499 6321	308	500	600		
W1	Rathbone Hotel		69%	£157	H	071-636 2001	72	12	10		
W1	The Ritz		86%	£249	HR	071-493 8181	130	60	60		
W1	St George's Hotel	Forte	65%	£150	H	071-580 0111	86	35	25		
W1	SAS Portman Hotel		77%	£195	H	071-486 5844	272	380	400		
W1	The Selfridge	MtCT	75%	£171	H	071-408 2080	295	300	296		
W1	Sherlock Holmes Hotel	Hilton	61%	£132	H	071-486 6161	125	80	60		
W1	Washington Hotel		70%	£178	H	071-499 7000	173	100	72		
W1	The Westbury	Forte	75%	£191	H	071-629 7755	244	120	110		
W2	Abbey Court			£148	PH	071-221 7518	22				
W2	Columbia Hotel			£58	H	071-402 0021	102	200	140		
W2	Craven Gardens Hotel			£66	H	071-262 3167	43	20			
W2	Hospitality Inn Bayswater	MtCT	60%	£103	H	071-262 4461	175	40	30		
W2	London Embassy	Jarvis	68%	£125	H	071-229 1212	192	70	120		
W2	London Metropole Hotel		69%	£155	H	071-402 4141	742	1,300	800	yes	
W2	Mornington Hotel		63%	£89	H	071-262 7361	68	14			
W2	Parkwood Hotel			£65	H	071-402 2241	18				
W2	Pembridge Court Hotel		65%	£120	H	071-229 9977	20		50		
W2	Royal Lancaster Hotel	Jarvis	75%	£169	H	071-262 6737	418	1,100	1,400		
W2	Stakis London Coburg			£122	H	071-221 2217	132				
W2	Whites Hotel	MtCT	77%	£191	H	071-262 2711	54	20	20		
W6	Novotel	Novotel	65%	£89	H	081-741 1555	635	900	800		
W8	Apollo Hotel			£68	H	071-835 1133	50	20			
W8	Atlas Hotel			£68	H	071-835 1155	50				
W8	Copthorne Tara	Copthorne	69%	£141	H	071-937 7211	829	500	360		
W8	Kensington Park Thistle	MtCT	67%	£150	H	071-937 8080	332	120	80		

Location	Hotel	Group	%	Room Price	Cat	Tel	Rooms	Conf	Banq	Leisure Centre	Swim Pool	Golf
W8	Kensington Close Hotel	Forte	59%	£109	H	071-937 8170	530	180	60			
W8	Kensington Palace Thistle	MtCT	67%	£110	H	071-937 8121	299	180	170			
W8	Hotel Lexham		78%	£56	H	071-373 6471	66					
W8	The Milestone		63%	£210	H	071-917 1000	57	25	25			
W9	Colonnade Hotel		79%	£80	H	071-286 1052	49					
W11	The Halcyon		67%	£235	HR	071-727 7288	43	20	40			
W11	Hilton Inter Kensington	Hilton	60%	£180	HR	071-603 3355	603	300	300			
W11	Portobello Hotel		66%	£120	H	071-727 2777	25					
W14	London Olympia Hilton	Hilton	61%	£125	H	071-603 3333	405	500	350			
WC1	Bonnington Hotel		66%	£95	H	071-242 2828	215	250	130			
WC1	Euro & George Hotels		65%	£47	H	071-387 8777	75					
WC1	Euston Plaza Hotel		69%	£110	H	071-383 4105	150	110	72			
WC1	Forte Crest Bloomsbury	Forte	63%	£121	H	071-837 1200	284	1,200	600			
WC1	Holiday Inn Kings Cross	Holiday Inns	69%	£145	H	071-833 3900	405	220	180	yes		
WC1	Kenilworth Hotel	Edwardian	63%	£180	H	071-637 3477	192	120	80		yes	
WC1	The Marlborough	Edwardian	69%	£167	H	071-636 5601	169	180	260			
WC1	Montague Park Hotel		64%	£150	H	071-637 1001	109					
WC1	President Hotel		68%	£66	H	071-837 8844	447	130	80			
WC1	Hotel Russell	Forte	78%	£141	H	071-837 6470	328	450	350			
WC1	St Giles Hotel		81%	£110	H	071-636 8616	600	45	110	yes		
WC2	Hampshire Hotel	Edwardian	65%	£247	HR	071-839 9399	124	80	70		yes	
WC2	Howard Hotel		70%	£254	HR	071-836 3555	135	150	130			
WC2	Moat House	QMH	65%	£135	H	071-836 6666	153	100	100			
WC2	Mountbatten Hotel	Edwardian	70%	£207	H	071-836 4300	127	80	60			
WC2	Royal Trafalgar Thistle	MtCT	65%	£141	H	071-930 4477	108	8				
WC2	The Savoy	Savoy Group	91%	£260	HR	071-836 4343	200	500	400	yes		
WC2	The Waldorf	Forte	83%	£195	HR	071-836 2400	292	420	420		yes	

London Airports (see also under Middlesex, Surrey and Sussex (West) in **Hotels by County** listings, England section)

Location	Hotel	Group	%	£		Phone					
Heathrow Airport	Excelsior Hotel	Forte	71%	£110	H	081-759 6611	839	800	800	yes	yes
Heathrow Airport	Forte Crest	Forte	68%	£105	H	081-759 2323	572	200	200	yes	yes
Heathrow Airport	Forte Posthouse (Ariel)	Forte	65%	£68	H	081-759 2552	186	12			
Heathrow Airport	Granada Lodge	Granada		£63	L	081-574 5875	46				
Heathrow Airport	Heathrow Hilton Hotel	Hilton	74%	£167	HR	081-759 7755	400	240	200	yes	yes
Heathrow Airport	Holiday Inn Crowne Plaza	Holiday Inns	74%	£167	H	(0895) 445555	374	220	170	yes	yes
Heathrow Airport	Jarvis Berkeley Internat	Jarvis	67%	£85	H	081-897 2121	56	120	120		
Heathrow Airport	Park Hotel	MtCT	61%	£111	H	081-759 2400	306	600	1,000		
Heathrow Airport	Radisson Edwardian International	Edwardian	76%	£184	H	081-759 6311	459	520	300	yes	yes
Heathrow Airport	Ramada Hotel Heathrow		66%	£115	H	081-897 6363	638	550	450	yes	yes
Heathrow Airport	Sheraton Skyline	Sheraton	73%	£174	H	081-759 2535	353	500	500	yes	yes
Heathrow Airport	Sheraton Heathrow Hotel	Sheraton	70%	£210	H	081-759 2424	440	80	70		
Gatwick Airport	Chequers Thistle	MtCT	63%	£106	H	(0293) 786992	78	70	100		
Gatwick Airport	Copthorne Effingham Park	Copthorne	72%	£126	H	(0342) 714994	122	600	600	yes	yes
Gatwick Airport	Copthorne London Gatwick	Copthorne	69%	£128	H	(0342) 714971	227	130	160		
Gatwick Airport	Europa Gatwick		63%	£93	H	(0293) 886666	211	150	120		yes
Gatwick Airport	Forte Posthouse	Forte	63%	£68	H	(0293) 771621	210	150	150		
Gatwick Airport	Forte Crest Gatwick	Forte	74%	£109	H	(0293) 567070	468	340	240	yes	yes
Gatwick Airport	Gatwick Moat House	QMH	62%	£90	H	(0293) 785599	121	180	150		
Gatwick Airport	Gatwick Concorde Hotel	QMH	61%	£104	H	(0293) 533441	116	100	100		
Gatwick Airport	Gatwick Hilton Internat	Hilton	72%	£159	H	(0293) 518080	550	500	500	yes	yes
Gatwick Airport	Holiday Inn Gatwick	Holiday Inns	68%	£118	H	(0293) 529991	217	300	200	yes	yes
Gatwick Airport	Ramada Hotel Gatwick		70%	£114	H	(0293) 820169	255	150	180	yes	yes
Gatwick Airport	Travel Inn			£43	L	(0582) 414341	120				
Horley	Langshot Manor	Whitbread	73%	£106	HR	(0293) 786680	7	18	18		

Hotels with Sporting Facilities

LONDON

Location	Hotel	Leisure Centre	Indoor Pool	Outdoor Pool	Squash	Tennis	Golf	Fishing	Riding	Croquet
E14	Britannia International	▲	▲							
NW1	The Regent London	▲	▲							
NW3	Regent's Park Marriott	▲	▲							
SE16	Scandic Crown Nelson Dock	▲	▲			▲				
SW1	The Berkeley	▲	▲							
SW1	Cadogan Hotel					▲				
SW1	Durley House					▲				
SW1	The Lowndes Hyatt					▲				
SW1	Scandic Crown Victoria	▲	▲							
SW5	Swallow International	▲	▲							
SW7	Rembrandt Hotel	▲	▲							
SW10	Hotel Conrad	▲	▲							
W1	Churchill Inter-Continental					▲				
W1	The Dorchester	▲	▲							
W1	Grosvenor House	▲	▲							
W1	Marble Arch Marriott		▲							
W1	May Fair Inter-Continental	▲	▲							
W1	Le Meridien	▲	▲		▲					
W2	London Metropole Hotel	▲	▲							
WC1	Holiday Inn Kings Cross	▲	▲		▲					
WC1	St Giles Hotel	▲	▲		▲					
WC2	The Savoy	▲	▲							

London Airport Heathrow

Location	Hotel	Leisure Centre	Indoor Pool	Outdoor Pool	Squash	Tennis	Golf	Fishing	Riding	Croquet
Heathrow	Excelsior Hotel	▲	▲							
Heathrow	Heathrow Hilton Hotel	▲	▲							
Heathrow	Holiday Inn Crowne Plaza	▲	▲				▲			
Heathrow	Radisson Edwardian Int'nal	▲	▲							
Heathrow	Ramada Hotel Heathrow	▲	▲							
Heathrow	Sheraton Skyline		▲							
Gatwick	Chequers Thistle			▲						
Gatwick	Copthorne Effingham Park	▲	▲			▲	▲			▲
Gatwick	Copthorne London Gatwick				▲	▲	▲			
Gatwick	Europa Gatwick			▲		▲				
Gatwick	Forte Posthouse			▲						
Gatwick	Forte Crest Gatwick	▲	▲							
Gatwick	Gatwick Hilton International	▲	▲							
Gatwick	Holiday Inn Gatwick	▲	▲							
Gatwick (Horley)	Langshott Manor									▲
Gatwick	Ramada Hotel Gatwick	▲	▲	▲						

Hotels with Facilities for Disabled Guests

Compiled in association with the **Holiday Care Service** charity (2 Old Bank Chambers, Station Road, Horley, Surrey RH6 9HW Tel 0293 774535 Fax 0293 784647). If writing to them please enclose a minimum of 38p in stamps. Readers can join Friends of Holiday Care Service through an annual contribution of £10.

All hotels in the first set of listings under each country are recommended in this Guide **and** have been inspected by the Holiday Care Service. The additional listings include hotels that have informed us that they have specially adapted rooms and facilities for disabled guests; these specific facilities have **not** been inspected by disabled guests for this Guide.

London

Copthorne Tara **W8**
Cumberland Hotel **W1**
Knightsbridge Green Hotel **SW3**
The Marlborough **WC1**
Le Meridien **W1**
Novotel **W6**
Sheraton Park Tower **SW1**
Tower Thistle **E1**
White House **NW1**

Additional:

Berners Park Plaza **W1**
Bonnington Hotel **WC1**
The Clifton-Ford **W1**
The Dorchester **W1**
Forum Hotel **SW7**
Holiday Inn Kensington **SW7**
Hotel Inter-Continental London **W1**
Hyde Park Hotel **SW1**
The Lanesborough **SW1**
The Langham Hilton **W1**
London Hilton on Park Lane **W1**
Marble Arch Marriott **W1**

RESTAURANT ROUND-UP

Please refer to the How to Use This Guide section (p18–19) at the front of the Guide for explanation of categories, pricing and star systems, crowns (Traditional or Modern), traditional Sunday Lunch, Dessert (Dsrt) symbol, and Restaurants with Rooms (RR). See also wine and cheese awards feature (from p 41). ★ after a Room Price indicates that only half-board terms are offered.

Location	Establishment	Cat	Star	Price	Seats	Private Rm	Crown	Open Sun	Sun L	Sea Food	Room Price	Des	Good Cheese	O/S Wine	New World	Open Air	National Cooking
E1	Bloom's	R		£40	150	40		All									
E1	The Hothouse	R		£50	78	45		All									
E1	Namaste	R		£35	72	40										yes	Indian
E1	Shampan	R	↑	£40	60	15		All									Indian
E8	Faulkners	R		£25	60			All									
EC1	Alba	R		£60	40					yes							Italian
EC1	Bubb's	R		£75	75	25											French
EC1	Café du Marché	R		£55	60	66											French
EC1	The Eagle	R	↑	£40	50												
EC1	The Hope & Sirloin	R		£40	32	20											
EC1	Mange-2	R		£70	65	25											
EC1	Le Mesurier	R		£65	25	25											French
EC1	The Peasant	R		£45	80	40		L				Dsrt					French
EC1	Quality Chop House	R		£40	40			All									British
EC1	Ravi Shankar	R	↑	£25	68			D									Indian
EC1	Stephen Bull's Bistro & Bar	R		£60	95	35						Dsrt			N/W		
EC2	Corney & Barrow	R		£75	30	28	T										
EC2	Sri Siam City	R		£55	140												Thai
EC2	Tatsuso	R	★	£80	120	10	M										Japanese
EC3	The Hospitality Suite	R		£75	30		M										French
EC3	Imperial City	R		£55	180	16							yes				Chinese
EC3	Luc's Restaurant & Brasserie	R		£50	150												French

Area	Restaurant		Price	Seats	Set	Cards				Cuisine
EC3	Poons in the City	R	£50	200	40					Chinese
EC3	Seoul	R	£30	30						Korean
EC4	Ginman	R	£50	72						Japanese
EC4	Miyama	R	£80	85	10	M				Japanese
EC4	Sweetings	R	£60	70						
EC4	Whittington's	R	£70	55			yes			
N1	Anna's Place	R	£45	40	50	All		yes		Swedish
N1	Casale Franco	R	£60	130	30			yes		Italian
N1	Frederick's	R	£65	140				yes		
N1	Granita	R	£50	62						
N1	Hodja Nasreddin	R	£25	48	35	All				Turkish
N1	Mojes Restaurant	R	£45	45		All				
N1	Nam Bistro	R	£45	50	30	All				Vietnamese
N1	Satay Hut	R	£30	90		D				Thai
N1	Sonargaon	R	£50	60		All				Indian
N1	Suruchi	R	£30	34		L				Indian
N1	Tuk Tuk Restaurant	R	£30	40	40					Thai
N3	Rani	R	£40	90	23	All				Indian
N4	Chez Liline	R	£45	44						
N5	Iznik	R	£45	54		L				Turkish
N8	Les Associés	R	£60	38		All	yes			French
N8	Florians	R	£50	60	23	All				Italian
N16	Beyoglu Ocakbasi	R	£30	36	40	All				Turkish
N16	Istanbul Iskembecisi	R	£30	80	25	All				Turkish
N16	01 Adana	R	£30	50		All				Turkish
N16	Rasa	R	£40	42	25	All				Indian
N16	Le Soir	R	£35	46						
N16	Yum Yum	R	£45	100		All				Thai
NW1	Asuka	R	£70	60		All				Japanese
NW1	Belgo	R	£40	75		L		yes		Belgian
NW1	Big Night Out	R	£55	70	30	All		yes		
NW1	Café Delancey	R	£40	200		L				
NW1	Camden Brasserie	R	£55	105		All			yes	
NW1	Cheng-Du	R	£60	70		All				Chinese

Location	Establishment	Cat	Star	Price	Seats	Private Rm	Crown	Open Sun	Sun L	Sea Food	Room Price	Des	Good Cheese	O/S Wine	New World	Open Air	National Cooking
NW1	China Jazz	R		£70	90			All									Chinese
NW1	Daphne	R		£45	85	30										yes	Greek
NW1	Fanari	R		£30	95	40		All								yes	Greek
NW1	Great Nepalese	R		£30	48												Indian
NW1	Hellas	R		£30	60											yes	Greek
NW1	Hudson's Restaurant	R		£65	45			All	SL			Dsrt					British
NW1	Lemonia	R		£30	140	40		L									Greek
NW1	Nontas	R		£30	50												Greek
NW1	Odette's	R		£65	60	30		L					yes		N/W	yes	Greek
NW1	Otafuku	R		£60	36											yes	Japanese
NW1	Ravi Shankar	R		£25	68	25		All							N/W		Indian
NW1	The Regent London	HR		£95	100			All									S E Asian
NW1	Singapore Garden	R		£45	65												Italian
NW1	Trattoria Lucca	R		£55	85	24											
NW1	Underground Café	R		£40	36												North African
NW2	Laurent	R		£60	30	14											
NW2	Quincy's	R		£75	112	8											
NW3	Benihana	R		£60	45			All									Japanese
NW3	Caffè Graffiti	R		£40	100			All								yes	Italian
NW3	Green Cottage	R		£60	46			All									Chinese
NW3	Jinkichi	R		£55	60			All									Japanese
NW3	Mr Ke	R	←	£55	75	15		All									Chinese
NW3	Qinggis	R		£70	55			All									Chinese
NW3	Wakaba	R		£45	140	24		All									Japanese
NW3	ZeNW3	R		£65	75			All									Chinese
NW4	Kaifeng	R		£30	60	30		L									Chinese
NW5	Le Petit Prince	R		£50	75			All									North African
NW6	Gung-Ho	R		£55	78			L	SL								Chinese
NW6	Peter's	R		£45	60			All									French
NW6	Singapore Garden	R		£45	100	60		All									S E Asian

Area	Restaurant			£										Cuisine
NW6	Vijay	R		£25	78			All						Indian
NW7	Good Earth	R		£55	90			All						Chinese
NW7	Hee's	R		£50	100	30		All						Chinese
NW8	Au Bois St Jean	R		£70	60	40		D					yes	French
NW8	L'Aventure	R		£65	45	60		All						French
NW8	Don Pepe	R		£50	45	20		L						Spanish
NW8	Greek Valley	R		£40	62	30		D					yes	Greek
NW8	Hilton Int'nal Regent's Park	HR		£70	42			All						Japanese
NW10	Sabras	R		£25	32			D						Indian
NW11	Bloom's	R		£40	70			D						
NW11	Tiger under the Table	R		£65	70		M	All						S E Asian
SE1	Bengal Clipper	R		£60	175			All						Indian
SE1	Blue Print Café	R		£75	86			L						
SE1	Butlers Wharf Chop-house	R		£60	115			L	SL		O/S	N/W	yes	
SE1	Café dell'Ugo	R		£60	75				Dsrt	yes			yes	Italian
SE1	Cantina del Ponte	R		£25	95			L						
SE1	Mutiara	R		£95	70			All		yes	O/S	N/W	yes	S E Asian
SE1	Le Pont de la Tour	R	←	£65	105	22	M	All	Dsrt	yes	O/S	N/W	yes	French
SE1	RSJ	R		£40	95	20		All					yes	
SE5	Silver Lake	R		£50	40									Chinese
SE6	Casa Cominetti	R		£35	50									Italian
SE14	Thailand Restaurant	R		£65	25									Thai
SE19	Luigi's	R		£50	65			All					yes	Italian
SE22	Sema	R		£45	70	25		L						Thai
SE22	Thistells	R		£60	30	20		All	SL	yes				
SW1	Al Bustan	R		£105	70			All					yes	Lebanese
SW1	The Berkeley	HR	★	£55	70	34	T		Dsrt	yes			yes	French
SW1	Café Fish	R		£70	90			All			O/S	N/W	yes	
SW1	Le Caprice	R	←	£40	70			All					yes	
SW1	Ebury Wine Bar	R		£80	80									
SW1	Fifth Floor Restaurant	HR		£90	110			All						
SW1	The Goring	HR		£75	75	50		All	SL	yes	O/S	N/W		British
SW1	Green's Rest'nt & Oyster Bar	R		£75	75	26		L	SL	yes	O/S	N/W		British
SW1	The Grenadier	R		£65	28			All	SL		O/S	N/W		British

Location	Establishment	Cat	Star	Price	Seats	Private Rm	Crown	Open Sun	Sun L	Sea Food	Room Price	Des	Good Cheese	O/S Wine	New World	Open Air	National Cooking
SW1	The Halkin	HR	★	£100	45	26	M	D				Dsrt					Italian
SW1	Hunan	R		£50	45			D					yes				Chinese
SW1	Hyatt Carlton, Rib Room	R		£110	63	35	T	All	SL					O/S	N/W		British
SW1	Hyatt Carlton, Chelsea Room	HR	↑	£115	63	35	M	All	SL					O/S	N/W		French
SW1	L'Incontro	R		£100	55		M										Italian
SW1	Isohama	R		£60	30			All									Japanese
SW1	Ken Lo's Memories of China	R		£75	150	20		D									Chinese
SW1	Kundan	R		£55	130	120											Indian
SW1	Kura	R		£90	25			D									Japanese
SW1	The Lanesborough	HR	★	£90	106		T	All	SL			Dsrt	yes	O/S	N/W		French
SW1	Mijanou	R	↑	£95	28	24						Dsrt		O/S	N/W	yes	Italian
SW1	Mimmo d'Ischia	R		£90	90	30											Italian
SW1	Mitsukoshi	R		£100	140	24											Japanese
SW1	Motcomb's	R		£60	70	22		L								yes	British
SW1	Olivo	R		£55	45												Italian
SW1	Overtons at St James's	R		£80	75	20	T			yes			yes			yes	
SW1	Pearl of Knightsbridge	R		£80	80	40		All				Dsrt	yes				Chinese
SW1	Pomegranates	R		£80	50	12		All							N/W		
SW1	La Poule Au Pot	R		£55	72			L									French
SW1	Quaglino's	R		£70	338	40											
SW1	Restaurant Marco-Pierre White, Hyde Park Hotel	R	★★★	£175	50		T					Dsrt	yes	O/S	N/W		
SW1	St James Court	HR		£90	65												French
SW1	Sale e Pepe	R		£70	70		T										Italian
SW1	Salloos	R		£70	55			D									Indian
SW1	Santini	R		£100	70	32											Italian
SW1	Shepherd's	R		£55	45	22		D									British
SW1	Sheraton Belgravia	HR		£70	80								yes				
SW1	Signor Sassi	R		£60	80								yes				Italian
SW1	Simply Nico	R	★	£65	45								yes				French

Postcode	Restaurant	Type	Rating	Price	Seats	Pvt	Hrs	Cards	SL	•	Dsrt	•	O/S	N/W	•	Cuisine
SW1	The Square	R	*↑	£80	75	30		All			Dsrt		O/S	N/W		
SW1	Suntory	R		£120	120	8	T										Japanese
SW1	Tate Gallery Restaurant	R		£55	100											British
SW1	Tophams Ebury Court	HR		£50	30	24							yes				British
SW1	Wilton's	R		£110	90	18	T	All		yes						
SW2	Bon Ton Roulet	R		£40	40	25		L								
SW3	Albero & Grana	R	←	£50	120			D			Dsrt					Spanish
SW3	The Argyll	R		£75	55	12										
SW3	Benihana	R		£120	140		M	All		yes						Japanese
SW3	Bibendum Oyster Bar	R		£70	44		M	All								
SW3	Bibendum	R	★		72	25	M	All			Dsrt		O/S	N/W		
SW3	Brasserie St Quentin	R		£55	80			All								French
SW3	La Brasserie	R		£55	130	25		All				yes	O/S		yes	French
SW3	The Capital	HR	**	£120	45	35	T	L			Dsrt					British
SW3	Dan's	R		£60	50			All							yes	Italian
SW3	Daphne's	R		£85	120	12		All							yes	
SW3	English House	R		£85	45	24		All								British
SW3	English Garden	R		£65	70			All								British
SW3	The Enterprise	R		£55	35	35		All							yes	
SW3	Foxtrot Oscar	R		£50	55	32	M	All	SL			yes				
SW3	Fulham Road	R	↑	£80	76	25			SL							
SW3	Good Earth	R		£55	160		M	All						N/W		Chinese
SW3	Grill St Quentin	R		£55	140		M	All								French
SW3	L'Hotel	HR		£40	49											
SW3	Joe's Café	R		£70	80		M	L				yes				
SW3	Khun Akorn	R		£65	70			All								Thai
SW3	Maroush II	R		£70	40	10										Lebanese
SW3	Monkeys	R		£80	90	24						yes				British
SW3	Poissonnerie de l'Avenue	R		£95	60	20				yes						French
SW3	S & P Thai	R		£40	70		T	D							yes	Thai
SW3	Sambuca	R		£70	110											Italian
SW3	San Frediano	R		£55	120											Italian
SW3	San Lorenzo	R		£100	130										yes	Italian
SW3	San Martino	R		£45		40		All							yes	Italian

Location	Establishment	Cat	Star	Price	Private Seats	Private Rm	Crown	Open Sun	Sun L	Sea Food	Room Price	Des	Good Cheese	O/S Wine	New World	Open Air	National Cooking
SW3	Sandrini	R		£65	75		M	All								yes	Italian
SW3	Scalini	R		£70	110			All										Italian
SW3	Le Suquet	R	*	£70	70	18		All		yes						yes	French
SW3	La Tante Claire	R	***	£140	42		T	All				Dsrt	yes	O/S			French
SW3	Thierry's	R		£60	70	34		All									French
SW3	Turner's	R	*	£100	50			All				Dsrt	yes	O/S			British
SW3	Waltons	R		£100	90	30	T	All	SL								
SW3	Zen Chelsea	R		£80	120	22		All									Chinese
SW3	Ziani	R		£65	57			All									Italian
SW4	Grafton Français	R		£65	64	28		All									French
SW4	Newton's	R		£55	70			All	SL							yes	
SW5	Krungtap	R		£25	35	40		All									Thai
SW5	Lou Pescadou	R		£50	55	10		All		yes						yes	French
SW5	Mr Wing	R		£65	120			All									Chinese
SW5	Noor Jahan	R		£40	60			All									Indian
SW6	Blue Elephant	R		£70	250	100		All									Thai
SW6	De Cecco	R		£40	68			All								yes	Italian
SW6	Mamta	R		£30	42			All									Indian
SW6	El Metro	R		£45	90			All								yes	Spanish
SW6	Nosh Brothers Bar & Restaurant	R		£65	85	40		All									
SW6	Samurai	R		£65	60			All									Japanese
SW6	Sushi Gen	R		£50	50			All									Japanese
SW6	Tandoori Lane	R		£35	58	10		All									Indian
SW6	Tien Phat	R		£30	65			All									Vietnamese
SW7	Bangkok	R		£40	60	24		All									Thai
SW7	Bistrot 190	R		£50	55	22		All									
SW7	Blakes Hotel	HR	←	£150	32	22	M	All	SL			Dsrt			N/W		
SW7	Bombay Brasserie	R	*	£70	175	100		All									Indian
SW7	La Bouchee	R		£35	85			All								yes	French
SW7	Café Lazeez	R		£60	130	60		All								yes	Indian

Area	Restaurant	Type		£			Cards	SL	Dress	A/C	O/S	N/W		Cuisine
SW7	Downstairs at 190	R		£60	70	28								
SW7	Gilbert's	R	←	£55	32									
SW7	The Gloucester	HR		£60	154	30	All		Drst				yes	
SW7	Hilaire	R	★↑	£85	50	25	All		Drst	yes				
SW7	Khan's of Kensington	R		£50	60		All							Indian
SW7	Khyber Pass	R		£30	36		All							Indian
SW7	Majlis	R		£35	32		All							Indian
SW7	Memories of India	R		£40	75	30	All						yes	Indian
SW7	Ognisko Polskie	R		£55	70	150	All							Polish
SW7	Pelham Hotel	HR		£50	30		All							British
SW7	Pun	R		£50	70	30	All							Chinese
SW7	Shaw's	R		£70	44									
SW7	Shezan	R		£70	100	100	All						yes	Indian
SW7	Tui	R		£45	52		All							Thai
SW9	Twenty Trinity Gardens	R	★↑	£45	54	20	All	SL					yes	French
SW10	Aubergine	R		£85	40				Drst	yes	O/S	N/W		French
SW10	Brasserie Koko	R	★	£40	32	6				yes	O/S	N/W		Japanese
SW10	The Canteen	R		£60	135	40	All		Drst		O/S	N/W	yes	
SW10	Chapter 11	R		£50	60									
SW10	Chez Max	R	←↑	£65	50		M						yes	
SW10	Chutney Mary	R	←↑	£60	130		All		Drst					Indian
SW10	Hotel Conrad	HR		£60	45	200							yes	
SW10	Formula Veneta	R		£50	60	30	L						yes	Italian
SW10	Glaister's Garden Bistro	R		£40	80	40	All						yes	
SW10	Harveys Café	R		£50	60	35	L							
SW10	Jake's	R		£45	70	45	L						yes	British
SW10	Ken Lo's Memories of China	R		£60	175	60	All							Chinese
SW10	Kingdom	R		£50	80	25	All							Chinese
SW10	Nikita's	R		£70	35	12								Russian
SW10	Buchan's	R		£45	70	50	All	SL						British
SW11	The Green Room	R		£50	40		D							
SW11	Lena's	R		£40	50		All						yes	Thai
SW11	Osteria Antica Bologna	R		£45	75		All						yes	Italian
SW11	Phuket	R		£60	60		All						yes	Thai

Location	Establishment	Cat	Star	Price	Seats	Private Rm	Crown	Open Sun	Sun L	Sea Food	Room Price	Des	Good Cheese	O/S Wine	New World	Open Air	National Cooking
SW11	Ransome's Dock	R		£65	65			L					yes		N/W	yes	Thai
SW13	Bangkok Garden	R		£35	50			All									Italian
SW13	Riva	R		£65	45			All					yes				
SW13	Sonny's	R		£65	100	20		L					yes				French
SW14	Le Braconnier	R		£60	30			L									
SW14	Crowthers	R		£65	32								yes				Thai
SW15	Bangkok Symphonie	R		£35	40			All									Japanese
SW15	Dan Dan	R	↑	£50	60	24		All									Italian
SW15	Del Buongustaio	R		£60	45								yes				Italian
SW15	Enoteca	R		£45	35	45											Italian
SW16	Royal China	R		£60	65		M	All									Chinese
SW16	Caterino's	R		£45	70			All									Italian
SW17	Oh'Boy	R		£40	42	15		All									Thai
SW17	Sree Krishna	R		£35	120	60		All					yes				Indian
SW18	Le Ptit Normand	R		£50	35	40							yes				French
W1	Al Hamra	R		£55	65											yes	Lebanese
W1	Alastair Little	R	★★	£85	55							Dsrt	yes		N/W		
W1	Arirang Korean Restaurant	R		£50	100	30		All									Korean
W1	Arisugawa	R		£60	100	20											Japanese
W1	The Athenaeum	HR		£85	60	40	T	All									
W1	Au Jardin des Gourmets	R		£75	150	50							yes	O/S			French
W1	Bahn Thai	R		£60	120	50		All									Thai
W1	Bentley's	R		£80	95	14				yes			yes				British
W1	Bistrot Bruno	R		£70	42												
W1	Britannia Inter-Cont, Shogun	HR		£90	65			D									Japanese
W1	Brown's Hotel	HR		£85	35			All									
W1	Café Royal Grill Room	R	★	£120	45	50	T					Dsrt			N/W		French
W1	Caravan Serai	R		£45	55	18	T	All						O/S			
W1	Chez Nico at Ninety Park Lane	R	★★★	£135	70	20						Dsrt	yes	O/S	N/W		French
W1	Chiang Mai	R		£40	60	25		All									Thai

Postcode	Restaurant	Cat	Rating	Price	Seats	Priv	Cards	Hrs	SL	yes	Dsrt	yes	O/S	N/W	Cuisine
W1	Chuen Cheng Ku	R		£35	400	160									Chinese
W1	Churchill Inter-Continental	HR		£80	90		M	All			Dsrt		O/S	N/W	
W1	Claridge's Restaurant	HR		£130	140	220	T	All							
W1	Claridge's, The Causerie	R		£85	40		T	All							
W1	The Connaught	HR	**	£160	75	22	T	All	SL			yes			French
W1	Cumberland Hotel, Mon	HR		£70	95	35	T	All					O/S	N/W	Japanese
W1	Define	R	←	£80	30	15									Japanese
W1	dell'Ugo	R		£40	180	14						yes			
W1	The Dog House	R		£45	30										
W1	The Dorchester, Grill Room	HR		£130	81	12	T	All	SL		Dsrt	yes	O/S	N/W	British
W1	Dorchester, Terrace Restaurant	R	**	£120	81	14	T	All					O/S	N/W	French
W1	Dorchester, Oriental Room	R		£120	79	12	T	All							Chinese
W1	Dorchester, Bar	R	←	£70	59	8	T	All			Dsrt				Italian
W1	Dragon's Nest	R		£45	130	60									Chinese
W1	Dragon Inn	R		£30	120										Chinese
W1	Efes Kebab House	R		£40	50	45		yes							Turkish
W1	L'Escargot	R	←	£70	85	45	T	All			Dsrt		O/S	N/W	French
W1	Est	R		£40	40										French
W1	L'Etoile	R		£80	60	30									French
W1	Four Seasons Hotel, Restaurant	HR	*	£120	55		T	All			Dsrt		O/S	N/W	
W1	Four Seasons Hotel, Lanes	R		£80	75		T	All					O/S	N/W	
W1	French House Dining Room	R		£45	30			D				yes			British
W1	Fuji	R		£70	54			L				yes			Japanese
W1	La Gaulette	R		£30	30										
W1	Le Gavroche	R	***	£160	60	50	T			yes	Dsrt		O/S		French
W1	Gay Hussar	R		£60	70	20									Hungarian
W1	Gopal's of Soho	R		£40	50	12		All							Indian
W1	Grahame's Seafare	R		£40	84	30				yes					
W1	Greenhouse	R	←	£80	90		T	All	SL						British
W1	alistair Greig's Grill	R		£90	65										
W1	Harbour City	R		£40	160	60		All							Chinese
W1	Hardy's	R		£50	80										
W1	Ikeda	R		£110	30	8		D							Japanese
W1	Ikkyu	R		£50	65										Japanese

Location	Establishment	Cat	Star	Price	Seats	Private Rm	Crown	Open Sun	Sun L	Sea Food	Room Price	Des	Good Cheese	O/S Wine	New World	Open Air	National Cooking
W1	Hotel Inter-Cont, Le Soufflé	HR	**↑	£150	70		T	L	SL			Dsrt	yes	O/S	N/W		French
W1	Jade Garden	R		£35	144			All									Chinese
W1	Kaspa	R		£70	60	12											
W1	Kaya	R		£70	70	40		D									Korean
W1	Lal Qila	R		£40	64			All									Indian
W1	Langan's Brasserie	R	↑	£85	220								yes				British
W1	Langan's Bistro	R		£65	38	25											
W1	The Lexington	R		£65	42												
W1	Lido	R		£40	140			All	SL								Chinese
W1	Lindsay House	R		£80	68	20		All									British
W1	Little Akropolis	R		£30	30	25										yes	Greek
W1	London Chinatown	R		£50	150	70		All									Chinese
W1	Maroush III	R		£70	88												Lebanese
W1	Masako	R		£100	80	35		All									Japanese
W1	May Fair Inter-Continental	HR		£80	65		T										French
W1	Le Meridien, Oak Room	HR	**	£135	50	300	T					Dsrt	yes				French
W1	Le Meridien, Terrace Garden	R		£65	130		T	L	SL								
W1	Ming	R	*	£55	70	26										yes	Chinese
W1	Mirabelle Restaurant	R	**	£110	100	30							yes	O/S			French
W1	Miyama	R		£75	67	17		D									Japanese
W1	Montcalm Hotel	HR		£80	60	16	T						yes				French
W1	Le Muscadet	R		£60	35		T										French
W1	Nakamura	R		£50	35	8		D									Japanese
W1	New Fook Lam Moon	R		£40	80			All									Chinese
W1	New Loon Fung	R		£60	400	30		All									Chinese
W1	New World	R		£35	600	250		All									Chinese
W1	Nico Central	R	*↑	£60	55	10	M					Dsrt	yes				French
W1	Ninjin	R		£60	54												Japanese
W1	Nusa Dua Restoran Indonesia	R		£35	60	12											S E Asian
W1	O'Keefe's	R		£45	37								yes				

	Name			£										Cuisine
W1	Odin's Restaurant	R		£65	60		T							
W1	Panda Si Chuen	R	★	£50	63	13								Chinese
W1	The Park Lane Hotel	HR		£70	60		M					yes	N/W		
W1	Pied à Terre	R	★★	£110	40										
W1	Ragam	R		£35	36	10		All		Dsrt				Indian
W1	Rasa Sayang	R		£40	200	20		All						S E Asian	yes
W1	La Reash	R		£35	70			All						North African
W1	Red Fort	R	←	£70	120	60		All						Indian
W1	The Ritz	HR		£120	100	65	T	All	SL	Dsrt	yes	O/S N/W	British	yes
W1	Saga	R		£100	48	12		All						Japanese
W1	St Moritz	R		£85	60					Dsrt				Swiss
W1	Les Saveurs	R	★★★	£55	80	10	T					O/S		French
W1	Shampers	R		£120	65	45					yes	O/S N/W		
W1	Soho Soho	R	←	£70	80	60					yes			
W1	Sri Siam	R		£55	55			D		Dsrt	yes			Thai
W1	Stephen Bull	R		£80	50									
W1	Topkapi	R		£35	56	45		All		Dsrt	yes	N/W		Turkish
W1	Villandry Dining Room	R		£45	70									
W1	Walsh's Seafood & Shellfish	R		£60	75	25			yes					
W1	White Tower	R		£70	76	18								Greek
W1	Yumi	R		£80	100	14								Japanese
W1	Zen Central	R		£95	150			All						Chinese
W1	Zoe	R		£65	70			L					Greek	yes
W2	L'Accento Italiano	R	←★	£55	22			All					Italian	yes
W2	Al San Vincenzo	R		£70	70	30		All		Dsrt	yes			Italian
W2	Four Seasons	R		£50	68			All						Chinese
W2	Halepi	R		£50	60			All						Greek
W2	Hsing	R		£50	88									Chinese
W2	Kalamaras	R		£40	110	30							Greek	yes
W2	Mandarin Kitchen	R		£50	85			All						Chinese
W2	Maroush	R		£70	120			All						Lebanese
W2	New Kam Tong	R		£35	120			All						Chinese
W2	Poons	R		£55	60			All						Chinese
W2	Rasa Sayang	R		£40				All					S E Asian	yes

Location	Establishment	Cat	Star	Price	Seats	Private Rm	Crown	Open Sun	Sun L	Sea Food	Room Price	Des	Good Cheese	O/S Wine	New World	Open Air	National Cooking
W2	Romantica Taverna	R		£40	120	70		All									Greek
W2	Royal China	R		£50	100	15		All									Chinese
W2	Standard	R		£40	130	50		All									Indian
W2	Tawana Thai Restaurant	R		£40	40	20		All									Thai
W2	Thai Kitchen	R		£50	40											yes	Thai
W2	Veronica's	R		£65	60	40										yes	
W4	Christian's	R		£60	42			L				Dsrt	yes			yes	French
W4	La Dordogne	R		£50	80	30		D					yes			yes	French
W4	Singapore	R		£35	60	16		All									S E Asian
W5	Charlotte's Place	R		£50	40	20											
W5	Momo	R		£50	24												Japanese
W5	Sala Thai	R		£35	60												Thai
W5	Wine & Mousaka	R		£40	92												Greek
W5	Young's Rendezvous	R		£40	100	80		All									Chinese
W6	The Brackenbury	R		£45	55	42		L	L							yes	British
W6	Los Molinos	R		£35	80												Spanish
W6	Mr Wong Wonderful House	R		£40	200	80		All									Chinese
W6	Nanking	R		£60	75	60		All								yes	Chinese
W6	River Café	R		£80	100		M	L								yes	Italian
W6	Snows on the Green	R		£70	60	24		L	SL								
W6	Sumos	R		£35	40	10		All									Japanese
W8	Al Basha	R		£70	140	65		D									Lebanese
W8	Arcadia	R		£65	80	16		L	SL							yes	
W8	The Ark	R		£45	75	27										yes	
W8	Boyd's	R		£70	40							Dsrt	yes		N/W		
W8	Byblos	R		£50	48			All									Lebanese
W8	Clarke's	R	★	£90	90								yes	O/S	N/W		
W8	Costa's Grill	R		£25	70	25										yes	Greek
W8	L'Escargot Doré	R		£80	50	25										yes	French
W8	Geales	R		£30	100	25				yes							

Area	Name	Cat		£	Seats	Priv	Open	SL		Dsrt		O/S N/W	Cuisine
W8	Kensington Place	R	★	£70	140		All				yes		British
W8	Launceston Place	R	←	£65	80	30	L	SL					British
W8	Malabar	R		£40	56	20	All						Indian
W8	La Paesana	R		£40	90								Italian
W8	Phoenicia	R		£50	100	50	All						Lebanese
W8	Le Quai St Pierre	R	←	£70	58				yes				French
W8	Shanghai	R		£60	90	30	D						Chinese
W8	Wodka	R		£45	60								Polish
W9	Supan	R		£35	30		L						Thai
W10	Brasserie du Marché aux Puces	R		£50	35	35						yes	
W10	Canal Brasserie	R		£40	67							yes	
W10	Jimmy Beez	R	←	£50	50					Dsrt		yes	
W11	L'Altro	R		£60	43	35	All		yes			yes	Italian
W11	Avenue West Eleven	R		£60	56		L						
W11	Chez Moi	R		£70	45	24	All						French
W11	The Halcyon	HR	★	£90	55		All	SL		Dsrt	yes	yes	
W11	Hilton Int Kensington, Hiroko	HR		£80	72	45	All	SL					Japanese
W11	Julie's	R		£70	100		D			Dsrt	yes	yes	
W11	Leith's	R		£115	75	40	All				yes	O/S	British
W11	Manzara	R		£25	40		All			Dsrt	yes	yes	Turkish
W11	192	R	←	£75	110	26	All						
W11	Orsino	R		£60	106	30	All						Italian
W12	Adam's Café	R		£30	60	24							North African
W12	Balzac Bistro	R		£50	80	60							French
W12	Rajput	R		£25	50		All						Indian
W12	The Rotisserie	R		£40	90		D				yes		
W13	Sigiri	R		£30	62	34	All						Sri Lankan
W14	Chinon	R		£65	50						yes		
W14	Cibo	R	★	£70	62		All			Dsrt	yes	yes	Italian
W14	Oliver's	R		£35	75		All	SL					British
WC1	Gonbei	R		£45	40	20							Japanese
WC1	Museum Street Café	R	★	£55	34		All			Dsrt	yes		Italian
WC1	Poons	R		£50	100							yes	Chinese
WC1	Wagamama	R		£25	104						yes		Japanese
WC2	Ajimura	R		£60	58	20							Japanese

Location	Establishment	Cat	Star	Price	Seats	Private Rm	Crown	Open Sun	Sun L	Sea Food	Room Price	Des	Good Cheese	O/S Wine	New World	Open Air	National Cooking
WC2	Bertorelli's	R		£60	90												Italian
WC2	Bhatti	R		£50	90	45		All								yes	Indian
WC2	Brixtonian Backayard	R		£50	36												
WC2	China City	R		£55	450			All									Chinese
WC2	Christopher's	R		£80	120	32		L							N/W		
WC2	Emerald Garden	R		£45	68	30		All									Chinese
WC2	L'Estaminet	R		£60	60	20											French
WC2	Fung Shing	R	★	£52	85	30		All									Chinese
WC2	Giovanni's	R		£65	38												Italian
WC2	Hampshire Hotel	HR		£75	55	70		All									
WC2	Hong Kong	R		£40	180	14		All									Chinese
WC2	Howard Hotel	HR		£100	93	60		All								yes	French
WC2	The Ivy	R	★	£70	110	60		All							N/W		
WC2	Joe Allen	R		£40	180			All							N/W		
WC2	Joy King Lau	R		£50	240	60		All									Chinese
WC2	Magno's Brasserie	R		£70	55												
WC2	Manzi's	R	★	£70	120	50				yes							
WC2	Mon Plaisir	R		£50	95	25											French
WC2	Neal Street Restaurant	R		£100	60	24	M	All									Italian
WC2	Now and Zen	R		£75	180			All									Chinese
WC2	Orso	R		£65	100			All									Italian
WC2	Le Palais du Jardin	R		£50	220	22		All									French
WC2	Poons	R		£30	50	30		All									Chinese
WC2	Poons	R		£30	130			All									Chinese
WC2	Rules	R		£60	140	48		All									British
WC2	The Savoy, River Room	HR	★	£130	140	80	T	All	SL			Dsrt	yes	O/S			French
WC2	The Savoy, Grill Room	R	★	£120	85		T		SL				yes	O/S	N/W		British
WC2	The Savoy, Upstairs	R		£50	28												
WC2	Sheekey's Restaurant	R		£65	90	36				yes							
WC2	Simpson's-in-the-Strand	R	★	£75	450	150	T	All	SL				yes				British
WC2	The Waldorf	HR		£90	60			D									

National Cuisines

Belgian

Belgo **NW1**

British

Bentley's **W1**
The Brackenbury **W6**
Buchan's **SW11**
The Capital **SW3**
The Dorchester, Grill Room **W1**
English House **SW3**
English Garden **SW3**
French House Dining Room **W1**
The Goring **SW1**
Greenhouse **W1**
Green's Restaurant & Oyster Bar **SW1**
Hudson's Restaurant **NW1**
Hyatt Carlton Tower, Rib Room **SW1**
Jake's **SW10**
Kensington Place **W8**
Langan's Brasserie **W1**

Launceston Place **W8**
Leith's **W11**
Lindsay House **W1**
Monkeys **SW3**
Motcomb's **SW1**
Oliver's **W14**
Pelham Hotel **SW7**
Quality Chop House **EC1**
The Ritz **W1**
Rules **WC2**
The Savoy, Grill Room **WC2**
Shepherd's **SW1**
Simpson's-in-the-Strand **WC2**
Tophams Ebury Court **SW1**
Waltons **SW3**
Wilton's **SW1**

Chinese

Cheng-Du **NW1**
China Jazz **NW1**
China City **WC2**
Chuen Cheng Ku **W1**
The Dorchester, Oriental Room **W1**
Dragon Inn **W1**
Dragon's Nest **W1**
Emerald Garden **WC2**
Four Seasons **W2**
Fung Shing **WC2**
Good Earth **NW7**
Good Earth **SW3**
Green Cottage **NW3**
Gung-Ho **NW6**
Harbour City **W1**
Hee's **NW7**
Hong Kong **WC2**
Hsing **W2**
Hunan **SW1**
Imperial City **EC3**
Jade Garden **W1**
Joy King Lau **WC2**
Kaifeng **NW4**
Ken Lo's Memories of China **SW1**
Ken Lo's Memories of China **SW10**
Kingdom **SW10**
Lido **W1**
London Chinatown **W1**

Mandarin Kitchen **W2**
Ming **W1**
Mr Ke **NW3**
Mr Wing **SW5**
Mr Wong Wonderful House **W6**
Nanking **W6**
New Fook Lam Moon **W1**
New Kam Tong **W2**
New Loon Fung **W1**
New World **W1**
Now and Zen **WC2**
Panda Si Chuen **W1**
Pearl of Knightsbridge **SW1**
Poons **W2**
Poons **WC1**
Poons in the City **EC3**
Poons **WC2**
Poons **WC2**
Pun **SW7**
Qinggis **NW3**
Royal China **SW15**
Royal China **W2**
Shanghai **W8**
Silver Lake **SE5**
Young's Rendezvous **W5**
Zen Chelsea **SW3**
Zen Central **W1**
ZeNW3 **NW3**

French

Les Associés **N8**
Au Bois St Jean **NW8**
Au Jardin des Gourmets **W1**
Aubergine **SW10**
L'Aventure **NW8**
Balzac Bistro **W12**
The Berkeley **SW1**
La Bouchée **SW7**
Le Braconnier **SW14**
La Brasserie **SW3**
Brasserie St Quentin **SW3**
Bubb's **EC1**
Café Royal Grill Room **W1**
Café du Marché **EC1**
Chez Moi **W11**
Chez Nico at Ninety Park Lane **W1**
Christian's **W4**
The Connaught **W1**
The Dorchester, The Terrace **W1**
La Dordogne **W4**
L'Escargot Doré **W8**
L'Estaminet **WC2**
L'Etoile **W1**
Four Seasons Hotel **W1**
Le Gavroche **W1**
Grafton Français **SW4**
Grill St Quentin **SW3**
The Hospitality Suite **EC3**
Howard Hotel **WC2**

Hyatt Carlton Tower **SW1**
Hotel Inter-Continental, Le Soufflé **W1**
Lou Pescadou **SW5**
Luc's Restaurant & Brasserie **EC3**
May Fair Inter-Continental **W1**
Le Meridien **W1**
Le Mesurier **EC1**
Mijanou **SW1**
Mirabelle Restaurant **W1**
Mon Plaisir **WC2**
Le Muscadet **W1**
Nico Central **W1**
Le P'tit Normand **SW18**
Le Palais du Jardin **WC2**
Peter's **NW6**
Poissonnerie de l'Avenue **SW3**
La Poule Au Pot **SW1**
Le Quai St Pierre **W8**
RSJ **SE1**
St James Court **SW1**
Les Saveurs **W1**
The Savoy **WC2**
Simply Nico **SW1**
Le Suquet **SW3**
La Tante Claire **SW3**
Thierry's **SW3**
Thistells **SE22**
Twenty Trinity Gardens **SW9**

Greek

Costa's Grill **W8**
Daphne **NW1**
Fanari **NW1**
Greek Valley **NW8**
Halepi **W2**
Hellas **NW1**
Kalamaras **W2**

Lemonia **NW1**
Little Akropolis **W1**
Nontas **NW1**
Romantica Taverna **W2**
White Tower **W1**
Wine & Mousaka **W5**

Hungarian

Gay Hussar **W1**

Indian

Bengal Clipper **SE1**
Bhatti **WC2**
Bombay Brasserie **SW7**
Café Lazeez **SW7**
Chutney Mary **SW10**
Gopal's of Soho **W1**
Great Nepalese **NW1**
Khan's of Kensington **SW7**
Khyber Pass **SW7**
Kundan **SW1**
Lal Qila **W1**
Majlis **SW7**
Malabar **W8**
Mamta **SW6**
Memories of India **SW7**
Namaste **E1**
Noor Jahan **SW5**

Ragam **W1**
Rajput **W12**
Rani **N3**
Rasa **N16**
Ravi Shankar **EC1**
Ravi Shankar **NW1**
Red Fort **W1**
Sabras **NW10**
Salloos **SW1**
Shampan **E1**
Shezan **SW7**
Sonargaon **N1**
Sree Krishna **SW17**
Standard **W2**
Suruchi **N1**
Tandoori Lane **SW6**
Vijay **NW6**

Italian

L'Accento Italiano **W2**
Al San Vincenzo **W2**
Alba **EC1**
L'Altro **W11**
Bertorelli's **WC2**
Caffe Graffitti **NW3**
Cantina del Ponte **SE1**
Casa Cominetti **SE6**
Casale Franco **N1**
Caterino's **SW16**
Cibo **W14**
Daphne's **SW3**
De Cecco **SW6**
Del Buongustaio **SW15**
Enoteca **SW15**
Florians **N8**
Formula Veneta **SW10**
Giovanni's **WC2**
The Halkin **SW1**
L'Incontro **SW1**
Luigi's **SE19**

Mimmo d'Ischia **SW1**
Museum Street Café **WC1**
Neal Street Restaurant **WC2**
Olivo **SW1**
Orsino **W11**
Orso **WC2**
Osteria Antica Bologna **SW11**
La Paesana **W8**
Riva **SW13**
River Café **W6**
Sale e Pepe **SW1**
Sambuca **SW3**
San Frediano **SW3**
San Lorenzo **SW3**
San Martino **SW3**
Sandrini **SW3**
Santini **SW1**
Scalini **SW3**
Signor Sassi **SW1**
Trattoria Lucca **NW1**
Ziani **SW3**

Japanese

Ajimura **WC2**
Arisugawa **W1**
Asuka **NW1**
Benihana **NW3**
Benihana **SW3**
Brasserie Koko **SW10**
Britannia Inter-Continental Hotel, Shogun
    W1
Cumberland Hotel, Mon **W1**
Dan Dan **SW15**
Defune **W1**
Fuji **W1**
Ginnan **EC4**
Gonbei **WC1**
Hilton International Kensington, Hiroko **W11**
Hilton International Regent's Park,
    Kashi Noki **NW8**
Ikeda **W1**
Ikkyu **W1**

Isohama **SW1**
Jinkichi **NW3**
Kura **SW1**
Masako **W1**
Mitsukoshi **SW1**
Miyama **EC4**
Miyama **W1**
Momo **W5**
Nakamura **W1**
Ninjin **W1**
Otafuku **NW1**
Saga **W1**
Samurai **SW6**
Sumos **W6**
Suntory **SW1**
Sushi Gen **SW6**
Tatsuso **EC2**
Wagamama **WC1**
Wakaba **NW3**
Yumi **W1**

Korean

Arirang **W1**
Kaya **W1**

Seoul **EC3**

Lebanese

Al Basha **W8**
Al Bustan **SW1**
Al Hamra **W1**
Byblos **W8**

Maroush **W2**
Maroush II **SW3**
Maroush III **W1**
Phoenicia **W8**

North African

Adam's Café **W12**
Laurent **NW2**

Le Petit Prince **NW5**
La Reash **W1**

Polish

Ognisko Polskie **SW7**

Wodka **W8**

Russian

Nikita's **SW10**

South East Asian

Mutiara **SE1**
Nusa Dua Restoran Indonesia **W1**
Rasa Sayang **W2**
Rasa Sayang **W1**

Singapore **W4**
Singapore Garden **NW6**
Singapore Garden **NW1**
Tiger under the Table **NW11**

Spanish

Albero & Grana **SW3**
Don Pepe **NW8**

El Metro **SW6**
Los Molinos **W6**

Sri Lankan

Sigiri **W13**

Swedish

Anna's Place **N1**

Swiss

St Moritz **W1**

Thai

Bahn Thai **W1**
Bangkok **SW7**
Bangkok Garden **SW13**
Bangkok Symphonie **SW15**
Blue Elephant **SW6**
Chiang Mai **W1**
Khun Akorn **SW3**
Krungtap **SW5**
Lena's **SW11**
Oh'Boy **SW17**
Phuket **SW11**
S & P Thai **SW3**

Sala Thai **W5**
Satay Hut **N1**
Sema **SE22**
Sri Siam **W1**
Sri Siam City **EC2**
Supan **W9**
Tawana Thai **W2**
Thai Kitchen **W2**
Thailand **SE14**
Tui **SW7**
Tuk Tuk **N1**
Yum Yum **N16**

Turkish

01 Adana **N16**
Beyoglu Ocakbasi **N16**
Efes Kebab House **W1**
Hodja Nasreddin **N1**

Istanbul Iskembecisi **N16**
Iznik **N5**
Manzara **W11**
Topkapi **W1**

Vietnamese

Nam Bistro **N1**

Tien Phat **SW6**

No one who
owns a copy
of the UK's
premier guide
to Hotels and
Restaurants
should be
without a copy of...

'Mobile Manners'

Cellnet's widely acclaimed guide to mobile etiquette in the 90's.

cellnet

Attempting to comply with the niceties of a courtesy code which has its origins in the remote and distant past – while using the most advanced personal communications technology of the nineties – can tax the most socially adept mobile user.

Many useful suggestions on how to avoid making a mobile faux pas can be found in 'Mobile Manners', Cellnet's tongue-in-cheek guide to mobile phone etiquette.

For your free copy of Mobile Manners...

call 0800 214000

England

Abberley   Elms Hotel   70%   £118

Tel 0299 896666   Fax 0299 896804   **H**

Stockton Road Abberley Hereford & Worcester WR6 6AT   Map 14 B1

The sweet, welcoming aroma of a year-round log fire greets guests in the
entrance hall of this substantial Queen Anne mansion just off the A443 and
surrounded by gardens that enjoy fine views of the countryside. Dotted
with antiques, the day rooms have a gracious, country-house feel enhanced
by board games and magazines. There's a mixture of antiques and
reproduction pieces in bedrooms that, whilst not freshly decorated, are
in good order and well appointed, with extras like fresh fruit, sherry and
books. Nine Coach House rooms are in similar style but without mini-bar
or remote-control for the TV. Bathrooms vary in size but all have
telephone, loudspeaker extension and generously-sized towels. No bathrobes
though. Beds are turned down in the evenings and room service is 24hr.
Queens Moat Houses. **Rooms** 25. *Garden, croquet, tennis, putting.*
AMERICAN EXPRESS *Access, Diners, Visa.*

Abbot's Salford   Salford Hall   66%   £95

Tel 0386 871300   Fax 0386 871301   **H**

Abbot's Salford Evesham Hereford & Worcester WR11 5UT   Map 14 C1

A fascinating Tudor building beside the A439 about eight miles west
of Stratford-upon-Avon. Once a guest residence for the monks of nearby
Evesham Abbey, it retains considerable historical and architectural interest.
Stained-glass windows depict coats of arms, and there's a half-timbered,
whitewashed wing and a fine walled garden. The central courtyard has
been glassed in to form a pleasant conservatory, giving striking views of its
gabled roofs. The lounge, once the Abbot's kitchen, displays original meat
hooks suspended from oak beams. Bedrooms, named after historical
characters connected with the hall and split between the main house and
the gate house, are mainly furnished with reproduction pieces; many have
exposed timberwork and mullioned windows. Conferences for up to 50.
No dogs. **Rooms** 34. *Garden, croquet, tennis, sauna, sun beds, snooker.*
AMERICAN EXPRESS *Access, Diners, Visa.*

Abingdon   Abingdon Lodge   61%   £88

Tel 0235 553456   Fax 0235 554117   **H**

Marcham Road Abingdon Oxfordshire OX14 1TZ   Map 15 D2

Clean-lined, modern low-rise hotel at the junction of the A34 and A415.
Day rooms include a distinctive octagonal bar. Several conference rooms
cater for up to 180 delegates. Twenty-six bedrooms reserved for non-
smokers. Children up to 12 stay free in parents' room. Ample car parking.
Rooms 63. *Garden.* AMERICAN EXPRESS *Access, Diners, Visa.*

> Consult page 20 for a full list of starred restaurants

Abingdon   Upper Reaches   62%   £106

Tel 0235 522311   Fax 0235 555182   **H**

Thames Street Abingdon Oxfordshire OX14 3TA   Map 15 D2

Six miles from Oxford, a former corn mill once operated by Benedictine
monks, standing on a virtual island between the Thames and the Abbey
Stream. Some bedrooms enjoy river views. The restaurant features
a working water wheel and mill race. River moorings for those guests who
wish to arrive by boat. Free parking for 70 cars. Forte Heritage. **Rooms** 25.
Terrace, fishing. AMERICAN EXPRESS *Access, Diners, Visa.*

Acle · Forte Travelodge · £45

Tel 0493 751970

L

Acle Norfolk NR13 3BE

Map 10 D1

At the junction of the A47 and the Acle bypass, to the east of Acle on the main road between Norwich and Great Yarmouth. *Rooms 40.*
AMERICAN EXPRESS *Access, Diners, Visa.*

Alcester · Arrow Mill · £72

Tel 0789 762419   Fax 0789 765170

I

Arrow Alcester Warwickshire B49 5NL

Map 14 C1

The Arrow Mill was listed in the Domesday Book, when it was a working flour mill valued at three shillings and sixpence! The stream-driven mill wheel still turns in the restaurant, and day rooms feature heavy beams and flagstones. Bedrooms of individual character use light, attractive fabrics and pine furniture. There's parking space for 200 cars, and a heliport. Dogs in kennels only. *Rooms 18. Garden, fishing. Closed 2 weeks Christmas.*
AMERICAN EXPRESS *Access, Diners, Visa.*

Alcester · Places of Interest

Coughton Galleries   Coughton Court Tel 0789 762642.
Ragley Hall   Tel 0789 762090.

Aldeburgh · Brudenell Hotel · 60% · £92

Tel 0728 452071   Fax 0728 454082

H

The Parade Aldeburgh Suffolk IP15 5BU

Map 10 D3

A traditional seaside esplanade hotel, where public rooms and many of the bedrooms look out on the briny. The elegant Music Room can accommodate up to 50 people for meetings and conferences. A dozen of the rooms are designated non-smoking. Under-16s can share their parents' room free. Forte Heritage. *Rooms 47.* AMERICAN EXPRESS *Access, Diners, Visa.*

Aldeburgh · Uplands · 60% · £60

Tel 0728 452420   Fax 0728 454872

H

Victoria Road Aldeburgh Suffolk IP15 5DX

Map 10 D3

A Regency house, just opposite the parish church and a stone's throw from the seafront, which maintains the best aspects of a snug guest house. Public areas include a rear conservatory which opens on to the landscaped gardens where there's a wing of chalets. Remaining bedrooms in the house retain some period features and have character and charm; all but three are en suite. No dogs. *Rooms 20. Garden.* AMERICAN EXPRESS *Access, Diners, Visa.*

Aldeburgh · Wentworth Hotel · 68% · £84

Tel 0728 452312   Fax 0728 454343

H

Wentworth Road Aldeburgh Suffolk IP15 5BD

Map 10 D3

Just back from the beach opposite the fishermen's huts and boats, the Wentworth has been in the same family ownership since 1920. This continuity has built up a reputation for service and civilised comfort which brings many repeat visits, and the Pritts are always looking for ways to improve and enhance their hotel, the latest testimony being additional bedrooms, a small conference room and more parking spaces. Many of the bedrooms look out to sea, and almost all have bathrooms en suite. There are two tastefully appointed lounges and a cosy bar. *Rooms 38. Garden. Closed 2 weeks from 27 Dec.* AMERICAN EXPRESS *Access, Diners, Visa.*

Aldeburgh   Places of Interest

Tourist Information   Tel 0728 453637.
Snape Maltings Concert Hall   Snape Tel 0728 452935.
Sizewell Visitor Centre   Nr Leiston Tel 0728 642139.

Alderley Edge   Alderley Edge Hotel   72%   £117

Tel 0625 583033   Fax 0625 586343   **HR**

Macclesfield Road Alderley Edge Cheshire SK9 7BJ   Map 6 B2

Friendly, well-drilled staff are a big plus at this Victorian hotel on the edge
of town. Fresh flowers abound in day rooms that include a comfortable
conservatory lounge overlooking the garden (part of which is given over
to a bird sanctuary). Soft floral schemes are favoured in the bedrooms,
of which the Executive (standard) rooms are rather on the small side, with
painted furniture, in contrast to spacious pine-furnished De Luxe rooms.
The latter also get various extras such as decanters of sherry, mini-bar,
teletext TV and spa bath; four are quite cottagey with beams and some
exposed stonework; all rooms include bathrobes and magazines. 24hr room
service. Children under 14 stay free in parents' room. No dogs. The Krug
room accommodates 120 for a theatre-style conference and 100 for a sit-
down banquet; a pair of other rooms is suitable for smaller meetings and
private parties. *Rooms 32. Garden.* AMERICAN EXPRESS *Access, Diners, Visa.*

Restaurant   £80

The effort that chef Brian Joy and his team put into making a meal here
an enjoyable experience is evident from the minute one is offered the
choice of home-made breads (fruit and nut, cheese, garlic and anchovy,
caraway and sun-dried tomato appear regularly). Similar attention to detail
is paid to sourcing ingredients for the extensive menus: typically, fine fresh
fish comes daily from the markets of Fleetwood and black pudding (for
breakfast or topping noisettes of lamb) from Bury market. 'Pearls of sun-
drenched Mediterranean melon set against a mosaic of exotic fruits and
berries doused in an elderflower and lemon cordial' sets the style for
flowery menu descriptions, but persevere to find well-thought-out dishes
like terrine of guinea fowl and cured ham marbled with pistachio and
prunes accompanied by endive leaves and a home-made apple chutney and
brioche; émincé of veal kidneys sautéed with candied aubergine and ginger,
with a juniper-flavoured sweet wine sauce. Desserts are as 'tempting'
as described – try the hot apple and cinnamon sponge pudding 'masked'
in a walnut custard. Aberdeen Angus beef is carved at the table at Sunday
lunchtimes, when the choice is either à la carte or a fixed-price menu.
An equally interesting light lunch menu is served Mon-Sat in the
conservatory. The cheese trolley usually offers a few choice British
offerings alongside Continental favourites. The sensational wine list is a real
labour of love – huge selection of champagnes (one of the largest in the
world?), magnums and half bottles, but equally important, a good choice
of wines under £15 per bottle. *Seats 80. Private Room 22. L 12-2 D 7-10.
Set L £13.25/£18.50 (Sun £18.50) Set D £23.*

Aldridge   Fairlawns   64%   £78

Tel 0922 55122   Fax 0922 743210   **H**

Little Aston Road Aldridge Walsall West Midlands WS9 0NU   Map 6 C4

Surrounded by farm land near the junction of the A452 and A454, John
Pette's well-cared-for hotel is based around an original Victorian house
with a couple of modern redbrick extensions. A comfortable dado-panelled
bar with leather armchairs and a rattan-furnished conservatory extension
is the main dayroom and there are several attractively decorated
conference/function rooms. Solid oak fitted units provide good, well-lit
work space in neat bedrooms which include six split-level suites with sofa

beds in the lounge area (good for families) and mezzanine bedrooms. Room service can provide hot food 24hrs a day. **Rooms** *35. Garden, croquet.* AMERICAN EXPRESS *Access, Diners, Visa.*

All Stretton   Stretton Hall Hotel   59%   £54

Tel 0694 723224   Fax 0694 724365   **H**
All Stretton nr Church Stretton Shropshire SY6 6HG   Map 6 A4

A major refurbishment was under way as we went to press, encompassing bedrooms and public rooms. There's due to be a new bar as well as a revamped residents' lounge. Banqueting/conferences for 70/30. Some rooms are suitable for family use. **Rooms** *14. Garden.* AMERICAN EXPRESS *Access, Diners, Visa.*

Alnwick   White Swan   58%   £70

Tel 0665 602109   Fax 0665 510400   **H**
Bondgate Within, Alnwick Northumberland NE66 1TD   Map 5 D1

A major decorative feature at this town-centre former coaching inn is that the hotel's staircase, revolving doors and some carved oak panelling all came from the *SS Olympic*, sister ship to the ill-fated *Titanic*. Other nautical references are to be found in the bar and lounges. Bedrooms are equipped with all the usual amenities – children under 14 stay free in parents' room. Additional bedrooms came on stream during the summer of 1994. Four conference rooms (up to 150 theatre-style). **Rooms** *58.* AMERICAN EXPRESS *Access, Visa.*

Alnwick   Places of Interest

Tourist Information   Tel 0665 510665.
Morpeth Chantry Bagpipe Museum   The Chantry, Bridge Street, Morpeth Tel 0670 519466.
   Historic Houses, Castles and Gardens
Alnwick Castle   Tel 0665 510777.
Cragside House & Country Park (NT)   Rothbury Tel 0669 20333.
Howick Hall Garden   Howick Tel 0665 577285.
Wallington House, Walled Garden and Grounds (NT)   Cambo, Morpeth Tel 0670 74283.

Alsager   Manor House   65%   £72

Tel 0270 884000   Fax 0270 882483   **H**
Audley Road Alsager Cheshire ST7 2QQ   Map 6 B3

Just three miles from Junction 16 of the M6 the Manor House is a modern hotel set in its own grounds, but since the site dates back in parts to the 17th century, old beams preserve a traditional feel in the restaurant, bars and several meeting rooms. Bedrooms are divided between the original part and a new wing; in the latter are two rooms adapted for disabled guests and two Executive rooms with jacuzzis. Children up to 14 stay free in parents' room. Conference facilities for 200. Compass Hotels. **Rooms** *57. Garden, indoor swimming pool, snooker.* AMERICAN EXPRESS *Access, Diners, Visa.*

Alsager   Place of Interest

Little Moreton Hall (NT)   Tel 0260 272018 *4 miles.*

Alston   Lovelady Shield   68%   £95

Tel 0434 381203   Fax 0434 381515   **HR**
Nenthead Road Alston Cumbria CA9 3LF   Map 5 D3

A long tree-lined drive leads to this secluded 1830s house set among the wild Pennine fells east of Alston on the A689. Bordered on one side by the river Nent, the hotel bottles its own mineral water (though this is from a source higher up in the hills). Public rooms include a delightful and peaceful lounge decorated in pale cream which co-ordinates tastefully with the pale blue of the upholstery. The adjacent bar has a convivial atmosphere. Bedrooms are of good size and are attractively homely in character with some fine old pieces of furniture and carefully co-ordinated colour schemes. Useful extras include shoe-shine kits. Bathrooms, though compact, are neat and have decent shower risers. Sustaining breakfasts, for which last orders are at 9am. *Rooms 12. Garden, croquet, tennis. Closed 4 Jan-5 Feb.* AMERICAN EXPRESS *Access, Diners, Visa.*

Restaurant £60

A charming, informal candlelit setting for a short, four-course fixed-price dinner which is simple in both style and presentation. A fruit cocktail, scrambled eggs with smoked salmon or Olde English-style potted lamb could start the meal; then comes a soup; a choice of three main courses (fish, poultry, meat); a couple of desserts and coffee with sweetmeats in the lounge. No smoking. *Seats 26. D 7-8.30. Set D £24.50*

Alton   Forte Travelodge £45

Tel 0420 562659   **L**

A31 Four Marks Winchester Road Alton Hampshire GU34 5HZ   Map 15 D3

On the A31 northbound, 5 miles south of Alton. Close to Winchester. *Rooms 31.* AMERICAN EXPRESS *Access, Diners, Visa.*

Alton   Grange Hotel   61% £65

Tel 0420 86565   Fax 0420 541346   **H**

London Road Alton Hampshire GU34 4EG   Map 15 D3

The two-acre garden, overlooked by the lounge and sun terrace, is quite a feature at the Levenes' friendly hotel. Croquet and putting are available, and a commercial company based at the hotel organises hot-air balloon trips. Individually appointed bedrooms include two honeymoon suites and the penthouse suite with a sunken bath. *Rooms 30. Garden, croquet, putting, coffee shop (9am-10.30pm).* AMERICAN EXPRESS *Access, Diners, Visa.*

Alton   The Swan   58% £88

Tel 0420 83777   Fax 0420 87975   **H**

High Street Alton Hampshire GU34 1AT   Map 15 D3

White-painted former coaching inn offering neat, practical accommodation alongside comfortable, unfussy public areas. Friendly staff. Banqueting and conference facilities for 100. Forte Heritage. *Rooms 36.* AMERICAN EXPRESS *Access, Diners, Visa.*

Alton   Places of Interest

Oates Memorial Library and the Gilbert White Museum   The Wakes, Selborne Tel 0420 50275.
   Historic Houses, Castles and Gardens
Jane Austen's House   Chawton Tel 0420 83262.
Jenkyn Place Garden   Bentley Tel 0420 23118.

Altrincham   Bowdon Hotel   65% £79

Tel 061-928 7121   Fax 061-927 7560   **H**

Langham Road Bowdon Altrincham Cheshire WA14 2HT   Map 6 B2

Victorian hotel with sympathetic extensions, on the B5161 and convenient for the motorway network (M56 exit 7 two miles). Neat, practical accommodation, several conference rooms and banqueting suites (capacity 130), a bar called *Silks* and an ample car park. Ramps have been added for visitors in wheelchairs. Children up to 14 stay free in parents' room. *Rooms 82.* AMERICAN EXPRESS *Access, Diners, Visa.*

Altrincham   Cresta Court   61%   £64

Tel 061-927 7272   Fax 061-926 9194   **H**

Church Street Altrincham Cheshire WA14 4DP   Map 6 B2

Handy for the motorway network, Manchester Airport and the North-West generally, the privately owned Cresta Court offers well-kept, up-to-date accommodation and a variety of air-conditioned conference and function rooms (max 300). Children up to 12 stay free in parents' room. *Rooms 139. Coffee shop (9am-6pm).* AMERICAN EXPRESS *Access, Diners, Visa.*

Altrincham   Francs   £40

Tel 061-941 3954   **R**

2 Goose Green Altrincham Cheshire   Map 6 B2

A French bistro offering a wide range of food, from sandwiches to *steak frites, potage* to *poisson en croute,* plus *plats du jour* – all with a breath of French air. Sunday lunch is always busy, with children under 10 fed free. All desserts are home-made. Outdoor eating on a terrace in good weather. Note that there is no connection with Francs in Chester. *Seats 75. Parties 40. L 12-3 D 5-11 (Sun 12-5). Set L (Sun) £7.50. Closed D Sun, all Bank Holidays.* AMERICAN EXPRESS *Access, Visa.*

Altrincham   George & Dragon   60%   £46

Tel 061-928 9933   Fax 061-929 8060   **H**

Manchester Road Altrincham Cheshire WA14 4PH   Map 6 B2

Smartly kept accommodation, Victorian-inspired bar-lounge. Children up to 16 stay free in parents' room. No room service. No dogs. *Rooms 46. Garden.* AMERICAN EXPRESS *Access, Diners, Visa.*

Altrincham   Places of Interest

Dunham Massey Hall and Garden (NT)   Tel 061 941 1025.
Ice Rink   Devonshire Road Tel 061 926 8316.

Note that all telephone numbers with area codes starting with 0 will start 01 from 16 April 1995.

Alveley   Mill Hotel   72%   £55

Tel 0746 780437   Fax 0746 780850   **H**

Birdsgreen Alveley nr Bridgnorth Shropshire WV15 6HL   Map 6 B4

From the starting point of a 16th-century mill, whose workings can still be seen in the pubby public bar, Franco D'Aniello has created a fine hotel with unusually spacious public areas that include a large, comfortably furnished lounge and roomy cocktail bar. Beautifully landscaped grounds provide plenty of photo opportunities – lake, rustic bridge, gazebo – making this a popular venue for weddings; there are also a number of well-planned function rooms. Upstairs, dado-panelled corridors are broad, and well-appointed bedrooms generally large with freestanding furniture, pleasing fabrics and phones at both desk and bedside. Superior rooms are particularly large and have either four-posters or elaborate bedhead drapes plus sofas and armchairs. Good bathrooms, with either corner or alcoved tubs, boast large bath sheets, mostly good shelf space, and often have twin basins; five have separate shower cubicles. A well-run hotel with notably friendly staff, 24hr room service and turn-down service in the evenings. Conference/banqueting facilities for up to 200; ample parking. No dogs. *Rooms 21. Garden, games room.* AMERICAN EXPRESS *Access, Diners, Visa.*

Alveston   **Alveston House**   65%   £80

Tel 0454 415050   Fax 0454 415425   **H**

Alveston nr Bristol Avon BS12 2LJ   Map 13 F1

Popular commercial hotel on the A38 close to Bristol and the M4 and M5.
The majority of bedrooms are singles, and the hotel is geared up to the
business trade with conference suites catering for up to 80 delegates. Ample
free parking. **Rooms** 30. Garden. AMERICAN EXPRESS *Access, Diners, Visa.*

Alveston   **Forte Posthouse**   62%   £68

Tel 0454 412521   Fax 0454 413920   **H**

Thornbury Road Alveston nr Bristol Avon BS12 2LL   Map 13 F1

11 miles north of Bristol, close to M4/M5 intersection, an extended Tudor
inn with a good conference trade (facilities for up to 100). **Rooms** 74.
Outdoor swimming pool, pitch & putt, children's play area. AMERICAN EXPRESS
Access, Diners, Visa.

Amberley   **Amberley Inn**   57%   £70

Tel 0453 872565   Fax 0453 872738   **H**

Amberley nr Stroud Gloucestershire GL5 5AF   Map 14 B2

High on Minchinhampton Common, this sturdy, stone-built inn enjoys
spectacular views of Woodchester Valley, particularly from the residents'
lounge. There are two bars, the oak-panelled Lounge and the locally
popular Country. Bedrooms share the views or overlook the garden. Four
especially pleasant rooms are in the Garden House. Children up to 16 stay
free in parents' room. **Rooms** 14. Garden. AMERICAN EXPRESS *Access,
Diners, Visa.*

Amberley   **Amberley Castle**   81%   £130

Tel 0798 831992   Fax 0798 831998   **HR**

Amberley nr Arundel West Sussex BN18 9ND   Map 11 A6

A real castle this, dating back to the 11th century, with its remarkably
complete curtain walls concealing the prettiest of gardens – very much the
creation of owner Martin Cummings, who is often mistaken for the
gardener. Just oozing history and with all sorts of fascinating details
to discover, Amberley nevertheless manages to defy the draughty castle
image with day rooms (dotted with antiques, the odd suit of armour and
rack of pikes) that are positively cosy. While husband Martin is out in the
garden it is Joy Cummings who has the flair for interior design, best seen
in individually decorated bedrooms that come with every comfort from
video players (the hotel has a library of films) and books to fruit and iced
water. Bathrooms all have spa baths and come with good toiletries,
bathrobes and generous towelling. High-quality staff provide a level
of service to match the surroundings. **Rooms** 14. Garden, croquet.
AMERICAN EXPRESS *Access, Diners, Visa.* MARTELL

Queen's Room Restaurant   £110

The 'baronial hall' dining room dates from the 13th century but is named
after Catherine of Braganza, whose visit here in 1685 is also
commemorated in a mural depicting her hunting in Arundel Park with
Charles II. Chef Paul Boschetti's highly accomplished cooking is rather
more up to date although the no-choice gourmet menu takes its inspiration
from old English recipes and the lunch menu offers one of a number
of traditional dishes (jugged hare, steak and oyster pie) and puds (jam roly-
poly, queen of puddings) each day. Home-smoked lobster in chervil butter
sauce, salad of Southdown lamb with mustard spices and mushrooms
cooked in honey (both signature dishes), chartreuse of Gressingham duck
with port and truffle sauce, and pan-fried turbot on a bed of creamed
potatoes with olive oil and thyme-scented juices give the style of the main

à la carte, which is available, though not generally offered, at lunchtime. New pastry chef Clare Jackson is responsible for a particularly moreish chocolate and cinnamon tart with an intriguing hint of fresh mint. *Seats 36. Parties 8. Private Room 48. L 12-2 D 7-9.30. Set L £13.50/£16.50 Set D £25.50.*

Ambleside   Kirkstone Foot   65%   £104★
Tel 053 94 32232   Fax 053 94 31110   H
Kirkstone Pass Road Ambleside Cumbria LA22 9EH   Map 4 C3

The original 17th-century manor house and its extensions and outbuildings offer hotel accommodation plus self-catering cottages and apartments (dogs welcome in the latter only). Many guests return year after year and the place has a homely feel, especially in the lounge and bar areas which look out on fine gardens and over Ambleside's rooftops. Bedrooms mainly have floral fabrics, colour co-ordinated schemes and smart modern furniture. They come in various sizes, among which front-facing rooms are decidedly superior. The three master bedrooms have king-size beds, and two rooms are particularly suitable for families. 1995 will see the start of a major refurbishment programme. ★Half-board terms only. *Rooms 16. Garden, croquet. Closed Jan.* AMERICAN EXPRESS *Access, Diners, Visa.*

Ambleside   Nanny Brow   62%   £130★
Tel 053 94 32036   Fax 053 94 32450   H
Clappersgate Ambleside Cumbria LA22 9NF   Map 4 C3

An interesting Edwardian building, built in 1908 in Tudor style a mile and a half from Ambleside on the A593 Coniston/Langdale road. Nanny Brow has fine, stepped gardens and views over the Brathay Valley. Lounge and bar retain a cosy feel with open log fires. Chintz decor predominates in the main-house bedrooms; those in the Garden Wing are generally larger, with good views. The ground-floor has access to a garden terrace, the first-floor suite to a private balcony. The hotel has its own ski boat, and fishing is available on a private stretch of the River Brathay. ★Half-board terms. *Rooms 18. Garden, spa bath, solarium, tennis, fishing. Closed 3 weeks Jan.* AMERICAN EXPRESS *Access, Diners, Visa.*

Ambleside   Rothay Manor   71%   £108
Tel 053 94 33605   Fax 053 94 33607   HR
Rothay Bridge Ambleside Cumbria LA22 0EH   Map 4 C3

A balconied Regency frontage is echoed by an elegant, restful interior of cool decor, deep-cushioned seating and garden views which are shared by the best, front-facing bedrooms. Of the three garden suites two are well suited to family use (children up to 10 stay free in parents' room) and two rooms (one suite) are equipped for disabled guests. A convenient location on the Coniston road is handy for Ambleside yet well protected from its bustle in secluded grounds. The Nixons have been here since it opened in 1967 and personal touches are evident throughout; service is very friendly and attentive. Guests have free use of a nearby leisure club (swimming pool, sauna, steam room, spa bath) and permits may be obtained for trout fishing. Traditional afternoon tea is served every day between 3.30 and 5.30. No dogs. *Rooms 18. Garden, croquet. Closed early Jan-mid Feb.* AMERICAN EXPRESS *Access, Diners, Visa.*

Restaurant   £70

The setting of polished mahogany tables and soft candle-light is thoroughly traditional, and both cooking and service are in keeping. Lunchtime sees a cold buffet Monday to Saturday, roasts on Sunday (book), while dinner is a fixed-price meal. Super prices (house wines at £9!) on a decent wine list; where there are no half bottles they are happy to serve half of a full bottle at 60% of the full bottle price – or you can buy the whole bottle and take some home. No smoking. *Seats 70. Parties 20. Private Room 36.*

L 12.30-2 (buffet only Mon-Sat) (Sun 12.30-1.30) D 8-9. Set L £14.50
(Sun) Set D £21/£24.

Ambleside   Wateredge Hotel   63%   £102

Tel & Fax 053 94 32332   **HR**

Waterhead Bay Ambleside Cumbria LA22 0EP   Map 4 C3

On the outskirts of Ambleside, the Wateredge is set right at the tip of Lake
Windermere and takes full advantage of its location with gardens
stretching down to the shore, a jetty and rowing boat – hence no children
under seven. It was originally a pair of fishermens' cottages but modern
extensions have added garden rooms with private balcony or patio and two
spacious ground-floor suites. A cosy bar, bright airy lounge and lake views
provide the unifying theme; the Cowap family and cheerful staff provide
the welcome. Guests have free membership of a nearby leisure club.
Rooms 23. Garden, boating, coarse fishing. Closed mid Dec-early Feb.
AMERICAN EXPRESS Access, Visa.

Restaurant   £65

Chefs Michael Cosgrove, Mark Cowap and Kathryn Cosgrove offer what
they describe as traditional farmhouse cuisine, making all their own breads,
pastries, ice creams, preserves and after-dinner truffles. Six courses include
some choice on a well-balanced menu which could result in seafood salad
of mussels, prawns, queenies, cockles and herring with a sour cream and dill
dressing, carrot and thyme soup served with wholemeal bread, a sorbet,
roast breast of goose with a morello cherry and pear chutney and a light
herb gravy, pineapple pavlova or blackcurrant, apple and raspbery pie, and
British cheeses to finish. Friendly service is again a plus, as is a non-smoking
policy. Lighter lunches (12-2pm) and afternoon teas (3-5pm) are served out
on the patio in warm weather, otherwise in the lounges – but in either case
there's a good view of the lake. ***Seats*** 45. Parties 12. D only 7-8.30.

Amesbury   Forte Travelodge   £45

Tel 0980 624966   **L**

A303 Amesbury Wiltshire SP4 7AS   Map 14 C3

At the junction of the A345 and the A303 eastbound, 8 miles north
of Salisbury on the major route for the West Country. ***Rooms*** 32.
AMERICAN EXPRESS Access, Diners, Visa.

Ampfield   Potters Heron Hotel   60%   £80

Tel 0703 266611   Fax 0703 251359   **H**

Ampfield nr Romsey Hampshire SO51 9ZF   Map 15 D3

White-painted thatched building on the A31 with ample free parking,
conference facilities for up to 140 and all-day informal eating in Potters
Pub. The majority of the bedrooms are designated non-smoking. Children
up to 16 stay free in parents' room. Lansbury. ***Rooms*** 54. Garden, keep-fit
equipment, sauna, children's playroom. AMERICAN EXPRESS Access, Diners, Visa.

Ampney Crucis   The Crown of Crucis   £60

Tel 0285 851806   Fax 0285 851735   **I**

Ampney Crucis Cirencester Gloucestershire GL7 5RS   Map 14 C2

A 400-year-old Cotswold village inn alongside the A417. The refurbished
oak-beamed bar and two-tier restaurant are housed in the old hostelry,
while bedrooms are in a purpose-built extension around a garden
courtyard. Most rooms enjoy a view over Ampney Brook to the village
cricket ground. 14 ground-floor rooms for the less active and four for non-
smokers; one room is equipped for disabled guests. Children under 6 share
parents' room free. Conference/banqueting 100/90. ***Rooms*** 25. Garden.
Closed 24-30 Dec. AMERICAN EXPRESS Access, Diners, Visa.

Andover   White Hart Inn   £79

Tel 0264 352266   Fax 0264 323767   ■

Bridge Street Andover Hampshire SP10 1BH   Map 14 C3

Former coaching inn with a history going back 300 years. Period character (c. 1900) created by pictures, posters and bric-a-brac in the day rooms. The Oak Room can host functions of up to 70 delegates. The inn changed hands just as we went to press. *Rooms 20.* AMERICAN EXPRESS *Access, Diners, Visa.*

Andover   Places of Interest

Cricklade Theatre   Tel 0264 365698.
Hawk Conservancy Park   Weyhill Tel 0264 772252.
Thruxton Motor Racing Circuit   Tel 0264 772696.
Finkley Down Farm Park   Tel 0264 352195

Ansty   Ansty Hall   70%   £100

Tel 0203 612222   Fax 0203 602155   **H**

Ansty nr Coventry Warwickshire CV7 9HZ   Map 7 D4

Just two minutes from Junction 2 of the M6, yet this mellow Caroline house dating from 1678 enjoys a peaceful rural setting. The entrance hall, with real log fire in winter, features wood panelling that is old rather than fine and the period day rooms tend to be multi-purpose – meeting room one day, lounge the next. Bedrooms are spacious with those in the original building sporting reproduction antique furniture, but perhaps the best are the 12 in a new wing (just a couple of years old) which come with comfortable wing armchairs and stylish individual decor. Almost all rooms have bedhead drapes or canopies. Dogs are only allowed in the six characterful stable-block bedrooms. 24hr room service. *Rooms 31. Garden.* AMERICAN EXPRESS *Access, Diners, Visa.*

Appleby-in-Westmorland   Appleby Manor Hotel   66%   £98

Tel 076 83 51571   Fax 076 83 52888   **HR**

Roman Road Appleby-in-Westmorland Cumbria CA16 6JB   Map 5 D3

A relaxing and friendly, family-owned hotel overlooking Appleby Castle and the Eden valley. Most of the original (1870s) architectural features remain, including the main fireplace and old hooks that used to carry rods to hang tapestries and pictures. Bright and cheerful bedrooms, whether those in the main house and modern wing or the seven in the coach house annexe, provide everything you need, from powerful hairdryers to in-house video films; four-poster beds attract a small supplement. Sink into one of the comfortable armchairs in the three lounges, warm yourself in front of a real log fire and sample one of the 71 single-malt whiskies on offer. Pool, snooker and table tennis in the games room. Lower tariff in November. Dogs in annexe rooms only. *Rooms 30. Garden, croquet, indoor swimming pool, spa bath, sauna, steam room, solarium, keep-fit equipment, games room. Closed 3 days Christmas.* AMERICAN EXPRESS *Access, Diners, Visa.*

Oak Room Restaurant   £50

A panelled room (with a hand-painted tiled fireplace) where no-nonsense British food is served in decent portions on fixed-price-only menus. Dishes such as beefsteak and oyster pudding, Gypsy Hill chicken (pastry-wrapped chicken breast stuffed with pigeon breast topped with leek butter) feature on the 'speciality' menus, with the likes of creamy soups, Solway salmon paté with dill mayonnaise, best end of lamb, pork loin medallions and whiting or sea bream on the tables d'hote. The commendable attitude to wine pricing continues – apart from four value-for-money fine wines, there's a fixed mark-up on the purchase price of every bottle. Sweets from a trolley or a choice of six local Cumbrian cheeses. Youngsters' menu served in the restaurant from 5-7.30pm. *Seats 70. Parties 30. L 12-1.45 .D 7-9. Closed 3 days Christmas. Set L & D from £17.95.*

Appleby-in-Westmorland   Tufton Arms   66%   £80

Tel 076 83 51593   Fax 076 83 52761   **H**

Market Square Appleby-in-Westmorland Cumbria CA16 6XA   Map 5 D3

An unusual and rather evocative conversion of a 16th-century building which became a Victorian pub, restored by the Milsom family with authentic pieces, period prints and atmospheric appeal. Clubby bar, restful drawing room, conservatory restaurant. More Victorian features and carefully updated bathrooms in the original bedrooms; a more modest modern wing is fitted out with the businessman in mind. In the centre of Appleby, by the A66. Residents can fish free on a stretch of the Eden. Shooting parties welcome. **Rooms** *19. Fishing, children's playground.* AMERICAN EXPRESS *Access, Diners, Visa.*

Applethwaite   Underscar Manor   74%   £150*

Tel 07687 75000   Fax 07687 74904   **HR**

Applethwaite Keswick Cumbria CA12 4PH   Map 4 C3

Overlooking Derwentwater and set in 40 acres of peaceful and tranquil grounds, the hotel is under the same direction (Pauline and Derek Harrison) as the *Moss Nook* restaurant near Manchester airport (*qv*). Just one mile from the Keswick roundabout on the A66, the hotel, an Italianate house built in Victorian times, retains many original architectural features – fireplaces, mouldings, plasterwork ceilings – with period furniture to match. Opulent fabrics, deep carpets and exquisite flower arrangements all add to this splendour, carried through to the luxurious and spacious bathrooms which command breathtaking views. Bathrooms are equally well appointed with smart fittings, decent toiletries and good towels. No children under 12. No dogs. Conference boardroom for 14. *Half-board terms only. **Rooms** 11. Garden.* AMERICAN EXPRESS *Access, Visa.*

Restaurant   £65

One of the dining rooms is a domed conservatory, which adds to the pleasure of the cooking here. Chefs Robert Thornton and Stephen Yare present menus with around six choices (less at lunctime) within each course. Over the years their style has evolved with many influences dictating the nature of dishes, but always relying on the best of local products (gamey Herdwick lamb, black pudding and wild mushrooms). They do their own smoking (incidentally banned in the restaurant), preserve fruits and make jams and marmalades, and a typical menu will consist of grilled Scottish langoustines wrapped in Savoy cabbage, breast of Gressingham duck served crisp with celeriac mousse, caramelised pineapple and a honey and vinegar sauce, and iced gingerbread parfait with white chocolate sorbet and tangerine sauce to finish. A 6-course *menu surprise* (£25) is available by entire table. Unusually, there are three Swiss wines on the list. Pleasant service, alfresco eating in fine weather. **Seats** *60. Parties 10. Private Room 20. L 12-1.30 D 7-8.30. Set L £18.50 Set D £25/£28.50.*

Ardley   Granada Lodge   NEW   £52

Tel 0869 346111   Fax 0869 345030   **L**

Granada Service Area Northampton Road Ardley nr Bicester Oxfordshire OX6 9RD   Map 15 D1

Oxford North/Cherwell Valley outlet. Between Oxford and Banbury, at the Cherwell Valley services by Junction 10 of M40. **Rooms** *64.* AMERICAN EXPRESS *Access, Diners, Visa.*

Arundel   Norfolk Arms   60%   £74

Tel 0903 882101   Fax 0903 884275   **H**

22 High Street Arundel West Sussex BN18 9AD   Map 11 A6

Arundel Castle is the seat of the Duke of Norfolk so it's natural to find the
Norfolk Arms occupying a prime site in the town's high street – it was
actually built by the 10th Duke some years ago. Bedrooms are bright, with
pale floral patterns and modern bathrooms. Newer rooms are in a detached
wing to the rear. Children up to 14 stay free in parents' room. Functions
and conferences for up to 100. Arundel Castle is an easy walk away.
Rooms 34. AMERICAN EXPRESS® *Access, Diners, Visa.*

Arundel   Places of Interest

Arundel Castle   Tel 0903 883136.
Denmans Garden   Fontwell Tel 0243 542808.
Arundel Wildfowl and Wetlands Trust   Tel 0903 883355.
Fontwell Park Racecourse   0243 543335.

Ascot   Berystede Hotel   67%   £150

Tel 0344 23311   Fax 0344 872301   **H**

Bagshot Road Sunninghill Ascot Berkshire SL5 9JH   Map 15 E2

Just to the south of Ascot, this Forte Grand hotel is based on a large
Victorian house standing in its own 6 acres of wooded grounds. As popular
with racegoers as business people, the public rooms and the best of the
bedrooms are in the original house and share its period feel. The majority
of the bedrooms, however, are in a modern extension – all are due
to be refurbished by March 1995. The hotel has its own conference centre,
including a business centre and catering for up to 120 delegates. *Rooms 91.
Garden, croquet, outdoor swimming pool, putting, games room.* AMERICAN EXPRESS®
Access, Diners, Visa.

Ascot   Hyn's   £50

Tel 0344 872583   **R**

4 Brockenhurst Road Ascot Berkshire   Map 15 E2

Peking, Szechuan and Cantonese all have their place on the menu (neatly
and clearly printed, and no numbers!). Most of the dishes will be familiar
to habitués of this most varied of cuisines, but a few are a little out of the
ordinary. There's also a small choice of Thai dishes. *Seats 90. Parties 10.
L 12-2.30 D 6-11. Closed 25 & 26 Dec. Set meals from £14.50.*
AMERICAN EXPRESS® *Access, Diners, Visa.*

Ascot   Royal Berkshire   74%   £168

Tel 0344 23322   Fax 0344 874240   **H**

London Road Sunninghill Ascot Berkshire SL5 0PP   Map 15 E2

Superb setting for this Queen Anne mansion, located between Ascot race
course and the Polo Club, previous occupants of which have included the
Churchill family and a certain Colonel Horlicks (of malted drink fame)
who developed the 15 acres of superb gardens and woodlands. Elegant
public areas. Bedrooms in the original house are spacious and stylish with
freestanding furniture and plenty of extras; those in the extensions are
a little simpler. The largest of the nine conference rooms can accommodate
up to 70 delegates theatre-style. Cooking in the State Room Restaurant
disappointed on our last visit. *Rooms 63. Garden, croquet, indoor swimming
pool, sauna, spa bath, tennis, squash, putting, helipad.* AMERICAN EXPRESS® *Access,
Diners, Visa.*

Ascot   Places of Interest

Racecourse   Tel 0344 22211.
Ascot Park Polo Club   Wood Hall Tel 0344 20399.

Ashbourne   Ashbourne Lodge Hotel   66%   £75

Tel 0335 346666   Fax 0335 346549   **H**

Derby Road Ashbourne Derbyshire DE6 1XH   **Map 6 C3**

On the A52 from Derby to Leek, this modern redbrick hotel is lent some
old-world style by rustic-designed public areas. Bedrooms are neat and
light but not over-large, although family rooms for two adults and two
children are available. Banqueting/conference facilities for 180/200. There's
an all-day brasserie (The Black Sheep) with a children's menu. No dogs.
Rooms 50. Garden. AMERICAN EXPRESS *Access, Diners, Visa.*

Ashbourne   Callow Hall   69%   £90

Tel 0335 343403   Fax 0335 343624   **H**

Mappleton Road Ashbourne Derbyshire DE6 2AA   **Map 6 C3**

Five minutes' drive from the centre of Ashbourne, the Spencer family's
Victorian mansion is an ideal retreat. Approached by a tree-lined drive
through 44 acres of woodland, it enjoys a mile of private fishing on the
nearby Bentley Brook. Besides fishing, it attracts shooting parties and is also
popular for small conferences. Quality antiques and family memorabilia are
the main features of the drawing room and homely little bar. Bedrooms
with tasteful design and elegant furnishings of the highest standard provide
plenty of extras – from books and magazines to fresh fruit and mineral
water; one spacious ground-floor room faces the house and is equipped for
disabled guests. Sumptuous tiled bathrooms boast bathrobes and locally
made toiletries. 1994 saw two new bedrooms and a ground-floor suite.
Children up to 12 stay free in their parents' room. No dogs. *Rooms 13.
Garden, game fishing. Closed 25 & 26 Dec.* AMERICAN EXPRESS *Access,
Diners, Visa.*

Ashford   Ashford International   71%   £98

Tel 0233 611444   Fax 0233 627708   **H**

Simone Weil Avenue Ashford Kent TN24 8UX   **Map 11 C5**

A smart hotel by Junction 9 of the M20. The lobby is part of a long, glass-
roofed boulevard which also houses an art gallery, golf shop, Avis car hire
desk, lively bar, restaurant with smart cocktail bar, and a brasserie with
tables spilling out on to the tiled concourse. A fountain and a large, four-
face hanging clock complete the rather pleasing Continental air. Spacious
bedrooms are well maintained and equipped. Queens Moat Houses.
*Rooms 200. Indoor swimming pool, sauna, solarium, whirlpool bath, beautician,
gym, brasserie (7am-11pm).* AMERICAN EXPRESS *Access, Diners, Visa.*

Ashford   Eastwell Manor   81%   £110

Tel 0233 635751   Fax 0233 635530   **HR**

Eastwell Park Boughton Aluph Ashford Kent TN25 4HR   **Map 11 C5**

There's an air of faded gentility at this Jacobean-style mansion set in 62
acres of grounds and built in the 1920s. The scale of the rooms is as grand
as the approach, with real log fires, flagstoned floors, oak panelling and
moulded plasterwork ceilings setting the tone. Bedrooms are comfortable
and well appointed, as are the bathrooms; although on our last visit
we thought that the decor throughout would benefit from being freshened
up. *Rooms 23. Garden, croquet, tennis, snooker, helipad.* AMERICAN EXPRESS
Access, Diners, Visa.

Restaurant £105

Patterned carpets and wallpaper in the Elizabeth-style dining room make an unexpected backdrop for the accomplished cooking of recently-arrived chef Ian Mansfield, who provides excellent-value set lunch and dinner menus as well as an extensive carte. Chilled turnip and leek soup scented with vanilla was an unusual but enjoyable variation on vichyssoise, while a salad of seasonal leaves with sun-dried tomatoes, shaved Parmesan, croutons and pine nuts owed much to London's current pre-occupation with Mediterranean food, as did a main course of roast cod with Puy lentils and a herb sauce. There's a confident touch about the cooking, also demonstrated in a tart of fresh goat's cheese, roasted peppers and pesto, which was well above average standard for a non-meat dish. Lemon tart with crème fraiche and strawberry sauce was classically executed. Good range of French and British cheeses, and good petits fours with the coffee. Courteous and friendly service. *Seats 80. Parties 10. Private Room 100. L 12.30-2 D 7.30-9.30 (Fri/Sat to 10). Set L £14.50 (Sun £18.00) Set D £24.50/£42/£36.50.*

Ashford Forte Posthouse 66% £68

Tel 0233 625790 Fax 0233 643176 **H**

Canterbury Road Ashford Kent TN24 8QQ Map 11 C5

Half a mile out of Ashford on the A28 to Canterbury and one mile from junction 9 of the M20. A modern hotel based around a 17th-century barn, now the restaurant. Conferences for up to 120 delegates. *Rooms 60. Garden.* AMERICAN EXPRESS *Access, Diners, Visa.*

Ashford Holiday Inn Garden Court 65% £72

Tel 0233 713333 Fax 0233 712082 **H**

Maidstone Road Hothfield Ashford Kent TN26 1AR Map 11 C5

A no-frills Holiday Inn offering only limited services and public areas, but spacious bedrooms with big beds and lightwood furniture. Good value, with free accommodation for children in parents' room and greatly reduced rates at weekends. Theatre-style conferences for up to 30 delegates. *Rooms 104. Keep-fit equipment.* AMERICAN EXPRESS *Access, Diners, Visa.*

Ashford Travel Inn £43

Tel 0233 712571 Fax 0233 713945 **L**

Maidstone Road (A20) Hothfield Common Ashford Kent TN26 1AP Map 11 C5

Rooms 40. AMERICAN EXPRESS *Access, Diners, Visa.*

Ashford Places of Interest

Tourist Information Tel 0233 629165.
Godinton Park Tel 0233 620773.

Ashford-in-the-Water Riverside Hotel 66% £85

Tel 0629 814275 Fax 0629 812873 **HR**

Fennel Street Ashford-in-the-Water Derbyshire DE4 1QF Map 6 C2

Sue and Roger Taylor's ivy-clad Georgian hotel is set in secluded grounds on the banks of the River Wye, near the centre of the village. Two comfortable sitting rooms, one with an inglenook fireplace, are complemented by an airy conservatory. Individually decorated bedrooms – some with four posters – all have heavy patterned drapes, which provide a homely feel. Luxury rooms, in a new wing, carry a small supplement. All are non-smoking. A cottage on the river is let on a self-catering basis. Light meals are served all day in the Terrace Room. *Rooms 15. Garden, croquet, fishing.* AMERICAN EXPRESS *Access, Visa.*

See over

Restaurant   £75

Chefs Simon Wild and Adrian Cooling have brought new energy and
vision to the hotel's smart dining rooms. Simple, traditional combinations,
such as melon with seasonal fruits, home-made soups with herbs or grilled
fillet steak, are mixed with more modern themes: salad of marinated
anchovies with a tapénade croute and ravigote sauce, home-cured beef with
fresh figs, Parmesan shavings and rocket, mushroom and tarragon sausage
with a tomato and red pepper coulis. Follow with home-made desserts
or smoked haddock rarebit on a tomato salad. Interesting wine list, with
a good selection of half bottles. *Seats 50. Parties 12. Private Room 20.
L 12-2 D 7-9.30.*

Ashford-in-the-Water   Places of Interest

Buxton Tourist Information   Tel 0298 25106.
Buxton Opera House   Water Street Tel 0298 71382.
Buxton Museum and Art Gallery   Terrace Road Tel 0298 24658.

Ashington   Mill House Hotel   £77

Tel 0903 892426   Fax 0903 892855   **I**
Mill Lane Ashington West Sussex RH20 3BZ   **Map 11 A6**

Comfortable, friendly and homely, this 300-year-old cottagey hotel
is clearly signposted on the northbound carriage of the A24 (it's less easy
to find from the London side). Some refurbishment during 1994 to the
public areas, which (like the bedrooms) are characterised by low ceilings
and uneven floors. Rooms are quite well equipped but simply decorated
and generally on the small side – two additional ones this year by the
purchase of the cottage next door. Children up to 11 are accommodated
free in parents' room (breakfast only charged). There are two four-poster
rooms. *Rooms 12. Garden. Closed 25 & 26 Dec.* AMERICAN EXPRESS *Access,
Diners, Visa.*

Ashington   The Willows   £55

Tel 0903 892575   **R**
London Road Ashington West Sussex RH20 3JR   **Map 11 A6**

Set back from the A24, this 15th-century farmhouse retains an inglenook
fireplace and old black beams. Chef/patron Carl Illes offers fixed-price
lunch and dinner menus which include a separate selection for vegetarians.
Dishes range from the simple and familiar (avocado prawns in a 'Maryrose'
sauce, grilled Dover sole, liver and bacon, fillet steak with creamy pepper
sauce) to the elaborate and less usual (ravioli filled with chicken mousse,
wild morel mushrooms and pistachios, served on a bed of warm beetroot
and a fresh horseradish sauce; pan-fried fillet of halibut wrapped in straw
potatoes on a bed of stewed leeks and a Pommery mustard grain sauce).
Chocaholics should be well satisfied by Willows truffle torte, baked white
chocolate cheesecake or chocolate and rum mousse – well-executed desserts
that remain on the menu. Ice cream lovers should seek out the Willows'
speciality of vanilla, caramel and dark chocolate ice creams laced with
Amaretto, Strega and Galliano, finished with whipped cream and frosted
nuts. *Seats 28. Parties 15. L 12-2 D 7-10. Closed L Sat, D Sun, all Mon.
Set L £12.50 (not Sun)/£15.50 Set D £18.25.* AMERICAN EXPRESS *Access, Visa.*

Askrigg   King's Arms Hotel   £70

Tel 0969 650258   Fax 0969 650635   **I**
Market Place Askrigg Wensleydale North Yorkshire DL8 3HQ **Map 5 D4**

Liz and Ray Hopwood's characterful, friendly inn has an unbroken history
dating back to 1760 when outbuildings, where now the Back Parlour is,
housed John Pratt's racing stables. Turner is known to have stayed here
while recording on canvas the tranquil Dales scenery of the early 1800s;
while today the main bar is universally recognised as 'The Drovers Arms'

as depicted on TV in *All Creatures Great and Small*. Each and every bedroom retains original features in keeping with the inn's manor house style, the many oak beams and uneven floors complemented by antique furniture, four-poster, half-tester and canopied brass beds, and colour co-ordinated fabrics of commensurate quality. Completion this year of the private residents' entrance and reception lounge has raised the entire King's Arms to a yet higher degree of comfort. Good bar snacks. ***Rooms 9.*** AMERICAN EXPRESS *Access, Visa.*

Aspley Guise · Moore Place · 70% · £85

Tel 0908 282000   Fax 0908 281888   **H**

The Squayre Aspley Guise nr Woburn Bedfordshire MK17 8DW   Map 15 E1

Junction 13 of the M1 is just one-and-a-half miles away, but this finely restored Georgian country house, built in 1786, stands in a peaceful village square. Day rooms have a friendly, club-like feel and are decorated in handsome period style with some original features remaining. Extensions include a sympathetically designed bedroom courtyard block, joined to the original house by a spacious glassed-in area where the reception and bar/lounge are located. Bedrooms are of a generous size, bright and airy, with lightwood furnishings and a good range of up-to-date accessories. Bathrobes and complimentary drinks in all rooms. Children up to 12 stay free in parents' room. ***Rooms 54. Garden, games room.*** AMERICAN EXPRESS *Access, Diners, Visa.*

Aston Clinton · Bell Inn · 78% · £176

Tel 0296 630252   Fax 0296 631250   **HR**

London Road Aston Clinton Buckinghamshire HP22 5HP   Map 15 E2

In the 17th century the Bell was a coaching inn and these origins are immediately apparent from its location (set back on the A41 London-Buckingham Road) and configuration – the former stables across the now flower-filled courtyard have discreetly become an integral block of bedrooms and suites. Now in its 50th year under the Harris family's ownership there's a unique blend of homely charm and serious professionalism, while an appealing mix of log-burning fire, fresh flowers and pine panelling sets the scene in the public rooms, where the mark of time and history is firmly stamped. The flagstoned smoking room with its brass ornaments and sporting pictures, and the elegant dining room are particularly notable. Enjoyable breakfasts. Conference (up to 120) and banqueting (up to 200) facilities. ***Rooms 21. Garden.*** AMERICAN EXPRESS *Access, Visa.*

Restaurant   ↑   £100

A new chef again this year, this time accompanied by marked improvements. Giles Stonehouse has worked in some prestigious kitchens, including the *Moulin de Mougins* under Roger Vergé. The Bell is now reaping the benefits. Begin with marinated goat's cheese salad or avocado and tarragon gateau with seared tiger prawns or a perfect shellfish salad (lobster, squid and langoustines) with a marvellous saffron dressing. To follow, perhaps local Aylesbury duck treated a number of ways – plain roast or a dodine with ceps, to name just two. Further options might include John Dory with sea asparagus or perfectly cooked lamb on a bed of Provençal vegetables. A dessert trolley groans with goodies and some fine cheese. A short 'bistro' menu is proving popular as a lighter option. Excellent service from an enthusiastic team under the direction of George Bottley. Wine is treated very seriously here, best illustrated by the 'wine menu', enabling you to accompany each of the three courses with a glass of different wine (choice of two). The wine list itself contains excellent house selections and a good sprinkling of half bottles, though compared to France and the rest of Europe, the New World is only meagrely represented. ***Seats 120. Parties 12. Private Room 20. L 12-1.45 D 7-9.45.*** *Set L £13.50/£17 (Sun £25) Set D £22.50.*

Aston Clinton   Place of Interest

Zoological Museum, British Museum (Natural History)   Akeman Street,
Tring Tel 044 282 4181 *3 miles.*

Axbridge   Oak House   £51

Tel 0934 732444   Fax 0934 733112   **I**

The Square Axbridge Somerset BS26 2AP   **Map 13 F1**

More ancient than it looks (it dates from the 13th century), the inn
overlooks the town square. The residents' lounge has a couple of inglenooks
providing cosy comfort in winter, and there's a restaurant and
an expanding bistro operation. Inexpensively furnished bedrooms are well
kept and offer the usual amenities. Three of the sparsely appointed
bathrooms have shower/WC only. *Rooms 10.* AMERICAN EXPRESS® *Access, Visa.*

Axbridge   Places of Interest

Tourist Information   Tel 0934 744071.
Cheddar Showcaves Museum and Exhibition   Tel 0934 742343.
Millfield School Polo Club   Gunthorpe Farm, Chapel Allerton Tel 0458
42291.

Aylesbury   Forte Posthouse   69%   £68

Tel 0296 393388   Fax 0296 392211   **H**

Aston Clinton Road Aylesbury Buckinghamshire HP22 5AA   **Map 15 D2**

A purpose-built modern hotel constructed around a central courtyard,
alongside the A41 three miles east of the town centre. Public areas are
open-plan and very smart. The tile-floored foyer leads to spacious lounges,
furnished in contemporary fashion and making good use of attractive,
colourful fabrics. Bedrooms are of a fair size and decorated in restful shades,
with solid furniture and fully tiled bathrooms. Half are designated non-
smoking. Ample banqueting facilities for 100, conferences up to 120.
Rooms 94. Garden, indoor swimming pool, gym, sauna, sun beds, beauty salon.
AMERICAN EXPRESS® *Access, Diners, Visa.*

Aylesbury   Hartwell House   86%   £165

Tel 0296 747444   Fax 0296 747450   **H R**

Oxford Road Aylesbury Buckinghamshire HP17 8NL   **Map 15 D2**

When Louis XVIII left here to assume his throne, Byron wondered 'why
wouldst thou leave calm Hartwell's green abode . . . Apician table and
Horatian Ode?'. Dating back to the 16th century, it's the epitome
of luxury, a magnificent country house set in 80 acres of parkland. Day
rooms have many notable features like rococo ceilings, choice antiques, oil
paintings and chandeliers. Wonderful plump-cushioned seating spreads
through the grandly proportioned reception rooms. Bedrooms show high
standards of luxury and comfort; sumptuously appointed in impressive
fashion, they employ antiques, rich fabrics and a host of pampering extras,
plus huge beds. Bright, neatly fitted bathrooms. Motivated staff provide
high levels of service. 100 yards from the main house is the Hartwell Spa,
modelled on an orangery inspired by Sir John Soane and incorporating fine
leisure facilities – the grand 50-foot swimming pool is surrounded by an
arched arcade and overlooked by a gallery where you will find the Spa Bar
and Buttery. The function Rooms are situated in a restored 18th-century
coach house and can accommodate up to 80 delegates; the rooms are
named after distinguished architects who have contributed to the evolution
of Hartwell House – James Gibbs, James Wyatt, Henry Keene and Eric
Throssell. There are also interesting rooms in the main house for private
dining. In addition to the leisure and meeting facilities Hartwell Court

houses the 16 most recent bedrooms and suites. No children under 8. Dogs are not allowed in the grounds, but good kennels are nearby. *Rooms 47. Garden, croquet, indoor swimming pool, spa bath, steam room, sauna, gym, beauty salon, solarium, fishing.* AMERICAN EXPRESS *Access, Diners, Visa.*

Restaurant

£100

If the food here impresses less than the surroundings it is at least in part because the surroundings are so impressive – the elegantly vaulted, pale yellow Soane room overlooking the croquet lawn and obelisk in parkland beyond, tail-coated waiters and fine table settings including Royal Doulton bone china. Fixed-price menus offer plenty of choice – about a dozen main dishes at night – with the likes of chicken consommé with quail's eggs and chervil, terrine of goose liver with Sauternes jelly and whole roast lobster salad with tomato and vegetable dressing among the starters and main dishes such as whole sea bass baked in a salt crust with a lime and ginger sauce, slices of beef fillet on a parsley cream and red wine sauce, and roast milk-fed pigeon on a potato galette with an apple and aubergine compote showing the style. Several interesting wines on a splendid and very comprehensive list that would benefit greatly if presented in a more orderly and user-friendly manner. Excellent half bottle choice. *Seats 70. Parties 8. Private Room 30. L 12.30-2 D 7.30-9.45. Set L £16.50/£22.40 Set D £38.*

Aylesbury   Places of Interest

Tourist Information Tel 0296 382308.
Limelight Theatre Queen's Park Centre, Queen's Park. Tel 0296 431272.
Leighton Buzzard Library Theatre Tel 0525 378310.
Buckinghamshire County Museum Tel 0296 88849.
Weedon Park Showground Tel 0296 83734.
  Historic Houses, Castles and Gardens
Claydon House Nr Winslow Tel 0296 730349.
Waddesdon Manor (NT) Waddesdon Tel 0296 651211/651282.

Bagshot   Pennyhill Park   75%

£134

Tel 0276 471774   Fax 0276 475570

H

London Road Bagshot Surrey GU19 5ET

Map 15 E3

Usefully located just off the A30, this well-equipped hotel and country club offers professional tuition in a number of sporting activities. Notable architectural features of the 19th-century house include the baronial-style foyer-lounge with stained-glass windows, exposed stone walls and slate floor, and the lounge, on two levels, with a beamed gallery upstairs and panelling downstairs. Bedrooms in the main building are spacious and charming, and those around the redeveloped courtyard vary from cosy and intimate to elegant mini-suites; all are named after flowers or shrubs, except for the luxurious Hayward suite. Children up to 14 stay free in parents' room. Parking for 120 cars, banqueting/conferences for 80/60. *Rooms 76. Garden, croquet, outdoor swimming pool, sauna, solarium, tennis, 9-hole golf course, riding, stabling, fishing.* AMERICAN EXPRESS *Access, Diners, Visa.*

Bakewell   Hassop Hall   74%

£93

Tel 0629 640488   Fax 0629 640577

H

Hassop nr Bakewell Derbyshire DE45 1NS

Map 6 C2

From Bakewell take the Sheffield road, then turn left on to the B6001 to Hassop and the Hall. Owned and run by Thomas Chapman since 1975, the Hall, originally the ancient seat of the Eyre family, stands among trees and parkland at the heart of the Peak District National Park. From the impressive approach you enter the marbled hallway with antiques and oil paintings. There is a chandeliered lounge in Regency style, a drawing room, a room for non-smokers and a relaxing oak-panelled bar. The large, luxurious bedrooms are individually decorated and furnished, with embroidered bed linen and splendidly appointed bathrooms. Dogs by arrangement only. ***Rooms*** *13. Garden, tennis, helipad. Closed 3 days Christmas.* AMERICAN EXPRESS® *Access, Diners, Visa.*

Bakewell   Places of Interest

Tourist Information   Tel 0629 813227.
Chatsworth House   Tel 0246 582204.
Haddon Hall   Tel 0629 812855.

Baldock   Forte Travelodge   £45

Tel 0462 835329   **L**
Great North Road Hinxworth nr Baldock Hertfordshire SG7 5EX   **Map 15 E1**

Southbound on the A1, north of Baldock. ***Rooms*** *40.* AMERICAN EXPRESS® *Access, Diners, Visa.*

Bamburgh   Lord Crewe Arms   £62

Tel 0668 214243   Fax 0668 214273   **H**
Front Street Bamburgh Northumberland NE69 7BL   **Map 5 D1**

New owners are feeling their way at the Lord Crewe, which stands virtually in the shadow of Bamburgh Castle. A new chef has been appointed, and future plans include negotiating to take shooting parties out of season. There are two cheerful bars, two lounges (one non-smoking) and 25 bedrooms, all but five en suite. TVs and drinks trays but no phones. No children under 5. ***Rooms*** *25. Closed 5 Jan-beginning Mar. Access, Visa.*

Bamburgh   Places of Interest

Bamburgh Castle   Tel 06684 208.
Grace Darling Museum   Tel 0665 720037.
Bamburgh Beach.

Banbury   Banbury House Hotel   62%   £93

Tel 0295 259361   Fax 0295 270954   **H**
27-29 Oxford Road Banbury Oxfordshire OX16 9AH   **Map 15 D1**

A handsome Georgian house offering all the modern comforts. Star of the accommodation is the Blenheim Suite with a four-poster bed and whirlpool bath. Functions (up to 90) and conferences (to 80) are a speciality. Access to the car park (free parking for 50 cars) is from Lucky Lane. Small, well-trained dogs only. Formerly a Moat House. ***Rooms*** *48.* AMERICAN EXPRESS® *Access, Diners, Visa.*

Many hotels offer reduced rates for weekend or out-of-season bookings. Always ask about special deals.

Banbury   Whately Hall   65%   £90

Tel 0295 263451   Fax 0295 271736   **H**
Banbury Cross Banbury Oxfordshire OX16 0AN   **Map 15 D1**

Dating from 1632, Whately Hall stands in gardens opposite Banbury Cross. The Cross is remembered in a nursery rhyme, and Jonathan Swift stayed here while writing *Gulliver's Travels*. Fine panelling, mullion windows and antiques give character to the day rooms. Bedrooms, some in a modern wing, all have well-lit, tiled bathrooms. Children up to 16 stay free in parents' room. Forte. ***Rooms*** *74. Garden, coffee shop (8.30am-5pm).* AMERICAN EXPRESS® *Access, Diners, Visa.*

Banbury   Places of Interest

Banbury Museum Tel 0295 259855.
Open Air Pool Tel 0295 62742.
Broughton Castle Tel 0295 262624.
Farnborough Hall Tel 0295 89202.
Upton House (NT) Edgehill Tel 0295 87266.

Barford   Glebe Hotel   68%   £110

Tel 0926 624218   Fax 0926 624625   **H**

Church Street Barford Warwickshire CV35 8BS   Map 14 C1

Built in the 1820s as a rectory, the Glebe became a hotel in 1948. Several extensions have been added over the last few years, including the spacious conservatory restaurant, the Glades leisure club and conference facilities for up to 150. Bedrooms, individually decorated in soft pastel shades, range from singles to four-posters, family rooms and the Shakespeare suite which has the bonus of a corner jacuzzi bath but the slight drawback of a view of the car park. Children up to 14 stay free in parents' room. Good service throughout. *Rooms 41. Garden, indoor swimming pool, keep-fit equipment, spa bath, sauna, steam room.* AMERICAN EXPRESS *Access, Diners, Visa.*

Barnard Castle   Jersey Farm Hotel   59%   £50

Tel 0833 38223   Fax 0833 31988   **H**

Darlington Road Barnard Castle Co Durham DL12 8TA   Map 5 D3

This informal and friendly little hotel stands a mile east of town on the A67 (turn off the A1(M) on to the B6275 for Piercebridge), surrounded by a working farm. John, Jean and Mark Watson offer a warm welcome in unpretentious surroundings – public areas are homely and unfussy and the bedrooms, in the old farmhouse and in extensions, are modest but comfortable. Superior rooms are larger, with more extras, and there are six suites. The conference centre can cater for banquets up to 150 and conferences up to 200. *Rooms 20. Garden. Access, Visa.*

Barnard Castle   Places of Interest

  Historic Houses, Castles and Gardens
Barnard Castle   Tel 0833 38212.
Bowes Museum Gardens   Tel 0833 690606.
Raby Castle   Staindrop Tel 0833 38212.

Barnby Moor   Ye Olde Bell   60%   £68

Tel 0777 705121   Fax 0777 860424   **H**

Barnby Moor nr Retford Nottinghamshire DN22 8QS   Map 7 D2

On the edge of Sherwood Forest, just a mile from the A1, Ye Olde Bell has been offering hospitality to travellers for hundreds of years. Old oak panelling, open fireplaces and diamond-pane leaded lights retain the character of the public rooms (refurbished during 1994) while bedrooms offer modern conveniences. Conferences for up to 250 delegates. Principal Hotels. *Rooms 55. Garden.* AMERICAN EXPRESS *Access, Diners, Visa.*

Barnham Broom   Barnham Broom Hotel   62%   £82

Tel 0603 759393   Fax 0603 758224   **H**

Honingham Road Barnham Broom nr Norwich Norfolk NR9 4DD   Map 10 C1

A large modern complex comprising hotel, golf and country club and conference centre (up to 200 delegates). The club bar and lounge overlook the grounds. All the bedrooms have writing desks and other extras include radios in the bathrooms. *Rooms 52. Indoor swimming pool, squash, sauna, spa bath, steam room, solarium, beauty salon, hairdressing, tennis, two championship golf courses, snooker, coffee shop (9.30am-9.30pm).* AMERICAN EXPRESS® *Access, Diners, Visa.*

Barnsley	Ardsley Moat House	59%	£81

Tel 0226 289401   Fax 0226 205374   **H**

Doncaster Road Ardsley Barnsley South Yorkshire S71 5EH   Map 6 C2

Extended 18th-century mansion (only the cocktail bar still shows period features) on the A635 to the east of town. Some bedroom decor looks a bit tired – the spacious Executive rooms are best. Extensive conference/function families for up to 300. Friendly staff. ***Rooms*** *73. Garden.* AMERICAN EXPRESS® *Access, Diners, Visa.*

Barnsley	Armstrongs	£55

Tel 0226 240113   **R**

6 Shambles Street Barnsley South Yorkshire S70 2SQ   Map 6 C2

Facing the Town Hall, Armstrongs is a little passé with pale drag-painted dado beneath rag-rolled walls. There is nothing old-fashioned about chef-patron Nicholas Pound's cooking, though, which is inventive without being gimmicky, and thoroughly enjoyable. Dinner might include the likes of grilled, marinated salmon with lemon-roasted peppers and saffron vinaigrette; chicken liver and apple tartlet with port sauce; braised tongue with mustard sauce; sweet and sour sauté of kidneys with vegetable julienne and orange segments, and thick cod fillets fried in oatmeal with parsnips and saffron broth. Leave room for puds like rhubarb ginger crumble, apricot crème brulée and iced butterscotch meringue cake. A similar lunch menu also includes a selection of lighter dishes for those wishing to eat less substantially (and more economically). A short fixed-price (£12.95) menu is available between 7 and 8pm. ***Seats*** *60. L 12-2 D 7-10. Closed L Sat, all Sun & Mon, Bank Holidays.* AMERICAN EXPRESS® *Access, Visa.*

Barnsley	Forte Travelodge	£45

Tel 0226 298799   **L**

520 Doncaster Road Stairfoot Roundabout Barnsley South Yorkshire   Map 6 C2

At the roundabout of A633 and A635, close to the centre of Barnsley. ***Rooms*** *32.* AMERICAN EXPRESS® *Access, Diners, Visa.*

Barnsley	Restaurant Peano	£60

Tel 0226 244990   **R**

102 Dodworth Road Barnsley South Yorkshire S70 6HL   Map 6 C2

Externally a rather dour Victorian house (about ½ mile from the town centre on the main road towards J37 of the M1) but inside bright and stylish with bright yellow walls sporting Mediterranean prints, bentwood and wicker chairs and crisp white napery. There is a comfortable bar area on the first floor. Michael Peano's style of cooking is difficult to categorise – his menus are constantly evolving and changing – but both French and Italian influences can be discerned in dishes that are never less than full of flavour and interest. A soup of yellow peppers flavoured with Parmesan cheese; foie gras-filled ravioli on a cabbage purée with Madeira sauce (a signature dish); goat's cheese wrapped in bread, pan-fried and served on a tomato and basil salad with balsamic vinegar dressing; pastry-wrapped breast of wood pigeon with wild mushroom mousse; beef arlesienne; Moroccan chicken, and pan-fried salmon with pommes frites demonstrate the range. Puds might include a crème brulée with banana and coconut, Italian orange pudding and a rich lemon tart. The shortish, but well-chosen, wine list is half French and half Italian. Ample own parking. ***Seats*** *45. L 12-2 D 7-9.30. Closed Sun, Mon, 2 weeks Sep. Set L & D* £*14.50.* AMERICAN EXPRESS® *Access, Visa.*

Barnsley   Places of Interest

Cannon Hall   Cawthorne Tel 0226 790270.
Wentworth Castle   Stainborough Tel 0226 285426.
Oakwell Football Ground   Tel 0226 295353.

Barnstaple   Imperial Hotel   60%   £71

Tel 0271 45861   Fax 0271 24448   **H**

Taw Vale Parade Barnstaple Devon EX32 8NB   Map 13 D2

A solid Edwardian building overlooking the river Taw. Meeting rooms
for up to 60 people. Forte. *Rooms 56.* AMERICAN EXPRESS *Access, Diners, Visa.*

Barnstaple   Lynwood House   £65

Tel 0271 43695   Fax 0271 79340   **RR**

Bishop's Tawton Road Barnstaple Devon EX32 9DZ   Map 13 D2

An elegant and spacious Victorian house run as a restaurant with rooms   ♔
by the Roberts family for 25 years. Ruth and 'No.2' son Matthew cook
in classical style; John and 'No. 3 son' Christian run the dining rooms,
which have traditional decor with large windows, polished mahogany
tables and discreet antique dividing screens. Seafood is the main speciality,
with dishes like crab pancakes, chunky fish soup, skate with capers and
brown butter, salmon mayonnaise and a medley of fish cooked in wine,
cream and cheese sauce and served on a bed of rice. Meaty choices could
include roast duckling and fillet steak, and a couple of vegetarian main
courses are offered. Good choice of desserts. A 'lighter meal' menu is also
available. No smoking. *Seats 50. Private Room 20. L 12-2 D 7-10.
Closed Sun except to residents. Set L £11.95/£13.95.* AMERICAN EXPRESS
Access, Visa.

Rooms   £61

Overnight guests are accommodated in five Executive bedrooms, all with
armchairs and plenty of creature comforts. Separate breakfast room; fresh
Scottish kippers.

> We endeavour to be as up-to-the-minute as possible, but inevitably
> some changes to key personnel may occur at restaurants and hotels
> after the Guide goes to press.

Barnstaple   Places of Interest

Tourist Information   Tel 0271 47177.
Arlington Court (NT)   Tel 0271 850296.
Marwood Hill   Marwood Tel 0271 42528.
**Museum of North Devon incorporating Royal Devon Yeomanry
    Museum**   Tel 0271 46747.
Exmoor Bird Gardens   South Stowford Tel 05983 352/412.

Barton Mills   Forte Travelodge   £45

Tel 0638 717675   **L**

Barton Mills Mildenhall Suffolk IP28 6AE   Map 10 B2

On the A11, at the 5 ways roundabout, 8 miles north-east of Newmarket.
Rooms 32. AMERICAN EXPRESS *Access, Diners, Visa.*

Barton Stacey — Forte Travelodge — £45

L

Tel 0264 720260

Barton Stacey nr Andover Hampshire SO21 3NP — Map 15 D3

On the A303 westbound – approximately 4 miles east of Andover. **Rooms** 20. AMERICAN EXPRESS® *Access, Diners, Visa.*

Barton-under-Needwood — Forte Travelodge — £45

L

Tel 0283 716784

Barton-under-Needwood Burton-on-Trent Staffordshire DE13 3EH — Map 6 C3

On the A38 southbound, 3 miles to the south of Burton-on-Trent. One room equipped for disabled guests. **Rooms** 40. AMERICAN EXPRESS® *Access, Visa.*

We welcome bona fide complaints and recommendations on the tear-out pages at the back of the book for readers' comments. They are followed up by our professional team.

Barton-under-Needwood (North) — Forte Travelodge — £45

L

Tel 0283 716343

Barton-under-Needwood Burton-on-Trent Staffordshire DE13 8EG — Map 6 C3

On the A38 northbound, 4 miles to the south of Burton-on-Trent. **Rooms** 20. AMERICAN EXPRESS® *Access, Diners, Visa.*

Basildon — Campanile Hotel — £44

L

Tel 0268 530810   Fax 0268 286710

Southend Arterial Road Pipps Hill Basildon Essex SS14 3AE — Map 11 B4

Take Junction 29 of the M25, then Basildon exit from A127. **Rooms** 98. AMERICAN EXPRESS® *Access, Diners, Visa.*

Basildon — Forte Posthouse — 59% — £68

H

Tel 0268 533955   Fax 0268 530119

Cranes Farm Road Basildon Essex SS14 3DG — Map 11 B4

Modern exterior, bright and pleasant accommodation, plus lake views from the conservatory-style bar. 5 rooms have been upgraded to Executive. Banqueting facilities for up to 250, conferences to 300. Formerly the *Forte Crest.* **Rooms** 110. AMERICAN EXPRESS® *Access, Diners, Visa.*

Basildon — Travel Inn — £43

L

Tel 0268 522227   Fax 0268 530092

Felmores East Mayne Basildon Essex SS13 1BW — Map 11 B4

Just off the M25 (J29). Half of the rooms are non-smoking; one room adapted for use by disabled guests. **Rooms** 32. Garden. AMERICAN EXPRESS® *Access, Diners, Visa.*

Basildon — Place of Interest

Towngate Theatre Pagel Mead Tel 0268 531343.

Basingstoke   Audleys Wood   75%   £123

Tel 0256 817555   Fax 0256 817500   **HR**

Alton Road Basingstoke Hampshire RG25 2JT   Map 15 D3

Alongside the A339 Alton road, close to Junction 6 of the M3. Built in the
late 1880s for Sir George Bradshaw (whose railway timetables made his
fortune) and set in seven wooded acres, the overtly Victorian house had
a varied history before being transformed into a hotel of some luxury (it
opened in 1989). A splendid carved oak fireplace graces the panelled
lounge, which also features a minstrel's gallery. Similar darkwood panelling
and a handsome fireplace are to be found in the bar. The majority of the
bedrooms are in sympathetically-designed extensions: roomy and tastefully
appointed, with marble-tiled bathrooms; main-house bedrooms are even
larger and more luxurious; 25 rooms are reserved for non-smokers. One
double room is suitable for the disabled. Children up to 14 can share their
parents' room at no charge; interconnecting rooms available. Friendly staff.
Mount Charlotte Thistle. *Rooms 71. Garden, croquet, pétanque, putting,
archery, golf practice net, helipad.* AMERICAN EXPRESS® *Access, Diners, Visa.*

Conservatory Restaurant   £66

Situated in what was the original palm house and conservatory, the striking
restaurant has a most unusual vaulted wood ceiling. Terence Greenhouse,
once Executive Head Chef on the *QE2*, is at the helm. An à la carte
is always offered, but lunchtimes also see both 2- or 3-course fixed-price
affairs and a hot 2-course business lunch. Both table d'hote and à la carte
menus are also offered at dinner, with daily specials and a couple
of interesting vegetarian dishes. All the menus are refreshingly described
in plain English, albeit rather flowery – dishes such as lozenge of exotic red
snapper marinaded in thyme and lemon, pot-roasted on a bed of leeks, with
a sharp herb and yoghurt cream or French crepe filled with an abundance
of fresh market vegetables, set on a pool of nutmeg cream. The style
is rather grand and the choice diverse. Good cheeses, both French and
English, served with walnut bread, chilled grapes and celery. Sunday lunch
offers a good choice (children under 10 half price). *Seats 66. Parties 12.
Private Room 40. L 12-1.45 (Sun from 12.30) D 7-9.45 (Sun to 9.15).
Closed 27-30 Dec, L Bank Holidays. Set L £13.75 & £14.95/£17.95
(Sun L 13.95) Set D from £20.*

Basingstoke   Forte Posthouse   64%   £68

Tel 0256 468181   Fax 0256 840081   **H**

Grove Road Basingstoke Hampshire RG21 3EE   Map 15 D3

Leave the M3 at Junction 6 and follow signs for Alton on the A339.
Accommodation includes 12 Executive rooms. Conference and banqueting
facilities for up to 180 delegates. *Rooms 84.* AMERICAN EXPRESS® *Access,
Diners, Visa.*

Note that all telephone numbers with area codes starting with 0
will start 01 from 16 April 1995.

Basingstoke   Forte Travelodge   £45

Tel 0256 843566   **L**

Winchester Road Basingstoke Hampshire RG22 6HN   Map 15 D3

2 miles from Junction 7 of the M3, off the A30 southbound, at the
Brighton Hill roundabout. *Rooms 32.* AMERICAN EXPRESS® *Access, Diners, Visa.*

Basingstoke   Hee's   £40

Tel 0256 464410   **R**

23 Westminster House Basingstoke Hampshire RG21 1CS   Map 15 D3

Decent MSG-free Szechuan and Peking cooking on the edge of Basingstoke's huge central shopping centre. Special cocktails liven things up, and cheerful staff provide attentive service. *Seats 80. L 12-2 D 6-11. Closed L Sun, 4 days Christmas. Set meals from £14.50.* AMERICAN EXPRESS *Access, Diners, Visa.*

Basingstoke   Hilton National   66%   £79

Tel 0256 460460   Fax 0256 840441   **H**

Old Common Road Black Dam Basingstoke Hampshire RG21 3PR   Map 15 D3

Bright, open-plan public areas, neat accommodation and numerous meeting rooms at a modern hotel a mile from Junction 6 of the M3 (follow the signs for Eastrop). Children up to 16 stay free in parents' room. Family rooms, indoor playroom. *Rooms 141. Indoor swimming pool, keep-fit equipment, sauna, assault course.* AMERICAN EXPRESS *Access, Diners, Visa.*

Basingstoke   The Ringway Hotel   65%   £64

Tel 0256 20212   Fax 0256 842835   **H**

Aldermaston Roundabout Ringway North Basingstoke Hampshire RG24 9NV   Map 15 D3

Bedrooms range from small singles to roomy, well-appointed suites. 26 rooms are designated non-smoking. Banquets and conferences for 140. A change of ownership was intended as we went to press. *Rooms 134. Indoor swimming pool, keep-fit equipment, sauna. Closed 1 week Christmas.* AMERICAN EXPRESS *Access, Diners, Visa.*

Basingstoke   Travel Inn   £43

Tel 0256 811477   Fax 0256 819329   **L**

Worting Road Basingstoke Hampshire RG22 6PG   Map 15 D3

Situated in the centre of a leisure park. *Rooms 49.* AMERICAN EXPRESS *Access, Diners, Visa.*

Basingstoke   Places of Interest

Tourist Information   Tel 0256 817618.
Stratfield Saye   Tel 0256 882882 *Home of the Duke of Wellington.*
The Vyne (NT)   Sherborne St. John Tel 0256 881337.
Basing House   Basing Tel 0256 467294.
Basingstoke Ice Rink   Tel 0256 840219.

Baslow   Cavendish Hotel   71%   £116

Tel 0246 582311   Fax 0246 582312   **HR**

Baslow Derbyshire DE45 1SP   Map 6 C2

Standing on the Chatsworth Estate and commanding very fine rural views, the Cavendish has a history going back several hundred years (for the last 20 of those years it has been under the personal direction of Eric Marsh). Solidly built of local stone, it has an exterior that is as characterful and traditional as the interior. The entrance hall is graciously inviting with fresh flower arrangements, antiques, porcelain and a roaring log fire in cooler weather. Adjoining it is a south-facing conservatory which fronts the lounge – a delightful room decorated in pale blues and yellows. The bar also has a log fire, is darker and more intimate with mahogany furniture and upholstery of striking blue and gold stripes. In addition to the main restaurant, there's an all-day informal eating outlet, the Garden Room. In the bedrooms, good beds ensure a peaceful night's sleep, and guests wake up to delightful views over the estate. Comfortable armchairs, writing desks and mini-bars with fresh milk help to make one's stay pleasurable. Bathrooms are bright with light varnished wood floors. Bathrobes and a range of toiletries are provided. 24hr room service. *Rooms 24. Garden, putting, fishing, gift shop (11-11), helipad.* *Access, Diners, Visa.*

Restaurant   £75

During the day, a bright, sunny dining room with super views over part of the Chatsworth estate. At night, the soft pastel colours of the decor come into their own with subtle light creating an elegant setting for imaginative and carefully constructed dishes. The choice is varied with a menu of supplementary dishes additional to the fixed-price options. Baked tuna steak in anchovy butter with a green peppercorn sauce; corn-fed chicken with wild mushrooms and polenta and venison casserole in a burgundy and rose petal sauce show the inventiveness. More classical are the likes of excellent lightly pan-fried scallops and scampi served with two sauces, tournedos Rossini and beautifully pink tender lamb roasted with fresh thyme. A superb selection of British cheeses can be taken instead of one of the enjoyable sweets of which passion fruit soufflé is a fine example. No smoking. *Seats 50. Parties 20. Private Room 18. L 12.30-2 D 7-10. Set L & D £20.75/£24.75.*

Baslow	**Fischer's Baslow Hall**	**★★**	**£96**
Tel 0246 583259 Fax 0246 583818			**RR**

Calver Road Baslow Derbyshire DE4 1RR   Map 6 C2

Following a major fire five years ago, Max and Susan Fischer had to then endure the effects of the recent recession; as a result, the initial prognosis for Baslow Hall was bleak. However, sheer determination and extremely hard work are, at last, reaping their rewards. Such as our Supreme Award of 1995 Restaurant of the Year. From humbler beginnings in Bakewell, the couple are now in possession of a most attractive hilltop property. Built in 1907 of local stone, the house stands on the village outskirts and is approached up a steep, snaking, tree-lined drive. Drinks and delicious canapés are taken in a lounge created from the former entrance hall. The room is dominated by a carved stone open fireplace and is furnished in a genteel country-house style. The pretty dining room, with candlelit tables and fine plaster ceiling is an apt setting for Max's superb culinary talents. His cooking (for fixed-price-only menus) demonstrates flair and endeavour. Flavours are deliberately distinct, ensuring stunning levels of complexity that enthral the palate. Visiting Sheffield market at 5am, he selects the cream of the crop to create his regularly changing menus. His influences are from the Mediterranean and the Orient as in a dish of fresh langoustines on saffron spaghetti or sautéed lamb's liver with ginger and lime. Fish is a speciality, a fine example being a fillet of sea bass with duxelles of black olives and a spinach sauce, or scallops, thinly sliced and lightly pan-fried to retain their soft sweetness then served on slivers of sautéed potato with a creamy chive sauce. Meat dishes too are brilliantly executed, as in a superlative gratinated roast saddle of lamb under a fragrant herb crust. The selection of cheeses (all in good condition) is from both home and abroad and precedes outstanding desserts such as a gratin of spring rhubarb served with prunes stuffed with apple and cinnamon, vanilla ice and a velvety sabayon. Superb value lunches offer a choice of four dishes at each stage; perhaps pan-fried lamb's kidneys with fresh parsley mousse followed by escalope of salmon, with tagliatelle à la crème and roast pears in caramel with chocolate sorbet to finish. Sunday lunch usually includes a traditional roast. No smoking. Well-chosen wines on the wine list, which is presented by style (dry, medium, sweet etc) with accompanying notes; for a restaurant of this class prices are not that unreasonable; half bottles in short supply. Simpler, but equally well-executed meals – including breakfast and afternoon tea – are served from 10am to 10pm (not Sun) in the 30-seater *Café Max,* a former living room

See over

off the entrance hall, and at four tables on the terrace in summer. *Seats 45.
Parties 8. Private Room 12. L 12-2 (Sun to 2.30) D 7-9.30 (Sat to 10).
Closed D Sun (except residents), 25 & 26 Dec. Set L £14.50/£16.50 (Sun
£18.50) Set D £36.* AMERICAN EXPRESS® *Access, Diners, Visa.* MARTELL

Rooms   £95

There are six bedrooms, all upstairs in the main house. Of these six, three
are on the small side but all are very tastefully decorated, with clever use
of bold, striking colour schemes to complement the mostly antique pine
furniture. Bathrooms have a plentiful supply of towels and toiletries though
only one has a shower. The latter forms part of a huge enamel bath that
stands in the centre of the room. Excellent breakfasts commence with
a refreshing exotic fruit salad and continue on to freshly baked warm
brioches and croissants. Banqueting rooms for 12, 30 and 40; conference
room for 40. No dogs.

Bassenthwaite	Armathwaite Hall	65%	£100
Tel 076 87 76551 Fax 076 87 76220			**H**
Bassenthwaite Lake nr Keswick Cumbria CA12 4RE			Map 4 C3

The Graves family has been in residence at Armathwaite since 1976, and
their commitment to making a welcoming haven means an ongoing
programme of refurbishment, most recently to the public rooms, ensuring
that the building lives up to its splendid setting. Lawns and parkland
bordered by woodlands lead down to the foreshore. Best bedrooms in the
historic stately house have fine views and plenty of space, while rooms
in the coach house/stable block are also spacious. There are extensive leisure
facilities, and the equestrian centre offers hacking and lessons. Families are
well catered for, with accommodation free for under-12s when sharing
parents' room; baby-sitting by arrangement, cots and high-chairs provided;
informal eating in the leisure club; activities such as a nature trail. A new
animal farm park with a variety of farm animals and rare breeds is open
between April and October. Two self-catering units are within the
grounds. A choice of conference rooms caters for up to 120. *Rooms 42.
Garden, croquet, tennis, indoor swimming pool, gym, sauna, steam room,
solarium, riding, spa bath, beauty and hair salons, snooker, 9-hole pitch & putt,
coarse and game fishing, mountain bikes, coffee shop (12.30-9.30).*
AMERICAN EXPRESS® *Access, Diners, Visa.*

Bassenthwaite Lake	Pheasant Inn	65%	£64
Tel 076 87 76234 Fax 076 87 76002			**H**
Bassenthwaite Lake nr Cockermouth Cumbria CA13 9YE			Map 4 C3

Originally a farm, the long and low Pheasant Inn nevertheless looks like
an archetypal Victorian roadside inn. It displays abundant period appeal:
open fires, beams hung with brasses, old prints and antique firearms. There
are three lounges (one non-smoking) and an atmospheric bar with tobacco-
brown walls. Well-kept gardens (where afternoon tea and bar snacks can
be taken) are an added summer attraction and are overlooked by tastefully
furnished bedrooms in varying styles. Adequate, simply fitted bathrooms
are the only obvious nod to modernity. One twin is in a bungalow adjacent
to the inn. No phones, TVs or dogs in bedrooms; no piped music or fruit
machines in the public rooms – just the pervading Lakeland peace and
quiet. *Rooms 20. Closed 25 Dec. Access.*

Bath	Apsley House	67%	£65
Tel 0225 336966 Fax 0225 425462			**H**
141 Newbridge Hill Bath Avon BA1 3PT			Map 13 F1

On the A431 a mile from the city centre on the road to Bristol, the house,
built in 1830 allegedly for the Duke of Wellington, is now in the hands
of Anne and Christopher Baker. Together they have restored some of the
period elegance, creating a hotel of charm and warmth. Fine paintings,

antiques and gilt-framed mirrors adorn the public rooms, hallways and splendid staircase. Bedrooms are pretty and homely, furnished with attractive floral fabrics and ornaments. Most bathrooms have separate shower installations with huge shower roses. *Rooms 7. Garden. Access, Visa.*

Bath	Bath Spa Hotel	87%	£195
Tel 0225 444424 Fax 0225 444006			**HR**
Sydney Road Bath Avon BA2 6JF			Map 13 F1

Without doubt one of Forte's flagship hotels, with surroundings, furnishings, a splendid health and leisure spa, and service to match. Carefully restored and extended, the Georgian mansion stands in landscaped grounds with panoramic views over the city, which is a ten-minute stroll away. Behind the elegant porticoed frontage is a good deal of style and luxury, complemented by super staff very capably directed by General Manager Robin Sheppard. A spacious entrance lobby with Oriental carpets over slate and stone diamond flooring, elaborate plasterwork ceiling, extravagant fresh flower display and antique long case clock sets the tone of public areas which include a gracious drawing room, the neo-classical Colonnade with murals and greenery, and clubby bar. At the far end of the Colonnade there is a display of mineral waters from around the world. Bedrooms (many non-smoking), including seven suites, are individually decorated in great style with a striking combination of check fabrics and floral prints. They offer a high degree of comfort, matched by particularly well-designed bathrooms in Grecian marble and mahogany, with padded towel seating, bathrobes and Penhaligon toiletries. Rather surprisingly (in such a grand hotel), families are made very welcome, with children under 16 sharing their parents' room free of charge, a day nursery provided for 2- to 9-year-olds, and consideration for junior palates. The fine function rooms (up to 140 theatre-style conferences, 120 for banqueting) are in keeping with the rest of the hotel. Extensive 24hr room service, ample parking. Dogs (basket and bowls provided) welcome; their owners can be accommodated on the ground floor with easy access to the grounds at the end of the corridor. Watch out for the mice, but do not be alarmed – they are all made of pastry and are the hotel's trademark! The tariff is now seasonal, with highest prices in Mar-Jun and Sept/Oct; useful reductions at other periods. *Rooms 98. Garden, croquet, indoor swimming pool, gym, sauna, spa bath, solarium, beauty & hair salons, tennis, valeting, coffee shop (7am-6pm), helipad.* AMERICAN EXPRESS *Access, Diners, Visa.*

Vellore Restaurant ↑

£90

The original ballroom makes for a fine setting in which to enjoy chef Jonathan Fraser's excellent cooking. His menus, using the best local and British produce, offer simple but quite robust dishes with style, variety and a high degree of skilful preparation, as well as pleasing presentation. A typical daily table d'hote offers three choices at each stage and might commence with a grand lobster ravioli with tarragon sauce, following with saddle of Avon farmed venison with mulled pears, celeriac and almonds, finally crowning it all with a crisp apple tart accompanied by calvados ice cream and a good choice of coffee. The one-price-meal à la carte could extend to a baked soufflé with smoked salmon, spinach and goat's cheese, wok-fried scallops with ginger and lime, pesto-crusted North Sea halibut with a white wine sauce, peppered duck breast served with a cassoulet of broad beans and lardons, dark rum tiramisu with caramelised banana, and cappuccino of chocolate. Exemplary amuse-gueule and petits fours, splendid coffee and caring service under maitre d' Francesco Di Bari. A jacket and tie is requested though they "do no insist". Contrary to the comments on the wine list, there is no equality between wines from Europe and the New World however well chosen the latter are (and there are indeed some good wines from which to choose). France provides the bulk of the list. Lunches and informal dinners – note the wines by the glass and bottle on the good-value list – are served in the 36-seat *Alfresco* (Colonnade), with honeyed woodstrip flooring, cane chairs and picture

See over

windows overlooking a patio garden (outside seating in summer) with fountain. Seasonal dishes with an eclectic cooking style (the Far East, Mediterranean and English – tiger prawns and won ton soup, home-made linguine with carbonara sauce, 'rich man's cod and chips' and Cadbury's chocolate burger); you can have just a starter and dessert, or the full three courses. Good selection of home-made breads (more mice!). *Seats 90. Parties 12. L (Sun only) 12-2 D 7-10; Alfresco 10am-10pm Set Sun L £19.50 Set D £34.*

Bath   Clos du Roy   £65

Tel 0225 444450   **R**

1 Seven Dials Sawclose Bath Avon BA1 1EN   Map 13 F1

Sited on the first floor under the prominent wrought-iron dome of the recent Seven Dials development near the Theatre Royal, Philippe Roy's smart restaurant is a fine setting for his culinary flair. Having originally opened the first *Clos du Roy* in Bath in 1984, he moved out to nearby Box before returning here in 1992. The interior plays around a musical theme – the white grand piano in the centre of the room is put to good use several nights a week. A picture window to the kitchen allows one to view chefs preparing the two-or three-course *menu du jour* (lunch, 6-7pm and post-theatre, in addition to a lower-priced carte at these times), which offers particularly good value and a choice of four dishes at each stage. At night, there's also a pair of fixed-price, three-course menus. Alongside these tables d'hote, the interesting evening à la carte might offer boneless quail salad garnished with roasted nuts and balsamic vinegar dressing or cassolette of scallops and artichoke salad served warm with a hazelnut oil dressing to start, then a good choice of fish main courses and perhaps ballotine of guinea fowl stuffed with prunes or marinated tenderloin of pork with star anise sauce; assiette gourmande, farmhouse cheeses, mousseline of fresh mint with bitter chocolate sauce and iced nougat parfait with red fruit coulis among the desserts. *Seats 65. L 12-2.30 D 6-11.30. Set L £8.95/£11.95 Set D £18.50/£22.50.* AMERICAN EXPRESS *Access, Diners, Visa.*

Bath   Fountain House   £120

Tel 0225 338622   Fax 0225 445855   **PH**

9/11 Fountain Buildings Lansdown Road Bath Avon BA1 5DV Map 13 F1

An 'all-suite hotel', Fountain House comprises one-, two-and three-bedroom suites with sitting room and smart, fully-equipped kitchen, within a Palladian mansion on the northern edge of the city centre. The idea is that one gets privacy and space with the level of service (except room service) one would expect of a conventional hotel – full maid service with fresh linen and kitchen servicing daily. Unfussy decor and good-quality furnishings are immaculately maintained. A basket of fresh bread, milk, yoghurt etc and a daily newspaper are delivered to the door each morning. Reception staff can organise most things from car hire and theatre tickets to a personal in-room fax or shooting on the owners' own 750-acre estate. Unlike in a serviced apartment there is no minimum stay and indeed many guests stay for just one night. There are no public rooms. Lock-up garages, laundry and drying room, iron and ironing board, cots and valet service all provided. *Suites 14.* AMERICAN EXPRESS *Access, Diners, Visa.*

Bath   Francis Hotel   67%   £112

Tel 0225 424257   Fax 0225 319715   **H**

Queen Square Bath Avon BA1 2HH   Map 13 F1

Forte Heritage hotel set in what were Georgian town houses overlooking the gardens of Queen Square in the centre of town. Public areas have a traditional feel – sofas and chesterfields in the clubby bar, old oil portraits and lacy cloths on the coffee tables in the residents' lounge. Bedrooms in the original building generally have freestanding furniture and the attractive Heritage colour scheme of red and green. Rooms in a newer wing are more functional (but spacious) with older style, shelf-type furniture and somewhat dated bathrooms. Limited own parking. *Rooms 93.* AMERICAN EXPRESS *Access, Diners, Visa.*

Bath   Garlands Restaurant   £60

Tel 0225 442283   **R**

7 Edgar Buildings George Street Bath Avon BA1 2EE   Map 13 F1

Tom and Jo Bridgeman have had Garlands for five years now and are well established in busy Bath. At the far end of the restaurant is a café/bar operation (see our *Just a Bite* Guide) and there's seating outside, weather permitting, for about 16. The main restaurant is small but that doesn't cramp the Bridgeman style. A recent innovation is Tom's Friday night gourmet special, a 5-course set meal for £15 which really allows him to flex his muscles. From the main, simpler menu you might be offered choices including a ragout of shellfish with lime and coriander, or chicken and hazelnut terrine with baby leeks and an orange compote, followed by cutlet of Scotch salmon with a Thai-style crust, or supreme of chicken poached with lemon balm, tarragon and coconut. Interesting wine list. Charming service led by Jo. *Seats 28. Parties 12. Private Room 40. L 12-2.15 D 7-10.30. Closed Mon, 25 & 26 Dec. Set L £10.95/£13.95 Set D £16.95/£19.50.* AMERICAN EXPRESS *Access, Diners, Visa.*

Bath   Hilton National   67%   £125

Tel 0225 463411   Fax 0225 464393   **H**

Walcot Street Bath Avon BA1 5BJ   Map 13 F1

Extensive refurbishments throughout the hotel have been ongoing during the last two years and are now complete, resulting in spacious and smart public areas, business centre and leisure club. Plaza rooms are best and a whole floor is reserved for non-smokers. Banqueting/conference facilities for 200/250. There's free parking for 20 cars on the forecourt. *Rooms 150. Indoor swimming pool, keep-fit facilities, sauna, steam room, solarium, coffee shop 9am-11pm.* AMERICAN EXPRESS *Access, Diners, Visa.*

Bath   The Hole in the Wall   ↑   NEW   £60

Tel 0225 425242   **R**

16 George Street Bath Avon BA1 2EH   Map 13 F1

Those with a longish memory will recall the Hole in the Wall under George Perry-Smith as one of the gastronomic hot spots of the 50s and 60s. The site has since gone through various owners and names and has recently been acquired by Chris Chown, proprietor of Plas Bodegroes in Pwllheli. Much of the scene is as before, including bits of original pottery. The main room features white walls, banquettes, rush floor covering and polished unclad tables, all combining to create a feel that is at once cheerful and fairly sober. A second room in contemporary style has been created by moving back the kitchen. The entrance to the restaurant is now from the level of the upper pavement, and no longer from the original 'hole in the wall' at roadside. The new chef is Adrian Walton, whose main menu (one price for everything in each course – the printed prices include service) is an amalgam of his ideas, Chris Chown's and George Perry-Smith's. Parsleyed ham with beetroot chutney, hot pot of shellfish with chilis, ginger and lemon grass, and salmon and mushroom cutlets with tartare sauce are very superior starters, and main courses include fashionable updates and revivals – braised lamb shank with garlic and lemon, spatchcocked poussin with apple and tarragon, cassoulet of duck leg confit, neck sausage, smoked pork and flageolet beans. Salmon in puff pastry with leeks, laverbread and chive sauce is derived from a Perry-Smith classic. Lemon tart, crème brulée and bara brith-and-butter pudding with whisky ice cream are among a fine set of puddings to round off a meal highlighted by careful technique and good honest flavours. At lunchtime there's also a two-or three-course business menu with a guaranteed service time of 50 minutes. Other pluses here are an efficient, involved young manager in Nigel Griffith and a smashing, cleverly compiled wine list with friendly prices (house champagne under £20, many bottles under £15) and an abundance of wines by the glass. Early visits suggest that the Hole in the Wall is all set to resume the place of honour it held in its heyday. **Seats** 75. Parties 18. L 12-2.30 D 6-11. Closed Sun, Bank Holiday Mon. Set L £9.50. Access, Visa.

Bath	**The New Moon**	**£50**
Tel 0225 444407		**R**
Seven Dials Sawclose Bath Avon BA1 1ES		Map 13 F1

There's a new manager (Mark Heather) and a new chef (Nicholas Peter) at the New Moon, but with reassuring regularity, the operation continues to run like clockwork, as the menu is a proven success. There's breakfast from 9-11.30, the brasserie menu all afternoon (12-7), lunch for a fiver (2 courses) 12-2.30 weekdays, dinner for a tenner (3 courses) 7 till late, Sunday to Wednesday, in addition to dinner à la carte. Except on Friday and Saturday nights, you can bring your own wine and not be charged corkage, though there's also a full wine list. So, with all these options, what of the food? Well, it's international, eclectic and fun. The simple brasserie menu might offer *tataki* of rare beef with pickled vegetables, wasabi and soya sauce, *bollito misto* with zampone and salsa verde, or bubble and squeak with fried egg, grilled bacon and crispy sage. Rice pudding comes with vanilla custard, apple and blackcurrant crumble tart with crème fraiche. The evening carte has most of the brasserie menu and then some – perhaps layers of monkfish and salmon steamed with fresh herbs and saffron dressing, then rump of lamb on char grilled polenta with sautéed shallots and sun-dried tomatoes, with a chocolate and cinnamon charlotte to finish. Other plus points are a non-smoking area, and outside seating for 30. **Seats** 70. Meals 9am-11.30pm. Closed 25 & 26 Dec, 1 Jan. Set D £10/£12.50. Set L £6/£8.50. AMERICAN EXPRESS Access, Visa.

Bath	**Lansdown Grove**	**65%**	**£90**
Tel 0225 315891 Fax 0225 448092			**H**
Lansdown Grove Bath Avon BA1 5EH			Map 13 F1

Owned by the same family since 1988, the Lansdown Grove, set in delightful gardens high up above the city, has benefited from continuity of care and attention. Individually decorated bedrooms reflect the good taste of the proprietor's wife with fresh, bright colour schemes and a variety of well-chosen fabrics. Furniture varies from limed oak to more traditional freestanding pieces. Public areas are equally well kept and include a comfortable residents' lounge of grand proportions. Children of all ages can stay free in parents' room, charged for meals as taken. Ample parking, plus a lock-up garage for 6 cars. **Rooms** 45. Garden. AMERICAN EXPRESS Access, Diners, Visa.

Bath	**Priory Hotel**	**79%**	**£170**
Tel 0225 331922 Fax 0225 448276			**HR**
Weston Road Bath Avon BA1 2XT			Map 13 F1

The Priory became a hotel as recently as 1969 (when it was created from a private residence) although of course its origins go back further to 1835, when it was built in Gothic style of lovely local Bath stone. Despite being centrally located in the city, the air is very much that of a country house hotel. An atmosphere of quiet elegance and luxurious comfort prevails, but it is in no way intimidating. The layout of the building is delightfully rambling, which adds to its charm. Bedrooms, named after flowers, are spotlessly maintained and equipped with numerous little extras. Parking for 26 cars. ***Rooms 21. Garden, outdoor swimming pool.*** *Access, Diners, Visa.*

Restaurant

£75

Michael Collom, at the helm since 1979, offers up classical French cooking with some English specialities, so you might be offered a well-cooked and well-balanced meal such as smoked mackerel salad with a dill vinaigrette dressing, followed by a poached breast of chicken with a watercress sauce, and caramelised oranges served with a pink grapefruit sorbet. Always some good-value special offers and bin ends on a solid list that has something for everyone at affordable prices. No smoking. ***Seats 70. Parties 10. Private Room 45. L 12-1.45 D 7-9.15. Set L £13.50/£17.50 Set Sun L £20.50 Set D £32/£38.***

Bath   Queensberry Hotel   75%   £98

Tel 0225 447928   Fax 0225 446065   **HR**

Russel Street Bath Avon BA1 2QF   Map 13 F1

In a quiet street just to the north of the town centre, this small hotel is part of an attractive terrace built by John Wood in 1772. Individually decorated rooms boast antique furniture, deep comfortable seating and homely touches like books, magazines, fruit and, in the spacious carpeted bathrooms, large towelling robes and quality toiletries. Day rooms include an elegant, intimate period drawing room and cosy bar overlooking secluded courtyard gardens. Full of charm and immaculately kept throughout. No dogs. ***Rooms 22. Garden. Closed 1 week Christmas.*** *Access, Visa.*

Olive Tree Restaurant

£55

Oriental rugs over white ceramic tiles, rag-rolled walls, modernistic (though comfortable) chairs and the crispest of white linen all add up to a cool sophistication which finds its match in Stephen Ross's contemporary menu. Hot goat's cheese and hazelnut tart, duck confit with lentils and smoked bacon, sauté of calf's kidneys with artichoke hearts, mushrooms and cream, and loin of venison roasted in pastry with green mustard sauce show his style. Fish dishes depend on what's good in the market, and there's always a vegetarian main course. Desserts are as tempting as the rest: rich rice pudding with black cherry purée, pink grapefruit and mint sorbet, hot apple feuilleté with cinnamon ice cream. Of some three dozen well-chosen wines more than half are priced under £15. No smoking. ***Seats 45. Private Room 25. L 12-2 D 7-10 Closed Sun & 2 wks Xmas/New Year. Set L £10.50 Set D £17.***

Bath   Royal Crescent Hotel   84%   £182

Tel 0225 319090   Fax 0225 339401   **HR**

16 Royal Crescent Bath Avon BA1 2LS   Map 13 F1

John Wood's magnificent crescent comprises 30 houses in a 500ft curve, and the two central houses are now this exceptional hotel. Day rooms, both here and in the Dower House to the rear of the enclosed garden (a delightful spot in summer), retain their 18th-century elegance along with some fine original oil paintings and a scattering of antiques. The best suites are very grand, with some fine architectural features, but even the most modest (a relative term here) have elaborate bedhead drapes or a half-tester along with antique furniture and extras like mineral water, fruit and a flowery plant. Bathrooms are suitably luxurious with towelling robes and quality toiletries. The Beau Nash suite has its own spa pool room. Standards of service match the surroundings with full evening maid service and valet parking (space for 30 cars). Other exclusive offerings include front row circle seats for Saturday night at the Theatre Royal. No dogs. ***Rooms 42. Garden, croquet, plunge pool.*** AMERICAN EXPRESS *Access, Diners, Visa.*   *See over*

Dower House Restaurant ★ ↑ £95

Unashamedly luxurious surroundings – elaborate gilt wall lights, marble busts and formal service – are more than matched by chef Steven Blake's sophisticated cooking. A marriage of traditional skills and a careful eye for presentation combine in well-conceived dishes that delight the palate as much as the eye and from the moment you start to nibble your amuse-gueule in the lounge you realise that the kitchen is producing something very special. Service, too, is all it should be – friendly, professional and informative. Our latest meal was an almost unqualified triumph: duck confit terrine with onions and foie gras was a rich but well-balanced dish, the centre of wine-braised onions showing a clever touch. In brochette of langoustines the sweetness and delicacy of the langoustines was matched beautifully with the light mousse encasing them whilst the light crumb coating provided a sensational alternative texture. The light cream sauce with chopped oyster mushrooms and chives rounded off a really fine dish. Rabbit with balsamic vinegar sauce and Solferino vegetables was another visual stunner, though the rich, piquant sauce veiled its balsamic content. Chocolate truffle box (with three light mousses) was a perfect dessert, followed by a good strong brew of coffee and an excellent selection of well-made petits fours. Very fine and well-balanced wine list with, it seems, more good drinking under £20 than in previous years, including a bargain house selection; good mix of Europe and the New World plus a splendid half bottle selection. Valet parking even for non-residents. *Seats 66. Parties 8. Private Room 80. L 12.30-2 D 7-9.30 (Sat till 10). Set L £14.50/£18.50 Set D £25.*

Bath   Places of Interest

Tourist Information   Tel 0225 462831.
Theatre Royal   Sawclose Tel 0225 448815.
   Historic Houses, Castles and Gardens
Claverton Manor   Tel 0225 460503 *American Museum in Britain.*
Crowe Hall Gardens   Widcombe Hill Tel 0225 310322.
Dyrham Park   near Junction 18 of M4 Tel 027582 2501.
Priston Mill   Nr Bath Tel 0225 23894.
Sally Lunn's House   Tel 0225 61634.
Bath Racecourse   Tel 0451 20517.
   Museums and Art Galleries
Museum of Costume Assembly Rooms   Tel 0225 461111 Ext 2785.
Roman Baths Museum   Tel 0225 461111 Ext 2785.
Number One Royal Crescent (Bath Preservation Trust)   Tel 0225 428126.
Victoria Art Gallery   Tel 0225 461111 Ext 2772.

Battle   Netherfield Place   78%   £100

Tel 0424 774455   Fax 0424 774024   **HR**

Battle East Sussex TN33 9PP   Map 11 C6

Surrounded by 30 acres of gardens and parkland, the Colliers' neo-Georgian, 1920s-built mansion offers peace and comfort in a relaxing atmosphere. Day rooms include an elegant lounge with antique walnut coffee tables and attractive soft furnishings in shades of pink and green, a cosy bar and small sun lounge giving on to a wisteria-draped patio. Bedrooms have considerable charm with reproduction antique furniture, well-chosen (often floral) fabrics and all sorts of extras from fresh fruit and flowers to mineral water, books and a jar of sweets. Good bathrooms, many with marble tiling, come with bathrobes, generous towelling and quality toiletries. The Pomeroy room has a four-poster bed and, along with the Mandeville Suite, attracts a supplement. Beds are turned down in the evening and room service is available throughout the day and evening. Children under 12 stay free in parents' bedrooms and get their own high tea from 5pm. Banqueting/conference facilities for 85/50. *Rooms 14. Garden, croquet, putting, tennis. Closed 3 weeks Christmas/New Year.*
AMERICAN EXPRESS *Access, Diners, Visa.*

Restaurant £70

Well stocked with soft fruits, vegetables and herbs, a one-acre, walled kitchen garden makes a considerable contribution to the kitchens here. Salmon and sole terrine, a trio of vegetable raviolis, duck breast with Grand Marnier and fresh ginger sauce and local halibut with prawn and watercress sauce demonstrate the style of well-balanced, fixed-price (lunch includes a half bottle of house wine) and evening à la carte menus. Good puds, like a delicious, individual apricot cheesecake were enjoyed on a recent visit. Sunday lunch is a buffet affair. Lots of space between tables in this redwood-panelled dining room. *Seats* 80. *Parties* 16. *Private Room* 40. L 12-2 D 7-9.30 (Sun to 9). Set L £14.50 (buffet) & £15.95 Set D £22.50.

Battle Places of Interest

Tourist Information Tel 04246 3721.
Battle Abbey Tel 04246 3792.
  Museums and Art Galleries
Battle Museum Langton House.
Buckleys Shop Museum Tel 04246 4269.
The Almonry Tel 04246 2727.

Battlefield Forte Travelodge NEW £45

Tel 0800 850 950 L
A49 Battlefield nr Shrewsbury Shropshire Map 6 B3

Opening winter '94. 4 miles north of Shrewsbury. AMERICAN EXPRESS® *Access, Diners, Visa.*

Bawtry The Crown 64% £62

Tel 0302 710341 Fax 0302 711798 H
High Street Bawtry South Yorkshire DN10 6JW Map 7 D2

A sturdy old coaching inn, over 300 years old, encompassing conference/function rooms for up to 150. Most bedrooms are in a modern wing: 18 non-smoking, one four-poster room, another equipped for disabled guests. Dogs welcome. Forte Heritage. *Rooms* 57. *Garden.* AMERICAN EXPRESS® *Access, Diners, Visa.*

Beacon Hill Forte Travelodge NEW £45

Tel 0449 721640 L
Beacon Hill A45/A140 Needham Market nr Ipswich Suffolk Map 10 C3

Rooms 40. AMERICAN EXPRESS® *Access, Diners, Visa.*

Beaconsfield Bellhouse Hotel 67% £120

Tel 0753 887211 Fax 0753 888231 H
Oxford Road Beaconsfield Buckinghamshire HP9 2XE Map 15 E2

De Vere hotel on the A40, close to junction 2 of the M40, with an impressive Spanish-style frontage. An ongoing programme of refurbishment was benefiting the bedrooms as we went to press. Half of the bedrooms are reserved for non-smokers. Six separate conference suites accommodate up to 450 delegates. Popular leisure club includes beauty therapy. Children up to 14 stay free in parents' room. *Rooms* 136. *Garden, indoor swimming pool, gym, squash, sauna, steam room, spa bath, sun beds, beauty salon, snooker.* AMERICAN EXPRESS® *Access, Diners, Visa.*

Beaconsfield   Places of Interest

Bekonscot Model Village   Tel 0494 672919.
Chiltern Open Air Museum Newland Park   Tel 02407 71117 *5 miles.*
Milton's Cottage   Tel 02407 2313.

Beanacre   Beechfield House   70%   £75

Tel 0225 703700   Fax 0225 790118   **H**

Beanacre nr Melksham Wiltshire SN12 7PU   **Map 14 B2**

Built in 1878 of Bath stone, the ornate house is surrounded by eight acres
of gardens containing many specimen trees, after which individual
bedrooms are named. A white marble fireplace in the reception area houses
a real log fire to welcome guests in winter. The two main day rooms are
appropriately furnished with reproduction period-style easy chairs plus
an incongruously modern, low-backed settee. Bedrooms vary in size but all
have pretty, matching fabrics and most an antique or two plus fruit,
flowers and mineral water. Good carpeted bathrooms. The National Trust
village of Lacock is a few minutes away. *Rooms 24. Garden, tennis, outdoor
swimming pool.* AMERICAN EXPRESS *Access, Diners, Visa.*

Bearsted   Tudor Park Golf & Country Club   67%   £109

Tel 0622 734334   Fax 0622 735360   **H**

Ashford Road Bearsted nr Maidstone Kent ME14 4NQ   **Map 11 C5**

The 18-hole golf course with its covered practice ground, shop and tuition
is a major attraction at this modern hotel near Junction 8 of the M20 and
just two miles from Leeds Castle. There are many other leisure facilities,
plus conference facilities for up to 275 delegates. The public rooms are
interestingly laid out and include an intimate piano bar, a garden restaurant
overlooking the golf course and a plum-coloured cocktail bar. Bedrooms
are of a good size and feature large, comfortable beds. Country Club
Hotels. *Rooms 120. Indoor swimming pool, spa bath, sauna, steam room,
solarium, gym, snooker, squash, tennis, car hire, coffee shop (10am-10pm),
beautician, children's play area, table tennis, golf (18), helipad.* AMERICAN EXPRESS
Access, Diners, Visa.

Beaulieu   Montagu Arms   67%   £96

Tel 0590 612324   Fax 0590 612188   **H**

Beaulieu New Forest Hampshire SO42 7ZL   **Map 14 C4**

At the head of the Beaulieu river, in the heart of the famous village, a fine
base for touring the New Forest, visiting the National Motor Museum
or viewing Lord Montagu's Beaulieu Palace. A welcoming, old creeper-clad
inn, cosy in winter with real fires and cool in good weather with a small
conservatory overlooking a paved terraced area; the latter is a fine spot for
afternoon tea in summer, overlooking a circular lawn and immaculately
kept, compactly terraced gardens. Public rooms include an intimate,
bookcase-lined bar, comfortable sitting room and a rather dark dining
room, only the front part of which benefits from the lovely garden views
at breakfast (on a recent visit breakfast was good but service distinctly
below par). Bedrooms range from a single overlooking the gardens to three
antique-furnished suites, one with two bathrooms, another with a corner
aspect and a four-poster bed heavily draped with floral fabric. Guests have
the use of the health and beauty centre and indoor swimming pool at sister
hotel *Careys Manor*, 6 miles away in Brockenhurst. Limited covered
parking. Bucklers Hard and Exbury Gardens (with 200 acres and a fine
display of azaleas and rhododendrons) are also nearby. *Rooms 24. Garden.*
AMERICAN EXPRESS *Access, Diners, Visa.*

Beaulieu   Places of Interest

Tourist Information   Tel 0590 612345 ext 278.
Beaulieu Abbey and National Motor Museum   Tel 0590 612123.

Bebington   Forte Travelodge   £45

Tel 051 327 2489   **L**
Bebington New Chester Road Eastham Wirral Merseyside L62 9AQ   Map 6 A2

On the A41 northbound, off Junction 5 of the M53. *Rooms 31.*
 Access, Diners, Visa.

Our inspectors *never* book in the name of Egon Ronay's Guides. They
disclose their identity only if they are considering an establishment for
inclusion in the next edition of the Guide.

Beccles   Waveney House   59%   £55

Tel 0502 712270   Fax 0502 712660   **H**
Puddingmoor Beccles Suffolk NR34 9PL   Map 10 D2

Situated in the heart of the Norfolk Broads, Waveney was built as a private
house around 1592, extended from 1750 onwards, and is now a Grade
I listed building. It's right on the river Waveney and there's a certain
amount of nautical chat in the bar and residents' lounge. Even bedrooms
have a shipboard feel with creaking floorboards, uneven walls and beams
beneath which to duck. One room has a four-poster bed. *Rooms 13.*
Garden, fishing, mooring. AMERICAN EXPRESS *Access, Diners, Visa.*

Beccles   Places of Interest

Marina Theatre   Lowestoft Tel 0502 573318.
Somerleyton Hall   Nr Lowestoft Tel 0502 730224/730308.
Kessingland Beach *4 miles south of Lowestoft.*
Lowestoft Beach.
Pleasurewood Hill American Theme Park   Corton Tel 0493 441611.

Beckingham   Black Swan   £50

Tel 0636 626474   **R**
Hillside Beckingham Lincolnshire LN5 0RF   Map 7 E3

A converted village pub with a country atmosphere and a charming
riverside garden where light summer lunches are served. The à la carte and
fixed-price menus provide an interesting selection of dishes, classically based
but often with original touches: soup (seafood or lemon saffron) garnished
with tarragon and fish quenelles, pheasant breast baked in filo pastry served
on a brown beer sauce, grilled fillet of beef served with a potato and leek
galette on a wild mushroom sauce. Soufflés are a speciality, and a hot rum
and raisin version with a rum sauce is a popular dessert. Children under 11
eat Sunday lunch free (one child per adult). No smoking. *Seats 36. L 12-2
(bookings only) D 7-10. Closed Mon, 25 & 26 Dec. Set L £14.75 (Sun
£12.50) Set D £14.75/£19.90. Access, Visa.*

Beckington   Forte Travelodge   NEW   £45

Tel 0373 830251   **L**

A36 Beckington nr Bath Avon   **Map 14 B3**

Around 11 miles south of Bath, 4 miles from Trowbridge and 6 miles from Warminster. AMERICAN EXPRESS® *Access, Diners, Visa.*

Bedford   Moat House   65%   £69

Tel 0234 355131   Fax 0234 340447   **H**

2 St Mary's Street Bedford Bedfordshire MK42 0AR   **Map 15 E1**

Modern tower block in a prime position in the town centre, overlooking the river Great Ouse and town bridge. Banqueting and conference facilities for 375/400. Informal eating in Mallards café/bar. Weekend tariff reductions. ***Rooms*** *100. Keep-fit equipment, sauna, spa bath.* AMERICAN EXPRESS® *Access, Visa.*

Bedford   Woodlands Manor   72%   £85

Tel 0234 363281   Fax 0234 272390   **H**

Green Lane Clapham Bedford Bedfordshire MK41 6EP   **Map 15 E1**

Two miles north of Bedford and set in its own grounds off the A6, Woodlands Manor is an impressive Victorian manor house. The porticoed entrance leads into a spacious and elegant hall with a carved stone fireplace, a wide polished-oak staircase and three groups of settees and armchairs creating the feel of a lounge. A further lounge, now with a small bar in one corner, offers additional seating on blue bird of paradise-patterned armchairs. Bedrooms include eight Executive rooms in a sympathetically added wing. These are larger than the remainder but all rooms are decorated and furnished to a high standard. Some bathrooms have white marble tiling, others are carpeted. Extras include satellite TV, hairdryers and trouser presses with mini-bars in the better rooms. There are three bedrooms in a separate cottage in the grounds. ***Rooms*** *25. Closed 3 days Christmas.* AMERICAN EXPRESS® *Access, Diners, Visa.*

Bedford   Places of Interest

Tourist Information   Tel 0234 215226.
Bowen West Community Theatre   Tel 0234 2193331.
The Swiss Garden   Old Warden, Biggleswade Tel 0234 228330.
Wrest Park House and Gardens   Silsoe, Nr Ampthill Tel 0525 60718.
Stagsden Bird Gardens   Tel 02302 2745.
   Museums and Art Galleries
Bromham Mill   Bromham Tel 0234 228330.
Cecil Higgins Art Gallery and Museum   Tel 0234 211222.
Bedford Museum   Tel 0234 53323.
The Shuttleworth Collection (Aviation History)   Old Warden,
   Biggleswade Tel 076 727 288.

Belford   Blue Bell Hotel   63%   £66

Tel 0668 213543   Fax 0668 213787   **H**

Market Square Belford Northumberland NE70 7NE   **Map 5 D1**

Creeper-clad, the Bell stands at the head of the village on a cobbled forecourt. In front are the old Market Place and stone cross, recently restored by English Heritage; the Norman parish church stands on a hill behind. The hotel's stone-flagged foyer leads to a stylish cocktail bar boasting a collection of miniature hand bells, and a restful residents' lounge. Bedrooms are classified by type and tariff from those in the annexe (with shower/WC's only) to superior and de-luxe rooms with full bathrooms and lovely views of the Blue Bell's 2-acre "garden of 10,000 blooms". Children are made truly welcome as two of the hotel's "Australian Directors" are, in fact, Mr and Mrs Shirley's own grandchildren. *Rooms 17. Garden.* AMERICAN EXPRESS® *Access, Visa.*

Belton	Belton Woods Hotel	72%	£115
Tel 0476 593200 Fax 0476 74547			**H**
Belton nr Grantham Lincolnshire NG32 2LN			Map 7 E3

Just off the A607, north of Grantham, a modern complex standing in 475 acres of grounds, with outstanding sports facilities that are matched by equally impressive accommodation. That accommodation has now been augmented by a new block of 40 bedrooms with the same standards and decor as the current rooms. Ambassador rooms (£140) are particularly spacious, and some of them, like the suites, have patios or balconies and views over the golf course. Leisure facilities have also been improved, with a new gym and beauty salon. A spacious, high-ceilinged lounge leading off the main foyer is filled with parlour plants and hanging baskets, and overlooks one of three golf courses (two 18-hole and one 9-hole). The cocktail bar on the first floor is more club-like, with easy chairs and rich decor; there's also a new conservatory and a 'spike bar' for golfers; the coffee shop has become *Plus Fours* restaurant. Excellent facilities for children include a children's playground and swimming pool, cots and baby-sitting. *Rooms 136. Garden, indoor swimming pool, spa bath, sauna, steam room, solarium, beauty salon, hairdressing, gym, games room, snooker, golf courses (2 18-hole, 1 9-hole), golf driving range, fishing, tennis.* AMERICAN EXPRESS® *Access, Diners, Visa.*

Belton   Place of Interest

Tourist Information   Tel 0476 66444.
   Historic Houses, Castles and Gardens
Belton House (NT)   Tel 0476 66116.
Fulbeck Hall   Tel 0400 72205.
Woolsthorpe Manor (NT)   Tel 0476 860338 *Birthplace of Sir Isaac Newton.*
Belvoir Castle   Tel 0476 870262.

Berkswell	Nailcote Hall	67%	NEW	£115
Tel 0203 466174 Fax 0203 470720				**H**
Nailcote Lane Berkswell Warwickshire CV7 7DE				Map 6 C4

A black and white timbered Jacobean building is at the heart of a hotel that enjoys a rural location (on the B4101) yet is just a few minutes from the Midlands motorway network and the NEC. Beyond a rug-strewn, oak-floored lobby the main day room in the original building is a small flagstone-floored cocktail bar; a further bar is attached to an informal atrium restaurant in a stylish barn conversion that also houses the leisure centre and half the bedrooms. Of good size and comfortably appointed, bedrooms in the main building have reproduction-style furniture. Four period rooms have real antiques, while those in the Barn conversion have pine pieces. Well-appointed bathrooms come with generously sized bath robes. *Rooms 38. Garden, croquet, golf (9), tennis, indoor swimming pool, children's splash pool, gym, solarium, spa bath, steam room, snooker.*

Berwick-upon-Tweed	Funnywayt'mekalivin		£50
Tel 0289 308827			**R**
41 Bridge Street Berwick-upon-Tweed Northumberland TD15 1ES			Map 3 D6

Elizabeth Middlemiss's unusually named restaurant has built up a loyal following, and the expansion continues: there are now three letting bedrooms. Menus continue to offer honest, robust, freshly made dishes in well-thought-out combinations. Thus you might eat a set dinner comprising Greek lentil soup, then smoked haddock savoury, wild venison braised with beetroot for main course, plum compote with cinnamon ice cream for pudding and Teviotdale cheese to round off. Lunch offers a short carte of similarly attractive cooking. Interesting, concise wine list. *Seats 32. Private Room 8. L 11.30-2.30 D at 8. Closed D Sun-Tue, 25 & 26 Dec, 1 Jan. Set D £22.50. Access, Visa.*

Berwick-upon-Tweed   Kings Arms   59%   £70

Tel 0289 307454   Fax 0289 308867   **H**

Hide Hill Berwick-upon-Tweed Northumberland TD15 1EJ   **Map 3 D6**

Dating from the 18th century, this town-centre hotel offers agreeable overnight accommodation that includes three rooms with four-posters. Solid oakwood furnishings give a reassuringly traditional feel, and there's plenty of room to relax in the chandelier-hung lounge and the cocktail bar. The Royal Suite is a popular venue for banquets and conferences. (max. 200). *Rooms 36. Coffee shop (9.30-5.30).* AMERICAN EXPRESS *Access, Diners, Visa.*

Berwick-upon-Tweed   Places of Interest

Tourist Information   Tel 0289 330733.
Lindisfarne Castle   Holy Island Tel 0289 89244 *Causeway flooded at high tide.*
Berwick Borough Museum & Art Gallery (EH)   Tel 0289 330933.
Manderston Duns   Tel 0361 83450 *15 miles.*
Paxton House   Tel 0289 86291.

Beverley   Beverley Arms   62%   £80

Tel 0482 869241   Fax 0482 870907   **H**

North Bar Within Beverley Humberside HU17 8DD   **Map 7 E1**

300-year-old coaching inn that retains a certain period interest. Bedrooms are mostly in a modern block. 20 are designated non-smoking. Children up to 14 stay free in parents' room. Ample free parking. Forte. *Rooms 57.* AMERICAN EXPRESS *Access, Diners, Visa.*

Beverley   Places of Interest

Art Gallery and Museum   Tel 0482 882255.
Beverley Minster   Tel 0482 868540.
Racecourse   Tel 0482 867488.

Bexley   Forte Posthouse   56%   £68

Tel 0322 526900   Fax 0322 526113   **H**

Black Prince Interchange Southwold Road Bexley Kent DA5 1ND   **Map 11 B5**

Beside the A2 this much extended former public house provides simple, no-frills accommodation in a purpose-built bedroom block. Self-contained business centre has up-to-date features. Two bars. *Rooms 102. Terrace, games room.* AMERICAN EXPRESS *Access, Diners, Visa.*

Bexleyheath   Swallow Hotel   71%   £96

Tel 081-298 1000   Fax 081-298 1234   **H**

1 Broadway Bexleyheath Kent DA6 7JZ   **Map 11 B5**

This comparatively recent addition to the Swallow chain, purpose-built and conveniently situated just off the A2, sports up-to-the-minute decor and state-of-the-art technology, providing all possible comforts and facilities. 52 of the well-proportioned bedrooms are reserved for non-smokers, two are especially adapted for the disabled guests. Conferences and banquets for up to 250. Parking for 80 cars. Dogs welcome. *Rooms 142. Terrace, indoor swimming pool, gymnasium, spa bath, steam room, solarium.* AMERICAN EXPRESS *Access, Diners, Visa.*

Bibury   The Swan   78%   £128

Tel 0285 740695   Fax 0285 740473   **HR**

Bibury Gloucestershire GL7 5NW   Map 14 C2

Liz Hayles and Alex Furtek run a really splendid hotel on the banks of the
River Coln. The setting, in neatly kept gardens, is a real delight, and the
first impressions continue throughout, from the foyer, where a grand piano
plays in the evenings, through to the comfortably furnished parlour (for
non-smokers) and the charming writing room, which was once the village
post office. Explore further through and one finds a splendid long bar with
pale oak panelling, leather tub chairs on flagstone floor, log fire and one
wall covered with a mural depicting various folk involved in the hotel's
transformation. Press on and the mood changes yet again in a stylish all-day
brasserie (an unexpected find in a sleepy Cotswold village) complete with
Italian wrought-iron furniture: a useful alternative to the hotel's rather
grand dining room and the place where late-risers will find breakfast.
There are all sorts of fine decorative fabrics throughout the hotel including
a collection of Charles Rennie Mackintosh chairs. Upstairs even the
standard bedrooms have great appeal with antique furniture and individual
decor; the best might have a four-poster bed, crystal chandelier, spa bath
or luxuriously large, old-fashioned freestanding tub. Fine toiletries and
bathrobes are standard. Quality of service from friendly, well-motivated
staff is high, with nice touches like the linen mat placed by the side of the
bed when rooms are serviced in the evenings. No dogs. *Rooms 18. Garden,
fishing, brasserie (10am-10pm). Closed 24 Dec-8 Jan.* **AMERICAN EXPRESS**
Access, Visa.

Restaurant   £100

Over the past year or so there have been several changes of head chef here,
so it is to be hoped that the new incumbent Guy Bossom will bring some
stability to the kitchen. His menus are certainly enticing and, alongside the
à la carte, the set-price dinner offers four courses after a Bibury trout
appetiser: perhaps a ravioli of red mullet with a garlicky sauce, carrot and
coriander soup, breast of Barbary duck with a confit of potato and a green
peppercorn cream, plus a white chocolate mousse with seasonal red fruits
and raspberry sorbet to finish. The à la carte dishes are similar in style:
eclectic cooking with Mediterranean influences, classical French and
modern British – as in fillet of red snapper with couscous, beef with a slice
of foie gras, truffle and Madeira juices, or a whole Dover sole with chive
and vermouth cream, ending with a warm bread-and-butter pudding and
apricot custard. *Seats 65. Parties 10. Private Room 12. L 12.30-2 D 7.30-9.45
Set Sun L £15.95 Set D £35.*

Bigbury-on-Sea   Burgh Island Hotel   66%   £174*

Tel 0548 810514   Fax 0548 810243   **H**

Burgh Island Bigbury-on-Sea Devon TQ7 4AU   Map 13 D3

Unique is an overworked word, but it certainly applies to Beatrice and
Tony Porter's 26-acre island and Art Deco hotel. They acquired the hotel
in 1985 and set about restoring it to its 1929 glory. That glory includes the
Palm Court with its Peacock Dome and cocktail bar, a glass sun lounge,
jet-black glass and pink mirrors on the staircase, and a magnificent
ballroom. Original Art Deco furniture graces day rooms and the
bedrooms, all of which are suites. The island boasts its own pub – the 14th-
century Pilchard Inn – and in the summer boat trips can be arranged.
There are also banqueting and conference facilities (100/120). Guests park
their cars in a lock-up garage on the mainland and are transported to the
island either by Land Rover or on a giant sea tractor. *Half-board only.
No dogs. *Rooms 14. Garden, sauna, solarium, tennis, keep-fit equipment, games
room, snooker, sea fishing. Closed mid-week during Jan & Feb.* **AMERICAN EXPRESS**
Access, Visa.

Bilbrough   **Bilbrough Manor**   75%   £105

Tel 0937 834002   Fax 0937 834724   **HR**

Bilbrough nr York North Yorkshire YO2 3PH   **Map 7 D1**

An attractive manor house among fine Georgian gardens in a quiet village
off the A64, six miles from York. Though the present house 'only' dates
from 1901, there's been an abode here for some 700 years, and it's probably
best known as the family home of Thomas Fairfax, Cromwell's right-hand
man. The Manor was restored by Colin and Sue Bell and opened
as a country house hotel in 1987. Day rooms include a foyer-bar and
a splendid lounge with lightwood panelling and comfortable sofas. Prettily
decorated bedrooms are light and airy with carefully matched colour
schemes and soft furnishings, but rather plain modern furniture. Compact,
carpeted bathrooms. No children under 10 (or dogs). A new chef joined
the hotel as we went to press. *Rooms 15. Garden, keep-fit equipment, sauna.
Closed 24-30 Dec.* AMERICAN EXPRESS *Access, Diners, Visa.*

Bilbrough   **Travel Inn (York)**   **NEW**   £43

Tel 0582 414341   **L**

Bilbrough Colton York North Yorkshire   **Map 7 D1**

On the A64 between Tadcaster and York. Meeting rooms. 6 miles from
York and 15 from Leeds. *Rooms 60.* AMERICAN EXPRESS *Access, Diners, Visa.*

If we recommend meals in a hotel or inn a separate entry is made for its
restaurant.

Billesley   **Billesley Manor**   75%   £151

Tel 0789 400888   Fax 0789 764145   **HR**

Billesley Alcester nr Stratford-upon-Avon Warwickshire B49 6NF   **Map 14 C1**

Signposted from the A46 about halfway between Stratford and Alcester,
this Queens Moat Houses-owned, 16th-century manor sits in 11 acres
of grounds that include a splendid topiary garden. Oak panelling is the
unifying theme of public areas that include a lounge, furnished with
slightly tired draylon sofas, and galleried cocktail bar plus a good indoor
swimming pool that in summer opens on to a sheltered patio. Bedrooms
in the original building are the more characterful but most are in two
newer wings of which the Topiary Wing is marginally to be preferred
as having fresher, more stylish decor. Rooms are properly serviced in the
evenings. Conference and banqueting facilities for up to 100. No dogs.
Rooms 41. Garden, croquet, tennis, pitch & putt, indoor swimming pool.
AMERICAN EXPRESS *Access, Diners, Visa.*

Stuart Restaurant   £85

Lots more oak here in the panelling and square, unclothed tables that are
surrounded by comfortable armed, button-back leather chairs –
encouraging one to linger over chef Mark Naylor's reliably good cooking.
Dishes such as goat's cheese salad with mango walnut dressing, breast
of Gressingham duck with confit of the leg and sweet spice sauce, best end
of lamb with lentils and roasted garlic, and brill with pesto, tagliatelle and
a champagne pimento sauce reflect modern trends and come in generous
portions. Good desserts such as pear and raisin "feuillette", hot raspberry
soufflé and crepes Suzette. Outdoor eating for 12 on a terrace. No children
under 6 after 7.30pm. *Seats 80. Parties 8. Private Room 40. L 12.30-2
D 7.30-9.30 (Fri & Sat to 10). Set L £17 Set D £26.*

Billingshurst   Forte Travelodge   £45

Tel 0403 782711   **L**

Staines Street Five Oaks Billingshurst West Sussex RH14 9AE   Map 11 A6

2 miles north-east of Billingshurst, on the A29 northbound, 8 miles south-west of Horsham. *Rooms 26.* AMERICAN EXPRESS *Access, Diners, Visa.*

Billingshurst   The Gables   £50

Tel 0403 782571   **R**

Pulborough Road Parbrook Billingshurst West Sussex RH14 9EU   Map 11 A6

Chef-patron Nicholas Illes is very much following the family tradition at this black and white timbered 15th-century restaurant just south of town on the A29; Dad runs *Cisswood House* at Lower Beeding (qv) and brother Carl the *Willows Restaurant* at Ashington (qv). They take it in turns to make early morning trips to the London markets to pick the best of ingredients for their respective kitchens. The same, seasonally-changing menu is served both at lunch and dinner (though differently priced) often with a good choice of dishes both simple – asparagus hollandaise, sole Colbert, liver and bacon with onion gravy – and more adventurous – char-grilled scallop salad with red pepper salsa, ginger, saffron and dill sauce. Partner Rebecca Gilroy runs front of house with charm and efficiency. No children on Friday or Saturday nights. *Seats 45. L 12.30-2 D 7.15-9 (Fri & Sat to 10). Closed L Sat, D Sun, all Mon, 2 weeks Jan/Feb. Set L £12.50/£14.95 Set Sun L £13.95 Set D £17.95.* AMERICAN EXPRESS *Access, Visa.*

Bingley   Bankfield Hotel   61%   £106

Tel 0274 567123   Fax 0274 551331   **H**

Bradford Road Bingley West Yorkshire BD16 1TU   Map 6 C1

On the A650 Bradford/Skipton road, a castellated Gothic frontage that "wouldn't look out of place on a Hollywood film set". Inside, handsome Victorian day rooms and mainly modern, decent-sized bedrooms, 29 of which have been recently refurbished. Conference facilities for up to 250 and winter dinner dances. Jarvis Hotels. *Rooms 103. Garden.* AMERICAN EXPRESS *Access, Diners, Visa.*

Birdlip   Kingshead House   £55

Tel 0452 862299   **RR**

Birdlip nr Gloucester Gloucestershire GL4 8JH   Map 14 B2

Judy and Warren Knock run a relaxed, informal and welcoming country restaurant which began life in the 17th century as a coaching inn. Judy offers fixed-price-only dinner menus that vary weekly plus lighter, value-conscious lunch options available in the bar as well as restaurant. On the dinner menu you might find swede and ginger soup and hot salt duck with lentils among the starters, then perhaps a scallop and crab brioche and a choice of about five main courses that includes one fish and one vegetarian (salmon with sorrel sauce, rack of lamb with pea purée and tomato sauce, herb pancake filled with cheese soufflé served with a red pepper sauce). Desserts are just as appealing, and the meal price includes coffee or tea and petits fours. Traditional (and other) dishes on the Sunday lunch menu. Popular culinary evenings have recently covered Castile and pre-Revolution Russia. Lots of half bottles on a concise and informative wine list with friendly prices. Diners taking a taxi home are entitled to taxi vouchers (£2.50 per person up to 4 per party). Smoking is discouraged by table cards. *Seats 32. L 12.30-1.45 D 7.30-9.45. Closed L Sat, D Sun, all Mon, 26 & 27 Dec, 1 Jan. Set Sun L £15.50 Set D £22.50/£24.50.* AMERICAN EXPRESS *Access, Diners, Visa.*

See over

Room £52

The one and only en-suite double bedroom is a delightful place to stop over for a night. Birdlip lies on the lovely Cotswold Way and is equidistant (8 miles) from Gloucester and Cheltenham. Accommodation closed at Christmas.

Birkenhead   Bowler Hat Hotel   65%   £70

Tel 051-652 4931   Fax 051-653 8127   **H**

2 Talbot Road Oxton Birkenhead Merseyside L43 2HH   **Map 6 A2**

One mile off the M53, junction 3, a large Victorian house with the majority of rooms in a redbrick extension to the rear. Children up to 12 stay free in parents' room. Function facilities for up to 240. Free parking for 100 cars. *Rooms 32. Garden.* AMERICAN EXPRESS *Access, Diners, Visa.*

Birkenhead   Places of Interest

Tourist Information   Woodside Visitors Centre Tel 051 647 6780.
Birkenhead Park   Tel 051 647 2366.
Williamson Art Gallery and Museum   Tel 051 652 4177.
Lady Lever Art Gallery   Port Sunlight Village Tel 051 645 3623.
Oval Sports Centre Bebington   Tel 051 645 0551.

Birmingham   Adil Tandoori   £25

Tel 021-449 0335   **R**

148-150 Stoney Lane Sparkbrook Birmingham West Midlands B11 8AJ   **Map 6 C4**

Basic balti house with a spreading reputation. Unlicensed, and the splendid nan bread does the work of knives and forks. *Seats 100. Parties 40. Private Room 25. Meals 12-12. Closed 25 Dec.* AMERICAN EXPRESS *Access, Diners, Visa.*

Changes in data sometimes occur in establishments after the Guide goes to press. Prices should be taken as indications rather than firm quotes.

Birmingham   Birmingham Metropole   72%   £156

Tel 021-780 4242   Fax 021-780 3923   **H**

National Exhibition Centre Birmingham West Midlands B40 1PP   **Map 6 C4**

A huge, modern hotel at the heart of the National Exhibition Centre site with over 800 rooms in three wings – Crown, Executive and Standard; it caters mainly for conference delegates and business folk. Decor is light and up-to-date, and the matching fabrics are contemporary in style; all rooms have smart, solid furniture and modern tiled bathrooms with good mirrors and showers. Twenty-six pairs of rooms interconnect, making them ideal for family or small business use. Children up to 12 stay free in parents' room. Public areas include a striking foyer (recently refurbished), a bar-lounge with mirrored columns and contemporary seating and decor plus three restaurants. 700 car parking spaces are available free to residents. The already impressive conference and banqueting facilities (catering for up to 2000 delegates) are being extended for 1995, and a new leisure complex will be added later in the year. *Rooms 802. Closed Christmas/New Year.* AMERICAN EXPRESS *Access, Diners, Visa.*

Birmingham	Campanile Hotel	£44

Tel 021-622 4925   Fax 021-622 4195   **L**

Irving Street Lee Bank Birmingham West Midlands B1 1DH   **Map 6 C4**

City-centre site, off Bristol Street, near Queensway. *Rooms 50.*
AMERICAN EXPRESS *Access, Diners, Visa.*

Birmingham	Chamberlain Hotel	53%	NEW	£35

Tel 021-627 0627   Fax 021-606 9001   **H**

Alcester Street Birmingham West Midlands B12 0PJ   **Map 6 C4**

With single rooms at £25 including breakfast – although it's worth the
extra £10 for a double to get a little more elbow room – price is the big
attraction at what was originally one of the Rowton Houses built in 1903
to provide decent, affordable accommodation for working men in 819
'cubicles'. Today, after £4m of refurbishment, there are just 250 rooms but
they are still small and offer fairly basic accommodation – TV, phone,
beverage kit (there is no room service) – with small en-suite shower/WC
rooms. Just eight rooms are larger and have bathtubs. The main public
room is a large Victorian-themed bar – also with keen prices. Breakfast
is a buffet affair where eggs only come scrambled and beverages from
a self-service machine. Conference/banqueting for 400/350. Secure, covered
parking at £2 per day is a big plus. *Rooms 250. News kiosk.*
AMERICAN EXPRESS *Access, Diners, Visa.*

Birmingham	Chung Ying	£40

Tel 021-622 5669   **R**

16 Wrottesley Street Birmingham West Midlands B5 6RT   **Map 6 C4**

The Chinese flock to this well-established, traditionally appointed
restaurant for its long Cantonese menu. The choice extends to well over
300 dishes, including more than 40 dim sum items and a 'special dishes'
section with stuffed peppers, crabmeat on straw mushrooms, frog's legs and
venison among the choice. Also of note are the casseroles: braised brisket
with spices, belly pork with yam, lamb with dried bean curd, duck's webs
and fish lips, chicken and liver. *Seats 220. Meals 12-11.30 (Sun to 11).
Closed 25 Dec.* AMERICAN EXPRESS *Access, Diners, Visa.*

Birmingham	Chung Ying Garden	£40

Tel 021-622 5669   **R**

17 Thorp Street Birmingham West Midlands B5 4AT   **Map 6 C4**

Sister and near neighbour of the original *Chung Ying*, this has more
modern decor, with pillars, plants and murals, and a similar menu.
Seats 300. Meals 12-11.30 (Sun to 11). Closed 25 Dec. AMERICAN EXPRESS
Access, Diners, Visa.

Birmingham	Copthorne Hotel	70%	£131

Tel 021-200 2727   Fax 021-200 1197   **H**

Paradise Circus Birmingham West Midlands B3 3HJ   **Map 6 C4**

Close to the International Convention Centre, and overlooking Centenary
Square, the hotel has a striking black glass exterior to complement the sleek
and contemporary public areas which include a marble-floored foyer and
raised bar-lounge. Connoisseur bedrooms offer guests extras to the standard
rooms, though all enjoy excellent bathrooms with large mirrors and plenty
of shelf space. Children up to 16 stay free in parents' room. Comprehensive
conference (200), banqueting (150) and fitness facilities, as well as a business
centre. Own limited free parking, and nearby multi-storey car park.
Summer of 1994 saw the ongoing refurbishment programme focusing
on the restaurants. *Rooms 212. Indoor swimming pool, gym, sauna, spa bath,
steam room, solarium, news kiosk.* AMERICAN EXPRESS *Access, Diners, Visa.*

Birmingham   Days of the Raj   £35
Tel 021-236 0445   R

51 Dale End Birmingham West Midlands B4 7LS   Map 6 C4

Northern Indian food served in relaxing surroundings. Specialities include mixed meat biryani, lamb chops masala and makhan chicken. Lunchtime buffet. *Seats 75. Private Room 35. L 12-2.30 D 7-11.30. Closed L Sat & Sun, 25 & 26 Dec. Set L £5.95.* AMERICAN EXPRESS *Access, Diners, Visa.*

Birmingham   Forte Crest   66%   £100
Tel 021-643 8171   Fax 021-631 2528   H

Smallbrook Queensway Birmingham West Midlands B5 4EW   Map 6 C4

Still known locally as the Albany, this high-rise hotel by the inner ring road is geared primarily to business people (facilities include 'in-house' pagers and a Business Support Centre) and conferences (up to 630 theatre-style in the largest of 11 meeting rooms). Bedroom decor tends to be rather masculine although Lady Crest rooms have softer schemes. Some two-thirds of the rooms are singles some of which have now been given larger beds. Bathrooms are compact but well thought-out with corner vanity units in marble and angled mirrors above – good for 'making up'. Comprehensive 24hr room service. Vouchers give free parking from 5pm-10am at the adjacent NCP multi-storey. Weekend tariff reductions. *Rooms 253. Indoor swimming pool, gym, squash, sauna, solarium, table tennis.* AMERICAN EXPRESS *Access, Diners, Visa.*

Birmingham   Forte Posthouse   60%   £68
Tel 021-357 7444   Fax 021-357 7503   H

Chapel Lane Great Barr Birmingham West Midlands B43 7BG   Map 6 C4

Practical, modern hotel on the A34, near Junction 7 of the M6. Conference and banqueting facilities for 150. *Rooms 192. Garden, indoor swimming pool, gym, sauna, solarium, spa bath, children's playroom and playground.* AMERICAN EXPRESS *Access, Diners, Visa.*

See the hotel by county listings for easy comparison of conference and banqueting facilities.

Birmingham   Granada Lodge   £51
Tel 021-550 3261   Fax 021-501 2880   L

Frankley Birmingham West Midlands B32 4AR   Map 6 C4

By Junctions 3/4 of M5. *Rooms 60.* AMERICAN EXPRESS *Access, Diners, Visa.*

Birmingham   Henry's   £45
Tel 021-200 1136   R

27 St Paul's Square Birmingham West Midlands B3 1RB   Map 6 C4

A short drive from the city centre is this purpose-built restaurant on split levels, serviced by friendly staff. As at its sister restaurant, the Cantonese menu is extensive and dishes are competently cooked, covering a range from satay and soups to scallops, sizzling dishes, shredded beef with fruity sauce, Singapore noodles and sweet and sour vegetarian wun tun. Set menus for 2 to 5+, and a set vegetarian menu (£12.50 per person). *Seats 140. Private Room 45. L 12-1.45 D 6-11. Closed Sun, Bank Holidays.* AMERICAN EXPRESS *Access, Diners, Visa.*

Birmingham   Henry Wong   £45

Tel 021-427 9799   **R**

283 High Street Harborne Birmingham West Midlands B17 9QH   Map 6 C4

Sister restaurant to *Henry's*, a bright and airy restaurant at the top end of Harborne, some four miles from the city centre with similar Cantonese menu. Sound cooking, good staff. *Seats 140. Parties 60. Private Room 40. L 12-1.45 D 6-11 (Fri & Sat to 11.30). Closed Sun, Bank Holidays. Set meals from £13.* AMERICAN EXPRESS *Access, Diners, Visa.*

Birmingham   Holiday Inn   70%   £128

Tel 021-631 2000   Fax 021-643 9018   **H**

Holliday Street Birmingham West Midlands B1 1HH   Map 6 C4

Located above an NCP car park in the city centre, this modern high-rise hotel with its numerous conference and meeting rooms (holding up to 160), smart public areas, choice of two bars and good leisure facilities is a popular venue for the business community. The bedrooms all have individually controllable air-conditioning and ample work space; Executive suites (4) boast king-size beds and fax machines. Bathrooms are well lit, with large mirrors and decent showers. ***Rooms** 288. Indoor swimming pool, keep-fit equipment, sauna, steam room, spa bath, solarium, kiosk.* AMERICAN EXPRESS *Access, Diners, Visa.*

Birmingham   Hyatt Regency   77%   £140

Tel 021-643 1234   Fax 021-616 2323   **HR**

2 Bridge Street Birmingham West Midlands B1 2JZ   Map 6 C4

A canalside setting in the heart of Birmingham for the impressive, mirrored 25-storey Hyatt Regency, which has a direct link to the International Convention Centre next door. Inside, the huge glazed atrium is the epitome of style and elegance, bedecked with plants, and awash with marble. The luxuriously appointed bedrooms include 12 suites; all are spacious and air-conditioned, featuring quality modern furniture and fashionably uncluttered decor, plus equally splendid, marble-floored bathrooms. Three rooms are adpated for the disabled, one floor of 17 rooms is reserved for non-smokers and three floors make up the Regency Club of superior rooms; the latter has its own Club Lounge on the 22nd floor. Floor-to-ceiling windows afford fine views over the Second City. Excellent leisure facilities. Young, smart and willing staff. Conference facilities for up to 240, banqueting to 200. Children up to 18 free in parents' room. Charged, valet parking in the hotel's 24hr-manned car park nearby. ***Rooms** 319. Garden, indoor swimming pool, gym, sauna, solarium, steam room, spa bath, business centre, café (6.30am-midnight).* AMERICAN EXPRESS *Access, Diners, Visa.*

Number 282   £80

A Brasserie on Broad Street is the tagline here, though 'broadsheet' might be even more appropriate with the day's news headlines, weather, entertainment and even a personalised message on the paper place mat. The menu itself (on the same sheet) is equally international, and might offer an adventurous leek vichyssoise with jellied beef tea and marjoram tempura, magret of duck marinated with ginger and lavender honey served with stir-fried bamboo, bean sprouts, baby corn and sugar peas, or roast pork fillet glazed with gorgonzola and served with soft polenta and smoked tomato-olive stew. Puddings could be lime-chocolate terrine with citrus fruit salad, or apple cobbler with vanilla ice cream and cinnamon sauce. Plenty of New World as well as European wines. Other eating venues include the all-day Court café and the Atrium itself. *Seats 80. Parties 20. L 12.30-2.30 D 6.30-11.30. Set L £12.75. Closed L Sat, all Sun.*

Birmingham	Midland Hotel	68%	£99

Tel 021-643 2601   Fax 021-643 5075

New Street Birmingham West Midlands B2 4JT

H

Map 6 C4

Purpose-built 130 years ago, the Midland was, as we went to press, due to close at the end of 1994 for major refurbishment, part of a £10m New Street development scheme. Reopening is scheduled for September 1996. *Rooms* 111. *Snooker. Closed Christmas period.* AMERICAN EXPRESS *Access, Diners, Visa.*

Birmingham	New Happy Gathering		£35

Tel 021-643 5247   Fax 021-643 4731

43 Station Street Birmingham West Midlands B5 4DY

R

Map 6 C4

The Chan family claims that theirs was the first (1970) Cantonese restaurant in Birmingham, and it can be found a short walk from Chinatown, above street level at the back of New Street Station. A tented fabric ceiling above the staircase and carved wood panels within the restaurant lend an opulent air, while traditional Chinese cuisine holds few surprises on the neatly laid-out menu. Two dozen or more dim sum and a dozen soups lead to meat, fowl and seafood sections with sizzling platters and vegetarian tofu alternatives. Set meals for two or more (set vegetarian meal for single diners); special banquets for six or more, special occasion menu for 2 or 3. *Seats* 90. *Private Room 100. L 12-2 D 5-11.30 (Fri to 12, Sun to 11) Sat all day 12-12. Closed 25 & 26 Dec. Set meals from £10.* AMERICAN EXPRESS *Access, Diners, Visa.*

Birmingham	Novotel	61%	£92

Tel 021-643 2000   Fax 021-643 9796

70 Broad Street Birmingham West Midlands B1 2HT

H

Map 6 C4

Almost next door to the International Convention Centre and the National Indoor Arena, a very modern Novotel with comfortable bedrooms and both leisure and business centres. Children up to 16 stay free in parents' room, breakfast included. Underground car park. Conference facilities for up to 300. No dogs. *Rooms* 148. *Gym, sauna, spa bath.* AMERICAN EXPRESS *Access, Diners, Visa.*

Birmingham	Plough & Harrow	59%	£95

Tel 021-454 4111   Fax 021-454 1868

135 Hagley Road Edgbaston Birmingham West Midlands B16 8LS

H

Map 6 C4

An attractive creeper-covered 17th century building, at the city end of the long Hagley Road, to which a modern bedroom block was added in 1974. Bed linen is splendidly crisp and white and towels large and soft. Bathrooms, though dated, do all have large tubs with showers above and bidets. Public areas (apart from bedroom corridors and it can be quite a trek to some rooms) are much more presentable with the main bar/lounge having plenty of good armchairs and a table spread with magazines. Friendly staff with the receptionists being particularly charming and helpful. Cooked breakfasts come fresh from the kitchen but the cold buffet is rather limited. Ample parking surrounds the hotel but it is not supervised. *Rooms* 44. AMERICAN EXPRESS *Access, Diners, Visa.*

Birmingham	Purple Rooms		£35

Tel 021-702 2193

1076 Stratford Road Hall Green Birmingham West Midlands B28 8AD

R

Map 6 C4

Set at the city end of a shopping parade on a dual carriageway leading through the suburbs towards Shirley. Silver service, the usual hot plates, a floating candle atop the pink-clothed tables, plus fairly-priced Indian and

Bangladeshi food. Sunday self-service buffet. No smoking in the middle dining room. *Seats 70. Private Room 25. L 12-2.30 D 6-12. Closed L Mon-Thu, 25 Dec. Set Lunch L £6.95.* AMERICAN EXPRESS *Access, Diners, Visa.*

Birmingham	**Rajdoot**	**£40**
Tel 021-643 8805		**R**
12 Albert Street Birmingham West Midlands B4 7UD		Map 6 C4

Rajdoot opened in Chelsea in 1966 and claims to be the first to use the tandoori in Europe. In the comfortable, quietly opulent Birmingham branch (as in the other outlets in Bristol, Manchester and Dublin) the clay oven turns out not only good lamb, chicken and prawn dishes but mackerel, quail, lamb's kidneys and vegetable shashlik. Among the curries is lamb and fish 'narial' – an interesting preparation including coconut milk and lemon. *Seats 76. Parties 40. L 12-2.30 D 6.30-11.30. Closed L Sun & Bank Holidays, all 25 & 26 Dec. Set L from £8 Set D from £14.50.* AMERICAN EXPRESS *Access, Diners, Visa.*

> 🍾 is our symbol for an outstanding wine list.

Birmingham	**Royal Alfaisal**	**£25**
Tel 021-449 5695		**R**
136-140 Stoney Lane Sparkbrook Birmingham West Midlands B11 8AQ		Map 6 C4

An all-day balti house where tables are laid, cafeteria-style, with absorbent papers in expectation of diners' dipping into Kashmiri cast-iron dishes with assorted tandoori nan. Breads, baked for five or more, are fully 18 inches across. Unlicensed. Bring your own: no corkage. Free secure parking. Just off the Stratford road (A34). *Seats 120. Parties 35. Private Room 50. Meals noon-midnight.* AMERICAN EXPRESS *Access, Diners, Visa.*

Birmingham	**Royal Angus Thistle**	**65%**	**£103**
Tel 021-236 4211 Fax 021-233 2195			**H**
St Chads Queensway Birmingham West Midlands B4 6HY			Map 6 C4

Modern city-centre hotel alongside the inner ring road, with easy parking. Summery day rooms, good-size bedrooms, up-to-date accessories. Work on a fitness room was due to start after we went to press. *Rooms 133.* AMERICAN EXPRESS *Access, Diners, Visa.*

Birmingham	**Shimla Pinks**	**£50**
Tel 021 633 0366		**R**
214 Broad Street Birmingham West Midlands B15 1AY		Map 6 C4

The cooking is Indian but the decor and atmosphere anything but; one enters into a roomy lounge with widely spaced dark blue sofas, beyond which the dining space is divided between a raised section with leather armchairs around crisply clothed tables and the main area with modernistic metal chairs and unclothed tables. Around the walls are old master paintings – but take a second look, they are not quite what they seem. The menu is more straightforward, with a good variety of well-explained dishes from throughout the sub-continent: karahi dishes from the north; kormas from Ceylon and Kashmir; achari chicken from Uttar Pradesh; chicken Jaipuri; chicken patia – originally from Persia. Dishes are well differentiated with good use of fresh herbs and spices. On Sunday and Monday nights, in addition to the à la carte, there is a 'banquet buffet' (although dishes are actually brought to the table) at £9.95. Shimla Pinks are the Indian version of Sloane Rangers. *Seats 140. L 12-2.30 D 6-11. Closed L Sat & Sun. Set L £6.95.*

Birmingham   Sloans   £60

Tel 021-455 6697   Fax 021-454 4335   **R**

**27 Chad Square Hawthorne Road Edgbaston Birmingham
West Midlands B15 3TQ**   Map 6 C4

Set in a small suburban shopping precinct, this smart, pale green, split-level restaurant is run in exemplary fashion by owner John Narbett and his friendly team. Lunch is a small-choice fixed-price menu of two or three courses, with Simon Booth's cooking based on English and French styles. Dishes are generally reasonably straightforward, shown by game terrine, eggs florentine, mustard-sauced breast of chicken and calf's liver with bacon and creamed potato. The evening carte is lengthier, in a similar vein. Scant New World representation on a mostly French wine list which is quite fairly priced; good selection of French regional and country wines. *Seats 66. L 12-2.15 D 7-10. Closed L Sat, all Sun, Bank Holidays, 1 week Christmas. Set L £11/£14.* AMERICAN EXPRESS *Access, Diners, Visa.*

Birmingham   Strathallan Thistle   63%   £85

Tel 021-455 9777   Fax 021-454 9432   **H**

225 Hagley Road Edgbaston Birmingham West Midlands B16 9RY   Map 6 C4

Circular modern building on the busy A465, very convenient for Edgbaston cricket ground and the International Convention Centre. Flexible conference facilities (up to 200 theatre-style). Easy, mainly covered parking. 24hr room service. ***Rooms** 167.* AMERICAN EXPRESS *Access, Diners, Visa.*

Birmingham   Swallow Hotel   77%   £140

Tel 021-452 1144   Fax 021-456 3442   **HR**

12 Hagley Road Five Ways Birmingham West Midlands B16 8SJ   Map 6 C4

An imposing Edwardian building, strikingly transformed into a quality luxury hotel. The foyer features sparkling Italian marble floors, rich mahogany woodwork and crystal chandeliers; there is a refined drawing room elegantly decorated with oil paintings, a quiet, dignified library and a handsome bar with colourful floral display throughout. The air-conditioned bedrooms are stylish, well-proportioned and comfortable; one room is well equipped for disabled guests. Beautiful fabrics are complemented by fine inlaid furniture and bathrooms are impressive, with marble tiling and a host of extras. An interestingly designed leisure club is based around an Egyptian theme. Attentive, professional staff. Parking for 70 cars. ***Rooms** 98. Indoor swimming pool, gym, spa bath, steam room, solarium, spa bath, hair & beauty salon.* AMERICAN EXPRESS *Access, Diners, Visa.*

Sir Edward Elgar Restaurant   £96

High-class service, personally supervised by deputy general manager Andrew Morgan, fits comfortably into the luxurious surroundings – murals and fine paintings covering the walls, pianist/singer six nights a week – of this split-level, Edwardian-themed restaurant. Luxury is not hard to find on the menu, either, with the likes of a caviar blini accompanying smoked salmon, lobster garnish to roasted Dover sole with a pepper sauce and Provençal herbs, and a bed of foie gras spätzle for the grilled maize-fed chicken. Other dishes might include spaghetti of vegetables and truffles, braised cod with red onions, potatoes and fresh thyme; a duo of veal with a potato and herb millefeuille, and English duck roasted with baby onions, lardons of bacon and small green lentils. In addition to the à la carte and table d'hote menus there is a special £25 post-theatre supper served until 10.45pm by prior arrangement only. Some keenly-priced wines on a list that favours France, but does less justice to other areas. No smoking. *Seats 55. Parties 10. Private Room 20. L 12.30-2.30 D 7.30-10.30. Closed L Sat. Set L £15.50/£19.50 (Sun £17.50) Set D £18.50/£25/£30 & £45.*

Langtry's £60

British cookery to traditional recipes produces daily lunchtime dishes from around the country: Hampshire cottage pie on Wednesday, boiled leg of Welsh mutton with caper sauce on Thursday and east-coast beer-battered cod and chips on Friday. Popular à la carte favourites also include Finnan haddock soup, mixed grill, home-made fruit cake with Lancashire cheese and English trifle. Outdoor seating for 16 in summer. *Seats 60. Parties 14. L 11.30-2.30 D 6.30-10.30. Closed Sun, Bank Holidays.*

Birmingham   Travel Inn £43
L
Tel 021 633 4820   Fax 021 633 4779
20 Bridge Street Birmingham West Midlands B1 2JH   Map 6 C4

Follow signs for ICC (5 minutes' walk) from M6, M5 & M42. Bridge Street is behind Central TV studios. Four meeting rooms for up to 30. *Rooms 54.* AMERICAN EXPRESS *Access, Diners, Visa.*

Birmingham Airport   Forte Posthouse   61% £68
H
Tel 021-782 8141   Fax 021-782 2476
Coventry Road Birmingham Airport Birmingham
West Midlands B26 3QW   Map 6 C4

30s' hotel with a modernised interior, standing on the A45 (take Junction 6 from the M42), one mile from the National Exhibition Centre and seven miles from the city centre. 12 Executive rooms; half the rooms are non-smoking. Conference and banqueting facilities for up to 150. *Rooms 136. Garden, snooker.* AMERICAN EXPRESS *Access, Diners, Visa.*

Birmingham Airport   Novotel   65% £92
H
Tel 021-782 7000   Fax 021-782 0445
Birmingham International Airport Birmingham West Midlands B26 3QL   Map 6 C4

In a prime site opposite the airport's main terminals, this Novotel has sound-proofed bedrooms and stylish day rooms. Major refurbishment was under way as we went to press. Children up to 16 stay free in parents' room. *Rooms 195. Restaurant (6am-midnight).* AMERICAN EXPRESS *Access, Diners, Visa.*

Birmingham   Places of Interest

Convention and Visitor Bureau City Arcade Tel 021-643 2514.
Convention and Visitor Bureau National Exhibition Centre Tel 021-780 4321.
Information Desk Birmingham Airport Tel 021-767 7145/6.
Birmingham Cathedral Tel 021-236 4333.
County Cricket Ground Edgbaston Tel 021-446 4422.
Aston Villa Football Ground Villa Park Tel 021-327 6604.
Ackers Park Trust Dry Ski Slope Small Heath Tel 021-771 4448.
Drayton Manor Park Nr Tamworth Tel 0827 287979.
Birmingham Nature Centre Tel 021-472 7775.
Dudley Zoo Tel 0384 252401.
   Theatres and Concert Halls
Birmingham Hippodrome Hurst Street Tel 021-622 7286.
Birmingham Repertory Theatre Broad Street Tel 021-236 4755.
Crescent Theatre Cumberland Street Tel 021-643 5858.
Midlands Arts Centre Cannon Hill Park Tel 021-440 4221.
City of Birmingham Symphony Orchestra Symphony Hall, International Convention Centre Tel 021-782 8282.
   Historic Houses, Castles and Gardens
Aston Hall Tel 021-327 0062.

Birmingham Botanical Gardens and Glasshouses   Edgbaston Tel 021-454 1860.
Castle Bromwich Hall Gardens   Tel 021-749 4100.
University of Birmingham Botanic Garden   Tel 021-414 5613.
   Museums and Art Galleries
Birmingham Museum and Art Gallery   Tel 021-235 2834.
Black Country Museum   Tipton Road, Dudley Tel 021-557 9643.
Museum of Science and Industry   Tel 021-236 1022.
The Patrick Collection (Autoworld)   Tel 021-459 9111.

Bishop's Tawton	**Halmpstone Manor**	**68%**	**£80**
Tel 0271 830321 Fax 0271 830826			**HR**
Bishop's Tawton Barnstaple Devon EX32 0EA			**Map 13 D2**

Ask directions to find the small 16th-century manor house, which stands
in gardens off a country lane and is at the heart of the Stanburys' working
farm. One is quickly made to feel at home by Jane and Charles' easy
friendliness while unwinding in front of a real fire in the spacious lounge
dotted with family photos and ornaments. There is a homely feel to the
shaggy-carpeted bedrooms too with all sorts of little comforts from fresh
fruit and decanter of sherry to magazines and mineral water along with
good armchairs and settees. Individually decorated in soft colours, rooms
are furnished with a mixture of antique and reproduction pieces; two have
four-poster beds. Bathrooms, two with shower and WC only, boast
bathrobes and generously sized towels. Rooms are properly serviced in the
evenings and excellent breakfasts start the day. No children under 12.
Rooms 5. Garden. Closed Jan. AMERICAN EXPRESS Access, Diners, Visa.

Restaurant   **£70**

First-rate local produce – Jane can probably tell you from which of the
neighbouring farms the lamb or beef on the menu originated – is the
backbone of short but often inventive fixed-price five-course dinners served
by candle-light in the pitch-pine-panelled dining room. Quail breast with
wild mushrooms, crab soufflé, monkfish with a seed mustard sauce and
fillet of beef served with caramelised shallots in a red wine sauce show her
style and range. No smoking. **Seats** 24. Parties 18. Private Room 30.
L by arrangement D 7-9.30. Set D £27.50.

Blackburn	**Moat House**	**58%**	**£65**
Tel 0254 264441 Fax 0254 682435			**H**
Preston New Road Blackburn Lancashire BB2 7BE			**Map 6 B1**

A modern Queens Moat Houses franchise with a distinctive gabled roof
and extensive conference facilities (for up to 350 theatre-style). Bedroom
refurbishment during 1994. **Rooms** 98. AMERICAN EXPRESS Access, Diners, Visa.

Blackburn	**Places of Interest**

Tourist Information   Tel 0254 53277.
Empire Theatre   Tel 0254 698859.
Gawthorpe Hall (NT)   Padiham Tel 0282 78511.
Blackburn Cathedral   Tel 0254 51491.
Blackburn Rovers Football Ground   Ewood Park Tel 0254 55432.
Blackburn Arena   Tel 0254 668686 *Ice Rink.*
Pendle Ski Club   Sabden Tel 0200 23939.
Ski Rossendale   Rawtenstall Tel 0706 228844.
   Museums and Art Galleries
Pendle Heritage Centre   Nelson, Nr Barrowford Tel 0282 695366.
Blackburn Museum and Art Gallery   Museum Street Tel 0254 667130.
**Towneley Hall Art Gallery and Museums and Museums of Local Crafts
   and Industries**   Burnley Tel 0282 24213.
Museum of Childhood   Church Street, Ribchester Tel 0254 878520.

Blackpool   Imperial Hotel   64%   £89

Tel 0253 23971   Fax 0253 751784   **H**

North Promenade Blackpool Lancashire FY1 2HB   Map 6 A1

A degree of Victorian grandeur survives at this Forte Grand hotel
overlooking the sea on the North Promenade. Generally good-sized
bedrooms offer all the usual modern conveniences. Conferences/banqueting
for 550/450. Children up to 14 stay free in parents' room. *Rooms 183.
Indoor swimming pool, keep-fit equipment, sauna, spa bath, steam room,
solarium.* AMERICAN EXPRESS *Access, Diners, Visa.*

Blackpool   Pembroke Hotel   67%   £129

Tel 0253 23434   Fax 0253 27864   **H**

North Promenade Blackpool Lancashire FY1 5JQ   Map 6 A1

A modern conference hotel with recently refurbished facilities for up to
900 delegates (theatre-style) and up to 650 for banqueting. In the main
holiday season families are well catered for, with a playroom, baby-sitting
and a supervised crèche (9am-9pm) as well as a separate children's menu.
A large swimming pool and Springs night club are among the leisure
amenities. The entrance to the large car park (for 328 cars) was being
revamped as we went to press. Metropole Hotels. *Rooms 274. Indoor
swimming pool, sauna, solarium.* AMERICAN EXPRESS *Access, Diners, Visa.*

Blackpool   September Brasserie   £65

Tel 0253 23282   **R**

15-17 Queen Street Blackpool Lancashire FY1 1PU   Map 6 A1

Above a hair studio (run by Pat Wood who moves upstairs to look after
front of house in the evenings) just off the promenade near North Pier, this
small, smart restaurant offers an adventurous menu of dishes all produced
singlehandedly by Michael Golowicz, whose previous experience has taken
in the Savoy and Sydney Opera House. He describes his cooking as 'creative
eclectic', which it certainly is. Trusted local suppliers allow him to produce
menus of great interest and variety, typified by butternut squash broth with
bacon, Jerusalem artichoke and mozzarella mousse on wild mushrooms,
fillet of sea bass with langoustines, couscous of corn-fed guinea fowl and
piccata of Wensleydale wild boar with Emmental and blueberries (dishes
don't come much more original than that!). September's highly individual
style and appeal continues through a helpfully annotated list of organic
wines. *Seats 40. L 12-2.30 D 7-9.30. Closed Sun, Mon, 26 Dec, 2 weeks
summer, 2 weeks winter.* AMERICAN EXPRESS *Access, Diners, Visa.*

Blackpool   Places of Interest

Tourist Information   Clifton Street Tel 0253 21623.
Tourist Information   Coronation Street Tel 0253 21891.
Tower   Tel 0253 22242
Pleasure Beach   Tel 0253 341033
North Pier   Tel 0253 21452
Central Pier   Tel 0253 23422
South Pier   Tel 0253 343096
Chingle Hall   Goosnargh Tel 0772 861082.
Stanley Park   Tel 0253 762341.
Blackpool Icedrome   Tel 0253 41707.
Blackpool Zoo   Tel 0253 65027.
   Theatres and Concert Halls
Winter Gardens and Opera House   Church Street Tel 0253 27786.

Blakeney   Blakeney Hotel   64%   £106

Tel 0263 740797   Fax 0263 740795   **H**
The Quay Blakeney nr Holt Norfolk NR25 7NE   **Map 10 C1**

Blakeney Point is part of the Heritage Coastline, in an area of outstanding
natural beauty, and is owned by the National Trust, so views of it across
the salt marshes from this family-owned-and-run hotel are valued
by conservationists, holidaymakers and business travellers alike. Most
rooms are in the main building but a few are in an annexe, some with
private patios. Back in the main house, one room has a four-poster bed
while all are comfortably furnished and have private bathrooms, TV,
telephone, tea and coffee facilities and a baby-listening service. Banquets and
conferences for up to 120/200. Car parking for 75. *Rooms 60. Garden,
indoor swimming pool, keep-fit equipment, sauna, spa bath, hair salon, snooker.*
AMERICAN EXPRESS *Access, Diners, Visa.*

Blakeney   Manor Hotel   58%   £56

Tel 0263 740376   Fax 0263 741116   **H**
Blakeney nr Holt Norfolk NR25 7ND   **Map 10 C1**

Privately-owned 17th-century former farmhouse on the north coast
of Norfolk, right next to salt marshes and a harbour inlet – ideal for
yachtsmen and bird-watchers. A flagstoned entrance hall leads into day
rooms that include a spacious lounge. Spotless bedrooms with candlewick
bedspreads and simple, white laminate units are arranged in converted
barns and stables around neat courtyards. Charming walled garden with
a seating area and a 400-year-old mulberry tree. No children under 10.
Rooms 37. Garden, bowling green. Closed 3-23 Jan. No credit cards.

Blakeney   Places of Interest

Holkham Hall   Tel 0328 710227.
Walsingham Abbey   Walsingham Tel 0328 820259.

> Many establishments are currently on the market, so ownership could
> change after we go to press.

Blanchland   Lord Crewe Arms   £70

Tel 0434 675251   Fax 0434 675337   **I**
Blanchland nr Consett Co Durham DH8 9SP   **Map 5 D2**

Wild and remote, and some 3 miles below Derwentwater in a deep valley,
Blanchland Abbey can trace its origins back to 1165; despite dissolution
in 1576, the layout of its surrounding village remains unchanged to this
day. At its heart is one of England's finest inns, containing remains of the
abbey lodge and kitchens and set in a cloister garden which is now
an ancient monument. Lord Crewe purchased the entire estate in 1704
from one Tom Forster, a Jacobite adventurer, whose sister Dorothy
is claimed still to be in residence. Bedrooms, needless to say, are splendidly
individual: suitably traditional in the old house with stone mullion
windows and restored fireplaces and mantels, yet up-to-date accessories
from colour TVs to bespoke toiletries and thoughtful extras from mending
kits to complimentary sherry. Altogether more contemporary are the style
and furnishings of rooms in the adjacent Angel Inn, which was once
a Wesleyan Temperance House, a mere newcomer dating from the 1750s.
In private (and caring) hands these last five years, the Lord Crewe Arms
today relives its centuries of pre-eminence. Good, substantial snacks in the
Crypt Bar. Children up to 14 stay free in parents' room. *Rooms 18. Garden.*
AMERICAN EXPRESS *Access, Diners, Visa.*

Blandford Forum   La Belle Alliance   £50

Tel 0258 452842   Fax 0258 480053   **RR**

Whitecliff Mill Street Blandford Forum Dorset DT11 7BP   **Map 14 B4**

Philip and Lauren Davison have owned and run La Belle Alliance for
ten years now, and have established both a strong local following and
a good network of suppliers, especially of fruit and vegetables, and of herbs,
which are grown for them by a neighbour. This attention to detail is also
apparent in the cooking of a range of set-price menus, which might include
such delights as poached quail's eggs on a nest of deep-fried leeks, glazed
with cheese and served with a watercress sauce, roast noisettes of English
lamb with a sauce of lamb stock and rosemary, and a sweet pear tart with
caramelised peach slices a chilled cider sauce. Carefully selected wine list
at fair prices. No smoking in the dining room. *Seats 32. Private Room 40.
L by arrangement only D 7-10. Closed Sun (open Bank Holiday weekend
Sun L), Mon, first 3 weeks Jan. Set D £13.95/£15.95 & £19.95.*
AMERICAN EXPRESS *Access, Visa.*

Rooms   £58

Six well-maintained bedrooms offer good creature comforts in attractive
surroundings.

Blandford Forum   Places of Interest

Tourist Information   Tel 0258 454770.
Royal Signal Museum   Blandford Camp Tel 0258 482248.
Milton Abbey   Milton Abbas Tel 0258 880484.

Blyth   Forte Travelodge   £45

Tel 0909 591775   **L**

Blyth Worksop Nottinghamshire   **Map 7 D2**

On the A1 southbound, 10 miles south of Doncaster. *Rooms 32.*
AMERICAN EXPRESS *Access, Diners, Visa.*

Blyth   Granada Lodge   £51

Tel 0909 591836   Fax 0909 591831   **L**

A1(M)/A614 Blyth Nottinghamshire S82 8HG   **Map 7 D2**

Rooms 39. **AMERICAN EXPRESS** *Access, Diners, Visa.*

Blyth   Places of Interest

Hodsock Priory   Tel 0909 591204.

Bodymoor Heath   Marston Farm   65%   £85

Tel 0827 872133   Fax 0827 875043   **H**

Dog Lane Bodymoor Heath nr Sutton Coldfield Warwickshire B76 9JD   **Map 6 C4**

Ten minutes' drive from Birmingham Airport and the NEC, Marston
Farm, set in 9 acres and beside the Fazeley canal, is just off Junction 9 of the
M42: follow signs to Kingsbury and Bodymoor Heath. A 17th-century
farmhouse forms the main body of the hotel, deriving both character and
intimacy from oak beams and inglenook fireplaces. In a converted barn are
20 uniform bedrooms and a boardroom with conference accommodation
for up to 45 and banqueting space for 110 (theatre-style 50). Satellite
TV now installed in bedrooms. Children free when sharing parents' room.
Greatly reduced rates at weekends. *Rooms 37. Garden, croquet, tennis,
fishing.* **AMERICAN EXPRESS** *Access, Diners, Visa.*

Bognor Regis   Royal Norfolk   60%   £70

Tel 0243 826222   Fax 0243 826325   **H**

The Esplanade Bognor Regis West Sussex PO21 2LH   **Map 11 A6**

With sea views and its own three acres of gardens, the hotel dates from the 1830s and has played host to visiting royalty throughout the years. Bedrooms, in various styles, are generally bright and pleasant. Forte Heritage. *Rooms 51. Garden.* AMERICAN EXPRESS *Access, Diners, Visa.*

Bollington   Mauro's   £60

Tel 0625 573898   **R**

88 Palmerston Street Bollington nr Macclesfield Cheshire SK10 5PW   **Map 6 C2**

The Mauro family run an authentic north Italian restaurant with a feast of flavours in the *antipasti alla caprese*, served from a trolley. Home-made noodles and ravioli are served several ways and market-fresh fish heads a list of daily specials. Lighter dishes on a good-value, 3-course lunch menu; open for Sunday lunch (£14.75) only on the first Sunday of the month. Exclusively Italian wines, as one might expect. *Seats 50. L 12-2 (Sat to 1.30) D 7-10 (Sat to 10.30). Closed Sun (see above) & Mon, 25 & 26 Dec, 3 weeks Aug/Sep. Set L £8.75.* AMERICAN EXPRESS *Access, Visa.*

Bolton   Beaumont Hotel   58%   £68

Tel 0204 651511   Fax 0204 61064   **H**

Beaumont Road Bolton Greater Manchester BL3 4TA   **Map 6 B2**

Modern hotel on the outskirts of Bolton, near Junction 5 of the M61. Two-level bedroom block. Conference/banqueting facilities for 120/90. Tariff reductions at weekends. Previously the Posthouse, now World of Forte brand. *Rooms 96. Garden, children's play area.* AMERICAN EXPRESS *Access, Diners, Visa.*

Bolton   Egerton House   63%   £88

Tel 0204 307171   Fax 0204 593030   **H**

off Blackburn Road Egerton Bolton Lancashire BL7 9PL   **Map 6 B2**

Victorian house set among trees and lawns just off the A666. Bright, comfortable lounge and bar, bedrooms graded either standard or superior. Guests have free use of the leisure facilities at the *Last Drop Village Hotel*, two minutes drive away. A self-contained function suite includes the Barn, catering for up to 150 delegates. Free bed and breakfast for under-12s. Owned by Macdonald Hotels since autumn 1993. Ample parking. *Rooms 32. Garden.* AMERICAN EXPRESS *Access, Diners, Visa.*

Bolton   Last Drop Village Hotel   68%   £88

Tel 0204 591131   Fax 0204 304122   **H**

Hospital Road Bromley Cross Bolton Lancashire BL7 9PZ   **Map 6 B2**

About 30 years ago, a collection of 18th-century moorland farm buildings was skilfully turned into a village with cottages, gardens, craft shops, a pub, a tea shop and, at its heart, a comfortable and well-equipped hotel (now owned by the McDonald group). Day rooms retain some original features, while bedrooms are mainly bright and modern with all the expected amenities. Children up to 12 stay free in parents' room. There are extensive conference facilities (in a choice of rooms) for up to 200 delegates. The hotel is well signed from the A666. *Rooms 83. Indoor swimming pool, gym, sauna, steam room, spa bath, squash, beauty and hair salons, coffee shop (10am-5.30pm).* AMERICAN EXPRESS *Access, Diners, Visa.*

Bolton — Pack Horse Hotel — 62% — £65

Tel 0204 27261   Fax 0204 364352   **H**

Nelson Square Bradshawgate Bolton Greater Manchester BL1 1DP   Map 6 B2

Redbrick building in the town centre, with comfortable accommodation,
cheerful bars and a thriving conference business (six rooms handling
up to 275 delegates). Children up to 14 stay free in parents' room. De Vere.
Rooms 72. AMERICAN EXPRESS *Access, Diners, Visa.*

Bolton — Places of Interest

Tourist Information   Tel 0204 364333.
Little Theatre   Hanover Street Tel 0204 24469.
Octagon Theatre   Howell Croft, South Bolton Tel 0294 20661.

Bolton Abbey — Devonshire Arms — 74% — £120

Tel 0756 710441   Fax 0756 710564   **H**

Bolton Abbey nr Skipton North Yorkshire BD23 6AJ   Map 6 C1

Traditional standards of hospitality are maintained at a much-extended
18th-century coaching inn which since 1753 has been in the hands of the
Dukes and Duchesses of Devonshire. Set in 12 acres of grounds in an area
of outstanding natural beauty, it is furnished and appointed with much
thought. Well-proportioned day rooms feature choice antiques and oil
paintings from the Devonshire family home of Chatsworth in Derbyshire.
The best bedrooms, in the main house, are individually themed and again
show carefully chosen furnishings and fabrics. Numerous little extras like
a decanter of sherry, magazines and flowers are a welcoming touch. The
majority of bedrooms in more recent wings are more uniform in size and
style, though they are equally inviting and comfortable. Good breakfasts
in the bar. Children up to 12 stay free in parents' room. Parking for 150
cars. Hotel residents have automatic membership of the latest feature,
a health, beauty and fitness centre which opened early in 1994. *Rooms 40.*
Garden, croquet, indoor swimming pool, all-weather tennis, spa bath, steam room,
solarium, gym, beauty therapy room, hairdressing salon, fishing.
AMERICAN EXPRESS *Access, Diners, Visa.*

Bonchurch — Winterbourne Hotel — 64% — £86

Tel 0983 852535   Fax 0983 853056   **H**

Bonchurch Isle of Wight PO38 1RQ   Map 15 D4

Charles Dickens wrote most of *David Copperfield* here, and the bedrooms
are named after characters in the novel. The setting is one of great charm,
with waterfalls in the garden and lovely sea views. Inside is no less
appealing, and the main day room has French windows opening on to the
terrace and garden. Bedrooms, most with sea views, vary considerably
in size and appointments, the best perhaps being five in the converted coach
house. Bonchurch is near Ventnor, on the southern tip of the island.
Rooms 19. Garden, outdoor swimming pool. Closed Nov-Feb. AMERICAN EXPRESS
Access, Diners, Visa.

Boreham Street — White Friars Hotel — 57% — £69

Tel 0323 832355   Fax 0323 833882   **H**

Boreham Street nr Herstmonceux East Sussex BN27 4SE   Map 11 B6

Built in 1721, and converted to a hotel in the 1920s; new owners took
over here in 1994. Day rooms and some bedrooms have old-fashioned
charm, complete with four-posters; nine rooms are in a separate cottage
block. Characterful, beamed conference room for up to 30 delegates
(banquets for 60). Two acres of gardens. The Cellar Bar was due to be
opened separately as a pub. *Rooms 20. Garden.* AMERICAN EXPRESS *Access,*
Diners, Visa.

Boroughbridge	The Crown	63%	£50

Tel 0423 322328   Fax 0423 324512

Horsefair Boroughbridge North Yorkshire YO5 9LB

H

Map 5 E4

Once a famous coaching inn, with stabling for more than 100 horses, now a comfortable hotel with conference facilities for 200 delegates. Smart day rooms include a oak dado-panelled reception/lounge and a bar. Ample car parking. Children up to 12 stay free in parents' room. *Rooms 42.* AMERICAN EXPRESS *Access, Diners, Visa.*

Borrowdale	Borrowdale Hotel	60%	£92*

Tel 076 87 77224   Fax 076 87 77338

Borrowdale Keswick-on-Derwentwater Cumbria CA12 5UY

H

Map 4 C3

A stone's throw from Derwentwater, three miles from Keswick on the B5289, stands a solid, greystone hotel whose style of hospitality resists change. Lovely enclosed garden overlooked by a bar and patio: chintz lounges with winter log fires, lake views and quiet, professional service. Free golf Mon-Fri at Keswick golf course. *Half-board terms only. *Rooms 34. Garden, children's playground. Closed 9 Jan to 6 Feb. Garden. Access, Visa.*

Borrowdale	Stakis Lodore Swiss Hotel	71%	£150*

Tel 07687 77285   Fax 07687 77343

Borrowdale Keswick Cumbria CA12 5UX

H

Map 4 C3

Holiday hotel set in 40 acres by Derwentwater; good family facilities and convenient for Keswick ferry ($\frac{1}{2}$ mile) and town ($3\frac{1}{2}$ miles). Picture windows afford splendid views from day rooms and the best, front-facing Club bedrooms. Several splendid family rooms (children are charged according to age; 6-16s £43 per night); daytime nursery open all year round; indoor children's play room and outdoor playground. The indoor swimming pool was being converted into a leisure centre as we went to press and the outdoor pool is no longer in use. Conference/banqueting facilities for 75. Free golf at Keswick golf club. No dogs in the hotel or garden. *Half-board terms only. *Rooms 70. Garden, gym, squash, sauna, steam room, solarium, sun bed, tennis, games room, nursery.* AMERICAN EXPRESS *Access, Diners, Visa.*

Bosham	Millstream Hotel	63%	£99

Tel 0243 573234   Fax 0243 573459

Bosham Lane Bosham West Sussex PO18 8HL

H

Map 15 D4

Part small manor house, part 18th-century malthouse, the peaceful Millstream is an attractive small hotel just a short walk from the heart of a picturesque sailing village, four miles from Chichester. A rattan-furnished bar and sunny lounge are agreeable places for a drink or a chat, as is the front lawn, past which the stream runs. Bedrooms, mostly furnished with reproduction antiques, include mini-safes and bathroom scales among their accessories; one room features a four-poster and some rooms boast jacuzzis. *Rooms 29. Garden.* AMERICAN EXPRESS *Access, Diners, Visa.*

Botley	Cobbett's		£65

Tel 0489 782068

15 The Square Botley Southampton Hampshire SO3 2EA

R

Map 15 D4

The whole menu is now on a set-price basis at Charles and Lucie Skipwith's delightful restaurant in an old timber-framed cottage. Lucie is a native of Bordeaux, and her roots are reflected in her French regional cuisine. The choice changes monthly. Poultry liver terrine served with a tomato and beetroot vinaigrette, broccoli mousseline with a Brie centre and poached salmon set in *sauce gribiche* are typical starters, while *plats principaux* could include roasted spring chicken sauced with ginger and pineapple, veal escalope *au pistou*, or sirloin steak flamed with brandy and topped with a knob of Stilton butter. The fish dish of the day (consult the slate in the bar) depends on the haul of the local boats. Finish in style with the *'symphonie de desserts* – a plate set with a cascade of tasters'* (supplement £5.50). ***Seats*** 40. *Private Room 14. L 12-2 D 7.30-10. Closed L Mon & Sat, all Sun, Bank Holidays, 2 weeks summer, 2 weeks winter. Set L & D £18.50/£23. Access, Visa.*

Boughton Monchelsea	**Tanyard Hotel**	**63%**	**£80**
Tel 0622 744705 Fax 0622 741998			**HR**
Wierton Hill Boughton Monchelsea nr Maidstone Kent ME17 4JT			**Map 11 C5**

From the B2163 at Boughton, turn down Park Lane opposite the Cock pub. Take the first right down Wierton Lane then fork right, and the Tanyard is on the left at the bottom of the hill. Once safely arrived you'll be subject to the caring attention of owner Jan Davies and enjoy beautiful views over the Kenton Weald. As the name suggests, the building was once a tannery, though it now operates as a cosy, charming small hotel with a house party atmosphere. The building itself still displays some original 14th-century beams both inside and out, as well as uneven floors and exposed brickwork. No children under six. No dogs. ***Rooms*** *6. Garden. Closed 2 weeks Jan.* AMERICAN EXPRESS *Access, Diners, Visa.*

Restaurant   £60

There are plenty of genuine or imitation Tudor rooms serving as restaurants: this one is model of how it should be done. The stone walls are unencumbered by unsuitable prints or other spurious decoration between the timbers. There are no superfluous drapes ruining the windows or wall-to-wall carpets hiding the flagstones. Furniture is simple. The cooking from Kevin Lea is contemporary in style and generous. Typical starters might be polenta, plum tomatoes, roast peppers and mozzarella baked and served with a baby spinach salad or cream of carrot and coriander soup. Main courses could be rack of lamb with mint and Madeira sauce or roast wood pigeon with cabbage and juniper sauce. For dessert you might find gooseberry crumble with lemon balm sauce or a terrine of milk, white and bitter chocolate. Flavours are thought through and nicely balanced. Service is friendly. ***Seats*** *30. L 12-2 D 7-9. Closed L Sat, all Sun & Mon. Set L £12.50/£15.50 Set D £23.*

Bournemouth	**Carlton Hotel**	**78%**	**£120**
Tel 0202 552011 Fax 0202 299573			**H**
East Overcliff Bournemouth Dorset BH1 3DN			**Map 14 C4**

A luxurious, well-run hotel of Edwardian origin, with independent status. Welcoming staff greet guests with a smile and the smart foyer sets the tone for the public areas; a walnut and mahogany-panelled library houses volumes of leather-bound books, cabinets filled with antiques and objets d'art, a bracket clock, and comfortable armchairs; a cocktail bar with leather chairs contains framed pencil sketches of the famous and antique mirrors; there's also a bright lounge which leads on to a sunny conservatory. Most of the suites and bedrooms have views of the coastline and bathrooms are designed to pamper. There's a health spa, a heated outdoor pool, and a games room with a full-size snooker table. The hotel has plenty of free covered car parking space. Conference/banqueting for 160/120. Children up to 14 stay free in parents' room. ***Rooms*** *70. Garden, outdoor swimming pool, gym, sauna, steam room, sun beds, beauty & hair salon, games room, snooker, boutique.* AMERICAN EXPRESS *Access, Diners, Visa.*

Bournemouth   Chine Hotel   65%   £85

Tel 0202 396234   Fax 0202 391737   **H**
Boscombe Spa Road Bournemouth Dorset BH5 1AX   **Map 14 C4**

In a fine position overlooking Poole Bay to the south, the 1874-built Chine
has benefited from the same conscientious family ownership since 1945.
Large bedrooms, nearly half with private balcony or patio, have light-oak
units and a pleasing pale-green colour scheme. Spacious public areas include
a cocktail bar open-plan to the large restaurant and a cosy residents' lounge
overlooking the pine-fringed outdoor swimming pool; landscaped gardens
extend down one side of the Boscombe Chine Gardens to the esplanade and
pier below. Business people are attracted by a number of well-equipped
conference rooms (in an adjacent building) and families appreciate the
playroom, games room, coin-operated laundry room and, during school
holidays, a children's activities organiser. Children up to 12 stay free
in parents' room. No dogs. Sister hotels are the *Haven* and *Sandbanks*
at nearby Poole. ***Rooms*** *97. Garden, outdoor & indoor swimming pool, sauna,
solarium, putting, games room.* AMERICAN EXPRESS *Access, Diners, Visa.*

Bournemouth   Langtry Manor   62%   £79

Tel 0202 553887   Fax 0202 290115   **H**
26 Derby Road East Cliff Bournemouth Dorset BH1 3QB   **Map 14 C4**

Built in 1877 for Lillie Langtry by Edward VII, when Prince of Wales, this
romantic manor is full of memorabilia of that heady era. Some suites
in particular recall the attachment – the Edward VII, the Jersey Lily, the
Lillie Langtry – and playing fair there's also an Alexandra suite! All suites
and rooms are individually decorated and furnished (a few are in the lodge
annexe). Further refurbishment and rationalisation of the smaller rooms
will ensure a maintenance of standards. ***Rooms*** *25. Garden.* AMERICAN EXPRESS
Access, Diners, Visa.

Bournemouth   Norfolk Royale   70%   £138

Tel 0202 551521   Fax 0202 299729   **H**
Richmond Hill Bournemouth Dorset BH2 6EN   **Map 14 C4**

The Norfolk Royale's splendid two-tier cast-iron verandah looks proudly
over the town, a testament to Bournemouth's Edwardian heyday. Twin
conservatories – one housing the pool and the other part of the all-day
Orangery restaurant (recently revamped) extend into the pretty garden
to the rear and several interconnecting rooms provide plenty of lounge/bar
space. Pretty, well-maintained bedrooms and good bathrooms. Four rooms
are reserved for non-smokers, others are equipped for lady travellers, yet
more are adapted for the disabled. Valet parking for 88 cars is a big plus
given the hotel's central location. Well-motivated staff. No dogs.
Banqueting/conferences for up to 100. ***Rooms*** *95. Indoor swimming pool,
sauna, spa bath, steam room.* AMERICAN EXPRESS *Access, Diners, Visa.*

Bournemouth   Ocean Palace   £45

Tel 0202 559127   Fax 0202 559130   **R**
8 Priory Road Bournemouth Dorset BH2 5DG   **Map 14 C4**

Behind the Bournemouth International Conference Centre and not far
from the seafront, this modern restaurant has a conservatory-style frontage,
simple decor and plain walls hung with contemporary Chinese artwork.
Hing Wong's cooking skills cover Peking and Szechuan styles, with special
vegetarian and seafood menus. Nearly 200 dishes on the menu including
popular sizzling dishes. ***Seats*** *150. Private Room 60. L 12-2.15 D 6-11.15.
Set L from £5.95 Set D from £14. Closed 3 days Christmas.* AMERICAN EXPRESS
Access, Diners, Visa.

Bournemouth   Palace Court   71%   £118

Tel 0202 557681   Fax 0202 554981   **H**

Westover Road Bournemouth Dorset BH1 2BZ   Map 14 C4

A high-rise hotel restored to its original between-the-wars splendour.
Spacious public areas are in 1930s' style: the front lounge with leather
armchairs in pale yellow and pale pink and the split-level lounge/bar on the
first floor in darker, more sophisticated tones. Conservatory-style windows
take advantage of views across the Solent to the Isle of Wight. A further
café/lounge has rattan furniture and ceiling fans slowly swishing overhead.
Decor in the bedrooms varies, but all have freestanding furniture, many
with walnut veneer pieces, and smartly-tiled bathrooms. Eight de luxe
rooms live up to their name with mirrored bedheads (containing cassette
players as well as radios) and bathrooms with spa baths, private mini-saunas
and exercise bicycles. Rooms at the front have balconies with outdoor
seating. Children up to 14 share parents' room free. 24hr room service can
provide hot meals even in the middle of the night. Conference/banqueting
facilities for 200/250 in 32 rooms. Ample garage parking (minimal charge)
and a car rental office. No dogs. *Rooms 110. Indoor swimming pool, gym, spa
baths, sauna, solarium, hair salon, café-bar (10am-11pm), night club.*
AMERICAN EXPRESS *Access, Diners, Visa.*

Bournemouth   Roundhouse Hotel   59%   £68

Tel 0202 553262   Fax 0202 557698   **H**

The Lansdowne Bournemouth Dorset BH1 2PR   Map 14 C4

Formerly a Forte Posthouse, this aptly named hotel is a circular building
on three floors above a spiral car park. Practical modern bedrooms and
roomy open-plan public areas. Conferences for up to 100. *Rooms 98.*
AMERICAN EXPRESS *Access, Diners, Visa.*

Bournemouth   Royal Bath Hotel   73%   £115

Tel 0202 555555   Fax 0202 554158   **HR**

Bath Road Bournemouth Dorset BH1 2EW   Map 14 C4

A splendid Victorian hotel combining traditional values (courteous and
helpful staff for example) and modern amenities such as the marvellous
Leisure Pavilion (opened in 1988) which features a heated kidney-shaped
swimming pool. There are also versatile conference facilities; the largest
of the seven rooms has a capacity of 500. The hotel stands in an
immaculately kept three-acre garden with clifftop views out to sea, enjoyed
by many of the bedrooms (some with terraces) which vary in style and size
but are all smartly furnished with good bathrooms that have large mirrors
and decent-sized towels. Excellent housekeeping, including a turn-down
service at night, is evident throughout. The vast public areas (bars and
lounges) are comfortable and well appointed, and breakfast in the Garden
Restaurant will not disappoint. Children up to the age of 14 years free
in parents' room. Supervised crèche daily in high season. Covered parking
for 70 cars. No dogs. De Vere Hotels. *Rooms 131. Garden, croquet, indoor
swimming pool, gym, sauna, spa bath, steam room, solarium, beauty & hair
salon, putting, snooker, children's playground, garage.* AMERICAN EXPRESS *Access,
Diners, Visa.*

Restaurant   £60

The Garden Restaurant is only open in the evenings and for Sunday lunch,
offering a cuisine with English, French and International inspiration.
Oscar's, a more intimate setting with Oscar Wilde memorabilia all round,
offers a French-orientated carte and set menus, which at lunchtime include
a roast carved from the trolley. *Garden: Seats 260. L (Sun only) 12.30-2.15
D 7-9.15. Set L £16.50 Set D £24. Oscar's: Seats 60. L 12.30-2.15
D 7-10.15.*

Bournemouth   Swallow Highcliff Hotel   70%   £120

Tel 0202 557702   Fax 0202 292734

St Michael's Road West Cliff Bournemouth Dorset BH2 5DU

H

Map 14 C4

An imposing Victorian hotel with a splendid clifftop location giving many of the rooms fine marine views. A funicular lift carries guests from hotel to promenade. Good-sized bedrooms in the main house have dark period-style furniture, those in the converted coastguard cottages smart lightwood pieces. Numerous public rooms include a terrace bar, a lounge for non-smokers and a night club. Magnificent conference facilities can cope with up to 450 delegates. Excellent family facilities in summer include a fenced-in outdoor play area and a creche. *Rooms 157. Garden, outdoor swimming pool, sauna, solarium, tennis, putting, games room, snooker.* AMERICAN EXPRESS *Access, Diners, Visa.*

Bournemouth   Places of Interest

Tourist Information   Westover Road Tel 0202 789789.
Pavilion Theatre   Westover Road Tel 0202 297297.
Pier Theatre   Bournemouth Pier Tel 0202 20250.
Westover Ice Rink   Tel 0202 293011.
Bournemouth, Christchurch (Friars Cliff), Hengistbury Beaches.

Bourton-on-the-Water   Dial House   61%   £79

Tel 0451 22244

The Chestnuts High Street Bourton-on-the-Water
Gloucestershire GL54 2AN

H

Map 14 C1

Built as a farmhouse in 1698 and converted to a hotel in 1989, Dial House stands opposite the middle bridge across the River Windrush. Lynn and Peter Boxall have carefully enhanced the interior with family antiques and understated decor adds to the charm of buildings and contents. Downstairs is the lounge with inglenooks, leather sofas and plentiful reading matter, upstairs bedrooms that include some with half-testers or four-posters. Four of the rooms overlook the garden. No children under eight. *Rooms 10. Garden, croquet.* AMERICAN EXPRESS *Access, Visa.*

Bowness-on-Windermere   Belsfield Hotel   62%   £108

Tel 053 94 42448   Fax 053 94 46397

Kendal Road Bowness-on-Windermere Cumbria LA23 3EL

H

Map 4 C3

There are splendid views from this hilltop Victorian building set in six acres of gardens, overlooking Lake Windermere, Bowness landing piers and the Belle Isle beyond. Accommodation ranges from singles to suites and family rooms (some with bunk beds, others with adjoining child's room). Lake view rooms attract a supplement. Good leisure facilities – the pool sports a sliding roof to take advantage of sunny days. On Saturday nights there's a dinner dance. Forte Heritage. *Rooms 64. Garden, indoor swimming pool, sauna, solarium, tennis, putting, snooker.* AMERICAN EXPRESS *Access, Diners, Visa.*

Bowness-on-Windermere   Gilpin Lodge   64%   £80

Tel 053 94 88818   Fax 053 94 88058

Crook Road Bowness-on-Windermere Cumbria LA23 3NE

HR

Map 4 C3

The Cunliffes' ancestral Lakeland home (set in 20 acres on the B5284 between Bowness and Kendal) offers a winning combination of warm welcome, home comforts and personal service. There's a wealth of books on gardening, cookery and Lakeland walks at both fireside and bedside and an abundance of floral displays, both fresh and dried. Cane chairs, pine furnishings, close-carpeted bathrooms and corner baths contribute to a cosseted feel. Not suitable for children under nine. Guests have free membership of the nearby Parkwood Country Club. No dogs. *Rooms 9. Garden, croquet, helipad.* AMERICAN EXPRESS *Access, Diners, Visa.*

Restaurant £60

Lunchtime is à la carte (fixed-price Sunday) while dinner brings a fixed-price five-course menu with plenty of choice. Christine Cunliffe and Christopher Davies combine classic skills with contemporary touches: rosette of salmon with a confit of chicory on a lemon and orange jus, caramelised onion and black pudding *tarte fine* on a shallot and mustard jus, roast duckling with a sesame, honey and Grand Marnier sauce, crepes Suzette, hot sticky fig and date pudding with an orange toffee sauce. Also lighter lounge lunches Mon-Sat. Courteous, attentive service. Fairly priced wine list. No smoking. *Seats 45. Parties 22. Private Room 16. L 12-2.30 D 7-8.45. Set L (Sun) £14 Set D £26.*

Bowness-on-Windermere   Linthwaite House   72% £110

Tel 053 94 88600   Fax 053 94 88601 **HR**

Bowness-on-Windermere Cumbria LA23 3JA   Map 4 C3

High standards of service combine with an amenable, unstuffy attitude in a hotel that enjoys an unsurpassed location on the B5284. With views of Lake Windermere and beyond to the Old Man of Coniston, Linthwaite's environment is conducive to relaxation with a unique, lived-in interior design which sees, for instance, old leather suitcases converted into practical coffee tables. Some smaller bedrooms' dimensions are similarly redeemed by Amanda Rosa's stylish interiors, with hand-made pine dressers and vanitory units providing the unifying theme; some rooms have lake views (room rates vary according to size and position). The best bathrooms, fully carpeted and brightly lit, feature mahogany panels and strong pulse showers. Free use of nearby leisure spa with pool, spa bath, sauna, steam room, squash and gym. No dogs. *Rooms 18. Garden, croquet, putting, practice golf hole, fly fishing. Closed 1 week after New Year.* AMERICAN EXPRESS *Access, Diners, Visa.*

Restaurant £68

Warming candle-light and polished mahogany tables create an intimate atmosphere for enjoying some very capable cooking in the modern British style. Speciality dishes include feuilleté of lamb's kidneys and shallots in a cognac sauce, cream of tomato and pimento soup, and paupiette of guinea fowl filled with a mousseline of walnuts and Brie presented on a pool of garlic and lemon sauce. There's always a vegetarian main course, and a selection of fine British cheeses is an alternative to desserts such as warm almond jalousie complemented by an Amaretto custard, or maple syrup ice cream in a brandy snap basket surrounded by a bitter chocolate sauce. Dinner comprises four courses plus canapés and coffee with petits fours. Lunches other than Sunday by arrangement, though soup and sandwiches are available during the week. The wine list is presented by style (dry crisp white, full red etc.) and not particularly easy to follow, though tasting notes help. Plenty of half bottles. No smoking. *Seats 48. Parties 8. Private Room 22. L (Sun) 12-1.30 D 7.15-9. Set Sun L £10.95 Set D £27.*

Bowness-on-Windermere   Old England Hotel   65% £126

Tel 053 94 42444   Fax 053 94 43432 **H**

Church Street Bowness-on-Windermere Cumbria LA23 3DF   Map 4 C3

Comfortable Georgian mansion with gardens rolling down to the lake where there is a private jetty for the hotel's motor boat (for hire by the hour) and for guests' rowing boats. The best rooms have lake views. 24 rooms are reserved for non-smokers, some are suitable for family use. Popular for conferences and banquets (up to 120) as well as holidaymakers. Forte Heritage. *Rooms 79. Garden, outdoor swimming pool, sauna, solarium, hairdressing, snooker, jetty.* AMERICAN EXPRESS *Access, Diners, Visa.*

Bracknell   Coppid Beech Hotel   72%   £125

HR

Tel 0344 303333   Fax 0344 301200

John Nike Way Bracknell Berkshire RG12 8TF

Map 15 E2

Of striking Swiss chalet design, the privately-owned Coppid Beech
is Berkshire's newest and largest hotel. A unique feature of the interior
is a triangular shaft extending to the full height of the building, lined with
aquaria (the largest in Europe apparently) and mirrors creating
a mesmerising, watery kaleidoscope. Extensive facilities include a lively
Bierkeller with live entertainment several nights a week, plush state-of-the-
art disco night club and Waves health and fitness centre. Well-thought-out
bedrooms (a significant number are full or junior suites) are well equipped
– there's even an account review and check-out facility available via the
advanced TV system – with large, comfortable beds. 24 hr room service
is extensive and beds are turned down at night. Children up to 16 share
parents' room free; youngsters are made to feel at home with the Bobby
Beech Nut club. Conference/banqueting facilities for 400/250. *Rooms 205.
Indoor swimming pool, gym, spa bath, sauna, solarium, steam room, dry ski slope,
ice rink, play area.* AMERICAN EXPRESS *Access, Diners, Visa.*

Rowans Restaurant   £70

A large, solidly comfortable restaurant with a menu that takes its
inspiration from a variety of European cuisines: gazpacho, creamed onion
soup, seared scallops on oxtail gravy, saltimbocca of monkfish with peppers
and creamed lobster gravy, loin of lamb niçoise, plain grills and a daily
roast carved from a trolley at lunchtime. Inventive vegetarian options
(blancmange of avocado with tomato salsa, potato lentil gateau with red
pimento cream). Desserts are chosen from a buffet display. Good choice
of British cheeses. Fair prices on a concise and interesting wine list that has
a good showing of well-chosen New World wines to balance the European
content. *Seats 125. Parties 8. Private Room 30. L 12-2.30 (Sun to 3)
D 6-10.30 (Sun 6.30-10). Set L £14.50 (Sun £15.95) Set D £22.50.*

Bracknell   Hilton National   69%   £127

H

Tel 0344 424801   Fax 0344 487454

Bagshot Road Bracknell Berkshire RG12 3QJ

Map 15 E2

In the heart of busy Bracknell, a modern hotel handy for the M3 (Junction
3) and M4 (Junction 10). Public areas have recently been refurbished;
bedrooms are due for the same treatment shortly. Large conference and
banqueting facilities for up to 400. Children up to 14 free in parents' room.
Rooms 167. Garden, keep-fit equipment, sauna, spa bath, coffee shop (24hrs).
AMERICAN EXPRESS *Access, Diners, Visa.*

Bracknell   Places of Interest

Tourist Information   Tel 0344 423149.
South Hill Park Arts Centre and Wilde Theatre   Tel 0344 472272.
John Nike Leisuresport Complex   Tel 0344 860033 *Ice Rink.*
Bracknell Ski Centre   Tel 0344 427435 *Dry Ski Slope.*

Bradford   Nawaab   £30

R

Tel 0274 720371

32 Manor Row Bradford West Yorkshire BD1 4QE

Map 6 C1

Set in a former banking house, atop Manor Row, with mushroom-
coloured walls and an ornamental elephant. The extensive Pakistani menu
covers tandoori specialities, balti dishes and around eight basic varieties
of curry. Chef's specialities include *machli makoni* (haddock, cream, cashew
nuts, coconut, pineapple), and several composite dishes – *nawaabi-e-khas*

comprises lamb, chicken, prawns, king prawns and chick peas. *Seats 120.
L 12-2 D 6-12 (Fri & Sat to 1.30am). Closed L Sat.* AMERICAN EXPRESS ®
Access, Visa.

Bradford   Restaurant 19   ★   £70
Tel 0274 492559   Fax 0274 483827   **RR**
19 North Park Road Heaton Bradford West Yorkshire BD9 4NT   Map 6 C1

It is for ten years now that chef Stephen Smith and partner Robert
Barbour, who looks after the front of house, have operated a splendid
restaurant with rooms in a quiet residential suburb north-west of the city
centre. The substantial Victorian town house stands on a corner
overlooking Lister Park. Both the bar and two candlelit dining rooms have
recently been beautifully redecorated – the bar in summery shades of blue
and gold, the dining rooms brightened with re-upholstered seats. The fine
collection of Russell Flint prints remain. The fixed-price four-course menus
change almost daily and consist of a choice of four starters, a soup, four
main dishes and four desserts or cheese. The selection is of modern, well-
balanced dishes with the emphasis very much on flavours and lightness.
Fashionable ingredients are skilfully combined, as in a starter of gently
poached salmon with tagliatelle, spring onions and a herby olive oil
dressing or locally smoked beef sirloin with a rocket salad, truffle oil and
Parmesan shavings. The soup course is served from a tureen brought to the
table, creamy fennel and courgette being a typical example. Main dishes are
wonderfully satisfying as in a plump breast of chicken neatly wrapped
in Parma ham and accompanied by cheesy sautéed polenta and a rissole
of the leg with sun-dried tomatoes and basil, crab cakes with a roulade
of Provençal vegetables and a pistachio and mint salsa, fillet of sea bass with
lemon grass and spring vegetables. These precede deliciously simple desserts
such as a chocolate parfait with sliced poached pear and a wickedly rich,
very dark hot chocolate sauce, rhubarb crumble, lemon tart or an apple
and calvados crème brulée with an apple sorbet. *Seats 36. Parties 12. L by
arrangement D 7-9.30 (Sat to 10.30). Closed Sun, 2 weeks Dec/Jan, 2 weeks
Sept. Set D £26.* AMERICAN EXPRESS ® *Access, Diners, Visa.*

Rooms   £70

The four bedrooms, furnished with cheerful, colourful chintzes and
antiques are supremely comfortable and well equipped. Bathrooms, with
top of the range fittings, are bright and spacious. Service has that
welcoming, homely touch that makes a stay here so much preferable
to larger establishments. Breakfasts are superb with requirements perfectly
met.

Bradford   Novotel   60%   £143
Tel 0274 683683   Fax 0274 651342   **H**
Merrydale Road Bradford West Yorkshire BD4 6SA   Map 6 C1

A faceless modern exterior houses comfortable and smart accommodation.
Conference/banqueting facilities for 300/180. Free parking for 200 cars.
Children up to 16 stay free in parents' room. *Rooms 131. Garden, outdoor
swimming pool.* AMERICAN EXPRESS ® *Access, Diners, Visa.*

Bradford   Stakis Norfolk Gardens Hotel   61%   £112
Tel 0274 734734   Fax 0274 306146   **H**
Hall Ings Bradford West Yorkshire BD1 5SH   Map 6 C1

A city-centre hotel with an adjacent car park and facilities for up to 700
banqueting or conference delegates. There are five bedroom floors, the
lower three being smarter and more up-to-date. *Rooms 120. Coffee shop
(24hr).* AMERICAN EXPRESS ® *Access, Diners, Visa.*

Bradford　　　Victoria Hotel　　58%　　£87

Tel 0274 728706　Fax 0274 736358　**H**

Bridge Street Bradford West Yorkshire BD1 1JX　Map 6 C1

Directly opposite Bradford's rail/bus interchange, the hotel's decor and proportions reflect its grand Victorian origins. There are lofty, pillared public rooms as well as a colourful bar with tented ceiling. Bedrooms are mostly quite smartly furnished. Forte Heritage. *Rooms 59.* AMERICAN EXPRESS *Access, Diners, Visa.*

Bradford　　　Places of Interest

Tourist Information　Tel 0274 753678.
Alhambra Theatre　Morely Street Tel 0274 752000.
Bradford Cathedral　Tel 0274 725958.
　Museums and Art Galleries
Colour Museum　Tel 0274 390955.
Cartwright Hall Art Gallery　Tel 0274 493313.
National Museum of Photography, Film and Television　Tel 0274 727488.
Also houses Britain's only IMAX cinema.
Mecca Leisure Ice Rink　Tel 0274 729091.
Bradford Northern RLFC　Tel 0274 733899

Bradford-on-Avon　　Woolley Grange　　75%　　£130

Tel 0225 864705　Fax 0225 864059　**HR**

Woolley Green Bradford-on-Avon Wiltshire BA15 1TX　Map 14 B3

'Families are most welcome' says the literature – and Woolley Grange does indeed live up to its reputation as one of the foremost family hotels in the land. Children stay free in their parents' rooms and certain rooms can be arranged together as interconnecting suites. The Den and Bear Garden are just part of the kiddies' kingdom, territory which now includes a flower and vegetable garden and a wreck room that was once a hen house (actually a rather grand Victorian building). The Grange is a handsome 17th-century country mansion whose comfortably lived-in day rooms are full of character, with antiques, paintings and real fires. There's a Victorian Gothic conservatory, an oak-panelled drawing room and various other rooms for whiling away a few quiet moments, and friendly young staff imbue the whole place with a friendly, relaxing feel that's a major part of the attraction. Bedrooms vary considerably in size but all have great character with a beamed bathroom here (mostly with Victorian-style fittings), a rugged stone fire breast there (about half have working gas coal fires), brass bedsteads, patchwork bedcovers, antiques and fresh flowers all helping to create an appealing 'country' feel. Don't miss the collection of interesting bicycles, which include a pre-war tandem, a modern penny farthing and a couple of Moultons. And be sure to say hello to Susie and Rosie, the Vietnamese pot-bellied pigs. The smallest doubles are priced considerably below the rate quoted above. *Rooms 20. Garden, croquet, outdoor swimming pool, tennis, games room.* AMERICAN EXPRESS *Access, Diners, Visa.*

Restaurant　　　　　　　　　　　£75

Colin White continues in fine form, producing dishes that are at once sophisticated and satisfying, rustic and urbane. Worldwide influences are apparent in menus that could include Thai fish soup, duck with a mango salsa, asparagus baked with prosciutto and gruyère, steamed sea bass with Chinese black beans and best end of lamb with globe artichoke ragout. A good selection of cheeses is an alternative to desserts like chilled lime mousse with passion fruit sauce or hot chocolate soufflé. In the conservatory or out on the terrace a less formal menu is served lunchtime and evening with such dishes as omelette Arnold Bennett, hamburger and griddled fishes with salsa verde. No smoking in the dining room. *Seats 54. Parties 40. Private Room 22. L 12.15-2 D 7.15-10. Set L £24 Set D £28.*

Bradford-on-Avon   Places of Interest

Tourist Information   Tel 02216 5797.
Iford Manor Gardens   Tel 02216 3146/2840/2364.

Braithwaite   **Ivy House**   66%   £68

Tel 076 87 78338   **H**
Braithwaite nr Keswick Cumbria CA12 5SY   Map 4 C3

Nick and Wendy Shill run a hotel of warmth and character in a small
17th-century house at the foot of the Lakeland fells. Walking is a favourite
pastime with guests, made more appealing by ample drying facilities and
log fires in the lounge. Fine old furniture and objets d'art are found in the
neat bedrooms, which include a honeymoon suite with four-poster. The
hotel is in the middle of the village just behind the Royal Oak pub.
No dogs. **Rooms** 12. Closed Jan. AMERICAN EXPRESS Access, Diners, Visa.

Bramhall   **Moat House**   63%   £85

Tel 061-439 8116   Fax 061-440 8071   **H**
Bramhall Lane South Bramhall Cheshire SK7 2EB   Map 6 B2

Built in 1972 and since expanded, this well-kept hotel appeals to both
leisure and business visitors. Conference and banqueting facilities for
110/170. Children up to 16 stay free in parents' room. Ample free parking.
Rooms 65. Keep-fit equipment, sauna, solarium. AMERICAN EXPRESS Access,
Diners, Visa.

Bramhope   **Forte Crest**   66%   £89

Tel 0532 842911   Fax 0532 843451   **H**
Bramhope nr Leeds West Yorkshire LS16 9JJ   Map 6 C1

16 acres of grounds, swimming pool, keep-fit amenities and conference
facilities for up to 160 in a hotel two miles from Leeds/Bradford Airport.
Children up to 15 free in parents' room. 82 rooms reserved for non-
smokers. **Rooms** 124. Garden, indoor swimming pool, gymnasium, sauna,
solarium, coffee shop (noon-10pm). AMERICAN EXPRESS Access, Diners, Visa.

Bramhope   **Jarvis Parkway Hotel**   62%   £116

Tel 0532 672551   Fax 0532 674410   **H**
Otley Road Bramhope nr Leeds West Yorkshire LS16 8AG   Map 6 C1

Built in 1939, the original building has a smart new colourful decor and
well-equipped leisure centre. As well as a few older rooms there is an
extension of attractive balconied bedrooms to the rear overlooking wooded
parkland. **Rooms** 105. Garden, indoor swimming pool, gym, sauna, spa bath,
steam room, solarium, beauty salon, tennis, games room. AMERICAN EXPRESS Access,
Diners, Visa.

Bramley   **Bramley Grange**   64%   £105

Tel 0483 893434   Fax 0483 893835   **H**
281 Horsham Road Bramley nr Guildford Surrey GU5 0BL   Map 15 E3

Based on a mock-Tudor Victorian house, Bramley Grange now extends
around three sides of a large garden (making it a popular venue for
weddings) with a wooded hillside completing the square. Half the
bedrooms are in the newest wing and feature limed oak furniture, plain
walls and co-ordinating fabrics. Other rooms are individually decorated,
from large rooms with antique furniture to a few small singles with
shower and WC only; all these original bedrooms were recently
refurbished. 'Standard' rooms attract a reduced weekday tariff; reductions

also at weekends. Banqueting/conference facilities for 120/80 in the Garden
Suite. *Rooms 45. Garden, croquet, tennis, putting.* AMERICAN EXPRESS
Access, Visa.

Brampton   Farlam Hall   75%   £170*

Tel 069 77 46234   Fax 069 77 46683   **HR**

Hallbankgate Brampton Cumbria CA8 2NG   Map 4 C2

The hotel stands on the A689 two miles from Brampton – not in Farlam
village. Set in lovely grounds complete with stream and ornamental lake,
the original 17th-century farmhouse was enlarged to form a manor house
in Victorian times. The Quinion and Stevenson families' latter-day
conversion to charming country house hotel features Victorian-design
wallpapers and authentically re-upholstered original pieces. Plants and fresh
flowers, books and board games enhance the lived-in feel. Individually
decorated bedrooms are a model of taste; most have space for a sitting area,
and bathrooms are modern and well equipped; the finest is a Victorian
recreation in dark mahogany. Splendid breakfasts and the charm and
courtesy of the resident hosts contribute greatly to a memorable stay.
No children under five. Function facilities for 45 (banqueting) and 25
(conference). Helipad facility with 24hrs' notice. *Half-board terms only.
Rooms 12. Garden. Closed 25-31 Dec.* AMERICAN EXPRESS *Access, Visa.*

Restaurant   £60

Guests are requested to arrive in the bar or front lounge in time to dine
between 8 and 8.30. This air of formality extends to dinner. Barry
Quinion's nightly fixed-price-only, 4-course menu changes daily and offers
self-styled "English Country House" cooking. A small choice of three dishes
at each course is typified by cream of carrot and parsley soup, hot Arbroath
smokies cooked with tomatoes and Jersey cream topped with a puff pastry
hat or cheese beignet with lemon mayonnaise and salad leaves to start,
followed by poached salmon and turbot with dill sauce and prawn tartlet,
roast breast of local pheasant with wild mushrom and port sauce
or medallions of beef fillet served with a potato and herb cake and a pink
peppercorn and brandy cream sauce. English cheeseboard with grapes,
celery and apple or the likes of chocolate terrine, apple, apricot and almond
pancake with banana ice cream, raspberry linzer torte, blackberry crème
brulée or coconut meringue with strawberries to follow. Short, diverse,
sensibly-priced wine list. Lunch (around £22.50) is served four times a year
(Mothering Sunday, Easter Day, Christmas Day and New Year's Day).
Snack lunches are available daily in the lounge to residents. No children
under 5. *Seats 45. Parties 20. D only 8-8.30. Set D £27.50 & £28.50.*

Brandon   Brandon Hall   65%   £97

Tel 0203 542571   Fax 0203 544909   **H**

Brandon nr Coventry Warwickshire CV8 3FW   Map 7 D4

An elegant mansion with a country house air, set in 17 acres of grounds.
Most of the accommodation (40 rooms) is in a modern extension. 20
bedrooms were refurbished during 1994. Families are well catered for.
Banqueting/conference facilities for up to 120. Forte Heritage. *Rooms 60.
Garden, squash, pitch & putt, archery.* AMERICAN EXPRESS *Access, Diners, Visa.*

Brands Hatch   Brands Hatch Thistle   70%   £80

Tel 0474 854900   Fax 0474 853220   **H**

Brands Hatch nr Dartford Kent DA3 8PE   Map 11 B5

A modern hotel standing on the A20, three miles from M25 and at the
main entrance to Brands Hatch racing circuit. Public rooms include
a spacious and quite elegant foyer with a polished granite tiled floor, pillars
and deep blue leather settees; opening from this is the Bugatti Bar. Best
bedrooms are those designated Executive, with remote-control teletext
TVs, bidets, dressing gowns and separate shower cubicle as well as the

standard hairdryers, trouser presses, room safes and individually controlled heating and ventilation. Minibars and tea-makers are also provided, and all the furniture is smartly contemporary. Conference/banqueting facilities for 270/250, and a hospitality suite at the track. Families are well catered for, and children up to 16 stay free in parents' room. **Rooms** *137. Garden, coffee shop (9.30am-10.30pm).* AMERICAN EXPRESS *Access, Diners, Visa.*

Brands Hatch   Place of Interest

Motor Racing Circuit   Fawkham Tel 0474 872331.

Branscombe   Masons Arms   64%   £54

Tel 0297 680300   Fax 0297 680500   **H**
Branscombe nr Seaton Devon EX12 3DJ   Map 13 E2

Surrounded by acres of unspoilt National Trust land and within a hop of the Devon Coastal Path, the Masons Arms is, unsurprisingly, popular with walkers. The 14th-century inn has slate floors, open fires and oak beams that were once the timbers of smugglers' boats. Guests may stay in the hotel itself, whose seven rooms are compact and quaint (two are without private bathrooms) or in the adjacent residential cottages, which have been sympathetically converted over the years. **Rooms** *21. Garden. Access, Visa.*

Branscombe   Place of Interest

Seaton Beach 5 miles.

Braunton   Otter's Restaurant   £50

Tel 0271 813633   **R**
30 Caen Street Braunton Barnstaple Devon EX33 1AA   Map 12 C2

Carol Cowie's realistically-priced set menu offers a choice of six or more dishes per course. She describes her cooking as 'English with French flair' and among her specialities are terrine of salmon with prawns and smoked salmon and fillet of venison served on a croute with a horseradish, cognac and cream sauce. Other typical dishes include fresh herb and spinach tagliatelle tossed in garlic butter and topped with Parma ham and Parmesan, twice-baked goat's cheese soufflé, sizzling snails, stir-fried julienne of beef fillet with oyster and soy sauces and prime Devon beef steaks. There's always a good choice of desserts, from honey-glazed orange and rum bread-and-butter pudding served with Devon clotted cream or a chocolate and Tia Maria mousse to fresh pineapple baked Alaska (another speciality) and an individual warm treacle sponge pudding served with vanilla custard. No smoking before 9.30 (but the bar is available). The restaurant stands in a little row of shops in the centre of the village, two miles from Saunton Sands. A riverside terrace is available for pre-dinner drinks or dining in the summer months. Unusually, all the dozen or so 'house recommended wines' are from Down Under – both Australia and New Zealand. There's a large free car park opposite the restaurant. **Seats** *40. D only 7-9.30. Closed Sun, Mon, 1 week Jan, 1 week Nov. Open L Mothers Day. Set D £15.50/£18.* AMERICAN EXPRESS *Access, Visa.*

Bray-on-Thames   The Waterside Inn   ★★★   £165

Tel 0628 20691   Fax 0628 784710   **RR**
Ferry Road Bray-on-Thames Berkshire SL6 2AT   Map 15 E2

"*Un restaurant avec chambres*". But *what* a restaurant with rooms! The Thameside setting is unsurpassed on a summer's day, when drinks can be taken on the terrace or on the electric launch *The Waterside Inn II*; and when the kitchen is on song the food is truly memorable. Michel Roux bought the Waterside with his brother in 1972, and his lieutenants – Head Chef Mark Dodson and Restaurant Manager Diego Masciaga – have been

at their posts since 1988. Time-honoured French cooking skills have been adapted to modern tastes, with the result that more dishes include *nage* or *jus* as opposed to old-fashioned sauces. Classic ingredients are still very much to the fore (foie gras, truffles, snails, lobster, turbot, tournedos, Bresse pigeon, Challans duck) but you'll also notice many herbs and spices making fresh, natural contributions to dishes: lemon thyme with a mussel soufflé; chive flavouring olive oil with grilled turbot; savory subtly enhancing *tournedos poelé, persillade à l'échalote, cordon d'escargots*. Desserts like warm raspberry soufflé or *ravioles au citrus et petit gratin de poires et bananes* put the finishing flourish on what should be a magnificent meal. A la carte is always available, plus a *menu gastronomique* at lunchtime during the week (priced very reasonably at £28), an evening *menu printemps* between October and April and a *menu exceptionnel* which (for 2 or more) offers smaller portions of dishes taken from the carte. The à la carte menu includes two main-course vegetarian dishes. The French-only wine list – '*c'est magnifique*' – has all the great names, and a few country wines. Surprisingly perhaps it's not all expensive, especially noting that prices are inclusive of service. The room is bright, elegant and inviting, though tables at the back do not enjoy the best of the views. An army of smartly turned-out staff provides constant, attentive service. No children under 12.
Seats 75. L 12-1.30 (Sun 12-2.30) D 7-10. Closed all Mon, L Tue, D Sun Oct-April, Bank Holidays (open L 25 Dec), 26 Dec-end Jan. Set L £28 Set D Oct-Apr £45 also Set L & D £62. Access, Diners, Visa.

Rooms   £110

Seven stylish and comfortable bedrooms, all en suite and some with river views, could persuade you to forget the drive home, and the fresh croissants will set you up for the day.

Brentwood	Forte Posthouse	61%	£68
Tel 0277 260260 Fax 0277 264264			**H**

Brook Street Brentwood Essex CM14 5NF   **Map 11 B4**

Comfortable modern redbrick hotel by the M25/A12. Conference/banqueting facilities for 120. Children up to 14 free in parents' room. Half the rooms are designated non-smoking. *Rooms 111. Garden, indoor swimming pool, gym, sauna, solarium, beauty salon.* AMERICAN EXPRESS *Access, Diners, Visa.*

Brentwood	Forte Travelodge	£45
Tel 0277 810819		**L**

A127 East Horndon nr Brentwood Essex CM13 3LL   **Map 11 B4**

Located 4 miles off Junction 29 of the M25 on the A127 eastbound, in the grounds of Halfway House. 4 miles south-east of Brentwood. *Rooms 22.* AMERICAN EXPRESS *Access, Diners, Visa.*

Brentwood	Moat House	67%	£114
Tel 0277 225252 Fax 0277 262809			**H**

London Road Brentwood Essex CM14 4NR   **Map 11 B4**

Originally a Tudor hunting lodge and mentioned by Pepys in his diaries, the hotel has since been considerably extended but very much in keeping with the original house. Three bedrooms in the main house have antique carved beds and a period feel, while other rooms are more modern, ranged motel-style around the garden. The hotel is easy to find, standing just half a mile from Junction 28 of the M25. *Rooms 33. Garden.* AMERICAN EXPRESS *Access, Diners, Visa.*

Set menu prices may not always include service or wine.

Bridlington   Expanse Hotel   60%   £59

Tel 0262 675347   Fax 0262 604928   **H**

North Marine Drive Bridlington Humberside YO15 2LS   Map 7 E1

Purpose-built in 1937, the Expanse is a traditional seaside hotel that has been owned by the Seymour family since 1948. Many of its guests are regulars, while others come for business meetings and conferences (banqueting for 120, three conference rooms for 80 in total). Public and lounge bars are agreeable places to relax, and quite a few of the bedrooms enjoy sea views; some have balconies. Children up to 15 stay free in parents' room. No dogs. **Rooms** *48.* AMERICAN EXPRESS *Access, Diners, Visa.*

Bridlington   Places of Interest

Burton Agnes Hall   Near Bridlington Tel 026289 324.
Bridlington North and South Beaches.

Bridport   Riverside Restaurant   £40

Tel 0308 22011   **R**

West Bay Bridport Dorset DT6 4EZ   Map 13 F2

The menu at this friendly, relaxed restaurant concentrates on locally caught fish and shellfish prepared plainly or with sauces. Red mullet, John Dory, Dover sole, lemon sole, plaice and sardines are grilled to order, and other choices could be skate with black butter and capers, deep-fried squid or baked brill Greek-style. Lobster is priced according to season and weight. There are a few meat dishes, too, such as Dorset air-dried ham, roast chicken and chili con carne. Breakfast, light snacks and Dorset cream teas are also served. In good weather tables are set outside on a patio overlooking the river. Opening times can vary with the seasons, so check when booking. **Seats** *70. L 11.30-2.30 (Sat & Sun to 4) D 6.30-8.45. Closed D Sun, all Mon (except Bank Holidays), late Nov-early Mar. Access, Visa.*

Bridport   Places of Interest

Mapperton House   Tel 0308 862645.
Parnham House & Gardens   Tel 0308 862204.

> Note that all telephone numbers with area codes starting with 0
> will start 01 from 16 April 1995.

Brierley Hill   Copthorne Hotel   71%   £122

Tel 0384 482882   Fax 0384 482773   **H**

The Waterfront Level Street Brierley Hill West Midlands DY5 1UR   Map 6 B4

Close to the M5 (J2/3), overlooking the canal marina and located next to the Merry Hill shopping complex with over 200 shops, the hotel opened in April 1993. It combines stylish public areas with well-designed bedrooms and suites; the large, circular, marble-floored lobby with a few scattered groups of lounge seating leads on to the combined bar/restaurant/coffee shop area which is on several split levels overlooking a stretch of canal. Mirrors in bedrooms (some 50 designated non-smoking) are cleverly placed to give both front and rear views (in 'lady' rooms one conceals an iron and ironing board). Connoisseur rooms get various extras, evening turn-down service and use of the Connoisseur lounge with complimentary Continental breakfast and beverages throughout the day. Purpose-built conference centre (250 theatre-style, 190 banquet), easy parking. Children up to 16 free in parents' room. **Rooms** *138. Patio, indoor swimming pool, gym, sauna, spa bath, solarium.* AMERICAN EXPRESS *Access, Diners, Visa.*

Brighouse   Forte Crest   68%   £98

Tel 0484 400400   Fax 0484 400068   **H**

Coalpit Lane Clifton Village Brighouse West Yorkshire HD6 4HW   **Map 6 C1**

A low-rise hotel set in landscaped gardens close to J25 of the M62. Two-thirds of the bedrooms are designated non-smoking. Children up to 16 stay free in parents' room. Good leisure facilities; seven meeting/banqueting rooms accommodating 20-200. *Rooms 94. Garden, croquet, indoor swimming pool, gym, sauna, spa bath, solarium.* AMERICAN EXPRESS *Access, Diners, Visa.*

Brightling   Jack Fuller's   £35

Tel 042 482 212   **R**

Brightling nr Robertsbridge East Sussex TN32 5HD   **Map 11 B6**

The name is visible only on the road from Robertsbridge to Brightling, so otherwise this former pub is easy to miss. It's fronted by a well-kept garden, and patio doors lead from the restaurant to a wide terrace (outside eating in summer) and another beautiful garden with panoramic views. Inside it's cosy and cheerful, and the owners add to the jolly atmosphere. Good local produce goes into the mainstay of the English menu: pies, puddings, casseroles and stews. Nursery puds like blackcurrant and apple crumble or sticky treacle tart demand cream or lovely thick custard. Note the number of English wines on the fairly-priced list. *Seats 72. Parties 35. Private Room 20. L 12-3 (Sun till 4) D 7-10. Closed D Sun, all Mon (except L Bank Hols), also Tue & Wed (Oct-March).* AMERICAN EXPRESS *Access, Diners, Visa.*

Brighton   Bedford Hotel   66%   £128

Tel 0273 329744   Fax 0273 775877   **H**

King's Road Brighton East Sussex BN1 2JF   **Map 11 B6**

The hotel comprises the lower floors of a tall seafront block. The facade has recently been renewed and there's now a terrace seating area with sea views. Bedrooms are large, with quality modern furniture and compact bathrooms, all with showers. Children up to 16 stay free in parents' room. Guests may use the leisure facilities of the *Metropole Hotel*, just 100 yards away. Banqueting/conference facilities for 300/450. Car park for 70 cars. *Rooms 129.* AMERICAN EXPRESS *Access, Diners, Visa.*

Brighton   Black Chapati   £45

Tel 0273 699011   **R**

12 Circus Parade New England Road Brighton East Sussex BN1 4GW   **Map 11 B6**

The decor is plain and minimalist, the only colour other than black being provided by a few abstract prints. Stephen Funnell's Indian-and-Orient-derived food is equally free of clichés, and Brighton is certainly the richer for it. Some dishes have a familiar ring – onion bhaji, Madras lamb curry – while others are distinctly unusual: breast of wood pigeon with udan noodles and coriander 'pesto', pan-fried rump of lamb with chick peas and masala cabbage, baked red mullet with tomatoes and ginger served with coconut rice. The chef's favourite drink, Breton cider, is an excellent accompaniment. Sunday lunch is a buffet. *Seats 30. Parties 12. L Sun 1-3 D 7-10.30. Closed D Sun, all Mon, 1 week June, 1 week Christmas. Set L £7.95.* AMERICAN EXPRESS *Access, Visa.*

Brighton   Brighton Metropole   70%   £160

Tel 0273 775432   Fax 0273 207764   **H**

King's Road Brighton East Sussex BN1 2FU   **Map 11 B6**

Very much geared to the business executive, the Metropole boasts massive and diverse conference facilities (for up to 1800 delegates) and vast exhibition space – 28 air-conditioned rooms in various sizes and configurations. The broad, deep foyer leads to an elegant drawing room with crystal chandeliers, finely detailed plasterwork and settees and armchairs round marble-topped tables. There is a second peaceful lounge and a dark, atmospheric cocktail bar. Good-size bedrooms, furnished in smart lightwood, include 16 suites with sea-facing balconies. Some rooms are large enough for settees as well as the standard two chairs and table. Good-value leisure breaks for families complete the appeal, with early suppers and a separate childrens' menu. Children up to 16 stay free in parents' room. *Rooms 328. Indoor swimming pool, sauna, steam room, solarium, spa bath, gym, sunbed, beauty salon, hairdressing, night club, coffee shop (24hr).* AMERICAN EXPRESS *Access, Diners, Visa.*

Brighton — The Brighton Thistle Hotel — 77% — £155

Tel 0273 206700   Fax 0273 820692 — **HR**

Kings Road Brighton East Sussex BN1 2GS — Map 11 B6

On the promenade two minutes' walk from the Royal Pavilion, the renamed Hospitality Inn has a strikingly modern exterior fronting an equally impressive interior with a large atrium lounge, under a glass roof four storeys above, filled with plants and trees and cleverly lit at night. Bart's Bar is a good spot to relax, and a brasserie, the Promenade, is open for lunch and dinner seven days a week. Good, if unexciting, standardised bedrooms are properly serviced in the evening and offer pleasing little extras like bathrobes, slippers and a bowl of fresh fruit. Notably smart staff are both friendly and helpful. Extensive 24hr room service. Free parking (for diners as well as residents) by voucher valid for the Town Hall car park under the hotel. Children up to 16 can stay free in their parents' room. *Rooms 204. Indoor swimming pool, gym, sauna, solarium, hairdressing.* AMERICAN EXPRESS *Access, Diners, Visa.*

La Noblesse Restaurant — £80

Subdued yet rich decor creates an atmosphere of quiet luxury in which to enjoy soundly cooked dishes from the lunch and evening table d'hote. Starters such as creamy celery and walnut soup or halibut and lobster terrine precede poached red snapper with spring onion sauce, breast of chicken filled with crab mousse served with lobster sauce, or (at a £2 supplement) fillet of beef topped with wild mushrooms. There are always a couple of vegetarian main courses, then creamy or fruity desserts. *Seats 50. L 12-2 D 7-10. Closed L Sat, all Sun, Bank Holidays. Set L & D £17.50.*

Brighton — China Garden — £55

Tel 0273 325124 — **R**

88 Preston Street Brighton East Sussex BN1 1HG — Map 11 B6

The 100-item menu at this smart roomy restaurant near the West Pier includes many Peking and Cantonese favourites: roast Peking duck for four (order 12 hours in advance), salt and pepper prawns, squid and lobster, grilled pork dumplings, Ying Yang Dover sole (one half stir-fried with vegetables, the other deep-fried with spices), Kung Po chicken, iron-griddle sizzlers, bean curd with minced beef and chili. *Seats 130. Private Room 40. Meals noon-11pm. Closed 25 & 26 Dec. Set meals from £15.50.* AMERICAN EXPRESS *Access, Diners, Visa.*

Brighton — Grand Hotel — 74% — £160

Tel 0273 321188   Fax 0273 202694 — **H**

King's Road Brighton East Sussex BN1 2FW — Map 11 B6

Brighton's best-known hotel – right on the seafront – is splendidly equipped for both the leisure and the conference markets. Hobden's Health Spa and the Midnight Blues night club (membership/admission to both included in room rate) are smartly contemporary, while the original luxury and grandeur survive in the coloured marble columns, the polished marble floors, the moulded plaster ceiling and the magnificent central staircase. In the lounge, heavy drapes, wing chairs, sofas and paintings give an elegant Victorian feel. Handsome furnishings and chintzy decor distinguish the bedrooms, which all offer full 24hr room service; de luxe rooms have sea views. There are rooms especially designed for lady executives, rooms with additional facilities for the disabled, 'romantic' rooms with double whirlpool baths and eight splendid suites. Top of the range is the Presidential Suite comprising two bedrooms, two sitting rooms and a private dining room. Afternoon tea is served in the airy conservatory, also overlooking the sea. De Vere Hotels. **Rooms** 200. *Indoor swimming pool, keep-fit equipment, sauna, spa bath, solarium, beauty & hair salon.* AMERICAN EXPRESS *Access, Diners, Visa.*

Brighton	Langan's Bistro	£70
Tel 0273 606933		**R**
1 Paston Place Brighton East Sussex BN2 1HA		Map 11 B6

The seaside branch of that small family of restaurants of which *Langan's Brasserie* in London is the most famous. Modern art-crammed walls follow the house style but this outpost is otherwise very much the domain of Mark (in the kitchen) and Nicole (front of house) Emmerson, who have been running things here since the beginning. The likes of warm scallop salad, country terrine, crab bisque, entrecote au vin rouge, grilled brill with leeks, and veal kidneys with a sorrel and Pommery mustard sauce feature on the short, constantly-changing carte; at lunchtimes this is supplemented by an even shorter prix-fixe. Sunday lunch is also a fixed-price menu only – about four choices of main dishes, always including a roast. Just two dozen wines offered with only the champagnes breaking the £20 barrier. **Seats** 42. *Parties 10. L 12.30-2.15 D 7.30-10.15. Closed L Sat, D Sun, all Mon, 26 Dec, 2 weeks Jan, 2 weeks Aug. Set L £12.50/£14.50 (Sun £14.50).* AMERICAN EXPRESS *Access, Diners, Visa.*

Brighton	La Marinade	£60
Tel 0273 600992		**R**
77 St George's Road Kemp Town Brighton East Sussex BN2 1EF		Map 11 B6

Popular, unpretentious little restaurant serving straightforward bistro food. Mussels in a curry sauce, snail-stuffed mushrooms, smoked fish, steaks, lobster, and chicken breast in a creamy calvados and mushroom sauce are typical of the style. Always a daily fish special. Good-value three-course lunches, including Sunday. No smoking in the upstairs dining room. **Seats** 36. *L 12-2 D 7-10. Closed L Sat, D Sun, all Mon. Set L £10.75.* AMERICAN EXPRESS *Access, Diners, Visa.*

Brighton	Old Ship Hotel	65%	£105
Tel 0273 329001 Fax 0273 820718			**H**
King's Road Brighton East Sussex BN1 1NR			Map 11 B6

A hotel of considerable charm and with a history dating back in part to the 15th century. A central location on the seafront is a big plus as is secure parking for 70 cars. Public areas include a surprisingly spacious oak-panelled lobby dotted with antiques, a pair of quiet lounges with Adam-style ceilings and the panelled Tettersell's Bar. The Paganini Ballroom is the largest of several rooms available for conferences or banquets (max 300/200). About two-thirds of the bedrooms (mostly those in the east wing) are smartly furnished with freestanding darkwood furniture, matching floral fabrics, breakfast table, good armchairs and up-to-date bathrooms. The remainder vary somewhat in age and style but all are at least acceptable. Friendly staff. 24hr room service. Children under 12 stay free in parents' room. A children's playroom operates at weekends. **Rooms** 152. AMERICAN EXPRESS *Access, Diners, Visa.*

Brighton   **Topps Hotel**   **69%**   **£79**

Tel 0273 729334   Fax 0273 203679   **HR**
17 Regency Square Brighton East Sussex BN1 2FG   **Map 11 B6**

Two Regency properties overlooking a square 100 yards from the seafront make a fine setting for a very friendly, agreeable hotel that tries to provide a real home from home. There's a simple lounge/reception where drinks are served and, upstairs, well-appointed bedrooms with fabric-lined walls and antiqued pine furniture offer a touch of luxury. All have armchairs or sofas, flowers, drinks trays and excellent bathrooms; five have seating areas, and the stars of the show are two four-poster rooms with balconies – perfect to catch the sun with breakfast. One extra single has been added since last year. No dogs. *Rooms 15. Closed 25 & 26 Dec.* AMERICAN EXPRESS *Access, Diners, Visa.*

Restaurant   **£50**

A two-hander with Paul Collins front of house and wife Pauline in the kitchen (they share the washing up) of a cosy basement restaurant. The fixed-price menu includes the first two courses plus coffee and service with puds like bread-and-butter pudding, trifle and toffee meringue being an optional extra. A thick vegetable soup made with chicken stock, salmon fishcakes with tomato sauce and scampi in filo parcels are typical of the half-dozen or so starters followed by a similar number of main dishes like rack of new season lamb with onion sauce; casserole of pigeon breast and prawn, sole and scallop pie. Steak and kidney pie, something of a speciality, is always available. Careful cooking ensures consistently enjoyable results with everything home-made, including the excellent bread. *Seats 24. Parties 10. Private Room 10. D only 7-9.30. Closed Sun & Wed, Jan & Christmas. Set D £18.95.*

Brighton (Hove)   **Quentin's**   **NEW**   **£50**

Tel 0273 822734   **R**
42 Western Road Hove East Sussex BN3 1JD   **Map 11 B6**

Cosy pine-decorated restaurant on the borders of Brighton and Hove. A monthly-changing carte is presented by chef Quentin Fitch, who enjoys cooking Thai and Middle-Eastern dishes, and these are often featured. Home-cured bresaola, Thai fishcakes or celery and walnut pie to start; lamb kebabs with mint and cucumber chutney, ribe-eye steak with chips or home-smoked salmon with fresh tagliatelle, cream and chives to follow. Delicious, simple desserts such as apple pie with home-made lavender ice cream. Bargain plats du jour for £4.95, including bread, mineral water and coffee. *Seats 46. Parties 20. Private Room 20. L 12-2.30 D 6.30-10.30. Closed Sun, Mon, last week Aug, 1 week Sep, 2 days Christmas.* AMERICAN EXPRESS *Access, Diners, Visa.*

Brighton (Hove)   **Sackville Hotel**   **61%**   **£75**

Tel 0273 736292   Fax 0273 205759   **H**
189 Kingsway Hove Brighton East Sussex BN3 4GU   **Map 11 B6**

Built as four private houses in 1904, but not opened as a hotel until 1930, this seafront hotel still retains many original decorative features. After the fresh coat of paint outside, the interior has had the treatment. The panelled bar-lounge has leather chesterfields and there is a small rattan-furnished sun lounge. Well-kept bedrooms mostly feature darkwood furniture and soft colour schemes. Two rooms have antiques and eight have sea-facing balconies. Guests can use the nearby King Arthur Sports Centre free, as they can Hove Golf Course. Ample parking. *Rooms 45.* AMERICAN EXPRESS *Access, Diners, Visa.*

Brighton (Hove)   Whitehaven Hotel   56%   £75

Tel 0273 778355   Fax 0273 731177   **H**

Wilbury Road Hove East Sussex BN3 3JP   Map 11 B6

Situated just off the seafront, the Whitehaven offers good standards
of cleanliness and repair at a small, modestly comfortable hotel.
Unrestricted street parking is another plus. No children under 8. One room
suitable for family use. No dogs. *Rooms* 17. *Garden.* **AMERICAN EXPRESS** *Access,
Diners, Visa.*

Brighton   Places of Interest

Tourist Information   Tel 0273 323755.
Sallis Benney Theatre   Grand Parade Tel 0273 604141.
Theatre Royal   Tel 0273 328488.
The Brighton Concert Centre   Tel 0273 203131.
The Dome Complex   Tel 0273 674357.
Royal Pavilion   Tel 0273 603005.
Brighton Museum and Art Gallery   Church Street Tel 0273 603005.
Brighton Cricket Ground   Eaton Road, Hove Tel 0273 732161.
Brighton Football Ground   Tel 0273 739535.
Brighton Racecourse   Tel 0273 682912/603580.
Brighton Ice Rink   Tel 0273 324677.
Euroski Dry Ski Slope   Tel 0273 688258.

Brimfield   Poppies Restaurant   ↑   £75

Tel 0584 711230   Fax 0584 711654   **RR**

The Roebuck Brimfield nr Ludlow Hereford & Worcester SY8 4NE   Map 14 A1

Set in a former coach house attached to the village pub (our Pub of the
Year in 1992), this is a restaurant with a touch of style, not just in the decor
– parquet floor, comfortably upholstered rattan and wicker chairs and
crisply white-clothed tables accented by some striking dark blue glass water
jugs and glasses – but also in the cooking. Carole Evans believes that food
should be fun but it takes some serious effort and talent in the kitchen
to produce dishes that are unfussy yet refined and thoroughly enjoyable.
A simple watercress soup just bursting with flavour, crab ravioli with
lemon grass sauce, roast brill with tomato and onion sauce, local venison
with a whimberry and kummel sauce, and apple pancakes flamed with
local cider brandy give a flavour (if not a taste) of what's on offer. British
farmhouse cheeses rate their own special menu with names like Longridge
Fell, Old Worcester White and Tornegus (winner of our British
Cheeseboard of the Year award 1995). There's a separate menu served
in the bar where, as in the restaurant, children are made most welcome.
Three-course set lunch served in the restaurant. Smashing wine list with
helpful tasting notes and a particularly good half-bottle selection, though
the New World is perhaps under represented. Polished service. *Seats 36.
Private Room 18. L 12-2 D 7-10. Closed Sun & Mon, 2 weeks Feb, 1 week
Oct, 25 & 26 Dec. Set L £18.* **AMERICAN EXPRESS** *Access, Visa.*

Rooms   £60

Three charming, immaculate bedrooms (all en-suite, two with showers and
one with a tub) furnished in limed oak offer everything from telephones
and remote-control TV to home-made fruit cake and beverage kit with
cafetière jug and real coffee. Wake up to breakfasts in which the local cow's
or ewe's milk yoghurt, bread, sausages, marmalade and honey are all home-
made (the latter from their own hives) and the eggs free-range. The rooms
are particularly suitable for children (by arrangement).

Brimfield   Place of Interest

Burford House Gardens   Tel 0584 810777.

Bristol   Aztec Hotel   74%   £102

Tel 0454 201090   Fax 0454 201593   **H**

Aztec West Business Park Almondsbury Bristol Avon BS12 4TS   **Map 13 F1**

A smart, professionally run, purpose-built, modern hotel in the Shire Inns group, owned by brewers Daniel Thwaites. It offers a good balance of facilities between mid-week conferences – a business centre provides secretarial services – and weekend family breaks. All bedrooms are of Executive standard with coffee tables, writing desk and fax point; 39 rooms are reserved for non-smokers. Syndicate rooms convert to family use at weekends with wall-mounted let-down beds; children under 14 are accommodated free in their parents' room. Day rooms are more than adequate, with lounges on two levels in the central 'lodge' and a smart snooker room. The hotel also has a fine leisure club and its own Black Sheep pub. Light meals and snacks are served in Danby's Bar, open from 9am-11pm; more formal dining in Quarterjacks restaurant. Regional specialities at breakfast include Somerset venison sausages and Alderley trout served with scrambled eggs. In a modern business park near Junction 16 of the M5 (south of the M4/M5 interchange). *Rooms 86. Garden, indoor swimming pool, gym, squash, sauna, solarium, steam room, snooker.* AMERICANEXPRESS *Access, Diners, Visa.*

Bristol   Berkeley Square Hotel   69%   £106

Tel 0272 254000   Fax 0272 252970   **H**

15 Berkeley Square Bristol Avon BS8 1HB   **Map 13 F1**

Flagship of the Bristol-based Clifton Hotels, the Berkeley Square Hotel is situated in the tranquil Georgian square where the BBC's *House of Elliott* is filmed. Well-equipped bedrooms vary from practical singles to spacious suites, their names drawn from eminent Bristolians. Thirteen rooms are designated non-smoking. Small lounge and restaurant at street level, with a state-of-the-art basement bar and café (7.30am-10pm). Small banquets and conferences (up to 50) can be accommodated. Covered parking for 20 cars. If you have to use a meter, the hotel's staff will 'keep an eye on it' until your departure. *Rooms 43.* AMERICANEXPRESS *Access, Diners, Visa.*

Bristol   Blue Goose   £45

Tel 0272 420940   **R**

344 Gloucester Road Bristol Avon   **Map 13 F1**

A large blue goose adorns the entrance to a roomy bistro with a menu of both domestic and foreign influences: carrot, orange and mint soup, twice-baked Stilton soufflé, Cornish mussels steamed in dry cider and black bean sauce, fillet of pork Cantonese-style, paupiette of chicken on a bed of lentils, millefeuille of polenta and aubergine. There's a 15-minute wait for individual caramelised rice pudding. Kind prices on the wine list (there's even champagne under £20). *Seats 80. D only 6.30-11.45. Closed Sun. Set D £13.50.* AMERICANEXPRESS *Access, Visa.*

Bristol   Bristol Marriott Hotel   73%   £137

Tel 0272 294281   Fax 0272 225838   **H**

2 Lower Castle Street Bristol Avon BS1 3AD   **Map 13 F1**

A city-centre high-riser that was once a Holiday Inn. Public areas are spacious and well laid-out. Good-sized, air-conditioned bedrooms offer large beds (two doubles in the twin-bedded rooms) and ample work space. Executive floor rooms are similar but with various extras – second telephone at the desk, mini-bar, bathrobe – and an exclusive Executive lounge with complimentary Continental breakfast and beverages. Children up to 19 stay free in parents' room. Three rooms equipped for disabled guests. Obliging staff and extensive 24hr room service. The Conference venue caters for up to 600 theatre-style; staffed business centre. Free

parking in an adjacent multi-storey car park. Half-price weekend tariff –
tremendous value. **Rooms** *289. Indoor swimming pool, gym, sauna, spa bath,
steam room, solarium, beauty salon, children's playroom, games room, news kiosk,
coffee shop 7am-11pm.* AMERICAN EXPRESS *Access, Diners, Visa.*

Bristol	**Forte Crest**	**67%**	**£109**
Tel 0272 564242 Fax 0272 569735			**H**
Filton Road Hambrook Bristol Avon BS16 1QX			**Map 13 F1**

City fringe hotel in 16 acres with its own lake. Health and fitness club;
large conference trade, with facilities for up to 500 delegates. Close to the
M32 (J1, take A4174) and M4 (from J19). Parking for 300 cars.
Rooms *197. Indoor swimming pool, gym, sauna, spa bath, solarium.*
AMERICAN EXPRESS *Access, Diners, Visa.*

Bristol	**Grand Hotel**	**62%**	**£94**
Tel 0272 291645 Fax 0272 227619			**H**
Broad Street Bristol Avon BS1 2EL			**Map 13 F1**

The central location, friendly staff and good porterage are plus points at the
Grand. Bedroom refurbishment is ongoing – rooms offer a good standard
of comfort and pleasing colour schemes. As we went to press a car park was
under construction due for completion in autumn 1994. Conferences (600)
and banquets (530) make up a lot of the Grand's business. 19 rooms are
reserved for non-smokers. Good breakfasts. Mount Charlotte Thistle.
Rooms *182.* AMERICAN EXPRESS *Access, Diners, Visa.*

Bristol	**Harveys Restaurant**		**£80**
Tel 0272 275034 Fax 0272 275003			**R**
12 Denmark Street Bristol Avon BS1 5DQ			**Map 13 F1**

The ancient cellars of Harveys Wine Merchants are home to a comfortable,
air-conditioned restaurant featuring the accomplished cooking of Ramon
Farthing, who brings a contemporary touch to classic skills. Lunch and
evening à la carte are similar, both with a range of interesting dishes like
slices of calf's liver layered between sheets of pasta and creamed leeks
surrounded by a Madeira sauce; lightly crisped fillet of sea bass on a bed
of garlic and nutmeg spinach leaves sauced with a light ratatouille butter
infusion; and (a speciality) breast of pigeon sliced on a bacon and potato
rösti with roasted goose liver, glazed shallots and a light sauce finished with
grenadine. Other specialities include home-cured bresaola in a splendid little
salad and hot orange soufflé served with a chocolate and Drambuie cream
and crisp biscuit twists. There's also a well-priced lunch table d'hote and
two fixed-price evening menus, the more expensive being a surprise
gourmet menu of six light courses "taking past and current menu
favourites, with an element of surprise". The thoroughly comprehensive
wine list is expertly laid out with each section wisely prefaced. The price
you see is the price you pay, since it includes both VAT and service –
smashing! Note the exceptional clarets, sherries and ports, but everything
is worth drinking here. Adjoining the restaurant is a fascinating wine
museum. **Seats** *120. Parties 14. Private Room 50. L 12-1.45 D 7-10.45.
Closed L Sat, all Sun and Bank Holidays. Set L £16.50 Set D £28 & £38.*
AMERICAN EXPRESS *Access, Diners, Visa.*

Bristol	**Hilton National**	**69%**	**£101**
Tel 0272 260041 Fax 0272 230089			**H**
Redcliffe Way Bristol Avon BS1 6NJ			**Map 13 F1**

Easy to find on the city's inner ring road near Temple Meads British Rail
station. The first-floor, open-plan reception area incorporates the bar and
lounge and there is a good business centre and small, unmanned leisure
centre on the same level. Bedrooms are either Executive (the price quoted),

Plaza rooms (£121) or Plaza suites (£151). One floor of rooms
is designated non-smoking. A buffet breakfast is served in a historic room
built originally as a kiln for the Phoenix glassworks in 1785 and one of the
last traces of Bristol's once-thriving glass industry. Children up to 16 stay
free in parents' room. Free parking (some covered) for 150 cars.
Rooms 201. *Indoor swimming pool, keep-fit equipment, sauna, spa bath, steam
room, solarium, news kiosk, coffee shop (all day).* AMERICAN EXPRESS *Access,
Diners, Visa.*

Bristol	Holiday Inn Crowne Plaza	72%	£130

Tel 0272 255010   Fax 0272 255040

H

Victoria Street Bristol Avon BS1 6HY

Map 13 F1

A strikingly modern, redbrick building standing on the site of the Old
City Wall, on the corner of Victoria Street and Temple Way, in the milieu
of Bristol's rapidly expanding, high-tech business quarter. Catering mainly
for the executive and conference market (for up to 200 delegates), the
modern bedrooms mix well-lit desk space, multipoint telephone and fax
line with uninspiring decor and plastic marble-look units in the bathrooms.
40 bedrooms are designated non-smoking and two on the first floor are
specially fitted for the disabled (there are also adapted toilets on the ground
floor); four air-conditioned, spacious suites have spa baths and bathrobes.
An open-plan foyer/lounge is noisy but reception and porterage are
effectively run. Children under 19 stay free in parents' room; seven family
rooms. Free underground parking (for 150) with direct lift access
to reception. 24hr room service. Conference/banqueting facilities for
200/180. No dogs. Previously the *Bristol Moat House.* Queens Moat Houses.
Rooms 132. *Keep-fit equipment, solarium.* AMERICAN EXPRESS *Access,
Diners, Visa.*

Bristol	Howard's	£50

Tel 0272 262921

R

1a Avon Crescent Bristol Avon BS1 6XQ

Map 13 F1

Just five minutes from the city centre in a Georgian listed building (cross
the old Hotwells swing bridge and follow signs to the *SS Great Britain*).
Gill and Chris Howard's restaurant continues to please. The appositely-
named chef David Roast makes everything on the premises, from bread
to petits fours, and presents seasonal à la carte menus with such dishes
as Thai chicken wrapped in filo leaves, pan-fried calf's liver with onion
compote, and a hot chocolate soufflé or crème brulée to finish. Lots of local
game and fish naturally, with extra dishes on the blackboard – try the
Cornish scallops and Tiger prawns or loin of venison. Vegetarians well
catered for; small selection of British cheeses, excellent coffee. Several wines
on the concise list are under £15. **Seats** 65. *Parties 25. Private Room 40.
L 12-2.30 D 7-11.30 Closed Sun, 25 & 26 Dec. Set L £13 Set D £15.*
AMERICAN EXPRESS *Access, Diners, Visa.*

Bristol	Hunt's	£60

Tel 0272 265580   Fax 0272 265580

R

26 Broad Street Bristol Avon BS1 2HG

Map 13 F1

Andy and Anne Hunt run their restaurant in small, intimate surroundings
a stone's throw away by St John's Gate. Daily menus (table d'hote at lunch,
à la carte at both lunch and dinner) feature a fine selection of fish according
to the market – perhaps grilled red mullet with bacon, potato and herb
vinaigrette, crab salad, Scottish scallops with hazelnut oil, white wine and
wild thyme, grilled monkfish with butter beans and salsa verde, baked sea
bass with lemon and dill. Baked goat's cheese with sweet onion marmalade
and buttered leeks, charcuterie with spiced plum sauce, maize-fed guinea
fowl with apples, calvados and sweet marjoram, veal cutlet with wild
green lavender and lemon butter are other typical choices. Among the
desserts you might well find a hot cranberry and Cointreau soufflé or trio

of chocolate hearts each with its own sauce. Vegetarians need to advise in advance. An improving and keenly priced wine list, though still light in the New World. *Seats 40. Parties 12. Private Room 26. L 12-2 D 7-10 (Sat to 10.30). Closed L Sat, all Sun & Mon, Bank Holidays, 1 week Easter, 1 week Aug, 2 weeks Christmas. Set L £10.50/£12.50. Access, Visa.*

Bristol — Jameson's Restaurant — £50

Tel 0272 276565 — **R**

30 Upper Maudlin Street Bristol Avon BS2 8DJ — Map 13 F1

Pretty, homely decor sets the scene at Carole Jameson's popular bistro, set on two levels and adorned with plenty of greenery. The lunchtime opening has now been rationalised to just Sundays, when an excellent value menu is offered. Cooking generally is of a good standard, with some imaginative combinations such as strudel of red mullet with spinach and tomatoes on a roasted red pepper sauce, alongside more classical dishes like lamb noisettes with a rosemary-scented sauce and roast garlic. There are usually a couple of vegetarian alternatives. Puddings are along the lines of chocolate rum mousse with coffee sauce, lemon soufflé, and gratin of soft fruits. Concise wine list and friendly service. *Seats 70. Private Room 40. L (Sun only) 12-4 D 6.30-10.30. Closed D Sun, Bank Holidays. Set D £13.95/£16.95. Access, Visa.*

Bristol — Restaurant Lettonie ★ — £80

Tel 0272 686456   Fax 0272 686943 — **R**

9 Druid Hill Stoke Bishop Bristol Avon BS9 1EW — Map 13 F1

Martin Blunos combines natural talent with true dedication to produce the kind of dishes that makes the effort of finding this small restaurant (just seven tables) in suburban Bristol well worthwhile. The house is in a shopping arcade, and the surroundings do not immediatley give a hint of the thought, skill and enterprise that go in to cooking. Everything on the menus bears the Blunos stamp of individuality, notably specialities like scrambled duck egg topped with Sevruga caviar served with blinis and a glass of iced vodka, roast rump of lamb scented with tarragon, and pumpkin ice cream. The set lunch menu offers three choices per course, the lower-priced dinner menu just two. Strong French showing on wine list, several bin ends (including vintage champagnes), otherwise only token representation from four countries. *Seats 24. L 12.30-2 D 7-9. Closed Sun & Mon, 2 weeks Aug, 2 weeks Christmas. Set L £15.95 Set D £19.50 (Tue-Thurs) & £29.95.* AMERICAN EXPRESS *Access, Visa.*

Bristol — Markwicks — £65

Tel 0272 262658 — **R**

43 Corn Street Bristol Avon BS1 1HT — Map 13 F1

Right in the heart of the old merchant quarter of the city, in some converted vaults, you'll find Stephen and Judy Markwick's elegant little restaurant. The slightly unusual decor – elegance combined with fun touches – is typical also of Stephen's cooking, which he performs with an assured hand and an element of panache. There are set menus as well as a carte, from which you might be offered tagliatelle with lamb's sweetbreads, Cumbrian air-dried ham and Madeira sauce, spinach, saffron and goats' cheese tartlet, venison soubise with juniper and port sauce, fillet of veal with morels, or baked cod with a pesto crust and tomato chili salsa. Delicious puddings such as fig and frangipane tart or chocolate délice with brandied grapes. Pastry dishes (either starters or puddings) are freshly baked and the appropriate waiting time is indicated on the menu. There's a very reasonably priced house selection on a carefully compiled wine list that includes some worthy bin ends. *Seats 40. Parties 8. Private Room 16. L 12-2 D 7-10.30. Closed L Sat, all Sun, Bank Holiday Mondays, 1 week Easter, 2 weeks Aug, 1 week Christmas. Set L £12.50/£15 Set D £19.50.* AMERICAN EXPRESS *Access, Visa.*

Bristol — Michael's Restaurant — £60

Tel 0272 276190 — **R**

129 Hotwell Road Bristol Avon BS8 4RU — Map 13 F1

Long-established and popular Clifton venue where notable Victorian decor, including antiques, and informal atmosphere contribute to the sense of occasion. An elaborate menu might include scallop and saffron terrine with a beurre blanc, or whole gobe artichoke with tiger prawns and a hollandaise sauce as starters (9 or 10 choices), followed by pigeon breasts with a confit of smoked garlic and wild mushrooms on a chive and bacon rösti with a Madeira jus, or sauté of fillet of beef with caramelised baby onions, glazed chestnuts and a red wine jus (from 10 or so main courses). For pudding, try an iced armagnac mousse with a caramel sauce and mango coulis, or chocolate marquise with a coffee grain sauce. Good selection of British farmhouse cheeses. No smoking in main dining room. *Seats 55. Private Room 40. L (Sun only) 12.30-2.30 D 7-11. Closed D Sun & Mon, 25 & 26 Dec, 1 Jan, 4 days Aug Bank Holiday. Set L from £9.95 Set D £23.95.* AMERICAN EXPRESS *Access, Visa.*

Bristol — Rajdoot — £40

Tel 0272 268033 — **R**

83 Park Street Bristol BS1 5PJ — Map 13 F1

Part of a small group of Indian restaurants offering comfort, good service and a consistently high standard of cooking. Dishes prepared in the tandoor are a speciality. *Seats 60. Parties 30. L 12-2.15 D 6.30-11.30. Closed L Sun, Bank Holidays, 25 & 26 Dec, 1 Jan.* AMERICAN EXPRESS *Access, Diners, Visa.*

> From April 1995 the area telephones code for Bristol changes from 0272 to 0117 plus the addition of 2 before six-digit numbers.

Bristol — Redwood Lodge Hotel & Country Club — 64% — £75

Tel 0275 393901   Fax 0275 392104 — **H**

Beggar Bush Lane Failand Bristol Avon BS8 3TG — Map 13 F1

Barely ten minutes from the city centre (via Clifton Bridge) and quite close to exit 19 of the M5, Redwood Lodge offers conference facilities (for up to 175 delegates) and an impressive choice of leisure activities, notably indoor and outdoor pools, five floodlit tennis courts and a dozen squash courts. The club bars or the Grill Room provide easy relaxation after exercise. Bedrooms, most of which are designated non-smoking, include 28 Executive rooms. Children up to 16 stay free in parents' room. Whitbread Country Club Resorts. *Rooms 108. Garden, croquet, indoor, outdoor & children's swimming pools, keep-fit equipment, sauna, solarium, beauty & hair salon, tennis, squash, badminton, snooker, children's playroom & playground, sports shop, 175-seat cinema, coffee shop (11am-10.30pm).* AMERICAN EXPRESS *Access, Diners, Visa.*

Bristol — Rodney Hotel — 64% — £87

Tel 0272 735422   Fax 0272 467092 — **H**

4 Rodney Place Clifton Down Road Bristol Avon BS8 4HY — Map 13 F1

Part of a Georgian terrace in the heart of Clifton village, the Rodney is just a stone's throw from Brunel's famed suspension bridge. At ground level, lounge, bar and restaurant are small and intimate, with mainly female staff to contribute a friendly welcome. Among the 50% of single bedrooms choose a "Superior" for extra space and a larger bed. The rooms take their names from the ships of Admiral Rodney's fleet at Saints in 1782. *Rooms 31.* AMERICAN EXPRESS *Access, Diners, Visa.*

Bristol   Stakis Bristol Hotel   61%   £114

Tel 0454 201144   Fax 0454 612022   **H**
Woodlands Lane Bradley Stoke Bristol Avon BS12 4JF   Map 13 F1

Modern low-rise hotel near junction 16 of the M5. Good-sized bedrooms, with one papered and one painted breeze-block wall, have all the usual amenities. Club rooms are standard rooms with a few extras added: miniature of whisky, mineral water, fruit, chocolate. Open-plan public areas offer plenty of comfortable seating for meeting and greeting. 24hr room service. *Rooms 111. Garden, indoor swimming pool, keep-fit facilities, sauna, spa bath, solarium.* AMERICAN EXPRESS *Access, Diners, Visa.*

Bristol   Swallow Royal Hotel   76%   £119

Tel 0272 255100   Fax 0272 251515   **HR**
College Green Bristol Avon BS1 5TA   Map 13 F1

Reopened in 1991 after many years of neglect, the hotel occupies one of the most favourable locations in Bristol. Standing next to the cathedral and overlooking the neat lawns of College Green, it was built in 1863. The original Victorian grandeur has now been enhanced by a decor with firmly traditional leanings but which also encompasses an elegantly fashionable touch. The polished red marble-floored foyer has beautiful lounges on each side furnished in a comfortable country house style with deep-cushioned settees arranged in well-spaced groups. Light refreshments and afternoon teas are served here. The cocktail bar features huge oriental murals at either end and a bar with gleaming glass and silverware. All the bedrooms apart from a few smaller inward facing rooms are spacious, with two armchairs and a writing desk. Every room has a whole host of the usual modern comforts from mini-bars with complimentary mineral water and fresh milk to irons and ironing boards for those who must press to impress. Coloured marble bathrooms have super-strong showers and most have bidets though a few have large corner baths instead where space is more limited. There are ten small suites with cosy sitting rooms and spa baths in the bathrooms. While staff provide good standards of general service, reception can be more akin to that found in less ambitious hotels. The breakfast hot buffet is very unexceptional, à la carte being preferable. *Rooms 242. Indoor swimming pool, sauna, solarium, spa bath, beauty & hair salons, keep-fit equipment. Closed 2 days Christmas.* AMERICAN EXPRESS *Access, Diners, Visa.*

Palm Court Restaurant   £70

The grand Palm Court extends up through three floors lined in Bath stone with curved balustrades and topped by stained-glass skylights. Menus follow the grand format, and might offer pan-fried red mullet on a lemon and tomato dressing, 'Brecon Court' venison cutlets with pear and sage chutney and iced raspberry parfait with raspberry sauce. Service is formal yet unfussy. *Seats 80. Parties 8. D only 7.30-10.30. Closed Sun, Bank Holidays. Set D £23.*

Bristol   Unicorn Hotel   63%   £70

Tel 0272 230333   Fax 0272 230300   **H**
Prince Street Bristol Avon BS1 4QF   Map 13 F1

The hotel stands on the old quayside overlooking the historic harbour and many bedrooms and day rooms enjoy fine waterfront views. Best of the bedrooms are Reserve Rooms on the sixth floor. 24hr room service. Children up to 12 stay free in parents' room. Separate conference facilities for up to 320 delegates. Free overnight parking. Rank Hotels. *Rooms 245.* AMERICAN EXPRESS *Access, Diners, Visa.*

Bristol   **Places of Interest**

Tourist Information   Tel 0272 260767.
Algars Manor   Iron Acton Tel 045422 372.
Bristol Cathedral   Tel 0272 264879.
Phoenix County Cricket Ground   Tel 0272 245216.
Mecca Leisure Centre - Ice Rink   Tel 0272 260343.
Bristol Zoo   Tel 0272 738951.
   Theatres and Concert Halls
Bristol Hippodrome   St. Augustine's Parade Tel 0272 265524.
Bristol New Vic and Bristol Old Vic Theatre Royal   King Street Tel 0272 277466.
   Museums and Art Galleries
Arnolfini Gallery   Tel 0272 299191.
Bristol Industrial Museum   Tel 0272 251470.
Bristol Museum and Art Gallery   Tel 0272 223571.
Maritime Heritage Centre and SS Great Britain   Tel 0272 260680.

Brixham   **Quayside Hotel**   59%   £52
Tel 0803 855751   Fax 0803 882733   **H**

King Street Brixham Devon TQ5 9TJ   Map 13 D3

The charming if maze-like feel given by narrow hallways and variously sized rooms betrays the hotel's origins as six fisherman's cottages. The former inhabitants would have approved of the little nautically-themed bar sharing downstairs space with a simple, 70s-furnished lounge. Upstairs, two bedrooms have four-poster beds while the best of the rest share a view over the picturesque inner harbour. Mainly very small bathrooms. The hotel's car park (30 spaces) is 400 yards away in Ranscombe Road. *Rooms 30. Patio. Closed 18-22 Dec, 29 Dec-8 Jan.* AMERICAN EXPRESS *Access, Diners, Visa.*

Broadhembury   **Drewe Arms**   £50
Tel 0404 841267   **R**

Broadhembury Devon EX14 0NF   Map 13 E2

Cooking with a Swedish accent in a small 15th-century thatched pub. Seafood features prominently on the blackboard menu in simple preparations like fillet of turbot with hollandaise, John Dory with orange and onion sauce or red mullet griddled with garlic. Also gravad lax, crab and lobster. Bar menu as an alternative. *Seats 40. Parties 20. L 12-2 D 7-10. Set L £16.95 Set D £16.95. Closed D Sun & 25 Dec. No credit cards.*

Broadway   **Broadway Hotel**   60%   £64
Tel 0386 852401   Fax 0386 853879   **H**

The Green Broadway Hereford & Worcester WR12 7AA   Map 14 C1

The Broadway began life as a monastic guest house, though most of the current building dates from around 1575, when it was a coaching inn. The interior courtyard now houses a pond, paved patio and white garden furniture rather than ostlers and horse troughs. Inside, the galleried lounge with its timbered gallery is an attractive feature. The bedrooms, decorated in pastel shades, are cosy, welcoming and immaculately maintained. *Rooms 20. Garden, fishing, riding.* AMERICAN EXPRESS *Access, Diners, Visa.*

Broadway   **Collin House**   65%   £86
Tel 0386 858354   **HR**

Collin Lane Broadway Hereford & Worcester WR12 7PB   Map 14 C1

A Cotswold-stone house about a mile north-west of Broadway signposted off the A44 Evesham road (turn right at Collin Lane). John Mills and his friendly staff offer a warm welcome and plenty of advice on what to see and do in the neighbourhood (a book of handwritten notes is placed in each bedroom). Rooms are spacious and have a cottagey feel with country furnishings and pretty floral fabrics. Two rooms have four-poster beds. In the winter months blazing log fires bring cheer to the lounge and bar. 'No children under 7 except by prior discussion with parents.' **Rooms** 7. *Garden, croquet, outdoor swimming pool. Closed 24-29 Dec. Access, Visa.*

Restaurant

£60

In the oak-beamed restaurant great store is set by fresh local ingredients. 'Cotswold suppers' (minimum charge £11) are offered every evening except Saturdays between 7 and 9pm., with the likes of macaroni cheese, oxtail casserole and bread-and-butter pudding with brandy and cream. For the more gastronomically minded, a proper dinner à la carte menu is served in the candle-lit dining room. Start, perhaps, with a cheese-topped pancake filled with puréed spinach and chicken or an asparagus and Parmesan soufflé with watercress sauce, followed by sea bass with a tomato and basil vinaigrette or lightly cooked venison with a gin and mulberry sauce. Tempting puddings might include treacle tart, date sponge pudding with butterscotch sauce and damson ice cream with an almond meringue. Tip-top bar and garden lunches (12-1.30) are an alternative to the fixed-price menu, and there's a traditional Sunday lunch (children welcome). The price of the three-course dinner is shown against the main course. Short wine list with all areas represented at fair prices. 'Fine wine' dinners are held every couple of months. Outdoor eating for 12 in the garden in good weather. **Seats** 24. L 12-1.30 D 7-9. Set L £14.50 (Sun £15) Set D £15-£23.

If we recommend meals in a hotel or inn a separate entry is made for its restaurant.

<table>
<tr><td>Broadway</td><td>Dormy House</td><td>69%</td><td>£106</td></tr>
<tr><td colspan="3">Tel 0386 852711   Fax 0386 858636</td><td>HR</td></tr>
<tr><td colspan="3">Willersey Hill Broadway Hereford & Worcester WR12 7LF</td><td>Map 14 C1</td></tr>
</table>

Privately owned converted 17th-century farmhouse just off the A214, with views over the Vale of Evesham. Beams, exposed stonework and tiled floors set the tone in the main house, whose two homely lounges have fine bay windows. Converted outbuildings house cottagey, comfortable bedrooms, many also with timbered ceilings; two rooms have four-posters. Delegates at the purpose-built conference centre (maximum 200) seem to appreciate the rustic, Cotswold-stone Barn Owl bar where less formal lunch and dinner menus are available (as well as afternoon tea). **Rooms** 49. *Garden, croquet, putting, keep-fit equipment, sauna, steam room, games room. Closed 25 & 26 Dec.* AMERICAN EXPRESS *Access, Diners, Visa.*

Restaurant

£90

A conservatory overlooks the garden and surrounding countryside, giving a brighter alternative to the more formal, dimly-lit dining room. Alan Cutler is now in charge of the kitchens, producing a wide range of English/French-inspired dishes on à la carte, table d'hote, gourmet and vegetarian menus (there's also a children's supper menu). Some dishes are simple – poached pear with Parma ham and an orange dressing, roast turbot with button mushrooms and button onions, steak with roast shallots and a red wine sauce; others a little more elaborate such as steamed sea bass topped with a tarragon mousse served with pan-fried scallops or lamb sweetbreads, kidney, liver, tongue and cutlet, each cooked in its own way with its own sauce. Philippe Olivier cheeses are served with walnut and raisin bread; sweets include a hot soufflé (notice required) and a banana flambé prepared at the table. Informative and fairly priced wine list with the ten wines under a tenner a particularly nice touch. Decent showing from the New World and a good sprinkling of half bottles. **Seats** 85. *Parties 18. L 12.30-2 (Sun to 2.30) D 7.30-9.30. Closed L Sat, 2 days Christmas. Set L £14/£16 Set D £25.50/£33.*

Broadway   Hunters Lodge   £65

Tel 0386 853247   **R**

High Street Broadway Hereford & Worcester WR12 7DT   **Map 14 C1**

A mellow, creeper-clad, Cotswold-stone building where cats sleep by a log
fire in the bar, candles are the only illumination in the beamed restaurant
and good, straightforward cooking is the order of the day. Typical dishes
from the à la carte include crispy roast duck with orange or apple sauce,
grilled Dover sole with lemon butter (or parcels of Dover sole and salmon
mousse in a fennel sauce) and pan-fried pork steak with Roquefort and
rosemary amongst the main dishes and starters like Finnan haddock
in a cheesy sauce, crispy crabmeat croquettes with a chicory salad, vegetable
strudel with yoghurt dressing and terrine of pork, chicken livers and
calvados. Homely puds – crème caramel, trifle, cheesecake – are displayed
on a side table. The set menus offer just two choices of starter and main
dish. An unambitious wine list but most at less than £20 and nearly 50%
also available in half-bottles. No children under 8 for dinner. "Half portions
for anyone – young or old!" *Seats 40. Private Room 20. L (Sat & Sun only)
12.30-1.45 D (Wed-Sat only) 7.30-9.45. Closed all Mon & Tue, 3 days
at Christmas, first 3 weeks Feb, first 3 weeks Aug. Set Sun L £15.*
AMERICAN EXPRESS *Access, Diners, Visa.*

Broadway   Lygon Arms   80%   £172

Tel 0386 852255   Fax 0386 858611   **HR**

High Street Broadway Hereford & Worcester   **Map 14 C1**

Part of the Savoy Group, the hotel is quintessentially English in all the best
possible ways. Enjoying a prominent position in the town since the 16th
century, the front is in fact deceptive as thoughtful extensions at the rear
go back some way, to accommodate the magnificent Country Club leisure
complex, its centrepiece being the swimming pool and circular spa bath,
overlooked by a gallery with comfortable seating that opens on to
an outdoor terrace. For the most part, the hotel's interior enjoys real old-
world charm of polished stone floors, low-beamed ceilings, wood panelling,
imposing open fireplaces (even lit in summer) and splendidly-maintained
bedrooms furnished with antiques and country-style fabrics, yet providing
modern amenities such as state-of-the-art satellite TV and wall safe. The
bathrooms are modern too, providing good toiletries, bathrobes (mini-
robes for children and their own toilet bag) and vases of flowers. In fact,
there are flowers everywhere – wonderful arrangements made up daily
in the flower room. This a good place to bring children, who are warmly
welcomed on arrival with their own play kits; there's a decent children's
room service menu (or they can eat informally in the cosy and atmospheric
hotel-owned *Goblets* wine bar next door), table tennis in the leisure
complex, baby-sitting at a very fair £3 per hour, and the family suites
sharing a bathroom are ideal. Staff, under the dedicated and watchful eye
of Managing Director Kirk Ritchie, succeed in being helpful and caring,
and discreet and courteous, exemplified by the nightly-turn down service,
the offer of a glass of sherry on arrival, and cleaning of car windscreens.
Standards of housekeeping are superb throughout, and breakfast in the
restaurant is a cut above the usual. Elegant conference facilities for up to 80.
Ample parking. *Rooms 65. Garden, roof terrace, indoor swimming pool, spa
bath, sauna, solarium, steam room, fitness studio, beauty salon, tennis, snooker,
table tennis, lock-up garage, wine bar, valeting, helipad.* **AMERICAN EXPRESS** *Access,
Diners, Visa.*

The Great Hall Restaurant   £80

With the arrival of new chef Roger Narbutt from London's *Dorchester*
as these pages go to press, we cannot yet comment on what his style
of cooking will be here, though we recognised his quality when previously
at *Sloans*, Birmingham and the *Bell Inn*, Belbroughton. However, we can
confidently predict that guests will still dine (at night by candle-light)

in imposing style in the Great Hall with its barrel ceiling, minstrels' gallery, heraldic frieze, and warmed by an open fire; that he will continue to serve a traditional pudding of the day, and that the superb range of English and Irish cheeses (winner of our British Cheeseboard of the Year in 1994) is not to be missed, while the wine list is sensibly pitched to suit all tastes and pockets. No children (under 3 at any time) after 8pm. *Seats 120. Parties 20. Private Room 96. L 12.30-2 D 7.30-9.15. Set L £19.50 Set D £29.75.*

Brockenhurst — Balmer Lawn Hotel — 65% — £85

Tel 0590 23116   Fax 0590 23864
Lyndhurst Road Brockenhurst Hampshire SO42 7ZB

H
Map 14 C4

A much-extended, four-storey former hunting lodge in the heart of the New Forest, with a distinctive mansard roof covered in copper. The hotel stands back from the A337 to Lyndhurst, half a mile from Brockenhurst. Rooms with a forest view and superior rooms attract a supplement. Children up to 16 stay free in parents' bedrooms; three family rooms. Plenty of leisure facilities both inside and out. Ladbroke Hotels, Hilton associate. *Rooms 55. Garden, croquet, indoor & outdoor swimming pools, gym, squash, sauna, spa bath, tennis, table tennis.* AMERICAN EXPRESS® *Access, Diners, Visa.*

Brockenhurst — Careys Manor — 65% — £99

Tel 0590 23551   Fax 0590 22799
Brockenhurst Hampshire SO42 7QH

H
Map 14 C4

A much-extended manor house eight miles from Junction 1 of the M27 (follow signs on the A337 for Lyndhurst and Lymington). In the high-ceilinged, airy modern lounge deep-cushioned seating offers relaxation, while more active moments can be passed in the Carat Club's leisure facilities. Most of the accommodation is in the garden wing (reached via rather characterless corridors) and includes more spacious Knightwood rooms with balconies or patios overlooking the walled garden; refurbishment was overdue on our most recent visit. Six rooms have four-posters. *Rooms 78. Garden, croquet, putting, mountain bikes, indoor swimming pool, gym, sauna, spa bath, steam room, solarium, beauty treatment.* AMERICAN EXPRESS® *Access, Diners, Visa.*

Brockenhurst — Le Poussin — ★ — £75

Tel 0590 23063
The Courtyard 49-55 Brookley Road Brockenhurst Hampshire
SO42 7RB

R
Map 14 C4

A charmingly intimate restaurant off a flowery courtyard (there are four tables for alfresco dining) reached via a passageway from the main street of the village. It's very much a family affair kept deliberately small, with Alex Aitken working single-handed in the kitchen while his wife Caroline and son Justin (who is also responsible for the well-selected wine list) run front of house in correct but friendly fashion. There are chicken prints on the walls, and the theme even extends to silver cruets on the elegantly set tables. The owners seek out the best of local produce, notably game, seafood and wild mushrooms. Pigeon, venison and rabbit in a port sauce is typical of the sometimes multi-partite dishes which are always interesting but never too elaborate. Terrines appear as both starters and desserts (white chocolate and strawberries); there are some fine British cheeses, and coffee comes with irresistible petits fours. No smoking. *Seats 24. Parties 10. L 12-1.30 D 7-9. Closed D Sun, all Mon & Tues, (in Jan Mon-Thur & Sun D). Set L £18.50 (3-course) Sun L £17 (2-course) Set D £20-£30. Access, Visa.* MARTELL COGNAC

Brockenhurst   Rhinefield House Hotel   68%   £105
Tel 0590 22922   Fax 0590 22800   **H**
Rhinefield Road Brockenhurst Hampshire SO42 7QB   Map 14 C4

A splendid neo-Elizabethan house built in the 1890s set in 40 acres
of ornamental gardens in the heart of the New Forest, reached via a long
drive signposted Rhinefield from the A35 west of Lyndhurst. The original
building houses time-share apartments and some impressive public rooms
used for meetings during the week and weddings at weekends. All but two
of the hotel bedrooms – large, and comfortable rather than luxurious – are
in a low-rise extension. Rooms looking out over the fine formal gardens,
which feature 'canals' and a maze in the style of Hampton Court Palace, are
charged at a higher rate. The main bar/lounge is spacious and an attractive
rattan-furnished Orangery offers additional lounge seating. 24hr room
service; beds turned down in the evening. The leisure club has striking
decor based on the lost city of Atlantis. Good breakfasts. Friendly staff.
*Rooms 34. Garden, outdoor swimming pool, plunge pool, gym, sauna, spa bath,
steam room, solarium, tennis, games room.* AMERICAN EXPRESS *Access, Diners, Visa.*

Bromborough   Travel Inn   £43
Tel 051 334 2917   Fax 051 334 0443   **L**
High Street Bromborough Cross Wirral Merseyside L62 7HZ   Map 6 A2

Situated on A41 North Wirral to Chester road, 1½ miles from Junction
5 of M53. *Rooms 32.* AMERICAN EXPRESS *Access, Diners, Visa.*

Brome   The Oaksmere   67%   £75
Tel 0379 870326   Fax 0379 870051   **H**
Brome Eye Suffolk IP23 8AJ   Map 10 C2

The Oaksmere is just off the A140 Norwich to Ipswich road, two miles
from Diss, and is set in its own grounds which even include a cricket pitch!
Ancient box and yew topiary surrounds the part-Tudor, part-Victorian
building. Stately oaks stand proudly, and the driveway is lined with lime
trees. Old rough-hewn beams, time-worn tiled floor and rustic furniture
feature in the atmospheric bar and the rebuilt Victorian conservatory
makes a most appealing lounge and morning coffee room. Bedrooms in the
Tudor part have exposed timbers and oak furniture while those in the
Victorian half are furnished with antiques. *Rooms 11. Garden.*
AMERICAN EXPRESS *Access, Diners, Visa.*

Never leave money, credit cards or valuables lying around in your
hotel room. Use the hotel safe or the mini-safe in your room.

Bromley   Bromley Court   66%   £89
Tel 081-464 5011   Fax 081-460 0899   **H**
Bromley Hill Bromley Kent BR1 4JD   Map 11 B5

A large modern accommodation and conference block adjoins the original
1820s' building at a popular hotel alongside the A21. The foyer serves as an
airy lounge, and there's a choice of attractive bars (one opens on to a patio
overlooking the well-tended gardens), plus a conservatory and coffee shop.
Bedrooms of varying sizes are smartly furnished in light wood or rattan,
and bathrooms with tubs also have shower risers. Families are well catered
for with baby-sitting, baby-listening and children's play area during family
Sunday lunch; children up to the age of 8 free in parents' room; family
rooms available. Saturday night dinner dances. Free membership of a local
health club, snooker club and night club. *Rooms 120. Garden, croquet,
putting, driving net.* AMERICAN EXPRESS *Access, Diners, Visa.*

Bromsgrove   Grafton Manor   70%   £125

HR

Tel 0527 579007   Fax 0527 575221

Grafton Lane Bromsgrove Hereford & Worcester B61 7HA   Map 14 B1

The Morris family have lived here since 1947 but it was only in the early 80s that they opened this mellow, red-brick Elizabethan manor house, first as a restaurant and later as a fully-fledged hotel. That the decor is sometimes less than pristine is more than compensated for by the warm welcome given to guests and the air of easy-going informality. The first-floor Great Parlour with its ribbed ceiling, red velvet walls, splendid old fireplace and brown draylon sofas and armchairs is the sole day room – there's a bar in one corner. All but one of the spacious bedrooms, which include two full suites, feature welcoming gas-log fires and offer extras like fresh fruit, mineral water and sherry. Furniture is antique – some pieces finer than others – and decor mostly William Morris. Six acres of grounds include a lake and water gardens. Dogs in kennels only. *Rooms 9. Garden.* AMERICAN EXPRESS *Access, Diners, Visa.*

Restaurant   £70

The same rich, gold, velvet fabric of the curtains also covers the walls of the 18th-century dining room here but the big attraction is Simon Morris's enthusiastic cooking that makes good use of both the hotel's extensive herb garden and local produce – Simon is a keen shot and provides much of the wild duck that features on the menu in season. His other great interest is Indian cuisine, thus the fixed-price menus might include the likes of lamb marinated in yoghurt and green herbs and chicken cooked with ginger, garden dill and coriander alongside gravad lax with mustard and dill sauce, Worcestershire pheasant with home-made medlar jelly and juniper berry sauce and fillet of pork with calvados and apple sauce. Puds are equally varied, Lord Grafton's whisky steamed pudding sharing the menu with tarte au citron and a stem ginger, Kahlua and coffee ice box cake. Excellent home-baked bread. No smoking. *Seats 42. Private Room 18. L 12.30-1.45 D 7.30-9 (Sat to 9.30, Sun at 7.30 only). Closed L Sat. Set L £20.50 (Sun L £16.95). Set D £22.50 & £28.50.*

Bromsgrove   Perry Hall   56%   £82

H

Tel 0527 579976   Fax 0527 575998

Kidderminster Road Bromsgrove Hereford & Worcester B61 7JN   Map 14 B1

In the centre of Bromsgrove, ivy-clad Perry Hall was once the home of the poet AE Housman (who wrote *A Shropshire Lad*). Bedrooms provide all the usual modern amenities. Free membership of local leisure club. The largest of the conference rooms can accommodate 120 delegates. Jarvis Hotels. *Rooms 58. Garden.* AMERICAN EXPRESS *Access, Diners, Visa.*

Bromsgrove   Pine Lodge Hotel   64%   £95

H

Tel 0527 576600   Fax 0527 878981

Kidderminster Road Bromsgrove Hereford & Worcester B61 9AB   Map 14 B1

Large hotel with Spanish hacienda looks and a courtyard garden just out of town on the A448 towards Kidderminster. The Iberian theme continues in the stylish foyer with its terracotta-tiled floor and timbered ceiling but the Terrace lounge (snacks served throughout the day) is furnished with Lloyd Loom chairs. Bedrooms (of which the majority are very spacious Club rooms) feature darkwood furniture and boldly patterned fabrics. Good breakfasts apart from the fried bread (best avoided) and rather solid croissants. 24hr room service. Conference facilities for up to 200. *Rooms 114. Patio, indoor swimming pool, gym, sauna, spa bath, solarium, snooker, indoor children's play room (weekends).* AMERICAN EXPRESS *Access, Visa.*

Bromsgrove   Stakis Country Court   69%   £120

Tel 021-447 7888   Fax 021-447 7273   **H**

Birmingham Road Bromsgrove Hereford & Worcester B61 0JB   Map 14 B1

Modern hotel built around a charming garden courtyard, complete with fountains and ponds, and offering large, well-designed bedrooms which include (with the businessman in mind) a spacious, well-lit work desk with second telephone, a comfortable sofa, glass-topped coffee table and mini-bar. Four rooms are adapted for the disabled; eight others are classified as Lady Executive rooms, and there are ten King Suites. Banqueting for 60, conferences for 80. There is one extra syndicate room this year, and thus one bedroom fewer. Good bathrooms have marble vanity units and generous towelling. *Rooms 140. Garden, indoor swimming pool, sauna, steam room, solarium, whirlpool bath, kiosk.* AMERICAN EXPRESS *Access, Diners, Visa.*

Bromsgrove   Places of Interest

Forge Mill Museum and Bordesley Abbey   Needle Mill Lane Tel 0527 62509.
Avoncroft Museum of Buildings   Stoke Heath Tel 0527 31363/31886.

Broughton   Broughton Park   65%   £93

Tel 0772 864087   Fax 0772 861728   **HR**

418 Garstang Road Broughton nr Preston Lancashire PR3 5JB   Map 6 B1

Half a mile from Junction 1 of the M55, Broughton Park is based on a handsome, redbrick Victorian manor house. An open-plan bar/lounge on three different levels serves equally well for the informal business meeting or a convivial drink before dinner. Bedrooms in the newer south wing are slightly to be preferred to those in the somewhat more dated east wing, though all are equally well equipped. Nine Executive rooms, three with four-poster beds, are the most spacious. Children up to 16 share parents' room free. Conference/banqueting facilities for 250/220. Whitbread Country Club Hotels. *Rooms 98. Garden, indoor swimming pool, gym, squash, sauna, spa bath, steam room, solarium, beauty salon, snooker, coffee shop (all day), helipad.* AMERICAN EXPRESS *Access, Diners, Visa.*

Courtyard Restaurant   £65

Within the original building, with a fine white marble fireplace, this pretty restaurant offers attentive service and competent cooking. The evening à la carte might encompass sautéed scallops with a tartare of beetroot, gravlax and cucumber, Manx crab potted with Lancashire cheese, saffron-marinated monkfish, braised poussin with a faggot of cabbage and Puy lentils and fennel juices, plus interesting desserts. Short daily tables d'hôte with four main dishes that always include a fish dish and daily roast. No smoking. Informal eating in the poolside restaurant. *Seats 110. Private Room 50. L 12-2 D 7-9.45. Closed L Sat. Set L £13.25 (Sun £10.95) Set D £18.95.*

Broxbourne   Cheshunt Marriott Hotel   66%   £80

Tel 0992 451245   Fax 0992 440120   **H**

Halfhide Lane Turnford Broxbourne Hertfordshire EN10 6NG   Map 15 F2

Three miles north of the M25 alongside the A10 and approached via the Broxbourne exit, this relatively new hotel offers smart open-plan public areas and bedrooms with either a king-size or two queen-size beds. Half overlook a pretty and peaceful inner courtyard with ground-floor rooms having patios. Power showers are a plus in the compact bathrooms. Three rooms are specially adapted for disabled guests. Ample parking. 24hr room service and 24hr reception. Children up to 12 stay free in parents' room. *Rooms 150. Garden, indoor swimming pool, keep-fit equipment, spa bath, bar snacks (11am-11pm).* AMERICAN EXPRESS *Access, Diners, Visa.*

Broxted   Whitehall   72%   £105

Tel 0279 850603   Fax 0279 850385   **HR**

Church End Broxted Essex CM6 2BZ   **Map 10 B3**

Leave the M11 at Junction 8 and take the road to Stanstead Airport; at the
terminal building roundabout follow signs to Broxted. Look out for the
village church and this gabled, 15th-century Elizabethan manor house
is next door. Attention to detail is the keynote here, from the comfortable
lounge with a log fire and views of the garden, to the spectacular timbered
dining room. Bedrooms are all of a good size and are bright and cheerful
with modern fabrics, table lamps and Oriental rugs. Staff are friendly and
housekeeping throughout is faultless. The beamed and galleried Barn House
is a most characterful function room, holding up to 120 people. Free
parking for 60 cars. No dogs. *Rooms 25. Closed 5 days Christmas. Garden,
outdoor swimming pool, tennis, helipad.* AMERICAN EXPRESS *Access, Diners, Visa.*

Restaurant   £80

Full of crooked timbers, the 600-year-old vaulted dining room is splendidly
atmospheric in contrast with young Liverpudlian Paul Flavell's cooking,
which is modern in style with light, delicate saucing and artistic, yet
unfussy, presentation. Typical dishes might be soufflé of haddock, champ
and whole grain mustard; spinach soup with tiger prawn won tons and
nutmeg croutons; casserole of veal sweetbreads with Madeira, morels and
shallots; venison on a potato and ginger rösti in a light *crème de mures* sauce.
Among the desserts could be hot raspberries in puff pastry on a tarragon
anglaise, or white chocolate and pistachio nut parfait on a butterscotch
sauce. There's a six-course *menu surprise*, a conventional three-course, multi-
choice menu or a short 3-course table d'hote (not available Sat or Sun) with
alternatives at each stage. Sunday lunch offers four choices per course. The
decent wine list is quite fairly priced, but with no notes you must rely
on the sommelier for guidance. When you see S.A., this stands for *Sans
année* (non-vintage). *Seats 60. Parties 20. L 12.30-2 D 7.30-9.30 (Sun
to 8.30). Closed 26-30 Dec. Set L £15.50/£19.50 (Sun £19.50)
Set D from £27.50.*

Broxton   The Birches Hotel   72%   £120

Tel 0829 731000   Fax 0829 250539   **H**

Carden Park Broxton nr Chester Cheshire CH3 9DQ   **Map 6 A3**

At the heart of Carden Park (main entrance on the A534 to the west of its
junction with the A41) with its golf course and wealth of other sporting
and leisure facilities, the hotel looks a little like an executive housing estate
with the high-quality bedroom accommodation (about 30% are full suites)
located within a number of detached, redbrick, two-storey buildings set
around brick-paved courtyards. All have the same stylish furniture and
fabrics plus facilities that include two telephone lines, high-tech TV with
numerous satellite channels, interactive CDI player for which games can
be hired (the golf game is particularly addictive), a mini 'butler's pantry'
with fridge and sink (room service offers Continental breakfast and
sandwiches throughout the day and evening), a small 'dressing room' area
and most have a fireplace – offering the possibility of a real fire – and
balcony. Bathrooms are appointed to the same high standard as the
bedrooms. Public areas are dispersed between the reception building, which
has a limited amount of lounge seating, an unusual 'bandstand' bar at the
centre of the restaurant and, about 50 yards from the main complex, the
Par 3 Brasserie which incorporates bar, brasserie and golf shop arranged
open-plan style under a pitched timber roof. *Rooms 82. Garden, croquet,
tennis, golf (18), driving range, golf shop, indoor swimming pool, keep-fit
equipment, spa bath, steam room, clay pigeon shooting, archery, bowls, boules,
mountain bikes, 4-wheel drive vehicles & course.* AMERICAN EXPRESS *Access,
Diners, Visa.*

Buckland

Buckland Manor 80%

Tel 0386 852626 Fax 0386 853557

£178

HR

Buckland nr Broadway Gloucestershire WR12 7LY

Map 14 C1

Oriental rugs strewn over parquet floors, fine paintings, an abundance of fresh flowers (even in the depths of winter when several log fires warm the day rooms), antiques and objets d'art all add up to a truly country-house atmosphere at this tranquil Cotswold-stone manor, which dates back to the 13th century. Largely antique-furnished bedrooms live up to the promise of the public areas with sofas, porcelain ornaments, fresh fruit, mineral water and flowering plants all contributing to the 'house-guest' feel. Bathrooms are equally well appointed, some with twin wash basins, many with walk-in showers in addition to the tub and all with generously sized bath robes and quality toiletries. No children under 12. No dogs. *Rooms* 14. *Garden, croquet, tennis, putting, outdoor swimming pool, helipad.* AMERICAN EXPRESS *Access, Visa.*

Restaurant

£95

Cream-painted panelling and stone-mullioned windows on three sides create a light airy room which, with tapestry upholstered chairs around widely spaced tables, combines elegance with comfort. In the kitchen, chef Martyn Pearn applies sound traditional skills to a well-judged à la carte that might include a freshly baked puff-pastry case of Cornish scallops and artichoke hearts and a pressed terrine of leeks and sweetbreads amongst the starters and main dishes such as rack of lamb in a garlic and herb crust with a glossy reduced sauce, breast of duck with a ginger and pineapple confit and glazed fillets of brill with leeks and mussels. For afters there are interesting puds – mango tarte tatin with coconut sorbet, hot chocolate and armagnac soufflé – or a good cheese selection. Sunday lunch is a fixed-price affair. No children under 8. No smoking. An excellent wine list, albeit presented in a confusing order, offers quality, fair prices and extensive tasting notes. *Seats* 40. *Parties* 10. *L* 12.30-1.45 *D* 7.30-9. *Set L* £18.50 (*Sun* £20.50).

Buckler's Hard

Master Builder's House

Tel 0590 616253 Fax 0590 616297

£85

I

Buckler's Hard nr Beaulieu Hampshire SO42 7XB

Map 15 D4

Master Builder Henry Adams should still recognise the house, as the 18th century building has been converted and extended sympathetically in meeting20th-century requirements. Maritime memorabilia are never far away; heavy beams and rustic furnishings make the welcoming bars popular with yachtsmen and tourists alike, while residents have their own homely lounge with easy chairs, period furniture and a large inglenook fireplace. Creaky floorboards and old-world charm make the six bedrooms in the main house appealing; rooms in a purpose-built block are plainer but well equipped. The hotel's grounds run down to the Beaulieu River. *Rooms* 23. *Garden.* AMERICAN EXPRESS *Access, Diners, Visa.*

Bunbury

Wild Boar 67%

Tel 0829 260309 Fax 0829 261081

£75

H

Whitchurch Road Bunbury nr Beeston Cheshire CW6 9NW

Map 6 B3

On the A49 Whitchurch to Warrington road, in the shadow of Beeston Castle, the Wild Boar is a handsome 17th-century hunting lodge with impressive, black and white timbered exterior. A lofty foyer-lounge and decent-sized bedrooms are in a modern, sympathetically designed building that adjoins the original. Children up to 12 stay free in parents' room. *Rooms* 37. *Garden.* AMERICAN EXPRESS *Access, Diners, Visa.*

Bunbury   Places of Interest

Beeston Castle   Nr Bunbury Tel 0829 260464.
Peckforton Castle   Tel 0829 260930.
Cholmondeley Castle Gardens   Malpas Tel 0829 720383.
Cheshire Polo Club   Mill Pool House, Park Road, Oulton Tel 0829 760650.
Oulton Park Motor Racing Circuit   Little Budworth Tel 0829 760301.

Burford   Bay Tree   67%   £95

Tel 099 382 2791   Fax 099 382 3008   **H**

Sheep Street Burford Oxfordshire OX8 4LW   Map 14 C2

Situated just off the main street, the charming Bay Tree was built in 1584
for Sir Lawrence Tanfield, Chief Baron of the Exchequer in the reign
of Elizabeth I. Much later it was a training school before becoming a hotel
in 1938. Oak beams, flagstones and good solid furnishings give the day
rooms a homely, traditional feel and bedrooms are in keeping (some have
four-posters that are said never to have left the building). Ten rooms are
in a cottage, while others overlook an attractive terraced garden; there are
also two suites and three junior suites. ***Rooms** 23. Garden, croquet.*
AMERICAN EXPRESS *Access, Diners, Visa.*

Burford   Forte Travelodge   NEW   £45

Tel 0800 850 950   **L**

A40 Burford Berry Barn Oxfordshire   Map 14 C2

Opening winter '94. AMERICAN EXPRESS *Access, Diners, Visa.*

Burford   Lamb Inn   £80

Tel 0993 823155   Fax 0993 822228   **IR**

Sheep Street Burford Oxfordshire OX18 4LR   Map 14 C2

The mellow charm of the 14th-century Lamb Inn, tucked down a quiet
side street in one of the Cotswolds' most attractive towns, is most appealing.
Public rooms range from a rustic bar at one end of the building to a chintz
lounge at the other with in between a combination of the two featuring
rugs on flagstone floor, a collection of brass ornaments over the fireplace,
a display of china figurines on a window shelf and antique furniture – all
polished and buffed to please the most exacting housekeeper. Real log fires
burn for most of the year and there is a very pretty walled garden to take
advantage of the elusive English summer. Cottagey, antique-furnished
bedrooms are equally appealing with old beams or pretty floral wall
coverings and matching curtains at the generally small windows.
Bathrooms vary from spacious to miracles of compactness, mostly with
Victorian-style brass fittings and wood-panelled tubs. TVs but no telephone
to disturb the peace. Dogs (£5 per night) by arrangement only. ***Rooms** 13.
Garden. Closed 25 & 26 Dec. Access, Visa.*

Restaurant   £70

A largely modern à la carte menu – kept sensibly short – is complemented
by a straightforward table d'hote that might offer broccoli and Stilton soup
or mussels in cream sauce, followed by sautéed lamb's kidneys with braised
shallots or baked trout fillet with ginger and lemon. Lunchtime snacks
served 12-2 in the bar and lounge (except three-course Sunday lunch which
commences with Bucks Fizz and offers a choice of roasts and 'the sweet
table'). No smoking. ***Seats** 56. Parties 18. L (Sun only) 12-2 D 7-9.30 (Sun
7.30-8.30 buffet only). Set Sun L £16 Set D £20.*

Burford   Places of Interest

Royal Air Force Polo Association   RAF Brize Norton, Carterton Tel
0993 842551 Ext 547.
Brize Norton Ski Slope   Carterton Tel 0993 824924.
Cotswold Wildlife Park   Tel 099 382 3006.

Burley   Burley Manor   61%   £74

Tel 0425 403522   Fax 0425 403227   **H**

Burley nr Ringwood Hampshire BH24 4BS   Map 14 C4

A Victorian manor house surrounded by 54 acres of parkland in the heart
of the New Forest. Families and dogs are encouraged. Period decor includes
stone fireplaces, a creaky staircase with carved balustrade and unusual
commode side-tables. Bedrooms are simply decorated and have smart, tiled
bathrooms; converted stable-block rooms are the largest and have the best
views over open fields, plus a couple of steps leading directly down to the
lawns. Riding stables in the grounds offer rides in the New Forest for both
novices and experts. Banquets for up to 60, conferences to 90. *Rooms 30.
Garden, croquet, riding stables, outdoor swimming pool, hairdressing, putting,
coarse fishing.* AMERICAN EXPRESS *Access, Diners, Visa.*

Burnham   Burnham Beeches Moat House   68%   £92

Tel 0628 603333   Fax 0628 603994   **H**

Burnham Buckinghamshire SL1 8DP   Map 15 E2

A lovely setting for an elegant Georgian building in ten acres of lawns,
with period public areas and smart modern bedrooms (children up to 16
stay free in parents' room). There are two four-poster rooms in the
Georgian part. Banqueting/conferences for 150/180. *Rooms 73. Garden,
indoor swimming pool, keep-fit equipment, sauna, spa bath, solarium, tennis.*
AMERICAN EXPRESS *Access, Diners, Visa.*

Burnham   Grovefield Hotel   63%   £80

Tel 0628 603131   Fax 0628 668078   **H**

Taplow Common Road Burnham Buckinghamshire SL1 8LP   Map 15 E2

A change of ownership at the Grovefield, which joined the Jarvis group
in the first half of 1994. So there's refurbishment gradually in the public
rooms and redecoration of the bedrooms. It's usefully located, about 15
minutes from Heathrow and close to Junction 7 of the M4, in the heart
of the Thames Valley. In its own seven acres of grounds, the setting is one
of the main assets. Main business is probably banqueting and conferences –
maximum capacity is now 170. Good facilities for children – high teas,
crèche, high chairs and activities like an egg hunt. *Rooms 38. Garden,
croquet, putting, bowling. Closed Christmas/New Year.* AMERICAN EXPRESS *Access,
Diners, Visa.*

Burnham Market   Hoste Arms   £72

Tel 0328 738257   Fax 0328 730103   **I**

The Green Burnham Market Norfolk PE31 8HD   Map 10 C1

A handsome 17th-century inn occupying a prime position overlooking the
green and parish church of a most picturesque village. Sound investment,
enthusiasm and positive aspirations over the past five years have
transformed the 'Hoste' into one of the most popular inns along the
Norfolk coast. Above-average pub food draws on supplies of fresh local and
seasonal produce from within a twenty mile radius. Upstairs beyond the
small gallery/lounge are fifteen bedrooms, two boasting four-
posters. Individually decorated, some with free standing pine, others with
antique pieces, all are being upgraded with designer colours, fabrics and

fittings to match more recent rooms. Spotless en-suite facilities and TVs, radios, tea-makers, telephones and hairdryers. First-rate breakfasts are served in the conservatory, which is also the venue for afternoon teas (free to residents). Ideally located for exploring the Norfolk coast and its many renowned bird reserves. **Rooms** 15. Garden. Access, Visa.

Burnley	Forte Travelodge	£42

Tel 0282 416039
Cavalry Barracks Barracks Road Burnley Lancashire BB11 4AS   **L**   Map 6 B1

At the junction between A671 and A679 on the outskirts of Burnley, close to Junction 10 of the M65. **Rooms** 32. AMERICAN EXPRESS Access, Diners, Visa.

Burnley	Oaks Hotel	63%	£88

Tel 0282 414141   Fax 0282 33401
Colne Road Reedley Burnley Lancashire BB10 2LF   **H**   Map 6 B1

A grand Victorian town house standing back from the A56 between Brierfield and Burnley, a short distance from Junction 12 of the M65 and surrounded by four acres of gardens. The house was originally built for a tea and coffee merchant, and the impressive staircase hall, one of the principal public rooms, features a magnificent stained-glass window depicting the coffee and tea trades. Other rooms, many still with original decorative features, including fine panelling, are very traditional, with red leather chesterfields. A galleried first-floor lounge area offers a greater degree of peace and quiet than some of the ground-floor rooms. Executive bedrooms are the best appointed and a few rooms are designated for family use. All rooms have queen-size beds and satellite TVs. **Rooms** 56. Garden, indoor swimming pool, keep-fit equipment, squash, sauna, spa bath, solarium, beauty salon, snooker. AMERICAN EXPRESS Access, Diners, Visa.

Burton-on-Trent, Dovecliffe Hall. See under Stretton, Staffs.

Burton-on-Trent	Riverside Inn	£65

Tel 0283 511234   Fax 0283 511441
Riverside Drive Branston Burton-on-Trent Staffordshire DE14 3EP   **I**   Map 6 C3

A privately-owned hotel on the banks of the River Trent, where it has fishing rights. Staff are friendly and helpful, and can direct visitors to local places of interest. Day rooms make good use of beams, linenfold panelling, copperware and greenery, and the bar has a little thatched roof. Modestly furnished bedrooms are not large but are very well kept, with pretty floral fabrics and the immaculate bathrooms (all with showers over tubs) boast quality toiletries. Conference/banqueting facilities for up to 150 delegates. Dogs and children welcome. **Rooms** 22. Garden, golf, fishing. AMERICAN EXPRESS Access, Visa.

Burton-on-Trent	Places of Interest

Tourist Information   Tel 0283 45454.
Bass Museum, Visitor Centre and Shire Horse Stables   Tel 0283 511000.
Heritage Brewery Museum   Tel 0283 69226.
Swadlincote   Tel 0283 217200.

Burtonwood	Forte Travelodge	£45

Tel 0925 710376
Burtonwood Warrington Cheshire WA5 3AX   **L**   Map 6 B2

On the westbound carriageway of the M62 at the Welcome Break Service Area between Junctions 7 and 9. **Rooms** 40. AMERICAN EXPRESS Access, Diners, Visa.

Bury   **Normandie Hotel**   64%   £83

Tel 061-764 3869   Fax 061-764 4866   **HR**

Elbut Lane Birtle nr Bury Greater Manchester BL9 6UT   Map 6 B1

To find the Normandie, a corner of France within a quintessentially
English part of the country, leave the M66 at Junction 2. Approach
Willow Street from Wash Lane, then turn right on the B6222, towards
Rochdale, away from Bury. Look out for signs to Old Birtle, and the hotel
is one mile up the narrow Elbut Lane. It makes an ideal base from which
to explore the countryside and at the same time is well situated for the
business communities of the North West. The hotel really came into being
in the late '60s, the dream of a homesick Frenchman, but has now been
in the capable and caring hands of mother-and-son team Gillian and Max
Moussa since 1985, with Joanna (sister to Max) joining the team last year.
Furnishings in the individually decorated bedrooms range from pastel-pale
to dramatic-dark, but all are comfortable and welcoming. Luxury rooms
are obviously larger and even more fully equipped. Standards
of housekeeping are high; staff are genuine, helpful and friendly. *Rooms 23.*
Garden. Closed 1 week Easter, 2 weeks Christmas. AMERICAN EXPRESS *Access,*
Diners, Visa.

Restaurant   ★   £80

The restaurant is much more than just an adjunct to the hotel, and the
Moussas proudly and personally lead a front of house team that provides
very 'correct' service. The cooking is still in the safe hands of Pascal
Pommier who has been in charge of the kitchen here since 1988. The
French menu is reassuringly main-stream in inspiration whilst
acknowledging modern trends. Rillettes of duck with haricots verts, spring
vegetable soup with ham hock, cauliflower mousse and cheese fritters
among the starters and main courses such as scallops with black noodles
and coriander, noisettes of venison with brandy and peppercorn sauce, and
breast of chicken with tarragon and Madeira sauce show the style. A very
moreish hot toffee pudding (from a list that could include warm rice
pudding with exotic fruits, caramel mousse and a dark chocolate marquise)
made a splendid finale to a recent meal. Long and wordy tasting notes
alongside most wines on the fine list, which is notable for its quality rather
than its quantity. *Seats 50. Parties 18. L 12-2 D 7-9.30 (Sat to 10).*
Closed L Sat & Mon, all Sun, Bank Holidays (except 25 Dec).
Set L £12.50/£15 Set D £18.95.

Bury   **Place of Interest**

Rochdale Art Gallery   Tel 0706 342154.

We publish annually, so make sure you use the current edition.
It's worth it!

Bury St Edmunds   **Angel Hotel**   66%   £85

Tel 0284 753926   Fax 0284 750092   **H**

Angel Hill Bury St Edmunds Suffolk IP33 1LT   Map 10 C2

Which came first, the hill or the hotel? Either way, the Angel is an integral
part of the town, and has been in continuous use as a hotel since 1452.
It comprises several adjacent buildings (the oldest part dating back to the
12th century) that gained a unifying facade in Georgian times, and is now
completely covered in Virginia creeper. Bedrooms come in all shapes and
sizes from large rooms with four-poster beds and antique furniture to small
singles with simple white-painted fitted units; all are in good order and
individually decorated – often quite stylishly. Bathrooms are decorated
to match each room. 24hr room service. Ample parking. *Rooms 42.*
AMERICAN EXPRESS *Access, Diners, Visa.*

Bury St Edmunds   Butterfly Hotel   62%   £62

Tel 0284 760884   Fax 0284 755476   **H**

Symonds Road Bury St Edmunds Suffolk IP32 7BW   Map 10 C2

Take the Bury East exit from the A45 to the Butterfly, a modern low-riser with modest accommodation. Delegate and private dining rooms for up to 50/22. Under-8s free in parents' room. No dogs. *Rooms 66.* AMERICAN EXPRESS® *Access, Diners, Visa.*

Bury St Edmunds   Suffolk Hotel   59%   £82

Tel 0284 753995   Fax 0284 750973   **H**

38 Buttermarket Bury St Edmunds Suffolk IP33 1DL   Map 10 C2

Handsome town-centre inn with all-day Suffolk pantry and Viking bar. Half the rooms are designated non-smoking. Under-16s free in parents' room. Forte Heritage. *Rooms 33. Coffee shop (10am-4pm).* AMERICAN EXPRESS® *Access, Diners, Visa.*

Bury St. Edmunds   Places of Interest

Tourist Information   Tel 0284 764667.
Ickworth House and Gardens (NT)   Tel 0284 735270.

Calbourne   Swainston Manor   66%   £76

Tel 0983 521121   Fax 0983 521406   **H**

Calbourne Isle of Wight PO30 4HX   Map 15 D4

Set in 32 acres of parkland, the manor is Georgian in appearance although much older in parts. Classical columns grace the spacious entrance hall and there is an elegantly proportioned drawing room. Bedrooms are of a good size and feature mahogany furniture and plenty of little extras – some now have a jacuzzi. Receptions are held in a 12th-century chapel adjoining the main building. Children up to 11 stay free in parents' room. *Rooms 17. Garden, indoor swimming pool, fishing.* AMERICAN EXPRESS® *Access, Diners, Visa.*

Calstock   Danescombe Valley Hotel   72%   £175*

Tel & Fax 0822 832414   **HR**

Lower Kelly Calstock Cornwall PL18 9RY   Map 12 C3

Where the Danescombe meets the Tamar on a wooded bend facing south, half a mile west of the village of Calstock is where you'll find the Danescombe Valley Hotel. Martin and Anna Smith are celebrating ten years in residence, a decade of welcoming guests to their tranquil, comfortable home. In addition to the five well-equipped bedrooms, just along the lane by the river there's also a cottage which is let on a self-catering basis, with special provision for dinner in the hotel. Breakfasts are "long, light and lazy affairs to provide a gentle start to the day". *Half-board terms only. Note unusual closing times. No children under 12. No dogs. Commission added if you pay by credit card. *Rooms 5. Garden, mooring. Closed Wed & Thu, also Nov-end Mar (but open 4 days Christmas)* AMERICAN EXPRESS® *Access, Diners, Visa.*

Restaurant   £70

Full bedrooms mean no non-resident dinner bookings can be taken, as the dining room (non-smoking) is not huge, so the lucky few can enjoy Anna's delightful cooking, arranged as a well-balanced, 4-course daily-changing set menu (though she is happy to discuss special needs). Local produce is used whenever possible, and a typical carefully composed meal might be locally smoked Tamar salmon served with a mixed leaf salad; guinea fowl stuffed with fennel and potatoes, roasted with olives and garlic and served with fresh vegetables from the valley; West Country unpasteurised farmhouse cheeses; compote of fruit with a ramekin of baked custard; and tea or coffee to finish. The very personal and well-presented wine list is arranged by grape variety, with an excellent Italian selection, and more than reasonable prices. **Seats** *12. Parties 8. D only at 7.30. Set D* £*27.50.*

Calstock   Place of Interest

Cotehele House (NT)   Tel 0579 50434.

Camberley   Frimley Hall   68%   £116
Tel 0276 28321   Fax 0276 691253   **H**
Portsmouth Road Camberley Surrey GU15 2BG   **Map 15 E3**

A short distance from Junction 3 of the M3, a turn-of-the-century Victorian manor house surrounded by splendid grounds that are floodlit at night. Magnificent stained-glass windows overlook an impressive carved wooden staircase – Victorian style that is carried through to the traditionally furnished bedrooms in the main house, two of which have four-poster beds. However, most of the bedrooms are located in a modern extension and are smaller, but equally appealing; 16 are designated non-smoking. Families are well catered for and children up to 16 stay free in parents' room. Conference and meeting rooms have Victorian character as well and cater for up to 60 delegates. Forte Heritage. **Rooms** *66. Garden.* AMERICAN EXPRESS® *Access, Diners, Visa.*

Camberley   Tithas   £30
Tel 0276 65803   **R**
31 High Street Camberley Surrey GU15 3RE   **Map 15 E3**

Mildly spicy, north Indian/Bengali cooking in modest surroundings. Meat and vegetarian set meals (thali) offer particularly good value. Specials include garlic chicken and lamb tikka masala. **Seats** *65. Private Room 16. L 12-2.30 D 6-12. Closed 25 & 26 Dec.* AMERICAN EXPRESS® *Access, Diners, Visa.*

Cambridge   Arundel House   60%   £58
Tel 0223 67701   Fax 0223 67721   **H**
53 Chesterton Road Cambridge Cambridgeshire CB4 3AN   **Map 15 F1**

Overlooking the river Cam and open parkland Arundel House is popular with business people as well as tourists. Privately owned, the hotel is well maintained throughout with pleasing traditional standards of accommodation. There is however, no provision of room service and no lifts, though the top floors enjoy splendid views. Recently added were a larger bar in the basement, a new conference room and 18 new bedrooms, all furnished to the same standard as the rest. Conference facilities for 50; own parking for 70. No dogs. **Rooms** *105. Garden, laundrette and ironing room. Closed 25 & 26 Dec.* AMERICAN EXPRESS® *Access, Diners, Visa.*

Cambridge   Cambridge Lodge Hotel   58%   £65
Tel 0223 352833   Fax 0223 355166   **H**
Huntingdon Road Cambridge Cambridgeshire CB3 0DQ   **Map 15 F1**

A mock-Tudor building standing in a secluded garden on the outskirts of the city. Three of the bedrooms have shower/washbasin only; top of the range is the bridal suite. The Garden Room is used for small meetings or conferences. **Rooms** *11. Garden. Closed 27-30 Dec.* AMERICAN EXPRESS® *Access, Diners, Visa.*

Cambridge   Cambridgeshire Moat House   63%   £78

Tel 0954 780555   Fax 0954 780010   **H**

Bar Hill Cambridge Cambridgeshire CB3 8EU   **Map 15 F1**

Well-designed modern hotel on the A604 with extensive leisure facilities, function suites, and a variety of bars and restaurants. Bedrooms are well equipped, with all the usual gadgets. Children up to 15 stay free in parents' room. *Rooms 98. Garden, golf (18), indoor swimming pool, keep-fit equipment, squash, spa bath, steam room, sun beds, tennis, pool table. Closed 25 & 26 Dec.* AMERICAN EXPRESS *Access, Diners, Visa.*

Cambridge   Charlie Chan   £45

Tel 0223 359336   **R**

14 Regent Street Cambridge Cambridgeshire CB1 2DB   **Map 15 F1**

The simply appointed ground-floor dining room and the much plusher Blue Lagoon upstairs offer the same selection of Chinese dishes. There are set meals for two or more, and the lengthy à la carte runs from a hot platter of prawns, wun tun, seaweed, squid, spring roll and spare ribs through soups, seafood, beef, pork and poultry (book the Peking roast duck in advance) to bean curd, vegetables and crushed red bean pancake. Reliable cooking, good serving staff. The Blue Lagoon provides a night-club ambience, with musical entertainment at weekends. *Seats 160. Parties 100. L 12-2.15 D 6-11.15. Closed 25 & 26 Dec. Set meals from £10.* AMERICAN EXPRESS *Access, Visa.*

Cambridge   Forte Posthouse   67%   £68

Tel 0223 237000   Fax 0223 233426   **H**

Lakeview Bridge Road Cambridge Cambridgeshire CB4 4PH   **Map 15 F1**

Well geared to the needs of private guests, families and business people, this smart modern hotel stands at the junction of the A45 and B1049. Half the bedrooms are designated non-smoking. *Rooms 118. Garden, indoor swimming pool, keep-fit equipment, sauna, spa bath, solarium.* AMERICAN EXPRESS *Access, Diners, Visa.*

Cambridge   Garden House   69%   £125

Tel 0223 63421   Fax 0223 316605   **H**

Granta Place Mill Lane Cambridge Cambridgeshire CB2 1RT   **Map 15 F1**

A modern hotel near the city centre, yet enjoying ample parking and riverside frontage; the hotel also owns the adjacent boatyard which hires out the punts to be seen on the Cam. The smart cocktail bar and lounge take full advantage of the setting, with the conservatory extensions and patio beyond. Standardised bedrooms offer good levels of comfort and most (attracting a supplement) overlook the river and meadows. Meeting rooms for up to 250 – the River Suite has its own entrance from the car park; the Peterhouse Theatre holds up to 180. No dogs. Queens Moat Houses. *Rooms 118. Garden, fishing, punting, gift shop, coffee shop (10.30am-10pm).* AMERICAN EXPRESS *Access, Diners, Visa.*

Cambridge   Gonville Hotel   62%   £85

Tel 0223 66611   Fax 0223 315470   **H**

Gonville Place Cambridge Cambridgeshire CB1 1LY   **Map 15 F1**

The refurbishment programme continues at this extended Victorian house, which overlooks the 25 acres of Parker's Piece. The ground floor is smartly attired in emerald green, brick red and cherry with an open-plan reception leading to a spacious and attractively bright and airy, Lloyd Loom-furnished bar/lounge at the rear. Smart, colourful bedrooms are up-to-date, with chintzy fabrics and well-co-ordinated decorative schemes. The hotel has its own free parking for 80 cars. Children up to 12 free in parents' room. Banqueting and conference facilities for up to 200. **Rooms 60.** AMERICAN EXPRESS® *Access, Diners, Visa.*

Cambridge   Holiday Inn   68%   £106

Tel 0223 464466   Fax 0223 464440
Downing Street Cambridge Cambridgeshire CB2 3DT

H
Map 15 F1

Modern behind its neo-classical facade, the Holiday Inn stands right in the heart of the city (follow signs towards Lion Yard). An escalator leads up from the marble-floored lobby to the first-floor reception desk and atrium-style, open-plan public areas. Air-conditioned bedrooms are the standard Holiday Inn product, combining comfort with practicality. Executive rooms get various extras plus the beds turned down in the evening. Half the accommodation is designated non-smoking. Children up to 19 stay free in parents' room. Free parking for 60+ cars. Several meeting rooms can cater for up to 150 delegates. **Rooms 199.** *Courtyard garden, indoor swimming pool.* AMERICAN EXPRESS® *Access, Diners, Visa.*

Cambridge   University Arms   65%   £115

Tel 0223 351241   Fax 0223 315256
Regent Street Cambridge Cambridgeshire CB2 1AD

H
Map 15 F1

Major refurbishment of the public rooms during 1994 at this imposing city-centre De Vere hotel. Conference facilities include a ballroom accommodating 300. Children under 14 free if sharing parents' room. Parking for 80 cars. **Rooms 115.** AMERICAN EXPRESS® *Access, Diners, Visa.*

Cambridge   Places of Interest

Tourist Information   Tel 0223 322640.
Cambridge and Newmarket Polo Club   Botolph Lane Tel 0223 314010.
Linton Zoo   Linton Tel 0223 891308.
  Theatres and Concert Halls
ADC Theatre   Park Street Tel 0223 355246.
Arts Theatre   St. Edward's Passage Tel 0223 355246.
Corn Exchange   Parsons Court, Wheeler Street Tel 0223 358977.
The Junction   Clifton Road Tel 0223 412600.
  Historic Houses, Castles and Gardens
Anglesey Abbey (NT)   Tel 0223 811200.
University Botanic Garden   Tel 0223 336265.
Wimpole Hall (NT)   Tel 0223 207257.
  Museums and Art Galleries
Cambridge and County Folk Museum   Tel 0223 355159.
Fitzwilliam Museum   Tel 0223 332900.
Kettles Yard   Tel 0223 352124.
The Scott Polar Research Institute   Tel 0223 336540.
Imperial War Museum   Duxford Airfield. Tel 0223 833963 or 835000 (*information line*).

Campsea Ashe   Old Rectory   £50

Tel 0728 746524
Campsea Ashe nr Woodbridge Suffolk IP13 0PU

RR
Map 10 D3

Stewart Bassett's comfortable Georgian house stands in its own grounds in a quiet village on the B1078 (from the A12). The welcome is genuinely warm and guests are shown into a drawing room where drinks are ordered and the meal announced. The meal is served by affable young girls; Stewart himself cooks and does the rounds towards the end of the evening. His is first-rate 'special occasion' home cooking, and in addition to dinners he now produces a splendid Sunday lunch. Starting with cream of mushroom soup or spinach and smoked salmon tart you could proceed to roast beef with all the trimmings, potato-topped fish pie or lentil and vegetable bake. Dessert could be fruit meringue or steamed syrup pudding with thick cream. No choice on the dinner menus. No smoking until after the meal. *Seats 45. Private Room 30. D 7.30-8.30, 25 & 26 Dec. Set D £17.* AMERICAN EXPRESS *Access, Diners, Visa.*

Rooms   £48

The nine bright, comfortable bedrooms include a Victorian room and two four-posters. Fine antiques, drawings and prints are featured. Children are "most welcome", but there are no special facilities. No smoking.

Cannock	Travel Inn	£43
Tel 0543 572721 Fax 0543 466130		**L**
Watling Street Cannock Staffordshire WS11 1SJ		**Map 6 C3**

Rooms 38. AMERICAN EXPRESS *Access, Diners, Visa.*

Canterbury	Canterbury Hotel	58%	£50
Tel 0227 450551 Fax 0227 780145			**H**
71 New Dover Road Canterbury Kent CT1 3DZ			**Map 11 C5**

Privately owned, city-centre hotel featuring a friendly pine-clad reception area and comfortably furnished bedrooms, with all the useful gadgets. Parking for 45 cars, small banquets (25) and conferences (40) accommodated. *Rooms 27.* AMERICAN EXPRESS *Access, Diners, Visa.*

Canterbury	Chaucer Hotel	61%	£97
Tel 0227 464427 Fax 0227 450397			**H**
63 Ivy Lane Canterbury Kent CT1 1TT			**Map 11 C5**

A large, traditional bar also serves as the lounge in a comfortable Forte Heritage hotel created from an extended Georgian house. Close to the city centre, just off the Ring Road. Conference/banqueting facilities for 100. Children up to 16 stay free in parents' room. *Rooms 42.* AMERICAN EXPRESS *Access, Diners, Visa.*

Canterbury	County Hotel	68%	£100
Tel 0227 766266 Fax 0227 451512			**HR**
High Street Canterbury Kent CT1 2RX			**Map 11 C5**

Although the hotel dates back to 1588, the atmosphere is one of Edwardian charm. There is an ongoing programme of refurbishment aimed at maintaining standards, both in the antique-filled day rooms and period-styled bedrooms. The High Street is pedestrianised, ensuring a quiet night's sleep – drivers should obtain directions to the rear (Stour Street), where covered parking is available at a supplementary charge. No dogs. *Rooms 73. Coffee shop (10.30am-11pm).* AMERICAN EXPRESS *Access, Diners, Visa.*

Sully's Restaurant   £65

The restaurant with its crimson velveteen-upholstered bar, pink tablecloths, abstract mural occupying one wall, and moulded ceiling, has the faded hallmarks of 60s' design. It is windowless and does not attract passing customers. The cooking is, however, of a high standard and worthy of the garish surroundings of what appears to be a restaurant which rarely buzzes with life. Pan-fried squab with braised lentils was perfectly cooked. You might eat a terrine of smoked salmon on a nest of marinated cucumber, followed by roast rib of Scottish beef and beef marrowbone from the two-course menu. An additional £3 for the three-course menu might bring you a whole poached pear filled with lemon cream and served with a cinnamon sauce. Service is relaxed and friendly. *Seats 50. Parties 10. Private room 150. L 12.30-2.30 D 7-10. Set L £12.50/£15 Set D £15.50-£18.*

Canterbury   Ebury Hotel   59%   £60

Tel 0227 768433   Fax 0227 459187   **H**

65 New Dover Road Canterbury Kent CT1 3DX   Map 11 C5

One mile south-east of the city centre, two Victorian houses, standing just back from the A2 road, with a large garden, an antique-furnished lounge and a small, indoor swimming pool. Light, airy bedrooms have recently been refurnished. Four self-catering flats and bungalows (not inspected) also available within the grounds. Family-owned and run. *Rooms 15. Garden, indoor swimming pool, spa bath, keep-fit equipment. Closed 14 Dec-14 Jan.* AMERICAN EXPRESS *Access, Visa.*

Canterbury   Falstaff Hotel   £85

Tel 0227 462138   Fax 0227 463525   **I**

8 St Dunstan's Street Canterbury Kent CT2 8AF   Map 11 C5

A centuries-old coaching inn whose day rooms get character from original beams, leaded windows and polished oak tables – and smartness from a recent extensive refurbishment. Bedrooms (many of them designated non-smoking) are neat and pretty and the majority use solid modern furniture that suits the feel of the place perfectly. Children under 16 are accommodated free in their parents' room, with meals charged as taken. Within easy walking distance of the town centre, next to the Westgate Towers. No dogs. Whitbread Lansbury. *Rooms 25.* AMERICAN EXPRESS *Access, Diners, Visa.*

Canterbury   Howfield Manor   68%   £83

Tel 0227 738294   Fax 0227 731535   **H**

Chartham Hatch Canterbury Kent CT4 7HQ   Map 11 C5

An attractive old manor house on the A28 to the west of Canterbury, once part of the estate of the Priory of St Gregory and still retaining interesting architectural features. Evidence of its long history can be seen in the huge inglenook fireplace in the lounge and priesthole in the bar, which also contains some striking trompe l'oeil murals. New-wing bedrooms are spacious and have good solid oak furniture, but those in the original house are more characterful with some exposed beams; all offer numerous little comforts and have smart, well-kept bathrooms. Conference/banqueting for 100/90. No children under 10. No dogs. *Rooms 13. Garden, helipad.* AMERICAN EXPRESS *Access, Visa.*

Canterbury   River Kwai   £40

Tel 0227 462090   **R**

49 Castle Street Canterbury Kent CT1 2PY   Map 11 C5

Thai restaurant in the centre of town offering the usual range of spicy salads, fiery curries and a range of one-dish rice or noodle dishes. *Pud Thai* – fried rice noodles with shrimps, crab meat, bean sprouts, ground peanuts, egg and chopped salted turnips – is a speciality. Good-value fixed-price menu at lunchtime. *Seats 70. Parties 30. L 12-2 D 6-10.30 (Fri & Sat to 11, Sun to 10). Closed L Mon, all Sun, 25 & 26 Dec, 1-3 Jan. Set L £7 Set D from £15.* AMERICAN EXPRESS *Access, Diners, Visa.*

Canterbury   Slatters Hotel   57%   £87

Tel 0227 463271   Fax 0227 764117   **H**

St Margarets Street Canterbury Kent CT1 2TR   Map 11 C5

Close to the city centre and cathedral, a Queens Moat Houses hotel with facilities for families (extra beds, baby-sitting) and business people (meeting rooms for up to 100). Small car park to the rear. *Rooms 31. Closed 25 & 26 Dec.* AMERICAN EXPRESS *Access, Diners, Visa.*

Canterbury   Places of Interest

Tourist Information   Tel 0227 766567.
Marlowe Theatre   St. Peter's Street Tel 0227 67246.
Canterbury Cathedral   Tel 0227 762862.
St. Lawrence Cricket Ground   Tel 0227 456886.
Lydden Hill Motor Racing Circuit   Tel 0304 830557.
Model Village   Westcliff, Ramsgate Tel 0843 592543 *15 miles.*
   Historic Houses, Castles and Gardens
Quex House   Birchington Tel 0843 42168.
Goodnestone Park Gardens   Nr Wingham Tel 0304 840218.
Chilham Castle   Nr Canterbury Tel 0227 730319.
   Zoos and Wildlife Parks
Howletts Zoo Park   Bekesbourne Tel 0227 721286.
Blean Bird Park   Honey Hill Tel 0227 471666.
Wingham Bird Park   Little Rusham Bird Farm, Wingham Tel 0227
   720836.

Carcroft   Forte Travelodge   £45   L
Tel 0302 330841

Great North Road Carcroft nr Doncaster South Yorkshire   Map 7 D2

On the A1 northbound, 6 miles north of Doncaster. **Rooms** *40.*
AMERICAN EXPRESS *Access, Diners, Visa.*

Carlisle   Granada Lodge   £51   L
Tel 069 74 73131   Fax 069 74 73669

M6 Junction 41/42 Southwaite Carlisle Cumbria CA4 0NT   Map 4 C2

Rooms *39.* AMERICAN EXPRESS *Access, Diners, Visa.*

Carlisle   Swallow Hilltop   59%   £80   H
Tel 0228 29255   Fax 0228 25238

London Road Carlisle Cumbria CA1 2PQ   Map 4 C2

Leave the M6 at Junction 42 and take the A6 to find this modern hotel
with conference rooms for up to 400. All bedrooms were undergoing
refurbishment as we went to press, due for completion in Spring 1995.
Rooms *92. Garden, indoor swimming pool, keep-fit equipment, sauna, spa bath.*
AMERICAN EXPRESS *Access, Diners, Visa.*

Carlisle   Places of Interest

Tourist Information   Tel 0228 512444.
Carlisle Castle   Tel 0228 31777.
Carlisle Cathedral   Tel 0228 48151.
Carlisle Racecourse   Tel 0228 22504.
Carlisle Ski Club   Tel 0228 31607.

Carlyon Bay   Carlyon Bay Hotel   68%   £128   H
Tel 0726 812304   Fax 0726 814938

Sea Road Carlyon nr St Austell Cornwall PL25 3RD   Map 12 B3

Set in 250 acres of sub-tropical gardens and grounds, including its own
championship golf course, the handsome creeper-clad hotel enjoys superb
views over the bay. It was built in 1930, and, while still first and foremost
a family holiday hotel, it also offers extensive conference/function facilities
(for up to 200/250 delegates). Large-windowed lounges, furnished
in traditional style, make the most of the splendid setting, as do most of the
light, attractive bedrooms (a supplement is charged for sea-facing rooms).
Families are particularly well catered for, with good outdoor facilities and
an indoor pool for youngsters. **Rooms** *73. Garden, croquet, 18-hole golf*

course, 9-hole approach golf course, tennis, helipad, indoor & outdoor swimming pools, spa bath, sauna, solarium, snooker, children's playground. AMERICAN EXPRESS® *Access, Diners, Visa.*

Carlyon Bay   Porth Avallen Hotel   60%   £81
Tel 0726 812802   Fax 0726 817097   H
Sea Road Carlyon Bay nr St Austell Cornwall PL25 3SG   Map 12 B3

About 2½ miles east of St Austell town centre and set high above Carlyon Bay, the Porth Avallen (built as a private house in the 1930s and now somewhat extended) enjoys some splendid views from its vantage point. The aim of the Perrett and Sim families is to offer peace and tranquillity in a well-ordered and modestly comfortable hotel. A small sun lounge and terrace beyond the oak-panelled lounge takes full advantage of the setting. Bedroom decor and furnishing varies in style considerably from one room to another, though all have private bathrooms and the usual gadgets. Best and largest are the five de luxe rooms. No dogs. *Rooms 24. Garden. Closed 1 week Christmas.* AMERICAN EXPRESS® *Access, Visa.*

Cartmel   Aynsome Manor   60%   £104*
Tel 053 95 36653   Fax 053 95 36016   H
Cartmel nr Grange-over-Sands Cumbria LA11 6HH   Map 4 C4

Half a mile north of the village in the vale of Cartmel is a welcoming house of 16th-century origins, run by the Varley family since 1981. Open fires, magazines and a porcelain doll collection create a homely atmosphere. Accommodation, divided between main house and converted stables across a cobbled courtyard, has an equally traditional feel and a redecoration programme keeps thing smart. *Half-board terms only. *Rooms 12. Garden. Closed 2-26 Jan.* AMERICAN EXPRESS® *Access, Visa.*

Cartmel   Uplands   £65
Tel & Fax 053 95 36248   RR
Haggs Lane Cartmel Cumbria LA11 6HD   Map 4 C4

A charming country house, some two miles from Grange-over-Sands, set in two acres of gardens with distant views over to Morecambe Bay. The spacious and comfortable lounge and the dining room next door are decorated in shades of pale pink, grey and blue. Walls are hung with large, mainly impressionist prints from the New York Metropolitan Museum of Art. Pine tables and attractive pickled pine chairs create an informal backdrop to Tom Peter's delicious, well-cooked three-course luncheons or four-course dinners. Meals commence with a freshly baked, warm malty-sweet brown loaf brought to the table with a board and bread-knife. The style is simple but flavours are carefully thought-out, complementing one another succesfully. A typical dinner menu in modern British style could start with poached asparagus in puff pastry with smoked salmon and hollandaise, or fresh scallops in a bacon, shallot and white wine sauce, and continue with a tureen of soup. The central dish could be baked brill with a leek and prawn sauce, local guinea fowl or loin of lamb served with plentiful vegetables. Finally a choice of four sweets or a cheese platter. No smoking. Coffee is served in the lounge. *Seats 28. Parties 12. L 12.30 for 1 D 7.30 for 8. Closed Mon, Jan & Feb. Set L £14.50 Set D £25.* AMERICAN EXPRESS® *Access, Visa.*

Rooms   £118*

Upstairs are five fine bedrooms all brightly decorated having white-painted furniture and light colour schemes. They are also well equipped – remote TVs, hairdryers, games and books. All are en suite, three having showers only. No children under 8. *Half-board.

Cartmel   Places of Interest

Holker Hall and Lakeland Motor Museum Cark-in-Cartmel Tel 05395
 58328.
Cartmel Racecourse Tel 05395 36340.

Castle Ashby   Falcon Hotel   £75
Tel 0604 696200   Fax 0604 696673   ⬛ I
Castle Ashby Northamptonshire NN7 1LF   Map 15 E1

The balance of its historic setting and up-to-date appointments marks out
the Falcon as both modern cottage hotel and traditional country inn.
Residents relaxing in the restful garden lounge with its attendant restaurant
or in the stone-vaulted basement bar (good bar snacks) enjoy high-quality
yet informal service from Neville Watson and his staff. Choice
of accommodation lies between brightly modernised hotel bedrooms
(recently refurbished) and those in a sleepy adjacent cottage which offers,
perhaps, the ultimate country village retreat. Super breakfasts and home-
made preserves. Two conference and meeting rooms cater for up to 30.
Rooms 14. *Garden.* AMERICAN EXPRESS *Access, Visa.*

Castle Cary   Bond's   63%   £80
Tel 0963 350464   Fax 0963 350464   **HR**
Ansford Hill Castle Cary Somerset BA7 7JP   Map 13 F2

Formerly the Half Moon coaching inn, Kevin and Yvonne Bond's listed
Georgian house is just off the A371, 300yds from Castle Cary station.
Creeper-clad without and cosily cosseting within, its emphasis on informal
good living is epitomised by glowing log fires in bar and lounge, and
period bedrooms, each with its own personal appeal, which lack nothing
in comfort. True personal service sets the seal on guests' well-being. Good
breakfasts amd light lunches (both now served to non-residents). House
parties, taking over the whole hotel and restaurant, are beginning to prove
popular (book well in advance). No children under 8, but babes in arms
welcome. No dogs. *Rooms* 7. *Garden. Closed 1 week Christmas. Access, Visa.*

Restaurant   £55

Yvonne's weekly-changing menu and nightly table d'hote contain a few   🍶
surprises and a good choice (spread across the menu options); her cooking
is substantial and nourishing, the dishes attractive. Start, perhaps, with crab
pasties on a saffron sauce or stir-fried chicken livers and chorizo in an
orange and mint dressing, following with monkfish tails in a sherry butter
glaze, herb-crusted lamb, a medley of fish with a carrot and coriander sauce
or grilled goose confit and black pudding with pear and bacon compote.
Seven or so puddings, from brandy snap basket with caramel ice cream
to rich figgy pudding with English custard. Interesting cheese selection and
a carefully chosen wine list that includes half a dozen good-value New
World wines. Light lunches. No smoking. *Seats 20. Parties 12. L by
arrangement D 7-9.30 (Sun & Mon last orders 7.30). Set D from £16.50.*

Castle Combe   Manor House   79%   £115
Tel 0249 782206   Fax 0249 782159   **HR**
Castle Combe nr Chippenham Wiltshire SN14 7HR   Map 14 B2

A well-run and charming country house hotel in an exceedingly attractive
and popular tourist village location. A manor house in Norman times, the
current building dates back in part to the 14th century. The surrounding
26 acres of grounds, gardens, river and woodland walks provide much
of the pleasure of staying here. Lounges and bar with log fireplaces give
it a cosy and relaxing air. This is matched in bedrooms divided between the
main building, and, by the driveway, a row of picturesque cottages. All are
charmingly decorated with individual style, antique furniture and comforts

in abundance. Comfortable armchairs and plenty of reading material all help to enchant you and two 'extras' which could combine happily are decanters of sherry and remote-control teletext TVs. Bathrooms are up-to-date with a profusion of toiletries, thick towels and bathrobes, good showers and extra telephones. Staff and management are friendly and eager to please. Such careful thought in so many aspects of this hotel makes it one to admire and appreciate. *Rooms 36. Garden, croquet, outdoor swimming pool, tennis, fishing, helipad.* AMERICAN EXPRESS *Access, Diners, Visa.*

Restaurant   £95

Chef Mark Taylor's high-quality food is superbly complemented by the professional service of restaurant manager Franco Campionni. Macaroni of oysters and champagne with fresh chives, royale of Scottish langoustines, velouté of split peas with pan-fried foie gras, smoked fillet of beef draped in a sauce of rosemary and tomato, roast best end of lamb with aubergine hollandaise and tarragon-scented jus are typical menu dishes. A 'Classical Section' on the menu also offers whole English duck roasted with fresh vanilla and tangerines, Dover sole, roast rib of beef Henry IV and locally smoked salmon served with lime. Gourmet vegetarians can work their way through a five-course dinner menu or order individual dishes as they take their fancy. Iced tiramisu soufflé and champagne and caramel mousse with orange salad among the desserts. Good British cheeses. Interesting choices for Sunday lunch include traditional Scottish roast beef. The restaurant describes its wine list as 'brief'; it is not! It's an excellent and varied list with helpful notes (including in many instances the percentage of grape varieties in a wine) and an outstanding Italian section. No smoking. *Seats 75. Parties 8. Private Room 30. L 12.30-2 D 7.30-10. Set L £16.95 (Sun £19) Set D £32.*

Castle Combe   Place of Interest

Castle Combe Motor Racing Circuit   Tel 0249 782417.

Castle Donington   Donington Thistle   70%   £118

Tel 0332 850700   Fax 0332 850823   **H**

East Midlands Airport Castle Donington Derbyshire DE74 2SH   Map 7 D3

Located within the perimeter of the East Midlands Airport, this modern two-storey redbrick hotel is also close to Donington Park motor racing circuit and the M1 (J23A, 24). A stone-tiled floor features in the spacious foyer and pine furniture in the bar. Bedrooms, all with double glazing and individually controlled heating, are decorated in restful shades with floral fabrics and lightwood units. Executive bedrooms, and the four suites, have mini-bars and various extras in the bathrooms like towelling robes and more luxurious toiletries. 24hr room service can rustle up a hot meal in the middle of the night. Children up to 15 stay free in parents' room. Conference/banqueting facilities for 220/180. Ample free parking. *Rooms 110. Indoor swimming pool, keep-fit equipment, sauna, spa bath, solarium, airport courtesy bus.* AMERICAN EXPRESS *Access, Diners, Visa.*

Castle Donington   Places of Interest

The Donington Motor Museum   Donington Park Tel 0332 810048.
Donington Park Motor Racing Circuit   Tel 0332 810048.

Cavendish   Alfonso's   £60

Tel 0787 280372   **R**

Cavendish nr Sudbury Suffolk CO10 8BB   Map 10 C3

Alfonso and Veronica Barricella have been providing authentic Italian food in their restaurant opposite the village green for more than 20 years. Among the favourites in their repertoire are minestrone, ravioli, *scaloppine al limone*, scampi *rondinella* (cooked in cointreau with onion, mushrooms, peppers wine and herbs, flamed in brandy and served on rice), and *rotondo*

Alfonso – fillet steak served on a crouton (croute?) with paté, artichoke, olive and brandy sauce. For dessert they whisk up an excellent zabaglione. No smoking (puffers can go to the bar). *Seats 30. L (Sun only) 12-2 D 7-9 (Fri/Sat to 9.30). Closed D Sun. Set L £12.50/£15 Set D £15.* AMERICAN EXPRESS *Access, Diners, Visa.*

Cawston   Grey Gables   £50

Tel 0603 871259   RR

Norwich Road Cawston Norwich Norfolk NR10 4EY   Map 10 C1

A small Georgian house (formerly Brandiston rectory) with a Victorian facade, about a mile south of Cawston, provides a homely setting for Rosalind Snaith's wholesome cooking. The short, fixed-price-only menu of three, four or five courses makes good use of seasonal produce in dishes such as ham and pease pudding, pumpkin soup, plum sorbet or smoked salmon, trout with almonds, Stilton puff pastry parcel with peppers, celery and onions (a speciality) and sautéed turkey with a green peppercorn sauce. Some 300 wines from around the world are on the super wine list that even advises (tongue in cheek) what to drink when under the weather! Fantastic prices – real value for money – lots of half bottles, and useful notes. Regional winner for East of England of our Cellar of the Year award 1995. No children under 5. *Seats 30. Private Room 24. L by arrangement D 7-8.30. Closed 24-26 Dec. Set D £17/£19/£21. Access, Visa.*

Rooms   £54

Eight peaceful bedrooms (six en suite) offer traditional furnishings together with hotel comforts like direct-dial telephone, TV, radio, and en-suite, carpeted bathrooms. Children up to 10 stay free in parents' room. Bedroom number 1 is the best and carries a small supplement. *Garden, lawn tennis.*

Chaddesley Corbett   Brockencote Hall   75%   £95

Tel 0562 777876   Fax 0562 777872   HR

Chaddesley Corbett nr Kidderminster Hereford & Worcester DY10 4PY   Map 6 B4

Surrounded by 70 acres of sheep-dotted pastureland, the Georgian-looking Brockencote Hall (it actually started life as a rather ugly early Victorian building, happily re-modelled after a fire some years ago) has spawned an almost identical building next door where most of the spacious bedrooms are now to be found. Stylish individual decor, fine cherrywood furniture and extras like sherry, fruit and mineral water make for very comfortable accommodation; one room has been specially adapted for disabled guests. Large bathrooms with alcoved tubs (three with spa baths and six with separate walk-in showers) are equally luxurious. A new conservatory lounge links the two buildings. Children under 12 share parents' room free. No dogs. *Rooms 17. Garden, croquet.* AMERICAN EXPRESS *Access, Diners, Visa.*

Restaurant   £80

The park and the lake provide classic English views from the elegant chandeliered restaurant, while Eric Bouchet satisfies the inner man with some very professional French cooking. Sound skills are applied to local and regional produce to create interesting, well-crafted dishes such as a starter of roast game birds in a rich port wine sauce garnished with roast parsnips in honey and topped with a puff pastry case, or a main course of pan-fried monkfish served on carrot spaghetti, garnished with ravioli of scallops and a light cream of smoked mussels. A good cheese trolley features both French and English cheeses. Three separate fixed-price-only dinner menus allow a certain amount of interchange, and the option to forego dessert. No smoking. *Seats 50. Parties 12. Private Room 28. L 12.30-1.30 D 7-9.30. Closed L Sat. Set L £13/£16.50 (Sun £16.50) Set D £18/£21.50 & £35.50.*

Chadlington   **The Manor**   **76%**   **£95**

Tel 0608 676711   **HR**
Chadlington Oxfordshire OX7 3LX   Map 14 C1

David and Chris Grant's mellow stone house, set in extensive grounds
in a pretty Cotswold village, has a wonderfully relaxing atmosphere and
the owners and staff couldn't be more helpful and attentive. Beyond the
panelled entrance lounge is a second lounge with an open fire where drinks
are served in the absence of any bar. Splendid bedrooms are the high point:
individually designed and tastefully furnished with antiques and period
pieces, they're full of little indulgences like fresh fruit and mineral water,
plus plentiful bath foam in the gold-tapped bathrooms. No dogs. *Rooms* 7.
Garden, helipad. Access, Visa.

Restaurant   **£60**

Chris Grant's five-course dinner menu changes daily, reflecting what's best
in the market, although favourite dishes often recur; space is limited and
non-residents should book ahead. Soup, perhaps celery and lovage,
is followed by an intermediate course such as venison patties, scrambled
eggs with smoked salmon hollandaise or spinach mousseline with tomato
sauce; lamb noisette with orange, ginger and garlic, saddle of lamb with
kidney sauce or red mullet with chive cream may be the main-course
options; finally, home-made sweets such as hazelnut meringue with
raspberry coulis or baked bananas with rum and raisins, and cheese and
biscuits to top it all off. You can forgive the fact that only France and
Germany are represented on the wine list when you observe the rock-
bottom prices here: they're verging on the silly, silly in the nicest possible
sense, because the customer is receiving the bargain of a lifetime, especially
if drinking vintage first-growth clarets. Lots of half bottles, exceptional
ports – sheer delight! Worthy winner of our 1994 Cellar of the Year
award. No smoking. *Seats* 25. *D only* 7-8.30. *Set D £25.50.*

Chagford   **Gidleigh Park**   **82%**   **£275★**

Tel 0647 432367   Fax 0647 432574   **HR**
Chagford Devon TQ13 8HH   Map 13 D2

Forty acres of magnificent grounds are the setting for this supreme country
house hotel, which lies in a fold of the Teign valley with splendid views
of Nattadon and Meldon Hills. The grounds themselves are a source
of great pride (in particular the water garden), but Paul and Kay
Henderson ensure that, inside or out, guests will enjoy the highest
standards. Most of the bedrooms, including two exquisite suites, are in the
main house, and there is a separate three-room cottage just across the river.
Quality antiques, enormous sofas, top-quality English fabrics and pleasing
floral arrangements are features of the panelled lounge and luxurious bar
(where fine wines are served by the glass from the Cruvinet machine):
discreet good taste is evident at every turn and service from the delightful
staff is exceptional. The tiny hamlet of Gidleigh, settled by King Harold's
mother, Gydda, dates from the eleventh century, but to find the hotel don't
go there. Take Mill Street out of Chagford Square. 150 yards past Lloyds
Bank, fork right. Straight on for two miles to the end of the lane. ★Half-
board terms only. *Rooms* 15. *Garden, croquet, bowls, game fishing, tennis.
Access, Visa.* **MARTELL COGNAC**

Restaurant   **£120**

The summer of 1994 saw a change of chef here, just too late for us to
do a full assessment for this edition of the guide. After nine hugely
successful years (two stars in last year's guide) Shaun Hill is handing over
to young Devonian Michael Caines (just 25 years old) whose background –
three years at *Le Manoir* under Raymond Blanc and most recently a stint
with Joël Robuchon in Paris – together with owner Paul Henderson's
knack of picking winners, bodes well for the maintenance of Gidleigh's
reputation for fine food. Michael will be introducing his own repertoire

of dishes but the format will remain the same with a fixed-price menu offering a choice of half a dozen starters and mains together with, at night, a no-choice seven-course speciality menu and at lunchtime a short table d'hote. Paul Henderson's wine list has long been acknowledged (certainly by this Guide) as one of the finest anywhere (in the world!). Prices are by no means stratospheric, indeed they're very fair, and in many cases provide a bargain – no greedy mark-ups here. On a remarkable and comprehensive list the Italian and American sections particularly stand out, but every wine oozes quality. Regional winner for the West Country of our Cellar of the Year award 1995. As we publish, Shaun Hill should be about to open his own restaurant, with a couple of bedrooms, at Ludlow in Shropshire – details available from Gidleigh Park. *Seats 40. Parties 8. Private Room 24. L 12.30-2 D 7-9. Set L £35/£45 Set D £45 & £50.*

Chagford   Great Tree Hotel   61%   £78

Tel 0647 432491   Fax 0647 432562

Sandy Park Chagford Devon TQ13 8JS

Map 13 D2

A driveway leads off the A382 two miles north of Chagford to the Eaton-Grays' relaxed hotel, a former hunting lodge in 18 acres of gardens and woodland, commanding splendid views of Dartmoor and the surrounding countryside. There's an old, rather Colonial character to the entrance hall with its ornate fireplace and a carved wooden staircase leading down to a raftered bar and lounge. Most of the bedrooms are at ground level with south-facing French windows. The Great Tree ambience is epitomised by complimentary sherry on arrival. Dogs welcome (£2.50 a day) but must be accompanied by valid vaccination certificates. The hotel has leased a 2½-mile stretch of the river Teign, and various other outdoor activities can be arranged. *Rooms 12. Garden, fishing.* AMERICAN EXPRESS *Access, Diners, Visa.*

Chagford   Mill End   63%   £80

Tel 0647 432282 Fax 0647 433106

Sandy Park Chagford Devon TQ13 8JN

Map 13 D2

The old flour mill, whose wheel still turns in the courtyard, has been a hotel since about 1929. It stands on the edge of Dartmoor in the beautiful valley of the river Teign, on whose banks the hotel has 600 yards of private fishing. Shooting is another popular pastime, while for quiet relaxation the chintzy sitting rooms have the appeal of a well-loved private house. Bedrooms are furnished with a mixture of traditional, antique and modern pieces. Children up to 16 sharing their parents' room are accommodated free; good facilities for young families including a long children's supper menu. The hotel is on the A382 (don't turn off towards Chagford). *Rooms 17. Garden, fishing, shooting. Closed 10 days mid-Dec, 10 days mid-Jan.* AMERICAN EXPRESS *Access, Diners, Visa.*

Chagford   Places of Interest

Okehampton Tourist Information   Tel 0837 53020.
Museum of Dartmoor Life   Tel 0837 522951.

Chapeltown   Greenhead House   £75

Tel 0742 469004

84 Burncross Road Chapeltown nr Sheffield South Yorkshire S30 4SF

Map 6 C2

A pretty little restaurant north of Sheffield run by Neil and Anne Allen. Neil offers an absorbing monthly-changing menu written in a distinctive hand. Meals are priced according to one's choice of main course – perhaps fillet steak with mixed mushrooms, scallops with pistou, casseroled guinea fowl with smoked bacon and red wine, or *cotriade* (a variation on a Breton fish stew, here using mixed fish poached in fish stock with potatoes, sorrel, leeks and cream, topped with a puff pastry lid). A typical selection of starters might include Stilton 'goyéres', smokey salmon quenelles, galantine of quail and smoked duck salad served with cauliflower florets, French beans, shallots and fresh tarragon in a dressing made with balsamic vinegar; mushroom soup or melon may follow as an inter-course offering. Leave room for English farmhouse cheeses served with grapes, apple and celery, mini éclairs, chocolate tears filled with truffle mousse, lemon tart or a Breton *far* flan made with prunes and calvados-flavoured crème fraiche. Carefully selected, diverse wine list with interesting bin ends. No smoking. **Seats 34.** *L by arrangement D 7-9. Closed Sun & Mon, 2 weeks Easter, 2 weeks Aug. 23 Dec-2 Jan. Set D from £26. Access, Visa.*

Charingworth	**Charingworth Manor**	**79%**	**£110**

Tel 0386 78555   Fax 0386 78353   **HR**

Charingworth nr Chipping Campden Gloucestershire GL55 6NS   Map 14 C1

The setting (54 acres of grounds) is glorious, and the view from the garden down across the valley is, quite simply, breathtaking. The gardens are always immaculately kept and most definitely worth strolling in or just relaxing in and taking afternoon tea in the sunshine. The main house, which dates back to the early 14th century, retains beams showing the original medieval decoration; the spacious sitting room has mullion windows, a patterned and painted oak beam ceiling, hand-stencilled walls, rugs on the polished wood floor and an imposing stone fireplace. Drinks are served here, straight from the cellar. The individually decorated bedrooms and suites feature antique furniture, and the Courtyard and Cottage rooms, created from the original stables and farm buildings, though more uniform and smaller, benefit from super bathrooms with separate walk-in shower, as well as bathtub. Thoughtful touches abound, such as fresh fruit, home-made biscuits and welcoming glasses of Madeira (naturally, since the hotel is owned by Blandy Brothers & Co). Don't forget to check out the Leisure Spa, and the impressive Long Room is an ideal venue for private functions (up to 36 sit-down). **Rooms** 24. *Garden, indoor swimming pool, sauna, steam room, solarium, billiards, tennis, helipad.* AMERICAN EXPRESS *Access, Diners, Visa.*

John Greville Restaurant   £80

Guests in the romantic dining room (in fact a series of interconnecting rooms) will enjoy chef William Marmion's à la carte menu, which has half a dozen choices in each section, plus a few daily specials. Presiding over a kitchen which overlooks the garden, his menu is pleasingly without gimmicks and written in plain English; starters such as terrine of game with orange chutney or grilled goat's cheese with roasted bell peppers, followed by breast of guinea fowl and green peppercorns or poached salmon with a tartlet of vegetables and chive butter sauce. Finish with sticky toffee pudding or vanilla cheesecake and a compote of berries. Good coffee, decent English cheeses and a very fine wine list that has many half bottles and quality wines by the glass (thanks to a wine preservation system) from around the world. **Seats 48.** *Parties 12. Private Room 36. L 12.30-2 D 7-9.30 (Sat, Sun to 10). Set L £17.50 Set D £29.50.*

Charlbury	**Bell Hotel**	**£75**

Tel 0608 810278   Fax 0608 811447   **I**

Church Street Charlbury Oxfordshire OX7 3PP   Map 14 C1

Historic Charlbury with its 7th-century St Mary's Church was royally chartered to hold cattle markets in 1256: the last one was held behind the Bell some 700 years later. With its own datestone of 1700, the mellow stone inn is full of character; the small flagstoned bar and attendant sun-lounge readily make guests much at home and in fair weather the patio looking down a long, sloping garden is a picturesque spot. Access to bedrooms is by steep staircases and narrow passageways, yet the rooms themselves are spacious and neatly appointed with matching fabrics and up-to-date accessories which include hair-dryers, trouser presses and welcome clock radios. The three smaller doubles have en-suite WC/showers only

and one single is not en-suite, though its adjacent bathroom is private.
Conference facilities in the converted stable block accommodate up to 55.
Children welcome (under-16s stay free in parents' room); cot and extra
beds provided. **Rooms** 14. Garden. [AMERICAN EXPRESS] Access, Diners, Visa.

Charlbury   The Bull at Charlbury

£40

R

Tel 0608 810689

Sheep Street Charlbury Oxfordshire OX7 3RR

Map 14 C1

Peter and Lucy Wearing are well established at this town-centre, Cotswold
stone pub, and the ground-floor restaurant has attracted much custom.
Dishes are selected à la carte, and you might choose king prawns in filo
pastry or a home-made soup with warm bread, followed by breast
of chicken marinated in lemon tea served au poivre, or salmon fillet with
a creamy asparagus sauce. Desserts are chosen from the Bull Sweet Stand.
Concise and well-priced wine list. **Seats** 50. Parties 25. D 7-9. Closed Mon,
4 days Christmas. Access, Visa.

Charlecote   Charlecote Pheasant   62%

£101

H

Tel 0789 470333   Fax 0789 470222

Charlecote nr Warwick Warwickshire CV35 9EW

Map 14 C1

Five miles from junction 15 of the M40, opposite the deer park
of Charlecote Manor, this hotel combines public rooms in old beamed
farmhouse buildings and bedrooms (including seven Executive rooms)
in a modern block. Conference and banqueting facilities up to 120.
Children up to 16 stay free in parents' room. **Rooms** 67. Garden, croquet,
tennis, outdoor swimming pool, keep-fit equipment, steam room, solarium.
[AMERICAN EXPRESS] Access, Diners, Visa.

Charnock Richard   Forte Travelodge

£45

L

Tel 0257 791746

**Welcome Break Mill Lane Chorley Charnock Richard Lancashire
PR7 5LR**

Map 6 B1

By the M6 service station, on the northbound carriageway between
Junctions 27 and 28. Formerly the Welcome Lodge. **Rooms** 100.
[AMERICAN EXPRESS] Access, Diners, Visa.

Chartham   Thruxted Oast

£73

PH

Tel 0227 730080

Mystole Chartham nr Canterbury Kent CT4 7BX

Map 11 C5

In peaceful countryside four miles from Canterbury, Tim and Hilary
Derouet's characterful little hotel started life in 1792 as a cluster of oast
houses. There are just three bedrooms (non-smoking) with beams, pine
roofs, pine furniture, patchwork quilts and many thoughtful little extras.
There's a very comfortable lounge, and breakfasts are served in the
farmhouse kitchen. The Oast is also home to the owners' picture-framing
business. No children under 8. No dogs. Check directions, as it's slightly off
the beaten track. **Rooms** 3. Garden, croquet. [AMERICAN EXPRESS] Access,
Diners, Visa.

Chedington   Chedington Court   71%

£150*

HR

Tel 0935 891265   Fax 0935 891442

Chedington nr Beaminster Dorset DT8 3HY

Map 13 F2

The gracious Jacobean manor, with its backdrop of beech trees and very
English setting in the valley of the River Parrett, has a history documented
at least back to 1316, and several well-known figures have been associated
with it over the years. The current facade owes much to William
Trevelyan Cox, who virtually rebuilt the house in 1840. It is now in the

loving and capable hands of Hilary and Philip Chapman. Ten acres
of grounds include sweeping lawns, ponds, a grotto and a water garden,
as well as a 1000-year-old yew tree. The interior lives up to the
expectations promised by the approach, with stone fireplaces (open log
fires), deep, comfortable upholstery, chandeliers, polished tables, and a piano
in the corner. Individually named bedrooms have a variety of bathroom
options (bath, shower, jacuzzi), and are furnished to a similarly high level
of comfort. The 9-hole golf course will have been expanded to 18 holes
by 1995. *Half-board terms only, though if notified by 10am that dinner
is not required, a reduction of 20% is made; "no service charge is added and
none is expected". The hotel is situated just off the A356, 4½ miles SE of
Crewkerne at Winyard's Gap. *Rooms 10. Garden, croquet, snooker, golf.
Closed 2 Jan-2 Feb.* AMERICAN EXPRESS® *Access, Visa.*

Restaurant £65

The light, airy dining room is fragrant with jasmine from the adjacent
conservatory at the appropriate time of year, but always provides a perfect
setting for Hilary Chapman's English (but French-inspired) 5-course,
nightly changing, menus. There are choices for starter and main course
(but not fish), as well as both pudding (sweet trolley) and cheese – a fine
range of British farmhouse cheeses. So you might put together a well-
balanced dinner comprising warm tomato and basil gateau with
an aubergine and pesto sauce, then steamed fillet of turbot topped with
vegetables and herbs, whole boned quails stuffed and pot roast with port
and shallots. Vegetarians are thoughtfully accommodated. Some exceptional
prices on a comprehensive wine list with a particularly fine German
section. Lots of half bottles. No children under 10 or after 7pm in the
restaurant. *Seats 25. Parties 8. Private Room 22. D only 7-9. Set D £27.50.*

Chedington   Hazel Barton £95
Tel 0935 891613   Fax 0935 891370 **PH**
Chedington nr Beaminster Dorset DT8 3HY Map 13 F2

For peace and quiet, and a home-from-home, this is a wonderful place
in which to stay. Not really a hotel, the house, built in the mid-19th
century, commands splendid views and has beautifully-maintained gardens
with a new pond added this year. Run in fine style by Beryl Schiller (her
superb breakfasts really epitomise the country house feel, other meals
by arrangement), the house's elegant lounges, with open log fires, are full
of genuine antiques, fine paintings, tasteful fabrics and delightful flower
arrangements, carried through to the four luxurious and individually
decorated bathrooms (some with separate showers). Here you'll find all the
pampering extras such as bathrobes, super towels and excellent toiletries.
There's a wood-panelled boardroom that seats up to 12, and 20 can
be seated in the dining room for a private party. No children under 7.
Rooms 4. Garden, croquet, snooker. Access, Visa.

If we recommend meals in a hotel or inn a separate entry is made for its
restaurant.

Chelmsford   Travel Inn   NEW £43
Tel 0582 414341   Fax 0582 400024 **L**
**Chelmsford Service Area Colchester Road Springfield Chelmsford
Essex CM2 5PY** Map 11 B4

20 minutes' drive from Junction 28 of M25, at the intersection of A12
(Chelmsford bypass) and A130. *Rooms 60.* AMERICAN EXPRESS® *Access,
Diners, Visa.*

Cheltenham   Hotel de la Bere   64%   £82

Tel 0242 237771   Fax 0242 236016   **H**

Southam Cheltenham Gloucestershire GL52 3NH   **Map 14 B1**

Three miles out of town on the Winchcombe road, convenient for the
racecourse. Lots of historic interest in a much-extended Tudor mansion,
including a cellar bar. Conference and leisure facilities (100/80) show the
modern side. *Rooms 57. Garden, outdoor swimming pool, squash, sauna,
solarium, tennis, badminton, snooker.* AMERICAN EXPRESS *Access, Diners, Visa.*

Cheltenham   Bonnets Bistro at Staithes   £50

Tel 0242 260666   **R**

12 Suffolk Road Cheltenham Gloucestershire GL50 2AQ   **Map 14 B1**

Paul Lucas takes care of the cooking at his smart bistro, while his wife
Heather looks after front of house. Paul's menu typically offers a mix
of traditional and modern dishes: smoked haddock with a light curry and
mango sauce, breast of chicken on a bed of leeks with a garlic cream sauce,
escalope of tuna with capers, shallots, lemon and a brown butter sauce,
tournedos of beef with red wine and thyme. Individual baked Alaska
is a favourite dessert. No children under 8. No smoking. *Seats 30.
Private Room 10. L 12-1.30 D 7-9.45. Closed Sun, Christmas.* AMERICAN EXPRESS
Access, Diners, Visa.

Cheltenham   Le Champignon Sauvage   ★   £75

Tel 0242 573449   **R**

24-26 Suffolk Road Cheltenham Gloucestershire GL50 2AQ   **Map 14 B1**

David and Helen Everitt-Matthias's well-respected restaurant has
unobtrusive decor in pale grey given a lift with a hint of pink and modern
prints. David's well-disciplined culinary imagination remains firmly based
around sound classic French skills, although modern touches take his
cooking into the firmament of star-winners. Dishes are presented in both
French and English on the clearly laid-out menus that change seasonally
and offer a short choice of around five dishes at each stage. An appetiser for
à la carte diners might be spiced pigeon breasts on a bed of beetroot and
barley and chocolate-enhanced sauce, scallop on ratatouille or cotechino
of venison and leek – enough to get the taste buds not just up and running
but well into top gear! David's skills in all areas of the kitchen are
demonstrated by dishes such as a terrine of pressed foie gras with mushy
peas and ham hock served with a warm green bean and black pudding
salad or fillet of Cockleford trout with a light fennel and broad bean
mousse and a watercress sauce – these are just starters! Follow, perhaps,
with fillet of Cotswold beef with oxtail tortelloni and a red wine shallot
sauce or roast Wye Valley salmon and squid with roast peppers, red onions
and a light tomato dressing. Fillet of cod is adorned with mussels and leeks
and accompanied by a cream sauce enhanced with Gewürztraminer; a dish
of rabbit comprises its leg braised with nuts and saddle wrapped
in pistachio mousse – involved dishes whose execution is invariably first-
class. Also tip-top are desserts such as iced honey and apricot terrine studded
with candied fruit, tiramisu, coconut blancmange with a gingerbread sauce
and candied nuts or light, bitter chocolate tart served with home-made
chocolate ripple ice cream – results matching the considerably fancier-
sounding French menu descriptions. Fine French cheeses complete the
Gallic picture. A multi-course Tasting Menu is also available for diners
before 8.30pm by prior arrangement. Three courses on the table d'hote
might offer a light potato and garlic soup with parsley cream or fillet
of brown trout with green beans and a ginger and lemon butter followed
by chicken fricassee with prunes, armagnac, noodles and walnuts or herb-
crusted lamb garnished with fennel and beetroot chutney; cheese or a daily
dessert and coffee to end a good-value meal. Vegetarians should advise
in advance. A lot of work has gone into the compilation of the revised

wine list which is most fairly priced (half are under £20 per bottle, many under £15); excellent balance, helpful tasting notes, worth exploring. *Seats 28. Parties 20. L 12.30-1.30 D 7.30-9.15. Closed L Sat, all Sun, Bank Holidays, 1 week Christmas. Set L £14.50/£17.50 Set D £18.50 & £24/£28.50.* AMERICAN EXPRESS *Access, Diners, Visa.*

| Cheltenham | Cheltenham Park | 68% | £114 |

Tel 0242 222021   Fax 0242 226935   **H**

Cirencester Rd Charlton Kings Cheltenham Gloucestershire GL53 8EA   Map 14 B1

South of town on the A435, a predominantly conference hotel (max. 350 delegates) based on a Georgian house which gives considerable style to smart public areas, particularly the foyer/reception and bar/lounge, both of which feature marbled columns. Good, well-equipped bedrooms featuring solid lightwood furniture are mostly in a new wing. The main meeting rooms have glass doors opening on to a patio enjoying fine views (shared by some bedrooms) across the adjacent Lilleybrook golf course to hills beyond – an ideal 'break-out' area for conferences in the summer months. 24hr room service. Children up to 16 stay free in parents' room. *Rooms 153. Garden.* AMERICAN EXPRESS *Access, Diners, Visa.*

| Cheltenham | Epicurean | ★ ★ | £100 |

Tel 0242 222466   Fax 0242 222474   **R**

81 The Promenade Cheltenham Gloucestershire GL51 1PJ   Map 14 B1

Patrick and Claire McDonald's smaller version of Sir Terence Conran's Butler's Wharf Gastrodrome occupies a Grade-II listed Regency terrace building, overlooking the fashionable inner promenade. Just opened, it's a bold enterprise and Claire's deft touch for interior design is clearly evident on every level: the ultra-modern basement continental Café Bar (open from 11-11) with high stools and lightwood counters serves tapas and tarts as well as a good selection of wines by the glass, while the ground-floor Bistro (bookings accepted), splendidly managed by Kevin Webley, has seating for around 40 and offers quality dishes at affordable prices: main courses (crab ravioli with ginger, grilled black pudding with lentils and onions, roast fishcake with a herb butter sauce) are around £7.50 each. However, it is for Patrick's serious cooking in the elegant and restful first-floor dining room that the above stars have been awarded. It's a lovely room with hand-painted wood panelling, a high ceiling with intricate cornices, pale beige curtains and carpet, offset by crisp white tablecloths with each table simply decorated by a pot of miniature white roses. Service, led by restaurant manager Max Palmer and sommelier Stephane Rodillon, with Claire also on hand in the evenings, is supremely professional, completely at ease with the style of presentation of dishes. Patrick and his brigade's cooking is British, albeit in a contemporary fashion, with modern techniques that owe much to classical training. The menu is purposely short, at present five choices in each section, though this may well expand to six later, when the restaurant has bedded in. To start, you will receive an appetiser, perhaps a gazpacho with caviar cream or an escabeche of salmon; first courses might include a quite perfect risotto of wild mushrooms and white truffle (moist without being cloying), lobster and langoustine ravioli or a stunning-looking plate of sea scallops with squid ink and ginger. For the main event you could choose roast salmon that arrives on a mound of unwatery spinach and surrounded by a concassé of tomatoes with a hint of basil, or a generous portion of braised beef topped with warm foie gras, accompanied by a rich red wine gravy and turned potatoes, carrots and onions. Delectable desserts: a tarte tatin (called caramelised apple here), chocolate tart or tangy and smooth glazed lemon tart; these are also preceded by a taster – a small cup of red berry soup in summer, a little bread-and-butter pudding or soufflé promised in winter. Excellent bread rolls and splendid coffee, accompanied by fine petits fours, end the meal with a flourish. There is also a £50 gourmet menu for an entire table, seven courses *en surprise,* while the bargain seasonal set lunch is presented verbally, depending on what's fresh from the markets. The restaurant wine list is of sensible length, though there's nothing outside France and the New World. Only in the Bistro and Café Bar do either Spain or Italy get a look-in. Plenty of parking outside (pay & display lunchtime, free in the evenings). *Seats 30. Parties 8. Private Room 16. L 12.30-2.30 D 7.30-10. Closed Sun, 2 weeks Jan, 1 week Aug. Set L £14/£17.50 Set D £27.50/£35.*

Cheltenham　　Golden Valley Thistle Hotel　　69%　　　£90

Tel 0242 232691　Fax 0242 221846　　　　　　　　　　**H**

Gloucester Road Cheltenham Gloucestershire GL51 0TS　　Map 14 B1

A 70s' hotel on the outskirts of Cheltenham, one mile from Junction 11 of the M5 (next to GCHQ) and two miles from the town centre. The bright, modern Garden Lounge has wicker furniture and its own patio. Extensive conference and banqueting facilities (up to 220 delegates accommodated theatre-style) have recently been completely refurbished. Free parking for up to 250. *Rooms 124. Garden, croquet, indoor swimming pool, gym, sauna, steam room, spa bath, solarium, beautician, tennis.* AMERICAN EXPRESS® *Access, Diners, Visa.*

> We do not accept free meals or hospitality – our inspectors pay their own bills.

Cheltenham　　　The Greenway　　80%　　　£110

Tel 0242 862352　Fax 0242 862780　　　　　　　　　　**HR**

Shurdington Cheltenham Gloucestershire GL51 5UG　　Map 14 B1

On the A46 at Shurdington a couple of miles south west of Cheltenham town centre, the creeper-clad Elizabethan manor opened as a hotel in 1947. The Elliotts have been in situ for fifteen years – owner Tony is a most engaging and effervescent *patron*, very professional, and with his young team runs an extremely efficient ship. Log fires in winter warm the flagstoned entrance foyer and large drawing room, both furnished with plenty of sofas and easy chairs, polished antiques, fine paintings and lovely flower arrangements. All the charming bedrooms, whether in the main house (reached via a splendid staircase) or in the restored coach house, have superb views; they are spacious and comfortable with antique furniture, stylish fabrics and excellent bathrooms (note the Floris toiletries and serious towels), most with tubs that have both hand and overhead showers. Housekeeping is immaculate (turndown service at night). Two meeting rooms (up to 35 theatre-style, 18 boardroom-style). No children under seven. No dogs. *Rooms 19. Garden, croquet, helipad. Closed 2-7 Jan.* AMERICAN EXPRESS® *Access, Diners, Visa.* MARTELL COGNAC

Restaurant　　　　　　　　　　　　　　　　　　£85

The Conservatory dining room, with delightful views of the sunken garden and lily pond (floodlit at night), offers enticing menus with interesting dishes created by chef Chris Colmer. Luncheon choice can be simple and familiar – potato and leek soup, boiled ham hock with parsley sauce, steak and chips – or more unusual, like cassoulet terrine filled with butter beans, duck confit and Toulouse sausage or pan-fried American sea bass with black pasta and little vegetables roasted with thyme. The evening selection offers equal variety: red pepper bavarois, poached smoked haddock with chive mash and a tarragon gratin, seared salmon with morel sauce, braised pig's trotter filled with a black pudding mousseline. Three vegetarian main courses are available, and puddings run from lemon curd tart to Stilton soufflé with glazed pears. Service is spot-on. There are few surprises on the wine list (mostly French), but with a bit of this and that from the New World, which perhaps represents the best value. *Seats 40. Private Room 20. L 12-2 D 7-9.30 (Sun to 8.30). Closed L Sat, L Bank Holidays. Set L £15/£17 Set D £25.*

Cheltenham   On The Park   76%   £96

Tel 0242 518898   Fax 0242 2511526   **HR**

Evesham Road Cheltenham Gloucestershire GL52 2AH   Map 14 B1

One of the many attributes of Darryl and Lesley-Anne Gregory's charming
town house opposite Pittville Park on the northern outskirts of town
(A435 Evesham Rd) is the luxurious and generous-sized bathrooms, some
almost rooms in themselves, with a wicker chair, marble-topped vanity
unit, bidet, old-fashioned tub and the usual pampering extras. Individually
designed bedrooms, each named after someone with Pittville connections,
are equally tasteful with fine bed linen, smart fabrics, genuine antiques,
collections of porcelain and decent paintings. The suites and four-poster
room are particularly well appointed. The civilised public areas certainly
do not suffer by comparison, notably a restful drawing room/bar and cosy
library/boardroom (seating up to 18), with French doors opening on to
a delightful enclosed and secluded garden, both elegantly furnished and
decorated. Note the splendid grandfather clock beside the reception desk,
and the super new loos. High levels of service and exemplary housekeeping
include the turn-down of beds and replacement of towels at night,
a welcoming decanter of mulled wine, mineral water and chocolates
on arrival. Super breakfasts are served with mini-boards of assorted breads
and toasts, pots of home-made jam and marmalade, good cafetière coffee
and large glasses of freshly squeezed orange juice. *Rooms 12. Garden.
Closed 1 week mid-Jan.* AMERICAN EXPRESS *Access, Diners, Visa.*

Restaurant   Tel 0242 227713   £70

Run on a concession basis by chef Eamonn and Nicola Webster, the dining
room, with its high ceiling and intricate cornices, is classically and
strikingly Regency in style, with each table graced by a tall, wrought-iron,
candelabra/floral display. There are both set and à la carte menus featuring
well-conceived dishes that owe much to classical training but are presented
in a more modern European fashion. Start with perhaps a well-made game
terrine, prettily served with clusters of home-made chutney and a tangy red
wine dressing, followed by a large portion of grilled brill unusually served
atop fried seaweed with a veal sauce, saffron potatoes and a good mixture
of al dente vegetables, and ending with a less than classical, but nonetheless
delightful apple *and* pear tarte tatin that comes with excellent clove ice
cream and butterscotch sauce. A sensibly short wine list has something for
everyone at fair prices. Service is both thoroughly pleasant and professional.
Light lunches can be taken in the garden. Traditional Sunday lunch.
*Seats 28. Parties 10. Private Room 18. L 12-2 (Sun to 2.30) D 7.30-9.30 (Sat
to 10). Set L £14.50 Set D £19.50.*

Note that all telephone numbers with area codes starting with 0
will start 01 from 16 April 1995.

Cheltenham   Queen's Hotel   69%   £109

Tel 0242 514724   Fax 0242 224145   **H**

The Promenade Cheltenham Gloucestershire GL50 1NN   Map 14 B1

In the heart of the elegant spa town of Cheltenham is the equally elegant
Queen's, built early (1838) in Queen Victoria's reign, and named in her
honour. The imposing white colonnaded hotel overlooks the Imperial
Gardens and the lofty foyer/lounge creates an air of Regency elegance
echoed in the magnificent stairwell and Napier Bar. Bedrooms (the best
of which are on the first floor) include six suites and several Executive
rooms; two rooms feature four-posters. All are well maintained and have
desk space, armchairs and the usual extras. Conference and banquet
facilities, catering for up to 200. 24hr room service. Free parking. Forte
Grand. *Rooms 74.* AMERICAN EXPRESS *Access, Diners, Visa.*

Cheltenham — Travel Inn — £43

Tel 0242 233847   Fax 0242 244887

L

Tewkesbury Road Uckington Cheltenham Gloucestershire GL51 9SL

Map 14 B1

10 minutes' drive from Cheltenham race course. *Rooms 40.* AMERICAN EXPRESS
Access, Diners, Visa.

Cheltenham — Places of Interest

Tourist Information   Tel 0242 522878.
Sudeley Castle   Winchcombe Tel 0242 602308.
Chedworth Roman Villa (NT)   Yanworth, Nr Cheltenham Tel 024289 256.
Cheltenham Art Gallery and Museum   Tel 0242 237431.
Pittville Pump Room Museum   Gallery of Fashion Pittville Tel 0242 512740.
Cheltenham Racecourse   Tel 0242 513014.
   Theatres and Concert Halls
Everyman Theatre   Tel 0242 512515.
Pittville Pump Room   Tel 0242 523690.
Playhouse Theatre   Tel 0242 522852.
Shaftesbury Hall Theatre   Tel 0242 22795.

Chelwood — Chelwood House — 63% — £75

Tel 0761 490730   Fax ext 504

HR

Chelwood Bristol Avon BS18 4NH

Map 13 F1

A former dower house, dating from the reign of Charles II, with lovely, unspoilt views across rolling countryside towards Bath, some 10 miles away. Owners Jill and Rudi Birk, who clearly love the place, have created a warm and welcoming atmosphere. The lounge, boasting fine listed panelling, opens to an attractive staircase leading to individually styled bedrooms which some may find over-fussy. The French, Chinese and Victorian themed rooms all have four-posters, and some humour is shown in naming the smallest one Lilliput. Home-made fruit compote is a feature of good, traditional breakfasts served in the sunny dining room.
No children under 8. No dogs. 200 yards south of the junction of A37 and A368. *Rooms 11. Garden, helipad. Closed first 2 weeks Jan.* AMERICAN EXPRESS
Access, Diners, Visa.

Garden Restaurant — £50

The conservatory-style 'restaurant in a garden', with plants and fountain, is decorated with murals. Typical offerings from Rudi, a Bavarian by birth, might include pigeon breast and crispy bacon salad or moules marinière to start, followed by steamed Cornish haddock on green tagliatelle with tarragon butter sauce or haunch of venison braised in red wine. If it's on the menu, try the Bavarian dish *herrentopf* – strips of beef tossed in butter with mushrooms, gherkins and tomato cream sauce and served with spätzle. Finish with hot Bavarian apple tart with cream or meringue chantilly with fresh pineapple, Kirsch and raspberry sauce. No smoking. *Seats 24. Parties 16. L (Sun) 12.30-1.15 D 7.30-9. Closed D Sun, first 2 weeks Jan. Set Sun L £10.50/£13.50 Set D £20.*

Chenies — Bedford Arms Thistle — 64% — £100

Tel 0923 283301   Fax 0923 284825

H

Chenies nr Rickmansworth Buckinghamshire WD3 6EQ

Map 15 E2

Redbrick hotel on the edge of the village, two miles from junction 18 of the M25. Banqueting facilities for 65, conferences up to 25. Two bars. 24hr room service in the recently refurbished bedrooms. *Rooms 10.*
AMERICAN EXPRESS *Access, Diners, Visa.*

Chenies   Place of Interest

Moor Park Mansion   Rickmansworth Tel 0923 776611.

Chessington   Travel Inn   £43
Tel 0372 744060   Fax 0372 720889   **L**
Leatherhead Road Chessington Surrey KT9 2NE   Map 15 E3

Adjacent to Chessington World of Adventure, 10 minutes' drive from
Hampton Court and both Sandown and Epsom race courses. *Rooms 42.*
AMERICAN EXPRESS® *Access, Diners, Visa.*

Chester   Abbots Well   62%   £89
Tel 0244 332121   Fax 0244 335287   **H**
Whitchurch Road Christleton Chester Cheshire CH3 5QL   Map 6 A2

One mile from the M53, an angular, low-rise modern hotel standing
in spacious grounds on the A41 east of Chester. Conference/banqueting
facilities for 230/200, health club. Jarvis. *Rooms 129. Garden, indoor
swimming pool, gym, sauna, spa bath, solarium.* AMERICAN EXPRESS® *Access,
Diners, Visa.*

Chester   Blossoms Hotel   63%   £97
Tel 0244 323186   Fax 0244 346433   **H**
St John Street Chester Cheshire CH1 1HL   Map 6 A2

Just off one of Chester's main shopping streets, Blossoms is a characterful
mix of 18th-century charm and modern amenities. Banqueting facilities for
up to 50, conferences for 100. Forte. *Rooms 64.* AMERICAN EXPRESS® *Access,
Diners, Visa.*

Chester   Chester Grosvenor   84%   £195
Tel 0244 324024   Fax 0244 313246   **HR**
Eastgate Street Chester Cheshire CH1 1LT   Map 6 A2

The distinctive frontage of this imposing hotel has graced the main street
in its present form since 1866, although hospitality had been provided
on the site from much earlier. It was acquired by the Grosvenor family
in 1800 and remains a jewel in their crown. The interior decor is as
graceful and elegant as you could wish, with sweeping staircases, the
magnificent Grosvenor chandelier, panelled library and draped drawing
room all providing an air of timelessness. Suites (8) and bedrooms are
equally luxurious, with attention to every possible detail. Handmade
furniture from Italy, silks and other fabrics from France and the USA,
combine with quality British craftsmanship to create a reassuring feeling
of solidity. Children up to 12 share their parents' room free; stylish
banqueting and conference facilities cater for up to 250 delegates; and there
is direct access to the hotel from Newgate Street car park. *Rooms 86.
Closed 25 & 26 Dec. Sauna, solarium, gym, valeting.* AMERICAN EXPRESS® *Access,
Diners, Visa.*

Arkle Restaurant   ★   £110

Named in honour of the triple Gold Cup-winning steeplechaser, this
thoroughbred restaurant is deep in the heart of the hotel beyond the library
lounge, where pre-prandial drinks are served, but with a skylight providing
natural illumination. Solidly luxurious, it boasts marbled columns, baronial
stone-clad walls and elegantly laid tables as highly polished as the service.
Lunchtime brings a fixed-price *menu du marché* (which always includes
a roast carved at the table from a silver trolley) supplemented by a couple
of fish dishes of the day while dinner is à la carte plus a six-course *menu
gourmand* temptingly described by the restaurant manager (or not, if you

See over

prefer to eat *en-surprise*). High-class cooking, under executive chef Paul Reed, produces such dishes as artichoke salad with oyster fritters, a pot-roast of wild rabbit with juniper-scented cabbage and mushroom sausage, and blanquette of John Dory with mustard seed and herb 'spatzelles' that combine the light modern style with a sound classical background. Tempting desserts like a delicious hot *soufflé aux pommes* or fine chocolate pastry leaves with grilled bananas vie for attention with a good cheese trolley featuring a wide selection of British farmhouse cheeses along with a few of the better-known French offerings. Perhaps the best bread trolley in the country generally carries about 14 different breads – all from the hotel's own bakery. A very extensive wine list has some vintage classics from France, a good German selection and lots of half bottles. *Seats 45. Parties 16. L 12-2.30 D 7-9.30. Closed L Mon, D Sun, Bank Holidays, 2 weeks from 25 Dec. Set L £18/£22.50 Set D £25/£37.*

La Brasserie £50

French-styled with a polished wood floor, painted glass dome ceiling, leather banquette seating and black bentwood chairs, this is the informal arm of the hotel which is open every day from early until late. Using, direct access from the street, some customers come in just for croissant and coffee, or a salad and glass of wine, though a complete meal can also be enjoyed. Starters include traditional fish soup with saffron rouille, black pudding with braised potatoes and onions, or polenta cakes with chargrilled vegetables. For a main course choose from beef and horseradish sausages with mashed potato, braised oxtail with root vegetables, grills, or cassoulet of monkfish with chicory, lemon and cucumber. Decent dessert trolley (try the orange and chocolate mousse) and good farmhouse cheeses. Sensible and not overly expensive wine list (house champagne under £25) with several bottles under £12 and half a dozen available by the glass. *Seats 90. Meals 7am-11.30pm. Closed 25 & 26 Dec.*

Chester **Chester Resort Hotel** **62%** **£70**

Tel 0244 851551   Fax 0244 851089 **H**
Backford Cross Chester Cheshire CH1 6PE Map 6 A2

North of the city at the A41/A5117 junction, this is a popular modern conference hotel, with facilities for 180 theatre-style and 200 banqueting. Children up to 16 stay free in parents' room. Ten rooms suitable for family use. *Rooms 113.* **AMERICAN EXPRESS** *Access, Diners, Visa.*

Consult page 20 for a full list of starred restaurants

Chester **Crabwall Manor** **76%** **£125**

Tel 0244 851666   Fax 0244 851400 **H**
Parkgate Road Mollington Chester Cheshire CH1 6NE Map 6 A2

Crabwall Manor is an imposing crenellated house set in 11 acres of beautifully laid out gardens and parkland, just north of the city on the A540. The site can be traced back to the Domesday Book, and a sense of history certainly pervades the place, combined with an awareness of the needs of the '90s. Service is professional and unobtrusive, with an attention to detail and homely touches that set it apart. A splendid stone staircase leads up to the individually decorated bedrooms which are unusually spacious and comfortable, all with sofa or pair of substantial armchairs plus proper breakfast table and good work space. Even more impressive are the large bathrooms, most with separate shower cubicle in addition to extra large bath tub and twin washbasins. All have bidets and good towels including bath robes. There is evening turn-down service and 24hr room service. Two bedrooms for non-smokers. Decent breakfasts. Banqueting/conferences for up to 100, parking for 100 cars. No dogs. *Rooms 48. Garden, croquet, snooker.* **AMERICAN EXPRESS** *Access, Diners, Visa.*

Chester — Forte Posthouse — 62% — £68

Tel 0244 680111   Fax 0244 674100 — **H**
Wrexham Road Chester Cheshire CH4 9DL — Map 6 A2

Modern redbrick hotel on the A483, two miles south of the city centre. Amenities include a health and fitness club, ample car parking and five conference rooms (theatre-style capacity up to 100). Executive rooms offer a few extras and attract a small supplement. Half the rooms are reserved for non-smokers. *Rooms 105. Indoor swimming pool, gym, sauna, spa bath, sun beds, children's playroom (weekends).* AMERICAN EXPRESS *Access, Diners, Visa.*

Chester — Francs — £40

Tel 0244 317952   Fax 0244 340690 — **R**
14 Cuppin Street Chester Cheshire CH1 2BN — Map 6 A2

Cheerful, bustling brasserie with old timber beams, ceiling fans and French rock music. The eating choice is wide, with anything from a quick snack to a a main-course meal available throughout the day. Good atmosphere, passable food. *Seats 110. Private Room 60. Meals 11-11. Set meals £9.85.* AMERICAN EXPRESS *Access, Visa.*

Chester — Moat House International Chester — 69% — £143

Tel 0244 322330   Fax 0244 316118 — **H**
Trinity Street Chester Cheshire CH1 2BD — Map 6 A2

Centrally located, large modern hotel with good leisure facilities and room for up to 600 conference delegates. Accommodation includes six penthouse suites. *Rooms 152. Gym, sauna, spa bath, solarium. Closed 24-26 Dec.* AMERICAN EXPRESS *Access, Diners, Visa.*

Chester — Mollington Banastre — 67% — £95

Tel 0244 851471   Fax 0244 851165 — **H**
Parkgate Road Chester Cheshire CH1 6NN — Map 6 A2

Comfortable accommodation (children up to 16 free in parents' room), plus good leisure and conference facilities (for up to 350 delegates) in an extended Victorian mansion surrounded by gardens. It stands a mile and a half from junction 16 of the M56. Ample free car parking. A golf course is due for completion during 1995. *Rooms 66. Garden, croquet, indoor swimming pool, gym, squash, sauna, solarium, whirlpool bath, beauty salon, hairdressing, coffee shop (11am-11pm).* AMERICAN EXPRESS *Access, Diners, Visa.*

Any person using our name to obtain free hospitality is a fraud.
Proprietors, please inform the police and us.

Chester — Rowton Hall — 64% — £88

Tel 0244 335262   Fax 0244 335464 — **H**
Whitchurch Road Chester Cheshire CH3 6AD — Map 6 A2

Built as a private residence in 1779, the hall stands three miles out of Chester on the A41, on the site of a Civil War battle. There's a spacious reception area and a lounge bar looking out on to the smart indoor pool. Rooms in the old house are stylish and individual, those in the adjoining wing more functional. Good amenities (Hamiltons Leisure Club) and conference facilities for up to 200 – also parking for 200 cars, with garaging available on request. *Rooms 42. Garden, croquet, indoor swimming pool, gym, sauna, spa bath, sun beds, squash, coffee shop (10am-10pm).* AMERICAN EXPRESS *Access, Diners, Visa.*

Chester   Places of Interest

Chester Visitor Centre   Tel 0244 351609.
Town Hall   Tel 0244 313126.
Gateway Theatre   Hamilton Place Tel 0244 340392.
The Boat Museum   Ellesmere Port Tel 051 355 5017 *Britain's premier canal museum.*
Grosvenor Museum   Grosvenor Street Tel 0244 321616.
Chester Cathedral   Tel 0244 324756.
Chester Racecourse   Tel 0244 323170.
Chester Zoo   Upton-by-Chester Tel 0244 380280.

Chester-le-Street   Lumley Castle   69%   £98

Tel 091 389 1111   Fax 091 389 1881   **H**
Chester-le-Street Co Durham DH3 4NX   Map 5 E2

"No ordinary hotel" – true! Set in spacious grounds, high above nearby Chester-le-Street (take the A167 towards Durham off the A1M North), parts of the castle date back to the 9th century. Authenticity abounds (have a look at the dungeons and the medieval banquet hall which is dominated by a giant stone fireplace and minstrel's gallery) and the interior oozes character, with furnishings that have been carefully chosen to harmonise. The lounge has period furniture, oil paintings and ornaments, and there are some 3000 books in the elegant library. Illuminated statues line the passage that leads to the function rooms (catering for banquet/conferences of up to 250/120), and the pillared and multi-domed Black Knight restaurant, which serves a good breakfast. Main bedrooms are spacious and appealing, with heavy drapes and beautiful decor combined with good antique furniture; feature Castle rooms have some added attractions like a raised sleeping area or a Queen Anne four-poster. The King James suite has a 20ft-high four-poster and a whirlpool bath. Most rooms, however, are in the courtyard and are smaller, and can also suffer from noise from either adjoining rooms or those above, but they are equally stylish, with decent bathrooms. Helpful and pleasant staff wear period costume. Children up to 12 stay free in parents' room. *Rooms 64. Garden, snooker, helipad.* *Closed 25 & 26 Dec, 1 Jan.* AMERICAN EXPRESS *Access, Diners, Visa.*

Chester-le-Street   Places of Interest

The North of England Open Air Museum   Beamish, Nr Chester-le-Street Tel 0207 231811.
Lambton Park Showground   Tel 091 388 5459.

> Our inspectors are full-time employees; they are professionally trained by us.

Chesterfield   Chesterfield Hotel   59%   £72

Tel 0246 271141   Fax 0246 220719   **H**
Malkin Street Chesterfield Derbyshire S41 7UA   Map 6 C2

A one-time railway hotel, just off the bypass. Purpose-built Peak Leisure Centre (with a large swimming pool) and conference suite for up to 200 delegates. Children under 16 stay free in parents' room. Accommodation includes 12 Executive rooms. No dogs. *Rooms 73. Indoor swimming pool, gym, sauna, spa bath, steam room, solarium, beauty salon, snooker.* AMERICAN EXPRESS *Access, Diners, Visa.*

Chesterfield	Forte Travelodge	£45
Tel 0246 455411		**L**
Brimington Road North Wittington Moor Chesterfield Derbyshire		**Map 6 C2**

By the A61 Chesterfield inner ring road on the northern outskirts of the town. **Rooms** 20. AMERICAN EXPRESS Access, Diners, Visa.

Chesterfield   Places of Interest

Tourist Information   Tel 0246 207777.
Bolsover Castle   Tel 0246 823349.
Hardwick Hall (NT)   Tel 0246 850430.
   Theatres and Concert Halls
Chesterfield Arts Centre   Tel 0246 208061.
Pomegranate Theatre   Tel 0246 232901.
The Winding Wheel   Tel 0246 209552.

Chichester	Comme Ca		£55
Tel 0243 788724			**R**
67 Broyle Road Chichester West Sussex PO19 4BD			**Map 11 A6**

North of town on the A286, and close enough to the Festival Theatre (3 minutes walk) to offer a straightforward pre-and post-theatre menu, this French restaurant with a bar is in a converted pub. Chef-patron Michel Navet cooks in a sound, classically-based style, offering a good choice of dishes from fish soup and goat's cheese in filo pastry to fillets of Dover sole sautéed with cream, mushrooms and prawns (a house speciality), calf's liver with a sage butter sauce and bacon, and grilled fillet of beef topped with Dijon mustard, caramelised and flambé (another speciality). Popular family Sunday lunches (special children's menu) and bar lunches. Six tables in the garden in good weather. **Seats** 48. L 12-2 D 5.30-10.30. Closed D Sun, all Mon, Bank Holidays. Set L £13.75/£16.75 (Sun £15.75) Set D £14.50/£16.50. AMERICAN EXPRESS Access, Visa.

Chichester	Dolphin & Anchor	63%	£102
Tel 0243 785121 Fax 0243 533408			**H**
West Street Chichester West Sussex PO19 1QE			**Map 11 A6**

Built in the 17th century, the Dolphin and the Anchor were rivals until united in 1910. Best bedrooms (which attract a supplementary charge) are at the front, with views of the cathedral opposite. Children up to 16 stay free in parents' room. Conference and banqueting ballroom (once the Liberal Assembly Rooms) caters for up to 180. Forte Heritage. **Rooms** 49. AMERICAN EXPRESS Access, Diners, Visa.

Chichester	The Droveway	£60
Tel 0243 528832		**R**
30a Southgate Chichester West Sussex PO19 1DR		**Map 11 A6**

Bookshelves, Old Master sketches and a new bar/lounge area at one end of this large upstairs room have transformed it from cavernous to almost cosy. Foodwise the main change this year is the introduction of a short fixed-price dinner menu (changing every few days) to supplement an appealing à la carte – salmon and sorrel chowder, brioche of scallops with Gewürztraminer sauce, capered halibut beurre blanc, jugged hare with bitter chocolate, noisettes of lamb with black trompette mushrooms. Short but varied list of puds or good, mostly English, cheese selection. Notably good coffees with names like Yemen Ismaili or Sumatra Mandeling plus a choice of loose leaf teas. Wine list concentrates on value for money. After-theatre (Chichester Festival) suppers by prior booking only. **Seats** 38. Private Room 8. L 12.30-2 D 7-10. Closed Sun, Mon, 1st 2 weeks Jan. Set L £11.50/£14 Set D £19.50. AMERICAN EXPRESS Access, Visa.

Chichester   Places of Interest

Tourist Information   Tel 0243 775888.
Chichester Festival Theatre   Oaklands Park Tel 0243 781312.
West Dean Gardens   Tel 0243 63301.
Chichester Cathedral   Tel 0243 782595.
The Roman Palace   Fishbourne Tel 0243 785859.
Royal Military Police Museum   Roussillon Barracks Tel 0243 786311.
Weald and Downland Open Air Museum   Singleton Tel 024 363 348.
Chichester Harbour   Area of outstanding natural beauty.

Chiddingfold   Crown Inn   £57

Tel 0428 682255   Fax 0428 685736   ▮

The Green Chiddingfold Surrey GU8 4TX   **Map 11 A5**

Established as a hostelry in 1285, the mellow half-timbered Crown is one
of the oldest recorded inns in England. Linenfold panelling, stained glass
in mullioned windows, creaking stairs and passages leading to atmospheric
bedrooms with sloping floors, bowed walls, beams and solid furniture
show its age. Annexe rooms are contrastingly light and modern. Some
rooms suitable for family use. ***Rooms** 8.* *Access, Diners, Visa.*

Childer Thornton   Travel Inn (Wirral South)   £43

Tel 051 339 8101   **L**

New Chester Road Childer Thornton South Wirral Cheshire L66 1QW   **Map 6 A2**

On A41, 400 yards south of M53 heading towards Chester. ***Rooms** 40.*
 Access, Diners, Visa.

Chilgrove   White Horse Inn   £60

Tel 0243 59219   Fax 0243 59301   **R**

High Street Chilgrove nr Chichester West Sussex PO18 9HX   **Map 15 E3**

Instead of a nice picture of a white horse, the pub sign here is a wine glass –
which is entirely appropriate as this wisteria-clad, 18th-century hostelry
boasts one of the finest wine lists in the country. But good wine deserves
good food and chef-partner Neil Rusbridger's essentially English cooking
fits the bill admirably. The three-course lunch and four-course dinner
menus are fixed-price affairs although dishes are also individually priced for
those wanting a lighter meal. Local game, Selsey crab and lobster are
specialities with the likes of local pigeon with wild mushrooms and potato
galette, civet of duck in Sauternes, blanquette of lamb with fresh asparagus
and the day's fish dish giving an idea of the half dozen or so main dishes
offered and which always include a vegetarian option such as a timbale
of baked aubergine and fresh basil. The list of desserts is recited at the table
and can include such adventurous ideas as chocolate ravioli with orange
sauce. Vegetables are particularly well handled. The sensational and
comprehensive world-wide wine list here has won so many accolades
(twice winner of our Cellar of the Year) that it sets a standard by which
others are judged. Lovers of German wines, for once, will not
be disappointed, nor will aficionados from all wine-growing regions for
that matter. Those with an eye for a bargain should come here, for prices
are so keen that Barry Phillips is almost giving away absolute gems.
***Seats** 70. Parties 24. Private Room 12. L 12-2 D 7-9.30. Closed D Sun, all
Mon, Feb, last week Oct. Set L £17.50 Set D £23 (4-course). Access,
Diners, Visa.*

Chippenham   Granada Lodge   £51
Tel 0666 837097   Fax 0666 837112   **L**

M4 Junction 17/18 Leigh Delamere Chippenham Wiltshire SN4 6LB   Map 14 B2

Rooms 35. AMERICAN EXPRESS *Access, Diners, Visa.*

Chipping   Gibbon Bridge Hotel   70%   £70
Tel 0995 61456   Fax 0995 61277   **H**

The Forest of Bowland Chipping Lancashire PR3 2TQ   Map 6 B1

Owned by the Simpson family for over 30 years, Gibbon Bridge, in the
remote Lancashire fells, was once a farmhouse. Converted sympathetically
to a hotel by local craftsmen using local materials whenever possible,
it is a tribute to the Simpsons' caring attitude. It stands on the banks of the
River Loud and is surrounded by 20 acres of lovingly tended gardens,
floodlit at night. Attention to detail even shows here, where a graceful
19th-century statue, stone bridges and gas lamps have been installed. Public
rooms and bedrooms are generously proportioned, the style being
reminiscent of a smart, modern hunting lodge, almost Bavarian in design
and concept. 22 of the bedrooms are magnificent, covering two floors with
a large ground-floor lounge and a separate upstairs bedroom. Some are
galleried and one has its own completely secluded and very private garden.
Two on the ground floor are equipped for disabled guests. Beds are king-
size with brass bedsteads, half-testers and four-posters being almost standard.
Excellent bathrooms with pretty floral suites are as thoughtfully equipped
as the bedrooms. There's a well-fitted health and gym area where you can
be cosseted to your heart's content. *Rooms 30. Garden, croquet, gym, steam
room, sauna, solarium, beauty salon, tennis.* AMERICAN EXPRESS *Access,
Diners, Visa.*

Chipping Campden   Cotswold House   70%   £95
Tel 0386 840330   Fax 0386 840310   **HR**

The Square Chipping Campden Gloucestershire GL55 6AN   Map 14 C1

A late-Georgian/early-Regency town house in the centre of town (yet with
a fine garden to the rear) run with great charm and easy-going hospitality
by the Greenstocks. There's a 'country house' feel to civilised day rooms,
which boast antiques, fresh flowers and nice architectural features like the
fine cantilevered spiral staircase that leads up to the bedroom floors. For
a change of mood there's a sort of countrified bar/café, also run by the
hotel, in a 17th-century building next door. Each bedroom is tastefully
themed as reflected in their names, Indian, Ribbons and Bows, Gothic,
Honeysuckle – some, like Paradise and Aunt Lizzie's room, are less obvious
than others. Antiques often feature in the decor and beds are turned down
at night. Just one small single has shower and WC only. Room service
operates throughout the day and evening. No children under 8. No dogs.
Rooms 15. Garden, croquet, café/bar (9.30am-10pm). Closed 24 – 28 Dec.
AMERICAN EXPRESS *Access, Visa.*

The Garden Room   £70

Its name inspired by the charming walled garden over which it looks, the
dining room here has some fine period features – Corinthian columns,
moulded ceiling – comfortable chairs around widely spaced tables and
a grand piano (sporting a fine flower display) that accompanies dinner
a couple of times a week. The main, fixed-price menu (there's also a short
'House Dinner') offers about seven choices at each stage with the likes
of a terrine of leeks set in a light ham mousseline, sausage of brill with
mussel and chive sauce, loin of new-season lamb garnished with vegetables
and with a garlic jus, compote of wild mushrooms with grilled polenta,
and the day's fish dish followed by puds like a mixed nut pithiviers
or honey bavarois with citrus fruits. Careful cooking produces pleasing
results and service is both attentive and friendly. A refreshing, sensibly

priced wine list is presented by grape style with helpful tasting notes – a good example of quality taking precedence over quantity with every wine well chosen and some top names featured. For once, France has to muck in with the rest of the world. No smoking. *Seats 30. Private Room 20. L (Sun only) 12-2. D 7.15-9.30. Set Sun L £15 Set D £25.*

Chipping Campden   Noel Arms   61%   £78

Tel 0386 840317   Fax 0386 841136

High Street Chipping Campden Gloucestershire GL55 6AT

H

Map 14 C1

When Charles II rested here in 1651 after defeat at the Battle of Worcester this renowned hostelry was already 300 years old. Many reminders of the past remain, including swords, shields and muskets in the foyer. There's a cosy beamed bar, a bright conservatory and an oak-panelled restaurant. Bedrooms are divided more or less evenly between those in a rustic style with antique furniture in the main part to a modern look in the wing. Some rooms have four-poster beds. Children up to 16 stay free in parents' room. *Rooms 26.* AMERICAN EXPRESS *Access, Diners, Visa.*

Many hotels offer reduced rates for weekend or out-of-season bookings. Always ask about special deals.

Chipping Campden   Seymour House   64%   £91

Tel 0386 840429   Fax 0386 840369

High Street Chipping Campden Gloucestershire GL55 6AH

H

Map 14 C1

In the main street of town, a mellow Cotswold-stone hotel with pretty garden to the rear. Bedrooms are the main strength here – varying in size and shape, some have characterful old beams and all but three (those awaiting refurbishment of which one has shower and WC all) boast reproduction antiques in a number of different styles. There are three full suites. Public rooms are, at the moment, limited to a single lounge with firm easy chairs and settees rather than deep armchairs and sofas apart from the restaurant where breakfast is taken and which features a 94-year-old vine. Limited room service throughout the day and evening but a thermos of fresh milk is provided for the beverage tray. *Rooms 16. Garden.* AMERICAN EXPRESS *Access, Visa.*

Chipping Campden   Places of Interest

Tourist Information   Tel 0386 840101.
Hidcote Manor Garden (NT)   Hidcote Bartrim Tel 0386 438333.
Kiftsgate Court Garden   Tel 0386 438777.

Chipping Norton   Crown & Cushion   £69

Tel 0608 642533   Fax 0608 642926

High Street Chipping Norton Oxfordshire OX7 5AD

I

Map 14 C1

Accommodation at this privately-owned former coaching inn (dating in parts from 1497) ranges from 11 'standard' rooms in the coach house annexe (one minute's walk away) up to suites with separate lounge, writing bureau, sofa and traditional cast-iron bath – prices vary considerbaly according to size of room. Top of the range are rooms with four-poster or half-tester beds; one room is on two levels with an old four-poster up a few steps from a separate lounge area. Public areas include a cosy lounge, beamed bar, numerous conference rooms (for up to 250) and a leisure club. *Rooms 40. Indoor swimming pool, gym, squash, sauna, solarium, snooker.* AMERICAN EXPRESS *Access, Diners, Visa.*

Chiseldon   Chiseldon House   67%   £83

Tel 0793 741010   Fax 0793 741059   **HR**

New Road Chiseldon nr Swindon Wiltshire SN4 0NE   Map 14 C2

Behind its listed Regency frontage, this former doctor's house has been considerably remodelled within to create a hotel of some charm but many contrasts. The original lounge and balconied bedrooms above are the pick for both comfort and outlook, while the bar and restaurant are condensed to the rear. Two stylish private rooms with seating for 16 to 20 are offered for seminars and dining. ***Rooms*** *21. Garden, outdoor swimming pool.* AMERICAN EXPRESS *Access, Diners, Visa.*

Orangery Restaurant   £65

A la carte and table d'hote menus feature dishes which are just that little bit different: quenelles of prawns and Camembert with a warm lime sauce, millefeuille of chicken livers on a bed of warm cranberries, darne of salmon with olives on a green pepper sauce, herb-crusted best end of lamb with a lemon and caper sauce. Vegetarian main courses available. British farmhouse cheeses. ***Seats*** *48. Private Room 20. L 12-2 D 7-9.30. Set L £11.95/£14.95 (Sun £11.95) Set D £16.95/£19.95.*

Chittlehamholt   Highbullen   60%   £105

Tel 0769 540561   Fax 0769 540492   **H**

Chittlehamholt nr South Molton Devon EX37 9HD   Map 13 D2

A splendid Victorian mansion standing in parkland on high ground between Exmoor and Dartmoor (M5 Junction 27, A361 to South Molton, B3226 5 miles, turn right to Chittlehamholt, through village half a mile to hotel). Bedrooms in comfortably traditional style are in the main house, an adjoining property in a country-style garden and a group of nearby cottages. Sports and leisure facilities are excellent (unlimited free golf, and a resident professional) while for less active moments the drawing room, conservatory and library are ideal spots. There's always plenty to do, but there are also restrictions – no children under eight, no dogs, no smoking in the restaurant or breakfast room, no credit cards. 85 acres of ancient woodland have recently been acquired adjacent to the hotel; below the wood, right on the river, is a four-bedroomed house suitable for a family group. ***Rooms*** *37. Garden, indoor & outdoor swimming pools, squash, sauna, spa bath, steam room, massage, solarium, hair & beauty salon, indoor & outdoor tennis, 9-hole golf course with resident professional, indoor putting, table tennis, snooker, sports shop, helipad.*

Chobham   Quails Restaurant   £55

Tel 0276 858491   **R**

1 Bagshot Road Chobham Surrey GU24 8BP   Map 15 E3

Very much a family affair with Chris and Debbie Wale in the kitchen and Carol and Robert Wale looking after front of house. The interior is light and airy (and air-conditioned) with sturdy country chairs around crisply-clothed tables, each sporting a mini-parlour plant. The regularly-changing à la carte menu is of French and modern British inspiration, shown by such dishes as brioche filled with oyster mushrooms in a tarragon and Madeira sauce, goat's cheese tartlet with toasted almonds and gooseberry, witch sole with saffron, Chardonnay and leeks, or maize-fed guinea fowl on a garlic and potato dauphine with a rosemary-infused jus. Desserts include fruit sorbets, steamed treacle pudding and nutty toffee tart. A small-choice two-course set dinner menu features a different French gastronomic menu each month. The price includes a half bottle of wine. Good Sunday lunches. There are many good wines at reasonable prices on the list; New World wines do not always state their country of origin. ***Seats*** *40. Parties 12 (8 at weekend). Private Room 40. L 12-2 D 7-10. Closed L Sat, D Sun, all Mon, 26 Dec. Set L (Sun) & D (not Sat & Sun) £12.95.* AMERICAN EXPRESS *Access, Diners, Visa.*

Chollerford   George Hotel   59%   £95

Tel 0434 681611   Fax 0434 681727
H
Chollerford nr Hexham Northumberland NE46 4EW
Map 5 D2

A riverside setting with delightful gardens and good leisure facilities (expanded this year). Most bedrooms have garden or river views and are furnished in an up-to-date fashion. Children up to 14 free in parents' room, two new family rooms, four Executive rooms. Banqueting/conferences for 100/60. Swallow Hotels. **Rooms** 50. *Garden, indoor swimming pool, spa bath, sauna, solarium, fishing, putting, nature trail, jogging track.* AMERICAN EXPRESS *Access, Diners, Visa.*

Christchurch   Splinters   £55

Tel 0202 483454   Fax 0202 483454
R
11 Church Street Christchurch Dorset BH23 1BW
Map 14 C4

A "Splinters" has existed here near the Priory in central Christchurch for over twenty years. The current incarnation is in the hands of Timothy Lloyd and Robert Wilson and modern pastel colour schemes, polished wooden floors and alcove-style seating plus even a table in their wine cellar create a cosy ambience to enjoy some quality cooking. Local fresh produce figures prominently on the menus, the simpler of which (lunchtime) runs from cream of tomato and basil soup, confit of onion tart and hot roast pigeon salad to salmon fish cakes with creamed leeks and sirloin steak with a red wine sauce. Many of the same dishes are included in the evening carte, with the recent imaginative addition of fillet of kangaroo with a Cajun cream. Among the desserts you might find white chocolate mousse with a raspberry coulis, or traditional steamed ginger pudding with honey custard. **Seats** 40. *Parties 10. Private Room 22. L 12-2.30 D 7-10.30. Set L £8.60. Closed 2 weeks Jan.* AMERICAN EXPRESS *Access, Diners, Visa.*

Christchurch   Travel Inn   £43

Tel 0202 485376   Fax 0202 474939
L
Somerford Road Christchurch nr Bournemouth Dorset BH23 3QG
Map 14 C4

Situated a few miles from both Mudeford and Boscombe beaches. One room is adapted for disabled guests. No dogs. **Rooms** 38. *Garden.* AMERICAN EXPRESS *Access, Diners, Visa.*

If we recommend meals in a hotel or inn a separate entry is made for its restaurant.

Churt   Frensham Pond Hotel   62%   £88

Tel 0252 795161   Fax 0252 792631
H
Churt nr Farnham Surrey GU10 2QB
Map 11 A5

Frensham Great Pond is a large lake with a busy weekend dinghy sailing club and the hotel overlooking it was originally built as a private residence in the 15th century. Nowadays it caters for both business and private visitors. Features include four conference suites and a leisure club with its own bar and restaurant. Most of the bedrooms are in an extension in the gardens to the rear. 24hr room service. No dogs. **Rooms** 51. *Garden, indoor swimming pool, sauna, solarium, squash, spa bath, keep-fit equipment, beauty salon, squash, games room, coffee shop (8am-10pm).* AMERICAN EXPRESS *Access, Diners, Visa.*

Cirencester   Fleece Hotel   64%   £90

Tel 0285 658507   Fax 0285 651017   **H**

Market Place Cirencester Gloucestershire GL7 2NZ   Map 14 C2

Timber-fronted Tudor inn in the centre of a town that once supported
a thriving wool trade. Accommodation includes single, double and twin
rooms, a family room, a four-poster and Executive room with jacuzzi.
Resort Hotels. **Rooms** 30. *Coffee shop (10am-3pm).* AMERICAN EXPRESS® *Access,
Diners, Visa.*

Cirencester   Stratton House   64%   £70

Tel 0285 651761   Fax 0285 640024   **H**

Gloucester Road Cirencester Gloucestershire GL7 2LE   Map 14 C2

On the A417 to the north of town this former wool merchant's house dates
back at least to the 17th century. It has been a hotel since 1947 and was
acquired by its current owners Forestdale Group in 1989. The period feel
has been retained in public areas like the flagstoned entrance hall, the
beamed bar with real log fire and leather tub chairs and the comfortable
lounge overlooking a walled garden. Pretty bedrooms are individually
decorated, those in the original building often retaining original fireplaces.
Good bathrooms offer large jars of shampoo and bath essence. Limited
room service. **Rooms** 41. *Garden, croquet.* AMERICAN EXPRESS® *Access,
Diners, Visa.*

Cirencester   Tatyan's   £45

Tel 0285 653529   **R**

27 Castle Street Cirencester Gloucestershire GL7 1QD   Map 14 C2

Szechuan, Hunan and Peking regional cooking provide the specialities
on a wide-ranging evening menu that includes ten prawn dishes. Order
Peking duck a day in advance. Good set lunch. Friendly and helpful service.
Seats 60. L 12-2 D 6-10.30. Closed L Sun in summer, all Sun in winter.
Set L £8.50 Set D £11.50/£14. AMERICAN EXPRESS® *Access, Diners, Visa.*

Cirencester   Places of Interest

Tourist Information   Tel 0285 654180.
Barnsley House Garden   Barnsley Tel 0285 740402.
Rodmarton Manor Garden   Tel 0285 841253.
Cirencester Park Polo Club   The Old Kennels, Cirencester Park
   Tel 0285 653225.

Clanfield   The Plough at Clanfield   £85

Tel 036 781 222   Fax 036 781 596   **IR**

Bourton Road Clanfield Oxfordshire OX8 2RB   Map 14 C2

Roses and wisteria clinging to the Cotswold stone walls of this small 16th-
century manor house make a pretty picture and the atmosphere within
is more that of an inn than a hotel; a single bar/lounge has a few old beams
and posts and draylon-covered wing chairs and settees in pink and blue.
Cosy bedrooms come with baby teddy bears to keep you company and
bathrooms – four with whirlpool tubs, two with shower and WC only –
are shared with families of plastic ducks along with towelling robes and
good toiletries. No dogs. **Rooms** 6. *Garden.* AMERICAN EXPRESS® *Access,
Diners, Visa.*

Tapestry Room Restaurant   £70

The menus in the Tapestry Room are many and diverse. The kitchen's
talents are best demonstrated in the seasonal Gourmand Menu of seven
dishes (any one of which you may change for something from the other
menus): parcel of smoked salmon and scrambled egg with truffles;

marinated goat's cheese salad; roast breast of duckling with a sage and
onion sauce; white chocolate and strawberry soufflé. Much simpler dishes
make up the à la carte Sunday brunch menu, among them duck liver
parfait, ham and cheese croissants, chicken chasseur, grilled salmon and
roast beef with Yorkshire pudding. *Seats 30. Private Room 12. L 12-2
D 7-10 (Sun to 9.30). Set L £10.95/£14.50 Set D from £19.50.*

Clawton	Court Barn	61%	£66
Tel 040 927 219 Fax 040 927 309			**H**
Clawton Holsworthy Devon EX22 6PS			Map 12 C2

Robert and Susan Wood have been running their charming little Manor
house (set in five acres of well-tended gardens) since 1986, and a steady
stream of returnees fills the relaxing day rooms and comfortable bedrooms,
all of which are non-smoking. Bathrooms were undergoing improvements
during 1994, and some bedrooms too. Three rooms are suitable for family
use, and children up to 14 stay free in parents' room. Cots, high-chairs and
baby-listening are available. Small receptions (40) and conferences (25) can
be accommodated, as can 16 cars. *Rooms 8. Garden, croquet, badminton,
tennis, pitch & putt, putting. Closed 1 week Jan.* AMERICAN EXPRESS *Access,
Diners, Visa.*

Claygate	Les Alouettes		£70
Tel 0372 464882			**R**
7 High Street Claygate Surrey KT10 0JW			Map 15 E2

'The new' Les Alouettes' pretty decor features a rose-entwined trellis
painted on the walls and their tableware is Royal Doulton bone china.
There's a good mix of straightforward dishes on the large à la carte –
Bayonne ham with melon, Dover sole (grilled or meunière), grills – along
with more adventurous creations such as a casserole of king scallops and
mussels braised with smoked bacon, vermouth and chives; millefeuille
of asparagus, shiitake and oyster mushrooms on a pesto sauce; baked turbot
with a crab and red pepper crust and minted hollandaise and honey-roast
Gressingham duck with cassis and apples. All dishes are based on good-
quality ingredients, carefully handled. There is now an additional fixed-
price 'brasserie menu' (Mon-Fri) that is particularly good value, especially
at lunchtime. Most wines on the initially offered, mainly French, wine list
are priced at less than £20, with the more famous and expensive names
reserved for a 'connoisseur' list available on request; house wines come
from the AC Cote de Provence, Chateau de Berne, with which Les
Alouettes is connected. *Seats 60. Parties 65. L 12-2.15 D 7-9.30 (Sat till 10).
Set L £9.95/£12.50 (Sun £14.50) Set D £14.95 (Sat £20). Closed L Sat,
all Sun, Bank Holidays, 2 weeks summer & 1 week Christmas.* AMERICAN EXPRESS
Access, Visa.

See the Restaurant Round-up for easy, quick-reference comparisons.

Clayton-le-Woods	Pines Hotel	65%	£55
Tel 0772 38551 Fax 0772 629002			**H**
Preston Road Clayton-le-Woods nr Chorley Lancashire PR6 7ED			Map 6 B1

Though the decor and furnishings are somewhat dated at this much-
extended Victorian house on the A6, just off the M6 (Junction 28/29), the
bedrooms are spacious and offer all modern facilities. Baskets of 'help-
yourself' fresh fruit are provided on bedroom landings. Four acres
of wooded grounds, ideal for business meetings and conferences (100), live
cabaret at weekends in the Dixon suite. No dogs. Free parking for 100 cars.
Rooms 39. Garden. Closed 25 & 26 Dec. AMERICAN EXPRESS *Access, Diners, Visa.*

Clearwell   Clearwell Castle   69%   £80

Tel 0594 832320   Fax 0594 835523   **H**

Clearwell nr Coleford Gloucestershire GL16 8LG   Map 14 B2

The site dates back to Roman times, but the current castle is of 18th-century origins, in Gothic Revival style, with a castellated exterior and stately halls. The bar is less stately, having instead a clubby appeal. Bedrooms combine four-posters and half-testers with up-to-date amenities. *Rooms* 14. *Garden, fishing, riding.* AMERICAN EXPRESS *Access, Diners, Visa.*

Clearwell   The Wyndham Arms   £60

Tel 0594 833666   Fax 0594 836450   **I**

Clearwell nr Coleford Gloucestershire GL16 8JT   Map 14 B2

John and Rosemary Stanford have completed 20 years as imperturbable hosts at the tranquil Wyndham, where accommodation is divided between original bedrooms in the evocative 600-year-old main building and a newly built stone extension where room sizes, decor and comforts are altogether more modern. Good bar snacks. *Rooms* 17. *Garden.* AMERICAN EXPRESS *Access, Diners, Visa.*

Cleethorpes   Kingsway Hotel   62%   £75

Tel 0472 601122   Fax 0472 601381   **H**

Cleethorpes Humberside DN35 0AE   Map 7 F2

A traditional seafront hotel, run by the Harris family for four generations. Regular refurbishment keeps things smart in the day rooms and in the bedrooms, most of which have solid reproduction furniture. One of the lounges is non-smoking. No children under five (5-14s free in parents' room). Garage parking (£1.50 overnight). No dogs. Leisure centre 300yds from hotel. *Rooms* 50. *Roof garden, garage. Closed 25 & 26 Dec.* AMERICAN EXPRESS *Access, Diners, Visa.*

Climping   Bailiffscourt   69%   £95

Tel 0903 723511   Fax 0903 723107   **HR**

Climping nr Littlehampton West Sussex BN17 5RW   Map 11 A6

Standing in 22 acres of gardens and grounds just 200 yards from the beach, Bailiffscourt was built by Lord Moyen in 1930 from recycled 13th-century building materials. The atmosphere is genuinely mellow with lots of old timbers, heavy iron-studded doors and old stone fireplaces. Old oak furniture and appropriate fabrics match the mood in bedrooms which, nonetheless, combine plenty of modern comforts; several boast four-posters and open log fires. Private dining and boardrooms can seat up to 80 for formal meals and 40 for conferences. *Rooms* 23. *Garden, outdoor swimming pool, tennis, pool table.* AMERICAN EXPRESS *Access, Diners, Visa.*

Restaurant   £80

Simon Rogan has emerged from his apprenticeship at the hands of both Marco Pierre White and Jean-Christophe Novelli to head his own brigade in the kitchens of Bailliffscourt. Traces of influence from both his mentors are to be found to good effect in his interesting and eclectic menu. Tagliatelle of oysters with muscadet, boulangère of scallops smoked *à la minute* with lemon and thyme or perhaps a salad of chicken winglets with duck gizzards to start; followed by confit of duck (perfect, crisp skin), noisettes of lamb with a fritter of its offal or sea bass en croute with a lobster sauce. Delicious desserts: a peach Melba of which Dame Nellie would have been proud, feuillantine of chocolate and at least two soufflés. Many dishes carry a supplement in the evening, boosting prices considerably. Light lunches are available in the bar (except Sun). No smoking. *Seats* 80. *Parties* 40. *Private Room* 40. L 12.30-2 D 7-9.45. *Set L £17.50 Set D £27.50.*

Clitheroe   Browns Bistro   £55

Tel 0200 26928   **R**

10 York Street Clitheroe Lancashire BB7 2DL   Map 6 B1

Bare boards and check cloths lend Browns a French café atmosphere, while
daily-changed blackboards emphasise the freshness of supplies. Fish and
shellfish from Manchester markets, Angus beef, complimentary *petits pains*
and salad bowl, generous portions – all enlivened by a general sense of fun.
House champagne at £16.50 and a marque at £25 set the tone for the very
fair prices on the wine list, which is littered with spelling mistakes and
hardly user-friendly; but, it is a good list and port lovers will not
be disappointed with the selection available by the glass. **Seats** 65.
*Parties 14. L 12-2 D 7-10. Closed L Sat, all Sun, 25 & 26 Dec, 1 Jan.
Access, Visa.*

Clitheroe   Place of Interest

Browsholme Hall   Tel 025486 330.

Coatham Mundeville   Hall Garth Golf & Country
                          Club Hotel   66%   £81

Tel 0325 300400   Fax 0325 310083   **HR**

Coatham Mundeville nr Darlington Co Durham DL1 3LU   Map 5E3

A nine-hole golf course and smart new leisure centre are the latest additions
to this hotel based around a 16th-century stone mansion just off the A167
within two minutes of the A1(M). Day rooms include three most civilised
country house-style lounges warmed by real fires in winter and with drinks
service from a dispenser bar, while for a change of mood there's a separate
Stables Bar with more lively, pubby atmosphere. Best of the bedrooms
perhaps are those furnished with antiques in the original building; the
majority, in a new wing, have darkwood freestanding pieces and co-
ordinating fabrics while those in the annexe above the bar feature solid
lightwood furniture. Three of these have shower and WC only. Bedroom
seating is generally limited to low armless easy chairs and a stool at the
desk. 24hr room service. **Rooms** 40. *Garden, tennis, golf (9), indoor
swimming pool, gym, sauna, steam room, spa bath, solarium. Closed 24-26 Dec.*
AMERICAN EXPRESS® *Access, Diners, Visa.*

Hugo's   £60

Choose between the dark red dining room or conservatory extension
to enjoy generally soundly cooked dishes from a fixed-price menu that
offers a good choice. Citrus pickled salmon, woodland mushrooms in filo
pastry with thyme sauce, fricassee of chicken in chive sauce, and pork loin
on celeriac rösti with apple and cider fondue show the style. Shorter lunch
menu. **Seats** 60. *Private Room 12. L 12-2 D 7-10. Closed D Sun, 24-26 Dec
(except Christmas Day Lunch). Set L £9.95 (Sun £10.95)
Set D £13.95/£17.95.*

Cobham   Hilton National   65%   £120

Tel 0932 864471   Fax 0932 868017   **H**

Seven Hills Road South Cobham Surrey KT11 1EW   Map 15 E3

Near Junction 10 of the M25, the hotel is based around Neville
Chamberlain's former home, now surrounded by various modern
extensions. Both public areas and bedrooms are well-kept, the latter with
good desk space (to which the telephone can be moved) and Plaza rooms
come with extras like mineral water, chocolates and miniatures of whisky.
The pool is small but with a 'jet stream' for more serious swimmers; the
fitness room is in a separate part of the building. Conferences are
an important part of the business during the week. **Rooms** 152. *Garden,*

tennis, indoor swimming pool, keep-fit equipment, squash, sauna, steam room, spa bath, solarium, dinner dance (Sat), helipad. AMERICAN EXPRESS® *Access, Diners, Visa.*

Cobham Woodlands Park 69% £130

Tel 0372 843933 Fax 0372 842704	H
Woodlands Lane Stoke d'Abernon Cobham Surrey KT11 3QB	Map 15 E3

The carefully restored (and much extended) former home of the match-making Bryant family is a magnificent example of late-Victorian country house style, set in ten acres of lawns. Particularly striking is the grand hall with its galleried landing, panelled walls and stained-glass ceiling; this is the residents' lounge, and other day rooms include the new Langtry's bar and brasserie. Bedrooms range from handsome suites with original built-in furniture in the main house to smaller but equally comfortable rooms in the wing; all offer an array of extras. The buffet breakfast provides decent quality and variety. Children up to 12 stay free in parents' room. Banqueting/conference facilities for 270/350. *Rooms 58. Garden, croquet, tennis. Closed 23-31 Dec.* AMERICAN EXPRESS® *Access, Diners, Visa.*

Cobham Place of Interest

Painshill Park and Gardens Tel 0932 868113.

Cockermouth Quince & Medlar £30

Tel 0900 823579	R
13 Castlegate Cockermouth Cumbria CA13 9EU	Map 4 C3

Next to Cockermouth Castle, a wood-panelled, candle-lit vegetarian restaurant, run on informal lines by Colin and Louisa Le Voi. Colin's menu is short but full of interest, with starters like asparagus and ricotta buckwheat pancakes and main courses which should arouse even carnivorous taste buds: mixed peppers, courgettes and black-eyed beans in a garlic, red grape and herb sauce, baked in a mould of carrot and courgette and served with a mixed side salad. Desserts lack nothing in appeal with the likes of iced Benedictine soufflé or dried apricots in brandy with vegan ice cream or natural yoghurt. No smoking. *Seats 26. Parties 14. D only 7-9.30. Closed Mon, also Sun in winter, 2/3 weeks Jan. Access, Visa.*

Cockermouth Place of Interest

Wordsworth House (NT) Tel 0900 824805.

Coggeshall White Hart 69% £82

Tel 0376 561654 Fax 0376 561789	HR
Market End Coggeshall Essex CO6 1NH	Map 10 C3

A centuries-old inn that still retains all its character with flagstone floors, low beams, inglenook fireplace and not one but two resident ghosts. One bay of the original (1420) Guildhall is now the residents' lounge, and careful renovation and refurbishment in recent years have added style and comfort to the atmospheric surroundings. Individually decorated bedrooms, 12 in an extension, offer little extras like fresh fruit and mineral water. *Rooms 18. Garden,* AMERICAN EXPRESS® *Access, Diners, Visa.*

Restaurant £60

A long, low and narrow dining room with sturdy beams and cheerful staff. An Italian menu ranges from a variety of pasta dishes (a speciality) to *fritto misto di mare,* scampi Newburg, veal escalope milanese and charcoal-grilled T-bone steak. Traditional Sunday lunch and a good selection of desserts. *Seats 70. L 12-2 D 7-9.45. Closed D Sun.*

Coggeshall   Places of Interest

Braintree Tourist Information   Tel 0376 550066
Paycocke's   Tel 0376 561305.

Colchester   Butterfly Hotel   61%   £62

Tel 0206 230900 Fax 0206 231095	**H**
Old Ipswich Road Ardleigh Colchester Essex CO7 7QY	**Map 10 C3**

Part of a small chain offering practical accommodation (there is separate
work space in all the bedrooms) and banqueting/conference facilities for
up to 50/80. Located on the A12/A120 near the Business Parks. No dogs.
Rooms 50. AMERICAN EXPRESS *Access, Diners, Visa.*

Colchester   Forte Posthouse   61%   £67

Tel 0206 767740 Fax 0206 766577	**H**
Abbotts Lane Eight Ash Green Colchester Essex CO6 3QL	**Map 10 C3**

Off the A604 to the north-west of the A12. Opened in spring '93 with
Posthouse's new Canadian log cabin-themed informal restaurant and good
leisure centre. More than half the bedrooms are designated non-smoking.
Children free when sharing parents' room. *Rooms 110. Terrace, indoor
swimming pool, gym, spa bath, sauna, steam room, solarium, beauty salon.*
AMERICAN EXPRESS *Access, Diners, Visa.*

Colchester   Places of Interest

Tourist Information   Tel 0206 712920.
Colchester Arts Centre   St. Marys-at-the-Walls, Church Street Tel 0206
   577301.
Mercury Theatre   Balkerne Gate Tel 0206 577301.
Colchester Museums   Tel 0206 712931.
Castle Park Cricket Ground   Tel 0206 574028.
Colchester Garrison Polo Club   East Mersea Tel 0206 383049.
Colchester Zoo   Stanway Tel 0206 331292.
Clacton Beach *13 miles SE Colchester.*
   Historic Houses, Castles and Gardens
Beth Chatto Gardens   Elmstead Market Tel 0206 822007.
Layer Marney Tower   Tiptree Tel 0206 330784.
St. Osyth Priory   St. Osyth Tel 0255 820492.

Colerne   Lucknam Park   83%   £145

Tel 0225 742777 Fax 0225 743536	**H R**
Colerne Wiltshire SN14 8AZ	**Map 14 B2**

Approached by a straight mile of beech-lined drive, a gracious Georgian
house in a tranquil setting, six miles from Bath on the southern edge of the
Cotswolds. The house has a particularly English feel and is luxuriously
fitted with sound taste. Day rooms are spacious and extremely elegant with
soft colours, choice antiques and oil paintings plus deep-cushioned sofas.
Sumptuously comfortable bedrooms are appointed to the highest standards
with handsome furnishings and fittings befitting a house of this stature.
Each is individually decorated in quintessential English style and most
of the marble-tiled bathrooms boast double double basins. Housekeeping
is immaculate. The leisure spa is conceived in the style of a Roman villa and
set in the old walled garden; there are two floodlit tennis courts. Four
individually decorated health and beauty rooms (for men and women)
were recently opened. Impeccably dressed, young staff. 24hr room service.
Banqueting/conference facilities for up to 80/150. No dogs, but kennelling
can be arranged. *Rooms 42. Garden, croquet, tennis, indoor swimming pool, spa
bath, sauna, solarium, steam room, gym, beauty & hair salon, snooker, helipad.*
AMERICAN EXPRESS *Access, Diners, Visa.*

Restaurant   £90

Discreet, polished service and a truly elegant dining room certainly set
expectations high for chef Michael Womersley's cooking. His menus are
fixed-price, offering an interesting selection of dishes that might include
a warm terrine of potato, sweetbreads and foie gras with a smooth onion
sauce, roast quail with green bean purée or home-smoked lobster to start,
followed by sautéed brill with a champagne sauce and fresh Périgord
truffles, pavé of veal with crispy noodles and a sorrel parsley sauce, supreme
of Trelough duck, and roast medallions of pork fillet with a rhubarb farce
and a Madeira sauce. Lunch is a two-or three-course affair offering equally
involved dishes – perhaps mussels, scallops and langoustine in a nest
of home-made tarragon noodles, sautéed fillet of pork with a Madeira,
lemon, lime and caraway sauce, and "lasagne" of seasonal fruits with
a Grand Marnier sauce. It's a help to know your wine vintages here, since
that's how the list is presented – by year. The better wines are quite steeply
priced; New World offers the best value. Water is bottled from their own
spring. No children under 8 for dinner (families can eat informally in the
leisure centre's Pavilion). No smoking. Gentlemen are required to wear
a jacket and tie in the evenings. *Seats* 85. *Parties* 8. *Private Rooms 8 to 28.
L 12.30-2 D 7.30-9.30 (Sat to 9.45). Set L £17.50/£22 (Sun £25)
Set D £39.50.*

Colsterworth   Forte Travelodge   £45

Tel 0476 861181	**L**
Colsterworth nr Grantham Lincolnshire NG33 5JJ	Map 7 E3

Located at the roundabout of the junction of the A1 (southbound) with
A151, 8 miles south of Grantham. ***Rooms*** *32.* AMERICAN EXPRESS *Access,
Diners, Visa.*

Coltishall   Norfolk Place Restaurant   **NEW**   £65

Tel 0603 738991	**R**
Point House High Street Coltishall Norfolk NR12 7AA	Map 10 C1

Just a two-hander at the moment with Phillipa Atkinson serving and Nick
Gill (once of *Hambleton Hall*) in the kitchen, where the emphasis is on fish
(often locally landed) and seasonal game from the surrounding area. The
four-course menu (choice of five main dishes) is all inclusive – not just
of coffee and service but of a sparkling aperitif cocktail, canapés (plus a plate
of whitebait last time we dined), an extra course like a small cup of chilled
soup before the main dish and good petits fours, home-made (as
is everything here including the bread). Terrine of foie gras with
burgundy-poached pears, sashimi of salmon and tuna with soy sauce and
ginger, whole roast lobster with a saffron tagliatelle, pot-roast guinea fowl
with white truffles and fresh tuna cooked with white wine, tomatoes and
thyme demonstrate the style. The cheese course is usually, but not always,
a selection of British farmhouse cheeses and puds might include a hot
soufflé of passion fruit, oranges and brandy, and ice cream profiteroles with
a chocolate truffle sauce. The setting, candle-lit tables in the oldest building
in the village, would be even more romantic were it not for some rather
intrusive 'background' music. Short but well-chosen list of wines to suit
most tastes and products. *Seats* 30. L by arrangement D 7.30-9.
Closed Sun-Tues, 3 days Christmas. AMERICAN EXPRESS *Access, Diners, Visa.*

Coniston   Sun Hotel   63%   £60

Tel 053 94 41248	**H**
Coniston Cumbria LA21 8HQ	Map 4 C3

The Old Man of Coniston creates a spectacular backdrop to this handsome
Victorian house in a hillside setting overlooking the village. Views from
a stylish, book-filled lounge are conducive to relaxation, while the adjacent

16th-century inn will appeal to the more convivial. Generally spacious bedrooms incorporate seating areas and are carpeted through to bright, airy bathrooms. Two rooms have four-posters. **Rooms** 11. *Garden. Closed Christmas. Access, Visa.*

Coniston   Places of Interest

Ravenglass Tourist Information   Tel 0229 717278.
Muncaster Castle and Gardens   Tel 0229 717614 *28 miles.*
The Owl Centre   Muncaster Castle Tel 0229 717393 *28 miles.*
Beatrix Potter Gallery (NT)   Main Street, Hawkshead Tel 05394 88444.
Brantwood House and Garden   (Home of John Ruskin) Coniston
   Tel 05394 41396.

Constantine Bay   Treglos Hotel   65%   £140*

Tel 0841 520727   Fax 0841 521163   **H**
Constantine Bay St Merryn Padstow Cornwall PL28 8JH   **Map 12 B3**

In the same ownership since 1965, this is a friendly, well-run hotel just five minutes from the sea, overlooking Constantine Bay and Trevose Golf Course. It's a popular place with many regular visitors, so balcony rooms are booked well in advance. All the public rooms except the bar have sea views; the three comfortable and traditional lounges are bright and airy. Bedrooms have simple white laminate units, large windows and compact bathrooms. There are four flats in the grounds which are let by the week. In the hotel jackets and ties are requested after 7pm. Special arrangements for families at the end of July and end of August. *Half-board terms only. **Rooms** 44. Garden, croquet, indoor swimming pool, spa bath, games room, children's playroom, snooker, lock-up garages. Closed 5 Nov-10 Mar. Access, Visa.*

Constantine Bay   Place of Interest

Constantine Bay, Harlyn Bay and Treyarnon Bay Beaches.

Cooden   Cooden Resort Hotel   60%   £76

Tel 0424 842281   Fax 0424 846142   **H**
Cooden Sea Road Bexhill-on-Sea East Sussex TN39 4TT   **Map 11 B6**

Right on the beach, with views across Pevensey Bay, this 30s' hotel caters well for both leisure and business guests. There are facilities for up to 160 conference delegates, a health and leisure club, a modern lounge, a cocktail bar and a tavern serving real ale. One of the bedrooms has been adapted for disabled guests; 12 are suitable for family use. Under-16s share parents' room free. **Rooms** 41. *Garden, croquet, indoor & outdoor swimming pools, gym, sauna, steam room, solarium, beauty & hair salon, helipad.* AMERICAN EXPRESS *Access, Diners, Visa.*

Cooden   Place of Interest

Bexhill Beach.

Copdock   Ipswich Moat House   64%   £74

Tel 0473 730444   Fax 0473 730801   **H**
London Road Copdock nr Ipswich Suffolk IP8 3JD   **Map 10 C3**

Modern hotel set in four acres of grounds just off the A12, three miles south of Ipswich. Ground-floor areas were refurbished during 1994. Besides practical, up-to-date accommodation the hotel offers extensive conference facilities (up to 500 delegates) and a well-equipped health and fitness club. Popular for weddings at weekends. **Rooms** 74. *Indoor swimming pool, keep-fit equipment, sauna, spa bath, solarium.* AMERICAN EXPRESS *Access, Diners, Visa.*

Corby   Carlton Manor Hotel   65%   £88

Tel 0536 401020   Fax 0536 400767   **H**

Geddington Road Corby Northamptonshire NN18 8ET   Map 7 E4

Substantial modern hotel at the junction of the A6116 and A43 to the
south-east of town. A spacious, uncluttered lobby sets the tone for unusually
large bedrooms (four luxury rooms and two suites are even bigger) with
good solid wood furniture and all the usual amenities including satellite
TV. Good-sized bathrooms offer ample shelf space and huge bath sheets.
Day rooms include two bars, a lounge with buttonback leather chesterfields
and a smart leisure centre. Standards of repair and housekeeping are high
throughout the hotel. *Rooms 68. Indoor swimming pool, gym, sauna, steam
room, spa bath, solarium, beauty salon, hair salon, snooker.* AMERICAN EXPRESS®
Access, Diners, Visa.

Corby   Rockingham Forest   60%   £65

Tel 0536 401348   Fax 0536 266383   **H**

Rockingham Road Corby Northamptonshire NN17 1AE   Map 7 E4

Off the A6116 to the north of town, this modern low-rise hotel was
originally privately built, which explains the more spacious public areas
and somewhat larger bedrooms than those found in most Posthouses – its
most recent incarnation. Two very large mini-suites are particularly good
value at a supplement of just £10. Meeting rooms for up to 250 theatre-
style. Half the bedrooms are designated non-smoking. Children free when
sharing parents' room. World of Forte. *Rooms 69. Garden.* AMERICAN EXPRESS®
Access, Diners, Visa.

Corfe Castle   Mortons House Hotel   62%   £80

Tel 0929 480988   Fax 0929 480820   **H**

45 East Street Corfe Castle Dorset BH20 5EE   Map 14 C4

An Elizabethan manor house, almost in the shadow of the castle, and linked
to it by tunnels. The entrance hall with its original minster stone fireplace
leads to a handsome oak-panelled drawing room with Indonesian friezes.
Bedrooms are in a sympathetic 1966 extension. *Rooms 17. Walled garden,
croquet.* AMERICAN EXPRESS® *Access, Diners, Visa.*

Corfe Castle   Place of Interest

Corfe Castle (NT)   Nr Wareham Tel 0929 480921.

If we recommend meals in a hotel or inn a separate entry is made for its
restaurant.

Cornhill-on-Tweed   Tillmouth Park   68%   £95

Tel 0890 882255   Fax 0890 882540   **H**

Cornhill-on-Tweed Northumberland TD12 4UU   Map 5 D1

Ronald and Sandra Dollery are now well settled in at this solid Victorian
mansion set high above the River Till. In the public rooms, decor and
artefacts all underline the hotel's role as a shooting and fishing venue, even
including a proper room for rods and guns and a drying room.
Individually decorated, antique-furnished bedrooms (the best, including
two garden rooms at a little distance from the main house, are very
spacious) combine comfort with modern amenities and good bathrooms
with wood-panelled tubs. *Rooms 13. Garden, croquet, snooker, clay pigeon
shooting.* AMERICAN EXPRESS® *Access, Diners, Visa.*

Corse Lawn   Corse Lawn House   71%   £90

Tel 0452 780771   Fax 0452 780840   **HR**

Corse Lawn nr Gloucester Gloucestershire GL19 4LZ   **Map 14 B1**

After 17 years Baba and Denis Hine continue in fine form at their
handsome Queen Anne house; their son Giles and his new wife Sue both
play a vital and enthusiastic role in running this most hospitable
of establishments. Day rooms are designed in a country house style and
spacious bedrooms (just two are rather smaller) are individually decorated,
with plain walls and attractive matching bedcovers, curtains and bedhead
drapes and furnished with antiques which include marble-topped
washstands to house beverage equipment (cafetière, ground coffee, loose tea,
vacuum flask of fresh milk and home-made biscuits). Full room service
is also available all day. The rooms are practical as well as pretty: there's
a proper leather-topped desk near a light fitting and extras like fruit,
mineral water and satellite TV. Good bathrooms, with ruffled blinds
to match the room, offer generous towelling and bathrobes. Breakfasts
include home-made marmalade and sausages plus home-cured bacon – the
sort of attention to detail one might expect from a place with such
an emphasis on good food. Kippers are on the menu (but not for room
service!) **Rooms** 19. *Garden, croquet, tennis, outdoor swimming pool, helipad.*
AMERICAN EXPRESS *Access, Diners, Visa.*

Restaurant   £75

Everything from the bread to delicious chocolates served with coffee
is home-made by Baba Hine and her team here, using only the best of fresh
ingredients to produce some thoroughly satisfying dishes. Menus in the
elegant L-shaped dining room are always full of interest, making the final
choice a tricky but pleasant task. Millefeuille of wild mushrooms, poached
gulls' eggs with samphire and hollandaise or hot crab sausage with tomato
sauce with chick peas could precede pigeon breasts in red wine, bourride
of mullet, monkfish, salmon and cod with mussels, or barbecued fillet
of pork with apple fritters; in addition, there's always a separate, interesting
vegetarian menu. A particularly good and varied pudding menu might
include chocolate indulgence (gateau, mousse, ice cream) and a super light
and fruity hot passion fruit soufflé. Less formal but equally good eating
is to be had in the bar/bistro which offers two menus – 'Baba's British Bill
of Fare' (she's English) and 'Denis's Menu Français' (he's French). Splendid
and comprehensive wine list with lots of half bottles, fair prices and helpful
introductory notes. **Seats** 50. *Private Room* 35. L 12-2 D 7-10. *Set L £15.95*
(Sun £17.95). Set D £23.50.

Never leave money, credit cards or valuables lying around in your
hotel room. Use the hotel safe or the mini-safe in your room.

Corsham   Methuen Arms   £59

Tel 0249 714867   Fax 0249 712004   **I**

2 High Street Corsham Wiltshire SN13 0HB   **Map 14 B2**

Housed around the remains of a 14th-century nunnery, and converted into
a brewery and coaching inn around 1608, there's abundant history here.
Among notable features in public areas are the 100-foot Long Bar
containing its own skittle alley, and outstanding examples of stonemasonry
through the ages to be found in the Winter's Court restaurant. Bedrooms
in the main, Georgian, house overlooking a fairly constant stream of traffic
are on the utilitarian side (several with WC/shower rooms only). To the
rear, and set around a courtyard facing the serene garden, the newer
bedrooms have a touch more elegance, enhanced in the honeymoon suites
by four-poster and half-tester beds. Banqueting/conferences for 120.
No dogs. **Rooms** 25. *Garden, skittle alley. Closed 26 Dec, 1 Jan.*
AMERICAN EXPRESS *Access, Visa.*

Corsham	Rudloe Park	64%	£80

Tel 0225 810555   Fax 0225 811412   **H**

Leafy Lane Corsham Wiltshire SN13 0PA   Map 14 B2

The Park's wooded drive leads off the A4 between Chippenham and Bath, at the top of Box Hill. It's a distinctive Bath-stone manor house standing in ten acres of award-winning gardens. Decor within is fittingly traditional, and the lounge-bar makes a comfortable setting in which to enjoy one of the impressive range of whiskies and cognacs. Bedrooms, with four-posters, half-testers or crown canopies, are traditionally furnished and full of homely touches like fresh fruit and complimentary sherry. *Rooms 11. Garden, croquet.* AMERICAN EXPRESS *Access, Diners, Visa.*

Corsham   Places of Interest

Chippenham Tourist Information   Tel 0249 657733.
Bowood House and Gardens   Calne Tel 0249 812102.
Corsham Court   Tel 0249 712214.
Sheldon Manor   Tel 0249 653120.

Coventry	Chace Hotel	61%	£91

Tel 0203 303398   Fax 0203 301816   **H**

London Road Toll Bar End Coventry West Midlands CV3 4EQ   Map 6 C4

On the A423, a Victorian main building with modern extensions. Children up to 14 stay free in parents' room. Banqueting/conference for 80/100. Forte. *Rooms 67. Garden, children's playground.* AMERICAN EXPRESS *Access, Diners, Visa.*

Coventry	Coventry Hill Hotel	60%	£68

Tel 0203 402151   Fax 0203 402235   **H**

Rye Hill Allesley Coventry West Midlands CV5 9PH   Map 6 C4

High-riser just outside the city on the A45. Conference facilities for 120. Formerly a Forte Posthouse (still in Forte ownership). *Rooms 184.* AMERICAN EXPRESS *Access, Diners, Visa.*

Coventry	De Vere Hotel	69%	£95

Tel 0203 633733   Fax 0203 225299   **H**

Cathedral Square Coventry West Midlands CV1 5RP   Map 6 C4

A large modern hotel, which overlooks the magnificent cathedral, and which enjoys direct access to the square through a conservatory. Attractive public areas include a spacious foyer and the Daimler bar-lounge decorated with pictures of one of Coventry's most famous cars. Generously-sized bedrooms are smart and well equipped, with plenty of working space and colourfully tiled bathrooms. Conference and banqueting facilities for up to 450. Children up to 14 stay free in parents' room. *Rooms 190.* AMERICAN EXPRESS *Access, Diners, Visa.*

Coventry	Forte Posthouse	66%	£68

Tel 0203 613261   Fax 0203 614318   **H**

Hinckley Road Coventry West Midlands CV2 2HP   Map 6 C4

Formerly the *Forte Crest*, this purpose-built hotel has a business centre, a fully equipped leisure club and a reduced tariff since last year. Banqueting/catering for up to 450, no room service. Parking for 200 cars. *Rooms 147. Gym, sauna, spa bath, steam room, solarium, beauty salon, putting, games room, coffee shop (7am-11pm).* AMERICAN EXPRESS *Access, Diners, Visa.*

Coventry   Hilton National   72%   NEW   £95

Tel 0203 603000   Fax 0203 603011   **H**

Paradise Way The Triangle Coventry Warwickshire CV2 2ST   Map 6 C4

Bedrooms at this large modern hotel by Junction 2 of the M6 come with air-conditioning, phones at the well-lit work/breakfast table as well as the bedside, special 'make up' desk with angled mirrors, iron and ironing board, glass-doored mini-bar and satellite TV; plus roomy bathrooms boasting marble floors and vanity units. Two rooms are equipped for the disabled. The spacious lobby with central flower display and three curved, free-standing reception counters, sets the tone for semi-open-plan public areas that combine comfort with a sense of style. Room service can provide hot meals 24 hours a day. Under-18s share parents' room free. Conference/banqueting facilities for 600/500; staffed business centre. *Rooms 172. Garden, indoor swimming pool, gym, sauna, steam room, spa bath, sun beds, beauty salon, hair salon.* AMERICAN EXPRESS *Access, Diners, Visa.*

Coventry   Novotel   62%   £55

Tel 0203 365000   Fax 0203 362422   **H**

Wilsons Lane Longford Coventry West Midlands CV6 6HL   Map 6 C4

Practical, modern accommodation close to Junction 3 of the M6. Banqueting/conferences for 120/200. *Rooms 100. Outdoor swimming pool, boules, children's playground.* AMERICAN EXPRESS *Access, Diners, Visa.*

Coventry   Travel Inn   NEW   £43

Tel 0203 636585   **L**

Rugby Road Binley Woods Coventry West Midlands CV3 2TA   Map 6 C4

5 minutes' drive from M6 on the right-hand side of A46 Eastern bypass, at the junction with Rugby Road. Two meeting rooms. *Rooms 52.* AMERICAN EXPRESS *Access, Diners, Visa.*

Coventry (North)   Campanile Hotel   £44

Tel 0203 622311   Fax 0203 602362   **L**

Wigston Road Walsgrave Coventry West Midlands CV2 2SD   Map 6 C4

Off the A4600 Hinckley Road, from Junction 2 of the M6. *Rooms 50.* AMERICAN EXPRESS *Access, Diners, Visa.*

Coventry (South)   Campanile Hotel   £44

Tel 0203 639922   Fax 0203 306898   **L**

Abbey Road Whitley Coventry West Midlands CV3 4BJ   Map 6 C4

Close to the A45 and A423, off the A46. *Rooms 50.* AMERICAN EXPRESS *Access, Diners, Visa.*

Coventry   Places of Interest

Tourist Information   Tel 0203 832303/832304.
Belgrade Theatre   Belgrade Square Tel 0203 553055.
Coventry Arts Centre   University of Warwick Tel 0203 417417.
Herbert Art Gallery and Museum   Jordan Well Tel 0203 832381.
Coventry Cathedral   Tel 0203 227597.
Coventry City Football Ground   Tel 0203 257171.
Coventry Sports Centre   0203 228601.

Cowan Bridge   Cobwebs   £60
Tel & Fax 052 42 72141   **RR**

Leck Cowan Bridge nr Kirkby Lonsdale Lancashire LA6 2HZ   Map 4 C4

At junction 36 of the M6 take the A65 towards Kirkby Lonsdale. Then at Cowan Bridge, follow signs for Leck, go under a railway bridge and on the left you'll come upon a charming Victorian house in a picturesque rural setting. Yvonne Thompson single-handedly cooks a balanced fixed-price, five-course dinner that might offer sole cornet filled with avocado, shrimps and salmon surrounded by a tomato sauce; turkey, duck, guinea fowl and pigeon with a spicy kumquat sauce (served with a selection of lightly cooked vegetables); cold lemon soufflé with cherries; a selection of local cheeses; and coffee and petits fours. Paul Kelly plays host and enthuses over a collector's wine list that's particularly strong on Alsace and the New World, with excellent-value house selections and half bottles. Booking essential. No smoking in the dining room. *Seats 24. D only 7.30 for 8. Closed Sun & Mon, Jan & Feb. Set D £25. Access, Visa.*

Rooms   £60

Five bedrooms in individual, charming style, with good creature comforts and excellent breakfasts.

Cowan Bridge   Hipping Hall Hotel   64%   £74
Tel 052 42 71187   Fax 052 42 72452   **H**

Cowan Bridge nr Kirkby Lonsdale Lancashire LA6 2JJ   Map 4 C4

Ian Bryant and Jocelyn Ruffle, here since 1988, pride themselves on creating a relaxed country-house atmosphere; guests meet for drinks round the fire and dine together at one table in the characterful, beamed Great Hall, complete with minstrel's gallery. There is also a help-yourself bar in the old stone-flagged conservatory. Bedrooms are bright, pretty and comfortable, with gleaming bathrooms. There are now direct-dial telephones in each room. The hall is the sole survivor of a 15th-century hamlet and stands on the A65 three miles east of Kirkby Lonsdale. No children under 12. *Rooms 7. Garden. Closed Jan & Feb. Access, Visa.*

Cranbrook   Hartley Mount   62%   £70
Tel 0580 712230   Fax 0580 715733   **H**

Hartley Road Cranbrook Kent TN17 3QX   Map 11 C5

A handsome Edwardian county manor house set in spacious gardens off the A229. There are views over farmland and the Weald of Kent from the hotel and a non-smoking policy in all rooms but the conservatory (where breakfast is served). The informal atmosphere is exemplified by a lack of formal reception facilities, as the owners Lionel and Lee Skilton prefer to greet guests personally. Bedrooms include a four-poster room with period bathroom and a very large family room. No dogs. *Rooms 7. Garden, croquet, tennis, mini-golf, pétanque.* AMERICAN EXPRESS *Access, Visa.*

Cranbrook   Kennel Holt Hotel   66%   £105
Tel 0580 712032   Fax 0580 715495   **H**

Goudhurst Road Cranbrook Kent TN17 2PT   Map 11 C5

Neil and Sally Chalmers have settled in well at this small, Elizabethan manor house with distinctive brick chimneys, just off the A262, three miles from Goudhurst. There are two beamed lounges, one with floral sofas and brick inglenook fireplace, the other, with oak panelling, acting as the bar. Bedrooms are now all en suite. Popular for weddings, with a marquee in the garden for larger affairs, and also well set up for small business meetings (up to 30). Parking for 30 cars. No dogs. *Rooms 9. Garden, croquet.* AMERICAN EXPRESS *Access, Diners, Visa.*

Cranbrook   Place of Interest

Sissinghurst Castle Garden (NT)   Tel 0580 712850.

Cranleigh   La Barbe Encore

£55

Tel 0483 273889

R

High Street Cranleigh Surrey GU6 8AE

Map 15 E3

Jean-Pierre Bonnet can be seen in the kitchen of his cheerful, friendly bistro producing generally mainstream French dishes – *oeuf en meurette*, guinea fowl terrine, blanquette of lamb, rumpsteak with shallots, crème brulée, sorbets. *Seats 60. Parties 30. L 12-2 D 7-10. Closed L Sat, D Sun, all Mon, Bank Holidays. Set L £6.95/£13.95/£15.95 Set D £17.50/£19.50.* AMERICAN EXPRESS *Access, Visa.*

Crathorne   Crathorne Hall   72%

£130

Tel 0642 700398   Fax 0642 700814

H

Crathorne nr Yarm Cleveland TS15 0AR

Map 5 E3

Set in 15 acres of grounds not far from the village centre and a short distance from the A19, Crathorne Hall was the last of the great stately homes built in the Edwardian era. Public rooms and the best of the bedrooms enjoy an elevated view over parkland with not a human habitation in sight. The drawing room is of classical proportions with a fine carved overmantel, large portraits in oil and brass chandeliers. Knoll sofas and buttoned leather Queen Anne style armchairs form part of a comfortable and very traditional decor. The cocktail bar has the air of a gentleman's club with its bottle-green walls, mahogany panelling and pillars and plush red velour chairs. Bedrooms are splendid though top floor and back rooms are smaller. Furniture is period style in keeping with the character of the building and all rooms are well equipped, superior rooms in particular. Bathrooms, some with bidets, have quality toiletries and bathrobes. Children under 14 share parents' room free. Conference/banqueting facilities for 200/130. *Rooms 37. Garden, croquet, helipad.* AMERICAN EXPRESS *Access, Diners, Visa.*

Crawley   George Hotel   64%

£76

Tel 0293 524215   Fax 0293 548565

H

High Street Crawley West Sussex RH10 1BS

Map 11 B5

An old gallows sign announces this town-centre former coaching inn. Some parts are beamed and atmospheric, others modern. About a quarter of the bedrooms were undergoing refurbishment during 1994. Forte Heritage. *Rooms 81.* AMERICAN EXPRESS *Access, Diners, Visa.*

Crawley   Places of Interest

Leonardslee Gardens   Lower Beeding Tel 0403 891212.
Gatwick Zoo   Charlwood Tel 0293 862312.

Crewe   Forte Travelodge

£45

Tel 0270 883157

L

Alsager Road Barthomley nr Crewe Cheshire CW2 5PT

Map 6 B3

At Junction 16 of the M6 and A500 between Nantwich and Stoke-on-Trent, off the junction roundabout signposted to Alsager. *Rooms 42.* AMERICAN EXPRESS *Access, Diners, Visa.*

Crick   Forte Posthouse Northampton/Rugby   64%   £68

Tel 0788 822101   Fax 0788 823955   **H**

Crick Northamptonshire NN6 7XR   Map 7 D4

Low-rise modern hotel near Junction 18 on the M1, 7 miles from Rugby. 14 meeting rooms, conference facilities for 185. An 'anytime' lounge has replaced the coffee shop. *Rooms 88. Garden, indoor swimming pool, gym, sauna, solarium.* AMERICAN EXPRESS® *Access, Diners, Visa.*

Crook   Wild Boar Hotel   60%   £84

Tel 0539 445225   Fax 0539 442498   **H**

Crook nr Windermere Cumbria LA23 3NF   Map 4 C3

Abundant character still pervades this old coaching inn, whose name commemorates the spot where Westmorland's last wild boar was killed (in King John's time). Public rooms are a mass of blackened beams, log fires and ancient oak furniture, the oldest dating from 1635. Much of this character is reflected in the main-house bedrooms with four-posters and two suites, one with a spa bath. A more modern wing offers rooms for non-smokers; bathrooms are generally on the small side. Children up to 15 stay free in parents' room. Free leisure facilities at a sister hotel a few miles away, discounted green fees at Windermere golf club (1 mile away). *Rooms 36. Garden.* AMERICAN EXPRESS® *Access, Diners, Visa.*

Crooklands   Crooklands Hotel   60%   £55

Tel 053 95 67432   Fax 053 95 67525   **H**

Crooklands nr Kendal Cumbria LA7 7NW   Map 4 C4

Just 1½ miles from the M6 (Junction 36) on the A65 in a peaceful rural location, the Crooklands is housed in a collection of farm buildings adjoining an original ale house. Superior rooms are in the more modern extension. *Rooms 30. Garden, snooker, coffee shop, carvery (7.30am-2pm & 7pm-9pm). Closed Christmas.* AMERICAN EXPRESS® *Access, Diners, Visa.*

Crosby-on-Eden   Crosby Lodge   66%   £85

Tel 0228 573618   Fax 0228 573428   **HR**

High Crosby Crosby-on-Eden nr Carlisle Cumbria CA6 4QZ   Map 4 C2

Since the Crosby-on-Eden by-pass was under construction as we went to press (due for completion in autumn 1994), the Sedgwicks kindly provide revised directions for finding Crosby Lodge: leave the M6 at Junction 44 and follow signs for Brampton. Approximately 3½ miles on, just off the A689, you should find this delightful crenellated Georgian country house, overlooking parkland and the river. The walled garden is ideal for a relaxing stroll. Indoors there's an elegant and professional air to the day rooms and bedrooms – those in the converted stable block are slightly less grand. Banqueting/conferences for 50/25. *Rooms 11. Garden. Closed 24 Dec-mid Jan.* AMERICAN EXPRESS® *Access, Visa.*

Restaurant   £65

There are extensive menus at lunch and dinner, cooked by Michael Sedgwick and served by Patricia. He describes the style as 'traditional with a continental influence' and this seems an apt turn of phrase, perhaps slightly underplaying the reality of such dishes as parcels of smoked Savoie ham filled with asparagus mousse and garnished with spiced pears, slices of smoked goose breast served with Cumberland sauce, pan-fried loin of pork with apricot sauce, fillet of lemon sole meunière with prawns, or grilled Solway salmon served with fresh asparagus and hollandaise sauce. Everything is home-made, from amuse-gueule to petits fours. Helpful notes against each wine on the diverse list. No children under 5 after 7.30pm.

See over

Jacket and tie required for gentlemen. No smoking. *Seats 50. Parties 40. Private Room 14. L 12-1.30 D 7.30-9 (Sun 7.15-8.45). Set L £15 Set D £26.50.*

Croydon   **Croydon Park**   **69%**   **£97**

Tel 081-680 9200   Fax 081-760 0426   **H**
7 Altyre Road Croydon Surrey CR9 5AA   **Map 11 B5**

A town-centre, roomy hotel opposite the Law Courts, with plenty of covered parking. The foyer is spacious but offers only limited seating, while the gas-lit Whistlers Bar (open 10am-11pm) is a more intimate spot. Bedrooms have queen-size beds and uniform decor, air-conditioning and compact bathrooms. Two floors are designated non-smoking and one room on the ground floor is equipped for disabled guests. There's a leisure centre, and conference/banqueting facilities for 300/200. Children up to 16 are accommodated free in parents' room. £70 weekend tariff. *Rooms 212. Indoor swimming pool, gym, squash, sauna, spa bath, sun beds.* AMERICAN EXPRESS® *Access, Diners, Visa.*

Croydon   **Forte Posthouse**   **61%**   **£68**

Tel 081-688 5185   Fax 081-681 6438   **H**
Purley Way Croydon Surrey CR9 4LT   **Map 11 B5**

Convenient location, aside the A23, with flexible conference facilities for 40 to 170 delegates. Half the bedrooms are designated non-smoking. *Rooms 83. 24hr coffee shop.* AMERICAN EXPRESS® *Access, Diners, Visa.*

Croydon   **Hilton National**   **69%**   **£105**

Tel 081-680 3000   Fax 081-681 6171   **H**
Waddon Way Purley Way Croydon Surrey CR9 4HH   **Map 11 B5**

Smart, new polished granite hotel with plenty of parking at the Croydon end of Purley Way. Quality public areas combine comfort and space with a considerable sense of style. Good bedrooms offer large beds and ample work space plus wing armchairs and proper breakfast table. White marble features in equally good bathrooms. Suites (actually just large rooms) have sophisticated wide-screen TVs that incorporate CD players and a video games feature, spa baths and separate shower cubicles in addition to the tub. Children up to 12 can stay free in parents' room. 24hr room service. *Rooms 168. Indoor swimming pool, gym, sauna, spa bath, steam room, solarium, beauty salon, coffee shop (10.30am-10.30pm).* AMERICAN EXPRESS® *Access, Diners, Visa.*

Croydon   **Selsdon Park**   **68%**   **£117**

Tel 081-657 8811   Fax 081-651 6171   **H**
Addington Road Sanderstead Croydon Surrey CR2 8YA   **Map 11 B5**

200 acres of parkland are the setting for ivy-clad Selsdon Park, whose amenities combine those of hotel, golf course, leisure club and conference venue. It's also a good place for weekending families, who enjoy special rates. The baronial-style entrance hall has stone walls, an elaborate plaster ceiling and leather armchairs that are also to be found in the oak-panelled bar-lounge with its heavily carved antique furniture and brass ornaments. Bedrooms come in a variety of sizes and styles from freestanding lightwood furniture to fitted units, and soft floral to bright fabrics. All have mini-bars and room safes in addition to the usual extras. The very best rooms enjoy views across the Surrey Hills. Regular dinner dances and baby-sitting by prior arrangement; golf-and tennis-mad parents will be in seventh heaven (coaches on site). Unusual 40m circuit indoor swimming pool. Reservable lock-up garages and car service to East Croydon station. *Rooms 170. Garden, croquet, golf (18-hole), putting green, driving range,*

indoor & outdoor swimming pools, gym, spa bath, sauna, solarium, beauty salon, tennis (grass & all-weather), boules, squash, snooker, children's playground, helipad. AMERICAN EXPRESS *Access, Diners, Visa.*

Croydon	**Travel Inn**	**£43**
Tel 081-686 2030 Fax 081-686 6435		**L**
Coombe Road Croydon Surrey CR0 5RB		**Map 11 B5**

Rooms 40. AMERICAN EXPRESS *Access, Diners, Visa.*

Cuckfield	**Murray's**	**£60**
Tel 0444 455826		**R**
Broad Street Cuckfield West Sussex RH17 5LJ		**Map 11 B6**

Several cottagey rooms, one reserved for non-smokers, provide a cosy setting in which to enjoy Sue Murray's skilled and imaginative cooking. Start, perhaps, with walnut roulade, aubergine charlotte or chili spare ribs, followed by chicken supreme with plum sauce, oxtail ragout or pigeon wrapped in cabbage. Relaxed and informal – "where children can be introduced to good food". Parking in the village car park opposite. Short wine list with almost all bottles under £20. **Seats 32. *Private Room 14. L 12-1.30 D 7.15-9.30. Closed L Sat, all Sun, Bank Holidays, 2 weeks Feb, 2 weeks Aug. Access, Visa.***

Cuckfield	**Ockenden Manor**	**71%**	**£98**
Tel 0444 416111 Fax 0444 415549			**H**
Ockenden Lane Cuckfield West Sussex RH17 5LD			**Map 11 B6**

Fresh flowers and a real log fire feature in the beamed entrance hall of an original Tudor building that has been sympathetically extended in the 19th and 20th centuries, the most recent addition being a block of eight bedrooms. There are attractive views of the South Downs from the rear of the hotel, which overlooks a grand garden. Day rooms include a pub-like, oak-panelled bar, a sunny sitting room and a non-smoking dining room. Bedrooms, five of which have four-poster beds, come in a variety of styles and include both reproduction and original antiques and many extras. **Rooms 22. *Garden.*** AMERICAN EXPRESS *Access, Diners, Visa.*

Cuckfield	**Places of Interest**

Wakehurst Place Garden (NT)   Tel 0444 892701 *7 miles.*
South of England Showground   Tel 0444 892700 *5 miles.*
All England Jumping Course   Hickstead Tel 0273 834315.

> Many establishments are currently on the market, so ownership could change after we go to press.

Dane End	**Green End Park**	**62%**	**£88**
Tel 0920 438344 Fax 0920 438523			**H**
Dane End nr Ware Hertfordshire SG12 0NY			**Map 15 F1**

Off the A602 between Ware and Stevenage, this 18th-century manor house stands peacefully in eight acres of gardens. There's an elegant air to the day rooms, which include an impressive bar with a patio, and a banqueting/conference facilities for up to 120/100 delegates. Bedrooms include two suitable for family occupation – children up to 5 stay free in parents' room. **Rooms 9. *Garden, croquet, tennis, putting.*** AMERICAN EXPRESS *Access, Diners, Visa.*

Darlington   Blackwell Grange Moat House   62%   £98

Tel 0325 380888   Fax 0325 380899   H
Blackwell Grange Darlington Co Durham DL3 8QH   Map 5 E3

17th-century mansion set in 15 acres of parkland, but contemporary comforts in the bedrooms, which include 11 grand, Georgian state rooms. 24hr room service. Good Locomotion Leisure Club and conference and banqueting suites for up to 250. Dinner dances on Saturdays. *Rooms 99. Garden, indoor swimming pool, spa bath, sauna, solarium, gym, putting, pétanque.* AMERICAN EXPRESS *Access, Diners, Visa.*

Darlington   St George Thistle   56%   £79

Tel 0325 332631   Fax 0325 333851   H
Teesside Airport nr Darlington Co Durham DL2 1RH   Map 5 E3

Redbrick, two-storey hotel serving the airport rather than the town. Smart, modern bedrooms. Banqueting facilities for 120, conferences for 160. Friday and Saturday night tariff rates are much reduced. *Rooms 57. Sauna, solarium.* AMERICAN EXPRESS *Access, Diners, Visa.*

Darlington   Sardis   £50

Tel 0325 461222   R
196 Northgate Darlington Co Durham DL1 1QU   Map 5 E3

On Northgate, smart and fashionable Sardis is a five-minute walk from the pedestrian town centre. It's bright inside with a high-windowed frontage and tables set on three tiers in an open-plan layout – crisp white table linen, good bread, Italian-derived menu, Italianate wine list, smooth, friendly service. *Seats 60. Parties 18. L 12-2.30 D 7-9.45. Closed Sun, Bank Holidays, 25 & 26 Dec, 1 Jan. Set L £9/£11 Set D £16. Access, Visa.*

Darlington   Swallow King's Head   57%   £90

Tel 0325 380222   Fax 0325 382006   H
Priestgate Darlington Co Durham DL1 1LW   Map 5 E3

Victorian hotel located above shops in the town centre. Conference and banquets are big business (up to 200 theatre-style in the Wellington Suite) and guests have free use of the nearby Dolphin Leisure Centre. *Rooms 85. Coffee shop (10am-5pm).* AMERICAN EXPRESS *Access, Diners, Visa.*

Darlington   Victor's   £55

Tel 0325 480818   R
84 Victoria Road Darlington Co Durham DL1 5JW   Map 5 E3

To the west and north of the station just off one of the inner ring road roundabouts, Victor's is a friendly, informal and totally unpretentious restaurant decorated in palest grey with simple lighting. Jayne Robinson gets all her supplies locally, and everything possible is made on the premises. Her cooking is honest and quite straightforward, with the emphasis on freshness and flavour. The three-course lunch offers particularly good value for money with appealing dishes such as tomato and fresh herb gratin, smoked haddock fish cakes with tarragon sauce or pork casseroled with juniper berries and apple. On the evening menu could be a warm salad of wild duck breast, steamed plaice with basil and orange butter sauce, and lamb's kidneys with coarse grain mustard and port. The lunchtime menu changes fortnightly, dinner monthly. Once a year, in June, they put kid on the menu. *Seats 30. L 12-2 D 7-10.30. Closed Sun & Mon, 1 week Christmas. Set L £8.50 Set D £20.* AMERICAN EXPRESS *Access, Diners, Visa.*

Darlington   Places of Interest

Tourist Information   Tel 0325 382698.
Darlington Arts Centre   Vane Terrace Tel 0325 483168.
Darlington Civic Theatre   Parkgate Tel 0325 486555.
Darlington Railway Centre and Museum   North Road Station Tel 0325
  460532.
Catterick Indoor Ski Slope   Tel 0748 833788.

Dartmouth   Carved Angel   ★★   £110

Tel 0803 832465   **R**
2 South Embankment Dartmouth Devon TQ6 9BH   Map 13 D3

One of the country's most celebrated and best-loved restaurants, where
a meal is always an occasion to savour. Partly it's the delightful quayside
setting, partly it's the room itself – elegant and airy behind a black-and-
white timbered frontage; but mostly of course it's the marvellous cooking,
by Joyce Molyneux and Nicky Coiley. They draw their inspiration from
Provincial France, from Europe, sometimes from farther afield, but the
foundation is always the pick of local produce, notably fish and shellfish,
beef and lamb, and game in winter. Fruits, vegetables and herbs come from
suppliers used by the Carved Angel for 20 years or more. This wonderful
produce is treated with the utmost respect in dishes sometimes absolutely
simple, sometimes more elaborate, but always with each ingredient playing
a full part. Provençal fish soup with rouille and garlic croutons is one of the
all-time favourites here, and other unfailing delights include salmon
in pastry (remembering Joyce's time at Bath's *Hole in the Wall*?), scallops
(perhaps with spiced lentils and coriander), calf's liver with a gin and lime
sauce, and hot passion fruit soufflé. Some of the dishes show many
influences on one plate: 'an aubergine plate' comprises aubergine with
coconut and yoghurt; spiced aubergine; aubergine marinaded with honey
and thyme; and a sesame brochette. The selection of Ticklemore cheeses
is another notable feature, and the inexpensive 'wines of the month'
selection is a nice touch and bonus to the already super and comprehensive
wine list. Note the bin ends. The dinner price includes 2 or 3 courses,
mineral water, sorbet or cheese, coffee, petits fours and service charge.
*Seats 45. Private Room 16. L 12.30-2 D 7.30-9. Closed D Sun, all Mon, Bank
Holidays except Good Friday, 6 weeks Jan/Feb. Set L £24/£29
Set D £40/£45. No credit cards.*

See the hotel by county listings for easy comparison of conference
and banqueting facilities.

Dartmouth   Royal Castle Hotel   £76

Tel 0803 833033   Fax 0803 835445   **I**
11 The Quay Dartmouth Devon TQ6 9PS   Map 13 D3

Right on the quay, in the centre of town, two Tudor merchants' houses
became a hostelry in the early 1700s and the castellated facade (a Regency
addition) explains the name. Antique furniture, Tudor fireplaces, oak beams
fashioned from ships' timbers and a 300-year-old cooking range are among
many reminders of the past, and in some of the bedrooms four-poster and
brass beds are in use. River-view rooms are the most sought after (and
attract a supplement); six now have jacuzzis. Children under 16 sharing
their parents' room can stay free. The owners are committed to "going
green": all purchasing is as 'green' as possible and they recycle as much
as they can. Mountain bikes are available for hire and guests are encouraged
to use public transport. **Rooms** *25. Limited covered parking. Access, Visa.*

Dartmouth   Stoke Lodge   60%   £71

Tel 0803 770523   Fax 0803 770851   **H**

Stoke Fleming Dartmouth Devon TQ6 0RA   Map 13 D3

In an area where tourism is one main industry and all things maritime another, Stoke Lodge offers the best of both worlds catering primarily for family holidays, and well situated at the top of the village to observe marine activity. Leisure facilities are good (a mixture of indoor and outdoor, in keeping with the climate), while public areas and bedrooms continue to be comfortable and well maintained. Parking for 50 cars. *Rooms 24. Garden, indoor & outdoor swimming pools, tennis, putting, keep-fit equipment, sauna, spa bath, solarium, outdoor play area, games room, giant chess. Access, Visa.*

Dartmouth   Places of Interest

Tourist Information   Tel 0803 834224.
Coleton Fishacre Garden (NT)   Coleton Tel 080425 466.

Daventry   Daventry Resort Hotel   70%   £100

Tel 0327 301777   Fax 0327 706313   **H**

Ashby Road Daventry Northamptonshire NN11 5SG   Map 15 D1

Located due north of Daventry town centre off a roundabout on the A361 and some 8 miles south of junction 18 of the M1. This is a large, sprawling, low-rise modern building geared almost exclusively to a business clientele – a business centre is located in one corner of the reception area. Automatic doors lead into a vast and elegant American-style lobby with highly-polished coloured marble floors, Chinese-style rosewood furniture and dark, flame-patterned long settees. Numerous Chinese table lamps provide low-key lighting, recessed lights and spots adding soft background illumination. The Cat's Whiskers Bar, although spacious, has a warm, clubby atmosphere created by effective soft lighting and attractive rosewood panelling. The night club area (Friday evenings) is at other times a conference room – one of many catering for 10-600 people. Bedrooms range from good-sized standard to Executive and suites. All have up-to-date quality fittings and are provided with useful extras. Two rooms have been specially designed for disabled guests, and almost half the accommodation is designated non-smoking. Children up to 16 can stay free in their parents' room. Bright, modern leisure facilities. *Rooms 138. Indoor swimming pool, children's swimming pool, gym, sauna, spa bath, solarium, beauty salon.* AMERICAN EXPRESS *Access, Diners, Visa.*

Dedham   Fountain House & Dedham Hall   £50

Tel 0206 323027   **RR**

Brook Street Dedham nr Colchester Essex CO7 6AD   Map 10 C3

Just outside the village, Dedham Hall stands in 5 acres of grounds. A loud clanging bell announces your arrival and drinks are taken in a tiny, cosy front lounge. The dining room has a charming, country cottage air of informality with its wheelback chairs and pretty pink decor. Tables have Wee Willie Winkie candle-holders and fresh flowers. The fixed-price menu changes weekly offering a choice of extremely simple but carefully prepared dishes. Stuffed mushrooms, smoked haddock florentine or lentil and ham soup could start the meal, followed by devilled lamb kidneys, baked trout with orange and walnut stuffing or breaded pork fillet with tomato sauce. Chocolate fondue (for 2) is a speciality dessert. Comprehensive selection of half bottles on a list that is particularly long on Italy, Germany and the New World, but short on champagnes. *Seats 32. Parties 14. Private Room 16. L Sun only 12.30-2 D 7-9.30. Closed D Sun, all Mon, Bank Holidays. Set D £18.50. Access, Visa.*

Bedrooms £57

There are six neat, homely bedrooms with residents having their own lounge and a convivial breakfast room. Further accommodation is used for the residential painting courses.

Dedham Maison Talbooth 78% £105

Tel 0206 322367 Fax 0206 322752 **H**

Stratford Road Dedham nr Colchester Essex CO7 6HN Map 10 C3

Maison Talbooth stands in an area of great beauty immortalised in the paintings of John Constable. When Gerald Milsom came here in 1952 it was a simple tea room, which has grown down the years into a tranquil hotel and restaurant (see entry below) of considerable renown. The *Pier at Harwich* is in the same ownership. All is calm and restful in the sunny lounge with its deep-cushioned armchairs, profusion of fresh flowers and views down Dedham Vale. The bedrooms, suites almost, strike a happy balance between the shameless luxury of fine co-ordinated fabrics and crown canopied beds and the quiet homeliness of abundant magazines, fresh fruit and a drinks tray. Bathrooms are superb, some with vast sunken tubs, all containing quality bath sheets and bespoke toiletries. The hotel lies just moments from the A12. *Rooms 10. Garden, croquet, helipad, giant chess.* AMERICAN EXPRESS *Access, Diners, Visa.*

Dedham Le Talbooth £100

Tel 0206 323150 **R**

Gunhill Dedham nr Colchester Essex CO7 6HP Map 10 C3

Alfresco dining under large canvas parasols is a fine summertime option at this beautifully located restaurant housed in a splendidly preserved half-timbered Tudor building right on the banks of the river Stour. The bar and lounges are very traditional, comfortable and welcoming and the dining room overlooks the terrace and river. Fixed-price menus of two or three courses are available lunchtime and evening and the à la carte offers a good choice of starters, mains and desserts. Lunchtime brings an hors d'oeuvre table, a daily roast and traditional dishes such as Irish stew, fish cakes or chicken forestière, and the evening fixed-price menu is similar. The carte has more modern elements, typified by grilled goat's cheese salad, duck served with a black olive and coriander sauce, or braised fillet of turbot in a Madeira cream sauce with cucumber and arame. Chateaubriand remains a favourite on this menu. Hot bitter chocolate soufflé is a speciality dessert. The wine list is notable for several reasons: wide-ranging, informative, good growers, the best vintages, but above all exceptionally keen prices – the restaurant's personal selection offers terrific value. *Seats 80. Private Room 24. L 12-2 D 7-9.30. Set L £12.50/£15 (Sun £19.95) Set D £16.50/£19.50.* AMERICAN EXPRESS *Access, Visa.* MARTELL

Dedham Place of Interest

Castle House (Home of painter Sir Alfred Munnings) Tel 0206 322127.

Denmead Barnard's £45

Tel 0705 257788 **R**

Hambledon Road Denmead Hampshire PO7 6NU Map 15 D4

A change of address just as we went to press for David and Sandie Barnard's home from home. The style of their operation remains broadly similar, though they no longer offer lunches except by prior arrangement. There are gourmet and à la carte menus as well as the set three-course meal, which will still include about three choices at each course. You might therefore enjoy a fresh home-made soup, followed by supreme of salmon, wrapped in pastry, baked and served with a hollandaise sauce, and home-made brown bread ice cream served with a raspberry sauce. *Seats 30. D only 7.30-10. Closed Sun & Mon, Bank Holidays, 1 week Christmas, 2 weeks Aug. Set D £13.50.* AMERICAN EXPRESS *Access, Visa.*

Derby   European Inn   NEW   £46
Tel 0332 292000   Fax 0332 293940   **L**
Midland Road Derby Derbyshire DE1 2SL   Map 6 C3

A brand new and attractive budget hotel with bright bedrooms and bathrooms. Two rooms are equipped for disabled guests. Breakfast is from a buffet selection and there are vending machines for alcohol, snacks and sundries; no restaurant. Two meeting rooms cater for up to 100. Reduced tariff at weekends. *Rooms 88.* AMERICAN EXPRESS *Access, Diners, Visa.*

Derby   Forte Posthouse   61%   £68
Tel 0332 514933   Fax 0332 518668   **H**
Pastures Hill Littleover Derby Derbyshire DE23 7BA   Map 6 C3

Neat, unfussy businessman's accommodation three miles west of the city centre on the A5250. Extensive grounds include a children's play area. Conference and banqueting for up to 60. *Rooms 62.* AMERICAN EXPRESS *Access, Diners, Visa.*

Derby   International Hotel   62%   £40
Tel 0332 369321   Fax 0332 294430   **H**
Burton Road Derby Derbyshire DE3 6AD   Map 6 C3

On the A5250 south-west of the city centre, the privately owned International, once a Victorian school, concentrates very much on conference and exhibition business. Bedrooms offer many extras and the suites boast spa baths. 24hr room service. Children up to 12 stay free in parents' room. Room rates much reduced from last year. *Rooms 62.* AMERICAN EXPRESS *Access, Diners, Visa.*

Derby   Midland Hotel   65%   £89
Tel 0332 345894   Fax 0332 293522   **H**
Midland Road Derby Derbyshire DE1 2SQ   Map 6 C3

Adjacent to Derby railway station, the Midland, built in 1841, has recently undergone major refurbishment with more planned. Its renaissance has resulted in a hotel that currently offers 50 standard and 50 brand new, smart, Executive rooms. The latter are in a rebuilt section and features include multiple phone points, fax and PC points, as well as splendid bathrooms with both steel baths and separate shower cubicles. There is ample seating and writing space too. All the hotel's bedrooms have attractive darkwood furniture. Standard rooms aren't as well equipped and their bathrooms are smaller and more functional. Children up to 11 stay free in parents' room. *Rooms 100. Garden, spa bath.* AMERICAN EXPRESS *Access, Diners, Visa.*

Derby   Places of Interest

Tourist Information   Tel 0332 255802.
Derby Playhouse   Eagle Centre Tel 0332 363275.
Guildhall Theatre   Market Place Tel 0332 255447.
Derby Cathedral   Tel 0332 41201.
Elvaston Castle Museum   Tel 0332 571342.
Royal Crown Derby Museum   Tel 0332 47051.
Derby Cricket Ground   Tel 0332 383211.
Derby County Football Ground   Tel 0332 40105.
Wingfield Park Showground   Belper Tel 0602 324653.
   Historic Houses, Castles and Gardens
Calke Abbey and Park (NT)   Tel 0332 863822.
Kedleston Hall   Tel 0332 842191.
Melbourne Hall and Gardens   Melbourne Tel 0332 862502.
Sudbury Hall (NT)   Tel 0283 585305.

Desborough   Forte Travelodge   £45

Tel 0536 762034   **L**

Harborough Road Desborough Northamptonshire   **Map 7 D4**

On the A6 southbound, 4 miles south-east of Market Harborough and 7 miles north of West Kettering. 3 miles from the A14 – the new A1/M1 link road. *Rooms 32.* *Access, Diners, Visa.*

Note that all telephone numbers with area codes starting with 0 will start 01 from 16 April 1995.

Diss   Weavers   £45

Tel 0379 642411   **R**

Market Hill Diss Norfolk IP22 3JZ   **Map 10 C2**

William and Wilma Bavin describe Weavers as a wine bar and eating house – versatility therefore seems to be the order of the day at what was originally a chapel for the Weaver's Guild, then a butcher's shop, and a wig maker's en route to becoming a restaurant. So history in the surrounding (oak timbers), modern British on the menu. Try perhaps apple, parsnip and Stilton soup, then locally-reared guineafowl, pot-roasted in a prune and leek sauce scented with Earl Grey tea, with tangy lemon cheese torte to finish. Interesting vegetarian dishes. No smoking before 2pm at lunchtime or 9.30pm in the evening. Extensive wine list with a few bargains to be had. *Seats 80. Parties 22. Private Room 50. L 12-2 D 7-9.30. Closed L Sat, all Sun, Bank Holidays, Xmas, 2 weeks end Aug. Set L £6.75/£8.45 Set D £10(not Sat)/£17.50. Access, Diners, Visa.*

Diss   Places of Interest

Bressingham Live Steam Museum and Gardens   Tel 0379 88386.
Banham Zoo   Banham Tel 0953 887476.

Doncaster   Campanile Hotel   £44

Tel 0302 370770   Fax 0302 370813   **L**

Doncaster Leisure Park Bawtry Doncaster South Yorkshire DN4 7PD   **Map 7 D2**

Close to the race course, off the A638. Closest motorway junction is Junction 3 of the M18, off Junction 2 of the A1(M). *Rooms 50.* AMERICAN EXPRESS *Access, Diners, Visa.*

Doncaster   Danum Swallow Hotel   64%   £86

Tel 0302 342261   Fax 0302 329034   **H**

High Street Doncaster South Yorkshire DN1 1DN   **Map 7 D2**

An Edwardian building in the centre of town; inside it's been thoroughly modernised (except for the Crystal Suite, which can accommodate up to 350 delegates in period style) with comfortable, spacious public areas and bedrooms which boast irons and ironing boards in addition to the usual amenities. *Rooms 66. Coffee shop (9am-5pm).* AMERICAN EXPRESS *Access, Diners, Visa.*

Doncaster   Grand St Leger   64%   £80

Tel 0302 364111   Fax 0302 329865   **H**

Bennetthorpe Doncaster South Yorkshire DN2 6AX   **Map 7 D2**

Just a five minute walk from the Doncaster Dome Leisure Park and with
the racecourse opposite and bloodstock sales yard behind, this 19th-century
building was once used as a hostelry for stable lads, but today, it provides
comfortable, unassuming accommodation. Pretty floral fabrics and
freestanding furniture feature in the cosy bedrooms. Day rooms include
a bar-lounge with a host of racing prints and photos. Banqueting up to 65.
Children under 12 free in parents' room. Greatly reduced rates at weekends.
Rooms 20. AMERICAN EXPRESS *Access, Diners, Visa.*

Doncaster   Moat House   64%   £88

Tel 0302 310331   Fax 0302 310197   **H**

Warmsworth Doncaster South Yorkshire DN4 9UX   **Map 7 D2**

Next to the junction of the A630 with the A1(M), this modern hotel
is stone-clad to fit in with surrounding buildings, most notably the 17th-
century Warmsworth Hall, which is now part of the hotel's extensive
conference/function facilities (up to 400 theatre-style). A spacious marble-
floored reception/lounge creates a good first impression for decent
standardised bedrooms in the main building. Best (Executive) rooms are
in the newest (3 years old) building reached via an underground corridor.
Good leisure centre. **Rooms** 100. *Indoor swimming pool, keep-fit equipment,
sauna, solarium.* AMERICAN EXPRESS *Access, Diners, Visa.*

Doncaster   Places of Interest

Tourist Information   Tel 0302 734309.
Civic Theatre   Waterdale Tel 0302 322817.
Comisbrough Castle   Tel 0709 863329.
Doncaster Racecourse   Tel 0302 320066.

Dorchester   The Mock Turtle   £54

Tel 0305 264011   **R**

34 High West Street Dorchester Dorset DT1 1UP   **Map 13 F2**

A charming restaurant formed from a number of interconnecting rooms
in a town house dating back to the late 17th century. Decor
is predominantly green with exposed stonework here and there, old
photographs, crisp white napery and a welcoming fire in the comfortable
lounge area. It's been run for five years by the Hodder family; Raymond's
menus are fixed-price only, but offer a good choice at both lunch and
dinner that is likely to please all tastes. Fish is a feature and there's usually
a long list of daily specials, perhaps including baked hake steak with garlic
butter or delice of halibut encrusted with local crab. Sound cooking
is complemented by friendly service. **Seats** 50. *Parties 20. L 12-2 D 7-9.30.
Closed L Mon (except Bank Holidays), L Sat, all Sun, 26 Dec.
Set L £10/£12.50 Set D £15.95/£18.95. Access, Visa.*

Dorchester   Places of Interest

Tourist Information   Tel 0305 267992.
Dorchester Arts Centre   Tel 0305 66926.
The Giant (NT)   Cerne Abbas *8 miles North.*
Pavillion Theatre   Tel 0305 783225.
Abbotsbury Swannery & Sub-Tropical Gardens   Abbotsbury Tel 0305
871387.
Historic Houses, Castles and Gardens
Danway House   Puddletown Tel 0305 269741.
Hardy's Cottage (NT)   Higher Bockhampton Tel 0305 262366.
Minterne Gardens   Minterne Magna Tel 0300 341370.

Wolfeton House   Tel 0305 263500.
  Museums and Art Galleries
The Dinosaur Museum   Icen Way Tel 0305 269741.
Tutankhamun Exhibition   Tel 0305 269741.
Dorset County Museum   Includes Thomas Hardy memorial room
  Tel 0305 262735.
Warmwell Leisure Resort Dry Ski Slope   Tel 0305 852911.

Dorchester-on-Thames	George Hotel	£70
Tel 0865 340404 Fax 0865 341620		**I**
High Street Dorchester-on-Thames Oxfordshire OX10 7HH		Map 15 D2

With a history spanning more than 500 years, the George is one of the
oldest inns in the land, and is currently undergoing refurbishment. Focal
point of the public area is a fine beamed bar. Bedrooms in the main
building have a solid, old-fashioned feel, some cosy and snug under oak
beams, two with four-posters. Other rooms have less character but are still
very adequate. Small meetings and seminars (for up to 70) are held in the
two rooms of a self-contained annexe; the beamed Stable room
is particularly characterful. *Rooms 18. Garden. Closed 1 week Christmas.*
AMERICAN EXPRESS *Access, Diners, Visa.*

Dorking	Forte Travelodge	£45
Tel 0306 740361		**L**
Reigate Road Dorking Surrey RH4 1QB		Map 15 E3

Half a mile east of Dorking town centre and 6 miles west of Reigate on the
A25. *Rooms 29.* AMERICAN EXPRESS *Access, Diners, Visa.*

Dorking	Partners West Street	£75
Tel 0306 882826		**R**
2 West Street Dorking Surrey RH4 1BL		Map 15 E3

With seating on two floors of a 16th-century building just off the main
street, Partners combines stylish decor with some sophisticated cooking of a
high standard. Rock oysters served warm with spinach, smoked bacon and
hollandaise sauce; fresh foie gras on a potato galette with wild mushrooms;
breast of pheasant cooked with root vegetables flavoured with thyme and
roasted monkfish on a pasta cake with globe artichoke, lentils and a red
wine jus demonstrate the range. Sweets like chocolate croissant pudding
and glazed lemon tart are supplemented by some good cheeses. There are
both à la carte and fixed-price menus. The wide-ranging wine list includes
five wines from Denbies wine estate (Dorking's own vineyard) and seven
different dessert wines by the glass. *Seats 45. Parties 12. Private Room 30.
L 12.30-2 D 7.30-9.30. Closed L Sat, D Sun, 25 & 26 Dec, 1 Jan.
Set L £11.95 Set D £19.95.* AMERICAN EXPRESS *Access, Diners, Visa.*

Dorking	White Horse	62%	£92
Tel 0306 881138 Fax 0306 887241			**H**
High Street Dorking Surrey RH4 1BE			Map 15 E3

Town-centre hotel developed from an old coaching inn, first recorded
as such in 1750 though parts date back to the 15th century. Oak beams and
log fires give a cosy, traditional feel to the day rooms, while in summer the
patio comes into its own. The outdoor pool has been filled in to create
more spacious gardens. Good modern bedrooms. Families are well catered
for. There's a choice of meeting and syndicate rooms holding up to 60
delegates (banqueting for up to 100). Leave the M25 at Junction 9 on to the
A24. Forte Heritage. *Rooms 68. Garden.* AMERICAN EXPRESS *Access,
Diners, Visa.*

Dorking   Places of Interest

Polesden Lacey (NT)   Nr Dorking Tel 0372 58203 or 52048.
Thorndike Theatre   Leatherhead Tel 0372 376211.

Dorrington	Country Friends	£65
Tel 0743 718707		**RR**
Dorrington nr Shrewsbury Shropshire SY5 7JD		**Map 6 A4**

A half-timbered house turned into a comfortable restaurant with rooms.
Chef-patron Charles Whittaker has changed the format, now offering two-
or three-course fixed-price menus lunchtime and evening. Trelough duck
is a speciality, sometimes appearing with a spiced plum and ginger sauce,
and venison is a seasonal favourite. Other choices might be twice-baked
courgette soufflé, fish quenelles with a smoked prawn sauce, chicken breast
in a wine and sweet pepper sauce served with home-made pasta, and lamb
with a tartlet of flageolet beans, baby onions and bacon. For pudding,
perhaps apple galette with mint custard, trio of chocolate or pineapple and
hazelnut ice cream. British cheeseboard, Welsh rarebit. Sunday lunch
is available only on certain occasions, such as Mothering Sunday. Light
lunches are served Mon-Sat in the bar. No smoking. *Seats 40. L 12-2 D 7-9
(Sat to 9.30). Closed Sun & Mon, Bank Holidays, last 2 weeks Jul, last week
Oct. Set L & D £20.50/£24.50 Set Sun L £15.50.* AMERICAN EXPRESS
Access, Visa.

Rooms   £98*

Three good-quality coach-house bedrooms are attractive with antiques,
if sparing with extras. Two are not en suite. None have phones or TVs.
*Room price includes dinner and a breakfast of Bucks Fizz and scrambled
eggs with smoked salmon. No dogs.

Set menu prices may not always include service or wine.

Dovedale	Izaak Walton Hotel	59%	£95
Tel 033 529 555 Fax 033 529 539			**H**
Dovedale nr Ashbourne Derbyshire DE6 2AY			**Map 6 C3**

Owned by the Duke of Rutland, the 17th-century farmhouse building,
where Izaak Walton once stayed, affords rolling views of Thorpe Cloud
and Dovedale in the Peak District Park. Fly fishing is available on a 4-mile
stretch of the River Dove, which flows through the estate. Leather
chesterfield sofas and open fires add comfort and warmth to the public
rooms; bedrooms are more noteworthy for the vistas without than the
space within. Conference facilities for up to 100. Under-16s stay free
in parents' room. Summer Sunday barbecues in the garden. *Rooms 34.
Garden, fishing, helipad.* AMERICAN EXPRESS *Access, Diners, Visa.*

Dovedale	Peveril of the Peak	60%	£102
Tel 033 529 333 Fax 033 529 507			**H**
Thorpe Dovedale nr Ashbourne Derbyshire DE6 2AW			**Map 6 C3**

Easily reached from the M1 and the M6, at the foot of the 900ft Thorpe
Cloud mountain in the heart of the Peak District, Peveril of the Peak has
been attracting ramblers and country lovers for over 100 years. The
"Dove", incidentally, is the river running through the hamlet. Probably
the original Thorpe Rectory (its origins are obscure), it features much local
Derbyshire stone in the public rooms. Bedrooms are traditional.
Banqueting/conferences for 70/80. Forte Heritage. *Rooms 47. Garden,
tennis.* AMERICAN EXPRESS *Access, Diners, Visa.*

Dover   Forte Posthouse   63%   £68

Tel 0304 821222   Fax 0304 825576   **H**

Singledge Lane Whitfield Dover Kent CT16 3LF   Map 11 D5

Modern low-riser on the Whitfield roundabout alongside the A2, 3 miles from the ferry terminal. Children up to 16 stay free in parents' room. Meeting rooms for up to 50. 24hr lounge menu. *Rooms 67. Garden, children's playroom (weekends).* AMERICAN EXPRESS *Access, Diners, Visa.*

Dover   Moat House   66%   £84

Tel 0304 203270   Fax 0304 213230   **H**

Townwall Street Dover Kent CT16 1SZ   Map 11 D5

A hotel near the sea catering well for both business and leisure visitors. Large beds in spacious bedrooms. Children under 15 stay free in parents' room. Banqueting/conference facilities for 120/80. *Rooms 79. Indoor swimming pool.* AMERICAN EXPRESS *Access, Diners, Visa.*

Dover   Travel Inn   £43

Tel 0304 213339   Fax 0304 214504   **L**

Folkestone Road Dover Kent CT15 7AB   Map 11 D5

Less than 10 minutes drive from the cross-Channel Ferry Port. *Rooms 30.* AMERICAN EXPRESS *Access, Diners, Visa.*

Dover   Places of Interest

Tourist Information   Tel 0304 205108.
Dover Castle   Tel 0304 201628.
Hoverspeed   Tel 0304 240241.
P&O   Tel 0304 203388.
Stenna Sealink   Tel 0233 647047.

We endeavour to be as up-to-the-minute as possible, but inevitably some changes to key personnel may occur at restaurants and hotels after the Guide goes to press.

Driffield   Bell Hotel   £75

Tel 0377 256661   Fax 0377 253228   **I**

Market Place Driffield Humberside YO25 7AP   Map 7 E1

Period charm and modern amenities combine in a coaching inn that's more than 250 years old. Large conference and function facilities (up to 250 delegates) are in the restored Old Town Hall, and further conversion houses a leisure complex with a small pool. Day rooms include the 18th-century wood-panelled Oak Room, the flagstoned Old Corn Exchange buffet/bar and a residents' lounge. Bedrooms boast antique furniture and up-to-date comforts. No children under 12. No dogs. *Rooms 14. Garden, indoor swimming pool, spa bath, steam room, massage, aromatherapy, sauna, solarium, keep-fit equipment, squash. Closed 24-30 Dec.* AMERICAN EXPRESS *Access, Diners, Visa.*

Driffield   Places of Interest

Burton Agnes Hall   Tel 091-261 1585.
Sledmere House and Gardens   Sledmere Tel 0377 236208.

Droitwich   Forte Travelodge   £45

Tel 0527 86545   **L**

Rashwood Hill Droitwich Hereford & Worcester WR9 8DA   **Map 14 B1**

Half a mile west of Junction 5 on the M5 and 2 miles north of Droitwich on the A38. **Rooms** *32*. AMERICAN EXPRESS *Access, Diners, Visa.*

Droitwich Spa   Chateau Impney   70%   £70

Tel 0905 774411   Fax 0905 772371   **H**

Droitwich Spa Hereford & Worcester WR9 0BB   **Map 14 B1**

Chateau Impney is a perfect example of classical French architecture in the chateau style so often executed outside France; and to find this elegant building in the heart of England gives a delicious *frisson* the first time you see it. The grand stone staircase, and fountains surrounded by fat, gilded cherubs enhance the impression. However, the principal business here is as a residential conference centre and banqueting suite (rather than as a setting for period masked balls); and the capacity has been expanded now to accommodate 1,000 delegates. Main-house bedrooms are spacious (but with surprisingly small bathrooms) while the separate Impney Court building offers newer but smaller accommodation. Nine apartments are also in a separate block. Children are only welcome by prior arrangement. No dogs. **Rooms** *120. Garden, sauna, gym, tennis, games room, helipad. Closed Christmas.* AMERICAN EXPRESS *Access, Diners, Visa.*

Droitwich Spa   Raven Hotel   66%   £130

Tel 0905 772224   Fax 0905 797100   **H**

Victoria Square Droitwich Spa Hereford & Worcester WR9 8DU **Map 14 B1**

Specialising in conferences and banqueting (for up to 150/250), the Raven also takes very good care of private guests, putting a premium on courtesy and professionalism. It's a handsome timber-framed building, parts of it going back to the 16th century. Overnight accommodation is more up-to-date than the exterior might suggest. **Rooms** *72. Garden.* AMERICAN EXPRESS *Access, Diners, Visa.*

Droitwich Spa   Places of Interest

Norbury Theatre   Friar Street Tel 0905 770154.
Hanbury Hall (NT)   Tel 052 784 214.
Droitwich Heritage Centre   Tel 0905 774312.

Dudley   Forte Travelodge   £45

Tel 0384 481579   **L**

Dudley Road Brierley Hill Dudley West Midlands DY5 1LQ   **Map 6 B4**

Situated on the A461 at Brierley Hill, 3 miles west of Dudley towards Stourbridge, very close to Merry Hill Centre. No adjacent restaurant facilities. **Rooms** *32.* AMERICAN EXPRESS *Access, Diners, Visa.*

Dulverton   Ashwick House   68%   £118*

Tel 0398 23868   Fax 0398 23056   **HR**

Dulverton Somerset TA22 9QD   **Map 13 D2**

Turn left at the post office in Dulverton, drive up to the moor, turn left after the cattle grid and follow the hotel sign. Richard Sherwood's Ashwick House, dating from the turn of the century, stands in isolation 1000 feet above the valley of the Barle, providing all the peace and fresh air anyone could want. The William Morris interior still boasts original wallpapers; although the present reconstruction dates only from 1980, an evocative Edwardian atmosphere has carefully been retained. Thus, beside your turned-down bed you'll find a goodnight sweet and an Edward Bear hot-water bottle. Bedrooms are spacious, with lovely parkland views and rather dated, chintzy decor. Fine days start with breakfast on the terrace. Sweeping lawns lead down to water gardens, thus no children under 8. No dogs. *Half-board terms. *Rooms 6. Garden, solarium. No credit cards.*

Restaurant   £60

Richard's capable one-man show extends to the kitchen and dinner, when a named, hand-written scroll menu is presented to each diner. Cooking is house party British, exemplified by apple and coriander soup, baked mushrooms stuffed with herbs and nuts, noisettes of spring lamb with a port wine sauce, chocolate mint pot and bread-and-butter pudding. No smoking. *Seats 30. Private Room 15. L (Sun only) 12.30-1.45 D 7.15-8.30. Set Sun L £14.75 Set D £21.75.*

Dulverton   Carnarvon Arms   60%   £80
Tel 0398 23302   Fax 0398 24022   **H**
Dulverton Somerset TA22 9AE   Map 13 D2

Purpose-built by the 4th Earl of Carnarvon in 1874 to accommodate railway passengers arriving at Dulverton station, the Carnarvon Arms is now very much geared to walkers, horse-riders (the hotel will put you in touch with nearby stables) and particularly fishermen, with just over five miles of trout and salmon fishing on the rivers Exe and Barle. The spacious lounges are large, old-fashioned and relaxing, with open fires, splendid views and flower displays. Bedrooms are modest but comfortable enough. Children up to 7 stay free in their parents' room. Owner Mrs Toni Jones has run the hotel for over 35 years. *Rooms 24. Garden, croquet, outdoor swimming pool, tennis, fishing, snooker, hair salon. Access, Visa.*

Dunbridge   Mill Arms Inn   £50
Tel 0794 340401   **R**
Dunbridge nr Romsey Hampshire SO51 0LF   Map 14 C3

Owner Niall Morrow continues with changes for the better at the Mill Arms, restructuring the menus virtually as we went to press. There's now a table d'hote menu at dinner from Mondays to Thursdays, offering fresh local produce cooked in a traditional style. The wine list was also revamped, to include a connoisseurs' selection. Sunday lunch is popular and booking is recommended. *Seats 60. Private Room 40. L 12-2.30 D 7-10 (Fri & Sat to 10.30). Set Sun L £7.95/£9.95.* AMERICAN EXPRESS *Access, Diners, Visa.*

Dunchurch   Forte Travelodge   £45
Tel 0788 521538   **L**
London Road Thurlaston Dunchurch nr Rugby Warwickshire CV23 9LG   Map 7 D4

Off the M45, on the A45 westbound, 3 miles south of Rugby town centre; 8 miles east of Coventry. *Rooms 40.* *Access, Diners, Visa.*

Dunkirk   Petty France Hotel   65%   £126
Tel 0454 238361   Fax 0454 238768   **H**
Dunkirk Badminton Avon GL9 1AF   Map 13 F1

This well-proportioned Georgian house set in eye-catching gardens alongside the A46 (4 miles north of M4 junction 18), is ideally situated mid-way between Bristol, Bath, Gloucester and Cheltenham. It thus satisfies tourists as well as business users of the banqueting and conference facilities (for up to 80). Day rooms are spacious and tranquil, and bedrooms are divided between the main house and a converted stable block; a traditional feel with period furniture and floral fabrics in the former gives way to cottagey curtains and lightwood fittings in the latter. *Rooms 20. Garden, croquet.* AMERICAN EXPRESS *Access, Diners, Visa.*

Dunstable	**Forte Travelodge**		**£45**

Tel 0525 211177

**Watling Street Hockliffe nr Leighton Buzzard Dunstable
Bedfordshire LU7 9LZ**

Map 15 E1

On the A5, 3 miles north of Dunstable. *Rooms 28.* AMERICAN EXPRESS *Access, Diners, Visa.*

Dunstable	**Old Palace Lodge**	**66%**	**£102**

Tel 0582 662201   Fax 0582 696422

Church Street Dunstable Bedfordshire LU5 4RT

Map 15 E1

A usefully situated hotel, on the A505 on the edge of the Chilterns, not far from junction 11 of the M1, nor from Luton airport. Creeper-clad and welcoming, it offers a choice of accommodation, all en-suite and a few non-smoking. Executive wing rooms have extra gadgets. In the absence of a lounge, the oak-panelled bar is the focal point of day rooms. *Rooms 49.* AMERICAN EXPRESS *Access, Diners, Visa.*

Dunstable	**Places of Interest**

Tourist Information   Tel 0582 471012.
Whipsnade Wildlife Park   Tel 0582 872171.

Dunster	**Luttrell Arms**	**64%**	**£107**

Tel 0643 821555   Fax 0643 821567

High Street Dunster nr Minehead Somerset TA24 6SG

Map 13 E1

A creeper-clad hotel of great historical interest, built in the 15th century as a guest house for the monks of Cleeve Abbey. Impressive architectural features include a superb Gothic hall (now the lounge) with a twelve-light window, hammer-beam roof and huge fireplace, and a timbered Tudor bar in the former kitchen. Bedrooms offer solid 20th-century comforts and functional modern bathrooms. Forte Heritage. *Rooms 27. Garden, garage.* AMERICAN EXPRESS *Access, Diners, Visa.*

Dunster	**Place of Interest**

Dunster Castle and Gardens (NT)   Nr Minehead Tel 0643 821314.

Durham	**Royal County Hotel**	**67%**	**£120**

Tel 091-386 6821   Fax 091-386 0704

Old Elvet Durham Co Durham DH1 3JN

Map 5 E3

A large business-orientated hotel created from a series of Jacobean town houses, close to the cathedral and castle and overlooking the River Wear. Attractively decorated bedrooms all have a mini-bar and a trouser press among the usual extras. One large room is adapted for disabled guests. Fine leisure facilities (with views over the river) attract weekend guests. Children under 14 free in parents' room. Swallow Hotels. *Rooms 150. Indoor swimming pool, spa bath, sauna, solarium, gym, beauty & hair salons, coffee shop (7am-9.30pm).* AMERICAN EXPRESS *Access, Diners, Visa.*

Durham	**Places of Interest**

Tourist Information   Tel 091-384 3720.
Auckland Castle   Bishop Auckland Tel 0388 601627.
Spectrum Leisure Centre Dry Ski Slope   Willington Tel 0388 747000.
Botanic Garden University of Durham   Tel 091-374 2671.
Durham Castle   Tel 091-374 3863.
Durham Light Infantry Museum and Durham Arts Centre   Tel 091-384 2214.
Durham Cathedral   Tel 091-386 4266.

Durham Ice Rink   Tel 091-386 4065.
Durham Country Cricket Club   Houghton-le-Spring Tel 091-512 0178.

Duxford	**Duxford Lodge**	**65%**	**£88**

Tel 0223 836444   Fax 0223 832271   **HR**

Ickleton Road Duxford nr Cambridge Cambridgeshire CB2 4RU   **Map 10 B3**

The hotel enjoys a peaceful setting in its own well-tended grounds in the sleepy village of Duxford, a short distance south of Cambridge and one mile from Junction 10 of the M11. The exterior is as inviting as the interior is comfortable and homely. The spacious bar contrasts with the small residents' lounge, both of which are furnished in attractive soft autumnal colour schemes. Walls are decorated with an extensive collection of fighter aircraft pictures – both prints and paintings, appropriate as the Imperial War Museum's Duxford Airfield is only a short distance away; the lodge itself was the wartime headquarters of Douglas Bader. Bedrooms, of which four are in an attractive garden wing, are all of a good size and neatly furnished. Colour schemes are restful and decor well maintained. Top-floor bedrooms have characterful sloping ceilings. There are four bridal suites, two of them with four-posters. ***Rooms*** *15. Garden. Closed 26-31 Dec.* AMERICAN EXPRESS *Access, Diners, Visa.*

Restaurant   **£50**

A handsome light-oak dado-panelled dual-aspect dining room where Ron Craddock produces menus that are wide-ranging, mostly of traditional French/English provenance but with a few Far Eastern touches such as beef and chicken satay or croquettes of crab with mango, lime and chili. Combinations and flavours are carefully thought out, as in Chicken Duxford – poached supreme of chicken cooked in a lavender-infused white wine and cream sauce. Other dishes are more familiar: Stilton mushrooms in puff pastry, rack of lamb, chef's pie of the day, sole meunière. Excellent desserts include a selection of home-made ice creams of which the English lavender is quite outstanding. ***Seats*** *36. Parties 12. Private Room 36. L 12-2 D 7-9.30. Closed L Sat. Set L £14.50 (Sun £9/£11.95) Set D £15.50.*

Easington	**Grinkle Park**	**70%**	**£80**

Tel 0287 640515   Fax 0287 641278   **H**

Easington Loftus nr Saltburn-by-Sea Cleveland TS13 4UB   **Map 5 E3**

Sweeping lawns and mature pines and rhododendrons surround a formidable mansion set in parkland just off the A174. The atmosphere inside is refined and quietly elegant, much as when it was a private house from the 1880s to 1947. The delightful Camellia Room, with picture windows, festoon blinds and wicker seating, has camellias actually growing up through the floor, and in the foyer-bar the roaring winter fire is reflected in the darkwood panelling. Bedrooms are named after local flora, birds and places; they're stylishly decorated, with light, restful colour schemes. ***Rooms*** *20. Garden, croquet, tennis, snooker.* AMERICAN EXPRESS *Access, Diners, Visa.*

East Boldon	**Forsters**		**£65**

Tel 091-519 0929   **R**

2 St Bedes Station Road East Boldon Tyne & Wear NE36 0LE   **Map 5 E2**

In the centre of Boldon, close to the A814 Sunderland to Gateshead road, Barry Forster's restaurant has a distinctive bottle-green exterior and stands in a small row of shops with limited parking at the front. Comprising a single room with a bar occupying the corner, it has pretty, peachy pastel decor. The few tables are quite closely spaced but this does not detract from the guest's comfort and appeal. An eclectic menu of imaginative and enjoyable food is offered. Starters might range from Cheddar cheese and chive soufflé to snails, mussels or Thai-style prawns. Main dishes include daily fresh fish from the market, roast breast of duck with black pudding and olive oil mash, roast loin of venison with braised cabbage, bacon and caraway, and grilled medallions of pork with creamy calvados sauce and Agen prunes. Sweets include sticky toffee pudding, chocolate marquise with coffee bean sauce and lemon crème brulée. Friendly service is provided by Sue Forster. No children under 8. Simple, jumbled wine list, sensibly priced. *Seats 28. D only 7-10. Set £15 (Tue-Fri). Closed Sun, Mon & Bank Holidays.* AMERICAN EXPRESS *Access, Diners, Visa.*

East Boldon   Places of Interest

South Shields Tourist Information   Tel 091-454 6612.
Old Customs House   Tel 091-454 0269.
Souter Lighthouse (NT)   Whitburn Tel 091-529 3161.

East Buckland   Lower Pitt   £50

Tel & Fax 0598 760243   **RR**
East Buckland Barnstaple Devon EX32 0TD   **Map 13 D2**

Just on the western edge of Exmoor National Park (two miles off the A361), an old stone farmhouse has been converted into a charming restaurant with rooms, owned and run since 1978 by the immensely capable and welcoming Jerome and Suzanne Lyons. Suzanne is in charge in the kitchens, and proudly credits local suppliers of excellent produce, which she uses to great effect. Typical starters might be sesame chicken: or baked smoked salmon creams served on a tossed leaf salad. For mains you might be offered *pavés de venaison*: venison marinaded with rosemary and shallots, pan-fried and finished with a Cumberland sauce; or prawns, stir-fried with cashew nuts, sesame oil, garlic, root ginger, lemon grass, peppers, mushrooms and seasonal vegetables. Delicious puddings along the lines of chocolate roulade or hazelnut meringue gateau filled with raspberry cream. Good English cheeses. Over twenty half bottles on the wine list. Three tables outside on a terrace in good weather. No smoking in restaurant. No children under 5 after 8.30pm. *Seats 32. Parties 16. Private Room 16. D only 7-8.30. Closed Sun & Mon (except residents), 25 Dec.* AMERICAN EXPRESS *Access, Visa.*

Rooms   £60

Three double rooms, all en-suite and all non-smoking, are comfortably furnished and equipped. No children under 5. Excellent breakfasts.

East Dereham   King's Head   £47

Tel 0362 693842   Fax 0362 693776   **I**
Norwich Street East Dereham Norfolk NR19 1AD   **Map 10 C1**

A modest but immaculately kept 17th-century coaching inn near the town centre and now under new ownership. A cosy red-carpeted bar, busy with locals, looks out past the patio to an attractive lawn (once the bowling green) with tables and chairs. Spotless bedrooms are gradually being upgraded by the new owners. Five rooms are located in the light and airy converted stable block; the remainder lying beyond gloomily-lit corridors in the main building. Families are made welcome. 15 miles from Norwich. *Rooms 15. Garden, tennis.* AMERICAN EXPRESS *Access, Diners, Visa.*

East Dereham   Phoenix Hotel   59%   £78

Tel 0362 692276   Fax 0362 691752   **H**
Church Street East Dereham Norfolk NR19 1DL   **Map 10 C1**

Now part of the World of Forte division, this bright redbrick 60s' hotel in the centre of town offers neat, practical bedrooms and function/conference suites accommodating up to 160. Forte Heritage. *Rooms 22.* AMERICAN EXPRESS *Access, Diners, Visa.*

East Grinstead   Gravetye Manor   84%   £200

Tel 0342 810567   Fax 0342 810080   **HR**

Vowels Lane East Grinstead West Sussex RH19 4LJ   Map 11 B5

The civilised hospitality and gracious charm of Peter Herbert and staff (for whom nothing is too much trouble) continue to provide an object lesson in how a country house hotel should be run. The care and attention to every last detail both within the splendidly transformed Elizabethan stone mansion (built in 1598) and in the 1000 acres of grounds is perfectly illustrated in the wing where four immaculate bedrooms were recently added and in the time and expense involved in restoring the William Robinson English garden to its former glory. Flower displays fill the gracious day rooms, which include a really delightful sitting room with oak panelling and an ornate moulded ceiling, and the entrance hall – now much brighter than in the past – with carefully selected chair patterns. Bedrooms, with their comfortable beds, antique furniture and sumptuous fabrics are models of good taste; books, magazines, post cards, bedside radios and TVs concealed behind tapestry screens are among a long list of thoughtful extras. The bathrooms, too, with his and her washbasins, bidet and power shower over the bath provide every conceivable need, and are havens of comfort. No children under 7, but babes in arms welcome – cots and baby-listening provided. Fly fishing on the lake between May and September. No dogs in the hotel; kennels at the head of the drive. The hotel stands 5 miles south-west of East Grinstead off the B2110 at the West Hoathly sign. **Rooms** *18. Garden, croquet, fishing. Access, Visa.* MARTELL

Restaurant   ★   £105

A comforting restaurant with an enviable reputation for consistently high standards, maintained over many years by a succession of talented chefs, the second chef generally inheriting the top job, thus ensuring a smooth transition. Add silky smooth service that is attentive without being overbearing and the room itself with mellow oak panelling under a Tudor ceiling and it all helps to create a memorable dining experience. A walled kitchen garden provides much of the produce in summer, their own smokehouse the smoked salmon, duck breast and the like and the spring which served the Manor since 1598 is still providing water for the tables. Well-balanced à la carte and table d'hote menus offer dishes with a strong English flavour, though often with a modern twist, like home-smoked haddock with poached egg and mustard seed butter sauce, pan-fried black pudding with apples, frisée salad and sherry vinegar jus, fillet of cod in yeast batter with potatoes mashed with olive oil and sauce rouille, saddle of local venison served on spatzli with light and dark peppercorn sauces, and roast chump of English lamb with tomato and rosemary fondue and rich port sauce. A warm Pithiviers and vanilla egg custard was a rather stolid, heavy affair on a recent visit and both canapés and petits fours rather mundane. Menu prices include service but not VAT. Our Cellar of the Year in 1994, the wine list is one to drool over. All the big names and best vintages are there, but so are more unusual offerings, with often unseen bins from Australia, Germany and Italy – all well represented, as are half bottles. Young sommelier Thierry Morigen knows his onions and is one of the hotel's panel that 'blind' tastes new wines considered for inclusion on updated lists. No smoking. *Seats 42. Parties 8. Private Room 18. L 12.30-2 D 7.30-9.30 (Sun to 9). Closed D 25 Dec to non-residents. Set L £20 (+vat) (Sun £28 +vat) Set D £26 (+vat).*

East Grinstead   Woodbury House   61%   £65

Tel 0342 313657   Fax 0342 314801   **H**

Lewes Road East Grinstead West Sussex RH19 3UD   Map 11 B5

Now under new ownership, a small hotel popular with business people, set in a Victorian house on the A22 just south of town. The bedrooms, which have attractive matching fabrics and rather nice reproduction antique furniture, all have good-sized, well-lit desks with sensible upright chairs, although easy chairs are of the low 'tub' variety. Tiled bathrooms, four with shower and WC only, are practical, with basic toiletries. Public areas include a spacious lounge, where the soft furnishings need some attention, and a combined bar/bistro with conservatory extension overlooking the road. **Rooms** 14. *Garden, bistro (12-2.30, 7-9.30). Closed 2 days between Christmas & New Year.* AMERICAN EXPRESS *Access, Diners, Visa.*

East Grinstead   Places of Interest

Hammerwood Park   Tel 0342 850594.
Lingfield Park Racecourse   Tel 0342 834800.

East Horsley	Thatchers Resort Hotel	62%	£102
Tel 0483 284291 Fax 0483 284222			**H**
Epsom Road East Horsley Surrey KT24 6TB			Map 15 E3

Weddings and conferences (for up to 60, banquets up to 95) are the staple business at this attractive mock-Tudor hotel set back from the road behind a lovely garden. Main public area is a comfortable open-plan bar lounge beyond a spacious parquet-floored reception area. Choose from prettily decorated accommodation in the main house, smaller motel-style rooms around the open-air pool and a few more cottagey bedrooms in an adjacent building. **Rooms** 59. *Garden, outdoor swimming pool.* AMERICAN EXPRESS *Access, Diners, Visa.*

East Stoke	Kemps Country House Hotel	56%	£78
Tel 0929 462563 Fax 0929 405287			**H**
East Stoke nr Wareham Dorset BH20 6AL			Map 14 B4

A quiet and welcoming country hotel converted from a Victorian rectory, situated on the A352 between Wareham and Wool. Five bedrooms are in the main building, four in a converted coach house; the best six pine-furnished rooms are in a recent addition, facing the Purbeck Hills. Two ground-floor rooms are suitable for disabled guests. Some rooms have whirlpool baths, and one boasts a modern four-poster. Children under 7 stay free in parents' room, meals charged as taken. Banqueting/conference facilities for 120/60. **Rooms** 15. *Garden.* AMERICAN EXPRESS *Access, Diners, Visa.*

East Stoke   Places of Interest

Athelhampton House and Gardens   Athelhampton Tel 0305 848363.
Clouds Hill (NT)   Near Wool Tel 0305 267992 *Cottage home of T E Lawrence.*
The Tank Museum Bovington Camp   Nr Wool Tel 0929 403329 or 403463.

Eastbourne	Cavendish Hotel	68%	£80
Tel 0323 410222 Fax 0323 410941			**H**
Grand Parade Eastbourne East Sussex BN21 4DH			Map 11 B6

Well-maintained and imposing seafront hotel with a modern corner extension. Large banqueting facilities (for up to 350) plus conferences for up to 220. Guests have special membership prices at the nearby David Lloyd sports and leisure club. Families are made welcome with helpful amenities provided; children up to the age of 7 are accommodated free in parents' room. **Rooms** 112. *Games room.* AMERICAN EXPRESS *Access, Diners, Visa.*

Eastbourne	Grand Hotel	75%	£120
Tel 0323 412345 Fax 0323 412233			**HR**
King Edward's Parade Eastbourne East Sussex BN21 4EQ			Map 11 B6

A renowned seafront hotel which maintains much of the style and grace of its Victorian origins. Marble pillars, crystal chandeliers, vast corridors and high-domed day rooms evoke a more leisurely, bygone age. Some of the sea-facing bedrooms have balconies and are huge, with bright furniture and up-to-date fabrics, while other rooms are smaller. 24hr room service, comprehensive leisure and exercise facilities, themed weekend breaks and children's hostesses keep the Grand apace with its more modern competitors. Families are well catered for. Function facilities for up to 400. De Vere Hotels. *Rooms 164. Garden, indoor & outdoor swimming pools, spa bath, sauna, steam room, solarium, beauty & hairdressing salons, keep-fit equipment, snooker.* *Access, Diners, Visa.*

Mirabelle Restaurant   £70

Imaginative menus executed with flair and served by polished and professional staff in elegant surroundings. Fixed-price lunch (2-or 3-course) and dinner (4-course, priced by choice of main course) menus offer a small but varied choice and in addition, an à la carte offers classic dishes with modern touches. Mussel soup with saffron, confit of duck leg on braised butter beans, liver and bacon with bubble and squeak, salmon on a tatin of endives with a red wine sauce and loin of venison wrapped in a pheasant mousseline and savoy cabbage show the eclectic style. At lunchtime there's always a traditional roast, served from a silver trolley. British and French cheeses, classic desserts. *Seats 50. Private Room 20. L 12.30-2.30 D 7-10.30. Closed Sun & Mon, Bank Holidays, 1st 2 weeks Jan. Set L £15.50/£18.50 Set D from £22.50.*

Eastbourne	Queen's Hotel	67%	£75
Tel 0323 722822 Fax 0323 731056			**H**
Marine Parade Eastbourne East Sussex BN21 3DY			Map 11 B6

Large white Victorian-built hotel overlooking the pier, sea and Carpet Gardens. Equally popular for conferences (up to 300 delegates) and leisure visits. Children up to 14 free in parents' room. Free parking for 80 cars. De Vere Hotels. *Rooms 108. Snooker.* AMERICAN EXPRESS *Access, Diners, Visa.*

Eastbourne	Wish Tower Hotel	66%	£85
Tel 0323 722676 Fax 0323 721474			**H**
King Edward's Parade Eastbourne East Sussex BN21 4EB			Map 11 B6

The hotel stands on the seafront opposite the Wish Tower, a martello tower that is now a Napoleonic and World War II museum. Bedrooms are in attractively up-to-date style, with modern comforts like double-glazing, and many enjoy sea views. A range of function facilities can cater for up to 120 banqueting, 100 conference delegates. Children up to 14 stay free in parents' room. Residents have free membership of the David Lloyd Tennis and Sports Leisure Centre. Principal Hotels. *Rooms 65.* AMERICAN EXPRESS *Access, Diners, Visa.*

Eastbourne   Places of Interest

Tourist Information   Tel 0323 411400.
Michelham Priory   Upper Dicker, Nr Hailsham Tel 0323 844224.
Towner Art Gallery and Local History Museum   Tel 0323 411688.
Tower No 73   (The Wish Tower) Tel 0323 410440.
Eastbourne and Bexhill Beaches.
Devonshire Park Centre (Tennis)   Tel 0323 415400.
   Theatres and Concert Halls
Congress Theatre   Devonshire Park Tel 0323 410000.
Devonshire Park Theatre   Tel 0323 410000.
Drusillas Zoo   Alfriston Tel 0323 870234.
Royal Hippodrome Theatre   Tel 0323 410000.

Eastleigh Forte Travelodge £45

Tel 0703 616813 **L**

Twyford Road Eastleigh nr Southampton Hampshire SO50 4LF **Map 15 D3**

On the Twyford Road, off the A335. Turn off between M3 and M27
Eastleigh North, following signs for town centre. 5 miles north
of Southampton and 6 miles south of Winchester. **Rooms** *32.*
AMERICAN EXPRESS *Access, Diners, Visa.*

Eastleigh Forte Posthouse
Southampton/Eastleigh 66% £68

Tel 0703 619700 Fax 0703 643945 **H**

Leigh Road Eastleigh Hampshire SO5 5PG **Map 15 D3**

Modern low-rise hotel just off A34, rebranded in 1994 from *Forte Crest.*
Features include a leisure centre and children's playground. **Rooms** *120.*
Indoor swimming pool, keep-fit equipment, spa bath, steam room, solarium,
beauty salon, pool table. AMERICAN EXPRESS *Access, Diners, Visa.*

Eccleshall St George Hotel £65

Tel 0785 850300 Fax 0785 851452 **I**

Castle Street Eccleshall Staffordshire ST21 6DF **Map 6 B3**

Behind the white-painted frontage of this 17th-century coaching inn
is a mixture of modern and old that includes an inglenook fireplace in the
bar – the focal point of the inn, with old beams and copper-topped tables.
Bedrooms are kept in immaculate order and have plenty of character, some
with fireplaces and exposed timbers. Small conferences are held in the first-
floor Old Library room. **Rooms** *10.* AMERICAN EXPRESS *Access, Diners, Visa.*

Edenbridge Honours Mill Restaurant £60

Tel 0732 866757 **R**

87 High Street Edenbridge Kent TN8 5AU **Map 11 B5**

A converted mill is the charming setting for some careful French cooking
from the kitchen of Martin Radmall. Well-balanced fixed-price menus
(Tues-Fri) are inclusive of coffee, petits fours and service; from three
choices at each stage one might choose *saucisson d'aiglefin fumé* (smoked
haddock) followed by *chevreuil au genièvre* (venison with juniper berries)
and cheese or dessert at both lunch and dinner, the latter including a half
bottle of house wine per person. Also offered is a fixed-price à la carte, with
fish mousse baba with mussels and langoustines, ragout of snails, wild
mushrooms and herb butter, pot au feu, lobster-stuffed chicken breast and
foie gras-stuffed pheasant with salmis sauce typifying the style. Among the
desserts you might find Sussex Pond pudding (a traditional steamed lemon
suet pudding), tarte tatin and fresh lime tart. Children welcome for Sunday
lunch. Quite pricy wine list, but there's a good choice of half bottles;
mostly French, with a nod to the New World. **Seats** *40. L 12.15-2*
D 7.15-10. Closed L Sat, D Sun, all Mon, 1-2 weeks after Christmas.
Set L £14.50 (Sun £22.50) & £31.75 Set D £25 & £31.75.
AMERICAN EXPRESS *Access, Visa.*

Edenbridge Places of Interest

Hever Castle Open Air Theatre Tel 0732 866114 *Open mid June-*
September.
Hever Castle & Gardens Tel 0732 865224.
Chiddingstone Castle Chiddingstone Tel 0892 870347.

Egham   Great Fosters   67%   £99

Tel 0784 433822   Fax 0784 472455   **H**

Stroude Road Egham Surrey TW20 9UR   Map 15 E2

The imposing facade of this stately Elizabethan house sets the tone for the quintessentially English public rooms with their ornate plaster ceilings, oak panelling and carved antique furniture. The best are on the first floor and feature richly embroidered fabrics and tapestry wall hangings; there are some period suites and four-poster rooms. Other rooms are plainer – some in the house, others in the conference centre. Get to Egham then follow the brown Historical Interest signs marked Great Fosters. No dogs. *Rooms 45. Garden, outdoor swimming pool, sauna, tennis, snooker.* AMERICAN EXPRESS *Access, Diners, Visa.*

Egham   Runnymede Hotel   74%   £145

Tel 0784 476171   Fax 0784 436340   **H**

Windsor Road Egham Surrey TW20 0AS   Map 15 E2

Leave the M25 at J13 and take the A308 Egham/Windsor road to find this riverside building whose rather unpromising redbrick exterior conceals a smart hotel with light, airy public areas and high levels of service – room service runs to cooked meals 24hrs a day and beds are turned down in the evening. Latest improvements include a conservatory extension to the lounge area and a £40,000 croquet lawn. The stylish Runnymede Spa leisure centre is particularly luxurious. The best (Executive) bedrooms are most appealing with yellow and blue colour scheme, good armchairs and fine marble bathrooms. Standard rooms are more variable in size (a few are on the small side) and decor, but all have the same amenities – air-conditioning, mini-bars, bathrobes – and benefit from the same high standards of housekeeping. Numerous, well-equipped conference rooms can cope with up to 400 delegates theatre-style. Children (£10 when sharing parents' room) are made welcome with their own menu in the hotel's informal restaurant, Charlie Bells, and a large children's pool in the Spa. Thorpe Park is only just down the road. *Rooms 171. Garden, croquet, tennis, putting, indoor swimming pool, children's pool, gym, dance studio, sauna, steam room, hydrotherapy bath, spa bath, solarium, beauty salon, hair salon, snooker, dinner-dance (Sat), helipad.* AMERICAN EXPRESS *Access, Diners, Visa.*

Egham   Places of Interest

Guards Polo Club   Windsor Great Park, Englefield Green Tel 0784 434212.
Thorpe Theme Park   Chertsey Tel 0932 569393.

Elcot   Jarvis Elcot Park   67%   £100

Tel 0488 58100   Fax 0488 58288   **HR**

Elcot nr Newbury Berkshire RG16 8NJ   Map 15 D2

The former, more simply named *Elcot Park* is now the subject of a refurbishment programme under its new ownership. The much-extended Georgian house is set back from the A4, halfway between Newbury and Hungerford. It stands in 16 acres of Kennet Valley woodland, its latest bedroom wing and leisure centre linked to the original by an impressive south-facing conservatory. There's a new bar area. Up-to-date bedrooms rooms include some equipped for disabled guests. 18 rooms are contained in a separate mews courtyard. Under-16s stay free in parents' room. *Rooms 75. Garden, tennis, indoor swimming pool, spa bath, sauna, solarium, gym, beauty salon, hot-air ballooning.* AMERICAN EXPRESS *Access, Diners, Visa.*

Orangery Restaurant and Conservatory   £70

Daily table d'hote and seasonal carte in the modern idiom from dependable chef Alex Robertson. Try pigeon terrine studded with pistachio nuts, roast fillet of monkfish wrapped in bacon, and dark chocolate and apricot marquise. Vegetarian choices, regional farmhouse cheeses and speciality teas. *Seats 100. L 12.30-2 D 7.30-9.30. Set meals £17.*

Elton   Loch Fyne Oyster Bar & Restaurant   £40

Tel 0832 280298   **R**

The Old Dairy Elton nr Peterborough Cambridgeshire PE8 5SG   **Map 7 E4**

100 yards from the A605 bypass to Oundle, eight miles from
Peterborough, an informal seafood restaurant and retail outlet
in a converted dairy building dating back to 1901. Scots pine, simple
furnishings and the freshest seafood ingredients brought down from
Scotland overnight. Rock oysters from their own oysterage, smoked fish
from their own smokehouse. *Bradhan rost* is a salmon smoked in a hot kiln;
here it is served with a whisky sauce. See also entries under Nottingham,
and Cairndow (Scotland). *Seats 85. Meals 9am-9pm (Fri & Sat to 10, Sun
to 5). Closed 25 & 26 Dec. Access, Visa.*

Ely   Forte Travelodge   £45

Tel 0353 668499   **L**

Witchford Road Ely Cambridgeshire CB6 3NN   **Map 10 B2**

On the roundabout at the junction of A10/A142. Situated on the outskirts
of Ely, 15 miles north of Cambridge. *Rooms 39.* AMERICAN EXPRESS *Access,
Diners, Visa.*

Ely   Lamb Hotel   62%   £77

Tel 0353 663574   Fax 0353 666350   **H**

2 Lynn Road Ely Cambridgeshire CB7 4EJ   **Map 10 B2**

Close to the Cathedral, the Lamb can trace its history back to the reign
of Richard II, although the present building is of somewhat later date.
It offers good, well-equipped accommodation in singles, doubles, family
rooms and four-poster rooms. A choice of bars, one of which (the Fenman)
is a popular local meeting place. Children under 14 share their parents'
room free. Queens Moat Houses. *Rooms 32.* AMERICAN EXPRESS *Access,
Diners, Visa.*

Ely   Old Fire Engine House   £50

Tel 0353 662582   **R**

25 St Mary's Street Ely Cambridgeshire CB7 4ER   **Map 10 B2**

The Old Fire Engine House was built in the 18th century, being converted
into a restaurant and art gallery in 1968. The main room has an uneven
tiled floor, kitchen tables and pew seating, others are more elegant. Home
cooking is plain English in style and includes such stalwarts as ham, leek
and potato soup, smoked salmon paté, roast beef and Yorkshire pudding
and home-cooked ham. Pike in white wine, casserole of pigeon and steak
and kidney pie are all considered specialities. Local asparagus, Norfolk
marsh samphire and Brancaster mussels also appear in season. The style
continues with sweets such as syllabub or meringues with cream. Few non-
French wines on the inexpensive list, which is accompanied by informative
notes. One room is reserved for non-smokers. Twelve seats in the garden
during good weather. *Seats 36. Private Room 24. L 12.30-2 D 7.30-9.
Closed D Sun, Bank Holidays, 2 weeks from Christmas Eve. Access, Visa.*

Ely   Places of Interest

Tourist Information   Tel 0353 662062.
Ely Cathedral   Tel 0353 667735.
   Museums and Art Galleries
Ely Museum   Tel 0353 666655.
The Stained Glass Museum   North Triforium, Ely Cathedral Tel 0353
   667735.
Oliver Cromwell's House   Tel 0353 662062.

Emsworth   Forte Travelodge   NEW   £45

Tel 0800 850 950   **L**

A27 Emsworth nr Havant Hampshire   Map 15 D4

8 miles west of Chichester on the A27. AMERICAN EXPRESS® *Access, Diners, Visa.*

Epping   Forte Posthouse   63%   £68

Tel 0992 573137   Fax 0992 560402   **H**

High Road Bell Common Epping Essex CM16 4DG   Map 11 B4

16th-century heritage still shows in the public rooms; bedrooms are
in a modern wing. Banqueting for 85, conferences facilities for 100.
Rooms *79.* AMERICAN EXPRESS® *Access, Diners, Visa.*

Erpingham   The Ark   £45

Tel 0263 761535   **R R**

The Street Erpingham Norfolk NR11 7QB   Map 10 C1

An old flint cottage set deep in rural Norfolk four miles north
of Aylesham off the A140. Sheila and Becky Kidd's very individual
cooking style shows many influences on fixed-price, handwritten menus
that change daily and derive from local suppliers and her own garden.
Typical dishes run from aubergine three ways, mushroom risotto and
a salad of crab, grapefruit and orange to Dover sole with parsley butter,
beef paupiettes with white wine and herb-roast leg of lamb with fennel
cream. Farmhouse cheese and a choice of four sweets. Vegetarian dishes are
always available – discuss when booking. Just a few non-French wines
on the decent and quite fairly priced wine list, notable for the house wine
priced at only £8. No smoking. *Seats 32. Private Room 18. L (Sun only)*
12.30-2 D 7-9.30 (Sat to 10). Closed D Sun & all Mon. Set L (Sun) £12.75
Set D £15.75/£18.50. No credit cards (could change).

Rooms   £90*

Three bedrooms, two with en-suite facilities, are available for overnight
stays, but only to non-smokers. Excellent breakfasts, with home-made
preserves. *Half-board terms only.

Esher   Good Earth   £55

Tel 0372 462489   **R**

14-18 High Street Esher Surrey KT10 9RT   Map 15 E2

Reliable cooking in comfortable surroundings, with speedy, attentive
service. The China-wide menu sticks mainly to familiar items, with the
occasional slightly less usual dish such as salmon steak (steamed or pan-
fried), beef with tangerine peel and hot sauce, bean curd with eight
precious gems or a vegetarian combination called faked yellow fish
comprising mashed split peas, Chinese mushrooms and spring onions.
Seafood and sizzling dishes are specialities. *See also outlets in London section.*
Seats 85. L 12-2.30 D 6-11. Closed 24-27 Dec. Set L from £12 Set D from
£17. AMERICAN EXPRESS® *Access, Diners, Visa.*

Esher   Places of Interest

Chessington World of Adventures   Tel 0372 727227.
Claremont Landscape Garden (NT)   Tel 0372 467806.
Kempton Park Racecourse   Tel 0932 782292.
Sandown Park Racecourse   Tel 0372 463072.
Ham Polo Club   20 Queens Road Tel 081 398 3263.
Sandown Ski School   Tel 0372 467132.

Eton   Antico   £55

Tel 0753 863977   Fax 0628 30045   **R**

42 High Street Eton Berkshire SL4 6BD   Map 15 E2

Behind a distinctive black-and-white, bow-windowed frontage that dates
back to the 18th century is a long-serving Italian restaurant with unusual,
Old-English decor. The menu is firmly traditional to match: familiar pasta
dishes, scampi, trout and Dover sole, ten ways with veal and desserts from
a trolley. *Seats 65. Parties 25. Private Rooms 12/25. L 12.30-2.30 D 7-10.30.
Closed L Sat, all Sun, Bank Holidays.* AMERICAN EXPRESS *Access, Diners, Visa.*

Eton   Christopher Hotel   £82

Tel 0753 852359   Fax 0753 830914   **I**

110 High Street Eton Berkshire SL4 6AN   Map 15 E2

In the middle of the High Street, close to the Thames; the former coaching
inn is just beyond the College on the right. Some bedrooms are in the main
house, others in courtyard chalets, all recently redecorated. Children up to
the age of 12 stay free in their parents' room. Three rooms suitable for
family use. Small banquets (30) and conferences (45). Dogs in courtyard
rooms only. *Rooms 34.* AMERICAN EXPRESS *Access, Diners, Visa.*

Evershot   Summer Lodge   78%   £120

Tel 0935 83424   Fax 0935 83005   **HR**

Evershot Dorchester Dorset DT2 0JR   Map 13 F2

A former Georgian dower house, sympathetically enlarged in keeping with
the original building, and fully justifying its name. Set in extensive, well-
maintained mature gardens, the impression is of staying in a country house
set in a rural landscape, yet the former main entrance leads, via a small
garden, to Evershot's main street. From a few windows there are views
over the picturesque village, while others look out over the gardens and
the surrounding rolling hills. A feature of the hotel is the wealth
of beautiful flower arrangements that adorn both public areas and
bedrooms, adding more colour to the already fresh and summery decor.
The main drawing room is spacious with ample, deep-cushioned sofas.
There is a further smaller, quieter lounge referred to as the reading room.
Both rooms have the welcoming touch of open fires. Bedrooms are
furnished with attractive light rattan furniture which complements the
pastel tones of the quality upholstery and drapes. Home-made biscuits and
tea/coffee facilities (among a host of extras) are provided for out-of-hours
service but the afternoon teas are unmissable including such delights
as moist lemon sponge cake and banana bread. Breakfasts, too, are
exceptionally good, with all requirements well catered for. All
is maintained in the highest order, bathrooms are pristine with ample thick
towels and quality bathtime products. Standards of service and hospitality
continue being second to none. *Rooms 17. Outdoor swimming pool, tennis.
Closed 2 weeks Jan.* AMERICAN EXPRESS *Access, Visa.*

Restaurant   ★   £100

With Edward Denny now installed as head chef, the quality of cooking has
moved up several gears. Current menus are a far cry from the early years
at Summer Lodge when there was no choice and only a roast as the main
course. The dining room, too, is now larger and grander. Amazing flower
arrangements create splashes of colour, while during the day and early
evening there are also fine views over the gardens. There is a high level
of sophistication to the cooking which, although classically based, is modern
and conservatively innovative. A dodine of duck, studded with pistachios
and with a layer of foie gras, is served with a tangy shallot and thyme
marmalade and goat's cheese soufflé comes with toasted almonds and
a smoked cheese sauce. For dinner there is an additional intermediate course
of either a soup or sorbet and these are followed by a main course choice

between the likes of roast loin of veal with a blackcurrant vinegar sauce, paupiettes of maize-fed guinea fowl with prunes and armagnac or fillet of beef with a red wine fumet and glazed with a hot sabayon. Delectable sweets range from a fruit-packed hot raspberry soufflé accompanied by a raspberry sorbet to English classics such as hot jam sponge with warm English cream. The selection of a dozen or so farmhouse cheeses is truly exceptional – almost all come from the West Country (Blue Vinney, Coleford Blue, Curworthy, Bulscombe goat's, Sharpham Brie) and all are served in prime condition with celery, apples and home-made raisin bread; most unusually, a half portion of cheeses is also offered. Sunday lunch is a four-course affair. Due acknowledgement is given to both suppliers and those who have helped compile the excellent wine list, with strength in depth in Europe and the New World. Good to see the support of local English wines (along with the cheeses) and a super selection of half bottles. Seating for 10 on the terrace in good weather. No children under 8 after 7.30pm. No smoking. **Seats** *50. Parties 20. Private Room 8. L 12.30-1.45 D 7.30-9. Set L £17.50/£19.50 (Sun £17.50) Set D £27.50.*

Eversley	**New Mill Restaurant**	**£80**
Tel 0734 732277 Fax 0734 328780		**R**
New Mill Road Eversley Hampshire RG27 0RA		Map 15 D3

It's the idyllic setting that is the big attraction here; a 16th-century watermill (the wheel still working) alongside the slow-moving, green-fringed Blackwater River. The main restaurant has an open fireplace, player-piano, quality table settings and, at one end, picture windows overlooking the river. Typical starters from the à la carte menu might include a twice-baked cheese soufflé, melon with Parma ham and smoked chicken salad with artichokes and quail's eggs, and main dishes like salmon with sorrel sauce, saddle of rabbit with seed mustard and tarragon sauce and steak and kidney pie plus a selection of chargrills. Prices reflect the surroundings (although service is included) but there are also table d'hote menus at lunchtime representing particularly good value. The low-beamed Grill Room offers a simpler, less expensive menu with less formal service (you can have just a single dish) and one can eat from this menu in the garden where ducks wander around between the tables. There is also a characterful bar with with flagstoned floor. On Sundays and Mondays the Grill Room menu only is available. A serious and comprehensive wine list has a couple of pages of suggested wines and tasting notes at keen prices; the rest of the classy list contains many of the great names. The New Mill is signposted from the A327. **Seats** *80. Private Room 40. L 12-2 D 7-10 (Sun 12.30-8). Closed L Sat (Sun & Mon Grill Room Menu only), 26 & 27 Dec, 1 Jan. Set L £12.50 Set D £19.50.* AMERICAN EXPRESS® *Access, Diners, Visa.*

Evesham	**Evesham Hotel**	**65%**	**£82**
Tel 0386 765566 Fax 0386 765443			**HR**
Cooper's Lane off Waterside Evesham Hereford & Worcester WR11 6DA			Map 14 C1

A largely Georgian hotel, with Tudor origins, set in several acres of secluded grounds on the edge of town and run in their own jolly style by the Jenkinson family for the last 18 years. The 'Jenkinson' humour breaks out all over the place from the 'seaside postcard' mural by the pool (Evesham-by-the-Sea) to the padlocked perfume in the (award-winning) public loos that also come with magazines and a portable radio in each cubicle. Bedrooms (keys are attached to a teddy bear) have a traditional feel with candlewick bedspreads and all sorts of extras from playing cards and a copy of Punch to rubber ducks and clothes-washing liquid in the bathroom. Some rooms have characterful beams and others a period feel with painted Georgian panelling. Public rooms centre around a comfortable, chintzy bar. "Well-behaved youngsters are as welcome as well-behaved grown-ups" according to the 'Junior à la carte' that also requests no pipes, cigars or bubble-gum in the restaurant, and there are all sorts of board games and other amusements about the place to keep younger guests amused plus an outdoor play area with swings, trampoline and slide. There is baby-listening and babysitting (by arrangement) plus cots (the first five come with a pack of nappies, wipes etc); extra beds are charged at £1.50 per year of the child's age (typical of the individual style of doing things here). Room service from 7am-11pm. Freephone reservation number: 0800 716969. *Rooms 40. Garden, croquet, indoor swimming pool, table tennis, indoor play area & outdoor playground.* Closed 25 & 26 Dec. AMERICAN EXPRESS® *Access, Diners, Visa.*

Cedar Restaurant £60

A jokey menu (changing weekly) but the setting is elegant (Regency style) and the results on the plate quite satisfactory with well-judged dishes like bacon-wrapped breast of chicken filled with tea-steeped prunes on a sherry and tarragon sauce; brochette of tuna marinated in wine, garlic and herbs with a tomato sauce; and slices of pork fillet flamed with brandy and served with Stilton and walnuts. Separate menus provide for vegetarians, children and those looking for simpler dishes – smoked salmon, grills, cold meats and salads. Good puds include treacle tart, a rich chocolate pot and an excellent apple millefeuille. At lunchtime there is a buffet option (£6.65) in addition to the regular menu. Ever idiosyncratic, the long wine list (it comes in five volumes) is strong in New World wines and includes offerings from as far afield as Zimbabwe, Sweden and Peru but none whatsoever from France or Germany, and an almost endless liqueur and spirit list runs from 'A' (Almedranda from Mexico) to 'Z' (Zubrowka Vodka). *Seats 55. Parties 8. Private Room 12. L 12.30-2 D 7-9.30.*

🍶 is our symbol for an outstanding wine list.

Evesham   Riverside Hotel   68%   £80

Tel 0386 446200   Fax 0386 40021   **HR**

The Parks Offenham Road Evesham Hereford & Worcester WR11 5JP   Map 14 C1

Vincent and Rosemary Willmott's white pebbledash house stands in three acres by the River Avon. It's a touch tricky to find, up a private road off Offenham Road (which is not accessible from the bypass). A colourful fresco of river life greets guests on entering, while downstairs an attractive lounge is decorated in corals and greens with plenty of comfortable seating. Bedrooms, with river views, are pretty and appealing, soft colours and co-ordinated fabrics being well employed. Staff are smartly attired, keen and obviously enjoy their jobs. The hotel is closed Sunday night and all Monday. No dogs. *Rooms 7. Garden, fishing. Access, Visa.*

Restaurant £55

Fine views over the River Avon from the dining room, where Rosemary Willmott offers fixed-price, hand-written, daily-changing menus with a good choice of dishes. English and French are the basis of her methods, but there are also some influences from further afield: spicy vegetable samosas with yoghurt and chutney, steamed fillet of sea bass with ginger and lime, tiger prawns in filo pastry with couscous and dips. Other dishes are more traditional, such as devilled herring roes, roast duckling with sage and onion stuffing, and rack of lamb with a mustard and herb crust. British cheeses. Treacle sponge, rich bitter chocolate and rum truffle torte, passion fruit mousse with shortbread – three tempting desserts. No smoking. *Seats 45. L 12.30-2 (Sun to 1.30) D 7.30-9. Closed D Sun, all Mon. Set L £15.95 (£17.95 Sun) Set D £21.95.*

Evesham   Places of Interest

Tourist Information   Tel 0386 446944.
Snowshill Manor (NT)   Broadway Tel 0386 852410.

Exeter — Buckerell Lodge — 67% — £84

Tel 0392 52451   Fax 0392 412114   **H**

157 Topsham Road Exeter Devon EX2 4SQ   Map 13 D2

'The Exeter Oasis' is how Buckrell Lodge is described, aptly so as it is set in its own well-maintained gardens in a leafy part of the city, yet just a mile from the centre. A thorough refurbishment of the hotel means that all rooms have benefited from the face-lift (the overall number reducing by two). Some rooms are in the main Regency house, others in the newer sympathetically added wing. Executive rooms have extras like bathrobes, fresh fruit and mineral water, and some also have a jacuzzi; others are designated Lady Executive, a few are adapted for the disabled, and 12 are reserved for non-smokers: most options have thus been anticipated by owners Bruce and Pat Jefford, who inspire their staff to high standards of service and care, making this a welcoming place to stay. Children up to 12 stay free in parents' room. Meeting rooms and a purpose-built conference centre (for up to 60 delegates). *Rooms 52. Garden.* AMERICAN EXPRESS *Access, Diners, Visa.*

Exeter — Forte Crest — 69% — £105

Tel 0392 412812   Fax 0392 413549   **H**

Southernhay East Exeter Devon EX1 1QF   Map 13 D2

1989-built hotel with cathedral views from some of the bedrooms. Conference facilities in seven rooms for up to 150 delegates. 40 of the bedrooms, where children up to 16 stay free with parents, are reserved for non-smokers. Weekend tariff reductions. Rooms for disabled guests. *Rooms 110. Indoor swimming pool, gym, sauna, spa bath, solarium.* AMERICAN EXPRESS *Access, Diners, Visa.*

Exeter — Rougemont Thistle Hotel — 63% — £79

Tel 0392 54982   Fax 0392 420928   **H**

Queen Street Exeter Devon EX4 3SP   Map 13 D2

Mount Charlotte Thistle have completed a major refurbishment of the public areas here and added "Thistle" to the formal name. "Rougement" is a reference to the red clay soil of the area and is an apt name for the red-brick building. It's usefully located in the city centre, close to the station and not very far from the oldest parts, around the cathedral. Conferences for up to 300. *Rooms 90.* AMERICAN EXPRESS *Access, Diners, Visa.*

Any person using our name to obtain free hospitality is a fraud.
Proprietors, please inform the police and us.

Exeter — Royal Clarence — 71% — £98

Tel 0392 58464   Fax 0392 439423   **H**

Cathedral Yard Exeter Devon EX1 1HD   Map 13 D2

On the green facing the 14th-century cathedral, the Royal Clarence claims to be the first inn in Britain to receive the title 'hotel'. Behind its white, Georgian facade the building contains several architectural styles and retains an atmosphere steeped in the past. Every one of the bedrooms is in Tudor, Georgian or Victorian style. A wealth of oak panelling, moulded friezes and covings, gilt-framed mirrors and period furniture contrive to unify the theme. By comparison, bathrooms are thoroughly modern, though smallish. The stately Georgian-style Clarence Room accommodates conferences/banquets for up to 120/90. No dogs. Parking is limited, but special overnight rates have been arranged with local car parks. Queens Moat Houses. *Rooms 56.* AMERICAN EXPRESS *Access, Diners, Visa.*

Exeter   St Olaves Court   63%   £78

Tel 0392 217736   Fax 0392 413054   **HR**

Mary Arches Street Exeter Devon EX4 3AZ   **Map 13 D2**

Though it is only some 300 yards from the cathedral, you might need
to ask directions when booking – or head for the city centre and the Mary
Arches car park between Bartholomew and Fore Streets. The front of the
Georgian building overlooks a pretty walled garden and circular pond
with fountain, and parking space for a few cars. A welcoming glass
of sherry and magazines are nice touches in the bedrooms, which also
provide trouser press, tea- and coffee-making facilities (shame about the
UHT milk/cream pots) and wall-mounted hairdryer, while several of the
bathrooms have jacuzzi baths, though towels are of postage-stamp size.
Notably good bread (toast) at breakfast, which also offers local sausages and
heather honey. **Rooms** *17. Garden.* AMERICAN EXPRESS *Access, Diners, Visa.*

Restaurant   £60

Relaxing dining rooms, decorated in pastel shades and a peaceful garden for
summer meals, combine to provide a comforting, old-fashioned feel. Not
so the food: terrine of Brixham fish in a saffron jelly, millefeuille of squid,
crab and lobster or fricassee of wild mushrooms with spinach noodles and
truffle oil all keep pace with current trends. Follow with fillets of Joh Dory
with a julienne of leeks, roasted local quail and home-made game sausage
with a beetroot jus or breast of duck with fresh fig and a port sauce. Short
list of beautifully presented desserts. Friendly service. **Seats** *55.* **Parties** *24.*
Private Room 18. L 12-2 D 6.30-9.30. Set D 10.50/£13.50.
Closed 1 week Christmas.

Exeter   Travel Inn   £43

Tel 0392 875441   Fax 0392 876174   **L**

398 Topsham Road Exeter Devon EX2 6HE   **Map 13 D2**

One mile from M5. From Junction 30 follow A379 on to A38 ring road.
Situated on a roundabout on the intersection between A38 (to Dawlish)
and A377 (to Exeter). **Rooms** *40.* AMERICAN EXPRESS *Access, Diners, Visa.*

Exeter   White Hart   61%   £78

Tel 0392 79897   Fax 0392 50159   **H**

South Street Exeter Devon EX1 1EE   **Map 13 D2**

An ancient inn at the heart of town, dating from the 15th century and
originally a resting place for monks. It's built around an attractive cobbled
courtyard, off which are various bars where exposed beams, timbers and
bulging walls abound. The residents' lounge in the oldest part sports
an uneven and unusual plasterwork ceiling. Much of the original structure
of the stables can be seen in the reception area. Most bedrooms are
in a modern extension and have a purpose-built look with functional fitted
units. Six rooms have shower and WC only. *Bottlescrue Bill's* Wine Bar
is off the car park and the cobbled wine garden comes into its own during
good weather. No dogs. **Rooms** *59. Closed 24 Dec-26 Dec.* AMERICAN EXPRESS
Access, Diners, Visa.

Exeter   Places of Interest

Tourist Information   Tel 0392 265297.
The Barnfield Theatre   Tel 0392 70891.
Northcott Theatre   Stocker Road Tel 0392 54853.
Exeter Maritime Museum   The Haven Tel 0392 58075.
Exeter Cathedral   Tel 0392 55573.
Exeter Racecourse   Tel 0392 832599.
Exeter Ski Club   Tel 0392 211322.
Westpoint Showground   Tel 0392 444777.

Historic Houses, Castles and Gardens
Killerton (NT) Tel 0392 881345.
University of Exeter Garden Tel 0392 263263.
Bickleigh Castle Tel 0884 855363 *13 miles.*

Exmouth	**Imperial Hotel**	**60%**	**£107**
Tel 0395 274761 Fax 0395 265161			**H**
The Esplanade Exmouth Devon EX8 2SW			Map 13 E3

Popular whitewashed Forte Heritage holiday hotel set in its own grounds
on the esplanade with many bedrooms overlooking the gardens and sea.
Children up to the age of 16 free in parents' room. ***Rooms** 57. Garden,
outdoor swimming pool, tennis.* AMERICAN EXPRESS *Access, Diners, Visa.*

Exmouth	**Place of Interest**

Budleigh Salterton Beach.

Eyton	**Marsh Country Hotel**	**65%**	**£100**
Tel 0568 613952			**HR**
Eyton Leominster Hereford & Worcester HR6 0AG			Map 14 A1

Personally run by the owners, with some part-time help, the Gillelands'
lovingly restored, 14th-century, black and white timbered home makes
a charming rural hideaway. Surrounded by $1\frac{1}{2}$ acres of splendid gardens –
one of their passions – the hotel is a couple of miles north of Leominster.
The main day room is a fine medieval hall with rug-strewn, flagstoned
floor and plenty of deep sofas and armchairs. The bar, with coal-burning
stove, is in the adjacent Solar Wing which also houses a small, characterful
meeting room on the first floor. Just five pretty bedrooms, mostly pine-
furnished, come with comforts like fresh fruit, mineral water and a bowl
of sweets in addition to TVs and direct-dial phones. No smoking
in bedrooms. No dogs. ***Rooms** 5. Garden, croquet.* AMERICAN EXPRESS *Access,
Diners, Visa.*

Restaurant	**£55**

Sunny yellow walls, a few old beams and comfortably upholstered, high-
backed chairs set around crisply clothed tables all combine to create
an elegant dining room with a cottagey feel. The fixed-price menu (with
four choices at each stage) might include an excellent goat's cheese and leek
soufflé and hot smoked mackerel pot with a beetroot and potato salad with
gooseberry mayonnaise amongst the starters and mains such as apricot-
stuffed saddle of lamb and lemon sole with a tarragon and mushroom
filling. Herefordshire duck is a regular feature and there is always
a vegetarian option. A well-stocked herb garden is put to good use with,
for example, sweet cicely appearing in an Alsatian rhubarb tart. Booking
essential as restaurant may not open in the absence of residents.
No smoking. ***Seats** 24. L Sun only 12.30-2 D 7.30-9. Set D £18.50.*

Fairford	**Bull Hotel**	**60%**	**£44**
Tel 0285 712535 Fax 0285 713782			**H**
Market Place Fairford Gloucestershire GL7 4AA			Map 14 C2

Visitors to the Bull have been many and varied since its first recorded
appearance as a hotel in 1745. It's right on the Market Square, and as such
would have provided refreshment to merchant men and travellers alike.
Perhaps, then, little has changed in some respects! Less obvious are signs
of its even earlier incarnation, as a monks' chanting house – though neither
did monks turn away a tired or hungry visitor. Inside, it's atmospheric and
attractive, and each room has its own feature, be it beams and sloping
ceilings, a four-poster bed or a sunken bath. Conference facilities for up to
80 delegates. ***Rooms** 20. Terrace, fishing.* AMERICAN EXPRESS *Access, Diners, Visa.*

Fairy Cross   Portledge Hotel   62%   £67

Tel 0237 451262   Fax 0237 451717   **H**

Fairy Cross nr Bideford Devon EX39 5BX   Map 12 C2

A Jacobean staircase, ancestral portraits and fine panelling and mouldings are among the period features. Boldly decorated day rooms, traditionally styled bedrooms, in which children up to 12 can stay free with parents. The Garden Restaurant is in its own seven-acre woodland site. Conference facilities for up to 100. **Rooms** 35. *Garden, outdoor swimming pool, tennis, crazy golf. Access, Visa.*

Fairy Cross   Place of Interest

Rosemoor Garden, The Royal Horticultural Society   Nr Great
 Torrington Tel 0805 24067.

Falmouth   Falmouth Hotel   63%   £96

Tel 0326 312671   Fax 0326 319533   **H**

Castle Beach Falmouth Cornwall TR11 4NZ   Map 12 B4

The advantages of the natural harbour that is Falmouth really blossomed in Victorian times, which is when this hotel – the town's first purpose-built – came into being. It's quite surprising to find an example of the French Chateau style in the depths of Cornwall but the rest of the setting – neat gardens, light and airy day rooms and especially the conservatory – are typically English. Half the bedrooms have a view of the sea (other rooms overlook the river), and three Executive bedrooms have balconies and whirlpool baths. There are also self-catering cottages (5) and apartments (24) within the grounds, and facilities for conferences and banquets (for up to 250), plus a leisure centre. Families with young children are admirably catered for. **Rooms** 73. *Garden, indoor swimming pool, sauna, spa bath, solarium, beauty & hair salon, putting, snooker.* AMERICAN EXPRESS® *Access, Diners, Visa.*

Falmouth   Greenbank Hotel   69%   £105

Tel 0326 312440   Fax 0326 211362   **H**

Harbourside Falmouth Cornwall TR11 2SR   Map 12 B4

The call of the sea is strong at the Greenbank, which looks across the vast natural harbour to Flushing on the far bank. The picture-windowed bar and the traditionally appointed lounges make the most of the marvellous setting, as do the majority of the bedrooms, many of them named after former resident captains and their vessels. Some rooms have balconies, including the honeymoon suites, which also have jacuzzis. The hotel is on the edge of the town centre: keep to the harbourside when approaching from Truro and follow the signs from the roundabout after Penryn. Covered parking for 30 cars. **Rooms** 61. *Garden, gym, sauna, solarium, beauty & hair salon. Closed 24 Dec-14 Jan.*

Falmouth   Pandora Inn   £40

Tel 0326 372678   **R**

Restronguet Creek Mylor Bridge Falmouth Cornwall TR11 5ST   Map 12 B4

Roger and Helen Hough have been at the Pandora for nearly 10 years, and have a strong local following as well as being popular with tourists. Parts of the building date back to the 13th century, and the flagstone floors, low beamed ceilings and nautical memorabilia all add to the sense of history. In the restaurant, there's good use of local ingredients (especially fish and shellfish) – moules marinière takes Helford mussels into the pot; locally caught sea bass is baked in the oven and served with a chive butter sauce. From further afield, there's a brochette of chicken and mango coated with honey-wine sauce served on a bed of rice. It's worth checking the board for daily specials, and there's a separate, simpler bar menu available at lunch and dinner. Excellent range of wines by the glass. Ask for directions when booking. *Seats 45. D only 7-10. Closed Sun in winter, 25 Dec. Access, Visa.*

Falmouth   Royal Duchy Hotel   66%   £109

Tel 0326 313042   Fax 0326 319420   **H**

Cliff Road Falmouth Cornwall TR11 4NX   **Map 12 B4**

Originally built in 1893, the hotel sits atop the cliffs between the town and Gyllyngvase beach commanding fine sea views. It's a good place for both exercise and relaxation; public rooms range from sun lounge to spacious dining room with live entertainment during the summer season. A small leisure area has plenty of facilities, and bedrooms have Regency-style freestanding furniture and modern accessories. Bathrooms are clean and functional. Friendly staff, typical of the Brend Hotel group. *Rooms 47. Garden, indoor swimming pool, children's pool, sauna, spa bath, solarium, games room.* AMERICAN EXPRESS *Access, Diners, Visa.*

Falmouth   St Michael's Hotel   63%   £86

Tel 0326 312707   Fax 0326 211772   **H**

Stracey Road Falmouth Cornwall TR11 4NB   **Map 12 B4**

Located directly opposite Gyllyngvase beach, this hotel provides basic yet comfortable accommodation for the tourist or business visitor. Banquets/conferences for 160/200. There's a spacious bar/lounge with a sun terrace which overlooks award-winning gardens. No dogs. *Rooms 66. Garden, indoor swimming pool, keep-fit equipment, sauna, spa bath, solarium, games room, outdoor play area.* AMERICAN EXPRESS *Access, Diners, Visa.*

Falmouth   Seafood Bar   £45

Tel 0326 315129   **R**

Quay Street Falmouth Cornwall TR11 3HH   **Map 12 B4**

Down a few steps in a steep passageway near the customs house quay, this lively bar serves the very freshest of seafood, from monkfish soup, Catalan prawns and Helford oysters to lemon sole, skate, squid, crab and spinach parcels and lobster. Also steaks (sirloin or oyster-stuffed carpetbagger fillet). *Seats 24. Parties 12. D only 7-10.30. Closed Sun in winter, 2 weeks Nov, 24-26 Dec. Access, Visa.*

Falmouth   Places of Interest

Tourist Information   Tel 0326 312300.
Falmouth Arts Centre   Church Street Tel 0326 314566.
Princess Pavillion   Melville Road Tel 0326 311277.

Fareham   Forte Posthouse   61%   £68

Tel 0329 844644   Fax 0329 844666   **H**

Cartwright Drive Titchfield Fareham Hampshire PO15 5RS   **Map 15 D4**

One of the newest (and largest) redbrick Posthouses, with a leisure centre and a range of meeting rooms (up to 140 people theatre-style, ample parking). Half the comfortable bedrooms are designated non-smoking and four have been purpose-built for disabled guests. From M27 Junction 9 (10 miles from both Portsmouth and Southampton) take the A27 south towards Fareham. *Rooms 126. Garden, indoor swimming pool, gym, sauna, solarium, snooker, children's playground.* AMERICAN EXPRESS *Access, Diners, Visa.*

Fareham   Red Lion Hotel   57%   £55

Tel 0329 822640   Fax 0329 823579   **H**

East Street Fareham Hampshire PO16 0BP   Map 15 D4

Now owned by Countryside Inns & Hotels, this former coaching inn
is equidistant from Portsmouth and Southampton. Some period character
remains. Function facilities for up to 100. Family-friendly, with cots and
beds free of charge. No dogs. *Rooms 43. Garden, sauna.* AMERICAN EXPRESS
Access, Diners, Visa.

Fareham   Solent Hotel   75%   £108

Tel 0489 880000   Fax 0489 880007   **HR**

Solent Business Park Whiteley Fareham Hampshire PO15 7AJ   Map 15 D4

In a most unexpected location – adjacent to Junction 9 of the M27 (10
miles from both Portsmouth and Southampton) – this gabled hotel dating
from 1990 almost has the feel of a New England inn, successfully balancing
wood and brick in its design and happily satisfying the contrasting needs
of business and leisure guests. The functions (max 250) are separated
physically in the building's design, but high standards of service do not
exclude one at the expense of another. All the bedrooms are of Executive
standard, in traditional style, with both working and relaxing space plus
comprehensive comforts – from bathrobes to mini-bars. Suites
accommodate syndicate, business and interview requirements in the week
and have ample space for families at weekends; children up to 16 are
accommodated free in their parents' room. Committed young staff and
expert management show good direction throughout. The *Parson's Collar*
pub in the grounds offers Daniel Thwaites ales and informal eating – a
place for parents to unwind while taking up the hotel's baby-listening
facility. A stylish leisure club has a private membership and access from
within the hotel; a floodlit tennis court is the latest feature. Plenty of easy
parking. Shire Inns. *Rooms 90. Garden, tennis, indoor swimming pool,
children's splash pool, gym, squash, sauna, spa bath, steam room, solarium, beauty
salon, snooker, helipad.* AMERICAN EXPRESS *Access, Visa.*

Woodlands Restaurant   £55

One room in the stone-floored dining area overlooks grass and woodlands
beyond, carefully segregating conference diners when required, leaving
other guests to enjoy the open fire in the main, split-level room.
An enterprising carte and table d'hote offer familiar favourites with
an interesting twist – speciality dishes include mussels with fettucine,
Cantonese-style fish and loin of venison. *Seats 100. Parties 30. L 12.30-2
D 7-10. Closed L Sat. Set L £9.95/£12.95 (Sun £6.50/£13.95)
Set D £14/£20.*

Fareham   Places of Interest

Tourist Information   Tel 0329 221342.
Titchfield Abbey   Titchfield Tel 0329 43016.
Porchester Castle   Porchester Tel 0705 378291.
Royal Navy Submarine Museum   Gosport Tel 0705 529217.
Fort Brockhurst   Gosport Tel 0705 581059.

Farnborough   Forte Crest   66%   £99

Tel 0252 545051   Fax 0252 377210   **H**

Lynchford Road Farnborough Hampshire GU14 6AZ   Map 15 E3

Handsome Edwardian building alongside A325. Day rooms have period
appeal, bedrooms are mainly modern. Banqueting and conference facilities
for 120/150. Children up to 15 free in parents' room. *Rooms 110. Garden,
indoor swimming pool, keep-fit equipment, spa bath, sauna, steam room, solarium,
beauty salon, coffee shop (12-10.30).* AMERICAN EXPRESS *Access, Diners, Visa.*

Farnham   Bishop's Table Hotel   62%   £85

Tel 0252 710222   Fax 0252 733494   **H**

27 West Street Farnham Surrey GU9 7DR   Map 15 E3

A small, Georgian town-centre hotel (next to the public library) with individually decorated bedrooms, most now including some antique furniture and French pine beds. The bridal suite features a Victorian half-tester bed. Kass and Mariam Verjee, a brother and sister team, run the place in friendly style. Peaceful, secluded garden with a magnificent cedar tree to the rear. Children up to 13 free in parents' room. Guests may park in the library car park next door during the evening and overnight. *Rooms 18. Garden. Closed 26 Dec-4 Jan.* AMERICAN EXPRESS *Access, Diners, Visa.*

Farnham   Bush Hotel   62%   £82

Tel 0252 715237   Fax 0252 733530   **H**

The Borough Farnham Surrey GU9 7NN   Map 15 E3

17th-century buildings cluster around a cobbled courtyard at a well-kept Forte hotel in the town centre. Most bedrooms are in a newer wing that overlooks the garden. *Rooms 66. Garden, coffee shop (10am-6pm).* AMERICAN EXPRESS *Access, Diners, Visa.*

Farnham   Krug's   £55

Tel 0252 723277   **R**

84 West Street Farnham Surrey GU9 7EN   Map 15 E3

A homely Austrian restaurant with a stag's head, log-burning stove and Alpine folksy tablecloths setting the scene for Gerhard Krug's competent and authentic national cooking. Dinner proceeds at a leisurely pace and dishes such as smoked bacon and cabbage soup, meat or cheese fondue and pan-fried pork fillet with soured cream and garlic sauce show the style. Fine home-cooked desserts include pancakes filled with apricot purée and praline or cinnamon-laced apfelstrudel. Note that Krug's is no longer open for lunch. *Seats 80. Private Room 40. D only 7-11. Closed Sun.* AMERICAN EXPRESS *Access, Visa.*

Farnham   Places of Interest

Farnham Tourist Information   Tel 0252 715109.
Aldershot Tourist Information   Tel 0252 20968.
Aldershot Military Museum   Tel 0252 314598.
Crosswater Farm and Gardens Churt.
Rural Life Centre   Tilford Tel 0252 795571.
Birdworld   Tel 0420 22140.
Aldershot Ice Rink   Tel 0252 336464.
Stainforth Ski Centre   Aldershot Tel 0252 25889.

Faugh   String of Horses Inn   £68

Tel 0228 70297   Fax 0228 70675   **I**

Heads Hook Faugh nr Carlisle Cumbria CA4 9EG   Map 4 C2

Substantial white-painted coaching inn with an unbroken 300-year history, in a tiny hamlet off the A69. The rustic bar and lounges sport a plethora of panelling, oak beams, polished brass and similar trappings. Those in the bedrooms are rather more surprising: Hollywood-style brass fittings, large corner baths and proprietor Eric Tasker's complimentary hangover kit; several rooms have four-poster beds. Family facilities; popular bar snacks and Sunday lunches. Breakfast can even extend to curry if that's your bent. *Rooms 14. Terrace, outdoor swimming pool (heated all year), keep-fit equipment, spa bath, sauna, solarium, games room. Closed 25 & 26 Dec.* AMERICAN EXPRESS *Access, Diners, Visa.*

Faversham   Read's   £75

Tel 0795 535344   Fax 0795 591200

R

Painter's Forstal Faversham Kent ME13 0EE

Map 11 C5

David and Rona Pitchford are well established in their smart little
restaurant just outside Faversham, David leading the way from the kitchen
and Rona charming the guests at front of house. There's a precise touch
to the cooking, a sureness of flavouring and saucing, a deftness to the
presentation on the plate. Set meals are well balanced, and Read's
Traditional Menu, for example, (available at lunch and dinner from
Tuesday to Friday) might offer (with no choices) savoury nibbles, then
a surprise appetiser at the table, next cream of celery soup with butter-fried
croutons, a main course of breast, drumstick and thigh of farmyard chicken
braised in red wine *coq au vin*-style and served with a selection of fresh
vegetables, a choice of sweet or cheese then finally coffee and sweet nibbles.
Other dishes typical of David's style might be a fillet of pink trout grilled
in an envelope of courgettes and served on a creamed lobster sauce, a tart
of Italian plum tomatoes baked in the oven with olive oil, shallots and fresh
basil, a fillet of brill on buttered leeks with a melange of vegetables, and
roast chump of new season English lamb with a millefeuille of aubergines
and rosemary-scented jus. Delicious desserts – chocoholics anonymous
speaks for itself, the Image is a selection of all the offerings for the
indecisive or the self-indulgent. The idea of offering a condensed list of 40
wines at £16 or under is an excellent one, though for the relevant tasting
notes you must search through the excellent main list. However, it's easy
to use and decently priced. There's a nice note on the lunch menu to the
effect that if you're short of time, just say, and Rona will pace your meal
accordingly. *Seats 40. Private Room 18. L 12-2 D 7-10. Closed Sun & Mon,
Bank Holidays. Set L £14.50 Set D £23.50/£32.* AMERICAN EXPRESS *Access,
Diners, Visa.* MARTELL

Fawkham   Brandshatch Place   65%   £90

Tel 0474 872239   Fax 0474 879652

H

Fawkham Valley Road Fawkham Kent DA3 8NQ

Map 11 B5

This redbrick Georgian house built for the Duke of Norfolk stands
opposite the Paddock entrance to Brands Hatch racing circuit. Plain public
rooms range from a pale pink lounge and bar area to a selection of meeting
and conference rooms. The self-contained leisure club is well equipped.
Bedrooms have up-to-date decor and include small seating areas and
remote-control TVs as standard features. Bathrooms are more basic and
functional. *Rooms 29. Garden, indoor swimming pool, gym, squash, sauna,
steam room, spa bath, solarium, snooker.* AMERICAN EXPRESS *Access, Diners, Visa.*

Fawkham   Places of Interest

Orchard Theatre Home Gardens   Dartford Tel 0322 34333.
Hesketh Park Cricket Ground   Dartford Tel 0322 225152.

We do not accept free meals or hospitality – our inspectors pay their
own bills.

Felixstowe   Orwell Moat House   69%   £75

Tel 0394 285511   Fax 0394 670687

H

Hamilton Road Felixstowe Suffolk IP11 7DX

Map 10 D3

Comfortable public rooms retain many period features at this Victorian
town-centre hotel opposite the railway station; bedrooms offer all the usual
modern comforts, and there are conference facilities for up to 220. 24hr
lounge service. Ample free parking. *Rooms 58. Garden.* AMERICAN EXPRESS
Access, Diners, Visa.

Felsted   Rumbles Cottage

£55

Tel 0371 820996

R

Braintree Road Felsted Essex CM6 3DJ

Map 11 B4

In the centre of Felsted, a whitewashed, 16th-century cottage with low, beamed ceilings and four dining rooms. It's run in a friendly and relaxed style by enthusiastic chef-proprietress Joy Hadley, whose eclectic, monthly-changing English menu offers a choice of five dishes per course. Among her specialities are Stilton, cauliflower and onion soup; salmon, cucumber and lemon bavarois; chicken and asparagus Wellington; twice-baked soufflés; Arabian lamb casserole, lavender ice cream, and Stilton, pear and sultana crumble – but don't expect to find them all on the same menu! Many of the vegetables, including white aubergines, salsify, curly kale, dwarf sugar peas and a variety of lettuces, come from Joy's own garden. There is always an unusual vegetarian dish. Frequent 'guinea pig menus' (£12.50) for tasting experimental dishes are also offered to adventurous diners at dinner Tue-Thu; £10 pasta menu Fri. All-British cheeses. *Seats 50. Parties 16. Private Room 22. L Sun only 12-2 D 7-9. Closed D Sun, all Mon. Set Sun L £12.50 Access, Visa.*
Also at:
Rumbles Castle Restaurant, 4 St James Street, Castle Hedingham, Essex (Tel 0787 461490)
Open L Sun only & D Wed-Sat.

Fenstanton   Forte Travelodge

£45

Tel 0954 230919

L

Fenstanton nr Cambridge Cambridgeshire

Map 15 F1

Located on the eastbound side of the A604, 4 miles south-east of Huntingdon and 10 miles north-west of Cambridge. ***Rooms** 40.*
AMERICAN EXPRESS® *Access, Diners, Visa.*

Ferndown   Dormy Hotel   71%

£105

Tel 0202 872121   Fax 0202 895388

H

New Road Ferndown nr Bournemouth Dorset BH22 8ES

Map 14 C4

Manager Derek Silk has kept standards high here since 1977. Guests will find plenty to please them: public rooms include an all-day bar and brasserie with well-upholstered rattan furniture, and a further bar with oak-panelled walls, red plush chesterfields and a real log fire. The leisure club's facilities are extensive: there's a club room with snooker, pool, darts and table tennis, and a children's games room with supervised activities during holiday periods; both the gym and pool are wonderfully light and airy. Bedrooms offer good standards of modern comfort; 18 rooms for non-smokers; children under 14 share parents' room free. Well geared-up for conferences with some 10 meeting rooms, the largest of which can accommodate up to 250 delegates in theatre style. De Vere. ***Rooms** 128. Garden, putting green, driving net, indoor swimming pool, gym, squash, sauna, steam room, spa bath, solarium, beauty salon, tennis, snooker, brasserie (10am-10pm), children's playground.* AMERICAN EXPRESS® *Access, Diners, Visa.*

Ferndown   Travel Inn (Poole/Ringwood)

£43

Tel 0202 874210   Fax 0202 897794

L

Ringwood Road Tricketts Cross Ferndown Dorset BH22 9BB

Map 14 C4

Between Ringwood and Poole on the A348, south of the Tricketts Cross roundabout. 15 minutes from Bournemouth. ***Rooms** 32.* AMERICAN EXPRESS®
Access, Diners, Visa.

Ferrybridge   Granada Lodge   £51

Tel 0977 672767   Fax 0977 672945   **L**

M62/A1 Junction 33 Ferrybridge West Yorkshire WF11 0AF   **Map 7 D1**

Rooms 35. AMERICAN EXPRESS® *Access, Diners, Visa.*

Findon   Findon Manor   61%   £70

Tel 0903 872733   **H**

Findon West Sussex BN14 0TA   **Map 11 A6**

A former rectory dating back in part to the 16th century and owned until
the 1930s by Magdalen College, Oxford. Reception is in the delightful
beamed lounge, beyond which there's a cosy little bar which serves as the
village local. Bedrooms vary in size and furnishings, the best having four-
posters and spa baths. The garden is a popular spot for tea in summer
or a game of croquet. *Rooms 10. Garden, croquet.* AMERICAN EXPRESS®
Access, Visa.

Fleet   Forte Travelodge   £45

Tel 0252 815578   **L**

Hartley Wintney Basingstoke Hampshire RG27 8BN   **Map 15 D3**

Located on the westbound carriageway of the M3 at the Welcome Break
Fleet service area, between Junctions 4A and 5. *Rooms 40.* AMERICAN EXPRESS®
Access, Diners, Visa.

Flitwick   Flitwick Manor   73%   £125

Tel 0525 712242   Fax 0525 712242   **H R**

Church Road Flitwick Bedfordshire MK45 1AE   **Map 15 E1**

A late 17th/early 18th-century house set in rolling parkland just a couple
of minutes from the M1 (Junction 12). The high-ceilinged music room (the
main day room) sets the tone of the hotel with homely touches like
magazines and chessboard set up ready for play. Bedrooms come in all
shapes and sizes from small singles to one with a large four-poster and
original panelling; all rooms get the same extras including ice and slices
of lemon with the well-stocked drinks tray, mineral water, fresh fruit,
home-made biscuits, books, magazines and fresh flowers. Bathrooms are
equally variable – two have shower and WC only, one with his 'n' hers
'kissing' bath tubs. Banqueting/conference facilities for 60. Recent
management changes have now, we hope, been finalised. *Rooms 15.
Garden, croquet, tennis, helipad.* AMERICAN EXPRESS® *Access, Visa.*

Restaurant   £100

Between the good canapés that arrive with the menu and nicely varied
petits fours with the coffee Duncan Poyser's fixed-price menu offers
a selection of thoroughly modern dishes: hot scallop soufflé scented with
thyme and served with girolle butter, mosaic of sweetbreads and crab with
grain mustard sauce, shin of veal braised with anise and orange, and baked
supreme of salmon set on a red bean pancetta and parsley broth set the tone.
Unusual menu reading, surprises on the plate too, with vegetables forming
an integral part of the garnish of each main dish. Plenty of interest for afters
too, with the likes of tarte tatin of figs with port ice cream and a warm
compote of griottines and raspberries topped with a hot soufflé of vanilla
flecked with bitter chocolate. The lunchtime selection (including Sunday
lunch) is more limited, but always interesting. *Seats 40. Parties 8.
Private Room 30. L 12.15-1.45 D 7.15-9.30 Set L £16.50/£19.50
(Sun £23.50) Set D £35.50.*

Folkestone   Paul's   £45

Tel 0303 59697   **R**

2a Bouverie Road West Folkestone Kent CT20 2RX   Map 11 C5

Locally supplied fresh fish is one of the specialities prepared by Paul and Penny Hagger in their popular, colourful restaurant. A typical example is fillets of Dover sole poached in cream with prawns and a little Chablis. Other typical dishes run from cream of watercress soup with toasted almonds and unusual haggis samosa to pheasant crumble, Barnsley chop with a honey and rosemary sauce, and calf's liver with a spicy paprika, garlic and cream sauce. There's always a decent choice for vegetarians. Sweets from the trolley. Keenly-priced wine list. *Seats 80. L 12-2.30 D 7.30-9.30 (Sat from 7). Closed 25/26 Dec. Set L & D £12.90/£15.65. Access, Visa.*

Folkestone   La Tavernetta   £45

Tel 0303 54955   **R**

Leaside Court Clifton Gardens Folkestone Kent CT20 2ED   Map 11 C5

Chef-partner Felice Puricelli has been providing sound Italian cuisine since 1965 in his friendly basement restaurant. The menu offers reliable favourites such as *tagliatelle amatriciana, petto di pollo cacciatore, scaloppa di vitello milanese* and *tiramisu. Seats 55. Private Room 22. L 12-2.30 D 6-10.30. Closed Sun, Bank Holidays. Set L from £9.50.* *Access, Diners, Visa.*

Folkestone   Places of Interest

Tourist Information   Tel 0303 58594.
Metropole Arts Centre   Tel 0303 55070.
Leas Cliff Hall   Tel 0303 53191.
Kent Battle of Britain Museum   Tel 0303 893140.
Eurotunnel – Le Shuttle   Tel 0303 27100.
Cheriton Cricket Ground   Tel 0303 53366.
Folkestone Racecourse   Tel 0303 66407.
Hoverspeed – Sea Cat   Tel 0304 240241.

Fontwell   Forte Travelodge   £45

Tel 0243 543973   **L**

A27/A29 Fontwell West Sussex BN18 0SB   Map 11 A6

On the A27, 5 miles north of Bognor Regis. *Rooms 32.* AMERICAN EXPRESS *Access, Diners, Visa.*

Fontwell   Places of Interest

Fontwell Park Racecourse   Tel 0243 543335.

Framlingham   The Crown   62%   £102

Tel 0728 723521   Fax 0728 724274   **H**

Market Hill Framlingham Suffolk IP13 9AN   Map 10 D2

A Forte Heritage hotel that stands out from the crowd with much 16th-century period charm. A flagstoned foyer/lounge and public bar have beamed ceilings and open fires, with a creaking staircase leading up to simple bedrooms furnished with freestanding oak units. The best bedroom has a panelled oak four-poster and floral print settee. Plenty of car parking at the back of the hotel. *Rooms 14.* AMERICAN EXPRESS *Access, Diners, Visa.*

Framlingham   Place of Interest

Framlingham Castle   Tel 0728 723330.

Freshford   Homewood Park   79%   £115

Tel 0225 723731   Fax 0225 723820   **HR**

Hinton Charterhouse Freshford Avon BA3 6BB   Map 13 F1

Just off A36, 5 miles south of Bath. Mainly Georgian, although the cellars
date back to the 13th century, Homewood Park enjoys 10 acres of its own
grounds within an area designated as being of outstanding natural beauty.
Oil paintings, Oriental rugs, a collection of bronze statuettes and some
framed Hermès scarves all contribute to the charm of relaxing day rooms,
kept to a high standard by owners Frank and Sara Gueuning. Bedrooms
vary in size (and price – the price quoted is for larger rooms with better
outlooks) but all share the same degree of comfort and sense of style: well-
chosen fabrics (often with elaborate bedhead drapes), the occasional antique,
cut-glass decanter of sherry, mineral water and pretty bathrooms decorated
to match the individual rooms. Two semi-suites attract only a slightly
higher tariff. Banqueting/conference facilities for 75/30. No dogs.
Rooms 15. Garden, tennis, croquet, helipad. AMERICAN EXPRESS *Access,
Diners, Visa.*

Restaurant   £75

There is a simple elegance to the twin dining rooms, which were recently
redecorated. One is encouraged by comfortable chairs and views out to the
garden to linger over chef Tim Ford's stylish cooking. Both table d'hote
and à la carte menus are offered, the former perhaps offering a well-
balanced meal of duck and pistachio nut terrine, pan-fried medallions of
cod with a red wine and balsamic vinegar dressing, rhubarb and ginger
cheesecake with lemon and ginger ice cream, and coffee with home-made
petits fours to finish. The carte might see Cornish lobster consommé
infused with star anise, accompanied by lobster and truffle ravioli; grilled
fillets of red mullet, sea bass and salmon with lemon couscous and a sweet
pepper sauce; a daily main-course fish dish; medallions of venison *en
crépinette* with tarragon mousse and beetroot tagliatelle; free-range chicken
stuffed with morels, served with a timbale of ratatouille and a carrot and
Sauternes sauce; with, perhaps, caramelised white chocolate crème brulée
with mint chocolate chip ice cream, poached pears on a creamy rice
pudding galette and a raspberry coulis or cheeses served with apricot and
rosemary bread to finish. There's a fair sprinkling of half bottles on the
conventional wine list; several countries are represented, but by a single
bottle. 12 seats on a terrace in good weather. No smoking. *Seats 55.
Parties 26. Private Room 40. L 12-1.30 D 7-9.30. Set L £17.50/£20
Set D £27.50.*

Freshwater   Farringford Hotel   57%   £88

Tel 0983 752500   **H**

Bedbury Lane Freshwater Isle of Wight PO40 9PE   Map 14 C4

Owners Mr and Mrs Cerise have been running the Farringford since 1980,
and have created a peaceful retreat with gardens bordering National Trust
downland. Day rooms at this 18th-century Gothic-style house include
a French-windowed drawing room, a small bar and a library with
Tennyson memorabilia (the poet once lived here.) Bedrooms (15 in the
main house, 4 accessed outside) are modest and neat, and there are also 24
bungalows and 4 flats in the grounds let on a self-catering basis. Families
with children are welcome, and baby-sitting and baby-listening can
be arranged. *Rooms 19. Outdoor swimming pool, garden, croquet, 9-hole golf
course, putting, bowling green, tennis, children's play area.* AMERICAN EXPRESS
Access, Diners, Visa.

Fressingfield   The Fox & Goose Inn   £65

Tel 037 986 247   **R**

Fressingfield nr Diss Suffolk IP21 5PB   Map 10 C2

Next to the churchyard and the village pond, the Fox & Goose was built
around 1500 as a Guildhall before becoming a pub. These days it's more

restaurant than pub with the single bar quickly filling up with diners looking at the menu when they are busy, but there is also a bar menu or you can just have a drink. The word eclectic might have been invented to describe a menu which ranges from Peking duck with pancakes and hoisin sauce, Japanese fish and vegetable tempura, and griddled squid with coriander houmus to sun-dried tomato and basil risotto, Caesar salad, Barbary duck confit with braised Puy lentils, and much else besides. The decor is very 'country' with old black beams and red-tiled floor in the main dining room (which was the kitchen in olden days) and a further room with sea-grass matting and 'stable' booths, used when busy. The atmosphere is informal and obliging, children are made welcome with their own menu plus a 'play box', crayons for drawing on the paper table cloths and, out in the garden, where one can also eat and drink, a see-saw and sandpit. An outstanding wine list comes in two parts, the 'short list' (with some 50 wines) and the 'long list' (we lost count) – just three are priced by the glass but if you fancy a glass of something from the 'short list' they will probably oblige. *Seats 50. Private Room 24. L 12-2.15 D 7-9.15. Set L £9.95/£13.50. Closed D Sun in winter (except by arrangement), Mon & Tue, 2 weeks Nov, 25 & 26 Dec. No credit cards.*

Frilford Heath	Dog House Hotel	£69
Tel 0865 390830 Fax 0865 390860		**I**
Frilford Heath nr Abingdon Oxfordshire OX13 6QJ		Map 15 D2

The 17th-century Dog House (a ten-minute drive from Oxford) has rooms in contemporary cottage style. Furniture is good-quality pine (one room has a pine four-poster), and accessories include remote-control teletext TV. Bathrooms have smart modern tiling, large mirrors and good lighting. Children's play area. Plenty of free parking. *Rooms 19. Garden.* AMERICAN EXPRESS *Access, Diners, Visa.*

Garforth	Hilton National	61%	£87
Tel 0532 866556 Fax 0532 868326			**H**
Wakefield Road Garforth nr Leeds West Yorkshire LS25 1LH			Map 7 D1

Stylish public areas raise expectations for the bedrooms, which although well kept, are small and fairly ordinary. Leisure centre. Meeting 2000 is a conference facility for up to 400 delegates. *Rooms 144. Garden, indoor swimming pool, keep-fit equipment, sauna, solarium, pool table.* AMERICAN EXPRESS *Access, Diners, Visa.*

Gateshead	Forte Travelodge	£45
Tel 091-438 3333		**L**
A194 Leam Lane Wardley Whitemare Pool nr Gateshead Tyne & Wear NE10 8YB		Map 5 E2

On the outskirts of Newcastle-upon-Tyne (4 miles to the south-east), 4 miles east of Gateshead town centre and 8 miles west of Sunderland. At the junction of A194M and A184. Heading north, take right-hand fork just past Washington Services on the A1. *Rooms 41.* AMERICAN EXPRESS *Access, Diners, Visa.*

Gateshead	Newcastle Marriott	70%	£108
Tel 091-493 2233 Fax 091-493 2030			**H**
MetroCentre Gateshead Newcastle Tyne & Wear NE11 9XF			Map 5 E2

Just off the A1 (Newcastle Western bypass) and opposite the MetroCentre (Europe's largest indoor shopping and leisure complex), the Marriott is tall and faced entirely in darkened glass. The spacious and modern white marble-floored foyer is stylishly appointed with wide brown leather settees and armchairs. Bedrooms have smart lightwood furniture and soft pastel colour schemes; all are well equipped – even to the extent of having video recorders with a selection of video cassettes for hire. Bathrooms have power showers and good towels. Ten highly distinctive, themed rooms are very original, well thought out and popular. Children up to 18 free in parents' room. Conference facilities for up to 450. Price reductions at weekends. *Rooms 150. Indoor swimming pool, spa bath, gym, solarium, sauna, steam room, beauty salon.* AMERICAN EXPRESS *Access, Diners, Visa.*

Gateshead   Springfield Hotel   63%   £93

Tel 091-477 4121   Fax 091-477 7213   **H**

Durham Road Low Fell Gateshead Tyne & Wear NE9 5BT   **Map 5 E2**

Jarvis business hotel by the A6127, 4 miles from A1(M) junction. Conference/banqueting facilities for 120/100. Children up to 5 stay free in parents' room. A secure car park was being constructed as we went to press. *Rooms 60.* AMERICAN EXPRESS *Access, Diners, Visa.*

Gateshead   Swallow Hotel   60%   £90

Tel 091-477 1105   Fax 091-478 7214   **H**

High West Street Gateshead Tyne & Wear NE8 1PE   **Map 5 E2**

A leisure club, ample secure car parking and conference facilities for up to 350 are among the amenities at this modern hotel three miles from the A1(M) and one mile from the city centre – check directions. Children up to 14 can stay free in their parents' room. *Rooms 103. Indoor swimming pool, keep-fit equipment, sauna, spa bath, steam room, solarium.* AMERICAN EXPRESS *Access, Diners, Visa.*

Gateshead   Places of Interest

Tourist Information   Tel 091-477 3478.
Caedmon Hall   Tel 091-477 3478.
Gibside Chapel and Grounds (NT)   Gibside Tel 0207 542255.
Bede Monastery Museum   Jarrow Tel 091-489 2106.
Wickham Thorns Farm Ski Slope   Dunston Tel 091-460 8746.
Gateshead International Sports Stadium   Tel 091-478 1687.

Gatwick Airport   Chequers Thistle   63%   £106

Tel 0293 786992   Fax 0293 820625   **H**

Brighton Road Horley Surrey RH6 8PH   **Map 15 E3**

At a roundabout on the A23 to the north of the airport, this white-painted building with beamed gables was indeed once a Tudor coaching inn, though inside only the beamed bar hints at its past. Standardised bedrooms, all in a two-storey 'system built' extension to the rear, are in good order with all the usual creature comforts and practical bathrooms. 24hr room service. There's free parking if you stay at the hotel prior to flying from Gatwick. *Rooms 78. Outdoor swimming pool, coffee shop (10am-10pm).* AMERICAN EXPRESS *Access, Diners, Visa.*

Gatwick Airport   Copthorne Effingham Park   72%   £126

Tel 0342 714994   Fax 0342 716039   **H**

West Park Road Copthorne West Sussex RH10 3EU   **Map 15 E3**

Follow signs to East Grinstead, off Junction 10 of the M23. Six sequoia trees, originally imported from Oregon to commemorate Wellington's victory at Waterloo, line the driveway. There's lots more of interest in the modernised stately home, including a large rotunda conference centre (catering for up to 600 delegates). Decent-sized bedrooms have reproduction furniture including a breakfast table. Best rooms have private balconies. 27 rooms reserved for non-smokers. Under-16s share parents' room free. *Rooms 122. Garden, croquet, golf (9), indoor swimming pool, children's splash pool, gym, squash, steam room, sauna, spa bath, solarium, beauty & hair salon, helipad.* AMERICAN EXPRESS *Access, Diners, Visa.*

Gatwick Airport   Copthorne London Gatwick   69%   £128

Tel 0342 714971   Fax 0342 717375   **H**

Copthorne nr Crawley West Sussex RH10 3PG   Map 15 E3

Set in 100 acres of gardens and woodland, the Copthorne is centred round
a 16th-century farmhouse. Oak beams and log fires keep the period feel
in the White Swan pub, and many of the bedrooms are also in traditional
style. Connoisseur rooms feature king-size beds and spa baths; rooms are
available for non-smokers (100) and disabled guests. There are several
places to eat, and a variety of conference and function rooms. Families are
well catered for, and under-12s can stay free in their parents' room. The
hotel is just six minutes from the airport, and two from the M23 (Junction
10, then A264 towards East Grinstead). *Rooms 227. Garden, croquet, jogging
track, children's playground, gym, sauna, solarium, squash, tennis.*
AMERICAN EXPRESS *Access, Diners, Visa.*

Gatwick Airport   Europa Gatwick   68%   £119

Tel 0293 886666   Fax 0293 886680   **H**

Balcombe Road Maidenbower nr Crawley West Sussex RH10 4ZR   Map 15 E3

Now owned by Britannia Hotels, the Europa is on the B2036 about 15
minutes from the airport. A modern low-rise hotel built in an unusual
hacienda style, it has whitewashed walls and terracotta roofs. Inside, it's just
as distinctive, and reception impresses first with its tall rafters, terrazzo
marble floor and dark mahogany furniture. There are two restaurants (the
Silk Trader serving Chinese food and the *Méditerranée*), a lounge bar for
lighter meals, a cocktail bar, numerous syndicate rooms and Studio 4 –
a well-equipped health and leisure centre (now with a dance studio). Smart
bedrooms with polished wood and autumnal colour schemes range up to
Executive rooms with sofa beds and work areas, and Club rooms with
whirlpool baths. Parking for 250 cars. *Rooms 211. Garden, indoor swimming
pool, gym, steam room, spa bath, sauna, solarium, dance studio, beautician,
hairdressing.* AMERICAN EXPRESS *Access, Diners, Visa.*

Our inspectors *never* book in the name of Egon Ronay's Guides. They
disclose their identity only if they are considering an establishment for
inclusion in the next edition of the Guide.

Gatwick Airport   Forte Crest Gatwick   74%   £109

Tel 0293 567070   Fax 0293 567739   **H**

North Terminal Gatwick Airport West Sussex RH6 0PH   Map 15 E3

Gatwick's most distinctive hotel is 100 yards from the north terminal and
has a covered walkway, leading directly into the unusual, eight-storey-high
atrium, under which a bright cocktail bar and café take on an open-air feel.
Public areas are modernistic, even a bit austere, and the uniformly
furnished bedrooms are stark, though well lit and comfortable, with
chrome fittings and black and white decor; striped bedcovers provide
a dash of colour; glazing is thoroughly efficient with little or no air traffic
noise. Children up to 16 stay free in parents' room. A surprisingly easy-to-
use, high-tech TV system displays messages, flight information, a running
total of the bill and even a check-out facility in addition to regular viewing.
Service throughout is helpful, knowledgeable, friendly and efficient. 24hr
room service. Guests booking in for even one night can park their cars for
15 days in the long-term car park. Banqueting/conference facilities for
up to 240/340. Staffed business centre. *Rooms 468. Indoor swimming pool,
sauna, solarium, gym, news kiosk, hair & beauty salon, coffee shop (5.30am –
1am).* AMERICAN EXPRESS *Access, Diners, Visa.*

Gatwick Airport   Forte Posthouse Gatwick   63%   £68
Tel 0293 771621   Fax 0293 771054   H
Povey Cross Road Horley Surrey RH6 0BA   Map 15 E3

On the A23 a mile north of the airport. Good modern bedrooms, choice of conference and meeting rooms (up to 150 delegates), large long-term car park. Courtesy airport coach every 30 minutes (6.15am-11.45pm). *Rooms 210. Outdoor swimming pool, coffee shop (7am-10pm), airport courtesy coach (from 6.15am).* AMERICAN EXPRESS *Access, Diners, Visa.*

Gatwick Airport   Gatwick Concorde Hotel   61%   £104
Tel 0293 533441   Fax 0293 535369   H
Church Road Lowfield Heath Crawley West Sussex RH11 0PQ   Map 15 E3

Queens Moat Houses hotel off the A23. Some of the bedrooms overlook the runways. Courtesy coach from airport and station. *Rooms 116.* AMERICAN EXPRESS *Access, Diners, Visa.*

Gatwick Airport   Gatwick Hilton International   72%   £159
Tel 0293 518080   Fax 0293 28980   H
Gatwick West Sussex RH6 OLL   Map 15 E3

A pedestrian walkway directly connects Gatwick's south terminal with this large hotel's four-storey central atrium; a full-size replica of *Jason*, Amy Johnson's biplane, hangs from the ceiling. Good-sized bedrooms have easy chairs, breakfast tables, large beds and all the extras one would expect from an international hotel; TVs even display flight information, very useful if your plane is delayed. Three floors are now set aside for non-smokers. The Jockey Bar's horse-racing theme harks back to the days when Gatwick racecourse was on this site. Conferences for up to 500. Lloyds Bank cashpoint machine. *Rooms 550. Indoor swimming pool, sauna, solarium, spa bath, steam room, gym, beauty salon, hairdressing, kiosk, car rental desk, business centre, 24hr coffee shop.* AMERICAN EXPRESS *Access, Diners, Visa.*

Gatwick Airport   Gatwick Moat House   62%   £90
Tel 0293 785599   Fax 0293 785991   H
Longbridge Roundabout Horley Surrey RH6 0AB   Map 15 E3

Five-storey hotel by a roundabout on the A23, half a mile north of the airport. Bedrooms have individual heat and air controls. First-floor bar and brasserie. Conferences up to 180. Airport courtesy coach; long-term car parking. Children up to 12 free in parents' room. *Rooms 121. Snooker.* AMERICAN EXPRESS *Access, Diners, Visa.*

We publish annually, so make sure you use the current edition. It's worth it!

Gatwick Airport   Holiday Inn Gatwick   68%   £118
Tel 0293 529991   Fax 0293 515913   H
Langley Drive Crawley West Sussex RH11 7SX   Map 15 E3

Modern hotel on the A23 four miles south of the airport. Good leisure and conference facilities (for up to 300) – six bedrooms have been made into syndicate rooms to increase capacity, and there's a business centre. *Rooms 217. Gym, indoor swimming pool, children's pool, spa bath, sauna, solarium, snooker, coffee shop (11am-11.30pm).* AMERICAN EXPRESS *Access, Diners, Visa.*

Gatwick Airport   **Ramada Hotel Gatwick**   **70%**   £114

Tel 0293 820169   Fax 0293 820259   **H**

Povey Cross Road Horley Surrey RH6 0BE   Map 15 E3

Well-signposted, large modern hotel just off the A23. Spacious and stylish public areas include the Brighton Belle bar (based on an old Pullman carriage) with walls that are lined with railway memorabilia; leather sofas, large brass table lamps and a marble-tiled floor make the foyer-lounge an attractive area. The best bedrooms are spacious and well equipped, with efficient sound-proofing, good air-conditioning and neutral decor. The extensive leisure centre includes two squash courts. Good, self-contained conference facilities for up to 150 delegates, and a business centre. Courtesy coaches to the airport. *Rooms* 255. *Garden, coffee shop (10am-11pm), beautician, indoor swimming pool, sauna, solarium, spa bath, gym, squash.* AMERICAN EXPRESS *Access, Diners, Visa.*

Gatwick Airport   **Travel Inn**   **NEW**   £43

Tel 0582 414341   **L**

North Terminal Longbridge Way Gatwick Airport Crawley W Sussex   Map 15 E3

From M23 head for the North Terminal. At the roundabout take the third exit (Longbridge Way) to find the lodge on the right-hand side. *Rooms* 120. AMERICAN EXPRESS *Access, Diners, Visa.*

Gayton   **Travel Inn**   £43

Tel 051-342 1982   Fax 051-342 8983   **L**

Chester Road Gayton Wirral Merseyside L60 3FD   Map 6 A2

A short drive from both Ellesmere Port and Wirral Leisure Park. *Rooms* 37. AMERICAN EXPRESS *Access, Diners, Visa.*

Gerrards Cross   **Bull Hotel**   **63%**   £125

Tel 0753 885995   Fax 0753 885504   **H**

Gerrards Cross Buckinghamshire SL9 7PA   Map 15 E2

Some glimpses still of coaching days; mostly modern bedrooms which children up to 14 share free with parents. 20 rooms are designated non-smoking. Conferences for up to 200. De Vere. *Rooms* 95. *Garden, croquet.* AMERICAN EXPRESS *Access, Diners, Visa.*

Gillingham   **Stock Hill House**   **74%**   £170★

Tel 0747 823626   Fax 0747 825628   **HR**

Stock Hill Gillingham Dorset SP8 5NR   Map 14 B3

A few miles south of the A303 on the A3081 on the village outskirts a long winding tree-lined drive leads to Peter and Nita Hauser's splendid Victorian country mansion. Set in 10 acres of well-tended wooded grounds the house has, over the years, been lovingly decorated to create an almost home-from-home ambience, made even more welcoming by the Hausers' warmth and hospitality. The entrance hall features a pair of virtually life-size upstanding Indian mules carved in 1840. They stand before a huge ornate gilt mirror. Such features, though to a lesser scale, are scattered throughout the hotel. Occupying a corner of the entrance hall is an intimate lounge area with an open fire. Immediately next door, the drawing room offers an equal level of cosy homeliness. Bedrooms are finished to a high standard with colourful designer chintzes and a smattering of antiques and unusual objets d'art. Creature comforts abound including fresh fruit, books and magazines. The carpeted bathrooms are spotless, a few have bidets. As Peter and Nita say, they aim to create something very special. They succeed. ★Half-board terms only. No children under 7. No dogs. *Rooms* 9. *Garden. Access, Visa.*

See over

Restaurant   ★ ↑   £80

An elegant dining-room with elaborate gilt-framed mirrors at either end
and well-spaced, beautifully laid tables. Over the past ten years since
moving from Sark, Peter Hauser has developed his own unique style. The
cuisine of his native Austria forms the core of his inspiration, robust
traditional cooking with a few modern embellishments. There is a simple
directness to his food, well shown in thinly sliced grilled (and just pink)
duck breast served with hazelnut oil and dressed watercress or superb
jellied ham hock terrine with celery rémoulade. To accompany the seven
or so starters is the most wonderful bread, delicately perfumed with lemon
zest. A middle course consists of a choice of two soups, for instance a very
fine cream of nettle soup with crisp buttery garlic croutons. Main dishes
can include sliced poached beef sirloin with a horseradish cream; Aga-
roasted rack of lamb with cassis; sautéed pork tenderloin with Bosnian rice
or casseroled wild rabbit with spätzli. Vegetables and herbs come more
often than not from the kitchen gardens. Sweets can be elaborate as in
a meringue Suchard or simple – like home-made sorbets with seasonal
fruits or classically Austrian as in Esterhazy torte – thin layers of meringue
and nougat with well-balanced berry sauce. Service is superb and very
charming. No smoking. **Seats** 24. Private Room 12. L 12.30-1.45
D 7.30-8.45. Closed L some weekdays. Set L £18.50 Set D £28.

Gillingham   Places of Interest

Stourhead (NT)   Stourton Tel 0747 840348.
Stourton House Garden   Stourton Tel 0747 840417.

Gittisham   Combe House   73%   £97
Tel 0404 42756   Fax 0404 46004   **H**
Gittisham nr Honiton Devon EX14 0AD   Map 13 E2

Owners Thérèse and John Boswell, here since 1970, are both very much
involved in the day-to-day running of their stately Elizabethan mansion,
which enjoys a peaceful, attractive setting on a 3000-acre estate. Peaceful
it certainly is, but not remote, being less than two miles from the A30.
Public rooms have carved panelling in the entrance hall, ancestral portraits
in the panelled drawing room, a charming pink sitting room, a cosy bar
with pictures of John's horse-racing activities and everywhere architectural
features, antiques and personal touches by painter and sculptress Thérèse
(and her mother). Bedrooms vary in size and price, larger rooms tending
to have better views and more interesting furniture and pictures. One suite
and two rooms have four-poster beds. The hotel owns fishing rights on the
River Otter, with a season running from April to the end of September.
Rooms 15. Garden, croquet, fishing. Closed 26 Jan – 9 Feb. **AMERICAN EXPRESS**®
Access, Diners, Visa.

Glastonbury   No. 3 Restaurant & Hotel   £75
Tel 0458 832129   **RR**
3 Magdelene Street Glastonbury Somerset BA6 9EW   Map 13 F1

A Georgian town house on the A39 next to the ruins of Glastonbury
Abbey. Apart from being a very pleasant restaurant with rooms, it offers
the rather surprising services of massage, aromatherapy and beauty
consultancy. Ann Tynan serves a fixed-price menu, basically to residents
and their guests, but to others when space is available. Typical dishes might
include leeks and home-grown walnuts with Roquefort sauce, scallops
in shrimp sauce, brill with lemon butter, salmis of game and fillet of beef
au poivre. Cornish lobster is a speciality. **Seats** 20. D only 7.30-9. Closed Sun,
Mon & Tues, all Dec & Jan. Set D £26. Access, Visa.

Rooms £65

Six stylish bedrooms with antiques and bathrooms en suite; some rooms are in a modern annexe at the bottom of the garden. No dogs. Rooms always available.

Gloucester   **Forte Posthouse**   **66%**   £68

Tel 0452 613311   Fax 0452 371036   **H**

Crest Way Barnwood Gloucester Gloucestershire GL4 7RX   Map 14 B1

Modern hotel (formerly a Forte Crest) on the A417, strong on conference (up to 100) and leisure facilities. *Rooms 123. Indoor swimming pool, sauna, spa bath.* AMERICAN EXPRESS *Access, Diners, Visa.*

Gloucester   **Hatherley Manor**   **65%**   £75

Tel 0452 730217   Fax 0452 731032   **H**

Down Hatherley Lane Gloucester Gloucestershire GL2 9QA   Map 14 B1

Once the moated manor house of a country estate, 17th-century Hatherley Manor stands in 40 acres of parkland two miles north of Gloucester (just off the A38). Private guests and conference delegates (up to 300) are both well catered for, the former in comfortable bars and a lounge, the latter chiefly in the Hatherley Suite with its own entrance, bar and servery kitchen kept well away from the hotel proper. A few standard bedrooms are in the old part, but the majority are in the 'de luxe' category in the Jacobean wing. A few are suitable for family use (baby-listening and baby-sitting by arrangement; children up to 11 stay free in parents' room) and there's a four-poster honeymoon suite. Plenty of free parking. *Rooms 56. Garden, croquet.* AMERICAN EXPRESS *Access, Diners, Visa.*

We welcome bona fide complaints and recommendations on the tear-out pages at the back of the book for readers' comments. They are followed up by our professional team.

Gloucester   **Hatton Court**   **72%**   £95

Tel 0452 617412   Fax 0452 612945   **H**

Upton Hill Upton St Leonards Gloucester Gloucestershire GL4 8DE   Map 14 B1

Hatton Court enjoys panoramic views over the Severn Valley from its elevated position in 37 acres of grounds about three miles out of town on the B4073. Day rooms, and 18 of the bedrooms, are in the original, creeper-clad 17th-century building and comprise a lounge (which incorporates the reception desk) and bar both with dado oak panelling and French-style reproduction easy chairs, the bar featuring a pair of blow-windowed 'shop front' cabinets displaying porcelain and craft goods. Bedrooms, of which most are in an adjacent building, come with teddy bears on the pillow to keep you company and lots of extras like fruit, mineral water, sweets and home-made biscuits. Almost all the bathrooms have large corner tubs (two have regular baths and two shower and WC only) with those in the 'superior' and 'executive' rooms having a spa feature and each gets its family of plastic ducks along with bathrobes and good toiletries. Staff are notably friendly and beds are turned down at night. No dogs. *Rooms 45. Outdoor swimming pool, keep-fit equipment, sauna, solarium.* AMERICAN EXPRESS *Access, Diners, Visa.*

Gloucester	Travel Inn (Witcombe)	£43

Tel 0452 862521   Fax 0452 864926   **L**
Witcombe nr Gloucester Gloucestershire GL3 4SS   Map 14 B1

Rooms 40. AMERICAN EXPRESS *Access, Diners, Visa.*

Gloucester	Travel Inn (Longford)	£43

Tel 0452 523519   Fax 0452 300924   **L**
Tewkesbury Road Longford Gloucester Gloucestershire GL2 9BE   Map 14 B1

Rooms 40. AMERICAN EXPRESS *Access, Diners, Visa.*

Gloucester   Places of Interest

Tourist Information   Tel 0452 421188.
Berkeley Castle   Berkeley Tel 0453 810332.
Westbury Court Garden (NT)   Westbury-on-Severn Tel 0452 760461.
Gloucester Cathedral   Tel 0452 24167.
Gloucester Ski Centre   Tel 0452 414300.
     Museums and Art Galleries
Nature in Art   (The International Centre for Wildlife Art) Tel 0452
     731422.
City Museum and Art Gallery   Tel 0452 24131.
The Robert Opie Collection   Museum of Advertising and Packaging,
     Gloucester Docks Tel 0452 302309.
     Zoos and Wildlife Parks
National Birds of Prey Centre   Tel 0531 820286.
Wildfowl and Wetlands Trust   Slimbridge Tel 0453 890333.

Goathland	Mallyan Spout	61%	£65

Tel 0947 86206   **H**
Goathland Whitby North Yorkshire YO22 5AN   Map 5 F3

The unusual name comes from a waterfall which cascades into a wooded
valley not far from this ivy-clad hotel in a remote village. It's a homely,
welcoming place with family owners; the three lounges and two bars
provide ample space for relaxation and have views of the garden. Cottage-
style bedrooms include six rooms in a converted coach house. The two best
rooms have balconies and views of the valley and moors beyond. Two
studio flats are also available for self-catering. *Rooms 24. Garden. Access,
Diners, Visa.*

Godalming	Inn on the Lake	£75

Tel 0483 415575   Fax 0483 860445   **I**
Ockford Road Godalming Surrey GU7 1RH   Map 15 E3

On the A3100 just south of Godalming, this charming country house inn
run by Joy and Martin Cummings is set in 2 acres of lovely gardens with
lawns leading down to the lake. Guests will find stylish accommodation
with thoughtful extras such as magazines, sewing kits, trouser presses and
hairdryers in the best bedrooms; six rooms have spa baths and balconies.
All rooms are now en suite, the overall number having been reduced
by one. One room is suitable for family use. There's a convivial pubby bar
with a bar snack menu and a welcoming log fire in winter. Function
facilities for up to 120. *Rooms 19. Garden.* AMERICAN EXPRESS *Access,
Diners, Visa.*

Godalming   Place of Interest

Vann House   Hambledon Tel 0428 683413.

Golant Cormorant Hotel 63% £92

Tel & Fax 0726 833426 **H**

Golant nr Fowey Cornwall PL23 1LL Map 12 C3

The riverside setting in a small fishing village just north of Fowey is a great
attraction, and the bedrooms, day rooms and swimming pool all enjoy the
views. The restaurant and drawing room have recently been redecorated
to give a more modern look. Boats may be hired for sea or river fishing,
and the area is also a centre for sailing and water-skiing. Bedrooms are airy,
warm and comfortable, and there's a honeymoon room. The swimming
pool, set higher than the hotel, has a sliding roof for summer days.
No children under 12. *Rooms 11. Garden, indoor swimming pool, sun beds.
Closed Jan.* AMERICAN EXPRESS® *Access, Visa.*

Goodwood Goodwood Park 67% £93

Tel 0243 775537 Fax 0243 533802 **H**

Goodwood nr Chichester West Sussex PO18 0QB Map 11 A6

Within the 12,000 acre grounds of Goodwood estate, a much modernised
and extended old house plays host to hotel, golf and country club rolled
into one. Residential conferences and banqueting are the mainstay of mid-
week business (there's a dedicated conference centre catering for up to 120),
while weekends are busy with guests who make full use of the extensive
leisure facilities. Theatre breaks include tickets to the nearby Chichester
Festival Theatre and racing breaks at Glorious Goodwood are also popular.
Families are well catered for; under-16s stay free in their parents' room;
informal eating in the Waterbeach Grill. No dogs. Free parking for 300
cars. Country Club Hotels. *Rooms 88. Garden, indoor swimming pool, sauna,
solarium, spa bath, beauty salons, snooker, tennis, squash, keep-fit equipment,
beauty salon, 18-hole golf course, driving range, golf shop, coffee shop
(9.30am-10pm).* AMERICAN EXPRESS® *Access, Diners, Visa.*

Goodwood Places of Interest

Goodwood House Tel 0243 774107.
Goodwood Racecourse Tel 0243 774107.

Gordano Forte Travelodge £45

Tel 0275 373709 **L**

Gordano nr Portbury Avon BS20 9XG Map 13 E1

Seven miles from Bristol city centre at Junction 19 of the M5 motorway
in the Gordano service area. *Rooms 40.* AMERICAN EXPRESS® *Access,
Diners, Visa.*

Goring-on-Thames The Leatherne Bottel ↑ £70

Tel 0491 872667 **R**

Goring-on-Thames Berkshire RG8 0HS Map 15 D2

Signposted off the B4009 north of Goring, Keith Read and Annie Bonnet's
delightful establishment has just about everything going for it. A little row
of white-painted cottages stands on the edge of an unspoilt stretch of the
Thames with a large terrace for summer eating among the roses and herbs;
there's even an Edwardian launch (the *Natasha* – available for charter for
drinks or picnics). Inside the restaurant, the atmosphere is highly civilised
yet relaxed and informal with a log fire burning in the bar between two
dining rooms which boast some glorious floral displays courtesy of Annie.
Keith's philosophy in the kitchen is to use the freshest possible ingredients
with the main component of dishes simply cooked and served with virgin
olive oil dressings, rather than sauces, that are profligate in their use
of spices and home-grown herbs – baby squid pan-fried crisp with lemon
grass, sesame seeds, home-grown chickweed and red chili and herb

vinaigrette; long-braised shoulder of lamb with white beans, tomatoes, rosemary and garlic with roast black pudding; salmon roasted with ginger accompanied by wild garlic leaves and nori seaweed. Main courses come with either locally grown vegetables, 'greens' (Keith's very fond of curly kale) or a salad that will contain upwards of 20 different leaves. The menu is individually priced and at lunchtime (Mon-Fri) they are happy to serve just a single dish. There's a variety of good home-made breads (white, granary, spinach and walnut, tomato and black olive) and fine British and Irish cheeses. Plenty of good drinking under £20 on the concise wine list. No half bottles, though within reason most wines can be served by the glass or more – you pay for what you consume. *Seats 60. Parties 8. Private Room 12. L 12.15-2 (Sat & Sun to 2.30) D 7.15-9 (Sat to 9.30). Closed 25 Dec.* AMERICAN EXPRESS *Access, Visa.*

Goudhurst	**Star & Eagle Inn**	**£45**
Tel 0580 211512		**I**
High Street Goudhurst Kent TN17 1AL		**Map 11 B5**

The bedrooms at this gabled 14th-century inn come in all shapes and sizes, and one sports a restored four-poster bed. In the public areas period appeal survives in exposed beams, open brick fireplaces and old settles. No dogs. This Whitbread hotel stands less than two miles from the A21. *Rooms 11. Garden.* AMERICAN EXPRESS *Access, Visa.*

Goudhurst	**Place of Interest**	
Bedgebury National Pinetum Tel 0580 211044.		

Grantham	**Forte Travelodge**	**£45**
Tel 0476 77500		**L**
Grantham Service Area Gonerby Moor Grantham Lincolnshire NG32 2AB		**Map 7 E3**

At the Welcome Break service area on the A1 – 4 miles north of Grantham, 10 miles south of Newark-on-Trent. *Rooms 40.* AMERICAN EXPRESS *Access, Diners, Visa.*

Grantham	**Granada Lodge**	**£39**
Tel 0476 860686 Fax 0476 861078		**L**
A1/A151 Colsterworth Grantham Lincolnshire NG33 5JR		**Map 7 E3**

Rooms 38. AMERICAN EXPRESS *Access, Diners, Visa.*

Grantham	**Swallow Hotel**	**67%**	**NEW**	**£98**
Tel 0476 593000 Fax 0476 592592				**H**
Swingbridge Road Grantham Lincolnshire NG31 7XT				**Map 7 E3**

A modern low-rise hotel on the Grantham side of the junction of the A1 with the A607 to Melton Mowbray; it features good-sized, smart bedrooms and a comprehensively-equipped leisure centre. *Rooms 90. Patio, indoor swimming pool, children's splash pool, sauna, steam room, spa bath, solarium.* AMERICAN EXPRESS *Access, Diners, Visa.*

Grasmere	**Michael's Nook**	**79%**	**£170***
Tel 053 94 35496 Fax 053 94 35765			**HR**
Grasmere nr Ambleside Cumbria LA22 9RP			**Map 4 C3**

Originally built as a summer home and named in remembrance of the humble home of the shepherd in Wordsworth's poem, this grand Victorian house stands a short distance back off the A591 surrounded by three acres of landscaped gardens and ten acres of woodland. Reg Gifford, the owner, opened it as a hotel in 1969 and since then it has firmly established itself as one of the premier country house hotels in the Lake District. The doorbell is rung to gain admittance into a beautiful entrance hall which is typical of the gracious and supremely comfortable day rooms. An Oriental carpet on the polished parquet floor, antiques, a ticking grandfather clock, potted plants and fresh flowers create an immediate sense of well-being. The drawing room, approached through double doors, is also immensely impressive, the flower arrangements arrestingly beautiful. Decor is classically elegant, with deep-cushioned settees and armchairs in which to relax. The bar, sometimes also visited by Reg's Great Danes Lucifer and Oberon, has a delightful farmhouse ambience with its china-filled antique Welsh dresser and polished oak tables and chairs. Log fires warm the bar and drawing room in inclement weather. A fine balustrade staircase leads up to the bedrooms which, again, are very traditional in character and decor. Exquisite satinwood suites grace some rooms and the original furniture has been restored in one room with mahogany, oak and even Chinese lacquer in others, together with a whole host of extras making for very comfortable rooms. Three de luxe and superior rooms on the second floor are approached by steps from the garden behind the house. Beautiful bathrooms have thick towels, flannels, bathrobes and a range of Floris toiletries. Guests can use the keep-fit facilities, sauna and solarium at the sister hotel, the *Wordsworth*. There's also free golf Mon-Fri at Keswick. No dogs. ★Half-board terms only. ***Rooms*** *14. Garden, croquet.* AMERICAN EXPRESS *Access, Diners, Visa.*

Restaurant ★ ↑ £100

Orders and pre-dinner drinks are dealt with in the charming, cosy bar with dinner taken in one of the two splendid dining rooms. The first room has a striking decor of red gloss walls, gilt-framed mirrors and a crystal chandelier. The oak room is grander with fine oak-panelled walls. Highly polished antique mahogany tables, crystal glassware and gleaming silver create an ambience of relaxed but traditional formality. Kevin Mangeolles' cooking reflects the high quality and painstaking attention to detail exhibited in the decor and upkeep. Dinner is a £46 six-course no-choice gourmet menu or a £38 well-balanced five-course 'recommended' menu. Kevin's base is traditional English, his influences modern, his inspiration international, the results of which are dishes of great appeal and finely judged combinations of texture and flavour: crab and artichoke salad served on a cucumber galette with a saffron dressing; creamed swede and bacon soup garnished with garlic croutons; escalope of salmon filled with a salmon mousse and wild mushrooms; braised boneless oxtail topped with foie gras garnished with Maxim potatoes, salsify and a Madeira sauce. Desserts are no less alluring and no less accomplished, as shown by a millefeuille of banana parfait layered with chocolate discs and a coffee caramel sauce. Classy and comprehensive wine list with a super selection of half bottles; New World wines make a good showing and probably represent the best value. No smoking. ***Seats*** *28. Private Room 40. L 12.30 for 1 D 7.30 for 8. Set L £27.50 Set D £38/£46.*

Grasmere	The Swan	65%	£138★
Tel 053 94 35551 Fax 053 94 35741			H
Grasmere nr Ambleside Cumbria LA22 9RF			Map 4 C3

The inn-like public areas, with their carved furniture, horse brasses, copper jugs and pewter, are little changed since Wordsworth mentioned The Swan in his poem *The Waggoner*. By contrast, the bedrooms, many with views of the surrounding fells, offer more up-to-date comfort; half-tester beds in five feature rooms (with views); eight courtyard rooms attract partial views and a reduced rate. After wet days walkers will appreciate the Drying Room – the Swan attracts more tourist than business trade. Forte Heritage. ★Half-board terms only. ***Rooms*** *36. Garden.* AMERICAN EXPRESS *Access, Diners, Visa.*

Grasmere   White Moss House   69%   £128*

Tel 053 94 35295   **HR**

Rydal Water Grasmere Cumbria LA22 9SE   Map 4 C3

Sue and Peter Dixon are always cooking, serving or greeting guests at their tiny Lakeland hotel, built in 1730 and once owned by William Wordsworth. It's a very quiet, intimate place, very popular with walkers, and the views over Rydal Water from its wooded hillside location are another bonus. Bedrooms in the main house are full of antique pieces, and Susan Dixon's homely touches abound. Above the hotel, the hideaway Brockstone Cottage has two bedrooms (one a four-poster) and a kitchen. Good breakfasts extend to kippers, Cumberland sausage and black pudding. Guests have free use of a nearby leisure club. *Half-board terms only. No dogs. **Rooms** 6. Garden, game fishing. Closed Dec-Feb. Access, Visa.*

Restaurant   £60

The availability of seats for non-residents is very limited, so booking is essential for Peter Dixon's splendid five-course dinners served at 8 in a little cottage-style room. His meal is always well planned and executed, with no choice except at the dessert stage. A typical dinner might start with broccoli and basil soup, continue with a soufflé of smoked haddock and halibut with Westmorland smoked cheese, and centre on roast Lakeland mallard with sage and onion stuffing and a damson, port and pinot noir sauce. Next comes a choice of three desserts, usually including something traditional like Mrs Beeton's chocolate pudding, then some first-rate British cheeses (the choice runs to about a dozen). There's plenty of value on the wine list, which is a nice blend of old and mature vintages, and the New World, the latter presented by grape variety. Many halves. No smoking. *Seats 18. Parties 8. D only 7.30 for 8. Closed Sun. Set D £27.50.*

Grasmere   Wordsworth Hotel   72%   £124

Tel 053 94 35592   Fax 053 94 35765   **HR**

Grasmere nr Ambleside Cumbria LA22 9SW   Map 4 C3

The hotel stands in two peaceful acres located in Grasmere village, next to the churchyard where Wordsworth is buried. The conservatory bar and adjacent lounge have bold floral fabrics, some cane seating and the best of the views. There's also a pub – the Dove and Olive Branch – and a leisure centre whose swimming pool opens on to a sun-trap terrace. Individually decorated bedrooms vary widely in size and aspect; the best are two suites with whirlpool baths and an antique-furnished four-poster room. Many rooms are suitable for family use, and baby-sitting and baby-listening are available; there's also a children's menu. Free golf at Keswick mid-week. **Rooms** 37. Garden, indoor swimming pool, keep-fit equipment, sauna, spa bath, solarium, games room. AMERICAN EXPRESS Access, Diners, Visa.

Prelude Restaurant   £75

There's a traditional feel to the dining room but many of the variations on Bernard Warne's menus have a modern ring: grilled scallop and sole sausage rolled in brioche with creamed leek, kebabs of fresh and smoked salmon with a stir-fry of vegetables, parcel of prime beef fillet with a Stilton duxelles set on Anna potatoes and served with wild mushroom consommé. Other dishes are more traditional, particularly on the Sunday luncheon menu, and desserts such as apple and sultana pie or iced ginger parfait on a duet of orange and chocolate sauces are alternatives to the fine British cheeses. No-nonsense easy-to-use wine list with plenty of bottles (over half the list, including most of the New World) under £20. *Seats 75. L 12.30-2 D 7-9 (Fri & Sat to 9.30). Set L £18.50 (Sun £13.50) Set D from £29.50.*

Grasmere   Place of Interest

Dove Cottage and Wordsworth Museum   Tel 05394 35544.

Grayshott   Woods Place   £50
Tel & Fax 0428 605555   R
Headley Road Grayshott nr Hindhead Surrey GU26 6LB   Map 11 A6

Continental cuisine with Swedish specialities is the attraction at Dana and
Eric Norrgren's former butcher's shop in a village just off the A3 south
of Hindhead. Homely cooking encompasses a range of hearty, relatively
uncomplicated dishes: gravlax (try it with a glass of ice-cold akvavit), fresh
and smoked salmon burger, prawn-stuffed sole with saffron sauce, saddle
of hare in a juniper-scented cream and pheasant breast with a creamy sauce
and walnuts show the style. Leave room for upside-down apple tart
or pancakes with blueberry ice cream. *Seats 36. Parties 16. L 12-2.30
D 7-12. Closed Sun & Mon.* AMERICANEXPRESS *Access, Diners, Visa.*

Great Ayton   Ayton Hall   70%   £85
Tel 0642 723595   Fax 0642 722149   H
Low Green Great Ayton nr Middlesbrough North Yorkshire TS9 6PW   Map 5 E3

Approached down a narrow tree-lined avenue, the Hall, a Grade II listed
building, stands in six acres of mature grounds. The entrance hall is also the
bar. It is dark and intimate, with red velour upholstered Gothic-style high-
back chairs around the curved walls. The drawing room is charming with
its very traditional furnishings and a baby grand in one corner. In the
dining room there's a steadily growing collection of some 500
commemorative plates adorning the walls. Bedrooms on the first floor are
named after James Cook's ships, following his association with the place,
while on the next floor bedrooms have Maori names. All are of good size
and are well equipped. Sherry, fresh fruit and mineral water are among the
pampering extras. The second-floor rooms also have a cosy atmosphere
created by the sloping ceilings, pickled pine furniture and brass bedsteads.
Carpeted bathrooms are neat, with shower facilities due to be added
shortly. *Rooms 9. Garden, croquet.* AMERICANEXPRESS *Access, Diners, Visa.*

Great Baddow   Pontlands Park   70%   £135
Tel 0245 476444   Fax 0245 478393   H
West Hanningfield Road Great Baddow nr Chelmsford Essex CM2 8HR   Map 11 B4

An extended mid-Victorian hotel with an attractive health and leisure
centre. Bedrooms in the wing are huge, with high ceilings, separate sitting
areas, large beds, quality reproduction furniture and bright, stylish fabrics.
Rooms in the main house are similar but smaller; all bathrooms boast
bidets, high-class toiletries and good carpeting and decor. Public areas
include a marble-effect entrance hall, a comfortable bar, an elegant lounge
and a bright little garden coffee shop with lots of plants and Lloyd Loom
chairs. Dogs in kennels only. Children not allowed in health centre during
members' hours. 10% service charge is added to all accommodation, food
and bar final bills (included in the room rate above). *Rooms 17. Garden,
indoor & outdoor swimming pools, sauna, spa bath, solarium, keep-fit equipment,
beauty & hair salons, dance studio, coffee shop (12-2, 7-9), helipad.
Closed 24-30 Dec.* AMERICANEXPRESS *Access, Diners, Visa.*

Great Baddow   Places of Interest
Hyde Hall Garden   Rettendon Tel 0245 400256.
Chelmsford Cathedral   Tel 0245 263660.
Essex County Cricket Ground (Chelmsford)   Tel 0245 252420.
Riverside Ice and Leisure Centre   Tel 0245 269417.
Great Leighs Showground   Tel 0245 361259.

Great Dunmow   Saracen's Head   58%   £97

Tel 0371 873901   Fax 0371 875743   **H**
High Street Great Dunmow Essex CM6 1AG   Map 10 B3

Forte hotel blending Tudor and Georgian architectural features with
a modern wing of bedrooms. Banqueting and conference facilities for
around 50. Families with children well catered for, with baby-sitting and
listening available. Ten minutes drive from Junction 8 of the M11.
Rooms 24. AMERICAN EXPRESS *Access, Diners, Visa.*

Great Dunmow   The Starr   £75

Tel 0371 874321   Fax 0371 876337   **RR**
Market Place Great Dunmow Essex CM6 1AX   Map 10 B3

The Starr is a small restaurant housed in a 400-year-old timber-framed
hostelry building overlooking Great Dunmow's market place and has been
run by Brian and Vanessa Jones since 1980. London markets and local
sources supply the raw materials for Mark Fisher's careful hand: steamed
mussels with apples and cider, crab bisque, wing of skate with butter and
capers, pithiviers of duck livers, quail wrapped in pastry with port sauce
and mushrooms, peppered loin of venison with cognac and cream are all
typical dishes. Menus are entitled starters & light luncheons (weekdays), à la
carte main courses, supper and dinner, so there's a wide choice on offer. Fish
features strongly and Sunday lunches are always popular. Great thought has
gone into the fine wine list, which has many attractions – not least
of which is value for money; plenty of half bottles and informative helpful
notes. No smoking. **Seats** 50. *Private Rooms* 36. L 12-1.30 D 7-9.30.
*Closed L Sat, D Sun, 1st week Jan. Set L £15 (Sun £21.50) Set D £21.50,
£32.50 & £35.* AMERICAN EXPRESS *Access, Visa.* **MARTELL**

Rooms   £75

Eight en-suite bedrooms, with names like the Oak Room, the Brass Room
and the Poppy Room, are in the old stable block and individually
furnished, mainly with antiques. The Oak Room and Pine Room are
superior; all rooms are non-smoking. Special weekend rates. Only "good"
dogs are welcome. Parking in the rear courtyard. 15 minutes from
Stanstead Airport. *Rooms closed 1 week Jan.*

Great Dunmow   Place of Interest

Saling Hall Garden   Great Saling Tel 0371 850141.

Great Gonerby   Harry's Place   ★   £95

Tel 0476 61780   **R**
17 High Street Great Gonerby nr Grantham Lincolnshire NG31 8JS   Map 7 E3

An elegant, double-fronted village-centre Georgian house is both home and
workplace to Harry and Caroline Hallam. With only three tables the
restaurant has all the charm and intimacy of a gracious, yet relaxed and
informal, country dining room. Deep salmon-pink walls, varnished
stripped-pine doors and tables, fresh flowers and innumerable pretty
ornaments and wall hangings create a beautiful and comfortable setting
enhanced by candle-light and the soft illuminations of four table lamps, the
latter arranged on side furniture. The menu changes according to supplies
and is short, only two choices per course, but is prepared with an eye for
detail resulting in food that is both visually delightful and sensational
on the palate. Raw materials, from herbs to meat and game – perhaps
Lincolnshire grey partridge, Yorkshire grouse or salt marsh teal – fish,
poultry and even the cheeses (try the Colston Bassett blue Stilton) are
purchased from top suppliers to ensure the best textures and flavours. Both
of these are combined with immense skill as in a very fine pastry tartlet
filled with a layer of soft, almost creamy sweetcorn topped by a lightly

poached egg and gratinated chive hollandaise made with a reduction of sherry vinegar and black pepper. Main courses could be a fillet of Scottish turbot sautéed with olive oil, lemon juice, with wine, Pernod, rosemary and fennel or a filleted loin of baby roe deer roasted to an almost melting pink tenderness. "Usually no children under 5" to spoil the unique atmosphere. No smoking. *Seats 10. L 12.30-2 D 7-9.30. Closed Sun & Mon (except by prior arrangement), 25 & 26 Dec, Bank Holidays. Access, Visa.*

Great Milton	Le Manoir aux Quat'Saisons	86%	£194

Tel 0844 278881   Fax 0844 278847 **HR**

Church Road Great Milton Oxfordshire OX44 7PD   Map 15 D2

Now you see it, now you don't! The continuing saga of whether the hotel should be allowed to display a sign in a field indicating its presence just before (from London) Junction 7 of the M40 (from Birmingham, leave at Junction 8) could only happen in this country. We should be shouting from the rooftops that Raymond Blanc's country house hotel and restaurant is one of the finest in the UK, and that it has just celebrated its tenth anniversary. The recent announcement that Richard Branson's *Virgin* empire has taken a 50% stake in the operation changes nothing – in fact it's more a guarantee that standards will be maintained and improved. The 15th-century manor house stands in beautifully tended landscaped gardens (note the sculptured bronzes exhibited in the herb garden and watery spots) and inside it's a model of refined elegance. The flagstoned entrance hall leads into luxurious and comfortable lounges that are immaculately furnished with antiques, fine paintings and splendid flower arrangements and warmed in winter by open fires. The theme continues in the individually decorated bedrooms, which provide every conceivable luxury, from a decanter of Madeira to a bowl of fresh fruit. Several garden-wing rooms have their own private terrace with wrought-iron patio furniture, while the medieval dovecote has been converted into a romantic honeymoon suite. There are jacuzzi and whirlpool baths in the magnificent bathrooms, not to mention huge towels, generous bathrobes and exquisite toiletries. Of course, all this would be wasted without service and excellent housekeeping to match, and this, under the direction of new General Manager Simon Rhatigan, proceeds smoothly and efficiently. Breakfasts, naturally, are quite delicious. Small conferences (40). Dogs in kennels. **Rooms** *19. Garden, croquet, tennis, outdoor swimming pool, limousine, helipad.* AMERICAN EXPRESS *Access, Diners, Visa.* MARTELL

Restaurant   ★ ★ ★   £195

Self-taught Raymond Blanc has come a long way since he first opened his own restaurant in Summertown, Oxford. His accolades are displayed in the hotel's foyer for everyone to see, and with his TV series, cook books and cookery school *Le Petit Blanc* (courses run by long-serving head chef Clive Fretwell), you wonder where the man gets his energy from. Quite simply, he is a genius, his cooking both creative and technically superb. He can't do it alone, and doesn't, assisted as he is by Clive and the brigade, so the kitchen is always in safe hands, as is the restaurant itself (in fact three very different dining areas), under the guidance of Alain Desenclos. One of the dining rooms is a large conservatory (smoking allowed here) with good air-conditioning, cane chairs and a pink and green colour scheme, and lovely floral arrangements. The grounds and three-acre kitchen garden provide most of the quality produce used – whether it's organic herbs, vegetables, or fruits – and head gardener Anne-Marie Owens gets a well-deserved mention on the menu. The style has changed little through the years – it has evolved, but still with the lightest of touches, perhaps with more influences from the Far East than before, adding exotic flavours to sound cooking practices. The seasonal menus are written in French with English translations; a three-course *menu du jour* offers two choices in each section, following an appetiser; perhaps pressed terrine of duck with foie gras and lentils, grilled fillet of John Dory in a light chicken jus with rosemary, and a William pear charlotte on a raspberry coulis. Or your table

could be tempted by the eight-course *menu gourmand* (a snip at £65!).
Seriously, this offers you the chance of sampling a selection of specialities
(without having to make up your mind), among which you might
be served a charlotte of aubergines and sweet peppers; quail's eggs, spinach,
Parmesan and black Périgord truffle ravioli; grilled fillet of brill; roasted
corn-fed Bresse pigeon; ending with three tasting desserts, including,
if you're lucky, an orange parfait wrapped in a fine nougatine box. Push the
boat out further and choose à la carte, say, roasted medallion of sea bass
filled with langoustines or scallops on a bed of fennel, olive and cardamom
sauce, or roasted best end of Highgrove (guess where it comes from?) lamb
with pan-fried sweetbreads, kidneys and liver. Desserts (try *Le Café Crème*)
and farmhouse cheeses, from both France and Great Britain, are a delight,
petits fours and chocolates mini-masterpieces. The wine list is a serious
tome, with bucketfuls of fine French wines, but also an excellent showing
from elsewhere, including a splendid selection of the best that the New
World has to offer. Good to see many lesser-known and value-for-money
French country wines on the list too. **Seats** *95. Parties 12.*
Private Room 46/62. L 12.15-2.15 (Sun 2.30) D 7.15-10.15. Set L £29.50
(not Sun) D £65.

Great Snoring	Old Rectory	61%	£87
Tel 0328 820597 Fax 0328 820048			**H**
Barsham Road Great Snoring nr Fakenham Norfolk NR21 0HP			Map 10 C1

Behind the church on the Barsham road, the Old Rectory retains some
pleasing architectural features, including stone-mullioned windows
bordered by frieze tiles. Day rooms are peaceful and old-fashioned and
there are some fine period furnishings in the handsomely proportioned
bedrooms. The Shelton Suites, brick-and-flint self-catering cottages in the
grounds, offer a greater degree of privacy and seclusion, each having its
own living room and kitchen; servicing and breakfast provisions are
provided daily. No children under 8 in the main house, although families
with babes in arms may find the cottages a wonderfully relaxing country
retreat. Six miles from the Norfolk coast. No dogs. **Rooms** *6. Garden.*
Closed 24-27 Dec. AMERICAN EXPRESS *Diners.*

Great Yarmouth	Carlton Hotel	67%	£79
Tel 0493 855234 Fax 0493 852220			**H**
Marine Parade Great Yarmouth Norfolk NR30 3JE			Map 10 D1

The Carlton has a fine seafront location directly opposite Wellington Pier.
The hotel's impressive interior houses conference facilities for up to 150.
Bonuses for individual guests include Penny's café-bar (offering a weekday
happy hour and a modern brasserie menu encompassing Tex-Mex) and
a hair salon. Bedrooms have bright colour schemes and smart tiled
bathrooms. Children up to 12 free in parents' room; families are well
catered for, with baby-sitting by arrangement and high-chairs for junior
diners. Covered parking for 20 cars. Free admission to a nearby leisure
centre. **Rooms** *95.* AMERICAN EXPRESS *Access, Diners, Visa.*

Great Yarmouth	Seafood Restaurant		£55
Tel 0493 856009			**R**
85 North Quay Great Yarmouth Norfolk NR30 1JF			Map 10 D1

Chris and Miriam Kikis have been running this friendly little restaurant
since 1979 and have built up a loyal following. It's actually housed
in a converted railway station and can be a little difficult for first-timers
to find, so ask for directions when booking (which is advised). Fresh fish
and seafood are the order of the day here – the mixed platter is always
popular, as are the other variations of giant prawns, crayfish, scampi,
scallops, squid, oysters, whitebait, plaice, cod, brill....There are steaks for
those who must; and the wine list accommodates most palates and pockets.
There's an unusual still wine from Champagne, Ruinart Chardonnay –

at a hefty £39.50. *Seats 40. L 12-1.45 D 7-10.30. Closed L Sat, all Sun, Bank Holidays (open Good Friday), 3 weeks Christmas.* AMERICAN EXPRESS *Access, Diners, Visa.*

Great Yarmouth   Places of Interest

Tourist Information   Tel 0493 846345.
Britannia Theatre   Tel 0493 842914.
Royalty Theatre   Tel 0493 842043.
Great Yarmouth Racecourse   Tel 0493 842527.
Thrigby Hall Wildlife Park and Gardens   Tel 0493 369477.

Greta Bridge	Morritt Arms	£68
Tel 0833 627232 Fax 0833 627392		**I**
Greta Bridge nr Barnard Castle Durham DL12 9SE		Map 5 D3

An old coaching inn, which enjoys a picturesque location appropriate to its characterful interior. The lounge bar is comfortable and old-fashioned, with groups of easy chairs, an antique barrel organ and a miniature traction engine, while the famous Dickens Bar depicts various characters from the novels in striking Gilroy murals. Bedrooms, some of which have fine views, are quaint and homely. New owners took over just as we went to press. *Rooms 17. Garden, children's playground.* AMERICAN EXPRESS *Access, Diners, Visa.*

Grimsby	Forte Posthouse	64%	£68
Tel 0472 350295 Fax 0472 241354			**H**
Littlecoates Road Grimsby Humberside DN34 4LX			Map 7 F1

Friendly and peaceful late-60s' hotel on the outskirts of town, overlooking a golf course. Business-oriented in the week (catering for conferences of up to 250 delegates), popular with families at weekends. Half the bedrooms are designated non-smoking. Formerly a Forte Crest. *Rooms 52.* AMERICAN EXPRESS *Access, Diners, Visa.*

Grimsby   Places of Interest

Tourist Information   Tel 0472 240180.
Leisure Centre Ice Rink   Tel 0472 242000.
Animal Gardens Mablethorpe   Tel 05074 73346.

Grimston	Congham Hall	75%	£110
Tel 0485 600250 Fax 0485 601191			**HR**
Lynn Road Grimston King's Lynn Norfolk PE32 1AH			Map 10 B1

A cricket ground (where the village team play most weekends in summer), orchards and Christine Forecast's renowned herb garden (over 400 varieties with 100 available 'potted-up' for sale) are all included in the 40 acres of peaceful parkland that surround this Georgian house a few miles east of King's Lynn. Civilised day rooms with sunny yellow decor are full of flowers and the air is heavy with pot pourri. Both the latter are also to be found in bedrooms, which vary considerably from some with inexpensive units, via pine and rattan and wicker pieces to some with antiques. The common decoration theme is of stylish matching fabrics set off against plain walls and all get comforts like books, magazines, apples from the orchard and bowls of sweets. Some bathrooms are relatively functional (although all get robes, generous towelling and good toiletries); others, like those in the best rooms in a recent extension, feel more luxurious and have good power showers over the tubs. There are two full suites, including the splendid, split-level Garden Suite. Personally run by the hospitable Forecasts with a team of friendly staff. No children under

12. Dogs in kennels only. **Rooms** *14. Garden, croquet, tennis, outdoor swimming pool, spa bath, cricket, helipad.* AMERICAN EXPRESS *Access, Diners, Visa.*

MARTELL

Orangery Restaurant £85

Pastoral views and a plant-fringed skylight make this a summery room, with peach-coloured walls and rattan chairs and elegantly laid tables. Several different fixed-price menus are offered at night – one of three courses (choice of three dishes at each stage), one of four courses (half a dozen choices) and the seven course Hobson's Choice menu which must be taken by the whole table. Between them they offer a wide selection of inventive dishes often reflecting the modern idiom. Confit of rabbit with grilled aubergine and pesto, salade niçoise with fresh sautéed tuna, marinated red mullet with saffron marmalade and tapénade croutons, and braised oxtail with a parsnip and potato purée show the range. Most of the vegetables come from their own kitchen garden in their season but herbs are less in evidence than one might expect. No children under 12. No smoking. **Seats** *50. Parties 8. Private Room 18. L 12.30-2 D 7.30-9.30. Closed L Sat. Set L £15 Set D £21.50-£36.*

Grindleford   **Maynard Arms**   £60

Tel 0433 630321 Fax 0433 630445	■
Main Road Grindleford Derbyshire S30 1HP	Map 6 C2

A solid-stone roadside inn located in the Peak National Park on a hillside outside the village. Public rooms include a spacious and attractive public bar – The Longshaw. The cocktail bar is equally smart with its deep green velour upholstery. Bedrooms, some with secondary glazing to help with heat retention in winter, are cottagey in style with pretty fabrics and old-fashioned furniture. Two have four-posters and all have a good selection of extras including remote TV, trouser press, hairdryer and radio-alarm. Bathrooms have gleaming dark blue wall tiling; three sport corner baths. **Rooms** *13.* AMERICAN EXPRESS *Access, Diners, Visa.*

Grizedale   **Grizedale Lodge**   61%   £70

Tel 05394 36532 Fax 05394 36572	HR
Grizedale nr Hawkshead Cumbria LA22 0QL	Map 4 C4

Jack and Margaret Lamb's hidden hotel, small and homely, welcomes so many annual returnees that you'll need to book well in advance. Comfortable rewards are found in the roomy lounge, cheery bar and spick-and-span cottage-style bedrooms; two rooms are in an extension; one is a family room with a double and two single beds; two have four-posters. No smoking. No dogs, but there are kennels nearby. Follow the Tourist Board signs from Hawkshead or Newby Bridge for Grizedale Forest Park and the Theatre in the Forest. **Rooms** *9. Garden. Closed 2 Jan-10 Feb. Access, Visa.*

Restaurant in the Forest £45

Margaret's home-style cooking is based on excellent local supplies, including Esthwaite trout and venison from the Forestry Commission. Farmhouse terrine, crisply roasted Derwentwater duckling and pork cooked with lemon and lime are typical dishes which are big in flavours and generous in serving. Home-made fudge accompanies coffee. No smoking. Monday lunch is limited to bar snacks. **Seats** *30. L 12.15-1.45 D 7-8.30 (Sun at 7). Set D £16.95.*

Guildford   **The Angel**   71%   £105

Tel 0483 64555 Fax 0483 33770	H
91 High Street Guildford Surrey GU1 3DP	Map 15 E3

In the centre of town, halfway up the steep pedestrianised High Street on the left, the Angel has a long and distinguished history on a site dating back as far as the 13th century. Nine of the eleven bedrooms are full suites and all are furnished to a high standard with reproduction antique furniture and a variety of stylish fabrics with bedhead drapes and quilted covers. Marble bathrooms boast large soft towels and bathrobes. The only day room is a small galleried lounge with ancient redbrick inglenook fireplace, old black timbers, a 17th-century parliament clock and deep, comfortable settees and armchairs, where drinks are served to residents and diners only. Beds are turned down in the evenings and excellent breakfasts (cooked to order from 7 to 11) are served in the cosy, wood-panelled Oak Room. Limited parking for residents behind the hotel, approached via Angel Gate off North Street. *Rooms 11.* AMERICAN EXPRESS *Access, Diners, Visa.*

Guildford	Forte Crest	68%	£119
Tel 0483 574444 Fax 0483 302960			**H**
Egerton Road Guildford Surrey GU2 5XZ			Map 15 E3

Darkwood panelling and a white marble fireplace lend a very civilised air to the public areas at this smart modern hotel on the outskirts of town (follow signs for Cathedral/University then the Surrey Research Park). It's very much geared-up to the requirements of business travellers and there are conference facilities for up to 120 delegates. Comprehensive 24hr room service. Children up to 16 stay free in parents' room. Considerable tariff reductions Fri & Sat. Hard by the A3 northbound. *Rooms 111. Garden, indoor swimming pool, gym, sauna, solarium.* AMERICAN EXPRESS *Access, Diners, Visa.*

Guildford	Mandarin	£35
Tel 0483 572293		**R**
13 Epsom Road Guildford Surrey GU1 3JT		Map 15 E3

Modern, cool decor with black lacquered chairs and spotlit tables add up to a quietly chic ambience in a friendly restaurant at the top of the town (opposite the Odeon cinema). Cooking covers Szechuan and Cantonese styles with both outstanding crispy aromatic duck and unusual deep-fried quail showing flair in the kitchen. Mongolian lamb and beef are filling hot pot dishes. No children under 5. *Seats 55. L 12.30-2.30 D 6-10.45. Closed L Sun, all 24-26 Dec. Set D from £17.50.* AMERICAN EXPRESS *Access, Diners, Visa.*

Guildford   Places of Interest

Tourist Information   Tel 0483 444007.
Yvonne Arnaud Theatre   Millbrook Tel 0483 64571.
Guildford Cathedral   Tel 0483 65287.
Woodbridge Road Cricket Ground   Tel 0483 572181.
Combined Services Polo Committee   Pirbright Tel 0483 798449.
Stoke Park Showground   Tel 0483 414651.
    Historic Houses, Castles and Gardens
Clandon Park and Garden (NT)   Tel 0483 222482.
Coverwood Lakes   Ewhurst Tel 0306 731103.
Hatchlands Park House and Gardens (NT)   East Clandon Tel 0483 222787.
Loseley House   Tel 0483 304440.
Wisley Garden   (The Royal Horticultural Society) Wisley Tel 0938 224234.
    Museums and Art Galleries
British Red Cross Museum and Archives   Barnett Hill, Wonersh. Tel 0483 898595.
Gallery 90   Ward Street Tel 0483 444741.
Guildford Museum   Tel 0483 444750.

Guiseley   Prachee   £45
Tel 0943 872531   **R**
6 Bradford Road Whitecross Guiseley West Yorkshire LS20 8NH   **Map 6 C1**

At a major intersection just to the north of the town centre this Indian
restaurant has smart decor and an extensive menu featuring a good number
of set meals as well as à la carte dishes. All is very carefully prepared and
highly enjoyable with clear spicing and particularly good bread. *Seats 56.
Parties 25. L 12-2 D 6-12. Closed 25 & 26 Dec. Access, Visa.*

Gulworthy   The Horn of Plenty   ★   £100
Tel & Fax 0822 832528   **RR**
Gulworthy nr Tavistock Devon PL19 8JD   **Map 12 C3**

Signposted off the A390 to the west of Tavistock, the 200-year-old house
stands in four acres of gardens and orchards. The welcome from Elaine and
Ian Gatehouse is warm and friendly, and new windows in the restaurant
give even better views of the Tamar Valley. The well-balanced fixed-price
menus are the responsibility of Peter Gorton, whose recent spell with
Robuchon in Paris has added new ideas and technique to his repertoire, and
of his new sous chef Kevin Bingham. Cream of fennel soup with herb
croutons, tempura fried sole with a Thai sauce and warm salad
of marinated duck with French beans and asparagus show the range
of starters, while main courses could include pan-fried sea bass on a bed
of braised leeks served with a sweet and sour sauce, breast of chicken filled
with calf's sweetbreads and pearl barley, or medallions of venison served
with apple compote and a black pepper cider sauce. Desserts remain a great
temptation – chocolate pavé with deep-fried grapes in champagne butter
is typical – and there's a selection of English and Continental cheeses. A new
pot luck menu (£17.50 three courses) has been a great success on Monday
nights. Pleasant, if unspectacular, wine list, quite reasonably priced. Mostly
French, but with a little New World. No children under 13. *Seats 48.
Private Room 12. L 12-2 D 7-9.30. Closed L Mon, 24-26 Dec. Set L £17.50
Set D £26.50.* AMERICAN EXPRESS *Access, Visa.*

Rooms   £92

Six of the seven pine-furnished bedrooms, each with its own balcony
overlooking the valley, are in the converted coach house. Direct-dial
phones, remote-control TVs and well-stocked mini-bars provide the
modern comforts. No children under 13. *Garden.*

Hackness   Hackness Grange   61%   £126
Tel 0723 882345   Fax 0723 882391   **H**
Hackness nr Scarborough North Yorkshire YO13 0JW   **Map 5 F3**

An attractive 19th-century house standing in its own grounds by the River
Derwent in the North York Moors National Park. Bedrooms are divided
between the main house and the courtyard. Free parking for 50 cars.
No dogs. *Rooms 28. Garden, croquet, indoor swimming pool, tennis, pitch and
putt, fishing.* AMERICAN EXPRESS *Access, Diners, Visa.*

Hadley Wood   West Lodge Park Hotel   66%   £112
Tel 081-440 8311   Fax 081-449 3698   **HR**
Cockfosters Road Hadley Wood nr Barnet Hertfordshire EN4 0PY   **Map 15 E2**

An extended 19th-century country house set in parkland that includes
an arboretum and a lake. Inside there's an orderly, civilised feel in the
lounge, plentifully supplied with armchairs, in the brick-walled bar and
in the four conference rooms (catering for up to 80 delegates). Bedrooms
are individually decorated and furnished, and the majority have small
entrance lobbies. The hotel is on the A111 halfway between the M25 (exit

24) and Cockfosters underground station. Free membership of, and taxi to, local leisure club. 24hr room service. Ample free parking. No dogs.
Rooms 45. *Garden, croquet, golf practice net, putting, bar billiards.*
AMERICAN EXPRESS *Access, Visa.*

Cedar Restaurant   £65

A split-level dining room furnished in a homely country style with pine furniture and pretty pink napery. Peter Leggat, now in his second year, produces daily-changing menus with a choice of one, two or three courses from a well-thought-out, varied selection of between 8 and 10 dishes for each course. There is a modern inflection to his style though it has to be said that conservative and traditional elements are very apparent, dictated by the tastes of the largely business and suburban clientele. The food is none the worse for this with noteworthy careful cooking. Anglesey mussel soup is a small bowl of plump, tender, shell-less molluscs in a fragrant, creamy broth while Gressingham duck is half the bird, crisply roasted and accompanied by shaped apple pieces in a light Calvados gravy. Other choices could be pork medallions with a wild mushroom sauce or Dover sole with herb butter (supplementary charge). Excellent, if slightly too cool, British cheeses are available as well as delicious sweets such as an 18th-century chocolate pie with coffee cream or Bowmans Farm ices. Friendly, old-fashioned service. **Seats** 75. *Parties* 24. *L* 12.30-2 *D* 7.15-9.45. *Set L £15/£17.50 (Sun £17.50) Set D £16.50/£19.50.*

Hagley   Travel Inn   £43
Tel 0562 883120   Fax 0562 884416   **L**
Birmingham Road Hagley nr Stourbridge West Midlands DY9 9JS   **Map 6 B4**

Birmingham City Centre 15 minutes' drive, Birmingham International Airport 20 minutes. **Rooms** 40. AMERICAN EXPRESS *Access, Diners, Visa.*

Hailey   The Bird in Hand   £55
Tel 0993 868321   Fax 0993 868702   **I**
Hailey nr Witney Oxfordshire OX8 5XP   **Map 14 C2**

A delightful "residential country inn" and popular eating pub in a rural setting surrounded by open fields, one mile north of Hailey on the B4022 between Witney and Charlbury. Sixteen spacious, cottage-style bedrooms (non-smoking) are in keeping with the original Cotswold-stone former coaching inn, in a U-shaped building on two storeys with wooden balconies, all overlooking an attractive grassed courtyard. Two twin-bedded, ground-floor rooms have facilities for disabled guests and a couple of large family rooms sleep up to five; matching floral fabrics, pine furnishings, thoughtful touches like full-length mirrors and cotton wool plus good housekeeping bring all rooms up to a good hotel standard. Light meals and a good pint can be enjoyed in the cosy stone-walled bar rooms (one of which features a fine inglenook) and on picnic tables outside on the patio and in the walled front garden. Residential weekday conferences are popular, with the Windrush dining room doubling as a conference room (for up to 35, theatre-style). **Rooms** 16. *Garden. Closed Christmas week.* *Access, Visa.*

Halifax   Holdsworth House   69%   £90
Tel 0422 240024   Fax 0422 245174   **H**
Holdsworth nr Halifax West Yorkshire HX2 9TG   **Map 6 C1**

Three miles north of Halifax stands a 17th-century manor house which the Pearson family have turned into a really charming hotel. Period appeal remains in the day rooms, notably the three handsome oak-panelled rooms that make up the restaurant. The entrance hall also features polished panelling, and the lounge opens on to an attractive courtyard. The best bedrooms are four split-level suites and the rest are both neat and comfortable with colourful fabrics and mainly period furniture. Two rooms specially adapted for disabled guests. Good facilities for children (under-10s free in parents' room). Characterful meeting rooms hold up to 100. **Rooms** 40. Garden. Closed Christmas/New Year. AMERICAN EXPRESS® Access, Diners, Visa.

Halifax   Places of Interest

Tourist Information   Tel 0422 368725.
Piece Hall   Tel 0422 58087.
Playhouse   Kings Cross Street Tel 0422 365998.
Toulston Polo Club   Bowers Hall, Barkisland Tel 0422 372529.
Sportsman Leisure Dry Ski Slope   Swalesmoor Tel 0422 40760.
Halifax RLFC   Tel 0422 361026

If we recommend meals in a hotel or inn a separate entry is made for its restaurant.

Hambleton   Hambleton Hall   84%   £147

Tel 0572 756991   Fax 0572 724721   **HR**
Hambleton nr Oakham Leicestershire LE15 8TH   Map 7 E3

In the small village of Hambleton, which is on a peninsula jutting out into Rutland Water, the Victorian hall is well placed to enjoy some fine views of the surrounding countryside. Very much a country house in style it is professionally run by general manager Jeffrey Crocket and his charming staff, who provide a high standard of friendly, personal service. Day rooms like the refined drawing room with its happy blend of elegance and homely comfort, and the warm red bar with inglenook fireplace receive the finishing touch with Anne Taylor's artistic floral displays – something of an institution here. Fresh flowers also add to the appeal of bedrooms where fine fabrics, antiques, armchairs and sofas combine in stylish individual schemes. Creature comforts range from home-made biscuits, mineral water and portable radio to extra-large towelling robes and huge bathsheets in the luxurious bathrooms. Rooms are properly serviced in the evening with curtains drawn, beds turned down and fresh towels for the bathroom. **Rooms** 15. Garden, tennis, outdoor swimming pool, helipad. AMERICAN EXPRESS® Access, Visa.

Restaurant   ★★   £110

Aaron Patterson and his team of young turks in the kitchen here are not only seriously ambitious but have the talents to match. First-rate ingredients, the *sine qua non* of good cooking, include a plentiful supply of game from the surrounding countryside and produce from the hotel's own recently revitalised walled kitchen garden (they even grow their own peaches along with the blackcurrants that turn up in the breakfast jam) as well as the result of Aaron's early morning trips to Covent Garden. A complimentary taster – foie gras rolled in chopped truffles perhaps – sets up the taste buds for dishes such as oven-baked oysters scented with rosemary and Beluga caviar, ravioli of fresh langoustines in a light truffle sauce, roast Gressingham duck with baby beetroot and turnips and a jasmine tea sauce, Norfolk squab pigeon with roasted garlic and a Gewürztraminer sauce and hot pistachio soufflé with banana ice. The full à la carte is served both sessions as is the no-choice set menu of the day and dishes like locally farmed chicken, cooked *en vessie* perfumed with black Perigord truffle in the 'Gourmet Corner'. An innovative wine list has plenty of good drinking under £20 and thirty 'wines of the moment' that are drinking particularly well. The rest of the list shows a sensible balance between France and Europe and the New World – California lovers are especially well catered for, as are those who wish to sample half bottles. **Seats** 80. Parties 10. Private Room 20. L 12-2 D 7-9.30. Set L & D £29.50.

Hampton Wick — Le Petit Max — £50

Tel 081-977 0236   **R**

97a High Street Corner Vicarage Road Hampton Wick Surrey KT2 5NB   Map 15 E2

With the opening in 1994 of *Chez Max* in Chelsea (see London section), the Renzlands have rationalised their operation here. Marc looks after the Surrey branch (with Graham Thompson at front of house), offering two sittings at Sunday lunchtime and usually two sittings in the evening. Be reminded that during the day from Monday to Saturday, an entirely separate workman's café style, *Bonzo's*, operates in the same premises. However, once safely installed at one of the few tightly squeezed tables, you'll have the opportunity of enjoying the likes of tartine of foie gras with rémoulade on a bed of mixed leaves dressed with walnut oil vinaigrette, roast wild salmon served with buttered vegetables, Jersey royals and sauce hollandaise, and *tarte tatin aux poires*. No children. **Seats** 35. L Sun only *12.30 & 3.45. D 7-10.30 (Fri & Sat to 11). Set L & D £21.50. Closed Mon, Bank Holidays. No credit cards.*

Hampton Wick — Place of Interest

Hampton Court Palace   Tel 081-781 9500

Hanchurch — Hanchurch Manor — £75

Tel 0782 643030   Fax 0782 643035   **H**

Hanchurch nr Stoke-on-Trent Staffordshire ST4 8JD   Map 6 B3

Road-building schemes in the immediate area have caused expansion plans to be put on hold at this distinctive Tudor-style mansion, which is reached by an attractive driveway and stands in nine acres of gardens with a fishing lake. Just five bedrooms are currently being let, each individually decorated and filled with thoughtful little extras. No children under 12. No dogs. The hotel was graded at 74% in our 1994 Guide. **Rooms** 9. Garden, fishing. *Closed 25 & 26 Dec, 1 Jan.* AMERICAN EXPRESS *Access, Diners, Visa.*

Handforth — Belfry Hotel — 69% — £85

Tel 061-437 0511   Fax 061-499 0597   **HR**

Stanley Road Handforth nr Wilmslow Cheshire SK9 3LD   Map 6 B2

Professionalism and service – luggage porterage is the norm, beds are turned down at night, room service is 24hrs – are the great strengths of a hotel run by the Beech family for over 30 years. Behind a rather utilitarian exterior public rooms include a very pink reception; spacious lounge with button-back leather chairs, reproduction antique table and glass chandeliers (that look a little incongruous given the rather functional architecture of the room); and a bar last decorated when grey, drag-painted woodwork was the fashion. Bedrooms are not large (though a number have been converted into good-sized singles as this is predominantly a business hotel) but have good freestanding furniture and pleasant, mostly Sanderson, fabrics. Bathrooms are practical rather than luxurious. Five full and four junior suites are more spacious and come with larger bathrooms. Courtesy coach to Manchester Airport. No dogs. **Rooms** 80. Garden. *Closed 25 Dec eve, all Jan 1.* AMERICAN EXPRESS *Access, Diners, Visa.*

Restaurant — £80

Little things, like remembering to bring a fresh napkin along with the finger bowl, exemplify the excellent service provided here under the watchful eye of long-serving restaurant manager James Moore. Equally reliable and satisfying is the cooking of Mark Fletcher and his brigade who cope with table d'hote, gourmet and extensive à la carte menus with confidence and without short cuts. The range includes something for everyone with simple dishes like parsnip and orange soup, liver and bacon (from a section of the menu called 'A return to the traditional English table') and grilled Dover sole; classics such as Caesar salad, beef Stroganoff and fillet of beef Rossini, and more exotic offerings like a casserole of snails in pastry with Pernod and garlic cream or monkfish cooked in a tempura batter with an orange and ginger butter sauce. A nice old-fashioned touch is the well stocked hors d'oeuvre trolley – a rarity these days. The room is comfortable rather than elegant, with a sunken area in the centre that comes into its own for the regular Friday night dinner dances. The wine list represents extremely good value (good to see a *marque* champagne under £30) with an excellent French section. The rest of Europe and the New World have more predictable offerings, but judged on price alone this is a really 'friendly list'. Regional winner for the North of England of our Cellar of the Year award 1995. *Seats 120. Private Room 40. L 12.30-2 D 7-10. Closed Bank Holidays. Set L £13 & £21.50 (Sun £14.75) Set D £16 & £21.50.*

Handforth	Handforth Chinese Restaurant	£45
Tel 0625 531670		**R**
8a The Paddock Handforth Cheshire SK9 3NE		Map 6 B2

A straightforward restaurant in a parade of shops in suburban Manchester serving good, honest Chinese food. Sound cooking and professional service are matched by some interesting dishes (fish slices smoked in tea leaves, mushrooms in garlic sauce with pancake wraps) supplementing more familiar choices. *Seats 85. L 12-2 D 5.30-11.30 (till 12 Fri & Sat). Closed L Sat & Sun, 25 & 26 Dec. Set L from £5.50 Set D from £15.* AMERICAN EXPRESS *Access, Visa.*

Harlow	Green Man	60%	£92
Tel 0279 442521 Fax 0279 626113			**H**
Mulberry Green Old Town Harlow Essex CM17 0ET			Map 15 F2

Forte Heritage hotel with the heart of a 14th-century coaching inn (the building is listed) and modern bedroom blocks. Two bars, but no lounge. Conference and banqueting facilities for 55/60. *Rooms 55. Garden.* AMERICAN EXPRESS *Access, Diners, Visa.*

Harlow	Moat House	68%	£80
Tel 0279 422441 Fax 0279 635094			**H**
Southern Way Harlow Essex CM18 7BA			Map 15 F2

Modern hotel with a squat, faceless exterior close to Junction 7 of M11 (one mile). Stylish, spacious public rooms and bedrooms. Conference facilities for 150; ample parking. Children under 12 share parents' room free. *Rooms 118. Games room, snooker.* AMERICAN EXPRESS *Access, Diners, Visa.*

Harlow	Places of Interest

The Playhouse   The High Tel 0279 24391.
Epping Forest District Museum   Tel 0992 716882.
Harlow Ski School   Tel 0279 21792.

Harome	Pheasant Hotel	68%	£115*
Tel 0439 771241			**H**
Harome nr Helmsley North Yorkshire YO6 5JG			Map 5 E4

The village smithy, the village shop and two cottages were transformed into a comfortable and relaxed hotel by the pond and millstream. Day rooms comprise a little oak-beamed bar, a restaurant and a lounge that opens on to a flagstoned terrace. Bedrooms include three suites in buildings around a courtyard and one with facilities for the disabled; to one side of this courtyard is a building housing the heated swimming pool. Two cottages (Foxglove and Holly), both a short walk away from the hotel, are also available for accommodation. No children under 12. Dogs by prior arrangement only. ★Half-board terms. *Rooms 12. Garden, indoor swimming pool. Closed Christmas Eve-end Feb. No credit cards.*

Harpenden   Glen Eagle Hotel   63%   £87

Tel 0582 760271   Fax 0582 460819   **H**

1 Luton Road Harpenden Hertfordshire AL5 2PX   Map 15 E2

A functional-looking redbrick hotel with ample free parking. Decent-sized bedrooms, 24hr room service, and several function rooms. The Glen Eagle stands on the A1081, near the railway station. *Rooms 50. Closed 26-31 Dec. Garden.* AMERICAN EXPRESS *Access, Diners, Visa.*

Harpenden   Moat House   68%   £113

Tel 0582 764111   Fax 0582 769858   **H**

Southdown Road Harpenden Hertfordshire AL5 1PE   Map 15 E2

Elegant redbrick Georgian house, just off A1081. Tastefully decorated day rooms and well-equipped bedrooms (13 of which are reserved for non-smokers). Family facilities. Banqueting/conferences for 120/170. *Rooms 53.* AMERICAN EXPRESS *Access, Diners, Visa.*

Harrogate   Café Fleur   £45

Tel 0423 503034   **R**

3 Royal Parade Harrogate North Yorkshire HG1 2SZ   Map 6 C1

Behind a red and gold frontage opposite the Crown Hotel, this is a friendly French brasserie-style restaurant with a wooden floor, cane-backed chairs and neatly set mahogany tables. A straightforward selection on the various menus runs from grilled sardines and chicken liver paté to pasta, fish pie, salmon with an orange and basil sauce, Toulouse sausages and oxtail casserole. Steak sandwich is a popular quick-snack speciality. Set menus include Petite Fleur, which is very cheap (and even cheaper before 7.30 Sun-Thurs). No smoking. *Seats 56. Parties 14. D only 6-9.30. Closed 25 & 26 Dec, 1 Jan. Set D from £4.95. Access, Visa.*

Harrogate   The Crown   67%   £90

Tel 0423 567755   Fax 0423 502284   **H**

Crown Place Harrogate North Yorkshire HG1 2RZ   Map 6 C1

Forte Heritage hotel originally built in 1740 as a coaching inn, but of the grander variety. Redecoration of public rooms during 1994. Free use of the *Majestic's* leisure facilities. Conferences/banquets for up to 450/300. *Rooms 121.* AMERICAN EXPRESS *Access, Diners, Visa.*

Harrogate   Drum & Monkey   £45

Tel 0423 502650   **R**

5 Montpellier Gardens Harrogate North Yorkshire HG1 2TF   Map 6 C1

Bustling fish restaurant on two floors with cramped tables. Simple dishes fare best on a menu that ranges from oysters, mussels and scallops to lobster (bisque, cocktail, cold with a salad, steamed with garlic butter, Thermidor and Drouant – cream and mustard sauce), sole, monkfish and the popular seafood pie. Lunch prices lower than dinner. *Seats 50. Parties 8. L 12-2.30 D 7-10.15. Closed Sun. Access, Visa.*

Harrogate **Hospitality Inn** **61%** **£92**

Tel 0423 564601 Fax 0423 507508 **H**

West Park Prospect Place Harrogate North Yorkshire HG1 1LB Map 6 C1

On the A61, a row of town-centre converted Georgian town houses, close to the parkland of The Stray. Children up to 14 free in parents' room. Busy conference and banqueting facilities for 150/100. No dogs. Mount Charlotte Thistle. *Rooms 71.* AMERICAN EXPRESS *Access, Diners, Visa.*

Harrogate **Imperial Hotel** **65%** **£85**

Tel 0423 565071 Fax 0423 500082 **H**

Prospect Place Harrogate North Yorkshire HG1 1LB Map 6 C1

Overlooking the Stray in the centre of town the hotel looks out over flower-filled borders with balconied first-floor bedrooms at the front making the most of the view. Public areas are smart with white marble-tiled floors, the bar and lounge merging into one having the same buttoned, dark red-upholstered settees and armchairs. Bedrooms with traditional style darkwood furniture are neat and come with a range of useful amenities. Bathrooms are simple, with vinyl floors. *Rooms 85. Snooker.* AMERICAN EXPRESS *Access, Diners, Visa.*

Harrogate **The Majestic** **64%** **£111**

Tel 0423 568972 Fax 0423 502283 **H**

Ripon Road Harrogate North Yorkshire HG1 2HU Map 6 C1

Completed in 1900 the hotel stands in 12 acres on a hillside directly above the town's major conference venue. Public rooms are impressively spacious with much marble in evidence. Bedrooms are gradually being refurbished, bringing them up to a more attractive standard. *Rooms 156. Garden, indoor swimming pool, gym, squash, sauna, spa bath, solarium, tennis, golf driving net, beauty & hair salons, snooker.* AMERICAN EXPRESS *Access, Diners, Visa.*

Harrogate **Miller's, The Bistro** ★ **£60**

Tel 0423 530708 **R**

1 Montpelier Mews Harrogate North Yorkshire HG1 2TG Map 6 C1

Forming part of an attractive mews development in the centre of town, the restaurant offers sheltered alfresco dining in a courtyard when the weather's favourable. The interior is cool and airy with mirrored walls, light wood and creamy napery creating a smart, modern appearance. The kitchen is tiny yet from it Simon Gueller produces some extremely accomplished cooking that is fashionably light and imaginative. Starters (all at £5) include a choice of a gratin of crab and pink grapefruit, risotto of ink with roast calamari or a mosaic of salmon and lobster with a gazpacho sauce and green peppercorns. A macaroni of scallops offers excellent al dente, unusually shaped pasta in a creamy coriander sauce with thin strips of ginger and very fresh flash-fried scallops. Meat and poultry main dishes are priced at £9.50 and range from pot-roast chicken, sauce Bois-Boudran and braised celery hearts to Scottish sirloin 'en crépinette' with wild mushrooms and caramelised shallots. Fish and shellfish at £10.50 include a salade niçoise with fresh tuna and smoked haddock with poached egg and new potatoes or a delicious escalope of turbot baked with a tomato and herb topping and accompanied by chateau potatoes coated in a gratinated sabayon of grain mustard. Desserts are no less delectable, including a featherlight raspberry mousse surrounded by a raspberry coulis, lemon tart and chocolate marquise. Charming service is led by Rena, Simon's wife. Booking is essential. *Seats 40. Parties 14. L 12-2 D 7-10. Closed Sun, Mon, Bank Holidays, 10 days Christmas.* AMERICAN EXPRESS *Access, Visa.*

Harrogate   Moat House   64%   £144

Tel 0423 500000   Fax 0423 524435   **H**

King's Road Harrogate North Yorkshire HG1 1XX   Map 6 C1

Large hotel conveniently sited right next door to the Exhibition and
Conference centre and linked directly to it. Modern, redbrick building
with lots of mirrored glass. Conference/banqueting facilities for 400/250.
Rooms 214. AMERICAN EXPRESS *Access, Diners, Visa.*

Harrogate   Old Swan Hotel   69%   £126

Tel 0423 500055   Fax 0423 501154   **HR**

Swan Road Harrogate North Yorkshire HG1 2SR   Map 6 C1

The present building dates back to 1840, and additional character to its
exterior is provided by a luxuriant growth of Virginia creeper. The
interior maintains much of its original Victorian ambience, though the
lounge bar has a somewhat more modern appearance with its pastel pink
walls, contrasting upholstery and mirror-fronted bar counter. Breakfasts are
served in the splendid Wedgwood room with its skylight supported
by pillars and elaborate plasterwork on the walls. Bedrooms overlooking
the lawns and flower beds at the front are sunny and spacious – not that
any rooms are small. All are tastefully decorated and boast a lot
of amenities but not satellite TV. This is the hotel where Agatha Christie
stayed in 1926 when she disappeared from public eye. Aspiring private eyes
return now for the Super Sleuth weekends held every few months.
Children under 12 stay free in parents' room. **Rooms** 135. *Garden, croquet,
tennis.* AMERICAN EXPRESS *Access, Diners, Visa.*

Library Restaurant   £70

An elegant and delightfully traditional room offering standards a cut above
many provincial hotels of this size. Appealing, modern dishes are offered,
such as warm salad of field mushrooms, avocado and pine kernels, escalope
of salmon with a brioche and crab crust, and iced parfait of coconut and
mango. Decent cheeses; the wine list has helpful notes. *Seats 30. Parties 10.
L 12.30-2 D 7-10. Set L from £9.95 Set D £18.*

Harrogate   Hotel St George   63%   £100

Tel 0423 561431   Fax 0423 530037   **H**

Ripon Road Harrogate North Yorkshire HG1 2SY   Map 6 C1

Edwardian-styled interiors and good-sized bedrooms behind an ivy-clad
facade. Extensive conference facilities (for up to 150 delegates) and
a modern leisure club. Swallow Hotels. **Rooms** 93. *Garden, indoor swimming
pool, keep-fit equipment, sauna, spa bath, steam room, solarium.* AMERICAN EXPRESS
Access, Diners, Visa.

Harrogate   Studley Hotel   64%   £95

Tel 0423 560425   Fax 0423 530967   **H**

28 Swan Road Harrogate North Yorkshire HG1 2SE   Map 6 C1

A large, well-tended rockery at the front and just about sufficient car-
parking at the rear are two differing but good features of this homely
town-centre hotel not far from the main conference venues. There's a lively
public bar on the ground floor and reception and the residents' bar are
on the first floor. Natural, polished lightwood is used to good effect
throughout. Bedrooms are cosy and attractively decorated. They have a lot
of the usual extras, from biscuits to satellite TV channels. Bathrooms are
carpeted. Housekeeping can falter at times, though staff are friendly and
helpful. Near the entrance to Valley Gardens. No children under 7.
Rooms 36. *Garden. Closed 2 days Christmas.* AMERICAN EXPRESS *Access,
Diners, Visa.*

Harrogate   Tannin Level   £35

Tel 0423 560595   Fax 0423 563077   **R**
5 Raglan Street Harrogate North Yorkshire HG1 1LE   Map 6 C1

Basement wine bar on the corner of Raglan Street and Princes Street with
brick walls, slate floors, old pews and assorted kitchen-style chairs, and
green boards on which are written the daily menu. This usually includes
an interesting, well-balanced mix of dishes with a French accent: home-
made soups (perhaps Moroccan lamb broth or green pea, courgette and
mint), paté and terrines (Stilton, leek and mushroom), many meaty main
courses (stincotto of ham shank and couscous, salsicotto sausage and
polenta) vegetarian options, good fresh fish and desserts. Simple, tasty fare,
well executed. Extensive list of wines plus a dozen by the glass. One of the
rooms is non-smoking. *Seats 75. Parties 30. Private Room 12. L 12-2
D 5.30-10 (Sat 6.30-10.30). Closed all Sun, 25 & 26 Dec, 1 Jan, L Bank
Holidays. Access, Visa.*

Harrogate   Places of Interest

Harrogate Tourist Information   Tel 0423 525666.
Harrogate Conference and Exhibition Centre   Tel 0423 500500.
Royal Pump Room Museum   Tel 0423 503340.
Harrogate Theatre   Tel 0423 502116.
Wetherby Racecourse   Tel 0937 582035.
Harrogate Ski Centre   Tel 0423 505457.
Great Yorkshire Showground   Tel 0423 561536.

Note that all telephone numbers with area codes starting with 0
will start 01 from 16 April 1995.

Harrow   Percy's   £70

Tel 081-427 2021   Fax 081-427 8134   **R**
66 Station Road North Harrow Middlesex HA2 7SJ   Map 15 E2

Almost next to North Harrow station and originally a wine bar, Percy's
is now a restaurant with a cool, summery decor. The Bricknell-Webbs
were, prior to this venture, turf accountants but now husband, Tony, looks
after the front of house while wife, Tina, cooks. She is completely self-
taught and uses produce originating primarily from the South-West. They
even have their own 40-acre farm in North Devon and as such are self-
sufficient in herbs and most vegetables. Game, in season, and fish are
particularly strong points, the fish arriving from day boats to ensure
as near-perfect freshness as possible. The cooking is involved, with
sometimes unusually interesting combinations. Starters, all at one price,
could be a prawn and mussel risotto – here made with wild red Camargue
rice and also containing arame seaweed, pumpkin and chestnuts; pan-fried
soft herring roes are served on toasted dill brioche with a red onion and
sour-cream dressing. Main courses are in two price brackets – the lower
one includes the likes of rabbit in pancetta cooked in coconut cream sauce
with coriander, curry and kaffir lime leaves and skate cooked with
gorgonzola, garlic, spicy onions, pink peppercorns and raspberry vinegar.
The higher band includes loin of lamb with crème fraiche and a garlic
sauce. Unconventional sweets, too, such as hazelnut meringue topped with
star-anise ice cream which has been laced with anise spirit, the whole then
smothered in unsweetened organic apricot sauce topped with toasted
hazelnut pieces. Organic coffee to finish. A no-smoking restaurant.
No children under 10. *Seats 80. Parties 14. L 12-3 D 6.30-10. Closed Sun &
Mon, Tues after Bank Holidays & 4 days at Christmas.* AMERICAN EXPRESS *Access,
Diners, Visa.*

Hartlebury   Forte Travelodge   £45

Tel 0299 250553   **L**

**Shorthill Nurseries Hartlebury Kidderminster Hereford & Worcester
DY11 6DR**   Map 14 B1

On the southbound carriageway of the A449, 6 miles south
of Kidderminster. *Rooms 32.* AMERICAN EXPRESS *Access, Diners, Visa.*

Hartlepool   Grand Hotel   59%   £68

Tel 0429 266345   Fax 0429 265217   **H**

Swainson Street Hartlepool Cleveland TS24 8AA   Map 5 E3

A balconied Victorian ballroom tops the function/conference facilities
at this handsome redbrick hotel opposite the main shopping centre. There's
an evening disco/jazz bar. *Rooms 47.* AMERICAN EXPRESS *Access, Diners, Visa.*

Hartshead Moor   Forte Travelodge   £45

Tel 0274 851706   **L**

Clifton Brighouse West Yorkshire HD6 4RJ   Map 6 C1

Located on the eastbound carriageway of the M62 at the Welcome Break
service area between Junctions 25 and 26. *Rooms 40.* AMERICAN EXPRESS
Access, Diners, Visa.

Our inspectors are full-time employees; they are professionally trained
by us.

Harvington   The Mill   65%   £85

Tel & Fax 0386 870688   **HR**

Anchor Lane Harvington nr Evesham Hereford & Worcester WR11 5NR   Map 14 C1

A Georgian mill, with lawns running down to a peaceful stretch of the
river Avon, now converted into a hotel run in friendly informal fashion
by partners Simon, Jane, Richard and Susan Greenhalgh. Small, button-
back armchairs in red or green furnish the low-ceilinged lounge (where
drinks are also served – there's no separate bar) given character by a couple
of old beams and some old bakery oven doors set above the gas coal fire.
Artificial plants and 'for-sale' pictures complete the decor. Pleasant, well-
kept bedrooms all face the morning sun and overlook the river. Cooked
breakfasts include some excellent fried bread. Not suitable for children
under 10. No dogs. Signposted off the B439 opposite Harvington village.
*Rooms 15. Garden, croquet, tennis, fishing, outdoor swimming pool.
Closed 6 days at Christmas.* AMERICAN EXPRESS *Access, Diners, Visa.*

Restaurant   £60

The choice of main dishes dictates the price of a three-course dinner (the
fixed-price lunch is a limited selection of the evening dishes) in the pretty,
pale-peach and grey restaurant. The likes of twice-baked cheese soufflé,
spinach roulade, guinea fowl au vin, Gressingham duck (with a rather
sweet orange and ginger sauce) and steak, kidney and oyster pudding are
competently cooked. Wines are listed twice – once by style (from dry
to sweet for whites and light to rich for reds) and again in ascending order
of price, although over three-quarters are under £20 so there is no need
to take out a second mortgage. A less formal lounge/terrace menu is served
weekdays and most Saturday lunchtimes. 24 *Seats 40. Private Room 14.
L 11.45-1.45 D 7-8.45. Set L £11.95/£13.95. Set Sun L £13.45
Set D from £21.*

Harwich   Pier at Harwich   £61

Tel 0255 241212   Fax 0255 322752   **RR**

The Quay Harwich Essex CO12 3HH   Map 10 C3

Overlooking the harbour (and within a mile of the ferry port), the first-floor restaurant is just the place to enjoy good, fresh seafood which comes both plain (dressed crab, oysters, sole meunière, fish and chips, grilled sea bass) and sauced (monkfish with a red pepper and tomato sauce, cod Mornay, timbale of salmon, prawns and spinach on a chive and vermouth butter sauce). Steaks and a chicken dish also on the menu. A succinct wine list at sensible prices includes a varied selection of half bottles. The *Ha'penny Pier* on the ground floor is a second, family-orientated restaurant also with a mainly fish menu. *Seats 70. Parties 30. Private Room 90. L 12-2 D 6-9.30. Set L £9/£11.75 (Sun £14.25) Set D £16. Closed D 25 & 26 Dec.* AMERICAN EXPRESS *Access, Diners, Visa.*

Rooms   £63

The third-floor accommodation comprises six bedrooms of varying standards, all with a nautical theme, some with views down the estuary. All have en-suite bathrooms and televisions.

Haslemere   Lythe Hill Hotel   71%   £112

Tel 0428 651251   Fax 0428 644131   **H**

Petworth Road Haslemere Surrey GU27 3BQ   Map 11 A6

1½ miles east of town on the B2131, Lythe Hill has been created from a collection of old farm buildings, which include a splendid Elizabethan house (where the five most characterful bedrooms are located), plus a few newer bits all set in 20 acres of grounds which encompass a croquet lawn, two lakes and a bluebell wood, with some glorious Surrey countryside beyond. A small lounge is supplemented by a comfortable cocktail bar but the great strength here are the bedrooms which include a dozen full suites and a number of large rooms with separate sitting area. All rooms and suites are individually decorated and furnished, mostly with reproduction antiques, and boast Italian marble bathrooms with bidet, bathrobe and generous towelling. Rooms are serviced in the evening and there is 24hr room service. Conference/banqueting facilities for 60/130. *Rooms 40. Garden, croquet, tennis, fishing, games room, helipad.* AMERICAN EXPRESS *Access, Visa.*

Haslemere   Morel's   ★   £90

Tel 0428 651462   **R**

23 Lower Street Haslemere Surrey GU27 2NY   Map 11 A6

Situated on a raised pavement on the road between the high street and the station, Morel's may not be particularly easy to find on a first visit; however, those in the know park in the main town car park just across the road (you'll have to ask for directions). The restaurant seems to cruise happily along in top gear nowadays, with Jean-Yves Morel directing operations in the kitchen and his wife Mary-Anne looking after front of house. The summery blues and pale creams of the once cottagey interior's decor are complemented by large vases of mixed flowers with stylish knotted blue tablecloths, carefully fanned white napkins, gleaming glassware and shining silver cutlery – all indications of an impeccably run establishment. A small dish of crudités is served with aperitifs in the comfortable, beamed bar with its well-upholstered sofas and armchairs. Typically, a ballotine of pigeon confit with lentils and balsamic vinaigrette may be served as an amuse-gueule to titillate the taste buds and indicate the kitchen's tip-top intentions; similarly, home-baked crusty white or brown rolls and butter made into a featherlight mousse get a meal off to a good start. Jean-Yves offers both a short, classic à la carte French menu (two or three courses at set prices, whatever one's choice) and a table d'hote (Tue-

Fri), the latter offering a choice of three dishes at each stage – perhaps Mediterranean fish soup, pigeon with crisp pasta and red wine sauce, and apricot and Amaretto liqueur soufflé. A recent carte offered *feuillette d'asperges au cerfeuil* (asparagus in puff pastry layers with chervil and lemon), a *paillasson* of crisp potatoes, duck confit, little onions and duck juices, a salad of goat's cheese baked in filo pastry with pine nuts and basil, and marinated salmon with citrus fruits and green peppercorns among the starters; main dishes included a daily fresh fish dish (perhaps turbot with langoustine sauce, monkfish or brill), breast of Gressingham duck with kumquats and an orange and Dubonnet sauce, *escalope de porc aux pommes caramelisées et au Calvados* (pork fillet with caramelised apple and Calvados sauce), and poussin roasted with whole garlic cloves and a sherry vinegar sauce. Blinis with smoked salmon, yoghurt and Danish caviar and *crépinette de queue de boeuf bourguignonne* (braised oxtail off the bone served with seedless grapes and the sauce enriched with port) are popular dishes that continually appear on menus, and the latter is considered a speciality. Excellent desserts include a dark and white chocolate marquise with coffee bean sauce, pear poached in red wine, spiced with cardamom and served with a curry ice cream (it doesn't taste like it sounds!), grandmother's crème brulée with sorbets, a selection in miniature (*assiette du chef*) or French cheeses. Some bargains on the mainly French wine list, with only Australia representing the New World. Excellent, attentive and highly professional service. No smoking in the dining room. *Seats 50. L 12.30-2 D 7-10. Closed L Sat, all Sun & Mon, 3 weeks end Sep, 25-28 Dec. Set L £17 Set D £19.50 (Tue-Fri) £25/£31.* [AMERICAN EXPRESS] *Access, Diners, Visa.* [MARTELL]

Hastings   **Cinque Ports Hotel Periquito**   **66%**   **£51**

Tel 0424 439222   Fax 0424 437277   **H**

Summerfields Hastings East Sussex TN34 1ET   Map 11 C6

A change of ownership for this hotel in the modern American low-rise style, with bright, spacious public areas furnished with good-quality period-style settees and armchairs. There are seven purpose-built conference rooms for up to 300 delegates. The hotel stands on the A21 leading into the town centre. Children up to 14 stay free in parents' room. *Rooms 40.* [AMERICAN EXPRESS] *Access, Diners, Visa.*

Hastings   **Röser's**   ★   **£65**

Tel 0424 712218   **R**

64 Eversfield Place St Leonards-on-Sea nr Hastings
East Sussex TN37 6DB   Map 11 C6

One of several restaurants facing the pier, it's Gerald Röser's high standards in the kitchen that put this one in a class of its own. A proper veal stock forms the base of many of the sauces and everything from the choice of breads to the selection of sorbets is home-made. Seafood – local line-caught sea bass, shellfish from Scotland – and seasonal game are both areas of speciality with the likes of home-made venison sausages with port sauce, seared scallops with saffron sauce and chargrilled vegetables, breast of wood pigeon with wild mushroom sauce and Hastings turbot with flat parsley sauce and red-wine butter. Soups are a strength too – a creamy potato soup with crisp julienne of vegetables proving much more refined (and moreish) than the mundane ingredients might suggest. Among the puds, Röser's chocolate mousse, made with the finest Belgian chocolate, and an apple millefeuille have become fixtures by popular demand and there are cheeses (mostly local) served with fresh fruit and nuts. Mostly booth seating behind the bow window with its ruffled Dutch blinds. Limited but high-quality New World wines on a classy list which boasts an impressive array of the best French growers. Regional winner for South of England of our Cellar of the Year award 1995. *Seats 40. Private Room 40. L 12-2 D 7-10. Closed L Sat, all Sun & Mon, Bank Holidays, 1 week Jan, 1 week Aug. Set L £13.95/£15.95 Set D £18.95.* [AMERICAN EXPRESS] *Access, Diners, Visa.*

Hastings   Royal Victoria Hotel   70%   £72

Tel 0424 445544   Fax 0424 721995   **H**

The Marina St Leonards-on-Sea nr Hastings East Sussex TN38 0BD   Map 11 C6

The seafront Royal Victoria retains the grand style of architecture that graced the Victorian age. An elegant marble staircase sweeps up from the foyer and in the first-floor piano lounge-cum-bar there are pillars, arches and ornate plaster mouldings, plus sea views. All the bedrooms are designated as suites, with either a separate sitting room or a large sitting area. Children up to 16 free in parents' room. Conferences/banquets for up to 150/120. Resort Hotels. *Rooms 50.* AMERICAN EXPRESS *Access, Diners, Visa.*

Hastings   Places of Interest

Tourist Information   Tel 0424 718888.
Stables Theatre   Tel 0424 423221.
Great Dixter House and Gardens   Northiam Tel 0797 253160.
Hastings Castle and 1066 Story   Tel 0424 717963.
Hastings Embroidery   Town Hall Tel 0424 722022.
Shipwreck Heritage Centre   Tel 0424 437452.
Sea Life Centre   Tel 0424 718776.
Museum and Art Gallery   Tel 0424 721202.

Hatch Beauchamp   Farthings Hotel   70%   £65

Tel 0823 480664   **H**

Hatch Beauchamp nr Taunton Somerset TA3 6SG   Map 13 E2

On the edge of the rolling Blackdown Hills just south of Taunton, and a few minutes from Junction 25 of the M5, lies the pretty village of Hatch Beauchamp and the equally pretty Farthings Hotel. New owners this year are David and Marie Barker, who bring over 20 years' experience in the trade to their new venture. They have made positive changes already, increasing the overall number of bedrooms (all en-suite), giving a face lift to the public areas and adding a seminar room to bring the banqueting/conference capacity up to 24. They see their market as a challenging mixture of business trade, special functions, a half-way house for travellers heading further west and destination tourists wishing to explore this relatively untouched part of the countryside (special weekend packages including cream teas are available). Early indications are that they have struck a good balance. *Rooms 8. Garden, croquet. Closed 2 weeks Jan. Access, Diners, Visa.*

Hatfield Heath   Down Hall   71%   £126

Tel 0279 731441   Fax 0279 730416   **H**

Hatfield Heath nr Bishops Stortford Hertfordshire CM22 7AS   Map 11 B4

Down Hall is a splendid Italianate mansion set in 100 acres of parkland with fine enclosed lawns. The handsome exterior is matched in the day rooms; the focal point is the main lounge with its Italian stone fireplace, huge crystal chandeliers and furniture ornate with ormolu, and the canopied bar boasts a green marble counter and matching tables. There are two restaurants and Sunday barbecues in summer. Bedrooms are divided between the main house and the sympathetically designed west wing; wing rooms have larger and more luxurious bathrooms, mini-bars and extra phones in the bathrooms and on the desks. Well geared up for conferences of up to 290. *Rooms 103. Garden, croquet, putting, indoor swimming pool, spa bath, sauna, tennis, snooker.* AMERICAN EXPRESS *Access, Diners, Visa.*

Hatherleigh   George Hotel   £65

Tel 0837 810454   Fax 0837 810901   **I**

Market Street Hatherleigh nr Okehampton Devon EX20 3JN   Map 13 D2

Originally a sanctuary for monks, later brew house, tavern, coaching inn and law court. The cob-and-thatch building still has old-fashioned appeal. Bedrooms are comfortable and traditionally furnished. *Rooms 11. Garden, outdoor swimming pool, snooker.* AMERICAN EXPRESS *Access, Visa.*

Hathersage   Hathersage Inn   £62

Tel 0433 650259   Fax 0433 651199   **I**

Hathersage Derbyshire S30 1BB   Map 6 C2

The ivy-clad, stone-built inn stands by Hathersage's steep main street and has been in the Bowie family for over 30 years. At the front, the Cricketers bar is full of local memorabilia while the neatly kept bedrooms are at the back of the building. Creature comforts include a drinks tray and fresh fruit. There are two four-poster honeymoon suite. Many special occasion breaks – it's a good base for exploring the Peak District. *Rooms 15.* AMERICAN EXPRESS *Access, Diners, Visa.*

Havant   Bear Hotel   59%   £60

Tel 0705 486501   Fax 0705 470551   **H**

East Street Havant Hampshire PO9 1AA   Map 15 D4

Historic town-centre coaching inn with modest accommodation and good parking. Conference facilities for up to 120, banqueting up to 100. Children up to 12 free in parents' room. Owned by Countryside Inns & Hotels. *Rooms 42.* AMERICAN EXPRESS *Access, Diners, Visa.*

Havant   Forte Posthouse   62%   £68

Tel 0705 465011   Fax 0705 466468   **H**

Northney Road Hayling Island Havant Hampshire PO11 0NQ   Map 15 D4

Practical modern hotel on the north shore of Hayling Island. Two bars, health and fitness club, free car park, conferences for up to 140. *Rooms 92. Indoor swimming pool, gym, sauna, spa bath, solarium.* AMERICAN EXPRESS *Access, Diners, Visa.*

Hawkchurch   Fairwater Head Hotel   65%   £110

Tel 0297 678349   **H**

Hawkchurch nr Axminster Devon EX13 5TX   Map 13 E2

The garden and the views over the Axe valley are major attractions at the Austin and Lowe families' peaceful Edwardian hotel, which numbers many loyal returnees among its guests. Housekeeping is diligent in both the main-house bedrooms and those in the wing; attention to detail includes fresh Devon milk for the tea and coffee-making facilities. A garden wing is not connected to the house but offers the most up-to-date rooms with compact bathrooms and views over the gardens. *Rooms 21. Garden, croquet, snooker. Closed Jan-Feb.* AMERICAN EXPRESS *Access, Diners, Visa.*

Hawkhurst   Tudor Court   61%   £66

Tel 0580 752312   Fax 0580 753966   **H**

Rye Road Hawkhurst Cranbrook Kent TN18 5DA   Map 11 C6

On the Rye road (A268) about a mile from Hawkhurst half way between Tunbridge Wells and the coast, this well-kept redbrick hotel has equally spruce gardens. Guests can enjoy a drink on the terrace or in the oak-panelled bar, or while away an hour or two with a book in the lounge. Comfortably appointed bedrooms include some with four-posters.

Children up to 12 free in parents' room. There's a conference suite and two syndicate rooms, catering for up to 70 delegates and plenty of parking. *Rooms 18. Garden, croquet, clock golf, tennis, children's play area.* AMERICAN EXPRESS *Access, Diners, Visa.*

Hawkhurst   Place of Interest

Bodiam Castle (NT)   Tel 0580 830436 *4 miles*

Haworth   Weavers   £50
Tel 0535 643822   R
15 West Lane Haworth nr Bradford West Yorkshire BD22 8DU   Map 6 C1

Follow signs for the Bronte Parsonage Museum (and use its car park – free after 6pm) to find a characterful restaurant in a row of old weaver's cottages. There's a light touch in the kitchen from chef/proprietors Colin and Jane Rushworth and mainly local produce is used. A good selection of soups usually features among starters like deep-fried monkfish skewer with Gruyère cheese and tomato sauce, mussels with white wine and cream, banana and blue cheese pastry, minced lamb and onion meatballs and 'Yorkshire pud wi' rich onion gravy' (or vegetarian gravy on request); fisherman's bake, pot-roasted, bacon-wrapped breast of chicken stuffed with orange, garlic and butter and served with a mushroom and tomato sauce, local calf's liver and hot pot of venison among the main courses. Crispy roast breast of Gressingham duck served on a rhubarb sauce is considered a speciality, along with roast fillet of pork with herb stuffing, 'cracklin', apple purée and scrumpy gravy. Afters include homely favourites. 'Sampler' menu served 6.45-7.15 Tue-Fri and Sunday lunch. Cheerful service completes the satisfying picture. *Seats 45. Parties 16. L (winter Sun only) 12-1.30 D 7-9. Closed D Sun & Mon, 2 weeks mid-Summer, 2 weeks after Christmas. Set 'sampler' meals £9.95/£11.95.* AMERICAN EXPRESS *Access, Diners, Visa.*

Rooms   £68

Four bedrooms, each with en-suite bathroom, combine antique pieces with modern touches like TV, video, direct-dial phone and trouser press. All have views over the Parsonage and village to the moors beyond. No food served during the day. No children under 5 or dogs. *Closed after Sunday lunch to Tuesday afternoon.*

Haworth   Place of Interest

Bronte Parsonage   Tel 0535 42323.

Haydock   Forte Travelodge   £45
Tel 0942 272055   L
Piele Road Haydock St Helens Merseyside WA11 9TL   Map 6 B2

On the A580 westbound, 2 miles west of Junction 23 on the M6. *Rooms 40.* AMERICAN EXPRESS *Access, Diners, Visa.*

Haydock   Haydock Forte Posthouse   65%   £68
Tel 0942 717878   Fax 0942 718419   H
Lodge Lane Newton-le-Willows Haydock Merseyside WA12 0JG   Map 6 B2

Smart, modern and well-organised hotel. Half the bedrooms are of the better Executive standard. Health club; conference/banqueting facilities for up to 200. *Rooms 136. Garden, indoor swimming pool, gym, sauna, spa bath, solarium.* AMERICAN EXPRESS *Access, Diners, Visa.*

Haydock   Haydock Thistle   67%   £107

Tel 0942 272000   Fax 0942 711092   **H**

Penny Lane Haydock St Helens Merseyside WA11 9SG   Map 6 B2

Neo-Georgian, low-rise lodge by Junction 23 of the M6 with spacious lounge and bedrooms. Leisure spa and conference facilities for up to 300 delegates. Children up to 16 stay free in parents' room. *Rooms 139. Garden, indoor swimming pool, gym, sauna, steam room, spa bath, solarium, beauty salon, games room, snooker.* AMERICAN EXPRESS *Access, Diners, Visa.*

Haydock   Place of Interest

Haydock Park Racecourse   Tel 0942 727345.

Hayes   Travel Inn   £43

Tel 081-573 7479   Fax 081-569 1204   **L**

362 Uxbridge Road Hayes Middlesex UB4 0HE   Map 15 E2

10 minutes' drive from Heathrow Airport. *Rooms 40.* AMERICAN EXPRESS *Access, Diners, Visa.*

Hayfield   Bridge End Restaurant   £65

Tel 0663 747321   Fax 0663 742121   **RR**

7 Church Street Hayfield Derbyshire SK12 5JE   Map 6 C2

Bridge End is in the middle of Hayfield, opposite the church, with the River Sett running through the village. The attractive 19th-century stone building is a very English canvas on which chef Jonathan Holmes paints an international picture. Menus change regularly and you might be offered for example Benjamin smokies: Arbroath smokies, prawns, smoked and fresh salmon, simmered in cream with dill, topped with cheese and grilled; or spiced baby black puddings with sautéed apples and rösti potatoes, served on a sage jus; followed by roast haunch of wild boar, marinated and served in a beetroot and mustard sauce, or guinea fowl, marinated in lime, fried in butter, and served with a fresh tomato sauce. Desserts are equally intense, such as a white chocolate parfait, bejewelled with crystallised ginger, paw paw, cherries and praline, served on a passion fruit sauce, or a more simple apple crumble served with cinnamon ice cream and custard. The 'unabridged' is a selection of all the desserts in miniature, and there's a separate cheese menu, complete with map! There's a good-value wine list with many wines under £15. House policy of reduced mark-ups on fine wines – other restaurants note! *Seats 50. Private Room 20. Sun L 12.30-2.30 D Tue-Sat 7.30-10. Closed D Sun, all Mon, 1st week Jan.* AMERICAN EXPRESS *Access, Diners, Visa.*

Rooms   £45

Four en-suite bedrooms in attractive cottage style with pine furnishings and bedsteads have a secure separate entrance. 5% dinner discount for residents. Children up to 5 stay free in parents' room.

Hayfield   Place of Interest

Lyme Park House and Gardens   Disley Tel 0663 762023.

Haytor   Bel Alp House   72%   £120

Tel 0364 661217   Fax 0364 661292   **H**

Haytor nr Bovey Tracey Devon TQ13 9XX   Map 13 D3

In a hillside location commanding splendid views over the rolling Devonshire countryside, this fine Edwardian house and its gardens have been much improved by Roger and Sarah Curnock since they arrived in 1983. Peace and quiet reign in the antique-furnished day rooms, amply supplied with armchairs, sofas and a host of pot plants. The atmosphere is more that of being a house guest in a large family home than of staying in a hotel. Light, airy bedrooms have plain walls, matching floral fabrics, more armchairs and pot plants, and carpeted bathrooms (two with the original Edwardian tubs on marble plinths) with quality toiletries. Housekeeping and repair are immaculate throughout. Smoking discouraged. The hotel lies two and a half miles west of Bovey Tracey off the B3387 before Haytor. *Rooms 9. Garden, croquet, snooker. Access, Visa.*

Heathrow Airport Excelsior Hotel 71% £110

Tel 081-759 6611   Fax 081-759 3421 **H**

Bath Road West Drayton Middlesex UB7 0DU Map 15 E2

A huge, modern hotel near the airport terminals with 248 Executive rooms, 16 suites, 100 non-smoking rooms and five equipped for wheelchair-bound guests. A spacious, marble-floored foyer sets the tone for the day rooms, which include two bars, one in plush and mahogany, and two restaurants. Children up to 14 free in parents' room. Conference/banqueting facilities for 800. Forte Grand. *Rooms 839. Indoor swimming pool, sauna, spa bath, solarium, beauty & hair salons, flower shop, coffee shop (noon–midnight).* AMERICAN EXPRESS *Access, Diners, Visa.*

Heathrow Airport Forte Crest 68% £105

Tel 081-759 2323   Fax 081-897 8659 **H**

Sipson Road West Drayton Middlesex UB7 0JU Map 15 E2

Familiar landmark by the M4 turn-off to Heathrow, ten storeys high and dating from the mid-70s. Chinese and Italian restaurants, a carvery, an informal American-style bar with juke box and pool table, and a traditional cocktail bar. Conference facilities for up to 200. *Rooms 572.* AMERICAN EXPRESS *Access, Diners, Visa.*

Heathrow Airport Forte Posthouse (Ariel) 65% £68

Tel 081-759 2552   Fax 081-564 9265 **H**

Bath Road Hayes Middlesex UB3 5AJ Map 15 E2

Six additional bedrooms have increased the sleeping capacity but reduced the scope of the meeting rooms at this hotel which for many years was the Ariel. *Rooms 186.* AMERICAN EXPRESS *Access, Diners, Visa.*

Heathrow Airport Granada Lodge £61

Tel 081-574 5875   Fax 081-574 1891 **L**

M4 Junction 2/3 Westbound Heston Middlesex TW5 9NA Map 15 E2

Rooms 46. AMERICAN EXPRESS *Access, Diners, Visa.*

Heathrow Airport Heathrow Hilton 74% £167

Tel 081-759 7755   Fax 081-759 7579 **HR**

Terminal 4 Heathrow Airport Hounslow Middlesex TW6 3AF Map 15 E2

An ultra-modern hotel with many striking features, notably the massive atrium covering the foyer and the major public areas. Central lifts split the ground floor – the entrance, foyer-lounge and reception area, to one side; the brasserie, Oscar's (the American-style restaurant), and an open-plan bar and lounge to the other. Adequately sized bedrooms have effective double-glazing, and provide a tranquil escape from the hustle of an international airport. They also all have multi-channel TV which, thanks to the miracles of modern technology, keeps one informed of airport activities and the state of one's bill at the touch of a button. Three rooms are specially designed for disabled guests. A well-equipped gym provides excellent facilities for the excesses suffered by the modern traveller. A covered walkway gives direct access to Terminal 4. There are banqueting/conference facilities for 200/240. Children up to the age of 18 stay free in parents' room. Valet parking. ***Rooms** 400. Indoor swimming pool, gym, sauna, steam room, solarium, news kiosk, coffee shop (24hrs).* AMERICAN EXPRESS® *Access, Diners, Visa.*

Zen Oriental £60

This modern dining room avoids the hubbub generated by airport life. Far Eastern, rather than strictly Chinese, most of the dishes will be recognisable to those familiar with the Zen concept. Dishes vary from the traditional, sesame prawn toasts or spare ribs, to the exotic and expensive – fresh lobster or whole sea bass; each with a choice of five sauces. However, our dish described as "assorted seafood in green curry sauce" contained only cuttlefish and tiger prawns – this was hardly a selection! The table d'hote menu may not be automatically produced, but can be a worthwhile alternative, as à la carte prices can be steep if you're not prudent. Three hours' free parking is available, for customers, in the main car park at the front of the hotel. *Seats 60. L 12-2 D 6-11. Closed L Sat, 25 Dec. Set L £12.50 Set D £23.50 & £28.*

Heathrow Airport   Holiday Inn Crowne Plaza   74%   £167

Tel 0895 445555   Fax 0895 445122   **H**

Stockley Road West Drayton Middlesex UB7 9NA   Map 15 E2

Holiday Inns' top-of-the-range Crowne Plaza brand offering higher levels of service – 24hr table service in the lounge/bar, extensive room service with a good range of hot meals available throughout the night, a turn-down service in the evenings, valet parking – and generally more comfort than one might expect to find in a more standard Holiday Inn. Spacious bedrooms, with a pleasing maroon and dark blue colour scheme, have proper armchairs and breakfast table plus plenty of work space – even more in the Business Study rooms that have a more masculine black and grey decor; half the rooms are non-smoking. Two rooms were specially designed for disabled guests during the recent major refurbishment. Poly-cotton bedding and shortish baths (but with good showers above them) in otherwise well-appointed bathrooms which include face cloths and towelling robes. Most luxurious of the bedrooms are the Directors and Presidential suites. Children up to the age of 19 are accommodated free in their parents' room; informal eating in the Café Galleria. There's a large swimming pool in the leisure centre, where there are also facilities for disabled guests and mothers with babies. Conference/banqueting facilities for up to 220/170; staffed business centre. Just north of the M4. ***Rooms** 374. Garden, golf (9), indoor swimming pool & children's pool, spa bath, gym, sauna, solarium, steam room, beauty salon, coffee shop (6.30am-12.30am), news kiosk, helipad.* AMERICAN EXPRESS® *Access, Diners, Visa.*

Heathrow Airport Jarvis Berkeley International 67%   £85

Tel 081-897 2121   Fax 081-897 7014   **H**

Bath Road Cranford Middlesex TW5 9QF   Map 15 E2

On the A4 two miles from Heathrow, the former *Berkeley Arms* has now been rebranded by Jarvis, and room rates have come down since last year. Practical bedrooms, state-of-the-art conference facilities for up to 120. ***Rooms** 56.* AMERICAN EXPRESS® *Access, Diners, Visa.*

Heathrow Airport   Park Hotel   61%   £111

Tel 081-759 2400   Fax 081-759 5278   **H**

Bath Road Longford West Drayton Middlesex UB7 0EQ   Map 15 E2

Triple-glazing and air-conditioning in all the bedrooms are big pluses at a low-rise Mount Charlotte hotel located between the A4 and the airport's runways. Banqueting for up to 1000. Major refurbishment is planned for 1995. ***Rooms** 306. Kiosk, coffee shop (10.30am-11.30pm).* AMERICAN EXPRESS® *Access, Diners, Visa.*

Heathrow Airport
Radisson Edwardian International   76%   £184

Tel 081-759 6311   Fax 081-759 4559   **H**

Bath Road Hayes Middlesex UB3 5AW   Map 15 E2

Behind its glass and marble facade the Edwardian International offers
abundant style, comfort, service and modern amenities five minutes from
the airport. Public areas include a vast foyer with carpet-strewn pink
marble floor, cocktail bar-cum-lounge with deep sofas in a variety of rich
fabrics and polo-themed bar sporting real saddles in place of bar stools.
Bedrooms, though not large, are visually appealing with decoratively
painted satinwood furniture and stylishly colourful matching bedcovers
and curtains. There are 17 luxurious suites with marble-lined bathrooms,
spa baths, separate impulse showers and twin washbasins with gold fittings;
some rooms have four-posters. 150 rooms are reserved for non-smokers.
An extensive room service menu is available 24hrs a day. Conferences
are an important part of the business here with a fully-equipped business centre
and a theatre-style capacity of 520 in a wide range of suites. Ample free
parking. *Rooms 459. Indoor swimming pool, gym, sauna, spa bath, solarium,
beauty & hair salon, news kiosk, brasserie (6am-11pm).* AMERICAN EXPRESS *Access,
Diners, Visa.*

Heathrow Airport   Ramada Hotel Heathrow   66%   £115

Tel 081-897 6363   Fax 081-897 1113   **H**

Bath Road Hounslow Middlesex TW6 2AQ   Map 15 E2

In one of the largest hotels on 'the strip' at Heathrow, the public areas were
in the midst of major refurbishment as we went to press in the summer
of '94. About half the bedrooms were still in rather dated 70s' style so until
their planned refurbishment is accomplished best go for the other half,
designated Executive, which were done up a couple of years ago with some
nice bird's-eye maple furniture and white marble trimmings in the
bathrooms. All rooms come with air-conditioning, Robo Bar, new multi-
channel TVs (with airport flight information) and, in the newer rooms,
no less than three telephones. Extensive 24hr room service and high-tech
conference facilities for up to 550 theatre-style. There's a courtesy coach
to the terminals and, by prior booking only, a square deal giving up to
three weeks' free parking when staying the night before you fly out.
*Rooms 638. Indoor swimming pool, gym, sauna, solarium, beauty & hair salons,
kiosk, coffee shop.* AMERICAN EXPRESS *Access, Visa.*

Heathrow Airport   Sheraton Heathrow Hotel   £210

Tel 081-759 2424   Fax 081-759 2091   **H**

Colnbrook bypass West Drayton Middlesex UB7 0HJ   Map 15 E2

Decent-sized bedrooms in a stylishly contemporary hotel a mile from the
airport. Undergoing a complete refurbishment programme as we went
to press. Graded at 70% in last year's Guide. *Rooms 415. Garden, courtesy bus
to airport.* AMERICAN EXPRESS *Access, Diners, Visa.*

Heathrow Airport   Sheraton Skyline   73%   £174

Tel 081-759 2424   Fax 081-750 9150   **H**

Bath Road Hayes Middlesex UB3 5BP   Map 15 E2

The focal point of this hotel on the A4 is the most unusual Patio Caribe,
a large indoor tropical garden complete with palm trees, swimming pool,
bar and music. Rooms range from standard to Executive categories, but all
are right up-to-the-minute, with air-conditioning, automated mini-bars,
computer links, sprinklers and smoke detector system (31 rooms are no-
smoking); rooms on the third floor are designated as de luxe and the
second-floor rooms were due for refurbishment this year. Conference and

banqueting facilities for up to 500. Children up to 16 stay free in parents' room. No dogs. *Rooms 353. Indoor swimming pool, gym, florist, gift shop, coffee shop (6am–1am).* AMERICANEXPRESS® *Access, Diners, Visa.*

Helford   Riverside   £80

Tel 0326 231443 Fax 0326 231103	**RR**
Helford nr Helston Cornwall TR12 6JU	Map 12 B4

In an idyllic setting by a wooded tidal creek, the Riverside is a pretty, cottagey restaurant with rooms run in welcoming style by Edward and Susie Darrell. The kitchen is at the heart of the enterprise, and Susie makes fine use of local produce, particularly seafood, for her four-course dinner menus. Warm mussel and fresh crab salad with a dill dressing, pan-fried scallops with baby asparagus and baby spinach or roast quail with a chicken liver parfait stuffing could start your meal, with steamed fillets of turbot with clams and a chive butter sauce, or best end of lamb in puff pastry with a rosemary-infused red wine sauce as the centrepiece. Next come English and French cheeses, then perhaps bread-and-butter pudding or an iced mango parfait with a passion fruit syrup. Smashing wine list with the New World particularly well represented and reasonably priced. Lots of old vintages, half bottles and asterisks (up to three) for strength of recommendation. No children under 10. *Seats 38. Parties 12. D only 7.30–9.30. Closed Nov–Feb. Set D £30. No credit cards.*

Rooms   £75

The six bedrooms boast antiques, Oriental carpets, fresh flowers, remote-control TV, mini bar, books and magazines but very deliberately no telephones. The terrace is the perfect spot for a splendid Continental breakfast with home-made croissants and marmalade. No dogs. *Garden.*

> Changes in data sometimes occur in establishments after the Guide goes to press. Prices should be taken as indications rather than firm quotes.

Helland Bridge   Tredethy Country Hotel   56%   £68

Tel 0208 841262 Fax 0208 841707	**H**
Helland Bridge Bodmin Cornwall PL30 4QS	Map 12 B3

Take the A389 from Bodmin, then the B3266 to Camelford to find this grey-stone country house, standing in a tranquil setting of nine wooded acres. Best bedrooms are in the light and sunny front half, whereas rooms at the back have views only of the courtyard and another wing. There are also ten self-catering cottages in the grounds. Small banquets/conferences for up to 50. Parking for 60 cars. No dogs. *Rooms 11. Garden, outdoor swimming pool, solarium.* AMERICANEXPRESS® *Access, Diners, Visa.*

Helland Bridge   Places of Interest

Bodmin Tourist Information   Tel 0208 76616.
Tintagel Castle (EH)   Tel 0840 770328 *18 miles.*
Trebarwith Strand Beach *12 miles.*
Lanhydrock   Bodmin Tel 0208 73320.
Pencarrow House and Garden   Nr Bodmin Tel 0208 841369.
Royal Cornwall Showground   Nr Wadebridge Tel 0208 812183.

Hellingley	Forte Travelodge	£45

Tel 0323 844556

Hellingly Hailsham East Sussex BN27 4DT
L
Map 11 B6

On the A22 at the Boship Roundabout, 2 miles north of Hailsham, 9 miles north of Eastbourne. *Rooms 40.* AMERICAN EXPRESS *Access, Diners, Visa.*

Helmsley	Black Swan	69%	£117

Tel 0439 770466   Fax 0439 770174

Market Place Helmsley North Yorkshire YO6 5BJ
H
Map 5 E4

Plenty of history at the Black Swan – it has been an Elizabethan coaching inn, a Tudor rectory, a Georgian private residence; if anything it has come full circle, offering hospitality to travellers in the second Elizabethan era. Day rooms, including several lounges, have heavy timbers, low beamed ceilings and cottagey decor. Residents have their own bar as well as the public bar, both being small, cosy and welcoming. Bedrooms are individually decorated and 12 are designated non-smoking; the restaurant is another smokeless zone. Forte Heritage. *Rooms 44. Garden.* AMERICAN EXPRESS *Access, Diners, Visa.*

Helmsley	Feversham Arms	66%	£70

Tel 0439 770766   Fax 0439 770346

1 High Street Helmsley North Yorkshire YO6 5AG
H
Map 5 E4

Rebuilt in 1855 on the site of the previous Board Inn, the hotel is a good base for touring the Yorkshire Moors and Dales. Bedrooms, all centrally heated, include some with four-posters, and a couple of rooms on the ground floor are suitable for less mobile guests. Day rooms offer a choice of lounge and bars. No children under 6, but 6-16s can share their parents' room free of charge. *Rooms 18. Garden, tennis, outdoor swimming pool.* AMERICAN EXPRESS *Access, Diners, Visa.*

Helmsley	Places of Interest

Rievaulx Abbey   Helmsley Tel 04396 228.
Rievaulx Terrace and Temples.

Hemel Hempstead	Boxmoor Lodge Hotel 57% NEW	£60

Tel 0442 230770   Fax 0442 252230

London Road Hemel Hempstead Hertfordshire HP1 2RA
H
Map 15 E2

Once a family home, Boxmoor Lodge has recently been extended to include a development of 18 chalet-style bedrooms in its grounds alongside the A41 north-west of Hemel Hempstead. The main house has a tiny bar-cum-reception area with a cosy beamed lounge down two steps. Bedrooms are smart, spacious and well maintained, and offer the usual extras like remote TV, trouser press, hairdryer and mineral water. Tariff reductions at weekends when there's a good-value family room. *Rooms 20. Garden.* AMERICAN EXPRESS *Access, Diners, Visa.*

Hemel Hempstead	Forte Posthouse 62% NEW	£67

Tel 0442 251122   Fax 0442 211812

Breakspear Way Hemel Hempstead Hertfordshire HP2 4UA
H
Map 15 E2

On the A414 near the M1 (J8), one of the newest Posthouses with Canadian log cabin-themed public areas and good leisure centre. Children free when sharing parents' room. *Rooms 146. Terrace, indoor swimming pool, gym, spa bath, sauna, steam room, solarium, beauty salon, hair salon.* AMERICAN EXPRESS *Access, Diners, Visa.*

Hemel Hempstead   Travel Inn   NEW   £43

Tel 0442 879149   Fax 0442 879147   **L**

Stoney Lane Bourne End nr Hemel Hempstead Hertfordshire HP1 2SB   Map 15 E2

Off the third exit of A41 (a new dual carriageway), 5 minutes' drive from Junction 20 of M25. Take the third exit for Bourne End Industrial Estate. Meeting rooms available for up to 30. *Rooms 60.* AMERICAN EXPRESS® *Access, Diners, Visa.*

Henley-on-Thames   Red Lion   62%   £100

Tel 0491 572161   Fax 0491 410039   **H**

Hart Street Henley-on-Thames Oxfordshire RG9 2AR   Map 15 D2

Bedroom refurbishment continues at this wisteria-clad hotel by the finishing post of the Henley Royal Regatta rowing course, right by the bridge. Antique pine panelling is a feature in some of the day rooms, and in the bar flagstones and a log fire produce a rustic air. Two small banqueting/conference suites cater for up to 70. Bedrooms (mostly 17th-century) generally combine period appeal with modern comfort. The Regatta Bar offers bar snacks and the restaurant overlooks the river. Families welcome. *Rooms 26.* AMERICAN EXPRESS® *Access, Visa.*

Henley-on-Thames   Places of Interest

Tourist Information   Tel 0491 578034.
Fawley Court   - Marian Fathers Historic House and Museum Tel 0491 574917.
Greys Court (NT)   Rotherfield Grey. Tel 0491 628529.
Stonor Park   Tel 0491 638587.

Hereford   Moat House   63%   £83

Tel 0432 354301   Fax 0432 275114   **H**

Belmont Road Hereford Hereford & Worcester HR2 7BF   Map 14 A1

A mile and a half from the city centre on the Abergavenny road. Accommodation divided between discreet motel-style units and a spacious new extension. Two family rooms, conference facilities for up to 300. *Rooms 60. Garden.* AMERICAN EXPRESS® *Access, Diners, Visa.*

Hereford   Travel Inn   £43

Tel 0432 274853   Fax 0432 343003   **L**

Holmer Road Holmer nr Hereford Hereford & Worcester HR4 9RS   Map 14 A1

Hereford race course and leisure centre 5 minutes' walk. *Rooms 40.* AMERICAN EXPRESS® *Access, Diners, Visa.*

Hereford   Places of Interest

Tourist Information   Tel 0432 268430.
New Hereford Theatre   Tel 0432 268785.
Hereford Cathedral   Tel 0432 359880.
   Historic Houses, Castles and Gardens
Dinmore Manor and Gardens   Leominster Tel 0432 830322.
Moccas Court, House and Parkland   Moccas Tel 0981 500381.
The Weir Garden (NT)   Swainshill Tel 0684 850051.
Hereford Racecourse   Tel 0432 273560.
   Museums and Art Galleries
Hereford City Museum and Art Gallery   Tel 0432 268121 ext 207.
Cider Museum and King Offa Cider Brandy Distillery   Hereford Cider Museum Trust Tel 0432 354207.
Churchill Gardens Museum   Tel 0432 267409.
The Old House   Tel 0432 268121.

Herne Bay   L'Escargot   £55

Tel 0227 372876   **R**

22 High Street Herne Bay Kent CT6 5LH   **Map 11 C5**

Here since 1984, Alain and Joyce Bessemoulin are charming hosts and their
friendly, informal restaurant has an uncomplicated appeal. Alain cooks
in a competent and unfussy fashion using good fresh ingredients in largely
classic French dishes: Burgundy snails, *paté de campagne,* calf's liver with
Dubonnet and orange sauce, breast of chicken *Argenteuil* and pork
Normandy-style are typical. Consult the blackboard for the day's fish
special. *Seats 40. L 12-1.30 D 7-9.30. Closed L Sat, Thur in winter, 1 week
Jan, 1 week Sep. Set L £6.95 Set D £13.95. Access, Visa.*

Herne Bay   Places of Interest

Brambles English Wildlife Rare Breeds Centre   Wealdon Forest Park
   Tel 0227 712379.
Margate Tourist Information   Tel 0843 220241.
Winter Gardens   Tel 0843 292795.
Bembon Brothers Theme Park   Tel 0843 227011.
Cliftonville Aquarium   Tel 0843 221951.

Hersham   The Dining Room   £50

Tel 0932 231686   **R**

10 Queens Road The Village Green Hersham Surrey KT12 5LS   **Map 15 E2**

Scrubbed pine tables, pews and Laura Ashley wallpaper give a country feel
to the five small dining rooms (one for non-smokers) of this friendly,
informal restaurant. The English menu ranges from traditional – steak and
kidney pudding, duck liver paté with Cumberland sauce – to more unusual
offerings like bacon-wrapped banana with peach chutney, black pudding
with tomato and coriander sauce, and duck and raspberry casserole under
a savoury crumble. Cooking is creative rather than refined with fairly
generous portions. *Seats 90. Parties 12. Private Room 30. L 12-2 (Sun
to 2.30) D 7-10.30 (Sat from 6.30). Set L £11.75 (Sun £11/£14) Set
D £12.75. Closed L Sat, D Sun, Bank Holidays & 1 week Christmas.*
AMERICAN EXPRESS® *Access, Visa.*

Herstmonceux   Sundial Restaurant   £90

Tel 0323 832217   **R**

Gardner Street Herstmonceux East Sussex BN27 4LA   **Map 11 B6**

In a setting equally pretty inside and out (this is a good spot for alfresco
eating in summer), the Bertolis have been welcoming diners to their most
civilised 17th-century, tile-hung cottage restaurant for over a quarter
of a century. Laure presides front of house although Giuseppe makes
frequent excursions from the kitchen to greet new and old customers alike.
There are no short cuts taken in the kitchen, where traditional values are
brought to bear on a largely classical French carte. Mousseline of salmon
and prawns, cheese soufflé, bouillabaisse with saffron and rouille, pastry
wrapped venison paté, chicken à la bourguignonne, turbot fillets rolled
with salmon in a beurre blanc sauce with fresh lobster garnish and Barbary
duck with a red wine and red berry sauce are just a small selection from
a fairly extensive choice. For a minimum of two people the five-course
menu surprise might be a good way of avoiding difficult choices. Puds and
Continental cheeses are temptingly displayed on a central buffet table.
Smoking is allowed only in the bar/lounge area. Apart from two
Australian wines, the list cocks a snook at the New World – there are none
at all! However, the French collection is particularly strong, with several
bottles under £20. *Seats 50. Private Room 20. L 12.30-2.30 D 7.30-9.30
(Sat to 10). Closed D Sun, all Mon, 2/3 weeks Aug/Sep, Xmas-mid Jan.
Set L £12.50/£15.50 (Sun £17.50) Set D £24.50.* AMERICAN EXPRESS® *Access,
Diners, Visa.*

Hertingfordbury   **White Horse Hotel**   63%   £107

Tel 0992 586791   Fax 0992 550809   **H**

Hertingfordbury Road Hertingfordbury Hertfordshire SG14 2LB   Map 15 F2

Once a coaching inn on the Cambridge-Reading run, now a mix
of Georgian facade, earlier interiors and modern bedroom blocks. Small
banquets/conferences (25/40) only. Forte Heritage. *Rooms 42. Garden.*
AMERICAN EXPRESS *Access, Diners, Visa.*

Hertingfordbury   **Place of Interest**

Hatfield House and Gardens   Hatfield Tel 0707 262823.

Hethersett   **Park Farm Hotel**   64%   £70

Tel 0603 810264   Fax 0603 812104   **H**

Hethersett nr Norwich Norfolk NR9 2PP   Map 10 C2

Five miles south of Norwich, the Gowing family's hotel has expanded
considerably over the years from the original Georgian farmhouse.
Bedrooms in various styles (Executives have four-posters and whirlpool
baths) are arranged around the landscaped gardens, some in the old
buildings, others in a renovated Norfolk barn. 28 of the rooms are
designated non-smoking. Also in outbuildings are a well-equipped leisure
complex and the six conference rooms. *Rooms 38. Garden, croquet, indoor
swimming pool, gym, sauna, spa bath, steam room, solarium, tennis, games room,
snooker, helipad.* AMERICAN EXPRESS *Access, Diners, Visa.*

Hetton   **Angel Inn**   £65

Tel 0756 730263   Fax 0756 730363   **R**

Hetton nr Skipton North Yorkshire BD23 6LT   Map 6 C1

Success has not come suddenly nor overnight to Denis Watkins and John
Topham, who apply rare expertise as much to the restaurant as they
do their acclaimed bar and brasserie (awarded a star in our 1994 *Pubs and
Inns* Guide). Dinners follow a fixed-price format of well-balanced multiple
choice. Seafood is well represented, in a starter of hot boudin of scallops and
scampi, served with charred salmon and a light lemon and ginger sauce,
or as a daily market-led main course. Alternative seasonal offerings might
be confit of duck leg cooked à la grecque and chargrilled breasts of wood
pigeon served on a crouton with wild mushrooms, lardons and flageolet
beans. Composition is consistently thoughtful and balanced, and skilfully
executed. To follow, hot sticky toffee pudding remains a firm Yorkshire
favourite; a more delicate alternative is to be found in roast glazed pears
with honey ice cream and a blackberry coulis. The Watkins' wine list is an
eclectic and personal one. Vacuum storage permits the diner the rare
luxury of sampling wines by the glass from the extensive cellar chosen
to complement each course. *Seats 50. L (Sun only) 12-1.30 D 7-9.30.
Closed L Mon-Sat, D Sun (except by arrangment). Set D £21.95. Access, Visa.*

Hexham   **Beaumont Hotel**   62%   £80

Tel & Fax 0434 602331   **H**

Beaumont Street Hexham Northumberland NE46 3LT   Map 5 D2

A compact and neatly-kept family-run hotel at the heart of town, handy
for both shopping and the historic Abbey. The glass-fronted foyer/lounge
and a convivial bar are the extent of day rooms at street level, with
a cocktail bar and boardroom on the first floor overlooking the abbey
gardens. Pastel papers and bright bedspreads enliven well-equipped
bedrooms (80% of them are non-smoking), the best of which sport large
Georgian-style windows. There are six rather smaller single rooms.

Children under 6 stay free in parents' room). No dogs. Conference/ banqueting for up to 80. **Rooms 23.** *Keep-fit equipment, sun beds. Closed 25 & 26 Dec.* AMERICANEXPRESS® *Access, Diners, Visa.*

Hexham   Places of Interest

Museum of Border History   Tel 0434 604011 *Not Weekends*
Hexham Racecourse   Tel 0434 603738.

Hickstead   Forte Travelodge   NEW   £45

Tel 0444 881377   **L**

A23 Hickstead West Sussex   Map 11 B6

10 miles north of Brighton on the A23. **Rooms 40.** AMERICANEXPRESS® *Access, Diners, Visa.*

High Wycombe   Forte Posthouse   65%   £68

Tel 0494 442100   Fax 0494 439071   **H**

Crest Road High Wycombe Buckinghamshire HP11 1TL   Map 15 E2

Low-riser by Junction 4 of the M40, with conference and banqueting facilities for around 100. **Rooms 106.** *Garden, children's playground, pool table.* AMERICANEXPRESS® *Access, Diners, Visa.*

High Wycombe   Places of Interest

Tourist Information   Tel 0494 421892.
Wycombe Sports Centre Swimming Pool   Tel 0494 446324.
   Historic Houses, Castles and Gardens
Hughenden Manor (NT)   Tel 0494 532580 *Home of Benjamin Disraeli.*
West Wycombe Park (NT)   West Wycombe Tel 0494 24411.
Chenies Manor House and Garden   Little Chalfont Tel 0494 762888
   8 miles on A404.

Higham   The Knowle   £68

Tel 0474 822262   **R**

School Lane Higham nr Rochester Kent ME3 7HP   Map 11 B5

Set in three acres of secluded gardens, making it a popular wedding venue on Saturdays, Lyn and Michael Baragwanath's large Victorian rectory is both an easygoing restaurant and a family home. Sit in the eclectically furnished bar to choose from an equally varied menu of dishes more notable for fresh ingredients and generous portions than modern fads. Cheese soufflé royale, peach Knowle (filled with a mixture of cheese, herbs, brandy and garlic), grilled Dover sole, chicken with ginger, pot-roast pheasant and various sauced steaks show the range. Lunchtimes (except Sunday) and Tuesday to Thursday evenings there is an additional 'Bistro' menu that is considerably less expensive than the standard carte. **Seats 60.** *Private Room 45. L 12.30-2 D 6.30-9.30. Closed L Sat, D Sun, all Mon. Set L £14.95. Access, Visa.*

Highclere   The Yew Tree   £50

Tel 0635 253360   **R**

Hollington Cross Andover Road Highclere nr Newbury Berkshire RG15 9SE   Map 15 D3

A delightful 15th-century inn just south of the village on the A343. Several cottagey interconnecting rooms form the restaurant where Jenny Wratten offers an intriguing menu. Her repertoire is firmly English, with many traditional and old-fashioned items: South Coast plaice on or off the bone, tweed kettle tart (salmon in a pastry case with a leek, chive and parsley sauce), hot crab ramekins, breast of duck with a honey and orange sauce. Finish with a savoury (perhaps herring roes on a toasted muffin), chocolate and brandy mousse or rhubarb and champagne jellies. There's a pretty patio for summer eating. Six cottagey rooms offer comfortable overnight accommodation. *Seats 50. Parties 25. Private Room 20. L 12-2.30 D 6.30-10 (7-9.30 Sun).* AMERICAN EXPRESS® *Access, Visa.*

Hinckley	Hinckley Island Hotel	64%	£89
Tel 0455 631122 Fax 0455 634536			**H**
The A5 Hinckley Leicestershire LE10 3JA			Map 7 D4

Adjacent to exit 1 of the M69, at the junction of the A5, this conference-oriented hotel covers some 15 acres. A huge statue of Neptune greets arrivals in the marble-floored, mirror-ceilinged foyer. Accommodation is all comfortable but the newer de luxe rooms are more spacious and more stylish than standard rooms. Children up to 16 stay free in parents' room. No dogs. The conference facilities can handle up to 400 delegates. *Rooms 270. Indoor swimming pool, gym, sauna, spa bath, steam room, solarium, beauty & hair salon, snooker, fishing, news kiosk, coffee shop (7am-10pm)* AMERICAN EXPRESS® *Access, Diners, Visa.*

Hinckley   Places of Interest

Nuneaton Tourist Information   Tel 0203 384027.
Arbury Hall   Tel 0203 382804 or 0676 40259 *8 miles.*
Twycross Zoo   Morton-Juxta-Twycross, Atherstone Tel 0827 880250.

Hintlesham	Hintlesham Hall	82%	£97
Tel 0473 652268 Fax 0473 652463			**HR**
Hintlesham nr Ipswich Suffolk IP8 3NS			Map 10 C3

A fine Tudor mansion to which an imposing Georgian facade and entrance arcade were latter added, Hintlesham enjoys a lovely setting in the rolling Suffolk countryside just to the south-west of Ipswich. The interior lives up to its impressive external appearance with no less than four elegant, comfortably furnished dayrooms – twin drawing rooms in one of which is the bar, a red-walled library with period-painted floor and various board games sharing space with the shelves of books, and the peaceful Garden Room – all well supplied with fresh flowers and well-chosen art works. Several categories of bedroom – from 'small doubles' to 'large principal rooms' and suites – vary in size rather than levels of comfort and decor (most are named after the predominant fabric design used) with all having a mixture of antiques and reproduction furniture, good armchairs and a generally luxurious feel. Many, including the 12 in a separate Courtyard block, feature characterful old timbers. Fine bathrooms, all but seven with separate walk-in showers, mostly have bidets and often feature white marble trimmings. All have bathrobes and quality toiletries. Notably friendly staff offer a high standard of care from automatic luggage porterage to 24hr room service. Good breakfasts begin with freshly squeezed orange or grapefruit juice. *Rooms 33. Garden, croquet, tennis, golf (18), outdoor swimming pool, game fishing, sauna, steam room, spa bath, solarium, snooker, helipad.* AMERICAN EXPRESS® *Access, Diners, Visa.*

Restaurant   £90

Depending on the number of diners, you eat either in the pine-panelled 'Parlour' or in the very grand, high-ceilinged 'Salon', although the decor here in shades of mauve may be something of an acquired taste. It takes no effort at all though to develop a taste for the uncomplicated cooking that emerges from Alan Ford's kitchen. Established combinations like carrot and orange soup, asparagus with hollandaise sauce and duck with cassis sauce share the menu with more inventive dishes such as medallions of pork with black pudding timbale and smoked bacon sauce and steamed turbot with braised endive and an orange and green peppercorn sauce plus such modish offerings as pithiviers of mozzarella, sun-dried tomato and spinach on a chive sauce, and seized fillet of haddock served with creamed polenta and a tomato and olive butter sauce. Super wine list with each country prefaced by knowledgeable notes. House recommendations well worth looking at, as is the entire list, which has been carefully and thoughtfully compiled. Decent prices ensure good drinking here! *Seats* 120. L 12-2 D 7-9.30. Set L £18.50 Set D £24.

Hinton   Hinton Grange   62%   £108

Tel 0272 372916   Fax 0272 373285   **HR**

Hinton nr Dyrham Wiltshire SN14 8HG   Map 13 F1

The Lindsay-Walkers' conversion of a stone farmhouse and outbuilding in six acres of grounds has brought a touch of country living only minutes from Bath and the M4 (from Junction 18). The main building comprises a 15th-century stone-flagged bar and a lounge in simple Chinese style; a conservatory houses both bar and heated swimming pool. Bedrooms in the surrounding buildings are Victorian-style recreations, with period washstands and bathing alcoves. There are antique four-posters and open fires (£7.95 charge for the thrill of being greeted by it lit, 2 hours' notice required). A lake has a tiny island with one tree and a summer house from which one can fish for trout. The Palm Court conservatory pool-side bar area is kept at tropical heat all year round, nurturing palm trees and orchids, and even providing bananas for the restaurant. Banqueting/ conference facilities for 55/25. No children under 16. Separate high-season tariff. *Rooms* 18. *Garden, croquet, 9-hole pitch & putt, indoor swimming pool, gym, sauna, solarium, tennis, fishing.* AMERICAN EXPRESS *Access, Diners, Visa.*

Inglenook Restaurant   £50

Informal surroundings for sound cooking by chef Neil Cooper, whose short à la carte is typified by a choice of home-made soups, smoked supremes of chicken and duck on celeriac purée with a light horseradish dressing, skate wing with orange and lemon sauce, herb-crusted best end of lamb, and a filo pastry money bag filled with apple and raspberries set on a puddle of warm butterscotch sauce; simpler dishes are always available on request, as is a good-value fixed-price menu. Vegetarians are well catered for. Seating for 15 on a terrace in summer. No children under 16. *Seats 60. Parties 12. Private Room 15. L 12.15-2.30 D 7-9.45. Set L £14.95 Set D £16.95.*

Hockley Heath   Nuthurst Grange   74%   £117

Tel 0564 783972   Fax 0564 783919   **HR**

Nuthurst Grange Lane Hockley Heath Warwickshire B94 5NL   Map 6 C4

The original redbrick house has been added to a number of times over the last 100 years, but the overall result is a surprisingly handsome building, helped by its setting in extensive landscaped grounds. The restaurant takes pride of place on the ground floor along with a pair of plush chesterfield-furnished lounges (one for non-smokers) where drinks are also served; there is no bar. Pretty, individually-decorated bedrooms are spacious and comfortable with sofas and armchairs alongside the freestanding, darkwood furniture, and extras ranging from books, chocolates and fruit to more mundane fly-spray and shoe-cleaning kit. Poly-cotton duvets are standard but more traditional bedding is available on request. Bathrooms all have 'air spa' baths, telephone extensions, bathrobes and personal room safes. "Suitable for children who are well behaved." Conference/banqueting for 80/95. No dogs. M40 J16 is northbound only, so, from the south, take M42 northbound and then exit at J4, proceeding via A3400 to Hockley Heath. *Rooms* 15. *Garden, croquet, helipad.* AMERICAN EXPRESS *Access, Diners, Visa.*

Restaurant   £60

The restaurant is very much the centrepiece of the hotel. Chef-proprietor David Randolph sources and handles fine, fresh produce with great care, creating dishes on the variety of fixed-price-only menus that are notable for honest, distinctive flavours and attractive presentation. A simpler, short choice table d'hote might offer broccoli and almond soup followed by whole roasted pigeon with a burgundy and thyme sauce, finishing with steamed date pudding with toffee sauce; the fixed-price à la carte extends to cover terrine of foie gras and leek, confit of duck with Chinese spices, lobster and Cheddar bisque, whole roasted, boneless quails with Jerusalem artichoke and Madeira, and breast of guinea fowl with smoked bacon and sauerkraut. Desserts might include an unusual tea mousse with oranges or warm strawberries with green peppercorns and a ginger ice-cream. Separate vegetarian menu. Fresh herbs come from their own Victorian walled garden. No smoking (puffers can use the lounge if desperate). The concise wine list features clarets, burgundies and a good house selection. Toilets equipped for disabled guests. *Seats 50. Parties 10. Private Rooms 95. L 12-2 D 7-9.30. Closed L Sat. Set L £16.50 & £18.90/£23.90 Set D £23.90 & £29.90-£45.*

Hockley Heath   Travel Inn (Solihull)   NEW   £43

| Tel 021 744 2942   Fax 021 733 7075 | L |

Stratford Road Hockley Heath nr Shirley Solihull West Midlands B90 4PT   Map 6 C4

On A3400 Birmingham to Stratford-upon-Avon road, 2 miles south of Junction 4 of M42. *Rooms 40.* AMERICAN EXPRESS *Access, Diners, Visa.*

Holbeton   Alston Hall   65%   £90

| Tel 0752 830555   Fax 0752 830494 | H |

Alston Cross Holbeton nr Plymouth Devon PL8 1HN   Map 13 D3

Alston Hall is set in four acres of parkland and offers lovely views across the South Hams to the sea. It's just outside the village, and it's a good idea to ask for directions when booking. Built in 1906, the Hall retains its Edwardian elegance, especially in the galleried and panelled Great Hall which gains illumination through lovely stained glass windows. Individually decorated bedrooms have attractive matching bedcovers and curtains and smart carpeted bathrooms. All are furnished and equipped to the same standard with superior rooms (£10 supplement) being larger and having the better views. Banqueting/conferences for up to 100; parking for 100. *Rooms 20. Garden, croquet, indoor swimming pool, keep-fit equipment, sauna, solarium, tennis.* AMERICAN EXPRESS *Access, Diners, Visa.*

Hollingbourne   Jarvis Great Danes   64%   £102

| Tel 0622 631163   Fax 0622 735290 | H |

Ashford Road Hollingbourne Kent ME17 1RE   Map 11 C5

Great Danes stands in 22 acres of grounds next door to Leeds Castle off Junction 8 of the M20. It has very extensive, up-to-the-minute conference facilities and also on site is the Sebastian Coe Health Park whose attractions include a running track and floodlit tennis courts. Some rooms suitable for family use; conferences for up to 600, theatre-style. *Rooms 126. Garden, indoor swimming pool, gym, sauna, solarium, tennis, 9-hole pitch & putt, helipad.* AMERICAN EXPRESS *Access, Diners, Visa.*

Hope Cove   Cottage Hotel   56%   £94*

| Tel 0548 561555 | H |

Hope Cove nr Kingsbridge Devon TQ7 3HJ   Map 13 D3

The village of Hope Cove rests in the curve of Bigbury Bay and this popular family hotel makes the most of the views. The sun terrace is the place to be in summer, while inside there are three lounges and a cocktail bar which was built from timbers salvaged from a wrecked windjammer, the *Herzogin Cecilie*. 25 bedrooms now have en-suite facilities and some have balconies. A few singles at the back miss out on the sea views and are

priced lower. Much reduced rates for children. *Half-board terms.
*Rooms 35. Garden, games room, tots' outdoor play area. Closed Jan.
No credit cards.*

Hope Cove	Lantern Lodge	59%	£69
Tel 0548 561280			**H**
Grand View Road Hope Cove nr Kingsbridge Devon TQ7 3HE			Map 13 D3

Overlooking the sea and the fishing village of Hope Cove, the Lantern
Lodge is a pleasant and popular clifftop hotel. It's easy to relax in the cosy
little bar or in the homely lounges with their antique pieces and choice
of TV or books. Individually furnished bedrooms (three with four-posters)
are well kept, with neat bath or shower rooms. Sea view rooms are priced
slightly higher. No children under ten. No dogs. *Rooms 14. Garden,
putting, indoor swimming pool, keep-fit equipment, sauna, sun beds.
Closed Dec-Feb. Access, Visa.*

Horley	Langshott Manor	73%	£106
Tel 0293 786680 Fax 0293 783905			**HR**
Langshott Horley Surrey RH6 9LN			Map 11 B5

Personally run by the Noble family, this small Elizabethan manor house
has enormous charm. Domestic-scale day rooms with mellow panelling,
old timbers and rug-strewn floors gain a real homely atmosphere from
family photos, fresh flowers (from the delightful gardens), objets d'art and
the house labrador dozing in front of the open-hearth fire with its
smouldering logs. Bedrooms are no less characterful or appealing with
antique furniture, stylish fabrics and all sorts of personal touches plus high-
quality beds with the finest Egyptian cotton bedding. Smoking is allowed
downstairs but not in the bedrooms. Three acres of "peaceful, English
gardens". An added attraction is a one-way courtesy car on departure
to nearby Gatwick airport and free parking for up to two weeks. No dogs.
Rooms 7. Garden, croquet. Closed 24-30 Dec. AMERICAN EXPRESS *Access,
Diners, Visa.*

Restaurant £65

A tiny dining room with just a few lace-clothed tables, so for non-residents
it is strictly by prior reservation only. Christopher, the son of the house, has
largely taken over from mother in the kitchen but the cooking remains
unpretentiously good and satisfying. The fixed-price-only menus generally
offer a choice of three or four dishes at each stage beginning with
mushroom soup, chicken liver paté and melon with port, perhaps to be
followed by pheasant with Calvados and cream, sole and salmon paupiettes,
rosemary lamb and filet mignon with mushrooms and Marsala. Vegetables
are simply cooked and desserts might include the likes of chocolate roulade
and bread-and-butter pudding. The well-chosen wine list is more than
adequate, the Nobles' native New Zealand being well represented.
No smoking. *Seats 14. Private Room 12. L by arrangement D 7-9.30.
Set L £15/£22 Set D £18/£25.*

Horndon-on-the-Hill	The Bell Inn & Hill House	£50
Tel 0375 642463 Fax 0375 361611		**RR**
High Road Horndon-on-the-Hill Essex SS17 8LD		Map 11 B4

Located in the village centre a few doors from one another, the two
establishments are in the same family ownership. The Bell, dating in part
from the 15th century, offers a blackboard menu and a friendly rustic,
pubby ambience including beams, unpolished wood tables and flagstone
floors, while Hill House next door has more formal dining in a pretty
pastel-coloured room. The Bell menu features both simple and more
unusual dishes: seafood broth, roast duck and avocado salad, lamb cutlets
baked in pastry with a haggis mousse. Starters at Hill House from a choice
of about nine could include smoked salmon and cream cheese parcels,

asparagus with lemon hollandaise or chicken and guinea fowl sausage. Main dishes from an ample and varied selection of about ten are typified by salmon baked with ginger, roast breast of duck with honey and peaches, and loin of pork with shiitake mushrooms and spring onions. This is imaginative cooking, skilfully executed and with very enjoyable results on the plate. Sweets follow in the same conservatively innovative style with apple and rhubarb crumble served with whisky anglaise or lime and ginger mousse. Diverse wine list. The Bell Inn has a marquee (available for functions) which can seat 120. *Bell Inn: **Seats** 40. Parties 12. Private Room 60. L 12-1.45 D 7.15-9.45. Closed 25 & 26 Dec. Hill House: **Seats** 32. Parties 12. L 12-2 D 7.30-9.45. Closed L Sat, all Sun & Mon, 25-31 Dec. Set meals from £14.95.* AMERICAN EXPRESS *Access, Visa.*

Rooms £54

Above and also to the rear of Hill House are 11 pretty, cottagey en-suite bedrooms, each thoughtfully equipped and neatly maintained.

Horsham   Travel Inn £43

Tel 0403 250141   Fax 0403 270797   **L**

57 North Street Horsham West Sussex RH12 1RB   **Map 11 A6**

Straightforward lodge accommodation with ample parking. 21 rooms reserved for non-smokers. ***Rooms** 40.* AMERICAN EXPRESS *Access, Diners, Visa.*

Horton   French Partridge £60

Tel 0604 870033   Fax 0604 870032   **R**

Horton nr Northampton Northamptonshire NN7 2AP   **Map 15 D1**

The Partridges have been serving good food at their friendly restaurant since 1963 and have many loyal customers. Bottle-green walls hung with oil paintings, black leather banquettes and polished mahogany tables create a sedate, traditional ambience. The fixed-price, constantly changing menu offers four courses (plus coffee) with a small choice at each stage; perhaps cream of watercress soup or marinated fresh salmon and sardine fillets with a new potato salad to start, followed by a second course of cheese fondue pancake or smoked haddock tart topped with a poached egg; main courses might offer a choice of chicken breast with mild curry sauce, escalope of turkey stuffed with Parma ham and cream cheese, 'old-fashioned' braised oxtail with herb dumplings or filo pastry-wrapped leg of farmed rabbit with pork and hazelnut stuffing. The choice extends at dessert to up to seven – from brown sugar meringues to iced orange soufflé with Grand Marnier and bombe cevenole (an ice cream pudding with vanilla shell and sweet chestnut filling) – plus a savoury like soft herring roes on toast. Fair prices on the interesting wine list that features a good selection of clarets and burgundies and an unusual choice of three viognier whites from the Rhone. Smoking is discouraged. The restaurant is on the B526 Northampton-Newport Pagnell road. ***Seats** 40. Parties 10. D only 7.30-9. Closed Sun & Mon, 2 weeks Christmas, 2 weeks Easter, first 3 weeks Aug. Set D £23. No credit cards.*

Horton-cum-Studley   Studley Priory   64% £98

Tel 0865 351203   Fax 0865 351613   **H**

Horton-cum-Studley nr Oxford Oxfordshire OX33 1AZ   **Map 15 D2**

Set in 13 acres of wooded grounds seven miles from Oxford, this striking Elizabethan manor house has impressive day rooms that include a splendid hall panelled in pitch pine, a lofty drawing room and a Victorian bar with oak panelling. Six bedrooms are in the main house (one with a four-poster dating from about 1700), while the majority are in the Jacobean wing reached through a labyrinth of corridors. These rooms are smaller and more modern. Children up to 16 share parents' room free of charge. Small conferences (for up to 45, theatre-style) are big business here, so you'll sometimes be sharing the drawing room with the delegates. *Rooms 19. Garden, croquet, tennis, clay-pigeon shooting, helipad.* AMERICAN EXPRESS *Access, Diners, Visa.*

Hove. For entries under Hove please refer to Brighton.

Hovingham	Worsley Arms	£98
Tel 0653 628234 Fax 0653 628130		**I**
Hovingham North Yorkshire YO6 4LA		Map 5 E4

Built in 1841 and described as late late-Georgian in style, the inn has from that day to this been in the hands of the Worsley family, owners of nearby Hovingham Hall. Inside are elegant, comfortable lounges and the lively, recently refurbished Cricketers Bar, HQ of the local team and hung with a photographic collection of Yorkshire's greatest in action. Spacious bedrooms echo the Georgian feel and all have traditionally appointed bathrooms with large bathsheets and generous toiletries. Picnic hampers provided on request for those intent on exploring Ryedale. *Rooms 22. Garden, squash, mountain bikes.* AMERICAN EXPRESS *Access, Barclaycard.*

Huddersfield	George Hotel	62%	£85
Tel 0484 515444 Fax 0484 435056			**H**
St George's Square Huddersfield West Yorkshire HD1 1JA			Map 6 C1

In the main square opposite the railway station, a large Victorian building with sizeable conference and banqueting rooms (up to 200 delegates) plus stylish, well-equipped bedrooms. Guests enjoy free admission to Huddersfield Sports Centre, whose facilities include an Olympic-size swimming pool. Children under 14 stay free in parents' room. *Rooms 60.* AMERICAN EXPRESS *Access, Diners, Visa.*

Huddersfield	Pennine Hilton National	66%	£96
Tel 0422 375431 Fax 0422 310067			**H**
Ainley Top Huddersfield West Yorkshire HD3 3RH			Map 6 C1

Above the town centre, conveniently located by junction 24 of the M62, a modern, low-rise hotel with attractive, contemporary-style bedrooms with small, but bright, bathrooms. Children up to 12 stay free in parents' room. Leisure Centre and conference facilities for up to 450. Ample free car parking. *Rooms 118. Indoor swimming pool, sauna, steam room, gym, coffee shop (7am-10pm).* AMERICAN EXPRESS *Access, Diners, Visa.*

Huddersfield   Places of Interest

Tourist Information   Tel 0484 430808.
Holmfirth Postcard Museum   Holmfirth Tel 0484 682231.
Huddersfield Art Gallery   Tel 0484 513808.

Hull	Campanile Hotel	£44
Tel 0482 25530 Fax 0482 587538		**L**
Beverley Road/Freetown Way Hull Humberside HU2 9AN		Map 7 E1

Off the A63, within the city centre, near the station. *Rooms 50.* AMERICAN EXPRESS *Access, Diners, Visa.*

Hull	Ceruttis	£60
Tel 0482 28501 Fax 0482 587597		**R**
10 Nelson Street Hull Humberside HU1 1XE		Map 7 E1

The Cerutti family have completed 20 years at their friendly harbourside restaurant, where seafood is naturally the speciality. Dover sole remains a favourite (grilled, meunière or six other ways) and several dishes, including fish cakes, scallops and scampi, are available as either starter or main course. King prawns – cold, or hot in garlic butter – are sold by the unit, and Ceruttis' fish grill is an appetising platter of lightly grilled mixed fish. A few meat dishes, but this really is a classic restaurant for seafoodies. *Seats 40. Private Room 24. L 12-2 D 7-9.30. Set D from £11.50. Closed L Sat, all Sun, Bank Holidays, 1 week Xmas. Access, Visa.*

Hull   Forte Crest   69%   £109

Tel 0482 225221   Fax 0482 213299   **H**

Castle Street Hull Humberside HU1 2BX   Map 7 E1

Alongside the impressive dock development, the best rooms in this purpose-built hotel have balconies and fine views over the marina. Conferences and banqueting for 120. Children up to 16 free in parents' room. *Rooms 99. Patio, indoor swimming pool, gym, sauna, solarium, beauty salon.* AMERICAN EXPRESS *Access, Diners, Visa.*

Hull   Forte Posthouse   62%   £68

Tel 0482 645212   Fax 0482 643332   **H**

Ferriby High Road North Ferriby Hull Humberside HU14 3LG   Map 7 E1

Comfortable modern hotel outside Hull, overlooking the remarkable suspension bridge. About half the bedrooms are reserved for non-smokers. Banqueting/conferences for up to 100. *Rooms 95.* AMERICAN EXPRESS *Access, Diners, Visa.*

Hull   Travel Inn   £43

Tel 0482 645285   Fax 0482 645299   **L**

Ferriby Road Hessle Hull Humberside HU31 0JA   Map 7 E1

North of the Humber Bridge. From M62 take A63 until you see the bridge; the left lane is signed to Humber Bridge and Beverley and the hotel is on the first roundabout. 5 minutes' drive from Hull city centre. *Rooms 40.* AMERICAN EXPRESS *Access, Diners, Visa.*

Hull   Places of Interest

Tourist Information   Tel 0482 223559.
Burton Constable Hall and Gardens   Tel 0964 562400.
   Theatres and Concert Halls
New Theatre   Tel 0482 20244.
Spring Street Theatre   Tel 0482 20491.
Truck Theatre   Tel 0482 225800.
   Museums and Art Galleries
Ferens Art Gallery   Tel 0482 222750.
Town Docks Museum   Tel 0482 222737.
University of Hull Art Collection   Tel 0482 465192.
Wilberforce House and Georgian Houses   Tel 0482 222737.
Hull City Football Ground   Tel 0482 51119.
Hull RLFC   Tel 0482 29040
Hull Kingston Rovers RLFC   Tel 0482 74648
Humberside Ice Arena   Tel 0482 25252.

Hungerford   Jarvis Bear Hotel   63%   £75

Tel 0488 682512   Fax 0488 684357   **H**

Charnham Street Hungerford Berkshire RG17 0EL   Map 14 C2

Just 3 miles from Junction 14 of the M4 on the A4 on the outskirts of town, one of England's most historic inns, once owned by Henry VIII, provides modern comforts in evocative surroundings. Accommodation includes four-poster rooms and courtyard rooms looking on the river Dunn. Guests have the use of free health facilities at the nearby Elcot Park

Hotel (3 miles away, under the same ownership) and squash, gym, saunas, snooker and skittles at the Meadowview Leisure Club (50 yards away). *Rooms* 41. *Garden.* AMERICAN EXPRESS *Access, Diners, Visa.*

Hunstrete	Hunstrete House	77%	£150
Tel 0761 490490 Fax 0761 490732			**HR**
Hunstrete Chelwood nr Bath Avon BS18 4NS			**Map 13 F1**

Off the A368 about equidistant from Bristol and Bath, the hotel stands in 92 acres of grounds fronted by a deer park. Built in the 18th century, the property now has new owners who have completed a major restoration programme, bringing Hunstrete closer to the upper echelons of classic English country house hotels. The inner hall (with no natural light) has an open fireplace with settees gathered round it to create a cosy corner while the other main rooms take full advantage of a glorious south-facing aspect. The library and, next door, the drawing room, as well as the now totally remodelled bar, are decorated in a fashionably traditional style with fine paintings, polished antiques and beautiful flower arrangements. Fine fabrics are used for drapes and upholstery too. Bedrooms, whether in the main house or across the sunny courtyard, are both smart and spacious. Each is furnished to a high standard, mirroring the day rooms with a fine collection of elegant furnishings. There is ample seating and a welcoming decanter of sherry too. Bathrooms are splendid, fitted with marble bath surrounds and having carpeted floors. Showers are first-rate and about half the bathrooms have bidets. All have a good supply of thick towels and quality toiletries. Staff are charming, forever with a smile it seems. Some are long-serving, having been here since its first days as a hotel in the late 70s. *Rooms* 24. *Garden, croquet, outdoor swimming pool, tennis.* AMERICAN EXPRESS *Access, Visa.*

Restaurant   £100

New chef Robert Clayton joined after our last visit and just as we went to press. Early menus read well: spring consommé with garden vegetables, pan-fried calf's liver with a purée of onion and thyme with a Madeira and almond sauce, apple and pear tart with caramel sauce. *Seats* 50. *Parties* 10. *Private Room* 30. L 12.30-2 D 7.30-9.30. Set L £15 (Set Sun L £19.50) Set D £23.50.

Huntingdon	Old Bridge Hotel	68%	£90
Tel 0480 52681 Fax 0480 411017			**HR**
1 High Street Huntingdon Cambridgeshire PE18 6TQ			**Map 7 E4**

As its name suggests, the hotel stands alongside an ancient bridge that crosses the River Great Ouse. A short distance from the town centre and on the ring road, its creeper-clad Georgian exterior is a welcome sign of hospitality. Public rooms comprise a spacious open-plan lounge with three steps leading down to the bar. The Terrace, a restaurant that opens out from the lounge, is where breakfast is taken – choice being from an extensive cold buffet selection and some carefully cooked items. Numerous summery murals decorate the walls. Well-co-ordinated colour schemes and comfortable period-style furniture give the place a genteel country-house atmosphere. Bedrooms are furnished in a similar manner, some with boldly exciting colour schemes and all with a good selection of extras. One room has a brass four-poster. Bathrooms are carpeted, and provide bathrobes, a good supply of thick towels and quality toiletries. One of the hotel's chief attributes is the charm and courtesy of the staff and this is apparent the minute you enter the lobby. Poste Hotels. *Rooms* 26. *Garden.* AMERICAN EXPRESS *Access, Diners, Visa.*

Restaurant   £80

Nick Steiger, formerly of the *Pheasant* at Keyston (see entry), also part of the small Poste Hotels group, has settled well into the more challenging role of chef-patron of this popular hostelry. The dining room with its limed oak panelling and black-and-gold-framed ancient prints is the setting for food that is an exciting and eclectic mix ranging from such starters as warm potato latkes with smoked salmon and sour cream and chicken teriyaki with daikon and sesame sauce or dariole of turbot in spinach with a Madeira sauce. Main dishes, too, are equally imaginative and well-thought-out; for instance, monkfish is roasted and comes with deep-fried chard and a Thai spice sauce and magret of duck breast has mashed turnips and a purée of apple and cinnamon as accompaniments. The selection of British cheeses is superb and sweets are such classic favourites as sticky toffee pudding, or a featherlight chocolate soufflé accompanied by a creamy rum and raisin ice cream. Quite simply the wine list is a wow! The 'house' selection for instance offers over twenty well-chosen wines from all areas (several available by the glass) under £20, including a quality champagne. Overall the entire list is very fairly priced, and there are many half bottles and magnums, as well as remnant bin ends from past lists; apposite tasting notes. Informal eating in The Terrace (jazz nights on the first Friday of the month) includes a lunchtime buffet. Courteous, attentive staff. *Seats 44. Parties 14. Private Room 28. L 12-2 D 7-10. Closed D 25 Dec. Set Sun L £18.95.*

Huntingdon   Places of Interest

Island Hall Godmanchester Tel 0480 459676.
The Cromwell Museum Tel 0480 425830.
Huntingdon Racecourse Tel 0480 453373.

We welcome bona fide complaints and recommendations on the tear-out pages at the back of the book for readers' comments. They are followed up by our professional team.

Huntsham   Huntsham Court   68%   £125

Tel 039 86 365 Fax 039 86 456	**HR**
Huntsham nr Bampton Tiverton Devon EX16 7NA	Map 13 D2

A rather gaunt Victorian Gothic pile run in friendly, very casual style by owners Mogens and Andrea Bolwig. Eating is communal, there's an honour system in the bar, and you just wander into the kitchen if you need anything. There's great atmosphere in the day rooms (log fires, a panelled great hall, splendid pieces of furniture) and in the roomy bedrooms, named after composers, there are Victorian beds and baths and pre-war radios with an authentic crackle – not a teasmaid in sight! The hotel is dedicated to music, with the classical variety played *forte* in the evening. The day starts with an excellent buffet breakfast. No dogs, however "good" or "small". Private house parties and group functions are a speciality and their mood is likely to determine the atmosphere. It's about as far away from the world of chain hotels as you could imagine. *Rooms 14. Garden, croquet, tennis, sauna, mini-gym, snooker.* AMERICAN EXPRESS *Access, Diners, Visa.*

Restaurant   £75

Five-course dinners (no choice, but variations possible in advance) are served by candle-light in leisurely fashion at an often convivial, communal table. Guests are welcome to browse around the wine cellars where they'll find the New World and Spain particularly well represented; fair prices and some wines charged by the glass from bottles left open on the table. *Seats 30. D only 8-10. Set D £25.30.*

Huntsham   Places of Interest

Tiverton Tourist Information   0884 255827.
Knightshayes Court (NT)   Nr Tiverton Tel 0884 254665.
Tiverton Castle   Tel 0884 253200.
The Tiverton Museum   Tel 0884 256295.

Hurley   Ye Olde Bell   65%   £100

Tel 0628 825881   Fax 0628 825939   **H**
High Street Hurley nr Maidenhead Berkshire SL6 5LX   Map 15 D2

Built in 1135 as a guest house for a Benedictine monastery, this black-and-white inn has claims to be England's oldest. You enter through a Norman arch to find a heavily beamed bar with comfortable armchairs, old brass and lots of character, while adjacent to it is the tiny Hogarth Bar. The comfortable bedrooms vary from handsome, traditionally furnished rooms in the inn and neighbouring Malt House to more modern ones in an annexe. There are some four-poster rooms. Children up to 14 stay free in parents' room. Function facilities include a tithe barn with medieval beams and rafters. Resort Hotels. *Rooms 36. Garden, croquet.* AMERICAN EXPRESS *Access, Diners, Visa.*

Hurstbourne Tarrant   Esseborne Manor   72%   £112

Tel 0264 736444   Fax 0264 736473   **HR**
Hurstbourne Tarrant nr Andover Hampshire SP11 0ER   Map 14 C3

An unpretentious yet stylish country house hotel lying in the heart of Watership Down country, set back off the A343 about a mile to the north of Hurstbourne Tarrant. It displays obvious attention to detail both in the public rooms and in the overnight accommodation, with fresh flowers, carved ducks, glossy magazines, family ornaments and some antiques. All the bedrooms have been decorated and furnished to a very high standard in both fabrics and materials, enjoying views of the well-kept gardens or rich farmland beyond. The six most spacious rooms are housed in a converted stable block, just a short distance across a courtyard. Extras provided include thick bath robes, books and fresh fruit. Bathrooms benefit from full-length mirrors, spacious surfaces and vividly coloured bath toys. No children under 12. No dogs. *Rooms 12. Garden, croquet, tennis.* AMERICAN EXPRESS *Access, Diners, Visa.*

Restaurant   £80

Andy Norman cooks good produce with skill and assurance. His interesting menus range from a "Springtime Treat" (£10.50 including a glass of wine) and two-course 'Quickie' lunch to a well-balanced dinner menu. Good warm bread rolls, friendly and cheerful service plus a cosy atmosphere make it a pleasurable environment in which to enjoy dishes such as sautéed herring roes on creamed spinach with a lightly curried sauce, Provençal beef stew, salmon and plaice coulibiac, liver and bacon with caramelised onions and a grain mustard gravy, and, for a rather spectacular finale, poached pear in puff pastry masked with a warm ginger and butterscotch sauce set on a cold lime custard. *Seats 30. L 12.30-2 D 7.30-9.30. Set L £14/£17.50 (Sun £17.50) Set D £15.50.*

Hythe   Hythe Imperial   71%   £105

Tel 0303 267441   Fax 0303 264610   **H**
Princes Parade Hythe Kent CT21 6AE   Map 11 C5

Right on the seafront at Hythe, the Imperial still manages to be set in 50 acres of grounds, and its wide frontage means that all bedrooms face the gardens and sea. Bedrooms range from singles to doubles to suites, some with jacuzzis, some with four-posters or half-testers. The polished mahogany reception area is adorned with brown leather chesterfields and leads through to comfortable bars and lounges. Pleasant staff and excellent leisure facilities that include go-karting and a children's play area with Scalextric. Families are particularly well catered for with baby-sitting, baby-listening and crèche facilities available on Saturday mornings; they can eat informally in the leisure centre bistro. Banqueting/conferences for 140/200. Sunday Plus is an interesting idea – extend a weekend stay (keeping the use of your room) until 5pm on Sunday for a nominal charge that includes Sunday lunch. No dogs. *Rooms 100. Garden, croquet, indoor swimming pool, gym, spa bath, sauna, solarium, steam room, beauty & hair salons, squash, tennis, games room, 9-hole golf course, putting, helipad, coffee shop (7.30am-10.30pm).* AMERICAN EXPRESS *Access, Diners, Visa.*

Hythe   Stade Court   62%   £80

Tel 0303 268263   Fax 0303 261803   **H**

West Parade Hythe Kent CT21 6DT   **Map 11 C5**

A small, welcoming entrance hall opens out on to a bamboo-furnished bar, and there's an upstairs lounge looking out to sea. There are also Channel views from many of the traditionally-styled bedrooms, the majority of which have little sun lounges. Children up to 16 can stay free in their parents' room. Free use of the extensive leisure facilities at sister hotel the *Hythe Imperial* 600 metres away, excluding golf (for which a green fee is charged). *Rooms 42. Garden, coffee shop (7.30am-10.30pm).* AMERICAN EXPRESS *Access, Diners, Visa.*

Hythe   Places of Interest

Lympne Castle Tel 0303 267571.
Port Lympne Zoo Park Lympne Tel 0303 64646.

> Note that all telephone numbers with area codes starting with 0 will start 01 from 16 April 1995.

Ide   Old Mill   £55

Tel 0392 59480   **R**

20 High Street Ide nr Exeter Devon EX2 9RN   **Map 13 D2**

Set menus and à la carte are available both lunchtime and evening in the tranquil surroundings of a converted 16th-century mill, just off the A30 Okehampton road roundabout, 2 miles west of Exeter. Fish dishes feature prominently on chef/proprietor Jon Cruwys's menus and "lobsters, steaks, sticky toffee pudding and ice creams" are considered as house specialities. *Seats 45. Private Room 8. L 12-1.30 D 7-9.30. Closed L Sat, all Sun, 26-29 Dec. Set L £8.95/£9.95 Set D £11.95/£14.* AMERICAN EXPRESS *Access, Visa.*

Ilford   Forte Travelodge   NEW   £45

Tel 0800 850 950   **L**

The Beehive Beehive Lane Ilford Essex IG4 5DR   **Map 11 B4**

AMERICAN EXPRESS *Access, Diners, Visa.*

Ilford   Travel Inn   NEW   £43

Tel 081 550 6451   **L**

Redbridge Lane East Ilford Essex IG4 5BG   **Map 11 B4**

Situated on Redbridge Lane East just off A12 and M11 Junction 3.
Rooms 40. AMERICAN EXPRESS *Access, Diners, Visa.*

Ilkley   Box Tree   ★   £85

Tel 0943 608484   Fax 0943 607186   **R**

37 Church Street Ilkley West Yorkshire LS29 9DR   **Map 6 C1**

Decor-wise, little has changed here over the years save a picture or two; the
cottagey restaurant (very pretty outside) is in fact a series of small, intimate
rooms with gilt-framed oils, wall cabinets of fine china, the odd cherub,
and a Baccarat glass tree on each table. The cooking and service are
exemplary with new chef Thierry Le Pretre-Granet settling in well since
his move from Devon. The cuisine, unsurprisingly, is a mixture of classical
French and modern British, with the emphasis on the finest and freshest
ingredients. Presentation is impressive, flavours equally so, and with saucing
spot-on, the dishes emanating from the kitchen are models of correctness.
Both lunch (3 courses) and dinner (four) offer fixed-price menus with
several choices in each section, typical examples being a steamed fillet
of turbot in a fish velouté with oysters and asparagus or sautéed duck foie
gras with a morel cream in a veal jus as starters, followed by Scottish wild
salmon with a red wine sauce or roast fillet of lamb flavoured with thyme
and olives in a lamb jus. Good desserts – a recent visit ended with
a delectable millefeuille of apricots and a refreshing plate of warm
strawberries in a caramelised orange sauce with crème fraiche ice cream.
After-meal coffees and teas, accompanied by excellent petits fours, are
treated very seriously with a huge range available. The wine list is quite
fairly priced, mostly French, though the small New World showing is very
well chosen. No smoking in restaurant. *Seats 50. Parties 35.*
*Private Room 15. L 12-2.30 D 7-10.30. Closed L Sat, D Sun, all Mon and last
2 wks Jan. Set L from £22.50 Set D £29.50.* AMERICAN EXPRESS *Access, Visa.*

Ilkley   Rombalds Hotel   61%   £84

Tel 0943 603201   Fax 0943 816586   **HR**

West View Wells Road Ilkley West Yorkshire LS29 9JG   **Map 6 C1**

Ian and Jill Guthrie are the enterprising owners of Rombalds, part
of a period sandstone terrace just yards from the edge of Ilkley Moor. The
main day room is a comfortable, traditionally furnished bar/lounge busy
with diners having pre-and post-prandial drinks. Bedrooms, which include
four suites, are modestly comfortable, mostly with inexpensive white
melamine furniture and functional bathrooms – about half with shower
and WC only. The coach-house meeting room combines character with
high-tech facilities. Friendly staff. 24hr room service. Children up to 12
stay free in parents' room. *Rooms 15. Garden. Closed 27-30 Dec.*
AMERICAN EXPRESS *Access, Diners, Visa.*

Restaurant   £65

Food is a very important part of life here, and perhaps the best-known
offering is the "Edwardian Breakfast" served every Sunday (and Boxing
Day) from 9am till 1. The hot and cold buffet (£4.65) is just the start of it,
and for £13.35 you can take in the buffet, fish starters (kippers, kedgeree,
Finnan haddock, smoked salmon) and the main grill of all things
breakfasty. There's a buffet and a short set menu each lunchtime, and
an additional more extensive evening carte. The dinner menu on Sunday
features the speciality of roast beef with a separate course of Yorkshire

pudding and onion gravy. Vegetarian main courses. No smoking. *Seats 36. Parties 10. Private Room 50. L 12-2 (Sun 9am-1) D 7-9.30 (Sun till 9). Set L £9.95 Set D £10/£12.95.*

Ilminster	Forte Travelodge	£45
Tel 0460 53748		**L**
Southfield roundabout Horton Cross Ilminster Somerset TA19 9PT		Map 13 E2

Located on the A303 at the intersection with the Ilminster bypass, west of the town centre. ***Rooms** 32.* AMERICAN EXPRESS® *Access, Diners, Visa.*

Ingatestone	Heybridge Hotel	68%	£89
Tel 0277 355355 Fax 0277 353288			**H**
Roman Road Ingatestone Essex CM4 9AB			Map 11 B4

Motel-style rooms stand round a central courtyard, and there are purpose-built conference facilities for up to 600 delegates. Just off the A12. Formerly the *Heybridge Moat House*. ***Rooms** 22. Garden.* AMERICAN EXPRESS® *Access, Diners, Visa.*

Ipswich	Belstead Brook Hotel	68%	£77
Tel 0473 684241 Fax 0473 681249			**H**
Belstead Road Ipswich Suffolk IP2 9HB			Map 10 C3

On the southern outskirts of Ipswich (ask for directions when booking), the 16th-century Belstead Brook is set in eight acres of gardens and woodland. Public rooms and the four-poster honeymoon suite are in the original house with most of the other well-appointed bedrooms in a modern extension. Accommodation ranges from studio singles via standard and Executive to presidential suites. Some of the suites have whirlpool baths. Children up to 12 stay free in parents' room. Purpose-built syndicate rooms cater for functions of up to 70. ***Rooms** 76. Garden, croquet, gym.* AMERICAN EXPRESS® *Access, Diners, Visa.*

If we recommend meals in a hotel or inn a separate entry is made for its restaurant.

Ipswich	Constable Country Hotel	63%	£68
Tel 0473 690313 Fax 0473 680412			**H**
London Road Ipswich Suffolk IP2 0UA			Map 10 C3

On the A1214, about two miles from Ipswich on the London side, this former Posthouse (still in Forte ownership) offers stylish public areas and decent-sized bedrooms. ***Rooms** 112. Outdoor swimming pool (May-Aug), children's play area.* AMERICAN EXPRESS® *Access, Diners, Visa.*

Ipswich	Marlborough Hotel	65%	£69
Tel 0473 257677 Fax 0473 226927			**H**
Henley Road Ipswich Suffolk IP1 3SP			Map 10 C3

Peacefully located north of the town centre, the Marlborough is in the same ownership as the *Angel*, Bury St Edmunds. The tasteful public areas and the comfortable bedrooms (the best have antique furniture) are both well kept. 24hr room service. ***Rooms** 22. Garden, croquet.* AMERICAN EXPRESS® *Access, Diners, Visa.*

Ipswich　　Novotel　　61%　　£65

Tel 0473 232400　Fax 0473 232414　　**H**
Greyfriars Road Ipswich Suffolk IP1 1UP　　Map 10 C3

Five minutes' walk from the pedestrianised town centre and only a brisk
ten minutes from the station: purpose-built facilities include all-day brasserie,
conferences for up to 200 (banquets 150) and 3 bedrooms for the disabled.
Under-16s stay free in parents' room, with breakfast also free. ***Rooms** 100.
Patio, brasserie (6am-midnight).* AMERICAN EXPRESS *Access, Diners, Visa.*

Ipswich　　Places of Interest

Tourist Information　Tel 0473 258070.
Christchurch Mansion and Wolsey Art Gallery　Christchurch Park Tel
　0473 253246.
Museum of East Anglian Life　Stowmarket Tel 0449 612229.
Wolsey Theatre　Tel 0473 53725.
　　Historic Houses, Castles and Gardens
Bucklesham Hall Gardens　Bucklesham Tel 047388 263.
Helmingham Hall and Gardens　Stowmarket Tel 047339 217/363
Otley Hall　- House and Garden, Otley Tel 047339 264.
Ipswich Town Football Ground　Tel 0473 219211.
Suffolk Ski Club　Wherstead Tel 0473 36737.
Suffolk Showground　Tel 0473 726847.

Ixworth　　Theobald's　　£60

Tel 0359 231707　　**R**
68 High Street Ixworth nr Bury St Edmunds Suffolk IP31 2HJ　　Map 10 C2

Simon and Geraldine Theobald set up their restaurant in a village seven
miles north of Bury St Edmunds in 1981; consistency has been the name
of their game ever since. Oak beams and log fires make a traditional
English setting for enjoying Simon's capable and confident cooking. The
price of a three-course meal is dictated by the price of the main dish (an
allowance is made for any course not required); at lunchtime there is also
a good-value table d'hote with three or so choices (more on Sundays)
at each stage. The cheapest main-course option is vegetarian (perhaps stir-
fried vegetables in a pastry case with ginger and soy sauce), continuing
with the likes of bacon-wrapped noisettes of hare with a blackcurrant-laced
game sauce, sea bass with roast fennel and a white port and mustard seed
sauce or pan-fried fillet steak with smoked bacon, mushrooms and port
wine sauce. An additional 'fish supper' (4 set courses £29.50 including half
a bottle of Chablis per person) is also offered on Friday evenings; game
features in season and good saucing is a notable highlight. You certainly
don't need long pockets to afford the wines on the fine list – prices are
a snip! Tasting notes accompany the 'especially recommended' selection.
Super drinking all round. No smoking during service – puffers can repair
to the lounge. No children under 7 at dinner. *Seats 36. L 12-1.30 D 7-9.30.
Closed L Sat, D Sun, all Mon, Bank Holidays. Set L £12.95/£15.95 (Sun
£16.95) Set D from £20.50 (vegetarian) & from £24.50. Access, Visa.*

Jervaulx　　Jervaulx Hall　　70%　　£130★

Tel 0677 460235　Fax 0677 460263　　**H**
Jervaulx Masham nr Ripon North Yorkshire HG4 4PH　　Map 5 D4

On the A6108 between Masham and Middleham, the hall stands in the
attractive grounds next to the ruins of the 12th-century abbey. A dignified
yet homely atmosphere prevails with watercolours, period furnishings,
ornaments and family photos in the quiet and appealing day rooms. Peace
is the main objective in the bedrooms and there's an abundance of quality
toiletries in the carpeted bathrooms. John and Margaret Sharp are the
resident hosts. ★Half-board terms. ***Rooms** 10. Garden. Closed Nov-Mar.
No credit cards.*

Jevington   Hungry Monk   £60

Tel 0323 482178   Fax 0323 483989   **R**

The Street Jevington nr Polegate East Sussex BN26 5QF   Map 11 B6

New this year at the Hungry Monk is a third private dining room. Seating just six, it is popular for small parties or families with children, and is a typical example of the thoughtfulness that Nigel and Sue Mackenzie put into the running of their friendly little restaurant. From the quaint exterior to the atmospheric interior, the charm of the place envelopes you. The fixed-price menu offers plenty of choice along the way, and might include crab fishcake with a mild curry sauce; fennel and potato soup served hot or cold; calf's liver with pink peppercorns on fresh *paglia e fieno*, rabbit stuffed with leeks in prosciutto with wild mushroom sauce, or a vegetarian option such as cabbage stuffed with polenta and mushrooms with a fresh tomato sauce. Delicious puddings like dark chocolate mousse with brandied cherries and cream, or rice pudding with prunes in armagnac complete the meal. Smoking is only allowed in the lounge. No children under 3. *Seats 40. Private Room 10. L Sun 12-2.15 (Mon-Sat by arrangement) D 7-10. Closed Bank Holiday Mons, 3 days Christmas. Set Sun L £20.90 Set D £20.90.* AMERICAN EXPRESS.

Kendal   The Moon   £35

Tel 0539 729254   **R**

129 Highgate Kendal Cumbria LA9 4EN   Map 4 C3

Valerie Macconnell's eye-catching bistro opposite the Brewery Arts Centre (where there is parking) was refurbished last year and the menu choice expanded. Attention to quality and loyalty to local produce remain paramount and make for Lakeland food at its best; the monthly-changing menu is still firmly vegetarian, with interesting choices such as mushroom and broad bean korma, pancakes with Cajun-spiced vegetables and topped with sour cream or filo pastry filled with goat's cheese, fennel and roasted red pepper, ably assisted by a gooseberry, apple and honey sauce. Meat and fish options might include prawn kebabs marinated in lime and coriander and served with a satay sauce; monkfish, whiting and prawn thermidor; chicken breast stuffed with lime, ginger and toasted hazelnuts and accompanied by a watercress sauce. The Moon hosts a pudding club once a month so there's an ever-changing choice of puddings, perhaps including spiced steamed fruit suet pudding and custard or sticky toffee pudding served with cream; a starters club has also been instigated. Children's portions. Short, sensibly-priced wine list. No smoking in the restaurant. *Seats 38 (upstairs 26). Parties 22. Private Room 40. D only 6.30-10 (Sat from 6). Closed 24 & 25 Dec, 1 Jan. Access, Visa.*

Kendal   Woolpack Hotel   59%   £65

Tel 0539 723852   Fax 0539 728608   **H**

Stricklandgate Kendal Cumbria LA9 4ND   Map 4 C3

17th-century former coaching inn (its ground floor was once Kendal's wool auction room) with old-fashioned original bedrooms, a modern annexe and a private car park at the rear. 30 rooms were due for refurbishment as we went to press. Children up to 12 stay free in parents' room. No dogs. *Rooms 54.* AMERICAN EXPRESS *Access, Diners, Visa.*

Kendal   Places of Interest

Tourist Information   Tel 0539 725758.
Levens Hall   Tel 05395 60321.
Sizergh Castle and Garden (NT)   Tel 05395 60070.
Kendal Ski Club   Tel 0539 33031.
  Museums and Art Galleries

Abbot Hall Art Gallery   Tel 0539 722464.
Abbot Hall Museum of Lakeland Life and Industry   Tel 0539 722464.
Kendal Museum of Natural History and Archaeology   Tel 0539 721374.

Kenilworth	Restaurant Bosquet	£75
Tel 0926 52463		**R**
97a Warwick Road Kenilworth Warwickshire CV8 1HP		Map 6 C4

Bernard and Jane Lignier have been here since 1981, and their cosy little restaurant has a strong local following. French in concept and execution, the menus nevertheless draw on good British produce, with an English translation below each French dish. Accurate saucing and good flavour/texture combinations are one of Bernard's strengths, as in red mullet and saffron soup, calf's liver with a lime sauce, terrine of pike and scallops with a butter sauce, or saddle of venison with chestnuts and mandarins in a port and game sauce. Dishes sometimes appear on both the carte and the fixed-price menu – the latter offers choices at each course and is not available on Saturdays. **Seats** 26. L by arrangement D 7-9.30. Closed Sun & Mon, 1 week Christmas, 3 weeks Aug. Set D £19.80 (exc Sat). AMERICAN EXPRESS Access, Visa.

Kenilworth	De Montfort Hotel	63%	£100
Tel 0926 55944 Fax 0926 57830			**H**
Kenilworth Warwickshire CV8 1ED			Map 6 C4

Modern De Vere hotel with spacious day rooms and a good standard of accommodation including some larger family rooms. Banqueting facilities up to 200, conferences to 300. **Rooms** 98. AMERICAN EXPRESS Access, Diners, Visa.

We do not accept free meals or hospitality – our inspectors pay their own bills.

Kenilworth	Simpson's	NEW	£50
Tel 0926 864567			**R**
101 Warwick Road Kenilworth Warwickshire CV8 1HL			Map 6 C4

'French café' chairs surround crisply clothed tables behind the twin 'shop' windows of this new restaurant in the main street while the walls sport menus from some of the famous restaurants where chef/patron Andreas Antona and head chef Andy Walters have worked. The fixed-price menu (shorter at lunchtime) offers a good choice of robust, mainly French dishes – duck and pork rillettes, Lyon sausage salad, bavette of beef with red wine shallot sauce, cassoulet de Toulouse – along with some more Mediterranean-style items such as gnocchi with pesto, cod with olive and tomato vinaigrette and spinach roulade with mascarpone cheese. Desserts range from chestnut charlotte and tiramisu to bread-and-butter pudding. One of the two rooms is designated non-smoking. Own parking to the rear. **Seats** 75. Private Room 85. L 12.30-2 D 7-10. Closed L Sat, D Sun, all Bank Holidays. Set L £10.95 (Sun £13.95) Set D £13.95/£16.95. Access, Diners, Visa.

Kenilworth   Place of Interest

Royal Showground   National Agricultural Centre, Stoneleigh Park Tel 0203 696969.

Kenton — Travel Inn £43

Tel 081-907 1671   Fax 081-909 1604   **L**

Kenton Road Kenton Middlesex HA3 8AT   Map 15 E2

Rooms 43. AMERICAN EXPRESS *Access, Diners, Visa.*

Keswick — Keswick Hotel   60%   £75

Tel 076 87 72020   Fax 076 87 71300   **H**

Station Road Keswick Cumbria CA12 4NQ   Map 4 C3

Solid Victorian hotel set in four acres of gardens, an easy walk from the town centre. Lovely lakeland views attract families and walkers as well as business trade. A fine Victorian conservatory has a grapevine and is an ideal place for afternoon tea. Guests can play golf free (Monday to Friday) at Keswick Club. *Rooms 66. Garden, putting.* AMERICAN EXPRESS *Access, Diners, Visa.*

Kettering — Kettering Park Hotel   71%   £110

Tel 0536 416666   Fax 0536 416171   **H**

Kettering Parkway Kettering Northamptonshire NN15 6XT   Map 7 E4

Styled inside and out in the manner of a large Jacobean manor house though actually built only recently, Kettering Park stands above a roundabout south of Kettering right next to the A1/M1 link road. Stone floors laid with Oriental carpets, oak panelling, deep-coloured, richly patterned upholstery, dark polished wood tables and furniture, tapestry wall hangings – all create an ambience that feels traditional and long-established. Public areas, structured on differing levels, flow into one another culminating in a spacious, well-laid-out bar/lounge. Bedrooms are well designed and up to date offering a good range of amenities. Executive rooms have a sitting area, all rooms have a writing desk. Decor features polished wood and well-matched, colourful fabrics. Bathrooms have excellent showers with a good selection of quality toiletries. The hotel's leisure facilities are magnificent. Banquets/conferences for up to 250 in 7 different suites. Families are well catered for. Plenty of parking. Shire Inns. *Rooms 88. Garden, indoor swimming pool, children's swimming pool, gym, squash, sauna, spa bath, steam room, solarium, snooker.* AMERICAN EXPRESS *Access, Diners, Visa.*

Kew — Wine & Mousaka £35

Tel 081-940 5696   **R**

12 Kew Green nr Richmond Surrey TW9 3BH   Map 15 E2

Sensibly-priced Greek restaurant opposite Kew Green and next to the Coach & Horses pub. The menu covers the usual favourites including both meat and vegetarian moussaka; other specialities include souvla (lamb cooked on the bone on a charcoal spit) and kleftiko. Triada comprises stuffed courgette, pepper and vine leaves with pork mince, rice and herbs. See also entry under London W5 (Ealing). *Seats 52. Parties 20. L 12-2.30 D 6-11. Set L & D £6.95. Closed Sun, Bank Holidays.* AMERICAN EXPRESS *Access, Diners, Visa.*

Keyston — The Pheasant   ↑   £50

Tel 0832 710241   Fax 0832 710340   **R**

Village Loop Road Keyston nr Bythorn Cambridgeshire PE18 0RE   Map 7 E4

Down a narrow country lane off the busy new A14 A1/M1 link the peaceful village of Keyston has, as its claim to fame, one of the most delightful inns in the country. Standing at its heart, the Pheasant, a long, low white-washed building with a thatched roof, looks much older than its 150 or so years. Inside there are heavy dark oak beams and thick walls

hung with old hunting prints. The interior is divided into a number
of inter-connecting rooms, of which the bar with its open log fireplace
is the focal point. The menu is the same here as in the Red Room
restaurant, the only difference being that in the latter tables are larger,
napkins are of linen and there is a no-smoking policy. Roger Jones,
formerly of Franco Taruschio's *Walnut Tree* at Abergavenny, is now well
established and has introduced, on a menu that changes about every ten
days, mouthwatering dishes, the majority with fashionably modern
Mediterranean (notably Italian) and Oriental influences. Saffron and leek
risotto or Parma ham with artichoke hearts and salsa verde could precede
sautéed chicken with a hot Thai curry sauce and basmati rice, casserole
of rabbit with creamy tagliatelle or tenderloin of pork with braised red
cabbage. Cheeses are all unpasteurised and British, from Neal's Yard Dairy.
Sweets include a delicious pecan and butterscotch steamed pudding
or poached pear with pistachio ice cream. Roast sirloin of beef with
Yorkshire pudding, roast potatoes and onion gravy at Sunday lunchtimes
only. If all wine lists were similar to this one, restaurant customers would
never have cause to complain – it offers fantastic value, choice and clarity –
this is the place to try a wine you don't know – you'll not be disappointed.
*Seats 100. Parties 18. Private Room 40. L 12-2 D 6.30-10 (Sun 7.30-9.30).
Closed D 25 & 26 Dec.* AMERICAN EXPRESS *Access, Diners, Visa.*

Kidderminster   Stone Manor   65%   £68

Tel 0562 777555   Fax 0562 777834   **H**

Stone nr Kidderminster Hereford & Worcester DY10 4PJ   **Map 6 B4**

Set in 25 acres of gardens, the mock-Tudor manor was built in 1926. Many
of the bedrooms overlook the rose gardens and swimming pool; some
rooms have four-posters. A choice of four suites can cater for up to 100
conference delegates. *Rooms 52. Garden, croquet, outdoor swimming pool,
tennis, putting.* AMERICAN EXPRESS *Access, Diners, Visa.*

Kidderminster   Places of Interest

Hartlebury Castle   Tel 0229 250410.
Harvington Hall   Tel 0562 777 267.
Dudmaston House and Garden (NT)   Quatt, Bridgnorth Tel 0746
   780866.
West Midland Safari and Leisure Park   Bewdley Tel 0299 402114.

We publish annually, so make sure you use the current edition.
It's worth it!

Kilve   Meadow House   70%   £75

Tel 0278 741546   Fax 0278 741663   **H**

Sea Lane Kilve nr Bridgwater Somerset TA5 1EG   **Map 13 E1**

Howard and Judith Wyer-Roberts operate a civilised home-from-home
at their former rectory in the foothills of the Quantocks, five minutes from
a quiet, fossil-strewn beach (the inspiration for Wordsworth's *On Kilve's
Beach*). Among the eight acres of hotel grounds there are immaculate
landscaped gardens with a stream feeding a duck pond. It's a peaceful setting
without and the main-house bedrooms are spacious, attractive and well
appointed within. Stable rooms across the car park have sitting rooms and
a pleasant, cottagey look. Antiques, original paintings and log fires are
features in the drawing room, lounge and study. Children under 10 share
parents' room free; sensible considerations are made for children.
Banqueting/conference facilities for 35/20. Turn right off the A39 at the
Hood Arms when coming from Bridgwater. *Rooms 10. Garden, croquet.*
AMERICAN EXPRESS *Access, Visa.*

King's Lynn   **Butterfly Hotel**   **62%**   **£62**

Tel 0553 771707   Fax 0553 768027   **H**

Beveridge Way Hardwick Narrows King's Lynn Norfolk PE30 4NB   Map 10 B1

A modern, town-fringe hotel at the A10/A47 roundabout; part of a small East Anglian group aiming at the middle market. Conferences up to 40; banqueting up to 28. *Rooms 70. Garden.* AMERICAN EXPRESS *Access, Diners, Visa.*

King's Lynn   **Duke's Head**   **60%**   **£88**

Tel 0553 774996   Fax 0553 763556   **H**

Tuesday Market Place King's Lynn Norfolk PE30 1JS   Map 10 B1

Forte Heritage hotel with an imposing 17th-century frontage. Singles, doubles and superior doubles. Children up to 16 stay free in parents' room. Conference facilites for up to 330. *Rooms 71.* AMERICAN EXPRESS *Access, Diners, Visa.*

King's Lynn   **Knights Hill Hotel**   **64%**   **£89**

Tel 0553 675566   Fax 0553 675568   **H**

Knights Hill Village South Wootton King's Lynn Norfolk PE30 3HQ   Map 10 B1

Set in 11 acres at the junction of the A148 and A149, 4 miles north-east of King's Lynn, stands a village complex of hotel, pub, leisure club and conference centre (up to 400 delegates). The sympathetic conversion of this collection of 17th-century farm buildings includes comfortable, well-appointed accommodation. A stylish extension to the original farmhouse houses the more up-to-date rooms with more modest (and older) bedrooms in the adjacent courtyard apartments, each with a private entrance. Rooms are generally spacious with attractive darkwood furniture, co-ordinating fabrics and en-suite facilities with showers over tubs. All the added comforts including satellite TV, and guests have free use of the Leisure Club. Children up to 15 stay free in parents' room. *Rooms 52. Indoor swimming pool, gymnasium, sauna, spa bath, steam room, solarium, tennis, snooker, helipad.* AMERICAN EXPRESS *Access, Diners, Visa.*

King's Lynn   **Places of Interest**

Tourist Information   Tel 0553 763044.
Houghton Hall   Tel 0485 569.
Oxburgh Hall (NT)   Swaffham Tel 036621 258.
Sandringham House and Grounds   Sandringham Tel 0553 772675.
Peckover House and Garden (NT)   Wisbech Tel 0945 583463.
Hunstanton Beach *14 miles King's Lynn.*

Kingham   **Mill House**   **66%**   **£80**

Tel 0608 658188   Fax 0608 658492   **H**

Kingham nr Chipping Norton Oxfordshire OX7 6UH   Map 14 C1

Privately-owned Cotswold hotel in a quiet pastoral setting complete with trout stream. Local stone and exposed beams give character to the day rooms, and features from earlier days include two fine old bread ovens. Most of the prettily decorated bedrooms enjoy pleasant views. The hotel is situated halfway between Stow-on-the-Wold and Chipping Norton. No children under five, but 5-12-year-olds can stay free in their parents' room. No dogs. *Rooms 23. Garden, croquet, fishing.* AMERICAN EXPRESS *Access, Diners, Visa.*

Kingsbridge   Buckland-Tout–Saints Hotel   £150*

Tel 0548 853055   Fax 0548 856261   **H**

Kingsbridge South Devon TQ7 2DS   Map 13 D3

Sitting in six acres of gardens and woodlands, this is an elegant Queen
Anne manor house, personally run by John and Tove Taylor and their son
George. Provisionally graded at 75%, with half-board terms only (£150
for two). Dinner is taken in a very grand pine-panelled room,
complementing the Great Hall and elegant drawing room, both beautifully
and tastefully furnished and decorated. Individually-styled bedrooms and
splendid bathrooms (smaller top rooms are less grand) have good pieces
of antique furniture, fine fabrics and lovely garden views. Meeting room
for up to 16. No children under 8. *Rooms* 12. *Garden, croquet, putting green.*
AMERICAN EXPRESS *Access, Diners, Visa.*

Kingston   Restaurant Gravier   £70

Tel 081-549 5557   **R**

9 Station Road Norbiton Kingston Surrey KT2 7AA   Map 15 E2

French cooking, with seafood a speciality, is the attraction at this well-liked
suburban restaurant, whose decor features exposed-brick walls and hop
swags. The short printed menu is more or less doubled by dishes of the day,
recited at the table, the result of Jean-Philippe Gravier's early morning trips
to Billingsgate. Joanne Gravier (the only English member of an otherwise
exclusively French team) rules in the kitchen with a sure touch, producing
excellent, generally quite straightforward dishes like mussels with garlic,
cream and white wine, clams provençale, salmon in champagne sauce, sea
bass *au beurre nantais* (a particularly good choice), sole normande and
lobster (*Thermidor, à l'armoricaine*, flambé with calvados). A couple of meat
dishes. Good desserts. Outside eating in fine weather. *Seats 40. L 12.15-2
D 7-10. Closed L Sat, all Sun, Bank Holidays, 1 week Aug, Christmas.
Set L £16.50.* AMERICAN EXPRESS *Access, Visa.*

Kington   Penrhos Court   £100

Tel 0544 230720   Fax 0544 230754   **RR**

Penrhos Kington Hereford & Worcester HR5 3LH   Map 9 D4

In six acres of grounds, standing on the hill between Lyonshall and Kington
on the A44, Martin Griffiths' and Daphne Lambert's restaurant is in the
beautifully restored 13th-century Cruck Hall, complete with flagstone
floors and heavy beams – a characterful setting for occasional medieval
banquets. Daphne offers daily-changing menus with a short choice, using
organic and locally produced produce whenever possible. Dishes like warm
chicken liver salad, mussels in white wine with saffron and fennel, sea
bream grilled with aromatic oils, escalope of salmon with black noodles,
sun-dried tomatoes, pine kernels and basil, duckling à la bigarade (with
orange and lemon) and chargrilled chicken with wild mushrooms, garlic
and coriander typify her style and dedication in the kitchen. Simple, but
well-executed desserts such as carrot cake with Greek yoghurt, chocolate
praline parfait with chocolate sauce and passion fruit sorbet. 4-course
Sunday lunches offer a small choice, but always include a traditional roast.
The diverse wine list continues to grow, tending to feature smaller
producers. No smoking. *Seats 70. Private Room 20. D only 7.30-9.
Closed Feb. Set L Sun £15 Set D £18.50/£22.50.* AMERICAN EXPRESS *Access,
Diners, Visa.*

Rooms   £90

Nineteen individually-styled bedrooms, named after birds, show some fine
taste. The latest eight rooms are in converted Elizabethan barns; of a fair
size, they use lightwood and mahogany furniture, co-ordinated
contemporary fabrics and bright, clean decor. Bathrooms (some with
shower/WC only) have attractive fittings and quality toiletries. Limited

hotel-style public areas, but high bedroom standards. The Swallow Room features a four-poster bed and private balcony. Children up to 10 free in parents' room. No dogs. *Garden.*

Kington   Place of Interest
Hergest Croft Gardens   Tel 0544 230160.

Kintbury   Dundas Arms   £65
Tel 0488 658263   Fax 0488 658568   **IR**
53 Station Road Kintbury nr Newbury Berkshire RG15 0UT   Map 14 C2

The Kennet and Avon canal runs by this 18th-century inn with roomy, traditionally-styled accommodation in a converted livery and stable block. Sliding picture windows offer access to a terrace with garden furniture; all rooms enjoy views over the water. *Rooms 5. Closed Christmas/New Year.* AMERICAN EXPRESS *Access, Visa.*

Restaurant   £65

Views over the canal from this comfortable dining room where chef/proprieter David Dalzell-Piper offers fresh local ingredients cooked with skill and confidence. These talents show up well on the understated, hand-written menu with dishes like boned quail filled with paté and served with sweet red pepper relish, grilled fillets of red mullet with saffron onions, cajun-spiced monkfish with tomato sauce, or roast breast of duck with mint and lemon or blood orange sauce. Luscious puddings and fine British cheeses. Always a super wine list, the more so at the giveaway prices the restaurant charges. *The* place to drink that special claret or burgundy you've never sampled before, though everything on the list is worth drinking. We repeat: exceptional value for money. *Seats 36. Parties 22. L 12-2 D 7.30-9.15. Closed D Mon, all Sun. Set L £16.50.*

Kinver   Berkleys   £55
Tel 0384 873679   **R**
5 High Street Kinver West Midlands DY7 2HG   Map 6 B4

In the Piano Room (a pianist plays Fri & Sat eves) Andrew Mortimer's short menu, with explanatory notes, is cautiously contemporary: calf's liver with orange vinegar butter sauce, braised pigeon with egg noodles, venison terrine with a ginger, apple and quince chutney, tiger prawns with sun-dried tomatoes, noisettes of boar with mango and blush grapefruit, fillet of turbot in puff pastry with vermouth sauce are typical dishes. Desserts from a trolley. The bistro, with a different selection of dishes, is open lunchtime and evening. *Seats 35. D only 7-10 (Bistro also 12-2 & 7-10, closed L Sat). Closed Sun (& bistro), Bank Holidays, first 2 weeks Feb.* AMERICAN EXPRESS *Access, Diners, Visa.*

Knaresborough   Dower House   63%   £66
Tel 0423 863302   Fax 0423 867665   **H**
Bond End Knaresborough nr Harrogate North Yorkshire HG5 9AL   Map 6 C1

An ivy-clad red-brick former dower house – the main building dates from Tudor times – that retains considerable appeal in period furnishings and features (notably a handsome Georgian staircase). Some of the bedrooms have an old-fashioned feel, while others, along with the conference (for up to 65) and leisure facilities, are modern. Children up to 16 stay free in parents' room. Dogs allowed by prior arrangement. *Rooms 32. Garden, indoor swimming pool, gym, sauna, steam room, spa bath, solarium.* AMERICAN EXPRESS *Access, Diners, Visa.*

Knaresborough   Places of Interest

Allerton Park   Tel 0423 330927.
Mother Shipton's Cave and Petrifying Well   Tel 0423 864600 *Oldest tourist attraction in Britain.*

Knutsford	**Brasserie Belle Epoque**	£60
Tel 0565 633060 Fax 0565 634150		**RR**
60 King Street Knutsford Cheshire WA16 2DT		Map 6 B2

The Mooneys may be celebrating their 21st anniversary here this year but that they are still full of energy and enthusiasm is evidenced by a complete change of menu and cuisine – note the name change and new lunchtime opening. Where dishes were formerly rather rich the new style is much lighter and more modern – home-made tagliatelle with roasted red pepper purée and fresh basil; Cheshire cheese sausages with sage and apple chutney; chargrilled tuna steak with tapénade; best end of lamb on onion polenta with gravy – although Lancashire favourites like tripe (cooked in cider and gratinated with crumbly Lancashire cheese) and black pudding (with calvados raisins and mash, and a mild curry and apple sauce) also find their place along with Bakewell tart and 'proper' custard. Within an eccentric and fascinating 1906 building, in one of the main streets of town, the interior is an evocation of the Parisian Belle Epoque with many original fittings and artefacts. In good weather a few tables are put out on the roof garden. *Seats 110. Parties 15. Private Room 80. L 12-2 D 7-10. Closed L Sat, all Sun, Bank Holidays, 1 week Jan.* AMERICAN EXPRESS *Access, Diners, Visa.*

Rooms   £40

Seven mostly antique-furnished bedrooms, with generally rather masculine decor, come with remote-control TVs and good bathrooms – all with tubs and generous towelling. Most rooms overlook an Italianate terrace and the herb garden.

Knutsford	**Cottons Hotel** 65%	£114
Tel 0565 650333 Fax 0565 755351		**H**
Manchester Road Knutsford Cheshire WA16 0SU		Map 6 B2

Five minutes from the M6 (junction 19) and just 15 from Manchester Airport, Cottons was designed with a New Orleans theme. There's plenty of free parking, versatile facilities for conferences (up to 200 delegates theatre-style) and a well-designed leisure club (including a floodlit tennis court) to which all guests have free membership during their stay. Two bars – the Bourbon Street and the Rose Revived – provide a choice for the thirsty. Considerable reductions for children, whether or not in parents' room. Shire Inns. *Rooms 82. Indoor swimming pool, gym, sauna, spa bath, solarium, tennis.* AMERICAN EXPRESS *Access, Diners, Visa.*

Knutsford	**Forte Travelodge**	£45
Tel 0565 652187		**L**
Chester Road Tabley Knutsford Cheshire WA16 0PP		Map 6 B2

On the A556 northbound, 15 miles south of Manchester city centre. East of Junction 19 of the M6. *Rooms 32.* AMERICAN EXPRESS *Access, Diners, Visa.*

Knutsford   Places of Interest

Tatton Park (NT)   Tel 0565 564822.
Tabley House Collection   Tel 0565 50888.
Tabley Showground   Tel 027 073 245.

Lacock   At The Sign of The Angel   £78

Tel 0249 730230   Fax 0249 730527   **IR**

6 Church Street Lacock nr Chippenham Wiltshire SN15 2LB   Map 14 B2

A 15th-century wool-merchant's house situated in a National Trust village
and run by the Levis family since 1953. Beams, creaking floors, huge
fireplaces and heavy oak furniture offer plenty of character in main-house
bedrooms; a couple of rooms are in the annexe, reached by a little bridge
across the garden stream. The lounge is shared by residents and diners.
Rooms 10. Garden. Closed 22-30 Dec. AMERICAN EXPRESS Access, Visa.

Restaurant   £80

A traditional roast, with a fish alternative, is the centrepiece of set dinners
served by candle-light. There's also a good à la carte selection, and dishes
from a solidly English repertoire could include Stilton and walnut paté,
grilled fillets of sole, pan-fried lamb's kidneys in Madeira sauce, beef and
tomato rissoles and roast duck with sage and apricot stuffing. For sweet,
meringues and treacle and walnut tart come with the option of clotted
cream. English cheeseboard. Few half bottles on a pleasant wine list that
offers fair prices. **Seats** 45. Parties 20. Private Room 20. L 12.30-2
D 7.30-8.30. Closed L Mon. Set L £16 Set D £22.50-£30.

Lacock   Places of Interest

Lacock Abbey (NT)   Tel 024973 227.
Fox Talbot Museum of Photography (NT)   Tel 024 973 459.

Lamorna Cove   Lamorna Cove Hotel   65%   £66

Tel 0736 731411   **H**

Lamorna Cove nr Penzance Cornwall TR19 6XH   Map 12 A4

Lamorna Cove is on the southern edge of the Penwith Peninsula about 15
minutes drive from Penzance (first take the Newlyn road, then the B3315
towards Porthcurno and Treen, from which the cove and hotel are
signposted). Set into the steeply sloping wooded hillside, it enjoys splendid
views. Malcolm and Lisa Gray, now well settled in, have an ongoing
programme of refurbishment although most of their original intentions
have now been accomplished resulting in a home-from-home full of style
and comfort. Rooms and suites are priced according to their view – cove,
valley, or both. Well equipped and maintained dayrooms and sun terraces
make ideal spots in which to relax. **Rooms** 15. Garden, outdoor swimming
pool. Access, Visa.

Lancaster   Forte Posthouse   69%   £68

Tel 0524 65999   Fax 0524 841265   **H**

Waterside Park Caton Road Lancaster Lancashire LA1 3RA   Map 6 A1

Well-designed, practical accommodation and smart public rooms in a low-
rise hotel overlooking the river Lune. Banqueting and conference facilities
for 100/120. **Rooms** 115. Indoor swimming pool, gym, sauna, spa bath,
solarium. AMERICAN EXPRESS Access, Diners, Visa.

Lancaster   Places of Interest

Tourist Information   Tel 0524 32878.
Judges' Lodgings Museum   Tel 0524 32808.
Frontierland Western Theme Park   Morecambe Tel 0524 410024.
   Theatres and Concert Halls
Dukes Theatre   Tel 0524 66645.
Nuffield Theatre Studio   Tel 0524 39026.
Leighton Hall   Carnforth Tel 0524 734474.

Land's End   Land's End Hotel   64%   £75

Tel 0736 871844   Fax 0736 871599   **H**

Land's End Sennen Cornwall TR19 7AA   Map 12 A4

Part of the Land's End complex that includes a museum, 'Man and the Sea'
exhibition, farm animal and craft area and a multi-sensory presentation
of Cornish history (well worth seeing) amongst other things, all of which
are free to hotel guests. Conversely, visitors to the centre have access to the
hotel's public rooms which consist of a smart reception/lounge with rugs
over woodblock floor, and a rattan-furnished Observatory Bar with
a breathtaking view of the Atlantic from its clifftop position. Bedrooms
have light, soft colour schemes with original pictures on the walls, limed
lightwood furniture and Lloyd Loom easy chairs and glass-topped tables.
Many have sea views. Good bathrooms except for the lack of shelf space.
Conference facilities can cope with up to 200 delegates theatre-style.
Formerly called the *State House*. **Rooms** *34. Terrace, children's playground,
gift shops, coffee shop (10am-5pm).* AMERICAN EXPRESS *Access, Visa.*

Lands End   Places of Interest

Minack Theatre   Porthcurno Tel 0736 810471.
Sennen Cove Beach.

Langar   Langar Hall   70%   £80

Tel 0949 60559   Fax 0949 61045   **HR**

Langar Nottinghamshire NG13 9HG   Map 7 D3

The village of Langar (signposted via Bingham on the A52 or Cropwell
Bishop on the A46) is tucked away in the lush vale of Belvoir, and the Hall
itself is virtually hidden behind the church. Built in 1830 of local sandstone,
it is now the family home of Imogen Skirving and as such is crammed full
of antiques and homely artefacts. Large oil paintings of past family
members line the wide stone staircase in the entrance hall, which has
an informality continued throughout the hotel. There's very much an air
of loving care, which applies to furnishings and guests equally. Public
rooms comprise a dark, intimate library and bright, sunny drawing room
both furnished in a comfortable, lived-in style. Bedrooms upstairs in the
main house vary in size and character; the newly converted courtyard
rooms are more up-to-date but all the rooms have oodles of appeal
including a wide selection of books and fine views over the extensive
grounds. **Rooms** *12. Garden, croquet.* AMERICAN EXPRESS *Access, Diners, Visa.*

Restaurant   £70

With pillars and a huge fireplace, the restaurant occupies what was an inner
hall. Silver candelabra and fresh flowers decorate tables which are large and
well-spaced. The cooking is supervised by Imogen Skirving though chef
Toby Garratt, who has been at Langar since 1992, adds his own style,
which could be described as modern British: duck liver parfait, toast and
chutney, or potato pancake, smoked eel and watercress as starters; roast cod,
leeks, mussels and saffron or boiled bacon and carrots with parsley sauce
as mains. Try prune and armagnac mousse or Italian chocolate cake
to finish, or Stilton from Colston Bassett, the neighbouring village.
Seats *30. Private Room 20. L 12.30-2 D 7-9.30. Closed Sun (residents only).*

Langdale   Langdale Hotel   71%   £132

Tel 05394 37302   Fax 05394 37694   **H**

Great Langdale nr Ambleside Cumbria LA22 9JD   Map 4 C3

Thirty-five acres of woodland make a secluded setting for a well-run hotel
and country club. Bedrooms, all doubles or twins, are in several satellite
blocks built of Lakeland stone, and there are some family rooms with bunk
beds. Decor is either modern or Edwardian with four-posters or canopied

beds, and there are some self-catering lodges for weekly rental. There's an open-plan bar-lounge, and a nearby slate-walled pub bar. Rooms overlooking Great Langdale Beck have private balconies. Children up to 3 stay free in their parents' room. Up to 14 they pay £20. Guests have full use of the hotel's considerable leisure facilities. *Seats 65. Garden, croquet, tennis, fishing, indoor swimming pool, children's splash pool, gym, squash, sauna, steam room, spa bath, solarium, sun beds, beauty salon, hair salon, children's playground, games room, snooker, shop, coffee shop (9am-11pm), helipad.* AMERICAN EXPRESS *Access, Diners, Visa.*

Langho	Northcote Manor	67%	£75
Tel 0254 240555 Fax 0254 246568			**HR**
Northcote Road Langho nr Blackburn Lancashire BB6 8BE			Map 6 B1

About ten miles from the M6 (Junction 31), the extended Victorian redbrick house looks down over the Ribble Valley, though not all the hotel's rooms enjoy this view. Inside, the atmosphere is almost 'olde worlde' with beams, oak panelling and roaring log fires (even on chilly summer nights). The entrance hall-cum-bar has two lounges leading off it and a fine staircase that ascends to the bedrooms, all now with bathrooms (as opposed to shower only) en suite. The spacious bedrooms are attractively decorated and furnished, retaining much of their original character, with good antiques, bric-à-brac, bold and colourful fabrics, and nice touches such as board games, magazines, music alarm and remote-control satellite TV. Bathrooms vary from modern to old-fashioned (with Victorian tiles and cast-iron tubs), all splendidly equipped, even boasting Nina Ricci toiletries. Under the direction of joint owners Craig Bancroft and Nigel Haworth (see below), service is of a high standard (for example afternoon tea and warm shortbread on arrival) with excellent housekeeping and maintenance. They have been in situ for ten years, and one of their long-term projects is to improve and expand the garden, starting with the planting of several thousand trees in surrounding fields to shield the property. Breakfasts are sensational, with freshly squeezed juices, seasonal fruits, local yoghurt, home-made jams and marmalade, as well as farm eggs, local sausages and black pudding. Banqueting for 100, conferences for 40, with the boardroom ideal for small numbers up to 26. No dogs. *Rooms 14. Garden, helipad. Closed 1 & 2 Jan.* AMERICAN EXPRESS *Access, Diners, Visa.*

Restaurant ↑ £80

The main dining room has an attractive bay window, which sets the tone for some quite splendid cooking. Nigel Haworth is a gifted and talented chef and leads by example, presenting dishes with a distinct Northern and local feel, a credit to both him and his suppliers (poultry from Goosnargh, fish from Fleetwood, Bury black pudding, mature farmhouse cheeses etc). The dinner menu is sensibly short, and yet manages to encompass something for everyone, starting with, say, the house specialities of prime fillet of beef with a dressing of garden herbs, mixed salad leaves with a truffle dressing or a black pudding and buttered pink trout on a mustard and watercress sauce. Main courses include Hindle Wakes (his version is corn-fed breast of chicken with a rhubarb and basil stuffing wrapped in bacon), or rack of new season lamb with sweetbreads and leeks and served with puréed potatoes. On a recent visit we enjoyed a spectacularly-made terrine of foie gras, duckling, potatoes and lentils wrapped in Savoy cabbage with a dribble of balsamic dressing, which preceded a plate of small individual Lancashire delicacies (including black pudding and potted shrimps), followed by a generous portion of salmon poached in duck fat on roast peppers with grilled potatoes and Parma ham – sounds bizarre but worked a treat! A small chocolate tart, not too bitter, not too sweet, with a dollop of chocolate ice cream was a fitting finale. The set-price lunch is a simpler affair, and Sunday has a traditional roast, but both show the same innovative and modern cooking principles as the more involved dishes in the evening. A decent and reasonably inexpensive wine list has plenty of half bottles. Representing the North of England in our British

Meat Chef of the Year competition, Nigel won the title in a fiercely
contested final held in London at the end of June. *Seats 100.*
Private Room 35. L 12-1.30 (2 Sun) D 7-9.30 (10 Sat). Set L £14.95.

Langley-on-Tyne	Langley Castle	65%	£70

Tel 0434 688888   Fax 0434 684019

H

Langley-on-Tyne nr Haydon Bridge Northumberland NE49 0LY

Map 5 D2

Surrounded by ten acres of woodland, this resplendent castle, built in 1350,
is full of architectural interest and has walls that are seven feet thick; the
main staircase houses some of the best-preserved 14th-century garderobes
in Europe and there's a chapel in the roof. Bedrooms are simply furnished
but given individuality by stylishly-draped half-tester beds. One of the en-
suite bathrooms has a sauna and another a whirlpool bath. A large, lofty
drawing room – gloriously characterful – boasts an open fireplace and
antique furniture. Banqueting/conference facilities for 120/160. The hotel
is on the A686, a mile or two south of Haydon Bridge. *Rooms 10. Garden,
sauna, spa bath.* AMERICAN EXPRESS *Access, Diners, Visa.*

Lavenham	Great House		£45

Tel 0787 247431

RR

Market Place Lavenham Suffolk CO10 9QZ

Map 10 C3

The Great House is 15th-century with a Georgian facade, and stands just
opposite the historic Guildhall in this well-preserved medieval town.
Frenchman Régis Crépy provides excellent food, served in cosy
surroundings on rural French and English menus, applying a modern touch
to the best local ingredients. *Paté de campagne aux pistaches, carré d'agneau
à l'ail, raie au beurre noir* and *tarte au citron à la crème* indicate the style;
parcels of cheese fondue, confit of duck with beans, tarte tatin and crème
brulée are considered specialities. Wide selection of French cheeses. Long,
brasserie-style lunch menu (not Sun) and both fixed-price (not D Sat) and
à la carte in the evening. French-style Sunday lunch, when there's a choice
of around six or dishes at each stage, is always popular. Seating for 25 on
a patio. Smoking is not encouraged. *Seats 40. Private Room 50. L 12-2.30
D 7-9.30 (Sat to 10.30). Closed D Sun, all Mon, 5-25 Jan. Set Sun
L £15.95, children £9 Set D £15.95 (not Sat).* AMERICAN EXPRESS *Access, Visa.*

Rooms

£68

There are four charming, traditionally furnished bedrooms all with either
a separate lounge or a sitting area; one room has two double beds. Thick
beams, antique furniture and floral fabrics create the look of village
England. Walled garden with swings. The tariff increases to £78
on Saturday nights and £88 on Bank Holidays; children under 3 share free
(cot supplied), 3- to 12-year-olds are charged £10.

Lavenham	The Swan	71%	£122

Tel 0787 247477   Fax 0787 248286

HR

High Street Lavenham nr Sudbury Suffolk CO10 9QA

Map 10 C3

A splendid example of Elizabethan architecture, the Swan has been
welcoming guests since the 15th century. Bristling with timbers, the cosy
alcoves meander one into another, creating charming public areas. The
lounge has long been the setting for relaxing afternoon tea, while the
earthy real-ale bar has the warm feel of a much-loved local. Walkways
overlooking pretty little gardens lead to the variously sized bedrooms,
designed to retain the period feel; stylish furniture and extras like fruit and
chocolates set the tone for the attention to detail in evidence
throughout the hotel; 18 rooms are reserved for non-smokers. If you want
to get the real feel of the place, ask for a room with a four-poster bed and
private sitting room. Breakfast is good and service is generally on the ball.
Banqueting/conference facilities for 40/50. Forte Heritage. *Rooms 47.
Garden, croquet.* AMERICAN EXPRESS *Access, Diners, Visa.*

Restaurant £75

The restaurant, built in 1965, is in keeping with the hotel's origins and has a lofty, open-raftered ceiling and a minstrel's gallery. Chef Andrew Barrass has a sure touch and his menus offer a good choice of carefully cooked dishes, simply conceived and elevated by imaginative touches. A recent, seasonal menu offered tiger prawns and crispy vegetables, chicken and leek broth, rosettes of English lamb, chateaubriand (for two), Dover sole fillets in champagne and breast of pheasant with wild mushrooms. Informal snacks served 9.30-5.30 in the lounge areas. No smoking. *Seats 70. Parties 12. Private Room 40. L 12.30-2 D 7-9.30. Set L £12.95/£14.95 (Sun £16.95) Set D £19.95.*

Lavenham   Place of Interest

The Priory Lavenham   Tel 0787 247417.

Leamington Spa   Courtyard by Marriott   65%   £80

Tel 0926 425522   Fax 0926 881322   **H**

Olympus Avenue Europa Way Leamington Spa Warwickshire CV34 6RJ   Map 14 C1

Roomy and practical accommodation in an industrial park, aimed mainly at the business traveller. Conference and banqueting facilities for up to 50. Children free in parents' room. Half the bedrooms are designated non-smoking. Free car parking. *Rooms 97. Keep-fit equipment.* AMERICAN EXPRESS *Access, Diners, Visa.*

Leamington Spa   Inchfield Hotel   63%   £78

Tel 0926 883777   Fax 0926 330467   **H**

64 Upper Holly Walk Leamington Spa Warwickshire CV32 4JL   Map 14 C1

A solid Victorian house, just five minutes from the town centre and about ten from the M40. Bedrooms are of a good standard, quietly stylish and equipped with the usual modern comforts. Children up to 12 stay free when sharing parents' room. No dogs. *Rooms 22. Garden.* AMERICAN EXPRESS *Access, Visa.*

Leamington Spa   Mallory Court   80%   £162

Tel 0926 330214   Fax 0926 451714   **HR**

Harbury Lane Bishop's Tachbrook Leamington Spa Warwickshire CV33 9QB   Map 14 C1

Two miles south of Leamington Spa, off the B4087 towards Harbury, and standing in 10 acres of beautifully landscaped gardens, Mallory Court has an air of luxury and refinement. It's one of the original country house hotels and still one of the very best, built in 1910 in the Elizabethan style of tall chimneys and stone-mullioned windows with leaded lights. A small entrance hall leads directly into the main lounge, complete with deep-cushioned couches and armchairs, quality drapes, deep carpets and fine period furniture; the drawing room boasts green leather chesterfields and there's a delightful conservatory sun-trap. Bedrooms are generally of a good size and impeccably designed, with stylish fabrics, light, fresh colours and quality freestanding furniture; some have four-posters. Extras in the rooms include bath robes, mineral water, flowers and magazines. The Blenheim suite is nothing short of luxurious with its own balcony, two tubs in the bathroom and a painted ceiling. Attentive staff and highly efficient housekeeping. Unsuitable for children under the age of nine. Parking includes six garage spaces. No dogs – kennelling nearby. *Rooms 10. Garden, croquet, outdoor swimming pool, squash, all-weather tennis. Closed first 10 days Jan.* AMERICAN EXPRESS *Access, Visa.* MARTELL COGNAC

See over

Restaurant ★ £120

With chef/proprietor Allan Holland in the kitchen it's not surprising that food and the dining room are given a high priority here. Oak panelling, yellow tablecloths and chintzy curtains set the scene with armed, leather dining chairs providing the comfort. The formerly confusing menu format has now been simplified to a conventionally priced à la carte, no-choice, five-course Gourmet menu (both available at lunchtime) and fixed-price lunch and dinner menus offering a choice of six or so dishes at each stage. Care in preparation and presentation is the keynote of dishes that generally stick to tried and trusted combinations: terrine of foie gras with Sauternes jelly and brioche, scallop mousse with leeks, scallops and ginger sauce, fillet of venison on red cabbage with a poivrade sauce and blackcurrants; feuilleté of William pear poached in vanilla syrup with caramel sauce. Occasional excursions away from the mainstream may include fillet of beef with polenta and salsa verde or braised rabbit with fresh pasta and prune sauce. Lobster terrine with herb sauce and braised turbot with leeks and wild mushrooms are considered specialities. Service lives up to the food – and the prices. Last year we described the wine list, perhaps rather unkindly, as 'safe'. It is, in fact, an excellent list with well-chosen wines at every step, and the practice of offering several wines by the glass should be followed by other country house hotels of this class. "No service charge is made or expected." No children under 9. *Seats 50. Private Room 25. L 12.30-2 D 7-9.45 (Sat to 10, Sun to 9). Set L £19.50/£23.50. Set D £30 & £60.*

Many establishments are currently on the market, so ownership could change after we go to press.

Leamington Spa   Regent Hotel   68%   £89

Tel 0926 427231   Fax 0926 450728   **HR**

77 The Parade Leamington Spa Warwickshire CV32 4AX   Map 14 C1

The Regent was the largest hotel in the world when built in 1819, and George IV, when still Prince Regent, graciously allowed it to be named after him. In the same family ownership since 1904, the hotel has benefited from ongoing refurbishment, which recently meant a new lift – and a face lift for the bar. Charmingly 'old-fashioned' touches include eiderdowns on the beds, the overnight cleaning of shoes left outside bedroom doors at night and genuinely friendly, helpful service from often long-serving staff. Free parking. 24hr room service. *Rooms 80. Games room.* AMERICAN EXPRESS *Access, Diners, Visa.*

Vaults Restaurant   £65

Head chef Roland Clark is happily still at the helm, presiding over à la carte and fixed-price menus which offer fairly traditional dishes. You might find trout with almonds, veal viennoise, supreme of chicken, noisettes of lamb, grilled sardines with garlic butter, tortelloni with mushrooms and cream and a reassuringly British hot rhubarb and cinnamon cobbler. The setting, as the name suggests, is the barrel-vaulted cellars of the hotel, most of it reserved for non-smokers. Good wine list with some bargains to be found among the erratically priced first-growth clarets. *Seats 50. Parties 20. Private Room 20. L 12.30-2.30 D 7.30-10.45 (Fri & Sat from 7). Closed Sun, 25 & 26 Dec. Set L £9.75/£11.75 Set D £16.50.*

Leamington Spa   Places of Interest

Tourist Information   Tel 0926 311470.
Offchurch Bury Polo Club   Red House Farm, Campion Hills Tel 0926 882883.

Ledbury   The Feathers   £79

Tel 0531 635266   Fax 0531 632001   **I**

High Street Ledbury Hereford & Worcester HR8 1DS   **Map 14 B1**

Between Malvern and Ross-on-Wye, a classic timber-framed former
coaching inn dating from 1564 with oddly-shaped, en-suite, double-glazed
bedrooms (including one with a four-poster), original Elizabethan wall
paintings, uneven, creaky floors and drunken staircases. Good snacks in the
hop-bedecked Fuggles Bar and small rear patio in good weather. Function
facilities in the ballroom complex for 130. *Rooms 11.* AMERICAN EXPRESS ®
Access, Diners, Visa.

Ledbury   Hope End   70%   £120

Tel 0531 633613   Fax 0531 636366   **HR**

Hope End Ledbury Hereford & Worcester HR8 1SQ   **Map 14 B1**

Elizabeth Barrett-Browning's former home, largely of 18th-century origin,
nestles in 40 acres of wooded parkland and a Georgian landscaped garden
which includes a temple, grotto and island ruin. Today's incumbents John
and Patricia Hegarty run this haven of tranquillity in suitably informal
fashion, setting piles of books by the deep sofas in front of the log-burning
stoves. Simply decorated bedrooms, one in a little rustic cottage, have
exposed beams along with country oak and antique stripped-pine furniture,
fresh flowers and yet more books; no TV unless requested. Cork and tile
bathrooms come with a selection of bath oils. The rate quoted is for
a standard room. Two small rooms are priced at £97, the best rooms
£140. No children under 12. No dogs. *Rooms 9. Garden.*
Closed mid Dec-1st week Feb. Access, Visa. MARTELL COGNAC

Restaurant   £70

Patricia Hegarty is the definitive home cook, her chutneys, breads and
jellies as integral a part of production as her nightly fixed-price dinner. The
kitchen garden provides vegetables, herbs and fruit for many dishes;
a typical meal might start with carrot and coriander seed soup or little
lamb meatballs with tomato and cinnamon sauce; continue with tenderloin
of pork with cider and sage sauce; and end with cheese and a dessert such
as bitter chocolate and orange baked custard, or demerara meringues with
a sauce of red fruits. Though not the easiest to use, the predominantly
French wine list (lots of mature clarets) is quite fairly priced; good half
bottle selection. No smoking. *Seats 24. Parties 8. D only 7.30. Set D £30.*

Ledbury   Place of Interest

Eastnor Castle   Tel 0531 2305/2894.

> From April 1995 the area telephones code for Leeds changes from
> 0532 to 0113 plus the addition of 2 before six-digit numbers.

Leeds   Adriano Flying Pizza   £30

Tel 0532 666501   Fax 0532 665470   **R**

60 Street Lane Roundhay Leeds West Yorkshire LS8 2DQ   **Map 6 C1**

Celebrating 20 years of good business in 1994, Adriano offers much more
than just pizzas. Apart from the carte of standard Italian main courses
(plenty of veal, chicken and steak dishes), the daily (except Monday) list
of fresh fish dishes is particularly worthy of note, along with the regular
lemon sole and *calamari fritti*. In good weather eat outside on the cobbled
pavement under a colourful awning. *Seats 140. Parties 20. L 12-2.30
D 6-11.30. Closed Easter Sun, 25 & 26 Dec, 1 Jan.* AMERICAN EXPRESS ®
Access, Visa.

Leeds — Bibis

£50
R

Tel 0532 430905   Fax 0532 340844

Minerva House 16 Greek Street Leeds West Yorkshire LS1 5RU

Map 6 C1

Smart, yet informal restaurant in Roman forum style squeezed in between city-centre office blocks. An extensive menu – everything from lobster ravioli with shrimp sauce and *osso buco alla milanese* to pizzas – is supplemented by daily specials. Cooking is distinctly above average, as is the service, which is particularly swift at lunchtime to meet the needs of the local business community. **Seats** 160. L 12-2.15 D 6-11.15. Closed Sun. AMERICAN EXPRESS *Access, Visa.*

Leeds — Brasserie Forty Four   ↑

£70
R

Tel 0532 343232   Fax 0532 343332

44 The Calls Leeds West Yorkshire LS2 7EW

Map 6 C1

Now well-established as one of the city's best eating houses, the restaurant enjoys an enviable riverside location with a balcony for alfresco dining. Originally a grain-mill it is located adjacent to and under *42 The Calls*, the hotel, with which it shares a similar modern design concept. Huge colourful artwork hangs on the white-painted brick walls and tables and chairs are of simple contemporary design. The menu reflects this simplicity of decor and is a lengthy selection of modern Mediterranean dishes augmented by a few of Oriental and American origin. To begin, saffron risotto comes with large chunks of lightly poached smoked haddock; a boudin of chicken is served with a creamy fennel and saffron sauce and sautéed foie gras is accompanied by shallots and balsamic vinegar. Main dishes range from such quite basic dishes as Toulouse sausages with lentils to baked breast of chicken with a herb and Parmesan crust, salmon escalope with linguini and a lemon butter sauce and prime rib of beef served off the bone and either blackened with Cajun spices or with a light wild mushroom gravy. Well-cooked vegetables are priced separately. Desserts include agreeably citrous crepes Suzette, classic lemon tart or an indulgent (for 2) chocolate fondue with Cointreau-laced chocolate, marshmallows and fresh fruit pieces. Splendid service. Booking essential. There's currently a 25% discount on food ordered between 6.30pm and 7.15pm or after 10pm Monday to Friday and at lunchtime a light and rapid menu is also available. **Seats** 112. Private Room 60. L 12-2.30 D 6.30-10.30. Closed L Sat, all Sun. Set L £7.95. AMERICAN EXPRESS *Access, Visa.*

Leeds — Darbar

£30
R

Tel 0532 460381

16-17 Kirkgate Leeds West Yorkshire LS1 6BY

Map 6 C1

Splendidly grand first-floor restaurant serving better-than-average Indian food with the emphasis on subtlety rather than heat. The lunchtime hot buffet offers terrific value for money. **Seats** 92. Parties 50. L 11.30-2 D 6-11.30. Closed 25 Dec. AMERICAN EXPRESS *Access, Diners, Visa.*

Leeds — Dawat

£30
R

Tel 0532 872279

4-6 Leeds Road Kippax nr Leeds West Yorkshire LS25 7LT

Map 6 C1

Indian home cooking Delhi-style – from lamb pasanda and king prawn pepper masala and kulfi plus tandoori specialities from owner Mrs Arora in two 19th-century cottages. **Seats** 26. Parties 16. D only 6.30-11. Closed Sun, 25 & 26 Dec. AMERICAN EXPRESS *Access, Visa.*

Leeds   42 The Calls   £140

Tel 0532 440099   Fax 0532 344100   **PH**

42 The Calls Leeds West Yorkshire LS2 7EW   Map 6 C1

Created from a derelict riverside grain mill, 42 The Calls provides a new
level of modern, sophisticated comfort for visitors to Leeds.
In a redevelopment area, it's the brainchild of Jonathan Wix. Its strong
point is the bedrooms: co-ordinated soft furnishings blend with the
building's original features like painted stone walls and warehouse beams.
Each room has a large work desk, three phones, a CD stereo system and
coffee percolator; one room is equipped for disabled guests. Bathrooms are
equally impressive. Minimal day rooms include a bright foyer and small
lounge. Excellent staff impress greatly and free valet parking is among the
services offered. 24hr room service. The top-floor Fletland suite seats
40 boardroom style, 55 theatre; a barge moored outside the hotel has been
converted for conference use. As we went to press we heard that Jonathan,
the co-owner here with Michael Gill, is changing the profile with the
arrival of *Pool Court at the Calls* as the main restaurant within the hotel. It's
due to open on 12th November 1994 (after this Guide is published),
so more about this development next year! Meanwhile, both the hotel
aspects and the next-door *Brasserie 44* (see entry above) remain unchanged.
Rooms *41. Coarse fishing. Closed 5 days Christmas.* AMERICAN EXPRESS *Access,*
Diners, Visa. MARTELL

From April 1995 the area telephones code for Leeds changes from
0532 to 0113 plus the addition of 2 before six-digit numbers.

Leeds   *Haley's Hotel*   72%   £102

Tel 0532 784446   Fax 0532 753342   **HR**

Shire Oak Road Headingley Leeds West Yorkshire LS6 2DE   Map 6 C1

An elegant Victorian town house down a quiet leafy lane off Headingley's
main thoroughfare. Transformed four years ago into a charming small
hotel it possesses a homely lounge-cum-bar which is furnished in an elegant
country house style with a couple of comfortable settees and groups
of chairs and armchairs. Bedrooms are the best feature. Each is decorated
differently, all in good taste with fine well co-ordinated fabrics which
include colourful quilted chintzes. Furniture is of good quality with lots
of polished natural wood. All expected amenities from tea/coffee-makers
to satellite TVs are provided. Each room also has its own 'Haley the Cat',
a delightful life-size kitty which guests leave outside the door when they
do not wish to be disturbed. Bathrooms are neat and thoughtfully
equipped. Large shower roses over the baths provide a reviving deluge
in the morning. ***Rooms*** *22. Garden. Closed 26-30 Dec.* AMERICAN EXPRESS
Access, Diners, Visa.

Restaurant   £60

A choice of two menus greets diners in this rather sombre dining room
decorated in shades of cream and brown. The fixed-price menu is of 3 or
4 courses while the à la carte offers a short imaginative selection of quite
capably prepared dishes ranging from curried parsnip soup with crispy
parsnips to beef fillet with a bubble and squeak cake and a garlic and shallot
confit. Sweets include traditional favourites such as warm treacle sponge
and custard or the likes of cherry and kirsch soufflé with cherry sorbet (20
minutes' wait). On the whole the young staff do their very best, the wine
waiter in particular being both enthusiastic and knowledgeable. ***Seats*** *50.*
Parties 10. Private Room 25. Sun L 12.30-2 D 7.15-9.45. Closed L Mon-Sat.
Set Sun L £11.95. Set D £18.95/£23.95.

Leeds   Hilton International   69%   £105

Tel 0532 442000   Fax 0532 433577   **H**

Neville Street Leeds West Yorkshire LS1 4BX   Map 6 C1

Escalators in glass 'antechambers' lead to the cool marble reception/lounge.
A modern, well-kept, well-run hotel. One bedroom is equipped for
disabled guests. Conference/banqueting facilities for 400/290. A leisure and
health complex was being built as we went to press. *Rooms 206. Garage,
coffee shop (10am-11pm).* AMERICAN EXPRESS *Access, Diners, Visa.*

Leeds   Holiday Inn   69%   £132

Tel 0532 442200   Fax 0532 440460   **H**

Wellington Street Leeds West Yorkshire LS1 4DL   Map 6 C1

Ten minutes walk westwards from the city centre the hotel stands en route
to the airport. Tall and only five years old it offers all the expected modern
comforts. The leisure facilities include a splendid blue-mosaic-tiled
swimming pool. *Rooms 125. Indoor swimming pool, children's pool, keep-fit
equipment, sauna, spa bath, solarium, snooker.* AMERICAN EXPRESS *Access,
Diners, Visa.*

Leeds   Leeds Marriott   74%   NEW   £141

Tel 0532 366366   Fax 0532 366367   **H**

4 Trevelyan Square Boar Lane Leeds West Yorkshire LS1 6ET   Map 6 C1

Part of an attractive new office development overlooking a pretty, part-
lawned quadrangle with fountain due east of the station at the junction
of Boar Lane and Briggate. Efficient car parking by the hall porters takes
the strain out of staying at a city-centre hotel. Boasting impressive public
rooms, the Marriott, opened in October '93, features a spacious foyer with
large, square stone pillars and rich mahogany panelling. John T's Bar has
a clubby, almost traditional ambience which is created in part by more
mahogany panelling, etched frosted glass windows and leather-upholstered
seating. Bedrooms are comfortable and up-to-date, each with at least
a double (queen-size) bed, some with two. Executive rooms have king-size
beds. Each has all the expected amenities, the latter have a mini-bar and
bathrobes, but all have fax points, remote satellite TVs and an efficient and
comprehensive provision of room service which includes a reasonable
breakfast. Bathrooms are supplied with plentiful towels and have good
showers. *Rooms 244. Indoor swimming pool, gym, sauna, solarium, spa bath,
news kiosk.* AMERICAN EXPRESS *Access, Diners, Visa.*

Leeds   Leodis Brasserie   NEW   £80

Tel 0532 421010   Fax 0532 430432   **R**

Victoria Mill Sovereign Street Leeds West Yorkshire LS1 4BJ   Map 6 C1

The ground floor of a former Victorian mill, just south of the city centre
in a fast-developing area now firmly on the circuit of Leeds' smart set.
Curved plate-glass screens, halogen spots and stylish modern furniture
contrast with the old timbers and exposed redbrick of the walls and arched
ceilings. The menu is appropriately modern with a lengthy, varied choice
of starters, mains and sweets. Yet there's no compromise in standards
in dishes like super-fresh flash-grilled scallops accompanied by a crisp
balsamic vinegar-dressed salad and ruby grapefruit segments (although the
bitter tartness of the citrus is perhaps not the perfect complement to the
scallops). A thick, well-chilled gazpacho comes with a selection of bowls
containing crunchy croutons, diced peppers, tomato and cucumber as well
as garlic-infused olive oil. Main dishes range from a roast breast of duck
with cider and apples, baked fillet of red snapper with a coriander, pine nut
and lime crumble to tender grilled venison medallions accompanied
by a neat tartlet of caramelised red cabbage, a blackcurrant sauce providing
a suitable counterpoint of sweetness and acidity. Sweets include a very rich

dark chocolate tart which comes with an equally rich chocolate sauce. Other choices could be lemon tart, rum and raisin mousse or sticky toffee pudding with toffee sauce. Charming service. Booking essential. *Seats 169. Parties 20. L 12-2 D 6-10 (Fri & Sat to 11). Closed L Sat, all Sun, L Bank Holidays, 25 & 26 Dec. Set L & D £11.95 (except Sat after 7.30).* AMERICAN EXPRESS *Access, Visa.*

Leeds	**Maxi's Chinese Restaurant**	**£40**
Tel 0532 440552 Fax 0532 343902		**R**
Bingley Street Leeds West Yorkshire LS3 1LX		**Map 6 C1**

The largest purpose-built Chinese restaurant in the North, serving Cantonese and Peking cuisine to 300 diners. Hardly worthy of a foodie pilgrimage, but worth knowing about; plenty of room for families and a couple of private suites for functions. *Seats 300. Meals 12-12. Set meals from £15.* AMERICAN EXPRESS *Access, Diners, Visa.*

Leeds	**Merrion Thistle Hotel 65%**	**£105**
Tel 0532 439191 Fax 0532 423527		**H**
Merrion Centre Wade Lane Leeds West Yorkshire LS2 8NH		**Map 6 C1**

Even more refurbishment at this modern hotel, located in the huge Merrion Centre which is itself sandwiched between the University and the old city centre. In total, some £6 million has been spent on the facelift. More of the previously rather small rooms have been enlarged, reducing the overall number but increasing the facilities within each – all the usual electrical gadgets and creature comforts are standard. Some rooms are designated with Executive status, others are especially equipped for lady guests. Good bathrooms. Free overnight parking in next door multi-storey car park. *Rooms 109.* AMERICAN EXPRESS *Access, Diners, Visa.*

Leeds	**New Asia**	**£35**
Tel 0532 343612		**R**
128 Vicar Lane Leeds West Yorkshire LS2 7NL		**Map 6 C1**

Mr Xuan Truong Hoang produces inexpensive Vietnamese specialities in slightly old-fashioned surroundings. Fine spring rolls made to order, mung bean flour (*luk dao fan*) noodles and *char siu*. There's a long list of seafood and over a dozen soups. *Seats 60. L 12-2 D 5-12. Set L from £4.20 Set D from £9.50. Access, Visa.*

> Many hotels offer reduced rates for weekend or out-of-season bookings. Always ask about special deals.

Leeds	**The Olive Tree**	**£55**
Tel 0532 569283		**R**
Oaklands Rodley Lane Leeds West Yorkshire LS13 1NG		**Map 6 C1**

George and Vasoulla Psarias have really put the Olive Tree on the map, thanks to their recent television appearances – though those in the know already went there for some above-average Greek cooking and a lively atmosphere. Unusually, vegetarians are well catered for (probably better than they are in Greece!). The à la carte is not particularly cheap but early diners (before 7.30pm Mon-Fri and all day Sun) can take advantage of a good-value set meal at £9.95. Greek coffee comes with some excellent Turkish delight. Every Tuesday there is a 'bouzouki' evening with live music and dancing at no extra charge. *Seats 150. Private Room 60. L 12-2 D 6-11. Closed L Sat, D Sun, 25 Dec, 1 Jan. Set L £9.95/£13.50 Set D £9.95 (till 7.30pm) & £13.50.* AMERICAN EXPRESS *Access, Visa.*

Leeds   Oulton Hall Hotel   75%   NEW   £115

Tel 0532 821000   Fax 0532 828066   **H**

Rothwell Lane Oulton Leeds West Yorkshire LS26 8HN   Map 6 C1

Acquired by De Vere in 1991 when it was in a state of advanced
dereliction, the hotel, which has been restored at huge expense, recreates
a semblance of the original Grade II classical Italianate mid-19th century
mansion and opened in June 1993. Surrounded by Leeds City Council golf
courses (reception is able to book guests on to these), the hotel also has its
own extensive leisure complex. A fine black-and-white tile-floored
entrance hall leads to a series of very impressive public rooms. The
beautifully proportioned and furnished library and drawing room open
one to another and share the services of a tail-coated butler. Here walls are
covered in fine damask and as elsewhere in the public areas, huge glittering
crystal chandeliers hang from the ornate ceilings. The galleried Great Hall
offers additional very comfortable seating and leads to the Calverley Bar
with its elegant red leather-upholstered seating. Doors open on to the south
terrace, which in turn overlooks a formal garden. The majority of the
bedrooms have very much an 'international air' being uniform in size and
equipped with a host of modern amenities including mini-bars and remote
satellite TVs. There is plenty of writing space and two comfortable
armchairs provide ample opportunity for relaxation. Beds too are
comfortable. Bathrooms feature good showers. Breakfasts are served in an
elegant room but are mediocre, with choices taken from a cold and hot
buffet service. Friendly staff. *Rooms 152. Garden, indoor swimming pool,
gym, sauna, solarium, spa bath, beauty salon, snooker.* AMERICAN EXPRESS *Access,
Diners, Visa.*

Leeds   Queen's Hotel   68%   £94

Tel 0532 431323   Fax 0532 425154   **H**

City Square Leeds West Yorkshire LS1 1PL   Map 6 C1

Right in the city centre and just opposite the station, Queen's was the
grandest hotel in Leeds when it was built in the 1930s and many original
features have been retained. Particularly impressive are the Palm Court
Lounge (returned to its first use having been a furniture room for many
years), large oval lobby with domed ceiling and clubby, mahogany-
panelled bar. Authentic 1930s furniture and light fittings distinguish
bedrooms, which also offer all the modern comforts including up-to-date
bathrooms. Five rooms adapted for use by the disabled. 62 designated non-
smoking. 24hr room service and free valet parking. Conference facilities
for 600. Forte Grand. *Rooms 190. Shop, Palm Court Lounge (7.30am-11pm).*
AMERICAN EXPRESS *Access, Diners, Visa.*

Leeds   Sang Sang   £50

Tel 0532 468664   **R**

7 The Headrow Leeds West Yorkshire LS1 6PU   Map 6 C1

Over 200 dishes are listed on the long menu at this popular Chinese
restaurant. All the favourites are represented including sizzling dishes,
noodles with mixed meat and Peking duck. *Seats 90. Parties 80.
Private Room 16. L 12-1.45 D 5.30-11. Closed Sun & Bank Holidays.
Set L from £4.95 Set D from £8.* AMERICAN EXPRESS *Access, Diners, Visa.*

Leeds   Sous le Nez en Ville   £55

Tel 0532 440108   Fax 0532 450240   **R**

Basement Quebec House Quebec Street Leeds West Yorkshire
LS1 2HA   Map 6 C1

A deservedly popular, intimate and informal cellar-like basement restaurant
with polished pine furniture and quarry-tiled floors. The menu
is imaginative and very enjoyable, comprising well-prepared dishes such

as rillettes of pork with apple chutney, roast French black pudding with
onions and green peppercorns to begin and some French classics such
as beef bourguignon and cassoulet among the selection of mostly modern
mains. Sweets, too, are a mixture of old favourites and the new. Sticky
toffee pudding with toffee sauce and steamed jam sponge and custard
feature alongside the likes of white chocolate paté with macaroons and
lemon syrup or iced Amaretto sponge with raspberry ice cream and
Amaretto sauce. Very cordial service even at peak times. Booking very
advisable. *Seats 75. Parties 16. Private Room 20. L 12-2.30 D 6-10.30 (Fri &
Sat to 11). Closed L Sat, all Sun, Bank Holidays. Set D (6-7.30) £12.95 incl ½
bottle of wine. Access, Visa.*

Leeds   Thai Siam   £40
Tel 0532 451608   R
68-72 New Briggate Leeds West Yorkshire LS1 6NU   Map 6 C1

Friendly service from traditionally clad staff in simple, uncluttered first-
floor surroundings. The Thai menu offers 60+ dishes, with a further two
dozen in the vegetarian section. MSG-free. *Seats 60. L 12-2.30 D 6-11
(Sun & Mon to 10.30). Set L from £5.50 Set D from £11. Access, Visa.*

Leeds   Places of Interest

Tourist Information Tel 0532 478302.
Harewood House and Bird Garden Tel 0532 886225/886238.
The Hollies Park Tel 0532 782030.
Museum of Leeds
Middleston Railway Moor Road Railway Station Tel 0532 710320.
City Varieties Music Hall Tel 0532 430808.
Civic Theatre Tel 0532 462453.
Grand Theatre and Opera House Tel 0532 459351.
Leeds Playhouse Tel 0532 442141.
International Pool Tel 0532 438696.
Headingley Cricket Ground Tel 0532 787394.
Leeds United Football Ground . Tel 0532 716037.
Leeds RLFC Tel 0532 786181
Pontefract Park Racecourse Tel 0977 703224.

Leicester   Belmont Hotel   65%   £89
Tel 0533 544773   Fax 0533 470804   H
De Montfort Street Leicester Leicestershire LE1 7GR   Map 7 D4

In the ownership of the Bowie family since 1934, the Belmont stands in a
quiet street just off the A6. Good-quality darkwood furniture is used in the
bedrooms, the larger of which are designated Executives. Among the day
rooms are two bars and a new brasserie. Children up to 16 stay free
in parents' room. *Rooms 65. Garden.* AMERICAN EXPRESS *Access, Diners, Visa.*

From April 1995 the area telephones code for Leicester changes from
0533 to 0116 plus the addition of 2 before six-digit numbers.

Leicester   Curry Pot   £45
Tel 0533 538256   R
78 Belgrave Road Leicester Leicestershire LE4 5AS   Map 7 D4

Tandoori restaurant offering a short menu of Indian favourites that are
a cut above the standard suggested by the rather dull exterior. Particularly
good samosas, chicken tikka and masala, plus lamb shahi korma. *Seats 55.
Parties 30. L 12-2 (Sat to 1.30) D 6-11 (Sat to 11.30). Closed Sun, 25 & 26
Dec. Set meals from £16.25.* AMERICAN EXPRESS *Access, Diners, Visa.*

Leicester   Forte Posthouse   64%   £68

Tel 0533 630500   Fax 0533 823623   **H**

Braunston Lane East Leicester Leicestershire LE3 2FW   Map 7 D4

Modern low-riser equidistant from Junction 21 of the M1 and the city centre. Conference/banqueting facilities for 100. *Rooms 172. Garden.* AMERICAN EXPRESS *Access, Diners, Visa.*

Leicester   Granada Lodge   £51

Tel 0530 244237   Fax 0530 244580   **L**

M1/A50 Junction 22 Markfield Leicester Leicestershire LE6 0PP   Map 7 D4

Rooms 39. AMERICAN EXPRESS *Access, Diners, Visa.*

Leicester   Holiday Inn   72%   £114

Tel 0533 531161   Fax 0533 513169   **H**

129 St Nicholas Circle Leicester Leicestershire LE1 5LX   Map 7 D4

At the hub of a major road interchange, near Junction 21 of the M1, Leicester's Holiday Inn is a tall building reaching high over the city. The marbled reception area makes a splendid first impression, and the lounge area that adjoins it is no less appealing. The rustic-style Hayloft restaurant with beams and agricultural accoutrements is an interesting contrast to the otherwise modern decor. Bedrooms provide plenty of space, large beds, fitted units and good tiled bathrooms. 76 are designated non-smoking. The well-equipped health and leisure club is a great family attraction at weekends. Free covered parking for residents. Conference facilities for 300. *Rooms 188. Indoor swimming pool, sauna, solarium, spa bath, steam room, news kiosk, coffee shop (7am-10.15pm).* AMERICAN EXPRESS *Access, Diners, Visa.*

Leicester   Jarvis Grand Hotel   66%   £106

Tel 0533 555599   Fax 0533 544736   **H**

Granby Street Leicester Leicestershire LE1 6ES   Map 7 D4

A city-centre Victorian building with ample parking, close to the railway station. Public rooms live up to the name and bedrooms are stylish and of a good size. 24hr room service; children up to 14 can stay free in parents' room. Two themed bars; carvery restaurant; vast banqueting and conference facilities for up to 450. Jarvis Hotels. *Rooms 92. Coffee shop (7-7).* AMERICAN EXPRESS *Access, Diners, Visa.*

Leicester   Leicester Forest Moat House   58%   £79

Tel 0533 394661   Fax 0533 394952   **H**

Hinckley Road Leicester Leicestershire LE3 3GH   Map 7 D4

Alongside the A47 four miles from the city centre, 3 miles from Junction 21 interchange of M69 and M1. Well-equipped bedrooms, a choice of bars and conference rooms for up to 65. Ample free car parking. *Rooms 34. Garden.* AMERICAN EXPRESS *Access, Diners, Visa.*

Leicester   Man Ho   £40

Tel 0533 557700   **R**

16 King Street Leicester Leicestershire LE1 6RJ   Map 7 D4

Comprising two houses in a low Georgian terrace behind New Walk Centre, Man Ho probably offers the best Chinese cooking in Leicester. Space, comfort and tastefully modern decor make a fine setting in which smartly-suited waitresses serve a mix of Peking, Cantonese and Szechuan cooking. Good choice à la carte or on various set menus. Sunday lunch (12-

4) sees a dim sum buffet (£10 adult, £6 child). *Seats 130. Private Room 60.*
L 12-2.30 D 6-11.30 (Sat & Sun 12-11.30). Closed 25 Dec. Set L from £6.50
Set D from £12. AMERICAN EXPRESS *Access, Visa.*

Leicester — Rise of the Raj — £35

Tel 0533 553885

R

6 Evington Road Leicester Leicestershire LE2 1HF

Map 7 D4

Indian cooking in a homely restaurant on two floors. The menu is fairly
standard, with many variations on lamb, chicken and prawns providing the
bulk of the dishes. Specialities include chicken or king prawn masala, lamb
pasanda and tandoori rainbow trout. Good-value thali (set meals), both
meat and vegetarian. Popular Sunday buffet (children half price). *Seats 70.*
Private Room 40. L 12-2 D 6-11.30 (open all day Sun). Closed 25 Dec.
AMERICAN EXPRESS *Access, Diners, Visa.*

Leicester — Stakis Country Court — 69% — £106

Tel 0533 630066   Fax 0533 630627

H

Braunstone Leicester Leicestershire LE3 2WQ

Map 7 D4

Ten minutes from the city centre, just off Junction 21 of the M1, at the
end of the M69, this modern, business-oriented hotel offers good-sized
bedrooms (all rooms have either one or two double beds), an extensive
range of conference facilities (for up to 90 with plans for expansion
to accommodate 200), a well-equipped leisure club and reduced rates for
families at off-peak weekends when businessmen are thin on the ground.
Children under 16 stay free in parents' room. *Rooms 141. Garden, indoor*
swimming pool, gym, sauna, spa bath, steam room, solarium, beauty salon.
AMERICAN EXPRESS *Access, Diners, Visa.*

Leicester — Places of Interest

Tourist Information   Tel 0533 511300/511301.
Haymarket Theatre   Tel 0533 539797
Phoenix Arts Theatre   Tel 0533 554854.
Bosworth Battlefield Visitor Centre & Country Park   Market Bosworth
Tel 0455 290429.
Leicester Cathedral   Tel 0533 625294.
The Leicestershire Museum and Art Gallery   New Walk Tel 0533
554100.
Leicestershire Museum of Technology   Tel 0530 510851.
Grace Road Cricket Ground   Tel 0533 831880.
Leicester City Football Ground   Tel 0533 555000.
Leicester Racecourse   Tel 0533 716515.
Outdoor Pursuits Centre Dry Ski Slope   Tel 0533 681426.
Braunstone Park Showground   Tel 0509 231665.
Mallory Park Motor Racing Circuit   Tel 0455 842931.

Lenham — Chilston Park — 71% — £95

Tel 0622 859803   Fax 0622 858588

H

Sandway Lenham nr Maidstone Kent ME17 2BE

Map 11 C5

Four miles from Junction 8 of M20, between Ashford and Maidstone, this
is a remarkable hotel set in 250 acres complete with a lake: 17th-century
diarist John Evelyn called it "a sweetly watered place", and the atmosphere
thus evoked is reverently maintained. The Grade I listed house contains
a treasure trove of antique furniture, oil paintings, water colours, rugs and
objets d'art. Over 200 candles are lit by tail-coated staff throughout the
public areas at dusk, evoking a sense of the past. The Marble Hall and
Drawing Room are fine examples of elegant comfort and each bedroom
in the house has its own very individual style and character; some have
open fires. The Hogarth Room has an 18th-century four-poster and
a splendid view of the lake. Bedrooms in the stable block are simpler but

not without charm. Characterful conference and meeting rooms (for up to 120). On balmy summer days, you can now take a punt across the lake. *Rooms 40. Garden, croquet, tennis, coarse fishing, snooker.* AMERICAN EXPRESS *Access, Diners, Visa.*

Letchworth	**Broadway Toby Hotel**	**59%**	**£60**
Tel 0462 480111 Fax 0462 481563			**H**
The Broadway Letchworth Hertfordshire SG6 3NZ			**Map 15 E1**

A smartly-kept hotel with a friendly, non-chain feel (even though it is in the Toby Restaurant Group, a division of Bass Taverns Ltd.). Well-furnished bedrooms and a calm cocktail bar-cum-lounge. Conference and banqueting facilities for up to 180. *Rooms 35.* AMERICAN EXPRESS *Access, Diners, Visa.*

Lewdown	**Lewtrenchard Manor**	**73%**	**£98**
Tel 056 683 256 Fax 056 683 332			**H R**
Lewdown nr Okehampton Devon EX20 4PN			**Map 12 C2**

James and Sue Murray create the atmosphere of a large and happy family home at their handsome 17th-century mansion, where hymn-writer and novelist the Rev. Sabine Baring Gould once lived. The setting is particularly peaceful and delightfully rural, and the bedrooms all enjoy fine views through leaded windows. The rooms vary in size, the larger with antique furniture including a couple with four-posters, but all benefit from well-chosen fabrics, fresh flowers, mineral water and, in the carpeted bathrooms, towelling robes, good toiletries and huge soft bath sheets. Room service offers drinks and light snacks throughout the day and evening and beds are turned down at night. No children under eight. *Rooms 8. Garden, croquet, fishing, clay-pigeon shooting, helipad.* AMERICAN EXPRESS *Access, Diners, Visa.*

Restaurant   £75

A grand room with oil portraits of some of the former occupants of the house gazing down at the crisply clothed tables where today's guests are offered a choice between Patrick Salvadori's varied menus. Salmon with watercress and a cream sauce or terrine of pork and asparagus with an apple and Madeira dressing could be your starter, with guinea fowl accompanied by a lemon butter sauce, brill with fennel and Pernod, or traditional roast beef to follow. Desserts could be simple – ice creams, strawberries with clotted cream – or more elaborate, like filo pancake filled with marinated pineapple and melon with a selection of fruit sauces. Service is a happy combination of friendliness and formality. No smoking. *Seats 35. Parties 8. Private Room 16. L by arrangement & Sun 12-2.30 D 7.15-9.30. Set L £16 Set D £25.*

Never leave money, credit cards or valuables lying around in your hotel room. Use the hotel safe or the mini-safe in your room.

Lewes	**Shelleys Hotel**	**60%**	**£140**
Tel 0273 472361 Fax 0273 483152			**H**
High Street Lewes East Sussex BN7 1XS			**Map 11 B6**

One of the original Mount Charlotte hotels (acquired in 1977), Shelleys is located on the main road through Lewes. Built originally (16th century) as an inn, it was later a manor house, military hospital and a number of flats. Children up to 16 stay free in parents' room. *Rooms 17. Garden, croquet.* AMERICAN EXPRESS *Access, Diners, Visa.*

Lewes   Places of Interest

Historic Houses, Castles and Gardens
Bateman's (NT)   Burwash Tel 0435 882302 *Rudyard Kipling lived here.*
Charleston Farmhouse   Fircle Tel 032 183 265 *Home of Vanessa and Clive Bell and Duncan Grant, leaders of the Bloomsbury movement.*
Firle Place   Tel 0273 858335.
Glynde Place   Tel 0273 858337.
Monk's House   Rodmell Tel 0273 479274 *Cottage home of Virginia and Leonard Woolf.*
Wilmington Priory and Long Man   Nr Newhaven Tel 0323 870537 *10 miles.*
Borowski Centre Dry Ski Slope   Newhaven Tel 0273 515402.
Drusillas Zoo   Alfriston Tel 0323 870656.

Lichfield   George Hotel   59%   £90

Tel 0543 414822   Fax 0543 415817   **H**
Bird Street Lichfield Staffordshire WS13 6PR   Map 6 C3

Regency style survives in the spacious, peaceful day rooms and the pastel-decorated bedrooms of this Jarvis hotel. The ballroom can accommodate up to 100 guests for a banquet or conference. Children up to 12 stay free in parents' room. ***Rooms 38.*** AMERICAN EXPRESS *Access, Diners, Visa.*

Lichfield   Places of Interest

Tourist Information   Tel 0543 252109.
Hanch Hall and Garden   Tel 0543 490308.
Lichfield Cathedral   Tel 0543 256120.
Samuel Johnson Birthplace Museum   Tel 0543 264972.
Lichfield Heritage Exhibition Treasury and Muniment Room   Tel 0543 256611.

Lifton   Arundell Arms   65%   £90

Tel 0566 784666   Fax 0566 784494   **HR**
Lifton Devon PL16 0AA   Map 12 C2

With 20 miles of its own water on the Tamar (and its tributaries), the 16th-century Arundell Arms is a haunt for serious fisherfolk, although come the autumn it's shooting parties who take over the country-furnished bar and rug-strewn, slate-floored sitting room. In the garden, a 250-year-old circular stone cockpit – one of the few remaining in England – is now a tackle shop and rod room. Anne Voss-Bark, owner here for more than 30 years, is herself a keen fisherwoman and co-author of the *Beginner's Guide to Fly Fishing.* Well-kept bedrooms, a few in an annexe across the street, have pleasant pastel colour schemes and all the usual modern amenities; some have period furnishings, others freestanding pine pieces, while the singles feature built-in furniture. Neat bathrooms, just a couple with shower and WC only. Children up to 16 stay free in parents' room. Banqueting for 110, conference facilities for 100. The village is now bypassed ("a great dark cloud has been lifted from the village") and can be reached in around 40 minutes from the end of the motorway at Exeter. ***Rooms 29.*** *Garden, fishing. Closed 2 days Christmas.* AMERICAN EXPRESS *Access, Diners, Visa.*

Restaurant   £75

An elegantly proportioned room with a central glass chandlier but stackable (though comfortably upholstered) banqueting chairs that don't quite live up to the overall style intended. Chef Philip Burgess has been running the kitchen here for some years and he keeps up to date with modern trends, evidenced in dishes like a salad of sweet peppers with Parmesan shavings, anchovies and a basil dressing, shallot soup with thyme cream, spiced ground beef fillet with coriander cream and polenta, and

grilled guinea fowl with raisin and pine nut fritters. Tamar salmon
is a speciality in season. A so-called à la carte menu is actually a fixed-price
(depending on the number of courses taken) affair, available both
lunchtime and evening, along with a less expensive table d'hote menu.
No children in the restaurant at dinner. Informal eating in the Arundell
Bar (12-2.30, 6.30-9.30). **Seats** 70. Private Room 30. L 12.30-2 D 7.30-9.30.
Set L £11.75/£14.75 (Sun £15.50) D £21.50/£26.

Lifton   Place of Interest

Launceston Castle   Launceston Tel 0566 2365.

Lincoln   D'Isney Place   £62

Tel 0522 538881   Fax 0522 511321   **PH**
Eastgate Lincoln Lincolnshire LN2 4AA   **Map 7 E2**

A delightful garden surrounds D'Isney Place, an 18th-century building
by the Cathedral offering an exceptionally warm and comfortable
atmosphere. David and Judy Payne run it as an up-market bed and
breakfast hotel. Well-loved antique furniture abounds and there's a homely
feel throughout. The rooms vary from large, with four-posters and spa
baths or steam showers, to compact and charming singles, one with
shower/WC only. Also available is a cottage with two double en-suite
bedrooms, living room, dining room and kitchen. All the bedrooms have
tables and breakfast is served to order in the rooms. Limited parking within
the grounds. **Rooms** 17. Garden. AMERICAN EXPRESS Access, Diners, Visa.

Lincoln   The Jew's House Restaurant   £55

Tel 0522 524851   **R**
15 The Strait Lincoln Lincolnshire LN2 1JD   **Map 7 E2**

At the bottom of a steep hill leading up to the cathedral, the Jew's House
dates back to 1180 (its fascinating history is related on the back of the
menu) although Richard Gibbs' largely French-inspired menu is rather
more up-to-date with the likes of grilled goat's cheese in puff pastry with
leeks, duck with kumquats or rack of lamb with a pine kernel and basil
crust. At lunchtime there are also lighter dishes in addition to the main à la
carte and it's worth checking out the blackboard for the day's fish dishes
and things like local samphire in season. Soufflé Grand Marnier
is a speciality dessert. There are just six tables in the rough stone-walled
dining room plus a little lounge on the first floor for pre- or post-prandial
drinks. Certainly the best restaurant in Lincoln, and indeed for miles
around. **Seats** 25. Parties 14. L 12-1.30 D 7-9.30. Closed L Mon, all Sun,
Bank Holidays (except Good Fri). Set L & D £18.50. AMERICAN EXPRESS Access,
Diners, Visa.

Lincoln   Lincoln Forte Posthouse   63%   £68

Tel 0522 520341   Fax 0522 510780   **H**
Eastgate Lincoln Lincolnshire LN2 1PN   **Map 7 E2**

A modern hotel right beside the cathedral and handy for visiting old
Lincoln. Well-equipped bedrooms. Conference and function facilities for
up to 80. **Rooms** 70. Garden. AMERICAN EXPRESS Access, Diners, Visa.

Lincoln   Travel Inn   £43

Tel 0522 525216   Fax 0522 542521   **L**
Lincoln Road Canwick Hill Lincoln LN4 2RF   **Map 7 E2**

On the junction of B1188 to Branston and B1131 to Bracebridge Heath.
Two miles from the city centre. **Rooms** 40. AMERICAN EXPRESS Access,
Diners, Visa.

Lincoln · White Hart · 69% · £100

Tel 0522 526222 Fax 0522 531798

Bailgate Lincoln Lincolnshire LN1 3AR

H c

Map 7 E2

An old Forte Heritage hotel in the heart of the city on a site where there has been an inn for over 600 years (Richard II stayed in 1387). Secure parking available opposite. *Rooms 48.* AMERICAN EXPRESS *Access, Diners, Visa.*

Lincoln · Places of Interest

Tourist Information   Tel 0522 529828.
Theatre Royal   Tel 0522 23303.
  Historic Houses, Castles and Gardens
Doddington Hall   Doddington Tel 0522 694308.
Lincoln Castle   Castle Hill Tel 0522 511068.
Tattershall Castle (NT)   Tattershall, Nr Woodhall Spa Tel 0526 42543.
The Old Hall   Gainsborough Tel 0427 612669.
Lincoln Cathedral   Tel 0522 530320.
City and County Museum   Tel 0522 530401.
Usher Gallery   Tel 0522 527890.
Market Rasen Racecourse   Tel 0673 843434 *16 miles.*
Cadwell Park Motor Racing Circuit   Nr Louth Tel 0507 343248.
Grange-de-Lings Showground   Tel 0522 522900.

See the hotel by county listings for easy comparison of conference and banqueting facilities.

Linton · Wood Hall · 76% · £95

Tel 0937 587271 Fax 0937 584353

Tripp Lane Linton nr Wetherby West Yorkshire LS22 4JA

HR

Map 6 C1

Almost at the top of a hill, surrounded by 100 acres of wooded parkland and with a Carmelite monastery at the rear, the hotel is approached from the centre of Linton along a very busy winding single-track road. Its high hillside position gives front bedrooms commanding views over the valley below. Dating from 1750, the house is fronted by an elegant semi-circular portico and intimate entrance hall has polished flagstone floors and beautiful floral arrangements creating a welcoming feeling. Public rooms are invitingly relaxing, particularly a classically proportioned drawing room with deep-cushioned settees, antiques and a few ornaments. The bar next door is more sombre, with dark oak-panelled walls. It features a baby grand as a dispensing counter. A new leisure complex has been added together with, above, a wing of new bedrooms. These are all uniformly spacious and attractively decorated. Front-facing bedrooms have the lightest and best aspects. Bedrooms in the original base vary in size though they tend to be larger and have more character. Bathrooms, however, are a little simpler. The new-wing bathrooms have excellent showers. All rooms are well equipped. Standards of room service are less than adequate and on our latest visit decor was showing signs of wear and tear. *Rooms 43. Garden, coarse fishing, indoor swimming pool, spa bath, solarium, beauty salon, steam room, gym, snooker.* AMERICAN EXPRESS *Access, Diners, Visa.*

Restaurant · £85

An elegantly appointed dining room with a fair menu of modern quasi-fashionable dishes. Typical are goat's cheese tortellini with spinach and a butter sauce, terrine of sea bass and parsley on a watercress salad, loin of venison on a potato and onion rösti with a prune and armagnac sauce or fillet of Scotch beef with a Stilton sabayon, button onions and a port wine sauce. Desserts can be uninspired and service somewhat half-hearted. *Seats 60. Parties 10. Private Room 30. L 12.30-2.30 D 7-9.30. Closed L Sat.*

Liskeard   Well House   74%   £90

Tel 0579 342001   **HR**

St Keyne Liskeard Cornwall PL14 4RN   Map 12 C3

From the church in St Keyne take the left fork to St Keyne Well to find
this tranquil spot set in small landscaped gardens that include an enchanting
duck pond. Built at the turn of the century by a tea-planter, it is the most
charming retreat, and owner Nick Wainford and his staff are never
anything but friendly, helpful and discreet. Off the tiled hall are a relaxing
drawing room and an inviting little bar; across the hall, the dining room
has magnificent bay windows overlooking the sun terrace and lawns.
Individually designed bedrooms and well-equipped bathrooms are
immaculately kept. First-rate breakfasts. **Rooms** 7. *Garden, croquet,
outdoor swimming pool, tennis. Access, Visa.*

Restaurant   £65

Lunch and dinner menus of 2, 3 or 4 courses plus canapés, coffee and petits
fours feature what's best and freshest from the local markets. Dishes run
from Cornish fish soup with garlic croutons and galantine of quail with
sun-dried tomatoes and wild mushrooms to calf's liver with creamed
tarragon potatoes, medallions of monkfish with pesto sauce and red pepper
coulis, and sirloin steak with an oyster mushroom compote and Madeira
jus. Vegetarian food cooked to order. West Country cheeses. **Seats** 32.
L 12.30-2 D 7.30-10. Set L & D from £19.95.

Liskeard   Place of Interest

Thorburn Museum and Gallery   Tel 0579 20325/21129 *Audio-visual
 gallery.*

Liverpool   Armadillo   £55

Tel 051-236 4123   **R**

20 Mathew Street Liverpool Merseyside L2 6RE   Map 6 A2

In the recently-christened 'Cavern Quarter' of town (the club made famous
by the Beatles was just a few doors away) this friendly, informal, bistro-
style eating place is now owned by local entrepreneur brothers John and
Frank Kenny. There has been no change of personnel in the kitchen,
however, which still produces dishes like spinach and cream cheese roulade,
chestnut paté, roast monkfish with smoked bacon and tomato sauce, rack
of lamb with filo parcel of spinach and apricot with dry vermouth sauce
and chicken with an orange and grapefruit sauce. There are always a couple
of vegetarian options. End perhaps with *tarte au citron* or rich raisin
pudding. Less formal lunch and early supper (5-6.30pm) menu with
no miminum charge – just have a starter, a slice of quiche or one of the
main dishes (all at £6.50). **Seats** 75. *L 12-3 Early Supper 5-6.45 (Not Sat)
D 7-10.30. Closed Sun, Mon, Bank Holidays.* AMERICAN EXPRESS *Access,
Diners, Visa.*

Liverpool   Atlantic Tower   65%   £105

Tel 051-227 4444   Fax 051-236 3973   **H**

Chapel Street Liverpool Merseyside L3 9RE   Map 6 A2

A city-centre hotel, rising like a great liner on the Liverpool skyline, with
public areas that include a bar inspired by Nelson's *Victory*. Well-equipped
bedrooms make good-sized singles but rather compact doubles and
twins, with no space between beds in the latter. Corner rooms are
larger and there are eight full suites. The hotel has its own car park.
Conference/banqueting facilities for 150/120. A major refurbishment of the
exterior is due for completion by the end of 1994. Mount Charlotte
Thistle. **Rooms** 226. *Garage.* AMERICAN EXPRESS *Access, Diners, Visa.*

Liverpool   Britannia Adelphi Hotel   68%   £94

Tel 051-709 7200   Fax 051-708 8326   **H**

Ranelagh Place Liverpool Merseyside L3 5UL   Map 6 A2

Leisure facilities and Spindles health club, conferences for up to 1000 delegates, six bars and a (refurbished) night club are among the amenities of a large hotel with many grand original Edwardian features. Bedrooms range from singles to suites and jacuzzi rooms. Children up to 16 stay free in parents' room. The hotel is next door to Lime Street station. *Rooms 391. Indoor swimming pool, sauna, spa bath, squash, hairdressing & beauty salon, snooker, coffee shop (11am-2am Mon-Sat).* AMERICAN EXPRESS *Access, Diners, Visa.*

Liverpool   Campanile Hotel   £44

Tel 051-709 8104   Fax 051-709 8725   **L**

Chaloner Street Queen's Dock Liverpool Merseyside L3 4AJ   Map 6 A2

Just outside the city centre. *Rooms 82.* AMERICAN EXPRESS *Access, Diners, Visa.*

Liverpool   Gladstone Hotel   60%   £91

Tel 051-709 7050   Fax 051-709 2193   **H**

Lord Nelson Street Liverpool Merseyside L3 5QB   Map 6 A2

Modern Forte hotel (formerly the Crest) to the rear of Lime Street Station. 24hr room service menu. Extensive conference facilities can cope with up to 600 delegates theatre-style. *Rooms 154.* AMERICAN EXPRESS *Access, Diners, Visa.*

Liverpool   La Grande Bouffe   £50

Tel 051-236 3375   **R**

48a Castle Street Liverpool Merseyside L2 7LQ   Map 6 A2

Informal basement restaurant, mainly self-service at lunchtime. Evening table service brings the likes of home-made black pudding, feta cheese salad, pot-roast of lamb with haricot beans and steamed monkfish à la niçoise. *Seats 60. Parties 16. Private Room 16. L 12-3, D 6-10.30. Closed L Sat, D Mon, all Sun & Bank Holidays.* AMERICAN EXPRESS *Access, Visa.*

Liverpool   Moat House   67%   £105

Tel 051-709 0181   Fax 051-709 2706   **H**

Paradise Street Liverpool Merseyside L1 8JD   Map 6 A2

Spacious bedrooms, large beds, smart public areas and a leisure centre with swimming pool. Conference/banqueting for 450/300. Children up to 16 stay free in parents' room. Nearly half the bedrooms are designated non-smoking. Follow road signs for Albert Dock and Paradise Street car park. *Rooms 251. Indoor swimming pool, gym, sauna, spa bath, solarium, news kiosk, coffee shop (10.30am-midnight).* AMERICAN EXPRESS *Access, Diners, Visa.*

Liverpool   St George's Hotel   58%   £62

Tel 051-709 7090   Fax 051-709 0137   **H**

St John's Precinct Lime Street Liverpool Merseyside L1 1NQ   Map 6 A2

Early 70s' Forte hotel in the centre of town. Additional parking (free to guests between 4pm and 10am) in adjacent multi-storey. *Rooms 155.* AMERICAN EXPRESS *Access, Diners, Visa.*

Liverpool   Travel Inn (West Derby)   £43

Tel 051 228 4724Fax 051 220 7610   **L**

Queens Drive West Derby Liverpool Merseyside L13 0DL   **Map 6 A2**

On the Liverpool ring road, 10 minutes' drive from the city centre and
M62. *Rooms 40.* AMERICAN EXPRESS *Access, Diners, Visa.*

Liverpool   Trials Hotel   65%   £105

Tel 051-227 1021   Fax 051-236 0110   **H**

56 Castle Street Liverpool Merseyside L2 7LQ   **Map 6 A2**

Listed, early-Victorian bank building – the extravagantly rococo former
banking hall makes a most impressive bar – opposite the law courts. All
the bedrooms are big enough to accommodate a comfortable three-piece
suite, some are very large and five are full suites. Amenities include mini-
bars (although room service is 24hrs), satellite TV and, in spacious
bathrooms, spa tubs. The reception/lounge features some nice, polished
mahogany dado panelling and chandeliers. There is no restaurant but
a period breakfast room, in need of some redecoration, where the cooked
breakfast is a better bet than the Continental alternative. There are
arrangements with several restaurants in town enabling guests to charge
meals to their hotel room. Staff are friendly and helpful. Valet parking.
Rooms 20. AMERICAN EXPRESS *Access, Diners, Visa.*

Liverpool   Places of Interest

Tourist Information   Tel 051-709 3631.
Croxteth Hall & Country Park   Tel 051-228 5311.
Speke Hall (NT)   Tel 051-427 7231.
Liverpool Cathedral   Tel 051-709 6271.
Metropolitan Cathedral of Christ the King   Tel 051-709 9222.
Aigburth Cricket Ground   Tel 051-427 2930.
Everton Football Ground   Goodison Park Tel 051-521 2020.
Liverpool Football Ground   Anfield Park Tel 051-263 2361.
Aintree Racecourse   Tel 051-523 2600.
Liverpool Aquarium   Tel 051-207 0001.
Knowsley Safari Park   Prescot Tel 051-430 9009.
Mersey Ferries   Tel 051-630 1030.
Beatles Story   Albert Dock Tel 051-709 1963.
   Theatres and Concert Halls
Empire Theatre   Tel 051 709 1555.
Everyman Theatre   Tel 051 709 4776.
Liverpool Playhouse   Tel 051 709 8478/9.
Neptune Theatre   Tel 051 709 7844.
   Museums and Art Galleries
Liverpool Museum and Planetarium   Tel 051-207 0001.
Merseyside Maritime Museum   Tel 051-207 0001.
Walker Art Gallery   Tel 051-207 0001.
Tate Gallery Liverpool   Tel 051-709 3223.
Pilkington Glass Museum   St. Helens Tel 0744 692014.

Lockington Hilton National E Midlands Airport 69%   £113

Tel 0509 674000   Fax 0509 672412   **H**

Derby Road Lockington Leicestershire DE7 2RH   **Map 7 D3**

Near Junction 24 of the M1 and just 1½ miles from the airport; Donington
Park race track is also nearby. A modern low-rise hotel with conference
facilities for up to 300. Children up to 14 stay free in parents' room.
*Rooms 152. Indoor swimming pool, sauna, spa bath, solarium, gym, beauty
salon, coffee shop (7am-11pm).* AMERICAN EXPRESS *Access, Diners, Visa.*

Lolworth · Forte Travelodge · £45

Tel 0954 781335

L

Huntingdon Road Lolworth Cambridgeshire CB3 8DR

Map 15 F1

On the A604 northbound, 3 miles north of Junction 14 on the M11,
5 miles north of Cambridge. *Rooms 20.* AMERICAN EXPRESS® *Access,
Diners, Visa.*

Long Crendon · The Angel Inn · £50

Tel 0844 208268

RR

Bicester Road Long Crendon Buckinghamshire HP18 9EE

Map 15 D2

A charming pub-restaurant dating back to the early 1500s. In one of the
eating rooms, which include a Lloyd Loom-furnished conservatory, one
can see part of the original wattle and daub construction. Chef-patron
Mark Jones's cooking has a strong Mediterranean slant – chargrilled
ciabatta with salsa verde and olives, crostini with various toppings,
brochette of lamb and beef with chargrilled vegetables, steak frites (from
a camp site in St Tropez, according to the menu), confit of duck with
Provençal beans – although the likes of Lancashire black pudding with
noodles and mustard sauce, bangers 'n' mash and Stilton-stuffed chicken
breast wrapped in bacon are also to be found. A variety of fresh fish dishes
depends upon twice-weekly deliveries direct from Billingsgate. A short
wine list puts the emphasis on New World wines, with about eight
available by the glass. Open for Sunday lunch, but not always – phone to
find out. *Seats 70. Private Room 40. L 12-2.30 D 6.30-10. Closed D Sun.
Access, Visa.*

Rooms · £40

Of the four en-suite bedrooms (two with shower and WC only) two are
particularly characterful with old black beams. Furniture varies from old
pine to some more modern pieces and all rooms have TV, direct-dial
phones and tea/coffee-making kit. No dogs.

Long Eaton · Sleep Inn · NEW · £50

Tel 0602 460000   Fax 0602 460726

L

Bostock Lane Long Eaton Nottingham Nottinghamshire NG10 5NL

Map 7 D3

Comprising spacious, brightly decorated double and family rooms this
American-inspired overnighter stands adjacent to the M1 at Junction 25.
Triple-glazed on the motorway side, the bedrooms have modern open-plan
design, all with good-sized shower cubicles; four rooms equipped for
disabled guests. Amenities include video recorders with a supply of rental
tapes; alcohol, soft drinks, snacks and toiletry items are available from
vending machines on the ground floor. Informal eating in an American-
themed brasserie. Weekend tariff reductions. Meeting rooms for up to 75.
Rooms 101. Closed 1 week Christmas. AMERICAN EXPRESS® *Access, Diners, Visa.*

Long Melford · Black Lion · 65% · £65

Tel 0787 312356   Fax 0787 374557

H

The Green Long Melford Sudbury Suffolk CO10 9DN

Map 10 C3

Count the Toby jugs and admire the maps and copper collection or relax
in deep sofas in the charming lounge. There's also a library, and games for
both adults and children. Bedrooms are bright and comfortable, attractive
fabrics complementing neutral walls and carpets. Each room has antique
pine furniture and an easy chair or sofa. *Rooms 9. Garden.
Closed 23 Dec-2 Jan.* AMERICAN EXPRESS® *Access, Visa.*

Long Melford · Bull Hotel · 65% · £102

Tel 0787 378494   Fax 0787 880307   **H**
Hall Street Long Melford Suffolk CO10 9JG   **Map 10 C3**

Built by a wealthy wool merchant in the 15th century, becoming a posting
house with the arrival of the coaching era, the real-Tudor Bull is now
a Forte Heritage Hotel combining character with comfort. 10 bedrooms
are designated non-smoking. 60-seat conference room, banquets for 120.
Parking for 25 cars. Children up to 14 stay free in parents' room.
Rooms 25. AMERICAN EXPRESS *Access, Diners, Visa.*

Long Melford · Chimneys · £80

Tel 0787 379806   **R**
Hall Street Long Melford Sudbury Suffolk CO10 9JR   **Map 10 C3**

A black and white timbered building in the centre of the village
as charming inside – a wealth of ancient timbers and mellow brickwork
setting off crisp white napery and bone china tableware – as out. Owner
Sam Chalmers is a consummate professional who, although no longer
cooking himself, ensures that the kitchen maintains a consistently high
standard. Salad of quail's eggs and asparagus with cheese and herb fritters,
terrine of smoked fish with a pepper purée, grilled turbot on a bed
of fennel and onions with tomato vinaigrette, and wild mushroom-stuffed
guinea fowl in puff pastry demonstrate the style of fixed-price menus
to which an à la carte menu is about to be added. Dinner or Luncheon Club
membership offers significant price advantages among other things like
wine tastings. A notable wine list includes a good selection of halves and
about 18 wines by the glass – everything from the house vin de pays to
1er cru Volnay and Puligny-Montrachet. **Seats** 50. L 12-2 D 7-9.30.
Closed D Sun. Set D £27.50. AMERICAN EXPRESS *Access, Diners, Visa.*

Long Melford · Places of Interest

Kentwell Hall (House, Garden & Maze)   Long Melford Tel 0787
310207.
Melford Hall (NT) House & Garden   Long Melford Tel 0787 880286.

Long Sutton · Forte Travelodge · £45

Tel 0406 362230   **L**
Wisbech Road Long Sutton Spalding Norfolk PE12 9AG   **Map 10 B1**

On the A17, 12 miles west of King's Lynn and 10 miles north of Wisbech.
Rooms 40. AMERICAN EXPRESS *Access, Diners, Visa.*

Longham · Bridge House · 61% · £52

Tel 0202 578828   Fax 0202 572620   **H**
2 Ringwood Road Ferndown Longham Dorset BH22 9AN   **Map 14 C4**

Anna Joannides is Greek Cypriot and her hotel on the Stour has a distinctly
Mediterranean air; the sunny reception and lounge have white walls with
tiles depicting Greek goddesses and the large bar opens on to a terrace
overlooking the water. Bedrooms have plain white walls and pink draylon
headboards; some large rooms have canopied or four-poster beds and many
rooms enjoy river views. Several conference suites are available for up to
120 delegates. No dogs. **Rooms** 37. *Garden, coarse fishing, children's play area.*
AMERICAN EXPRESS *Access, Diners, Visa.*

Longhorsley   Linden Hall   75%   £123

Tel 0670 516611   Fax 0670 88544   **H**

Longhorsley nr Morpeth Northumberland NE65 8XF   Map 5 D2

An imposing, listed Georgian house stands at the centre of a much-extended
hotel surrounded by 450 acres of mature park and woodland. For the
individual guest there are choices of the imposing Inner Hall, drawing
room and two bars (one of them a pub in the grounds) in which to relax,
generally uninterrupted by users of the Health Spa and Conference Centre
(capacity 300). The latest Garden Rooms (opened in 1993) are set
in enclosed courtyards closest to the indoor pool and afford a high degree
of seclusion. State-of-the-art satellite TVs, complimentary fruit, decanted
sherry and all-enveloping bathrobes are all the high-quality trappings
of gracious living; in contrast, the restaurant food and somewhat
impersonal service perhaps don't measure up. Children up to 14 share
parents' room free. Afternoon tea served from 4-5.30pm. *Rooms 50.
Garden, tennis, croquet, putting, indoor swimming pool, sauna, solarium,
beauty & hair salon, snooker, mountain bikes, coarse fishing, all-weather cricket
pitch.* AMERICAN EXPRESS® *Access, Diners, Visa.*

Longridge   Paul Heathcote's Restaurant   ★★   £90

Tel 0772 784969   **R**

104-106 Higher Road Longridge nr Preston Lancashire PR3 3SY   Map 6 B1

The whisper of good things emanating from an unfashionable corner
of Lancashire which heralded Paul Heathcote's first stellar entry into the
Guide in 1992 has risen since into a crescendo of universal appreciation.
Both the quality and sheer inspiration of his cooking brought early
comparisons in these pages to *Sharrow Bay* (where he once worked), the
former *Pool Court* in Pool-in-Wharfedale, *21 Queen Street* in Newcastle and
the *Old Vicarage* at Ridgeway. Today, his style of "Modern British
Cooking" is arguably the most innovative in the whole of England, earning
him the sobriquet from a national Sunday newspaper of "Cook of the
North". But this is rather more than simply the story of one man's success.
Paul Heathcote has by degrees gathered around him a coherent team both
in the kitchen and front of house who take pride in excellence as a part
of everyday life, yet apart from one none of them has yet passed a 35th
birthday. Exceptional among them is Head Chef, Andrew Barnes, whose
initiation to the stoves was as "plongeur" in one of Heathcote's earlier
kitchens. In Paul's dynamic world of self-belief, here is proof positive that
anything is possible. And so it proves. Both the lunch and à la carte menus
change quite frequently so as to reflect the availability of seasonal raw
materials: duck and maize-fed chicken from nearby Goosnargh, or beef
from Dornoch. The Gourmet menu (still a snip at £32.50) offers six set
courses containing perhaps ten times as many consituent parts. Breads
of onion, sage and cheese or walnut, dates and rosemary accompany
a chilled tomato and chervil juice of pure clarity and subtle complexity.
A pig's trotter filled with ham and sage has a pea purée, onion sauce and
a garnish of mange tout beignets. Roast red mullet lies over leaf spinach
and fondant potato with vegetable mirepoix and a red pepper sauce.
A sorbet is optional: flavoured with lemon and rosemary, it transpires to be
irresistible. The breast of Goosnargh duck is a minor masterpiece
of composition, encompassing caramelised apples, cider potatoes and
dumplings made from the leg, with spring cabbage and a succulent, simple,
translucent jus. Alongside Swaledale and Jersey Blue is served Mrs
Kirkham's local 3-day curd, leaf and ash-wrapped goat's cheese while,
to finish, an *assiette gourmande* might include a bread-and-butter pudding,
syrup sponge with crème anglaise, summer pudding with clotted cream
and a miniature strawberry shortcake. We have found no fault this year
with the kitchen's creativity translating into simple, unqualified success
on the plate. An almost complete absence of traditionally-minded "classic"
saucing contributes to an appreciation of down-to-earth honest flavours
obtained from unquestionably fine, and predominantly local, ingredients. If,

as now appears plain, this is to be Heathcote's "stock in trade" then there is no alternative than thoroughly to applaud it, as scarcely a plate returns to the "plonge" with more than a crumb or two on it. Half a mile past the White Bull pub (follow signs for Jeffery Hill), this relaxed, sophisticated restaurant has entered another dimension from where Paul Heathcote started out, albeit with star quality from day one, only four years ago. To say simply that the food just improves is frankly to be a little condescending; the modest boy from Bolton has indeed made good. Our Chef of the Year in 1994 has indubitably earned his second star. An improved wine list has most areas represented. Well-chosen wines (good mix of established growers and lesser names); no tasting notes, so seek advice from Paul Wiltshire, an excellent sommelier. *Seats 50. Parties 18. L 12-2 (Sun to 2.30) D 7-9.30. Closed L Tues, Wed, Thurs, Sat (but open those L in Dec), all Mon. Set L £20 (Sun £22.50) Set D £35.* AMERICAN EXPRESS *Access, Visa.*

Looe	**Talland Bay Hotel**	67%		£92
Tel 0503 72667 Fax 0503 72940				**H**
Talland Bay nr Looe Cornwall PL13 2JB				**Map 12 C3**

New owners plan some refurbishment during the winter of 1994/95 at this white-painted hotel set high above Talland Bay. The general style and tune of the hotel will remain unchanged and Maureen Le Page (manageress for nearly 15 years) remains, a familiar face to greet returning guests. The main lounge boasts a real log fire whenever there is the slightest chill in the air and a smaller non-smoking lounge also houses a small library. Fresh flowers abound even in the bedrooms, which vary considerably in size and furnishings with everything from inexpensive melamine units to antiques. Many of the practical bathrooms come with bidets and all have hot water bottles hanging up behind the door. Beds are turned down at night. The hotel is surrounded by $2\frac{1}{2}$ acres of terraced gardens, and the area around the heated outdoor pool is particularly delightful. *Rooms 21. Garden, croquet, outdoor swimming pool, keep-fit equipment, sauna, solarium, games room. Closed Jan.* AMERICAN EXPRESS *Access, Diners, Visa.*

Looe	**Places of Interest**

Monkey Sanctuary   Tel 0503 262532.

Loughborough	**Friendly Hotel**	63%	**NEW**	£96
Tel 0509 211800 Fax 0509 211868				**H**
New Ashby Road Loughborough Leicestershire LE11 0EX				**Map 7 D3**

New low-rise redbrick hotel on the A512 near Junction 23 of the M1. There are a few standard rooms, most being in Friendly Hotels' Premier category with extras like teletext and mini-bar. 12 suites have small sitting rooms. A third of the rooms are designated non-smoking. Public areas are open-plan in style and there is a small leisure centre. *Rooms 94. Indoor swimming pool, gym, spa bath, sauna, solarium.* AMERICAN EXPRESS *Access, Diners, Visa.*

Loughborough	**King's Head**	58%		£96
Tel 0509 233222 Fax 0509 262911				**H**
High Street Loughborough Leicestershire LE11 2QL				**Map 7 D3**

Neat and comfortable hotel in the Jarvis group, being thoroughly refurbished as we went to press. Banqueting/conferences for 120. Children up to 12 stay free in parents' room. *Rooms 78. Pool table.* AMERICAN EXPRESS *Access, Diners, Visa.*

Loughborough	**Place of Interest**

The Bell Foundry Museum   Tel 0509 233414.

Lower Beeding   Cisswood House   66%   £96

Tel 0403 891216   Fax 0403 891621   **HR**

Sandygate Lane Lower Beeding nr Horsham West Sussex RH13 6NF   Map 11 A6

Built in the late 1920s by the then chairman of Harrods, using many
of that store's craftsmen, the mock-Tudor house has since been twice
sympathetically extended to create this hotel, owned and run by Othmar
and Elizabeth Illes since 1979. Oak timbers and panelling feature in public
rooms that include a comfortable bar and separate residents' lounge that
sometimes becomes part of an adaptable function suite. Traditionally
furnished bedrooms have plain walls with a variety of different fabrics and
all have a breakfast table and good desk space. Rooms are generally
of a good size but the nine in the most recent extension are particularly
spacious and have separate walk-in showers in their bathrooms. Room
service throughout the day and evening. Conference and banqueting rooms
cater for up to 200/130. No dogs. Eight miles from Gatwick Airport.
*Rooms 34. Garden, croquet, indoor swimming pool. Closed 10 days
Christmas/New Year.* AMERICAN EXPRESS® *Access, Diners, Visa.*

Restaurant   £55

Taking turns with his two sons (both of whom have their own restaurants
in the area), Othmar Illes makes regular trips to the London markets,
ensuring that only the best quality ingredients arrive at the kitchen, where
they are sympathetically handled in fairly straightforward dishes that are
served in generous portions. Foie gras terrine, moules marinière, crab and
avocado salad with sun-dried tomatoes, half a roast duck with sage and
onion stuffing, Dover sole Colbert, filo-wrapped salmon with sole
mousseline stuffing and watercress sauce, and grilled liver and bacon show
the style from a fixed-price menu (the same, though differently priced
at lunch and dinner) that offers a good choice. Puds range from 'floating
island' and pecan pie to a refined apple and almond crumble served with
a very alcoholic Kirsch cream sauce. The dining room looks out through
leaded light windows on to a peaceful, mature garden. Quite fair prices
on the decent wine list, notable for its good Italian selection. *Seats 60.
Private Room 30. L 12.15-2 D 7-9.30 (Sat to 10). Closed Sun.
Set L £16.50/£18.50 Set D £18.25/£20.50.*

Lower Beeding   South Lodge   76%   £130

Tel 0403 891711   Fax 0403 891766   **HR**

Brighton Road Lower Beeding West Sussex RH13 6PS   Map 11 A6

A fine house built by a noted Victorian explorer and botanist, Frederick
Duncan Godman, with 90 acres of grounds full of rare trees and shrubs,
including the largest rhododendron in England. The nearby Mannings
Heath Golf Club is in the same ownership and the hotel's guests have
members' rights there. Day rooms still have a strong Victorian feel with
lots of carved oak panelling and some nice ribbed ceilings. Good-sized
bedrooms, which include four full suites, are appealing and comfortable
with individual decor and proper armchairs and/or sofas; one room
is equipped with extra handrails for disabled guests. Italian marble
bathrooms are particularly luxurious, most with separate showers and twin
wash basins and all with bidets and bathrobes. Bedrooms are properly
serviced in the evening, room service is 24hr and staff are notably friendly
and helpful. Conference/banqueting rooms for up to 85/80. No dogs.
*Rooms 39. Garden, croquet, tennis, golf (18), putting, pétanque, coarse fishing,
snooker, helipad.* AMERICAN EXPRESS® *Access, Diners, Visa.*

Restaurant   £100

From the windows there are fine views across the lawns to the countryside
beyond; inside, the dining room features some fine Victorian oak dado
panelling topped with dresser-like affairs displaying a collection
of decorative plates. The evening à la carte is full of interest with starters

like lemon and dill tortellini filled with crab and salmon on a light shellfish soup or roasted peppers topped with grilled goat's cheese with tomato, basil and virgin olive oil. Main dishes might include a tournedos of wild salmon with a casserole of scallops, mussels and asparagus, or crispy aromatic duck on creamed pistachios with olive oil, braised lentils and a sherry sauce. A less expensive option might be chef John Elliott's three-or five-course, no-choice 'signature menu'. Lunchtime there's a set menu only with about four choices at each stage. Puds are nicely varied with Spotted Dick, croissant butter pudding and a millefeuille of fresh summer berries among the selection on our last visit. The very decent (but expensive) wine list would benefit from fewer spelling mistakes (Tattinger, Rothchild, La Flaive etc). No smoking. *Seats* 40. *Parties 10. Private Room 30. L 12-2.30 (Sun to 3) D 7-10 (Sat to 10.30). Set L £16 (Sun £18.50) Set D £25 & £32.*

Lower Beeding　　Places of Interest

Leonardslee Gardens　Tel 0403 891212.
The High Beeches Gardens　Nr Handcross Tel 0444 400589.
Nymans Garden (NT)　Handcross Tel 0444 400321 or 400002.

Lower Slaughter　Lower Slaughter Manor　80%　　£180★

Tel 0451 820456　Fax 0451 822150　　**·H·R**

Lower Slaughter nr Bourton-on-the-Water Gloucestershire GL54 2HP　　**Map 14 C1**

A peaceful Georgian manor surrounded by its own grounds which include the finest 15th-century dovecote in the country, on the edge of one of the prettiest villages in the Cotswolds. It is the home of experienced hoteliers Peter and Audrey Marks, who personally welcome guests and whose family photos add to the country house feel of antique-furnished public areas that boast some fine plasterwork ceilings, particularly in the panelled drawing room, and impressive chimney pieces. Bedrooms are well appointed, with chintzy floral fabric favoured for the drapes, matching padded headboards and fabric-draped kidney-shaped dressing tables. Numerous extras include fruit, magazines, toffees, home-made biscuits, sherry and mineral water. Roomy bathrooms, many with twin washbasins and bidets and some with separate walk-in showers (others have splendid 'deluge' shower heads over the tub in addition to a hand-held attachment for hair washing) are well supplied with towelling and toiletries and decorated to match their bedrooms. Bedrooms in the coach house have been totally refurbished since last year bringing them up to the same high standard as those in the main house. No children under 10. No dogs. ★Half-board terms. *Rooms* 14. *Garden, croquet, tennis, putting, indoor swimming pool, sauna.* AMERICAN EXPRESS *Access, Visa.*

Restaurant　　↑　　　　　　　　　　　　　　　£80

The room is elegant, the service correct and formal and Julian Ehlers' cooking classy and refined which all adds up to a most satisfactory dining experience. A well-balanced, fixed-price dinner offers a good choice (the lunch menu is only slightly shorter) of dishes that are often creative but never gimmicky. Devonshire squab roasted with carrots and scallions served on *pain d'épice* with a ginger wine sauce, and warm "confied" fillets of salmon served with white haricot beans and an aged sherry vinaigrette both caught the eye on a recent menu and it was good to find the parsley and shallot ravioli (a notable success we mentioned last year) again on the menu but this year served with some pan-fried langoustines. A nicely varied selection of puds usually includes one of Julian's exemplary hot soufflés. Stupendous wine list with much improved Australian and New Zealand sections to complement the existing Californian choice (winner of last year's award). France is not ignored, and indeed the entire list is expertly chosen, enabling serious drinking at fair prices. No children under 10. No smoking. *Seats* 26. *Private Room 16. L 12-2 (Sun 12.30-2.30) D 7-9 (Fri & Sat tO 9.45). Set L £17.95 Set D £28.50.*

Lower Swell   Old Farmhouse   £60

Tel 0451 830232   Fax 0451 870962

Lower Swell Stow-on-the-Wold Gloucestershire GL54 1LF   Map 14 C1

A very relaxed and unpretentious place with everything under the personal
supervision of Dutch owner Erik Burger. The premises were a working
farm until the 1960s, and the original 16th-century farmhouse contains the
bar-lounge and restaurant. Above are neat country-style bedrooms, two
of which share a bathroom. Further bedrooms are in former stables
opening on to the car park; best rooms are in the old coach house, where
there's also a quiet residents' lounge with TV, magazines and board games.
Slightly higher tariff Fri and Sat nights. Mountain bikes are available for
hire and air-pistol shooting can be arranged in a corner of the garden.
Lower Swell is one mile west of Stow on the B4068. **Rooms** 14. Garden.
Closed 2 weeks Jan. Access, Visa.

Lower Wick   Forte Travelodge   **NEW**   £45

Tel 0800 850 950

M5 Welcome Break Lower Wick nr Dursley Gloucestershire G11 6DD   Map 13 F1

Opening winter '94 at Michaelwood Welcome Break, between Junctions
13 and 14 of M5, approximately 8 miles north-east of Bristol.
AMERICAN EXPRESS Access, Diners, Visa.

Ludlow   Dinham Hall   64%   £90

Tel 0584 876464   Fax 0584 876019

By the Castle Ludlow Shropshire SY8 1EJ   Map 6 B4

Georgian town house in a quiet street opposite Ludlow Castle. The lounge
features an intriguing oversized fireplace (with real log-fire in winter) that
incorporates medieval carvings, Georgian panels and even a bit of Art
Deco. The bar is part of an informal brasserie. Pleasant bedrooms, which
vary in size, are mostly furnished with solid darkwood 'hotel' furniture and
all have fridges and tea and coffee-making kit – room service is available
but not advertised. Bathrooms – nearly all with shower and WC only –
come with thigh-length bathrobes. Decent cooked breakfasts but the cold
selection is a bit limited. New owners took over just before we went to
press. **Rooms** 13. Garden, sauna, keep-fit equipment. AMERICAN EXPRESS
Access, Visa.

Ludlow   Feathers Hotel   70%   £98

Tel 0584 875261   Fax 0584 876030

Bull Ring Ludlow Shropshire SY8 1AA   Map 6 B4

The stunning timber-framed facade dates from 1620 and inside there are
other fine architectural features, most notably perhaps the panelled first-
floor lounge with carved overmantle and remarkable Tudor ceiling. The
real appeal of this historic town-centre hotel is due to the loving care
lavished on it since the 1940s by the Edwards family – adding an antique
here, a pair of gilt-framed mirrors on a landing there, some new oak
panelling somewhere else – and numerous long-serving staff who ensure
that everything runs smoothly. It's difficult to generalise about bedrooms
that range from fairly plain standard rooms (but with all the usual
amenities) with fitted units to luxurious Comus rooms with air-
conditioning and locally-made oak furniture. Bathrooms are equally varied,
some having older-style tiling, others colourful Spanish tiles, separate
shower cubicles and twin wash basins. All come with towelling robes and
hot water bottles and most have bidets. **Rooms** 40. Snooker. AMERICAN EXPRESS
Access, Diners, Visa.

Ludlow	Forte Travelodge	£45
Tel 0584 711695		**L**
Woofferton Ludlow Shropshire SY8 4AL		Map 6 A4

On the A49, 4 miles south of Ludlow at the junction of the A456 and the B4362. 8 miles north of Leominster. *Rooms 32.* AMERICAN EXPRESS *Access, Diners, Visa.*

Ludlow	Place of Interest

Ludlow Racecourse   Tel 0584 77221.

Luton	Chiltern Hotel	60%	£92
Tel 0582 575911 Fax 0582 581859			**H**
Waller Avenue Luton Bedfordshire LU4 9RU			Map 15 E1

A former Forte Crest (still Forte-owned) halfway between the M1 (junction 11) and Luton town centre. Caters well for families; also popular for functions and conferences (up to 250). Long-hours brasserie, 24hr room service. *Rooms 91.* AMERICAN EXPRESS *Access, Diners, Visa.*

Luton	Hotel Ibis	60%	£51
Tel 0582 424488 Fax 0582 455511			**H**
Spittlesea Road Luton Bedfordshire LU2 9NZ			Map 15 E1

Purpose-built, redbrick hotel opposite Luton airport's main runway. No frills, clean accommodation at a budget price, with many rooms suitable for family use. One child per person free in parents' room. *Rooms 98. Coffee shop (6.30am-10.30pm).* AMERICAN EXPRESS *Access, Diners, Visa.*

Luton	Leaside Hotel	55%	£45
Tel 0582 417643 Fax 0582 34961			**H**
72 New Bedford Road Luton Bedfordshire LU3 1BT			Map 15 E1

Near the town centre but a touch tricky to find (ask for a map showing directions), Leaside is a modest but very agreeable little hotel run since 1980 by Carole and Martin Gillies. The building is Victorian, and a certain period charm survives in the panelled bar. In the club room guests can relax over a frame of snooker. Many bedrooms are smallish singles, but the basic needs are supplied and housekeeping is good. Lounge with open fire and snooker; the lounge bar opens on to a terrace surrounded by trees. Access to the car park at the back is via Old Bedford Road and Villa Road. *Rooms 15. Garden, snooker. Closed 25 & 26 Dec, 1 Jan.* AMERICAN EXPRESS *Access, Diners, Visa.*

Note that all telephone numbers with area codes starting with 0 will start 01 from 16 April 1995.

Luton	Luton Gateway Hotel	57%	£76
Tel 0582 575955 Fax 0582 490065			**H**
641 Dunstable Road Luton Bedfordshire LU4 8RQ			Map 15 E1

Practical accommodation (75% single rooms) in a modern building at Junction 11 of the M1. This was formerly a Forte Posthouse and is still owned by Forte. *Rooms 117.* AMERICAN EXPRESS *Access, Diners, Visa.*

Luton   Strathmore Thistle   63%   £106

Tel 0582 34199   Fax 0582 402528   **H**

Arndale Centre Luton Bedfordshire LU1 2TR   Map 15 E1

High-rise hotel next to town-centre shopping and railway station. Banqueting facilities for up to 250, conferences to 300. Video-monitored car park. *Rooms 150. Coffee shop (11am–11pm).* AMERICAN EXPRESS *Access, Diners, Visa.*

Luton   Places of Interest

Tourist Information   Tel 0582 401579.
St. Georges Theatre   Tel 0582 21628.
Luton Hoo   Tel 0582 22955.
Luton Museum and Art Gallery   Tel 0582 36941.
Stockwood Craft Museum and Gardens   Tel 0582 38714.
Luton Town Football Ground   Tel 0582 411622.

Lutterworth   Denbigh Arms   66%   £65

Tel 0455 553537   Fax 0455 556627   **H**

High Street Lutterworth Leicestershire LE17 4AD   Map 7 D4

An extended Georgian coaching inn right on the high street just over a mile from Junction 20 and the M1. The Fielding Room, largest of three function rooms, can accommodate 50 for a meeting, 40 for a banquet. Good housekeeping and pleasant, friendly staff. Now part of Sands Hotel Group. *Rooms 34.* AMERICAN EXPRESS *Access, Diners, Visa.*

Lutterworth   Place of Interest

Stanford Hall   Tel 0788 860250.

Lyme Regis   Alexandra Hotel   58%   £94

Tel 0297 442010   Fax 0297 443229   **H**

Pound Street Lyme Regis Dorset DT7 3HZ   Map 13 E2

Built in 1735 as a dower house and converted to a hotel at the beginning of this century, the Alexandra occupies a fine hillside position with a pathway to the beach. Most of the individually-decorated bedrooms overlook Lyme Bay and Cobb Harbour. *Rooms 26. Garden. Closed Christmas–early Feb.* AMERICAN EXPRESS *Access, Diners, Visa.*

Lymington   Gordleton Mill   65%   £80

Tel 0590 682219   Fax 0590 683073   **HR**

Silver Street Hordle nr Lymington Hampshire SO41 6DJ   Map 14 C4

Creeper-clad 17th-century mill, a couple of miles west of town, with the mill stream running through gardens past a delightful terrace before disappearing under the building. Just seven bedrooms, one a suite with small sitting room, and with the same polished pine furniture, attractive decor and lots of extras like fruit, mineral water, magazines and a welcoming bottle of champagne that is delivered to the room as one settles in. All the bathrooms have spa tubs, except one with a shower cubicle in the room and en-suite loo, nice large towels and generous quantities of toiletries. Beds are turned down at night. Room service is limited to tea and coffee (which is free) and sandwiches served throughout the day and evening. There is no bar but drinks are served in one of the low-ceilinged lounges (one for non-smokers) where some of the original mill workings can be seen and which are also used by diners. Excellent breakfasts come with home-made preserves *Rooms 7. Closed 1st 2 weeks Jan.* AMERICAN EXPRESS *Access, Diners, Visa.*

See over

Provence Restaurant ★   £95

Taking over from a star chef must be a daunting task but Didier Heyl
is more than up to the task, earning his own laurels with a high-class menu
that takes its inspiration from not only Provence but also the other
culinary regions of France. The à la carte (there's a shorter version
at lunchtime) ranges from foie gras, slightly smoked and served hot
on a bed of choucroute – the influence of Didier's native Alsace, a ballotine
of knuckle of pork, and pan-fried scallops glazed with Belgian cherry lager
to a classic Provençal bouillabaisse, a dish of rabbit cooked in three different
ways, and a 'poule au pot' made with 'Blackfeet' chicken breast and legs
(stuffed with mushrooms) in its own stock with root vegetables, croutons
and whipped cream. Puds might include a hot pistachio soufflé with bitter
chocolate sauce and Didier's own version of the classic poire Belle Hélène.
A good cheese trolley includes both French and British offerings. Sunday
to Thursday nights there is also a good-value, no-choice Evening
in Provence menu that includes a different glass of Provençal wine with
each of three courses. To sample the six-course menu gastronomique one
must come on Friday or Saturday evening or for Sunday lunch. The room,
with lots of windows taking advantage of the garden and waterside setting,
has an appealing French rustic style enhanced by an all-French team front
of house. One might question why all the wines are listed in French (yes,
we know the restaurant styles itself 'gastronomique français', but le vin
d'Angleterre blanc, rouge & doux looks pretty silly), but one cannot deny the
list is excellent: comprehensive, fairly priced, lots of half bottles and a good
house selection. No children under 7. No smoking. *Seats 40. Parties 12.
Private Room 30. L 12-2.30 D 7-10. Set L £12.50/£15 (Sun £19.50)
Set D £21.50 (Sun-Thur) £39 gastronomique Fri & Sat plus Sun L.*

Lymington   **Passford House**   70%   £110

Tel 0590 682398   Fax 0590 683494   **H**

Mount Pleasant Lane Lymington Hampshire SO41 8LS   **Map 14 C4**

On the edge of the New Forest between Lymington (2 miles) and Sway,
this elegant white house was originally the home of Lord Arthur Cecil.
Two bedroom wings and a leisure centre have since been added, but the
traditional look survives in the lounges – one oak-panelled with an open
fire, another with French windows opening on to a patio and ornamental
pool. Upstairs there are bright and airy bedrooms (15 designated De Luxe)
with mostly white furniture; carpeted bathrooms have showers and useful
toiletries. The purpose-built Dolphin leisure centre has a good range
of facilities. Children are catered for admirably, with cots, high-chairs,
a separate play area and separate meal times; first child under 12 sharing
parents' room is accommodated free; 13 family rooms. *Rooms 55. Garden,
indoor & outdoor swimming pools, sauna, solarium, spa bath, keep-fit equipment,
tennis, putting, games room.* AMERICAN EXPRESS *Access, Visa.*

Lymington   **Stanwell House**   65%   £75

Tel 0590 677123   Fax 0590 677756   **H**

High Street Lymington Hampshire SO41 9AA   **Map 14 C4**

The hotel dates from the 18th century, but careful modernisation has
extended its scope. Attractive day rooms include a smart cocktail bar and
a chintzy lounge. Behind the restaurant is a paved garden which opens
on to a small function/conference suite. Well-equipped bedrooms
(including one with a four-poster) are named after Bordeaux wine
chateaux. Children up to 10 stay free in parents' room. No dogs.
Now under new ownership. *Rooms 37. Garden. Access, Visa.*

Lymington   **Place of Interest**

Spinners Garden   Tel 0590 673347.

Lympsham   Batch Farm Country Hotel   56%   £52

Tel 0934 750371   Fax 0934 750501   **H**

Lympsham nr Weston-super-Mare Somerset BS24 0EX   Map 13 E1

The setting is 50 acres of open farmland through which flows the River Axe. Origins of the former farmhouse are evident in the beams which adorn the bar and residents' lounges. The neat, practical bedrooms in an extension enjoy views of either the Mendip or Quantock hills. Space and facilities for families, but not their pets (no dogs). The adjoining Somerset Suite is a popular venue for functions up to 70. Lympsham is about 3 miles from Junction 22 of M5. Personally run by owners Mr and Mrs Brown. *Rooms 8. Garden, croquet, coarse fishing. Closed Christmas.* AMERICAN EXPRESS *Access, Diners, Visa.*

Lympstone   River House   £70

Tel 0395 265147   **R R**

The Strand Lympstone Devon EX8 5EY   Map 13 E3

There are lovely views over the river Exe to Powderham Castle from Michael and Shirley Wilkes' restaurant with rooms, and when the tide is in the water laps against the walls. Dinner is the main attraction, offering two to five courses at various fixed prices, with fish dishes always a good bet. At least five different vegetables, prepared in an interesting and varied manner, accompany main courses. Vegetarians are well catered for, there's a good choice of puddings, and home-made fudge, praline and chocolates are a treat with coffee. Sunday lunch is a popular affair, with a choice of four dishes per course (always including a roast); weekday lunches are simpler. *Seats 34. Private Room 14. L 12-1.30 D 7-9.30 (Sat to 10.30). Closed D Sun, all Mon, Bank Holidays. Set L Sun £16/£20 Set D from £21.95.* AMERICAN EXPRESS *Access, Visa.*

Rooms   £87

The two pretty bedrooms have en-suite bathrooms and many thoughtful extras. No children under six. No dogs.

Lyndhurst   The Crown   65%   £89

Tel 0703 282922   Fax 0703 282751   **H**

High Street Lyndhurst New Forest Hampshire SO43 7NF   Map 14 C4

A solid gabled building in the high street opposite the church (follow the one-way traffic signs). Ample lounge areas provide space to relax with pleasant views of the gardens; the bar is a fine period piece with library-style wood panelling. Decent-sized bedrooms have stylish repro and antique furniture and good bathrooms. Children under 16 are accommodated free when they share a room with a parent. The New Forest surrounds the village, and walking and cycling are popular pastimes. *Rooms 40. Garden.* AMERICAN EXPRESS *Access, Diners, Visa.*

Lyndhurst   Lyndhurst Park   63%   £60

Tel 0703 283923   Fax 0703 283019   **H**

High Street Lyndhurst Hampshire SO43 7NL   Map 14 C4

On the edge of town – where it meets the New Forest – the Georgian origins of this now much-extended hotel (it boasts the largest conference/function facilities in the area – up to 500 theatre-style) are largely lost except in the cocktail bar and chandeliered reception hall – both recently refurbished in warm red tones. Apart from a small lounge the other main public room is a characterfully rustic bar. Bedrooms, which come in a variety of pretty schemes with polycotton duvets, are notably well-kept and appealing, often with brass bedheads and always with well-lit dressing/work table. Good, fully tiled and carpeted bathrooms each come with a huge bottle of shampoo and a family of plastic ducks. 24hr room service can provide a cooked meal throughout the day and evening with sandwiches and drinks overnight. *Rooms 59. Garden, tennis, outdoor swimming pool, sauna, games room.* AMERICAN EXPRESS *Access, Diners, Visa.*

Lyndhurst   Parkhill Hotel   69%   £95
Tel 0703 282944   Fax 0703 283268 ·

HR

Beaulieu Road Lyndhurst Hampshire SO43 7FZ   Map 14 C4

Set within its own 12 acres of grounds, themselves surrounded by the New Forest, that include a well-stocked lake, this 18th-century country house could not have a more peaceful location. Improvements continue to be made both to the civilised and comfortable day rooms, which boast antiques, ornaments and real fires in winter, and to the bedrooms which, although varying considerably in size and shape, are almost all furnished with antique pieces and most have benefited from recent redecoration with attractive individual schemes. Green plants are everywhere and comforts like mineral water, fresh fruit and rooms being properly serviced in the evening are standard. Bathrooms also vary considerably in size and age of fittings but all are in good order and come with bathrobes, generous towelling and large bottles of Badedas for the tub – just two have only showers. Four rooms are in a separate Coach House and it is only here and in the self-contained Cottage suite (which has its own private walled garden) that dogs are allowed. Staff are friendly and obliging. *Rooms 20. Garden, croquet, putting, coarse fishing, outdoor swimming pool.* AMERICAN EXPRESS *Access, Diners, Visa.*

Cedar Restaurant   £60

A pretty restaurant, spacious and light, with a new conservatory extension. The cooking, which is nouvellish in style but with sensible portions, overcomes the somewhat precious language of the menu – dishes are 'complimented by' or 'with a pool' of sauces that are 'laced' or 'scented' with this and that – to prove most acceptable on the plate. Saucing is particularly good. Roulade of salmon and prawns with lime mayonnaise; terrine of smoked pheasant, wood pigeon and Parma ham; noisettes of lamb with garlic crust and herb purée; brill with mustard and apple crust and coriander butter sauce show the style. Good cheese trolley, variable coffee. No smoking. *Seats 120. Private Room 36. L 12-2 D 7-9. Set L £15/£17.50 (Sun £16) Set D £23.50.*

Lyndhurst   Places of Interest

Furzey Gardens   Minstead Tel 0703 812464.
New Forest Museum and Visitor Centre   Lyndhurst Tel 0703 283914.
Rhinefield (New Forest) Polo Club   Manor Farm Cottage, Minstead Tel 0703 813678.
New Park Showground   Brockenhurst Tel 0590 22400.

Lynmouth   Rising Sun Inn   £79
Tel 0598 53223   Fax 0598 53480

I

Harbourside Lynmouth Devon EX35 6EQ   Map 13 D1

Medieval character in the form of oak panelling, uneven floors and crooked ceilings survives in a 14th-century thatched inn overlooking the picturesque harbour (leave the M5 at Junction 23 signposted to Minehead and follow the A39 to Lynmouth). Bedrooms are in keeping, being snug and cottagey. Shelley's Cottage, where the poet spent his honeymoon with his 16-year-old bride, consists of a double bedroom with four-poster bed, a sitting room and a private garden. The inn owns a stretch of river for salmon fishing. No children under five. *Rooms 16. Garden, fishing.* AMERICAN EXPRESS *Access, Diners, Visa.*

Lynton — Lynton Cottage — 65% — £78

Tel 0598 52342   Fax 0598 52597

H

North Walk Lynton Devon EX35 6ED

Map 13 D1

A family-run hotel on the cliff 500 feet above Lynmouth Bay offering spectacular sea views from the day rooms (and all but three bedrooms). Well modernised and smartly kept, it's a warm, friendly place, particularly the bar, with comfortable, old-fashioned seats and Victorian pine panelling. Bedrooms are individually decorated and range from cosy and small to airy and spacious. Well-appointed bathrooms. No children under ten, except babes in arms. *Rooms 17. Garden, bar billiards. Closed Jan.* AMERICAN EXPRESS® *Access, Diners, Visa.*

Lytham — Clifton Arms — 63% — £76

Tel 0253 739898   Fax 0253 730657

H

West Beach Lytham Lancashire FY8 5QJ

Map 6 A1

Best bedrooms at this redbrick Victorian building on the seafront (A584) are the 'Executives' at the front, overlooking the Ribble Estuary; standard rooms are smaller. Winged armchairs and settees fill the lounge. Children up to 16 can share their parents' room at no charge. Conference/banqueting facilities for 150. *Rooms 42. Sauna, solarium, spa bath, keep-fit equipment.* AMERICAN EXPRESS® *Access, Diners, Visa.*

Lytham St Annes — Dalmeny Hotel — 60% — £69

Tel 0253 712236

HR

19 South Promenade St Annes Lytham St Annes Lancashire FY8 1LX

Map 6 A1

A seaside hotel of wide appeal, in the ownership of the Webb family since 1945. There are several restaurants, ample roomy lounges and bars, leisure facilities, family recreational activities and accommodation that runs from singles to apartments with kitchens. Outdoor car park for 60 cars, underground park for 40. Friendly, helpful staff add to the pleasure. A new wing of of 45 bedrooms plus a glass-canopied restaurant was under construction as we went to press. *Rooms 91. Indoor swimming pool, gym, squash, solarium, beauty and hair salon, children's playroom, games room, coffee shop (8am-10.30pm). Closed 24-26 Dec.* AMERICAN EXPRESS® *Access, Visa.*

C'est La Vie — £60

The main restaurant for non-residents serves an à la carte selection that ranges from crab bisque and chicken liver parfait to pan-fried salmon with a basil butter sauce, duck breast marinated in orange juice, soya, ginger and honey, braised oxtail and rack of lamb. *C'est La Vie* is in a vaulted basement. There's also a popular carvery and a barbecue restaurant. *Seats 45. L 12-2 D 6.30-9. Closed Sun, Mon, 3 days Christmas.*

Lytham St. Anne's — Place of Interest

Church Road Cricket Ground   Tel 0253 733422.

Macclesfield — Sutton Hall — £85

Tel 0260 253211   Fax 0260 252538

I

Bullocks Lane Sutton Macclesfield Cheshire SK11 0HE

Map 6 B2

Originally an endowment to a monastery in the 11th century, then a 16th-century baronial residence, then a nunnery until 30 years ago, Sutton Hall now describes itself as a public house, restaurant and hotel. It's full of old-world atmosphere: black oak beams, flagstones and open log fires characterise the day rooms, and all the bedrooms feature lace-draped four-posters, Gothic windows and sturdy English furniture. Banqueting/conference facilities for 60/30. *Rooms 10. Garden. Access, Visa.*

Macclesfield   Places of Interest

Tourist Information   Tel 0625 21955.
Macclesfield Silk Museum and Heritage Centre   Tel 0625 613210.
Paradise Mill Silk Museum   Tel 0625 618228.
   Historic Houses, Castles and Gardens
Capesthorne Hall and Gardens   Tel 0625 861221.
Gawsworth Hall   Tel 0260 223456.
Hare Hill Garden (NT)   Hare Hill, Over Alderley Tel 0625 828981.
Jodrell Bank   Arboretum Tel 0477 71339.

Madingley	**Three Horseshoes**	**£65**
Tel 0954 210221 Fax 0954 212043		**R**
High Street Madingley nr Cambridge Cambridgeshire CB3 8AB		**Map 15 F1**

Richard Stokes' kitchen was being revamped during 1994 so that by the
time you read this, he should have an even better base from which
to produce his interesting Italian/Mediterranean-influenced menus, available
in the bar or the attractive restaurant/conservatory. Try duck confit with
roast tomatoes, olives and fig salad, then pan-fried fillet of lamb with basil
polenta and a risotto of chanterelles and asparagus, and finish with
an unusual chocolate tagliatelle with nougatine and mascarpone ice cream
in an almond biscuit basket and hot chocolate sauce. Wonderful cheeses
from Neal's Yard Dairy. Concise, well annotated wine list. *Seats 94. L 12-2
D 6.30-10. Closed D Sun. Set L £16.95.* *Access,
Diners, Visa.*

Maiden Newton	**Le Petit Canard**	**£55**
Tel 0300 320536		**R**
Dorchester Road Maiden Newton Dorset DT2 OBE		**Map 13 F2**

Geoff and Lin Chapman describe their cooking as "pretty much global" but
will narrow it down to "Pacific Rim" if you insist! Whatever, it translates
as a light modern touch to ingredients drawn from far and near –
chargrilled kangaroo fillet with mustard and shallot sauce, slow-roasted
black bean and cracked pepper duck on sautéed Chinese leaf, fish from
Brixham, local vegetables, West Country artisan cheese. Pear and almond
napoleon with caramel drizzles would complete a 3-course set meal. The
menu changes monthly and the wine list is updated weekly by computer,
ensuring a well-priced selection of bin ends and half bottles. No children
under 6. *Seats 28. Private Room 32. D only 7-9. Closed Sun & Mon.
Set D £19.95. Access, Visa.*

Maidenhead	**Fredrick's**	**75%**	**£155**
Tel 0628 35934 Fax 0628 771054			**H R**
Shoppenhangers Road Maidenhead Berkshire SL6 2PZ			**Map 15 E2**

In a quiet residential road, yet only minutes from Junction 8/9 of the M4,
Fredrick Losel's attractive redbrick hotel offers luxury and high-quality
service to a predominantly senior executive clientele. The reception area,
with strikingly modern chandeliers, marble waterfall and complimentary
glass of champagne on check-in, sets the tone of public rooms that include
a verdant winter garden looking out over a patio, and a sumptuous cocktail
bar. A novel feature of the decoratively more restrained bedrooms is that
beds are set upon solid plinths. Standard rooms have a pair of easy chairs
around a breakfast table while the five larger rooms have settees in separate
sitting areas. All have mini-bars, satellite TV and well-appointed bathrooms
– most with bidets. Three single rooms have shower and WC only. Rooms
are properly serviced in the evenings and staff are notably smart. 24hr
room service. Free parking for 90 cars. Conference facilities for up to 100.
No dogs. *Aghadoe Heights* in Killarney is a sister hotel. **Rooms** *37. Garden,
croquet, helipad. Closed 24-30 Dec.* *Access, Diners, Visa.*

Restaurant   £100

An overtly luxurious room – gilt and crystal chandeliers, painted wall panels, monogrammed china and glassware – is matched by formal service under the eye of maitre d' Tony Guttilla and Brian Cutler's highly professional cooking based on classic French and English methods. Top-quality produce is the starting point for stylishly presented dishes like grilled squid on roasted peppers, samosas of vegetables, walnuts and figs, sea bass baked in a salt crust and roast rack of lamb for two. Sunday lunch includes roast rib of beef served from the trolley. Home-made ices and sorbets among the desserts. *Seats 60. Parties 15. L 12-2 D 7-9.45. Closed L Sat. Set L £19.50 (Sun £23.50) Set D £28.50.*

Maidenhead   Holiday Inn   66%   £147

Tel 0628 23444   Fax 0628 770035   **H**
Manor Lane Maidenhead Berkshire SL6 2RA   Map 15 E2

Set in 18 acres of grounds close to junction 8/9 of the M4 and junction 4 of the M40, this hotel is usefully situated for visitors to the Thames Valley area. Top-notch, large conference and banqueting facilities (for up to 400) include the characterful, reconstructed Elizabethan Shoppenhangers Manor house in the grounds. Straightforward accommodation, but good leisure facilities, including a children's pool. Playroom provided for children at weekends; families can eat informally in the poolside café. *Rooms 189. Garden, indoor swimming pool, spa bath, sauna, solarium, squash, gymnasium, snooker, coffee shop (7am-11pm).* AMERICAN EXPRESS *Access, Diners, Visa.*

Maidenhead   Places of Interest

Cliveden (NT)   Taplow, Nr Burnham Tel 0628 605069.
Stanley Spencer Gallery   King's Hall, Cookham-on-Thames Tel 062 85 20890/20043.
Courage Shire Horse Centre   Maidenhead Thicket Tel 0628 824848.

Maidstone   Larkfield Priory   62%   £58

Tel 0732 846858   Fax 0732 846786   **H**
812 London Road Maidstone Kent ME20 6HJ   Map 11 B5

Leave the M20 at Junction 4 taking the A228 Tonbridge road, then the Maidstone road from the first roundabout, to find a Forte Heritage hotel centred around a Victorian priory. A popular conference venue with facilities for up to 80 delegates. The well-equipped Larkfield Leisure Centre is half a mile away. All the usual amenities in the bedrooms, which include, at a premium, a four-poster room. *Rooms 52. Garden.* AMERICAN EXPRESS *Access, Diners, Visa.*

Maidstone   Mandarin Chef   £35

Tel 0622 755917   **R**
35 Lower Stone Street Maidstone Kent   Map 11 B5

Friendly service and sound Chinese cooking by chef Ken Lai make this a popular place with a regular clientele. Peking and Cantonese regions are well represented with dishes such as braised beef fillet, sweet and sour pork, hot and sour soup, pickled cabbage, diced chicken with cashew nuts in yellow bean sauce and baked crab in ginger and spring onion sauce. Town-centre site with modern decor in assorted blues. Ring ahead for an off-the-menu feast of specials. The well-priced special lunch is available Mon-Fri. *Seats 75. L 12-2.15 D 5.30-11.30. Set L from £7 Set D from £14.* AMERICAN EXPRESS *Access, Diners, Visa.*

Maidstone   Stakis Country Court Hotel   67%   £110

Tel 0622 734322   Fax 0622 734600   **H**

Bearsted Weavering Maidstone Kent ME14 5AA   **Map 11 B5**

Next to the M20 at Junction 7, the hotel is set around a landscaped courtyard. Spacious bedrooms have double beds, modern furnishings, speed-dial phones, smart tiled bathrooms and good showers. Ladies rooms and rooms adapted for disabled guests are available. Leisure club and extensive high-tech meeting and conference facilities. Ample car parking. *Rooms 139. Garden, indoor swimming pool, gym, sauna, spa bath, solarium, beauty salon.* AMERICAN EXPRESS *Access, Diners, Visa.*

Maidstone   Travel Inn   NEW   £43

Tel 0622 752515   **L**

London Road Maidstone Kent ME16 0HG   **Map 11 B5**

From M20 J5 take the London Road and head towards Maidstone. Half a mile from the junction (Aylesford). Six miles from Leeds Castle; two minutes' drive from Allington Castle and Lock (NT). *Rooms 40.* AMERICAN EXPRESS *Access, Diners, Visa.*

Maidstone   Places of Interest

Tourist Information   Tel 0622 673581.
Hazlitt Theatre   Tel 0622 58611.
Boughton Monchelsea Place   Boughton Monchelsea Tel 0622 743120.
Leeds Castle and Culpeper Gardens   Tel 0622 765400.
Tyrwhitt-Drake Museum of Carriages   Tel 0622 54497.
The Moat Cricket Ground   Tel 0622 54545.
Kent County Showgrounds   Tel 0622 30975.
Leeds Castle   Aviary and Culpeper Garden Tel 0622 65400.
Mereworth Parrot Park   Seven Mile Lane, Mereworth Tel 0622 812045.

Maldon   Blue Boar   59%   £75

Tel 0621 852681   Fax 0621 856202   **H**

3 Silver Street Maldon Essex CM9 7QE   **Map 11 C4**

An ancient inn (parts go back to the 14th century) located just off the High Street, notable for its elegant Georgian facade, heavy oak beams, open fires and timbered wings overlooking a stable yard. The majority of bedrooms (17) are designated non-smoking. Forte Heritage. *Rooms 28. Garden.* AMERICAN EXPRESS *Access, Diners, Visa.*

Maldon   Francine's   £50

Tel 0621 856605   **R**

1a High Street Maldon Essex CM9 7PB   **Map 11 C4**

An unpretentious restaurant, sited in one of Maldon's oldest buildings. The minuteness of John Brotherton's kitchen is not something he lets constrain him. Care is taken over the preparation of French-inspired dishes using the freshest of produce. The menu, now fixed-price 2 or 3 courses with coffee, changes on the first Tuesday of each month. Crab pancakes, parsnip soup, Madeira-sauced breast of duck, halibut with a mushroom and herb crust and fillet of beef on a bed of crisp noodles and red wine sauce. To finish, perhaps lemon-flavoured custard creams or individual apple charlotte. John's wife Sara produces meals from her native Thailand on the third and fourth Wednesdays of each month. *Seats 24. L by arrangement D 7.30-9.30. Closed Sun & Mon, Bank Holidays exc Christmas Day lunch, 2 weeks Feb, 2 weeks Aug. Access, Visa.*

Maldon   Places of Interest

Tourist Information   Tel 0621 856503.
Oakwood Arts Centre   Tel 0621 56503.

Malmesbury   Old Bell Hotel   64%   £75

Tel 0666 822344   Fax 0666 825145   **H**

Abbey Row Malmesbury Wiltshire SN16 OBW   Map 14 B2

The Old Bell has claims to be England's oldest hotel. Founded by the
Abbot of Malmesbury in the reign of King John, it was originally a guest
house for visitors to the Abbey library. Behind a wisteria-clad facade public
rooms are either ancient (there's an 800-year-old chimney in one of the
lounges) or Edwardian (cocktail bar and dining room). Bedrooms in the
main building come in all shapes and sizes, while those in the converted
stables are more uniformly modern. Families are well catered for; children
up to 10 stay free in parents' room. No dogs. As we went to press we heard
that the Old Bell had been purchased by Luxury Family Hotels, with
management from Nigel Chapman (*Woolley Grange*, Bradford-on-Avon)
and Nicholas Dickinson (formerly Managing Director at *Le Manoir aux
Quat' Saisons*). An extensive programme of upgrading should see all of the
bedrooms refurbished in the coming year or so. It is the new owners' stated
intention to follow Woolley Grange's unusually successful combination
of family facilities and high-quality dining themes at the newly restored
Old Bell. *Rooms 37. Garden.* AMERICAN EXPRESS *Access, Visa.*

Malvern   Abbey Hotel   62%   £75

Tel 0684 892332   Fax 0684 892662   **H**

Abbey Road Malvern Hereford & Worcester WR14 3ET   Map 14 B1

A mix of impressive, ivy-clad exterior and modern bedrooms in an
extension block. Conference/banqueting facilities for up to 350/300 but the
hotel is also much used by tourists to the area. Children under 14
accommodated free in parents' room. De Vere Hotels. *Rooms 107.*
AMERICAN EXPRESS *Access, Diners, Visa.*

Malvern   Anupam   £40

Tel 0684 573814   Fax 0684 893945   **R**

85 Church Street Malvern Hereford & Worcester WR14 2AE   Map 14 B1

Indian cooking of a dependable quality, plus efficient service and a list
of complementary wines compiled by the nearby *Croque-en-Bouche*. The
standard menu is supplemented by interesting chef's specials such as chicken
with ground almonds, fresh ginger and coriander leaves Jaipur style, West
Coast prawns with spinach and garlic. A good selection for vegetarians.
Seats 54. L 12.30-2 D 6-12. Closed 25 & 26 Dec. Set meals from £11.95.
AMERICAN EXPRESS *Access, Diners, Visa.*

Malvern   Colwall Park Hotel   62%   £86

Tel 0684 540206   Fax 0684 540847   **H**

Walwyn Road Colwall Malvern Hereford & Worcester WR13 6QG   Map 14 B1

At the foot of the Malvern Hills, in the centre of Colwall village on the
B4218 between Malvern and Ledbury, this mock-Tudor hotel offers
simple, well-kept accommodation. Public rooms include a street-facing
lounge bar with comfortable chairs and sofas, and a quiet, traditionally
furnished lounge. Bedrooms are light and spacious, with quality furniture
and functional bathrooms without frills. Families are well catered for.
Special interest breaks are regularly organised. Conference/banqueting for
120/100. *Rooms 20. Garden, croquet. Closed 3-10 Jan.* AMERICAN EXPRESS
Access, Visa.

Malvern   The Cottage in the Wood   65%   £95

Tel 0684 573487   Fax 0684 560662   **HR**

Holywell Road Malvern Wells Hereford & Worcester WR14 4LG   **Map 14 B1**

A particularly relaxing, family-run hotel with a glorious setting looking out over the Severn Plain from high on the steep wooded slopes of the Malvern Hills. It comprises three distinct buildings; the public rooms and eight cottagey bedrooms are in a fine Georgian dower house, with further accommodation in the nearby Beech Cottage and Coach House (with access to balconies or patios). Children are charged at £1.50 per year of their age. Private conference room for up to 18. **Rooms** 20. Garden. AMERICAN EXPRESS® Access, Visa.

Restaurant   £65

Kathryn Young's Options lunch menu offers "light bites" with a roll and butter or "mega bites". In the first category come gammon and pineapple puffs, mushroom kiev, tuna burger and tempura, in the latter bacon chops, cold poached salmon, liver stroganoff and fillet or sirloin steak. This is available (along with a set menu) every day except Sunday, when a traditional four-course menu is served (£12.95, half price for children). The evening à la carte selection is typified by pork and beetroot pirozhki, smoked salmon cheesecake, faggots provençale, coconut plaice and lamb with Stilton and mint. Desserts could include hazelnut pinwheels, soured cream apple pie and layered tropical fruit terrine. Good English cheeses. No smoking until coffee in the bar or lounge. There are four vineyards within 15 miles and all feature on the wine list – in fact, there's probably no other establishment in the country that promotes English wines to this extent. A lot of work has gone into the comprehensive list, which is both keenly priced and well annotated. Even China is represented. **Seats** 50. Parties 20. Private Room 14. L 12.30-2 D 7-9 (Winter Sun-Thur to 8.30). Set L £9.95 (Sun £12.95).

Malvern   Croque-en-Bouche   ★   £90

Tel 0684 565612   **R**

221 Wells Road Malvern Wells Hereford & Worcester WR14 4HF   **Map 14 B1**

Two miles south of Malvern on the A449, Robin and Marion Jones's late-Victorian house attracts visitors from near and far with its winning combination of terrific cooking and superb wines. Dinner is a five-course affair which starts with soup (perhaps split green pea with leek and sorrel) and continues with a choice of three second courses. These include the fishy part of the meal with the likes of Cornish skate with a mango, ginger and coriander salsa or salmon smoked by the restaurant with applewood and fennel. The main (next) course also provides a triple choice, typically honey-roast Barbary duck, bulgar-stuffed leg of lamb and grilled marinated escalopes of venison. Well-made sauces, potato gratin and spot-on garnishes enhance these dishes, which are followed by salad leaves, British cheeses and fine desserts (a £4 supplement gets you six 'tastes' from the dessert list). Equally impressive as Marion's kitchen is Robin's cellar. Past winner on several occasions of our awards, the lists – there are two, one red and one white – require careful reading. Marvel not only at the realistic and generous prices (remind yourself that these include VAT and service), but also at the very apposite tasting notes written with passion, knowledge and humour. Terrific drinking from everywhere – worth seeking advice. Incidentally, half-size copies of the lists are available to buy – £3 gets you a better read than many a paperback. No smoking. A true one-off among restaurants, and very much a two-hander by Robin and Marion. Book, and be punctual – to keep the Joneses happy, and to get to grips with that wine list! **Seats** 24. Parties 6. Private Room 6. D only 7.30-9 (Sat to 9.30). Closed Sun-Tue, Christmas/New Year, 2 weeks Sep. Set D £32.50. Access, Visa. MARTELL COGNAC

Malvern   Foley Arms   61%   £78

Tel 0684 573397   Fax 0684 569665   **H**

14 Worcester Road Great Malvern Hereford & Worcester WR14 4QS   **Map 14 B1**

Said to be the town's oldest hotel (built as a coaching inn in 1810), the Foley Arms stands at the top of the town, commanding magnificent views over the Severn valley. Public areas include two homely lounges (one non-smoking), a pubby bar and a summer dining terrace. Good-sized bedrooms, the best with fine views, are comfortable and unfussy, with duvets and freestanding units. Under-16s stay free in parents' room. Own parking. *Rooms 28. Garden, giant chess.* AMERICAN EXPRESS *Access, Diners, Visa.*

Malvern   Places of Interest

Tourist Information   Tel 0684 892289.
Little Malvern Court   Nr Great Malvern Tel 0684 892988.

Manchester   Britannia Hotel   66%   £123

Tel 061-228 2288   Fax 061-236 9154   **H**

Portland Street Manchester Greater Manchester M1 3LA   **Map 6 B2**

Converted from a cotton warehouse and resplendent with its over-the-top furnishings, the Britannia, a hotel since 1982, is a peculiar mix of showy public rooms (note the fine cantilever staircase) and simply decorated bedrooms. Fancier suites are split-level and bedecked in floral prints. Two discos, together with numerous bars and restaurants, keep up the lively pace. *Rooms 362. Indoor swimming pool, keep-fit equipment, sauna, solarium, beauty & hair salons, coffee shop (11am-2am).* AMERICAN EXPRESS *Access, Diners, Visa.*

Manchester   Charterhouse Hotel   72%   £109

Tel 061-236 9999   Fax 061-236 0674   **H**

Oxford Street Manchester Greater Manchester M60 7HA   **Map 6 B2**

In the heart of the business district, the terracotta building was designed by Sir Alfred Waterhouse, famously associated with the Natural History Museum in London. Much of the original Victorian architecture – ornate plasterwork, intricate cornicing, lofty columns and stained-glass windows – has been retained, especially in the vast open-plan public areas, which feature contemporary seating, heavy drapes and greenery in modern country house style. The Mongolian restaurant is an interesting recent addition. Bedrooms vary in size and are individually decorated with tastefully co-ordinated fabrics; there are thirteen suites. Fully carpeted bathrooms have gold taps, low basins, good-quality toiletries and a telephone. Children up to 12 stay free in their parents' room; cots and extra beds provided. Conference and banqueting facilities. *Rooms 58. Closed Christmas period.* AMERICAN EXPRESS *Access, Diners, Visa.*

Manchester   Copthorne Hotel   70%   £128

Tel 061-873 7321   Fax 061-873 7318   **H**

Clippers Quay Salford Quays Manchester Greater Manchester M5 3DL   **Map 6 B2**

Standing next to the quays in the Salford Docks redevelopment area (just a mile from the city centre) is a modern redbrick hotel. A high ceiling, exposed brickwork and polished tile floor combine to give an up-to-date feel to the foyer, with other day rooms continuing the contemporary theme. The Clippers Bar has tinted mirror walls and is a genuinely comfortable place to relax. The most popular bedrooms overlook the quay and have large bay windows, allowing in plenty of natural light; coloured-wood furniture and bathrooms tiled in two colours continue the bright theme. Superior 'Connoisseur' rooms on the top floor have recently been updated and two suites added. Two bedrooms are specifically adapted for use by wheelchair-bound guests and sixty are non-smoking. 24hr room and lounge service. Conference and function facilities for up to 150. No dogs. *Rooms 166. Indoor swimming pool, sauna, solarium, spa bath, steambath, gym.* AMERICAN EXPRESS *Access, Diners, Visa.*

Manchester   Forte Posthouse   60%   £68

Tel 061-998 7090   Fax 061-946 0139   **H**

Palatine Road Northenden Manchester Greater Manchester M22 4FH   **Map 6 B2**

Mid-70s, high-rise hotel, 3 miles from the airport, 7 miles from the city centre, close to junction 9 of M63. Cosy day rooms and comfortable bedrooms. Banqueting/conference facilities for 100/150. *Rooms 190. Garden.* AMERICAN EXPRESS *Access, Diners, Visa.*

Manchester   Gaylord   £50

Tel 061-832 4866   Fax 061-832 6037   **R**

Amethyst House Spring Gardens Manchester Greater Manchester M2 1EA   **Map 6 B2**

Under new ownership (but with the same chef since 1988), Gaylord is one of Manchester's best Indian restaurants, offering tandoori, Mughlai and Kashmiri cuisine. Outstanding dishes include home-made cottage cheese (in kebabs, in pakoras, with spinach, with peas or in kulcha (leavened bread)), lamb korma badami, and a splendidly rich chicken tikka masala. Lotus roots are an unusual item in the vegetable section. In the city centre by the main post office, but not too easy to find (approach via King Street if coming by car, as it's half a block from the Market Street precinct). Excellent value lunches. *Seats 90. L 12-2.30 D 6-11.30. Set L £5.95 Set D from £11.95. Closed 25 Dec & 1 Jan.* AMERICAN EXPRESS *Access, Diners, Visa.*

Manchester   Granada Lodge   £51

Tel 061-410 0076   Fax 061-655 3358   **L**

M62 Junction 18/19 Birch Manchester Greater Manchester OL10 2QH   **Map 6 B2**

Rooms 37. AMERICAN EXPRESS *Access, Diners, Visa.*

> If we recommend meals in a hotel or inn a separate entry is made for its restaurant.

Manchester   Holiday Inn Crowne Plaza   73%   £124

Tel 061-236 3333   Fax 061-228 2241   **H**

Peter Street Manchester Greater Manchester M60 2DS   **Map 6 B2**

A grand town-centre hotel (adjacent to the G-Mex centre) restored at great expense to its past glory with ornate ceilings, arches and pillars. The foyer area is vast, with a glass roof and hanging plants crowning white columns. Cane chairs and comfortable couches adorn the adjoining terrace lounge. The high-ceilinged Octagon, one of three bars, is decorated in similar style; there are also three restaurants. Corridors that lead to the bedrooms are wide and reminiscent of a former age of spacious and luxurious hotels. Bedrooms, many recently refurbished, are generously sized and have a high standard of decor, with tiled bathrooms throughout; one room is adapted for disabled guests and two more are due to come on line in 1994. Extensive conference and banqueting (including kosher) facilities for up to 700. *Rooms 303. Indoor swimming pool, sauna, solarium, spa bath, steam room, gym, squash, beauty & hair salon, osteopath, news kiosk, shop (7am-8pm), coffee shop (11-3, 5.30-10.30).* AMERICAN EXPRESS *Access, Diners, Visa.*

Manchester   Jarvis Piccadilly   73%   £119

Tel 061-236 8414   Fax 061-228 1568.   **H**

Piccadilly Plaza Manchester Greater Manchester M60 1QR   Map 6 B2

In the heart of the city opposite Piccadilly Gardens, a high-rise hotel that
is considerably smarter inside than the surroundings would suggest. Fast
lifts lead up to an elegant reception area on the second floor, with
an expanse of sparkling, coloured-marble flooring, and the Club Bar, both
of which set the standard for decor throughout. The Verandah Restaurant
on the open-plan third floor has good views over Piccadilly Gardens; the
Belvedere lounge bar is open until the wee small hours. Other refreshment
outlets include the Portland Arms, Harveys Wine Bar and the Viennese
Coffee House. On the lower ground floor there's a well-equipped leisure
club centred around a good-sized pool. Bedrooms – 175 singles, 34 twins,
57 double and 9 suites – are also generously sized with darkwood furniture
contrasting against lighter, contemporary colour schemes and well-lit
bathrooms. The top, Ambassador floor has its own check-in and a butler.
Very extensive conference and banqueting facilities. Jarvis Hotels.
*Rooms 275. Indoor swimming pool, gym, spa bath, sauna, solarium, steam room,
beauty & hair salon, coffee shop (10am-9pm, Sun till 6).* AMERICAN EXPRESS
Access, Diners, Visa.

🍾 is our symbol for an outstanding wine list.

Manchester   Market Restaurant   £55

Tel 061-834 3743   **R**

**Edge Street/104 High Street Smithfield City Centre Manchester
Greater Manchester M4 1HQ**   Map 6 B2

Close to the city centre, in what is now the garment district, the O'Gradys'
friendly, homely restaurant has enormous appeal. Decorwise it's like
stepping back in time with everything from the crockery and green wicker
chairs to the light fittings and background music dating back to the 1940s
– even the wine carafes are old-fashioned milk bottles. In contrast the
monthly-changing menu takes its inspiration from all over the place.
Starters might include middle-eastern tabouleh, air-dried ham with melon,
pitta bread with houmus and aubergine 'caviar' and John Tovey's recipe for
spiced minced lamb with 'custard topping' while main dishes range from
duck breast with cranberry relish and port gravy, daube of beef, and lamb
kebab with Greek yoghurt and pine nuts to broccoli and cheese ravioli
with tomato and basil sauce (there are always a couple of interesting
vegetarian choices). Puds are important here too, as is fitting for the home
of the famous Pudding Club, whose members meet six times a year
to indulge in a feast of desserts like steamed puddings, fruit pies, chocolate
confection, syllabubs and the like all helped down with lashings of real
custard and extra thick cream. For those with more savoury tastes there
is now a Starters Society. Sounds silly, but note the beers on a wine list that
has fair prices, but few half bottles. *Seats 42. Private Room 24. D only
6-9.30 (Sat from 7). Closed Sun, Mon, Tue, 1 week Christmas, 1 week Easter,
Aug.* AMERICAN EXPRESS *Access, Visa.*

Manchester   Novotel   62%   £65

Tel 061-799 3535   Fax 061-703 8207   **H**

Worsley Brow Worsley Manchester Greater Manchester M28 2YA   Map 6 B2

Modern hotel in its own grounds by Junction 13 of the M62. Ample free
parking. Banqueting/conferences for up to 200/220. Novotel policy is that
two children under 16 are accommodated free, with breakfast included,
when sharing their parents' room. *Rooms 119. Garden, outdoor swimming
pool.* AMERICAN EXPRESS *Access, Diners, Visa.*

Manchester   Penang Village   £45

Tel 061-236 2650   R

56 Faulkner Street Manchester Greater Manchester   Map 6 B2

Hot, rich and spicy dishes run the gamut of Malaysian cuisine in a first-floor restaurant on the south corner of Chinatown, near the Chinese Arch. Chicken satay or one of the range of soups is a popular prelude to a wide range of main courses including, as specialities, grilled king prawns or fish fillets with sambal sauce, sizzling chili beef or a squid curry. Hot, 4-course buffet lunch Tue-Thur (£6). Plenty of vegetarian options. Charming service from sarong-clad waitresses. *Seats 70. Parties 80. L 12-2 D 5.30-11.30. Set L £5/£6.50 Mon & Fri, £6.50 Tue-Thur Set D from £15.* AMERICAN EXPRESS *Access, Diners, Visa.*

Manchester   Portland Thistle   69%   £130

Tel 061-228 3400   Fax 061-228 6347   H

3/5 Portland Street Manchester Greater Manchester M1 6DP   Map 6 B2

In the heart of the city overlooking Piccadilly Gardens, the Portland is within easy reach of most of the city's amenities. As we went to press, the hotel was undergoing complete refurbishment of the ground floor, including the foyer, bars and restaurants. The Executives are the best of the bedrooms. Conference rooms hold up to 300. Valet parking. 24hr room service. Children up to 12 stay free in parents' room. Good leisure facilities. *Rooms 205. Indoor swimming pool, keep-fit equipment, sauna, steam room, spa bath, solarium.* AMERICAN EXPRESS *Access, Diners, Visa.*

Manchester   Quan Ju De   £60

Tel 061-236 5236   Fax 061-236 1663   R

44 Princess Street Manchester Greater Manchester M1 6DE   Map 6 B2

Authentic Peking restaurant whose chef (Jian Ping Ma) and team came from the parent restaurant in Peking. Despite the bright, simple decor and trendy modern artwork, the menu has plenty of traditional dishes, with roasted duck in 'authentic Beijing-style' and crispy aromatic duck as the specialities. Grilled dumplings, hot and sour seafood clear soup, a speciality of plaice fillet in rice wine sauce, and teppan beef served on a sizzling platter also feature on a balanced menu of commendable brevity. Good spicing and competent handling of raw materials are the hallmarks. Tempting banquets for two or more include a vegetarian version. Pianist Tues-Sat eves. *Seats 120. Parties 80. Private Room 48. L 12-2.30 D 6-11.30. Closed Sun & Bank Holidays. Set L from £4.80 Set D from £18.50.* AMERICAN EXPRESS *Access, Visa.*

> Any person using our name to obtain free hospitality is a fraud.
> Proprietors, please inform the police and us.

Manchester   Rajdoot   £40

Tel 061-834 2176   R

Carlton House 18 Albert Square Manchester Greater Manchester M2 5PR   Map 6 B2

Rajdoot is a small chain of restaurants (established in 1966) serving well-prepared Indian food in comfortable surroundings. Tandoori dishes are a speciality, with mackerel, quail and lamb kidneys joining more familiar variations on lamb, chicken and prawns. Other branches are in Birmingham, Bristol and Dublin. *Seats 67. L 12-2.30 D 6-11.30. Closed L Sun, 25 & 26 Dec. Set L £8 Set D £15.50.* AMERICAN EXPRESS *Access, Diners, Visa.*

Manchester   Ramada Hotel   73%   £117

Tel 061-835 2555   Fax 061-835 0731   **H**

Blackfriars Street Manchester Greater Manchester M3 2EQ   Map 6 B2

A tall modern hotel with extensive conference and banqueting facilities (up to 400 guests). Day rooms include a large, luxurious lounge off the marble-clad lobby. The muted, pastel-shaded bedrooms are all spacious (mini-suite size), with seating areas, desk space, all the expected modern accessories and bright, well-equipped bathrooms. Children up to 16 stay free in parents' room. *Rooms 200. Gift shop.* AMERICAN EXPRESS *Access, Diners, Visa.*

Manchester   Sachas Hotel   64%   £83

Tel 061-228 1234   Fax 061-236 9202   **H**

Tib Street Piccadilly Manchester Greater Manchester M4 1SH   Map 6 B2

Formerly a C&A store, now a bright hotel with major conference facilities (up to 650 delegates) and a health club. Bedrooms vary from inner ones with neither windows nor natural light to superior versions with whirlpool baths and four-poster beds. There are lively eating and drinking spots in the basement (the pizzeria is open 6pm-2am). Sister hotel to the *Britannia* *Rooms 223. Indoor swimming pool, keep-fit equipment, sauna, solarium, beauty & hair salons, night club.* AMERICAN EXPRESS *Access, Diners, Visa.*

Manchester   Siam Orchid   £60

Tel 061-236 1388   Fax 061-236 8830   **R**

54 Portland Street Manchester Greater Manchester M1 4QU   Map 6 B2

A friendly Thai restaurant on the edge of Manchester's Chinatown, a few steps from both the *Britannia* and *Piccadilly* hotels. A long menu covers the whole Thai range from soups and satay to fish cakes, spicy salads, curries of several hues, noodle platters, rice platters and many variations on pork, chicken, beef, crab, fish, prawns, lobster, squid and eggs. There's plenty of choice, too, for vegetarians, plus a business lunch menu (£7) and other set menus for four or more. Mainly bought-in Continental desserts. Sister to *Royal Orchid* (see entry). *Seats 55. L 11.30-2.30 D 6.30-11.30 (Fri from 6pm, Sat 11.30am-11.30pm, Sun 11.30am-11pm). Closed 25 Dec, 1 Jan. Set L from £5 Set D £16-£27.* AMERICAN EXPRESS *Access, Visa.*

Set menu prices may not always include service or wine.

Manchester   Sonarga   £45

Tel 061-861 0334   **R**

269 Barlow Moor Road Chorlton-cum-Hardy Manchester Greater Manchester   Map 6 B2

On the edge of south Manchester's residential fringe at Chorlton-cum-Hardy, the broad-fronted Sonarga is more Armani that original Veeraswamy, presenting much more than the oft-seen good shopfitting job. A well-judged modern style of Bangladeshi cooking and service is offered and the kitchen appears eager to offer new ideas without forsaking traditional values. The menu is overhauled thoroughly at least once a year. Sonarga supreme dishes need to be ordered a day in advance, such as *koowazi* lamb – a whole leg, marinated then roasted, served for four or more. Other unusual dishes include salmon *kaljeera* and chicken *jaratree*. Undoubtedly one of the best Indian restaurants in the area. Fried chicken and chips appears in a short section of the menu labelled "something English". *Seats 64. D 5.30-12 (Fri to 12.30, Sat 3.30-12.30, Sun 3.30-11.30). Closed L Mon-Fri, 25 Dec. Set D £15.95. Access, Visa.*

Manchester   That Café   £45

Tel 061-432 4672   **R**

1031 Stockport Road Levenshulme Manchester Greater Manchester M19 2TB   Map 6 B2

A friendly, unpretentious restaurant by the A6, south of the city.
An à la carte menu operates six evenings a week, with a short set menu
as an additional offering Tuesday to Thursday. Dishes on both are
straightforward, from the day's soup, bruschetta and chicken liver and
brandy paté to chicken with celery, rabbit casserole, rack of lamb and the
fish of the day (consult the mirrors in the dining room). Vegetarian main
courses always available. *Seats 80. Private Room 35. L (Sun only) 12.30-3
D 7-10.30. Closed D Mon, 1 week Aug, 25-28 Dec. Set L £10.95
Set D £12.95.* AMERICAN EXPRESS *Access, Visa.*

Manchester   Victoria & Albert Hotel   73%   £141

Tel 061-832 1188   Fax 061-834 2484   **HR**

Water Street Manchester Greater Manchester M3 4JQ   Map 6 B2

Between their TV studios and the river Irwell, Granada's flagship hotel
is a cleverly converted mid-19th-century warehouse. Original oak-timbered
ceilings and cast-iron pillars feature in the smart galleried reception area,
'Watsons' bar/lounge with its comfortable Victorian drawing room
atmosphere and conservatory overlooking the river, and in the all-day
French-style café/bistro. Bedrooms, which vary in size and shape, also boast
timbered ceilings and some exposed brickwork; each is named after, and
subtly themed with stills from, a different Granada TV drama or series.
King-or queen-sized beds and a high level of equipment – the TV offers
account review, quick check-out and breakfast ordering facilities – make
for a comfortable stay aided by keen staff offering an above average level
of service. Children under 16 years free in parents' room. No dogs.
Conference facilities for up to 250. *Rooms 132. Garden, keep-fit equipment,
sauna, solarium, coffee shop (10am-midnight), news kiosk.* AMERICAN EXPRESS
Access, Diners, Visa.

Sherlock Holmes Restaurant   £65

John Benson-Smith cooks with style and wit throughout a menu which
never lacks interest. Some dishes are as simple as could be – Yorkshire
pudding with onion gravy, chicken liver paté, roast beef carved from the
trolley, poached salmon hollandaise – while others are a good deal more
elaborate, typified by a hot, spicy Thai salad of prawns, mango, apricot and
cashew nuts, or pan-fried grey mullet with smoked salmon, mushrooms,
cherry tomatoes and a red wine sauce. Very good desserts, excellent home-
baked bread. *Seats 130. Parties 40. Private Room 16. L 12-2 D 7-10.
Closed L Sat. Set Sun L £14.95 Set D (pre-and post-theatre) £15.*

Manchester   Woodlands   £55

Tel 061-336 4241   **R**

33 Shepley Road Audenshaw Manchester Greater Manchester M34 5DJ   Map 6 B2

Set in a solid Victorian house alongside B6169. Chef William Mark
Jackson's menus are based on sound, classical French traditions and offer
a good choice – five or six on the table d'hote (not available Saturday),
eight or so on the carte at each stage. The style is straightforward – ham
and mushroom filo cracker with a cream sauce, chicken livers marinated
in Oriental spices, grilled supreme of chicken with a citrus butter sauce
on the table d'hote; the carte extends to encompass the likes of salmon
mousseline with deep-fried goujons of plaice with a chive sauce and
medallions of venison cooked with chestnuts, mushrooms and glazed
onions. Lesley Ann Jackson runs front of house with friendliness and
efficiency. Descriptive, mainly French wine list. Smoking is discouraged (as

are credit cards). Accommodation (£60) is now offered in three rooms that recently came into operation. *Seats 40. Parties 24. L 12-2 D 7-9.30 (Sat to 10). Closed 1st week Jan & Easter, 2 weeks mid-Aug. Set L & D £15.65. Access, Visa.*

Manchester	Yang Sing	★	£50
Tel 061-236 2200 Fax 061-236 5934			**R**
34 Princes Street Manchester Greater Manchester M1 4JY			Map 6 B2

The class of cooking and the length of the menus make this the most appealing Chinese restaurant in town, and its popularity remains undiminished. Tanks of live carp, eels and lobsters testify to the importance chef/proprietor Harry Yeung places on freshness and quality of ingredients. Some 40 different dim sum (even more on Sundays) can be chosen from trolleys parked in the middle of the restaurant or ordered from the waiting staff. A selection of pastries (all from their own kitchen) or fresh fruit for afters. On the ground floor is a Chinese Fondue Restaurant where dishes are cooked in a stock (rather than oil) that is drunk as a soup after the main ingredients of the dish have been eaten. Banquets for up to 200 guests can be held in the largest of several private rooms. *Seats 140. Parties 40. Private Room 200. Meals 12-11.30. Closed 25 Dec. Set meals from £27 for two.* AMERICAN EXPRESS *Access, Visa.*

Manchester   Places of Interest

Tourist Information   Tel 061-234 3157/3158.
Manchester Cathedral   Tel 061-773 2959.
Heaton Hall   Tel 061-236 9422.
Granada Studios Tour   Water Street Tel 061-833 0880.
Old Trafford Cricket Ground   Warwick Road Tel 061-848 7021.
Oldham Ski Centre   Tel 061-678 4055.
   Theatres and Concert Halls
Contact Theatre   Tel 061-274 4400.
Library Theatre   Tel 061-236 7110.
Manchester Opera House   Tel 061-831 7766.
Palace Theatre   Tel 061-236 9922.
Royal Exchange   Tel 061-833 9833.
   Museums and Art Galleries
City Art Gallery   Tel 061-236 5244.
Gallery of English Costume   Tel 061-224 5217.
The Museum of Science and Industry   Tel 061-832 2244.
Manchester Museum   Tel 061-275 2634.
Whitworth Art Gallery   Tel 061-273 4865.
Art Gallery   Oldham Leisure Services Tel 061-678 4651.
   Football Grounds
Manchester City   Tel 061-226 1191.
Manchester United   Tel 061-872 1661.
Oldham Athletic   Tel 061-624 4972.

Manchester Airport	Etrop Grange	66%	£111
Tel 061 499 0500 Fax 061 499 0790			**H**
Outwood Lane Manchester Airport Greater Manchester M22 5NR			Map 6 B2

The hotel is based on a small Georgian house, whose ground floor has been opened up to create public spaces that though not extensive are stylishly furnished with ribbon-hung pictures and rather low-hanging crystal chandeliers (six-footers need to duck). The bar is essentially the corridor leading to the dining room and there is a small conservatory. Bedrooms are generally a bit on the small side but are well equipped (mini-bar, room safe etc) and all have armchairs and/or sofas. They are stronger on decor – fine fabrics, mostly antique beds – than practicality in that where there is a desk it is often rather small and sometimes there is no upright chair; similarly, bathrooms come with wood-panelled tubs and lacy shower curtains but minimal shelf space. Helpful staff, particularly the porters, but service lacks polish – not removing afternoon tea tray when turning down bed in the evening, for example. Good choice of cooked breakfasts including Manx kippers with herb butter and fresh limes, and kedgeree in addition to the fry-up that comes with a brace of free-range eggs. Juices are freshly squeezed. Room service is 24hrs. *Rooms 41. Courtesy car to airport.* AMERICAN EXPRESS *Access, Diners, Visa.*

Manchester Airport   Forte Crest   65%   £109

Tel 061-437 5811   Fax 061-436 2340   **H**
Ringway Road Wythenshawe Greater Manchester M90 3NS   Map 6 B2

Between terminals A & B, 8 miles from the city centre. Banqueting and conference facilities for 120/200, plus a leisure centre. 24hr room service. *Rooms 290. Garden, indoor swimming pool, gym, sauna, café (6.30am-11pm).* AMERICAN EXPRESS *Access, Diners, Visa.*

Manchester Airport   Four Seasons Hotel   68%   £121

Tel 061-904 0301   Fax 061-980 1787   **H**
Hale Road Hale Barns nr Altrincham Greater Manchester WA15 8XW   Map 6 B2

A privately owned hotel two miles from the airport (at junction 6 of the M56). Smart modern bedrooms overlook central courtyard gardens. The top-of-the-range suites have lounges and jacuzzis. Well geared up for business people with up-to-date conference facilities (maximum 120) and secretarial support services available. There's a good choice of spots in which to relax, including the Lobby Bar, Vivaldi's cocktail bar, Mulligans snug and Mollenski's conservatory. Children up to 12 stay free in parents' room. *Rooms 94.* AMERICAN EXPRESS *Access, Diners, Visa.*

Manchester Airport   Hilton International   71%   £159

Tel 061-436 4404   Fax 061-436 1521   **H**
Outwood Lane Manchester Airport Greater Manchester M90 1WP   Map 6 B2

Convenient for both the airport and the motorway network, this modern hotel caters admirably for travellers and general businessmen alike with its good business and meeting facilities (for up to 300), which have recently been expanded and refurbished. Similar investment in the leisure facilities means there's now a huge gym, which is well-used, and a solarium has been added. The third recipient of a facelift is the bar. Plaza bedrooms are larger and more impressive than the standard rooms, but all are smartly furnished with contemporary fabrics and have surprisingly spacious bathrooms. Double-glazing features throughout, so noise is not a problem, despite the location. *Rooms 222. Garden, indoor swimming pool, children's pool, gym, solarium, spa bath, sauna, steam room, coffee shop (8am-midnight).* AMERICAN EXPRESS *Access, Diners, Visa.*

Manchester Airport   Moss Nook   £80

Tel 061-437 4778   Fax 068 498 8089   **RR**
Ringway Road Moss Nook Manchester Greater Manchester M22 5WD   Map 6 B2

Well signed from the airport (one mile away). Red suede walls, heavy drapes, stained glass, silver plate, heavy crystal glassware, and lace slips over the tablecloths lend an air of opulence. The French-style à la carte menu is supplemented by a *menu surprise* (five small courses at lunchtime, seven in the evening). Luxury ingredients and an outsize menu typify the style. Everyone should leave room for the grand selection of desserts, while chocoholics should head straight for the chocolate medley. Outdoor terrace seating for 20 in good weather. Mostly French wines on the list, with only a nod elsewhere. No children under 8. *Seats 65. Parties 10. L 12-1.30 D 7-9.30 Closed L Sat, all Sun & Mon, Bank Holidays, 2 weeks from 26 Dec. Set L £16.50 Set D £28.* AMERICAN EXPRESS *Access, Diners, Visa.*

Room   £140*

An adjacent, self-contained cottage has one double bedroom with two en-suite bathrooms, a lounge, TV and telephone. The makings of a Continental breakfast are provided. No children under 12. Accommodation closed for 2 weeks from Christmas Eve. *Price for two including dinner.

Market Drayton   Goldstone Hall   60%   £75

Tel 0630 661202   Fax 0630 661585   **H**

Goldstone Market Drayton Shropshire TF9 2NA   Map 6 B3

South of Market Drayton, follow brown and white signposts from the A459 for Goldstone Hall Gardens. Set in five acres of mature gardens, the proprietor-run hall is an accumulation of centuries of building, with possible Anglo-Saxon origins, and is furnished with the family collection of antiques. Bedrooms are individually designed, with period furniture, and several have large Victorian brass bedsteads. One room has a period four-poster, another is in Louis XIV style. Separate conference and banqueting rooms. *Rooms 8. Garden, croquet, snooker.* AMERICAN EXPRESS *Diners, Access, Visa.*

Market Drayton   Place of Interest

Market Drayton Pool   Tel 0630 2619.

Market Harborough   Three Swans Hotel   65%   £72

Tel 0858 466644   Fax 0858 433101   **H**

21 High Street Market Harborough Leicestershire LE16 7NJ   Map 7 D4

Charles I slaked his thirst here in 1645, by when this splendid coaching inn was already more than 200 years old. Several bars ensure that today's visitors don't go thirsty, and there's an attractive conservatory/lounge and a patio. Bedrooms are in the main building or a block across the courtyard. All are of a good size, decorated in restful pastels and furnished with smart modern units; all have private bathrooms with tubs, shower and toiletries. Two bedrooms are equipped for disabled guests. Friendly staff. The Old School House self-contained conference centre caters for up to 100 delegates, with further rooms in the main building. Tariff reductions at weekends. No dogs. *Rooms 36. Coffee shop (9am-3pm).* AMERICAN EXPRESS *Access, Diners, Visa.*

Market Harborough   Places of Interest

Deene Park House and Gardens   Nr Corby Tel 078085 278 or 361.
Kirby Hall   Nr Corby Tel 0536 203230.
Rockingham Castle   Corby Tel 0536 770240.
Rutland Polo Club   Barnsdale House, Great Easton Tel 0536 770238.

Markington   Hob Green   70%   £90

Tel 0423 770031   Fax 0423 771589   **H**

Markington nr Harrogate North Yorkshire HG3 3PJ   Map 6 C1

870 acres of farm and woodland make a fine setting for a mellow stone hotel, and the gardens have won many prizes as well as providing pleasant views of the rolling Yorkshire countryside. The garden room is bright and summery, while the hall and drawing room have a traditional appeal that's helped along by antiques and log fires. Books, magazines and games are available for relaxation. Bedrooms are individually appointed in homely style and furniture is an agreeable mix of period and modern. Most have a little sitting area. *Rooms 12. Garden.* AMERICAN EXPRESS *Access, Diners, Visa.*

Markyate — Hertfordshire Moat House — 57% — £78

Tel 0582 840840   Fax 0582 842282   **H**
London Road Markyate Hertfordshire AL3 8HH   Map 15 E1

Only one mile from the M1 (Junction 9) alongside the A5, a modern hotel with adequate bedrooms and bathrooms, a good gym and a thriving conference trade (for up to 300). Tariff reductions at weekends. *Rooms 89. Gym, solarium.* AMERICAN EXPRESS *Access, Diners, Visa.*

Marlborough — Ivy House — 61% — £68

Tel 0672 515333   Fax 0672 515338   **H**
High Street Marlborough Wiltshire SN8 1HJ   Map 14 C2

Resident owners David Ball and Josephine Scott offer purpose-built conference facilities (up to 80 delegates) as well as hotel amenities at their Grade II listed Georgian house, which was once a school for boys known as Marlborough Academy. Bedrooms, some with separate sitting areas, are spread between the main house, the conference block and an annexe across the High Street. Children up to 10 stay free in parents' room. *Rooms 33. Coffee shop (8am-9.30pm).* AMERICAN EXPRESS *Access, Visa.*

Marlow — Compleat Angler Hotel — 73% — £164

Tel 0628 484444   Fax 0628 486388   **HR**
Marlow Bridge Marlow Buckinghamshire SL7 1RG   Map 15 E2

A famous Marlow landmark in a glorious riverside setting by the weir. Said to be where Izaak Walton wrote his definitive angling work (after which the hotel is named), it dates in part back to the 16th century, but has been extended over the years. The latest extension houses eighteen bedrooms, twelve of which overlook the river. Creaking floorboards feature in the original rooms, which include riverside rooms at a supplement. Each room bears the name of a fishing fly. On the ground floor the marble-floored foyer leads to a panelled bar with a conservatory, opening on to a small balcony that also overlooks the river. Children up to 15 stay free in parents' room. Forte Grand. *Rooms 62. Garden, croquet, tennis, fishing.* AMERICAN EXPRESS *Access, Diners, Visa.*

Valaisan Restaurant — £115

Adequate cooking in the classic mould with some modern adaptations, good cheeses and decent wine list. Superb views and professional service from an able team. *Seats 96. Parties 20. L 12.30-2.30 (Sun to 3) D 7-10. Set L from £17.95/£22.95 (Sun £28.50) Set D £29.50.*

Marlow — Place of Interest

Bisham Abbey Sports Centre   Tel 0627 476911.

Marston Moretaine — Forte Travelodge — £45

Tel 0234 766755   **L**
Beanscroft Road Marston Moretaine Bedfordshire MK43 0PZ   Map 15 E1

On the A421 northbound, 3 miles from Junction 13 of the M1, 6 miles south-west of Bedford. *Rooms 32.* AMERICAN EXPRESS *Access, Diners, Visa.*

Matlock — Riber Hall — 71% — £98

Tel 0629 582795   Fax 0629 580475   **HR**
Matlock Derbyshire DE4 5JU   Map 6 C2

Twenty minutes from Junction 28 of the M1, an atmospheric Elizabethan manor house graced with antiques, beams and fresh flowers. There's a lovely conservatory and walled garden, making it a wonderfully peaceful location. Bedrooms are located in converted stables across a courtyard where the original beams and rough stone walls remain; all are filled with thoughtful extras, centrally heated and have period four-poster or half-tester beds. Best rooms face south and east and overlook the large garden. Bathrooms are well equipped, neat and warm; five of them sport whirlpool baths. A tennis trainer ball machine is available on the all-weather tennis court. No children under 10. No dogs. *Rooms 11. Garden, tennis.* AMERICAN EXPRESS® *Access, Diners, Visa.*

Restaurant £66

An additional dining room and lounge (for non-smokers) came into use in the summer of 1994, offering more visitors the chance to enjoy chef Jeremy Brazelle's sound cooking. Luncheon is fixed-price, with dishes running from duck liver mousse paté with orange or chicken and mushroom brioche via a selection of sorbets to game pie, stir-fried Oriental salmon and medallions of beef on a brandy and peppercorn sauce. Desserts might include parfait of walnuts and Tia Maria on a hot chocolate sauce, or apple and cinnamon pie on a warm *crème anglaise*. Similar style in the evening. Vegetarian dishes available on a separate menu (£18.50). Tasting notes available alongside every wine (even half bottles) on a list that gives only a cursory nod to the New World. *Seats 60. Private Room 40. L 12-1.30 D 7-9.30. Set L £11.50/£14.50.*

Matlock Bath	New Bath Hotel	63%	£108
Tel 0629 583275 Fax 0629 580268			**H**
New Bath Road Matlock Bath Derbyshire DE4 3PX			Map 6 C3

10 miles from junction 28 of the M1, tucked away down a narrow, twisting gorge, the New Bath is set in five acres of landscaped gardens overlooking the river Derwent. Good leisure facilities include an outdoor swimming pool fed by a thermal spring. Conference/banqueting for up to 200 and family facilities reflect the midweek/weekend balance of business. Forte Heritage. *Rooms 55. Garden, indoor & outdoor swimming pools, sauna, solarium, tennis, putting.* AMERICAN EXPRESS® *Access, Diners, Visa.*

Matlock Bath   Place of Interest

Gullivers Kingdom Matlock Bath   Tel 0629 580540.

Mawnan	Budock Vean Hotel	65%	£144
Tel 0326 250288 Fax 0326 250892 .			**H**
Mawnan nr Falmouth Cornwall TR11 5LG			Map 12 B4

There's a resident golf professional at Budock Vean, but there are plenty of other activities also on offer at this elegant sporting hotel set in 65 acres of sub-tropical gardens, which include a private foreshore to the Helford river. A new management team, formerly at *Polurrion* in Mullion, joined last year. Spacious bedrooms include some with sitting rooms. There are also three self-catering cottages in the grounds, two adjoining with a private garden, and a larger separate one. 2% surcharge when paying by credit card. *Rooms 58. Garden, indoor swimming pool, tennis, golf (18), putting, table tennis, coarse fishing, snooker. Closed Jan-Feb. Access, Diners, Visa.*

Mawnan	Meudon Hotel	69%	£106
Tel 0326 250541 Fax 0326 250543			**H**
Mawnan nr Falmouth Cornwall TR11 5HT			Map 12 B4

The Pilgrim family, here for 30 years, put the accent on peace, quiet and personal service, with no conferences or even large parties to intrude. Sub-tropical gardens, laid out by 'Capability' Brown, are a major attraction of staying here and are at their flowering best between March and June; the gardens lead down to a private beach. The house itself was built at the turn of the century, and the new wing, connected at first-floor level, is in matching stone. The main lounge is very comfortable and appealing, with

paintings, photographs, fresh flowers and antiques. Bedrooms are
individually appointed in elegant style, with furnishings and fittings
of a uniformly high standard; all overlook the gardens. Two balcony suites
have their own sitting rooms. Residents can enjoy free golf at the Falmouth
Golf Club (two miles away) and both sea and river fishing are available.
A really charming and friendly place where most of the guests are regulars.
Rooms 32. Garden, hair salon, snooker. Closed Jan & Feb. Access, Diners, Visa.

Mawnan   Nansidwell   70%   £98

Tel 0326 250340   Fax 0326 250440   **HR**

Mawnan nr Falmouth Cornwall TR11 5HU   Map 12 B4

A traditional country hotel with ample supplies of friendliness, peace and
beautiful scenery. Built at the turn of the century, although the wisteria
clad exterior looks older, it enjoys an idyllic location in five acres
of gardens surrounded by National Trust land between Helford River and
the sea. Day rooms have a comfortably lived-in feel, with family photos
creating a genuinely homely atmosphere. Individually decorated bedrooms
with 'country' and near-antique furniture vary considerably in size but all
boast fresh flowers and generous quantities of books and magazines.
No room service. *Rooms 12. Garden, tennis, sun beds, boules. Closed Jan.
Access, Visa.*

Restaurant   £66

An appealing dining room with decorative plates adorning yellow rag-
painted walls and views over the terraced gardens. Equally appealing are
Anthony Alcott's well-executed dishes from a fairly sophisticated menu that
includes speciality fish dishes such as smoked haddock and spinach
cannelloni, fillets of lemon sole with fresh asparagus and lime butter sauce,
and medallions of monkfish with a ragout of lobster and chanterelles. Roast
best end of lamb with a tomato and garlic crumb, veal escalope on a curry
and mushroom sauce, and roast breast of wild duck with port and glazed
apples could be among the meaty options. *Seats 38. Parties 10. L 12.30-1.45
D 7-9. Set L £12.75 (Sun £14.75) Set D £25.*

Mawnan   Places of Interest

Glendurgan Garden (NT)   Helford River Tel 0208 74281.
Trebah Garden   Tel 0326 250448.

Medmenham   Danesfield House   78%   £135

Tel 0628 891010   Fax 0628 890408   **HR**

Medmenham Marlow Buckinghamshire SL7 3ES   Map 15 D2

Danesfield is the third house since 1664 to occupy this spectacular setting,
overlooking the Thames, and it was completed in this incarnation towards
the end of the last century. The Tudor-style architecture is a nod to the
site's early inhabitants, complete with clock tower, crenellations and
twisted redbrick Elizabethan chimney stacks. A large stone terrace and
formal parterre gardens (including an Italian water garden) take full
advantage of the hotel's views. The tapestry-hung Grand Hall is baronial
in scale with hammerbeam roof and minstrel's gallery (now a snooker
room); other day rooms include a wicker-furnished atrium and bar with
leather seating and loggia. Bedrooms come in one of three colours –
apricot, blue or pink – with everything coloured and themed
appropriately. Friendly staff offer good levels of service with rooms
properly serviced in the evenings and a 24hr room service menu. Parking
for over 100 cars, banqueting/conferences for 120/200. Children up to 14
free in parents' room. No dogs. *Rooms 89. Garden, croquet, outdoor
swimming pool, squash, tennis, snooker, helipad.* AMERICAN EXPRESS *Access,
Diners, Visa.*

Oak Room

£100

The panelled Oak Room has a fine ribbed plaster ceiling and a loggia extension where breakfast is served. The short but reasonably well-balanced à la carte changes weekly and might include the likes of terrine of quail and girolles accompanied by a grain mustard and apple chutney, or deep-fried won tons of marinated scallops, spring onions and sweet and sour sauce as starters; and for a main course pan-fried brill topped with fish mousse served with a dusting of curry powder, diamonds of carrot and mangetout, new potatoes and a white wine butter sauce; or roasted lamb rump sliced around a tian of aubergine, courgette, onion and tomato, served with gratin potatoes and a thyme sauce. For dessert, try perhaps a rich chocolate truffle torte with a compote of raspberries. *Seats 50. Parties 10. L 12-2 D 7-10 (Sun to 9.30). Set L £15.50/£19.50 Set D £29.50/£32.50.*

Melbourn   Pink Geranium   ↑

£105

R

Tel 0763 260215   Fax 0763 262110

Station Road Melbourn nr Royston Hertfordshire SG8 6DX

Map 15 F1

In one of the prettiest and most romantic cottage restaurants in the country Steven Saunders remains firmly at the helm despite his several related but outside interests. This ensures a consistency of standards from a dedicated and highly professional team headed by new chef Philip Guest. Approached through a well-tended garden, the restaurant is pink outside and pink inside. Rose-pink geraniums feature in the curtains and upholstery as well as in the wide borders around the walls. The effort is to create a cosy, traditional ambience. The menu keeps firmly abreast of the times while retaining a strong element of classicism. For example, a single raviolo of spinach with Parmesan is served topped with finely shredded fresh basil and a light basil and garlic oil; a winter suet pudding of braised venison has caramelised shallots and roasted chestnuts. Tenderloin of lamb is steamed to pink perfection having first been rolled in fresh herbs; it is then served sliced on a fried potato galette and accompanied by a slice of Mediterranean vegetable cake – courgettes, aubergines and plum tomatoes layered in alternating thin slices – and a delicate garlic cream. Sweets range from the simple, steamed chocolate pudding with chocolate sauce, to the elaborate – crisp rounds of nougatine layered with lightly caramelised bananas, smooth coconut sorbet and surrounded by a creamy coffee anglaise. No children in the dining room after 8pm, however a crèche facility is offered (or a private room for families with children). Limousine service offered at taxi prices – distance no object. *Seats 70. Parties 12. Private Room 55/18. L 12-2.30 D 7-10.30. Closed D Sun, all Mon, 26-29 Dec. Set L £14.95/£17.95 (Sun £18.95) Set D £29.95.* AMERICAN EXPRESS® *Access, Visa.*

Melbourn   Place of Interest

Bassingbourn Ski Club   Royston Tel 0462 34107.

Melksham   Toxique

£65

R

Tel 0225 702129

187 Woodrow Road Melksham Wiltshire SN12 7AY

Map 14 B3

Take the Calne road from the town-centre mini roundabout, turn left after ½ mile into Forest Road and continue for nearly a mile – eventually you'll find Toxique. However, you must book in advance as it's 'famine or feast round these parts', meaning it's closed when not busy and very busy when booked up. Nevertheless, Peter Jewkes and chef-partner Helen Bartlett's slightly eccentric restaurant with its farmhouse look and unusual decor (cheap chairs and tables disguised with loose covers, an abstract mural) is worth a visit. A fixed-price-only menu offers 6 dishes at each stage: perhaps a warm salad of pan-fried scallops and pancake strips with an orange vinaigrette or chestnut and almond soup with lemon grass to start, followed by spring lamb with charred sweet peppers and tomatoes, aubergine and sautéed potatoes, poached crab-stuffed hake with fennel, green sauce and fragrant rice, plus a handful of straightforward vegetarian options. A few more involved dishes may attract a small supplement. Saucing is a strong point (try their pan-fried breast of Trelough duck with orange muscat sauce if it's on the menu), as is service from the busy owner. Two diners can order a plate of sampling desserts (also for a small supplement). No smoking at the table (but it's allowed in the bar area). Several less well-known wines and growers on the good wine list; interesting sweet wine section but just one champagne. Outside tables for drinks in good weather. Accommodation is also offered (£80 half-board for two) in four rooms. An unusual find in an area poorly served by decent restaurants. *Seats* 30. *Parties* 20. *Private Room* 20. *L Sun only 12.30-2 D 7-10. Closed D Sun, all Mon & Tues, 2 weeks Jan/Feb. Set L (Sun only) £13.50/£16.50 Set D £24.50.* AMERICAN EXPRESS *Access, Visa.*

Melksham   Place of Interest

Devizes Tourist Information   Tel 0380 729408.

Mellor   Millstone Hotel   £88

Tel 0254 813333   Fax 0254 812628   **I**

Church Lane Mellor nr Blackburn Lancashire BB2 7JR   **Map 6 B1**

Ten minutes from Junction 31 of the M6, next to St Mary's church in a quiet village off the A59, this small, friendly hotel effectively mixes modern conveniences with the charm of a traditional roadside inn. One of the two bars also acts as the village local. Four single bedrooms have recently been combined to provide two doubles, as part of an ongoing programme of improvement. Bedrooms are neat and well maintained. Children up to the age of 16 are free in parents' room. Shire Inns. *Rooms* 19. *Patio.* AMERICAN EXPRESS *Access, Diners, Visa.*

Melmerby   Village Bakery   £30

Tel 0768 881515   Fax 0768 881848   **R**

Melmerby Penrith Cumbria CA10 1HE   **Map 4 C3**

A converted barn with a bright, airy conservatory and pine furniture, run since 1976 by Andrew and Lis Whitley, and overlooking the green of a beautiful fellside village, ten miles east of Penrith on the A686 Alston road. The owners are committed to providing food produced by organic methods. All the breads and pastries are produced on the premises in a wood-fixed brick oven, and any fruit and vegetables not coming from their garden are obtained from local organic supplies. Breakfast is served until 11am (raspberry porridge, kippers, free-range eggs, croissants, spicy buns, full fried breakfast and a version for vegetarians). Lunch starts at noon, with last orders at 2: soup comes first, then brown lentil and red wine moussaka, hot prawn salad, Cumberland sausage or the Baker's lunch with bread and North Country cheeses; for dessert, fruit pie, sherry trifle or perhaps Christmas pudding. Also savoury snacks, sandwiches and a memorable cream tea. Children's portions are reduced by a third. No smoking. *Seats* 40. *Meals 8.30-5 (Sun from 9.30). Closed 25-27 Dec, 1 Jan. Access, Diners, Visa.*

Melton Mowbray   George Hotel   57%   £45

Tel 0664 62112   Fax 0664 410457   **H**

High Street Melton Mowbray Leicestershire LE13 0TR   **Map 7 D3**

The entrance hall at this very old former coaching inn was once the archway through which the stage coaches drove. The arrival and departure clock still stands on display, and another traditional touch is provided by four-posters in some of the bedrooms. Special rates for families in adjoining rooms. There are two bars, one with beams and hunting prints, and a patio. New owners since last year, and reduced room rates. *Rooms* 22. AMERICAN EXPRESS *Access, Diners, Visa.*

Meriden   De Vere Manor Hotel   64%   £85

Tel 0676 522735   Fax 0676 522186   **H**

Main Road Meriden West Midlands CV7 7NH   Map 6 C4

Impressive, extended Georgian-style building with comfortable bedrooms in a smart modern wing. Popular for conferences and banquets (400/300), but no leisure facilities. Children up to 12 free in parents' room. 2 rooms are specially equipped for disabled guests. *Rooms 74.* AMERICAN EXPRESS *Access, Diners, Visa.*

Meriden   Forest of Arden Hotel   70%   £123

Tel 0676 522335   Fax 0676 523711   **H**

Maxstoke Lane Meriden West Midlands CV7 7HR   Map 6 C4

Just over a mile off the A45 (west of Coventry), near the M6/M42 intersection, this purpose-built resort-style hotel, golf and country club stands at the end of a country lane in 400 acres of rolling countryside. The Mediterranean-style interior is welcoming, and the lounge and reception areas were refurbished during 1994. Bedrooms are comfortable and furnished in contemporary fashion; bathrooms are carpeted and have good-quality showers. Extensive leisure facilities are housed in the impressive Country Club and include a large pool. A supervised crèche can be provided by arrangement (as can baby-sitting); families may eat informally in the poolside grill and bar. Country Club Hotels. *Rooms 154. 2 golf courses, fishing, indoor swimming pool, sauna, steam room, spa bath, solarium, squash, tennis, snooker, fitness studio, beauty salon, dance studio.* AMERICAN EXPRESS *Access, Diners, Visa.*

Mickleton   Three Ways Hotel   59%   £68

Tel 0386 438429   Fax 0386 438118   **H**

Mickleton nr Chipping Campden Gloucestershire GL55 6SB   Map 14 C1

Standing at the heart of a Cotswold village between Broadway and Stratford, this is a privately-run hotel built from mellow, local stone. Bedrooms are practical rather than luxurious, with modest en-suite facilities. Although the decor is dated, cleanliness is a strong point. Friendly and relaxing atmosphere; family facilities (children up to 16 stay free in parents' room). Three conference/function suites, one opening onto a patio. Three Ways is the home of the Pudding Club, whose members meet regularly in winter to overdose on heavyweight hot puds served with 'lashings of custard'. *Rooms 41. Garden.* AMERICAN EXPRESS *Access, Diners, Visa.*

Note that all telephone numbers with area codes starting with 0 will start 01 from 16 April 1995.

Middle Wallop   Fifehead Manor   61%   £80

Tel 0264 781565   Fax 0264 781400   **H**

Middle Wallop nr Stockbridge Hampshire SO20 8EG   Map 14 C3

Standing in well-kept gardens and grounds on the A343, the manor has a long and interesting history that includes a spell as a nunnery. Central to the house is the medieval dining hall with its mullioned windows and there is a small bar plus a lounge. Large bedrooms in the main house have good-size bathrooms; smaller singles (with showers only) are in an annexe, but colour schemes are used throughout, and the furniture is mostly modern, although a few antiques help contribute to the friendly and informal atmosphere. Fine cooked breakfasts. *Rooms 16. Garden. Closed 2 weeks Christmas.* AMERICAN EXPRESS *Access, Diners, Visa.*

Middlecombe   Periton Park   66%   £78

Tel 0643 706885   **H**

Periton Road Middlecombe nr Minehead Somerset TA24 8SW   Map 13 D1

Beautifully situated at the northern edge of Exmoor National Park, Periton Park (built in 1875) is set in its own gardens against a backdrop of woodland and streams. It's not surprising, then, that outdoor pursuits of the huntin', shootin' and fishin' variety are the main guest occupations. There are log fires in winter, endless views in summer, and a warm welcome all year round from owners Richard and Angela Hunt. Each bedroom (all en suite) has its own character and all enjoy splendid views; two are for non-smokers, and one ground-floor room, with French windows opening on to the garden, allows dogs. The rooms have been upgraded and all have been redecorated. No children under 12. *Rooms 8. Garden, croquet, shooting, riding, fishing.* AMERICAN EXPRESS *Access, Visa.*

Middlesbrough   Hotel Baltimore   62%   £85

Tel 0642 224111   Fax 0642 226156   **H**

250 Marton Road Middlesbrough Cleveland TS4 2EZ   Map 5 E3

Popular executive hotel south of the town centre on the A172, handy for Teesside airport (9 miles). Bedrooms are double-glazed and have colour TV and radio, direct-dial telephones and tea/coffee making facilities. Banqueting/conferences for 100/140. Free secured parking. *Rooms 31.* AMERICAN EXPRESS *Access, Visa.*

Middlesbrough   Hospitality Inn   59%   £93

Tel 0642 232000   Fax 0642 232655   **H**

Fry Street Middlesbrough Cleveland TS1 1JH   Map 5 E3

High-rise hotel in the town centre. Five banqueting and conference suites have a maximum capacity of 400. Mount Charlotte Thistle. *Rooms 180.* AMERICAN EXPRESS *Access, Diners, Visa.*

Middlesbrough   Places of Interest

Tourist Information   Tel 0642 243425.
Ormesby Hall (NT)   Tel 0642 324188.
Middlesbrough Football Ground   Ayresome Park Tel 0642 819659.
Redcar Racecourse   Redcar Tel 0642 484068.
   Theatres and Concert Halls
Little Theatre   Tel 0642 818971.
Redcar Bowl   Tel 0642 231212.
Town Hall Crypt   Tel 0642 221866.
   Museums and Art Galleries
Captain Cook Birthplace Museum   Tel 0642 311211.
Cleveland Crafts Centre   Tel 0642 226351.
Cleveland Gallery   Tel 0642 225408.
Guisborough Priory   Guisborough Tel 0287 38301.
Middlesbrough Art Gallery   Linthorpe Road Tel 0642 247445.

Middleton Stoney   Jersey Arms   £72

Tel 0869 343 234   Fax 0869 343 565   **I**

Middleton Stoney nr Bicester Oxfordshire OX6 8SE   Map 15 D1

A 17th-century Cotswold-stone inn alongside the B430 (between Junctions 9 & 10 of the M40) offering comfortable accommodation in cottagey style. Bedrooms are divided between the main house (where wooden beams and creaking floors abound) and the courtyard, where they are a little more up-to-date; the Lily Langtry Suite has a four-poster bed and sitting room. Day rooms include a low-ceilinged bar warmed by an open fire and a lounge with half panelling and comfortable seating. No dogs. *Rooms 16. Garden.* AMERICAN EXPRESS *Access, Diners, Visa.*

Middleton-in-Teesdale   Teesdale Hotel   £61

Tel 0833 40264   Fax 0833 40651

I

Market Place Middleton-in-Teesdale nr Barnard Castle Co Durham DL12 0QG

Map 5 D3

At the centre of this rather austere stone-built village deep in the High Pennines, the Streit family have been practising their own brand of hospitality for 18 years. Over those years the day rooms have been carefully modernised throughout, tastefully furnished and immaculately kept. Individually decorated bedrooms are for the most part full of colour and natural light, with those on the first floor being the best, with neatly-kept (if rather basic) en-suite bathrooms; one large family room, where children under 5 share with parents free. Bar snacks are recommended. *Rooms* 12. *Access, Visa.*

Midhurst   Angel Hotel   £65

Tel 0730 812421

IR

North Street Midhurst West Sussex GU29 9DN

Map 11 A6

Behind a non-committal white-painted Georgian facade the Angel is a warm and welcoming place. Public rooms are largely centred around the two bars and restaurants with a relatively quiet residents' lounge at the front. Furnishings throughout are a mix of well-maintained polished antiques, deep relaxing armchairs and settees with paintings and prints on the walls – the usual traditional trappings that befit a well-cared-for establishment such as this. Bedrooms, all on upper floors, are in either the original building or a purpose-built modern block to the rear. All are of a good size and comfortably appointed possessing all the expected extras. Bathrooms too are up to date and kept in good order. *Rooms* 21. *Garden.* AMERICAN EXPRESS *Access, Diners, Visa.*

The Cowdray Room and Brasserie   £60

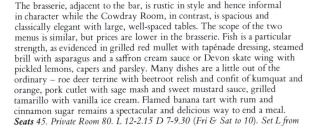

The brasserie, adjacent to the bar, is rustic in style and hence informal in character while the Cowdray Room, in contrast, is spacious and classically elegant with large, well-spaced tables. The scope of the two menus is similar, but prices are lower in the brasserie. Fish is a particular strength, as evidenced in grilled red mullet with tapénade dressing, steamed brill with asparagus and a saffron cream sauce or Devon skate wing with pickled lemons, capers and parsley. Many dishes are a little out of the ordinary – roe deer terrine with beetroot relish and confit of kumquat and orange, pork cutlet with sage mash and sweet mustard sauce, grilled tamarillo with vanilla ice cream. Flamed banana tart with rum and cinnamon sugar remains a spectacular and delicious way to end a meal. *Seats 45. Private Room 80. L 12-2.15 D 7-9.30 (Fri & Sat to 10). Set L from £11.50 (Sun £14.95) Set D £16.*

Midhurst   Spread Eagle   69%   £87

Tel 0730 816911   Fax 0730 815668

H

South Street Midhurst West Sussex GU29 9NH

Map 11 A6

The characterful 15th-and 17th-century buildings combine here with friendly staff and pleasing decor to form a most appealing hotel. The lounge bar with log fire, polished ship's timbers and fresh flowers has great charm, as do the other public areas, including the residents' lounge with its high, beamed ceiling. Bedrooms are individually decorated with quiet good taste and are furnished with a mixture of reproduction and antique pieces. Many, including the five four-poster rooms, have old exposed timbers or mellow wood panelling. Two family suites are available in the adjoining Market House. Children up to 10 stay free in parents' room. Smart bathrooms offer huge towels and good toiletries. The 17th-century

Jacobean Hall is a characterful setting for banquets and meetings (for around 100/60). Weekday snacks in the lounge bar. *Rooms 41. Garden.* AMERICAN EXPRESS *Access, Diners, Visa.*

Midhurst   Places of Interest

Petworth House (NT)   Petworth Tel 0798 42207.
Cowdray Park Polo Club   Cowdray Estate Office Tel 0730 812423.

Milford-on-Sea	Rocher's	£65
· Tel 0590 642340	·	R
69-71 High Street Milford-on-Sea Hampshire SO41 0QG		Map 14 C4

Behind the pink-washed exterior of this high-street restaurant the atmosphere is friendly and inviting, with Rebecca providing charming service while French husband Alain Rocher works single-handedly in the kitchen. Dishes on the fixed-price menu (there's also a shorter, less expensive menu available during the week) are listed in French but come with clear English descriptions. The territory is largely familiar with noisettes of lamb with rosemary, magret of duck with blackcurrant sauce, boeuf bourguignon, supreme of chicken with creamy garlic sauce, crème caramel and coupe belle Hélène showing the style. Good fish is supplied by local fishermen. Reliably good cooking has attracted a strong local following and with just seven tables booking is advisable. An all French wine list is strong on wines from Alain's native Loire valley. No children under 10 (13 at dinner). *Seats 30. L (Sun only) 12.30-1.45 D 7.15-9.45. Closed D Sun (except Sun before Bank Holidays), all Mon & Tue, 2 weeks Jun. Set Sun L £13.50 Set D £16.50 (except Sat & Bank Holiday Sundays) & £19.40/£22.90.* AMERICAN EXPRESS *Access, Visa.*

Milford-on-Sea	South Lawn	66%	£84
Tel 0590 643911 Fax 0590 644820	·		H
Lymington Road Milford-on-Sea nr Lymington Hampshire SO41 0RF			Map 14 C4

The high proportion of repeat business here says much for the standards of maintenance, service and hospitality provided by Ernst and Jennifer Barten, owners since 1971 of this rambling black-and-white former dower house. Fresh flowers make a colourful show both outside and in the roomy lounge, and the bedrooms have views over paddocks and garden. Three rooms are on the ground floor, the rest on the first. No children under seven. No dogs. *Rooms 24. Garden. Closed 20 Dec-20 Jan. Access, Visa.*

Milton Common	Belfry Hotel	60%	£93
Tel 0844 279381 Fax 0844 279624	·		H
Brimpton Grange Milton Common nr Thame Oxfordshire OX9 2JW			Map 15 D2

Driving from London on the M40, the hotel is next to Junction 7 but from the Birmingham approach take Junction 8. The original building has been much extended over the years and as a result offers bedrooms that differ in style and character. There are small, old-fashioned rooms and larger, brighter more modern rooms. They share a spacious dark oak-panelled bar and an attractive small leisure centre. *Rooms 77. Garden, indoor swimming pool, gym, sauna, solarium. Closed 24-31 Dec.* AMERICAN EXPRESS *Access, Diners, Visa.*

Milton Keynes	Forte Crest	68%	£109
Tel 0908 667722 Fax 0908 674714			H
500 Saxon Gate Milton Keynes Buckinghamshire MK9 2HQ			Map 15 E1

Modern hotel in the centre of town, next to the huge covered shopping centre. 24hr room service. Free car park. Banqueting facilities for up to 110, conferences to 150. *Rooms 151. Indoor swimming pool, gym, sauna, solarium.* AMERICAN EXPRESS *Access, Diners, Visa.*

Milton Keynes — Friendly Hotel — £84

Tel 0908 561666   Fax 0908 568303   **H**
Monksway Two Mile Ash Milton Keynes Buckinghamshire MK8 8LY   Map 15 E1

Practical, modern low-rise hotel at the junction of the A5 and A422.
Twelve Premier Plus suites with small kitchenette and fax machine
in a small lounge are favoured by both business people and families.
Children stay free in parents' room. Conference facilities for up to 150.
Rooms 88. Indoor swimming pool, gym, sauna, spa bath, steam room, solarium.
AMERICAN EXPRESS *Access, Diners, Visa.*

Milton Keynes — Travel Inn — £43

Tel 0908 663388   Fax 0908 607481   **L**
Secklow Gate West Central Milton Keynes Buckinghamshire MK9 3BZ   Map 15 E1

5 minutes' drive from M1 Junction 14, following H6 route, in the centre
of the city. Conference facilities for up to 20 in the Gallery Room.
Rooms 38. AMERICAN EXPRESS *Access, Diners, Visa.*

Milton Keynes — Places of Interest

Tourist Information   Tel 0908 691995.
Chicheley Hall   023065 252.
The Stables Theatre   Tel 0908 314466.
Stowe Landscape Gardens (NT)   Nr. Buckingham Tel 0280 822850.
Bladerunner Ice Arena   Childs Way Tel 0908 692660.

Minster Lovell — Old Swan — 67% — £90

Tel 0993 774441   Fax 0993 702002   **H**
Minster Lovell nr Witney Oxfordshire OX8 5RN   Map 14 C2

A half-timbered Cotswold inn close to the Windrush river retaining many
of its original pub features. There are three lounges with polished flagstone
floors and open log fires, and a beamed restaurant opening on to
a picturesque rear garden. Sixteen superior bedrooms offer a comfortable
and relaxing stay, while the smaller bedrooms of the adjacent conference
centre are offered at a lower rate when not in use by resident delegates.
No dogs. *Rooms 57. Garden, croquet, putting, tennis, fishing, punting.*
AMERICAN EXPRESS *Access, Diners, Visa.*

Monk Fryston — Monk Fryston Hall — 65% — £90

Tel 0977 682369   Fax 0977 683544   **H**
Monk Fryston nr Leeds North Yorkshire LS25 5DU   Map 7 D1

There has been a dwelling on this site since William the Conqueror's time,
though the present building looks back only a couple of centuries.
It remained a private residence until purchased by the Duke of Rutland,
who turned it into a hotel in 1954. The grey stone walls and mullioned
windows gracefully absorb the new wing added in 1986. In the grounds,
formal gardens embrace an ornamental lake; indoors, open log fires and
fine oak panelling set the scene. An oak staircase leads up to bright,
traditionally furnished bedrooms, all of which have tiled and carpeted
bathrooms. Rooms in the new wing have more modern furnishings, but all
are well equipped and maintained. *Rooms 28. Garden.* AMERICAN EXPRESS
Access, Visa.

Monkton Combe — Combe Grove Manor — 71% — £168

Tel 0225 834644   Fax 0225 834961   **H**
Brassknocker Hill Monkton Combe Bath Avon BA2 7HS   Map 13 F1

Perched high up above the Limpley Stoke valley and set within its own 68
acres of wooded grounds, the manor has extensive leisure facilities
belonging to the associated country club (which even offers 7-day morning

crèche facilities for parents with youngsters). Elegant day rooms and the best of the bedrooms – individually decorated in some style with reproduction period-style furniture – are in the original Georgian house beneath which, in the old cellars reached via some external steps, is an informal bar and bistro decorated in ancient Roman style. The majority of more standardised bedrooms are some 50 yards away in the Garden Lodge, designed to take full advantage of the splendid view (just four rooms are rear-facing) with most having a private patio or balcony. Beds are turned down at night. 24hr room service. Conference/banqueting facilities for 100/80 in the Tapestry Room of the Garden Lodge and in the Roman Room in the Manor House. No dogs. 2 miles from Bath city centre and 18 miles from M4 Junction 18. *Rooms 41. Garden, croquet, indoor & outdoor swimming pools, gym, sauna, spa baths, steam room, solarium, beauty salon, aerobics studio, indoor & outdoor tennis, golf (5-hole), putting, golf driving range, crazy golf, bowling green, crèche, coffee shop (10am-11pm).* AMERICAN EXPRESS® *Access, Diners, Visa.*

Montacute	King's Arms Inn	£64
Tel 0935 822513 Fax 0935 826549		■
Montacute Somerset TA15 6UU		Map 13 F2

A 16th-century hamstone inn, standing opposite the church in a picturesque and unspoilt village, that was once an ale-house owned by the abbey; a change of ownership took place in 1993. Today's comfortable, modernised little inn offers characterful accommodation in en-suite rooms, either standard or deluxe, the best with a four-poster or half-tester bed. The Windsor room is a relaxing lounge; the Pickwick Bar remains the centre of village life, with real ales and bar snacks. Follow a relaxing night with a decent buffet-style breakfast and a walk on the National Trust's wooded St Michael's Hill behind the hotel. No dogs. *Rooms 11. Garden.* AMERICAN EXPRESS® *Access, Diners, Visa.*

Montacute	Place of Interest

Montacute House (NT)   Tel 0935 823289.

Morcott	Forte Travelodge	£45
Tel 0572 87719		■L
Glaston Road Morcott nr Uppingham Leicestershire LE15 8SA		Map 7 E4

On the A47 eastbound, 4 miles east of Uppingham. *Rooms 40.* AMERICAN EXPRESS® *Access, Diners, Visa.*

Morden	Forte Travelodge	£45
Tel 081-640 8227		L
Epsom Road Morden Surrey SM4 5PH		Map 15 E2

On A24 Epsom Road, 8 miles south of central London. From A3 take A298 to Merton, turn right towards Lower Morden; at roundabout follow Lower Morden Lane to T-junction and turn left to A24. *Rooms 32.* AMERICAN EXPRESS® *Access, Diners, Visa.*

Moreton-in-Marsh	Annie's	£60
Tel 0608 651981		R
3 Oxford Street Moreton-in-Marsh Gloucestershire GL56 0LA		Map 14 C1

In a romantic cottagey setting of candle-light and soft music, David Ellis is in the kitchen while Anne runs front of house in the most friendly fashion. David's is French and English country cooking, quite straightforward and without pretension: salmon fish cakes with a white wine and salmon cream sauce, tiger prawns in filo pastry, roast poussin with a lemon mustard sauce, lamb fillet with Provençal vegetables and a port wine sauce. Pecan pie with toffee ice cream could be among the desserts. Sunday lunch always includes a traditional roast. *Seats 30. Private Room 10. L (Sun only) 12-2 D 7-10 Set Sun L £17.50 Set D (Mon-Fri) £19. Closed D Sun, 2 weeks Jan/Feb.* AMERICAN EXPRESS® *Access, Diners, Visa.*

Moreton-in-Marsh — Manor House — 66% — £75

Tel 0608 50501 Fax 0608 51481	**H**
High Street Moreton-in-Marsh Gloucestershire GL56 0LJ	Map 14 C1

Parts of this roadside, Cotswold-stone manor house set in an attractive garden date back to 1545, but others are nearly new. The hall and lounges both have a period feel, while the bar is more modern. Even in the bedrooms there's a choice between traditional and modern. *Rooms 39. Garden, indoor swimming pool, sauna, spa bath, putting.* AMERICAN EXPRESS® *Access, Diners, Visa.*

Moreton-in-Marsh — Marsh Goose — £65

Tel 0608 52111	**R**
High Street Moreton-in-Marsh Gloucestershire GL56 0AX	Map 14 C1

The Marsh Goose is, in a way, one of the Cotswolds' best kept secrets. Those in the know are already utterly dedicated, and first-timers are usually bowled over by what they find behind the honey stone walls: the approach to the restaurant is as modest, unassuming and low key as the driving force here, chef Sonya Kidney. She doesn't seek publicity, but her menus are an excellent advertisement for her skills, and even in a part of the country densely populated by quality restaurants, her cooking stands out for its reliability and individual flair. A well-thought-out pricing structure offers, at lunch, a simple no-choice set meal (perhaps mushroom and Madeira soup, fillet of halibut with saffron cream sauce and mussels, and warm mincemeat and frangipane tart) or a carte of about five light choices per course. For the three-course dinner menu she moves into top gear – seven or eight choices per course, some attracting a small supplement but otherwise the price is fixed. There's always a thoughtful vegetarian alternative. You could enjoy grilled scallops wrapped in pancetta served with an olive and parsley salad (succulent scallops, their inherent slight sweetness offset by the sharper salad); followed by roast best end of English lamb served with aubergine, tomato and coriander, and finish with a wicked and glorious black coffee jelly in a brandy snap basket with clotted cream, caramelised walnuts and butterscotch sauce. Good Sunday lunch. Smoking in the bar area only. Short, but diverse wine list; a good choice of dessert wines is offered by the glass. Regional winner, Dessert of the Year 1995. *Seats 60. Parties 22. Private Room 15. L 12.30-2.30 D 7.30-9.45. Closed D Sun, all Mon, 26 Dec, 1 Jan. Set L £13.50 (Sun £17) Set D £23.* AMERICAN EXPRESS® *Access, Visa.*

Moretonhampstead — White Hart Hotel — £63

Tel 0647 40406 Fax 0647 40565	**I**
The Square Moretonhampstead Devon TQ13 8NF	Map 13 D2

A landmark in a small former woollen town, the inn was originally a Georgian posting house. Owner Peter Morgan with his managers and staff keep up high standards of hospitality for both residents (comfortable, old-fashioned bedrooms, a cosy lounge where afternoon tea is served) and locals (in the oak-beamed bar with its polished wood and gleaming copper). Though the style is mainly traditional, the bathrooms boast telephone extensions and modern power showers. Children up to 10 are accommodated free in their parents' room. *Rooms 20. Garden.* AMERICAN EXPRESS® *Access, Diners, Visa.*

Moretonhampstead — Place of Interest

Castle Drogo (NT)   Chagford Tel 064743 3306.

Morley   Breadsall Priory   69%   £108

Tel 0332 832235   Fax 0332 833509   **H**

Moor Road Morley nr Derby Derbyshire DE7 6DL   Map 6 C3

Very much geared to the conference and leisure market, Breadsall Priory
is usefully located just north of Derby. Although its origins lie in the 13th
century (evident in the gracious proportions and tiled-and-arched reception
area) the design and facilities are all totally up to date, as befits its target
market. Bedrooms are well equipped and comfortably furnished. No dogs.
Country Club Hotels. *Rooms 91. Garden, croquet, indoor swimming pool,
gym, squash, sauna, spa bath, steam room, solarium, beauty salon, tennis, two
golf courses (18), putting green, golf driving range, snooker, helipad.*
AMERICAN EXPRESS *Access, Diners, Visa.*

Morley   Place of Interest

American Adventure Theme Park   Nr Ilkeston Tel 0773 531521.

Morston   Morston Hall   73%   £130*

Tel & Fax 0263 741041   **H**

Morston Holt Norfolk NR25 7AA   Map 10 C1

Dating back to the 17th century, Morston Hall is a substantial flint house
with secluded grounds to the front and side including a tranquil walled
garden with ancient ice-house in one corner. It stands on the A149 coast
road close to Morston's tidal quay from where boats depart for the seal
sanctuary at Blakeney Point, which is due north. Now in their third year,
Galton Blackiston, his wife Tracy and partner Justin Fraser have combined
their experience and talents to create a hotel offering country hospitality
at its best. The welcome is apparent as soon as you enter the rug-strewn
flagstone-floored hall. Fresh flowers and smiles greet you and there
is genuine warmth in the welcome. To one side of this entrance hall
is a comfortable, relaxing and homely lounge with more flowers, most
from the garden. The conservatory has recently been enlarged. The
bedrooms, some with dual-aspect windows, are large, sunny, bright and
traditional, overlooking the gardens and rolling farmland beyond. Each
room is equipped with almost every conceivable amenity – even a back-
scratcher! Good bathrooms and in the morning excellent fruit among the
breakfast offerings. One more room with dressing room and bathroom
is due on stream towards the end of 1994. *Half-board terms only.
Rooms 4. Closed Jan 1-late Feb.* AMERICAN EXPRESS *Access, Visa.*

Mottram St Andrew   De Vere Mottram Hall   70%   £140

Tel 0625 828135   Fax 0625 829284   **H**

Mottram St Andrew Prestbury Cheshire SK10 4QT   Map 6 B2

De Vere Hotels' impressive Georgian mansion, adjacent to the A538, stands
in 270 acres of mature parkland. Extensive leisure facilities include
a championship golf course and clubhouse. Spacious day rooms in the
original Mottram Hall feature restored Adam ceilings and fine panelling.
Most of the bedrooms are in newer extensions. Banqueting/conferences for
180/275. *Rooms 133. Garden, indoor swimming pool, gymnasium, squash,
sauna, spa bath, solarium, beauty salon, snooker, tennis, golf (18).*
AMERICAN EXPRESS *Access, Diners, Visa.*

Moulsford-on-Thames   Beetle & Wedge   71%   £95

Tel 0491 651381   Fax 0491 651376   **HR**

Moulsford-on-Thames Oxfordshire OX10 9JF   Map 15 D2

An enviable Thameside location, immortalised in *The Wind in the
Willows*, is approached down a narrow lane off the A329. Once the home
of Jerome K Jerome of *Three Men in a Boat* fame it is now in the very
capable hands of Katie and Richard Smith (our 1995 Hosts of the Year).

The past few months have seen many subtle changes to the appearance
with the addition of a splendid dining room and entrance lobby. A pretty
and cosy new bar area has been created adjacent to the entrance, affording
fine river views. The lounge continues to be decidedly homely and very
comfortable, and in inclement weather a fire wards off chills. Bedrooms,
most with river views, are very desirable, possessing both charm and style.
Antique pine furniture and sleep-inducing bedding characterise all, while
the deep-carpeted bathrooms have splendid freestanding cast-iron Victorian
bathtubs as well as such modern conveniences as bidets. In the summer,
a water garden with long-established water lilies comes into its own with
light grills, salads and fish served al fresco. Banqueting/conferences for
up to 64/50. Own parking for 30 cars. **Rooms** *10. Garden, fishing.*
AMERICAN EXPRESS *Access, Diners, Visa.*

The Dining Room   ★   £100

The choice nowadays is whether to eat in the simple conviviality of the
Boathouse Brasserie which has the appeal of the charcoal grill and
an imaginative, varied choice of well-prepared dishes or in the formal
elegance of the wall-to-wall-windowed dining room where Richard Smith
supervises a cuisine that's both sophisticated and very fashionable. There
is also an inner dining room decorated in pretty shades of pink, a room
eminently suitable for dining when the weather becomes cooler. Kate
Smith is assisted front of house by the utterly captivating Mercedes, who
hails from Cahors in south-western France. Starters, from a daily-changing
menu, range from a wonderful stir-fry of bean sprouts with delicately
spiced cuttlefish with coriander and a seared scallop to a hot Stilton soufflé
with a creamy wild mushroom sauce and sautéed foie gras with Lyonnaise
onions. Main dishes are mouthwateringly good – sea-fresh halibut escalope
melting on the fork and accompanied by a small handful of plump
langoustines and satisfyingly rich lobster sauce or roast best end of new
season's English lamb with rosemary and girolles. Side dishes served
alongside are delicious vegetables such as fresh asparagus with hollandaise,
rösti potatoes, leeks and fennel. A range of superb desserts include the likes
of hot *beignets soufflés* with warm lemon curd or a perfectly formed hot
Cointreau soufflé with a raspberry sauce. Cafetière coffee and excellent
petits fours complete a superbly satisfying repast. Hardly any non-French
wines on an otherwise outstanding list. Few half bottles, but note the house
policy: paying for what you drink out of a full bottle plus a small
supplement – commendable. No smoking. **Seats** *30. Private Room 50.
L 12.30-2 D 7.30-10. Closed D Sun, all Mon. Set L £17.50 (Mon-Fri) Sun
£24.50.*

Boathouse Brasserie   ↑   £70

Perched on the banks of the Thames, a skilfully converted boathouse
enables diners from the upper dining room to sit on a terrace (6 tables)
overlooking the water. On a lower level is a further dining room with
a bar counter and glowing charcoal grill. Decor throughout is rustic with
uneven terracotta floors, rough redbrick walls and heavy beams and struts
overhead. An imaginative and varied menu can cause problems when
it comes to choosing as everything sounds so good. Starters merge into
main dishes with no distinct boundary between the two. Thus crispy duck
and frisée salad; rösti with ham, raclette and a fried egg; duck and pork
rillettes with grilled bread are available under both headings. An artichoke
heart filled with sautéed wild mushrooms is topped with a creamy
hollandaise while other starters could be moules marinière, or a skate salad
with cherry tomatoes and ravigote sauce followed perhaps by a seafood
risotto with saffron, guinea fowl with cabbage and cardoons or a fricassee
of red mullet, John Dory and scallops with pan-fried baby onions and leeks.
From the charcoal grill come fish such as whole Dover sole or monkfish
tails, the latter with scallops and a red pepper sauce; and meat dishes could
be venison medallions with fresh figs, mushrooms and a port wine sauce
or a simple but good sirloin steak béarnaise. Excellent sweets and cafetière
coffee together with highly personable staff make this an occasion
to remember. **Seats** *50. Parties 16. L 12-2 D 7.30-10. Closed 25 Dec.*

Moulton   Black Bull   £55

Tel 0325 377289   **R**

Moulton nr Richmond North Yorkshire DL10 6QJ   **Map 5 E3**

The Pagendam family, here since 1963, have built a wide and still growing
reputation for the food served at their splendid pub/restaurant a mile south
of Scotch Corner. That reputation rests largely, but by no means
exclusively, on fish, shellfish and Aberdeen Angus beef. The last appears
as one of the centrepieces of Sunday lunch, and also on the main menu
in grilled fillet or sirloin, peppered fillet, fillet under pastry
or chateaubriand for two. On the seafood front are sole, scallops, sea bass,
lobster, Dublin Bay prawns and plenty more besides. As well as the carte
there's a lunchtime prix-fixe, Sunday lunch and a lunchtime (Mon-Sat) bar
snack selection. *Seats 100. Parties 10. Private Room 36. L 12-2.30 (Sun to 3)
D 6.45-10.15. Closed D Sun, 24-27 Dec. Set L £13.75 (Sun £15).*
AMERICAN EXPRESS *Access, Visa.*

Moulton   Places of Interest

North Yorkshire County Showground East Cowton Tel 0609 773429.
Catterick Bridge Racecourse Tel 0748 811478.

Mousehole   Lobster Pot   57%   £80

Tel 0736 731528   Fax 0736 731140   **H**

Mousehole nr Penzance Cornwall TR19 6QX   **Map 12 A4**

Mousehole is the epitome of a quaint Cornish fishing village, and the
Lobster Pot by natural extension an archetypal atmospheric hotel.
It overlooks the harbour, whose activity can be watched from most of the
public rooms and some of the well-maintained bedrooms. There's extra
accommodation in four cottages across the narrow street. Very much
a holiday, rather than a business, base with families well catered for.
Rooms 25. Closed 2-31 Jan & Mon-Wed in Feb. Access, Visa.

Much Birch   Pilgrim Hotel   64%   £90

Tel 0981 540742   Fax 0981 540620   **H**

Much Birch nr Hereford Hereford & Worcester HR2 8HJ   **Map 14 A1**

Set back from the A49 between Hereford and Ross-on-Wye, this much-
extended former rectory stands in four acres of grounds with views over
Golden Valley and the Black Mountains. Stone walls, oak furniture and
a log-burning stove give character to the bar, and the bedrooms have good-
quality furnishings, armchairs and useful desk space. Children aged 10 or
under are accommodated free in parents' room. Half the bedrooms are
designated non-smoking. *Rooms 20. Garden, croquet, 3-hole pitch & putt.*
AMERICAN EXPRESS *Access, Diners, Visa.*

Mudeford   Avonmouth Hotel   59%   £107

Tel 0202 483434   Fax 0202 479004   **H**

95 Mudeford Christchurch Dorset BH23 3NT   **Map 14 C4**

Forte Heritage hotel with a private jetty, slipway and moorings at the end
of lawns leading down to Christchurch Harbour. Best bedrooms (with
a small supplement) have balconies and/or sea views. *Rooms 41. Garden,
outdoor swimming pool, games room.* AMERICAN EXPRESS *Access, Diners, Visa.*

Mullion   Polurrian Hotel   66%   £66

Tel 0326 240421   Fax 0326 240083   **H**

Mullion Helston Cornwall TR12 7EN   **Map 12 B4**

On a cliff above a secluded beach and cove, Polurrian is a family holiday
hotel par excellence, with a wide range of activities on the premises and
many more in the neighbourhood. Comfortable lounges take full

advantage of the views and so do many of the bedrooms (rooms without the view are priced £20 lower). Free accommodation and breakfast for 6-14 year olds sharing adults' room, with meals charged as taken. For under-5s, high tea is also free if parents have booked on dinner, bed & breakfast terms. 200 yards from the hotel are six bungalows let out on a weekly self-catering basis. *Rooms 39. Garden, indoor & outdoor swimming pools, tennis, keep-fit equipment, squash, badminton, sauna, spa bath, solarium, putting, sea fishing, boating, snooker, coffee shop (7.30am-8.30pm). Closed Jan & Feb. Access, Visa.*

Nantwich	Churche's Mansion	NEW	£70
Tel 0270 625933 Fax 0270 74256			**R**
Hospital Street Nantwich Cheshire CW5 0RY			Map 6 B3

The restaurant is housed in a four-gabled 16th-century building with original oak beams, exposed brickwork, open fireplaces and complementary furnishings. No grumbles about chef Graham Tucker's fine English cooking, though service on one occasion was less than perfect (45 minutes' wait from entering premises to the first course being served is too long and was the least of several niggles) when the restaurant was only half full. That said, you certainly receive value for money here, both at lunch and dinner when sensible-length menus, including vegetarian, are offered. Starters might offer a feuilleté of scallops and oysters with leek, ginger and local asparagus; lobster and turbot sausage on a saffron tagliatelle with tomato and pesto sauce; or a creamed parsnip, apple and lemon soup with nutmeg gnocchi, while main courses (there's a traditional roast of the day at lunchtime) include cassoulet of guinea fowl, roast Gressingham duck with a Jerusalem artichoke and potato pie and wild mushrooms, or braised Mediterranean-style monkfish. Look out for local crayfish in summer. Pleasant desserts (warm bread-and-butter pudding with apricot ice cream, apple and cinnamon strudel with blackberry sorbet), carefully chosen British cheeses and four sorts of cafetière coffee round off the meal in fine style. Prices on the concise wine list are very fair. No smoking in the dining rooms. No children under 10 at dinner; families welcome for Sunday lunch (half price, half portions offered). *Seats 50. Private Room 24. L 12-2.30 D 7-9.30. Closed D Sun & all Mon, 2nd week Jan. Set L £11.50/£14 Set D £22. Access, Diners, Visa.*

Nantwich	Rookery Hall	79%	£150
Tel 0270 610016 Fax 0270 626027			**HR**
Worleston nr Nantwich Cheshire CW5 6DQ			Map 6 B3

The Hall was built in about 1815 and 50 years later was given a new rear and a Schloss-like tower by a homesick banker from Bavaria. Surrounded by extensive grounds, with some lovely walks by the river, the old Hall retains the spacious reception rooms with character highlighted by moulded ceilings, fine antiques and panelling. A bar has recently been added. Other stylish additions of recent years are the Coach House, a self-contained conference centre (for up to 100 delegates) converted from Georgian stables with bedrooms built around the courtyard, and the west wing. All bedrooms are luxuriously furnished and some offer fresh flowers; fruit and sherry greet guests on arrival and well-designed bathrooms have excellent overhead showers and good toiletries. There's 24hr room service. Not particularly easy to find – it's on the B5074. *Rooms 45. Garden, croquet, tennis, putting, coarse fishing, helipad. Closed 26-30 Dec.* *Access, Diners, Visa.*

Restaurant

£85

Several equally elegant dining rooms here – one has old oak panelling, another fine polished mahogany and a third (which is also the breakfast room) is in pretty country house style – in which to enjoy David Alton's intelligently constructed menus. Modern European is his style, and both à la carte and table d'hôte (three choices per course) are offered. Shellfish sausage on a prawn dill butter, baked breast of chicken with a rich wild mushroom, brandy and peppercorn sauce, and casseroled loin of spring lamb with tarragon dumplings and baby vegetables glazed with cider butter are fine examples of his skills. Leave room for a dessert (fruit délices, sticky toffee pudding, pastry case with poached pear and brandy-soaked raisins) or a selection of British and French cheeses served with home-baked hazelnut bread. **Seats** 30. Parties 8. Private Room 60. L 12-2 D 7-9.45. Set L £12.50/£16.50 Set D £25.

Nantwich   Places of Interest

Crewe Tourist Information Centre   Tel 0270 583191
Lyceum Theatre   Heath Street, Crewe Tel 0270 211149.

Neasham   Newbus Arms   £60

Tel 0325 721071 Fax 0325 721770	H

Neasham Road Neasham Darlington Co Durham DL2 1PE — Map 5 E3

New owners here just as we went to press, hence the absence of grading for this creeper-clad establishment dating from the 1780s. **Rooms** 15. Garden, squash. AMERICAN EXPRESS Access, Diners, Visa.

Needham Market   Pipps Ford   60%   £55

Tel 0449 760208 Fax 0449 760561	H

Needham Market nr Ipswich Suffolk IP6 8LJ — Map 10 C3

Raewyn Hackett-Jones welcomes guests personally to her 16th-century farmhouse in a delightful garden just off the A45/A140 roundabout. Winter log fires burn in huge inglenooks, and a fine breakfast featuring home-produced honey, eggs and bread is served in the plant-filled conservatory. Bedrooms, all named after flowers, are split between the house and adjacent Stables Cottage, up a steep spiral staircase. In the main house, Sweet Pea and Forget-Me-Not share a shower room. Hollyhock has a four-poster. No phones or TV in the bedrooms. No children under 5. No dogs. No smoking. **Rooms** 6. Garden, outdoor swimming pool, tennis, coarse fishing. Closed mid Dec-mid Jan. No credit cards.

Nether Langwith   Goff's Restaurant   £60

Tel 0623 744538	RR

Langwith Mill House Nether Langwith nr Mansfield Nottinghamshire NG20 9JF — Map 7 D2

An old, dilapidated cotton mill forms a striking landmark alongside the A632 about a mile east of the village. Five years ago the Goffs converted the adjacent Mill House into a charming homely restaurant with rooms. The front entrance is actually at the back (when approached from the road) and on the ground floor there's a simple, cosy lounge and two pretty, candlelit dining rooms – one spacious, the other intimate. On offer is an imaginative menu that changes monthly, supplemented by a short selection of daily specials. Fish is delivered from Abergavenny on Tuesdays and features the likes of sea and freshwater bream with sautéed onions and potatoes in a chive butter sauce, and grilled tuna on sautéed spinach with herb butter. Other dishes range from egg, bacon and tomato soup and pan-fried calf's liver with a rich currant sauce to loin of pork stuffed with pesto and accompanied by a Madeira sauce with tomato and basil or breast of duck with wild mushroom ragout. Desserts include such popular standards as sticky toffee pudding. **Seats** 45. Parties 12. Private Room 28. L 12-2.30 D 7-9.30. Closed L Sat, D Sun, all Mon, Tue after Bank Holidays, 1 week Sep, 1 week Mar. AMERICAN EXPRESS Access, Diners, Visa.

Rooms   £50

The two bedrooms are spacious and comfortable. Storage heaters provide ample heat on chilly nights and remote control TV, books, magazines and fresh fruit are among the homely extras.

New Alresford   Hunters   £55

Tel 0962 732468   **RR**

32 Broad Street New Alresford Hampshire SO24 9AQ   Map 15 D3

Wine bar/brasserie with two distinctive bow-fronted windows, awnings and candle-light within, run by the Birmingham family. Morning coffee is served from 11, followed an hour later by the luncheon menu of starters, light snacks and main courses. Ramekin of hot smoked haddock with cheese and chives, chicken liver parfait, sausages and mash, grilled sea bream beurre blanc and confit of duck leg with tarragon and cream sauce show the style. Sunday lunch in winter is a simpler affair. In the evenings there are table d'hote (not Sat) and à la carte menus whose offerings range from tuna salad with quail's eggs and gazpacho purée and duck terrine with red onion confit to steamed halibut with delmonico potatoes and a celery and sun-dried tomato sauce, and noisettes of lamb with a roasted red pepper and thyme sauce (the chef specialises in sauces). Lemon crème brulée and baked banana in filo pastry are typical desserts. The Garden Room is a popular venue for parties, accommodating up to 80 guests. *Seats 30. Parties 12. Private Room 80. L 12-2 D 7-10. Closed Sun except lunch in winter, six days at Christmas. Set D £11.95/£13.95.* AMERICAN EXPRESS *Access, Diners, Visa.*

Rooms   £48

The three bedrooms, all with shower and WC en suite, are in an old Georgian building.

New Barnet   Mims   ↑   £75

Tel 081-449 2974   **R**

63 East Barnet Road New Barnet Hertfordshire EN4 8RN   Map 15 F2

The surprises here are on the plate rather than in the unprepossessing surroundings. In a parade of shops right next to a petrol station partners Mostafa Abouzahrah and Ali Al-Sercy, the chef, have created a verdant jewel of a restaurant. In a more fashionable location it would doubtless receive more attention and approbation. Decor inside is simple – striking green walls with alabaster wall lights, rattan and polished pine chairs and a split-level wood-block floor. Menus change daily, fixed-price for lunch, and à la carte for dinner. Dishes are imaginative and can be artistically presented as in roast duck with mashed roast parsnips which arrives with a tall central tower of deep-fried parsnip slivers, the crisp duck and vegetables arranged around the plate; or sea-fresh sea bass very lightly baked, retaining all its softness and succulence, served skin-side up on a bed of soft artichoke noodles and topped with alternate layers of fried celeriac crisps and deep-fried baby cabbage leaves. Flavours are wonderfully distinct and unsullied by over-elaboration, sauces are delicate jus. Charming and attentive service. No children under 6 after 7pm. Special parking arrangements behind the garage next door during the evenings and all day Sunday. *Seats 40. Parties 8. L 12-2.30 D 6.30-11 Sun meals 12-10.30. Closed L Sat, all Mon, 1 week Sept & 25-30 Dec. Set L £9.50/£14. Access, Visa.*

New Milton   Chewton Glen   89%   £207

Tel 0425 275341   Fax 0425 272310   **HR**

Christchurch Road New Milton Hampshire BH25 6QS   Map 14 C4

Half way between Bournemouth and Lymington, Martin and Brigitte Skan's magnificent 'hotel, health and country club' justly enjoys a worldwide reputation not only for what it offers today, but for consistently maintaining the highest standards since 1966. Great hotels rely on the quality of their staff and here they are unquestionably professional, courteous and efficient, superbly directed by the Skans and their new managing director Peter Crome (previously General Manager at the *St Andrews Old Course Hotel* in Scotland and Manager of *The Savoy* in London before that). Set in 70 acres of grounds, including a superlative croquet lawn, the hotel has evolved over the years into one of the country's finest, pioneering styles and setting standards that others have followed; the most recent example is the stunningly-designed leisure and health club whose centrepiece swimming pool of magnificent proportions epitomises the quality to be found throughout. It is hard to imagine that the leisure facilities here can be bettered anywhere else in the UK; hotel guests share the facilities with non-resident club members. The newest garden bedrooms with balconies and terraces are equally luxurious, complementing those that guests have relaxed in for many years, with high-quality fabrics, beautiful colour schemes, period furniture and bathrooms, complete with fresh flowers, that positively pamper; it goes without saying that fruit, sherry, mineral water, home-made biscuits and 24hr room service are all provided. Such elegance is also apparent in the public areas where the tastefully decorated rooms with their exquisite antiques, fine paintings and memorabilia still provide the atmosphere of a large, modern private house. No children under seven; child-sitting by arrangement; families can eat informally in the balcony lounge of the health club or formally (at a price – hamburger, chips and peas £16!) in the restaurant between 6 and 7. Breakfast, as befits an establishment of this calibre, is fit for a king, ranging from freshly-baked pastries to stewed prunes, kedgeree and kippers. No dogs. Elegant conference/banqueting facilities for 110/120. Minimum two nights' weekend stay at certain times of year. ***Rooms*** *58. Garden, croquet, indoor & outdoor swimming pools, solarium, sauna, steam room, spa bath, beauty & hair salon, gym, golf (9), indoor & outdoor tennis, putting, snooker, valeting, boutique, helipad.* ~~AMERICAN EXPRESS~~ *Access, Diners, Visa.* MARTELL

Marryat Room Restaurant ★ £100

Chef Pierre Chevillard handles first-rate ingredients with admirable assurance and produces sauces with subtle flavours and perfect textures. Both lunch and dinner see fixed-price and à la carte menus offered, with lighter dishes tending to feature on the former; all menus are refreshingly written in unpretentious English. A three-course table d'hote in spring might offer smoked eel, smoked salmon and bacon salad with creamy horseradish dressing followed by breast of chicken on a bed of leeks with a cashew nut and truffle oil dressing, with caramelised lemon tart and poached cherries to finish; an alternative table d'hote incorporates fancier ingredients such as wild mushrooms, New Forest venison, turbot and lobster, but there are only alternatives at each stage on both menus. A la carte sees a varied choice, showing off Chevillard's prowess at combining complementary flavours; dishes might include cream of pheasant and chestnut soup, double-baked Emmental soufflé with fondue sauce, steamed, crab-filled Savoy cabbage with a 'nage' of local cockles among the starters; to follow, Dover sole, Black Angus cote de boeuf with a rich marrowbone sauce or fillet of English lamb wrapped in crispy shredded potatoes and served with a tarragon jus. Terrine of duck foie gras flavoured with green walnut wine and fillet of turbot served on a tapénade crouton are considered speciality dishes. Interesting vegetarian options; both English and French cheeses. Sunday lunch sees a diverse choice that includes roast sirloin of Scottish beef with Yorkshire pudding. Desserts are tempting to the point of indulgence: hot coffee soufflé with home-made mocha ice cream, sweet spiced savarin with poached peaches and pears, Valrhona chocolate tart served warm with a pistachio sauce. Lovely petits fours served with various styles of coffee show that attention is really paid to detail; throughout the meal one feels that the kitchen's intentions are consummated. Summer eating here is delightful, both on an outdoor terrace area where tables are laid out overlooking the gardens (and swimming pool) and in the delightful conservatory dining room. Great care has gone into the compilation of the very comprehensive wine list that not only features the best French growers and vintages, but also takes the rest of the world's wine-producing countries seriously. Marvellous New World selection; prices fair(ish!). The restaurant is now all no-smoking. No children under 7. **Seats** 120. Parties 8. L 12.30-2 D 7.30-9.30. Set L £17.50/£22.50 (Sun £25) Set D £25 & £39.

Newark	**Forte Travelodge**	**£45**
Tel 0636 703635		**L**
North Muskham Newark Nottinghamshire NG23 6HT		Map 7 D3

Situated on the A1 southbound. Three miles north of Newark-on-Trent. **Rooms** 30. AMERICAN EXPRESS Access, Diners, Visa.

Newark	**Gannets Café-Bistrot**	**£40**
Tel 0636 702066		**R**
35 Castlegate Newark Nottinghamshire NG24 1AZ		Map 7 D3

David and Hilary Bower have been running Gannets very successfully since 1979 and have built up a strong local following. The bistrot is on the first floor (with a separate side entrance) while the café occupies the ground floor, and during 1994 was undergoing expansion. There are separate kitchens for each operation as well as separate menus both devised and overseen (and often cooked) by Hilary, and in the bistrot you might find dishes such as salad of fillet of pork beef with ginger, potted crab with cream and brandy, baked fillet of cod with a red pesto crust, breast of chicken with linguini and a coriander and cumin sauce, summer pudding with cream, banoffi pie and Colston Bassett Stilton with wheat wafers. Concise, international, reasonably-priced wine list. No smoking. **Seats** 40 (café 36). L 12-2 D 6.30-9.30 (café 10am-4.30pm). Closed all Sun, Mon & Tue (not café), 1 week Christmas (café 25 & 26 Dec). Access, Visa.

NEW CHEF

Newark	**Grange Hotel**	**58%**	**£53**
Tel 0636 703399 Fax 0636 702328			**H**
73 London Road Newark Nottinghamshire NG24 1RZ			Map 7 D3

An unassuming, family-run Victorian hotel on the edge of town. Accommodation runs from singles to family rooms and a four-poster room. Free parking at the back of the hotel. No dogs. **Rooms** 15. Garden. Closed 24 Dec-3 Jan. Access, Visa.

Newbury	**Chequers Hotel**	**66%**	**£92**
Tel 0635 38000 Fax 0635 37170			**H**
Oxford Street Newbury Berkshire RG13 1JB			Map 15 D2

A handsome Georgian facade conceals an even older town-centre coaching inn. Good standards of comfort and modern amenities. Forte Heritage. **Rooms** 56. Garden. AMERICAN EXPRESS Access, Diners, Visa.

Newbury	**Donnington Valley Hotel**	**74%**	**£95**
Tel 0635 551199 Fax 0635 551123			**H**
Old Oxford Road Donnington nr Newbury Berkshire RG16 9AG			Map 15 D2

Alongside its own golf course this very modern, privately-owned hotel conceals a surprisingly stylish interior behind a rather less remarkable redbrick exterior. Beneath a vast, steeply-pitched timber ceiling the main, split-level public areas boast a real log fire, Oriental carpets over parquet floor and numerous comfortable sofas and armchairs with intriguing antique knick-knacks dotted about. The effect created is one of Edwardian elegance (though with modern comfort as the whole hotel is air-conditioned), a theme that extends to the bedrooms, many of which have period-style inlaid furniture and hand-painted tiles in the good bathrooms. There is a turn-down service in the evenings and extensive 24hr room service. Children up to 12 stay free in parents' room. Some rooms are equipped for disabled guests. Purpose-built conference facilities cater for up to 200 delegates. **Rooms** 58. *Garden, golf (18), putting, fishing, shooting.* AMERICAN EXPRESS *Access, Diners, Visa.*

Newbury   Foley Lodge   71%   £115

Tel 0635 528770   Fax 0635 528398   **H**

Stockcross Newbury Berkshire RG16 8JU   **Map 15 D2**

Just over a mile from Newbury, off the A4 to Hungerford (take M4 J13), this former Victorian hunting lodge is approached via a winding, tree-lined drive. The entrance is through a glass conservatory with black-and-white tiled floor and wicker chairs, overlooking the landscaped gardens. A "modern Victorian" ambience is cleverly created in both the public rooms and bedrooms by using fringed floral drapes and smart reproduction antiques. There is a high standard of accommodation throughout, with rooms in a new block being equally comfortable. Top of the range is the luxurious Sycamore Suite with a four-poster bed. A bright and airy octagonal pagoda is an unusual setting for the bubbling, circular swimming pool. Meeting rooms for up to 220 persons. Children up to the age of 12 free in parents' room, with meals charged as taken. **Rooms** 69. *Garden, croquet, indoor swimming pool.* AMERICAN EXPRESS *Access, Diners, Visa.*

Newbury   Hilton National   69%   £111

Tel 0635 529000   Fax 0635 529337   **H**

Pinchington Lane Newbury Berkshire RG14 7HL   **Map 15 D2**

Modern low-rise hotel one mile south of Newbury with a variety of conference rooms (catering for up to 100) and a leisure complex. Best of the bedrooms are the Plaza rooms, with bigger beds and more accessories than the others; non-smoking rooms available. Children up to 12 stay free in parents' room. **Rooms** 109. *Indoor swimming pool, keep-fit facilities, sauna, steam room.* AMERICAN EXPRESS *Access, Diners, Visa.*

Newbury   Millwaters   67%   £75

Tel 0635 528838   Fax 0635 523406   **H**

London Road Newbury Berkshire RG13 4UT   **Map 15 D2**

Eight charming acres of gardens surround Millwaters, the specific waters being those of the rivers Kennet and Lambourn which meander through the gardens. Conference and banqueting (for up to 50) are the mainstays, in addition to fishing. Bedrooms and dayrooms are all comfortably furnished. Tariff reductions at weekends (when weddings are popular). **Rooms** 30. *Garden, croquet, fishing.* AMERICAN EXPRESS *Access, Diners, Visa.*

If we recommend meals in a hotel or inn a separate entry is made for its restaurant.

Newbury   Regency Park Hotel   70%   £103

Tel 0635 871555   Fax 0635 871571   **H**

Bowling Green Road Thatcham Newbury Berkshire RG13 3RP   **Map 15 D2**

Five minutes from Newbury (signposted off the A4 Reading road), and standing in 5 acres of grounds, the original Edwardian house is now rather lost within more modern extensions. Spacious bedrooms offer guests comfortable, carefully planned accommodation in rooms that are light and well appointed. Picture windows in the sun lounge overlook the patio and an ornamental fountain. There's a staffed business centre in the hotel grounds which can cater for up to 170 delegates. Keen, helpful management and a variety of special weekend themes and special rates throughout the year. **Rooms** 50. *Garden, news kiosk.* AMERICAN EXPRESS *Access, Diners, Visa.*

Newbury — Stakis Newbury Hotel — 67% — £108

Tel 0635 247010 Fax 0635 247077 — **H**

Oxford Road Newbury Berkshire RG16 8XY — **Map 15 D2**

Just off Junction 13 of the M4, the Stakis Newbury is well designed for business people. Bedrooms feature good desk/work space, and there are four conference/seminar rooms with up-to-date equipment catering for up to 60. **Rooms 112.** *Indoor swimming pool, gymnasium, sauna, spa bath, steam room, solarium.* AMERICAN EXPRESS *Access, Diners, Visa.*

Newbury — Places of Interest

Tourist Information The Wharf Tel 0635 30267.
Watermill Theatre Bagnor Tel 0635 45834.
Westridge Open Centre Tel 0635 253322.
Highclere Castle Tel 0635 253210 *Home of the Earl and Countess of Carnarvon.*
Sandham Memorial Chapel (NT) Burghclere, Nr Newbury Tel 0635 27 394/292.
Newbury Racecourse Tel 0635 40015.
Chieveley Showground Tel 0635 247111.

Newby Bridge — The Swan — 61% — £88

Tel 053 95 31681 Fax 053 95 31917 — **H**

Newby Bridge nr Ulverston Cumbria LA12 8NB — **Map 4 C4**

Attractively situated opposite the five-arched stone bridge over the River Leven by Windermere's southern shore, the Swan is a comfortable family hotel and fisherman's haunt, popular also for themed weekend breaks. In addition to one suite and four de luxe bedrooms with balconies and a river view, there are five spacious family rooms (children £18 per night) and bright, neatly-kept bathrooms throughout. Facilities for conferences of up to 65 delegates; ample parking. No dogs. **Rooms 36.** *Garden, croquet, coarse fishing, mooring, helipad, coffee shop (12-2.45, 3.30-5.30, 6.45-9.45).* AMERICAN EXPRESS *Access, Diners, Visa.*

Newby Wiske — Solberge Hall — 69% — £60

Tel 0609 779191 Fax 0609 780472 — **H**

Newby Wiske nr Northallerton North Yorkshire DL7 9ER — **Map 5 E4**

Leisure and business visitors are both well looked after at the Hall, a country mansion dating from 1824 and set in 16 acres of gardens and woodland. The views are impressive and inside there's a delightful wood-panelled foyer with a blue-and-white-tiled fireplace, a homely lounge and a comfortable bar. Bedrooms are good-sized, some having four-posters, with plenty of thoughtful extras. Children under 14 stay free in parents' room. **Rooms 25.** *Garden, clay-pigeon shooting, snooker.* AMERICAN EXPRESS *Access, Diners, Visa.*

Newby Wiske — Place of Interest

Thirsk Racecourse Tel 0845 522276.

Newcastle-under-Lyme — Clayton Lodge — 60% — £91

Tel 0782 613093 Fax 0782 711896 — **H**

Clayton Road Newcastle-under-Lyme Staffordshire ST5 4AF — **Map 6 B3**

On the A519, a mile from the M6 (J15) this Jarvis-owned conference and meeting hotel has views over the Lyme Valley. The largest of the several conference rooms can accommodate 270. Well-equipped bedrooms, where children up to 16 stay free with parents. The club bar has been refurbished in the style of a gentleman's club. **Rooms 49.** AMERICAN EXPRESS *Access, Diners, Visa.*

Newcastle-under-Lyme   Forte Posthouse   60%   £68

Tel 0782 717171   Fax 0782 717138   **H**

Clayton Road Newcastle-under-Lyme Staffordshire ST5 4DL   Map 6 B3

100 yards from Junction 15 of the M6, this Posthouse provides decent modern accommodation for all the family, keep-fit amenities and conference facilities for up to 120. Children up to 16 stay free in parents' room. *Rooms 119. Indoor swimming pool, splash pool, gym, sauna, solarium, sun beds, children's playroom (weekends), playground, helipad.* **AMERICAN EXPRESS** *Access, Diners, Visa.*

Our inspectors are full-time employees; they are professionally trained by us.

Newcastle-under-Lyme   Places of Interest

Tourist Information Tel 0782 711964.
New Victoria Theatre Tel 0782 717954.

Newcastle-upon-Tyne   The Blackgate Restaurant   £70

Tel 091-261 7356   **R**

Milburn House The Side Quayside Newcastle-upon-Tyne Tyne & Wear
NE1 3JE   Map 5 E2

One of Newcastle's oldest restaurants, with an unbroken history since 1905, the Blackgate is housed in the bottom of Milburn House, just off Dean Street. Chef Douglas Jordan enjoys the celebration of British cooking in deceptively simple dishes with a carefully constructed range and balance of flavours. A "Menu Select" at lunch and early evening produces skilfully cooked main dishes at bargain prices: roast cod fillet with potato and courgette purée and first-class marinated rib of beef, pan-fried and served with anchovy butter. À la carte are salmon and leek casserole, and pot-roast pigeon with epicurean sauce, medallion of salmon baked in lime and pistachio crust, and pepped duck breast with mandarin and garlic marmalade. Fine British puddings such as apricot and sultana Bakewell and brown bread trifle, and good local cheeses from Dunsyre Blue to Haltwhistle. *Seats 43. Parties 12. Private Room 12. L 12-2 D 6.30-10. Closed L Sat, all Sun, D Mon, Bank Holidays, 24-29 Dec.* **AMERICAN EXPRESS** *Access, Diners, Visa.*

Newcastle-upon-Tyne   Copthorne Hotel   73%   £130

Tel 091 222 0333   Fax 091 230 1111   **H**

The Close Quayside Newcastle-upon-Tyne Tyne & Wear NE1 3RT   Map 5 E2

To the west of the Tyne Bridge and built straight alongside the Tyne, the hotel makes the most of its riverside location. All the bedrooms are at the front, some with balconies. Stylishly modern in design with an impressive marble-floored five-floor atrium at its heart, space and high standards of comfort are its hallmarks. Here, in what is also a lounge, there are tan leather seats and burr-walnut tables while in Claspers Bar, named after the rower, the ambience is a little more clubby. Classic bedrooms are well-equipped but Connoisseur bedrooms have the edge on comfort with king-size beds, bathrobes and more in the way of little extras. All rooms are fully air-conditioned and have satellite TVs though the movies are not free. Excellent power showers in the bathrooms. Free overnight parking in the multi-storey car park which occupies the rear of the hotel. Executive conference and banqueting facilities (150/200), a business centre and *Waves the Club* fitness and leisure centre are further services offered. *Rooms 156. Gym, sauna, spa bath, steam room, solarium, news kiosk, shop.* **AMERICAN EXPRESS** *Access, Diners, Visa.*

Newcastle-upon-Tyne   County Thistle   68%   £104

Tel 091-232 2471   Fax 091-232 1285   **H**

Neville Street Newcastle-upon-Tyne Tyne & Wear NE99 1AH   Map 5 E2

A handsome Victorian building opposite Central station. Popular for conferences (up to 200). Choice of restaurants and bars. Decent bedrooms, studios being the best equipped. *Rooms 115.* AMERICAN EXPRESS *Access, Diners, Visa.*

Newcastle-upon-Tyne   Courtney's   £55

Tel 091-232 5537   **R**

5-7 The Side Quayside Newcastle-upon-Tyne Tyne & Wear NE1 3JE   Map 5 E2

Michael and Kerensa Carr's small split-level restaurant in what can be described as the city's gastronomic quarter is simple and without frills, but therein lies its success. No surplus of staff here, just a couple of well-mannered and keen enthusiasts assisting the owners (Michael does the cooking, which is precise and correct). A blackboard indicates the evening specials of the day and the lunchtime fixed-price menu in addition to the regular menu. There's a distinctive English slant to the cooking with a range of dishes from starters such as smoked chicken and Gruyère filo with a leek sauce or poached egg Benedict to main courses that include supreme of salmon with a saffron cream sauce or chopped lamb steak with a rosemary gravy. For dessert, try the floating islands with praline, an unusual and crunchy interpretation of a classic sweet or a strawberry syllabub. Vegetarians are well catered for. Inexpensive wines with a good house selection. *Seats 28. L 12-2 D 7-10.30. Closed L Sat, all Sun, Bank Hols, 2 weeks May. Set L £14.50.* AMERICAN EXPRESS *Access, Visa.*

Newcastle-upon-Tyne   Fisherman's Lodge   £85

Tel 091-281 3281   Fax 091-281 6410   **R**

7 Jesmond Dene Jesmond Newcastle-upon-Tyne
Tyne & Wear NE7 7BQ   Map 5 E2

In a deep wooded valley two miles from Newcastle city centre, Fisherman's Lodge has been among the best known of north-eastern restaurants for many years (it opened in 1979). Variety is allied to fine cooking throughout the various menus, which include one for vegetarians. 'Chef's classics' put the emphasis on seafood with dishes such as lobster with garlic butter, surf and turf, and grilled salmon with scallops, asparagus tips and a sorrel sauce. Specialities, which change daily, increase the choice, and desserts include home-made ice creams. Short, lunchtime snack menu of starter-size portions also offered. No children under 10 after 8pm. No smoking in the dining room (it's permitted with coffee in the lounge). Patio/garden seating for 30 in good weather. *Seats 65. Parties 14. Private Room 40. L 12-2 D 7-11. Closed L Sat, all Sun, Bank Holidays. Set L £17 Set D £25.* AMERICAN EXPRESS *Access, Diners, Visa.*

If we recommend meals in a hotel or inn a separate entry is made for its restaurant.

Newcastle-upon-Tyne   Forte Crest   61%   £95

Tel 091-236 5432   Fax 091-236 8091   **H**

New Bridge Street Newcastle-upon-Tyne Tyne & Wear NE1 8BS   Map 5 E2

City-centre hotel with a business centre and many meeting/conference rooms (for up to 550). Computer link-up and satellite TV in all rooms. Free overnight (only) parking in the adjacent council car park. *Rooms 166.* AMERICAN EXPRESS *Access, Diners, Visa.*

Newcastle-upon-Tyne King Neptune £45

Tel 091-261 6657 R

34 Stowell Street Newcastle-upon-Tyne Tyne & Wear NE1 4XB Map 5 E2

The Mak brothers are first-generation Geordie Chinese and take great pride in their Peking and Szechuan cooking. Seafood is a particularly strong point, with a dozen prawn dishes, scallops, oysters, squid, crab and fish fillets. The King Neptune banquets, rising in complexity from "Jade" through "Pearl" to "Diamond", encompass sizzling steak in black pepper Peking sauce, baked lobster with Szechuan sea-spiced chili (a speciality) and deep-fried duck slices with champagne hot and sour sauce. Booking is usually essential, even on Sundays. The restaurant is in the heart of Newcastle's Chinatown. *Seats 120. Private Room 65. L 12-1.45 D 6.30-10.45 (Sat 6-11.30). Closed 25 Dec, 1 Jan. Set L from £6.50 Set D from £14.80.* AMERICAN EXPRESS *Access, Diners, Visa.*

Newcastle-upon-Tyne Moat House 59% £68

Tel 091-262 8989 Fax 091-263 4172 H

Coast Road Wallsend Newcastle-upon-Tyne Tyne & Wear NE28 9HP Map 5 E2

Modern low-riser set in its own grounds on the Silverlink Business Park, by the A19 just north of the Tyne Tunnel. Plenty of free car parking, numerous large conference rooms (up to 400 delegates) and a health complex. Good tariff reductions at weekends; children under 14 stay free in parents' room. *Rooms 147. Keep-fit equipment, spa bath, sauna, plunge pool, steam room, solarium, games room.* AMERICAN EXPRESS *Access, Diners, Visa.*

Newcastle-upon-Tyne Novotel 63% £65

Tel 091-214 0303 Fax 091-214 0633 H

Ponteland Road Kenton Newcastle-upon-Tyne Tyne & Wear NE3 3HZ Map 5 E2

Very modern Novotel just off the A1 on the western by-pass. Spacious bedrooms, air conditioning, facilities for disabled guests. Conferences for up to 250. Children up to 15 stay free in parents' room. Ample free car parking. *Rooms 126. Indoor swimming pool, gym, sauna, restaurant (6am-midnight).* AMERICAN EXPRESS *Access, Diners, Visa.*

Newcastle-upon-Tyne Swallow Hotel 63% £90

Tel 091-232 5025 Fax 091-232 8428 H

Newgate Arcade Newcastle-upon-Tyne Tyne & Wear NE1 5SX Map 5 E2

A modern hotel in the city centre, with assets that include an ample free car park, conference facilities and a sixth-floor cocktail bar affording panoramic views. Children up to 14 stay free in parents' room. *Rooms 93.* AMERICAN EXPRESS *Access, Diners, Visa.*

Newcastle-upon-Tyne Swallow Gosforth Park 73% £120

Tel 091-236 4111 Fax 091-236 8192 H

High Gosforth Park Newcastle-upon-Tyne Tyne & Wear NE3 5HN Map 5 E2

A splendid modern hotel in 12 acres of wooded parkland next to Newcastle racecourse and just off the A1. Neat, well-tended grounds form a good first impression. Stylish day rooms include an elegant foyer/lounge and two bars, and there are good conference (up to 600 delegates) and leisure facilities. Accommodation includes luxury suites, studios and spacious Executive rooms. The standard bedrooms are not large, but nevertheless attractive with modern lightwood furniture and an armchair, their bathrooms tidy and well equipped. 100 rooms are designated non-smoking. Free parking for 300 cars. *Rooms 178. Garden, indoor swimming pool, gym, squash, sauna, spa bath, solarium, hairdressing, tennis, helipad, courtesy car.* AMERICAN EXPRESS *Access, Diners, Visa.*

Newcastle-upon-Tyne   21 Queen Street   ★ ↑   £95

Tel 091-222 0755   Fax 091-230 5875   **R**

21 Queen St Princes Wharf Quayside Newcastle-upon-Tyne Tyne &
Wear NE1 3UG   Map 5 E2

Terence Laybourne is owner and chef at this smart, sophisticated restaurant,
which stands light and pastel-elegant behind a sombre Victorian front not
far from the waterside to the east of the Tyne bridges. There's
a comfortable bar in which to contemplate the menu over an aperitif, front
of house being very well orchestrated by young manager Nicholas Shottel
(the recommended house aperitif is a glass of Charles de Fere Tradition
with peach liqueur). The kitchen's style is based on classical French training,
but the menus extend far beyond France to incorporate ideas from the near
and far East. This is very intelligent cooking, with the happiest marriage
of flavours and textures, and a degree of innovation that shows confidence,
even exuberance, but never anything but the firmest of grasps on what will
and will not work. Some of the very best dishes are relatively simple –
broad bean and Parmesan salad with country ham, sauté of salmon and
asparagus with chervil butter, roast lamb with mustard, herbs and
Lyonnaise potatoes – while others are more elaborate, including medallions
of Kielder venison with a compote of lentils and spices, assiette of duck
cooked five ways, or a classic tournedos Rossini. Terrine of ham knuckle
and foie gras served with pease pudding is a splendid example of European
community spirit! Desserts maintain the high quality of earlier courses,
shown by pear and almond soufflé, a chocolate extravaganza or a warm
'minestrone' of red fruits with mascarpone sorbet, black pepper and basil.
Lunchtime also sees a two- or three-course fixed-price menu that is simpler
but every bit as appealing. There are more than 20 wines under £20 in the
house selection – the rest of the list is also keenly priced. **Seats** 50. L 12-2
D 7-10.45. Closed L Sat, all Sun, Bank Holidays, 2 weeks Aug.
Set L £15/£17. AMERICAN EXPRESS Access, Diners, Visa.

Newcastle-upon-Tyne   Places of Interest

Tourist Information   Tel 091-261 0691.
Gulbenkian Studio Theatre   Tel 091-232 9974.
Theatre Royal   Tel 091-232 2061.
Tyne Theatre   Tel 091-232 1551.
Seaton Delaval Hall and Gardens   Whitley Bay Tel 091-237 3040/1493.
Newcastle Cathedral   Tel 091-232 1939.
Newcastle United Football Ground   St. James' Park Tel 091-232 8361.
Newcastle Racecourse   Tel 091-236 2020.
Whitley Bay Ice Rink   Tel 091-252 6240.
Cullercoats Beach   7 Miles.
   Museums and Art Galleries
Trinity Maritime Centre   Tel 091-261 4691.
Laing Art Gallery   Tel 091-232 7734.
Hancock Museum   Tel 091-222 7418.
Hunday National Tractor and Farm Museum   Newton Tel 0661 842553.
Cherryburn, Berwick Museum   Mickley, Nr Stocksfield Tel 0661
   843276 Thomas Berwick Birthplace Trust.

Newcastle-upon-Tyne Airport   Moat House   62%   £105

Tel 0661 824911   Fax 0661 860157   **H**

Woolsington Newcastle-upon-Tyne Tyne & Wear NE13 8DJ   Map 5 E2

Low-rise modern redbrick hotel just north of the Tyne Tunnel.
Conference/banqueting facilities for 400/350. Children up to the age of 12
are accommodated free in parents' room. 22 rooms are reserved for non-
smokers, all are sound-proofed. Free parking throughout your holiday
if you stay the night here before flying off from the airport – courtesy
transport to the terminal is provided. **Rooms** 100. AMERICAN EXPRESS Access,
Diners, Visa.

Newlyn   Higher Faugan Country House Hotel   62%   £84

Tel 0736 62076   Fax 0736 51648   **H**

Newlyn nr Penzance Cornwall TR18 5NS   Map 12 A4

Built by Stanhope Forbes at the turn of the century, this sturdy greystone house stands at the end of a winding drive in 10 acres of lawns and woodland. Day rooms are peaceful and traditional, and the best bedrooms feature Victorian or Edwardian furnishings; rooms with superior views attract a small supplement. Children under 12 sharing parents' room stay free. ***Rooms** 11. Garden, outdoor swimming pool, tennis, keep-fit equipment, putting, solarium, snooker, games room.* AMERICAN EXPRESS *Access, Diners, Visa.*

Newmarket   Heath Court Hotel   62%   £70

Tel 0638 667171   Fax 0638 666533   **H**

Moulton Road Newmarket Suffolk CB8 8DY   Map 10 B3

Modern hotel (formerly a Moat House) behind the town clock tower, with well-appointed bedrooms, a lounge with board games and magazines and versatile function rooms (up to 120 for conferences). Children up to 14 stay free in parents' room. ***Rooms** 47.* AMERICAN EXPRESS *Access, Diners, Visa.*

Newmarket   White Hart   60%   £49

Tel 0638 663051   Fax 0638 667284   **H**

High Street Newmarket Suffolk CB8 8JP   Map 10 B3

A redbrick hotel in the High Street opposite the Jockey Club. The lounge bar, with its cane furniture, mirrors, plants and muted lights, complements the robust public bar, which has stained-glass panels, deep sofas, a panelled serving area and racing pictures. Comfortable bedrooms have either an art deco or a country look. Conferences for up to 120 delegates. ***Rooms** 23.* AMERICAN EXPRESS *Access, Visa.*

Newmarket   Places of Interest

The National Horseracing Museum   Tel 0638 667333.
Newmarket Racecourse   Tel 0638 663482.

Newport Pagnell   Forte Travelodge   £45

Tel 0908 610878   **L**

Welcome Break Newport Pagnell Buckinghamshire MK16 8DS   Map 15 E1

By the M1 service station, on the northbound carriageway between Junctions 14 and 15. Formerly the *Welcome Lodge. **Rooms** 92.* AMERICAN EXPRESS *Access, Diners, Visa.*

Newquay   Hotel Bristol   64%   £80

Tel 0637 875181   Fax 0637 879347   **H**

Narrowcliff Newquay Cornwall TR7 2PQ   Map 12 B3

The Young family, at the helm since the hotel opened in 1927, put courtesy and comfort high on their list of priorities. The redbrick Bristol enjoys a fine situation overlooking the sea and the beach (some distance below the cliff), and there are splendid views from many of the bedrooms; these come in various styles, some traditional, others more modern. There are also some self-catering holiday houses. Day rooms provide ample space to relax over a drink, a chat or one of the board games available from reception. Conferences (for up to 300 delegates) and banquets (up to 260) are catered for. Parking for 100 cars & 5 lock-up garages available behind the hotel. ***Rooms** 74. Indoor swimming pool, sauna, solarium, beauty & hair salon, games room.* AMERICAN EXPRESS *Access, Diners, Visa.*

Newquay   Hotel Riviera   63%   £84

Tel 0637 874251   Fax 0637 850823   **H**

Lusty Glaze Road Newquay Cornwall TR7 3AA   **Map 12 B3**

Popular for family holidays, functions and conferences (for around 150), this well-appointed modern hotel overlooks a lovely stretch of coastline. Three bars, a lounge and a garden provide plenty of space to relax, and in summer there's evening entertainment. Most of the bedrooms enjoy sea views. Free parking for 60 cars. *Rooms 50. Garden, outdoor swimming pool, squash, sauna, games room, snooker, children's playroom and play area.* AMERICAN EXPRESS *Access, Diners, Visa.*

Newquay   Place of Interest

Trerice (NT)   Tel 0637 875404.

Newton Abbot   Passage House   65%   £75

Tel 0626 55515   Fax 0626 63336   **H**

Hackney Lane Kingsteignton Newton Abbot Devon TQ12 3QH   **Map 13 D3**

Follow the racecourse signs from the A380 to find this modern hotel, which enjoys fine views along the Teign estuary. Contemporary decor, spacious bedrooms, friendly staff and purpose-built spa and conference facilities. Some self-catering apartments have recently come on stream. *Rooms 38. Garden, indoor swimming pool, keep-fit equipment, sauna, spa bath, steam room, solarium, coarse fishing.* AMERICAN EXPRESS *Access, Diners, Visa.*

Newton Abbot   Places of Interest

Ugbrooke House   Chudleigh Tel 0626 852179.
Outdoor Seasonal Pool   Tel 0626 61101.
Newton Abbot Racecourse   Tel 0626 53235.
Shaldon Wildlife Trust   Shaldon Tel 0626 872234 *7 miles.*
Teignmouth and Meadfoot Beaches.

Newton Solney   Newton Park   67%   £111

Tel 0283 703568   Fax 0283 703214   **H**

Newton Solney Burton-on-Trent Derbyshire DE15 0SS   **Map 6 C3**

Three miles from the centre of Burton-on-Trent, the 17th-century, creeper-clad Newton Park enjoys a peaceful setting in landscaped grounds overlooking the river. Conference facilities for up to 120 delegates, some family rooms. Jarvis Hotels. *Rooms 50. Garden. Closed Christmas.* AMERICAN EXPRESS *Access, Diners, Visa.*

Nidd   Nidd Hall   76%   £120

Tel 0423 771598   Fax 0423 770931   **H**

Nidd nr Harrogate North Yorkshire HG3 3BN   **Map 6 C1**

Follow the signs to Nidd on the B6165 a few miles north of Harrogate off the A61. A long tree-lined drive leads up to this stately mansion set in 45 acres of parkland which includes a splendid three-acre lake used for fishing and boating. The entrance hall, surmounted by a glass cupola, is impressive with its white marble floor and very summery yellow ragged walls hung with copies of old masters. Public rooms are very spacious and comfortable with ample seating. The decor is of a reasonably high standard, the style reminiscent of a lived-in country house. Best of the bedrooms are in the main house, those at the front enjoying wonderful vistas, through the trees and over the seemingly uninhabited surrounding countryside. The quite separate courtyard rooms were converted a few years ago from stables and are pleasant enough but not quite as appealing as the 38 in the hall. All are attractively furnished in a traditional style with a plethora of colourful fabrics and mahogany furniture, and all are well equipped. Breakfasts are of average quality with a hot and cold buffet though special requests are eagerly complied with. *Rooms 59. Garden, croquet, indoor swimming pool, gym, sauna, sun beds, beauty salon, squash, tennis, snooker, table tennis, boating.* AMERICAN EXPRESS *Access, Diners, Visa.*

North Huish   **Brookdale House**   69%   NEW   £80

Tel 0548 821661 Fax 0548 821606	H
North Huish nr South Brent Devon TQ10 9NR	Map 13 D3

New owners Gill and Michael Mikkelsen are keen to please at their Tudor-Gothic style Victorian rectory set in $2\frac{1}{2}$ acres of gardens (which include a pretty waterfall), within the beautiful South Hams area. The main day room is a most civilised lounge, with real log fire when needed, where drinks are also served. Antique-furnished bedrooms vary somewhat in size; three are in an adjacent cottage, but all are equally appealing with decor featuring soft floral fabrics set off by plain walls. Fresh fruit, flowers and magazines add a homely touch and in the evening beds are turned down, curtains drawn and bedside lights turned on. Room service is offered throughout the day and evening and good cooked breakfasts make a good start to the day. *Rooms 8. Garden. Closed 2 weeks mid Jan.* AMERICAN EXPRESS *Access, Diners, Visa.*

Consult page 20 for a full list of starred restaurants

North Petherton   **Walnut Tree Inn**   65%   £68

Tel 0278 662255 Fax 0278 663946	H
Fore Street North Petherton nr Bridgwater Somerset TA6 6QA	Map 13 E2

A carefully modernised, 18th-century coaching inn on the A38 (one mile from J25 M5), with conference and function facilities. Business people will appreciate the good work space in both standard and larger Executive bedrooms, while more romantically-inclined weekenders may plump for one of the spacious four-poster suites. Friendly service from resident proprietors. Conference/banqueting facilities for 80/75. Weekend tariff reductions. *Rooms 28. Garden, solarium.* AMERICAN EXPRESS *Access, Diners, Visa.*

North Stifford   **Stifford Moat House**   61%   £83

Tel 0375 390909 Fax 0375 390426	H
High Road North Stifford nr Grays Essex RM16 1UE	Map 11 B4

On the A13 one mile east of the M25 (Junction 30/31), this is a well-equipped hotel catering for both business and leisure visitors (up to 530 delegates in 13 rooms, theatre-style). Originally a Georgian country house, it stands in $6\frac{1}{2}$ acres of well-maintained grounds. Children up to 16 stay free in parents' room. Rates much reduced since last year. *Rooms 96. Garden, tennis, pétanque. Closed 27-30 Dec.* AMERICAN EXPRESS *Access, Diners, Visa.*

North Stoke   **Springs Hotel**   70%   £110

Tel 0491 836687 Fax 0491 836877	H
Wallingford Road North Stoke Oxfordshire OX9 6BE	Map 15 D2

The thirty acres of grounds which surround the mock-Tudor building include a spring-fed lake from which it gets its name. Public areas include a panelled lounge of old-world appeal and a small cosy bar. Bedrooms generally are spacious and pleasantly appointed with quality fabrics, smart furniture and subtle colours: best are those with private balconies. 24hr room service. No dogs. The hotel stands halfway between the M4 (J8/9) and the M40 (J6) between Goring and Crowmarsh on the B4009. *Rooms 36. Garden, croquet, outdoor swimming pool, sauna, tennis.* AMERICAN EXPRESS *Access, Diners, Visa.*

Northampton   Courtyard by Marriott   65%   £63

Tel 0604 22777   Fax 0604 35454   **H**

Bedford Road Northampton Northamptonshire NN4 7YF   Map 15 D1

Five minutes from Junction 15 of the M1, just off the A45 alongside the A428, one mile from the town centre. Large bedrooms, competitively priced, with desks plus fax and data sockets. Children free in parents' room. Modern meeting rooms for up to 30. Plenty of free, secure parking. *Rooms 104. Keep-fit equipment, coffee shop (7am-10.15pm).* AMERICAN EXPRESS® *Access, Diners, Visa.*

Northampton   Forte Travelodge   £45

Tel 0604 758395   **L**

Upton Way Northampton Northamptonshire NN5 6EG   Map 15 D1

On the western outskirts of Northampton, on the ring road off the A45. Two miles from Junction 15A on the M1. *Rooms 40.* AMERICAN EXPRESS® *Access, Diners, Visa.*

Northampton   Moat House   63%   £107

Tel 0604 22441   Fax 0604 230614   **H**

Silver Street Northampton Northamptonshire NN1 2TA   Map 15 D1

A tall and distinctive blue and white building in the town centre. Numerous function and meeting rooms (the largest, the Buckingham Suite, can accomodate 600) make it a popular conference venue. Considerable tariff reductions at weekends. Children up to 11 stay free in parents' room. *Rooms 138. Sauna, spa bath, solarium, beauty salon, hairdressing.* AMERICAN EXPRESS® *Access, Diners, Visa.*

Northampton   Stakis Country Court   68%   £112

Tel 0604 700666   Fax 0604 702850   **H**

100 Watering Lane Collingtree Northampton Northamptonshire NN4 0XW   Map 15 D1

Just a few hundred yards from Junction 15 of the M1, this very modern business-oriented hotel is built around a central courtyard with a fountain. Large bedrooms, all with king-size beds, are bright and summery with floral fabrics; each has a spacious work desk in addition to the usual unit furniture. Expansion of the leisure facilities this year means the addition of a fully equipped gym and a dance studio. Midweek trade tends to be business oriented while the weekends are more family-minded. *Rooms 139. Garden, indoor swimming pool, gym, sauna, spa bath, solarium, beautician.* AMERICAN EXPRESS® *Access, Diners, Visa.*

Northampton   Swallow Hotel   72%   £99

Tel 0604 768700   Fax 0604 769011   **H**

Eagle Drive Northampton Northamptonshire NN4 0HN   Map 15 D1

Overlooking Delapre Lake and golf course, a low-rise, purpose-built hotel that combines a modern, redbrick exterior with a smart interior stylishly employing black leather, white marble and a distinct Japanese influence. Most of the seating areas are open-plan, but there's also a small lounge that serves mainly as a quiet reading or writing room. Bedrooms are equally modern and all offer a couple of smartly upholstered armchairs and all the usual modern extras. Half the bathrooms have bidets and all are provided with a selection of toiletries; two rooms are equipped for the disabled. Children up to 14 free if sharing parents' room; families can eat informally in one of the two restaurants. A new bar area, Italian restaurant and conservatory were being developed as we went to press. The small but sunny pool has tall windows overlooking a lake. A purpose-built residential management development centre is attached to the hotel; conference/

banqueting facilities for 220/200. Three miles from Junction 15 of the M1. *Rooms 120. Garden, indoor swimming pool, sauna, sun beds, spa bath, steam room, keep-fit equipment, coffee shop (10am-10.30pm), helipad.* AMERICAN EXPRESS *Access, Diners, Visa.*

Northampton	Travel Inn	£43
Tel 0604 832340 Fax 0604 831807		**L**
Harpole Turn Weedon Road Northampton Northamptonshire NN7 4DD		Map 15 D1

Meeting rooms available, 2 miles off Junction 16 of the M1. *Rooms 51.* AMERICAN EXPRESS *Access, Diners, Visa.*

Northampton	Westone Moat House	59%	£69
Tel 0604 406262 Fax 0604 415023			**H**
Ashley Way Weston Favell Northampton Northamptonshire NN3 3EA			Map 15 D1

Built in 1914, the Westone is a warm, honey-coloured stone mansion set in its own grounds off the A4500 to the east of town. Public rooms have some interesting architectural features and bedrooms are well equipped with modern comforts. Children up to 12 stay free in parents' room. Theatre-style conferences for up to 180. *Rooms 66. Garden, keep-fit equipment, sauna, solarium, putting. Closed Christmas/New Year.* AMERICAN EXPRESS *Access, Diners, Visa.*

Northampton   Places of Interest

Tourist Information   Tel 0604 22677.
Central Museum and Art Gallery   Guildhall Road Tel 0604 39415.
The Canal Museum   Stoke Bruerne, Nr Northampton Tel 0604 862229.
Wantage Road Cricket Ground   Tel 0604 32917.
Towcester Racecourse   Tel 0327 50969.
Skew Bridge Ski School   Rushden, Nr Wellingborough Tel 0933 59939/53808.
CLA Game Fair Showground   Castle Ashby Tel 071 235 0511.

Northleach	Old Woolhouse	★	£90
Tel 0451 860366			**R**
Market Place Northleach Gloucestershire GL54 3EE			Map 14 C2

Time has definitely not marched on here, and the restaurant is all the better for it. Why change a successful formula? A husband and wife team, Jacques Astic in the kitchen, Jenny at front of house; a lovely Cotswold-stone building, intimate within with a low ceiling and old timbers, an open fireplace, antiques, and tables set with gleaming silver and household china. The kitchen is domestic in size, indeed the entire restaurant is no larger than a country house dining room, but therein lies the charm of the place. The menu, usually read out at 8pm, changes daily depending on the freshest ingredients available; fish, for instance, relies on the catch delivered, producing, perhaps, a dish of turbot, mussels and scallops with a very spicy sauce. Jacques is not averse to cooking offal: calf's sweetbreads and kidneys in cassis are a house speciality. *Poulet au porto* is a favourite, as are desserts such as *tarte aux pruneaux* and almond meringue daquoise with an apricot sauce. First-class bread and coffee, plus super wines – ask, there are some real bargains to be had. *Seats 18. D only 8.15-9.30. Closed Sun & Mon (except by arrangement), 1 week Christmas. Set D £35. No credit cards.*

Northleach	Wickens		£55
Tel 0451 860421			**R**
Market Place Northleach Gloucestershire GL54 3EJ			Map 14 C2

Right in middle of one side of the Market Square of this quintessentially Cotswold village is Chris and Joanna Wicken's typically English restaurant. Menus change with the seasons, at least weekly, and each month they also carry a red and white wine selection. From the light luncheon menu you can put together as many – or as few courses as you like. Typical spring dinner offerings might be herring fillets marinaded with juniper berries and served on a bed of mixed leaves tossed in walnut oil dressing, then Cotswold lamb casseroled in a nut brown ale with apricots and root vegetables and topped with horseradish dumplings, with one of Joanna's luscious puddings to finish. There's usually a witty literary quote on the menu. Extensive range of English wines on the list. No smoking. *Seats 36. Parties 22. Private Room 20. L 12.15-1.30 (summer only) D 7.20-9. Closed Sun & Mon, Bank Holidays. Set D £19.50.* AMERICAN EXPRESS® *Access, Visa.*

Northleach   Place of Interest

Cotswold Countryside Collection Fossewa Tel 0451 60715.

Northwich   Friendly Floatel   56%   £73

Tel 0606 44443   Fax 0606 42596   **H**

London Road Northwich Cheshire CW9 5HD   Map 6 B2

A novel hotel that floats in the basin where the Rivers Dane and Weaver meet in the centre of town. Cabins (bedrooms) are not large but practical and ship-shape with good, well-lit workspace. All but the six Premier Plus rooms (two with four-posters) have shower and WC only; one room is equipped for disabled guests. Ask for a river view, there's no extra charge. Main day room is a pleasant panelled bar with rattan furniture. Landlubbers should note that although normally rock steady there can be some movement in rough weather. Although not advertised, room service is available 24hrs. Children under 12 share parents' room free. *Rooms 60. Keep-fit equipment, sauna, solarium.* AMERICAN EXPRESS® *Access, Diners, Visa.*

Northwich   Hartford Hall   63%   £73

Tel 0606 75711   Fax 0606 782285   **H**

School Lane Hartford Northwich Cheshire CW8 1PW   Map 6 B2

Mock-Victorian is the style of the day rooms at this 16th-century gabled house just off the A556 (M56 Junction 7, M6 Junction 19). Good desk space in the bedrooms, where children up to 7 can stay free in their parents' room. Two conference/banqueting rooms (max. capacity 100). *Rooms 20. Garden.* AMERICAN EXPRESS® *Access, Diners, Visa.*

Northwich   Place of Interest

Arley Hall and Gardens   Arley Tel 0565 777353.

Norton   Hundred House Hotel   £69

Tel 0952 71353   Fax 0952 71355   **IR**

Norton nr Shifnal Shropshire TF11 9EE   Map 6 B4

A creeper-covered, red-brick Georgian inn standing alongside the A442. Personally run by the Phillips family, it has great charm, with mellow brick walls, stained glass, colourful patchwork, leather upholstery and (hanging from the ceiling beams) dozens of bunches of dried flowers and herbs, all from Sylvia's splendid garden, which you are encouraged to visit. Enchanting antique-furnished bedrooms have lots of nice touches like patchwork bedcovers (often on antique brass beds), fresh flowers and pot pourri. All have good en-suite bathrooms and room service of drinks and light snacks is available throughout the day and evening. *Rooms 10. Garden.* AMERICAN EXPRESS® *Access, Diners, Visa.*

Restaurant   £65

There's a distinctly modern touch to the dishes on Stuart Phillips' sensibly short à la carte menu. Char-grilled vegetables marinated with coriander

and served with red onion crostini, terrine of cold rabbit with a creamy
sage sauce (their own herbs are well used and appear in the little posy
of flowers on each table), pan-fried fillet steak with balsamic sauce and
char-grilled leeks, and roast lamb steak with sun-dried tomatoes and braised
fennel show the style. Fish dishes, baked salmon with chive beurre blanc
for example, appear on the list of the day's specials. Notably good puds
range from tarte tatin and mango Pavlova with coconut ice cream and
tamarillo sauce to Bakewell tart and hot banana papillote and custard.
Seats 60. Parties 12. Private Room 30. L 12-2.30 D 6.15-10 (Sun 7-9).

Norwich	**Adlard's** ★	**£85**

Tel 0603 633522

79 Upper St Giles Street Norwich Norfolk NR2 1AB

R

Map 10 C1

A strong contender for the title of best restaurant in East Anglia, Adlard's
is a classic example of a restaurant run by a thoroughly dedicated chef-
patron and his wife – David and Mary Adlard. The decor is a sombre affair
but quite stylish with a dark green scheme, tables on various levels and oil
paintings adorning the walls. Crisp white linen tablecloths add a classic
touch and a cosy and welcoming air pervades the whole restaurant. David
Adlard's French-based cooking is highly capable, producing accomplished
dishes that make the most of seasonal produce; in fact, his professorial look
gives a clue to his passionate zeal in sourcing and synergising ingredients.
Lunchtime brings a two- or three-course fixed-price menu that offers
remarkable value for money with such dishes as a tart of softly boiled
quail's eggs with mushroom duxelles and a brunoise of smoked salmon,
roast wild pigeon with chutney and herb salad, or escalope of spring lamb
Burgundy-style with *pommes purées.* The evening choice is also four or five
dishes per course, with either individual prices per course or a set price for
three or four courses. Hot foie gras with a main dish of breast of duck and
leg confit with Puy lentils, sherry vinegar sauce and grapes could be your
starter, with braised vegetables and gratin dauphinois, or sea bass with
sorrel 'Troisgros' served with fennel and tagliatelle. Superb cheeses
or a salad, then perhaps dark and white chocolate mousse with citrus syrup,
or a tulip of armagnac and prune ice cream with hot spiced compote
of prunes. The wine list is unusual in as much as French wines are relegated
to the back. It's a super list, fairly-priced, with plenty of half-bottles and
a marvellous New World selection. David's meals are a total delight, from
canapés and home-baked rolls to the petits fours served with coffee, and
Mary does a great job at front of house. Regional winner, Dessert of the
Year 1995. *Seats 40. L 12.30-1.45 D 7.30-10.30. Closed L Sat, all Sun &
Mon, 25 Dec. Set L £10/£13 Set D £24.50/£29.* AMERICAN EXPRESS
Access, Visa. MARTELL

Norwich	**Brasted's**	**£60**

Tel 0603 625949

8-10 St Andrew's Hill Norwich Norfolk NR2 1DS

R

Map 10 C1

John Brasted's cosy little restaurant is now ten years old; tucked away
in the old part of the city, it's only a short walk from both the Cathedral
and the Castle. Candy-striped fabrics cover the ceiling and walls to create
an intimate effect (a refurbishment was imminent as we went to press).
Chef Adrian Clarke's carefully-planned menus offer English dishes "with
a French influence" and feature daily fresh fish dishes and beef stroganoff
as specialities. Thoughtful shopping and classic combinations might include
roast tomato soup finished with a basil purée, Spanish cured ham served
with celeriac salad or melon, lamb's kidneys in a sherry and mustard sauce
set on a creamed potato nest, breadcrumb-coated loin of pork served with
an apple sauce fortified with calvados and diced prunes, or skate wing with
black butter and capers. The thoughtful and fairly-priced wine list includes
a vintage chart and notes on the house selection. *Seats 22. Parties 16. L 12-2
D 7-10. Closed L Sat, all Sun, Bank Holidays & 24 Dec-2 Jan.
Set L £8.50/£12.50.* AMERICAN EXPRESS *Access, Diners, Visa.*

Norwich   Forte Posthouse   63%   £68

Tel 0603 56431   Fax 0603 506400   **H**

Ipswich Road Norwich Norfolk NR4 6EP   Map 10 C1

Modern building in secluded grounds just off the A140, to the south
of town. 44 non-smoking rooms. Under-16s share their parents' room free;
46 rooms have an extra bed. The largest of several conference rooms can
hold up to 100 delegates theatre-style. *Rooms 116. Garden, indoor swimming
pool, gym, sauna, spa bath, solarium, outdoor children's play area.*
AMERICAN EXPRESS *Access, Diners, Visa.*

Norwich   Forte Travelodge   NEW   £45

Tel 0603 57549   **L**

A11/A47 interchange Norwich southern bypass Norwich Norfolk   Map 10 C1

AMERICAN EXPRESS *Access, Diners, Visa.*

Norwich   Friendly Hotel   60%   £83

Tel 0603 741161   Fax 0603 741500   **H**

2 Barnard Road Bowthorpe Norwich Norfolk NR5 9JB   Map 10 C1

Modern, purpose-built, low-rise hotel 4 miles west of the city centre, on the
A1074, offering straightforward accommodation. Fully-equipped leisure
centre; conference and banqueting facilities for up to 200. Easy parking.
Rooms 80. Indoor swimming pool, gym, spa bath, sauna, steam room, solarium.
AMERICAN EXPRESS *Access, Diners, Visa.*

Norwich   Greens Seafood Restaurant   £60

Tel 0603 623733   Fax 0603 615268   **R**

82 Upper St Giles Street Norwich Norfolk NR2 1LT   Map 10 C1

Local supplies of fresh fish form the basis of the menu at Dennis
Crompton's popular restaurant with appropriate nautical decor. Avocado
and Cromer crab or a selection of shellfish could precede salmon, skate,
plaice, sea bass, cod or Dover sole, grilled, steamed or deep-fried and served
with herb butter, garlic butter or a sauce. Simple sweets; well-chosen,
fairly-priced wines. *Seats 48. L 12.15-2.15 D 7-10.45. Closed L Sat & Mon,
all Sun, Bank Holidays, 1 week Christmas. Set L £13 Set D from £21.*
Access, Visa.

We publish annually, so make sure you use the current edition.
It's worth it!

Norwich   Marco's   £80

Tel 0603 624044   **R**

17 Pottergate Norwich Norfolk NR2 1DS   Map 10 C1

Here since 1970, Marco Vessalio still greets diners from the door of his
kitchen, the master of all he surveys; his is quintessential provincial Italian
food, steadfastly untrendy, with wonderful ingredients unfailingly well
cooked. Rice terrine with sole fillet and pesto sauce, tagliolini with smoked
salmon or gnocchi with a wild mushroom sauce could be your starter,
followed perhaps by sea bass and endives, chicken saltimbocca alla romana
or beef fillet in a crusty potato base in Barbera wine sauce. Desserts include
a classic zabaglione and Italian style bread-and-butter pudding (*budino dolce
di pane*) served with a glass of Prosecco wine. Champagnes apart, it's an all-
Italian wine list (and why not?) with sensible tasting notes. No smoking
in the dining room, but you may indulge in the Marco Polo bar lounge.
*Seats 20. Parties 10. L 12.30-2 D 7-10. Closed Sun & Mon, Bank Holidays.
Set L £14.* AMERICAN EXPRESS *Access, Diners, Visa.*

Norwich	Hotel Nelson	65%	£83
Tel 0603 760260 Fax 0603 620008			**H**
Prince of Wales Road Norwich Norfolk NR1 1DX			**Map 10 C1**

Keep one eye open for the railway station, opposite which stands this modern red-brick hotel alongside the River Wensum. Picture windows in the spacious lounge overlook the water and one of the two bars displays memorabilia of Nelson's flagship *Victory*. Best bedrooms include a sitting area and some have private balconies. One twin-bedded room is adapted for the use of disabled guests, with its own car-parking space and entrance from the car park. The largest of five conference rooms can accommodate up to 90 delegates. A new leisure centre, with indoor pool, sauna, steam room, solarium and gym, opened in the summer of 1994. *Rooms 132. Garden.* AMERICAN EXPRESS *Access, Diners, Visa.*

Norwich	Hotel Norwich	62%	£70
Tel 0603 787260 Fax 0603 400466			**H**
121 Boundary Road Norwich Norfolk NR3 2BA			**Map 10 C1**

Modern, privately-run redbrick hotel on the outer ring road (A47) north-east of the city. Roomy, well-equipped bedrooms with ample writing surfaces, some undergoing refurbishment as we went to press. Popular for functions, with facilities for around 300 in 13 different rooms. Children under 16 stay free in parents' room. 24hr room service. Sister establishment to the *Hotel Nelson* (see entry). *Rooms 108. Indoor swimming pool, spa bath, sauna, solarium, keep-fit equipment, coffee shop (7am-10pm).* AMERICAN EXPRESS *Access, Diners, Visa.*

Norwich	Norwich Sport Village Hotel	63%	£69
Tel 0603 788898 Fax 0603 406845			**H**
Drayton High Road Hellesdon Norwich Norfolk NR6 5DU			**Map 10 C1**

Practical, roomy bedrooms are at the centre of a very extensive sports complex situated just off the outer Norwich ring road on the A1067 to Fakenham. All the rooms have en-suite facilities, half showers, half tubs. Children up to 16 share parents' room free. Sporting facilities are the most impressive feature, with over 60 sports and activities available. They include seven squash courts and no less than a dozen tennis courts, seven of them indoors. Hotel guests share the lively open-plan bar, bistro and restaurant with the other users of the complex. The Aquapark swimming complex includes a competition pool, a shallow, warm playpool with two slides and rapids and a paddling pool for toddlers. There's a soft play area for the very young. All the rooms are suitable for families and cots, potties, nappies, high-chairs and baby food can be provided; supervised crèche for six hours a week. No dogs. Conference facilities for thousands. Dinosaur Park (open mid Apr-Nov) is 9 miles away on the A1067 Fakenham road. *Rooms 55. Garden, indoor swimming pool, gym, squash, sauna, steam room, solarium, spa bath, multi-sports hall, aerobics, beauty & hair salon, tennis, badminton, snooker.* AMERICAN EXPRESS *Access, Diners, Visa.*

Norwich	Sprowston Manor	69%	£102
Tel 0603 410871 Fax 0603 423911			**H**
Sprowston Park Wroxham Road Norwich Norfolk NR7 8RP			**Map 10 C1**

Built around a 16th-century manor house, once the home of the Gurney banking family, this extended hotel by the A1151 contains a wealth of up-to-date facilities. A leisure club is at the heart of the most recent development, resplendent with palms and stone balustrades. Meeting and conference rooms (catering for up to 150 theatre-style) are kept discreetly apart from the main hotel day rooms, with a separate entrance to the ballroom. Bedrooms benefit from views of the surrounding parkland, home to the adjacent Sprowston Golf Club; they also combine stylish fitted furniture and floral fabrics with up-to-date accessories including mini-bars and wall safes. Eight bedrooms are in the original manor house. Children under 16 stay free in parents' room. *Rooms 97. Garden, golf (18), indoor swimming pool & children's splash pool, spa bath, sauna, solarium, beauty salon, gym.* AMERICAN EXPRESS *Access, Diners, Visa.*

Norwich   Places of Interest

Tourist Information   Tel 0603 666071.
Norwich Cathedral   Tel 0603 626290
Norwich City Football Ground   Carrow Road Tel 0603 612131.
Fakenham Racecourse   Nr Norwich Tel 0328 862388.
Norfolk Ski Club   Tel 0692 650442.
Royal Norfolk Showground   New Costessey Tel 0603 748931.
   Theatres and concert halls
Norwich Puppet Theatre   Tel 0603 615564.
Theatre Royal   Tel 0603 623562.
Little Theatre   Sheringham Tel 0263 822347.
   Historic Houses, Castles and Gardens
Blickling Hall (NT)   Aylsham Tel 0263 733084.
The Fairhaven Garden Trust   South Walsham Tel 060549 449.
Felbrigg Hall (NT)   Cromer Tel 026 375 444.
Mannington Hall   Saxthorpe Tel 026 387 4175.
Norwich Castle   Tel 0603 222222.
Raveningham Hall Gardens   Raveningham Tel 050846 206.
   Museums and Art Galleries
Colman's Mustard Museum   Tel 0603 627889.
Norwich Castle Museum   Tel 0603 223624.
Sainsbury Centre for Visual Arts University of East Anglia
   Tel 0603 592470.

Norwich Airport **Stakis Ambassador Hotel 65%**	**£79**
Tel 0603 410544 Fax 0603 789935	**H**
Cromer Road Norwich Airport Norwich Norfolk NR6 6JA	Map 10C1

Modern redbrick hotel whose aeronautical associations include the Concorde Bar and a replica Spitfire in the garden. Practical accommodation in decent-sized bedrooms; the honeymoon suites feature four-poster beds and jacuzzis. Purpose-built facility for conferences and banquets (up tp 350/500). *Rooms 108. Indoor swimming pool, gym, sauna, steam room, solarium, whirlpool bath.* AMERICAN EXPRESS *Access, Diners, Visa.*

Nottingham **Forte Crest 70%**	**£95**
Tel 0602 470131 Fax 0602 484366	**H**
St James's Street Nottingham Nottinghamshire NG1 6BN	Map 7 D3

Large city-centre hotel whose bedrooms employ bold, up-to-date fabrics, smart, freestanding furniture and restful colour schemes; higher-floor rooms have good views. Bathrooms are fully tiled and well lit, with showers as well as tubs. Public areas include a striking foyer with white floor tiles and contrasting black woodwork. Large conference and function rooms (catering for up to 600). Family facilities. Free NCP parking. A health and fitness club is planned for 1995. *Rooms 130.* AMERICAN EXPRESS *Access, Diners, Visa.*

Nottingham **Forte Posthouse 61%**	**£68**
Tel 0602 397800 Fax 0602 490469	**H**
Bostocks Lane Sandiacre Nottingham Nottinghamshire NG10 5NJ	Map 7 D3

One of the original Posthouses, in a residential area close to Junction 25 of the M1. Practical accommodation plus conference/meeting rooms. *Rooms 91. Garden.* AMERICAN EXPRESS *Access, Diners, Visa.*

Nottingham	**Higoi**		**£50**
Tel 0602 423379			**R**
57 Lenton Boulevard Nottingham Nottinghamshire NG7 2FQ			**Map 7 D3**

Japanese chef Mr Kato, assisted by his English wife, continues to educate customers in the delights of his native cooking. Helpful and informative staff will guide you through the complete range of specialities and menus, including good-value vegetarian, children's (£3.99) and *dombure* one-pot lunches and a bento box dinner. Teriyaki, shogoyaki and tempura dinners are preceded by selected hors d'oeuvre; choice of à la carte or set meals (book two days ahead for the multi-course Kaiseki feast). On the Nottingham-Derby road (turn left at the Savoy cinema). *Seats 35. L 12-2 D 6.30-10. Closed L Mon, Tue, all Sun & Bank Holidays. Set L from £5.90 Set D from £15.95.* AMERICAN EXPRESS *Access, Diners, Visa.*

Nottingham	**Holiday Inn Garden Court**	**65%**	**£80**
Tel 0602 500600 Fax 0602 500433			**H**
Castle Marina Park Nottingham Nottinghamshire NG7 1GX			**Map 7 D3**

Spacious rooms with large beds are a big plus at this bright modern hotel off the A6005, near the marina; good value, too – particularly for families, as the room price covers up to four occupants. Significant tariff reductions at weekends. *Rooms 100.* AMERICAN EXPRESS *Access, Diners, Visa.*

> From April 1995 the area telephones code for Nottingham changes from 0602 to 0115 plus the addition of 2 before six-digit numbers.

Nottingham	**Loch Fyne Oyster Bar**		**£25**
Tel 0602 508481			**R**
17 King Street Nottingham Nottinghamshire NG1 2AY			**Map 7 D3**

Produce from its illustrious Scottish progenitor (see under Cairndow, Scotland) travels overnight to its offshoot in the centre of Nottingham. Loch Fyne oysters and shellfish take their place alongside more humble offerings of mussel stew and Arbroath smokies, with Cheddar, Bonnet and Dunsyre Blue to follow. See also under Elton. *Seats 45. Parties 20. Meals 9-8.30 (Thurs to Sat to 10.30). Closed Sun. Access, Visa.*

Nottingham	**Man Ho**		**£40**
Tel 0602 474729			**R**
35 Pelham Street Nottingham Nottinghamshire NG1 2EA			**Map 7 D3**

A city-centre restaurant specialising in the cooking of Canton, Peking and Szechuan. At lunchtime, the busiest period, the emphasis is very much on the selection of some 60 dim sum dishes. This is one of only two city-centre restaurants offering these classic 'light snacks'. Service, though charming, can be a mite absent-minded. *Seats 270. Meals 12-12.* AMERICAN EXPRESS *Access, Diners, Visa.*

Nottingham	**Moat House**	**59%**	**£90**
Tel 0602 602621 Fax 0602 691506			**H**
Mansfield Road Nottingham Nottinghamshire NG5 2BT			**Map 7 D3**

Major refurbishment recently at this modern block hotel to the north of the city centre, covering public rooms, club bar and dining rooms as well as the bedrooms. Conferences/banqueting for up to 200/160. Not to be confused with the *Royal Moat House* nearer the heart of the city. *Rooms 172. Closed 28 & 29 Dec.* AMERICAN EXPRESS *Access, Diners, Visa.*

Nottingham — Noble House

£60

Tel 0602 501105

R

31 Greyfriar Gate Nottingham Nottinghamshire NG9 1EF

Map 7 D3

Friendly and helpful service complemented by stylish, swish black and pink decor all add to the ambience of this sophisticated Peking-style restaurant opposite Broad Marsh Centre. An extensive menu (including some sixteen 'sizzling' dishes) is based on good raw materials that are well handled in choices like sweet and sour fish, fried beef with pickled cabbage, peppered salted scallops or squid, and lamb with yellow bean sauce. Highchairs and booster seats for adventurous junior diners. *Seats 80. L 12-2 D 6-11.30 (Sun 12-11.30). Closed 3 days Christmas. Set L from £6 Set D from £14.* AMERICAN EXPRESS *Access, Diners, Visa.*

Nottingham — Novotel 62%

£70

Tel 0602 720106 Fax 0602 465900

H

Bostock Lane Long Eaton Nottingham Nottinghamshire NG10 4EP

Map 7 D3

Practical, modern accommodation just off junction 25 of the M1. Up to two children under 16 stay free of charge (inc breakfast) when sharing their parents' room. 30 rooms are reserved for non-smokers. Half of the rooms have been redecorated, and air-conditioning installed. The hotel restaurant is open for à la carte service from 6am-midnight. Conference facilities for up to 200. *Rooms 105. Garden, outdoor swimming pool.* AMERICAN EXPRESS® *Access, Diners, Visa.*

Nottingham — Ocean City

£40

Tel 0602 410041 Fax 0602 240369

R

100-104 Derby Road Nottingham Nottinghamshire NG1 5FB

Map 7 D3

A cavernous restaurant just out of the city centre; highly popular with the local Chinese community. The long Cantonese menu is strong on sizzling dishes and assorted seafood that includes lobster, crab and monkfish; these are well complemented by some more unusual and rarely seen dishes on the freshly cooked lunchtime dim sum selection. *Seats 250. Parties 12. L 12-2.30 (Mon & Tue to 4) D 6-12 (Mon-Fri), Sat 12-12, Sun 12-10.30. Closed 25 Dec. Set L from £5.90 Set D from £13.* AMERICAN EXPRESS® *Access, Diners, Visa.*

Nottingham — Royal Moat House 70%

£107

Tel 0602 414444 Fax 0602 475667

H

Wollaton Street Nottingham Nottinghamshire NG1 5RH

Map 7 D3

An internal atrium planted with tropical trees and plants is a major attraction at this strikingly modern city-centre hotel next to the Theatre Royal. Several bars and restaurants fringe this unique feature, and there's also a sunken lounge off the black marble foyer; the Penthouse Bar offers panoramic views over the city. Bedroom size varies from roomy doubles and twins to rather more compact singles. Decor is light and contemporary in style and all rooms have a mini-bar and the usual modern comforts. 24hr room service. Conference facilities for up to 600 delegates. Free multi-storey car parking. No dogs. *Rooms 201. Squash, hairdressing, kiosk, coffee shop (10am-6pm), beauty salon.* AMERICAN EXPRESS *Access, Diners, Visa.*

Nottingham — Rutland Square Hotel (By the Castle) 69%

£78

Tel 0602 411114 Fax 0602 410014

H

St James Street Nottingham Nottinghamshire NG1 6FJ

Map 7 D3

Reached by following the signs to the castle, this city-centre hotel, housed in a tall stylish red-brick Georgian-style building, has the added convenience of parking in the adjacent NCP, with charges included in the room rates. Top-floor bedrooms have been converted to Executive rooms, each with trouser press and bath robes, while on the ground floor public rooms have been re-arranged to provide additional lounge space and the bar has been moved to a mezzanine glass-roofed side wing. No dogs. *Rooms* 104. AMERICAN EXPRESS *Access, Diners, Visa.*

Nottingham   Sonny's   ↑   £60

Tel 0602 473041   **R**

3 Carlton Street Hockley Nottingham Nottinghamshire NG1 1NL   **Map 7 D3**

With the exception of floors, bar counter and chairs (which are black), the decor is cool, bright and white. Walls have vertical wood-strip cladding and are hung with a few examples of minimalist contemporary art. With a frontage that is all window there are white pull-down blinds to shield diners from the glare of the sun and the stare of the passer-by: an appropriately laid-back, modern setting for a short, progressive, modern menu. Examples include starters such as thin slices of seared, rare, very tender beef accompanied by a palate-tingling sweet chili relish; chopped salmon with onions, capers, dill and gherkin or mackerel *en papillote* with ginger, spring onions and lemon grass. Main courses provide further cause for indecision as such stunning and mouthwatering examples as roast monkfish with a warm caper and anchovy salsa, lamb and pancetta sausage with polenta and a roasted tomato sauce or Thai red vegetable curry with jasmine rice are on offer. Sweets fully live up to and even surpass expectations – wonderfully rich slice of moist chocolate truffle cake with a coarsely crushed amaretti crust and a smooth raspberry sauce; coconut, lemon grass and mint parfait or mango tarte tatin with ginger ice cream are other delicious alternatives. *Seats* 80. Parties 11. L 12-2.30 D 7-10.30 (*Fri & Sat to 11*). Closed 25 & 26 Dec, 1 Jan. Set L £10.95 Set D £13.95. AMERICAN EXPRESS *Access, Visa.*

Nottingham   Stakis Victoria Hotel   62%   £92

Tel 0602 419561   Fax 0602 484736   **H**

Milton Street Nottingham Nottinghamshire NG1 3PZ   **Map 7 D3**

19th-century Edwardian building in a central position. Accommodation ranges from singles to family rooms and suites. Nine conference rooms (recently refurbished) handle from 6 to 200 delegates. *Rooms* 166. AMERICAN EXPRESS *Access, Diners, Visa.*

Nottingham   Strathdon Thistle   66%   £103

Tel 0602 418501   Fax 0602 483725   **H**

44 Derby Road Nottingham Nottinghamshire NG1 5FT   **Map 7 D3**

Neat, practical bedrooms and comfortable day rooms in a modern hotel in the heart of the city near the Cathedral, directly opposite the Albert Hall conference and exhibition centre and Playhouse theatre. Choice of bars and 24hr room service. Children up to 14 free in their parents' room. Guests have free use of the leisure facilities at the sister hotel the *Donington Thistle* at Castle Donington (see entry). Banqueting/conferences for 100/150. Limited parking only (use the NCP nearby). *Rooms* 68. AMERICAN EXPRESS *Access, Diners, Visa.*

Nottingham   Travel Inn   NEW   £43

Tel 0582 414341   **L**

Phoenix Park Babbington Nottingham Nottinghamshire   **Map 7 D3**

Less than one mile from J26 of M1 on the A610 towards Nottingham. Four miles from the city centre. Due to open in February 1995. *Rooms* 60. AMERICAN EXPRESS *Access, Diners, Visa.*

Nottingham   Places of Interest

Tourist Information   Tel 0602 470661.
Nottingham Playhouse   Tel 0602 419419.
Theatre Royal   Tel 0602 482626.
Newstead Abbey   Tel 0623 793557 *Home of the poet Byron.*
Wollaton Hall   Tel 0602 281333/281130.
Nottingham Forest Football Ground   City Ground Tel 0602 822202.
Notts County Football Ground   Meadow Lane Tel 0602 861155.
Holme Pierrepoint National Water Sports Centre   Adbolton Lane
   Tel 0602 821212.
Nottingham Racecourse   Tel 0602 580620.
Nottingham Ice Stadium   Tel 0602 484526.
Nottingham Sutton Centre Ice Rink   Sutton-in-Ashfield, Nr Nottingham.
   Tel 0623 554554.
Carlton Forum Ski Slope   Tel 0602 872333.
   Museums and Art Galleries
D H Lawrence Birthplace Museum   Tel 0773 763312.
The Lace Centre   Nottingham Tel 0602 413539.
Museum of Costume and Textiles   Tel 0602 483504.
Nottingham Castle Museum   Tel 0602 483504.

Nuneaton	**Forte Travelodge**	**£45**
Tel 0203 382541		**L**
Nuneaton nr Coventry Warwickshire CV10 7TF		**Map 6 C4**

On the A444, 3 miles from Junction 3 of M6 and 15 miles from the
Birmingham NEC. No restaurant facilities nearby. **Rooms 40.**
AMERICAN EXPRESS *Access, Diners, Visa.*

Nuneaton	**Forte Travelodge**	**NEW**	**£45**
Tel 0800 850 950			**L**
Yeoman St Nicholas Park Drive Nuneaton Warwickshire			**Map 6 C4**

Opening autumn '94. AMERICAN EXPRESS *Access, Diners, Visa.*

Nuneaton	**Travel Inn**	**£43**
Tel 0203 343584 Fax 0203 327156		**L**
Coventry Road Nuneaton Warwickshire CV10 7PJ		**Map 6 C4**

20 minutes' drive from Birmingham International Airport; children
up to 16 free in parents' room. **Rooms 48.** AMERICAN EXPRESS *Access,
Diners, Visa.*

Nutfield	**Nutfield Priory**	**71%**	**£127**
Tel 0737 822066 Fax 0737 823321			**H**
Nutfield Redhill Surrey RH1 4EN			**Map 11 B5**

East of Redhill on the A25, Nutfield Priory is an extravagant Victorian-
Gothic pile built on a ridge commanding extensive views over the Surrey
and Sussex countryside. Day rooms include the galleried main hall that
comes complete with stained-glass windows and pipe organ, panelled
library with some fine carving on the ribbed ceiling, and the bar set within
a country house-style lounge. Individually decorated bedrooms have
considerable appeal with elaborate bedhead drapes or canopies and a variety
of furniture from rattan to reproduction antique pieces. A number
of beamed rooms are particularly characterful. All have room safes and
good bathrooms decorated to match individual bedrooms. A popular
conference venue with 10 different meeting rooms and guests have free
membership of the separately run Fredericks sports and leisure club situated
within the hotel's grounds. No dogs. **Rooms 52.** *Garden, indoor swimming
pool, sauna, solarium, spa bath, steam room, gym, beauty salon, badminton,
squash, snooker. Closed a few days between Xmas and New Year.*
AMERICAN EXPRESS *Access, Diners, Visa.*

Oakham   Barnsdale Lodge Hotel   65%   £70

Tel 0572 724678   Fax 0572 724961   **H**

The Avenue Rutland Water nr Oakham Leicestershire LE15 8AH   **Map 7 E3**

Edwardian in style but originally a 16th-century farmhouse, Barnsdale
Lodge stands alongside the A606 two miles east of Oakham by Rutland
Water. Antiques and solid oak furniture are found in the day rooms, and
there are period prints and ornaments in the little lounge. Some of the
bedrooms enjoy views over Rutland Water; one room has a half-tester bed.
The largest of the conference suites is the Barn, with a maximum capacity
of 300. A conservatory was added in 1994 and 12 additional bedrooms are
due to come on stream for the 1995 season. **Rooms** 17. *Access, Visa.*

Oakham. Hambleton Hall – see under Hambleton.

Oakham   Whipper-in Hotel   66%   £94

Tel 0572 756971   Fax 0572 757759   **HR**

Market Place Oakham Leicestershire LE15 6DT   **Map 7 E3**

17th-century town-centre hotel whose bedrooms – tastefully decorated
with individual schemes and a mixture of antique and reproduction
furniture – outshine public areas where some refurbishment would
be welcome. Of two pubby bars one offers some sofas and armchairs
to supplement a small lounge. **Room** 24. *Courtyard.* AMERICAN EXPRESS® *Access,
Diners, Visa.*

Restaurant   £60

Hunting prints around the walls, a couple of old beams and comfortable
high-backed chairs create a cosy 'county' setting for some sound cooking.
Terrine of chicken and game with woodland mushrooms; pan-fried pigeon
breast on a potato and celeriac rösti with port sauce; marinated Barbary
duck breast served Chinese style with stir-fried vegetables; noisettes
of lamb with an apricot and thyme mousseline on a sharp raspberry sauce
and scallops served with a Savoy cabbage parcel on a saffron sauce are
typical dishes. Good vegetables are given as much care as the rest of the
meal. Pleasant service. **Seats** 38. *Private Room 20. L 12.30-2 D 7.30-9.30.
Set L £6.95 Set D £9.95.*

Odiham   George Hotel   £72

Tel 0256 702081   Fax 0256 704213   **I**

High Street Odiham nr Basingstoke Hampshire RG25 1LP   **Map 15 D3**

First granted a licence in 1540, the privately-owned George has kept a good
deal of its period character. Timber framing can be seen throughout, and
in the Oak Room – a popular place for afternoon tea or private parties –
the wattle and daub walls are exposed. The oak-panelled, flagstone-floored
restaurant was at one time an assize court. Main-house bedrooms have
creaking floors, beams and antiques, while rooms in the converted barn and
coach house are modern behind original exteriors. Four-poster rooms
attract a small supplement and in one of them some Elizabethan wall
paintings are carefully protected. One mile from the M3 (junction 5).
Rooms 18. *Garden.* AMERICAN EXPRESS® *Access, Diners, Visa.*

Old Burghclere   Dew Pond   £70

Tel 0635 278408   **R**

Old Burghclere Newbury Berkshire RG15 9LH   **Map 15 D3**

Very much a family restaurant with the cooking done by Keith Marshall,
wife Julie at front of house and her brother looking after the drinks side,
the 16th-century house stands in Watership Down surrounded by beautiful
countryside. Inside, the two dining rooms are comfortably and pleasantly
furnished with good pictures, objets d'art and newly upholstered chairs –

there's even an open fire. The fixed-price menu (there's now a cheaper and less extensive variation during the week as well) changes every eight weeks with several choices in each course; game dishes (rillettes of pheasant, saddle of venison or roast brace of quail, feature whenever possible with ingredients coming from a local farm, otherwise a typical meal might consist of spiced mussel broth, flavoured with saffron, coriander and chili, best end of lamb roasted and served with gratin dauphinois, ratatouille and a garlic cream sauce, with apple and caramel tart to finish, the latter served with caramel ice cream and crème anglaise. For an extra £2 why not try the grand plated selection of all the desserts in miniature? Good farmhouse British cheeses (Wedmore and Devon Oke for example), Colombian coffee and a fairly-priced wine list with a dozen good wines under £15 and plenty of half bottles. No longer open for lunch, except for private functions. *Seats* 40. *Private Room* 25. *Parties* 50. D 7-10. *Closed Sun & Mon, 1st 2 weeks Jan, 2 weeks mid-Aug. Set D £16.50/£23. Access, Visa.*

Old Harlow   **Travel Inn**   **£43**

Tel 0279 442545   Fax 0279 452169   **L**

Cambridge Road Old Harlow Essex CM20 2EP   **Map 11 B4**

Riverside location, 15 miles from Stanstead Airport. ***Rooms** 38.*
AMERICAN EXPRESS *Access, Diners, Visa.*

See the Restaurant Round-up for easy, quick-reference comparisons.

Old Minster Lovell **Lovells at Windrush Farm ↑ NEW**   **£80**

Tel & Fax 0993 779802   **RR**

Old Minster Lovell Oxfordshire OX8 5RN   **Map 14 C2**

Set in 80 acres of grounds, Lovells has very much the appearance of a fine and substantial farmhouse. The dual-aspect dining room is part of a more recent addition and is small and elegant with ornately swagged heavy white drapes at the windows, part-lined in deep blue chintz matching the dark blue candles on the tables. Robert Marshall-Slater works virtually single-handed in the kitchen, producing daily-changing fixed-price menus that are exciting and well thought-out, reflecting his extensive experience with the likes of Peter Kromberg at the Inter-Continental in London and at the Arkle restaurant at the Chester Grosvenor. Lunch is a three-course affair while for dinner there are seven beautifully balanced courses, the meal beginning with deep-fried light cheesy beignets followed perhaps by two delicious scallops wrapped in Parma ham, pan-fried and served on a bed of home-grown oak leaf lettuce with a little dribble of Tuscan olive oil. Next might come a delightful little tea cup sitting in a saucer. In it is a wonderfully creamy, thick shallot soup subtly flavoured with slices of fresh truffle poached in veal stock. As a fish course, a slice of poached wild salmon comes surrounded by a rich but not overpowering lobster bisque, without the cream, and a topping of interleaved tomato and courgette slices. The main dish could consist of a sliced breast of duck served on a mixture of butter beans and fresh broad beans with asparagus spears in a sauce of the cooking juices. The cheeses follow, mostly French and each carefully described. A typical selection could be St Killian, Camembert, Crottin de Chavignol, Camembert au Calvados, Fourme d'Ambert and Fougéru, all in first-class condition. To cleanse the palate these are followed by a chaud-froid such as a lime sorbet with hot peach tea. To complete a meal of marvellous achievement there's a selection of plated miniature desserts – a well-risen hot apple soufflé, an iced apple nougat with toasted almonds and a roasted, virtually caramelised apple with a fine caramel sauce. Some good wines on a rather randomly-organised list. Service is extremely pleasant. Booking is essential. *Seats* 18. *Parties* 10. L 12-2 D 8-9.30. *Closed Mon, 3 weeks Jan. Set L £13.50 (Sun £16.50) Set D (7-course) £27.50.* AMERICAN EXPRESS *Access, Diners, Visa.*   *See over*

Rooms   £145

Just two rooms at present, though more are planned. They're full
of thoughtful extras and equipped to a standard you could expect of a much
grander place. One has shower/WC only. Big towels, fine soaps, bathrobes.
Splendid breakfasts.

Oldbury   Forte Travelodge   £45
Tel 021-552 2967   **L**

Wolverhampton Road Oldbury Warly West Midlands B69 2BH   **Map 6 C4**

On the A4123 northbound off Junction 2 of the M5, on the outskirts
of Birmingham. *Rooms 33.* AMERICAN EXPRESS *Access, Diners, Visa.*

Oldham   Travel Inn   NEW   £43
Tel 061 681 1373   **L**

The Broadway Chadderton Oldham Greater Manchester OL9 8DW **Map 6 B2**

From Junction 18 of M62, take Middleton turning on to M66; at the end
of M66 turn right on to A576 towards Higher Blackley. Turn left at next
traffic lights on to A6104; the lodge is situated at the junction with A663.
Rooms 40. AMERICAN EXPRESS *Access, Diners, Visa.*

Ormesby St Margaret   Ormesby Lodge   58%   £46
Tel 0493 730910   Fax 0493 733103   **H**

**Decoy Road Ormesby St Margaret nr Great Yarmouth Norfolk
NR29 3LG**   **Map 10 D1**

A small family-run hotel five miles north of Great Yarmouth and within
a mile or so of several beaches. The building is Victorian, and some of the
original feel survives in the bar/lounge. Bedrooms vary in their decor and
furnishings but all are in good order and nearly all have private bathroom
facilities. Parking for 30 cars. *Rooms 8. Garden.* AMERICAN EXPRESS *Access,
Diners, Visa.*

Oswestry   Forte Travelodge   £45
Tel 0691 658178   **L**

Oswestry Shropshire SY11 4JA   **Map 8 D2**

At the Mile End service area on the A5/A483 roundabout outside
Oswestry. *Rooms 40.* AMERICAN EXPRESS *Access, Diners, Visa.*

Oswestry   Wynnstay Hotel   66%   £65
Tel 0691 655261   Fax 0691 670606   **H**

Church Street Oswestry Shropshire SY11 2SZ   **Map 8 D2**

In the town centre opposite St Oswalds church, this is a typical Georgian
building with stylish day rooms. Besides the restaurant and lounge there
are conference facilities for up to 190, plus a 200-year-old crown bowling
green as an unusual leisure offering. Best of the bedrooms have whirlpool
baths. Children up to 13 free in parents' room. Work started in the
summer of 1994 on a swimming pool and a leisure centre. *Rooms 27.
Garden, bowling, coffee shop (9.30am-10pm).* AMERICAN EXPRESS *Access,
Diners, Visa.*

Otley   Chevin Lodge   64%   £75
Tel 0943 467818   Fax 0943 850335   **H**

York Gate Otley West Yorkshire LS21 3NU   **Map 6 C1**

Set in fifty acres of woodlands and lakes and built of Finnish pine, the
Lodge is the largest log construction in the country. Bedrooms are in either
the main building or smaller log lodges scattered amongst the trees. Despite
the rusticity, rooms have all the usual modern conveniences. Executive
lodges have separate lounges. The well-equipped Woodlands Suite has

facilities for up to 120 conference delegates. Guests have free membership of a private leisure club 5 minutes drive away. ***Rooms 50***. *Garden, jogging trail, mountain bikes, sauna, solarium, tennis, fishing, games room.* AMERICAN EXPRESS *Access, Visa.*

Oundle   **Talbot Hotel**   **62%**   £82

Tel 0832 273621 Fax 0832 274545	**H**
New Street Oundle Northamptonshire PE8 4EA	Map 7 E4

Built as a monks' hostel, and rebuilt in the 17th century with stones from nearby Fotheringhay Castle, the Talbot is quite splendid with its transom windows and bell-capped gables. In 1638 the oak staircase descended by Mary Queen of Scots on the day of her execution in 1587 was installed. Conference/banqueting facilities for up to 100. Forte Heritage. ***Rooms 40***. *Garden.* AMERICAN EXPRESS *Access, Diners, Visa.*

> We endeavour to be as up-to-the-minute as possible, but inevitably some changes to key personnel may occur at restaurants and hotels after the Guide goes to press.

Oxford   **Al-Shami**   £30

Tel 0865 310066 Fax 0865 311241	**R**
25 Walton Crescent Oxford Oxfordshire OX1 2JG	Map 15 D2

Between Somerville and Worcester Colleges, this Lebanese restaurant is open long hours and serves authentic dishes including charcoal grills of lamb, chicken and minced meat and the usual wide range of hot and cold hors d'oeuvre. The wine list includes a dozen Lebanese varieties plus arak. Set menus can be arranged for parties of six or more, and there are one or two dishes for vegetarians. ***Seats 50***. *Meals 12-12. No credit cards.*

Oxford   **Bath Place**   £80

Tel 0865 791812 Fax 0865 791834	**RR**
4 & 5 Bath Place Holywell Street Oxford Oxfordshire OX1 3SU	Map 15 D2

A major coup for Yolanda Fawsitt at the quaint Bath Place was the arrival at Easter 1994 of chef Jeremy Blake O'Connor (whose previous venture at Moreteyne Manor ended with a major fire). He has a free rein with the menu and seems to have settled in extremely well. Previous regulars at Bath Place have been pleasantly surprised at his meals, an early example of which started with a succulent raviolo of salmon and scallops set on a bed of lightly braised chicory, served in an olive oil sauce flavoured with aromatic herbs and tomatoes, an excellent combination of textures and flavours. For main course, aiguillettes of Scottish sirloin of beef with a shallot, cognac and green peppercorn sauce, served with a vegetable tartelette, timbale of spinach and a fondant potato was perfectly balanced and displayed a sure touch. Unusually, a choice of plated cheeses or a hot cheese savoury – twice-baked Gruyère soufflé with a cheese sauce, served with an endive and watercress salad, or for pudding a feuillette of strawberries with pastry cream, strawberry sorbet and raspberry coulis. The simple set menus (no choice) are sometimes surcharged for guests of residents. Inexpensive wines on a list of 80 bottles offer good drinking under £20. No smoking. ***Seats 30***. *L 12-2 D 7-10 (Fri & Sat to 10.30). Closed L Tue, D Sun, all Mon. Set L £12/16.50/Sun £19.50 (Sun £19.50) Set D £21.95/£24.50.* AMERICAN EXPRESS *Access, Visa.*

Rooms   £100

Ten small, neat comfortable bedrooms, well equipped, set around the courtyard. The classification as a restaurant with rooms reflects the absence of separate public rooms, and the establishment's concentration on being food-led.

Oxford   Cherwell Boathouse   £45

Tel 0865 52746   Fax 0865 391459   **R**

Bardwell Road Oxford Oxfordshire OX2 6SR   Map 15 D2

Park your car or moor your punt, and enjoy a leisurely meal in the
friendly surroundings of a converted boathouse on the River Cherwell. The
evening menu is three-course, fixed-price, weekly-changing. Creamy mussel
soup or Greek salad with feta cheese could be your starter, with baked
monkfish and green salsa, or loin of free-range pork with a wild mushroom
sauce to follow. There's always a starter and a main course for vegetarians
(peppers stuffed with creamy fennel and goat's cheese) and a trio of British
cheeses is an alternative to coffee and walnut ice cream or sticky toffee
pudding. A la carte at lunchtime (but set Sunday lunch). Prices on the
excellent wine list are still ridiculously low and superb value for money.
Some of the half bottles equate to the cost of a glass in other establishments.
The outside eating area will be enlarged for 1995. *Seats 50. L 12-2
D 7-10.30. Closed L Tues, D Sun, all Mon, Dec 24-30. Set Sun L £16
Set D £16.* AMERICAN EXPRESS *Access, Diners, Visa.*

Oxford   Eastgate Hotel   61%   £122

Tel 0865 248244   Fax 0865 791681   **H**

High Street Oxford Oxfordshire OX1 4BE   Map 15 D2

Comfortably refurbished behind its 18th-century facade, the Eastgate stands
at the Magdalen College end of the High (reception entrance is in Merton
Street). Pick of the accommodation is the four-poster Ruskin Suite. Forte
Heritage. *Rooms 43.* AMERICAN EXPRESS *Access, Diners, Visa.*

Oxford   Restaurant Elizabeth   ↑   £75

Tel 0865 242230   **R**

82 St Aldate's Oxford Oxfordshire OX1 1RA   Map 15 D2

Dating from the 15th century, the first-floor dining areas are very
traditional and intimate, a most appropriate setting for the classical dishes
that are the cornerstone of Salvador Rodriguez's cooking. Perennially
popular with (better-off!) students, local residents and tourists alike, it's
very much an Oxford institution. Mousse Paquita (salmon, prawns and
avocado), breast of wood pigeon with a juniper and port sauce, and
champagne sorbet comprise a typical good value set lunch menu. The carte,
too, is full of classics like escargots, carré d'agneau, and an excellent crème
brulée. Prices on the wine list are inclusive of service, so what you see
is what you pay! A classic list (nothing from the New World) with decent
showings from both Spain and Germany alongside France. Owner Antonio
Lopez has been smoothly in charge since 1966. *Seats 40. L 12.30-2.30
D 6.30-11 (Sun 7-10.30). Closed Mon, 24-30 Dec, Good Friday, 24-31 Dec.
Set L £15.* AMERICAN EXPRESS *Access, Diners, Visa.* MARTELL

Oxford   15 North Parade   £70

Tel 0865 513773   **R**

15 North Parade Avenue Oxford Oxfordshire OX9 1JH   Map 15 D2

Enthusiastic and dedicated owner Georgina Wood's son, Sean, has been
joined by his colleague Ben Gorman to produce an exciting, innovative and
eclectic menu. The restaurant, located in a narrow lane just north of the
city centre, is decorated in a cool, modern manner and has a herbaceous-
bordered walled patio at the rear for alfresco dining, weather permitting.
The menu introduces refreshingly fashionable concepts, dishes being
characterised by clear well-balanced flavours. A starter of crab spring roll
comprises crisp deep-fried filo pastry wrapped around a delicious fresh crab
mixture. It comes on a bed of spring and red onion salsa. Otherwise there's
parsleyed ham and ox tongue terrine and for main course chunks
of monkfish on a skewer with peppers and a pesto of pumpkin seeds and

coriander. Other dishes could be a generous half-pound chopped rumpsteak hamburger accompanied by a spicy yellow catsup, red onion relish and chunky chips or a lamb, saffron zucchini and marjoram tagine with three-rice timbale. To finish there are delightful sweets such as hot double chocolate brownie, warm cherry and kirsch savarin or a peach tarte tatin. Everything including the bread is prepared with great care and served by charming staff. *Seats* 55. *L* 12-2 *D* 7-11. *Closed D Sun, all Mon, some Bank Holidays, last 2 weeks Aug. Set L £15.75 Set D from £19.50. Access, Visa.*

Oxford   Moat House   62%   £123

Tel 0865 59933   Fax 0865 310259

Wolvercote Roundabout Oxford Oxfordshire OX2 8AL   Map 15 D2

Modern business hotel two miles north of the city centre at the junction of A34 and A40. Bedrooms were being refurbished during 1994. Good leisure centre, conference facilities for up to 150, banqueting to 110. Extensive free car parking. *Rooms 155. Indoor swimming pool, gym, squash, sauna, spa bath, solarium, putting, snooker, coffee shop (7am-10.30pm). Closed New Year.* AMERICAN EXPRESS *Access, Diners, Visa.*

Oxford   Old Parsonage   70%   £135

Tel 0865 310210   Fax 0865 311262

1 Banbury Road Oxford Oxfordshire OX2 6NN   Map 15 D2

On a site dating back to the 14th century, the Old Parsonage was established in 1660 and underwent a major transformation in order to open as a small hotel of quality and individuality early in 1991. Great style and taste have been employed in its refurbishment, creating an effect that's very easy on the eye. Bedrooms, though not large, are stylishly appointed with striking soft furnishings, muted colours and harmonious fittings. Accessories include mini-bars, hairdryers and remote-control radio and TVs with satellite stations. Stunning marble-fitted bathrooms have two showers, soft towels, fine toiletries and telephone extensions. A clubby bar has walls hung with hundreds of pictures and there's a small lounge. Young, efficient staff. No dining room as such, but light meals are served in the bar, including such dishes as tomato, avocado and mozzarella salad, king prawns served with spicy mayonnaise and fillet of sirloin steak with French fries and salad. A good selection of wine is available by bottle, half bottle and glass. *Browns* restaurant (under the same ownership as the hotel) is two minutes away. *Rooms 30. Garden, punting. Closed 23-27 Dec.* AMERICAN EXPRESS *Access, Diners, Visa.*

Note that all telephone numbers with area codes starting with 0 will start 01 from 16 April 1995.

Oxford   Randolph Hotel   68%   £126

Tel 0865 247481   Fax 0865 791678

Beaumont Street Oxford Oxfordshire OX1 2LN   Map 15 D2

Built in 1864 in neo-Gothic style, the Randolph is named after Dr Francis Randolph, a benefactor of the Ashmolean Museum opposite. The grand, oak-panelled foyer with high vaulted ceiling and sweeping staircase sets the tone for the day rooms, which include an elegant, chandeliered lounge, clubby bar with red leather armchairs, and Spires restaurant where good breakfasts are served under a splendid plasterwork ceiling. Bedrooms vary in size from small to spacious and include a number of suites. The hotel has a number of suites catering for anything from 20 to 300 conference visitors. Free covered parking for 70 cars. Forte Grand. *Rooms 109. Kiosk, coffee shop (10-8).* AMERICAN EXPRESS *Access, Diners, Visa.*

Oxford   Travel Inn   NEW   £43

Tel 0582 414341   **L**

Arlington Business Park Cowley Oxford Oxfordshire   **Map 15 D2**

Three miles from the city centre, in the Arlington Business Park, situated just off A4142. Two miles from M40. *Rooms 60.* AMERICAN EXPRESS *Access, Diners, Visa.*

Oxford   Places of Interest

Tourist Information   Tel 0865 726871.
Oxford United Football Ground   Manor Ground Tel 0865 61503.
Kirtlington Park Polo Club   Bicester Tel 0869 50777.
Oxford University Polo Club   c/o Wolfson College Tel 0865 274100.
Oxford Ice Rink   Tel 0865 248076.
Oxford Cathedral   Tel 0865 276155.
    Theatres and Concert Halls
Apollo Theatre   Tel 0865 244554.
Pegasus Theatre   Tel 0865 722851.
Oxford Playhouse   Tel 0865 247134.
    Historic Houses, Castles and Gardens
Waterperry Gardens   Nr Wheatley Tel 0844 339226.
Kingston House   Kingston Bagpuiz, Nr Abingdon Tel 0865 820259.
    Museums and Art Galleries
The Ashmolean Museum of Art and Archaeology   Tel 0865 278000.
Museum of Modern Art   Tel 0865 722733.
Museum of Oxford   Tel 0865 815559.
The Oxford Story   Tel 0865 728822.
The Pitt Rivers Museum   Tel 0865 270927.

Padstow   The Seafood Restaurant   ★ ↑   £80

Tel 0841 532485   Fax 0841 533344   **RR**

Riverside Padstow Cornwall PL28 8BY   **Map 12 B3**

Rick Stein has for 20 years been chef-patron at what has become one of the country's best known seafood restaurants, one totally deserving of an emphasis on *The* in its title. His understanding of his craft and raw materials helps produce food of quality to make a meal here an experience to both savour and admire. Drinks taken in the conservatory come served with a simple jar of Greek black and green olives, freshly baked baguettes and brown bread – all quality hallmarks showing attention to detail. Dishes are essentially straightforward, allowing the peak freshness of the produce to shine through, and many show a French influence: fish and shellfish with *rouille, mouclade* with leeks (a speciality from La Rochelle region), *fruits de mer* served in the shell on ice, *grillade* of monkfish and Dover sole with a *sauce vierge* of sun-dried tomatoes, garlic and tarragon and a purée of potatoes with Provençal olive oil. Lobsters are kept in chilled seawater tanks until ordered. Sweets keep up the enjoyment level, notably baked-to-order apple tart, crème brulée and a moist, dark chocolate gateau with a bitter chocolate sorbet, a white chocolate and praline truffle and a mint-flavoured *crème anglaise.* Keen prices on a splendid and well-balanced wine list that includes helpful tasting notes. *Seats 70. Parties 12. L 12.30-2.15 D 7-10. Closed Sun, May Day & last week Dec to 2 Feb. Set L £20.25 Set D £27.85.* AMERICAN EXPRESS *Access, Visa.* MARTELL

Rooms   £73

Ten individually decorated bedrooms above the restaurant provide some very comfortable accommodation; light and airy colour schemes plus televisions, mini-bar and tea/coffee making facilities are standard features. Two rooms have private balconies with views of the harbour. All rooms have stylish bathrooms en suite, most with good shower baths. Breakfast taken in the restaurant includes English, kippers or Continental, the nearby delicatessen providing many of the items.

St Petroc's House   Tel 0841 532700

A small, 8-bedroom hotel (from £50 per double) 150 yards up the hill from the restaurant. It has a 30-seat Bistro (closed Monday) offering a daily-changing, 3-course menu ar £15.45 including coffee (typically carrot and green coriander soup, salmon steak with a white wine, parsley and butter sauce, and strawberries with balsamic vinegar).

Padstow   Place of Interest

Polzeath Beach.

Paignton   Palace Hotel   60%   £103

Tel 0803 555121   Fax 0803 527974   **H**

Esplanade Road Paignton Devon TQ4 6BJ   Map 13 D3

Traditional seaside hotel overlooking the pier and Torbay beyond. Good leisure amenities and conference facilities for up to 50. Forte Heritage. *Rooms 52. Garden, outdoor swimming pool, keep-fit equipment, sauna, spa bath, solarium, beautician, hair salon, tennis, pool table.* AMERICAN EXPRESS *Access, Diners, Visa.*

Paignton   Redcliffe Hotel   62%   £92

Tel 0803 526397   Fax 0803 528030   **H**

Marine Drive Paignton Devon TQ3 2NL   Map 13 D3

A round tower is the central feature of this distinctive turn-of-the-century hotel on Paignton seafront, dividing Paignton and Preston beaches. Day rooms enjoy the view, as do some of the bedrooms, which include seven low-ceilinged rooms of character in the tower; family suites also available. An indoor leisure complex was completed last year. Conference/banqueting for 150/210. A private tunnel leading to the beach is of particular appeal to children. No dogs. 24hr room service. *Rooms 58. Garden, indoor & outdoor swimming pool, mini-gym, sauna, steam room, spa bath, solarium, hair salon (not Mon), putting, games room, children's playground.* AMERICAN EXPRESS *Access, Visa.*

Paignton   Places of Interest

Tourist Information   Tel 0803 558383.
Compton Castle   Tel 0803 872112.
Paignton Zoo   Tel 0803 557479.
Paignton Sands Beach.

Painswick   Painswick Hotel   70%   £97

Tel 0452 812160   Fax 0452 812059   **H**

Kemps Lane Painswick Gloucestershire GL6 6YB   Map 14 B2

Tucked away down the narrow streets behind the church in one of the most architecturally interesting Cotswold villages, the Painswick Hotel is a grand Palladian mansion. Numerous intriguing features include an Italianate loggia overlooking the croquet lawn in gardens that also enclose a 'grotto' built by a vicar (this was once the Rectory) to amplify his sermons and an elaborate ribbed ceiling in the former chapel, now the bar. Elegant day rooms – some occasionally used for meetings – boast some fine antiques and paintings. It's run in relaxed style by Somerset and Helene Moore, who create a friendly atmosphere. Accommodation varies from spacious rooms with some notable antiques, objets d'art and stylish fabrics in the original building to smaller rooms with more modest pieces and some modern furniture in a newer wing but all have extras like magazines, mineral water and bathrobes. Top of the range are two rooms with four-posters, one with feminine floral canopies, the other with a more solid,

masculine, oak version. Breakfasts with freshly squeezed orange juice and some lovely smoky bacon start the day. *Rooms 20. Garden, croquet.*
AMERICAN EXPRESS *Access, Visa.* MARTELL COGNAC

Parkgate   Ship Hotel   58%   £60

Tel 051-336 3931   Fax 051-353 0051   **H**

The Parade Parkgate The Wirral Cheshire L64 6SA   **Map 6 A2**

A small stone-fronted Forte hotel overlooking the Dee estuary; the Birdwatchers bar (serving real ale) has picture windows from which to observe the wildlife on the salt marshes. The two front bedrooms have four-poster beds and the best views. Ample free car parking. *Rooms 26. Closed 23-30 Dec.* AMERICAN EXPRESS *Access, Diners, Visa.*

Parkham   Penhaven Country House   64%   £112

Tel 0237 451388   Fax 0237 451878   **H**

Parkham nr Bideford Devon EX39 5PL   **Map 12 C2**

Maxine and Alan Wade are the friendly hosts at a small 19th-century hotel whose setting in the Devon countryside includes nine acres of woodland and gardens. Inside, all is spick and span, from the bar with its log fire to the bedrooms – these range from standard to 'super-de-luxe' and six cottage suites. All rooms have both bath and shower. No smoking in the restaurant. No children under ten. Turn left at Horns Cross on the A39; 1½ miles into Parkham village then first left. *Rooms 12. Garden.* AMERICAN EXPRESS *Access, Diners, Visa.*

> If we recommend meals in a hotel or inn a separate entry is made for its restaurant.

Paulerspury   Vine House   £55

Tel 0327 811267   Fax 0327 811309   **RR**

100 High Street Paulerspury Northamptonshire NN12 7NA   **Map 15 D1**

A 300-year-old village-centre limestone cottage a few miles south of Towcester and a mile off the A5 is now a restaurant with rooms that exudes charm and hospitality, thanks to involved owners Marcus and Julie Springett. A tiny, cosy bar serves for pre-dinner drinks, while the dining room is spacious, bright and, though modernised, still retains much of its original charm. Marcus offers a short, daily-changing menu using the freshest seasonal produce and creating rich, satisfying flavours in robust, imaginative dishes. Faced with home-smoked cod and butter bean terrine with a saffron dressing, the first young nettles with potato and lobster soup and lamb croquettes with apricot pickle, choosing a starter is a pleasant but difficult task, and main courses such as fillet of turbot with a compote of red peppers or breast of duckling with 'mushie' peas and mint sauce also pose a selection problem. Fruity desserts are typified by pears set in honey jelly with home-bottled blackberries served with a warm creamy rice pudding. Easy to use wine list with helpful tasting notes – several bottles under £15. Julie serves in polite, discreet style. Tell her when booking if you want a no-smoking table. *Seats 45. Private Room 12. L 12-2.30 D 7-10.30. Closed L Mon & Sat, all Sun, 26-30 Dec. Set L £13.95 Set D £19.50. Access, Visa.*

Rooms   £62

There's a quiet lounge for residents, who have the pleasure of sleeping in one of the 6 prettily decorated bedrooms. Though not large they are well equipped and each has neat en-suite facilities. One boasts a four-poster. No dogs.

Penkridge   William Harding's House   £50

Tel 078 571 2955

R

Mill Street Penkridge Stafford Staffordshire ST19 5AY

Map 6 B3

Leave the M6 at Junction 12 or 13 and take the A449. Built as a stable in 1693 and occupied by Cromwell's men during the Civil War, this is a small, cottagey restaurant run by Fiona and Eric Bickley. Eric's frequently-changing menu is a fixed-price-only affair and offers a good choice – perhaps 'ragoo' of langoustines and scallops, savoury poached pears on fresh pineapple with a warm tayberry sauce or sautéed chicken livers in filo pastry to start, followed by a duo of game with venison medallions and pheasant breast, slivers of lamb's liver with a hint of sage and a sharp orange purée or a melée of halibut and monkfish wrapped with salmon on a julienne of winter vegetables. To finish, 'British rural cheeses' and a choice of desserts displayed on the sideboard. Sunday lunch is a relaxed occasion and offers a choice of four dishes for each course, including a roast meat; diners are coaxed into lingering awhile. Puddings and British cheeses are served from a sideboard. Supper Club first Thursday of every month, with multiple returns 'for seconds' of puddings!. No children under 15. *Seats* 24. *Parties* 16. *Private Room* 16. L (*First & last Sun in month only*) *at* 1pm D 7.30-9.30. *Closed D Sun & Mon. Set Sun L £11.95 Set D £18.95. Access, Visa.*

Penrith   Forte Travelodge   £45

Tel 0768 66958

L

Redhills Penrith Cumbria CA11 0DT

Map 4 C3

A quarter of a mile west of Junction 40 of the M6, 15 miles east of Keswick on the A66. *Rooms* 32. AMERICAN EXPRESS® *Access, Diners, Visa.*

Penrith   North Lakes Hotel   71%   £114

Tel 0768 68111   Fax 0768 68291

H

Ullswater Road Penrith Cumbria CA11 8QT

Map 4 C3

A modern hotel, by Junction 40 of the M6, which comfortably divides its time between mid-week conferences and a weekend base for Lakeland visitors. Facilities for both categories are purpose-built around a central lodge of local stone and massive railway-sleeper beams, which houses bar, lounges and coffee shop. Newest Executive-style bedrooms have raised work areas with fold-away beds, while interconnecting syndicate rooms convert handily for family use at holiday times. Two rooms are specially adapted for disabled guests. Children up to 14 free in parents' room. 24hr room service. Conference and banqueting facilities for up to 250 and a staffed business centre. Activities for children every weekend and during school holidays. An extension to the leisure club is planned. Shire Inns. *Rooms* 84. *Garden, indoor swimming pool & children's splash pool, sauna, spa bath, solarium, gym, squash, snooker.* AMERICAN EXPRESS® *Access, Diners, Visa.*

Penrith   Places of Interest

Acorn Bank Garden (NT)   Temple Sowerby Tel 07683 61893.
Dalemain Dacre   Tel 07684 86450.

Penzance   Abbey Hotel   67%   £85

Tel 0736 66906   Fax 0736 51163

HR

Abbey Street Penzance Cornwall TR18 4AR

Map 12 A4

The truly delightful Abbey Hotel is perched above and overlooks the quay in a quiet backwater of town (on entering Penzance take the road marked Sea Front, pass a large car park on the left, turn right just before the bridge, then turn left up the slipway). Jean and Michael Cox's house is a model of good taste, replete with their collections of antiques and fine art, deep armchairs and abundant reading material. Stylish bedrooms retain the building's uniqueness and charm, using colour and light to great advantage where space is limited. "Not a family hotel." *Rooms 7. Garden, croquet. Closed 3 or 4 days at Christmas.* AMERICAN EXPRESS *Access, Visa.*

Restaurant   £60

Do book as, with only six tables, non-residents are only welcomed as space allows, but don't expect any great sense of occasion. A table d'hote offers three choices per course nightly. Mushroom and pepper bake, courgette and blue cheese soup or quenelles of salmon à la creme (a speciality) could precede lobster-sauced lemon sole, supreme of chicken filled with crab and a lemon and thyme sauce, or the vegetarian option, perhaps aubergine, mixed nuts and garlic bake. Choice of three sweets. *Seats 18. Parties 10. D only 7.30-8.30. Set D £22.50.*

Penzance   Harris's   £70
Tel 0736 64408   **R**
46 New Street Penzance Cornwall TR18 2LZ   **Map 12 A4**

Owner Roger Harris buys fresh fish from Newlyn Harbour for his friendly little restaurant opposite the Sir Humphrey Davy statue. Moules marinière, grilled red mullet and grilled or poached John Dory make regular appearances along with some equally appealing meat dishes: corn-fed chicken in filo pastry with glazed apple and calvados sauce, rack of lamb, fillet steak grilled or with a Madeira sauce. Ask about the special 'Taste of Cornwall' menu which is sometimes featured. Vegetarians should give notice on the morning of their visit. Additional lighter lunchtime menu (salmon pancakes, crab salad or florentine, goujons of sole, liver and bacon). *Seats 30. Private Room 24. L 12-2 D 7-10. Closed Sun, winter Mons, 25 & 26 Dec, 1 Jan, 2 weeks Nov.* AMERICAN EXPRESS *Access, Visa.*

Penzance   Places of Interest

Tourist Information   Tel 0736 62207.
The Acorn Theatre   Tel 0736 65520.
St. Michael's Mount (NT)   Marazion Tel 0736 710507.
Trengwainton Garden (NT)   Tel 0736 63021.
Penzance and District Museum and Art Gallery   Tel 0736 63625.
Porthmeor Beach *5 miles NW Penzance.*

Our inspectors *never* book in the name of Egon Ronay's Guides. They disclose their identity only if they are considering an establishment for inclusion in the next edition of the Guide.

Peterborough   Butterfly Hotel   63%   £70
Tel 0733 64240   Fax 0733 65538   **H**
**Thorpe Meadows Longthorpe Parkway Peterborough Cambridgeshire
PE3 6GA**   **Map 7 E4**

One of a small chain of modern, low-rise brick-built East Anglian hotels. Peterborough's Butterfly sits at the water's edge, overlooking Thorpe Meadows rowing lake. Neat, practical accommodation ranges from studio singles to four suites. Conferences (80), banqueting (50). *Rooms 70.* AMERICAN EXPRESS *Access, Diners, Visa.*

Peterborough — Forte Posthouse — 60% — £68

Tel 0733 240209   Fax 0733 244455   **H**

Great North Road Norman Cross Peterborough Cambridgeshire PE7 3TB   Map 7 E4

Popular business hotel at the Norman Cross roundabout on the A1. Good leisure facilities and the usual good Forte value. Meeting rooms for up to 50. Children up to 16 stay free in parents' room. *Rooms 90. Indoor swimming pool, gym, sauna, spa bath, solarium.* AMERICAN EXPRESS *Access, Diners, Visa.*

Peterborough — Forte Travelodge — £45

Tel 0733 231109   **L**

Alwalton Village nr Peterborough Cambridgeshire PE7 3UR   Map 7 E4

On the A1 Great North Road southbound, 3 miles from the centre of Peterborough. *Rooms 32.* AMERICAN EXPRESS *Access, Diners, Visa.*

Peterborough — Peterborough Moat House — 64% — £80

Tel 0733 260000   Fax 0733 262737   **H**

Thorpe Wood Peterborough Cambridgeshire PE3 6SG   Map 7 E4

Two miles west of the city centre by the Thorpe Wood golf course and Nene Country Park, a modern redbrick hotel offering extensive leisure and air-conditioned conference facilities; the largest room can take up to 400 delegates. 45 of the bedrooms are reserved for non-smokers. Children up to 15 stay free in parents' room. *Rooms 125. Indoor swimming pool, gym, sauna, spa baths, steam room, solarium, games room.* AMERICAN EXPRESS *Access, Diners, Visa.*

Peterborough — Swallow Hotel — 69% — £105

Tel 0733 371111   Fax 0733 236725   **H**

Lynch Road Peterborough Cambridgeshire PE2 0GB   Map 7 E4

Modern, low-rise hotel by the A605, two minutes from the A1 (take Alwalton-Chesterton-Business Park & Showground sign). Spacious public areas are bright and airy. Extensive leisure and conference facilities for up to 300. *Rooms 163. Garden, indoor swimming pool, keep-fit equipment, sauna, spa bath, steam room, solarium, beauty & hair salon.* AMERICAN EXPRESS *Access, Diners, Visa.*

Peterborough — Travel Inn — £43

Tel 0733 235794   Fax 0733 391055   **L**

Ham Lane Orton Meadows Peterborough Cambridgeshire PE2 0UU   Map 7 E4

4 minutes' drive from the city centre. Take Peterborough exit from A1, then A605, following signs to Nene Park. Meeting rooms for up to 24. *Rooms 40.* AMERICAN EXPRESS *Access, Diners, Visa.*

Peterborough — Places of Interest

Tourist Information   Tel 0733 317336.
Key Theatre   Tel 0733 52439.
Lady Lodge Arts Centre   Tel 0733 237073.
Peterborough Cathedral   Tel 0733 43342.
Peterborough Museum and Art Gallery   Tel 0733 43329.
East of England Ice Rink   Tel 0733 260222.
East of England Showground   Tel 0733 234451.
Peakirk Wildfowl Trust   Tel 0733 252271.

Petersfield — Langrish House — 63% — £55

Tel 0730 266941   Fax 0730 260543   **H**
Langrish Petersfield Hampshire GU32 1RN
Map 15 D3

Built around the heart of a 16th-century farmhouse and converted
to a hotel in 1979, the house stands in rolling countryside three miles out
of Petersfield off the A272. Bedrooms have peaceful pastoral views,
traditional furnishings and a few homely extras. The large cellar (now
a bar) was reputedly excavated by Royalist prisoners taken at the Civil
War's Battle of Cheriton after which they ended up in their own prison!
Rooms 18. Garden. Closed Christmas and New Year's Eve. AMERICAN EXPRESS
Access, Diners, Visa.

Pickering — White Swan — £76

Tel & Fax 0751 472288   **I**
The Market Place Pickering West Yorkshire YO18 7AA
Map 5 E4

A charming town-centre inn where guests can find quiet (in the elegant
lounge) or conviviality (in the oak-panelled bar and snug). Gradual,
continuous improvement of bedrooms sees the addition of good-quality
pine furniture and personally selected antique pieces where once were
hardwood and melamine. Deirdre Buchanan and her loyal staff provide the
warmest of welcomes, and decent bar food is produced by a quietly
competent kitchen. *Rooms 13. Access, Visa.*

Pingewood — Kirtons Farm Hotel & Country Club — 60% — £87

Tel 0734 500885   Fax 0734 391996   **H**
Pingewood Reading Berkshire RG3 3UN
Map 15 D2

Unexceptional standardised bedrooms (those in the new wing are best),
except that each has a balcony overlooking the lake where the European
water-ski championships are sometimes held. Residential conferences
(facilities for up to 140) are the main business during the week but
at weekends it's the extensive leisure facilities of the adjacent country club
(also available to hotel guests) that are the big attraction. 24hr room
service. Near Junction 11 of the M4 but ask for detailed directions when
booking. *Rooms 81. Indoor swimming pool, gym, squash, spa baths, sauna,
steam room, solarium, beauty & hair salon, snooker, tennis, water-skiing.*
AMERICAN EXPRESS *Access, Diners, Visa.*

> Many establishments are currently on the market, so ownership could
> change after we go to press.

Plumtree — Perkins Bar Bistro — £50

Tel 0602 373695   **R**
Old Railway Station, Station Road Plumtree Nottinghamshire
NG12 5NA
Map 7 D3

Tony and Wendy Perkins have been providing meals for the discerning
at their converted railway station for 12 years now – and standards have
not slipped. Up a short driveway, and set in a mature garden, one is cut off
from the sounds of modern life. Start with grilled sardines provençale,
asparagus with hollandaise sauce or delicious trout fillet marinated
in Sauvignon; herb-crusted rack of lamb with a rosemary sauce, fried
goujons of plaice with garlic mayonnaise or one of the many game dishes
offered in their season. Friendly and efficient service. *Seats 93. Parties 30.
Private Room 30. L 12-2.30 D 6.30-9.45. Closed Sun, Mon, 1 week
Christmas.* AMERICAN EXPRESS *Access, Diners, Visa.*

Plymouth   **Boringdon Hall**   70%   £75

Tel 0752 344455   Fax 0752 346578   **H**

Colebrook Plympton Plymouth Devon PL7 4DP   **Map 12 C3**

1587 saw the transformation of older buildings (originally a monastery) into today's handsome and stately manor house, and Sir Francis Drake was guest of honour at the inaugural grand banquet. It is said that Queen Elizabeth stayed a year later when touring the West Country. A spectacular bar in the Great Hall provides a focal point, overlooked by both restaurant and minstrel's gallery. Above, tower bedrooms feature carved four-posters and matching period furniture. Extensions, externally clad in original stone, stand around a courtyard alongside the leisure club (the latter is not the only modern feature, for Boringdon also boasts conference facilities for up to 120 delegates). Children up to the age of 12 free in parents' room. *Rooms 40. Garden, indoor swimming pool, keep-fit equipment, sauna, tennis.* AMERICAN EXPRESS *Access, Diners, Visa.*

Plymouth   **Campanile Hotel**   £44

Tel 0752 601087   Fax 0752 223213   **L**

Marsh Mills Longbridge Road Plymouth Devon PL6 8LD   **Map 12 C3**

Off a roundabout junction on the A38, heading towards Cornwall. *Rooms 50.* AMERICAN EXPRESS *Access, Diners, Visa.*

Plymouth   **Chez Nous**   ★   £95

Tel 0752 266793   Fax 0752 660428   **R**

13 Frankfort Gate Plymouth Devon PL1 1QA   **Map 12 C3**

It's really quite surprising that no-one else has picked up on Jacques and Suzanne Marchal's phrase of 'Cuisine Spontanée' – it's so apt for our times and, cleverly, as right for the '90s as it was when they set up in 1980. The attractive red, white and blue dining room tells you at once that you're in a corner of France, as does the menu, quirkily priced as 2850p rather than in pounds sterling! So what will you get for your pence? Well, it all depends on the market, of course, but typical offerings would be *mousse de foies de volaille et sa brioche aux noix*, or *croustades de ris d'agneau au Madère*, followed by *filet de turbot aux poivrons doux*, or *mignons de porc au tamarin*. Vegetables or salad to accompany, French cheeses or classic desserts to follow, coffee (an extra 200p!) to conclude. A well-balanced list of mainly French wines with decent house selections and good half bottles. Convenient local parking. *Seats 28. L 12.30-2 D 7-10.30. Closed Sun & Mon, Bank Holidays, 3 weeks Feb, 3 weeks Sep. Set meals £28.50.* AMERICAN EXPRESS *Access, Diners, Visa.* MARTELL

Plymouth   **Copthorne Hotel**   70%   £103

Tel 0752 224161   Fax 0752 670688   **H**

Armada Way Plymouth Devon PL1 1AR   **Map 12 C3**

The Copthorne is an attractive hotel, with the light and elegant decor in the foyer setting the overall tone; other public areas include a restaurant, brasserie (open 10.30-10.30), Gallery cocktail bar and lounge. Bedrooms include Classic (singles), Connoisseur and suites all with contemporary fitted furniture and plenty of writing space; there are rooms for non-smokers and one for disabled guests; tiled bathrooms have good counter space and large, well-lit mirrors. Children up to 16 stay free in parents' room. 24hr room service. Rooms on the fourth floor have recently been refurbished. Ample free parking. Greatly reduced weekend rates (Fri-Sun). Facilities for banquets and conferences (up to 75) and Plymsoles (geddit?) leisure club. The hotel is at North Cross roundabout, opposite the university. *Rooms 135. Indoor swimming pool, gym, sauna, steam room, solarium, pool table.* AMERICAN EXPRESS *Access, Diners, Visa.*

Plymouth   Forte Posthouse   65%   £68

Tel 0752 662828   Fax 0752 660974   **H**

Cliff Road The Hoe Plymouth Devon PL1 3DL   **Map 12 C3**

High-riser with fine views from its prime position on the Hoe.
Conferences for up to 100, banqueting to 80. No room service. *Rooms 106.
Garden, outdoor swimming pool.* AMERICAN EXPRESS *Access, Diners, Visa.*

Plymouth   Moat House   70%   £92

Tel 0752 662866   Fax 0752 673816   **H**

Armada Way Plymouth Devon PL1 2HJ   **Map 12 C3**

Day rooms at this high-rise hotel, in particular the Penthouse restaurant and
bar, command spectacular views of the Hoe and Plymouth Sound. So do
many of the good-sized, picture-windowed bedrooms, which have double
beds (twins have two double beds), seating areas and plenty of writing
space. On the ground floor the large, bright reception area includes the
relaxing International Bar. Conference and banqueting facilities for up to
425. Children under 16 are accommodated free if sharing their parents'
room. Ample free parking below the building. *Rooms 212. Indoor
swimming pool, gym, sauna, steam room, solarium, games room.* AMERICAN EXPRESS
Access, Diners, Visa.

Plymouth   Novotel   62%   £54

Tel & Fax 0752 221422   **H**

Marsh Mills Roundabout Plymouth Devon PL6 8NH   **Map 12 C3**

Practical modern accommodation and conference/banqueting facilities (for
up to 240 delegates) on the A38 two miles from the town centre.
Rooms 100. Garden. AMERICAN EXPRESS *Access, Diners, Visa.*

Plymouth   Places of Interest

Tourist Information   Tel 0752 264849.
Athenaeum Theatre   Tel 0752 266079.
Theatre Royal   Tel 0752 668.
City Museum and Art Gallery   Tel 0752 264878.
Plymouth Argyle Football Ground   Home Park Tel 0752 562561.
Dartmoor Wildlife Park   Sparkwell Tel 0755 37209.
   Historic Houses, Castles and Gardens
Saltram House (NT)   Tel 0752 336546.
Antony House, Woodland Garden and Natural Woods(NT)   Torpoint
   Tel 0752 812191.
Mount Edgcumbe House & Country Park   Tel 0752 822236.

Changes in data sometimes occur in establishments after the Guide
goes to press. Prices should be taken as indications rather than firm
quotes.

Pocklington   Feathers Hotel   £50

Tel 0759 303155   Fax 0759 304382   **I**

Market Place Pocklington Humberside YO4 2UN   **Map 7 D1**

A friendly market-town inn, 15 minutes drive from York, useful to know
in the area. Main-house rooms include a conservatory, and a bridal suite
with a four-poster bed. Six rooms with bow-fronted windows are in the
stone-clad annexe. Two family rooms. Two conference rooms for up to 85
delegates. Free parking for up to 60 cars. No dogs. *Rooms 12. Garden.*
AMERICAN EXPRESS *Access, Diners, Visa.*

Podimore   Forte Travelodge   £45

Tel 0935 840074   **L**

Podimore nr Yeovil Somerset BA22 8JG   Map 13 F2

On the A303, 6 miles north of Yeovil and adjacent to the junction with the A37. *Rooms 31.* AMERICAN EXPRESS *Access, Diners, Visa.*

Polperro   Kitchen at Polperro   £55

Tel 0503 72780   **R**

The Coombes Polperro Cornwall PL13 2RQ   Map 12 C3

Park in the village car park and walk down to Ian and Vanessa Bateson's lovely little restaurant. The cooking is enjoyable and unpretentious, the menus interesting and varied and always with seafood at centre stage. Crab is *the* special special, in half an avocado, in a classic cocktail, in a filo pastry parcel, dijonnaise. . . . Prawns also appear in many preparations, and daily specials could include chargrilled sole, swordfish steak and scallops with a sweet yellow pepper sauce. Meaty dishes, too, plus a good selection of vegetarian main courses such as mushroom ravioli or mixed bean goulash. No children under ten. *Seats 24. Parties 6. D only 7-9.30. Open main season Tues-Sat plus Bank Holidays; other times variable. Access, Visa.*

Pool-in-Wharfedale   Pool Court

Pool Bank Pool-in-Wharfedale Otley West Yorkshire LS21 1EH   Map 6 C1

As we went to press, we heard that after 28 years Michael and Hanni Gill were moving Pool Court lock, stock and barrel and that this change will occur as the Guide is published. Pool Court Restaurant with Rooms in its familiar guise at Pool-in-Wharfedale closed on 30th September 1994. However, *Pool Court At The Calls* was due to open in Leeds on 12th November 1994. More about this one next year! (See under Leeds, *42 The Calls*).

Poole   Haven Hotel   69%   £120

Tel 0202 707333   Fax 0202 708796   **HR**

Banks Road Sandbanks Poole Dorset BH13 7QL   Map 14 C4

Follow signs to the Swanage ferry to find the Haven, right by the water's edge at the entrance to the world's second largest natural harbour giving most of the bedrooms (many with balconies) fine views either of Brownsea Island and the Purbeck hills or across the Solent to the Isle of Wight. Comfortable rather than luxurious, with lightwood furniture and matching bedcovers and curtains, the rooms are immaculately kept, as in the whole hotel. Inviting public areas include the beamed Marconi lounge (he made the first wireless telegraph broadcast from here) with leather chesterfields, and a splendid conservatory with comfortably upholstered 'garden' furniture and waterside terrace beyond. The exceptionally comprehensive leisure centre includes both indoor and outdoor pools, just a few steps beyond which is the hotel's own sandy beach. A visit (particularly by other hoteliers) to the luxurious gents loos is recommended. There's also a fine, purpose-built business centre adjacent to the hotel catering for up to 170. No children under 5, but 5- to 12-year-olds stay free in parents' room. No dogs. *Rooms 94. Indoor & outdoor swimming pools, gym, squash, sauna, spa bath, steam room, solarium, beauty salon, hairdressing, tennis.* AMERICAN EXPRESS *Access, Diners, Visa.*

Sea View Restaurant   £55

Large, 20s-style dining room with short but well-balanced table d'hote dinner menu supplemented by a varied grill menu. Well-thought-out dishes are reliably cooked and swiftly served – from starters like salad of monkfish tails with grapefruit and avocado or a whole quail with an apricot farce baked in a filo pastry wrapping, to main courses that might encompass paupiette of beef filled with foie gras mousse or a ragout of angler fish and tiger prawns set on home-made noodles and a basil and tomato sauce. To finish, perhaps a millefeuille of sablé biscuits layered with butterscotch mousse and served with a fudge sauce or iced chocolate parfait with coffee anglaise. Lunch is a buffet/carvery affair, including Sunday when a traditional roast is always offered. No children after 7pm. Light lunches are also available in the informal conservatory and on the terrace, from where there are views of Poole Bay and Studland. *Seats 150. Parties 24. L 12.30-2 D 7-9.30. Set L £14.50 Set D £22.*

La Roche £80

The more intimate à la carte restaurant is where chef Karl Heinz Nagler is given full rein to his undoubted skills. The sophisticated black-edged decor is a suitable foil to equally sophisticated dishes such as a fruit soup enriched with sparkling wine and topped with champagne sorbet, steamed, lettuce-wrapped scallops garnished with truffle ravioli, crispy leeks and a truffle vinaigrette, rack of lamb with a ratatouille galette and a basil lamb jus, and a light and fruity chocolate and strawberry soufflé. The carefully chosen wine list features French wines and a few examples from the New World. No children under 10 years. *Seats 30. Parties 8. D only 7-10.30. Closed Sun, Mon, 25 & 26 Dec.*

Poole	**Mansion House**	**74%**	**£110**
Tel 0202 685666 Fax 0202 665709			**HR**
11 Thames Street Poole Dorset BH15 1JN			Map 14 C4

Facing St James Church across a tiny square, the marble-pillared portico and tall, arched windows of the Mansion House epitomise Georgian elegance. It is only a stone's throw from bustling Poole quay, yet it affords an oasis of calm within. The best bedrooms are generously proportioned and airy, although some others are rather less so. Each is decorated in individual style and furnished with fine antiques, to which today's more modern necessities have been sympathetically added. More thoughtful, homely extras extend to mineral water, fresh fruit and boiled sweets in the rooms plus complimentary early morning tea tray and choice of newspaper. 'Limited' 24hr room service. Children up to 12 stay free in parents' room. No dogs. *Rooms 28.* AMERICAN EXPRESS *Access, Diners, Visa.*

Benjamins Restaurant £65

A smart dining club, also open to the public, where non-residents (or non-members) pay 15% supplement to the 'modern English' fixed-price menu prices. Crab mousse, creamy mussels with wine, blue cheese and walnut soufflé, a daily roast (carved from a silver trolley), simply grilled Dover sole, daily fresh fish dishes and duet of venison and pigeon are typical of the style; good vegetarian options and traditional puddings complete the picture. A popular hors d'oeuvre table is laid out on Saturday evening and Sunday lunch; the latter sees an unusually wide choice with a choice of roasts. The clubby atmosphere successfully avoids stuffiness and service is good. JJ's Bistro offers more informal fare, but is only open to members and residents. Very fair prices on the carefully compiled wine list. *Seats 100. Parties 14. Private Room 40. L 12.30-2 D 7.30-9.30 (Sat from 7). Closed L Sat, D Sun. Set L £10-£16.50 (Sun L £12.95) Set D £16.95/£24.95.*

Poole	**Quay Thistle Hotel**	**63%**	**£80**
Tel 0202 666800 Fax 0202 684470			**H**
The Quay Poole Dorset BH15 1HD			Map 14 C4

Rebranded by Mount Charlotte, this former Hospitality Inn overlooks the harbour and is signposted from the town centre. Neat, practical bedrooms include 20 reserved for non-smokers. *Rooms 68. Patio.* AMERICAN EXPRESS *Access, Diners, Visa.*

Poole   **Sandbanks Hotel**   59%   £120

Tel 0202 707377   Fax 0202 708885   **H**

15 Banks Road Sandbanks Poole Dorset BH13 7PS   Map 14 C4

Ideal for families, with an attractive patio and garden leading on to a sandy beach, and complete holiday services that include organised activities, a children's restaurant and a nursery. 17 rooms are specifically designated as family rooms. Four tiers of balconied bedrooms look either out to sea or across Poole Bay and the open-plan bar, vast sun lounge and dining rooms also enjoy panoramic views over the sea. Much money and effort has recently been expended on maintenance. Adult guests may use the leisure facilities at the *Haven Hotel* (see entry). No dogs. *Rooms 105. Garden, indoor swimming pool, sauna, steam room, solarium, spa bath, gym, crèche (daily in summer), children's outdoor play area, coffee shop (8am-11pm).* AMERICAN EXPRESS *Access, Diners, Visa.*

Poole   **Places of Interest**

Tourist Information   Tel 0202 673322.
Poole Arts Centre   Tel 0202 685222.
Guildhall Museum   Tel 0202 675151.
Waterfront Poole   Tel 0202 675151/683138.
Icetrax Ice Rink   Tel 0202 716000.
Sandbanks Beach.

Porlock   **Oaks Hotel**   65%   £75

Tel & Fax 0643 862265   **HR**

Porlock Somerset TA24 8ES   Map 13 D1

An Edwardian country house in an elevated position among lawns and trees (oaks, of course!), with views down to Porlock Bay. Tim and Anne Riley, here since 1986, are the most welcoming of hosts, and the lounge, with its flowers, books and magazines, is an easy place for relaxing. There's also an intimate bar. Bedrooms are light and pretty with a mix of pine and some nice old-fashioned pieces. Service is a strong point and the whole place is kept crisp and fresh. *Rooms 10. Closed Jan & Feb. Garden.* AMERICAN EXPRESS *Access, Diners, Visa.*

Restaurant   £45

Anne's daily-changing menus are unpretentious and offer fine value. Start with soup (perhaps cream of celery, apple and tomato), a smoked salmon pancake or cheese soufflé; follow with the fish/shellfish course; continue with saddle of lamb, orange-sauced breast of duck or beef olives; and round things up with a sorbet, ice cream, treacle tart or a selection of local cheeses. Fair prices on a concise wine list. No smoking. *Seats 24. Parties 12. D only 7-8.30. Set D £20.*

Porth   **Trevelgue Hotel**   62%   £96*

Tel 0637 872864   Fax 0637 876365   **H**

Porth nr Newquay Cornwall TR7 3LX   Map 12 B3

A budget family holiday hotel *par excellence* that is sufficiently well endowed with facilities to easily overcome the vagaries of British weather. With the rolling downs of north Cornwall behind, a 180° sea vista to the front and a large, sandy beach just down the hill, the Trevelgue has a head start with its position. Self-styled as a "parents' haven" and "children's paradise", its continued success (after 13 years) is achieved by providing almost everything that families need – at no extra cost – in order to have a peaceful stay away from the comforts of home. From babes in arms to the most energetic of teenagers, due consideration is given to their requirements; you name it and they've generally thought of it, and they bring it off with panache. The arrangements for children's high tea and for parents to enjoy their modest evening meal are particularly impressive (the

wine list is very keenly priced). Cots, high-chairs, bunk beds, bikes,
buggies, back packs, baby walkers, baby baths, sterilisers, bottle warmers
and bouncy chairs can all be provided if booked in advance. The hotel
is spacious enough never to feel like a nursery and the management have
cleverly made the adult attractions as inviting as those for their junior
guests. Accommodation is in 42 spacious (if somewhat spartan) family
suites with 28 further rooms for additional family members. Guests
without children are not encouraged. Half-board, weekly terms only
in season. Winner of our Family Hotel of the Year award in our *..and Baby
Comes Too* Guide 1994. **Rooms** *70. Garden, tennis, children's sports in high
season, squash, golf practice net, 3-hole golf course, mini-golf, giant chess,
croquet & boules, skittles, air rifle range, children's adventure playground,
outdoor & indoor swimming pools, health and beauty salon, pool, disco, table
tennis, BMX track. Hotel closed Nov-end Mar (booking office open).
Access, Visa.*

Portloe	Lugger Hotel	59%	£104
Tel 0872 501322 Fax 0872 501691			**H**
Portloe Truro Cornwall TR2 5RD			**Map 12 B3**

17th-century inn, smugglers' haunt, boat-builders' shed, and since 1950
a cosy, friendly little waterside hotel run by the hospitable Powell family.
The sea and tiny beach are virtually on the doorstep, and in fine weather
the cocktail bar terrace is a popular spot. Oak-beamed lounge, library, well-
equipped bedrooms divided between the original building and a modern
addition. No children under 12. **Rooms** *19. Closed mid Nov – early Feb.*
AMERICAN EXPRESS *Access, Diners, Visa.*

Portsmouth	Forte Posthouse	65%	£68
Tel 0705 827651 Fax 0705 756715			**H**
Pembroke Road Southsea Portsmouth Hampshire PO1 2TA			**Map 15 D4**

Near the Hovercraft terminal at Southsea, a modern hotel with leisure and
business centres (conferences for up to 220, banqueting up to 180).
Formerly called *Forte Crest.* **Rooms** *163. Indoor swimming pool, gymnasium,
sauna, spa bath, steam room, solarium.* AMERICAN EXPRESS *Access, Diners, Visa.*

Portsmouth	Hilton National	66%	£70
Tel 0705 219111 Fax 0705 210762			**H**
Eastern Road Farlington Portsmouth Hampshire PO6 1UN			**Map 15 D4**

Modern low-rise hotel alongside M27 just off the A2050 to Southsea, and
ten minutes from Portsmouth city centre. Well-equipped bedrooms
(children up to 14 stay free in parents' room), leisure centre, free parking.
Rooms *178. Indoor swimming pool, keep-fit facilities, sauna, spa bath, floodlit
tennis, snooker.* AMERICAN EXPRESS *Access, Diners, Visa.*

> Any person using our name to obtain free hospitality is a fraud.
> Proprietors, please inform the police and us.

Portsmouth	Hospitality Inn	61%	£79
Tel 0705 731281 Fax 0705 817572			**H**
South Parade Southsea Portsmouth Hampshire PO4 0RN			**Map 15 D4**

Seafront hotel with some Victorian features, but mainly modern bedrooms.
13 rooms reserved for non-smokers. Children up to 16 share parents' room
free. Popular for conferences and functions for up to 250 people. Mount
Charlotte Thistle Hotels. **Rooms** *115.* AMERICAN EXPRESS *Access, Diners, Visa.*

Portsmouth   Pendragon Hotel   59%   £49

Tel 0705 823201   Fax 0705 750283   **H**

Clarence Parade Southsea Portsmouth Hampshire PO5 2HY   Map 15 D4

Now privately owned, the Pendragon has reduced its room rates this year, though facilities remain the same. Banqueting/conferences for up to 100, family rooms and children's menu. Sea views over the Solent add to the appeal. *Rooms 49. Patio.* AMERICAN EXPRESS *Access, Diners, Visa.*

Portsmouth   Portsmouth Marriott Hotel   73%   £96

Tel 0705 383151   Fax 0705 388701   **H**

North Harbour Cosham Portsmouth Hampshire PO6 4SH   Map 15 D4

The hotel stands alongside the junction of the A3 and M27, a short drive from the ferry terminals and the town centre. Public areas in atrium-style include swimming pool, lounge, bar and split-level restaurant. Bedrooms on seven floors are roomy, with high standards of housekeeping, stylish wooden furniture, modern fabrics and good-sized beds – all doubles and many king-size. Compact bathrooms have good showers (but smallish baths) and plenty of toiletries. Leisure facilities include a snooker room and well-kept secluded garden with barbecue. Banqueting and conference facilities up to 450 (300 in one suite). The rate quoted is for a standard room. Premier rooms are priced at £116. Rates include parking. *Rooms 170. Garden, indoor swimming pool, keep-fit equipment, squash, volleyball, basketball, sauna, spa bath, solarium, snooker, children's playroom & playground.* AMERICAN EXPRESS *Access, Diners, Visa.*

Portsmouth   Places of Interest

Tourist Information   Tel 0705 832464.
Kings Theatre   Tel 0705 820527.
New Theatre Royal   Tel 0705 864611.
Portsmouth Cathedral   Tel 0705 823300.
Portsmouth Football Ground   Fratton Park Tel 0705 731204.
   Museums and Art Galleries
Charles Dickens' Birthplace Museum   Tel 0705 827261.
Portsmouth Naval Heritage Trust   Tel 0705 861533.
HMS Victory   HM Naval Base Tel 0705 819604.
Mary Rose Ship Hall and Exhibition   HM Naval Base Tel 0705 750521.
The Royal Naval Museum   HM Naval Base Tel 0705 733060.
D-Day Museum   Tel 0705 827261.
HMS Warrior 1860   HM Naval Base Tel 0705 291379.

Poundsgate   Leusdon Lodge Hotel   61%   NEW   £60

Tel 03643 304   Fax 03643 599   **HR**

Leusdon Poundsgate nr Newton Abbot Devon TQ13 7PE   Map 13 D3

Not easy to find this oasis of a hotel, perched high on the moors above Newton Abbot, so phone for directions. The views from the public rooms and many of the bedrooms will make the effort worthwhile. The home comforts and delightful welcome will make you feel like a guest in a private house. Delicious cream teas. A good centre for walking in Dartmoor National Park. *Rooms 7. Garden, croquet.* AMERICAN EXPRESS *Access, Visa.*

Restaurant   £55

Good simple cooking using the best ingredients: lovage soup, melon with West Country air-dried ham or smoked trout paté served with proper wholemeal toast to start; perhaps fillets of sole with a mushroom sauce or well-prepared pork poivrade to follow. There are always interesting vegetarian options. For dessert the hot chocolate soufflé is a must. Beautiful views of the Dart valley from the dining room. *Seats 18. Parties 8. L by arrangement. D 7.30-8.45. Set D £19.50.*

Powburn   Breamish Country House Hotel   67%   £72

Tel 066 578 266   Fax 066 578 500   **H**

Powburn Alnwick Northumberland NE66 4LL   **Map 5 D1**

Resident owners Doreen and Alan Johnson offer hospitality and
tranquillity in abundance at their Georgian-style building, originating
in the 17th century as a farmhouse and converted in the 19th century
to a hunting lodge. Five acres of gardens and woodland provide the setting,
and trees from those woods furnish the names of the individually decorated
bedrooms. *Rooms 11. Garden. Closed Jan-14th Feb. Access, Visa.*

Powerstock   Three Horseshoes Inn   £50

Tel 0308 85328   **RR**

Powerstock Bridport Dorset DT6 3TF   **Map 13 F2**

The Three Horseshoes is a stone and thatch country inn with simple
country furnishings and open fires, reached by narrow winding lanes. Its
restaurant comprises two pine-panelled rooms, one small and cosy, the
other more roomy and airy. Fish is what chef-licensee Pat Ferguson is best
known for, and the blackboard menu offers several examples of freshly
caught produce, simply prepared and presented. Meat-eaters are also well
provided for. Cooking is generally in traditional British mode, especially
the puddings. Very popular for Sunday lunches – essential to book,
especially in winter. Tables in the garden for summer eating. *Seats 60.
L 12-2 D 7-10 (to 9 Sun). Set L £10.95/£12.95.* AMERICAN EXPRESS
Access, Visa.

Rooms   £50

Four large, traditionally-styled rooms have central heating, en-suite
bathrooms and lovely views. Delightful garden. Families with children are
welcome; cots available.

Prestbury   Bridge Hotel   63%   £84

Tel 0625 829326   Fax 0625 827557   **H**

New Road Prestbury nr Macclesfield Cheshire SK10 4DQ   **Map 6 B2**

Old-world charm and modern convenience meet in a privately owned
hotel next to the church in the centre of a pretty village. Day rooms retain
some feel of the 17th-century origins, while most of the bedrooms are
in a modern redbrick extension overlooking the River Bollin. Banqueting
and conference facilities for up to 100. *Rooms 23. Garden.* AMERICAN EXPRESS
Access, Diners, Visa.

Prestbury   The White House Manor   £112

Tel 0625 829376   Fax 0625 828627   **HR**

The Village Prestbury Cheshire SK10 4HP   **Map 6 B2**

Each bedroom has been decorated on a different theme here, with the
accent on quality. There are no public areas as such (thus no hotel grading),
just a small conservatory lounge and honesty bar where you can take
a leisurely breakfast, though it's just as often served in the privacy of your
own room. The very individually furnished bedrooms range from the
most elegant 'Crystal Room' which has a locally crafted four-poster bed,
crystal chandelier and and whirlpool bath to the sporty 'Minerva' that
includes a Turkish steam room and power shower, as well as antique
sporting equipment. Then there's the 'Glyndebourne' with a music centre
and comprehensive library of modern and classical music, or 'The Studio'
featuring art. Room service is available throughout the day and evening
and in addition there are extensive bar and beverage facilities in the
bedrooms, as well as remote-control TV, hairdryer and decent toiletries.
Small meeting rooms 5/40, conferences (60 theatre-style) and banqueting
(120 sit-down) in the restaurant. *Rooms 9. Garden.* AMERICAN EXPRESS
Access, Diners, Visa.

Restaurant £65

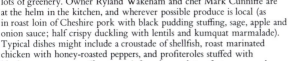

A few minutes' walk from the hotel, in the centre of the village, the pretty restaurant features exquisite table settings, Macclesfield silk and lace, and lots of greenery. Owner Ryland Wakeham and chef Mark Cunniffe are at the helm in the kitchen, and wherever possible produce is local (as in roast loin of Cheshire pork with black pudding stuffing, sage, apple and onion sauce; half crispy duckling with lentils and kumquat marmalade). Typical dishes might include a croustade of shellfish, roast marinated chicken with honey-roasted peppers, and profiteroles stuffed with blueberry cream on cheese sauce. A fine cheese platter features several British farmhouse varieties (Dunsyre Blue, Bonchester, Pencarreg); few half bottles on the wine list that has a good selection of New World wines, helpful tasting notes and quite reasonable prices. *Seats 75. Parties 28. Private Room 40. L 12-2 D 7-10. Closed D Sun, L Mon. Set L £11.95 Set D £16.50.*

Preston   **Forte Posthouse**   **63%**   £68

Tel 0772 259411   Fax 0772 201923   **H**

The Ringway Preston Lancashire PR1 3AU   Map 6 B1

Tall redbrick hotel with neatly designed bedrooms, and conference facilities for up to 120. Free parking for guests' cars in an adjacent multi-storey. *Rooms 121.* AMERICAN EXPRESS *Access, Diners, Visa.*

Preston   **Novotel**   **62%**   £55

Tel 0772 313331   Fax 0772 627868   **H**

Reedfield Place Walton Summit Preston Lancashire PR5 6AB   Map 6 B1

Practical modern accommodation (half the rooms designated non-smoking) and conference facilities for 180. Children up to 16 stay free in parents' room. Situated on the A6, and handy for the M6 (J29) and M61 (J9). Free parking for up to 140 cars. *Rooms 100. Outdoor swimming pool.* AMERICAN EXPRESS *Access, Diners, Visa.*

Preston   **Travel Inn**   £43

Tel 0772 720476   Fax 0772 729971   **L**

Blackpool Road Lea Preston Lancashire PR4 0XL   Map 6 B1

Rooms 40. AMERICAN EXPRESS *Access, Diners, Visa.*

Preston   **Places of Interest**

Tourist Information   Tel 0772 53731.
Hoghton Tower   Tel 025 485 2986.
Harris Museum and Art Gallery   Tel 0772 58248.
Camelot Theme Park   Chorley Tel 0257 455044.

Puckrup   **Puckrup Hall Hotel & Golf Club**   **75%**   £97

Tel 0684 296200   Fax 0684 850788   **HR**

Puckrup Tewkesbury Gloucestershire GL20 6EL   Map 14 B1

Formerly a small Regency hotel, the original building (which still contains 16 of the bedrooms) is now just an annexe (linked by glass walkway) to a splendid new hotel. Exceptionally well designed and built to a high standard, it boasts many nice architectural and decorative features showing great attention to detail. A marble 'compass' floor, with mural-painted dome above, is at the centre of a reception area that sports faux-marble columns and some classical statuary. Lots of other appealing public areas include an Orangery, a cocktail bar with baronial light fittings, a clubby golfer's bar with oak panelling and leather armchairs, and a modernistic coffee shop. The last two are part of a smart golf club/leisure centre that also houses the crèche (mornings during the week and all day at weekends). Well-designed bedrooms come with good lightwood, freestanding furniture, proper armchairs, phones at both desk and bedside, extras like mineral water and books, and, when the beds are turned down at night, a cuddly hedgehog is left on your pillow to keep you company and to take home as a souvenir. Smart bathrooms have panelled tubs with good showers above, marble-effect vanity units, large bathtubs and quality toiletries. There are two full suites and eight 'junior' suites with charming circular sitting areas opening on to furnished balconies. An extensive room service menu can provide a choice of hot dishes 24 hours a day. *Rooms 84. Garden, croquet, golf (18), putting, coarse fishing, indoor swimming pool, gym, sauna, steam room, spa bath, solarium, beauty salon, indoor children's playroom, helipad.* AMERICAN EXPRESS *Access, Diners, Visa.*

Balharries Brasserie/The Regency Room   £45/90

Two restaurants here now. The main Balharries Brasserie (named after the head chef – quite a distinction!) is stylishly informal in decor and offers a wide-ranging menu with everything from hoisin chicken and magic mushrooms to pizzas, grills, omelettes, burgers and sandwiches. The 'à la carte' restaurant (The Regency Room) remains in the original building with its period setting but now operates only for dinner from Wednesday to Saturday, with a classy menu typified by dishes such as scallop terrine with a ginger salsa dressing, warm quail salad with orange, pigeon pithiviers with creamed watercress and caramelised shallots, roast sea bass with carrots and nettles, and collops of beef with foie gras and sherry. No smoking in the Regency Room. **Brasserie:** *Seats 110. Private Room 24. L 12.30-2.30 D 6.30-10 (Fri & Sat to 10.30). Set Sun L £8.55/10.55 Set D £18.50.*

Puddington	**Craxton Wood**	**70%**	**£95**

Tel 051-339 4717   Fax 051-339 1740
Parkgate Road Puddington South Wirral Cheshire L66 9PB

HR

Map 6 A2

Craxton Wood is usefully located, just 6 miles from Chester, 2 miles from both the M56 and M53, and easily accessible from either Manchester or Liverpool airports and their business communities. That said, the hotel itself is an oasis of calm, where old-fashioned standards of service and comfort hold sway and where owner/manager Mr Petranca has been greeeting guests since 1967. Extensive wooded grounds (floodlit at night), lawns and rose gardens provide a peaceful setting and the spacious bedrooms are reassuringly traditional, with reproduction furniture, conservative decor and neat, bright bathrooms. By contrast, the bar is done out in modern greys, pinks and pastel blues, though the main feature here is the splendid view that can be had of the gardens. The lounge is more traditional in style and very formal, with the highly polished furniture that characterises the bedrooms. Children under 6 stay free in parents' room. Parking for 45 cars, banqueting/conferences for 50/35. No dogs. No food, even for residents, after breakfast on Sunday and Bank Holidays. *Rooms 14. Garden. Closed first week Jan, last 2 weeks Aug.* AMERICAN EXPRESS *Access, Diners, Visa.*

Restaurant   £70

The French menu with English translations might offer you a salad of smoked duck with herbs and orange segments then monkfish tail, roasted and served on puréed leeks and spinach with a red pepper sauce, with chocolate mousse on a pistachio sauce to finish, though there is plenty of choice at each course. There's a separate vegetarian menu and a good range of English and French cheeses. *Seats 85. Parties 50. L 12.30-2 D 7.30-10. Set L (inc wine) & D £19.85/£29.85. Closed Sun, Bank Holidays.*

Puddington   Place of Interest

Ness Gardens   Liverpool Botanic Gardens Between Neston and Burton
Tel 051 336 7769.

Pulborough   Chequers Hotel   61%   £69

Tel 0798 872486   Fax 0798 872715   **H**

Church Place Pulborough West Sussex RH20 1AD   Map 11 A6

An intimate hotel, formed from a charming little Queen Anne house and
adjacent stone building, which has been run, and lovingly cared for, by the
Searancke family for over 30 years. Recent changes include development
of a patio garden and complete refurbishment of some rooms (2 are now
designated non-smoking, as is the restaurant). Small car park (for 16 cars);
banqueting/conference facilities for 30/20. **Rooms** 11. *Garden, coffee shop
(9.30am-5.30pm).* *Access, Diners, Visa.*

Pulborough   Stane Street Hollow   £60

Tel 0798 872819   **R**

Codmore Hill Pulborough West Sussex RH20 1BG   Map 11 A6

Converted from two 16th-century cottages, René and Ann Kaiser's long-
established, charming restaurant is built of solid Sussex stone. René's
cooking has been reliably solid for over 18 years; his menu changes in its
entirety every four weeks, offering the likes of a creamy lentil soup with
a hint of curry and garlic croutons, smoked salmon and eel with fresh
horseradish cream or sweet-pickled herrings on a warm potato salad with
apples and gherkins to start, followed by casseroled rabbit with thyme,
Normandy-style fillet of pork, rack of lamb, lamb's sweetbreads with fresh
sorrel and cream and duck breast with orange sauce. Vegetarians may
be enticed by a wholemeal tartlet filled with spinach and pine kernels,
topped with a watercress-flavoured cheese soufflé. There's a choice of seven
dishes at each course including *assiette René* which offers a taster
in miniature of four of the desserts – from rhubarb cheesecake to meringue
with blackcurrant sorbet and purée. Lunch is a simpler, fixed-price 2-course
affair with no choice (cassolette of duckling, pheasant and bacon with
lentils, apple and blackberry pancake), except on Sundays when the whole
works comes into play, including roast rib of beef. Splendid value
on a sound wine list which features plenty of half bottles. **Seats** *32. Private
Rooms 16 & 24. L 12.30-1.15 (Sun to 1.30) D 7.15-9.15. Closed L Sat,
D Sun, all Mon & Tue, 2 weeks June, 2 weeks Nov, 24-27 Dec. Set L £8.50
(Sun £12.50/£15.50). No credit cards.*

Pulborough   Place of Interest

Parham Elizabethan House & Gardens   Parham Park Tel 0903 742021.

Purton   Pear Tree   74%   £92

Tel 0793 772100   Fax 0793 772369   **HR**

Church End Purton nr Swindon Wiltshire SN5 9ED   Map 14 C2

Formerly the vicarage for the parish church of St Mary's and actually
moved, stone by stone, from beside the church to its present site on the
outskirts of the village in 1910; now carefully extended – a charming,
galleried atrium joins old and new – the Pear Tree is an immaculately kept
and well-run hotel. Pink is the predominant colour scheme for the day
rooms while bedrooms favour pastel hues and come with all sorts of extras
from fresh flowers, sherry and mineral water to teletext on the TV and
towelling robes and quality toiletries which vary according to the gender
of the guest – in the otherwise fairly standard bathrooms. Ask about the
special 'Let Off Steam' weekends arranged in conjunction with the Swindon
and Cricklade Railway. **Rooms** *18. Garden, croquet.* *Access,
Diners, Visa.*

See over

Restaurant   £65

Janet Pichel-Juan produces interesting English menus in a delightful
conservatory setting, making excellent use of local meat produce. Lunch
and dinner show a similar style and range: ham and parsnip soup with
wholemeal croutons, puff pastry case of lamb's sweetbreads in a dark
grapefruit sauce, steamed fillets of brill with laverbread and saffron,
pheasant with sultanas, grapes and a calvados cream sauce, grilled Scotch
beef topped with walnut butter on a bed of diced bacon and peppers. The
vegetarian option is always of interest, too – perhaps sesame seed pie
of curried cauliflower, quorn and leeks – and the short dessert list always
includes a 'traditional pudding of the day'. Four *marque* champagnes at £30
or less bear witness to a fairly priced wine list that has helpful notes on each
wine. Lots of Chardonnays and Cabernet Sauvignons. *Seats* 60. *Parties* 14.
Private Room 50. *L* 12-2 *D* 7-9.30. *Closed L Sat. Set L* £17.50
Set D £27.50.

Quorn   The Quorn   72%   £92

Tel 0509 415050   Fax 0509 415557   **H**

66 Leicester Road Quorn Leicestershire LE12 8BB   Map 7 D3

With gardens reaching down to the river Soar, the Quorn offers ease
of access with a touch of the country thrown in. The mahogany-panelled
entrance hall with its flagstones, Oriental rugs and carved stone fireplace,
has a very welcoming look, and a splendid wooden staircase featuring oil
paintings and a brass chandelier heightens the country house feel. Bedrooms
in a modern purpose-built part are prettily decorated and tastefully
furnished; appointments include air-conditioning, two armchairs and
remote-control TV (some with teletext). There are various attractive
function rooms, from the 12-seater Snug to the mahogany-panelled
Charnwood Suite which can hold 120. Staff are very jolly and friendly.
The hotel is in the centre of Quorn, a village which is now by-passed
by the A6. *Rooms* 19. *Garden, coarse fishing, helipad.* AMERICAN EXPRESS *Access,
Diners, Visa.*

Quorn   Quorn Grange   67%   £94

Tel 0509 412167   Fax 0509 415621   **HR**

Wood Lane Quorn Leicestershire LE12 8DB   Map 7 D3

A short drive off the A6 brings you to this extended, ivy-clad Victorian
house. Stylish bedrooms offer garden views and are tastefully appointed
using contemporary fabrics offset against plain walls. Impressive, brightly
lit bathrooms have huge mirrors, marble surrounds and powerful showers.
A bar-lounge is housed in a bright, plant-filled conservatory. *Rooms* 17.
Garden. AMERICAN EXPRESS *Access, Diners, Visa.*

Restaurant   £60

Dining room windows are hung with Austrian blinds – a quietly elegant
setting for chef Gordon Lang's serious cooking. Toasted goat's cheese salad
or a little casserole of chicken and scampi could start the meal, followed
perhaps by salmon with soy, coriander and crab, rack of lamb or duckling
with a spinach and celeriac gateau. *Seats* 50. *Parties* 12. *Private Room* 30.
L 12-2.30 *D* 7-9.30 (Sat to 10, Sun to 9). *Closed L Sat. Set L from* £7.95
(Sun £9.95) *Set D from* £15.95.

Ramsbottom   Village Restaurant   £45

Tel 0706 825070   **R**

Market Place Ramsbottom nr Bury Lancashire BL0 9HT   Map 6 B1

Several changes here, though Ros Hunter still does the cooking (without
salt) while partner Chris Johnson looks after front of house and the superb
wines. The old restaurant has closed – it's now an informal bistro with pew

seating and only opens from lunch Wednesday to lunch Sunday,
a traditional affair with usually sirloin of beef as the centrepiece. Ingredients
are first class, lunch is à la carte from the blackboard, supper (not dinner
in these parts!) offers three courses at different fixed prices, typical examples
being carrot and cumin soup, home-cured beef, venison, fillet of silver hake
and real puddings (rhubarb and mace, crème brulée, chocolate rum pot,
and rich tipsy trifle). There's always an interesting vegetarian option,
a marvellous selection of mature and strong cheeses, and a short and
carefully chosen wine list with a further several hundred wines available (at
an additional £4.95 corkage) from the basement food and wine shop.
*Seats 32. Parties 8. L 12-2.30 (Sun at 1.30) D 7.45. Closed D Sun, all Mon &
Tues. Set L from £9.95 (Sun £14.95).*   *Access, Diners, Visa.*

Ravenstonedale   Black Swan Inn   £66

Tel 053 96 23204   ▮ I

Ravenstonedale nr Kirkby Stephen Cumbria CA17 4NG   Map 5 D3

At the top of an unspoilt village near the M6 (J38), the Black Swan
is a turn-of-the-century Lakeland stone inn with welcoming resident
owners in Gordon and Norma Stuart. It's a great base for walking and
fishing holidays, and relaxation is easy in the quaint stone-walled bars, the
sitting rooms or the sheltered garden. Main bedrooms in traditional style
are supplemented by more modern additions in the old stables, where
ramps and wide doorways offer good access for disabled guests. *Rooms 16.
Garden, lake and river fishing, tennis.* AMERICAN EXPRESS *Access, Diners, Visa.*

Reading   Forte Posthouse   64%   £68

Tel 0734 875485   Fax 0734 311958   ▮ H

500 Basingstoke Road Reading Berkshire RG2 0SL   Map 15 D2

Near Junction 11 of the M4. Good leisure amenities. Banqueting and
conference facilities for 110. Parking for 300. *Rooms 138. Garden, indoor
swimming pool, gym, sauna, spa bath, solarium.* AMERICAN EXPRESS *Access,
Diners, Visa.*

Reading   Forte Travelodge   £45

Tel 0734 750618   ▮ L

387 Basingstoke Road Reading Berkshire RG2 0JE   Map 15 D2

On the A33 southbound, close to Reading town centre. 1 mile north
of Junction 11 of the M4. *Rooms 36.* AMERICAN EXPRESS *Access, Diners, Visa.*

Reading   Granada Lodge   NEW   £52

Tel 0800 555 300   ▮ L

**Granada Reading Service Area M4 Burghfield Reading Berkshire RG3
3UQ**   Map 15 D2

Between Junctions 11 & 12 of M4. Under construction as we went
to press; due to open around Easter 1995. *Rooms 40.* AMERICAN EXPRESS *Access,
Diners, Visa.*

Reading   Holiday Inn Reading   71%   £106

Tel 0734 391818   Fax 0734 391665   ▮ H

Richfield Avenue Caversham Bridge Reading Berkshire RG1 8BD   Map 15 D2

Situated right on the edge of the Thames by the side of Caversham Bridge,
this three-storey hotel is ultra-modern in design with a mixture of red brick
and sloping roofs. Much trade comes from the business community
(banquets for 180, conferences for 200) – unsurprisingly, given its location
and good communication links – but it is also a useful tourist stopover.
Large, open-plan public rooms include a cocktail bar in the sunken lounge,
and a spotless white marble foyer. Limed lightwood furniture graces the
uniformly decorated bedrooms. Eight suites have private balconies with

river views, good-sized sitting rooms and better quality furnishings. Parking for 200 cars. Queens Moat Houses. *Rooms 111. Indoor swimming pool, sauna, solarium, gym.* AMERICAN EXPRESS® *Access, Diners, Visa.*

Reading   Ramada Hotel   68%   £117

Tel 0734 586222   Fax 0734 597842   **H**

Oxford Road Reading Berkshire RG1 7RH   **Map 15 D2**

A large modern redbrick hotel in the central area of town offering well-equipped bedrooms (all have individually controllable air-conditioning), the best of which are 32 Executives (worth the small premium) with better-quality lightwood furniture giving plenty of work space and a second telephone at the desk. Seven rooms are designated as Lady Guest rooms; one room for the disabled; the presidential Suite is top of the range. Public areas were refurbished last year. *Froggies* is an informal café/bar; buffet-only breakfast. Conference/banqueting facilities for 220/150. Free valet parking is available in a supervised reserved section of a nearby multi-storey car park. Children under 18 stay free in parents' room. *Rooms 194. Indoor swimming pool, gym, sauna, spa bath, sun beds, beauty salon.* AMERICAN EXPRESS® *Access, Diners, Visa.*

Reading   Places of Interest

Tourist Information   Tel 0734 566226.
Bulmershe College Dry Ski Slope   Tel 0734 663387.
Carters Ski Centre   Tel 0734 55589
   Historic Houses, Castles and Gardens
The Old Rectory   Burghfield Tel 073529 2206.
Englefield House and Garden   Theale Tel 0734 302221.
Stratfield Saye House   Tel 0256 882882.
Mapledurham House   Tel 0734 723350.

Redditch   Campanile Hotel   £44

Tel 0527 510710   Fax 0527 517269   **L**

Far Moor Lane Winyates Green Redditch Hereford & Worcester B98 0SD   **Map 14 C1**

Near A435/A4032 intersection, off M42 Junction 3. *Rooms 50.* AMERICAN EXPRESS® *Access, Diners, Visa.*

Reeth   Burgoyne Hotel   66%   £60

Tel & Fax 0748 884292   **HR**

The Green Reeth Richmond North Yorkshire DL11 6SN   **Map 5 D3**

An intentionally personalised and intimate small hotel has been created here by partners Derek Hickson and Peter Carwardine with echoes of, and obliquely paying homage to, an early *Sharrow Bay*. Once the home of the Burgoyne Johnson family, the imposing ivy-faced house stands in a prominent position overlooking the village green with commanding views of Swaledale and the surrounding hills shared by all but one of its bedrooms. The warmth of welcome, abundant comfort in elegant if slightly fussy day rooms and the personal attention which cossets each and every guest echoes the pleasure and pride which Peter and Derek take in having one stay in their house. In the tastefully modernised bedrooms plain, rich fabrics, freestanding furniture, easy chairs and magazines engender the feeling of well-being; remote-control TV and radio/alarm clocks are provided, but phones have been avoided. Where the bathrooms of three of the rooms cannot practically be incorporated en-suite, towelling robes and slippers are provided for a short step across the corridor. *Rooms 8. Garden. Closed 3 Jan – 1st weekend in Feb.* AMERICAN EXPRESS® *Access, Visa.*

Restaurant   £55

Dinner is a nightly-changed five-course affair where guests foregather in the
lounge (there is no bar) to choose their first and middle courses. Peter
Carwardine's cooking, reliable and solidly English, is matched by Derek
Hickson's smooth, professional service. Space is strictly limited and non-
residents, though warmly welcomed, are nonetheless required to book.
Seats 32. Parties 12. Private Room 12. D at 7.45. Set D £21 (5 course).

Reigate	**La Barbe**	**£60**
Tel 0737 241966		**R**
71 Bell Street Reigate Surrey RH2 7AN		**Map 15 E3**

An informal, bistro-like setting with high-backed settles and pine fittings,
on the edge of the town centre. French menus combine classics like garlic
snails, duck breast in blackcurrant sauce and a casserole of beef and morels
with more adventurous dishes such as wild mushroom, apple, shallot and
herb pie, or lamb cutlets presented with a courgette mousse and garlic
sauce. Main courses are accompanied by a selection of vegetables and the
speciality gratin dauphinois. Dishes are helpfully cross-referenced with
recommended bottles on the well-described wine list. *Seats 65. L 12-2
D 7-10. Closed L Sat, all Sun, Bank Holidays. Set L £16.45/£17.95/£16.95
Set D £19.95/£21.95.* AMERICAN EXPRESS *Access, Visa.*

Reigate	**Bridge House**	**61%**	**£82**
Tel 0737 246801 Fax 0737 223756			**H**
Reigate Hill Reigate Surrey RH2 9RP			**Map 15 E3**

On the A217, just off Junction 8 of the M25, 15 minutes from Gatwick
Airport. From its position high on Reigate Hill, this modern hotel enjoys
impressive views across the valley. Bedrooms are of a good size, with smart
darkwood units; the best rooms have south-facing balconies and good
views, while rear rooms have poor outlooks but are very quiet.
Considerably reduced stand-by room rates after 6pm and at weekends.
No dogs. *Rooms 39.* AMERICAN EXPRESS *Access, Diners, Visa.*

Reigate	**The Dining Room**	**NEW**	**£65**
Tel 0737 226650			**R**
59a High Street Reigate Surrey RH2 9AE			**Map 15 E3**

Smart new first-floor restaurant above the high street shops. A short à la
carte (supplemented by particularly good value fixed-price options)
is determinedly modern in style with the likes of chilled roasted peppers
with baby mozzarella; a tart of porcini mushrooms on a bed of dressed
Japanese leaves; pan-fried John Dory with a raw tomato coulis and herb
vinaigrette; seared beef fillet with Anna potatoes and a wild mushroom
casserole, and breast of duck with its own confit and lentils – all produced
in workmanlike fashion by chef Anthony Tobin in the kitchen. Desserts
range from a terrine of summer fruits with strawberry sauce and a rich
chocolate torte and a caramel 'Paris-Brest' with vanilla ice cream. Just two
dozen, well-chosen wines from Bibendum with none, apart from the fizz,
above £22. Smoking allowed only in the small bar area. *Seats 50. L 12-2
D 7-10. Closed L Sat, all Sun, 2 weeks Christmas, 1 week Easter & 1 week
August. Set L £9.95 Set D £13.95.* AMERICAN EXPRESS *Access, Diners, Visa.*

Renishaw	**Sitwell Arms**	**61%**	**£60**
Tel 0246 435226 Fax 0246 433915			**H**
39 Station Road Renishaw nr Eckington Derbyshire S31 9WR			**Map 7 D2**

A roadside inn, dating back in parts to the 18th century, featuring
a purpose-built block of bedrooms, each of a good, comfortable standard.
Two large bars form the greater part of the public areas. *Rooms 30.*
AMERICAN EXPRESS *Access, Diners, Visa.*

Retford   Forte Travelodge   £45
Tel 0777 838091   **L**
Markham Moor nr Retford Nottinghamshire DN22 0QU   **Map 7 D2**

On the A1 northbound, 14 miles north of Newark-on-Trent, with access
from both northbound and southbound carriageways. *Rooms 40.*
AMERICAN EXPRESS *Access, Diners, Visa.*

Richmond   Burnt Chair   £55
Tel 081-940 9488   **R**
5 Duke Street Richmond Surrey TW9 1HP   **Map 15 E2**

A small restaurant, just around the corner from Richmond Theatre, with
closely-packed, crisply-clothed tables behind a gauze-draped shop front.
Formerly an accountant, chef/patron Weenson Andrew Oo has
an enthusiasm for food and wine (the wine list comes with personal tasting
notes) that finds expression in an interesting à la carte with a distinctly
Provençal flavour: roasted red pepper and tomato soup; niçoise tart with
salad leaves and sweet pepper vinaigrette; daube of wild beef (the calves are
given the run of the Welsh hills for a couple of years); roasted salmon with
beurre blanc; magret of duck with bacon, lentils and a garlic potato purée.
A short fixed-price menu is available till 8pm (7pm Fri & Sat) and after the
performance for theatre-goers. A special combined theatre/supper ticket
is available from the box office offering 2 courses from the fixed-price
menu for £7 (£9 Fri & Sat) along with a stalls or dress circle seat.
*Seats 31. L 12-2.30 D 6-11. Closed L Sat & Mon, all Sun, 1 week Christmas,
1 week Aug. Set D £15 till 8pm (7pm Fri & Sat). Access, Visa.*

Richmond   Petersham Hotel   65%   £130
Tel 081-940 7471   Fax 081-940 9998   **HR**
Nightingale Lane Richmond Surrey TW10 6UZ   **Map 15 E2**

Distinctive French Gothic-style building dating from 1865 with
an elevated position on Richmond Hill affording fine views of a tranquil
bend of the River Thames. An impressive cantilever staircase (the largest
in the country) extends from the black-and-white tiled floor of the
lobby/reception to a painted ceiling five floors above. Bedrooms vary
considerably in size and shape with the largest having the best views and
reproduction antique furniture; others incorporate more modest shelf-type
fitted units. Bathrooms are often beyond an open arch, in which case there
is a separate loo. Public rooms include two small lounges furnished
in traditional style and a cocktail bar in pastel shades. No dogs. *Rooms 54.*
AMERICAN EXPRESS *Access, Diners, Visa.*

Nightingales   £65

Smart, comfortable dining room in shades of pink and blue where smooth,
professional service complements reliably good cooking from head chef
Tim Richardson's kitchen. The intelligently compiled à la carte offers
something for everyone with English dishes like kidney soup with Madeira
and roast pheasant with traditional accompaniment, classics such as omelette
Arnold Bennett, salade niçoise and beef Wellington, and in the modern
idiom ravioli of wild duck and hare, charcoal-grilled fresh tuna with
ratatouille and olive oil dressing, and Cornish scallops cooked in the shell
with Noilly Prat and cinnamon. Good puds range from a daily 'hot English
Pudding' via cherry yoghurt mousse to a properly made hot soufflé.
Sunday lunchtimes there is a fixed-price menu only (choice of five main
dishes) and only at this meal are children specifically catered for, with those
under 10 paying half price with special menu alternatives offered. One no-
smoking room. *Seats 70. Parties 14. Private Room 36. L 12.15-2.15 (Sun
to 2.45) D 7-9.45 (Sun to 8.45). Closed 25 & 26 Dec. Set L £17.50/£22.50
(Sun £20).*

| Richmond | **Richmond Gate Hotel** | 65% | £113 |

Tel 081-940 0061   Fax 081-332 0354

Richmond Hill Richmond Surrey TW10 6RP

H

Map 15 E2

High up on Richmond Hill, overlooking the edge of 2500-acre Richmond Park and the Thames, the hotel was originally a collection of four 18th-century buildings. The original, Morshead House, contains intimate public rooms and eight luxury double rooms of grand proportions, some with four-posters. In a newer extension, to the rear, bedrooms are equally attractive and comfortable, though more uniform in design. Under-7s stay free in parents' room. Functions/conferences for up to 60. No dogs. *Rooms 64. Garden, croquet, squash.* AMERICAN EXPRESS® *Access, Diners, Visa.*

| Richmond | **River Terrace** | | £65 |

Tel 081-332 2524   Fax 081-332 6136

The Tower Bridge Street Richmond Surrey TW9 1TQ

R

Map 15 E2

Lovely Thames views from this Georgian building right on Richmond Bridge. Eat inside in the new conservatory (seating about 40) or out on the terrace from a short menu offering the likes of pan-fried scallops on a bed of leeks and bacon, braised rabbit with capers and red peppers on a bed of spinach, and orange and cardamom brulée. Concise, reasonably-priced international wine list. **Seats** 200. *Private Room 50. L 12-3 (Sun to 4) D 7-10.30 (Fri & Sat to 11). Closed D Sun & all Mon (both winter only), 26-30 Dec.* AMERICAN EXPRESS® *Access, Diners, Visa.*

| Ridgeway | **Old Vicarage** | ★★ | £90 |

Tel 0742 475814   Fax 0742 477079

Ridgeway Moor Ridgeway nr Sheffield Derbyshire S12 3XW

R

Map 6 C2

Close to the village centre and set back from the road, the Old Vicarage is a substantial Victorian house surrounded by lawns and mature trees. As there's only the most discreet of name plates by the entrance gate it is advisable to obtain precise directions when booking. The welcome is warm and the decor is pleasingly unfussy in a country-house style with a charming, homely sitting room where pre-dinner drinks and wonderfully involved canapés are served. The dining room, candle-lit at night, is decorated in soft pastel shades offset by beautiful oil paintings and verdant prospects of the gardens, creating a romantic and elegant setting for stunning cooking from Tessa Bramley and fellow head chef Rupert Staniforth. An appetiser of thinly sliced, delicately sautéed scallops with tiny, fresh marjoram leaves with a lime dressing and asparagus spears is a marvellous beginning and a clear indication of the supreme effort and care taken in both preparation and presentation. The use of home-grown produce, particularly herbs (and even their minuscule flowers), creates a myriad of delightful taste sensations. There has of late been a shift away from some of the Oriental influences of last year, the kitchen instead pursuing a course of providing slightly more robust, but still remarkably delicate and refined dishes imbued with the Bramley hallmarks of subtlety and sophistication – a fillet of turbot may sit on a bed of vegetable julienne, accompanied by a brilliant, pale pink, translucent rhubarb butter sauce infused with a hint of star anise. Traditional oxtail soup, mussels in smoked salmon cream with spring onion potato pancakes or caramelised and roasted tomato tart with spinach sauce are typical of the starters. Main dishes could include pork fillet, hot-smoked over sage and served on creamed polenta with broccoli, prunes and pancetta; fillet of Angus beef is presented with ox tongue and vegetables tossed in a mustard dressing and calf's liver might come with a potato and parsnip purée and shallot compote. Truly memorable desserts include the ever-popular hot chocolate pudding with hot fudge sauce and English custard; another choice could be a trio of pear desserts with a baked caramelised pear, a basket of pear sorbet and a pear and star anise brulée. A choice of seven or so cheeses come exclusively from around the British Isles – the Grubb family's Cashel Blue

from Co Tipperary in Ireland, Humphrey Errington's ewe's milk Lanark
Blue from Scotland and Alison Blunt's Flower Marie goat's cheese from
East Sussex are all favourites. Coffee is served with hand-made chocolates
and petits fours. A cosy and – if weather permits – beautifully bright and
sunny conservatory makes a charming setting for Tessa Bramley's Bistro,
her second dining room and one which has a fixed-price menu chalked
up on a blackboard against the wall. Prices here may be lower and the food
marginally simpler in style but the attention to detail and the quality of the
cooking is just as apparent as in the main dining room. Pot-roasted chicken
with glazed vegetables is one of those dishes one dreams of – the chicken
meltingly tender and accompanied by potatoes, parsnips and carrots cooked
with a rich, partly caramelised glaze and a delicious cream sauce. There are
some good and inexpensive regional and country wines on the sound wine
list, though there are few New World wines; plenty of half bottles,
though. Two rooms for meetings and private dining. No smoking.
Seats 35 (Bistro 30). *Parties* 12. *Private Room* 16. L (*reservations only*)
*12.30-2.30 D 7-10.45. Closed D Sat (Bistro only), all Mon, 1 week after
Christmas. Set meals £27.50 (Sun L £18.50), Bistro £17.50.*
AMERICAN EXPRESS *Access, Visa.*

Ripley	**Boar's Head Hotel**	**66%**	**£85**

Tel 0423 771888   Fax 0423 771509
Ripley nr Harrogate North Yorkshire H53 3AY

HR
Map 6 C1

Dating back to 1830 when the Lord of the Manor rebuilt the village next
to his castle (open to the public during the summer), this former coaching
inn was refurbished by the present Lord some three years ago and turned
into a fairly up-market hotel. Oil paintings and furniture from the castle
help to create the country house feel in tranquil drawing and morning
rooms and the individually decorated bedrooms, which favour plain walls
and stylish matching fabrics. Antique furniture features in rooms in the
main building and in the larger rooms in another house across the cobbled
square, while those in the former stable block are furnished with white-
painted wicker pieces. Nice touches include porcelain ornaments and
wooden toy catamarans in bathrooms that boast large soft towels and
quality toiletries. **Rooms** 25. Garden, tennis, coarse fishing. AMERICAN EXPRESS
Access, Visa.

Restaurant

£70

Service in the warm, red dining room is rather less polished than chef
David Box's accomplished cooking for the short but well-balanced fixed-
price menu. Starters might include goose livers on a sage and onion croute
with black pepper sauce, tagliolini with Parma ham and basil, and a terrine
of fresh fruits with spearmint and elderflower granita; main courses, grilled
scallops with baby spinach on a saffron sauce, breast of Gressingham duck
with orange and lime sauce and grilled fillet of beef with spring vegetables.
In between comes a choice of soup or sorbet. A good-value set lunch
is replaced by a menu of individually priced light dishes in high season. The
excellent wine list has exceedingly kind prices (including 10+ champagnes
under £30 and lots of good drinking under £20); good representation
from Europe and the New World plus useful notes, many dessert wines
and half bottles. *Seats* 38. *Parties* 14. *Private Room* 10. L 12-2 D 7-9.30.
Set L £14/£17.90 (Sun £14.50).

Ripley	**Michels'**	★	**£90**

Tel 0483 224777
13 High Street Ripley Surrey GU23 6AQ

R
Map 15 E3

Erik and Karen Michel opened their popular restaurant in 1986 and have
not only survived the lean times of the late '80s but have sprung into the
'90s with even more aplomb. Erik's cooking has gained in assurance,
it seems, so that locals-in-the-know have to vie wtih destination diners for
a seat at his table. The setting – an elegant dining room within an equally

elegant Georgian-fronted Clock House – is ideal for Erik's style of cooking, and his artistry is not restricted to the plate, extending also to the paint palette. The Michels use locally grown produce whenever possible, picking wild mushrooms in season, growing their own herbs, baking the delicious range of breads daily. Menus change with the seasons, the surprise menu changing daily of course. The extensive carte might include as starters an unusual cream of nettle soup, or seafood sausages with oysters in ink and saffron sauce, or roast quail, boned and set on a toasted brioche with quail liver mousse served on lamb's lettuce in a truffle dressing in an intricate and pretty presentation. For main course try the robust roast loin of wild boar with horseradish and caper sauce, or pan-fried sea bass with salsify and shrimps (another unusual but successful combination of flavours), the crustacean sauce flavoured with thyme and lemon. The dessert menu, which we are delighted to see still includes last year's award-winning (in this Guide) savarin baba, might also challenge you with a hot tarte tatin of caramelised peppered pineapple with vanilla ice cream and crème de cacao sauce or lemon mousse in a crisp ground almond pastry, served with cherries cooked in their own juice and kirsch. Karen Michel guides you through these delights charmingly at front of house. *Seats 50. Parties 12. Private Room 12. L 12.30-1.30 D 7.30-9 (Sat 7-9.30). Closed L Sat, D Sun, all Mon, 25 & 26 Dec, 1st week Jan. Set L £19.50 Set D £21.50/28.* AMERICAN EXPRESS *Access, Visa.*

Ripon   **Ripon Spa Hotel**   **62%**   **£72**

Tel 0765 602172   Fax 0765 690770   **H**

Park Street Ripon North Yorkshire HG4 2BU   **Map 5 E4**

A comfortable hotel dating from 1909, with good staff and commendably high standards of housekeeping. The prize-winning gardens are a major plus, and the setting is secluded considering its proximity to the city centre. Another asset comes in the shape of the high-ceilinged bedrooms. Rooms are individually decorated and furnished, and two have four-posters. Two de luxe rooms have whirlpool baths. Most of the bedrooms enjoy garden views. The hotel has several conference/function rooms, with a capacity of up to 180. Children up to 12 stay free in parents' room (breakfast will be charged). *Rooms 40. Garden, croquet.* AMERICAN EXPRESS *Access, Diners, Visa.*

Ripon   **Places of Interest**

Fountains Abbey & Studley Royal Gardens (NT)   Tel 0765 86333.
Newby Hall & Gardens   Nr Ripon Tel 0423 322583.
Ripon Cathedral   Tel 0765 2072.
Ripon Racecourse   Tel 0765 602165.
Lightwater Valley Action Park   Tel 0765 85321.

Roade   **Roadhouse Restaurant**   **£55**

Tel 0604 863372   **R**

16 High Street Roade Northamptonshire NN7 2NW   **Map 15 D1**

Once the local ale house, Christopher and Susan Kewley's village restaurant with pink rag-roll-effect walls and a couple of old beams offers a shortish menu of dishes soundly cooked by Chris: roulade of spinach stuffed with leeks, mussels marinière, peppered steak with brandy and cream sauce, baked cod with herb vinaigrette and tagliatelle, grilled duck breast with a confit of the leg and a red wine and ginger sauce. Game is considered a speciality in season. The keenly-priced lunch menu is based on less expensive dishes from the evening à la carte. Service is unhurried. There is a small bar for pre-dinner drinks. *Seats 45. L 12.30-1.45 D 7-9.30. Closed L Sat, D Sun, all Mon, Bank Holidays, 2 weeks Jul/Aug & 1 week Dec. Set L £14.50 (Sun £15.75).* AMERICAN EXPRESS *Access, Visa.*

Rochester   Bridgewood Manor Hotel   68%   £105

Tel 0634 201333   Fax 0634 201330   **H**

Bridgewood Roundabout Maidstone Road Rochester Kent ME5 9AX   Map 11 B5

Virtually beside Junction 3 of the M2, this modern brick-built hotel offers up-to-date meeting and conference facilities as well as a good base for the local tourist attractions. General manager Gail Callaway and her staff provide friendly and helpful service. Public areas including a spacious reception lounge and bar have an ecclesiastical decorative inspiration. Bedrooms (30 designated non-smoking) have all the expected features, remote TV, trouser presses and compact, clean, functional bathrooms. 24hr room service. Children up to 16 stay free in parents' room. A central courtyard area provides a sheltered al fresco area in the summer months. There's a wide range of facilities in the self-contained leisure club. Marston Hotels. **Rooms** 100. *Patio, indoor swimming pool, gym, sauna, spa bath, solarium, hair & beauty salon, tennis, snooker.* AMERICAN EXPRESS *Access, Diners, Visa.*

Rochester   Forte Posthouse   62%   £68

Tel 0634 687111   Fax 0634 684512   **H**

Maidstone Road Rochester Airport Rochester Kent ME5 9SF   Map 11 B5

Up-to-date comfort near Junction 3 of the M2 and Junction 6 of the M20. Children stay free in parents' bedrooms. **Rooms** 105. *Indoor swimming pool, gym, sauna, spa bath, solarium, steam room, beauty salon, coffee shop (7am-10.30pm).* AMERICAN EXPRESS *Access, Diners, Visa.*

Rochester   Places of Interest

Tourist Information   Tel 0634 843666.
Cobham Hall   Cobham Tel 0472 823371.
Rochester Castle (EH)   Tel 0634 402276.
Rochester Cathedral   Tel 0634 43364.
Charles Dickens Centre   Tel 0634 844176.
Alpine Ski Centre   Chatham Tel 0634 827979.
Oast House Theatre   Gillingham Tel 0634 372121.
Doddington Place Gardens   Sittingbourne Tel 079586 385.
The Ice Bowl   Gillingham Tel 0634 388477.

Rolleston-on-Dove   Brookhouse Hotel   62%   £85

Tel 0283 814188   Fax 0283 813644   **H**

Brookside Rolleston-on-Dove nr Burton-on-Trent Staffordshire DE13 9AA   Map 6 C3

Standing by the village brook, the William and Mary listed brick building dates from around 1690 and was converted to a hotel in 1976. Bedrooms are all individually styled, featuring antique furniture, and many have four-posters, half-testers or Victorian brass beds trimmed with Nottingham lace; several are in an adjacent converted barn. Two extra rooms this year, one of them a suite. No children under 12. **Rooms** 21. *Garden.* AMERICAN EXPRESS *Access, Diners, Visa.*

Romaldkirk   Rose & Crown   £74

Tel 0833 650213   Fax 0833 650828   **IR**

Romaldkirk Co Durham DL12 9EB   Map 5 D3

An imposing 18th-century coaching inn in a most picturesque village setting, and a fine base for touring, walking, fishing and shooting. The main bar has a fine stone fireplace, wood panelling, old black and white photos of the village, a grandfather clock and some alarming-looking traps. Wrought iron-legged tables are surrounded by roundback chairs or bench seating, and on the dining side of the room there are exposed stone walls, beams and old farm implements. A residents' lounge, heavily endowed with more stripped stone and beams, features wing chairs and period furniture, books, magazines and board games. Everywhere there are local watercolours. Creaking floorboards, beams, stripped stone walls, well-chosen antique furniture and contemporary fabrics feature in the refurbished and improved bedrooms; duvets can be swapped for sheets and blankets. Front views overlook the village green. Five further rooms, in an annexe, are more uniform in size and design, with modern furniture and fittings. Excellent snacks and real ales served all sessions in the bar and Crown Room; six tables are outside in front of the hotel. Children under 5 stay free in parents' room. Service is friendly and smiling throughout. *Rooms* 12. *Closed 25 & 26 Dec. Access, Visa.*

Restaurant £65

In the part-panelled restaurant there are elegantly clothed tables (enhanced by a recent complete refurbishment) and a civilised air. Chef Christopher Davy's fixed-price, four-course dinners make excellent use of local produce, typified by roast breast of farm duckling with a Seville orange sauce, or chargrilled noisettes of local lamb with a tomato and aubergine casserole. Flanking these main courses could be chicken liver paté, cream of leek soup, brown bread ice cream and dark chocolate pot. Roast ribs of English beef with Yorkshire pudding is a favourite centrepiece of the Sunday lunch menu. No smoking. *Seats 24. Parties 12. L (Sun only) 12-1.30 D 7.30-9 (Sun open for residents only). Set L (Sun) £11.50 Set D £22.*

Romsey **Old Manor House** ★ £90

Tel 0794 517353 **R**

21 Palmerston Street Romsey Hampshire SO51 8GF **Map 14 C3**

The Old Manor House is exactly that, so it's somewhat unexpected to encounter Italian and French dishes – until you realise that Mauro Bregoli is keeping his national heritage alive in this corner of England. That's not to say that he doesn't take full advantage of local produce like Test valley trout, Lymington lobster or fresh local asparagus, to serve alongside his more familiar *arrosto di vitellone tonnato*, braised ox cheek with polenta, or stuffed leg of duck with blackberry sauce. Additionally, he tracks down wild mushrooms and game (the latter get shot!), hunts truffles, hangs and smokes meat in the restaurant's giant chimney breast, and is a dab hand at making fresh pasta (perhaps tagliolini with warm fresh tomatoes, basil and extra virgin olive oil). Naturally, the dessert menu features a tiramisu, as well as home-made amaretto ice cream or crème brulée with raspberries. Alongside the splendid and lengthy wine list (note the exceptional depth of clarets) there's an inexpensive and well-chosen house selection featuring wines from France, Italy and the New World. *Seats 42. Parties 10. Private Room 22. L 12-2 D 7-9.30. Closed D Sun, all Mon, 1 week Christmas. Set meals £13.50/£17.50.* AMERICAN EXPRESS® *Access, Visa.*

Romsey **White Horse Hotel** **63%** £102

Tel 0794 512431 Fax 0794 517485 **H**

Market Place Romsey Hampshire SO51 8ZJ **Map 14 C3**

Georgian facade, oak beams, bedrooms (both period and modern) in a Forte Heritage hotel right on the market place. Courtyard seating. Banqueting facilities for 90, conferences up to 40. *Rooms 33.* AMERICAN EXPRESS® *Access, Diners, Visa.*

Romsey **Places of Interest**

Paultons Romany and Village Life Museums and Theme Park Paultons Park, Ower Tel 0703 814442.
Rapids of Romsey Tel 0794 830333.
Wellow Vineyards Tel 0794 830880.
Historic Houses, Castles and Gardens
Broadlands Tel 0794 516878 *Home of Lord Mountbatten.*
Hillier Gardens and Arboretum Ampfield Tel 0794 68787.
Mottisfont Abbey Garden (NT) Mottisfont Tel 0794 41220/40757.

Rosedale Abbey   Milburn Arms   60%   £70

Tel & Fax 0751 417312   **H**

Rosedale Abbey nr Pickering North Yorkshire YO18 8RA   **Map 5 E3**

Country hotel and village pub, the Milburn Arms enjoys a tranquil and
beautiful setting in the North Yorks moors. Plants, ornaments, books and
games make the lounge a nice place to spend an hour or two, and in the bar
an extensive range of snacks and meals is served. Individually-decorated
bedrooms have good bathrooms and some also have fine views; dogs
in ground-floor annexe rooms only. A favoured spot in summer is the
peaceful garden, opposite the village green, with tables set out under
a splendid 150-year-old cedar. *Rooms 11. Garden. Closed 2 days Christmas.
Access, Diners, Visa.*

Ross-on-Wye   Chase Hotel   64%   £75

Tel 0989 763161   Fax 0989 768330   **H**

Gloucester Road Ross-on-Wye Hereford & Worcester HR9 5LH   **Map 14 B1**

Large Georgian house – although the impressive entrance hall with colour-
tiled floor and marble columns supporting stone arches looks more
Victorian – set in well-kept grounds that make it a popular wedding venue.
There's no separate lounge but the bar is smart and comfortable. Attractive
bedrooms feature co-ordinating fabrics with floral curtains and striped
bedcovers in several different colours. The furniture is sturdy light oak.
Fully-tiled bathrooms have decent toiletries. Decorative order is excellent
throughout. The four Executive rooms are the most spacious – two have
four-poster beds. Best stick to the cold buffet at breakfast. *Rooms 39.
Garden.* AMERICAN EXPRESS *Access, Diners, Visa.*

Ross-on-Wye   Forte Travelodge   NEW   £45

Tel 0800 850 950   **L**

**M50/A40 Welcome Break Ross Spur Northbound Ross-on-Wye
Hereford & Worcester**   **Map 14 B1**

Opening winter '94. AMERICAN EXPRESS *Access, Diners, Visa.*

Ross-on-Wye   Pengethley Manor   67%   £115

Tel 0989 730211   Fax 0989 730258   **H**

Pengethley Park nr Ross-on-Wye Hereford & Worcester HR9 6LL   **Map 14 B1**

Pengetheley is to be found at the end of a long drive off the A49 Ross (10
minutes to the south) to Hereford (20 minutes north) road. Fifteen acres
of estate with a par 3 golf course, trout lake, vineyard and landscaped
gardens enhance the tranquil country setting. There is also plenty
of activity for sportsmen. Banqueting for up to 75 and conference rooms
accommodating 50 kept discreetly separate. One purpose-built bedroom for
disabled guests; children up to 16 stay free in parents' room with meals
charged as taken. *Rooms 25. Garden, croquet, outdoor swimming pool, golf (9),
trout lake, snooker, outdoor chess.* AMERICAN EXPRESS *Access, Diners, Visa.*

Ross-on-Wye   Pheasants   £70

Tel 0989 565751   **R R**

52 Edde Cross Street Ross-on-Wye Hereford & Worcester HR9 7BZ   **Map 14 B1**

Down a side street, this former pub is now a homely restaurant with warm,
red rag-rolled walls, a few old beams, some gentle jazz/swing in the
background and a distinctly unhurried atmosphere. It's a two-handed affair
with New Zealander Adrian Wells serving (and in charge of the wines)
and chef-patronne Eileen Brunnarius in the kitchen. Cooking is good
dinner-party style with the likes of a creamed spinach tartlet with quail
eggs and a butter sauce, smoked duck breast with melon, pork fillets with
prunes and a cider sauce, and sesame chicken with cashew nut sauce on the

fixed-price and à la carte menus. Lunch is a less formal affair with a
blackboard menu. Puds might include a pear tatin with caramel and ginger
wine sauces and a raw sugar meringue with apple cheese. Good farmhouse
cheeses come with Herefordshire cider cake and such names as Yemen
'Ismaila' and Rose Pouchong are to be found amongst the teas and coffees
on offer. A very personal selection of wines, with helpful tasting notes,
always lists a dozen each of reds and whites by the glass. If in doubt ask
Adrian the style of wine you prefer and leave the choice in his safe,
knowledgeable hands. *Seats* 22. *Private Room* 4. *L 12.30-1.30. D 7-10.
Closed Sun & Mon, L between Nov & mid Mar (except by arrangement),
25 Dec-2 Jan. Set D £18.50.* AMERICAN EXPRESS *Access, Diners, Visa.*

Rooms   £40

Two modestly furnished bedrooms (no TV or phone) share a good
bathroom with Eileen and her ever-growing herd of hippopotami. Hearty
breakfasts make a good start to the day.

Ross-on-Wye   Places of Interest

Tourist Information   Tel 0989 562768.
Goodrich Castle   Tel 0600 890538.
Hill Court Gardens   Hom Green Tel 0989 763123.

Rotherham   Campanile Hotel   £44

Tel 0709 700255   Fax 0709 545169   **L**
Lowton Way off Denby Way Hellaby Industrial Estate Rotherham South
Yorkshire S66 8RY   Map 7 D2

Off M18 Junction 1, past M1 Junction 32. *Rooms* 50. AMERICAN EXPRESS
Access, Diners, Visa.

Rotherham   Moat House   69%   £84

Tel 0709 364902   Fax 0709 368960   **H**
Moorgate Road Rotherham South Yorkshire S60 2BG   Map 7 D2

By the A618, south of town, close to Rotherham General Hospital,
a modern, angular redbrick hotel. Leisure facilities (no pool) and conference
suites (for up to 250); elegant banqueting room for up to 200. Children
up to 5 share parents' room free. 21 rooms reserved for non-smokers.
Rooms 80. *Gym, spa bath, sauna, steam room, solarium, helipad.*
Closed 25-30 Dec. AMERICAN EXPRESS *Access, Diners, Visa.*

Rotherham   Travel Inn   £43

Tel 0709 543216   Fax 0709 531546   **L**
Bawtry Road Rotherham South Yorkshire S65 3JB   Map 7 D2

On A631 near Wickersley, between Junction 1 of M18 and Junction 33 of
M1. 10 minutes from Sheffield and Doncaster. *Rooms* 37. AMERICAN EXPRESS
Access, Diners, Visa.

Rotherham   Places of Interest

Tourist Information   Tel 0709 823611.
Rotherham Arts Centre   Tel 0709 373866.

Rotherwick   Tylney Hall   79%   £118

Tel 0256 764881   Fax 0256 768141   **HR**
Rotherwick nr Hook Hampshire RG27 9AZ   Map 15 D3

Signposted from the B3349 west of Junction 5 of the M3, Tylney Hall
is a grand mansion built about 100 years ago but incorporating some much
older architectural features like the ornate Italian ceiling of one of the
lounges. Indeed, fine ceilings are a feature of the extensive public rooms

here and come in various styles, Tudor in the dining room, delicate and refined in the Wedgwood room and baronial in the ballroom that also features a minstrel's gallery and massive stone fireplace. The building is set in 66 acres of grounds with fine Gertrude Jekyll gardens that include cascading waterfalls, fountains, ornamental lakes and woodland walks. There are no small bedrooms here and many are very spacious. All share the same pink and pale green colour scheme, though in various styles, with a mixture of antique and reproduction furniture and all have good armchairs and/or settees. Levels of service are high with notably attentive, friendly staff and the moving of telephones from desk to bedside when rooms are serviced in the evenings is a nice touch. 24hr room service. For guests seeking extra privacy there are three cottage suites in the grounds overlooking a small lake. Conference/banqueting facilities in a variety of rooms, catering for 150/100. No dogs. *Rooms 91. Garden, croquet, tennis, indoor & outdoor swimming pools, gym, sauna, spa bath, snooker, helipad.* AMERICAN EXPRESS *Access, Diners, Visa.*

Oak Room   £95

Impeccable service from engaging maitre d' Ignacio Gonzalez and his team adds lustre to the cooking in the mellow oak-panelled dining room. Careful cooking of first-rate raw materials is the hallmark of Stephen Hine's à la carte that includes the likes of fresh foie gras on toasted tomato brioche with onion marmalade, warm asparagus with chervil butter sauce, Gressingham duck with plum and Oriental spice sauces and venison with cabbage rösti and a red wine and thyme sauce. The lunchtime table d'hote concentrates on English Fayre. Pretty hefty mark-ups on the decent wine list (the cheapest champagne is over £35 with service); good balance between Europe and the New World; plenty of half bottles. Outdoor dining for 24 on the terrace in summer. Regional winner, British Cheeseboard of the Year 1995. *Seats 100. Parties 10. L 12.30-1.45 D 7.30-9.30 (Fri & Sat to 10). Set L £19 (Sun £17) Set D £27.*

Rothley	**Rothley Court**	**67%**	**£100**
Tel 0533 374141 Fax 0533 374483			**H**
Westfield Lane Rothley Leicestershire LE7 7LG			**Map 7 D3**

By the B5328 west of Rothley (six miles outside Leicester), this imposing 13th-century manor stands in six acres of grounds, surrounded by lawns and open farmland. As you would expect from Forte Heritage, much historical character is retained including an 11th-century chapel built by the Holy Order of the Knights Templar. Day rooms feature some fine oak panelling, buttoned-leather chairs, exposed floorboards and stone fireplaces, while the main staircase boasts two fine stained-glass windows. Manor bedrooms vary in size with antique furniture and subdued colour schemes, while annexe rooms are more uniform; feature rooms, like the King Henry III suite in a separate cottage, attract a justifiable 20% supplementary charge. *Rooms 36. Garden.* AMERICAN EXPRESS *Access, Diners, Visa.*

Rowde	**George & Dragon**	**£30**
Tel 0380 723053		**R**
High Street Rowde Wiltshire SN10 2PN		**Map 14 C3**

Inspired, inventive and realistically-priced cooking emanates from the kitchen of Tim and Helen Withers' village pub, and blackboards abundantly proclaim what's on offer. Fresh fish is a speciality, and depending on availability you might find any or all of grilled Dover sole, roast hake with peppers and pesto, salmon hollandaise, red mullet with orange and anchovy, and squid stuffed with lemon, garlic and parsley. There's also a long and appealing list of land-derived goodies, from wild mushroom soup and hot cheese soufflé to lamb and aubergine daube, pork with prunes and cold roast sirloin salad with potatoes and pickles. Puddings could include rhubarb fool, crème brulée and chocolate ginger roulade with lemon grass custard. An inexpensive wine list (lots of wines under

£10, plenty available by the glass) has helpful tasting notes. *Seats 35.*
L 12-2 D 7-10. Closed Sun, Mon, 25,26 Dec 1 Jan. Set L £10. Access, Visa.

Rowsley   Peacock Hotel   64%   £87

Tel 0629 733518   Fax 0629 732671   **H**

Rowsley Matlock Derbyshire DE4 2EB   Map 6 C2

A small hotel with the river Derwent running through the gardens, so its's
no surprise to find plenty of anglers among the guests – there's trout and
grayling fishing on the Derwent and an additional 12 rods on the Wye.
Dating back to the 17th century, the hotel has an appeal that is enhanced
by mellow, antique-filled public rooms including a beamed bar with rough
stone walls, while individually decorated bedrooms offer all the usual
modern comforts. Children up to 16 stay free in parents' room. This Jarvis
hotel stands on the A6 five miles north of Matlock and three miles south
of Bakewell. *Rooms 14. Garden, fishing.* AMERICAN EXPRESS *Access, Diners, Visa.*

Ruckhall   Ancient Camp Inn   £48

Tel 0981 250449   **I**

Ruckhall nr Eaton Bishop Hereford & Worcester HR2 9QX   Map 14 A1

On the site of a former Iron Age fort, the inn stands atop an escarpment
overlooking a wide bend in the river Wye. Ruckhall (not on many maps)
is signposted on the main A465 leaving Hereford towards Abergavenny.
Conversion by owners David and Nova Hague retains original stonework
and flagstone floor to create an intimate atmosphere, cheered in winter
by huge log fires. Nova's home-made bar meals are served lunchtime and
evening (but not on Mondays). Three neat bedrooms to the rear have
showers/WC only; of two at the front one has a private sitting room, the
other an en-suite bath elevated to maximise its river view. All are centrally
heated. No children under eight. No dogs. *Rooms 5. Garden, fishing.*
Access, Visa.

Rugeley   Forte Travelodge   £45

Tel 0889 570096   **L**

Western Springs Road Rugeley Staffordshire WS15 2AS   Map 6 C3

On the A51/B5013, 8 miles east of Stafford in the centre of the town, next
to the bus station. Take Junctions 13/14 from the M6 southbound
at Stafford or Junction 11 northbound at Cannock. *Rooms 32.*
AMERICAN EXPRESS *Access, Diners, Visa.*

Runcorn   Campanile Hotel   £44

Tel 0928 581771   Fax 0928 581730   **L**

Lowlands Road Runcorn Cheshire WA7 5TP   Map 6 A2

Take Junction 12 off the M56 to the A557 ring road. Close to the station.
Rooms 53. AMERICAN EXPRESS *Access, Diners, Visa.*

Runcorn   Forte Posthouse   62%   £68

Tel 0928 714000   Fax 0928 714611   **H**

Wood Lane Beechwood Runcorn Cheshire WA7 3HA   Map 6 A2

A modern hotel not far from Junction 12 of the M56, overlooking the
Frodsham Hills and Weaver Valley. Ample free car parking, a leisure club
and very extensive conference facilities (a choice of 19 rooms holding up to
500 delegates theatre-style). 86 rooms are designated non-smoking.
Rooms 135. Garden, indoor swimming pool, gym, sauna, spa bath, steam room,
solarium, beauty salon, outdoor children's play area. AMERICAN EXPRESS *Access,*
Diners, Visa.

Rushden — Forte Travelodge   £45

Tel 0933 57008   **L**

Rushden Northamptonshire NN10 9AP   Map 15 E1

Located on the A45 eastbound near Rushden, 14 miles east
of Northampton and 10 miles south of Kettering. *Rooms 40.*
AMERICAN EXPRESS *Access, Diners, Visa.*

Rusper — Ghyll Manor   68%   £93

Tel 0293 871571   Fax 0293 871419   **H**

High Street Rusper nr Horsham West Sussex RH12 4PX   Map 11 A5

Surrounded by 40 acres of landscaped gardens on the main road to Rusper,
two miles east of the A24 from Dorking. Bedrooms are split between the
main, original house, two cottages and a converted stable mews set around
a cobbled courtyard and high-beamed function room. Those in the
extensions are modern and larger than those in the house, which have
a few antiques and period detail. Beamed ceilings and open fires add to the
atmosphere. Three additional bedrooms this year. Children up to 16
accommodated free in parents' room; cots and baby-listening available.
Forte Heritage. *Rooms 25. Garden, croquet, tennis.* AMERICAN EXPRESS *Access,
Diners, Visa.*

Rye — George Hotel   62%   £92

Tel 0797 222114   Fax 0797 224065   **H**

High Street Rye East Sussex TN31 7JP   Map 11 C6

Former coaching inn dating in parts back to 1575. Day rooms are
comfortably traditional, and most of the bedrooms have old beams – three
are suitable for family use. The Georgian ballroom is a popular choice for
banqueting functions (up to 100) and conferences (up to 80). Forte
Heritage. *Rooms 22.* AMERICAN EXPRESS *Access, Diners, Visa.*

Rye — Landgate Bistro   £60

Tel 0797 222829   **R**

5/6 Landgate Rye East Sussex TN31 7LH   Map 11 C6

Skilled cooking in the simple surroundings of a popular bistro
in a picturesque tourist town. Fish is very much a speciality on chef/patron
Toni Ferguson-Lees' menu, shown by squid braised with white wine,
tomatoes and garlic, scallops and John Dory with an orange and vermouth
sauce and steamed fillet of wild salmon with chive hollandaise. One of the
most popular dishes is 'very fishy stew', a selection of local fish poached
in stock and served with aïoli, garlic bread and a salad. There's no shortage
of choice for meat-eaters, with such dishes as salad of confit of duck with
green lentils, wild rabbit with garlic and thyme, guinea fowl with sherry
and mushrooms and fillet of beef in pastry with béarnaise sauce. Among
the sweets could be Jamaican chocolate cream, lemon tart or cherries with
a bay leaf custard in a biscuit cup. *Seats 30. D only 7-9.30.
Closed Sun & Mon. Set D (Tue-Thur) £14.90.* AMERICAN EXPRESS *Access,
Diners, Visa.*

Rye — Mermaid Inn   60%   £106

Tel 0797 223065   Fax 0797 225069   **H**

Mermaid Street Rye East Sussex TN31 7EU   Map 11 C6

Rebuilt in 1420 (on foundations dating back to 1156), the Mermaid stands
among the cobbled streets of ancient Rye. Once famous for its smuggling
associations, it remains strong on romantic, old-world appeal, with low
beams, antique furnishings, Elizabethan illustrations and linenfold panelling.

Five of the bedrooms have four-posters, six are suitable for family use.
No children under 8. No dogs. Free parking at the rear of the inn.
Rooms 28. AMERICAN EXPRESS *Access, Diners, Visa.*

Rye   Places of Interest

Tourist Information   Tel 0797 226696.
Lamb House   Tel 0797 226696 *Home of Henry James.*
Camber Sands Beach *3 miles E of Rye.*

Saffron Walden	Saffron Hotel	57%	£55
Tel 0799 522676 Fax 0799 513979			**H**
10-18 High Street Saffron Walden Essex CB10 1AY			Map 10 B3

A listed building of 16th-century origin, in the centre of a historic and
charming market town. There's an old-fashioned panelled bar with exposed
brickwork and timbers. Bedrooms, a few with four-posters, vary in size
and style, but their decor and appointments are generally quite modest.
Some rooms are reached by winding passages with head-threatening beams.
Children up to ten stay free in parents' room. *Rooms 20. Garden.*
AMERICAN EXPRESS *Access, Diners, Visa.*

Saffron Walden   Places of Interest

Audley End House and Park (EH)   Tel 0799 22399.
Mole Hall Wildlife Park   Widdington, Newport Tel 0799 40400.

St Albans	Noke Thistle	68%	£90
Tel 0727 854252 Fax 0727 841906			**H**
Watford Road St Albans Hertfordshire AL2 3DS			Map 15 E2

Practical accommodation in what was once the farm of Burston Manor. Set
in its own grounds near the M1, M10 and M25. Banqueting for up to 55,
conferences to 60. Residents have membership of the vast St Albans
Health & Racquet Club and nearby Mentmore Golf Club. Children up to
14 stay free in parents' room. Informal eating in the Baltimore Bean
Company American-themed saloon. Reduced weekend tariff. *Rooms 111.
Garden, gym.* AMERICAN EXPRESS *Access, Diners, Visa.*

St Albans	St Michael's Manor	63%	£94
Tel 0727 864444 Fax 0727 848909			**H**
Fishpool Street St Albans Hertfordshire AL3 4RY			Map 15 E2

The manor house, which dates from the 16th century, stands in five acres
of attractive gardens complete with a lake. Well-proportioned day rooms
have a traditional feel, particularly the Oak Lounge, part of the original
Tudor structure, with fine plastered ceilings dated 1586. The restaurant has
a bright conservatory (Victorian in style but dating from 1987) that's
popular for private parties. The grounds contain many specimen trees, after
which all the bedrooms are named. Best of the rooms are doubles with
four-posters and garden views. *Rooms 22. Garden.* AMERICAN EXPRESS *Access,
Diners, Visa.*

St Albans	Sopwell House Hotel	69%	£124
Tel 0727 864477 Fax 0727 844741			**H**
Cottonmill Lane Sopwell St Albans Hertfordshire AL1 2HQ			Map 15 E2

South-east of the city centre, Sopwell House, once the country home
of Earl Mountbatten, still retains a good degree of its original Georgian
elegance even though in the last few years it has undergone considerable
enlargement. Eleven acres of part-wooded, part-landscaped gardens provide
a peaceful rural setting. Substantial conference facilities (for up to 400),
a new bedroom wing and a splendid leisure complex are all fairly recent
additions and the owner plans yet more improvements to upgrade the

quality of what is on offer. Public rooms, which lead off a highly polished stone-floored foyer, begin with an elegant, quite clubby bar furnished with brown leather chesterfields, heavy bottle green drapes and a carved Georgian-style darkwood bar counter; this sets the tone for the drawing room and library. 22 of the bedrooms have four-posters and these, together with a number of other rooms, have a traditional ambience. The remainder are a little more modern in style, furnished with lightwood units. Decor in all is well co-ordinated and tasteful. Extras include satellite TV. Bathrooms in cream or white marble are excellent, each with a power shower, scales and useful toiletries. **Rooms** *92. Garden, croquet, indoor swimming pool, gym, sauna, spa bath, steam room, solarium, beauty salon, hair salon, snooker, brasserie (10am-10pm).* AMERICAN EXPRESS *Access, Diners, Visa.*

St Albans — Places of Interest

Tourist Information   Tel 0727 864511.
Abbey Theatre   Tel 0727 57861.
The Gardens of the Rose   Chiswell Green Tel 0727 50461.
St Albans Cathedral   Tel 0727 60780.
Dunstable Road Showground   Redbourne Tel 0582 792626.
   Museums and Art Galleries
St Albans Organ Museum   Tel 0727 51557/73896.
The Verulamium Museum   St Michael's Tel 0727 54659 or 866100 Ext 2912.
The Mosquito Aircraft Museum   Salisbury Hall, London Colney Tel 0727 22051.

St Austell	Boscundle Manor	65%	£110
Tel 0726 813557 Fax 0726 814997			H
Tregrehan St Austell Cornwall PL25 3RL			Map 12 B3

Secluded grounds make a peaceful setting for this lovely little 18th-century manor house, whose owners Andrew and Mary Flint have been in residence since 1978, opening for the summer season only. Seven bedrooms are in the main house, one in the Garden Room above the swimming pool and two in a cottage at the top of the garden; all the doubles (8) have spa baths. Although more suited to residents wanting a quiet holiday, self-entertaining families might find this a pleasant home-from-home, run like a private house. No functions, no lunches for non-residents, just good old peace and quiet. **Rooms** *10. Garden, croquet, golf practice area, outdoor swimming pool, keep-fit equipment, helipad.* Closed end Oct-end Mar. *Access, Visa.*

St Austell	White Hart		£63
Tel 0726 72100 Fax 0726 74705			I
Church Street St Austell Cornwall PL25 4AT			Map 12 B3

Although the centrally located White Hart is steeped in history (it dates back to 1735) it offers every modern comfort to holidaymakers and business travellers. Banqueting/conference facilities for up to 60. The saloon bar is the focal point of the day rooms. **Rooms** *18. Closed 25 & 26 Dec.* AMERICAN EXPRESS *Access, Diners, Visa.*

St Ives (Cambs)	Slepe Hall	61%	£60
Tel 0480 463122 Fax 0480 300706			H
Ramsey Road St Ives Cambridgeshire PE17 4RB			Map 10 B2

A Grade II listed building dating from 1848 and a private boarding school for girls until its conversion in 1966. Now a small, comfortable hotel, it's kept in excellent order by Jan and Colin Stapleton. Several bedrooms feature four-poster or half-tester beds, and among the public areas is the Brunel Suite, which can cater for 220 conference delegates or banqueters. **Rooms** *16. Garden. Closed 24-29 Dec.* AMERICAN EXPRESS *Access, Diners, Visa.*

St Ives (Cornwall)   Garrack Hotel   62%   £91

Tel 0736 796199   Fax 0736 798955   **H**
Burthallan Lane St Ives Cornwall TR26 3AA   Map 12 A3

Run by the Kilby family for 30 years, the creeper-clad Garrack stands
in two acres of gardens overlooking Porthmeor beach and the distant
sweep of St Ives Bay. The main lounge is a busy family room with games
and books, and there are two other more formal lounges plus a pleasant
cocktail bar. Bedrooms in the main house are traditionally furnished and
vary in size; those in the extension are more modern and roomy. Some
rooms have four-posters, some spa baths and there are also family rooms
with bunk beds. *Rooms 18. Garden, indoor swimming pool, keep-fit
equipment, sauna, solarium, spa bath, coffee shop (11am-10pm).*
AMERICAN EXPRESS *Access, Diners, Visa.*

St Ives (Cornwall)   Pig 'n' Fish   £45

Tel 0736 794204   **R**
Norway Lane St Ives Cornwall TR26 1LZ   Map 12 A3

In a simply appointed restaurant above a back-street craft market chef-
patron Paul Sellars prepares fine seafood dishes, many with a French
or Italian accent. Lunchtime is fixed-price, dinner à la carte, and typical
dishes include warm mussel salad with parsley pesto, shellfish open ravioli
with olive oil, lemon and garlic, grilled cod with mashed potato and wild
garlic leaves, brill hollandaise and sautéed monkfish with smoked pancetta,
rocket and roasted red peppers. Many dishes are highly original – witness
pot-roast skate with butter beans and salsa verde. Tempting sweets such
as lemon soufflé pudding with cinnamon sauce, or chocolate marquise with
peanut brittle wafer. *Seats 30. L 12.30-1.30 D 7-9.30. Set L £14/£17.50.
Closed Sun & Mon, Nov to mid-Mar. Access, Visa.*

St Ives   Places of Interest

Tourist Information   Tel 0736 796297.
The Barbara Hepworth Museum   (The Tate Gallery) Tel 0736 796226.
Paradise Park   Hayle Tel 0736 753365.
Porthmeor Beach *10 miles.*

St Margaret's   Wallett's Court   60%   £50

Tel 0304 852424   Fax 0304 853430   **HR**
West Cliffe St Margaret's Dover Kent CT15 6EW   Map 10 B2

Wallett's Court is a lovely old country manor house, just outside
St Margaret's on the B2058 (off the A258 Dover/Deal road), and it has
a history documented back to the Domesday Book, explained for interested
visitors on a frieze in one of the dining rooms and evident also in the
atmosphere of the house. The main building is dated 1627, on either side
of the porch, and feels as though it has also always been in good and caring
hands, whether those belonged to Queen Eleanor of Aquitaine or Chris and
Lea Oakley, who have been here since 1977 and are now ably assisted
by son Craig. Three bedrooms are in the main house and carry a small
supplement (one, the Seaview Room, just gives you that glimpse, as do
south-east facing ground-floor public rooms) while the remainder are
in two separate sympathetic conversions (the former granary) across the
gravel drive and beautifully manicured lawn. All are comfortably
furnished and well maintained. The lounge and bar are beamed and feature
an upright Steinway whose ivories talented guests may tinkle.
A conservatory extension, brought on stream just as we last visited, not
only increases the dining area from two interconnecting rooms to three,
but also offers a most attractive additional lounge furnished with muslin
drapes and soft cushions on rattan chairs. Excellent breakfasts offer locally
cured and made bacon and sausages, free-range eggs, locally smoked fish,
and home-made preserves as well as healthy options like home-made muesli

and herbal teas, all served with just the right balance of efficiency and relaxation. **Rooms** 10. *Garden, tennis. Closed 4 days Christmas, 1 week last Jan. Access, Visa.*

Restaurant   £55

Chris Oakley draws on his early days at *Le Poulbot* (he retired down here but missed the stove!) to produce set menus of three courses during the week but five (with choices) on Saturdays, served in the candle-lit, beamed, non-smoking dining rooms. The menu changes daily, and draws strongly on local produce, carefully cooked with some well-thought-out flavour and texture combinations. Thus you might start with a smooth and densely flavoured spinach and watercress soup, served (if you wish, not if you don't) with a splash of cream and croutons, or a Kentish platter of oak-smoked duck breast and wood pigeon served with a traditional Cumberland sauce; moving on to a slice of moist wild salmon laid on a sweet basil sauce with tomato and golden puff pastry; then a good sharp orchard sorbet before rack of new season's local lamb with its own gravy and Kentish Bramleys; or a vegetarian option of harlequin tomatoes (two beefsteak tomato halves stuffed separately with carrot and cauliflower purées, served on a Bramley purée – apples and love apples, presumably). There's a choice of puddings displayed, such as whisky chocolate mousse topped with raspberry syllabub and fresh raspberries, summer pudding, hot bread-and-butter pudding, or a platter of about eight British and Continental cheeses. Coffee and Belgian chocolates close the proceedings. Good, well-annotated wine list. Charming service led by Craig Oakley. **Seats** 60. *Parties 30. Private Room 30. D only 7-9. Closed Sun (except residents). Set D £20 (Sat £25).*

St Martin's	St Martin's Hotel	69%	£186★
Tel 0720 22092 Fax 0720 22298			**HR**
St Martin's Isles of Scilly TR25 0QW			**Map 12 A2**

Following a flight by Skybus helicopter or plane from the mainland (or a 2½hr sea crossing from Penzance) that arrives on St Mary's Island nearby, the hotel launch transfers guests to St Martin's island, 28 miles out in the Atlantic; the hotel will make all travel arrangements to suit guests – there are many options via Penzance, Exeter, Plymouth and Newquay. The island provides the ultimate escape for solitude seekers, an equally novel activity centre for families (under-14s stay free in parents' room) and the last word in privacy for a conference (max 100) or private dinner (up to 60). Public rooms include the first-floor sunset lounge which affords wonderful views westward towards Tresco. ★Half-board terms only for high season, but the off-season B&B tariff has been changed since last year, with improved options for eating. Now under new ownership, but the management has remained the same. **Rooms** 24. *Garden, indoor swimming pool, fishing, snooker, sailing and scuba-diving instruction. Closed Nov.* AMERICAN EXPRESS *Access, Diners, Visa.*

Tean Restaurant   £55

Refurbished last year, the restaurant makes good use of local fish which is landed right on the hotel's quay. Lobster is a speciality and game and home-grown vegetables also feature on the choice of table d'hote menus – *menu du jour* and *menu gourmet*, from which diners can easily mix and match. The former menu offers standard favourites, while the latter might extend to quenelles of cream cheese and apricots with Parma ham or warm monkfish salad with a spicy lime dressing, followed by a fish dish and then grilled fillet of halibut 'accompanied by pearls of the vineyard and a rosemary fish sauce' or 'roast loin of lamb filled with a pistachio and apricot farce edged by a burgundy sauce'. Daily vegetarian dish. No smoking. Lighter bar lunches. **Seats** 60. *Parties 16. L in bar only D 7.15-9. Set D £16.50 & £26.50.*

St Mary's — Hotel Godolphin — 58% — £72

Tel 0720 22316   Fax 0720 22252
Church Street St Mary's Isles of Scilly TR21 0JR

H
Map 12 A2

In the hands of the Mumford family since 1967, the hotel stands
in a delightful town-house garden just a minute from the harbour beach.
It has a welcoming, homely appearance that is reinforced inside, where
a panelled entrance hall leads to a comfortable lounge area with gold velour
seating around a marble fireplace. There is also a cosy bar. Most of the
simply furnished bedrooms have functional bathrooms without showers;
three are not en suite and four are suitable for family use. No dogs.
Rooms 31. *Garden, sauna. Closed mid Oct-mid Mar. Access, Visa.*

St Mary's — Tregarthen's Hotel — 60% — £110*

Tel 0720 22540   Fax 0720 22089
St Mary's Isles of Scilly TR21 0PP

H
Map 12 A2

Founded in 1840 by a Captain Tregarthen, owner of the steam packet *Little
Western*, this friendly hotel with a loyal following of regular guests stands
in terraced gardens overlooking the harbour. Day rooms include the Little
Western bar serving good snacks at lunchtime and a roast on Sunday.
Bedrooms, some looking out to sea, are neat and comfortable. The Port
Light – a double room with private bathroom and sitting room, lies across
the garden, 30 yards from the hotel entrance. One bathroom boasts
a Victorian cast-iron tub. *Half-board terms. No children under five.
No dogs. *Rooms* 29. *Garden. Closed 3rd week Oct-3rd week Mar.*
AMERICAN EXPRESS *Access, Diners, Visa.*

St Mawes — Idle Rocks Hotel — 64% — £128

Tel 0326 270771   Fax 0326 270062
Tredenham Road St Mawes Cornwall TR2 5AN

HR
Map 12 B4

On the water's edge in the lovely Roseland Peninsula the privately owned
(but not personally run) Idle Rocks is a popular destination for both
residents and passers-by. Public rooms – including a panelled bar and
armchair-filled lounge – enjoy harbour views. Pretty bedrooms in the main
building – bedhead drapes, ribbon-hung pictures, antique and reproduction
furniture – are not large but have good carpeted bathrooms with
darkwood panelled tubs; three, including two tiny singles, have shower
and WC only. More spacious bedrooms, with equally good facilities, are
in a nearby annexe. There are also some cottages and apartments nearby, let
on a self-catering basis. Twice a week, weather permitting, trips are
available on the hotel's own 55-foot ketch. *Rooms* 24. *Access, Visa.*

Waters Edge Restaurant — £65

Fish is naturally popular here, though there's also plenty of choice for meat
eaters from Alan Vickops's à la carte and table d'hote menus. A typical
starter would be quail and duck breast salad with garlic croutons and a sun-
dried tomato dressing, then grilled fillet of salmon on a herb butter sauce,
with strawberry and Grand Marnier layered shortbread hearts on a red
berry coulis to finish. *Seats* 65. *Parties* 20. *L Sun only 12-2.30 D 7-9.15. Set
Sun L £11.50. Set D £18.95.*

St Mawes — Rising Sun — 62% — £89

Tel 0326 270233
The Square St Mawes Truro Cornwall TR2 5DJ

H
Map 12 B4

A popular and lively place on the waterfront in the centre of the village.
The small conservatory frontage houses a lounge bar, and there's a public
bar that's a favourite with the locals. Residents can retreat to their own
little lounge at the back (six seats, with TV). Bedrooms are smart and

simple, with pine furniture and neat, practical bathrooms. Children up to
12 stay free with parents in the family room. *Rooms 11. Terrace.*
AMERICAN EXPRESS *Access, Visa.*

St Mawes   Hotel Tresanton   69%   £70

Tel 0326 270544   Fax 0326 270002
Lower Castle Road St Mawes Cornwall TR2 5DR

H
Map 12 B4

The pretty village of St Mawes is a popular holiday destination, and
travellers are assured of a warm welcome from Graham and Maureen
Brockton at the Tresanton. For afternoon tea the vagaries of the English
weather are accommodated by comfortable sofas and open fires; the better
days by lovely gardens and a terrace. All the bedrooms enjoy sea views,
and four have little balconies. No children under 10. *Rooms 21. Garden.*
Closed 1 Nov-4 Mar (open 10 days Christmas). AMERICAN EXPRESS *Access,*
Diners, Visa.

Salcombe   Marine Hotel   68%   £152

Tel 0548 844444   Fax 0548 843109
Cliff Road Salcombe Devon TQ8 8JH

H
Map 13 D3

In a splendid setting by the Salcombe estuary, the Marine makes the most
of its location with picture windows in the roomy, comfortable public
areas. There's also a sun deck with plenty of loungers. Best bedrooms are
on the patio floor – pretty in pink, with pink-washed furniture. All but six
rooms enjoy the views. Good leisure facilities. Children up to seven stay
free in parents' room. Dogs in selected rooms only. *Rooms 51. Garden,*
indoor swimming pool, keep-fit equipment, sauna, spa bath, solarium, beauty
& hair salon, sea fishing, mooring, games room. AMERICAN EXPRESS *Access,*
Diners, Visa.

Salcombe   Soar Mill Cove   66%   £128

Tel 0548 561566   Fax 0548 561223
Soar Mill Cove nr Salcombe Devon TQ7 3DS

H
Map 13 D3

As you would expect from its location – spectacular sea views in one of the
tourist industry's hotspots – Soar Mill Cove is most definitely a holiday and
family hotel – indeed, Keith Makepeace goes so far as virtually to guarantee
no conference trade, so guests can be totally relaxed. Care for their well-
being has extended this year to the creation of individual gardens in front
of six of the rooms, though all rooms in this one storey, garden-facing
purpose-built hotel already have patios as well as direct access to the
meadows and the beach beyond. Inside, bedrooms and bathrooms are
comfortable and well maintained, as are public areas, though your stay here
will essentially be of an outdoor nature. The National Trust sandy beach
and cliff walks prove highly popular daytime activities. Families with
young children are admirably catered for (ages 1-6 charged 20% of tariff,
6-15 30%); high tea at 5.30pm is designed to leave adult residents in peace
in the dining room during dinner. *Rooms 16. Garden, indoor & outdoor*
swimming pools, tennis, putting, games room, laundry room.
Closed Nov-mid Feb. Access, Visa.

Salcombe   South Sands   60%   £134*

Tel 0548 843741   Fax 0548 842112
Cliff Road Salcombe Devon TQ8 8LL

H
Map 13 D3

Salcombe is one of the most southerly towns in England, and South Sands
is well placed to get the best of the sunshine, with great views out to sea.
Under the same ownership (the Edwards family, with John and Bridget
in charge here) as the *Tides Reach* (see below) but even closer to the shore
with the sandy beach reaching right up to the terrace walk, the South
Sands caters more for younger children with ten family suites and a special
high tea for youngsters served in the terrace bar/coffee shop from 5pm.

Generally good-sized bedrooms, half with freestanding pine and half with white melamine fitted furniture, are uncluttered, with carpeted, fully tiled bathrooms. Friendly staff. *Half-board terms only, but B&B in early and late season. *Rooms 31. Terrace, indoor swimming pool, spa bath, steam room, solarium, moorings, children's playroom, pool room, coffee shop (10.30-6.30). Closed Nov-Feb. Access, Visa.*

Salcombe	Spinnakers	£50
Tel 0548 843408		**R**
Fore Street Salcombe Devon TQ8 8JG		Map 13 D3

The waterside restaurant and bar (downstairs in the Salcombe Apartment building) is a popular spot since most of the tables have views of the estuary. There's also seating for about 36 outside on the terrace. David and Sandra May serve up informal meals at lunchtime, with a more formal service in the evenings. Unpretentious atmosphere, plenty of local fish and a few meat alternatives. *Seats 60. Parties 20. Private Room 30. L 12-2 D 7-9.30. Closed D Sun, also all Mon & Tue in winter, all Dec & Jan. Set D £12.95. Access, Visa.*

Salcombe	Tides Reach	71%	£144*
Tel 0548 843466 Fax 0548 843954			**H**
South Sands Salcombe Devon TQ8 8LJ			Map 13 D3

There's a modern yet somehow timeless air at the Tides Reach, a popular holiday destination since it was built and where the Edwards family maintain consistently high standards. It nestles snugly in the valley immediately behind South Sands beach, with clear views over the estuary and the Bolt Head. All the elegant public areas – the marble-floored, plant-filled conservatory-style entrance, the restful lounge, the stylish Aquarium Bar – enjoy sea views, as do all but three bedrooms. These range from five singles with small double beds to junior and family suites, penthouse rooms (most have balconies) and extra large Premier and Honeymoon rooms. All rooms have all the usual electrical gadgets. The sunbathing deck next to the pool and a grass area around an ornamental pond are both glorious suntraps. Very friendly and willing staff and excellent leisure facilities on-site or nearby, some at a small extra charge. A small public ferry chugs its way from South Sands beach into the town and there are spectacular coastal walks straight from the hotel. No children under 8. *Half-board terms only in high season. *Rooms 38. Garden, indoor swimming pool, sauna, spa bath, solarium, keep-fit equipment, beauty and hairdressing salons, snooker, squash, sailing, windsurfing (with tuition), water skiing, moorings, boat house & dinghy park. Closed Nov-Feb.* AMERICAN EXPRESS *Access, Diners, Visa.*

Salcombe	Place of Interest

Overbecks Museum and Garden (NT)   Tel 0548 842893.

Note that all telephone numbers with area codes starting with 0 will start 01 from 16 April 1995.

Salisbury	Rose & Crown	56%	£95
Tel 0722 327908 Fax 0722 339816			**H**
Harnham Road Harnham Salisbury Wiltshire SP2 8QJ			Map 14 C3

A 13th-century, half-timbered inn whose gardens border the river Avon. Public areas and five characterful bedrooms are in the original building; other rooms, including family rooms, are in a modern extension. Children up to 12 stay free in parents' room. Queens Moat Houses. *Rooms 28. Garden.* AMERICAN EXPRESS *Access, Diners, Visa.*

Salisbury White Hart 63% £97

Tel 0722 327476 Fax 0722 412761 **H**

1 St John Street Salisbury Wiltshire SP1 2SD **Map 14 C3**

City-centre hotel with an impressive pillared portico and elegant Georgian facade, but modest bedrooms. Plenty of free parking. Banquets/conferences for 60/100. Handy for the Cathedral and main shops. Forte Heritage. *Rooms 68.* AMERICAN EXPRESS *Access, Diners, Visa.*

Salisbury Places of Interest

Tourist Information Tel 0722 334956.
  Theatres and Concert Halls
Medieval Hall Tel 0980 610304.
Salisbury Arts Centre Tel 0722 21744.
Salisbury Playhouse Tel 0722 20333.
  Historic Houses, Castles and Gardens
Fitz House Garden Tel 0722 716257.
Heale Gardens and Plant Centre Tel 0722 73504.
The King's House Tel 0722 332151.
Old Sarum Tel 0722 335398.
Wilton House Wilton Tel 0722 743115.
Stonehenge Nr Amesbury.
Salisbury Cathedral Tel 0722 22457.
Salisbury and South Wiltshire Museum and Stonehenge Gallery Tel 0722 332151.
Salisbury Racecourse Tel 0722 326461.

Saltash Granada Lodge £45

Tel 0752 848408 Fax 0752 848346 **L**

A38 bypass Saltash Cornwall PL12 6LF **Map 12 C3**

Rooms 31. AMERICAN EXPRESS *Access, Diners, Visa.*

Samlesbury Swallow Trafalgar 60% £95

Tel 0772 877351 Fax 0772 877424 **H**

Preston New Road Samlesbury Lancashire PR5 0UL **Map 6 B1**

Heading east from Junction 31 of the M6 and alongside the A59 at its intersection with the A677 Blackburn road is a practical, modern business-orientated hotel with good leisure facilities and conference capacities of up to 250. Parking for 300 cars. *Rooms 78. Garden, indoor swimming pool, spa bath, sauna, steam room, solarium, keep-fit equipment, squash.* AMERICAN EXPRESS *Access, Diners, Visa.*

Samlesbury Tickled Trout 63% £95

Tel 0772 877671 Fax 0772 847463 **H**

Preston New Road Samlesbury nr Preston Lancashire PR5 OUJ **Map 6 B1**

A modern hotel on the banks of the Ribble, west of junction 31 of the M6. Bedrooms and public rooms were being refurbished during 1994. Quiet bedrooms (most overlook the river) have fitted furniture, modern fabrics and the usual accessories. Children up to 14 stay free in parents' room. Conference facilities for up to 100. *Rooms 72. Indoor swimming pool, fishing.* AMERICAN EXPRESS *Access, Diners, Visa.*

Sandbach Chimney House 62% £80

Tel 0270 764141 Fax 0270 768916 **H**

Congleton Road Sandbach Cheshire CW11 0ST **Map 6 B2**

Although only moments from the M6 (Junction 17), the mock-Tudor Chimney House has a remarkably peaceful rural setting within eight acres of wooded grounds. Open-plan public areas focus on a back-to-back pair of original fireplaces. Conference facilities for up to 100 theatre-style. No dogs. *Rooms 48. Garden, sauna, solarium.* AMERICAN EXPRESS *Access, Diners, Visa.*

Sandiway   Nunsmere Hall   77%   £138

Tel 0606 889100   Fax 0606 889055

HR

Tarporley Road Sandiway Cheshire CW8 2ES

Map 6 B2

Almost surrounded by a 60-acre lake, turn-of-the-century Nunsmere Hall enjoys a delightfully secluded setting in Delamere Forest. A fine galleried entrance hall sets the tone for appealing day rooms which include a comfortable, oak-panelled bar, leather-furnished library and a lounge with a huge floral centrepieces. Notably large, antique-furnished bedrooms are individually decorated, with comfortable sitting areas. Sybaritic bathrooms, many with separate shower cubicle, in addition to a large tub, all have bidets, generous towelling and attractive basins sunk into marble-topped wash stands. Rooms are properly serviced in the evenings and there is 24hr room service. No dogs. *Rooms 32. Garden, croquet, golf practice net, archery, helipad.* AMERICAN EXPRESS *Access, Diners, Visa.*

Garden Room Restaurant   £70

The restaurant features brass chandeliers hanging from the moulded plaster ceiling and floor-length undercloths on tables which boast pretty, high-quality tableware. Chef Paul Kitching's attractively presented offerings tend to be modern in style with the likes of confit of smoked salmon, smoked haddock and poached salmon with a herb and yoghurt vinaigrette, or roast saddle of venison with grilled black pudding, truffle-scented pancakes and a Madeira and truffle-scented game stock. Desserts might include chocolate mousse with ginger shortcakes or an apple-flavoured crème brulée with Shrewsbury biscuits, sugared hazelnuts and a cinnamon Chantilly cream. British farmhouse cheeses are served with home-made date and walnut bread. Particularly good *amuse gueule* arrive with the menu. A lighter menu is served in the lounge or on the terrace throughout the day. No smoking. *Seats 48. Parties 12. Private Room 42. L 12-2 D 7-10. Set L £14.95 (Sun £17.95) Set D £25.*

Saunton   Saunton Sands   67%   £128

Tel 0271 890212   Fax 0271 890145

H

Saunton nr Braunton Devon EX33 1LQ

Map 12 C1

A family-oriented resort hotel commanding panoramic views over the North Devon coastline: five miles of golden sands beckon, and if you resist the glorious outdoors there are extensive indoor leisure facilities instead. Bedrooms are neat, light and airy. Children's facilities include a crèche, play areas, entertainment, plenty of cots, baby-sitting, baby-listening and high teas. Three conference suites accommodate 20-200. Parking for over 100 cars. 24-hour room service. No dogs, but kennels can be arranged nearby. *Rooms 96. Garden, croquet, tennis, squash, indoor & outdoor swimming pools, spa bath, sauna, solarium, snooker, hair and beauty salons, indoor and outdoor play areas.* AMERICAN EXPRESS *Access, Diners, Visa.*

Sawbridgeworth   Manor of Groves Hotel   70%   £103

Tel 0279 600777   Fax 0279 600374

H

High Wych Sawbridgeworth Hertfordshire CM21 0LA

Map 11 B4

A long winding drive leads through a golf course to a gracious Georgian Manor house which looks out over the course and the rest of the 150 acres of surrounding mature parkland. Previous owners the Sharers have left and the hotel has new management. Standards of decor aren't what they used to be, particularly in the public areas, where marble floors lack their mirror-like shine and carpets are stained with age and neglect. Bedrooms retain a certain charm in that they have good aspects from the windows and they are of a good size and prettily decorated. They are however not too well provided with extras and there are scarcely any homely touches – not a potted plant or even a dried flower arrangement in sight. The marble bathrooms are in quite good order. **Rooms** *32. Garden, tennis, golf (18), outdoor swimming pool, gym, sauna, solarium, snooker.* AMERICAN EXPRESS® *Access, Diners, Visa.*

Scalby   **Wrea Head**   65%   £99

Tel 0723 378211 Fax 0723 371780	**H**
Scalby nr Scarborough North Yorkshire YO13 0PB	**Map 5 F3**

Built in 1881, Wrea Head stands in 14 acres of wooded and landscaped grounds that were once part of a deer park. It's signposted off the A171 and reached by a narrow driveway. A fine oak-panelled hall features a wall-long stained-glass window, there's a minstrel's gallery in the lounge, and the bar is notable for an unusual terracotta frieze. Individually appointed bedrooms are generally neat and comfortable, with delightful views. Free use of leisure facilities at *Hackness Grange* (see entry under Hackness), 3 miles away. No dogs. **Rooms** *21. Garden, croquet.* AMERICAN EXPRESS® *Access, Visa.*

Scarborough   **The Crown**   63%   £90

Tel 0723 373491 Fax 0723 362271 ·	**H**
Esplanade Scarborough North Yorkshire YO11 2AG	**Map 5 F4**

Crowning the cliffs overlooking South Bay, this gracious hotel caters to both tourist and business trade (conference facilities for up to 200 delegates). Forte Heritage. **Rooms** *78. Snooker, solarium, hair salon.* AMERICAN EXPRESS® *Access, Diners, Visa.*

Scarborough   **Lanterna**   £45

Tel 0723 363616	**R**
33 Queen Street Scarborough North Yorkshire YO11 1HQ	**Map 5 F4**

Run for 20 years by the Arecco family, Lanterna offers a menu of straightforward Italian dishes, from *tonno e fagioli* and spaghetti (bolognese, carbonara, napoletana) to scampi, chicken breast in four ways, veal escalopes and steaks. **Seats** *36. D only 7-9.30. Closed Sun & Mon, 25 & 26 Dec. Access, Visa.*

Scarborough   **Places of Interest**

Tourist Information   Tel 0723 373333.
Royal Opera House   Tel 0723 36999.
St. Joseph Theatre in the Round   Tel 0723 370541.
Whitby Abbey   Whitby Tel 0947 603568.
Filey Bay Beach *7 miles from Scarborough.*

Scole   **Scole Inn**   £63

Tel 0379 740481 Fax 0379 740762	**I**
Ipswich Road Scole nr Diss Norfolk IP22 4DR	**Map 10 C2**

Built in 1655 by a wool merchant, this grand-looking redbrick inn is Grade 1 listed for its architectural interest. Splendid brick gables front and rear show a Dutch influence. Bedrooms in the Georgian stable block are quieter and more modern than those in the main building, which face the busy A140. These rooms, though, are full of character, many having carved oak doors, old timbers and fireplaces plus four-poster or half-oak doors, old timbers and fireplaces plus four-poster or half-tester beds. The beamed, pubby bar is also full of atmosphere with a vast brick fireplace, dark oak furniture and an 'old English Inn' ambience. **Rooms** *23.* AMERICAN EXPRESS® *Access, Diners, Visa.*

Scotch Corner   Forte Travelodge   £45

Tel 0748 823768   **L**

Scotch Corner Skeeby nr Richmond North Yorkshire DL10 5EQ   Map 5 D3

On the A1 northbound, ½ mile south of Scotch Corner. **Rooms** *40.*
AMERICAN EXPRESS *Access, Diners, Visa.*

Seahouses   Olde Ship Hotel   £66

Tel 0665 720200   Fax 0665 721383   **I**

9 Main Street Seahouses Northumberland NE68 7RD   Map 5 D1

Alan and Jean Glen, here since 1969, have emphasised the nautical charm
of their characterful old inn overlooking the picturesque harbour and Farne
Islands. The tiny cabin bar and handsome saloon bar house marine antiques,
while the long gallery lounge has a collection of model ships. It's very
much a traditional pub, a social centre for regulars and locals, and it has
a lawn and summerhouse for fair-weather use. Good bar food is served
at lunchtime, and in the evening there are sandwiches and a four-course
dinner menu. A small function room with its own bar can accommodate
up to 30. Homely bedrooms; two have four-poster beds. No children
under 10. No dogs. **Rooms** *15. Garden. Closed Dec & Jan.* AMERICAN EXPRESS
Access, Visa.

Seahouses   Place of Interest

Beadnell Bay Beach *4 miles South.*

Seale   Hog's Back Hotel   64%   £109

Tel 0252 782345   Fax 0252 783113   **H**

Seale nr Farnham Surrey GU10 1EX   Map 15 E3

A tile-hung, gable-fronted hotel set high up on the Hog's Back on the A31,
with day rooms smart in pastel and pale wood, a leisure centre and
conference facilities for up to 140 in the Summit Conference Centre. 14
more bedrooms have recently been added. Children up to 14 stay free
in parents' room. Jarvis Hotels. **Rooms** *89. Garden, indoor swimming pool,
keep-fit equipment, sauna, spa bath, solarium, beauty salon.* AMERICAN EXPRESS
Access, Diners, Visa.

Seaton Burn   Holiday Inn Newcastle   70%   £130

Tel 091-236 5432   Fax 091-236 8091   **H**

**Great North Road Seaton Burn nr Newcastle-upon-Tyne Tyne & Wear
NE13 6BP**   Map 5 D2

One of the earliest Holiday Inns set in 13 acres of grounds, off
a roundabout on the A1 seven miles north of the city, six miles from the
Metrocentre and five from the airport. The lobby, with its polished stone
floor, is imposing and other day rooms include a bar that overlooks the
indoor pool. Bedrooms offer modern extras, compact bathrooms with
superb showers and a good supply of thick towels. Conference facilities for
up to 400; ample parking. Children up to 19 share their parents' room free
of charge. **Rooms** *150. Garden, indoor swimming pool, sauna, solarium, spa
bath, keep-fit equipment, kiosk.* AMERICAN EXPRESS *Access, Diners, Visa.*

Seaton Burn   Horton Grange   £80

Tel 0661 860686   Fax 0661 860308   **RR**

Seaton Burn Newcastle-upon-Tyne Tyne & Wear NE13 6BU   Map 5 D2

Located on the perimeter of a large working farm complex, the Grange
was once the landowner's private home. Virtually equidistant from city
centre and Newcastle airport, it is best approached by following the airport
signs from the A19 junction with the A1 western by-pass. The house,
converted by owners Andrew and Sue Shilton, manages to combine

elegance with homeliness: traditional decor and furnishings, fine handcut crystal and 18th-century English plate in fact produce a relaxing and unstuffy atmosphere in which to enjoy chef Steve Martin's fixed-price, five-course dinner, for which the menu changes nightly. As a preliminary, there might be canapés of smoked salmon mousse, and miniature vegetable spring rolls. A typical starter, oak-smoked chicken and pigeon with salad leaves and baby corn brushed with a blue cheese dressing, is full of well-balanced flavours – soft, deep-red pigeon breast and crunchy salad – and comes with good home-made bread and unsalted butter. Crab bisque laced with cognac has a good grainy texture from the crab shells. For main course, try fillet of Scotch beef with a red onion compote served on rösti potato with a red wine vinegar and beef jus and wild mushrooms. Desserts might include warm caramelised rice pudding with William pear and a cardamom-scented custard. *Seats 30. Parties 24. Private Room 8. L residents only D 7-8.30. Closed D Sun (except residents), 25 & 26 Dec. Set D £32. Access, Visa.*

Rooms   £80

Five spacious bedrooms in the main house contain a treasure trove of heirlooms and antique pieces and has spacious, well-aired bathrooms. Facing the Grange's own herb garden and just yards from the front door is the Peach House which contains a further four rooms, described as "single suites". They each have a bright private sitting room for those "with masses of paperwork to do". These are offered at a more economical rate of £60 (including dinner).

Seaview	Seaview Hotel	62%	£60

Tel 0983 612711   Fax 0983 613729   **HR**

High Street Seaview Isle of Wight PO34 5EX   Map 15 D4

The epitome of a small, family-run seaside hotel. Nicholas and Nicola Hayward run this charming little hotel-cum-local inn set just back from the sea front with a most appealing efficiency. A small patio with pub-style white iron tables and chairs at the front of the hotel is a delightful sun trap from which one can watch the world, his boat, spouse and children go by; it leads into a narrow hallway, either side of which are a busy bar and a restaurant. To the rear are two snug lounges (one for non-smokers), another popular nautically-themed bar with bare boards and an open-air yard. Public rooms buzz in season, yet are snug in winter. Upstairs, the bedrooms (some with views over the Solent) are all individually decorated with predominantly blue and yellow colour schemes and feature interesting pictures, objets d'art and spotless bathrooms. *Rooms 16. Sea fishing, family apartment. Closed 25 Dec.* AMERICAN EXPRESS *Access, Visa.*

Restaurant   £50

An intimate dining room with close-set tables, candle-lit in the evenings; unmessed-about-with local flat fish, crab and lobster are probably the best bet. Snacks are served in the adjacent bar or out on the terrace. Realistically priced wines. *Seats 32. L 12-2 D 7.30-9.30. Closed D Sun (except Bank Holiday weekends).*

Seavington St Mary	The Pheasant	69%	£70

Tel 0460 240502   Fax 0460 242388   **H**

Water Street Seavington St Mary nr Ilminster Somerset TA19 0QH   Map 13 F2

A setting of landscaped gardens with abundant trees and shrubs imbues Edmondo and Jacqueline Paoloni's converted 17th-century farmhouse with distinctive charm and character. Look for signs for Seavington St Michael from the South Petherton end of the A303 Ilminster bypass. Hand-crafted reproductions of 18th- and 19th-century fine wood furniture feature in all the individually styled bedrooms: two in the main house with beams galore, the rest in cottages across the garden. No dogs. *Rooms 8. Garden. Closed 26 Dec-5 Jan.* AMERICAN EXPRESS *Access, Diners, Visa.*

Sedgemoor   Forte Travelodge   £45
Tel 0934 750831   L

Welcome Break Sedgemoor Weston-super-Mare Avon BS24 0JL   Map 13 E1

Situated on the M5 northbound, 2 miles north from Junction 22, 6 miles
south of Weston-super-Mare. Access to the southbound carriageway is at
Junction 22. Ask for directions – you'll probably need them! *Rooms 40.*
AMERICAN EXPRESS *Access, Diners, Visa.*

Sedlescombe   Brickwall Hotel   56%   £60
Tel 0424 870253   Fax 0424 870785   H

Sedlescombe nr Battle East Sussex TN33 0QA   Map 11 C6

A Tudor mansion overlooking the village green originally built for the
local ironmaster. Deep-red velour fireside chairs, oak panelling, exposed
beams, and a log fire give character to the bar, and the residents' lounge
is equally friendly. Some bedrooms boast four-posters and black beams.
Rooms 23. Garden, outdoor swimming pool (Apr–Oct). AMERICAN EXPRESS *Access,
Diners, Visa.*

> If we recommend meals in a hotel or inn a separate entry is made for its
> restaurant.

Sevenoaks   Royal Oak   66%   £70
Tel 0732 451109   Fax 0732 740187   HR

High Street Sevenoaks Kent TN13 1HY   Map 11 B5

A former coaching inn with a handsome flintstone Georgian facade. Rich,
bold colours perfectly complement the fabric of the building. Traditional
or antique furniture is used in the bedrooms, which are decorated
in individual, often striking style. Neat, bright bathrooms. Among the day
rooms are a cosy pub-like bar (where imaginative bar snacks are served
in a candle-lit section with scrubbed pine tables and comfortable, well-
upholstered seats), a beautifully furnished drawing room and a conservatory
where morning coffee and afternoon tea may be taken. *Rooms 39. Tennis.*
AMERICAN EXPRESS *Access, Diners, Visa.*

Restaurant   £65

A charming and comfortable restaurant comprising several rooms that are
partially panelled and cleverly lit, creating a relaxing atmosphere. A la carte
and fixed-price menus provide plenty of choice and straightforward
descriptions: baked filo case filled with various cheeses, a bowl of steaming
hot oxtail, roast rack of lamb sitting on a bed of lentils, warm treacle tart.
James Butterfill's fixed-price menus offer particularly good value. Outdoor
eating in good weather on a creeper-clad patio. *Seats 60. Parties 24.
L 12.30–2 D 7.30–10.30. Closed L Sat. Set L £8.95/10.95
Set D £10.95/13.95.*

Sevenoaks   Places of Interest

Tourist Information   Tel 0732 450305.
Lullingstone Castle   Eynsford Tel 0322 862114.
  Historic Houses, Castles and Gardens
Emmetts Garden   Tel 0732 75429.
Great Comp Gardens   Borough Green Tel 0732 882669.
Ightham Mote (NT)   Ivy Hatch, Ightham Tel 0732 810378.
Knole (NT)   Tel 0732 450608.
Chartwell (NT)   Tel 0732 866368 *Home of Winston Churchill.*
Squerryes Court   Westerham Tel 0959 62345.

Shaftesbury	Grosvenor Hotel	62%	£92

Tel 0747 852282   Fax 0747 854755   **H**

The Commons Shaftesbury Dorset SP7 8JA   **Map 14 B3**

Centrally located former coaching inn based around a cobbled courtyard.
Homely, traditional feel. Conference/banqueting facilities for 150/120.
Children under 16 stay free when sharing a room with their parents and
eat for half-price. Under-5s even eat free. Forte Heritage. *Rooms 35.*
AMERICAN EXPRESS *Access, Diners, Visa.*

Shaftesbury	Royal Chase Hotel	60%	£83

Tel 0747 853355   Fax 0747 851969   **H**

Shaftesbury Dorset SP7 8DB   **Map 14 B3**

To the south of the town centre on a roundabout where the A30 and A350
intersect, a friendly, family-run hotel. Until 1922 the building was used
as a monastery and the present bar was once the chapel. Much has changed
since those days and now the hotel offers a cosy library lounge and
a popular indoor leisure area. Best of the bedrooms are the Crown rooms.
Bathrooms in the older parts of the building are quite compact. Staff are
friendly and obliging. Conference/banqueting facilities for 140/160.
Families are well catered for, particularly in holiday periods; informal
eating in the Country Kitchen. *Rooms 35. Garden, indoor swimming pool,
sauna, steam room, solarium, children's playground.* AMERICAN EXPRESS *Access,
Diners, Visa.*

Shaftesbury   Place of Interest

Wincanton Racecourse   Tel 0963 32344.

Shanklin	Cliff Tops Hotel	64%	£99

Tel 0983 863262   Fax 0983 867139   **H**

Park Road Shanklin Isle of Wight PO37 6BB   **Map 15 D4**

A modern hotel, one of the Isle of Wight's largest, with fine sea views and
bright, spacious day rooms. It stands high above Sandown Bay, and
a public lift leads down to the seafront. There's a choice of bars, a leisure
club, conference rooms for up to 240 delegates and plenty of facilities for
children. Most of the bedrooms have balconies. *Rooms 88. Garden, indoor
swimming pool, gym, sauna, spa bath, steam room, solarium, beauty & hair
salon, snooker, children's play area.* AMERICAN EXPRESS *Access, Diners, Visa.*

Shanklin Old Village	The Cottage	£60

Tel 0983 862504   Fax 0983 867512   **R**

8 Eastcliff Road Shanklin Old Village Isle of Wight PO37 6AA   **Map 15 D4**

Three old cottages in a cul de sac on the town side of Shanklin's old village,
visible from the main road. Neil Graham and partner Alan Priddle have
been in the kitchen and at front of house respectively for 20 years. Neil's
daily-changing table d'hote at lunchtime (perhaps venison paté with
Cumberland sauce, plaice bonne femme, puds and coffee) and evening à la
carte menus are a careful mix of English and French. The carte offers a long
list of starters and classic main courses, all elegantly scripted on the
handwritten menu. A filo of fishes with spinach and cream sauce, smoked
duck breast with gooseberry relish, tomato and cumin soup, veal
dijonnaise, medallions of beef with pink peppercorns and cream sauce,
salpicon of lamb (roasted best end of lamb coated with minted béarnaise)
and vegetarian strogonoff typify the style. All puddings and desserts are
home-made – from banana and almond flan to tipsy cake and raspberry
pavlova. There's a pretty courtyard garden seating just six for summer
eating. No smoking in the restaurant, but there are two lounges for puffers.

No children under 15. *Seats* 32. *Parties* 10. *L* 12-2 *D* 7.30-9.45.
Closed D Sun, all Mon, 26 Dec, 4 weeks Feb/Mar and Oct. Set L £7.50.
AMERICAN EXPRESS *Access, Diners, Visa.*

Shanklin   Places of Interest

Sandown Tourist Information   Tel 0983 403886.
Morton Manor Gardens   Brading Tel 0983 4061-68.
Nunwell House & Gardens   Brading Tel 0983 407240.
Osborne House   East Cowes Tel 0983 200022.
Carisbrooke Castle   Newport Tel 0983 522107.

Sheffield   Charnwood Hotel   64%   £90

| Tel 0742 589411   Fax 0742 555107 | H |
| 10 Sharrow Lane Sheffield South Yorkshire S11 8AA | Map 6 C2 |

A Georgian mansion just south of the city centre – ask for directions –
converted to a hotel in 1985. Bedrooms, where some promised
refurbishment will be welcome, feature brass bedheads and darkwood units
incorporating a mini-bar. Carpeted bathrooms offer good shelf space and
generously sized towels. Day rooms include several small lounges – one
in period style, another the conservatory-style Garden Room – plus
an appealing fin de siècle Parisian-style brasserie. Good cooked breakfasts.
Friendly staff. *Rooms 22.* AMERICAN EXPRESS *Access, Diners, Visa.*

> From April 1995 the area telephones code for Sheffield changes
> from 0742 to 0114 plus the addition of 2 before six-digit numbers.

Sheffield   Forte Posthouse   65%   £68

| Tel 0742 670067   Fax 0742 682620 | H |
| Manchester Road Sheffield South Yorkshire S10 5DX | Map 6 C2 |

A modern, stilted tower-block building recently regraded from Forte
Crest. Half the rooms are non-smoking. Good leisure facilities and
conference/banqueting amenities supported by secretarial services; ample
free car parking. Children up to 16 free in parents' room; facilities for
families. 24hr room service. 5 miles from M1 junction 33, on the A57.
Rooms 136. Indoor swimming pool, spa bath, sauna, solarium, gym.
AMERICAN EXPRESS *Access, Diners, Visa.*

Sheffield   Grosvenor House   67%   £67

| Tel 0742 720041   Fax 0742 757199 | H |
| Charter Square Sheffield South Yorkshire S1 3EH | Map 6 C2 |

Prominent tower-block hotel with direct access from its own car park.
Rooms on the higher floors have good views over the city. Large
conference/banqueting facilities; two boardrooms seat up to 20.
Rooms 103. AMERICAN EXPRESS *Access, Diners, Visa.*

Sheffield   Holiday Inn Royal Victoria   67%   £109

| Tel 0742 768822   Fax 0742 724519 | H |
| Victoria Station Road Sheffield South Yorkshire S4 7YE | Map 6 C2 |

Large redbrick Victorian building with well-proportioned, high-ceilinged
day rooms. 20 bedrooms are designated non-smoking. Conference and
banqueting facilities for up to 400. Children up to 19 free in parents' room.
Ample free car parking. *Rooms 100.* AMERICAN EXPRESS *Access, Diners, Visa.*

Sheffield   Moat House   68%   £103

Tel 0742 375376   Fax 0742 378140   **H**
Chesterfield Road South Sheffield South Yorkshire S8 8BW   Map 6 C2

On the outskirts of town, by the A61 towards Chesterfield, this large,
modern, redbrick hotel is wearing well since being opened by the Duke
of Devonshire in 1989. Large bedrooms have solid lightwood units
providing good work space plus a couple of easy chairs around a coffee
table and decent-sized bathrooms with ample shelf space. Public areas
include a separate lounge off the spacious, marble-floored lobby and a bar
with a large stained-glass feature – though more comfortable perhaps is the
cocktail bar in the restaurant area. The leisure centre includes a well-
equipped gym and aerobics studio and conference facilities can
accommodate up to 500 delegates theatre-style. Cooked breakfasts are
collected from a buffet but a freshly fried egg was quickly and cheerfully
provided after a recent overnight inspection. *Rooms 94. Garden, indoor
swimming pool, gym, sauna, spa bath, steam room, sun beds, beauty salon.*
AMERICAN EXPRESS *Access, Diners, Visa.*

Sheffield   Nirmal's   £40

Tel 0742 724054   **R**
189-193 Glossop Road Sheffield South Yorkshire S10 2GW   Map 6 C2

Blackboard specials, which don't change very often, supplement the regular
North Indian menu at this well-established restaurant on the edge of the
city centre. A good plan though is to allow the friendly, chatty owner Mrs
Gupta to guide you towards the more unusual and interesting dishes. Good
range of vegetarian options. *Seats 80. Private Room 50. L 12-2.30 D 6-12
(Fri & Sat to 1). Closed L Sun, all 25 & 26 Dec. Set L £6.95/£12.50
Set D from £12.50.* AMERICAN EXPRESS *Access, Diners, Visa.*

Sheffield   Novotel   63%   £65

Tel 0742 781781   Fax 0742 787744   **H**
Arundel Gate Sheffield South Yorkshire S1 2PR   Map 6 C2

Sheffield's newest hotel, and the most central, being opposite City Hall and
close to both the Crucible and Lyceum Theatres. Cheerful, open-plan
public areas are matched by practical, well-planned bedrooms that all come
with extra sofa-beds (ideal for families) and WCs separate from the
bathroom. 24hr room service. 75% of rooms are reserved for non-smokers.
Rooms 144. Indoor swimming pool, keep-fit equipment. AMERICAN EXPRESS *Access,
Diners, Visa.*

Sheffield   St George Swallow Hotel   64%   £96

Tel 0742 583811   Fax 0742 500138   **H**
Kenwood Road Sheffield South Yorkshire S7 1NQ   Map 6 C2

Up-to-date accommodation, conference facilities (for up to 200) and
a smart leisure club in a much-extended country house set in 11 acres
of landscaped gardens (including an ornamental lake), two miles from the
city centre. 48 single bedrooms have recently been converted into 24
doubles. *Rooms 117. Garden, indoor swimming pool, keep-fit equipment, sauna,
spa bath, steam room, solarium, coffee shop (10am-10pm).* AMERICAN EXPRESS
Access, Diners, Visa.

Sheffield   Places of Interest

Tourist Information   Tel 0742 734671/734672.
Sheffield Cathedral   Tel 0742 753434.
Roche Abbey   Maltby Tel 0709 812739.
   Theatres and Concert Halls
Crucible Theatre   Tel 0742 79922.
Leadmill   Tel 0742 754500.

Merlin Theatre   Tel 0742 551638.
   Museums and Art Galleries
Graves Art Gallery   Tel 0742 734781.
Kelham Island Industrial Museum   Tel 0742 722106.
Mappin Art Gallery   Tel 0742 726281.
Ruskin Gallery   Tel 0742 734781.
Sheffield United FC   Bramhall Lane Tel 0742 738955.
Sheffield Wednesday FC   Hillsborough Tel 0742 343122.
Sheffield Eagles RLFC   Tel 0742 610326.
Sheffield Ski Village   Tel 0742 769459.
Don Valley Stadium   Tel 0742 560607.

Shepperton   Moat House   61%   £118

Tel 0932 241404   Fax 0932 245231   **H**

Felix Lane Shepperton Middlesex TW17 8NP   Map 15 E2

A peaceful location by the Thames is a big plus at this modern hotel set
in 11 acres of grounds and with its own private mooring. Conference
facilities for up to 300 delegates. 24hr room service. *Rooms 180. Sauna,
solarium, keep-fit equipment, putting, mooring, 9-hole pitch & putt.
Closed 1 week Christmas.* AMERICAN EXPRESS *Access, Diners, Visa.*

Shepperton   Warren Lodge   £82

Tel 0932 242972   Fax 0932 253883   **I**

Church Square Shepperton Middlesex TW17 9JZ   Map 15 E2

Close to the Thames, on the corner of a pretty village square in the middle
of a conservation area, this 18th-century inn offers clean, basic
accommodation in a picturesque setting. There are views of the river not
only from the wood-beamed bar but also from six rooms in a newer wing
which lead on to a courtyard, motel-style. Modestly decorated bedrooms
are kept in good order. Small banquets (65) and conferences (18) only.
Parking for 16, no dogs. *Rooms 50. Garden. Closed 5 days
Christmas/New Year.* AMERICAN EXPRESS *Access, Diners, Visa.*

> 🍾 is our symbol for an outstanding wine list.

Shepton Mallet   Blostin's Restaurant   £50

Tel 0749 343648   **R**

29 Waterloo Road Shepton Mallet Somerset BA4 5HH   Map 13 F1

Nick and Lynne Reed's dark, candle-lit bistro offers consistently well-
cooked meals with 2- or 3-course fixed-price menus supplemented by an
additional list of à la carte seasonal specialities. Fish soup, warm chicken and
smokey bacon salad, escalope of salmon with sorrel sauce and crispy duck
with bacon, mushrooms and burgundy sauce might feature on the former,
with stir-fried squid, grilled goat's cheese, poached smoked haddock, loin
of venison with wild mushrooms, monkfish wirth saffron sauce and herb-
crusted rack of lamb with rosemary sauce on the latter. The ubiquitous
sticky toffee pudding with butterscotch sauce appears among the desserts
alongside treacle and walnut tart with clotted cream and home-made ice
creams. Separate vegetarian menu. *Seats 30. D only 7-9.30.
Closed Sun & Mon, 2 weeks Jan, 2 weeks Jun. Set D £13.95/£14.95.
Access, Visa.*

Shepton Mallet   Places of Interest

Tourist Information   Tel 0749 345258.
Wookey Hole Caves and Mill Wookey Hole   Nr Shepton Mallet.
Royal Bath & West Showground   Tel 0749 823211.

Sherborne   Eastbury Hotel   67%   £75

Tel 0935 813131   Fax 0935 817296   **H**

Long Street Sherborne Dorset DT9 3BY   **Map 13 F2**

Built in 1740, the Eastbury is a fine Georgian town house with well-proportioned rooms. Public areas comprise an elegant entrance hall, a comfortably furnished lounge, a library and an intimate cocktail bar with an ornately carved counter. Bedrooms, named after English flowers, have smart polished-wood furniture and pretty fabrics. Bathrooms offer showers and tubs, plus good soaps and toiletries. No dogs. Families are well catered for – children up to 10 stay free sharing with two adults. Conference and banqueting facilities for 80/100. *Rooms 15. Garden. Access, Visa.*

Sherborne   Sherborne Hotel   58%   £66

Tel 0935 813191   Fax 0935 816493   **H**

Horsecastles Lane Sherborne Dorset DT9 6BB   **Map 13 F2**

The former *Posthouse*, still owned by Forte, has been renamed. On the A30 just outside Sherborne, the low-rise modern building has its own grounds and gardens. *Rooms 59. Golf driving net, croquet, playground.* AMERICAN EXPRESS *Access, Diners, Visa.*

Shere   Kinghams   NEW   £55

Tel 0483 202168   **R**

Gomshall Lane Shere Surrey GU5 9HB   **Map 15 E3**

Cottagey restaurant (dating back to 1620) where service is less formal than the crisply clothed tables and elaborately folded napkins. It's run by two brothers, Jason front of house and Paul in the kitchen producing enjoyable, generally uncomplicated dishes such as duck, pheasant and blackcurrant terrine; Mediterranean fish soup; rack of lamb with herb crust and rosemary gravy; escalope of veal with wild mushrooms and Marsala sauce; gooey chocolate pudding and hazelnut Pavlova. A blackboard that displays a £10 two-course menu at lunchtimes and on Tuesday-Thursday evenings is used for fish dishes on Friday night and additional specialities on Saturday night. One of the separate rooms is reserved for non-smokers and in summer there is seating for 60 in the garden. Ample parking. *Seats 45. Private Room 25. L 12-2.30 D 6.30-9.30. Closed D Sun & all Mon. Set L £10 Set D £10 (Tues-Thur). Closed 25 & 26 Dec.* AMERICAN EXPRESS *Access, Visa.*

Shifnal   Park House   71%   £109

Tel 0952 460128   Fax 0952 461658   **H**

Park Street Shifnal nr Telford Shropshire TF11 9BA   **Map 6 B4**

Originally two adjacent country houses of completely different architectural styles, Park House has nevertheless managed to retain much of the atmosphere of a private house. An elegant garden suite and individually stylish private rooms accommodate conferences of up to 200 delegates. Bedrooms use quality furniture and fabrics, and plentiful extras include decanters of sherry and baskets of fresh fruit. Children under 12 stay free in parents' room. Near Junction 4 of the M54. *Rooms 54. Garden, indoor swimming pool, spa bath, sauna, solarium, fishing.* AMERICAN EXPRESS *Access, Diners, Visa.*

Shifnal   Places of Interest

Boscobel House   Tel 0902 850244.
Weston Park   Weston-under-Lizard Tel 095276 207.

Shinfield   L'Ortolan   ★★★   £140

Tel 0734 883783   Fax 0734 885391   **R**

Old Vicarage Church Lane Shinfield nr Reading Berkshire RG2 9BY   **Map 15 D2**

Where does the man get his relentless energy from? After eight years in situ, John Burton-Race's enthusiasm for cooking involved and masterly dishes shows no signs of abating. However, don't think the operation here is a one-man band – it's not, with John's right-hand man, Nigel Marriage, supporting him in the kitchen, together with a dedicated brigade, including wiz pastry chef Michael Taylor. Then there's front of house under the aegis of Christine (Marie Christine really) Burton-Race, a combination of French charm and professionalism, and English sang-froid. Her team is no less proficient, marshalled into an efficient and knowledgeable unit – witness the description of the French cheeses (now joined by some British farmhouse varieties) that are always in tip-top condition. As the address implies, the building is indeed the old vicarage, now flanked by two conservatories (one an adjunct of the dining room, the other a drawing room for pre-prandial drinks or after-dinner coffee and exquisite petits fours – a fitting end to memorable dining). The dining conservatory and the front of the restaurant overlook a delightful garden and terrace, the perfect spot on a balmy day. And yet the restaurant is only a few minutes from Junction 11 of the M4, just an hour's drive from London. What of the cooking? Well, it's exciting and creative, remarkable in fact, starting with perfect *amuse-gueule* preparing the taste buds for what is to follow from a choice of menus (check which are not available at weekends). Menu dishes (two courses à la carte £45) are written in French with descriptive English translations that actually inform you of what you are about to eat. For instance, you are told that a *brandade de morue, sauce vierge* is freshly salted cod, poached in milk, resting on steamed potato, topped with thin strips of bacon and served with a sauce vierge. Unhelpfully, however, it doesn't tell you what *sauce vierge* is! (It's a seasoned frothy butter sauce with lemon juice). Another starter, one of John's signature dishes, unfortunately attracting a surcharge, is lasagne of langoustines (layered langoustines in their mousse between fresh pasta leaves with truffle oil). For a main course look no further than corn-fed squab pigeon roasted with honey, with sherry vinegar added to its caramelised cooking juices, or a slice of sea bass steamed in champagne with oyster jus and topped with a *paysanne* of leeks. Desserts are truly mouthwatering – the delicate caramel mousse served in a dome of toffee (*dome de mousse, caramel brûlée*), a L'Ortolan speciality, is still on the menu, as is the *assiette chocolatière*, small portions of various chocolate desserts. Equally impressive are the tarts (apple, bilberry, raspberry etc), all served with delicious home-made ice creams. It's also worth noting that many of the specialist suppliers are local (crayfish, fresh snails, eggs etc) ensuring that the quality of raw materials is top-notch, so vital to cooking as exceptional as this. The wine list is exemplary, but you must search carefully for bargains, though the house selection is both well chosen and fairly priced. Most wine-producing countries get a look in, but the list is predominantly French, to be expected at a restaurant which rivals the best in France. *Seats 65. Parties 12. Private Room 25. L 12-2.15 D 7-10. Closed D Sun, all Mon, last 2 weeks Aug, last 2 weeks Feb. Set L £22 (not Sun) and £32. Set D £32 & £40.* AMERICAN EXPRESS *Access, Diners, Visa.* MARTELL COGNAC

Shipdham   Shipdham Place   64%   £65

Tel 0362 820303   **H**

Shipdham nr Thetford Norfolk IP25 7LX   **Map 10 C1**

Situated on the A1075, half way between East Dereham and Watton, this old rectory dates back in part to 1630 and there's a Victorian addition too. Day rooms include an elegant morning room, and a TV lounge in the old part has stripped pine panelling. Good breakfasts are served in the delightful old kitchen. More old pine, antiques and rattan easy chairs characterise the pretty bedrooms. One room is suitable for family use, and nursery teas are provided. *Rooms 8. Garden.* AMERICAN EXPRESS *Access, Diners, Visa.*

Shorne   Inn on the Lake   61%   £70

Tel 0474 823333   Fax 0474 823175   **H**

Shorne nr Gravesend Kent DA12 3HB   **Map 11 B5**

A modern stopover set in landscaped grounds with ornamental lakes. Two lounge bars open off the reception area, one quieter with settees, the other with conference chairs and often occupied for that purpose. Of the pleasant and practical bedrooms, a few on the first floor overlook the lakes and have balconies. Banqueting/conference facilities for 500/700. *Rooms 78. Garden.* AMERICAN EXPRESS *Access, Diners, Visa.*

Shrewsbury   Lion Hotel   62%   £92

Tel 0743 353107   Fax 0743 352744   **H**

Wyle Cop Shrewsbury Shropshire SY1 1UY   **Map 6 A3**

A town-centre Forte Heritage hotel with characterful, beamed bedrooms and other period features amid the modern day rooms and conference facilities (up to 200 delegates). Children up to 15 stay free in parents' room. *Rooms 59.* AMERICAN EXPRESS *Access, Diners, Visa.*

Shrewsbury   Prince Rupert Hotel   64%   £83

Tel 0743 236000   Fax 0743 357306   **H**

Butcher Row Shrewsbury Shropshire SY1 1UQ   **Map 6 A3**

Queens Moat Houses hotel in the medieval city centre (access from Fish Street or Church Street). Bedrooms include two four-poster suites, and four rooms are suitable for family use: children up to 16 stay free in parents' room. Valet parking. Banqueting and conference facilities for up to 110. *Rooms 65.* AMERICAN EXPRESS *Access, Diners, Visa.*

Shrewsbury   Places of Interest

Tourist Information   Tel 0743 50761.
The Music Hall   The Square Tel 0743 50671.
Quarry Swimming Centre   Tel 0743 236583.
   Historic Houses, Castles and Gardens
Attingham Park (NT)   Attingham Tel 0743 77 203.
Hodnet Hall Gardens   Hodnet Tel 063 084 202.
Pitchford Hall   Condover Tel 06944 205.
Shipton Hall   Much Wenlock Tel 074 636 225.

Sidmouth   Belmont Hotel   63%   £106

Tel 0395 512555   Fax 0395 579101   **H**

The Esplanade Sidmouth Devon EX10 8RX   **Map 13 E2**

Serving a mixture of family and business customers, standing in substantial grounds on the seafront, the Belmont was built as a private residence in 1820, becoming a hotel exactly a century later. Attention to detail lavished by owners the Brend family pays dividends, and there's an air of elegance in the public rooms. There are views over the bay from its roomy lounges and from many of its bedrooms. Some rooms have private balconies, and de luxe rooms offer numerous cosseting extras such as bathrobes. Guests have free use of the leisure facilities of the sister hotel next door, the *Victoria* (see entry). Parking for 45 cars, banqueting/ conferences for 120/90. No dogs. *Rooms 54. Garden, putting.* AMERICAN EXPRESS *Access, Diners, Visa.*

Sidmouth   Fortfield Hotel   59%   £70

Tel & Fax 0395 512403

Sidmouth Devon EX10 8NU   Map 13 E2

Andrew and Annabel Torjussen own and run an Edwardian redbrick hotel
overlooking a cricket ground and the sea beyond. A light, sunny lounge
makes the most of the location, and a number of bedrooms have balconies.
Smoking not encouraged. Payments by credit card are surcharged by 2½%.
Rooms 55. Garden, indoor swimming pool, sauna, solarium, games room.
AMERICAN EXPRESS *Access, Diners, Visa.*

Sidmouth   Hotel Riviera   65%   £118

Tel 0395 515201   Fax 0395 577775

The Esplanade Sidmouth Devon EX10 8AY   Map 13 E2

A handsome Regency facade fronts a terrace of three-storey houses in the
middle of the esplanade overlooking Lyme Bay. The Regency Bar
is a relaxing spot for a drink, while cream teas can be enjoyed in the lounge
or out on the patio. A programme of bedroom and bathroom
refurbishment has recently been completed; most rooms have bay views;
two rooms are specially equipped for disabled guests. Concessionary green
fees at two nearby golf courses. Banqueting/conference facilities for 90.
Rooms 27. Terrace. AMERICAN EXPRESS *Access, Diners, Visa.*

Sidmouth   Victoria Hotel   67%   £142

Tel 0395 512651   Fax 0395 579154

The Esplanade Sidmouth Devon EX10 8RY   Map 13 E2

Named after Queen Victoria, a frequent visitor to her neighbouring
residence, the hotel was actually opened early in the reign of Edward VII.
Lounges are roomy and relaxing, and most of the well-appointed bedrooms
face south and the sea (many have French windows leading to private
balconies). The swimming pool complex is a great attraction, including
as it does a barbecue, bar and buttery. Families are well catered for with
good leisure facilities, baby-sitting and considerations for children in the
dining room. Room service is available at any hour. No dogs. *Rooms 65.
Garden, indoor & outdoor swimming pools, sauna, spa bath, solarium,
hairdressing, tennis, putting, snooker & games room, lock-up garages.*
AMERICAN EXPRESS *Access, Diners, Visa.*

Sidmouth   Place of Interest

Jacobs Ladder Beach.

We do not accept free meals or hospitality – our inspectors pay their
own bills.

Silchester   Romans Hotel   64%   £80

Tel 0734 700421   Fax 0734 700691

Little London Road Silchester nr Reading Hampshire RG7 2PN   Map 15 D3

Built in the early years of this century, this handsome Lutyens house stands
amid trim lawns and mature grounds with two hard tennis courts. Inside,
polished floors, oak panelling and ornate mouldings take the eye in the day
rooms, while bedrooms in the main house have space, comfort and mainly
period furniture. Extension rooms are smaller. Not far from the M3 (leave
at Junction 6) and the M4 (Junction 11). Children up to 15 stay free
in parents' room. *Rooms 23. Garden, outdoor swimming pool, tennis.
Closed 25 Dec & 1 Jan.* AMERICAN EXPRESS *Access, Diners, Visa.*

Silloth-on-Solway   Skinburness Hotel   67%   £70

Tel 069 73 32332   Fax 069 73 32549   **H**

Silloth-on-Solway nr Carlisle Cumbria CA5 4QY   Map 4 C2

The delightfully isolated Skinburness Hotel is ideally placed (on the shores
of the Solway Firth) for those wishing to explore the rugged beauty of this
part of England. The interior recreates a Victorian atmosphere by use
of brass lamps and ceiling fans, cane furniture and a picturesque
conservatory. Accommodation is divided between plainly decorated Green
Rooms and generally more comfortable Red Rooms which provide the
extra space required by vacationing families. Special terms for golfers who
wish to play at the local championship course. A leisure centre is planned
for the near future. *Rooms 25. Garden, keep-fit equipment, sauna, solarium,
snooker.* AMERICAN EXPRESS *Access, Diners, Visa.*

Silverton   Silverton Restaurant   £50

Tel 0392 860196   **R**

Fore Street Silverton Devon BX5 4HP   Map 13 D2

On the first floor of the Silverton Inn on the main street, this informal
restaurant – paper cloths, some dark blue banquettes, a few old beams,
candles and lots of fresh flowers – is only open for dinner three nights
a week plus a Sunday brunch. Mathew Mason (who spent several years
with Shaun Hill at *Gidleigh Park*) presents a short blackboard menu (just
five starters and five main dishes) which might include grilled red mullet
with plum tomatoes and deep-fried ginger, loin of pork with celeriac and
morels and always rump steak. Particularly good puds like cassis parfait,
chocolate marquise and individual cherry Bakewell tart with clotted
cream. *Seats 45. L Sun only 12-3 D 7-11. Set D £15/£17.50.
Closed D Sun, all Mon-Wed. Access, Visa.*

Many hotels offer reduced rates for weekend or out-of-season bookings.
Always ask about special deals.

Simonsbath   Simonsbath House   64%   £90

Tel 064 383 259   **H**

Simonsbath Somerset TA24 7SH   Map 13 D1

Owned and run by Mike and Sue Burns for the last ten years, Simonsbath
dates from 1654. Right in the centre of the Forest of Exmoor, its location
is tranquil; inside you'll find oak panelling and velvet drapes, log fires, fresh
flowers, comfortable sofas and plenty of books – in short, a mellow,
inviting home from home. Individually decorated bedrooms contain
a mixture of modern pieces and some four-posters. Self-catering cottages.
No children under 10. No dogs. *Rooms 7. Garden. Closed Dec & Jan.*
AMERICAN EXPRESS *Access, Diners, Visa.*

Sindlesham   Reading Moat House   70%   £126

Tel 0734 351035   Fax 0734 351642   **H**

Mill Lane Sindlesham nr Wokingham Berkshire RG11 5DF   Map 15 D2

Standing in its own grounds near the M4 (Junction 10 is closest), a late-80s'
hotel built in sympathy with the next door 19th-century mill house that
now houses the hotel's own free-house pub (*The Poacher*) and night club.
Features include a stylish, pine-panelled, marble-floored foyer, a roomy
lounge bar and smartly appointed bedrooms and bathrooms. Two
bedrooms are specially equipped for disabled guests. 24hr room service.
Conference/banqueting facilities for 80/200; car parking for 360.
Secretarial business facilities. *Rooms 96. Garden, gym, sauna, steam room,
fishing.* AMERICAN EXPRESS *Access, Diners, Visa.*

Sissinghurst   Rankins   £65

Tel 0580 713964   **R**

The Street Sissinghurst Kent TN17 2JH   Map 11 C5

A charming, white clapboard cottage is the setting for Hugh Rankin to produce short but invariably interesting and enjoyable fixed-price evening meals and Sunday lunches. Dishes are very much his own: crab and lentil soup with julienne of clementine, steamed broccoli florets with prawns and chive hollandaise, pan-fried pigeon breasts with a rich mushroom sauce. There's always a vegetarian main course (perhaps puff pastry tart of roast Mediterranean vegetables with olives and salsa verde), and to round things off there are some hard-to-resist puddings and desserts. *Seats 30. L (Sun only) 12.30-1.30 D 7.30-9. Closed Mon, Tues, Bank Holidays, 1 week Oct, 1 week May. Set L £15.95 Set D £18.95. Access, Visa.*

Six Mile Bottom   Swynford Paddocks   74%   £107

Tel 0638 570234   Fax 0638 570283   **H**

Six Mile Bottom nr Newmarket Cambridgeshire CB8 0UE   Map 10 B3

The poet Byron was a regular visitor to this elegant country mansion, which stands on the A1304 in a 60-acre stud farm (this is very much horse-racing territory, and Newmarket is only six miles away). The dado-panelled and galleried hall/reception sets the period tone and from there you can progress to a large bar/lounge with stylishly draped curtains, comfortable easy chairs and a grand piano. The bedrooms have attractive matching bedcovers and curtains and many extras, including books and mini-bars; four 'superior' rooms are particularly spacious with bigger bathrooms and showers as well as tubs. *Rooms 15. Garden, croquet, all-weather tennis, putting, giant chess. Closed 4 days between Christmas & New Year.* AMERICAN EXPRESS *Access, Diners, Visa.*

Skipton   Forte Travelodge   £45

Tel 0756 798091   **L**

Gargrave Road Skipton North Yorkshire BD23 1UD   Map 6 C1

At the roundabout junction of the A65 and A59. *Rooms 32.* AMERICAN EXPRESS *Access, Diners, Visa.*

Never leave money, credit cards or valuables lying around in your hotel room. Use the hotel safe or the mini-safe in your room.

Skipton   Randell's Hotel   65%   £83

Tel 0756 700100   Fax 0756 700107   **H**

Keighley Road Snaygill Skipton North Yorkshire BD23 2TA   Map 6 C1

A purpose-built hotel, just south of the town centre; the Trans-Pennine Waterway passes to the rear. Spacious bedrooms are light and contemporary with fully-tiled private facilities; one room has facilities for the disabled. 16 new rooms have recently been added and Ladies Rooms are now available; family rooms have a double and two single beds, family suites have communicating rooms with room for two adults and four children. Day rooms include an open-plan lobby and a first-floor bar. There's also a well-equipped leisure centre, conference/banqueting facilities for 400/350 and a terrace overlooking the canal. Splendid facilities for youngsters, including the state-registered Playzone supervised nursery (for under-7s) with outdoor play area. 24hr room service. Children up to 16 stay free in parents' room. *Rooms 76. Indoor swimming pool, gym, squash, sauna, spa bath, steam room, solarium, hair & beauty salons, coffee shop (7am-10pm), snooker.* AMERICAN EXPRESS *Access, Diners, Visa.*

Slaidburn   Hark to Bounty Inn   £40

Tel 0200 446246   **I**

Slaidburn nr Clitheroe Lancashire BB7 3EP   Map 6 B1

The inn dates back in parts to the 13th century and is steeped in history – it
was called The Dog until 1875 when it acquired its current name during
a hunt. Another attractive feature is a remarkable courtroom which kept
that function until 1937. Nowadays, still keeping its old jury benches and
witness box (now a bar counter), it's used for banquets or conferences (up
to 50 delegates). Bedrooms are modest and cottagey in style; one has
WC/shower only. To the rear, a sheltered garden runs down to a little
river. The surrounding Forest of Bowland is a most attractive area, and this
is an ideal base from which to explore it. *Rooms 8. Garden, games room.*
AMERICAN EXPRESS *Access, Diners, Visa.*

Sleaford   Forte Travelodge   £45

Tel 0529 414752   **L**

Holdingham Sleaford Lincolnshire NG34 8PN   Map 7 E3

On the roundabout at the junction of the A17/A15, one mile north
of Sleaford on the bypass. *Rooms 40.* AMERICAN EXPRESS *Access, Diners, Visa.*

Slough   Copthorne Hotel Slough/Windsor   71%   £135

Tel 0753 516222   Fax 0753 516237   **H**

Cippenham Lane Slough Berkshire SL1 2YE   Map 15 E2

Conveniently situated next to junction 6 of the M4 and a 15-minute drive
from Heathrow, the Copthorne owes 80% of its trade to corporate business.
All the elegant public areas – the polished granite-floored reception area,
the comfortable, spacious lounge and relaxing bar – are Art Deco in style;
so, too, the variously sized conference rooms, which can handle up to 250
delegates. All bedrooms – whether Classics, Connoisseurs or suites, are
decorated to the same high standard with lightwood units and co-
ordinating fabrics. Tiled bathrooms offer showers and tubs, plus good soaps
and toiletries. 24hr room service. First-rate leisure club. Plenty of free
parking. No dogs. *Rooms 219. Indoor swimming pool, gym, sauna, spa bath,
steam bath, solarium, snooker.* AMERICAN EXPRESS *Access, Diners, Visa.*

Slough   Courtyard by Marriott   60%   £84

Tel 0753 551551   Fax 0753 553333   **H**

Church Street Chalvey Slough Berkshire SL1 2NH   Map 15 E2

At the first roundabout towards Slough from Junction 6 of the M4, this
was the first of Marriott's new (to England) hotels aimed primarily at the
weekday business traveller, although the weekend tariff (£48) is also very
attractive to families on the move. Children up to 12 free in parents' room.
There's no porterage or room service but food and drink may be taken
to rooms from the cheerful 'Number One' all-day bar/brasserie or 24hr
vending machines. Uncluttered bedrooms are well equipped and good
bathrooms have both under-floor heating and heated mirrors. *Rooms 148.
Keep-fit equipment, brasserie (6.30am-6.30pm).* AMERICAN EXPRESS *Access,
Diners, Visa.*

Slough   Heathrow/Slough Marriott Hotel   73%   £131

Tel 0753 544244   Fax 0753 540272   **H**

Ditton Road Langley Slough Berkshire SL3 8PT   Map 15 E2

Next to Junction 5 of the M4, a purpose-built hotel with good modern
leisure and conference facilities (for up to 400) plus stylish day rooms.
Bedrooms have at least one double bed and are decorated in soft shades
with lightwood units. 70 rooms were being refurbished during 1994,
as was the bar area. All have tiled, if rather small, bathrooms. The Leisure

Club was also being upgraded. Children up to 18 stay free in parents' room. *Rooms 352. Indoor swimming pool, gym, sauna, spa bath, steam room, solarium, beauty & hair salons, all-weather floodlit tennis, games room, coffee shop (6.30am-11pm), courtesy airport coach.* AMERICAN EXPRESS *Access, Diners, Visa.*

Slough   Place of Interest

Ice Arena   Montem Lane Tel 0753 821555.

Solihull	**Jarvis George Hotel**	**66%**	**£111**
Tel 021 711 2121 Fax 021 711 3374			**H**
The Square Solihull West Midlands B91 3RF			**Map 6 C4**

The oldest part of this town-centre hotel dates back to the 16th century and houses the beamed Club Room bar which is furnished exclusively with comfortable tub and wing armchairs. Most bedrooms are in modern wings extending around three sides of a 16th-century bowling green. Standard rooms are just that, but there are also Executive bedrooms with bird's-eye maple veneered furniture and phones at both desk and bedside plus Town House Suites – some junior suites with separate sitting area and ten with galleried bedrooms reached via spiral staircases – off a 'street'-themed corridor with flagstone floor and exterior styled doors. These rooms boast personal fax machines, large working tables and executive stress-relieving toys along with various other extras. Children up to 12 share parents' room free. *Rooms 127.* AMERICAN EXPRESS *Access, Diners, Visa.*

Solihull	**Moat House**	**69%**	**£105**
Tel 021-711 4700 Fax 021-711 2696			**H**
Homer Road Solihull West Midlands B91 3QD			**Map 6 C4**

Purpose-built in 1990, this large hotel stands just out of the town centre. A marble-floored entrance hall leads to the reception, main lounge and a raised bar area. Light decor throughout, with seating comfortable and contemporary in both design and colour. Bedrooms are equally stylish, using co-ordinating fabrics and mainly darkwood freestanding furniture. Modern health and fitness club. Conference and banqueting facilities for up to 200. A large car park (free) surrounds the hotel. *Rooms 115. Garden, indoor swimming pool, gym, sauna, steam room, spa bath, solarium.* AMERICAN EXPRESS *Access, Diners, Visa.*

Solihull	**Regency Hotel**	**64%**	**£95**
Tel 021-745 6119 Fax 021-733 3801			**H**
Stratford Road Shirley Solihull West Midlands B90 4EB			**Map 6 C4**

The luxurious leisure club is a major feature at this Regency-style building on the A34, half a mile from Junction 4 of the M42. Children under 14 share parents' room free. Conference/banqueting facilities for up to 150. *Rooms 112. Garden, indoor swimming pool, plunge pool, gym, sauna, steam room, spa bath, solarium, coffee shop (10am-10pm).* AMERICAN EXPRESS *Access, Visa.*

Solihull	**St John's Swallow Hotel**	**63%**	**£95**
Tel 021-711 3000 Fax 021-705 6629			**H**
651 Warwick Road Solihull West Midlands B91 1AT			**Map 6 C4**

Comfortable, well-appointed hotel with a distinctive gabled facade, massive conference/banqueting and good leisure facilities. Children up to 14 accommodated free in parents' room; six family rooms and two rooms equipped for disabled guests. Many of the rooms have recently been refurbished. Parking for 400 cars. Five minutes drive from the M42. *Rooms 177. Garden, indoor swimming pool, spa bath, sauna, solarium, steam room, keep-fit equipment.* AMERICAN EXPRESS *Access, Diners, Visa.*

Solihull   Travel Inn   £43

Tel 021-744 2942   **L**

Stratford Road Shirley Solihull West Midlands B90 4PT   **Map 6 C4**

Rooms 40. AMERICAN EXPRESS® *Access, Diners, Visa.*

Solihull   Places of Interest

Baddesley Clinton (NT)   Tel 0564 783294.
Solihull Ice Rink   Tel 021-742 5561.

Somerton   Lynch Country House Hotel   69%   £45

Tel 0458 272316   Fax 0458 272590   **H**

4 Behind Berry Somerton Somerset TA11 7PD   **Map 13 F2**

Set in the heart of lush Somerset countryside, the Grade II listed house
is surrounded by ten acres with 2800 trees, a small lake and formal gardens.
Bedrooms contain books, magazines and tourist maps; appointments are
individual, from Victorian bedsteads to a Georgian four-poster. A bed and
breakfast hotel only, with the breakfast room overlooking the grounds and
lake. Self-catering cottages also available. *Rooms 6. Garden, croquet.
Closed 25 & 26 Dec. Access, Visa.*

Sourton   Forte Travelodge   £45

Tel 0837 52124   **L**

Sourton Cross nr Okehampton Devon EX20 4LY   **Map 13 D2**

On the A30, at the junction with A386, 4 miles west of Okehampton.
Rooms 32. AMERICAN EXPRESS® *Access, Diners, Visa.*

South Cave   Forte Travelodge   £45

Tel 0430 424455   **L**

Beacon service area South Cave Hull Humberside   **Map 7 E1**

Located at the Beacon service area on the eastbound carriageway of the
A63, 12 miles west of Kingston-upon-Hull and 1½ miles east of Junction 38
of the M62. *Rooms 40.* AMERICAN EXPRESS® *Access, Diners, Visa.*

We welcome bona fide complaints and recommendations on the tear-out
pages at the back of the book for readers' comments. They are followed
up by our professional team.

South Milford   Forte Posthouse Leeds/Selby   65%   £68

Tel 0977 682711   Fax 0977 685462   **H**

South Milford nr Leeds North Yorkshire LS25 5LF   **Map 7 D1**

At the junction of the A1 and A63, between York and Leeds (close to J33
of M62). Modern hotel with a variety of conference facilities for up to 120;
ample parking. Children up to 16 stay free in parents' room. 43 rooms are
no-smoking. All-day, informal lounge snacks. *Rooms 105. Garden, indoor
swimming pool, 9-hole pitch & putt, tennis, children's playroom (weekends),
playground.* AMERICAN EXPRESS® *Access, Diners, Visa.*

South Mimms — Forte Posthouse — 60% — £68

Tel 0707 643311   Fax 0707 646728   **H**

Bignells Corner South Mimms nr Potters Bar Hertfordshire EN6 3NH   Map 15 E2

Up-to-date accommodation just off to the left of the South Mimms service area on the M25. A room is set aside for children at weekends and there's also a playground. *Rooms 120. Gym, sauna, spa bath, solarium, pool table.* AMERICAN EXPRESS *Access, Diners, Visa.*

South Mimms — Forte Travelodge — £45

Tel 0707 665440   **L**

Bignells Corner South Mimms nr Potters Bar Hertfordshire EN6 3QQ   Map 15 E2

Located at Junction 23 of the M25 at the Welcome Break service area. Central London 15 miles. *Rooms 52.* AMERICAN EXPRESS *Access, Diners, Visa.*

South Molton — Whitechapel Manor — 76% — £120

Tel 0769 573377   Fax 0769 573797   **HR**

South Molton Devon EX36 3EG   Map 13 D2

Follow the Whitechapel sign from a roundabout on the A361 near South Molton to find this delightfully peaceful Elizabethan manor house fronted by terraced lawns and enjoying a fine view across the Yeo Valley. A fine Jacobean carved oak screen separates the entrance from the Great Hall, which is cosier than it sounds with period-style knole sofas around the fireplace under a time-bowed William and Mary ceiling. The other day room is a blue leather-furnished bar with logs slowly smouldering in the inglenook. There's a scattering of antiques both downstairs and in the bedrooms which range from small to large – some with small, separate sitting/dressing rooms that are also ideal for a child's bed – with soft colour schemes and extras like games compendium and jug of iced water from their own spring. Bathrooms, decorated to match the rooms, all have panelled tubs with showers above, generously sized bottles of bath oil and towelling robes. Room service is limited to drinks throughout the day and evening, Continental breakfast and afternoon tea. Run by the hospitable John and Patricia Shapland since 1987. £15 charge for all children. No dogs. *Rooms 10. Garden, croquet.* AMERICAN EXPRESS *Access, Diners, Visa.*
MARTELL COGNAC

Restaurant — £80

Patricia Shapland shares the cooking with chef Martin Lee, producing enjoyable dishes that are a happy compromise between simplicity and elaboration. Good local produce features in offerings like sautéed Cornish scallops with ribbons of vegetable and a balsamic vinegar dressing, best end of Devon lamb with garlic cream sauce and fillet of Devon beef with roast shallots and Madeira sauce. Other dishes might include a hot Gruyère cheese soufflé, calf's sweetbreads with an aubergine purée and red wine sauce, and breast of Barbary duck with rösti and cep sauce. Asterisked dishes indicate not the usual supplement but a reduction in price from a fixed-price 3/4-course menu. Coffee is served with petits fours in the Great Hall or bar. A sensible wine list has something to suit most tastes and pockets. No smoking. *Seats 24. Private Room 8. L 12-1.45 D 7-8.45. Set L & D £18 & £26-£37.*

South Normanton — Swallow Hotel — 69% — £100

Tel 0773 812000   Fax 0773 580032   **H**

Carter Lane East South Normanton Derbyshire DE55 2EH   Map 7 D3

Modern, low-rise hotel near Junction 28 of the M1 with spacious public areas and large, conference facilities for a maximum of 200 delegates. Two of the bedrooms have been specially designed for disabled guests. *Rooms 161. Indoor swimming pool, keep-fit equipment, sauna, spa bath, steam room, solarium.* AMERICAN EXPRESS *Access, Diners, Visa.*

South Normanton   Place of Interest

Sherwood Forest Visitor Centre   Tel 0623 824490.

South Witham   Forte Travelodge

£45

| Tel 0572 767586 | **L** |

New Fox South Witham Lincolnshire LE15 8AU   **Map 7 E3**

Northbound on the A1, 9 miles south of Grantham. *Rooms 32.*
AMERICAN EXPRESS *Access, Diners, Visa.*

Southall   Asian Tandoori Centre

£15

| Tel 081-574 2597 | **R** |

114 The Green Southall Middlesex UB2 4BQ   **Map 15 E2**

Simple Indian canteen serving hearty, unsophisticated food throughout the
day. Particularly good peshwari stuffed nan. Unlicensed; non-smoking area.
Seats 80. Meals 9am-10.30pm (Fri-Sun to 11pm).
Also at:
157 The Broadway, Southall. Tel 081-574 3476   **Map 15 E2**

Southampton   Browns Restaurant

£70

| Tel 0703 332615 | **R** |

**Frobisher House Nelson Gate Commercial Road Southampton
Hampshire SO1 0GX**   **Map 15 D4**

A bright, friendly restaurant near the Mayflower Theatre, with go-ahead
owners in Richard and Patricia Brown. Patricia's menus (à la carte plus
daily chef's choices and a *menu surprise*) cover a fair range, from grilled
goat's cheese salad and a splendid spinach and anchovy soufflé to halibut
with asparagus butter, a little stew of stuffed calamari with poached salmon,
loin of lamb with roasted vegetables and a tri-partite duck dish of roast
breast, confit leg and boudin served in a sauce flavoured with thyme and
oranges. To finish, perhaps hazelnut tart, hot strawberry soufflé
or a 'naughty but nice' trio of chocolate desserts. No children under 12.
*Seats 26. L 12-2.30 D 7-11 (Sat to 11.30). Closed L Sat, Bank Holidays, last
2 weeks Aug. Set L & D £12.50/£16.50 (Sun L £15)
Set D £10.50/£14.95.* AMERICAN EXPRESS *Access, Diners, Visa.*

Southampton   Dolphin Hotel   60%

£82

| Tel 0703 339955   Fax 0703 333650 | **H** |

High Street Southampton Hampshire SO9 2DS   **Map 15 D4**

This Forte Heritage hotel is a modernised 18th-century coaching inn with
conference facilities for 90. Free use of nearby Posthouse health and fitness
club. Children up to 16 stay free in parents' room. *Rooms 73.*
AMERICAN EXPRESS *Access, Diners, Visa.*

Southampton   Forte Posthouse   58%

£68

| Tel 0703 330777   Fax 0703 332510 | **H** |

Herbert Walker Avenue Southampton Hampshire SO1 0HJ   **Map 15 D4**

Ten-storey tower-block hotel with views of the liners' berths from some
rooms. Well-equipped bedrooms, spacious nautical bar, children's playroom
(at weekends) and playground. Banqueting/conferences for up to 200.
Rooms 128.'Indoor swimming pool, gymnasium, sauna, spa bath, solarium.
AMERICAN EXPRESS *Access, Diners, Visa.*

Southampton — Hilton National — 68% — £94

Tel 0703 702700   Fax 0703 767233   **H**
Bracken Place Chilworth Southampton Hampshire SO16 3RB 4HB   Map 15 D4

Up-to-date leisure and business facilities in a modern redbrick Hilton hotel by the A33 and M27 (approach from Junction 5). 50 Plaza bedrooms and suites feature a queen-size bed, welcome drink, chocolates, mini-bar, bathrobe and slippers, fresh fruit and attract a considerable supplement. Two rooms equipped for disabled guests; 21 rooms reserved for non-smokers. Children under 16 share parents' room free. 24hr room service. Banqueting/conference facilities for 150/220; ample parking. *Rooms 135. Garden, indoor swimming pool, gym, sauna, steam room, solarium, beauty salon, deli, coffee shop (9am-6pm).* AMERICAN EXPRESS *Access, Diners, Visa.*

Southampton — Kuti's — £45

Tel 0703 221585   **R**
37 Oxford Street Southampton Hampshire SO1 1DP   Map 15 D4

Kuti's has moved from London Road to Oxford Street, where it continues to offer a fine range of Bangladeshi-style Indian cooking. Besides the familiar chicken, lamb and prawn variants you'll find some more unusual items including half-a-dozen ways with duck and preparations of trout, sea bass and the exotic *ayre* fish and *chitol* fish. *Seats 74. L 12-2.15 D 6-11.30. Closed 25 & 26 Dec. Set L £8.50 (buffet Sun-Fri) Set D £10.95.* AMERICAN EXPRESS *Access, Visa.*

Southampton — Novotel — 62% — £65

Tel 0703 330550   Fax 0703 222158   **H**
1 West Quay Road Southampton Hampshire SO1 0RA   Map 15 D4

Very modern hotel convenient for railway station, ferries and Ocean Village. Geared to business use in the week (with conference facilities for up to 450, banqueting up to 350), children up to 16 stay free in parents' room. *Rooms 121. Indoor swimming pool, keep-fit facilities, sauna, games room.* AMERICAN EXPRESS *Access, Diners, Visa.*

Southampton — Polygon Hotel — 65% — £72

Tel 0703 330055   Fax 0703 332435   **H**
Cumberland Place Southampton Hampshire SO9 4GD   Map 15 D4

Close by the civic centre, a 30s' structure in red brick overlooking Watts Park. Banqueting/conference facilities for 400/500 (parking for 150). Free use of *Forte Posthouse* health and fitness club in Herbert Walker Avenue. Forte. *Rooms 119.* AMERICAN EXPRESS *Access, Diners, Visa.*

> See the Restaurant Round-up for easy, quick-reference comparisons.

Southampton — Southampton Park Hotel — 64% — £66

Tel 0703 223467   Fax 0703 332538   **H**
12 Cumberland Place Southampton Hampshire SO15 2WY   Map 15 D4

Functional modern building overlooking Watts Park. Well-equipped bedrooms (front ones have balconies), are gradually being refurbished – the ground floor is complete. Roomy lounge areas, two restaurants, a cocktail bar, conference rooms (up to 200 delegates) and a leisure club. *Rooms 72. Terrace, indoor swimming pool, sauna, spa bath, steam room, solarium.* AMERICAN EXPRESS *Access, Diners, Visa.*

Southampton   Travel Inn   £43

Tel 0703 732262   Fax 0703 740947   **L**

Romsey Road Nursling Southampton Hampshire SO1 9XJ   Map 15 D4

From J3 of M27 take M271 towards Romsey; at next roundabout take
third exit (to Southampton); the hotel is 1½ miles along on the right-hand
side. *Rooms 32.* AMERICAN EXPRESS *Access, Diners, Visa.*

Southampton   Places of Interest

Tourist Information   Tel 0703 221106.
Maritime Museum   Seafront Tel 0703 223941.
Exbury Gardens   Exbury Tel 0703 891203.
Lepe Country Park   Exbury Tel 0703 899108.
New Forest Butterfly Farm   Ashurst Tel 0703 293367.
Southampton City Art Gallery   Tel 0703 231375.
Northlands Road Cricket Ground   Tel 0703 333788.
Southampton Football Ground   The Dell Tel 0703 220505.
Calshort Activities Centre   Fawley Tel 0703 891380/892077.
Southampton Ski Centre   Bassett Tel 0703 760604.
   Theatres and Concert Halls
Mayflower Theatre   Tel 0703 330083.
Mountbatten Theatre   Tel 0703 832453.
Nuffield Theatre   Tel 0705 581576.

Southport   New Bold Hotel   58%   £51

Tel 0704 532578   Fax 0704 532528   **H**

Lord Street Southport Merseyside PR9 0BE   Map 6 A1

Family-owned and family-run, the Bold stands on the town's leafy main
boulevard. Modern bedrooms include two for family use and a bridal suite
with sunken bath; back rooms are the quietest. A public bar serves
traditional beers and Raphael's bar/café has long-hours opening and live
entertainment. Reception is upstairs, and the front door leads straight into
the bar. *Rooms 23. Access, Visa.*

Southport   Prince of Wales Hotel   65%   £74

Tel 0704 536688   Fax 0704 543488   **H**

Lord Street Southport Merseyside PR8 1JS   Map 6 A1

On Southport's tree-lined main street, with modern amenities and some
of Southport's Victorian atmosphere remaining both inside and out.
Conferences are the main business, with a maximum capacity of 450
theatre-style. Children up to 16 stay free in parents' room. Parking for 90
cars. Forte. *Rooms 104. Garden, 24hr lounge service.* AMERICAN EXPRESS *Access,
Diners, Visa.*

> Note that all telephone numbers with area codes starting with 0
> will start 01 from 16 April 1995.

Southport   Places of Interest

Tourist Information   Tel 0704 533333.
Atkinson Art Gallery   Tel 0704 533133.
Rufford Old Hall (NT)   Rufford Tel 0704 821254.
Martin Mere Wildfowl Trust   Tel 0704 895181 *6 miles.*
Royal Birkdale Golf   Tel 0704 67920.
Trafalgar Road Cricket Ground   Birkdale Tel 0704 69951.
Southport Zoo   Tel 0704 538102.

Southsea   Bistro Montparnasse   £55

Tel 0705 816754   **R**

103 Palmerston Road Southsea Hampshire PO5 3PS   Map 15 D4

Fresh fish, careful cooking and attractive presentation of a fiercely modern menu are the hallmarks of Peter and Gillian Scott's warm and welcoming French bistro, conveniently close to Southsea's main shopping area and the ferries to France and Spain. Gillian offers a well-thought-out and often inventive choice on her à la carte menu, which change monthly. The eclectic mix of dishes runs from home-made breads and focaccia served with tapénade and houmus to fettuccine with radicchio, walnuts and raisins, falafel with tabbouleh, aubergine and roasted garlic custard tart, osso buco with gremolata, steak and wild mushroom pie, oak-smoked fillet of beef with Roquefort polenta and caramelised onions, hot treacle sponge pudding and custard, and Sauternes and lemon cake with syllabub. A special blackboard set menu at £12.50 is also offered on weekdays; the minimum à la carte charge is also £12.50 (there is no longer a fixed-price meal charge). An upstairs room has recently been redecorated and is now used for private dining parties. *Seats 50. Private Room 20. D only 7-10. Closed Sun & Mon, 2 weeks Jan. Set D £12.50 (not Sat).* AMERICAN EXPRESS® *Access, Visa.*

Southsea   Places of Interest

Southsea Castle Portsmouth Tel 0705 827261.
D Day Museum Clarence Parade Tel 0705 827261.
Pyramids Complex *Fun pools* Tel 0705 294444.
Sea Life Centre Tel 0705 734461.

Southwell   Saracen's Head   62%   £80

Tel 0636 812701   Fax 0636 815408   **H**

Market Place Southwell Nottinghamshire NG25 0HE   Map 7 D3

The 16th-century half-timbered inn still shows many original features, including a fine wall painting. Characterful public areas and bedrooms that offer all the usual modern comforts and conveniences. Banqueting/conferences for up to 120. Forte Heritage. *Rooms 27.* AMERICAN EXPRESS® *Access, Diners, Visa.*

Southwell   Place of Interest

Southwell Minster Tel 0636 812649.

Southwold   The Crown   £63

Tel 0502 722275   Fax 0502 724805   **IR**

90 High Street Southwold Suffolk IP18 6DP   Map 10 D2

Restored town-centre Georgian inn in the ownership of Adnams, the Southwold brewers. To the front, facing the High Street, the Parlour serves as half lounge, half dining area; the front bar and attendant restaurant exude refinement. Bedrooms are "small" but well equipped, with antique or decent reproduction pieces and bright fabrics and furnishings; all have private bathrooms though three are not strictly en suite (their private bathrooms are across a corridor); one family room has a double and two single beds; another pair of rooms adjoin. Function facilities for 22 (banqueting), 40 (theatre-style conference). Car parking is limited. *Rooms 12. Closed 1 week Jan.* AMERICAN EXPRESS® *Access, Diners, Visa.*

Restaurant   £50

Andrew Mulliss's daily menus take their inspiration from far and wide. For starters, perhaps emincé of pigeon breast strogonoff with a timbale of wild rice or whole roast quail with a light mustard sauce, following with steamed fillet of turbot Andalusian-style, Malay-spiced vegetable stir-fry with saffron rice or sautéed escalope of venison with soft peppercorn sauce. Traditional roast Sunday lunch. Affordable prices on a remarkable Adnams wine list which has tasting notes alongside each wine and reviews of vintages. There are gems everywhere you look – the global list is very comprehensive and deserves careful scrutiny. No smoking. In addition to the restaurant menu there are first-rate snacks in the bar, where over 20 wines are offered by the glass – a superb service. **Seats 22 + Parlour 16.** *Parties 8. L 12.30-1.45 D 7.30-9.30. Set L £12.75/£14.75 Set D £17.25/£19.25.*

Southwold	The Swan	65%	£81

Tel 0502 722186   Fax 0502 724800   **HR**

Market Place Southwold Suffolk IP18 6EG   **Map 10 D2**

The ancient Swan, rebuilt in 1660 after a fire that destroyed most of the town, stands facing the market square and backs on to Adnams Brewery. An old long-case clock and fresh flowers grace the flagstoned foyer and an abundance of sofas the period drawing room. Main-house bedrooms are traditional in style with freestanding furniture, including the odd antique, while simpler chalet-style rooms surround a garden to the rear. Banquets/conferences for up to 80/50. Good bar snacks. **Rooms 45.** *Garden, croquet.* AMERICAN EXPRESS® *Access, Diners, Visa.*

Restaurant £65

An elegant, pink dining room and a choice of fixed-price only menus. Chef David Goode offers a varied range of dishes that include British classics like a trio of game, pigeon and chicken terrines set over a Cumberland sauce or steamed Scottish salmon with a hollandaise sauce. Sauté of cod with a caper onion crust, braised leg of lamb steak and venison haunch with a Stilton creamed sauce are other possibilities, with Spotted Dick and custard a favourite among the desserts. No smoking. **Seats 50.** *Private Room 40. L 12-1.45 D 7-9.30. Closed lunchtime Mon-Fri Jan-Easter. Set L £11.50/£13.95 (Sun £12.50/£16.50) Set D from £17.50.*

Southwold	Place of Interest

Southwold Beach.

Spark Bridge	Bridgefield House	60%	£60

Tel 0229 885239   Fax 0229 885379   **HR**

Spark Bridge Ulverston Cumbria LA12 8DA   **Map 4 C4**

To describe Bridgefield House as modest is to decry neither its homeliness nor the warmth of the proprietors' welcome. A decade of steady improvements has established a hotel of some charm in a superb location overlooking the Crake valley (on the back lane from Lowick Bridge to Spark Bridge). Bedrooms, though spacious, are modestly appointed with mostly freestanding furniture, telephones and clock radios; TVs there are not. "Well-disciplined dogs are welcome." Facilities for families are limited but the Glisters' accommodating attitude promises a relaxing stay; junior gourmets will be over the moon, sports freaks less so. **Rooms 5.** *Garden. Closed 25 Dec eve. Access, Visa.*

Restaurant £60

Dinner at candle-lit dark mahogany tables is courteously overseen by David Glister. His wife Rosemary's daily-changing six-course, fixed-price-only menus are a labour of love and offer a small choice only at starter and pudding stages. A typical menu might start with duck livers sautéed in Grand Marnier with kumquats, a platter of prawns, cockles, mussels and herring pieces or filo pastry tartlets filled with herb and cream cheese paté, following this with fennel soup with sesame toasts; strips of fillet steak with blackcurrants and green peppercorns might be accompanied by copious vegetables (sauté potatoes, mixed vegetable casserole with puréed tomato sauce, Jerusalem artichokes roasted in oatmeal and steamed

mangetout and baby sweetcorn). Sliced purple plums in a cinnamon cream
flan, crushed meringues with a hazelnut, creme de cacao and bitter
chocolate cream or raspberries and strawberries in a Drambuie and honey
cream flummery among the puddings, with perhaps sautéed lamb
sweetbreads in Madeira on toast or Gala apple with Lancashire cheese and
walnuts as a savoury conclusion. Coffee and truffles to finish. Concise wine
list, plenty of half bottles and decent prices, with Australia the pick of the
bunch. Booking essential. *Seats 24. Parties 6. D only 7.30 for
8. Set D £20.*

Staddlebridge	McCoy's	70%	£99
Tel 0609 882671 Fax 0609 882660			**HR**
Staddlebridge North Yorkshire DL6 3JB			Map 5 E3

The hotel stands at the intersection of the A19 and the A172 with entry
via the southbound lane of the latter. It's an extraordinary place, not for the
more conservative-minded, but then there are hotels a-plenty catering
to their tastes. Here is a unique establishment run with care and dedication
by three brothers, Eugene, Peter and Tom McCoy. On the ground floor
there's a long narrow lounge and in the next room a spacious bar. Both are
decorated in a very laid-back and original style – settees from around the
40s, one or two virtually coming apart, are piled with huge scatter
cushions covered in flamboyantly colourful fabrics. The bar with its
multicoloured foil wallpaper and palms has an ambience that wouldn't
be amiss in some tropical climes. Bedrooms too are striking. Wallpaper
by Hubert de Givenchy and a mix of furniture from antique pine to simply
painted pieces create a splendid setting with comfortable seating and even
more comfortable beds. Windows have secondary glazing to reduce
possible noise levels. Bathrooms have huge shower roses and good soaps.
In the morning superb breakfasts range from a platter of unusual fruit
to eggs from their own free-range black hens. *Rooms 6. Garden.*
Closed 25 & 26 Dec, 1st Jan. AMERICAN EXPRESS *Access, Diners, Visa.* MARTELL

Restaurant   ★ ↑   £85

The extremely popular bistro in the cellar appears to have gone a long way
to reviving interest, both local and from further afield, in dining
at McCoy's. The key to this success has been more informal dining and the
opportunity for relatively inexpensive meals. The restaurant on the ground
floor, now open for dinner only, offers a glittering candle-lit experience
with maroon mirrored-lined walls and beautiful pink napery. The menu
is more sophisticated than in the bistro and cleverly innovative, Tom and
Eugene McCoy's style since the very beginning. The quality of the cooking
emanating from the same kitchen is of the same high standard in both
places though, by the very nature of the ingredients and some details
of preparation, the cooking in the restaurant can reach even higher levels
at times. Thus a celery and red pepper soup – a thick potage with celery
and Far Eastern spices – is simply delicious as would suit either the
restaurant or bistro. Langoustine pasta with a shellfish sauce, foie gras with
brioche and grapes stewed in Madeira or stunning pan-fried scallops topped
with caviar and served in a red wine sauce are eminently suitable for the
restaurant. Main dishes include such long-time favourites as honey-roasted
pigeon with lentils and two boned roasted quail served on a bed of rösti
potatoes with grapes and a Madeira sauce as well as the likes of halibut with
fried lettuce and tarragon sauce or pan-fried venison with wild mushrooms
and smoked bacon. As well as new desserts such as crunchy caramelised
fresh pineapple served hot with a creamy coconut ice cream and vanilla
sauce there are perennial favourites like crêpe San Lorenzo with a filling
of amaretti biscuits in Grand Marnier and vanilla cream and the
outstanding choc-o-block Stanley – a chocolate fondant with sponge soaked
in Tia Maria with a coffee bean sauce or "thin, thin oh so very thin" layers
of puff pastry, crème patissière and strawberries. Excellent cheeses and
to finish superb coffee and home-made chocolate truffles. Fabulous service.
Booking essential. *Seats 50. Parties 15. Private Room 30. D only 7-9.30.
Closed Sun & Mon, 25 & 26 Dec, 1 Jan.*

Stafford   De Vere Tillington Hall   63%   £90

Tel 0785 53531   Fax 0785 59223   **H**

Eccleshall Road Stafford Staffordshire ST16 1JJ   Map 6 B3

Half a mile from the M6 (J14), this modern De Vere hotel adds good
leisure and conference facilities (200 maximum) to decent bedrooms that
range from singles to four-poster rooms. A programme of refurbishment
is due to be completed by the end of 1994. Children up to 14 share adult
accommodation free, paying for meals as taken. *Rooms 90. Garden, indoor
swimming pool, gym, sauna, spa bath, solarium, beauty salon, tennis, snooker.
Closed 28 & 29 Dec.* AMERICAN EXPRESS *Access, Diners, Visa.*

Stafford   Places of Interest

Tourist Information   Tel 0785 40204.
**Shugborough (NT) House & Garden & Staffordshire County Museum &
Park Farm**   Tel 0889 881388.
Wolseley Garden Park   Wolseley Bridge Tel 0889 574888.
County Showground   Weston Road Tel 0785 58060.

We endeavour to be as up-to-the-minute as possible, but inevitably
some changes to key personnel may occur at restaurants and hotels
after the Guide goes to press.

Stamford   The George of Stamford   72%   £100

Tel 0780 55171   Fax 0780 57070   **HR**

71 St Martins Stamford Lincolnshire PE9 2LB   Map 7 E3

The George must be one of England's most famous old coaching inns, and
it declares its history from the moment you approach its prime town-
centre site. You can still just visualise a coach-and-four going through
to the cobbled courtyard, though the ostler would be surprised to see that
the livery stables now house a business centre, and instead of waiting for
coaches, visitors to the London Room and York Bar are enjoying a pint
of Adnams. Open fires, exposed stonework walls, flagstone floors and
beams all add to the atmosphere. Bedrooms are quirky and quaint (owing
to the age of the building), several have four-posters and some overlook the
courtyard, but all are well equipped and maintained. Poste Hotels.
Rooms 47. Garden, croquet. AMERICAN EXPRESS *Access, Diners, Visa.*

Restaurant   £85

Chris Pitman has been Executive Chef (and Hotel Manager) here for
twenty years and his aim is to use the best of British raw ingredients,
presented in inspired international ways to a discerning clientèle. Thus you
might choose Scotch salmon and smoked haddock tartare with a salad
of artichoke and French beans, or pan-fried pigeon breast on chargrilled
polenta with a sauce of lentils and port from the à la carte dinner menu.
There's a Light Quick Lunch menu available in the restaurant (not
Sundays) taking some dishes from the carte such as spicy Thai crabcake
with beansprouts and a lime leaf and coconut sauce, or lamb's sweetbreads
with filo pastry, caramelised shallots and Madeira sauce. Desserts and
cheeses live up to the standards. The more expensive the wine (to the
hotel), the lower the mark-up, which is commendable practice that
everyone should follow. This really is a super and interesting world-wide
list, with bargains at every turn. There are tasting notes where necessary,
even a 'magnum' list, not to mention bin ends at giveaway prices. *Seats 80.
Parties 12. Private Room 50. L 12.30-2.30 D 7.15-10.30 (Garden Lounge
12-10.30pm). Set L £15.50/£18.50 (Mon-Sat).*

Stamford   Places of Interest

Tourist Information   Tel 0780 55611.
Burghley House   Tel 0780 52451.
Stamford Brewery Museum   Tel 0780 52186.
Tallington Dry Ski Slope   Tel 0788 344990.

Standish   Almond Brook Moat House   63%   £89

Tel 0257 425588   Fax 0257 427327   **H**

Almond Brook Road Standish nr Wigan Greater Manchester WN6 0SR   Map 6 B1

Two hundred yards from Junction 27 of the M6, this Moat House includes
banqueting/conference facilities for up to 270 and a leisure centre among its
facilities. Neat, well-maintained bedrooms. Families are well catered for;
under-14s sharing with parents are free. *Rooms 122. Garden, indoor
swimming pool, keep-fit equipment, sauna, solarium. Closed 24-30 Dec.*
AMERICAN EXPRESS *Access, Diners, Visa.*

Standish   Places of Interest

Wigan Pier   Wigan Tel 0942 323666 *4 miles.*
Wigan International Pool   Wigan Tel 0942 43345.

Stanstead Abbots   Briggens House   70%   £106

Tel 0279 792416   Fax 0279 793685   **H**

Stanstead Road Stanstead Abbots nr Ware Hertfordshire SG12 8LD   Map 15 F2

A large, stately home-from-home, a few miles off the M11, set in 45 acres
of grounds with its own 9-hole golf course. High standards of service are
typified by the smart, uniformed doormen. A magnificent carved wood
staircase leads up from the entrance hall with its glass chandelier to 22
bedrooms in the main house; 32 more are in the converted coach house
and have lower ceilings, but all are equally tastefully decorated with a good
range of extras included as standard. Swagged drapes and stylish
reproduction antiques give an elegant air. In summer, tables are set on the
expansive lawns outside the French windows leading off the lounge.
Function facilities for 100. Children under 12 free in parents' room. Queens
Moat Houses. *Rooms 54. Garden, croquet, outdoor swimming pool, tennis, golf
(9), bowls, fishing, coffee shop (9-7.30). Closed 1 week Christmas.*
AMERICAN EXPRESS *Access, Diners, Visa.*

Stanstead Abbots   Places of Interest

Hill House   Ware Tel 0920 870013.
Trading Places Gallery   New Road, Ware Tel 0920 469620.

Stanton St Quintin   Stanton Manor   64%   £82

Tel 0666 837552   Fax 0666 837022   **HR**

Stanton St Quintin nr Chippenham Wiltshire SN14 6DQ   Map 14 B2

"Your home in Wiltshire" proclaims the brochure, and indeed Elizabeth
and Philip Bullock are the friendliest and most welcoming of hosts at their
stone manor house. The present main house dates from the 19th century,
though some buildings are much older, notably a 14th-century dovecote.
Bedrooms are individually appointed in traditional style. Children up to 18
stay free in parents' room. Two minutes from the M4 (J17). *Rooms 10.
Garden. Closed 1st 2 weeks Aug, New Year.* AMERICAN EXPRESS *Access, Visa.*

Restaurant   £50

Simple dishes appeal on a short à la carte, to which the manor's own
kitchen garden contributes seasonal fruit and vegetables – and much of the
rest is supplied locally. Soup, smoked goose breast or a mosaic of fresh fruits

could precede paupiettes of sole, roulade of pork or loin of venison
on a rich blackcurrant shallot sauce. Vegetarian menu. No smoking.
Seats 30. Parties 14. Private Room 30. L 12-2 D 7-9.30.
Set L & D £15/£18. Closed Sun (open Sun dinner residents only).

Changes in data sometimes occur in establishments after the Guide
goes to press. Prices should be taken as indications rather than firm
quotes.

| Stapleford | Stapleford Park | 86% | £142 |

Tel 0572 787522   Fax 0572 787651   **HR**

Stapleford nr Melton Mowbray Leicestershire LE14 2EF   Map 7 E3

Set in 500 acres of rolling parkland, Stapleford dates back to the 16th
century with later additions creating a most impressive architectural
jumble. It was refurbished and transformed into a hotel, at no small
expense, by the much-missed Bob Payton of *Chicago Pizza Pie Factory*
fame, and the grandeur of the public rooms – acres of polished mahogany
panelling, high ceilings, fine Adam reception room, majestic galleried inner
hall, library bar – is tempered by the informal atmosphere created by keen
young staff (who all sport name badges). Upstairs, luxuriously appointed
bedrooms have been individually decorated not only by recognised
designers such as Nina Campbell and David Hicks but also by more
surprising names like Turnbull & Asser (a very masculine room with shirt
fabric-inspired wall coverings), Tiffany's (the jewellers), Crabtree & Evelyn
(who also supply all the toiletries to the hotel) and Max Pike (the plumber,
whose room features a splendid, freestanding Victorian tub). Bathrooms are
marbled, with towelling robes and huge bath sheets. Children up to 10 stay
free in parents' room. Conference/banqueting in the Sherard Suite for
200/150. The latest development (due to open just after we went to press)
was the conversion of The Garden Cottage on the estate – less than 100yds
from the main house – to become a self-contained conference suite with its
own kitchen and dining room plus four bedrooms themed by Coca Cola,
MGM, Range Rover and IBM. *Rooms 42. Garden, croquet, coarse fishing,*
tennis, clay pigeon shooting, basketball, American horseshoes, helipad.
AMERICAN EXPRESS *Access, Diners, Visa.* MARTELL

Restaurant   £75

Depending on the number of diners either the Grinling Gibbons room
with its wealth of ornate carving or (and always at lunchtime) the Old
Kitchen with stone walls and high vaulted ceiling is used. Each table gets
a whole home-baked loaf on a marble bread board to accompany evening
dishes with a distinctly trendy sound: beef carpaccio with potato and
anchovy cream; grilled prawns wrapped in Parma ham with three aïolis;
charred sea bass with herb fettuccine and extra virgin olive oil; chicken
with grilled vegetables and balsamic vinaigrette. Puddings range from
bread-and-butter to baked figs with frozen honey and vanilla yoghurt and
an all-American chocolate pecan pie. An all-day (9am-11pm) lounge menu
– burgers, sandwiches and salads – adds some entrées like pasta of the day,
fish cakes and grilled chicken which are served in the dining room
at lunchtime. Sunday lunches bring a traditional roast menu in winter and
a barbecue on the terrace in summer (whatever the weather). You wouldn't
expect the wine list to be conventional – and it isn't! Unusually, it's
presented by taste and grape variety, fairly priced (even a *marque*
champagne is under £30, a rare occurrence in a grand hotel such as this)
and apart from the excellent Californian choices, it has plenty of appeal
elsewhere. Outdoor eating for 48 on the terrace. No smoking. *Seats 70.*
Parties 8. Private Room 50. L 12-2.30 D 7-9.30 (Fri & Sat to 10.30).
Set L £19.95.

Steeple Aston — Hopcrofts Holt Hotel — 63% — £80

Tel 0869 40259   Fax 0869 40865   **H**
Steeple Aston nr Oxford Oxfordshire OX6 3QQ   Map 15 D1

Once a coaching inn, the hotel has now expanded its role with Executive accommodation and purpose-built conference rooms which can cater for up to 200 delegates. Just off the A4260 between Banbury and Oxford. Mount Charlotte Thistle. *Rooms 88.* AMERICAN EXPRESS *Access, Diners, Visa.*

Stevenage — Forte Posthouse — 58% — £67

Tel 0438 365444   Fax 0438 741308   **H**
Old London Road Broadwater Stevenage Hertfordshire SG2 8DS   Map 15 E1

On the B197 to the north of town. One of the smaller Posthouses, with public rooms in a 15th-century building and bedrooms in more modern extensions. No 'Executive' rooms. Children free when sharing parents' room. *Rooms 54.* AMERICAN EXPRESS *Access, Diners, Visa.*

Stevenage — Novotel — 60% — £65

Tel 0438 742299   Fax 0438 723872   **H**
Knebworth Park Stevenage Hertfordshire SG1 2AX   Map 15 E1

Reduced room rates this year at this modern, open-plan hotel at Junction 7 of the A1(M). Banqueting facilities for up to 120, conferences up to 150. *Rooms 100. Outdoor swimming pool.* AMERICAN EXPRESS *Access, Diners, Visa.*

Stevenage — Travel Inn — NEW — £43

Tel 0438 351318   **L**
Corey's Mill Lane Stevenage Hertfordshire SG1 4AA   Map 15 E1

Close to the A1(M) Junction 8, on the intersection of A602 Hitchin Road and Corey's Mill Lane. *Rooms 40.* AMERICAN EXPRESS *Access, Diners, Visa.*

Stevenage — Places of Interest

Tourist Information   Tel 0438 369441.
Gordon Craig Theatre   Tel 0438 316291.
Benington Lordship Gardens   Tel 0438 85668.
Shaw's Corner (NT)   Ayot St. Lawrence Tel 0438 820307 *Home of George Bernard Shaw.*
Welwyn Roman Baths   Tel 0707 271362.
Knebworth House   Knebworth Tel 0438 812661.
Stevenage Ice Rink   Tel 0438 740750.
Welwyn Garden City Ski Centre   Tel 0707 331056/330780.
Silver Leys Polo Club Troopers   Drivers End. Codicote Tel 0438 820414.

Stilton — Bell Inn — £64

Tel 0733 241066   Fax 0733 245173   **R**
Great North Road Stilton nr Peterborough Cambridgeshire PE7 3RA   Map 7 E4

Reputedly the oldest coaching inn on the Great North Road (and once refuge to highwayman Dick Turpin), the Bell boasts a Roman well in the courtyard and an impressive 15th-century stone frontage. Modern additions include hotel reception glassed in under the original archway and two rear wings of bedrooms with today's trappings, tokens of antiquity sadly confined to the odd four-poster bed. Separate conference/banqueting for up to 100 in the Marlborough Suite. No dogs. *Rooms 19. Garden. Closed 25 & 26 Dec.* AMERICAN EXPRESS *Access, Diners, Visa.*

See over

Restaurant   £45

The delightful, galleried restaurant with vaulted ceiling and exposed rafters
is more in character with the original Old Bell. Weekly table d'hote menus
and à la carte conclude with good Stilton cheese (it was first sold
to travellers here in the 1720s), plum bread and vintage port. Vegetarian
options. Snacks at lunchtime in the stone-flagged bar. *Seats 40. Parties 20.
Private Room 12. L (2nd week Dec-1st week Jan only) 12-2 (Sun from 12.30)
D 7-9.30 (Sun to 9). Set Sun L £9.95 Set D £14.50.*

Stockbridge   Grosvenor Hotel   57%   £70

Tel 0264 810606   Fax 0264 810747   **H**

High Street Stockbridge Hampshire SO20 6EU   **Map 14 C3**

On the A30 in the village centre, the Grosvenor (owned by Countryside
Inns) has kept many of its original Georgian features, including
a colonnaded porch. The bar is one of the focal points of Stockbridge life.
Bedrooms in the original house are larger than those in the converted
stables. Banqueting and conference facilities for around 70. *Rooms 25.
Garden, sauna, snooker.* AMERICAN EXPRESS *Access, Diners, Visa.*

Stockbridge   Places of Interest

Houghton Lodge House and Gardens   Tel 0264 810177.
Museum of Army Flying   Middle Wallop Tel 0264 384421.

Stockport   Alma Lodge   61%   £95

Tel 061-483 4431   Fax 061-483 1983   **H**

149 Buxton Road Stockport Cheshire SK2 6EL   **Map 6 B2**

Two miles from the M6 (Junction 12) on the A6 to the south of Stockport,
this early Victorian house has been greatly extended to create a Jarvis-
owned business-oriented hotel. Some original features of the old house –
wood panelling and open fires – survive in the public rooms. All bedrooms
now also have showers. Banqueting/conference facilities for up to 250.
Children up to 16 accommodated free in parents' room. *Rooms 52.*
AMERICAN EXPRESS *Access, Diners, Visa.*

Stockport   Forte Travelodge   £45

Tel 0625 875292   **L**

London Road South Adlington Stockport Cheshire SK12 4NA **Map 6 B2**

On the A523, 5 miles south of Stockport and 5 miles north of Macclesfield.
Rooms 32. AMERICAN EXPRESS *Access, Diners, Visa.*

Stockport   Travel Inn   £43

Tel 061-499 1944   Fax 061-437 4910   **L**

Finney Lane Heald Green Stockport Cheshire SK8 2QH   **Map 6 B2**

1 mile from Manchester Airport. *Rooms 41.* AMERICAN EXPRESS *Access,
Diners, Visa.*

Stockport   Travel Inn   NEW   £43

Tel 061-480 2968   Fax 061-477 8320   **L**

Buxton Road Stockport Cheshire SK2 6NB   **Map 6 B2**

On the A6 in the centre of Stockport, 10 minutes' drive from Junction 12
of M63. *Rooms 40.* AMERICAN EXPRESS *Access, Diners, Visa.*

Stockport   Places of Interest

Tourist Information   Tel 061-474 3320/3321.
Bramhall Hall   Bramhall Tel 061-485 3708.
Stockport Art Gallery   War Memorial Building Tel 061-474 4453.

Stockton-on-Tees   Swallow Hotel   67%   £96

Tel 0642 679721   Fax 0642 601714   **H**

10 John Walker Square Stockton-on-Tees Cleveland TS18 1AQ   Map 5 E3

Practical, town-centre business hotel with an Egyptian-themed leisure centre and an all-day brasserie – Matchmakers (closed Sun) – named after John Walker, the man who invented the match and who came from Stockton. Banqueting/conference facilities for 250/300. Head for Stockton town centre and follow signs to the multi-storey car park, whose 6th floor is for hotel residents. *Rooms 124. Indoor swimming pool, keep-fit equipment, sauna, spa bath, steam room, solarium.* AMERICAN EXPRESS *Access, Diners, Visa.*

Stockton-on-Tees   Places of Interest

Preston Park Museum   Tel 0642 781184.
Sedgefield Racecourse   Tel 0642 557081.
Billingham Ice Rink   Billingham Tel 0642 554449.

Stoke Gifford   Forte Travelodge   **NEW**   £45

Tel 0272 501530   **L**

The Beaufort Arms North Road Stoke Gifford nr Bristol Avon   Map 13 F1

5 miles north-east of Bristol. Take Junction 19 of M4 or Junction 16 of M5. AMERICAN EXPRESS *Access, Diners, Visa.*

Stoke-on-Trent   Haydon House Hotel   65%   £62

Tel 0782 711311   Fax 0782 717470   **H**

Haydon Street Basford Stoke-on-Trent Staffordshire ST4 6JD   Map 6 B3

A family-owned Victorian hotel with friendly atmosphere, dependable accommodation and six de luxe suites, each with its own entrance, in adjacent Glebe Mews. Classy Victorian-style day rooms with antique clock collection. Take the A500 from M6 (J15 or 16) to the A53 turn-off. The hotel stands on the A53 at Basford. *Rooms 25. Closed 1 week Jan.* AMERICAN EXPRESS *Access, Diners, Visa.*

Stoke-on-Trent   North Stafford Hotel   61%   £90

Tel 0782 744477   Fax 0782 744580   **H**

Station Road Stoke-on-Trent Staffordshire ST4 2AE   Map 6 B3

Red-brick Victorian hotel with cheerful, generally good-sized bedrooms and conference/seminar facilities for up to 450. Children up to 14 stay free in parents' room. *Rooms 69.* AMERICAN EXPRESS *Access, Diners, Visa.*

Set menu prices may not always include service or wine.

Stoke-on-Trent   Stakis Stoke-on-Trent Grand   68%   £96

Tel 0782 202361   Fax 0782 286464   **H**

Trinity Street Hanley Stoke-on-Trent Staffordshire ST1 5NB   Map 6 B3

The Stakis Grand, situated at Hanley town centre and close to Stoke Festival Park, combines a busy conference trade (max 300) with good family facilities and a leisure club. Two ground-floor rooms are equipped for disabled guests. Children up to 15 stay free in parents' room. Bennett's pubby lounge/bar is open all day (except Sunday). Vastly reduced tariff for 14 day+ stays. Staffed business centre. *Rooms 128. Indoor swimming pool, keep-fit equipment, sauna, spa bath, steam room, solarium.* AMERICAN EXPRESS *Access, Diners, Visa.*

Stoke-on-Trent   Stoke-on-Trent Moat House   70%   £119

Tel 0782 219000   Fax 0782 284500   **H**

Etruria Hall Festival Way Etruria Stoke-on-Trent Staffordshire ST1 5BQ   **Map 6 B3**

Ten minutes drive from the M6, and equidistant from Junctions 15 and 16, the hotel stands by the A53 at the heart of the 1986 Garden Festival park. Day rooms, leisure club and smart up-to-date bedrooms are in a sympathetically designed stone-clad complex which reflects within it many of the original hall's features. There are no fewer than 23 conference rooms, which can handle 500+ delegates. Free car parking for 350 cars. Children up to 16 stay free in parents' room. *Rooms 143. Indoor swimming pool, gym, sauna, spa bath, solarium, beauty salon, snooker, coffee shop (8am-10pm).* AMERICAN EXPRESS *Access, Diners, Visa.*

Stoke-on-Trent   Places of Interest

Tourist Information   Tel 0782 411222.
Biddulph Grange Garden (NT)   Biddulph Tel 0782 517999.
Stoke City Football Club   Victoria Ground Tel 0782 413511.
Port Vale Football Ground   Vale Park, Burslem Tel 0782 814134.
North Staffordshire Ski Club   Kidsgrove Tel 0782 784908.
Alton Towers   Alton Tel 0538 702200.
Festival Park Leisure Complex   Tel 0782 283838.
   Museums and Art Galleries
Chatterley Whitfield Mining Museum   Tel 0782 813337.
City Museum and Art Gallery   Tel 0782 202173.
Wedgwood Museum   Josiah Wedgwood and Sons Ltd
   Tel 0782 204218/204141.
Gladstone Pottery Museum   Tel 0782 319232.
Minton Museum   Tel 0782 744766.
Sir Henry Doulton Gallery   Tel 0782 575454.

Stokesley   Chapters   65%   £59

Tel 0642 711888   Fax 0642 713387   **HR**

27 High Street Stokesley North Yorkshire TS9 5AD   **Map 5 E3**

Alan Thompson's plans continue apace – the most recent innovation is the Personal Appearance suite on the first floor comprising hairdresser, solarium, beautician, reflexologist, hypnotherapist, and masseur. Special weekend breaks available on a half-board basis. *Rooms 13. Garden, bistro (12-11pm). Closed 25 Dec, 1 Jan.* AMERICAN EXPRESS *Access, Diners, Visa.*

Restaurant   £40

Assisted by Catherine Richardson, Alan continues to turn out interesting menus using fresh local produce whenever possible, but presented with an international twist. Thus you might try Scottish rope-grown mussels marinière, confit of Barbary duckling, the breast pan-fried and served with puréed celeriac on a port sauce, and a peach and kiwi cheesecake to finish. *Seats 36. L by arrangement D 7-9.30 (Sat to 10). Closed Sun.*

Ston Easton   Ston Easton Park   88%   £153

Tel 0761 241631   Fax 0761 241377   **HR**

Ston Easton nr Bath Avon BA3 4DF   **Map 13 F1**

Equidistant from Bath and Bristol, the magnificent listed Grade 1 Palladian house was built in 1740 and contains some exceptional architectural features. Extensively restored and refurbished while owned by the Smedley family, it is set in the only remaining Humphrey Repton landscape in Somerset – the hotel's gardens, including wells, a ruined grotto and bridges spanning the river Norr, and an 18th-century ice house, are not to be missed. On the river bank 75 yards from the house is the Gardener's Cottage comprising two separate suites, each with a large twin/double-bedded room, living room and private bathroom. The magnificence of the

gardens is reflected in the wonderful floral displays you'll find in the salon
– note the ornate plasterwork and trompe l'oeil murals – and in the library,
which contains listed mahogany bookcases. Tastefully-decorated bedrooms,
some with four-posters of the Chippendale and Hepplewhite periods, have
luxurious bathrooms, boasting fine fittings (Rudge & Co, Czech & Speake)
and Crabtree & Evelyn toiletries. Impeccable staff provide excellent service
(beds turned down and towels changed when guests are dining), and a real
English country house-style breakfast will not disappoint. Children of seven
years onwards and babes in arms welcome, and kennelling for dogs
is available (free of charge) though dogs are not allowed in bedrooms
or public rooms. The house offers perhaps a unique glimpse into the
'Upstairs, Downstairs' world of the 18th-century: ask to see 'downstairs'
which has a kitchen museum, linen room, servants' hall, billiard room and
wine cellars, all in use today. Period meeting rooms (36 theatre-style) and
banqueting (the house's original dining room, now called the Yellow
Room) for 24. **Rooms 21.** *Garden, croquet, tennis, bicycle hire, snooker, lounge
snack service* (7.30am-11pm), *helipad.* AMERICAN EXPRESS *Access, Diners, Visa.*

Restaurant   ↑   £95

The main dining room, with fine wood panelling painted in soft colours
and bamboo-style furniture, was the old parlour. Relying on the best and
freshest produce, including vegetables, herbs and fruit from the walled
kitchen garden, chef Mark Harrington cooks with style, imagination and
consistency. First-course choice is headed by soup 'freshly prepared each day
from fruits, herbs and garden vegetables'; other starters could include
grilled oysters and smoked bonito with a champagne glaze, roulade of foie
gras with a Sauternes jelly or gateau of feta cheese and sun-dried tomatoes
in a Provençal dressing. There's usually a choice of five main courses,
typified by poached roulade of turbot and langoustine Newburg or fillet
of veal and wild mushrooms baked in brioche and puff pastry, and always
including a vegetarian dish. Several enticing cold desserts and one hot (this
to be ordered with the main course). Fine British cheeses, and quite
wonderful wine list with the New World well represented (note the
outstanding Penfolds collection). Well laid-out mostly by vintage, the best
growers, plenty of half bottles – seek advice, it's worth it! No smoking.
Lunch can be taken on the terrace in fine weather. **Seats 40. Parties 8.**
*Private Room 24. L 12.30-2 D 7.30-9.30 (Fri & Sat to 10). Set L £26
Set D £38.50.*

See the hotel by county listings for easy comparison of conference
and banqueting facilities.

Stonehouse	**Stonehouse Court**	**68%**	£75
Tel 0453 825155 Fax 0453 824611			**H**
Bristol Road Stonehouse Gloucestershire GL10 3RA			**Map 14 B2**

Conveniently situated about a mile from Junction 13 of the M5,
Stonehouse Court is an imposing 17th-century building (Grade II listed) set
in six acres of secluded gardens. Bedrooms are split between spacious rooms
with mullioned windows in the main house and more uniform ones
in redbrick extensions. Children occupying parents' room are
accommodated free of charge. Day rooms include a large panelled lounge
with fine carved stone fireplace, abundant seating and a bar with green
leather chesterfield sofas. Conference/banqueting facilities for up to 120.
Friendly management. New owners Arcadian have improvement plans for
1995. **Rooms 36.** *Garden, putting, snooker, fishing, helipad.* AMERICAN EXPRESS
Access, Visa.

Stonehouse   **Place of Interest**

Slimbridge Wildfowl Trust   Tel 0453 890333.

Stonham   Mr Underhill's   ★   £75

Tel 0449 711206   **R**

Stonham nr Stowmarket Suffolk IP14 5DW   Map 10 C3

On the A140, close to its junction with the A1120, the Bradleys' typical
Suffolk 'three-box' house is older than it appears from the outside with old
timbers much in evidence internally. The whole effect, with Bauhaus chairs
around crisply clothed tables and the work of local artists supplementing
their own art collection around the warm red walls, is very pleasing. Chris
Bradley works single-handedly in the kitchen on his daily-changing no-
choice menu (discussed when looking to sort out likes and dislikes) priced
for starter and main dish with cheese, desserts (three or four choices) and
coffee (which comes with good home-made petits fours) as optional extras.
First-rate ingredients are sympathetically handled in dishes that are
essentially uncomplicated yet thoroughly satisfying. A salad of warm
asparagus bound together with a purée of broad beans followed
by a slightly pink rack of lamb with an *herbes de Provence* gateau before
a delightful cream tart flavoured with cinnamon constituted a perfectly
balanced meal enjoyed recently. Judy Bradley looks after front of house
(with help when they are busy) with great charm. No smoking until
coffee. Quality not quantity on the wine list; some excellent choices at fair
prices, with apposite tasting comments alongside the bottles listed; and, yes,
there is an Australian Underhill shiraz on the list! *Seats* 24. *Parties* 16. *L by
arrangement D 7.30-9. Closed D Sun, all Mon, Bank Holidays (open 25 & 26
Dec). Set D from £25. Access, Diners, Visa.*

If we recommend meals in a hotel or inn a separate entry is made for its
restaurant.

Stonor   Stonor Arms   £80

Tel 0491 638345   Fax 0491 638863   **RR**

Stonor nr Henley-on-Thames Oxfordshire RG9 6HE   Map 15 D2

A converted 18th-century village pub offering two levels of food: informal
yet serious lunchtime snacking in Blades Brasserie and a more formal menu
in the elegant restaurant proper and conservatory room. Aperitifs and
canapés are served in a spacious drawing room graced with antiques and
comfortable sofas. Stephen Frost uses fresh produce from local sources, fish
from Cornwall and some meats and vegetables from their own farm
or estates in Scotland. Ballotine of quail with braised red cabbage and
juniper sauce, terrine of lamb's sweetbreads, bacon and potato, pan-fried
breast of duckling with apple purée and ginger sauce, bacon-wrapped
rabbit stuffed with prunes, hot dark chocolate soufflé with white chocolate
sorbet, poached fruit savarin – mouthwatering stuff. The brasserie menu
is similarly enticing: duck rillettes with pear chutney, salmon tartare with
mustard cream, fillet of spotted bass on a bed of spinach and grapefruit
sauce, thin apple tart with clotted cream and caramel sauce. Outdoor eating
in summer. The excellent and comprehensive wine list will satisfy the most
assiduous drinker in both price and depth of choice; there are several
vintages of Chateau Batailley (Pauillac) and a dozen Olivier Leflaive
burgundies, as well as helpful notes alongside the 'recommended' wines.
Seats 20 (restaurant) 40 (brasserie). *Parties* 10. *Private Rooms* 12/24.
*Restaurant: L by arrangement D 7-9.30, Blades: L & D 12-2 & 7-9.30 7 days.
Restaurant closed D Sun. Set D £29.50.* AMERICAN EXPRESS *Access, Visa.*

Rooms   £93

A wing of bedrooms, numbering nine (including two suites – £137.50 per
night), is furnished to a high standard with some antiques. Cots and Z-beds
for children are additional charges. No dogs. *Garden.*

Storrington   Abingworth Hall   70%   £96

Tel 0798 813636   Fax 0798 813914   **HR**

Thakeham Road Storrington West Sussex RH20 3EF   **Map 11 A6**

Built before World War 1, but with more of a 1930s' feel, Abingworth
Hall is set back from the B2139 in eight acres of gardens, north
of Storrington. Day rooms include a cosy, oak-panelled drawing room well
stocked with books and magazines, a spacious bar and a rattan-furnished
conservatory. Bedrooms vary considerably in size, the best (and largest)
coming with antique furniture and separate 'walk-in' showers in the
bathrooms; others tend to have standard, darkwood hotel furniture.
Hairdryers, radio alarms and magazines are standard, but bathrooms and
trouser presses are reserved for the best rooms and more of the TVs have
remote control. Limited room service is offered throughout the day and
evening. No dogs. **Rooms** *20. Garden, croquet, tennis, putting, coarse fishing,
helipad.* AMERICAN EXPRESS *Access, Visa.*

Restaurant   £65

A table d'hote menu offering three choices at each stage is supplemented
at night by a short à la carte. Generally straightforward dishes – Caesar
salad, duck and orange paté, whole lemon sole grilled with Paris butter,
duck breast with blackcurrants and cassis, lemon tart, zabaglione – are
carefully prepared and reliably cooked by Peter Cannon, who has been chef
here for more than 10 years. Realistically priced wines. **Seats** *50.
Private Room 16. L 12.30-1.45 D 7.15-9. Set L £12.50 Set D £19.50.*

Storrington   Little Thakeham   77%   £150

Tel 0903 744416   Fax 0903 745022   **HR**

Merrywood Lane Storrington West Sussex RH20 3HE   **Map 11 A6**

A Lutyens house with Gertrude Jekyll garden, the latter restored over the
last few years, both individually attract admirers but it's the way the two
complement each that is the glory of Little Thakeham. Over the last 15
years the Ractliffs have filled the public rooms with period 'arts and crafts'
furniture and objets d'art with a small first-floor gallery displaying
a collection of turn-of-the-century porcelain, glass and silverware that
is available for sale. Bedrooms are furnished with antiques from earlier
periods and individually decorated with a variety of stylish fabrics. Two
full suites have sofa-beds in their lounges, making them suitable for
families. Bathrooms that come with robes and bathsheets mostly have only
hand-held showers at the tub – just two have 'power' showers. No room
service is advertised, guests are encouraged to make use of the day rooms,
but drinks and sandwiches are available in rooms throughout the day and
evening – meals in suites only (of which there are two). **Rooms** *9. Garden,
outdoor swimming pool, tennis, helipad. Closed 2 weeks Christmas/New Year.*
AMERICAN EXPRESS *Access, Diners, Visa.*

Restaurant   £90

The dining room features a huge inglenook fireplace – one of several in the
house. A new chef, Joanne Docherty, is producing sensibly short (4-5 main
dishes) fixed-price menus (four courses at night) that now include
Mediterranean-influenced dishes – pastrami with tomatoes and olives,
bruschetta with roasted peppers and balsamic vinegar dressing – along with
the likes of Thakenham asparagus with lemon butter, rack of Southdown
lamb with rosemary and garlic, grilled lemon sole and Barbary duck with
ginger and honey. Straightforward wine list with many of the top French
names present; bits and bobs from elsewhere. There's a delightful terrace
for summer dining. **Seats** *30. Private Room 24. L 1-2 D 7-9. Closed D Sun,
L Mon. Set L £16.50/£21.50 Set D (4-course) £32.50.*

Storrington Manleys £85

Tel 0903 742331

Manleys Hill Storrington West Sussex RH20 4BT

Map 11 A6

Well-established restaurant in a pretty Queen Anne cottage at the foot
of the South Downs. Inside, the beamed ceiling is a foil for smart table
settings and crisp napery, and there's always a posy of fresh flowers on each
table. Chef-patron Karl Löderer's cooking is sophisticated and accomplished
with dishes like a 'gateau' of sole, crab, scallops and brill topped with puff
pastry and served with a chive sauce (or pan-fried scallops, crab mousse and
deep-fried mussels with a langoustine sauce); blinis with smoked salmon,
caviar and dill cream; turbot roasted with a crust of shellfish and potatoes
and served with a langoustine sauce, plus specialities from his native Austria
– *Gedunsteter zwiebel rost-braten mit mais Dukate* (braised sirloin steak with
crisp onions and a sweetcorn galette), *Salzburger Nockerln* (lemon and
orange flavoured soufflé cooked in honey and rum). The fixed-price lunch
and dinner menus offer a choice of four or so dishes at each stage and are
fully inclusive of service, coffee, amuse-bouche and nice, varied petits fours.
The equivalent of an à la carte menu (available at lunchtime if you ask)
comes at a fixed price (£26) that covers the first two courses. Sunday lunch
always includes a traditional roast and a fish option. France, Germany and
even Austria (but nothing from the rest of Europe) are well represented
on the wine list, whereas the New World has but three bottles, and one
of those is a dessert wine; good selection of half bottles, though. **Seats** 48.
*Parties 36. Private Room 22. L 12-2 D 7-9.15 (to 10 Sat). Closed D Sun
& all Mon, 1st 2 weeks Jan. Set L £18.60 (Sun £23.50) Set D £26.50.*
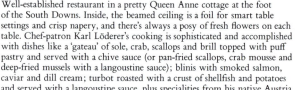 *Access, Visa.*

Room £75

For overnight guests a luxurious suite, with every modern comfort,
overlooks the garden and Downs beyond. Continental breakfast is served
in the suite. No dogs.

Storrington Old Forge £55

Tel & Fax 0903 743402

6a Church Street Storrington West Sussex RH20 4LA

Map 11 A6

A converted beamed forge is the relaxing setting for adventurous cooking
from chef-patron Clive Roberts, who offers monthly-changing menus. The
choice is nothing if not original, typified by parfait of bacon and black
pudding or smoked salmon parcels filled with a smoked eel mousse and
served with a spring onion and ginger vinaigrette among the starters; and
main courses such as sliced goose breast with a sauce of pink grapefruit and
green peppercorns. Completing the meal could be British farmhouse
cheeses, home-made ices or something more elaborate like an iced bombe
of sultanas and apricots served with a dried apricot sauce. French wines take
a back seat on this refreshing list that offers terrific value for money and
the opportunity to experiment in the New World. California house wines
are a steal. **Seats** 24. *Parties 18. L 12.30-1.30 D 7.15-9. Closed L Sat & Tues,
D Sun, all Mon, 1 week spring, 3 weeks autumn. Set L £12/£14.50
Set D £16/£20.50.* *Access, Diners, Visa.*

Storrington Place of Interest

St. Mary's House and Gardens Bramber Tel 0903 816205.

Stourbridge Bon Appétit £55

Tel 0384 375372

38 Market Street Stourbridge West Midlands DY8 1AG

Map 6 B4

Pleasant, unpretentious yet homely restaurant on two floors of a small town
house on the edge of the town centre. Careful, uncomplicated cooking
is the formula that has attracted a strong local following – booking

is advisable. Starters such as broccoli and Stilton flan, or ragout of duck
livers and garlic mushrooms in sherry cream sauce are followed by main
dishes like fillet of sole with herb crust and vermouth sauce, baked
moussaka and roast loin of pork with parsnip purée and baked apple, but
leave room for some good puds: summer fruit brulée, rum bread-and-
butter pudding, steamed sponge pudding with two sauces. Fixed-price
menus (particularly good value at lunchtimes and Tuesday-Thursday
evenings when prices are almost half those on Friday and Saturday nights)
offer a choice of half a dozen dishes at each stage. *Seats 60. Private Room 40.
L 12.30-2 D 7.30-10. Closed L Sat, all Sun (except L in winter) & Mon.
Set L £9.75/£11.75 & £17.50/£19.75 Set D £17.50/£19.75, also
Tue-Thur £9.75/£11.75.* AMERICAN EXPRESS *Access, Visa.*

Stourbridge	Talbot Hotel	59%	£50
Tel 0384 394350 Fax 0384 371318			**H**
High Street Stourbridge West Midlands DY8 1DW			Map 6 B4

A charming redbrick town-centre inn with many reminders of its
coaching-days origins back in the 17th century. There are heavy doors
to the coach entrance and some handsome timbers and moulded ceilings
in the day rooms. A marvellous old staircase winds up to bedrooms, which
vary in t!.eir size and furnishings. Some look out over the interior
courtyard. *Rooms 25. Coffee shop (9am-11pm).* AMERICAN EXPRESS *Access, Visa.*

Stourbridge	Places of Interest

Hagley Hall   Nr Stourbridge Tel 0562 882408.
Broadfield House Glass Museum   Barnett Lane, Kingswinford Tel 0384
    252401.

Stourport-on-Severn	Moat House	62%	£73
Tel 0299 827733 Fax 0299 878520			**H**
Hartlebury Road Stourport-on-Severn Hereford & Worcester DY13 9LT			Map 6 B4

Well set up for business or pleasure, the Moat House stands in a wooded
20-acre site. Banqueting and conference facilities for 350/250. Children
up to 14 stay free in parents' room. Take the Hartlebury Road out
of Stourport; the hotel is half a mile along on the left. *Rooms 68. Garden,
golf (8-hole), outdoor swimming pool, gym, squash, sauna, tennis, games room.*
AMERICAN EXPRESS *Access, Diners, Visa.*

Stourport	Place of Interest

Eastgrove Cottage Garden Nursery   Sankyns Green, Nr Shrawley
    Tel 0299 896389.

Stow-on-the-Wold	Fosse Manor	60%	£97
Tel 0451 830354 Fax 0451 832486			**H**
Fosse Way Stow-on-the-Wold Gloucestershire GL54 1JX			Map 14 C1

Resident proprietors Bob and Yvonne Johnston and their loyal staff run
a family haven that attracts many repeat visits. Built in the style
of a Cotswold manor house, it stands in its ivy coat in grounds set back
from the A429 (originally the Fosse Way) about a mile south of Stow-on-
the-Wold. Bedrooms (including several suitable for family occupation)
overlook colourful gardens and the bright look of the day rooms
is enhanced throughout by potted plants, fresh flowers and spotless
housekeeping. Children up to 16 stay free in their parents' room and family
facilities include supervised play times for children in a playroom and
playground on high days and holidays. *Rooms 20. Garden, sauna, spa bath,
solarium, beauty salon. Closed 22-30 Dec.* AMERICAN EXPRESS *Access, Diners, Visa.*

Stow-on-the-Wold   Grapevine Hotel   68%   £108

Tel 0451 830344   Fax 0451 832278   **HR**

Sheep Street Stow-on-the-Wold Gloucestershire GL54 1AU   Map 14 C1

Charming Cotswold-stone hotel (note the characterful bar) where owner
Sam (Sandra) Elliott is constantly making improvements. Winnie the
parrot has left home (no, he hasn't flown away, just got better digs!) and
been replaced by refurbishment throughout: in the cosy reception/lounge,
corridors, stairs – mind your head on the low beams – and two of the main
hotel bedrooms (welcoming glass of sherry on arrival), several with
exposed stonework and original beams. Further bedrooms in the garden
wing, and pine-furnished Rafters' rooms, the best having mini-bar and
trouser press in addition to the normal extras. Immaculate housekeeping,
friendly staff. No dogs. **Rooms** 23. Patio (*front & back*).
Closed 24 Dec-11 Jan. AMERICAN EXPRESS *Access, Diners, Visa.*

Restaurant   £50

A 70-year-old trailing ceiling vine (grapes were already fully ripe in mid-
July!) is the prominent feature in this pretty pink conservatory dining
room, where the cooking has a distinct British slant as in a turbot terrine
spiked with crab and tarragon with a cucumber and yoghurt cream,
or grilled pork cutlet with a warm spiced apple and raisin compote,
finishing with either a good selection of British farmhouse cheeses,
or a traditional pudding: syrup sponge and rich vanilla sauce, pear and
almond tart, and sticky toffee pudding with caramel sauce. Lighter lunches
(also served in the bar) and a traditional Sunday lunch menu with choices
that includes a glass of Bucks Fizz. **Seats** 42. L 12-2 D 7-9.30. Set L (*Sun
only*) £12.95 Set D £17.95.

Stow-on-the-Wold   Unicorn Hotel   59%   £103

Tel 0451 830257   Fax 0451 831090   **H**

Sheep Street Stow-on-the-Wold Gloucestershire GL54 1HQ   Map 14 C1

17th-century origins with some period appeal (steep tiled roof, dormer
windows and original beams). Forte. **Rooms** 20. AMERICAN EXPRESS *Access,
Diners, Visa.*

Stow-on-the-Wold   Wyck Hill House   74%   £98

Tel 0451 831936   Fax 0451 832243   **HR**

Burford Road Stow-on-the-Wold Gloucestershire GL54 1HY   Map 14 C1

Two miles south of Stow off the A424 this hilltop manor house, built early
in the 18th century, stands in 100 acres of its own grounds and gardens
commanding fine views across the Windrush Valley. Day rooms combine
comfort with a carefully created lived-in feel; rugs over time-worn
floorboards in the cedar-panelled library and inner hall with its fine
galleried staircase, leather armchairs in the clubby bar and dark oil portraits
and various items of porcelain that look deceptively as if they have always
been part of the house. Generally spacious bedrooms are either in the main
house (traditionally furnished with antique and reproduction pieces and
floral fabrics), the Orangery some 100 yards away (bright summery rooms
with rattan furniture and orange patterned soft furnishings, each with
French windows opening on to a patio) or, at a similar distance from the
main building, in the coach house where pine-furnished rooms open
directly on to a central courtyard. Rooms are all of a similar standard
except that de luxe rooms get the better views and a couple of little extras
like sherry, sweets and shortbread. Some rooms boast king-size and
four-poster beds. Attentive, friendly staff. **Rooms** 31. Garden, riding.
AMERICAN EXPRESS *Access, Diners, Visa.*

Restaurant £95

A contrast in styles here between the richly opulent inner dining room with red damask fabric-covered walls and huge central flower display and a large conservatory which takes full advantage of the panoramic views. Plenty of choice too on Ian Smith's confidently handled, modish à la carte: roulade of spinach and wild mushrooms with grilled scallops on a lime and ginger sauce; tartlets of sautéed pheasant with a confit of shallots and chestnuts; pot-roasted rabbit; halibut with a lemon and thyme crust; noisettes of lamb sautéed with garlic, rosemary, shallots and cocotte potatoes. Plain grills are also available, and on Saturday there's a light luncheon menu offering the likes of toasted club sandwiches, escalope of salmon, cold beef or a salad of avocado and prawns. Table d'hote lunch other days, with a bumper Sunday lunch. Splendid desserts such as Bramley apple and sultana tart, coffee fondant pudding and fritters of pineapple and figs. Rather too many bin ends on the wine list, which contains few surprises and not many bargains. No smoking. **Seats** 70. Parties 8. Private Room 32. L 12.30-2 D 7.30-9.30. Set L £9.50/£11.95 (Sun £17.50) Set D £29.50.

Stowmarket Forte Travelodge £45

Tel 0449 615347 — **L**

Stowmarket Suffolk IP14 3PY — Map 10 C3

On the A45 westbound, 10 miles north of Ipswich with Bury St Edmunds also within easy reach. **Rooms** 40. AMERICAN EXPRESS® Access, Diners, Visa.

Stratfield Turgis Wellington Arms £60

Tel 0256 882214 Fax 0256 882934 — **I**

Stratfield Turgis Basingstoke Hampshire RG27 0AS — Map 15 D3

Hard by the A33 behind a handsome white Georgian facade, a charming old inn with a mix of the old and new. A small and pubby L-shaped bar leads directly round into a friendly drawing room in country-house style. Fifteen bedrooms in the original building include two "luxury doubles" (one a suite with a heavily-carved four-poster and spa bath), while the other 20 are in a two-storey modern extension to the rear, uniformly decorated in Laura Ashley pastel shades plus modern light oak furniture. A couple of modern suites serve as both small meeting rooms and family rooms with pull-down additional beds. Good light meals and snacks in the public bar/lounge. Next door to the Duke of Wellington's estate (Stratfield Saye House, where river fishing can be arranged) and close to Wellington Country Park (ideal for family outings). The Long Room caters for banquet/conferences of up to 60/80. Busy Mon-Thurs with business travellers but more restful at weekends, when reduced rates apply. **Rooms** 35. Garden, fishing. AMERICAN EXPRESS® Access, Diners, Visa.

Stratford-upon-Avon Alveston Manor 65% £115

Tel 0789 204581 Fax 0789 414095 — **H**

Clopton Bridge Stratford-upon-Avon Warwickshire CV37 7HP — Map 14 C1

A Midsummer Night's Dream was first performed here in the seven acres of lovely gardens that are dominated by a large cedar tree. A converted manor house, with a gabled exterior, tall chimney stacks and leaded windows, behind which there remains a good deal of traditional decor and period charm in the day rooms. Bedrooms, though, are mainly modern; 'feature' and 'luxury' rooms attract only a small supplement; all rooms were refurbished early last year. Children under 16 stay free in parents' room. Banqueting/conference facilities for 150. Free use of a local leisure centre. Forte Grand. **Rooms** 106. Garden, croquet, pitch & putt. AMERICAN EXPRESS® Access, Diners, Visa.

**Stratford-upon-Avon, Billesley Manor.
See entry under Billesley.**

Stratford-upon-Avon	**Dukes Hotel**	65%	£70

Tel 0789 269300   Fax 0789 414700

H

Payton Street Stratford-upon-Avon Warwickshire CV37 6UA

Map 14 C1

Two Georgian town houses dating from 1820 make up a civilised,
privately-owned hotel not far from the town centre, shops and theatres.
Friendly armchairs, antique furniture and ornaments make a homely, lived-
in lounge, and there's a small bar. Bedrooms are neat and comfortable, with
period pieces; there are two four-poster rooms and two suites. No children
under 12. No dogs. **Rooms** 22. *Garden, croquet. Closed Christmas
to New Year.* AMERICAN EXPRESS *Access, Visa.*

Stratford-upon-Avon	**Ettington Park**	76%	£145

Tel 0789 450123   Fax 0789 450472

H

Alderminster Stratford-upon-Avon Warwickshire CV37 8BS

Map 14 C1

An imposing neo-Gothic stately home with a Grade 1 preservation listing.
It stands five miles south of Stratford on the A34 to Oxford, in mature
parkland by the Stour. The interior of the house fully lives up to the
promise of the setting and is being refurbished this year. Notable features
include a lovely plant-filled conservatory entrance, a fine Victorian
drawing room, a richly panelled library bar and a very elegant and
relaxing lounge. Bedrooms are no less impressive, with plenty of space,
well-chosen antiques, light, restful colour schemes and all sorts of little
personal touches. The majority of rooms enjoy fine country views. The
Long Gallery is one of the most characterful meeting rooms in the country,
with book-lined walls and a high, wood-panelled vaulted ceiling; it holds
up to 65 delegates. Similarly, there are other interesting rooms like the
14th-century chapel with stained-glass windows, suitable for private dining
and board meetings. Children up to 12 stay free in parents' room. No dogs.
Rooms 48. *Garden, croquet, tennis, indoor swimming pool, keep-fit equipment,
sauna, solarium, steam room, spa bath, coarse fishing, riding, clay-pigeon
shooting, helipad.* AMERICAN EXPRESS *Access, Diners, Visa.*

Stratford-upon-Avon	**Falcon Hotel**	63%	£116

Tel 0789 205777   Fax 0789 414260

H

Chapel Street Stratford-upon-Avon Warwickshire CV37 6HA

Map 14 C1

Behind a classic timbered facade there's a blend of old and new. The
beamed and panelled Oak Bar is as old as the building (1640), while the
conference rooms (for up to 200) are thoroughly up-to-date. 20 bedrooms,
including a four-poster suite, are in the original part, the rest in a modern
section. Children up to the age of 16 can stay and have breakfast free
of charge if sharing a room with an adult. 27 rooms are designated non-
smoking. Ample car parking. Queens Moat Houses. **Rooms** 73. *Garden.*
AMERICAN EXPRESS *Access, Diners, Visa.*

Stratford-upon-Avon	**Forte Posthouse**	59%	£68

Tel 0789 266761   Fax 0789 414547

H

Bridgefoot Stratford-upon-Avon Warwickshire CV37 7LT

Map 14 C1

Popular tourist, family and business base overlooking the river Avon,
opposite the theatre. Some rooms are of Executive standard. **Rooms** 60.
Children's playground. AMERICAN EXPRESS *Access, Diners, Visa.*

Stratford-upon-Avon   Liaison   NEW   £60

Tel 0789 293400   Fax 0789 297863   R

1 Shakespeare Street Stratford-upon-Avon Warwickshire CV37 6RN   Map 14 C1

Having taken a break since leaving their former restaurant (of the same name) in Solihull, partners Patricia Plunkett (in the kitchen) and Ank Van Der Tuin (front of house) have returned with renewed enthusiasm to create this chic, modern restaurant within what was originally a Methodist chapel, though more recently a motor museum. The fixed-price menu offers five choices at each stage: roulade of chicken and duck with a compote of exotic fruits; wild mushroom soup with chervil; boned guinea fowl on a confit of lentils, apple and celeriac; chargrilled chicken with roasted shallots on a sweet pepper pancake; tiramisu; parcel of mountain cheeses served hot with a ginger and walnut dressing surrounded by a salad of figs. In addition there is a gourmet menu (two choices) at lunchtime and until 7.30pm an informal single-dish Liaison Lights menu with the likes of a lobster club sandwich with crème fraiche, caviar and melon, Pernod-spiked bouillabaisse and warm brioche filled with mango and pine kernels. Full meals begin with freshly made canapés and end with good petits fours, both served on glass cake stands. *Seats 55. L 12-2.30 D 6-10.30. Closed L Sat, all Sun, 2 weeks Jan. Set L £13.50 D £19.50.* AMERICAN EXPRESS *Access, Diners, Visa.*

Stratford-upon-Avon Moat House International 71%   £141

Tel 0789 414411   Fax 0789 298589   H

Bridgefoot Stratford-upon-Avon Warwickshire CV37 6YR   Map 14 C1

A purpose-built, modern hotel close to the centre of town (on the A34) with a wealth of facilities to keep the conference trade happy. Spacious public rooms beyond the redesigned entrance area include a simply furnished residents' lounge and another that overlooks the River Avon. Uniform bedrooms are of a good size and comfortable, with smart dark furniture. Some of the rooms have views of the Royal Shakespeare Theatre and river; 64 on the third floor are reserved for non-smokers; eight are triple rooms for families (children up to 15 stay free in their parents' room). Piano Bar. Superb Metropolitan health and fitness centre. Conference and banqueting facilities for up to 450. *Rooms 247. Garden, gym, indoor swimming pool, spa bath, sauna, steam room, solarium, beautician, hairdressing, mooring, helipad, disco, shopping arcade, news kiosk.* AMERICAN EXPRESS *Access, Diners, Visa.*

Stratford-upon-Avon   The Opposition   £50

Tel 0789 269980   R

13 Sheep Street Stratford-upon-Avon Warwickshire CV37 9EF   Map 14 C1

Nigel Lambert's busy bistro offers a winning combination of good food, fair prices and convivial atmosphere that puts it ahead of most of the opposition. Light dishes and starters head the menu, including garlic mushrooms or snails, trio of salmon with a horseradish cream, and chicken liver paté. Greek and Niçoise salads may be ordered as either starter or main course, and hot mains range from pasta and pizza to chargrilled burger, Cajun-style chicken and a bowl of chili. Banoffi pie is the speciality dessert. *Seats 50. Parties 10. L 12-2 D 5.30-11 (Sun till 10). Closed 25, 26 Dec. Access, Visa.*

Stratford-upon-Avon   Shakespeare Hotel   69%   £110

Tel 0789 294771   Fax 0789 415111   H

Chapel Street Stratford-upon-Avon Warwickshire CV37 6ER   Map 14 C1

A Forte Heritage hotel with a central location (next to the town hall) and a long history. The gabled and timbered facade is typical of its 17th-century origins, and inside are beams and flagstones, open fires and period furnishings. Floral fabrics and smart darkwood furniture are used in the bedrooms, which include five suites and three four-poster rooms. Children up to 14 stay free in parents' room. Bedroom refurbishment is planned for the end of 1994. Function facilities for up to 100. *Rooms 63. Garden.* AMERICAN EXPRESS® *Access, Diners, Visa.*

Stratford-upon-Avon	**Stratford House**	**62%**	**£71**
Tel 0789 268288 Fax 0789 295580			**H**
18 Sheep Street Stratford-upon-Avon Warwickshire CV37 6EF			Map 14 C1

Approximately one hundred yards from the Royal Shakespeare Theatre and the river Avon, this quiet little hotel in a Georgian house is a comfortable, friendly home from home, its appeal enhanced by owner Sylvia Adcock's antiques, pictures and china. An open fire warms the lounge, and there's a bright conservatory restaurant and bar. In warm weather the walled garden comes into its own. Neat bedrooms use floral fabrics and darkwood units. Families are welcome, with most facilities provided. Charged parking in a nearby car park. *Rooms 11. Garden. Closed 4 days at Christmas.* AMERICAN EXPRESS® *Access, Diners, Visa.*

Stratford-upon-Avon	**Welcombe Hotel**	**74%**	**£125**
Tel 0789 295252 Fax 0789 414666			**H**
Warwick Road Stratford-upon-Avon Warwickshire CV37 0NR			Map 14 C1

A large and handsome Jacobean-style mansion a mile and a half from the centre of Stratford. The parkland that surrounds it includes two lakes and an 18-hole, par 70 golf course, whose clubhouse is a popular spot for a drink or a snack. There's an Italian garden, a rose garden, a winter garden and a water garden. In the main building is the oak-panelled bar, named after sometime owner the historian Sir George Trevelyan. In the oak-panelled lounge, deep sofas and armchairs provide abundant comfort, and a log fire burns in the ornate black marble fireplace. Individually furnished bedrooms in the main house have antiques and period pieces, plus marble bathrooms with separate showers. Some of the suites are most impressive – the Lady Caroline (Trevelyan) comprises four-poster bedroom, drawing room, study and a luxurious bathroom where you can wallow in the bathtub and watch a TV soap at the same time. Rooms in a garden wing are smaller but equally comfortable. Breakfasts are disappointing. Owners since 1983 are Orient Express Hotels. *Rooms 76. Garden, tennis, golf (18), games room. Closed 28 Dec-3 Jan.* AMERICAN EXPRESS® *Access, Diners, Visa.*

Stratford-upon-Avon	**White Swan**	**62%**	**£117**
Tel 0789 297022 Fax 0789 268773			**H**
Rother Street Stratford-upon-Avon Warwickshire CV37 6NH			Map 14 C1

The exterior of this old inn is little changed since Shakespeare's day and public rooms are full of atmosphere, with old beams, timbers and a well-preserved wall painting dating from 1550 in the bar. Bedrooms, except for two antique-furnished rooms in the original building, are in rear extensions of various ages (the newest some 60 years old) and though varying widely in size and shape share the same solid oak furniture, pleasant matching bedcovers and curtains and the usual modern amenities. *Rooms 37.* AMERICAN EXPRESS® *Access, Diners, Visa.*

Stratford-upon-Avon	**Windmill Park**	**64%**	**£98**
Tel 0789 731173 Fax 0789 731131			**H**
Warwick Road Stratford-upon-Avon Warwickshire CV37 0PY			Map 14 C1

Four linked blocks provide practical accommodation in a modern redbrick hotel on the A439 (leave the M40 at Junction 15). Fully-equipped leisure centre; conference facilities for up to 360; many large family and

interconnecting bedrooms, with under-12s staying free in parents' room.
*Rooms 103. Tennis, indoor swimming pool, gym, sauna, spa bath, steam room,
solarium.* AMERICAN EXPRESS *Access, Diners, Visa.*

Stratford-upon-Avon   Places of Interest

Tourist Information   Tel 0789 293127.
The Teddy Bear Museum   Tel 0789 293160.
The Shakespeare Birthplace Trust's Properties
   The Shakespeare Centre Tel 0789 204016.
Stratford-upon-Avon Racecourse   Tel 0789 267949.
   Theatres and Concert Halls
Royal Shakespeare Theatre   Tel 0789 295623.
Swan Theatre   Tel 0789 295623.
The Other Place   Tel 0789 292565.

Streatley-on-Thames   Swan Diplomat   68%   £134

Tel 0491 873737   Fax 0491 872554   **HR**

High Street Streatley-on-Thames Berkshire RG8 9HR   Map 15 D2

This charming hotel (the welcome is friendly and professional) spreads
itself along the south bank of the River Thames, enabling the public rooms,
including the pine-clad bar and the comfortable lounges, to have extensive
views of the river, the boats and the ducks. Likewise, over half the
bedrooms overlook the water, many of these with their own balconies.
Two are reserved for non-smokers. The attractively decorated bedrooms
are furnished with traditional-style mahogany pieces, combining comfort
with all mod cons. Breakfast can be a disappointment, relying too much
on a hot (actually in our most recent experience only warm) self-service
buffet. The Continental alternative (£8) offered tired croissants, with
standard butter and preserves. For the energetic, the well-equipped
Reflexions fitness centre, incorporated in the building, is available free for
guests. Moored alongside is the Magdalen College Barge which, as well
as looking picturesque, provides an unusual setting for meetings and
cocktail parties. Spacious car park. 24hr room service. *Rooms 46. Garden,
indoor 'fitness' swimming pool, sauna, solarium, gym, bicycles, rowing boats,
moorings.* AMERICAN EXPRESS *Access, Diners, Visa.*

Riverside Restaurant   £80

Something of a garden house feel here with trellis ceiling and faux-rattan
chairs, but it's the riverside setting that's still the main attraction. Executive
chef Christopher Cleveland is a consummate professional and under his
guidance the kitchen reliably produces both a well-crafted à la carte (dinner
only) and table d'hote. Dinner brings the more elaborate dishes, typified
by terrine of salmon and broccoli with a champagne vinegar dressing
or a mousse of corn-fed chicken served with a ravioli of vegetables and
a paprika/yoghurt sauce. There are simple classics, too, such as best end
of lamb with stuffed tomatoes (dish for two), daily 'fishmonger's
recommendations', vegetarian mains and starters, and desserts like warm
apple and cinnamon pancakes with a compote of red fruits or chilled white
and dark chocolate terrine accompanied by a trio of sauces. A rather good
and comprehensive wine list has plenty of half bottles. House wines apart,
quite pricey. Breakfast, a lighter lunch and afternoon tea are served in the
Duck Room brasserie, which also enjoys river views. *Seats 75.
Private Room 32. L 12.30-2 D 7.30-9.30 (Sat from 7). Closed L Sat.
Set L £12.50 (Duck Room) & £19.95 Set D £27.50.*

Street   Bear Hotel   63%   £60

Tel 0458 42021   Fax 0458 840007   **H**

53 High Street Street Somerset BA16 0EF   Map 13 F1

On the edge of town, just off the A39, the late-Victorian stone-built Bear
retains its intimate air in the small fire-lit residents' lounge and livelier bar
and patio. There's a sturdy, old-fashioned feel to the main-house bedrooms;

seven in the Rose Cottage annexe are more modern. Well-equipped
conference and function facilities for up to 120. 24hr room service.
No dogs. *Rooms* 17. *Garden, outdoor swimming pool. Closed 25 Dec.*
AMERICAN EXPRESS *Access, Visa.*

Stretton   Ram Jam Inn   £57
Tel 0780 410776   Fax 0780 410361   IR
Great North Road Stretton nr Oakham Leicestershire LE15 7QX   Map 7 E3

Hard by a service station nine miles north of Stamford on the northbound
lane of the A1 (southbound drivers take the B668 exit to Oakham and
follow signs), the Ram Jam Inn, named after a special brew produced in its
early days, is a very pleasing alternative to the mass of commercial hotels
and eating places along the A1. Public rooms are devoted completely
to informal, yet smartly furnished eating areas (bar, snack, outdoor terrace
and restaurant). All the bedrooms overlooking the garden and orchard are
individually and tastefully decorated with limed pine furniture, and are
surprisingly quiet considering the proximity to the road. *Rooms* 10.
Garden, coffee shop (7am-10pm). Closed 25 Dec. AMERICAN EXPRESS *Access,
Diners, Visa.*

Restaurant   £35

Coffee, breakfast, snacks and full meals are all available in a pleasantly light
dining room overlooking the orchard. Between chefs as we went to press.
Seats 30. *Private Room 25. L 12-2.30 D 7-10 (light meals 7am-10pm).*

Stretton   Dovecliffe Hall   68%   £85
Tel 0283 531818   Fax 0283 516546   HR
Dovecliffe Road Stretton nr Burton-on-Trent Staffordshire DE13 0DJ   Map 6 C3

A fine Georgian house in eight acres of gardens surrounded by farmland,
Dovecliffe is as much a restaurant with rooms as a hotel. The two elegant
lounges may seem excessively spacious for just seven bedrooms but come
into their own for perusing the dinner menu or taking post-prandial
brandies. Beneath the fine central staircase the reception desk doubles
as a bar counter. Bedrooms, most large but with one small single with
shower and WC only, are comfortably furnished and come with various
thoughtful extras such as fruit, mineral water and bathrobes. *Rooms* 7.
*Garden, helipad. Closed 1 week Spring, 2 weeks summer, 1 week Christmas.
Access, Visa.*

Restaurant   £65

Uncomplicated, but not uninteresting, cooking based on good raw
materials is a formula that has attracted a strong local following to this
elegantly proportioned, high-ceilinged restaurant where the ebullient
owner Nicholas Hine is very much in evidence greeting diners – many
by name. Dinner brings a sort of à la carte (the choice of main course
determines the price of a three-course meal) plus a table d'hote menu, while
lunch is a more limited (but good-value) fixed-price affair. Chargrilled
venison on red cabbage with port sauce, supreme of chicken with creamed
potatoes and pink peppercorn sauce, pan-fried calf's liver with smoked
bacon and sweet and sour onions, and grilled fillet of trout with lemon
butter typify main dishes that come with simple but accurately cooked
vegetables. Bread-and-butter pudding made with double cream and
Cointreau-soaked raisins and served with crème anglaise and caramel
is considered a speciality pudding. A decent wine list offers six or seven
wines and no less than seven vintage ports by the glass. Three tables
on a terrace in good weather. *Seats* 85. *Parties 24. Private Room 60.
L 12-1.45 D 7-9.30. Closed D Sun, all Mon, L Sat. Set L £9.50/£11.50
(Sun £13.95) Set D £17.50.*

Stroud   Oakes   ★ ↑   £80

Tel 0453 759950   **R**

169 Slad Road Stroud Gloucestershire GL5 1RG   Map 14 B2

Standing proudly overlooking the B4070 and Slad valley just north
of town, this immaculate former girls' college has one of the regions finest
tables. Chris Oakes and wife Caroline have matured into highly
professional and accomplished restaurateurs, producing a consistently
polished, controlled but seductive product. His cooking shows great
economy and finesse with an almost religious respect for raw ingredients
and the best quality produce, with vivid colours and intense clean flavours
dominating each plate. A dish of goat's cheese fried in olive oil and
tomatoes topped with a pine kernel and pesto crust was simplicity itself,
but wonderful; as was a large feta ravioli with spinach and tomato
vinaigrette. Main courses such as roasted breast of chicken with an intense
but balanced hazelnut sauce and a rich sticky osso buco with each knuckle
topped with a pungent purée of garlic and lemon zest are accompanied
by exemplary vegetables. Pricey desserts are indulgently rich, the coffee
good and served with petits fours. Set menus with no choice for 3 courses
are excellent value. Interesting, affordable wines with a good choice
by glass and half bottle. *Seats 34. L 12.30-1.45 D 7.30-9.30. Closed D Sun,
all Mon, Bank Holidays. Set L £10 Set D £16.* AMERICAN EXPRESS *Access, Visa.*

Stroud   Places of Interest

Tourist Information   Tel 0453 765768.
Misarden Park Gardens   Tel 028582 309.
Painswick Rococo Garden   Painswick Tel 0452 813204.

Stuckton   The Three Lions   £60

Tel 0425 652489   Fax 0425 656144   **R**

Stuckton nr Fordingbridge Hampshire SP6 2HF   Map 14 C4

In a rural setting on the edge of the New Forest, June and Karl Wadsack's
converted pub is a mecca for lovers of good food, fine wine and
conviviality. Blackboard menus proclaim a daily-changing choice of dishes
making good use of local ingredients: pigeon breast, venison sausage and
lentils, Poole Bay sole (grilled or meunière), roast duck with apricot and
hazelnut stuffing and a Bramley apple sauce. Many influences from further
afield are also apparent, with typical examples including steamed sea bass
Chinese style, Wiener schnitzel and Indonesian nasi goreng. Choc pot,
apple strudel and bread-and-butter pudding are favourite desserts. A snack
menu is also available. June's wine list is superbly balanced with exceptional
offerings from Germany, Alsace and particularly Australia. Other countries
well-represented too and there's an extensive selection of dessert wines.
Prices reasonably friendly. No children under 14. No smoking. *Seats 55.
Parties 10. L 12.15-1.30 D 7.15-9 (Sat to 9.30). Closed D Sun, all Mon
2 weeks Jul-Aug, 1 week Oct, 1 week Christmas. Access, Visa.*

Stuckton   Place of Interest

Rockbourne Roman Villa   Nr Fordingbridge Tel 072 53 541.

Studland Bay   Knoll House   63%   £165★

Tel 092 944 251   Fax 092 944 423   **H**

Studland Bay nr Swanage Dorset BH19 3AH   Map 14 C4

Given up as a lordly residence in 1932 when the ferry road was built
passing by the front of the hotel and cutting through the Studland estate,
the hotel has now been in the ownership of the Ferguson family for the
past 35 years. They have greatly extended the original country house,
creating a popular summertime retreat for families, particularly those with
younger children; weekly terms only are offered in high season. There

is a special children's dining room serving 'real' food, with non-slip floor and an attendant, specially dedicated kitchen as well as a host of amenities including a splendid outdoor Swedish-designed play area complete with a large pirate ship, climbing frame, chutes and more. The beach is a few hundred yards away across the road and can be glimpsed through the trees from the front bedrooms. All rooms are comfortably homely and possess clean, simple bathrooms, though a number are not en suite. The permutations for those requiring different types of rooms are almost endless, with many interconnected rooms and simple suites. For adults there's a child-free lounge as well as a spacious bar and restaurant with much-sought-after window tables. The leisure centre is compact but comprehensively equipped. No televisions are provided, though they can be hired and there is a separate television lounge. Baby listening involves housekeepers who 'patrol the corridors' from 7.30 to 11pm. Winner of our Family Hotel of the Year award in 1990 – and it's still in the top league. *Half-board terms. **Rooms** 70. *Garden, tennis, golf (9 hole), indoor & outdoor swimming pool, gym, sauna, steam room, spa bath, solarium, children's playroom, games rooms, outdoor playground, gift shop, self-service launderette, writing/bridge room. Closed Nov-Easter. No credit cards.*

Studland Bay   Place of Interest

Swanage Beach.

Sturminster Newton   Plumber Manor   £55
Tel 0258 472507   Fax 0258 473370   **RR**
Hazelbury Bryan Road Sturminster Newton Dorset DT10 2AF   Map 14 B4

The restaurant is definitely the centre of attraction at the Prideaux-Brune family's home in the heart of Hardy country. Built in 1665 from local stone, the house is surrounded by lawns shaded by fine old trees. Brian Prideaux-Brune's fixed-price, three-course dinner menus might start with quail in filo pastry with leek purée and Denhay ham or smoked duck breast with plum sauce, followed by an optional set fish course (perhaps monkfish *en brochette*) and then chicken *indienne*, medallions of beef with mushrooms and paprika, fillet of pork with avocado, brandy and cream or beef Wellington. A selection of sweets is served from a trolley. Sunday lunch, for which there's a good choice, is popular. Decent wines. A fine base for a weekend touring Hardy country. Small conference rooms for up to 40, and popular for boardroom meetings of up to 12. **Seats** 60. *Private Room 50. L (Sun only) 12.30-1.30 D 7.30-9.30. Closed Feb. Set L (Sun only) £17.50 Set D £20/£25.* AMERICAN EXPRESS *Access, Diners, Visa.*

Rooms   £80

The 16 rooms are spacious and well appointed, most having antique furniture. Six are in the main house, four more in the courtyard; the rooms in a converted stone barn are more modern and even larger, with window seats overlooking a stream and the garden. Full English breakfast plus fresh fish. Free stabling is provided on a do-it-yourself basis. *Garden, croquet, tennis.*

Sudbury   Mabey's Brasserie   £55
Tel 0787 374298   **R**
47 Gainsborough Street Sudbury Suffolk CO10 7SS   Map 10 C3

More bistro than brasserie (it's only open at usual meal times) with pine and pews and a new blue colour scheme, there is also now a separate dining room for smokers. The menu, written on blackboards above the open kitchen, is varied, if a little less eclectic that it used to be, with deep-fried parcels of Cambazola cheese, gravad lax with dill sauce, chicken and vegetable terrine and warm salad of crispy Chinese-style duck among the starters; various chargrilled dishes included in the mains: chicken breast with noodles and sesame sauce, calf's liver and bacon with black pudding, chump of lamb with tarragon sauce; plus cod baked with a herb crust and salmon on salad with basil vinaigrette and new potatoes. Vegetables, like the bread, are extras. Puds range from summer pudding and vanilla crème brulée to Earl Grey tea and lemon sorbet. Air-conditioned. *Seats 50. Private Room 35. L 12-2 D 7-10. Closed Sun & Mon, 5 days at Christmas.* AMERICAN EXPRESS® *Access, Visa.*

Sudbury	Mill Hotel	58%	£93
Tel 0787 375544 Fax 0787 373027			**H**
Walnut Tree Lane Sudbury Suffolk CO10 6BD			Map 10 C3

The old mill stands on the banks of the Stour by a large mill pond. Bedrooms are either old-fashioned or extension-modern. Children up to 14 may stay free in parents' room. Extensive room service menu includes 24hr sandwich availability. Note the old 16-ft millwheel behind glass in the bar-lounge. *Rooms 56. Garden, coarse fishing.* AMERICAN EXPRESS® *Access, Diners, Visa.*

Sudbury   Places of Interest

Tourist Information   Tel 0787 881320.
Gainsborough's House   Gainsborough Street Tel 0787 72958.
Colne Valley Railway   Castle Hedingham Tel 0787 61174.
   Historic Houses, Castles and Gardens
Hedingham Castle   Castle Hedingham Tel 0787 60261.

Sunderland	Swallow Hotel	70%	£105
Tel 091-529 2041 Fax 091-529 4227			**H**
Queen's Parade Seaburn Sunderland Tyne & Wear SR6 8DB			Map 5 E2

A smart, modern hotel sited north of Sunderland right on the seafront overlooking a long stretch of good sand with amusement arcades a little further along. A uniformed bell boy greets you at the entrance and carries your luggage to your room. Reception is in a part of a spacious lounge area done out, as is the whole place, in a smart, colourful, contemporary style. The Mariner bar, as its name implies, has a nautical theme. Best of the bedrooms overlook the sea. These are spacious and have sitting areas; all rooms are well equipped with, in addition to the usual facilities, an iron and board, mini-bar and satellite TV. Reasonable breakfasts are taken in the sunny restaurant. 24hr room service and guarded parking. *Rooms 66. Indoor swimming pool, keep-fit equipment, sauna, spa bath, solarium.* AMERICAN EXPRESS® *Access, Diners, Visa.*

Sunderland   Places of Interest

Tourist Information   Tel 091-565 0960/0990.
Sunderland Empire Theatre   Tel 091-514 2517.
Hylton Castle   Tel 091-548 0152.
Washington Old Hall (NT)   Washington Tel 091-416 6879.
Sunderland Football Ground   Roker Park Tel 091-514 0332.
Sunderland Ice Rink and Leisure Centre   Tel 091-514 2511.
Silksworth Dry Ski Slope   Tel 091-522 9119.
Washington Waterfowl Park   Washington Tel 091-416 5454.

Surbiton	Chez Max		£65
Tel 081-399 2365			**R**
85 Maple Road Surbiton Surrey KT6 4AW			Map 15 E2

Chef-patron Max Markarian's conservatory-roofed suburban restaurant is a haven of enjoyable French cooking. Some of his dishes are familiar classics – moules marinière, trout breton – while many have individual touches, among them breast of guinea fowl with a lime and raisin sauce

or spicy duck in filo pastry with apricot sauce. *Seats 40. L 12.30-2
D 7.30-10. Closed L Sat, all Sun & Mon 24-30 Dec. Set L £15.95
Set D £11.95/£14.95).* AMERICAN EXPRESS *Access, Diners, Visa.*

Sutton	Heen's	£50
Tel 081-643 1221		**R**ᵉ
14 Mulgrave Road Sutton Surrey SM2 6LE		Map 15 E3

Smartish Chinese restaurant opposite Sutton railway station, run by the
urbane John Man and his unusually communicative and attentive team.
Fresh lobster and crab (both kept live) are something of a speciality – each
is served either in black bean sauce, chili and garlic sauce or with ginger
and spring onion – on a menu that also includes the usual range from bang
bang chicken and crispy duck to stir-fried king prawns with orange and
various sizzling dishes. *Seats 80. Parties 30. L 12-2.30 D 6-11.15.
Closed 2 days at Christmas. Set L & D from £13 (min 2 persons).*
AMERICAN EXPRESS *Access, Diners, Visa.*

Sutton	Holiday Inn London Sutton	70%	£129
Tel 081-770 1311 Fax 081-770 1539			**H**
Gibson Road Sutton Surrey SM1 2RF			Map 15 E3

This redbrick town-centre hotel with ample free parking offers practical
and convenient accommodation. Well laid-out bedrooms have the usual
Holiday Inn virtues of large beds, plenty of well-lit work space and good
easy chairs around a substantial breakfast table. Bathrooms are user-friendly,
too, with thermostatically-controlled showers over tubs, good shelf space
and large towels. Executive Club bedrooms and suites have various extras
and include seven Study Rooms equipped with fax machines. There's
a separate staffed business centre. Four rooms are specially designed for
guests in wheelchairs. Good breakfasts; light snacks in the Balcony Lounge
overlooking the health and leisure club where there's a separate children's
splash pool. Modern conference facilities for up to 220. Children under 19
can share their parents' room at no charge; vast tariff reductions
at weekends. Ask for a map showing directions from M25. *Rooms 116.
Indoor swimming pool, spa bath, sauna, solarium, steam room, beautician,
keep-fit equipment, snooker, coffee shop (9am-6pm).* AMERICAN EXPRESS *Access,
Diners, Visa.*

Sutton	Partners Brasserie	£50
Tel 081-644 7743		**R**
23 Stonecot Hill Sutton Surrey SM3 9HB		Map 15 E3

In a parade of shops on the A24, this is the sister restaurant to *Partners West
Street* (see under Dorking), offering a nicely varied carte of well-thought-
out dishes: gratin of lobster and scallop in a Sauternes sauce, pasta noodles
with sun-dried tomatoes, roasted crispy duck with turnip dauphinois and
a port sauce, chargrilled sirloin with wild mushroom casserole, bread-and-
butter pudding with cinnamon custard, tangy lemon tart with raspberry
coulis. Sound cooking and friendly staff have earned a loyal local
following. Just 20 wines, but selected from around the world and
realistically priced. *Seats 32. Parties 12. L 12-2 D 7-9.30. Closed L Sat, all
Sun & Mon, 25 Dec-2 Jan. Set L & D £7.50/£9.95.* AMERICAN EXPRESS *Access,
Diners, Visa.*

Sutton	Places of Interest

Epsom Polo Club   Tel 0372 362593.
Epsom Racecourse   Tel 0372 726311.

Sutton Coldfield   Forte Travelodge

£45

Tel 021-355 0017

L

Boldmere Road Sutton Coldfield West Midlands B72 5UP

Map 6 C4

4 miles from both Junctions 5 and 6 of the M6. Situated on Boldmere
Road (B4142), off the A452, between Chester Road and Jockey Road.
2 miles from Sutton Coldfield and 6 miles from Birmingham. *Rooms 32.*
AMERICAN EXPRESS *Access, Diners, Visa.*

Sutton Coldfield   Moor Hall   62%

£90

Tel 021-378 2442   Fax 021-378 4637

H

Moor Hall Drive Four Oaks Sutton Coldfield West Midlands B75 6LN

Map 6 C4

In a rural setting, but handy for the motorway network, the extended
Edwardian building is surrounded by a golf course. It has its own leisure
centre, plus facilities for up to 200 delegates. There are two bars, and the
bedrooms include suites and Executive rooms. Families welcome.
Rooms 75. Garden, indoor swimming pool, gym, sauna, solarium.
AMERICAN EXPRESS *Access, Diners, Visa.*

Sutton Coldfield   New Hall   78%

£129

Tel 021-378 2442   Fax 021-378 4637

HR

Walmley Road Sutton Coldfield West Midlands B76 8QX

Map 6 C4

A mile or so south of town, off B4148, surrounded by 26 acres of beautiful
grounds, New Hall is said to be the country's oldest moated building.
Dating from the 13th century, the sympathetically restored house is now
a luxury hotel of some note. Though owned corporately by Mount
Charlotte Thistle, it is run along personal lines by Ian and Caroline Parkes,
who have an obvious love of the place. Day rooms include an elegantly
furnished lounge and feature panelling, ornate ceilings and latticed
windows. Bedrooms in the main house are largest and most are
sumptuously appointed, but the majority of rooms are in an unobtrusive
modern wing built around a courtyard. There is generally a high standard
of decor and furnishing; all the bathrooms are luxuriously fitted out.
Immaculately turned-out, professional staff. No children under eight.
A choice of sumptuous meeting rooms can accommodate up to 40
delegates. No dogs. Seven miles from Birmingham city centre; 10 miles
from the National Exhibition Centre. Guests can play golf,
by arrangement, at the Belfry. *Rooms 60. Garden, croquet, golf driving net,
putting, tennis, helipad.* AMERICAN EXPRESS *Access, Diners, Visa.*

Restaurant

£95

Mellow oak panelling, stone-mullioned windows with leaded lights
featuring some heraldic stained-glass, and quality table settings all add
to the appeal of the dining room. As we went to press (August) we heard
of the new appointment of head chef Simon Radley (previously at the
Chester Grosvenor) who will probably continue the French-influenced
modern English cooking style. The well-balanced and user-friendly wine
list offers a good choice between Europe and the New World; both the
Discovery and House sections have interesting wines at fair prices, and
there's a good showing of both half bottles and wines by the glass.
No smoking. *Seats 60. Parties 10. Private Room 15. L 12.30-2 (Sun to 2.15)
D 7-10 (Sun to 9.30). Closed L Sat. Set Sun L £16.50 Set D £25.45.*

Sutton Coldfield   **Penns Hall**   66%   £112

Tel 021-351 3111   Fax 021-313 1297   **H**

Penns Lane Walmley Sutton Coldfield West Midlands B76 8LH   **Map 6 C4**

Ample grounds with a splendid lake are the setting for Penns Hall, a 17th-century house carefully adapted and extended into a comfortable hotel and conference venue. A covered walkway across the lake leads to the Sebastian Coe Health Park, complete with running track. Special event facilities in a variety of rooms holding up to 650. Easy access from Junction 9 of the M42 (4 miles), linking to the M6 (J6) and M40 (J4). Jarvis. *Rooms 114. Garden, indoor swimming pool, squash, gym, spa bath, sauna, solarium, beauty salon, steam room, snooker, children's playground.* AMERICAN EXPRESS® *Access, Diners, Visa.*

Sutton Scotney North   **Forte Travelodge**   £45

Tel 0962 761016   **L**

Sutton Scotney North nr Winchester Hampshire S021 3JY   **Map 15 D3**

At the Northside Welcome Break service area on the A34 northbound, 8 miles east of Andover. Easy access to M3 and M4. *Rooms 31.* AMERICAN EXPRESS® *Access, Diners, Visa.*

Sutton Scotney South   **Forte Travelodge**   £45

Tel 0962 760779   **L**

Sutton Scotney South nr Winchester Hampshire SO21 3JY   **Map 15 D3**

At the Southside Welcome Break service area on the A34 southbound, 8 miles north of Winchester city centre. *Rooms 40.* AMERICAN EXPRESS® *Access, Diners, Visa.*

Swavesey   **Forte Travelodge**   £45

Tel 0954 789113   **L**

Cambridge Road Swavesey nr Cambridge Cambridgeshire   **Map 15 F1**

8 miles north-west of Cambridge on the eastbound carriageway of the A604. *Rooms 36.* AMERICAN EXPRESS® *Access, Diners, Visa.*

> Note that all telephone numbers with area codes starting with 0 will start 01 from 16 April 1995.

Swindon   **Blunsdon House**   69%   £93

Tel 0793 721701   Fax 0793 721056   **H**

Blunsdon Swindon Wiltshire SN2 4AD   **Map 14 C2**

From Junction 15 of the M4 take the A419 Cirencester road. After about 7 miles turn right to Broad Blunsdon. The driveway and frontage have recently enjoyed a face-lift, enhancing the first impression as you approach the hotel. A farm guest house in 1958, a country club in 1960, and a fully licensed hotel since 1962 – and the Clifford family have been here from the beginning. It's now a popular conference rendezvous (up to 300 delegates) with extensive leisure club facilities. There are ample lounges and bars, while all the bedrooms are reasonably roomy and many have pleasant views. Decoration and appointments are of smart modern business standard, and bathrooms all have shower attachments; some have spa baths. Families are well catered for; children up to 16 stay free in parents' room. No dogs. *Rooms 88. Garden, indoor swimming pool, children's splash pool, gym, squash, sauna, steam room, spa bath, solarium, beauty salon, tennis, golf (9), putting, games room, snooker, crèche.* AMERICAN EXPRESS® *Access, Diners, Visa.*

Swindon   **De Vere Hotel**   69%   £115

Tel 0793 878785   Fax 0793 877822   **H**

Shaw Ridge Leisure Park Whitehill Way Swindon Wiltshire SN5 7DW   Map 14 C2

Follow the signs to Shaw Ridge Leisure Park, some 2½ miles from the M4 (junction 16), or Link Centre. Brick-built and fronted by a clock tower and futuristic leisure club (recently expanded gym facilities), it offers extensive and well-equipped conference and banqueting areas. Two floors of well-equipped bedrooms are built around a central courtyard; half the bedrooms are reserved for non-smokers. Two rooms are specially equipped for disabled guests. 24hr room service. **Rooms** *154. Garden, indoor swimming pool, gym, sauna, steam room, spa bath, solarium, beauty salon, snooker, news kiosk, coffee shop (7.30am-10pm).* AMERICAN EXPRESS *Access, Diners, Visa.*

Swindon   **Forte Crest**   62%   £89

Tel 0793 831333   Fax 0793 831401   **H**

Oxford Road Stratton St Margaret Swindon Wiltshire SN3 4TL   Map 14 C2

Modern low-rise hotel on the A420, near the A419 roundabout. Very much geared-up to the need of the business traveller with secretarial services, in-house pager facilities, 24hr room service and meeting rooms for up to 50 people theatre-style. **Rooms** *91. Snooker.* AMERICAN EXPRESS *Access, Diners, Visa.*

Swindon   **Forte Posthouse**   63%   £68

Tel 0793 524601   Fax 0793 512887   **H**

Marlborough Road Swindon Wiltshire SN3 6AQ   Map 14 C2

70s' hotel set in five acres of grounds between Junction 15 of the M4 and the town centre. Three 80-seat conference rooms plus six 8-people syndicate rooms. **Rooms** *100. Garden, indoor swimming pool, keep-fit equipment, sauna, spa bath, solarium.* AMERICAN EXPRESS *Access, Diners, Visa.*

Swindon   **Swindon Marriott**   71%   £105

Tel 0793 512121   Fax 0793 513114   **H**

Pipers Way Swindon Wiltshire SN3 1SH   Map 14 C2

A modern purpose-built hotel standing in mature woodland next to a golf course. It's easily found when approaching from junction 15 of the M4, and only half a mile from the Old Town. Scandinavian-influenced public areas overlook the Leisure Area and are open-plan, with central beams and pine ceilings. Contemporary-style bedrooms have plenty of natural light and individual temperature control; children up to 16 stay free in parents' room. There are three suites and twelve rooms with king-size beds; 24hr room service is available. Conferences and banqueting for up to 280. Ample free parking. **Rooms** *153. Indoor swimming pool, keep-fit equipment, squash, sauna, spa bath, steam bath, solarium, beauty and hair salon, tennis, shop.* AMERICAN EXPRESS *Access, Diners, Visa.*

Swindon   **Wiltshire Hotel**   62%   £79

Tel 0793 528282   Fax 0793 541283   **H**

Fleming Way Swindon Wiltshire SN1 1TN   Map 14 C2

Swindon's only central hotel, a short walk from bus and railway stations and with ample free parking in an adjacent public car park. Meeting rooms from 22 to 230, with banqueting for up to 200. Mount Charlotte Thistle. **Rooms** *95.* AMERICAN EXPRESS *Access, Diners, Visa.*

Swindon   Places of Interest

Tourist Information   Tel 0793 530328/526161.
Wyvern Theatre   Tel 0793 24481.
Buscot Park (NT)   Faringdon Tel 0367 240786.
Great Western Railway Museum   Tel 0793 526161.
Swindon Town Football Ground   County Ground Tel 0793 430430.
Ice Rink Link Centre   Tel 0793 871212.

Swinfen   Swinfen Hall   70%   £85

Tel 0543 481494   Fax 0543 480341   **H**

Swinfen nr Lichfield Staffordshire WS14 9RS   **Map 6 C4**

Splendid Palladian mansion set back from the A38 about two miles south
of Lichfield. The ornate entrance hall is a 'wedding cake' confection
in cream, pale blue and gold with fluted columns supporting a minstrel's
gallery; beyond is a more restrained lounge with French windows opening
on to a fine stone terrace overlooking formal gardens. A leather
chesterfield-furnished bar is more Edwardian in style. First-floor bedrooms
tend to be spacious (some very) with reproduction antique furniture and
stylish fabrics, while those on the second floor are smaller with standardised
lightwood furniture but the same pleasing soft furnishings. Details of
repair (a number of fitted carpets need re-stretching for example) and
housekeeping need attention. Rooms are not serviced at night but there
is 24hr room service. No dogs. *Rooms 19. Garden, croquet. Closed 4 days
between Christmas and New Year.* AMERICAN EXPRESS *Access, Visa.*

Tadcaster   Forte Travelodge   £45

Tel 0973 531823   **L**

Tadcaster nr York North Yorkshire   **Map 7 D1**

On the eastbound carriageway of the A64, 7 miles south-west of York and
5 miles north-east of Tadcaster. *Rooms 40.* AMERICAN EXPRESS *Access,
Diners, Visa.*

We publish annually, so make sure you use the current edition.
It's worth it!

Tadworth   Gemini Restaurant   £55

Tel 0737 812179   **R**

28 Station Approach Tadworth Surrey KT20 5AH   **Map 15 E3**

Robert and Debbie Foster are now well established in their friendly little
restaurant located in a parade of shops near the station. Debbie is at front
of house while Robert concentrates on the kitchen, from where he produces
a selection of set price menus, in French style but described in English.
Typical dishes might be pan-fried sweetbreads and kidneys in a spring
onion sauce au gratin, or warm crab tartelette surrounded by baby leaves
and avocado, drizzled with a coriander vinaigrette as starters; then as main
courses stir-fry of monkfish, tiger prawns and scallops in a Pernod sauce
or breast of corn-fed guinea fowl on a bed of bubble and squeak with
whisky and almonds. For dessert try a rum and sultana crème brulée,
or a light mango bavarois mousse circled by its own sauce. English and
French cheeses are served with walnuts and apples. From Tuesday
to Thursday evenings it's possible to opt for just two courses at £17.50.
Traditional roast Sunday lunchtime. No children under 10. *Seats 40.
L 12-2 D 7-9.30. Closed L Sat, D Sun, Mon, 1 week after Christmas, 2 weeks
June. Set L £10.50/£12.50 (Sun £14.50) Set D £17.50 (Tues-Thurs
only)/£21.50. Access, Visa.*

Tamworth   Granada Lodge   £51

Tel 0827 260123   Fax 0827 260145   **L**

M42/A5 Junction 10 Tamworth Staffordshire B77 5PH   Map 6 C4

Rooms 63. AMERICAN EXPRESS® *Access, Diners, Visa.*

Tamworth   Travel Inn   £43

Tel 0827 54414   Fax 0827 310420   **L**

Bitterscote Bonehill Road Tamworth Staffordshire B78 3HQ   Map 6 C4

From Junction 9 of M42 take A446, following signs to Lichfield. After half a mile take A4091 Tamworth. Continue for approximately 6 miles on to a dual carriageway; at next roundabout take the fourth exit. *Rooms 40.* AMERICAN EXPRESS® *Access, Diners, Visa.*

Taplow   Cliveden   92%   £235

Tel 0628 668561   Fax 0628 661837   **H R**

Taplow nr Maidenhead Berkshire SL6 0JF   Map 15 E2

Where do you start when describing such a remarkable and majestic hotel as this? Its history – a former home of a Prince of Wales, several dukes and the Astor family, Cliveden (also a Stately Home and gardens owned by The National Trust, and therefore open to visitors at certain times) has been at the centre of Britain's social and political life for over three centuries. Its location – overlooking the Thames in the valley below and set in over 350 acres of parkland and gardens, with a series of estate walks, some winding down to the river, where the hotel's own launch and electric canoe are moored on the reach, one of the most beautiful and unspoilt stretches of the river. Naturally, the boats are available for hire, whether for a summer picnic, a barbecue on one of the hotel's islands or just a trip down (or up) the river. During the summer guests can join the daily 6pm champagne river trip before supper. Or the mansion itself, built in 1666, with the terrace, the dominant feature of the south facade, looking down on the 17th-century parterre, scene of the *son et lumière* due to commence in the summer of 1995. Inside, the magnificent Great Hall with its lavish carved wood interior and stone fireplace, an apt setting for the works of art, tapestries and armour; the main staircase; the panelled library (nice spot for afternoon tea); the Adam-style boudoir (once Nancy Astor's sitting room); the French Rococo dining room where the staff wear white gloves (start the day with a traditional English breakfast here); the east and west wing corridors – all featuring wonderful portraits and paintings. Even the *porte cochère* houses something interesting: George Bernard Shaw's silver-topped cane. Each air-conditioned bedroom and suite (four full, six 'junior' – given their size, a relative term!) have been named after someone connected to the house and are sumptuously and stylishly furnished and decorated, offering every conceivable need and luxury, including guest slippers. Bathrooms (most with his and hers washbasins) are simply stunning. Honeymooners even receive monogrammed bedside mats! In the suites you'll find a music centre and a video recorder (the hotel provides a very comprehensive video – plenty for the children too – and compact disc collection), not to mention fresh fruit, afternoon tea, and Bucks Fizz before supper. New this year is the Clutton wing, offering additonal bedrooms, the air-conditioned Macmillan meeting room, and Cliveden Club members-only restaurant, converted from the original stables, and retaining existing stalls and feeding troughs to create an authentic atmosphere. This wing connects with the Garden wing with its state-of-the-art and fully air-conditioned Churchill boardroom that opens directly on to its own terrace and overlooks the luxurious Pavilion Leisure complex (watch your step on the slippery surface surrounding the indoor pool!) with its own Conservatory restaurant, housed in the original walled garden. Children under 2 are not allowed to use the facilities at any time, those up to the age of 12 until noon. However, there is a crèche and organised programmes for them, though probably not riding the hotel's own horses. Service, from impeccably dressed staff, is outstanding, from the moment you pass the Fountain of Love, up the gravel approach after a long drive through the estate, to be met by tail-coated doormen; housekeeping is of the highest order. Banqueting for up to 160, conferences for 36. Even dogs are admirably catered for. **Rooms** *37. Garden, indoor and outdoor swimming pools, childrens' splash pool, hot tub, spa pool, saunas, plunge pool, steam room, gym, treatment rooms, hairdressing, croquet, indoor and outdoor tennis, squash, badminton, snooker, riding, coarse fishing, boating, valeting, laundry service, Bentley limousine.* AMERICAN EXPRESS *Access, Diners, Visa.*

Terrace Dining Room   £120

Once the main drawing room of the house, the setting here is undoubtedly one of the finest in the country with sweeping views across the parterre and for many miles beyond. Table settings are immaculate, service smooth, correct and professional. Cooking is a mixture of traditional English (Colchester oysters, Scotch salmon, grilled Dover sole with parsley butter, mixed grill, calf's liver and bacon, hot bread-and-butter pudding, summer pudding with elderflower ice cream) and classical French, offering such dishes as terrine of foie gras, fillet of sea bass with a truffle couscous and langoustine butter sauce, and roast corn-fed chicken with a truffle and morel cream sauce, with a hint of Mediterranean in the carpaccio of beef and fillets of red mullet with pesto noodles. Lots of seasonal changes – game (venison, grouse, snipe, partridge, pheasant or woodcock), shellfish, local vegetables and soft fruit and the hotel's new air-conditioned and temperature-controlled van makes daily trips to the markets, ensuring the freshest and best produce (see below). The varied wine list includes the excellent English Chiltern Valley wines, several (pricey!) vintage Australian Penfolds Grange wines, plenty of half bottles. No smoking. "A donation of £2 to The National Trust is charged to each guest. Service is neither included nor anticipated". Worthy winner of our Kitchen of the Year Award 1995. **Seats** *70. Parties 12. Private Room 50. L 12.30-2.30 D 7-10.30. Set L £26 (Sun £34) Set D £43.*

Waldo's   ★   £105

Of the hotel's two restaurants (this one has a separate kitchen), chef Ron Maxfield gives full rein to his talents here. This is his showcase, with cooking that is perhaps more modern and innovative than upstairs, relying on the finest ingredients. You descend a flight of stairs, pass a wall of old servants' bells, and enter a lobby adorned with photos of the rich and famous (kings and queens, dukes and duchesses, Chaplin, Roosevelt, Lloyd George and Shaw) who stayed at the house in the Astor period. In the Gents cloakroom there are drawings of Christine Keeler and Mandy Rice-Davies by Dr Stephen Ward – the main protagonists in the Profumo affair that led to the downfall of the Macmillan government in 1964. A pianist plays in the pine-panelled bar; the restaurant itself is small, intimate and clubby. Great attention is paid to presentation, and flavours are intense in such dishes as Cornish crab with lime and pimentos, grilled scallops and a warm potato and chive salad; lasagne of lobster and langoustine with a truffle-scented dressing; or grilled fillet of Scotch beef with smoked foie gras, girolles and artichokes poivrade. Puddings (a hot mirabelle soufflé with liquorice ice cream or warm caramelised apple and filo pastry tart on a bilberry sauce with cinnamon ice cream) are splendid creations and show Ron's team's talents to the full. Same wine list and contributions as the dining room. No smoking. **Seats** *26. Parties 6. D only 7-10.30. Closed Sun & Mon. Set D £40, £47 & £60.*

Taunton	**The Castle**	**76%**	**£102**
Tel 0823 272671 Fax 0823 336066			**H R**
Castle Green Taunton Somerset TA1 1NF			Map 13 E2

You will not find a more quintessentially English hotel than this. Steeped in history, the original Norman castle (note the West front clad with burgeoning wisteria at the right time of year) dates back many centuries, and inside there's a careful balance of the old and the new. Handsome stonework, tapestries, English chintz and fine art all feature in the evocative public areas; the great oak staircase adds to the feeling of grandeur. Such surroundings deserve the highest standards of service, and you will not be disappointed here. The first evidence of this is when greeted on arrival by charmingly friendly and efficient staff; they are obviously well motivated, mainly due to the fact that two generations of the Chapman family (with Kit at the helm) have been in situ and know how things should be done. Of necessity (it's hard to modernise and knock down 15-foot thick walls), not all the bedrooms are as spacious and plush as the Bow or garden suites with their deep sofas, canopied beds and heavy fabrics, indeed some of the singles are on the small side, though they are all smartly furnished and decorated in their own individual style with those extra bits and bobs to make your stay even more comfortable. Good bathrooms (with decent toiletries) invite a long soak! Cars can be pampered as well: locked in the garage for a tenner or washed for a fiver! *Rooms 35. Garden.* AMERICAN EXPRESS *Access, Diners, Visa.* MARTELL COGNAC

Restaurant   ★ ↑   £80

Phil Vickery, here since 1990, is maintaining the great Castle tradition for fine British cooking. There's a wide choice of menus, all dependent on first-rate suppliers (deservedly listed for all to see – if you like the cheese for instance you'll know where to get it from) and written in straightforward, unpretentious English. From the simplest luncheon could come chilled plum tomato and tarragon soup with herb cream, braised ox tongue with gherkins and walnut oil creamed potatoes, plus a summer pudding with clotted cream. Move on to the higher-priced menus and you might find some more exotic influences at work: seared salmon with a spice crust, couscous and spring onion crème fraiche (and that's just a starter!); grilled red mullet with pasta ribbons and cherry tomato dressing or braised shoulder of lamb with thyme, garlic and spring vegetables. There's a fine British cheeseboard and some splendid desserts, as you would expect from the winning creator of our 1995 Dessert of the Year. Look out for baked egg custard tart with nutmeg ice cream, rhubarb and walnut crumble or hot chocolate pudding with bitter chocolate sauce. Service from a young and committed team is most professional. Sunday lunch is a traditional 3-course meal with roast sirloin of beef and Yorkshire pudding as the centrepiece. More informal lunchtime eating (not Sunday) in the Minstrel's Bar. A marvellously informative, clear and well-presented wine list has great depth. The house and table wines offer remarkable value, but then the entire list is most fairly priced; even the simplest suppliers get a mention. No smoking. *Seats 60. Private Room 28. L 12.30-2 D 7.30-9. Set L £14.50/£16.50 & £28.50/£32.50 (Sun £16.50, children half price) Set D £19.90/£23.90 & £28.50/£32.50.*

Taunton	**County Hotel**	**61%**	**£81**
Tel 0823 337651	Fax 0823 334517		**H**
East Street Taunton Somerset TA1 3LT			Map 13 E2

Usefully located in the town centre, this white-fronted former coaching inn offers comfortable Superior rooms, more functional Standards, and convenient free parking. Extensive conference facilities seating up to 400, and banqueting for up to 350. Forte Heritage. *Rooms 66.* AMERICAN EXPRESS *Access, Diners, Visa.*

Taunton	**Forte Posthouse**	**66%**	**£68**
Tel 0823 332222	Fax 0823 332266		**H**
Deane Gate Avenue Taunton Somerset TA1 2UA			Map 13 E2

Two miles from the town centre, close to Junction 25 of the M5. Modern conference facilties for up to 280. *Rooms 97. Keep-fit equipment, sauna.* AMERICAN EXPRESS *Access, Diners, Visa.*

Taunton — Porters Wine Bar — £40

Tel 0823 256688   **R**

49 East Reach Taunton Somerset TA1 3EX   Map 13 E2

The menu changes several times a week, offering straightforward, enjoyable dishes such as chicken liver and port paté, deep-fried Camembert with redcurrant and raspberry sauce, lasagne with salad and sautées, loin of pork Normandy and red mullet fillets with ginger and spring onions. Three vegetarian choices; sticky toffee pudding a favourite sweet. A dozen wines available by the glass. Four courtyard tables in good weather and a non-smoking area to the rear of the restaurant. *Seats 50. Parties 30. L 12-2 D 7-9.45. Closed L Sat, all Sun, Bank Holidays. Access, Visa.*

Taunton — Travel Inn — £43

Tel 0823 321112   Fax 0823 322054   **L**

81 Bridgwater Road Taunton Somerset TA1 2DU   Map 13 E2

Close to Junction 25 of the M5. *Rooms 40.* AMERICAN EXPRESS *Access, Diners, Visa.*

Taunton — Places of Interest

Tourist Information   Tel 0823 274785.
Brewhouse Theatre   Tel 0823 83244.
Forde Abbey and Gardens   Nr Chard Tel 0460 20231.
Hestercombe House and Gardens   Cheddon Fitzpaine Tel 0823 337222.
Somerset County Museum   Tel 0823 255504.
County Cricket Ground   Tel 0823 272946.
Royal Naval Equestrian Association   Orchard House, Hatch Beauchamp Tel 0823 480223.
Taunton Racecourse   Tel 0823 337172.
Wellington Sports Centre   Wellington Tel 0823 473010.
Cricket St. Thomas Wildlife Park   Chard Tel 0460 30755.

Teffont Evias — Howard's House Hotel — 68% — £108

Tel 0722 716392   Fax 0722 716820   **HR**

Teffont Evias Dinton nr Salisbury Wiltshire SP3 5RJ   Map 14 C3

In a sleepy hamlet of medieval origins the families Firmin and Ford have studiously converted their Tudor stone farmhouse into a very comfortable private house hotel. They are direct descendants of Christopher Mayne, who bought the manor in 1692 (it was built some 70 years earlier). Two acres of gardens now provide flowers for bedrooms and day rooms, as well as herbs for the kitchen. A little gem of a place. *Rooms 8. Garden, croquet.* AMERICAN EXPRESS *Access, Diners, Visa.* MARTELL COGNAC

Restaurant — £75

Paul Firmin's fixed-price dinner menus, which offer six or more choices per course, are well balanced and carefully executed. You might start with marinated pigeon breasts with calvados jus and a compote of apples and onions, or mousseline of prawns with cucumber and a shellfish beurre blanc, before moving on to pan-fried scallops with coriander and a niçoise vinaigrette, or noisettes of lamb with spiced beans, tomato, thyme and a red wine jus. Finish with pear and almond tart with amaretto crème anglaise, or blackcurrant mousse with shortbread and a liquorice cream. The wine list is carefully compiled, concise and very fairly priced. Five tables on a terrace for outdoor eating. *Seats 34. L (Sun only) 12.30-2 D 7.30-10. Set L £17.50 Set D £29.50/£32.50.*

Teignmouth — Thomas Luny House

£60
PH

Tel 0626 772976

Teign Street Teignmouth Devon TQ14 8EG

Map 13 D3

Built by the marine artist Thomas Luny in the late 18th century, this small Georgian town house has been charmingly restored by John and Alison Allan. This means that one is essentially a guest in their home, socialising with them and fellow guests in the well-appointed drawing room that displays family photos, and sharing the non-smoking evening meal around a large polished dining table. The simple, carefully prepared set dinner (£14.50 – for residents and their guests only) is a joint effort by the Allens and there is a short, modestly-priced list of wines. Four antique-furnished bedrooms have been decorated with great style and quality and have excellent co-ordinating bathrooms (one has shower and WC only). All rooms have direct-dial telephones and remote-control TV, plus homely touches like fresh flowers, books and mineral water. It all adds up to a delightful alternative to a conventional hotel. Follow signs to the quay and turn into Teign Street just before the port entrance. The room rate includes afternoon tea. No children under 12. No dogs. *Rooms 4. Garden. Closed mid Dec-1st Feb. No credit cards.*

Telford — Forte Travelodge

£45
L

Tel 0952 251244

Admaston Road Shawbirch Crossroads Telford Shropshire TF1 3QA

Map 6 B3

On the A5223 at the junction of the A442 and B5063, 2 miles from Junction 6 of the M54. 6 miles north-west of Telford town centre. *Rooms 40.* AMERICAN EXPRESS *Access, Diners, Visa.*

Telford — Holiday Inn Telford/Ironbridge   68%

£109
H

Tel 0952 292500   Fax 0952 291949

St Quentin Gate Telford Shropshire TF3 4EH

Map 6 B3

With easy access to the M54 (Junction 4) and town centre, this modern low-riser is adjacent to Telford Racquet and Exhibition Centre. Business centre serves conferences (max 290) and banqueting up to 180. Health and leisure club. Ample free parking. *Rooms 100. Indoor swimming pool, gym, sauna, spa bath, steam room, solarium, beautician.* AMERICAN EXPRESS *Access, Diners, Visa.*

Our inspectors are full-time employees; they are professionally trained by us.

Telford — Madeley Court   67%

£90
H

Tel 0952 680068   Fax 0952 684275

Madeley Telford Shropshire TF7 5DW

Map 6 B3

Public areas, which include a small oak-panelled lounge/bar, are in the oldest (13th-century) part of a predominantly Elizabethan hotel that, although within the Madeley area of Telford, is next to a small lake and has a rural setting. Bedrooms are divided between eight characterful, antique-furnished, historic rooms in the old building (two in a 16th-century gatehouse) and those in the new East and South wings, the former with rag-rolled fitted units, the latter with darkwood freestanding furniture. Individually decorated, and in some style, all rooms have neat bathrooms (just hand-held showers with the tubs in all except the South wing rooms) and jugs of iced water. Conference facilities (capacity 200) are in a converted 16th-century mill. *Rooms 47. Patio.* AMERICAN EXPRESS *Access, Diners, Visa.*

Telford   Moat House   67%   £94

Tel 0952 291291   Fax 0952 292012   **H**

Forgegate Telford Shropshire TF3 4NA   Map 6 B3

Close to the town centre and easily accessible from the motorways, this is a modern hotel with good conference (12 rooms catering for up to 500 delegates) and leisure facilities. Comfortable atrium lounge and Forgegate Bar. Children up to 16 free in parents' room. *Rooms 148. Indoor swimming pool, gym, sauna, spa bath, solarium.* AMERICAN EXPRESS *Access, Diners, Visa.*

Telford   Telford Hotel Golf & Country Club   64%   £94

Tel 0952 585642   Fax 0952 586602   **H**

Great Hay Sutton Hill Telford Shropshire TF7 4DT   Map 6 B3

Standing south of the town centre above Ironbridge Gorge, the hotel combines comfortable, modern accommodation with golf and country club facilities and a state-of-the-art conference centre for up to 200 delegates. Under-16s stay free in parents' room; good family facilities at weekends (the hotel is convenient for the seven Ironbridge museums), plus a children's menu and play area in the Racquets coffee shop. Queens Moat Houses. *Rooms 86. Garden, indoor swimming pool, gym, golf course, golf driving range, spa bath, sauna, solarium, steam room, hair and beauty salons, coffee shop (9am-9.30pm).* AMERICAN EXPRESS *Access, Diners, Visa.*

Telford   Places of Interest

Tourist Information   Tel 0952 291370.
Benthall Hall (NT)   Broseley Tel 0952 882159.
Ironbridge Gorge Museum   Tel 0952 453522.
Telford Ice Rink   Tel 0952 291511.
Telford Ski Slope   Tel 0952 586791.

Tetbury   Calcot Manor   75%   £115

Tel 0666 890391   Fax 0666 890394   **HR**

Tetbury Gloucestershire GL8 8YJ   Map 14 B2

A warm welcome awaits you at this fine hotel, situated in secluded grounds, three miles west of Tetbury on the A4135. The manor house complex, built of Cotswold stone, dates in part from the 14th century. The atmosphere is one of peaceful relaxation: spacious lounges, opening on to terraces and lawns, are tastefully decorated and furnished with deep armchairs and sofas; gentle log fires further soften the scene. The bedrooms vary in size from large (de luxe) to very adequate (standard), and are in the throes of being re-decorated to a very high standard. The best have bathrooms with spa baths, and luxurious bath robes. Some particularly characterful rooms are in former stables set around a courtyard that boasts a new fountain and arbour feature. Also new this year are four splendid family suites which have been created out of an old barn (leaving the tranquil atmosphere of the main house undisturbed), with high-tech features such as "piped" children's videos and sophisticated baby-listening devices, alongside Beatrix Potter books. An enclosed garden adjacent to the family rooms has a play "train". Children's high teas are served from 5.30pm. No dogs. Banqueting/conference facilities for up to 60/40. *Rooms 20. Garden, outdoor swimming pool.* AMERICAN EXPRESS *Access, Diners, Visa.*

Restaurant   £60

New chef Alec Howard has now established a short carte designed to please both the adventurous and those with simpler tastes. The Italian Pink dining room, candle-lit in the evening, with a splendid butcher's table (where the home-made bread is displayed and cut) and linen napery, gives him the perfect stage. Fresh fish from Cornwall, local organic beef and a well-kept British cheeseboard show his enthusiasm. For dinner, double-baked cheese soufflé with mustard sauce (light and delicious) and maize-fed chicken with turnip gratin and a garlic sauce are two dishes that dwell in the memory. Desserts might include bread-and-butter pudding with cinnamon custard, or chocolate marquise with a grapefruit and orange sauce. Simple one-course lunches are available in addition to the à la carte; and a good selection of wines by the glass. Knowledgable and friendly service. A terrace provides 4 tables for outdoor eating. No smoking in the dining room. *Seats 50. Private Room 35. L 12.30-2 D 7.30-9.30. Set Sun L £15.*

Tetbury	The Close	72%	£88

Tel 0666 502272   Fax 0666 504401

8 Long Street Tetbury Gloucestershire GL8 8AQ

Map 14 B2

The original house was built in the 16th century for a local wool merchant and became a hotel in 1974. It presents a relatively modest face to the main street, but the rear elevation, which forms one side of a delightful walled garden hidden away from the market-town bustle, is more impressive. Rag, drag and stipple painting take the eye in the day rooms and in the bedrooms, which vary in size and shape; some feature old beams, one is in Art Deco style, none lacks in comfort. Beds are turned down at night. 22 car parking spaces at the rear of the hotel. Now managed by Virgin's Voyager Hotels. No dogs. *Rooms 15. Garden, croquet.* AMERICAN EXPRESS *Access, Diners, Visa.*

Tetbury	Snooty Fox Hotel	69%	£80

Tel 0666 502436   Fax 0666 503479

Market Place Tetbury Gloucestershire GL8 8DD

Map 14 B2

A 16th-century former coaching inn with steep stone gables and original wooden pillars, the Snooty Fox stands in the town centre opposite the Market House. Lounge space is plentiful and the two rooms (one for non-smokers) are peaceful and traditional in character with deep sofas, magazines, oil paintings and prints of the Beaufort Hunt, with which the hotel has long associations. The bar, with its imposing copper fire hood, is a contrastingly lively spot and a popular locals' rendezvous for its real ales and 'Snooty Snacks'. Family antiques and portraits continue the period tone in the individually designed bedrooms, all of which are upstairs – where little extras like a basket of fruit, jar of sweets and bottles of mineral water are typical thoughtful touches. The bathrooms are carpeted and light, and boast luxurious bathrobes and towels. No dogs. Hatton Hotels. *Rooms 12.* AMERICAN EXPRESS *Access, Diners, Visa.*

Tetbury   Places of Interest

Tourist Information   Tel 0666 503552.
Chavenage House   Tel 0666 502329.
Beauford Polo Club   Down Farm, Westonbirt Tel 0666 88214.

Tewkesbury	Royal Hop Pole	66%	£95

Tel 0684 293236   Fax 0684 296680

Church Street Tewkesbury Gloucestershire GL20 5RT

Map 14 B1

One of the smaller hotels in the Forte chain, and one of the oldest in the county, the Royal Hop Pole is mentioned by Charles Dickens in *The Pickwick Papers*. Sympathetic conversion has provided an elegant drawing room and rear-facing bar. Best of the bedrooms feature a four-poster and executive extras, but many may plump for the oak-beamed character of the older rear bedrooms, where bathroom space is at a premium. A walled garden runs down to the River Avon and the hotel's private mooring. *Rooms 29. Garden, mooring.* AMERICAN EXPRESS *Access, Diners, Visa.*

Tewkesbury   Tewkesbury Park   62%   £93

Tel 0648 295405   Fax 0684 292386   **H**

Lincoln Green Lane Tewkesbury Gloucestershire GL20 7DN   **Map 14 B1**

Just 5 minutes from Junction 9 of the M5, Tewkesbury Park is more country club than country house, and conferences (up to 150 people) are big business. Well-appointed bedrooms afford views of the Malvern Hills. Good facilities for families with a supervised crèche in the leisure club throughout the week. Chidren's playroom and playground. Children up to 16 free in parents' room. No dogs. Country Club Hotels. *Rooms 78. Garden, indoor swimming pool, gym, squash, sauna, steam room, spa bath, solarium, beauty salon, tennis, golf, snooker, coffee shop (10am-10.30pm).* AMERICAN EXPRESS *Access, Diners, Visa.*

Thame   Spread Eagle   65%   £84

Tel 0844 213661   Fax 0844 261380   **H**

Cornmarket Thame Oxfordshire OX9 2BW   **Map 15 D2**

A square-fronted redbrick former coaching inn standing in the centre of town. To the rear is ample free car parking as well as the reception. Public rooms are divided between the small lounge area in the entrance lobby and the quite separate bars across the cobbled yard in the original part of the hotel. Decor throughout is mellow and quite in keeping with the hotel's character. Bedrooms in the main house have period charm while bedrooms in a wing extending into the car park have the advantage of French windows which open on to a sunny, west-facing lawn and flower beds. Equipped with the usual trappings of a modern hotel, the rooms are well maintained and staff give the impression of being only too willing to please. One bedroom is equipped for disabled guests. 24hr room service. Children under 15 are accommodated free of charge in parents' room, but there are also special rates for adjoining rooms. Tariff reductions Fri-Sun. Also banqueting suites and syndicate rooms holding up to 250. No dogs. *Rooms 33. Garden. Closed 28-30 Dec.* AMERICAN EXPRESS *Access, Diners, Visa.*

Thetford   The Bell   62%   £83

Tel 0842 754455   Fax 0842 755552   **H**

King Street Thetford Norfolk IP24 2AZ   **Map 10 C2**

An old coaching inn overlooking the Ouse with many architectural features dating back to the 15th century. Bedrooms in the old part are beamed, several boasting four-posters; wing rooms are more up-to-date. No charge for under-16s sharing parents' room. The function facility houses banqueting for 60, conferences up to 80. Forte Heritage. *Rooms 47. Terrace, coffee shop (10-5).* AMERICAN EXPRESS *Access, Diners, Visa.*

Thetford   Places of Interest

Euston Hall   Thetford Tel 0842 766377.
Kilverstone Wildlife Park   Tel 0842 755369.
Snetterton Motor Racing Circuit   Snetterton Tel 095 387 303.

Thornaby-on-Tees   Forte Posthouse   60%   £68

Tel 0642 591213   Fax 0642 594989   **H**

Low Lane by Stainton Village nr Thornaby-on-Tees Cleveland TS17 9LW   **Map 5 E3**

An older-style Posthouse in the village of Stainton. 70 of the bedrooms are designated non-smoking. Conferences for up to 100 delegates. Ample free parking. *Rooms 135. Garden, sunbeds.* AMERICAN EXPRESS *Access, Diners, Visa.*

Thornbury   **Thornbury Castle**   **80%**   £105

Tel 0454 281182   Fax 0454 416188   **H**

Thornbury nr Bristol Avon BS12 1HH   Map 13 F1

History abounds at Thornbury Castle, its gardens and vineyard surrounded
by high walls. Henry VIII appropriated the castle as a royal demesne for
many years, after which Mary Tudor spent some time here before
returning it to the descendants of the original owner, the Duke
of Buckingham. Bedrooms, some reached via stone and spiral staircases, are
full of character with many features (Tudor fireplaces, oriel windows,
shutters, intricate ceilings) retained. Several, with fine views, have four-
poster beds decked out with bold country fabrics; all greet arriving guests
with a bowl of fruit and decanter of sherry, and provide good bathrooms
offering pampering extras. Baronial public rooms (candle-lit each evening,
which adds to the atmosphere) are impressive, none more than the panelled
lounge with its magnificent stone fireplace, high mullioned windows and
Tudor portraits on the walls. The room rate quoted above is the minimum
for a twin/double; de luxe rooms are priced at £200. No children under
12. No dogs. Convenient motorway access from M4 (J20/21) and
M5 (J14/16). *Rooms 18. Garden, croquet, helipad. Closed 2 days early Jan.*
AMERICAN EXPRESS *Access, Diners, Visa.*

Thornton Heath   **Mamma Adele**   £50

Tel 081-683 2233   **R**

23 Brigstock Road Thornton Heath Surrey CR7 7JJ   Map 11 B5

An agreeable little family restaurant with a real taste of Italy. Kam Memon
runs front of house with urbane good humour, and Adele is always happy
to prepare a full meal or just a plate of pasta (the latter includes not only
familiar variations but some one-offs such as vodka and Stilton). Seasonal
specials add to the choice, and there's always something for vegetarians.
Leave room for Mamma's home-made sweets. The wine list includes plenty
of decent Italian bottles. *Seats 32. L 12-2.30 D 6.30-10.30 (Sat 7-11.30).
Closed L Mon & Sat, all Sun, Bank Holidays, 2 weeks Jan. Set meals £12.95.*
AMERICAN EXPRESS *Access, Diners, Visa.*

Thornton-le-Fylde   **River House**   £75

Tel 0253 883497   Fax 0253 892083   **RR**

Skippool Creek Thornton-le-Fylde nr Blackpool Lancashire FY5 5LF   Map 6 A1

"To invite a person into your house is to take charge of their happiness for
as long as they are under your roof" is how the River House's brochure
begins. Not, perhaps an original sentiment but a sincere one, especially
as manifested at Bill and Carole Scott's very original establishment. It enjoys
a delightful location opposite Skippool Creek and offers confidently cooked
food in a relaxed setting. The menu's influence is French, and though some
menu favourites recur there's always plenty of choice. Try perhaps salmon
Angélique (goujons of salmon with a white wine and cream sauce), then
eye of loin of lamb with a light garlic and rosemary sauce, followed
by a rib-stickingly good English steamed pudding. Bill's menu comes with
the proviso of availability being dependant on supply, so you can be sure
that if it's on, it's good, and if possible it will be home-made. The wine list
is extensive, interesting and very reasonably priced. *Seats 40. Parties 30.
Private Room 12. L & D by arrangement. Set L & D £18.50 (Sun L £12.75).
Closed D Sun, some Bank Holidays. Access, Visa.*

Rooms   £100

Five individually decorated and named rooms offer traditional comfort and
modern amenities. Well-behaved children are welcome. *Garden, croquet.*

Thrapston — Forte Travelodge — £45

Tel 0832 735199

L

Thrapston Bypass Thrapston Northamptonshire

Map 7 E4

On the A14 (the new A1/M1 link road), 8 miles east of Kettering. Corby 8 miles, Wellingborough 10 miles. *Rooms 40.* AMERICAN EXPRESS ® *Access, Diners, Visa.*

Thrussington — Forte Travelodge — £45

Tel 0664 424525

L

Thrussington Leicestershire LE7 8TF

Map 7 D3

On the A46 southbound, 8 miles north of Leicester city centre. *Rooms 32.* AMERICAN EXPRESS ® *Access, Diners, Visa.*

Thundridge — Hanbury Manor — 85% — £161

Tel 0920 487722   Fax 0920 487692

HR

Thundridge nr Ware Hertfordshire SG12 0SD

Map 15 F1

A very handsome and substantial Jacobean-style mansion surrounded by 200 acres of golf course and mature parkland. Its varied history includes a period as a convent during which additional wings and a cloister were added. A long, sweeping drive leads directly from the A10 to the front entrance, where a valet is on hand to park your car. A genuinely warm greeting is extended in the entrance hall, to the right of which is the magnificent galleried oak hall with its huge tapestries, open fireplace, panelled walls and lofty ceiling from whose beams are suspended immense crystal chandeliers. The library serves as a peaceful retreat during the day but in the evening it is often used as an overflow for the splendidly elegant bar with its pale cream walls and richly coloured upholstery. Bedrooms include 25 fine suites; all have good views over the grounds and are furnished with impeccable taste. Each is thoughtfully equipped with the likes of mini-bar, trouser press and hairdryer, with dressing gowns in the superb marble bathrooms. The latter have bidets in some and good quality toiletries are common to all. One bedroom has been adapted for use by disabled guests. The hotel boasts a palatial indoor swimming pool and leisure complex that rivals the best. Very friendly, obliging staff. 24hr room service. Children up to 12 share parents' room free. Conference and banqueting facilities for up to 150 in a selection of ten rooms including the unusual Poles Hall. One night's deposit is requested to guarantee accommodation. 25 miles from central London. *Rooms 96. Garden, croquet, golf (18), tennis, squash, putting, indoor swimming pool, spa bath, sauna, solarium, gym, snooker, beautician, crèche, news kiosk, helipad.* AMERICAN EXPRESS ® *Access, Diners, Visa.*

Zodiac Restaurant and Conservatory — £125

The Zodiac room features fine oil paintings and a splendid plaster ceiling, which, with careful scrutiny, reveals the twelve signs. Open for dinner only, it offers a complex and elaborate menu with Albert Roux of Le Gavroche as consultant and Rory Kennedy the Executive Chef. Sauces are greatly reduced, resulting in intense, attention-grabbing flavours. Oysters, gently warmed and meltingly soft, are served in the shell with a rich, creamy wild mushroom and sorrel sauce, while red mullet fillets are served cooked in a highly-seasoned oil with deep-fried aubergine slices. Less successful on a recent visit was a fillet of veal accompanied by a very dark, powerful sauce that lacked sophistication and sadly unbalanced the dish. The sweets were a slightly disappointing selection of fruit tarts and millefeuilles or an à la carte selection that included a gateau St Honoré with too-thick custard-filled choux balls and a hard toffee-covered biscuit base. A vegetarian menu is available. Better news on the wine front: a much-improved and informative wine list has helpful notes and includes several French collections (Krug, Latour, Domaine de la Romanée-Conti) as well as a good New World showing; there are plenty of half bottles and the best growers are well represented – this is an outstanding list, even going so far as to preview wines purchased for the future. Regional winner for the Home Counties of our Cellar of the Year award 1995. *The Conservatory* restaurant opens for breakfast, lunch and some dinners. It offers a lighter version of the dinner menu in bright, airy surroundings with views over the golf course. Risotto with calf's liver, garlic and parsley and roast halibut with root vegetables and red wine ginger sauce are typical. Booking is essential. Light snacks may be taken in all-day *Vardon's* (10am-10pm) above the health club; outdoor eating on a terrace. "5% service is included in menu prices." No smoking in the restaurants. No children under 8 in the Zodiac restaurant. *Seats 40. Parties 8. Private Room 8. D 7.30-9.30 (Fri & Sat from 7, to 9.45). Closed D Sun except Bank Holiday weekends. Set D £25 & £45.*

Thurlestone	Thurlestone Hotel	69%	£162
Tel 0548 560382 Fax 0548 561069			H
Thurlestone Kingsbridge Devon TQ7 3NN			Map 13 D3

The elegance of the 20s combines with the amenities of the 90s in a handsome family-owned hotel in a lovely setting with spectacular sea views. Splendidly geared to family holidays (particularly at half-term breaks, when dancing, competitions, film shows and parties are all laid on), with an excellent leisure club; the hotel also has an off-peak trade in conferences (for up to 140). Day rooms make the most of the location, likewise half the smart, well-equipped bedrooms. Accommodation is graded as de luxe (sea view, video player, private bar, undercover parking, no dogs allowed), sea view and country view. Children up to 12 can stay free of charge in their parents' room, but a minimum charge of £12 is made for breakfast and children's supper. Gentlemen are requested to wear jackets and ties for dinner in the (no-smoking) restaurant. Ample parking. *Rooms 68. Garden, indoor & outdoor swimming pools, gym, squash, sauna, solarium, beauty & hair salon, tennis, golf (9), putting, badminton, games room, snooker, children's playroom and playground, coffee shop (8am-10pm), helipad. Access, Visa.*

Thurrock	Granada Lodge		£59
Tel 0708 891111 Fax 0708 860971			L
M25 Junction 30/31 Dartford Crossing Thurrock Essex RM16 3BG			Map 11 B5

Rooms 35. AMERICAN EXPRESS *Access, Diners, Visa.*

Tickton	Tickton Grange	62%	£60
Tel 0964 543666 Fax 0964 542556			H
Tickton nr Beverley Humberside HU17 9SH			Map 7 E1

A family-owned Georgian house standing just off the A1035 east of Beverley in 3½ acres of rose gardens, where afternoon teas are served in the summer. Day rooms retain a traditional appeal, and bedrooms are decorated in a fresh, light style. There are two suites, one with a Georgian four-poster bed. Tickton truffles are offered as a welcome. The Whymant family run the hotel along friendly and informal lines. *Rooms 18. Garden, croquet.* AMERICAN EXPRESS *Access, Diners, Visa.*

Tintagel	Trebrea Lodge	66%	£62
Tel 0840 770410			HR
Trenale Tintagel Cornwall PL34 0HR			Map 12 B2

A little inland from the village on a slight rise, this civilised country hotel dates back 600 years, although the facade is Georgian. It's furnished throughout with antiques (one of the partners owns an antique shop in London); there's an elegant and sunny first-floor drawing room and cosy 'honesty' bar (the only place in the house apart from one bedroom where one may smoke) where a log fire burns for most of the year. Appealing bedrooms, all enjoying fine views across fields to the sea in the distance, are individually decorated, with good bathrooms; about half have shower and WC only. One room has recently been graced with a four-poster. No smoking. No children under 5. *Rooms 7. Garden.* AMERICAN EXPRESS® *Access, Visa.*

Restaurant   £40

Dinner, served at 8pm in the small candle-lit oak-panelled dining room, is a simple no-choice affair that allows the excellent, often local, ingredients to speak for themselves. A typical menu might be tarragon eggs *en cocotte*, grilled lamb chops with redcurrant, orange and mint sauce, apples with orange caramel sauce and Cornish Yarg and Stilton. Chef/proprietor Sean Devlin numbers marinated home-cured beef among his specialities. The short wine list has no half bottles but good house wine is available by the glass. *Seats 14. Set D £14.75.*

Tiverton Forte Travelodge	£45
Tel 0884 821087	**L**
Sampford Peverell Service Area nr Tiverton Devon EX16 7HD	Map 13 D2

At Junction 27 of the M5, 7 miles east of Tiverton. *Rooms 40.* AMERICAN EXPRESS® *Access, Diners, Visa.*

Toddington Granada Lodge	£51
Tel 0525 875150 Fax 0525 878452	**L**
Toddington Service Area M1 Southbound nr Dunstable Bedfordshire LU5 6HR	Map 15 E1

Rooms 43. AMERICAN EXPRESS® *Access, Diners, Visa.*

Tonbridge Goldhill Mill	£65
Tel 0732 851626 Fax 0732 851881	**PH**
Golden Green Hadlow Tonbridge Kent TN11 0BA	Map 11 B5

Check directions when booking at this superior bed-and-breakfast hotel with luxurious accommodation. Originally a watermill, it enjoys an idyllic location beside a river surrounded by twenty acres including mature gardens and ponds containing freshwater crayfish (a breakfast speciality in summer months). Amiable hosts Shirley and Vernon Cole ensure that you relax in what has been their family home since the late 1930s. The house is stylishly decorated – a beamed farmhouse kitchen (used for breakfast) resplendent with working mill wheel, a drawing room with wood-burning stove, a small TV/video lounge. Three individually decorated bedrooms (non-smoking, like the rest of the house) beautifully furnished in chintzy soft furnishings offer an abundance of extras, remote-control TVs, bowls of fruit and fresh floral displays. One room has a four-poster. Lavishly appointed bathrooms include jacuzzi baths in two rooms and excellent toiletries. In the grounds, the Ciderpass Cottage is open all year for self-catering accommodation. No children or dogs. *Rooms 3. Garden, croquet, floodlit tennis court. Closed 15 Jul-31 Aug. Access, Visa.*

Tonbridge Rose & Crown 59%	£79
Tel 0732 357966 Fax 0732 357194	**H**
125 High Street Tonbridge Kent TN9 1DD	Map 11 B5

A 16th-century coaching inn with traditionally furnished bedrooms in the old part, modern rooms in the garden wing. 20 of the rooms are designated non-smoking. Children up to 16 stay free in parents' room. Conference/banqueting facilities for 120/80. Forte Heritage. *Rooms 50. Garden.* AMERICAN EXPRESS® *Access, Diners, Visa.*

Torquay | Grand Hotel | 68% | £115

Tel 0803 296677   Fax 0803 213462
Sea Front Torquay Devon TQ2 6NT

Map 13 D3

Large, white-painted Edwardian hotel where Agatha Christie
honeymooned, on the seafront just 100 yards from Torquay railway
station. Recently refurbished bedrooms have a variety of pleasant colour
schemes, good easy chairs and darkwood furniture. There are sea-views
from about half the rooms, of which those designated 'Riviera' are the most
spacious. Beds are turned down at night and room service is 24hrs. Glass-
fronted display cabinets feature in the entrance/reception area, which leads
into a large central lobby with lounge seating. The main day room,
though, is Boaters bar with sun lounge beyond. The more pubby Pullman
bar is reached from outside the hotel. A family-oriented hotel: there
is a nanny-supervised playroom during school holidays and a climbing
frame out in the garden in addition to the usual availability of cots, high-
chairs etc. Children under 12 sharing parents' room stay free. *Rooms 112.
Garden, tennis, indoor & outdoor swimming pools, keep-fit equipment, solarium,
spa bath, hair salon.* AMERICAN EXPRESS *Access, Diners, Visa.*

Torquay | Homers Hotel | 64% | £60

Tel 0803 213456   Fax 0803 213458
Warren Road Torquay Devon TQ2 5TN

Map 13 D3

A small Victorian hotel, perched high above Torbay, where new owners
have undertaken considerable refurbishment, most notably in the variously
sized bedrooms that are now much more tastefully decorated than
formerly, with extravagantly-sized padded headboards that co-ordinate
with bedcovers and curtains. A tray of mineral water, biscuits and sweets
is left at the bedside when rooms are serviced in the evening. The great
majority of rooms share a panoramic view of the bay. Genteel day rooms
have been opened up to each other but still retain a period feel with
reproduction-style easy chairs and lots of parlour plants. The bar is in
an alcove off this main lounge, part of which is reserved for non-smokers.
A terrace looks down on to a stepped garden that affords direct access
to Torquay's famous Rock Walk Gardens. *Rooms 15. Garden.*
AMERICAN EXPRESS *Access, Diners, Visa.*

Torquay | Imperial Hotel | 83% | £145

Tel 0803 294301   Fax 0803 298293
Parkhill Road Torquay Devon TQ1 2DG

Map 13 D3

Branded a 'Forte Grand', the Imperial really is a grand hotel. Built in the
mid-19th century (although the recently redecorated exterior looks
younger) an imposing marble-floored lobby with fluted Corinthian
pilasters and glittering chandeliers sets the tone for extensive public areas
that boast many fine period features: the colonnade with painted panels,
luxurious Palm Court lounge with Lloyd Loom-furnished Sun Deck
beyond, bar with deeply comfortable leather armchairs and Regency
Lounge with dancing to a live band every Friday and Saturday night.
Outside, ranks of sunloungers surround the pool and, from the hotel's
elevated position high above the bay, terraced gardens reach right down
to the shore. Most of the bedrooms have their own entrance lobbies and
more than half have good-sized, furnished balconies overlooking the bay.
Traditionally furnished either with reproduction antique or freestanding
darkwood pieces, they come in a variety of bright, tasteful colour schemes
and all have good bathrooms, with generous towels and bathrobes.
Numerous staff, under executive director Harry Murray who has been
running things here for over 17 years, offer high levels of service with
a proper concierge, evening turn-down and extensive 24hr room service.
For younger guests there is the Seagull Club – with its own suite of rooms
– and all sorts of activities from painting and model making to dressing-up

and video games organised during the summer and other holiday periods. A £5 million refurbishment of the public areas and exterior has just been completed. *Rooms 167. Garden, tennis, indoor & outdoor swimming pools, gym, squash, sauna, solarium, spa bath, beauty salon, snooker.* AMERICAN EXPRESS *Access, Diners, Visa.*

Torquay	Livermead Cliff Hotel	60%	£60
Tel 0803 299666 Fax 0803 294496			**H**
Sea Front Torquay Devon TQ2 6RQ			Map 13 D3

Right by the sea, with 20 steps leading to safe beaches, this is not surprisingly a popular family holiday spot. It's also geared up to the conference trade (for up to 70 delegates), so it's quite a busy place all year round. Picture windows in the lounge look out to sea. Parents with offspring are well catered for with cots, baby-sitting, baby-listening and children's high tea available. Children up to 15 stay free in parents' room. Good housekeeping (some bedrooms recently redecorated), friendly staff. *Rooms 64. Garden, outdoor swimming pool, solarium, laundry room.* AMERICAN EXPRESS *Access, Diners, Visa.*

Torquay	Livermead House	60%	£90
Tel 0803 294361 Fax 0803 200758			**H**
Sea Front Torquay Devon TQ2 6QJ			Map 13 D3

Charles Kingsley was an early guest here, and today's water babies will appreciate the swimming pools. The sea is also at hand, providing panoramic views from the hotel's picture windows. There's plenty to keep visitors occupied both inside and out, and for relaxation there's a choice of lounges and bars. Well-kept bedrooms, the best of them facing the sea. A new conference and banqueting facility – the Regency Suite – can accommodate 250 for functions, 300 for meetings. Free parking for 100 cars. No dogs. *Rooms 65. Garden, adults' and childrens' outdoor swimming pool, keep-fit equipment, squash, sauna, solarium, putting, snooker.* AMERICAN EXPRESS *Access, Diners, Visa.*

Torquay	Orestone Manor	58%	£90
Tel 0803 328098 Fax 0803 328336			**H**
Rockhouse Lane Maidencombe Torquay Devon TQ1 4SX			Map 13 D3

Take the Teignouth road out of Torquay to find this hotel run by the Staples family. Situated high above Babbacombe Bay and once the home of artist John Calcott Horsley, it enjoys fine views of the sea. Clean and comfortable public rooms and all the bedrooms have been recently decorated, and most have sea views. Bed and breakfast terms are available only in country facing rooms and for a maximum of two nights, thus providing the hotel restaurant with a captive audience. Cots are available for a small surcharge, but their occupants are denied access to the dining room in the evening. *Rooms 18. Garden, outdoor swimming pool, children's splash pool. Closed Jan.* AMERICAN EXPRESS *Access, Diners, Visa.*

Torquay	Osborne Hotel	65%	£86
Tel 0803 213311 Fax 0803 296788			**H**
Hesketh Crescent Meadfoot Beach Torquay Devon TQ1 2LL			Map 13 D3

The Osborne describes itself as a country house hotel by the sea, and its location within a well-maintained Regency crescent on the hillside ensures good views over the bay. Bedrooms and apartments offer a high level of comfort, while there are good business facilities (conference/banqueting for 80/60) and leisure pursuits available both within the hotel and nearby. No dogs. *Rooms 23. Garden, indoor & outdoor swimming pools, tennis, brasserie (11am-11pm).* AMERICAN EXPRESS *Access, Visa.*

Torquay   Palace Hotel   68%   £110

H

Tel 0803 200200   Fax 0803 299899

Babbacombe Road Torquay Devon TQ1 3TG   Map 13 D3

Lounges have been refurbished and bedrooms upgraded at the Palace, which is set in 25 acres of gardens and woodland stretching to the sea. It opened in 1921 as a hotel offering some of the finest sporting facilities in the land and still admirably provides the active guest with some of the best (golf, swimming, tennis and squash professionals on hand). Music or entertainment is provided nightly, and families are very well catered for. Out of season the hotel is often busy with conferences (handling up to 2000 delegates theatre-style and offering a full range of services). Six large bedroom suites have splendid views, individual decor and good-quality furniture; other rooms are simpler but comfortable with handsome period bathrooms. Children up to three free in parents' room. Parking for 150. No dogs. *Rooms 140. Garden, croquet, indoor & outdoor swimming pools, squash, sauna, hairdressing, indoor & outdoor tennis, 9-hole golf course, snooker, nanny, children's playroom, hair salon, helipad.* AMERICAN EXPRESS *Access, Diners, Visa.*

Torquay   Table Restaurant   ↑   £70

R

Tel 0803 324292

135 Babbacombe Road Babbacombe Torquay Devon TQ1 3SR   Map 13 D3

In the Babbacombe suburb to the east of town, this restaurant is quite charming, with sunny yellow decor and a glittering chandelier at the centre of a small room. Working single-handedly in the kitchen Trevor Brooks nevertheless manages to offer four or five choices at each stage of his fixed-price menus. Red mullet soup with saffron and tomato, galantine of salmon with seared scallops on a lemon chive butter sauce, Chinese vinegar-glazed duck breast with black pepper and tarragon jus, and roast saddle and braised neck fillet of lamb with a barley risotto on a rosemary-scented sauce are typical of Trevor's well-conceived, carefully executed dishes. Fish dishes vary daily according to the market: salmon from the Dart or Teign with Cajun spices and wasabi butter is a summer speciality. Warm chocolate tartlet, rhubarb and ginger crème brulée and a lemon meringue dessert vie for attention with some good local cheeses for afters. No children under 10 years. No smoking. *Seats 20. D only 7.30-9.30. Closed Mon, 2 weeks Feb, 2 weeks Sept. Set D £26. Access, Visa.*

Torquay   Places of Information

Tourist Information   Tel 0803 297428.
Torre Abbey   Tel 0803 293593 *Includes Dame Agatha Christie Memorial Room.*
Wessex Ski Club   Tel 0803 313350.
Odicombe, Anstey's Cove and Meadfoot Beaches.

Towcester   Forte Travelodge   £45

L

Tel 0327 359105

East Towcester Bypass Towcester Northamptonshire NN12 0DD   Map 15 D1

Off Junction 15A of the M1 towards Oxford, on the A43, 8 miles south of Northampton. *Rooms 33.* AMERICAN EXPRESS *Access, Diners, Visa.*

Tresco   Island Hotel   67%   £170*

HR

Tel 0720 422883   Fax 0720 423008

Tresco Isles of Scilly TR24 0PU   Map 12 A2

Tresco, England's "Island of Flowers", is privately owned and maintained, its lanes free of traffic. Guests arriving at the quay (2½ hours from Penzance) or heliport (20 minutes from Penzance) are transported by tractor-drawn charabanc to the island's only hotel, set in beautifully tended gardens by the shore. Picture windows make the most of this spectacular location and the panoramic sea views: should the mists close in there's a Terrace Bar (with a wide range of snacks) and a Quiet Room stacked with books, magazines and games. Some bedrooms enjoy sea views, while others overlook the gardens. Special holiday packages for gardeners, bird-watchers and others. ★Half-board terms only. No dogs. *Rooms 40. Garden, outdoor swimming pool, fishing, boating, bowling green, games room, tennis. Closed Nov-end Feb.* AMERICAN EXPRESS® *Access, Visa.*

Restaurant £60

Table d'hote and à la carte menus place strong emphasis on local seafood (Scillonian scallops, Bryher crab), and there's chicken, Dorset veal and Devonshire beef from the grill and a cold buffet. Traditional farmhouse cheeses. Luxurious Sunday buffet (£27.50, includes lobster). Children under 12 can eat half-price from the carte. No smoking. *Seats 110. Private Room 10. L 12-2.15 D 7-9. Set D £24.*

Tresco   Place of Interest

Tresco Abbey Gardens   Tel 0720 22849.

Tring   Travel Inn £43
Tel 0442 824819   Fax 0442 890787 L
Tring Hill Tring Hertfordshire HP23 4LD   Map 15 E2

On the A41 heading out towards Aylesbury. Nearest motorway Junctions 11, M1 and 20 M25. No family rooms, but special second room rates for children at weekends. 15 minutes from Whipsnade Zoo. No dogs. *Rooms 30. Garden, children's play area. Closed 24 & 25 Dec.* AMERICAN EXPRESS® *Access, Diners, Visa.*

Troutbeck   Mortal Man Inn £95*
Tel 053 94 33193   Fax 053 94 31261 I
Troutbeck nr Windermere Cumbria LA23 1PL   Map 4 C3

The name of the inn is derived from a painting by one Julius Caesar Ibbetson, who died in 1817, which contains the inscription 'O mortal man that lives by bread...'. A good motif for a very hospitable inn set in the glorious lakeland which inspired so many poets and travellers, and still borne out after 20 years by resident owners Christopher and Annette Poulsom. Join the regulars in the Village Bar or relax in the residents' bar and sunny lounge overlooking the Troutbeck Valley. Bedrooms are smart, bathrooms compact and housekeeping praiseworthy. No children under five. ★Half-board terms only. *Rooms 12. Garden. Closed mid Nov-mid Feb. No credit cards.*

Troutbeck   Place of Interest

Holebird Garden   Tel 09662 6238.

Truro   Alverton Manor   70% £95
Tel 0872 76633   Fax 0872 222989 H
Tregolls Road Truro Cornwall TR1 1XQ   Map 12 B3

An impressive Victorian Gothic building on the A390 from St Austell. Conferences are an important part of the hotel's business and one of the rooms was once a chapel (the building then being a convent). Apart from the restaurant, the only day room is an elegantly proportioned and comfortable lounge that also incorporates the bar. Excellent, individually decorated bedrooms are the great strength here with stylish fabrics, good-quality reproduction antique furniture and extras like sherry and mineral water. Bathrooms, three with shower and WC only, are equally good, with robes and generous towelling. 24hr room service. There are plans to add a leisure complex. No dogs. *Rooms 34. Garden, snooker.* AMERICAN EXPRESS *Access, Diners, Visa.*

Truro   Places of Interest

Tourist Information   Tel 0872 74555.
City Hall   Tel 0872 76461.
Trelissick Garden (NT)   Tel 0872 862090.
Trewithen House and Gardens   Probus Tel 0726 882764.
Truro Cathedral   Tel 0872 76782.
Flambards Theme Park   Culdrose Manor Tel 0326 574549.

Tuckenhay	Floyd's Inn (Sometimes)	£125

Tel 0803 732350   Fax 0803 732651   **IR**

Bow Creek Tuckenhay Totnes Devon TQ9 7EQ   Map 13 D3

There's an air of laid-back eccentricity about food writer and broadcaster Keith Floyd's pub-cum-restaurant-with-rooms set alongside a small quay on the heavily wooded, and very beautiful, Bow Creek. The rusticated bar (on the top floor, which is at road level, of a building dating back to 1550) consists of several interconnecting rooms and offers an eclectic 'Canteen Menu' (caviar, Thai red duck curry, corned beef hash) plus a menu reflecting Keith's current culinary interest – Italian on our last visit, but it will have changed by the time you read this! The restaurant is one floor below, and at quay level there is a dispense bar for alfresco drinkers; there is also a lunchtime barbecue in summer, weather permitting. The three bedrooms in an adjacent building – 'Floyd's Barn' – are tremendous fun (but watch out for the rather frisky Alsatian dogs that roam free along the quay). One room has a strong nautical theme (rough-hewn timber shelves suspended by ropes, deckchair seating, old drum table and an old brass ship's telegraph standing at the foot of the bed); another, the 'Dukes Room', furnished with antiques (including an out-of-tune piano) and with rather masculine decor; and the third, the Khun Akorn room, with Thai decor and satin sheets. All sorts of extras, from complimentary drinks (including champagne) and chocolate bars in the fridge, plus books, fruit, tooth picks and even a packet of cigarettes. Bathrooms, two with separate walk-in showers in addition to the tub, have mirrored walls, Floris toiletries, slippers and towelling robes. Choose between an extensive cooked breakfast or a Continental version, plus boiled egg, served in your bedroom. Overnight guests also get to choose a jar or two of home-made preserves to take away as a souvenir. *Rooms 4. Sunbed, snooker.* AMERICAN EXPRESS *Access, Visa.*

George's Restaurant   £100

George is a teddy bear who sits in front of a glass of wine at table three, a packet of Capstan Full Strength tucked into his yellow-checked waistcoat and sporting a 'Floyd' bow tie. A split-level room with terrace overlooking the creek for pre-dinner drinks, it has just five tables, where diners choose from a daily-changing, fixed-price menu that is mainstream, French-inspired rather than the more adventurous menu served in the bar above. With only three choices at each stage, a typical night's menu might be smoked salmon bavarois, puff pastry filled with venison and morels, and a mushroom risotto with artichoke and chicken livers for starters, noisettes of lamb with asparagus and mint hollandaise, roast duck with pink peppercorn sauce, and bourride as the main dishes. Then there is a selection of British (mostly local) cheeses and/or puds like crème brulée, chocolate tart with cinnamon ice cream, raspberry parfait and sticky toffee pudding. Sound cooking and unfussy presentation achieve most satisfactory results. *Seats 26. Parties 6. L 12-2 D 7-9. Closed L Sat, D Sun and all Tue.* Set L £25 Set D £42.50.

Tunbridge Wells   Cheevers   £60

Tel 0892 545524   Fax 0892 535956   **R**

56 High Street Tunbridge Wells Kent TN1 1XF   Map 11 B5

In the last 12 months, while the menu has remained in the same mode and the quality of the cooking and service as high in quality as ever, various cost formulae have been tried, apparently successfully, to improve custom during the week. At present, the fixed-price dinner menu is £25 on Friday and Saturday. From Tuesday through to Thursday, and at lunchtime, all starters are £4, all main courses £9.55 and all desserts £4. The menus change weekly, though variations from one week to another can be small. Rack of lamb with one crust or another remains a signature dish. Recent sightings include: salad of quail's eggs and bacon; wild salmon poached with sorrel; quenelles of pike with a dill dressing; clafoutis; and warm chocolate pudding with vanilla ice cream. Though this is some of the best cooking in Kent and the under-stated decor is creditable, the bleak view which greets the customers at the end of the restaurant – an air-conditioning unit, a screen hiding the entrance to the kitchen and a staircase leading to the loos – leaves a poor impression. The closeness of tables underlines the feeling that the owners could benefit from (and deserve) larger premises. *Seats 32. Parties 16. L 12.30-2 (Sat to 1.45) D 7.30-10.30. Closed Sun & Mon, 1 week Christmas (phone to check). Set D £25.* AMERICAN EXPRESS *Access, Visa.*

> Consult page 20 for a full list of starred restaurants

Tunbridge Wells   Downstairs at Thackeray's   £45

Tel 0892 537559   **R**

85 London Road Tunbridge Wells Kent TN1 1EA   Map 11 B5

Downstairs, with its own separate courtyard entrance, this delightful little place with cosy, close-set tables and fresh flowers has the friendly relaxed feel of a bistro, still of course under the watchful eye of Bruce Wass, though with Peter Lucas in the kitchen. The menu is primarily modern European, with dishes such as baked aubergine and pesto, poached egg on a brioche case with Arbroath smokies and hollandaise, or spinach-wrapped vegetable terrine on a tomato and red pepper coulis priced as starters or main courses. Robust main courses like oxtail braised in red wine served with basil dumplings vie for attention alongside grilled fresh tuna with spinach and sweet red peppers. Delicious desserts like anise parfait with fresh fruit salad or apricot compote with chestnut ice cream round off the meal, and there's a good selection of British and Irish farmhouse cheeses. Booking is advisable. *Seats 34. L 12.30-2.30 D 7.30-9.30. Closed Sun & Mon, Bank Holidays, 5 days Christmas. Set L £6.50/£8.50 Set D £9.85. Access, Visa.*

Tunbridge Wells   Royal Wells Inn   64%   £80

Tel 0892 511188   Fax 0892 511908   **H**

Mount Ephraim Tunbridge Wells Kent TN4 8BE   Map 11 B5

The royal coat of arms atop the family-run Royal Wells is a proud memento of the days when, during her childhood, Queen Victoria used to stay here. Inside, there's a stylish reception/lounge with columns, marble-effect wallcoverings and matching fabrics as well as a light and attractive bar area. Best bedrooms are on the top floor – these have brass beds, quality pine furniture, Laura Ashley fabrics and up-to-date, tiled bathrooms; two rooms have four-posters. The hotel bus is a delightful 1909 Commer, once owned by the founder of the AA, Lord Lonsdale. Conference/banquet facilities for up to 90. *Rooms 20. Closed 25 & 26 Dec.* AMERICAN EXPRESS *Access, Diners, Visa.*

Tunbridge Wells   Spa Hotel   72%   £84

Tel 0892 520331   Fax 0892 510575   **HR**

Mount Ephraim Tunbridge Wells Kent TN4 8XJ   Map 11 B5

The Spa was built in 1766 as a country mansion for Sir George Kelly and
remained a private home for its first century. It became a hotel in 1880 and
has been in the same family ever since. Sister hotel to *The Goring*
in London, it stands in 15 acres of gardens and parkland that include two
lakes. The foyer opens on to a spacious lounge with Corinthian columns,
darkwood panelling and a gas log fire at each end; half is reserved for non-
smokers. The Equestrian Bar is a favourite place for a drink or bar food.
Bedrooms vary in size and decor, but all feature freestanding furniture.
De luxe rooms have king-sized beds and tend to be larger, with views
across the gardens. As part of the ongoing programme of refurbishment the
York Suite, one of the function rooms, has recently had a face-lift.
Although conferences (for up to 300) form most of the weekday business,
there is an atmosphere of a moderately grand hotel run along traditional
lines, with excellent leisure facilities. Children up to 16 free in parents'
room. ***Rooms*** *76. Garden, croquet, indoor swimming pool, gym, sauna, spa
bath, solarium, beauty & hair salon, tennis, children's adventure playground.*
AMERICAN EXPRESS *Access, Diners, Visa.*

Chandelier Restaurant   £60

In the large, high-ceilinged Regency dining room, good-quality produce
is best enjoyed in the simpler dishes. Lunchtime roasts are carved and
served formally from a trolley. There's a weekly list of 'old traditionals'
such as a Tuesday meal of split ham and pea soup, roast best end of lamb,
with onion sauce or beef cobbler, with steamed chocolate pudding with
banana custard to finish – just the sort of food to keep the climate at bay!
Separate vegetarian menu, and table d'hote and à la carte menu at dinner.
Seats *90. L 12.30-2 D 7-9.30. Closed L Sat. Set L £12.50. Set D £15.50.*

Tunbridge Wells   Thackeray's House   ★   £90

Tel 0892 511921   **R**

85 London Road Tunbridge Wells Kent TN11 1EA   Map 11 B5

Chef/patron Bruce Wass has recently improved this pretty restaurant
facing the common, in a house where William Makepeace Thackeray once
lived. The former bar has become part of the restaurant making room for
extra tables to cope with busy weekend custom. The new area is just far
enough removed from the main restaurant to allow for a private dinner
party. The new bar upstairs is a great improvement on the former, rather
cramped one. Cooking is in contemporary, Anglo-French rustic mode.
Country paté with onion marmalade, grilled turbot with red wine sauce
and 'crispy' fried garlic, duck confit with flageolet beans and thyme, and
iles flottantes are typical. Best end of lamb with Dijon mustard and a fresh
herb crust is a signature dish. Simpler dishes are sometimes better – roast
red mullet fillet with capers, orange and saffron was overwhelmed by its
accompaniments. There is a good variety of British cheeses, considerately
served. The wine list is above average, with a good selection of French
classics. ***Seats*** *40. Private Room 40. L 12.30-2.30 D 7-10. Closed D Sun, all
Mon, Bank Holidays, 5 days Christmas. Set L £10/£14.75 (Sun £18.50)
Set D £17.50/£21.50. Access, Visa.*

Tunbridge Wells   Places of Interest

Tourist Information   Tel 0892 515675.
Assembly Hall   Tel 0892 30613.
Trinity Arts Centre   Tel 0892 44699.
Neville Road Cricket Ground   Tel 0892 20846.
Bowles Outdoor Pursuits Centre   Tel 0892 64127.
   Historic Houses, Castles and Gardens
Scotney Castle Garden (NT)   Lamberhurst Tel 0892 890651.

Penshurst Place   Penshurst, Tonbridge Tel 0892 870307.
Moorlands Gardens   Friars Gate, Nr Crowborough Tel 0892 652474.

Turners Hill	Alexander House	79%	£150

Tel 0342 714914   Fax 0342 717328   **HR**
East Street Turners Hill West Sussex RH10 4QD   Map 11 B5

An imposing country mansion set in 135 acres on the B2110 between
Turners Hill and East Grinstead. Distinguished buildings have occupied the
site since the 14th century and the oldest part of the present house dates
from the early 17th century. Numerous grand day rooms feature many
high-quality antiques, paintings (including *A Jamaica Bay* by Noel Coward)
and other decorative features like the painted silk chinoiserie panels in the
main salon and a pair of ornate French ormolu lamps in the foyer. A bar
has recently been created in what was the kitchen. Many bedrooms have
traditional yew furniture and boast original paintings plus many little
extras like fresh flowers, fruit and magazines. Smart, friendly staff.
No children under 7. No dogs. Handy for Gatwick (9 miles). *Rooms 15.
Garden, croquet, keep-fit equipment, tennis, snooker, limousine service, valeting.*
AMERICAN EXPRESS *Access, Diners, Visa.*

Restaurant   £120

An elegant room in a striking shade of pinky orange with a high level
of service from attentive staff (some in tail-coats) and quality of tableware
(fine Royal Worcester china). The chef's style is classical and modernised
French and English, and the à la carte menu makes use of high-quality,
often luxurious ingredients: paté of duck and goose liver with brioche,
glazed scallops and crayfish, grilled lobster with hot butter sauce or a light
cheese sauce, wild salmon baked in filo pastry with truffles and mushrooms,
steak Diane. Classic desserts, too, such as soufflé Grand Marnier, crepes
Suzette and strawberry sablé. There are also table d'hote menus and
a separate vegetarian menu. No smoking. *Seats 60. Private Room 55.
L 12.30-2 D 7.30-9.30 (Sun to 9). Set L £14.75/£16.75 (Sun £18.95)
Set D £24.95.*

Tutbury	Ye Olde Dog & Partridge Inn	£73

Tel 0283 813030   Fax 0283 813178   **I**
High Street Tutbury nr Burton-on-Trent Staffordshire DE13 9LS   Map 6 C3

In the middle of the main village street, the inn has kept much of its 15th-
century character, and its half-timbered frontage with diamond-leaded
windows is a pretty subject for a picture postcard. Inside, the welcome
is warm: there are two traditional bars and a restaurant where a busy buffet
and carvery operate and a pianist plays nightly. Three bedrooms with
black-and-white panelling and creaking floorboards are in the main
building, the rest in an adjacent Georgian house with a central spiral
staircase. Four-poster and half-tester rooms are available. *Rooms 17. Garden.
Closed 25 Dec, 1 Jan.* AMERICAN EXPRESS *Access, Visa.*

Twickenham	Hamiltons	£50

Tel 081-892 3949   **R**
43 Crown Road St Margarets Twickenham Middlesex TW1 3EJ   Map 15 E2

The approach to Hamiltons is heralded by its distinctive red and gold
exterior and stained glass windows, though once it has drawn you in, you
are relaxed by the calmer, welcoming apricot/cream shades. David Poole,
at the stove since 1987, cooks an Anglo-French menu, sometimes à la carte
and sometimes set: Tuesday to Friday lunchtimes see a fixed-price menu
with soup or salad to start followed by just one daily-changing dish.
Typical dishes might be smoked haddock and chive fishcakes on a creamy
chive sauce (as either a starter or a light main course), grilled venison
sausages with bubble and squeak on a port wine sauce, cassoulet of chicken
and ham, crisp shortbread filled with berries and vanilla cream on a vanilla

sauce, and rich dark chocolate and orange curaçao truffle with almond sauce. Live jazz during family Sunday lunchtimes. *Seats 48. Parties 16. Private Room 8. L 12-2.30 (Sun to 3.30) D 7-10.30 (Fri & Sat to 11). Closed L Sat, D Sun, all Mon, Bank Holidays, 1 week New Year. Set L £10.95 (£14.50 Sun).* AMERICAN EXPRESS *Access, Visa.*

Twickenham   McClements Bistro   NEW   £60

Tel 081-744 9610   Fax 081-890 1372   **R**

2 Whitton Road Twickenham Middlesex TW1 1BJ   **Map 15 E2**

John McClements' second venture is a charming bistro, as small and cosily friendly as his original restaurant down the road. Decorated in soft pastel shades, it features a fortnightly-changing menu prepared by head chef Philip Rickerby. The choice is extensive over a range of full-flavoured, well-prepared dishes. Offal's a great passion of Mr McClements and here appears even with the warm, freshly baked rolls in the form of duck rillettes, made with the gizzards. Starters range from a wild mushroom risotto with Parmesan shavings and black pudding en croute with a Dijon mustard sauce to a terrine of ham and parsley in jelly, scallops roasted with caramelised chicory or sautéed eel with shallots and red wine sauce. Main courses include stuffed lamb's heart and lamb's tongue and a baked potato with tripe provençale, a rich *assiette du boucher*. There's also roast cod with pig's trotter bitoks and garlic mash. Less offally dishes include crispy breast of duck with lime and orange and boned baby chicken cooked with caramelised chicory. Superb desserts to finish such as tarte tatin, a pyramid of profiteroles or a stunning tarte au citron. *Seats 40. Parties 10. Private Room 12. L 12-2.30 D 7-10.30 (Fri & Sat to 11). Closed 10 days August. Set L & D £9.95. Access, Visa.*

Twickenham   McClements Restaurant   ★   £65

Tel 081-755 0176   Fax 081-890 1372   **R**

12 The Green Twickenham Middlesex TW2 5AA   **Map 15 E2**

A tiny place with a simplicity of decor converted by pink chiffon drapes and Austrian blinds at the single large front window. Walls have a few sepia-tinted prints but the rest of the decor is a very pale grey. The food here is more strongly seafood-orientated than previously, though John McClements' passion for offal still makes an appearance, as in grilled scallops with black pudding, cassoulet of Dublin Bay prawns with duck gizzard and stuffed pig's trotter served with a slice of crispy cooked cod. Other more conventional choices from a short but imaginative and well-put-together carte include a plate of three salmons (gravad lax, tartare and smoked) leek and potato soup with poached oysters or confit of stuffed duck. Whatever the choice the execution is superb with great care taken to ensure the correct balance of flavours and textures. The gratin of fresh, boned eel is a particular favourite starter, the eel skinned and steamed then glazed under a hollandaise crust. Crispy-cooked sea bass is served with a delicate soya butter sauce under a 'hair-net' of deep-fried vegetables. Simple desserts to finish include the likes of a tangy lemon tart and crème brulée as well as a hot soufflé with calvados sauce. Staff provide the kind of friendly service you'd expect from such a homely little restaurant. *Seats 14. Parties 8. Private Room 20. L 12-2.30 D 7-10.30). Closed Sun & Mon. Access, Visa.*

Uckfield   Horsted Place   79%   £136

Tel 0825 750581   Fax 0825 750459   **HR**

Little Horsted Uckfield East Sussex TN22 5TS   **Map 11 B6**

Off the A26 to the south of Uckfield, Horsted Place is a fine example of high-Victorian architecture with its distinctive chequered brickwork, splendidly exuberant Pugin staircase and grounds laid out by Geoffrey Jellicoe. Day rooms, which are off an elegant central hall running the length of the house, include a library and large lounge, boasting two real fires in winter. Individually decorated in some style, bedrooms vary somewhat in size but all are furnished with good reproduction antiques and offer all sorts of comforts from books and magazines to fruit and mineral water. Guests have access to the adjacent championship golf course (under the same ownership as the hotel and home to the European Open for the next few years) and Glyndebourne is just five minutes down the road. Conference/banqueting facilities in the Horsted Management Centre for 100/30. No children under 8. No dogs. **Rooms** 17. *Garden, croquet, indoor swimming pool, tennis, golf (18), fishing, helipad.* AMERICAN EXPRESS *Access, Diners, Visa.*

Pugin Dining Room £95

Designed by the eponymous architect (also responsible for the Houses of Parliament) in one of his more restrained moments, this luxuriously appointed dining room is an appropriate setting for Allan Garth's sensibly short menu of dishes that are a well-judged balance between interest, lack of complication and modern trends. Roasted scallops with olives, capers, figs and anchovies, warm rabbit with raisin and balsamic dressing, casserole of wild duck in a port wine sauce with bacon and button onions, and a parcel of veal, Parma ham and sage with noodles on a butter sauce give the style; vegetarian options. All smoking of food is done on the premises. No notes and too many spelling mistakes on an otherwise decent wine list, though wines are somewhat inconsistently priced (champagne Louis Roederer Cristal 1985 at £180 – surely not?). Outdoor seating for 16 on a terrace. No children under 8 after 8pm. **Seats** 36. Parties 12. *Private Room 30. L 12-2 D 7.30-9.30. Set L £14.95/£18.50 (Sun £18.50) Set D £28.50.*

Uckfield   Places of Interest

Sheffield Park Garden (NT)   Tel 0825 790655.
Bluebell Railway   Sheffield Park Station Tel 082 572 2370 *Talking Timetable 3777.*

Ullswater   Leeming House   75%   £115

Tel 076 84 86622 Fax 076 84 86443	**HR**
Watermillock Ullswater nr Penrith Cumbria CA11 0JJ	Map 4 C3

Surrounded by 20 acres of beautifully landscaped gardens on the northern shore of Ullswater, Leeming House dates from the early 1800s. Public rooms lead off a long, pillared entrance hall and, in keeping with the character of the building, are classically traditional in decor and furnishings. The library, with book-filled shelves, and the adjoining sitting and drawing rooms have comfortable deep-cushioned settees and armchairs arranged in well-spaced groupings. The bar is dark and clubby with wood-panelled walls. The drawing room and a wide, tiled conservatory which connects a wing of newer bedrooms have good views over the gently sloping grounds, with glimpses of the lake through a fine collection of trees. Best bedrooms, too, have excellent views (a 10% supplement is payable). Fourteen have balconies and five ground-floor rooms have patios; eleven rooms are reserved for non-smokers. Possessing a tasteful floral decor with smart darkwood furniture they are all elegantly furnished and comprehensively equipped (including one for disabled guests). Bathrooms have lovely old-fashioned fittings as well as good toiletries and bathrobes. Dogs in bedrooms only. Forte Grand. **Rooms** 40. *Garden, fishing, helipad.* AMERICAN EXPRESS *Access, Diners, Visa.*

Restaurant £80

A long, beautifully proportioned dining room with fine south-facing views over the grounds to the lake. Familiar classics on the menu (chicken liver parfait, Manx kipper and whisky terrine with creamed horseradish, cold cooked meats, steamed ginger pudding) are interspersed with a few innovations (anyone for hot Sage Derby and pine nut fritters with tomato and basil coulis?). The choice for dinner is three or six courses while lunchtime has a slightly shorter, three-course menu. Sunday lunch sees traditional roast sirloin of Angus beef served with light Yorkshire pudding and creamed shiitake mushrooms. Friendly service. No smoking. No very young children in the evening. **Seats** 80. Parties 10. Private Room 30. L 12.30-1.45 D 7.30-8.45. Set L £16.25 (Sun) Set D £28.50/£35.50.

Ullswater   Old Church Hotel   67%   £90

Tel 076 84 86204   Fax 076 84 86368   **HR**

Watermillock Ullswater Cumbria CA11 0JN   Map 4 C3

Kevin and Maureen Whitemore provide a warm welcome for guests at their pleasant lakeside hotel, which was built in 1754 on the site of a 12th-century church. Both lounges are built for relaxation and packed with board games and periodicals. Maureen's bold colour schemes brighten the bedrooms (priced according to the view), with crown canopies and half-testers framing really comfortable beds. Excellent breakfasts. No dogs. **Rooms** 10. Garden. Closed Nov-Mar. Access, Visa.

Restaurant   £60

The smaller lounge doubles as an aperitif bar where guests gather prior to dinner (availability is limited for outside diners and booking is essential). Kevin's menu (order by 7) offers a short, straightforward selection: avocado, bacon and watercress salad, hot smoked salmon with tagliatelle, cream of sweetcorn soup, chicken supreme with a tomato and basil or lemon and fennel sauce, rack of Lakeland lamb (a speciality). Helpful tasting notes for each carefully-chosen wine on a concise list that has many of the top growers. No smoking. **Seats** 30. D only 6-8. Set D £20.

Ullswater   Rampsbeck Country House Hotel   65%   £80

Tel 07684 86442   Fax 07684 86688   **HR**

Watermillock Ullswater Cumbria CA11 0LP   Map 4 C3

An 18th-century country house with 18 acres of gardens and grounds and marvellous views from its setting on Ullswater. Tom and Marion Gibb generate a warm air of hospitality that resides in the lounge, with its grandfather clocks, log fire and flowers, and the bar, which gives on to the patio and garden. All the spick-and-span bedrooms enjoy lake or garden views, and there's a small supplement for rooms with a private balcony overlooking the lake. No children under 5. **Rooms** 20. Garden, croquet, fishing, mooring. Closed 6 weeks Jan/Feb. Access, Visa.

Restaurant   £55

Modern classical cooking by Andrew McGeorge produces fine, well-constructed dishes using the pick of local suppliers. Steamed fillets of brill with sautéed spinach, tomato sauce and quenelles of ratatouille; veal fillet, sweetbreads and ragout of kidneys served in a tartlet with a pickled walnut sauce; and loin of venison with a chartreuse-flavoured game jus and a baked pithiviers of foie gras show a style which is at once imaginative and disciplined. The wine list is presented by style, each wine accompanied by fruity (but fruitless) tasting comments. Very keen prices. No smoking in the restaurant. There's also a light and interesting bar lunch menu, and cream teas are served in the lounge. **Seats** 36. Private Room 20. L 12-1.30 D 7-8.30. Set L £19.95 Set D £25 & £32.50.

Ullswater   Sharrow Bay   82%   £250*

Tel 076 84 86301   Fax 076 84 86349   **HR**

Howtown Ullswater Cumbria CA10 2LZ   Map 4 C3

Francis Coulson and Brian Sack have together created the epitome of gracious country living at the original country house hotel, nestling beneath Barton Fell. The hotel is bordered on three sides by 12 acres of gardens, in an idyllic location on the very edge of Lake Ullswater; the main house's satellites – the Lodge Gatehouse, Garden Cottage, Bank House

(1 mile away) and Thwaite Cottage, Tirril (4 miles distant and with
no room service) – are equally desirable, offering every conceivable
pampering comfort. Success feeds on success and such is the renown of this
hotel that there are times, particularly at the peak of the season, when space
comes under pressure. The hotel is in a National Park and petty bureaucrats
envious of or blind to the hotel's potential veto the alteration of even
a single stone. The erection of a Victorian conservatory was deemed
acceptable however, though size was strictly delineated and thus has helped
in creating additional seating (though without a lake view). This view is to
be had from the main lounge with its picture windows; here, as in the
second lounge and conservatory, are deep-cushioned settees and armchairs,
fresh flowers, fine ornaments and paintings. There is no bar proper,
so drinks are served in the lounges. Bedrooms upstairs in the main house
do not all have their bathrooms en suite, but all the remainder do. Each
and every bedroom is furnished to the highest standards of comfort and
luxury with fine embroidered linen sheets on sleep-inducing mattresses.
Fine porcelain and tassels (two of Francis' passions) are everywhere, and
plants and books adorn the tables. Most bedrooms have sitting areas and
bathrooms with exquisite toiletries and thick, cosseting towels. Breakfasts
are as much of an institution here as the famed afternoon teas, lunches and
dinners. Newly-baked croissants, brioches, freshly-squeezed orange juice
and a cooked breakfast *sans pareil* are all guaranteed to set you up for
at least a day's fell walking. Staff, under the supervision of managers (and
co-directors) Nigel Lawrence and Nigel Lightburn, are long serving and
very dedicated, each ensuring that every guest is properly cared for and
that the hotel is kept in absolute gleaming, ship-shape order. No children
under 13. ★Half-board terms only. **Rooms** 28. *Garden. Closed Dec-Feb.
No credit cards.* [MARTELL]

Restaurant ★   £95

Last year, the menu welcomed guests to Francis and Brian's 46th season (in
1994) and then advised that 'Cooking is Art and all Art is Patience'. Haste
is not something that immediatley springs to mind when seated in either
of the two delightful dining rooms. The lakeside dining room has splendid
views over the water, while next door in the Victorian panelled studio
dining room there is a genteel ambience and tables are spaciously arranged.
Fixed-price meals are ordered in one of the lounges and then you file past
a sample tray of that mealtime's desserts (having them described as you go).
The menu has changed little in its format down the years, and each dish
from the almost overwhelming choice is still described in florid detail;
choose, perhaps, roast quail served on Sharrow noodles with a dariole
of leek and wild mushroom and a Madeira and truffle sauce or grilled
scallops from the Kyle of Lochalsh served with a tarragon-dressed salad
with soy-scented sauce to commence a five-course lunch. Follow with a fish
course (fillet of halibut with white wine sauce with a delicate cheese soufflé
suissesse) and then Sharrow fruit sorbet. Main courses at dinner might
include noisettes of English lamb (accompanied by a sauce 'made with the
goodness of the lamb'), roast saddle of local venison, galette of salmon,
grilled fillet of sea bass and fried calf's liver with onion marmalade
in a pastry casing with smoked bacon and a cassis sauce. The preparation
of dishes is essentially simple, but made more complex by the elaborate
accompanying garnishes. As if these were not enough, vegetables are
plentiful, perhaps including young carrots, mangetout, cauliflower, red
cabbage and both Parisienne and new potatoes. Follow that, if you can,
with a choice of up to a dozen desserts – superb Old English Regency
syllabub, lemon posset with raspberries, traditional bread, butter and
marmalade pudding and apricot sauce, and 'the famous and original icky
sticky toffee sponge with cream' are typical – and a selection of 'Great
British cheeses' (foresaken at lunchtime). From the wonderful selection
of breads to begin through to the delightful petits fours at the end eating
here is an experience to be savoured. Marvellous and varied wine list with
an impressive array of wines by the glass (a choice of 24), many half bottles
and plenty of good drinking under £20; check out the bin ends.
No smoking. No childen under 13. **Seats** 64. *Parties 10. L 1-1.30 D 8-8.30.
Set L £30.75 Set D £40.75.*

Ulverston   Bay Horse Inn   £65
Tel 0229 583972   Fax 0229 580502   RR
Canal Foot Ulverston Cumbria LA12 9EL   Map 4 C4

A mile and a half from Ulverston, follow the signs for Canal Foot to find
this old pub with a sympathetic conversion that includes an intimate
conservatory restaurant with picturesque views over the Leven estuary.
Chef Robert Lyons pays homage to co-owner John Tovey at Miller Howe
on a menu, directing you to the master's cookbooks for some recipes, some
of which are quite inspired. Try for example fresh crab and sweetcorn
custard baked and served on a tomato and basil sauce, veal cutlet pan-fried
with field mushrooms, sun-dried tomatoes and mozzarella, served with
a rich Madeira sauce and Cape brandy pudding with crème fraiche
to finish. Coffee is served with home-made truffles in the lounge. There are
two wine lists, though customers choose mainly from the outstanding New
World list (80+), which features many gems at keen prices. No children
under 12. No smoking. *Seats 50. Private Room 30. L 12.30 D 7.30 for 8.
Closed L Sun & Mon, Jan. Set L £14.50. Access, Visa.*

Rooms   £120*

Overnight accommodation is provided in six (seven from December 1994)
attractive en-suite bedrooms, five of which open on to a small terrace with
a view of the estuary. No children under 12. *Half-board terms.

Ulverston   Place of Interest

The Laurel and Hardy Museum   Tel 0229 582292.

Upper Slaughter   Lords of the Manor   75%   £115
Tel 0451 820243   Fax 0451 820696   HR
Upper Slaughter nr Bourton-on-the-Water Gloucestershire GL54 2JD   Map 14 C1

Eight acres of parkland with a lake make a delightfully peaceful and very
English setting for this hotel, a 12th-century rectory with Victorian and
20th-century additions. Also very English are the bedrooms with chintzy
fabrics, nice antique pieces and restful watercolours on the walls. Bottles
of mineral water, a bowl of fruit and welcoming decanter of sherry add the
homely touches. Bathrooms, which match the individually decorated
bedrooms, boast high-class toiletries and generously sized robes. Room rates
vary – a small double is £98, while the four-posters are £185. Various day
rooms – there are three lounges in addition to the bar – have a nice
country-house feel with lots of fresh flowers and real log fires in winter
in addition to antiques, Oriental rugs and bric-a-brac assembled over the
years by owner James Gulliver. Attentive staff offer good standards
of service. No dogs. *Rooms 29. Garden, croquet, fishing. Closed 1-15 Jan.*
AMERICAN EXPRESS *Access, Diners, Visa.*

Restaurant   £90

A pleasing room, with yellow walls, crisp white napery and quality
tableware looking out on to the walled garden, where a patio makes a fine
spot for drinks or coffee (or even a meal) when the weather allows. Chef
Robert-Clive Dixon's style is 'country cooking with a modern influence',
evidenced by dinner dishes such as roast sweetbreads with onions and
tomato confit, turbot braised with wild mushrooms, ham hock, potato,
cabbage and salami, or roast duckling with a spicy pearl barley risotto and
an apricot and pear chutney. Desserts could include baked prune and
almond tart with cinnamon ice cream or honey nougatine glacé
on a passion fruit sauce. Lunchtime sees well-priced set menus, or you can
have just a bite from the short à la carte choice. Considerable effort has
gone into the comprehensive wine list, which has fairly-priced house
recommendations, and very helpful background notes; excellent selection

See over

of wines (all types) and ports by the glass. No smoking. *Seats 60. Parties 10. Private Room 60. L 12.30-2 (Sun to 2.30) D 7.30-9.30. Set L £10.95/£12.95 Set D £28.50.*

Uppingham   The Lake Isle   £60

Tel 0572 822951   Fax 0572 822951   **RR**

16 High Street East Uppingham Leicestershire LE15 9PZ   Map 7 E4

Just off the town centre, David and Claire Whitfield's charming, informal restaurant is in an 18th-century property reached by way of flower-decked Reeves Yard. Chef David gathers the ingredients for his short multi-course menus from near and far with twice-weekly deliveries from the Paris Rungis market, fish from Grimsby and Cornwall, plus herbs from his own walled garden. A sure touch is evident in dishes like sun-dried tomato and pimento soup, mushrooms stuffed with ham, Dijon mustard and pesto, roast loin of pork with walnuts, thyme and sherry and steamed paupiettes of sole with a smoked salmon and dill sauce. 'Healthy food choices' on the lunchtime menu might include salmon and smoked haddock fish cakes with a tomato and basil sauce, an individual caraway tartlet filled with smoked salmon and scrambled egg, or spicy lentil and potato cakes. A fine choice of British cheeses is served with walnut bread and a bowl of nuts. The splendid and well-chosen wine list has fair prices and probably the best half-bottle selection in the country; the New World is treated with respect. *Seats 40. Parties 22. Private Room 10. L 12.30-2 D 7-10. Closed L Mon, D Sun except to residents. Set L £10.95/£13.50 Set D £21.* *Access, Diners, Visa.*

Rooms   £66

The twelve bedrooms vary in size and style and are named after French wine regions (the Dom Perignon is large and has a whirlpool bath). All have direct-dial phones, colour TVs and thoughtful extras like fruit, mineral water and a decanter of sherry. Two double-bedded Cottage Suites are also available, one of which is self-contained and suitable for long stays. Good breakfasts in the restaurant or Continental served in the room.

Uttoxeter   Forte Travelodge   £45

Tel 0889 562043   **L**

Ashbourne Road Uttoxeter Staffordshire ST14 5AA   Map 6 C3

On the outskirts of Uttoxeter, 5 miles south of Alton Towers Leisure Park, at the junction of A50/B5030. *Rooms 32.* AMERICAN EXPRESS *Access, Diners, Visa.*

Uttoxeter   Place of Interest

Alton Towers   Tel 0538 702200.
Uttoxeter Racecourse   Tel 0889 562561.

Ventnor   Royal Hotel   60%   £66

Tel 0983 852186   Fax 0983 855395   **H**

Belgrave Road Ventnor Isle of Wight PO38 1JJ   Map 15 D4

Neat gardens front a Victorian sandstone hotel, now independently owned. Bedrooms have lightwood fitted units and colourful floral curtains. Small banquets/conferences for up to 40. *Rooms 54. Garden, outdoor swimming pool, games room.* AMERICAN EXPRESS *Access, Diners, Visa.*

Ventnor   Places of Interest

Tourist Information   Tel 0983 853625.
The Winter Gardens   Tel 0983 855111.
Appuldercombe House   (Ruins and Park) Wroxall Tel 0983 852484.

Veryan   Nare Hotel   70%   £124

Tel 0872 501279   Fax 0872 501856   **HR**

Carne Beach Veryan nr Truro Cornwall TR2 5PF   Map 12 B3

Standing above the mile-long sandy Carne Beach, the Nare has been
transformed from a simple, seaside hotel to a model of good taste and
a haven of tranquillity. Lounges and drawing room face extensive patios
and garden and have country house appeal with antique furniture. The
very best of the bedrooms have easy chairs and sofas, with beautiful views
out to sea and over the hotel lawns from picture windows and balconies.
Expect fruit and flowers on arrival and join fellow guests for
complimentary afternoon tea. Despite the hotel's location and sports
amenities (a new indoor swimming pool and spa bath were installed last
year), the hotel is not really suitable for families. A drying/boot room
is very useful for walkers. Concessionary vouchers are given to guests who
wish to play golf at Truro Golf Club. *Rooms 35. Garden, indoor & outdoor
swimming pool, spa bath, sauna, sun beds, tennis, gym, snooker, coffee shop
(12-2, 7.15-9), sports boat, sail boards. Closed 6 weeks Jan-mid Feb.
Access, Visa.*

Restaurant   £70

Appealing sea views through windows with swathed pelmets; standard
fare, using good local produce and seafood, is served in healthy-sized
portions. Flambé dishes (charged as a supplement to the table d'hote) are
popular and hors d'oeuvre, desserts and cheese are served on well-laden
trolleys. A light lunch is served in the Gwendra Room and adjacent terrace
during the week; traditional Sunday lunch is in the dining room. Jacket
and tie preferred in the evening. No children under 7 in the dining room
at night (the early evening children's menu is £10!). Minimum à la carte
charge £28 per person. Picnic lunches available. *Seats 70. Parties 12.
Private Room 20. L 12.30-2 D 7.15-9.30. Set L (Sun) £13.50
Set D (5-course) £25.*

Wadhurst   Spindlewood   59%   £63

Tel 0580 200430   Fax 0580 201132   **HR**

Wallcrouch Wadhurst East Sussex TN5 7JG   Map 11 B6

Small family-run Victorian hotel in five acres of gardens just east of town
on the B2099. Pleasant bedrooms are furnished in traditional style with
antiqueish and some more utilitarian pieces; all come with beverage kits,
hairdryers, remote-control TVs and radio-alarms. Carpeted bathrooms have
tubs but no showers (except for one with shower and WC only) although
for hair-washing there are flexible attachments that fit over the taps.
No separate lounge but some easy chairs in the bar with its bay window
overlooking the gardens. "Children with well-behaved parents" are
welcomed. No dogs. *Rooms 8. Garden, helipad. Closed 4 days Christmas.
Access, Visa.*

Restaurant   £65

The same regularly changing fixed-price menu is served at both lunch and
dinner in a spacious period dining room with nice ribbed ceiling and real
log fire in winter. Half a dozen dishes at each stage are supplemented
by several soups and fish dishes each day to provide plenty of choice.
Home-made soups, individual seafood quiche, hot mushroom mousse
in a leek and almond broth, jugged or loin of hare with peppercorn sauce,
pan-fried calf's liver, grilled fillet of beef with apple, grapes and red wine
sauce, and a selection of both hot and cold puddings (orange and Grand
Marnier crepe soufflé, apricot mousse gateau), show the range. Long-
serving chef Harvey Lee Aram's cooking includes good home-baked bread
rolls. Additionally – Monday to Friday – snack lunches are served in the
bar. Traditional Sunday lunches. Ten seats in the verandah. *Seats 40.
Private Room 24. L 12.15-1.30 D 7.15-9. Closed L Bank Holidays & 25 Dec.
Set L & D £23.20 (Sun L £14.95).*

Wakefield   Campanile Hotel   £44

Tel 0924 201054   Fax 0924 201055   **L**

Monckton Road Wakefield West Yorkshire   **Map 6 C1**

Canalside location, 15 minutes' drive outside Leeds. Nearest motorway
junction is J39 from the M1, taking A636 Denby Dale road. *Rooms 77.*
AMERICAN EXPRESS *Access, Diners, Visa.*

Wakefield   Cedar Court   59%   £91

Tel 0924 276310   Fax 0924 280221   **H**

Denby Dale Road Calder Grove Wakefield West Yorkshire WF4 3QZ   **Map 6 C1**

Modern, purpose-built business hotel on the roundabout at Junction 39
of the M1, 12 miles south of Leeds. Open-plan day rooms, practical
accommodation including several suites and a dozen Executive rooms;
satellite TVs throughout; phone extensions in bathrooms; some whirlpool
baths. Conference/banqueting facilities up to 400. Children stay free
in parents' room. Free parking for up to 350 cars. No dogs. *Rooms 150.
Garden.* AMERICAN EXPRESS *Access, Diners, Visa.*

Wakefield   Forte Posthouse   64%   £68

Tel 0924 276388   Fax 0924 276437   **H**

Queen's Drive Ossett Wakefield West Yorkshire WF5 9BE   **Map 6 C1**

Modern low-rise hotel near Junction 40 of the M1. Facilities for up to 150
delegates in the largest of several conference rooms. 24hr lounge menu.
Parking for 160 cars. *Rooms 99. Garden.* AMERICAN EXPRESS *Access,
Diners, Visa.*

Wakefield   Granada Lodge   £51

Tel 0924 830569   Fax 0924 830609   **L**

M1 Junction 38/39 Woolley Edge Wakefield West Yorkshire WF4 4LQ   **Map 6 C1**

Rooms 31. AMERICAN EXPRESS *Access, Diners, Visa.*

Wakefield   Swallow Hotel   58%   £88

Tel 0924 372111   Fax 0924 383648   **H**

Queen Street Wakefield West Yorkshire WF1 1JU   **Map 6 C1**

A tall hotel, with splendid views from bedrooms on the upper floors, near
the Cathedral in the city centre. Public rooms are on the first and second
floors. The largest of several conference rooms can take up to 200 delegates.
Parking for 40 cars. Guests have free membership of a local gym/sauna
centre and snooker club. *Rooms 63.* AMERICAN EXPRESS *Access, Diners, Visa.*

Wakefield   Places of Interest

Theatre Royal and Opera House   Drury Lane Tel 0924 366556.
Nostell Priory (NT)   Tel 0924 863892.
Wakefield Cathedral   Tel 0924 373923.
   Museums and Art Galleries
Wakefield Art Gallery   Wentworth Terrace Tel 0924 375402 or 295796.
Yorkshire Mining Museum and Underground Tours   Caphouse Colliery,
   New Road, Overton Tel 0924 848806.
Yorkshire Sculpture Park   Bretton Hall, West Bretton Tel 0924
   830579/830302.
Featherstone Rovers RLFC   Tel 0977 702386.
Wakefield Trinity RLFC   Tel 0924 372445.

Walberton   Avisford Park   66%   £106

Tel 0243 551215   Fax 0243 552485   **H**

Yapton Lane Walberton Arundel West Sussex BN18 0LS   Map 11 A6

From Arundel, follow the A27 towards Chichester and turn left on to the
B2132 to find this Georgian manor house set in 62 acres of grounds. The
day rooms at this former boys' school are large, as befits a hotel whose
principal business is conference delegates. The Garden Lodge Business
Centre is linked by an enclosed walkway and comprises a Grand Hall
(holding up to 350), 24 Executive bedrooms, two suites and an Italian
restaurant. Banquets for 250. No dogs. *Rooms 126. Garden, croquet, indoor
swimming pools, sauna, solarium, snooker, 9-hole golf course, tennis, squash.*
AMERICAN EXPRESS *Access, Diners, Visa.*

Walkington   Manor House   72%   £93

Tel 0482 881645   Fax 0482 866501   **HR**

Northlands Walkington Beverley Humberside HU17 8RT   Map 7 E1

In a wonderfully peaceful location surrounded by the Yorkshire Wolds,
3 minutes from Beverley on the B1230, stands this late-Victorian house run
by Derek and Lee Baugh along the lines of a private house with family
guests. The bedrooms, all with king-size beds, offer fine country views and
are decorated in soft tones. Comfortable seating, flowers, magazines and
ornaments add to the homely appeal. Bathrooms squeeze with difficulty
into 19th-century rooms, but are well equipped. Day rooms include
an elegant drawing room with fine antiques, oil paintings and seating made
for relaxation. Friendly staff and notably good housekeeping. No children
under 12. *Rooms 7. Garden. Closed 25, 26 Dec, 1 Jan. Access, Visa.*

Restaurant   £75

An elegant blue dining room and adjoining conservatory provide a choice
of environments in which to enjoy Derek Baugh's cooking. Fixed-price-
only menus are described in refreshingly straightforward English and the
style gives classical dishes modern elaboration: nine Bridlington queenies
in the half-shell cooked in nine different flavours and sauces(!); salmis
of rabbit, peppered chicken liver, sweetbreads and wild mushrooms
on a creamy leek ragout; breast of chicken seared in chervil butter with
a julienne of vegetables and a mild apricot korma sauce. Mixed grill Manor
House is an up-to-date version of an old favourite with bacon, kidney,
steak, cutlet, liver, sausage, cherry tomatoes, mushrooms, onion rings, fried
quail's egg, mignonette potatoes and maitre d'hotel butter. Coffee is served
with chocolate truffles. Simpler lunches and a good-value nightly table
d'hote. There are several inexpensive, 'well-worth-drinking' wines
on a pleasing list that's mostly French, with a dip into the rest of Europe
and the New World. *Seats 50. Parties 24. Private Room 20. D only
7.30-9.15. Closed Sun. Set D from £15.*

> 🍾 is our symbol for an outstanding wine list.

Wallingford   George Hotel   60%   £80

Tel 0491 836665   Fax 0491 825359   **H**

High Street Wallingford Oxfordshire OX10 0BS   Map 15 D2

Dick Turpin took rooms at this historic coaching inn and during the Civil
War Royalist troops were billeted here. Now, in a less turbulent phase, the
George mixes tradition with basic modern hotel amenity. Nine of the
bedrooms are reserved for non-smokers. A self-contained suite can
accommodate up to 120 conference delegates. Children up to 12 stay free
in parents' room. Free use of the nearby Didcot Wave leisure centre.
Mount Charlotte Thistle. *Rooms 39.* AMERICAN EXPRESS *Access, Diners, Visa.*

Wallingford   Shillingford Bridge Hotel   61%   £68

Tel 0865 858567   Fax 0865 858636

Ferry Road Shillingford nr Wallingford Oxfordshire OX10 8LX

H

Map 15 D2

The Thameside location has been well utilised with public rooms, now all
attractively refurbished, overlooking a wide, slow-flowing stretch of the
river as it passes under Shillingford Bridge. Bedrooms too have benefited
from the hand of the decorator with much use of soft pastel colours and
a generally pretty, floral decor. Three have four-posters and virtually all
have good westward views over the river. Large sliding patio windows are
an appealing feature of a few spacious bedrooms in a separate converted
wooden house. Bathrooms have economy size bottles of family shampoo
and bath foam and come ready occupied by a family of ducks – the yellow
plastic species. **Rooms** *42. Garden, outdoor swimming pool, squash, coarse
fishing, mooring.* AMERICAN EXPRESS *Access, Diners, Visa.*

Wallingford   Place of Interest

Corn Exchange   Market Place Tel 0491 39336.

Walsall   Boundary Hotel   61%   £71

Tel 0922 33555   Fax 0922 612034

Birmingham Road Walsall West Midlands WS5 3AB

H

Map 6 C4

This former *Posthouse*, still owned by Forte, is found by taking Junction
7 of the M6, then the A34 to the ring road intersection. It's a modern
purpose-built hotel offering facilities for small banquets (25) and
conferences (45). **Rooms** *98.* AMERICAN EXPRESS *Access, Diners, Visa.*

Walsall   Friendly Hotel   60%   £84

Tel 0922 724444   Fax 0922 723148

20 Wolverhamptom Rd West Bentley Walsall West Midlands WS2 0BS

H

Map 6 C4

By Junction 10 of the M6, this was one of Friendly Hotel's first purpose-
built units; low-rise, open-plan public areas, small leisure centre, practical
standardised bedrooms and 12 suites with small lounges and personal fax
machines. One room equipped for disabled guests. Meeting rooms for up to
180. **Rooms** *153. Garden, indoor swimming pool, gym, sauna, steam room, spa
bath, sun beds.* AMERICAN EXPRESS *Access, Diners, Visa.*

> If we recommend meals in a hotel or inn a separate entry is made for its
> restaurant.

Walsall Wood   Baron's Court Hotel   62%   £55

Tel 0543 452020   Fax 0543 361276

Walsall Wood Walsall West Midlands WS9 9AH

H

Map 6 C4

Tudor-inspired styling and fittings feature throughout the ground-floor
areas of this unusual hotel on the A461. Bedrooms employ Queen Anne-
style furniture and soft decor. Executive rooms are larger and have
whirlpool baths. Total refurbishment was due for completion as this Guide
came out. Banquets/conferences for up to 200. **Rooms** *100. Indoor
swimming pool, keep-fit equipment, sauna, spa bath, steam room, solarium.*
AMERICAN EXPRESS *Access, Diners, Visa.*

Walsall   Places of Interest

Museum and Art Gallery and Garman Ryan Collection   Tel 0922
653135.
Walsall Leather Centre Museum   Tel 0922 721153.

Waltham Abbey — Swallow Hotel — 66% — £110

Tel 0992 717170   Fax 0992 711841 — **H**

Old Shire Lane Waltham Abbey Essex EN9 3LX — Map 15 F2

Just north of Junction 26 of the M25, this is one of Swallow's newest hotels. Public rooms and bedrooms radiate from an impressive lobby bar and lounge area which is dominated by a huge, glittering funnel-shaped fountain. Neat, well-equipped bedrooms offer 24hr room service. Children up to 14 stay free in parents' room. Good leisure facilities. Ample free parking. *Rooms 163. Garden, croquet, indoor swimming pool, children's swimming pool, keep-fit equipment, sauna, spa bath, solarium, courtesy mini-bus, helipad.* AMERICAN EXPRESS *Access, Diners, Visa.*

> Note that all telephone numbers with area codes starting with 0 will start 01 from 16 April 1995.

Wansford-in-England — The Haycock — 70% — £85

Tel 0780 782223   Fax 0780 783031 — **HR**

Wansford-in-England Peterborough Cambridgeshire PE8 6JA — Map 7 E4

A lovely 17th-century honey-coloured stone coaching inn in 6 acres of grounds next to the junction of A1 and A47. It has been much extended, in sympathetic style, the most recent additions being a large conference/ballroom (a lovely setting for functions with its soaring oak beams, enormous fireplace and private garden, catering for up to 200) and the stone-walled Orchard Room with all-day bar and coffee-shop menu. Other day rooms include a pubby bar and two traditional lounges. Bedrooms in the older parts of the building are full of character, but all have been decorated with great style and flair by Julia Vanocci using high-quality fabrics and furnishings; one ground-floor twin room has a wide door and handrails for disabled guests. Bathrooms are equally luxurious. Extensive grounds feature award-winning gardens which stretch along the banks of the river Nene and the village cricket pitch. The variety of food on offer in both bar (excellent bar snacks), Orchard Room (7am-11pm with a fine lunchtime buffet) and restaurant caters for all tastes and pockets; outdoor barbecue daily in summer with seating for 100. Poste Hotels. *Rooms 50. Garden, croquet, fishing, pétanque, helipad.* AMERICAN EXPRESS *Access, Diners, Visa.*

Restaurant — £70

Candelabras and highly-polished silver add to the mellow, traditional atmosphere of the twin dining rooms here. Richard Brandrick's and Peter Grant's menu is pretty traditional too, with the likes of 'cheffy's' steak and kidney pie and jugged hare with sausage meat balls (both considered specialities), plus the daily roast sirloin of prime English beef that always features on the silver trolley. An extra charge of £3.50 (reduced from £3.95 last year) for fresh vegetables and potatoes obviously reduces the perceived value of main-course menu prices. Other offerings might include terrine of local game with a thyme and port sauce or salmon quenelles on a spinach and watercress sauce to start, followed by roast rack of lamb carved at the table (served with redcurrant tartlets) or poached fillets of plaice stuffed with salmon mousse and a white wine, cream and dill sauce. Home-made desserts or British cheeses from Neal's Yard. Coffee served in a cafetière with decaffeinated as an option. A wine list doesn't need to be long to be considered outstanding, if, as is the case here, it has been carefully compiled to complement the style of restaurant and offers both helpful notes and giveaway prices! *Seats 100. Parties 10. Private Room 30. L 12-2.30 D 7-10.30. Set L £13.95.*

Wantage   Bear Hotel   58%

£60

H

Tel 023 57 66366   Fax 023 57 68826

Market Square Wantage Oxfordshire OX12 8AB

Map 14 C2

Since the 16th century the Bear has been a notable feature on the market square of the town where Alfred the Great was born (his statue is another landmark). The cobbled courtyard evokes some of the atmosphere of the past, and a few of the bedrooms are furnished with some older pieces, including brass bedsteads. A few rooms are suitable for family use. The Ascot Suite provides conference facilities for up to 80. No dogs. **Rooms** *34.* AMERICAN EXPRESS *Access, Diners, Visa.*

Wareham   Priory Hotel   72%

£100

HR

Tel 0929 551666   Fax 0929 554519

Church Green Wareham Dorset BH20 4ND

Map 14 B4

The former priory of Lady St Mary stands in landscaped gardens that reach down to the River Frome. Two beautifully decorated lounges overlook the gardens, and there is a small traditional bar. Bedrooms vary in size but all are thoughtfully equipped: each has mineral water, fresh fruit, books and magazines, plus bathrobes, clothes brushes and hairdryers. One room has a four-poster and a whirlpool bath and all feature handsome antique furniture. The Boathouse, converted from a 16th-century clay barn, contains two bedrooms and two luxurious suites. Moorings are available for guests arriving by boat. No dogs. **Rooms** *19. Garden, croquet, coarse & game fishing.* AMERICAN EXPRESS *Access, Diners, Visa.*

Restaurant

£75

Two rooms: ground-floor dining room for breakfast and lunch; Abbots Cellar in vaulted stone cellars for candle-lit dinner. Seasonal produce, local and British, is the basis of Michael Rust's appealing menus, which apply modern accents to traditional methods: hot black pudding on braised lentils in a rich onion gravy; marinated salmon with lemon juice, dill and wholegrain mustard; Dover sole with saffron potatoes, cucumber and rosemary butter sauce; medallions of venison with celeriac pearls, chestnuts and a rich port wine sauce. Steak Diane and crêpes Suzette are prepared at the table; roasts carved at the table; desserts from the trolley; English cheeses. Many clarets on decent wine list which also has a good selection of New World wines. Plenty of half bottles, fair prices. **Seats** *66. Private Room 24. L 12.30-2.30 D 7.30-10. Set L £12.95/£14.95 (Sun £16.95). Set D £22.50/£26.50.*

Wareham   Springfield Country Hotel   60%

£100

H

Tel 0929 552177   Fax 0929 551862

Grange Road Stoborough nr Wareham Dorset BH20 5AL

Map 14 B4

Set in six acres of stylishly landscaped gardens off the A351, a pleasant redbrick hotel with an appealing modern exterior. The spacious foyer is dominated by a splendid stag's head and there are two cosy bars. Bedrooms are agreeable and neatly maintained, all featuring a uniform pink decor, and include doubles, twins and singles, plus a number of family rooms and suites; bidets and avocado suites in the compact bathrooms. The recently added function suite and impressive leisure club is approached across an uncovered, grassy patch from the hotel and has bars, an informal restaurant and banqueting/conference facilities for 160/200; squash and indoor bowls promised for the end of 1994. Good family facilities, including high teas. Outdoor pool heated May-Oct. **Rooms** *32. Garden, tennis, indoor & outdoor swimming pool, gym, squash, sauna, steam room, solarium, badminton, games room (snooker, pool & table tennis), children's playroom & playground.* AMERICAN EXPRESS *Access, Visa.*

Wareham   Place of Interest

Tank Museum   Bovington Camp Tel 0929 403329.
Swanage Beach *9 miles SE of Wareham.*

Warminster   Bishopstrow House   79%   £123

Tel 0985 212312   Fax 0985 216769

HR

Boreham Road Warminster Wiltshire BA12 9HH   Map 14 B3

An elegant, ivy-clad Georgian house in a lovely setting at the end
of a private drive. The entrance hall, morning room and dining rooms are
stylish and formal, with fine oil paintings, French and English antiques,
Persian carpets and deep, inviting armchairs. Flower displays add splendid
splashes of colour. Spacious bedrooms are in three places: main house,
garden rooms and courtyard rooms reached by long corridors. Rooms are
either standard or de luxe. Fruit, biscuits, plants and magazines are provided
and some of the bedrooms feature spa baths or separate showers. A stunning
indoor swimming pool looks out on to the gardens. Conference facilities
for up to 60. Sister hotel to *Charingworth Manor* (see entry under Chipping
Campden). **Rooms** *32. Garden, indoor & outdoor swimming pools, indoor &
outdoor tennis, game fishing, sauna, helipad.* AMERICAN EXPRESS® *Access,
Diners, Visa.*

The Temple Restaurant   £80

Garden views accompany inventive modern cooking by Chris Suter.
Refreshingly straightforward menu descriptions in English belie the effort
and invention that go into his dishes: pan-fried John Dory with white
asparagus and a warm balsamic vinaigrette, warm salad of honey-roast duck
leg confit with Puy lentils, fricassée of free-range chicken with morel
mushrooms, roast best end of lamb with herb crust. To finish, farmhouse
cheeses, home-made ice creams and sorbets (plain or in splendid creations
like rhubarb and strawberry gratin with rhubarb sorbet). An excellent and
well-balanced wine list, constantly revised, does have some reasonably
priced wines, but on the whole mark-ups are as expected in a hotel of this
standard. **Seats** *65. Parties 8. Private Room 22. L 12-2 D 7.30-9.30.
Set L £12.30 Set D £31.*

Warminster   Granada Lodge   £51

Tel 0985 219639   Fax 0985 214380

L

A36/A350 Warminster Wiltshire BA12 7RU   Map 14 B3

Rooms 31. AMERICAN EXPRESS® *Access, Diners, Visa.*

Warminster   Place of Interest

Longleat House and Wildlife Park   Tel 09853 551/328.

Warrington   Holiday Inn Garden Court   65%   £70

Tel 0925 838779   Fax 0925 838859

H

Woolston Grange Avenue Woolston Warrington Cheshire WA1 4PX   Map 6 B2

By Junction 21 of the M6, one of the 'junior' Holiday Inns offering good
bedrooms (over half for non-smokers), with limited public areas. Children
up to 19 stay free in parents' room. Parking for 114 cars. **Rooms** *99. Patio,
games room.* AMERICAN EXPRESS® *Access, Diners, Visa.*

Warrington   Lord Daresbury Hotel   67%   £105

Tel 0925 267331   Fax 0925 601496

H

Chester Road Daresbury Warrington Cheshire WA4 4BB   Map 6 B2

Conveniently located by junction 11 of the M56, this modern, conference-
oriented hotel (meeting rooms for up to 500 delegates) also offers extensive
leisure amenities. Half the rooms are reserved for non-smokers; some are

designated as Lady Executive rooms. A £500,000 bedroom upgrading programme was under way as we went to press. De Vere Hotels. *Rooms 140. Garden, indoor swimming pool, gym, sauna, spa bath, steam bath, solarium, beauty and hair salon, squash, snooker, children's play area, coffee shop (7.45am–5.45pm).* AMERICAN EXPRESS *Access, Diners, Visa.*

Warrington	**Travel Inn**	**£43**
Tel 0925 414417 Fax 0925 414544		**L**
Winwick Road Warrington Cheshire		**Map 6 B2**

Close to Junction 9 of the M62. *Rooms 40.* AMERICAN EXPRESS *Access, Diners, Visa.*

Warrington	**Places of Interest**

Tourist Information   Tel 0925 36501.
Museum & Art Gallery   Tel 0925 44400/30550.
Warrington RLFC   Tel 0925 35338.

Warwick	**Hilton National**	**66%**	**£106**
Tel 0926 499555 Fax 0926 410020			**H**
Stratford Road Warwick Warwickshire CV34 6RE			**Map 14 C1**

Conferences for up to 400 are catered for at this low-rise modern hotel on the A429 by Junction 15 of M40. Executive rooms and four-bedded family rooms available. 24hr room service. One bedroom is equipped for disabled guests. *Rooms 181. Indoor swimming pool, keep-fit equipment, sauna, steam room, sun beds.* AMERICAN EXPRESS *Access, Diners, Visa.*

Warwick	**Places of Interest**

Tourist Information   Tel 0926 492212.
Doll Museum   Tel 0926 495546.
Warwickshire Museum   Tel 0926 410410 ext 2021.
Warwick Racecourse   Tel 0926 491553.
  Historic Houses, Castles and Gardens
Charlecote Park (NT)   Tel 0789 470277.
Warwick Castle   Tel 0926 495421.
Packwood House (NT)   Hockley Heath Tel 0564 782024.

Washington	**Campanile Hotel**	**£44**
Tel 091-416 5010 Fax 091-416 5023		**L**
Emerson Road Washington nr Newcastle-upon-Tyne Tyne & Wear NE37 1LE		**Map 5 E2**

Off the A1(M) between the A1231 and A195. *Rooms 77.* AMERICAN EXPRESS *Access, Diners, Visa.*

Washington	**Forte Posthouse**	**59%**	**£68**
Tel 091-416 2264 Fax 091-415 3371			**H**
Emerson District 5 Washington Tyne & Wear NE37 1LB			**Map 5 E2**

Just south of Washington Services on A1(M), a practical modern hotel that's popular with business visitors, who obviously appreciate good-value rooms and conference facilities. Children under 16 free in parents' room. *Rooms 138. 18-hole pitch & putt, children's playroom & playground.* AMERICAN EXPRESS *Access, Diners, Visa.*

Washington   Granada Lodge   £51

Tel 091-410 0076   Fax 091-410 0057   **L**

A1(M) Washington nr Newcastle-upon-Tyne Tyne & Wear DH3 2SJ   Map 5 E2

Rooms 35. AMERICAN EXPRESS *Access, Diners, Visa.*

Washington   Moat House   66%   £94

Tel 091-417 2626   Fax 091-415 1166   **H**

Stone Cellar Road High Usworth District 12 Washington Tyne & Wear
NE37 1PH   Map 5 E2

First-class leisure facilities are the main attraction at a modern Moat House
standing by a championship golf course. Large bedrooms have all the usual
modern accessories. Popular with business people during the week and
sportsmen and families at weekends. Conference/banqueting suites for
200/180. *Rooms 106. Garden, indoor swimming pool, 18-hole golf course,
pitch & putt, golf driving range, spa bath, sauna, solarium, keep-fit equipment,
squash.* AMERICAN EXPRESS *Access, Diners, Visa.*

Washington   Travel Inn (Sunderland)   £43

Tel 091-548 9384   Fax 091-548 4148   **L**

Wessington Way Castletown Washington nr Sunderland Tyne & Wear
SR5 3HR   Map 5 E2

Adjacent to Sunrise Business Park, at the junction of A19 and A1231.
Rooms 40. AMERICAN EXPRESS *Access, Diners, Visa.*

Waterhouses   Old Beams   ★ ↑   £80

Tel 0538 308254   Fax 0538 308157   **RR**

Leek Road Waterhouses Staffordshire ST10 3HW   Map 6 C3

An 18th-century former inn on the A523 transformed by Nigel and Ann
Wallis into a country restaurant of enormous charm. Oak beams, open fires
and Windsor chairs feature within while the sunny conservatory boasts
a splendid mural. Add an abundance of fresh flowers and urbane service,
supervised by Ann, and the scene is set for Nigel's well-balanced dinner
menus that manage to give ample variety within the half-dozen choices
(4-5 at lunchtime) offered at each stage. Ravioli of fresh oysters, pan-fried
foie gras on Calvados sauce, turbot mousse on real caviar sauce, and a brace
of quails in pastry with couscous (a refined version of the North African
dish) demonstrate his versatility. Desserts could include hot pistachio
or strawberry soufflé, millefeuille of chocolates and roast figs with ice
cream and a sweet red wine sauce. The less expensive lunch menu avoids
the more luxurious ingredients. Consistently high standards are evident
throughout, from an excellent venison terrine served as the complimentary
starter at a recent meal via home-made bread and tangy between-course
sorbet to the petits fours that arrive with coffee. Several good wine-makers
appear on the excellent wine list that has helpful tasting notes (but rather
too many spelling mistakes!); good half-bottle selection. No smoking
at table. *Seats 50. Private Room 20. L 12-2 D 7-9.30. Closed L Sat, D Sun,
all Mon. Set L £10.95 (except Sun) & £17.50 Set D £18.50 (except Sat) &
£32.50.* AMERICAN EXPRESS *Access, Diners, Visa.* MARTELL

Rooms   £87

Just across the road in a converted smithy are the five luxurious bedrooms
(large Premier or small De Luxe), each named after one of the famous
Staffordshire potteries. Individually decorated with flair and style the
rooms boast hand-made beds from Heal's, beautiful hand-embroidered
Egyptian cotton bedding and splendid bathrooms with towelling robes,
huge monogrammed bath sheets and Badedas for the tub. Continental

breakfasts – with croissants hot from the oven, freshly squeezed orange juice and home-made preserves – can be served in the room, cooked breakfasts in the restaurant. No smoking. No dogs.

Wateringbury   Wateringbury Hotel   59%   £61

Tel 0622 812632   Fax 0622 812720   **H**

Tonbridge Road Wateringbury nr Maidstone Kent ME18 5NS   **Map 11 C5**

Rooms at this tile-hung roadside inn range from singles to a four-poster suite. There's a cane-furnished conservatory, a cocktail bar and two function rooms (catering for up to 50 delegates). *Rooms 40. Garden, sauna.* AMERICAN EXPRESS *Access, Diners, Visa.*

Watford   Hilton National   64%   £105

Tel 0923 235881   Fax 0923 220836   **H**

Elton Way Watford Hertfordshire WD2 8HA   **Map 15 E2**

Practical accommodation, a leisure centre and extensive conference facilities (for up to 500). Children under the age of 14 are accommodated free in parents' room, but their time in the leisure centre is limited. 24hr room service. Ample free parking. *Rooms 195. Indoor swimming pool, gym, sauna, spa bath, steam room, beauty salon, coffee shop (8am-11pm).* AMERICAN EXPRESS *Access, Diners, Visa.*

Watford   Jarvis International   60%   £109

Tel 081-950 6211   Fax 081-950 5804   **H**

A41 Watford By-pass Watford Hertfordshire WD2 8HQ   **Map 15 F2**

Acquired by Jarvis one and a half years ago, the hotel is undergoing a gradual and major refurbishment programme. To date, the public areas and the Sebastian Coe leisure centre have been completed. Also in place are the 17 'summit' conference rooms designed to hold from 2 to 45 delegates. Bedrooms are next in line. *Rooms 160. Garden, tennis, indoor swimming pools, sauna, spa bath, solarium, beauty salon.* AMERICAN EXPRESS *Access, Diners, Visa.*

Watford   Places of Interest

Palace Theatre   Tel 0923 35455.
Watford Football Ground   Vicarage Road Tel 0923 30933.
Watford Ski School   Garston Tel 0923 676559.

Wath-in-Nidderdale   Sportsman's Arms   £60

Tel 0423 711306   **RR**

Wath-in-Nidderdale Pateley Bridge nr Harrogate North Yorkshire HG3 5PP   **Map 6 C1**

Making optimum use of seasonal market availability, an ever-enthusiastic Ray Carter produces nightly dinners in a classic style as he has done here for 15 years. Pier-fresh Whitby fish, Dales lamb and free-range chickens are served with flavour-led vegetables both common and exotic. Perennially popular, his summer pudding has been passed on to many protegés, whilst the nightly cheese selection is peerless also. Almost giveaway prices on a fine wine list (house wines at £9.50, five champagnes under £30). Splendid selection from the New World, though none of these are available in half bottles. *Seats 50. Parties 8. Private Room 8. Sun L 12-2.30 D 7-10 (Sun to 8.30). Closed 25 Dec. Set Sun L £11.75 Set D £18.75 (Set Sun D £13.50 at 7.30pm). Access, Visa.*

Rooms   £47

Stripped pine doors are the unifying theme of the single corridor of bedrooms which are of modest size and appointment; returning guests appreciate rather the total peace and quiet and the absence of room telephones. Whilst all are equipped with wash basins only two out of seven have full en-suite facilities: two WCs and two separate bathrooms are shared by the rest. A long, leisurely and very large breakfast is served at 9.

Watlington   Well House

Tel 0491 613333

34-40 High Street Watlington Oxfordshire OX9 5PY

£60

RR

Map 15 D2

In a quiet village 12 miles south-east of Oxford and two miles from the M40 (J6), five little properties, some dating back to the 15th century, have been carefully altered to produce a delightful restaurant with rooms. Owners Patricia and Alan Crawford are particularly friendly hosts and meals in the beamed dining room, with its exposed brick fireplace and well-spaced tables, are very relaxed affairs. Patricia's cooking is sound and very straightforward, offered on both table d'hote and carte at lunch and dinner: oxtail soup, cheese and parsley fritters, lamb's liver with onion confit, spiced aubergine pancakes (there's a separate vegetarian menu), roast monkfish wrapped in bacon on a sweet pepper sauce, chocolate velvet cake, lemon roulade. Scant recognition of the New World on the predominantly French wine list, but Germany gets a look in. No smoking. A simpler snackier menu is available at lunchtime in the little bar. *Seats* 40. *L* 12.30-2 *D* 7-9.15 (*Sat to 9.30*). *Closed L Mon & Sat, D Sun, 1 week from 26 Dec. Set meals £14.50/£18.50.* AMERICAN EXPRESS *Access, Diners, Visa.*

Rooms

£66

Ten bedrooms all have their own shape and character; there's a quiet lounge with an open fireplace and a bar with an old well and access to the rear terrace. Cots and high-chairs provided for junior guests.

Weedon   Crossroads Hotel   55%

Tel 0327 340354   Fax 0327 340849

High Street Weedon Northamptonshire NN7 4PX

£52

H

Map 15 D1

Not the establishment of TV fame but a well-run lodge located on the busy intersection of the A5 and A45, with efficient triple-glazing for the rooms where it matters. A new reception area-cum-lounge with floral-patterned chairs and fake marble (vinyl) tables. The remainder of the public areas are in the original building and comprise a large, characterful bar (full of pubby artefacts) with a south-facing balcony (only 3 tables). Bedrooms are all in a U-shaped motel-style block (except for 10 in the main building). Attractively furnished and neatly maintained. Bathrooms are on the small side. *Rooms* 48. *Garden, tennis, brasserie (7am-6pm).* *Closed 25 & 26 Dec.* AMERICAN EXPRESS *Access, Diners, Visa.*

Wells   Ritcher's

Tel 0749 679085

5 Sadler Street Wells Somerset BA5 2RR

£55

R

Map 13 F1

In an alley between shops in the town centre, Nick Hart and Kate Ritcher offer a choice of casual eating in the pine-furnished downstairs bistro and more formal dining in the comfortable upstairs restaurant – both outlets making wide use of prime local produce. Typical items on the bistro menu run from grilled Somerset Camembert salad and moules marinière to sautéed chicken with cream and tarragon, goose egg bénédictine, salmon with lemon mayonnaise and individual venison and guinea fowl pie with a blackcurrant and orange pickle. From the restaurant come the likes of salmon and prawn sausage with a leek and cream fricasse, oven-baked loin of pork en croute with an apple stuffing and sauce béarnaise, and individual cointreau and dark chocolate mousse with a fresh orange and honey dressing. Tables outside in the bistro. No children under ten in the restaurant. *Restaurant: Seats* 14. *L* 12-2 (*booking only*) *D* 7-9 (*Sat to 9.30*). *Closed Sun, Mon, 26 Dec, 1 Jan. Set L £12.50/£14.50*

*Set D £14.50/£17.50. Bistro: **Seats** 18. Parties 12. L 12-2 (Sat to 2.30)
D 7-9 (Sat to 9.30). Set L £4.95/£6.95 Set D £10.50/£12.50.
Closed 26 Dec, 1 Jan. Access, Visa.*

Wells   Places of Interest

Tourist Information   Tel 0749 72552.
Wells Cathedral   Tel 0749 74483.
   Historic Houses, Castles and Gardens
The Bishop's Palace   Tel 0749 78691.
Milton Cottage and Gardens   Tel 0749 72168.
Pear Tree House   Litton Tel 076121 220.

Welwyn   Clock Hotel   54%   £73

Tel 0438 716911   Fax 0438 714065   **H**

The Link Welwyn Hertfordshire AL6 9XA   **Map 15 E1**

Enjoying a prominent position on a roundabout alongside the northbound
carriageway of the A1(M), from which it's approached via Junction
6, a hotel that's popular with business folk. Friendly Hotels. *Rooms 95.
Gym. Closed 3 days at Christmas.* AMERICAN EXPRESS *Access, Diners, Visa.*

Wembley   Hilton National   65%   £139

Tel 081-902 8839   Fax 081-900 2201   **H**

Empire Way Wembley Middlesex HA9 8DS   **Map 15 E2**

Practical modern accommodation, within easy walking distance
of Wembley Arena, Stadium and Conference Centre. Carvery-style
restaurant and a bar that gets very busy on match and concert dates.
10 conference rooms catering for up to 350 delegates. The new health club
is now on stream, and the standard rooms are next for refurbishment.
***Rooms** 306. News kiosk.* AMERICAN EXPRESS *Access, Diners, Visa.*

Wentbridge   Forte Travelodge   £45

Tel 0977 620711   **L**

Barnsdale Bar Wentbridge nr Pontefract West Yorkshire WS8 3JB   **Map 7 D1**

Located on the A1 southbound at the Barnsdale Bar service area, south
of Wentbridge. 6 miles south of Junction 33 of M62, 8 miles north
of Doncaster. ***Rooms** 56.* AMERICAN EXPRESS *Access, Diners, Visa.*

Wentbridge   Wentbridge House   64%   £75

Tel 0977 620444   Fax 0977 620148   **H**

Wentbridge nr Pontefract West Yorkshire WF8 3JJ   **Map 7 D1**

Only half a mile from the A1, the house, dating from 1700, possesses
beautifully laid-out grounds. A new owner has retained the services
of long-serving general manager Otto Hinderer. He is also gradually
refurbishing the hotel, at the same time carefully retaining all its former
great charm and character. Thus the bar now has fine damask-covered
walls, creating, with the polished bar counter and gleaming glassware,
a smart and yet convivial ambience. New carpets throughout the public
areas retain their distinctive Fleur de Lys design. Bedrooms are cosy and
homely, furnished mostly with dark Stag furniture and pretty floral fabrics.
All the usual amenities are on hand, including bottles of mineral water.
One bedroom has fine oak panelling as well as the only four-poster built
by the Mouseman of Thirsk. Neat, carpeted bathrooms. Excellent
housekeeping. ***Rooms** 12. Garden. Closed 25 Dec eve.* AMERICAN EXPRESS *Access,
Diners, Visa.*

Weobley   Ye Olde Salutation Inn   £54

Tel 0544 318443   Fax 0544 318216

Market Pitch Weobley Hereford & Worcester HR4 8SJ   Map 14 A1

Remarkable transformation by dedicated young owners of this 14th-century ale and cider house has created stylish overnight accommodation with a unifying Victorian theme. Three large bedrooms (one with a four-poster) have en-suite WC/shower rooms, while the two erstwhile smaller doubles have been knocked into one, also en suite. The entire restaurant and an area of the lounge/bar is no-smoking. Commendable breakfasts. No children under 12, except infants (by arrangement). *Rooms 4. Closed 25 Dec.* AMERICAN EXPRESS *Diners, Access, Visa.*

West Bexington   Manor Hotel   59%   £76

Tel 0308 897616   Fax 0308 897035

Beach Road West Bexington nr Bridport Dorset DT2 9DF   Map 13 F2

"Where country meets coast", says their literature, and indeed Richard and Jayne Childs' manor house stands in a garden on a gentle slope near the famous Chesil Bank shingle beach, overlooking Lyme Bay. Stone walls and oak panelling are much in evidence. Day rooms include lounge/reading room, cellar bar, restaurant and conservatory. Pretty, cottagey bedrooms, most with sea views, are furnished with old pine and enhanced with books and ornaments. Families are very well catered for. Conference/banqueting for 40/65. *Rooms 13. Garden, children's playground. Closed 25 Dec.* AMERICAN EXPRESS *Access, Diners, Visa.*

West Bromwich   Moat House   59%   £84

Tel 021-553 6111   Fax 021-525 7403

Birmingham Road Bromwich West Midlands B70 6RS   Map 6 C4

A squarish modern hotel with good-sized bedrooms and conference facilities for up to 180 theatre-style. Take Junction 1 from M5, close to the M6 interchange. *Rooms 172. Coffee shop (8am-4pm), news kiosk.* AMERICAN EXPRESS *Access, Diners, Visa.*

West Bromwich   Places of Interest

Art Gallery and Museum   Wednesbury Tel 021-556 0683.
West Bromwich Albion Football Ground   The Hawthorns Tel 021-525 8888.

> We do not accept free meals or hospitality – our inspectors pay their own bills.

West Chiltington   Roundabout Hotel   61%   £80

Tel 0798 813838   Fax 0798 812962

Monkmead Lane West Chiltington nr Pulborough West Sussex RH20 2PF   Map 11 A6

"Nowhere near a roundabout", a Tudor-style hotel with leaded windows, whitewashed walls and attractive, cottagey exterior. The cartwheel chandelier in the entrance hall, fairy lights over the bar and armchairs upholstered in tapestry style characterise the public rooms. Attractive oak furniture and tapestries feature in the bedrooms, the roomiest of which are classified as Executive (although decorated in essentially the same style) and some have four-poster beds. Tiled bathrooms are modest, but well kept. Children up to 12 stay free in parents' room. *Rooms 24. Garden.* AMERICAN EXPRESS *Access, Diners, Visa.*

West Didsbury   The Lime Tree   £45

Tel 061-445 1217   **R**

8 Lapwing Lane West Didsbury Manchester, Gtr Manchester M20 8WS   **Map 6 B2**

Well-established, busy bistro – wood-block floor, unclothed tables, candles in bottles – where a frequently-changing menu of robust dishes is served with cheerful informality. Guinea fowl filled with leek and mushroom mousse on an oyster mushroom sauce, calf's liver with Dijon mustard sauce and red onion confit, and fillet of salmon on an asparagus and chive sauce typify the mains with the likes of baked goat's cheese with Cumberland sauce, wild mushroom and spinach salad and melon with tropical fruit to start and tarte au citron, sticky toffee pudding and chocolate roulade to finish. Sunday lunch is a fixed-price affair that comes at almost half price for children. *Seats* 80. *Private Room 40. L (Sun only) 12-2.30 D 6.30-10.30. Closed Bank Holidays. Set Sun L £10.50.* AMERICAN EXPRESS *Access, Visa.*

West Runton   The Links Country Park Hotel
& Golf Club   62%   £165★

Tel 0263 838383   Fax 0263 838265   **H**

Sandy Lane West Runton nr Cromer Norfolk NR27 9QH   **Map 10 C1**

Set in 35 acres of coastal parkland, midway between Sheringham and Cromer on the A149, the privately-owned Links is a large Edwardian mock-Tudor building. Conferences and banquets (for up to 200) are a growing part of the business, but private guests are well looked after in comfortable day rooms and decently-equipped bedrooms (satellite TV, 24hr room service). The Garden Rooms are larger. Suitable for sports-orientated families (all facilities free to residents); children under 16 free in parents' room. ★Half-board terms only. *Rooms 40. Garden, indoor swimming pool, tennis, 9-hole golf course, sauna.* AMERICAN EXPRESS *Access, Visa.*

Weston-on-the-Green   Weston Manor   61%   £105

Tel 0869 350621   Fax 0869 350901   **H**

Weston-on-the-Green Oxfordshire OX6 8QL   **Map 15 D1**

An imposing castellated manor house standing in 13 acres of gardens and grounds on the B430 six miles north of Oxford. Accommodation is divided between the main house and smaller, more modern rooms in the former coach house. Most characterful of the day rooms is the Baronial Hall dining room complete with minstrel's gallery. Themed party weekends are a regular feature. *Rooms 36. Garden, outdoor swimming pool, squash.* AMERICAN EXPRESS *Access, Diners, Visa.*

Weston-super-Mare   Grand Atlantic   64%   £82

Tel 0934 626543   Fax 0934 415048   **H**

Beach Road Weston-super-Mare Avon BS23 1BA   **Map 13 E1**

Modernised Victorian hotel standing in pleasant gardens with views across the broad, sandy sweep of Weston Bay. Winter conference trade, summer holiday makers. Popular venue for wedding receptions. *Rooms 76. Outdoor swimming pool (Jul & Aug only).* AMERICAN EXPRESS *Access, Diners, Visa.*

Weston-super-Mare   Places of Interest

Clevedon Court (NT)   Nr Clevedon.
The Manor House   Walton-in-Gordano Tel 0272 872067.
Weston-Super-Mare Beach.
Avon Ski Centre   Churchill Tel 0934 852335.

Weston-under-Redcastle   Hawkstone Park   61%   £75

Tel 0903 200611   Fax 0903 200311   H
Weston-under-Redcastle Shrewsbury Shropshire SY4 5UY   Map 6 B3

In the world of golf Hawkstone is known as the course where Sandy Lyle
learnt his game. There are in fact *two* courses, and a historic park with
splendid cliffs and grottoes, monuments and follies. In the handsome
restored inn are a pub, cocktail bar, lounge and restaurant, plus function
suites (up to 200 banqueters or conference delegates). Comfortable
bedrooms, fully-tiled bathrooms, children up to 14 stay free in parents'
room. No dogs. *Rooms 59. Garden, outdoor swimming pool, golf, putting,
tennis, sauna, solarium.* AMERICAN EXPRESS *Access, Diners, Visa.*

Westonbirt   Hare & Hounds   59%   £80

Tel 0666 880233   Fax 0666 880241   H
Westonbirt nr Tetbury Gloucestershire GL8 8QL   Map 14 B2

A former farmhouse built of Cotswold stone and standing in ten acres
of gardens and woodland by the A433. Jeremy and Martin Price have run
it since Coronation year (1953), and its old-fashioned charm and homely
atmosphere remain a great attraction. Sturdy oak and leather are used for
furnishings, and some of the bedrooms have four-posters. Five rooms are
in the garden cottage, with their own adjacent parking. Children up to 16
can stay free in their parents' room. *Rooms 30. Garden, croquet, tennis,
squash, games room.* AMERICAN EXPRESS *Access, Visa.*

Wetheral   Crown Hotel   70%   £106

Tel 0228 561888   Fax 0228 561637   H
Wetheral nr Carlisle Cumbria CA4 8ES   Map 4 C2

Originally an 18th-century coaching inn, the Crown stands above the river
Eden, tucked away from the village itself, yet only minutes from junction
42/43 of the M6 (via the A69/B6263). Behind the bright white frontage,
there's a warm and welcoming hotel. *Waltons*, the pubby bar, exudes
atmosphere and serves a good pint of Thwaites (who own Shire Inns),
while the garden-facing lounge is suitably relaxing. Bedroom
accommodation is attractive and well-maintained with bright modern
bathrooms. Both the conference facilities (for up to 150, complete with
business centre) and the smart leisure club (complete with children's splash
pool) are purpose-built and discreetly separate. Pleasant conservatory
restaurant. Children under 16 stay free in parents' room. Two cottages
in the grounds are let on a self catering basis. Free parking for 80 cars. Shire
Inns. *Rooms 51. Garden, indoor swimming pool, sauna, solarium, spa bath,
keep-fit equipment, squash, snooker.* AMERICAN EXPRESS *Access, Diners, Visa.*

Wetherby   Sheba   £35

Tel 0937 583694   R
Swan Cottage 36 North Street Wetherby West Yorkshire LS22 4NN   Map 7 D1

Reliable Bangladeshi restaurant using no animal fats. Speciality home-style
pasanda and tikkas. One of the specialities is *moghul-e-azam*, combining king
prawn curry, chicken tikka mussalam and lamb tikka resala. They also
do balti dishes. *Seats 40. D only 5.30-midnight. Closed 25 Dec. Access, Visa.*

Wethersfield   Dicken's   £60

Tel 0371 850723   R
The Green Wethersfield Essex CM7 4BS   Map 10 B3

Set in the heart of the village next to the village hall the restaurant oozes
charm and character. Drinks and orders are taken in a cosy bar at the front.
The dining room at the rear is a gem – a gallery with two tables for two

overlook the main body. There are beams everywhere and rough plaster walls painted salmon pink. The food is truly eclectic, with Oriental and Mediterranean influences. Flavours are clean and results enjoyable. Starters could be a dish of garganelli pasta with a sauce of tomato and basil with artichoke hearts and capers followed perhaps by baked cod with *petits pois à la française*. A short selection of sweets includes the likes of chocolate and lime parfait or sticky toffee pudding. Friendly service. ***Seats** 45*.
Private Room 18. L 12.30-2 D 7.30-9. Closed D Sun, all Mon & Tues. AMERICAN EXPRESS *Access, Diners, Visa.*

Weybridge   Casa Romana   £65

Tel 0932 843470   Fax 0932 854221   **R**

2 Temple Hall Monument Hill Weybridge Surrey KT13 8RH   **Map 15 E3**

Etchings of old Rome adorn the walls of a comfortable Italian restaurant where diners sit on colourful striped chairs. The à la carte has been reduced in length, sticking mainly to familiar dishes but with the occasional exotic foray – calf's liver with mango, breast of chicken with peaches, kiwi fruit and a champagne and cream sauce. Popular for Sunday lunch when a choice of roasts is offered plus sweets and cheeses from a trolley. Good Italian wines, though vintages are rarely shown on the list; a dozen or so fine French bottles complete the choice. ***Seats** 90. L 12-3 D 7-10.45 (Sun to 10). Closed L Sat, 25 & 26 Dec. Set L £16.50 (Sun £14.95) Set D £16.50.* AMERICAN EXPRESS *Access, Diners, Visa.*

Weybridge   Oatlands Park   69%   £128

Tel 0932 847242   Fax 0932 842252   **H**

146 Oatlands Drive Weybridge Surrey KT13 9HB   **Map 15 E3**

A late 18th-century mansion, in 10 acres of parkland, whose porticoed entrance leads into a most impressive galleried lounge with trompe l'oeil marble columns and tapestry hangings under a large glass dome. Bedrooms of various sizes are furnished in mahogany. Children up to 15 stay free in parents' room. Weekly residential conferences (for up to 300) are the main business. Sister to the *Swiss Cottage Hotel* in London. ***Rooms** 117. Garden, coffee lounge (10am-11pm), tennis.* AMERICAN EXPRESS *Access, Diners, Visa.*

Weybridge   Ship Thistle   63%   £116

Tel 0932 848364   Fax 0932 857153   **H**

5 Monument Green Weybridge Surrey KT13 8BQ   **Map 15 E3**

Originally an 18th-century coaching inn, now much extended with conference/banqueting facilities for up to 140. Open-plan public rooms have a few antiques to add period character. Free parking for 50 cars. ***Rooms** 39. Terrace.* AMERICAN EXPRESS *Access, Diners, Visa.*

Weymouth   Perry's   £60

Tel 0305 785799   **R**

The Harbourside 4 Trinity Road Weymouth Dorset DT4 8TJ   **Map 13 F3**

Down by the attractively busy Old Harbour, Perry's not unsurprisingly specialises in local seafood. Consult the blackboard for daily specials of lobster, crab, oysters, bass, brill, sole etc. On the printed menu you might find game terrine, mushroom samosas, rosette of beef on a bed of pot-roasted vegetables, and supreme of duckling in filo pastry with ginger, lime and corn syrup. Desserts include Sharrow Bay's sticky toffee pudding. The covered terrace at the back of the restaurant is popular in summer. ***Seats** 54. Private Room 40. L 12-2 D 7-9.30. Set L £10/£12.50. Closed L Mon & Sat; D Sun except high season. Access, Visa.*

Weymouth   Places of Interest

Weymouth Tourist Information   Tel 0305 772444.
Weymouth Beach.
Nothe Fort   Barrack Road Tel 0305 787243.

Wheatley   Forte Travelodge

£45

L

Tel 0865 875705

London Road Wheatley nr Oxford Oxfordshire OX9 1JH

Map 15 D2

On the outskirts of Wheatley on the A418, Junction 8 of the M40. 5 miles east of Oxford City Centre. *Rooms 24.* AMERICAN EXPRESS *Access, Diners, Visa.*

Whimple   Woodhayes Hotel   75%

£90

HR

Tel 0404 822237

Whimple nr Exeter Devon EX5 2TD

Map 13 E2

Katherine Rendle and her family run their delightfully situated Georgian home-from-home just off the A30 Exeter to Honiton Road with great style and panache. Surrounded by park-like gardens, an apple orchard and sheep grazing in the distance, the setting is rural and peaceful, although Exeter is only eight miles away. The guests' wishes come first, and afternoon tea with mouthwatering cakes included in the tariff is a typically personal touch; their policy of no nasty extras on bills (teas, coffees, sandwiches and light laundry are not charged as extra) is "greatly appreciated" by their guests. There are two lounges, one with green, pale blue and apricot decor and soft sofas, the second with a grey scheme, a small library and even deeper sofas. For a peaceful drink, head for the flagstoned bar with its old pine furniture. Spacious bedrooms have solidly traditional furniture. Housekeeping is good and the breakfasts are excellent. An adult, friendly country retreat, with no children under 12 to disturb the peace. No dogs. *Rooms 6. Garden, croquet, tennis.* AMERICAN EXPRESS *Access, Diners, Visa.*

Restaurant

£65

Katherine discusses her menus with guests and special diets are gladly catered for (Katherine has been a vegetarian herself for 26 years!). Dinners are party occasions in the lovely dining room where tables are sensibly spaced and French doors lead out on to a paved terrace. Six fixed courses could include such dishes as frisée and walnut or fresh pear and avocado salad with a soured cream dressing, then sorrel soup or vegetable consommé, followed by red mullet with fennel and Pernod or Dover sole with prawns and coriander; a meat course might offer pan-fried calf's liver with juniper berries and lime or fillet of beef with polenta and salsa verde. Only the dessert course offers a choice, perhaps including crème brulée, chocolate marquise with caramelised oranges and home-made ice creams or sorbets; finally, local Denhay mature Cheddar and Colston Basset Stilton served with oatcakes, grapes and walnuts. Concise wine list with a dozen house selections (most available by the glass on request). Four tables outside for residents' afternoon tea (although Katherine will be happy to accommodate non-residents who ring ahead). Due to the size of the operation, dinner is only open to non-residents when the accommodation is not full. *Seats 18. L by arrangement for residents only (£15) D 7-9.30. Set D £25.*

Whitewell   Inn at Whitewell

£60

I

Tel 020 08 222

Whitewell Forest of Bowland nr Clitheroe Lancashire BB7 3AT

Map 6 B1

Richard Bowman, lessee of the Duchy of Lancaster, and his staff imbue this ancient stone inn with warmth, personality and a pleasing quirkiness. It's set amid the wild beauty of North Lancashire, overlooking the River Hodder and standing next to the village church. A stone-floored tap room and a library with good books and pictures are both mellow and civilised.

Bedrooms feature luxurious fabrics, Bang & Olufsen music systems and video recorders; some have antique furniture, peat fires and Victorian baths. Telephones are available for most rooms on request. Food in both bar and restaurant; good breakfasts. "Dogs with kind natures and good manners are very welcome . . . but no Alsatians, Rottweilers or moody dogs in public rooms." **Rooms** *10. Garden, coarse & game fishing, games room.* AMERICAN EXPRESS *Access, Diners, Visa.*

Whitstable — Whitstable Oyster Fishery Company — £45

Tel 0227 276856   Fax 0227 770666 — **R**

The Royal Native Oyster Stores Horsebridge Beach Whitstable Kent CT5 1BU

Map 11 C5

Sole (their pun not ours!) producers of Royal Whitstable Natives, the actual Fishery Company houses the restaurant within what was originally the oyster storage area. Nowadays the bivalves are held in the original tidal tanks, along with other live shellfish. There's a succinct piscatorial menu chalked on a board, offering for example scallops in bacon or squid pan-fried with garlic as alternative starters to the delectable oysters. Simply dressed crab, and chargrilled salmon fillet with dill mayonnaise are typical main courses. **Seats** *67. Private Room 30. L 12-2.30 D 7-9.30. Closed D Sun, all Mon, 25 & 26 Dec, 1 Jan.* AMERICAN EXPRESS *Access, Diners, Visa.*

Wickham — Old House Hotel — 66% — £80

Tel 0329 833049   Fax 0329 833672 — **HR**

The Square Wickham Hampshire PO17 5JG

Map 15 D4

A splendid Georgian town house overlooking the village square at the junction of the A32 and B2177. It's run with dedication by Richard and Annie Skipwith, who have created a civilised and unpretentious hotel. Polished wood floorboards, rugs and period furniture grace the two lounges, one of which is panelled; solid period pieces are also to be found in the warm, comfortable and prettily decorated bedrooms. Nine of the bathrooms also now have stand-up showers as well as baths. One meeting room (or private dining room) with seating around a large oval table. No dogs. **Rooms** *12. Garden. Closed 2 weeks Aug, 10 days Christmas.* AMERICAN EXPRESS *Access, Diners, Visa.*

Restaurant — £70

Classical and modern elements meet in the kitchen, and Annie Skipwith's background in Provence is a major influence on chef Nick Harman, here since 1986. The surroundings are relaxed and friendly, and the short menu (written in French with English translations) changes weekly, offering dishes such as crab bisque, game terrine, calf's liver with a Dubonnet sauce, Dover sole and Hungarian-style pork fillet – there are four choices at each stage. Fish comes from a fishing fleet at Portsmouth, maize-fed poultry from over the Channel in Brittany. Home-made ices are regulars on the dessert menu, perhaps alongside tarte tatin, meringue with seasonal fruits or Nico's chocolate marquise. Service is included in the fixed-price menus. **Seats** *40. Parties 22. Private Room 14. L 12.30-1.30 D 7-9.45. Closed L Sat & Mon, D Sun, Bank Holidays. Set meals £20/£25.*

Willerby — Grange Park — 67% — £86

Tel 0482 656488   Fax 0482 655848 — **H**

Main Street Willerby nr Hull Humberside HU10 6EA

Map 7 E1

Adjacent to the A164 and Willerby Shopping Park, Grange Park is a much-extended Victorian house standing in 12 acres of grounds four miles from the centre of Hull. Besides comfortable modern accommodation it offers extensive purpose-built conference facilities (up to 500 in 4 suites and 10 syndicate rooms). Families are quite well catered for with a children's playground and (limited) crèche facilities. Guests have free use of the Club Tamarisk, whose attractions include a gymnasium and

pool. Hydrotherapy and aromatherapy treatment rooms are planned.
Rooms 104. Garden, indoor swimming pool, gym, helipad. AMERICAN EXPRESS
Access, Diners, Visa.

Willerby   Willerby Manor   62%   £89

Tel 0482 652616   Fax 0482 653901   **H**

Well Lane Willerby nr Hull Humberside HU10 6ER   Map 7 E1

An extended Victorian house set in three acres of landscaped gardens,
attracting mid-week business clientele and functions at weekends.
Everglades Bar is conservatory in style, overlooks the garden and offers
an informal menu. A variety of rooms provide conferences and banqueting
facilities for up to 500; ample parking. Most of the bedrooms are
in a modern annexe, and half have king-size beds. Weekend room rates are
considerably reduced. Part of a local, family-owned wine merchant
business. *Rooms 38. Garden. Access, Visa.*

Williton   White House   £65

Tel 0984 632306   **RR**

Williton Somerset TA4 4QW   Map 13 E1

On the main road through the village, the White House has been run since
1967 by Dick and Kay Smith, who also share the cooking. British, French,
American and Asian influences can all be found on the nightly-changing
menu, from which guests can opt for 3, 4 or 5 courses. Top local suppliers
provide the finest raw materials, and the Smiths do the rest. Speciality
dishes cover the whole range: grilled marinated pigeon breast with hot
beetroot, soufflé suissesse, black-baked chicken with mango salsa and sweet
potato purée, fillet of beef 'Alice Waters', spiced aubergine gratin, *délice
au chocolat*, Anton Mosimann's bread-and-butter pudding. English cheeses
are served with home-made oatmeal biscuits. A mostly French and fairly-
priced wine list (note the good selection of half bottles) has personal and
informed tasting notes. *Seats 26. D only 7 for 7.30, 8.30 for 9.
Set D £22.50/£25/£27.50. Closed Nov-May. No credit cards.*

Rooms   £68

Residents may choose between a bedroom in the main house or those in the
former stables with individual access. Twelve rooms in all, nine of them
en suite.

Wilmington   Home Farm   58%   £56

Tel 0404 831246   Fax 0404 831411   **H**

Wilmington nr Honiton Devon EX14 9JR   Map 13 E2

A thatched former farmhouse (a working farm until 1950) with a five-acre
garden, a cobbled courtyard, a flagstoned bar and a homely lounge with
piano, books and board games. Bedrooms are divided between the main
house and the Garden and Courtyard wings. *Rooms 13. Garden.*
AMERICAN EXPRESS *Access, Visa.*

Wilmslow   Harry's   £50

Tel 0625 528799   **R**

70 Grove Street Wilmslow Cheshire   Map 6 B2

A simple, single doorway leads up to the first-floor location where those
in the know enjoy excellent Cantonese-inspired dishes served by friendly,
helpful staff. Fresh seafood, stir-fries and sizzling platters are among the
specialities, and a whole page of the menu is given over to Harry's
Suggestions, which could include prawns with honey coconut milk balls,
chili calamari, baked lobster (with ginger and spring onion, spicy Szechuan
sauce or butter consommé) and veal braised in a clay pot. *Seats 80.
Private Room 50. D only 5.30-11.30 (Fri/Sat to 11.45). Closed Mon, 25 Dec.
Set D from £15.* AMERICAN EXPRESS *Access, Visa.*

Wilmslow   Moat House   58%   £109

Tel 0625 529201   Fax 0625 531876   **H**

Altrincham Road Wilmslow Cheshire SK9 4LR   **Map 6 B2**

A modern hotel in Swiss chalet style offering modest accommodation, with good, on-the-spot leisure club facilities, conference facilities for 300 and a nightclub. Courtesy coaches to Manchester Airport, a mile away. Free long-term parking (up to two weeks) for overnight guests on production of flight tickets. Reduced rates at weekends. *Rooms 125. Indoor swimming pool, gym, squash, sauna, spa bath, solarium, beautician.* AMERICAN EXPRESS *Access, Diners, Visa.*

Wilmslow   Stanneylands   70%   £85

Tel 0625 525225   Fax 0625 537282   **HR**

Stanneylands Road Wilmslow Cheshire SK9 4EY   **Map 6 B2**

The Beech family's redbrick hotel stands in attractive gardens in the Bollin Valley, three miles from Manchester International Airport and ten from the city itself. Original Edwardian day rooms include an oak-panelled lounge and a cosy bar-lounge with an open fire. Individually decorated bedrooms with solid, freestanding furniture benefit from pleasant views. 24hr room service. Two characterful private rooms hold up to 100. No dogs. *Rooms 33. Garden.* AMERICAN EXPRESS *Access, Diners, Visa.*

Restaurant   £80

The twin oak-panelled dining rooms are clubby and comfortable with discreet, efficient service from long-serving restaurant manager Jacques Franke and his team. The kitchen produces dishes in the contemporary English style on à la carte and fixed-price menus: smoked salmon waffles topped with a fried quail's egg on a lemon sauce; celeriac and horseradish mousse with a salad of green beans in a tapénade dressing; calf's liver grilled and accompanied by a lemon and black pudding hash; loin of lamb baked with a mousse of wild mushrooms and root vegetable salsa beside a polenta cake. A catholic wine list should please everyone; decent prices, good growers and a fair sprinkling of New World wines. *Seats 80. Parties 25. Private Room 100. L 12.30-2 D 7-10. Closed 1 Jan, Good Friday, 26 Dec, D Sun (except to residents). Set L £9.50/£12.50 Set D (6 courses) £25.*

Wilmslow   Place of Interest

Quarry Bank Mill, Museum of the Cotton Textile Industry Styal
   Tel 0625 527468.

Wimborne   Les Bouviers   £60

Tel 0202 889555   **R**

Oakley Hill Merley Wimborne Dorset BH21 1RJ   **Map 14 C4**

There's no doubting chef-patron James Coward's commitment to producing "first-class food and service" and he is never backward in coming forward with his substantial successes in the catering competition world. His cottagey and sunny restaurant has ceiling fans, floral drapes and a conservatory that really comes into its own in good weather. Local produce is used whenever possible, and everything from bread to sorbets and petits fours on his enterprising menus is made on the premises. The style is a mix of French and English, demonstrated by the dual language menu that offers dishes like wild rabbit terrine studded with pistachio and orange, encircled with a frisée salad and topped with market vegetables, whole Dover sole, venison Lorraine with bitter chocolate and juniper berry sauce, and attractively presented desserts. Cheese soufflés, lemon grass brulée and 'speciality fish served at the table' are considered specialities. Now open for more traditional French than English Sunday lunch. Good-value gourmand menu. No smoking. *Seats 50. L 12-2 D 7-10. Closed L Sat, D Sun, 1 week Christmas. Set L £8.95/£11.95 (Sun £16.95) Set D from £21.95.* AMERICAN EXPRESS *Access, Diners, Visa.*

Wimborne   Places of Interest

Wimborne Minster Tel 0202 884753.
  Historic Houses, Castles and Gardens
Cranborne Manor Gardens Cranborne Tel 07254 248.
Edmondsham House and Gardens Cranborne Tel 07254 207.
Kingston Lacey (NT) Tel 0202 883402.

Winchester   Forte Crest   69%   £89

Tel 0962 861611   Fax 0962 841503   **H**

Paternoster Row Winchester Hampshire SO23 9LQ   Map 15 D3

A modern hotel just across from the cathedral. Among the day rooms are
a coffee shop with lots of light pine, a lounge with dark leather seating and
a cocktail bar. Bedrooms boast smart Italian furniture and Executive rooms
overlook the cathedral. Children stay free in parents' room. Banquets for
80+, conferences up to 100. *Rooms 94. Coffee shop (10am-10pm).*
AMERICAN EXPRESS *Access, Diners, Visa.*

Winchester   Lainston House   75%   £140

Tel 0962 863588   Fax 0962 776672   **H**

Sparsholt Winchester Hampshire SO21 2LJ   Map 15 D3

Well-signposted off the A272 to the west of Winchester, this fine William
and Mary house glories in 63 acres of classic English parkland. The
entrance hall/reception is particularly welcoming in winter, when a log fire
smoulders in a large Delft tile fireplace; those in the comfortable lounge
with its floral fabrics and brass chandeliers sport flowers. The remaining
public room is the library lounge boasting some fine carved cedar
panelling. Main-house bedrooms have high ceilings and elegant
proportions, the 14 in the Chaudleigh Court extension have more
uniformity but perhaps the best are the six newest rooms created out of the
former stable block. These are very sumptuous with some fine antiques and
luxurious bathrooms that even boast TVs. All rooms have quality
furnishings and stylish decor but only the de luxe rooms get extras like
mineral water and fruit and in many the TV control does not, oddly, allow
the set to be turned on and off remotely. Friendly staff and good cooked
breakfasts. Various conference and function rooms (catering for up to 80
theatre-style) include a restored half-timbered barn; ample parking.
Rooms 37. Garden, tennis, croquet, snooker, game fishing, helipad.
AMERICAN EXPRESS *Access, Diners, Visa.*

Winchester   The Old Chesil Rectory   NEW   £50

Tel 0962 851555   **R**

Chesil Street Winchester Hampshire SO23 8HU   Map 15 D3

The building dates back to 1450 and has enormous appeal with its old
timbers, mellow brickwork and open fire in winter. On two floors, with
crisp white linen upstairs and less formal unclothed tables downstairs, there
are also two menus – fixed-price or 'bistro' (the latter not Fri & Sat nights)
– although one can eat from either or mix and match wherever you sit.
Chef-patron Nicholas Ruthven-Stuart's cooking has an honesty and
genuineness that is most appealing with the likes of gravad lax salad with
grilled scallops; langoustine ravioli; curried apple soup with sour cream;
entrecote with grain mustard sauce; casserole of venison and guinea fowl;
confit of duck with lentils, shallots and red wine sauce, and the day's fish
dish, which depends upon what's good in the market. Prune and armagnac
ice cream is considered a speciality among good desserts that may also
feature chocolate St Emilion, crème brulée and bread-and-butter pudding.
Good selection of wines by the glass. *Seats 56. Private Room 30. L 12-2.30
D 6-9.30. Closed Sun & Mon. Set L from £10.95 Set D from £16.50.*
Access, Visa.

Winchester   Royal Hotel   67%   £85

Tel 0962 840840   Fax 0962 841582   **H**
St Peter Street Winchester Hampshire SO22 8BS   Map 15 D3

Hidden away just 100 yards from the High Street, this former Benedictine
convent changed hands last year; the new owners have undertaken
a programme of refurbishment. Its modest frontage conceals a secluded
walled garden overlooked by lounge, bar terrace and a modern extension
of smart, up-to-date bedrooms. There are four four-poster rooms and
a family room sleeps up to 5. A striking marble-floored foyer leads
to separate function and meeting rooms accommodating up to 150
delegates. The terrace barbecue is a popular summer feature. Under-16s stay
free in parents' room. **Rooms** 75. Garden. AMERICAN EXPRESS Access,
Diners, Visa.

Winchester   Wykeham Arms   £75

Tel 0962 853834   Fax 0962 854411   **IR**
75 Kingsgate Street Winchester Hampshire SO23 9PE   Map 15 D3

Sandwiched between the Cathedral and Winchester College by the 18th-
century Kingsgate Arch the Wykeham Arms has become something of an
institution in its 250-year history. Local pub, comfortable accommodation,
discerning restaurant, used by destination travellers, passers-through, locals
and simply those-in-the-know. Not everyone knows of the special
relationship the inn has with the cathedral, for which its customers have
helped raise £60,000 towards a music foundation. The areas that are
typically "inn" are quintessentially so: open log fires, rooms decorated with
tankards and artefacts from days gone by. Bedrooms are stylish and have
modern comforts. No children under 14 overnight or in restaurant.
No specifically non-smoking bedrooms but guests are requested to abstain.
Rooms 7. Garden, sauna. AMERICAN EXPRESS Access, Visa.

Restaurant   £55

The kitchen is run by four lady cooks headed by Vanessa Booth and
proprietor Graeme Jameson admits he is lucky with his team. They turn
out a splendid variety of dishes on menus that change twice daily, with
a different emphasis at lunch and dinner. Some interesting combinations are
to be found, such as salmon, leek and ginger terrine, Stilton and quince
paté, Oriental marinated crisp vegetable salad as starters; then strips
of lamb's liver pan-fried with sage and bacon, accompanied by potato and
apple cakes and a Dijon mustard sauce, or Wyke cottage pie with crusty
bread, or rack of lamb roasted with parsnip dauphinoise and a rosemary
and redcurrant glaze. For dessert try the unusual carrot and ginger pudding
with butterscotch sauce, or apricot and Grand Marnier fool. 20 of the
wines, from a well-chosen list, are also available by the glass. For summer
eating and drinking there is a neat walled garden and patio. Booking
is absolutely essential. No-smoking room. **Seats** 72. Parties 8. L 12-2.30
D 6.30-8.45. Closed Sun, 25 Dec.

Winchester   Places of Interest

Tourist Information   Tel 0962 840500/848180.
Theatre Royal   Tel 0962 842122.
Avington Park   Tel 0962 78202.
Hinton Ampner (NT)   Nr New Alresford Tel 0962 771305.
Winchester Cathedral   Tel 0962 53137.
Marwell Zoo   Colden Common Tel 0962 777406.
   Museums and Art Galleries
Museums   Peninsula Barracks Tel 0962 864176.
Winchester Cathedral Triforium Gallery
**Gurkha, Light Infantry Royal Green Jackets and Royal Hussars
   Museum, Peninsula Barracks**   Tel 0962 864176.
Winchester City Museum   Tel 0962 848269.
Guildhall Gallery   Tel 0962 52874.
The Great Hall (King Arthur's Table)   Tel 0962 846476.

Windermere   Holbeck Ghyll   72%   £130

Tel 053 94 32375   Fax 053 94 34743   **HR**

Holbeck Lane Windermere Cumbria LA23 1LU   Map 4 C3

If approaching from Windermere on the A591, take the right turning
signposted Troutbeck after the Brockhole Visitor Centre. This is about half
way to Ambleside, so if coming from the other direction it's the first sign
to the left. Commanding a majestic view over Lake Windermere, this was
once the hunting lodge of Lord Lonsdale, whose name adorns the
ceremonial belt of British Boxing Championships. Today, as the home
of Patricia and David Nicholson, it possesses a timeless, lived-in feel with
the welcoming scents of fresh flowers in summer and pine logs glowing
in the inglenook in cold weather. Patricia and her housekeepers run
an immaculate house where thoughtful decor even matches tissue boxes
and pin cushions to the theme of each individually decorated bedroom.
As the latest stage of steady improvements, two smaller doubles have been
extended into suites with their own access to the garden. All the bathrooms
are now stylishly tiled with smart mahogany fittings, bathrobes and quality
toiletries. An ebullient David Nicholson fronts operations with verve and
good humour, taking pride in his bespoke snooker room which converts
for use as a boardroom and in his purchase of five more acres of mature
woodland which has enabled construction of the new tennis courts.
Rooms 14. Garden, tennis, putting, snooker. AMERICAN EXPRESS *Access,
Diners, Visa.*

Restaurant   £55

In the oak-panelled restaurant the menu changes every day, offering
a tempting variety of dishes based on prime local produce and with English
and French influences. Duck confit flaked between potato and white turnip
galettes or mussels and prawns in a mildly spiced coconut sauce could
precede soup, poached egg with kedgeree or a water ice, with a main
course of baked turbot with julienne of carrots and leeks, segments of pink
grapefruit and spears of asparagus, or a traditional pot roast of beef served
with baby Yorkshire puddings and herb dumplings. Some of the desserts
are also fairly elaborate – how about a duo of chocolate and pecan cookie
ice cream and dark chocolate truffle ice cream on a white chocolate sauce
with fresh strawberries? Decent wine list with the New World offering
the best value; good selection of half bottles. No children under 9. *Seats 38.
Parties 12. Private Room 14. D only 7-8.45. Set D £27.50/£30.*

Windermere   Merewood Hotel   66%   £90

Tel 05394 46484   Fax 05394 42128   **H**

Ecclerigg Windermere Cumbria LA23 1LH   Map 4 C3

Almost midway between Windermere and Ambleside on the A591, the
hotel dates from 1812 and is approached up a long, quite steeply inclined
drive that twists through part of the 25 acres of secluded grounds. From its
elevated position there are good views of the lake from public rooms and
from the six large front-facing bedrooms. The conservatory bar with its
mosaic-tiled floor, mahogany panelling and brown leather chesterfields has
a smart Edwardian ambience. The drawing room and library, next door
to it, are both used as lounges and in keeping with the character of the
building have traditional suites of furniture. Bedrooms, some with pine,
others with mahogany furniture, are of a good size and have a colourful,
homely decor. New owners intend to continue the hotel's conference-based
angle; facilities for up to 40 delegates. *Rooms 20. Garden.* AMERICAN EXPRESS
Access, Diners, Visa.

Windermere   Miller Howe   70%   £150*

Tel 053 94 42536   Fax 053 94 45664   **H**

Rayrigg Road Windermere Cumbria LA23 1EY   Map 4 C3

John Tovey's Miller Howe, an impressive Edwardian country house, stands well above Lake Windermere, with probably the grandest and most stunning views of any hotel in the Lake District. Built alongside the A592, it has well-tended grounds which sweep down almost to the water's edge. The hotel's public rooms and best bedrooms all share the panoramic vista with sunsets over the distant Cumbrian mountains particularly glorious. A heavy wooden door leads from the porch into a homely entrance hall lined with numerous past awards. Unusual objets d'art, sculptures ancient and modern, oil paintings and fine antique pieces put together unfussily create a comfortable, welcoming, lived-in feel. All three lounges have been revamped in keeping with the hotel's Edwardian origins. In the conservatory the bright decor comprises cushioned white garden furniture and window sills of potted plants. Bedrooms, though not large, have a cosy, rather old-fashioned appeal that's changed little down the years. White laminate built-in units are used in even the best rooms, compensated for in the high standards of cleanliness and amenities on offer: books, games, small stereo system with classical music cassettes, trouser press, even umbrellas. The best bedrooms overlook the lake and have balconies with seating at white wrought-iron tables. Binoculars are provided too. Pretty ornaments add to the bedrooms' sense of homeliness. Compact bathrooms have lots of extras, all of good quality – thick towels, classy toiletries and bathrobes. Coming down for breakfast guests are greeted at the foot of the stairs with a complimentary Bucks Fizz which is followed by a very extensive menu that will leave you replete till lunchtime at the earliest. *Half-board only. **Rooms** 13. Garden. Closed early Dec-early Mar.* AMERICAN EXPRESS *Access, Visa.* MARTELL

Set menu prices may not always include service or wine.

Windermere   Rogers Restaurant   £55

Tel 053 94 44954   **R**

4 High Street Windermere Cumbria LA23 1AF   Map 4 C3

Roger Pergl-Wilson is the sole cook and his wife Alena the most affable of hostesses at their cosy corner of France in the heart of the English Lakes (located opposite Windermere Information Centre). Dishes are straightforward, robust in flavour, and highly enjoyable. Mousses sometimes appear among the starters (hot parsnip with roasted peppers and pesto sauce, celeriac with Stilton cream), while main courses run from pan-fried Windermere char with lemon and parsley to calf's liver with bacon, sage and Marsala, prune-stuffed loin of pork and sautéed chicken with cider and cream. Desserts are very hard to resist – apple and apricot crumble with custard, St Emilion chocolate brandy pudding with coffee cream – and there are good French and English cheeses. Particularly good-value, 3-course table d'hote includes canapés and coffee with petits fours. Phone about the regular Thursday French nights and other special events. Some fair prices on the decent wine list that has a sprinkling from the New World including Moldavia. **Seats** 44. Private Room 26. D only 7-9.30. *Closed Sun except on Bank Holiday weekends, 1 week summer, 1 week Christmas. Set D £12.50.* AMERICAN EXPRESS *Access, Diners, Visa.*

Windermere   Places of Interest

Tourist Information   Tel 053 94 46499.
Lake District National Park Centre   Brockhole Tel 053 94 46601.
Windermere Steamboat Museum   Tel 053 94 45565.

Windsor   Castle Hotel   67%   £156

Tel 0753 851011   Fax 0753 830244   **H**

High Street Windsor Berkshire SL4 1LJ   **Map 15 E2**

Period atmosphere and modern facilities behind a Georgian facade.
Children up to the age of 16 free in parents' room; baby-sitting and
listening. Forte Grand. **Rooms** *104. Coffee shop (8am-11pm).*
AMERICAN EXPRESS *Access, Diners, Visa.*

Windsor   Oakley Court   78%   £177

Tel 0628 74141   Fax 0628 37011   **HR**

Windsor Road Water Oakley nr Windsor Berkshire SL4 5UR   **Map 15 E2**

Set in 35 acres of landscaped grounds that slope gently down to the banks
of the Thames, Oakley Court – a grand Victorian manor – is only about
half an hour from central London. The spacious lounges have open log
fires, chandeliers and original, ornate plasterwork ceilings. The panelled
library has over 500 volumes with which to while away the hours.
Bedrooms are most appealing, with almost all rooms in separate extensions
(the Riverside and Garden Wings) close to the main house; many are
particularly spacious and boast splendid red granite bathrooms; the six
luxurious suites in the original house have a more traditional, period feel.
Informal eating in the 30-seater Boaters Brasserie (closed L Sun) offers the
likes of salmon and crab cakes with spring onions served with a tomato
sauce (£3.75/£6.50) or Oriental savoury parcels served with a spicy dip
(£5.50/£10.50). Boats for hire from the hotel's private jetty; weekend
summer steam boat service to Windsor. Queens Moat Houses. Parking for
200. **Rooms** *92. Garden, billiards, croquet, 9-hole golf, boating, fishing.*
AMERICAN EXPRESS *Access, Diners, Visa.*

Oak Leaf Restaurant   £100

Long-serving chef Murdo MacSween has recently left. Expect an
international menu offering gingered gravad lax with coriander and lime
pickle garnished with deep-fried spring onions, or sauté of scallops coated
with sesame seeds, followed by breast of duck with creamed turnips and
prune chutney, or corn-fed chicken stuffed with a pepper mousse, served
with ribbons of leek and a smoked chicken and cream sauce. All main
courses include appropriate vegetables, though an additional selection is also
available. There is a separate section of lighter dishes such as salad
of Chinese-style vegetables with mackerel and sole parcels and a hot sesame
sauce; and vegetarian options like spiced vegetable salad with ricotta cheese
and spinach pastries. Desserts are equally intricate, as shown in pear poached
in white wine filled with blackcurrant mousse, or a parfait of three
chocolates served with apricot preserve. Good coffee with petits fours,
or herb/fruit teas. The excellent wine list is in two parts: country of origin
and grape variety, so appears twice as large as it really is. There's a hotel
wine committee, made up of hotel representatives and wine merchants, that
recommends certain bins on the list – happily, not always the expensive
ones. **Seats** *70. Parties 16. L 12.30-2 D 7.30-10. Set L 19.75/£22.50
Set D £29/£36.*

Windsor   Places of Interest

Tourist Information   Tel 0753 852010.
   Theatres and Concert Halls
Farrer Theatre   Eton College Tel 0753 866278.
Windsor Arts Centre   Tel 0753 859336.
Theatre Royal   Tel 0753 853888.
   Historic Houses, Castles and Gardens
The Savill Garden Wick Lane   Englefield Green Tel 0753 860222.
Dorney Court   Tel 0628 604638.
The Valley Gardens   (Windsor Great Park) Tel 0753 860222.

Windsor Castle   Tel 0753 831118.
St George's Chapel   Tel 0753 865538.
Royal County of Berkshire Polo Club   North Street, Winkfield Tel 0433
   886555.
Windsor Racecourse   Tel 0753 865234.

Winkleigh **Pophams**	£30
Tel 0837 83767	**R**
Castle Street Winkleigh Devon EX19 8HQ	**Map 13 D2**

The most intimate of restaurants squeezed into a tiny village shop which
is also a morning coffee shop and deli. Melvyn Popham produces daily-
changing lunch menus in his tiny kitchen. Duck breasts, marinated
overnight in honey, soy sauce, ginger and sherry vinegar and baked in the
oven, are a popular speciality, while other typical dishes range from
chicken liver terrine to salmon stuffed with spinach and mushrooms baked
in pastry and chicken with Parmesan and a curry cream sauce. Prune and
brandy ice cream, port and claret jelly and fresh lemon tart are hard-to-
resist sweets. Unlicensed, so bring your own wine – no corkage. *Seats 10.
Parties 10. L only 12-3. Closed Sun, 25 Dec & all Feb. Access, Visa.*

Winkton **Fisherman's Haunt Hotel**	£59
Tel 0202 484071 Fax 0202 478883	**I**
Salisbury Road Winkton Christchurch Dorset BH23 7AS	**Map 14 C4**

James Bochan has been here for 20 years, dispensing hospitality
to fishermen and non-anglers alike – the hotel stands on the B3347
Christchurch Ringwood road about 2 miles from Bournemouth (Hurn)
Airport, and the River Avon is just across the road. The building's 17th-
century origins are not all that evident, but the bars, one featuring an old
well with spring water, have a certain personality as well as real ale.
Bedrooms, furnished in various styles, are spread around the main building
(largest rooms), an old coach house and a nearby cottage. *Rooms 20.
Garden. Closed 25 Dec.* AMERICAN EXPRESS *Access, Diners, Visa.*

Winsford **Royal Oak Inn**	£90
Tel 064 385 455 Fax 064 385 388	**I**
Winsford Somerset TA24 7JE	**Map 13 D2**

At the centre of a sleepy Exmoor village resistant to street lighting and
noise, Charles Steven's lovely 13th-century thatched inn doubles as village
local and celebrated haunt for the hunting and fishing folk who throng the
place, especially in winter. The hotel waters run through the village and
additional beats, fishing tuition and the hire or purchase of fishing tackle
can be arranged. Residents enjoy the privacy of cosy chintz lounges and
cottagey main-house bedrooms which nestle under thatched eaves. Five
double bedrooms and a family cottage are in a sympathetically converted
annexe around the rear courtyard. Children under 10 stay free in parents'
room. A large selection of home cooking is available, from bar snacks
to full meals. *Rooms 15. Garden, fishing.* AMERICAN EXPRESS *Access,
Diners, Visa.*

Winterbourne **Grange Resort Hotel** 68%	£100
Tel 0454 777333 Fax 0454 777447	**H**
Northwoods Winterbourne Avon BS17 1RP	**Map 13 F1**

Seven miles from Bristol, but only a few minutes from M4 (J19) and
M5 (J16); nevertheless, you should obtain directions when booking. The
much-extended Victorian building stands in 18 acres of mature parkland,
just outside the village. Conference facilities (up to 150 delegates) occupy
much of the main house with bedrooms and leisure club in attendant
modern blocks; 19 rooms for non-smokers; children up to 16 share
parents' room free. Six Executive rooms have larger work space and bay

windows overlooking the grounds. No dogs. Resort Hotels. *Rooms 52.*
Garden, indoor swimming pool, sauna, spa bath, solarium, beauty salon, helipad.
AMERICAN EXPRESS *Access, Diners, Visa.*

Winteringham   Winteringham Fields   ★   £90

Tel 0724 733096   Fax 0724 733898   **RR**

Silver Street Winteringham Humberside DN15 9PF   **Map 7 E1**

Six miles west of the Humber Bridge (south) and some eight miles north
of Scunthorpe is perhaps an unusual spot to find such a fine restaurant,
located in a 16th-century house once owned by the Marquis
of Lincolnshire. Many of the original features, such as old ships' beams,
oak panelling and open fireplaces, have been retained, adding character
to dining here, and in summer you can take advantage of the conservatory
or terrace in the pretty garden. It's run in exemplary fashion by Germain
(he cooks) and Annie Schwab, and you will enjoy both the style
of cooking, which has a distinct Continental feel, and the fabulous wine list.
Menus change with the seasons, as do their covers – a nice touch, though
it's worth noting that several signature dishes are retained from month
to month. Wherever possible local or home-grown produce is used and
with the proximity of Grimsby, there's always a daily supply of fresh fish.
Also in season, there's plenty of game around, and this is treated with
particular respect as you would expect from a European! There are
a variety of menus to choose from, for instance an entire table might plump
for the *menu surprise*, six courses that change daily, say, a confit of duckling,
oxtail soup, halibut with potato crust and beetroot sauce, rolled rack
of Lincolnshire lamb, exceptional cheeses (30 plus at any one time), and
ending with a dessert of four styles of apple: sorbet, soufflé, mousse and
tarte tatin. Or, choose the 3-course *menu du jour* – no choice at dinner, but
three at lunchtime, when the dishes are perhaps simpler. Favourites on the
à la carte menu include a gateau of polenta and calf's sweetbreads with
bitter orange preserve, skate wings with braised shallots and light beer, and
hot Winteringham corn tart with butterscotch. Each wine-growing area
is helpfully prefaced by a wine writer's overview; the list is splendidly
diverse and constantly revised with perhaps the best bargains to be found
in the monthly selections, though there's good value throughout.
No smoking in the restaurant. Regional Winner for North of England of
our British Cheeseboard of the Year award 1995. *Seats 36. Parties 12.*
Private Room 10. L 12-1.30 D 7.30-9.30. Closed L Mon & Sat, all Sun,
Bank Holidays, 2 weeks Xmas, 1st week Aug. Set L £15.75 D £27/£42.
AMERICAN EXPRESS *Access, Visa.* **MARTELL**

Rooms   £92

Seven luxurious bedrooms of character, including a four-poster and a suite,
are individually and stylishly decorated with period furniture. Four are
in the main house, three in the converted courtyard stables. Start the day
with a super breakfast! No children under 8. No dogs. No smoking.

Winteringham   Places of Interest

Scunthorpe Tourist Information   Tel 0724 282301.
Scunthorpe Civic Theatre   Tel 0724 85912.
Normanby Hall and Country Park   Normanby Tel 0724 720588.

Wishaw   The Belfry   73%   £125

Tel 0675 470301   Fax 0675 470178   **H**

Lichfield Road Wishaw Warwickshire B76 9PR   **Map 6 C4**

This large, ivy-clad hotel in the De Vere group stands amid two
international standard golf courses (the Derby & Championship Brabazon)
set in 360 acres of grounds. Golf is big business (the shop has been
expanded), so too conferences, and the facilities for both are extensive. The
largest of the eight bars, with a pubby feel, overlooks one of the courses

and has special spike-proof flooring. Also notable among the public areas
is a sunken amphitheatre-style lounge with a glass roof and abundant
greenery. Smart and stylish bedrooms with solid period furnishings are
in four wings and are named after famous golfers. Choice of four
restaurants. Children up to 14 can stay free in parents' room. *Rooms 219.
Garden, croquet, golf (2x18), floodlit driving range, putting green, gym, indoor
swimming pool, spa bath, sauna, steam room, solarium, beautician, squash, tennis,
children's playground, night club.* AMERICAN EXPRESS *Access, Diners, Visa.*

Witherslack	Old Vicarage	68%	£98
Tel 053 955 2381 Fax 053 955 2373			**H R**
Church Road Witherslack Cumbria LA11 6RS			**Map 4 C4**

The Reeve and Burrington-Brown families are well established in their
delightful Georgian former vicarage and offer warmth and hospitality
within a most attractive setting. Well-appointed bedrooms are either in the
Old House or the aptly-named Orchard House – the orchard in question
being of damsons and apples – and offer welcome relaxation from touring
the Lake District. Super breakfasts. *Rooms 15. Garden, croquet, tennis.
Access, Visa.*

Restaurant

£60

An appetite built up sampling the delights of the great British outdoors can
be satisfied by the limited-choice dinner prepared by Stanley Reeve, assisted
by the newly-recruited Paul Axford, who trained with Richard Shepherd
in London. Local suppliers are proudly credited on the menus, and their
wares contribute to dishes such as ragout of scallops with a white wine
sauce and fresh dill linguini or venison and Cumbrian ale casserole with
a herb pastry crust. For pudding, try damson ice cream in a brandy snap
basket and a red berry compote, or apricot and frangipane flan. The
cheeseboard continues to be a highlight, emphasising as it does hand-made
specialities from the north of England. Breads, ices and chocolates are also
all home-made. Quite a concise and varied wine list with an excellent
selection of half bottles; fair prices. *Seats 35. Parties 18. Private Room 10.
L Sun only 12.30 for 1 D at 7.30 for 8. Set L £13.50 Set D £22.50*

Witney	Witney Lodge	62%	£91
Tel 0993 779777 Fax 0993 703467			**H**
Ducklington Lane Witney Oxfordshire OX8 7TJ			**Map 14 C2**

Just outside Witney at the junction of the A40 and A415, a modern hotel
with an attractive stone frontage. Bright, practical accommodation, rustic-
style bar-lounge, purpose-built leisure centre with a decent-size indoor pool.
Popular for conferences (up to 140) and banquets (130). Family facilities
include a splash pool for toddlers alongside the bright, daylight pool. 24hr
room service. No dogs. *Rooms 74. Gym, indoor swimming pool, spa bath,
sauna, solarium, snooker.* AMERICAN EXPRESS *Access, Diners, Visa.*

Wiveliscombe	Langley House	66%	£79
Tel 0984 623318 Fax 0984 624573			**H R**
Langley Marsh Wiveliscombe nr Taunton Somerset TA4 2UF			**Map 13 E2**

Peter and Anne Wilson's pale-peach Georgian house (with 16th-century
origins) nestles in lovely countryside at the foot of the Brendon Hills; drive
half a mile north of Wiveliscombe on the road to Langley Marsh. It's
a pretty place with four acres of landscaped gardens, cobbled courtyard and
attractive, lived-in drawing rooms. Bedrooms are particularly stylish and
appealing with well-planned colour schemes and lots of little extras. The
Wilsons' personal care and attention are of a high order and breakfasts are
super. *Rooms 8. Garden, croquet.* AMERICAN EXPRESS *Access, Visa.*

Restaurant £65

The beamed, candle-lit restaurant with its silver and crystal table settings enhances the air of well-being to which Peter's dinner menus, changing nightly, do full justice. Produce is first-rate, carefully cooked and (puddings apart) presented without choice; a walled kitchen garden provides the freshest of ingredients. A typical four-course menu might comprise terrine of vegetables with a chilled tomato coulis, sea bass with Provençal breadcrumbs on a bed of leeks with beurre blanc, rosettes of Somerset lamb fillet with a tartlet of onion and cassis purée, and one of a selection of half-a-dozen desserts, including perhaps bread-and-butter pudding, terrine of dark and white chocolates and spiced apple, raisin and cinnamon shortcake. West Country cheeses (with walnut and banana bread) are offered for those who want the complete experience! Some excellent wines (depth in Bordeaux and Burgundy) on a pleasing list; New World offers particularly good value. No smoking. *Seats 16. Parties 6. Private Room 20. L by arrangement D 7.30-8.30 (Sat at 8.30 only). Set D from £22.50.*

Woburn	Bedford Arms	68%	£97

Tel 0525 290441   Fax 0525 290432   **H**

George Street Woburn nr Milton Keynes Bedfordshire MK17 9PX   Map 15 E1

On a crossroads in the heart of the village, the hotel has recently been undergoing a major refurbishment programme. Public areas were the first to be completed and there is now a smart new reception area. The Tavistock bar has a historical air with its redbrick walls, heavy oak timbers and horsebrasses, while the cocktail bar is elegantly appointed. Bedrooms in a purpose-built block at the rear were the last to be redecorated. Now transformed into rooms with a pleasing well co-ordinated decor, they do, however, lack the character and charm of the ten original bedrooms in the main house. Tasteful decor includes fine inlaid furniture and shell hand-basins. Satellite TVs and mini-bars are included among the extras. Mount Charlotte Thistle. *Rooms 55.* AMERICAN EXPRESS *Access, Diners, Visa.*

Woburn	Bell Inn	57%	£65

Tel 0525 290280   Fax 0525 290017   **H**

21 Bedford Street Woburn Bedfordshire MK17 9QD   Map 15 E1

A privately-owned hotel with a mixture of Tudor, Georgian and Victorian buildings standing on either side of the street. To one side are a beamed bar and restaurant, to the other reception and a residents' lounge. The bar is a popular spot for snacks. A conference room can accommodate up to 30 theatre-style. Bedrooms retain much of the character of the original buildings and all have en-suite facilities. Children up to 16 share family rooms without charge. No dogs. *Rooms 25. Closed 25-30 Dec.* AMERICAN EXPRESS *Access, Diners, Visa.*

Woburn	Paris House		£90

Tel 0525 290692   Fax 0525 290471   **R**

Woburn Park Woburn Bedfordshire MK17 9QP   Map 15 E1

Located just off the A4012, Paris House has a splendid setting in the middle of a deer park. The eye-catching half-timbered house is fronted by a well-tended garden where, in fine weather, aperitifs and coffee are served. Inside, the dining room has bold ivy-patterned wallpaper and some large abstract paintings. Peter Chandler, chef/patron since 1983, offers a menu of modernised classical cooking, the execution of which is belied by the simple descriptions. You might be offered a tartlet of leeks and smoked haddock with a red pepper sauce, or confit of crispy duck with blackcurrants, lamb cutlets in tarragon vinegar, salmon in champagne, iced prune and armagnac soufflé, or tarte fine aux pommes with honey sauce. Moderately priced wine list. *Seats 44. L 12-2 D 7-9.30. Closed D Sun, all Mon, Bank Holidays, Feb. Set L £23 (Sun £25) Set D £36.* AMERICAN EXPRESS *Access, Diners, Visa.*

Woburn   Place of Interest

Woburn Abbey   Tel 0525 290666.

Wokingham   Stakis St Anne's Manor   69%   £144

Tel 0734 772550   Fax 0734 772526   **H**

London Road Wokingham Berkshire RG11 1ST   Map 15 D2

A converted and extended manor house situated in 25 acres of grounds
close to the A329(M). Well-appointed bedrooms (with ongoing
refurbishment) and comfortable public areas. Good leisure amenities.
Banqueting/conference facilities for 300/250 with plans to build a separate
dedicated conference centre within the next year. *Rooms 130. Garden,
indoor swimming pool, sauna, spa bath, steam room, solarium, tennis.*
AMERICAN EXPRESS *Access, Diners, Visa.*

Wolverhampton   Goldthorn Hotel   62%   £65

Tel 0902 29216   Fax 0902 710419   **H**

Penn Road Wolverhampton West Midlands WV3 0ER   Map 6 B4

A 19th-century house with large, modern extensions in distinctly
contrasting architectural style gives a mix of atmospheres, similarly
mirrored in the styles of bedrooms. One mile south of the town centre
on the A449, half a mile from the Wolverhampton ring road. Conference
facilities for up to 140. Parking for 120. No dogs. *Rooms 92. Garden.*
AMERICAN EXPRESS *Access, Diners, Visa.*

Wolverhampton   Mount Hotel   60%   £85

Tel 0902 752055   Fax 0902 745263   **H**

Mount Road Tettenhall Wood Wolverhampton West Midlands WV6 8HL   Map 6 B4

Eight miles from Junction 10 of the M6 and two miles from the centre,
a solid, 1870s redbrick building with modern bedroom wings, set
in extensive gardens. Banqueting/conference facilities include the Grand
Library complete with Italian rococo-style ceiling and minstrel's gallery.
Free parking. Jarvis Hotels. *Rooms 56. Garden.* AMERICAN EXPRESS *Access,
Diners, Visa.*

Wolverhampton   Novotel   61%   NEW   £65

Tel 0902 871100   Fax 0902 870054   **H**

Union Street Wolverhampton West Midlands WV1 3JN   Map 6 B4

Difficult to miss on the town centre ring road, the large new Novotel
features the usual plain but practical bedrooms and airy open-plan public
areas. An outdoor swimming pool operates from May to September.
Rooms 132. Outdoor swimming pool. AMERICAN EXPRESS *Access, Diners, Visa.*

Wolverhampton   Victoria Hotel Periquito   67%   £52

Tel 0902 29922   Fax 0902 29923   **H**

Lichfield Street Wolverhampton West Midlands WV1 4DB   Map 6 B4

Next to the town's Grand Theatre and opposite the station this is a smart,
modern hotel with a marble-tiled foyer and lively bar. Bright furnishings
are used throughout, trying hard to compensate for some compact single
bedrooms and generally small bathrooms. Short on amenities, the hotel
aims largely at the conference and function trade, catering for up to 200
and 150 respectively. *Rooms 117.* AMERICAN EXPRESS *Access, Diners, Visa.*

Wolverhampton   Places of Interest

Tourist Information   Tel 0902 312051.
Grand Theatre   Tel 0902 29212/714775.
Civic Hall   Tel 0902 312030.
Bantock House   Bantock Park, Bradmore Tel 0902 24548.

Central Art Gallery and Museum Tel 0902 312032.
Wolverhampton Wanderers Football Ground Molineux Stadium
Tel 0902 712181.
Wolverhampton Racecourse Tel 0902 24481.
Historic Houses, Castles and Gardens
Chillington Hall Tel 0902 850236.
Moseley Old Hall (NT) Tel 0902 782808.
Wightwick Manor (NT) Tel 0902 761108.

Woodbridge	Seckford Hall	68%	£99
Tel 0394 385678 Fax 0394 380610			**H**
Woodbridge Suffolk IP13 6NU			Map 10 D3

Family-owned and run since 1950, this imposing Elizabethan manor house
is reached by following the A12 Woodbridge by-pass (don't turn off into
the town) until a distinctive sign announces the hotel on the left. The house
is embraced by 34 acres of gardens and woodlands which include
an ornamental fountain and lawns leading down to a willow-fringed lake.
Its interior is characterised by period features such as linenfold panelling,
heavily beamed ceiling, huge fireplace and carved wooden doors of the
Great Hall (lounge), offset by its plush velvet furnishings and richly
coloured carpet. Bedrooms are comfortably furnished more in private
house than hotel style, four have four-poster beds (one dates back to 1587)
and some are in a courtyard complex that includes an inspired conversion
of an old tithe barn into a delightful heated swimming pool.
Banqueting/conference facilities for 100. Tudor Bar. Adjacent 18-hole golf
course. *Rooms 32. Garden, indoor swimming pool, solarium, spa bath, gym,*
fishing, helipad, coffee shop (10am-10pm). Closed 25 Dec. AMERICAN EXPRESS
Access, Diners, Visa.

Woodford Bridge	Prince Regent Hotel	63%	£85
Tel 081-505 9966 Fax 081-506 0807			**H**
Manor Road Woodford Bridge Essex IG8 8AE			Map 11 B4

The main house is Georgian, although now much extended to include
substantial function and conference facilities for up to 400 delegates. Smart,
up-to-date bedrooms are in a converted Victorian abbey joined to the
original building. *Rooms 51. Garden.* AMERICAN EXPRESS *Access, Diners, Visa.*

Woodhall Spa	Dower House	62%	£60
Tel 0526 352588 Fax 0526 354045			**H**
Manor Estate Woodhall Spa Lincolnshire LN10 6PY			Map 7 E2

In over two acres of grounds on a private road, an Edwardian hotel
sheltered from the nearby town centre. Comfortable armchairs around
a log fire in the entrance hall give winter visitors a warm welcome, while
summer guests will enjoy the garden views from the lounge and bar.
Traditional bedrooms (six en suite, one with a bathroom down the
corridor) are spacious and quiet. Children under 5 share parents' room free.
Rooms 7. Garden. AMERICAN EXPRESS *Access, Diners, Visa.*

Woodstock	Bear Hotel	66%	£123
Tel 0993 811511 Fax 0993 813380			**HR**
Park Street Woodstock Oxfordshire OX2 1SZ			Map 15 D2

Longstanding landmark of local catering, the origins of the creeper-clad
coaching inn going back to the 12th century. It stands in a quiet side street
before the gates to Blenheim Palace. Bedrooms come in all shapes and sizes
with decorations ranging from antique to modern. There is plenty
of period charm, including heavy black beams and a Cotswold-stone
fireplace with roaring log fire in the downstairs lounge-bar. Forte Heritage.
Rooms 45. AMERICAN EXPRESS *Access, Diners, Visa.*

See over

Restaurant

£60

Darkwood reproduction furniture, white napery and original oak beams
make a good contrast in the dining room. The short, seasonal menu offers
the likes of smoked haddock and spinach mousse, game terrine en croute
with a wild berry compote, rosette of salmon with a light strawberry sauce,
salmis of local game with braised red cabbage, braised beef and casserole
of veal with herb and prune dumplings. Desserts include Spotted Dick with
custard, chocolate and mint pot and a hot soufflé of the day. *Seats 75.
Parties 65. L 12.30-2.30 (Sun 12-2.30) D 7-10 (Sun to 9.30).
Set L £14.95/£16.95 (Sun £18.50) Set D £25.95.*

Woodstock	**Feathers Hotel**	**73%**	**£114**

Tel 0993 812291   Fax 0993 813158   **HR**

Market Street Woodstock Oxfordshire OX7 1SX   **Map 15 D2**

Eight miles north of Oxford in the centre of historic Woodstock, the
Feathers stands almost next to the gates of Blenheim Palace. Converted
from four separate houses, it offers a range of comfortable, characterful
accommodation behind its 17th-century Cotswold-stone frontage. All
bedrooms have elaborately draped curtains and a useful range of extras that
includes mineral water, chocolates, fresh flowers, magazines and tea
on arrival. Some rooms have draped awnings over the beds, while the best
have four-posters. Bathrooms are luxuriously fitted in marble throughout,
with bathrobes and an abundance of toiletries provided. The upstairs
drawing room with a library and open fire is the most inviting of the day
rooms and a cosy bar has flagstone flooring and an open fireplace. During
warm weather the courtyard garden is a delightful spot for light meals
(which are also served in the Whinchat Bar). Service is courteous and
efficient. Mountain bikes are available free of charge to guests. ***Rooms** 17.
Garden.* AMERICAN EXPRESS *Access, Diners, Visa.*

Restaurant

£75

A quiet, sophisticated air pervades the dining room, where à la carte and
fixed-price menus provide a choice of interesting options. David Lewis's
style is modern British, typified by baked goat's cheese with sun-dried
tomato vinaigrette, marinated queen scallops with chili and shallot dressing,
and confit leg and roasted breast of Norfolk duckling with caramelised
garlic and honey. British cheeses are served with walnut, onion and herb
bread; desserts range from sorbets served with their own compotes
to shortbread tartlet of orange with chocolate and peppermint. The decent
wine list is greatly enhanced by offering several fine wines by the glass.
Lighter eating in the Whinchat Bar. *Seats 60. Private Room 60.
L 12.30-2.15 D 7.30-9.30. Set L £15.50/£18.50 (Sun £19.50)
Set D £23.50.*

Woodstock	**Places of Interest**

Tourist Information   Tel 0993 811038.
Blenheim Palace   Tel 0993 811325.
Oxfordshire County Museum   Tel 0993 811456.

Woody Bay	**Woody Bay Hotel**	**59%**	**£66**

Tel 05983 264   **H**

Woody Bay Devon EX31 4QX   **Map 13 D1**

Martin and Colette Petch can offer guests at their 100-year-old hotel two
major attractions: spectacular views from its woody site overlooking the
bay and an abundance of peace and quiet (there are no phones in the
bedroom, but TVs are available on request). All but two of the rooms
enjoy the views and those two are slightly discounted. There are two four-
poster rooms and a family suite. Leave the A49 at Martinhoe Cross (or
go via the Valley of Rocks coastal toll road). ***Rooms** 15. Access, Visa.*

Woolacombe   Woolacombe Bay Hotel   65%   £170★

·Tel 0271 870388   Fax 0271 870613   **H**

South Street Woolacombe Devon EX34 7BN   Map 12 C1

Family summer holidays, winter breaks and conferences (for up to 250 delegates) are the main business at this imposing Edwardian hotel, whose lawns and gardens reach down to three miles of golden sands. The attractions extend outside the immediate vicinity, as guests enjoy preferential rates at both Saunton Sands Golf Club and Eastacott Meadows riding stables. Public rooms are fairly grand, bedrooms (including a new twin and a new family room) bright and roomy, with mostly modern furnishings. There are self-catering suites, apartments and flats. No dogs. ★Half-board terms only. *Rooms 63. Garden, croquet, indoor & outdoor swimming pools, keep-fit equipment, squash, sauna, spa bath, steam room, solarium, hairdressing, tennis, pitch & putt, indoor bowls, billiards room, children's playroom and organiser in high season. Closed Jan.* AMERICAN EXPRESS® *Access, Diners, Visa.*

Woolacombe   Place of Interest

Woolacombe Sands. *Blue flag beach.*
Exmoor.

Woolton Hill   Hollington House   81%   £110

Tel 0635 255100   Fax 0635 255075   **HR**

Woolton Hill nr Newbury Berkshire RG15 9XR   Map 15 D2

Australians John and Penny Guy have brought an air of homely informality to this fine Edwardian mansion set in 14 acres of woodland gardens to the south of Newbury (follow signs to Hollington Herb Garden from the A343). It has just been discovered that the gardens are an early example of Gertrude Jekyll's work and the hunt is on for the original planting scheme with a view to restoration. The several lounges and galleried oak-panelled inner hall are comfortably relaxing with books, magazines, fresh flowers and, in winter, real log fires. Personal touches include John's collection of model ships in glass cases and Penny's splendid appliqué and patchwork cushions. Spacious, individually decorated bedrooms are most appealing, with antique and reproduction pieces and sybaritic bathrooms (most with whirlpool tubs and separate walk-in showers) with huge bath sheets, oversized bathrobes and every little extra one can imagine. New this year is a small indoor swimming pool, snooker room and games area (table tennis etc) created out of old stables. Good breakfasts. No dogs. *Rooms 20. Garden, indoor & outdoor swimming pool, tennis, putting.* AMERICAN EXPRESS® *Access, Visa.*

The Oak Room   £80

A fine room with oak panelling, Tudor-style ribbon ceiling and high quality table settings. For the second year running, a new chef was awaited as we went to press but a recent meal, with the sous chef in charge, was more than satisfactory. Looking at the wine list (a weighty tome indeed!) you could be forgiven for thinking you were in Australia, which consumes many, many pages! It's a magnificent selection, certainly the best in the UK and probably the best anywhere outside Australia – a worthy winner of our New World Cellar of the Year award 1995. In fact the entire list is quite outstanding, with great depth, many half bottles, magnums, dessert wines and ports – again, the majority from Oz. *Seats 50. Parties 45. Private Room 45. L 12-2.30 D 7-9.30. Set L £12/£15.*

Worcester   Brown's   £75

Tel 0905 26263   **R**

24 Quay Street Worcester Hereford & Worcester WR1 2JJ   Map 14 B1

A spacious, high-ceilinged restaurant converted from a corn mill, with large picture windows overlooking the river and a capacious public car

park. Dinner is a fixed-price (fully inclusive), three-course affair
of wholesome dishes with a fashionable ring: sauté of monkfish with
Japanese dressing, tagliatelle with roasted bell peppers, saffron and basil,
roast guinea fowl with mushrooms and rosemary. Also fresh fish of the
day, a vegetarian special and home-made water ices among the desserts.
Lunch is a simpler meal along the same lines. No children under 8.
*Seats 95. L 12.30-1.45 D 7.30-9.45. Closed Bank Holiday Mon, 1 week
Christmas. Set L £15 Set D £30.* AMERICAN EXPRESS *Access, Diners, Visa.*

Worcester	Fownes Hotel	70%	£85
Tel 0905 613151 Fax 0905 23742			**H**
City Walls Road Worcester Hereford & Worcester WR1 2AP			Map 14 B1

On the site of a famous glove factory, by an attractive canalside walk just
a short distance from the cathedral and city centre. Victorian character
is evident in the stylish and spacious interior; public rooms include a large
foyer, a smart cocktail bar and an intimate library, where dark green walls
and green leather wing chairs allow both the books and the collection
of Royal Worcester china to be seen to advantage. Spacious bedrooms, all
sited away from the busy main road, are well equipped, with freestanding
mahogany furniture and quiet colour schemes. Good desk space and seating
are provided. One bedroom is equipped for disabled guests. The John
Fownes suite caters for conferences of up to 120. Children up to 16 may
share parents' room free. **Rooms 61. Garden, gym, sauna.** AMERICAN EXPRESS
Access, Diners, Visa.

Worcester	Giffard Hotel	61%	£56
Tel 0905 726262 Fax 0905 723458			**H**
High Street Worcester Hereford & Worcester WR1 2QR			Map 14 B1

Decent accommodation in concrete 1960s' hotel opposite the cathedral.
Conferences and banqueting cater for up to 150. Residents can use the
adjacent NCP for only £2 a day. Forte. **Rooms 103. Snooker.**
AMERICAN EXPRESS *Access, Diners, Visa.*

Worcester   Places of Interest

Tourist Information   Tel 0905 726311/723471.
Swan Theatre   Tel 0905 27322.
Worcester Arts Workshop   Tel 0905 21095.
The Greyfriars (NT) House & Gardens   Tel 0905 23571.
Spetchley Park Gardens   Tel 0905 65224/213.
Worcester Cathedral   Tel 0905 28854.
   Museums and Art Galleries
City Museum and Art Gallery   Tel 0905 763763.
The Dyson Perrins Museum of Worcester Porcelain   Worcester Royal
   Porcelain Works Tel 0905 23221.
The Elgar Birthplace   Crown East Lane, Lower Broadheath Tel 0905
   333224.
New Road Cricket Ground   Tel 0905 787394.
Worcester Racecourse   Tel 0905 25364.

Worfield	Old Vicarage	67%	£85
Tel 0746 716497 Fax 0746 716552			**HR**
Worfield Bridgnorth Shropshire WV15 5JZ			Map 6 B4

Set in two acres of grounds overlooking fields and farmland, Peter and
Christine Iles's redbrick Edwardian parsonage reflects the peace and quiet
of its village setting. Twin conservatories jutting out into the garden house
a relaxing lounge. Individually designed bedrooms, each named after a local
village, sport reproduction furniture, pretty soft furnishings and copious
extras. Four rooms in the Coach House have superior fittings (larger
showers, jacuzzis, safes) and open on to a private garden with unspoilt
views across the valley to the river Worfe; six of the bedrooms are for

non-smokers and one is adapted for the use of wheelchair-bound guests. Staff are particularly friendly and families with children are welcome – no charge for extra beds or a cot in parents' room; high tea at 6pm; children up to 10 can stay free in parents' room. *Rooms 14. Garden, croquet.* *Access, Diners, Visa.*

Restaurant £72

Set-price menus run through a repertoire of modern English cooking, and chef John Williams can be relied on to deliver the goods. Dishes are interesting without being unduly complicated, good examples being beetroot and cider soup, terrine of pork and black pudding with home-made apple chutney, and braised shank of Shropshire lamb with creamed leeks and a Madeira-scented sauce. Desserts are just as tempting (chocolate, fruit and nut tart served with poire William sabayon) and there's a notable selection of traditional and new British cheeses. A quite wonderful wine list with a liberal sprinkling of half bottles, good balance throughout the world and prices that encourage you to drink well! Regional winner for Midlands/Heart of Engalnd of our Cellar of the Year award 1995. *Seats 45. Parties 10. Private Room 16. L 12-2 D 7-9 (Sun at 7). Set L £17.50 (Sun £12.50) Set D £21.50/£26.50 (Fri & Sat £26.50/£31.50).*

Worksop   Forte Travelodge £45

Tel 0909 501528   **L**

St Anne's Drive Dukeries Mill Worksop Nottinghamshire S80 3QD   Map 7 D2

At the junction of the A57 and A60, west of Worksop, on the town bypass. *Rooms 40.* *Access, Diners, Visa.*

Worksop   Place of Interest

Clumber Park (NT)   Tel 0909 476592.

Worthing   Beach Hotel   64% £77

Tel 0903 234001   Fax 0903 234567   **H**

Marine Parade Worthing West Sussex BN11 3QJ   Map 11 A6

In a prime seafront position, the Beach offers modest comfort behind a long terraced frontage. Public rooms are on a scale large enough to handle conferences of up to 200. The majority of the double-glazed bedrooms are singles; most are generally light and spacious with a traditional look. Some rooms have their own balconies directly overlooking the sea. No dogs. *Rooms 84. Coffee shop (10am-10pm).* AMERICAN EXPRESS *Access, Diners, Visa.*

Worthing   Chatsworth Hotel   57% £77

Tel 0903 236103   Fax 0903 823726   **H**

Steyne Worthing West Sussex BN11 3DU   Map 11 A6

A conference-orientated hotel in a one-way system (turn left after the pier) with fine creeper-covered Georgian facade, overlooking Steyne Gardens and the sea. Well-kept bedrooms are not luxurious, but include the extras one now expects as standard. Children under 14 sharing with two adults charged for meals only. The games room contains two full-size snooker tables. *Rooms 105. Games room.* AMERICAN EXPRESS *Access, Diners, Visa.*

Worthing   Places of Interest

Tourist Information   Tel 0903 210022.
Connaught Theatre   Tel 0903 35333.
Pavilion Theatre   Tel 0903 820500.
Highdown Gardens   Goring-by-Sea Tel 0903 48067.
Worthing Museum and Art Gallery   Chapel Road Tel 0903 39999 Ext 121 *Saturday 204229.*

Worthington   Kilhey Court   65%   £95

Tel 0257 472100   Fax 0257 422401   **H**

Chorley Road Worthington Wigan Lancashire WN1 2XN   **Map 6 B1**

Built by a Wigan brewer in 1884, the main building stands in ten acres of woodland alongside the A5106, near Standish. Additions such as the conference and business centres (catering for up to 150, with ample parking), a leisure club with a small pool, a bedroom block and the reception area lack much of the house's original elegance. Bedrooms are provided with a work desk and mini-bar, and finished in white ash and floral fabrics – putting practicality ahead of luxury. Rural tranquillity and proximity to the M61 and M6 are major assets. 24hr room service. Informal eating in Courts café/bar (closed Mon-Wed). *Rooms 55. Garden, night club (Fri & Sat), indoor swimming pool, sauna, solarium, keep-fit equipment, spa bath, fishing, outdoor children's playground.* AMERICAN EXPRESS *Access, Diners, Visa.*

Wrotham Heath   Forte Posthouse
                    Maidstone/Sevenoaks   67%   £68

Tel 0732 883311   Fax 0732 885850   **H**

London Road Wrotham Heath nr Sevenoaks Kent TN15 7RS   **Map 11 B5**

Located on the A20 close to Junction 2A of the M26, offering spacious, well-designed public areas and good leisure facilities. The bar and lounge areas are in an open-plan arrangement, one section of the lounge overlooking an inner courtyard with an ornamental pool. Meeting room for 60. *Rooms 106. Garden, indoor swimming pool, sauna, solarium, whirlpool bath, gym.* AMERICAN EXPRESS *Access, Diners, Visa.*

Wrotham Heath   Travel Inn   £43

Tel 0732 884214   Fax 0732 780368   **L**

London Road Wrotham Heath nr Sevenoaks Kent TN15 7RX   **Map 11 B5**

10 minutes' drive from Brands Hatch and the town centres of Sevenoaks and Maidstone. *Rooms 40.* AMERICAN EXPRESS *Access, Diners, Visa.*

Wroxton St Mary   Wroxton House Hotel   66%   £105

Tel 0295 730482   Fax 0295 730800   **H**

Wroxton St Mary nr Banbury Oxfordshire OX15 6QB   **Map 14 C1**

On the Stratford side of Banbury (A422), three village houses dating from the 17th century have been sympathetically linked by a modern clocktower wing built of local honey-coloured stone to make this genuinely friendly hotel. Reception and a sunken lounge flank the flagstoned foyer, beyond which is a period-style bar featuring open fires in winter, or masses of flowers in summer. Bedrooms are individually decorated, with original timbers preserved in some of the older rooms; the balance in a newer block use stylish darkwood furniture. Children under 10 free in their parents' room; family facilities provided. *Rooms 32. Garden.* AMERICAN EXPRESS *Access, Diners, Visa.*

Wych Cross   Ashdown Park Hotel   77%   NEW   £110

Tel 0342 824988   Fax 0342 826206   **HR**

Wych Cross nr East Grinstead East Sussex RH18 5JR   **Map 11 B6**

From the A22 at Wych Cross take the minor road signposted Hatfield to find this extensive Victorian mansion, opened as a hotel in late 1993. The setting is splendid with the hotel's own 187 acres of mature parkland, which boasts a herd of wild deer, surrounded by the Ashdown Forest. From the porte-cochère you enter into a grand, galleried entrance hall/reception with the welcoming aroma of a log fire that burns year round in a large stone fireplace. Day rooms include a row of three stately

lounges and a cocktail bar from which an open stairway leads down
to a convivial snooker room with two full-sized tables as well as bar
billiards for less serious cue men. Five grades of bedroom differ only in size
and outlook as all have the same reproduction antique-style furniture,
comfortable easy chairs and extras like mineral water and fresh fruit;
bathrooms all come with robes, generous towelling and quality toiletries.
Keen staff are aiming at high levels of service with rooms properly serviced
in the evenings and 24hr room service. A large chapel (the house was once
a nunnery – it's also been an American university and a training centre for
one of the big banks) has been imaginatively converted into a pair of fine
conference/function rooms holding up to 180 theatre-style. Under the same
ownership as *Tylney Hall,* Rotherwick (qv). ***Rooms*** *95. Garden, croquet,
tennis, bowling green, 9-hole pitch & putt, indoor swimming pool, gym, squash,
sauna, snooker.* AMERICAN EXPRESS *Access, Diners, Visa.*

Anderida Restaurant   £80

The name comes from that given by the Romans to the forest that
surrounds the hotel and which can be seen in the distance from the tall,
stone-mullioned windows of the large dining room. The kitchen is in the
experienced and safe hands of John McManus who uses only the best-
quality ingredients for dishes like a warm salad of baked English goat's
cheese with pesto, aubergine and tomato charlotte, terrine of seasonal game
with pistachio and home-made chutney, roast monkfish with red wine
sauce and confit of shallots and breast of free-range chicken baked
in a paper parcel with white wine and sweetbreads. Good, clear-flavoured
sauces and attractive, unfussy presentation are notable features. One of the
British cheeses on the list is produced especially for the hotel. The
introduction to the diverse selection on the wine list promises "a high
standard of quality, interest and, hopefully, value for money". The cheapest
champagne at £33 (without service), representing a hefty 100%+ mark-up,
is not a good start! But full marks for a well-rounded list that includes
many French country wines, a decent selection from the New World, the
exceptional English Chiltern Valley dessert wine and plenty of half bottles.
No children under 5 after 7pm. ***Seats*** *120. Parties 10. Private Room 24.
L 12.30-2 D 7.30-10 (Sun to 9.30). Set L £15 (Sun £17.95) Set D £25.*

Wylam   **Laburnum House**   £65

Tel 0661 852185   **RR**

Main Street Wylam Northumberland NE41 8AJ   Map 5 D2

A delightful little restaurant in a Tyneside village, with inviting wicker
chairs set at attractively laid tables. Traditional and modern elements are
both to be found on a menu that changes frequently and always offers
variety and reliable standards of cooking: fried squid with salsa dip, herring
fillets provençale, chicken paté with Cumberland sauce, fillet of turbot
with crab sauce, guinea fowl with honey and apple, fillet of beef *au poivre.*
Sorbets, ice creams, strawberry shortcake and steamed chocolate pudding
with hot chocolate sauce are among a tempting variety of desserts. ***Seats*** *40.
Parties 12. D only 6.30-10. Closed Sun, 26 Dec, 1 & 2 Jan. Set D £15.50.*
AMERICAN EXPRESS *Access, Visa.*

Rooms   £50

Four neat bedrooms, all doubles and all quite large; three have private
shower rooms and one a bathroom.

Wymondham   **Number Twenty Four**   £45

Tel 0953 607750   **R**

24 Middleton Street Wymondham Norfolk NR18 0BH   Map 10 C2

Town-centre restaurant with recently enlarged premises (no 26 next door
can be hired for private functions), but reservations still need to be made
well in advance for Saturday nights. The newer dining room is spacious
and prettily decorated, while the original dining rooms are tiny, almost

cottagey. Chef/proprietor Richard Hughes offers a lunchtime blackboard menu with individually priced dishes as well as a three-course fixed-priced menu of virtually the same dishes. There are a few more choices on the evening three-course menu. Local ingredients are put to good use in dishes such as terrine of local pheasant and chicken served with a confit of red onion and orange, noisettes of pork with a grain mustard crust and apple and cider cream gravy and Pickerings' black pudding, and escalope of Lowestoft cod with a Welsh rarebit topping and a parsley cream. Good vegetarian options. Try a glass of Somerset royal cider brandy with desserts such as warm apple and ginger tart, nougatine glacé, baked orange custard or 'the grand dessert' – a little of everything. Sound, reliable, imaginative cooking without pretensions in friendly, informal surroundings. Also open from 10-2.30 Mon-Sat for lighter snacks. No smoking before 9.30. *Seats* 75. *Parties* 20. *Private Room* 60. *L* 10-2.30 *D* 7.30-9.30. *Closed Sun & Mon, 25-31 Dec. Set L £8.50/£10.50 Set D £14.95. Access, Visa.*

Yattendon	Royal Oak	£80

Tel 0635 201325   Fax 0635 201926

The Square Yattendon nr Newbury Berkshire RG16 0UF   Map 15 D2

A redbrick wisteria-clad inn in the village square, where Cromwell dined before the battle of Newbury in 1644. Characterful beamed bars are almost exclusively given over to expensive bar meals. The recently refurbished hotel reception/lounge is also used for pre-and post-prandial drinks by restaurant diners. Five pretty bedrooms have all mod cons and all sorts of extras in bathrooms, of which two are private but not en suite (just across the hall). Refurbishment of bedrooms has been promised for some time. On our last visit the restaurant food was disappointing, service friendly but unskilled, housekeeping in the dining room unimpressive. No dogs. **Rooms** 5. *Garden.* AMERICAN EXPRESS *Access, Diners, Visa.*

Yelverton	Moorland Links	65%	£74

Tel 0822 852245   Fax 0822 855004

Yelverton nr Plymouth Devon PL20 6DA   Map 12 C3

A low-rise hotel, signposted off the A386 between Plymouth and Tavistock, within the Dartmoor National Park. Main day rooms include a lounge, the Gun Room bar and a ballroom giving on to the lawns. Individually decorated bedrooms are spacious and comfortable, with well-equipped, carpeted bathrooms. A new wing of 15 bedrooms was due to be completed just as we went to press. Conference facilities for up to 120, banqueting up to 200. Children up to 16 stay free in parents' room. Forestdale Hotels. **Rooms** 45. *Garden, tennis, helipad. Closed 1 week Christmas.* AMERICAN EXPRESS *Access, Diners, Visa.*

Yelverton	Place of Interest

Buckland Abbey   (NT and Plymouth City Council) Tel 0822 853607.

Yeovil	Little Barwick House	£55

Tel 0935 23902   Fax 0935 20908

Barwick Village nr Yeovil Somerset BA22 9TD   Map 13 F2

Christopher and Veronica Colley's house is a listed Georgian dower house facing west with delightful sloping gardens, just off the A37 two miles south of Yeovil. Veronica's four-course, fixed-price menu offers a small choice of dishes, using top-quality local produce in simple preparations. Grilled trout, salad of sautéed chicken livers, cream smokies or baked stuffed red pepper could start your meal, followed by a main course of butter-roast poussin, sole from West Bay, or roast loin of venison with blackcurrant and port sauce. Game in season, vegetarian options. No smoking. **Seats** 40. *Private Room* 20. *D only* 7-9 (*Sat to 9.30*). *Closed Sun (except residents), 3 weeks Jan. Set D £16.50/£21.90.* AMERICAN EXPRESS *Access, Visa.*

Rooms £72

Six spotlessly kept bedrooms (no smoking) with simple decor and furnishings promise peace and quiet in an abundantly calm rural setting. Exemplary breakfasts are served in the sunlit morning room.

Yeovil   The Manor Hotel   63%   £87

Tel 0935 231161   Fax 0935 706607   **H**
Hendford Yeovil Somerset BA20 1TG   Map 13 F2

Close to the town centre, an old mansion dating from 1735 with converted stables offering modern bedroom facilities. Conferences and private dining for up to 60; attractive conservatory opening to enclosed formal garden. Forte Heritage. *Rooms 41. Garden.* AMERICAN EXPRESS *Access, Diners, Visa.*

Yeovil   Places of Interest

Tourist Information   Tel 0935 71279.
Octagon Theatre   Tel 0935 22884.
Fleet Air Arm Museum and Concorde Exhibition   Yeovilton Tel 0278 75595.
Yeovil Ski Centre   Tel 0935 21702.
  Historic Houses, Castles and Gardens
Brympton d'Evercy   Tel 0935 862528.
Clapton Court Gardens and Plant Centre   Crewkerne Tel 0460 73220/72200.
Lytes Cary Manor (NT)   Somerton Tel 045822 3297.

York   Abbey Park Resort Hotel   57%   £75

Tel 0904 658301   Fax 0904 621224   **H**
The Mount York North Yorkshire YO2 2BN   Map 7 D1

One mile from the city centre, this hotel offers modern facilities behind a Georgian facade. Accommodation comprises singles, doubles, twins and family rooms – some rooms enjoy fine views of the city. *Rooms 85.* AMERICAN EXPRESS *Access, Diners, Visa.*

York   Dean Court Hotel   63%   £100

Tel 0904 625082   Fax 0904 620305   **H**
Duncombe Place York North Yorkshire YO1 2EF   Map 7 D1

Originally built to provide homes for the clergy of York Minster (opposite the west front of which it stands) Dean Court is now a privately owned hotel. The public areas boast some fine yew-veneered furniture and fittings, there's a delightful tearoom-conservatory and a private dining/conference room, the McLeod Suite. Bedrooms are light and airy, and those at the front have fine views of the Minster and its close. 24hr room service. Valet parking (the car park is just three minutes walk away). Children up to 16 stay free in parents' room. No dogs. *Rooms 42. Coffee shop (9.30am-6.30pm).* AMERICAN EXPRESS *Access, Diners, Visa.*

York   Forte Posthouse   65%   £68

Tel 0904 707921   Fax 0904 702804   **H**
Tadcaster Road York North Yorkshire YO2 2QF   Map 7 D1

Bright and airy day rooms surround a central lawn at a practical modern hotel on the A1036, south of the city. Banqueting for 65 and conferences for up to 120 theatre-style. *Rooms 139. Garden.* AMERICAN EXPRESS *Access, Diners, Visa.*

York   Grange Hotel   74%   £98

Tel 0904 644744   Fax 0904 612453

HR

Clifton York North Yorkshire YO3 6AA

Map 7 D1

A fine Regency town house, carefully restored from a group of flats, just
400 yards north of the city walls on the A19 road to Thirsk. The relaxed,
homely atmosphere is exemplified by the elegant morning room – plump
cushions on the couches, a fine open fire, oil paintings hanging on the walls
and fresh flowers. The bedrooms may not be large but are individually
furnished with fine-quality fabrics, antique furniture and English chintz;
two ground-floor rooms may be suitable for the disabled. The young
management and friendly staff have high hotel-keeping standards and help
make this a good alternative to uniform, commercial rivals. Baby-sitting
can be arranged in advance and there's a couple of high-chairs in the
Brasserie (easiest access is via the rear car park). Meeting rooms for
up to 60. *Rooms 30. 24hr lounge service.* AMERICAN EXPRESS *Access, Diners, Visa.*

Ivy Restaurant   £60

A new chef last year, but the cooking continues in a similar vein, though
now with fixed-price menus only. Pressed terrine of leeks with sweet
pepper dressing, smoked haddock salad with new potatoes and chive
dressing, and braised ham hocks on Savoy cabbage with carrots and parsley
at lunch, plus warm scallop and bacon salad with red wine vinaigrette and
breast of chicken filled with white pudding on braised garlic lentils and
vegetarian options at dinner. Simpler fare is offered in the 45-seat, brick-
vaulted Brasserie converted from the old cellars. *Seats 65. Private Room 70.
L 12.30-2.30 D 7-10 (Brasserie 12-3, 6-11). Set L £12.50 (Sun £15)
Set D £19.50. Closed L Sat.*

York   Judges Lodging   64%   £95

Tel 0904 638733   Fax 0904 679947

H

9 Lendal York North Yorkshire YO1 2AQ

Map 7 D1

Close to York Minster, within the footstreet zone, a fine Georgian town
house which was the official residence of the Assize Court judges from
1806. It remained such until 1977, when it was restored and opened
as a hotel. Two curved stone stairs lead you from the courtyard to the
lovely central door, beyond which is a beautifully proportioned hall with
a small lounge area. Arched redbrick ceilings add character to the cellar bar
and the bedrooms are delightful, with antiques, fine paintings, prints and
lots of extras. Family facilities. Own parking. The manager for the last 14
years, Mr Brown, has recently become the new owner and undertaken
a programme of total bedroom refurbishment. *Rooms 12. Garden.*
AMERICAN EXPRESS *Access, Diners, Visa.*

York   Melton's   £50

Tel 0904 634341   Fax 0904 629233

R

7 Scarcroft Road York North Yorkshire YO2 1ND

Map 7 D1

Lucy and Michael Hjort and Elizabeth Cooper please all-comers with
a short, eclectic menu that mixes the adventurous with more standard fare,
making use of local suppliers when possible. Warm blinis with beetroot
and soured cream, goat's cheese gnocchi with basil sauce and salami with
fennel in a salad of sun-dried tomatoes could be your starter, preceding
ox tongue with mashed potatoes and spinach, salmon and smoked eel in red
wine or roast leg of lamb marinated as game. Tuesday, Wednesday and
Thursday evenings bring, respectively, seafood, pudding and vegetarian
specialities. Good-value fixed-price lunches (including Sundays) and early
dinners (leave by 7.45pm). Desserts might include a white chocolate parfait
with lime syrup or bread-and-butter pudding. Super value, too, is provided
by the excellent wine list (maximum mark-up £10 a bottle); lots of half
carafes/half bottles and decent wines by the glass. *Seats 40. Parties 30.*

Private Room 15. L 12.-2 D 5.30/6.15 & 7-10. Closed D Sun, L Mon, 3 weeks from Christmas Eve. Set L & early D from £11.50. Access, Visa.

York	**Middlethorpe Hall**	**79%**	**£149**

Tel 0904 641241   Fax 0904 620176

HR

Bishopthorpe Road York North Yorkshire YO2 1QB

Map 7 D1

This lovely William and Mary house, magnificently restored by Historic House Hotels, stands in well-tended grounds alongside York racecourse just 1½ miles from the city centre. Its classical exterior is complemented by a carefully decorated and furnished interior; first impressions as you enter the hall are the chequerboard flagged floor, a log fire, fine paintings and a splendid carved oak staircase. A wealth of fine-quality furniture includes some good antiques, carefully chosen to match the period, and the chandeliered drawing room boasts numerous beautifully upholstered sofas and armchairs. Bedrooms are of a similarly high standard, with plenty of extras; Edwardian-style bathrooms are graced by brass fittings as well as high-class toiletries, generous towels and bathrobes. Standards of housekeeping are as high as ever. Banquets/conferences for 50/68. No children under eight; no dogs. Smart meeting and conference facilities. ***Rooms*** *30. Garden, croquet.* AMERICAN EXPRESS *Access, Diners, Visa.*

Restaurant

£100

Kevin Francksen knows his market through and through, and the same attention to detail evident in the establishment as a whole is apparent in his cooking. Menus are well priced, well balanced and well cooked, and sometimes the choices presented are hard to make. Perhaps try game terrine with spicy poached pear, bouillabaisse of red mullet, salmon, mussels and prawns, with banana and poppy seed parfait to finish. Service is formal and professional, in keeping with the setting. Plenty of half bottles on the decent wine list that presents both a house selection and sommelier's suggestions. Grill Room open 7.30-9.45 (Fri & Sat, summer only). No children under 8. No smoking. ***Seats*** *60. Parties 8. Private Room 50. L 12.30-1.45 D 7.30-9.45. Set L £14.90/£16.90 Set D £24.95/£27.95/£32.95.*

York	**Mount Royale**	**66%**	**£75**

Tel 0904 628856   Fax 0904 611171

H

119 The Mount York North Yorkshire YO2 2DA

Map 7 D1

Located just a short distance outside the city walls on one of the principal routes into the centre, the privately owned hotel offers comfortable, homely accommodation with very pleasant staff in attendance. The best and quietest rooms overlook the beautifully maintained gardens at the rear– though front rooms are all triple glazed. Public rooms include a very snug bar with dark oak panelling originally from a church. There's also a brighter cocktail bar-cum-coffee lounge with bamboo furniture. It serves as one of two lounges; the other, more laid-back and relaxing and is located in a more modern extension to the side. Bedrooms vary in size and character but all are furnished to a good standard with many thoughtful extras provided. Four garden rooms are very spacious and have patio doors that open on to a small verandah overlooking, and with access to, the gardens. ***Rooms*** *23. Garden, outdoor swimming pool, sauna, steam room, solarium, snooker. Closed 24-30 Dec.* AMERICAN EXPRESS *Access, Diners, Visa.*

York	**19 Grape Lane**		**£75**

Tel 0904 636366

R

19 Grape Lane York North Yorkshire YO1 2HU

Map 7 D1

The restaurant is housed in a characterful timbered building close to York Minster on the corner of Coffee Yard (off Stonegate) and Grape Lane. The lunch menu is chalked up on blackboards and includes simple salads and soups to begin with and equally simple main dishes to follow such as cod in a herb crust and beef in red wine. There's also an even lighter menu of sandwiches and other light snacks. *Seats 34. Parties 22. Private Room 22. L 12-1.45 D 7-10 (Sat to 10.30). Closed Sun & Mon, Christmas, 2 weeks Jan/Feb, 2 weeks Sep. Set D £19.95. Access, Visa.*

York	Novotel	62%	£85

Tel 0904 611660   Fax 0904 610925   **H**

Fishergate York North Yorkshire YO1 4AD   **Map 7 D1**

Modern redbrick hotel in the city centre (A19 Selby road), by the side of the River Ouse. All rooms have a double and a single bed. Four bedrooms equipped for disabled guests. Two children under 16 may share their parents' room free of charge, breakfast included. Conference/banqueting facilities for 210/130; parking for 150. *Rooms 124. Indoor swimming pool.* AMERICAN EXPRESS *Access, Diners, Visa.*

York	Royal York Hotel	67%	£110

Tel 0904 653681   Fax 0904 623503   **H**

Station Road York North Yorkshire YO2 2AA   **Map 7 D1**

Adjacent to the railway station with its own covered entrance from it, and fronted by three acres of well-tended gardens, the hotel, built in 1878, is a fine example of solidly-built Victorian architecture. The entrance hall features a grand staircase flanked by two impressive Italian crystal chandeliers. Spacious public rooms include a basement bar, Tiles, its walls covered in original and now listed, Birmantoft tiles. There's also a leisure complex. Bedrooms are very smartly decorated with front-facing rooms enjoying good views of the cathedral. *Rooms 145. Garden, croquet, putting, gym, sauna, steam room, solarium, hair salon.* AMERICAN EXPRESS *Access, Diners, Visa.*

York	Stakis York	65%	£122

Tel 0904 648111   Fax 0904 610317   **H**

Tower Street York North Yorkshire YO1 1SB   **Map 7 D1**

A modern redbrick hotel standing in the shadows of Clifford's Tower in the heart of the city. Bedrooms, all doubles or twins, are comprehensively equipped with satellite TV, mini-bars and the usual modern amenities. Bathrooms are neat but compact. A branch of Henry J Bean's is to open here in November 1994 (on the site of an Italian pasta joint). *Rooms 128.* AMERICAN EXPRESS *Access, Diners, Visa.*

York	Swallow Hotel	64%	£105

Tel 0904 701000   Fax 0904 702308   **H**

Tadcaster Road York North Yorkshire YO2 2QQ   **Map 7 D1**

A mile from the city centre on the A1036, the Swallow stands in its own grounds overlooking the historic Knavesmire racecourse. The purpose-built Swallow Management Centre has proved a popular addition to the facilities which include a leisure club and parking for 200+ cars. Banqueting/conferences for 120/170. Children up to 14 free in parents' room. Special weekend breaks for families. *Rooms 112. Garden, croquet, indoor swimming pool, steam room, spa bath, sauna, solarium, keep-fit equipment, pitch & putt, coffee shop (10am-10pm).* AMERICAN EXPRESS *Access, Diners, Visa.*

York	Viking Hotel	69%	£132

Tel 0904 659822   Fax 0904 641793   **H**

North Street York North Yorkshire YO1 1JF   **Map 7 D1**

Tall, modern Queens Moat Houses hotel and conference centre standing in a convenient central location by the river Ouse. Style and comfort are not lacking in the brick-walled reception, the lounge and the bar, the last two with river views. A choice of conference suites can handle up to 350 delegates. Bedrooms are well lit and amply furnished. No dogs. Limited underground garaging (£5 a night). *Rooms 188. Gym, sauna, spa bath, solarium, golf practice net.* AMERICAN EXPRESS *Access, Diners, Visa.*

York   Places of Interest

Tourist Information   Tel 0904 621756.
Grand Opera House   Tel 0904 628877.
Theatre Royal   Tel 0904 23568.
York Minster   Tel 0904 623608.
York Racecourse   Tel 0904 620911.
Flamingo Land Zoo and Family Fun Park   Malton Tel 065 386287.
  Historic Houses, Castles and Gardens
Assembly Rooms   Tel 0904 61361.
Beningbrough Hall   Tel 0904 470666.
Castle Howard   Tel 065 384 333.
Merchant Adventurers' Hall   Tel 0904 654818.
Treasurer's House (NT)   Tel 0904 624247.
Sutton Park   Sutton-on-the-Forest Tel 0347 810249.
  Museums and Art Galleries
The Arc Archaeological Resource Centre   Tel 0904 654324.
Fairfax House   Tel 0904 655543.
Jorvik Viking Centre   Tel 0904 643211.
National Railway Museum   (Science Museum) Tel 0904 621261.
York Castle Museum   Tel 0904 653611.
York City Art Gallery   Tel 0904 623839.
York Story   Tel 0904 628632.

Yoxford	Satis House	63%	£75

Tel 0728 668418   **H**
Yoxford Saxmundham Suffolk IP16 3EX   Map 10 D2

The Grade II listed country house is set in three acres of parkland alongside the A12. Charles Dickens was a friend of the original owner and Pip Gargery mentions the house in *Great Expectations*. The entrance hall is paved with York stone and leads to public rooms furnished with antiques. Two of the bedrooms are older in style with large, solid wood half-tester double beds and Edwardian baths and fittings, while others are more modern. No children under 14 or dogs. Malaysian food is a speciality in the restaurant (D only, closed Sun & Mon) and their Kenduri feast is always popular. *Rooms 7. Garden, croquet, keep-fit equipment, sauna, solarium, spa bath.* AMERICAN EXPRESS *Access, Diners, Visa.*

Note that all telephone numbers with area codes starting with 0 will start 01 from 16 April 1995.

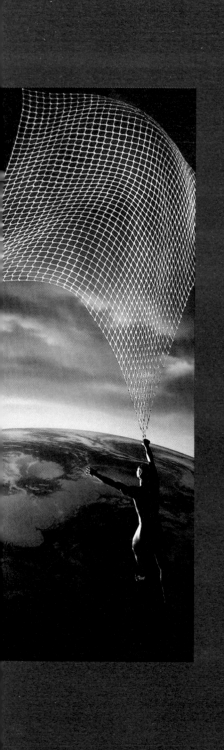

BIG
on choice.

Choosing the right tariff is important if you're to get the best value from your mobile phone.

Cellnet offers a wide tariff choice so you can choose the best combination of affordability and network features.

What's more, we make it easy to identify the tariff that is ideal for your needs.

For further information call
0800 214000

cellnet

Choosing the right tariff is important if you're to get the best value from your mobile phone.

primetime™

plus

Cellnet's digital service is ideal for international business users who need to keep in touch – and be contactable – in the UK and abroad.

**For further information call
0800 214000**

primetime ™

**Cellnet's premier TACS
business service. Ideal
for the business user
needing to make more
than 2 calls a day
during working hours.**

citytime ™

**Ideal for frequent
business users who
make most of their
calls from in and
around London,
but who still need
to be able to make
and receive calls
from anywhere in
the country.**

lifetime ™

**Ideal for less frequent
users (1 or 2 calls per
day) – personal or
business – who are
likely to receive more
calls than they make.**

**For further information call
0800 214000**

Scotland

Aberdeen   Ardoe House   70%   £108

Tel 0224 867355   Fax 0224 861283   **H**

South Deeside Road Royal Deeside Grampian AB1 5YP   Map 3 D4

A few minutes' drive from the centre of Aberdeen, Ardoe House enjoys a secluded setting at the end of a winding drive. Its style is Scottish Baronial, and day rooms retain all their best original features, with carved oak panelling and handsome ceiling work. The drawing room and cocktail bar are warm and inviting, and there's a choice of rooms available for conferences and banquets (for up to 300/200). Bedrooms are comfortable and well appointed, whether in the main building (some reached by a fine oak staircase past a stained-glass window) or in the sympathetically designed modern section, where the majority are located. Children up to 12 stay free in parents' room. *Rooms 71. Garden, croquet, putting.* AMERICAN EXPRESS *Access, Diners, Visa.*

Aberdeen   Atlantis   £65

Tel 0224 591403   **R**

Malacca Hotel 349 Gt Western Road Aberdeen Grampian AB1 6NN   Map 3 D4

Having moved from Bon Accord Crescent last year, the Atlantis is now happily installed in the 21-roomed Malacca Hotel. Although many more meat dishes are now offered, the strength is still in fresh seafood, bought whenever possible from Aberdeen's renowned fish market. Chef Mark Ronaldson favours a simple approach to preserve the fresh flavours and textures. Orkney oysters and mussels are favourite starters, with sole, salmon and king prawns among the most popular main courses. Dishes come plain or sauced: véronique for king prawns, green peppercorns for monkfish, herb butter to accompany fillets of lemon sole stuffed with a salmon and leek mousse. The cold seafood platter for two (£60) is a generous selection of all the seafood presented with four different dips. Sunday lunchtime three-course carvery (£7.50). *Seats 40. Parties 20. L 12-2 D 6-10.* AMERICAN EXPRESS *Access, Diners, Visa.*

Aberdeen   Caledonian Thistle   68%   £135

Tel 0224 640233   Fax 0224 641627   **H**

Aberdeen Grampian AB9 1HE   Map 3 D4

City-centre hotel with Regency-style day rooms, double-glazed bedrooms and a choice of eating places – the café/bar is open 10am-midnight. Children up to 12 share parents' room free. Conference/banqueting for 35/25. *Rooms 80. Sauna.* AMERICAN EXPRESS *Access, Diners, Visa.*

Aberdeen   Copthorne Hotel   68%   £135

Tel 0224 630404   Fax 0224 640573   **H**

122 Huntly Street Aberdeen Grampian AB1 1SU   Map 3 D4

City-centre hotel behind a converted warehouse facade. Good standards of accommodation in Classic and Connoisseur rooms and suites. 24hr room service. Conference facilities for 200+. No dogs. *Rooms 89.* AMERICAN EXPRESS *Access, Diners, Visa.*

Aberdeen   The Courtyard on the Lane   NEW   £60

Tel 0224 213795   **R**

1 Alford Lane Aberdeen Grampian AB1 1YD   Map 3 D4

Tucked away in a back alley by the junction of Holburn and Union Streets, this first-floor restaurant offers some highly enjoyable cooking from Tony Heath – formerly one half of the excellent team at *Farleyer House* in Aberfeldy. The à la carte menu (slightly simpler and significantly cheaper at lunchtime) is not long but sufficiently well thought-out that you do not feel short of choice. Starters might include a pastry case of boneless

quail with oyster mushrooms in a tarragon and Madeira sauce and a stew
of squid and mussels on a bed of noodles along with simpler dishes like
plain smoked Tay salmon or melon and Parma ham. Grilled fillets
of turbot and monkfish with a Chablis and saffron sauce; breast of chicken
filled with smoked ham and banana in a grain mustard sauce and Aberdeen
Angus fillet steak with rösti potatoes, caramelised shallots and a red wine
sauce typify the main courses. Good puds like caramelised apple tart with
caramel sauce and butterscotch ice cream, and tiramisu. Service, under
partner Shona Drysdale, is notably friendly and efficient. There's
an informal bistro on the ground floor that is also open for Saturday lunch.
*Seats 30. L 12-2 D 7-9.30. Closed L Sat, all Sun & Mon, 2 weeks July, 25 &
26 Dec, 1 & 2 Jan.* AMERICAN EXPRESS *Access, Visa.*

Aberdeen	**Gerard's**	£70
Tel 0224 639500		**R**
50 Chapel Street Aberdeen Grampian AB1 1SN		Map 3 D4

Reliable, sound cooking – French and international – is the hallmark
of Gerard Flecher's city-centre restaurant, off the west end of Union Street.
Very good value business lunches offer an unusually wide choice, from
cream soup of the day with garlic bread to vol-au-vent of rabbit and
venison with French mustard served with noodles. Dinner brings a *menu
complet* and a varied à la carte choice that includes classics such as garlic
snails and moules marinière along with more innovative suggestions like
veal, chicken and duck piccatas in a cheese, egg and lemon batter served
with creamed pasta, or monkfish escalopes wrapped with prune and
smoked ham, skewered and grilled. Predominantly French wine list with
twenty or so fine reserve wines. *Seats 90. Parties 30. Private Room 24.
L 12-2.30 D 6-10.30. Closed Sun, Local Bank Holidays. Set L £9.95 &
£12.50 Set D £22.85.* AMERICAN EXPRESS *Access, Diners, Visa.*

Aberdeen	**Holiday Inn Crowne Plaza**	69%	£132
Tel 0224 713911 Fax 0224 714020			**H**
Oldmeldrum Road Buicksburn Aberdeen Grampian AB2 9LN			Map 3 D4

There's a courtesy coach provided between Aberdeen Airport and this
modern hotel, where all the bedrooms have double beds and the usual
range of electric gadgets. Well equipped for leisure and for conferences
(500 theatre-style). *Rooms 144. Indoor swimming pool, keep-fit equipment,
sauna, steam room, solarium.* AMERICAN EXPRESS *Access, Diners, Visa.*

Aberdeen	**The Marcliffe at Pitfodels**	NEW	78%	£115
Tel 0224 861000 Fax 0224 868860				**HR**
North Deeside Road Pitfodels Aberdeen AB1 9PA				Map 3 D4

Aberdeen's latest and best hotel is set in six acres of landscaped grounds
on the western outskirts of the city, newly built, but in traditional style,
by experienced local hoteliers Stewart and Sheila Spence. Day rooms like
the rug-strewn, flagstoned lobby and richly furnished lounge with its red
walls, real fire and scattering of antiques, demonstrate Sheila's flair for
interior design. Bedroom decor is particularly striking with innovative
combinations of floral patterns, checks and colourful Mediterranean prints
used to great effect. Well-designed and spacious with quality furniture –
antiques in the Master bedrooms that boast such extras as video machines
and decanters of sherry – and comfortable armchairs, all rooms have desk
as well as bedside phones, mini-bars with fresh milk for the discreetly
hidden beverage kit (there's also 24hr room service) and trouser press
incorporating iron and ironing board. Good bathrooms feature a third tap
at the washbasin dispensing specially purified drinking water. Immaculate
staff, kitted-out in the hotel's own tartan, are numerous and attentive,
providing a high level of service. Good breakfasts include 'Aberdeen
Rowies', a local speciality a bit like a flat croissant. No dogs. *Rooms 42.
Garden, snooker.* AMERICAN EXPRESS *Access, Diners, Visa.* MARTELL COGNAC

See over

Conservatory Restaurant and Invery Room £90

A choice of eating here: the smart yet informal, split-level (divided
by stone balustrade) Conservatory with terrace offering a short but varied
à la carte – steak and mushroom pie with Guinness, grilled salmon with
sun-dried tomato and herb butter, chargrilled steaks – and the opulent,
formal, dinner-only Invery Room. The latter, sporting a handsome antique
sideboard, offers a fixed-price, four-course menu that shares some dishes
with the Conservatory plus the likes of a warm salad of West Coast scallops
flavoured with tomatoes and balsamic vinaigrette, chargrilled halibut
with chive butter sauce and medallions of beef with wild mushroom
and Madeira sauce. Cooking generally is uncomplicated but not
unsophisticated; and the raw materials are first-rate. Price quoted is for the
no-smoking Invery Room. *Invery Room: **Seats** 30. Parties 10. Private Room
24. D only 7-10. Closed Sun. Set D £33.50. Conservatory: **Seats** 70. L 12-
2.15 D 6.30-10.*

Aberdeen   Silver Darling £65

Tel 0224 576229 **R**

Pocra Quay North Pier Aberdeen Grampian AB2 1DQ Map 3 D4

A French speciality 'barbecued seafood' restaurant overlooking the city and
old port from the farthest point of the North Quay. Most of the fish
is prepared in full view of diners through a large kitchen window, cooked
on the barbecue and served with fennel, tomatoes and a herb butter sauce.
Besides this there's a wide choice, from Mediterranean crab soup, pasta
with seafood and basil, and a cold soufflé with smoked salmon and fromage
blanc to trout poached in Sancerre, fried brill flambé with whisky and
gigot of monkfish braised with smoked bacon, stuffed with wild
mushrooms, garlic and thyme and served with a crab sauce. Short, carefully
annotated all-French wine list. Booking is essential at this very popular
place, which has plans to expand during 1995. ***Seats** 35. Parties 30. L 12-2
D 7-10. Closed L Sat & all Sun, 2 weeks Christmas.* AMERICAN EXPRESS *Access,
Diners, Visa.*

Aberdeen   Stakis Tree Tops   63% £128

Tel 0224 313377   Fax 0224 312028 **H**

161 Springfield Road Aberdeen Grampian AB9 2QH Map 3 D4

In a residential area on the western edge of the city, a hotel offering singles,
doubles, twins, Executive rooms, family rooms and a suite, all complete
with the expected up-to-date accessories. There's a well-equipped leisure
club and large, comprehensive conference facilities catering for up to 1000
delegates. Children up to 15 stay free in parents' room. 30% of the rooms
are non-smoking. ***Rooms** 110. Indoor swimming pool, gym, spa bath, sauna,
tennis.* AMERICAN EXPRESS *Access, Diners, Visa.*

Aberdeen   Travel Inn £43

Tel 0224 821217 **L**

Murcar Bridge of Don Aberdeen Grampian AB2 8BP Map 3 D4

Rooms 40. AMERICAN EXPRESS *Access, Diners, Visa.*

Aberdeen   Places of Interest

Tourist Information   Tel 0224 632727.
St Andrew's Cathedral   Tel 0224 640290.
St Machar's Cathedral   Tel 0224 485988.
St Mary's R.C. Cathedral   Tel 0224 640160.
Aberdeen F.C. Pittodrie   Tel 0224 632328.
Caimhill Ski Slope   Tel 0224 311781.
Alford Slope   Tel 09755 63024.

Beach Leisure Centre   Tel 0224 649930.
  Theatres and Concert Halls
Aberdeen Music Hall   Tel 0224 641222.
Aberdeen Arts Centre   Tel 0224 635208.
Capitol Theatre   Tel 0224 583141.
Haddo House Hall   Tel 06515 851770 *By Tarves 10 miles.*
His Majesty's Theatre   Tel 0224 641122.
  Historic Houses, Castles and Gardens
Castle Fraser (NT)   Sauchen. Tel 0330 3463.
Cruickshank Botanic Gardens   Tel 0224 272704.
Crathes Castle Garden   Banchory. Tel 0330 44525.
Drum Castle   Tel 0330 811204.
Duthie Park and Winter Gardens   Tel 0224 276276.
Kildrummy Castle Gardens   Alford Tel 09755 71277.
Seaton Park   Don Street. Tel 0224 276276.
Pitmedden Garden (NT)   Udny. Tel 065 1842352.
  Museums and Art Galleries
Art Gallery/James Dun's House   Tel 0224 635208/646333.
Peacock Artspace   Tel 0224 639539.
Maritime Museum/Provost Ross's House   Tel 0224 585788.
University Marischal Museum   Tel 0224 273131.
Grampian Transport Museum   Alford. Tel 09755 62292.
Crombie Woollen Mill   Woodside Tel 0224 483201.

Aberdeen Airport Aberdeen Marriott Hotel 70%	£141
Tel 0224 770011 Fax 0224 722347	**H**
Riverview Drive Farburn Dyce Aberdeen Grampian AB2 0AZ	Map 3 D4

Low-rise hotel two miles from the airport built around a central leisure area with kidney-shaped pool. Standardised bedrooms are spacious and practical rather than luxurious – poly-cotton sheets, open hanging space. 24hr room service. Executive rooms get various extras. One room is equipped for disabled guests. Children up to 19 share parents' room free. Conference and banqueting facilities for 400/350; parking for 200. Courtesy coach to and from the airport. Guests may use the squash courts at the *Skean Dhu* hotel nearby. 4 miles from the city centre. *Rooms 154. Indoor swimming pool, keep-fit equipment, sauna, spa bath, solarium, gift shop (7.30am-9pm), coffee shop (all day).* AMERICAN EXPRESS *Access, Diners, Visa.*

Aberdeen Airport Airport Skean Dhu Hotel 65%	£123
Tel 0224 725252 Fax 0224 723745	**H**
Argyll Road Dyce Aberdeen Grampian AB2 0DU	Map 3 D4

Conveniently close to the aiport terminal, this Mount Charlotte Thistle hotel combines roomy, well-equipped bedrooms with a busy conference trade (up to 450 delegates). Children stay free in parents' room. *Rooms 148. Garden.* AMERICAN EXPRESS *Access, Diners, Visa.*

Aberfeldy Farleyer House 70%	£120
Tel 0887 820332 Fax 0887 829430	**HR**
Weem Aberfeldy Perthshire Tayside PH15 2JE	Map 3 C4

A 16th-century croft enlarged in the 1700s to house the Bailiff and transformed again in the 18th century to become Dower House to nearby Menzies Castle, Farleyer House enjoys a fine position overlooking the Tay valley to the west of town on the B846. The elegant drawing room and library bar with inner sanctum are comfortably furnished in country house style with deep armchairs and a relaxed atmosphere. Bedrooms vary somewhat in size and appeal with some built-in furniture plus a good scattering of antiques and individual decor; some Club rooms have recently come on stream. Rooms are properly serviced in the evenings and breakfasts come with freshly squeezed orange juice. Guests have use of the

leisure facilities (including an indoor swimming pool) at the nearby
Kenmore Club. Children under 10 stay free in parents' room. Dogs
in kennels only. **Rooms** 11. *Garden, croquet, golf (6-hole), helipad.*
AMERICAN EXPRESS *Access, Diners, Visa.*

Menzies Restaurant £75

Polished tables, dark green decor and floral curtains give a traditional look
to the dining room. The fixed-price dinner menu offers no choice,
although alternatives can be had from the menu of the hotel's informal
Scottish Bistro, except for the number of courses taken. Sliced River Tay
salmon flavoured with coriander, wild mushroom soup, loin of venison
with Highland beef fillet, and Scottish cheeses or raspberry crème brulée
with honey ice cream make up a typical meal. Herb-baked turbot with
saffron sauce is a speciality. From the bistro – choose as few or as many
courses as you like – could come mushroom and garlic pancakes, Provençal
fish soup, rack of lamb, roast duck breast, hot chocolate pudding and ratafia
of figs with honey ice cream. No smoking. **Seats** 24. Private Room 30.
D 7.30 for 8 (Bistro 10-2 & 6-9.15). Closed Sun-Thur in winter.
Set D £27/£32.

Aberfeldy   Places of Interest

Tourist Information   Tel 0887 820276.

We endeavour to be as up-to-the-minute as possible, but inevitably
some changes to key personnel may occur at restaurants and hotels
after the Guide goes to press.

Aberfoyle   Braeval Old Mill   ↑   £75

Tel 0877 382711   Fax 0877 382400   **R**
Braeval by Aberfoyle Central FK8 3UY   Map 3 B5

An old stone mill by the junction of the A81 and A821 just east of town.
Inside, the floor is flagstoned, the walls rough stone (softened by some arty
fabric wall-hangings) and the tables are now clothed. The overall effect
is most pleasing and is enhanced by charming service. There is no choice
for the first three of four courses on the fixed-price menu, thus allowing
chef-patron Nick Nairn to concentrate fully on each of the well-conceived
dishes on the day's menu. Typical of his modern style might be a lobster
lasagne followed by a salad of herbs, olive oil croutons and tapénade before
some local wild boar with cabbage stir-fried with garlic and juniper and
a bitter chocolate sauce, or fettucine of olives, tomato, Parmesan and pesto;
salmon, chili and cod fishcake with red pepper sauce, and roast fillet of beef
with shallots, bacon and red wine gravy. Vegetarian options are available
given notice. There is a choice at the pud stage with the likes of strawberry
Pavlova, caramelised apple tart and a particularly delicious mango mousse
enjoyed at a recent meal. No children under 10 years. Keen prices
on a smashing wine list that embraces most of the world's wine-producing
regions. Many half bottles. **Seats** 34. *L weekdays by arrangement, Sun
12.30-1.30 D 7-9.30. Closed D Sun & Mon, Bank Holidays, 1 week Feb,
1 week May/Jun, 1 week Nov. Set L £18.50 Set D £27.50.* AMERICAN EXPRESS
Access, Visa. MARTELL

Aberfoyle   Places of Interest

Tourist information   Tel 08772 352.

Abington — Forte Travelodge £45

Tel 0864 2782

L

Abington Biggar Strathclyde ML12 6RG

Map 4 B1

At the junction of the A74 with the M74 at the Welcome Break Service Area, Abington. **Rooms 54.** AMERICAN EXPRESS Access, Diners, Visa.

Achiltibuie — Summer Isles 64% £90

Tel 0854 622282 Fax 0854 622251

HR

Achiltibuie by Ullapool Highland IV26 2YG

Map 2 B2

A friendly family-run hotel in a particularly beautiful spot. Public areas include a sitting room with TV, honesty bar and games, plus a small study with a telephone. There are no TVs or phones in the neat, light bedrooms, three of which are in Norwegian pine-log cabins a few steps from the main building (the rate for these is £75). The Log House Suite, also in Norwegian pine, is a self-contained house that can accommodate 5. Owners Mark and Geraldine Irvine will be happy to give advice about fishing, bird-watching and walking. Children under 8 by arrangement. *Rooms 12. Garden, coffee shop (10.30am-9pm in high season). Closed mid Oct-Easter. No credit cards.* MARTELL COGNAC

Restaurant £75

There are spectacular views of the Summer Isles to be had from the dining room, where Chris Firth-Bernard makes good use of top-quality local produce, seafood and shellfish in particular. The five-course dinner starts with an interesting soup, perhaps mushroom and mustard with Madeira, continues with the likes of goujons of monkfish or beef carpaccio and majors on a main course such as Summer Isles lobster with baked fillet of cod on a bed of seafood, or haunch of roe deer with traditional accompaniments. Choice of five puddings, British cheeses, coffee. For those choosing wines by price the wine list is easy to use (wines are listed from lowest to highest price); however, there are no introductory or tasting notes, so you must rely on the staff's knowledge on each wine for advice – you might need it (unless you've got half an hour to disentangle the list)! There's some representation from the New World and a good selection of half bottles. No smoking. *Seats 26. Parties 8. D only at 8. Set D £32.*

Note that all telephone numbers with area codes starting with 0 will start 01 from 16 April 1995.

Advie — Tulchan Lodge 77% £350★

Tel 0807 510200 Fax 0807 510234

H

Advie nr Grantown-on-Spey Highland PH26 3PW

Map 2 C3

The immaculately maintained Tulchan Lodge is one of the finest Edwardian shooting lodges in Scotland, and it continues to offer some of the best fishing on 8 miles of the Spey – both banks (each beat has its own ghillie and luxurious fishing cabin where lunch is served) – and shooting on the 25,000-acre estate (grouse, pheasant, duck flighting and roe deer stalking). It was constructed, apparently, without regard to labour and cost, designed to offer every possible amenity and comfort, and there's still a similar philosophy holding true today, the atmosphere being much more that of a country house weekend party than a hotel. Dinner, for residents only, is served butler style at a single large polished table. No children under 14. ★Full-board terms only. Mid-April to September is the summer fishing season, October to January it is open only for shooting parties and February to April it is closed altogether. Dogs in kennels only. *Rooms 9. Garden, game fishing, shooting, snooker, tennis. Closed Feb-Apr. No credit cards.*

Airth   Airth Castle   68%   £100

Tel 0324 831411   Fax 0324 831419

Airth by Falkirk Central FK2 8JF

H

Map 3 C5

Lovely views over the Forth Valley from this carefully restored castle, dating in parts from the 14th century (to get there, take Junction 7 off the M9, then the A905 to Kincardine Bridge). Some bedrooms and two of the conference rooms (up to 400 delegates) are in a recent extension. Public areas are splendid, with fine proportions, ornate ceilings and elegant traditional furniture. Modern-day facilities are provided in bedrooms that range from spacious Executive-style to romantic four-poster. 36 rooms are suitable for family use, nominal charges for children under 12 (or under 3 in a cot). Leisure amenities are in the country club at the end of the drive. No dogs. *Rooms 75. Garden, indoor swimming pool, sauna, solarium, spa bath, keep-fit equipment, children's play areas.* AMERICAN EXPRESS *Access, Diners, Visa.*

Airth   Place of Interest

Bannockburn Museum (NT)   Tel 0780 812664   *11 miles.*

Alexandria   Cameron House   81%   £150

Tel 0389 55565   Fax 0389 59522

Loch Lomond Alexandria Strathclyde G83 8QZ

HR

Map 3 B5

Cameron House has a wonderful setting, right on the shores of Loch Lomond in 100 acres of lawns, gardens and woodland. The majestic Georgian building offers a mixture of traditional elegance (in the day rooms and bedrooms) and state-of-the-art technology (in the splendidly equipped Leisure Club and the bar). Bedrooms and bathrooms are generously laid out and provide all comforts, and service throughout is exemplary. Extensive range of outdoor sports as well as the Leisure Club. Families are well catered for, with a daily crèche (normally to 5pm, but extended to 9pm on Thurs & Fri), early suppers at 6pm and baby-sitting available. No dogs. *Rooms 68. Garden, croquet, indoor swimming pools, steam room, sauna, solarium, spa bath, squash, badminton, snooker, gym, hairdressing, beauty salon, crèche, kiosk, 9-hole golf course, tennis, watersports centre, marina, fishing, mountain bikes.* AMERICAN EXPRESS *Access, Diners, Visa.*

Georgian Room   £80

The main hotel dining room (there's also a Brasserie for lighter, more casual meals) is sumptuous and graceful, an ideal backdrop for Jeff Bland's sophisticated Scottish cooking with a modern touch. Two of his signature dishes are ravioli of salmon and asparagus, and hot pear soufflé with dark chocolate, ably demonstrating his skill. Other unusual dishes might be layers of Scottish seafood garnished with vegetables and silver birch wine; artichoke filled with woodland mushrooms and asparagus in a pastry case; or parfait of malt whisky with warm fruits and almond biscuit. There are fixed price and à la carte menus. No children under 14. *Seats 42. Parties 10. Private Room 42. L 12-2 D 7-10. Closed L Sat. Set L £13.95/£16.50 Set D £32.50/£38.50.*

Alexandria   Place of Interest

Balloch Castle Country Park   Tel 0389 58216.

Altnaharra   Altnaharra Hotel   60%   £113*

Tel & Fax 054 981 222

Altnaharra by Lairg Highland IV27 4UE

H

Map 2 B2

A renowned base for salmon and trout fishing, this remote 19th-century inn keeps fishing records that go back over 100 years. Ghillies can be hired, there's a tackle shop and a chalet provides rod racks, deep freeze and drying facilities. Fishing tuition may be available by advance arrangement. Healthy walks in lovely country are another popular option. There are no TVs or telephones in the airy bedrooms, among which are two annexe cottages ideal for anglers' families. *Half-board terms only. *Rooms 18. Garden, game fishing. Closed Nov-early Mar. Access, Visa.*

Alyth — Drumnacree House — £55

Tel 082 83 2194 — **RR**

St Ninians Road Alyth Perthshire Tayside PH11 8AP — Map 3 C4

Chef-patron Allan Cull is never short of enthusiasm and a good deal of skill is evident in his short, fixed-price dinner menu. This might commence with stir-fried lamb's kidneys or warm Arbroath smokie mousse, followed by pan-fried fillet of Tay sea trout with beurre blanc and chive sauce or Parma ham-wrapped supreme of pigeon with a brandy and honey sauce. A steak is also usually on the menu and Cajun dishes are considered a speciality. Desserts might include little chocolate pots with Grand Marnier, steamed sticky gingerbread pudding and bread-and-butter pudding. Coffee is served with home-made truffles. Eleanor Cull looks after the front of house with its pretty pink linen and candles. *Seats 30. Parties 23. Private Room 12. D only 7-9.30. Closed all Sun & Mon (to non-residents), 23-31 Dec. Set D £18.50. Access, Visa.*

Rooms — £62

Six neat, no-smoking bedrooms offer modest comfort with duvets, TVs, tea and coffee kit and en-suite shower rooms. No charge for children under 5. Good breakfasts might include kedgeree, kippers and home-made black pudding. *Garden.*

Annan — Warmanbie Hotel — 59% — £74

Tel 0461 204015 — **H**

Annan Dumfries & Galloway DG12 5LL — Map 4 C2

Home of the Duncan family since 1953, this Georgian house set in 45 acres of wooded grounds by the river Annan was converted to a hotel in 1983. There's still a homely, private house feel about the day rooms, and a traditional look to the bedrooms, which offer easy chairs, books, mini-bars and tea-makers; room 1 has a mahogany four-poster with matching furniture and a Victorian bathtub. A holiday cottage (Warmanbie Lodge) on the estate sleeps four people in two bedrooms. Under-16s stay in their parents' room for £6.95 including breakfast. Free fishing on a private stretch of the Annan. *Rooms 7. Garden, game fishing.* AMERICAN EXPRESS® *Access, Visa.*

Anstruther — Cellar — £70

Tel 0333 310378   Fax 0333 312544 — **R**

24 East Green Anstruther Fife KY10 3AA — Map 3 D5

Warming fires and natural stone walls create an aptly charming setting for Peter Jukes's cooking at this characterful restaurant, tucked away behind the harbour. Fish from nearby Pittenweem is the mainstay of his menu, in which simplicity and sophistication are skilfully and sensitively combined to produce dishes like langoustines baked whole in the shell with hot herb and garlic butter, or try their speciality dish, served as a starter, of crayfish and mussel bisque gratinée. Other starters might include a tempting trio of cold cured Scottish salmons: light oak-smoked; marinated gravad lax and hot-kiln-roasted smoked, served with a dill and sweet mustard sauce. Main dishes on a recent menu offered turbot and West Coast scallops braised in Chardonnay and enriched with cream, or, more simply, fresh tuna with a crushed black peppercorn sauce. Medallions of fillet of beef cooked in the pan with oyster mushrooms and served with a cream of Dijon mustard sauce might be the alternative on an otherwise exclusively seafood menu. A selection of their own desserts, or cheeses,

followed by coffee and petits fours rounds off the meal very nicely.
Booking is essential. Some generous prices on the wine list enable you
to drink well without having to dig too deep into your pockets. Very
carefully chosen wines from some of the best wine-makers worldwide.
*Seats 30. L 12.30-1.30 D 7.30-9. Closed Sun, Mon, 10 days Christmas. Set
D £28.50.* AMERICAN EXPRESS *Access, Visa.*

Anstruther   Place of Interest

Scottish Fisheries Museum Tel 0333 310628.

Appin   Invercreran County House Hotel   67%   £120

Tel 063 173 414   Fax 063 173 532   **H**

Appin by Oban Highland PA38 4BJ   **Map 3 B4**

A long, low-level hotel built in the 70s, standing in rugged countryside off
the A828 Oban-Fort William road. A semi-circular part at the centre of the
building is fronted by balconied terracing and houses a colourful lounge
and the dining areas; drinks service comes from a neat dispense bar.
Downstairs are master bedrooms with spacious tiled bathrooms, all with
showers and bidets. No children under five; 5-10s stay free in parents'
room. Dogs in kennels only. *Rooms 9. Garden, sauna. Closed 1 Nov-1 Mar.
Access, Visa.*

Ardentinny   Ardentinny Hotel   59%   £86

Tel 036 981 209   Fax 036 981 345   **H**

Loch Long Ardentinny nr Dunoon Strathclyde PA23 8TR   **Map 3 B5**

A former droving inn on the A880 by Loch Long, Ardentinny offers
comfortable accommodation with the bonus of stunning views of the loch
and surrounding forests and mountains. There's a selection of malt whiskies
to be had in the Viking and Lauder bars, where yachtsmen and fishermen
take their ease. Bedrooms are neat and bright, the best (designated 'Fyne'
and attracting a supplement) being slightly larger, with better views and
some extras; some have showers only. Considerable tariff reductions mid-
Mar to end May. Bar food is recommended. *Rooms 11. Garden, fishing,
hotel boat, mountain bikes. Closed Nov-mid Mar.* AMERICAN EXPRESS *Access,
Diners, Visa.*

Ardentinny   Place of Interest

Younger Botanic Garden Benmore Tel 0369 6261 *7 miles.*

Consult page 20 for a full list of starred restaurants

Arduaine   Loch Melfort Hotel   63%   £90

Tel 0852 200233   Fax 0852 200214   **H**

Arduaine by Oban Argyll Strathclyde PA34 4XG   **Map 3 B5**

There are magnificent views over the Sound of Jura from the Loch
Melfort, which has been in the capable hands of resident owners Philip and
Rosalind Lewis since 1989. Next door are the Arduaine Gardens (National
Trust) so there's plenty outdoors to attract the eye. Inside is equally
enticing, with comfortable, well-maintained public rooms and bedrooms
either in the main house or the Cedar Wing (joined to the main house
by a covered walkway), with patios or balconies. The Chartroom Bar
is a favourite with yachtsmen. No dogs in the main house or public rooms.
Small conferences (up to 20). *Rooms 26. Garden, mooring, book & gift shop.
Closed Jan & Feb. Access, Visa.*

Arisaig Arisaig House 75% £135

Tel 068 75 622 Fax 068 75 626 **HR**

Beasdale Arisaig Highland PH39 4NR Map 3 A4

Three miles east of the village, Arisaig House enjoys an idyllic location surrounded by some of the most gently beautiful scenery in Scotland and with fine views across Arisaig Sound. Originally Victorian, the house was virtually rebuilt after a fire in the 1930s, thus the day rooms are light and airy with plain white walls that make a perfect background for well-chosen antiques, objets d'art and an abundance of fresh flowers – the latter all from their own 20 acres of grounds. Personally run by the unobtrusively hospitable Smithers family, the whole place has an air of peace and tranquillity. Bedrooms vary in size from two full suites to a single room whose bathroom is private but not en suite. There's a variety of furniture too, from antiques to more contemporary pieces but all rooms are immaculately kept with tasteful decor and humanising touches like books, fresh flowers and fruit. Bathrooms all have tubs but only hand-held showers; generous towelling includes bath robes and toiletries are of good quality. Conserves at breakfast are all home-made with soft fruits from the kitchen garden. No children under 10 years. **Rooms** 14. *Garden, croquet, snooker, helipad. Closed Dec-Mar. Access, Visa.*

Restaurant £85

Dinner is fixed-price but with an unusual format in that chef David Wilkinson (the son-in-law of the house) proposes his own five-course menu but with a list of alternatives should your tastes and his not quite coincide. Cooking is refined yet not overcomplicated with dishes such as fresh asparagus with puff pastry and butter sauce; pork and duck rillettes; cream of Jerusalem artichoke soup; brandy-flamed breast of Norfolk duck with a honey-scented sauce; whole lemon sole with parsley butter, and marinated venison with red wine and chestnut sauce demonstrating the style. Good puds might include fresh figs poached in port with cinnamon ice cream and a very moreish passion fruit mousse with coconut ice cream. Lunch is a much less formal affair, also served in the bar or out on the terrace – the ideal spot if the weather allows. The New World doesn't get a look in on the rather pedestrian wine list. No smoking. No children under 10 years. **Seats** 36. *Parties 10. L 12.30-2 D 7-9. Set D £29.50.*

Arisaig Old Library Lodge £55

Tel 0687 450651 Fax 0687 450219 **RR**

Arisaig Highland BH39 4NH Map 3 A4

On the road to the Isles, where it borders Loch Non Seall with fine views as far as the Inner Hebrides, the Broadhursts' 200-year-old stable has been converted into a pleasing little restaurant with white-painted rough stone walls, cork floor and black-painted tables. Over the last 10 years or so self-taught cook Alan Broadhurst has managed to develop a network of local sources for some of the excellent produce to be found hereabouts, most notably the first-rate seafood (which usually gets exported direct to the Continent) like langoustines, sole, crab, mussels and Mallaig scallops. Venison, duck and chicken also appear on the short (about five choices at each stage), fixed-price dinner menus in dishes that are uncomplicated but not uninteresting – mussel and fennel soup, venison with herbs and rowanberry and red wine sauce, scallops on a leek purée. Puds are homely and the bread home-baked. Eight different wines are served by the glass – either large or small – from a decent list. Lunch is a less formal affair that also includes salads and 'toasties'. **Seats** 28. *Parties 12. L 11.30-2.30 D 6.30-9.30. Closed Nov-one week before Easter. Set D £19.50. Access, Visa.*

Rooms £59

The six bedrooms, four of them chalet-style to the rear of the main building, are spacious, clean and bright with the modern conveniences of remote-control TV, direct-dial phones and tea and coffee-making kit. All are en suite with two having shower and WC only. Good, freshly cooked breakfasts begin with freshly squeezed orange juice.

Auchencairn   Balcary Bay Hotel   64%   £84

Tel 055 664217   Fax 055 664272   **HR**

Auchencairn nr Castle Douglas Dumfries & Galloway DG7 1QZ   Map 4 B3

On the shore road two miles south of Auchencairn this sophisticated, white pebbledash, early 17th-century house has a glorious location on the edge of Balcary Bay. Its seclusion made it a haunt of smugglers in years gone by and today one can see the salmon nets jutting out into the bay towards Heston Isle, where the contraband was landed. It's now a comfortable hotel run in friendly fashion by the Lambs, and peace and quiet are major attractions. Day rooms include the spacious oak-timbered general lounge with chintzy cushions enlivening the brown dralon easy chairs, a pretty non-smoking lounge and a small cocktail bar with terrace from which to enjoy the view. Floral patterns are favoured in the individually decorated bedrooms (the majority having bay views) with darkwood 'Stag' furniture and good en-suite bathrooms. A bowl of fresh fruit welcomes guests and beds are turned down at night. *Rooms* 17. *Garden, snooker. Closed mid Nov-Feb. Access, Visa.*

Restaurant   £60

Fish dishes, fresh from Scottish rivers and seas whenever possible, feature on the menu in the pale green dining room although there are also plenty of meat dishes – lamb en croute, duck with soy and honey sauce, chicken cooked in basil and aniseed. In addition to the à la carte there's a daily changing fixed-price dinner with a couple of choices at each stage other than the sorbet. One of each of the day's half-dozen or so desserts is displayed on a sideboard. *Seats* 50. *L by arrangement D 7-8.30 (till 9 high season). Set D £18.75.*

Auchencairn   Collin House   68%   £76

Tel 0556 640292   Fax 0556 640276   **HR**

Auchencairn nr Castle Douglas Dumfries & Galloway DG7 1QN   Map 4 B3

Dating from 1750, pink-painted Collin House is easily spotted in its elevated position to the east of town from which it enjoys fine views across the Solway Firth. It's the sort of place where guests soon get to know each other over pre-dinner drinks served in the civilised, homely drawing room with its open fire, flowers, books and a nice collection of paintings. Spacious bedrooms, furnished with a variety of antiques, are light and airy with homely extras justifying the brochure promise of 'unpretentious comfort'. Good-sized bathrooms (one is huge) offer large bathsheets and good toiletries. Breakfasts, which include haggis, kippers and smoked haddock amongst the options, are worth getting up for. *Rooms* 6. *Garden. Closed 3-4 weeks in Jan/Feb. Access, Visa.*

Restaurant   £65

Fresh flowers and bronze animals grace the polished, antique tables of the red dining room where John Wood's short (a couple of choices at each stage plus a soup course) fixed-price menu offers sound, uncomplicated cooking. Salad of smoked duck breast with an orange and cognac dressing; dill-marinated Orkney herrings with mustard sauce; carrot, apple and ginger soup; fillet of Galway beef with Madeira sauce, and salmon in a buttery court bouillon show the style, with the likes of sticky toffee pudding or chocolate and whisky parfait for afters. Booking is essential for non-residents. No smoking. No children under 10. *Seats* 16. *D only 7.30 for 8. Set D £26.*

Auchterarder   Auchterarder House   75%   £130

Tel 0764 663646   Fax 0764 662939   **HR**

Auchterarder Tayside PH3 1DZ   Map 3 C5

Just 1½ miles north of Auchterarder on the B8062, this baronial-style
mansion was built in 1832. Nowadays it's a hotel popular with corporate
clients and boasting many fine features: carved oak panelling in the central
hall, ribbed ceilings and marble fireplace in the day rooms, a characterful
billiard room bar, and charming conservatory. The Brown family have
added the warm welcome and many homely touches like original
paintings, an abundance of fresh flowers and numerous objets d'art.
Bedroom decor varies, but all have extras both luxurious (like a cut-glass
decanter of good sherry) and practical (iron and ironing board). Many
of the bathrooms include bidets and separate showers. **Rooms** 15. *Garden,
croquet, pitch & putt, putting green.* AMERICAN EXPRESS *Access,
Diners, Visa.*

Restaurant   £95

A richly, if somewhat somberly, decorated room in Victorian style with
heavy woodwork, dark green flock wallpaper and elaborately moulded and
ribbed ceiling, but Audrey Brown's pretty posies of fresh flowers brighten
things up on tables immaculately laid with fine china and glassware and
boasting silver candelabra. David Hunt's fixed-price dinner menu leans
heavily on good Scottish produce in dishes like West Coast mussel stew
spiked with Pernod and garnished with herb dumplings; red deer from
Perthshire with a chicken, barley and tarragon timbale and red wine sauce,
braised turbot with a light pesto and a warm dill and tomato dressing, and
Aberdeen Angus beef collops served with langoustine tails in a gingered
shellfish and coriander sauce. Interesting puds might include a baked
chocolate spiced pudding with honey ice cream and toddie sabayon, and
an iced terrine of young rhubarb and orange with a marmalade sauce.
When he's in the mood, proprietor Ian Brown might accompany dinner
at the grand piano in the main hall. The fine old cellars house some
exceptional wines on a splendid and comprehensive list. Some idiosyncratic
notes, keen prices. **Seats** 50. *Parties* 8. *Private Room* 15. *L by arrangement
D 7-9.30. Set Sun L £15 Set D £37.50/£45/£50.*

Auchterarder   Gleneagles Hotel   86%   £220

Tel 0764 662231   Fax 0764 662134   **H**

Auchterarder Tayside PH3 1NF   Map 3 C5

Gleneagles – the very name conjures up an image and a reputation, neither
of which are let down by the reality of the place. More than just an hotel,
though a grand hotel in every sense; more than just a sports complex,
though one of the best in the world. The famous names associated with the
latter aspect are legendary, of course – Jack Nicklaus, Mark Phillips, Jackie
Stewart – as are those in the grand arcade of shops: Harvey Nichols,
Mappin & Webb, Burberry's, the Royal Bank of Scotland. Accommodation
ranges from the Royal Lochnagar Suite and the Monarch's Suite, to three
other grades of suite, on to four grades of bedroom – we quote a basic
price. There are even special rates for dogs, horses and hawks! The country
club encompasses Champneys Health Spa where you can relax and recover
from all the choosing. Dining facilities range from the formal Strathearn
Restaurant to the more relaxed Country Club Brasserie. Conferences of up
to 360 delegates can take equal advantage of all that's on offer. It's one
of a kind. **Rooms** 234. *Garden, croquet, indoor swimming pool, sauna, steam
room, solarium, whirlpool bath, gym, hairdressing, tennis, squash, golf courses,
pitch & putt, jogging trails, bowling green, riding, clay-pigeon shooting, coarse
and game fishing, falconry, mountain bikes, children's playground, snooker,
valeting, shopping arcade, bank, post office.* AMERICAN EXPRESS *Access,
Diners, Visa.*

Auchterarder   Places of Interest

Tourist Information   Tel 0764 663450.

Auchterhouse   Old Mansion House   68%   £95

Tel 082 626 366   Fax 082 626 400   **HR**

Auchterhouse by Dundee Tayside DD3 0QN   Map 3 C5

A 16th-century whitewashed Scottish baronial house skilfully converted
by Nigel and Eva Bell to a charming and relaxed hotel. Some nice
architectural features include the vaulted entrance hall, an open Jacobean
fireplace and a splendidly ornate 17th-century plasterwork ceiling in the
original drawing room. Pleasantly furnished bedrooms – two are family
suites with separate children's bedrooms – have good bathrooms well
stocked with toiletries. The house is on the B954 seven miles from Dundee.
*Rooms 6. Garden, croquet, outdoor swimming pool, squash. Closed 25 & 26 Dec,
1st week Jan.* AMERICAN EXPRESS *Access, Diners, Visa.*

Restaurant   £70

Much local produce is used for the varied carte that is supplemented
by a separate vegetarian menu. Cullen skink (smoked haddock and potato
soup), smoked Tay salmon, whole prawn tails in an English mustard cheese
sauce with leeks and carrots, collops in the pan with sherry and pickled
walnuts, and chocolate marquise with a coffee sauce show the style. Also
bar lunch and supper menus. No under-10s at night. No smoking. *Seats 50.
Private Room 22. L 12-1.45 D 7-9.30 (Sun to 9). Set L £11.95/£13.95.*

Aviemore   Aviemore Highlands Hotel   61%   £70

Tel 0479 810771   Fax 0479 811473   **H**

Aviemore Centre Aviemore Highland PH22 1PJ   Map 3 C4

On the A9 Perth to Inverness road, a modern hotel popular for both
business and pleasure, with banqueting/conference facilities for up to 120,
and plenty of free parking. 24hr room service. *Rooms 103. Garden, sun
beds.* AMERICAN EXPRESS *Access, Diners, Visa.*

Aviemore   Stakis Aviemore Four Seasons   70%   £100

Tel 0479 810681   Fax 0479 810534   **H**

Aviemore Highland PH22 1PF   Map 3 C4

A seven-storey hotel at the heart of the skiing centre, a mile from the A9,
with views of the Spey Valley and the Cairngorms. Centrally-heated
bedrooms with smart darkwood furniture range from singles to triples.
The main day room is a bright, picture-windowed lounge. Half the
bedrooms are designated non-smoking. Two conference rooms (120 + 40).
The coffee shop has been converted into a brasserie. *Rooms 88. Garden,
indoor swimming pool, gym, sauna, spa bath, steam bath, solarium, ski school.*
AMERICAN EXPRESS *Access, Diners, Visa.*

Aviemore   Stakis Coylumbridge Resort Hotel   62%   £98

Tel 0479 810661   Fax 0479 811770   **H**

Aviemore Highland PH22 1QN   Map 3 C4

Skiing is the thing at Aviemore, but this sprawling modern hotel caters
admirably for all sorts of activities for both adults and children. There's
a sports hall for children, a fun house and an outdoor play area. It's also
geared up for large conferences (maximum 750 delegates). Most of the
bedrooms are big enough for family use, and baby-sitting, baby-listening
and (at busy times) a crèche are provided. A couple of rooms are suitable
for disabled guests. *Rooms 175. Two indoor swimming pools, sauna, steam
bath, solarium, beauty & hair salon, tennis, archery, target shooting.*
AMERICAN EXPRESS *Access, Diners, Visa.*

Aviemore   Places of Interest

Tourist Information Tel 0479 810363.
Strathspey Steam Railway   Tel 0479 810725.
Aviemore Mountain Resort Centre Ice Rink   Tel 0479 810624.
Caird Sport Dry Ski Slope   Tel 0479 810310.
Cairngorm Reindeer Centre   Tel 0479 861228.
Cairngorm Chairlift Company   Tel 0479 861261.

Ayr   Fouters Bistro   £40

Tel 0292 261391   R

2a Academy Street Ayr Strathclyde KA7 1HS   Map 4 A1

Fran and Laurie Black have celebrated 21 years at Fouters, a cheerful bistro
in vaulted basement premises down a cobbled lane opposite the Town Hall.
Scottish produce (especially local seafood, and game in season) is cooked
in French style with consistently enjoyable results. So you might be offered
a salad of smoked trout from the Fence Bay Fisheries, or a freshly baked
brioche filled with brown *champignons de Paris* and North Atlantic
shrimps; followed by Scottish salmon with asparagus or a steak *belle
forestière*. Light lunches, blackboard specials, good-value bistro menus and
plenty of half bottles on the wine list. *Seats 38. L 12-2 D 6.30-10.30 (Sun
7-10). Set L £4.95/£6.95/£8.50. Closed L Sun, all Mon, 25 & 27 Dec, 1-3
Jan.* AMERICAN EXPRESS *Access, Diners, Visa.*

Ayr   Jarvis Caledonian Hotel   64%   £116

Tel 0292 269331   Fax 0292 610722   H

Dalblair Road Ayr Strathclyde KA7 1UG   Map 4 A1

Town-centre hotel with leisure facilities and a conference suite (for up to
175). Many bedrooms suitable for families (children up to 16 stay free
in parents' room). Within easy reach of eight golf courses, thus popular for
sporting breaks. *Rooms 114. Indoor swimming pool, gym, sauna, spa bath,
solarium.* AMERICAN EXPRESS *Access, Diners, Visa.*

> If we recommend meals in a hotel or inn a separate entry is made for its
> restaurant.

Ayr   The Stables   £45

Tel 0292 283704   R

Queen's Court 41 Sandgate Ayr Strathclyde KA7 1BD   Map 4 A1

In a shopping area of restored Georgian and Victorian buildings Edward
Baines and his chef William McFadzean demonstrate the art of traditional
Scottish cooking. Anything from light snacks to full meals is available:
scones with Arran jam, apple flans, chocolate fudge cake and clootie
dumplings; haggis; fish and meat prepared in the family smokehouse;
steaks; salads. Chicken stovies are made with potatoes, turnips, onions and
carrots. Ham and haddie pie is a traditional dish of bacon and smoked
haddock. Tweed kettle is a casserole of salmon, mushrooms, celery and
onions spiced with mace and cooked in white wine. The wine list includes
a number of traditional country wines, one made from the sap of the silver
birch. No reservations. No smoking in the main dining room. *Seats 50.
Meals 10-4.45 (Sun – Jul/Aug/Sep only – from 12.30). Closed 25 & 26 Dec,
1 & 2 Jan. No credit cards.*

Ayr (Monkton)	Travel Inn	£43

Tel 0582 482224   **L**
Kilmarnock Road Monkton Strathclyde KA9 2RJ   Map 4 A1

5 miles from Ayr, on A77/A78 roundabout by Prestwick Airport. *Rooms 40.* AMERICAN EXPRESS® *Access, Diners, Visa.*

Ayr   Places of Interest

Tourist Information   Tel 0292 284196.
Gaiety Theatre   Tel 0292 264639.
Ayr Racecourse   Tel 0292 264179.
Ayr Ice Rink   Tel 0292 263024.
   Historic Houses, Castles and Gardens
Burns Cottage   Alloway. Tel 0292 441215.
Blairquhan Castle and Gardens   Straiton Nr Maybole. Tel 065 57 239.
Culzean Castle Garden and Country Park (NT)   Maybole. Tel 065 56 274.

Ballachulish	Ballachulish Hotel	60%	£80

Tel 08552 606   Fax 08552 629   **H**
Ballachulish Argyll Highland PA39 4JY   Map 3 B4

Just off the A82, three miles north of Glencoe and some 12 miles south of Fort William, this is one of Scotland's oldest hotels. Set above Loch Linnhe at the base of picturesque mountains, the hotel has panoramic views from all the public areas. Bedrooms are called Lairds or Chieftains, the latter being superior and enjoying the best of the light, space and views. Guests have free use of the leisure centre at the sister hotel *The Isles of Glencoe* about two miles away. Families are well catered for. *Rooms 30. Garden, sea fishing. Access, Visa.*

Ballachulish	Isles of Glencoe Hotel	59%	£85

Tel 085 52 603   Fax 085 52 770   **H**
Ballachulish Highland PA39 4HL   Map 3 B4

"Almost afloat" on the shore of Loch Leven, this new, clean-cut purpose-built hotel makes a useful overnight stop with comfortable uncluttered bedrooms, although their narrow sloping windows fail to make the best of the views – the loch and ancient burial island of the Clan McDonald on one side and mountains on the other. Friendly young staff. Men and women share changing facilities for the basic leisure centre. Much-reduced rates for children sharing parents' room. *Rooms 39. Indoor swimming pool, spa bath, sauna, steam room, coffee shop (10am-10pm). Access, Visa.*

Ballachulish   Places of Interest

Tourist Information   Tel 085 52 296

Ballater	Craigendarroch Hotel	74%	£125

Tel 033 97 55858   Fax 033 97 55447   **H**
Braemar Road Ballater Grampian AB35 5XA   Map 3 C4

Seven miles from Balmoral on the banks of the River Dee, this fine hotel in Scottish baronial style offers comfort, peace and a wealth of sports and leisure amenities in a setting of peace and beauty. Fair-sized bedrooms are bright and modern, with plenty of toiletries in the bathrooms, and views of the Dee valley to wake up to. Thoughtful extras abound, from sewing kit to shortbread, playing cards to sherry. There are two bars (one with regular live music nights) and three restaurants. No dogs, but excellent facilities for children, including a daily crèche and the Acorn Club for 5 to

15-year-olds. *Rooms 49. Garden, indoor swimming pool, gym, squash, sauna, spa bath, solarium, beauty & hair salon, tennis, dry ski slope, snooker.* AMERICAN EXPRESS *Access, Diners, Visa.*

Ballater   Tullich Lodge   71%   £190*

Tel 033 97 55406   Fax 033 97 55397   **HR**
Ballater Grampian AB35 5SB   Map 3 C4

An imposing but delightful pink granite mansion overlooking the Dee on the A93 Aberdeen-Braemar road. Hector Macdonald and Neil Bannister have been here since 1968, running a hotel of great atmosphere and real character which attracts a large number of regularly-returning guests. Crenellations and towers are outward distinguishing features, while inside antiques, pictures and handsome furnishings grace the drawing room and chintzy little sitting room (the perfect place to retire with a book); an old Broadwood piano in the drawing room 'responds kindly to early 19th-century music'. Bedrooms are individually decorated in keeping with the rest of the place, and the Tower Room, on the third floor, provides not only exercise but a splendid Victorian bathroom; televisions are available on request only; however, a wireless is in every room. High tea is served to children at 5pm in the kitchen, and both picnic lunches and packed dinners ('for the train') can be provided. *Half board only. Rooms 10. Garden. Closed Dec-Mar.* AMERICAN EXPRESS *Access, Diners, Visa.*

Dining Room   £60

In the mahogany-panelled dining room (no smoking; jacket and tie requested) Neil prepares no-choice four-course dinners based on sound classic and modern British methods. Typical recent offerings have included mussels *au gratin*, avocado pear with tomato vinaigrette and collops of venison on warmed watercress among the starters, then perhaps cullen skink or consommé before a main course of poached halibut with anchovy butter, grilled monkfish and bacon on a skewer or roast leg of lamb with rowan jelly. The fourth course is a fruit-based dessert or Scottish cheeses, and coffee is included in the meal price. *Seats 26. Parties 24. L at 1 D 7.30-9. Set L in the bar £7 Set D £23.*

Ballater   Places of Interest

Tourist Information   Tel 03397 55306.
Balmoral Castle   Tel 03397 42334 Open May to July. *8 miles.*
Braemar Castle   Tel 03397 41219.

Banchory   Raemoir House   71%   £95

Tel 0330 824884   Fax 0330 822171   **HR**
Raemoir Banchory Grampian AB31 4ED   Map 3 D4

Sixteen miles south west of Aberdeen and 2½ miles north of Banchory on the A980 is Raemoir House, an 18th-century mansion set in a 3500-acre estate which has been in the Sabin family since 1943. Ongoing attention to refurbishment ensures that standards are maintained at the same time as the cosy ambience. Rich red brocade chairs, panelled walls and valuable antiques enhance the traditional look of the morning room, and the bar is fashioned from a Tudor four-poster. Bedrooms are all different in size and character, but most have inviting chaises longues, day beds or armchairs. Six rooms are in the historic 16th-century Ha'Hoose immediately behind the mansion. There are five self-catering apartments converted from the original coach-house and stables. *Rooms 25. Garden, croquet, sauna, sun beds, keep-fit equipment, tennis, game fishing, pitch & putt, shooting. Closed 2 weeks Jan.* AMERICAN EXPRESS *Access, Diners, Visa.*

The Macintyre Room   £70

The emphasis in Derek Smith's largely international menu is on Scottish produce and the more local the better. You can't beat Raemoir pheasant braised in claret for instance! Other examples could be a feuilleté of Dee salmon with a watercress and lime reduction, or roast baron of Scottish lamb with an orange and apricot confit and a rosemary jus. Both table d'hote and à la carte are offered, plus one of the longest vegetarian menus outside a 'dedicated' vegetarian restaurant that we've seen. Fine Scottish cheese trolley. *Seats 64. Parties 16. Private Room 80. L 12.30-2 D 7.30-9. Set L £14.50 (Sun) Set D £24.50.*

Banchory	Tor-na-Coille Hotel	66%	£85
Tel 0330 822242 Fax 0330 824012			**H**
Inchmarlo Road Banchory Grampian AB31 4AB			Map 3 D4

Built as a private house in 1873 and run as a hotel since the turn of the century, Tor-na-Coille retains much of its Victorian character. The function room can accommodate 90 people for a banquet or conference. Bedrooms are furnished with antiques. The hotel copes very well with children (under-12s stay free in parents' room) and the owner's nanny is able to help out by arrangement. *Rooms 23. Garden, croquet, squash. Closed 25-27 Dec.* AMERICAN EXPRESS *Access, Diners, Visa.*

🍾 is our symbol for an outstanding wine list.

Banchory	Places of Interest

Tourist Information   Tel 03302 2000.

Bearsden	Fifty Five BC		£50
Tel 041-942 7272 Fax 041-942 9650			**R** *
128 Drymen Road Bearsden Glasgow Strathclyde G61 3RB			Map 3 B6

Restaurant and bar with great family appeal. The style is modern with worldwide influences, so you'll find filo basket of smoked haddock, roast monkfish and grilled langoustines sharing the restaurant menu with sweet and sour vegetables, pan-fried pigeon and chargrilled Scottish steaks. On the bar menu are snackier items such as crispy potato skins, quiche and the 55BC Quarter Pounder, plus a selection of sandwiches. *Seats 24. L 12-2 D 7-10. Closed 1 & 2 Jan. Access, Visa.*

Bearsden	Place of Interest

Bearsden Ski Club   Tel 041-942 2933.

Beattock	Auchen Castle	64%	£54
Tel 06833 407 Fax 06833 667			**H**
Beattock nr Moffat Dumfries & Galloway DG10 9SH			Map 4 C2

Set high above, and signposted from, the A74 about a mile north of Beattock, this impressive, early Victorian, Scottish baronial mansion enjoys fine views across Annandale to the Moffat hills. A well-run, friendly hotel with day rooms including a comfortable chintzy lounge and convivial bar. Bedrooms in the main house vary considerably both in size, decor (the best quite stylish) and furniture which ranges from simple fitted units and new but traditional-style, freestanding pieces to a couple with antiques. Ten rooms are in a separate red cedarwood chalet and have fitted units, patchwork bedspreads and good views. These rooms have shower and WC only. Owner Robert Beckh also has an unusual collection of old vehicles – "Tonka toys for grown-ups" – that guests can try out within the hotel's 50 acres of grounds. *Rooms 25. Garden, game fishing. Closed 3 weeks Christmas/New Year.* AMERICAN EXPRESS *Access, Diners, Visa.*

Beattock   Places of Interest

Dumfries Tourist Information   Tel 0387 53862. At Dumfries 25 miles.
Drumlanrig Castle and Country Park   Tel 0848 31682.
  Museums and Art Galleries
Dumfries Museum   Tel 0387 53374.
Gracefield Arts Centre   Tel 0387 62084.
Robert Burns Centre   Tel 0387 64808.
Burns House   Tel 0387 55297.

Blairgowrie   Kinloch House   70%   £145*
Tel 0250 884237   Fax 0250 884333   **HR**
Kinloch by Blairgowrie Tayside PH10 6SG   Map 3 C5

Highland cattle graze in the 25 acres of parkland and policies (Scottish for
the pleasure-grounds around a mansion) that surrounds a creeper-clad 19th-
century house which has been turned into a relaxing country hotel
by David and Sarah Shentall. Public areas include oak-panelled hall and
first-floor galleries and a period drawing room; most guests seem to prefer
the convivial atmosphere of the comfortable bar or the charm of the plant-
filled conservatory with its Lloyd Loom chairs and tables. All the
rooms are now traditionally furnished and boast particularly luxurious bathrooms.
Extras include books, magazines, ironing boards and bathrobes. Shooting
parties and fishermen appreciate the Sportsman's room, which offers
everything from a deep freeze to dog bowls. Room service is limited.
*Half-board terms only. Three miles west of Blairgowrie, on the A923
to Dunkeld. *Rooms 21. Garden, croquet, fishing. Closed 2 weeks Dec.*
AMERICAN EXPRESS *Access, Diners, Visa.*

Restaurant   £70

A civilised dining room where chef Bill McNicoll's daily-changing menus
bring a good choice of dishes, both simple and more elaborate – from
smoked salmon parcels with lemon mayonnaise or seasonal game paté
to pan-fried sirloin steak and herb-crusted supreme of halibut on a bed
of spinach and a tomato butter sauce. Desserts from a trolley. Also informal
lunches with interesting open sandwiches. Sunday lunch sees a small choice
that usually includes good beef dishes. Marvellous selection of half bottles
on the carefully compiled wine list that is most fairly priced; though
there are not that many New World wines, they do represent quality.
No children under 7 at night. Jackets and ties are requested in the evening.
No smoking. *Seats 55. Parties 12. Private Room 30. L 12.30-2 D 7-9.15.
Set L £13.95 Set D £24.90.*

Blairgowrie   Places of Interest

Tourist Information   Tel 0250 872960.

Bonnyrigg   Dalhousie Castle   62%   £120
Tel 0875 820153   Fax 0875 821936   **H**
Bonnyrigg nr Edinburgh Lothian EH19 3JB   Map 3 C6

Built around 1450 (though it's thought there was a dwelling on this site
even earlier) from locally quarried red sandstone, Dalhousie is a real castle
complete with tower, crenellations and dungeons, which now house the
restaurant. Notable features of the public areas include more fine Gothic-
style fan vaulting in the entrance hall and a 'wedding cake' moulded ceiling
in the wood-panelled library that is the main day room. Bedrooms vary
considerably in furnishings and decor, but all have en-suite bathrooms.
Functions and meetings are a major part of the business here – facilities for
up to 120. *Rooms 25. Garden.* AMERICAN EXPRESS *Access, Diners, Visa.*

Bonnyrigg   Places of Interest

Tourist Information   Tel 031 660 6814.

Bridge of Allan   Royal Hotel   59%   £66

Tel 0786 832284   Fax 0786 834377   **H**
Henderson Street Bridge of Allan Central FK9 4HG   Map 3 C5

Built in 1842 in what was then a spa town (now most notably home
to Stirling University), the Royal stands half a mile from the railway
station and one mile from the M9 (junction 11). Bedrooms offer all the
usual accessories including satellite TV, and all have modern bathrooms.
There's a plush bar, an oak-panelled lounge and several conference rooms
(maximum capacity 150). **Rooms** *32. Garden.* AMERICANEXPRESS *Access,
Diners, Visa.*

Cairndow   Loch Fyne Oyster Bar   £35

Tel 049 96 264   Fax 049 96 234   **R**
Clachan Farm Cairndow Strathclyde PA26 8BH   Map 3 B5

Knock back a few oysters or push the boat out for a feast of shellfish, all
of local origin. Their own smokehouse produces a wonderful platter
of smoked trout, eel, salmon, mussels, cod's roe and mackerel. Other
attractions range from herring fillets in four marinades (dill, sherry,
tomato, spices) to seafood chowder, kippers, salmon steak and venison.
Carefully chosen, short wine list. Situated at the head of Loch Fyne, with
seats outside for fine weather. **Seats** *80. Parties 50. Meals 9-9 (Nov to Mar
9-6). Closed 25 & 26 Dec, 1 Jan.* AMERICANEXPRESS *Access, Visa.*

Callander   Roman Camp   69%   £95

Tel 0877 330003   Fax 0877 331533   **H R**
off Main Street Callander Tayside FK17 8BG   Map 3 B5

Starting life as a modest 17th-century manor house, subsequent alterations
and extensions have give the Roman Camp something of a French chateau-
like appearance, complete with a pair of towers, one hiding a 'secret' chapel.
The hotel's drive begins in the main street of town but the building
is surrounded by fine gardens bordering the River Teith. When the house
was turned into a hotel in the 1930s, much of the original furniture and
objets d'art (there's even the remains of a wreath from Queen Victoria's
coffin on display) remained in place both in the public rooms – which
include a mellow panelled library with fine Tudor-style ceiling, and
civilised drawing room – and in the bedrooms, which feature a mixture
of antique and painted pieces. There are three full suites, seven 'superior'
(larger) rooms of which three are in more modern style, and four 'standard'
rooms of which two have shower and WC only. Other bathrooms have
suites from various periods, with some of the tubs in need of resurfacing.
All rooms get extras like sherry, fresh fruit, mineral water and fresh
flowers. Beds are turned down at night and room service is available
throughout the day and evening. **Rooms** *14. Garden, game fishing.*
AMERICANEXPRESS *Access, Diners, Visa.*

Restaurant   £95

The timbered ceiling of the dining room gives it a somewhat Austrian feel,
although painted with traditional Celtic patterns. Both the à la carte and
no-choice, four-course tasting menu feature dishes in the modern idiom –
red mullet with grilled vegetables marinated in olive oil and balsamic
vinegar; saddle of hare with beetroot marmalade, celeriac purée and
blackcurrant sauce; rack of lamb with herb crust on a garlic and button
onion confit with Stilton tart – competently handled by the kitchen.
No smoking. **Seats** *40. Parties 12. Private Room 32. L 12-2 D 7-9.
Set L £12.50/£17 Set D £30.*

Callander   Places of Interest

Tourist Information   Tel 0877 30342.
Rob Roy and Trossachs Visitor Centre   Tel 0877 30342.

Canonbie — Riverside Inn £72

Tel 038 73 71512 **IR**

Canonbie Dumfries & Galloway DG14 0UX — Map 4 C2

Overlooking the river Esk in the small village of Canonbie just north of the border, the white-painted Riverside Inn is in immaculate order inside and out. The carpeted bar, furnished with country chairs grouped around sewing-machine tables, is happily free of piped music, fruit machines and the like. Six en-suite bedrooms (two with shower and WC only) have pretty, matching bedcovers and curtains – and even loo roll and tissue box covers – and boast extras like fresh fruit, mineral water, books and magazines plus TV but no telephone. For residents there is a domestic-scale sitting room. *Rooms 6. Garden. Closed 2 weeks Nov, 2 weeks Feb. Access, Visa.*

Restaurant £55

Robert and Susan Phillips share the cooking duties for the beamed dining room here. Concentrating on good local produce, their fixed-price dinner menu offers a choice of four main dishes such as crispy roast farm duck with soft peppercorn and strawberry sauce; chargrilled Aberdeen Angus steak, fillet of salmon in olive oil with red peppers and sun-dried tomatoes, with starters like baked garlic oysters and air-dried Cumbrian ham. Leave room for such puds as dark treacle pudding, rhubarb and ginger ice cream and lime and grapefruit meringue pie. At lunchtimes (except Sunday) and in the evenings there is a substantial blackboard menu in the bar. No smoking. No children under 10 years. *Seats 24. D only 7.30-8.30. Closed 25 & 26 Dec, 1 Jan. Set D £22.*

Chapel of Garioch — Pittodrie House 65% £110

Tel 0467 681444   Fax 0467 681648 **H**

Chapel of Garioch nr Inverurie Highland AB51 9HS — Map 2 D3

Fishing, stalking, shooting and riding are all available locally, combining with facilities on the premises to make this a fine base for sporting holidays. The house dates largely from the 17th century (rebuilt from 15th-century origins) and the reception rooms are very traditional and homely, with antiques, family portraits and log fires. The wine bar is stocked with more than ninety malt whiskies. Bedrooms are either in the main building (motley fabrics, antiques) or in a 1990-built wing, with reproduction furniture and decent modern bathrooms. There are banqueting and conference facilities for 130/150. *Rooms 27. Garden, croquet, squash, tennis, snooker, clay-pigeon shooting, helipad.* AMERICAN EXPRESS *Access, Diners, Visa.*

Any person using our name to obtain free hospitality is a fraud.
Proprietors, please inform the police and us.

Cleish — Nivingston House 65% £90

Tel 0577 850216   Fax 0577 850238 **H**

Cleish Kinross Tayside KY13 7LS — Map 3 C5

Formerly a farmhouse, with parts dating back to 1725, stone-built Nivingston House enjoys a tranquil setting in 12 acres of gardens at the foot of the Cleish Hills (yet only two miles from J5 of the M90). Public rooms include a quiet drawing room and a cosy, plush bar whose attractions include 50 malts. Pretty bedrooms with Laura Ashley fabrics and wallpapers are well kept, like the whole hotel, and there are neat bathrooms, a few of which have shower and WC only. Children up to 13 stay free in parents' room. *Rooms 17. Garden, croquet, putting. Closed 1st 2 weeks Jan.* AMERICAN EXPRESS *Access, Visa.*

Colbost — Three Chimneys Restaurant — £60

Tel 047 081 258   **R**

Colbost by Dunvegan Isle of Skye Highland IV55 8ZT   Map 2 A3

New this year at the Three Chimneys, Eddie and Shirley Spear's charming restaurant housed in a former crofter's cottage, is an all-day menu, expanding the already popular main lunchtime session. Morning coffee, afternoon tea and light meals therefore offer more opportunites to sample the delights of Shirley's cooking (and Ann Knight's baking) – see our *Just a Bite Guide*. At whatever time of day you visit, you can be assured of excellent local produce (suppliers are both cherished and credited) prepared and cooked with care and conscientiousness. In the evening, dinner is fixed price, usually four courses for £25 though more elaborate celebratory or seafood menus are also offered. A typical meal could therefore be home-made soup with a selection of freshly baked bread, succulent scallop mousse, a main course of pan-fried breast of wood pigeon with a prune and port sauce and baked red cabbage, then to finish either fine Scottish cheeses or a dessert such as hot marmalade pudding with Drambuie custard. Brownie points for offering not only a serious complete vegetarian four-course set dinner, but even incorporating choices within those courses – other chefs and restaurateurs, take note! The wine list is an excellent complement to the cooking, reasonably priced throughout. No smoking. *Seats 30. Parties 18. L 12.30-2 D 7-9. Closed Sun (open Sun before Bank Holidays), Nov-Mar. Set D from £25. Access, Visa.*

Colbost — Places of Interest

Dunvegan Castle   Tel 047 022 206.
Skye Silver   Tel 047 081 263.
Colbost Folk Museum   Tel 047 022 296.

Contin — Craigdarroch Lodge — 56% — £98

Tel & Fax 0997 421265   **H**

Contin by Strathpeffer Highland IV14 9EH   Map 2 B3

Built as a shooting lodge in the early part of the 19th century, Craigdarroch stands along a tree-lined drive off the A835 at the foot of the mountains. It's a great base for touring, walking and all kinds of outdoor activities – much of its business now revolves around special golfing packages. On site are a bar and lounge, plus a range of leisure pursuits. Bedrooms are modest but provide the basic comforts. *Rooms 13. Garden, indoor swimming pool, sauna, solarium, tennis, snooker. Closed Jan & Feb. No credit cards.*

Craigellachie — Craigellachie Hotel — 68% — £95

Tel 0340 881204   Fax 0340 881253   **HR**

Craigellachie Grampian AB3 9SS   Map 2 C3

A hundred years old and still going strong, this solidly built hotel on the A95 stands in the village where the Spey and the Fiddich rivers meet. Public areas include an airy lounge with lace-draped grand piano, antique sideboard and plenty of armchairs and sofas, plus a small library and snug green bar with a good choice of local malt whiskies. Floral chintzy fabrics decorate the bedrooms, which have smart modern bathrooms and either antique or contemporary traditional-style furniture. *Rooms 30. Garden, tennis, sauna, solarium, keep-fit equipment, games room.* AMERICAN EXPRESS *Access, Diners, Visa.*

Ben Aigen Restaurant — £70

The restaurant puts great reliance on local produce for its Scottish-based menus: cured Spey salmon, savoury haggis dumplings, light mousse of West Coast prawns and Arbroath smokies, roast gigot of Scottish lamb, cranachan, seasonal fruits glazed with a Glayva sabayon. Scottish cheeses are served with oatcakes. Small lunchtime à la carte, set-price Sunday lunch. No smoking. *Seats 40. Parties 10. Private Room 25. L 12.30-2 D 7.30-9.30. Set Sun L £13.50 Set D £25.50*

Craignure   Isle of Mull Hotel   56%   £84

Tel 068 02 351   Fax 068 02 462   **H**

Craignure Isle of Mull Argyll Strathclyde PA65 6BB   **Map 3 A5**

A long, low modern building where all bedrooms look out across the Sound of Mull. Day rooms offer plenty of space to relax, and one of the lounges has access to a patio. Two bars. Children up to the age of 6 stay free in parents' room. The gardens run down to the sea. *Rooms 60. Garden. Closed Nov-Mar.* AMERICAN EXPRESS *Access, Visa.*

Craignure   Places of Interest

Tourist Information   Tel 06802 377.

Crieff   Crieff Hydro   64%   £96*

Tel 0764 655555   Fax 0764 653087   **H**

Crieff Tayside PH7 3LQ   **Map 3 C5**

An enormous Victorian building, now a family hotel par excellence with an impressive range of leisure activities to keep everyone busy and fit – from indoor cinema and table tennis room to outdoor riding school and golf course. Most of the bedrooms are of a decent size, furnished with either lightwood units or more traditional or antique pieces; nine two-storey family chalets are in the woods behind. Table licence only, no bar. Banqueting for up to 250 and conference facilities for up to 300 people. Plans include a new wing of bedrooms, due for completion in the middle of 1995. No dogs (a few kennels are provided, but require prior booking). *Half-board terms only. *Rooms 194. Garden, croquet, indoor swimming pool, whirlpool, spa bath, sauna, steam room, sun beds, boutique, hairdressing and beauty salon, tennis, squash, badminton, 9-hole golf course, putting, bowling green, snooker, riding school, football pitch, cinema, playroom, playground, coffee shop (10am-11.30pm).* AMERICAN EXPRESS *Access, Diners, Visa.*

Crieff   Places of Interest

Tourist Information   Tel 0764 652578.
Visitors Centre   Tel 0764 654014.
Stuart Crystal   Tel 0764 654004.
Glen Turret Distillery   Tel 0764 652424.
Drummond Castle Gardens   Muthill. Tel 0764 681321.

Crinan   Crinan Hotel   69%   £115

Tel 054 683 261   Fax 054 683 292   **HR**

Crinan by Lochgilphead Strathclyde PA31 8SR   **Map 3 B5**

At the northern end of the canal connecting Loch Fyne with the Atlantic stands a tiny fishing village and the Ryans' hotel, which has been constructed in such a way that every window has a view either westwards up the Jura sound or down over the canal's 15th, and final, lock. Major local attractions include the renowned Argyll Gardens and seal colonies (boat trips arranged). Interiors by Mrs Ryan (alias Frances MacDonald the well-known artist) add colour to Italian varnished pine bedrooms of which the pick have private balconies. *Rooms 22. Garden. Closed 1 week Christmas. Access, Visa.*

Westward Restaurant   £65

The hotel's main restaurant, newly decorated in soft, gentle colours, makes use of the finest seafood and prime Aberdeen Angus beef. The four-course dinner menu starts with a choice of about five starters (three fishy), then perhaps trout, sole and prawn mousseline, before the centrepiece dish, a choice typically of River Add salmon with hollandaise or charcoal-grilled sirloin steak. Scottish cheddar or a lemon meringue pie is a favourite way to finish; Mount Kenya coffee served in the lounge. No smoking until after main course. Light lunches are served in the bar at the east end of the hotel. A really enthusiastic wine list covers the full spectrum and is revised all the time. The knowledgeable tasting notes indicate that the writer samples every bottle in the cellar – lucky person! *Seats 50. D only 7-9. Set D £25.50.*

Lock 16 Restaurant ★

£95

On the hotel's top floor, this specialist seafood restaurant depends very much on the local fishing fleet which comes in (late afternoon) to unload at the quayside below. A bad catch and the restaurant might not open (it's closed on Sunday and Monday anyway), so it's always best to check. On a good day the fishermen will land jumbo prawns from Corryvreckan, lobsters from the Sound of Jura, Princess clams from Loch Fyne and mussels from Loch Craignish, so you can reasonly expect dishes such as Crinan seafood stew, moules marinière and wild salmon. How the freshest of fresh seafood is cooked is down to chef/proprietor Nick Ryan, but it's safe to say that he's a traditionalist and doesn't muck about too much with accompaniments, allowing the fish to taste of just that. Don't miss the hot lime soufflé with chocolate sauce, and either the whole Stilton or whole mature Scottish farmhouse cheddar, served with oatcakes. Jacket and tie for gentlemen. *Seats 20. L on request only. D at 8. Closed Sun & Mon, Oct-April. Set D £40.*

Cromarty   Royal Hotel

£50

Tel 0381 600217

I

Marine Terrace Cromarty Highland IV11 8YN

Map 2 C3

A terrace of 18th-century coastguard's cottages on the waterfront has been converted into a hotel of considerable charm, with welcoming hosts in Stewart and Yvonne Morrison. A fire burns brightly in the homely lounge, off which runs a sun lounge with wicker chairs. There are two bars, one with pool and darts, and a function suite with a capacity of 120. Immaculate, individually decorated bedrooms in traditional style boast sea views and cotton sheets. ***Rooms*** *10. Garden.* AMERICAN EXPRESS *Access, Visa.*

Cumbernauld   Travel Inn

£43

Tel 0236 725339   Fax 0236 736380

L

4 South Muirhead Road Cumbernauld Strathclyde G67 1AX

Map 3 C5

Just off A80 in town centre. ***Rooms*** *37.* AMERICAN EXPRESS *Access, Diners, Visa.*

Cumbernauld   Westerwood Hotel   73%

£100

Tel 0236 457171   Fax 0236 738478

HR

St Andrews Drive Westerwood Cumbernauld Strathclyde G68 0EW

Map 3 C5

Set on a hill above the A80, Westerwood is a modern hotel and country club with a golf course (designed by Dave Thomas and Severiano Ballesteros) that boasts a 40ft waterfall at the 15th green and wonderful views over the Campsie Hills. For après-golf choose between the hotel's luxurious lounge and cocktail bar with fabric-covered walls and indoor garden or the less formal tartan-carpeted country club. Artificial trees are a novel form of decor in good standard bedrooms. Beds are turned down at night and staff are friendly and helpful. Families are well catered for and can eat informally by the lovely indoor pool or in the clubhouse. Children under 3 may share parents' room free (£30 for over-3s). Banqueting/conference facilities for 180/200. ***Rooms*** *49. Garden, golf (18), bowling green, pétanque, tennis, indoor swimming pool, snooker, gym, sauna, spa bath, steam room, solarium, hairdressing, coffee shop (10am-6pm), golf shop, helipad.* AMERICAN EXPRESS *Access, Diners, Visa.*

Old Masters Restaurant

£70

An unusual circular dining room with dark-green watered-silk-effect walls and tented ceiling from which hangs a large brass chandelier. Tom Robertson's sophisticated menus offer River Tay salmon carved

on a trolley, pan-fried quail breasts on a confit of green lentils and smoked
bacon with a port wine sauce, smoked haddock chowder, lasagne
of Scottish salmon and spinach with creamed fennel, medallion of beef fillet
with a horseradish crust and a burgundy truffle essence, and tempting
desserts. Reduced menu at Sunday lunchtime when the central attraction
is prime roast Scottish beef. Service is as smooth and confident as the
cooking. *Seats* 70. *Parties* 8. *Private Room* 24. *L Sun only 12-2.45
D 6.45-9.45. Open Fri & Sat only Jan & Feb. Closed Mon & Tue all year. Set
Sun L £12.95 Set D £15/£21.50.*

Cupar	**Ostlers Close**	**£60**
Tel 0334 655574		**R**
25 Bonnygate Cupar Fife KY15 4BU		Map 3 C5

Wild mushrooms garnered from nearby forests, herbs and salad ingredients
from his own garden and other good local produce give Jimmy Graham's
careful cooking a head start at an unpretentious restaurant hidden down
an alleyway off Bonnygate. The short, interesting menus change almost
daily, but typically might offer a choice of soups, pan-fried chicken livers
on a potato and herb galette, fillets of monkfish on a bed of seakale with
a pesto sauce, and a trio of organic pork dishes at lunch; dinner could see
fillets of mixed seafood in a light cheese herb batter on a red pepper sauce,
seafood broth, terrine of goat's cheese and potato, roast saddle of roe
venison with wood pigeon breast in a shallot and red wine sauce and
honey, Drambuie and oatmeal ice cream, hot sticky toffee pudding with
butterscotch sauce or Scottish cheeses to finish. Thoughtful wine list with
a fine selection under £20. No children under 6 in the evening, but half
portions and plainer food offered at lunch. *Seats 26. L 12.15-2 D 7-9.30.
Closed Sun & Mon, first 2 weeks Jun. Set £12/£15 D £19/£25.*
AMERICAN EXPRESS *Access, Visa.*

Cupar   Places of Interest

Tourist Information Tel 0334 52874.
Douglas Bader Gardens Tel 0334 53722 ext 437.
Scottish Deer Centre Bow-of-Fife Tel 033 781 391.

Dalguise, Kinnaird House. See entry under Dunkeld.

Dirleton	**Open Arms Hotel**	**67%**	**£115**
Tel 0620 85241 Fax 0620 85570			**H**
Dirleton nr North Berwick Lothian EH39 5EG			Map 3 D5

There's a cosy and friendly atmosphere at this small, family-run hotel, well
situated for holiday makers and well equipped for conferences, banquets,
receptions (marquee on the lawn) and outside catering. Children up to
5 stay free in parents' room. *Rooms* 7. *Garden. Access, Visa.*

Drumnadrochit	**Polmaily House**	**63%**	**£86**
Tel 0456 450343			**HR**
Drumnadrochit Highland IV3 6XT			Map 2 B3

New owners John and Sonia Whittington-Davis have made several
improvements to this converted private house set in gardens and woodlands
on the A831 west of Drumnadrochit. Central heating has been installed,
and family rooms and a king-size suite created; there's also a children's play
area. Public rooms include a library, a drawing room and a little bar.
No dogs. *Rooms 10. Garden, croquet, tennis, outdoor swimming pool.
Access, Visa.*

Urquhart Restaurant   £45

Light lunches are served by the pool, in the garden or in the restaurant.
Dinner features a lot of local produce, as in baked trout with almond
butter, salmon in pastry with vermouth and dill sauce, and braised pheasant

with whisky and juniper. Also lamb, sirloin steak and venison served plain charcoal-grilled or sauced. Smoking is allowed in the drawing room but not in the restaurant. *Seats 40. Parties 12. L 12-2.30 D 7.30-9.30. Set D £16.*

Drybridge	Old Monastery Restaurant	£55
Tel 0542 832660		**R**
Drybridge Buckie Grampian AB56 2JB		Map 2 C3

On a hill three miles inland from Buckie, the former monastery enjoys delightful views over the Moray Firth (turn off the A98 at Buckie junction on to the Drybridge road. Follow the road for 2½ miles – do *not* turn right into Drybridge village). Maureen Gray offers a warm welcome front of house, while Douglas in the kitchen uses the best of the local larder with fish from the Spey, seasonal game and Aberdeen Angus beef. Popular choices include scampi and scallops Thermidor, steaks and medallions of Highland venison with a raspberry and redcurrant sauce. Venison might also appear smoked with a gooseberry and mint jelly. There are plenty of half bottles on a well-priced wine list. *Seats 45. L 12-1.30 D 7-9.30 (Sat to 10). Closed Sun & Mon, 3 weeks Jan, 2 weeks Nov.* AMERICAN EXPRESS *Access, Visa.*

Drybridge	Places of Interest

Banff Boyndie Bay beach   Inverboyndie.
Buckle Maritime Museum   Tel 0542 32121.

Dryburgh	Dryburgh Abbey	65%	£100
Tel 0835 22261 Fax 0835 23945			**H**
St Boswells Dryburgh Borders TD6 0RQ			Map 4 C1

On the A68 at St Boswells take the B6404, drive through the village and follow the signs to Scott's View and Earlston (B6356). The red sandstone hotel, especially popular with the shooting and fishing fraternity, stands next to the historic ruins of Dryburgh Abbey and alongside the River Tweed. It has recently been restored and refurbished to a high standard, with both the attractive public areas (two lounges – one on the first floor next to the restaurant – and a bar) and bedrooms (named after fishing flies) offering comfort and space. From the Garden View rooms to the four-poster room and suites which enjoy views across the wooded grounds to the abbey or the river, all provide hairdryer, trouser press, and teletext remote-control TV, as well as decent bathrooms. Minor niggles on a recent visit were noisy plumbing and poor lighting. Up to 150 can be accommodated in the function suite, and there's also a private dining room/boardroom. *Rooms 26. Garden, indoor swimming pool, putting, fishing, helipad. Access, Visa.*

Dryburgh	Places of Interest

Jedburgh Tourist Information   Tel 0835 63435 *8 miles.*
Jedburgh Abbey   Tel 0835 63925.
Mary Queen of Scots House   Tel 0835 63331.

Drymen	Buchanan Highland Hotel	62%	£110
Tel 0360 60588 Fax 0360 60943			**H**
Main Street Drymen by Loch Lomond Central G63 0BQ			Map 3 B5

This former coaching inn now has a thouroughly modern air – as in the relaxing conservatory – whilst not forgetting its origins, as in the arched and beamed lounge bar. The bedrooms are well equipped and maintained and there's an excellent leisure centre (the Buchanan Club) as well as a versatile range of conference and banqueting suites (up to 150 delegates and 120 for a function). Children up to 12 stay free in parents' room. Six rooms are reserved for non-smokers. Baby-sitting and baby-listening are available. ***Rooms*** *51. Garden, indoor swimming pool, gym, squash, sauna, spa bath, beauty salon, tennis, golf (9), bowling green, coffee shop (10am-9pm).* AMERICAN EXPRESS® *Access, Diners, Visa.*

Drymen   Place of Interest

Ben Lomond   Tel 041 552 8391 *11 miles.*

Dulnain Bridge   Auchendean Lodge   62%   £54

Tel 0479 851 347   **HR**

Dulnain Bridge Grantown-on-Spey Highland PH26 3LU   Map 2 C3

Built as an Edwardian hunting and fishing lodge, this owner-run country hotel is set in spectacular scenery a mile south of Dulnain Bridge on the A95. A range of activities – canoeing on the Spey, skiing in the Cairngorms, shooting, fishing and hiking – is available locally. There's period furniture in two open-fired lounges and individually-styled bedrooms (five en-suite) have electric blankets, radio/alarms and TVs, but no phones. 200 acres of woods and 1½ acres of gardens surround the hotel. ***Rooms*** *8. Garden, pitch & putt. Closed 4 weeks Nov or Jan.* AMERICAN EXPRESS® *Access, Diners, Visa.*

Restaurant   £55

Dinner is a daily-changing, four-course affair making good use of local game, fish, garden vegetables and wild mushrooms – a passion of chef Eric Hart. Those mushrooms could appear on toast, in mushroom and sherry soup or in a cream sauce with baked haddock. Other choices could include sweet-cured herring or gravad lax, salmon with sorrel hollandaise, calvados-sauced pheasant and wild venison casserole. To finish, perhaps sticky date pudding, orange pancake with malt whisky butter or banana ice cream with burnt honey sauce. Good Scottish cheeses. The menu states that "credit card commission is charged extra". Snacks or picnics provided if prior notice given. No smoking. ***Seats*** *20. D only 7.30-9. Set D £23.50.*

Our inspectors *never* book in the name of Egon Ronay's Guides. They disclose their identity only if they are considering an establishment for inclusion in the next edition of the Guide.

Dulnain Bridge   Muckrach Lodge   59%   £78

Tel 0479 851257   Fax 0479 851325   **H**

Dulnain Bridge Grantown-on-Spey Highland PH26 3LY   Map 2 C3

Captain and Mrs Watson's Victorian hunting lodge sits in ten acres of its own grounds with fine views of the Dulnain valley all around. It's a fine base for touring the beautiful Speyside country, and a most pleasant place for just sitting back and relaxing. The feel is friendly and informal in both lounge and bar, and there are soothing views from most of the bedrooms, which include a four-poster room. Carpeted bathrooms offer good towelling and all sorts of bits and bobs from cotton wool balls to a nail brush. The former steading (stables) now houses two full suites, one especially adapted for wheelchair-bound guests. No dogs. Children under five years stay free in parents' room. ***Rooms*** *12. Garden, fishing, helipad. Closed 3 weeks Nov.* AMERICAN EXPRESS® *Access, Diners, Visa.*

Dumbarton — Forte Travelodge — £45

L

Tel 0389 65202

Milton Dumbarton Strathclyde G82 2TY

Map 3 B5

On the A82 westbound, 8 miles west of Glasgow, 1 mile east of Dumbarton centre. *Rooms 32.* AMERICAN EXPRESS® *Access, Diners, Visa.*

Dunblane — Cromlix House — 82% — £160

HR

Tel 0786 822125   Fax 0786 825450

Kinbuck by Dunblane Central FK15 9JT

Map 3 C5

The 3000-acre estate is in the hands of the family who have been here for 500 years and their collection of fine furniture, paintings and porcelain continues to grace this sturdy Victorian mansion set in glorious countryside to the north of Dunblane. The collection of fishing rods, croquet mallets and wellies in the entrance hall indicates the atmosphere as that of a treasured family home. Day rooms such as the leather-furnished library and morning room with its floral-patterned linen covers on armchairs and settees, combine elegance with comfort. Spacious, antique-furnished bedrooms (eight are full suites) often have period light fittings and other features that give something of an Edwardian feel. Bathrooms, with fittings from various periods, are all large and boast quality toiletries and towelling. *Rooms 14. Garden, tennis, shooting, fishing.*
Closed mid Jan–mid Feb. AMERICAN EXPRESS® *Access, Diners, Visa.* 🐂 MARTELL COGNAC

Restaurant — £90

A room of great elegance with fluted pilasters and ornate gilt light fittings matched by fine bone china and rat's-tail silver cutlery with pistol-grip knives. Fixed-price dinners, with just a couple of choices at each stage, make use of the best local produce, carefully prepared and eye-catchingly presented. Typical items include filo pastry tartlet with sautéed scallops and halibut with a caviar sauce, carrot and turnip soup, baked Tay salmon with horseradish and herb crust on a shellfish bisque with green grapes, and collops of pork topped with apples and goat's cheese over a tarragon and cabbage sauce. For dessert, perhaps pear and Grand Marnier tarte or individual sticky toffee pudding with treacle sauce and double cream. No smoking. *Seats 62. Private Room 40. L 12.30-1.15 D 7-8.30. Set L £17/£24 Set D £35.*

Dunblane — Stakis Dunblane — 61% — £111

H

Tel 0786 822551   Fax 0786 825403

Perth Road Dunblane Central FK15 0HG

Map 3 C5

Handsome Victorian building set high above the main road to Perth in 44 acres of grounds. The main attraction is the leisure facility, and bedrooms range from singles, twins and doubles to family rooms, suites and 33 Club rooms with whirlpool baths. Conferences are also big business, with room for up to 500 theatre-style. *Rooms 214. Garden, indoor swimming pool, keep-fit equipment, sauna, solarium, beauty salon, tennis, putting, playroom.* AMERICAN EXPRESS® *Access, Diners, Visa.*

> Set menu prices may not always include service or wine.

Dunblane — Places of Interest

Tourist Information Tel 0786 824428.
Dunblane Cathedral Tel 0786 824254.
Leighton Library Tel 0786 822850.
Doune Motor Museum Carse of Cambus. Tel 0786 841203.

Dundee   **Angus Thistle**   **69%**   £107

Tel 0382 26874   Fax 0382 322564   **H**

Marketgait Dundee Tayside DD1 1QU   Map 3 C5

A modern, six-storey hotel in the heart of the city offering a good standard of bedroom accommodation (including five suites) and conference facilities for up to 500 delegates; some rooms have views across the Tay Estuary. 24hr room service. ***Rooms** 58.* AMERICAN EXPRESS *Access, Diners, Visa.*

Dundee   **Invercarse Hotel**   **59%**   £80

Tel 0382 69231   Fax 0382 644112   **H**

371 Perth Road Dundee Tayside DD2 1PG   Map 3 C5

The privately-owned Invercarse is an extended Victorian house set on a hill (some three miles west of the city centre) affording views across the Tay to the Fife hills beyond. Bedrooms vary in size; children up to 12 can share parents' room free. There's a lounge bar with views, and a leather-furnished cocktail bar. Conference/banqueting for 200/280. ***Rooms** 38. Garden.* AMERICAN EXPRESS *Access, Diners, Visa.*

Dundee   **Travel Inn**   **NEW**   £43

Tel 0582 414341   **L**

Discovery Quay Riverside Drive Dundee Tayside   Map 3 C5

Situated on the waterfront opposite the mainline railway station, 2 minutes' walk from the city centre. ***Rooms** 40.* AMERICAN EXPRESS *Access, Diners, Visa.*

> Note that all telephone numbers with area codes starting with 0 will start 01 from 16 April 1995.

Dundee   **Travel Inn (Dundee West)**   £43

Tel 0382 561115   **L**

Kingsway West Invergowrie Dundee Tayside DD2 5JU   Map 3 C5

Rooms 40. AMERICAN EXPRESS *Access, Diners, Visa.*

Dundee   **Places of Interest**

Tourist Information   Tel 0382 27723.
St Paul's Cathedral   Tel 0382 24486.
Camperdown Country Wildlife Park   Tel 0382 623555.
University Botanic Garden   Tel 0382 66939.
Olympia Leisure Centre   Tel 0382 203888.
Shaw's Dundee Sweet Factory   Tel 0382 610369.
Tay Road Bridge Observation Platforms.
   Theatres and Concert Halls
Dundee Repertory Theatre   Tel 0382 23530.
Whitehall Theatre   Tel 0382 22684.
Steps Film Theatre   Tel 0382 23141/24938.
   Museums and Art Galleries
Barrack Street Museum   Tel 0382 23141.
Broughty Castle Museum   Tel 0382 23141.
McManus Galleries   Tel 0382 23141.
Mills Observatory   Tel 0382 67138.
Seagate Gallery and Printmakers Workshop   Tel 0382 26331.
H.M. Frigate Unicorn   Tel 0382 200900.
R.R.S. Discovery   Tel 0382 201245.

Dunfermline   King Malcolm Thistle   65%   £93

Tel 0383 722611   Fax 0383 730865   **H**

Queensferry Road Dunfermline Fife KY11 5DS   Map 3 C5

Fifteen miles from the centre of Edinburgh and a short drive from Junction 2 of the M90. Modern bedrooms have all the expected amenities plus 24hr room service. The Malcolm Suite can accommodate up to 150 delegates theatre-style. Children up to 14 stay free in parents' room. *Rooms 48. Garden.* AMERICAN EXPRESS *Access, Diners, Visa.*

Dunfermline   Places of Interest

Tourist Information   Tel 0383 720999.
Knockhill Motor Racing Circuit   Tel 0383 723337.

Dunkeld   Kinnaird   76%   £170

Tel 0796 482440   Fax 0796 482289   **H R**

Kinnaird Estate by Dunkeld Tayside PH8 0LB   Map 3 C5

On the B898 just north of Dunkeld, about four miles off the A9, the 18th-century Kinnaird House, surrounded by its 9,000-acre estate, has a splendid position overlooking the river Tay. In the caring hands of owner Constance Ward, the house flourishes and continues to attract a regular clientele who like to enjoy style and comfort. Day rooms, furnished almost entirely with antiques, include the red cedar-panelled drawing room, where fresh flowers and family mementos and pictures create a homely feel, and a clubby snooker room. No children under 12. Dogs in (heated) kennels only. *Rooms 9. Garden, croquet, tennis, game fishing, snooker. Closed Feb.* AMERICAN EXPRESS *Access, Visa.* MARTELL

Restaurant   £90

John Webber's modern British menus enjoy a sophisticated setting in Kinnaird's elegant dining room. In addition to the set lunches (priced for two and three courses), dinner really displays his art at the highest level. There are about six choices at each course offering a good range, such as open ravioli of sautéed pigeon breast with red wine and lentils, or a salad gateau of Arbroath smokies with potato and green beans on a light dill dressing as starters. Main courses could include a grilled sausage of guinea fowl set on celeriac purée and Madeira sauce, or sautéed fillet of turbot set on crisp potato with red wine and thyme butter. Try a chocolate pithiviers set on a rum and coffee sauce to finish. There are plenty of half bottles on an excellent wine list, which includes inexpensive French country wines and a page of house suggestions. No smoking. Gentlemen should wear jackets and ties. *Seats 35. Parties 8. Private Room 24. L 12.30-1.45 D 7-9.30. Set L £19.50/£24 Set D £38.*

Dunoon   Chatters   £50

Tel 0369 6402   **R**

58 John Street Dunoon Strathclyde TA23 8BJ   Map 3 B5

Rosemary MacInnes is now comfortably established at Chatters, and has made a few changes. First the kitchen was extended, and now an extension is being built (as we go to press), to accommodate a lounge/conservatory. This is where you'll be able to relax with drinks before and/or after dinner. The menu balance has changed too, with less emphasis on morning and afternoon coffees and teas, more on à la carte lunches and dinners. Chef David Craig, also on board since the start, makes good use of local seafood and game, and in addition to delicious desserts there's a fine array of cheeses. *Seats 30. L 12-2.30 D 6-9.30. Closed Sun, January. Access, Visa.*

Duror   Stewart Hotel   59%   £80

Tel 063 174 268   Fax 063 174 328   **H**

Glen Duror Appin Argyll Highland PA38 4BW   Map 3 B4

The hospitable Lacy family (here since 1986) and their young staff offer a friendly welcome at their Victorian house, which stands in five acres of terraced gardens with beautiful views of Loch Linnhe. The oldest part was built 120 years ago in the style of a hunting lodge. An open fire warms the simple yet pleasant bar and upstairs there's a quiet and spacious lounge. Bedrooms are in a new wing; they are simple and neat, with views (most), modest modern furniture and tiny bathrooms. Children up to 15 stay free in parents' room. The hotel is signposted off the A828 six miles south of Ballachulish on the way to Oban. *Rooms 19. Garden. Closed mid Oct-Easter.* AMERICAN EXPRESS *Access, Diners, Visa.*

East Kilbride   Stuart Hotel   62%   £80

Tel 03552 21161   Fax 03552 64410   **H**

Cornwall Way East Kilbride Strathclyde G74 1JR   Map 3 C6

A modern hotel whose day rooms include two bars and a function suite with an unusual brass ceiling. Biggest and best bedrooms are Executives. Informal eating in Archies lounge bar and Jellowickis bar and grill. Conference facilities for up to 200, banqueting for 150. 24hr room service. *Rooms 39.* AMERICAN EXPRESS *Access, Diners, Visa.*

East Kilbride   Travel Inn   £43

Tel 03552 22809   Fax 03552 30517   **L**

Brunel Way The Murray East Kilbride Strathclyde G75 0JY   Map 3 C6

Take A725 from Junction 5 of M74, following signs for East Kilbride, then A726 towards Paisley; turn left at roundabout, then left into Brunel Way. *Rooms 40.* AMERICAN EXPRESS *Access, Diners, Visa.*

East Kilbride   Westpoint Hotel   74%   £115

Tel 03552 36300   Fax 03552 33552   **H**

Stewartfield Way East Kilbride Strathclyde G74 5LA   Map 3 C6

Part of the Craigendarroch Group – see *Craigendarroch* and *Cameron House* hotels – this modern hotel is unusual in both design and location. Situated on a new industrial estate, it lies close enough to Glasgow to attract the business community, though it appears the hotel's major appeal is in its superb leisure facilities, accessible by a covered walkway. There are also banqueting and conference rooms for up to 120/140. There are nice touches in the public areas such as large floral displays and daily newspapers laid out, and the bedrooms lack nothing in style or quality. Executive bedrooms especially are models of good taste, with spacious sitting areas and splendid bathrooms (separate walk-in power shower), with marble-effect tiling, robes and fine Scottish toiletries. Among the thoughtful extras in the bedrooms are a sherry decanter, sweets, pot pourri, fruit and flowers, and a full turn-down service is carried out. The TV cabinet houses a mini-bar (with fresh milk), sliding hospitality tray and swivelling remote-controlled hi-tech set that provides teletext and satellite. Standard breakfast includes a pleasant buffet. 24hr room service and all-day lounge menu. No dogs. *Rooms 74. Indoor swimming pool, gym, squash, sauna, steam room, spa bath, solarium, beauty salon, snooker.* AMERICAN EXPRESS *Access, Diners, Visa.*

East Kilbride   Places of Interest

The Ice Bowl Ice Rink   Tel 03552 44065.

Edinburgh   Alp-Horn   £45

Tel 031-225 4787   **R**

167 Rose Street Edinburgh Lothian EH2 4LS   **Map 3 C6**

Just off Charlotte Square and two minutes from Princes Street, a Swiss
restaurant with a chalet atmosphere (Rose Street is pedestrianised – best
to park in Charlotte Square or George Street). Cheese and beef fondues (for
two or more) are well-executed specialities, and air-dried Swiss beef and
ham (*assiette de Grisons*), veal sausage (*kalbsbratwurst*), venison with apple
and cranberry sauce and spätzli, plus *eminé de veau zurichoise* with rösti
potatoes are also faithful to their origins. *Supreme de volaille Sophia Loren*
is a breadcrumbed breast of chicken filled with ham and cheese, garnished
with asparagus, served with rösti. *Emmentaler Schafsvoressen* is an old Swiss
peasant dish – a saffron-flavoured lamb stew served with a beetroot side
salad. Apfel strudel is made on the premises. Lunchtimes see an excellent
value 'square deal lunch' of two courses and a shortened à la carte. Try the
Swiss wines, even though they may seem expensive alongside the rest
of the wine list. Separate room for non-smokers. *Seats 66. Parties 45.
Private Room 28. L 12-2 D 6.30-10. Closed Sun, 25 & 26 Dec, 1st week Jan.
Set L £5.50.* AMERICAN EXPRESS *Access, Diners, Visa.*

Edinburgh   Atrium   ↑   £60

Tel 031-228 8882   **R**

Cambridge Street Edinburgh Lothian EH1 2ED   **Map 3 C6**

Within the atrium of Saltire Court – a smart new office building next
to the Usher Hall in Edinburgh's Theatre district – the restaurant's post-
modern decor is quite stunning with railway sleeper tables, raw linen-
draped chairs and glass torches based on an ancient glass drinking horn, set
in wrought-iron sconces imparting an almost medieval atmosphere. Some
of the dishes on Andrew Radford's twice-daily-changing menu (four or five
choices at each stage) are almost equally stunning; for example a brilliant
dish of lemon sole topped with a tomato gratin in a langoustine and
coriander broth sampled at a recent meal. Other dishes that demonstrate
Andrew's modern style might include duck and salami salad with truffle
oil; sausage (spicy Italian) and mash with Parma ham and lentil jus; roast
cod, salsa gratin and spinach; and maize-fed chicken, with polenta,
mousserons and parsley. Puds tend to be variants of his old favourites like
sticky toffee pudding, lemon soufflé tart and apple, pear and date crumble.
Service is a happy blend of informality and professionalism. There is also
a short snack menu at lunchtime and for pre-theatre diners between 6-7pm.
There's not much order on the wine list, though it has very well-chosen
wines which are keenly priced (3 *marque* champagnes under £30).
*Seats 60. L 12-3 D 6-10.30. Closed L Sat, all Sun, 1 week Christmas. Access,
Diners, Visa.*

Edinburgh   L'Auberge   £75

Tel 031-556 5888   Fax 031-556 2588   **R**

56 St Mary Street Edinburgh Lothian EH1 1SX   **Map 3 C6**

Daniel Wencker's long-established and comfortable French restaurant is in
Edinburgh's 'old town', off the Royal Mile near John Knox House.
Although chef Fabrice Bresulier's menu features French classics, much
emphasis is put on the good-value tables d'hote at lunchtime and in the
evening (4-course). A straightforward lunch might comprise salmon terrine
with yoghurt and herb cream, then lamb cutlets with rosemary and honey,
finishing with a gratin of strawberries with Chartreuse. In the evening the
menu extends to encompass dishes like a tulip of thinly-sliced, gravlax-style
salmon with a little Provençal touch ("au parfum de fenouil"), aiguillettes
of home-smoked duck breast with a warm crottin (goat's cheese) and
hazelnut salad, and supreme of Scotch salmon en croute served with a beer-
flavoured butter cream sauce. Crème brulée, tarte au citron, crepes suzettes,
armagnac-flavoured chocolate mousse among the desserts. Sunday lunch

sees a fixed-price, three-course set menu. The New World receives only a cursory representation on the otherwise good French wine list that includes an interesting selection of half bottles. *Seats 55. Parties 20. L 12.15-2 D 6.30-9.30. Closed 26 Dec, 1 & 2 Jan. Set L £8.50/£10 & £13.50 (Sun £13.50) Set D £16.85/£19.85.* AMERICAN EXPRESS *Access, Diners, Visa*

Edinburgh   The Balmoral   83%   £171

Tel 031-556 2414   Fax 031-557 3747

HR

Princes Street Edinburgh Lothian EH2 2EQ

Map 3 C6

At the top of Forte's tree in Scotland, the Balmoral wears its total refurbishment from the early '90s very comfortably indeed. Opulence, comfort, courtesy, elegance are the watchwords here – definitely a place in which to be cosseted, and nothing is too much trouble for the very professional staff. Bedrooms (with marble bathrooms) and suites are excellently equipped and maintained, modern conveniences blending discreetly with traditional furnishings. There is good provision for non-smoking, lady executive and disabled guests. We quote a standard price: there are superior, deluxe and suites above that. Public areas are of a similarly high standard, encompassing the Palm Court Lounge, coffee shop, bars, brasserie and the main restaurant, so that any style of refreshment can be provided. Room service is available around the clock. There are ten function suites, the largest taking 400, the total facility being for 800. *Rooms 189. Indoor swimming pool, gym, sauna, steam room, sunbeds, beauty & hair salon, cashmere & crystal shop, coffee shop (9-5).* AMERICAN EXPRESS *Access, Diners, Visa.*

The Grill, No 1 Princes Street   ↑   £110

Very much the grand hotel dining room, where discretion and attention to detail (both in decor and in food presentation) are impeccable. On the à la carte menu the prices are written out as words not figures (slightly prolonging the shock), although the better value set lunch menus are expressed in a more straightforward manner. Many dishes are indicated with a thistle device as being a "Taste of Scotland" Try perhaps terrine of foie gras, chicken and leeks, layered with spinach and surrounded by lamb's lettuce, or a chartreuse of asparagus with a frisée salad, crispy smoked duck and a walnut dressing, then for main courses roast saddle of rabbit with a ragout of broad beans and a rabbit confit, in a duo of champagne cream and Leith claret sauces, or courgette flowers filled with a crab mousse served on a cushion of fresh samphire, finished in a carrot and Chateau Challon sauce. An extensive range of excellent quality fish and meat can be simply grilled, and with eight hours' notice, two people can share pressed Rouennais duck, its preparation finished at table. The separate vegetarian menu is of similar style, and the lunch menus read more simply. The wine list is concise for an establishment of this calibre, travels the world and reaches to the upper price bracket. *Seats 45. Parties 8. L 12-2.15 D 7-10.30. Closed L Sat & Sun. Set L £18.50/£21.50 Set D £35.*

Bridges Brasserie   £35

A brasserie in the Continental style, with an all-day menu of salads, sandwiches, appetisers (stuffed mushrooms, quiche, paté) and main courses (fish and chips, grilled rib-eye steak). Also a wide selection of cakes and pastries, coffees and teas. *Seats 80. Meals 7am-11pm.*

Edinburgh   Barnton Thistle   63%   £107

Tel 031-339 1144   Fax 031-339 5521

H

Queensferry Road Edinburgh Lothian EH4 6AS

Map 3 C6

On the A90, handy for airport and city centre, providing modern comfort for both leisure and business visitors. Conference/banqueting facilities for 130/100. *Rooms 50.* AMERICAN EXPRESS *Access, Diners, Visa.*

Edinburgh   Braid Hills Hotel   61%   £89

Tel 031-447 8888   Fax 031-452 8477   **H**

134 Braid Road Edinburgh Lothian EH10 6JD   Map 3 C6

A lofty, baronial hotel whose upper-floor bedrooms afford sweeping views
over Edinburgh. A strong group and function clientele enjoys neatly kept,
well-equipped rooms serviced by obliging staff. *Rooms 68. Garden.*
AMERICAN EXPRESS *Access, Diners, Visa.*

Edinburgh   Caledonian Hotel   79%   £240

Tel 031-225 2433   Fax 031-225 6632   **HR**

Princes Street Edinburgh Lothian EH1 2AB   Map 3 C6

Built at the turn of the century by the Caledonian Railway Company, the
'Caley' is virtually a national monument. In the hands of Queens Moat
Houses it has maintained traditional standards of hospitality and service
while moving with the times in terms of comfort and amenities. The
carpeted foyer leads to a grand, gracefully proportioned and elegant lounge,
furnished with plush shot-silk sofas. This is a popular meeting place for
afternoon tea, and light snacks are served throughout the day. Carriages
restaurant and bar retains the redbrick former station entrance as an inside
wall. Bedrooms are individually styled, featuring well-chosen furniture and
luxurious drapes; 5th-floor rooms are smaller than some of the others; 41
rooms are reserved for non-smokers. De luxe rooms and those with a view
of the Castle attract a supplement; there are also 22 suites. Towelling robes
are provided in all the bathrooms, which include a TV/radio speaker;
elegant antique-style fittings in Executive rooms. Plus factors are the
number of telephone extensions in the rooms, 24hr lounge service and
a turn-down service. Families are particularly well catered for; children
up to 16 stay free in parents' room. No dogs. Conference facilities for up to
400; banqueting for 200+. Free parking for 40 cars. *Rooms 239.*
AMERICAN EXPRESS *Access, Diners, Visa.*

La Pompadour   £100

Opened in 1925 and named after Louis XV's mistress, the Pompadour
is elegant and formal; ornate plasterwork frames large wall paintings
of delicate flowers, a pianist plays soothing music and excellent staff
provide impeccable service. Chef Tony Binks presents a menu of traditional
Scottish dishes at lunchtime, while in the evening there's an à la carte
selection with a French slant: oysters with creamed leeks and Brie glazed
with a champagne sabayon, fillets of Dover sole gratinated with a liaison
of Chablis and Dijon mustard, maize-fed poussin stuffed with Roquefort
cheese, apple and Chateau de Born prunes. Chef Binks also offers a multi-
course tasting menu with such dishes as creamed cauliflower and broad
bean soup with Gruyère and almond dumplings; River Tay salmon stuffed
with oyster mushrooms bound in natural yoghurt, with a panaché of fennel
and corn with fine egg noodles; and pot-roast guinea fowl with root
vegetables, spiced savoy cabbage and black-eye beans. Desserts from the
trolley, Scottish and French farmhouse cheeses. A decent though quite pricy
wine list, but it's a pity that the New World wines are not deemed worthy
enough of an introduction, as are the European countries. *Seats 70.*
L 12.30-2 D 7.30-10.30. Closed L Sat, all Sun. Set L £27 Set D £35

Carriages Restaurant   £60

Carriages is open for breakfast (winner of our Breakfast of the Year award
1995), lunch and dinner seven days a week, serving a range of familiar,
fairly straightforward dishes on à la carte and table d'hote menus. Chicken
liver paté, avocado and prawn salad, seafood pasta and lamb hot pot
accompany the day's roast at lunchtime, along with some Scottish
favourites like haggis or Musselburgh pie. In the evening, steaks are a very
popular choice (plain grilled, with bordelaise, pepper or chasseur sauce, or
in classic entrées such as steak Diane and tournedos Rossini. *Seats 150.*
L 12-2.30 D 6.30-10. Set L £14.50/£17.25 (Sun £16.25) Set D £24.50.

Edinburgh   **Capital Moat House**   66%   £111

Tel 031-334 3391   Fax 031 334 9712   **H**
Capital Moat House Clermiston Road Edinburgh Lothian EH12 6UG   Map 3 C6

Located in north east Corstorphine, the hotel is quite a way from the City centre. Taken over by Queens Moat House in 1991, it has been going through major refurbishment and a new wing of bedrooms was completed in early 1994. The Terrace restaurant, an attractive conservatory-style dining room, is the hotel's most striking feature, offering exceptional views of the surroundings. Refurbished Executive bedrooms are unusually large, with an attractive, discreet pink decor and well-designed bathrooms. Standard ones tend to be smaller and more ordinary. The hotel has a well-equipped leisure centre. Children up to 14 can stay free in their parents' room. *Rooms 110. Indoor swimming pool, gym, sauna, solarium, spa bath, beauty salon.* AMERICAN EXPRESS *Access, Diners, Visa.*

Edinburgh   **Carlton Highland**   68%   £154

Tel 031-556 7277   Fax 031-556 2691   **H**
North Bridge Edinburgh Lothian EH1 1SD   Map 3 C6

Besides well-equipped bedrooms and comfortable day rooms the Carlton Highland (located between Princes Street and the Royal Mile) has a fine leisure club, conference facilities for up to 350 and a night club with dancing and live entertainment several nights a week. One room is equipped for disabled guests. Children up to 15 stay free in their parents' room. Scottish Highland Hotels. *Rooms 197. Indoor swimming pool, gym, sauna, spa bath, steam room, solarium, squash, snooker, hair & beauty salon, coffee shop (10am-6pm).* AMERICAN EXPRESS *Access, Diners, Visa.*

Edinburgh   **Channings**   64%   £125

Tel 031-315 2226   Fax 031-332 9631   **H**
South Learmonth Gardens Edinburgh Lothian EH4 1EZ   Map 3 C6

A few minutes' walk from the city centre is a series of fine, adjoining Edwardian town houses run as a comfortable, privately-owned hotel with a country house feel. Traditional features – oak panelling, high moulded ceilings, ornate fireplaces, antique furniture and prints – remain in the peaceful lounges, while the bedrooms (some overlooking old Edinburgh) are individually furnished in a more contemporary manner. Staff are friendly and there's a relaxed ambience throughout. Children up to 15 years can stay free in their parents' rooms. *Rooms 48. Terrace. Closed 24-28 Dec.* AMERICAN EXPRESS *Access, Diners, Visa.*

Edinburgh   **Denzlers 121**   £50

Tel 031-554 3268   **R**
121 Constitution Street Leith Edinburgh Lothian EH6 7AE   Map 3 C6

Sister restaurant to the *Alp-Horn* and with a similarly Swiss menu but without the chalet-style decor. Externally forbidding former bank premises down amongst the bonded warehouses of Leith (5 minute taxi ride from the centre of Edinburgh); inside is bright and welcoming, while outside the parking is easy in the evening. Solidly traditional Swiss favourites like veal zurichoise, air-dried beef and ham (*bunderplatti*) and cheese fondues (minimum 2 persons) share the menu with the likes of smoked salmon served on toast with prawns in cream horseradish sauce and saddle of hare garnished with croutons, bacon and mushrooms, served with spätzli. Puds include *apfel strudel* and *coupe Nesselrode* (fresh chestnut purée piped over vanilla ice cream and meringue topped with cream). The set lunch offers very good value (*oeuf en cocotte*, pigeon pie) and includes a drink. Short, diverse wine list includes three Swiss wines. *Seats 65. Parties 15. L 12-2 D 6.30-10. Closed L Sat, all Sun, Mon, 1st week Jan. Set L £7.50* AMERICAN EXPRESS *Access, Diners, Visa.*

Edinburgh   Forte Posthouse   62%   £68

Tel 031-334 0390   Fax 031-334 9237   **H**

Corstorphine Road Edinburgh Lothian EH12 6UA   Map 3 C6

On the A8 halfway between airport and city centre, with both
Murrayfield (for the rugby) and the zoo nearby. Conference facilities for
up to 120 delegates. *Rooms 200.* AMERICAN EXPRESS *Access, Diners, Visa.*

Edinburgh   Forte Travelodge   £45

Tel 031-441 4296   **L**

Dreghorn Link City Bypass Edinburgh Lothian EH13 9QR   Map 3 C6

On the eastbound carriageway of the A720 Edinburgh City bypass
at Dreghorn (Colmton exit) and 5 miles south-west of the city centre.
Rooms 40. AMERICAN EXPRESS *Access, Diners, Visa.*

Edinburgh   George Inter-Continental Hotel   74%   £202

Tel 031-225 1251   Fax 031-226 5644   **H**

19 George Street Edinburgh Lothian EH2 2PB   Map 3 C6

Very conveniently located for the shopping on Edinburgh's Princes Street.
The classical facade conceals a grand entrance lobby complete with elegant,
fluted Corinthian columns, polished marble floors and a raised seating area
behind a wooden balustrade from where one can observe the busy comings
and goings. Other public areas include the clubby Gathering of the Clans
bar sporting clan mementoes and curios from the whisky trade. Luxurious
bedrooms have comfortable settees or armchairs and quality freestanding
furniture (mostly in yew), teletext TVs, in-house movies and beverage
facilities neatly hidden away in cabinets. Conference/banqueting facilities
for 220/170. Five nights a week there's a Scottish evening with a five-
course banquet and entertainment. *Rooms 195. News kiosk, 24hr lounge
service.* AMERICAN EXPRESS *Access, Diners, Visa.*

Edinburgh   Granada Lodge   £51

Tel 031-653 2427   Fax 031-653 6106   **L**

A1 Musselburgh Bypass Musselburgh Edinburgh Lothian EH21 8RE   Map 3 C6

Rooms 44. AMERICAN EXPRESS *Access, Diners, Visa.*

Many establishments are currently on the market, so ownership could
change after we go to press.

Edinburgh   Greenside Hotel   £70

Tel 031-557 0022   **PH**

9 Royal Terrace Edinburgh Lothian EH7 5AB   Map 3 C6

Relatively close to the centre, the hotel benefits from a quiet location, with
bedrooms overlooking the Royal Terrace gardens in front or the flowery
rear gardens which the owners take great pride in keeping up themselves.
Bedrooms are roomy, furnished with taste and sparkling clean.
A comfortable lounge is used for watching television and the owner cooks
a very good breakfast. *Rooms 13.* AMERICAN EXPRESS *Access, Diners, Visa.*

Edinburgh   Hilton National   68%   £156

Tel 031-332 2545   Fax 031-332 3805   **H**

69 Belford Road Edinburgh Lothian EH4 3DG   Map 3 C6

A modern hotel just a few minutes walk from Princes Street. Public areas
centre on a glitzy, split-level cocktail bar; a more pubby bar is to be found
in what was an old flour mill. Business centre, several conference rooms
(125 in largest room). *Rooms 144.* AMERICAN EXPRESS® *Access, Diners, Visa.*

Edinburgh   Holiday Inn Garden Court   65%   £101

Tel 031-332 2442   Fax 031-332 3408   **H**

107 Queensferry Road Edinburgh Lothian EH4 3HL   Map 3 C6

Located on the A90 a mile from the city centre. Formerly a Crest hotel,
bedrooms are somewhat smaller than the normal Holiday Inn standard and
36 of the single rooms have shower and WC only. More than half the
bedrooms are reserved for non-smokers. Meeting rooms for up to 60.
Ample free parking. *Rooms 119. Garden, gym.* AMERICAN EXPRESS® *Access,
Diners, Visa.*

Many hotels offer reduced rates for weekend or out-of-season bookings.
Always ask about special deals.

Edinburgh   Howard Hotel   74%   £180

Tel 031-557 3500   Fax 031-557 6515   **H**

36 Great King Street Edinburgh Lothian EH3 6QH   Map 3 C6

Created out of three interconnected town houses in the Georgian 'New
Town' area of the city, the rather dour exterior of the Howard conceals
a hotel of quiet luxury and considerable comfort. The dark greens, blues
and purples of the Highland's heather predominate in bedrooms which
boast a mixture of antiques and painted furniture. Dishes of fruit and nuts,
mineral water, bowls of pot pourri and the like are common to all rooms
and all, except four rather small singles, get a second phone at the desk.
Bathrooms, again except for the singles, come with separate shower
cubicles, many boast twin washbasins and three or four have wonderful
old-fashioned freestanding tubs – others have nice chunky reproduction-
style suites with brass fittings. The main day room is the very model
of a refined Edinburgh drawing room. Staff are most helpful and friendly.
Good cooked breakfasts are served in the basement restaurant. *Rooms 16.
Garden.* AMERICAN EXPRESS® *Access, Diners, Visa.*

Edinburgh   Indian Cavalry Club   £45

Tel 031-228 3282   Fax 031-225 1911   **R**

3 Atholl Place Edinburgh Lothian EH3 8HP   Map 3 C6

Modern Indian cooking with an emphasis on steaming; the menu
unusually suggests side dishes as suitable accompaniments for main-course
dishes and also suggests wines to match. Stylish setting, with enormous
swagged curtains and black-and-white checked floor in the high-ceilinged
ground-floor Officers' Mess and a marquee-style Club Tent downstairs;
military-uniformed waiters provide attentive service. Buffet-style choice
of main courses at lunchtime; interesting seafood banquet for two or more.
Also at: 8-10 Eyre Place (Tel 031-556 2404). The informal Pakora Bar,
serving a mix of western and Indian cooking in a bistro-style atmosphere,
is at Glenville Place (Tel 031-225 9199). *Seats 80. Private Room 40.
L 12-2.30 D 5.30-midnight. Set L from £6.95 Set D from £9.95 (vegetarian)
& £15.95.* AMERICAN EXPRESS® *Access, Diners, Visa.*

Edinburgh   Kalpna   £35

Tel 031-667 9890   **R**

2 St Patrick Square Edinburgh Lothian EH8 9EZ   Map 3 C6

Gujerati and South Indian vegetarian food has few finer homes than
Kalpna, a non-smoking restaurant in the student area. Their elephant logo
was designed to show that you can be big, strong and intelligent without
eating meat. Here you will feast on bhel poori, dosa masala, wok-fried
vegetables with ginger, nuts and a sweet/sour sauce, special rice dishes like
basmati with coconut, lentils, lemon and coriander, stuffed paratha bread,
carrot-based halva with almonds and cardamom and gulab jaman. The
lunchtime buffet is a snip at £4, and there are various price options in the
evening with a choice of set thali meals. On Wednesdays there's a regional
gourmet buffet (£8.50). The short wine list includes Veena, a light
Riesling blended with Indian spices. A sister restaurant, *Spices*, at 110, West
Bow Street, Grassmarket, is not exclusively vegetarian. *Seats 60. Parties 30.
L 12-2 D 5.30-11. Closed L Sat, all Sun, Dec 25 & New Year's Day.
Set L from £4. Access, Visa.*

Edinburgh   Kelly's   £55

Tel 031-668 3847   **R**

46 West Richmond Street Edinburgh Lothian EH8 9DZ   Map 3 C6

Just off the Pleasance and particularly convenient for the new Festival
Theatre, with opening times that cater for pre-theatre suppers, Jeff and
Jacquie Kelly have run their restaurant in a former baker's shop in a
Georgian block since 1986. The room is small and L-shaped, with wall
lamps, plants, tubular chairs and pink napery. Cooking is modern and
British on the short, one-price dinner menu that typically offers mushroom
and watercress broth, rabbit terrine, grilled goat's cheese, smoked haddock
roulade, sautéed scallops and monkfish, hazelnut mousseline-stuffed supreme
of chicken, fillet steak with horseradish and caper cream sauce, and
vegetable gateau with Brie-filled crescents and a sweet pimento sauce.
Scottish lamb is a favourite in Jacquie's kitchen – try it encrusted with
pistou (made with tarragon rather than the more usual basil) and
accompanied by caramelised aubergine and onion confit. Popular puddings
might encompass dark chocolate roulade and an almond vacherin filled
with strawberries and cream; British and French cheeses. No smoking
before 9.30 pm. *Seats 34. D only 5.30-9.30. Closed Sun & Mon, 1st week
Jan, all Oct. Set D £21.* AMERICAN EXPRESS *Access, Visa.*

Edinburgh   King James Thistle   70%   £99

Tel 031-556 0111   Fax 031-557 5333   **H**

St James Centre 107 Leith Street Edinburgh Lothian EH1 3SW Map 3 C6

Accommodation is first rate at this luxurious hotel in a position that's ideal
for both business and tourist visitors. Double-glazing keeps traffic noise
at bay, and bedrooms have good writing areas and mini-bars. En-suite
bathrooms are well equipped, with powerful showers. Children up to 12
stay free in parents' room. Public areas are split between the ground and
third floors. The street-level foyer-lounge is elegant, with marble-effect
floor, chandelier and comfortable winged armchairs. The American-
themed bar, brasseries and cocktail bar are reached by means of a swift and
efficient lift. The hotel is linked to the St James shopping centre, which
is easily accessible from the third floor. Conference/banqueting facilities for
250. Regular evening entertainment includes a long-popular two-hour
haggis ceremony. The hotel has parking for only 20 cars, but there's
a special deal with the NCP opposite. *Rooms 147.* AMERICAN EXPRESS *Access,
Diners, Visa.*

Edinburgh — Martin's — £75

Tel 031-225 3106 — **R**

70 Rose Street North Lane Edinburgh Lothian EH2 3DX — Map 3 C6

Between Frederick Street and Castle Street, in cobbled North Lane off Rose Street (vehicles must enter via Frederick Street as it's a one-way system), Martin's is run by Martin and Gay Irons, who nurture their customers in a charming atmosphere that features clever lighting and lots of fresh flowers. Chef Forbes Stott produces short, daily-changing menus utilising good ingredients (most of the vegetables are organically grown and Martin's father provides the herbs from his own garden) that are simply but carefully cooked in dishes like a warm salad of smoked salmon, mussels and chorizo, sautéed scallops and monkfish with cucumber, olive, pepper and avocado salsa, roast breast of Barbary duck with courgette spaghetti and cinnamon sauce, baked halibut with a Provençal crust and tomato coulis, pear, pistachio and apricot strudel, and elderflower and basil sorbet. Good-value, fixed-price-only, two-course lunches offer a small yet interesting choice: perhaps a feuilleté of venison and duck liver with broad beans and balsamic vinegar followed by lemon sole fillets with capers, lemon and parsley. Unpasteurised Scottish and Irish cheeses are served on a board. No background music, no smoking and no children under 8. Fair mark-ups on the fine wine list (not surprising it's fine since the two main suppliers are Zubair's Raeburn Fine Wines and Bill Baker's Reid Wines); good half-bottle selection. *Seats 28. Private Room 8. L 12-2 D 7-10 (Fri & Sat to 10.30). Closed L Sat, all Sun & Mon, 4 weeks Dec/Jan, 1 week Jun, 1 week Sept. Set L £10.95.* AMERICAN EXPRESS *Access, Diners, Visa.*

Edinburgh — Ristorante Raffaelli — £45

Tel 031-225 6060 — **R**

10 Randolph Place Edinburgh Lothian EH3 7TA — Map 3 C6

A sophisticated setting for all-day service of generally mainstream Italian cooking. Good home-made pasta features in a dish like tagliatelle with porcini mushrooms; other choices might include four-cheese or seafood risotto, grilled sea bass with barbecue sauce, medallions of venison with Barolo and polenta or grilled T-bone of veal with garlic and rosemary. Snacks in the wine bar next door. *Seats 60. Parties 20. Meals 12.15-9.30 (Sat from 6.30, Fri & Sat to 10). Closed L Sat, all Sun, Bank Holidays, 25 & 26 Dec, 1 Jan.* AMERICAN EXPRESS *Access, Diners, Visa.*

Edinburgh — Ristorante Tinelli — £35

Tel 031-652 1932 — **R**

139 Easter Road Edinburgh Lothian EH7 5QA — Map 3 C6

Unassuming, modestly comfortable restaurant where chef-patron Giancarlo Tinelli's North Italian fare is offered on a short but varied menu. Bresaola, fish soup, tortelli with a trio of ricotta, chestnut and pumpkin fillings, king prawns mornay, baked rabbit with a cream and rosemary sauce sit beside more familiar dishes such as risotto alla bolognese, scampi and scaloppine alla veneziana. The three-course lunchtime menu is selected from highlighted dishes on the evening menu. *Seats 35. L 12-2.30 D 6.30-11. Closed Sun & Mon (except at Christmas and during Festival), 25-27 Dec, 1-5 Jan. Set L £8.95.* AMERICAN EXPRESS *Access, Visa.*

Edinburgh — Roxburghe Hotel — 64% — £110

Tel 031-225 3921 Fax 031-220 2518 — **H**

38 Charlotte Square Edinburgh Lothian EH2 4HG — Map 3 C6

On the corner of Charlotte Square and noisy George Street; inward-facing rooms can suffer from extraneous noise. The smart interior manages to mix both country and town house feels. Decor in the bedrooms varies widely, but they are generally in good order. Children up to 14 stay free in parents'

room; informal eating in the 'Melrose on the Square' bistro. Conference/
banqueting facilities for 200/225. Only meter parking around the square.
Rooms 75. *Coffee shop (7.30am-8pm).* AMERICAN EXPRESS *Access, Diners, Visa.*

Edinburgh   Royal Terrace Hotel   70%   £157

Tel 031-557 3222   Fax 031-557 5334   **H**

18 Royal Terrace Edinburgh Lothian EH7 5AQ   Map 3 C6

Glittering chandeliers, sumptuous carpets and elaborately draped curtains
grace the elegant reception and lounge areas at a hotel consisting of six
linked houses on a famous cobbled terrace built to commemorate King
George IV's visit to the city in 1822. Bedrooms vary in size but all are
given an appealing period feel by plaster-panelled walls and many have
stylish bedhead drapes. Rooms range from singles to four-poster rooms and
suites. Bathrooms mostly have spa baths and a few boast luxurious impulse
showers. Children up to 14 stay free in parents' room. Paved and
landscaped gardens to the rear run the length of the hotel. The hotel is ten
minutes walk from Princes Street. Banqueting for 60, conferences for 80.
On-street parking (40p per hour daytime, free overnight). **Rooms** 93.
*Garden, indoor swimming pool, gym, sauna, spa bath, solarium, beauty salon,
outdoor chess.* AMERICAN EXPRESS *Access, Diners, Visa.*

Edinburgh   Scandic Crown   63%   £155

Tel 031-557 9797   Fax 031-557 9789   **H**

80 High Street The Royal Mile Edinburgh Lothian EH1 1TH   Map 3 C6

The hotel enjoys a prime location on the historic Royal Mile, and behind
its old turreted facade it's all modern and contemporary in Scandinavian
style with open-plan public areas. There are different varieties of spacious
bedrooms "with the best beds in town": standard, club and de luxe –
though you might consider that the price for a rack rate single at £98 (for
an attic room) excessive – we did! All the more so, when noting there
were no porters available either on arrival or departure, cooked breakfast
in bedrooms was unavailable, and unusually, room safes were charged for,
and did not have instructions on how to use – all examples of disappointing
standards of service. On the plus side, adjacent car parking with direct
access to the hotel is free to guests. There are several conference and
syndicate rooms, catering for up to 220 delegates. Plans for the immediate
future include extending the leisure facilities. **Rooms** 238. *Indoor swimming
pool, gym, sauna, solarium.* AMERICAN EXPRESS *Access, Diners, Visa.*

Edinburgh   Shamiana   £40

Tel 031-228 2265   **R**

14 Brougham Street Edinburgh Lothian EH3 9JH   Map 3 C6

Around the corner from the King's Theatre is an Indian restaurant with
decidedly untypical black, white and grey-tiled decor. North-West Indian
Kashmiri cuisine is the speciality with subtle spicing ringing the changes
from run-of-the-mill Indian cooking. Shahi murgh (royal chicken) and
Shahi jahar kurzi (royal lamb) are festive dishes requiring 24 hours notice.
Seats 43. *L 12-2 D 6-11.30. Closed L Sat & Sun, all 25 Dec, 1 Jan.
Set L from £5.95.* AMERICAN EXPRESS *Access, Diners, Visa.*

Edinburgh   Sheraton Grand Hotel   79%   £169

Tel 031-229 9131   Fax 031-228 4510   **H**

1 Festival Square Edinburgh Lothian EH3 9SR   Map 3 C6

Recent sympathetic refurbishment throughout has transformed the
Sheraton Grand into a first-class modern hotel with classical elegance
featuring its own tartan, commissioned from Hunters of Brora, makers
of fine Scottish fabrics. A grand staircase now leads to the second level,
housing the bar and lounge area, shopping gallery, boardroom and meeting
rooms, two of which have fine views of the castle. There are three floors

of superior Grand/Castle View rooms in country-house style offering bathrobes and an evening turn-down service, but all the rooms have tasteful American cherrywood furniture, tartan checks and prints of old Edinburgh, as well as the usual facilities of remote-control satellite TV, mini-bar, and hospitality tray. Bathrooms are on the small side. Two rooms are equipped for disabled guests. Excellent service from the committed and attentive staff, also attired in tartan. Children up to 17 share parents' room free. Conference and banqueting facilities for 485. No dogs. *Rooms 261. Indoor 'leisure' pool, gym, sauna, spa bath, sun beds, 24hr lounge service, news kiosk, shop.* AMERICAN EXPRESS *Access, Diners, Visa.* 🐂

Edinburgh	**Stakis Grosvenor Hotel**	**64%**	**£98**
Tel 031-226 6001 Fax 031-220 2387			**H**
Grosvenor Street Edinburgh Lothian EH12 5EF			Map 3 C6

Usefully located hotel of Victorian origin, set in a gracious street. Main business comes from conferences and banquets, for up to 500. No dogs. *Rooms 136.* AMERICAN EXPRESS *Access, Diners, Visa.*

Edinburgh	**Swallow Royal Scot**	**65%**	**£120**
Tel 031-334 9191 Fax 031-316 4507			**H**
111 Glasgow Road Edinburgh Lothian EH12 8NF			Map 3 C6

Five miles west of the city centre, two miles from the airport, a large 70s' hotel with a leisure club and conference/banqueting facilities for 350/250. Children up to 14 stay free in parents' room. *Rooms 259. Indoor swimming pool, keep-fit equipment, sauna, steam room, spa bath, solarium, hair salon, dinner dance (Sat).* AMERICAN EXPRESS *Access, Diners, Visa.*

Edinburgh	**Szechuan House**		**£30**
Tel 031-229 4655			**R**
12 Leamington Terrace Edinburgh Lothian EH10 4JN			Map 3 C6

This unpretentious little restaurant serves authentic Szechuan cooking, with spicy items underlined on the menu. These include bang bang chicken, steamed lamb and steamed beef in the starters, and various seafood, poultry and meat dishes among the mains. *Seats 150. Parties 25. Private Room 25. L Fri only 12-2 D 5-12. Closed Mon & 2 days at Chinese New Year. Access, Visa.*

Edinburgh	**Travel Inn**		**£43**
Tel 031-661 3396 Fax 031-652 2789			**L**
228 Willowbrae Road Edinburgh Lothian EH8 7NG			Map 3 C6

2 miles east of the city centre, by the A1, to the rear of Holyrood Park. *Rooms 39.* AMERICAN EXPRESS *Access, Diners, Visa.*

Edinburgh	**Vintners Room, The Vaults**		**£55**
Tel 031-554 6767			**R**
87 Giles Street Leith Edinburgh Lothian EH6 6BZ			Map 3 C6

The old sale room of the Vintners' Guild with its 17th-century Italian plasterwork (smoke-blackened from the candles that provide the only illumination) is home to Tim Cumming's appealingly robust, well-executed cooking. Market-fresh produce gets skilful handling in dishes like asparagus and cheese tartlet, lemon sole with prawns and vermouth sauce, and guinea fowl with bacon, lentils and red wine. Sticky toffee pudding, crème brulée and hot pear and almond tart among the desserts. Informal lunch in the wine bar offers a 2-or 3-course, fixed-price menu with a small but always interesting choice. The setting is more formal in the evening. Fair prices

and lots of half bottles (and plenty by the glass) on a sound wine list.
No smoking. *Seats 60. Private Room 36. L 12-2.30 D 7-10.30. Closed Sun,
2 weeks Christmas. Set L £8.75/£11.75.* AMERICAN EXPRESS *Access, Visa.*

Edinburgh   Places of Interest

Tourist Information   Tel 031-557 1700.
Edinburgh Airport Tourist Information   Tel 031 333 2167.
British Rail, Waverley Station   Tel 031-556 2451.
Busline LRT   Tel 031-554 4494 3858. **FMT**   031-556 84864
St. Giles Cathedral   Tel 031-225 4363.
St Mary's R.C. Cathedral   Tel 031-556 1798.
Clan Tartan Centre   Tel 031-553 5161.
Hearts F.C.   Tel 031-337 6132.
Hibs F.C.   Tel 031-661 2159.
Meadowbank Sports Centre and Stadium   Tel 031-661 5351.
Hillend Ski Centre   Tel 031-445 4433.
Central Cycle Hire   Tel 031-228 6333.
Portobello Swimming Pool   Tel 031-669 4077
Royal Commonwealth Pool   Tel 031-667 7211
Murrayfield Ice Rink   Tel 031-337 6933.
Edinburgh Zoo   Tel 031-334 9171.
Ingliston Motor Racing Circuit   Tel 041-641 2553.
Camera Obscura   Tel 031-226 3709.
Edinburgh Experience   Tel 031-556 4365.
   Theatres and Concert Halls
Church Hill Theatre   Tel 031-447 7597.
Festival Fringe: Enquiries Tel 031-226 5257.
International Festival Box Office   Tel 031-226 4001.
Kings Theatre   Tel 031-229 1201.
Netherbow Arts Centre   Tel 031-556 9579.
Playhouse Theatre   Tel 031-557 2590.
Royal Lyceum Theatre   Tel 031-229 7404.
Queens Hall   Tel 031-668 2019.
Traverse Theatre   Tel 031-226 2633.
Usher Hall   Tel 031-228 1155.
   Historic Houses, Castles and Gardens
Dalkeith Country Park   Tel 031-663 5684.
Edinburgh Castle   Tel 031-225 9846.
Edinburgh Dungeon   Tel 031-225 1331.
Craigmillar Castle   Tel 031-661 4445.
Dalmeny House   South Queensferry Tel 031-331 1888.
Edinburgh Butterfly and Insect World   Lasswade Tel 031-663 4932.
Hopetoun House   South Queensferry Tel 031-331 2451.
The Georgian House   Tel 031-225 2160.
Lennoxlove   Haddington. Tel 062 082 3720.
Palace of Holyroodhouse   Tel 031-556 7371.
Royal Botanic Garden   Tel 031-552 7171.
   Museums and Art Galleries
The Fruitmarket Gallery   Tel 031-225 2383.
Edinburgh Crystal Visitor Centre   Penicuik Tel 0968 675128.
Collective Gallery   Tel 031-220 1260.
Edinburgh Gallery   Tel 031-557 5227.
Royal Scottish Academy   Tel 031-225 6671.
Edinburgh University Collection of Historical Instruments
   Tel 031-447 4791.
Huntly House Museum and Museum of Childhood   Tel 031-225 2424.
National Gallery of Scotland   Tel 031-556 8921.
Scottish National Portrait Gallery   Tel 031-556 8921.
Scottish National Gallery of Modern Art   Tel 031-556 8921.
Royal Museum of Scotland   Tel 031-225 7534.
Scottish Whisky Heritage Centre   Tel 031-220 0441.

Elgin　　　Mansion House　　67%　　　£100

Tel 0343 548811　Fax 0343 547916　　**H**
The Haugh Elgin Moray Grampian IV30 1AW　　Map 2 C3

Set in gardens next to the river Lossie, the turreted mansion built in the mid-19th century is within a stone's throw of the town centre. The chandeliered entrance hall makes a good first impression, and spruce day rooms comprise the piano lounge (a favourite pre-dinner meeting place), the Wee Bar and the Still Room with its whisky collection. Good-sized bedrooms offer a lot of extras, including a welcoming glass of sherry and a mini-bar. A staircase connects the bedrooms to the Country Club, whose facilities include an all-day snack bar. No dogs. Now under the ownership and direction of James and Joan Stirrat. *Rooms 22. Garden, indoor swimming pool, sauna, spa bath, sun beds, gym, snooker, beauty and hair salons, coffee shop (10am-10pm).* AMERICAN EXPRESS *Access, Diners, Visa.*

Elgin　　　Places of Interest

Tourist Information　Tel 0343 542666.
The Glenfiddich Distillery　Dufftown. Tel 0340 20373.
Elgin Cathedral　Tel 0343 547171.

Eriska　　　Isle of Eriska　　73%　　　£155

Tel 063 172 371　Fax 063 172 531　　**HR**
Eriska Ledaig by Oban Strathclyde PA37 1SD　　Map 3 B5

On its own 280 acre island (reached via a private vehicle bridge) the Buchanan-Smiths' Scottish baronial-style mansion is at the heart of what is virtually a private nature reserve; it's a nightly ritual to feed the badgers that come up to the French doors of the bar each evening. After 21 years, Beppo Buchanan-Smith has largely taken over the running of Eriska from parents Robin and Sheena although the former is still often the caring, attentive host front of house and the latter retains overall control of the kitchen. Physically the hotel has a lot of appeal – chintzy drawing room with real log fires and baby grand (well supplied with sheet music to encourage its use), panelled central hall with fine pargeted frieze, spacious, traditionally furnished bedrooms (all recently recarpeted and now with real linen sheets) with every sort of comfort from proper sofas and armchairs to hot water bottles and fresh flowers everywhere – but the real secret of Eriska is the way it combines a family-run country house atmosphere with the highest standard of professional service that extends to bedrooms being serviced three times a day and a room service menu that provides a choice of hot meals 24 hrs a day. That 60% of guests are returnees (an enviable statistic) is no surprise. A leisure centre was being planned as we went to press. *Rooms 17. Garden, fishing, riding, tennis, shooting, putting, windsurfing, water-skiing. Closed Dec-Feb.* AMERICAN EXPRESS *Access, Visa.*

Restaurant　　　　　　　　　　　　　　　　　　　£85

A dado-panelled dining room with candle-lit, polished wooden tables and exemplary service delivered with an entirely appropriate degree of friendliness. Dinner is a fixed-price, multi-course affair with just a couple of choices at most stages; a typical night's offerings might be Eriska sausage salad with herb dressing or asparagus hollandaise to start followed by soup or a fish dish (Loch Etive prawns pan-fried with sesame seeds perhaps) before the main decision between a fish dish and the nightly roast carved from the trolley. A choice of puds and we're on the home stretch with just a savoury like Kentish rarebit to negotiate before the cheese trolley arrives and then it's off to collect coffee and petits fours from the main hall. Alan Clark, a young man who hails from nearby Oban, does a good job in the kitchen providing food designed first and last to be enjoyed. No guidance notes on the wine list, but it's quite fairly priced and clearly laid out. Several French country wines under a tenner. *Seats 40. Parties 12. D only 8-9. Set D £35.*

Erskine   Forte Posthouse   62%   £68

Tel 041-812 0123   Fax 041-812 7642   **H**

by Erskine Bridge Strathclyde PA8 6AN   Map 3 B6

Practical modern accommodation close to the M8 on the south side
of Erskine Bridge. Conference facilities for up to 600, banqueting to 450.
*Rooms 166. Indoor swimming pool, keep-fit equipment, sauna, spa bath,
solarium, beauty salon, pitch and putt, children's playground.* AMERICAN EXPRESS
Access, Diners, Visa.

Ettrickbridge   Ettrickshaws   62%   £76

Tel 0750 52229   **H**

Ettrickbridge Selkirk Borders TD7 5HW   Map 4 C1

New owners have recently taken over this turn-of-the-century country
house set in spectacular countryside west of Selkirk and on the B7009.
Open fires warm the drawing room and bar, and both they and the
traditionally appointed bedrooms enjoy the views. Note that the hotel now
accepts children under nine and is open all year. *Rooms 6. Garden, game
fishing. Access, Visa.*

Fairlie   Fins Restaurant   NEW   £55

Tel 0475 568989   **R**

Fencefoot Farm Fairlie nr Largs Strathclyde   Map 3 B6

Part of a fish farm and smokery just south of town on the A78, the
restaurant is in a 350-year-old barn with whitewashed rough-stone walls,
green-painted concrete floor and pine tables. Not surprisingly the menu
is almost entirely seafood (just one starter and Aberdeen steaks for
carnivores) with the likes of Jura monkfish tails casseroled with leeks and
Pernod, reel-caught lobster, Colonsay cod with orange and lemon butter
sauce, and a seafood platter that includes the products of their own
smokehouse. Starters include gravad lax, moules marinière and local oysters
that reassuringly spend three days in their own purification plant. Lunch
is a less formal affair with such things as seafood omelette and smoked
salmon and prawn quiche. Homely puds. *Seats 32. L 12-2.30 D 7-10.
Closed D Sun, all Mon, 25 & 26 Dec.* AMERICAN EXPRESS *Access, Diners, Visa.*

Falkirk   Hotel Cladhan   60%   £69

Tel 0324 27421   Fax 0324 611436   **H**

Kemper Avenue Falkirk Central FK1 1UF   Map 3 C5

Behind the somewhat unprepossessing modern exterior the Cladhan's
interior is stylish and attractive. Public areas are open-plan and designed
in a striking modern style with an art deco influence. The bedrooms are
light and airy, with good-quality fitted furniture and thermostatically
controlled heating. Most rooms overlook the Callender estate and gardens.
The hotel can cater for banquets and conferences for up to 200. *Rooms 37.
Garden.* AMERICAN EXPRESS *Access, Diners, Visa.*

Falkirk   Pierre's   £50

Tel 0324 635843   **R**

140 Grahams Road Falkirk Central FK2 7BQ   Map 3 C5

Self-styled as 'Falkirk's French connection', patron Pierre Renjard obviously
imagines himself and his customers to be in a pleasant little corner
of France. The menus stick in the main to tried and tested favourites from
the French bistro repertoire: *huitres (de Loch Fyne!), grenouilles en matelote,*
mussels, *soupe de poissons,* French onion soup, *sole meunière,* duck breast with
honey sauce and ginger, profiteroles and Gaelic coffee on the à la carte.
Good-value business lunch (grilled sardines and garlic butter, sautéed

chicken with tarragon and grapes, poached banana in orange and cinnamon sauce) and Taste of France menus in addition to the à la carte. *Seats 40. Parties 25. L 12-2 D 6.45-9.30. Closed L Sat, all Sun & Mon, 2 weeks Jan, 2 weeks July. Set L £5.50 Set D £11.85 (£9.85 before 7.30pm).* AMERICAN EXPRESS *Access, Diners, Visa.*

Falkirk   Places of Interest

Tourist Information   Tel 0324 20244.
  Museums and Art Galleries
Kinneil Museum and Roman Fortlet   Tel 0506 824318.
Falkirk Museum   Tel 0324 24911.

Forfar Royal Hotel 57%	£70
Tel & Fax 0307 462691	**H**
Castle Street Forfar Tayside DD8 3AE	Map 3 C4

A modest entrance conceals a thriving, compact, well-kept hotel complete with leisure centre, ballroom and roof garden. Bedrooms, apart from one four-poster room, are small, but neat and practical. No dogs. Conferences for up to 220. *Rooms 19. Indoor swimming pool, sauna, spa bath, solarium, hair salon, coffee shop (10am-10pm).* AMERICAN EXPRESS *Access, Diners, Visa.*

Forfar   Places of Interest

Tourist Information   Tel 0307 467876.
Edzell Castle and Gardens   Nr Brechin. Tel 031-244 3101 *18 miles.*
Barrie's Birthplace (NT)   Kirriemuir. Tel 0575 72646 *6 miles.*

Fort William Crannog Seafood Restaurant	£50
Tel 0397 705589	**R**
Town Pier Fort William Highland PH33 7NG	Map 3 B4

Converted ticket office and bait store in a quayside setting with views down Loch Linnhe. Scrubbed tables and a simple, mainly fish menu (including a vegetarian dish of the day). Langoustines (caught by their own fishing boat) and smoked salmon from their own smokehouse are specialities. Try cranachan (toasted oats with whisky, whipped cream and raspberries) or vacherin (meringue, whipped cream, ginger and Cointreau) to finish. *Seats 70. Private Room 20. L 12-2.30 D 6-9.30. Closed 25 Dec, 1 Jan. Access, Visa.*

Fort William The Factor's House	£85
Tel 0397 705767 Fax 0397 702953	**RR**
Torlundy Fort William Highland PH33 6SN	Map 3 B4

Dinner at this former manager's house at the foot of Ben Nevis is mostly for residents, but outsiders can join in. Soup is followed by, for example, roast lamb or salmon en croute. Charcoal grilled sirloin is always on the menu. Children's meal served between 6 and 7pm. *Seats 20. Parties 10. D only 7-9.30. Closed Mon, also mid Nov-mid Mar. Set D £23.* AMERICAN EXPRESS *Access, Visa.*

Rooms	£82

Bedrooms have views of either Ben Nevis or the surrounding hills. Guests have the use of the facilities of Inverlochy Castle. *Rooms 7. Garden, tennis.*

Fort William Inverlochy Castle 90%	£240
Tel 0397 702177 Fax 0397 702953	**HR**
Torlundy Fort William Highland PH33 6SN	Map 3 B4

What makes Inverlochy special is the very highest standard of service from staff who evince a genuine interest in the comfort and well-being of guests, and a constant programme of refurbishment means that standards throughout are always maintained. 1994 completed 25 years as a country house hotel, and although it was built in 1863 with tower and turrets this castle was always designed for comfort rather than defence. Perhaps the grandest of the five day rooms is the Great Hall with ornate Venetian crystal chandeliers hanging from a frescoed ceiling depicting chubby cherubs cavorting amongst the clouds. Highly polished antiques abound both in the public areas and in the luxurious bedrooms above, each individually decorated, often in summer shades, with proper sofas and armchairs, fresh flowers, books and sybaritic bathrooms (the smallest would be large by most hotel standards) many with bidets and separate showers, the others all having 'power' showers over tubs – and finished with marble. Generous towelling, robes and quality toiletries are standard. Children under 4 are free in parents' room. Dogs in kennels only. *Rooms* 17. *Garden, croquet, tennis, fishing, snooker, valeting. Closed Dec-Feb.* AMERICAN EXPRESS *Access, Diners, Visa.* 🐂 MARTELL

Restaurant   ★   £100

Simon Haigh is now well established in the kitchen here, routinely providing sophisticated dishes that are full of interest without being in any way contrived. First-rate raw materials form the basis of dishes such as chilled oysters with watercress cream; ballotine of foie gras with a Sauternes jelly and french bean salad; braised escalope of turbot with broad bean, tomato, basil and a scallop mousse; loin of venison with roasted pears, walnuts and a peppery port sauce, and caramelised lemon tart with poached figs and pears. The fixed-price dinner menu is short (just four choices at each stage plus a soup course) but well-balanced while the lunch menu (two or three options) is supplemented by a more snacky, individually-priced light lunch menu. There are two highly civilised dining rooms – the larger with polished wooden tables and a couple of monumental, heavily carved sideboards, the smaller with clothed tables – both with the same fine china and silverware. Service is never less than exemplary – as one would expect from Inverlochy. There is a pleasing number of half bottles on the comprehensive wine list that has a good New World section, complementing several mature clarets and top growers from Burgundy. *Seats* 40. *Private Room* 14. L 12.30-2 D 7-9.30. *Set L £23.50/£27.50 Set D £39.95.*

Fort William   Mercury Hotel   58%   £93

Tel 0397 703117   Fax 0397 700550   **H**
Achintore Road Fort William Highland PH33 6RW   Map 3 B4

Modern hotel with half of its standardised bedrooms enjoying views across Loch Linnhe. Very spacious and smart bar/lounge. Children up to 13 stay free in parents' room. *Rooms* 86. *Sauna, pool table.* AMERICAN EXPRESS *Access, Diners, Visa.*

Fort William   Places of Interest

Tourist Information   Tel 0397 703781.
Ben Nevis 5 *miles*

Gairloch   Creag Mor   66%   £76

Tel 0445 2068   Fax 0445 2044   **H**
Charleston Gairloch Highland IV21 2AH   Map 2 B3

Larry and Betty Nieto offer year-round hospitality in the spectacular setting of Wester Ross, where their hotel stands in landscaped grounds overlooking Old Gairloch harbour. The two-level Gallery Lounge enjoys marvellous views and also houses an exhibition of watercolours. In the Bothan Bar and cocktail bar there's a choice of more than 100 whiskies. Bedrooms are neat, bright and well equipped for a comfortable stay. Informal eating in the Buttery. *Rooms* 17. *Garden, games room, coffee shop (8am-10pm). Access, Visa.*

Gairloch   Places of Interest

Tourist Information Tel 0445 2130.
Inverewe Garden Tel 044586 356.

Garve   Inchbae Lodge   57%   £56

Tel 09975 269   Fax 09975 269   **HR**
Inchbae by Garve Highland IV23 2PH   Map 2 B3

In a superb setting by the River Blackwater (north-west of Garve on the
A834), stands Leslie and Charlotte Mitchell's friendly and hospitable little
hotel, which was once a hunting lodge. The small, rustic bar is also the
'local' and in the lounge, where a real fire burns most of the year, the
modern low-backed settees are arranged so as to encourage conversation
amongst guests. There are lots of board games and jigsaw puzzles for the
occasional rainy day. Bedrooms, half in the main house and half in an
adjacent red cedar chalet, are modestly appointed – no TV, radio
or telephone and all but three have shower and WC only – but well-kept
and quite attractive with pine furniture and a plum and pale green colour
scheme. Breakfast choices include locally smoked haddock. *Rooms 12.
Garden, fishing. Closed 25 & 26 Dec. No credit cards.*

The Dining Room   £60

The menu (fixed-price only) is short, just two choices at each stage plus
a soup course, but changes daily and allows Les to concentrate on dishes
that make good use of some of the excellent local ingredients: really peaty,
rum-cured smoked salmon stuffed with wild poached salmon and
mayonnaise, loin of wild venison cooked pink and served with a tarragon
sauce, corn-fed chicken with bacon and a Stilton cream sauce. Charlotte
is responsible for the puds – raspberry and peach brulée perhaps,
or a delicious chocolate brioche pudding, a sort of bread pudding equivalent
of *pain au chocolat* – and sweeties served with good coffee in the lounge.
No smoking. A bar menu provides snacks and light meals every lunchtime
and evening. *Seats 30. Parties 8. Private Room 30. D only 7-8.30.
Closed 25 & 26 Dec. Set D £21.*

Gatehouse of Fleet   Cally Palace   69%   £118*

Tel 0557 814341   Fax 0557 814522   **H**
Gatehouse of Fleet Dumfries & Galloway DG7 2DL   Map 4 B2

The 18-hole golf course is now up and running at this 18th-century
mansion with lofty public rooms decorated in Louis XIV style and a plush
cocktail bar. Bedrooms have pleasant decor, good bathrooms and
thoughtful extras; two rooms are equipped for disabled guests. Conference
facilities (for up to 80) are well patronised, and the hotel is also popular for
family holidays and special occasions. No dogs. *Half-board terms.
Rooms 56. Garden, croquet, golf (18), indoor swimming pool, sauna, spa bath,
solarium, tennis, games room, indoor carpet bowls, children's play room &
playground, fishing. Closed 4 Jan to end Feb. Access, Visa.*

Gatehouse of Fleet   Murray Arms Inn   £70

Tel 0557 814207   Fax 0557 814370   **I**
Anne Street Gatehouse of Fleet Dumfries & Galloway DG7 2HY   Map 4 B2

A warm, friendly old posting inn (established over 300 years) whose
hospitable day rooms include the Burns Room, where the poet reputedly
wrote *Scots Wha Hae*. There's also a little cocktail bar. Bedrooms, all
centrally heated, are by no means grand but lack nothing to a good
night's rest. These, and the bathrooms, are kept in very good order.
A cottage in the garden consists of a twin or double bedroom, sitting room
(with bed/settee) and bathroom, making it very suitable for families.

See over

Children up to 14 free in parents' room. The inn stands on the A75 Dumfries to Stranraer road. **Rooms** *13. Garden, croquet, coffee shop* *(noon-9.45pm).* AMERICANEXPRESS *Access, Diners, Visa.*

Gatehouse of Fleet   Places of Interest

Tourist Information   Tel 0557 814212.

Giffnock   Macdonald Thistle   64%   £85

Tel 041-638 2225   Fax 041-638 6231   **H**

Eastwood Toll Giffnock nr Glasgow Strathclyde G46 6RA   Map 3 B6

Modern commercial hotel convenient for Glasgow Airport (six miles) and the city centre (five miles). Conference facilities for up to 160, banqueting up to 130. 24hr room service. Reduced tariff at weekends. **Rooms** *56. Terrace, sauna, solarium.* AMERICANEXPRESS *Access, Diners, Visa.*

Glamis   Castleton House   71%   £90

Tel 0307 840340   Fax 0307 840506   **HR**

By Glamis Forfar Angus Tayside DD8 1SJ   Map 3 C4

On the A94 three miles from Glamis Castle, a Victorian house has been turned by William and Maureen Little into a charming country hotel with the emphasis on comfort, service and good food. The six bedrooms, all with en-suite facilities, are furnished with high-quality reproduction pieces, and there are showers above the dark-panelled tubs. The hotel can arrange fishing, shooting and stalking. Banqueting for up to 60. No dogs. **Rooms** *6. Garden, putting.* AMERICANEXPRESS *Access, Visa.*

Restaurant   £50

William uses local produce plus fruit and vegetables from his own garden on a varied menu that might include smoked trout with horseradish cream, game terrine with prunes and armagnac, roulade of smoked salmon and monkfish with vermouth sauce, pot-roast breast of pheasant with winter vegetables and sherry consommé, hot pear and almond tart with warm custard, and iced hazelnut mousse with praline sauce. Good-value, five-course, no-choice 'chef recommends' menu in addition to the carte. No smoking. Informal eating in the Conservatory restaurant from 12pm-10pm. **Seats** *28. L 12-2.30 D 7-9.30. Set L £11.75.*

Glamis   Places of Interest

Glamis Castle   Tel 030 784 242/3.
Folk Museum   Tel 030 784 288.

Glasgow   Amber   £40

Tel 041-339 6121   **R**

130 Byres Road Glasgow Strathclyde G12 8TD   Map 3 B6

Under colonial fans and red-tinged lights, menus, music and cutlery may appear Westernised but the cooking is authentic at this, one of Glasgow's favourite Chinese restaurants. Lunch choices offer remarkable value without compromising quality and the chef's specialities include seafood and aromatic crispy duck. Peking and Cantonese dishes. **Seats** *70. L 12-2 D 5-11.30 Meals Sat 12-12. Closed 3 days Chinese New Year. Set L from £4.50 Set D from £12.* AMERICANEXPRESS *Access, Diners, Visa.*

Glasgow   Ashoka West End   £30

Tel 041-339 0936   Fax 041-337 3385   **R**

1284 Argyle Street Glasgow Strathclyde G3 8AB   Map 3 B6

Indian restaurant on the corner of Glasgow's longest and shortest streets. Dozens of variations on lamb, chicken and prawn; thalis and set meals for 2 or more featuring tandoori, karahi, korma and a large vegetarian selection. There's a new healthy option menu with dishes cooked without excessive fats and oils, decreasing the fat content by almost 80% and the calorific value by over 50%. There are five other branches (three in Glasgow plus Johnstone and Paisley) as well as three bar/diners in Glasgow. Own jokey newspaper – The Delhi Record. *Seats 60. Parties 30. Private Room 36. D only 5-12.30 (Fri & Sat to 1). Closed 25 Dec, 1 Jan. Set meals (2 persons) from £18.75.* AMERICAN EXPRESS *Access, Diners, Visa.*

Glasgow — Brasserie on West Regent Street — £45
Tel 041-248 3801   Fax 041-248 8197 — **R**
176 West Regent Street Glasgow Strathclyde G2 8HF — Map 3 B6

Part of the *Rogano* stable, with the familiar tartan carpet and smart, white-aproned staff, the Brasserie prepares fresh local and seasonal produce in both traditional and modern styles. Wild mushrooms with garlic butter, seafood bisque, poached salmon hollandaise and rack of lamb with shallot jus show the style. A couple of vegetarian main dishes are always available – perhaps vegetable and nut risotto with pimento sauce and saffron pasta with feta cheese and red chili peppers. There are also 'something lighter' and 'after-theatre' menus offering such dishes as French onion soup, smoked chicken in puff pastry and Cumberland sausages with onion gravy. *Seats 100. Private Room 50. Meals 12-11. Closed Sun, Bank Holidays. After-theatre supper £9.75.* AMERICAN EXPRESS *Access, Diners, Visa.*

Glasgow — Buttery — £75
Tel 041-221 8188   Fax 041-204 4639 — **R**
652 Argyle Street Glasgow Strathclyde G3 8UF — Map 3 B6

Tastefully converted Victorian city-centre pub now operating on two floors. Chef Stephen Johnston offers some unusual dishes such as an individual pigeon and blackberry pie with an oatmeal glaze, or home-made ravioli filled with Italian sausage in a black olive and basil sauce, or grilled fillet of brill on a sharp dark peppercorn butter. For dessert, try the creamy warm praline and bread pudding on a vanilla pod sauce, the luscious hickory chocolate mousse with nut shortbread dusted with cinnamon, or strawberry délice with bee's pollen yoghurt. The Belfry Bistro in the basement is open 12-2.30 and 6-10.30. A recent very useful addition is their own car park. *Seats 50. Parties 12. Private Room 8. L 12-2.30 D 7-10.30. Closed L Sat, all Sun, Bank and local Holidays. Set L £14.75.* AMERICAN EXPRESS *Access, Diners, Visa.*

Glasgow — Café Gandolfi — £35
Tel 041-552 6813   Fax 041-332 4264 — **R**
64 Albion Street Glasgow Strathclyde G1 1NY — Map 3 B6

All-day à la carte eating in a bistro-style café in the old merchant district. Snacks until noon, then the full menu. No under-14s after 8pm. *Seats 60. Parties 12. Meals 9am-11.30pm (Sun from noon). No credit cards.*

Glasgow — Copthorne Hotel — 64% — £125
Tel 041-332 6711   Fax 041-332 4264 — **H**
George Square Glasgow Strathclyde G2 1DS — Map 3 B6

Overlooking busy George Square with Queen Street railway station adjacent, the Copthorne is well situated for passers-through as well as destination visitors. Bedrooms range from Classic or Connoisseur to suites, and all offer 24hr room service; under-16s stay free in parents' room. Conference/banqueting for up to 100. *Rooms 140.* AMERICAN EXPRESS *Access, Diners, Visa.*

Glasgow D'Arcy's £45

Tel 041-226 4309 **R**

Basement Courtyard Princes Square Glasgow Strathclyde G1 4PR Map 3 B6

Part café, part restaurant in the Princes Square shopping centre. Popular dishes from around the world: stuffed mushrooms, deep-fried Camembert, seafood terrine with mustard and dill sauce, veal milanese, moules marinière, steaks. Free glass of wine if you order before 7. *Seats 72. Parties 16. Meals 9.30am-midnight (Sun 11-6). Closed 25 & 26 Dec, 1 & 2 Jan. Set Sun L £5.95 Set D £7.95/£9.95.* AMERICAN EXPRESS *Access, Diners, Visa.*

Glasgow Devonshire Hotel £120

Tel 041-339 7878 Fax 041-339 3980 **PH**

5 Devonshire Gardens Glasgow Strathclyde G12 0UX Map 3 B6

Ring the doorbell to gain admittance to this discreet, luxurious hotel at one end of an imposing Victorian terrace set back from the main road out of the city towards the west. The atmosphere is deliberately quiet and restful with dark, rich tones in the hallway and mellow autumnal shades used in the recently refurbished lounge that also doubles up as the bar with drinks set out on a side table. There is also a small dining room (just four tables) that is mainly for residents only. Spacious, antique pine-furnished bedrooms are individually decorated in considerable style and all boast proper armchairs and/or sofas along with little extras like magazines and mineral water. Bathrooms, decorated to match the bedrooms, are of a good size too, with power showers over the tubs (one room has shower and WC only), telephone extensions, bath robes and generous towelling. Room service offers a choice of hot meals 24 hours a day. There's no car park but easy, unrestricted street parking right outside. Children up to 10 stay free in parents' room. *Rooms 14.* AMERICAN EXPRESS *Access, Diners, Visa.*

Glasgow Forte Crest 74% £119

Tel 041-248 2656 Fax 041-221 8986 **H**

Bothwell Street Glasgow Strathclyde G2 7EN Map 3 B6

Classic re-styling in marble and primary colours, customer-conscious staff and strong management all contribute to the Forte Crest's position among Glasgow's top hotels. Day rooms are stylish and relaxed while in the bedrooms touches of luxury are provided by mini-bars, remote-control TV and comprehensive grooming accessories. Bathrooms are smartly fitted and brightly lit. The hotel has no leisure amenities, but guests are offered some elite services: same-day laundry, valeting, multi-lingual reception staff and valet parking. There are excellent facilities for conferences, with room for up to 800 delegates theatre-style and first-class support services. *Rooms 257.* AMERICAN EXPRESS *Access, Diners, Visa.*

Glasgow Glasgow Hilton 78% £140

Tel 041-204 5555 Fax 041-204 5004 **HR**

1 William Street Glasgow Strathclyde G3 8HT Map 3 B6

Now comfortably established in the city, it's sometimes hard to remember when the Hilton wasn't here. The eye-catching decor, standards of service and watchpoints like Minsky's Deli – not to mention the very shape of the tall, glass and granite building – could almost make you believe you were Stateside rather than Clydeside. Air-conditioned bedrooms (with sealed windows) have standardised decor and furnishings, but an extra £25 on the room-only rate brings Executive status with extras like bathrobe and slippers, and use of the top-floor Executive lounge with complimentary Continental breakfast, afternoon tea and evening drink. One floor caters specifically to Japanese guests with signs and room information in the appropriate language, green tea added to the beverage tray and a *yukata*

(Japanese pyjamas) provided as standard. A traditional Japanese breakfast is also available. Extensive 24hr room service and conference/banqueting facilities for up to 1100. Valet parking. *Rooms 319. Indoor swimming pool, gym, sauna, steam room, solarium, beauty & hair salons, news kiosk, coffee shop (6.30am-11pm).* AMERICAN EXPRESS *Access, Diners, Visa.* 🐄

Camerons Restaurant

£95

Designed to resemble several interconnecting rooms from a grand Scottish country house, the decor here is amongst the most appealing of any modern hotel restaurant. There's plenty to like about the menu too with dishes like a light broth of Western Isles seafood and summer vegetables with seaweed pastry twists; cream of snow pea soup with fresh ginger; warm foie gras salad with grapes and raspberry vinaigrette; John Dory baked over dried fennel with a light tomato dressing; a medley of Highland game with forest mushrooms on a rich game jus; and lightly smoked new season lamb with polenta, charred aubergine (the kitchen has just acquired a brand new chargrill) and fresh vegetable tips, combining a light, modern style with the best of Scottish produce. The kitchen, under Londoner Michael Mizzen, makes a professional job of translating menu descriptions to the plate; good selection of interesting vegetarian options. The wine list is presented by grape variety and even includes an Israeli kosher section. The New World is well represented, there's a good house selection under £15 and plenty of half bottles. *Seats 60. Private Room 25. L 12-2 D 7-11. Closed L Sat, all Sun. Set L £16.50/£19.*

Glasgow Glasgow Marriott 73% £110

Tel 041-226 5577 Fax 041-221 9202 **H**

Argyle Street Anderston Glasgow Strathclyde G3 8RR Map 3 B6

One-time *Holiday Inn*, close to the city centre (by Junction 19 of the M8); the extensive public areas (part of which overlook the indoor pool) have recently been refurbished. Good-sized bedrooms all offer large beds, breakfast table and ample work space plus mini-bars and individually controllable air-conditioning; one room is equipped for disabled guests. A small supplement brings Executive status with extras like bath robe and slippers, fresh fruit, complimentary wine and a turn-down service in the evening. Comprehensive 24hr room service and extensive conference/banqueting facilities for 720/600 (parking for 180+). *Rooms 298. Indoor swimming pool, gym, squash, sauna, spa bath, solarium, hair salon, kiosk, coffee shop (10am-6pm).* AMERICAN EXPRESS *Access, Diners, Visa.*

Glasgow Glasgow Thistle 67% £130

Tel 041-332 3311 Fax 041-332 4050 **H**

36 Cambridge Street Glasgow Strathclyde G2 3HN Map 3 B6

Situated next to the pedestrianised shopping centre this modern hotel (formerly the *Hospitality Inn*) is particularly suited to business customers, with conference suites to hold up to 1500 and a free 250-space car park for residents. Especially roomy de luxe bedrooms and efficient 24hr room service. The bedroom refurbishment is still ongoing. Children up to 14 stay free in parents' room. Dogs welcome. *Rooms 307.* AMERICAN EXPRESS *Access, Diners, Visa.*

Glasgow Jurys Pond Hotel 59% £86

Tel 041-334 8161 Fax 041-334 3846 **H**

2 Shelly Road Great Western Road Glasgow Strathclyde G12 0XP Map 3 B6

Overlooking the boating pond from which it takes it name, this is the first Scottish outlet for the Irish-based Jurys group (it was previously the Stakis). Good leisure and conference facilities, the latter for up to 150. 60 bedrooms are designated non-smoking. Well set up for families (under-12s stay free in parents' room). The hotel stands on the Great Western Road three miles

west of the city centre (leave the M8 at junction 17 and follow the A82 for
2½ miles). *Rooms 133. Indoor swimming pool, children's pool, gym, sauna, spa
bath, solarium. Closed 24-29 Dec.* AMERICAN EXPRESS *Access, Diners, Visa.*

Glasgow	Kelvin Park Lorne Hotel	63%	£87
Tel 041-334 4891 Fax 041-334 1659			**H**
923 Sauchiehall Street Glasgow Strathclyde G3 7TE			Map 3 B6

10 minutes from the city centre, a Queens Moat Houses hotel with a choice
of accommodation (standard Executive, superior Executive and suites) and
six conference suitesfor up to 360 delegates. *Rooms 99. Coffee shop
(11.30-10). Closed 25 & 26 Dec.* AMERICAN EXPRESS *Access, Diners, Visa.*

Glasgow	Loon Fung		£45
Tel 041-332 1240 Fax 041-332 3705			**R**
417 Sauchiehall Street Glasgow Strathclyde G2 3JD			Map 3 B6

Colourful carvings of the dragon and phoenix (Loon Fung) decorate one
end of this smart restaurant, which takes pride in its authentic Cantonese
cooking. It's open all day, with a business lunch Mon-Fri, and dim sum (30
varieties) available until 7. Sliced abalone with oyster sauce, Cantonese
roast duck, deep-fried squid, steamed scallops and sizzling platters
of Cantonese-style fillet steak take centre stage in the evening. Vegetarian
meals available. Special banquets can be ordered by prior arrangement.
*Seats 120. Parties 30. Private Room 40. Meals 12-11.30. Set L £5.70
Set D from £10.* AMERICAN EXPRESS *Access, Visa.*

Glasgow	Mata Hari		£40
Tel 041-332 9789			**R**
17 West Princes Street Glasgow Strathclyde GB4 9BS			Map 3 B6

Malaysian cooking in a basement restaurant with a no-smoking section.
Dishes to try include chicken, beef and king prawn satay (also mushroom
for vegetarians), *kari daging istimewa* (rump steak slices cooked with
aubergine and 'tropical spices', *rendang ayam* (chicken with 'exotic' spices
and lemon grass), *ikan halia* (chunks of fish cooked with shredded ginger,
chili and soya bean sauce) and *acar* (mixed vegetable pickle with sesame
seeds in a spiced lemon grass sauce). Hot and sour tom yum soup and char
koay teow (stir-fried noodles with chicken, shrimps, chili, egg and bean
sprouts) are considered specialities. Desserts include coconut pancakes and
rambutan stuffed with pineapple. *Seats 60. Private Room 15. D only 6-10.30
(Fri & Sat to 11.30). Closed Sun, 25 & 26 Dec, 1 Jan. Set L from £5
Set D £17.50.* AMERICAN EXPRESS *Access, Diners, Visa.*

Glasgow	Moat House International	69%	£134
Tel 041-204 0733 Fax 041-221 2022			**H**
Congress Road Glasgow Strathclyde G3 8QT			Map 3 B6

Adjacent to the Scottish Exhibition Centre (follow signs from J19 of the
nearby M8), with fine views across the Clyde. Historical connections with
Glasgow's shipbuilding past are recalled by the vast mural which dominates
one end of the spacious, glass-walled public areas. On ground and
mezzanine floors conference and banqueting suites will hold up to 1000,
serviced by a self-contained business centre. The chief recreation area is the
Waterside health and leisure club. Roomy bedrooms are identically
equipped with maple-effect fitted furniture and marble-finish bathrooms;
state-of-the-art TV includes a breakfast order facility, bill check and
automatic payment service. Under-13s stay free in their parents' room and
there are various family facilities. Ample parking space. *Rooms 282. Indoor
swimming pool, gym, spa bath, sauna, solarium, coffee shop (7am-11pm).*
AMERICAN EXPRESS *Access, Diners, Visa.*

Glasgow   One Devonshire Gardens   82%   £155

HR

Tel 041-339 2001   Fax 041-337 1663

1 Devonshire Gardens Glasgow Strathclyde G12 0UX   Map 3 B6

One Devonshire is one of a kind. Owned by Ken McCulloch and superbly run by Beverly Payne, this is a hotel of real style and distinction. It's an unusual spot at which to find such insulated comforts, situated as it is at the junction of the Great Western and Hyndland Roads; rooms at the rear are therefore quieter. Every creature comfort imaginable (within a hotel context!) seems to be available in bedrooms, bathrooms or public rooms as appropriate, creating an air of opulence and luxury that somehow doesn't overawe. Quality is evident throughout, whether it's the level of service provided (courteous porterage, immaculate housekeeping and cheerful turning-down of beds at night), the facilities offered in the bedrooms (hi-tech TV and CD player, mini-bar, fresh flowers, books, magazines, quality toiletries, and luxurious hooded bathrobes), or the standard and degree of comfort in the lounge and bar, where you can unwind and relax in serene splendour, surrounded by antiques and good paintings. You really feel valued and cosseted in a manner that only a truly professional hotelier and his staff can achieve. Having said 'one of a kind', we look forward to Ken's new hotel openings of *The Malmaisons* in Edinburgh and Glasgow (both due as we publish), repeating the successful formula, albeit a little differently. Here, up to 50 can be catered for conference-style (32 banquet) in either the boardroom, study or private dining room. Children under 14 may stay free in their parents' room. **Rooms** *27. Patio garden.*
AMERICAN EXPRESS *Access, Diners, Visa.* MARTELL

Restaurant   £80

Sophisticated decor sees the crisp, spotlit whiteness of damask tablecloths set against a background of midnight blue with dense medieval-tapestry patterned drapes and wallpaper. There's a new chef, Andrew Fairlie, since last year but the market-driven, fixed-price menu format is unchanged except that there is now a little more choice. Very much in the modern idiom, typical dishes might include grilled and marinated vegetables with rocket, balsamic dressing and shaved Parmesan; crab ravioli; grilled goat's cheese with roasted egg plant; steamed turbot with potato salad and gazpacho sauce; breast of pigeon with shallot and garlic confit on a bed of Puy lentils and pan-fried calf's liver with sage-mashed potatoes and a green peppercorn sauce; all are based on first-rate ingredients cooked with flair and skill. Puds are fairly mainstream: lemon tart, chocolate marquise and gratin of strawberries. Good selection of home-made breads. Sunday lunch always includes prime roast joints of Scottish roast beef carved at your table. Prices are quite steep on the excellent wine list (good to see the New World well represented); fortunately there are many half bottles.
Seats *44. Parties 8. Private Room 32. L 12.30-2 D 7-10.30. Closed L Sat.*
Set L £21.50 Set D £37.50.

See the Restaurant Round-up for easy, quick-reference comparisons.

Glasgow   La Parmigiana   £50

R

Tel 041-334 0686

447 Great Western Road Glasgow Strathclyde G12 8HH   Map 3 B6

An unpretentious family-run trattoria, rather smarter than most. The menu follows a fairly familiar path, with sections for starters, pasta, main courses (including fresh fish from the market) and desserts (William pears cooked in moscato wine and a mousse of strawberry and kirsch are a little bit different). Popular three-course lunch offers a good choice (considering the admirably low price); booking advisable. **Seats** *55. L 12-2.30 D 6-11. Closed L Bank Holidays, all Sun, 25/26 Dec & 1/2 Jan. Set L £6.80.*
AMERICAN EXPRESS *Access, Diners, Visa.*

Glasgow   The Puppet Theatre   ↑   NEW   £75

Tel 041-339 8444   Fax 041-339 7666   **R**

11 Ruthven Lane Glasgow Strathclyde G12 9BQ   Map 3 B6

Venture down a narrow lane opposite Hillhead Metro station in Glasgow's
West End to find one of the city's newest and most chic restaurants. The
first choice to make is whether to eat in the dark green, candle-lit,
labyrinthine interior (one wall features a detail from the ceiling of the
Sistine Chapel, another is mirrored, and there is an intimate padded booth)
or the eccentrically-shaped conservatory to the rear of the early 19th-
century building. Even more difficult is the decision about what to choose
from a menu that is full of good things – skewered scallops with lentils and
coriander; consommé of smoked salmon with langoustine and vegetable
tortellinis; seared marinated beef fillet with radish, cucumber and roasted
peanuts; steamed fillet of sea bass with hot and sweet peppers; calf's liver
with lime and caramelised onions; rich venison pie; and side dishes like
aubergine and polenta cakes, and carrot and celeriac mousse. Puds range
from the exotic – roast baby pineapple with vanilla and cinnamon – to
a jam tart with clotted cream custard. Raw materials used are first-rate, as is
their preparation in Douglas Painter's kitchen. Just two dozen well-chosen
wines on offer, almost all (except the fizz) at less than £20 a bottle.
*Seats 72. Private Room 22. L 12-2.30 D 7-11. Set L £11.95/£13.95 Set Sun
L £15.95.* AMERICAN EXPRESS *Access, Diners, Visa.*

Glasgow   Ristorante Caprese   £35

Tel 041-332 3070   **R**

217 Buchanan Street (basement) Glasgow Strathclyde G1 2JZ   Map 3 B6

Cheerful, inexpensive and atmospheric basement Italian restaurant close
to the Royal Concert Hall. The menu holds few surprises but cooking
is enjoyably robust and homely. House specialities include veal cordon bleu,
steak pizzaiola and chicken Kiev. Also daily blackboard dishes and
vegetarian choices. *Seats 60. Private Room 25. L 12-2.30 D 5.30-11.
Closed L Sat, all Sun, Bank Holidays. Set L £5.50.* AMERICAN EXPRESS *Access,
Diners, Visa.*

We welcome bona fide complaints and recommendations on the tear-out
pages at the back of the book for readers' comments. They are followed
up by our professional team.

Glasgow   Rogano   £75

Tel 041-248 4055   Fax 041-248 2608   **R**

11 Exchange Place Glasgow Strathclyde G1 3AN   Map 3 B6

Popular as ever and as firmly traditional as its setting of art deco ocean-liner
decor, Rogano is a Glasgow institution. Fish and seafood feature very
strongly on the menu – from fish soup, oysters, mussels and sashimi
to lobster, langoustines, salmon, scallops and monkfish. Parma ham with
fresh figs, fillet of Angus beef with peppercorns and cognac, breast
of duckling with apricots, port and cinnamon, malt whisky parfait with
prunes and Earl Grey syrup complete the picture. Downstairs, the all-day
Café Rogano is more informal. No smoking at lunch and dinner until 2pm
or 9pm (when hand-made Davidoffs are proffered). Park in Exchange
Square or on Queen Street. *Seats 55. Parties 16. Private Room 16. L 12-2.30
D 6.30-10.30 (Sun 6 to 10) (Café 12-11, to midnight Fri & Sat, Sun 6-10
only). Closed L Sun, all Bank Holidays. Set L £16.50.* AMERICAN EXPRESS *Access,
Diners, Visa.*

Glasgow   Stakis Grosvenor   66%   £117
Tel 041-339 8811   Fax 041-334 0710   **H**
Grosvenor Terrace Glasgow Strathclyde G12 0TA   **Map 3 B6**

At the west end of the city, just opposite the Botanical Gardens, a Victorian frontage conceals a totally refurbished hotel. Conference/banqueting for up to 400, 50% non-smoking bedrooms and 14 spacious family rooms (under-12s stay free) are among the facilities. The coffee shop is now the West End Piano Bar. *Rooms 95.* AMERICAN EXPRESS *Access, Diners, Visa.*

Glasgow   Swallow Hotel   62%   £92
Tel 041-427 3146   Fax 041-427 4059   **H**
517 Paisley Road West Glasgow Strathclyde G51 1RW   **Map 3 B6**

A mile west of the city centre at junction 23 of the M8, near Ibrox Park, a busy modern hotel with conference facilities for 300+, a leisure club and parking for 150 cars. Almost half the bedrooms are designated non-smoking. Recently refurbished in many areas. *Rooms 117. Indoor swimming pool, gym, sauna, spa bath, steam room.* AMERICAN EXPRESS *Access, Diners, Visa.*

Glasgow   Tinto Firs Hotel   62%   £85
Tel 041-637 2353   Fax 041-633 1340   **H**
470 Kilmarnock Road Glasgow Strathclyde G43 2BB   **Map 3 B6**

A modern, if modest, hotel in the suburbs (three miles from the city centre) with club class bedrooms and two suites. Banqueting for 130, conferences up to 200. Friendly staff create a relaxed atmosphere. Free parking for 40 cars. 24hr room service. Mount Charlotte Thistle. *Rooms 27. Garden.* AMERICAN EXPRESS *Access, Diners, Visa.*

Glasgow   Town House   66%   £110
Tel 041-332 3320   Fax 041-332 9756   **H**
54 West George Street Glasgow Strathclyde G2 1NG   **Map 3 B6**

Created out of the turn-of-the-century former Royal Academy of Music and Drama building, the Town House enjoys a conveniently central location opposite the Stock Exchange and not far from both the Queen's Street and Central railway termini. Some nice architectural features include the vaulted lobby and bas-reliefs (honouring famous composers) adorning the staircase. There is a coffee lounge at lobby level but the main day room for residents is a cosy, armchair-furnished bar on the first floor. Bedrooms, individually decorated in some style, are generally of good size and smart bathrooms come with generous towelling and good toiletries. Small details of repair and housekeeping need attention in some bedrooms. Service is friendly enough but a little lacking in polish. Not everything on the breakfast menu was available on a recent overnight stay. Beds are turned down at night and room service is offered throughout the day and evening. There are five period meeting/function rooms. *Rooms 34.* AMERICAN EXPRESS *Access, Diners, Visa.*

Glasgow   Two Fat Ladies   £55
Tel 041-339 1944   **R**
88 Dumbarton Road Glasgow Strathclyde G11 6NX   **Map 3 B6**

Chef-patron Calvin Matheson specialises in seafood on menus that change four times a year at his relaxed restaurant near the City Art Gallery. Starters such as garlicky steamed mussels, pan-fried squid or home-cured gravad lax precede main courses which draw their inspiration from home and away: cod and prawn fishcake with parsley sauce, chargrilled whole sea bass with tomato salsa, fillet of halibut teriyaki, baked salmon in filo

pastry with ginger and soya butter sauce. A la carte or set menus available.
*Seats 30. L 12-2.30 D 5.30-10.30. Closed L Mon, all Sun, 12 days at start
of year. Set L £7.75 Set D £9.75. No credit cards.*

Glasgow   Ubiquitous Chip   £75

| **Tel 041-334 5007   Fax 041-337 1302** | **R** |

12 Ashton Lane Glasgow Strathclyde G12 8SJ   Map 3 B6

A former Victorian coach house and stables in a cobbled lane near the
university. The main restaurant is in the covered courtyard (with rampant
greenery) and offers an inventive, daily-changing menu that combines
a strong Scottish slant with modern touches – vegetarian haggis and neeps,
shellfish bisque with cream and fresh ginger, Oban-landed squid cooked
in its own ink and served with balsamic onion and lemon zest vinaigrette,
pan-fried 'gravellachs' scallops on a roasted potato cake with stewed garlic,
and heather honey and Scotch whisky parfait are typical items
on a summer menu. More traditional dishes included langoustines with
mayonnaise, braised oxtail ragout, Aberdeen Angus steak au poivre (or
with onion and leek marmalade) and Scots burnt cream – the long list
of handwritten dishes seems endlessly enticing. Cooking is more bistro-ish
than refined, with generously-sized portions. The 'Upstairs at the Chip' bar
offers a less expensive all-day menu along similar lines; several tables are set
on a balcony overlooking the restaurant courtyard below. Good selection
of Scottish cheeses (priced either individually or as a mixed platter).
Vegetarians are unlikely to be disappointed. Alongside the comprehensive
and most fairly-priced wine list (which features the New World
as prominently as Europe) are 100 single Highland malt whiskies that will
gladden many hearts and satisfy the serious connoisseur. Friendly staff and,
generally, exemplary service. *Seats 140. Parties 60. Private Room 30.
L 12-2.30 D 5.30-11 (Upstairs open 12-11). Closed 25 & 31 Dec, 1 & 2 Jan.
Set L £10.*   AMERICAN EXPRESS, Access, Diners, Visa.

Glasgow   Places of Interest

Tourist Information   Tel 041-204 4400.
Caledonian MacBrayne Ferries   Tel 0475 33755.
City Tours   Tel 041-332 1607.
ScotRail   Tel 041-332 9811.
Glasgow Airport   Tel 041-887 1111.
Glasgow Cathedral   Tel 041-552 3205.
St Mary the Virgin Cathedral   Tel 041-339 6691.
Glasgow Ski Centre Club   Tel 041-427 4991.
Kelvin Hall Int. Sports Arena   Tel 041-357 2525.
Celtic F.C.   Celtic Park Tel 041-556 2611.
Rangers F.C.   Ibrox Stadium Tel 041-427 8811.
Calderpark Zoo   Tel 041-771 1185.
    Theatres and Concert Halls
Citizens Theatre   Tel 041-429 0022.
Glasgow Royal Concert Hall   Tel 041-332 6633.
Glasgow Film Theatre   Tel 041-332 6535.
Greenock Arts Guild Theatre   Tel 0475 23038.
Royal Scottish Academy of Music   Tel 041-332 5057.
Scottish Exhibition and Conference Centre   Tel 041-248 3000.
The Tramway   Tel 041-227 5511.
City Halls   Tel 041-227 5511 .
Kings Theatre   Tel 041-227 5511.
Mitchell Theatre   Tel 041-227 5511.
Pavilion Theatre   Tel 041-332 1846.
SNO Henry Wood Hall   Tel 041-226 3868.
Theatre Royal   Tel 041-332 9000.
Third Eye Centre   Tel 041-332 7521.
Tron Theatre   Tel 041-552 4267.
    Historic Houses, Castles and Gardens
Greenbank Garden   Tel 041-639 3281.

Botanic Gardens Tel 041-334 2422.
The Hill House Helensburgh. Tel 0436 3900.
Hutcheson's Hall Tel 041-552 8391.
Pollock House & Park (Burrell Collection in Pollock Park)
Tel 041-632 0274.
Provands Lordship Tel 041-552 8819.
The Tenement House Tel 041-333 0183.
Museums and Art Galleries
Art Gallery and Museum Tel 041-357 3929.
Burrell Collection Tel 041-649 7151.
Dome of Discovery Tel 041-427 1792.
Hunterian Art Gallery Tel 041-330 5431.
Hunterian Museum Tel 041-330 4221.
McLean Museum and Art Gallery Greenock Tel. 0475 23741.
McLellan Galleries Tel 041-351 1854.
Museum of Tranport Tel 041-357 3929.
Peoples's Palace Tel 041-554 0223.
Paisley Museum and Art Galleries Paisley. Tel 041-889 3151.
Police Museum Tel 041-204 2626.

Glasgow Airport   Forte Crest   68%   £95

Tel 041-887 1212   Fax 041-887 3738   **H**
Abbotsinch nr Paisley Strathclyde PA3 2TR   Map 3 B6

The only hotel located directly beside Glasgow Airport. All the bedrooms
are sound-proofed, double-glazed and air-conditioned. Many rooms have
recently been refurbished and half the rooms are reserved for non-smokers.
24hr room service. Children up to 15 share parents' room free.
Banqueting/conference facilities for 450/500. Ask about occasional special
rates to include long-stay car parking and weekend tariff reductions.
Rooms 307. AMERICAN EXPRESS *Access, Diners, Visa.*

Glasgow Airport   Stakis Glasgow Airport   61%   £114

Tel 041-886 4100   Fax 041-885 2366   **H**
Inchman Road Renfrew Glasgow Airport Strathclyde PA4 5EJ   Map 3 B6

A modern hotel on the A8, some five minutes from the airport. Bedrooms
offer practical comforts, and nine suites accommodate up to 1000 for
conferences. *Rooms 141. Garden, golf-driving range.* AMERICAN EXPRESS *Access,
Diners, Visa.*

Glasgow Airport   Travel Inn   NEW   £43

Tel 041-842 1563   **L**
Whitecart Road Glasgow Airport Paisley Glasgow PA3 2TH   Map 3 B6

Close to Airport Terminal. 24hr check-in and meeting rooms. *Rooms 80.*
AMERICAN EXPRESS *Access, Diners, Visa.*

Glencarse   Newton House Hotel   58%   £80

Tel 073 886 250   Fax 073 886 717   **H**
Glencarse nr Perth Tayside PH2 7LX   Map 3 C5

Set back in gardens from the A85 four miles east of Perth, this is a
substantial double-fronted dower house dating from 1840 It's well kept
throughout, comfortable and genteel. There's a little lounge and a cocktail
bar, and bedrooms ranging from small singles to more roomy doubles and
twins. *Rooms 10. Garden, playground, news kiosk.* AMERICAN EXPRESS *Access,
Diners, Visa.*

Glenelg   Glenelg Inn   £72

Tel 059 982 273   Fax 059 982 373   **IR**

Glenelg by Kyle of Lochalsh Highlands IV40 8JR   Map 3 B4

It's a spectacular and somewhat precipitous drive to reach this old inn, idyllically set on the shore of Glenelg Bay, that has been sympathetically refurbished by local man Christopher Main. To a convivial, rustic bar have been added, within the original stable block, six spacious bedrooms individually decorated and furnished with antiques. Each has its own smart bathroom and a view over to Skye. The Master bedroom attracts a supplement, but is particularly well appointed with little in the way of modern paraphernalia to spoil the uncluttered homeliness. One room is above the bar and attracts a suitably lower tariff. Residents socialise after dinner in the Morning Room with its Victorian paintings and photos, green leather chesterfield, stag's head and various antiques and objets d'art – a comfortable retreat. Stay for two nights and there is a free excursion on one of the hotel's own boats – either a large motor yacht or a rigid inflatable; seven nights' stay earns a full day's Loch fishing along with other 'extras'. **Rooms** 6. *Garden, fishing, boat trips. Closed mid-Oct to Easter* (*bars open*), *except to party bookings. No credit cards.*

Restaurant   £50

The intimate dining room has a civilised air with candles and fresh flowers on the tables and a real fire on chilly evenings. Local seafood, venison and hill-bred lamb are the mainstays of the fixed-price menu. Typical main dishes might include Milanese lamb cutlets with a crispy lemon coating, monkfish with almonds, apple and cream, roasted Arnisdale venison in a rich gravy and salmon with a cornichon vinaigrette. Simpler starters (eggs florentine, smoked salmon, stuffed mushrooms, French onion soup) and tempting desserts such as crème renversé, fresh fruit en papillote and raspberry cheesecake, along with a cheeseboard offering "three very good cheeses". Straightforward snacks at lunchtime – it's worth building up an appetite for dinner… **Seats** 20. *D only 7.30-9. Set D £19.*

Glenrothes   Balgeddie House   65%   £97

Tel 0592 742511   Fax 0592 621702   **· H**

Balgeddie Way Glenrothes Fife KY6 3ET   Map 3 C5

Until recently surrounded by farmland, this 18th-century Georgian house was converted to a hotel in 1989 and is now part of a suburb of Glenrothes new town. Bedrooms on the first floor are superior and spacious, with fine modern bathrooms, those on the second floor are twins, with sloping ceilings. There's a choice of bars – cocktail for pre-dinner drinks, the Paddock serving bar lunches and suppers and the Lodge with machines and pool table – and a lounge. Outside there's a lawn the size of a football pitch and eight acres of landscaped gardens complete with palm trees. Children stay free in their parents' room. Functions/conferences for up to 70. **Rooms** 18. *Garden.* AMERICAN EXPRESS *Access, Diners, Visa.*

Glenrothes   Places of Interest

Glenrothes Tourist Information   Tel 0592 754954.
Kirkcaldy Tourist Information   Tel 0592 267775.
Adam Smith Theatre   Kirkcaldy Tel 0592 260498.
Falkland Palace & Garden (NT)   Tel 0337 57397.
Kirkcaldy Ice Rink   Tel 0592 52151.
Crystals Arena Ice Rink   Tel 0592 773774.
    Museums and Art Galleries
Burntisland Edwardian Fair   Tel 0592 260732.
Kirkcaldy Museum and Art Gallery   Tel 0592 260732.

| **Gourock** | **Stakis Gantock Hotel** | **64%** | **£101** |

Tel 0475 634671   Fax 0475 632490

Cloch Road Gourock Strathclyde PA15 1AR

H

Map 3 B5

Friendly staff, smart day rooms and well-equipped bedrooms including Executive suites. Fine views across the Clyde. Extensive banqueting and conference facilities, including two boardrooms, plus good leisure centre. *Rooms 99. Indoor swimming pool, gym, sauna, steam room, spa bath, solarium, floodlit tennis, children's playground.* AMERICAN EXPRESS *Access, Diners, Visa.*

| **Gourock** | **Places of Interest** |

Tourist Information   Tel 0475 39467.

| **Gretna Green** | **Forte Travelodge** | | **£45** |

Tel 0461 337566

Gretna Green Dumfries & Galloway CA6 5HQ

L

Map 4 C2

On the A74M northbound, 8 miles north of Carlisle on the main route to Glasgow, 2 miles north of Gretna. *Rooms 41.* AMERICAN EXPRESS *Access, Diners, Visa.*

| **Gullane** | **Greywalls Hotel** | **76%** | **£150** |

Tel 0620 842144   Fax 0620 842241

Muirfield Gullane Lothian EH31 2EG

HR

Map 3 C5

Built in 1901, Greywalls is one of the few examples of Lutyens' architecture north of the Border. In a lovely position next to Muirfield Golf Course, the house has a perfect unity of design. The Library is a very fine room with lightwood panelling, grand piano, 'His Master's Voice' gramophone and an open fire; to the north you glimpse the Firth of Forth, to the south Gertrude Jekyll's rose garden. There's a clubby bar and a delightful sun room. Bedrooms are generally of fine proportions and full of light; little personal touches like books and portable radios make the hotel a home from home. Enchanting cottage-style rooms in the lodge. Good breakfast, friendly service. On the A198 at the east end of Gullane village. *Rooms 22. Garden, croquet, tennis. Closed Nov-Mar.* AMERICAN EXPRESS *Access, Diners, Visa.*

Restaurant

£80

Paul Baron, here since 1990, is a careful chef, with neat presentation being one of his hallmarks; attention to detail (everything from bread to petits fours is home-made) is another, particularly in sourcing the good local beef and salmon that appears in dishes such as pan-fried mignons of beef topped with caramelised onions and a herb crust or simply grilled salmon served with sorrel butter. The dining room is delightful and has been recently refurbished; menus are organised daily and offer fixed-price, four-course meals with a choice of around four dishes at each stage. Red pimento terrine wrapped in Cumbrian air-dried ham with a shallot and plum tomato compote, followed by seafood casserole served in puff pastry with a saffron-infused white wine sauce and then délice of strawberries with strawberry sorbet might comprise a typical meal. Booking is essential for dinner. Traditional roast Sunday lunch. The French content on the easy-to-use wine list is excellent, the rest less so, and £30+ (including service) for a non-marque champagne is a bit steep! *Seats 50. Parties 12. Private Room 20. L 12.30-2 D 7.30-9. Set L £17 (Sun £20) Set D £33.*

| **Gullane** | **La Potinière** | **★** | **£75** |

Tel 0620 843214

Main Street Gullane Lothian EH31 2AA

R

Map 3 C5

A two-hander with Hilary Brown in the kitchen and David combining the role of host and waiter – they share the washing up! The downside to this is that one eats at a fixed hour from a no-choice menu and at the pace of the slowest diners (which can be a bit tedious if there is a large party) without even the dirty plates being removed until the whole room has finished. However, everything is more than compensated by Hilary's fine cooking with thoughtfully composed dishes brought together in well-balanced menus. Soup could be a cream of sweet peppers with orange, coming before a fish dish like fillets of sole layered with pistou on a bed of spinach with a sweet and sour sauce. Next comes the main dish, perhaps a supreme of pigeon with pearl barley and wild mushrooms or a leg of guinea fowl with an apricot stuffing; after which a salad is served. Then the day's cheese with a pud such as a soufflé glacé à l'orange or citron surprise (a soufflé-like topping over a tangy lemon curd base) to finish. Lunch follows the same format except that you have to choose between cheese and dessert. A splendid floral display (David's department) dominates the centre of the small, pretty dining room and bunches of dried flowers hang from rustic ceiling beams. It's a good idea to book well in advance, especially at weekends, but it's always worth trying at the last moment – on our last visit (anonymous of course) we managed to get a table at less than 24 hours' notice. The fabulous wine list has changed little – even the keen prices! – except for the new and enlarged champagne section that boasts ten *marques* under £30. No smoking. No credit cards. **Seats** *30. L at 1 D at 8. Closed L Fri & Sat, D Sun-Thur, all Wed, 25 & 26 Dec, 1 & 2 Jan, 1 week Jun, Oct. Set L £18.25 (£19.25 Sun) Set D £28.50. No credit cards.*

MARTELL

Harray Loch	Merkister Hotel	59%	£59
Tel 085 677 366 Fax 085 677 515			H
Harray Loch Orkney KW17 2LF			Map 2 C1

First and last a fishing hotel, with great sport on Loch Harray and three other lochs. The brown trout fishing is among the best in the world, and boats, outboards and ghillies can be arranged. Deep-freezing facilities are available, and smoking of the fish can be organised. Owner Angus MacDonald is a keen fisherman himself, and is always willing to give guidance, and his wife Elma runs the hotel with great charm. Centre of affairs is the bar, while a new feature is the conservatory built on to the front of the hotel. Bedrooms, all now en suite, are modest but well kept. Birdwatchers are also attracted here, and the hotel has a bird hide in the grounds. Ask for a map showing directions from Stromness ferry terminal when booking. **Rooms** *14. Garden, game fishing.* AMERICAN EXPRESS *Access, Visa.*

Helmsdale	Navidale House	60%	£65
Tel 043 12 258			H
Helmsdale Highland KW8 6JS			Map 2 C2

Beautifully situated in six acres of woods and gardens on the Moray Firth, this friendly former hunting lodge, now a favourite with anglers, is on the A9 just north of Helmsdale. The bar is small and cosy, the lounge rather old-fashioned. Bedrooms in the main house are pleasantly furnished, with period pieces and functional tiled bathrooms. Five rooms are in a lodge in the grounds. Children up to the age of 10 stay free in parents' room. **Rooms** *14. Garden, croquet, squash, game fishing. Closed Nov & Dec. Access, Visa.*

Ingliston	Norton House	66%	£120
Tel 031-333 1275 Fax 031-333 5305			H
Ingliston nr Edinburgh Lothian EH28 8LX			Map 3 C5

Set on the western outskirts of Edinburgh, conveniently located for the airport, and in its own parkland with sweeping lawns and tall trees, Norton House's grand Victorian origins are instantly clear. Inside, wood panelling and marble work continue the ambience created by the approach. The Oak Room bar is in the main building while the Tavern is in converted stables within the grounds. It has a parquet floor, pew seating and a regular clientele of locals. Bedrooms are comfortably furnished, well equipped and range from standard to suite. Families are well catered for, especially around Christmas and Easter. A Voyager hotel. *Rooms 47. Garden, croquet, outdoor play area.* AMERICAN EXPRESS *Access, Diners, Visa.*

Inverness   Bunchrew House   67%   £105

Tel 0463 234917   Fax 0463 710620   **H**

Bunchrew Inverness Highland IV3 6TA   Map 2 C3

A couple of miles out of town on the A682, Bunchrew House is a fine-looking Scottish baronial mansion set alongside the Beauly Firth in 20 acres of woodland. The bar and appealing, restful lounge both feature dark brown painted panelling and real fires in winter. About half the comfortable bedrooms have reproduction antique furniture while five more recently created rooms have good quality darkwood pieces. Individually decorated in a variety of pleasant fabrics, all rooms have mini-bars (although there is room service throughout the day and evening) and poly-cotton bedding. The atmosphere is relaxed and friendly with obliging staff. Beds are turned down at night. *Rooms 11. Garden, fishing. Closed 2 weeks Jan.* AMERICAN EXPRESS *Access, Visa.*

Inverness   Caledonian Hotel   69%   £99

Tel 0463 235181   Fax 0463 711206   **H**

33 Church Street Inverness Highland IV1 1DX   Map 2 C3

Alongside the river Ness, a smart city-centre hotel with good conference (for up to 350 delegates) and leisure facilities plus modern public rooms. Ample parking. Children free up to the age of 15 in parents' room. Jarvis Hotels. *Rooms 106. Indoor swimming pool, gym, sauna, spa bath, solarium, beauty salon, snooker.* AMERICAN EXPRESS *Access, Diners, Visa.*

Inverness   Culloden House   73%   £165

Tel 0463 790461   Fax 0463 792181   **HR**

Inverness Highland IV1 2NZ   Map 2 C3

An impressive mansion in Georgian style run since 1981 by resident owners Marjory and Ian McKenzie. History abounds in the house (Bonnie Prince Charlie once seized it), the 40 acres of lawns and parkland and the surrounding countryside. The traditional feel is preserved within the chandeliered hall, and in the grandly proportioned lounge and dining room with their ornate plasterwork, friezes and carved fireplace surrounds. Accommodation ranges from single rooms via standard twins and triples to king-size doubles, four-posters and twins with jacuzzis. Four stylish no-smoking suites are in the imposing Garden Mansion 200 yards from the main building (don't be alarmed if you find a little wild roe deer grazing outside your window in the morning when you wake up). No children under ten. *Rooms 23. Garden, tennis, sauna, solarium, snooker.* AMERICAN EXPRESS *Access, Diners, Visa.*

Restaurant   £80

Lunch in the elegant Adam Room is à la carte and dinner an inclusive affair of five courses. Michael Simpson's style combines Scottish country house and French, exemplified by chicken liver paté with oatcakes, grilled West Coast scallops glazed with a light onion and herb butter, and the speciality venison in pastry with port wine sauce. There's always an interesting vegetarian main course (Crowdie cheese and pine kernels in a filo pastry parcel in a pimento sauce) and some fruity, creamy desserts. The wine list, though not particularly user-friendly, has a good selection of half bottles and several good-value wines if you look carefully. *Seats 50. Private Room 35. L 12.30-2 D 7-9. Set D £32.50.*

Inverness   Dunain Park   69%   £120

Tel 0463 230512   Fax 0463 224532   **HR**

Inverness Highland IV3 6JN   **Map 2 C3**

Ann and Edward Nicoll's handsome Georgian hunting lodge stands in six
acres of gardens and woodland a mile from Inverness on the A82 road
to Loch Ness. Various styles of accommodation are available, top of the
range being six suites in the main building with spacious sitting rooms
and Italian marble bathrooms. Two rooms are in cottages in the
grounds. *Rooms 14. Garden, croquet, indoor swimming pool, sauna.
Closed 3 weeks Jan/Feb.* AMERICAN EXPRESS *Access, Diners, Visa.*

Restaurant   £65

The walled garden provides Ann with many vegetables, fruit and herbs for
use in the kitchen. Her cooking is Scottish with French influences, based
on seasonal local produce: mousseline of smoked haddock and whiting,
salmon baked in sea salt served with a white port, lime and ginger sauce,
terrine of chicken and guinea fowl layered with venison and pigeon,
Highland beef Wellington. A short light lunch menu is also available.
Sweets from the buffet. No smoking in the dining room. A choice of 85
malt whiskies puts the icing on the cake. *Seats 36. Parties 12. L 12.30-1.30
D 7-9 Set L £16.50.*

Inverness   Kingsmills Hotel   67%   £125

Tel 0463 237166   Fax 0463 225208   **H**

Culcabock Road Inverness Highland IV2 3LP   **Map 2 C3**

One mile from the centre of town (next to Inverness golf course) and
surrounded by inspiring countryside, the 18th-century house was
extensively remodelled to create a modern hotel. Top of the range
of bedrooms are seven grander 'Presidential' rooms. One room equipped
for disabled guests; thirteen reserved for non-smokers. Children up to 14
share parents' room free; 11 family rooms available, five with bunk beds,
six larger rooms with extra beds. Six self-catering 'holiday villas' are
100yds from the hotel. The leisure club includes an informal refreshment
area. Conference facilities for up to 60, banqueting up to 80. 24hr room
service. Swallow Hotels. *Rooms 79. Garden, indoor swimming pool,
mini-gym, sauna, steam room, spa bath, solarium, beauty & hair salon
(aromatherapy by appointment), 3-hole pitch & putt, children's playground.*
AMERICAN EXPRESS *Access, Diners, Visa.*

Inverness   Mercury Hotel   62%   £102

Tel 0463 239666   Fax 0463 711145   **H**

Millburn Road Inverness Highland IV2 3TR   **Map 2 C3**

Modern, purpose-built hotel set at the foot of the North Kessoch Bridge,
which connects Inverness with the Black Isle. The fifth floor has recently
been upgraded to Executive status. Banqueting and conferences (for up to
230) are a large part of the Mercury's business. Parking for 150 cars.
Mount Charlotte Thistle. *Rooms 118. Garden.* AMERICAN EXPRESS *Access,
Diners, Visa.*

Inverness   Places of Interest

Tourist Information   Tel 0463 234353.
Eden Court Theatre   Tel 0463 221718.
Cawdor Castle   Tel 066 77 615.
Culloden Battlefield and Museum   Tel 0463 790607 *7 miles.*
St Andrew's Cathedral   Tel 0463 233535.
Inverness Museum and Art Gallery   Tel 0463 237114.
Inverness Ice Centre   Tel 0463 235711.
Clan Tartan Centre   Holm Woolen Mills Tel 0463 223311.

Inverurie   Thainstone House   76%   £116

HR

Tel 0467 621643   Fax 0467 625084

Inverurie nr Aberdeen Grampian AB51 5NT   Map 3 D4

An extended 19th-century Palladian mansion with grand portal entrance
from which broad stairs lead up to the main public areas. These include
a galleried reception area, elegant lounge with Adam-style ceiling, and
comfortable cocktail bar which in winter boasts a real fire in its black
marble fireplace. There is a more pubby, informal bar on the ground floor.
Bedrooms come with reproduction mahogany furniture, good armchairs
and a variety of stylish, often rather masculine, decorative schemes although
rather surprisingly there are no pictures on the walls. Extras include
a decanter of sherry and a bottle of mineral water left at the bedside when
beds are turned down in the evening. Smart bathrooms are equipped with
good showers above tubs which have a convenient thermostatically
controlled filling system. Towelling robes and large bathsheets are
provided but shelf space is limited. Well turned-out staff offer high-quality
service with friendly smiles. Extensive 24hr room service. No dogs.
*Rooms 46. Garden, indoor swimming pool, gym, spa bath, steam room, snooker,
helipad.* AMERICAN EXPRESS *Access, Diners, Visa.*

Simpsons   £80

A long Georgian-style room, with dark blue, damask-effect walls and
elaborate drapes at tall windows, provides a suitably sophisticated setting
for chef Bill Gibb's stylish cooking. The main four-course dinner menu
might include a light scallop mousse, game terrine in a Grand Marnier jelly
and roast monkfish with stir-fry vegetables and a sweet pepper sauce
amongst the starters followed by a choice of soups before mains like breast
of duck on a bed of spinach with a calvados and crème de cassis sauce, pan-
fried turbot with a horseradish crust in a lemon grass sauce with
langoustines or a delicious fricassee of rabbit served in a pastry case with
winter vegetables and a champagne and coriander sauce. Puds are nicely
varied and there is a good selection of Scottish and French cheeses. The less
expensive three-course table d'hote menu is not available on Friday and
Saturday although there is sometimes a £22.50 option on theme nights.
The good-value lunch menu is largely composed of dishes from the dinner
menu. No children under 9 at night. No smoking. *Seats 42.
Private Room 24. L 12-2 D 7-9.30. Set L £14.50 (Set Sun L £16.50)
Set D £19.50 (except Fri & Sat).*

If we recommend meals in a hotel or inn a separate entry is made for its
restaurant.

Irvine   Hospitality Inn   68%   £85

H

Tel 0294 74272   Fax 0294 77287

46 Annick Road Irvine Strathclyde KA11 4LD   Map 4 A1

A Moorish theme pervades the central concourse, lounge and bar. Superior
bedrooms are round the atrium and the pool. Children up to 16 stay free
in parents' room, paying for meals as taken. Conference facilities for up to
320, banqueting to 220. Full secretarial service available. Ample car
parking. Mount Charlotte Thistle. *Rooms 127. Indoor swimming pool, spa
bath, golf (9-hole), putting.* AMERICAN EXPRESS *Access, Diners, Visa.*

Irvine   Place of Interest

The Galleon Ice Rink   Kilmarnock. Tel 0563 24014 *10 miles.*

Johnstone   Forte Travelodge   NEW   £45

Tel 0800 850 950   **L**

A737 Johnstone nr Paisley Strathclyde   **Map 3 B6**

Opening winter '94. AMERICAN EXPRESS *Access, Diners, Visa.*

Kelso   Ednam House   64%   £74

Tel 0573 224168   Fax 0573 226319   **H**

Bridge Street Kelso Borders TD5 7HT   **Map 5 D1**

A town-centre Georgian house with lawns reaching down to the River
Tweed, a homely open fire, sporting paintings, cosy armchairs and waders
and waterproofs in the hall. It's a popular fishing hotel, and outside high
season the large majority of guests are salmon fishers (Feb/Mar &
Oct/Nov). The bars (where lunches are served Monday to Saturday) are
convivial and the lounges are quietly traditional. Well-kept bedrooms
match modern comforts with old-fashioned courtesies. Children under
8 share parents' room free of charge. *Rooms 32. Garden, croquet, fishing,
helipad. Closed 24 Dec-12 Jan. Access, Visa.*

Kelso   Sunlaws House   72%   £134

Tel 0573 450331   Fax 0573 450611   **H**

Heiton Kelso Borders TD5 8JZ   **Map 5 D1**

An imposing Scottish country house three miles from Kelso on the A698,
at the south end of Heiton village, offering peace, quiet and plenty
of sporting activities. Log fires keep things cosy in the entrance hall, the
elegantly draped drawing room, the library bar and the central hall with
its ornate carved wooden fireplace. The two best bedrooms also have log
fires, along with antique furnishings. Other main-house rooms use good-
quality darkwood pieces, while those in the converted stable block tend
to have fitted units. Bathrooms are decorated to match their individually
styled bedrooms where beds are turned down at night. The hotel has its
own trout loch, and various sporting activities can be arranged for guests.
Rooms 22. Garden, croquet, tennis, clay-pigeon shooting, game fishing.
AMERICAN EXPRESS *Access, Diners, Visa.*

Kelso   Places of Interest

Tourist Information   Tel 0573 23464.
Tait Concert Hall   Tel 0450 75991.
Kelso Museum   Tel 0573 25470.
   Historic Houses, Castles and Gardens
Floors Castle   Tel 0573 23333.
Mellerstain   Gordon. Tel 0573 81225.

Kenmore   Kenmore Hotel   62%   £97

Tel 0887 830205   Fax 0887 830262   **H**

Kenmore Tayside PH15 2NU   **Map 3 C5**

Reputedly Scotland's oldest inn (1572), the Kenmore is a magnet for
anglers (they have two miles of private beats on the Tay, which flows past
the inn). The various cosy public rooms, one called the Poets Parlour
to commemorate a visit by Robert Burns, are made even more inviting
by real fires. Bedrooms, 14 in a Victorian gatehouse opposite, vary
considerably in decor and furnishings. The hotel, which recently changed
hands, is situated at the east end of Loch Tay on the A827. Guests can use
the facilities of the nearby Kenmore Country Club. *Rooms 39. Game
fishing, tennis.* AMERICAN EXPRESS *Access, Visa.*

Kentallen of Appin — Ardsheal House — 64% — £160*
Tel 063 174 227   Fax 063 174 342 — HR
Kentallen of Appin Highland PA38 4BX — Map 3 B4

A 1½-mile private drive that borders Ardsheal Bay and Loch Linnhe finds
this beautifully located 18th-century house. A motley collection of antiques
and period pieces furnishes the various small, lived-in day rooms – oak-
panelled entrance hall, TV lounge (there are more in bedrooms), library
lounge, pine-boarded snooker room and tiny bar in what used to be the
butler's pantry – and bedrooms that have something of an Edwardian feel.
New owners Neil and Philippa Sutherland (actually 'old' owners as the
house was formerly in their family for three generations) are not due
to take over personally until the end of 1995; in the meantime things will
carry on much as before, with the present chef George Kelso in the kitchen
and his wife Michelle as manageress. Located on the A828 five miles south
of Ballachulish bridge between Glencoe and Appin. *Half-board terms
only. *Rooms 13. Garden, tennis, snooker. Closed mid Jan–mid Feb, and mid
week during winter months except Christmas and New Year.* AMERICAN EXPRESS®
Access, Visa.

Restaurant — £80

George Kelso's excellent cooking continues here. There's a garden feel
in the conservatory dining room, and much use is made of the
vegetables, herbs and fruits that come from the two-acre kitchen garden.
Seafood, naturally, features on the daily-changing menus – there are always
two choices for each course – perhaps pressed terrine of salmon, lemon sole
and leeks served with a champagne and caviar sauce or a tartlet of local
mussels, asparagus and courgettes served with basil cream sauce to start,
followed by soup (cullen skink), roast saddle of local venison with braised
lentils and smoked bacon, or braised fillet of halibut with sherry vinegar.
It's hard to choose a dessert when such delights as caramelised lemon tart,
bread and butter pudding or banana and rum soufflé are on offer. Those
that cannot make up their mind can settle for fresh fruit or cheese! Some
keen prices on the wine list, which has a good selection from the New
World and plenty of half bottles. In fine weather there are a couple
of tables on the lawn, especially suitable for light lunches. No smoking
in the dining room. *Seats 40. Parties 20. L 12-1.45 D 8 for 8.30.*
Set L £17.50 Set D £32.50.

Kentallen of Appin — Holly Tree — 65% — £76
Tel 063 174 292   Fax 063 174 345 — H
Kentallen of Appin Highland PA38 4BY — Map 3 B4

The Holly Tree has evolved from a former railway station, and retains
some of the more interesting features of that original incarnation. However,
the level of comfort and hospitality available nowadays far exceeds
anything any railways board ever offered! Comfortable seats and generous
fabrics and furnishings make this a delightful spot from which to enjoy the
splendid views of Loch Linnhe and the hillside behind. Children under
5 stay free in parents' room; families well catered for. *Rooms 10. Garden.*
Access, Visa.

Kilchrenan — Ardanaiseig — 74% — £160
Tel 08663 333   Fax 08663 222 — HR
Kilchrenan by Taynuilt Strathclyde PA35 1HG — Map 3 B5

There's ten miles of winding single-track road (an attractive drive in itself)
to negotiate before reaching the noted rhododendron – and azalea-filled
woodland gardens that surround this Scottish baronial-style mansion
gloriously set on the edge of Loch Awe. Day rooms include a grand,
elegantly proportioned drawing room and cosy library bar – both with
real log fires when it's chilly. Bedrooms – the most spacious have either

loch or garden views – are individually decorated, some more recently than others, and furnished with antiques. Extras include mineral water, fresh fruit and bathrobes. Bathrooms, all with hand showers over plastic tubs, offer good-quality toiletries but smallish towels. No children under eight. *Rooms 14. Garden, croquet, tennis, fishing, hotel boat, games room, snooker, riding, helipad. Closed Oct-Apr.* AMERICAN EXPRESS® *Access, Diners, Visa.*

Restaurant   £80

New chef Simon Bailey continues the essentially simple style, with carefully prepared dishes such as smoked salmon with horseradish cream, loin of spring lamb with a rosemary jus, fillet of beef with Madeira sauce, grilled supreme of salmon, smooth chicken liver parfait, and breast of corn-fed chicken served on creamed leeks. Good cheeses served with celery, crackers and grapes. The table d'hote dinner comprises five courses (with only alternative choices) and there is a short list of grills. Splendid views of the Loch from the dark red dining room. Traditional Sunday lunch includes roast sirloin of Highland beef with Yorkshire pudding and a rich onion gravy. No children under eight after 7.30. No smoking. *Seats 30. Parties 8. L 12-2.30 D 7.30-9. Set L £12.50 Set D £30.*

Kilchrenan   Taychreggan Hotel   66%   £67

Tel 08663 211   Fax 08663 244   **HR**

Kilchrenan by Taynuilt Strathclyde PA35 1HQ   **Map 3 B5**

With a glorious location on the edge of Loch Awe, this former drovers' inn (they spent the night here before swimming their cattle across the Loch) was modestly extended in the 1970s to enclose a charming cobbled courtyard. Refurbishment has spread from the lounges to some of the bedrooms, best of which is the Johnson Room with a four-poster bed and an excellent loch view. In the bar is a "shamefully large selection" of finest malt whiskies. Hill walking is a favourite pastime, and there are 13 munros (peaks over 3000ft) in the vicinity. No children under 14. *Rooms 15. Garden, croquet, coarse and game fishing, boating.* AMERICAN EXPRESS® *Access, Visa.*

Restaurant   £70

Hugh Cocker prepares both à la carte and fixed-price menus for the restaurant, where antique tables are set against a collection of modern paintings. The five-course menu could start with chicken liver parfait and proceed via soup or a sorbet to a main course such as mignons of beef with pleurotte mushrooms. A sweet is followed by cheese, then coffee and petits fours. One of the chef's specialities is darne of Mull salmon grilled, with anchovy butter or *sauce vierge*. No children under 12. No smoking. *Seats 36. L 12.30-2.15 D 7.30-8.45. Set L £14/£17 Set D £15/ £19/£26.50.*

Kildrummy   Kildrummy Castle   70%   £120

Tel 09755 71288   Fax 09755 71345   **H**

Kildrummy Alford Grampian AB33 8RA   **Map 3 C4**

Built in 1900 as a rather grandiose castellated country house, the hotel has a lovely setting overlooking the ruins of a 13th-century castle, and gardens which feature specimen trees, alpine plants and rare shrubs. (Grampian has more than 70 castles, many just a short drive from the hotel.) The baronial entrance hall contrasts with the Adam elegance of the sunny drawing room. Two carved lions act as sentries on a splendidly ornate staircase which leads to the bedrooms. These are less grand than the day rooms but are comfortable, spacious and warm; an ongoing programme of refurbishment continues to improve the rooms – those in the attic with sloping ceilings are charming. Children up to 14 stay free in their parents' room and are offered their own menu in the lounge, plus an outdoor playground. Long-serving owner Thomas Hanna strongly motivates his staff, who are outgoing and friendly. Trout and salmon fishing are available on a 3½-mile stretch of the river Don, and local centres organise shooting, stalking, riding and pony trekking. *Rooms 15. Garden, snooker, fishing, children's playground. Closed Jan.* AMERICAN EXPRESS *Access, Visa.*

Kilfinan   Kilfinan Hotel   £72

Tel 070 082 201   Fax 070 082 205   **IR**

Kilfinan by Tighnabruaich Strathclyde PA21 2AP   Map 3 B5

A delightful Swiss/Scottish couple, Rolf and Lynne Mueller, run this remote white-stoned coaching inn amid magnificent scenery on the east shore of Loch Fyne, reached down a single-track road (B8000, off the A886) between Strachur and Tighnabruaich. The Dunoon ferry is less than an exhilarating hour's drive across the moors. Purchased about ten years ago by the Laird of Kilfinan, so that it would not fall into the hands of developers, the inn has exclusive access to beautiful Kilfinan Bay (about 20 minutes walk through the garden and the estate) and is well placed for traditional outdoor pursuits. Two bars, neither of them a lounge, are both cosy and characterful with log fires, and the bedrooms – some antique-furnished – offer all the usual little luxuries, including good-quality toiletries in the carpeted en-suite bathrooms; one room overlooks St Finnan's graveyard, a surprisingly pleasant view. Incidentally, don't be alarmed by the brown peat-coloured water – 'at least it hasn't been filtered seven times by humans!'. Good walking country begins right outside the door. *Rooms 11. Garden, fishing, snooker, helipad. Closed Feb.* AMERICAN EXPRESS *Access, Visa.*

Restaurant   £70

Crisp table linen, cutlery and glassware gleaming in the candle-light, and a glowing log fire make the twin dining rooms particularly appealing. Rolf brings Swiss precision into his cooking, exemplified in the fixed-price-only dinner menu that offers a small choice at each of the four courses: a recent menu offered fillet of rabbit set on spinach with a Madeira sauce, neep brose, langoustine tails in a garlic and herb sauce, and lime and rum syllabub or a selection of local cheeses to finish, plus good coffee served with petits fours. 3-course Sunday lunch always includes a traditional roast; lighter lunches are served in the Lamont Room and the Lounge. Outdoor eating for 20 in the garden in good weather. *Seats 22. Parties 10. Private Room 24. L Sun only 12-2 D 7.30-9.30. Set Sun L £12.50 Set D £25.*

Note that all telephone numbers with area codes starting with 0 will start 01 from 16 April 1995.

Killiecrankie   Killiecrankie Hotel   64%   £138*

Tel 0796 473220   Fax 0796 472451   **H**

Killiecrankie by Pitlochry Tayside PH16 5LG   Map 3 C4

Four acres of landscaped gardens overlook the river Garry and the Pass of Killiecrankie (turn off the A9 north of Pitlochry). There's something of the feeling of an inn about the little hotel, which was built as a manse in 1840. The reception hall and small panelled bar (which has a suntrap extension) have displays of stuffed animals and an upstairs lounge offers various board games plus a variety of books as distractions. Pine-furnished bedrooms are fresh and bright. Bar menu for informal lunches and suppers. *Half-board terms. **Rooms 10. Garden, croquet. Closed Jan & Feb.** Access, Visa.*

Killiecrankie   Place of Interest

Blair Castle   Tel 079 681 207.

Kilmarnock Forte Travelodge NEW £45

Tel 0563 73810 L

A71 Kilmarnock Strathclyde Map 4 A1

Rooms 40. AMERICAN EXPRESS® *Access, Diners, Visa.*

Kilmore Glenfeochan House 70% £124

Tel 063 177 273　Fax 063 177 624 HR

Kilmore Oban Strathclyde PA34 4QR Map 3 B5

Built in 1875 (though some parts are probably much older), the house
stands in a beautiful, peaceful spot at the head of Loch Feochan, five miles
south of Oban, on a 350-acre estate of hills, lochs, rivers and farmland. The
eight-acre garden contains a Victorian arboretum with over 100
rhododendrons. Inside, all is spick and span, from the entrance hall and
stairway featuring pitch pine to the drawing room with a fine moulded
ceiling and complementary antiques. Bedrooms have plain walls, floral
curtains and more antiques. TVs and radios are provided, but no phones;
no smoking. The Tulip Room has an en-suite round bathroom in the
turret. Self-catering accommodation is available in the farmhouse.
No children under ten. No dogs. *Rooms 3. Garden, fishing. Closed Nov-Feb.
Access, Visa.*

Restaurant £70

Guests gather for dinner at 8 and non-residents can join them by prior
arrangement. Patricia Baber is an excellent cook and her short dinner
menus (discussed at breakfast time) make as much use as possible of produce
from the estate or local sources: salmon is served fresh or cured
traditionally and smoked over oak, and other favourites include Jura
venison, lobster, and guinea fowl roasted and served with a damson and gin
sauce. *Seats 10. D only at 8. Set D £30.*

Kilwinning Montgreenan Mansion House Hotel 70% £92

Tel 0294 557733　Fax 0294 585397 H

Montgreenan Estate Torranyard by Kilwinning Strathclyde KA13 7QZ Map 3 B6

The Mansion House was built in 1817 by one Dr Robert Glasgow, and
once completed it was described as 'a very desirable residence'. Current
owners the Dobson family believe this still to be true, as do their many
returning regulars. It stands in 45 acres of gardens and grounds (four miles
north of Irvine on the A736) and many period features, including marble
and brass fireplaces and decorative plasterwork, have been retained. Day
rooms are of quite grand proportions, the lounge-library being particularly
appealing. There are several conference rooms (maximum capacity 100).
Bedrooms, furnished with reproduction pieces or antiques, range from
standard singles to suites. Children up to 12 stay free in parents' room.
Rooms 21. Garden, croquet, tennis, 5 practice golf holes, putting, snooker.
AMERICAN EXPRESS® *Access, Diners, Visa.*

Kilwinning Place of Interest

Brodick Castle, Garden and Country Park　Isle of Arran. Tel 0770 2202
via ferry from Ardrossan.

Kinclaven by Stanley Ballathie House 74% £150

Tel 0250 883268　Fax 0250 883396 HR

Kinclaven by Stanley Tayside PH1 4QN Map 3 C5

Built in 1850 in the baronial style, Ballathie was a private residence until
1971 when it became a hotel – it is still in the same safe hands today. The
lawns slope down to the edge of the River Tay and the house is set at the

heart of its own 15,000 acre estate yet it's only about 20 minutes from
Perth. Some fine ceilings and marble fireplaces feature in the numerous,
comfortable and stylishly decorated day rooms that include an elegantly
proportioned drawing room, clubby leather-furnished bar and spacious
inner hall from which a grand oak staircase leads to the bedrooms. These
vary considerably in size from large master rooms to a few compact singles
amongst the standard rooms but all are individually decorated to the same
high standard and all are equally well appointed. Banqueting/conference
facilities for 60/120. *Rooms 37. Garden, tennis, fishing, putting, shooting.
Closed 25 & 26 Dec.* AMERICAN EXPRESS *Access, Diners, Visa.*

Restaurant   £70

Wonderful views across the River Tay from the elegant high-windowed
dining room. The daily-changing set menus often feature local and Scottish
ingredients, though influences are drawn from further afield: marinated
brill in Oriental spices, ratatouille and coriander samosas with a mixed leaf
salad, warm salad of wood pigeon with chanterelles, smoked bacon and
a sherry vinegar dressing, steamed fillet of halibut with saffron noodles,
asparagus and a shellfish sauce. Finish with nougatine wafers with dark
chocolate mousse and crème fraiche. Lunch brings a good value à la carte
during the week and a fixed-price menu on Sunday. Chef Kevin
MacGillivray is happy to suggest special menus at lunch or dinner for party
bookings. Quite fair prices on a sensible wine list. No smoking. *Seats 60.
Parties 14. Private Room 32. L 12-2 D 7-9. Set L (Sun only) £12.75
Set D £22.59/£25.*

Kingussie   The Cross   £70
Tel 0540 661166   Fax 0540 661080   **RR**
Tweed Mill Brae Ardbroilach Road Kingussie Highland PH21 1HX   Map 3 C4

From the traffic lights in Kingussie, travel uphill along Ardbroilach Road
for 250m; then turn left down Tweed Mill Brae to find Tony and Ruth
Hadley's converted old tweed mill by the River Gynack. White-painted
rough stone walls and a timbered ceiling contrast with immaculately crisp
white linen and luxurious table settings in the cleverly lit dining room.
Ruth's sympathetic and refined use of the best of Scottish produce is evident
in the limited-choice, fixed-price dinner (four courses during the week and
seven on Saturday's 'Gastronomic Menu') that might include West Coast
seafood salad (with asparagus, scallops, prawns and monkfish) or game
sausage with onion confit, then capsicum and tomato soup, followed
by saddle of mountain hare, fillet of Aberdeen Angus beef or poached
Lochinver turbot with dill and grain mustard sauce; finally, good Scottish
cheeses or the likes of poached pears with a chocolate fudge sauce and
honey and cinnamon ice cream, or baked lime cheesecake. Home hot-
smoked salmon, venison 'francatelli' and chocolate whisky 'laird' are
considered specialities. Vegetarians should notify in advance. Past winner
of our Cellar of the Year, the current wine list offers fabulous drinking
at very fair prices. Germany and the New World are well-represented
alongside France – some guidance notes, but ask Tony Hadley for advice.
Outdoor eating for 12 on a terrace overlooking the river. No children
under 12. No smoking. *Seats 28. L 12.30-2 D 7-9 Closed Tues, 1-27 Dec,
5 Jan-1 Mar. Set D £27.50 (Sat £35). Access, Visa.* MARTELL

Rooms   £150*

Upstairs, beyond a resident's lounge that successfully mixes antiques with
Scandinavian-style seating, are nine individually styled bedrooms that
generally combine pine and antique furniture to good effect. Good
bathrooms, mostly with bidet and separate shower cubicle in additon to the
tub, boast large towels and good-quality toiletries. No TVs. No smoking
in the bedrooms, only in the lounge. The waterside terrace makes a good
spot for Continental breakfast that comes with lovely home-made jams.
No dogs. *Half-board terms only. Garden.

Kingussie   Places of Interest

Tourist Information   Tel 0540 661297.
Kincraig Highland Wildlife Park   Tel 0540 651270.
Waltzing Waters   Newtonmore Tel 0540 673752.

Kinlochbervie   Kinlochbervie Hotel   64%   £84

Tel 0971 521275   Fax 0971 521438   **H**
Kinlochbervie by Lairg Highland IV27 4RP   Map 2 B2

Almost at the northernmost tip of mainland Scotland 47 miles from Lairg,
Kinlochbervie is a modern hotel set high up on a hill, boasting splendid
seaward views. Six bedrooms (and a first-floor residents' lounge crammed
with literature for walkers and fishermen) also benefit from the aspect. All
rooms have showers as well as baths. A convivial bar and bistro adjacent
are popular with locals. No smoking in the restaurant. Parking for 40 cars.
Rooms 14. *Sea fishing and loch fishing. Closed 1 Nov-31 Mar.*
AMERICAN EXPRESS *Access, Diners, Visa.*

Kinross   Granada Lodge   £51

Tel 0577 64646   Fax 0577 64108   **L**
M90 Junction 6 Kinross Tayside KY13 7NQ   Map 3 C5

Rooms 35. AMERICAN EXPRESS *Access, Diners, Visa.*

Kinross   Windlestrae Hotel   62%   £95

Tel 0577 863217   Fax 0577 864733   **H**
The Muirs Kinross Tayside KY13 7AS   Map 3 C5

Windlestrae – its name is derived from 'tall grasses swaying gently in the
breeze by Loch Leven' – is a relaxing retreat set in landscaped gardens,
offering a warm welcome from Terry and Jean Doyle. The lounges (one
split-level) are comfortable, as are the bedrooms, while the leisure club
is equipped to a high standard. Conferences/banquets for up to 250; parking
for 80. *Rooms* 45. *Garden, indoor swimming pool, gym, sauna, steam room, spa
bath, solarium, beauty and hair salon.* AMERICAN EXPRESS *Access, Diners, Visa.*

Kirkmichael   Log Cabin Hotel   59%   £66

Tel 0250 881288   Fax 0250 881402   **H**
Kirkmichael Tayside PH10 7NB   Map 3 C4

A mecca for outdoor activists (fishing, shooting, stalking and walking –
bring your camera!). The hotel is built of Norwegian pine logs and stands
half a mile from A924 between Pitlochry and Blairgowrie. Quite modest
accommodation (TVs on request), but in keeping with the surroundings.
Rooms 13. *Garden, games room, snooker, game fishing, shooting, craft shop.*
AMERICAN EXPRESS *Access, Diners, Visa.*

Kirknewton   Dalmahoy Hotel, Golf & Country Club   78%   £123

Tel 031-333 1845   Fax 031-333 3203   **HR**
Kirknewton Lothian EH27 8EB   Map 3 C6

Situated by the Pentland Hills, seven miles west of Edinburgh just off the
A71, surrounded by two mature golf courses and with a well-equipped
leisure centre, Dalmahoy is not only conveniently placed but also offers
plenty of diversions. The imposing house has been carefully restored to its
original Georgian splendour but the bedrooms enjoy every modern
comfort. Banqueting/conference facilities for up to 190, parking for up to
400. Children up to the age of 15 accommodated free in parents' room.
Informal eating in the poolside Terrace restaurant. Country Club Hotels.
Rooms 116. *Garden, 18-hole golf courses, putting, tennis, indoor swimming*

pool, squash, sauna, solarium, snooker, gym, spa bath, beautician, coffee shop (9.30am-10pm). AMERICAN EXPRESS *Access, Diners, Visa.*

Pentland Restaurant £70

Chef Gary Bates offers a set menu in the stately dining room, but there's plenty of choice at each course – with plenty of supplementary prices. Try a starter of West Coast seafood with a white wine sauce and chives, roast local wood pigeon garnished with a warm shallot and saffron vinaigrette, and finish with a baked apple and frangipane galette or a selection of farmhouse cheeses. Wines are fairly priced, mostly from Europe. *Seats 120. Parties 20. L 12-2 D 7-9.45. Closed L Sat. Set L £14.50 (Sun £13.95) Set D £23.50.*

Kirknewton   Place of Interest

Epsom Polo Club Dalmohay Estate Office. Tel 031-333 1331.

Kyle of Lochalsh   Lochalsh Hotel   63%   £87
Tel 0599 4202   Fax 0599 4881   **H**
Ferry Road Kyle of Lochalsh Highland IV40 8AF   Map 2 B3

A privately owned, white-painted building opposite the ferry terminal and looking over the sea to Skye. Beauty spots abound locally, and a day's sightseeing can conclude agreeably with a dram or two in the cocktail bar. Bedrooms are fresh, bright and comfortable. *Rooms 38. Garden.* AMERICAN EXPRESS *Access, Diners, Visa.*

Kyle of Lochalsh   Places of Interest

Tourist Information   Tel 0599 4276.
Eilean Donan Castle   Wester Ross. Tel 059 985 202.
Lochalsh Woodland Garden   Tel 059981 219.

Langbank   Gleddoch House   68%   £130
Tel 0475 540711   Fax 0475 540201   **H**
Langbank Strathclyde PA14 6YE   Map 3 B5

The large windows of Gleddoch House look out on to a 360-acre estate and beautiful countryside over to the Clyde, and inside there's plenty to please the eye too. In the main lounge area there are leather easy chairs in which to relax, and dado panelling and more leather chairs give a period feel to the baize-lined bar, which offers a hundred different brands of whisky. The rooms are all named after Scottish birds, each engraved on the door-plate. Children under 12 stay free in parents' room. Banqueting/conference facilities for 120/150. *Rooms 33. Garden, squash, sauna, snooker, golf (18), riding, fishing, helipad.* AMERICAN EXPRESS *Access, Diners, Visa.*

Lerwick   Shetland Hotel   62%   £78
Tel 0595 5515   Fax 0595 5828   **H**
Holmsgarth Road Lerwick Shetland ZE1 0PW   Map 2 D2

Close to the town centre and overlooking the harbour (where the ferries from Aberdeen dock), the Shetland is a skilfully designed modern hotel that caters well for both the summer tourist and year-round business. Bedrooms are uniformly light and spacious, with private bathrooms throughout. There is a bright, comfortable bar and an impressive function hall. Banqueting facilities available for up to 200 and conferences for 300 delegates. *Rooms 64. Garden.* AMERICAN EXPRESS *Access, Diners, Visa.*

Lerwick   Places of Interest

Tourist Information   Tel 0595 3434.

Letham   Fernie Castle   60%   £70

Tel 0337 81381   Fax 0337 81422   **H**

Letham by Cupar Fife KY7 7RU   **Map 3 D4**

Set in 25 acres of woodland grounds alongside the A914, the original 1300s
L-shaped castle has been altered and extended in most centuries since.
Public rooms include a rough-stone vaulted cocktail bar in the oldest part
of the building and a small, comfortable first-floor residents lounge in the
Georgian section. Modestly comfortable bedrooms divide roughly 50:50
between 'large' and 'small' rooms, six of the latter with shower and
WC only, mostly furnished with G-Plan pieces and decorated in a variety
of styles. Newish owners are about to begin a progressive programme
of bedroom refurbishment. *Rooms 15.* AMERICAN EXPRESS *Access, Visa.*

Linlithgow   Champany Inn   ★   £100

Tel 050 683 4532/4388   Fax 050 683 4302   **R**

Champany Linlithgow Lothian EH49 7LU   **Map 3 C5**

Quite simply, you'll not find better Aberdeen Angus beef than here,
provided and cut to order by butcher Nigel Best, and hung on the bone
in the restaurant's own chill rooms for at least three weeks. Clive and Anne
Davidson's restaurant is situated 2 miles north-east of Linlithgow where the
A904 meets the A803. The buildings at Champany corner date from the
16th century, the time of Mary Queen of Scots, born two miles away
at Linlithgow Palace. Whether you choose from the charcoal grill – cuts
are on display, and steaks can be cut to your own specification and
charged by the ounce – or one of the fixed-price menus, remember that
lovely old saying "the nearer the bone the sweeter the meat". In any event,
there is no substitute for quality, be it a salmon bagger (thick cut sirloin
with a pouch of smoked salmon), T-bone, entrecote, or even lamb
in season, all mouth-watering examples of Scottish produce at its best. You
could also indulge in seafood specialities such as Shetland salmon hollandaise
or lobster (from the restaurant's seawater pool), and for a starter try the
home-smoked salmon, local oysters, or a prawn bisque. If there's any room
left for a dessert the sweet trolley features cheesecake, crème brulée,
chocolate mousse and fresh fruit tart as well as fresh fruits and a variety
of home-made ice creams, or else try the superb Stilton with home-made
oatcakes. On the fantastic and fairly-priced wine list (past winner of Cellar
of the Year) there are inexpensive own-label house wines, the best South
African selection in the country and burgundies to suit every taste and
pocket. You can eat outside in the garden in fine weather. No children
under eight. *Seats 55. Parties 14. L 12.30-2 D 7-10. Closed L Sat, all Sun,
25 Dec, 1 Jan. Set L £13.75/£18.25 Set D £27.50/£35.* AMERICAN EXPRESS
Access, Diners, Visa.

Linlithgow   Champany Inn Chop & Ale House   £50

Tel 050 683 4532   **R**

Champany Linlithglow Lothian EH49 7LU   **Map 3 C5**

With the installation of a new purpose-built kitchen due for completion
by the end of 1994, you can see the chefs at work when you walk into this
much less formal eaterie, where the same outstanding Aberdeen Angus
steaks are served (though less expensive and cut a bit smaller) as at its sister
restaurant, together with various burgers, deep-fried Scottish prawn tails
(scampi), chargrilled grain-fed chicken and a cold buffet with help-yourself
salad bar. For afters go for the home-made, hot malted waffles
or Champany's own cheesecake served with apricot purée. Ten tables set
in a courtyard for alfresco dining. Own label wines. *Seats 46. L 12-2 (Sat &
Sun to 2.30) D 6.30-10 (from 6 Sat). Closed 25 Dec & 1 Jan.* AMERICAN EXPRESS
Access, Diners, Visa.

Linlithgow   Places of Interest

Tourist Information Tel 0506 844600.
Linlithgow Palace Tel 0506 842896.

Lochinver   Inver Lodge Hotel   70%   £120

Tel 057 14 496   Fax 057 14 395   **H**
Lochinver Highland IV27 4LU   Map 2 B2

Built at the beginning of 1988, the hotel is set high above the village
in a scene of exceptional peace and beauty. It's an ideal base for fishing (10
rods on local rivers, 10 more with boats on the lochs, drying room, deep
freeze), bird-watching and hill walking, and after the day's activity the
lounge and cocktail bar offer comfort and conviviality. Generously sized
bedrooms – each named after a nearby mountain or loch – feature bold
earth tones and colourful fabrics. Two rooms, Suilven and Canisp, have
dining tables and sofas. Children up to 16 are accommodated free
in parents' room. *Rooms 20. Garden, sauna, solarium, fishing, snooker, gift
shop, helipad. Closed mid Oct-mid Apr.* AMERICAN EXPRESS *Access, Diners, Visa.*

Lochinver   Places of Interest

Tourist Information Tel 05714 330.

Markinch   Balbirnie House   74%   £125

Tel 0592 610066   Fax 0592 610529   **HR**
Balbirnie Park Markinch by Glenrothes Fife KY7 6NE   Map 3 C5

A large Georgian mansion to which the Victorians added a massive classical
portico, Balbirnie is surrounded by fine gardens (including some rare
rhododendrons) at the centre of a 400-odd-acre country park that includes
a golf course to which hotel guests have priviliged access. Backed-up by an
efficient team of smartly kitted-out staff, the Russell family run the hotel
on friendly, personal lines. Day rooms include a well-stocked (both with
books and malts) library bar, peaceful drawing room and architecturally
fine Long Gallery. Only a few bedrooms are less than spacious and all are
individually decorated in great style and comfort with lots of extras from
sherry and mineral water to towelling robes in good bathrooms that
feature panelled tubs and white marble shelving. Just a couple of rooms are
a bit close to the kitchen extractor fan. Beds are turned down at night and
room service is 24hrs. *Rooms 30. Garden, snooker.* AMERICAN EXPRESS *Access,
Diners, Visa.*

Restaurant   £65

Depending on the needs of private functions, you sit in one or other of two
high-ceilinged period dining rooms. Both the four-course set dinner and
less formal lunchtime à la carte (three-course set lunch on Sunday) feature
chargrilled steaks along with a balanced choice of sauced dishes like roast
halibut with sauce choron and piccata of pork with an apple and clove
crust and a calvados reduction at dinner, and chicken 'El Mehicano' and
steak, Guinness and mushroom pie at lunchtime. Cooking is workmanlike
rather than inspired. Wines, on an extensive list, are usefully coded for
dryness/sweetness (whites) or lightness/fullness (reds). *Seats 100.
Private Room 56. L 12-2 D 7-9.30. Set Sun L £13.75 Set D £25/£35.*

Maryculter   Maryculter House   65%   £108

Tel 0224 732124   Fax 0224 733510   **H**
South Deeside Road Maryculter Grampian AB1 0BB   Map 3 D4

A fine location on the banks of the river Dee makes Maryculter a popular
wedding venue, especially with a new function suite for up to 180 people.
The oldest room (now a rattan-furnished cocktail bar/lounge) has high
stone walls and dates back to the 13th century. The other main public

room is the Victorian-styled Poachers Bar which opens on to a riverside patio. Bedrooms, including those in an extension, feature pine furniture and pretty fabrics with matching curtains and duvet covers. Considerable weekend tariff reductions. Children up to 12 stay free in parents' room. *Rooms 23. Garden. Closed 26 & 27 Dec.* AMERICAN EXPRESS *Access, Diners, Visa.*

Maybole	Ladyburn	73%	£140
Tel 06554 585 Fax 06554 580			**HR**
By Maybole Strathclyde KA19 7SG			Map 4 A2

Set in 23 acres ($4\frac{1}{2}$ of which are well-kept gardens) near the Kilkerran estate, signposted off the B741 2 miles south of Crosshill. The family home of the Hepburns, it is run by owner/manager/chef Jane Hepburn in country-house style with family photos and pictures in the day rooms (a very pleasant drawing room with pale pink and pale green armchairs and Chinese lacquered pieces and an equally pleasant library for smokers) along with fresh flowers, ornaments and objets d'art that are to be found throughout the hotel. Bedrooms (no smoking) feature plain cream walls setting off antique furniture, more flowers, fruit, books, ornaments and Royal Doulton bone china for tea and coffee-making facilities. Bathrooms (3 with large showers only) have generous bottles of bath oil plus huge bath sheets. Rooms are properly serviced at night. There is no bar, but drinks are served in the drawing room or library. No children under 14. *Rooms 8. Garden, croquet. Closed 4 weeks between Jan & Mar.* AMERICAN EXPRESS *Access, Visa.*

Dining Room   £60

Dried flowers in the fireplaces, lacy cloths over yellow undercloths, bone china and fresh flowers help create a pleasant dining room. Jane cooks in a simple, homely style making exclusive use of local supplies and preparing everything except bread on the premises. Speciality dishes include roast sirloin, Aunt Ella's chicken and mushroom pie and Ladyburn tart. Vegetarians should make their requirements known when booking. The wine list is short but varied with a good sprinkling of half bottles. No smoking. *Seats 25. L 12.30-1.30 D 7.30-8.30. Closed L Sun, all Mon. Set L from £10 Set D from £23.*

Melrose	Burts Hotel	£72
Tel 089 682 2285 Fax 089 682 2870		**I**
Market Square Melrose Borders TD6 9PN		Map 4 C1

On the A6091, 3 miles from the A7 and 2 miles from the A68 in the heart of Border country and below the Eildon Hills, lies Melrose. At its heart is Burts Hotel, which has been in the Henderson family's capable hands since 1971. It's a useful centre from which to explore the area, whether you favour stately homes, salmon fishing or something in between. However you've spent your day, there's a warm welcome back at the hotel, along with impeccably maintained bedrooms. *Rooms 21. Garden, snooker. Closed 24-26 Dec.* AMERICAN EXPRESS *Access, Diners, Visa.*

Melrose	George & Abbotsford Hotel	56%	£70
Tel 089 682 2308 Fax 089 682 3363			**H**
High Street Melrose Borders TD6 9PD			Map 4 C1

A Victorian look has been restored to this town-centre former coaching inn, once a haunt of Sir Walter Scott. Glass-shaded brass chandeliers, red plush upholstery and dado panelling set the tone in the day rooms; separate conference rooms accommodate up to 180. Neat bedrooms range from standards with shower/WC only to four-poster rooms. Children up to 16 stay free in parents' room. *Rooms 30. Garden.* AMERICAN EXPRESS *Access, Diners, Visa.*

Melrose   Places of Interest

Tourist Information   Tel 089 682 2555.
Teddy Melrose Teddy Bear Museum   Tel 089 682 2464.
  Historic Houses, Castles and Gardens
Abbotsford House   Tel 0896 2043 *Home of Sir Walter Scott.*
Mertoun Gardens   St Boswells. Tel 0835 23236.
Priorwood Garden   Tel 089 682 2555.
Thirlestane Castle   Lauder Tel 0578 722430.

## Milngavie	**Black Bull Thistle**	**59%**	**£92**
Tel 041-956 2291 Fax 041-956 1896			**H**
Main Street Milngavie Strathclyde G62 6BH			Map 3 B5

A useful stopover on the A81 six miles north of the centre of Glasgow. Children up to 10 stay free in parents' room. Conferences and functions for up to 120. *Rooms 27.* ᴀᴍᴇʀɪᴄᴀɴ ᴇxᴘʀᴇss® *Access, Diners, Visa.*

## Muir-of-Ord	**Dower House**	**£65**
Tel & Fax 0463 870090		**RR**
Highfield Muir-of-Ord Highland IV7 7XN		Map 2 B3

One mile out of Muir-of-Ord on the A862 Dingwall road, the Dower House stands in three acres of mature grounds and has been personally run by Robyn and Mena Aitchison since 1988. Robyn's dinner in the ornate dining room comprises four courses with only a few choices. Perhaps steamed monkfish with lemon grass or black pudding with sautéed apples and mustard vinaigrette to start, followed by cream of Jerusalem artichoke soup; then breast of duck with peppered pineapple and lime sauce or mixed seafood in a puff pastry case; finally, gratiné of preserved summer fruits, chocolate crepe with orange armagnac mousse or Scottish cheeses; home-made truffles with coffee complete the picture. No children under 5 in the dining room after 7.30pm (they can have supper from 5.30pm). One is asked to advise in advance for luncheon arrangements; Sunday lunch usually features good Scottish meat dishes but not necessarily cooked in a traditional manner (fish may also appear). No smoking. Eight seats in the garden in fine weather. *Seats 26. L 12.30-2 D 7.30-9. Closed 1 week Oct, 25 Dec. Set L (by arrangement) £15 Set D £28. Access, Visa.*

Rooms   £90

The five bedrooms are comfortable and cottagey, and all have Victorian-style bathrooms with cast-iron baths and brass fittings, plus "colour television if required". One has its own sitting room. No dogs. *Garden, croquet, children's playground.*

## Nairn	**Clifton Hotel**	**70%**	**£96**
Tel 0667 453119 Fax 0667 452836			**HR**
Viewfield Street Nairn Highland IV12 4HW			Map 2 C3

Turn west at the only roundabout on the A96 through Nairn to find the Clifton Hotel, a delightful town house just minutes from the beach, next door to the Nairn Pottery studios and run since 1952 by J. Gordon Macintyre, hotelier and patron of the arts. The house bears witness to his individual taste, with hand-chosen antiques, fresh and dried flowers and fragrant pot-pourri making public rooms cosy and attractive. There are antiques, too, in the bedrooms, where TVs and telephones do not intrude. *Rooms 12. Garden. Closed Nov-Mar.* ᴀᴍᴇʀɪᴄᴀɴ ᴇxᴘʀᴇss® *Access, Diners, Visa.*

Restaurant   £60

Charles Macintyre offers a daily-changing menu, handwritten in French, but he uses local produce when possible to produce a classic Auld Alliance choice. So *turbot grillé à l'aneth* or *gigot d'agneau à la moutarde* clearly display their origins. Slightly more unusual combinations also appear, such as *mousse de saumon au tabouleh* or *salade de lentilles noires et tapénade*. The confident touch in the cooking pays dividends. Delicious puddings and cheeses. The separate Green Room (serenely colour co-ordinated in green and white including the flowers!) is non-smoking, and is used sometimes for lunch, and for private parties. Breakfast is served right up until noon! *Seats 40. Parties 12. Private Room 12. L 12.30-1 D 7-9.30.*

Nairn	**Golf View Hotel**	**67%**	**£88**
Tel 0667 452301 Fax 0667 455267			**H**
Seabank Road Nairn Highland IV12 4HD			**Map 2 C3**

Since reverting to private ownership a couple of years ago this late-Victorian hotel has benefited from considerable refurbishment. Public areas all share the same decor with elaborate floral drapes, brass chandeliers and co-ordinating soft furnishings while well-kept bedrooms (all with proper armchairs and/or sofas) have a variety of bright fabrics for the matching bedcovers and curtains. Only the unwrapped bars of soap jar somewhat in otherwise good bathrooms – several with separate walk-in shower and twin basins. The garden – where a new leisure centre should have been completed as we go to press – extends down to a sandy beach on the Firth of Forth opposite the Black Isle. Sunsets here can be quite spectacular. Continuity since the change of ownership has been assured by the hospitable Greta Anderson, who has been running things for over 16 years. **Rooms** 47. *Garden, tennis.* AMERICAN EXPRESS *Access, Diners, Visa.*

Nairn	**Newton Hotel**	**65%**	**£70**
Tel 0667 453144 Fax 0667 454026			**H**
Inverness Road Nairn Highland IV12 4RX			**Map 2 C3**

At the bottom of a winding, tree-lined private drive, this imposing building is set in 27 acres with sweeping views overlooking the Nairn golf course and the Moray Firth beyond. The high-ceilinged rooms within the main house are more interesting than the newer, more contemporary ones in the adjacent Newton Court, a converted granary and stables. Bar meals are served in a conservatory extension to the cocktail bar. The peaceful setting, well-chosen antiques and velvet upholstery recall the gracious Victorian era. Families welcome: up-to-4s share parents' accommodation free, 5s-14s have a 50% reduction. Functions for up to 80. **Rooms** 44. *Garden, croquet, putting, sauna, sun beds.* AMERICAN EXPRESS *Access, Diners, Visa.*

Nairn	**Places of Interest**

Tourist Information   Tel 0667 52753.
Cawdor Castle   Cawdor Tel 06677 615 *6 miles.*

Newburgh	**Udny Arms Hotel**	**60%**	**£76**
Tel 035 86 89444 Fax 035 86 89012			**H**
Main Street Newburgh Grampian AB41 0BL			**Map 2 D3**

The Victorian facade is on the main street but at the back there are pleasant views over a golf course and the Ythan estuary. Day rooms vary: perhaps the most appealing is the mellow cocktail bar with its pine-board banquettes, scrubbed pine tables and Windsor chairs. Bedrooms are furnished mainly in traditional style and are all en suite; the best rooms overlook the picturesque estuary. Children under 12 stay free in parents' room; informal eating in the bistro and café/bar. Theatre-style conferences for up to 130. Parking for 200 cars. **Rooms** 26. *Garden.* AMERICAN EXPRESS *Access, Diners, Visa.*

Newhouse   Travel Inn

£43

L

Tel 0698 860277   Fax 0698 861353

Glasgow Road Newhouse nr Motherwell Strathclyde ML1 5SY

Map 3 C6

Rooms 40. AMERICAN EXPRESS *Access, Diners, Visa.*

Newton Stewart   Kirroughtree Hotel   76%

£120*

HR

Tel 0671 402141   Fax 0671 402425

Newton Stewart Dumfries & Galloway DG8 6AN

Map 4 A2

In eight acres of grounds set well back from the A75, the public rooms of the 18th-century Kirroughtree hotel are still rather obviously opulent with much flock wallpaper, ormolu-mounted furniture, onyx and gilt coffee tables and the like. Upstairs, however, the new owners have transformed the formerly rather tacky bedrooms into high-class accommodation (not all may yet be finished so ask for 'new' rooms when booking). The number of rooms has reduced as smaller rooms have been merged, pure cotton sheets replace the poly-cotton variety, furniture is now new high-quality mahogany in traditional style with proper dining table for room service meals, stylish soft furnishings include sofas and armchairs, and extras run to mineral water, sherry, fruit and bathrobes. In the evening beds are turned down, curtains drawn and bedside lights switched on. Now in the same ownership as the *North West Castle* at Stranraer and *Cally Palace* at Gatehouse of Fleet. No children under 10 in hotel or restaurant. *Half-board terms only. **Rooms** 17. Garden, croquet, tennis, badminton, putting. Closed 2 Jan-early Mar. Access, Visa.*

Restaurant

£65

Twin dining rooms – one in red (reserved for smokers) and one in blue – with plush banquette seating around watered-silk-effect walls. Foodwise, Ian Bennett continues to please with his sensibly short, daily-changing menus (à la carte at lunchtime, fixed-priced for dinner) that feature good, often local, ingredients in dishes as varied as pigeon choucroute, curried apple soup, venison 'grand veneur', grey mullet with crispy celeriac and ginger sauce, and guinea fowl with cranberries and limes. For afters go for an artistically presented pud like caramelised lemon and banana tart or some good Scottish cheeses that always include a selection of local goats' and ewes' milk cheeses along with things like Mull of Kintyre truckle cheddar. No children under 10. Few half bottles on the decent wine list – quite a lot of good drinking under £20, and two *marque* champagnes under £30. **Seats** 60. Private Room 20. L 12.30-1.30 D 7-9.30. Set D £22.50.

Newton Stewart   Places of Interest

Tourist Information   Tel 0671 402431.

Newtonmore   Ard-na-Coille Hotel   67%

£126*

HR

Tel 0540 673214   Fax 0540 673453

Kingussie Road Newtonmore Highland PH20 1AY

Map 3 C4

On the A86 at the north end of Newtonmore and high in the forest, amongst its two acres of pine woodland, Nancy Ferrier's and Barry Cottam's former shooting lodge is today a tranquil and intimate country hotel. Edwardian-style public rooms and sunny terrace have an open outlook towards the Cairngorm mountains. Most of the guest bedrooms have a southerly aspect and all enjoy uninterrupted views of the Spey Valley. Each is different in decor and period furniture; all are immaculately kept. Dogs in two rooms only, by prior arrangement. *Half-board terms only. Minimum stay of two nights at peak weekends. **Rooms** 7. Garden. Closed mid-Nov-end Dec. Access, Visa.*

See over

Restaurant £65

Five-course set dinner, prepared by the proprietors, is served at 7.45pm after much care with cooking and presentation and equal emphasis on local produce. Salad of Argyll smoked ham and venison, curried parsnip soup and poached Oban Bay langoustines with a shellfish and whisky sauce typify the balance of ingredients and flavours. A wide selection of cheeses could then precede an amaretto torte served with a raspberry coulis. An exemplary and very well-balanced wine list with helpful notes, a good selection of half bottles but, most important of all, fair prices; there are many New World wines as well (listed by grape variety) – it's worth coming here just to drink! *Seats 18. Parties 16. Private Room 6. D at 7.45. Set D £27.50.*

Newtown St Boswells   Le Provençale   £40

Tel 0835 23284   **R**
Monksford Road Newtown St Boswells Borders TD6 0SB   Map 4 C1

Frenchman René Duzelier in the kitchen and his Scottish wife Elizabeth at front of house make a fine team in their spotless little restaurant just off the A68. The daily-changing menu is handwritten with English descriptions in a distinctive French script. Straightforward cooking covers dishes like garlic snails, cream of vegetable soup, boeuf en croute, coq au vin, fillets of haddock in vermouth and, to finish, oranges in Grand Marnier or bread-and-butter pudding. No smoking. *Seats 40. L 12-2 D 5-10. Closed Sun & Mon, 2 weeks Jan, 3 weeks Jul, 2 weeks Nov. Set L £6.10 & £12.55. No credit cards.*

North Berwick   Marine Hotel   64%   £97

Tel 0620 892406   Fax 0620 894480   **H**
Cromwell Road North Berwick Lothian EH39 4LZ   Map 3 D5

Fine coastal views of the Firth of Forth are enjoyed from this imposing Victorian hotel with a long golfing tradition (it overlooks the 16th green of the North Berwick Championship Westlinks Course and there are dozens of courses nearby). Bedrooms are more practical than luxurious, save for those in the turret. Banqueting for 300; conferences up to 350. Forte. *Rooms 83. Outdoor swimming pool, sauna, sun bed, tennis, putting, snooker, children's playground.* AMERICAN EXPRESS *Access, Diners, Visa.*

North Berwick   Places of Interest

Tourist Information   Tel 0620 2197.
Malleny Garden (NT)   Balerno Tel 031449 2283.

North Middleton   Borthwick Castle   66%   £95

Tel 0875 820514   Fax 0875 821702   **H**
North Middleton nr Gorebridge Lothian EH23 4QY   Map 3 C6

Built in 1430 and beseiged by Cromwell in 1650, historic Borthwick Castle with its tall twin towers once held Mary Queen of Scots as a prisoner. She escaped, dressed as a page boy, from a window of the vast stone-vaulted main hall, which boasts a 40-foot Gothic arch, minstrel's gallery and hooded fireplace. Spiral staircases within the massive stone walls lead to bedrooms offering more atmosphere than luxury. Top of the range is the Mary Queen of Scots four-poster 'double bedchamber'. Most bathrooms have shower and WC only. Probably the most genuinely atmospheric medieval castle hotel in the country (follow Historic Buildings sign on the A7). *Rooms 10. Garden, croquet. Closed Jan, Feb.* AMERICAN EXPRESS *Access, Diners, Visa.*

North Queensferry   Queensferry Lodge   63%   £70

Tel 0383 410000   Fax 0383 419708   **H**

St Margaret's Head North Queensferry nr Inverkeithing Fife KY11 1HP   Map 3 C5

A modern family-run hotel overlooking the Forth and its famous bridges.
Bedrooms are quite generous on space and accessories, and sparkling
bathrooms have good showers over the tubs and ample towelling. A tourist
information office is manned from 10 to 6 throughout the year, and
in a Scottish crafts shop you can find out all about the area. Conference and
banqueting facilities for 150/200. Plans for the next couple of years include
another 30 bedrooms and a leisure complex. *Rooms 32.* AMERICAN EXPRESS
Access, Visa.

Oban   Alexandra Hotel   59%   £90

Tel 0631 62381   Fax 0631 64497   **H**

Corran Esplanade Oban Strathclyde PA54 5AA   Map 3 B5

Built in the late 1860s, the hotel stands on the esplanade a short stroll from
the town centre. Modest accommodation, two lounges and a cocktail bar.
Trips can be arranged on the hotel's motor cruiser, the *Ocean Ranger.*
Function facilities for up to 120. A new leisure centre opened in Easter
1994, adding considerably to the hotel's attractions. *Rooms 60. Garden,
indoor swimming pool, solarium, steam room, gym, snooker, games room.
Closed Jan.* AMERICAN EXPRESS *Access, Visa.*

Oban   Columba Hotel   60%   £79

Tel 0631 62183   Fax 0631 64683   **H**

North Pier Esplanade Oban Strathclyde PA34 5QD   Map 3 B5

An Edwardian sandstone building on the North Pier, with views across the
bay to the Western Isles. Three bars offer a choice for a relaxing drink, and
conference suites can cater for up to 300 delegates. Children up to 14 stay
free when sharing parents' room. *Rooms 51. Closed Nov-Mar.*
AMERICAN EXPRESS *Access, Visa.*

Oban   Knipoch Hotel   72%   £124

Tel 085 26 251   Fax 085 26 249   **HR**

by Oban Strathclyde PA34 4QT   Map 3 B5

The Craig family have been hands-on owners since 1981 of an elegant
Georgian hotel standing six miles south of Oban on the A816 halfway
along the shore of Loch Feochan, an arm of the sea stretching four miles
inland. Lounges and bars are filled with family heirlooms, and there are
plenty of magazines to read in the leathery comfort of fireside armchairs.
Well-proportioned bedrooms have period furniture and particularly well-
appointed bathrooms. A purpose-built bedroom extension blends well with
the original. Good housekeeping. No dogs. *Rooms 17. Garden.
Closed mid Nov-mid Feb.* AMERICAN EXPRESS *Access, Diners, Visa.*

Restaurant   £80

Dinner is three or five courses featuring excellent produce from garden,
loch and the hotel's own smokery; their salmon is cured, marinated
in juniper, rowan, Barbados sugar, herbs and whisky then smoked over oak
for three days. Smoked scallops are another speciality. Highland potato
soup and home-baked bread could precede halibut and sole with
champagne sauce, salmon steak hollandaise or duck with port wine sauce.
Centrepiece of the gourmet menu is chateaubriand with béarnaise and
a generous selection of vegetables. Next comes cheese, then dessert
(strawberry in a brandy snap tuile, Cointreau crepes) and coffee with petits
fours. There's an excellent and comprehensive wine list, very fairly priced,
with tasting notes alongside each wine. Much is from France, though

See over

Germany, Italy and Spain are well represented; some from the New
World. Winner of our Scotland regional Cellar of the Year award 1995.
*Seats 44. Parties 24 Private Room 12. L by arrangement D 7.30-9.
Set D £27.50.*

Oban   Places of Interest

Tourist Information   Tel 0631 63122.
Highland Theatre   Tel 0631 62444.
Gateway Leisure Centre   Tel 0631 62345.
Easdale Island Folk Museum   Tel 0852 300370.
Oban Distillery   Tel 0631 64262.
Sealife Centre   Barcaldine Tel 063172 386.
Ardchattan Gardens   Ardchattan Priory Tel 063175 274.
Argyll Boat Cruises   Tel 0631 65687.

Oldmeldrum   Meldrum House   65%   £95

Tel 0651 872294   Fax 0651 872464   **H**

Meldrum House Oldmeldrum Grampian AB1 0AE   **Map 2 D3**

Friendly new local owners here following a two-year closure, although all
the antique furniture, paintings and objets d'art remain very much
as before. In a substantial Scottish Baronial mansion, a welcoming, year-
round log fire burns in the spacious entrance hall, off which is a small,
rough-stone, barrel-vaulted bar that dates back to the 13th century. The
drawing room, by contrast, is in elegant yet homely country-house style.
All but one of the antique-furnished bedrooms are very large with fine
views over the grounds and pretty, rather than stylish, soft furnishings.
Somewhat dated bathrooms are a weak point perhaps with three having
shower and WC only and some of the tubs in others in need of resurfacing.
The entrance to the estate (there's an attractive drive past a lake to reach the
house) is at the junction of the A947 and B9170 just out of town. *Rooms 9.
Garden, fishing. Access, Visa.*

Onich   Allt-nan-Ros Hotel   63%   £95

Tel 085 53 250   Fax 085 53 462   **HR**

Onich nr Fort William Highland PH33 6RY   **Map 3 B4**

The great glory of this white pebbledash, early Victorian shooting lodge
on the A82 is its fabulous panoramic view (shared by all but one of the
bedrooms) across Lochs Levin and Linnhe to the mountains beyond.
On a clear day one can see as far as the Isle of Mull. Inside, all is neat and
well ordered; the bar, with a real fire in its white marble fireplace
in winter, opens on to a lounge with picture windows. Bedrooms all
feature good darkwood, freestanding furniture and a variety of pretty
fabrics with curtains, polycotton duvets and even ribbon-tied lampshades
all matching. Two rooms are in a converted stable annexe. Good, freshly-
cooked breakfasts with nice smoky bacon. The hotel's name means 'Burn
of the Roses', a reference to the stream which runs through the garden.
Rooms 21. Garden, putting. Closed mid Nov-Christmas, 3 Jan-mid Feb.
AMERICAN EXPRESS *Access, Diners, Visa.*

Restaurant   £55

Short, fixed-price dinner menu with a typical main-course selection being
lamb with roasted shallots and a basil sauce, fillets of sole and cod with
a white wine and rosemary cream sauce, and venison with purée potatoes
and a blackcurrant jus. Lighter lunches. Picture windows take full
advantage of the view. *Seats 45. Parties 25. L 12.30-2 D 7-8.30. Set L £8
Set D £19.50.*

Onich   Lodge on the Loch   63%   £137*

Tel 085 53 237   Fax 085 53 463   **H**

Creag Dhu Onich nr Fort William Highland PH33 6RY   Map 3 B4

A friendly little hotel set amid spectacular loch and mountain scenery just off the A82 (five miles north of Glencoe, twelve miles south of Fort William). Plump-cushioned sofas make for easy relaxation in the lounge, and there's a modern bar. Best bedrooms are the Chieftains with loch views. Guests have free membership of "The Isles Club" with a pool, sauna, steam room and turbopool, 3 miles away at sister hotel the *Isles of Glencoe*. *Half-board terms only (children up to 16 enjoy considerable reductions). **Rooms** 18. Garden. Closed mid Nov-mid Dec, early Jan-early Feb. Access, Visa.*

Onich   Onich Hotel   61%   £77

Tel 0855 821214   Fax 0855 821484   **H**

Onich nr Fort William Highland PH33 6RY   Map 3 B4

A general upgrading of the bedrooms this year shows Iain and Grace Young's commitment to maintaining standards and customer loyalty in their popular hotel. Its location virtually at the head of Loch Linnhe makes it an ideal spot to stay and indulge in all sorts of strenuous outdoor activities of the climbing and hill walking variety, followed by less strenuous indoor ones such as relaxing in the spa bath or the bar! There are early suppers for exhausted youngsters, substantial bar snacks for midday refuelling, and a general feeling of warmth and welcome for everyone. **Rooms** 27. Closed 1 week Christmas, 1 week Jan. Garden, keep-fit equipment, spa bath, solarium, pool table. AMERICAN EXPRESS Access, Diners, Visa.

Peat Inn   The Peat Inn   ★ ↑   £85

Tel 0334 840206   Fax 0334 840530   **RR**

Peat Inn by Cupar Fife KY15 5LH   Map 3 C5

Six miles from St Andrews and just an hour's drive from Edinburgh, this is no ordinary restaurant. Originally a coaching inn, it sits at the crossroads in the centre of a tiny village named after the inn, and its heart is chef/patron David Wilson's kitchen. With his wife Patricia (who designed the sumptuous bedrooms – see below) he has run this restaurant in true French country style for over twenty years; formal yet friendly, with a reception lounge with open log fire, carved sideboard, high-backed tapestry chairs, and rough white plaster walls. There are three separate dining rooms in which to enjoy the modern cooking, which very much reflects the produce available locally. This has two beneficial effects – a guarantee of freshness and quality, and encouragement to local suppliers and growers. You have three choices: the daily-changing menu of the day, a tasting menu of seven speciality dishes (slightly smaller portions than normal, and for an entire table only) which changes about every six weeks, and à la carte that runs with the seasons. Several dishes (fish soup, lobster salad with a citrus vinaigrette, breasts of pigeon with wild mushrooms in a red wine sauce with brandy and juniper and venison with port) appear frequently, because if they didn't, some regular customers might feel disappointed. Always ask what the selection of the day's fish is: a recent visit enabled us to sample an aromatic smoked fish soup with lobster, grilled salmon with Thai spices and celeriac purée and roast monkfish on a bed of potato and onion in a meat juice – all this after a delicious appetiser of warm onion tart, and followed by braised duck leg on a bed of a cabbage with coriander, Scottish cheeses and a trio of caramel desserts. Other sweet temptations include a feuilleté of white chocolate ice cream with a dark chocolate sauce or a little pot of chocolate and rosemary. The magnificent wine list deserves to be scrutinised carefully. David is such an enthusiast that should you need help in choosing, he'll probably end up sitting alongside you! Seriously, it's well worth experimenting here. **Seats** 48. Private Room 24. L 12.30 for 1 D 7-9.30. Closed Sun & Mon, 25 Dec, 1 Jan. Set L £18.50 Set D from £28. AMERICAN EXPRESS Access, Diners, Visa. MARTELL

See over

Rooms   £135

... and these are no ordinary bedrooms! Overlooking the garden, they are
in fact suites (seven split level and one ground level suitable for disabled
guests) with an upstairs sitting room, where a super Continental breakfast,
consisting of freshly squeezed orange juice, fresh grapefruit compote,
yoghurt, hot croissants etc, is served. Excellent coffee and tea (the latter
comes in decent-sized cups). The rooms have been furnished by design
graduate Patricia and provide the utmost comfort – smart co-ordinating
fabrics, good French period furniture (a cabinet hides the remote-control
teletext TV, Scottish mineral water and a variety of games), luxurious
Italian marble bathrooms with Czech & Speake fittings and toiletries,
bathrobes, and even slippers. There are fresh flowers, fruit, home-made
biscuits, books and magazines, as well as direct-dial telephone, radio/alarm
and hairdryer – these rooms are among the best you'll find anywhere.

Peebles	Cringletie House	65%	£92
Tel 0721 730233 Fax 0721 730244			**HR**
Peebles Borders EH45 8PL			Map 4 C1

Owned and run since 1971 by the Maguire family, Cringletie is a baronial-
style mansion which was built in 1861 for the Wolfe family, and it still
offers a family welcome today. Set well back from the A703, three miles
north of Peebles, it provides peace and quiet and enjoys views of the distant
Meldon and Moorfoot Hills. Marbled fireplaces, fresh flowers from the
gardens and antiques enhance the traditional decor. Most impressive of the
day rooms is the panelled drawing room with fine painted ceiling. Well-
maintained bedrooms offer traditional comforts. **Rooms** *13. Garden, croquet,
tennis, putting. Closed Jan & Feb. Access, Visa.*

Restaurant   £60

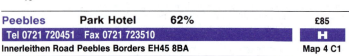

Aileen Maguire, ably assisted since 1981 by Sheila McKellar, offers well-
balanced set menus with choices at the main courses, drawing as much
produce as possible from the lovely walled kitchen garden. So you might
enjoy a five-course dinner comprising smoked haddock mousseline with
spinach sauce; then tomato and courgette soup; for main course medallions
of venison with whisky cream sauce with a selection of vegetables, and
a delicious nougatine meringue slice to finish. Prices are extremely
favourable on a sound wine list. No smoking in the dining room. **Seats** *56.
Parties 12. Private Room 27. L 1-1.45 D 7.30-8.30. Sun L £15
Set D £23.50.*

Peebles	Park Hotel	62%	£85
Tel 0721 720451 Fax 0721 723510			**H**
Innerleithen Road Peebles Borders EH45 8BA			Map 4 C1

A handsome, whitewashed building on the A72. Views of gardens and hills
are enjoyed by many of the bedrooms, which include one with a four-
poster. Guests may use the extensive leisure facilities of the *Peebles Hotel
Hydro*, also operated by Peebles Hotel Hydropathic Ltd and less than half
a mile away. **Rooms** *24. Garden, putting.* AMERICAN EXPRESS® *Access,
Diners, Visa.*

Peebles	Peebles Hotel Hydro	70%	£103
Tel 0721 720602 Fax 0721 722999			**H**
Innerleithen Road Peebles Borders EH45 8LX			Map 4 C1

In Scottish border country, Peebles Hotel Hydro is a complete resort: once
installed, you are unlikely to need anything throughout your stay that
is not available on-site. The list of facilities in Bubbles leisure centre
is seemingly endless, and Pieter Van Dijk, in charge since 1972, keeps
abreast of new trends and options, bringing them on stream as appropriate.

Despite the up-to-date technology, the hotel is true to its Edwardian origins in terms of grandeur and elegance in public rooms and bedrooms, even down to weekend dances in the ballroom – or there's a disco for the younger element. Families are well catered for. Banqueting, conference and function facilities for up to 400. *Rooms 137. Garden, croquet, indoor swimming pool, sauna, steam room, solarium, spa bath, gym, beautician, hairdressing, tennis, squash, badminton, pitch & putt, putting, riding, games room, snooker, coffee shop (11am-11pm), kiosk, children's playground & playroom.* AMERICAN EXPRESS *Access, Diners, Visa.*

Peebles	Tontine Hotel	57%	£80
Tel 0721 720892 Fax 0721 729732			**H**
High Street Peebles Borders EH45 8AJ			**Map 4 C1**

Modest, practical accommodation at an agreeable hotel established in 1808. Under-15s stay free in parents' room. Forte Heritage. *Rooms 37.* AMERICAN EXPRESS *Access, Diners, Visa.*

Peebles   Places of Interest

Tourist Information   Tel 0721 720138.
Traquair Castle   Innerleithen Tel 0896 830323.
Robert Smails Printing Works   Innerleithen

Perth	Number Thirty Three		£55
Tel 0738 633771			**R**
33 George Street Perth Tayside PH1 5LA			**Map 3 C5**

Choose between the light meal menu of the oyster bar (ideal for theatre-goers) and the more substantial dishes offered in the dining area beyond at this art deco nearly-all-seafood restaurant near the centre of town. The former might include seafood soup, grilled tomato and mozzarella salad, Scottish oysters and a platter of assorted fresh, smoked and marinated fish and shellfish, the latter pan-fried lemon sole with herb butter, Loch Sween scallops in a vermouth sauce, roast duckling and grilled fillet steak. Both menus show the list of puds, sticky toffee pudding with butterscotch soufflé and iced maple and ginger meringue gateau being typical. *Seats 42. Parties 10. L 12.30-2.30 D 6.30-9.30. Closed Sun & Mon, 10 days Christmas/New Year.* AMERICAN EXPRESS *Access, Visa.*

Perth	Royal George Hotel	62%	£97
Tel 0738 624455 Fax 0738 30345			**H**
Tay Street Perth Tayside PH1 5LD			**Map 3 C5**

A Georgian jumble of a hotel close to the city centre with some rooms facing the river Tay. Refurbished day rooms are quite extensive and offer many quiet, comfortable seating areas. Functions for up to 100 in the ballroom. A limited room service is offered. Forte Heritage. *Rooms 42. Garden.* AMERICAN EXPRESS *Access, Diners, Visa.*

Perth	Stakis City Mills Hotel	60%	£90
Tel 0738 628281 Fax 0738 643423			**H**
West Mill Street Perth Tayside PH1 5QP			**Map 3 C5**

Right in the heart of Perth, the Stakis is based on a watermill dating back to the 15th century. Single, double and twin rooms, plus a couple of family rooms have all been refurbished in the last two years. Satellite TV and in-house movies. Conferences up to 140 theatre-style. *Rooms 76.* AMERICAN EXPRESS *Access, Diners, Visa.*

Perth   Places of Interest

Tourist Information   Tel 0738 638353.
Perth Theatre   Tel 0738 621031.
St Ninian's Cathedral   Tel 0738 621373.
Perth Museum and Art Gallery   Tel 0738 632488.
Dewars Ice Rinks   Tel 0738 637810.
Perth Showgrounds   Tel 0738 623780.
Perth Hunt Racecourse   Tel 0738 651597.
Caithness Glass Visitor Centre   Inveralmond Tel 0738 637373.
   Historic Houses, Castles and Gardens
Branklyn Garden (NT)   Tel 0738 625535.
Megginch Castle Gardens   Errol. Tel 0821 642222.

Peterhead	Waterside Inn	67%	£93
Tel 0779 471121 Fax 0779 470670			**H**
Fraserburgh Road Peterhead Grampian AB42 7BN			Map 2 D3

Turn left at a grassy roundabout as you approach Peterhead from Aberdeen (A92) and follow signs to St Fergus to find this modern hotel which seems set to educate its guests in more than just the three 'Rs', including (but not restricted to) refuge, refresh, revitalise, relax, relive, reward – aiming ultimately for you to return. There's certainly plenty to do in the well-equipped leisure centre or the immediate area (the unspoilt far north-east coast of Scotland), and special breaks are offered at various times of the year. There's a series of bars to suit every taste, and several conference rooms (maximum capacity 250). 40 studio bedrooms in a separate block are compact and functional, while those in the main building are more spacious and luxurious; children stay free in parents' room. *Rooms 110. Garden, indoor swimming pool, keep-fit equipment, sauna, steam room, spa bath, sunbeds, snooker, grill room (7am-10pm Tue-Sat).* AMERICAN EXPRESS *Access, Diners, Visa.*

Peterhead   Places of Interest

Tourist Information   Tel 0779 471904.
Arbuthnot Museum   Tel 0779 477778.

Pitlochry	Green Park Hotel	58%	£78
Tel 0796 473248 Fax 0796 473520			**H**
Cluny Bridge Road Pitlochry Tayside PH16 5JY			Map 3 C4

Graham and Anne Brown have been at the Green Park for over 25 years and their attention to detail shows throughout. Some bedrooms have recently been refurbished, while the lounge and bar also continue to provide comfort and loch views. Neat, well-tended gardens lead right down to the shore of Loch Faskally, and when it's fine you can have light meals or snacks in the garden. Children under 5 free in parents' room. *Rooms 37. Garden, putting, game fishing, games room. Closed Nov-Mar. Access, Visa.*

Pitlochry	Pitlochry Hydro Hotel	64%	£102
Tel 0796 472666 Fax 0796 472238			**H**
Knockard Road Pitlochry Tayside PH16 5JH			Map 3 C4

Set high above Pitlochry, the Hydro is a sturdily-built, well-maintained and well-run late-Victorian hotel. Its attractions are supplemented by good leisure facilities, mostly housed in the Hydro Club. Bedrooms, including a couple of suites, have modern tiled bathrooms. Children up to 14 stay free in parents' room. No dogs. *Rooms 62. Garden, croquet, putting, indoor swimming pool, gym, spa bath, sauna, solarium, snooker. Closed Jan-early Feb.* AMERICAN EXPRESS *Access, Diners, Visa.*

Pitlochry   Places of Interest

Tourist Information   Tel 0796 472215.
Pitlochry Theatre Festival   Tel 0796 472680. *May-Oct.*
Blair Castle   Blair Atholl. Tel 0796 481207.

Port Appin   Airds Hotel   75%   £266*

Tel 063 173 236   Fax 063 173 535   **HR**
Port Appin Appin Strathclyde PA38 4DF   Map 3 B5

With glorious views across Loch Linnhe this 250-year old former ferry inn
conceals a most civilised and comfortable hotel behind its modest white
painted facade. Although not grand in scale the public areas lack nothing
when it comes to comfort with lots of overstuffed armchairs and sofas,
fresh flowers, books, magazines and real fires in the two charming lounges,
an intimate bar (not much used) and a small flower-filled conservatory
by the entrance. Bedrooms vary considerably in size with the smallest
being rather compact but others feeling quite spacious. The best have
proper armchairs, the smaller more modest seating but all get homely
touches with fresh flowers and porcelain ornaments. Most feature antique
furniture. Good bathrooms come with robes, generous towelling and
plenty of quality toiletries and, like the bedrooms, are properly serviced
in the evening. Expect a warm welcome from the Allen family, who have
been here for nearly 20 years. *Half-board terms only. **Rooms** 12. Garden.
Closed 10-31 Jan.* AMERICAN EXPRESS *Access, Visa.* MARTELL

Restaurant   £80

A long, low-ceilinged dining room, with elegantly laid tables – napkins
neatly tied with a tartan bow – of which those in the window are the most
sought after. Betty and Graeme Allen (mother and son) share the work
in the kitchen producing sophisticated yet uncomplicated dishes for their
daily-changing, four-course, fixed-price menu. Sautéed scallops with
shiitake mushrooms and a sweet and sour sauce, smooth chicken liver
terrine with crab apple and orange jelly and toasted brioche, fillet of wild
salmon on a bed of honeyed aubergines with hollandaise sauce, and roast
loin of rabbit stuffed with morels on a bed of spinach with a tarragon and
mushroom sauce typify the style. Light lunches are served in the lounge. A
sensational wine list of great depth with quality bottles at every turn; very
fair prices and, unusually for a Scottish country hotel, an exceptional Italian
section; Germany and the New World are also well represented; many
half bottles. **Seats** *36. L by arrangement, D at 8. Set D £35.*

Port William   Corsemalzie House   61%   £75

Tel 0988 860254   Fax 0988 860213   **H**
Port William by Newton Stewart Dumfries & Galloway DG8 9RL   Map 4 A3

The McDougalls have been at Corsemalzie since 1981 but the stone
mansion has been in its secluded forty acres of woodland for over
a century. Apart from creature comforts, the main attractions are of the
fishing and shooting variety (rights on the renowned Rivers Bladnoch and
Tarff as well as on the nearby lochs), and the comfortable lounges make
an ideal place to relax after such strenuous activity. Bedrooms are generally
of a decent size; all have private bath or shower. Children under 13 free
in parents' room. Parking for 35 cars. Banqueting/conferences
for 70/95. **Rooms** *14. Garden, putting, game fishing, shooting.
Closed 25 & 26 Dec, 8 Jan-5 Mar. Access, Visa.*

Portpatrick   Knockinaam Lodge   73%   £104

Tel 0776 810471   Fax 0776 810435   **HR**
Portpatrick nr Stranraer Dumfries & Galloway DG9 9AD   Map 4 A2

An air of contentment surrounds this most welcoming and comfortable
country house, which for the last 10 years has been as much the home

of Marcel and Corinna Frichot as of their numerous returning guests. An eclectic clock collection graces most public rooms, which include a warmly panelled bar complete with stag's head, and open-fire-warmed sitting rooms with a wealth of plump-cushioned sofas, magazines and board games. Bedrooms are equally gracious, prettily decorated but not over-fussy, and bathrooms include a splendid tub used by Winston Churchill. Excellent breakfasts and delightful service. Children up to 12 stay free in parents' room. The lodge nestles in a secluded cove with private beach (follow signs from the A77). **Rooms 10.** *Garden. Closed 2 Jan-25 Mar.* AMERICAN EXPRESS *Access, Diners, Visa.* MARTELL

Restaurant £80

Stuart Muir's French menus make good use of home-grown and local produce: alternatives for the first course could be *filet de bourgeois grillé à la citronnelle sa nage aux herbes,* or *demi pintade fermier roti en casserole son jus au cresson de fontaine*; mains could be goujonnettes of sole or beef in red wine; lastly a choice of dessert or Jacques Vernier farmhouse cheese. Bar snacks supplement the lunchtime menu. No smoking in the dining room. **Seats** 26. Parties 10. L 12.30-2 D 7.30-9. Set L £22 Set D £32.

Portree	Rosedale Hotel	56%	£70
Tel 0478 613131 Fax 0478 612531			**H**
Beaumont Crescent Portree Isle of Skye Highland IV51 9DB			Map 2 A3

Situated right on the quayside of a quaint, picturesque fishing harbour, the Rosedale enjoys splendid views across the bay. The building was originally a group of fishermen's homes, and the conversion provides simple but comfortable accommodation in well-kept en-suite bedrooms reached by narrow stairs and corridors. Some of the accommodation is in Beaumont House a little way along the waterfront. The lounges and an atmospheric bar (both to be refurbished by the end of 1994) provide ample space for relaxation. The cooking shows promise, although it is not without faults. **Rooms** 23. *Garden. Closed Oct-April. Access, Visa.*

Portree   Places of Interest

Tourist Information   Tel 0478 612137.
An Tuireann Arts Centre   Tel 0478 613306.
Old Skye Crofter's House Folk Museum   Luib Tel 0471 822427.
Skye Woollen Mill   Tel 0478 612889.
The Museum of the Isles   Isle of Skye. Tel 04714 305.
Talisker Distillery   Carbost Tel 0478 640203 *20 miles.*

Quothquan	Shieldhill Hotel	73%	£134
Tel 0899 20035 Fax 0899 21092			**H**
Quothquan Biggar Strathclyde ML12 6NA			Map 3 C6

Surrounded by the rolling farmland of the Clyde Valley, the oldest part of this crenellated, stone-built mansion dates back to the 12th century. Inside all is relaxed and comfortable in country-house style with the main oak-panelled drawing room boasting fresh flowers, magazines and plenty of deep armchairs. Bedrooms vary considerably in size – the largest is a huge split-level affair with a vast, sunken spa bath within the room – but all have antique furniture, good easy chairs and extras like mineral water and a decanter of sherry. Several rooms have (gas coal) fireplaces. Each has been individually decorated with pretty Laura Ashley fabrics and wall coverings that extend to the matching bathrooms (two with shower & WC only). Good breakfasts begin with freshly squeezed orange juice. New owners took over in the spring of 1994, then, just as we went to press, a new chef also. No children under 11, no dogs and no smoking in the bedrooms. **Rooms** 11. *Garden.* AMERICAN EXPRESS *Access, Diners, Visa.*

Quothquan   Place of Interest

New Lanark Conservation Village   Tel 0555 661345 *8 miles.*

Rockcliffe | Baron's Craig | 65% | £90

Tel 0556 630225 Fax 0556 630328 | **H**
Rockcliffe by Dalbeattie Dumfries & Galloway DG5 4QF | Map 4 B3

Rockcliffe is a small village overlooking the mouth of Rough Firth, just where it joins the Solway Firth, and Baron's Craig is perfectly situated to take full advantage of the splendid views thus afforded. The house, built of local granite in the 1800s, is elegantly proportioned and public rooms are light, airy and comfortably furnished. Bedrooms are modern and well equipped, all have en-suite facilities, all bathrooms now have showers and three new family rooms have been created. Parking for 30 cars. Small conferences (up to 20) can be accommodated. *Rooms 22. Garden, golf practice net, putting, sailing, windsurfing, water-skiing. Closed Nov-Easter. Access, Visa.*

Rockcliffe | Places of Interest

Kircudbright Tourist Information Tel 0557 30494.
Threave Garden nr Castle Douglas Tel 0556 502575 *12 miles.*

Rothes | Rothes Glen Hotel | 65% | £110

Tel 0340 831 254 Fax 0340 831 566 | **H**
Rothes nr Elgin Grampian AB38 7AH | Map 2 C3

Forty acres of grounds at the head of the Glen of Rothes provide rural peace at a baronial house designed by the architect of Balmoral Castle. Inside, there's an elegant lounge with ribbed ceiling and white marble fireplace, plus a bar and TV room. Antique furniture graces most of the variously-sized bedrooms that provide the normal amenities, including mini-bar. Two rooms have shower only. *Rooms 16. Garden, putting. Closed Christmas-Jan.* AMERICAN EXPRESS *Access, Diners, Visa.*

St Andrews | The Grange Inn | | £45

Tel 0334 472670 Fax 0334 478703 | **R**
Grange Road St Andrews Fife KY16 8LJ | Map 3 D5

Part of a group of pretty little old cottages about a mile out of town to the south-east and with fine views over St Andrews and the Tay Estuary to the Angus Hills beyond, the Grange Inn is now almost exclusively a restaurant, although there is still a tiny atmospheric bar with flagstone floor, ancient fireplace and beamed ceiling. Three separate dining rooms (two for non-smokers) are cottagey with bare stone walls, paper napkins and a charming mix of rustic and antique furniture. The menu sticks mainly to fairly straightforward grills and the excellent local seafood with details of the day's catch appearing on a blackboard menu along with seasonal items like asparagus. Sticky toffee pudding, banoffi pie and chocolate mousse exhaust the pudding menu although there is also always some Stilton and a couple of Scottish cheeses to be had along with wheat wafers or oatcakes. Friendly, welcoming atmosphere. *Seats 75. Private Room 35. L 12.30-2.15 D 6.30-9.15.* AMERICAN EXPRESS *Access, Diners, Visa.*

St Andrews | Rufflets Country House | 65% | £130

Tel 0334 472594 Fax 0334 478703 | **H**
Strathkinness Low Road St Andrews Fife KY16 9TX | Map 3 D5

They are justly proud of their ten acres of award-winning gardens (complete with topiary and a stream) at this 1920s-built hotel on the B939 a mile and a half west of St Andrews. Inside, the hotel is as well kept as the gardens, with pretty floral fabrics and wallpapers and mostly traditional darkwood furniture. Three particularly attractive rooms are in a rose-covered cottage in the grounds. Children up to 10 stay free in parents' room. Public areas include an appealing entrance hall, lounge, little bar and formal drawing room. ***Rooms** 25. Garden, putting.* AMERICAN EXPRESS® *Access, Diners, Visa.*

St Andrews   Rusacks Hotel   74%   £114

Tel 0334 474321   Fax 0334 477896   **H**

Pilmour Links St Andrews Fife KY16 9JQ   **Map 3 D5**

Standing by the 18th fairway of the world-famous Old Course, this grand Victorian hotel not surprisingly attracts golf-lovers from near and far. The sun lounge provides a quiet retreat and fairway views, and the golf-themed Champion's Bar is a good place to relive the triumphs and disasters of the day's golf. Many fine features survive both in the day rooms (marble columns, crystal chandeliers) and in the bedrooms, many of which sport antiques. Smart bathrooms have generous towelling bathrobes. Room rates vary from that quoted (twins, doubles) to £134 (double luxurious), £174 (course views) and £254 (suites). Well-turned-out staff provide a high level of service that includes valet parking, luggage porterage and proper bedroom service in the evenings. Forte Grand. ***Rooms** 50. Sauna, solarium.* AMERICAN EXPRESS® *Access, Diners, Visa.*

St Andrews   St Andrews Old Course Hotel   82%   £210

Tel 0334 474371   Fax 0334 477668   **H**

St Andrews Fife KY16 9SP   **Map 3 D5**

Arguably one of the most famous golfing hotels in the world, set beside the infamous 17th Road Hole, and by the clubhouse of the Royal and Ancient, it also has views to the bay, the city and behind that, the Highlands: almost a microcosm of all things quintessentially Scottish. Once you've recovered from the splendour of the setting, enter the hotel proper to have your breath taken away again by the sheer sumptuousness and elegance of the surroundings. Chandeliers and sofas to sink into typify the comfort, stencilled coving and book-lined walls the artistry that has gone into the creation of a haven of peace and luxury. Attention to detail in the bedrooms is equally meticulous, with traditional wooden furniture, TVs hidden away in cabinets and footstools with the comfortable armchairs. High-class toiletries and generously-sized bathrobes add to the exuberance in the marble bathrooms. Indoor leisure activities are centred on the Spa, the luxuriously equipped health and beauty centre, based around the stunning glass-covered, pillared and frescoed pool area. Golfing guests wishing to play the Old Course should apply to the hotel's golf steward. The hotel also provides fine facilities for banqueting and conferences (up to 300 people). Children up to 12 stay free in parents' room. Special children's menu available. ***Rooms** 125. Garden, indoor swimming pool, gym, steam room, solarium, golf shop, coffee shop 10am-10pm.* AMERICAN EXPRESS® *Access, Diners, Visa.*

St Andrews   Places of Interest

Tourist Information   Tel 0334 472021.
Buchanan Theatre   Tel 0334 476161.
Earlshall Castle and Gardens   Leuchars Tel 0334 839205.
British Golf Museum   Tel 0334 478880.
East Sands Leisure Centre   Tel 0334 476506.

St Fillans   Four Seasons Hotel   60%   £70

Tel & Fax 0764 685 333   **HR**

St Fillans nr Crieff Tayside PH26 2NF   **Map 3 C5**

Unremarkable at first sight, except for its stunning location at the head of Loch Earn, the Four Seasons is the sort of hotel that improves with acquaintance – a process that begins with a warm welcome from a member of the Scott family. Residents and diners share a small bar which has Oregon pine and natural stone features, and there is also a small, genteel lounge and on the first floor a tiny library that also offers various board games. Modestly furnished bedrooms are bright, cheerful and generally of good size; six are in chalets above and to the rear of the hotel. Super breakfasts come with rolls hot from the oven, home-made bread and freshly squeezed orange juice. Children up to 6 stay free in parents' room. *Rooms 18. Garden. Closed early Dec-end Feb.* *Access, Diners, Visa.*

Restaurant £55

Fabulous views from the dining room here (tables in the window are much sought after) and some pretty good cooking too from Andrew Scott (the son of the house) and his small team. Everything is home-made, from the bread and the oatcakes that accompany a board of well-kept cheeses to the chutney that comes with an excellent pork terrine that is rather more sophisticated than the 'country-style' label might suggest. Other dishes from the daily changing, fixed-price dinner might include smoked Tay salmon, new season's roast sea bass with garlic and tomato, fillet of salmon surrounded by a dill mousse and wrapped in filo pastry, roast leg of lamb, and breast of wood pigeon and saddle of venison with turnips and whisky. Portions are generous almost to a fault. If you're counting calories best not to look at the sweet trolley. *Seats 40. Private Room 30. L 12.15-2.15 D 7-9.30. Set Sun L £12.50.*

Scarista	Scarista House	67%	£84
Tel 0859 550238 Fax 0859 550277			**HR**
Scarista Isle of Harris Highland PA85 3HX			Map 2 A3

The Callaghans' former manse on the Atlantic coast of Harris (15 miles south-west of Tarbert on the A859) must be one of the most remote hotels in Britain. Ruggedly beautiful countryside and endless deserted beaches are a magnet for walkers, bird-watchers and fishermen, who also appreciate the warm welcome and homely comforts of Scarista House. One of the two lounges is lined with books and there is a record collection available for guests' use. Bedrooms in the annexe are larger and more modern than those in the main house, which have a touch more character; three are reserved for non-smokers. No children under 8. Well-trained dogs are welcome so long as they do not disturb the hill sheep. *Rooms 8. Garden. Closed mid Oct-Apr. No credit cards.*

Restaurant £55

Jane Callaghan's simple, hearty dinners are served in a candle-lit dining room and are based on good local produce using only free-range eggs and meat, and avoiding farmed seafood. The choice is fixed, so advise in advance of any dislikes ("or, indeed, any likes"). Watercress soup, lamb fillet with Puy lentils with saffron potatoes and braised endive, and orange cake with orange flowerwater salad made up a recent menu. Scottish cheeses. Bread, cakes and preserves are all home-made. *Seats 20. Private Room 8. L by arrangement. D at 8.15. Set D £25.*

Scone	Murrayshall House	72%	£130
Tel 0738 551171 Fax 0738 552595			**HR**
Scone Tayside PH2 7PH			Map 3 C5

Golf is a major attraction at this turn-of-the-century stone mansion, with an 18-hole golf course, a professional on hand to give tuition, driving range, a golf shop and a clubhouse with bar. Fabric-covered walls feature in the stylish day rooms, dark blue damask to match the soft furnishings in the quiet lounge and a bold floral pattern in the lounge bar. Best bedrooms are those in the original part of the house, those in the newer wing being somewhat smaller, but all offer many extras like fresh flowers, fruit, magazines and mineral water. Rooms are properly serviced in the evenings as are the bathrooms, which boast robes and large bath sheets. Children up to 10 stay free in parents' room. *Rooms 19. Garden, tennis, bowling, golf (18), driving range.* AMERICAN EXPRESS *Access, Diners, Visa.*

See over

Old Masters Restaurant   £60

A luxuriously appointed hotel restaurant with light lunch menu and
evening à la carte. Typical dinner dishes could include parfait of chicken
livers with redcurrant sauce, fish stew, chicken with a tomato, stem ginger
and coriander sauce, beef and Irish stout casserole and roast deer with sweet
and sour cabbage. Also sandwiches and light meals in the clubhouse.
*Seats 60. Parties 12. Private Room 30. L 12-2 D 7-9.30. Set L (business) from
£6.95 Set D £17.50.*

Scone   Place of Interest

Scone Palace   Tel 0738 552300.

Scourie   Eddrachilles Hotel   60%   £72

Tel 0971 502080   Fax 0971 502477   **H**

Badcall Bay Scourie Highland IV27 4TH   Map 2 B2

This 200-year-old hotel enjoys a setting of outstanding peace and rugged
beauty in a 320-acre estate at the head of Badcall Bay. Handa Island bird
sanctuary is a few miles to the north, and boat trips can be made from
nearby Tarbet. To the south are Britain's highest waterfalls, of Eas-coul-
Aluin. It's also a great base for walking, exploring, climbing and fishing
and packed lunches are available for serious outdoor types. Seven of the
neatly-kept bedrooms have shower/WC only. No children under 3. No
dogs. *Rooms 11. Garden, boat hire. Closed Nov-Feb. Access, Visa.*

Scourie   Scourie Hotel   60%   £68

Tel 0971 502396   Fax 0971 502423   **H**

Scourie Highland IV27 4SX   Map 2 B2

Built by the second Duke of Sutherland as a coaching inn, this is now
a fishing hotel *par excellence*. Brown trout, sea trout and salmon are all
to be found in the 50 hotel-controlled beats in the 25,000 acres of grounds,
and boats can be supplied for many of the beats. Packed lunches are
available. Tales swapped in the lounges and cocktail bar are naturally fairly
fishy. Bedrooms, including two garden suites, are modern and well kept,
with fitted furniture and good-sized bathrooms (two rooms are without
en-suite facilities). There are no TVs, but the views from the windows are
very watchable. Children from 3 to 12 stay free in parents' room, being
charged only for meals as taken; no children under 3. *Rooms 20. Garden,
game fishing. Closed Nov-Mar.* AMERICAN EXPRESS *Access, Diners, Visa.*

Selkirk   Philipburn House   60%   £90

Tel 0750 20747   Fax 0750 21690   **H**

Linglie Road Selkirk Borders TD7 5LS   Map 4 C1

Set back from the A707/A708 junction, a mile from the town centre
on the Peebles road, this extended 18th-century house has been turned into
a delightful family hotel with a Tyrolean-style interior. The Hill family,
owners since 1971, cater for all kinds of visitors – business, fishing, tourist,
family – and friendly hospitality is their watchword. Bedrooms – in the
house, by the pool or in the 'log cabin' – feature pine, pretty fabrics and
a host of extras. Parents will appreciate the privacy provided by many
separate but connecting children's rooms. An extension to the bar should
be available by February 1995. *Rooms 16. Garden, outdoor swimming pool,
games room, children's playground, crèche. Access, Visa.*

Selkirk   Places of Interest

Tourist Information   Tel 0750 20054.
Bowhill   Tel 0750 20732.
Halliwell's House Museum   Tel 0750 20096.

Skeabost Bridge   Skeabost House   60%   £77

Tel 0470 532202   Fax 0470 532454   **H**

Skeabost Bridge by Portree Isle of Skye Highland IV51 9NP   Map 2 A3

Twelve acres of woodland and gardens surround a former hunting lodge
on Loch Snizort. It's a comfortable place, with the same family owners
since 1970, and relaxation is easy in the lounges, the flagstoned sun lounge,
the cosy bar and the billiard room. A new attraction, opened in mid-1994,
is a 60-seat conservatory with its own kitchen. Pretty bedrooms include
one with a four-poster and a few in the nearby Garden House. One
is a large family room. The hotel owns eight miles of the river Snizort,
which runs through the grounds, and has a boat on a nearby loch.
*Rooms 26. Garden, golf (9-hole), fishing, snooker. Closed 1 Nov-Easter.
Access, Visa.*

Skeabost Bridge   Place of Interest

Edinbane Pottery   Tel 0470 582234.

Skelmorlie   Manor Park   61%   £75

Tel & Fax 0475 520832   **H**

Skelmorlie nr Largs Strathclyde PA17 5HE   Map 3 B6

Situated between Skelmorlie and Largs on the A78 coast road, just
a quarter of an hour from Greenock and the M8 motorway, the hotel was
built in 1840. There are spectacular views from the 15 acres of grounds and
water gardens, immaculately landscaped, and from the Adam-designed
house – note the intricate cornices, oak staircase and galleried landing.
Seven bedrooms are in the main building, the rest in the nearby Stables
Court. In the Cowal suite Churchill and Eisenhower met to plan the D-
Day landings; 150 delegates can be accommodated theatre-style. No dogs.
Rooms 23. Garden. AMERICAN EXPRESS *Access, Diners, Visa.*

Sleat   Kinloch Lodge   67%   £80

Tel 0471 833214   Fax 0471 833277   **HR**

Sleat Isle of Skye Highland IV43 8QY   Map 3 A4

Kinloch Lodge is a white stone building at the head of Loch Na Dal in the
south of the island. Built in 1680 as a farmhouse, it is now the home
of Lord and Lady Macdonald, and guests are made to feel like family
friends. Its isolated position makes it a haven of peace and the views are
truly outstanding. Two stylish drawing rooms enjoy the spectacular setting
and are adorned with ancestral portraits, fine antiques, porcelain pieces and
each with a roaring fire provide the perfect spot for afternoon tea or a pre-
dinner drink. Bedrooms, mostly rather small, are comfortable and quiet,
with no phones or TVs to disturb the peace; prices vary to reflect their size
and outlook (prices are also greatly reduced during low season – March
and April, mid-October and November). Furniture is a mixture of antique
and modern pieces and the two rooms not en suite have bathrooms across
the corridor. Children by arrangement only. *Rooms 10. Garden, stalking,
fishing. Closed 1 Dec-28 Feb. Access, Visa.*

Dining Room   £75

Expert home cooking by Lady Macdonald and three others. Local
ingredients, hearty portions, friendly staff. Some typical dishes from the
five-course, limited-choice menu: herb profiteroles filled with bacon and
cream cheese; spinach, apple and turmeric soup; roast leg of lamb with
Reform sauce, fillet of salmon in filo parcels with dill butter; marmalade
creamy rice brulée. No smoking in the dining rooms. Coffee with fudge
is served in the drawing rooms. Concise, carefully selected wine list. The
hotel holds regular cookery demonstrations. *Seats 30. Parties 15. D at 8.
Set D £25.*

Sleat   Places of Interest

Clan Donald Centre   Armadale Castle Tel 04714 305.
Kylerhea Otter Haven.

South Queensferry **Forth Bridges Moat House 61%**   £114

Tel & Fax 031-331 1199   **H**

South Queensferry Lothian EH30 9SF   Map 3 C5

Five miles from Edinburgh airport, a 60s' hotel with spectacular views
of both Forth Bridges and good leisure facilities. Conference/banqueting
facilities for 250. Children up to 14 stay free in parents' room. *Rooms 108.
Garden, indoor swimming pool, gym, squash, sauna, spa bath, hair salon,
snooker, coffee shop 9-7.* AMERICAN EXPRESS *Access, Diners, Visa.*

South Queensferry   Places of Interest

Dalmeny House   Tel 031-331 1888.
Hopetoun House   Tel 031-331 2451.

Spean Bridge   Old Station Restaurant   £45

Tel 0397 712535   **R**

Station Road Spean Bridge Highland PH34 4EP   Map 3 B4

Trains still stop (just four a day) at this railway station where the former
ticket office and waiting rooms that line the platform have been turned
into a most appealing restaurant by Richard (in the kitchen) and Helen
(front of house) Bunney. The sensibly short (about five dishes at each stage)
à la carte nevertheless offers plenty of variety with mains ranging from
a simple chargrilled Aberdeen Angus steak to grilled teriyaki salmon fillet,
duck breast with apricot and lemon sauce, and a spiced aubergine and
mushroom casserole. Notable among the starters is the soup of the day
– a subtle cream of chestnut on our last visit – while puds might include
a whisky marmalade ice cream along with a good sticky toffee pudding.
Smoking is allowed only in the pre-dinner drinks area. *Seats 30. Parties 10.
Private Room 12. L 12-2.30 D 6-9. Closed L Mon-Fri, D Mon-Wed
in Winter, 25 & 26 Dec, 1 Jan. Access, Visa.*

> If we recommend meals in a hotel or inn a separate entry is made for its
> restaurant.

Stewarton   Chapeltoun House   71%   £99

Tel 0560 482696   Fax 0560 485100   **H**

Stewarton-Irvine Road Stewarton Strathclyde KA3 3ED   Map 3 B6

Chapeltown House was built at the turn of the century for a Glasgow
merchant and his English bride and still retains many original features, the
pale pink-washed walls and stone balustrades of the exterior highlighting its
serene position amid 20 well-kept acres of gardens. The oak-panelled
entrance hall, friezes, plasterwork and teak floors all add to the sense
of occasion and, to its many regulars, of homecoming. Bedrooms range
in style and character from the super-king-size four-poster room, with bay
windows to catch the early morning sun, to master and superior rooms,
but all have thoughtful extras. No children under 12. *Rooms 8. Garden.
Closed 1st 2 weeks Jan.* AMERICAN EXPRESS *Access, Visa.*

Stirling — Granada Lodge

£51
L
Map 3 C5

Tel 0786 815033   Fax 0786 815900
M90/M80 Junction 9 Stirling Central FK7 8EU

Rooms 37. AMERICAN EXPRESS *Access, Diners, Visa.*

Stirling — Places of Interest

Tourist Information   Tel 0786 475019.
MacRobert Arts Centre   Tel 0786 461081.
Stirling Castle   Tel 0786 450000.
Smith Art Gallery and Museum   Tel 0786 471917.
Regimental Museum of Argyll and Sutherland Highlanders
   Tel 0786 475165.

Stornoway — Cabarfeidh Hotel   64%

£80
H
Map 2 A2

Tel 0851 702604   Fax 0851 705572
Manor Park Stornoway Isle of Lewis Highland PA87 2EU

An early-70s hotel (the name means stag's head) with a rather faceless exterior belying the inviting interior, a brisk walk from the Ullapool ferry terminal on the largest of the Outer Hebrides islands. The Viking Bar (with a longship for a counter), a cocktail bar and a restaurant divided into three differently styled areas comprise the public rooms. Cheerful bedrooms, all en suite. Banquets and conferences for up to 200/250. Spectacular scenery and an abundance of peace are major assets. *Rooms 46. Garden.* AMERICAN EXPRESS *Access, Diners, Visa.*

Stornoway — Places of Interest

Tourist Information   Tel 0851 703088.

Strachur — Creggans Inn   61%

£98
H
Map 3 B5

Tel 036 986 279   Fax 036 986 637
Strachur Strathclyde PA27 8BX

Sir Fitzroy and Lady Maclean's white-painted inn stands amid magnificent scenery by Loch Fyne on the Road to the Isles. It's a great part of the world for fishing, walking and touring, after which a glass of the hotel's own Old MacPhunn ten-year-old vatted malt goes down well in either bar. There's a peaceful sitting room and a large garden lounge, both with delightful views. Decor varies in the small but charming bedrooms, almost all of which have bathrooms en suite. *Rooms 21. Garden, fishing.* AMERICAN EXPRESS *Access, Diners, Visa.*

Strachur — Places of Interest

Crarae Glen Garden   Minard. Tel 0546 86614.
Inveraray Castle   Tel 0499 2203 *20 miles.*
Argyll Wildlife Park   Inveraray Tel 0499 2264.
European Sheep and Wool Centre   Lochgoiliead Tel 03013 247
   10 miles.

Stranraer — North West Castle   68%

£70
H
Map 4 A2

Tel 0776 704413   Fax 0776 702646
Portrodie Stranraer Dumfries & Galloway DG9 8EH

Tastefully extended since being built in 1820, the hotel stands opposite the ferry port. It was once the home of the Arctic explorer Sir John Ross, whose name is commemorated in the panelled bar, and was the first hotel in the world to have its own indoor curling rink. Bedrooms include six suites, and many rooms have enough space for an extra bed or cots. Conference and banqueting facilities for 150 delegates; enquire about special arrangements for residents at two local golf courses and nearby squash courts. Sister establishment to the *Cally Palace Hotel* in Gatehouse of Fleet and *Kirroughtree Hotel*, Newton Stewart. **Rooms** *71. Garden, indoor swimming pool, curling rink, sauna, solarium, spa bath, gym, snooker, coffee shop (10am-10pm), gift shop. No credit cards.*

Stranraer   Places of Interest

Tourist Information   Tel 0776 702595.
  Historic Houses, Castles and Gardens
Castle Kennedy and Lochinch Gardens   Tel 0776 2024.
Logan Botanic Garden   Tel 0776 860231.
Glenwhan Gardens   Dunragit Tel 0581 400222.

Strathblane   Kirkhouse Inn   £72

Tel 0360 770621   Fax 0360 770896   ■

Glasgow Road Strathblane Central G63 9AA   Map 3 B5

On the A81 Stirling and Aberfoyle road, ten miles north of Glasgow, this roadside inn is at the foot of the Campsie Fells and thus popular with walkers. It's an ideal touring centre as Loch Lomond, the Trossachs, Glasgow and Stirling are all within 30 minutes by car. Sprucely kept public areas include a busy public bar and quieter lounge and restaurant. Pastel colours are used in the bedrooms, which include a honeymoon suite with a sunken bath. 24hr room service. Children up to 12 stay free in parents' room. Adventure weekends are a big attraction. **Rooms** *15. Garden, fishing, pool table.* AMERICAN EXPRESS *Access, Diners, Visa.*

Talladale   Loch Maree Hotel   £80

Tel 044 584 288   Fax 044 584 241   ■

Achnasheen Talladale Highland IV2 2HC   Map 2 B3

A purpose-built fishing hotel beautifully situated on the banks of the loch between Gairloch and Kinlochewe. The glorious outdoors is certainly a major attraction, and inside things have changed dramatically from the former time-warp Victorian cosiness. One twin room is equipped for disabled guests. Four additional bedrooms are planned by the end of 1994. The hotel owns eight boats (complete with mandatory ghillies) for sea trout and salmon fishing on the loch; tackle and gifts available in the hotel shop. **Rooms** *30. Garden, fishing, boating. Access, Visa.*

Tarbert   Stonefield Castle   58%   £90★

Tel 0880 820836   Fax 0880 820929   H

Loch Fyne Tarbert Strathclyde PA29 6YJ   Map 3 B6

Sixty acres of grounds surround the 19th-century former baronial home and many of the rooms command spectacular views over Loch Fyne. It's great walking country, and many outdoor sporting activities are available in the vicinity. Day rooms are in comfortable, traditional style, so too the bedrooms in the main house. Wing rooms are more ordinary but certainly adequate. Two miles north of Tarbert – look out for hotel signs. ★Half-board terms. **Rooms** *32. Garden, outdoor swimming pool (summer only), fishing, sauna, sun beds, snooker.* AMERICAN EXPRESS *Access, Diners, Visa.*

Tarbert   Places of Interest

Tourist Information   Tel 0880 820429.

Tiroran   Tiroran House   70%   £186*

HR

Tel & Fax 068 15 232

Tiroran Isle of Mull Strathclyde PA69 6ES   Map 3 A5

The splendid wild landscapes of the Isle of Mull provide a perfect backdrop
to Tiroran House, a traditional Scottish sporting lodge that is a warm and
friendly hotel as well as still the home of Robin and Sue Blockey. It has its
own 15 acres of gardens and woodland, run through with streams, and
spectacular views of Loch Scridain. The house naturally takes full advantage
of the setting, with big picture windows and roaring log fires, and
is furnished with antiques and family silver. Six bedrooms of individual
decor and charm are in the main house, the rest are in adjacent pine
cottages. Biscuits, cheese and a half bottle of wine are typical of the
thoughtful touches that await arriving guests; breakfast, too, is exemplary.
No phones, no TVs, no children under ten. *Half-board terms only.
*Rooms 9. Garden, croquet, games room. Closed early Oct-mid May.
No credit cards.*

Restaurant   £70

Sue Blockey concentrates on using good fresh seasonal produce to the best
effect, though non-residents will only be able to sample the results if there
are some bedrooms unoccupied. Salads, herbs, fruits and vegetables come
from her own garden when possible. The set dinner menu has choices for
starters and puddings but not for main courses, but a well-balanced summer
offering could be Dansyre Blue cheese tartlets with a white wine and chive
sauce, followed by wild Mull salmon with sauce Choron, then gooseberry
fool with brandy soufflé and orange shortbread with coffee and chocolates
to finish. Excellent bread is baked daily and fine Scottish cheeses and Stilton
are fitting additions. Lunch, for residents only, is served on the verandah;
packed lunches are also provided on request. Short but imaginative wine
list with informative tasting notes. *Seats 20. Parties 8. D at 7.45.
Closed L except residents. Set D £28.50.*

Tiroran   Places of Interest

Iona Community Tel 06817 407
Fingal's Cave Staffa Tel 041-552 8391.

Tobermory   Tobermory Hotel   57%   £64

H

Tel 0688 2091   Fax 0688 2254

53 Main Street Tobermory Isle of Mull Strathclyde PA75 6NT   Map 3 A4

Ring the bell to gain access to this small, carefully maintained hotel on the
waterfront of Tobermory Bay. Owners Martin and Kay Sutton put
hospitality top of their list, and two cosy lounges furnished with floral sofas
and easy chairs, well-chosen ornaments and pictures offer welcoming
touches like magazines and fresh flowers. Compact bedrooms (all non-
smoking) include some king-size beds. The bathrooms are well kept; nine
are currently en suite. Two ground-floor rooms have been adapted to the
needs of guests in wheelchairs. *Rooms 17. Access, Visa.*

Tobermory   Places of Interest

Tourist Information Tel 0688 2182

Troon   Marine Highland Hotel   67%   £145

H

Tel 0292 313066   Fax 0292 314444

Crosbie Road Troon Strathclyde KA10 6HE   Map 4 A1

This handsome Victorian sandstone structure overlooks the 18th fairway
of Royal Troon championship golf course. Accommodation options are
standard, de luxe or top-of-the-range Ambassador suites. Families welcome,
with entertainment during festive periods, baby-sitting and baby-listening

offered; children up to 14 share parents' room free. Good conference facilities for up to 220. Leave the A77 and follow the B789 to Troon. Scottish Highland Hotels. **Rooms** 72. *Indoor swimming pool, gym, squash, sauna, steam room, solarium, beauty salon, putting, snooker, helipad, brasserie (11am-11pm).* AMERICAN EXPRESS *Access, Diners, Visa.*

Troon   Piersland House   64%   £94

Tel 0292 314747   Fax 0292 315613   **H**

15 Craigend Road Troon Strathclyde KA10 6HD   Map 4 A1

A sandstone and timbered building dating from 1890 and originally owned by the grandson of whisky man Johnnie Walker. From the reception, stairs lead up to a galleried landing with exposed roof timbers. Further pleasing architectural features are to be found in the bar/lounge, which boasts stone-mullioned windows, an embroidered frieze and a ribbed ceiling. Bedrooms are individually and prettily appointed; newly opened are four cottage suites next to the hotel. Banqueting/conference facilities for up to 150/110. The hotel stands opposite Royal Troon golf club, with upwards of a dozen more courses in the neighbourhood. **Rooms** 23. *Garden, putting.* AMERICAN EXPRESS *Access, Diners, Visa.*

Troon   Places of Interest

Tourist Information   Tel 0292 317696.

See the hotel by county listings for easy comparison of conference and banqueting facilities.

Turnberry   Turnberry Hotel   84%   £200

Tel 0655 31000   Fax 0655 31706   **HR**

Turnberry Strathclyde KA26 9LT   Map 4 A2

When Turnberry opened in 1906 it became the world's first hotel and golf resort, and the country club and health spa keep it today in the forefront of sporting hotels. It is also established as a top-flight conference and banqueting venue (up to 150 delegates in the self-contained Turnberry Suite). The hotel overlooks the famous links of Ailsa and Arran, to the islands of that name and towards the Mull of Kintyre beyond. Day rooms combine comfort and splendour at a high level, and bedrooms, too, are notably stylish, with luxuriously equipped bathrooms. There are ten suites, with luxury apartments including four-posters and jacuzzis. The *Clubhouse* offers an informal setting for simple eating, from sandwiches and salads to the daily roast. The *Bay at Turnberry* offers health-conscious menus and is open from April to October, as is the Halfway House by the 10th tee on the Ailsa Course. There are several other bars, including the Deck lounge above the spa. **Rooms** 132. *Garden, indoor swimming pool, gym, spa bath, sauna, solarium, beauty & hair salon, 2 18-hole golf courses, 12-hole pitch & putt, health spa, tennis, squash, riding, snooker, helipad.* AMERICAN EXPRESS *Access, Diners, Visa.*

Restaurant   £90

The à la carte menu is strong on luxury items – caviar, foie gras, lobster, champagne-poached turbot, sweetbreads braised in Amontillado – while the fixed-price dinner menu has a daily roast along with dishes with a contemporary ring such as turbot and scallop mousse with a caviar and dill butter sauce, terrine of Scottish salmon and supreme of chicken with asparagus mousse, grilled with a trio of sweet pepper coulis. Sunday lunch comprises a glass of champagne, three courses, coffee and petits fours. **Seats** 180. *Parties* 10. *Private Room* 110. *L (Sun only) 1-2.30 D 7.30-10. Set Sun L £19.50 Set D £37.50.*

Tweedsmuir   Crook Inn   59%   £52

Tel 089 97 272   Fax 089 97 294   **H**

Tweedsmuir nr Biggar Borders ML12 6QN   Map 4 C1

Standing on the A701 Moffat-Edinburgh road and set in the ruggedly
beautiful Tweed valley, the Crook is a good base for walking, climbing
and touring holidays. Guests can also enjoy free fishing on 30 miles of the
River Tweed. Burns wrote *Willie Wastle's Wife* in what is now the bar,
and locally-born John Buchan set many of his novels in the area. Neat
bedrooms are simple in their appointments, with no TVs or telephones.
There are a few Art Deco features in the lounge and some of the
bathrooms. The success of the glass-making centre in the former stable
block has led to the subsequent creation of the Upper Tweed Heritage
Centre. Light meals can be enjoyed in the garden. *Rooms 7. Garden, fishing,
putting, coffee shop.* AMERICAN EXPRESS *Access, Diners, Visa.*

Uig   Uig Hotel   59%   £75

Tel 0470 542205   Fax 0470 542308   **H**

Uig Isle of Skye Highland IV51 9YE   Map 2 A3

On a hillside at the north end of the island, the former coaching inn
(a hotel since 1946) is handy for the ferry to Uist and Harris. You come
here to enjoy the peace and solitude, the wonderful scenery, the walks and
the wildlife. Day rooms are neat and homely, and provide fine sea views.
The conservatory has been turned into a coffee shop. Comfortable
bedrooms with smart co-ordinated colour schemes include six in Sobhraig
House, a converted steading next to the hotel. Self-catering apartments are
available. Popular for bridge congresses, plus garden and wildlife tours.
Rooms 16. Garden, pony trekking. Closed mid Oct-week before Easter.
AMERICAN EXPRESS *Access, Diners, Visa.*

Ullapool   Altnaharrie Inn   73%   £250★

Tel 0854 633230   **HR**

Ullapool Wester Ross Highland IV26 2SS   Map 2 B2

A small launch transfers you from the quayside at Ullapool across Loch
Broom. The trip takes approximately 10 minutes and transports you to the
crock of gold at the end of a rainbow. Wisteria-clad and painted white
with a cottage garden at the front, the impression from the sea as you
approach is of a delightful house surrounded by trees nestling below
heather-clad hills. The welcome extended by Fred Brown as you walk
up the path to the front door is as warm and charming as the wonderful
interior. The smell of log fires mingles with the heady perfume of gigantic
lily blooms in the entrance hall, which doubles as a small but comfortable
lounge. There's a further, more spacious lounge upstairs. Decor throughout
is a very tasteful mix of styles – the rough white-painted walls hung with
all manner of artwork, beautiful paintings and craftwork. Books abound
as do vases of simply arranged but stunning flowers. Bedrooms, whether
upstairs in the main house or in the little cottages close by in the grounds,
are brightly decorated, spotless and possess all the charm and style you'd
expect from a very well-run small country hotel. While there are no radios
or TVs, little extras which are provided include fresh fruit and water.
Candles and torches are there for night-time use when the generator
is switched off. Bathrooms are equally bright and immaculately
maintained. Fine toiletries more than compensate for the sometimes peaty
appearance of the water, which is inevitable in such a remote location.
Rooms are serviced to a very professional and high standard with beds
turned down at night and bathrooms tidied up with fresh towels provided.
Breakfasts in the morning are a simpler extension of the previous night's
dinner with a wonderful selection of carefully prepared items, from
porridge to venison sausages and buttery croissants, home-made jams and
marmalades – a meal that will help sustain you almost till dinner-time.

See over

The ferry leaves shortly after breakfast returning to Ullapool where cars
are parked in a private quayside car park. This is a strictly no-smoking
hotel. No children under 7. ★Half-board terms only. *Rooms 8. Garden.
Closed mid Nov-week before Easter.* AMERICAN EXPRESS MARTELL COGNAC

Restaurant   ★ ★ ★   £120

The cooking is every bit as special as the location, the best tables being
those able to best enjoy the wonderful view across the loch and taking full
advantage of the setting sun. A supremely romantic restaurant with
gleaming glassware, candles and vases of fresh flowers decorating the highly
polished tables and original artwork on the walls. Fred Brown together
with a young, dedicated team looks after the front of house while Gunn
Eriksen, only very rarely emerging from her kitchen, virtually
singlehandedly produces dishes of great visual appeal and artistry. Her raw
material sources are the wealth of local produce with fish delivered direct
from the fishing boats and shellfish stored live in creels on the sea-bed.
There is no choice for dinner but guests are asked, at the time of booking,
whether they have any dislikes, dietary requirements or food allergies.
Returning guests have an alternative choice too, though with food this
exceptional who cares if you have to sit down to the same meal? Gunn has
a passion for cooking hard-to-find, uncommon ingredients fashioning them
into dishes that totally captivate the palate. Distinct natural flavours and
sauces that are simple, being mostly the reduced pan juices with a few
discreet additions, are what you'll find here. Menus are of five courses and
well balanced. The only choice comes at the dessert stage when there are
three on offer though it is quite usual for all three to be offered at once.
A typical menu will begin with a fillet of young turbot with spinach, baby
leeks, morels and a champagne-vinegar butter sauce followed by a clear
soup with vegetable vermicelli and langoustines fried in butter. A main
dish of quail fillets with mushrooms, grapes and foie gras served on a bed
of cabbage has two sauces, one of juniper and cream, the other of the pan
juices and a dash of burgundy. Afterwards comes a selection of fine cheeses.
Desserts include an apple cooked in fine, crisp pastry with a calvados ice
cream and caramel sauce, a slice of lemon tart and layers of hazelnut cake
and coffee ice cream with chocolate and a compote of raspberries. Super
coffee and chocolates rounds off an exceptional evening. An excellent wine
list with lots of half bottles and a very well chosen house selection. Best
value probably outside France. *Seats 18. Parties 14. D only 8pm (Light lunch
available to residents only). Set D £50.*

Consult page 20 for a full list of starred restaurants

Consult page 20 for a full list of starred restaurants

Ullapool   Ceilidh Place   £96

Tel 0854 612103   Fax 0854 612886   ■

14 West Argyle Street Ullapool Highland IV26 2TY   Map 2 B2

Literally meaning 'Meeting Place', Jean Urquhart's Ceilidh Place is much
more: bookshop, arts centre with gallery, coffee shop, evening restaurant
and venue for theatre, music and poetry all housed in a cosy collection
of welcoming rooms. Such is the extent of the live entertainment that the
single little TV is more than adequate. The pretty bedrooms are
comfortable and spotless; ten rooms now have en-suite facilities. Eleven
additional rooms in a separate building across the street offer more spartan,
budget accommodation with shared facilities. It is in this clubhouse that
most of the evening entertainment takes place. Ceilidh Place can arrange
sea angling, skiing tow-boats, loch fishing and pony trekking. Families are
well catered for. *Rooms 13. Garden, book shop, coffee shop (9am-9.30pm)
Closed 2 weeks Jan.* AMERICAN EXPRESS *Access, Diners, Visa.*

Ullapool   Places of Interest

Tourist Information   Tel 0854 612135.

Uphall   Houstoun House   68%   £115

Tel 0506 853831   Fax 0506 854220   **H**

Uphall Lothian EH52 6JS   **Map 3 C5**

Three buildings, the main one distinctively gabled, set in 20 acres of fine gardens that include yew hedges and copper beeches of great antiquity. The hotel offers comfortable and roomy accommodation in bedrooms that are either contemporary in style or more traditional, some with four-posters. Tower bedrooms retain some of the original 17th-century panelling. Day rooms also vary in age and character; there's a pleasantly modern lounge overlooking the tree-lined drive and three panelled dining rooms. Conference/banqueting facilities for 350/250; a new conference and function centre was due to open in October 1994. Hotel guests may play on the golf course that surrounds the hotel. ***Rooms** 30. Garden.* AMERICAN EXPRESS® *Access, Diners, Visa.*

Whitebridge   Knockie Lodge   71%   £130★

Tel 0456 486276   Fax 0456 486389   **HR**

Whitebridge Highland IV1 2UP   **Map 3 B4**

Just 20 minutes from Fort Augustus but a world away from the tourist-beaten track, Knockie Lodge enjoys a glorious setting high above Loch Nan Lann. Built as a hunting lodge in 1789, it is immensely civilised, with a timelessly tranquil atmosphere nurtured by the warm hospitality of Ian and Brenda Milward, here since 1983. Peat and log fires warm the antique-filled hall and appealing morning room (where the honesty bar is to be found) with family photos and ornaments adding to the charm. Traditionally furnished bedrooms (some with antiques) are prettily decorated and boast fresh flowers, mineral water and lots of books. All have direct-dial phones but no radio or TV. No children under ten. ★Half-board terms only – the rate quoted is for a small twin. Superior twins are £160, superior doubles £180. ***Rooms** 10. Garden, fishing, sailing, snooker. Closed end Oct–end Apr.* AMERICAN EXPRESS® *Access, Diners, Visa.*

Restaurant   £70

Chris Freeman's no-choice five-course dinners, served in a delightful panelled room, make good use of local supplies including salmon and lamb. Goujons of haddock, marinated salmon with melon, Highland lentil soup, stuffed quail baked in filo on a bed of creamed spinach, clootie dumpling and caramelised pear cake show the style. The cheeseboard and coffee round off the meal. No smoking. ***Seats** 22. D at 8. Set D £27.50.*

Note that all telephone numbers with area codes starting with 0
will start 01 from 16 April 1995.

Wales

Abercynon   Llechwen Hall   £69

Tel 0443 742050   Fax 0443 742189   **I**

Abercynon nr Llanfabon Mid Glamorgan CF37 4HP   Map 9 C6

About 1½ miles from Abercynon, (signposted from the A4054), Llechwen
Hall is a 17th-century farmhouse, converted to a gentleman's residence
in 1905, to country hotel five years ago. The name means "a place
of shelter" or "refuge", and seems very appropriate, as the atmosphere
evoked here is warm and welcoming. There are period pieces in both day
rooms and bedrooms, one of which has a four-poster. A lively local trade
adds welcoming warmth to the bars and restaurant and there are
banqueting and conference facilities (for up to 80) in the Nelson suite.
Rooms 11. Garden. AMERICAN EXPRESS *Access, Diners, Visa.*

Aberdovey   Plas Penhelig   62%   £80

Tel 0654 767676   Fax 0654 767783   **H**

Aberdovey Gwynedd LL35 0NA   Map 8 C3

A wooded driveway leads from the A493 to the house, whose seven acres
of award-winning grounds include a walled kitchen garden. The views are
splendid, whether over the gardens or out across the Dovey estuary. Inside,
the feel is Edwardian in the oak-panelled hall and in the south-facing
lounge, while bedrooms are more modern in aspect; larger rooms have
a table and two chairs. The terrace is an agreeable spot for an alfresco drink
and the terrace bar is open for snack lunches. *Rooms 11. Garden, croquet,
putting, tennis. Closed 23 Dec-1 Mar. Access, Visa.*

Aberdovey   Trefeddian Hotel   58%   £100*

Tel 0654 767213   Fax 0654 767777   **H**

Aberdovey Gwynedd LL35 0SB   Map 8 C3

Trefeddian stands back from the A493, half a mile north of Aberdovey,
with fine views across Cardigan Bay. Day rooms, which include lounge,
reading room and bar, offer a choice of peace and quiet or conviviality.
Neat, practical bedrooms include several with balconies. There's plenty
of information on what to do in the area. *Half-board terms only in the
hotel. Self-catering accommodation is also available in a house, flat and
bungalow. Family facilities (including three new family rooms and
children's playroom and playground). *Rooms 46. Garden, indoor swimming
pool, tennis, pitch & putt, solarium, snooker. Closed 2 Jan-9 Mar. Access, Visa.*

Abergavenny   Llanwenarth Arms Hotel   £59

Tel 0873 810550   Fax 0873 811880   **I**

Brecon Road Abergavenny Gwent NP8 1EP   Map 9 D5

A refurbished roadside inn (on the A40) some 3 miles to the west
of Abergavenny standing on an escarpment above the Usk valley. Residents
enjoy the use of their own lounge and a Victorian-style conservatory
furnished with comfortable cane furniture. Bedrooms, approached by way
of a sheltered courtyard, are attractively furnished and immaculately kept,
each one enjoying its fair share of the view across to Sugar Loaf mountain.
Good bar snacks. No dogs. *Rooms 18. Garden.* AMERICAN EXPRESS *Access,
Diners, Visa.*

Abergavenny   Walnut Tree Inn   ★   £77

Tel 0873 852797   Fax 0873 859764   **R**

Llandewi Skirrid Abergavenny Gwent NP7 8AW   Map 9 D5

Leave Abergavenny by the B4521 to find this delightful restaurant, which
was once a coaching inn for scholars seeking the spires of Oxford. Ann and
Franco Taruschio have been spreading their culinary gospel for over 30
years and what started as an inn with three tables is now a restaurant of

international repute. The long carte, of up to 20 dishes at each course, is easily handled by Franco's well-trained kitchen team. The market sets the menu, with simply described titles and none of the flowery descriptions that can appear at more pretentious establishments. Asparagus and tarragon soup (decorated with a frond of that herb, but curiously lacking its flavour); bruschetta of seafood; warm salad of fennel with dried tomatoes, crispy globe artichokes and *crescente* bread (seriously delicious); local salmon with rhubarb and ginger; lamb sweetbreads with mushrooms, Marsala and Parma ham (on a recent visit the perfectly cooked sweetbreads were completely overpowered by a pepper sauce); home-made Italian cheeses in peak condition. At lunchtime meals are only served in the rustic bistro/bar. In the evening the dining room proper is opened, with its brown linen napery. Space is at a premium, so booking is essential. *Seats 46. L 12.15-3 D 7.15-10. Closed Sun & Mon, Christmas, 2 weeks Feb. No credit cards.*

Abergavenny Places of Interest

Tourist Information Tel 0873 857588.
Abergavenny Showground Tel 0873 853152.

Aberkenfig New Garden £35

Tel 0656 724361 **R**

40 Pandy Road Aberkenfig nr Bridgend Mid Glamorgan Map 9 C6

Stylishly modern behind an unassuming frontage, New Garden offers a mainly Cantonese menu that keeps the crowds rolling in. Stuffed crab claws, black bean mussels or honey-roast spare ribs could precede soup, then perhaps grilled fish with crabmeat sauce, a filling hot pot dish or one of a dozen ways with duck. Various set meals for 2 or more. *Seats 160. Parties 100. L 12-2 D 5.30-12. Closed L Sun, 3 days Christmas. Set meals from £13.* AMERICAN EXPRESS *Access, Diners, Visa.*

Abersoch Porth Tocyn Hotel 69% £94

Tel 0758 713303 Fax 0758 713538 **HR**

Bwlchtocyn Abersoch Gwynedd LL53 7BU Map 8 B3

Run in commendable style since 1948 by the Fletcher-Brewer family, the hotel has gained a reputation for attentive hospitality. Once a row of lead-miners' cottages, it stands high above Cardigan Bay; it's about 2½ miles south of Abersoch, through the hamlets of Sarn Bach and Bwlchtocyn. The chintzy lounges contribute just the right degree of homeliness. Bedrooms, though generally small, are individually furnished in a similar style, many with restful sea views (these rooms attract a small supplement), all with private bathrooms and showers. Families with children are well catered for (children stay free in parents' room) – ask for their 'useful information for families' info sheet which sets out their aims and expectations. Flexibility is the key here. *Rooms 17. Garden, outdoor swimming pool, tennis. Closed mid Nov-week before Easter. Access, Visa.*

Restaurant £60

The focal point of Louise Fletcher-Brewer's self-styled "dinner party cooking" is her short-choice two- or five-course dinner menu that is completely changed each day. In practice, the style is less 'cordon bleu' than one might expect, with hazelnut and goat's cheese soufflé, pan-fried crab cakes with lime and coriander, ragout of lamb's liver and kidney with a Jerusalem artichoke mousse, honey-baked ham with a Welsh mustard sauce, poached paupiettes of sole and sea trout with a red pepper butter sauce, coffee crunch cheesecake and Spotted Dick with a sabayon sauce all typical dishes. There's always an intercourse fresh soup (perhaps sweet potato and leek or carrot and ginger), Welsh and other cheeses and coffee with home-made petits fours. Lunch is casual, maybe alfresco by the pool, with an all-you-can-eat hot and cold buffet on Sundays. No children under 7 after 7.30pm in the dining room; high tea provided earlier for youngsters. With the most expensive wine at less than £40 (vintage Krug apart), mark-ups are fair on the list, 20% of which is available in half bottles. **Seats** 50. Parties 20. L 12.30-2 D 7.30-9.30. Set L (Sun) £14.50 Set D £18/£24.

Abersoch   Riverside Hotel   59%   £72

Tel 0758 712419   Fax 0758 712671   **H**

Abersoch Gwynedd LL53 7HW   Map 8 B3

John and Wendy Bakewell, now in their 26th year at the Riverside, say that like monks they took a solemn vow of hospitality when they made the move from farming all that time ago. They have remained true to their word, as the many returning visitors will attest. Family-run and family-friendly, the hotel is well situated on the Lleyn peninsula. The River Soch actually flows next to the garden. Bedrooms are neat, modern and functional. Reduced rates for children with many facilities supplied including cots, high-chairs and a laundry room. No dogs. **Rooms** 12. Garden, indoor swimming pool (open Apr-end of Sept). Closed mid Nov-Mar. AMERICAN EXPRESS Access, Visa.

Aberystwyth   Conrah Country Hotel   63%   £79

Tel 0970 617941   Fax 0970 624546   **H**

Chancery Aberystwyth Dyfed SY23 4DF   Map 9 B4

Tucked away at the end of a long drive lined by rhododendrons, three miles south of Aberystwyth, set in 22 acres of grounds and woods, the Conrah puts peace, friendliness and fine views high on the agenda, and the three drawing rooms provide them in abundance. 11 of the bedrooms are in the main house, the rest around a courtyard. All are comfortable and cheerful, with en-suite bathrooms. No children under 5 (or dogs). **Rooms** 20. Garden, croquet, indoor swimming pool, sauna, table tennis. Closed 1 week Christmas. AMERICAN EXPRESS Access, Diners, Visa.

Aberystwyth   Places of Interest

Tourist Information   Tel 0970 612125.
Aberystwyth Arts Centre   Tel 0970 623232.
Llywernog Silver-Lead Mine Museum   Ponterwyd Tel 0970 85620.
Strata Florida Abbey   Tel 0974 831261 10 miles.
Vale of Rheidol Railway   Brecon Mountain Railway Tel 0970 675993/625819.

Bangor   Forte Travelodge   NEW   £45

Tel 0248 370345   **L**

A5/A55 Llandegai nr Bangor Gwynedd LL57 4BG   Map 8 B2

Three or so miles from Bangor, a former Pavilion Lodge where several smaller rooms have been joined to create eight family rooms (each with a double bed and sofa bed). Two rooms for disabled guests. Restaurant on site. **Rooms** 30. AMERICAN EXPRESS Access, Diners, Visa.

Bangor   Places of Interest

Bangor Information Centre   Tel 0248 352786.
Theatr Gwynedd   Bangor Tel 0248 351708 7 miles.
Cathedral Church of St. Deiniol   Bangor Tel 0248 351693.

Barry   Bunbury's   £50

Tel 0446 732075   **R**

14 High Street Barry South Glamorgan CF6 8EA   Map 9 C6

30s' sounds and setting behind the Barry Hotel. The main menu covers a good range of dishes, in individual and often fairly adventurous style.

There's also a lunchtime blackboard menu with dishes priced at around £4. *Seats 32. L 10.30-2.30 D 7.30-10 (Sat to 10.30). Closed Sun & Mon, Bank Holidays. Access, Visa.*

Barry	**Mount Sorrel Hotel**	**59%**	**£85**
Tel 0446 740069 Fax 0446 746600			**H**
Porthkerry Road Barry South Glamorgan CF62 7XY			Map 9 C6

Converted from two Victorian houses 30 years ago, with more recent additions for extra accommodation, meeting rooms (conferences for up to 150) and leisure facilities. Comfortable day rooms, very acceptable bedrooms (children up to 16 stay free when sharing with parents); two suites have interconnecting rooms and six other rooms are suitable for families. *Rooms 43. Indoor swimming pool, keep-fit equipment, sauna.* AMERICAN EXPRESS *Access, Diners, Visa.*

Barry   **Places of Interest**

Knap Swimming Pool   Tel 0446 735175.
Barry Island Pleasure Park   Tel 0446 741250.

Beaumaris	**Bulkeley Arms**	**59%**	**£67**
Tel 0248 810415 Fax 0248 810146			**H**
Castle Street Beaumaris Anglesey Gwynedd LL58 8AW			Map 8 B1

A sturdy Georgian building opposite the pier with splendid views across the Menai Straits to Snowdonia. Families and individual guests are equally well catered for; informal eating in the Castle Bar bistro which has recently been refurbished as have several of the delightful bedrooms, which are thus reduced slightly in number. Banquets/conferences for 140/180; plenty of parking; dogs welcome. *Rooms 38. Garden.* AMERICAN EXPRESS *Access, Visa.*

Beaumaris   **Places of Interest**

Beaumaris Castle   Tel 0248 810361.
Beaumaris Gaol Museum   Tel 0248 810921.
Pencarreg Glyn Garth   Nr Beaumaris Tel 0248 713545.

Our inspectors are full-time employees; they are professionally trained by us.

Beddgelert	**Royal Goat Hotel**	**60%**	**£68**
Tel 076 686 224 Fax 076 686 422			**H**
Beddgelert Gwynedd LL55 4YE			Map 8 B2

The Roberts family play host to the regulars who come for Snowdonia's fishing, walking and climbing. Beyond the white-painted facade an entrance hall/reception has heavily carved furniture and brass ornaments, more of which feature in the comfortable residents-only bar; there's plenty of lounge space and two dining rooms. Some of the bedrooms have four-posters; 18 rooms reserved for non-smokers. Children up to 12 stay free in parents' room. Function facilities for up to 100 theatre-style. *Rooms 34. Garden, games room, indoor children's playroom, fishing, coffee shop (7.30am-midnight).* AMERICAN EXPRESS *Access, Diners, Visa.*

Beddgelert   **Places of Interest**

National Trust Information Point   Tel 076 686 293.
Sygun Copper Mine   Tel 076 686 595.

Betws-y-Coed   Royal Oak   59%   £78

Tel 0690 710219   Fax 0690 710603   **H**

Holyhead Road Betws-y-Coed Gwynedd LL24 0AY   Map 8 C2

A solid stone edifice across from the river Llugwy where there's
a traditional and welcoming air in both the reception and bar with studded
brown leather and antique oak furniture. Bedrooms have restful autumnal
decor, simple modern furniture and two armchairs; six annexe rooms have
glossy laminated furniture with eye-catching mirrored bedheads. No dogs.
Rooms *27. Garden, coffee shop (7.30am-8.45pm).* AMERICAN EXPRESS *Access,
Diners, Visa.*

Betws-y-Coed   Places of Interest

Plas-y-Brenin National Centre for Mountain Activities   Capel Curig
Tel 06904 214.
Swallow Falls   Tel 0690 710796.

Bontddu   Bontddu Hall   62%   £90

Tel 0341 430661   Fax 0341 430284   **H**

Bontddu nr Dolgellau Gwynedd LL40 2SU   Map 8 C3

One of the main attractions at Michael and Margaretta Ball's unspoilt
Victorian Gothic country mansion is, quite simply, peace and quiet, though
its setting in Snowdonia means there's also plenty of activity in the area for
those so desiring – golf, hill walking, pony trekking, seafishing, the narrow
gauge railway. For those of a more cerebral than physical inclination, there
are splendid, elegant, period day rooms from which to enjoy the stunning
views. Bedrooms, the majority also offering fine views over the Mawddach
estuary, include a four-poster room and one with a spa bath. Six lodge
suites are in the hotel grounds. No children under 3, but up-to-16s stay free
in parents' room. **Rooms** *20. Garden. Closed Nov-Mar.* AMERICAN EXPRESS
Access, Diners, Visa.

Brechfa   Ty Mawr   £50

Tel 0267 202332   Fax 0267 202437   **RR**

Brechfa nr Carmarthen Dyfed SA32 7RA   Map 9 B5

Tiny Brechfa village stands by the Marlais river bridge below the 1200-
year-old forest which covers its steep valley. Once part of the managed
estate with a history traceable back at least to early Elizabethan times,
Ty Mawr ("The Big House") also has a big heart, personified in Dick and
Beryl Tudhope's warm hospitality. Their philosophy of "simplicity with
style" is evidenced both by the restaurant's gleaming and immaculately
restored interior and in the style and quality of Beryl's food. At dinner her
hat-shaped dominicans (a Ty Mawr speciality twice-baked cheese soufflé),
mushroom and tarragon puffs and salmon terrine with parsley pesto
exhibit an assured range of skills with a leaning deliberately away from
undue fussiness. New season's Welsh lamb – with a timbale of wild rice
and apricots and minted yoghurt – and Towy salmon with ginger and
a soy and sesame dressing do fine justice to the best seasonal tastes of Wales
to accompany perhaps, a Seyval/Reichensteiner 1992 from the ever-
improving vineyard at Llanerch. Coffee and Amaretto parfait, a crisp
baklava or a plate of Welsh cheese provide fine finishings. The 3-course
dinner, including coffee and sweetmeats, is priced according to choice
of main course. Booking is essential. **Seats** *35. Parties 10. Private Room 24.
L 12-1.30 D 7-9.30. Closed L Mon-Wed, L Sun, last 2 weeks Jan, last week
Nov. Set L £12.50.* AMERICAN EXPRESS *Access, Visa.*

Rooms   £68

The five bedrooms, all with private facilities, are also immaculate with
varnished pine furniture, country decor and crisp duvets and bed-linen.

With no phones, radio or TV to intrude, residents laud their sheer tranquillity. Quiet children welcome overnight. A new designated conference room accommodates 25.

Bridgend — Forte Travelodge — £45

Tel 0656 659218 — **L**

Sarn Park Service Area nr Bridgend Mid Glamorgan CF32 9RW — Map 9 C6

Located on the M4 at Junction 36 at the Welcome Break Service Area. Situated midway between Cardiff and Swansea, 2 miles from Bridgend. *Rooms 40.* AMERICAN EXPRESS *Access, Diners, Visa.*

If we recommend meals in a hotel or inn a separate entry is made for its restaurant.

Capel Coch — Tre-Ysgawen Hall — 76% — £110

Tel 0248 750750 Fax 0248 750035 — **HR**

Capel Coch nr Llangefni Anglesey Gwynedd LL77 7UR — Map 8 B1

A long tree-lined drive off the B5111, about five miles north of Llangefni, leads to this substantial Victorian mansion. It has been extensively refurbished over the last few years by Pat Craighead with, for example, lots of elaborate coving and ceiling roses added to the high-ceilinged public rooms, all of which lead off a spacious galleried central hall with skylight high above. Bedrooms, all individually decorated in considerable style, vary in size from ample to huge, the largest having new, high-quality mahogany furniture, the others a variety of antique pieces. Carpeted bathrooms, all with towelling robes and good toiletries, also vary from large with spa bath and bidet to some rather smaller with deep burgundy suites and limited shelf space. Decent breakfasts make a good start to the day. Room service is 24hrs and luggage porterage always offered. The hotel no longer has its own shooting, but it can be arranged in the area. Conference/banqueting facilities for up to 150/120. *Rooms 20. Garden, kennels.* AMERICAN EXPRESS *Access, Diners, Visa.*

Restaurant — £75

The main dining room is a large extension jutting out into the garden; when less busy a smaller, more cosy room is used. Warm quail salad with raspberry vinaigrette, roast monkfish tail with crispy leeks and white wine sauce, rack of Welsh lamb on a bed of ratatouille, noodles in a cream sauce with strips of chicken, mushrooms and peppers, sponge-wrapped chocolate mousse with chocolate ice cream and a brandy sabayon of seasonal fruits typify the freshly prepared, soundly cooked dishes to be found on the à la carte (dinner only) and short table d'hote menus. Pleasant, friendly service. *Seats 64. Parties 12. Private Room 30. L 12-2.30 D 7-9.30. Set L £14 Set D £19.95.*

Cardiff — Angel Hotel — 66% — £118

Tel 0222 232633 Fax 0222 396212 — **H**

Castle Street Cardiff South Glamorgan CF1 2QZ — Map 9 D6

Between the Castle and Arms Park rugby stadium, the distinctive Angel has kept its individual character for over 100 years. Liveried doormen show guests into the foyer, where chandeliers, pillars and a mural of clouds and cherubs make a good impression. Bedrooms are generally roomy, and there are several function rooms catering for up to 300 theatre-style in the galleried Dragon Suite (parking for 70). Executive rooms attract a supplement and there are weekend tariff reductions Fri-Sun (two nights minimum stay at busy periods). 24hr room service. Children under 16 share parents' room free. Queens Moat Houses. *Rooms 91. Gym, sauna, solarium, beauty salon, snooker.* AMERICAN EXPRESS *Access, Diners, Visa.*

Cardiff   **Armless Dragon**   £50

Tel 0222 382357   **R**

97 Wyeverne Road Cathays Cardiff South Glamorgan CF2 4BG   **Map 9 D6**

A popular bistro whose monthly-changing à la carte is supplemented
by 1-, 2- or 3-course lunch menus with two choices per course and a drink
included. Fish is a favourite, and the day's selection posted on the board can
be poached, grilled, fried or served in one of four sauces. On the meat front
could come Barbary duck breast with lemon and almond sauce, pheasant,
venison or fillet steak, and there's always something for vegetarians.
Laverballs and mushrooms are a standing dish among the starters. *Seats 45.
L 12.15-2.15 D 7.15-10.30. Closed L Sat, all Sun & Mon, 25 & 26 Dec,
1 Jan. Set L £5.90/£7.90/£9.90.* AMERICAN EXPRESS *Access, Diners, Visa.*

Cardiff   **Campanile Hotel**   £44

Tel 0222 549044   Fax 0222 549000   **L**

Caxton Place Pentwyn Cardiff South Glamorgan CF2 7HA   **Map 9 D6**

Closest M4 junction is J29; off the Pentwyn interchange of the A48(M).
Rooms 50. AMERICAN EXPRESS *Access, Diners, Visa.*

Cardiff   **Cardiff International**   **67%**   £80

Tel 0222 341441   Fax 0222 223742   **H**

Mary Ann Street Cardiff South Glamorgan CF1 2EQ   **Map 9 D6**

A striking modern hotel opposite Cardiff International Arena and next
to the National ice rink. Victorian brick and cast iron are cleverly
matched, and an arcade-style interior echoes the architecture of Cardiff's
markets. Bedrooms, all twin or double-bedded, include two floors
upgraded to Executive standard; eight rooms are equipped for the disabled.
Smart and keen staff. Children up to 12 accommodated free in their
parents' room. Banqueting/conference facilities for 40/40. 24hr room
service. Free, covered parking for up to 55 cars; car rental outlet on site.
No dogs. *Rooms 143.* AMERICAN EXPRESS *Access, Diners, Visa.*

Cardiff   **Cardiff Marriott Hotel**   **68%**   £130

Tel 0222 399944   Fax 0222 395578   **H**

Mill Lane Cardiff South Glamorgan CF1 1EZ   **Map 9 D6**

A stylish city-centre hotel especially convenient for St David's Hall, the
national rugby stadium and the central railway station. Modish decor
of much steel and glass incorporates a view of the indoor pool and leisure
areas from the spacious open-plan lounge. Large American-configuration
bedrooms (with two double beds in all twin rooms) provide comfortable
easy chairs and plenty of well-lit work space, and include non-smoking and
Executive floors. Conference and banqueting facilities for 300. Special
weekend leisure breaks include free accommodation for children up to 16
years when sharing parents' room. Formerly the *Holiday Inn*. *Rooms 182.
Indoor swimming pool, gym, squash, sauna, spa bath, solarium, beauty salon.*
AMERICAN EXPRESS *Access, Diners, Visa.*

Cardiff   **Copthorne Hotel**   **70%**   £119

Tel 0222 599100   Fax 0222 599080   **H**

Culverhouse Cross Cardiff South Glamorgan CF5 6XJ   **Map 9 D6**

A large new five-storey hotel to the west of town off the A48 (take
Junction 33 M4) near the HTV studios. Lots of wood panelling and rich
autumnal colour schemes predominate in appealing public areas, some
of which overlook the hotel's own small lake. All the good-sized bedrooms
are well laid out with large desks (to which the phone is easily movable)
with comfortable armchairs in addition to breakfast table and proper
armchair. Good bathrooms feature polished red-granite vanitory units.

Rooms on the Connoisseur Floor get extras like bathrobes and slippers plus use of an Executive lounge with free soft drinks and Continental breakfast. Two rooms are equipped for disabled guests. Children up to 12 stay free in parents' room. Banqueting/conference facilities for 200/300 (parking for 225). *Rooms 135. Indoor swimming pool, gym, sauna, spa bath, steam room, solarium, snooker.* AMERICAN EXPRESS *Access, Diners, Visa.*

Cardiff	Forte Crest	69%	£95
Tel 0222 388681 Fax 0222 371495			**H**
Castle Street Cardiff South Glamorgan CF1 2XB			Map 9 D6

City-centre hotel located between the River Taff and Arms Park, undergoing refurbishment in 1994. A business centre supports conferences of up to 180 delegates. *Rooms 155. Snooker.* AMERICAN EXPRESS *Access, Diners, Visa.*

Cardiff	Forte Posthouse	63%	£68
Tel 0222 731212 Fax 0222 549147			**H**
Pentwyn Road Cardiff South Glamorgan CF2 7XA			Map 9 D6

Modern hotel near Junction 29 of the M4 (take A48(M) for 3 miles then Pentwyn exit), four miles from the city (12 from the airport), set in 6 acres of grounds. Standard and Executive rooms, the latter featuring a few more comforts. Conference facilities (up to 140) with ample parking. *Rooms 139. Indoor swimming pool, gym, sauna, steam room, spa bath, solarium, snooker, beauty salon.* AMERICAN EXPRESS *Access, Diners, Visa.*

Cardiff	Forte Travelodge		£45
Tel 0222 549564			**L**
Circle Way East Llanederyn Cardiff South Glamorgan CF3 7ND			Map 9 D6

4 miles north-east of Cardiff city centre. Off the A48(M) on the road to Coed-y-Gores. 3 miles from Junction 29 of the M4. *Rooms 32.* AMERICAN EXPRESS *Access, Diners, Visa.*

Cardiff	Moat House	70%	£130
Tel 0222 732520 Fax 0222 549092			**H**
Circle Way East Llanederyn Cardiff South Glamorgan CF3 7XF			Map 9 D6

Travelling west on the M4, leave at Junction 29 and take the A48(M). Heading east from West Wales, take the A470 at Junction 32 to arrive at this Moat House, set in its own grounds east of Cardiff. It's smart, comfortable and practical behind its unexciting modern exterior. Day rooms are in open plan, providing plenty of space in which to unwind. The conference complex (for up to 300 delegates) is on the first floor. Good-sized bedrooms, with extra touches of luxury plus evening maid service in Executive rooms. *Rooms 135. Indoor swimming pool, keep-fit equipment, spa bath, sauna, solarium. Closed Christmas/New Year.* AMERICAN EXPRESS *Access, Diners, Visa.*

Cardiff	Le Monde		£40
Tel 0222 387376			**R**
60 St Mary Street Cardiff South Glamorgan			Map 9 D6

One of a trio of atmospheric restaurants-cum-wine bars, this one appeals primarily to fish-eaters with a wide array of shell, sea and freshwater fish. Its siblings are *La Brasserie* (0222 372164) specialising in grilled meats and seasonal game and offering a £5 set lunch, and *Champers* (0222 373363) with a Spanish slant to both menu and wine list – over 100 Riojas! *Champers* is open Sunday evening to 12.30am and seats about 150. *Seats 70. L 12-2.30 D 7-12. Closed Sun, 25 Dec.* AMERICAN EXPRESS *Access, Diners, Visa.*

Cardiff   Park Hotel   70%   £113

Tel 0222 383471   Fax 0222 399309   **H**

Park Place Cardiff South Glamorgan CF1 3UD   Map 9 D6

Following the major refurbishment at the Park of all bedrooms and
function rooms (conferences for up to 300), the next to be similarly treated
are the ground-floor public rooms. The Park's impressive stone-clad facade
is a striking landmark on Cardiff's pedestrianised Queen Street and today's
lack of traffic is a bonus for those occupying the best, front-facing
bedrooms. Entry, however, is from Park Place and vehicular access (to the
rear) is tricky. Mount Charlotte Thistle. ***Rooms** 119.* AMERICAN EXPRESS *Access,
Diners, Visa.*

Cardiff   Travel Inn   £43

Tel 0633 680070   Fax 0633 681143   **L**

Newport Road Castleton nr Cardiff South Glamorgan CF3 8UQ   Map 9 D6

On the old A48, 3 miles from Junction 28 of M4 heading towards Cardiff,
next to the Coach & Horses Beefeater. Two rooms are equipped for
disabled guests, 30 for non-smokers. Family suite. No dogs. ***Rooms** 47.
Garden, children's playground.* AMERICAN EXPRESS *Access, Diners, Visa.*

Cardiff   Places of Interest

Cardiff Tourist Information   Tel 0222 227281.
Caerphilly Tourist Information   Tel 0222 851378.
Cardiff Arms Park   Tel 0222 390111.
Cathedral Church of St. Peter and St. Paul   Tel 0222 561545.
The National Museum of Wales   Tel 0222 397951.
Welsh Folk Museum   St. Fagans Tel 0222 569441.
Wales Empire Pool   Tel 0222 382296.
Sophia Gardens Cricket Ground   Tel 0222 343478.
Wales National Ice Rink   Tel 0222 383451.
   Theatres and Concert Halls
Chapter Arts Centre   Tel 0222 396061.
New Theatre   Tel 0222 394844.
Sherman Theatre   Tel 0222 230451.
St. David's Hall   Tel 0222 371236.
   Historic Houses, Castles and Gardens
Caerphilly Castle   Tel 0222 883143 *5 miles.*
Cardiff Castle   Tel 0222 822083.
Castle Coch Tongwynlais   Tel 0222 810101.
Dyffryn Botanic Garden   Tel 0222 593328.

Carmarthen   Ivy Bush Royal   59%   £60

Tel 0267 235111   Fax 0267 234914   **H**

Spilman Street Carmarthen Dyfed SA31 1LG   Map 9 B5

Once a favoured retreat of Lord Nelson and Lady Hamilton, today a Forte
Heritage hotel on the West Wales heritage trail, popular with coach tours
and conferences (max 200). Note the stained glass window in the lounge
commemorating the formation of the first Circle of Bards. Children up to
16 stay free in parents' room. ***Rooms** 75. Garden.* AMERICAN EXPRESS *Access,
Diners, Visa.*

Carmarthen   Places of Interest

Tourist Information   Tel 0267 231557.
Carmarthen Museum   Tel 0267 231691.
Pembrey Beach *20 miles.*

Chepstow   **Castle View Hotel**   £60

Tel 0291 620349   Fax 0291 627397   **I**

16 Bridge Street Chepstow Gwent NP6 5EZ   Map 9 D6

This friendly little hotel was built in the 17th century as a private residence, perhaps with stones from neighbouring Chepstow Castle, which commands the Wye riverbank opposite. Ivy-covered now, and genuinely welcoming, it's immaculately kept by Martin and Vicky Cardale. Original walls and timbers may still be seen, both in the public area and in some bedrooms, most of which feature smart mahogany pieces. One room, with its own lounge and sleeping up to four, is in a small cottage next door and there are two spacious family rooms overlooking the garden. Good variety of snacks in the bar. *Rooms 13. Garden.* AMERICAN EXPRESS *Access, Diners, Visa.*

Chepstow   **Leadon's Brasserie**   £45

Tel 0291 627402   **R**

6 Station Road Chepstow Gwent NP6 5EP   Map 9 D6

A recent move from the centre of town to roomier premises (turn off the A48 at the sign to Chepstow Station) has served to extend Wayne Leadon's loyal following, though some of the intimacy of his former brasserie appears to be lacking. The food's great strength is its consistency, allied to careful composition. Chicken tikka parcels with mint raita, or delicately sautéed kidneys in sherry cream sauce serve as curtain-raisers to fish specialities which might include sea bass with shrimps, ginger and thyme; alternatively lamb noisettes with béarnaise or a chateaubriand for two. Good desserts, breads and coffee; service, though, can be patchy. *Seats 44. L 12-2 D 6-9. Closed 25 & 26 Dec, 1 Jan. Set D £12.95 (orders before 7.30).*

Chepstow   **St Pierre Hotel & Country Club Hotel**   **70%**   £100

Tel 0291 625261   Fax 0291 629975   **H**

St Pierre Park Chepstow Gwent NP6 6YA   Map 9 D6

Flagship in Wales for the newly-titled Country Club Resorts group of Whitbread hotels, St Pierre enjoys an enviable reputation for its golfing (two 18-hole courses) and very extensive recreational facilities set in 400 acres of mature parkland just two miles from the Severn Bridge (M4 J22). Recently completed restyling of the 14th-century mansion at the hotel's heart has produced a spacious and well-lit foyer and reception lounge beyond which you can relax in a fine oak-panelled bar and lounge overlooking the final greens. Access for banqueting, conferences (for up to 220) and ever-present golf societies is kept sensibly apart, through the Trophy Bar. Poolside grill and sports bar and the self-contained leisure centre all remain interconnected in the new layout. A varied choice of bedrooms ranges from ground-floor courtyard suites and mansion bedrooms overlooking the park to the dozen detached lodges, ranging from three to six bedrooms, in St Pierre's Lakeland Village, which is much favoured for golf or house parties and family get-togethers. Children up to 16 years are accommodated free in parents' room – cots available. Direct reservation line is (0291) 624444. *Rooms 142. Garden, indoor swimming pool, gym, golf, croquet, jogging track, cycle track, squash, badminton, sauna, spa bath, solarium, beauty salon, tennis, bowling, coffee shop (10am-10pm).* AMERICAN EXPRESS *Access, Diners, Visa.*

Chepstow   **Places of Interest**

Tourist Information   Tel 0291 623772.
Chepstow Castle   Tel 0291 624065.
Chepstow Museum   Tel 0291 625981.
Chepstow Racecourse   Tel 0291 622260.
Caldicot Castle   Tel 0291 420241 *5 miles.*

Chirk   Starlings Castle   £50

Tel & Fax 0691 718464   **RR**

Bronygarth Chirk nr Oswestry Clwyd SY10 7NU   Map 8 D2

The address is of little help in finding the Pitts' 17th-century sandstone
farmhouse in its isolated position high up on the Welsh side of the border
not far from Offa's Dyke; best ask for directions – they will happily fax
you a map. Once found, the reward is a delightfully civilised, slightly rustic
away-from-it-all hideaway with the bonus of Anthony Pitt's highly
accomplished cooking. The menu, with five or so choices at each stage,
changes frequently with dishes that are at the same time sophisticated and
unpretentious: *fromage de tete* with *sauce ravigote*, house charcuterie, pot-
roast ox heart with flageolet beans, grilled salmon with olive, parsley and
lemon vinaigrette and the tenderest venison steak you'll ever eat served
on a parsnip potato cake with black truffle hollandaise and a rich sauce
made from the marinade. Puds like hot chocolate soufflé and poached pears
with lemon and white wine or a selection of Welsh and Borders farmhouse
cheeses. The dining room has recently moved into a converted barn with
rough stone walls, flagstone floor and wood-burning stove; another such
stove warms a homely bar/lounge with drinks-laden dresser, comfortably
'lived-in' sofas and armchairs, worn carpet, magazines, newspapers and
music centre. *Seats 60. Private Room 50. L (Sun only) 12-2.30 D 7-10.*
AMERICAN EXPRESS *Access, Diners, Visa.*

Rooms   £55

Antique-furnished bedrooms come with non-remote TVs, beverage kits
and comforts like thick duvets, hot water bottles and collections of books.
Eight rooms share two bathrooms (silk dressing gowns are provided for
the trip) while two new rooms have en-suite facilities. Families welcome;
high-chairs, cots and Z-beds provided.

Chirk   Places of Interest

Chirk Castle Tel 0691 777701.

Clydach   The Drum and Monkey   £50

Tel 0873 831980   **R**

Clydach Blackrock Abergavenny Gwent   Map 9 D5

Skilful conversion of a derelict pub alongside the A465 has created
a refined restaurant and lounge bar whose views of Clydach Gorge are
superb. Jon West's cooking skills are to the fore throughout a varied menu
of dishes both plain (chicken liver paté, veal escalope with warm tomato
salad, grilled steaks, jam sponge) and a little more outré, such as rillettes
of chicken with fresh mango and curried mayonnaise, mousseline of lemon
sole with garlic prawns and tarragon butter, or breast of guinea fowl with
a timbale of the leg meat. Lighter bar snacks daily; early evening menu
£12.45 for three courses. Check directions when booking. *Seats 50.
Private Room 25. L 12-2 D 6-9.30. Set D £12.45. No credit cards.*

Colwyn Bay   Café Niçoise   £45

Tel 0492 531555   **R**

124 Abergele Road Colwyn Bay Clwyd LL29 7PS   Map 8 C1

Traditional and modern French cooking in Carl and Lynne Swift's
romantic setting with French background music. Typical dishes on Carl's
à la carte could include salade niçoise, locally smoked salmon with
marinated vegetables and *sauce gribiche*, noisettes of Welsh lamb with pan-
fried aubergine and rosemary, and good locally-caught sea bass in season.
Good-value, three-course table d'hote offers a choice of around four dishes
at each stage. Vegetarian options. After-theatre tables can be arranged.
*Seats 32. L 12-2 D 7-10. Closed L Mon-Wed, all Sun, 1 week Jan, 1 week
June. Set meals £10.50/£12.95 (not D Fri & Sat).* AMERICAN EXPRESS
Access, Visa.

Colwyn Bay   Colwyn Bay Hotel   61%   £53

Tel 0492 516555   Fax 0492 515565   **H**

Penmaenhead Colwyn Bay Clwyd LL29 9LD   Map 8 C1

All the bedrooms enjoy sea views at this distinctive hotel (formerly called *Seventy Degrees*), which stands on a clifftop above Colwyn Bay. Children up to 12 stay free in parents' room. Conference facilities for up to 200 delegates. Easy access from the A55. ***Rooms** 43.* **AMERICAN EXPRESS** *Access, Diners, Visa.*

Colwyn Bay   Places of Interest

Tourist Information   Tel 0492 530478.
Bodnant Garden   Tal-y-Cafn Tel 0492 650460.
Bodelwyddan Castle   Bodelwyddan Tel 0745 583539 *10 miles.*
Welsh Mountain Zoo   Tel 0492 532938.

Conwy   Sychnant Pass Hotel   60%   £60

Tel 0492 596868   Fax 0492 870009   **H**

Sychnant Pass Road Conwy Gwynedd LL32 8BJ   Map 8 C1

Self-styled as "a little bit of Switzerland in Wales", the three acres of grounds (just within the Snowdonia National Park) around this substantial white-pebbledash house include a stream, a pond and woods. It's lovely walking country, but when the weather's not so kind the lounge and bar are good places to relax. Fine views can be enjoyed from the bedrooms, the best and largest of which are those in the original part of the house, where furnishings are traditional; other rooms have modern units. One ground-floor room is adapted for disabled guests. The Conwy Tunnel considerably eases access to this pleasant location. Children up to 12 stay free in parents' room. ***Rooms** 13. Garden, keep-fit equipment, sauna, spa bath.* **AMERICAN EXPRESS** *Access, Diners, Visa.*

Conwy   Places of Interest

Tourist Information   Tel 0492 592248.
Conwy Castle   Tel 0492 592358.
Aberconwy House   Tel 0492 592246
Smallest House   Quayside

Coychurch   Coed-y-Mwstwr Hotel   70%   £95

Tel 0656 860621   Fax 0656 863122   **HR**

Coychurch nr Bridgend Mid Glamorgan CF35 6AF   Map 9 C6

High above the Vale of Glamorgan, the "whispering trees" of this Victorian hotel's name are easily heard among the 17 acres of ancient woodland in which Coed-y-Mwstwr stands, one of the most attractively positioned country mansions in South Wales. True to its Victorian origins, decor and furnishings are a blend of homely charm and elegant period style: private suites and function rooms have high ceilings, chandeliers, oak panelling and huge fireplaces. Bedrooms throughout are spacious and comfortable with crown-canopied beds and carpeted bathrooms containing bathrobes and a good supply of toiletries. Children up to 14 stay free in parents' room. Conference/banqueting facilities for 185/160. Leave the M4 at Junction 35. Now under the management of Voyager Hotels. ***Rooms** 23. Garden, outdoor swimming pool, tennis, snooker.* **AMERICAN EXPRESS** *Access, Diners, Visa.*

Eliot Room   £75

The setting is one of high-beamed ceiling, chandeliers and wood-panelled walls, and Gareth Passey's fixed-priced lunch and dinner menus are equally serious affairs, designed to reflect the best ingredients of the locality. The à la carte features the likes of mousseline of chicken and scallops with parsley purée and warm butter sauce or quenelles of smoked pork paté with toasted herb brioche to start, followed by grilled sea bream with a garlic and peppercorn crust on a sauce of fresh mussels or double entrecote cut from prime Llandovery meat or best end of lamb with a caraway-scented mousse and concassé of wild mushrooms and kidneys. The involved nature of dishes extends to desserts: bread-and-butter pudding layered with caramelised apples and served with cinnamon custard or orange and hazelnut pâté on a chocolate sauce with a raspberry coulis; simplicity returns in traditional sponge pudding topped with home-made jam and 'English custard'. Interesting Welsh cheeses among the selection. No children after 8pm. *Seats 50. Parties 16. Private Room 24. L 12-2.15 D 7.15-10.15 (Sat to 10.30, Sun to 9.30). Set L £12.95/£15.95 (Sun) Set D £24 (5-course).*

Crickhowell	Bear Hotel	£52
Tel 0873 810408 Fax 0873 811696		**I**
High Street Crickhowell Powys NP8 1BW		Map 9 D5

Dating back to the 15th century and once a stopping-off point on the London-West Wales coaching route, the Bear bristles with personality and continues its tradition of hospitality as the focal point of the market town. The evocative, busy bars, with low black beams, sturdy old furniture and open fires, are good places for a snack, a drink or a chat with locals, and upstairs there's a quiet residents' lounge. Bedrooms, some grouped round a Tudor-style courtyard, have good-quality furniture and warm, well-chosen fabrics. Top of the range is a four-poster room with jacuzzi. Three rooms, including one suite, are in an annexe. *Rooms 28. Garden.* AMERICAN EXPRESS *Access, Visa.*

Crickhowell	Gliffaes Country House Hotel	63%	£65
Tel 0874 730371 Fax 0874 730463			**H**
Crickhowell Powys NP8 1RH			Map 9 D5

Fishing is the favourite pastime at this distinctive late-Victorian Italianate house (spot the campanile) that is set in 29 acres of grounds (include 7 acres of gardens) and overlooks a mile of water on the left bank of the Usk, west of Crickhowell. Many other outdoor activities have a following here, while the sitting room and drawing room are splendid places for doing nothing. Bedrooms are spacious and attractively furnished with old or antique pieces. Dogs permitted in the lodge. *Rooms 22. Garden, croquet, fishing, tennis, snooker. Closed 5 Jan-24 Feb.* AMERICAN EXPRESS *Access, Diners, Visa.*

Crickhowell	Places of Interest

Tretower Court & Castle   Tel 0874 730279.

Cross Hands	Forte Travelodge	£45
Tel 0269 845700		**L**
A48 Cross Hands nr Llanelli Dyfed SA14 6NW		Map 9 B5

On the A48 eastbound, 11 miles east of Carmarthen. *Rooms 32.* AMERICAN EXPRESS *Access, Diners, Visa.*

Eglwysfach	Ynyshir Hall	70%	£110
Tel 0654 781209 Fax 0654 781366			**HR**
Eglwysfach Machynlleth Powys SY20 8TA			Map 8 C3

A Georgian manor house, once owned by Queen Victoria, set on the Dovey estuary by an extensive bird reserve. Owner Rob Reen is an accomplished artist, whose work is to be found the in bedrooms, each named after a famous painter, and throughout the immaculate day rooms which also feature a collection of Oriental rugs. An artist's eye is also

evident in the stylish decor of the bedrooms, which are furnished with
antiques and come with magazines, books and mineral water (best rooms
also get sherry) amongst other comforts. Top of the range (£125) are the
suites – the Degas and Renoir (both non-smoking) and the Vermeer with
an 1860 walnut bed and blue-tiled bathroom. Breakfast includes freshly
squeezed orange juice and home-made conserves. No children under
9 years. *Rooms 8. Garden, pitch & putt.* AMERICAN EXPRESS *Access, Diners, Visa.*

Restaurant   £60

Rob's artistic output also features on the walls of the dining room with its
well-spaced, crisply-clothed tables. Dishes on Tony Pierce's fixed-price
menu are modern British, interesting and innovative, but never remotely
outrageous: warm timbale of chicken mousse with leaf spinach and a truffle
oil dressing; paupiettes of guinea fowl with poached apricots, bacon and
thyme; roulade of salmon and basil on a chive and potato purée with leeks
and roast fish sauce; hot pistachio soufflé; layered white, milk and dark
chocolate terrine with Grand Marnier sauce. Three-course Sunday lunch,
bar lunches (soup, Welsh rarebit, a fish dish) on other days. House wines
are well chosen and offer good value though one could reasonably expect
to see a champagne under £40! Not the case here. However, it's a good list
with the New World making a fair appearance. *Seats 40. Private Room 18.
L 12.30-1.30 D 7-8.45. Set L £16 Set D £26.*

Ewloe	**St David's Park Hotel**	**69%**	£97
Tel 0244 520800 Fax 0244 520930			**H**
St David's Park Ewloe Clwyd CH5 3YB			Map 8 D2

Smart, modern hotel, with some neo-Georgian features, at the junction
of the A55 and A494. Inside, the several areas that make up the bar/lounge
include a couple of 'rooms' with fireplaces, floral armchairs and busy
wallpaper giving something of a Victorian feel, plus an airy orangery with
black-and-white tiled floor. Spacious, well-planned bedrooms have good,
solid oak furniture and roomy bathrooms (rooms with interconnecting
doors can suffer from unwanted neighbourly noise); 30 rooms for non-
smokers. The seven 'junior suites' have separate walk-in showers and extras
like robes and slippers. Beds are turned down at night and room service
is 24hrs. The breakfast buffet is well stocked but the cooked items can
sometimes suffer from the self-service format. The new Northop Country
Park golf and country club is just 5 minutes away from the hotel –
courtesy transport provided. Banqueting/conferencing for 220/270 (ample
parking). *Rooms 121. Garden, tennis, golf (18), indoor swimming pool, gym,
spa bath, steam room, sauna, solarium, beautician, games room, snooker.*
AMERICAN EXPRESS *Access, Diners, Visa.*

Fishguard	**Fishguard Bay Hotel**	**59%**	£60
Tel 0348 873571 Fax 0348 873030			**H**
Quay Road Goodwick Fishguard Dyfed SA64 0BT			Map 9 A5

Ten acres of woodland stand at the back while Cardigan Bay is straight
ahead as well as the ferry service to Rosslare. A popular venue for
functions, with conferences and banquets for up to 300. Best and brightest
bedrooms have bay-facing balconies: only seven rooms don't have en-suite
bathrooms. Children up to 14 stay free in their parents' room. *Rooms 62.
Garden.* AMERICAN EXPRESS *Access, Diners, Visa.*

Gowerton	**Cefn Goleu Park**	**69%**	£80
Tel 0792 873099			**HR**
Cefn Stylle Road Gowerton West Glamorgan SA4 3QS			Map 9 B6

Bought by Emma and Claude Rossi in 1987, the manor house, which
stands in 48 acres of gardens, has been restored with love, patience and the
skills of local craftsmen. A stunning vaulted central hall contains unique
showcases of china dolls, and is ringed by a minstrel's gallery leading to four

master bedrooms with Victorian elegance recreated. No children under 10. No dogs. *Rooms 4. Garden. Closed 2 weeks Jan. Access, Visa.*

Restaurant £60

From Claude and Bernard's kitchen come hearty, full-flavoured dishes such as langoustines fried in garlic butter, chicken with walnuts, sirloin steak with whisky sauce, veal escalope with orange sauce. Desserts from a trolley might include a choice of gateaux, tiramisu, praline vacherin and crepe Suzette. Sunday lunchtime brings soup, melon or local cockles, around four main courses that usually include a choice of roasts and a fish dish, and the sweet trolley. The table d'hote represents good value and offers a fair choice. Smoking is not encouraged. 30 seats on a patio in good weather. *Seats 48. Parties 28. Private Room 20. L (Sun only) 12.30-2 D 7.30-9.30. Closed D Sun, all Mon. Set Sun L £12.50 Set D £13.50 (Tue-Fri).*

Gwbert-on-Sea	Cliff Hotel	60%	£70

Tel 0239 613241 Fax 0239 615391	**H**
Gwbert-on-Sea Cardigan Dyfed SA43 1PP	Map 9 B4

Thirty acres of private headland provide outstanding sea views from this privately owned hotel, whose convivial atmosphere is augmented by friendly staff and high-profile management. There's a wealth of recreational facilities, both on and off site, for all the family (under-12s free in parents' room); fishing on a private stretch of the River Teifi, conference and banqueting (max 220). Self-catering apartments offering full use of the hotel facilities are also available. *Rooms 73. Garden, fishing, outdoor swimming pool, gym, squash, sauna, golf (9), snooker.* *Access, Diners, Visa.*

Halkyn	Forte Travelodge	£45

Tel 0352 780952	**L**
A55 Halkyn Clwyd CH8 8RF	Map 8 D1

On the A55 westbound 13 miles west of Chester, *Rooms 31.* *Access, Diners, Visa.*

Holyhead	Trearddur Bay Hotel	65%	NEW	£96

Tel 0407 860301 Fax 0407 861181	**H**
Holyhead Anglesey Gwynedd LL65 2UN	Map 8 B1

A family-run and family-friendly coastal hotel on the western tip of Anglesey just two miles from Holyhead and the Irish ferry terminal. Smart public areas provide a choice between the lively Dragon Bar with its attendant conservatory (where children are served early high teas) and the more sedate cocktail bar and lounge overlooking the bay. A self-contained indoor swimming pool is in the garden, while for hardier types the real thing, and a safe, sandy beach, are just across the road. The majority of bedrooms, agreeably modernised and decorated in muted colours, share views of the sand dunes and rocky coastline; those facing west with new private balconies are certainly the pick. Friendly, cheerful staff, children welcome; cots and bunk beds available. *Rooms 31. Garden, indoor swimming pool, games room.* *Access, Diners, Visa.*

Lake Vyrnwy Hotel. See under Llanwddyn.

Lamphey	Court Hotel	67%	£95

Tel 0646 672273 Fax 0646 672480	**H**
Lamphey Pembroke Dyfed SA71 5NT	Map 9 A5

Much extended and improved since its opening as a hotel in 1978, The Court is peacefully situated in extensive grounds just a mile from the south Pembrokeshire coast (take the A48 from the M4 to Carmarthen, then

A477 Pembroke Road, at Milton village turn left off Lamphey).
A handsomely-proportioned staircase dominates the reception hall, from
which radiate remodelled day rooms. The pick is a cocktail bar leading
to the new conservatory and patio which make a fine-weather alternative
for breakfast service, as well as children's high teas. Nonetheless, the
Georgian elegance of the Court's origins is carefully retained and reflected
also in main-house bedrooms which are spacious, elegantly furnished and
enjoy fine views. A new wing here offers rooms of self-styled de-luxe
standards. Remaining bedrooms are in fact purpose-designed studios in the
Westminster annexe where sitting rooms, sofa beds and breakfast tables are
ideally suited for family use. Despite privacy of access and proximity
of parking, their short distance from the main house and recreation
facilities is generously reflected in the price. Children up to 16 stay free
in parents' room, cots available. Conference/banqueting facilities for up to
50. *Rooms* 35. *Garden, outdoor swimming pool, keep-fit equipment, sauna, spa
bath, solarium, tennis, helipad.* AMERICAN EXPRESS *Access, Diners, Visa.*

Lamphey   Places of Interest

Pembroke National Park Tourist Information   Tel 0646 682148.
Tenby Tourist Information   Tel 0834 842402.
Colby Woodland Garden (NT)   Amroth, Tenby Tel 0558 822800/0834
  811725 *13 miles.*
**National Museum of Gypsy Caravans, Romany Crafts and
  Lore**   Pembroke Tel 0646 681308.
Manor House Wildlife and Leisure Park   Tenby Tel 0646 651201.
Tenby Museum and Picture Gallery   Tel 0834 842809.
Tenby Beach
Torch Theatre   Milford Haven Tel 0646 695267 *15 miles.*

Llanarmon Dyffryn Ceiriog   Hand Hotel   £58

Tel 069 176 666   Fax 069 176 262   **I**
Llanarmon Dyffryn Ceiriog nr Llangollen Clwyd LL20 7LD   Map 8 D2

Originally a 16th-century farmhouse, the Hand stands in beautiful
countryside in a picturesque village at the head of the Ceiriog Valley.
An old black range in reception, antiques in lounge and bar plus a log fire
all add up to a cosy, traditional atmosphere. Bedrooms are neat and simple,
with plain walls and white fitted furniture. The hotel has its own all-
weather tennis court and fishing can be arranged. *Rooms* 13. *Garden, tennis.*
AMERICAN EXPRESS *Access, Diners, Visa.*

Llanarmon Dyffryn Ceiriog   West Arms Hotel   £78

Tel 069 176 665   Fax 069 176 622   **I**
Llanarmon Dyffryn Ceiriog nr Llangollen Clwyd LL20 7LD   Map 8 D2

Nestling in the lovely Ceiriog Valley, this 400-year-old country inn offers
cosy comfort within and well-manicured gardens without. Slate-flagged
floors, vast inglenooks and beams offset by period furnishings preserve the
atmosphere of a bygone age. Though six of the bedrooms are now fairly
modern, the rest retain exposed beams, brass bedsteads and antique
furniture, to which neatly added bathrooms provide the requisite modern
comforts. A private garden suite accommodates meetings and dinner parties
for up to 70 guests. Families are well looked after. *Rooms* 12. *Garden,
fishing. Closed 2 weeks Jan/Feb.* AMERICAN EXPRESS *Access, Diners, Visa.*

Llanberis   Y Bistro   £50

Tel 0286 871278   **R**
43-45 High Street Llanberis Gwynedd LL55 4EU   Map 8 B2

The menu at Danny and Nerys Roberts' friendly restaurant is written
in both English and Welsh. Local ingredients make a good showing,

appearing in black pudding with apple sauce, loin of lamb with a port and redcurrant sauce, and pan-fried beef rump with a creamy Stilton sauce. Snowdon pudding is a steamed suet pudding with a sherry sauce. The menu price includes canapés, side salad, home-baked bread, coffee and florentines. *Seats 50. Private Room 22. D only 7.30-9.30 (Sat to 9.45). Closed Sun & Mon except Bank Holidays. Set D £18.50/£21.50. Access, Visa.*

Llanberis   Places of Interest

Museum of the North, Power of Wales   Tel 0286 870636.
Snowdon Mountain Railway   Tel 0286 870223.
Welsh Slate Museum   Tel 0286 870630.

Llandeilo   Cawdor Arms   65%   £42

Tel 0558 823500   **H**

Rhosmaen Street Llandeilo Dyfed SA19 6EN   Map 9 C5

Clearly signposted at the end of the M4, and attractively situated in the Vale of Towy, the hotel bears the Cawdor family coat of arms as its emblem. Handsome proportions and a slightly faded elegance are hallmarks of the Georgian day rooms, and bedrooms include the four-poster Rose and Victorian suites and Howard's Room, where Howard Hughes stayed in 1927 after making a forced landing on his transatlantic flight. As we went to press, the hotel had just been purchased by a new company, Gwestau Sîr Gâr. *Rooms 17. Access, Diners, Visa.*

Llandeilo   Places of Interest

Dolaucothi Gold Mines (NT) *12 miles*   Tel 0558 650359.

Llandrillo   Tyddyn Llan   66%   £88

Tel 0490 440264   Fax 0490 440414   **HR**

Llandrillo nr Corwen Clwyd LL21 0ST   Map 8 C2

This lovely Georgian house is where the Kindreds live. Once a shooting lodge for the Dukes of Westminster, it stands amid beautifully tended gardens in the Vale of Edeyrnion above the Dee (on which it has four miles of fishing rights) and below the Berwyn mountains in some of the finest countryside in Wales. It is also a special place developed and extended over the last ten years to his own design by Peter Kindred and replete with antiques, period furniture and unusual art, some of it his own. No more house-proud proprietor could be found either than Bridget and it shows in the immaculate condition of everything within from fresh flowers and pot pourri to bathroom towels and bed linen. Residents are made instantly welcome and at home: each individually furnished bedroom reflects the calm of Tyddyn Llan's idyllic setting and nothing appears too much trouble for hosts whose hospitality transcends mere hotelkeeping. *Rooms 10. Garden, croquet, fishing. Closed Feb. Access, Visa.*

Restaurant   £60

Dinner begins, as it were, in the bar and lounge with an informal introduction to the highlights of a nightly-changed fixed-price menu which places high emphasis on original and forceful flavours. Balsamic dressing and sautéed peppers enliven the delicate hot fish terrine; leeks, crispy bacon and pungent red wine jus bring to life a chicken breast of unquestionable quality; and a gratin of soft summer fruits is richly augmented by its Grand Marnier sabayon and a pistachio biscuit. The display of local Welsh cheeses, a fairly priced list of quality wines and the studied informality of genuinely warm service all enhance the natural pleasures of dining in the kindred spirit. *Seats 70. Parties 20. Private Room 44. L 12.30-2 D 7.30-9.30 (Sun 7-8.30). Set L £10.50/£12.50 (Sun £13.50) Set D £21.50/£23.50.*

Llandudno	**Bodysgallen Hall**	77%	£155

Tel 0492 584466   Fax 0492 582519 · **HR**

Llandudno Gwynedd LL30 1RS   Map 8 C1

A 13th-century tower is the oldest part of a building that has seen additions in most centuries since with the latest dating from 1905. Set in over 200 acres of grounds that include some fine formal gardens, the house has been carefully restored by Historic House Hotels and furnished in true country house style with antiques and oil paintings to complement the mellow oak panelling, ornate pargeting and other original features of day rooms which boast numerous sofas plump with feather-filled cushions. Bedrooms, which include nine one-or two-bedroom Cottage Suites around a charming garden, vary considerably in size and shape but all are decorated and furnished to the same high standard with antique, fabric-draped pieces plus flowering plants, porcelain ornaments and comforts like mineral water and home-made biscuits. One cottage suite has ramps for disabled guests. Cork-floored bathrooms feature huge bath sheets and luxurious toiletries. Attentive, friendly staff. Due for completion by early 1995 is a leisure complex, 200m away from the house, surrounded by mature woodland; this will comprise indoor pool, gym, sauna, solarium, spa and a buttery bar. No children under 8; dogs only in the Cottage Suites. Banqueting/conference facilities for 40/50. Signposted from the A470 just out of town. **Rooms** 28. *Garden, croquet, tennis, helipad.* AMERICAN EXPRESS *Access, Diners, Visa.*

Restaurant   £85

The twin dining rooms have fine views over the estate from stone-mullioned windows; inside, young, confident chef Mair Lewis and her team offer a fixed-price menu with plenty of choice. Dishes such as locally-smoked salmon (attracting a small supplement), warm salad of duck confit with wild mushrooms and a tomato and walnut dressing, and fillet of smoked trout with orange and horseradish sauce feature among the starters, with poached fillet of salmon wrapped in spinach with prawns and a grilled scallop and grilled fillet of beef with deep-fried garlic and turned vegetables indicating the main-course style. Sunday lunch also offers a good choice, perhaps even offering a selection of three roasts, usually including a leg of Welsh lamb. Leave room for queen of puddings, hot Bakewell tart with sweet butterscotch sauce or dark chocolate and hazelnut mousse on a coffee bean sauce. The lunchtime menu always includes a daily roast and a glass of house wine. A splendid wine list, but why are New World wines still listed by style (unlike Europe)? No matter, they are keenly priced and, alongside several marque champagnes, the house selection and cellarman's choice (all at £15) represent terrific value; lots of half bottles. Regional winner for Wales of our Cellar of the Year award 1995. No smoking. No children under 8. **Seats** 80. *Parties 12. Private Room 40.* L 12.30-2 D 7.30-9.30. Set L £13.90/£15.90 (Sun £16.50) Set D £27.50/£29.95.

Llandudno	**Empire Hotel**	69%	£70

Tel 0492 860555   Fax 0492 860791 · **H**

Church Walks Llandudno Gwynedd LL30 2HE   Map 8 C1

Len and Elizabeth Maddocks have been here since 1962 and their dedication is obvious throughout. The exterior of the Empire was undergoing major renovation as we went to press, following on the recent refurbishments to the interior (main lounge and bedrooms). This still results in a wide choice of rooms, from budget singles to de luxe rooms in the Victorian house next to the main building; antiques, cast-iron beds, silk drapes and marble-floored bathrooms with whirlpool baths are features. Multi-channel TV and video recorders (large library of films available) and personal safes in all rooms. **Rooms** 58. *Indoor & outdoor swimming pools, spa bath, sauna, steam room, roof garden and sun terrace, beauty salon. Closed 17-29 Dec.* AMERICAN EXPRESS *Access, Diners, Visa.*

Llandudno   St George's Hotel   61%   £75

Tel 0492 877544   Fax 0492 878477   **H**

St George's Place Llandudno Gwynedd LL30 2LG   **Map 8 C1**

Situated right on the promenade, Llandudno's oldest hotel offers up-to-date conferences and banqueting facilities for up to 250 and the Shape Club offers top-to-toe health, hair and cosmetic care. Many bedrooms afford views of the sea and Great Orme, and the best have balconies. Under-12s stay free in their parents' room. **Rooms** *86. Keep-fit equipment, sauna, spa bath, steam room, solarium, beauty & hair salon. Closed 10 days Jan.* AMERICAN EXPRESS *Access, Diners, Visa.*

Llandudno   St Tudno Hotel   69%   £75

Tel 0492 874411   Fax 0492 860407   **HR**

The Promenade Llandudno Gwynedd LL30 2LP   **Map 8 C1**

Martin and Janette Bland came here in 1972, since when their charming seafront hotel has been known for its friendliness and good service. Either side of the entrance hall the bar/lounge and sitting room (reserved for non-smokers) are Victorian in style – parlour plants, original fire places – in contrast to a bright coffee lounge to be found beyond the reception desk where fresh flowers compete with the receptionists' smiles. A small bottle of sparkling wine greets guests in bedrooms that, though generally not large, are individually decorated in pretty co-ordinating fabrics and wall coverings with a good eye for detail. Rooms are properly serviced in the evenings as are the bathrooms with their generous towelling and good toiletries. In 1861 Alice Liddell, later to be immortalised in Lewis Carroll's *Alice's Adventures in Wonderland*, spent a holiday here. Very much family-friendly. High tea is served at 5.30 in the coffee lounge. Limited parking. **Rooms** *21. Patio, indoor swimming pool.* AMERICAN EXPRESS *Diners, Access, Visa.*

Garden Room Restaurant   £65

Painted greenery and trellis work on the walls together with potted plants and conservatory-style furniture provide the garden feel promised in the restaurant's name. David Harding's cooking is 'modern British with Welsh and classic French influences', so among his dishes you'll find such diverse choices as hotpot of Conwy mussels with cider, parsley and cream, collops of pork with prunes and a brandy sauce, oxtail and Madeira soup, daube of beef, gin and tonic sorbet, and hot treacle and oatmeal tart with egg sauce. Organically-produced Welsh cheese. Traditional roasts are included among the Sunday lunch choice. Something from somewhere for everyone on the interesting wine list, which has helpful and personal tasting notes, plenty of half bottles and fair prices – inexpensive house wines and a champagne under £20! No smoking. **Seats** *55. L 12.30-1.45 D 7-9.30 (Sun to 9). Set L £11.50/£13.50 (Sun £14.50) Set D (5-course) £26.*

Llandudno   Places of Interest

Tourist Information   Tel 0492 876413.
Mostyn Art Gallery   Tel 0492 874151.
Llandudno Dry Ski Slope   Tel 0492 874707.
Alice in Wonderland Visitor Centre   Tel 0492 860082.

Llangammarch Wells Lake Country House Hotel 68%   £80

Tel 059 12 202   Fax 059 12 457   **HR**

Llangammarch Wells Powys LD4 4BS   **Map 9 C4**

Standing in 50 acres of parkland and enjoying genuine tranquillity, this mainly Edwardian hotel has grandly proportioned day rooms including a drawing room where traditional Welsh teas are served. In the summer, teas are also served in the garden overlooking the River Irfon. Bedrooms have fine views and are individually styled with a combination of antiques and restful colour schemes. Smart, efficient staff mirror the owners'

enthusiasm. Fishing is available on three rivers and the hotel's lake.
Rooms 19. Garden, pitch & putt, tennis, fishing, snooker. AMERICAN EXPRESS®
Access, Visa.

Restaurant

£65

Fixed-price, five-course dinners with a choice of three or four dishes at each
stage are typified by cream of courgette and pimento soup, warm terrine
of monkfish with sun-dried tomatoes, dill and crabmeat on a saffron and
dill sauce, honey-roast poussin with almonds and loin of Welsh lamb with
a mint and walnut crust and Puy lentils. Home-made ice cream among the
desserts. Popular Sunday lunches. No children under 8 in the evening.
Plenty of choice on the varied wine list. *Seats 50. L 12.45-1.45
(non-residents by arrangement only) D 7-8.45. Set L £15.50 (Sun)
Set D £24.50.*

Llangefni, Tre-Ysgawen Hall. See entry under Capel Coch.

Llangefni   Places of Interest

Holyhead Tourist Information   Tel 0407 762622.
Wylfa Nuclear Power Station   Tel 0407 710471 *10 miles.*

Llangollen   Hand Hotel   55%   £65

Tel 0978 860303   Fax 0978 861277   **H**

Bridge Street Llangollen Clwyd LL20 8PL   Map 8 D2

Country hotel with gardens reaching down to the river Dee. Simple,
attractive rooms (many refurbished in 1994). Three rooms suitable for
family use. Banqueting and conference facilities for up to 80. *Rooms 57.
Garden, fishing.* AMERICAN EXPRESS® *Access, Diners, Visa.*

Llangollen   Royal Hotel   59%   £82

Tel 0978 860202   Fax 0978 861824   **H**

Bridge Street Llangollen Clwyd LL20 8PG   Map 8 D2

Looking just a little like a fairy-tale castle, the Royal overlooks a 14th-
century stone bridge on the banks of the Dee. Simple bedrooms, two bars
and a comfortable lounge. Banqueting/conferences for up to 80. Forte
Heritage. *Rooms 33.* AMERICAN EXPRESS® *Access, Diners, Visa.*

Llangollen   Places of Interest

Tourist Information   Tel 0978 860828.
European Centre for Traditional and Regional Cultures
    Tel 0978 861292.
Llangollen Railway   Tel 0978 860951.
Valle Crucis Abbey   Tel 0978 860326 *2 miles.*
Chirk Castle   Tel 0691 777701 *6 miles.*

Llangybi   Cwrt Bleddyn Hotel   71%   £100

Tel 0633 450521   Fax 0633 450220   **H**

Tredunnock nr Usk Gwent NP5 1PG   Map 9 D6

A large house standing in 17 acres of countryside three miles from
Caerleon, between Llangybi and Tredunnock, Cwrt Bleddyn can trace its
heritage back to the 14th century. Some original features date back just
to the 17th century but the interior is modernised to a great extent,
including 25 spacious bedrooms and 11 suites. The lounge and private

meeting rooms feature carved panelling and fireplaces and the sun lounge/cocktail bar has a spectacular high-domed glass ceiling. Good family facilities; coffee shop in leisure club 11am-11pm. Conference facilities for up to 200. *Rooms 36. Garden, indoor swimming pool, gym, sauna, steam room, solarium, spa bath, beauty salon, hair salon, games room, tennis, squash.* AMERICAN EXPRESS *Access, Diners, Visa.*

Llanrug	Seiont Manor	71%	£100
Tel 0286 673366 Fax 0286 672840			**H**
Llanrug Caernarfon Gwynedd LL55 2AQ			Map 8 B2

Developed from the farmstead of a Georgian manor house, the hotel stands on the A4086. 150 acres of parkland provide pleasant walks, and Snowdonia National Park and the Isle of Anglesey are both a short drive away. Fishing is available on the river Seiont, and guests have complimentary access to a nearby golf course. Public rooms, including a traditional oak-panelled bar, a lounge and a very comfortable library (the last two serving morning coffee, lunch and afternoon tea), are also furnished in a manner that befits the ancient character of the building. Bedrooms are in two purpose-built blocks which extend from the original stone building and are in a style sympathetic to it. Rooms have either little balconies or patio doors, are of a good size and all boast antique or good-quality period furniture. Conference facilities for up to 100 delegates. Voyager Hotels (a Virgin company) have managed Seiont Manor since April 1994. *Rooms 28. Garden, indoor swimming pool, keep-fit equipment, sauna, fishing.* AMERICAN EXPRESS *Access, Diners, Visa.*

Llanrug   Places of Interest

Caernarfon Tourist Information   Tel 0286 672232.
Caernarfon Castle   Tel 0286 677617 *World Heritage Listed Site.*
Penrhyn Castle (NT)   Nr Bangor Tel 0248 353084.
Segontium Roman Fort Museum   Caernarfon Tel 0286 675625.

Llansanffraid Glan Conwy	Old Rectory	73%	£90
Tel 0492 580611 Fax 0492 584555			**HR**
Llanrwst Road Llansanffraid Glan Conwy Gwynedd LL28 5LF			Map 8 C1

Standing above the A470, the Old Rectory (dating from 1740) enjoys splendid views across the Conwy estuary from Conwy Castle to Snowdonia. Personally run by the Vaughans, with Michael presiding over front of house in chatty, friendly style. The main day room is a comfortable, pine-panelled lounge where drinks are also served – there is no separate bar. Antique-furnished bedrooms come with all sorts of homely comforts from fresh flowers and fruit to piles of books and magazines. Each room also has an iron and ironing board plus tea- and coffee-making kit, although room service of beverages and sandwiches is available throughout the day and evening. Dogs, children (not under 5) and smokers are all restricted to two rooms in an adjacent converted stable block. *Rooms 6. Garden. Closed 14 Dec-1 Feb.* AMERICAN EXPRESS *Access, Diners, Visa.*

Restaurant   £70

A most civilised dining room, originally two rooms but now joined by twin arches, with collections of silverware and decanters on antique side tables, fine china in glass-fronted cabinets, chandeliers and some fine paintings on the walls – an ideal setting in which to enjoy Wendy Vaughan's excellent four-course set dinners unhurriedly served by Michael. Concentrating on local produce like Welsh black beef and mountain lamb, a typical dinner might be a freshly-baked walnut and tomato tart with warm walnut oil dressing, pepper and anchovy-stuffed fillet of beef with a balsamic vinegar sauce, then a choice between a sorbet and some Welsh farmhouse cheeses before choosing between a couple of delicious desserts. Everything from the bread rolls to the nibbles served with pre-dinner

drinks is freshly prepared and cooked with a sure touch. No smoking.
Seats 16. D only 7.30 for 8. Set D £27.50.

Llanvihangel Gobion   Llansantffraed Court   66%   £75

Tel 0873 840678   Fax 0873 840674   **H**

Llanvihangel Gobion nr Abergavenny Gwent NP7 9BA   Map 9 D5

A neo-classical Lutyens house with strong Georgian influences standing
on the B4598 Abergavenny road; extensive parkland surrounds the house
on the fringe of the Usk valley with the Black Mountains as a backdrop.
Most characterful of the bedrooms are on the top floor, with oak beams
and dormer windows. Children up to 5 stay free in parents' room. The
lounge and bar provide ample space for a relaxing chat or drink.
Conference/banqueting for 70/120. Now managed by the Mount Charlotte
Thistle group. *Rooms 21. Garden, helipad.* AMERICAN EXPRESS *Access,
Diners, Visa.*

Note that all telephone numbers with area codes starting with 0
will start 01 from 16 April 1995.

Llanwddyn   Lake Vyrnwy Hotel   67%   £73

Tel 0691 73692   Fax 0691 73259   **HR**

Lake Vyrnwy Llanwyddyn Montgomery Powys SY10 0LY   Map 8 C3

The magnificent, if austere, stone mansion high on a wooded hillside looks
across 1,100 acres of man-made lake set amid 24,000 acres of the Vyrnwy
Estate. Built at the same time as the dam in 1890 (drinking water from
here is still supplied to Liverpool 68 miles away) this is indeed a magical
spot and, now as then, "a retreat for all country lovers". True to their
Victorian origins, the generously proportioned public rooms, have
an ageless feel, with chintz sofas, Bechstein piano, tapestries and oil
paintings gracing the lounge, while a clubby atmosphere in the bar
is enhanced by pitch pine, leather armchairs and sporting prints. For
an informal drink, the spectacular views can be enjoyed from the balcony
of the adjacent Tavern. The majority of bedrooms share this aspect; each
is individually designed with much antique and period furniture
in evidence and many special features of unique appeal, from private sitting
areas and balconies to four-poster beds and jacuzzi baths. Conference
facilities accommodate up to 120; banqueting for 50. Children welcome
overnight; cots provided. *Rooms 38. Garden, tennis, shooting, fishing, boat
hire, sailing, bicycles, helipad.* AMERICAN EXPRESS *Access, Diners, Visa.*

Restaurant   £65

The kitchens' home production runs from breakfast marmalade to petits
fours at dinner, with the estate and gardens providing their fair share
of seasonal produce. A timbale of wild salmon and scallops, fillet of Welsh
black beef with Madeira sauce and gratin of fruits with Grand Marnier
sabayon typify nightly choices from a fixed-price varied-choice menu.
Contrived daily to catch the seasons' every mood, results may be as varying
as the ever-changing view, though pleasure can equally be derived from
both in this unparalleled setting. *Seats 120. Private Room 50.
L 12.30-1.45 D 7.30-9.15. Set D £22.50*

Llanwddyn   Places of Interest

Powysland Museum & Montgomery Canal Centre   The Canal Wharf,
Welshpool Tel 0938 554656.
Montgomeryshire Showground   Welshpool Tel 0938 554818.
Powis Castle (NT)   Welshpool Tel 0938 554336.
Glebe House Garden   Welshpool Tel 0938 553602.

Llanwnda   Stables Hotel   57%   £42

Tel 0286 830711   Fax 0286 830413   **H**

Llanwnda nr Caernarfon Gwynedd LL54 5SD   **Map 8 B2**

Three miles south-west of Caernarfon on the A499, this is a modest single-storey hotel set around original Victorian stables which now house a small bar and restaurant. Children up to 12 stay free in parents' room. Four-room suite also available. **Rooms** 14. *Garden, outdoor swimming pool, helipad.* AMERICAN EXPRESS® *Access, Visa.*

Changes in data sometimes occur in establishments after the Guide goes to press. Prices should be taken as indications rather than firm quotes.

Llyswen   Llangoed Hall   81%   £130

Tel 0874 754525   Fax 0874 754545   **HR**

Llyswen Brecon Powys LD3 0YP   **Map 9 D5**

This site has played host to a number of distinguished buildings over the centuries, including, it is thought, the home of the first Welsh Parliament. The house as it stands now dates from the 1600s, but was completely restored and largely redesigned earlier this century by Sir Clough Williams-Ellis, who later went on to build Portmeirion, the renowned Italianate village in North Wales. Sir Bernard Ashley bought the hotel in 1987, and has masterminded its restoration to its current Edwardian splendour, with marvellous results. The Great Hall and other public rooms boast open fires, original paintings, large sofas and some fine antiques. The feeling of space and luxury is enhanced by the sweeping staircase leading to the bedrooms, each individually decorated and all having thoughtful touches such as decanters of sherry, Welsh spring water and bowls of fruit. The wallpaper and sumptuous fabrics hint at the owner's other interests! Luxurious bathrooms with hand-held showers and huge towels retain something of the old-fashioned quality – even the tubs fill at a leisurely pace, and Floris toiletries add to the classy feel. Delicious traditional breakfast includes a vegetarian option of Glamorgan sausages. Conference and banqueting for 30/40. **Rooms** 23. *Garden with maze, tennis, croquet, fishing, snooker, helipad.* AMERICAN EXPRESS® *Access, Diners, Visa.*

Restaurant   £105

An elegant room with fluted pilasters and some fine pictures from Sir Bernard's personal collections around pale yellow walls. Posies of fresh flowers adorn immaculately set tables that are matched by a keen eye for presentation in Nigel Morris's kitchen. Choose from the 'petit' à la carte – just five options at each stage but a well-balanced selection – or the day's equally well-composed, no-choice, five-course dinner menu. Roast sea scallops with chargrilled vegetables, a trio of foie gras terrines, fillet of monkfish with ginger-scented noodles (a nice light hand with the ginger), breast of free-range Trelough duck roasted with cinnamon (again well judged), 'tart tatin' of pear and a plate of apple desserts demonstrate the style. Lunch offers a limited choice, set-price menu. Smooth, professional service. No smoking. **Seats** 46. *Private Room* 14/22. *L* 12.15-2.15 *D* 7.15-9.30. *Set L £16 (Sun £16.75) Set D £35.50*

Llyswen   Places of Interest

Brecon Tourist Information   Tel 0874 622485.
Builth Wells Tourist Information   Tel 0982 553307.
Wyeside Arts Centre   Builth Wells Tel 0982 552555.
Royal Welsh Showground   Llanelwedd Tel 0982 553683.

Machynlleth   **Wynnstay Arms**   57%   £53

Tel 0654 702941   Fax 0654 703884   **H**

Maengwyn Street Machynlleth Powys SY20 8AE   Map 8 C3

Town house hotel, well placed in the valley of the River Dovey as a base from which to visit Snowdonia. Family owned, the Wynnstay takes pride in offering a warm welcome to visitors and locals. Convivial bar. Children up to 14 stay free in parents' room. *Rooms 20.* AMERICAN EXPRESS *Access, Diners, Visa.*

Machynlleth   **Places of Interest**

Centre for Alternative Technology   Llwyngwern Quarry
   Tel 0654 702400 $2\frac{1}{2}$ miles.

Merthyr Tydfil   **Baverstock Hotel**   57%   £55

Tel 0685 386221   Fax 0685 723670   **H**

Heads of the Valley Road Merthyr Tydfil Mid Glamorgan CF44 0LX   Map 9 C5

Modern hotel in an elevated position on the A465. A good deal of business comes from conferences and meetings in a variety of rooms (50 residential, 400 daytime; ample parking). Reduced rates at weekends when businessmen are thin on the ground. Under new ownership. *Rooms 53. Garden, games room, helipad.* AMERICAN EXPRESS *Access, Diners, Visa.*

Merthyr Tydfil   **Places of Interest**

Ynysfach Engine House   Tel 0685 721858/83704.
Cyfarthfa Castle Museum and Art Gallery   Tel 0685 723112.

Miskin   **Miskin Manor**   70%   £95

Tel 0443 224204   Fax 0443 237606   **H**

Penddylan Road Pontyclun Miskin Mid Glamorgan CF7 8ND   Map 9 C6

Built of mellow grey Welsh stone, the present manor dates from the 1850s. Overlooking both the M4 (1 mile from Junction 34) and the river Ely, the hotel stands in 20 acres of garden and woodland. Oak linenfold panelling, a predominant feature of the elegantly proportioned day rooms, is now lightened by recent interior refurbishing in bright colours which reflect their pastoral aspect. Individually furnished bedrooms, notable for their size and luxurious appointment, each have their share of the view. Crown-canopied beds, two four-posters and a suite occupied in the 1920s by the future Edward VIII imbue this fine house with a tangible legacy of its own history. A short walk from the hotel, the self-contained Health and Leisure club with playroom and crèche is shared, at no charge for residents, with local members. *Rooms 32. Garden, indoor swimming pool, gym, squash, spa bath, steam room, sauna, solarium, beauty salon, badminton, coffee shop (10am-10pm), creche (9am-3pm Mon-Fri).* AMERICAN EXPRESS *Access, Diners, Visa.*

Mumbles   **Norton House**   65%   £65

Tel 0792 404891   Fax 0792 403210   **HR**

17 Norton Road Mumbles Swansea West Glamorgan SA3 5TQ   Map 9 C6

The Power family's enviable reputation for hospitality draws a faithful clientele to their wisteria-clad former master mariner's house just a few hundred yards from the seashore. Focal point of the day rooms is the mirror-lined bar with its unusual umbrella-vaulted ceiling, though residents seeking peace and quiet have use of a first-floor lounge over the old coach house. Here, bedroom conversions are practical and neatly appointed with those on the ground floor having access to their own patios and gardens.

See over

Four main-house rooms have four-poster beds, generous seating areas, newly restyled bathrooms and welcoming extras which include complimentary sherry. *Rooms 15. Garden. Closed 25 & 26 Dec.* AMERICAN EXPRESS *Access, Diners, Visa.*

Restaurant   £65

The influence and enthusiasm of first son Mark Power brings touches of originality to dinner menus which, though written in Welsh, have a broad, traditional English and French base. Laverbread-stuffed mushrooms appears alongside prawn-filled pancakes; grilled beef fillet is served with herby Yorkshire pudding and sherry gravy; steamed chocolate pudding with Grand Marnier sauce remains a firm favourite. Equally traditional restaurant furnishings, flambé and liqueur trolleys and the proprietors' personally-selected wine list are all reminiscent of the private entertaining which Norton House's style still echoes. *Seats 36. Parties 10. Private Room 16. L by arrangement D 7.15-9.30 (sun 7-9). Set D £19.50/23.50.*

Mumbles   Place of Interest

Caswell Bay Beach

Newport   Celtic Manor   75%   £117
Tel 0633 413000   Fax 0633 412910   **H**
The Coldra Newport Gwent NP6 2YA   Map 9 D6

Just one minute from Junction 24 of the M4, this 19th-century manor house is set in a 300-acre estate. Well set up for both business and pleasure, the hotel maintains high standards of decor, maintenance and service. Six conference suites cater for up to 350 delegates, and the leisure facilities are impressive. By spring of 1995 there should be a tennis club and the Ian Woosnam Golfing Academy. There is an elegant drawing room and a large patio conservatory which is used for breakfast. Bedrooms are of a good size and feature triple glazing, freestanding darkwood furniture with ample writing space, attractive window seating and smartly tiled, well-lit bathrooms. *Rooms 73. Garden, indoor swimming pool, gym, sauna, solarium, helipad.* AMERICAN EXPRESS *Access, Diners, Visa.*

Newport   Hilton National   61%   £80
Tel 0633 412777   Fax 0633 413087   **H**
The Coldra Newport Gwent NP6 2YG   Map 9 D6

In an attractive woodland setting, the hotel entrance is just 100 yards from Junction 24 of the M4. Facilities much geared to business conferences (up to 500), exhibitions, seasonal coach parties and banqueting (400), swing over to more general family use at weekends with swimming, games room and evening entertainment. Children up to 18 can stay free in parents' 3-bedded rooms with no breakfast charge for those under 12. Cots available free of charge. *Rooms 119. Indoor swimming pool, keep-fit equipment, sauna, steam room, games room.* AMERICAN EXPRESS *Access, Diners, Visa.*

Note that all telephone numbers with area codes starting with 0 will start 01 from 16 April 1995.

Newport   Stakis Cardiff-Newport Hotel   69%   £113

Tel 0633 413737   Fax 0633 413713   **H**

Chepstow Road Langstone Newport Gwent NP6 2LX   Map 9 D6

Stakis hotel built round a courtyard garden. Roomy overnight
accommodation, leisure centre, self-contained facilities for business
meetings. Children up to 12 free in parents' room. 35 non-smoking rooms.
Ample free parking. Previously the *Stakis Country Court*. **Rooms** *139.
Indoor swimming pool, gym, sauna, steam room, spa bath, solarium.*
AMERICAN EXPRESS *Access, Diners, Visa.*

Newport (Magor)   Granada Lodge   £52

Tel 0633 880111   Fax 0633 881896   **L**

Magor Newport Gwent NP6 3YL   Map 9 D6

At the Magor Service Area by Junction 23 of M4. Children under 16 share
parents' room free. Direct-dial (credit card) telephones and satellite TV in
the rooms. 24hr room service. No dogs. **Rooms** *43.* AMERICAN EXPRESS *Access,
Diners, Visa.*

Newport   Places of Interest

Tourist Information   Tel 0633 842962.
Dolman Theatre   Tel 0633 263670.
Newport Centre   Tel 0633 259676.
Tredegar House   Tel 0633 815880.
Cathedral Church of St. Woolos   Tel 0633 63338.
Museum and Art Gallery   Tel 0633 840064.
Roman Legionary Museum   Caerleon Tel 0633 423.

Northop   Soughton Hall   79%   £119

Tel 0352 840811   Fax 0352 840382   **HR**

Northop nr Mold Clwyd CH7 6AB   Map 8 D2

Watch out for the sheep as you drive down a long avenue of lime trees
to approach this creeper-clad, former Bishop's Palace dating from 1714.
The grandeur of some of the public rooms, like the high-ceilinged first-
floor sitting room with its decorated beams and tapestry wall hangings,
is moderated by personal touches like family photos and objets d'art at what
is the Rodenhursts' family home as well as a hotel. A real log fire warms
the entrance hall and there is a tiny bar hidden behind a 'secret' door in the
small library. Antiques abound, particularly in the bedrooms, which come
with all sorts of extras such as fresh fruit, mineral water and comfortable
armchairs plus various ornaments all of which help to create a 'house guest'
ambience. Antiques also feature in some of the good bathrooms, all
of which have views of the surrounding countryside. Breakfast is taken
in the original servants' hall which still features an old black range. Golf
can be arranged at a new course adjacent to the hotel. **Rooms** *12. Garden,
snooker, tennis, archery. Closed first 2 weeks Jan.* AMERICAN EXPRESS *Access, Visa.*

Restaurant   £75

Depending upon the number of diners you eat either in the grand, high-
ceilinged State Dining Room or the more intimate South Parlour. In either
event the lead crystal glassware and Royal Doulton china that grace the
candle-lit, polished wooden tables are of the best quality. Dish descriptions
on the à la carte menu tend to be a bit florid but cooking is essentially
sound. A dome of seasonal melon accompanied by a ginger, strawberry and
kiwi syrup with an orgy of citrus fruits, topped with a refreshing water ice,
and roast fillet of Welsh lamb perfumed with coriander and rosemary
enhanced by a purée of garlic and lentil potatoes and finished with a garlic
and tarragon jus, demonstrate the style, both literary and culinary. The
fixed-price dinner menu is not always available. A well-thought-out wine

list with something for everyone from everywhere at fair prices. Note the collection of rare South African wines not usually available in this country. *Seats 40. Private Room 50. L by arrangement D 7.30-9.30 (Sat to 10, Sun to 8). Set L £14.95 Set D £21.50.*

Northop   Places of Interest

Mold Tourist Information   Tel 0352 759331.
Clwyd Theatre   Mold Tel 0352 755114 *4 miles.*

Northop Hall   Forte Travelodge   £45
Tel 0244 816473   **L**
Northop Hall Mold Clwyd CH7 6HB   Map 8 D2

Located on the A55 eastbound, 3 miles north east of Mold. **Rooms** *40.* AMERICAN EXPRESS *Access, Diners, Visa.*

Pant Mawr   Glansevern Arms   £55
Tel 055 15 240   **I**
Pant Mawr nr Llangurig Powys SY18 6SY   Map 9 C4

On the A44, four miles west of Llangurig, personally owned and managed for 27 years by Mr Edwards and family, the Glansevern Arms commands a magnificent position overlooking the upper reaches of the Wye. An intimate bar and lounge soak in the glorious hill scenery by day and glow with warmth from log fires at night. Residents equally enjoy the peace and quiet afforded by bedrooms with private sitting areas, uninterrupted by any phones, where the views should provide a greater attraction than television. **Rooms** *7. Closed 1 week Christmas. No credit cards.*

Pant Mawr   Places of Interest

Newtown Tourist Information   Tel 0686 625580.
Gregynog House and Gardens   Newtown Tel 0686 650224 *28 miles.*
Robert Owen Memorial Museum   Newtown Tel 0686 626345.
W H Smith Museum   Newtown Tel 0686 626280.

Penally   Penally Abbey   65%   £92
Tel 0834 843033   Fax 0834 844714   **HR**
Penally nr Tenby Dyfed SA70 7PY   Map 9 B5

Set in five acres of gardens and woodland overlooking sand dunes and Carmarthen Bay, Penally Abbey is a Gothic-style stone-built mansion with an adjoining coach house. There's a tiny bar, a vine-shaded conservatory and a homely lounge where guests can play various musical instruments. Four bedrooms have four-posters (two are in the Coach House), others pine wardrobes and period wash-stands. Cheerful staff and welcoming hosts. Good breakfasts. No dogs. **Rooms** *11. Garden, croquet, small indoor swimming pool, games room.* AMERICAN EXPRESS *Access, Visa.*

Restaurant   £50

Elleen Warren makes excellent use of prime local ingredients on her fixed-price dinner menus. Dressed crab, breast of duck with tomato and basil sauce, skate wings in lemon butter and Stilton-stuffed fillet of beef wrapped in bacon and finished with red wine show the style. No children under seven. No smoking. *Seats 46. Parties 20. Private Room 12. D only 7.30-9.30. Set D £23.50.*

Pencoed   Forte Travelodge   £45

Tel 0656 864404   **L**

Old Mill Felindre Road Pencoed nr Bridgend Mid Glamorgan CF3 5HU   **Map 9 C6**

Head north on the A473 from Junction 35 of the M4, taking first right
into Felindre Road. 10 minutes from Bridgend. *Rooms 40.* AMERICAN EXPRESS
Access, Diners, Visa.

Penmaenpool   George III Hotel   £88

Tel 0341 422525   Fax 0341 423565   **I**

Penmaenpool nr Dolgellau Gwynedd LL40 1YD   **Map 8 C3**

Magnificent views are shared by all but two of the bedrooms at the
Cartwright family's 17th-century inn at the head of the Mawddach estuary.
Focal point of the day rooms is the Dresser Bar (the bar counter is made
from part of an old Welsh dresser), where wooden tables are polished, brass
ornaments gleam and a welcoming fire burns in the grate. There's also
a cellar bar (actually at ground level) and a cosy residents' lounge.
Bedrooms, half of them in the adjacent Victorian former railway station,
are pretty and traditional, bathrooms smart and modern. *Rooms 11.*
Fishing. Access, Visa.

Port Talbot   Travel Inn   £43

Tel 0639 813017   Fax 0639 823096   **L**

Baglan Road Port Talbot West Glamorgan SA12 8ES   **Map 9 C6**

Rooms 40. AMERICAN EXPRESS *Access, Diners, Visa.*

Port Talbot   Places of Interest

Aberdulais Falls   nr Neath Tel 0639 636674.
Afan Lido Swimming Pools   Tel 0639 884141.

Porthkerry   Egerton Grey   68%   £85

Tel 0446 711666   Fax 0446 711690   **H**

Porthkerry nr Cardiff South Glamorgan CF6 9BZ   **Map 9 C6**

This handsome former rectory, standing in 7 acres of woodland at the
fringe of the Vale of Glamorgan, is hidden in a lush valley at the foot of a
single track road; rather surprisingly, it is just two minutes' drive from
Cardiff Wales Airport. Follow the signs to Rhoose from the M4 at
Junction 33, and the hotel is indicated off the airport perimeter road. A
parquet-floored foyer leads to elegantly-proportioned day rooms: the
lounge with deep-cushioned sofas, family portraits and grand piano; a
restful library replete with magazines and board games; and a mahogany-
furnished breakfast room that doubles (as required) for conferences or
private dining (capacity 20). Bedrooms abound with antique furniture,
including a vast four-poster in the honeymoon suite. The decor of each is a
striking mix of bold colour schemes and plush fabrics with thick carpeting
running through to spacious, well-lit bathrooms, the pick of which feature
Edwardian baths, with exposed brasswork and huge deluge shower heads.
On our last visit, however, we felt that shortcomings in housekeeping were
generally indicative of a lack of attention to detail. The general standard of
service on our most recent visit was distinctly below par. *Rooms 10.*
Garden, tennis. AMERICAN EXPRESS *Access, Diners, Visa.*

Portmeirion   Hotel Portmeirion   74%   £132

Tel 0766 770228   Fax 0766 771331   **HR**

Portmeirion Gwynedd LL48 6ER   **Map 8 B2**

Portmeirion was created (and opened in 1926) by Sir Clough Williams-
Ellis on the secluded, Aber Iâ peninsula on the Traeth Bach estuary, though
it was 1973 before the whole fairy-tale village, comprising 50 buildings   *See over*

arranged round a central piazza, was completed. The hotel is based on an early-Victorian villa near the shore and contains some stunning public rooms: among others the black and white marble-floored hall and the Indian-themed Jaipur Bar particularly take the eye. Guests stay either in the main hotel building with the pick of the sea views or in the surrounding suites and cottages that make up the village, all within very comfortable walking distance of the hotel. Five de luxe suites in the Anchor and Fountain building overlook the swimming pool and estuary. No dogs. Conference/banqueting facilities for up to 120. *Rooms 34. Garden, outdoor swimming pool, golf (18), tennis, sea fishing, coffee shop (10am-5pm), village shops (closed Jan-Mar). Closed early Jan-early Feb.* AMERICAN EXPRESS *Access, Diners, Visa.*

Restaurant   £65

The stunning, light, spacious, curvilinear dining room (added to the hotel during the 1930s) with fine vistas across the estuary is a fitting backdrop for Craig Hindley's light touch in the kitchen, utilising first-rate local raw materials in modern style with international influences. Paté of game with pickled vegetables and honey apples, or terrine of vegetables with a basil and olive dressing are typical starters; guinea fowl with candied orange, raisins and a jasmine tea sauce, or salmon baked in a herb crust with cucumber and ginger typical main courses. The trio of chocolate puddings is a popular dessert. The fixed-price dinner menus offer about six choices at each stage, the good-value lunch menu about half that number. The fairly-priced wine list is both well balanced and well annotated. It's quite fun to read the Welsh names of the famous wine growing areas of the world! No smoking. *Seats 100. Parties 16. Private Room 35. L 12.30-2 D 7-9.30. Set L £10/£13.50 (Sun £16) Set D £20/£25. Closed L Mon.*

Portmeirion   Places of Interest

Portmeirion Village   Tel 0766 770228.
Gloddfa Slate Mine   Blaenau Ffestiniog Tel 0766 830664.
Ffestiniog Railway   Porthmadog Tel 0766 831654.
Llechwedd Slate Caverns   Tel 0766 830306.

Presteigne   Radnorshire Arms   £92

Tel 0544 267406   Fax 0544 260418   ▌■▐
High Street Presteigne Powys LD8 2BE   Map 9 D4

Built in 1616 by Sir Christopher Hatton, a favourite of Queen Elizabeth I, the main house on Presteigne's historic High Street is a magnificent example of 17th-century magpie architecture. It opened as a coaching inn in 1792, and the town's stocks in front of it remained in use until 1851. Fine Jacobean panelling in the lounge, and black oak beams, high-backed settles and log fires in the hotel bar are splendidly evocative of a bygone era, to which the main-house bedrooms (despite up-to-date additions of telephones, TVs and en-suite bathrooms) add their own sense of history. Across the garden, however, a rear extension of chalet-style bedroom accommodation does rather spoil the period piece. Designated conference facility for 20. Children under 16 accommodated free in parents' room. *Rooms 16. Garden.* AMERICAN EXPRESS *Access, Diners, Visa.*

Pwllheli   Plas Bodegroes   £75

Tel 0758 612363   Fax 0758 701247   ▌RR▐
Nefyn Road Pwllheli Gwynedd LL53 5TH   Map 8 B2

A small Georgian house, hidden away in woodland two miles out of town on the Nefyn road, is the idyllic setting for Chris and Gunna Chown's stylish restaurant with rooms. Duck-green walls crammed with contemporary Welsh art and lit by mini-spotlights suspended from wires strung across the ceiling create a modern setting for some modish cooking. Ballotine of duck with red onion confit, warm monkfish salad with mushrooms and Carmarthen ham, chargrilled lamb kebab with sherry vinegar sauce, grilled goat's cheese with celery and walnut salad and warm chocolate tart are typical of the appealing dishes Chris creates out of largely local ingredients for his fixed-price, five-course menu that offers about five choices at each stage. A fine wine list, fairly priced (no less than three *marque* champagnes under £30) and with helpful guidance – look no further than the excellent house selection, but should you do so, you'll be well rewarded. No smoking. *Seats 35. Private Room 16. D only 7-9.30 (Sun to 9). Closed Mon & Nov-Feb. Set D £30.* AMERICAN EXPRESS *Access, Visa.*

Rooms £140*

Gunna's Scandinavian flair for interior design is evident in the eight immaculate, individually styled bedrooms that combine charm and style. Rooms at the top of the house are given added character by some exposed beams and all have smart modern bathrooms. Enjoy the garden from the wisteria-draped veranda or there's croquet for the more energetic. No smoking in bedrooms. *Half-board terms only. Accommodation closed Monday nights (note other seasonal closures – see above).

Reynoldston Fairyhill 65% £85

Tel 0792 390139 Fax 0792 391358 **HR**

Reynoldston Gower Swansea West Glamorgan SA3 1BS Map 9 B6

The hotel is set in beautiful countryside at the heart of the peninsula (best located by following signs to Gower from J47 of the M4); its own 24 acres include a meandering trout stream and lake, and abundant wild life. Within, Fairyhill's quiet intimacy is perhaps its greatest asset to which new proprietors, brother and sister Andrew Hetherington and Jane Camm, contribute a homely style of personal service. The newly-refurnished drawing room and leafy patio are an idyllic setting for afternoon tea or pre-dinner drinks, and there's a more modest, yet convivial, bar. Bedroom accoutrements include remote-control TVs and CD players (reception has a record library); fresh fruit on arrival and beds turned down during dinner. Conversion of some bathrooms from WC/shower only to full baths with showers is virtually complete. Splendid country breakfasts. No children under 8. Now open year-round. *Rooms 11. Garden, fishing.* AMERICAN EXPRESS *Access, Visa.*

Restaurant £55

Partner Paul Davies runs the kitchen with Kate Cole, offering lunch daily and a fixed-price dinner, with a balanced range of choices which changes every night. Champions of local produce on offer are Penclawdd cockles as an appetiser, laverbread (in a tartlet with smoked bacon) among first courses, and poached sewin in season (with cucumber sauce, perhaps) to follow. Tagliatelle with fennel and aubergine and beef fillet béarnaise are typical alternatives. Choice of desserts such as tarte tatin or floating islands is requested early and individually prepared to order. The comprehensive wine list is the work of a true enthusiast; future plans include bottling their own spring water. *Seats 70. Parties 40. Private Room 16. L (Sun only) 12.30-1.15 D 7.30-9. Set L (Sun) £12.50 Set D £22.50.*

Rossett Llyndir Hall 71% £110

Tel 0244 571648 Fax 0244 571258 **H**

Llyndir Lane Rossett nr Wrexham Clwyd LL12 0AY Map 8 D2

Ten minutes drive from the centre of Chester, this 'Strawberry Gothic' hall is surrounded by beautiful parkland. Bedrooms are well sized and furnished with antique pieces, the effect being both tasteful and elegant without being ostentatious. Most of the rooms are in a sympathetic new building. Some rooms are suitable for family use and children up to 14 stay free in parents' room. A gracious and sunny drawing room looks out over the lush lawns. Banquet and conference facilities for up to 90/150. *Rooms 38. Garden, indoor swimming pool, spa bath, steam room, solarium, coffee shop (7am-10pm, till 11 weekends).* AMERICAN EXPRESS *Access, Diners, Visa.*

Rossett   Places of Interest

Wrexham Tourist Information   Tel 0978 357845.
Bersham Industrial Heritage Museum Centre   Bersham
   Tel 0978 261529 *8 miles.*
Chirk Castle (NT)   Tel 0691 777701.
Erddig (NT)   Tel 0978 355314.
Bangor-on-Dee Racecourse   Tel 0978 780323 *10 miles.*

Ruthin	Ruthin Castle	62%	£82
Tel 0824 702664 Fax 0824 705978			**H**
Corwen Road Ruthin Clwyd LL15 2NU			**Map 8 C2**

Thirty-eight acres of gardens and parkland surround ancient Ruthin Castle,
where relics of the past include a drowning pool, whipping pit and
dungeons. The castle has known attack, siege and virtual destruction, but
more peaceful diversions today centre around the cocktail bar, splendid
lounge, or comfortable bedrooms appointed in traditional style. The Great
Hall is the scene of regular medieval banquets, which guests may attend.
Conference/banqueting facilities for up to 150, with ample parking.
No dogs. *Rooms 60. Garden, snooker, fishing, helipad.* AMERICAN EXPRESS *Access,
Diners, Visa.*

Ruthin   Places of Interest

Ruthin Tourist Information and Craft Centre   Tel 0824 703992.
Cathedral Church of St. Asaph   Tel 0745 583597 *16 miles.*

St David's	St Non's Hotel	56%	£64
Tel 0437 720239 Fax 0437 721839			**H**
St David's Dyfed SA62 6RJ			**Map 9 A5**

Named appropriately after the mother of St David, this friendly family
hotel half a mile from the town centre offers some of the best children's
terms around: under-6s stay free in parents' room and enjoy free breakfast
and high tea. Other bonuses include five ground-floor bedrooms for the
less mobile, and free golf at the picturesque St David's 9-hole course.
Rooms 24. Garden. AMERICAN EXPRESS *Access, Diners, Visa.*

St David's	Warpool Court	62%	£104
Tel 0437 720300 Fax 0437 720676			**H**
St David's Dyfed SA62 6BN			**Map 9 A5**

Bordering National Trust parkland, Warpool Court enjoys spectacular
scenery and panoramic views over St Brides Bay to the offshore islands
beyond. Equally eye-catching within is the Ada Williams collection
of unique armorial and ornamental hand-painted tiles which bedeck the
public areas and a number of the bedrooms. Private rooms for conferences
accommodate up to 70 people. Children under 14 stay free in parents'
room (a children's menu is also provided); outdoor playground for
children. Free golf at the St David's course. The hotel was built in the 1860s
as St David's Cathedral School. *Rooms 25. Garden, croquet, tennis, covered
outdoor swimming pool (Easter-Oct), keep-fit equipment, sauna, games room,
children's play area. Closed January.* AMERICAN EXPRESS *Access, Diners, Visa.*

St David's   Places of Interest

Haverfordwest Tourist Information   Tel 0437 763110.
County Showground   Haverfordwest Tel 0437 764331.
St David's Bishop's Palace   Tel 0437 720517.
Cathedral Church of St David and St Andrew   Tel 0437 720202.

Museums and Art Galleries
Scolton Manor Museum   Spittal Tel 0437 731328.
Graham Sutherland Gallery   Haverfordwest Tel 0437 751297.

Swansea   Forte Crest   69%   £95

Tel 0792 651074   Fax 0792 456044   **H**

39 The Kingsway Swansea West Glamorgan SA1 5LS   Map 9 C6

High-riser in the city centre, updated from its 60s' look. Leisure and
business centres (conference facilities for 200+). Two-thirds of the
bedrooms are designated non-smoking. Children up to 15 stay free
in parents' room. Free overnight parking in NCP opposite. *Rooms 99.
Indoor swimming pool, gym, sauna, solarium.* AMERICAN EXPRESS *Access,
Diners, Visa.*

Swansea   Hilton National   65%   £78

Tel 0792 310330   Fax 0792 797535   **H**

Phoenix Way Enterprise Park Llansamlet Swansea West Glamorgan
SA7 9EG   Map 9 C6

Two-storey, purpose-built redbrick hotel three miles from the city centre
and two from the M4 (Junctions 44 or 45). Conference facilities for up to
200. 24hr room service. Refurbished during 1994. *Rooms 120. Keep-fit
equipment, sauna, sunbeds.* AMERICAN EXPRESS *Access, Diners, Visa.*

Swansea   Langland Court Hotel   £78

Tel 0792 361545   Fax 0792 362302   **I**

31 Langland Court Road Langland Swansea West Glamorgan SA3 4TD   Map 9 C6

Take the A4067 coastal road from Swansea to Mumbles (five miles) and
follow signs to Langland Bay (turn left at Newton Church) to find this
comfortable clifftop inn. Public areas take the form of a Tudor-style
residence, to which *Polly's*, the Dylan Thomas-themed wine bar, adds much
character. Period-style main-house bedrooms mostly have fine views of the
Bristol Channel, while further rooms occupy the former coach house (dogs
allowed here only) across the road; top of the range are Tudor-style rooms
with four-posters. Some attic rooms have third-bed alcoves and convertible
couches. Children up to 16 stay free in parents' room. Popular for
conferences and functions (for up to 150). *Rooms 21. Garden.*
AMERICAN EXPRESS *Access, Diners, Visa.*

> If we recommend meals in a hotel or inn a separate entry is made for its
> restaurant.

Swansea   Number One   £55

Tel 0792 456996   **R**

1 Wind Street Swansea West Glamorgan SA1 1DE   Map 9 C6

The atmosphere at Kate Taylor's bistro is convivial and it's immensely
popular, so booking is advised. There's nothing pretentious about either the
surroundings or her no-nonsense cooking. Fish and shellfish are popular
choices – sweet-cured herring with potato and mustard salad, fillets
of monkfish in Ricard sauce – while meat dishes might include roast
haunch of venison with poached pear and port or fillet steak en croute.
Separate menus for desserts and cheese. Good-value 2- and 3-course lunches
with a small choice (perhaps rillettes of pork followed by home-made
faggots and peas or fillet of hake with *sauce vierge*, then bread-and-butter
pudding). "Coffee ad lib." *Seats 40. L 12-2.30 D 7-9.30. Closed D Mon
& Tue, all Sun. Set L £9.50/£11.95.* AMERICAN EXPRESS *Access, Visa.*

Swansea   Swansea Marriott   67%   £102

Tel 0792 642020 Fax 0792 650345   **H**
Maritime Quarter Swansea West Glamorgan SA1 3SS   Map 9 C6

Modern, four-storey redbrick hotel in the Maritime Quarter. Good-size
bedrooms (50% non-smoking) look out over either the bay or the marina.
Children up to 18 stay free in parents' room. Ample free parking.
Rooms 118. Indoor swimming pool, keep-fit equipment, spa bath, sauna.
AMERICAN EXPRESS *Access, Diners, Visa.*

Swansea   Places of Interest

Tourist Information Tel 0792 468321.
Clyne Gardens Tel 0792 401737.
Caswell Bay Beach.
Pembrey Motor Racing Circuit Tel 0554 891042.
Pembrey Sands Beach.
St Helen's Cricket Ground Tel 0792 466321.
Singleton Park Showground Tel 0792 302429.
  Theatres and Concert Halls
Brangwyn Hall Tel 0792 470002.
Dylan Thomas Theatre Tel 0792 473238.
Grand Theatre Tel 0792 462028.
Taliesin Arts Centre Tel 0792 295438.
  Museums and Art Galleries
Cery Richards Gallery Tel 0792 295438.
Glynn Vivian Art Gallery Tel 0792 655006/651738.
Maritime and Industrial Museum Tel 0792 470371/650351.
Parc Howard Museum and Art Gallery Llanelli Tel 0554 773538
  16 miles.

Talsarnau   Maes-y-Neuadd   72%   £109

Tel 0766 780200 Fax 0766 780211   **HR**
Talsarnau nr Harlech Gwynedd LL47 6YA   Map 8 C2

Signposted off the B4573 between Talsarnau and Harlech, Maes-y-Neuadd
enjoys a tranquil setting on one side of an almost secret valley with fine
views across the Snowdonia National Park. The oldest part of the building,
now the bar with stone inglenook and leather upholstery, dates from the
15th century with later additions from the 16th and 19th. Other day
rooms include a central lobby/lounge with large skylight and bedrooms
vary considerably in style from a small single with shower and WC only,
a few with pine furniture, others with antique pieces and a four-poster with
oak furniture to a splendidly large room (one of four in the adjacent stable
block) with black beams, high pitched ceiling and log-burning stove. All
have armchairs and/or sofas and bathrooms (three with spa baths) offer
good towelling and robes. Meeting rooms for up to 40, banqueting for
up to 50 (which can also be arranged on the nearby Ffestiniog Railway).
Personally run in friendly fashion by Malcolm and Olive Horsfall and
Mike and June Slatter, who pursue a policy of continual improvement
to the hotel. *Rooms 16. Garden, croquet, helipad.* AMERICAN EXPRESS *Access,
Diners, Visa.*

Restaurant   £70

Peter Jackson's dinner menu is officially a five-course affair but add the
complimentary starter and the fact that one is encouraged to sample the
outstanding Welsh cheeses plus *both* puds (perhaps raspberry soufflé
pancake and baked fruit in filo) before rounding off with one of their
unusual ice creams and it can be more like eight or nine. The well-
balanced, daily-changing menu offers a small choice at some stages;
between a warm quail and scallop salad or terrine of leeks and laverbread
to start, perhaps to be followed by a soup (carrot, potato and oatmeal 'cawl'

– Welsh for broth) and a fish dish (shallow-fried brill with brown butter and cucumber) before deciding between collops of venison with a herb crust, escalope of pork with a creamy tarragon sauce and apple gateau or a vegetarian option (aubergine gateau with a tomato fondue). A variety of home-baked breads testifies to the care taken in the kitchen, where good use is also made of the extensive herb garden. Three-course Sunday lunch includes a traditional roast and a fish dish among the choices. Peter represented Wales in the British Meat Chef of the Year competition – see pages 28–39. Few surprises on the wine list – something suitable for all tastes at affordable prices. No smoking. No children under 7 at dinner. *Seats* 50. *Parties* 12. *Private Room* 12. L 12.15-1.45 D 7-9.15. *Set L £8.75/£11.75 (Sun £14.50) Set D £14.50 & £27.50.*

Talsarnau   Places of Interest

Tourist Information Harlech   Tel 0766 780658.
Theatr Ardudwy Harlech   Tel 0766 780667.
Harlech Castle   Tel 0766 780552.

Talyllyn   Tynycornel Hotel   59%   £90

Tel 0654 782282   Fax 0654 782679   **H**
Talyllyn Tywyn Gwynedd LL36 9AJ   Map 8 C3

Fishing is the main attraction here, but the marvellous setting on Talyllyn Lake in Snowdonia National Park makes it a popular base for hikers and lovers of all aspects of the great outdoors. The hotel has its own fleet of small boats for hire. The atmosphere is cosy and relaxed in the lounge and bar. Accommodation is comfortable and functional. Children up to the age of 12 stay free in parents' room. Banqueting/conference facilities for up to 66. *Rooms 16. Garden, outdoor swimming pool, sauna, solarium, fishing.* AMERICAN EXPRESS *Access, Diners, Visa.*

Talyllyn   Place of Interest

Talyllyn Railway and Narrow-gauge Railway Museum   Tel 0654 710472.

Tintern Abbey   Beaufort Hotel   60%   £92

Tel 0291 689777   Fax 0291 689727   **H**
Tintern Abbey nr Chepstow Gwent NP6 6SF   Map 9 D5

Stone-built hotel whose front rooms look out on to the ruins of 800-year-old Tintern Abbey in the Wye valley. Children under 16 stay free in parents' room. Banqueting/conference facilities for 120/60. 7 miles from Junction 22 of M4. Jarvis Hotels. *Rooms 24. Garden, fishing, games room.* AMERICAN EXPRESS *Access, Diners, Visa.*

Tintern Abbey   Royal George   59%   £72

Tel 0291 689205   Fax 0291 689448   **H**
Tintern Abbey nr Chepstow Gwent NP6 6SF   Map 9 D5

The beautiful Wye Valley is the setting for Tony and Maureen Pearce's friendly hotel at the foot of a lovely wooded hillside. A trout stream runs alongside, and the ruins of Tintern Abbey are just a short walk away. The hotel began life in 1598 as the Irons Master's cottage for the nearby mines and was converted into a coaching inn in the 17th century. There are hints of the building's previous lives in its present appearance and versatility: there's ample bar and lounge space (one lounge is stocked with board games) and a large function room. Some of the bedrooms have balconies overlooking the gardens. One child under 14 free in parents' room; ten rooms are suitable for family occupation. *Rooms 19. Garden, fishing.* AMERICAN EXPRESS *Access, Diners, Visa.*

Tintern Abbey   Places of Interest

Tourist Information   Tel 0291 689431.
Tintern Abbey   Tel 0291 624647.

Trellech   The Village Green   £45

Tel 0600 860119   **RR**

Trellech nr Monmouth Gwent NP5 4PA   Map 9 D5

Bob and Jane Evans's once-derelict, 450-year-old village inn remains in the
forefront of today's fashion toward combining bistro-style food with more
traditional restaurant concepts. Customer preference has narrowed the
dividing line between bistro and à la carte to a large degree with the main
courses changed daily on large blackboard menus to complement popular
starters such as chef's terrine with onion chutney and gravad lax with dill
mustard dressing. Tuscan fish stew, roast duck with lychees and stincotto
(from the pork hock) served over tagliatelle are recent additions
to a commendably adventurous range. Sweets still include, on request,
a little-of-everything *assiette gourmande*. **Seats** 70. *Parties 12.
Private Room 24. L 12-1.45 D 7-9.45 (Sat to 10). Closed D Sun, all Mon
(except D Bank Holiday Mondays), 10 days Jan. Set Sun L £11.75.
Access, Visa.*

Rooms   £45

An adjacent stable conversion houses two small bedroom suites with
kitchenettes let on a self-catering or bed-and-breakfast basis. The rooms
have TV but no 'phones, and en-suite WC/shower rooms only. Children
accommodated free.

Trellech   Places of Interest

Tourist Information Monmouth   Tel 0600 713899.
Nelson Collection and Local History Centre Monmouth   Tel 0600
    713519.

Welsh Hook   Stone Hall   £55

Tel 0348 840212   Fax 0348 840815   **RR**

Welsh Hook Wolfscastle nr Haverfordwest Dyfed SA62 5NS   Map 9 A5

Hidden down country lanes (in woodland) 1½ miles off the A40 (signed
from Wolfscastle), the restaurant's interior is as Welsh as one would hope
to find at such an address as this, replete with exposed stone alcoves and
roof timbers, flagged floors and metre-thick walls. By the huge hooded
range there are even bread ovens built into the original inglenook. For ten
years now, Martine Watson has brought her own native Gallic touch
to a menu alive with colour and flavours. Her menu, of course, is French:
gateau d'aubergine, courgette et champignons provençal is brought alive by sun-
dried tomatoes and a richly tarragon-flavoured coulis. *Filet de turbot et sa
crêpe aux algues* is baked in its seaweed-flavoured pancake, wrapped
in creamy crab sauce and dotted with parsley and pink peppercorns.
Though kitchen personnel (inevitably) and culinary persuasion have
inexorably changed over the decade, Mme Watson's calm professional
influence has remained steadfast. **Seats** 34. *Parties 10. Private Room 30.
D only 7.30-9.30. Closed Mon, restricted opening Jan/Feb (phone to check).
Set D £15.* AMERICAN EXPRESS® *Access, Visa.*

Rooms   £63

Residents enjoy use of their own lounge and five en-suite bedrooms (three
doubles and two singles) all of which are immaculately kept. Children,
made welcome overnight, are offered their own supper at 6pm. The
resident cats are great favourites: no dogs admitted.

Whitebrook   Crown at Whitebrook   £65

Tel 0600 860254   Fax 0600 860607   **RR**

Whitebrook nr Monmouth Gwent NP5 4TX   Map 14 A2

Deep in the steeply wooded Whitebrook Valley, the original inn has
resurfaced as a modern, white-painted rectangular building run since 1988
by Roger and Sandra Bates as a restaurant with rooms offering a relaxed,
informal atmosphere with high standards of personal service.
A comfortable lounge (which houses the reception desk and small dispense
bar) leads on to a cottagey, beamed dining room with wheelback chairs
and pink and blue tablecloths. A fixed-price dinner menu offers a choice
of seven or eight dishes at each stage with the likes of pan-fried fillet of red
mullet served on stir-fried chicory with mussels and dill; sautéed lamb's
kidneys served in a short pastry case with black pudding and fried onions;
mallard breast, cooked pink, served with spiced pear and rillettes of duck
with a game jus; baked fillet of salmon on a bed of spinach served with
wild mushroom tortellini and a red wine sauce; thin apple tart served with
caramel ice cream and vanilla sauce; light rhubarb mousse with crisp
ginger biscuits and rhubarb orange sauce. Sandra makes everything herself
from the bread, gravad lax, ice creams and sorbets, to the stocks that are
at the heart of some excellent sauces, while Roger is the chatty host front
of house. Lunchtime brings a shorter, simpler prix-fixe plus a varied light
lunch menu also served in the lounge. A well-rounded and fairly-priced
wine list has plenty of half bottles and helpful notes. *Seats 30.*
*Private Room 12. L 12-2 D 7-9. Closed L Mon, D Sun (except for residents),
25 & 26 Dec, 2 weeks Jan, 2 weeks Aug. Set L £14.95 Set D £24.95.*
AMERICAN EXPRESS *Access, Diners, Visa.*

Rooms   £80

Twelve well-kept, modestly furnished bedrooms (some recently
refurbished) with compact en-suite bathrooms offer good overnight
accommodation. All have direct-dial phones, remote-control TV, radio-
alarm, hairdryer and tea/coffee-making facilities. The terrace makes
a good spot for breakfast if the weather is kind.

Wrexham   Forte Travelodge   £45

Tel 0978 365705   **L**

Wrexham Bypass Rhostyllen Wrexham Clwyd LL14 4EJ   Map 8 D2

At the A483/A5152 roundabout, 4 miles south of Wrexham and 6 miles
east of Llangollen. *Rooms 32.* AMERICAN EXPRESS *Access, Diners, Visa.*

Wrexham   Travel Inn   £43

Tel 0978 853214   Fax 0978 856838   **L**

Chester Road Gresford nr Wrexham Clwyd LL12 8PW   Map 8 D2

Two miles from Wrexham, on the B5445 Chester Road, off the A483 dual
carriageway near the village of Gresford. *Rooms 38.* AMERICAN EXPRESS *Access,
Diners, Visa.*

We welcome bona fide complaints and recommendations on the tear-out
pages at the back of the book for readers' comments. They are followed
up by our professional team.

45 LITRES OF
NATURAL SPRING WATER
FREE!

YOUR CHOICE OF WATER COOLER
FREE FOR 7 DAYS

FLOOR STANDING
WATER COOLER

This latest, very attractive cooler offers a choice of cold and room temperature, or cold and Hot Natural Mineral Water. Which ever model you choose, this cooler will take up little more than one square foot of floor space.

CRYSTAL
NATURAL MINERAL WATER

TEL UK : 01993 883593 · FAX: 01993 883652
TEL LONDON & SOUTH EAST : 0181 314 1144 · FAX: 0181 690 1616

**THE CRYSTAL SPRING WATER COMPANY LIMITED
ST. GEORGE'S WELL, SILK HILL, SWAN LANE,
LONG HANBOROUGH, WITNEY, OXFORDSHIRE OX8 8BT**

Channel Islands
& Isle of Man

Alderney

Braye   First & Last   £30

Tel 0481 823162   **R**

Braye Alderney   Map 13 F4

The only restaurant on the island to benefit from the sea view, with
a panoramic dining room on the first floor. The blue decor is strongly
marine. As you would expect in this location, fish is the order of the day,
such as fresh sardines in garlic butter, bouillabaisse (also available as a half
portion), moules marinière. There are also plenty of steaks and omelettes,
and a concise wine list. In the evening, red lanterns are lit for a more
romantic atmosphere. No small children in the evening. *Seats 75.*
Parties 50. L 12.30-1.45 D 7-11.30. Closed Mon, Oct-Apr. AMERICAN EXPRESS
Access, Diners, Visa.

St Anne   Hotel Chez André   63%   £62

Tel 0481 822777   Fax 0481 822962   **H**

Victoria Street St Anne Alderney   Map 13 F4

The Marks family are now happily settled at the Hotel Chez André, with
manager Steven Marks taking a firm hold of the reins. The homely lounge
and breakfast conservatory adjacent to the restaurant are attractive features.
En-suite bedrooms have trouser press, satellite TV, hairdryer and tea/coffee
facilities. *Rooms 11.* AMERICAN EXPRESS *Access, Visa.*

St Anne   Georgian House   £45

Tel & Fax 0481 822471   **R**

Victoria Street St Anne Alderney   Map 13 F4

There are several nice touches which make the Georgian House stand out:
one is a courtesy car between the house and the harbour (book it when you
make your table reservation); another is The Garden Beyond, the peaceful,
fragrant garden area complete with open air bar and grill, designed to take
full advantage of the kind climate. But whether you're indoors or out,
at lunch (more simple) or at dinner (more elaborate), you can relish
a friendly welcome from owners Elizabeth and Stephen Hope, and positive
cooking from chef Eddie Nash. The blackboard might announce whole
Alderney plaice, or wing of skate with black butter and capers, fresh local
lobsters and crab, Georgian House mixed grill, bangers and mash with
onion gravy – an eclectic mix to suit most tastes. The evening carte might
include salmon tartare, Parma ham with pickled vegetables, breast
of chicken stuffed with prawns, excellent steaks from the grill and always
three or four choices for vegetarians. There are sufficient visitors from
France for one version of the menu not only to be written in French but
priced in Francs! Sunday lunch is worth booking. Much more than a pub –
a gem! A star entry in our Pub Guide. *Seats 48. Parties 40.*
Private Room 24. L 12-2.30 D 7-10. Closed D Tue. Set Sun L £8.75.
AMERICAN EXPRESS *Access, Diners, Visa.*

St Anne   Inchalla Hotel   64%   £73

Tel 0481 823220   Fax 0481 823551   **HR**

The Val St Anne Alderney   Map 13 F4

Set in its own secluded grounds with lovely views across the English
Channel and to the bird sanctuary island of Burhou, Inchalla has been
in the capable and attentive hands of Valerie Willis since 1982.
A conservatory has been added to the lounge, and most of the well-
maintained and well-equipped bedrooms have been refurbished. There's
a small car park. The use of jacuzzi, sauna and solarium is by appointment
only with a £5 charge. *Rooms 9. Garden, sauna, spa bath, solarium.*
Closed 2 weeks Christmas. AMERICAN EXPRESS *Access, Visa.*

Restaurant

£55

The restaurant has also been refurbished, and whereas parties have always been welcome if pre-booked for lunch, it's now the intention to offer a regular lunch-time service. The set dinner might provide a trio of smoked fish with a light salmon mousse and dill dressing served on a crisp salad, followed by roast best end of lamb with rosemary and garlic, with a choice of desserts to complete your meal. Good-value bottles on the short wine list. *Seats* 30. *L 12-2 D 7-8.45. Closed D Sun. Set D £13.75.*

ALDERNEY   Place of Interest

Tourist Information   Tel 0481 822994.

Guernsey

Castel	La Grande Mare	75%	£113
Tel 0481 56576 Fax 0481 56532			**HR**
Vazon Bay Castel Guernsey GY5 YLL			Map 13 E4

Situated on Guernsey's west coast with seaward aspects over the broad sandy sweep of Vazon Bay and the Atlantic (the ocean in question!) beyond, La Grande Mare further enjoys its own 100 acres of land, complete with 9-hole golf course (it is after all styled as a hotel, golf and country club). The pastel-washed building, in a style appealingly somewhere between a traditional Guernsey farmhouse and a Mediterranean villa and bedecked with balconies, is set around an outdoor pool and patio. Inside, public rooms are relaxed and welcoming: arched windows, limed oak furniture and exposed brickwork enhance the Continental feel created by rugs and soft upholstery. However, it is in the bedroom accommodation that La Grande Mare is particularly unusual and innovative, in that it ranges from rooms (some with four-posters) to studios, to luxury exclusive penthouse suites, to one- or two-bed apartments, to a villa for eight. All bathrooms are spacious, extensively equipped and meticulously maintained; all suites have facilities for fixing light snacks; all ten apartments have a fully fitted kitchen: and since special breaks for 2-7 nights are available (with or without golf and fishing), you really can tailor-make your own ideal stay from the various alternatives. As well as the self-catering facilities, there is a full 24hr room service and although bed and breakfast rates are available (and quoted in our guide price), half-board terms are preferred. This truly is a most unusual place to stay, with excellent standards of housekeeping and service throughout (as befits the thought and attention to detail which obviously went into the original concept and design). *Rooms 34. Croquet, outdoor swimming pool, splash pool, spa bath, golf (9), fishing.* AMERICAN EXPRESS *Access, Diners, Visa.*

Restaurant

£75

The icing on the cake at La Grande Mare was surely the arrival, just after we went to press last year, of chef Adrian Jones, bringing a pedigree which includes stints at some of the best training grounds in the country. He has settled in well, understood the market quickly and added his own touches to owner Simon Vermeulen's concept. Thus you can expect to find the best of all worlds: a modern interpretation of classical themes but using fresh local produce in peak condition, or 'British with European influences'. Menus are carefully structured to offer a range from two or three well-balanced courses at lunchtime to an evening menu gourmand of seven courses, plus of course a carte. But it is the set dinner menu that is particularly attractive, popular and cleverly presented: the full five courses, coffee and a complementary glass of wine per course is £34.50, but from the same carte you can have just two courses and coffee for a mere

See over

£16.50. The full meal might comprise a prettily presented sea bass salad with a saffron dressing; then a granita to prepare you for a simple-sounding but delicious tasting roasted free-range chicken on a bed of celeriac; a dessert chosen from the carte – perhaps a strawberry sablé with honeycomb and lemon ice cream, or an unusual but wickedly tempting chocolate and praline rozenne. Next comes a well-kept selection of British farmhouse cheeses – some of the best names around: Appleby Cheshire, Montgomery Cheddar, for example; and finally coffee and petits fours to finish. The atmosphere, as befits seriously-intentioned food, manages to be slightly formal and fairly relaxed at the same time. Service, led by the charming Vito Scaduto, is as professional as you would expect. At the appropriate times meals can be taken on the terrace; and there's a non-smoking section. Sensible notes on a 'grand' wine list featuring plenty of the best names. Look carefully for bargains; house selection could be widened. *Seats* 75. *L 12-2 D7-9.30. Set L £11.50/£14.95 (Sun £13.95) Set D £16.50/£18.95 & £34.50/£39.50.*

Castel   Hougue du Pommier   £71

| Tel 0481 56531   Fax 0481 56260 | **I** |
| Castel Guernsey | Map 13 E4 |

'Apple Tree Hill' is the meaning of the name, so it's no surprise to find this lovely inn set in an old orchard. Quiet bedrooms, which overlook the well-kept gardens, are comfortable, with remote-control colour TV and tea/coffee facilities. The solar heated swimming pool is remote and sheltered by trees. Six new deluxe bedrooms were being built as we went to press which, with other alterations, will bring the total number to 43. Children up to 5 stay free in parents' room. Parking for 70 cars. Banqueting for 50. *Rooms 38. Garden, outdoor swimming pool, sauna, solarium, golf (18), games room.* AMERICAN EXPRESS *Access, Diners, Visa.*

L'Erée   The Taste of India   £35

| Tel 0481 64516 | **R** |
| Sunset Cottage L'Erée Guernsey GY7 9LN | Map 13 E4 |

One of the few Indian restaurants on the island, it is well located at the end of Rocquaine Bay near Lihou island right on the west coast. The menu is strong on tandoori and there's also a section called Exquisite Dishes, which are the restaurant specialities. Try the Cobo Bay special: lamb cooked in a kahari with garlic, ginger, fresh coriander and the final touch – flamed in brandy! Dishes are prepared with quality ingredients and a delicate mix of spices. There is also a branch in St Peter Port (Tel 0481 723730). *Seats 35. L 12-2 D 6-11. Set Sun L £9.95 Set D £15/£18. Closed L Mon, all 25 Dec.* AMERICAN EXPRESS *Access, Diners, Visa.*

Forest   Mallard Hotel   67%   £66

| Tel 0481 64164   Fax 0481 65732 | **H** |
| Forest Guernsey | Map 13 E4 |

Conveniently located near the airport (there's a courtesy bus between the two, or from hotel to harbour), this hotel offers good accommodation at kind prices. Public rooms are particularly large and the big attraction is of course the outdoor solar-heated swimming pool with plenty of sun beds and outdoor tables. Bedrooms are comfortable, with trouser press, hairdryer, colour TV and tea/coffee facilities. Rooms overlooking the swimming pool have balconies facing south. Rooms facing the back of the building are quieter. Perfect for families. Parking for 200 cars. Banqueting/conferences for up to 150. During 1994 the cinema will have doubled to four screens. *Rooms 47. Garden, outdoor swimming pool, keep-fit equipment, sauna, spa bath, solarium, tennis, golf (9 hole), games room, 4 screen cinema. Closed Christmas, January. Access, Visa.*

Pleinmont   Imperial Hotel   £56

Tel 0481 64044   Fax 0481 66139   **I**

Pleinmont Torteval Guernsey GY8 0PS   Map 13 E4

Attractive little hotel ideally located at the south end of Rocquaine Bay,
also overlooking the harbour at Portelet. Bar, restaurant and most of the
bedrooms benefit from a beautiful view of the bay. Four rooms have
attractive balconies with patio furniture, all have clean and bright
accommodation with tea/coffee facilities, colour TV and direct-dial
telephone. Children are welcome if well behaved, with a nominal food
charge. Special rates include a car hire. *Rooms 17. Garden, café
10.30am-11pm. Closed Dec-Mar. Access, Visa.*

St Martin   Hotel Bon Port   66%   £88

Tel 0481 39249   Fax 0481 39596   **H**

Rue Gros Jean Moulin Huet Bay St Martin Guernsey GY4 6EW   Map 13 E4

The modern Bon Port has good views over two of the island's prettiest
bays (Moulin Huet, often painted by Renoir, and Petit Port) and is quiet
and comfortable. Bedrooms (including four suites) are well maintained and
equipped – best ones have sea views and balconies. The Gate House cottage
alongside the main building has one double and two single bedrooms and
is let by the week on a self-catering basis. No children under 14. *Rooms 18.
Garden, outdoor swimming pool. Access, Visa.*

St Martin   St Margaret's Lodge   63%   £76

Tel 0481 35757   Fax 0481 37594   **H**

Forest Road St Martin Guernsey   Map 13 E4

Midway between the airport and St Peter Port, the lodge is close to the
south coast with its beaches and cliff paths. The modern interior includes
a comfortable lounge and lounge bar. Bedrooms, all with en-suite facilities,
include three suites, six rooms are reserved for non-smokers. Guests can
take a twice-daily courtesy coach for shopping in town. Banqueting and
conference facilities have recently been expanded – there's a new function
room for 120, a small syndicate room, conference suites and private dining
room. *Rooms 47. Garden, croquet, outdoor swimming pool, sauna, solarium.*
AMERICAN EXPRESS *Access, Diners, Visa.*

St Martin   La Trelade Hotel   61%   £68

Tel 0481 35454   Fax 0481 37855   **H**

Forest Road St Martin Guernsey GY4 6UB   Map 13 E4

Predominantly a holiday hotel, set in three acres of grounds close to the
airport and with easy access to the south coast bays. Lounges, bars and
simple bedrooms are all clean and comfortable. Friendly staff. Families are
well catered for with a children's playground and baby-listening available.
Children up to 16 pay for meals but not accommodation in parents' room.
Rooms 45. Garden, outdoor swimming pool, putting, games room.
AMERICAN EXPRESS *Access, Diners, Visa.*

St Peter Port   Absolute End   £50

Tel 0481 723822   Fax 0481 729129   **R**

St George's Esplanade St Peter Port Guernsey   Map 13 E4

On the seafront about a mile from the town centre, this is a pretty, cottagey
restaurant specialising in fish and shellfish though there's also plenty
of choice for meat-eaters and vegetarians. The choice runs from calamari
salad, oysters florentine and grilled sardines as typical starters, to beef
medallion with Madeira sauce and veal medallion with hollandaise and

asparagus (neatly described as *black and white*), scallops meunière, or brill
à la cardinale (local fish baked in a foil with wine, peppers, mussels and
prawns, served in a lobster sauce) as main courses. Desserts are of the
profiteroles/banana split/crepes Suzette school. *Seats 60. Parties 20.
Private Room 20. L 12-2 D 7-10. Closed Sun, Jan. Set L £11.*
AMERICAN EXPRESS *Access, Diners, Visa.*

St Peter Port   Braye Lodge   £70
Tel 0481 723787   Fax 0481 712876   H
Ruette Braye St Peter Port Guernsey   Map 13 E4

A coat of paint and a fresh smile, but as yet no progress on the planned
expansion which we reported last year, hence the absence of grading.
Rooms 25. Garden, outdoor swimming pool. Closed November. **AMERICAN EXPRESS**
Access, Diners, Visa.

St Peter Port   Duke of Richmond   63%   £65
Tel 0481 726221   Fax 0481 728945   H
Cambridge Park St Peter Port Guernsey GY1 1UY   Map 13 E4

The hotel began life in 1790 as Grover's Hotel. A regular visitor was the
third Duke of Richmond, who was Master of Ordnance here from 1781-
1795 (during which time he was instrumental in building the Martello
watchtowers which give Guernsey's coastline such character). When the
hotel was eventually renamed, it honoured its former patron, with the
permission of the present incumbent of the title. The hillside location
provides many excellent views from many of the bedrooms, some
of which have balconies. Inland rooms are the cheapest, while top of the
range is the penthouse suite. Conference/banqueting facilities for 100/240.
Children under 12 free if sharing parents' room. *Rooms 75. Terrace, outdoor
swimming pool.* **AMERICAN EXPRESS** *Access, Diners, Visa.*

St Peter Port   La Frégate   64%   £108
Tel 0481 724624   Fax 0481 720443   H
Les Cotils St Peter Port Guernsey   Map 13 E4

Set in its own peaceful gardens above St Julian's Avenue, La Frégate is an
18th-century manor house providing high standards of comfort and service
along with views of the harbour from most of the bedrooms. Some rooms
have double-glazed patio doors opening on to private balconies.
No children under 14. Park for 20 cars. Banquets for 50. No dogs.
Rooms 13. Terrace. **AMERICAN EXPRESS** *Access, Diners, Visa.*

St Peter Port   Louisiana   £60
Tel 0481 713157   Fax 0481 712191   R
South Esplanade St Peter Port Guernsey   Map 13 E4

The menu here isn't completely Cajun/Creole (for a start, vegetarians are
well catered for!) as there's a fair sprinkling of traditional French and Italian
dishes too, but whatever your taste there's a lively atmosphere and some
good cooking. Seafood is well represented as in roast lobster Baton Rouge,
or marinated Guernsey scallops, or linguine bayou (with local cream and
crab). Meat too is well treated – try calf's liver flambé Monte Carlo
or Cajun prime rib steak Mardi Gras (blackened, then served with
a béarnaise sauce). Toothsome puddings range from Mississippi mud cake
to tiramisu to pears Louis XV prepared at the table. Sunday lunch
is popular. The first floor now operates as the Baton Rouge Brasserie with
a similar but slightly simpler menu. *Seats 100. Private Room 25. L 12-2.30
D 6.30-10.30. Closed Mon, Bank Holidays. Set L £8/£10 (Sun £9.95)
Set D £12.95/£15.95.* **AMERICAN EXPRESS** *Access, Visa.*

St Peter Port	**Le Nautique**		£50
Tel 0481 721714			**R**
The Quay Steps St Peter Port Guernsey			Map 13 E4

Long-established French restaurant standing on the seafront, overlooking the harbour and marina, with a reassuringly unchanged menu. Fish is the pick of the menu, as you might expect. Sole comes grilled, meunière or with a champagne and lobster sauce; lobster itself is offered grilled and flambéed with whisky, Thermidor or cold with mayonnaise and salad; monkfish is presented with dugléré or orange and pepper sauce. Duck, lamb and steaks are also popular and there's a selection of three vegetarian dishes. Service is polished and efficient, booking essential. Smart dress is preferred. Smoking only allowed in the bar. Children not allowed under 5 or after 8.30. Short wine list with many bottles also offered in halves. *Seats 68. Parties 30. Private Room 30. L 12-2 D 7-10. Closed Sun, 1st 2 weeks Jan.* AMERICAN EXPRESS *Access, Diners, Visa.*

St Peter Port	**Old Government House**	**68%**	£108
Tel 0481 724921 Fax 0481 724429			**H**
Ann's Place St Peter Port Guernsey GY1 4AZ			Map 13 E4

OGH, as it's affectionately known, offers traditional standards of decor and service, and the classically elegant entrance hall is a reminder of the days when it actually was the Governor's residence. Bedrooms and public rooms are well maintained. The Governor's Bar is cosy and intimate with its military memorabilia and the Centenary Bar, opened in 1958 to mark 100 years of the hotel's existence, features dancing to the hotel band Monday to Saturday in summer and weekends in winter. Best bedrooms are in a modern wing. Conference/banqueting facilities for 200. *Rooms 72. Garden, outdoor swimming pool, gym, sauna, spa bath, solarium, coffee shop 10am-9pm.* AMERICAN EXPRESS *Access, Diners, Visa.*

St Peter Port	**St Pierre Park**	**71%**	£135
Tel 0481 728282 Fax 0481 712041			**H**
Rohais St Peter Port Guernsey GY1 1FD			Map 13 E4

The St Pierre Park was built in 1983 on the edge of the main town, in 45 acres of parkland. Refurbishment of the bedrooms and corridors has now been completed, and some rooms are especially suitable for families. All are well equipped. Most impressive of all is the leisure complex, with its Tony Jacklin-designed 9-hole golf course, three outdoor tennis courts, a 25m indoor swimming pool and a fully-equipped health suite. Public rooms are airy and elegant. The lounge/bar and some bedrooms overlook the garden and ornamental lake. Banqueting/conferences for 280/220. Children under 12 stay free in their parents' room. *Rooms 135. Garden, croquet, indoor swimming pool, gym, sauna, steam room, spa bath, solarium, beauty & hair salons, tennis, 9-hole golf course, snooker, coffee shop (10am-10.30pm), outdoor play area.* AMERICAN EXPRESS *Access, Diners, Visa.*

GUERNSEY   Places of Interest

Tourist Information   Tel 0481 723552.
Aquarium   Tel 723301
Auberge du Val Herb Garden   Tel 63862.
Castle Cornet   Tel 726518.
26 Cornet Street   (Nat Trust of Guernsey) Tel 728451.
Fort Grey Shipwreck Museum   Tel 726518.
German Occupation Museum   Tel 38205.
German Underground Hospital   Tel 39100.
German Botanical Gardens   Tel 36690.
Guernsey Clockmakers   Tel 36360.
Guernsey Coppercraft   Tel 65112.
Guernsey Folk Museum   Tel 55384.

Guernsey Museum & Art Gallery   Tel 726518.
Guernsey Shires   Tel 43923.
Guernsey Toys   Tel 723871.
Guernsey Woodcarvers   Tel 65373.
Hauteville House   (Maison de Victor Hugo) Tel 721911.
La Valette Underground   Tel 722300.
Military Museum.
Le Friquet Butterfly Centre   Tel 54378.
Le Planel Dolls   Tel 64326.
Le Tricoteur   Tel 64040.
Les Rouvets Tropical Vinery   Tel 63566.
Manor Railways   Tel 38655.
Moulin Huet Pottery   Tel 37201.
Oatlands Craft Centre   Tel 44282.
Philatelic Bureau   (GPO) Tel 726241.
Sausmarez Manor   Tel 35571.
The Dolls House Collection   Tel 35904.
The Rose Centre   Tel 36580.
The Strawberry Farm   Tel 64428.
The Telephone Museum   Tel 711221.
Wild Sub-Tropical Gardens   Tel 35571.

Herm

Herm	**White House**	**64%**	**£102★**
Tel 0481 722159 Fax 0481 710066			**HR**
Herm			**Map 13 E4**

"Paradise is this close" says the White House's brochure, and indeed at this,
the only hotel on the island, there is comfortable accommodation for those
who want to escape the hurly-burly of mainland life. The hotel produces its
own electricity and there are no televisions or telephones in the bedrooms;
a small butane cooker is used to heat up the kettles. The best bedrooms
have sea view and balcony. The hotel is self-contained with a succession
of homely lounges, an elegant sea view restaurant and the Ship Inn, a pub
with a Carvery dining room. ★Half-board terms only. Self-catering
cottages and flats also available. ***Rooms** 38. Garden, croquet, outdoor
swimming pool, tennis. Closed Oct-Mar. Access, Visa.*

Restaurant

£40

The White House has its own oyster farm so it will come as no surprise
that the specialities on the set menu are largely seafood, though meat-eaters
are also well catered for and vegetarians are not neglected. Try salad
of smoked duckling with quail's egg and herb croutons, then baked fillet
of fresh hake with a cheese and chive crust, and hazelnut baskets filled with
marshmallow and rum cream set on a coffee sauce to finish. The gourmet
menu, well priced with a choice of five courses, is only available
on Saturday nights and carries owner Michael Hester's personal
recommendations for accompanying wines. Meals are served in an elegant
dining room where smoking is not allowed. ***Seats** 118. Parties 12.
L 12.30-2 D 7-9.30. Set Sun L £9.95. Set D £15.25/£16.25.*

Jersey

Bouley Bay   Water's Edge Hotel   64%   £104

Tel 0534 862777   Fax 0534 863645   **H**

The Slipway Bouley Bay Trinity Jersey JE3 5AS   Map 13 F4

A unique location on the island, as it stands alone in Bouley Bay with a beautiful view, direct access to the pebble beach and outdoor swimming pool. Bar and dining rooms both overlook the sea. Bedrooms are comfortable – the best ones have small balconies and sea views. Children up to 12 stay free in parents' room (meals charged as taken). Children's menu and early suppers available. Banqueting/conferences for 130/65. Dogs welcome. 24hr room service. *Rooms 51. Garden, outdoor swimming pool, sauna, sunbeds, coffee shop (10am-5pm), Black Dog Bar (12-2, 6.30-8). Closed Nov-Easter.* AMERICAN EXPRESS *Access, Diners, Visa.*

Gorey   Jersey Pottery Garden Restaurant   ↑   £60

Tel 0534 851119   Fax 0534 856403   **R**

Gorey Village Gorey Jersey JE3 9EP   Map 13 F4

Colin Jones has been running the Garden Restaurant at the Jersey Pottery for an amazing 40 years. It's an attractive restaurant, set in a flowery conservatory with garden furniture, umbrellas, and climbing vines. The extensive menu offers any number of seafood dishes, some slightly more unusual such as *cappucini*, freshly picked crab meat with thin slices of smoked salmon in a brandy-flavoured Marie Rose sauce, or salmon Cameron – an escalope of salmon interleaved with home-made pasta. Beautiful fresh seafood salads and plateaux de fruits de mer using locally caught seafood are a speciality. The next-door self-service café offers cold dishes (mainly seafood salads), pastries and afternoon teas. Children are very welcome in both restaurants. *Seats 300. Parties 40. Meals 11.30-4.30. Closed Sun (also Sat in winter), Bank Holidays, 10 days Christmas.* AMERICAN EXPRESS *Access, Diners, Visa.*

Gorey   Moorings Hotel   62%   £88

Tel 0534 853633   Fax 0534 857618   **H**

Gorey Pier Gorey Jersey JE3 6EW   Map 13 F4

A small, friendly, waterfront hotel tucked between Mont Orgueil Castle and Gorey Harbour, just a short distance from Grouville Bay. Two bars provide a choice for relaxing over a drink, and there's a lounge and roof garden. Bedrooms are furnished in simple style, with colour TV, radio, hairdryer, trouser press, direct-dial telephone and tea/coffee-making facilities. Banqueting/conferences for 60/30. No dogs. *Rooms 16.* AMERICAN EXPRESS *Access, Visa.*

🍷 is our symbol for an outstanding wine list.

Gorey   Old Court House Hotel   64%   £89

Tel 0534 854444   Fax 0534 853587   **H**

Gorey Village Grouville Jersey JE3 9EX   Map 13 F4

Parts of the Old Court House (specifically the restaurant) date back to the 15th century although the overall appearance is modern. Bedrooms and public areas are well equipped and maintained, making it a popular destination for family holidays. New-wing bedrooms have balconies, while the pleasant older rooms are more spacious. *Rooms 58. Garden, outdoor swimming pool, sauna, solarium. Closed Nov-Mar.* AMERICAN EXPRESS *Access, Diners, Visa.*

Grouville   Grouville Bay Hotel   62%   £80

Tel 0534 851004   Fax 0534 857416

H

Grouville Jersey JE3 9BB

Map 13 F4

Located right next to the Royal Jersey Golf course, the hotel has no golf
concession but enjoys attractive views over the greens. In the other
direction there are views of the 12th-century Mont Orgueil Castle.
Bedrooms face either the golf course and the sea (with balconies), or the
garden and the interior of the island – 40% are suitable for family use.
Footpath to the nearby beach. Early suppers for children, plenty of high-
chairs and babysitting are all available. Comfortable public rooms.
*Rooms 56. Garden, outdoor swimming pool, children's swimming pool and
playroom, snooker, games room. Closed Oct–Apr.* AMERICAN EXPRESS *Access,
Diners, Visa.*

Havre des Pas   Ommaroo Hotel   59%   £85

Tel 0534 23493   Fax 0534 59912

H

Havre des Pas St Helier Jersey JE2 4UQ

Map 13 F4

Traditional seaside hotel (popular with families) some of whose rooms have
sea-facing balconies. All rooms now have en-suite facilities. Child-friendly.
Relaxing lounges and bars. *Rooms 85. Garden.* AMERICAN EXPRESS *Access,
Diners, Visa.*

Havre des Pas   Hotel de la Plage   66%   £80

Tel 0534 23474   Fax 0534 68642

H

Havre des Pas St Helier Jersey JE2 4UQ

Map 13 F4

On the outskirts of St Helier and situated right on the seafront, this
is a well-run modern hotel with picture windows to enhance the views.
Day rooms are in various styles: subdued and modern in the split-level
lounge-bar, tropical in the Caribbean Bar, bamboo in the sun lounge. Sea-
facing bedrooms have balconies; inland-view rooms are cheaper. All have
en-suite bathrooms with the usual electric gadgets and bathrobes. Snacks
are served all day in the lounges, in the bedrooms or on the terrace.
No dogs. *Rooms 78. Keep-fit facilities, solarium, games room.
Closed end Oct–early Apr.* AMERICAN EXPRESS *Access, Diners, Visa.*

Portelet Bay   Portelet Hotel   66%   £100

Tel 0534 41204   Fax 0534 46625

H

Portelet Bay St Brelade Jersey JE3 8AU

Map 13 F4

The Portelet was built in the 30s and retains some Art Deco features,
notably at the entrance. It also aims to observe the sentiments of that era
in terms of courtesy and attention to detail. Most popular of the public
rooms is the sun lounge overlooking the pool to St Brelade's Bay beyond.
Elsewhere there's a quiet residents' lounge and a 70s-style cocktail bar.
Many of the bedrooms have private balconies. Free early-morning tea
or coffee and paper, mini-bus to town. No dogs. *Rooms 86. Garden, outdoor
swimming pool, tennis, putting, games room. Closed Oct–Apr.* AMERICAN EXPRESS
Access, Diners, Visa.

Rozel Bay   Chateau la Chaire   74%   £110

Tel 0534 863354   Fax 0534 865137

HR

Rozel Bay Jersey JE3 6AJ

Map 13 F4

Built in 1843 just above the charming harbour of Rozel Bay, the hotel's
public rooms retain the proportions and elegance of the last century, from
the welcoming reception hall, with its large staircase, to the high-ceilinged
rococo lounge or the intimate, oak-panelled dining room. There's
an unusual suite on the ground floor which has a mezzanine level within it.
All the bedrooms benefit from stylish decor. Executive rooms on the first

floor have comfortable sitting areas and jacuzzi bathtubs. Regular double bedrooms are much smaller, with the charming cosiness of lower ceilings under slanted roofs and small windows. Complimentary water, fruit basket and biscuits in all bedrooms. Banqueting for 65, parking for 25 cars. No children under 7. *Rooms 14. Garden.* AMERICAN EXPRESS *Access, Diners, Visa.*

Restaurant £70

From the oak-panelled dining room with a traditional atmosphere extends a contemporary conservatory with a view of the hotel terrace and surrounding trees. Here a simple menu is well executed with a strong emphasis on fresh seasonal fish and shellfish. The conservatory is non-smoking, and there are 30 seats outside on the terrace. Well-stocked wine list. *Seats 65. Parties 30. L 12.30-2 D 7-10 Set L £11.75/£14.25 D £19.50/£25.*

St Aubin	Old Court House Inn	£80
Tel 0534 46433 Fax 0534 45103		**I**
St Aubin Harbour St Aubin Jersey		Map 13 F4

The Old Court House was actually more than simply that – the court house itself occupied the rear of the building while the front part was a merchant's house. The tall building overlooks the harbour (presumably so that maritime transgressors could quickly be brought to book!), the best view of all being from the penthouse suite with its private sun terrace. All bedrooms are well furnished and equipped. Popular spots for eating and drinking on the terrace and in the bars. No children under 10. *Rooms 10.* AMERICAN EXPRESS *Access, Diners, Visa.*

St Brelade	Atlantic Hotel	71%	£130
Tel 0534 44101 Fax 0534 44102			**H**
La Moye St Brelade Jersey JE3 8HE			Map 13 F4

Simon Dufty from *Longueville Manor* is now running the Atlantic Hotel for Managing Director Patrick Burke, and it reopened in April 1994 after an extended winter break, emerging into the spring sunshine with everything shiny and new. The extensive refurbishment has resulted in new public areas, specifically the entrance, reception, library, cocktail bar, lounges and restaurant. The bedrooms are equally well equipped and maintained, with all the usual extras. The Garden Studios on the ground floor are larger than the standard bedrooms, two suites are bigger again. Another major feature is the Palm Club, a well-equipped health and leisure centre. Banqueting/conferences for 60. No dogs. *Rooms 50. Garden, indoor & outdoor swimming pools, keep-fit equipment, sauna, spa bath, sun beds, tennis. Closed Jan & Feb.* AMERICAN EXPRESS *Access, Diners, Visa.*

St Brelade	Hotel Chateau Valeuse	65%	£76
Tel 0534 46281 Fax 0534 47110			**HR**
St Brelade Jersey JE3 8EE			Map 13 F4

Well-situated, on the South-facing St Brelade's Bay, the hotel is set back from the main road. Bedrooms (some with seaward balconies) are all simply and comfortably furnished. Impeccably maintained gardens surround the pool. No children under five. *Rooms 33. Garden, outdoor swimming pool, putting. Closed mid Oct-Apr. Access, Visa.*

Restaurant £50

A carte (not Sundays) and set menus appeal to residents and day visitors alike. Lots of seafood prepared in classical ways, plus grills and flambés. *Seats 70. Parties 50. L 12.45-1.45 D 8-9. Closed D Sun. Set L £9/£14.50 (Sun £11) Set D £14.50.*

St Brelade   La Place Hotel   67%   £110

Tel 0534 44261   Fax 0534 45164   **H**

Route du Coin La Haule St Brelade Jersey JE3 8BF   Map 13 F4

Just four miles from St Helier and only seven minutes from the airport,
La Place is for those who like rural surroundings. It was once a farmhouse
but is now much enlarged by modern extensions. The main public rooms
are part of the original, 400-year-old building. There's a delightful open-air
seating area in a south-facing courtyard, a bright bar with green bamboo
furniture and two lounges, one of which has a black-beamed ceiling, a pink
granite fireplace, antique furniture and polished brass ornaments. Bedrooms
include seven around the pool. Children up to 12 stay free in parents'
room. There's parking for 35 cars, and banqueting/conference facilities for
90/45. *Rooms 40. Garden, outdoor swimming pool, sauna, spa bath, sunbeds.*
AMERICAN EXPRESS *Access, Diners, Visa.*

St Brelade   Sea Crest   64%   £90

Tel 0534 46353   Fax 0534 47316   **HR**

Petit Port St Brelade Jersey JE3 8HH   Map 13 F4

Owners Julian and Martha Bernstein run this relaxing white-painted
modern hotel, which overlooks a rocky bay at the south-west end of the
island, and their attention to detail is apparent in personal touches
throughout. Bedrooms, five with balconies, overlook the bay so guests can
often watch spectacular sunsets. Children under 5 stay free in parents' room.
No dogs. *Rooms 7. Garden, outdoor swimming pool. Closed Feb.*
AMERICAN EXPRESS *Access, Visa.*

Restaurant   £70

Set menus change every couple of weeks so that with the carte as well
there's plenty of choice available in the pretty dining room, which also
looks seawards. There's good use of seafood (crab, prawns, mussels, scallops,
tuna) and more than a mere nod to France in dishes like Breton fish soup
with rouille, or pan-fried French black sausage and crispy bacon served
on mixed leaves with a grain mustard dressing. Tables on the terrace for
summer eating. *Seats 60. Parties 25. L 12.30-2 (Sun to 3) D 7.30-10.
Closed all Mon, also D Sun in winter. Set L £11.50 Set D £18.50.*

St Brelade's Bay   Hotel L'Horizon   72%   £160

Tel 0534 43101   Fax 0534 46269   **H**

St Brelade's Bay Jersey JE3 8EF   Map 13 F4

L'Horizon faces due south over the long stretch of St Brelade's Bay so takes
full advantage of the sunshine, and leisure facilities also shine here. Club
L'Horizon is a well-equipped centre for relaxing or keeping fit, and a 40ft
motor yacht, *Clipper L'Horizon,* is available for day charter. Public areas
include a bar with picture windows and beach views, a drawing room,
a library and three restaurants. Good-sized bedrooms, nearly all with sea
views, have decent-quality furniture and well-equipped bathrooms.
Banqueting/conference facilities for 240/150. No dogs. Parking for 127
cars. 24hr room service. Now owned by Arcadian (who bought Clipper).
*Rooms 106. Terrace, indoor swimming pool, keep-fit equipment, sauna, steam
room, spa bath, solarium, beauty and hair salons, coffee shop (10am-11pm).*
AMERICAN EXPRESS *Access, Visa.*

St Brelade's Bay   St Brelade's Bay Hotel   70%   £140

Tel 0534 46141   Fax 0534 47278   **H**

St Brelade's Bay Jersey JE3 8EF   Map 13 F4

Family owned and run for five generations by the Colleys and set in seven
acres of award-winning gardens, the St Brelade's Bay Hotel is a popular
spot for family holidays, especially as there's a resident lifeguard at the two

heated freshwater swimming pools. Although the exterior looks modern the interior has a timeless elegance with moulded ceilings and chandeliers, comfortable sofas and chairs and an abundance of fresh flowers. First- and second-floor rooms are traditional, while those on the third floor are more modern; all are attractively and tastefully decorated and furnished. Sea view rooms have a balcony, on the other side rooms overlook the gardens. Families are well catered for. *Rooms 72. Garden, croquet, outdoor swimming pool, children's swimming pool, keep-fit equipment, sauna, sunbeds, games room, tennis, putting, snooker. Closed mid Oct–mid Apr. Access, Visa.*

St Helier — Apollo Hotel — 63% — £87
Tel 0534 25441   Fax 0534 22120   **H**
9 St Saviour's Road St Helier Jersey JE2 4LA   Map 13 F4

A modern two-storey hotel built round a courtyard. Public areas provide plenty of space to relax: there are two bars (one in pub style), a coffee shop serving snacks throughout the day, an indoor leisure centre and a sun-trap terrace. Bedrooms, some with balconies, include many suitable for family occupation. Children up to 5 stay free in parents' room. Parking for 60 cars. Banqueting/conference facilities for 180/120. No dogs. *Rooms 85. Terrace, indoor swimming pool, gym, sauna, spa bath, solarium.* AMERICAN EXPRESS *Access, Diners, Visa.*

St Helier — Beaufort Hotel — 60% — £93
Tel 0534 32471   Fax 0534 20371   **H**
Green Street St Helier Jersey   Map 13 F4

The cool marble reception area sets the scene at this friendly modern hotel in town. Free parking is a bonus; indoor leisure facilities and outdoor sun terrace are both popular. Relaxing day rooms, comfortable bedrooms; all have the usual electrical gadgets. *Rooms 54. Indoor swimming pool, spa bath, games room (summer).* AMERICAN EXPRESS *Access, Diners, Visa.*

St Helier — La Capannina — £60
Tel 0534 34602   Fax 0534 77628   **R**
65 Halkett Place St Helier Jersey   Map 13 F4

Italian restaurant with a menu mostly written in French! Daily specials often feature local seafood; flambés are popular. Extensive wine list. *Seats 130. Parties 40. Private Room 20. L 12-2 D 7-10. Closed Sun, Bank Holidays, 1 week Christmas.* AMERICAN EXPRESS *Access, Diners, Visa.*

St Helier — De Vere Grand — 68% — £125
Tel 0534 22301   Fax 0534 37815   **HR**
Esplanade St Helier Jersey JE4 8WD   Map 13 F4

Rebranded but otherwise reassuringly unchanged, the De Vere Grand has a long, gabled frontage – a distinctive feature on the seafront – and the entrance is appropriately impressive, with ornate coloured pillars and a marble floor. The smart period-style bar and lounge have fine views and so do balconied front bedrooms, which attract a hefty surcharge. It's a busy hotel catering for both holiday and business visitors (conference/banqueting facilities for 180/275). Families are well provided for with free accommodation for under-14s in their parents' room, plus baby-sitting and special children's meals also available. Good leisure facilities. *Rooms 115. Terrace, indoor swimming pool, keep-fit equipment, sauna, steam room, spa bath, solarium, beauty & hair salons, snooker.* AMERICAN EXPRESS *Access, Diners, Visa.*

Regency Room — £75

The elegant Regency Room offers only table d'hote menus and is the main hotel dining room. Try a starter of salmon tartare with quail's eggs, followed by hollandaise-glazed brill tartlets, then sliced duck breast with an olive sauce, with sweets and coffee to finish. Separate vegetarian and vegan menus. *Seats 250. Private Room 21. D only 7.30-9.30. Set D £16.50/£19.50.*

Victoria's   £75

Mainly à la carte (though the table d'hote menus from the Regency Room are also available sometimes) and slightly more sophisticated. Dancing to live music each evening. *Seats 150. L 12.30-2 D 7.30-10.30. Set L £14.75. Closed D Sun.*

♔

St Helier   Hotel de France   £120

Tel 0534 38990   Fax 0534 35354   **H**
St Saviour's Road St Helier Jersey   Map 13 F4

An unfortunate fire in spring 1994 resulted in damage to 50 bedrooms and the normal reception area. A temporary reception has been arranged and life goes on as usual in the rest of the hotel but the rebuilding was not due for completion before we went to press, hence the absence of grading this year (was 71% in our 1994 guide). *Rooms 323. Terrace, outdoor and indoor swimming pool, keep-fit equipment, squash, sauna, spa bath, solarium, beauty & hair salon, games room, snooker, news kiosk (8-12, 4-7).* AMERICAN EXPRESS® *Access, Diners, Visa.*

St Helier   Pomme d'Or Hotel   65%   £90

Tel 0534 78644   Fax 0534 37781   **H**
The Esplanade St Helier Jersey JE2 3NF   Map 13 F4

An attractive location right on the harbour, overlooking the marina, adds to the appeal here. Cool, refreshing decor in air-conditioned public areas and comfortable bedrooms. Free use of the tropical Aquadome at the sister hotel the *Merton* (St Saviour). Conference/banqueting facilities for 300. No dogs. *Rooms 147. Coffee shop (7am-11pm).* AMERICAN EXPRESS® *Access, Diners, Visa.*

St Ouen   The Lobster Pot   £65

Tel 0534 482888   Fax 0534 481574   **RR**
L'Etacq St Ouen Jersey JE3 2FB   Map 13 F4

A popular spot with tours and coaches where booking is recommended for weekends. The location is attractive, overlooking St Ouen's Bay, and the original granite farmhouse dates back to the 17th century. The fish and shellfish are landed about 200 yards away, so it can't be much fresher nor more local! All manner of seafood is served in traditional French style, as are the extensive meat and poultry options, but most people are here for the lobsters, served grilled, à la nage, Newburg or Thermidor. *Seats 90. Private Room 45. L 12.30-2 D 7.30-10. Set L £9.95 (Sun £10.50) Set D £14.50.* AMERICAN EXPRESS® *Access, Diners, Visa.*

Rooms   £70

Thirteen large bedrooms with the usual modern amenities of TV, trouser press, hairdryer and even a small bar area with tea and coffee facilities and a small refrigerator. The best rooms naturally have a sea view. Good for families. Parking for 65 cars. No dogs.

St Peter   Mermaid Hotel   64%   £93

Tel 0534 41255   Fax 0534 45826   **H**
Airport Road St Peter Jersey JE3 7BN   Map 13 F4

A modern hotel located near the airport and built next to a natural lake. Bedrooms all have the expected facilities and though not large they benefit from south-facing balconies with a lake view. The hotel is self-contained with restaurants, bar, pub and impressive leisure facilities. No dogs.

Children under 5 free in parents' room – early suppers provided. Parking for 100 cars. Banqueting/conferences for 120/80. **Rooms** *68. Garden, croquet, golf (9 hole) outdoor & indoor swimming pools, keep-fit equipment, sauna, spa bath, solarium, tennis, putting.* AMERICAN EXPRESS *Access, Diners, Visa.*

St Saviour — Longueville Manor — 80% — £155

Tel 0534 25501   Fax 0534 31613

HR

St Saviour Jersey JE2 7SA

Map 13 F4

Malcolm and Ragnhild Lewis and Sue Dufty are still keeping it in the family (3rd generation, 40 years) at the most prestigious hotel on Jersey. Warmth of welcome and elegant decor combine to make the Manor seem accessible yet special at the same time. The carved-panelled dining room and lounge, part of the architectural interest of the house, are beautifully complemented by stylish yet not overdone furnishings. Bedrooms (each named after a rose) are of course up to the standard of the rest, each with its own style, some with original stone fireplaces. Bathrooms feel more like anterooms, with strong attention to detail. Master bedrooms, located at the front of the building, closer to the road, tend to be smaller and not as quiet. Fifteen acres of grounds provide peaceful walks and of course tables are set outside near the swimming pool for light lunches, afternoon teas or cocktails. Charming staff lavish care and attention on the guests. No children under 7. **Rooms** *32. Garden, croquet, outdoor swimming pool, tennis.* AMERICAN EXPRESS *Access, Diners, Visa.*

Restaurant

£90

The two dining rooms cater for different moods, from the solemn atmosphere of the 13th-century carved-panelled oak room to the more relaxed armchairs of the light and airy second room. Chef Andrew Baird has been in residence since 1971 and is thoroughly at home, producing table d'hote, à la carte, dégustation and vegetarian menus using some home-grown herbs and vegetables. You might choose terrine of venison with toasted brioche and onion marmalade, poached turbot on a mustard seed cream, then a praline soufflé with chocolate ice cream. The tasting menu, served to complete tables only, is a balanced meal of nine courses including coffee, and really displays Andrew's talents to the full, while the carte is equally extensive. Impressive cheese trolley of farmhouse British and French selections. Patchy wine list, mostly French, next to nothing from the New World. Good selection of half bottles. Seating for 20 on the terrace. **Seats** *65. Parties 30. Private Room 65. L 12.30-2 D 7.30-9.30. Set L £15/19 (£18 Sun) Set D £30/£50.*

St Saviour — Merton Hotel — 60% — £80

Tel 0534 24231   Fax 0534 68603

H

Belvedere Hill St Saviour Jersey JE2 7RP

Map 13 F4

Located right outside St Helier, on a sloped street off the A3, a spacious hotel with basic comfortable accommodation and the amazing Aquadome complex of indoor and outdoor swimming pools. Good for children, with entertainment for them in the evening. **Rooms** *330. Garden, indoor and outdoor swimming pool, children's swimming pool, squash, tennis, coffee shop (10.30-2, 3-6, 9.30-12), games room.* AMERICAN EXPRESS *Access, Diners, Visa.*

JERSEY — Places of Interest

Tourist Information   Tel 0534 500777.
Battle of Flowers Museum   St Ouen Tel 482408.
Berni Gallery   St Helier Tel 68080.
Channel Island Military Museum   St Ouen Tel 23136.
Elizabeth Castle   St Helier Tel 23971.
Fantastic Tropical Gardens   St Peter Tel 481585.
Fort Regent Leisure Centre   St Helier Tel 500000.
German Command Bunker   St Brelade Tel 482089.
German Underground Hospital   St Lawrence Tel 863442.

Jersey Butterfly Centre St Mary Tel 481707.
Jersey Flower Centre St Lawrence Tel 865665.
Jersey Museum St Helier Tel 30511.
Jersey Zoo, Trinity Tel 864666.
Les Mielles Visitor Centre St Ouen Tel 483651.
La Hougue Bie Grouville Tel 853823.
Le Moulin de Quètivel St Peter Tel 45408.
Living Legend St Peter Tel 485496.
Micro World St Ouen Tel 483390.
Mont Orgueil Castle Gorey Tel 853292.
Samarès Manor St Clement Tel 70551.
St Matthews (Glass) Church St Lawrence Tel 20934.
St Peter's Bunker Museum St Peter Tel 481048.

Sark

Sark	Aval du Creux Hotel	57%	£70
Tel 0481 832036 Fax 0481 832368			**HR**
Sark			**Map 13 E4**

Eight miles east of Guernsey is the island of Sark, a peaceful retreat with
forty miles of coastline, bracing walks and no traffic. Peter and Cheryl
Tonks' friendly little hotel, originally a farmhouse, is a good place for
family holidays, with four of the bedrooms of a suitable size for families.
Children up to 3 stay free in parents room and early suppers are available.
There are two lounges and a small bar hung with local pictures. Half board
terms preferred – we quote B&B rate. ***Rooms*** *12. Garden, outdoor swimming
pool, boules. Closed Oct–Apr.* AMERICAN EXPRESS *Access, Visa.*

Restaurant   £55

As well as hotel residents and Sark visitors, folk from Guernsey have been
known to make a day trip by boat to Sark, principally to have lunch
at Aval du Creux and often for the lobsters. Seafood in general plays the
leading role here, with local crab served hot in a shell with cheese glaze,
as well as oysters, scallops and monkfish. There are also well-prepared meat
dishes, and on the lighter lunch menu omelettes, pancakes and baguettes
filled with seafood or the 'carpetbagger', with ham, chicken, cheese and
salad. That bracing sea air does give you an appetite, not to mention all the
walking! ***Seats*** *40. L 12-2 D 7-9. Set L £4.95/£6.95 (Sun £8.95)
Set D £15.95.*

Sark	Dixcart Hotel	64%	£78
Tel 0481 832015 Fax 0481 832164			**HR**
Sark GY9 OSD			**Map 13 E4**

Sark's longest established hotel was originally a 16th-century longhouse, the
main dwelling in one of the 40 feudal Tenements which still warrant
a seat in Sark's parliament. The absence of cars and continued existence
of ancient ranks really makes a stay here seem like a step back in time
(complete with exposed beams and brickwork), though domestic comforts
are modern. Homely lounge and bar for the occasional rainy day and fifty
acres of land with private access to the Dixcart Bay beach. Children
welcome if well behaved. Open all year. ***Rooms*** *15. Garden, playroom.*
AMERICAN EXPRESS *Access, Diners, Visa.*

Restaurant   £40

The restaurant's beautiful view over the sloping gardens is peaceful and
relaxing. The table d'hote menu features plenty of local seafood (bream,
brill, Herm oysters, Guernsey scallops, sole, sea bass), or more unusually,

a starter of Sark rabbit napped with redcurrant sauce or from further afield wild Scotch salmon poached in white wine and lemon, served with a whisky and crab sauce. Simple steaks attract a supplement. Well-priced wine list. *Seats 65. L 12-1.30 D 7-9 (high season to 9.30). Set L £13.25 (Sun £10.75) Set D £13.50.*

Sark   Hotel Petit Champ   61%   £68

Tel 0481 832046   Fax 0481 832469   **H**

Sark GY9 0SF   Map 13 E4

Splendid sea views are a feature at this small hotel, owned and run by Chris and Caroline Robins since 1991, in a quiet setting on carless Sark's west coast. Built as a private residence towards the end of the last century, the Petit Champ became a hotel in 1948. There's a tiny bar, leafy sun lounge and a quiet, homely lounge. Bedrooms are best described as cosy, and are undisturbed by TVs or telephones; some rooms have sliding patio doors. No children under seven. No dogs. Half-board terms preferred – we quote B&B rate. *Rooms 16. Garden, outdoor swimming pool, putting, horse & carriage hire, bicycle hire, sea fishing, yacht charters. Closed Oct-Easter.* AMERICAN EXPRESS *Access, Diners, Visa.*

Sark   La Sablonnerie   66%   £60

Tel 0481 832061   Fax 0481 832408   **HR**

Sark   Map 13 E4

As there are no cars on the island, the hotel provides a horse-drawn carriage to bring guests from the harbour to Little Sark, the southern part of the island connected by a narrow natural bridge with breathtaking views. The lovely beach of La Grande Grève is just a short walk away. The hotel is a lesson in *savoir vivre*, and charming owner Elizabeth Perrée has celebrated 21 years at the helm. The heart of the hotel is the cosy bar with low ceiling, granite walls and blue velvet decor. The hotel is surrounded by beautifully kept gardens and its own farm which supplies fruit, vegetables and dairy products for the restaurant, mostly organic. The bright, comfortable bedrooms are individually decorated with simple pine furniture; about half of them are not ensuite; six are reserved for non-smokers. A lovely tea garden located a few yards from the main building is open all day for light meals and afternoon teas. *Rooms 22. Closed mid Oct-Easter. Garden.*

Restaurant   £55

The main dining room has warm red decor, simple pine furniture and candle-light in the evening. Dinner begins with large plates of canapés in the bar, followed by perhaps smoked chicken and spinach roulade, consommé célestine, supreme of fresh salmon and lobster quat'saisons, and desserts with Sark cream. Succulent, flavoursome, delicious. *Seats 40. Parties 20. L 12-2.30 D 7-9.30. Set L £16.80 Set D £20.50.*

Sark   Stocks Hotel   61%   £72

Tel 0481 832001   Fax 0481 832130   **HR**

Sark GY9 0SD   Map 13 E4

Management of Stocks has now formally passed to the next generation with son Paul Armorgie and his wife at the helm of this granite-built hotel, which lies in a quiet wooded valley overlooking Dixcart Bay, 20 minutes walk from the harbour. There's a homely atmosphere in the lounge, and comfortable, unfussy bedrooms are decorated with darkwood furniture and floral fabrics. No TVs in the rooms. Seated banquets for 70, but Stocks is not in any way a business hotel. *Rooms 24. Garden, outdoor swimming pool, coffee shop (10am-10pm). Closed Oct-Mar.* AMERICAN EXPRESS *Access, Diners, Visa.*

See over

Cider Press Restaurant

£50

Both table d'hote and à la carte menus are offered, the former changing daily and the latter monthly, with local fish, shellfish and meat always featuring. Try for instance a sausage of Sark rabbit meat and wild mushrooms, layered over spring leaves and scented with a tarragon dressing, or noisettes of monkfish wrapped in local spinach leaves, poached in white wine and served in a saffron cream sauce. For pudding there might be a mandarin and marzipan parfait served with a tangy citrus dressing. There are 60 seats on the front lawn. Coffee, lunch, cream teas and light evening meals are served in the *Courtyard Bistro*; children's supper menu served here from 5-7pm. No children under 7 nor after 7pm in the main dining room. *Seats 60. Parties 12. Private Room 8. L 12-2.30 D 7-9. Set L £5.50/£7.95 (Sun £7.95). Set D £10.50/£15.95/£23.50.*

SARK   Place of Interest

Tourist Information   Tel 0481 832345.

Isle of Man

Ballasalla   La Rosette
£75

Tel 0624 822940

R

Main Road Ballasalla Isle of Man

Map 4 A4

Local seafood, including crab and queenies (little scallops), and straightforward meat dishes get simple classic treatment in a French-style café-bistro. The fish, up to about eight varieties, are cooked in one of three ways – plain grilled, baked in garlic, or with a cream and champagne sauce. The restaurant is 5 minutes drive from the airport. *Seats 45. Parties 16. L 12-3 D 7-10. Closed Sun, 1st 2 weeks Jan. Set L from £15 Set D £30.* AMERICAN EXPRESS *Access, Visa.*

Douglas   Palace Hotel   65%
£95

Tel 0624 662662   Fax 0624 625535

H

Central Promenade Douglas Isle of Man

Map 4 B4

The excellent leisure complex, with its own bar/café, the cinemas, the night club and the public casino provide plenty of entertainment for guests at the seafront Palace, one of the focal points of the island's night life. Other day rooms are smart and spacious, and bedrooms are quite well equipped; they range from singles through twins and doubles to sea view Executive rooms and sea view suites. Ample parking. Banqueting and conference facilities for 300+. Pleasant, helpful staff. No dogs. *Rooms 133. Indoor swimming pool, sauna, spa bath, solarium, beauty & hair salon, casinos, night club, cinemas, coffee shop (7am-10pm).* AMERICAN EXPRESS *Access, Diners, Visa.*

Douglas   Sefton Hotel   63%
£68

Tel 0624 626011   Fax 0624 676004

H

Harris Promenade Douglas Isle of Man

Map 4 B4

A turn-of-the-century seafront hotel with smart rooms behind its grand white frontage. The spacious interior is modern with just a hint of days gone by. There are good sea views from the lounge and the best bedrooms. Rooms now include four family suites and nine Executives. Popular for weekend and special breaks (golf, rambling, bird-watching etc). There is a secret door leading to the adjacent Gaiety Theatre. Conference and banqueting facilities for 100. No dogs. Private car park. *Rooms 80. Indoor swimming pool, keep-fit equipment, sauna, spa bath, steam room, solarium, beauty salon, coffee shop (9.45am-11.30pm).* AMERICAN EXPRESS *Access, Diners, Visa.*

Ramsey   Grand Island Hotel   67%   £96

Tel 0624 812455   Fax 0624 815291   **H**

Bride Road Ramsey Isle of Man   **Map 4 B4**

One mile north of Ramsey on the Bride Road, the handsome white-painted hotel looks down past terraced lawns to Ramsey Bay. Originally a Georgian manor house, it has a traditional look and feel, and there are a few antiques among the furnishings. Bedrooms are done out prettily, with pinks and blues predominating. There are extensive conference facilities (for up to 300) and a new bistro. Parking for 100. *Rooms 56. Garden, croquet, indoor swimming pool, sauna, spa bath, steam room, beauty & hair salon, putting, snooker, coarse fishing.* AMERICAN EXPRESS *Access, Diners, Visa.*

Ramsey   Harbour Bistro   £45

Tel 0624 814182   **R**

5 East Street Ramsey Isle of Man   **Map 4 B4**

Informal eating in a friendly bistro near the quay. Seafood is quite a feature on the menu with fresh local supplies every day, and dishes available as starter or main course: the famous local queenie scallops cooked with Provençal sauce, with bacon, onion and black pepper or with creamed garlic sauce on a bed of spinach, fisherman's pie, poached or deep-fried plaice fillets, sautéed or deep-fried king prawns. Also plenty for meat-eaters (lots of ways with steak) and indulgent desserts – "to hell with the calorie count". *Seats 50. L 12-2 D 6.30-10.30. Closed D Sun, 2 weeks Jan, 1 week Oct. Set L (Sun) £9.95. Access, Visa.*

Note that all telephone numbers with area codes starting with 0 will start 01 from 16 April 1995.

Recommended by

EGON RONAY'S GUIDES

1995

Hotels & Restaurants	Pubs & Inns
Europe	Just a Bite
Family Hotels & Restaurants	Paris
Oriental Restaurants	Ireland
New Zealand & South Pacific	Australia

Northern Ireland

Aghadowey   Greenhill House   £42
Tel 0265 868241   **PH**
24 Greenhill Road Aghadowey Coleraine Co Londonderry BT51 4EU   **Map 22 C1**

The Hegartys bought their pleasant Georgian farmhouse in 1969 because they wanted the land and, although graciously framed by mature trees and lovely countryside views, it is still very much the centre of a working farm. Elizabeth Hegarty greets arrivals at her guest house with an afternoon tea in the drawing room that includes such an array of home-made tea breads, cakes and biscuits that dinner plans may well waver. Rooms, including two large family rooms, are unostentatious but individually decorated with colour co-ordinated towels and linen; good planning makes them exceptionally comfortable and there are many thoughtful touches – fresh flowers, fruit basket, chocolate mints, tea/coffee-making facilities, hairdryer, bathrobe, proper clothes hangers, even a torch. A 5-course set dinner is available (by arrangement) to residents (£26 for two) at 6.30pm, except on Sundays; no wines are provided. *Rooms 6. Garden. Closed Nov-Feb. Access, Visa.*

Annalong   Glassdrumman Lodge   69%   £95
Tel 039 67 68451   Fax 039 67 67041   **HR**
85 Mill Road Annalong Co Down BT34 4RH   **Map 22 D2**

Situated just off the A2 coast road, with lovely views over the sea or back into the Mournes, this former farmhouse now has luxurious bedrooms with fresh flowers, fruit, mineral water and exceptionally well-appointed bathrooms. Service is a high priority, including 24hr room service, overnight laundry and a secretarial service, and breakfast a speciality – you can even go and choose your own newly-laid egg if you like. Beaches, walking, climbing, and fishing available locally. No tariff reductions for children. *Rooms 10. Garden, tennis, riding.* AMERICAN EXPRESS *Access, Diners, Visa.*

Memories Restaurant   £60

In the French-style restaurant good use is made of organically grown vegetables and naturally reared beef and pork from the hotel farm and seafood from local ports. Individual wines by the glass are chosen to go with each course of the daily-changing menu (£12-£14 per person extra). No smoking in the dining room. *Seats 50. Private Room 20. L by reservation only to residents. D at 8. Set D 25.*

Ballymena   Galgorm Manor   71%   £110
Tel 0266 881001   Fax 0266 880080   **HR**
136 Fenaghy Road Ballymena Co Antrim BT42 1EA   **Map 22 D1**

Next to a natural weir on the River Maine, which runs through the 85 acres of grounds, this Georgian manor has recently been acquired by new owners, who have made a good job of refurbishing the public areas with rich fabrics, warm colour schemes and a scattering of antiques to create an unashamedly luxurious atmosphere. The 'designer-rustic' Gillies Bar in a converted outbuilding offers a change of mood. As we went to press work was beginning to bring the bedrooms, which are all in a new wing, up to the standard of the day rooms. Bathrooms all have separate shower cubicles in addition to the tub. There are also six self-catering cottages in the grounds. 24hr room service. An equestrian centre to the rear of the house includes a show-jumping course, eventing cross-country practice area, specially constructed gallops and numerous rides through the estate. The new Great Hall banqueting and conference centre caters for up to 300/500 on two floors. *Rooms 23. Garden, riding, game fishing.* AMERICAN EXPRESS *Access, Diners, Visa.* MARTELL COGNAC

Restaurant £68

A fine room with glittering chandeliers, elaborately draped curtains and Arcadian murals depicting the four seasons. The dinner menu – priced by the course (ie starter £4.95, main £14.50) – offers starters such as confit of duck with wild cranberries and rocket salad, papaya wrapped in smoked Parma ham or venison terrine with the likes of roast pheasant with onion and sage sauce, pan-fried halibut in a white wine and cream sauce and rack of lamb with bubble and squeak garnish to follow; dishes are competently cooked. Lunch brings a shorter, fixed-price menu and there's always a traditional roast on Sundays. Several good wines and growers on the concise wine list, though few half bottles. *Seats 73. Private Room 14. L 12-2.30 D 7-9.45 (Sun 6 to 9). Set L £12.50 (Sun £14.95).*

Belfast   Antica Roma £65

Tel 0232 311121   Fax 0232 310787   **R**

67 Botanic Avenue Belfast Co Antrim BT7 1JL   Map 22 D2

Impressive decor based on ancient Rome – mosaic floor, classical murals, columns, distressed stucco – combines with more sophisticated Italian cooking at this fashionable restaurant in the university district. The evening à la carte includes the likes of wild mushrooms with crushed chili peppers, garlic and olive oil on toasted bread; gratinated oak-smoked crab claws in a light bisque sauce; chicken liver salad with croutons, mushrooms and pine nuts in a walnut oil dressing; fillet of salmon on a spinach and sorrel purée with orange sauce and sliced scallops; saltimbocca and duck *al limone*. Good puds include *mandorle alla barese* (rich almond cake with layers of mocha and praline butter cream and chocolate ganache) and *frutta candita* (fresh fruit deep fried in a light batter and served hot with puréed fruit dips). Regional winner for Northern Ireland of our Dessert of the Year award 1995. No à la carte at lunchtime but two good-value set menus each provide a choice of four main dishes. Particularly good Italian section on the wine list with some recherché offerings. *Seats 160. Private Room 70. L 12-3 D 6-11. Set L £9.95/£12.95. Closed L Sat & all Sun, 3 days at Christmas & 31 Dec.* AMERICAN EXPRESS *Access, Visa.*

Belfast   Bengal Brasserie £35

Tel 0232 640099   **R**

339 Ormeau Road Belfast Co Antrim BT7 3GL   Map 22 D2

About a mile south of the city centre, this recently refurbished Indian restaurant is situated in a modern shopping arcade. Sound Bengali cooking includes a list of daily blackboard specials such as scampi masala, tandoori duck and Indian river fish as well as a wide choice on the main menu with lamb and chicken dishes jostling for space beside prawns, lobster, crayfish and 'European dishes' (steaks with sauces, omelettes, chicken Kiev). Friendly, helpful staff. *Seats 46. Private Room 50. L 12-1.45 D 5.30-11.15 (Sun to 10.15). Closed 25 Dec, Set meal £15.95. Access, Diners, Visa.*

Belfast   Dukes Hotel   67% £98

Tel 0232 236666   Fax 0232 237177   **H**

65 University Street Belfast Co Antrim BT7 1HL   Map 22 D2

A Victorian facade covers a bright modern hotel in a residential area close to Queen's University and the Botanical Gardens. Black leather and chrome feature in the foyer seating. There are function facilities for up to 140 and a health club. Pastel decor and impressionist prints set the tone in the bedrooms, all double-glazed and some designated non-smoking. Children up to 16 stay free in parents' room. Much reduced weekend rates. *Rooms 21. Keep-fit equipment, sauna.* AMERICAN EXPRESS *Access, Diners, Visa.*

Belfast   Europa Hotel   £120

Tel 0232 327000   Fax 0232 327800

H

Great Victoria Street Belfast Co Antrim BT2 7AP

Map 22 D2

New owners, Hastings Hotels have undertaken a major programme
of refurbishment at the city-centre, high-rise Europa. As we went to press
95% of the rooms had been improved and a large extension was being
added to the front of the building. No dogs. *Rooms 184. Closed 25 Dec.*
AMERICAN EXPRESS *Access, Diners, Visa.*

Belfast   Manor House Cantonese Cuisine   £40

Tel 0232 238755

R

43-47 Donegall Pass Belfast Co Antrim BT7 1DQ

Map 22 D2

The main menu at this family-run Cantonese restaurant runs to more than
300 items, and there are others on the vegetarian and Peking-style set
menus (book 3 days ahead for the vegetarian party menu). Sound cooking
over the whole range, which adds fish head and duck's web to all the
familiar favourites. *Seats 80. Private Room 50. Meals 12-12.
Closed 25 & 26 Dec, 12 Jul. Set L from £5.50 Set D from £14.50. Access,
Diners, Visa.*

Belfast   Plaza Hotel   64%   £82

Tel 0232 333555   Fax 0232 232999

H

15 Brunswick Street Belfast Co Antrim BT2 7GE

Map 22 D2

Ultra-modern city-centre business hotel with well-equipped bedrooms, all
with satellite TV, hairdryer and trouser press as standard, and five
conference suites (capacity 70 theatre-style, 100 restaurant-style). There are
14 rooms reserved for non-smokers. Children up to 10 stay free in parents'
room; four rooms have extra beds. No dogs. *Rooms 76.* AMERICAN EXPRESS
Access, Diners, Visa.

Belfast   Roscoff   ★   £75

Tel 0232 331532   Fax 0232 312093

R

Lesley House Shaftesbury Square Belfast Co Antrim BT2 7DB

Map 22 D2

Via Albert Roux in London plus spells in Canada and California, Paul and
Jeanne Rankin arrived in Belfast some five years ago and opened the chicest
restaurant in town. Since then it's been one success after another, firstly
maintaining standards and consistently cooking the best food in the area,
then bringing on young chefs (witness the present sous chef, the very
talented Jane McMeekin who started here as an unpaid pastry commis and
has gained several internal promotions), presenting a TV series, and writing
a recipe book. The last two require opinions, which the couple are
certainly not short of – in fact, they've had a go at us, but we don't mind!
The bottom line is that they run a fine restaurant and their travels reflect
Paul's style of cooking which is modern and innovative. His influences are
divers, producing dishes such as foie gras wontons with wild mushrooms
and wilted rocket, spiced sole tempura with lobster and coriander aïoli, and
fresh figs in Merlot with honey almond ice cream. Complementing the
good food (the set lunch is a real bargain) is a most fairly priced and
interesting wine list; service by keen and bright (in both senses) staff is
noticeably slick. *Seats 70. L 12.15-2.15 D 6.30-10.30. Set L £14.50
Set D £19.50. Closed L Sat, all Sun, 11 & 12 July, 24, 25 & 26 Dec, 1 Jan.*
AMERICAN EXPRESS *Access, Diners, Visa.* MARTELL

Belfast   Speranza   £40

Tel 0232 230213   Fax 0232 236752

R

16 Shaftesbury Square Belfast Co Antrim BT2 7DB

Map 22 D2

Large, bustling pizzeria/restaurant on two floors with red check tablecloths
and rustic chalet-style decor. The menu offers a range of huge crisp-based

pizzas and about a dozen pasta dishes (all at around a fiver) plus a few chicken and other meat dishes between £6.95 and £10.95 (for the fillet steak). Attentive service from boys and girls smartly kitted out in bright red cummerbunds with matching bow ties. For children there are high-chairs and a special menu written on colouring mats (crayons supplied) that are entered each week into a prize draw for a toy. In the same ownership as *Antica Roma* and *Villa Italia* (qv). *Seats 170. D only 5-11.30. Closed Sun, 3 days at Christmas & 11, 12 Jul. Access, Visa.*

Belfast	Stormont Hotel	69%	£127
Tel 0232 658621 Fax 0232 480240			**H**
587 Upper Newtownards Road Stormont Belfast Co Down BT4 3LP			Map 22 D2

Way out of town on the Newtownards Road, opposite Stormont Castle, this modern hotel is always busy and bustling, having various function rooms in addition to the Confex Centre with its 10 purpose-built trade and exhibition rooms. Public areas centre around a sunken lounge (sometimes used as a conference 'break-out' area) off which is a cosy cocktail bar. A mezzanine lounge has huge glass windows overlooking the castle grounds. The majority of bedrooms have been completely refurbished in recent times and are spacious, comfortable and practical with good, well-lit work space and modern easy chairs. Good bathrooms feature marble tiling. A few rooms are more dated and await refurbishment but are equally well equipped with satellite TV etc. Smart, helpful staff offer attentive lounge service and there's a 24hr room-service menu. Good breakfasts are served in the informal all-day brasserie. *Rooms 106.* AMERICAN EXPRESS *Access, Diners, Visa.*

Belfast	Strand Restaurant		£35
Tel 0232 682266 Fax 0232 663189			**R**
12 Stranmillis Road Belfast Co Antrim BT9 5AA			Map 22 D2

Anne Turkington's popular restaurant/wine bar has been refurbished with Charles Rennie Mackintosh inspiration, and the eating area has been opened out somewhat. Food is served throughout the day, and one-plate meals at a bargain £3.95 are served from noon till 11pm Mon-Thur and noon till 7 Fri and Sat (cod and chips, French onion flan, chili con carne, liver and bacon hot pot). Sunday lunch (£6.95) features roast beef. A la carte, the selection runs from soup, oyster fritters and devilled kidneys to burgers, fillets of pink trout, pork gorgonzola and aubergine parmigiana. *Seats 80. Parties 20. Private Room 25. L Sun 12-3 D Sun 5-10 Meals Mon-Sat 12-12. Closed 25 & 26 Dec, 12 & 13 July.* AMERICAN EXPRESS *Access, Diners, Visa.*

Belfast	Villa Italia		£45
Tel 0232 328356 Fax 0232 234978			**R**
39 University Road Belfast Co Antrim BT7 1ND			Map 22 D2

Sister restaurant to *Speranza* (see above) but with a little less emphasis on pizzas and more on pasta and other Italian dishes. A shade more upmarket too, although still informal in style, with quieter background music and less rustic decor. Service is equally friendly and efficient. *Seats 110. D only 5-11.30 (Sat from 4, Sun 4-10). Closed 25, 26 & 31 Dec, 12 July & Easter Sun.* AMERICAN EXPRESS *Access, Visa.*

Belfast	The Warehouse		£45
Tel 0232 439690 Fax 0232 230514			**R**
35-39 Hill Street Belfast Co Antrim BT1 2LB			Map 22 D2

A popular and lively "bar with wine and restaurant", whose menus cover a fair range of tasty, straightforward dishes. From the evening table d'hote (available on both floors) could come leek and potato soup, peppered pork chop, salmon and monkfish tart, hot bread and butter pudding, chocolate biscuit cake and home-made ice creams. Similar à la carte selection in the restaurant at lunchtime, plus informal lunchtime menu and evening snack menu in the wine bar. Live music Fri and Sat nights. *Seats 90. Private Room 45. Wine bar open for drinks 11.30-11 L 12-3 D 6-9. Closed D Mon, L Sat, all Sun, Bank Holidays. Set D £13.50/£16.50. Access, Diners, Visa.*

Belfast	Welcome Restaurant	£40
Tel 0232 381359		**R**
22 Stranmillis Road Belfast Co Antrim BT9 5AA		**Map 22 D2**

The entrance is topped by a pagoda roof, and inside dragons, screens and lanterns establish that this is indeed a Chinese restaurant. The menu runs to over 100 items, mainly familiar, popular dishes, and there are special menus for individuals and small parties. *Seats 80. Parties 25. Private Room 30. L 12-2 D 5-11.30 (Sun to 10.30). Closed L Sat & Sun, 24-26 Dec. Set meals from £12.* AMERICAN EXPRESS *Access, Diners, Visa.*

Belfast	Wellington Park	59%	£94
Tel 0232 381111 Fax 0232 665410			**H**
21 Malone Road Belfast Co Antrim BT9 6RU			**Map 22 D2**

Redesigned foyer, amalgamated bar and restaurant areas and bedroom upgrades have kept the Wellington Park up to date. The locality and a thriving conference business (capacity 150 theatre-style) ensure a lively atmosphere, but one of the three bars is kept exclusively for residents. Children up to 12 stay free in parents' room. Residents have free use of Queens University's sports centre, 5 minutes from the hotel. No dogs. *Rooms 50.* AMERICAN EXPRESS *Access, Diners, Visa.*

Belfast	Places of Interest

Tourist Information   Tel 0232 246609
Mount Stewart House and Gardens (NT)   Greyabbey Tel 02477 88387
   17 miles
Ulster Museum and Botanic Gardens   Tel 0232 381251
Belfast Zoo   Tel 0232 776277 *5 miles North*
Malone House Art Gallery and Gardens   Upper Malone Rd
   Tel 0232 681246
Dixon Park   Upper Malone Rd Tel 0232 320202
Transport Museum   Tel 0232 451519
Down Royal Racecourse   Lisburn Tel 0846 621256 *6 miles*
   Theatres and Concert Halls
Grand Opera House   Great Victoria St Tel 0232 241919
Lyric Theatre   Ridgeway St Tel 0232 381081
Ulster Hall   Bedford St Tel 0232 323900
Group Theatre   Bradford St Tel 0232 229685

Belfast International Airport	Novotel	62%	£75
Tel 08494 22033 Fax 08494 23500			**H**
Belfast International Airport Co Antrim BT29 4AB			**Map 22 D2**

The only hotel actually at the international airport, which is about 17 miles to the north of the city centre. Opened in 1993, the hotel offers practical, standardised bedrooms, open-plan public areas and conference facilities for up to 250 delegates (theatre-style), banqueting for 180. For children there is a 'kids corner' with Lego table and video by the informal restaurant and a small outdoor play area in addition to the usual amenities. Children under 16 stay free in parents' room. 24hr room service. *Rooms 108.* AMERICAN EXPRESS *Access, Diners, Visa.*

Bushmills   Bushmills Inn   58%   £78

Tel 02657 32339   Fax 02657 32048   **H**

25 Main Street Bushmills Co Antrim BT57 8QA   Map 22 C1

After the Giant's Causeway, the world's oldest distillery at Bushmills is the biggest attraction in the area (and well worth a visit; mid-week is most interesting); the Bushmills Inn also attracts year-round local support. The exterior, including a neat garden at the relocated (back) main entrance, creates a welcoming impression that extends into the hall, with its open fire and country antiques, and other public areas that encompass several bars and a large dining room. Bedrooms are quite modest, individually decorated and comfortably furnished; some family rooms are remarkable for their ingenious use of space. A beamed loft provides a splendid setting for private functions (up to 85 people) and the 'secret library' a unique venue for special occasions. *Rooms 11. Garden, fishing. Access, Visa.*

Bushmills   Places of Interest

Giant's Causeway Tourist Information   Tel 02657 31855/31582
Dunluce Castle
The Old Bushmills Distillery   Tel 02657 31521

Carrickfergus   The Wind-Rose Wine Bar

Tel 09603 64192   Fax 09603 51164   **R**

The Marina Carrickfergus Co Antrim BT38 8BE   Map 22 D2

Overlooking the marina, a well-appointed formal restaurant on the upper floor is approached by an exterior spiral staircase and has clear views across Belfast Lough (booking essential). The ground-floor wine bar below has a pubby atmosphere with a strongly nautical theme and provides simple bar food. *Seats 85. Open 12-12. Bar Food L 12-2.30 snacks 2.30-5 D 5-9. Closed L Sat, D Sun & Mon, 25 & 26 Dec. Access, Visa.*

Comber   La Mon House   59%   £85

Tel 0232 448631   Fax 0232 448026   **H**

The Mills 41 Gransha Road Comber Co Down BT23 5RF   Map 22 D2

Public areas in this low-rise modern hotel include a bar featuring copper-topped tables, a small residents' lounge (which may be in private use), carvery restaurant and a fun bar with disco (Fri). Practical bedrooms have simple fitted furniture; nine large rooms have balconies and there are eight small singles with shower only. Families will enjoy the country health club and outdoor areas. Banqueting facilities for 450, conference up to 1100 theatre-style. Regular Saturday night dinner dances. In the countryside, 5 miles from Belfast city centre. No dogs. *Rooms 38. Garden, indoor swimming pool, gymnasium, sauna, solarium, whirlpool bath, putting.* AMERICAN EXPRESS *Access, Visa.*

Comber   Places of Interest

Down Country Museum   Downpatrick Tel 0396 615218
Mount Stewart   Newtownards Tel 024774 387
Wildfowl and Wetlands Centre   Castle Espie Tel 0242 874146 *3 miles*
Nendrum Monastery   Mahee Island
Rowallane Garden   Tel 0238 510131
Downpatrick Racecourse   Downpatrick Tel 0396 612054
Newtownards Priory *3 miles*
Ballycopeland Windmill *8 miles*
Northern Ireland Aquarium   Portaferry Tel 02477 28062
    26 miles
Grey Abbey *10 miles*

Crawfordsburn — Old Inn — £90

Tel 0247 853255   Fax 0247 852775   **I**

15 Main Street Crawfordsburn Co Down BT19 1JH   Map 22 D2

Located off the main Belfast to Bangor road, this 16th-century inn is in a pretty village setting and is supposed to be the oldest in continuous use in all Ireland. Its location is conveniently close to Belfast and its City Airport. Oak beams, antiques and gas lighting emphasise the natural character of the building, an attractive venue for business people (conference facilities for 150, banqueting for 90) and private guests alike. Individually decorated bedrooms vary in size and style, most have antiques, some four-posters and a few have private sitting rooms; all are non-smoking. Romantics and newly-weds should head for the recently refurbished honeymoon cottage. Free private car parking for overnight guests. No dogs. *Rooms 34. Garden. Closed 24-26 Dec.* AMERICAN EXPRESS *Access, Diners, Visa.*

Downpatrick — Tyrella House — £35

Tel 0396 851422   **PH**

Clanmaghery Road nr Ballykinler Downpatrick Co Down BT30 8SU   Map 22 D2

Set snugly in mature woodland (although only a few hundred yards from the beach), a delightful period house on a 300-acre working farm. While not exactly grand, the house has many attractive features, including a spacious hall and well-proportioned reception rooms – a gracious drawing room is elegantly furnished with antiques and the matching dining room provides a lovely setting for Sally Corbett's home cooking (dinner only for residents at 8pm – £21). Bedrooms vary interestingly in size and shape, all overlook pleasant gardens and the house retains the warmth of a family home. With access to some of the best riding country in Ireland, horses are a particular enthusiasm here and hunting, stabling and cross country tuition are available. No children under 8; no dogs (kennels provided); no smoking throughout. Take the A2 Ardglass road out of Clough for 4 miles; look for the blue gates with Gate Lodge on the right. *Rooms 3. Private beach, horse riding/hunting. Phone for Christmas closures. No credit cards.*

Dunadry — Dunadry Inn — 64% — £105

Tel 0849 432474   Fax 0849 433389   **H**

2 Islandreagh Drive Dunadry Co Antrim BT41 2HA   Map 22 D2

Originally a paper mill founded early in the 18th century, later a linen mill, now a well-known riverside hotel 15 minutes from Belfast city centre and 10 from the airport. Best bedrooms are on the ground floor, with access to the gardens. Executive rooms feature computer points and fax machines. The Copper Bar under the main staircase is a popular spot for a drink and the lunchtime buffet. Extensive conference facilities. Children up to 5 stay free in parents' room. No dogs. *Rooms 67. Garden, croquet, crazy golf, game fishing, bicycles, indoor swimming pool, keep-fit equipment, spa bath, sauna, steam room, solarium. Closed 24-27 Dec.* AMERICAN EXPRESS *Access, Diners, Visa.*

Dunadry — Place of Interest

Antrim Round Tower

Dunmurry — Forte Crest Belfast — 67% — £80

Tel 0232 612101   Fax 0232 626546   **H**

300 Kingsway Dunmurry Co Antrim BT17 9ES   Map 22 D2

Business-oriented hotel a short drive from Belfast city centre and airport. Accommodation includes Lady Crest rooms, non-smoking rooms and rooms designated as family-size. Children up to 12 stay free in parents' room. 24hr room service. Conference/meeting facilities for up to 450. Free parking for 200 cars. **Rooms** 82. *Keep-fit equipment, squash.* AMERICAN EXPRESS *Access, Diners, Visa.*

Garvagh	MacDuff's Restaurant, Blackheath House	£50

Tel & Fax 0265 868433	**RR**

112 Killeague Road Garvagh nr Coleraine Co Londonderry BT51 4HH | **Map 22 C1**

A basement restaurant under a fine, immaculately kept Georgian house, MacDuff's is characterful, comfortable and convivial. There's a small separate reception area and it is run by staff who cope well under the busiest of circumstances. The generally relaxed atmosphere is carried through to a comforting ring of familiarity on Margaret Erwin's menu in starters like Stilton puffs with hot, sweet and sour sauce and twice-baked soufflé with summer salad – popular perennials kept on the menu by requests from regulars. Spicing is a feature, but traditional main courses like grilled wild local salmon with hollandaise are also given a further lift, as in a garnish of crispy dulse; local catches feature in a classic seafood symphony with halibut, fat prawns and mussels in a light wine sauce. Good desserts might include hazelnut meringue with raspberries (including a generous 'wee dram' of Drambuie in the cream) or simple Jamaican banana, split and grilled with rum and sugar. No children under 12. No smoking. On the A29 four miles north of Garvagh. **Seats** 45. *Parties 10. Private Room 12. D only 7-9.30. Closed Sun & Mon. Closed 4/5 days at Christmas. Access, Visa.*

Rooms £60

Accommodation is available in five large, comfortably furnished en-suite rooms with lovely views over the gardens and surrounding countryside.

Garvagh   Place of Interest

Leslie Hill Farm Park   by Ballymoney Tel 0265 666803

Helen's Bay	Deanes on the Square ↑	£60

Tel 0247 852841	**R**

7 Station Square Helen's Bay Co Down BT19 1TN | **Map 22 D2**

When the railways arrived in the 1860s the first Marquis of Dufferin and Ava built his own station – in Scottish baronial style. Still a functioning railway station, the building is now a novel restaurant and home to some exciting cooking by Michael Deane. Dishes like smoked salmon sausage with basil pesto, marinated duck with tandoori sausage and soya, and tender slices of venison on rösti potato surrounded by strips of pheasant and chicken in a mustard sauce are full of flavour and if you think whiting is a dull fish try Michael's creamed whiting with baby capers as a starter. Portions are generous and presentation attractive yet unfussy. No à la carte but a couple of fixed-price menus, both with choices, or try the multi-course tasting menu – most fun when you allow each dish to be a surprise when it arrives. From part of the restaurant you can see into the kitchen and some windows look out on to the platform. There is a small bar in the basement. **Seats** 40. *L Sun 12.30-2.30 D 7-10. Set L £15 Set D from £18 & £30. Closed D Sun & all Mon, 2 weeks Jan & 1 week July.*

Holywood	Culloden Hotel 72%	£152

Tel 0232 425223 Fax 0232 426777	**HR**

142 Bangor Road Craigavad Holywood Co Down BT18 0EX | **Map 22 D2**

Originally a palace of the bishops of Down, this splendid 19th-century building in Scottish Baronial style stands in 12 acres of gardens overlooking Belfast Lough. Antiques, stained glass, fine plasterwork and paintings grace the day rooms (though the Gothic Bar is in modern mode). Good-sized, well-furnished bedrooms are mostly in an extension. There are two restaurants, an inn in the grounds, various function suites and a well-appointed health and fitness club. No dogs. **Rooms** *89. Garden, indoor swimming pool, keep-fit equipment, squash, sauna, spa bath, solarium, tennis, snooker. Closed 24-25 Dec.* AMERICAN EXPRESS® *Access, Diners, Visa.*

The Mitre Restaurant £65

Comfortable and relaxing, with friendly, efficient service. The menu is quite extensive, ranging from traditional grills and classics such as scampi provençale or garlic snails to more contemporary creations like pan-fried monkfish with vegetable tagliatelle and a tomato/Pernod sauce. Sunday lunch always features a roast on the fixed-price menu. Separate vegetarian menu. There is also a grill bar in the complex, 'The Cultra Inn'. *Seats 150. Parties 20. Private Room 50. L 12.30-2.30 D 7-9.45 (Sun to 8.30). Closed L Sat. Set L & D £17.*

Holywood   Sullivans £55

Tel & Fax 0232 421000   **R**

Sullivan Place Holywood Co Down BT18 9JF   **Map 22 D2**

Bright and cheerful with sunny yellow walls and colourfully upholstered chairs, Sullivans operates as a coffee shop during the day (Devon scones, pecan pie and lunchtime savouries like venison terrine, salmon and leek quiche and soup) before turning into a fully-fledged restaurant at night. After only a short time the accomplished cooking of young chef/patron Simon Shaw (formerly at *Roscoff* in Belfast) has already gained such a loyal following that booking is advisable at weekends. Dishes like a duck confit with sweet chilis, vegetable strudel, warm pigeon salad with lentils and leeks, monkfish with saffron vinaigrette and rack of lamb with green peppercorn cream come in portions substantial enough to satisfy local appetites. Desserts range from rice pudding with fruit compote to mango tart with lemon sorbet. There's a short à la carte in addition to the prix fixe. Unlicensed, but there are a couple of wine merchants nearby. **Seats** *40. L 10-4 D 6.30-9.30. Set D (Tue-Thur only) £14.95. Closed D Mon, all Sun & Bank Holidays. Access, Visa.*

Holywood   Place of Interest

Ulster Folk and Transport Museum   Cultra Tel 0232 428428

Larne   Magheramorne House   63% £66

Tel 0574 279444   Fax 0574 260138   **H**

59 Shore Road Magheramorne Larne Co Antrim BT40 3HW   **Map 22 D1**

53 acres of woodland overlooking Larne Lough provide a fine setting for a late-Victorian house which offers fresh, bright bedrooms, banqueting/conference facilities for up to 180 and free parking for 150 cars. Extensive Victorian gardens. No dogs. **Rooms** *22. Garden.* AMERICAN EXPRESS® *Access, Diners, Visa.*

Larne   Places of Interest

Ballylumford Dolmen   Island Magee
Carrickfergus Castle   *12 miles*

Londonderry   Beech Hill House Hotel   59% £85

Tel 0504 49279   Fax 0504 45366   **HR**

32 Ardmore Road Londonderry Co Londonderry BT47 3QP   **Map 22 C1**

More hotel than country house, Beech Hill has rapidly become a favourite venue for local private functions, with banqueting and conference facilities for 80. Spacious, well-proportioned public areas include a lounge/bar comfortably furnished in somewhat clubby style. Bedrooms, all recently refurnished, vary considerably in size and comfort. Children under 10 may share their parents' room at no charge. No dogs. **Rooms** *17. Garden, tennis. Closed 25 & 26 Dec.* AMERICAN EXPRESS® *Access, Visa.*

Ardmore Room Restaurant   ↑   £50

In what was once the billiard room, the restaurant overlooks mature gardens and is the prettiest and most intimate room in the hotel – a fitting setting for the fine food for which head chef Noel McMeel has established a well-deserved reputation since the hotel opened in 1991. Classical dishes are handled with confidence and flair and the saucing is excellent. Start, perhaps, with a spot of role reversal in poached pear with a timbale of Cashel Blue cheese and raspberry vinaigrette, or a more traditional terrine of duck, flavoursome and chunky, served in a ring of delicious chopped port and apple jelly. Breads, including tea breads typical of the area, come warm from the oven and main dishes, such as pan-fried, marinated monkfish accompanied by a spaghetti of vegetables with a ginger and balsamic vinaigrette, have great verve. Good vegetable selection and pretty desserts. **Seats** *40. Parties 20. Private Rooms 18 & 30. L 12-2.30 D 6-10. Set L £11.95 (Sun £12.95) Set D £17.95.*

Londonderry   Everglades Hotel   59%   £80

Tel 0504 46722   Fax 0504 49200   **H**

Prehen Road Londonderry Co Londonderry BT47 2PA   Map 22 C1

South of the town on the banks of the River Foyle, this modern low-rise hotel is a popular venue for conferences and banqueting (350/250) besides providing bright, practical accommodation. Top of the bedroom range are two suites with jacuzzis and turbo showers. Children up to 12 stay free in parents' room. **Rooms** *52. Garden. Closed 24 & 25 Dec.* AMERICAN EXPRESS ® *Access, Diners, Visa.*

Londonderry   Places of Interest

Tourist Information   Tel 0504 267284
Derry's Walls
St Columb's Cathedral   off London St Tel 0504 262746
O'Doherty's Tower   Magazine St Tel 0504 265238
Display Centre   Butcher St Tel 0504 362016
Ulster-American Folk Park   Omagh Tel 0662 243292
Brachmore Stone Circus   nr Cookstown

> If we recommend meals in a hotel or inn a separate entry is made for its restaurant.

Newcastle   Slieve Donard Hotel   63%   £99

Tel 03967 23681   Fax 03967 24830   **H**

Downs Road Newcastle Co Down BT33 0AG   Map 22 D2

Imposing red-brick Victorian railway hotel facing the Irish Sea (next to the Royal County Down Golf Club) with the Mountains of Mourne in the background, 'The Slieve' caters mainly to conferences in winter and holidaymakers, tour groups and weddings in the summer. A grand, galleried entrance hall sets the tone for public areas which include a large elegant lounge with conservatory extension (sometimes used for functions), cosy library sitting room and a bar named after Charlie Chaplin, who once stayed here. Bedrooms vary in shape and size but, apart from the third currently being refurbished, share the same blue and peach colour scheme, polycotton duvets and dark mahogany furniture. The only advertised room service is breakfast, and that is not available for conference delegates. Good leisure centre. Parking for 200 cars. **Rooms** *120. Garden, indoor swimming pool, gymnasium, solarium, spa bath, steam room, beauty salon, putting, tennis, shop.* AMERICAN EXPRESS ® *Access, Diners, Visa.*

Newcastle   Places of Interest

Seaforde Gardens   Tel 0396 87225 *5 miles*
Castle Ward   Strangford Tel 0396 86204 *15 miles*

Portaferry   Portaferry Hotel   63%   £80

Tel 02477 28231   Fax 02477 28999   **HR**

10 The Strand Portaferry Co Down BT22 1PE   Map 22 D2

Formed out of an 18th-century terrace on the seafront, where the ferry
crosses the neck of Strangford Lough, the Portaferry has been substantially
remodelled over recent years to create a delightful small hotel run with
a winning combination of charm and professionalism by John and Marie
Herlihy. Public areas include a tweedy bar and several tastefully decorated
little lounges sporting pictures of the surrounding area by local artists.
Light, airy bedrooms come with lightwood furniture and matching floral
bedcovers and curtains, neat bathrooms with huge bath sheets. No dogs.
Rooms 14. *Closed 24 & 25 Dec.* AMERICAN EXPRESS *Access, Diners, Visa.*

Restaurant   £65

The secret of Anne Truesdale's cooking is the use of the best local produce
in dishes that are essentially simple, although not without interest. Lamb
from the mountains of Mourne and Ulster beef feature but it's seafood that
takes pride of place with amazingly plump scallops from the Lough (pan-
fried with garlic and bacon perhaps or baked in white wine and cheese),
Murlough Bay mussels, prawns from Portavogie, Ardglass crab (in filo
pastry with tomato and basil sauce), goujons of monkfish (with fresh lime
sauce), salmon (wild Irish in season) and lobsters from their own tanks.
Vegetables, often organically grown, are well handled too. At lunchtime
there is a fairly extensive bar menu that is also served in the dining room
except on Sundays, when there is a fixed-price menu that always features
a traditional roast. *Seats* 80. *L 12.30-2.30 D 7-9. Set L (Sun only) £12.95.
Closed 24 & 25 Dec.*

Portballintrae   Bayview Hotel   58%   £65

Tel 02657 31453   Fax 02657 32360   **H**

2 Bayhead Road Portballintrae nr Bushmills Co Antrim BT57 8RZ   Map 22 C1

Overlooking the tiny harbour and the bay, the long pebbledash hotel
building stands half a mile from the main A2 coastal route. Functions and
conferences (up to 300) are quite big business, but residents have their own
sitting room, and there's also a convivial bar. Bedrooms include one semi-
suite with a small sitting room area and generally have modern bathrooms.
Six cottages are a short distance from the hotel; these are let as self-catering
or as three-bedroom suites. Dogs by prior arrangement only. *Rooms* 16.
Indoor swimming pool, sauna, solarium, snooker. Access, Visa.

Portrush   Ramore   ★   £55

Tel 0265 824313   **R**

The Harbour Portrush Co Antrim BT56 8BN   Map 22 C1

The sheer cosmopolitan buzz of this waterside restaurant, with its sleek,
chic black-and-chrome decor, smoothly operating open kitchen flanked
by huge baskets of freshly baked breads and serried ranks of highly
professional staff, is apt to take the uninitiated by surprise. It's trendier than
one might expect to find in Portrush town and a tribute to the remarkable
style of chef George McAlpin and the family team that their bright, airy
restaurant continues to attract flocks of enthusiastic diners from throughout
Ireland and beyond. Local seafood still predominates, but a keen feeling for
the mood of the moment imbues the cooking with unusual immediacy
in starters like tempura prawns (Dublin Bay prawns fried in spiced batter
with pepper salsa and garlic parsley butter) or Italian summer salad (cos,

rocket, Parma ham, avocado, cherry tomatoes, boiled eggs and croutons topped off with shavings of fresh Parmesan); the wide variety of modestly priced main dishes (collops of peppered fillet steak, supreme of duck, rack of Irish lamb) includes a handful of interesting 'complete dishes' such as a local version of paella or Thai chicken (succulent chargrilled breast on a bed of oriental vegetables with a sesame and mushroom soya vinaigrette and frites) – remarkable value at £7.50. Desserts are a speciality: there is always a hot soufflé on the list – perhaps hot fresh fruit and Grand Marnier – and daily blackboard specials like an excellent tangy lemon tart. Very good coffee, served with petits fours. *Seats 80. D only 6.30-10.30 (lunchtime wine bar downstairs). Closed Sun & Mon, 25 & 26 Dec. Access, Visa.*

Portrush — Place of Interest

Dunluce Castle *3 miles*

Templepatrick — Templeton Hotel — 66% — £100

Tel 084 94 32984   Fax 084 94 33406

882 Antrim Road Templepatrick Ballyclare Co Antrim BT39 0AH   Map 22 D2

An eye-catching modern hotel a mile from the M2 and handy for Belfast airport. Spacious bedrooms are equipped with the expected up-to-date amenities, and the four Executive rooms have additionally mini-bars and jacuzzis. Day rooms take various decorative themes – sleek black and gold for the cocktail bar, Scandinavian for the banqueting hall (catering for up to 350), echoes of medieval knights in the restaurant. New conference suite for up to 50 in a separate annexe. 24hr room service. Free parking for 125 cars. *Rooms 20. Garden. Closed 25 Dec.* AMERICAN EXPRESS *Access, Diners, Visa.*

Our inspectors *never* book in the name of Egon Ronay's Guides. They disclose their identity only if they are considering an establishment for inclusion in the next edition of the Guide.

Recommended by

EGON RONAY'S GUIDES

1995

YOUR GUARANTEE
OF
QUALITY AND INDEPENDENCE

- Establishment inspections are anonymous
- Inspections are undertaken by qualified Egon Ronay's Guides inspectors
- The Guides are completely independent in their editorial selection
- The Guides do not accept advertising, hospitality or payment from listed establishments

---

Hotels & Restaurants
Europe
Family Hotels & Restaurants
Oriental Restaurants
New Zealand & South Pacific

Pubs & Inns
Just a Bite
Paris
Ireland
Australia

Egon Ronay's Guides are available from all good bookshops or can be ordered from Leading Guides, 35 Tadema Road, London SW10 0PZ
Tel: 071-352 2485 / 352 0019   Fax: 071-376 5071

Republic of Ireland

When calling from outside the Republic omit the initial
zero and prefix the number with 010-353.
For example, Sheen Falls Lodge, Kenmare 010-353 64 41600.

Prices quoted are expressed in Irish Punts.

Adare   Adare Manor   81%   £220

Tel 061 396566   Fax 061 396124   **HR**

Adare Co Limerick   Map 23 B5

Home, for two centuries, of the Dunraven family, this magnificent neo-
Gothic mansion is set in 900 acres on the banks of the river Maigue. Its
splendid chandeliered drawing room and the glazed cloister of the dining
room look over formal box-hedged gardens towards the Robert Trent
Jones golf course (currently still being developed and not available for play,
although arrangements are made with a club nearby). Other grand public
areas include the gallery, modelled after the Palace of Versailles, with its
Flemish choir stalls, fine stained-glass windows and hand-carved
bookshelves. Gracious bedrooms have individual hand-crafted fireplaces,
fine locally-made mahogany furniture, cut-glass table lamps and impressive
marble bathrooms with strong showers over huge bathtubs. Children
under 12 are accommodated free in their parents' room. No dogs.
*Rooms 64. Garden, indoor swimming pool, gymnasium, sauna, games room,
snooker, golf driving range, riding, fishing, clay-pigeon shooting.*
AMERICAN EXPRESS *Access, Diners, Visa.* MARTELL

Restaurant   ↑   £85

Dining in style comes easy at Adare: after taking an aperitif in the drawing
room overlooking the parterre gardens and developing golf course beyond,   ♛
move through to the elegant panelled dining room with views of the river
Maigue and consider chef de cuisine Gerard Costelloe's imaginative fare
on a choice of table d'hote or à la carte menus. Local produce, including
vegetables from the estate's own gardens, features in dishes like garden leaf
salad, a colourful, piquant combination of mixed leaves tossed in a creamy
blue cheese dressing and scattered with crisp deep-fried beetroot 'chips', or a
main course 'stew' of Irish seafood – salmon, sole, monkfish, scallops – in
a tangy lemon sauce. Desserts range from homely (individual blackberry
and apple crumble, crème anglaise) to the richly exotic (chocolate marquise
on a marmalade sauce). Tempting selection of home-made breads; excellent
service. *Seats 65. Private Room 25. L 12.30-2.30 (Sun to 3) D 7.30-9.30.
Set L £21 Set D £32.50.*

Adare   Dunraven Arms Hotel   72%   £133

Tel 061 396633   Fax 061 396541   **HR**

Adare Co Limerick   Map 23 B5

Sporting activities, including golf, fishing and especially hunting and all
things equestrian, are a particular attraction here at 'the fox-hunting centre
of Ireland' but the Dunraven Arms also attracts a wide range of guests,
including business clients and many travellers who are tempted
by imaginative bar food to break a journey here. Meticulously maintained
public areas have a timeless, traditional atmosphere with old furniture lifted
by softly bright classical colour combinations in the decor in everything
from the busy pubby bar to the serenity of the residents' drawing room,
known as 'the library'. Bedrooms are individually furnished to a high
standard with excellent bathrooms, antiques and many thoughtful extras,
like fresh flowers, fruit and mineral water. The turn-down service includes
fresh towels and chocolates on the pillow. No tea/coffee-making facilities,
but room service is prompt. Frequent functions create a buzz around the
hotel, but newer rooms away from public areas are quiet. Children up to 4
may stay free in their parents' room. 24hr room service. *Rooms 44. Garden,
tennis, shop.* AMERICAN EXPRESS *Access, Diners, Visa.*

The Maigue Room   £55

Banqueting and dining are kept separate at the Dunraven Arms and head
chef Mark Phelan is building up an excellent reputation for his elegant
restaurant, named after the local river. Table d'hote or à la carte menus
might typically start with a variation on a traditional local dish like black

pudding, pan-fried and imaginatively served with featherlight apple fritters
and a colourful red onion confit, or a stunningly pretty warm terrine
of trout and fresh prawn tails in a vermouth-scented beurre blanc with dill.
Main courses also highlight the quality of local produce, including the
finest roast beef (carved from a trolley in the evening). Delicious desserts
like good old lemon meringue pie, lightly baked and served with
an orange sauce. Lovely brown soda bread, aromatic coffee. *Seats 60.
Parties 20. Private Room 35. L 12.30-2.30 D 7.30-9.30. Bar Food 12-6pm.
Set L £11.50 Set D £21.50. Closed Good Friday.*

Adare	The Mustard Seed ↑	£60
Tel 061 396451		**♿ R**
Main Street Adare Co Limerick		**Map 23 B5**

Picturesque surroundings in this olde-worlde thatched cottage and a warm
welcome from the proprietor, Dan Mullane, provide the perfect ambience
for Michael Weir's confident, creative cooking. Four-course dinner menus
based firmly on the best of local and seasonal produce present difficult
choices but, once the decisions are made, the cosy little reception/bar makes
an enjoyable place to anticipate the pleasures ahead: an Oriental terrine
of layered pork, leeks and spinach is a sight to behold on a bed or puréed
apples sharpened with balsamic vinegar, while a salad of crisp green beans,
with quails' eggs, slivers of Parmesan and black olives in a chive nut oil is,
quite simply, moreish. Smoked haddock chowder comes with a spicy
rouille and irresistible home-baked breads, while main courses feature game
in season, local free-range duck and elegant fish dishes such as trio of fish –
baked escalope of salmon with steamed sole and pan-fried scallops on a
chive and spring onion sauce. Good farmhouse cheeses and imaginative
variations on homely desserts, like delicious banoffi pie with caramel sauce
and banana coulis. To finish, home-made petits fours and fragrant coffee.
*Seats 50. Parties 18. Private Room 30. D only 7-10. Set D £25.
Closed Sun & Mon, Bank Holidays, Feb.* AMERICAN EXPRESS® *Access, Diners, Visa.*

Adare	Woodlands House Hotel 60%	£50
Tel 061 396118 Fax 061 396073		**H**
Adare Co Limerick		**Map 23 B5**

From small beginnings in 1983 the Fitzgerald family have developed their
hotel to its present stage, with facilities for weddings, banquets and
conferences for up to 350. Roomy public areas include two bars and
a strikingly decorated lobby/lounge with comfortable seating and
a colourful mural, while both banqueting suites and the restaurant overlook
well-maintained gardens and countryside. Bedrooms, including two suites
and most with a pleasant outlook, vary in age and amenities (the older ones
are due for refurbishment during '94) but are well maintained; twenty-six
new rooms were planned to come on stream in Autumn 1994. No dogs.
Rooms 57. Garden. Closed 24 & 25 Dec. AMERICAN EXPRESS® *Access, Diners, Visa.*

Adare	Place of Interest

Castle Matrix   Rathkeale Tel 069 64284

Ahakista	Hillcrest House	£33
Tel 027 67045		**PH**
Ahakista Durrus Co Cork		**Map 23 A6**

Comfortable accommodation and home-cooked food are the main
attractions at this neat farmhouse, situated on a working farm overlooking
Dunmanus Bay. Of the four rooms, three are upstairs and en suite while
one double (with bath) is on the ground floor with direct access to parking
facilities. Suitable for families. Residents' dinner is £24 for two. *Rooms 4.
Games room. Closed Nov-Apr. No credit cards.*

Ahakista   Shiro   ★   £80

Tel 027 67030   **RR**

Ahakista nr Bantry Co Cork   Map 23 A6

A visit to the remote Shiro Japanese Dinner House, situated in a fine, meticulously maintained Georgian house overlooking Dunmanus Bay, is likely to be both unique and unforgettable. The dining room may only accommodate small numbers, but both the welcome and the food are big-hearted. Often referred to as an experience which defies description, Kei Pilz's authentic Japanese food is so exquisite in both preparation and presentation that it remains in the mind as a finely detailed patchwork, an impressionistic mirage of culinary delights. With great charm Werner Pilz guides newcomers through the menu, which changes daily and may consist of three short courses – perhaps *zensai* (flower-decked appetisers), *moriawase* (delicate egg dishes and sushi) and *suimono* (a seasonal soup), followed by a choice of eight main courses including a selection of lightly-battered deep-fried *tempura* dishes, *sashimi* (seasonal raw fish, served with soy sauce and *wasabi* – hot green mustard) and *yakitori* (chicken breast, liver and vegetables on bamboo skewers, with a traditional spicy sauce). Several dishes are suitable for vegetarians. A selection of home-made ices, including green tea, dramatically arranged with some colourful fruit against a black plate and followed by a choice of teas and coffees, rounds off the experience. There's a pleasant, short wine list that lists French classics alongside the *sake*. 5% supplement for paying by credit card. Bookings only. *Seats 18. Private Room 10. D only 7-9. Set D £33.* AMERICAN EXPRESS *Access, Diners, Visa.*

Rooms   £36

A charming traditional cottage (sleeping two) in the grounds is available for self-catering.

Ardee   The Gables   £60

Tel 041 53789   **RR**

Dundalk Road Ardee Co Louth   Map 22 C3

In what might still seem, relative to other areas which have developed so dramatically over the last few years, something of a culinary desert, this bourgeois restaurant is enormously popular. Owner-chef Michael Caine uses the best of local ingredients without allowing the forces of fashion to intrude on a French menu distinctly reminiscent of the 60s, with huge servings and rich sauces, typically in dishes like French snails with garlic butter, fresh Clogherhead prawns thermidor, honey roast duckling with port and orange sauce and breast of chicken stuffed with smoked salmon and crab, finished with butter, cream and Chablis – to the evident satisfaction of an appreciative local clientele who like things just the way they are. *Seats 34. D only 7-10. Set D £19.95. Closed Sun & Mon, 2 weeks Jun & 2 weeks Nov, 25 & 26 Dec.* AMERICAN EXPRESS *Access, Visa.*

Rooms   £34

Accommodation is offered in five rooms, all en suite. *Garden.*

Athy   Tonlegee House   £55

Tel & Fax 0507 31473   **RR**

Athy Co Kildare   Map 23 C4

Just outside town, Mark and Marjorie Molloy's restored Georgian home offers good cooking, a warm welcome, excellent bedrooms and a favourable price/quality ratio. Dinner is a five-course affair (priced according to the choice of main dish), or six if opting for the selection of four Irish farmhouse cheeses (the small extra charge includes a glass of port). The likes of duck liver parfait with toasted brioche and onion confit, venison pithiviers, ravioli of crab with grain mustard and shellfish

See over

sauce are among the starters, and guinea fowl with wild mushroom sauce
or breast of Barbary duck with a confit of its leg and a port and caper sauce
might be included in the main-course options. All are prepared with a skill
and care that extends to a choice of home-baked breads and desserts like
pear and almond tart cooked to order. The day's fish and seasonal game
dishes are recited when the menu is offered. Diners and overnight guests
share a comfortable period sitting room. *Seats 40. L by arrangement
D 7-9.30 (to 10.30 Fri & Sat). Set D from £20. Closed D Sun
(residents only), 24-26 Dec and Good Friday. Access, Visa.*

Rooms £58

Five spacious, antique-furnished bedrooms have been individually decorated
with attractive fabrics and offer various homely comforts in addition
to remote-control TV, direct-dial telephones and good, large en-suite
bathrooms. Breakfast, using free-range eggs, makes an excellent start to the
day.

Aughrim   Aughrim Schoolhouse Restaurant £45
Tel 0905 73936 R
Aughrim nr Ballinasloe Co Galway Map 23 B4

The work of conversion from schoolhouse to a charming country
restaurant can be followed in a scrapbook kept by the fire in the reception
area. Geraldine Dolan and Mícheál Harrison produce intelligent menus
of interesting modern dishes which have quickly won a fair following.
Cheese and spinach tartlet, confit of duck salad, hot crab claws with lemon
pasta and Hungarian goulash soup are typical starters, followed perhaps
by poached salmon with a basil white wine sauce, roasted breast and
braised leg of pheasant or sirloin steak with green peppercorn or béarnaise
sauce. Good vegetables; 'bonnofie' pie a speciality dessert. *Seats 50.
L 12.30-3 (Sun only + Tue-Sat July-Aug) D 6.30-11. Closed D Sun
Oct-May, all Mon, 24-26 Dec. Set Sun L £9.50 Set D £16.50.*
AMERICAN EXPRESS *Access, Visa.*

Aughrim   Place of Interest
Battle of Aughrim Centre Tel 0905 73939

Ballina   Downhill Hotel   65% £86
Tel 096 21033   Fax 096 21338 H
Ballina Co Mayo Map 22 B3

Set in landscaped gardens overlooking the river Brosna, with extensive
leisure and conference facilities and good fishing nearby as major
attractions. The purpose-built conference centre and hospitality rooms
accommodate groups from 10 to 400 and the leisure centre has a 50ft oval
swimming pool; nightly entertainment in Frog's Pavilion piano bar. Good
facilities for families include cots, high-chairs, baby-listening, baby-sitting
(by arrangement), playroom and a supervised crèche. Easy parking for 300.
A steam room and plunge pool were planned for the end of 1994.
*Rooms 50. Garden, indoor swimming pool, keep-fit equipment, squash, sauna,
spa bath, solarium, tennis, games room, snooker. Closed 3 days Christmas.*
AMERICAN EXPRESS *Access, Diners, Visa.*

Ballina   Mount Falcon Castle   60% £88
Tel & Fax 096 21172 HR
Ballina Co Mayo Map 22 B3

The castle was built in neo-Gothic style in 1876, and the 100 acres
of grounds extend to the banks of the River Moy (fishing is available either
here or on Lough Conn). Woodland walks unfold the beauty of the
surroundings, while back inside huge log fires and convivial company

make for instant relaxation. Simple bedrooms are furnished with antiques. Constance Aldridge, who has owned the castle and greeted visitors for over 50 years, is an indispensible part of the charm of the place. **Rooms** 10. *Garden, tennis, game fishing, games room. Closed Christmas week, Feb & Mar.* AMERICAN EXPRESS *Access, Diners, Visa.*

Restaurant   £50

Local produce, much of it from the estate farm and walled gardens, is the basis of confident, uncomplicated country house cooking. Soup, salmon, leg of lamb, spicy chicken, crème caramel and bread-and-butter pudding typify the menu. Guests gather around one table in the dining room. Lunch available by arrangement. **Seats** 28. *D only at 8. Set D £22.*

Ballyconneely	Erriseask House	64%	£80
Tel 095 23553 Fax 095 23639			**HR**
Ballyconneely Clifden Co Galway			Map 23 A4

In a stunning shoreside location seven miles south of Clifden, with immediate access to miles of empty beaches, brothers Christian and Stefan Matz have been running this discreet hotel since 1988 and their success is doing much, not only for their own reputation, but for the growing recognition of culinary clustering in the Clifden area. Except for the raw beauty of its setting and a tendency to mount unusual art exhibitions, the hotel is understated, cool, continental in style throughout the public areas. Bedrooms, which are neatly decorated in somewhat neutral tones, follow suit – the atmosphere suggests a reversal of the usual priorities, more restaurant with rooms than hotel with interesting food. **Rooms** 13. *Garden. Closed Nov-Easter.* AMERICAN EXPRESS *Access, Diners, Visa.*

Restaurant   £60

The restaurant is formally well appointed but has more warmth than elsewhere – a hint, perhaps, of the passion and perfectionism which Stefan Matz brings to his cooking. In concept and balance, choice of prime ingredients and the skill with which he blends originality with classical and modern French cuisine to create memorable meals, Stefan is making a serious contribution to the developing Irish food scene. His attention to detail in wonderful little amuse-bouche, petits fours and fragrant home-baked breads, for example, is outstanding but the bold strokes are equally well conceived in dishes that are as flavoursome as they are beautifully presented – terrine of duck foie gras with glazed apples, pigeon breast in a sherry vinegar sauce, veal medallions with wild mushrooms and home-made pasta. Good French and Irish farmhouse cheeseboard and lovely classic desserts. Light lunches only. No smoking. **Seats** 35. *Parties 12. Private Room 20. D 6.30-9.30. Set D £17.50/£21.90 & £29.*

Ballyconnell	Slieve Russell Hotel	78%	£140
Tel 049 26444 Fax 049 26474			**H**
Ballyconnell Co Cavan			Map 22 C3

Hotel, golf and country club and major conference venue, Slieve Russell stands in a lovely fishing area and takes its name from a nearby mountain. A marbled colonnade and grand central staircase set a tone of subdued luxury in the day rooms, where guests have a good choice of eating and drinking outlets. Spacious bedrooms have extra-large beds, with good amenities including trouser press as standard and large marble bathrooms, all with jacuzzi air baths. The championship golf course is in full swing and excellent leisure facilities adjoining the hotel include a 20 metre pool. **Rooms** 150. *Indoor swimming pool, children's pool, gymnasium, squash, sauna, spa bath, steam room, tennis, golf (18, snooker, creche, hair & beauty salon).* AMERICAN EXPRESS *Access, Diners, Visa.*

Ballycotton   Bayview Hotel   NEW   67%   £80

Tel 021 646746   Fax 021 646824   **H**

Ballycotton Co Cork   Map 2 B6

Although in the present ownership since 1974, this hotel has recently been
completely re-built. It now combines a unique seafront location beside
Ballycotton harbour with a carefully judged design that retains traditional
features like human proportions and open fires, and also incorporates
modern conveniences of warmth and up-to-date bathrooms. Built to take
full advantage of the wonderful location, all rooms have lovely sea/harbour
views and well-designed bathrooms while suites, which occupy corner sites
on two floors, have especially good views on two sides, and all the top
floor has a pleasingly cosy 'cottage attic' feeling. All rooms have space for
a cot (no charge) or extra bed and there is baby-listening (baby-sitting
by arrangement), high-chairs and an early evening meal for children.
Public areas are spacious and, although not ostentatious, quality is evident
in the furnishing throughout; the dining room, which can be divided
if required, is particularly attractive and, like the rest of the hotel, also
enjoys the magnificent views. Facilities for small conferences (up to 50,
theatre-style) and plenty of parking. Tennis facilities available at a nearby
hotel. No dogs. *Rooms 35. Garden. Closed Nov-Easter.* AMERICAN EXPRESS
Access, Visa.

Ballydehob   Annie's Restaurant   £55

Tel 028 37292   **R**

Main Street Ballydehob Co Cork   Map 23 A6

Faces light up when Annie Barry's tiny restaurant is mentioned. It's all
so laid back: the way Levis' old grocery/bar across the road serves aperitifs
while you wait for your table and, quite likely, digestifs afterwards,
to relieve pressure on space. Set 4-course dinners change daily and, although
understandably leaning towards local seafood, give a wide range of choices
at each course, including a vegetarian dish of the day. Lamb kidneys in filo,
baked fresh wild salmon with lemon and fresh herb sauce, followed
by roasted almonds and Baileys ice cream or local Gubbeen cheese typify
the style. *Seats 24. D only 6.30-9.30. Set D £22. Closed Sun, Mon, first three
weeks Oct + ring in winter to check opening times. Access, Visa.*

Ballyferriter   Tigh an Tobair (The Well House)   £35

Tel 066 56404   **R**

Ballyferriter Co Kerry   Map 23 A5

In an area otherwise surprisingly badly served, this pleasant, informal
restaurant is an oasis for parched travellers. Walk through the grocery shop
at the front and you will find an unpretentious little restaurant arranged,
quite literally, around a deep well (glass-topped for safety but still clearly
visible) and furnished with the unmistakable tiled tables and chunky wares
of Louis Mulcahy's nearby pottery. The emphasis is very much on simple
home cooking in traditional dishes like Irish stew and Dublin coddle, good
thick soups and big, wholesome salads and sandwiches made with home-
made bread. *Seats 30. Parties 8. Meals 10-8. Closed Jan & Feb. Access, Visa.*

Ballyhack   Neptune Restaurant   £50

Tel 051 89284   **R**

Ballyhack New Ross Co Wexford   Map 23 C5

Instead of sweeping away on the Wexford road to the right when leaving
the Passage East Car Ferry, turn left and look up towards the restored
Ballyhack Castle and, just below it, one of the South-East's most attractive
little informal bistro/restaurants will beckon. There are three distinct
rooms and a patio that overlooks the harbour. The emphasis is, not
surprisingly, on seafood; whether it is Neptune creamy fish soup, shrimp

and ginger hotpot or scallops in orange and gin sauce with rice for a light lunch, a 'tourist' restricted-choice menu dinner at £11.90, the works from the à la carte – light game terrine, perhaps, hot crab brehat – or a delicious Sunday lunch. Pierce and Valerie McAuliffe's light and airy restaurant with its Mediterranean colours, water views and unexpectedly reasonable prices will draw you back. Interesting short wine list – and one of very few Irish restaurants to encourage BYO. Lunch Sunday, other days by arrangement. *Seats* 45. *Private Room* 30. *L (Sun only) 12.30-3 D 6.30-10 (Sat to 10.30). Closed Mon (except Jul & Aug), 1 Nov-end Mar. Set Sun L £6.50/£10.50 Set D £11.90.* AMERICAN EXPRESS *Access, Diners, Visa.*

| **Ballylickey** | **Ballylickey Manor House** | **67%** | **£99** |

Tel 027 50071   Fax 027 50124   **H**

Ballylickey Bantry Co Cork   Map 23 A6

Ballylickey has been the Graves' family home for four generations and run as a hotel for over four decades. The main house, which is impressively furnished with antiques, has views over Bantry Bay and five spacious suites with well-appointed bathrooms. Ten acres of award-winning gardens afford a splendid setting for an outdoor swimming pool and garden restaurant, in addition to simpler accommodation in seven chalets, all with en-suite rooms. *Rooms 5 in main house. Garden, outdoor swimming pool, fishing, croquet. Closed early Nov-end Mar.* AMERICAN EXPRESS *Access, Visa.*

| **Ballylickey** | **Larchwood House** | **£60** |

Tel 027 66181   **RR**

Pearsons Bridge Ballylickey Bantry Co Cork   Map 23 A6

Owner-chef Sheila Vaughan and her husband Aidan have been steadily building up a reputation for good food and accommodation at Larchwood since they opened in 1990. Although located in a private home, the restaurant is cleverly designed to take full advantage of views over garden and river to the mountains beyond and also to allow maximum privacy in a limited space. Five-course, fixed-price-only menus offer a wide selection, priced according to the choice of main course and highlighting the best of local produce, particularly a good range of fish: seafood and apple soup, rhubarb sorbet, paupiettes of sole with mustard sauce and pigeon breasts with blackcurrant sauce are typical, followed by warm chocolate cake with caramel sauce, perhaps, or local farmhouse cheeses. Excellent breakfasts also offer an unusual range of options, including several fish choices and a cheese plate. *Seats 20. Parties 13. D only 6.30-10. Set D from £18. Closed Sun, 1 week Christmas.* AMERICAN EXPRESS *Access, Diners, Visa.*

Rooms   £36

Accommodation is offered in four comfortable en-suite rooms, including two family rooms. Rooms at the back have lovely views. No dogs. *Garden.*

| **Ballylickey** | **Seaview House Hotel** | **70%** | **£100** |

Tel 027 50462   Fax 027 51555   **HR**

Ballylickey Bantry Co Cork   Map 23 A6

Since converting her family home to a hotel in the mid-70s, Miss Kathleen O'Sullivan has built up an impressive reputation – not only for consistently high standards of essentials like comfort and housekeeping, but also for her personal supervision and warmth of welcome. Spacious, well-proportioned public rooms include a graciously decorated drawing room, a library and comfortable television room, while generously-sized bedrooms are all individually decorated and some have sea views. Family furniture and antiques enhance the hotel throughout and a ground-floor room has been thoughtfully equipped for disabled guests. *Rooms 17. Garden. Closed mid Nov-mid Mar.* AMERICAN EXPRESS *Access, Visa.* MARTELL

Restaurant £55

Overlooking the garden, with views over Bantry Bay, several well-appointed rooms linked by arches and furnished with antiques and fresh flowers combine to make an elegant restaurant with plenty of privacy. Set five-course dinner menus change daily and offer a wide choice on all courses, with the emphasis firmly on local produce, especially seafood, in dishes ranging from a simple fresh crab salad or a scallop mousse with vermouth sauce to John Dory with a mussel and spinach sauce. No children under 5 in dining room; separate arrangements are made for them. *Seats 45. Parties 20. L (Sun only) 12.45-2 D 7-9.30. Set Sun L £12 Set D £23.*

Ballymote   Temple House   61% £70
Tel 071 83329   Fax 071 83808   **H**
Ballymote Co Sligo   Map 22 B3

Temple House is a magnificent Georgian mansion set in 1000 acres of parkland with terraced gardens, a working farm and a lake well known for the size of its pike. Imposing, even austere externally, the house is warm and welcoming behind its front door, in spite of the grand scale of the outer hall (note the trophies of outdoor pursuits) and the elegant inner hall. There are four centrally heated double bedrooms – two of them very large, all very comfortable – and a single with shower. Deb Perceval does the cooking, using home-grown or home-reared produce to good effect in her no-choice dinners (residents only). Guests gather for drinks in a cosy sitting room with an open fire, and coffee is served in the drawing room afterwards. The day starts with the double delight of marvellous views and a super breakfast. High tea for kiddies is served at 6.30 – children's room rates are negotiable. No perfumes or aerosols, please, owing to Mr Perceval's chemical sensitivity. *Rooms 5. Garden, coarse fishing, snooker, lake boats (3). Closed Dec-Mar (except shooting parties Dec & Jan).* AMERICAN EXPRESS *Access, Visa.*

Ballynahinch   Ballynahinch Castle   71% £104
Tel 095 31006   Fax 095 31085   **H**
Recess Ballynahinch Co Galway   Map 22 A3

Renowned as a fishing hotel, this crenellated Victorian mansion can be both more impressive and more relaxed than anticipated – the fish, the grandeur and the wonderful setting may attract the first-time visitor, but it is the unstuffy atmosphere combined with a high level of comfort, friendliness and an invigorating mixture of residents and locals at the bar at night that brings people back. Under the present management, renovations and extensions have been completed with unusual attention to period detail, a policy also generally carried through successfully in furnishing both public areas and bedrooms. Most bedrooms and some reception rooms – notably the dining room – have lovely romantic views down through ancient woodland to the Ballynahinch River below; four bedrooms and seven bathrooms have recently been refurbished. Facilities for small conferences (25). Kennels provided for dogs. "Well-behaved and controlled" children welcome. *Rooms 28. Garden, croquet, tennis, fishing, shooting, bicycles. Closed all Feb.* AMERICAN EXPRESS *Access, Diners, Visa.*

Ballyvaughan   Gregans Castle   71% £99
Tel 065 77005   Fax 065 77111   **HR**
Ballyvaughan Co Clare   Map 23 B4

The Haden family (Peter, Moira, and son Simon-Peter) run this friendly, welcoming hotel, which stands three miles from the village in the Burren's limestone landscape overlooking Galway Bay. The building has an austere, grey appearance, but there's a deal of comfort and style within. Public rooms include an elegant, traditional drawing room, the Corkscrew Bar and the library, which is home not only to books but also to an important collection of murals of Burren flora. Rooms, which vary in size and shape but are all decorated to a high standard, some with four-posters, have a refreshing emphasis on peace and quiet, without radios or televisions. No dogs. **Rooms** *22. Garden. Closed Nov-Mar. Access, Visa.*

Restaurant   £75

Before settling into the elegant dining room, relax in the bar and order from Margaret Cronin's carefully constructed five-course menus which change daily but are always based on the best of local ingredients, notably lamb and seafood, in dishes like whole black sole with a chive sauce, fillets of John Dory with herb butter, and roast rack of Burren lamb with a rosemary jus. Good locally-made Irish farmhouse cheeses. Light meals are served all day in the bar. **Seats** *60. Private Room 40. L 12-3 (in bar) D 7-8.30. Set D £27.*

Ballyvaughan   Places of Interest

Tourist Information   Tel 065 81171
Aillwee Cave   Tel 065 77036
Cliffs of Moher
The Burren
Dunguaire Castle   Kinvara Tel 091 37108
Thoor Ballylee   by Gort. W B Yeats' home. Tel 091 31436

Baltimore   Chez Youen   £75
Tel & Fax 028 20136   **R**
The Pier Baltimore Co Cork   Map 23 B6

Youen Jacob has been delighting visitors to Baltimore with his distinctly Breton style of seafood cooking since 1978 and it's a case of *plus ça change*: concessions will be made to non fish-eaters in the shape of an occasional vegetable soup or melon with port and perhaps a steak with green peppercorn sauce, but it is the dramatic presentation of seafood in the shell which draws admiring sighs. Lobster is very much a speciality and available all year round and the shellfish platter on the £32 dinner menu includes Dublin Bay prawns, oysters or Baltimore shrimps, crab and velvet crab as well as lobster – all served in shell, this dish is indeed a sight to behold. The wines are all very carefully selected by Youen himself in France and much of it shipped in March (directly after bottling) for drinking the following summer. Booking essential. **Seats** *45. Parties 12. Private Room 50. L 12.30-2.30. D 6-11. Open Easter-end Sept. Closed all Nov, 24 & 25 Dec. Set L from £12.50 Set D from £21.50.* AMERICAN EXPRESS *Access, Diners, Visa.*

Bantry   Bantry House   £90
Tel 027 50795   **PH**
New Street Bantry Co Cork   Map 23 A6

Owned by the White family since 1739 and seat of the four Earls of Bantry (1816–1891), Bantry House is in one of the most beautiful settings in the British Isles, with unforgettable views over Bantry Bay. In 1945 it earned the distinction of being the first house in Ireland to be opened to the public but, although undeniably grand, it has a uniquely informal atmosphere. Guest accommodation available in the East and West wings overlooks the famous Italian Garden behind the house, with its fountain, parterres and 'stairway to the sky' and includes a suite and a family floor, all with en-suite bathrooms and direct-dial telephones. Facilities include a residents' sitting room, a billiard room and television room. Admission to the house and gardens is free to residents and dinner is available for residents by arrangement Apr-Oct, Mon-Fri. **Rooms** *7. Garden, games room, shop.* AMERICAN EXPRESS *Access, Diners, Visa.*

Bantry   Place of Interest

Bantry House   Tel 027 50047

Barna   Ty Ar Mor   £60

Tel 091 92223   **R**

The Pier Barna Co Galway   Map 23 B4

Close your eyes and imagine you're in Brittany when you visit this little seafood restaurant, last in a row of cottages on the quay at Barna.

In summer Hervé Mahe puts a few tables out on the terrace so guests can enjoy the view – on colder days sitting by the cosy turf fire contemplating the pleasures ahead, as read off a large and scrupulously legible blackboard menu, has more appeal. The place has natural charm with its stone walls and flagstones, narrow winding stairs to an upper room with bigger windows, home-laundered linen and haunting background jazz. All this and good food too, as M Mahe and his Breton chef Philippe Dano turn out even the simplest of dishes with Gallic flair – a wonderful 'salade', zesty with radishes, grated carrot, a punchy dressing and a basket of hot baguettes and butter, perhaps, or six fat oysters nestling on a bed of cracked ice and glistening seaweed, lobster fresh from the sea and cooked to order. Look out for the typically French 'prix-fixe' value in limited choice 3-course menus (lunch, £8.50; dinner £12.50). Breton crepes are a lunchtime speciality (served from 1 to 4). *Seats 55. Parties 10. Private Room 30. L 12-2.15 D from 7pm. Closed 15 Jan-14 Feb. Set L £8.50 Set D £12.50. Access, Visa.*

Note that all telephone numbers with area codes starting with 0 will start 01 from 16 April 1995.

Beaufort   Dunloe Castle   71%   £96

Tel 064 44111   Fax 064 44583   **H**

Beaufort nr Killarney Co Kerry   Map 23 A5

In a glorious, verdant setting of parkland, only the empty shell of the keep from the original 13th-century castle remains at this modern hotel. Nevertheless, the building gives a good first impression and all public areas, including the cocktail bar and restaurant, have been refurbished. The main public room is a spacious, comfortably furnished first-floor drawing room with some well-chosen antiques and lovely views of the Gap of Dunloe. All bedrooms have good bathrooms; twenty new junior suites were created last winter. 24hr room service. Sister hotel to *Hotel Europe* (Killarney, 2½ miles away) and *Ard-na-Sidhe* (Caragh Lake). Banqueting/conference facilities for 200/300. *Rooms 120. Garden, indoor swimming pool, sauna, tennis, riding, putting, game fishing, cycling. Closed Oct-Apr.* AMERICAN EXPRESS *Access, Diners, Visa.*

Birr   Dooly's Hotel   60%   £50

Tel 0509 20032   Fax 0509 21332   **H**

Birr Co Offaly   Map 23 C4

Right on Emmet Square, in the centre of Georgian Birr, this attractively old-fashioned hotel is one of Ireland's oldest coaching inns, dating back to 1747. It's a good holiday centre with plenty to do locally – Birr Castle gardens are very near, also golfing, fishing, riding and river excursions. Public rooms include two characterful bars and are traditionally furnished and well maintained. Pleasant, modest bedrooms are all en suite; some may be noisy when there's a function in the night-club. Children up to 7 share parents' room at no charge. *Rooms 18. Garden, coffee shop (9.30am-10pm), night club, coarse fishing. Closed 25 Dec.* AMERICAN EXPRESS *Access, Diners, Visa.*

Birr   Tullanisk

£76

Tel & Fax 0509 20572

PH

Birr Co Offaly

Map 23 C4

George and Susie Gossip have run their carefully restored 18th-century Dower House in the demesne of the Earls of Rosse (still resident at Birr Castle) as a delightful country house hotel since 1989. The house is beautiful, interesting and comfortable, the surrounding gardens and parkland lovely and full of wildlife, of which a fair cross-section may make an appearance while you watch from the big mahogany dining table at dinner. George is an excellent chef and enjoys producing memorable no-choice dinners (£22 per head for non-residents) and breakfasts live up to the promise of the night before and more. **Rooms** 7. *Garden, croquet, table tennis. D only 8.30. Closed 4 days at Christmas. Access, Visa.*

Birr   Places of Interest

Birr Castle   Tel 0509 20056
Charleville Forest Castle   Tullamore Tel 0506 21279 *20 miles*

Blacklion   MacNean Bistro

£40

Tel 072 53022

R

Blacklion Co Cavan

Map 22 C2

A modest little room on Blacklion's main street is the setting for some excellent and imaginative cooking by Vera Maguire and her son Nevan. Courgette flowers filled with sole and dill mousse is a typical starter, which could precede braised leg and fried saddle of rabbit, steamed monkfish with shallots and burgundy sauce, or even fried fillet of ostrich served on rösti accompanied by organic vegetables. Splendid desserts (typically roast pear with caramel sauce, passion fruit ice cream and a compote of berries) finish the meal in fine style. **Seats** 35. *L (Sun only) 12.30-3.30 light meals 3-6 D 5-10. D Tue-Sun (winter Thur-Sun only). Closed all Mon. Set L (Sun) £10. Set D from £18.50. Access, Visa.*

Blacklion   Places of Interest

Enniskillen Keep *10 miles*
Castle Coole   Tel 0365 322690 *15 miles*
Florence Court   Tel 0365 348249 *5 miles*

Prices quoted for the Republic of Ireland are in Irish punts.

Blackrock   Ayumi-Ya

£40

Tel 01 283 1767   Fax 01 662 0221

R

Newpark Centre Newtownpark Avenue Blackrock Co Dublin

Map 23 D4

Situated in a small shopping centre, Ayumi-Ya opened in 1983 and offers a wide range of authentic Japanese dishes. Diners are given the choice of western or Japanese-style seating when booking – also the time to opt for a teppanyaki table if you want food cooked in front of you. In addition to teppanyaki and an à la carte menu for old hands, set menus ranging from vegetarian, through the Ayumi-Ya dinner course to a special seasonal dinner make the choices easier. Staff are very ready with advice, and owner Akiko Hoashi uses the menu to impart a few tips on how to order and even how to eat ('Japanese customers tend to make noise when sipping soup'). No children after 8.15. The Dublin *Ayumi-Ya* (qv) is slightly more geared to western tastes. **Seats** 40. *Private Room 25. D only 7-11 (Sun 6-10). Closed 24-26 Dec, Good Friday, 1 Jan. Set D £13.50 (Sun £10.25).* AMERICAN EXPRESS *Access, Diners, Visa.*

Blackrock   Clarets   ↑   £70
Tel 01 288 2008   Fax 01 283 3273   R
63 Main Street Blackrock Co Dublin   Map 23 D4

An unpretentious, comfortable and welcoming restaurant where Alan
O'Reilly offers creative, interesting cooking. There may be a special tasting
menu one week, or a theme menu based on a specific cuisine another, but
there will always be imaginative, carefully cooked food at fair prices.
Mousseline of seafood in a ginger sauce, salad of Stilton and avocado, brill
with scallop mousse and angel hair pasta and fillet of veal on a bed of rösti
with a wild mushroom sauce show the style. Game is a speciality in season;
breads are good, also their tangy lemon tart. **Seats** *50. L 12.30-2.30 D 7-10.
Closed L Sat, all Sun & Mon, Bank Holidays. Set L £10.95 Set D £18.95.*
AMERICAN EXPRESS *Access, Visa.*

Blarney   Blarney Park Hotel   63%   £110
Tel 021 385281   Fax 021 381506   H
Blarney Co Cork   Map 23 B6

About half an hour's drive out of Cork city, this modern, low-rise hotel has
good conference and family facilities, including a particularly well-
equipped leisure centre with a high and winding 40-metre water slide.
Bright, spacious public areas include a recently refurbished lounge area
on two levels, each with its own open fire, with a pleasant outlook over
extensive grounds at the back of the hotel. Bedrooms are organised along
the corridors with good-sized doubles on one side and smallish twins
(especially suitable for children) opposite. Children under two stay free (no
charge for cots), extra beds are available by arrangement; there are fun-
packs provided in children's rooms, a creche operates all year round and
children's entertainment can be arranged at any time when five or more
children are resident. Conference facilities for 350, with an efficient
secretarial service. Nearby attractions include Blarney Castle, with its
famous Blarney Stone and Blarney Woollen Mills. 24hr room service.
No dogs. **Rooms** *76. Garden, indoor swimming pool, children's splash pool,
gym, sauna, steam room, tennis, games room, snooker.* AMERICAN EXPRESS *Access,
Diners, Visa.*

We endeavour to be as up-to-the-minute as possible, but inevitably
some changes to key personnel may occur at restaurants and hotels
after the Guide goes to press.

Blessington   Downshire House   59%   £66
Tel 045 65199   Fax 045 65335   H
Downshire House Blessington Co Wicklow   Map 23 D4

It's difficult not to be charmed by the friendly atmosphere and
unpretentious comfort of this substantial village hotel built in 1800 and run
by Rhoda Byrne since 1959. One enters into the recently refurbished bar-
lounge, where all the seats are small armchairs, before finding the reception
desk at the head of a broad flight of stairs leading down to the function
room – a modern addition. Decoratively modest bedrooms – plain white
walls, candlewick bedspreads, functional fitted furniture – nevertheless offer
all the modern comforts including remote-control TV, hairdryer, direct-
dial phones and beverage kit plus crisp, pure cotton bedding. Bathrooms
are a little dated and boast only unwrapped soap on the toiletries front but,
like the whole hotel, are immaculately kept. **Rooms** *25. Garden, croquet,
tennis. Closed mid Dec-early Jan. Access, Visa.*

Blessington   Place of Interest

Russborough   Tel 045 65239

Boyle   Cromleach Lodge   78%   £118

Tel 071 65155   Fax 071 65455   **HR**

Ballindoon Castlebaldwin nr Boyle Co Sligo   **Map 22 B3**

The views over Lough Arrow from Christy and Moira Tighe's modern,
purpose-built small hotel are almost heart-breakingly beautiful and it has
been designed to make the most of them. Spacious, thoughtfully furnished
rooms all share the wonderful views and are individually decorated and
finished to the highest of international standards, each with queen-size and
single bed, safe, mini-bar, tray with tea- and coffee-making facilities
(including a teapot) and fresh milk always in the fridge, remote-control
TV, comfortable armchairs, writing and dressing areas. In addition to the
usual hairdryer in the room there's a trouser press, ironing board and ice
machine on the landing (a full laundry/ironing service is also offered).
Large, well-lit and thoughtfully appointed, tiled bathrooms have full-size
bath with strong over-bath shower, efficient extraction, piles of big, warm
towels on heated rails and quality toiletries. Standards of housekeeping are
exceptional. Not really suitable for children – Cromleach is really
a carefully honed adult preserve (and all the better for it). *Rooms 10.*
Garden, game fishing, boating. Closed 3 days Christmas, 3 weeks Jan.
AMERICAN EXPRESS *Access, Visa.* MARTELL

Restaurant   ★   £75

The excellent restaurant continues to develop, with a more relaxed air
of confidence now adding to the enjoyment of Moira Tighe's talents in the
kitchen. In addition to the 5-course set dinner menu, an 8-course tasting
menu is prepared daily for residents at the same price, reinforcing this
establishment's well-earned reputation for providing not only excellence,
but also outstanding value for money. The dining areas are beautifully
appointed and immaculately maintained, with crisp linen, elegantly
understated Rosenthal china, silver and modern crystal, while fresh flowers
on the table provide a single, striking splash of colour. Moira Tighe's real
love of cooking shines through in her impeccably sourced ingredients and
talented renditions of great modern classics; she has a rare lightness of touch
– notably in excellent saucing – also seen in the work of pastry chef Sheila
Sharpe, who is producing outstanding results in dishes like tartlet of quail
breasts on armagnac cream – boneless, tender pink-cooked quail
breastsin a little wisp of a featherlight pastry case, set in a pool of pale,
interesting sauce. Simplicity goes gourmet in, for example, a tasting trio
of soups, served in tiny cups and accompanied by a selection of four home-
made breads, and local meat is seen to advantage in creative main courses
like fillet of lamb with crab risotto or fillet of beef with a piquant sauce
of Cashel blue cheese. Organically grown vegetables and side salads, served
separately, are treated with imagination and respect. But Moira's meals are
designed to end on a triumphant note: her desserts are renowned and the
Tasting Selection is specially recommended. No smoking. *Seats 50.*
Parties 12. Private Room 20. L by arrangement D 7-9 (Sun 6.30-8).
Set L £16.95 Set D £29.50.

Boyle   Place of Interest

Clonalis House   Castlerea Tel 0907 20014 *15 miles*

Bray   Tree of Idleness   £65

Tel 01 286 3498   **R**

Seafront Bray Co Wicklow   **Map 23 D4**

The original Tree of Idleness was situated in Bellapais, Cyprus, with views
of the coastline and the hillside citrus groves. This one, on the seafront
at Bray, continues the Greek-Cypriot tradition and in the capable hands

of owner Susan Courtellas and chef Ismail Basaran is firmly established among Ireland's favourite restaurants. Dips and dolmades, moussaka and souvlaki, halloumi and calamares account for only part of the menu, and other choices include spinach ravioli filled with crab mousse served with a carrot sauce, chicken saffron, roast pheasant with grapes and chestnuts and fillet steak with a red wine sauce and truffles. Supplementing the à la carte menu is a table d'hote (not available Saturday), the latter's whose price depends on the main course. A truly exceptional wine list with a huge choice, especially among red bordeaux; most wine-producing regions are covered and the top growers are chosen; ports include some from the Russian Massandra collection. *Seats* 50. *Parties* 25. D only 7.30-11 (Sun to 10). *Closed Mon, Bank Holidays, 1 week Christmas, 2 weeks Sep. Set D from £17.* AMERICAN EXPRESS® *Access, Diners, Visa.*

Bray   Place of Interest

Killruddery House and Gardens   Tel 01 286 3405

Bunclody   Clohamon House   £80
Tel 054 77253   Fax 054 77956   PH
Bunclody Co Wexford   Map 23 C5

Set in 180 acres of rolling farmland in the scenic Slaney valley, with a wonderful view across the River Slaney to Mount Leinster, Sir Richard and Lady Levinge's enchanting 18th-century family home is a haven backed by beechwoods and gardens with many rare trees and shrubs. Graciously proportioned rooms are enhanced by family furniture and portraits going back over 250 years, but there is a lovely family atmosphere as guests gather at the fireside in the chintzy drawing room for drinks, knowing that Maria Levinge is in the kitchen whipping up one of her wonderfully imaginative dinners, to be served at an elegant, polished table lit by candle-light. Thoughtfully decorated rooms vary, but have a full complement of antiques and characterful bathrooms complete with toiletries; comfortable beds are turned down as you dine and a very good chocolate left on the pillow. On the premises, Connemara ponies are a major interest – Maria manages an internationally renowned stud – and there is a private stretch of salmon and trout fishing on the Slaney. Self-catering accommodation in converted outbuildings includes a barn which is suitable for the disabled. Dogs welcome – kennels provided. Busy around the time of the Wexford Opera Festival in late Oct/early Nov. *Rooms 4. Garden, riding, fishing. Closed mid Nov-1 Mar. Access, Visa.*

Bundoran   Le Chateaubrianne   NEW   £55
Tel 072 42160   R
Sligo Road Bundoran Co Donegal   Map 22 B2

Since opening in 1993, Brian and Anne Loughlin's correct, impeccably furnished yet warm, welcoming and family-friendly restaurant has made quite an impact on the north-west dining scene. Well-trained staff ensure that everything runs smoothly and Anne makes an excellent hostess, keeping a close eye on the comfort of guests from the moment they are shown into the bar and presented with daily-changing menus to the moment of reluctant departure. Comfortable chairs and well-appointed tables – white linen over a colourful undercloth, linen napkins, quality cutlery and fine, plain glasses – provide an appropriate setting for Brian Loughlin's fine food. Typically, a tartelette of baby mushroom and smoked bacon in a creamy garlic sauce might see a light, crisp pastry case piled high with lightly-cooked mushroom quarters and crunchy diced smoked bacon in a sauce with a good bite of garlic in it. Local ingredients predominate, cooked with a nicely judged balance of simplicity and imagination, as in Donegal lamb on a bed of wild mushrooms with a rosemary jus – a thick slice, served pink and juicy with a light, herby stuffing, the piquancy of rosemary and the richness of the mushrooms complementing the meat without dominating. Seafood is handled with similar flair, and imaginatively cooked, plentiful vegetables are left on the table in their serving dishes. Good desserts range from homely puddings (such as an individual, steamed dark chocolate pudding set in a pool of orange chocolate sauce) to classic crème brulée served on a fruit compote. Delicious cafetière coffee and petits fours. *Seats 45. Parties 14. Private Room 20. L 12.30-2.30 D 6.30-10. Closed Tues in winter, 1st two weeks Nov. Set L £10 Set D £17.50. Access, Visa.*

Bunratty   Fitzpatricks Shannon Shamrock   60%   £137
Tel 061 361177   Fax 061 471252   **H**
Bunratty Co Clare   Map 23 B4

A low-rise modern hotel alongside Bunratty Castle with a leisure centre and banqueting facilities for up to 150. Only four miles from Shannon airport, this would make a good base for touring Clare and the Burren; children under 12 charged £5 if sharing parents' room. *Rooms 115. Indoor swimming pool, sauna, steam room. Closed 25 Dec.* AMERICAN EXPRESS *Access, Diners, Visa.*

Bunratty   MacCloskey's   £70
Tel 061 364082   **R**
Bunratty House Mews Bunratty Co Clare   Map 23 B4

Gerry and Marie MacCloskey have established a successful formula over a dozen years at their atmospheric restaurant in the cellars of 17th-century Bunratty House. A five-course fixed-price menu offers straightforward dishes such as asparagus beurre blanc, grilled kidneys on a bed of braised onions, cod with parsley and lemon butter, duck with orange sauce and steak with green peppercorns. Icky sticky pudding, passion fruit mousse or honey and lime cheesecake to finish. *Seats 60. Private Room 22. D only 7-10. Closed Sun & Mon, 20 Dec-25 Jan, Good Friday. Set D £28.50. Access, Visa.*

Bunratty   Place of Interest
Bunratty Castle and Folk Park   Tel 061 361511

Caherdaniel   Derrynane Hotel   62%   £70
Tel 066 75136   Fax 066 75160   **HR**
Caherdaniel Co Kerry   Map 23 A6

In a spectacular location on the southern stretch of the Ring of Kerry, this unprepossessing 1960s' hotel offers a warm welcome and good facilities for family holidays. Accommodation is simple but a high standard of housekeeping, good value for money and lovely sea views ensure satisfaction. 12 family rooms have bunk beds; supervised crèche in the evenings. *Rooms 75. Garden, outdoor swimming pool, games room. Closed Oct-Apr.* AMERICAN EXPRESS *Access, Diners, Visa.*

Restaurant   £45

The bar and restaurant overlook the open-air swimming pool and are well placed to take advantage of the magnificent sea views. Good, fresh ingredients are used to produce enjoyable 'home-cooked' food and attractive desserts at very reasonable prices. Children's menu; high-chairs provided. *Seats 100. L 12.30-2 D 7-9. Set L £7.50 Set D £18.50.*

Caherdaniel   Loaves & Fishes   £55
Tel 066 75273   **R**
Caherdaniel nr Derrynane Co Kerry   Map 23 A6

Helen Mullane and Armel Whyte set up this charming little restaurant in 1990. The style is comfortably cottagey, with an old range, low ceilings and random plate collection and an interesting little bar/reception area at the back with light filtering through a stained-glass skylight. Armel's imaginative, shortish à la carte menu offers plenty of interest, starting, perhaps, with a platter of smoked wild fish with a cucumber pickle or country terrine of pork with garlic and a tomato and mustard-seed relish (for serious garlic-lovers). Well-balanced main courses include favourites like crab claws on a beurre blanc, sirloin steak and local Kerry lamb, with a rosemary scented potato stuffing and port jus, perhaps, and fish, typically darne of salmon with a creamed Noilly Prat sauce. Good desserts include a tangy lemon tart. *Seats 32. Private Room 12. D only 7-9.30. Closed Mon Jun-Aug, Mon & Tues Sep, Halloween to Easter. Access, Visa.*

Cahirciveen   Brennan's Restaurant   £55

Tel 066 72021   **R**

13 Main Street Cahirciveen Co Kerry   Map 23 A6

The Brennans moved from Castlequin into new premises in the main street in 1993 and, although not totally settled in on the evening of a recent inspection, the wagon is starting to roll. The place has a sense of style, menus are interesting and imaginative use of fresh local ingredients seems to be their hallmark. Opening hours have recently been extended, giving owner-chef Conor Brennan a chance to improve the image of daytime food on the Ring of Kerry. *Seats 30. Parties 20. L 12-2.30 D 7-10 snacks 10-5 (except Sundays), early bird dinner 6-7.30. Closed 24-26 Dec, Nov & Feb for dinner. Access, Visa.*

Caragh Lake   Hotel Ard-na-Sidhe   70%   £96

Tel 066 69105   Fax 066 69282   **H**

Caragh Lake nr Killorglin Co Kerry   Map 23 A5

The beautiful lakeside setting and the peace and quiet are major pluses at this splendid Victorian mansion on the edge of Caragh Lake. In the house there are 12 good-sized bedrooms furnished with antiques and a further eight rooms with private patios are available in the garden house (recently refurbished). Sister hotel to *Hotel Europe* (Killarney) and *Dunloe Castle* (Beaufort), whose sporting facilities are available to Ard-na-Sidhe guests. *Rooms 20. Garden, game fishing. Closed Oct-Apr.* AMERICAN EXPRESS *Access, Diners, Visa.*

Caragh Lake   Caragh Lodge   65%   £99

Tel 066 69115   Fax 066 69316   **H**

Caragh Lake nr Killorglin Co Kerry   Map 23 A5

Owner Mary Gaunt is in personal charge at this Victorian fishing lodge, which stands in delightful gardens on the shore of Caragh Lake. Boating, fishing and swimming are favourite pastimes, there's a tennis court in the grounds and five championship golf courses are a short drive away. Peaceful antique-furnished day rooms. Bedrooms in main house or garden cottages. Small dogs allowed with prior notice. *Rooms 10. Garden, sauna, tennis, game fishing, rowing boat, bicycles. Closed mid Oct-Easter. Access, Visa.*

Carlingford   Jordan's Bar & Restaurant   £55

Tel 042 73223   **R**

Carlingford Co Louth   Map 22 D3

Harry and Marian Jordan take turns in the kitchen of their warmly decorated restaurant, but the day always starts with a baking session to produce their delicious brown soda bread and white yeast rolls. Menus are nicely balanced between the traditional and modern, and local produce is used wherever possible. They grow their own herbs and even produce their own butter. Typical dishes run from terrine of fresh salmon, pigeon breast with a herb salad and natural, baked or jellied oysters to hake with samphire sauce, crubeens (pig's trotters) and shank of lamb wrapped in puff pastry and accompanied by a rosemary sauce. Half the wines are priced at under £12.50. Seven letting bedrooms (£48 for 2) with period-style pine furniture, lough views and business facilities came on stream last summer. No smoking. *Seats 34. Parties 12. Private Room 16. L (Sun only) 12.30-2.30 D 7-10. Closed 25 & 26 Dec, 2 weeks mid Jan. Set L £12 Set D £19.50.* AMERICAN EXPRESS *Access, Diners, Visa.*

Carlingford   Place of Interest

Carlingford Castle

Carne   Lobster Pot   £50

Tel 053 31110   Fax 053 31401   **R**

Carne Co Wexford   **Map 23 D5**

Long and low outside, cosy and comfortable within, the Lobster Pot is restaurant, bar and pub rolled into one. The menu sticks mainly to familiar seafood dishes, from prawn cocktail to grilled or poached wild salmon, pan-fried Dover sole, seafood mornay and lobster from the tank. Also a 'landlubber's choice' of chicken, crispy duck and various steaks. Smoking discouraged. Tables outside in the summer. *Seats 28. Parties 16. Private Room 30. L 12.30-2.30 (Sun only Sep-end May) D 6-9. Bar Menu all day. Closed L Mon-Sat also L Sun Jun-Sep (except bar meals), D Tue-Sat in winter, Good Friday, 25 Dec, all Jan.* AMERICAN EXPRESS *Access, Visa.*

Carrick-on-Shannon   Hollywell House   £50

Tel & Fax 078 21124   **PH**

Liberty Hill Carrick-on-Shannon Co Leitrim   **Map 22 B3**

Just across the bridge at Carrick-on-Shannon, with lovely views down through the garden to the river, this fine period house offers comfortable en-suite rooms furnished with antiques (two with river views), but it is Tom and Rosaleen Maher's hospitality which makes Hollywell outstanding. Good breakfasts, with home-made bread and preserves, but no evening meals except by special arrangement. No dogs. *Rooms 3. Garden, fishing. Closed 16 Dec-10 Jan. No credit cards.*

Carrick-on-Shannon   Places of Interest

Lough Rynn Estate and Gardens   Mohill Tel 078 31427 *10 miles*
Strokestown Park House   Strokestown Tel 078 33013 *12 miles*

Carrickmacross   Nuremore Hotel   72%   £120

Tel 042 61438   Fax 042 61853   **H**

Carrickmacross Co Monaghan   **Map 22 C3**

The championship-length golf course is a great attraction at this modern low-rise hotel on the N2, and last Summer saw the opening of a brand new pavilion with bar, snack menu and changing facilities. Many of the bright, airy bedrooms overlook a lake. Banqueting for up to 500, conferences for 300 theatre-style. No dogs. *Rooms 69. Garden, indoor swimming pool, gymnasium, squash, sauna, spa bath, solarium, tennis, golf (18), games room.* AMERICAN EXPRESS *Access, Diners, Visa.*

Carrigtwohill   Niblicks   £38

Tel 021 883667   **R**

Fota Island Golf Club Carrigtwohill Co Cork   **Map 23 B6**

Take the Cobh turning off the N25 about five miles east of Cork to find the club house, converted from an old farm, of a new golf course within which, under a barn-like roof, is an informal restaurant run by Michael Ryan (brother of Declan at *Arbutus Lodge*). The menu makes no formal distinction between starters and main dishes though some can be either and are dual priced. An eclectic selection ranges from seafood chowder, a plate of tapas and hot New York steak sandwich to fettucine with wild mushrooms and grilled salmon with chive and white wine sauce. Puds include the likes of millefeuille of passion fruit and cassis ice cream, and yoghurt and cardamom cream with orange confit. The menu gets a bit shorter after 3pm and dinner, in similar style, is served only on Friday and Saturday. Roast lamb usually features at Sunday lunch. A balcony overlooking an ornamental lake makes an ideal spot for summer eating. The style of the menu makes it easy to eat for considerably less than the price for two quoted above. *Seats 100. L 12.30-6 D 6.30-9.30 (Fri & Sat only). Closed D Sun-Thurs, 25 & 26 Dec.* AMERICAN EXPRESS *Access, Diners, Visa.*

Cashel	Cashel House	76%	£145
Tel 095 31001 Fax 095 31077			**HR**
Cashel Co Galway			Map 22 A3

Standing in secluded beauty at the head of Cashel Bay, the Victorian house is set in award-winning gardens running down to a private beach. Dermot and Kay McEvilly have been the welcoming, professional hosts since 1968, and their hotel won instant renown a year later when General and Madame de Gaulle stayed for two weeks. Turf and log fires add a cosy glow to the gracious day rooms, where antiques and fresh flowers take the eye. Bedrooms are individually decorated, and the Garden Suite rooms are particularly stylish, with separate seating areas and access to the patio. Service is excellent and breakfast includes a wide range of home-made produce, from soda bread and marmalade to black pudding. *Rooms 32. Garden, tennis, sea & game fishing, boating, horse riding (inc dressage). Closed 10-31 Jan.* AMERICAN EXPRESS *Access, Diners, Visa.*

Restaurant £70

Fixed-price five-course dinners in the sunny restaurant feature the best of home-grown and local produce prepared without undue elaboration or fuss. From a typical winter menu you might choose garlic mussels, smoked salmon or veal and quail terrine to start, then one of two soups, a sorbet, and scallop-stuffed sole, salmon with leek sauce, lobster (£7.20 per pound supplement) or roast sirloin of beef with béarnaise sauce. Home-made ice cream and tarte tatin are sweet alternatives to a selection of Irish cheeses. Lunch in the bar. *Seats 70. Parties 12. Private Room 10. L 1-2 (in the bar) D 7.30-8.30 (Sun 7.30-9). Set D from £28.*

Cashel	Chez Hans	£70
Tel 062 61177		**R**
Rockside Cashel Co Tipperary		Map 23 C5

Seafood features strongly on the menu at this former Wesleyan chapel at the foot of the Rock of Cashel, but meat-eaters are in no way the poor relations! Hans-Peter Matthià puts a contemporary stamp on classic recipes: escalope of salmon with a lemon butter sauce, gratin of Dublin Bay prawns with mangetout and a saffron sauce, breast of free-range chicken with Cashel Blue cheese and leek sabayon. Other favourites, simple and straightforward, include oak-smoked salmon, Rossmore oysters, sole meunière and steak with a peppercorn sauce. *Seats 60. D only 6.30-10. Closed Sun & Mon, Bank Holidays, 3 weeks Jan. Access, Visa.*

Cashel	Zetland House	65%	£115
Tel 095 31111 Fax 095 31117			**H**
Cashel Co Galway			Map 22 A3

On the edge of Cashel Bay, Zetland House was a sporting lodge when built in the early 19th century. It's still a favoured base for outdoor pursuits, notably fishing and rough shooting. Cosy sitting rooms; most bedrooms have spectacular sea views. *Rooms 20. Garden, croquet, tennis, fishing, snooker. Closed Nov-Easter.* AMERICAN EXPRESS *Access, Diners, Visa.*

Cashel   Places of Interest

Cahir Castle Cahir Tel 052 41011
GPA Bolton Library   Tel 062 61944
Thurles Racecourse   Tel 0504 22253 *16 miles*

Castleconnell   Castle Oaks House Hotel   64%   £72

Tel 061 377666 Fax 061 377717	**H**
Castleconnell Co Limerick	Map 2 B5

In the picturesque waterside village of Castleconnell, six miles from
Limerick off the Dublin road, this attractive, well-located hotel makes
an excellent venue for local functions, but is of special interest to fisherfolk
as it has its own stretch of the River Shannon that runs alongside well-
maintained woodland paths in the grounds. Public areas in the hotel are
nicely proportioned – notably the pretty blue and yellow dining room,
a pleasant breakfast location. Bedrooms vary considerably in size and
appointments, ranging from elegant and spacious with half-tester bed and
garden view to a rather cramped double with a dated bathroom and
overlooking a flat roof, but it is generally a comfortable hotel, with helpful
staff and a family-friendly attitude. There's an exceptionally well-equipped
leisure centre (creche Mon-Fri 10-2) in the large wooded grounds, plus
a large complex of 24 self-catering holiday houses. Banqueting/conference
for 300/350; parking for 200. 24hr room service. No dogs. *Rooms 11.
Garden, indoor swimming pool, solarium, sauna, spa bath, steam room, beauty
salon, tennis, pitch & putt, fishing. Closed 25 Dec.* AMERICAN EXPRESS *Access,
Diners, Visa.*

Castledermot   Kilkea Castle   70%   £225

Tel 0503 45156 Fax 0503 45187	**H R**
Kilkea Castledermot Co Kildare	Map 23 C4

The oldest inhabited castle in Ireland, Kilkea was built in 1180 by Hugh
de Lacy. Steeped in history, it has been renovated and converted with skill
and sensitivity that allow it to retain its inherent elegance and grandeur.
Rooms, many with wonderful views over the formal gardens and
surrounding countryside, are splendidly furnished to incorporate modern
comforts in a manner appropriate to their age and style and the adjoining
leisure centre, although architecturally discreet, offers state-of-the-art
facilities. Outdoor sports include clay pigeon shooting, archery, tennis
and fishing on the nearby River Greese. An 18-hole championship golf
course was due to open in September 1994. *Rooms 40. Garden, tennis,
indoor swimming pool, sauna, jacuzzi, steam room, sun bed, gymnasium.
Closed 4-5 days Christmas.* AMERICAN EXPRESS *Access, Diners, Visa.*

De Lacy's   £75

The first-floor restaurant is appropriately grand with magnificent views
over the countryside and a bright, airy atmosphere. Scottish chef George
Smith has a distinctive style and the lengthy descriptions on the menu give
an indication of the complexity of what is to follow. But the quality
of ingredients shines through and, in specialities such as the roast of the day,
there are excellent simpler alternatives available. Local produce features
strongly, much of it taken from the gardens below, where guests can take
coffee in summer and wander around to see the old fruit trees, vegetables
and herbs. Salads and vegetables are a speciality and desserts beautiful and
sophisticated, to match their surroundings. Typical main-course dishes
include salmon topped with a fish mousseline, wrapped in pastry, baked
and served with a crayfish sauce, or loin of venison pan-fried with herbs,
carved on rösti glazed with game essence and served with a poached pear.
*Seats 65. Parties 14. L 12.30-2.30 D 7-9.30. Closed 25 Dec. Set L £15
Set D £28.*

Castlelyons — Ballyvolane House

£80

PH

Tel 025 36349   Fax 025 36781

Castlelyons Co Cork

Map 23 B5

This gracious house, set in lovely wooded grounds and surrounded by its own farmland, dates back to 1728 and was modified to its present Italianate style in the mid-19th century. The impressive pillared hall with its baby grand piano sets the tone but, despite the elegance of the house and its period furnishings the owners, Jeremy and Merrie Green, are well known for their special brand of informal hospitality. The atmosphere is very relaxed: well-proportioned reception rooms are warmed by huge log fires, and residents' dinner is cooked by Merrie and taken communally around a lovely mahogany table, with stories relating to the house abounding. Bedrooms vary in size and outlook but all are warm and comfortable, furnished with antiques and with roomy bathrooms en-suite – one has an original Edwardian bath reached by mahogany steps. *Rooms 6. Garden, croquet, fishing.* AMERICAN EXPRESS *Access, Visa.*

Castletownshend — Mary Ann's Bar & Restaurant

£50

R

Tel 028 36146   Fax 028 36377

Castletownshend nr Skibbereen Co Cork

Map 23 B6

The building dates from the 11th century, but Mary Ann's has been in business for a mere 150 years. It's best known for its bar food (served both sessions seven days a week), which runs from sandwiches and salads to sirloin steaks by way of soups, scallops and chicken Kiev. Dinner in the restaurant also has a strong following, with typical choices including seafood tagliatelle, turbot hollandaise en croute, a hot shellfish platter, rack of lamb and fillet of beef with a red wine sauce. The Vine Room in the garden seats 20 and an outdoor stone patio seats a further 90 in good weather. *Seats 50. L 12.30-2.30. D from 6 (restaurant 6.30). Closed Mon Nov-Mar (except Christmas period). Set L £13.50 (winter Sun only) Set D £19.95. Access, Visa.*

Clifden — Abbeyglen Castle   60%

£83

H

Tel 095 21201   Fax 095 21797

Sky Road Clifden Co Galway

Map 22 A3

Take the N59 from Galway City to Clifden, then Sky Road out of Clifden to find the hotel, 300 yards on the left in 12 acres of grounds. Owner Paul Hughes personally welcomes guests, many of whom return year after year, to his crenellated hotel. Steps lead down from the hotel to landscaped gardens and an outdoor pool and tennis court. Public areas include a spacious drawing room for residents and a relaxing pubby bar with open peat fire. Refurbishment continues in the good-sized bedrooms. No children under 10. Local fishing facilities are a major attraction. *Rooms 40. Garden, outdoor swimming pool, sauna, tennis, pitch and putt, snooker, table tennis. Closed 10 Jan-1 Feb.* AMERICAN EXPRESS *Access, Diners, Visa.*

Clifden — Ardagh Hotel   60%

£75

HR

Tel 095 21384   Fax 095 21314

Ballyconneely Road Clifden Co Galway

Map 22 A3

Quiet family-run hotel on the edge of Ardbear Bay, a couple of miles south of Clifden. Day rooms include a roomy and comfortable bar, two lounges and a top-floor sun room. Golf, fishing and riding can be arranged. No dogs. *Rooms 21. Closed Nov-end Mar.* AMERICAN EXPRESS *Access, Diners, Visa.*

See over

Restaurant   £55

The first-floor restaurant has lovely views to add to the enjoyment
of Monique Bauvet's imaginative way with local produce. Farmhouse
terrine with summer fruits, seafood chowder, saffron-sauced brill, lobster
(grilled fresh from the tank) and pot-roasted rack of spring lamb show
their style. Lighter meals in the bar. *Seats 50. Parties 30. D only 7.15-9.30.
Set D from £23.*

Clifden   Destry Rides Again   £40

Tel 095 21722   **R**

Clifden Co Galway   **Map 22 A3**

Decor at the Foyles' entertaining little restaurant (named after a Marlene
Dietrich film) is predictably wacky – an old Georgian fanlight decorates
one wall and has a real skull balanced on top, a collection of silver food
domes and a variety of 'boys in the backroom' memorabilia all create
atmosphere. Dishes on the shortish menu have a modern ring, exemplified
by vermicelli with smoked chicken and mozzarella, chargrilled halibut
with black olives and horseradish, roast Barbary duck with raspberry and
ginger, and grilled pork fillet coated in spices with hot and sour sauce.
Desserts include good home-made ices and a rich 'Lethal Chocolate Pud',
made to a secret recipe. Confident, classy cooking and great fun. Short,
user-friendly, keenly-priced wine list, with plenty available by the glass.
Wheelchair facilities. *Seats 32. Parties 16. L 12-3 D 6-10 (in winter open
only for dinner Thu-Sat 7-9). Access, Visa.*

Clifden   Foyles Hotel   61%   £79

Tel 095 21801   Fax 095 21458   **H**

The Square Clifden Co Galway   **Map 22 A3**

Formerly known as the Clifden Bay Hotel Edmund Foyle (twin brother
of Paddy, see *Quay House*) decided to change the name recently when
a German visitor complained that he could not see the bay from his
window – and high time, too, as it's been owned by, managed by and
home to the Foyle family since 1917. It's a comfortable, friendly,
undemanding, old-fashioned hotel with rooms which are all ensuite but
vary considerably in size and appointments, rather grand corridors and
public areas which were in the process of re-arrangement at the time
of going to press – the bar (where food is available all day) is moving
to the back of the hotel and a new upmarket restaurant is to take its place
beside the front door. The residents' dining room, which opens on to
a sheltered, private courtyard, will remain. *Rooms 30. Closed 1 Nov-Easter
weekend.* AMERICAN EXPRESS *Access, Diners, Visa.*

Clifden   O'Grady's Seafood Restaurant   £50

Tel 095 21450   **RR**

Market Street Clifden Co Galway   **Map 22 A3**

Mike O'Grady's traditional seafood restaurant has well-spaced tables, some
in alcoves but all with a degree of privacy. Try starting with a speciality
like Jack's smoked fish bisque – smooth, creamy but with just the right
amount of texture and smokiness to be interesting, served with a choice
of good home-made white yeast bread or wholemeal soda. Sophisticated
main courses from a wide choice, predominantly but not exclusively
seafood, on the à la carte dinner menu might include grilled fillet of turbot
with a compote of rhubarb and champagne butter cream or best end
of lamb on a jus of wild mushrooms with a hint of pesto, while lunch
offerings are simpler – marinière-style mussels, perhaps, or braised kidneys
with a creamy mushroom and pink peppercorn sauce. Follow with 'sinful
desserts' or farmhouse cheese. An informal piano bistro serves one-plate
specialities. No children under 5. *Seats 50. Parties 21. Private Room 12.
L 12.30-2.30 D 6.30-10. Closed Sun (Mar-Jun), Feb-mid Mar.
Set L £6/£8.95 Set D £12/£18.* AMERICAN EXPRESS *Access, Visa.*

Rooms £36

Accommodation is of a high standard with eleven en-suite bedrooms available nearby in Sunnybank House. Gardens, outdoor swimming pool, sauna and tennis. Tel 095 21437 for details.

Clifden   The Quay House   NEW £50

Tel 095-21369   **RR**

Beach Road Clifden Co Galway   Map 22 A3

Paddy and Julia Foyle (*Rosleague Manor, Destry Rides Again*) seem finally to have put down roots at this lovely quayside restaurant with rooms. Simultaneously elegant and delightfully wacky (who else would hang one of an otherwise sobre set of prints upside down?), there's a comfortable drawing room for aperitifs and chat, with newly-added conservatory off it for afternoon teas and such, while the restaurant itself comprises two rooms across the hall which can be opened up or separate, but is nicest as one space so that the unusual triangular fireplace halfway up the far end wall can be enjoyed by all (a thoughtfully placed mirror makes this possible from most angles). Paddy and Julia supervise service, while Dermot Gannon, who moved down with them from *Destry*, turns out little gems like deep-fried calamari with chili and grilled pepper salad or sautéed lamb's kidneys and sweetbreads with red onion confit, served with a choice of wholemeal yeast bread and focaccia, fresh from the Aga. Seafood is the star, of course, as in chargrilled halibut with tarragon and garlic butter, but local meats are not overlooked – Connemara lamb is always a winner, typically roasted with wild thyme and garlic, but also beef which is carefully sourced from a Midland farmer and transformed into something like 'prime steer beef fillet, flame-grilled, with Italian potato cakes'. Finish, perhaps, with a dessert such as Lethal Chocolate Pudding, a secret invention imported from *Destry*. **Seats** 70. *Parties* 10. *Private Room 30. L 12-3 D 7-9.30. Closed 2 weeks Christmas, Sun & Mon Oct-Apr. Set D £19.50 ('Highdays & Holidays only'). Access, Visa.*

Rooms £50

Six lovely airy, stylishly decorated rooms with large individualistic bathrooms are available for weary diners to retire to. Front ones enjoy a quayside outlook, with or without water depending on the tide, while others overlook gardens. Children under 7 may stay free in their parents' room and an early evening meal is available by arrangement.

Clifden   Rock Glen Manor   67% £90

Tel 095 21035   Fax 095 21737   **HR**

Ballyconneely Road Clifden Co Galway   Map 22 A3

A mile and a half from Clifden on the Ballyconneely road, this lovely, restful 19th-century shooting lodge is tucked away over a secluded anchorage in what must surely be one of the most beautiful hotel locations in Ireland. John and Evangeline Roche, who have owned Rock Glen for over 20 years, describe it as "an oasis of tranquillity" and they are right. Comfortable, chintz-covered sofas and chairs in front of a welcoming turf fire tempt guests into a drawing room which, along with the bar and conservatory area beside it, enjoys lovely hill and sea views. Fourteen of the rooms, all in a regular ongoing programme of improvement and refurbishment, are on the ground floor and the standard of comfort is high throughout. Golf, horse riding, fishing, mountain climbing and beaches are all available nearby. Children welcome "if well behaved". No dogs. *Rooms 29. Garden, croquet, tennis, putting green, fishing, snooker. Closed end Oct-mid Mar.* AMERICAN EXPRESS *Access, Diners, Visa.*

Restaurant £60

Clever use of mirrors creates a feeling of spaciousness in this pleasant, traditionally decorated room and uniformed staff move swiftly to ensure that every comfort has been anticipated. Meanwhile, John Roche prepares local produce such as mussels steamed in the shell and served with white wine and spring onion sauce, perhaps, followed by freshly caught fish, typically John Dory, simply grilled and served on a shrimp sauce, or Connemara lamb with rosemary and mint. Finish off with a banana crème brulée, perhaps, or a plate of farmhouse cheeses. Next morning's breakfast sees the room transformed, with fresh juice and freshly baked brown bread on the table and a very fine breakfast menu to choose from, including a selection of fish and a vegetarian breakfast. Informal bar snacks served from 12 to 5. No smoking. *Seats 60. Parties 10. Private Room (alcove) 10. D only 7-9. Set D £22. Closed end Oct-mid Mar.*

Clifden   Place of Interest

Connemara National Park   Tel 095 41054

Clonmel   Clonmel Arms   61%   £86

Tel 052 21233   Fax 052 21526   **H**

Sarsfield Street Conmel Co Tipperary   **Map 23 C5**

Some of the bedrooms at the town-centre Clonmel Arms are suitable for family occupation, and children under 12 can stay free in their parents' room. There are extensive banqueting and conference facilities (for up to 600), two restaurants and two bars. *Rooms 31. Terrace, coffee shop (10am-10pm). Closed 25 Dec.* AMERICAN EXPRESS *Access, Diners, Visa.*

Clonmel   Places of Interest

Ormond Castle   Carrick-on-Suir Tel 051 40787
Clonmel Racecourse   Powerstown Park Tel 052 22611

Collooney   Glebe House   £45

Tel 071 67787   **RR**

Collooney Co Sligo   **Map 22 B2**

Marc and Brid Torrades rescued Glebe House from dereliction to open it as a restaurant in 1990 and, while it does not yet have the level of sophistication that many of the established country houses have achieved, their warmth of hospitality and willingness to please are likely to win the hearts of many a guest. Judging by their performance to date, each passing year will see big improvements. Chef Brid uses the best of local produce in hearty, generous dishes such as duck rillettes with onion marmalade or smoked salmon in a dill sauce topped by a featherlight fleuron of puff pastry followed, perhaps, by paupiettes of lemon sole stuffed with colourful julienne vegetables or a vegetarian pancake in a light mustard sauce. Good vegetables are served up in dishes left on the table for guests to help themselves. Classic desserts include a surprise dessert plate; balanced selection of French and Irish farmhouse cheeses. *Seats 35. Parties 20. Private Room 30. L by arrangement D 6.30-9.30. Set D £16.25. Closed 2 weeks (perhaps Jan).*

Rooms   £30

Accommodation is available in four spacious, individually decorated rooms, all en suite, two with baths. *Garden.*

Collooney   Markree Castle   60%   £97

Tel 071 67800   Fax 071 67840   **H**

Collooney Co Sligo   **Map 22 B2**

Charles Cooper, the 10th generation of his family to live in Markree, has made a fine job of restoring pride and splendour to a castle which had for some years been empty and neglected. Space and character both abound, the place is well heated (huge fires everywhere) and there's a beautiful dining room with some exquisite Italian plasterwork. The views are superb, and the setting, in meadows, woods and gardens reaching to the river Unsin, guarantees peace and quiet. They serve an excellent afternoon tea. *Rooms 15. Garden, fishing, riding. Closed Feb.* AMERICAN EXPRESS *Access, Diners, Visa.*

Cong	Ashford Castle	88%	£270

Tel 092 46003   Fax 092 46260

HR

Cong Co Mayo

Map 22 B3

With its origins dating back to the early 13th century and set amid 350 acres of magnificent parkland (including a golf course) on the nothern shores of Lough Corrib, this splendid castle has been lovingly restored – its recent history is depicted for all to see by photographic and written memorabilia displayed in various parts of the building. Throughout, there's rich panelling, intricately carved balustrades, suits of armour and fine paintings. Whether you wish to relax in the elegant drawing room, wander around the halls and galleries, or retire to the Dungeon Bar after dinner and listen to the delightful Annette Griffin singing traditional Irish folk songs and playing the harp to the accompaniment of Carol Coleman's piano, there's a unique atmosphere throughout. Managing Director Rory Murphy has been in situ for over 20 years and, with the assistance of William (Bill) Bucklcy, runs a truly fine hotel, backed up by excellent professional and committed staff. Spacious bedrooms (including several suites) offer attractive views and every conceivable luxury, from flowers and fresh fruit on arrival to slippers, bathrobes and Molton Brown toiletries in the splendid bathrooms; throughout the rooms you'll find period furniture, fine fabrics and superb housekeeping that includes a turn-down service. Discreet conference facilities (several EEC ministerial conferences have been held here) accommodate up to 110 theatre-style and 75 for banquets. The hotel is committed to excellence, in standards of both service and ambience. *Dromoland Castle* in Newmarket-on-Fergus (see entry) is a sister hotel. *Rooms 83. Garden, croquet, golf (9), tennis, equestrian centre, jaunting-car, fishing, lake cruising, bicycles, boutique, snooker.* AMERICAN EXPRESS *Access, Diners, Visa.*

Connaught Room   ↑

£110

Part of the original Georgian House built in 1715, the handsome, panelled dining room with chandeliers and vast windows is only open at night and is sometimes used for theme evenings. Executive chef Denis Lenihan presides over both restaurants (see George V below) and here presents an à la carte menu with supplementary daily specials. Meat and poultry are sourced from local farms, so you can rely on the quality of raw materials, and fish comes from the West coast. A typical meal might include tartare of lightly smoked lamb fillet served with tapénade, fillet of turbot with scallops on a parsley dressing and a plate of assorted chocolate desserts. Fine selection of breads, cheeses and good coffee. Service is both caring and supremely professional. There are a few French wines quite reasonably priced for a hotel of this class, though look outside France for the best value. *Seats 40. D only 7-9.30.*

George V Room

£100

A much larger room also with handsome panelling and chandeliers. Service is again outstanding, and here fixed-price menus with several choices in each course are offered. Dinner is usually a five-course affair. Start with poached Cleggan lobster served on a truffle oil dressing, followed by carrot soup, roast rack of Connemara hill lamb and a confit of shallots, finishing with local farmhouse cheeses and a lightly frozen prune and armagnac soufflé. 15% service is added to all prices. *Seats 135. L 1-2.15 D 7-9.30. Set L £19 Set D £34.*

Cong	Place of Interest

Ballinroe Racecourse   Tel 092 41052

We publish annually, so make sure you use the current edition.
It's worth it!

Cork   Arbutus Lodge   70%   £80

Tel 021 501237   Fax 021 502893   **HR**

Montenotte Cork Co Cork   Map 23 B6

Considerable improvements and refurbishment have taken place in most
of the bedrooms at this former home of a Lord Mayor of Cork, high above
the city with views of the River Lee and the surrounding hills. The hotel
gets its name from the Arbutus tree, one of the many rare trees and shrubs
growing in the spectacular terraced gardens. The house is full of genuine
antique furniture (note the four-poster in the Blue Room) and some
marvellous art, both old and new, the modern paintings by Irish artists
much in demand by galleries and museums. Declan and Patsy Ryan, here
since 1961, extend a warm welcome to all their guests, ably backed up by
charming staff. Whether you choose to relax in the cosy lounge or the
panoramic bar with its own terrace, you'll feel at home and the cleverly
designed and smartly decorated bedrooms, utilising all possible space,
provide both comfort and tranquillity. Bathrooms boast quality towels,
bathrobes and toiletries and you'll start the day with as good a breakfast
as you'll encounter anywhere. Conference facilities for up to 120.
Rooms 20. Garden, tennis. *Access, Diners, Visa.*

Restaurant   ★   £80

Alongside Myrtle Allen (see entry for *Ballymaloe House*), Declan Ryan has
trained and brought on more chefs in this country than anyone. Back
in the kitchen from early morning until service commences, he has
currently moulded together an enthusiastic young team headed by the
talented Helen Ward, who is just 21! Here is a restaurant that has remained
loyal to its roots – no slavish copying of French trends but a reliance
on local produce including herbs and soft fruit from the hotel's own garden
and traditional Cork dishes – spicy beef, tripe and drisheen. Game in season
and the freshest of fish are also a feature (inspect the seafood tank in the
bar) and always a fine example of the kitchen's style is the nightly-
changing, seven-course tasting menu – no mini-portions, but enough
to satisfy the hungriest of souls – spiced beef and mushroom filo parcels,
nage of scallops and prawns, escalope of salmon on sorrel sauce, very tender
roast mallard with blackcurrants, finishing with chocolate and rum log
or gargantuan floating islands. Ask for the ingredients of the 'fence reducer
sorbet', sometimes served as a palate cleanser! Service is as caring and
professional as you'll find anywhere, the cheeseboard promotes Irish cheeses
in tip-top condition, and the sweet trolley will tempt even the faint-
hearted. A variety of breads is baked on the premises daily, and the wine
list has been lovingly nurtured for three decades. Years ago, on his wine
trips to France, Declan discovered several fine and relatively unknown
growers from whom he still buys. *Seats 50. Parties 30. Private Room 25.
L 1-2 D 7-9.30. Closed Sun, 1 week Christmas. Set L £14.50
Set D £21.50/£27.75.*

Cork   Bully's   £25

Tel 021 273555   Fax 021 273427   **R**

40 Paul Street Cork Co Cork   Map 23 B6

Pizzas from the wood-burning oven are one of the specialities of Eugene
Buckley's popular little place. They come in a dozen varieties, top of the
range being Bully's special – a half-folded version with bolognese sauce,
ham, onion and mushrooms. Also on the menu are home-made pasta, grills,
omelettes and seafood dishes. Also at Douglas Village, Co Cork. Tel 021
892415; and Bishops Town. Tel 021 546838. *Seats 40. Parties 20. Meals
12-11.30. Closed 25 & 26 Dec, Good Friday. No credit cards.*

Cork   Cliffords   ★   £70

Tel 021 275333   **R**

18 Dyke Parade Cork Co Cork   **Map 23 B6**

Style and quality are the keynotes here, in terms not only of cooking but
also of service and decor. The building itself, once the civic library,
is Georgian, but the whole place has been elegantly modernised, and
Michael and Deirdre Clifford's collection of contemporary Irish art adorns
the walls. The dining area is striking in its simplicity, with comfortable
high-back chairs, high-quality linen and single flowers floating in glass
bowls. Michael's cooking is controlled and confident, with inventive use
of the best of local produce. The dinner menu changes monthly, though
some specialities put in regular appearances. Typifying his style are a warm
salad of grilled scallops with an aubergine mousse, Clonakilty black
pudding with poached free-range egg, cabbage and smoked kassler, velouté
of celeriac and wild mushrooms, monkfish tails 'en papillote' with ginger
and spring onions and pan-fried fillet of beef with braised salsify and a rich
Fleurie sauce. There's always a fresh fish of the day, plus game in season and
some very hard-to-resist chocolate desserts. Provided you don't drink
vintage first-growth clarets, the modest wine list is reasonably priced.
Seats 40. Parties 10. Private Room 20. L 12.30-2.30 D 7.30-10.30.
Closed L Sat & Mon, all Sun, Bank Holidays, 2 weeks Aug. Set L £13.50
Set D £29. AMERICAN EXPRESS *Access, Diners, Visa.*

> If we recommend meals in a hotel or inn a separate entry is made for its
> restaurant.

Cork   Crawford Gallery Café   £45

Tel 021 274415   **R**

Emmet Place Cork Co Cork   **Map 23 B6**

In the city centre next to the Opera House, this is an offshoot of the
renowned Ballymaloe House at Shanagarry. Ballymaloe desserts, ice cream
or petits fours round off a meal whose centrepiece could be chicken pie,
braised lamb with colcannon or the day's catch from Ballycotton. Snackier
items include bruschetta and open sandwiches. Also open for breakfast.
Seats 70. Private Room 200. Meals Mon-Sat 9-5. Closed Sun, Bank Holidays,
1 week Christmas. Access, Visa.

Cork   Fitzpatrick Silver Springs   65%   £107

Tel 021 507533   Fax 021 507641   **H**

Tivoli Cork Co Cork   **Map 23 B6**

On the side of a steep hill overlooking the river and the main Dublin road,
about 2 miles out of town, the modern Silver Springs is also a major
convention centre with a large, up-to-date facility built in 1990 a little
further up the hill above the hotel (banqueting for 750, conferences
up to 1000). Even further up the hill are an extensive leisure centre and
nine-hole golf course. Within, the hotel public areas are spacious and
include a large public bar with live music from Thursday to Sunday
evenings. Recently refurbished bedrooms, all double-glazed, have
lightwood fitted furniture, good easy chairs and practical bathrooms. 'Club'
rooms are larger and there are two 'full' and three 'junior' antique-furnished
suites. 24hr room service. Children under 12 share their parents' room
at no charge. No dogs. *Rooms 109. Garden, indoor swimming pool,*
gymnasium, aerobic studio, solarium, sauna, spa bath, steam room, 9-hole golf
course, squash, indoor & outdoor tennis, snooker, helipad, courtesy coach.
Closed 25 Dec. AMERICAN EXPRESS *Access, Diners, Visa.*

Cork   Flemings   £55

Tel 021 821621   Fax 021 821800   **RR**

Silver Grange House Tivoli Cork Co Cork   Map 23 B6

Just a short drive from Cork on the Dublin road, Flemings is a large Georgian family house standing in five acres of gardens. Those acres include a kitchen garden which provides much of the fruit, vegetables and herbs needed in the restaurant, a light, handsome double room with marble fireplaces, comfortably upholstered chairs and well-dressed waiters. Michael Fleming's cooking is French, his menus sometimes fractured French with English translations: timbale of fish and shellfish in an orange and champagne sauce, confit of smoked chicken, pan-fried scallops with a lemon and ginger-flavoured white wine sauce, rich venison stew with vegetables and herbs garnished with gnocchi. Always a roast at Sunday lunchtime. Not a lengthy wine list, but it's full of choice bottles and the best growers. *Seats* 50. *Parties* 22. *Private Room* 36. *L* 12.30-2.30 *D* 6.30-11. *Set L* £12.50 *Set D* £20. *Closed Good Friday, 24-26 Dec.* AMERICAN EXPRESS *Access, Diners, Visa.*

Rooms   £55

Accommodation is available in four spacious rooms, comfortably furnished in a style appropriate to the age and graciousness of the house. All have en-suite bathrooms. *Garden.*

Cork   Forte Travelodge   £42

Tel 021 310722   Fax 021 310707   **L**

Jct South Ring Road/Kinsale Road Cork Airport Blackash Co Cork   Map 23 B6

1½ miles south of Cork city centre on the main airport road, 1 mile from it. The room rate of £31.95 (without breakfast) could include up to 3 adults, a child under 12 and a baby in a cot. One room is suitable for disabled guests. *Rooms* 40. AMERICAN EXPRESS *Access, Diners, Visa.*

Cork   Imperial Hotel   66%   £121

Tel 021 274040   Fax ext 2507   **H**

South Mall Cork Co Cork   Map 23 B6

On the main commercial and banking street of town the Imperial's neo-classical facade conceals something of a mixture of styles. The marble-floored lobby and some of the bedroom corridors, which feature a number of fine antiques, retain their original 19th-century grandeur, the cocktail bar (with nightly pianist) and restaurant have been given a 1930s' theme and the public bar remembers Cork's history as a shipbuilding centre. Bedrooms, apart from a few that are furnished with antiques in traditional style, are determinedly modern with white fitted units, glass and chrome coffee tables and contemporary lights. About half the rooms have novel wall-mounted 'clothes grooming cabinets' that are designed to deodorise and dewrinkle garments. 12 of the bathrooms have shower and WC only. Room service is available but not advertised. A recent acquisition is secure covered parking for about 80 cars, three minutes' walk from the hotel. *Rooms* 101. *Closed 1 week at Christmas.* AMERICAN EXPRESS *Access, Diners, Visa.*

Cork   Isaacs   £35

Tel 021 503805   **R**

48 MacCurtain Street Cork Co Cork   Map 23 B6

An 18th-century warehouse has been carefully adapted into a fine restaurant serving an eclectic menu conceived by chef Canice Sharkey. Lunchtime brings some snacky items (French bread with ham, cheese and pickle; selection of patés and terrines) but otherwise a fairly similar selection to the evening, including perhaps salad of smoked chicken with apples and home-dried tomatoes, salmon and potato cakes, grilled king prawns and sirloin steak with rosemary and garlic potatoes. Sauternes and olive oil cake with winter fruit salad is an intriguing dessert. Short vegetarian menu. **Seats 90. Parties 30. L 12-2.30 D 6.30-10.30 (Sun to 9).** *Closed L Sun, 5 days Christmas.* AMERICAN EXPRESS *Access, Visa.*

Cork — Ivory Tower Restaurant — £55

Tel 021 274665 — **R**

35 Princes Street Cork Co Cork — **Map 23 B6**

Situated in the first-floor front of a period office building just off one of Cork's main shopping streets. The atmosphere is friendly and informal – bare-board floor, unclothed tables, work of local artists on the walls – and chef/patron Seamus O'Connell's cooking is certainly individualistic. A cassoulet of smoked chicken seemed to have been crossed with Irish stew being full of chunks of root vegetables and arriving in an appetite-challenging bowlful. Mussel, saffron and orange soup was well judged with the orange element nicely subdued; other dishes included peppered shark with ratatouille; smoked salmon sausages, scallops and prawns with red onion beurre blanc; and venison and blackberry osso buco. There are always several vegetarian options. Lunch prices are lower than in the evening. Two or three home-made breads vary from day to day. **Seats 36.** *L 12-4 D 6.30-11. Set D varies, from £14.50. Closed Sun & Mon. No credit cards.*

Cork — Jacques — £55

Tel 021 277387   Fax 021 270634 — **R**

9 Phoenix Street Cork Co Cork — **Map 23 B6**

Jacques has recently been modernised and extended, and table service has replaced the previous self-service arrangement. Nothing has changed on the food side, so the evenings still bring a good choice of dishes both traditional and modern, from garlicky crab claws, warm scallop salad and lamb's kidneys with grapes and croutons to roast duck, bacon-wrapped pheasant, pork Dijon and Eastern-style shark kebab. Simpler lunchtime menu – bruschetta, crostini, soup, open sandwiches, fish cakes, half-a-dozen desserts. **Seats 60. Parties 20. L 11.30-3 D 6-10.30. Closed D Mon, all Sun, Bank Holidays, 10 days Christmas.** AMERICAN EXPRESS *Access, Diners, Visa.*

Prices quoted for the Republic of Ireland are in Irish punts.

Cork — Jurys Hotel — 66% — £140

Tel 021 276622   Fax 021 274477 — **H**

Western Road Cork Co Cork — **Map 23 B6**

Modern low-rise riverside hotel about half a mile from the centre of town on the Killarney road. Public areas include a choice of two bars, both with live music nightly: the convivial, pubby Corks Bar that is popular with locals and a cocktail bar with waterfall feature in the open-plan, split-level restaurant area. Decor in the well-kept bedrooms is gradually being changed from abstract to more appealing floral patterns with matching curtains and quilted bedcovers. TVs are multi-channel with the remote controls rather annoyingly wired to the bedside units. Extras include fruit and mineral water. Good, well-lit bathrooms all have vanity units, sometimes in white marble, offering good shelf space. Room service is 24hr and beds are turned down at night. Conference/banqueting facilities for 700/520. No dogs. **Rooms 185.** *Garden, indoor & outdoor swimming pool, children's splash pool, keep-fit equipment, sauna, spa bath, squash. Coffee shop (7am-11pm).* AMERICAN EXPRESS *Access, Diners, Visa.*

Cork   Lotamore House   60%   £48

Tel 021 822344   **H**

Tivoli Cork Co Cork   Map 23 B6

Once the home of the Cudmore family, a large house only a few minutes' drive from the city centre; set in mature gardens which soften the view over what is now a commercial harbour. Although not grand, the house was built on a large scale with airy bedrooms that have slightly dated but well-maintained bathrooms and are comfortably furnished to sleep three, with room for an extra bed or cot (no extra charge). A large drawing room has plenty of armchairs and an open fire and, although only breakfast and light meals are offered, Fleming's Restaurant (see entry) is next door. Conference facilities for up to 20. **Rooms** *20. Garden.* *Closed 2 weeks Christmas.* AMERICAN EXPRESS *Access, Diners, Visa.*

Cork   Lovetts   £72

Tel 021 294909   Fax 021 508568   **R**

Churchyard Lane off Well Road Douglas Cork Co Cork   Map 23 B6

The Lovett family's comfortable, confident restaurant is situated in a fashionable residential area to the south of the city (convenient for the airport) and has a loyal local following. Portraits by 19th-century Cork artist John Butler Brennan provide a perennial talking point and a lively background for Margaret Lovett and Marie Harding's imaginative cooking. Seafood is its main strength, but the best of all local seasonal produce features throughout the menus: wild salmon even comes straight from the rod. Start, perhaps, with black pudding mousse with a grain mustard sauce or grilled Galway Bay mussels with garlic butter, followed by main courses such as escalopes of salmon with lemon or white wine sauce, other daily fresh fish options and classic meat dishes. Separate vegetarian menu. More informal bar food also available at lunchtimes. Diverse wine list. **Seats** *45. Private Room 24. L 12.30-2 D 7-10. Closed L Sat, all Sun, Bank Holidays. Set L £14.50 Set D £21.* AMERICAN EXPRESS *Access, Diners, Visa.*

Cork   Metropole Hotel   58%   £88

Tel 021 508122   Fax 021 506450   **H**

MacCurtain Street Cork Co Cork   Map 23 B6

Recent refurbishment has given the 100-year-old 'Met' a new lease of life. That the hotel is the epicentre of Cork's annual jazz festival is reflected in the numerous photos and sketches of the stars who have performed here displayed in the bar. On the bedroom front it is only those on the top two floors that we recommend, those being the ones that have been refurbished, partly with dark stained pine furniture (some retain the old units revamped); they all have good bathrooms that although brand new are given a period feel by the tiling, wood-panelled tub and generously sized, chunky wash basins. Bedroom size and shape varies considerably and the view from some is a bit grim. The best have views over the River Lee as it flows through the centre of town. 24hr room service. Banqueting for 300, conference facilities for 500. A leisure centre was planned for the end of 1994. **Rooms** *108.* AMERICAN EXPRESS *Access, Diners, Visa.*

Cork   Michael's Bistro   NEW   £45

Tel 021 276887   **R**

4 Mardyke Street Cork Co Cork   Map 23 B6

Situated next door to Michael Clifford's eponymous restaurant (see entry), with its entrance around the corner and its own separate (but communicating) kitchen under Denis Cogan, the new bistro's colour scheme alone, with its violets, pinks and black, would alert aficionados to the common ownership. The Bistro is smaller and more intimate, however, seating a couple of dozen on smart black chairs at rather small tables plus an extra four on stools at a little bar by the door (better for a drink while waiting for a table); prints of food photographs from Michael's cookery book line the walls and the menu is much more informal, incorporating starters like tagliatelle with mushrooms and ham in a cream herb sauce along with a signature dish of warm salad of Clonakilty black pudding with glazed apples. Main courses are homely, typically Irish stew with boiled potatoes or potato and crab cakes served with garden greens in a creamy parsley sauce. Desserts include a nicely gooey caramelised banana crepe with butterscotch sauce and excellent ice creams, or there's a farmhouse cheese plate. Small outdoor eating area for just four diners. *Seats 27. L 12-2.30 D 6-10.30. Closed Sun, Bank Holidays, 2 weeks Aug. Access, Visa.*

Cork	**Morrisons Island Hotel**	**68%**	**£119**
Tel 021 275858 Fax 021 275833			**H**
Morrisons Quay Cork Co Cork			Map 23 B6

Overlooking the River Lee, in Cork's business district, this 'all-suite' hotel – in France it would be called a *hotel résidence* – is designed for the business person with each suite having a separate lounge (with kitchenette): ideal for meeting or entertaining. Actually four are junior suites (large rooms with separate sitting area) without the kitchenette and there are four larger penthouse suites with balconies and completely separate kitchens, two with two bedrooms. Decorwise it's fairly simple with lightwood units in the bedrooms and darkwood in the sitting rooms with tweedy soft furnishings. Downstairs there's a smart marble-floored lobby and cosy bar that with several sofas doubles as a lounge area. Room service is 24hr, as is porterage, and there is free secure parking. *Rooms 40. Closed 4 days at Christmas.* AMERICAN EXPRESS *Access, Diners, Visa.*

Cork	**O'Keeffe's**		**£65**
Tel 021 275645			**R**
23 Washington Street West Cork Co Cork			Map 23 B6

A hospitable restaurant, run since 1990 by Marie and Tony O'Keeffe. Their à la carte menu changes every month and offers the likes of pork and spinach terrine with onion marmalade, boned pig's trotter stuffed with a mousse of Clonakilty white pudding and rolled in garlic breadcrumbs or tomato, onion and anchovy tart with mozzarella cheese to start, followed by prawn and scallop stir-fry, tripe and onions with fried polenta, or noisettes of venison with a port and cranberry sauce. Small choice of desserts or Irish cheeses to finish. Sauces are a strength, presentation is good and portions are generous; Marie's culinary influences are wide-ranging, with fresh local ingredients taking pride of place in the kitchen. *Seats 33. L by arrangement D 6.30-10. Closed Sun, Bank Holidays, 10 days Christmas.* AMERICAN EXPRESS *Access, Diners, Visa.*

Cork	**Rochestown Park Hotel**	**67%**	**£85**
Tel 021 892233 Fax 021 892178			**H**
Rochestown Road Douglas Cork Co Cork			Map 23 B6

Take the south ring road to Douglas and keep a sharp lookout for the hotel's signs (they're small and brown) to find the bright yellow building. Public rooms are in the original Georgian house, formerly a seminary for trainee priests and once home to the Lord Mayors of Cork, with bedrooms in modern extensions. Standard bedrooms have been designed with the business person very much in mind and have practical fitted furniture including a well-lit desk with a second phone. Extras include mineral water, bowl of fruit, mints and towelling robes in bathrooms that all boast bidets. 20 Executive rooms are very large and have spa baths. Public areas include comfortable sitting areas off the marble-floored lobby, a bar with rattan-furnished conservatory and a snug residents' bar for late-night drinkers. The hotel's pride and joy is a most impressive leisure centre; the 'cooked' breakfasts are, however, nothing to be proud of. Seven acres of mature gardens are open to residents. **Rooms** *63. Garden, indoor swimming pool, children's splash pool, gymnasium, solarium, sauna, spa bath, steam room, hydro-massage pool, aerobics studio, thalassotherapy clinic.* AMERICAN EXPRESS *Access, Diners, Visa.*

Cork	Seven North Mall	£60
Tel 021 397191 Fax 021 300811		**PH**
7 North Mall Cork Co Cork		**Map 23 B6**

This elegant house dating from 1750 belongs to the family of Cork city architect Neil Hegarty and is run by his wife, Angela, who offers guests tea on arrival. It's centrally situated on a tree-lined south-facing mall overlooking the River Lee. Rooms are all spacious, individually furnished in a pleasingly restrained style in keeping with the house itself and with bathrooms cleverly added to look as if they have always been there. Some rooms have river views and there is a ground-floor room especially designed for disabled guests. Excellent breakfasts. A nice touch is the personalised map of the city centre given to guests, which shows clearly all the best restaurants, pubs, museums, galleries and theatres, mostly reassuringly near. **Rooms** *5. Closed 18 Dec-6 Jan. Access, Visa.*

Cork   Places of Interest

Tourist Information   Tel 021 273251
The Queenstown Story   Cobh Tel 021 813591
Jameson Heritage Centre   Midleton Tel 021 613594
Triskell Arts Centre   off South Main Street Tel 021 272022
Crawford School of Art and Gallery   Emmet Place Tel 021 966777
GAA Athletic Grounds   Pairc Chaoimh Tel 021 963311
Cork City Gaol   Tel 021 542478
Church of St Francis   Liberty Street
St Finbarre's Cathedral   Sharman Crawford Street
St Colman's Cathedral   Cobh
Everyman Palace   MacCurtain Street Tel 021 501673
Opera House   Emmet Place Tel 021 270022
   Historic Houses, Castles and Gardens
Blarney Castle House and Gardens   Tel 021 385252
Dunkathel   Glanmire Tel 021 821014 *4 miles*
Riverstown House   Glanmire Tel 021 821205 *4 miles*
Fota Wildlife Park   Carrigtwohill nr Cobh Tel 021 812678

Crossmolina	Enniscoe House	63%	£88
Tel 096 31112 Fax 096 31773			**H**
Castlehill nr Crossmolina Ballina Co Mayo			**Map 22 B3**

Generations of the same family have lived here on the shores of Lough Conn since the 17th century and the mature woodland, antique furniture and family portraits all contribute to today's enjoyment of Irish hospitality and country house life. The current owner, Susan Kellett, has established a Research and Heritage Centre in converted yard buildings behind the house. One service offered by the Centre is tracing family histories. The main bedrooms have four-posters or canopied beds and fine views of park and lake. **Rooms** *6. Garden, game fishing. Closed mid Oct-end Mar.* AMERICAN EXPRESS *Access, Visa.*

Delgany	Glenview Hotel	63%	£90
Tel 01 287 3399 Fax 01 287 7511			**H**
Glen o' the Downs Delgany Co Wicklow			**Map 23 D4**

New owners have now been in situ for two years and continue to make major improvements to this hotel that nestles beneath Sugarloaf Mountain. There are 30 acres of gardens and dramatic views of the Glen o' the Downs.

Redecoration has been completed throughout and the building now encompasses a conference area with state-of-the-art facilities (catering for up to 300) at one end and extra bedrooms at the other. Well-equipped bedrooms have tea and coffee-making facilities, hairdryer and trouser press as standard and children under 5 stay free in parents' room. A new leisure centre with swimming pool, gymnasium, steam room and jacuzzi was due to be finished by March 1995. **Rooms** *37. Garden.* AMERICAN EXPRESS *Access, Diners, Visa.*

Dingle — Beginish Restaurant £55

Tel 066 51588   Fax 066 51591

R

Green Street Dingle Co Kerry

Map 23 A5

Two lofty rooms provide the main seating here, while a small conservatory overlooking the lovely garden can be used as a private room. The restaurant takes its name from one of the Blasket islands and is a comfortable spot for enjoying the talents of Pat Moore. Her menu leans heavily towards seafood, the final choice depending on the day's catch and her own inspiration. Typical items on the dinner carte run from smoked mackerel paté and mussels beurre blanc to poached lobster, turbot with olive oil-scented potato pureé and a chive sauce, and pan-fried medallions of monkfish with a fennel confit and tomato basil sauce. Some meat choices, too, and delicious desserts like choux puff with fresh fruit or rhubarb soufflé tart. Good farmhouse cheese selection. **Seats** *52. Private Room 18. L 12.30-2.15 D 6-9.30. Closed Mon, mid Nov-Mar.* AMERICAN EXPRESS *Access, Diners, Visa.*

Dingle — Dingle Skellig Hotel 61% £86

Tel 066 51144   Fax 066 51501

H

Dingle Co Kerry

Map 23 A5

Pleasant, practical and comfortable behind its unprepossessing 60s' facade, the Dingle Skellig is a popular place with families on holiday. Children are very well looked after, and there's also plenty to keep grown-ups active and amused. The sea views are quite a feature, and there's special anti-glare glass in the conservatory restaurant. Bedrooms are of a reasonable size, with several designated for family occupation. No dogs. **Rooms** *110. Garden, indoor swimming pool, sauna, solarium, beauty & hair salon, tennis, games room, snooker, deep-sea fishing. Closed mid Nov-mid Mar.* AMERICAN EXPRESS *Access, Diners, Visa.*

Dingle — Doyle's Seafood Bar & Townhouse £50

Tel 066 51174   Fax 066 51816

RR

4 John Street Dingle Co Kerry

Map 23 A5

Local seafood is the main attraction at this family-run restaurant with flagstone floors and old pine furniture. Menus are made up daily according to the catch landed by the Dingle boats, and lobster, selected from a tank in the bar, is a speciality. Cooking is straightforward, emphasising the freshness of the product. Start, perhaps, with sweet and sour marinated herrings, crab cocktail (or soup), millefeuille of warm oysters with Guinness sauce or home-cured gravad lax. Main courses include another wide selection of fish and seafood – from grilled mussels with garlic stuffing to turbot served on the bone with *sauce ravigote*; twice-baked cheese soufflé and rack of lamb may be the only alternatives to seafood. Finish with a homely dessert such as raspberry meringue cake or choose from a small selection of Irish farmhouse cheeses. Shorter-choice, simpler set-price dinner menu served from 6 to 7pm only. The wine list is strong on whites and includes a sensibly priced Australian selection. **Seats** *50. Parties 12. D only 6-9. Closed Sun, also mid Nov-mid Mar. Set D to 7pm £13.50. Access, Diners, Visa.*

 See over

Rooms £62

High-quality accommodation (open 7 days) includes a residents' sitting
room and eight stylish bedrooms furnished with antiques and luxurious
bathrooms. Breakfasts include "boiled real eggs" and the restaurant's own
fine smoked salmon (also available for take-away) served with scrambled
eggs – they wouldn't dream of letting you go on your way without
a proper breakfast. New accommodation suites had just come on line as we
went to press.

Dingle　　**Greenmount House**　　　£40

Tel 066 51414　　　**PH**

Greenmount Dingle Co Kerry　　Map 23 A5

John and Mary Curran's neat modern guesthouse is handy to everything
but has enough height to afford views over Dingle – and an enviable
reputation for hospitality, comfort, excellent housekeeping and outstanding
breakfasts, which are served in a stylish conservatory overlooking the
harbour. Individually decorated rooms all have new bathrooms (shower
only), direct-dial telephones and many thoughtful touches including electric
blankets, TVs, clock radios, hairdryers, fresh fruit and flowers. No children
under 8 years. No dogs. Own parking. *Rooms 8. Garden. Closed 22-28 Dec.
Access, Visa.*

Dingle　　**The Half Door**　　　£55

Tel 066 51600　Fax 066 51206　　**R**

John Street Dingle Co Kerry　　Map 23 A5

Cosy and welcoming, with a genuine cottage atmosphere enhanced
by exposed stone walls, copper pots and original white tiles around the
chimney breast. There's a sunny conservatory area to the rear. Denis
O'Connor's menu majors on seafood, so the choice varies with the season
and the catch. Seafood bisque, steamed mussels, or sautéed oysters masked
with a chive sauce could be your starter, followed perhaps by grilled brill,
salmon en croute or baked fillet of plaice with a mustard sauce. Good
simple sweets. *Seats 50. Parties 12. Private Room 20. L 12.30-2.30 D 6-10.
Closed Tue, Halloween-2nd week Dec & early Jan-Easter.* AMERICAN EXPRESS
Access, Diners, Visa.

🍷 is our symbol for an outstanding wine list.

Dingle　　**Lord Baker's Bar & Restaurant**　　　£60

Tel 066 51277　　　**R**

Main Street Dingle Co Kerry　　Map 23 A5

Tom Baker – businessman, councillor, auctioneer and poet, and
affectionately known as Lord Baker – acquired these premises in 1890 and
they've gradually developed from general supplier and function caterer to a
popular and thriving restaurant and bar. Locally made tapestries are an eye-
catching display in the main eating area, beyond which is a conservatory
extension leading into the garden. Choose between the full restaurant menu
and the less formal bar menu, which offer similar choices from seafood
soup, garlic prawns and chicken liver paté to seafood mornay and steaks.
Particularly favoured for Sunday lunch. *Seats 85. Parties 25. L 12.30-2.30
D 6-10. Closed 25 Dec. Set L (Sun) £10.50 Set D £13.50/£16.50.*
AMERICAN EXPRESS *Access, Diners, Visa.*

Dingle　　**Place of Interest**

Great Blasket Island　Tel 066 13111

Donegal Town   Harvey's Point Country Hotel   63%   £99

Tel 073 22208   Fax 073 22352   H

Lough Eske Donegal Town Co Donegal   Map 22 B2

Situated in a marvellous location close to Donegal town on the shores
of Lough Eske, Jody Gysling's low-rise, purpose-built hotel has
a predictably Swiss-German atmosphere. The chalet-style buildings make
good use of wood, with pergolas and covered walkways joining the
residential area to the main bars and restaurants. Views over the lough are
lovely and the waterside location brings an atmosphere of serenity which
is emphasised by the good nature of everybody involved in this family-run
business, ranging from the host himself down to his trusty dogs.
Continental-style rooms, all on the ground floor with direct access
to verandah and gardens, feature show-wood furniture and are well
equipped with satellite TV, video and mini-bars as well as direct-dial
phones, hairdryers, tea/coffee facilities and, in Executive rooms, four-poster
beds and trouser presses. Banqueting and conference facilities for 200/300.
No children under 10. Easy parking. *Rooms 20. Garden, tennis, fishing.
Closed end Nov–Easter.* AMERICAN EXPRESS *Access, Diners, Visa.*

Dublin   Aberdeen Lodge   £65

Tel 01 283 8155   Fax 01 283 7877   PH

53 Park Avenue off Ailesbury Road Dublin 4   Map 23 D4

Located in a smart, peaceful south Dublin suburb, Aberdeen Lodge stands
on an avenue lined with well-established trees. The Halpins have converted
two substantial Edwardian properties to create a discreet, comfortable
private hotel. There's a simple lounge on the ground floor along with
an attractive and spacious breakfast/dining room (dinner is available
to residents by prior arrangement). Bedrooms, their windows double-
glazed, are identically furnished, each with custom-built modern pieces;
rear ones overlook a cricket and rugby ground. The usual comforts like
trouser presses and hairdryers are provided and bathrooms have full
facilities, showers being quite powerful. Enjoyable breakfasts include the
likes of scrambled eggs and smoked salmon. No dogs. *Rooms 16.*
AMERICAN EXPRESS *Access, Diners, Visa.*

Dublin   Anglesea Town House   £90

Tel 01 668 3877   Fax 01 668 3461   PH

63 Anglesea Road Dublin 4   Map 23 D4

A fine, creeper-clad south Dublin Edwardian residence run with enormous
dedication and flair by Helen Kirrane with the help of her charming
daughters. The minute you enter, the heady perfume of pot pourri greets
and all around are beautiful ornaments and furnishings. A drawing room
is the epitome of cosy homeliness with its fine, comfortable seating and
numerous books and yet more tasteful ornaments. Bedrooms feature
lacework, heavy drapes and a comforting, motherly decor. Bathrooms,
some with shower only, are spotless, like the rest of the house. Bedding has
a wonderful 'all-through' freshly laundered smell. In the mornings guests
are treated to what is without doubt the most stunning breakfast in the
British Isles. To begin, a large bowl of fresh fruit salad is brought, then
a bowl of dried fruit compote and one of baked fruit in creamy yoghurt.
Next comes a bowl of warm baked cereal (oats, fruits, nuts soaked
in orange juice overnight then freshly baked with cream). You help
yourself to all these along with a glass of freshly squeezed orange juice.
The main course follows – specialities are kedgeree and Anglesea omelette
(a soufflé omelette with smoked salmon and three different cheeses). Other
options include kidneys, sole, plaice, salmon or trout as well as more usual

offerings. To accompany, hot buttered toast, home-baked breads and limitless amounts of good tea or coffee. To finish, a selection of small dainty cakes such as a moist frangipane tart. A quite extraordinary place. No dogs. *Rooms* 7. *Garden.* AMERICAN EXPRESS *Access, Diners, Visa.*

Dublin — Ariel House — £85

Tel 01 668 5512   Fax 01 668 5845

PH

52 Lansdowne Road Ballsbridge Dublin 4

Map 23 D4

A substantial listed Victorian mansion, built in 1850, has for the past 35 years been home to the O'Brien family. It has also been one of Dublin's most charming private house hotels. Unusually for such premises there's a cosy 'wine bar' close to the reception desk where a selection of wines can be enjoyed. The drawing room and bedrooms, in the original house, are furnished with beautiful pieces of Victorian furniture. Rooms are spacious and well-equipped and each has its own character. There is, however, a wing of ten standard bedrooms at rear which are modern and more functional in style and overlook the neat, well-tended garden. All bedrooms have full tub facilities (both bath and shower). Each also has a trouser press with iron and board, a hairdryer and an array of useful extras. Breakfast is served in a pretty conservatory on highly polished mahogany tables. Smoking discouraged. Free parking. No dogs. *Rooms 28. Closed 2 weeks Christmas.* AMERICAN EXPRESS *Access, Visa.*

Dublin — Ayumi-Ya Japanese Steakhouse — £40

Tel 01 662 2233   Fax 01 662 0221

R

132 Lower Baggot Street Dublin 2

Map 23 D4

One section of the menu at this informal basement restaurant, an offshoot of the Blackrock original, is given over to teppanyaki – beef, chicken, salmon, prawns, tofu, Tokyo burger – griddled and served with a choice of sauces. Other favourites include tonkatsu (deep-fried breadcrumbed pork), mixed vegetable stir-fry and egg noodles with meat, seafood or vegetables. The evening selection is more extensive. Japanese-style seating for 8. *Seats 40. Parties 20. L 12.30-2.30 D 6.30-11.30. Closed all Sun. Set L & D from £6.95.* AMERICAN EXPRESS *Access, Diners, Visa.*

Dublin — Berkeley Court — 76% — £191

Tel 01 660 1711   Fax 01 661 7238

H

Lansdowne Road Dublin 4

Map 23 D4

The flagship of the Doyle Hotel Group, the luxurious Berkeley Court has an impressively large split-level lobby-lounge with mirrored columns, brass-potted parlour palms and reproduction furniture in a mixture of styles. There are two bars – the Royal Court and the popular Conservatory – and two restaurants. The Court Lounge is a civilised spot for afternoon tea. Ballroom, boardroom and several suites provide function facilities for up to 300 (banquet) and 400 (conference) people. Accommodation includes a proportion of spacious Executive suites with classic furnishings and the sumptuously appointed Penthouse Suite. One floor of rooms (29) is designated non-smoking. *Rooms 207. Keep-fit equipment, hair salon, news kiosk, boutique.* AMERICAN EXPRESS *Access, Diners, Visa.*

Dublin — Blooms Hotel — 60% — £121

Tel 01 671 5622   Fax 01 671 5997

H

6 Anglesea Street Temple Bar Dublin 2

Map 23 D4

Modern city-centre hotel near Trinity College and Dublin Castle. An alternative to the pubby bar is a small cocktail bar integrated to the restaurant (newly decorated in bright yellow); otherwise the only sitting area is a rather shabby lounge off the marbled lobby. Bedrooms, by contrast, are pleasant and well-kept with triple-glazed windows and extras like a complimentary quarter bottle of wine and evening newspaper. Bathrooms are a little dated but generally of good size and quite adequate; all have low stools and telephone extensions and some have bidets. No dogs. **Rooms 86.** *Night club. Closed 24, 25 & 26 Dec.* AMERICAN EXPRESS *Access, Diners, Visa.*

Dublin	**Burlington Hotel**	**70%**	**£154**

Tel 01 660 5222   Fax 01 660 8496   **H**

Upper Leeson Street Dublin 4   Map 23 D4

Part of the Doyle Hotel Group, the Burlington is Ireland's largest hotel and always bustles with commercial business. Public rooms are on a grand scale, with large chandeliers in the main lobby/lounge area, a convivial bar (Buck Mulligan's) and a disco. Bedrooms are thoughtfully designed and well-equipped, with good working space for the business guest and neat tiled bathrooms with ample shelf space and bathrobes. The Burlington has a good reputation for banquets and has conference facilities for up to 1000. No dogs. **Rooms 450.** *Hair salon, kiosk, boutique.* AMERICAN EXPRESS *Access, Diners, Visa.*

Dublin	**Central Hotel**	**57%**	**£139**

Tel 01 679 7302   Fax 01 679 7303   **H**

1 Exchequer Street Dublin 2   Map 23 D4

Privately-owned hotel whose plus points include a central location, nightly live music in the Tavern, the owner's collection of contemporary Irish art around the walls and free use of a nearby office car park overnight (7.30pm-8.30am) and at weekends. Bedrooms vary widely in size and shape but all are furnished in similar style with functional lightwood units. About half the bathrooms have shower and WC only. No dogs. **Rooms 70.** *Closed 25 & 26 Dec.* AMERICAN EXPRESS *Access, Diners, Visa.*

Dublin	**Chapter One**	**£70**

Tel 01 873 2266   Fax 01 873 2330   **R**

18/19 Parnell Square Dublin 1   Map 23 D4

A characterful vaulted cellar restaurant underneath the Dublin Writers Museum. Menus lean slightly towards Russian/Scandinavian themes, offering starters like warm salads, baked goat's cheese and duck livers with garlic croutons alongside blinis and gravad lax; main courses might include roast duck with apricot sauce and endives, or griddled calf's liver with black olives, rosemary, red onion and a balsamic vinegar gravy. Good pastry dishes among the desserts. Concise wine list. The Museum Coffee Shop, upstairs, serves more informal food all day. Pre-theatre dining (6-7) £12.50. **Seats 100.** *Private Rooms 16-40. L 12-2.30 D 5.45-11. Closed L Sat, all Sun, Bank Holidays (except coffee shop). Set L £11.50 Set D £15.50.* AMERICAN EXPRESS *Access, Diners, Visa.*

Dublin	**The Chili Club**	**£45**

Tel 01 677 3721   **R**

1 Anne's Lane South Anne Street Dublin 2   Map 23 D4

Just off bustling South Anne Street, in Dublin's most fashionable shopping area, this intimate, low-ceilinged restaurant provides an oasis of serenity. Anna, the Thai chef, cooks the hot and spicy food of her homeland to be 'as traditional as the market will allow'. Satays, sweet and sours and even most of the curries are easy on the palate, but the soups have the expected Thai kick. **Seats 42.** *Parties 15. Private Room 16. L 12.30-2.30 D 7-11. Closed L Sat, all Sun, L Bank Holidays all Good Friday. Set L £7.95 Set D £18.* AMERICAN EXPRESS *Access, Diners, Visa.*

Dublin   Clarence Hotel

Tel 01 677 6178   Fax 01 677 7487   **HR**

6 Wellington Quay Dublin 2   Map 23 D4

Built in 1890 and recently purchased by the rock band *U2*, the Clarence is in the middle of a very major transformation into a top-grade modern hotel, albeit with a 1930s' decorative theme. It has always been the traditional stopping place for country folk 'coming to town' as it's just down the road from Heuston station, however this staid image is gradually being changed. The Kitchen nightclub has opened in the basement and there will be a new residents' lounge off the lobby; at the rear of the ground floor is the smart, all-day brasserie called The Tea Room. The hotel's bedrooms will be closed for a complete revamp until Spring 1995, but the rest of the hotel's facilities will remain open during that time. **Rooms** *45. Closed 25-28 Dec.* *Access, Diners, Visa.*

The Tea Room   **NEW**   £70

Snappy, 1930s' decor and evocative background music are in tune with the style of the hotel and the restaurant is attracting a stylish, mostly young clientele. The floor area is broken up into different levels, including a balcony approached by steep, potentially dangerous, stairs – but that's no bother to the friendly, fit young staff who zip up and down with trays, looking good in long black aprons. Nicholas Healy (ex-*Dunderry Lodge*) has taken over the restaurant management to good effect and Michael Martin (ex-*La Stampa*) is producing interesting and generally well-delivered menus, with strong vegetarian options. A wide range of starters from the carte might include excellent foie gras with Sauternes sauce, served on a herbed crouton with a little choucroute garnish, although galantine of duck was spoilt on a recent visit by an overpoweringly acidic tomato and ginger chutney. Roast scallops and lentils was a masterful dish on the other hand, prettily presented with a flourish of savoury tuile sprinkled with sesame seeds. Scallops also drew praise in a risotto of squid ink, with roast scallops, saffron sauce – excellent flavours, golden crisp scallops, while fish and chips was less well received – several small pieces of sole with a scattering of hand-cut designer chips for £12.95, which is more than the early evening, 3-course menu (6-8pm £12.50). Imaginative vegetarian options might include baked artichoke with sweetcorn, spiced lentil sauce, or tagliatelle with white truffle oil, wild mushrooms and a morel cream sauce. Typical desserst are a classic crème brulée and an assiette gourmandise (with a strong emphasis on chocolate), or there's an Irish cheeseboard option. Children are not encouraged. Afternoon tea is served from 3 to 5, 7 days a week. Valet parking (£2). **Seats** *130. L 12-2.30 D 6-11 (Sun to 10). Set D £12.50 (6-8 not Sat).*

> Set menu prices may not always include service or wine.

Dublin   The Commons Restaurant   £85

Tel 01 475 2597   Fax 01 478 0551   **R**

Newman House 85/86 St Stephen's Green Dublin 2   Map 23 D4

In the basement of Newman House, one of Dublin's most historic buildings, this spacious restaurant is unique among city-centre restaurants as it looks out on to mature trees in a large courtyard (where tables are set out for aperitifs in fine weather) and has access to a further five acres of private gardens beyond. Soothing decor is in classic dark blues and creams, with stone floors warmed by the earthy toes of oriental rugs, fresh flowers and a stimulating collection of specially commissioned paintings by Irish artists. Michael Bolster, second chef under Gerard Kirwan until the spring of 1994, has taken on the mantle of chef de cuisine and, on the basis of recent visits, is cooking confidently with no great change of style. The best of local produce – notably fish but also a good choice of meats and game in season – imaginative use of offal (typically in fillet of veal with a ragout of sweetbreads, red wine and roast garlic) and, occasionally, unusual offerings such as kid provide a sound base for dishes which are usually colourful and lively. A few minor lapses, as in a rather dull tomato and fennel soup remarkable only for the unexpected addition of saffron, are quickly forgotten in the context of the high standard of cooking and presentation generally experienced throughout a meal. A good choice of delicious, freshly-baked breads starts a meal off on the right track. From a three-course (five-course at dinner) table-d'hote and carte, typical first courses might include a good mixed leaf salad with a judicious sprinkling of mixed herbs and either lightly char-grilled tender pieces of lamb fillet (pink and juicy within) topped with substantial shavings of fresh Parmesan and a piquant dressing with whiskey or, perhaps, grilled monkfish with a zappy lime and ginger pickle. Imaginative, simply presented main courses might include perfectly pan-fried halibut set on an emerald bed of finely slivered mangetout surrounded by an artistic splash of lobster cream, or firm-fleshed roast fillet of monkfish, sliced and fanned over a bed of mixed lentils and finely diced vegetables in a pool of dark red wine beurre blanc. An unfussy selection of accompanying vegetables includes two styles of potato – typically new boiled potatoes and 'marquise', a nest of puréed potato enclosing a tasty spoonful of colourful finely diced mixed vegetable. Elegant, refreshingly understated desserts could include a simple hazelnut praline parfait with a dark chocolate sauce or lovely featherlight puff pastry in a feuillette of fresh fruit in a scented mango coulis; in the evening there's also a selection of Irish cheeses. Delicious Java coffee is served with a crunchy brandysnap petit four. 15% service is automatically applied to the bill. *Seats 60. Parties 12. Private Room 20. L 12.30-2.15 D 7-10. Closed L Sat, all Sun, Bank Holidays, 25 & 26 Dec. Set L £17 Set D £27.50.* AMERICAN EXPRESS ® *Access, Diners, Visa.* MARTELL

Dublin   Hotel Conrad   75%   £222

Tel 01 676 5555   Fax 01 676 5424   H

Earlsfort Terrace Dublin 2   Map 23 D4

Opposite the National Concert Hall, just off St Stephen's Green, the Conrad is very much a modern international-style hotel with an impressive array of business facilities. It caters largely to a corporate clientele – although concessions to the locality include Alfie Byrne's bar, themed along the lines of a traditional Dublin pub. Bedrooms, while decoratively uninspiring, are eminently comfortable and well planned with large beds, good easy chairs, decent work space, three telephones (including sockets for fax), and every modern comfort. Excellent marble bathrooms have large tubs with good showers above them, comprehensive toiletries and ample towelling with generously-sized bathrobes. Levels of service are high, from free valet parking and comprehensive 24hr room service to a proper turn-down service in the evenings, when a bottle of mineral water and a hand-made Irish chocolate are left at the bedside. Breakfast is the best meal of the day. Banqueting for 150, conference facilities for 250. Conrad is the international branch of Hilton USA, which is not to be confused with the now British (Ladbroke-owned) Hilton chain. No dogs. *Rooms 191. Hair salon, news kiosk, brasserie (7am-11.30pm).* AMERICAN EXPRESS ® *Access, Diners, Visa.*

Dublin   Cooke's Café   ↑   £65

Tel 01 679 0536   Fax 01 679 0546   R

14 South William Street Dublin 2   Map 23 D4

A heart-of-the-city restaurant that has deservedly been a phenomenal success ever since opening in mid-1992. Johnny Cooke's the chef (along with Harry McKeogh) and he heads a dedicated team who work in a tiny, open-plan kitchen separated from an equally none-too-large, very informal dining room by a tall screen which features a mural in the same 'distressed' classical Italianate style as the rest of the room. Tables are close and there are several sittings, so the timing of bookings, which are essential, can be critical. The menu will be familiar to those conversant with the current vogue for new-wave cooking. Here it is mostly Italian. Presentation, too, forms an integral part of the experience, as in delicious lightly fried squid rings served in the middle of an extra large plate and sitting on a square of spicy arrabbiata sauce with roasted garlic (although on a recent visit the promised hot spiciness was lacking). To accompany, if required, a small wicker basket overflowing with superb home-baked breads is offered along with an olive oil dip. A cream of red bell pepper soup garnished with goat's cheese; mussels steamed with garlic, wine, leeks, herbs and butter and Caesar salad are all typical starters. Main dishes are quite diverse, ranging from tortelloni with Parmesan, gorgonzola cream and melted appenzeller cheese to calf's liver with a sage and pancetta butter and a plump, tender partridge roasted and served on a creamy celeriac purée and surrounded by a delicately fragrant lemon thyme butter. Simply prepared, very fresh vegetables are available separately. Desserts include good home-made ice creams and such sugary delights as honey chocolate cake or a very similar chocolate marzipan cake and pecan tart. Sunday brunch menu (£13·95). In fine weather there are tables outside on the pavement. Service does its best to cope with the often crowded conditions. According to the menu, discretionary gratuities cannot be processed on credit cards. *Seats 40. Parties 12. Private Room 45. Meals 12.30-4 & 6-11 (Fri & Sat to 11.30), Sun 12.30-3.30 & 6-9.30. (May-Sept 8am-midnight). Set L £12.95. Set D (6-7.30, Mon-Fri) £13.95. Closed Bank Holidays.* AMERICAN EXPRESS *Access, Diners, Visa.*

Dublin	**Le Coq Hardi**	★	**£95**

Tel 01 668 9070 Fax 01 668 9887	**R**
35 Pembroke Road Ballsbridge Dublin 4	**Map 23 D4**

John and Catherine Howard run a classic restaurant in a classic Georgian building at the end of a terrace. Inside are high ceilings and handsome mirrors, brasswork and ornate plasterwork, and the immaculately set tables put the seal on a setting that's entirely fitting for John's serious French-based cooking. Many of his dishes are from the traditional repertoire – terrine of foie gras with brioche, cod boulangère, Venetian-style lamb's liver, entrecote with a shallot and bone marrow sauce. 'Le Coq Hardi' is a breast of chicken filled with potato, wild mushrooms and herbs, wrapped in bacon, oven-roasted and finished with Irish whiskey sauce. Other dishes are more contemporary in style, such as warm salad with game, pink grapefruit and pine nuts, strudel of vegetables on a light curry sauce with mint, or darne of salmon steamed with tomato, black olives, olive oil and sea salt. Bread-and-butter pudding with Irish whiskey custard is a favourite dessert. Particularly famous for its Bordeaux cellar, which includes an 1870 Chateau Mouton Rothschild for the modest sum of £5000+, do not ignore the exceptional selection of cognacs and armagnacs, nor the rest of the list that has plenty of good wines from outside France; really, though, this is a connoisseur's list to drool over. *Seats 50. Private Room 34. L 12-2.30 D 7-11. Closed L Sat, all Sun, Bank Holidays, 1 week Christmas, 2 weeks Aug. Set L £16 Set D £28.50.* AMERICAN EXPRESS *Access, Diners, Visa.*

Dublin	**The Davenport Hotel**	76%	**£180**

Tel 01 661 6800 Fax 01 661 5663	**H**
Merrion Square Dublin 2	**Map 23 D4**

The original, imposing neo-classical facade of architect Alfred G Jones's Merrion Hall fronts one of Dublin's most elegant hotels, opened last year. Only a stone's throw from Trinity College and the National Gallery, the impressive exterior of The Davenport is carried through into the marble-pillared lobby, an atrium encircled by Georgian windows which soars up through six storeys to the domed roof and cupola. Rooms beyond are on a more human scale, with relatively low ceilings creating an unexpectedly intimate atmosphere throughout the hotel. Colour schemes tend to be bold, giving each area a specific character – the Presidents Bar is masculine, club-like, for example, the restaurant lighter and more feminine – with stylish drapes and quality materials, notably marble and a variety of woods, used throughout. Although not individually decorated there is considerable variety among the bedrooms (some Lady Executive designated), which tend to have a homely, almost country atmosphere which is emphasised by the irregular shapes in some rooms and (well-furnished) bathrooms. Nice touches include a safe as well as trouser press, air-conditioning, good American over-bath showers, bath robes, turn-down service and an attractive Irish-made range of toiletries. 24hr room service. Private 24hr valet parking. Banqueting/conference facilities for 400/300. Guests have use of the private Riverview Racquets and Fitness Club at members' rates. **Rooms** *120.* AMERICAN EXPRESS® *Access, Diners, Visa.*

Dublin	**Dobbins Wine Bistro**	**£60**
Tel 01 676 4670		**R**
15 Stephen's Lane Dublin 2		**Map 23 D4**

Probably best visited in a group, this clubby city-centre 'Nissen-hut' operates well under the close supervision of owner John O'Byrne and has a dark, curved ceiling (offset somewhat by the bright conservatory area at the far end, which is very popular in summer), sawdust-strewn floor and a series of tables for 2-4 in intimate booths along the wall; low lighting and an abundance of bottles add to an away-from-it-all atmosphere which means this is a place to approach with caution if you have to go back to work after lunch. Gary Flynn's tempting menus might include starters such as grilled goat's cheese with pesto or fresh West Coast crab with roasted peppers, followed by pan-fried spring lamb's liver with a croustade of kidney and wild mushroom or (boned) breast of quail with spinach and smoked bacon in a pastry parcel. Details are good: generous, plain wine glasses; lovely home-baked brown bread and white rolls; lightly cooked vegetables included whole baby carrots, plus a choice of sautéed or new potatoes; interesting desserts and particularly creamy, flavoursome ice cream; lots of freshly brewed coffee. Ten tables on a patio for outdoor eating. *Seats* 80. *Parties* 20. *Private Room* 40. L 12.30-3 D 7.30-11.30. *Closed L Sat, all Sun & Mon, Bank Holidays, Christmas week. Set L £14.50 Set D £21.50.* AMERICAN EXPRESS® *Access, Diners, Visa.*

Dublin	**Doyle Montrose Hotel**	**65%**	**£106**
Tel 01 269 3311 Fax 01 269 1164			**H**
Stillorgan Road Dublin 4			**Map 23 D4**

A major facelift has given the Montrose a smart modern appearance. Located alongside the N11, a few miles south of the city centre, it now also has an attractive 'old Ireland' themed pub with its own entrance. Spacious public areas include a large open-plan bar and lounge. Bedrooms are furnished in an identical smart, contemporary style with Executive rooms differing only in being larger. A good selection of amenities includes an iron and ironing board. Acceptable breakfasts are cooked to order – quite a rarity in a large hotel. **Rooms** *179. Beauty salon, hair salon, news kiosk/shop.* AMERICAN EXPRESS® *Access, Diners, Visa.*

Dublin	**Doyle Tara Hotel**	**61%**	**£106**
Tel 01 269 4666 Fax 01 269 1027			**H**
Merrion Road Dublin 4			**Map 23 D4**

Formerly the *Tara Tower*, the hotel has recently undergone some major changes (with more planned as we went to press). On the ground floor, the spacious lobby and open-plan bar are due for refurbishment, while at the rear there are now 32 splendid new Executive rooms decorated in a smart, modern style. All rooms have the same amenities but the standard rooms at the front enjoy the best views over Dublin Bay. The hotel is very convenient for the Dun Laoghaire ferry. **Rooms** 114. *News kiosk/shop.* AMERICAN EXPRESS *Access, Diners, Visa.*

Dublin   L'Ecrivain   £70

Tel 01 661 1919   Fax 01 661 0617   R
112 Lower Baggot Street Dublin 2   Map 23 D4

As the name implies, this unpretentious little basement restaurant serves French food and has a writers' theme, with portraits of famous Irish writers by local artist Liam O'Neill hanging on the terracotta-painted walls. A tiny reception lounge with a comfy sofa welcomes diners, who can look forward to fresh seasonal produce, especially the fish that comes from south and west Cork on the day the catch is landed; everything is expertly cooked by chef/patron Derry Clarke and his small team in the kitchen. Seasonal vegetarian and à la carte menus are supplemented by good-value set lunch and dinner offerings with a selection of five starters and main courses to choose from. Look out for dishes such as pan-fried black and white puddings with pureéd mash and jus, grilled goat's cheese with a crisp salad and pesto in a filo basket and west coast mussel broth with smoked bacon, followed by steamed brill with lemon grass, rosemary, roasted sweet peppers and aged balsamic vinegar, or generous slices of tender rib of beef with mushrooms and light tarragon puffs. Desserts, recited at the table, could include pear and almond tart, crème brulée and Paris-Brest. Excellent Irish farmhouse cheeses, generous cups of various coffees and intimate service from Sally-Anne Clarke and her team. The decent wine list has the added benefit of wines costing £20 or more not attracting the service charge – a commendable practice that more restaurants should follow. **Seats** 40. L 12.30-2 D 6.30-11. Closed L Sat, all Sun. Set L £13.50 Set D £22.95. AMERICAN EXPRESS *Access, Diners, Visa.*

> When telephoning establishments in the Republic from *outside*
> the Republic, dial 010-353 then the number we print without
> initial zero: e.g. Cliffords in Cork is 010-353 21 275333.

Dublin   Ernie's   £80

Tel 01 269 3260   Fax 01 269 3969   R
Mulberry Gardens Donnybrook Dublin 4   Map 23 D4

The Evans family has owned this elegant south-city restaurant since 1984 and its most remarkable feature is the late Ernie Evans's personal collection of paintings (mostly of Irish interest and many of his beloved Kerry), which take up every available inch of wall space – closely followed by the pretty little central courtyard garden which makes an especially attractive feature when floodlit at night. The interior was extensively refurbished last year. Chef Sandra Earl is very much in control in the kitchen, producing refreshingly updated versions of the classics. Feuillette of mussels with smoked bacon and dill, warm parcel of crab and mozzarella, and pan-fried medallions of monkfish with tagliatelle, wild mushrooms and seed mustard sauce are all typical of her style and desserts include comfort food like apple and prune tart with Calvados ice cream as well as elegant concoctions appropriate to a grand finale. **Seats** 60. L 12.30-2.30 D 7.15-10.15. Closed L Sat, all Sun & Mon, Bank Holidays, 1 week Xmas. Set L £13.50 Set D £22.50. AMERICAN EXPRESS *Access, Diners, Visa.*

Dublin   Les Frères Jacques

£80

Tel 01 679 4555   Fax 01 679 4725

R

74 Dame Street Dublin 2

Map 23 D4

Situated opposite Dublin Castle, a stone's throw from Trinity College, this
discreet two-storey French restaurant has dark green and cream decor,
Parisian prints, pristine white table linen and fine glasses full of promise.
Although the menus are given unstuffily in English, everything else is
uncompromisingly French. A well-balanced choice on the menus will
always include well-sourced local poultry and meat. Sample this in a starter
of duck confit on a bed of sautéed garlic potatoes, perhaps, or in main
courses such as roast lamb en croute with a minted béarnaise and rosemary
juices or roast pork steak with baby vegetables, potato cake and sherry
sauce. Lobster is a speciality, in starters like cassolette of fresh lobster
thermidor or, as a dramatic main course, roast lobster with Irish whiskey.
A la carte seafood suggestions given at the end of the lunch and dinner
menus depend on daily market availability. Desserts are sophisticated – a
trio of exotic fruit sorbets nestled in a brandysnap basket, perhaps, or a dark
chocolate truffle cake laced with vanilla and coffee sauce; the French
cheeseboard is a further temptation. Special house recommendations on the
wine list are good value. *Seats 55. Private Rooms 15 (downstairs)/40
(upstairs). L 12.30-2.30 D 7.30-10.30 (Fri & Sat to 11). Closed L Sat, all Sun,
Bank Holidays, 25-29 Dec. Set L £13 Set D £20.* AMERICAN EXPRESS
Access, Visa.

Dublin   Furama

£75

Tel & Fax 01 283 0522

R

88 Donnybrook Road Dublin 4

Map 23 D4

Like eating inside a gleaming black lacquered box, with the dining area
reached via a small wooden bridge over an ornamental pool with goldfish.
Furama offers a selection of familiar Cantonese as well as a few Szechuan
dishes, capably cooked and served by hardworking, very pleasant staff.
There's a special fish menu offering scallops, mussels, black sole, sea bass and
lobster (from a tank); the scallops may come sliced in a black bean sauce,
while the sole can be steamed with ginger and scallions. Sweets – like
much of the menu – are aimed at Western palates with various ices
dominating the choice. *Seats 100. Parties 25. L 12.30-2 D 6-11.30 (Fri &
Sat to 12, Sun 1.30-11). Set D £17. Closed 24-26 Dec, Good Friday.*
AMERICAN EXPRESS *Access, Diners, Visa.*

Many hotels offer reduced rates for weekend or out-of-season bookings.
Always ask about special deals.

Dublin   George's Bistro & Piano Bar

£70

Tel 01 679 7000   Fax 01 679 7560

R

29 South Frederick Street Dublin 2

Map 23 D4

In a side street between the Dail and Trinity College, a bistro popular
with the post-theatre crowd. Straightforward menu of dishes based on top-
quality ingredients, correctly cooked. Steaks, racks of lamb and Dover
sole are favourite main courses, with something like avocado with crab
or garlic mushrooms to start. The other attraction is live music (piano with
female vocal), which tends to inhibit conversation but fuels the late-night
buzz. *Seats 90. Private Room 50. L 12-3 D 7-1am. Closed Sun & Mon, Bank
Holidays, 1 week Christmas. Set L £9 Set D £18.50.* AMERICAN EXPRESS *Access,
Diners, Visa.*

Dublin   Georgian House   56%   £86

Tel 01 661 8832   Fax 01 661 8834   **H**

20 Lower Baggot Street Dublin 2   Map 23 D4

Bedrooms in the original building have character and charm while those
in the recently built separate bedroom extension at the rear are more
modern and functional. Conveniently close to the city centre, the hotel also
has direct access to its own pub, Maguire's, next door. Children up to 4 stay
free in parents' room. 24hr room-service. No dogs. *Rooms 33.*
AMERICAN EXPRESS *Access, Diners, Visa.*

Dublin   Glenveagh Town House   £60

Tel 01 668 4612   Fax 01 668 4559   **PH**

31 Northumberland Road Ballsbridge Dublin 4   Map 23 D4

A large Georgian house within comfortable walking distance of the city
centre (it has off-street parking – a very useful feature). Bedrooms are
pleasantly decorated and sport duvets and remote-control TVs. Bathrooms
have excellent showers. Breakfasts are available from 8am though earlier
meals can be arranged. The selection is a familiar one but includes black
and white pudding among its offerings. There's a comfortable drawing
room at the front. Friendly, caring staff. No dogs. *Rooms 11.*
Closed 21-27 Dec. Access, Visa.

Dublin   Good World   £40

Tel 01 677 5373   **R**

18 South Great George's Street Dublin 2   Map 23 D4

A city-centre restaurant much favoured by Dublin's Chinese community,
who flock here at lunchtime for an excellent selection of carefully prepared
dim sum. These come in steamer baskets of stainless steel rather than
bamboo but this is no way affects their quality. Mixed meat dumplings and
char siu buns are noteworthy as are the long, slippery rice-flour envelopes
of the various cheung funs. The regular menu features a standard selection
of classic Cantonese dishes, but it's the dim sum that are primarily
of interest here. No smoking in the downstairs dining room. *Seats 95.*
*Parties 40. Private Room 20. Meals 12.30pm-3am. Closed 25 & 26 Dec. Set L
£5.50 Set D £13.50.* AMERICAN EXPRESS *Access, Diners, Visa.*

Dublin   The Grafton Plaza Hotel   64%   £90

Tel 01 475 0888   Fax 01 475 0908   **H**

Johnsons Place Dublin 2   Map 2 D4

Modern, well-designed and not without a certain style, the Grafton Plaza is
located by Grafton Street and St Stephen's Green, putting shopping areas,
parks, museums and theatres within easy walking distance. Decor is bright
and stylish, and bedrooms of various sizes are well appointed with Irish-
made carpets and furniture (except for some antiques) also of Irish origin.
Hairdryers, multi-channel TVs, tea-makers, quality toiletries and good shelf
space in the bathrooms. No private parking, but guests can use a nearby
multi-storey park. No dogs. *Rooms 75. Closed 24-26 Dec.* AMERICAN EXPRESS
Access, Diners, Visa.

Dublin   Gresham Hotel   64%   £140

Tel 01 874 6881   Fax 01 878 7175   **H**

Upper O'Connell Street Dublin 1   Map 23 D4

A prime position on Upper O'Connell Street and free, secure valet parking
are major attractions of this famous north-city hotel. The comfortably
furnished, chandelier-lit lobby/lounge is a popular meeting place, especially
for morning coffee or afternoon tea, and Toddy's Bar (named after
an illustrious former manager) is an all-day eating spot. Front bedrooms are

best, with smart modern bathrooms, and there are nine full suites.
Banqueting/conference facilities for 200/325. *Rooms 200.*
Closed 25 & 26 Dec. AMERICAN EXPRESS *Access, Diners, Visa.*

Dublin   Grey Door   £50

| Tel 01 676 3286   Fax 01 676 3287 | RR |

22 Upper Pembroke Street Dublin 2   Map 23 D4

Conveniently close to the main south city-centre shopping and business
areas, the Grey Door is discreetly set in a fine Georgian terrace near
Fitzwilliam Square. Russian influences feature strongly, especially in the
dinner menu of the cosy, small-roomed ground-floor restaurant decorated
in classical pale grey and primrose yellow. Starters include blinis with
mushrooms, smoked salmon or caviar. Seafood *moskova* is a mixture
of poached turbot and salmon wrapped in spinach and served with
a tomato and basil vinaigrette. Main dishes range from planked steak
Hussar (a sirloin steak cooked on oak planks, served with garlic butter,
duchesse potatoes and sweet pickle) to a chicken breast, breadcrumbed and
fried after being stuffed with vodka and garlic butter. Fish dishes could
be monkfish *nantaise* – the fish pan-fried and marbled with roast vegetables
and served on a mushroom butter sauce. Lunchtime sees a simple 3-course
set menu; in the basement *Blushers* bistro offers simpler evening fare.
*Seats 50. L 12.30-2.15 D 7-11 (Bistro 6-11.30). Set L £14.50. Closed L Sat,
all Sun & Bank Holidays.* AMERICAN EXPRESS *Access, Diners, Visa.*

Rooms   £99

Seven bedrooms are spacious and appointed to a high standard, with
mahogany furniture and fine fabrics in pale blues and reds; thoughtfully
designed bathrooms have powerful over-bath showers and generous towels.
There is an elegant, period drawing room for residents' use, traditionally
furnished with a marble fireplace and antiques. Staff are friendly and
helpful.

Dublin   Hibernian Hotel   70%   £135

| Tel 01 668 7666   Fax 01 660 2655 | HR |

Eastmoreland Place Ballsbridge Dublin 4   Map 23 D4

A Victorian redbrick building, once a nurses' home, tucked away in a quiet
residential area. Handy for the centre of Dublin, though not quite as central
as the fondly-remembered *Royal Hibernian* (now the site of a shopping mall
on Dawson Street). The public areas, including two reception lounges,
can double up to receive small conferences/receptions; they are cosy, with
open fireplaces and well furnished with decent pictures and plenty
of comfortable seating as well as pretty floral arrangements; the perfect spot
for afternoon tea, offering a haven of peace and tranquillity. The hotel's
trademark is a huge glass bowl of liquorice allsorts and jelly babies on the
reception counter, a theme carried through to the bedrooms, where
it becomes a novel alternative to fresh fruit. Bedrooms, by no means lavish
but quite adequately furnished, offer remote-control TV, trouser press,
hairdryer, bathrobe, slippers; quality Crabtree & Evelyn toiletries (plus
emergency shaving kit and dental care) are to be found in the compact
bathrooms, though the towels are on the small side. Super-friendly staff
provide just the right level of service, which includes a nightly bed turn-
down service; an added bonus is that of real loose-leaf tea for a refreshing
breakfast drink. Children under 12 stay free in their parents' room. Under
the same ownership as *Grey Door* (see entry). Secure parking. *Rooms 30.
Patio garden.* AMERICAN EXPRESS *, Access, Diners, Visa.*

Restaurant   £55

Relaxing dining in an elegantly appointed room decorated in deep
terracotta, dark green and cream or under stylish cream parasols on the
terrace – an oasis of tranquillity in the city. French chef Frederic Souty

produces limited but lively daily-changing à la carte and table d'hote menus; the former may offer a choice of about four first and main courses, typically artichokes and wild mushrooms tossed in garlic or gratin of mussels and raspberry vinegar followed by soup and sorbet at dinner. Well-balanced main courses might include confit of goose with morel and cognac essence or roast noisettes of venison with a redcurrant jus. French cheeseboard. *Seats 40. Parties 15. Private Room 25. L 12.30-2.30 D 6.30-10 (Fri & Sat to 11). Set Sun L £12.95. Set D £21.95. Closed L Sat, Good Friday, Christmas.* AMERICAN EXPRESS *Access, Diners, Visa.*

Dublin	Imperial	£40
Tel & Fax 01 677 2580		**R**
13 Wicklow Street Dublin 2		Map 23 D4

Smartly decorated Chinese restaurant with pink and gold marble effect walls and much polished brass in evidence, creating a smartly upmarket interior. An ornamental pool has golden carp (not on the menu). The regular menu features a familiar selection of mainly Cantonese dishes. Lunchtime and especially on Sundays there's a good selection of dim sum available. Standards of service are excellent. *Seats 180. Parties 50. Private Room 70. Meals 12.30pm-11.45pm. Set L £6 Set D £15.* AMERICAN EXPRESS *Access, Visa.*

Dublin	Ivy Court	£55
Tel 01 492 0633 Fax 01 492 0634		**R**
88 Rathgar Road Dublin 6		Map 23 D4

Swiss chef Joseph Frei cooks an eclectic and imaginative range of dishes in his delightful restaurant almost due south of the city centre. Walls have large Breughel-inspired murals while the menu offers such varied starters as quick-fried ribbons of squid, surprisingly mildly flavoured with garlic and chilis, or traditional black pudding with onion jam and redcurrant jelly. Main dishes include enjoyable pasta dishes as well as sole fillets creole served with fried banana, rice and a mild curry sauce; half a roast boned and stuffed duckling with a raspberry coulis or veal emincé with Swiss-style rösti potatoes. There's an attractive courtyard, out front, used for fine-weather dining. No smoking in downstairs dining room. Children welcome before 8pm. Early bird set dinner (5.30-7, £11.25) Mon-Fri. *Seats 80. Parties 12. Private Room 26. (Dec only) £11.50. D only 5.30-11.30. Closed 25 Dec, Good Friday. Access, Diners, Visa.*

Dublin	Jurys Christchurch Inn	55%	£56
Tel 01 475 0111 Fax 01 470 4888			**H**
Christchurch Place Dublin 8			Map 23 D4

Budget hotel within walking distance of the city centre run on the same lines as sister hotel *Jurys Galway Inn* (see entry, Galway). Spacious rooms, some with views over Christchurch cathedral and its environs, accommodate up to four people for a flat-rate room tariff. Basic requirements are well provided for, with good-sized beds, neat bathrooms with over-bath showers, decent towels and toiletries, direct-dial phone and colour TV. One floor of rooms is designated non-smoking. Children up to 14 stay free in parents' room. No room service. Multi-storey car park nearby. *Rooms 183. Closed 24-26 Dec.* AMERICAN EXPRESS *Access, Diners, Visa.*

Dublin	Jurys Hotel and Towers	76%	£162
Tel 01 660 5000 Fax 01 660 5540			**H**
Pembroke Road Ballsbridge Dublin 4			Map 23 D4

With its close proximity to the Lansdowne Road (rugby and soccer) ground, the main hotel can get seriously busy on match days with fans clamouring to gain access to the bars. The traditional Dubliner Pub to the right of the bright and airy foyer has a comfortable raised seating area, while the other, the Pavilion Lounge, is to the rear under a glass pyramid with rockery, greenery and trickling water. In addition, the hotel has two restaurants, a long-hours Coffee Dock, and from May-October 2½ hours of sparkling Irish cabaret that has played to well over 2 million people during the last 30 years. Most of the bedrooms in the main hotel, including four rooms (two in each part of the hotel) specially adapted for the disabled, have undergone refurbishment recently and provide decent comfort and facilities. Away from all this hustle and bustle, The Towers is a separate hotel within a hotel! With its own security, hospitality lounge, boardroom and reading room you can escape the scrum and relax in total peace and tranquility. Here, the superior bedrooms (£224) and suites, with their own dressing room, and furnished to a high standard, even offer a modern rocking armchair, as well as fresh fruit and chocolates on arrival. There are well-stocked 'robo' bars that charge you at a touch, several telephone extensions, and a turn-down service at night. Smartly-tiled bathrooms have good toiletries, bathrobes and an overhead (and sometimes overpowering) shower above the bathtub. 24hr room service has the odd lapse, with orders taking a long time to arrive (or not at all!) and trays becoming becalmed – sometimes not cleared away for several hours. Children under 12 stay free in their parents' room. Extensive banqueting (600) and conference (850) facilities. Ample parking. No dogs. *Rooms 390. Garden, indoor and outdoor swimming pools, spa bath, beauty and hair salons, masseuse, shop, airline desk, coffee shop (6.30am-4.30am, to 10.45pm Sun).* AMERICAN EXPRESS *Access, Diners, Visa.*

Dublin	**Kapriol**	£65
Tel 01 475 1235		**R**
45 Lower Camden Street Dublin 2		**Map 23 D4**

A popular Italian restaurant near the famous *Bleeding Horse* pub and within walking distance of many of the main hotels. Egidia and Giuseppe Peruzzi provide a warm greeting, a very friendly atmosphere and a menu of traditional Italian dishes which has barely changed in 20 years. Pasta is all home-made, and main-course specialities include sea trout baked in foil, chicken involtini, veal escalopes stuffed with chopped fillet steak and casseroled, and venison in a rich wine sauce (Oct-Mar). *Seats 30. D only 7.30-12. Closed Sun, Bank Holidays, 2 weeks Aug.* AMERICAN EXPRESS *Access, Diners, Visa.*

Dublin	**Langkawi Malaysian Restaurant**	£40
Tel 01 668 2760		**R**
46 Upper Baggot Street Dublin 4		**Map 23 D4**

Decorated throughout with a batik theme, Langkawi offers a selection of far eastern dishes with Malay, Chinese and Indian influences. Chef Alexander Hosey brings street credibility to his mee goreng 'hawker' style (£8.95) – the type of popular food sold cheaply in outdoor markets in Malaysia and Singapore – as well as subtlety to some of his more exotic dishes. range from mild satay to 'devil's curries' for fireproof palates: ayam (chicken breast) and daging babi (pork). The inspiration for the latter comes from "a blending of locally produced spices and seasoning of Portuguese influence in the region of the city of Malacca". *Seats 50. L 12.30-2 D 6-12. Closed L Sat & Sun, 24-27 Dec, Good Friday.* AMERICAN EXPRESS *Access, Diners, Visa.*

Dublin	**Lobster Pot**	£70
Tel 01 668 0025		**R**
9 Ballsbridge Terrace Dublin 4		**Map 23 D4**

A welcoming and comfortable first-floor dining room with a cosy ambience and very genial, long-serving staff. A tray of the day's fresh fish is brought to the table – Galway oysters, mussels, Dublin Bay prawns, plaice, monkfish, black soles and lobster are among the selection. Although specialising in fish they also have an extensive choice of meat dishes including wild duck and excellent steaks. Cooking is soundly classical and traditional and is none the worse for it. Results are extremely enjoyable as in scampi, deliciously moist under their crisp breadcrumb coating and accompanied by a well-made tartare sauce. Salmon and turbot are poached or grilled; plaice and sole grilled on the bone, the latter also available *bonne femme*. Individual preferences are well catered for. The sweet trolley can be admired for its simplicity; typically, a blackcurrant mousse is a perfect blend of light, smooth egg and cream mixture, the blackcurrant glaze providing the correct balance of sweet tartness. *Seats 40. Parties 16. L 12.30-2.30 D 6.30-10.30. Closed L Sat, all Sun, Bank Holidays & 1 week Christmas.* AMERICAN EXPRESS *Access, Diners, Visa.*

Dublin   Locks   £85

Tel 01 454 3391   Fax 01 453 8352   **R**

1 Windsor Terrace Portobello Dublin 8   Map 23 D4

Generous portions of imaginative food are served in Claire Douglas's restaurant down by the canal in the residential Portobello district. Bouillabaisse, ravioli of spinach with prawns in a blue cheese sauce, roast duck with pineapple sauce and suckling pig with apples and horseradish show the style. Steaks are the popular simpler choice. *Seats 47. Private Room 30. L 12.30-2 D 7.15-11. Closed L Sat, all Sun, Bank Holidays, 1 week Christmas. Set L from £13.95 Set D £21.* AMERICAN EXPRESS *Access, Diners, Visa.*

Dublin   Marine Hotel   64%   £84

Tel 01 832 2613   Fax 01 839 0442   **H**

Sutton Cross Dublin 13   Map 23 D4

Standing right at Sutton Cross at the isthmus of Howth some 10kms from the city centre, the Marine has a large car park at the front while at the rear lawns lead right down to the waters of Dublin Bay. Public rooms include a delightful sun lounge overlooking the lawns and an attractive bar with brass fittings and gilt-edged furniture. Both bedroom floors have just been completely refurbished. Decor is appealing with richly coloured floral fabrics and smart darkwood furniture. All are well equipped (hairdryer, trouser press, remote TV). Bathrooms, too, are neat, all with showers, some with shower/WC only. Friendly and helpful staff. *Rooms 26. Garden, indoor swimming pool, sauna. Closed 25 & 26 Dec.* AMERICAN EXPRESS *Access, Diners, Visa.*

Set menu prices may not always include service or wine.

Dublin   Merrion Hall   £70

Tel 01 668 1426   Fax 01 668 4280   **PH**

56 Merrion Road Ballsbridge Dublin 4   Map 23 D4

The recent addition of the adjacent property has doubled the capacity of this charming, immaculately maintained, family-run guesthouse on the main ferry road just south of the city centre. The main sitting room is very comfortable, encapsulating perfectly the friendly and homely ambience generated by the Sheeran family. There's now an additional sitting room identical in size to the original one. It is used primarily in the busier summer months. Bedrooms are pretty and well equipped. Four are triple rooms while a further four have both a double and a single bed. The excellent breakfast selection features a self-service buffet including home-made yoghurt, poached fruits, fresh fruit salad and a cheeseboard. No dogs. *Rooms 15. Closed 2 weeks from 21 Dec. Access, Visa.*

Dublin   Le Mistral   ★   £80

Tel 01 478 1662   Fax 01 478 2853   **R**

16 Harcourt Street Dublin 2   Map 23 D4

Despite its cellar setting and other-worldly history – the restaurant
is located in the now whitewashed basement of a house once inhabited
by Bram Stoker (creator of Dracula) and still contains the old black range
used in his kitchen – Le Mistral brings a touch of warm, herb-scented
Provençal sunshine to Dublin. Larger-than-life proprietor Philippe Misischi
is a wonderfully Poirot-like character who exudes such potent Gallic
hospitality and charm that would-be critics are disarmed even before
orders are taken. Christophe Cassière, who has been chef de cuisine since
the spring of 1994, works closely with M. Misischi in association with his
friend Raymond Blanc; M. Blanc (see Le Manoir aux Quat'Saisons under
Great Milton, England) has made several guest appearances in the kitchen
and is actively involved with menu planning on an ongoing basis – a
unique situation for an Irish restaurant and a partnership which is creating
some exciting results. Based on the results of his daily visits to the market,
a choice of both table d'hôte (three courses at lunch, four in the evening)
and a short (but unusual) carte is offered plus there's always a selection
of daily fresh fish – a wonderfully tempting selection offered at its best,
with understandable leanings towards Mediterranean seafood. Typically,
the daily tray could include oysters, scallops, prawns (the French variety,
to be butterflied and grilled, perhaps), truly wild salmon, monkfish, red
mullet and much more. These maritime treasures are balanced by some
of the earthy ones also keenly appreciated by the French: rabbit, that most
underestimated of meats, served, perhaps, in medallions on a warm salad
with a piquant grain mustard sauce; pigeon, also generally undervalued
in Ireland, roast and served with braised cabbage enlivened by green
Chartreuse; pig's trotters, well-known as hearty pub food in some areas, but
here typically served caramelised as a first course, the tender meat stripped
from the bone, formed into a roundel, seasoned quite sharply and dressed
with fine Provençal breadcrumbs. Balance is achieved with visually
beautiful dishes like a terrine of Bresse guinea fowl, its meat dramatically
layered with colourful diced vegetables en gelée and perfectly partnered
by a richly flavoured, deep red, plum tomato coulis. Main courses are
served with a choice of side salad or the day's vegetables and, while fish
is served with wonderfully aromatic sauces (monkfish with a thyme-and
rosemary-scented *petit jus de volaille*), apparently simple offerings such
as supreme of grilled free-range chicken are not only unexpectedly
flavoursome but might arrive at the table spilling with bright green broad
beans, smoked bacon and the tiniest of baby onions. Classic desserts such
as a deeply dark chocolate marquise perfectly balanced by a pale *crème
anglaise* or a terrine of fresh fruits served with orange caramel please
by their unaffected simplicity and flavour. The excellent cheeseboard
is unashamedly French. Freshly brewed coffee is served by the cup. Service
is attentive throughout and attracts an automatic surcharge of 12½%.
Seats 60. *Parties* 16. *Private Room* 40. L 12-2.30 D 7-11 *(Fri & Sat to 11.30).
Set L £12.95 Set D £18.95. Closed L Sat, all Sun, Bank Holidays & 5 days
Christmas.* AMERICAN EXPRESS *Access, Diners, Visa.*

Dublin   Mont Clare Hotel   66%   £146

Tel 01 661 6799   Fax 01 661 5663   **H**

Merrion Square Dublin 2   Map 23 D4

Sister hotel to the *Davenport* (qv) across the road and with a similar clubby
feel although a little less grand and more intimate in style. The bar is a fine
example of a traditional Dublin pub complete with bare-board floor,
enough mahogany to stock a rain forest and lots of atmosphere. The only
other sitting area is in a small alcove off the smart marble-floored lobby.
Bedrooms are generally not large but have warm decor in stylish dark reds
and blues with darkwood furniture, air-conditioning and telephones
at both desk and bedside with a third in the good marble bathrooms.

Guests have use of the private Riverview Racquets and Fitness Club at members' rates. Free valet parking. **Rooms** *74.* AMERICAN EXPRESS® *Access, Diners, Visa.*

Dublin   No 31   £68

| Tel 01 676 5011   Fax 01 676 2929 | **PH** |

31 Leeson Close off Leeson Street Lower Dublin 2   Map 23 D4

In a small mews close to the city centre (and most Dublin restaurants and nightlife), the Bennetts have opened up their stylish home to offer charming and exclusive bed and breakfast accommodation. You press an intercom at heavy, varnished light oak doors set in a high perimeter wall to gain admittance. The instant you enter, the impression is of a well-designed modern house. It was built by the architect Sam Stephenson and was his home for 30 years. Here he entertained celebrities of politics and culture. Cool white, with good use of light and space, typifies the decor. The lounge, with a mirror mosaic-lined bar in the corner, features an eye-catching square sunken seating area, black leather upholstery contrasting with the white. Around the walls are numerous works of art. Upstairs, there's a large refectory table where Mary Bennett produces excellent breakfasts between 8.30 and 10. These include vegetarian options, freshly baked scones, home-made preserves and freshly squeezed fruit juices. Bedrooms are bright, simply appointed and homely, one with its own patio. Remote-control TVs, radio-alarms and hot drink facilities are standard. Secure, locked parking is also provided, as is a laundry service. **Rooms** *5. Patio. Closed 25 Dec. Access, Visa.*

Dublin   Oisíns   £95

| Tel & Fax 01 475 3433 | **R** |

31 Upper Camden Street Dublin 2   Map 23 D4

The menu at this modest little first-floor restaurant is rendered in both Irish and English, listing a short but interesting selection of dishes with a traditional provenance: Dublin coddle (a stew of bacon, sausages, potatoes and onions), crubeens (pig's trotters), Irish stew with dumplings, carrageen moss. Friendly service, regular live music. The wine list has an Irish table wine from Mallow. **Seats** *40. D only 6.30-10.30. Closed Sun & Mon in winter, Bank Holidays, 24 Dec-end 1st week Jan.* AMERICAN EXPRESS® *Access, Diners, Visa.*

Dublin   Old Dublin Restaurant   £60

| Tel 01 454 2028   Fax 01 454 1406 | **R** |

90/91 Francis Street Dublin 8   Map 23 D4

An evening à la carte has increased the menu options at this welcoming, comfortable restaurant, whose various rooms feature marble fireplaces and good pictures. Eamonn Walsh's cooking takes its main influences from Russia and Scandinavia: gravlax, borsch, blinis with salted salmon, prawns, herrings or mushroom salad, chicken Kiev, Georgian lamb kebabs. House specialities such as prawn-stuffed turbot Odessa, salmon coulibiac and planked sirloin Hussar carry a supplement on the fixed-price menu. Good cheeseboard; all desserts home-made. Early bird menu (6-7) £10. **Seats** *65. Parties 30. Private Room 16. L 12.30-2.30 D 6-11. Closed L Sat, all Sun, Bank Holidays, 3 days Christmas. Set L from £12.50 Set D from £19.* AMERICAN EXPRESS® *Access, Diners, Visa.*

Dublin   101 Talbot   £32

| Tel 01 874 5011 | **R** |

101 Talbot Street Dublin 1   Map 23 D4

Upstairs in a busy shopping street, close to O'Connell Street and the Abbey and Gate Theatres, this bright, airy restaurant has a rather arty cheap and cheerful atmosphere which harmonises well with the wholesome

Mediterranean-influenced and spicy Eastern food. Pasta, vegetarian, fish and meat dishes all appear on the menu: tagliatelle with pesto, hazelnut rissoles, Chinese-style stir-fried vegetables, poached salmon, baked haddock with avocado/hollandaise sauce, pan-fried lamb's liver, medallions of pork with an orange and rum sauce. Open all day for tea, coffee, soup, pasta and snacks. *Seats 90. L 12-3 D 6.30-11 (light meals 10am-11pm). Closed D Mon, all Sun, Bank Holidays.* AMERICAN EXPRESS *Access, Diners, Visa.*

Dublin   Pasta Fresca   £30

Tel 01 679 2402   **R**

2-4 Chatham Street Dublin 2   Map 23 D4

Bustling Italian restaurant/wine bar/deli just off the smart Grafton Street shopping area. Friendly waiting staff serve an all-day selection of straightforward food – pasta, pizza, salads, burgers and a few more substantial meat dishes. *Seats 85. Meals 8am-11.30pm. Closed Good Friday, 25 & 26 Dec. Set L £4.95 Set D £8.50. Access, Visa.*

Prices quoted for the Republic of Ireland are in Irish punts.

Dublin   Patrick Guilbaud   ★ ↑   £100

Tel 01 676 4192   Fax 01 660 1546   **R**

46 James Place off Lower Baggot Street Dublin 2   Map 23 D4

Approaching this purpose-built restaurant, you might wonder if you are in the right street, so unprepossessing does the building look from a distance. But once inside there's no mistake – a comfortable reception lounge with several striped sofas, lots of greenery in both the plant-filled atrium and high-ceilinged dining room, decent art (mostly abstract paintings), and, above all, very smartly attired and professional staff. For well over a decade this has been *the* place in which to enjoy classical French cuisine with a light, modern approach. The seemingly ageless Patrick is on hand to offer advice on the menus as well as engaging customers in conversation, whether on golf – one of his passions – or France's chances in the Five Nations rugby championship, especially against Ireland at Lansdowne Road! For an eponymous restaurant, somewhat unusually Patrick is not the chef/patron – the cooking is left to a team of French chefs, led by Guillaume Le Brun (visible in a glass-fronted kitchen); indeed, most of the staff are French. The ingredients, naturally, are mostly Irish, notably as in seafood dishes, such as pan-fried king scallops served with seasonal salad and bacon, Dublin Bay prawns in crisp pastry cases served with mango and capers, or steamed sea bass on a saffron purée with red pepper oil. Also highly recommended as starters are the home-made lemon pasta with salmon and hot lobster tourte with chive sauce, while game dishes in season (roast wild venison with sauce poivrade and morello cherries or roast breast of pheasant with parcels of mushrooms) are eagerly awaited by regulars. The table d'hote lunch and dinner menus (both exclusive of a service charge of 15%, as is the à la carte) are particularly good value, and though there's a somewhat limited choice at dinner (four courses and coffee), lunch offers four selections among both starters and main courses. And for a table whose occupants cannot make up their minds, why not try the *menu surprise* (£45 per person)? Desserts (a tart lemon mousse, berry cheesecake or poached pear in red wine) and French cheeses are quite splendid, as is the variety of breads offered, the amuse-gueule, the coffee and petits fours. Service is impeccable. As you would expect, the wine list is predominantly French, but not exclusively so, and – for a restaurant of this class – prices are reasonable; note the old classics in the 'Specialist Cellar'. The restaurant is now air-conditioned. *Seats 60. Parties 20. Private Room 30. L 12.30-2 D 7.30-10.15. Closed Sun & Mon, Bank Holidays.* Set L £18.50 Set D £25 & £45. AMERICAN EXPRESS *Access, Diners, Visa.* MARTELL

Dublin   Pizzeria Italia   £25

Tel 01 677 8528   **R**

23 Temple Bar Dublin 2   **Map 23 D4**

A tiny one-room pizza-bar and restaurant run since 1986 by the Alambi
family. Efficient, humorous staff and delicious, herby aromas set the tone:
traditional minestrone is convincingly home-made and pizzas and classic
pasta dishes feature alongside steaks and the likes of *pollo cacciatore* (chicken
cooked in red wine with mushrooms, onion, tomato and oregano) and
crème caramel. *Seats 18. Meals 12-11. Closed Sun & Mon, Bank Holidays,
2 weeks June, 2 weeks from 24 Dec. No credit cards.*

Dublin   Il Primo   £45

Tel 01 478 3373   **R**

16 Montague Street Dublin 2   **Map 23 D4**

Simply appointed little Italian restaurant opposite the Children's Hospital
(Harcourt Street). Dishes range from hot garlic crostini with sun-dried
tomatoes and basil, Roman salad with cold meats and duck liver terrine
with roasted peppers to perky salads, pizzas and pasta. Any wine under
£30 is available by the glass. *Seats 44. Parties 30. L 12-3 D 6-11 (Fri, Sat
to 11.30). Closed Sun, Bank Holidays.* AMERICAN EXPRESS *Access, Diners, Visa.*

Dublin   Raglan Lodge   £77

Tel 01 660 6697   Fax 01 660 6781   **PH**

10 Raglan Road Ballsbridge Dublin 4   **Map 23 D4**

Built in 1861 and epitomising the grand Victorian town-house style, the
lodge stands in a select tree-lined avenue off one of the main routes to the
city centre. Helen Moran has been here just over two years and has created
a charming, hospitable environment. Thirteen white granite steps lead
up to the main door, painted a distinctive and cheering sunshine yellow.
There's a lounge on the lower ground floor, though it is little used, while
on the ground floor there's a fine breakfast room wherein to enjoy the likes
of slices of smoked salmon bordered by soft scrambled eggs. The seven
high-ceilinged bedrooms are spotlessly maintained and feature creature
comforts like sweet-smelling warm bedding, thick towels, good soaps and
crystal-clear reception of all the major television channels. No dogs.
Rooms 7. Garden. Closed 1 week Christmas. AMERICAN EXPRESS *Access, Visa.*

Dublin   Rajdoot   £48

Tel 01 679 4274   **R**

26 Clarendon Street Westbury Centre Dublin 2   **Map 23 D4**

Part of a small UK chain (although the latest branch is on the Costa del
Sol) of reliable restaurants specialising in tandoori and North Indian
Moghlai cooking. The latter tends to produce mild and subtly spiced dishes
like chicken pasanda – the breast stuffed with flaked almonds, mint and
cherries with a sauce of cashew nuts and almonds. Luxurious, somewhat
exotic decor. *Seats 92. L 12-2.30 D 6.30-11.30. Set L from £6.95
Set D from £17.50. Closed Sun, L Bank Holidays, 25 & 26 Dec, Good
Friday.* AMERICAN EXPRESS *Access, Diners, Visa.*

Dublin   Roly's Bistro   ↑   £50

Tel 01 668 2611   Fax 01 660 8535   **R**

7 Ballsbridge Terrace Ballsbridge Dublin 4   **Map 23 D4**

The combination of proven individuals – restaurateur Roly Saul and chef
Colin O'Daly – makes for a successful restaurant, deservedly popular since
opening. On two floors, upstairs perhaps has a more authentic bistro
atmosphere, while the ground floor is a little more sedate, and there's a real
buzz about the place, so much so that staff can sometimes become distracted

and unobservant, especially when you're trying to attract their attention! First comes an excellent variety of breads, followed by an eclectic selection of dishes from crab bisque and guinea fowl terrine to roast pork with apple sauce and Dublin Bay grilled black sole. Less succesful and quite unusual are vegetable gnocchi (potato and pea rissoles!), but spot on are spicy stir-fry chicken and Cajun-style steamed fillet of plaice on a bed of spinach with sun-dried tomatoes and a dash of chili. Good accompanying salads and vegetables as well as the puddings (super orange crème brulée), coffee and inexpensive wines – there are several under £10 a bottle. Regional winner for Republic of Ireland of our Dessert of the Year award 1995. **Seats** *120. Parties 12. Private room 65. L 12-3 D 6-10 (Sun to 9). Closed Good Friday, 25 & 26 Dec. Set L £10.50.* **AMERICAN EXPRESS** *Access, Visa.*

Dublin   Royal Dublin Hotel   63%   £108

Tel 01 873 3666   Fax 01 873 3120   **H**

40 Upper O'Connell Street Dublin 1   Map 23 D4

A modern hotel on Dublin's most famous street, with practical overnight accommodation, an all-day brasserie and a business centre with full facilities. Children under 12 stay free in parents' room. Secure parking for 35 cars in a basement garage. **Rooms** *117. Brasserie (7am-midnight).* **AMERICAN EXPRESS** *Access, Diners, Visa.*

Dublin   Ryans of Parkgate Street   £55

Tel 01 671 9352   Fax 01 671 3590   **R**

28 Parkgate Street Dublin 8   Map 23 D4

This professionally-run, well-appointed little restaurant over the famous pub is popular with locals and, as it is handy for Heuston station just across the bridge, a visit can be a treat before or after a journey. Robert Moorehouse, chef since the restaurant first opened in 1989, prepares interesting menus and presents them with confidence. Typical starters from a choice of eight on the à la carte dinner menu might include lamb's sweetbreads with radicchio, sorrel and mustard sauce or goat's cheese wrapped in spinach baked in filo pastry. Main courses also offer a choice of eight, including, perhaps, feuillette of Dublin Bay prawns and monkfish with lemon and garlic sauce or roast rack of lamb, thyme sauce, served with potato cutlet. Desserts include particularly good ice creams and there's always an Irish farmhouse cheese plate. **Seats** *32. L 12.30-2.30 D 7-10 (Sat to 10.30). Closed L Sat, D Mon, all Sun, Bank Holidays, Good Friday, 25 Dec. Set L £13.* **AMERICAN EXPRESS** *Access, Visa.*

Dublin   Sachs Hotel   62%   £98

Tel 01 668 0995   Fax 01 668 6147   **H**

19-29 Morehampton Road Donnybrook Dublin 4   Map 23 D4

The night club at this small hotel in a Georgian terrace is a popular attraction, and a different kind of exercise is available (free to residents) at a leisure centre a short drive away. Bedrooms are individually appointed in period style, and double-glazing keeps things peaceful at the front. Conference/function facilities. **Rooms** *20. Closed 25 Dec.* **AMERICAN EXPRESS** *Access, Diners, Visa.*

Dublin   Señor Sassi's   £58

Tel 01 668 4544   **R**

146 Upper Leeson Street Dublin 4   Map 23 D4

Busy, bustling restaurant with densely packed marble-topped tables and currently fashionable Mediterranean/Californian style dishes; salad of warm squid with ginger and soy, loin of lamb with aubergine and balsamic vinegar jus, fillet steak with caramelised onions and mash, paillard of salmon with wilted greens and herb salsa, bruschetta of chargrilled vegetables. The daytime menu is in brasserie style with dishes ranging from

£1.90 (for country broth with hot bruschetta) to £7.50 (steak with red wine jus and braised cabbage). *Seats 65. Private Room 30. L 12-3 D 6-11.30 (Fri & Sat 7-12, Sun 5.30-10.30). Set L £9.50. Closed L Sun & Mon, Good Friday, 25 & 26 Dec, 1 Jan.* AMERICAN EXPRESS *Access, Diners, Visa.*

Dublin	Shalimar	£50
Tel 01 671 0738 Fax 01 677 3478		**R**
17 South Great George's Street		**Map 23 D4**

Smart, comfortable restaurant opposite the Central Hotel serving standard Indian fare in friendly fashion. *Seats 110. L 12-2.30 (Sun to 3) D 6-12 (Fri & Sat to 12.30, Sun 5-12). Closed L Sat, 25 & 26 Dec, Muslim Holidays. Set L £6.95.* AMERICAN EXPRESS *Access, Diners, Visa.*

Dublin	Shelbourne Hotel	74%	£243
Tel 01 676 6471 Fax 01 661 6006			**H**
St Stephen's Green Dublin 2			**Map 23 D4**

Situated on St Stephen's Green, Europe's largest garden square, the Shelbourne has been at the centre of Dublin life since opening its doors early in the 19th century. The Irish Constitution was drafted in what is now one of the many function rooms. The hotel has retained much of its original grandeur, with a magnificent faux-marbre entrance hall and a sumptuous lounge where morning coffee and afternoon tea are taken. The famous Horseshoe Bar and the newer Shelbourne Bar are among the favourite gathering places for Dubliners, especially on a Friday night, and many a scandal has originated from their walls. Spacious, elegantly furnished superior and de-luxe rooms and suites have traditional polished wood furniture and impressive drapes, while standard rooms in a newer wing are smaller. All rooms are well appointed, with bathrobes, mini-bars and three telephones as standard. Valet parking. 12 function rooms can cater for up to 500 for a reception. Children up to 16 stay free in parents' room. As we went to press, a major refurbishement programme was nearing completion. Forte Grand. *Rooms 164. Beauty salon, gents' hairdressing, news kiosk.* AMERICAN EXPRESS *Access, Diners, Visa.*

Dublin	La Stampa	£55
Tel 01 677 8611 Fax 01 677 3336		**R**
35 Dawson Street Dublin 2		**Map 23 D4**

Noisy (but unobtrusively), bustling, lively and frenetic – just how a restaurant of this *genre* should be. Sited in a spacious high-ceilinged room with large mirrors and plain wood floor, there's a Renaissance feel about the place, which also has a fully licensed bar where drinks can be enjoyed while waiting for a table. What's more, the staff smile and besides being genuinely cheerful are efficient as well; combine this with decent food at fair prices, and you have a winning and successful formula, as here. Chef Paul Flynn spent several years working in top London restaurants, and though the dishes on the menu are altogether more rustic and substantial than served in those establishments, his background and pedigree stand him in good stead. Starters include freshly made pasta strips with a chunky tomato sauce, chopped Toulouse sausage and coriander (also available as a main course), an authentic Caesar salad, or a spicy terrine of duck with onion compote, while main courses might feature roast monkfish with basil purée, tomato and pepper olive oil, boiled bacon with traditional Irish colcannon (curly kale and mashed potato) and a caper and parsley sauce, or herb-crusted roast rack of lamb served with Provençal tomatoes and potato dauphinois in a light garlic sauce. Desserts are no less abundant in the true sense of the world – try the sticky toffee pudding or chocolate truffle cake, pronounced "wicked" by two adults on a recent visit. Fine coffee and very drinkable house wines on an inexpensive wine list. *Seats 160. Parties 20. Private Room 50. L 12.30-2.30 D 6.30-11.30. Closed L Sat & Sun, Good Friday, 2 days Christmas. Set L £12.50.* AMERICAN EXPRESS *Access, Diners, Visa.*

Dublin   Stauntons on the Green   £88

Tel 01 478 2133   Fax 01 478 2263   **PH**

83 St Stephen's Green South Dublin 2   Map 23 D4

The front bedrooms of Stauntons on the Green overlook the beautiful St Stephen's Green while the rear-facing rooms have almost equally attractive views over the hotel's private gardens and Victorian Iveagh Gardens beyond. Recently acquired, this mid-terrace Georgian property comprises three houses of fine classical proportions. It is gradually undergoing a major programme of upgrading which will lift it from its current guesthouse status. Completion is due sometime in 1995. Currently there's a traditional rear-facing sitting room while upstairs, bedrooms are fitted with simple units and have tea/coffee facilities and remote-control TVs. Bathrooms, all with showers, have good toiletries. No dogs. *Rooms* 32. *Garden. Closed 25 & 26 Dec.* AMERICAN EXPRESS *Access, Diners, Visa.*

Dublin   Stephen's Hall Hotel   65%   £143

Tel 01 661 0585   Fax 01 661 0606   **HR**

14/17 Lower Leeson Street Dublin 2   Map 23 D4

Situated in a thriving business and tourist area just off St Stephen's Green and run on the same lines as *Morrison's Island* in Cork (see entry), this is Dublin's first all-suites hotel. Each suite has its own lobby and kitchenette in addition to a dining area and sitting room. Suite types range from studios (double bed, kitchen, bathroom) to three townhouses each with two single and a double bed, two bathrooms, sitting room, kitchen, dining room, balcony and private entrance to the street. All are well furnished in a pleasingly understated modern Irish style, with thoughtfully planned bathrooms and well-designed furniture. In addition to full room service and 24-hour porter service, a special shopping service is available for guests who wish to cook in their suite; all meals, including breakfast, can also be taken in the restaurant. *Rooms* 37. *Free secure parking. Closed 1 week Christmas, but ring to confirm.* AMERICAN EXPRESS *Access, Diners, Visa.*

The Bistro   £45

The semi-basement restaurant is bright and warmly decorated, with simple table settings. A new menu style had just been introduced as we went to press. Live music Fri and Sat nights. *Seats 48. Parties 20. Private Room 40. L 12.15-2.30 D 6.15-9.30 (Fri & Sat to 10). Closed L Sat, all Sun.*

Dublin   Ta Se Mohogani Gaspipes   £45

Tel 01 679 8138   **R**

17 Manor Street Stoneybatter Dublin 7   Map 23 D4

A nonsense name for a stylish little American restaurant featuring live jazz on Friday and Saturday. Lunchtime brings pasta, omelettes, burgers and New York strip sirloin steak, while in the evening there's pasta plus specialities like chicken cutlet milanese or oriental-style sautéed pork medallions. Also daily fish, international and dessert specials ("your waitperson will inform you"). Vegetarian dishes, too. *Seats 40. Parties 16. L 12-3 D 7-11 (Fri & Sat to 1.30 am), Sun 1-4 (brunch menu). Closed Mon, 2 weeks Aug, Bank Holidays. Access, Diners, Visa.*

Dublin   The Westbury   79%   £189

Tel 01 679 1122   Fax 01 679 7078   **HR**

Off Grafton Street Dublin 2   Map 23 D4

Part of the Doyle Hotel Group since 1985, the Westbury is located within walking distance of many Dublin landmarks. The major shops are also close at hand, and the hotel has its own shopping mall. Among the day rooms are the Terrace Bar and the Sandbank Seafood Bar. Pinks and blues are key colours in the bedrooms, which offer a high standard of comfort and accessories; they range from modernised singles to luxury penthouse suites. Business gatherings and banquets (to a maximum of 170) are accommodated in elegantly furnished boardrooms and function suites. Here, as elsewhere, the Westbury has the atmosphere of a top-class hotel with legions of staff providing a good level of service. *Rooms 203. Gymnasium, beauty & hair salon, news kiosk, coffee shop (10am-10pm, Sun to 3pm).* AMERICAN EXPRESS *Access, Diners, Visa.*

Russell Room   £85

The traditional French menu holds few surprises, though the cooking is sound and both service and surroundings suitably stylish. Seafood makes a strong showing, and flambéed crepes Suzette is a completely apposite dessert for the setting. A three-course table d'hote lunch (four courses at dinner) offers a choice of five or so dishes at each course. *Seats 100. Parties 40. L 12.30-2.30 D 6.30-10.30 (Sun to 9.30). Set L £18.50 Set D £23.50.*

Dublin   Zen   ↑   £50

Tel 01 497 9428   **R**

89 Upper Rathmines Road Dublin 6   Map 23 D4

An unusual Chinese restaurant in many respects, not least that the south-city premises occupy what was once a Church of England meeting hall – the lofty hammer-beam roof is still evident. Purchased by the present owner in the 60s, the building started its new life as a snooker and slot machines hall, but the advent of the national lottery put a stop to that! The other reason it's unusal is because it's owned by an Irishman, Dennis O'Connor, who doesn't speak a word of Chinese, yet imports his chefs and staff directly from Beijing. They eventually arrive after many months of bureaucratic red tape. The cooking is mainly Szechuan with the particularly hot and spicy dishes asterisked on the menu, such as the hot (in both senses) appetizer of dumplings in a ginger, garlic and chili sauce, guaranteed to burn (in a tasteful manner) the roof of your mouth! For the less adventurous there are more conventional starters: sesame prawn toast, crispy spring rolls and orange-flavoured sliced beef. Main dishes include succulent and carefully prepared prawns (fried with cashew nuts or in a garlic sauce), steamed whole black sole in ginger sauce or various sizzling meats. Aromatic or smoked duckling arrive less highly seasoned, or you could give a day's notice and order crispy Beijing duck, roasted whole, its skin and meat mixed with spring onions and bean paste, then rolled in wheat pancakes. For those undecided there are several set dinners from which to choose, or else one can ask for a cross-section of specialities. Charming service can sometimes be a little hesitant; incidentally, the house white wine goes extremely well with the style of cooking. *Seats 85. Parties 12. Private room 14. L 12.30-2.30 D 6-11.30. Closed L Mon-Wed & Sat, 25 & 26 Dec, Good Friday. Set D from £17.50.* AMERICAN EXPRESS *Access, Diners, Visa.*

Dublin   Places of Interest

Tourist Information   Tel 01 284 4768
Dublin Airport   Tel 01 844 5387
Bank of Ireland   College Green Tel 01 661 5933
Trinity College (Book of Kells) and Dublin Experience
   University of Dublin Tel 01 677 2941
The Curragh   Co Kildare Tel 01 289288
Dublin Zoo   Phoenix Park Tel 01 677 1425
Fairyhouse Racecourse   Ratoath Tel 01 825 6777
Irish Whiskey Corner   Bow Street Distillery Tel 01 872 5566
Leopards Town   Fox Rock Tel 01 893607
Gaelic Athletic Association (GAA)   Tel 046 23638
Croke Park Football Ground   Hurling and Gaelic Football
   Tel 01 836 3222

Irish Rugby Union   Tel 01 668 4601
Lansdowne Road Rugby Ground   Baub Bridge Tel 01 668 4601
  Theatres and Concert Halls
Abbey and Peacock Theatres   Lower Abbey Street Tel 01 878 7222
Andrew's Lane Theatre   Exchequer Street Tel 01 679 5720
Gaiety Theatre   South King Street Tel 01 677 1717
Gate Theatre   Cavendish Row Tel 01 874 4045
Olympia Theatre   Dame Street Tel 01 677 7744
Tivoli Theatre   Francis Street Tel 01 454 4472
National Concert Hall   Earlsfort Terrace Tel 01 671 1888
Point Depot (Exhibitions and Concerts)   North Wall Quay
  Tel 01 836 6000
Irish Film Centre   Eustace Street Tel 01 679 3477
  Museums and Art Galleries
Dublinia, Christchurch   Tel 01 475 8137
Chester Beatty Library and Gallery of Oriental Art   Shrewsbury Road
  Tel 01 269 2386
Civic Museum   South William Street Tel 01 679 4260
Dublin Writer's Museum   Parnell Square North Tel 01 872 2077
Fry Model Railway Museum   Malahide Castle Tel 01 845 2758
Irish Museum of Modern Art/Royal Hospital   Kilmainham
  Tel 01 671 8666
Guinness Brewery   James's Gate Tel 01 453 6700 ext 5155
Hugh Lane Municipal Gallery   Parnell Square Tel 01 874 1903
National Gallery of Ireland   Merrion Square West Tel 01 661 5133
National Museum of Ireland   Kildare Street Tel 01 661 8811
National Wax Museum   Granby Row, Parnell Square Tel 01 872 6340
Natural History Museum   Merrion Street Tel 01 661 8811
  Historic Houses, Castles and Gardens
Ashtown Castle   Phoenix Park Tel 01 661 3111
Drimnach Castle   Longmile Road Tel 01 450 2530 *4 miles*
Dublin Castle   Dame Street Tel 01 677 7129
Joyce Tower   Sandycove Tel 01 280 9265
Kilmainham Gaol   Kilmainham Tel 01 453 5984
Malahide Castle   Malahide Tel 01 845 2655
Marsh's Library   St Patrick Close Tel 01 454 3511
National Botanic Gardens   Glasnevin Tel 01 837 7596
Newbridge House   Donabate Tel 045 31301
Newman House   St Stephen's Green Tel 01 475 7255
Number Twenty Nine   Lower Fitzwilliam Street Tel 01 702 6165
Powerscourt Townhouse   South William Street Tel 01 679 4144
Royal Hospital   Kilmainham Tel 01 671 8666
  Cathedrals & Churches
Christ Church Cathedral   Christ Church Place Tel 01 677 8099
St Patrick's Cathedral   Patrick's Close Tel 01 475 4817
Whitefriar Street Carmelite Church   Aungier Street Tel 01 475 8821
Pro Cathedral   Marlborough Street Tel 01 287 4292

Dublin Airport	**Forte Crest**	**57%**		**£129**
Tel 01 844 4211 Fax 01 842 5874				**H**
Dublin Airport Co Dublin				**Map 22 D3**

Conference facilities for 160, 10 meeting rooms, ample car parking and
24hr room service in a modern hotel within the airport complex. Some
non-smoking rooms, some of family size (children up to 16 stay free
in parents' room). ***Rooms** 188. Closed 25 Dec.* AMERICAN EXPRESS *Access,
Diners, Visa.*

Dun Laoghaire   Chestnut Lodge   £50

Tel 01 280 7860   Fax 01 280 1466   PH

2 Vesey Place Monkstown Dun Laoghaire   Map 23 D4

Built in 1844, the building is a very fine example of classical Regency architecture. From its position almost at the end of a row of similar houses on a hillside, there are glimpses of the sea visible through the chestnut trees which were planted in a small park across the road at the front. This is very much a family home with breakfast taken communally at a beautiful highly polished mahogany dining table in the drawing room. Here, after a very comfortable night's sleep in one of the spacious, warm and well-appointed bedrooms, you can enjoy freshly squeezed orange juice, a choice of fresh fruit salad, yoghurts, stewed fruits and cereals before tucking into a delicious traditional Irish cooked breakfast finished off by oven-warmed croissants and home-made preserves. Very usefully located close to the Dun Laoghaire/Holyhead ferry terminal. No dogs. *Rooms 4. Access, Visa.*

Dun Laoghaire   Restaurant na Mara   £75

Tel 01 280 0509   Fax 01 284 4649   R

1 Harbour Road Dun Laoghaire Co Dublin   Map 23 D4

Railway buffs will be fascinated by this elegant harbourside restaurant, as it is the old Kingstown terminal building and is owned by Irish Rail Catering Services. In 1970 a preservation order was issued by the local authority. The interior has classical decor throughout in soft soothing tones. French-influenced menus are a mixture of traditional and modern styles, with a strong emphasis on the sea in dishes like lobster bisque, seafood sausage, oysters raw or served warm with smoked salmon and paloise sauce, grilled black sole, brill Grand Duc and Dublin Bay prawns in garlic butter, mornay or curried. Flambéed specialities feature and there is a short choice of meat and vegetarian dishes. Well-chosen wines (mostly French) at fair prices, with some helpful notes; several good champagnes. *Seats 75. Private Room 36. L 12.30-2.30 D 7-10.30. Closed Sun, 1 week Christmas, Bank Holidays. Set L from £13.50 Set D £23.* AMERICAN EXPRESS *Access, Diners, Visa.*

We welcome bona fide complaints and recommendations on the tear-out pages at the back of the book for readers' comments. They are followed up by our professional team.

Dun Laoghaire   Royal Marine Hotel   64%   £85

Tel 01 280 1911   Fax 01 280 1089   H

Marine Road Dun Laoghaire Co Dublin   Map 23 D4

Imposing Victorian hotel set in four acres of grounds overlooking the ferry port yet just moments from the main street of town. Grand day rooms feature faux-marble columns, high ceilings and elaborate coving. Upstairs, it's a hotel of two halves with the best rooms, off broad chandelier-lit corridors in the original building, having nice lightwood furniture and smart bathrooms; eight of the rooms here are particularly large, with four-poster beds, antique furniture and spacious bathrooms boasting chunky Victorian-style fittings. The remaining bedrooms are in the 1960s' Marine Wing and offer ageing shelf-type fitted units and a textured finish to the walls. Substantial cooked breakfast. No dogs. *Rooms 104. Garden.* AMERICAN EXPRESS *Access, Diners, Visa.*

Dun Laoghaire   Places of Interest

Tourist Information   Tel 01 280 6984/5/6
National Maritime Museum   Haigh Terrace Tel 01 280 0969
James Joyce Tower   Sandycove Tel 01 280 9265

Dundalk   Ballymascanlon House   59%   £77

Tel 042 71124   Fax 042 71598   **H**

Ballymascanlon Dundalk Co Louth   Map 22 D3

Two miles out of Dundalk on the Belfast road, this Victorian mansion is set
in 130 acres of parkland. Bedrooms vary considerably in size, the largest
being arranged around a glass-domed circular landing. There is a well-
planned leisure complex, good golf course and conference facilities for 250.
*Rooms 36. Garden, indoor swimming pool, gymnasium, squash, sauna, solarium,
floodlit tennis, golf (9). Closed 24-27 Dec.* AMERICAN EXPRESS *Access, Diners, Visa.*

Dundalk   Places of Interest

Tourist Information   Tel 042 35484
Basement Gallery   Town Hall Tel 042 32276
Dundalk Racecourse   Dowdallshill Tel 042 34419
Moyry Castle
Kilnasaggart Pillar Stone

Dunderry   Dunderry Lodge Restaurant   £75

Tel 046 31671   **R**

Dunderry Navan Co Meath   Map 22 C3

Although set in a comfortably furnished, characterful old stone building,
formally set tables with white linen and fine glasses create a sense
of occasion at this well-known country restaurant. Owner-chef Paul Groves
uses home-grown and local produce to good effect in menus which are
imaginative without being pretentious. Both table d'hote (a small choice
at each of three courses, or four with soup) and carte are offered. From the
latter, start with a turntable of Oriental appetisers (for two), including
satay, wun tuns, spring rolls, chili prawns, tandoori fish and sushi rice,
a grilled game sausage with sweet and sour red cabbage and a juniper jus
or ravioli of oysters on a light thyme sauce; continue with puff pastry-
wrapped, pan-fried scallops with parsley, bacon and garlic, fried wild
mallard on creamed celeriac and a Madeira sauce or Parma ham-wrapped
teal filled with pistachio. Leave room for the famous dessert trolley that
groans with a wide range of temptations – from floating islands and
chocolate mousses to ices set in a bowl of hazelnut meringue gateau. Sunday
lunch offers exceptional value; there's always a roast. Interesting and unusual
selection of wines. No children under 6. *Seats 40. Parties 12. L Sun
12.30-2.30 (other days by arrangement) D 7-9.30. Closed L Sat, D Sun,
all Mon, Bank Holidays, 2nd week Jan, 1st week Aug. Set L £13.50
Set D £13.95/£15.95.* AMERICAN EXPRESS *Access, Visa.*

Dundrum   Dundrum House   66%   £92

Tel 062 71116   Fax 062 71366   **H**

Dundrum Co Tipperary   Map 23 B5

The Crowe family take great pride in their hotel, a large Georgian house
set in 150 acres through which a trout-filled river runs. Public rooms
include a lofty reception hall, a comfortable drawing room furnished with
wing chairs and, in the old chapel, a bar with live music every night
in summer. Spacious, simply decorated bedrooms are furnished with
antiques. The 150-acre County Tipperary Golf and Country Club
is incorporated within the extensive grounds. *Rooms 55. Garden, tennis,
riding, golf (18), fishing, snooker.* AMERICAN EXPRESS *Access, Diners, Visa.*

Dunkineely   Castle Murray House   69%   £44

Tel 073 37022   Fax 073 37330   **HR**

Dunkineely Co Donegal   Map 22 B2

Since they opened in September 1991 some hidden force has gradually drawn the cognoscenti to Thierry and Clare Delcros' dramatically situated small clifftop hotel a few miles west of Donegal town. Overlooking the ruins of the castle after which it is named, with stunning views of the rugged Donegal coastline and crashing seas, the location is truly breathtaking – and this sturdily built and well-run establishment lives up to it. On to the original structure the Delcros have built well-judged additions including a long and comfortable stone-floored semi-conservatory along the front (imaginatively lit at night and well placed to make the most of the view) and a second phase of spacious bedrooms, furnished simply but to a high standard with pristine white-tiled bathrooms to match. A cosy bar and residents' sitting room beside the dining room opened last year. *Rooms 10. Access, Visa.*

Restaurant   £55

The large, well-appointed dining room has tweed-curtained, double-glazed windows on two sides to take full advantage of the views and a big continental-style table-height log fire, providing an appropriate setting for Thierry Delcros' excellent French cooking. Menus change by the season, with a stronger emphasis on seafood in summer, and pricing by choice of main course allows semi à la carte flexibility of choice with set menu economy, but their understated language does nothing to prepare the diner for the richly imaginative treats Thierry has in store – or for his sure-handed skill in the execution in, typically, mussels in garlic butter finished unexpectedly with melted cheese and served fiercely hot with a crispy seaweed garnish. In addition to a wide range of seafood, main courses might offer an unusual combination like kebabs of duck fillet, wrapped in bacon, tightly packed on wooden skewers and served on a little bed of crisp cabbage. Pretty desserts, a mixed French and Irish farmhouse cheese selection and good coffee. *Seats 45. Parties 15. D only 7-9.30. Closed Mon & Tues Nov-Easter, 24 & 25 Dec, 2 weeks Feb.*

Dunlavin   Rathsallagh House   67%   £110

Tel 045 53112   Fax 045 53343   **HR**

Dunlavin Co Wicklow   Map 23 C4

Joe and Kay O'Flynn's delightful, rambling country house (built in the former stables of a Queen Anne house which burned down in 1798) has an award-winning walled kitchen garden, 280-acre farm and seemingly endless rolling parkland. Fishing and deer-stalking are easily arranged (also hunting in season) and the new 18-hole golf course is a further attraction – or you can simply catch up with your reading by the fireside in the delightfully lived-in drawing room. Rooms are generally spacious and quite luxurious in an understated way, with lovely country views; some smaller, simpler rooms in the stable yard have a special cottagey charm. Three bedrooms were added last year. There is a completely separate private conference facility for up to 50 theatre-style (25 boardroom-style) in a courtyard conversion at the back. Outstanding breakfasts are served in the traditional way from a huge sideboard. No children under 12. *Rooms 17. Garden, croquet, indoor swimming pool, tennis, golf (18), snooker, helipad. Closed 23-26 Dec.*  *Access, Diners, Visa.*

Restaurant   £65

Take in the easy-going atmosphere in the old kitchen bar while reading the menu, then settle down in the traditional dining room and enjoy the evening shadows falling on parkland and the hills beyond. Good home cooking is the order of the day, allowing the freshness and quality of prime local produce to come through. Typical offerings on the limited choice four-course menu might include mushroom and thyme soup, grilled Wexford scallops or woodland salad with quails' eggs, followed by Duncannon turbot with béarnaise or spicy bacon and garlic potatoes. Roast local beef is a speciality, also Wicklow lamb. Leave some room for a tempting dessert from the trolley, or some Irish farmhouse cheese. Snacks are also served all day in the bar. *Seats 50. Private Room 15. L by arrangement for groups, not Sun. D 7.30-9. Closed Mon in winter, 3 days Christmas, 1 week from 2 Jan. Set L £14.95 Set D £25-£30.*

Dunworley	Dunworley Cottage	£60
Tel 023 40314		**R**
Butlerstown Clonakilty Dunworley Co Cork		Map 23 B6

Katherine Norén's remote stone cottage is a haven of serious cooking, favouring organic produce and catering for special dietary needs. Many dishes have become specialities, including nettle soup, Clonakilty black or white/black pudding served with sherry sauce and lingonberries, home-made smoked salami, seafood casserole and steaks pan-fried and served with garlic butter, fried onions, mushrooms and a green peppercorn sauce. Apfel strudel, home-made ice creams and petits fours, farmhouse cheeses to finish. Children's menu (Swedish meatballs the favourite) or half-portions at half prices. *Seats 50. Private Room 20. L 1-3 D 6.30-10. Closed Mon & Tue, also Nov and Jan-Feb. Set D £20.* AMERICAN EXPRESS *Access, Diners, Visa.*

Durrus	Blairs Cove House Restaurant	£60
Tel 027 61127		**R**
Blairs Cove Durrus nr Bantry Co Cork		Map 23 A6

Converted from the characterful outbuildings of the 17th-century Blairs Cove House, in a lovely waterside location overlooking Dunmanus Bay, Sabine and Philippe de Mey's restaurant has been delighting guests with its unique style since 1981. The renowned buffet groans under an abundance of starters (local seafood, patés and salads), then a wide range of main courses that includes locally caught fish – warm salad of scallops, perhaps, or John Dory with vegetables, lemon and soya dressing – and specialities like rack of lamb or steak cooked over an open wood-fired grill in the restaurant. To finish, irresistible desserts and local farmhouse cheeses are dramatically displayed on top of the grand piano. The loos are up a long flight of stairs. Well-equipped, self-catering accommodation is available on the premises and nearby. Look for the blue entrance gate, 1½ miles outside Durrus, on the Goleen/Barley Cove road. *Seats 59. D only 7.30-9.30. Closed Sun (also Mon Sep-Jun), Nov-Feb. Set D £24.* AMERICAN EXPRESS *Access, Diners, Visa.*

Ennis	Auburn Lodge	61%	£70
Tel 065 21247 Fax 065 21202			**H**
Galway Road Ennis Co Clare			Map 23 B4

Low-rise modern hotel on the N17 20 minutes from Shannon airport. Practical accommodation, friendly staff and versatile conference/function facilities for up to 500. Ample free parking. No dogs. *Rooms 100. Garden, tennis.* AMERICAN EXPRESS *Access, Diners, Visa.*

Ennis	Old Ground Hotel	66%	£99
Tel 065 28127 Fax 065 28112			**H**
Ennis Co Clare			Map 23 B4

This famous old ivy-clad hotel next to Ennis cathedral is handy for Shannon Airport and a convenient base for touring Clare. Some of the ground-floor bedrooms are suitable for disabled guests, and conference facilities for up to 250 (banquets 180) are provided. Children under 16 may stay free in their parents' room. Forte Heritage. *Rooms 58.* AMERICAN EXPRESS *Access, Diners, Visa.*

Ennis   West County Inn   59%   £55

Tel 065 28421   Fax 065 28801   **H**
Clare Road Ennis Co Clare   Map 23 B4

"Hospitality is our strength" is the motto of this bright modern hotel, and that extends to families, disabled guests (some rooms expecially fitted out) and conference delegates. 1994 saw the completion of a programme of refurbishment in the bedrooms. The West County also has a snooker room, and guests may use free of charge the leisure centre at the sister hotel *Clare Inn* (Newmarket-on-Fergus). *Rooms 110. Tennis, Snooker.* AMERICAN EXPRESS® *Access, Diners, Visa.*

Ennis   Places of Interest

Tourist Information   Tel 065 28366
Graggaunowen Bronze Age Project   Quin Tel 061 367178
Knappogue Castle   Quin Tel 061 361511

Enniskerry   Curtlestown House   £50

Tel 01 282 5083   Fax 01 286 6509   **R**
Curtlestown Enniskerry Co Wicklow   Map 23 D4

A charming country restaurant in a little farmhouse half an hour's drive from Dublin. Colin Pielow's traditional menus change with the seasons, game being a winter stalwart, with fish taking centre stage in summer. Poached salmon with watercress sauce, chicken chasseur, braised saddle of rabbit and peppered sirloin steak show his admirably straightforward style. Sunday lunch is much more a family affair than the evenings. One room is reserved for non-smokers. *Seats 45. Parties 20. Private Room 25. L (Sun only) 12.30-2.30 D 8-10. Closed Mon & D Sun. Set Sun L £12 Set D from £18. Access, Diners, Visa.*

> We welcome bona fide complaints and recommendations on the tear-out pages at the back of the book for readers' comments. They are followed up by our professional team.

Enniskerry   Enniscree Lodge   59%   £77

Tel 01 286 3542   Fax 01 286 6037   **HR**
Glencree Valley Enniskerry Co Wicklow   Map 23 D4

The views are really wonderful from this friendly old inn, which has a cosy bar for winter, a terrace for sunny weather and good all-day bar food. Bedrooms are comfortably furnished in country style and most enjoy the beauty of the setting; bathrooms are slightly dated but neat and functional. A residents' lounge doubles as a small function room. Children up to 12 may stay free in parents' room. *Rooms 10. Closed Mon-Thur in Jan & Feb.* AMERICAN EXPRESS® *Access, Diners, Visa.*

Restaurant   £60

Chef Paul Moroney succeeds with a combination of traditional and contemporary cuisine in this attractive restaurant overlooking Glencree. Dishes on a winter menu included potato and parsnip boxty with a purée of spiced apple, terrine of rabbit and pigeon, Wicklow lamb in a mustard crust with mint chutney, and roast pheasant with garden herb stuffing and juniper berry sauce. *Seats 40. Parties 12. L 12.30-2.30 D 7.30-9.30 (Sat to 10, Sun to 9). Set L £14 Set D £14.50.*

Enniskerry   Places of Interest

Powerscourt Gardens and Waterfall   Tel 01 286 7676
Fernhill Gardens   Sandyford Tel 01 295 6000 *3 miles*

Fahan   Restaurant St John's   £55

Tel 077 60289   **R**

Fahan Innishowen Co Donegal   Map 22 C1

In a substantial period house overlooking Lough Swilly, Reg Ryan's warm welcome is underlined by a glowing open fire in the bar area and the decor throughout is comfortably unassertive, leaving the mind clear to enjoy Phil McAfee's confident cooking to the full. A two-tier system offers a five-course restricted choice £16 menu, or more choice at £20. Start perhaps with smoked chicken salad with hazelnut oil and balsamic vinegar or gravad lax with a dill sauce, followed by a home-made soup – typically carrot and tarragon or a chowder - then a tossed mixed leaf salad. Main courses might include tender crisp-skinned roast duckling, cooked on the bone but served off it, lamb with a home-made gooseberry mint jelly or a wide choice of fish – turbot, brill, John Dory – with fennel sauce. Details – delicious home-baked bread, imaginative vegetables, desserts with the emphasis on flavour rather than show, such as peaches in brandy with vanilla ice cream and wonderful choux petits fours with spun sugar served with freshly brewed coffee – all add up to a great dining experience. There's a good selection of half bottles and New World wines on the comprehensive wine list at friendly prices. *Seats 40. Private Room 22. No smoking in rear dining room. D only 7-9.30. Closed Sun-Tue, 2 days Christmas, Good Friday.* AMERICAN EXPRESS® *Access, Diners, Visa.*

Ferrycarrig Bridge   Ferrycarrig Hotel   61%   £90

Tel 053 22999   Fax 053 41982   **HR**

Ferrycarrig Bridge nr Wexford Co Wexford   Map 23 D5

All bedrooms in this well-run modern waterside hotel overlook the Slaney estuary and there is a path leading to Ferrycarrig Castle. Comfortably furnished public rooms include the Dry Dock bar and two restaurants, all enjoying the views. Stylish bedrooms have well-equipped bathrooms with plenty of shelf space. There's conference space for up to 400, ample free parking and up-to-date leisure facilities. *Rooms 40. Garden, gymnasium, sauna, steam room, solarium, whirlpool bath, beauty salon.* AMERICAN EXPRESS® *Access, Diners, Visa.*

The Conservatory   £60

Renovations and extensions continue at Ferrycarrig, but the Conservatory restaurant remains a pleasant spot beside a paved garden, making good use of the waterside location. Well regarded locally and perhaps best known for Sunday lunch, the kitchen (under head chef Mairead Kennedy since 1992) is at its best when stretched on the à la carte. Local produce is highlighted in, for example, a zesty starter pf crab meat enhanced with root ginger, spring onion and pimento, bound with dairy cream and served with a tossed salad; this might be followed by a choice of local beef, pork or seafood and a more unusual choice such as new season's guinea fowl, boned and wrapped in smoky bacon, roasted and served on a piquant cranberry and orange vinaigrette. Desserts range from the homely, as in warm rhubarb and ginger tart with crème anglaise, to more sophisticated offerings and there's always a farmhouse cheeseboard. Also The Boat House restaurant (à la carte D only 6.30-9, seats 45). *Seats 90. L 12.30-2.15 D 7-9. Set Sun L £9.50 Set D £19.50. Closed D Sun, all Mon & Tue.* AMERICAN EXPRESS® *Access, Diners, Visa.*

Foulksmills Horetown House £50

Tel 051 63771   Fax 051 63633

R

Foulksmills Co Wexford

Map 23 C5

Horetown House is best known as a residential equestrian centre with
a relaxed country atmosphere. Residents generally use the dining room
in the main house (where a hearty farmhouse dinner is offered as an
alternative to the more formal table d'hote). Alternatively, the Cellar
Restaurant, which is cosy and atmospheric, with an open fire, whitewashed
arches and sturdy country furniture, is open to non-residents and very
popular in the area, especially for Sunday lunch (2 sittings). Proprietor Ivor
Young and his head chef David Cronin can be relied on to produce meals
based on quality ingredients, including local salmon, wild Wicklow
venison and other game in season. Mid-week early bird (6.30-7.30) menu:
£16. **Seats** 45. Parties 10. Private Room 30. L (Sun only) 12.30-2.30 D 7-9.
Set L £9.50 Set D from £19.50. Closed D Sun, all Mon, Bank Holidays,
Christmas week. Access, Visa.

Furbo Connemara Coast Hotel 71% £120

Tel 091 92108   Fax 091 92065

H

Furbo Co Galway

Map 23 B4

Snuggled down into rocks between Barna and Spiddal, on the sea side
of the road, this pleasingly unobtrusive, low-rise modern hotel has been
developed with an environmentally considerate design policy already
successfully applied at the sister hotel, *Connemara Gateway*, at Oughterard.
Spacious public areas include an impressive foyer/lounge area, large
restaurant and banqueting/conference rooms (capacity up to 500/750)
overlooking the sea and a well-equipped leisure centre. Most bedrooms
have sea views and, although not individually decorated, are comfortably
furnished with neat en-suite bathrooms. Good family facilities include six
interconnecting rooms, a playroom (supervised at weekends and
throughout the summer season), a children's entertainment programme and
a new outdoor play area and games/snooker room added in 1994.
Rooms 113. Terrace, tennis, indoor swimming pool, children's splash pool, gym,
solarium, sauna, spa bath, steam room, news kiosk. Closed 25 & 26 Dec.
AMERICAN EXPRESS Access, Diners, Visa.

Galway Ardilaun House 66% £94

Tel 091 21433   Fax 091 21546

H

Taylors Hill Galway Co Galway

Map 23 B4

The original house was built in 1840 and contains handsomely
proportioned day rooms looking out over the attractive grounds.
Sympathetic extensions have been added over the past 30 years or so,
providing unpretentious, traditionally furnished bedrooms of various sizes,
and a conference facility for up to 400 delegates. Friendly, helpful staff.
No dogs. **Rooms** 90. Garden, gymnasium, sauna, solarium, snooker.
Closed 6 days Christmas. AMERICAN EXPRESS Access, Diners, Visa.

Galway Brennans Yard 64% £90

Tel 091 68166   Fax 091 68262

H

Lower Merchants Road Galway Co Galway

Map 23 B4

A new hotel created from stylishly converted old warehousing in Galway
city's 'Left Bank' area. First impressions are of an attractive building with
unexpectedly cramped entrance, but the second phase of development,
which will include the foyer as originally planned, has yet to be completed.
Public rooms currently in operation include a pleasantly bright if smallish
dining room (also to be extended) and, at the back, the striking Oyster Bar
for informal meals, especially local seafood. Individually decorated
bedrooms make up in style what is lacking in space – well-planned, clean-

lined rooms have old stripped pine pieces, locally-made pottery and neat, functional bathrooms; three rooms have both a double and single bed; family facilities are provided. Direct-dial phones, radio and TV, tea/coffee-making facilities, hairdryer and toiletries included as standard. A large extension is planned for 1995. **Rooms 24.** *Closed 2 weeks Christmas.* AMERICAN EXPRESS *Access, Diners, Visa.*

Galway	Casey's Westwood Restaurant	£60
Tel 091 21442/21645		**R**
Dangan Upper Newcastle Galway Co Galway		Map 23 B4

Bernie and Mary Casey have been running this popular eating place since 1982 and the long, low building houses a number of bars and restaurant areas to suit various occasions. An evening in the main restaurant starts in the cocktail lounge, where orders are taken before you settle into a comfortable carver or banquette at a well-appointed table to enjoy son John Casey's sound cooking; there's no doubting John's commitment or his imaginative flair in the kitchen. His menus offer a wide choice – perhaps offering a timbale of smoked salmon and cream cheese with mango mayonnaise, stuffed fillet of pork with wild mushroom sauce and feuilleté of grapes with a Kirsch sabayon at lunchtime, from a three-course menu with three choices at each stage. Four-course dinners see more involved dishes, from ravioli of chicken and cheese with smoked bacon and basil sauce to half a roast pheasant served with a purée of parsnip and chocolate and raspberry sauce, and blackberry and blackcurrant délice with home-made fig and port ice cream – flavours galore! Vegetables are imaginative, desserts unusual and prettily presented and home-made petits fours are served with coffee. Low-cholesterol and vegetarian dishes available. *Seats* 120. L 12.30-2.15 D 6.30-10. *Closed Good Friday, 24-26 Dec. Set L £10.95 Set D £19.50.* AMERICAN EXPRESS *Access, Visa.*

Galway	Corrib Great Southern Hotel	68%	£128
Tel 091 755281 Fax 091 751390			**H**
Dublin Road Galway Co Galway			Map 23 B4

Overlooking Galway Bay, a large, modern hotel on the edge of the city, offering a wide range of facilities for both business guests and family holidays. Bedrooms vary considerably; refurbished rooms are much improved and new, spacious 'superior' rooms are well planned with good attention to detail and stylish bathrooms. Children under 2 stay free in parents' room, £20 per night for under-12s; baby-sitting arranged on request. The (smallish) swimming pool has a lifeguard at all times and, in summer only, children's entertainment and a crèche are provided. New state-of-the-art business/convention centre has facilities for groups of 8 to 850, with banqueting for up to 700. Public areas include a cosy residents' lounge and O'Malleys Pub, a big, lively bar with sea views. **Rooms 180.** *Indoor swimming pool, steam room, spa bath, snooker, helipad.* AMERICAN EXPRESS, *Access, Diners, Visa.*

Galway	Glenlo Abbey	68%	£115
Tel 091 26666 Fax 091 27800			**H**
Bushy Park Galway Co Galway			Map 23 B4

An 18th-century abbey conversion whose newest rooms include six suites with whirlpool baths. All the rooms have king-size beds, personal safes and roomy, well-designed marble bathrooms. There are two bars – the Kentfield for cocktails and the convivial Oak Cellar, and a variety of function rooms. An 18-hole golf course with clubhouse and restaurant were added last summer; two tennis courts, a gymnasium and sauna were promised for the end of 1994. 134-acre waterfront position, with 800-metre frontage on to the river Corrib. **Rooms 43.** *Garden. Closed 24-29 Dec.* AMERICAN EXPRESS *Access, Diners, Visa.*

Galway   Great Southern   69%   £113

Tel 091 64041   Fax 091 66704   **H**

Eyre Square Galway Co Galway   **Map 23 B4**

Overlooking Eyre Square right in the heart of Galway, this historic railway
hotel (built in 1845) has retained many of its original features, and old-
world charm mixes easily with modern facilities. Refurbished public rooms
are quite grand and include O'Flahertys Pub bar as well as a cocktail
lounge. Bedrooms, which vary somewhat but are generally spacious, are
traditionally furnished with dark mahogany units, brass light fittings and
smart fabrics. Various rooms offer conference facilities for up to 450
(banquets 350). Roof-top swimming pool with magnificent views over the
city. *Rooms 116. Indoor swimming pool, sauna, steam room, hair salon.*
AMERICAN EXPRESS *Access, Diners, Visa.*

Galway   Jurys Galway Inn   55%   £61

Tel 091 66444   Fax 091 68415   **H**

Quay Street Galway Co Galway   **Map 23 B4**

The emphasis at the Galway Inn is firmly on value for money; run on the
same lines as the new *Jurys Christchurch Inn* in Dublin, this 'inn' offers
a good standard of basic accommodation without frills. Rooms, almost all
with lovely views, are large (sleeping up to four people) with everything
required for basic comfort and convenience – neat en-suite bathroom, TV,
phone – but no extras. Beds are generous, with good-quality bedding, but
wardrobes are open; don't expect tea/coffee-making facilities or room
service, either. Public areas include an impressive, well-designed foyer with
seating areas, a pubby bar with a good atmosphere and a self-service
informal restaurant. Obviously a good place for family accommodation and
budget-conscious travellers; booking some way ahead is advised.
Rooms 128. Closed 24-28 Dec. AMERICAN EXPRESS *Access, Diners, Visa.*

Galway   The Malt House   £50

Tel 091 63993   Fax 091-751796   **R**

Olde Malt Mall off High Street Galway Co Galway   **Map 23 B4**

Since changing hands in 1993, this welcoming old restaurant and bar off
High Street has kept its character but seems to have benefited from
a renewal of vigour – the style is much the same but, whether you drop
in for a bowl of home-made soup (which comes with a particularly good
brown bread for a mere £1.60) or have a full lunch or dinner from the
decidedly traditional restaurant menu, it is served with enthusiasm.
*Seats 55. Private Room 16. L 12.30-3 D 6.30-10.30. Closed L Sun, 3 days
Christmas. Set L £7/£9.50. Set D £13.95/£16.50.* AMERICAN EXPRESS *Access,
Diners, Visa.*

Galway   Places of Interest

Tourist Information   Tel 091 63081
Thoor Ballylee   Gort Tel 091 31436 *W B Yeats' home*
Coole   Gort Tel 091 31804 *Nature Reserve*
Galway Racecourse   Ballybrit Tel 091 53870
Aran Islands   Tel 091 63081

Glasson   Glasson Village Restaurant   £50

Tel 0902 85001   **R**

Glasson Athlone Co Westmeath   **Map 22 C3**

An attractive stone building (once a barracks) in a pretty village off the
main road in Goldsmith country. The atmosphere is friendly, and the place
really bustles at Sunday lunchtime. Owner-chef Michael Brooks
is something of a seafood specialist, so on the dinner menu you might find
goujons of lemon sole with garlic butter, hot terrine of salmon and hake

with a sweet red pepper sauce, seafood soup and the fresh fish dish of the day. Other choices could include a warm salad of spicy lamb sausages, tandoori-style julienne of chicken with mint sauce and roast rack of lamb *persillé*. Lobsters and oysters are kept in a tank in the reception area.
Seats 55. Parties 12. Private Room 14. L 12.30 & 2.15 (Sun only, 2 sittings) D 7-10.15. Closed D Sun, all Mon, 3 weeks Oct, 4 days Christmas. Set L £9.75 Set D £16.75. Access, Diners, Visa.

Glasson	Wineport Restaurant	£40
Tel 0902 85466 Fax 0902 85466		**R**
Glasson nr Athlone Co Westmeath		Map 22 C3

In an idyllic waterside location on Lough Ree, just outside Athlone, this relaxed, well-appointed restaurant is decorated on a stylish nautical theme and seems to offer the best of every world, with a cosy reception area and open fire at one end and views over the lough from most tables. Thérèse Gilsenan's confident cooking puts flesh on simple but imaginative seasonal menus for different occasions – all-day food in summer, early dinners (called the Tee-Bird Menu in honour of regulars from Glasson Golf Club), Sunday brunch and à la carte dinner menu -- in dishes like warm duck liver, sweet and sour dressing (crisp, colourful mixed leaves, crusted juicy pink livers, judiciously light vinaigrette) with freshly baked brown and white breads, a traditional Sunday roast (pink-cooked lamb, perhaps, with home-made redcurrant and mint jelly), fresh cod fillet updated with an unusual but not overpowering basil and pine nut sauce, delicious home-made ices and warm fruit pies, aromatic freshly-brewed coffee. All this and great service, a wonderful view and often a pair of visiting swans to boot. An enterprising 'pot-luck' system of browsing through the bottles in stock rather than consulting a list provides entertainment and safeguards the budget, as most sell at a flat rate of £8.95, with half of any bottle for £5.50; there's also a smaller selection of classics at £18.95. *Seats 45. Parties 30. L Sun only 12-4 D 5.30-10 (except June-Aug Meals 12-10). Closed 25 & 26 Dec. Set D £12.50.* AMERICAN EXPRESS *Access, Diners, Visa.*

Glen of Aherlow	Aherlow House	63%	£53
Tel 062 56153 Fax 062 56212			**H**
Glen of Aherlow nr Tipperary Co Tipperary			Map 23 B5

Standing four miles from Tipperary in the middle of a forest, Aherlow House was originally a hunting lodge. The decorative inspiration is Tudor, and beyond the heavy oak doors the atmosphere is set by darkwood beams and log fires. A large terrace outside the bar commands views of the glen. Well-appointed, individually furnished bedrooms include two suitable for families (under-tens free in parents' rooms). Conference/function facilities. No dogs. *Rooms 10. Closed Mon-Thu Nov-mid Dec & mid Jan to early March.* AMERICAN EXPRESS *Access, Diners, Visa.*

Glen of Aherlow	Place of Interest
Tipperary Racecourse Tel 062 51357	

Glendare	The Rectory	NEW	£65
Tel 028 33072			**R**
Glendare Co Cork			Map 22 B6

Situated in a lovely south-facing waterside location, this beautifully proportioned Georgian residence has been restored to its former elegance and now provides a delightful setting for a fine restaurant. Throughout the reception and dining areas, bold, deep wall colours are picked up in the soft-hued floral curtains that frame long views over Glandora Harbour towards islands of Adam and Eve, while crisp white linen, fine glass glasses, fresh flowers, comfortable balloon-back mahogany chairs and traditionally uniformed staff all set the scene for Ciarán Scully's skilful cooking. Carefully sourced ingredients – including fish caught from their own boat and landed just below the restaurant each day – feature on a well-balanced table d'hote menu that changes weekly and a carte varied every few weeks according to seasonal availability, in first courses like tender lamb's liver, pan-fried until just pink and served on a Marsala jus with piquant, naturally sweet-sour onion confit, a puffball of featherlight Yorkshire pudding, or unusual steamed skate wings with a parsley and caper sauce, the white flesh scattered jewel-like with glistening diced carrot and leek. Good home-made breads (brown soda with white sesame seed rolls) accompany good soups – a smooth, carefully balanced combination such as smoked salmon with leek, perhaps – or alternatively a crisp, colourful mixture of garden salads and fresh herbs. Strong seafood main courses – typically four of nine on the carte, including turbot, monkfish, John Dory and wild salmon -are balanced by imaginative meat and poultry including, perhaps, roast saddle of rabbit with baby vegetables, sun-dried tomatoes, Parma ham and Madeira jus, or juicy sliced breast of chicken stuffed with a mousseline of salmon and prawn encircling a crisp tri-colour spaghetti of vegetables, served on a light prawn sauce – a complex dish and a delight to the eye which could disappoint in less skilful hands, but Ciarán Scully balances colours, textures and flavours with the skill of a master juggler. Organically grown vegetables, always a selection of at least five, are served on individual gratin dishes. Tempting desserts include a baked rhubarb compote with simple country flavours in contrast to the sophistication of, say, dark, milk and white chocolate marquise with hazelnut fudge sauce and lemon and orange jelly. Farmhouse cheeses are all local and there's an unusually wide selection of speciality teas and tisanes plus good coffee to accompany imaginative petits fours. *Seats 80. Parties 12. Private Room 40. D only 7-9.30. Set D £21.50. Closed 25 Dec.* AMERICAN EXPRESS *Access, Diners, Visa.*

Goleen Harbour   Heron's Cove Restaurant   £35

Tel 028 35225   Fax 028 35422   **RR**

Goleen Harbour West Cork Co Cork   Map 23 A6

Owner-chef Sue Hill runs a tidy ship at her chameleon-like waterside restaurant, which converts from its daytime persona as a practical, inexpensive stop-off place with rugged wooden tables and menus to match – hearty soups, home-made bread, home-cooked ham, farmhouse cheeses, seafood specials and afternoon teas – to a romantic candle-lit evening restaurant with embroidered cloths, linen napkins and silver cutlery. As the atmosphere is transformed, so too is the menu, now sophisticated and frequently changing. What the two faces of Heron's Cove have in common is the freshness of good local ingredients and a refreshing determination to keep prices reasonable. Lobster and oyster tanks. Good choice of sensibly-priced wines. *Seats 30. Private Room 24. Meals 12-9.45pm. Set L (Sun) £8.75 Set D £14.50/£17.50. Closed Oct-May.* AMERICAN EXPRESS *Access, Diners, Visa.*

Rooms   £33

Three en-suite rooms are available for bed & breakfast throughout the year (but booking essential Oct-Apr). Self-catering accommodation also available. Seaside terrace. *Garden.*

Gorey   Marlfield House   81%   £154

Tel 055 21124   Fax 055 21572   **HR**

Gorey Co Wexford   Map 23 D5

Built in 1820 and standing in lovely gardens and woodland, the mansion has been owned and run by the Bowe family since 1978. Fine beaches and many tourist spots are within a walk or short drive, but it's equally pleasant to 'stay put' and relax in the sumptuous, stylish day rooms. These include a semi-circular hall (note the splendid 18th-century marble fireplace) and an elegant lounge. Bedrooms are individually decorated and vary from charming smaller rooms at the top of the house – some with four-posters

and all with good facilities and beautiful bedding including fine, broderie
anglaise-trimmed, cotton sheets – to a very grand series of six luxurious
suites on the ground floor, each different but all with elaborate use
of exclusive fabrics, carefully chosen antiques and pictures and
appropriately large, well-appointed bathrooms. Colours throughout the
house are rich and subtle and beautiful fresh flowers abound. No dogs.
Rooms *19. Garden, sauna, tennis, helipad. Closed 10 Dec-1 Feb.*
AMERICAN EXPRESS *Access, Visa.*

Restaurant® £90

In one of the loveliest formal dining rooms of any Irish country house,
trompe l'oeil greenery leads effortlessly into a conservatory richly hung
with well-maintained plants and through to the garden with its immaculate
lawns and borders backed by mature trees. Kevin Arundel took over
as head chef in the spring of 1994 and, working closely with the owner
Mary Bowe, produces sophisticated seasonal menus firmly based on local
produce, much of it grown under Ray Bowe's supervision in a neat kitchen
garden almost within sight of the dining room window. Local game
features in season, and the area is famous for its soft fruit, especially
strawberries which take pride of place on high summer dessert menus;
there is always fresh fish straight from Courtown harbour and also mussels
from Wexford in season. A typical dinner might start with tartare
of smoked salmon with a cucumber and lemon dressing, followed
by a classic French onion soup and pan-fried monkfish and cod on a bed
of fennel, with a chive and tomato sauce. Garden vegetables are just that,
appearing in side dishes and vegetarian alternatives like a little quiche
of mixed vegetables topped with blue cheese and a lovage cream sauce.
Sophisticated desserts like iced praline and armagnac parfait with
a blackcurrant and cassis coulis or pear and cinnamon crème brulée
compete for attention with Irish farmhouse cheeses, including one of the
longest-established and best, locally-made St Killian from Carrighbyrne.
Formal luncheon is available in the dining room and, in addition, a library
snack menu offers superior bar food. The wine list is long on French
classics (with notes on Bordeaux and Burgundy vintages) but short on half
bottles, and there's only a modest section on the New World. **Seats** *60.
L 12.30-1.45 D 7-9.30. Set L £17.50 Set D £28.*

> If we recommend meals in a hotel or inn a separate entry is made for its
> restaurant.

Greencastle   Kealy's Seafood Bar   £45

Tel 077 81010   **R**

The Harbour Greencastle Co Donegal   Map 22 C1

Unexpected sophistication awaits the visitor to this rugged commercial
fishing port – James and Tricia Kealy's bar is more cocktail than
fisherman's and, although tables are simply laid with paper napkins and
inexpensive cutlery and glasses, it is immediately obvious that the food
is taken seriously. Wholesome all-day snacks give way to a good value
four-course dinner menu, often including popular dishes lifted out of the
ordinary by giving them a new twist – avocado may come with pesto and
sun-dried tomatoes, for instance, poached salmon with a wild mushroom
sauce, even the ubiquitous seafood cocktail, though simply described as 'a
mixture of white fish', has been known to conceal large chunks of lobster.
Sirloin steak is offered as a concession to non-fish eaters, vegetables are
served simply and generously on a platter and desserts range from homely
and hot (apple pie, crepes suzette) to sophisticated cold (passion fruit
delight); black plates are used to good effect for fish and desserts.
No smoking room. **Seats** *40. Parties 25. Private Room 20. L 12.30-5
D 7-9.30. Closed Mon, 1 week Mar, 1 week Oct, Good Friday, 25 Dec.*
AMERICAN EXPRESS *Access, Diners, Visa.*

Greystones   The Hungry Monk   £55

Tel 01 287 5759   **R**
Greystones Co Wicklow   Map 23 D4

On the first floor, over a building society, this characterful little restaurant
is unassuming from the street and the contrast inside is remarkable:
a glowing fire and candlelight – even at Sunday lunch, now sensibly
extended to make a very Irish lunch ("not brunch but linner", says genial
host Pat Keown!), with last orders at 8pm – add to the warm welcome.
Well-appointed tables with fresh flowers, delicious home-baked bread,
serious wine glasses and, of course, a plethora of monk-related pictures and
bric-a-brac complete the picture. Menus, changed seasonally, keep an eye
on fashions and inject popular dishes with a dash of originality – as
in warm salad of garlic mushrooms or roast lamb with a herb crust and
minted lamb jus – but top-quality ingredients are the vital link, including
game in season and daily seafood blackboard specials, from nearby
Greystones harbour. Best of all, perhaps, are the prices – value for money
is a priority here and the size of the bill is often a welcome surprise. A quite
splendid and very fairly-priced wine list features an inexpensive house
section, and a really comprehensive world-wide selection with the New
World well represented, as are Italy, Spain and Portugal. *Seats 40.
Parties 20. L Sun only 12.30-8 D 7-11. Closed D Sun & Mon, 25 Dec, Good
Friday.Set L Sun £10.95 Set D (not Sat) £14.95.* AMERICAN EXPRESS *Access,
Diners, Visa.*

Hodson Bay   Hodson Bay Hotel   65%   £90

Tel 0902 92444   Fax 0902 92688   **H**
Hodson Bay Athlone Co Roscommon   Map 22 C3

Large, lively, lakeside hotel offering extensive conference and leisure
facilities. Golfing is available in the Athlone Golf Club, located next to the
hotel, boating and watersports on Lough Ree and River Shannon and
a wide number of pursuits in the hotel's excellent leisure and activity
centre. Practical en-suite bedrooms, large foyer-lounge, dining room plus
self-service food area, waterside bar. Expansion plans are afoot to increase
the number of bedrooms to 100. *Rooms 46. Garden, tennis, indoor
swimming pool, gymnasium, keep-fit equipment, sauna, solarium, fishing.*
AMERICAN EXPRESS *Access, Diners, Visa.*

Hodson Bay   Place of Interest

Athlone Castle   Athlone Tel 0902 92912

Howth   Adrian's   £50

Tel 01 839 1696   **R**
3 Abbey Street Howth Co Dublin   Map 23 D4

In the temporary absence of his daughter (and head chef) Catriona, Adrian
Holden had been in the kitchen of this small family-run restaurant himself
for some months, but no discernible change of style was evident on our
most recent visit. Menus change frequently, offering interest, variety and
careful use of fresh produce. Crudités and a tasty dip are on the table
to welcome new arrivals and a basket of home-made breads, warm from
the oven, follows very shortly afterwards. From the £16 dinner menu,
pasta with spinach and pesto makes a lively starter – good home-made pasta
and a zesty sauce – and smoked Gubbeen cheese and smoked salmon
presents a pleasing alternative to plain smoked salmon. Vegetarian tastes are
always considered on the main course options, as in broccoli hollandaise
with mushroom ragout, and local seafood is strong but dependent on the
weather – but Adrian is known for buying his meat well, so rack of lamb
or pork and chicken satay should not disappoint. Vegetables tend to be
reliably simple and plentiful; desserts can be variable: sometimes stunning,
sometimes less so. Daytime menus offer more flexibility, although there are

also 2/3-course set lunches. Children are not encouraged. *Seats 46.*
Parties 12. Private Room 15. Meals 12.30-10 L 12.30-3 (Sun 2-5.30 supper)
D 7.30-10 (Mon-Fri 6-8 early supper). Set L £6.50/£7.90 (Sun £9.95)
Set D £16. Closed 25 & 26 Dec. AMERICAN EXPRESS *Access, Diners, Visa.*

Howth   Deer Park Hotel   64%   £80

Tel 01 832 2624   Fax 01 839 2405   **H**

Howth Co Dublin   **Map 23 D4**

Located high up on the Howth peninsula and surrounded by 1200 acres
that includes five golf courses (18, 9 and 12-hole par 3, 18-hole pitch and
putt, plus a new 9-hole course). Deer Park also enjoys excellent views to the
north and east with Howth harbour, Ireland's Eye and Lambay islands
in one direction, Dublin in the other. Built in 1973, it has a fairly modern
appearance. There's a bright, airy first-floor residents' lounge with a terrace
for fine weather, while on the ground floor the bar offers excellent views
to the east and Dublin. Bedrooms are of good size, offering smart
darkwood furniture. Some have their own fridge and toaster as well as the
usual tea/coffee facilities. Bread and cereals can be provided for those with
early planes to catch from Dublin airport. Vinyl-floored bathrooms, all
with showers, have enamel baths. *Rooms 50. Garden, golf.* AMERICAN EXPRESS *Access, Diners, Visa.*

Howth   Howth Lodge Hotel   65%   £90

Tel 01 832 1010   Fax 01 832 2268   **H**

Howth Co Dublin   **Map 23 D4**

Built 175 years ago and since considerably enlarged (but keeping the
original style), with the whole frontage painted a distinctive black and
white, Howth Lodge offers good standards of accommodation as well as a
very fine leisure centre across the road (note that the gym is only available
to fully experienced users). On the ground floor, public areas are open-plan,
featuring a spacious lounge with bamboo furniture that leads to a cosy,
beamed bar with stripped bare floorboards at the rear. There are 13 older
bedrooms in the original building, but the majority are in a purpose-built
modern block completed last year. All bedrooms are well equipped,
double-glazed and offer at least a partial view of the sea. The new
bedrooms are excellent – of good size and very prettily decorated. Front
rooms have traditional-style darkwood furniture, while the rear rooms
have lightwood pieces. Bathrooms are bright and clean; six have bidets.
Rooms 46. Garden, indoor swimming pool, plunge pool, beauty salon, solarium,
sauna, spa bath, steam room, gym. Closed 3 days Dec. AMERICAN EXPRESS *Access,*
Diners, Visa.

Howth   King Sitric   £70

Tel 01 832 6729   Fax 01 839 2442   **R**

East Pier Harbour Road Howth Co Dublin   **Map 23 D4**

Howth is home to one of the largest fishing fleets in Ireland, so King Sitric,
a very well-established fish restaurant, is perfectly placed on the harbour
front. Warm salad with grilled herring, baked crab gateau, moules
marinière, poached lemon sole, queen scallops, sole meunière or Colbert,
lobster taken from the tank, grilled or poached turbot, poached salmon,
oysters from Galway Bay... these and many more classics you'll find
on Aidan MacManus's mouthwatering menus. Lunch in the seafood bar
provides great views and excellent value for money. Joan MacManus is a
charming hostess. King Sitric is not only an outstanding seafood restaurant
but boasts one of the finest wine lists in Ireland with excellent house
recommendations, an especially splendid selection of Chablis and Alsace,
and a comprehensive choice of other whites and red wines, many of which
are served at the restaurant's special 'wine evenings'. *Seats 60.*
Private Room 22. L 12.30-3 (summer and pre-Christmas only) D 6.30-11.
Closed Sun, Bank Holidays, 10 days Jan & Easter. Set D £22. AMERICAN EXPRESS
Access, Diners, Visa.

Howth   Place of Interest

Howth Castle Gardens   Tel 01 832 2624

Inistioge   The Motte   £60

Tel 056 58655   **R**

Inistioge Co Kilkenny   Map 23 C5

Set in one of Ireland's prettiest villages, everything about Tom Reade-
Duncan and Alan Walton's intimate, characterful little restaurant is just
right – the antiques, artistic candle-lit table settings and warm, welcoming
atmosphere. The menu, which is changed with the seasons according
to availability of produce and sensibly limited to a choice of about six
on each course, is interesting and chef Alan Walton follows through with
style. Start, perhaps, with crab and ginger strudel, a sausage of crabmeat
quite sharply scented with ginger, wrapped in filo and partnered with
a mellow balsamic vinaigrette or hare terrine, followed by crisp-skinned
pink-fleshed Barbary duck with a sumptuous confit of garlic and flageolet
beans or fillets of plaice with a crispy herb and pine nut crust. Details are
excellent: three kinds of olives to nibble over aperitifs and three kinds
of bread, served with nice little chunks of butter in a pottery bowl, good
choice of imaginatively presented vegetables, farmhouse cheese selection,
delicious gimmick-free desserts, lovely aromatic coffee. *Seats 24. Parties 8.
D only 7-10 (Sun to 9). Set D £18.50. Closed Bank Holidays, Christmas
week.* AMERICAN EXPRESS *Access, Diners, Visa.*

Innishannon   Innishannon House Hotel   63%   £95

Tel 021 775121   Fax 021 775609   **H**

Innishannon Co Cork   Map 23 B6

Built in 1720 for a wealthy farmer, Innishannon House enjoys a romantic
setting in gardens and parkland on the Bandon River (fishing available here
and on the Brinny). Bedrooms, all en suite, are individual in their size,
shape and furnishings; some overlook the river, others the gardens.
A newly created, airy suite features a period bathroom. There's a cosy
residents' bar (snacks served all day), a restaurant, sitting room and
conservatory. Popular afternoon teas. *Rooms 14. Garden, fishing, boating.*
AMERICAN EXPRESS *Access, Diners, Visa.*

Innishannon   Place of Interest

Timoleague Castle Gardens   Tel 023 46116 *10 miles*

Kanturk   Assolas Country House   72%   £104

Tel 029 50015   Fax 029 50795   **HR**

Kanturk Co Cork   Map 23 B5

Only an hour from Cork city, Assolas is well situated as a base for visiting
West Cork and Kerry. The charming creeper-clad house goes back to the
17th century and is currently home to three generations of Bourkes,
including the manager, Joe, and his wife Hazel, a very talented chef.
An exceptional welcome is backed up by open log fires, elegant furnishings
and antiques, excellent housekeeping and a high level of comfort
throughout. Of the nine bedrooms, three in the main house are designated
'Superior' and are large, with the finest views; three are in a restored old
stone building in the courtyard. Despite its undeniable elegance, Assolas has
all the warmth and hospitality of a family home – best summed up,
perhaps, by the collection of wellington boots in the hall for anyone who
feels like seeking out the otters along the riverbank. No dogs in the house.
Rooms 9. Garden, croquet, tennis, fishing. Closed Nov-mid March.
AMERICAN EXPRESS *Access, Diners, Visa.*

Restaurant   ★   £65

They do things properly at Assolas and the deep red walls, polished antique
furniture and neatly uniformed staff provide a fitting background for Hazel
Bourke's wonderful food, much of it produce from their own beautifully
maintained walled kitchen garden (in which herbs, vegetables and soft fruit
grow) or from trusted local suppliers – allowing maximum variety for
residents. Start, perhaps, with Union Hall prawns and scallops in a puff
pastry case, typically followed by a pink grapefruit sorbet or dressed Assolas
greens. Local lamb, served with a rosemary flavoured jus and Hazel's mint
jelly, might tempt from a choice of five main courses, which always
includes an imaginative vegetarian option. Simplest desserts are sometimes
the best – superb blackcurrant ice cream or a shimmering jewel-like
compote of garden fruits – and the local farmhouse cheeseboard is kept
in immaculate condition. Coffee and petits fours are served beside the fire
in the drawing room. There are no New World wines on an otherwise
decent wine list that features many top growers. No children under 7.
Seats 25. Private Room 20. D only 7-8.30. Set D £27.

Kenmare   d'Arcy's   £70

Tel 064 41589   Fax 064 41589   **RR**

Main Street Kenmare Co Kerry   Map 23 A6

Matthew d'Arcy moved across the road from the *Park Hotel* in 1992 to set
up in this converted bank and his wife Aileen provides a warm welcome.
There's a real fire glowing where the main banking hall used to be and the
vault at the back is opened up on busy nights. Staff are informal and
friendly and the menu longish and ambitious. Ravioli of prawn mousse
with a sweet pepper-scented butter or leek and chicken timbale could start
your meal, with rolled fillet of black sole (accompanied by a spinach
mousse and sea urchin sauce) or stuffed guinea fowl to follow. Desserts
include an excellent orange and Cointreau soufflé. Previously known as
The Old Bank House. *Seats 40. Private Room 25. D 7-9 (from 5 to 10.30
high season). Set D £15. Closed Mon, Tues & Wed in winter. 24-26 Dec, last
2 weeks Jan.* AMERICAN EXPRESS *Access, Diners, Visa.*

Rooms   £30

Five neat, comfortably furnished rooms are individually decorated in
homely style. Smallish bathrooms (some with shower only, just two en
suite) have plenty of thick towels and toiletries supplied. Sitting room with
TV.

Kenmare   Dromquinna Manor Hotel   60%   £85

Tel 064 41657   Fax 064 41791   **H**

Blackwater Bridge nr Kenmare Co Kerry   Map 23 A6

About three miles out of town and beautifully situated in extensive
grounds leading down to the private foreshore and a little quay and newly
built marina (the setting for their informal summer Old Boathouse Bistro
restaurant), this Victorian manor boasts a unique tree-house apartment
as well as many more orthodox attractions, including a Great Hall with
original oak panelling. Generously proportioned bedrooms are individually
decorated, all en suite, some with four-poster or brass beds. A generally
relaxed atmosphere pervades the hotel. *Rooms 28. Garden, keep-fit
equipment, games room, tennis, mooring, fishing.* AMERICAN EXPRESS *Access,
Diners, Visa.*

Kenmare   Hawthorn House   £36

Tel 064 41035   Fax 064 41932   **PH**

Shelbourne Road Kenmare Co Kerry   Map 23 A6

Kevin and Trina Murphy took over this comfortable, centrally situated
modern guesthouse in 1992 and the high standards established by the

previous owner Gerry Browne (manager of *Sheen Falls Lodge Hotel*) are being maintained. Individually furnished rooms are all en suite (some shower only), with tea/coffee-making facilities, and some have TV. Good breakfasts. Children up to 8 stay free in parents' room. No dogs. *Rooms 8. Garden.* ![AMERICAN EXPRESS] *Access, Visa.*

Kenmare   The Horseshoe

£35

Tel 064 41553

R

3 Main Street Kenmare Co Kerry

Map 23 A6

Behind its unassuming exterior The Horseshoe hides a pleasantly rustic old-fashioned bar. Behind this again, there's a cosy, informal restaurant with open fire, oil-clothed tables, (real) cattle stall divisions and an unpretentious menu backed up by owner-chef Irma Weland's simple, wholesome food. Old favourites like deep-fried mushrooms with garlic mayonnaise take on a new lease of life in Irma's hands (crisp, light, very hot and full of contrasts), and, while steaks and fish are reliable, a vegetarian main course such as tagliatelle with creamy leek, mushroom and garlic sauce can be memorable. A daily specials board makes good use of the freshest ingredients. Good desserts may include a moreish caramelised apple and pear flan. Tables outside in summer. *Seats 35. Parties 8. Private Room 30. Meals 12-10pm. Closed Tues in winter, 25 Dec. No credit cards.*

Kenmare   Packie's

£270

Tel 064 41508

R

Henry Street Kenmare Co Kerry

Map 23 A6

Owner-chef Maura O'Connell Foley packs in the crowds with cooking that's short on pretension and long on flavour. The sunny influences of California and the Med combine with domestic traditions on a menu typified by smoked salmon with red onion and caper sauce, grilled crubeens (pig's trotters) with mustard pickle, fillet of brill with carrot and wine sauce and warm fish mousse with oysters and chive sauce. Among the desserts you might find chocolate pots, tiramisu or baked bananas with butterscotch sauce. *Seats 35. D only 5.30-10. Closed Sun, Nov-Easter. Access, Visa.*

Kenmare   Park Hotel Kenmare   87%

£270

Tel 064 41200   Fax 064 41402

HR

Kenmare Co Kerry

Map 23 A6

In late Victorian times the gentry travelled from various parts of the country by train, stopping at Kenmare, and the hotel was built in 1897 by the Great Southern and Western Railway Company for passengers to stay overnight, before continuing their journey the next day. The company sold the hotel in the late 70s, and since then, under the direction of Francis Brennan, it has enjoyed an enviable reputation – indeed, it was our Hotel of the Year in 1988. Set in eleven acres of unspoilt gardens on the shores of Kenmare Bay, and yet only a short walk from town, the hotel is particularly renowned for its fine antiques, stained-glass windows, marvellous paintings, attention to detail (an expert Dutch gilder spends the entire off-season painstakingly restoring every crevice in the ornate plasterwork and cornices), comfortable and elegant day rooms, and beautiful flower arrangements. On a cold day one can relax in front of a crackling log fire, or in summer and autumn take a stroll in the grounds and admire the changing colours. Bedroom refurbishment ensures that guests can sleep both soundly and in supreme comfort – the nine suites and most of the rooms are very spacious indeed with wonderful views, and offer every conceivable luxury, from bathrobes, slippers and exquisite toiletries in the marble bathrooms to fresh fruit, mineral water and books. Quality bed linen, good furniture, fine fabrics and excellent towels, backed up by superb housekeeping, complete the picture. Breakfast is a quite wonderful experience, including a 'healthy' alternative prepared in accordance with the recommendations of the world's heart associations. Special 'programmes' for Christmas and New Year – ask for their brochure. Children up to 10 may share their parents' room at no charge. Banqueting for 30, conference facilities for 50. No dogs. **Rooms 50.** *Garden, croquet, tennis, golf (18), games room. Closed mid Nov-22 Dec, 4 Jan-Easter.* AMERICAN EXPRESS *Access, Diners, Visa.* MARTELL

Restaurant ★ £90

The Park's warm welcome and special magic continue right from the ever-burning fire in the hall through to the beautifully appointed, yet surprisingly relaxed, high-ceilinged dining room with its wonderful views. Formal touches such as antiques are amusingly offset by quirks of personal taste – no designer co-ordinations here. Enjoy an aperitif in the bar, where the door opens to give a view of the mountains beyond, framed by palm trees stirring in the wind. If you're lucky enough to sit at a window table the view broadens to include the upper reaches of the estuary and hotel lawn. Both daily-changing tables d'hote (3-course at lunch, 4-course at dinner) and carte are available, the former offering a choice of three dishes at each stage, the latter tempting with dishes described in refreshingly plain English on a menu that uses a watercolour of Kenmare's rich scenery as a backdrop. Chef Brian Cleere works with obvious confidence and verve in his recently revamped kitchen, often presenting breathtakingly beautiful dishes, and also understanding when to let the natural flavours and textures speak for themselves. Typically, a table d'hote lunch doesn't stint on the involved nature of dishes, starting with cassoulet of snails, Parma ham and oyster mushrooms with a thyme sauce, followed by poached fillet of turbot with a ravioli of lobster and prawns with a tomato and herb bouillon; strawberry sablé with a blackcurrant coulis and amaretto sauce to finish. The carte might offer home-made fettuccine with Atlantic oysters, ribbons of wild smoked salmon, leek sauce and caviar, terrine of guinea fowl and pigeon with a truffle vinaigrette, seafood (including lobster) from Kenmare Bay, pan-fried fillet of beef with a chartreuse of oxtail, onion confit and a red wine glaze and half a dozen or so tempting desserts. A selection of Irish cheeses is served with home-made walnut bread and a glass of port – a very civilised way to end an enjoyable meal in a delightful setting. Service under Jim McCarthy mirrors the balance shown in the kitchen – superbly professional complemented by the right amount of friendliness. The exceptional wine list offers several French classics of different vintages, as well as a comprehensive Californian section of over 30 bins; the Australian, Italian and Spanish sections present perhaps the best value. *Seats 80. Private Room 30. L 1-1.45 D 7-8.45. Set L £18.50 Set D £37.*

Kenmare	Sheen Falls Lodge	87%	£230
Tel 064 41600 Fax 064 41386			**HR**
Kenmare Co Kerry			Map 23 A6

There are several remarkable aspects of this hotel, not the least being that only a small part – the original 17th-century house – is not new, though you wouldn't know it from looking at the rest of the buildings. So cleverly has it been designed, and so beautifully does it blend into its surroundings – on one side the cascading waters from the Sheen River, on the other woodland and gardens overlooking Kenmare Bay – that it's really not apparent that the hotel has only been open for three years. On the site of a country estate dating back to the 1600s, including a long stretch of the river (private salmon fishing arranged), there are over 300 acres of grounds featuring lawns, semi-tropical gardens and tranquil woodland walks. Inside, the spacious foyer features marbled columns and a welcoming fire; there's also a mahogany-panelled library with deep green leather sofas, relaxing lounges, and a snooker room with arguably the finest views you'll ever cue in! Really spacious bedrooms, featuring natural wood and fine fabrics, include a self-contained apartment and eight suites (one suitable for disabled guests); all have equally spectacular views and feature amenities such as three telephones, personal safe, remote-control satellite TV and video recorder, iron and trouser press, mineral water and a bowl of fresh fruit daily. Naturally, there's a nightly turn-down service, and in the marble bathrooms with his and hers washbasins you'll find bathrobes, slippers, hairdryer, excellent toiletries and decent-sized towels. The state-of-the-art William Petty Conference Centre, named after the original landowner, can accommodate up to 140 delegates and lies in the basement, almost undetected and unnoticed by other guests, alongside the superbly equipped leisure facilities. **Rooms** *40. Garden, croquet, gymnasium, sauna, spa bath, steam room, solarium, tennis, riding, bicycles, clay-pigeon shooting, coarse & game fishing, games room, boutique, helipad. Closed 5 Dec-23 Dec, Jan-mid Feb.* AMERICAN EXPRESS *Access, Diners, Visa.*

La Cascade Restaurant　　★　　　　　　　　　£90

Chef Fergus Moore's sophisticated menus are as attractive as the glorious views of the falls, which are floodlit at night. Both a daily, four-course table d'hote dinner and an extravagant à la carte are offered and should please even the most discerning diner. Typical starters might include coriander-scented lasagne of prawns with buttered juices, oven-roasted quail on a tatin of glazed apple, and slivers of fresh lobster with a concassé of tomato and red onion and a sea urchin rouille; main courses continue the involved theme with dishes like lightly wood-smoked fillet of beef on a fumet of Hermitage and shallots, fillets of black sole with sesame prawns and a red wine butter sauce, plus a vegetarian choice of agnolotti of wild mushrooms on a bed of steamed couscous finished with white butter and chervil. Local wild Atlantic salmon is cured and smoked on the premises, served with a sour cream and fresh herb dressing to start or (fresh) chargrilled and served with a purée of new potatoes with saffron and truffle oil dressing. Finish, perhaps, with chocolate marjolane, baked kumquat and orange pekoe tart with a mascarpone cream or compote of cherries with a brulée of sweet rice. Irish farmhouse cheeses are served with Parmesan biscuits. Excellent service is now led by Frances Hayden. Weekday food is waitress-served in the lounge from 11am-11pm (oysters, open sandwiches, fish casserole, stir-fried chicken, tasting plate of desserts), and afternoon tea (£8.50) from 3-5pm. The impressive wine list is notable for its good selection of half bottles; yes, it's quite expensive, but not too outrageous for a hotel of this class. Visit the marvellous cellars, which are also used for private parties, tastings and after-dinner imbibing! **Seats** *120. Parties 16. Private Room 24. L Sun only 1-2 D 7.30-9.30. Set Sun L £17.50 Set D £35.*

Kilcoran	Kilcoran Lodge	58%	£68
Tel 052 41288　Fax 052 41994			**H**
Kilcoran Cahir Co Tipperary			Map 23 C5

On the N8, 5 miles from the town of Cahir in the Cork direction. Set in 20 acres of grounds, this former hunting lodge overlooks the Suir Valley. Conference/banqueting facilities for 300/220. **Rooms** *23. Indoor swimming pool, keep-fit equipment, sauna, spa bath, solarium, riding, coarse & game fishing.* AMERICAN EXPRESS *Access, Diners, Visa.*

Kilkenny	Kilkenny Kitchen		£20
Tel 056 22118　Fax 056 65905			**R**
Kilkenny Design Centre Castle Yard Kilkenny Co Kilkenny			Map 23 C5

Situated in the Design Centre, a collection of craft shops and studios in the beautifully built outbuildings opposite the Castle, the Kilkenny Kitchen offers good home cooking on the premises and, in the shape of crusty home-made breads and delicious cakes (also to take away). Both hot and cold meals are much admired for their variety and general wholesomeness. Typical dishes on the daily menu are salmon terrine, vegetarian quiche, chicken Wellington and braised steak. Among the desserts (all home-made) are Irish whiskey gateau and apple Bakewell tart. Afternoon tea is delicious. **Seats** *170. Light meals 9-5 L 12-4 (Sun 10-5). Closed Good Friday, Christmas, Sun Jan-April.* AMERICAN EXPRESS *Access, Diners, Visa.*

Kilkenny — Lacken House — £60

RR

Tel 056 61085   Fax 056 62435

Dublin Road Kilkenny Co Kilkenny

Map 23 C5

One of Kilkenny's leading restaurants (and guesthouses) is run by highly respected chef Eugene McSweeney and his wife Breda; they have built up their reputation over the last ten years. Situated on the edge of the town in a Victorian house with a pleasant, well-proportioned drawing room/bar, the basement restaurant has rather small tables, but the quality of the food is more than adequate compensation. Eugene's dinner menu is in a progressive Irish mode and changes frequently, offering a well-balanced choice based on the classics but with concesssion to current trends; typical dishes might include fanned melon and orange with lemon grass syrup, Clonakilty black pudding with onion marmalade and wholegrain mustard sauce, braised duckling with mandarin sauce or poached salmon and hake in dill cream; Lacken House 'dessert plate' to finish. The choice is small, but only the freshest of local produce is used, much of it organic, particularly the vegetables. A varied Irish farmhouse cheese plate includes local specialities, notably Blue Abbey and Croghan goat's cheese. *Seats 35. D only 7-10.30. Closed Sun & Mon, 1 week Christmas. Set D £22.* AMERICAN EXPRESS *Access, Diners, Visa.* MARTELL COGNAC

Rooms

£55

Eight bedrooms, all with shower or bath, provide simple accommodation; children up to 4 stay free in parents' room; children under 12, sharing parents' room, £10 B&B. Breakfast is excellent and is served either in the dining room or via room service. *Garden.*

Kilkenny — Newpark Hotel — 58% — £97

H

Tel 056 22122   Fax 056 61111

Castlecomer Road Kilkenny Co Kilkenny

Map 23 C5

The leisure centre and the banqueting/conference facilities supplement acceptable overnight accommodation at a 60s' hotel on the N77. All-day snack service in the lobby. 24 new family-size bedrooms were added last year. *Rooms 84. Indoor swimming pool, children's pool, keep-fit equipment, sauna, spa bath, steam room, solarium, tennis.* AMERICAN EXPRESS *Access, Diners, Visa.*

Kilkenny — Places of Interest

Tourist Information   Tel 056 21755
Dunmore Cave   Tel 056 67726
Gowran Park Racecourse   Tel 056 26110
Irish National Design Centre   Tel 056 22118
Jerpoint Abbey   Tel 056 24623
Kilkenny Castle   Tel 056 21450
Rothe House   Parliament Street Tel 056 22893

Killarney — Aghadoe Heights Hotel — 70% — £145

HR

Tel 064 31766   Fax 064 31345

Aghadoe Killarney Co Kerry

Map 23 A5

Low-rise concrete and glass hotel of 1960s' origin refurbished in varying styles but to a generally high standard in public areas and the views over Lake Killarney and the mountains beyond are wonderful, especially from the elegantly appointed dining room. Leisure facilities, although conspicuous from the road, do not intrude. Bedrooms and bathrooms are neat, although not large. Conference/banqueting facilities for 130/100. Sister hotel to *Fredrick's* in Maidenhead, England. *Rooms 60. Garden, indoor swimming pool, gymnasium, sauna, spa bath, steam room, solarium, beauty salon, tennis, fishing, boutique, helipad.* AMERICAN EXPRESS *Access, Diners, Visa.*

See over

Fredrick's Restaurant   ↑   £100

In this luxuriously appointed first-floor dining room with dramatic (probably unrivalled) views over the Lakes of Killarney, chef Robin Suter is running a very fine kitchen with dinner menus changing daily and lunch menus every week. The style is formal, imaginative, distinctly French and based on superb quality produce – everything positively zings with freshness and portions are unexpectedly generous. Try, perhaps, avocado with fresh crab and grapefruit (colourful, light and beautifully presented with a generous amount of white crabmeat) or cassolette of Kerry seafood and linguini (an excellent mixture of shellfish – fresh prawns, crab claws, mussels – white fish and salmon with home-made pasta in an outstandingly flavoursome light creamy sauce). An exceptional selection of freshly baked breads, handed separately, will undoubtedly prove irresistible. Typical main courses on the lunch menu might include tournedos of cod with tomato and thyme sauce (the cod is wrapped in streaky bacon, making a very substantial dish) or succulent grilled lamb cutlets maitre d'hotel prettily presented with a small salad and cherry tomato garnish. An imaginative vegetable selection might typically include new potatoes, pommes almondines, braised fennel, batons of carrot, very light crisp onion rings and crisply cooked broccoli. Fritters are a favourite dessert, mixed fruit perhaps, very light and crisp, followed by fragrant cafetière coffee and delicious home-made petits fours. Lively Sunday lunch with a buffet and a jazz band. An interesting wine list includes some selected for exceptional value, from £13-£19.50, a collection of 'Wild Geese' wines from Irish-connected families, and a good selection of half bottles. *Seats 84. Parties 24. Private Room 70. L 12.15-2 D 7-9.30. Set L £17.50 D £29.50.*

> Never leave money, credit cards or valuables lying around in your hotel room. Use the hotel safe or the mini-safe in your room.

Killarney   Cahernane Hotel   66%   £110

Tel 064 31895   Fax 064 34340   **HR**

Muckross Road Killarney Co Kerry   Map 23 A5

Killarney's lakes and mountains create a majestic backdrop for a fine hotel that was once the residence of the Earls of Pembroke. Inside, Conor O'Connell and his staff create a warm, friendly atmosphere, and standards of service, comfort and housekeeping are high. There is a choice between traditional master bedrooms in the main house and simpler but spacious and well-appointed rooms in a sympathetic modern wing. Children under 12 may stay free in parents' room. *Rooms 48. Garden, hairdressing, tennis, pitch & putt, game fishing, boutique. Closed 31 Oct-1 Apr.* AMERICAN EXPRESS Access, Diners, Visa.

The Herbert Room Restaurant   £65

In the smartly refurbished Herbert Room Eddie Hayes offers a choice of menus for dinner – four courses plus coffee and petits fours on the table d'hote, or a wide-ranging à la carte. The former tends to be more traditional, with dishes such as mussels provençale, beef consommé, paupiettes of Dover sole with prawn tails and entrecote steak with mushrooms. Other choices – paillard of salmon with lemon aïoli, fettucine with crabmeat sauce – move into the slightly more adventurous realms of the carte, where you could find snails cooked in port, served on black pasta with a sauce of gorgonzola, cream and wild mushrooms, or a vegetarian Buddhist stew. On this menu, too, are classics like sole véronique and steak Diane. Light lunches are served in the lounge. Something for everyone on the well-rounded wine list, though a bottle of mineral water will set you back £4 and champagne £40! *Seats 90. Parties 30. Private Room 14. D 7-9.30. Set D £24.*

Killarney   Dingles Restaurant   £45

Tel 064 31079   **R**

40 New Street Killarney Co Kerry   Map 23 A5

Genuine hospitality and congenial surroundings are the keynotes at Gerry and Marion Cunningham's relaxed restaurant and it is obviously a favourite rendezvous for locals who appreciate Gerry's easy welcome as much as Marion's excellent uncomplicated food, which is based on the best ingredients and delivered with admirable simplicity. Open fires, ecclesiastical furniture and old plates on the walls create a characterful ambience in which to enjoy anything from a home-made burger with freshly cut chips cooked in olive oil to a 4-course dinner. *Seats 45. D only 6-10.30. Closed Sun (except holiday w/ends). 20 Dec-1 Mar.* AMERICAN EXPRESS *Access, Diners, Visa.*

Killarney   Hotel Europe   72%   £96

Tel 064 31900   Fax 064 32118   **H**

Killorglin Road Fossa Killarney Co Kerry   Map 23 A5

A large modern hotel next to Killarney Golf and Fishing Club, catering equally well for private guests and conference delegates (up to 500 theatre style). The mountain and lake views are quite a feature, and most of the spacious bedrooms have balconies to make the most of the setting. Day rooms include a lounge with a pine ceiling copied from an English castle. There's an excellent health and fitness centre. *Rooms 205. Garden, indoor swimming pool, gymnasium, solarium, sauna, spa bath, beauty salon, hair salon, fishing, tennis, riding, games room, snooker room, news kiosk, boutique, helipad. Closed Nov-Mar.* AMERICAN EXPRESS *Access, Diners, Visa.*

Killarney   Foley's Townhouse   £80

Tel 064 31217   Fax 064 34683   **RR**

23 High Street Killarney Co Kerry   Map 23 A5

A Killarney landmark since the late 40s, Foley's is another example of the winning Kerry format – a front-of-house bar which gradually develops into a fully-fledged restaurant further back – in this case a cosy bar with an open fire, furnished to encourage lingering, backed by rather business-like rows of tables indicating clearly the level of turnover which might be expected in high season. With Denis and Carol Harnett here since 1967, the well-established feel of Foley's is reassuringly disregarding of fashion and, although emanating from modern, well-equipped and scrupulously clean kitchens, Carol Harnett's menus reflect this in style and content, in dishes like soup of the day (mushroom, perhaps – a thick country purée), sole on the bone and scallops in potato-piped shells, both served surprisingly with roast potato and mixed side salads reminiscent of the 60s. On such an outstanding and comprehensive wine list it's a shame that half bottles are in such short supply. House wines, however, are well chosen and very fairly priced, while the classics feature many of the great houses. Families are made welcome with good facilities for tots and their parents. *Seats 95. Private Room 25. L (bar food) 12.30-3 D 5-11. Closed 24-26 Dec. Private Room 25.* AMERICAN EXPRESS *Access, Visa.*

Rooms   £70

Foley's Townhouse is the culmination of Carol Harnett's long-held ambition to provide top-class accommodation at the restaurant – twelve rooms are individually decorated to a high standard and much thought has gone into planning each room to maximise use of space and comfort, including double-glazing to reduce traffic/late-night noises; special care was taken with the bathrooms, which are all exceptionally well appointed with unusual colour schemes, quality tubs and washbasins, special tiles and all the touches more usually found in leading hotels. Guests use a separate entrance and public areas include a residents' lounge and a private dining room. Banqueting/conference facilities for up to 95/25. No dogs. Accommodation closed 1 Nov-1 Mar.

Killarney   Gaby's Seafood Restaurant   £60

Tel 064 32519   Fax 064 32747   **R**

27 High Street Killarney Co Kerry   Map 23 A5

Although only in the present purpose-built premises since 1992, chef Geert Maes has been indispensable to the Killarney dining scene since 1976. The new restaurant is larger and has a bar area near the door, with a little garden at the back. Within, the space is cleverly broken into several levels, creating an unexpectedly initimate atmosphere that is enhanced by plants and good lighting. Whether for an informal lunch (home-made soups, open sandwiches, seafood platter) or a leisurely dinner (cassolette of prawns and monkfish, grilled lobster), this is a place where respect for fresh local produce can be depended upon – seafood is the speciality, but it is reassuringly dependent on availability. A most fairly priced wine list offers an outstanding worldwide selection and, unusually for a seafood restaurant (though it does serve steaks and lamb), includes a super repertoire of red wines as well. *Seats* 65. *L* 12.30-2.30 *D* 6-10. *Closed all Sun & L Mon, 3 weeks Feb.* AMERICAN EXPRESS *Access, Diners, Visa.*

Killarney   Great Southern   69%   £129

Tel 064 31262   Fax 064 31642   **H**

Killarney Co Kerry   Map 23 A5

Situated close to the town centre (3 minutes' walk), this former railway hotel is a substantial building set in 36 acres of gardens that curve around the main building and bedroom extensions. The entrance hall is impressive, with Ionic columns, chandeliers and a large seating area. Bedrooms vary considerably in size and style; many have been recently refurbished (as have the main public areas). Leisure facilities are good and the hotel offers a variety of function facilities, taking conferences of up to 1000 theatre-style and banquets up to 650. The Punch Bowl cocktail bar overlooks the hotel gardens. *Rooms* 180. *Garden, indoor swimming pool, splash pool, sauna, spa bath, gymnasium, tennis, hairdressing, baby-sitting. Closed 6 weeks Jan/Feb.* AMERICAN EXPRESS *Access, Diners, Visa.*

Killarney   Kathleen's Country House   £60

Tel 064 32810   Fax 064 32340   **PH**

Tralee Road Killarney Co Kerry   Map 23 A5

Just a mile from the centre of Killarney, this family-run establishment is peacefully set in well-maintained gardens and equally well-known for the warmth of Kathleen O'Regan-Sheppard's welcome and her scrupulous attention to detail. Public areas are spacious and individually decorated bedrooms with views exceptionally well appointed, all with fully-tiled bath and shower en suite, direct-dial phone, trouser press, tea/coffee facilities, individually controlled central heating, radio alarm clock, orthopaedic beds, TV and hairdryer. Good breakfasts are cooked to order and served in an attractive dining room overlooking the garden and unspoilt countryside. All rooms non-smoking. No children under 10. No dogs. *Rooms* 17. *Garden, croquet. Closed Dec-Feb.* AMERICAN EXPRESS *Access, Visa.*

Killarney   The Killarney Park Hotel   73%   £130

Tel 064 35555   Fax 064 35266   **H**

Kenmare Place Killarney Co Kerry   Map 23 A5

This newish hotel with classical lines enjoys a central setting in attractive gardens set with mature trees. First impressions are carried through to the smart foyer, which is spacious, with fires, plenty of comfortable seating and,

in common with most of the other public areas, notably the bar,
a pleasingly bold colour scheme with fabrics mixed to good effect. The
restaurant is more restrained and has a cosy area especially appropriate for
winter dining. Although not individually furnished, bedrooms are planned
in groups to have variety in shape and size as well as colour schemes; all are
spacious, several very large and especially suitable for families, and marbled
bathrooms are well appointed. Banqueting/conference facilities for
160/150. The leisure centre "Club at the Park" opens out on to its own
furnished patio. No dogs. *Rooms 66. Garden, indoor swimming pool,
children's pool, gymnasium, steam room, keep-fit equipment.* AMERICAN EXPRESS ®
Access, Diners, Visa.

Killarney	**Killarney Towers Hotel**	**57%**	**£120**
Tel 064 31038 Fax 064 31755			**H**
College Square Killarney Co Kerry			Map 23 A5

Very centrally located, this new hotel has quite spacious, identical, but
comfortably furnished bedrooms with tea-making facilities, multi-channel
TV and neat en-suite bathrooms. 55 more rooms have been opened in the
last year. Children under 3 share parents' room free; 3- to 12-year-olds half
price. Two bars include a residents' lounge and the lively Scruffy's pub.
Lock-up car park. *Rooms 157.* AMERICAN EXPRESS ® *Access, Diners, Visa.*

Killarney	**Randles Court Hotel**	·	**£120**
Tel 064 35333 Fax 064 35206			**H**
Muckross Road Killarney Co Kerry			Map 23 A5

Well situated – it is convenient for Muckross House and Killarney
National Park but also within walking distance of the town centre – this
attractive Edwardian house underwent extensive refurbishment before
opening as an owner-run hotel in 1992. Period features including fireplaces
and stained glass windows have been retained however and comfortably
furnished public areas include a small bar, spacious drawing room with log
fire, murals and antiques and an elegant restaurant opening on to a sheltered
patio. Bedrooms have direct-dial telephones, satellite television, radio,
hairdryer and well-appointed bathrooms; children under 5 may stay free
in their parents' room. *Rooms 37. Patio. Closed 6Jan-17 Mar.*
AMERICAN EXPRESS *Access, Visa.*

Killarney	**The Strawberry Tree**	**£65**
Tel & Fax 064 32688		**R**
24 Plunkett Street Killarney Co Kerry		Map 23 A5

Owner-chef Evan Doyle and restaurant manager Denis Heffernan have
been running this first-floor restaurant to growing acclaim since 1983 and
now, as the first Irish restaurant to make an absolute commitment to using
wild, free-range and organic produce in 1993, a new standard has been set.
The ambience is comfortably cottagey but sophisticated, with open stone
and whitewashed walls, open fires and low ceilings with elegantly
appointed tables and thoughtfully written menus which give a hint
of serious goings-on in the kitchen. Wild salmon is home-smoked over oak
and apple wood, producing a pale, unusually subtle smoke, real (that is,
organic) vegetable soups come with wonderful warm breads and corned
beef and cabbage is served, unusually, as a starter – and, more unusually
still, they can tell you exactly where the beef came from. A sorbet might
be made of gorse and wild mint, a duet of wild foods could be pan-fried
breast of wood-pigeon with home-made rabbit sausages. Desserts include
a good bread-and-butter pudding and home-made ices, such as lemon balm
and honey. Fragrant coffees or herbal teas come with irresistible petits
fours. The excellent house wine selection is made democratically each year
by friends and regulars. *Seats 30. Parties 14. L by arrangement D 6.30-10.30.
Set Early Bird menu (6.30-8) £14.95. Closed Jan/Feb.* AMERICAN EXPRESS *Access,
Diners, Visa.*

Killarney   Torc Great Southern   63%   £94

Tel 064 31611   Fax 064 31824   **H**

Park Road Killarney Co Kerry   Map 23 A5

Modern, low-rise hotel half a mile from the town centre on the main Cork road. Well-run, with views of the Kerry mountains, it makes a good base for a holiday in the area. 20 bedrooms were refurbished last year and a new bar was added. *Rooms 94. Garden, indoor swimming pool, table tennis, creche. Closed Oct-end Mar.* AMERICAN EXPRESS *Access, Diners, Visa.*

Killarney   West End House   £50

Tel 064 32271   Fax 064 35979   **R**

New Street Killarney Co Kerry   Map 23 A5

Situated opposite St Mary's church, this pleasant restaurant has a somewhat Tyrolean atmosphere and features an unusual open fire, built high into the wall of the bar end of the restaurant to cast warmth right across the room. Table settings are perhaps inappropriate for an otherwise upmarket restaurant: paper mats and foil-wrapped butter even at dinner. A starter such as pink grapefruit segments gratinated with brown sugar, a dash of rum and little balls of rum sorbet could equally well end a meal; presentation is attractive without ostentation and cooking of hearty dishes like soups (onion with port or leek and potato with country bacon) with home-made brown bread and rack of Kerry lamb is sound. Accommodation also available: three rooms, at around £40 per night. *Seats 60. Parties 20. Private Room 25. L 12-2 D 6-10. Closed Mon. Set D £16.50. Access, Visa.*

Killarney   Places of Interest

Tourist Information   Tel 064 31633
Killarney National Park   Tel 064 31947
Ross Castle   Tel 064 32402
Crag Cave   Castle Island Tel 066 41244

Killiney   Court Hotel   68%   £97

Tel 01 285 1622   Fax 01 285 2085   **H**

Killiney Bay Killiney Co Dublin   Map 23 D4

Half an hour from the city centre by car or DART railway, this extended Victorian mansion looks over landscaped gardens to Killiney Bay. The most recent additions include a new cocktail bar and conservatory and the reception area has also been enlarged and modernised. Bedrooms, most with sea views, are spacious and pleasantly decorated with darkwood furniture and co-ordinated fabrics; under-12s stay free in parents' room. An international conference centre has facilities for up to 300. No dogs. *Rooms 86. Garden.* AMERICAN EXPRESS *Access, Diners, Visa.*

Killiney   Fitzpatrick's Castle   68%   £160

Tel 01 284 0700   Fax 01 285 0207   **H**

Killiney Co Dublin   Map 23 D4

Dating back to 1741 and converted by the present owners in 1974, this imposing castle hotel is half an hour's drive from Dublin city centre and, despite its size and style, has a surprisingly lived-in atmosphere. Extensive facilities include two large lounges, two restaurants, a basement disco and a conference suite for up to 550 delegates. Roomy bedrooms, including some mini-suites, have darkwood furniture and draped curtains. *Rooms 90. Garden, indoor swimming pool, gymnasium, squash, sauna, steam room, hair & beauty salon, tennis.* AMERICAN EXPRESS *Access, Diners, Visa.*

Killiney Place of Interest

Ayesha Castle Tel 01 285 2323

Killorglin Nick's Restaurant

£65

Tel 066 61219 Fax 066 61233

R

Lower Bridge Street Killorglin Co Kerry

Map 23 A5

Nick and Anne Foley's popular seafood restaurant always has a good buzz
and Nick's cooking, which relies entirely on daily catches for its seafood
and local suppliers for lamb, beef and organically grown vegetables,
is mainly traditional French. From a wide seafood selection, boosted
by daily specials, could come oysters, lobster, plaice, sole and salmon, plus
grilled fillets of brill, turbot and John Dory with lemon butter sauce.
Elsewhere on the menu you might find asparagus with hollandaise,
ballotine of duck with cherry relish, chicken Cordon Bleu, pork or lamb
cutlets and various steaks. A really splendid wine list – note the extensive
selection from the Loire particularly, but also Alsace and Burgundy. Even
though Nick's is predominantly a seafood restaurant, red wine drinkers will
not be disappointed, nor supporters of the New World. *Seats 80. Parties 50.
Private Room 35. D only 6-10 Set D £23/£25. Closed Nov, Mon & Tue
Jan-Easter, Mon & Tues.* AMERICAN EXPRESS *Access, Diners, Visa.*

Kinnegad The Cottage

£25

Tel 044 75284

R

Kinnegad Co Westmeath

Map 22 C3

Baking is a speciality at this neat, homely cottage restaurant, so afternoon
tea is a good time to drop in for scones, cakes and preserves. Sandwiches,
salads and omelettes are popular orders for light meals, while at the luxury
end of the menu are fresh and smoked salmon. *Seats 30. Parties 14.
Private Room 26. L 12-3 D 6-8. Closed D Sat, all Sun, 10 days Christmas.
No credit cards.*

Kinsale Actons Hotel   60%

£100

Tel 021 772135 Fax 021 772231

H

Pier Road Kinsale Co Cork

Map 23 B6

Overlooking the harbour, this attractive quayside hotel was created from
several substantial period houses. Conference/banqueting facilities for up to
300. Children up to 14 stay free in parents' room. Forte Heritage.
Rooms *57. Indoor swimming pool, gymnasium, sauna, solarium.*
AMERICAN EXPRESS *Access, Diners, Visa.*

Kinsale Blue Haven Hotel

£84

Tel 021 772209 Fax 021 774268

IR

3 Pearse Street Kinsale Co Cork

Map 23 B6

Serious fishermen and trenchermen alike should head for the small, cosy,
blue-and-white Blue Haven hotel near the quay, where not only is there
a 36' ocean-going angling boat for hire, but also good food and
comfortable accommodation after a hard day's sport. Bedrooms are all in a
new wing, and all are neat with smart white furniture and pictures by local
artists. All have en-suite facilities, some with baths, some with just showers.
The bar serves a wide choice of imaginative food – from a choice of soups
to sandwiches and good seafood – and is very attractive, with wood
panelling, natural stone and a log fire, and has many snug corners. It opens
on to a cane-furnished conservatory which, in turn, leads on to a patio. The
entrance has been upgraded and a new wine shop/delicatessen opened just
off the lobby. Cots, high-chairs and baby-sitting can all be arranged
on request. No dogs. ***Rooms*** *18. Bar & conservatory (10.30am-9.30pm),
teas & light snacks (3-5pm), sea fishing. Closed 25 Dec.* AMERICAN EXPRESS *Access,
Diners, Visa.*

See over

Restaurant   £60

The diner is left with no doubt as to the specialities of the characterful
restaurant, which has a strong maritime theme and overlooks an attractive
courtyard garden. Chef Stanley Matthews kicks off with starters of seafood
chowder, wild smoked salmon or baked Rossmore oysters glazed with
hollandaise, followed by Oriental seafood Kashmiri, grilled Dover sole
on the bone or scallops on a skewer with bacon and mushrooms. Seafood
is balanced by dishes like sautéed herbed goat's cheese or Jack Barry's lamb's
kidneys, smoked chicken salad, Mitchelstown venison or prime fillet steaks.
Good local farmhouse cheeses, including Carrigaline. A well-rounded wine
list offers very fair prices with little over £20. *Seats 45. Parties 18. D only
7-10.30. Closed 25 Dec.*

Kinsale   Chez Jean-Marc   ↑   £55

Tel 021 774625   Fax 021 774680   **R**

Lower O'Connell Street Kinsale Co Cork   **Map 23 B6**

A cheerful yellow outside, beamed and country-cosy within, this is a
warm, welcoming place offering excellent food and efficient service. Jean-
Marc Tsai's cooking is traditional French with Oriental accents (Sun night
Chinese menu). From the classic repertoire come French onion soup,
garlicky baked mussels, duck à la bigarade and roast pheasant with shallots
and brandy sauce and *pommes darphin*. Striking a more exotic note are salad
Mikado, Thai stir-fry and roast monkfish steak on a bed of scallops and
creamed tagliatelle flavoured with a hint of curry. Desserts are simple and
delicious. The wine list includes a good choice of house bottles. *Seats 55.
Parties 15. L (Sun only, low season) 12.30-3 D 6.45-10.30 (winter 7-10).
Closed D Sun, all Mon (winter), 3 days Christmas, weekdays Feb.*
AMERICAN EXPRESS® *Access, Diners, Visa.*

Kinsale   Man Friday   £55

Tel 021 772260   **R**

Scilly Kinsale Co Cork   **Map 23 B6**

A popular and convivial restaurant housed in a series of little rooms high
above the harbour. Seafood is the natural speciality, with oysters cold
or poached, crab au gratin, sweet and sour scampi, black sole (grilled
or Colbert) and monkfish with a prawn sauce among the wide choice. That
choice extends outside the fishy realms to the likes of Robinson Crusoe's
warm salad (mixed leaves, croutons and bacon), deep-fried Brie with
a plum and port sauce, Swiss-style veal escalope and roast rack of lamb with
rosemary and a red wine sauce. Strawberry crème brulée, chocolate terrine,
grape pudding or home-made ice creams round things off. Consistency is a
keynote here, and it's owner-chef Philip Horgan (in charge since 1978)
who maintains it. *Seats 80. Private Room 35. L by arrangement only (groups)
D 7-10. Closed Good Friday, 24-26 Dec.* AMERICAN EXPRESS® *Access, Visa.*

Kinsale   Max's Wine Bar   £40

Tel 021 772443   **R**

Main Street Kinsale Co Cork   **Map 23 B6**

Wendy Tisdall is coming up for 20 years at her charming little restaurant,
where highly varnished tabletops reflect fresh flowers and plants and
menus are always light and tempting. Duck liver paté with plum sauce,
half a dozen oysters or spinach pasta with fresh salmon could start a meal,
or there are some speciality salads – Caesar, baked goat's cheese, crudités
with a garlic or curry dip. Next might come the day's fish catch, poached
chicken, beefburgers or rack of lamb, with bread-and-butter pudding,
lemon pancakes or chocolate rum mousse to finish in style. The early bird
menu offers particularly good value for money (6.30-8pm £12).
No smoking in the conservatory (10 seats). *Seats 40. Parties 12. L 1-3
D 6.30-10.30. Closed Nov-Feb. Set D £12. Access, Visa.*

Kinsale   The Old Bank House

£80

Tel 021 774075   Fax 021 774296

PH

11 Pearse Street Kinsale Co Cork

Map 23 B6

A Georgian building of some character, formerly a branch of the Munster and Leinster Bank. Individually furnished bedrooms are spacious, elegant and comfortable, with good antiques and well-appointed bathrooms. Public areas, including breakfast room and sitting room, are non-smoking. Babies are accommodated, but 2-9 year olds are not encouraged. *Rooms 9. Closed 3 days Christmas.* AMERICAN EXPRESS ® *Access, Visa.*

Kinsale   Old Presbytery

£44

Tel 021 772027

PH

Cork Street Kinsale Co Cork

Map 23 B6

Victorian antiques, many of rural interest, are a feature of Ken and Cathleen Buggy's peaceful, comfortable home. The six bedrooms are decorated in traditional style, with big beds and Irish linen, and there's a comfortable sitting room with an open fire. Breakfast is a splendid spread, with a choice of 52 items including freshly baked bread, home-made preserves and yoghurts, apricots and figs in cider, pickled herrings and cheese. "Children and dogs are not turned away if at the door, but are not really encouraged." The old kitchen has been turned into a small restaurant, where Ken produces short, daily-changing dinner menus with old-fashioned unusual soups, Continental salads and freshly caught fish among the specialities. Restaurant only open to non-residents. *Seats 14. D only 7.30-8.30. Closed Sun, 1 week Christmas. Set D £18. No credit cards.*

Kinsale   Scilly House   65%

£90

Tel 021 772413   Fax 021 774629

H

Scilly Kinsale Co Cork

Map 23 B6

An old house of great charm and character overlooking the harbour and Kinsale Bay. The style is American country, with old pine furniture, antiques, traditional American quilts, floral prints and folk art. Public rooms include a bar/library with grand piano, a cosy sitting room and a dining room with views over the garden down to the sea. There are views, too, from most of the individually appointed bedrooms, which include one suite. No children under 12. *Rooms 7. Garden. Closed 1 Nov-15 Apr.* AMERICAN EXPRESS ® *Access, Visa.*

Kinsale   Place of Interest

Charles Fort   Tel 021 772263

Laragh   Mitchell's of Laragh

£45

Tel & Fax 0404 45302

RR

The Old Schoolhouse Laragh Co Wicklow

Map 23 D4

Jerry and Margaret Mitchell's lovingly restored old cut-granite schoolhouse, with leaded window panes, open fires and country pine furniture, provides adults with a tranquil haven from the crowds which nearby Glendalough tends to attract – and very good home cooking to boot. Menus, changed with the seasons, might include sautéed lambs' kidneys, piquant with whiskey and orange, or crisp hot button mushrooms on toast, fragrant in lemon and garlic, followed by tender, juicy roast lamb with home-made mint jelly, perhaps, or a real old-fashioned steak and kidney pie, or salmon in filo, with a dill mayonnaise. "All types of food are served all day to our visitors from all around the world", says Margaret, so one can eat quiche for breakfast or a fry-up for dinner if it takes one's fancy. Margaret's home baking is a great strength and, not surprisingly perhaps, afternoon tea (£3.50) is a speciality. No children under 12. *Seats 30. Private Room 20. Meals 9am-10pm (Sun 9pm). Set Sun L £10.50*

See over

Set D £15.50. Closed from D Sun to L Wed in winter, Bank Holidays, 4 weeks in winter, 2 days at Christmas. AMERICAN EXPRESS® *Access, Visa*

Rooms   £36

Accommodation is offered in five neat en-suite twin rooms with pleasant rural outlook. Two more rooms and a guest sitting room were added in summer '94. No dogs.

Leenane   Delphi Lodge   £70

Tel 095 42211   Fax 095 42296   **PH**

Leenane Co Galway   **Map 22 A3**

Set in a spectacular, unspoilt valley and surrounded by Connacht's highest mountains, this early 19th-century sporting lodge was built by the Marquis of Sligo in one of the most beautiful (and wettest) parts of Ireland. The current owners, Peter and Jane Mantle, have restored and sensitively extended the house which now has eleven guest bedrooms, which vary considerably in size and layout in keeping with the age of the house, but all are ensuite, with lovely views over the lake or woodlands and mountains. A comfortable family atmosphere prevails and, although quite grandly furnished with antiques, sporting paraphernalia and abundant reading matter everywhere ensure the relaxed comfort of guests. Dinner, for residents only, is served at a long mahogany table, presided over by the captor of the day's biggest salmon. Just across the road, four restored cottages offer self-catering accommodation. ***Rooms** 11. Garden, fishing, snooker. Closed 1 Nov-31 Jan. Access, Visa.*

Leenane   Killary Lodge   59%   £56

Tel 095 42276   Fax 095 42314   **H**

Leenane Co Galway   **Map 22 A3**

Superbly located in woodland with beautiful views through to Killary Harbour, this unusual hotel is owned by Jamie and Mary Young, who also run the renowned Little Killary Adventure Centre nearby, and provides the best of both worlds for people attracted to the idea of a healthy outdoor activity holiday but also willing to pay for the comfort of a hotel rather than returning to a bleak hostel at the end of a long day in the fresh air. Rooms, mostly twin but also some singles and doubles, all with shower or bath en-suite, are comfortably furnished and have phones but no television (as a matter of policy). Children up to 14 stay free in parents' room. Activities such as horse riding, canoeing, orienteering, archery, sailing and tennis are available; no experience is necessary, as trained guides will ease guests into new activities to suit their individual pace. Relaxation is the aim. ***Rooms** 18. Garden, tennis, games room, shop. Closed Dec & Jan. Access, Visa.*

Leenane   Portfinn Lodge   £55

Tel 095 42265   Fax 095 42315   **RR**

Leenane Co Galway   **Map 22 A3**

Rory and Maeve Daly have been running this seafood restaurant at the head of Killary Harbour since 1988 and the dining area is shared between a room of the main house and an adjoining conservatory, both with western window tables (on a good evening) offering views of the sun sinking behind the mountains. Very good moist brown soda bread with sunflower seeds is on the table to welcome guests; thereafter seafood takes pride of place although the menu actually offers quite a wide choice, including a number of Oriental dishes. A typical meal might start with a roulade of stuffed smoked salmon, or a seafood bisque followed, perhaps, by monkfish and scallops with a tomato, garlic, basil and brandy sauce or roast duck with Grand Marnier sauce. Finish with something like 'Dad's gooey meringue pudding', or stay safe with an Irish cheeseboard. ***Seats** 36. Parties 10. Private Room 40. D only 5.30-9 (flexible). Closed 1 Nov-Easter. Set D £16.50. Access, Visa.*

Rooms   £35

Eight neat purpose-built en-suite rooms, all sleeping three and one with
four beds; accessible (but not specially equipped) for disabled guests.

Leighlinbridge   The Lord Bagenal Inn   £45
Tel 0503 21668   R
Leighlinbridge Co Carlow   Map 23 C4

Food, wine and hospitality are all dispensed in good measure at this
renowned old inn just off the main M9 Waterford-Carlow road. The style
of cooking is always evolving, and more modern dishes are joining old
favourites like the oysters and mussels, the crabs and the scallops, the home-
made patés, the steaks and the fine fresh fish. The whole family is made
very welcome and there's a special children's menu. Booking is advised for
Sunday lunch. Also a new tourist menu and plenty of vegetarian dishes.
Farmhouse cheeses. There are surprisingly few half bottles on an otherwise
enterprising and comprehensive wine list that provides helpful notes and is
fairly priced. Regional winner for Ireland of our Cellar of the Year award
1995. *Seats* 90. *Parties 25. Private Room 40. L 12.30-2.30 D 6-10.30 (bar
food 12.30-10.30). Closed 25 Dec, Good Friday. Set L £9.50
Set D £11.50/£14.95. Access, Diners, Visa.*

Leighlinbridge   Place of Interest

Altamont   by Tullow Tel 0503 59128

Letterfrack   Rosleague Manor   72%   £90
Tel 095 41101   Fax 095 41168   HR
Letterfrack Connemara Co Galway   Map 22 A3

Owned and managed by the welcoming Foyle family, the Georgian manor
stands in 30 acres of gardens overlooking Ballinakill Bay. Character and
comfort are in generous supply, the former including carefully chosen
antiques and paintings, the latter assisted by central heating and peat fires.
Bedrooms are nearly all of a very good size (with separate seating areas
or mini-suites) and all have good bathrooms. There are two drawing
rooms and a conservatory bar. ***Rooms*** *20. Garden, sauna, tennis, billiards,
fishing. Closed Nov-Easter.* AMERICAN EXPRESS *Access, Visa.*

Restaurant

Nigel Rush's four-course dinner menus are served at round antique tables
under chandeliers in a delightfully civilised room. Local produce (some
of it home-grown) is put to excellent use in dishes that range from fresh
prawn mayonnaise, duck liver paté and marinated mushrooms in red wine,
honey and herbs among the starters to potato and walnut soup as a second
course, then grilled wild salmon with scallion butter, guinea fowl with
brandy and raisins, and medallions of pork in cider sauce. Only cold dishes
at lunchtime. Home-made ice creams feature among the sweets. Teas and
coffees are served in the drawing rooms. No smoking in the dining room.
*Seats 60. Parties 8. Private Room 10. L 1-2.30 D 8-9.30 (Sun to 9).
Set D from £25.*

Letterfrack   Place of Interest

Kylemore Abbey   Connemara Tel 095 41146

Limerick   Castletroy Park Hotel   74%   £139
Tel 061 335566   Fax 061 331117   HR
Dublin Road Limerick Co Limerick   Map 23 B5

Located on the Dublin road on the outskirts of town, this well-designed
red-brick hotel meets every business need. The new university concert hall
and foundation building, just three minutes' walk away, will greatly

enhance Limerick's growing reputation as a major conference centre, and with its own state-of-the-art conference and leisure facilities the hotel is ideally situated to benefit. A welcoming atmosphere warms the wood-floored entrance hall and conservatory, while the Merry Pedlar 'pub', which also serves bistro-style food, offers traditional and authentic Irish hospitality and a decent pint. Bedrooms are large with plenty of writing space, good lighting and up-to-date features – satellite TV, fax and computer points, two phones, minibar and trouser press; bathrooms are on the small side. Executive rooms offer more extras including king-size bed, bathrobe and turn-down service plus several other complimentary items. Whether your needs require facilities for a conference (up to 450) or a private boardroom, the hotel can cater for both and also provides a fully-equipped business centre. Note the amenities available in the superbly equipped leisure centre. Good buffet breakfast served in the restaurant. 24hr room service. No dogs. *Rooms 107. Garden, terrace, indoor swimming pool, children's splash pool, gymnasium, keep-fit equipment, solarium, sauna, spa bath, steam room, beauty salon, tennis, leisure centre.* Closed 24 & 25 Dec. AMERICAN EXPRESS *Access, Diners, Visa.*

McLaughlin's Restaurant   £65

Widely regarded as one of the leading restaurants in the area, McLaughlin's tries hard to be cosy, with candle light and shelves of old books to soften the surroundings – although the atmosphere is still inclined to be impersonal, with a rather businesslike approach by staff ('Smoking or non-smoking, madam?'), a reminder that the restaurant is located in a large hotel. On the four-course dinner menu Pat O'Sullivan, head chef since late 1992, presents reliable *cuisine moderne* starting, perhaps, with a tasty *amuse-bouche* such as a miniature barbecued kebab, followed by country-style terrine with Cumberland sauce or a millefeuille of wild mushrooms in a red wine sauce, then a choice of soups or citrus sorbet. Main-course choices tend to lean towards fish or, perhaps, a roast rack of lamb with a duxelles of mushrooms. Rather jumpy service is characterised by persistent over-use of a jumbo peppermill. Informal lunch and evening meals are available from an international bar menu at the hotel's Merry Pedlar 'pub'. *Seats 70. Parties 30. L 12.30-2 D 7-9.30. Set L £14.50 Set D £22. Closed L Sat, D Sun.*

Limerick   Greenhills Hotel   62%   £119

Tel 061 453033 Fax 061 453307	H
Ennis Road Limerick Co Limerick	Map 23 B5

Continual improvement is the aim at this family-run hotel and, although older rooms (due for refurbishment this year) seem quite dated they have a pleasant outlook over garden or tennis court and are all well equipped, with telephone, tea/coffee-making facilities, trouser press and television. Newer rooms are larger and more comfortable, with well-finished, fully-tiled bathrooms. Public areas include a leisure centre, spacious lobby and a pleasant bar. Under-4s may stay free in parents' room. No dogs. *Rooms 60. Garden, indoor swimming pool, children's pool, gymnasium, sauna, steam room, solarium, beauty salon, tennis. Closed 25 Dec.* AMERICAN EXPRESS *Access, Diners, Visa.*

Limerick   Jurys Hotel   68%   £116

Tel 061 327777 Fax 061 326400	H
Ennis Road Limerick Co Limerick	Map 23 B5

Centrally situated just across the bridge from Limerick's main shopping and business area, Jurys prides itself on hospitality and service as well as convenience. A good impression is created in the spacious lobby area and carried through the public areas, including the pleasant Limericks Bar (which features the history of the famous rhyming verse), two restaurants and extensive leisure facilities, while a continuous programme of refurbishment has ensured that standards are maintained. Service is a priority, friendly staff provide 24 hour room service. Newer bedrooms are larger and more stylishly decorated with smarter bathrooms but, although slightly dated, older rooms are kept in good repair and are equally well equipped (including trouser press and multi-channel TV; tea/coffee-making facilities available on request). *Rooms 96. Garden, indoor swimming pool, children's splash pool, gym, sauna, steam room, spa bath, tennis, coffee shop (7am-10pm). Closed 25 & 27 Dec.* AMERICAN EXPRESS *Access, Diners, Visa.*

Limerick — Restaurant de La Fontaine — £60

Tel 061 414461   Fax 061 411337 — **R**

12 Upper Gerald Griffin Street Limerick Co Limerick — **Map 23 B5**

Appropriately named after the great writer of fables, Alain Bras' first-floor restaurant has an other-worldliness which strikes the first-time visitor immediately on climbing wide carpeted stairs – distinctly reminiscent of the approach to 1950s' picture houses – to the reception area. Once inside, it could be provincial France, a feeling strongly reinforced by chef Bernard Brousse's evocative *cuisine grand'mère* in dishes such as venison terrine, accompanied by delicious little Puy lentils, and excellent robust country main courses like rabbit with cabbage. An exceptional French wine list (for other countries you must ask). The entrance has recently been converted into a 30-seat wine bar, where lunches and apéritifs are served. *Seats 40. L 12.30-2.30 D 7-10. Set L £10 Set D £21.50. Closed L Sat, all Sun, Bank Holidays & Christmas.* AMERICAN EXPRESS *Access, Diners, Visa.*

Limerick — Limerick Inn Hotel — 68% — £117

Tel 061 326666   Fax 061 326281 — **H**

Ennis Road Limerick Co Limerick — **Map 23 B5**

The helipad in front of this low-rise modern hotel attracts considerable attention from passing traffic and there is usually a bit of a buzz around the large, airy reception area and public rooms. Good-sized rooms at the back of the hotel have a pleasant outlook over countryside, have well-designed bathrooms and are equipped to a high standard, including trouser press complete with iron and ironing board in addition to hairdryer, phone, tea/coffee-making facilities and multi-channel TV while superior rooms and suites also have mini-bars. Conference and business facilities for up to 600 delegates include secretarial services. Good health and leisure facilities; resident hair stylist and beautician. *Rooms 153. Garden, indoor swimming pool, gymnasium, sauna, solarium, steam room, whirlpool bath, tennis, putting, snooker, coffee shop (7.30am-10.30pm). Closed 25 Dec.* AMERICAN EXPRESS *Access, Diners, Visa.*

Limerick — Quenelle's Restaurant — NEW — £55

Tel 061 411111 — **R**

Corner of Mallow & Henry Street Limerick Co Limerick — **Map 23 B5**

Kieran and Sindy Pollard burst on to the Limerick dining scene in the summer of 1993 and their interesting little three-level city-centre restaurant overlooking the river is already making its mark. Although especially popular at lunchtime, when a bargain three-course menu draws the crowds, a calmer evening visit is required to do justice to Kieran's confident, adventurous cooking and a more elegant table presentation. A typical 5-course menu might include parcels of wild boar (in season), a choice of soups and also an unusual, amusingly presented sorbet and a full range of local produce in the main-course choices, including excellent steak given a new twist with a nutty bacon crust, perhaps an interesting vegetarian option such as vegetables crepes with a cheese and basil sauce and, of course, a selection of local seafood. Imaginative desserts might include an excellent classic crème caramel delicately decorated with fresh fruit fans and there's a good selection of farmhouse cheeses. Attention to detail is outstanding throughout, from the presentation of little amuse-bouches on arrival, through garnishing side vegetables with a dainty filo moneybag parcel filled with a julienne of vegetables, to the minted truffles served with coffee. **Seats** 35. L 12-2.15 D 7-10. Closed L Sat, all Sun & Mon, 24-26 Dec, Good Friday. Set L £5.20 Set D £19.75. Access, Visa.

Limerick	**Two Mile Inn Hotel**	**63%**	£78
Tel 061 326255 Fax 061 453783			H
Ennis Road Limerick Co Limerick			Map 23 B5

Actually just three miles from the centre of Limerick, this striking modern hotel features an enormous lobby with a large seating area, rather like an airport lounge, but the hotel as a whole is imaginatively laid out and other areas are surprisingly intimate. Bedrooms are attractively arranged around garden areas which afford a feeling of quietness and privacy and are furnished with deck chairs and sunshades in summer. Conference centre, with banqueting for up to 350. No dogs. **Rooms** 123. Garden, shop. Closed 24-26 Dec. AMERICAN EXPRESS Access, Diners, Visa.

Limerick	**Places of Interest**

Tourist Information   Tel 061 317522
City Gallery of Art   Upper Mallow Street Tel 061 310663
City Museum   John Square Tel 061 417826
King John's Castle   Tel 061 411201
St John's Cathedral   Tel 061 414624
St Mary's Cathedral   Tel 061 310293
Limerick Racecourse   Tel 061 29377
Cratloe Woods House   Cratloe Tel 061 327028 *5 miles*
Lough Gur Interpretative Centre   Lough Gur Tel 061 85186 *6 miles*

Lough Eske	**Ardnamona House**	£60
Tel 073 22650 Fax 073 22819		PH
Lough Eske Donegal Town Co Donegal		Map 22 B2

Beautifully situated in outstanding gardens overlooking Lough Eske, the secluded position of this attractive, rambling house belies its close proximity to Donegal town. Front rooms are most desirable, with lovely views over the lough to the mountains beyond, but all are individual with private bathrooms and a peaceful outlook through rhododendrons and azaleas which have received international acclaim. It is, in fact, a gardener's paradise (with a garden trail, guide leaflet and all plants labelled) but this serene place also offers miles of walks through ancient oak forests full of mosses and ferns, private boating and fishing on the lake. No smoking. **Rooms** 5. Garden, fishing. Closed Christmas & New Year. Access, Visa.

Maddoxtown	**Blanchville House**	£50
Tel 056 27197		PH
Dunbell Maddoxtown Co Kilkenny		Map 23 C5

Easily recognised by the folly in its grounds, this elegant Georgian house is on a working farm and, while conveniently close to the crafts and culture of Kilkenny city, has all the advantages of peace and restfulness associated with the country – and similarly Tim and Monica Phelan aim to provide guests with 20th-century comfort to balance 19th-century style. The house has a lovely, airy atmosphere, with matching, well-proportioned dining and drawing rooms on either side of the hall and pleasant, comfortably furnished bedrooms (most en-suite, two with private bathrooms) overlooking lovely countryside. Dinner is available to residents by arrangement and, like the next morning's excellent breakfast, is taken at the communal mahogany dining table. **Rooms** 6. Garden. Closed 1 Nov-1 Mar. Access, Visa.

Malahide — Bon Appétit £80

Tel & Fax 01 845 0314 R
9 St James Terrace Malahide Co Dublin Map 22 D3

An elegant Georgian terrace house, overlooking the estuary, has been the
setting for both the home and business of Catherine and Patsy McGuirk
since 1989. Aperitifs are served in the ground-floor drawing room/bar,
notable for its pleasing local watercolours, while the cosy restaurant,
decorated in warm tones of red and dark green, is in the basement. Chef
Patsy serves classical French food based on top-quality fresh ingredients
(Dingle Bay scallops, Carlingford lobster, Kilmore crab, east coast mussels),
with a handful of daily specials added for variety. Thus, snails in garlic
butter and fillets of sole Walewska sit happily alongside crispy duckling
with potato, herb and Grand Marnier stuffing and *gigot de lapin braisée
à l'essence de Cabernet Sauvignon et filet roti aux herbes et moutard.* The super
wine list has many fine French classics, most of which are accompanied
by tasting notes (of varying help!); the best value is outside these, with lots
of good drinking under £20. *Seats 55. Private Room 20. L 12.30-2 D 7-11.
Closed L Sat, all Sun, Bank Holidays, 1 week Christmas. Set L £10
Set D £22.* AMERICAN EXPRESS *Access, Diners, Visa.*

Malahide — Eastern Tandoori £40

Tel 01 845 4154/5 R
1 New Street Malahide Co Dublin Map 22 D3

Although it's on the first floor, overlooking the new Malahide marina
development, the atmosphere at this out-of-town branch of the well-known
city centre restaurant is distinctly other-worldly, with an all-Indian staff,
authentic furnishings and sound effects. Choose from four set menus
at varying prices, or from the à la carte: between them they offer a wide,
well-balanced choice of dishes ranging from gently aromatic to fiery hot,
suiting the novice without offending old hands. Old favourites are there
in mild onion bhajee, served with a small salad, various tandoori dishes –
chicken tikka, mackerel, even quail and crab claws – and several jalfrezi
dishes such as beef, lamb or chicken, hot with chili, fresh ginger and
coriander. Chef's recommendations are more interesting, some desserts
garnished with the classic silver leaf, and side dishes like tarka dal (lentils
with fresh coriander) and aloo jeera (dry potatoes with cumin seed) are
good. Wine is pricy, but Cobra Indian beer suits the food better anyway.
*Seats 64. Parties 20. D only 6-11.30. Set D from £14.95. Closed 25 Dec,
Good Friday.* AMERICAN EXPRESS *Access, Diners, Visa.*

Prices quoted for the Republic of Ireland are in Irish punts.

Malahide — Grand Hotel 66% £90

Tel 01 845 0000   Fax 01 845 0987 H
Malahide Co Dublin Map 22 D3

Polished double doors in the splendid cream-painted frontage lead into
a pillared entrance hall resplendent with fine crystal chandeliers, marble
fireplace, comfortable, well-spaced settees and winged armchairs. At the
rear of the ground floor is Matt Ryan's bar, a split-level room decorated
in a distinctive 20s' Mackintosh style, while to the left of the entrance
is the Griffin bar, open evenings only and due for refurbishment. Newer
bedrooms contrast markedly with the older ones (although almost all have
now been refurbished) in having smart pickled pine furniture and a host
of amenities as well as being double-glazed and possessing bright, well-
equipped bathrooms. *Rooms 100. Garden. Closed 25 & 26 Dec.*
AMERICAN EXPRESS *Access, Diners, Visa.*

Malahide Roches Bistro £55

Tel 01 845 2777 **R**

12 New Street Malahide Co Dublin **Map 22 D3**

Family-run by sisters Orla Roche and Niamh Boylan, this is probably the
nearest to a French local restaurant to be found in Co Dublin. Set
in Malahide's attractive main street, it's a small, intimate place with cheerful
blue and white check linen and an open fire in winter. The wide-ranging
set menus change daily and show a strong bias towards French country
cooking and lots of seafood dishes – all cooked in an open kitchen, watched
by guests taking an aperitif or coffee at the dividing bar. Go for specialities
like crab soufflé à la crème or seafood pancakes or try an unusual
combination like monkfish with fresh mint. Meat-lovers will find strip
loin steak with pink and green peppercorns thick, tender and piquant.
Apple and frangipane tart is a speciality and there's a good selection
of farmhouse cheeses, then as much freshly brewed coffee as you like. Early
bird menu (6-7.30) £12.95. The short French wine list is mostly under
£20. *Seats 35. Parties 30. L 12-2.30 D 6-10.30. Closed L Mon Jan-Jun,
D Mon & Tue (& Wed in winter), all Sun, Bank Holidays, 2 weeks Jan.
Set L £10.95 Set D £18.95.* AMERICAN EXPRESS *Access, Diners, Visa.*

Malahide Place of Interest

Malahide Castle Tel 01 845 2655

Note that all telephone numbers with area codes starting with 0
will start 01 from 16 April 1995.

Mallow Longueville House 72% £110

Tel 022 47156   Fax 022 47459 **H R**

Mallow Co Cork **Map 23 B5**

Three miles west of Mallow on the N72 Killarney Road, this handsome
Georgian house built in 1720 has been run as a hotel since 1969 by the
O'Callaghan family, descendants of the original occupants. While grandly
proportioned, the gracious house has an easy informality which makes
it seem natural to be surrounded by gilt-framed mirrors, family portraits
and impressive fireplaces with log fires burning. Bedrooms are stylishly
furnished with antiques, good fabrics and thoughtfully equipped modern
bathrooms. Breakfast offers a fine choice, both hot and cold, including
home-made bread. No dogs. *Rooms 16. Garden, game & coarse fishing, games
room, snooker. Closed 20 Dec-mid March.* AMERICAN EXPRESS *Access, Visa.*

Presidents' Restaurant ↑ £65

William O'Callaghan's creative, imaginative cooking is surveyed
by previous Presidents of Ireland, who look down from the walls of an
elegant, lofty room. Produce from their private fishing on the Blackwater
and his father's farm and gardens supplies most of his needs in the kitchen.
Specialities on the short, well-chosen menus (fixed-price or à la carte)
include home-smoked salmon timbale, ravioli of Castletownbere prawns
and noisettes of Longueville lamb filled with tarragon mousse. Garden
vegetables, served in little bouquets, are what they claim to be and have
great depth of flavour. Desserts often come from the garden too, as in
summer fruit soup. A highly unusual and very tempting alternative
is caramelised pear on a slice of brioche with beer ice cream. The surprise
menu (£35) is available from 7-9 and only to an entire party. Irish
farmhouse cheeses are excellent and home-made chocolates and petits fours
come with the coffee. *Seats 45. Parties 15. Private Room 20. L 12.30-2
D 7-9. Set L £15 Set D £26/£35.*

Mallow   Places of Interest

Annes Grove Gardens   Castletownroche Tel 022 26145
Mallow Racecourse   Mount Ruby Tel 022 21565

Maynooth   Moyglare Manor   75%   £136

Tel 01 628 6351   Fax 01 628 5405   **HR**

Moyglare Maynooth Co Kildare   Map 23 C4

Traffic-wise, Maynooth can be something of a bottleneck, but Moyglare
itself is a couple of miles down the road past the church. A long tree-lined
avenue leads to the fine Georgian house, which has a lovely garden and
overlooks peaceful parkland and mountains beyond. Owned by Norah
Devlin and managed by Shay Curran, the hotel is stuffed full of antiques,
objets d'art, paintings and all manner of lamps. The public rooms are
a veritable Aladdin's Cave of memorabilia and comfortable furnishings – a
tranquil doze in front of the marble fireplace in the lounge is to
be recommended. Period-style bedrooms, several with four-posters or half-
testers, are individually furnished, but if you want a TV to interrupt
or spoil your surroundings you must ask – they are available on request.
A ground-floor garden suite is particularly grand. Bathrooms have been
modernised and provide generously-sized towels and decent toiletries. Look
out for the freshly-baked scones and bread which accompany excellent
cafetière coffee at breakfast. No children under 12. No dogs. *Rooms 17.
Garden, tennis. Closed 3 days Christmas.* AMERICAN EXPRESS, *Access, Diners, Visa.*

Restaurant   £75

The setting is romantic, with candles or Victorian lamps on the tables, and
the menu features many fish dishes. Try a seafood terrine with champagne
sauce, crab claws in garlic butter or poached fillets of brill served with
a perfect hollandaise sauce. Hormone-free sirloin steak comes grilled with
a green peppercorn sauce, while pork is done the traditional way – with
a potato and herb stuffing and apple sauce. Lunch menus offer less choice.
There's a good cheeseboard and a choice of sweets (white chocolate terrine
perhaps), followed by either tea or coffee accompanied by home-made
petits fours. Sample the home-made bread, and if you like your wine list
classic there are many fine bottles from which to choose – 25 vintages
of Chateau d'Yquem alone! – though half bottles are thin in the cellar.
No smoking. *Seats 80. Private Room 50. L 12.30-2.15 (Sun 12-2.30) D 7-9.
Closed L Sat. Set L £11.95 Set D £21*

Maynooth   Place of Interest

Castletown House   Celbridge Tel 01 628 8252

Midleton   Farm Gate   £50

Tel 021 632771   **R**

The Coolbawn Midleton Co Cork   Map 23 B6

Sisters Marog O'Brien and Kay Harte have been running this unique shop
and restaurant to growing acclaim since 1985 and it's a joy to behold. The
shop at the front overflows with wonderful local produce – organic fruit
and vegetables, cheeses, honey – and a vast selection of their own fine home
baking, while the evocatively decorated, comfortable, old-pine-furnished
and modern sculpture-enhanced restaurant at the back changes, chameleon-
like, from a bustling daytime persona characterised by wholesome savoury
fare and irresistible baking, to a far more sophisticated evening scene (on
Friday and Saturday) complete with string quartet. A typical menu might
offer celery soup, pan-fried salmon with a fennel and olive sauce, stuffed
or steamed mussels, duck with sage and onion stuffing, rosemary-flavoured
leg of lamb and pan-fried fillet beef with a 'famous Jameson' sauce. Alfresco

eating for 20 in the garden. *Seats* 60. *Meals 9-5.30 L 12-4 D (Fri & Sat only) 7.30-9.30. Closed all Sun, Bank Holidays, 25 Dec, Good Friday. Set D £16.50. Access, Visa.*

Midleton   Place of Interest

Jameson Heritage Centre   Tel 021 613594

Mountrath   Roundwood House   58%   £64

Tel 0502 32120   Fax 0502 32711   **HR**

Mountrath Co Laois   Map 23 C4

A "love it or loathe it" kind of place, with some visitors objecting to the very air of eccentricity which makes the majority of guests love Frank and Rosemarie Kennan's small, early Georgian Palladian villa enough to keep coming back for more. Don't expect curtains at your bedroom windows, but the big wooden shutters (correct for a house of this period) will be snugly closed while you communally enjoy Rosemarie's unpretentious good home cooking around a large polished mahogany table in their lovely dining room. Old-fashioned bathrooms have all that is needed, including towels that are mismatched but plentiful and, like the rest of the house, lovely and warm; there will also be a water bottle tucked into your bed when you finally make it there. Frank is the host, dispensing pre-dinner drinks in front of the huge drawing room fire and letting guests in on the local scene. In the morning, guests wake to a chorus of birdsong from the surrounding woods and children, especially, will enjoy visiting the yard to see if there are any chicks or kittens around, or perhaps to collect a warm egg for breakfast. Tariff reductions for stays of two nights or more; children under 12 pay 50% of tariff when sharing with their parents. Stabling available. *Rooms 6. Garden, croquet. fishing.*

Restaurant   £60

Non-residents can book for Sunday lunch (when separate tables are laid), or dinner if there is room. Rosemarie's food continues to make friends – lovely home cooking, cooked on the Aga, is the norm. Roasts with fresh herbs, simple, lightly cooked vegetables, gratins of potato (with more than a generous hint of garlic), farmhouse cheeses with home-made biscuits, a choice of wickedly gooey or wholesome desserts. Finish with coffee by the fireside. *Seats 26. Parties 16. Set L (Sun only) £11 Set D £19.* AMERICAN EXPRESS® *Access, Diners, Visa.*

Mountrath   Place of Interest

Damer House   Roscrea Heritage Centre Tel 0505 21850 *16 miles*

Moycullen   Cloonnabinnia House Hotel   61%   £55

Tel 091 85555   Fax 091 85640   **H**

Ross Lake Moycullen Co Galway   Map 23 B4

Situated in landscaped gardens overlooking Ross Lake, this unpretentious 1960s' hotel owes its charm to the warmth and genuine hospitality of the Kavanagh family. The atmospheric bar, popular with locals and guests alike, is often the scene for much talk of fishing. Public areas generally are a homely mixture of old and new, with comfort and a relaxed atmosphere the keynotes. Modest bedrooms are all en suite, with lovely views; function rooms (conferences 300/banquets 240) are downstairs, well away from residents and with a separate entrance. Four rooms are designated non-smoking. Children under 12 stay free in parents' room. Three self-catering cottages are also available. *Rooms 14. Garden, fishing, hunting, shooting. Closed Nov-Mar. Access, Visa.*

Moycullen   Drimcong House Restaurant   ★   £65

Tel 091 85115   R

Moycullen Co Galway   Map 23 B4

Gerry Galvin, and his wife Marie have been running their renowned restaurant just west of Moycullen on the Galway-Clifden road since 1984, and it is still one of the most remarkable establishments in the country. Gerry's classical skills are put to the test nightly in inventive cooking based firmly on the best local ingredients, with both 3/5-course dinner menus and the à la carte changing regularly to make best use of produce at its peak. The choice is remarkable for a small restaurant, including a 5-course vegetarian menu (£16.50) and, unusually for any restaurant (but typical of a chef who has establishment a special reputation for encouraging the young), children who are old enough to cope are made particularly welcome in a special 3-course menu 'for pre-teenage people' (£8.50). There is ample time to inwardly digest the menus in the comfortable, book-strewn bar before moving through to the oak-polished formality of the dining room that overlooks gardens on two sides. A typical evening's offerings might include grilled goat's cheese with a zinging mixed leaf salad, followed by a choice of soup or sorbet, while main courses usually include local Connemara lamb – roast, perhaps, with wild garlic – and fish of the day, typically baked hake in a chervil cream sauce, giving an ever-so-subtle flavour of anise to complement the fresh-from-the-boat fish. A la carte options might extend to grilled oysters with garlic and Gruyère or quenelles of pike in a shellfish sauce to start, with main courses like confit of duck with mushroom croute and satsuma sauce or roast quail and pigeon with grapes and shallots to follow. Tempting desserts tend to be classical – frozen amaretto soufflé in raspberry sauce, grape and almond tart – although a dessert 'pizza' shows signs of reinventing the wheel! Always an excellent Irish farmhouse cheeseboard, served with home-baked biscuits. The modest wine list offers wines in two sections: under and over £14. *Seats 50. Private Room 32. D only 7-10.30. Closed Sun, Mon, Bank Hols, Jan & Feb. Set D £15.95/£18.95.* AMERICAN EXPRESS *Access, Diners, Visa.*
MARTELL

Moydow   The Vintage   £45

Tel 043 22122   R

Moydow Co Longford   Map 22 C3

Former cookery teacher Regina Houlihan has developed The Vintage bar into quite a catering enterprise, looking after both local functions and serving dinner three nights a week (plus Sunday lunch). The four-course Sunday lunch menu may be a seafood platter followed by home-made soup, then roast rib of beef, and a pudding to follow. The evening dinner menu offers a reasonable choice, possibly including tagliatelle alfredo, stuffed quail with chicken mousseline, fillet of brill Japanese-style and pan-fried chicken with wild mushroom sauce. A la carte dishes are also available. Garden, outdoor eating. *L 1-3 (Sun only) D 7-10.30 (Thur-Sun only). Set Sun L £8·95 Set D £13.95.* AMERICAN EXPRESS *Access, Visa.*

Mullingar   Crookedwood House   £55

Tel 044 72165   Fax 044 72166   R

Crookedwood Mullingar Co Westmeath   Map 22 C3

Noel and Julie Kenny have plans to add accommodation to the excellent restaurant at their 200-year-old former rectory overlooking Lough Derravaragh. Noel's menus change with the seasons and feature the best of local produce. From a winter selection come grilled breast of wood pigeon on rösti with onion marmalade, cream of parsnip and nutmeg soup, roulade of sole and smoked salmon, and a duet of pheasant and venison with a wild mushroom and juniper berry sauce. Good simple desserts, Irish farmhouse cheeses. *Seats 35. Parties 14. Private Room 25. L (Sun only) 12.30-2 D 7-10. Closed D Sun & Mon, Bank Holidays, 2 weeks Nov. Set L £12.50 Set D £17.95.* AMERICAN EXPRESS *Access, Diners, Visa.* MARTELL

Mullingar   Place of Interest

Tullynally Castle and Gardens   Castlepollard Tel 044 61159 *16 miles*

Navan   Ardboyne Hotel   60%   £75

Tel 046 23119   Fax 046 22355   **HR**

Dublin Road Navan Co Meath   **Map 22 C3**

A friendly, well-run modern hotel standing in its own grounds on the
outskirts of town. Bedrooms, all with compact tiled bathrooms, are simple
and practical, with fitted furniture and good desk/dressing table space.
There's a bright, comfortable lounge and a warm, convivial bar. All-day
snacks are available in the bar/foyer area. Children are more than welcome,
and under-12s can stay free in their parents' room. **Rooms** *27. Garden, disco
(Fri & Sat). Closed 24-27 Dec.* AMERICAN EXPRESS *Access, Diners, Visa.*

Terrace Restaurant   £55

Simple, straightforward dishes are available on several menus, including à la
carte, tourist, luncheon, table d'hote and early bird. 'Chef Recommends'
on the carte include prawns provençale, wiener schnitzel, shish kebab and
sirloin steak. Sweets from the buffet. **Seats** *150. Private Room 50.
L 12.30-2.30 D 5.30-10 (Sun till 9). Set L £10.95 Set D £12.50/£17.50.*

Navan   Places of Interest

Hill of Tara   Tel 046 25903
Navan Racecourse   Tel 046 21350
Butterstream Garden   Trim Tel 046 36017

Newbawn   Cedar Lodge   62%   £75

Tel 051 28386   Fax 051 28222   **H**

Carrigbyrne Newbawn Co Wexford   **Map 23 C5**

14 miles from Wexford on the main Rosslare-Waterford road, this family-
run hotel stands in lush countryside beneath the slopes of Carrigbyrne
Forest. Redbrick walls, wooden ceilings and open fires create a warm and
welcoming atmosphere in the public rooms and paintings and frescos
by local artists provide interesting focal points. Bedrooms are practical and
neatly appointed. Conference/function suite for up to 100 (banquets 70)
in adjoining low-rise wings. **Rooms** *18. Garden. Closed 25 & 26 Dec, Jan.
Access, Visa.*

Newbawn   Place of Interest

John F Kennedy Arboretum   Tel 051 88171

Newbay   Newbay Country House   £60

Tel 053 42779   Fax 053 46318   **PH**

Newbay nr Wexford Co Wexford   **Map 23 D5**

A comfortable family-run country house dating from 1822 but
incorporating earlier outbuildings. The outside impression is a touch
stern, but the real atmosphere is very warm and relaxed. Day rooms are
of imposing proportions, with interesting antiques, amply sized country
furniture and displays of dried flowers arranged by Mientje (Min) Drum.
Bedrooms are spacious, comfortable and individually furnished with four-
poster beds but without TVs or phones. Paul Drum's food (for residents
only), offers no choice and is served at one large table. The house is situated
2 miles from Wexford and not far from the ferry port of Rosslare.
No dogs. **Rooms** *6. Garden. Closed mid Nov-mid Mar except for groups
or by prior appointment.* AMERICAN EXPRESS *Access, Diners, Visa.*

Newbridge   Hotel Keadeen   68%   £85

Tel 045 31666   Fax 045 34402   **H**

Ballymany Newbridge Co Kildare   Map 23 C4

Leave the M7 at exit 10 and head back towards Newbridge to find 'the inn
on the Curragh', a well-kept hotel in a garden setting near the famous
racetrack. Conferences and functions (up to 800) are big business, but
private guests are well catered for in good-sized bedrooms furnished
in a variety of styles. No dogs. *Rooms 37. Garden. Closed 25-27 Dec.*
AMERICAN EXPRESS *Access, Diners, Visa.*

Newbridge   Places of Interest

Punchestown Racecourse   Naas Tel 045 97704
Naas Racecourse   Tel 045 97391
Japanese Gardens   Tully Tel 045 21251 *5 miles*
Irish National Stud   Tully Tel 045 21617 *5 miles*
Emo Court and Gardens   Emo Tel 0502 26110 *10 miles*

Newmarket-on-Fergus   Clare Inn Hotel   64%   £87

Tel 061 368161   Fax 061 368622   **H**

Dromoland Newmarket-on-Fergus Co Clare   Map 23 B4

Outstanding leisure facilities are provided at the modern, low-rise Clare
Hotel, which stands in the middle of Dromoland's 18-hole golf course
(£14 green fee). The leisure centre (free to guests; children under 16
must be accompanied, no children after 7pm) includes a fully-equipped
gymnasium, and deep-sea fishing can be arranged from the hotel's
catamaran, the *Liscannor Star*. The Castlefergus Bar, with weekend
entertainment, is a good place to unwind, and there are residents' lounges,
two restaurants and a children's playroom. Bedrooms are of a decent size,
most of them suitable for family occupation. Children up to 4 are
accommodated free, while under-12s are charged £10, which includes
B&B and high tea. Conference facilities for up to 400. Nine miles from
Shannon Airport on the main Limerick/Galway road. *Rooms 121. Garden,
indoor swimming pool, gymnasium, sauna, steam room, spa bath, sun bed,
solarium, tennis, pitch & putt, crazy golf, croquet, lawn bowling, outdoor
draughts, games room, coffee shop (12.30-10pm).* AMERICAN EXPRESS *Access,
Diners, Visa.*

Newmarket-on-Fergus   Dromoland Castle   79%   £262

Tel 061 368144   Fax 061 363355   **HR**

Newmarket-on-Fergus Co Clare   Map 23 B4

The castle's history can be traced back to the 16th century when the estate
belonged to the O'Brien clan, direct descendants of Brian Boru, High King
of Ireland; hence the name of the magnificent and newly built conference
venue, comprising a great hall, gallery, boardrooms and business centre
catering for up to 450 delegates. Close to Shannon airport, the hotel is set
among 370 acres of woods and parkland (a stroll through the walled
garden is also a must) that include a championship golf course, the eighth
green of which is overlooked by the library bar. If the outside is imposing,
the public rooms inside are surprisingly intimate and relaxed, with roaring
log fires, elegant and comfortable seating, many period antiques and a huge
collection of family portraits, not to mention the fine fabrics, glittering
chandeliers, intricate plasterwork and high ceilings. There is a variety
of bedrooms, some necessitating long walks down corridors; many of the
rooms have recently been refurbished and the best are extremely spacious
with lovely views of either the lake or the grounds. Each is beautifully
appointed with high-quality fabrics, excellent bed linen and impressive
furniture, and all the usual extras that you would expect from a hotel
of this class: flowers, fresh fruit and mineral water on arrival, together with
bathrobes, slippers, toiletries and decent towels in the good bathrooms

(some of which are on the small side). Standards of service, under the direction of General Manager Mark Nolan, are high and housekeeping is exemplary (a nightly turn-down of beds can be expected, of course). Children up to 12 stay free in their parents' rooms. No dogs. The new Brian Boru conference and banqueting centre handles up to 450 for conferences & receptions up to 1000. Sister hotel to *Ashford Castle*, Cong (see entry). **Rooms** *73. Garden, golf, riding, fishing, clay-pigeon shooting, shooting, archery, tennis, snooker, bicycles.* AMERICAN EXPRESS *Access, Diners, Visa.*

The Earl of Thomond Room   ↑   £115

The elegance of the castle is perhaps best illustrated by the grandness of the dining rooms: high ceilings, chandeliers and splendid drapes matched by fine china, gleaming crystal and linen cloths. In the evenings you'll be further seduced by a traditional Irish harpist and maybe even a fiddler, together with the dishes of long-serving executive head chef Jean-Baptiste Molinari. He presents a variety of menus: a four-course table d'hote, say pan-fried scallops 'niçoise' style, beef consommé, supreme of chicken roasted with a confit of shallots in a thyme-scented jus and a choice of dessert; a £45 6-course Taste of Ireland (also written in Gaelic) featuring such dishes as rabbit paté, plaited fillet of sole braised with cider and cabbage and hot brown bread soufflé; or à la carte – home-made lamb ravioli with a creamy sauce of herbs and meat juices, braised fillet of turbot with a champagne sauce and Beluga caviar, ending with a dark chocolate gateau filled with a compote of banana or apple and Calvados pie (prepared by chef-patissière Elma Campion). Much work goes into the composition of the menus, reflected by the high standard of execution, and it's a real pleasure to encounter such professional, courteous and knowledgeable staff. The good-quality bread, coffee and petits fours complete the satisfaction one will experience here. Prices on the the good wine list are not modest – you will have to hunt carefully for bargains! **Seats** *90. Parties 10. Private Rooms 24 & 60. L 12.30-2 D 7.30-10. Set L £18 Set D £33.*

Newport	**Newport House**	**67%**	£124

Tel 098 41222 Fax 098 41613	**HR**
Newport Co Mayo	**Map 22 A3**

A creeper-clad Georgian house stands in large gardens adjoining the town and overlooking the Newport river and quay – an unusual location for one of the most attractive and hospitable country houses in Ireland, run by Kieran and Thelma Thompson. Fishing is the major attraction, with salmon and sea trout fishing on the river and nearby loughs. Golf, riding and pony trekking are also available locally, but the appeal of the house itself with its beautiful central hall and sweeping staircase (now clad in a hand-woven McMurray carpet from Connemara) and gracious drawing room is enough to draw guests without sporting interests. Bedrooms, like the rest of the house, are furnished in style with antiques and fine paintings and bathrooms which can be eccentric but work well; most of the rooms are in the main house, a few in the courtyard. The day's catch is weighed and displayed in the hall and a cosy fisherman's bar provides the perfect venue for a reconstruction of the day's sport. **Rooms** *20. Garden, sea & game fishing, snooker. Closed 7 Oct-18 Mar.* AMERICAN EXPRESS *Access, Diners, Visa.*

Restaurant   £70

A high-ceilinged dining room overlooking the gardens and decorated in restrained period style provides an elegant setting for John Gavin's confident cooking, based on the best of local produce, much of it coming from the organically-worked walled kitchen garden. Home-smoked salmon makes a perfect starter on a 6-course dinner menu, followed by soup (cream of vegetable or carrot and coriander) and, perhaps, pan-fried quail with mousseline of chicken and a tarragon sauce or pan-fried salmon with lemon and chive cream sauce. Oysters (either *au naturel* or baked Rockefeller) are usually offered as an additional course. Vegetables and salads are as fresh as it is possible to be and there's a choice of farmhouse cheese or a fine dessert menu (Baileys soufflé with chocolate sauce, rhubarb tartlet with fruit coulis and vanilla sauce) to finish. Though Italian wines are sandwiched between Jura and Provence, the predominantly French wine list is otherwise clearly laid out and easy to use; however, there are no tasting notes, not much from the New World and nothing from California. No smoking in the dining room. *Seats 39. Parties 16. Private Room 35. D only 7.30-9.30. Set D £28.*

Oughterard   Connemara Gateway Hotel   66%   £108

Tel 091 82328   Fax 091 82332   **H**

Oughterard Co Galway   **Map 22 B3**

Originally a typical 60s' motel, the Connemara Gateway has been cleverly extended and developed to make the discreetly stylish modern building it is today. Warmth, comfort and a relaxed atmosphere are the keynotes and, although the decor is generally low-key, the work of local artists, including impressive wallhangings on Celtic themes in the reception area, create a nice feeling of continuity – an idea successfuly developed in the cosy bar, which is based on a rural agricultural theme and has a welcoming turf fire – definitely a cut above the average modern hotel bar. Rooms vary considerably in age and appointments, but local tweed is used to advantage in most and the emphasis is on homely comforts, such as properly organised tea and coffee facilities; similarly, bathrooms, although variable, have nice touches like hanging space for guests' hand laundry. Children up to 12 stay free in parents' room and good family facilities include an indoor swimming pool, children's entertainment in high season and high teas (6pm) and videos (7pm) every evening. Bicycle hire nearby. Banqueting/conference facilities for up to 120/100. No dogs. *Rooms 62. Garden, croquet, indoor swimming pool, sauna, solarium, snooker, tennis, children's indoor play room and playground. Closed end Dec-Jan (open New Year).* AMERICAN EXPRESS *Access, Diners, Visa.*

Oughterard   Currarevagh House   65%   £91

Tel 091 82313 · Fax 091 82731   **HR**

Oughterard Co Galway   **Map 22 B3**

Harry and June Hodgson, fifth generation and here for nearly 30 years, practise the art of old-fashioned hospitality in their Victorian manor house set in parkland, woods and gardens by Lough Corrib. Day rooms are homely and traditional, and the drawing room is the perfect setting for afternoon tea. Bedrooms are peaceful, with no phones or TV. The hotel has sporting rights over 5000 acres and fishing facilities that include boats and ghillies. *Rooms 15. Garden, tennis, fishing, mooring, swimming, hotel boats. Closed Nov-Mar. No credit cards.*

Restaurant   £50

A succulent meat dish is the centrepiece of no-choice five-course dinners prepared by June Hodgson from the pick of local produce. That dish might be haunch of venison with brandy and apple sauce, rack of lamb with honey and Guinness or roast beef with Yorkshire pudding. Preceding it could be duck liver paté and poached salmon, or cold consommé indienne and smoked salmon *en choux*, with a dessert, Irish cheeses and coffee to complete a really satisfying meal. No smoking. Snack lunches. *Seats 28. D only at 8. Set D £18.*

Oughterard   Sweeney's Oughterard House   59%   £98

Tel 091 82207   Fax 091 82161   **H**

Oughterard Co Galway   **Map 22 B3**

Unobtrusive newer extensions do not detract from the old-fashioned charm of this 200-year-old hotel just across the road from a particularly pretty stretch of the Owenriff River. The cottagey impression extends to cosy public rooms, furnished with antiques, and well manicured lawns provide a perfect setting for tea on a sunny afternoon. Bedrooms, where under-12s may stay free with their parents, vary considerably in size and appointments. **Rooms** 20. Garden. Closed 22 Dec-15 Jan. AMERICAN EXPRESS® Access, Diners, Visa.

Oughterard   Place of Interest

Aughnanure Castle   Tel 091 82214

Oysterhaven   The Oystercatcher   £65

Tel 021 770822   **R**

Oysterhaven Begooly Co Cork   **Map 23 B6**

Bill and Sylvia Patterson, both originally from Scotland, run a most attractive, cottagey restaurant known for its charming atmosphere and consistently excellent food. Oysters naturally make appearances on the dinner menu – simmered in garlic butter with almonds, in sausages on a saffron sauce and in angels on horseback. Wild mushrooms in a brioche is another speciality dish, and you might also find gateau of foie gras with apples, scallops on a julienne of vegetables, pig's trotter stuffed with veal sweetbreads and Madeira-sauced chateaubriand. Fine fresh cheeses, and a selection of savoury alternatives to "the sweet things in life". There's a good all-round wine list with plenty of excellent drinking under £20. **Seats** 30. Parties 20. Private Room 20. L by arrangement for parties of 7 or more D 7.30-9.30 (bookings only in winter). Closed for a month early each year – phone for details. Set D £22.95. AMERICAN EXPRESS® Access, Visa.

Parknasilla   Great Southern   72%   £161

Tel 064 45122   Fax 064 45323   **H**

Parknasilla Sneem Co Kerry   **Map 23 A6**

Overlooking Kenmare Bay (on which the hotel's own *Parknasilla Princess* offers pleasure cruises) and set in 200 acres of sub-tropical parkland, this late-Victorian building blends well with its exotic surroundings. An air of tranquillity is immediately conveyed by a sense of space, antiques and fresh flowers in the foyer and the tone of restful luxury is continued through all the public areas to elegantly decorated bedrooms. Good indoor leisure facilities are matched by a wide range of outdoor attractions, including a series of scenic walks through the estate. Banqueting for 70. No dogs. **Rooms** 84. Garden, indoor swimming pool, outdoor Canadian hot-tub, sauna, spa bath, steam room, tennis, golf (9), riding, games room, snooker, sea-fishing, water sports, bicycles, clay-pigeon shooting, archery. Closed Jan-Mar. AMERICAN EXPRESS® Access, Diners, Visa.

Parknasilla   Place of Interest

Derrynane National Historic Park   Caherdaniel Tel 066 75113

Rathmullan   Rathmullan House   62%   £104

Tel 074 58188   Fax 074 58200   **HR**

Rathmullan nr Letterkenny Co Donegal   **Map 22 C1**

For more than 30 years Bob and Robin Wheeler have run their extended Georgian mansion, which stands in lovely tranquil gardens running down to the shore of Lough Swilly. Open fires warm the antique-furnished day rooms, which include a period drawing room, library and cellar bar. Not the least of the distinctive features here is the unique pool complex with Egyptian Baths. Accommodation ranges from well-appointed master suites to family rooms and budget rooms without bathrooms. Outstanding breakfasts. **Rooms** 23. Garden, indoor swimming pool, steam room, tennis. Closed Nov-mid Mar. AMERICAN EXPRESS® Access, Diners, Visa.

The Pavilion £60

Liam McCormick's famous tented Pavilion restaurant makes a delightful setting for one of the best hors d'oeuvre buffet displays in the country (a speciality on Sundays) although the temptation is to try too many things from a selection of fishy starters including eels, smoked salmon and various terrines (both sliced to order), lots of salads and vegetarian options. Main-course choices also take vegetarians seriously and are understandably strong on seafood; good soups, interesting sauces and accompaniments. Desserts usually include carrageen pudding, which also appears with a choice of fruits on the breakfast buffet, and coffee is served with petits fours in the drawing room. Booking essential for both lunch and dinner. *Seats 60. Parties 20. Private Room 20. L (Sun only) 1-1.45. D 7.30-8.45. Set Sun L £12 Set D £22. Closed Nov-mid Mar.*

Rathmullan Places of Interest

Glebe House and Gallery Church Hill Letterkenny Tel 074 37071
Glenveagh National Park Tel 074 37088

Rathnew Hunter's Hotel 60% £80

| Tel 0404 40106 Fax 0404 40338 | HR |
| Newrath Bridge Rathnew Co Wicklow | Map 23 D4 |

The Gelletlie family and their forebears have been running this delightfully old-fashioned coaching inn since 1820, so it is not surprising that it should encompass a mixture of styles, including some interesting antiques. The current owner, Maureen Gelletlie, adds just the right element of eccentricity to the very real charm of the place. Rooms vary considerably; co-ordinated schemes are not to be expected, but all rooms were being upgraded to include en-suite facilities as we went to press. More important is the meticulously maintained garden leading down to a river at the back, with its wonderful herbaceous borders – the perfect place for their famous afternoon tea, an aperitif or coffee after a meal. Inclement weather is also anticipated, with a welcoming open fire in the cosy bar. Friendly, informal service is excellent. *Rooms 17. Garden. Closed 25-28 Dec.* AMERICAN EXPRESS *Access, Diners, Visa.*

Restaurant £55

Several steps back in time, the restaurant overlooks the garden and everything about it, including the service, is refreshingly old-fashioned. Long-standing chef John Sutton offers daily-changing 3- and 4-course set menus; try oak-smoked fresh trout fillets, roast Wicklow lamb with fresh herbs, vegetables from the garden and nursery puddings such as apple and blackberry tart or lemon meringue pie. Prices are fair on a cosmopolitan wine list. *Seats 54. Parties 14. L 1-2.30 (Sat & Sun to 3) D 7.30-9. Set L £13.50 Set D £19.50*

Rathnew Tinakilly House 76% £110

| Tel 0404 69274 Fax 0404 67806 | HR |
| Rathnew Wicklow Co Wicklow | Map 23 D4 |

A substantial Victorian mansion built in the 1870s for Captain Robert Halpin, Commander of the *Great Eastern*, which laid the first telegraph cable linking Europe and America. It's set in seven acres of gardens overlooking a bird sanctuary and sweeping down to the Irish Sea. The building has been extensively renovated both inside and out, with the addition of a period-style wing comprising fifteen suites and half suites, and run as a hotel by William and Bee Power since 1983. Furnished to a high standard with antiques, good pictures and an interesting collection of Halpin memorabilia, the interior is a model of good taste with a deal of old world charm – a fine mix of Victorian style and modern comforts. Comfortably furnished period bedrooms vary; the best are large, with four-posters and lovely sea views; ground-floor rooms have direct access to the garden. Children are welcome, with cots, high-chairs and baby-sitting provided by arrangement. The new wing houses fifteen bedrooms, the restaurant and conference and banqueting facilities for up to 150. Friendly, professional service. Very good breakfasts; all-day snacks, including afternoon tea, served in the residents' lounge. No dogs. **Rooms** *29. Garden, tennis, putting green, croquet.* AMERICAN EXPRESS *Access, Diners, Visa.* MARTELL

Restaurant   £75

"Splendid fresh food in elegant Victorian surroundings" rings true – the best of old and new combine in John Moloney's cooking. His creative seasonal menus are based on the best of local produce, especially seafood; fresh fruit and vegetables are grown on the premises. For a light lunch, try a smoked salmon salad and cheeses with some of Bee's renowned brown bread; alternatively, the set lunch menu might offer duck liver parfait with Melba toast and tomato chutney followed by poached salmon with Noilly Prat and herbs from their own garden; a fresh fruit mousse on a raspberry coulis to finish. The four-course table d'hote dinner changes daily, offering the likes of grilled goat's cheese in a poppyseed crust with salad, a freshly made soup (perhaps tomato and orange or cream of leek and potato), pan-fried fillet of beef with red wine and chanterelles, with blackcurrant parfait in sponge biscuit and a selection of fruit sauces to finish. A French and Irish (when available) cheeseboard is also offered. The wine list covers a diverse range and there's a good selection of half bottles. **Seats** *70. Private Room 40. L 12.30-2 D 7.30-9 (Sun to 8). Set L £17.50 Set D £28.50.*

Recess	Lough Inagh Lodge	68%	£104
Tel 095 34706 Fax 095 34708			H
Inagh Valley Recess Connemara			Map 22 A3

Once a sporting lodge in common ownership with *Ballynahinch Castle*, this small hotel is set in spectacular scenery on the shores of Lough Inagh, 42 miles from Galway. Completely refurbished by the present owners and opened as a hotel in 1990, it combines the advantages of the old and the new – in large, well-proportioned rooms, interesting period detail and lovely fireplaces with welcoming log fires, balanced by modern comfort and practicality. Public areas include two drawing rooms, each with an open fire, a lovely dining room with deep-green walls and graceful spoonback Victorian mahogany chairs and a very appealing bar, with a big turf fire and its own back door and tiled floor for dripping fisherfolk. Bedrooms, some with four-posters, are all well appointed and unusually spacious with views of lake and countryside and walk-in dressing rooms leading to well-planned bathrooms. While it has special appeal to sportsmen, Lough Inagh is a good base for touring Connemara and there is golf and pony trekking nearby. Children up to 12 stay free in parents' room. **Rooms** *12. Garden, fishing. Closed Oct-Apr.* AMERICAN EXPRESS *Access, Diners, Visa.*

Renvyle	Renvyle House	63%	£118
Tel 095 43511 Fax 095 43515			H
Renvyle Co Galway			Map 22 A3

Once owned by Oliver St Gregory, this famous Lutyens-esque house is approached by a stunning scenic drive along a mountain road with views down into a blue-green sea of unparallelled clarity. However, once reached, the hotel itself seems to be snuggling down for shelter and has only limited views. Public areas celebrate the house's glorious past, when it was visited by the rich and famous including Sir Winston Churchill; the bar, which is the scene of many a late-night revel, has a particularly poignant atmosphere and also a memory-laden back corridor, lined with photographs and press cuttings. There's a pleasant lounge/sun room leading on to a sunny verandah near the swimming pool and an interesting, well-appointed dining room (Lutyens-style furniture still casts its spell over much of the house), but bedrooms are very variable and although there are two pleasant suites with little balconies overlooking the pool, and a number of other good-sized rooms of character, many would disappoint guests attracted by the illustrious history of the place. Beyond protective boulders on the sea side, there is little sign of the storm damage suffered several years ago, although the golf course has been upgraded since. Conference facilities for up to 120, banqueting for 150. *Rooms 65. Garden, croquet, outdoor swimming pool, tennis, golf (9), putting, bowling green, riding, fishing, snooker, bicycles. Closed 1 Jan-mid Mar.* AMERICAN EXPRESS *Access, Diners, Visa.*

Riverstown	Coopershill House	69%	£88
Tel 071 65108 Fax 071 65466			**HR**
Coopershill Riverstown Co Sligo			Map 22 B3

Standing at the centre of a 500-acre estate, this immaculate Georgian mansion has been home to seven generations of the O'Hara family since it was built in 1774 and now successfully combines the spaciousness and elegance of the past with modern amenities and the warmest of welcomes. The rooms retain their original regal dimensions and are furnished in period style with family portraits and antiques. Spacious bedrooms all have en-suite bathrooms and most have four-poster or canopy beds; no smoking in the bedrooms. Peace and tranquillity sum up the atmosphere: no TVs or radios, but books and personal touches like fresh flowers and mineral water. A splendid breakfast starts the day at this most hospitable of country hotels. No dogs in the house. *Rooms 7. Garden, croquet, outdoor tennis, coarse and game fishing, games room, boating. Closed end Oct-mid Mar (except for house parties).* AMERICAN EXPRESS *Access, Diners, Visa.*

Restaurant   £50

Antique polished tables, silver candelabra and a log fire in the white marble fireplace provide a fitting setting for Lindy O'Hara's good home cooking. A no-choice 5-course menu might include cheese parcels, a traditional soup, stuffed pork with fresh apricot sauce, a good choice of farmhouse cheeses and, perhaps, lemon mousse. No smoking. *Seats 14. D only 8 for 8.30. Set D £22.*

Rosses Point	The Moorings		£45
Tel 071 77112			**R**
Rosses Point Co Sligo			Map 22 B2

With an almost waterside location (there's a road between it and the sea), views over Sligo Bay and a cosy dining room with open beams and traditional furniture, The Moorings makes an attractive venue and, not surprisingly, Sunday lunch is a speciality. Local seafood predominates in old favourites – Galway Bay oysters on ice, chowder, coquilles St Jacques, poached sea trout with lobster and brandy sauce, monkfish in garlic butter. Popular food, freshly cooked at reasonable price. *Seats 90. Parties 20. Private Room 45. L 12.30-2.30 (Sun only) D 5.30-9.30. Set L £8.50. Closed Mon low season, 1 week in winter, 24-28 Dec.* AMERICAN EXPRESS *Access, Visa.*

Rosslare	Great Southern	62%	£91
Tel 053-33233 Fax 053 33543			**H**
Rosslare Co Wexford			Map 23 D5

Its position overlooking Rosslare harbour makes this modern hotel a useful stopover for ferry users and there's plenty to keep children happy with a crèche, playground and their own restaurant. Public rooms are light and spacious, with ample seating; many of the simply-furnished bedrooms are suitable for family occupation. Up to 150 conference delegates can be accommodated theatre-style, 200 for a banquet. Ask for their helpful golfer's guide to local courses. *Rooms 99. Garden, indoor swimming pool, keep-fit equipment, tennis, sauna, steam room, snooker, hairdressing, children's play area. Closed Jan-Mar.* AMERICAN EXPRESS *Access, Diners, Visa.*

Rosslare   **Kelly's Strand Hotel**   71%   £84

Tel 053 32114   Fax 053 32222   **H**
Rosslare Co Wexford   Map 23 D5

William J Kelly really started something in 1895 when he established a tea
room here. A century on, the place is out on its own as a family resort
hotel, with an almost endless list of ways to keep guests as busy, as relaxed
and as entertained as they choose. Heading the facilities is the excellent
Aqua leisure club (including an outdoor Canadian hot tub), and there's also
live entertainment every night and plenty of diversions for children.
Bright, fresh bedrooms are in practical modern style. No dogs. **Rooms** *99.*
Garden, croquet, bowls, indoor swimming pools, gymnasium, squash, sauna, spa
bath, solarium, beauty & hair salon, indoor & outdoor tennis, badminton, bicycles,
games rooms, crazy golf, snooker, crèche, children's play area, table tennis, giant
chess and draughts. Closed early Dec-late Feb. AMERICAN EXPRESS *Access, Visa.*

Rosslare   **Places of Interest**

Ferry Terminal Tourist Information   Tel 053 33622
Windsurfing Centre   Tel 053 32101

Rossnowlagh   **Sand House Hotel**   69%   £88

Tel 072 51777   Fax 072 52100   **H**
Rossnowlagh Co Donegal   Map 22 B2

Improvements continue at the crenellated Sand House hotel, which sits
right by a large sandy beach overlooking immense Donegal Bay and the
Atlantic Ocean. The Atlantic conservatory lounge takes full advantage
of views that are also enjoyed by many of the bedrooms (those with the
very best views attract a small supplement). Mary and Brian Britton,
together with their son and staff, extend a warm welcome, reinforced by a
fire in the Victorian-style lobby. Bedrooms, immaculate like the rest of the
hotel, are individually decorated with expensive, stylish fabrics; furniture
varies from antiques to fairly modest fitted units, and superior rooms have
chaises longues. A delightful, peaceful hotel, as the many regular guests will
testify. Banqueting/conference facilities for 60. Good golf and riding
facilities nearby. **Rooms** *40. Garden, tennis, mini-golf, croquet, surfing,*
canoeing, board sailing, sea, game & coarse fishing, games room, indoor children's
play room, helipad. Closed late Oct-Easter. AMERICAN EXPRESS *Access, Diners, Visa.*

Rossnowlagh   **Smugglers Creek Inn**   £40

Tel 072 52366   **IR**
Rossnowlagh Co Donegal   Map 22 B2

Perched high on the cliffs overlooking the wonderful golden strand
at Rossnowlagh, an imaginatively restored pub and restaurant. Visitors have
the endless fascination of watching the powerful Atlantic rollers come
in from afar to spend themselves on the beach far below – and all this
while sitting in considerable comfort, with open fires and delicious bar
food from which to choose. Accommodation is offered in five rooms,
all en suite, interestingly decorated and with sea views. Rooms vary
considerably and most are on the small side – one corner room, with
windows in two walls, is slightly larger than average and has even better
views. **Rooms** *5. Garden. Closed Good Friday (bar only), 24 & 25 Dec,*
Mon & Tue in winter. Access, Visa.

Restaurant   £40

Across the corridor from the bar, the rustic/nautical atmosphere
is continued in the stone-floored restaurant, furnished with pleasing
informality using stripped-pine dressers and old country kitchen furniture
to advantage and lots of plants. Tables near the window have splendid sea
views, while those at the back are in a cosy non-smoking area. All share
cheerful service and a wide menu that works the smugglers' theme

to death. There's a predictable emphasis on seafood in dishes like deep-fried squid (crispy rings with provençale sauce), Smugglers sea casserole (scallops, salmon and prawns mornay) or classic pan-fried sole on the bone. Simple meat dishes cater for carnivorous tastes and there are always vegetarian options. No children after 9pm. *Seats 50. Parties 10. Private Room 24. L (Restaurant Sun only, bar snacks daily from 1-6pm) 12.30-2.30 D 6.30-9.30. Set L £8.75 (Sun only). Access, Visa.*

Roundwood	Roundwood Inn	£60
Tel 01 281 8107		R
Roundwood Co Wicklow		Map 23 D4

Set amidst spectacular scenery in the highest village in the Wicklow Hills, this 17th-century inn is furnished in traditional style with wooden floors, darkwood furniture and huge log fires throughout. Excellent bar food is available every day and includes, typically, soup, sandwiches, fresh or smoked salmon, Galway Bay oysters, chicken in the basket, goulash and Irish stew. The restaurant menu leans towards bigger dishes like rack of Wicklow lamb, roast wild Wicklow venison and other game in season. Booking is advisable for Sunday lunch, when roast suckling pig is a long-standing attraction. German influences are evident in long-established specialities like wiener schnitzel, triple liqueur parfait and a feather-light fresh cream gateau which is not to be missed. A mainly European wine list, strongest in France and Germany, starts at under £10 for the house selection and ascends to 40 times that for a 1967 Pauillac. *Seats 45. Parties 35. Private Room 32. L 1-2.30 D 7.30-9.30 (Sat to 10). Closed D Sun, all Mon, 25 Dec, Good Friday. Set L £13.95. Access, Visa.*

Sandycove	Bistro Vino	£40
Tel 01 280 6097		R
56 Glastmile Road Sandycove Co Dublin		Map 23 D4

In the rather sad culinary desert that this part of south Dublin has become in recent years, Bistro Vino is something of an oasis. It's a buzzy little first floor restaurant near the seafront at Sandycove (only a stone's throw from the old Mirabeau) and clearly a big hit with the locals who appreciate the moderate prices, unpretentiously good, lively food and informal atmosphere. A not over-ambitious (and all the better for it) à la carte menu is offered, plus an early evening set menu. Typically, a warm salad of marinated wood pigeon comprises a delicious combination of slivered pigeon breast, mixed leaves, sun-dried tomatoes and toasted pine kernels with a zesty olive oil dressing and crusty garlic bread. Seafood is strong, as in a dish of mixed shellfish in a tomato, cream and black pepper sauce, served with angel hair pasta. Nice tarts and homely puds on the blackboard dessert menu. Beware the steep stairs as you leave. No children under 12. *Seats 45. Parties 35. D only 5-11.30. Closed 25 Dec, Good Friday. Set D £9.95 (Early Bird 5-7pm). Access, Visa.*

Scotshouse	Hilton Park	£111
Tel 047 56007 Fax 047 56033		PH
Scotshouse nr Clones Co Monaghan		Map 22 C3

Magnificent woodlands and gardens make a lovely, peaceful setting for 18th-century Hilton Park. The mansion has been in the Madden family for over 250 years and Johnny and Lucy are the eighth generation to live here. They run it very much as a family home which takes in guests, and it's full of interest, with heirlooms, family portraits and four-poster beds. Large bedrooms, some with dressing rooms and characterful bathrooms, afford wonderful views. Lucy cooks an excellent no-choice five-course dinner in traditional country house style, with most of the raw materials produced in their own grounds or locally. The estate covers 600 acres, including three lakes where swimming, boating and fishing keep visitors occupied. A fine breakfast starts the day, served in the bright, charming Green Room.

Enter the estate by the main entrance on the Clones-Scotshouse road and look out for a black gate with silver falcons. Children between eighteen months and six years of age are not encouraged. No dogs. *Rooms 5. Garden, golf (9), shooting, coarse & game fishing, boating. Closed Oct-Easter except for parties by arrangement. Access, Visa.*

Scotshouse   Place of Interest

Castle Leslie   Glasloughby Monaghan Tel 047 88109

Shanagarry   Ballymaloe House   66%   £120

Tel 021 652531   Fax 021 652021   **HR**

Shanagarry Co Cork   Map 23 C6

Part of an old castle that became a farmhouse, modernised through the centuries, but with the 14th-century keep remaining in its original form. The hotel is situated in the middle of a 400-acre farm, both owned and run by Ivan and Myrtle Allen, and part of a group of family enterprises that includes a cookery school, craft shop and the *Crawford Gallery Café* in Cork (see entry). Two miles from the coast, near the small fishing village of Ballycotton, the main house provides the day rooms, a large drawing room with an open fire and a TV room, complete with video recorder. Throughout, there's an interesting collection of modern Irish paintings with works by Jack B Yeats in the dining room. Thirteen bedrooms in the main building are traditionally furnished, and a further five modern, garden rooms open on to a lawn. Another eleven rooms, more cottagey in character, surround the old coachyard, with some on ground level suitable for wheelchairs. Teenagers especially will appreciate the self-contained 16th-century Gatehouse which has its own small entrance hall and a twin-bedded room with its bathroom up a steep wooden staircase. Ballymaloe is a warm and comfortable family home, especially welcoming to children of all ages (high tea is served at 5.30pm), who can rely on the Allen (grand)children to relay the latest news from the farm or share the sandpit and pool. For the delightful breakfasts, all the ingredients are local or home-made, with even the oatmeal used for porridge ground in an old stone mill down the road. *Rooms 30. Garden, croquet, outdoor swimming pool, tennis, golf (9), children's outdoor play area. Closed 24-26 Dec.* AMERICAN EXPRESS *Access, Diners, Visa.* MARTELL COGNAC

Restaurant   ★   £80

Perhaps more than anyone else in the country, Myrtle Allen has nurtured, encouraged and cajoled chefs from her kitchen to spread their wings further afield after first achieving high standards here. Wherever you go in Ireland, you're likely to come across an individual who at some time has cooked alongside this doyenne of Irish chefs. There are several smallish interconnecting dining rooms, any of which can be used privately, all furnished with antiques, and a conservatory with a black-and-white tiled floor, Lloyd Loom furniture and lots of greenery. With the bread home-baked, the fish caught locally (sometimes the menu is deliberately late to see what the fishing boats have brought in), and the salads and vegetables picked that day, you can certainly rely on the ingredients being fresh and wholesome – indeed, much produce comes from their own farm. With Irish and French as the main influences, the cooking is simple, enhancing the quality of the raw materials. Typically, nightly-changing menus might feature Ballycotton fish soup, hot dressed crab, brill *en papillote* with fresh herbs, a selection of patés, hot buttered lobster, fillet of sole with spinach butter sauce, roast stuffed loin of Shanagarry pork with apple sauce and red cabbage, or roast chicken with *pipérade*. Try some Irish cheeses before the dessert (perhaps an apricot tart or praline gateau) and linger awhile over some excellent cafetière coffee. Ivan Allen has built up a fine wine cellar over many years with some exceptional vintage Bordeaux and an increasing awareness of quality New World wines. *Seats 90. Private Room 30. L 12.30-2 (Sun buffet at 1) D 7-9.30 (Sun buffet at 7.30). Set Sun L £16.50. Set D £30.*

Shannon Great Southern 64% £114

Tel 061 471122 Fax 061 471982 **H**

Shannon Airport Shannon Co Clare Map 23 B4

Situated directly opposite the main terminal building, a modern airport
hotel, totally refurbished three years ago. Soundproofed bedrooms include
11 Executive rooms and three suites. Fourteen rooms designated non-
smoking. Conference facilities for up to 170, banqueting for 140.
Rooms 115. Garden, coffee shop. Closed 25 & 26 Dec. AMERICAN EXPRESS *Access,
Diners, Visa.*

Shannon Oakwood Arms Hotel 63% £96

Tel 061 361500 Fax 061 361414 **H**

Shannon Co Clare Map 23 B4

A family-owned, redbrick hotel (opened in 1991) that creates a good first
impression with its neatly laid-out flower beds. If the mock-Tudor style
of the hotel is somewhat surprising in this setting, its aviation theme is less
so: the lounge bar and function room both honour the memory of the
pioneer female pilot Sophie Pearse, who came from the area, and the
restaurant is named after Howard Hughes's famous flying boat, *The Spruce
Goose*. Public areas are quite spacious and comfortably furnished and,
although not individually decorated, bedrooms have all the necessary
comforts and are double-glazed. *Rooms 46. Patio. Closed 25 Dec.*
AMERICAN EXPRESS *Access, Diners, Visa.*

Shannon Place of Interest

Airport Tourist Information Tel 061 61664/61565

Skerries Red Bank Restaurant £60

Tel 01 849 1005 Fax 01 849 1598 **R**

7 Church Street Skerries Co Dublin Map 22 D3

Terry McCoy – wit, wag, owner and chef – creates imaginative, generous
dishes based on local seafood in his well-known north Dublin restaurant
located in a converted bank. Have a drink and read the menu in the
comfortable reception area, then settle down to specialities such as baked
crab 'Loughshinney' (blended with dry sherry and served in its own shell),
whole Dublin Bay prawns cooked in fish stock and served with garlic
butter or black sole 'Red Bank' (stuffed with mussels and prawns). There's
always a choice of soups (try the cockle and mussel consommé or smoked
haddock and leek) on the carte, alongside the long list of fish dishes.
To complete the picture, loin of pork, rack of lamb, breast of duck and
steaks make regular appearances with interesting sauces. Tempting desserts,
including a very good baked chocolate cheesecake, are served from the
trolley and there's a farmhouse cheeseboard. Three-course Sunday lunches
and table d'hote both offer a good choice. Menus change with the seasons
and favour organic produce whenever available. There's something for
everyone on the fairly priced wine list, which has useful notes
to complement menu items; good drinking under £20. Not really suitable
for children under 8. Smoking is permitted in the dining room, but the
'ban smoking in restaurants completely' campaign has an eager proponent
in Mr McCoy. *Seats 45. Parties 14. Private Room 10. L (Sun only)
12.30-2.15 D 7-10. Closed D Sun, all Mon, 4 days Christmas, 2 weeks Nov.
Set L £13.75 Set D £17.95/£21.* AMERICAN EXPRESS *Access, Diners, Visa.*

Skerries Place of Interest

Ardgillan Castle Balbriggan Tel 01 849 2212

Sligo   **Sligo Park**   **58%**   £99

Tel 071 60291   Fax 071 69556   **H**

Pearse Road Sligo Co Sligo   **Map 22 B2**

In the absence of any real competition, this modern hotel set in seven acres of parkland on the southern edge of town attracts a high proportion of the area's business. Bedrooms are adequate and children up to four may stay free in their parents' room; 4-under 12s pay 50% when sharing; 17 rooms were recently refurbished – insist on one when booking. The hotel's main strengths are its conference and banqueting facilities, which can cater for up to 500 (theatre-style conferences), and a particularly good leisure centre. *Rooms 90. Garden, indoor swimming pool & children's splash pool, gym, solarium, sauna, spa bath, steam room, tennis, snooker.* AMERICAN EXPRESS *Access, Diners, Visa.*

If we recommend meals in a hotel or inn a separate entry is made for its restaurant.

Sligo   **Truffles Restaurant**   £25

Tel 071 44226   **R**

The Mall Sligo Co Sligo   **Map 22 B2**

Bernadette O'Shea's 'new age pizza' restaurant is unusual, to say the least: a delightfully wacky dining room with amusing trompe l'oeil decorations and a peat fire setting the tone. Thoroughly original treatments for the humble pizza (served in 8″ and 10″ sizes) include a variety of eclectic ingredients – the Californian Classic will include sun-dried tomatoes and roasted garlic, the Mexicano, spicy sausage and fresh hot chili peppers and so on, but the best of all is the Irish Cheese Board, a surprisingly light taste experience adding melting goat's cheese, Cashel blue, smoked Brie, cream cheese, cottage cheese, Irish mozzarella and fresh herbs to a crisp base and fresh tomato sauce. Home-made soups, garlic bread, filled stromboli bread, wonderful main course salads – including Italian, Roquefort and Greek – based on locally grown organic produce, and a choice of fresh pastas (made with free-range eggs) are other attractions. It's a small, eccentric place ("service charge not included, but anticipated"), now deservedly popular, so book ahead. The wine bar upstairs is open from 7pm (Sun 5-10pm). *Seats 38. Parties 10. D only 5-10.30 (Sun to 10). Closed Mon, 3 days Christmas, 4 days Easter.*

Sligo   **Places of Interest**

Tourist Information   Tel 071 61201
Lissadell House Drumcliffe   Tel 071 63150
Parkes Castle   Tel 071 64149
Sligo Racecourse   Cleveragh Tel 071 62484/60094

Spiddal   **Boluisce Seafood Bar**   £45

Tel 091 83286   Fax 091 83285   **R**

Spiddal Connemara Co Galway   **Map 23 B4**

Kevin and Monica MacGabhaun have kept more or less to the formula operated so successfully by the Glanville family for 20 years. Seafood is of course the star of the show in both the first-floor restaurant and the downstairs bar: seafood chowder, mussels in cream sauce, oysters natural or baked, Atlantic black sole, Galway Bay salmon, lobster thermidor. Also good steaks and stir-fries in the bar; children's portions. *Seats 60. Parties 10. Meals 12-10 (Sun 12.30-10). Closed Good Friday, 24-26 Dec.* AMERICAN EXPRESS *Access, Visa.*

Spiddal   **Bridge House Hotel**   **59%**   **£65**

Tel 091 83118   **H**

Spiddal Connemara Co Galway   **Map 23 B4**

The relaxed atmosphere of this comfortable, unpretentious family-run hotel
has been attracting a loyal clientele since 1959 and, although a major
refurbishment of the front of the hotel and foyer was under way as we
went to press, it seems unlikely that it will signal any major change
of direction. En-suite bedrooms are neat and homely. French windows
open on to the back garden from the bar and dining room. The Stirrup
Room grill is open all day for informal food. No children under 3 (or
dogs). *Rooms 14. Garden. Closed Christmas-mid Feb.* AMERICAN EXPRESS®
Access, Visa.

Stillorgan   **China-Sichuan Restaurant**   **£50**

Tel 01 288 4817   Fax 01 288 0882   **R**

4 Lower Kilmacud Road Stillorgan Co Dublin   **Map 23 D4**

The China Sichuan Food Authority sponsors this smart, civilised restaurant
five miles south of Dublin city centre, and many of the dishes are hot with
spices and chili. Among these (denoted on the menu by an asterisk) are
orange-flavoured sliced cold beef, fried prawns in garlic sauce and fried
lamb shreds in aromatic sauce. Wines include Great Wall white and red
from China. *Seats 50. Parties 20. L 12.30-2.30 (Sun & Bank Holidays
1-2.30) D 6-11. Closed 25-27 Dec. Set L from £6 Set D £16.50.*
AMERICAN EXPRESS® *Access, Visa.*

Straffan   **Barberstown Castle**   **70%**   **£110**

Tel 01 628 8157   Fax 01 627 7027   **H R**

Straffan Co Kildare   **Map 23 C4**

Next door to the Kildare Hotel & Country Club (with whom they share
golf and leisure facilities), Barberstown Castle is a historically fascinating
place – parts of it go back to the early 13th century (with many later
additions) – and it can lay claim to continuous occupation for over 40
years. Under the present ownership since 1987, the castle has been
thoroughly renovated and refurbished in keeping with its age and style and
now offers very comfortable accommodation in ten well-appointed,
individually decorated en-suite rooms – some in the oldest part, the Castle
Keep, others in the 'new' Victorian wing. Public areas, including two
drawing rooms and an elegant bar, have been renovated with the same
care and there are big log fires everywhere. A separate function room
in converted stables has banqueting facilities for 160, conferences 200.
Rooms 10. Closed 24-26 Dec. AMERICAN EXPRESS® *Access, Visa.*

Castle Restaurant   **£65**

A series of whitewashed rooms in the semi-basement of the old Castle
Keep, with a great atmosphere heightened by fires, candles in alcoves and
on tables, and wall lighting; the table style is appropriately simple: plain
white cloths and ladderback oak chairs. Head chef Tom Rowe has
established quite a reputation for the restaurant since his arrival in 1991,
turning out tasty starters like sautéed lamb's kidneys with bacon and red
wine or warm black and white pudding salad – an imaginative alternative
to several fashionable dishes – and an unusually richly flavoured mushroom
soup, all served with excellent dark, moist wholemeal soda bread. Main
courses might include a big plate of mixed seafood with a tomato and dill
sauce, or pork steak enlivened with a piquant mixture of honey, ginger and
spring onions. A good selection of simply prepared vegetables is left on the
table for guests to help themselves. Desserts range from a very rich
chocolate truffle cake to a refreshing fruit salad plate with sabayon, served
with a tuile and a ball of creamy Bailey's ice cream; farmhouse cheeses are
served with home-made biscuits and big, juicy grapes. Lovely cafetière
coffee to finish. In addition to the dinner and à la carte menus, a special

tasting menu is available to complete parties. Bar meals at weekday lunchtimes. Smoking discouraged. **Seats** *55.Parties 15. Private Room 35. L 1-2.30 (Sun only) D 7.30-9.30 (Sun 7-8.30). Closed 3 day Christmas. Set L £15.50 (£11.50 children) Set D £22.50 & £25.*

Straffan	**Kildare Hotel**	**87%**	**£250**

Tel 01 627 3333 Fax 01 627 3312	**HR**

Straffan Co Kildare	Map 23 C4

Already affectionately known as the K Club (attached to the hotel is the country club which is centred around the golf course designed by Arnold Palmer), the hotel is best reached from Dublin (17 miles) via the N7, taking a right at Kill to Straffan. Reputedly, previous owners of the original (*Straffan*) house were dogged by bad luck, but those myths have now been discarded with the creation of this magnificent complex, surrounded by beautifully landscaped gardens (ask for the garden walk leaflet), with the River Liffey running through the grounds. The new buildings blend in tastefully with the old house (indeed it's hard to see the 'join') and inside there's much opulence, highlighted by sumptuous furnishings, fine period antiques and an outstanding collection of paintings, including several by Jack B Yeats, who has a room devoted to his works. Each of the spacious bedrooms has been individually designed – note the different *trompe l'oeil* designs, also apparent in the bar – and no two of the marble bathrooms (luxury toiletries, bathrobes, slippers and huge towels) are the same. All rooms are lavishly and handsomely furnished; on arrival, guests are treated to a bowl of fruit, hand-made chocolates and mineral water; satellite TV, video recorder, mini-bar and personal safe are standard amenites, along with handily-placed telephones. Such luxury, of course, requires levels of service, housekeeping and maintenance to match, a task that General Manager Ray Carroll and his motivated team of staff achieve admirably. There are two meeting rooms in the main house, one an imposing boardroom, and up to 600 can be accommodated in the indoor tennis arena, part of the sports centre, which is easily transformed to suit the occasion. Also available, adjoining the hotel, are self-contained, two-bedroomed courtyard apartments and a three-bedroomed lodge. **Rooms** *45. Garden, indoor swimming pool, gymnasium, squash, sauna, solarium, hair & beauty salon, golf (18), tennis, snooker, bicycles, coarse and game fishing, clay-pigeon shooting.* AMERICAN EXPRESS *Access, Diners, Visa.*

The Byerley Turk   £100

The restaurant's name, perhaps unfamiliar to those who do not follow horse-racing sport, comes from one of the three Arab stallions in the male line of every thoroughbred horse in the world; its impressively draped tall windows, marble columns and rich decor in tones of deep terracotta, cream and green harmonise perfectly with the style of the original house. The room is cleverly shaped to create semi-private areas and make the most of window tables, laid with crested china, monogrammed white linen, gleaming modern crystal and silver. Chef Michel Flamme's leanings towards classical French cuisine are tempered by traditional Irish influences and, with his kitchen garden now in full production, by local and home-grown seasonal produce, as in warm asparagus salad with garden leaves in a walnut dressing or supreme of chicken with a stew of broad beans scented with garlic and basil. An additional Seasonal Fayre Menu offers sophisticated dishes and the 3-course table d'hote dinner menu might include roast monkfish accompanied by a cream of lobster sprinkled with mussels, followed by roast spring lamb with a vegetable parcel and finishing, perhaps, with a plate of caramel desserts or a selection of Irish and French cheeses. The modest (but not modestly priced) wine list would benefit from a clearer layout and some notes. The Legend Restaurant in the golf club offers a buffet lunch (£15.95) in summer and table d'hote in winter; à la carte in the evenings. **Seats** *70. Parties 30. Private Room 44. L 12.30-2 D 7-10. Set Sun L £22 Set D £37.*

Straffan   Places of Interest

Steam Museum   Tel 01 627 3155
Castletown House   Celbridge Tel 01 628 8252
Irish National Stud   Tully Tel 045 21617 *15 miles*
Japanese Gardens   Tully Tel 045 21251 *15 miles*

Swords   Le Chateau   £55

Tel 01 840 6533   **R**

River Mall Main Street Swords Dublin Co Dublin   **Map 22 D3**

In a shopping mall near Dublin airport, John Dowd's cooking easily
outclasses the surroundings. The menu is mainly French with a few more
original offerings – such as pasta Tara, a well-balanced dish of home-made
pasta with garlic, cream, bacon and baby mushrooms – added for good
measure. No children after 8.30pm. *Seats 60. Parties 20. D only 7-11.
Closed Sun, Mon in winter, Bank Holidays, 1 week Christmas/New Year.
Set D £19.75.* AMERICAN EXPRESS *Access, Diners, Visa.*

Swords   Forte Travelodge   £42

Tel 01 840 9233   **L**

N1 Dublin/Belfast Road Swords Bypass nr Dublin Co Dublin **Map 22 D3**

On the southbound carriageway of the Swords bypass at Swords
roundabout, 1½ miles north of Dublin airport, 16 miles north of Dublin
city centre. The room rate of £31.95 (without breakfast) could include
up to 3 adults, a child under 12 and a baby in a cot. *Rooms 40.*
AMERICAN EXPRESS *Access, Diners, Visa.*

Swords   The Old Schoolhouse   £50

Tel 01 840 4160   Fax 01 840 5060   **R**

Coolbanagher Swords Co Dublin   **Map 22 D3**

Set in a quiet backwater away from the main road, this old stone building
has been sympathetically restored and converted to make a delightful
restaurant. There are always daily specials on the blackboard: warm scallop
and bacon salad, baked crab with brandy and cream, Galway oysters and
particularly good fish from nearby harbours Skerries and Howth. Other
typical à la carte dishes might be venison tartlets glazed with grain
mustard, goat's cheese filo parcel with cider cream, a choice of up to four
home-made soups, rack of lamb, roast half Barbary duckling with orange
and black cherry sauce and a couple of vegetarian options. Steaks of 6, 8 or
10 ounces are served with a choice of sauces. Interesting desserts like apple
pie, strawberry mousse in dark chocolate cups, profiteroles with caramel
sauce and sunken chocolate soufflé with Amaretto prunes. *Seats 70. Parties
20. Private Rooms 10/20. L 12.30-2.30 D 6.30-10.30. Closed L Sat, all Sun,
Bank Holidays, 3 days Christmas. Set L £10.95/£12.95 Set D £19.50.*
AMERICAN EXPRESS *Access, Diners, Visa.*

Swords   Place of Interest

Newbridge House   Donabate Tel 01 843 6534 *4 miles*

Thomastown   Mount Juliet Hotel   84%   £215

Tel 056 24455   Fax 056 24522   **HR**

Mount Juliet Thomastown Co Kilkenny   **Map 23 C5**

The imposing 18th-century Mount Juliet House stands in 1500 acres
of parkland and formal gardens through which flow the rivers Kings and
Nore; a traditional stone bridge crosses the latter for access to the hotel. Its
exquisite interior is no less striking: public rooms feature wonderful

moulded plasterwork and the Parlour boasts a colourful marble fireplace.
The bedrooms and generously proportioned suites are individually styled,
with soft floral fabrics, solid oak furniture and deep-cushioned sofas; most
have fine Adam fireplaces. Bathrooms are equally luxurious, with many
extras. Three large suites are in Ballylinch House; Rose Garden lodges
(eight two-bedroomed apartments) are also in the grounds of the
estate. Recreational facilities include the Iris Kellett equestrian centre,
a magnificent Jack Nicklaus-designed golf course (home of the 1994 Irish
Open) and golf academy, an impressive new leisure centre abutting the
clubhouse and one of Ireland's oldest cricket clubs. Children under 12 stay
free in their parents' room. Meeting rooms for up to 50, banqueting for
140. **Rooms** 56. *Garden, croquet, indoor swimming pool, health and beauty
treatments, sauna, steam room, exercise room, tennis, game fishing, golf (18),
archery, clay-pigeon shooting, riding, snooker, bicycles, helipad.* AMERICAN EXPRESS
Access, Diners, Visa.

Lady Helen Dining Room   £66

Although grand, this gracefully elegant, high-ceilinged room, softly
decorated in pastel shades and with sweeping views over the grounds,
is not forbidding and has a pleasant atmosphere. To match these beautiful
surroundings, enthusiastic new chef Rory Morahan is developing his Celtic
kitchen theme, with "fine dining" in the evening offering both four-course
table d'hote and à la carte featuring grills. In the sporting centre, Hunter's
Yard, the 64-seat *Loft* restaurant offers a very popular £18 Sunday brunch
buffet style and all-day (7am-9.30pm) menu during the week. The wine
list is unambitious for an aspiring hotel such as this; only three modest
clarets under £30, just three white burgundies that pre-date the '90s
vintages and few half bottles. **Seats** 55. *Parties 8. Private Room 40. D 7-10.
Set D £33.*

Tralee	Ballyseede Castle Hotel	60%	£85
Tel 066 25799 Fax 066 25287			**H**
Tralee Co Kerry			Map 23 A5

Just off the Killarney road, this 15th-century castle was once the chief
garrison of the Fitzgeralds, Earls of Desmond. Granite pillars and wrought-
iron gates stand at the entrance and impressive public rooms include
a lobby with Doric columns, two drawing rooms with fine plasterwork
and a dining room overlooking ancient oaks. Bedrooms are spacious and
comfortable; bathrooms vary considerably. Conference/banqueting for
180/80. Golf, fishing, riding and shooting available nearby. Children up to
the age of 10 stay free in their parents' room. No dogs. **Rooms** 15. *Garden.
Access, Diners, Visa.*

Tralee	Brandon Hotel	61%	£96
Tel 066 23333 Fax 066 25019			**H**
Princes Street Tralee Co Kerry			Map 23 A5

This pleasantly situated modern hotel is in the heart of medieval Tralee,
overlooking a park and the famous Siamsa Tire folk theatre. Recently
refurbished throughout, public areas are impressively roomy and, while
some bedrooms are on the small side, all are comfortably furnished and
have neat, fully-tiled bathrooms with plenty of shelf space and
thermostatically-controlled bath taps. The well-equipped leisure centre
includes a beauty salon and there are conference and banqueting facilities
for 1100/550). Parking for 500 cars. No dogs. **Rooms** *160. Indoor swimming
pool, gym, solarium, sauna, steam room, beauty salon.* AMERICAN EXPRESS *Access,
Diners, Visa.*

Tralee   Places of Interest

Kerry The Kingdom   Tel 066 27777
Tralee Racecourse   Tel 066 26188
Listowel Racecourse   Tel 068 21144

Tuam   Cré na Cille   £50

Tel 093 28232   **R**

High Street Tuam Co Galway   **Map 22 B3**

Venetian blinds, darkwood tables with place mats, simple cutlery and paper
napkins create quite a businesslike lunchtime atmosphere that is enhanced
by the crush of people coming in from the street – perhaps more Toulouse
than Tuam. Evenings are more formal and the setting softer, but the
common link is chef Cathal Reynolds's confident use of local ingredients
in generously served food at remarkably keen prices. Typical dishes include
hearty duck liver paté or pan-fried Irish Brie in a vermouth sauce followed
by brill fillets in a saffron cream sauce or a vegetarian dish of the day. Good
baked desserts, typically in classic tarts – frangipane, Bakewell – given
a modern twist. *Seats 45. Private Room 30. L 12.30-2.30 D 6-10.
Closed Sun, 24-27 Dec, Bank Holidays.* AMERICAN EXPRESS *Access, Diners, Visa.*

Waterford   Dwyer's Restaurant   £55

Tel 051 77478   **R**

8 Mary Street Waterford Co Waterford   **Map 23 C5**

In a backstreet near the bridge Martin Dwyer's comfortable, low-key
converted barracks provides an undemonstrative background for his
quietly confident cooking. A limited choice 3-course early evening menu
is extremely good value, or there's a more flexible table d'hote with
a wider choice, plus a good à la carte menu. The Dwyer style is original
without being gimmicky, with careful attention to flavour and texture
contrasts/combinations. Typical dishes on a winter evening included spiced
carrot soup, lamb's kidneys with black pepper, monkfish with smoked
salmon sauce, roast breast of pheasant mousseline with port wine sauce and
medallions of fillet steak sauced with onion and thyme leaves. Desserts such
as marquise of three chocolates, pear and almond tart or hot bananas and
ginger with ice cream are equally irresistible. *Seats 30. Parties 10. D only
6-10 (early evening menu 6-7.30). Closed Sun, 1 week Christmas, Good
Friday, 2 weeks July. Set D £13.* AMERICAN EXPRESS *Access, Diners, Visa.*

Waterford   Granville Hotel   69%   £83

Tel 051 55111   Fax 051 70307   **H**

1 Meagher Quay Waterford Co Waterford   **Map 23 C5**

On the quay by the River Suir, the Granville is kept in tip-top condition
by owners Liam and Ann Cusack and their staff. The style throughout the
day rooms is traditional, and there are many reminders of the hotel's
history: the Thomas Francis Meagher bar honours an early owner, the
Bianconi restaurant salutes another owner (the man who started Ireland's
first formal transport system) and the Parnell meeting room remembers
where Charles Stewart Parnell made many famous speeches. Stylishly
decorated bedrooms of various sizes all have good bathrooms. Children
under 12 stay free in parents' room. No dogs. *Rooms 74.* AMERICAN EXPRESS
Access, Diners, Visa.

Waterford   Jurys Hotel   61%   £106

Tel 051 32111   Fax 051 32863   **H**

Ferrybank Waterford Co Waterford   **Map 23 C5**

Large modern hotel dominating a hillside on the opposite side of the River
Suir to Waterford town. The spacious lobby/lounge features a long white
marble reception desk, a pair of fine Waterford crystal chandeliers and
a comfortable sitting area. Of the five floors of bedrooms, all of which
share the same fine view over the city, only the top floor (which is very
dated) has yet to benefit from refurbishment with darkwood furniture,
matching floral curtains, polycotton duvets and smart new bathrooms with
white marble vanity units providing good shelf space. Up to two children
under 12 stay free in parents' room; 20 rooms have both a double and

single bed. 24hr room service. Activity club and video room for children (Mon-Fri) during school summer holidays. 38 acres of garden. Banqueting for 600, conference facilities for 700. No dogs. *Rooms 98. Garden, indoor swimming pool, plunge pool, gym, solarium, sauna, spa bath, steam room, hair salon, tennis, children's outdoor play area. Closed 24 & 27 Dec.* AMERICAN EXPRESS *Access, Diners, Visa.*

Waterford   Prendiville's Restaurant & Guesthouse   £60

Tel 051 78851   Fax 051 74062   RR

Cork Road Waterford Co Waterford   Map 23 C5

Peter and Paula Prendiville serve imaginative food at reasonable prices and with professionalism at their converted gate lodge, which is just out of the centre and a short drive from the crystal factory. Paula plans her menus around the best of fresh local ingredients, and her dishes show a deal of controlled creativity: escalopes of warm smoked salmon with chives, cucumber and cream; deep-fried tempura-battered squid with an aïoli dip; roast honey-glazed duck breast served with wine-poached pears; fillet of lamb baked in a potato crust with a beer and onion gravy. Irish farmhouse cheeses; tempting desserts. *Seats 50. Private Room 20. L 12.30-2.15 D 6.30-10.30. Closed Sun, Good Friday, 24-26 Dec. Set L £10.50 Set D (till 8pm) £13.25.* AMERICAN EXPRESS *Access, Diners, Visa.*

Rooms   £46

Nine recently redecorated simply-furnished rooms are available, seven with en-suite facilities and all with phones. Some have crochet bedspreads and seven rooms have TVs. Children up to 5 stay free in their parents' room, 5-10's pay for breakfast only.

Waterford   Tower Hotel   59%   £114

Tel 051 75801   Fax 051 70129   H

The Mall Waterford Co Waterford   Map 23 C5

Opposite, and taking its name from, an ancient Viking tower, the hotel has recently been extended and refurbished. The now spacious lobby copes well with tour groups and a large plush bar overlooks the River Suir. Apart from a couple of singles, bedrooms are of good size and similarly decorated and furnished with plain walls and simple darkwood furniture whether in the old or new part of the building. All have good easy chairs and modern bathrooms. 24hr room service. Banqueting for 600, conference facilities for 500. *Rooms 141. Indoor swimming pool, children's splash pool, gymnasium, solarium, sauna, spa bath, steam room. Closed 25 & 26 Dec.* AMERICAN EXPRESS *Access, Diners, Visa.*

Waterford   Waterford Castle   74%   £220

Tel 051 78203   Fax 051 79316   HR

The Island Ballinakill Waterford Co Waterford   Map 23 C5

From the town centre, head for Dunmore East and follow the signs to the hotel, which is situated on its own island. A small chain car ferry transports you across the water to the imposing 18th-century castle with a carved granite arch entrance and studded oak doors. The great hall has a roped-off coat of arms hand-woven into the carpet, a cavernous fireplace, again with the Fitzgerald coat of arms on the chimney breast, old panelling, a fine ribbon plaster ceiling and antique leather chairs, as well as many portraits on the walls. The stylish drawing room has several comfortable sofas and genuine antiques, which also feature in some bedrooms, notably the suites. Others are a combination of the old and the new, but nearly all command fine views of the surrounding parkland and water. Bathrooms, offering good toiletries and bathrobes, have freestanding Victorian bath tubs with gold fittings (but no protective shower curtains), painted washbasins and loos with wooden seats and overhead cisterns and chains! First-rate breakfast includes fresh orange juice and leaf tea. Two conference rooms can accommodate up to 30. The indoor swimming pool is housed

separately, a few hundred yards from the hotel. Staff seem to lack direction.
Dogs in kennels only. *Rooms 19. Garden, indoor swimming pool, tennis, golf*
(18), bicycles. AMERICAN EXPRESS *Access, Diners, Visa.*

Restaurant   £80

Chef Paul McCluskey has been cooking here for several years, and the   ♛
spectacular dining-room setting – old oak panelling, plaster ceiling, oil
paintings and Regency-striped chairs – presents the perfect backdrop for
his sound cooking. Pity then about the intrusive piped music that
is inappropriate for a hotel of this standing. Both lunch and dinner menus
change daily, the latter priced almost double, with only a soup or sorbet
in addition. A typical offering might consist of asparagus in puff pastry on
a butter sauce, cream of carrot and bacon soup, pan-fried fillets of brill
with tomato and chives, finishing with a chocolate cup on a coffee bean
sauce. Service is pleasant enough, the bread good and the coffee strong.
The wine list is safe without being particularly outstanding. *Seats 60.*
Private Room 26. L 12.30-2 D 7-10 (Sun to 9). Set L £17.50 Set D £32.50.

Waterford   Places of Interest

Tourist Information   Tel 051 75788
Waterford Cathedral   Tel 051 74757
Waterford Crystal Glass Factory   Kilbarry Tel 051 73311
Waterford Racecourse   Tramore Tel 051 81425

Westport   The Olde Railway Hotel   63%   £65

Tel 098 25166   **H**

The Mall Westport Co Mayo   **Map 22 A3**

Beautifully situated along the tree-lined Carrowbeg River on the Mall
in the centre of Westport, the Olde Railway Hotel is the real McCoy. Once
described by William Thackeray as 'one of the prettiest, comfortablist
hotels in Ireland', it was built in 1780 as a coaching inn for guests of Lord
Sligo. Now, in the hands of the Rosenkranz family, who have owned
it since 1983, it retains considerable character and is well known for its
antique furniture and a pleasing atmosphere of slight eccentricity, although
concessions to the present generation of traveller have been made in the
form of en-suite bathrooms, satellite television and private car parking, also
a secretarial service including use of fax machine and computer. Public
areas include a conservatory dining room quietly situated at the back of the
hotel and a rather splendid recently restored function room with original
stone walls. The large bar, which is the public face of an essentially private
hotel, is popular for bar food and the main entrance is from the mall.
Children up to 12 stay free in parents' room. *Rooms 24. Closed 25 Dec.*
AMERICAN EXPRESS *Access, Visa.*

Wexford   White's Hotel   62%   £76

Tel 053 22311   Fax 053 45000   **H**

George Street Wexford Co Wexford   **Map 23 D5**

Recent developments at this historic hotel (whose look is now largely
modern) are centred mainly around the new fitness and leisure centre.
There's also a new night club (the Cairo Club) and refurbishment work has
been carried out in many areas. Bedrooms are practical, with fitted units
and neat, fully-tiled bathrooms. Conference/banqueting facilities for up to
600/450. No dogs. *Rooms 82.* AMERICAN EXPRESS *Access, Diners, Visa.*

Wexford   Places of Interest

Tourist Information   Tel 053 23111
Westgate Heritage Centre   Tel 053 42611
Johnstown Castle Demesne and Agricultural Museum   Tel 053 42888
Irish National Heritage Park   Ferry Carrig Tel 053 41733
Wexford Racecourse   Tel 053 23102

Wicklow   Old Rectory   59%   £90

Tel 0404 67048   Fax 0404 69181   **HR**

Wicklow Co Wicklow   **Map 23 D4**

Since 1977 Paul and Linda Saunders have been welcoming hosts at their delightful early-Victorian rectory on the edge of town, near the famous Mount Usher gardens (2 miles away). It's decorated with great individuality throughout; the cosy sitting room has a white marble fireplace and traditional furnishings are brought to life by some unusual collections, notably ex-fireman Paul's display of helmets and related paraphernalia. Colourfully decorated bedrooms are all en suite and have many homely extras including fresh flowers. There's an outstanding choice at breakfast (Irish, Scottish or Swiss menus). *Rooms 5. Garden. Closed Nov-1 Apr.* AMERICAN EXPRESS *Access, Diners, Visa.*

Restaurant   £60

Linda Saunders presents a blend of Victorian and modern, French and Irish in the Orangery dining room area. Most guests choose the special gourmet menu, a no-choice meal which might typically comprise salmon trout quenelles, melon sorbet, pheasant en croute with ginger wine sauce and chocolate and Cointreau mousse in a little chocolate pot accompanied by candied oranges. A particularly unusual and imaginative feature is a floral dinner menu (served only during the Co. Wicklow Garden Festival, May-Jun) containing such delights as gravad lax with chive flowers, hot marigold muffins and cheesecake with a garland of frosted pansy and lilac flowers. No smoking. *Seats 12 à la carte (20 for set menu). Parties 8. D only at 8. Set D £26.*

Wicklow   Places of Interest

Tourist Information   Tel 0404 69117
Mount Usher Gardens   Ashford Tel 0404 40116

Youghal   Aherne's Seafood Restaurant   £60

Tel 024 92424   Fax 024 93633   **RR**

163 North Main Street Youghal Co Cork   **Map 23 C6**

The current owners are the third generation of the FitzGibbon family to run this renowned restaurant and bar on the N25. Local seafood is very much the star of the show, appearing famously in chowder, moules marinière, a hot potato and smoked salmon gratin and Youghal Bay lobster served thermidor or hot and buttered. If your budget doesn't stretch to lobster, try the pasta with smoked salmon and cream, grilled cod with herb butter or a trio of seafood with a shellfish sauce. The all-day bar menu offers snackier items as in open fishy sandwiches on home-made brown bread, salads and even a house pizza. Lovely desserts might include chocolate and orange bavarois, lemon cheesecake or sherry trifle. The wine list, perhaps surprisingly, has almost as many reds as whites. Prices are fair, with several bottles under £15. *Seats 60. Private Room 20. L 12.30-2.15 D 6.30-9.30 Bar food 10.30-10.30. Closed 5 days Christmas. Set L £15 Set D £25.* AMERICAN EXPRESS *Access, Diners, Visa.*

Rooms   £100

Aherne's ten stylish en-suite bedrooms are individually decorated to a very high standard and furnished with antiques.

Youghal   Places of Interest

Myrtle Grove   Tel 024 92274
Lismore Castle Gardens   Lismore Tel 058 54424 *17 miles*

Hotel Groups

Overleaf is a listing of major hotel groups each of which has to a lesser or greater extent a definable corporate identity. We have included budget hotel chains (some coming under the banner of the major groups) which, while not given our normal percentage grading, nevertheless offer a convenient stop-over.

A brief description of the main characteristics of each group is given as well as head office addresses, and phone and fax numbers for general enquiries and central reservations.

In the subsequent tables we list those hotels (in groups or privately owned) recommended in this Guide. Conference and banqueting facilities are highlighted; the numbers quoted are for the maximum number of delegates for a theatre-style conference or diners at a banquet in one room. Leisure centres are listed if they are part of the hotel and feature at least an indoor heated swimming pool, sauna, solarium, whirlpool bath and keep-fit equipment. These conference and banqueting facilities have not been evaluated by our inspectors.

Prices quoted are for high season and include a cooked breakfast for two adults. Research conducted up to July 1994.

0800 telephone numbers are freephone.

Campanile Hotels

Head Office: Unit 8, Red Lion Court, Alexandra Road, Hounslow, Middlesex
TW3 1JS Tel 081-569 5757

Reservations 081-569 6969

A chain of 15 modern, purpose-built, functional hotels – part of a 350-strong group throughout Europe; as we went to press, the latest (by Dartford Tunnel) was due to open in early 1995. All are open 365 days. Liverpool has 24hr reception. All bedrooms are either twin or double, have remote-control colour TV, fully fitted bathrooms, radio-alarms. Each hotel has rooms designed for the disabled. A standard tariff of £35.75 per room (£29.50 at weekends) applies though there is a third person supplement of £7.50 (children under 12 are free, cots available). Two sets of communicating rooms per hotel (no extra charge). Bistro-style restaurants feature a children's menu. Buffet breakfasts, either Continental or full English, are £4.25 per person, from 7-9am (from 8 at weekends). Each hotel has conference facilities for 30. All major credit cards accepted. Last check-in time 11pm.

Copthorne Hotels

Head Office: Victoria House, Victoria Road, Horley, Surrey RH6 7AF
Tel 0293 772288   Fax 0293 772345

Reservations: 0800 414741

Primarily a business hotel group of 12 UK hotels, but locations may be convenient for family weekend breaks; Plymouth is an example, London good value. Standard rooms (Classics) offer good-sized bedrooms each with a double bed, colour TV with movie and/or satellite channel (only the hotel in Slough/Windsor has the children's channel), en-suite bath and shower as well as the other usual facilities that are expected of a modern hotel. Executive rooms (Connoisseur) have larger, more comfortable bedrooms and, usually, a better outlook. Extras include fresh fruit and magazines, while bathrooms offer bathrobes and better-quality toiletries. Under-16s share parents' room free of charge, except at the Copthorne Tara in London. Dogs are generally not welcome in rooms. Effingham Park, Gatwick Airport has a crèche facility as part of its leisure centre, also an outside play area for children. Recent group expansion has been into Europe rather than within the UK. All major credit cards accepted.

Country Club Hotels

Head Office: Oakley House, Oakley Road, Leagrave, Luton, Bedfordshire
LU4 9QH Tel 0582 422994 Fax 0582 400024 or 405680

Central Reservations: Tel 0582 562256   Fax 0582 400024

Country Club Resorts

A feature of Whitbread's newly renamed flagship group is that all but two (Redwood Lodge, Bristol, Avon and Broughton Park, Lancashire) of the ten have at least one 18-hole golf course. Additionally, all feature a comprehensive range of leisure and sports facilities including swimming pools, saunas, solarium, tennis and squash courts and fitness studios. Tudor Park, Bearsted (Kent), St Pierre Park, Chepstow (Gwent) and Tewkesbury Park (Gloucestershire) feature a children's play area. Redwood Lodge has a cinema; Forest of Arden, Meriden (W Midlands) has a dance studio. Under-16s stay free if sharing parents' room; occupying their own room they are charged 70% of adult rate; Z-beds and cots provided at no charge. All major credit cards accepted.

Lansbury Collection

Once 43-strong, there are now only 18 Lansbury brand, mainly business-orientated hotels. The character is fairly traditional, but they differ considerably in style ranging from old coaching inn (The Falstaff, Canterbury) to mock-Tudor (Chimney House Hotel, Sandbach, Cheshire). Under-16s stay free if sharing with parents; a Z-bed or cot can be supplied (subject to availability). All major credit cards accepted.

Travel Inns

Travel Inn Reservations: Tel 0582 414341   Fax 0582 405680

There are now 60-odd Travel Inns (plus more expected to open in 1995), all located next to separate, themed eating chains where breakfast is served (7-9am weekdays, 8-10am weekends and Bank Holidays). All rooms have bath and shower, always a double bed with duvet, remote-control TV, tea- and coffee-making facilities, radio/alarm and adequate writing/work space. At the time of going to press, Travel Inns operated a price of £33.50 per room (exc breakfast) irrespective of whether taken as a single, double or for family occupancy. Two children under 16 are accommodated free when sharing with adults. Payment is on arrival and reception closes at 11pm. Every Travel Inn has a room specially adapted for disabled guests. Family-size rooms are not available at Basildon and Harlow (Essex), Birmingham (W Midlands), Cannock (Staffs), Cardiff, Longford (Gloucester), Northampton (Northants) or Tring (Herts); at these locations a second room may be booked (at weekends only – Fri, Sat & Sun) for under-16s at a charge of around half the standard tariff. No-smoking rooms are available. No dogs except guide dogs. Only Access and Visa credit cards accepted.

De Vere Hotels

Head Office: De Vere House, Chester Road, Daresbury, Warrington, Cheshire WA4 4BN

Reservations: Tel 0925 265050   Fax 0925 601264

On the whole, these are quite distinctive hotels, some grand, others not, each with its own style and character based on comfort and tradition. Properties range from the Grand hotels on the seafront in Eastbourne and Brighton to the Belfry in Wishaw, Warwickshire and the Belton Woods Hotel near Grantham in Lincolnshire with their magnificent golf courses. Standards of service are generally high. Leisure clubs are free to guests; many have splash pools (no children under 8 in the spa baths). Under-14s share their parents' room at no charge, but meals are charged as taken (except at Tillington Hall, Stafford where breakfast is included). Tillington Hall is convenient for Alton Towers and special deals are regularly offered for families. No dogs are allowed at Belton Woods, The Royal Bath (Bournemouth) or The Belfry. All major credit cards accepted.

Radisson Edwardian Hotels

Head Office: 140 Bath Road, Hayes, Middlesex UB3 5AW
Tel 081-897 6644 Fax 081-899 3533

Reservations: Tel 081-564 8888   Fax 081-759 8422

A London-based group of nine hotels ranging from The Hampshire in Leicester Square and the Radisson Edwardian International (the only one with a swimming pool) at London Heathrow to the more modest but still comfortable Kenilworth and Grafton Hotels. They're aimed mainly at the business and group markets (only babies can share their parents room at no charge), but the convenient locations may suit families with babes in arms or slightly older children. Baby-sitting can be arranged. All major credit cards accepted.

Forte Hotels

Head Office: Forte Hotels (Exclusive, Grand, Heritage, Crest, Posthouse), 166 High Holborn London WC1V 6TT Tel 071-836 7744

Central Reservations (local call cost): 0345 404040 (leisure breaks)
Fax 0296 81391
Business Guarantee Line: Freephone 0800 404040

The UK's largest network of hotels encompasses six categories of hotels that range from the Exclusive, Grand and Heritage brands down to the budget Travelodges. The Forte Crest and Forte Posthouse brands are the two primarily aimed at the businessman. Heritage hotels are mid-priced and of varied appeal; they are generally situated in small towns and more rural locations, often with a coaching inn history. The World of Forte is a mixed bag, not all of which are recommended in this guide; however, there are some interesting properties in the group but they don't necessarily fit in with the branding applied to others in the Forte empire. Free parking (for up to 15 days) at Forte's 15 airport hotels. Children under 16 stay free (plus under-5s eat free) when sharing with their parents at all Forte hotels; at Crest hotels up to three children under 16 may stay in a separate room when accompanied by two adults.

Forte Exclusive, Grand & Heritage

Reservations: (local call cost) 0345 404040

World of Forte

Head Office: Great West House, Great West Road, Brentford, Middlesex TW8 9DF Tel 081-568 4540

Reservations: (local call cost) 0345 404040

Forte Crest

Reservations: (local call cost) 0345 404040

Incorporating some of the best former Posthouses and most of the original Crests, a chain of modern business-orientated hotels. Over half have fully-equipped business centres. All offer 24hr room service for both Executive and standard rooms. All major credit cards accepted.

Forte Posthouse

Reservations: 0800 404040

A leading UK chain of around 60 mostly purpose-built modern hotels. Many have health and fitness centres. The extremely competitive room rate is the main attraction; constant for two years, the 'room only' prices have only just been raised to £56 Sun-Thurs (£59.50 in 14 of the outlets); prices come down quite drastically at weekends (Fri & Sat). Some family rooms have up to four beds; cots and Z-beds are available on request. Unsupervised children's playrooms are provided weekends and almost all the sites have outdoor play areas. Half the sites have indoor swimming pools. Executive rooms are sometimes available for a small supplement. All major credit cards accepted.

Forte Travelodge

Head Office: Unit 2, Cartel Business Centre, Stroudley Road, Basingstoke, Hampshire RG24 8FW Tel 0256 812828

Travelodge Reservations: 0800 850950

Roadside budget 'lodge' accommodation offering simple, modern rooms in over 100 locations conveniently sited along major routes. Room rates, payable in advance, are currently £33.50 per room (excluding breakfast). All have en-suite bathrooms with shower, colour television, radio/alarms and tea- and coffee-making facilities. Rooms sleep three adults, a child under 12 on a sofa bed and a baby in a cot (supplied on request). Every Travelodge has a room equipped for the disabled. The lodges do not have a restaurant as almost all are adjacent to a high-profile Forte catering outlet. Receptions open at 3pm (answerphone before that time). All major credit cards accepted.

Friendly Hotels

Head Office: Premier House, 10 Greycoat Place, Westminster, London SW1P 1SB

Reservations: 0800 591 910 Conferences Tel 0800 289 235

A small chain of 27 mixed-quality hotels that extends into Europe (including Copenhagen and Caen). The range covers the Floatel in Nantwich, Cheshire to modern, purpose-built low-risers in Norwich and Milton Keynes; some of the latest openings have not yet been inspected and are not included; other hotels in the group are updates of older-style buildings or budget lodges (Stop Inns), many of which do not come up to our standards. Generally modest accommodation is offered and children under 14 stay free (meals charged as taken) when sharing their parents' room. Premier Plus Rooms offer a higher standard with welcome drink, trouser press, teletext TV, mini-bar, hairdryer and personal toiletries. Good leisure facilities in most of the hotels. All major credit cards accepted.

Granada Lodges

Head Office: Toddington Service Area, M1 Service Area Southbound, Toddington, Near Dunstable, Bedfordshire LU5 6HR
Tel 0525 873881 Fax 0525 875358

Reservations: 0800 555 300 (24hr 7 days)

A chain of 26 budget hotels located close to major routes (the latest opening was at Oxford North, by the new M40 Cherwell Valley Services at Junction 10; Reading is currently under construction, to open in Spring 1995). All rooms are doubles or twins and have private bath and shower, colour TV with satellite channels, radio/alarm and tea- and coffee-making facilities; phones also now feature. In-room continental breakfast is available, otherwise meals may be taken in the adjacent service area restaurant. Family rooms are available and two children under 16 sharing with two adults are accommodated free (excluding breakfast). Every lodge has rooms for the disabled. Prices are from £39.95 (Sun-Thurs, reduced on Fri & Sat) for twin, double or family rooms; higher tariffs at Heston (London Heathrow) and Thurrock (Dartford Crossing). Payment is on arrival; cot supplied at no extra charge (as are non-allergenic pillows). 50% of lodges have outdoor play areas for children. No dogs. All major credit cards accepted.

Hilton Hotels

Head Office: Hilton International Hotels (UK), Chancel House, Neasden Lane, London NW10 2XE Tel 081-459 8031
Hilton National (UK), Millbuck House, Clarendon Road, Watford, Herts WD1 1DN Tel 0923 246464
Hilton UK Reservations, PO Box 137, Watford, Herts WD1 1DN

Reservations: Tel 0923 238877 Fax 0923 815594
Conference Reservations Tel 0923 250222

The Hilton Hotel group is now a mix of Hilton International (London-based), 25 Hilton National (Milton Keynes and Swindon are the very latest openings and not yet inspected) and a further eight associate hotels around the country. Croydon, Basingstoke, Bracknell, Watford, Southampton, Newbury, East Midlands/Nottingham, Leeds, Leeds Garforth, Newport and Swansea are designated as Happy Family Hotels, many with 3- or 4-bedded rooms. Hilton International and Hilton National hotels have superior rooms designated either Executive or Plaza – these are to a higher specification than standard rooms. They include large teletext TVs, a welcome tray with miniature spirits, chocolates, bathrobes, additional toiletries and lounge seating. Apart from all but one of the London hotels (the London Hilton on Park Lane), the majority of Hilton hotels have leisure centres that include swimming pools, fitness rooms and saunas. All major credit cards accepted.

Holiday Inns

European Head Office Woluwe Office Park 1, Rue Neerveld 101, 1200 Brussels, Belgium
Tel 010 32 2 773 5511   Fax 010 32 2 772 0272
UK: Area Director, c/o Holiday Inn Crowne Plaza, Stockley Road, West Drayton, Middlesex UB7 9NA 0895 445555

Holiday Inn Worldwide Reservations: Tel 0800 897 121 Fax: Guest relations Tel 010 31 020 606 5456

Top of the Holiday Inn range are the Crowne Plazas in Aberdeen, Bristol, London Heathrow and Manchester. Standard Holiday Inns offer large double beds and good bathrooms as well as free accommodation for children and young adults (up to the age of 19) when sharing with parents. All have good leisure facilities and well-equipped conference rooms. Holiday Inn Weekender breaks offer special rates for weekend and longer stays. All major credit cards accepted.

Holiday Inn Garden Court

Central Reservations: 0800 897 121

Under Bass plc the original Holiday Inn concept has been expanded to include Holiday Inn Garden Courts, an economy version offering excellent-value accommodation but more limited hotel facilities. Outlets in Ashford, Edinburgh, Nottingham and Warrington/Chester, Brent Cross (North London) and London (Welbeck Street, converted from an existing hotel). All major credit cards accepted. A new outlet opened in Aylesbury just after we went to press and has not yet been inspected.

Jarvis Hotels

Head Office: Wye House, London Road, High Wycombe, Buckinghamshire HP11 1LH Tel 0494 473800 Fax 0494 471666

Linkline Reservations: (local call cost) Tel 0345 581 237 Fax 071-589 8193
Conference Reservations: Tel 071-581 3466 Fax 071-589 8193

A nationwide network of middle-range hotels – a mixed portfolio, but usually dependable. With the acquisition last year of Resort Hotels, the Jarvis group is now the fifth largest hotel operator in the UK. Purpose-built Summit meeting rooms are a major attraction for the group. Trouser presses and hairdryers are supplied in all rooms; Executive bedrooms have a better standard of decor and extras such as fruit and chocolates plus more toiletries in the bathrooms. Up to two children under 16 may share their parents' room at no charge (meals charged as taken). Embassy Leisure Breaks offer special rates for weekend and longer stays. Many of the hotels have leisure clubs, some with children's splash pools. Great Danes in Hollingbourne, Kent is near Leeds Castle and features a Sebastian Coe Health Park plus an outdoor play area. Clayton Lodge in Newcastle-under-Lyme is convenient for Alton Towers. All major credit cards accepted.

Marriott Hotels

Scott's Hotels Limited, Executive Office, Ditton Road, Langley, Berkshire SL3 8PT Tel 0753 544255 Fax 0753 585484

Worldwide Reservations: Freephone (UK) Tel 0800 221 222   Fax 071-591 1128
Conferences & Groups Tel 071-591 1100   Fax 071-591 1128

The Marriott corporation run the London Marriott and Cheshunt Marriott, while the remainder are operated under franchise by Scott's Hotels who were previously associated with Holiday Inns. Staff have been trained to the high corporate standards demanded by Marriott, the aim of the group being to attract senior management in the business market during the week and family and leisure business at weekends. Bedrooms are spacious, with large desks and comfortable sofas. The Bristol, Heathrow/Slough, Marble Arch and Leeds Marriotts have Executive floors with private lounges and complimentary canapés. There are 18 hotels in the group including four **Courtyard by Marriott** (Leamington Spa, Lincoln, Northampton, Slough) outlets, which offer more moderately priced accommodation but still have good-sized rooms with separate seating and dressing areas, plus mini-gyms. All major credit cards accepted.

Mount Charlotte Thistle Hotels

Head Office: Mount Charlotte Thistle Hotels, 2 The Calls, Leeds, West Yorkshire LS2 7JU Tel 0532 439111

Central Reservations: Tel 071-937 8033   Fax 071-938 3658
National Conference Sales: Tel 071-938 1755   Fax 071-938 3674

Next to the Forte Hotels group, Mount Charlotte Thistle hotels are the most widespread throughout the country with hotels from Plymouth in Devon to Wick in the north of Scotland, and including many in London, from the enormous Tower Thistle at Tower Bridge to the country house-style Cannizaro House in Wimbledon. Overall, the quality of bedroom accommodation is good for the price; children are accommodated in a variety of ways – from Z-beds and sofa beds to additional single beds; under-14s share their parents' room during the week (subject to availability of suitable rooms at the time of booking, with meals charged as taken). The majority of hotels offer Executive bedrooms: these are larger rooms, more recently decorated and each having a number of useful extras. Lady guests have specially designated rooms. The large, modern Hospitality Inn in Brighton has a seafront location, convenient for the Lanes; the Golden Valley Thistle in Cheltenham is a good base from which to tour the Cotswolds; motor racing enthusiasts could head for the modern Donington or Brands Hatch Thistle hotels. All major credit cards accepted.

Novotel

Head Office: Novotel UK, 1 Shortlands, Hammersmith, London W6 8DR Tel 081-748 4580 Fax 081-741 0672

Resinter Reservations: 071-724 1000 Fax

A multinational hotel chain that includes 18 UK properties located on the outskirts of cities and close to motorway junctions; room prices at most of the hotels were recently brought down to a considerably more competitive level. Bedrooms, are somewhat plainly decorated, large and functional. The standard is identical in all and is designed for practical comfort and rest. Each has a bed/settee as well as a double bed. There is ample writing space among the usual modern facilities offered. Accommodation and breakfast are free for two children under 16 sharing their parents' room. Food and room service are available at any time from 6am to midnight and most bars follows the same hours. Only Newcastle, Sheffield and York hotels have indoor swimming pools; Bradford, Manchester, Nottingham, Plymouth, Preston, Stevenage and Wolverhampton have outdoor pools. Birmingham, Newcastle and Sheffield have fitness centres. The hotel in York is a good family base for visiting the Viking Centre and National Railway Museum. Major credit cards accepted in most Novotels but not all.

Principal Hotels

Head Office: Principal House, 11 Ripon Road, Harrogate, North Yorkshire HG1 1JA Tel 0423 530797

Reservations: Tel 0800 454 454   Fax 0423 500086

After a two-year period of uncertainty, the Principal Hotel Group was finally sold in March 1994. This group of 22 hotels (not all recommended in this Guide) – most located in town or city centres – is characterised by an attractive, traditional style and decor. Standard rooms are well equipped, with all the usual amenities. Executive rooms have bathrobes and a trouser press. Sky TV (with the cartoon channel) in most hotels. Special 'Flexibreak' half-board rates for stays of two nights or more (can be spread over more than one hotel). All major credit cards accepted. Under-4s free; 4-13s £9.50 per night when sharing with two adults; half price if sharing their own room.

Queens Moat Houses

Head Office: Queens Court, 9 Eastern Road, Romford, Essex RM1 3NG
Tel 0708 730522 Fax 0708 762691

Reservations: Tel 0800 289 330/331/332   Fax 0708 761033

With properties as diverse as the Royal Crescent in Bath, Eastwell Manor in Ashford, the Rose and Crown in Salisbury and the Newmarket Moat House, there is no longer a characteristic pattern to the 100+ UK hotels currently in the Queens Moat Houses group (one of the three largest UK hotel groups, alongside Forte and Mount Charlotte Thistle). It was only a relatively short time ago that the group name was synonymous with pleasant enough but, on the whole, rather lacklustre hotels offering acceptable standards of accommodation, but now QMH is now firmly into the luxury hotel league as well (Eastwell Manor, Ashford). 25 of the hotels have swimming pools. Bournemouth, Plymouth, Stoke on Trent (convenient for Alton Towers) and Telford (Ironbridge Museums and Gorge) are the most 'family-friendly'; last year, Plymouth even offered a Baby & Toddlers Delight weekend with all the necessary accoutrements provided. Many QMH hotels near airports (except Gatwick where only a reduced rate is offered and Stansted where it's only free while resident) give free car parking for up to 15 nights – Shepperton (Heathrow 5 miles), Manchester (4 miles), Birmingham (7 miles), Glasgow (3 miles), Edinburgh (5 miles); enquire about courtesy transfer facilities. All major credit cards taken.

Shire Inns

Head Office: Shire Inns Ltd, Colne Road, Reedley, Burnley,
Lancashire BB10 2NG
Tel 0282 414141   Fax 0282 415322

A small group of elegant hotels owned and run by Daniel Thwaites brewers, thus many have a separate pub in their grounds. The range, from south to north, covers Fareham, Bristol, Kettering, Knutsford, Blackburn, Burnley (nr Brierfield), Penrith and Carlisle. Some are extended from older properties, while others – like Kettering, Bristol and Fareham are modern, custom-built hotels cleverly sited to attract a good business clientele. Adjacent health clubs (open to hotel guests as well as a private membership), often with squash and tennis courts, help enliven the hotels at weekends when Weekend Refreshers offer reduced tariffs for two-night stays (if one night is a Saturday then a third night is given free of charge). Children under 16 share their parents' room at no charge (breakfast included); if they occupy their own room they are charged 50% of the adult tariff. Some family rooms include bunk beds. Children's menu, cots, high-chairs and baby-listening are all offered. The Montcalm in Marble Arch, London is an associate hotel. Bristol, Kettering Park, Penrith and Fareham feature children's splash pools as a part of their indoor swimming pools. Dogs welcome. All major credit cards accepted.

Stakis Hotels

Head Office: 3 Atlantic Quay, York Street, Glasgow G2 8GH
Tel 041-221 0000 Fax 041-204 1111

Hotel Reservations: 0800 262 626   Fax 041-304 1111
Conference Call: 0800 833 900

Located close to major business centres and trunk routes as well as in country settings, the hotels offer spacious, comfortable accommodation and 10 currently have a self-contained business centre. Guests have free use of the sports and leisure facilities. Originally based in Scotland, but now with over 30 hotels scattered throughout the UK. The Stakis Lodore

Swiss and Stakis Aviemore Coylumbridge Resort Hotel are particularly family-friendly. A Short Breaks and Family Holiday brochure highlights those group hotels that offer family facilities. All major credit cards accepted.

Swallow Hotels

Head Office: Swallow House, 19 Parsons Road, Washington, Tyne & Wear NE37 1QS Tel 091-419 4545 Fax 091-415 1888

Central Reservations: Tel 091-419 4666   Fax 091-415 1777

Based in the North East but with new hotels and acquisitions in the south this is a chain of hotels that continues to improve its image. Hotels of the standing of the Birmingham Swallow are much to be admired. 28 of the 35 current hotels have leisure clubs; most include an indoor heated swimming pool, sauna and/or steam room, solarium and spa bath; mini-gyms also feature in many. Dundee, Newcastle and Carlisle have outdoor children's play areas. Children of 14 years and under sharing a room with two adults are accommodated and served a cooked breakfast free of charge. Some family rooms have three or four beds (bunks). The Swallow Highcliff at Bournemouth is particularly family-friendly. All major credit cards accepted.

Voyager Hotels

No central reservations number

Part of Richard Branson's Virgin Group, Voyager Hotels are a mixture of interesting properties: Norton House in Ingliston 6 miles from Edinburgh (Lothian), Crathorne Hall near Yarm in Cleveland (North Yorkshire border) and Rhinefield House in Brockenhurst (Hampshire); there is one additional hotel outside the UK – La Residencia in Deia, Majorca. Children under 14 stay free in their parents' room (one child per paying adult – special rates for single-parent families); meal are charged as taken; children in their own room are charged 75% of adult rate. Only Rhinefield House has a swimming pool (both indoor and outdoor); hotel amenities are shared with occupants of their time-share facilities. The Close in Tetbury, (Glos) is now under a management contract to Voyager, as are three hotels owned by Welsh Water. Ask about their standby rate after 5pm – a nice touch from the owners of Virgin airline. All major credit cards accepted.

**On the BIG network, you're safer –
wherever life takes you.**

Recognising the important
contribution mobile phones can
make to personal security, Cellnet
introduced Lifetime, the low cost
tariff for personal users who need
a mobile mainly to help them cope
with life's little surprises.

Making mobile communications
more affordable and more
accessible, Lifetime is ideal if you
only need a phone to make 1or 2
calls a day – or give you peace of
mind in an emergency.

Whether you're on the 'school run'
and your car breaks down; you've
missed the last bus; or you have a
flat tyre, with Cellnet you can
summon help fast – around the
country, around the clock.

When things are not going to plan –
it's nice to be connected to the
BIG network.

For further information call
0800 214000

HOTELS LISTED BY COUNTY

ENGLAND

Swimming pool refers to indoor swimming pools only. See the How to Use This Guide section for explanation of our percentage rating system, room pricing and categories.

Key: QMH (Queens Moat Houses), MtCT (Mount Charlotte Thistle), Whitbread (Country Club Hotels)

Avon

Location	Hotel	Group	%	Room Price	Cat	Tel	Rooms	Conf	Banq	Leisure Centre	Swim Pool	Golf
Alveston	Alveston House		65%	£80	H	(0454) 415050	30	80	75			
Alveston	Forte Posthouse	Forte	62%	£68	H	(0454) 412521	74	100	120			
Bath	Apsley House		67%	£65	H	(0225) 336966	7					
Bath	Bath Spa Hotel	Forte	87%	£195	HR	(0225) 444424	98	140	120	yes	yes	
Bath	Fountain House			£120	PH	(0225) 338622	14					
Bath	Francis Hotel	Forte	67%	£112	H	(0225) 424257	93	80	70			
Bath	Hilton National	Hilton	67%	£125	H	(0225) 463411	150	250	200	yes	yes	
Bath	Lansdown Grove		65%	£90	H	(0225) 315891	45	120	84			
Bath	Priory Hotel		79%	£170	HR	(0225) 331922	21	70	70			
Bath	Queensberry Hotel	QMH	75%	£98	HR	(0225) 447928	22	25	25			
Bath	Royal Crescent Hotel		84%	£182	HR	(0225) 319090	42	65	80			
Beckington	Forte Travelodge	Forte		£45	L	(0373) 830251						
Bristol	Aztec Hotel	Shire Inns	74%	£102	H	(0454) 01090	86	220	200	yes	yes	
Bristol	Berkeley Square Hotel		69%	£106	H	(0272) 254000	43	16	50			
Bristol	Bristol Marriott Hotel	Marriott	73%	£137	H	(0272) 294281	289	600	600	yes	yes	
Bristol	Forte Crest	Forte	67%	£109	H	(0272) 564242	197	500	425	yes	yes	
Bristol	Grand Hotel	MtCT	62%	£94	H	(0272) 291645	182	600	530	yes	yes	

Town	Hotel	Group	%	Rate	Type	Tel					
Bristol	Hilton National Bristol	Hilton	69%	£101	H	(0272) 260041	201	300	275		yes
Bristol	Holiday Inn Crowne Plaza	QMH	72%	£130	H	(0272) 255010	132	200	180		yes
Bristol	Redwood Lodge Hotel & CC	Country Club	64%	£75	H	(0275) 393901	108	175	250	yes	yes
Bristol	Rodney Hotel		64%	£87	H	(0272) 735422	31				
Bristol	Stakis Bristol Hotel	Stakis	61%	£114	H	(0454) 201144	111	80	100	yes	yes
Bristol	Swallow Royal Hotel	Swallow	76%	£119	HR	(0272) 255100	242	250	230	yes	yes
Bristol	Unicorn Hotel		63%	£70	H	(0272) 230333	245	320	300		
Chelwood	Chelwood House		63%	£75	HR	(0761) 490730	11	24	45		
Dunkirk	Petty France Hotel		65%	£126	H	(0454) 238361	20	25	80		
Freshford	Homewood Park		79%	£115	HR	(0225) 723731	15	30	75		
Gordano	Forte Travelodge	Forte		£45	L	(0275) 373709	40				
Hunstrete	Hunstrete House	Arcadian	77%	£150	HR	(0761) 490490	24	70	50		
Monkton Combe	Combe Grove Manor		71%	£168	H	(0225) 834644	41	100	80	yes	yes
Sedgemoor	Forte Travelodge	Forte		£45	L	(0934) 750831	40				
Stoke Gifford	Forte Travelodge	Forte		£45	L	(0272) 501530					
Ston Easton	Ston Easton Park		88%	£153	HR	(0761) 241631	21	40	24		
Thornbury	Thornbury Castle		80%	£105	H	(0454) 281182	18				
Weston-super-Mare	Grand Atlantic	Forte	64%	£82	H	(0934) 626543	76	250	250		
Winterbourne	Grange Resort Hotel	Jarvis	68%	£100	H	(0454) 777333	52	150	150		yes

Bedfordshire

Town	Hotel	Group	%	Rate	Type	Tel					
Aspley Guise	Moore Place		70%	£85	H	(0908) 282000	54	50	50		
Bedford	Moat House	QMH	65%	£69	H	(0234) 355131	100	400	375		
Bedford	Woodlands Manor		72%	£85	L	(0234) 363281	25	40	60		
Dunstable	Forte Travelodge	Forte		£45	L	(0525) 211177	28				
Dunstable	Old Palace Lodge		66%	£102	H	(0582) 662201	49	50	40		
Flitwick	Flitwick Manor		73%	£125	HR	(0525) 712242	15	60	60		
Luton	Chiltern Hotel	Forte	60%	£92	H	(0582) 575911	91	250	220		
Luton	Hotel Ibis		60%	£51	H	(0582) 424488	98	100	70		
Luton	Leaside Hotel		55%	£45	H	(0582) 417643	15				
Luton	Luton Gateway Hotel	Forte	57%	£76	H	(0582) 575955	117	80			
Luton	Strathmore Thistle	MtCT	63%	£106	H	(0582) 34199	150	300	270		

Location	Hotel	Group	%	Room Price	Cat	Tel	Rooms	Conf	Banq	Leisure Centre	Swim Pool	Golf
Marston Moretaine	Forte Travelodge	Forte		£45	L	(0234) 766755	32					
Toddington	Granada Lodge	Granada		£51	L	(0525) 873881	43					
Woburn	Bedford Arms	MtCT	68%	£97	H	(0525) 290441	55	60	40			
Woburn	Bell Inn		57%	£65	H	(0525) 290280	25	30	45			

Berkshire

Location	Hotel	Group	%	Room Price	Cat	Tel	Rooms	Conf	Banq	Leisure Centre	Swim Pool	Golf
Ascot	Berystede Hotel	Forte	67%	£150	H	(0344) 23311	91	120	120			
Ascot	Royal Berkshire	Hilton	74%	£168	H	(0344) 23322	63	75	70		yes	
Bracknell	Coppid Beech Hotel		72%	£125	HR	(0344) 303333	205	400	225		yes	
Bracknell	Hilton National	Hilton	69%	£127	H	(0344) 424801	167	400	265			
Bray-on-Thames	The Waterside Inn			£110	RR	(0628) 20691	7					
Elcot	Jarvis Elcot Park	Jarvis	67%	£100	HR	(0488) 58100	75	120	100	yes	yes	
Eton	Christopher Hotel			£82	I	(0753) 852359	34	45	30			
Hungerford	Jarvis Bear Hotel	Jarvis	63%	£75	H	(0488) 682512	41	60	60			
Hurley	Ye Olde Bell	Jarvis	65%	£100	H	(0628) 825881	36	140	120			
Kintbury	Dundas Arms			£65	IR	(0488) 58263	5					
Maidenhead	Fredrick's		75%	£155	HR	(0628) 35934	37	100	140			
Maidenhead	Holiday Inn	Holiday Inns	66%	£147	H	(0628) 23444	189	400	400		yes	
Newbury	Chequers Hotel	Forte	66%	£92	H	(0635) 38000	56	65	120			
Newbury	Donnington Valley Hotel		74%	£95	H	(0635) 551199	58	200	180		yes	yes
Newbury	Foley Lodge		71%	£115	H	(0635) 528770	69	220	200	yes	yes	
Newbury	Hilton National	Hilton	69%	£111	H	(0635) 529000	109	100	150			
Newbury	Millwaters		67%	£75	H	(0635) 528838	30	50	50			
Newbury	Regency Park Hotel		70%	£103	H	(0635) 871555	50	170	120			
Newbury	Stakis Newbury Hotel	Stakis	67%	£108	H	(0635) 247010	112	60	50		yes	
Pingewood	Kirtons Farm Country Club		60%	£87	H	(0734) 500885	81	140	105	yes	yes	
Reading	Forte Posthouse	Forte	64%	£68	H	(0734) 875485	138	110	80	yes	yes	
Reading	Forte Travelodge	Forte		£45	L	(0734) 750618	36				yes	

Location	Hotel	Operator	%	Price	Cat	Phone	Rooms			F1	F2	F3	F4
Reading	Granada Lodge		71%	£52	L	(0800) 555300	40		180				
Reading	Holiday Inn Reading	QMH	68%	£106	H	(0734) 391818	112	200	150			yes	yes
Reading	Ramada Hotel		70%	£117	H	(0734) 586222	194	220	200		yes		yes
Sindlesham	Reading Moat House	QMH	71%	£126	H	(0734) 351035	96	80	180			yes	yes
Slough	Copthorne Slough/Windsor	Copthorne	60%	£135	H	(0753) 516222	219	250			yes		yes
Slough	Courtyard by Marriott		73%	£84	H	(0753) 551551	148	50				yes	yes
Slough	Heathrow/Slough Marriott	Marriott	68%	£131	HR	(0753) 544244	349	350	400			yes	yes
Streatley-on-Thames	Swan Diplomat		92%	£134	HR	(0491) 873737	46	90	80		yes		yes
Taplow	Cliveden		67%	£235	H	(0628) 668561	37	36	160			yes	yes
Windsor	Castle Hotel	Forte	78%	£156	HR	(0753) 851011	104						
Windsor	Oakley Court	QMH	69%	£177	HR	(0628) 74141	92	160	200			yes	yes
Wokingham	Stakis St Anne's Manor	Stakis	81%	£144	HR	(0734) 772550	130	400	300		yes	yes	yes
Woolton Hill	Hollington House Hotel			£110	I	(0635) 255100	20	38	45	yes			yes
Yattendon	Royal Oak			£80		(0635) 201325	5						

Buckinghamshire

Location	Hotel	Operator	%	Price	Cat	Phone	Rooms			F1	F2	F3	F4
Aston Clinton	Bell Inn		78%	£176	HR	(0296) 630252	21	120	200				
Aylesbury	Forte Posthouse	Forte	69%	£68	H	(0296) 393388	94	120	100				yes
Aylesbury	Harwell House	Historic House	86%	£165	HR	(0296) 747444	47	80	60			yes	yes
Beaconsfield	Bellhouse Hotel	De Vere	67%	£120	H	(0753) 887211	136	450	288			yes	yes
Burnham	Burnham Beeches Moat House	QMH	68%	£92	H	(0628) 603333	73	180	150			yes	yes
Burnham	Grovefield Hotel	Jarvis	63%	£80	H	(0628) 603131	38	170	120				
Chenies	Bedford Arms Thistle	MtCT	64%	£100	H	(0923) 283301	10	25	65				
Gerrards Cross	Bull Hotel	De Vere	63%	£125	H	(0753) 885995	95	200	160				
High Wycombe	Forte Posthouse	Forte	65%	£68	H	(0494) 442100	106	100	90				
Long Crendon	The Angel			£40	RR	(0844) 208268	4						
Marlow	Compleat Angler Hotel	Forte	73%	£164	HR	(0628) 484444	62	120	120				yes
Medmenham	Danesfield House		78%	£135	HR	(0628) 891010	89	200	120				
Milton Keynes	Forte Crest	Forte	68%	£109	H	(0908) 667722	151	150	110			yes	yes
Milton Keynes	Friendly Hotel	Friendly		£84	H	(0908) 561666	88	120	100			yes	yes
Milton Keynes	Travel Inn	Whitbread		£43	L	(0908) 663388	38						
Newport Pagnell	Forte Travelodge	Forte		£45	L	(0908) 610878	92						

Cambridgeshire

Location	Hotel	Group	%	Room Price	Cat	Tel	Rooms	Conf	Banq	Leisure Centre	Swim Pool	Golf
Cambridge	Arundel House		60%	£58	H	(0223) 67701	88	35	100			
Cambridge	Cambridgeshire Moat House	QMH	63%	£78	H	(0954) 780555	98	180	180		yes	yes
Cambridge	Cambridge Lodge		58%	£65	H	(0223) 352833	11	30	50			
Cambridge	Forte Posthouse	Forte	67%	£68	H	(0223) 237000	118	70	50	yes	yes	
Cambridge	Garden House	QMH	69%	£125	H	(0223) 63421	118	250	250		yes	yes
Cambridge	Gonville Hotel		62%	£85	H	(0223) 66611	60	200	200			
Cambridge	Holiday Inn	Holiday Inns	68%	£106	H	(0223) 464466	199	150	100		yes	
Cambridge	University Arms	De Vere	65%	£115	H	(0223) 351241	115	300	250			
Duxford	Duxford Lodge		65%	£88	HR	(0223) 836444	15	36	45			
Ely	Forte Travelodge	Forte		£45	L	(0353) 668499	39					
Ely	Lamb Hotel	QMH	62%	£77	H	(0353) 663574	32	65	65			
Fenstanton	Forte Travelodge	Forte		£45	L	(0954) 230919	40					
Huntingdon	Old Bridge Hotel	Poste Hotels	68%	£90	HR	(0480) 52681	26	50	110			
Lolworth	Forte Travelodge	Forte		£45	L	(0954) 781335	20					
Peterborough	Butterfly Hotel	Butterfly	63%	£70	H	(0733) 64240	70	80	50			
Peterborough	Forte Travelodge	Forte		£45	L	(0733) 231109	32					
Peterborough	Forte Posthouse	Forte	60%	£68	H	(0733) 240209	90	50	40			
Peterborough	Peterborough Moat House	QMH	64%	£80	H	(0733) 260000	125	400	400	yes	yes	
Peterborough	Swallow Hotel	Swallow	69%	£105	H	(0733) 371111	163	300	300	yes	yes	
Peterborough	Travel Inn	Whitbread		£43	L	(0733) 235794	40					
St Ives	Slepe Hall		61%	£60	H	(0480) 463122	16	220	220			
Six Mile Bottom	Swynford Paddocks		74%	£107	H	(0638) 570234	15	30	45			
Stilton	Bell Inn			£64	IR	(0733) 241066	19	100	100			
Swavesey	Forte Travelodge	Forte		£45	L	(0954) 789113	36					
Wansford-in-England	The Haycock	Poste Hotels	70%	£85	HR	(0780) 782223	50	250	200			

Cheshire

Town	Hotel	Group	%	Price	Type	Phone						
Alderley Edge	Alderley Edge Hotel		72%	£117	HR	(0625) 583033	32	120	100			
Alsager	Manor House		65%	£72	H	(0270) 884000	57	200	150		yes	yes
Altrincham	Bowdon Hotel		65%	£79	H	061-928 7121	82	130	130		yes	
Altrincham	Cresta Court		61%	£64	H	061-927 7272	139	300	300			
Bramhall	George & Dragon		60%	£46	H	061-928 9933	46		70			
Broxton	Moat House	QMH	63%	£85	H	061-439 8116	65	110	170			
Bunbury	Birches Hotel		72%	£120	H	(0829) 731000	82	200	150	yes	yes	
Burtonwood	Wild Boar		67%	£75	H	(0829) 260309	37	80	85			
	Forte Travelodge	Forte		£45	L	(0925) 710376	40					
Chester	Abbots Well	Jarvis	62%	£89	H	(0244) 332121	129	230	200	yes	yes	
Chester	Blossoms Hotel	Forte	63%	£97	H	(0244) 323186	64	100	50	yes	yes	
Chester	Chester Grosvenor		84%	£195	HR	(0244) 324024	86	250	220		yes	yes
Chester	Chester Resort Hotel	Jarvis	62%	£70	H	(0244) 851551	113	180	200			
Chester	Crabwall Manor		76%	£125	H	(0244) 851666	48	90	100			
Chester	Forte Posthouse	Forte	62%	£68	H	(0244) 680111	105	100	80	yes	yes	
Chester	Moat House International	QMH	69%	£143	H	(0244) 322330	152	600	350			
Chester	Mollington Banastre		67%	£95	H	(0244) 851471	64	350	300	yes	yes	
Chester	Rowton Hall		64%	£88	H	(0244) 335262	42	200	200	yes	yes	
Childer Thornton	Travel Inn	Whitbread		£43	L	051-339 8101	40					
Crewe	Forte Travelodge	Forte		£45	L	(0270) 883157	42					
Handforth	Belfry Hotel		69%	£75	HR	061-437 0511	80		180			
Knutsford	Brasserie Belle Epoque			£40	RR	(0565) 633060	7	85	120			
Knutsford	Cottons Hotel	Shire Inns	65%	£114	H	(0565) 650333	82	200	150		yes	
Knutsford	Forte Travelodge	Forte		£45	L	(0565) 652187	32					
Macclesfield	Sutton Hall			£85	I	(0260) 253211	10	30	60			
Mottram St Andrew	De Vere Mottram Hall	De Vere	70%	£140	H	(0625) 528135	133	275	180		yes	yes
Nantwich	Rookery Hall		79%	£150	HR	(0270) 610016	45	100	60			
Northwich	Friendly Floatel	Friendly	56%	£73	H	(0606) 44443	60	80	70			
Northwich	Hartford Hall		63%	£73	H	(0606) 75711	20	100	100			
Parkgate	Ship Hotel		58%	£60	H	051-336 3931	26					
Prestbury	Bridge Hotel	Forte	63%	£84	H	(0625) 829326	23	100	100			

Location	Hotel	Group	%	Room Price	Cat	Tel	Rooms	Conf	Banq	Leisure Centre	Swim Pool	Golf
Prestbury	White House Manor			£112	HR	(0625) 829376	9	60	120			
Puddington	Craxton Wood		70%	£95	HR	051-339 4717	14	35	50			
Runcorn	Campanile Hotel	Campanile		£44	L	(0928) 581771	53					
Runcorn	Forte Posthouse	Forte	62%	£68	H	(0928) 714000	135	500	450		yes	
Sandbach	Chimney House	Lansbury	62%	£80	H	(0270) 764141	48	90	90			
Sandiway	Nunsmere Hall		77%	£138	HR	(0606) 889100	32	50	60			
Stockport	Alma Lodge	Jarvis	61%	£95	H	061-483 4431	52	250	250			
Stockport	Forte Travelodge	Forte		£45	L	(0625) 875292	32					
Stockport	Travel Inn			£43	L	061-480 2968	40					
Stockport	Travel Inn			£43	L	061-499 1944	41					
Warrington	Holiday Inn Garden Court	Whitbread	65%	£70	H	(0925) 838779	99					
Warrington	Lord Daresbury Hotel	Holiday Inns	67%	£105	H	(0925) 267331	140	500	300	yes	yes	
Warrington	Travel Inn	De Vere		£43	L	(0582) 482224	40					
Wilmslow	Moat House	Whitbread	58%	£109	H	(0625) 529201	125	300	300	yes	yes	
Wilmslow	Stanneylands	QMH	70%	£85	HR	(0625) 525225	33	100	100		yes	

Cleveland

Location	Hotel	Group	%	Room Price	Cat	Tel	Rooms	Conf	Banq	Leisure Centre	Swim Pool	Golf
Crathorne	Crathorne Hall	Voyager	72%	£130	H	(0642) 700398	37	200	130			
Easington	Grinkle Park		70%	£80	H	(0287) 640515	20	60				
Hartlepool	Grand Hotel		59%	£68	H	(0429) 266345	47	200	160			
Middlesbrough	Hotel Baltimore		62%	£85	H	(0642) 224111	31	140	100			
Middlesbrough	Hospitality Inn	MtCT	59%	£93	H	(0642) 232000	180	400	400			
Stockton-on-Tees	Swallow Hotel	Swallow	67%	£96	H	(0642) 679721	125	300	250	yes	yes	
Thornaby-on-Tees	Forte Posthouse	Forte	60%	£68	H	(0642) 591213	135	100	100			

Cornwall

Location	Hotel	Group	%	Room Price	Cat	Tel	Rooms	Conf	Banq	Leisure Centre	Swim Pool	Golf
Calstock	Danescombe Valley Hotel		72%	£175	HR	(0822) 832414	5					

Location	Hotel	%	£	Code	Phone	No.			Facilities
Carlyon Bay	Carlyon Bay Hotel	68%	£128	H	(0726) 812304	73	250	220	yes yes
Carlyon Bay	Porth Avallen Hotel	60%	£81	H	(0726) 812802	24	100	100	yes yes yes
Constantine Bay	Treglos Hotel	65%	£140	H	(0841) 520727	44	60	120	yes yes
Falmouth	Falmouth Hotel	63%	£96	H	(0326) 312671	73	250	250	yes
Falmouth	Greenbank Hotel	69%	£105	H	(0326) 312440	61	80	120	yes yes
Falmouth	Royal Duchy Hotel	66%	£109	H	(0326) 313042	46	150	180	yes yes
Falmouth	St Michael's Hotel	63%	£86	H	(0326) 312707	66	200	160	yes yes yes
Golant	Cormorant Hotel	63%	£92	H	(0726) 833426	11		35	yes
Helford	Riverside		£75	RR	(0326) 231443	6			
Helland Bridge	Tredethy Country Hotel	56%	£68	H	(0208) 841262	11	50	40	
Lamorna Cove	Lamorna Cove Hotel	65%	£66	H	(0736) 731411	15			
Land's End	Land's End Hotel	64%	£75	H	(0736) 871844	34	100	200	
Liskeard	Well House	74%	£90	HR	(0579) 342001	7		30	
Looe	Talland Bay Hotel	67%	£92	H	(0503) 72667	21	30	70	
Mawnan	Budock Vean Hotel	65%	£144	H	(0326) 250288	58	80	100	yes
Mawnan	Meudon Hotel	69%	£106	H	(0326) 250541	32		65	
Mawnan	Nansidwell	70%	£98	HR	(0326) 250340	12			
Mousehole	Lobster Pot	57%	£80	H	(0736) 731528	25			
Mullion	Polurrian Hotel	66%	£66	H	(0326) 240421	39	100	120	yes yes
Newlyn	Higher Faugan Country House	62%	£84	H	(0736) 62076	11			
Newquay	Hotel Bristol	64%	£80	H	(0637) 875181	74	300	260	yes yes
Newquay	Hotel Riviera	63%	£84	H	(0637) 874251	50	120	150	
Padstow	Seafood Restaurant		£73	RR	(0841) 532485	10			
Penzance	Abbey Hotel	67%	£85	HR	(0736) 66906	7			
Portloe	Lugger Hotel	59%	£104	H	(0872) 501322	19		37	
St Austell	Boscundle Manor	65%	£110	H	(0726) 813557	10			yes
St Austell	White Hart		£63	I	(0726) 72100	18	60	46	
St Ives	Garrack Hotel	62%	£91	HR	(0736) 796199	18	30	35	yes
St Mawes	Idle Rocks Hotel	64%	£128	H	(0326) 270771	24			
St Mawes	Rising Sun	62%	£89	H	(0326) 270233	11			
St Mawes	Hotel Tresanton	69%	£70	H	(0326) 270544	21			
Saltash	Granada Lodge		£51	L	(0752) 848408	31			Granada
Tintagel	Trebrea Lodge	66%	£62	HR	(0840) 770410	7		16	

Location	Hotel	Group	%	Room Price	Cat	Tel	Rooms	Conf	Banq	Leisure Centre	Swim Pool	Golf
Truro	Alverton Manor		70%	£95	H	(0872) 76633	34	200	180			
Veryan	Nare Hotel		70%	£124	HR	(0872) 501279	35	50	90		yes	

Isles of Scilly:

Location	Hotel	Group	%	Room Price	Cat	Tel	Rooms	Conf	Banq	Leisure Centre	Swim Pool	Golf
St Martin's	St Martin's Hotel		69%	£186	HR	(0720) 22092	24	100	60		yes	
St Mary's	Hotel Godolphin		58%	£72	H	(0720) 22316	31					
St Mary's	Tregarthen's Hotel		60%	£110	H	(0720) 22540	29					
Tresco	Island Hotel		67%	£170	HR	(0720) 422883	40					

Cumbria

Location	Hotel	Group	%	Room Price	Cat	Tel	Rooms	Conf	Banq	Leisure Centre	Swim Pool	Golf
Alston	Lovelady Shield		68%	£95	HR	(0434) 381203	12	12	36			
Ambleside	Kirkstone Foot		65%	£104	H	(053 94) 32232	16		50			
Ambleside	Nanny Brow		62%	£130	HR	(053 94) 32036	18	50	35			
Ambleside	Rothay Manor Hotel		71%	£108	HR	(053 94) 33605	18	25	36			
Ambleside	Wateredge Hotel		63%	£102	HR	(053 94) 32332	23					
Appleby-in-Westmorland	Appleby Manor Hotel		66%	£98	HR	(076 83) 51571	30	35			yes	
Appleby-in-Westmorland	Tufton Arms		66%	£80	H	(076 83) 51593	19	100	80			
Applethwaite	Underscar Manor		74%	£150	HR	(076 87) 75000	11	14	40			
Bassenthwaite	Armathwaite Hall		65%	£100	H	(076 87) 76551	42	100	120	yes	yes	
Bassenthwaite Lake	Pheasant Inn		65%	£64	H	(076 87) 76234	20		55			
Borrowdale	Borrowdale Hotel		60%	£92	H	(076 87) 77224	34	30	100		yes	
Borrowdale	Stakis Lodore Swiss Hotel	Stakis	71%	£150	H	(076 87) 77285	70	75	75	yes	yes	
Bowness-on-Windermere	Belsfield Hotel	Forte	62%	£108	HR	(053 94) 42448	64	130	160	yes	yes	
Bowness-on-Windermere	Gilpin Lodge		64%	£80	HR	(053 94) 88818	9	20	20			
Bowness-on-Windermere	Linthwaite House		72%	£110	HR	(053 94) 88600	18	47	60			
Bowness-on-Windermere	Old England Hotel	Forte	65%	£126	H	(053 94) 42444	78	100	60			
Braithwaite	Ivy House		66%	£68	H	(076 87) 78338	12					

Location	Hotel	Group	%	Price	Type	Phone	Rooms				
Brampton	Farlam Hall		75%	£170	HR	(069 77) 46234	12	25	45		
Carlisle	Granada Lodge	Granada	59%	£51	L	(069 74) 73131	39				
Carlisle	Swallow Hilltop	Swallow	60%	£80	H	(0228) 29255	92	400	400	yes	yes
Cartmel	Aynsome Manor		60%	£104	H	(053 95) 36653	12				yes
Cartmel	Uplands			£118	RR	(053 95) 36248	5				
Coniston	Sun Hotel		63%	£60	H	(053 94) 41248	11	20	75		
Crook	Wild Boar Hotel		60%	£84	H	(0539) 445225	36	30			
Crooklands	Crooklands Hotel		60%	£55	H	(053 95) 67432	30	150	100		
Crosby-on-Eden	Crosby Lodge		66%	£85	HR	(0228) 573618	11	25	50		
Faugh	String of Horses Inn			£68	I	(0228) 70297	14	20	60		
Grasmere	Michael's Nook		79%	£170	HR	(053 94) 35496	14	35	50		
Grasmere	The Swan	Forte	65%	£138	H	(053 94) 35551	36	16			
Grasmere	White Moss House		69%	£128	HR	(053 94) 35295	6				
Grasmere	Wordsworth Hotel		72%	£124	HR	(053 94) 35592	37	130	110	yes	yes
Grizedale	Grizedale Lodge		61%	£70	HR	(053 94) 36532	9				
Kendal	Woolpack Hotel	Principal	59%	£65	H	(0539) 723852	54	150	120		
Keswick	Keswick Hotel		60%	£75	H	(076 87) 72020	66	80	150	yes	yes
Langdale	Langdale Hotel		71%	£132	H	(053 94) 37302	65	90	120	yes	yes
Newby Bridge	The Swan		61%	£88	H	(053 95) 31681	36	65			
Penrith	Forte Travelodge	Forte		£45	L	(0768) 66958	32				
Penrith	North Lakes Hotel	Shire Inns	71%	£114	H	(0768) 68111	84	250	220	yes	yes
Ravenstonedale	Black Swan Inn		67%	£66	I	(053 96) 23204	16		50		
Silloth-on-Solway	Skinburness Hotel		67%	£70	H	(069 73) 32332	25	200	170		
Spark Bridge	Bridgefield House		60%	£60	HR	(0229) 885239	5		30		
Troutbeck	Mortal Man Inn			£95	I	(053 94) 33193	12				
Ullswater	Leeming House	Forte	75%	£115	HR	(076 84) 86622	40	30	80		
Ullswater	Old Church Hotel		67%	£90	H	(076 84) 86204	10				
Ullswater	Rampsbeck Country House		65%	£80	HR	(076 84) 86442	20	20			
Ulverston	Sharrow Bay		82%	£250	HR	(076 84) 86301	28				
Wetheral	Bay Horse Inn & Bistro			£120	RR	(0229) 583972	6				
Wetheral	The Crown	Shire Inns	70%	£106	HR	(0228) 561888	51	150	150	yes	yes
Windermere	Holbeck Ghyll		68%	£110	H	(053 94) 32375	14	30	50		yes
Windermere	Merewood Hotel		66%	£90	H	(053 94) 46484	20	40			

Location	Hotel	Group	%	Room Price	Cat	Tel	Rooms	Conf	Banq	Leisure Centre	Swim Pool	Golf
Windermere	Miller Howe		70%	£150	H	(053 94) 42536	13	10				
Witherslack	Old Vicarage		68%	£98	HR	(053 95) 52381	15	15	18			

Derbyshire

Location	Hotel	Group	%	Room Price	Cat	Tel	Rooms	Conf	Banq	Leisure Centre	Swim Pool	Golf
Ashbourne	Ashbourne Lodge Hotel		66%	£75	H	(0335) 346666	50	200	180			
Ashbourne	Callow Hall		69%	£90	H	(0335) 343403	16	50	50			
Ashford-in-the-Water	Riverside Hotel		66%	£85	HR	(0629) 814275	15	20	50			
Bakewell	Hassop Hall		74%	£93	H	(0629) 640488	13	60	100			
Baslow	Cavendish Hotel		71%	£116	HR	(0246) 582311	24	25	50			
Baslow	Fischer's Baslow Hall			£120	RR	(0246) 583259	6	40	40			
Castle Donington	Donington Thistle	MtCT	70%	£118	H	(0332) 850700	110	220	180		yes	
Chesterfield	Chesterfield Hotel		59%	£72	L	(0246) 271141	73	200	225	yes	yes	yes
Chesterfield	Forte Travelodge	Forte				(0246) 455411	20					
Derby	European Inn		61%	£45	H	(0332) 292000	88	100	50			
Derby	Forte Posthouse	Forte	62%	£46	H	(0332) 514933	62	60	200			
Derby	International Hotel		65%	£68	H	(0332) 369321	62	70	150			
Derby	Midland Hotel		59%	£40	H	(0332) 345894	100	150	120			
Dovedale	Izaak Walton Hotel		60%	£89	H	(033 529) 555	34	100	70			
Dovedale	Peveril of the Peak	Forte		£95	H	(033 529) 333	47	80	110			
Grindleford	Maynard Arms			£102	I	(0433) 630321	13	80	12			
Hathersage	Hathersage Inn			£60	I	(0433) 650259	15	20	50			
Hayfield	Bridge End Restaurant			£60	RR	(0663) 747321	4	20	40			
Matlock	Riber Hall		71%	£45	HR	(0629) 582795	11					
Matlock Bath	New Bath Hotel	Forte	63%	£98	H	(0629) 583275	55	130	200			
Morley	Breadsall Priory	Country Club	69%	£108	H	(0332) 832235	91	120	100	yes	yes	
Newton Solney	Newton Park	Jarvis	67%	£111	H	(0283) 703568	50	120	100		yes	yes
Renishaw	Sitwell Arms		61%	£60	H	(0246) 435226	30	160	150			

Location	Hotel	Group	%	£	Code	Phone				Facilities
Rowsley	Peacock Hotel	Jarvis	64%	£87	H	(0629) 733518	14	20	24	yes
South Normanton	Swallow Hotel	Swallow	69%	£100	H	(0773) 812000	161	200	200	yes

Devon

Location	Hotel	Group	%	£	Code	Phone				Facilities
Barnstaple	Imperial Hotel	Forte	60%	£71	H	(0271) 45861	56	60	60	
Barnstaple	Lynwood House		61%	£61	RR	(0271) 43695	5	60	60	
Bigbury-on-Sea	Burgh Island Hotel		66%	£174	H	(0548) 810514	14	120	100	
Bishop's Tawton	Halmpstone Manor		68%	£80	HR	(0271) 830321	5	14	14	
Branscombe	Masons Arms		64%	£54	H	(0297) 80300	21	100	100	
Brixham	Quayside Hotel		59%	£52	H	(0803) 855751	30	30	20	
Chagford	Gidleigh Park		82%	£275	HR	(0647) 432367	15		24	
Chagford	Great Tree Hotel		61%	£78	H	(0647) 432491	12		30	
Chagford	Mill End		63%	£80	H	(0647) 432282	16	45		
Chittlehamholt	Highbullen		60%	£105	H	(0769) 540561	37			yes yes
Clawton	Court Barn		61%	£66	I	(040 927) 219	8	25	40	
Dartmouth	Royal Castle Hotel			£76	H	(0803) 833033	25	100	100	
Dartmouth	Stoke Lodge		60%	£71	H	(0803) 770523	24	100	100	yes
East Buckland	Lower Pitt			£50	RR	(0598) 760243	3			
Exeter	Buckerell Lodge		67%	£84	H	(0392) 52451	52	60	130	
Exeter	Forte Crest	Forte	69%	£105	H	(0392) 412812	110	150	120	
Exeter	Rougemont Thistle Hotel	MtCT	63%	£79	H	(0392) 54982	90	300	208	
Exeter	Royal Clarence	QMH	71%	£98	H	(0392) 58464	56	120	90	yes
Exeter	St Olaves Court			£78	HR	(0392) 217736	17			
Exeter	Travel Inn	Whitbread		£43	L	(0392) 87541	40			
Exeter	White Hart		61%	£78	H	(0392) 79897	59	70	70	
Exmouth	Imperial Hotel	Forte	60%	£107	H	(0395) 274761	57	20	20	
Fairy Cross	Portledge Hotel		62%	£67	H	(0237) 451262	35			
Gittisham	Combe House		73%	£97	H	(0404) 42756	15	34	22	
Gulworthy	The Horn of Plenty			£92	RR	(0822) 832528	7	16	50	
Hatherleigh	George Hotel		65%	£65	I	(0837) 810454	11	50	75	
Hawkchurch	Fairwater Head Hotel		65%	£110	I	(029 77) 349	21			
Haytor	Bel Alp House		72%	£120	H	(0364) 661217	9			

Location	Hotel	Group	%	Room Price	Cat	Tel	Rooms	Conf	Banq	Leisure Centre	Swim Pool	Golf
Holbeton	Alston Hall		65%	£90	H	(0752) 830555	20	80	100	yes	yes	yes
Hope Cove	Cottage Hotel		56%	£94	H	(0548) 561555	35	50	95			yes
Hope Cove	Lantern Lodge		59%	£69	H	(0548) 561280	14		30		yes	
Huntsham	Huntsham Court		68%	£125	HR	(0398) 6365	14	50	35			
Lewdown	Lewtrenchard Manor		73%	£98	HR	(056 683) 256	8	80	60			
Lifton	Arundell Arms		65%	£90	HR	(0566) 784666	29	100	110			
Lympstone	River House			£87	RR	(0395) 265147	2					
Lynmouth	Rising Sun Inn			£79	I	(0598) 53223	16					
Lynton	Lynton Cottage		65%	£78	H	(0598) 52342	17	30	20			
Moretonhampstead	White Hart Hotel			£63	I	(0647) 440406	20	80	90			
Newton Abbot	Passage House		65%	£75	H	(0626) 55515	40	120	125	yes	yes	
North Huish	Brookdale House		69%	£80	H	(0548) 82402	8	40	40			
Okehampton	Forte Travelodge	Forte		£45	L	(0837) 52124	32					
Paignton	Palace Hotel		60%	£103	H	(0803) 555121	52	50	40		yes	
Paignton	Redcliffe Hotel		62%	£92	H	(0803) 526397	58	150	210	yes	yes	
Parkham	Penhaven Country House		64%	£112	H	(0237) 451388	12		40			
Plymouth	Boringdon Hall		70%	£75	H	(0752) 344455	40	120	110		yes	yes
Plymouth	Campanile Hotel	Campanile		£44	L	(0752) 601087	50					
Plymouth	Copthorne Hotel	Copthorne	70%	£103	H	(0752) 224161	135	75	100		yes	
Plymouth	Forte Posthouse	Forte	65%	£68	H	(0752) 662828	106	80	80			
Plymouth	Moat House	QMH	70%	£92	H	(0752) 662866	212	425	400	yes	yes	
Plymouth	Novotel	Novotel	62%	£54	H	(0752) 221422	100	240	160		yes	
Poundsgate	Leusdon Lodge Hotel		61%	£60	HR	(036 43) 304	7	10	10			
Salcombe	Marine Hotel		68%	£152	H	(0548) 844444	51	75	120	yes	yes	
Salcombe	Soar Mill Cove		66%	£128	H	(0548) 561566	16				yes	
Salcombe	South Sands Hotel		60%	£134	H	(0548) 843741	31		80		yes	
Salcombe	Tides Reach		71%	£144	H	(0548) 843466	38			yes	yes	
Saunton	Saunton Sands		67%	£128	H	(0271) 890212	96	200	175	yes	yes	
Sidmouth	Belmont Hotel		63%	£106	H	(0395) 512555	54	90	120		yes	
Sidmouth	Fortfield Hotel		59%	£70	H	(0395) 512403	55	100	120			yes

Town	Hotel	Chain	%	Rate	Cat	Phone								
Sidmouth	Hotel Riviera		65%	£118	H	(0395) 515201	27	90	90			yes		
Sidmouth	Victoria Hotel		67%	£142	H	(0395) 512651	62	100	120	yes	yes	yes		
South Molton	Whitechapel Manor		76%	£120	HR	(0769) 573377	10	10	40					
Teignmouth	Thomas Luny House			£60	PH	(0626) 772976	4							
Thurlestone	Thurlestone Hotel		69%	£162	H	(0548) 560382	68	140	150	yes	yes	yes		yes
Tiverton	Forte Travelodge	Forte		£45	L	(0884) 821087	40							
Torquay	Grand Hotel		68%	£115	H	(0803) 296677	112	300	300	yes	yes			
Torquay	Homers Hotel		64%	£60	H	(0803) 213456	15	50	50					
Torquay	Imperial Hotel	Forte	83%	£145	H	(0803) 294301	167	400	280	yes	yes			
Torquay	Livermead Cliff Hotel		60%	£60	H	(0803) 299666	64	70	120					
Torquay	Livermead House Hotel		60%	£90	H	(0803) 294361	65	300	250					
Torquay	Orestone Manor		58%	£90	H	(0803) 328098	18	12	50					
Torquay	Osborne Hotel		65%	£86	H	(0803) 213311	23	80	60		yes	yes		
Torquay	Palace Hotel		68%	£110	H	(0803) 200200	140	2,000	550	yes	yes	yes		yes
Tuckenhay	Floyd's Inn (Sometimes)			£125	IR	(0803) 732350	4							
Whimple	Woodhayes Hotel		75%	£90	HR	(0404) 822237	6							
Wilmington	Home Farm		58%	£56	H	(0404) 831246	13							
Woody Bay	Woody Bay Hotel		59%	£66	H	(059 83) 264	15	16						
Woolacombe	Woolacombe Bay Hotel		65%	£170	H	(0271) 870388	63	250	200	yes	yes			
Yelverton	Moorland Links		65%	£74	H	(0822) 852245	45	120						

Dorset

Town	Hotel	Chain	%	Rate	Cat	Phone								
Blandford Forum	La Belle Alliance		78%	£58	RR	(0258) 452842	6		42					
Bournemouth	Carlton Hotel		65%	£120	H	(0202) 552011	70	160	120					
Bournemouth	Chine Hotel		59%	£85	H	(0202) 396234	97	120	160		yes			
Bournemouth	Roundhouse Hotel	Forte	62%	£68	H	(0202) 553262	98	100	100					
Bournemouth	Langtry Manor		70%	£79	H	(0202) 553887	25	100	100					
Bournemouth	Norfolk Royale		71%	£138	H	(0202) 551521	95	100	100		yes	yes		
Bournemouth	Palace Court		73%	£118	H	(0202) 557681	110	200	250	yes	yes	yes		
Bournemouth	Royal Bath Hotel	De Vere	70%	£115	HR	(0202) 555555	131	500	448	yes	yes	yes		
Bournemouth	Swallow Highcliff Hotel	Swallow	71%	£120	H	(0202) 557702	157	450	275	yes	yes	yes		
Chedington	Chedington Court			£150	HR	(0935) 891265	10	22	22					yes

Location	Hotel	Group	%	Room Price	Cat	Tel	Rooms	Conf	Banq	Leisure Centre	Swim Pool	Golf
Chedington	Hazel Barton			£95	PH	(0935) 891613	4	12				
Christchurch	Travel Inn	Whitbread		£43	L	(0202) 485376	38					
Corfe Castle	Mortons House Hotel		62%	£80	H	(0929) 480988	17	20				
East Stoke	Kemps Country House Hotel		56%	£78	H	(0929) 462563	15	60	120			
Evershot	Summer Lodge		78%	£120	HR	(0935) 83424	17	20	50			
Ferndown	Dormy Hotel	De Vere	71%	£105	H	(0202) 872121	128	250	150	yes	yes	yes
Ferndown	Travel Inn (Poole/Ringwood)	Whitbread		£43	L	(0202) 874210	32					
Gillingham	Stock Hill House		74%	£170	HR	(0747) 823626	8					
Longham	Bridge House		61%	£52	H	(0202) 578828	37	120	100			
Lyme Regis	Alexandra Hotel		58%	£94	H	(0297) 442010	27		70			
Mudeford	Avonmouth Hotel	Forte	59%	£107	H	(0202) 483434	41	60	120			
Poole	Haven Hotel		69%	£120	HR	(0202) 707333	94	170	160		yes	
Poole	Mansion House		74%	£110	HR	(0202) 685666	28	40	100			
Poole	Quay Thistle Hotel	MtCT	63%	£80	H	(0202) 666800	68	60	50			
Poole	Sandbanks Hotel		59%	£120	H	(0202) 707377	105	150	250	yes	yes	
Powerstock	Three Horseshoes Inn			£50	RR	(0308) 485328	4					
Shaftesbury	Grosvenor Hotel	Forte	62%	£92	H	(0747) 852282	35	150	120			
Shaftesbury	Royal Chase Hotel		60%	£83	H	(0747) 853355	35	140	160		yes	
Sherborne	Eastbury Hotel	Arcadian	67%	£75	H	(0935) 813131	15	80	100			
Sherborne	Sherborne Hotel	Forte	%	£	H	(0935) 813191	59	80	100			
Studland Bay	Knoll House		63%	£165	H	(092 944) 251	70				yes	yes
Sturminster Newton	Plumber Manor			£80	RR	(0258) 472507	16	40	60			
Wareham	Priory Hotel		72%	£100	HR	(0929) 551666	19	20	45			
Wareham	Springfield Country Hotel		60%	£100	H	(0929) 552177	32	200	160	yes	yes	
West Bexington	Manor Hotel		59%	£76	H	(0308) 897616	13	40	65			
Winkton	Fisherman's Haunt Hotel			£59	I	(0202) 484071	20		100			

Durham

Location	Hotel	Group	%	Room Price	Cat	Tel	Rooms	Conf	Banq	Leisure Centre	Swim Pool	Golf
Barnard Castle	Jersey Farm Hotel		59%	£50	H	(0833) 38223	20	200	150			

Town	Hotel	Group	%	Price	Code	Phone	Rooms	Cap1	Cap2			
Blanchland	Lord Crewe Arms Hotel		63%	£70	H	(0434) 675251	18	35	20			
Chester-le-Street	Lumley Castle		69%	£98	H	091-389 1111	64	120	250			
Coatham Mundeville	Hall Garth Golf & CC		66%	£81	HR	(0325) 300400	40	300	220	yes	yes	
Darlington	Blackwell Grange Moat House	QMH	62%	£98	H	(0325) 380888	99	250	250	yes	yes	yes
Darlington	St George Thistle	MtCT	56%	£79	H	(0325) 332631	57	160	120			
Darlington	Swallow King's Head	Swallow	57%	£90	H	(0325) 380222	85	200	250			
Durham	Royal County Hotel	Swallow	67%	£120	H	091-386 6821	150	120	120	yes	yes	yes
Greta Bridge	Morritt Arms			£68	I	(0833) 627232	15	150	150			
Middleton-in-Teesdale	Teesdale Hotel			£61	I	(0833) 40264	12					
Neasham	Newbus Arms			£60	H	(0325) 721071	15	120	80			
Romaldkirk	Rose and Crown			£74	IR	(0833) 650213	12					

Essex

Town	Hotel	Group	%	Price	Code	Phone	Rooms	Cap1	Cap2			
Basildon	Campanile Hotel	Campanile	59%	£44	L	(0268) 530810	98					
Basildon	Forte Posthouse	Forte		£68	H	(0268) 533955	110	300	250			
Basildon	Travel Inn	Whitbread		£43	L	(0268) 522227	32		50			
Brentwood	Forte Posthouse	Forte	61%	£68	H	(0277) 260260	111	120	120		yes	
Brentwood	Forte Travelodge	Forte		£45	L	(0277) 810819	22					
Brentwood	Moat House	QMH	67%	£114	H	(0277) 225252	33	50	120			
Broxted	Whitehall		72%	£105	HR	(0279) 850603	25	120	120			
Chelmsford	Travel Inn	Whitbread		£43	L	(0582) 414341	60					
Coggeshall	White Hart Hotel		69%	£82	HR	(0376) 561654	18	30	80			
Colchester	Butterfly Hotel	Butterfly	61%	£62	H	(0206) 230900	50	80	50			
Colchester	Forte Posthouse	Forte	61%	£67	H	(0206) 767740	110	50	50		yes	
Dedham	Fountain House/Dedham Hall			£57	RR	(0206) 323027	6					
Dedham	Maison Talbooth		78%	£105	H	(0206) 322367	10					
Epping	Forte Posthouse	Forte	63%	£68	H	(0992) 573137	79	100	85		yes	
Great Baddow	Pontlands Park		70%	£135	H	(0245) 476444	17	50	200			
Great Dunmow	Saracen's Head	Forte	58%	£97	H	(0371) 873901	24	50	50			
Great Dunmow	The Starr			£75	RR	(0371) 874321	8	40	50			
Harlow	Green Man	Forte	60%	£92	H	(0279) 442521	55	60	55			
Harlow	Moat House	QMH	68%	£80	H	(0279) 422441	118	150	150			

Location	Hotel	Group	%	Room Price	Cat	Tel	Rooms	Conf	Banq	Leisure Centre	Swim Pool	Golf
Harwich	Pier at Harwich			£63	RR	(0255) 241212	6					
Horndon-on-the-Hill	Bell Inn			£54	I	(0375) 673154						
Horndon-on-the-Hill	Hill House			£54	RR	(0375) 642463	11	40	32			
Ilford	Forte Travelodge	Forte		£45	L	081-550 6451	40					
Ilford	Travel Inn	Whitbread		£43	L		22					
Ingatestone	Heybridge Hotel		68%	£89	H	(0277) 355355	28	600	550			
Maldon	Blue Boar	Forte	59%	£75	H	(0621) 852681	96	35	25			
North Stifford	Stifford Moat House	QMH	61%	£83	H	(0375) 390909	38	530	150			
Old Harlow	Travel Inn	Whitbread		£43	L	(0279) 442545	20					
Saffron Walden	Saffron Hotel		57%	£55	L	(0799) 522676	35	100	80			
Thurrock	Granada Lodge	Granada		£59	L	(0708) 891111						
Waltham Abbey	Swallow Hotel	Swallow	66%	£110	H	(0992) 717170	163	250	230		yes	
Woodford Bridge	Prince Regent Hotel		63%	£85	H	081-505 9966	51	400	300			

Gloucestershire

Location	Hotel	Group	%	Room Price	Cat	Tel	Rooms	Conf	Banq	Leisure Centre	Swim Pool	Golf
Amberley	Amberley Inn		57%	£70	H	(0453) 872565	14	30	25			
Ampney Crucis	Crown of Crucis			£60	I	(0285) 851806	25	100	90			
Bibury	The Swan		78%	£128	HR	(0285) 740695	18	80	80			
Bourton-on-the-Water	Dial House		61%	£79	H	(0451) 22244	10					
Charingworth	Charingworth Manor		79%	£110	HR	(0386) 78555	24		36	yes		yes
Cheltenham	Cheltenham Park		68%	£114	H	(0242) 222021	154	350	275			yes
Cheltenham	Golden Valley Thistle	MtCT	69%	£90	HR	(0242) 232691	124	220	300		yes	
Cheltenham	The Greenway		80%	£110	H	(0242) 862352	19	30	20			
Cheltenham	Hotel de la Bere	Forte	64%	£82	H	(0242) 237771	57	100	80			
Cheltenham	On The Park		76%	£64	H	(0242) 518898	8	16	20			
Cheltenham	Queen's Hotel	Forte	69%	£109	H	(0242) 514724	74	200	200			
Cheltenham	Travel Inn	Whitbread		£43	L	(0242) 233847	40					
Chipping Campden	Cotswold House		70%	£95	HR	(0386) 840330	15	20	45			

County	Hotel	Chain	%	Price	Type	Telephone							
Chipping Campden	Noel Arms		61%	£78	H	(0386) 840317	26	50	60				
Chipping Campden	Seymour House	Jarvis	64%	£91	H	(0386) 840429	16	35	90	yes			
Cirencester	Fleece Hotel		64%	£90	H	(0285) 658507	30	60	60				
Cirencester	Stratton House		64%	£70	H	(0285) 651761	41	180	150				
Clearwell	Clearwell Castle		69%	£80	H	(0594) 832320	14	40	140				
Clearwell	Wyndham Arms			£60	I	(0594) 833666	17						
Corse Lawn	Corse Lawn House		71%	£90	HR	(0452) 780771	19	40	75				
Fairford	Bull Hotel		60%	£44	H	(0285) 712535	20	80	80				
Gloucester	Forte Crest		66%	£68	H	(0452) 613311	123	80	90				
Gloucester	Hatherley Manor		65%	£75	H	(0452) 730217	56	300	250				
Gloucester	Hatton Court		72%	£95	H	(0452) 617412	45	60	80				
Gloucester	Travel Inn	Whitbread		£43	L	(0452) 523519	40						
Gloucester	Travel Inn	Whitbread		£43	L	(0452) 862521	40						
Lower Slaughter	Lower Slaughter Manor		80%	£180	HR	(0451) 20456	14	24	30	yes			
Lower Swell	Old Farmhouse Hotel			£60	I	(0451) 830232	14	25	25				
Lower Wick	Forte Travelodge	Forte		£45	L	(0800) 850950							
Mickleton	Three Ways Hotel		59%	£68	H	(0386) 438429	41	90	110				
Moreton-in-Marsh	Manor House		66%	£75	H	(0608) 50501	39	95	100	yes			
Painswick	Painswick Hotel		70%	£97	H	(0452) 812160	20	40	70				
Puckrup	Puckrup Hall		75%	£97	HR	(0684) 296200	84	275	220				
Stonehouse	Stonehouse Court	Arcadian	68%	£75	H	(0453) 825155	36	120	120				
Stow-on-the-Wold	Fosse Manor Hotel		60%	£97	H	(0451) 830354	20	40	72				
Stow-on-the-Wold	Grapevine Hotel		67%	£98	H	(0451) 830344	23	70					
Stow-on-the-Wold	Unicorn Hotel	Forte	59%	£103	H	(0451) 830257	20	25					
Stow-on-the-Wold	Wyck Hill House		74%	£98	HR	(0451) 831936	31	50					
Tetbury	Calcot Manor		75%	£115	HR	(0666) 890391	20	40	60				
Tetbury	The Close		72%	£88	H	(0666) 502272	15	40	60				
Tetbury	Snooty Fox Hotel		69%	£95	H	(0666) 502436	12	25	50				
Tewkesbury	Royal Hop Pole Hotel	Forte	66%	£95	H	(0684) 293236	29	12					
Tewkesbury	Tewkesbury Park	Country Club	62%	£93	H	(0684) 295405	78	150	140	yes		yes	yes
Upper Slaughter	Lords of the Manor		75%	£115	HR	(0451) 820243	29	45	60			yes	yes
Westonbirt	Hare & Hounds		59%	£80	H	(0666) 880233	30	100	150				

Greater Manchester

Location	Hotel	Group	%	Room Price	Cat	Tel	Rooms	Conf	Banq	Leisure Centre	Swim Pool	Golf
Bolton	Beaumont Hotel	Forte	58%	£68	H	(0204) 651511	96	120	90			
Bolton	Egerton House	Macdonalds	63%	£88	H	(0204) 307171	32	150	150			
Bolton	Last Drop Village Hotel	Macdonalds	68%	£88	H	(0204) 591131	83	200	200	yes		yes
Bolton	Pack Horse Hotel	De Vere	62%	£65	H	(0204) 27261	72	375	230			
Bury	Normandie Hotel & Rest		64%	£83	HR	061-764 3869	23	18	70			
Manchester	Britannia Hotel	Hidden	66%	£123	H	061-228 2288	362	300	250		yes	
Manchester	Charterhouse Hotel		72%	£109	H	061-236 9999	58	180	130			
Manchester	Copthorne Hotel	Copthorne	70%	£128	H	061-873 7321	166	150	130	yes	yes	
Manchester	Forte Posthouse	Forte	60%	£68	H	061-998 7090	190	150	100			
Manchester	Granada Lodge	Granada		£51	L	061-655 3403	37					
Manchester	Holiday Inn Crowne Plaza	Holiday Inn	73%	£124	H	061-236 3333	303	700	700	yes	yes	
Manchester	Novotel	Novotel	62%	£65	H	061-799 3535	119	220	220			
Manchester	Jarvis Piccadilly	Jarvis	73%	£119	H	061-236 8414	271	700	700	yes	yes	
Manchester	Portland Thistle	MtCT	69%	£130	H	061-228 3400	205	300	250	yes	yes	
Manchester	Ramada Hotel		73%	£117	H	061-835 2555	200	350	400			
Manchester	Sachas Hotel		64%	£83	H	061-228 1234	223	650	650	yes	yes	
Manchester	Victoria & Albert Hotel	Granada	73%	£141	HR	061-832 1188	132	250	200			
Manchester Airport	Etrop Grange		66%	£111	H	061-499 0500	41	65	80			
Manchester Airport	Forte Crest	Forte	65%	£109	H	061-437 5811	290	200	120	yes	yes	
Manchester Airport	Four Seasons Hotel		68%	£121	H	061-904 0301	94	120	100			
Manchester Airport	Hilton International	Hilton	71%	£159	H	061-436 4404	222	300	220	yes	yes	
Manchester Airport	Moss Nook			£140	RR	061-437 4778	1					
Oldham	Travel Inn	Whitbread		£43	L	061-681 1373	40					
Standish	Almond Brook Moat House	QMH	63%	£89	H	(0257) 425588	122	150	120		yes	

Hampshire

Location	Hotel	Chain	%	Price	Cat	Phone	Rooms				
Alton	Forte Travelodge	Forte	61%	£45	L	(0420) 562659	31		120		
Alton	Grange Hotel		58%	£65	H	(0420) 86565	30	100	100		
Alton	The Swan	Forte		£88	H	(0420) 83777	36	100	100		
Ampfield	Potters Heron Hotel	Lansbury	60%	£80	H	(0703) 266611	54	140	120		
Andover	White Hart Inn			£79	I	(0264) 352266	20	70	70		
Barton Stacey	Forte Travelodge	Forte		£45	L	(0264) 720260	20		40		
Basingstoke	Audleys Wood	MtCT	75%	£125	HR	(0256) 817555	71	55	40		
Basingstoke	Forte Posthouse	Forte	64%	£68	H	(0256) 468181	84	180	180		
Basingstoke	Forte Travelodge	Forte		£45	L	(0256) 843566	32				
Basingstoke	Hilton National	Hilton	66%	£79	H	(0256) 460460	141	150	130		yes
Basingstoke	The Ringway	Hilton	65%	£64	H	(0256) 20212	134	140	140		yes
Basingstoke	Travel Inn	Whitbread		£43	L	(0256) 811477	49				
Beaulieu	Montagu Arms		67%	£96	H	(0590) 612324	24	45	120		yes
Brockenhurst	Balmer Lawn Hotel	Hilton	65%	£85	H	(0590) 23116	55	100	100		yes
Brockenhurst	Careys Manor		65%	£99	H	(0590) 23551	78	100	160	yes	
Brockenhurst	Rhinefield House	Voyager	68%	£105	H	(0590) 22922	34	150	100		
Buckler's Hard	Master Builder's House			£85	I	(0590) 616253	23	40	50		
Burley	Burley Manor		61%	£74	H	(0425) 403522	30	90	60		
Eastleigh	Forte Travelodge	Forte		£45	L	(0703) 616813	32				
Eastleigh	Forte Posthouse Southampton	Forte	66%	£68	H	(0703) 619700	120	250	160		yes
Emsworth	Forte Travelodge	Forte		£45	L	(0800) 850950					
Fareham	Forte Posthouse	Forte	61%	£68	H	(0329) 844644	126	140	120	yes	yes
Fareham	Forte Travelodge	Forte		£55	L	(0329) 822640	43	80	100		
Fareham	Red Lion		75%	£108	H	(0489) 880000	90	250	250		yes
Farnborough	Solent Hotel	Shire Inns	66%	£99	H	(0252) 545051	110	150	120	yes	yes
Fleet	Forte Crest	Forte	59%	£45	L	(0252) 815578	40				
Fleet	Forte Travelodge	Forte		£60	H			140	120	yes	yes
Havant	Bear Hotel		62%	£68	H	(0705) 486501	42	80	100		yes
Havant	Forte Posthouse	Forte		£68	H	(0705) 465011	92	140	120	yes	yes
Hurstbourne Tarrant	Eseborne Manor		72%	£112	HR	(0264) 736444	12	12	40		
Lymington	Gordleton Mill		65%	£80	HR	(0590) 682219	7	30	70	yes	
Lymington	Passford House		70%	£110	H	(0590) 682398	55	80	150		yes

Location	Hotel	Group	%	Room Price	Cat	Tel	Rooms	Conf	Banq	Leisure Centre	Swim Pool	Golf
Lymington	Stanwell House	Arcadian	65%	£75	H	(0590) 677123	37	100	100			
Lyndhurst	The Crown		65%	£89	H	(0703) 282922	40	50	80			
Lyndhurst	Lyndhurst Park		63%	£60	H	(0703) 283923	59	500	300			
Lyndhurst	Parkhill Hotel		69%	£95	HR	(0703) 282944	20	60	120			
Middle Wallop	Fifehead Manor		61%	£80	H	(0264) 781565	16	40	25			
Milford-on-Sea	South Lawn		66%	£84	H	(0590) 643911	24		70			
New Alresford	Hunters			£48	RR	(0962) 732468	3					
New Milton	Chewton Glen		89%	£207	HR	(0425) 275341	58	110	120	yes	yes	yes
Odiham	George Hotel			£72	I	(0256) 702081	18	10	56			
Petersfield	Langrish House		63%	£55	H	(0730) 266941	18	60	100			
Portsmouth	Forte Posthouse	Forte	65%	£68	H	(0705) 827651	163	220	180	yes	yes	
Portsmouth	Hilton National	Hilton	66%	£70	H	(0705) 219111	118	230	200	yes	yes	
Portsmouth	Hospitality Inn	MtCT	61%	£79	H	(0705) 731281	115	250	250			
Portsmouth	Pendragon Hotel	Forte	59%	£49	H	(0705) 823201	49	100	100			
Portsmouth	Portsmouth Marriott Hotel	Marriott	73%	£96	H	(0705) 383151	170	450	450	yes	yes	
Romsey	White Horse Hotel	Forte	63%	£102	H	(0794) 512431	33	40	90			
Rotherwick	Tylney Hall		79%	£114	HR	(0256) 764881	91	150	100	yes	yes	
Silchester	Romans Hotel		64%	£80	H	(0734) 700421	24	50	45			
Southampton	Dolphin Hotel	Forte	60%	£82	H	(0703) 339955	73	90	120			
Southampton	Forte Posthouse	Forte	58%	£68	H	(0703) 330777	128	200	200	yes	yes	
Southampton	Hilton National	Hilton	68%	£94	H	(0703) 702700	135	220	150		yes	
Southampton	Novotel	Novotel	62%	£65	H	(0703) 330550	121	450	350		yes	
Southampton	Polygon Hotel	Forte	65%	£72	H	(0703) 330055	119	500	400			
Southampton	Southampton Park Hotel		64%	£66	H	(0703) 223467	72	200	150	yes	yes	
Southampton	Travel Inn	Whitbread		£43	L	(0703) 732262	32					
Stockbridge	Grosvenor Hotel		57%	£70	H	(0264) 810606	25	70	70			
Stratfield Turgis	Wellington Arms			£60	I	(0256) 882214	35	80	60			
Sutton Scotney North	Forte Travelodge	Forte		£45	L	(0962) 761016	31					
Sutton Scotney South	Forte Travelodge	Forte		£45	L	(0962) 760779	40					
Wickham	Old House Hotel		66%	£80	HR	(0329) 833049	12	10	40			

Winchester	Forte Crest	Forte	69%	£89	H	(0962) 861611	94	100	84		
Winchester	Lainston House		75%	£140	H	(0962) 863588	37	80	90		
Winchester	Royal Hotel		67%	£85	H	(0962) 840840	75	150	120		
Winchester	Wykeham Arms			£75	IR	(0962) 853834	7	10			

Isle of Wight

Bonchurch	Winterbourne Hotel		64%	£86	H	(0983) 852535	17		35		
Calbourne	Swainston Manor		66%	£76	H	(0983) 521121	17	250	250		yes
Freshwater	Farringford Hotel		57%	£88	H	(0983) 752500	19	30	110		
Seaview	Seaview Hotel		62%	£60	HR	(0983) 612711	16				
Shanklin	Cliff Tops Hotel		64%	£99	H	(0983) 863262	88	250	200	yes	
Ventnor	Royal Hotel		60%	£66	H	(0983) 852186	54	40	40		yes

Hereford & Worcester

Abberley	Elms Hotel	QMH	70%	£118	H	(0299) 896666	25	60	75		
Abbot's Salford	Salford Hall		66%	£95	H	(0386) 871300	34		65		
Brimfield	Poppies Restaurant			£60	RR	(0584) 711230	3				
Broadway	Broadway Hotel		60%	£64	H	(0386) 852401	20	20			
Broadway	Collin House		65%	£86	HR	(0386) 858354	7		34		
Broadway	Dormy House		69%	£106	HR	(0386) 852711	49	200	160		
Broadway	Lygon Arms	Savoy Group	80%	£172	HR	(0386) 852255	65	80	96		
Bromsgrove	Grafton Manor		70%	£125	HR	(0527) 579007	9	12	45		yes
Bromsgrove	Perry Hall	Jarvis	56%	£82	H	(0527) 579976	58	70	100		
Bromsgrove	Pine Lodge Hotel		64%	£95	H	(0527) 576600	114	200	200		
Bromsgrove	Stakis Country Court	Stakis	69%	£120	H	021-447 7888	140	80	60	yes	
Buckland	Buckland Manor		80%	£178	HR	(0386) 852626	13				
Chaddesley Corbett	Brockencote Hall		75%	£90	HR	(0562) 777876	17	20	45		
Droitwich	Chateau Impney		70%	£70	H	(0905) 774411	120	1,000	400	yes	yes
Droitwich	Forte Travelodge	Forte		£45	L	(0527) 86545	32				

Location	Hotel	Group	%	Room Price	Cat	Tel	Rooms	Conf	Banq	Leisure Centre	Swim Pool	Golf
Droitwich Spa	Raven Hotel		66%	£130	H	(0905) 772224	72	150	250			
Evesham	Evesham Hotel		65%	£92	HR	(0386) 765566	40	12	12		yes	
Evesham	Riverside Hotel		68%	£80	HR	(0386) 446200	7					
Eyton	Marsh Country Hotel		65%	£100	HR	(0568) 613952	5	36	24			
Hartlebury	Forte Travelodge	Forte		£45	L	(0299) 250553	32					
Harvington	The Mill at Harvington		65%	£85	HR	(0386) 870688	15	40	40			
Hereford	Moat House	QMH	63%	£83	H	(0432) 354301	60	300	250			
Hereford	Travel Inn	Whitbread		£43	L	(0432) 274853	40					
Kidderminster	Stone Manor		65%	£68	H	(0562) 777555	52	150	250			
Kington	Penrhos Court			£100	RR	(0544) 230720	19	70	70			
Ledbury	The Feathers			£79	I	(0531) 635266	11	150	130			
Ledbury	Hope End		70%	£120	HR	(0531) 633613	9					
Malvern	Abbey Hotel	De Vere	62%	£75	H	(0684) 892332	107	350	300			
Malvern	Colwall Park Hotel		62%	£86	H	(0684) 540206	20	120	100			
Malvern	The Cottage in the Wood		65%	£95	HR	(0684) 573487	20	18	14			
Malvern	Foley Arms		61%	£78	H	(0684) 573397	28	150	100			
Much Birch	Pilgrim Hotel		64%	£90	H	(0981) 540742	20	45				
Redditch	Campanile Hotel	Campanile		£44	L	(0527) 510710	50					
Ross-on-Wye	Chase Hotel		64%	£75	H	(0989) 763161	39	300	300			
Ross-on-Wye	Forte Travelodge	Forte		£45	L	(0800) 850950						
Ross-on-Wye	Pengethley Manor		67%	£115	H	(0989) 730211	25	50	75			yes
Ross-on-Wye	Pheasants			£40	I	(0989) 565751	2					
Ruckhall	Ancient Camp Inn			£48	I	(0981) 250449	5					
Stourport-on-Severn	Moat House	QMH	62%	£73	H	(0299) 827733	68	250	350			
Weobley	Ye Olde Salutation Inn		70%	£54	I	(0544) 318443	4					
Worcester	Fownes Hotel	Jarvis	70%	£85	H	(0905) 613151	61	120	120			yes
Worcester	Giffard Hotel	Forte	61%	£56	H	(0905) 726262	103	150	120			

Hertfordshire

Town	Hotel	Group	%	£	Class	Phone	Rooms					
Baldock	Forte Travelodge	Forte		£45	L	(0462) 835329	40					
Broxbourne	Cheshunt Marriott Hotel	Marriott	66%	£80	H	(0992) 451245	150	200	140	yes	yes	
Dane End	Green End Park		62%	£88	H	(0920) 438344	9	100	120			
Hadley Wood	West Lodge Park Hotel		66%	£112	HR	081-440 8311	45	80	65			
Harpenden	Glen Eagle Hotel		63%	£87	H	(0582) 760271	50	80	130			
Harpenden	Moat House	QMH	68%	£113	H	(0582) 764111	53	170	120			
Hatfield Heath	Down Hall		71%	£126	H	(0279) 731441	103	290	270		yes	
Hemel Hempstead	Boxmoor Lodge		57%	£60	H	(0442) 230770	20	40	64			
Hemel Hempstead	Forte Posthouse	Forte	62%	£67	H	(0442) 251122	146	60	50	yes	yes	
Hemel Hempstead	Travel Inn			£43	L	(0442) 879149	60					
Herringfordbury	White Horse Hotel	Forte	63%	£107	H	(0992) 586791	42	40	25			
Letchworth	Broadway Toby Hotel		59%	£60	H	(0462) 480111	35	180	180			
Markyate	Hertfordshire Moat House	QMH	57%	£78	H	(0582) 840840	89	300	300			
Rushden	Forte Travelodge	Forte		£45	L	(0933) 57008	40					
St Albans	Noke Thistle	MtCT	68%	£90	H	(0727) 854252	111	60	55			
St Albans	St Michael's Manor		63%	£94	H	(0727) 864444	22	36	110			
St Albans	Sopwell House		69%	£124	H	(0727) 864477	92	400	350			
Sawbridgeworth	Manor of Groves		70%	£103	H	(0279) 600777	32	80	140		yes	yes
South Mimms	Forte Posthouse	Forte	60%	£68	H	(0707) 643311	120	170	120	yes	yes	
South Mimms	Forte Travelodge	Forte		£45	L	(0707) 665440	52					
Stansted Abbots	Briggens House	QMH	70%	£106	H	(0279) 792416	54	100	100			
Stevenage	Forte Posthouse	Forte	58%	£67	H	(0438) 365444	54	60	45			
Stevenage	Novotel	Novotel	60%	£65	H	(0438) 742299	100	150	120			
Stevenage	Travel Inn	Whitbread		£43	L	(0438) 351318	40					
Thundridge	Hanbury Manor		85%	£161	HR	(0920) 487722	96	100	100	yes	yes	yes
Tring	Travel Inn	Whitbread		£43	L	(0442) 824819	30					
Watford	Hilton National	Hilton	64%	£105	H	(0923) 235881	195	500	400	yes	yes	yes
Watford	Jarvis International	Jarvis	60%	£109	H	081-950 6211	160	250	250	yes	yes	
Welwyn	Clock Hotel	Friendly	54%	£73	H	(0438) 716911	95	200	300			

Humberside

Location	Hotel	Group	%	Room Price	Cat	Tel	Rooms	Conf	Banq	Leisure Centre	Swim Pool	Golf
Beverley	Beverley Arms	Forte	62%	£80	H	(0482) 869241	57	60	60			
Bridlington	Expanse Hotel		60%	£59	H	(0262) 675347	48	81	120			
Cleethorpes	Kingsway Hotel		62%	£75	H	(0472) 601122	50	15	24			
Driffield	Bell Hotel			£75	I	(0377) 256661	14	250	280			
Grimsby	Forte Posthouse	Forte	64%	£68	H	(0472) 350295	52	250	250		yes	
Hull	Campanile Hotel	Campanile		£44	L	(0482) 25530	50					
Hull	Forte Crest	Forte	69%	£109	H	(0482) 225221	99	120	120	yes	yes	
Hull	Forte Posthouse	Forte	62%	£68	H	(0482) 645212	95	100	100			
Hull	Travel Inn	Whitbread		£43	L	(0482) 645285	40					
Pocklington	Feathers Hotel			£50	I	(0759) 303155	12	85	60			
South Cave	Forte Travelodge	Forte	62%	£45	L	(0430) 424455	40					
Tickton	Tickton Grange		72%	£60	H	(0964) 543666	18	86	86			
Walkington	Manor House		67%	£93	HR	(0482) 881645	7	50	40			
Willerby	Grange Park		62%	£86	H	(0482) 656488	104	500	500	yes	yes	
Willerby	Willerby Manor			£89	H	(0482) 652616	38	500	400			
Winteringham	Winteringham Fields			£92	RR	(0724) 733096	7					

Kent

Location	Hotel	Group	%	Room Price	Cat	Tel	Rooms	Conf	Banq	Leisure Centre	Swim Pool	Golf
Ashford	Ashford International	QMH	71%	£98	H	(0233) 611444	200	400	400	yes	yes	
Ashford	Eastwell Manor	QMH	81%	£110	HR	(0233) 635751	23	85	80			
Ashford	Forte Posthouse	Forte	66%	£68	H	(0233) 625790	60	120	100			
Ashford	Holiday Inn Garden Court	Holiday Inns	65%	£72	H	(0233) 713333	104	30				
Ashford	Travel Inn	Whitbread		£43	L	(0233) 712571	40					
Bearsted	Tudor Park	Country Club	67%	£109	H	(0622) 734334	120	278	216	yes	yes	yes
Bexley	Forte Posthouse	Forte	56%	£68	H	(0322) 526900	102	80	60			
Bexleyheath	Swallow Hotel	Swallow	71%	£96	H	081-298 1000	142	250	250	yes	yes	yes
Boughton Monchelsea	Tanyard Hotel		63%	£80	HR	(0622) 744705	6				yes	

County	Hotel	Group	%	£	Type	Phone	Rooms					
Brands Hatch	Brands Hatch Thistle	MtCT	70%	£80	H	(0474) 854900	137	270	250			
Bromley	Bromley Court		66%	£89	H	081-464 5011	120	150	200			
Canterbury	Canterbury Hotel		58%	£50	H	(0227) 450551	27	40	25			
Canterbury	Chaucer Hotel	Forte	61%	£97	H	(0227) 464427	42	100	100			
Canterbury	County Hotel		68%	£100	HR	(0227) 766266	73	180	130			
Canterbury	Ebury Hotel		59%	£60	H	(0227) 768433	15				yes	
Canterbury	Falstaff Hotel	Lansbury	68%	£85	I	(0227) 462138	24	50	50			
Canterbury	Howfield Manor		68%	£83	H	(0227) 738294	13	100	90			
Canterbury	Slatters Hotel	QMH	57%	£87	H	(0227) 463271	31	100	100			
Chartham	Thruxted Oast			£73	PH	(0227) 730080	3					
Cranbrook	Hartley Mount		62%	£70	H	(0580) 712230	7	20	65			
Cranbrook	Kennel Holt Hotel		66%	£105	H	(0580) 712032	9	30	25			
Dover	Forte Posthouse	Forte	63%	£68	H	(0304) 821222	67	50	50			
Dover	Moat House	QMH	66%	£84	H	(0304) 203270	79	150	120	yes		
Dover	Travel Inn	Whitbread		£43	L	(0304) 213339	30					
Fawkham	Brandshatch Place	Arcadian	65%	£90	I	(0474) 872239	29	100	100	yes	yes	
Goudhurst	Star & Eagle Inn			£45	I	(0580) 211512	11	20	60			
Hawkhurst	Tudor Court		61%	£66	H	(0580) 752312	18	70	60			
Hollingbourne	Jarvis Great Danes	Jarvis	64%	£102	H	(0622) 631163	126	600	320	yes	yes	yes
Hythe	Hythe Imperial		71%	£105	H	(0303) 267441	100	200	140	yes	yes	yes
Hythe	Stade Court		62%	£80	H	(0303) 268263	42	60	100			
Lenham	Chilston Park		71%	£95	H	(0622) 859803	40	120	120			
Maidstone	Larkfield Priory	Forte	62%	£58	H	(0732) 846858	52	100	65			
Maidstone	Stakis Country Court Hotel	Stakis	67%	£110	H	(0622) 734422	139	100	60	yes		
Maidstone	Travel Inn	Whitbread		£43	L	(0622) 752515	40					
Rochester	Bridgewood Manor Hotel		68%	£105	H	(0634) 201333	100	150	150	yes	yes	
Rochester	Forte Posthouse	Forte	62%	£68	H	(0634) 687111	105	40	80	yes	yes	
St Margaret's	Wallett's Court		60%	£50	HR	(0304) 852424	10					
Sevenoaks	Royal Oak		66%	£70	HR	(0732) 451109	39	35	100			
Shorne	Inn on the Lake		61%	£70	H	(0732) 823333	78	700	500			
Tonbridge	Goldhill Mill			£65	PH	(0732) 851626	3					
Tonbridge	Rose & Crown	Forte	59%	£79	H	(0732) 357966	48	120	80			
Tunbridge Wells	Royal Wells Inn		64%	£80	H	(0892) 511188	20	90	90			
Tunbridge Wells	Spa Hotel		72%	£84	HR	(0892) 520331	76	300	200	yes		

Location	Hotel	Group	%	Room Price	Cat	Tel	Rooms	Conf	Banq	Leisure Centre	Swim Pool	Golf
Wateringbury	Wateringbury Hotel	Forte	59%	£61	H	(0622) 812632	40	80	80			
Wrotham Heath	Forte Posthouse Maidstone	Whitbread	67%	£68	H	(0732) 883311	106	60	60	yes	yes	yes
Wrotham Heath	Travel Inn			£43	L	(0732) 884214					yes	

Lancashire

Location	Hotel	Group	%	Room Price	Cat	Tel	Rooms	Conf	Banq	Leisure Centre	Swim Pool	Golf
Blackburn	Moat House	QMH	58%	£65	H	(0254) 264441	98	350	300			
Blackpool	Imperial Hotel	Forte	64%	£89	H	(0253) 23971	183	550	450	yes	yes	
Blackpool	Pembroke Hotel	Metropole	67%	£93	H	(0253) 23434	274	900	650		yes	
Broughton	Broughton Park	Country Club	65%	£93	HR	(0772) 864087	98	250	220		yes	
Burnley	Forte Travelodge	Forte		£45	L	(0282) 416039	32					
Burnley	Oaks Hotel	Shire Inns	63%	£88	H	(0282) 414141	56	150	120	yes	yes	
Charnock Richard	Forte Travelodge	Forte		£45	L	(0257) 791746	100					
Chipping	Gibbon Bridge Country House		70%	£70	H	(0995) 61456	30	70	200			
Clayton-le-Woods	Pines Hotel		65%	£55	H	(0772) 38551	39	100	230			
Cowan Bridge	Cobwebs			£60	RR	(052 42) 72141	5					
Cowan Bridge	Hipping Hall		64%	£74	H	(052 42) 71187	7	14	20			
Lancaster	Forte Posthouse	Forte	69%	£68	H	(0524) 65999	115	120	100	yes	yes	
Langho	Northcote Manor		67%	£75	HR	(0254) 240555	14	40	100			
Lytham	Clifton Arms		63%	£76	H	(0253) 739898	42	150	150			
Lytham St Annes	Dalmeny Hotel		60%	£69	HR	(0253) 712236	91	200	200	yes	yes	
Mellor	Millstone Hotel	Shire Inns		£88	I	(0254) 813333	19	30	60			
Preston	Forte Posthouse	Forte	63%	£68	H	(0772) 259411	121	120	100			
Preston	Novotel	Novotel	62%	£55	H	(0772) 313331	98	180	130			
Preston	Travel Inn	Whitbread		£43	L	(0772) 720476	40					
Samlesbury	Swallow Trafalgar	Swallow	60%	£95	H	(0772) 877351	78	250	180	yes	yes	
Samlesbury	Tickled Trout	Macdonalds	63%	£95	H	(0772) 877671	72	100	100		yes	
Slaidburn	Hark to Bounty Inn			£40	I	(0200) 446246	8	50	50			
Thornton-le-Fylde	River House			£100	RR	(0253) 883497	5		40			
Whitewell	Inn at Whitewell			£60	I	(020 08) 222	10	200	150			
Worthington	Kilhey Court	Principal	65%	£95	H	(0257) 472100	55	180	350			yes

Leicestershire

Town	Hotel	Group	Rating	Cat	Phone	Price	Rooms				
Hinckley	Hinckley Island Hotel		64%	H	(0455) 631122	£89	270	400	350	yes	
Leicester	Belmont Hotel		65%	H	(0533) 544773	£89	65	150	120	yes	
Leicester	Forte Posthouse	Forte	64%	H	(0533) 630500	£68	172	100	100		
Leicester	Granada Lodge	Granada		L	(0530) 244237	£51	39				
Leicester	Holiday Inn	Holiday Inns	72%	H	(0533) 531161	£114	188	300	280	yes	
Leicester	Jarvis Grand Hotel	Jarvis	66%	H	(0533) 555599	£106	92	450	450	yes	
Leicester	Leicester Forest Moat House	QMH	58%	H	(0533) 394661	£79	34	65	80		
Leicester	Stakis Country Court	Stakis	69%	H	(0533) 630066	£106	141	90	70	yes	yes
Lockington	Hilton National E Midlands	Hilton	69%	H	(0509) 674000	£113	152	300	200	yes	yes
Loughborough	Friendly Hotel	Friendly	63%	H	(0509) 211800	£96	94	225	200	yes	yes
Loughborough	King's Head	Jarvis	58%	H	(0509) 233222	£96	78	120	120		
Lutterworth	Denbigh Arms	Jarvis	66%	H	(0455) 553537	£65	34	60	50		
Market Harborough	Three Swans Hotel		65%	H	(0858) 466644	£72	36	100	85		
Melton Mowbray	George Hotel		57%	H	(0664) 62112	£45	22	35	78		
Oakham	Barnsdale Lodge Hotel		65%	HR	(0572) 724678	£70	17	300	300		
Oakham	Hambleton Hall		84%	HR	(0572) 756991	£147	15	30	60		
Oakham	Whipper-In Hotel		66%	HR	(0572) 756971	£94	24	50	60		
Quorn	Quorn Grange		67%	HR	(0509) 412167	£94	17	120	170		
Quorn	The Quorn Country Hotel		72%	H	(0509) 415050	£92	19	100	150		
Rothley	Rothley Court	Forte	67%	H	(0533) 374141	£100	36	100	150		
Stapleford	Stapleford Park		86%	HR	(0572) 787522	£142	42	200	150		
Stretton	Ram Jam Inn			IR	(0780) 410776	£57	7	40			
Thrussington	Forte Travelodge	Forte		L	(0664) 424525	£45	32				
Uppingham	Forte Travelodge	Forte		L	(0572) 87719	£45	40				
Uppingham	The Lake Isle			RR	(0572) 822951	£66	12	10			

Lincolnshire

Town	Hotel	Group	Rating	Cat	Phone	Price	Rooms				
Belton	Belton Woods Hotel	De Vere	72%	H	(0476) 593200	£115	136	350	350	yes	yes
Colsterworth	Forte Travelodge	Forte		L	(0476) 861181	£45	32				
Grantham	Forte Travelodge	Forte		L	(0476) 77500	£45	40				

Location	Hotel	Group	%	Room Price	Cat	Tel	Rooms	Conf	Banq	Leisure Centre	Swim Pool	Golf
Grantham	Granada Lodge	Granada		£39	L	(0476) 860686	38					
Grantham	Swallow Hotel	Swallow	67%	£98	H	(0476) 593000	90	200	160	yes	yes	
Lincoln	D'Isney Place		63%	£62	PH	(0522) 538881	17					
Lincoln	Forte Posthouse	Forte		£68	H	(0522) 520341	70	80	80			
Lincoln	Travel Inn	Whitbread		£43	L	(0522) 525216	40					
Lincoln	White Hart	Forte	69%	£100	H	(0522) 526222	48	90	120			
Sleaford	Forte Travelodge	Forte		£45	L	(0529) 414752	40					
South Witham	Forte Travelodge	Forte		£45	L	(0572) 767586	32					
Stamford	The George of Stamford	Poste Hotels	72%	£100	HR	(0780) 55171	47	45	90			
Woodhall Spa	Dower House		62%	£60	H	(0526) 352588	7	20	26			

Merseyside

Location	Hotel	Group	%	Room Price	Cat	Tel	Rooms	Conf	Banq	Leisure Centre	Swim Pool	Golf
Bebington	Forte Travelodge	Forte		£45	L	051-327 2489	31					
Birkenhead	Bowler Hat Hotel		65%	£70	H	051-652 4931	32	240	250			
Bromborough	Travel Inn			£43	L	051-334 2917	32					
Gayton	Travel Inn	Whitbread		£43	L	051-342 1982	37					
Haydock	Forte Posthouse	Forte	65%	£68	H	(0942) 717878	136	200	200	yes	yes	
Haydock	Forte Travelodge	Forte		£45	L	(0942) 272055	40					
Haydock	Haydock Thistle	MtCT	67%	£107	H	(0942) 272000	139	300	220	yes	yes	
Liverpool	Atlantic Tower	MtCT	65%	£105	H	051-227 4444	226	120	150	yes	yes	
Liverpool	Britannia Adelphi Hotel		68%	£94	H	051-709 7200	391	1,000	700	yes	yes	
Liverpool	Campanile Hotel	Campanile		£44	L	051-709 8104	82					
Liverpool	Gladstone Hotel	Forte	60%	£91	H	051-709 7050	154	600	400			
Liverpool	Moat House	QMH	67%	£105	H	051-709 0181	251	450	300	yes	yes	
Liverpool	St George's Hotel	Forte	58%	£62	H	051-709 7090	155	300	280			
Liverpool	Trials Hotel		65%	£105	L	051-227 1021	20	140	90			
Liverpool (West Derby)	Travel Inn	Whitbread		£43	L	051-228 4724	40					

Location	Hotel	Group	Occ.	Price	Class	Telephone	Rooms				
Southport	New Bold Hotel		58%	£51	H	(0704) 532578	23				
Southport	Prince of Wales Hotel	Forte	65%	£74	H	(0704) 536688	104	450	350		

Middlesex

Location	Hotel	Group	Occ.	Price	Class	Telephone	Rooms				
Hayes	Travel Inn	Whitbread		£43	L	081-573 7479	40				
Heathrow Airport	Excelsior Hotel Forte		71%	£110	H	081-759 6611	839	800	800	yes	yes
Heathrow Airport	Forte Crest	Forte	68%	£105	H	081-759 2323	572	200	200	yes	
Heathrow Airport	Forte Posthouse (Ariel)	Forte	65%	£68	L	081-759 2552	186	12			
Heathrow Airport	Granada Lodge	Granada		£63	L	081-574 5875	46				
Heathrow Airport	Heathrow Hilton Hotel	Hilton	74%	£167	HR	081-759 7755	400	240	200	yes	yes
Heathrow Airport	Holiday Inn Crowne Plaza	Holiday Inns	74%	£167	H	(0895) 445555	374	220	170	yes	yes
Heathrow Airport	Jarvis Berkeley Inter	Jarvis	67%	£85	H	081-897 2121	56	120	120		
Heathrow Airport	Park Hotel	MtCT	61%	£111	H	081-759 2400	306	600	1,000		
Heathrow Airport	Radisson Edwardian Inter	Edwardian	76%	£184	H	081-759 6311	459	520	300	yes	yes
Heathrow Airport	Ramada Hotel Heathrow		66%	£115	H	081-897 6363	638	550	450	yes	yes
Heathrow Airport	Sheraton Skyline	Sheraton	73%	£174	H	081-759 2535	353	500	500	yes	yes
Heathrow Airport	Sheraton Heathrow Hotel	Sheraton	70%	£210	H	081-759 2424	440	80	70		
Kenton	Travel Inn	Whitbread	61%	£43	L	081-907 1671	43				
Shepperton	Moat House	QMH		£118	H	(0932) 241404	180	300	300		
Shepperton	Warren Lodge			£82	I	(0932) 242972	50	18	65		
Wembley	Hilton National	Hilton	65%	£139	H	081-902 8839	306	350	350		

Norfolk

Location	Hotel	Group	Occ.	Price	Class	Telephone	Rooms				
Acle	Forte Travelodge	Forte	62%	£45	L	(0493) 751970	40				
Barnham Broom	Barnham Broom Hotel		64%	£82	H	(0603) 759393	52	200	250	yes	yes
Blakeney	Blakeney Hotel		58%	£106	H	(0263) 740797	60	200	120	yes	yes
Blakeney	Manor Hotel			£56	H	(0263) 740376	37	12	60		
Burnham Market	Hoste Arms			£72	I	(0328) 738257	15	30	70		
Cawston	Grey Gables			£54	RR	(0603) 871259	8		24		
East Dereham	King's Head			£47	I	(0362) 693842	15	60	45		

Location	Hotel	Group	%	Room Price	Cat	Tel	Rooms	Conf	Banq	Leisure Centre	Swim Pool	Golf
East Dereham	Phoenix Hotel	Forte	59%	£78	H	(0362) 692276	22	150	120			
Erpingham	The Ark			£90	RR	(0263) 761535	3					
Great Snoring	Old Rectory		61%	£87	H	(0328) 820597	6					
Great Yarmouth	Carlton Hotel		67%	£79	H	(0493) 855234	95	150	140			
Grimston	Congham Hall		75%	£110	HR	(0485) 600250	14		50			
Hethersett	Park Farm		64%	£70	H	(0603) 810264	37	150	100		yes	
King's Lynn	Butterfly Hotel	Butterfly	62%	£62	H	(0553) 771707	70	50	15	yes		
King's Lynn	Duke's Head	Forte	60%	£88	H	(0553) 774996	71	330	230			
King's Lynn	Knights Hill Hotel		64%	£89	H	(0553) 675566	52	350	180	yes	yes	
Long Sutton	Forte Travelodge	Forte		£45	L	(0406) 362230	40					
Morston	Morston Hall		73%	£130	H	(0263) 741041	4					
Norwich	Forte Travelodge	Forte		£45	L	(0603) 57549						
Norwich	Forte Posthouse	Forte	63%	£68	H	(0603) 56431	116	100	70	yes	yes	
Norwich	Friendly Hotel	Friendly	60%	£83	H	(0603) 741161	80	200	200	yes	yes	
Norwich	Hotel Nelson		65%	£83	H	(0603) 760260	132	90	90		yes	
Norwich	Hotel Norwich		62%	£69	H	(0603) 787260	108	340	260	yes	yes	
Norwich	Norwich Sport Village Hotel		63%	£69	H	(0603) 788898	55	2,000	1,500	yes	yes	yes
Norwich	Sprowston Manor		69%	£102	H	(0603) 410871	97	150	100	yes	yes	
Norwich Airport	Stakis Ambassador Hotel	Stakis	65%	£79	H	(0603) 410544	108	500	350	yes	yes	
Ormesby St Margaret	Ormesby Lodge		58%	£46	H	(0493) 730481	8		90			
Scole	Scole Inn			£63	I	(0379) 740481	23	50	50			
Shipdham	Shipdham Place		64%	£65	H	(0362) 820303	8	20	20			
Thetford	The Bell	Forte	62%	£83	H	(0842) 754455	47	80	60			
West Runton	Links Country Park Hotel		62%	£165	H	(0263) 838383	40	200	150		yes	

Northamptonshire

Location	Hotel	Group	%	Room Price	Cat	Tel	Rooms	Conf	Banq	Leisure Centre	Swim Pool	Golf
Castle Ashby	Falcon Inn			£75	I	(0604) 696200	14	30	40			
Corby	Carlton Manor Hotel		65%	£88	H	(0536) 401020	68	190	180	yes	yes	

Location	Hotel	Group	%		Phone					
Corby	Rockingham Forest Hotel	Forte	60%	H	(0536) 401348	69	250	250		
Crick	Forte Posthouse Northampton	Forte	64%	H	(0788) 822101	88	185	120	yes	yes
Daventry	Daventry Resort Hotel	Jarvis	70%	H	(0327) 301777	138	600	350	yes	yes
Desborough	Forte Travelodge	Forte		L	(0536) 762034	32				
Kettering	Kettering Park Hotel	Shire Inns	71%	H	(0536) 416666	88	250	200	yes	yes
Northampton	Courtyard by Marriott	Marriott	65%	H	(0604) 22777	104	30	60		
Northampton	Forte Travelodge	Forte		L	(0604) 758395	40				
Northampton	Moat House	QMH	63%	H	(0604) 22441	142	600	500		
Northampton	Stakis Country Court	Stakis	68%	H	(0604) 700666	139	320	200	yes	yes
Northampton	Swallow Hotel	Swallow	72%	H	(0604) 768700	120	220	200	yes	yes
Northampton	Travel Inn	Whitbread		L	(0604) 832340	51				
Northampton	Westone Moat House	QMH	59%	H	(0604) 406262	66	180	180		
Oundle	Talbot Hotel	Forte	62%	H	(0832) 273621	39	100	100		
Paulerspury	Vine House			RR	(0327) 811267	6	12	30		
Thrapston	Forte Travelodge	Forte		L	(0832) 735199	40				
Towcester	Forte Travelodge	Forte		L	(0327) 359105	33				
Weedon	Crossroads Hotel	Forte	55%	H	(0327) 340354	48	50	120		

Northumberland

Location	Hotel	Group	%		Phone					
Alnwick	White Swan		58%	H	(0665) 602109	58	150	120		
Bamburgh	Lord Crewe Arms		63%	H	(0668) 214243	25		60		
Belford	Blue Bell Hotel		66%	H	(0668) 213543	17	120	80		
Berwick-upon-Tweed	Kings Arms		59%	H	(0289) 307454	36	180	200		
Chollerford	George Hotel	Swallow	59%	H	(0434) 681611	50	70	100	yes	
Cornhill-on-Tweed	Tillmouth Park		68%	H	(0890) 882255	13		80		
Hexham	Beaumont Hotel		62%	H	(0434) 602331	23	100	100		
Langley-on-Tyne	Langley Castle		65%	H	(0434) 688888	10	160	120		
Longhorsley	Linden Hall		75%	H	(0670) 516611	54	300	300		yes
Powburn	Breamish Country House Hotel		67%	H	(0665) 578266	11	15	40		
Seahouses	Olde Ship Hotel			I	(0665) 720200	15		30		
Wylam	Laburnum House			RR	(0661) 852185	4				

Nottinghamshire

Location	Hotel	Group	%	Room Price	Cat	Tel	Rooms	Conf	Banq	Leisure Centre	Swim Pool	Golf
Barnby Moor	Ye Olde Bell	Principal	60%	£68	H	(0777) 705121	55	250	200			
Blyth	Forte Travelodge	Forte		£45	L	(0909) 591775	32					
Blyth	Granada Lodge	Granada		£51	L	(0909) 591836	39					
Langar	Langar Hall		70%	£80	HR	(0949) 60559	12	20	50			
Long Eaton	Sleep Inn			£50	L	(0602) 460000	101	75				
Nether Langwith	Goff's Restaurant			£53	RR	(0623) 744538	2	20	40			
Newark	Grange Hotel		58%	£53	H	(0636) 703399	15	20	44			
Newark-on-Trent	Forte Travelodge	Forte		£45	L	(0636) 703635	30					
Nottingham	Forte Posthouse	Forte	61%	£68	H	(0602) 397800	91	50	50			
Nottingham	Forte Crest	Forte	70%	£95	H	(0602) 470131	130	600	600			
Nottingham	Holiday Inn Garden Court	Holiday Inns	65%	£80	H	(0602) 500600	100	50	20			
Nottingham	Moat House	QMH	59%	£90	H	(0602) 602621	172	200	160			
Nottingham	Novotel	Novotel	62%	£70	H	(0602) 720106	105	200	120			
Nottingham	Royal Moat House	QMH	70%	£107	H	(0602) 414444	201	600	500			
Nottingham	Rutland Square Hotel		69%	£78	H	(0602) 411114	104	300	200			
Nottingham	Stakis Victoria Hotel	Stakis	62%	£92	H	(0602) 419561	166	200	200			
Nottingham	Strathdon Thistle	MtCT	66%	£103	H	(0602) 418501	68	150	100			
Nottingham	Travel Inn	Whitbread		£43	L	(0582) 414341	60					
Retford	Forte Travelodge	Forte		£45	L	(0777) 838091	40					
Southwell	Saracen's Head	Forte	62%	£80	H	(0636) 812701	27	120	120			
Worksop	Forte Travelodge	Forte		£45	L	(0909) 501528	40					

Oxfordshire

Location	Hotel	Group	%	Room Price	Cat	Tel	Rooms	Conf	Banq	Leisure Centre	Swim Pool	Golf
Abingdon	Abingdon Lodge		61%	£88	H	(0235) 553456	63	180	136			
Abingdon	Upper Reaches	Forte	62%	£106	H	(0235) 522311	25	75	60			
Ardley	Granada Lodge			£52	L	(0869) 346111	64					

Location	Hotel	Chain	%	Price	Class	Phone	Rooms				
Banbury	Banbury House Hotel		62%	£93	H	(0295) 259361	48	70	90		
Banbury	Whately Hall	Forte	65%	£90	H	(0295) 263451	74	100	90		
Burford	Bay Tree		67%	£95	H	(0993) 822791	23	120	100		
Burford	Forte Travelodge	Forte		£45	L	(0800) 850950	13				
Chadlington	Lamb Inn		76%	£80	IR	(0993) 823155	7				
Charlbury	The Manor			£95	HR	(0608) 676711	14	55	55		yes
Chipping Norton	Bell Hotel			£75	l	(0608) 810278	40	250	160	yes	yes
Clanfield	Crown & Cushion			£69	l	(0608) 642533	6		20		
Dorchester-on-Thames	The Plough at Clanfield			£85	IR	(036 781) 222	18	50	70		
Frilford Heath	George Hotel			£70	l	(0865) 340404	19	30	100		
Great Milton	Dog House Hotel			£69	l	(0865) 390830	19	40	40		
Hailey	Le Manoir aux Quat'Saisons		86%	£194	HR	(0844) 278881	19	250	35		
Henley-on-Thames	The Bird In Hand			£45	l	(0993) 868321	16	35	70		
Horton-cum-Studley	Red Lion		62%	£100	H	(0491) 572161	26	60	60		
Kingham	Studley Priory		64%	£98	H	(0865) 351203	19	100	70		
Middleton Stoney	Mill House Hotel & Restaurant		66%	£80	H	(0608) 658188	23	50	70		
Milton Common	Jersey Arms			£72	H	(0869) 343234	16	12	50		
Minster Lovell	Belfry Hotel		60%	£93	H	(0844) 279381	77	250	180		yes
Moulsford-on-Thames	Old Swan		67%	£90	H	(0993) 774441	57	30	40		
North Stoke	Beetle & Wedge		71%	£95	HR	(0491) 651381	10	50	64		
Old Minster Lovell	Springs Hotel		70%	£110	H	(0491) 836687	36	50	30		
Oxford	Lovells at Windrush Farm			£145	RR	(0993) 779802	10				
Oxford	Bath Place Hotel & Restaurant			£100	RR	(0865) 791812			35		
Oxford	Eastgate Hotel	Forte	61%	£122	H	(0865) 248244	43	120	80		
Oxford	Moat House	QMH	62%	£123	H	(0865) 59933	155	150	110	yes	yes
Oxford	Old Parsonage		70%	£135	H	(0865) 310210	30				
Oxford	Randolph Hotel	Forte	68%	£126	H	(0865) 247481	109	300	200		
Oxford	Travel Inn	Whitbread		£43	L	(0582) 414341	60				
Steeple Aston	Hopcrofts Holt Hotel	MtCT	63%	£80	H	(0869) 40259	88	200	250		
Stonor	Stonor Arms			£93	RR	(0491) 638345	9		24		
Thame	Spread Eagle		65%	£84	H	(0844) 213661	33	250	200		
Wallingford	George Hotel	MtCT	60%	£80	H	(0491) 836665	39	120	100		
Wallingford	Shillingford Bridge Hotel		61%	£68	H	(0865) 858567	42	80	150		
Wantage	Bear Hotel		58%	£60	H	(023 57) 66366	34	80	60		

Location	Hotel	Group	%	Room Price	Cat	Tel	Rooms	Conf	Banq	Leisure Centre	Swim Pool	Golf
Watlington	Well House			£66	RR	(0491) 613333	10	12	50			
Weston-on-the-Green	Weston Manor		61%	£105	H	(0869) 350621	36	50	80			
Wheatley	Forte Travelodge	Forte		£45	L	(0865) 875705	24					
Witney	Witney Lodge		62%	£91	H	(0993) 779777	74	140	130		yes	
Woodstock	Bear Hotel	Forte	66%	£123	HR	(0993) 811511	45	70	25			
Woodstock	Feathers Hotel		73%	£114	HR	(0993) 812291	17	30	60			
Wroxton St Mary	Wroxton House Hotel		66%	£105	H	(0295) 730482	32	60				

Shropshire

Location	Hotel	Group	%	Room Price	Cat	Tel	Rooms	Conf	Banq	Leisure Centre	Swim Pool	Golf
All Stretton	Stretton Hall Hotel		59%	£54	H	(0694) 723224	14	30	70			
Alveley	Mill Hotel		72%	£55	H	(0746) 780437	21	200	200			
Battlefield	Forte Travelodge	Forte		£45	L	(0800) 850950						
Dorrington	Country Friends			£98	RR	(0743) 718707	3	20	45			
Ludlow	Dinham Hall		64%	£90	H	(0584) 876464	13	30	30			
Ludlow	Feathers Hotel		70%	£98	H	(0584) 875261	40	80	100			
Ludlow	Forte Travelodge	Forte		£45	L	(0584) 711695	32					
Market Drayton	Goldstone Hall		60%	£75	H	(0630) 661202	8	60	60			
Norton	Hundred House Hotel			£69	IR	(095 271) 353	10					
Oswestry	Forte Travelodge	Forte		£45	L	(0691) 658178	40					
Oswestry	Wynnstay Hotel		66%	£65	H	(0691) 655261	27	190	150			
Shifnal	Park House	Macdonalds	71%	£109	H	(0952) 460128	54	200	200		yes	
Shrewsbury	Lion Hotel	Forte	62%	£92	H	(0743) 353107	59	200	160			
Shrewsbury	Prince Rupert Hotel	QMH	64%	£83	H	(0743) 236000	65	110	110			
Telford	Forte Travelodge	Forte		£45	L	(0952) 251244	40					
Telford	Holiday Inn Telford	Holiday Inns	68%	£109	H	(0952) 292500	100	290	180	yes	yes	
Telford	Madeley Court		67%	£90	H	(0952) 680068	47	200	200		yes	
Telford	Moat House	QMH	67%	£94	H	(0952) 291291	148	500	400	yes	yes	yes
Telford	Telford Hotel		64%	£94	H	(0952) 585642	86	200	200	yes	yes	yes

Location	Hotel	Chain	%	Price	Type	Phone				
Weston-under-Redcastle	Hawkstone Park		61%	£75	H	(0939) 200611	59	200	200	yes
Worfield	Old Vicarage		67%	£85	HR	(0746) 716497	14	24	45	

Somerset

Location	Hotel	Chain	%	Price	Type	Phone			
Axbridge	Oak House		63%	£51	I	(0934) 732444	9		35
Castle Cary	Bond's		68%	£80	HR	(0963) 350464	7		20
Dulverton	Ashwick House		60%	£118	HR	(0398) 23868	6		
Dulverton	Carnarvon Arms	Forte	64%	£80	H	(0398) 23302	24	100	100
Dunster	Luttrell Arms			£107	H	(0643) 821555	27		
Glastonbury	No. 3 Restaurant & Hotel		70%	£65	RR	(0458) 832129	6		24
Hatch Beauchamp	Farthings Hotel	Forte		£65	H	(0823) 480664	8	24	
Ilminster	Forte Travelodge			£45	L	(0460) 53748	32		
Kilve	Meadow House		70%	£75	H	(0278) 741546	10	20	35
Lympsham	Batch Farm Country Hotel		56%	£52	H	(0934) 750371	8	75	85
Middlecombe	Periton Park		66%	£78	H	(0643) 706885	8	24	40
Montacute	King's Arms Inn			£64	I	(0935) 822513	11		20
North Petherton	Walnut Tree Inn		65%	£68	H	(0278) 662255	28	80	75
Podimore	Forte Travelodge	Forte		£45	L	(0935) 840074	31		
Porlock	Oaks Hotel		65%	£75	HR	(0643) 862265	10		12
Seavington St Mary	The Pheasant		69%	£70	H	(0460) 240502	8		
Simonsbath	Simonsbath House		64%	£90	H	(064 383) 259	7	30	25
Somerton	Lynch Country House Hotel		69%	£45	H	(0458) 272316	5		
Street	Bear Hotel		63%	£60	HR	(0458) 42021	17	120	120
Taunton	Castle Hotel		76%	£102	H	(0823) 272671	35	90	90
Taunton	County Hotel	Forte	61%	£81	H	(0823) 337651	66	400	350
Taunton	Forte Posthouse	Forte	66%	£68	H	(0823) 332222	97	280	170
Taunton	Travel Inn	Whitbread		£43	L	(0823) 321112	40		
Williton	White House			£68	RR	(0984) 632306	12		
Winsford	Royal Oak Inn			£90	I	(064 385) 455	15		
Wiveliscombe	Langley House		66%	£79	HR	(0984) 23318	8	24	20
Yeovil	Little Barwick House			£72	RR	(0935) 23902	6	20	40
Yeovil	The Manor	Forte	63%	£87	H	(0935) 231161	41	60	

Staffordshire

Location	Hotel	Group	%	Room Price	Cat	Tel	Rooms	Conf	Banq	Leisure Centre	Swim Pool	Golf
Barton-under-Needwood	Forte Travelodge (N)	Forte		£45	L	(0283) 716343	20					
Barton-under-Needwood	Forte Travelodge (S)	Forte		£45	L	(0283) 716784	40					
Burton-on-Trent	Riverside Inn			£65	I	(0283) 511234	22	150	150			yes
Cannock	Travel Inn	Whitbread		£43	L	(0543) 572721	38					
Eccleshall	St George Hotel			£65	H	(0785) 850300	10		65			
Hanchurch	Hanchurch Manor			£75	H	(0782) 643030	5	12				
Lichfield	George Hotel	Jarvis	59%	£90	H	(0543) 414822	38	100	100			
Newcastle-under-Lyme	Clayton Lodge	Jarvis	60%	£91	H	(0782) 613093	49	240	200			
Newcastle-under-Lyme	Forte Posthouse	Forte	60%	£68	H	(0782) 717171	119	120	100	yes		
Rolleston-on-Dove	Brookhouse Hotel		62%	£85	H	(0283) 814188	21	14	50		yes	
Rugeley	Forte Travelodge	Forte		£45	L	(0889) 570096	32					
Stafford	De Vere Tillington Hall	De Vere	63%	£90	H	(0785) 53531	90	200	174	yes	yes	
Stoke-on-Trent	Haydon House Hotel		65%	£62	H	(0782) 711311	25	100	80			
Stoke-on-Trent	North Stafford Hotel	Principal	61%	£90	H	(0782) 744477	69	450	425			
Stoke-on-Trent	Stakis Stoke-on-Trent	Stakis	68%	£89	H	(0782) 202361	127	300	250	yes	yes	
Stoke-on-Trent	Stoke-on-Trent Moat House	QMH	70%	£119	H	(0782) 219000	143	550	500	yes	yes	
Stretton	Dovecliffe Hall		68%	£85	HR	(0283) 531818	7	50	85			
Swinfen	Swinfen Hall		70%	£85	H	(0543) 481494	19	180	120			
Tamworth	Granada Lodge	Granada		£51	L	(0827) 260123	63					
Tamworth	Travel Inn	Whitbread		£43	L	(0827) 54414	40					
Turbury	Ye Olde Dog & Partridge Inn			£73	I	(0283) 813030	17	16				
Utoxeter	Forte Travelodge	Forte		£45	L	(0889) 562043	32					
Waterhouses	Old Beams			£87	RR	(0538) 308254	5		30			

Suffolk

Location	Hotel	Group	%	Room Price	Cat	Tel	Rooms	Conf	Banq	Leisure Centre	Swim Pool	Golf
Aldeburgh	Brudenell Hotel	Forte	60%	£92	H	(0728) 452071	47	50	80			

Town	Hotel	Group	%	Price	Type	Phone					
Aldeburgh	Uplands		60%	£60	H	(0728) 452420	20				
Aldeburgh	Wentworth Hotel		68%	£84	H	(0728) 452312	38				
Barton Mills	Forte Travelodge	Forte		£45	L	(0638) 717675	32				
Beacon Hill	Forte Travelodge	Forte		£45	L	(0449) 721640	40				
Beccles	Waveney House		59%	£55	H	(0502) 712270	13	130	95		
Brome	Oaksmere		67%	£75	H	(0379) 870326	11	80	70		
Bury St Edmunds	Angel Hotel		66%	£85	H	(0284) 753926	42	120	120		
Bury St Edmunds	Butterfly Hotel	Butterfly	62%	£62	H	(0284) 760884	66	50	30		
Bury St Edmunds	Suffolk Hotel	Forte	59%	£82	H	(0284) 753995	33	24	80		
Campsea Ashe	Old Rectory			£48	RR	(0728) 746524	9		35		
Copdock	Ipswich Moat House	QMH	64%	£74	H	(0473) 730444	74	500	400	yes	
Felixstowe	Orwell Moat House	QMH	69%	£75	H	(0394) 285511	58	200	200	yes	
Framlingham	The Crown	Forte	62%	£102	H	(0728) 723521	14			yes	
Hintlesham	Hintlesham Hall		82%	£97	HR	(0473) 652334	33	80	120	yes	yes
Ipswich	Belstead Brook Hotel		68%	£77	H	(0473) 684241	76	60	70		
Ipswich	Constable Country Hotel	Forte	63%	£68	H	(0473) 690313	112	120	100		
Ipswich	Marlborough Hotel		65%	£69	H	(0473) 257677	22	40	71		
Ipswich	Novotel	Novotel	61%	£65	H	(0473) 232400	100	200	150		
Lavenham	Great House		71%	£68	RR	(0787) 247431	4		50		
Lavenham	The Swan	Forte		£122	HR	(0787) 247477	47	50	40		
Long Melford	Black Lion		65%	£65	H	(0787) 312356	9	16	120		
Long Melford	Bull Hotel	Forte	65%	£102	H	(0787) 378494	25	60	120		
Needham Market	Pipps Ford		60%	£55	H	(0449) 760208	6	20	40		
Newmarket	Heath Court Hotel		62%	£70	H	(0638) 667171	47	100	100		
Newmarket	White Hart		60%	£49	H	(0638) 663051	23	120	100		
Southwold	The Crown			£63	IR	(0502) 722275	12	40	22		
Southwold	The Swan		65%	£81	HR	(0502) 722186	45	50	80		
Stowmarket	Forte Travelodge	Forte		£45	L	(0449) 615347	40				
Sudbury	Mill Hotel		58%	£93	H	(0787) 375544	56	80	80		
Woodbridge	Seckford Hall		68%	£99	H	(0394) 385678	32	100	100	yes	
Yoxford	Satis House		63%	£75	H	(0728) 668418					

Surrey

Location	Hotel	Group	%	Room Price	Cat	Tel	Rooms	Conf	Banq	Leisure Centre	Swim Pool	Golf
Bagshot	Pennyhill Park		75%	£134	H	(0276) 471774	76	60	80			
Bramley	Bramley Grange		64%	£105	H	(0483) 893434	45	80	120		yes	
Camberley	Frimley Hall	Forte	68%	£116	H	(0276) 28321	66	60	130			
Chessington	Travel Inn			£43	L	(0372) 744060	42					
Chiddingfold	Crown Inn	Whitbread		£57	I	(0428) 682255	8					
Churt	Frensham Pond Hotel		62%	£88	H	(0252) 795161	51	200	130	yes	yes	
Cobham	Hilton National	Hilton	65%	£120	H	(0932) 864471	152	300	250	yes	yes	
Cobham	Woodlands Park		69%	£130	H	(0372) 843933	58	350	270			
Croydon	Croydon Park		69%	£97	H	081-680 9200	212	300	200	yes	yes	
Croydon	Forte Posthouse	Forte	61%	£68	H	081-688 5185	83	170	170			
Croydon	Hilton National	Hilton	69%	£105	H	081-680 3000	168	400	350	yes	yes	
Croydon	Selsdon Park		68%	£117	H	081-657 8811	170	150	200	yes	yes	yes
Croydon	Travel Inn	Whitbread		£43	L	081-686 2030	40					
Dorking	Forte Travelodge	Forte		£45	L	(0306) 740361	29					
Dorking	White Horse	Forte	62%	£92	H	(0306) 881138	68	60	100			
East Horsley	Thatchers Resort Hotel	Jarvis	62%	£102	H	(0483) 284291	59	60	95		yes	
Egham	Great Fosters		67%	£99	H	(0784) 433822	45	60	200			
Egham	Runnymede Hotel		74%	£145	H	(0784) 436171	171	400	350	yes	yes	
Farnham	Bishop's Table Hotel		62%	£85	H	(0252) 710222	18	20	50			
Farnham	Bush Hotel	Forte	62%	£82	H	(0252) 715237	66	60	60			
Gatwick Airport	Chequers Thistle	MtCT	63%	£106	H	(0293) 786992	78	70	100			
Gatwick Airport	Forte Posthouse	Forte	63%	£68	H	(0293) 771621	210	150	150			
Gatwick Airport	Gatwick Moat House	QMH	62%	£90	H	(0293) 785599	121	180	150			
Gatwick Airport	Ramada Hotel Gatwick		70%	£114	H	(0293) 820169	255	150	180	yes	yes	
Godalming	Inn on the Lake			£75	I	(0483) 415575	19	120	120			
Guildford	The Angel		71%	£105	H	(0483) 64555	11	80	70			
Guildford	Forte Crest	Forte	68%	£119	H	(0483) 574444	111	120	112	yes	yes	

Location	Hotel	Chain	%	£	Type	Phone	Rooms				
Haslemere	Lythe Hill Hotel		71%	£112	H	(0428) 651251	40	60	130		
Horley	Langshott Manor		73%	£106	HR	(0293) 786680	7	18	18		
Morden	Forte Travelodge	Forte		£45	L	081-640 8227	32				
Nutfield	Nutfield Priory	Arcadian	71%	£127	H	(0737) 822066	52	60	110	yes	yes
Reigate	Bridge House		61%	£82	H	(0737) 246801	39	40	200		
Richmond	Petersham Hotel		65%	£130	HR	081-940 7471	54	50	36	yes	yes
Richmond	Richmond Gate Hotel		65%	£113	H	081-940 0061	64	60	50		
Seale	Hog's Back Hotel	Jarvis	64%	£109	H	(0252) 782345	89	140	120	yes	yes
Sutton	Holiday Inn London Sutton	Holiday Inns	70%	£129	H	081-770 1311	116	200	250	yes	yes
Weybridge	Oatlands Park		69%	£128	H	(0932) 847242	117	300	220	yes	
Weybridge	Ship Thistle	MtCT	63%	£116	H	(0932) 848364	39	140	130	yes	yes

East Sussex

Location	Hotel	Chain	%	£	Type	Phone	Rooms				
Battle	Netherfield Place		78%	£100	HR	(0424) 774455	14	50	85		
Boreham Street	White Friars Hotel		57%	£69	H	(0323) 832355	20	30	60		
Brighton	Bedford Hotel		66%	£128	H	(0273) 329744	129	450	300		
Brighton	Brighton Metropole	MtCT	70%	£160	H	(0273) 775432	328	1,800	1,200	yes	yes
Brighton	Brighton Thistle Hotel		77%	£155	HR	(0273) 206700	204	350	320		yes
Brighton	Grand Hotel	De Vere	74%	£160	H	(0273) 321188	200	850	600	yes	yes
Brighton	Old Ship Hotel		65%	£105	H	(0273) 329001	152	300	200	yes	
Brighton	Topps Hotel		69%	£79	HR	(0273) 729934	15				
Brighton (Hove)	Sackville Hotel		61%	£75	H	(0273) 736292	45	250	250		
Brighton (Hove)	Whitehaven Hotel		56%	£75	H	(0273) 778355	17				
Cooden	Cooden Resort Hotel	Jarvis	60%	£76	H	(0424) 842281	41	160	120	yes	
Eastbourne	Cavendish Hotel	De Vere	68%	£80	H	(0323) 410222	112	220	350	yes	
Eastbourne	Grand Hotel	De Vere	75%	£120	H	(0323) 412345	164	400	400	yes	yes
Eastbourne	Queen's Hotel	Principal	67%	£75	H	(0323) 722822	108	300	250		
Eastbourne	Wish Tower Hotel		66%	£85	H	(0323) 722676	65	100	120		
Hastings	Cinque Ports Hotel	Jarvis	66%	£51	H	(0424) 439222	40	300	250		
Hastings	Royal Victoria Hotel	Forte	70%	£72	H	(0424) 445544	50	150	120		
Hellingly	Forte Travelodge	MtCT		£45	L	(0424) 844556	40				
Lewes	Shelleys Hotel		60%	£140	H	(0273) 472361	17	50	60		

Location	Hotel	Group	%	Room Price	Cat	Tel	Rooms	Conf	Banq	Leisure Centre	Swim Pool	Golf
Rye	George Hotel	Forte	62%	£92	H	(0797) 222114	22	80	100			
Rye	Mermaid Inn		60%	£106	H	(0797) 223065	28	50	80			
Sedlescombe	Brickwall Hotel		56%	£60	HR	(0424) 870253	23		120		yes	yes
Uckfield	Horsted Place		79%	£136	HR	(0825) 750581	17	100	30			
Wadhurst	Spindlewood		59%	£63	HR	(0580) 200430	8	25	60			
Wych Cross	Ashdown Park Hotel		77%	£110	HR	(0342) 824988	95	180	150		yes	

West Sussex

Location	Hotel	Group	%	Room Price	Cat	Tel	Rooms	Conf	Banq	Leisure Centre	Swim Pool	Golf
Amberley	Amberley Castle		81%	£130	HR	(0798) 831992	14	40	48			
Arundel	Norfolk Arms		60%	£74	H	(0903) 882101	34	100	100			
Ashington	Mill House Hotel			£77	I	(0903) 892426	12	40	30			
Billingshurst	Forte Travelodge	Forte	60%	£45	L	(0403) 782711	26					
Bognor Regis	Royal Norfolk	Forte		£70	H	(0243) 826222	51	65	100			
Bosham	Millstream Hotel		63%	£99	H	(0243) 573234	29	50	100			
Chichester	Dolphin & Anchor	Forte	63%	£102	H	(0243) 785121	49	180	180			
Climping	Bailiffscourt		69%	£95	HR	(0903) 723511	23	40	80			
Crawley	George Hotel	Forte	64%	£76	H	(0293) 524215	81		100			
Cuckfield	Ockenden Manor		71%	£98	H	(0444) 416111	22	50	50			
East Grinstead	Gravetye Manor		84%	£200	HR	(0342) 810567	18	12	20			
East Grinstead	Woodbury House		61%	£65	H	(0342) 313657	14	20	45			
Findon	Findon Manor		61%	£70	H	(0903) 872733	10	40	26			
Fontwell	Forte Travelodge	Forte		£45	L	(0243) 543973	32					
Gatwick Airport	Copthorne Effingham Park	Copthorne	72%	£126	H	(0342) 714994	122	600	600	yes	yes	yes
Gatwick Airport	Copthorne London Gatwick	Copthorne	69%	£128	H	(0342) 714971	227	130	160			
Gatwick Airport	Europa Gatwick		63%	£93	H	(0293) 886666	211	150	120		yes	
Gatwick Airport	Forte Crest Gatwick	Forte	74%	£109	H	(0293) 567070	468	340	240	yes	yes	
Gatwick Airport	Gatwick Hilton Intern	Hilton	72%	£159	H	(0293) 518080	550	500	500	yes	yes	
Gatwick Airport	Gatwick Concorde Hotel	QMH	61%	£104	H	(0293) 533441	116	100	100		yes	

Location	Hotel	Group	%	Price	Code	Phone	Rooms						
Gatwick Airport	Holiday Inn Gatwick	Holiday Inns	68%	£118	H	(0293) 529991	217	300	200	yes			yes
Gatwick Airport	Travel Inn	Whitbread		£43	L	(0582) 414341	120					yes	yes
Goodwood	Goodwood Park	Country Club	67%	£93	H	(0243) 775537	88	120	120	yes		yes	yes
Hickstead	Forte Travelodge	Forte		£45	L	(0444) 881377	40						
Horsham	Travel Inn	Whitbread		£43	L	(0403) 250141	40						
Lower Beeding	Cisswood House		66%	£96	HR	(0403) 891216	34	200	130			yes	yes
Lower Beeding	South Lodge		76%	£130	HR	(0403) 891711	39	85	80				
Midhurst	Angel Hotel			£65	IR	(0730) 812421	21	80	100				
Midhurst	Spread Eagle		69%	£87	H	(0730) 816911	41	60	100				
Pulborough	Chequers Hotel		61%	£69	H	(0798) 872486	11	20	30				
Rusper	Ghyll Manor	Forte	68%	£93	H	(0293) 871571	25	100	100				
Storrington	Abingworth Hall		70%	£96	HR	(0798) 813636	20	50	55				
Storrington	Little Thakeham		77%	£150	HR	(0903) 744416	9	12	60				
Storrington	Manleys			£75	RR	(0903) 742331	1						
Turners Hill	Alexander House		79%	£150	HR	(0342) 714914	15	55	55				
Walberton	Avisford Park	Stakis	66%	£106	H	(0243) 551215	126	350	250	yes		yes	
West Chiltington	Roundabout Hotel		61%	£80	H	(0798) 813838	24	30	55				
Worthing	Beach Hotel		64%	£77	H	(0903) 234001	84	70	200				
Worthing	Chatsworth Hotel		57%	£77	H	(0903) 236103	107	150	150				

Tyne & Wear

Location	Hotel	Group	%	Price	Code	Phone	Rooms						
Gateshead	Forte Travelodge	Forte		£45	L	091-438 3333	41						
Gateshead	Newcastle Marriott Hotel	Marriott	70%	£108	H	091-493 2233	150	450	300	yes		yes	
Gateshead	Springfield Hotel	Jarvis	63%	£93	H	091-477 4121	60	120	100				
Gateshead	Swallow Hotel	Swallow	60%	£90	H	091-477 1105	103	350	350			yes	yes
Newcastle-upon-Tyne	Copthorne Hotel	Copthorne	73%	£130	H	091-222 0333	156	200	150			yes	yes
Newcastle-upon-Tyne	County Thistle	MtCT	68%	£104	H	091-232 2471	115	130	200				
Newcastle-upon-Tyne	Forte Crest	Forte	61%	£95	H	091-232 6191	166	550	350				
Newcastle-upon-Tyne	Moat House	QMH	59%	£68	H	091-262 8989	147	400	300	yes			
Newcastle-upon-Tyne	Novotel	Novotel	63%	£65	H	091-214 0303	126	200	160				
Newcastle-upon-Tyne	Swallow Gosforth Park	Swallow	73%	£120	H	091-236 4111	178	600	500			yes	yes
Newcastle-upon-Tyne	Swallow Hotel	Swallow	63%	£90	H	091-232 5025	93	100	85			yes	yes

Location	Hotel	Group	%	Room Price	Cat	Tel	Rooms	Conf	Banq	Leisure Centre	Swim Pool	Golf
Newcastle-upon-Tyne A'port	Moat House	QMH	62%	£105	H	(0661) 824911	100	400	350			
Seaton Burn	Holiday Inn	Holiday Inns	70%	£130	H	091-236 5432	150	400	280	yes		yes
Seaton Burn	Horton Grange			£80	RR	(0661) 860686	9					
Sunderland	Swallow Hotel	Swallow	70%	£105	H	091-529 2041	66	220	220	yes		yes
Washington	Campanile Hotel	Campanile		£44	L	091-416 5010	77					
Washington	Forte Posthouse	Forte	59%	£68	H	091-416 2264	138	100	80			
Washington	Granada Lodge	Granada		£51	L	091-410 0076	35					
Washington	Moat House	QMH	66%	£94	H	091-417 2626	106	200	180	yes		yes
Washington	Travel Inn (Sunderland)	Whitbread		£43	L	091-548 9384	40					

Warwickshire

Location	Hotel	Group	%	Room Price	Cat	Tel	Rooms	Conf	Banq	Leisure Centre	Swim Pool	Golf
Alcester	Arrow Mill			£72	I	(0789) 762419	18	60	100			
Ansty	Ansty Hall		70%	£100	H	(0203) 612222	31	80	80			
Barford	Glebe Hotel		68%	£110	H	(0926) 624218	41	150	130			
Billesley	Billesley Manor	QMH	75%	£151	HR	(0789) 400888	41	100	100		yes	
Bodymoor Heath	Marston Farm		65%	£85	H	(0827) 872133	37	50	110	yes	yes	
Brandon	Brandon Hall	Forte	65%	£97	H	(0203) 542571	60	120	120			
Charlecote	Charlecote Pheasant	QMH	62%	£101	H	(0789) 470333	67	120	120			
Hockley Heath	Nuthurst Grange		74%	£117	HR	(0564) 783972	15	80	95			
Hockley Heath	Travel Inn (Solihull)	Whitbread		£43	L	021-744 2942	40					
Kenilworth	De Montfort Hotel	De Vere	63%	£100	H	(0926) 55944	98	300	200			
Leamington Spa	Courtyard by Marriott	Marriott	65%	£80	H	(0926) 425522	94	50	50			
Leamington Spa	Inchfield Hotel		63%	£78	H	(0926) 883777	22	35	60			
Leamington Spa	Mallory Court		80%	£162	HR	(0926) 330214	10		50			
Leamington Spa	Regent Hotel		68%	£89	HR	(0926) 427231	80	100	180			
Nuneaton	Forte Travelodge	Forte		£45	L	(0203) 382541	40					
Nuneaton	Forte Travelodge	Forte		£45	L	(0800) 850950						
Nuneaton	Travel Inn	Whitbread		£43	L	(0203) 343584	48					

Location	Hotel	Operator	%	Rate		Phone						
Stratford-upon-Avon	Alveston Manor	Forte	65%	£115	H	(0789) 204581	106	150	150			
Stratford-upon-Avon	Dukes Hotel		65%	£70	H	(0789) 269300	22	65	48			
Stratford-upon-Avon	Ettington Park	Arcadian	76%	£145	H	(0789) 450123	48	210			yes	
Stratford-upon-Avon	Falcon Hotel	QMH	63%	£116	H	(0789) 205777	73	150	100	yes	yes	
Stratford-upon-Avon	Forte Posthouse	Forte	59%	£68	H	(0789) 266761	60	150	100			
Stratford-upon-Avon	Moat House International	QMH	71%	£141	H	(0789) 414411	247	450	450	yes		
Stratford-upon-Avon	Shakespeare Hotel	Forte	69%	£110	H	(0789) 294771	63	120	100	yes		
Stratford-upon-Avon	Stratford House		62%	£71	H	(0789) 268288	11					
Stratford-upon-Avon	Welcombe Hotel	Forte	74%	£125	H	(0789) 295252	76	120	180			yes
Stratford-upon-Avon	White Swan		62%	£117	H	(0789) 297022	37	40	20			
Stratford-upon-Avon	Windmill Park		64%	£98	H	(0789) 731173	103	360	350	yes	yes	
Warwick	Hilton National	Hilton	66%	£106	H	(0926) 499555	181	400	350	yes	yes	yes
Wishaw	The Belfry	De Vere	73%	£125	H	(0675) 470301	219	350	300	yes	yes	yes

West Midlands

Location	Hotel	Operator	%	Rate		Phone						
Aldridge	Fairlawns		64%	£78	H	(0922) 55122	35	80	80			
Berkswell	Nailcote Hall		67%	£115	H	(0203) 466174	38	100	130		yes	yes
Birmingham	Birmingham Metropole		72%	£156	H	021-780 4242	802	2,000	1,440	yes	yes	yes
Birmingham	Campanile Hotel	Campanile		£44	L	021-622 4925	50					
Birmingham	Chamberlain Hotel		53%	£35	H	021-627 0627	250	400	350			
Birmingham	Copthorne Hotel	Copthorne	70%	£131	H	021-200 2727	212	200	150	yes	yes	
Birmingham	Forte Crest	Forte	66%	£100	H	021-643 8171	251	630	560	yes	yes	
Birmingham	Forte Posthouse	Forte	60%	£68	H	021-357 7444	192	150	150	yes	yes	
Birmingham	Granada Lodge	Granada		£51	L	021-550 3261	60					
Birmingham	Holiday Inn	Holiday Inns	70%	£128	HR	021-631 2000	288	160	200	yes	yes	
Birmingham	Hyatt Regency		77%	£140	H	021-643 1234	319	240	200	yes	yes	
Birmingham	Midland Hotel		68%	£99	H	021-643 2601	111	200	170			
Birmingham	Novotel	Novotel	61%	£92	H	021-643 2000	148	300	150			
Birmingham	Plough & Harrow	Forte	59%	£95	H	021-454 4111	44	70	80			
Birmingham	Royal Angus Thistle	MtCT	65%	£103	H	021-236 4211	133	180	180			
Birmingham	Strathallan Thistle	MtCT	63%	£85	H	021-455 9777	167	200	150			
Birmingham	Swallow Hotel	Swallow	77%	£140	HR	021-452 1144	98	25	20			yes

Location	Hotel	Group	%	Room Price	Cat	Tel	Rooms	Conf	Banq	Leisure Centre	Swim Pool	Golf
Birmingham	Travel Inn	Whitbread		£43	L	021-633 4820	54					
Birmingham Airport	Forte Posthouse	Forte	61%	£68	H	021-782 8141	136	150	120			
Birmingham Airport	Novotel	Novotel	65%	£92	H	021-782 7000	195	40	30			
Brierley Hill	Copthorne Hotel	Copthorne	71%	£122	H	(0384) 482882	138	250	190		yes	
Coventry	Chace Hotel		61%	£91	H	(0203) 303398	67	100	80			
Coventry	Coventry Hill Hotel	Forte	60%	£68	H	(0203) 402151	184	120	150			
Coventry	De Vere Hotel	De Vere	69%	£95	H	(0203) 633733	190	450	450	yes	yes	
Coventry	Forte Posthouse	Forte	66%	£68	H	(0203) 613261	147	450	450	yes	yes	
Coventry	Hilton National		72%	£107	H	(0203) 603000	172	600	500	yes	yes	
Coventry	Novotel	Novotel	62%	£55	H	(0203) 365000	98	200	120			
Coventry (North)	Travel Inn	Whitbread		£43	L	(0203) 636585	52					
Coventry (South)	Campanile Hotel	Campanile		£44	L	(0203) 622311	50					
Coventry (South)	Campanile Hotel	Campanile		£44	L	(0203) 639992	50					
Dudley	Forte Travelodge	Forte		£45	L	(0384) 481579	32					
Dunchurch	Forte Travelodge	Forte		£45	L	(0788) 521528	40					
Hagley	Travel Inn	Whitbread		£43	L	(0562) 883120	40					
Meriden	Forest of Arden Hotel	Country Club	70%	£123	H	(0676) 522335	154	200	220	yes	yes	yes
Meriden	Manor Hotel	De Vere	64%	£85	H	(0676) 522735	74	400	300			
Oldbury	Forte Travelodge	Forte		£45	L	021-552 2967	33					
Solihull	Jarvis George Hotel	Jarvis	66%	£111	H	021-711 2121	127	200	180	yes	yes	
Solihull	Moat House	QMH	69%	£105	H	021-711 4700	115	200	160	yes	yes	
Solihull	Regency Hotel		64%	£95	H	021-745 6119	112	150	150			
Solihull	St John's Swallow Hotel	Swallow	63%	£95	H	021-711 3000	177	800	650	yes	yes	
Solihull	Travel Inn	Whitbread		£43	L	021-744 2942	40					
Stourbridge	Talbot Hotel		59%	£50	H	(0384) 394350	25	650	120			
Sutton Coldfield	Forte Travelodge	Forte		£45	L	021-355 0017	32					
Sutton Coldfield	Moor Hall	MtCT	62%	£90	L	021-308 3751	75	200	200			
Sutton Coldfield	New Hall	Jarvis	78%	£129	HR	021-378 2442	60	50	50		yes	
Sutton Coldfield	Penns Hall	Jarvis	66%	£112	H	021-351 3111	114	700	600	yes	yes	
Walsall	Boundary Hotel	Forte	61%	£71	H	(0922) 33555	98	45	25			

Town	Hotel	Group	%	£	Type	Phone						
Walsall	Friendly Hotel	Friendly	60%	£84	H	(0922) 724444	153	180	120	yes	yes	
Walsall Wood	Baron's Court Hotel		62%	£55	H	(0543) 452020	100	200	120	yes	yes	
West Bromwich	Moat House	QMH	59%	£84	H	021-553 6111	172	180	120			
Wolverhampton	Goldthorn Hotel		62%	£65	H	(0902) 29216	92	140	132			
Wolverhampton	Mount Hotel	Jarvis	60%	£85	H	(0902) 752055	56	200	150			
Wolverhampton	Novotel	Novotel	61%	£65	H	(0902) 871100	132	200	120			
Wolverhampton	Victoria Hotel Periquito		67%	£52	H	(0902) 29922	117	200	150			

Wiltshire

Town	Hotel	Group	%	£	Type	Phone						
Amesbury	Forte Travelodge	Forte		£45	L	(0980) 624966	32					
Beanacre	Beechfield House		70%	£75	H	(0225) 703700	24	40	50			
Bradford-on-Avon	Woolley Grange		75%	£130	HR	(0225) 864705	20	40	70			
Castle Combe	Manor House		79%	£115	HR	(0249) 782206	36	60	90			
Chippenham	Granada Lodge	Granada		£45	L	(0666) 837097	35					
Chiseldon	Chiseldon House		67%	£83	HR	(0793) 741010	21		20			
Colerne	Lucknam Park		83%	£145	HR	(0225) 742777	42	150	80		yes	
Corsham	Methuen Arms			£59	I	(0249) 714867	25	30	120			
Corsham	Rudloe Park		64%	£80	H	(0225) 810555	11		110		yes	
Hinton	Hinton Grange		62%	£108	HR	(0272) 372916	18	25	55		yes	yes
Lacock	At The Sign of The Angel			£78	IR	(0249) 730230	10					
Malmesbury	Old Bell Hotel	Arcadian	64%	£75	H	(0666) 822344	37	110	110			
Marlborough	Ivy House Hotel		61%	£68	H	(0672) 515333	33	80	80			
Purton	Pear Tree		74%	£92	HR	(0793) 772100	18	70	50			
Salisbury	Rose & Crown	QMH	56%	£95	H	(0722) 327908	28	80	50			
Salisbury	White Hart	Forte	63%	£97	HR	(0722) 327476	68	100	60			
Stanton St Quintin	Stanton Manor		64%	£82	H	(0666) 837552	10	30	60			
Swindon	Blunsdon House		69%	£93	H	(0793) 721701	88	300	250	yes	yes	
Swindon	De Vere Hotel	De Vere	69%	£115	H	(0793) 878785	154	450	280	yes	yes	
Swindon	Forte Posthouse	Forte	63%	£68	H	(0793) 524601	100	80	60	yes	yes	
Swindon	Forte Crest	Forte	62%	£89	H	(0793) 831333	91	50	80			
Swindon	Swindon Marriott Hotel	Marriott	71%	£105	H	(0793) 512121	153	280	250	yes	yes	
Swindon	Wiltshire Hotel	MtCT	62%	£79	H	(0793) 528282	95	230	200	yes	yes	

Location	Hotel	Group	%	Room Price	Cat	Tel	Rooms	Conf	Banq	Leisure Centre	Swim Pool	Golf
Teffont Evias	Howard's House		68%	£108	HR	(0722) 716392	9					
Warminster	Bishopstrow House		79%	£123	HR	(0985) 212312	32	65	65			yes
Warminster	Granada Lodge	Granada		£51	L	(0985) 219639	31					

North Yorkshire

Location	Hotel	Group	%	Room Price	Cat	Tel	Rooms	Conf	Banq	Leisure Centre	Swim Pool	Golf
Askrigg	King's Arms Hotel			£70	I	(0969) 650258	9					
Bilbrough	Bilbrough Manor		75%	£105	HR	(0937) 834002	15	30	65			
Bilbrough	Travel Inn (York)	Whitbread		£43	L	(0582) 414341	60					
Bolton Abbey	Devonshire Arms		74%	£120	H	(0756) 71041	40	150	100		yes	
Boroughbridge	The Crown		63%	£50	H	(0423) 322328	42	200	150			
Goathland	Mallyan Spout		61%	£65	H	(0947) 86206	24	70	70			
Great Ayton	Ayton Hall		70%	£85	H	(0642) 723595	9	80	60			
Hackness	Hackness Grange		61%	£126	H	(0723) 882345	28	20	70		yes	
Harome	Pheasant Hotel		68%	£115	H	(0439) 71241	12				yes	
Harrogate	The Crown	Forte	67%	£90	H	(0423) 567755	121	450	300			
Harrogate	Hospitality Inn	MtCT	61%	£92	H	(0423) 564601	71	150	100			
Harrogate	Imperial Hotel	Principal	65%	£85	H	(0423) 565071	85	200	120			
Harrogate	Majestic Hotel	Forte	64%	£111	H	(0423) 568972	156	600	800	yes	yes	
Harrogate	Moat House	QMH	64%	£144	H	(0423) 500000	214	400	250			
Harrogate	Old Swan Hotel		69%	£126	HR	(0423) 500055	135	300	500			
Harrogate	Hotel St George	Swallow	63%	£100	H	(0423) 561431	93	150	180	yes	yes	
Harrogate	Studley Hotel		64%	£95	H	(0423) 560425	36	15				
Helmsley	Black Swan	Forte	69%	£117	H	(0439) 70466	44	50	40			
Helmsley	Feversham Arms		66%	£70	H	(0439) 70766	18		20			
Hovingham	Worsley Arms Hotel			£84	I	(0653) 628234	22	55	70			
Jervaulx	Jervaulx Hall		70%	£130	H	(0677) 460235	10		20			
Knaresborough	Dower House		63%	£66	H	(0423) 863302	32	65	100	yes	yes	

Location	Hotel	Chain	Price	%	Type	Phone					
Markington	Hob Green		£90	70%	H	(0423) 770031	12	12	80		
Monk Fryston	Monk Fryston Hall		£90	65%	H	(0977) 682369	28	50	100		
Newby Wiske	Solberge Hall		£60	69%	H	(0609) 779191	25	100	100		yes
Nidd	Nidd Hall		£120	76%	H	(0423) 771598	59	250	150		
Pickering	White Swan		£76		I	(0751) 472288	13			yes	
Reeth	Burgoyne Hotel		£60	66%	HR	(0748) 884292	8				
Ripley	Boar's Head Hotel		£80	66%	HR	(0423) 771888	25				
Ripon	Ripon Spa Hotel		£72	62%	H	(0765) 602172	40	180	160		
Rosedale Abbey	Milburn Arms		£70	60%	H	(0751) 417312	11	30	65		
Scalby	Wrea Head Country Hotel		£99	65%	H	(0723) 378211	21	180	180		
Scarborough	The Crown		£90	63%	H	(0723) 373491	78	200	100		
Scotch Corner	Forte Travelodge	Forte	£45		L	(0748) 823768	40				
Skipton	Forte Travelodge	Forte	£45		L	(0756) 798091	32				
Skipton	Randell's Hotel		£83	65%	H	(0756) 700100	76	400	350		yes
South Milford	Forte Posthouse Leeds/Selby	Forte	£68	65%	H	(0977) 682711	105	120	100		yes
Staddlebridge	McCoy's		£99	70%	HR	(0609) 882671	6	30	60		
Stokesley	Chapters		£59	65%	HR	(0642) 711888	13	40	60		
Tadcaster	Forte Travelodge	Forte	£45		L	(0973) 531823	40				
Wath-in-Nidderdale	Sportsman's Arms		£47		RR	(0423) 711306	7				
York	Abbey Park Resort Hotel	Jarvis	£75	57%	H	(0904) 658301	85	120	120		
York	Dean Court Hotel		£100	63%	H	(0904) 625082	42	50	74		
York	Forte Posthouse	Forte	£68	65%	H	(0904) 707921	139	120	65		
York	Grange Hotel		£98	74%	HR	(0904) 644744	30	60	80		
York	Judges Lodging		£95	64%	H	(0904) 638733	12	30	30		
York	Middlethorpe Hall		£149	79%	HR	(0904) 641241	30	68	50		
York	Mount Royale		£75	66%	H	(0904) 628856	23				
York	Novotel	Novotel	£85	62%	H	(0904) 611660	124	210	130		yes
York	Royal York Hotel	Principal	£110	67%	H	(0904) 653681	145	280	250		
York	Stakis York	Stakis	£122	65%	H	(0904) 648111	128	180	120		
York	Swallow Hotel	Swallow	£105	64%	H	(0904) 701000	112	170	120	yes	yes
York	Viking Hotel	QMH	£132	69%	H	(0904) 659822	188	350	300		yes

Location	Hotel	Group	%	Room Price	Cat	Tel	Rooms	Conf	Banq	Leisure Centre	Swim Pool	Golf
South Yorkshire												
Barnsley	Ardsley Moat House	QMH	59%	£81	H	(0226) 289401	73	300	300			
Barnsley	Forte Travelodge	Forte		£45	L	(0226) 298799	32					
Bawtry	The Crown	Forte	64%	£62	H	(0302) 710341	57					
Carcroft	Forte Travelodge	Forte		£45	L	(0302) 330841	40					
Doncaster	Campanile Hotel	Campanile	64%	£44	L	(0302) 370770	50					
Doncaster	Danum Swallow Hotel	Swallow	64%	£86	H	(0302) 342261	66	350	300			
Doncaster	Grand St Leger		64%	£80	H	(0302) 364111	20		65			
Doncaster	Moat House	QMH	64%	£88	H	(0302) 310331	100	400	350	yes	yes	
Rotherham	Campanile Hotel	Campanile		£45	L	(0709) 700255	50					
Rotherham	Moat House	QMH	69%	£84	H	(0709) 364902	80	250	200			
Rotherham	Travel Inn	Whitbread		£43	L	(0709) 543216	37					
Sheffield	Charnwood Hotel		64%	£90	H	(0742) 589411	22	100	90			
Sheffield	Forte Posthouse	Forte	65%	£68	H	(0742) 670067	136	500	250	yes	yes	
Sheffield	Grosvenor House	Forte	67%	£67	H	(0742) 720041	103	500	450			
Sheffield	Holiday Inn Royal Victoria	Holiday Inns	67%	£109	H	(0742) 768822	100	400	350			
Sheffield	Moat House	QMH	68%	£103	H	(0742) 375376	94	500	350	yes	yes	
Sheffield	Novotel	Novotel	63%	£65	H	(0742) 781781	144	250	180	yes	yes	
Sheffield	St George Swallow Hotel	Swallow	64%	£96	H	(0742) 583811	117	200	200	yes	yes	
West Yorkshire												
Bingley	Bankfield Hotel	Jarvis	61%	£106	H	(0274) 567123	103	300	250			
Bradford	Restaurant 19			£70	RR	(0274) 492559	4		30			
Bradford	Novotel	Novotel	60%	£143	H	(0274) 683683	131	300	180			
Bradford	Stakis Norfolk Gardens	Stakis	61%	£112	H	(0274) 734734	120	700	700			
Bradford	Victoria Hotel	Forte	58%	£87	H	(0274) 728706	59	200	160			
Bramhope	Forte Crest	Forte	66%	£89	H	(0532) 842911	124	160	130	yes	yes	

Location	Hotel	Chain	%	Price	Code	Tel		Rooms					
Bramhope	Jarvis Parkway Hotel	Jarvis	62%	£116	H	(0532)	672551	103	300	225			yes
Brighouse	Forte Crest	Forte	68%	£98	H	(0484)	400400	94	200	180		yes	yes
Ferrybridge	Granada Lodge	Granada	61%	£51	L	(0977)	670488	35					
Garforth	Hilton National	Hilton	69%	£87	H	(0532)	866556	144	400	250		yes	yes
Halifax	Holdsworth House		69%	£90	H	(0422)	240024	40	100	100			
Hartshead Moor	Forte Travelodge	Forte		£45	L	(0274)	851706	40					
Haworth	Weavers			£68	RR	(0535)	643822	4					
Huddersfield	George Hotel	Principal	62%	£85	H	(0484)	515444	60	220	260			
Huddersfield	Pennine Hilton National	Hilton	66%	£96	H	(0422)	375431	118	450	400		yes	yes
Ilkley	Rombalds Hotel		61%	£84	HR	(0943)	603201	15	50	50			
Leeds	42 The Calls			£140	PH	(0532)	440099	22	55	50			
Leeds	Haley's Hotel		72%	£102	HR	(0532)	784446	22	30	25			
Leeds	Hilton International	Hilton	69%	£105	H	(0532)	442000	206	400	290		yes	yes
Leeds	Holiday Inn	Holiday Inns	69%	£132	H	(0532)	442200	125	200	150		yes	yes
Leeds	Leeds Marriott Hotel	MtCT	74%	£141	H	(0532)	366366	244	300	300			
Leeds	Merrion Thistle Hotel	MtCT	65%	£105	H	(0532)	439191	109	80	80			
Leeds	Oulton Hall Hotel	De Vere	75%	£115	H	(0532)	821000	152	330	300		yes	yes
Leeds	Queen's Hotel	Forte	68%	£94	H	(0532)	431323	190	600	600			
Linton	Wood Hall		76%	£95	HR	(0937)	587271	43	100	110			yes
Otley	Chevin Lodge		64%	£75	H	(0943)	467818	50	120	130			
Wakefield	Campanile Hotel	Campanile	59%	£44	L	(0924)	201054	77					
Wakefield	Cedar Court			£91	H	(0924)	276310	150	400	400		yes	yes
Wakefield	Forte Posthouse	Forte	64%	£68	H	(0924)	276388	99	150	140			
Wakefield	Granada Lodge	Granada		£51	L	(0924)	830569	31					
Wakefield	Swallow Hotel	Swallow	58%	£88	H	(0924)	372111	63	200	190			yes
Wentbridge	Forte Travelodge	Forte		£45	L	(0977)	620711	56					
Wentbridge	Wentbridge House	Forte	64%	£75	H	(0977)	620444	12	120	135			

SCOTLAND

Swimming pool refers to indoor swimming pools only. See the How to Use This Guide section for explanation of our percentage rating system, room pricing and categories.
Key: QMH (Queens Moat Houses), MtCT (Mount Charlotte Thistle), Whitbread (Country Club Hotels)

Borders

Location	Hotel	Group	%	Room Price	Cat	Tel	Rooms	Conf	Banq	Leisure Centre	Swim Pool	Golf
Dryburgh	Dryburgh Abbey Hotel		65%	£100	H	(0835) 22261	26	180	125	yes		
Ettrickbridge	Ettrickshaws Hotel		62%	£76	H	(0750) 52229	6		24			
Kelso	Ednam House		64%	£74	H	(0573) 224168	32	150	150			
Kelso	Sunlaws House		72%	£134	H	(0573) 450331	22	30	40			yes
Melrose	Burts Hotel		56%	£72	I	(089 682) 2285	21	30	50			
Melrose	George & Abbotsford Hotel		65%	£70	H	(089 682) 2308	30	180	160			
Peebles	Cringletie House		62%	£92	HR	(0721) 730233	13					
Peebles	Park Hotel			£85	H	(0721) 720451	24	80	120			
Peebles	Peebles Hotel Hydro	Forte	70%	£103	H	(0721) 720602	137	400	350	yes	yes	
Peebles	Tontine Hotel		57%	£80	H	(0721) 720892	37	40	90			
Selkirk	Philipburn House		60%	£90	H	(0750) 20747	16	40	40		yes	
Tweedsmuir	Crook Inn		59%	£52	H	(089 97) 272	7	40	50			

Central

Location	Hotel	Group	%	Room Price	Cat	Tel	Rooms	Conf	Banq	Leisure Centre	Swim Pool	Golf
Airth	Airth Castle		68%	£100	H	(0324) 831411	75	400	280	yes		
Bridge of Allan	Royal Hotel		59%	£66	H	(0786) 832284	32	150	120			
Drymen	Buchanan Highland Hotel		62%	£110	H	(0360) 60588	51	150	120		yes	yes
Dunblane	Cromlix House		82%	£160	HR	(0786) 822125	14	40	40			

Town	Hotel	Chain	%	£	Type	Phone	Rooms				
Dunblane	Stakis Dunblane	Stakis	61%	£111	H	(0786) 822551	214	500	400	yes	yes
Falkirk	Hotel Cladhan		60%	£69	L	(0324) 27421	37	200	200	yes	yes
Stirling	Granada Lodge	Granada		£51	L	(0786) 815033	37				
Strathblane	Kirkhouse Inn			£72	I	(0360) 770621	15	40			

Dumfries & Galloway

Town	Hotel	Chain	%	£	Type	Phone	Rooms				
Annan	Warmanbie Hotel		59%	£74	H	(0461) 204015	7				
Auchencairn	Balcary Bay Hotel		64%	£84	HR	(055 664) 217	17	50	50		
Auchencairn	Collin House		68%	£76	HR	(055 664) 292	6				
Beattock	Auchen Castle		64%	£54	H	(068 33) 407	25	40	80		
Canonbie	Riverside Inn			£72	IR	(038 73) 71512	6				
Gatehouse of Fleet	Cally Palace		69%	£118	H	(0557) 814341	56	80		yes	yes
Gatehouse of Fleet	Murray Arms Inn			£70	I	(0557) 814207	13	120	100		
Gretna Green	Forte Travelodge	Forte		£45	L	(0461) 337566	41				
Newton Stewart	Kirroughtree Hotel		76%	£120	HR	(0671) 402141	17	20	20		
Port William	Corsemalzie House		61%	£75	H	(0988) 860254	14	95	70		
Portpatrick	Knockinaam Lodge		73%	£104	HR	(0776) 810471	10				
Rockcliffe	Baron's Craig		65%	£90	H	(0556) 630225	22	20			
Stranraer	North West Castle		68%	£70	H	(0776) 704413	71	100	180	yes	yes

Fife

Town	Hotel	Chain	%	£	Type	Phone	Rooms				
Dunfermline	King Malcolm Thistle	MtCT	65%	£93	H	(0383) 722611	48	150	120		
Glenrothes	Balgeddie House		65%	£97	H	(0592) 742511	18	70	70		
Letham	Fernie Castle		60%	£70	H	(0337) 810381	15	160	140		
Markinch	Balbirnie House		74%	£125	HR	(0592) 610066	30	150	120		
North Queensferry	Queensferry Lodge		63%	£70	H	(0383) 410000	32	150	200		
Peat Inn	The Peat Inn			£135	RR	(0334) 840206	8				
St Andrews	Rufflets Country House		65%	£130	H	(0334) 472594	25	50	70		
St Andrews	Rusacks Hotel	Forte	74%	£114	H	(0334) 474321	50	120	150		
St Andrews	St Andrews Old Course Hotel		82%	£210	H	(0334) 474371	125	300	220	yes	

Location	Hotel	Group	%	Room Price	Cat	Tel	Rooms	Conf	Banq	Leisure Centre	Swim Pool	Golf
Grampian												
Aberdeen	Ardoe House		70%	£108	H	(0224) 867355	71	300	200			
Aberdeen	Caledonian Thistle	MtCT	68%	£135	H	(0224) 640233	80	35	25			
Aberdeen	Copthorne Hotel	Copthorne	68%	£135	H	(0224) 630404	89	220	200			
Aberdeen	Holiday Inn Crowne Plaza	Holiday Inns	69%	£132	H	(0224) 713911	144	500	432	yes	yes	
Aberdeen	The Marcliffe at Pitfodels		78%	£115	HR	(0224) 861000	42	420	350		yes	
Aberdeen	Stakis Tree Tops	Stakis	63%	£128	H	(0224) 313377	110	1,000	800	yes	yes	
Aberdeen	Travel Inn	Whitbread		£43	L	(0224) 821217	40					
Aberdeen Airport	Aberdeen Marriott Hotel	Marriott	70%	£141	H	(0224) 770011	154	400	350	yes	yes	
Aberdeen Airport	Airport Skean Dhu Hotel	MtCT	65%	£123	H	(0224) 725252	148	450	420	yes	yes	
Ballater	Craigendarroch Hotel		74%	£125	H	(033 97) 55858	49	100	100		yes	
Ballater	Tullich Lodge		71%	£190	HR	(033 97) 55406	10					
Banchory	Raemoir House		71%	£95	HR	(0330) 824884	25	50	80			
Banchory	Tor-na-Coille Hotel		62%	£65	H	(033 02) 2242	23	90	90			
Chapel of Garioch	Pittodrie House		65%	£110	H	(0467) 681444	27	150	130			
Craigellachie	Craigellachie Hotel		68%	£95	HR	(0340) 881204	30	45	60			
Elgin	Mansion House		67%	£100	H	(0343) 548811	22	200	200	yes	yes	
Inverurie	Thainstone House Hotel		76%	£116	HR	(0467) 621643	46	400	200	yes	yes	
Kildrummy	Kildrummy Castle		70%	£120	H	(097 55) 71288	15					
Maryculter	Maryculter House		65%	£108	H	(0224) 732124	23	200	180			
Newburgh	Udny Arms Hotel		60%	£76	H	(035 86) 89444	26	130	85			
Oldmeldrum	Meldrum House		65%	£95	H	(0651) 872294	9					
Peterhead	Waterside Inn		67%	£93	H	(0779) 471121	110	200	250	yes	yes	
Rothes	Rothes Glen Hotel		65%	£110	H	(0340) 831254	16	200	250			yes
Highland												
Achiltibuie	Summer Isles		64%	£90	HR	(0854) 622282	12					
Advie	Tulchan Lodge		77%	£350	H	(0807) 510200	9					

Location	Hotel	Chain	%	Price	Phone	Type	Rooms				
Altnaharra	Altnaharra Hotel		60%	£113	(054 981) 222	H	18				
Appin	Inverceran Country House		67%	£120	(063 173) 414	H	9	50			
Arisaig	Arisaig House		75%	£135	(068 75) 622	HR	14	12	24		
Arisaig	Old Library Lodge & Rest			£59	(0687) 450651	RR	6				
Aviemore	Aviemore Highlands Hotel		61%	£70	(0479) 810771	H	103	120	100		
Aviemore	Stakis Aviemore 4 Seasons	Stakis	70%	£100	(0479) 810681	H	88	160	180	yes	yes
Aviemore	Stakis Coylumbridge Resort	Stakis	62%	£98	(0479) 810661	H	175	750	610	yes	yes
Ballachulish	Ballachulish Hotel		60%	£80	(085 52) 606	H	30	100	80		
Ballachulish	Isles of Glencoe Hotel		59%	£85	(085 52) 603	H	39	70	120		
Contin	Craigdarroch Lodge		56%	£98	(0997) 421265	H	13				yes
Cromarty	Royal Hotel		63%	£50	(0381) 600217	I	10	120	120		
Drummadrochit	Polmaily House		62%	£86	(0456) 450343	HR	10		40		
Dulnain Bridge	Auchendean Lodge		59%	£54	(0479) 851347	HR	8	80	76		
Dulnain Bridge	Muckrach Lodge		59%	£78	(0479) 851257	H	12				
Duror	Stewart Hotel			£80	(063 174) 268	RR	19				
Fort William	The Factor's House			£82	(0397) 705767	HR	7				
Fort William	Inverlochy Castle	MtCT	90%	£240	(0397) 702177	HR	17		30		
Fort William	Mercury Hotel		58%	£93	(0397) 703117	H	86	15			
Gairloch	Creag Mor		66%	£76	(0445) 2068	HR	17		50		
Garve	Inchbae Lodge		57%	£56	(099 75) 269	IR	12		30		
Glenelg	Glenelg Inn		60%	£72	(059 982) 273	IR	6				
Helmsdale	Navidale House		67%	£65	(043 12) 258	H	14	16	60		
Inverness	Bunchrew House		69%	£105	(0463) 234917	H	11		16		
Inverness	Caledonian Hotel	Jarvis	73%	£99	(0463) 235181	H	106	350	220	yes	
Inverness	Culloden House		69%	£165	(0463) 790461	HR	23	50	50		
Inverness	Dunain Park		67%	£120	(0463) 230512	HR	14				
Inverness	Kingsmills Hotel	Swallow	62%	£125	(0463) 237166	H	79	60	80	yes	
Inverness	Mercury Hotel	MtCT	64%	£102	(0463) 239666	H	118	230	210		
Kentallen of Appin	Ardsheal House		65%	£160	(063 174) 227	HR	13		40		
Kentallen of Appin	Holly Tree		64%	£76	(063 174) 292	H	10		40	yes	yes
Kingussie	The Cross		65%	£150	(0540) 661166	RR	9			yes	yes
Kinlochbervie	Kinlochbervie Hotel		64%	£84	(0971) 521275	H	14				
Kyle of Lochalsh	Lochalsh Hotel		63%	£87	(0599) 4202	H	38	80	80		
Lochinver	Inver Lodge Hotel		70%	£120	(057 14) 496	H	20				

Location	Hotel	Group	%	Room Price	Cat	Tel	Rooms	Conf	Banq	Leisure Centre	Swim Pool	Golf
Muir-of-Ord	Dower House			£90	RR	(0463) 870090	5					
Nairn	Clifton Hotel		70%	£96	HR	(0667) 453119	12		26			
Nairn	Golf View Hotel		67%	£88	H	(0667) 452301	47	140	120			
Nairn	Newton Hotel		65%	£70	H	(0667) 53144	44	60	70			
Newtonmore	Ard-na-Coille Hotel		67%	£126	HR	(0540) 673214	7					
Onich	Allt-Nan-Ros Hotel		63%	£95	HR	(085 53) 250	21					
Onich	Lodge on the Loch		63%	£137	H	(085 53) 237	18					
Onich	Onich Hotel		61%	£77	H	(0855) 821214	27		40			
Portree	Rosedale Hotel		56%	£70	H	(0478) 613131	23					
Scarista	Scarista House		67%	£84	HR	(0859) 550238	8					
Scourie	Eddrachilles Hotel		60%	£72	H	(0971) 502080	11					
Scourie	Scourie Hotel		60%	£68	H	(0971) 502396	20					
Skeabost Bridge	Skeabost House		60%	£77	H	(0470) 532202	26					yes
Sleat	Kinloch Lodge		67%	£80	HR	(0471) 833214	10		15			
Stornoway	Cabarfeidh Hotel		64%	£80	H	(0851) 702604	46	250	200			
Talladale	Loch Maree Hotel			£80	I	(044 584) 288	30		50			
Uig	Uig Hotel		59%	£75	H	(0470) 542205	16	12				
Ullapool	Altnaharrie Inn		73%	£250	HR	(0854) 633230	8					
Ullapool	Ceilidh Place			£96	I	(0854) 612103	13	30	110			
Whitebridge	Knockie Lodge		71%	£130	HR	(0456) 486276	10					

Lothian

Location	Hotel	Group	%	Room Price	Cat	Tel	Rooms	Conf	Banq	Leisure Centre	Swim Pool	Golf
Bonnyrigg	Dalhousie Castle		62%	£120	H	(0875) 820153	25	70	120			
Dirleton	Open Arms Hotel		67%	£115	H	(0620) 85241	7	100	100			
Edinburgh	The Balmoral	Forte	83%	£171	HR	031-556 2414	189	400	800	yes		
Edinburgh	Barnton Thistle	MtCT	63%	£107	H	031-339 1144	50	130	100		yes	
Edinburgh	Braid Hills Hotel		61%	£89	H	031-447 8888	68	100	180			

Location	Hotel	Chain	%	£	Type	Phone					
Edinburgh	Caledonian Hotel	QMH	79%	£240	HR	031-225 2433	239	400	220		
Edinburgh	Capital Moat House	QMH	66%	£111	H	031-334 3391	110	350	350	yes	yes
Edinburgh	Carlton Highland		68%	£154	H	031-556 7277	197	350	250	yes	yes
Edinburgh	Channings		64%	£125	H	031-315 2226	48	35	20		
Edinburgh	Forte Travelodge	Forte		£45	L	031-441 4296	40				
Edinburgh	Forte Posthouse	Forte	62%	£68	H	031-334 0390	200	120	100	yes	yes
Edinburgh	George Inter-Continental		74%	£202	H	031-225 1251	195	220	170	yes	yes
Edinburgh	Granada Lodge	Granada		£51	L	031-653 2427	44				
Edinburgh	Greenside Hotel			£70	PH	031-557 0022	13				
Edinburgh	Hilton National	Hilton	68%	£156	H	031-332 2545	144	125	90		
Edinburgh	Holiday Inn Garden Court	Holiday Inns	65%	£101	H	031-332 2442	119	60	50	yes	yes
Edinburgh	Howard Hotel		74%	£180	H	031-557 3500	16	45	40	yes	yes
Edinburgh	King James Thistle Hotel	MtCT	70%	£99	H	031-556 0111	147	250	250		
Edinburgh	Roxburghe Hotel		64%	£110	H	031-225 3921	75	225	200		
Edinburgh	Royal Terrace Hotel		70%	£157	H	031-557 3222	93	80	60	yes	yes
Edinburgh	Scandic Crown Hotel	Scandic	63%	£155	H	031-557 9797	238	220	120	yes	yes
Edinburgh	Sheraton Grand Hotel	Sheraton	79%	£169	H	031-229 9131	261	485	485	yes	yes
Edinburgh	Stakis Grosvenor Hotel	Stakis	64%	£98	H	031-226 6001	136	500	500		
Edinburgh	Swallow Royal Scot	Swallow	65%	£120	H	031-334 9191	259	300	250	yes	yes
Edinburgh	Travel Inn	Whitbread		£43	L	031-661 3396	39				
Gullane	Greywalls Hotel		76%	£150	HR	(0620) 842144	22	35	50		
Ingliston	Norton House	Voyager	66%	£120	H	031-333 1275	47	300	180		
Kirknewton	Dalmahoy Hotel, Golf & CC	Country Club	78%	£123	HR	031-333 1845	116	190	120	yes	yes
North Berwick	Marine Hotel	Forte	64%	£97	H	(0620) 892406	83	350		yes	yes
North Middleton	Borthwick Castle		66%	£95	H	(0875) 820514	10	60	65		
South Queensferry	Forth Bridges Moat House		61%	£114	H	031-331 1199	108	250	200	yes	yes
Uphall	Houstoun House	QMH	68%	£115	H	(0506) 853831	30	350	250	yes	yes

Orkney

Location	Hotel	Chain	%	£	Type	Phone					
Harray Loch	Merkister Hotel		59%	£59	H	(085 677) 366	14	80			

Location	Hotel	Group	%	Room Price	Cat	Tel	Rooms	Conf	Banq	Leisure Centre	Swim Pool	Golf
Shetland												
Lerwick	Shetland Hotel		62%	£78	H	(0595) 5515	64	300	200			
Strathclyde												
Abington	Forte Travelodge	Forte		£45	L	(0864) 2782	54					
Alexandria	Cameron House		81%	£150	HR	(0389) 55565	68	300	275	yes	yes	yes
Ardentinny	Ardentinny Hotel		59%	£86	H	(036 981) 209	11		35			
Arduaine	Loch Melfort Hotel		63%	£90	H	(0852) 200233	26	20				
Ayr	Jarvis Caledonian Hotel	Jarvis	64%	£116	H	(0292) 269331	114	175	200	yes	yes	
Ayr (Monkton)	Travel Inn	Whitbread		£43	L	(0800) 850950	40					
Craignure	Isle of Mull Hotel		56%	£84	H	(068 02) 351	60					
Crinan	Crinan Hotel		69%	£115	HR	(054 683) 261	22	65	65			
Cumbernauld	Travel Inn	Whitbread		£43	L	(0236) 725339	37					
Cumbernauld	Westerwood Hotel		73%	£100	HR	(0236) 457171	49	200	180	yes	yes	yes
Dumbarton	Forte Travelodge	Forte		£45	L	(0389) 65202	32					
East Kilbride	Stuart Hotel		62%	£80	H	(035 52) 21161	39	200	150			
East Kilbride	Travel Inn	Whitbread		£43	L	(035 52) 222809	40					
East Kilbride	Westpoint Hotel		74%	£115	HR	(035 52) 36300	74	140	120			
Eriska	Isle of Eriska		73%	£155	HR	(063 172) 371	17	30		yes	yes	
Erskine	Forte Posthouse	Forte	62%	£68	H	041-812 0123	166	600	450	yes	yes	
Giffnock	Macdonald Thistle	MtCT	64%	£85	H	041-638 2225	56	160	130			
Glasgow	Copthorne Hotel	Copthorne	74%	£125	H	041-332 6711	140	100	80			
Glasgow	Devonshire Hotel			£120	PH	041-339 7878	14	50	30			
Glasgow	Forte Crest	Forte	73%	£119	H	041-248 2656	257	800	800			
Glasgow	Glasgow Marriott Hotel	Marriott	67%	£110	H	041-226 5577	298	720	600	yes	yes	
Glasgow	Glasgow Thistle Hotel	MtCT		£130	H	041-332 3311	307	1,500	1,200			
Glasgow	Glasgow Hilton	Hilton	78%	£140	HR	041-204 5555	319	1,100	950	yes	yes	

Town	Hotel	Group	%	£		Telephone							
Glasgow	Jurys Pond Hotel	Jurys	59%	£86	H	041-334 8161	133	150	120	yes	yes		
Glasgow	Kelvin Park Lorne Hotel	QMH	63%	£87	H	041-334 4891	99	360	300	yes	yes		
Glasgow	Moat House International	QMH	69%	£134	H	041-204 0733	282	1,000	1,000		yes		yes
Glasgow	One Devonshire Gardens		82%	£155	HR	041-339 2001	27	50	50				
Glasgow	Stakis Grosvenor	Stakis	66%	£117	H	041-339 8811	95	400	400	yes	yes		
Glasgow	Swallow Hotel	Swallow	62%	£92	H	041-427 3146	117	320	300	yes	yes		
Glasgow	Tinto Firs Hotel	MtCT	62%	£85	H	041-637 2353	27	200	130		yes		
Glasgow	Town House		66%	£110	H	041-332 3320	34	160	130				
Glasgow Airport	Forte Crest	Forte	68%	£95	H	041-887 1212	307	500	450				
Glasgow Airport	Stakis Glasgow Airport	Stakis	61%	£114	H	041-886 4100	141	1,000	1,000		yes		
Glasgow Airport	Travel Inn	Whitbread		£43	L	041-842 1563	80		80				
Gourock	Stakis Gantock Hotel	Stakis	64%	£101	H	(0475) 634671	99	180	80	yes	yes		
Irvine	Hospitality Inn	MtCT	68%	£85	H	(0294) 74272	127	320	220	yes	yes		
Johnstone	Forte Travelodge	Forte		£45	L	(0800) 850950							
Kilchrenan	Ardanaiseig		74%	£160	HR	(086 63) 333	14			yes		yes	
Kilchrenan	Taychreggan Hotel		66%	£67	HR	(086 63) 211	15	24	50				
Kilfinan	Kilfinan Hotel			£72	IR	(0700) 82201	11	50	38				
Kilmarnock	Forte Travelodge	Forte		£45	L	(0563) 73810	40						
Kilmore	Glenfeochan House		70%	£124	HR	(063 177) 273	3						
Kilwinning	Montgreenan Mansion House		70%	£92	H	(0294) 557733	21	100	100				yes
Langbank	Gleddoch House		68%	£130	H	(0475) 540711	33	150	120				
Maybole	Ladyburn		73%	£140	HR	(065 54) 585	8		20				
Milngavie	Black Bull Thistle	MtCT	59%	£92	H	041-956 2291	27	100	120				
Newhouse	Travel Inn	Whitbread		£43	L	(0698) 860277	40						
Oban	Alexandra Hotel		59%	£90	H	(0631) 62381	60	120	120				
Oban	Columba Hotel		60%	£79	H	(0631) 62183	51	300	250			yes	
Oban	Knipoch Hotel		72%	£124	HR	(085 26) 251	17						
Port Appin	Airds Hotel		75%	£266	HR	(063 173) 236	12						
Quothquan	Shieldhill		73%	£134	H	(0899) 20035	11	25	32				
Skelmorlie	Manor Park		61%	£75	H	(0475) 520832	23	150	130				
Stewarton	Chapeltoun House		71%	£99	H	(0560) 482696	8	80	55				
Strachur	Creggans Inn		61%	£98	H	(036 986) 279	21	50	85				
Tarbert	Stonefield Castle		58%	£90	H	(0880) 820836	32	160	120				
Tiroran	Tiroran House		70%	£186	HR	(068 15) 232	9						

Location	Hotel	Group	%	Room Price	Cat	Tel	Rooms	Conf	Banq	Leisure Centre	Swim Pool	Golf
Tobermory	Tobermory Hotel		57%	£64	H	(0688) 2091	17					
Troon	Marine Highland Hotel		67%	£145	H	(0292) 313066	72	220	160	yes	yes	
Troon	Piersland House		64%	£94	H	(0292) 31747	23	100	114		yes	
Turnberry	Turnberry Hotel		84%	£200	HR	(0655) 31000	132	150	250	yes	yes	yes

Tayside

Location	Hotel	Group	%	Room Price	Cat	Tel	Rooms	Conf	Banq	Leisure Centre	Swim Pool	Golf
Aberfeldy	Farleyer House		70%	£120	HR	(0887) 820332	11	25	30			yes
Alyth	Drummacree House			£62	RR	(082 83) 2194	6		50			
Auchterarder	Auchterarder House		75%	£130	HR	(0764) 663646	15	50	50			
Auchterarder	Gleneagles Hotel		86%	£220	H	(0764) 662231	234	360	240	yes	yes	yes
Auchterhouse	Old Mansion House		68%	£95	HR	(082 626) 366	6	20	22			
Blairgowrie	Kinloch House		70%	£145	HR	(0250) 884237	21	15	30			
Callander	Roman Camp Hotel		69%	£95	HR	(0887) 330003	14	50	45			
Cleish	Nivingston House		65%	£90	H	(0577) 850216	17	40	80			
Crieff	Crieff Hydro		64%	£96	H	(0764) 655555	194	300	250	yes	yes	yes
Dundee	Angus Thistle	MtCT	69%	£107	H	(0382) 26874	58	500	450			
Dundee	Invercarse Hotel		59%	£80	H	(0382) 69231	38	200	280			
Dundee	Travel Inn (Dundee West)	Whitbread		£43	L	(0382) 561115	40					
Dundee	Travel Inn	Whitbread		£43	L	(0582) 414341	40					
Dunkeld	Kinnaird		76%	£170	HR	(0796) 482440	9					
Forfar	Royal Hotel		57%	£70	H	(0307) 62691	19	220	160	yes	yes	
Glamis	Castleton House		71%	£90	HR	(0307) 840340	6		60			
Glencarse	Newton House Hotel		58%	£80	H	(0738) 860250	10	60	50			
Kenmore	Kenmore Hotel		62%	£97	H	(0887) 830205	39	20	70			
Killiecrankie	Killiecrankie Hotel		64%	£138	H	(0796) 473220	10					
Kinclaven by Stanley	Ballathie House		74%	£150	HR	(0250) 883268	37	120	60			
Kinross	Granada Lodge	Granada		£51	L	(0577) 64646	35					
Kinross	Windlestrae Hotel		62%	£95	H	(0577) 863217	45	250	220	yes	yes	

Location	Hotel	Chain				Phone						
Kirkmichael	Log Cabin Hotel		59%	£66	H	(0250) 881288	13	50	90			
Perth	Royal George Hotel	Forte	62%	£97	H	(0738) 24455	42	100	80			
Perth	Stakis City Mills Hotel	Stakis	60%	£90	H	(0738) 628281	76	140	140			
Pitlochry	Green Park Hotel		58%	£78	H	(0796) 473248	37	80	100	yes		
Pitlochry	Pitlochry Hydro Hotel		64%	£102	H	(0796) 472666	62	120	60			
Scone	Murrayshall House		72%	£130	HR	(0738) 51171	19	60	80		yes	
St Fillans	Four Seasons Hotel		60%	£70	HR	(0764) 685333	18	90	100			yes

WALES

Swimming pool refers to indoor swimming pools only. See the How to Use This Guide section for explanation of our percentage rating system, room pricing and categories.
Key: QMH (Queens Moat Houses), MtCT (Mount Charlotte Thistle), Whitbread (Country Club Hotels)

Location	Hotel	Group	%	Room Price	Cat	Tel	Rooms	Conf	Banq	Leisure Centre	Swim Pool	Golf
Clwyd												
Chirk	Starlings Castle			£46	RR	(0691) 718464	10					
Colwyn Bay	Colwyn Bay Hotel		61%	£53	H	(0492) 516555	43	200	180			
Ewloe	St David's Park Hotel		69%	£97	H	(0244) 520800	121	270	220	yes	yes	yes
Halkyn	Forte Travelodge	Forte		£45	L	(0352) 780952	31					
Llanarmon Dyffryn Ceiriog	Hand Hotel			£58	I	(069 176) 666	13	25	70			
Llanarmon Dyffryn Ceiriog	West Arms Hotel			£78	I	(069 176) 665	12	75	60			
Llandrillo	Tyddyn Llan		65%	£88	HR	(0490) 440264	10	50	90			
Llangollen	Hand Hotel	MtCT	55%	£65	H	(0978) 860303	57	80	80			
Llangollen	Royal Hotel	Forte	59%	£82	H	(0978) 860202	33	80	80			
Northop	Soughton Hall		79%	£119	HR	(0352) 840811	14	60	120			
Northop Hall	Forte Travelodge	Forte		£45	L	(0244) 816473	40					
Rossett	Llyndir Hall		71%	£110	H	(0244) 571648	38	150	90	yes	yes	
Ruthin	Ruthin Castle		62%	£82	H	(0824) 702664	60	200	150			
Wrexham	Forte Travelodge	Forte		£45	L	(0978) 365705	32					
Wrexham	Travel Lodge			£43	L	(0978) 853214	38					
Dyfed												
Aberystwyth	Conrah Country Hotel		63%	£79	H	(0970) 617941	20	40	70			
Brechfa	Ty Mawr			£68	RR	(0267) 202332	5	25	50		yes	

Town	Hotel	Group	%	Price	Cl	Phone						
Carmarthen	Ivy Bush Royal	Forte	59%	£60	H	(0267) 235111	75	200	200			
Cross Hands	Forte Travelodge	Forte		£45	L	(0269) 845700	32		300			
Fishguard	Fishguard Bay Hotel		59%	£60	H	(0348) 873571	62	300	300			yes
Gwbert-on-Sea	Cliff Hotel		60%	£70	H	(0239) 613241	70	220	189			
Lamphey	Court Hotel		67%	£95	H	(0646) 672273	35	65	80		yes	
Llandeilo	Cawdor Arms		65%	£42	H	(0558) 823500	17	80	130			
Penally	Penally Abbey		65%	£92	HR	(0834) 843033	12	80	46		yes	
St David's	St Non's Hotel		56%	£64	H	(0437) 720239	24	14				
St David's	Warpool Court		62%	£104	H	(0437) 720300	25	70	120		yes	
Welsh Hook	Stone Hall			£63	RR	(0348) 840212	5					

Glamorgan, Mid

Town	Hotel	Group	%	Price	Cl	Phone						
Abercynon	Llechwen Hall		70%	£69	I	(0443) 742050	11	80	80			
Bridgend	Forte Travelodge	Forte		£45	L	(0656) 659218	40					
Coychurch	Coed-y-Mwstwr Hotel		70%	£95	HR	(0656) 860621	23	185	160			
Merthyr Tydfil	Baverstock Hotel		57%	£55	H	(0685) 386221	53	250	280			
Miskin	Miskin Manor	Select	70%	£95	H	(0443) 224204	32	200	150	yes		
Pencoed	Forte Travelodge	Forte		£45	L	(0656) 864404	40					

Glamorgan, South

Town	Hotel	Group	%	Price	Cl	Phone						
Barry	Mount Sorrel Hotel		59%	£85	H	(0446) 740069	43	150	150			
Cardiff	Angel Hotel	QMH	66%	£118	H	(0222) 232633	91	300	300			yes
Cardiff	Campanile Hotel	Campanile	67%	£44	L	(0222) 549044	50					
Cardiff	Cardiff International		68%	£80	H	(0222) 341441	143	55	40	yes		
Cardiff	Cardiff Marriott Hotel	Marriott	68%	£130	H	(0222) 399944	182	300	300	yes		yes
Cardiff	Copthorne Hotel	Copthorne	70%	£119	H	(0293) 599100	135	300	200	yes		yes
Cardiff	Forte Posthouse	Forte	63%	£68	H	(0222) 731212	150	140	120	yes		yes
Cardiff	Forte Travelodge	Forte		£45	L	(0222) 549564	32					
Cardiff	Forte Crest	Forte	69%	£95	H	(0222) 388681	155	180	180			yes

Location	Hotel	Group	%	Room Price	Cat	Tel	Rooms	Conf	Banq	Leisure Centre	Swim Pool	Golf
Cardiff	Moat House	QMH	70%	£130	H	(0222) 732520	135	300	255	yes	yes	
Cardiff	Park Hotel	MtCT	70%	£113	H	(0222) 383471	119	300	300			
Cardiff	Travel Inn	Whitbread		£43	L	(0633) 680070	47					
Porthkerry	Egerton Grey		68%	£85	H	(0446) 711666	10	40	40			

Glamorgan, West

Location	Hotel	Group	%	Room Price	Cat	Tel	Rooms	Conf	Banq	Leisure Centre	Swim Pool	Golf
Gowerton	Cefn Goleu Park		69%	£80	HR	(0792) 873099	4	10	28			
Mumbles	Norton House		65%	£65	HR	(0792) 404891	15	20	16			
Port Talbot	Travel Inn	Whitbread		£43	L	(0639) 813017	40					
Reynoldston	Fairyhill		65%	£85	HR	(0792) 390139	11					
Swansea	Forte Crest	Forte	69%	£95	H	(0792) 651074	99	230	180	yes	yes	
Swansea	Hilton National	Hilton	65%	£78	H	(0792) 310330	120	200	140			
Swansea	Langland Court Hotel			£78	I	(0792) 361545	21	150	160			
Swansea	Swansea Marriott Hotel	Marriott	67%	£102	H	(0792) 642020	118	250	180	yes	yes	

Gwent

Location	Hotel	Group	%	Room Price	Cat	Tel	Rooms	Conf	Banq	Leisure Centre	Swim Pool	Golf
Abergavenny	Llanwenarth Arms Hotel			£59	I	(0873) 810550	18		70			
Chepstow	Castle View Hotel			£60	I	(0291) 620349	13					
Chepstow	St Pierre Hotel		70%	£100	H	(0291) 625261	147	220	220	yes	yes	yes
Llangybi	Cwrt Bleddyn Hotel		71%	£100	H	(0633) 450521	36	200	160	yes	yes	
Llanvihangel Gobion	Llansantffraed Court	MtCT	66%	£75	H	(0873) 840678	21	70	120			
Newport	Celtic Manor		75%	£117	H	(0633) 413000	73	350	350		yes	
Newport	Hilton National	Hilton	61%	£80	H	(0633) 412777	119	500	400	yes	yes	
Newport	Stakis Country Court Hotel	Stakis	69%	£113	H	(0633) 413737	139	90	70	yes	yes	
Newport (Magor)	Granada Lodge			£52	L	(0633) 880111	43					

Location	Hotel	Chain	Feature	%	Price	Type	Phone	Rooms			
Tintern Abbey	Beaufort Hotel			60%	£92	H	(0291) 689777	24	60	120	
Tintern Abbey	Royal George	Jarvis		59%	£72	H	(0291) 689205	19	90	120	
Trellech	Village Green				£45	RR	(0600) 860119	2			
Whitebrook	Crown at Whitebrook				£80	RR	(0600) 860254	12			

Gwynedd

Location	Hotel	Chain	Feature	%	Price	Type	Phone	Rooms			
Aberdovey	Plas Penhelig			62%	£80	H	(0654) 767676	11	45	60	
Aberdovey	Trefeddian Hotel			58%	£100	H	(0654) 767213	46			yes
Abersoch	Porth Tocyn Hotel			69%	£94	HR	(0758) 713303	17			
Abersoch	Riverside Hotel			59%	£72	H	(0758) 712419	12	20	30	yes
Bangor	Forte Travelodge	Forte			£45	L	(0248) 370345	30			
Beaumaris	Bulkeley Arms			59%	£67	H	(0248) 810415	38	180	140	
Beddgelert	Royal Goat Hotel			60%	£68	H	(076 686) 224	34	100	130	
Betws-y-Coed	Royal Oak			59%	£78	H	(0690) 710219	27	25	100	
Bontddu	Bontddu Hall			62%	£90	H	(0341) 430661	20	120	120	
Capel Coch	Tre-Ysgawen Hall			76%	£110	HR	(0248) 750750	19	150	120	
Conwy	Sychnant Pass Hotel			60%	£60	H	(0492) 596868	13	40	40	
Holyhead	Treaddur Bay Hotel			65%	£96	H	(0407) 860301	31	120	40	yes
Llandudno	Bodysgallen Hall		Historic House	77%	£155	HR	(0492) 584466	28	50	40	
Llandudno	Empire Hotel			69%	£70	H	(0492) 860555	58	36	45	yes
Llandudno	St Tudno Hotel			69%	£75	HR	(0492) 874411	21			yes
Llandudno	St George's Hotel			61%	£75	H	(0492) 877544	86	250	250	
Llanrug	Seiont Manor			71%	£100	H	(0286) 673366	28	100	100	yes
Llansanffraid Glan Conwy	Old Rectory			73%	£90	HR	(0492) 580611	6			
Llanwnda	Stables Hotel			57%	£42	H	(0286) 830711	14	80	120	
Penmaenpool	George III Hotel				£88	I	(0341) 422525	11		34	
Portmeirion	Hotel Portmeirion			74%	£132	HR	(0766) 770228	34	100	120	yes
Pwllheli	Plas Bodegroes				£140	RR	(0758) 612363	8			
Talsarnau	Maes-y-Neuadd			72%	£109	HR	(0766) 780200	16	40	50	
Talyllyn	Tynycornel Hotel			59%	£90	H	(0654) 782282	16	60	66	

Powys

Location	Hotel	Group	%	Room Price	Cat	Tel	Rooms	Conf	Banq	Leisure Centre	Swim Pool	Golf
Crickhowell	Bear Hotel		63%	£52	I	(0873) 810408	28	60	60			
Crickhowell	Gliffaes Country House Hotel		70%	£65	H	(0874) 730371	22	16	80			
Eglwysfach	Ynyshir Hall		67%	£110	HR	(0654) 781209	8	20	26			
Lake Vyrnwy	Lake Vyrnwy Hotel		68%	£73	HR	(069 173) 692	38	140	140			
Llangammarch Wells	Lake Country House Hotel		81%	£80	HR	(059 12) 202	19	80	85			
Llyswen	Llangoed Hall		57%	£130	HR	(0874) 754525	23	30	40			
Machynlleth	Wynnstay Arms			£53	H	(0654) 702941	20	40	80			
Pant Mawr	Glansevern Arms			£55	I	(055 15) 240	7					
Presteigne	Radnorshire Arms	Forte		£92	I	(0544) 267406	16	30				

CHANNEL ISLANDS

Swimming pool refers to indoor swimming pools only. See the How to Use This Guide section for explanation of our percentage rating system, room pricing and categories.
Key: QMH (Queens Moat Houses), MtCT (Mount Charlotte Thistle), Whitbread (Country Club Hotels)

Location	Hotel	Group	%	Room Price	Cat	Tel	Rooms	Conf	Banq	Leisure Centre	Swim Pool	Golf

Alderney

Location	Hotel	Group	%	Room Price	Cat	Tel	Rooms	Conf	Banq	Leisure Centre	Swim Pool	Golf
St Anne	Chez Andre		63%	£62	H	(0481) 822777	11		75			
St Anne	Inchalla Hotel		64%	£73	HR	(0481) 823220	9	40	50	70		

Guernsey

Location	Hotel	Group	%	Room Price	Cat	Tel	Rooms	Conf	Banq	Leisure Centre	Swim Pool	Golf
Castel	La Grande Mare Hotel		75%	£113	HR	(0481) 56577	34	30	80			yes
Castel	Hougue du Pommier			£71	I	(0481) 56531	43		50			yes
Forest	Mallard Hotel		67%	£66	I	(0481) 64164	47	150	80			yes
Pleinmont	Imperial Hotel			£56	H	(0481) 64044	17					
St Martin	Hotel Bon Port		66%	£88	H	(0481) 39249	14	20	60			
St Martin	St Margaret's Lodge		63%	£76	H	(0481) 35757	47	150	120			
St Martin	La Trelade Hotel		61%	£68	H	(0481) 35454	45	60	200			
St Peter Port	Braye Lodge			£70	H	(0481) 723787	25					
St Peter Port	Duke of Richmond		63%	£65	H	(0481) 726221	75	100	240			
St Peter Port	La Fregate		64%	£108	H	(0481) 724624	13		50			
St Peter Port	Old Government House		68%	£108	H	(0481) 724921	72	110	220			
St Peter Port	St Pierre Park		71%	£135	H	(0481) 728282	135	220	280	yes	yes	yes

Herm

Location	Hotel	Group	%	Room Price	Cat	Tel	Rooms	Conf	Banq	Leisure Centre	Swim Pool	Golf
Herm	White House		64%	£102	HR	(0481) 722159	38					

Jersey

Location	Hotel	Group	%	Room Price	Cat	Tel	Rooms	Conf	Banq	Leisure Centre	Swim Pool	Golf
Bouley Bay	Water's Edge Hotel		64%	£104	H	(0534) 862777	51	65	130			
Gorey	Moorings Hotel		62%	£88	H	(0534) 853633	16	30	60			
Gorey	Old Court House Hotel		64%	£89	H	(0534) 854444	58					
Grouville	Grouville Bay Hotel		62%	£80	H	(0534) 851004	56		150			
Havre des Pas	Hotel de la Plage		66%	£80	H	(0534) 23474	78	20	15			
Havre des Pas	Ommaroo Hotel		59%	£85	H	(0534) 23493	85	150	150			
Portelet Bay	Portelet Hotel		66%	£100	H	(0534) 41204	86	150	140			
Rozel Bay	Chateau la Chaire		74%	£110	HR	(0534) 863354	14		65			
St Aubin	Old Court House Inn			£80	I	(0534) 46433	10		50			
St Brelade	Atlantic Hotel		71%	£130	H	(0534) 44101	50	60	60			
St Brelade	Hotel Chateau Valeuse		65%	£76	HR	(0534) 46281	33		70	yes	yes	
St Brelade	La Place Hotel		67%	£110	H	(0534) 44261	40	45	90			
St Brelade	Sea Crest		64%	£90	HR	(0534) 46353	7		70			
St Brelade's Bay	Hotel L'Horizon	Arcadian	72%	£160	H	(0534) 43101	106	150	240	yes	yes	
St Brelade's Bay	St Brelade's Bay Hotel		70%	£140	H	(0534) 46141	72					
St Helier	Apollo Hotel		63%	£87	H	(0534) 25441	85	120	180	yes	yes	
St Helier	Beaufort Hotel		60%	£93	H	(0534) 32471	54	70	40		yes	
St Helier	De Vere Grand	De Vere	68%	£125	HR	(0534) 22301	115	180	275	yes	yes	
St Helier	Hotel de France			£120	H	(0534) 38990	323			yes	yes	
St Helier	Pomme d'Or Hotel		65%	£90	RR	(0534) 78644	147	300	300			
St Ouen	The Lobster Pot			£70	RR	(0534) 482888	13		100			
St Peter	Mermaid Hotel		64%	£93	H	(0534) 41255	68	80	120		yes	yes

St Saviour	Longueville Manor	80%	£155	HR	(0534) 25501	32	50	75	
St Saviour	Merton Hotel & Leisure Centre	60%	£80	H	(0534) 24231	330			yes

Sark

Sark	Aval Du Creux	57%	£70	HR	(0481) 832036	12		40	
Sark	Dixcart Hotel	64%	£76	HR	(0481) 832015	15			
Sark	Hotel Petit Champ	61%	£68	H	(0481) 832046	16			
Sark	La Sablonnerie Hotel	66%	£60	HR	(0481) 832061	22		40	
Sark	Stocks Hotel	61%	£72	HR	(0481) 832001	24		70	

Isle of Man

Douglas	Palace Hotel	65%	£95	H	(0624) 662662	133	320	300	yes
Douglas	Sefton Hotel	63%	£68	H	(0624) 626011	80	100	100	yes
Ramsey	Grand Island Hotel	67%	£96	H	(0624) 812455	56	300	200	yes

NORTHERN IRELAND

Swimming pool refers to indoor swimming pools only. See the How to Use This Guide section for explanation of our percentage rating system, room pricing and categories.

Key: QMH (Queens Moat Houses), MtCT (Mount Charlotte Thistle), Whitbread (Country Club Hotels)

Co Antrim

Location	Hotel	Group	%	Room Price	Cat	Tel	Rooms	Conf	Banq	Leisure Centre	Swim Pool	Golf
Ballymena	Galgorm Manor		71%	£110	HR	(0266) 881001	23	500	300			
Belfast	Dukes Hotel		67%	£98	H	(0232) 236666	21	130	140			
Belfast	Europa Hotel			£130	H	(0232) 327000	184	1,200	600			
Belfast	Plaza Hotel		64%	£82	H	(0232) 333555	76	100	100			
Belfast	Stormont Hotel		69%	£127	H	(0232) 658621	106	500	350			
Belfast	Wellington Park		59%	£94	H	(0232) 381111	50	180	120			
Belfast Airport	Novotel	Novotel	62%	£75	H	(084 94) 22033	108	250	180			
Bushmills	Bushmills Inn		58%	£78	H	(026 57) 32339	11	85	85			
Dunadry	Dunadry Inn		64%	£105	H	(0849) 432474	67	350	300			
Dunmurry	Forte Crest Belfast	Forte	67%	£80	H	(0232) 612101	82	450	350	yes	yes	
Larne	Magheramorne House		63%	£66	H	(0574) 279444	22	180	180			
Portballintrae	Bayview Hotel		58%	£65	H	(026 57) 31453	16	300	220			
Templepatrick	Templeton Hotel		66%	£100	H	(084 94) 32984	20	400	350		yes	

Co Down

Annalong	Glassdrumman Lodge	69%	£95	HR	(039 67) 68451	10	16	60	
Comber	La Mon House	59%	£85	H	(0232) 448631	38	1,100	450	yes
Crawfordsburn	Old Inn		£90	I	(0247) 853255	34	150	90	yes
Downpatrick	Tyrella House		£35	PH	(0396) 851422	3			
Holywood	Culloden Hotel	72%	£152	HR	(0232) 425223	89	500	300	yes
Newcastle	Slieve Donard Hotel	63%	£99	H	(039 67) 23681	110	1,000	440	yes
Portaferry	Portaferry Hotel	63%	£80	HR	(024 77) 28231	14			

Londonderry

Aghadowey	Greenhill House		£42	PH	(0265) 868241	6			
Garvagh	MacDuff's Restaurant, Blackheath		£60	RR	(0265) 868433	5			
Londonderry	Beech Hill House Hotel	59%	£85	HR	(0504) 49279	17	350	250	
Londonderry	Everglades Hotel	59%	£80	H	(0504) 46722	52	350	250	

REPUBLIC OF IRELAND

Swimming pool refers to indoor swimming pools only. See the How to Use This Guide section for explanation of our percentage rating system, room pricing and categories.
Key: QMH (Queens Moat Houses), MtCT (Mount Charlotte Thistle), Whitbread (Country Club Hotels)

Location	Hotel	Group	%	Room Price	Cat	Tel	Rooms	Conf	Banq	Leisure Centre	Swim Pool	Golf
Co Cavan												
Ballyconnell	Slieve Russell Hotel		78%	£140	H	(049) 26444	150	800	450	yes	yes	yes
Co Clare												
Ballyvaughan	Gregans Castle		71%	£99	HR	(065) 77005	22					
Bunratty	Fitzpatricks Shannon Shamrock		60%	£137	H	(061) 361177	115	200	150	yes		
Ennis	Auburn Lodge		61%	£70	H	(065) 21247	100	500	400		yes	
Ennis	Old Ground Hotel	Forte	66%	£99	H	(065) 28127	58	250	180			
Ennis	West County Inn		59%	£55	H	(065) 28421	110	200	500			
Newmarket-on-Fergus	Clare Inn Hotel		64%	£87	H	(061) 368161	121	400	350			
Newmarket-on-Fergus	Dromoland Castle		79%	£262	HR	(061) 368144	73	450	450		yes	yes
Shannon	Oakwood Arms Hotel		63%	£96	H	(061) 361500	46	200	250			
Shannon Airport	Great Southern	Great Southern	64%	£114	H	(061) 471122	115	170	140	yes		yes
Co Cork												
Ahakista	Hillcrest House			£33	PH	(027) 67045	4					
Ahakista	Shiro			£36	RR	(027) 67030	1					

County	Hotel	Chain		£	Type	Phone						
Ballycotton	Bayview Hotel		67%	£80	H	(021) 646746	35					
Ballylickey	Ballylickey Manor House		67%	£99	H	(027) 50071	5					
Ballylickey	Larchwood House		70%	£36	RR	(027) 66181	4					
Ballylickey	Seaview Hotel		70%	£100	HR	(027) 50462	17	35				
Bantry	Bantry House			£90	PH	(027) 50047	7					
Blarney	Blarney Park Hotel		63%	£110	H	(021) 385281	76	340	350	yes	yes	
Castlelyons	Ballyvolane House			£80	PH	(025) 36349	6		25			
Cork	Arbutus Lodge		70%	£80	HR	(021) 501237	20	120	180			
Cork	Fitzpatrick Silver Springs		65%	£107	H	(021) 507533	110	1,000	750	yes	yes	
Cork	Flemings			£55	RR	(021) 821621	4					
Cork	Forte Travelodge	Forte		£42	L	(021) 310722	40					
Cork	Imperial Hotel		66%	£121	H	(021) 274040	101	600	350			
Cork	Jurys Hotel	Jurys	66%	£140	H	(021) 276622	185	520	700	yes	yes	
Cork	Lotamore House		60%	£48	H	(021) 822344	20	20	20			
Cork	Metropole Hotel		58%	£88	H	(021) 508122	108	500	300			
Cork	Morrisons Island Hotel		68%	£119	H	(021) 275858	40	15	15			
Cork	Rochestown Park Hotel		67%	£85	H	(021) 892233	63	150	150	yes	yes	
Cork	Seven North Mall			£60	PH	(021) 397191	5					
Goleen Harbour	Herons Cove Restaurant			£33	RR	(028) 35225	3					
Innishannon	Innishannon House Hotel		63%	£95	H	(021) 775121	14	200	150			
Kanturk	Assolas Country House		72%	£104	HR	(029) 50015	9	20	20			
Kinsale	Actons Hotel	Forte	60%	£100	H	(021) 772135	57	400	300	yes	yes	
Kinsale	Blue Haven Hotel			£84	HR	(021) 772209	18					
Kinsale	The Old Bank House			£80	PH	(021) 774075	9					
Kinsale	Old Presbytery			£40	H	(021) 772027	6					
Kinsale	Scilly House		65%	£90	H	(021) 772413	7	25				
Mallow	Longueville House		72%	£110	HR	(022) 47156	16	20				
Shanagarry	Ballymaloe House		66%	£120	HR	(021) 652531	30					
Youghal	Aherne's Seafood Restaurant			£100	RR	(024) 92424	10					yes

Location	Hotel	Group	%	Room Price	Cat	Tel	Rooms	Conf	Banq	Leisure Centre	Swim Pool	Golf
Co Donegal												
Dunkineely	Castle Murray House		69%	£44	HR	(073) 37022	10	25				
Lough Eske	Ardnamona House			£60	PH	(073) 22650	5					
Lough Eske	Harvey's Point Country Hotel		63%	£99	H	(073) 22208	20	300	200			
Rathmullan	Rathmullan House		62%	£104	HR	(074) 58188	23	300			yes	
Rossnowlagh	Sand House Hotel		69%	£88	H	(072) 51777	40	75				
Rossnowlagh	Smugglers Creek Inn			£40	IR	(072) 52366	5					
Co Dublin												
Dublin	Aberdeen Lodge			£65	PH	(01) 283 8155	16					
Dublin	Anglesea Town House			£90	PH	(01) 668 3877	7					
Dublin	Ariel House			£85	PH	(01) 668 5512	28					
Dublin	Berkeley Court	Doyle	76%	£191	H	(01) 660 1711	207	400	300			
Dublin	Blooms Hotel		60%	£121	H	(01) 671 5622	86	30				
Dublin	Burlington Hotel	Doyle	70%	£154	H	(01) 660 5222	450	1,000	1,000			
Dublin	Central Hotel		57%	£139	H	(01) 679 7302	70	80	70			
Dublin	Clarence Hotel		60%	£50	HR	(01) 677 6178	45	60	60			
Dublin	Hotel Conrad		75%	£222	H	(01) 676 5555	191	250	150			
Dublin	Davenport Hotel		76%	£180	H	(01) 661 6799	120	300	400			
Dublin	Doyle Montrose Hotel	Doyle	65%	£106	H	(01) 269 3311	179	90				
Dublin	Doyle Tara Hotel	Doyle	61%	£106	H	(01) 269 4666	114	200	165			
Dublin	Georgian House		56%	£86	H	(01) 661 8832	33					
Dublin	Glenveagh Town House			£60	PH	(01) 668 4612	11					
Dublin	Grafton Plaza Hotel		64%	£90	H	(01) 475 0888	75	20	36			
Dublin	Gresham Hotel	Ryan	64%	£140	H	(01) 874 6881	200	325	200			

Town	Chain	Hotel	Rating	Rate	Cat	Phone	Rooms	Min	Max	Leisure	Golf
Dublin		Grey Door	70%	£99	RR	(01) 676 3286	7				
Dublin		Hibernian Hotel	74%	£135	HR	(01) 668 7666	30	40	55	yes	
Dublin	Jurys	Jurys Hotel and Towers		£162	H	(01) 660 5000	390	850	600	yes	
Dublin		Jurys Christchurch Inn	55%	£56	H	(01) 475 0111	183				
Dublin		Marine Hotel	64%	£84	H	(01) 832 2613	26	150	200	yes	
Dublin		Merrion Hall		£70	PH	(01) 681426	15				
Dublin		Mont Clare Hotel	66%	£146	H	(01) 661 6799	74	150	120		
Dublin		Number 31		£68	PH	(01) 676 5011	5				
Dublin		Raglan Lodge		£77	PH	(01) 660 6697	7				
Dublin		Royal Dublin Hotel	63%	£108	H	(01) 873 3666	117	250	230		
Dublin		Sachs Hotel	62%	£98	H	(01) 668 0995	20	170	150		
Dublin	Forte	Shelbourne Hotel	74%	£243	H	(01) 676 6471	164	500	300		
Dublin		Stauntons on the Green		£88	PH	(01) 478 2133	32				
Dublin		Stephen's Hall Hotel	65%	£143	HR	(01) 661 0585	37				
Dublin	Doyle	The Westbury	79%	£189	H	(01) 679 1122	203	300	170	yes	
Dublin	Forte	Forte Crest	57%	£129	H	(01) 844 4211	188	160	150		
Dublin Airport		Chestnut Lodge		£50	PH	(01) 280 7860	4				
Dun Laoghaire	Ryan	Royal Marine Hotel	64%	£85	H	(01) 280 1911	104	700	400	yes	
Dun Laoghaire		Deer Park Hotel	64%	£80	H	(01) 832 2624	50	140	100		yes
Howth		Howth Lodge Hotel	65%	£90	H	(01) 832 1010	46	200	200	yes	yes
Howth		Court Hotel	68%	£97	H	(01) 285 1622	86	300	300	yes	yes
Killiney		Fitzpatrick's Castle	68%	£160	H	(01) 284 0700	90	550	400	yes	
Killiney		Grand Hotel	66%	£90	H	(01) 845 0000	100	900	600		
Malahide	Forte	Forte Travelodge		£42	L	(01) 840 9233	40				

Co Galway

Town	Chain	Hotel	Rating	Rate	Cat	Phone	Rooms	Min	Max
Ballyconneely		Erriseask House	64%	£80	HR	(095) 23553	13		
Ballynahinch		Ballynahinch Castle	71%	£114	H	(095) 31006	28	25	
Cashel		Cashel House	76%	£145	HR	(095) 31001	32		
Cashel		Zetland House	65%	£115	H	(095) 31111	20		
Clifden		Abbeyglen Castle	60%	£99	H	(095) 21201	40	230	200

Location	Hotel	Group	%	Room Price	Cat	Tel	Rooms	Conf	Banq	Leisure Centre	Swim Pool	Golf
Clifden	Ardagh Hotel		60%	£83	HR	(095) 21384	21					
Clifden	Foyles Hotel		61%	£79	H	(095) 21801	30					
Clifden	O'Grady's Seafood Restaurant			£36	RR	(095) 21450	11					
Clifden	The Quay House			£50	RR	(095) 21369	6					
Clifden	Rock Glen Manor		61%	£90	HR	(095) 21035	29				yes	
Furbo	Connemara Coast Hotel		71%	£120	H	(091) 92108	113					
Galway	Ardilaun House		66%	£95	H	(091) 21433	90	400	250			
Galway	Brennans Yard		64%	£90	H	(091) 68166	24					
Galway	Corrib Great Southern Hotel	Great Southern	68%	£128	H	(091) 755281	180	850	700		yes	
Galway	Glenlo Abbey		68%	£115	H	(091) 26666	43	48	75			
Galway	Great Southern	Great Southern	69%	£113	H	(091) 64041	116	450	350		yes	
Galway	Jurys Galway Inn		55%	£61	H	(091) 66444	128					
Leenane	Delphi Lodge			£70	PH	(095) 42211	11					
Leenane	Killary Lodge		59%	£56	H	(095) 42276	18	35				
Leenane	Portfinn Lodge			£35	RR	(095) 42265	8					
Letterfrack	Rosleague Manor		72%	£90	H	(095) 41101	20					
Moycullen	Cloonabinnia House Hotel		61%	£55	H	(091) 85555	14					
Oughterard	Connemara Gateway Hotel		66%	£108	HR	(091) 82328	62	180	130		yes	
Oughterard	Currarevagh House		65%	£91	H	(091) 82312	15					
Oughterard	Sweeney's Oughterard House		59%	£98	H	(091) 82207	20					
Recess	Lough Inagh Lodge		68%	£104	H	(095) 34706	12	24				
Renvyle	Renvyle House		63%	£118	H	(095) 43511	65	120	150			
Spiddal	Bridge House Inn		59%	£65	H	(091) 83118	14					yes

Co Kerry

Location	Hotel	Group	%	Room Price	Cat	Tel	Rooms	Conf	Banq	Leisure Centre	Swim Pool	Golf
Beaufort	Dunloe Castle		71%	£96	H	(064) 44111	120	300	200			
Caherdaniel	Derrynane Hotel		62%	£70	HR	(066) 75136	75					
Caragh Lake	Hotel Ard-na-Sidhe		70%	£96	H	(066) 69105	20				yes	

Location	Hotel	Chain	Rating	Price	Type	Phone	Rooms					
Caragh Lake	Caragh Lodge		65%	£99	H	(066) 69115	10		120			
Dingle	Dingle Skellig Hotel		61%	£86	H	(066) 51144	115				yes	
Dingle	Doyle's Seafood Bar & Townhouse			£62	RR	(066) 51174	8					
Dingle	Greenmount House			£40	PH	(066) 51414	8					
Kenmare	d'Arcy's			£30	RR	(064) 41589	5					yes
Kenmare	Dromquinna Manor Hotel		60%	£85	H	(064) 41657	28					
Kenmare	Hawthorn House			£36	PH	(064) 41035	8					
Kenmare	Park Hotel Kenmare		87%	£270	HR	(064) 41200	50	50	30			yes
Kenmare	Sheen Falls Lodge		87%	£230	HR	(064) 41600	40	120	120		yes	
Killarney	Aghadoe Heights Hotel		70%	£145	HR	(064) 31766	60	100	130		yes	
Killarney	Cahernane Hotel		66%	£110	HR	(064) 31895	48					
Killarney	Hotel Europe		72%	£96	HR	(064) 31900	205	500	600	yes	yes	
Killarney	Foley's Townhouse			£70	RR	(064) 31217	12	25	95			
Killarney	Great Southern	Great Southern	69%	£129	H	(064) 31262	180	1,000	650	yes	yes	
Killarney	Kathleen's Country House			£60	PH	(064) 32810	17					
Killarney	Killarney Towers Hotel		57%	£120	H	(064) 31038	157					
Killarney	Killarney Park Hotel		73%	£130	H	(064) 35555	66	150	160	yes	yes	
Killarney	Randles Court Hotel			£120	H	(064) 35333	37		130			
Killarney	Torc Great Southern	Great Southern	63%	£94	H	(064) 31611	94				yes	
Killarney	Great Southern	Great Southern	72%	£161	H	(064) 45122	84	80	70	yes	yes	
Parknasilla	Ballyseede Castle Hotel		60%	£85	H	(066) 25799	15	180	80	yes	yes	
Tralee	Brandon Hotel		61%	£96	H	(066) 23333	160	1,100	550	yes	yes	

Co Kildare

Location	Hotel	Chain	Rating	Price	Type	Phone	Rooms					
Athy	Tonlegee House		70%	£58	RR	(0507) 31473	5		200			
Castledermot	Kilkea Castle		75%	£225	HR	(0503) 45156	45	200	70		yes	
Maynooth	Moyglare Manor		68%	£136	HR	(01) 628 6351	17	40	600			
Newbridge	Hotel Keadeen		70%	£85	H	(045) 31666	37	800	160			
Straffan	Barberstown Castle		70%	£110	HR	(01) 628 8157	10	200	44	yes		
Straffan	Kildare Hotel		87%	£250	HR	(01) 627 3333	45	70		yes	yes	yes

Location	Hotel	Group	%	Room Price	Cat	Tel	Rooms	Conf	Banq	Leisure Centre	Swim Pool	Golf
Kilkenny	Lacken House			£55	RR	(056) 61085	8	12				
Kilkenny	Newpark Hotel		58%	£97	H	(056) 22122	84	600	350	yes	yes	
Maddoxtown	Blanchville House			£50	PH	(056) 27197	6	30				
Thomastown	Mount Juliet Hotel		84%	£215	HR	(056) 24455	56	50	140	yes	yes	yes

Co Laois

Location	Hotel	Group	%	Room Price	Cat	Tel	Rooms	Conf	Banq	Leisure Centre	Swim Pool	Golf
Mountrath	Roundwood House		58%	£64	HR	(0502) 32120	6	12				

Co Leitrim

Location	Hotel	Group	%	Room Price	Cat	Tel	Rooms	Conf	Banq	Leisure Centre	Swim Pool	Golf
Carrick-on-Shannon	Hollywell House			£50	PH	(078) 21124	3					

Co Limerick

Location	Hotel	Group	%	Room Price	Cat	Tel	Rooms	Conf	Banq	Leisure Centre	Swim Pool	Golf
Adare	Adare Manor		81%	£220	HR	(061) 396566	64		220		yes	
Adare	Dunraven Arms		72%	£133	HR	(061) 396633	43	300	250			
Adare	Woodlands House Hotel		60%	£50	H	(061) 396118	57	350	270			
Castleconnell	Castle Oaks House Hotel		64%	£72	H	(061) 377666	11	350	300	yes	yes	
Limerick	Castletroy Park Hotel		74%	£139	HR	(061) 335566	107	400	300	yes	yes	
Limerick	Greenhills Hotel		62%	£119	H	(061) 453033	60	600	400	yes	yes	
Limerick	Jurys Hotel	Jurys	68%	£116	H	(061) 327777	96	200	130	yes	yes	
Limerick	Limerick Inn Hotel	Ryan	68%	£117	H	(061) 326666	153	600	800	yes	yes	
Limerick	Two Mile Inn		63%	£78	H	(061) 326255	125	350	350	yes	yes	

Co Louth

Town	Hotel	%	Price	Code	Phone	Rooms					
Ardee	The Gables		£34	RR	(041) 53789	5					
Dundalk	Ballymascanlon House	59%	£77	H	(042) 71124	36	250	300	yes	yes	

Co Mayo

Town	Hotel	%	Price	Code	Phone	Rooms					
Ballina	Downhill Hotel	65%	£86	H	(096) 21033	50	500	450	yes	yes	
Ballina	Mount Falcon Castle	60%	£72	HR	(096) 21172	10	40	140			
Cong	Ashford Castle	88%	£270	HR	(092) 46003	83					yes
Crossmolina	Enniscoe House	63%	£88	H	(096) 31112	6					
Newport	Newport House	67%	£124	HR	(098) 41222	20	150	150			
Westport	The Olde Railway Hotel	63%	£65	H	(098) 25166	24					

Co Meath

Town	Hotel	%	Price	Code	Phone	Rooms					
Navan	Ardboyne Hotel	60%	£75	HR	(046) 23119	27	700	400			

Co Monaghan

Town	Hotel	%	Price	Code	Phone	Rooms					
Carrickmacross	Nuremore Hotel	72%	£120	H	(042) 61438	69	300	500	yes	yes	yes
Scotshouse	Hilton Park		£111	PH	(047) 56007	5				yes	yes

Co Offaly

Town	Hotel	%	Price	Code	Phone	Rooms					
Birr	Dooly's Hotel	60%	£50	H	(0509) 20032	18					
Birr	Tullanisk		£76	PH	(0509) 20572	7					

Co Roscommon

Town	Hotel	%	Price	Code	Phone	Rooms					
Hodson Bay	Hodson Bay Hotel	65%	£90	H	(0902) 92444	46	500	400	yes		

Location	Hotel	Group	%	Room Price	Cat	Tel	Rooms	Conf	Banq	Leisure Centre	Swim Pool	Golf
Co Sligo												
Ballymote	Temple House		61%	£70	H	(071) 83329	5					
Boyle	Cromleach Lodge		78%	£118	HR	(071) 65155	10					
Collooney	Glebe House		60%	£30	RR	(071) 67787	4					
Collooney	Markree Castle			£97	H	(071) 67800	15	40	100			
Riverstown	Coopershill House		69%	£88	HR	(071) 65108	7					
Sligo	Sligo Park		58%	£95	H	(071) 60291	90			yes	yes	
Co Tipperary												
Clonmel	Clonmel Arms		61%	£83	H	(052) 21233	31	600	400			
Dundrum	Dundrum House		66%	£92	H	(062) 71116	55	400	350			yes
Glen of Aherlow	Aherlow House		63%	£53	H	(062) 56153	10	280	220			
Kilcoran	Kilcoran Lodge		58%	£68	H	(052) 41288	23	300	220	yes	yes	
Co Waterford												
Waterford	Granville Hotel		69%	£83	H	(051) 55111	74	300	200			
Waterford	Jurys Hotel	Jurys	61%	£106	H	(051) 32111	98	700	600	yes	yes	
Waterford	Prendiville's			£46	RR	(051) 78851	9					
Waterford	Tower Hotel		59%	£114	H	(051) 75801	141	500	600	yes		
Waterford	Waterford Castle		74%	£220	HR	(051) 78203	19	16			yes	yes
Co Wexford												
Bunclody	Clohamon House			£80	PH	(054) 77253	4					
Ferrycarrig Bridge	Ferrycarrig Hotel		61%	£90	HR	(053) 22999	40	400	400			

Location	Hotel	Chain	%	Price	Type	Phone					
Gorey	Marlfield House		81%	£154	HR	(055) 21124	19	20	30		
Newbawn	Cedar Lodge		62%	£75	H	(051) 28386	18	100	70		yes
Newbay	Newbay Country House			£60	PH	(053) 42779	6	150	200		yes
Rosslare	Great Southern	Great Southern	62%	£91	H	(053) 33233	99	20	200	yes	
Rosslare	Kelly's Strand Hotel		71%	£84	H	(053) 32114	99	600	450		
Wexford	White's Hotel		62%	£76	H	(053) 22311	82				

Co Wicklow

Location	Hotel	%	Price	Type	Phone					
Blessington	Downshire House	59%	£66	H	(045) 65199	25	100	250		
Delgany	Glenview Hotel	63%	£90	H	(01) 287 3399	37	300	200		
Dunlavin	Rathsallagh House	67%	£110	HR	(045) 53112	17	50		yes	yes
Enniskerry	Enniscree Lodge	59%	£77	HR	(01) 286 3542	10				
Laragh	Mitchell's of Laragh	60%	£36	RR	(0404) 45302	5	50	30		
Rathnew	Hunter's Hotel	76%	£80	HR	(0404) 40106	17	20			
Rathnew	Tinakilly House	59%	£116	HR	(0404) 69274	29	150	100		
Wicklow	Old Rectory		£90	HR	(0404) 67048	5				

Hotels with Sporting Facilities

ENGLAND

Location	Hotel	Leisure Centre	Indoor Pool	Outdoor Pool	Squash	Tennis	Golf	Fishing	Riding	Croquet
Avon										
Alveston	Forte Posthouse			▲						
Bath	Bath Spa Hotel	▲	▲			▲				▲
Bath	Hilton National	▲	▲							
Bath	Priory Hotel				▲					
Bristol	Aztec Hotel	▲	▲		▲					
Bristol	Bristol Marriott Hotel	▲	▲							
Bristol	Forte Crest	▲	▲							
Bristol	Hilton National Bristol	▲	▲							
Bristol	Redwood Lodge Country Club	▲	▲	▲	▲	▲				▲
Bristol	Stakis Bristol Hotel	▲	▲							
Bristol	Swallow Royal Hotel	▲	▲							
Dunkirk	Petty France Hotel									▲
Freshford	Homewood Park					▲				
Hunstrete	Hunstrete House					▲				▲
Monkton Combe	Combe Grove Manor	▲	▲	▲		▲				▲
Ston Easton	Ston Easton Park					▲				▲
Thornbury	Thornbury Castle									▲
Weston-super-Mare	Grand Atlantic			▲						
Winterbourne	Grange Resort Hotel		▲							
Bedford										
Flitwick	Flitwick Manor					▲				▲
Berkshire										
Ascot	Berystede Hotel			▲						▲
Ascot	Royal Berkshire			▲	▲	▲				▲
Bracknell	Coppid Beech Hotel			▲						
Elcot	Jarvis Elcot Park	▲	▲			▲				
Hurley	Ye Olde Bell									▲
Maidenhead	Fredrick's									▲
Maidenhead	Holiday Inn		▲		▲					
Newbury	Donnington Valley Hotel						▲	▲		
Newbury	Foley Lodge		▲							
Newbury	Hilton National	▲	▲							
Newbury	Millwaters							▲		▲
Newbury	Stakis Newbury Hotel	▲	▲							
Pingewood	Kirtons Farm Country Club	▲	▲			▲	▲			
Reading	Forte Posthouse	▲	▲							
Reading	Holiday Inn Reading	▲	▲							
Reading	Ramada Hotel	▲	▲							
Sindlesham	Reading Moat House						▲			
Slough	Copthorne Hotel Slough/Windsor	▲	▲							
Slough	Heathrow/Slough Marriott Hotel	▲	▲							
Taplow	Cliveden	▲	▲	▲	▲	▲		▲	▲	▲
Windsor	Oakley Court						▲	▲		
Wokingham	Stakis St Anne's Manor	▲				▲				
Woolton Hill	Hollington House Hotel	▲	▲	▲		▲				

Location	Hotel	Leisure Centre	Indoor Pool	Outdoor Pool	Squash	Tennis	Golf	Fishing	Riding	Croquet
Buckinghamshire										
Aylesbury	Forte Posthouse			▲						
Aylesbury	Hartwell House		▲			▲	▲			
Beaconsfield	Bellhouse Hotel	▲	▲		▲	▲				
Burnham	Burnham Beeches Moat House		▲			▲				
Burnham	Grovefield Hotel									▲
Gerrards Cross	Bull Hotel									▲
Marlow	Compleat Angler Hotel					▲		▲		▲
Medmenham	Danesfield House				▲	▲	▲			▲
Milton Keynes	Forte Crest	▲	▲							
Milton Keynes	Friendly Hotel	▲	▲							
Cambridgeshire										
Cambridge	Cambridgeshire Moat House		▲		▲	▲	▲			
Cambridge	Forte Posthouse	▲	▲							
Cambridge	Garden House								▲	
Cambridge	Holiday Inn		▲							
Peterborough	Forte Posthouse		▲							
Peterborough	Peterborough Moat House	▲	▲							
Peterborough	Swallow Hotel	▲	▲							
Six Mile Bottom	Swynford Paddocks						▲			▲
Cheshire										
Alsager	Manor House		▲							
Broxton	Birches Hotel	▲	▲		▲	▲				▲
Chester	Abbots Well	▲	▲							
Chester	Crabwall Manor									▲
Chester	Forte Posthouse	▲	▲							
Chester	Mollington Banastre	▲	▲		▲					▲
Chester	Rowton Hall	▲	▲			▲				▲
Knutsford	Cottons Hotel	▲	▲			▲				
Mottram St Andrew	De Vere Mottram Hall		▲			▲	▲	▲		
Nantwich	Rookery Hall					▲				
Runcorn	Forte Posthouse		▲							
Warrington	Lord Daresbury Hotel	▲	▲		▲					
Wilmslow	Moat House	▲	▲		▲					
Cleveland										
Crathorne	Crathorne Hall									▲
Easington	Grinkle Park						▲		▲	▲
Stockton-on-Tees	Swallow Hotel	▲	▲							
Cornwall										
Carlyon Bay	Carlyon Bay Hotel		▲	▲		▲	▲			▲
Constantine Bay	Treglos Hotel		▲							▲
Falmouth	Falmouth Hotel	▲	▲							
Falmouth	Royal Duchy Hotel		▲							
Falmouth	St Michael's Hotel	▲	▲							
Golant	Cormorant Hotel		▲							
Helland Bridge	Tredethy Country Hotel			▲						
Lamorna Cove	Lamorna Cove Hotel			▲						
Liskeard	Well House			▲		▲				
Looe	Talland Bay Hotel			▲						▲
Mawnan	Budock Vean Hotel	▲					▲			
Mawnan	Meudon Hotel								▲	
Mawnan	Nansidwell					▲				

Location	Hotel	Leisure Centre	Indoor Pool	Outdoor Pool	Squash	Tennis	Golf	Fishing	Riding	Croquet
Mullion	Polurrian Hotel	▲	▲	▲	▲	▲				▲
Newlyn	Higher Faugan Country House			▲		▲				
Newquay	Hotel Bristol	▲								
Newquay	Hotel Riviera				▲	▲				
Porth	Trevelgue Hotel	▲	▲		▲	▲	▲	▲		
St Austell	Boscundle Manor			▲			▲			
St Ives	Garrack Hotel	▲								
Veryan	Nare Hotel	▲	▲			▲				

Cumbria

Location	Hotel	Leisure Centre	Indoor Pool	Outdoor Pool	Squash	Tennis	Golf	Fishing	Riding	Croquet
Alston	Lovelady Shield						▲			
Ambleside	Kirkstone Foot									▲
Ambleside	Nanny Brow								▲	▲
Ambleside	Rothay Manor Hotel									▲
Appleby-in-Westmorland	Appleby Manor Hotel	▲								
Appleby-in-Westmorland	Tufton Arms							▲		
Bassenthwaite	Armathwaite Hall	▲	▲				▲	▲	▲	
Borrowdale	Stakis Lodore Swiss Hotel	▲	▲		▲	▲				
Bowness-on-Windermere	Belsfield Hotel	▲	▲			▲				
Bowness-on-Windermere	Gilpin Lodge									▲
Bowness-on-Windermere	Linthwaite House								▲	▲
Bowness-on-Windermere	Old England Hotel			▲						
Carlisle	Swallow Hilltop	▲	▲							
Faugh	String of Horses Inn		▲							
Grasmere	Michael's Nook									▲
Grasmere	White Moss House							▲		
Grasmere	Wordsworth Hotel	▲	▲							
Langdale	Langdale Hotel	▲	▲		▲	▲		▲		▲
Newby Bridge	The Swan							▲	▲	
Penrith	North Lakes Hotel	▲	▲		▲					
Ravenstonedale	Black Swan Inn						▲	▲		
Ullswater	Old Church Hotel							▲		
Ullswater	Rampsbeck Country House							▲		▲
Wetheral	The Crown	▲	▲							
Windermere	Holbeck Ghyll						▲			
Witherslack	Old Vicarage						▲			▲

Derbyshire

Location	Hotel	Leisure Centre	Indoor Pool	Outdoor Pool	Squash	Tennis	Golf	Fishing	Riding	Croquet
Ashford-in-the-Water	Riverside Hotel								▲	▲
Bakewell	Hassop Hall						▲			
Baslow	Cavendish Hotel						▲			
Castle Donington	Donington Thistle		▲							
Chesterfield	Chesterfield Hotel	▲	▲							
Dovedale	Izaak Walton Hotel						▲			
Dovedale	Peveril of the Peak						▲			
Matlock	Riber Hall						▲			
Matlock Bath	New Bath Hotel		▲	▲			▲			
Morley	Breadsall Priory	▲	▲		▲	▲	▲			▲
Rowsley	Peacock Hotel								▲	
South Normanton	Swallow Hotel	▲	▲							

Devon

Location	Hotel	Leisure Centre	Indoor Pool	Outdoor Pool	Squash	Tennis	Golf	Fishing	Riding	Croquet
Bigbury-on-Sea	Burgh Island Hotel						▲		▲	▲
Chagford	Gidleigh Park						▲		▲	▲
Chagford	Great Tree Hotel								▲	▲
Chagford	Mill End								▲	
Chittlehamholt	Highbullen	▲	▲	▲	▲	▲	▲	▲		▲

Location	Hotel	Leisure Centre	Indoor Pool	Outdoor Pool	Squash	Tennis	Golf	Fishing	Riding	Croquet
Clawton	Court Barn					▲				▲
Dartmouth	Stoke Lodge	▲	▲	▲		▲				
Exeter	Forte Crest		▲							
Exmouth	Imperial Hotel				▲	▲				
Fairy Cross	Portledge Hotel				▲	▲				
Gittisham	Combe House								▲	▲
Hatherleigh	George Hotel			▲						
Hawkchurch	Fairwater Head Hotel									▲
Haytor	Bel Alp House									▲
Holbeton	Alston Hall	▲	▲	▲		▲				▲
Hope Cove	Lantern Lodge		▲							
Huntsham	Huntsham Court					▲				▲
Lewdown	Lewtrenchard Manor								▲	▲
Lifton	Arundell Arms								▲	
Lynmouth	Rising Sun Inn								▲	
Newton Abbot	Passage House	▲	▲							
Paignton	Palace Hotel			▲		▲				
Paignton	Redcliffe Hotel	▲	▲							
Plymouth	Boringdon Hall				▲	▲	▲			
Plymouth	Copthorne Hotel		▲							
Plymouth	Forte Posthouse			▲						
Plymouth	Moat House	▲	▲							
Poundsgate	Leusdon Lodge Hotel									▲
Salcombe	Marine Hotel	▲	▲							
Salcombe	Soar Mill Cove		▲	▲		▲				
Salcombe	South Sands Hotel		▲							
Salcombe	Tides Reach	▲	▲		▲					
Saunton	Saunton Sands	▲	▲	▲	▲	▲				▲
Sidmouth	Fortfield Hotel					▲				
Sidmouth	Victoria Hotel	▲	▲	▲	▲	▲				
South Molton	Whitechapel Manor									▲
Thurlestone	Thurlestone Hotel	▲	▲	▲	▲	▲	▲			
Torquay	Grand Hotel	▲	▲	▲		▲				
Torquay	Imperial Hotel	▲	▲		▲	▲				
Torquay	Livermead House Hotel		▲			▲				
Torquay	Livermead Cliff Hotel		▲							
Torquay	Osborne Hotel		▲	▲		▲				
Torquay	Palace Hotel	▲	▲	▲		▲	▲			▲
Whimple	Woodhayes Hotel									▲
Woolacombe	Woolacombe Bay Hotel	▲	▲	▲	▲	▲				▲
Yelverton	Moorland Links					▲				

Dorset

Location	Hotel	Leisure Centre	Indoor Pool	Outdoor Pool	Squash	Tennis	Golf	Fishing	Riding	Croquet
Bournemouth	Carlton Hotel			▲						
Bournemouth	Chine Hotel		▲	▲						
Bournemouth	Norfolk Royale		▲							
Bournemouth	Palace Court	▲	▲							
Bournemouth	Royal Bath Hotel	▲	▲							▲
Bournemouth	Swallow Highcliff Hotel		▲			▲				
Chedington	Chedington Court						▲			▲
Chedington	Hazel Barton									▲
Evershot	Summer Lodge			▲		▲				
Ferndown	Dormy Hotel	▲	▲		▲	▲	▲			
Gillingham	Stock Hill House									
Longham	Bridge House								▲	
Mudeford	Avonmouth Hotel			▲						
Poole	Haven Hotel			▲	▲	▲				
Poole	Sandbanks Hotel	▲	▲							
Shaftesbury	Royal Chase Hotel		▲							

Location	Hotel	Leisure Centre	Indoor Pool	Outdoor Pool	Squash	Tennis	Golf	Fishing	Riding	Croquet
Sherborne	Sherborne Hotel									▲
Studland Bay	Knoll House		▲	▲		▲	▲			
Wareham	Priory Hotel								▲	
Wareham	Springfield Country Hotel	▲	▲	▲		▲				

Durham

Location	Hotel	Leisure Centre	Indoor Pool	Outdoor Pool	Squash	Tennis	Golf	Fishing	Riding	Croquet
Coatham Mundeville	Hall Garth Country Club	▲	▲			▲	▲			
Darlington	Blackwell Grange Moat House	▲	▲							
Durham	Royal County Hotel	▲	▲							
Neasham	Newbus Arms				▲					

Essex

Location	Hotel	Leisure Centre	Indoor Pool	Outdoor Pool	Squash	Tennis	Golf	Fishing	Riding	Croquet
Brentwood	Forte Posthouse			▲						
Broxted	Whitehall				▲	▲				
Colchester	Forte Posthouse	▲	▲							
Dedham	Maison Talbooth									▲
Great Baddow	Pontlands Park	▲	▲							
North Stifford	Stifford Moat House						▲			
Waltham Abbey	Swallow Hotel		▲							▲

Gloucestershire

Location	Hotel	Leisure Centre	Indoor Pool	Outdoor Pool	Squash	Tennis	Golf	Fishing	Riding	Croquet
Bibury	The Swan							▲		
Bourton-on-the-Water	Dial House									▲
Charingworth	Charingworth Manor	▲	▲							▲
Cheltenham	Golden Valley Thistle		▲		▲	▲				▲
Cheltenham	The Greenway									▲
Cheltenham	Hotel de la Bere				▲	▲	▲			
Chipping Campden	Cotswold House									▲
Cirencester	Stratton House									▲
Clearwell	Clearwell Castle							▲	▲	
Corse Lawn	Corse Lawn House				▲	▲				
Fairford	Bull Hotel						▲			
Gloucester	Forte Crest	▲								
Gloucester	Hatherley Manor									▲
Gloucester	Hatton Court				▲					
Lower Slaughter	Lower Slaughter Manor				▲		▲			
Moreton-in-Marsh	Manor House	▲								
Painswick	Painswick Hotel									▲
Puckrup	Puckrup Hall						▲			
Stonehouse	Stonehouse Court						▲			
Tetbury	Calcot Manor				▲					
Tetbury	The Close									▲
Tewkesbury	Tewkesbury Park	▲	▲		▲	▲	▲			
Upper Slaughter	Lords of the Manor								▲	
Westonbirt	Hare & Hounds					▲	▲			▲

Greater Manchester

Location	Hotel	Leisure Centre	Indoor Pool	Outdoor Pool	Squash	Tennis	Golf	Fishing	Riding	Croquet
Bolton	Last Drop Village Hotel	▲	▲		▲					
Manchester	Britannia Hotel		▲							
Manchester	Copthorne Hotel	▲	▲							
Manchester	Holiday Inn Crowne Plaza	▲	▲		▲					
Manchester	Novotel			▲						
Manchester	Hotel Piccadilly	▲	▲							
Manchester	Portland Thistle	▲	▲							

Location	Hotel	Leisure Centre	Indoor Pool	Outdoor Pool	Squash	Tennis	Golf	Fishing	Riding	Croquet
Manchester	Sachas Hotel	▲	▲							
Manchester Airport	Forte Crest	▲	▲							
Manchester Airport	Hilton International	▲	▲							
Standish	Almond Brook Moat House		▲							

Hampshire

Location	Hotel	Leisure Centre	Indoor Pool	Outdoor Pool	Squash	Tennis	Golf	Fishing	Riding	Croquet
Alton	Grange Hotel									▲
Basingstoke	Hilton National			▲						
Basingstoke	The Ringway			▲						
Brockenhurst	Balmer Lawn Hotel			▲	▲	▲	▲			▲
Brockenhurst	Careys Manor	▲	▲			▲				▲
Brockenhurst	Rhinefield House				▲		▲			
Burley	Burley Manor					▲			▲	▲
Eastleigh	Forte Posthouse Southampton	▲								
Fareham	Forte Posthouse	▲	▲							
Fareham	Solent Hotel	▲	▲		▲	▲				
Farnborough	Forte Crest	▲	▲							
Havant	Forte Posthouse	▲	▲							
Hurstbourne Tarrant	Esseborne Manor					▲				▲
Lymington	Gordleton Mill								▲	▲
Lymington	Passford House	▲	▲	▲						
Lyndhurst	Lyndhurst Park			▲		▲				
Lyndhurst	Parkhill Hotel			▲						
New Milton	Chewton Glen	▲	▲	▲		▲	▲			▲
Portsmouth	Forte Posthouse	▲	▲							
Portsmouth	Portsmouth Marriott Hotel	▲	▲		▲					
Rotherwick	Tylney Hall			▲	▲		▲			▲
Silchester	Romans Hotel				▲	▲				
Southampton	Forte Posthouse	▲	▲							
Southampton	Hilton National			▲						
Southampton	Novotel			▲						
Southampton	Southampton Park Hotel	▲	▲							
Stratfield Turgis	Wellington Arms						▲			
Winchester	Lainston House					▲	▲			▲

Hereford & Worcester

Location	Hotel	Leisure Centre	Indoor Pool	Outdoor Pool	Squash	Tennis	Golf	Fishing	Riding	Croquet
Abberley	Elms Hotel						▲			▲
Abbot's Salford	Salford Hall						▲			▲
Broadway	Collin House			▲						▲
Broadway	Dormy House									▲
Broadway	Lygon Arms			▲		▲				▲
Bromsgrove	Stakis Country Court	▲	▲							
Buckland	Buckland Manor					▲				▲
Chaddesley Corbett	Brockencote Hall									▲
Droitwich	Chateau Impney						▲			
Evesham	Evesham Hotel			▲						▲
Evesham	Riverside Hotel							▲		
Eyton	Marsh Country Hotel									▲
Harvington	The Mill at Harvington			▲		▲		▲		▲
Kidderminster	Stone Manor				▲	▲				▲
Ledbury	The Feathers				▲					
Malvern	Colwall Park Hotel									▲
Much Birch	Pilgrim Hotel									▲
Ross-on-Wye	Pengethley Manor						▲	▲	▲	▲
Ruckhall	Ancient Camp Inn							▲		
Stourport-on-Severn	Moat House			▲	▲	▲	▲			

Location	Hotel	Leisure Centre	Indoor Pool	Outdoor Pool	Squash	Tennis	Golf	Fishing	Riding	Croquet
Hertfordshire										
Broxbourne	Cheshunt Marriott Hotel	▲	▲							
Dane End	Green End Park					▲				
Hadley Wood	West Lodge Park Hotel									▲
Hatfield Heath	Down Hall			▲		▲				▲
Hemel Hempstead	Forte Posthouse	▲	▲							
Sawbridgeworth	Manor of Groves				▲	▲	▲			
South Mimms	Forte Posthouse	▲	▲							
St Albans	Sopwell House	▲	▲							▲
Stanstead Abbots	Briggens House			▲		▲	▲	▲		
Stevenage	Novotel			▲						
Thundridge	Hanbury Manor	▲	▲		▲	▲	▲			▲
Watford	Hilton National	▲	▲							
Watford	Jarvis International		▲			▲				
Humberside										
Driffield	Bell Hotel		▲		▲					
Hull	Forte Crest	▲	▲							
Tickton	Tickton Grange									▲
Willerby	Grange Park	▲	▲							
Isle of Wight										
Bonchurch	Winterbourne Hotel			▲						
Calbourne	Swainston Manor		▲				▲			
Freshwater	Farringford Hotel			▲		▲				▲
Shanklin	Cliff Tops Hotel	▲	▲							
Ventnor	Royal Hotel			▲						
Isles of Scilly										
St Martin's	St Martin's Hotel			▲			▲			
Tresco	Island Hotel			▲		▲	▲			
Kent										
Ashford	Ashford International	▲	▲							
Ashford	Eastwell Manor						▲			▲
Bearsted	Tudor Park	▲	▲		▲	▲	▲			
Bexleyheath	Swallow Hotel		▲							
Bromley	Bromley Court									▲
Canterbury	Ebury Hotel		▲							
Chartham	Thruxted Oast									▲
Cranbrook	Hartley Mount									▲
Cranbrook	Kennel Holt Hotel									▲
Dover	Moat House		▲							
Fawkham	Brandshatch Place	▲	▲		▲					
Hawkhurst	Tudor Court					▲				▲
Hollingbourne	Jarvis Great Danes	▲	▲			▲	▲			
Hythe	Hythe Imperial	▲	▲		▲	▲	▲			▲
Lenham	Chilston Park					▲		▲		▲
Maidstone	Stakis Country Court Hotel	▲	▲							
Rochester	Bridgewood Manor Hotel	▲	▲			▲				
Rochester	Forte Posthouse		▲							
Sevenoaks	Royal Oak					▲				
St Margaret's	Wallett's Court					▲				
Tonbridge	Goldhill Mill					▲				▲
Tunbridge Wells	Spa Hotel	▲	▲			▲				▲
Wrotham Heath	Forte Posthouse Maidst/S'oaks	▲	▲							

Location	Hotel	Leisure Centre	Indoor Pool	Outdoor Pool	Squash	Tennis	Golf	Fishing	Riding	Croquet
Lancashire										
Blackpool	Imperial Hotel	▲	▲							
Blackpool	Pembroke Hotel		▲							
Broughton	Broughton Park		▲		▲					
Burnley	Oaks Hotel	▲	▲		▲					
Chipping	Gibbon Bridge Country House						▲			▲
Lancaster	Forte Posthouse	▲	▲							
Lytham St Annes	Dalmeny Hotel		▲			▲				
Preston	Novotel				▲					
Samlesbury	Swallow Trafalgar	▲	▲		▲					
Samlesbury	Tickled Trout		▲						▲	
Whitewell	Inn at Whitewell								▲	
Worthington	Kilhey Court	▲	▲						▲	
Leicestershire										
Hinckley	Hinckley Island Hotel	▲	▲						▲	
Leicester	Holiday Inn	▲	▲							
Leicester	Stakis Country Court	▲	▲							
Lockington	Hilton Nat E Midlands Airport	▲	▲							
Loughborough	Friendly Hotel	▲	▲							
Oakham	Hambleton Hall					▲	▲			
Quorn	The Quorn Country Hotel								▲	
Stapleford	Stapleford Park						▲		▲	
Lincolnshire										
Belton	Belton Woods Hotel	▲	▲			▲	▲	▲	▲	
Grantham	Swallow Hotel	▲	▲							
Merseyside										
Haydock	Forte Posthouse	▲	▲							
Haydock	Haydock Thistle	▲	▲							
Liverpool	Britannia Adelphi Hotel	▲	▲		▲					
Liverpool	Moat House	▲	▲							
Norfolk										
Barnham Broom	Barnham Broom Hotel		▲			▲	▲	▲		
Blakeney	Blakeney Hotel		▲							
Dereham	King's Head						▲			
Grimston	Congham Hall			▲			▲			▲
Hethersett	Park Farm	▲	▲				▲			▲
King's Lynn	Knights Hill Hotel	▲	▲				▲			
Norwich	Forte Posthouse	▲	▲							
Norwich	Friendly Hotel	▲	▲							
Norwich	Hotel Norwich	▲	▲							
Norwich	Norwich Sport Village Hotel	▲	▲		▲	▲				
Norwich	Sprowston Manor	▲	▲				▲			
Norwich Airport	Stakis Ambassador Hotel	▲	▲							
West Runton	The Links Country Park		▲				▲			
Northamptonshire										
Corby	Carlton Manor Hotel	▲	▲							
Crick	Forte Posthouse Northampton	▲	▲							

Location	Hotel	Leisure Centre	Indoor Pool	Outdoor Pool	Squash	Tennis	Golf	Fishing	Riding	Croquet
Daventry	Daventry Resort Hotel	▲	▲							
Kettering	Kettering Park Hotel	▲	▲							
Northampton	Stakis Country Court	▲	▲							
Northampton	Swallow Hotel	▲	▲							
Weedon	Crossroads Hotel				▲	▲				

Northumberland

Location	Hotel	Leisure Centre	Indoor Pool	Outdoor Pool	Squash	Tennis	Golf	Fishing	Riding	Croquet
Chollerford	George Hotel		▲							
Longhorsley	Linden Hall		▲			▲				

Nottinghamshire

Location	Hotel	Leisure Centre	Indoor Pool	Outdoor Pool	Squash	Tennis	Golf	Fishing	Riding	Croquet
Langar	Langar Hall									▲
Nottingham	Novotel			▲						
Nottingham	Royal Moat House				▲					

Oxfordshire

Location	Hotel	Leisure Centre	Indoor Pool	Outdoor Pool	Squash	Tennis	Golf	Fishing	Riding	Croquet
Burford	Bay Tree									▲
Chipping Norton	Crown & Cushion	▲	▲							
Great Milton	Le Manoir aux Quat'Saisons			▲		▲				▲
Horton-cum-Studley	Studley Priory					▲				▲
Kingham	Mill House Hotel							▲		
Milton Common	Belfry Hotel	▲								
Minster Lovell	Old Swan					▲			▲	
Moulsford-on-Thames	Beetle & Wedge								▲	
North Stoke	Springs Hotel			▲	▲					▲
Oxford	Moat House	▲	▲		▲					
Wallingford	Shillingford Bridge Hotel			▲	▲			▲		
Weston-on-the-Green	Weston Manor				▲	▲				
Witney	Witney Lodge	▲								

Shropshire

Location	Hotel	Leisure Centre	Indoor Pool	Outdoor Pool	Squash	Tennis	Golf	Fishing	Riding	Croquet
Alveley	Mill Hotel							▲		
Market Drayton	Goldstone Hall									▲
Shifnal	Park House							▲		▲
Telford	Holiday Inn Telford/Ironbridge	▲	▲							
Telford	Moat House	▲	▲							
Telford	Telford Hotel	▲	▲				▲			
Weston-under-Redcastle	Hawkstone Park			▲			▲	▲		
Worfield	Old Vicarage									▲

Somerset

Location	Hotel	Leisure Centre	Indoor Pool	Outdoor Pool	Squash	Tennis	Golf	Fishing	Riding	Croquet
Dulverton	Carnarvon Arms				▲		▲	▲		▲
Hatch Beauchamp	Farthings Hotel									▲
Kilve	Meadow House									▲
Lympsham	Batch Farm Country Hotel								▲	▲
Middlecombe	Periton Park							▲	▲	▲
Porlock	Oaks Hotel								▲	
Somerton	Lynch Country House Hotel									
Street	Bear Hotel		▲							
Winsford	Royal Oak Inn							▲		

Location	Hotel	Leisure Centre	Indoor Pool	Outdoor Pool	Squash	Tennis	Golf	Fishing	Riding	Croquet
Staffordshire										
Burton-on-Trent	Riverside Inn						▲	▲		
Hanchurch	Hanchurch Manor							▲		
Newcastle-under-Lyme	Forte Posthouse	▲	▲							
Stafford	De Vere Tillington Hall	▲	▲				▲			
Stoke-on-Trent	Stakis Stoke-on-Trent	▲	▲							
Stoke-on-Trent	Stoke-on-Trent Moat House	▲	▲							
Swinfen	Swinfen Hall									▲
Suffolk										
Beccles	Waveney House							▲		
Copdock	Ipswich Moat House	▲	▲							
Hintlesham	Hintlesham Hall		▲			▲	▲	▲	▲	
Ipswich	Belstead Brook Hotel									▲
Ipswich	Constable Country Hotel				▲					
Ipswich	Marlborough Hotel									▲
Lavenham	The Swan									
Needham Market	Pipps Ford				▲		▲	▲		▲
Southwold	The Swan									▲
Sudbury	Mill Hotel							▲		
Woodbridge	Seckford Hall		▲					▲		
Yoxford	Satis House	▲								
Surrey										
Bagshot	Pennyhill Park					▲	▲	▲	▲	▲
Bramley	Bramley Grange						▲			
Churt	Frensham Pond Hotel	▲	▲		▲					
Cobham	Hilton National		▲		▲	▲				
Cobham	Woodlands Park									▲
Croydon	Croydon Park	▲	▲		▲					
Croydon	Hilton National	▲	▲							
Croydon	Selsdon Park	▲	▲	▲	▲	▲	▲			
Egham	Great Fosters					▲	▲			
Egham	Runnymede Hotel	▲	▲				▲			▲
Gatwick Airport	Chequers Thistle				▲					
Gatwick Airport	Forte Posthouse		▲							
Gatwick Airport	Ramada Hotel Gatwick	▲	▲		▲					
Guildford	Forte Crest		▲							
Haslemere	Lythe Hill Hotel						▲	▲		▲
Horley	Langshott Manor									▲
Nutfield	Nutfield Priory	▲	▲		▲					
Richmond	Richmond Gate Hotel				▲					▲
Seale	Hog's Back Hotel	▲	▲							
Sutton	Holiday Inn London Sutton	▲	▲							
Weybridge	Oatlands Park					▲				
Sussex, East										
Battle	Netherfield Place						▲			▲
Brighton	Brighton Metropole	▲	▲							
Brighton	Brighton Thistle Hotel		▲							
Brighton	Grand Hotel	▲	▲							
Cooden	Cooden Resort Hotel	▲	▲	▲						▲
Eastbourne	Grand Hotel	▲	▲	▲						

Location	Hotel	Leisure Centre	Indoor Pool	Outdoor Pool	Squash	Tennis	Golf	Fishing	Riding	Croquet
Lewes	Shelleys Hotel									▲
Sedlescombe	Brickwall Hotel				▲					
Uckfield	Horsted Place	▲				▲	▲	▲		▲

Sussex, West

Location	Hotel	Leisure Centre	Indoor Pool	Outdoor Pool	Squash	Tennis	Golf	Fishing	Riding	Croquet
Amberley	Amberley Castle									▲
Climping	Bailiffscourt				▲		▲			
East Grinstead	Gravetye Manor						▲			
Findon	Findon Manor									▲
Gatwick Airport	Copthorne Effingham Park	▲	▲		▲		▲			▲
Gatwick Airport	Copthorne London Gatwick				▲	▲				
Gatwick Airport	Europa Gatwick				▲	▲				
Gatwick Airport	Forte Crest Gatwick	▲	▲							
Gatwick Airport	Gatwick Hilton International	▲	▲							
Gatwick Airport	Holiday Inn Gatwick	▲	▲							
Goodwood	Goodwood Park				▲		▲	▲	▲	
Lower Beeding	Cisswood House				▲					
Lower Beeding	South Lodge						▲	▲	▲	▲
Rusper	Ghyll Manor						▲			▲
Storrington	Abingworth Hall						▲			▲
Storrington	Little Thakeham					▲	▲			
Turners Hill	Alexander House						▲			
Walberton	Avisford Park	▲	▲	▲	▲	▲				▲

Tyne & Wear

Location	Hotel	Leisure Centre	Indoor Pool	Outdoor Pool	Squash	Tennis	Golf	Fishing	Riding	Croquet
Gateshead	Newcastle Marriott Hotel	▲	▲							
Gateshead	Swallow Hotel	▲	▲							
Newcastle-upon-Tyne	Copthorne Hotel	▲	▲							
Newcastle-upon-Tyne	Moat House	▲								
Newcastle-upon-Tyne	Novotel		▲							
Newcastle-upon-Tyne	Swallow Gosforth Park		▲				▲	▲		
Seaton Burn	Holiday Inn	▲	▲							
Sunderland	Swallow Hotel	▲	▲							
Washington	Moat House		▲				▲	▲		

Warwickshire

Location	Hotel	Leisure Centre	Indoor Pool	Outdoor Pool	Squash	Tennis	Golf	Fishing	Riding	Croquet
Alcester	Arrow Mill							▲		
Barford	Glebe Hotel	▲	▲							▲
Billesley	Billesley Manor		▲				▲			▲
Bodymoor Heath	Marston Farm						▲	▲	▲	
Brandon	Brandon Hall				▲					
Charlecote	Charlecote Pheasant					▲	▲			▲
Leamington Spa	Mallory Court				▲	▲	▲			
Stratford-upon-Avon	Alveston Manor									▲
Stratford-upon-Avon	Dukes Hotel									
Stratford-upon-Avon	Ettington Park			▲			▲	▲	▲	▲
Stratford-upon-Avon	Moat House International	▲	▲							
Stratford-upon-Avon	Welcombe Hotel						▲	▲		
Stratford-upon-Avon	Windmill Park	▲	▲				▲			
Warwick	Hilton National		▲							
Wishaw	The Belfry	▲	▲		▲	▲	▲			▲

Location	Hotel	Leisure Centre	Indoor Pool	Outdoor Pool	Squash	Tennis	Golf	Fishing	Riding	Croquet
West Midlands										
Aldridge	Fairlawns			▲						▲
Berkswell	Nailcote Hall		▲				▲	▲		▲
Birmingham	Copthorne Hotel	▲	▲							
Birmingham	Forte Crest	▲	▲		▲					
Birmingham	Forte Posthouse	▲	▲							
Birmingham	Holiday Inn	▲	▲							
Birmingham	Hyatt Regency	▲	▲							
Birmingham	Swallow Hotel	▲								
Brierley Hill	Copthorne Hotel	▲	▲							
Coventry	Forte Posthouse	▲	▲							
Coventry	Hilton National	▲	▲							
Coventry	Novotel			▲						
Meriden	Forest of Arden Hotel	▲	▲			▲	▲	▲	▲	
Solihull	Moat House	▲	▲							
Solihull	Regency Hotel	▲								
Solihull	St John's Swallow Hotel	▲	▲							
Sutton Coldfield	Moor Hall									
Sutton Coldfield	New Hall					▲				▲
Sutton Coldfield	Penns Hall	▲	▲		▲					
Walsall	Friendly Hotel	▲	▲							
Walsall Wood	Baron's Court Hotel	▲	▲							
Wolverhampton	Novotel			▲						
Wiltshire										
Beanacre	Beechfield House			▲		▲				
Bradford-on-Avon	Woolley Grange			▲		▲				
Castle Combe	Manor House			▲		▲			▲	▲
Chiseldon	Chiseldon House					▲				
Colerne	Lucknam Park	▲	▲						▲	
Corsham	Rudloe Park									
Hinton	Hinton Grange			▲			▲	▲	▲	▲
Swindon	Blunsdon House	▲	▲		▲	▲				
Swindon	De Vere Hotel	▲	▲							
Swindon	Forte Posthouse	▲	▲							
Swindon	Swindon Marriott Hotel	▲	▲		▲	▲				
Warminster	Bishopstrow House		▲	▲		▲			▲	
Yorkshire, North										
Bolton Abbey	Devonshire Arms				▲		▲		▲	▲
Great Ayton	Ayton Hall									▲
Hackness	Hackness Grange				▲		▲			▲
Harome	Pheasant Hotel									
Harrogate	Majestic Hotel	▲	▲		▲	▲				
Harrogate	Old Swan Hotel						▲			▲
Harrogate	Hotel St George	▲	▲							
Helmsley	Feversham Arms				▲	▲				
Hovingham	Worsley Arms Hotel					▲				
Knaresborough	Dower House	▲	▲							
Nidd	Nidd Hall	▲	▲		▲	▲				▲
Ripley	Boar's Head Hotel					▲		▲		
Ripon	Ripon Spa Hotel									▲
Scalby	Wrea Head Country Hotel									▲
Skipton	Randell's Hotel	▲	▲							

Location	Hotel	Leisure Centre	Indoor Pool	Outdoor Pool	Squash	Tennis	Golf	Fishing	Riding	Croquet
South Milford	Forte Posthouse Leeds/Selby	▲				▲				
York	Middlethorpe Hall									▲
York	Mount Royale			▲						
York	Novotel		▲							
York	Royal York Hotel									▲
York	Swallow Hotel	▲	▲							▲

Yorkshire, South

Location	Hotel	Leisure Centre	Indoor Pool	Outdoor Pool	Squash	Tennis	Golf	Fishing	Riding	Croquet
Doncaster	Moat House	▲	▲							
Sheffield	Forte Posthouse	▲	▲							
Sheffield	Moat House	▲	▲							
Sheffield	Novotel		▲							
Sheffield	St George Swallow Hotel	▲	▲							

Yorkshire, West

Location	Hotel	Leisure Centre	Indoor Pool	Outdoor Pool	Squash	Tennis	Golf	Fishing	Riding	Croquet
Bradford	Novotel		▲							
Bramhope	Forte Crest	▲	▲							
Bramhope	Jarvis Parkway Hotel	▲	▲			▲				
Brighouse	Forte Crest	▲	▲							▲
Garforth	Hilton National	▲	▲							
Huddersfield	Pennine Hilton National	▲	▲							
Leeds	Holiday Inn	▲	▲							
Leeds	Leeds Marriott Hotel	▲	▲							
Linton	Wood Hall		▲						▲	
Otley	Chevin Lodge						▲		▲	
Oulton	Oulton Hall Hotel	▲	▲							

SCOTLAND

Location	Hotel	Leisure Centre	Indoor Pool	Outdoor Pool	Squash	Tennis	Golf	Fishing	Riding	Croquet
Borders										
Dryburgh	Dryburgh Abbey Hotel	▲						▲		
Ettrickbridge	Ettrickshaws Hotel							▲		
Kelso	Ednam House							▲		▲
Kelso	Sunlaws House				▲	▲		▲		▲
Melrose	Burts Hotel							▲		
Peebles	Cringletie House					▲				▲
Peebles	Peebles Hotel Hydro	▲	▲		▲	▲			▲	▲
Selkirk	Philipburn House			▲						
Tweedsmuir	Crook Inn							▲		
Central										
Airth	Airth Castle	▲								
Drymen	Buchanan Highland Hotel	▲			▲	▲	▲			
Dunblane	Cromlix House					▲		▲		
Dunblane	Stakis Dunblane	▲	▲			▲				
Strathblane	Kirkhouse Inn							▲		
Dumfries & Galloway										
Annan	Warmanbie Hotel							▲		
Beattock	Auchen Castle							▲		
Gatehouse of Fleet	Cally Palace	▲				▲	▲	▲		▲
Newton Stewart	Kirroughtree Hotel						▲			
Port William	Corsemalzie House							▲		
Portpatrick	Knockinaam Lodge							▲		
Stranraer	North West Castle	▲	▲							
Fife										
St Andrews	St Andrews Old Course Hotel	▲	▲				▲			
Grampian										
Aberdeen	Ardoe House									▲
Aberdeen	Holiday Inn Crowne Plaza	▲	▲							
Aberdeen	The Marcliffe at Pitfodels							▲		
Aberdeen	Stakis Tree Tops	▲	▲			▲				
Aberdeen Airport	Aberdeen Marriott Hotel	▲	▲							
Aberdeen Airport	Airport Skean Dhu Hotel			▲						
Ballater	Craigendarroch Hotel	▲			▲	▲				
Banchory	Raemoir House					▲		▲	▲	▲
Banchory	Tor-na-Coille Hotel				▲					
Chapel of Garioch	Pittodrie House				▲	▲				▲
Craigellachie	Craigellachie Hotel				▲					
Elgin	Mansion House	▲	▲							
Inverurie	Thainstone House Hotel	▲	▲							
Kildrummy	Kildrummy Castle							▲		
Oldmeldrum	Meldrum House						▲			
Peterhead	Waterside Inn	▲	▲							

Location	Hotel	Leisure Centre	Indoor Pool	Outdoor Pool	Squash	Tennis	Golf	Fishing	Riding	Croquet
Highland										
Advie	Tulchan Lodge					▲		▲		
Altnaharra	Altnaharra Hotel							▲		
Aviemore	Stakis Aviemore Four Seasons	▲	▲							
Aviemore	Stakis Coylumbridge Resort	▲	▲		▲	▲				
Ballachulish	Ballachulish Hotel							▲		
Contin	Craigdarroch Lodge		▲			▲				
Drumnadrochit	Polmaily House				▲	▲				
Dulnain Bridge	Muckrach Lodge							▲		
Duror	Stewart Hotel								▲	
Fort William	Inverlochy Castle					▲		▲		▲
Garve	Inchbae Lodge							▲		
Glenelg	Glenelg Inn							▲		
Harray Loch, Orkney	Merkister Hotel							▲		
Helmsdale	Navidale House				▲			▲		▲
Inverness	Bunchrew House							▲		▲
Inverness	Caledonian Hotel	▲	▲							
Inverness	Culloden House					▲				
Inverness	Dunain Park		▲							▲
Inverness	Kingsmills Hotel	▲	▲							
Kentallen of Appin	Ardsheal House					▲				
Kinlochbervie	Kinlochbervie Hotel							▲		
Lochinver	Inver Lodge Hotel							▲		
Nairn	Golf View Hotel					▲				
Nairn	Newton Hotel									▲
Scourie	Scourie Hotel							▲		
Skeabost Bridge	Skeabost House						▲	▲		
Sleat	Kinloch Lodge							▲		
Talladale	Loch Maree Hotel							▲		
Whitebridge	Knockie Lodge							▲		
Lothian										
Bonnyrigg	Dalhousie Castle							▲		
Edinburgh	The Balmoral	▲	▲							
Edinburgh	Capital Moat House	▲	▲							
Edinburgh	Carlton Highland	▲	▲		▲					
Edinburgh	Royal Terrace Hotel	▲	▲							
Edinburgh	Scandic Crown Hotel	▲	▲							
Edinburgh	Sheraton Grand Hotel	▲	▲							
Edinburgh	Swallow Royal Scot	▲	▲							
Gullane	Greywalls Hotel						▲			▲
Ingliston	Norton House									▲
Kirknewton	Dalmahoy Hotel Country Club	▲	▲		▲	▲	▲			
North Berwick	Marine Hotel				▲		▲			
North Middleton	Borthwick Castle									▲
South Queensferry	Forth Bridges Moat House	▲	▲		▲					
Strathclyde										
Alexandria	Cameron House	▲	▲		▲	▲		▲		▲
Ardentinny	Ardentinny Hotel								▲	
Ayr	Jarvis Caledonian Hotel	▲	▲							
Cumbernauld	Westerwood Hotel	▲	▲				▲	▲		
East Kilbride	Westpoint Hotel	▲	▲		▲					
Eriska	Isle of Eriska						▲		▲	▲
Erskine	Forte Posthouse	▲	▲							
Glasgow	Glasgow Hilton	▲	▲							

Location	Hotel	Leisure Centre	Indoor Pool	Outdoor Pool	Squash	Tennis	Golf	Fishing	Riding	Croquet
Glasgow	Glasgow Marriott Hotel	▲	▲		▲					
Glasgow	Jurys Pond Hotel	▲	▲							
Glasgow	Moat House International	▲	▲							
Glasgow	Swallow Hotel	▲	▲							
Gourock	Stakis Gantock Hotel	▲	▲				▲			
Irvine	Hospitality Inn		▲					▲		
Kilchrenan	Ardanaiseig	▲					▲	▲		▲
Kilchrenan	Taychreggan Hotel							▲		▲
Kilfinan	Kilfinan Hotel							▲		
Kilmore	Glenfeochan House							▲		
Kilwinning	Montgreenan Mansion House					▲				▲
Langbank	Gleddoch House				▲		▲			
Maybole	Ladyburn									▲
Oban	Alexandra Hotel		▲							
Strachur	Creggans Inn							▲		
Tarbert	Stonefield Castle					▲		▲		
Troon	Marine Highland Hotel	▲	▲		▲					
Troon	Piersland House									▲
Turnberry	Turnberry Hotel	▲	▲		▲	▲	▲		▲	

Tayside

Location	Hotel	Leisure Centre	Indoor Pool	Outdoor Pool	Squash	Tennis	Golf	Fishing	Riding	Croquet
Aberfeldy	Farleyer House							▲		▲
Auchterarder	Auchterarder House									▲
Auchterarder	Gleneagles Hotel	▲	▲		▲	▲	▲	▲	▲	▲
Auchterhouse	Old Mansion House				▲	▲	▲			
Blairgowrie	Kinloch House									▲
Callander	Roman Camp Hotel							▲		
Cleish	Nivingston House									▲
Crieff	Crieff Hydro	▲	▲		▲	▲	▲		▲	▲
Dunkeld	Kinnaird					▲		▲		▲
Forfar	Royal Hotel	▲	▲							
Kenmore	Kenmore Hotel						▲	▲		
Kinclaven by Stanley	Ballathie House						▲	▲		
Kinross	Windlestrae Hotel	▲	▲							
Kirkmichael	Log Cabin Hotel							▲		
Pitlochry	Green Park Hotel							▲		
Pitlochry	Pitlochry Hydro Hotel	▲	▲							▲
Scone	Murrayshall House					▲	▲			

WALES

Location	Hotel	Leisure Centre	Indoor Pool	Outdoor Pool	Squash	Tennis	Golf	Fishing	Riding	Croquet
Clwyd										
Ewloe	St David's Park Hotel	▲	▲			▲	▲			
Llanarmon Dyffryn Ceiriog	West Arms Hotel							▲		
Llandrillo	Tyddyn Llan							▲		
Llangollen	Hand Hotel							▲		▲
Llangollen	Royal Hotel							▲		
Northop	Soughton Hall						▲			
Rossett	Llyndir Hall	▲	▲							
Ruthin	Ruthin Castle							▲		
Dyfed										
Aberystwyth	Conrah Country Hotel		▲							▲
Gwbert-on-Sea	Cliff Hotel				▲	▲	▲	▲		
Lamphey	Court Hotel		▲				▲			
Penally	Penally Abbey		▲							▲
St David's	Warpool Court		▲				▲			▲
Gwent										
Chepstow	St Pierre Hotel	▲	▲			▲	▲	▲		
Llangybi	Cwrt Bleddyn Hotel	▲	▲		▲	▲				
Newport	Celtic Manor		▲							
Newport	Hilton National	▲	▲							
Newport	Stakis Country Court Hotel	▲	▲							
Tintern Abbey	Beaufort Hotel							▲		
Tintern Abbey	Royal George							▲		
Gwynedd										
Aberdovey	Plas Penhelig						▲			▲
Aberdovey	Trefeddian Hotel		▲				▲			
Abersoch	Porth Tocyn Hotel			▲		▲				
Abersoch	Riverside Hotel		▲							
Beddgelert	Royal Goat Hotel							▲		
Holyhead	Trearddur Bay Hotel		▲							
Llandudno	Bodysgallen Hall						▲			▲
Llandudno	Empire Hotel	▲	▲							
Llandudno	St Tudno Hotel		▲							
Llanrug	Seiont Manor		▲			▲		▲		
Llanwnda	Stables Hotel				▲					
Penmaenpool	George III Hotel						▲	▲		
Portmeirion	Hotel Portmeirion						▲	▲	▲	
Talsarnau	Maes-y-Neuadd									▲
Talyllyn	Tynycornel Hotel						▲	▲		
Glamorgan, Mid										
Coychurch	Coed-y-Mwstwr Hotel				▲		▲			▲
Miskin	Miskin Manor	▲	▲		▲					
Glamorgan, South										
Barry	Mount Sorrel Hotel		▲							
Cardiff	Cardiff Marriott Hotel	▲	▲		▲					

Location	Hotel	Leisure Centre	Indoor Pool	Outdoor Pool	Squash	Tennis	Golf	Fishing	Riding	Croquet
Cardiff	Copthorne Hotel	▲	▲							
Cardiff	Forte Posthouse	▲	▲							
Cardiff	Moat House	▲	▲							
Porthkerry	Egerton Grey					▲				

Glamorgan, West

Location	Hotel	Leisure Centre	Indoor Pool	Outdoor Pool	Squash	Tennis	Golf	Fishing	Riding	Croquet
Reynoldston	Fairyhill								▲	
Swansea	Forte Crest	▲	▲							
Swansea	Swansea Marriott Hotel	▲	▲							

Powys

Location	Hotel	Leisure Centre	Indoor Pool	Outdoor Pool	Squash	Tennis	Golf	Fishing	Riding	Croquet
Crickhowell	Gliffaes Country House Hotel							▲	▲	▲
Lake Vyrnwy	Lake Vyrnwy Hotel							▲	▲	
Llangammarch Wells	Lake Country House Hotel							▲	▲	
Llyswen	Llangoed Hall							▲	▲	▲

CHANNEL ISLANDS AND ISLE OF MAN

Location	Hotel	Leisure Centre	Indoor Pool	Outdoor Pool	Squash	Tennis	Golf	Fishing	Riding	Croquet
Guernsey										
Castel	La Grande Mare Hotel			▲			▲	▲		▲
Castel	Hougue du Pommier			▲			▲			
Forest	Mallard Hotel			▲		▲	▲			
St Martin	Hotel Bon Port			▲						
St Martin	St Margaret's Lodge			▲						▲
St Martin	La Trelade Hotel			▲						
St Peter Port	Braye Lodge			▲						
St Peter Port	Duke of Richmond			▲						
St Peter Port	Old Government House			▲						
St Peter Port	St Pierre Park	▲	▲			▲	▲			▲
Herm										
Herm	White House			▲		▲				▲
Jersey										
Bouley Bay	Water's Edge Hotel			▲						
Gorey	Old Court House Hotel			▲						
Grouville	Grouville Bay Hotel			▲						
Portelet Bay	Portelet Hotel			▲		▲				
St Aubin	Old Court House Inn			▲						
St Brelade	Atlantic Hotel	▲	▲	▲		▲				
St Brelade	Hotel Chateau Valeuse			▲						
St Brelade	La Place Hotel			▲						
St Brelade	Sea Crest			▲						
St Brelade's Bay	Hotel L'Horizon	▲	▲							
St Brelade's Bay	St Brelade's Bay Hotel			▲		▲				
St Helier	Apollo Hotel	▲	▲							
St Helier	Beaufort Hotel	▲								
St Helier	De Vere Grand	▲	▲							
St Helier	Hotel de France	▲	▲		▲	▲				
St Peter	Mermaid Hotel		▲	▲		▲	▲			▲
St Saviour	Longueville Manor			▲		▲				▲
St Saviour	Merton Hotel	▲	▲		▲	▲				
Sark										
Sark	Aval Du Creux			▲						
Sark	Hotel Petit Champ			▲						
Sark	Stocks Hotel			▲						
Isle of Man										
Douglas	Palace Hotel	▲	▲							
Douglas	Sefton Hotel	▲	▲							
Ramsey	Grand Island Hotel	▲	▲						▲	▲

NORTHERN IRELAND

Location	Hotel	Leisure Centre	Indoor Pool	Outdoor Pool	Squash	Tennis	Golf	Fishing	Riding	Croquet
Co Antrim										
Ballymena	Galgorm Manor							▲	▲	
Bushmills	Bushmills Inn							▲		
Dunadry	Dunadry Inn	▲	▲					▲		▲
Dunmurry	Forte Crest Belfast			▲						
Portballintrae	Bayview Hotel		▲							
Co Down										
Annalong	Glassdrumman Lodge					▲			▲	
Comber	La Mon House	▲	▲							▲
Holywood	Culloden Hotel		▲		▲	▲				
Newcastle	Slieve Donard Hotel		▲			▲	▲			
Co Londonderry										
Londonderry	Beech Hill House Hotel				▲					

REPUBLIC OF IRELAND

Location	Hotel	Leisure Centre	Indoor Pool	Outdoor Pool	Squash	Tennis	Golf	Fishing	Riding	Croquet
Co Cavan										
Ballyconnell	Slieve Russell Hotel	▲	▲		▲	▲	▲			
Co Clare										
Bunratty	Fitzpatricks Shannon Shamrock	▲	▲							
Ennis	Auburn Lodge						▲			
Ennis	West County Inn						▲			
Newmarket-on-Fergus	Clare Inn Hotel			▲		▲	▲		▲	▲
Newmarket-on-Fergus	Dromoland Castle					▲	▲	▲	▲	
Co Cork										
Ballylickey	Ballylickey Manor House			▲					▲	▲
Blarney	Blarney Park Hotel	▲	▲							
Castlelyons	Ballyvolane House								▲	▲
Cork	Arbutus Lodge						▲			
Cork	Fitzpatrick Silver Springs	▲	▲	▲		▲				
Cork	Jurys Hotel	▲	▲	▲	▲					
Cork	Rochestown Park Hotel	▲	▲							
Innishannon	Innishannon House Hotel							▲		
Kanturk	Assolas Country House						▲	▲		
Kinsale	Actons Hotel	▲	▲							
Kinsale	Blue Haven Hotel							▲		
Mallow	Longueville House							▲		
Shanagarry	Ballymaloe House				▲		▲	▲		▲
Co Donegal										
Lough Eske	Ardnamona House							▲		
Lough Eske	Harvey's Point Country Hotel						▲	▲		
Rathmullan	Rathmullan House			▲			▲			
Rossnowlagh	Sand House Hotel						▲		▲	
Co Dublin										
Dublin	Jurys Hotel and Towers			▲	▲					
Dublin	Marine Hotel			▲			▲			
Dublin Airport	Forte Crest			▲						
Howth	Deer Park Hotel						▲			
Howth	Howth Lodge Hotel	▲	▲							
Killiney	Court Hotel							▲		
Killiney	Fitzpatrick's Castle	▲	▲		▲	▲				
Co Galway										
Ballynahinch	Ballynahinch Castle						▲	▲		▲
Cashel	Cashel House						▲	▲	▲	
Cashel	Zetland House						▲	▲		▲
Clifden	Abbeyglen Castle			▲			▲			
Clifden	Rock Glen Manor						▲	▲		▲

Location	Hotel	Leisure Centre	Indoor Pool	Outdoor Pool	Squash	Tennis	Golf	Fishing	Riding	Croquet
Furbo	Connemara Coast Hotel		▲			▲				
Galway	Corrib Great Southern Hotel		▲							
Galway	Great Southern		▲							
Leenane	Delphi Lodge							▲		
Leenane	Killary Lodge					▲				
Letterfrack	Rosleague Manor					▲		▲		
Moycullen	Cloonnabinnia House Hotel							▲		
Oughterard	Connemara Gateway Hotel	▲				▲				▲
Oughterard	Currarevagh House					▲		▲		
Recess	Lough Inagh Lodge							▲		
Renvyle	Renvyle House			▲		▲	▲	▲	▲	▲
Spiddal	Bridge House Inn									

Co Kerry

Location	Hotel	Leisure Centre	Indoor Pool	Outdoor Pool	Squash	Tennis	Golf	Fishing	Riding	Croquet
Beaufort	Dunloe Castle		▲			▲		▲	▲	
Caherdaniel	Derrynane Hotel			▲						
Caragh Lake	Hotel Ard-na-Sidhe							▲		
Caragh Lake	Caragh Lodge					▲		▲		
Dingle	Dingle Skellig Hotel		▲			▲				
Kenmare	Dromquinna Manor Hotel					▲		▲		
Kenmare	Park Hotel Kenmare					▲	▲			
Kenmare	Sheen Falls Lodge					▲		▲	▲	
Killarney	Aghadoe Heights Hotel	▲	▲			▲		▲		
Killarney	Cahernane Hotel					▲		▲		
Killarney	Hotel Europe		▲			▲		▲	▲	
Killarney	Great Southern	▲	▲			▲				
Killarney	Kathleen's Country House								▲	
Killarney	Killarney Park Hotel		▲							
Killarney	Torc Great Southern		▲							
Parknasilla	Great Southern	▲	▲			▲		▲	▲	
Tralee	Brandon Hotel	▲	▲							

Co Kildare

Location	Hotel	Leisure Centre	Indoor Pool	Outdoor Pool	Squash	Tennis	Golf	Fishing	Riding	Croquet
Castledermot	Kilkea Castle		▲			▲				
Maynooth	Moyglare Manor					▲				
Straffan	Kildare Hotel	▲	▲		▲	▲	▲	▲		

Co Kilkenny

Location	Hotel	Leisure Centre	Indoor Pool	Outdoor Pool	Squash	Tennis	Golf	Fishing	Riding	Croquet
Kilkenny	Newpark Hotel	▲	▲			▲				
Thomastown	Mount Juliet Hotel	▲	▲			▲	▲	▲	▲	▲

Co Laois

Location	Hotel	Leisure Centre	Indoor Pool	Outdoor Pool	Squash	Tennis	Golf	Fishing	Riding	Croquet
Mountrath	Roundwood House							▲	▲	

Co Leitrim

Location	Hotel	Leisure Centre	Indoor Pool	Outdoor Pool	Squash	Tennis	Golf	Fishing	Riding	Croquet
Carrick-on-Shannon	Hollywell House							▲		

Location	Hotel	Leisure Centre	Indoor Pool	Outdoor Pool	Squash	Tennis	Golf	Fishing	Riding	Croquet
Co Limerick										
Adare	Adare Manor			▲				▲	▲	
Adare	Dunraven Arms					▲				
Castleconnell	Castle Oaks House Hotel	▲	▲							
Limerick	Castletroy Park Hotel	▲	▲			▲				
Limerick	Greenhills Hotel	▲	▲			▲				
Limerick	Jurys Hotel	▲	▲			▲				
Limerick	Limerick Inn Hotel	▲	▲			▲				
Limerick	Two Mile Inn									
Co Louth										
Dundalk	Ballymascanlon House	▲	▲		▲	▲				
Co Mayo										
Ballina	Downhill Hotel	▲	▲		▲	▲				
Ballina	Mount Falcon Castle						▲			
Cong	Ashford Castle					▲	▲	▲	▲	▲
Crossmolina	Enniscoe House							▲		
Newport	Newport House									▲
Westport	The Olde Railway Hotel								▲	
Co Monaghan										
Carrickmacross	Nuremore Hotel	▲	▲			▲	▲	▲		
Scotshouse	Hilton Park							▲	▲	
Co Offaly										
Birr	Dooly's Hotel							▲		
Co Roscommon										
Hodson Bay	Hodson Bay Hotel		▲				▲	▲		
Co Sligo										
Ballymote	Temple House							▲		▲
Boyle	Cromleach Lodge							▲		
Collooney	Markree Castle							▲		
Riverstown	Coopershill House						▲	▲		▲
Sligo	Sligo Park	▲	▲			▲				
Co Tipperary										
Dundrum	Dundrum House						▲	▲	▲	▲
Glen of Aherlow	Aherlow House								▲	
Kilcoran	Kilcoran Lodge	▲	▲					▲	▲	

Location	Hotel	Leisure Centre	Indoor Pool	Outdoor Pool	Squash	Tennis	Golf	Fishing	Riding	Croquet
Co Waterford										
Waterford	Jurys Hotel		▲			▲				
Waterford	Tower Hotel	▲	▲							
Waterford	Waterford Castle		▲				▲	▲		
Co Wexford										
Bunclody	Clohamon House								▲	▲
Gorey	Marlfield House					▲				
Rosslare	Great Southern	▲	▲			▲				
Rosslare	Kelly's Strand Hotel	▲	▲	▲	▲	▲			▲	
Co Wicklow										
Blessington	Downshire House					▲				▲
Dunlavin	Rathsallagh House				▲	▲	▲			▲
Rathnew	Tinakilly House					▲				▲

Hotels with Facilities for Disabled Guests

Compiled in association with the **Holiday Care Service** charity (2 Old Bank Chambers, Station Road, Horley, Surrey RH6 9HW Tel 0293 774535 Fax 0293 784647). If writing to them please enclose a minimum of 38p in stamps. Readers can join Friends of Holiday Care Service through an annual contribution of £10.

All hotels in the first set of listings under each country are recommended in this Guide **and** have been inspected by the Holiday Care Service. The additional listings include hotels that have informed us that they have specially adapted rooms and facilities for disabled guests; these specific facilities have **not** been inspected by disabled guests for this Guide.

England

Avon, Bristol **Bristol Marriott**
Berkshire, Bracknell **Coppid Beech Hotel**
Berkshire, Elcot **Elcot Park**
Berkshire, Newbury **Hilton National**
Berkshire, Newbury **Millwaters**
Berkshire, Newbury **Regency Park Hotel**
Berkshire, Slough **Copthorne**
Cambridgeshire, Cambridge **Arundel House**
Cambridgeshire, Cambridge **Gonville**
Cambridgeshire, Cambridge **Holiday Inn**
Cambridgeshire, Cambridge **University Arms**
Cambridgeshire, Peterborough **Butterfly**
Cambridgeshire, Peterborough **Moat House**
Cambridgeshire, Peterborough **Swallow Hotel**
Cheshire, Chester **Crabwall Manor**
Cumbria, Ambleside **Rothay Manor**
Cumbria, Appleby-in-Westmorland **Appleby Manor**
Cumbria, Bassenthwaite **Armathwaite Hall**
Cumbria, Bassenthwaite Lake **Pheasant Inn**
Cumbria, Grasmere **Wordsworth**
Devon, Plymouth **Boringdon Hall Hotel**
Devon, Plymouth **Campanile Hotel**
Devon, Plymouth **Copthorne Hotel**
Devon, Plymouth **Novotel**
Devon, Plymouth **Plymouth Moat House**
Dorset, Bournemouth **Norfolk Royale Hotel**
Dorset, Poole **Haven Hotel**
Co Durham, Chester-le-Street **Lumley Castle**
Co Durham, Darlington **Blackwell Grange Moat House**
Co Durham, Durham **Royal County Hotel**
Co Durham, Romaldkirk **Rose and Crown**
Essex, North Stifford **Stifford Moat House**
Gloucestershire, Cirencester **Stratton House Hotel**
Gtr Manchester, Manchester **Copthorne**
Gtr Manchester, Manchester **Novotel Manchester West**
Gtr Manchester, Manchester Airport **Manchester Airport Hilton**
Gtr Manchester, Standish **Almond Brook Moat House**
Hampshire, Southampton **Novotel**
Hampshire, Southampton **Polygon**
Hampshire, Southampton **Travel Inn Southampton**
Hereford & Worcester, Hereford **Hereford Moat House**
Hereford & Worcester, Ross-on-Wye **Pengethley Manor**
Hertfordshire, Broxbourne **Cheshunt Marriott**
Kent, Ashford **Ashford International Hotel**
Kent, Ashford **Forte Posthouse**
Kent, Bearsted **Tudor Park**
Kent, Brands Hatch **Brands Hatch Thistle**
Kent, Canterbury **County Hotel**
Kent, Dover **Dover Moat House**

Kent, Maidstone **Stakis Country Court**
Kent, Wateringbury **Wateringbury Hotel**
Lancashire, Preston **Novotel**
Leicestershire, Hinckley **Hinckley Island Hotel**
Leicestershire, Loughborough **Quorn Grange**
Merseyside, Haydock **Haydock Thistle**
Middlesex, Shepperton **Warren Lodge Hotel**
Norfolk, Kings Lynn **Butterfly**
Norfolk, West Runton **Links Country Park Hotel & Golf Club**
Northumberland, Langley **Langley Castle**
Northumberland, Longhorsley **Linden Hall**
Norfolk, Norwich **Friendly Hotel**
Norfolk, Norwich **Hotel Nelson**
Norfolk, Norwich **Hotel Norwich**
Norfolk, Norwich **Sprowston Manor**
Nottinghamshire, Nottingham **Holiday Inn Garden Court**
Nottinghamshire, Nottingham **Novotel**
Oxfordshire, Abingdon **Abingdon Lodge**
Oxfordshire, Wallingford **Springs Hotel**
Oxfordshire, Witney **Witney Lodge**
Shropshire, Worfield **Old Vicarage**
Suffolk, Aldeburgh **Brudenell Hotel**
Suffolk, Aldeburgh **Uplands**
Suffolk, Bury St Edmunds **Butterfly**
Suffolk, Ipswich **Novotel**
Suffolk, Needham Market **Pipps Ford**
Suffolk, Newmarket **Newmarket Moat House**
Surrey, Bramley **Bramley Grange**
Surrey, Egham **Runnymede Hotel**
Surrey, Horley **Forte Posthouse Gatwick**
Surrey, Seale **Hog's Back**
East Sussex, Boreham Street **Whitefriars Hotel**
East Sussex, Brighton **Bedford Hotel**
East Sussex, Brighton **Brighton Metropole**
East Sussex, Hastings **Cinque Ports Hotel**
East Sussex, Hastings **Royal Victoria Hotel**
West Sussex, Gatwick Airport **Chequers Thistle**
West Sussex, Gatwick Airport **Copthorne Effingham Park**
West Sussex, Gatwick Airport **Copthorne London Gatwick**
West Sussex, Gatwick Airport **Forte Crest**
West Sussex, Gatwick Airport **Gatwick Concorde**
West Sussex, Gatwick Airport **Gatwick Hilton International**
West Sussex, Gatwick Airport **Gatwick Moat House**
West Sussex, Gatwick Airport **Holiday Inn**
West Sussex, Goodwood **Goodwood Park**
Tyne & Wear, Newcastle **Copthorne**
Tyne & Wear, Newcastle **Holiday Inn**
Tyne & Wear, Newcastle **Novotel**
Tyne & Wear, Sunderland **Friendly Hotel**
Tyne & Wear, Washington **Washington Moat House**
Warwickshire, Warwick **Hilton International**
West Midlands, Birmingham **Copthorne**
West Midlands, Birmingham **Novotel**
West Midlands, Birmingham Airport **Novotel Birmingham Airport**
West Midlands, Brierley Hill **Copthorne Merry Hill**
West Midlands, Coventry **Novotel**
West Midlands, Wolverhampton **Novotel**
North Yorkshire, Bolton Abbey **Devonshire Arms**
North Yorkshire, Hackness **Hackness Grange**
North Yorkshire, Jervaulx **Jervaulx Hall**
North Yorkshire, Ripley **Boar's Head Hotel**
North Yorkshire, York **Grange**
North Yorkshire, York **Novotel**
South Yorkshire, Sheffield **Novotel**
West Yorkshire, Leeds **Holiday Inn**
West Yorkshire, Otley **Chevin Lodge**

Additional:

Berkshire, Newbury **Donnington Valley Hotel**
Buckinghamshire, Marlow **Compleat Angler Hotel**
Cambridgeshire, Wansford-in-England **The Haycock**
Cheshire, Chester **Moat House International Chester**
Cheshire, Chester **Rowton Hall**
Cheshire, Northwich **Friendly Floatel**
Cheshire, Prestbury **Bridge Hotel**
Cheshire, Warrington **Holiday Inn Garden Court**
Cheshire, Wilmslow **Stanneylands**
Cornwall, St Ives **Garrack Hotel**
Cumbria, Bowness-on-Windermere **Belsfield Hotel**
Cumbria, Penrith **North Lakes Hotel**
Cumbria, Ullswater **Leeming House**
Derbyshire, Ashbourne **Callow Hall**
Derbyshire, Derby **European Inn**
Derbyshire, Long Eaton **Sleep Inn**
Derbyshire, Morley **Breadsall Priory**
Devon, Sidmouth **Hotel Riviera**
Dorset, Christchurch **Travel Inn**
Dorset, East Stoke **Kemps Country House Hotel**
Essex, Basildon **Travel Inn**
Essex, Ingatestone **Heybridge Hotel**
Gloucestershire, Ampney Crucis **Crown of Crucis**
Gloucestershire, Cheltenham **Cheltenham Park**
Gloucestershire, Chipping Campden **Noel Arms**
Gloucestershire, Mickleton **Three Ways Hotel**
Gtr Manchester, Manchester **Holiday Inn Crowne Plaza**
Gtr Manchester, Manchester **Hotel Piccadilly**
Gtr Manchester, Manchester **Ramada Hotel**
Hampshire, Ampfield **Potters Heron Hotel**
Hampshire, Basingstoke **Audleys Wood**
Hampshire, Eastleigh **Forte Posthouse Southampton**
Hampshire, Fareham **Forte Posthouse**
Hampshire, Lymington **Passford House**
Hampshire, Middle Wallop **Fifehead Manor**
Hampshire, Milford-on-Sea **South Lawn**
Hampshire, Portsmouth **Hilton National**
Hampshire, Southampton **Hilton National**
Hereford & Worcester, Bromsgrove **Stakis Country Court**
Hereford & Worcester, Chaddesley Corbett **Brockencote Hall**
Hereford & Worcester, Worcester **Fownes Hotel**
Hertfordshire, Hadley Wood **West Lodge Park Hotel**
Hertfordshire, Harpenden **Glen Eagle Hotel**
Humberside, Willerby **Grange Park**
Kent, Bexleyheath **Swallow Hotel**
Lancashire, Chipping **Gibbon Bridge Country House**
Leicestershire, Market Harborough **Three Swans Hotel**
Middlesex, Heathrow Airport **Excelsior Hotel**
Middlesex, Heathrow Airport **Heathrow Hilton Hotel**
Middlesex, Heathrow Airport **Holiday Inn Crowne Plaza Heathrow**
Middlesex, Heathrow Airport **Ramada Hotel Heathrow**
Norfolk, Norwich **Norwich Sport Village Hotel**
Northamptonshire, Daventry **Daventry Resort Hotel**
Northamptonshire, Northampton **Courtyard by Marriott**
Northamptonshire, Northampton **Swallow Hotel**
Oxfordshire, Hailey **The Bird in Hand**
Somerset, Dulverton **Carnarvon Arms**
Somerset, Middlecombe **Periton Park**
Staffordshire, Barton-under-Needwood **Forte Travelodge**
Staffordshire, Stoke-on-Trent **Stakis**
Surrey, Croydon **Croydon Park**
Surrey, Egham **Great Fosters**
Surrey, Guildford **Forte Crest**
Surrey, Sutton **Holiday Inn**
West Sussex, Brighton **Brighton Thistle Hotel**
West Sussex, Lower Beeding **South Lodge**
West Sussex, Midhurst **Angel Hotel**

Tyne & Wear, Gateshead **Swallow Hotel**
Warwickshire, Bodymoor Heath **Marston Farm**
Warwickshire, Stratford-upon-Avon **Welcombe Hotel**
Warwickshire, Wishaw **The Belfry**
West Midlands, Birmingham **Swallow Hotel**
West Midlands, Meriden **Manor Hotel**
West Midlands, Solihull **Moat House**
West Midlands, Walsall **Friendly Hotel**
North Yorkshire, Harome **Pheasant Hotel**
North Yorkshire, Skipton **Randell's Hotel**
South Yorkshire, Sheffield **Moat House**
West Yorkshire, Brighouse **Forte Crest**
West Yorkshire, Halifax **Holdsworth House**
West Yorkshire, Leeds **42 The Calls**
West Yorkshire, Leeds **Queen's Hotel**
Wiltshire, Swindon **Blunsdon House**
Wiltshire, Swindon **De Vere Hotel**
Wiltshire, Swindon **Marriott**

Scotland

Fife, Markinch **Balbirnie House**
Grampian, Aberdeen Airport **Airport Skean Dhu Hotel**
Highland, Dulnain Bridge **Muckrach Lodge**
Highland, Kentallen of Appin **Holly Tree Hotel**
Highland, Onich **Lodge on the Loch**
Lothian, Edinburgh **Caledonian Hotel**
Lothian, Edinburgh **Forte Travelodge**
Lothian, Edinburgh **Holiday Inn Garden Court**
Lothian, Edinburgh **Sheraton Hotel**
Lothian, Edinburgh **Stakis Grosvenor Hotel**
Shetland, Lerwick **Shetland Hotel**
Strathclyde, Dumbarton **Forte Travelodge**
Strathclyde, Glasgow **Glasgow Hilton**
Strathclyde, Glasgow **Hospitality Inn**
Strathclyde, Glasgow **Moat House International**
Strathclyde, Irvine **Hospitality Inn**
Strathclyde, Oban **Alexandra House**
Tayside, Crieff **Crieff Hydro**
Tayside, Kinclaven by Stanley **Ballathie House**
Tayside, Pitlochry **Pitlochry Hydro**

Additional:

Borders, Dryburgh **Dryburgh Abbey Hotel**
Dumfries & Galloway, Gatehouse of Fleet **Cally Palace**
Grampian, Aberdeen **The Marcliffe at Pitfodels**
Grampian, Aberdeen Airport **Aberdeen Marriott Hotel**
Highland, Inverness **Kingsmills Hotel**
Highland, Inverness **Caledonian Hotel**
Highland, Talladale **Loch Maree Hotel**
Highland, Dulnain Bridge **Muchrach Lodge**
Highland, Aviemore **Stakis Coylumbridge Resort Hotel**
Lothian, Edinburgh **Carlton Highland**
Lothian, North Berwick **Marine Hotel**
Strathclyde, Glasgow **Glasgow Thistle Hotel**
Strathclyde, Glasgow **Glasgow Marriott Hotel**
Strathclyde, Tobermory **Tobermory Hotel**
Strathclyde, Troon **Piersland House**
Tayside, Kinross **Windlestrae Hotel**
Tayside, Kirkmichael **Log Cabin Hotel**

Wales

Clywd, Llangollen **Hand Hotel**
Dyfed, Fishguard **Fishguard Bay Hotel**
S Glamorgan, Cardiff **Cardiff Marriott**
S Glamorgan, Cardiff **Copthorne Hotel**
W Glamorgan, Swansea **Hilton National Swansea**
W Glamorgan, Swansea **Swansea Marriott Hotel**
Gwent, Abergavenny **Llanwenarth Arms Hotel**
Gwent, Llangybi **Cwrt Bleddyn Hotel**
Gwynedd, Beaumaris **Bulkeley Arms**
Gwynedd, Capel Coch **Tre-Ysgawen Hall**
Gwynedd, Llanwnda **Stables Hotel**
Gwynedd, Penmaenpool **George III Hotel**
Gwynedd, Talsarnau **Maes-y-Neuadd**
Powys, Llangammarch Wells **Lake Country House Hotel**

Additional:

Clwyd, Ewloe **St David's Park Hotel**
Clwyd, Llanarmon Dyffryn Ceiriog **West Arms Hotel**
S Glamorgan, Cardiff **Cardiff International**
S Glamorgan, Cardiff **Travel Inn**

Channel Islands

Guernsey, St Peter Port **St Pierre Park**

Additional:

Guernsey, Forest **Mallard Hotel**
Jersey, St Helier **De Vere Grand**

Isle of Man

Additional:

Douglas **Sefton Hotel**

Northern Ireland

Co Antrim, Larne **Magheramorne House**

Republic of Ireland

Co Clare, Ballyvaughan **Gregans Castle**
Co Clare, Ennis **West Country Inn**
Co Cork, Cork **Jurys House**
Co Dublin, Dublin **Jurys Hotel**
Co Dublin, Dublin **Montrose Hotel**
Do Dublin, Dublin Airport **Forte Crest**
Co Galway, Galway **Corrib Great Southern Hotel**
Co Limerick, Limerick **Castleray Park Hotel**
Co Limerick, Limerick **Limerick Inn**
Co Limerick, Limerick **Two Mile Inn**
Co Kerry, Kenmare **Sheen Falls Lodge**
Co Tipperary, Dundrum **Dundrum House**

Beautifully Situated Hotels

England

Avon, Freshford **Homewood Park** (HR)
Avon, Hunstrete **Hunstrete House** (HR)
Avon, Monkton Combe **Combe Grove Manor** (H)
Avon, Ston Easton **Ston Easton Park** (HR)
Avon, Thornbury **Thornbury Castle** (H)
Bedfordshire, Flitwick **Flitwick Manor** (HR)
Berkshire, Elcot **Jarvis Elcot Park** (HR)
Berkshire, Taplow **Cliveden** (HR)
Berkshire, Windsor **Oakley Court** (HR)
Berkshire, Woolton Hill **Hollington House Hotel** (HR)
Buckinghamshire, Aylesbury **Hartwell House** (HR)
Buckinghamshire, Marlow **Compleat Angler Hotel** (HR)
Buckinghamshire, Medmenham **Danesfield House** (HR)
Cheshire, Nantwich **Rookery Hall** (HR)
Cheshire, Puddington **Craxton Wood** (HR)
Cheshire, Sandiway **Nunsmere Hall** (HR)
Cleveland, Crathorne **Crathorne Hall** (H)
Cleveland, Easington **Grinkle Park** (H)
Cornwall, Calstock **Danescombe Valley Hotel** (HR)
Cornwall, Carlyon Bay **Carlyon Bay Hotel** (H)
Cornwall, Carlyon Bay **Porth Avallen Hotel** (H)
Cornwall, Golant **Cormorant Hotel** (H)
Cornwall, Lamorna Cove **Lamorna Cove Hotel** (H)
Cornwall, Land's End **Land's End Hotel** (H)
Cornwall, Liskeard **Well House** (HR)
Cornwall, Looe **Talland Bay Hotel** (H)
Cornwall, Mawnan **Budock Vean Hotel** (H)
Cornwall, Mawnan **Meudon Hotel** (H)
Cornwall, Mawnan **Nansidwell** (H)
Cornwall, Mullion **Polurrian Hotel** (H)
Cornwall, Portloe **Lugger Hotel** (H)
Cornwall, St Mawes **Hotel Tresanton** (H)
Cornwall, Veryan **Nare Hotel** (HR)
Cumbria, Alston **Lovelady Shield** (HR)
Cumbria, Ambleside **Rothay Manor Hotel** (HR)
Cumbria, Applethwaite **Underscar Manor** (HR)
Cumbria, Bassenthwaite **Armathwaite Hall** (H)
Cumbria, Borrowdale **Borrowdale Hotel** (H)
Cumbria, Borrowdale **Stakis Lodore Swiss Hotel** (H)
Cumbria, Brampton **Farlam Hall** (HR)
Cumbria, Cartmel **Aynsome Manor** (H)
Cumbria, Crosby-on-Eden **Crosby Lodge** (HR)
Cumbria, Grasmere **Michael's Nook** (HR)
Cumbria, Grasmere **Wordsworth Hotel** (HR)
Cumbria, Grizedale **Grizedale Lodge** (HR)
Cumbria, Ullswater **Leeming House** (HR)
Cumbria, Ullswater **Old Church Hotel** (HR)
Cumbria, Ullswater **Rampsbeck Country House Hotel** (HR)
Cumbria, Ullswater **Sharrow Bay** (HR)
Cumbria, Windermere **Merewood Hotel** (H)
Derbyshire, Ashbourne **Callow Hall** (H)
Derbyshire, Bakewell **Hassop Hall** (H)
Derbyshire, Baslow **Cavendish Hotel** (HR)
Derbyshire, Baslow **Fischer's Baslow Hall** (RR)
Derbyshire, Dovedale **Izaak Walton Hotel** (H)
Derbyshire, Matlock **Riber Hall** (HR)
Devon, Bishop's Tawton **Halmpstone Manor** (HR)
Devon, Chagford **Gidleigh Park** (HR)
Devon, Chagford **Great Tree Hotel** (H)
Devon, Chagford **Mill End** (H)
Devon, Chittlehamholt **Highbullen** (H)

Devon, Fairy Cross **Portledge Hotel** (H)
Devon, Gittisham **Combe House** (H)
Devon, Hawkchurch **Fairwater Head Hotel** (H)
Devon, Haytor **Bel Alp House** (H)
Devon, Holbeton **Alston Hall** (H)
Devon, Hope Cove **Cottage Hotel** (H)
Devon, Hope Cove **Lantern Lodge** (H)
Devon, Huntsham **Huntsham Court** (HR)
Devon, Lewdown **Lewtrenchard Manor** (HR)
Devon, North Huish **Brookdale House** (H)
Devon, Poundsgate **Leusdon Lodge Hotel** (HR)
Devon, Salcombe **Marine Hotel** (H)
Devon, Salcombe **Soar Mill Cove** (H)
Devon, Saunton **Saunton Sands** (H)
Devon, South Molton **Whitechapel Manor** (HR)
Devon, Thurlestone **Thurlestone Hotel** (H)
Devon, Torquay **Osborne Hotel** (H)
Devon, Whimple **Woodhayes Hotel** (HR)
Devon, Woody Bay **Woody Bay Hotel** (H)
Dorset, Chedington **Chedington Court** (HR)
Dorset, Evershot **Summer Lodge** (HR)
Dorset, Gillingham **Stock Hill House** (HR)
Dorset, Poole **Haven Hotel** (HR)
Dorset, Studland Bay **Knoll House** (H)
Dorset, West Bexington **Manor Hotel** (H)
Essex, Broxted **Whitehall** (HR)
Gloucestershire, Amberley **Amberley Inn** (H)
Gloucestershire, Charingworth **Charingworth Manor** (HR)
Gloucestershire, Cheltenham **The Greenway** (HR)
Gloucestershire, Corse Lawn **Corse Lawn House** (HR)
Gloucestershire, Lower Slaughter **Lower Slaughter Manor** (HR)
Gloucestershire, Stow-on-the-Wold **Wyck Hill House** (HR)
Gloucestershire, Tetbury **Calcot Manor** (HR)
Gloucestershire, Upper Slaughter **Lords of the Manor** (HR)
Hampshire, Burley **Burley Manor** (H)
Hampshire, Hurstbourne Tarrant **Esseborne Manor** (HR)
Hampshire, Lyndhurst **Parkhill Hotel** (HR)
Hampshire, New Milton **Chewton Glen** (HR)
Hampshire, Rotherwick **Tylney Hall** (HR)
Hampshire, Winchester **Lainston House** (H)
Hereford & Worcester, Abberley **Elms Hotel** (H)
Hereford & Worcester, Bromsgrove **Grafton Manor** (HR)
Hereford & Worcester, Buckland **Buckland Manor** (HR)
Hereford & Worcester, Chaddesley Corbett **Brockencote Hall** (HR)
Hereford & Worcester, Ledbury **Hope End** (HR)
Hereford & Worcester, Malvern **The Cottage in the Wood** (HR)
Hereford & Worcester, Ruckhall **Ancient Camp Inn** (I)
Hertfordshire, Hatfield Heath **Down Hall** (H)
Hertfordshire, Sawbridgeworth **Manor of Groves** (H)
Hertfordshire, Thundridge **Hanbury Manor** (HR)
Humberside, Walkington **Manor House** (H)
Isle of Wight, Freshwater **Farringford Hotel** (H)
Isles of Scilly, St Martin's **St Martin's Hotel** (HR)
Isles of Scilly, Tresco **Island Hotel** (HR)
Kent, Boughton Monchelsea **Tanyard Hotel** (HR)
Kent, Canterbury **Howfield Manor** (H)
Kent, Cranbrook **Kennel Holt Hotel** (H)
Kent, Lenham **Chilston Park** (H)
Lancashire, Whitewell **Inn at Whitewell** (I)
Leicestershire, Oakham **Hambleton Hall** (HR)
Leicestershire, Rothley **Rothley Court** (H)
Leicestershire, Stapleford **Stapleford Park** (HR)
Norfolk, Great Snoring **Old Rectory** (H)
Norfolk, Morston **Morston Hall** (H)
Northumberland, Cornhill-on-Tweed **Tillmouth Park** (H)
Northumberland, Langley-on-Tyne **Langley Castle** (H)
Northumberland, Longhorsley **Linden Hall** (H)
Nottinghamshire, Langar **Langar Hall** (HR)
Oxfordshire, Chadlington **The Manor** (HR)

Oxfordshire, Horton-cum-Studley **Studley Priory** (H)
Oxfordshire, Moulsford-on-Thames **Beetle & Wedge** (HR)
Oxfordshire, North Stoke **Springs Hotel** (H)
Somerset, Dulverton **Ashwick House** (HR)
Somerset, Kilve **Meadow House** (H)
Somerset, Middlecombe **Periton Park** (H)
Somerset, Porlock **Oaks Hotel** (HR)
Somerset, Winsford **Royal Oak Inn** (I)
Suffolk, Hintlesham **Hintlesham Hall** (HR)
Surrey, Bagshot **Pennyhill Park** (H)
Surrey, Churt **Frensham Pond Hotel** (H)
Surrey, Haslemere **Lythe Hill Hotel** (H)
Surrey, Richmond **Petersham Hotel** (HR)
Warwickshire, Alcester **Arrow Mill** (I)
Warwickshire, Billesley **Billesley Manor** (HR)
Warwickshire, Hockley Heath **Nuthurst Grange** (HR)
Warwickshire, Leamington Spa **Mallory Court** (HR)
Warwickshire, Stratford-upon-Avon **Ettington Park** (H)
Warwickshire, Stratford-upon-Avon **Welcombe Hotel** (H)
West Midlands, Sutton Coldfield **New Hall** (HR)
East Sussex, Battle **Netherfield Place** (HR)
East Sussex, Wych Cross **Ashdown Park Hotel** (HR)
West Sussex, Amberley **Amberley Castle** (HR)
West Sussex, Climping **Bailiffscourt** (HR)
West Sussex, East Grinstead **Gravetye Manor** (HR)
West Sussex, Lower Beeding **South Lodge** (HR)
West Sussex, Storrington **Abingworth Hall** (HR)
West Sussex, Storrington **Little Thakeham** (HR)
West Sussex, Turners Hill **Alexander House** (HR)
Wiltshire, Beanacre **Beechfield House** (H)
Wiltshire, Bradford-on-Avon **Woolley Grange** (HR)
Wiltshire, Castle Combe **Manor House** (HR)
Wiltshire, Colerne **Lucknam Park** (HR)
Wiltshire, Purton **Pear Tree** (HR)
Wiltshire, Teffont Evias **Howard's House** (HR)
Wiltshire, Warminster **Bishopstrow House** (HR)
North Yorkshire, Bilbrough **Bilbrough Manor** (HR)
North Yorkshire, Hackness **Hackness Grange** (H)
North Yorkshire, Jervaulx **Jervaulx Hall** (H)
North Yorkshire, Markington **Hob Green** (H)
North Yorkshire, Nidd **Nidd Hall** (H)
North Yorkshire, Scalby **Wrea Head Country Hotel** (H)
North Yorkshire, York **Middlethorpe Hall** (HR)
West Yorkshire, Linton **Wood Hall** (HR)
West Yorkshire, Otley **Chevin Lodge** (H)
West Yorkshire, Oulton **Oulton Hall Hotel** (H)

Scotland

Borders, Dryburgh **Dryburgh Abbey Hotel** (H)
Borders, Ettrickbridge **Ettrickshaws Hotel** (H)
Borders, Kelso **Ednam House** (H)
Borders, Kelso **Sunlaws House** (H)
Borders, Peebles **Cringletie House** (HR)
Borders, Peebles **Peebles Hotel Hydro** (H)
Central, Airth **Airth Castle** (H)
Central, Dunblane **Cromlix House** (HR)
Dumfries & Galloway, Beattock **Auchen Castle** (H)
Dumfries & Galloway, Gatehouse of Fleet **Cally Palace** (H)
Dumfries & Galloway, Newton Stewart **Kirroughtree Hotel** (HR)
Dumfries & Galloway, Port William **Corsemalzie House** (H)
Dumfries & Galloway, Portpatrick **Knockinaam Lodge** (HR)
Dumfries & Galloway, Rockcliffe **Baron's Craig** (H)
Fife, Markinch **Balbirnie House** (HR)
Grampian, Ballater **Tullich Lodge** (HR)
Grampian, Banchory **Raemoir House** (HR)
Grampian, Chapel of Garioch **Pittodrie House** (H)

Grampian, Kildrummy **Kildrummy Castle** (H)
Grampian, Maryculter **Maryculter House** (H)
Grampian, Oldmeldrum **Meldrum House** (H)
Highland, Achiltibuie **Summer Isles** (HR)
Highland, Advie **Tulchan Lodge** (H)
Highland, Altnaharra **Altnaharra Hotel** (H)
Highland, Arisaig **Arisaig House** (HR)
Highland, Drumnadrochit **Polmaily House** (HR)
Highland, Dulnain Bridge **Auchendean Lodge** (HR)
Highland, Duror **Stewart Hotel** (H)
Highland, Fort William **Inverlochy Castle** (HR)
Highland, Fort William **Mercury Hotel** (H)
Highland, Garve **Inchbae Lodge** (HR)
Highland, Glenelg **Glenelg Inn** (IR)
Highland, Helmsdale **Navidale House** (H)
Highland, Inverness **Bunchrew House** (H)
Highland, Inverness **Culloden House** (HR)
Highland, Inverness **Dunain Park** (HR)
Highland, Kentallen of Appin **Ardsheal House** (HR)
Highland, Kentallen of Appin **Holly Tree** (H)
Highland, Onich **Allt-Nan-Ros Hotel** (HR)
Highland, Onich **Lodge on the Loch** (H)
Highland, Onich **Onich Hotel** (H)
Highland, Scarista **Scarista House** (HR)
Highland, Scourie **Eddrachilles Hotel** (H)
Highland, Sleat **Kinloch Lodge** (HR)
Highland, Talladale **Loch Maree Hotel** (I)
Highland, Ullapool **Altnaharrie Inn** (HR)
Highland, Whitebridge **Knockie Lodge** (HR)
Lothian, Gullane **Greywalls Hotel** (HR)
Lothian, North Berwick **Marine Hotel** (H)
Lothian, North Middleton **Borthwick Castle** (H)
Orkney, Harray Loch **Merkister Hotel** (H)
Strathclyde, Ardentinny **Ardentinny Hotel** (H)
Strathclyde, Arduaine **Loch Melfort Hotel** (H)
Strathclyde, Crinan **Crinan Hotel** (HR)
Strathclyde, Eriska **Isle of Eriska** (HR)
Strathclyde, Kilchrenan **Ardanaiseig** (HR)
Strathclyde, Kilchrenan **Taychreggan Hotel** (HR)
Strathclyde, Kilmore **Glenfeochan House** (HR)
Strathclyde, Kilwinning **Montgreenan Mansion House** (H)
Strathclyde, Langbank **Gleddoch House** (H)
Strathclyde, Oban **Knipoch Hotel** (HR)
Strathclyde, Port Appin **Airds Hotel** (HR)
Strathclyde, Skelmorlie **Manor Park** (H)
Strathclyde, Strachur **Creggans Inn** (H)
Strathclyde, Tarbert **Stonefield Castle** (H)
Strathclyde, Tiroran **Tiroran House** (H)
Strathclyde, Turnberry **Turnberry Hotel** (HR)
Tayside, Aberfeldy **Farleyer House** (HR)
Tayside, Auchterarder **Auchterarder House** (HR)
Tayside, Auchterarder **Gleneagles Hotel** (H)
Tayside, Dunkeld **Kinnaird** (HR)
Tayside, Killiecrankie **Killiecrankie Hotel** (H)
Tayside, Kinclaven by Stanley **Ballathie House** (HR)
Tayside, Pitlochry **Green Park Hotel** (H)
Tayside, St Fillans **Four Seasons Hotel** (HR)

Wales

Clwyd, Llanarmon Dyffryn Ceiriog **Hand Hotel** (I)
Clwyd, Llanarmon Dyffryn Ceiriog **West Arms Hotel** (I)
Clwyd, Llandrillo **Tyddyn Llan** (HR)
Clwyd, Northop **Soughton Hall** (HR)
Clwyd, Rossett **Llyndir Hall** (H)
Dyfed, Aberystwyth **Conrah Country Hotel** (H)
Dyfed, Gwbert-on-Sea **Cliff Hotel** (H)

Dyfed, St David's **Warpool Court** (H)
Gwynedd, Aberdovey **Plas Penhelig** (H)
Gwynedd, Abersoch **Porth Tocyn Hotel** (HR)
Gwynedd, Beaumaris **Bulkeley Arms** (H)
Gwynedd, Beddgelert **Royal Goat Hotel** (H)
Gwynedd, Bontddu **Bontddu Hall** (H)
Gwynedd, Conwy **Sychnant Pass Hotel** (H)
Gwynedd, Holyhead **Trearddur Bay Hotel** (H)
Gwynedd, Llandudno **Bodysgallen Hall** (HR)
Gwynedd, Llansanffraid Glan Conwy **Old Rectory** (HR)
Gwynedd, Penmaenpool **George III Hotel** (I)
Gwynedd, Portmeirion **Hotel Portmeirion** (HR)
Gwynedd, Talsarnau **Maes-y-Neuadd** (HR)
Powys, Crickhowell **Gliffaes Country House Hotel** (H)
Powys, Eglwysfach **Ynyshir Hall** (HR)
Powys, Lake Vyrnwy **Lake Vyrnwy Hotel** (HR)
Powys, Llangammarch Wells **Lake Country House Hotel** (HR)
Powys, Llyswen **Llangoed Hall** (HR)
Powys, Pant Mawr **Glansevern Arms** (I)
South Glamorgan, Porthkerry **Egerton Grey** (H)
West Glamorgan, Reynoldston **Fairyhill** (HR)

Channel Islands

Jersey, Rozel Bay **Chateau la Chaire** (HR)
Jersey, St Brelade's Bay **Hotel L'Horizon** (H)
Jersey, St Saviour **Longueville Manor** (HR)
Sark, Sark **Hotel Petit Champ** (H)
Sark, Sark **Stocks Hotel** (HR)

Northern Ireland

Co Antrim, Ballymena **Galgorm Manor** (HR)

Republic of Ireland

Co Clare, Ballyvaughan **Gregans Castle** (HR)
Co Clare, Newmarket-on-Fergus **Dromoland Castle** (HR)
Co Cork, Ahakista **Hillcrest House** (PH)
Co Cork, Ballylickey **Ballylickey Manor House** (H)
Co Cork, Ballylickey **Larchwood House** (RR)
Co Cork, Ballylickey **Seaview Hotel** (HR)
Co Cork, Bantry **Bantry House** (PH)
Co Cork, Goleen Harbour **Herons Cove Restaurant** (RR)
Co Cork, Innishannon **Innishannon House Hotel** (H)
Co Cork, Kanturk **Assolas Country House** (HR)
Co Cork, Mallow **Longueville House** (HR)
Co Cork, Shanagarry **Ballymaloe House** (HR)
Co Donegal, Dunkineely **Castle Murray House** (HR)
Co Donegal, Rathmullan **Rathmullan House** (HR)
Co Donegal, Rossnowlagh **Smugglers Creek Inn** (IR)
Co Dublin, Howth **Deer Park Hotel** (H)
Co Galway, Ballyconneely **Erriseask House** (HR)
Co Galway, Ballynahinch **Ballynahinch Castle** (H)
Co Galway, Cashel **Cashel House** (HR)
Co Galway, Clifden **Abbeyglen Castle** (H)
Co Galway, Clifden **Ardagh Hotel** (HR)
Co Galway, Clifden **Rock Glen Manor** (HR)
Co Galway, Letterfrack **Rosleague Manor** (HR)
Co Galway, Oughterard **Currarevagh House** (HR)
Co Galway, Renvyle **Renvyle House** (H)
Co Kerry, Beaufort **Dunloe Castle** (H)

Co Kerry, Caherdaniel **Derrynane Hotel** (HR)
Co Kerry, Caragh Lake **Hotel Ard-na-Sidhe** (H)
Co Kerry, Caragh Lake **Caragh Lodge** (H)
Co Kerry, Dingle **Dingle Skellig Hotel** (H)
Co Kerry, Kenmare **Sheen Falls Lodge** (HR)
Co Kerry, Killarney **Aghadoe Heights Hotel** (HR)
Co Kerry, Killarney **Cahernane Hotel** (HR)
Co Kerry, Killarney **Hotel Europe** (H)
Co Kerry, Parknasilla **Great Southern** (H)
Co Kildare, Maynooth **Moyglare Manor** (HR)
Co Kildare, Straffan **Kildare Hotel** (HR)
Co Kilkenny, Thomastown **Mount Juliet Hotel** (HR)
Co Limerick, Adare **Adare Manor** (HR)
Co Monaghan, Scotshouse **Hilton Park** (PH)
Co Roscommon, Hodson Bay **Hodson Bay Hotel** (H)
Co Sligo, Riverstown **Coopershill House** (HR)
Co Tipperary, Dundrum **Dundrum House** (H)
Co Tipperary, Glen of Aherlow **Aherlow House** (H)
Co Waterford, Waterford **Waterford Castle** (HR)
Co Wexford, Ferrycarrig Bridge **Ferrycarrig Hotel** (HR)
Co Wexford, Gorey **Marlfield House** (HR)
Co Wicklow, Delgany **Glenview Hotel** (H)
Co Wicklow, Dunlavin **Rathsallagh House** (HR)
Co Wicklow, Laragh **Mitchell's of Laragh** (RR)
Co Wicklow, Rathnew **Hunter's Hotel** (HR)
Co Wicklow, Wicklow **Old Rectory** (HR)

Country House Hotels

This is a select category of small hotels offering civilised comfort, good service and fine food in an attractive and peaceful rural setting. Most of them are imposing country mansions converted and run with loving care by dedicated owners who are often a husband-and-wife team. They have no more than 35 bedrooms; all have recommended in-house restaurants, many of which are of star standard.

England

Avon, Freshford **Homewood Park**
Avon, Hunstrete **Hunstrete House**
Avon, Ston Easton **Ston Easton Park**
Berkshire, Taplow **Cliveden**
Berkshire, Woolton Hill **Hollington House Hotel**
Cornwall, Mawnan **Nansidwell**
Cumbria, Bowness-on-Windermere **Linthwaite House**
Cumbria, Grasmere **Michael's Nook**
Cumbria, Ullswater **Sharrow Bay**
Derbyshire, Baslow **Cavendish Hotel**
Devon, Chagford **Gidleigh Park**
Devon, Lewdown **Lewtrenchard Manor**
Devon, South Molton **Whitechapel Manor**
Dorset, Chedington **Chedington Court**
Dorset, Evershot **Summer Lodge**
Gloucestershire, Charingworth **Charingworth Manor**
Gloucestershire, Cheltenham **The Greenway**
Gloucestershire, Lower Slaughter **Lower Slaughter Manor**
Gloucestershire, Puckrup **Puckrup Hall**
Hereford & Worcester, Buckland **Buckland Manor**
Hertfordshire, Thundridge **Hanbury Manor**
Humberside, Walkington **Manor House**
Leicestershire, Oakham **Hambleton Hall**
Norfolk, Grimston **Congham Hall**
Oxfordshire, Great Milton **Le Manoir aux Quat'Saisons**
Surrey, Horley **Langshott Manor**
Warwickshire, Leamington Spa **Mallory Court**
East Sussex, Battle **Netherfield Place**
West Sussex, Amberley **Amberley Castle**
West Sussex, East Grinstead **Gravetye Manor**
West Sussex, Storrington **Little Thakeham**
Wiltshire, Bradford-on-Avon **Woolley Grange**
North Yorkshire, Bilbrough **Bilbrough Manor**

Scotland

Central, Dunblane **Cromlix House**
Dumfries & Galloway, Portpatrick **Knockinaam Lodge**
Grampian, Ballater **Tullich Lodge**
Highland, Arisaig **Arisaig House**
Highland, Fort William **Inverlochy Castle**
Strathclyde, Alexandria **Cameron House**
Strathclyde, Eriska **Isle of Eriska**

Wales

Clwyd, Northop **Soughton Hall**
Gwynedd, Capel Coch **Tre-Ysgawen Hall**
Gwynedd, Llandudno **Bodysgallen Hall**
Powys, Llyswen **Llangoed Hall**

Republic of Ireland

Co Cork, Kanturk **Assolas Country House**
Co Galway, Letterfrack **Rosleague Manor**
Co Sligo, Boyle **Cromleach Lodge**
Co Sligo, Riverstown **Coopershill House**
Co Wexford, Gorey **Marlfield House**
Co Wicklow, Rathnew **Hunter's Hotel**

15 Minutes off a Motorway

Eating in the motorway service areas may cut out extra travelling time, but it also cuts out any possibility of pleasing the discerning palate.

Yet throughout the land outstanding eating is available just a short drive from the motorway network, and the list that follows pinpoints STARRED RESTAURANTS that need no more than a 15-minute detour. And if you're looking for somewhere to spend the night in style, we also feature 70%+ within a similar range.

So even when time is important, you don't have to leave out the good things - just leave the motorway! For further details of these establishments, see individual entries in the main section of the Guide.

England

A1M

J1	Newcastle-upon-Tyne **Swallow Gosforth Park** (H)
	Newcastle-upon-Tyne **21 Queen Street** (R*†)
	Seaton Burn **Holiday Inn** (H)

M1

J12	Flitwick **Flitwick Manor** (HR)
J13	Aspley Guise **Moore Place** (H)
J15	Northampton **Swallow Hotel** (H)
J16	Daventry **Daventry Resort Hotel** (H)
J22	Leicester **Holiday Inn** (H)
J23	Quorn **The Quorn Country Hotel** (H)
J24	Castle Donington **Donington Thistle** (H)
J25	Nottingham **Forte Crest** (H)
	Nottingham **Royal Moat House** (H)
J47	Leeds **Haley's Hotel** (HR)

M3

J3	Ascot **Royal Berkshire** (H)
	Bagshot **Pennyhill Park** (H)
J5	Rotherwick **Tylney Hall** (HR)
J6	Basingstoke **Audleys Wood** (HR)
J8	Winchester **Lainston House** (H)

M4

J4	Heathrow Airport **Excelsior Hotel** (H)
	Heathrow Airport **Holiday Inn Crowne Plaza Heathrow** (H)
	Heathrow Airport **Radisson Edwardian International** (H)
	Heathrow Airport **Sheraton Heathrow Hotel** (H)
	Heathrow Airport **Sheraton Skyline** (H)
J6	Slough **Copthorne Hotel Slough/Windsor** (H)
	Slough **Heathrow/Slough Marriott Hotel** (H)
	Windsor **Oakley Court** (HR)
J8/9	Bray-on-Thames **The Waterside Inn** (RR***)
	Maidenhead **Fredrick's** (HR)
	Taplow **Cliveden** (HR*)
J10	Sindlesham **Reading Moat House** (H)
J11	Reading **Holiday Inn Reading** (H)
	Shinfield **L'Ortolan** (R***)
J13	Newbury **Donnington Valley Hotel** (H)
	Newbury **Foley Lodge** (H)
	Newbury **Regency Park Hotel** (H)

	Woolton Hill **Hollington House Hotel** (HR)
J15	Swindon **Swindon Marriott Hotel** (H)
J16	Purton **Pear Tree** (HR)
J17	Beanacre **Beechfield House** (H)
	Castle Combe **Manor House** (HR)
J18	Bath **Bath Spa Hotel** (HR†)
	Bath **Priory Hotel** (HR)
	Bath **Royal Crescent Hotel** (HR*†)
	Colerne **Lucknam Park** (HR)

M5

J2/3	Brierley Hill **Copthorne Hotel** (H)
J4	Bromsgrove **Grafton Manor** (HR)
	Chaddesley Corbett **Brockencote Hall** (HR)
J5	Abberley **Elms Hotel** (H)
	Droitwich **Chateau Impney** (H)
J7	Worcester **Fownes Hotel** (H)
J9	Corse Lawn **Corse Lawn House** (HR)
J11	Cheltenham **Le Champignon Sauvage** (R*)
	Cheltenham **Epicurean** (R**)
	Cheltenham **The Greenway** (HR)
	Cheltenham **On The Park** (HR)
	Gloucester **Hatton Court** (H)
J13	Painswick **Painswick Hotel** (H)
	Stroud **Oakes** (R*†)
J14	Thornbury **Thornbury Castle** (HR)
J16	Bristol **Aztec Hotel** (H)
J25	Hatch Beauchamp **Farthings Hotel** (H)
	Taunton **Castle Hotel** (HR*†)
J29	Whimple **Woodhayes Hotel** (HR)
J31	Exeter **Royal Clarence** (H)

M6

J2	Coventry **Hilton National** (H)
J2/3	Ansty **Ansty Hall** (H)
J6	Birmingham **Copthorne Hotel** (H)
	Birmingham **Holiday Inn** (H)
	Birmingham **Hyatt Regency** (HR)
	Birmingham **Swallow Hotel** (HR)
	Sutton Coldfield **New Hall** (HR)
J15	Hanchurch **Hanchurch Manor** (H)
J17	Nantwich **Rookery Hall** (HR)
J19	Alderley Edge **Alderley Edge Hotel** (HR)
J32	Longridge **Paul Heathcote's Restaurant** (R**)
J40	Penrith **North Lakes Hotel** (H)
	Ullswater **Leeming House** (HR)
	Ullswater **Sharrow Bay** (HR*)
	Wetheral **The Crown** (H)
J43	Brampton **Farlam Hall** (HR)

M11

J8	Broxted **Whitehall** (HR)
	Hatfield Heath **Down Hall** (H)

M20

J8	Lenham **Chilston Park** (H)
J9	Ashford **Ashford International** (H)
	Ashford **Eastwell Manor** (R)
J11	Hythe **Hythe Imperial** (H)

M23

J9	Horley **Langshott Manor** (HR)
J10	East Grinstead **Gravetye Manor** (HR*)
	Gatwick Airport **Forte Crest Gatwick** (H)
	Gatwick Airport **Gatwick Hilton International** (H)
	Gatwick Airport **Ramada Hotel Gatwick** (H)
	Turners Hill **Alexander House** (HR)
J11	Cuckfield **Ockenden Manor** (H)
	Lower Beeding **South Lodge** (HR)

M25

J3	Brands Hatch **Brands Hatch Thistle** (H)
J9	Sutton **Holiday Inn London Sutton** (H)
J13	Egham Runnymede Hotel (H)
J14	Heathrow Airport **Heathrow Hilton Hotel** (HR)

M27

J9	Fareham **Solent Hotel** (HR)
J12	Portsmouth **Portsmouth Marriott Hotel** (H)

M40

J4	Marlow **Compleat Angler Hotel** (HR)
	Medmenham **Danesfield House** (HR)
J7	Great Milton **Le Manoir aux Quat'Saisons** (HR***)
J9	Oxford **Old Parsonage** (H)
J15	Billesley **Billesley Manor** (HR)
	Leamington Spa **Mallory Court** (HR*)
	Stratford-upon-Avon **Ettington Park** (H)
	Stratford-upon-Avon **Moat House International** (H)
	Stratford-upon-Avon **Welcombe Hotel** (H)

M42

J4	Hockley Heath **Nuthurst Grange** (HR)
J6	Birmingham **Birmingham Metropole** (H)
	Meriden **Forest of Arden Hotel** (H)
J9	Wishaw **The Belfry** (H)

M50

J1	Puckrup **Puckrup Hall** (HR)
J2	Ledbury **Hope End** (HR)

M53

J5	Puddington **Craxton Wood** (HR)
J12	Chester **Chester Grosvenor** (HR*)
	Chester **Crabwall Manor** (H)

M54

J4	Shifnal **Park House** (H)

M56

J5   Manchester Airport **Hilton International** (H)
J6   Handforth **Belfry Hotel** (HR)
     Wilmslow **Stanneylands** (HR)

M62

J26 Bradford **Restaurant 19** (RR*)

M63

J9   Manchester **Charterhouse Hotel** (H)
     Manchester **Copthorne Hotel** (H)
     Manchester **Holiday Inn Crowne Plaza** (H)
     Manchester **Hotel Piccadilly** (H)
     Manchester **Ramada Hotel** (H)
     Manchester **Yang Sing** (R*)

Scotland

M8

J2   Edinburgh **The Balmoral** (HR↑)
      Edinburgh **Caledonian Hotel** (HR)
      Edinburgh **George Inter-Continental Hotel** (H)
      Edinburgh **Howard Hotel** (H)
      Edinburgh **King James Thistle Hotel** (H)
      Edinburgh **Royal Terrace Hotel** (H)
      Edinburgh **Sheraton Grand Hotel** (H)
J17   Glasgow **One Devonshire Gardens** (HR)
J17/18 Glasgow **Forte Crest** (H)
      Glasgow **Glasgow Hilton** (HR)
      Glasgow **Town House** (H)
J18   Glasgow **Glasgow Marriott Hotel** (H)

M9

J9   Dunblane **Cromlix House** (HR)
     Linlithgow **Champany Inn** (R*)

M80

J4   Cumbernauld **Westerwood Hotel** (HR)

Wales

J24 Llangybi **Cwrt Bleddyn Hotel** (H)
     Newport **Celtic Manor** (H)
J32 Cardiff **Moat House** (H)
     Cardiff **Park Hotel** (H)
J34 Miskin **Miskin Manor** (H)
J35 Coychurch **Coed-y-Mwstwr Hotel** (HR)

RESTAURANT ROUND-UP

ENGLAND

Please refer to the **How to Use This Guide** section (p18–19) at the front of the Guide for explanation of categories, pricing and star systems, crowns (Traditional or Modern), traditional Sunday Lunch, and Restaurants with Rooms (RR). See also wine and cheese awards feature (from p 41). ★ after a Room Price indicates that only half-board terms are offered.

Location	Establishment	Cat	Star	Price	Private Seats	Rm	Crown	Open	Sun L	Sea Food	Room Price	Des	Good Cheese	O/S Wine	New World	Open Air	National Cooking
Avon																	
Bath	Bath Spa Hotel	HR	↑	£90	90	120	T	All	SL			Dsrt				N/W	yes	
Bath	Clos du Roy	R		£65	65			All					yes				yes	French
Bath	Garlands Restaurant & Café/Bar	R		£60	28	40		All									yes	
Bath	Hole in the Wall	R	↑	£60	75											N/W		
Bath	The New Mocn	R		£50	80			All					Dsrt				yes	
Bath	Priory Hotel	HR		£75	70	45		All	SL					yes			yes	
Bath	Queensberry Hotel	HR		£55	45	25	M										yes	
Bath	Royal Crescent Hotel	HR	★↑	£95	65	48	T	All	SL			Dsrt		yes	O/S	N/W	yes	British
Bristol	Blue Goose	R		£45	80	80												
Bristol	Harveys Restaurant	R		£80	120	50	T					Dsrt		yes	O/S	N/W		British
Bristol	Howard's	R		£50	65									yes				
Bristol	Hunt's	R		£60	40	26												
Bristol	Jameson's Restaurant	R	★	£50	70	40		L	SL									
Bristol	Restaurant Lettonie	R		£80	24									yes		N/W		French
Bristol	Markwicks	R		£65	40	16								yes				
Bristol	Michael's Restaurant	R		£60	55	40		L	SL					yes				
Bristol	Rajdoot	R		£40	60			D										Indian

Location	Restaurant	Type	Rating	Price	N1	N2	T	Cards	SL	Dinner		O/S N/W		Cuisine
Bristol	Swallow Royal Hotel	HR		£70	80		T	L						
Chelwood	Chelwood House	HR		£50	24			All					yes	
Freshford	Homewood Park	HR		£75	55	40		All					yes	German
Hunstrete	Hunstrete House	HR		£100	50	30	T	All					yes	
Ston Easton	Ston Easton Park	HR	↑	£95	40	24	T	All	SL	Dsrt	yes	O/S N/W	yes	

Bedfordshire

Location	Restaurant	Type	Rating	Price	N1	N2	T	Cards	SL	Dinner		O/S N/W		Cuisine
Flitwick	Flitwick Manor	HR		£100	40	30	T	All	SL		yes		yes	
Woburn	Paris House	R		£90	44	16		L						

Berkshire

Location	Restaurant	Type	Rating	Price	N1	N2	T	Cards	SL	Dinner		O/S N/W		Cuisine
Ascot	Hyn's	R		£50	90			All					yes	Chinese
Bracknell	Coppid Beech Hotel	HR		£70	125	30		All				O/S N/W	yes	
Bray-on-Thames	The Waterside Inn	RR	★★★	£165	75		T	All	SL	£110 Dsrt		O/S		French
Elcot	Jarvis Elcot Park	HR		£70	100			All			yes	O/S		
Eton	Antico	R		£55	60	25					yes			Italian
Goring-on-Thames	The Leatherne Bottel	R	↑	£70	60	12		All			yes	O/S N/W	yes	
Kintbury	Dundas Arms	IR		£65	36					£65	yes		yes	
Maidenhead	Fredrick's	HR		£100	60	120	T	All			yes	N/W		
Old Burghclere	Dew Pond	R		£40	40	25		L			yes	N/W		
Shinfield	L'Ortolan	R	★★★	£140	65	25	T	All	SL	Dsrt	yes	N/W		
Streatley-on-Thames	Swan Diplomat	HR		£80	75	32		All	SL			N/W		
Taplow	Cliveden, Terrace Dining Room	HR		£120	70	42	T	yes		Dsrt		O/S N/W		
Taplow	Cliveden, Waldo's Restaurant	R	★	£105	26	12	T	All		Dsrt		N/W		
Windsor	Oakley Court	HR		£100	70			All	SL	Dsrt	yes	O/S N/W		
Woolton Hill	Hollington House Hotel	HR		£80	45			All	SL			O/S N/W	yes	

Buckinghamshire

Location	Restaurant	Type	Rating	Price	N1	N2	T	Cards	SL	Dinner		O/S N/W		Cuisine
Aston Clinton	Bell Inn	HR	↑	£100	120	20		All	SL			O/S N/W	yes	

Location	Establishment	Cat	Star	Price	Seats	Private Rm	Crown	Open	Sun L	Sea Food	Room Price	Des	Good Cheese	O/S Wine	New World	Open Air	National Cooking
Aylesbury	Hartwell House	HR		£100	70	30	T	All	SL				yes	O/S	N/W		
Long Crendon	The Angel	RR		£50	70	40				yes						yes	
Marlow	Compleat Angler Hotel	HR		£115	96	120		All	SL		£40						
Medmenham	Danesfield House	HR		£100	50	120	T	All							N/W		

Cambridgeshire

Location	Establishment	Cat	Star	Price	Seats	Private Rm	Crown	Open	Sun L	Sea Food	Room Price	Des	Good Cheese	O/S Wine	New World	Open Air	National Cooking
Cambridge	Charlie Chan	R		£45	160			All					yes				Chinese
Duxford	Duxford Lodge	HR		£50	36	36		All	SL			Dsrt	yes			yes	
Elton	Loch Fyne Oyster Bar	R		£40	85			L		yes						yes	
Ely	Old Fire Engine House	R		£50	36	24		All	SL				yes				
Huntingdon	Old Bridge Hotel	HR		£80	44	28		All	SL			Dsrt	yes	O/S	N/W		
Keyston	Pheasant Inn	R	←	£50	90	30		All	SL			Dsrt	yes	O/S	N/W		
Madingley	Three Horseshoes	R		£65	94	50		All	SL				yes		N/W	yes	
Stilton	Bell Inn	IR		£45	40	100		All	SL				yes			yes	
Wansford-in-England	The Haycock	HR		£70	100	30		All	SL		£64		yes	O/S	N/W	yes	British

Cheshire

Location	Establishment	Cat	Star	Price	Seats	Private Rm	Crown	Open	Sun L	Sea Food	Room Price	Des	Good Cheese	O/S Wine	New World	Open Air	National Cooking
Alderley Edge	Alderley Edge Hotel	HR		£80	80	22	T	All	SL			Dsrt	yes	O/S	N/W	yes	
Altrincham	Francs	R		£40	75			L								yes	
Bollington	Mauro's	R	★	£60	50												Italian
Chester	Chester Grosvenor, Arkle Rest	HR		£110	45		T	L				Dsrt	yes	O/S	N/W		
Chester	Chester Grosvenor, La Brasserie	R		£50	90								yes				
Handforth	Francs	R		£40	110	60		All									French
Handforth	Belfry Hotel	HR		£50	120	40		All	SL				yes	O/S	N/W		
Handforth	Handforth Chinese Restaurant	R		£45	85			D					yes	O/S			Chinese
Knutsford	Brasserie Belle Epoque	RR		£60	110	80	T				£40		yes	O/S			

Location	Restaurant	Cat.	Price	Seats	T	Meals		Accom.					Cuisine
Nantwich	Churche's Mansion	R	£60	50		L						yes	
Nantwich	Rookery Hall	HR	£85	30	†	All		Dsrt	yes			yes	
Prestbury	White House Manor	HR	£65	75				Dsrt	yes			yes	
Puddington	Craxton Wood	HR	£70	120	T				yes		yes		
Sandiway	Nunsmere Hall	HR	£70	48	T	All			yes		N/W	yes	French
Wilmslow	Harry's	R	£50	80	T	D			yes			yes	Chinese
Wilmslow	Stanneylands	HR	£80	100	T	L			yes	O/S	N/W		British

Cornwall

Location	Restaurant	Cat.	Price	Seats	T	Meals		Accom.					Cuisine
Calstock	Danescombe Valley Hotel	HR	£70	12		D			yes				
Falmouth	Seafood Bar	R	£45	24		D	yes		yes	O/S			
Helford	Riverside	RR	£80	38		All	yes	£75	yes	O/S	N/W		
Liskeard	Well House	HR	£65	32	T	All			yes			yes	
Mawnan	Nansidwell	HR	£66	38	T	All		Dsrt	yes				
Mylor Bridge	Pandora Inn	R ★↑	£40	45									
Padstow	Seafood Restaurant	RR	£80	70			yes	£73	yes	O/S	N/W		
Penzance	Abbey Hotel	HR	£60	20			yes	Dsrt	yes				
Penzance	Harris's	R	£70	35	T	D	yes		yes				
Polperro	Kitchen at Polperro	R	£55	24									
St Ives	Pig'n'Fish	R	£45	30		D	yes	Dsrt					
St Mawes	Idle Rocks Hotel	HR	£65	65		All			yes			yes	
Tintagel	Trebrea Lodge	R	£40	14		D							
Veryan	Nare Hotel	HR	£70	20		All			yes				

Cumbria

Location	Restaurant	Cat.	Price	Seats	T	Meals		Accom.					Cuisine
Alston	Lovelady Shield	HR	£60	26		All			yes				
Ambleside	Rothay Manor Hotel	HR	£70	70	T	L			yes			yes	British
Ambleside	Wateredge Hotel	HR	£65	45		All			yes			yes	
Appleby-in-Westmorland	Appleby Manor Hotel	HR	£50	70		All			yes		N/W		
Applethwaite	Underscar Manor	HR	£65	60	T	All		Dsrt	yes				British

Location	Establishment	Cat	Star	Price	Private Seats	Rm	Crown	Open	Sun L	Sea Food	Room Price	Des	Good Cheese	O/S Wine	New World	Open Air	National Cooking
Bowness-on-Windermere	Gilpin Lodge	HR		£60	45	16		All	SL			Dsrt	yes				
Bowness-on-Windermere	Linthwaite House	HR		£68	48	22		All	SL				yes			yes	
Brampton	Farlam Hall	HR		£60	45		T	D					yes				
Cartmel	Uplands	RR		£65	28			All	SL		£118*		yes				
Cockermouth	Quince & Medlar	R		£30	26			D					yes				
Crosby-on-Eden	Crosby Lodge	HR		£65	50	14		All									
Grasmere	Michael's Nook	HR	*†	£100	28	40	T	All				Dsrt	yes	O/S	N/W		
Grasmere	White Moss House	HR		£60	18								yes	O/S	N/W		
Grasmere	Wordsworth Hotel	HR		£75	75	100		All	SL				yes	O/S	N/W		
Grizedale	Grizedale Lodge	HR		£45	30			All								yes	
Kendal	The Moon	R		£35	38	40		D									
Melmerby	Village Bakery	R		£30	40			L									
Spark Bridge	Bridgefield House	HR		£60	24			D					yes		N/W		British
Ullswater	Leeming House	HR		£80	80	30	T	All	SL							yes	
Ullswater	Old Church Hotel	HR		£60	20			D					yes		N/W	yes	British
Ullswater	Rampsbeck Country House Hotel	HR		£55				All					yes				
Ullswater	Sharrow Bay	HR	*	£95	36	20	T	All	SL		£120*	Dsrt	yes	O/S	N/W	yes	
Ulverston	Bay Horse Inn & Bistro	RR		£65	64	30		All				Dsrt	yes	O/S	N/W		British
Windermere	Holbeck Ghyll	HR		£55	38	14		D					yes		N/W		
Windermere	Roger's Restaurant	R		£55	44	26		D				Dsrt	yes				
Witherslack	Old Vicarage	HR		£60	35	10		D	SL			Dsrt	yes		N/W		

Derbyshire

Location	Establishment	Cat	Star	Price	Private Seats	Rm	Crown	Open	Sun L	Sea Food	Room Price	Des	Good Cheese	O/S Wine	New World	Open Air	National Cooking
Ashford-in-the-Water	Riverside Hotel	HR		£75	50	20		All					yes			yes	
Baslow	Cavendish Hotel	HR		£75	50	18	T	All		yes			yes				
Baslow	Fischer's Baslow Hall	RR	**	£100	40	12	T	L	SL		£120	Dsrt	yes	O/S		yes	
Hayfield	Bridge End Restaurant	RR		£65	50	20		L	SL		£45						

Location	Restaurant			£						£						
Matlock	Riber Hall	HR		£66	60	40		All			Dsrt	yes	O/S		yes	
Ridgeway	Old Vicarage	R	**	£90	35	45		L				yes	O/S		yes	
Devon																
Barnstaple	Lynwood House	RR		£65	50	20	T	All	yes	£61	Dsrt	yes			yes	
Bishop's Tawton	Halmpstone Manor	HR		£70	24	30		L	yes			yes			yes	
Braunton	Otters Restaurant	R		£50	40						Dsrt					Swedish
Broadhembury	Drewe Arms	R		£50	40			L				yes				
Chagford	Gidleigh Park	HR		£120	40	24	T	All	yes		Dsrt	yes	O/S	N/W		
Dartmouth	Carved Angel	R	**	£110	45	16	T	L	yes			yes	O/S	N/W		
East Buckland	Lower Pitt	RR		£60	32	16						yes				
Exeter	St Olaves Court	HR		£60	50	18				£50	Dsrt	yes				
Gulworthy	The Horn of Plenty	RR	*	£100	50	12	T	All	SL	£92	Dsrt	yes		N/W	yes	
Huntsham	Huntsham Court	HR		£75	30			D								
Ide	Old Mill	R		£55	45							yes				
Lewdown	Lewtrenchard Manor	HR		£75	35	16	T	All	yes		Dsrt	yes				
Lifton	Arundell Arms	HR		£70				All						N/W		
Lympstone	River House	RR		£95	34	14		All	yes	£87	Dsrt	yes		N/W		
Plymouth	Chez Nous	R	*	£55	28							yes				
Poundsgate	Leusdon Lodge Hotel	HR		£50	18	30		L	yes		Dsrt	yes				
Salcombe	Spinnakers	R		£50	60			L				yes				
Silverton	Silverton Inn	R		£80	45	8		All				yes				
South Molton	Whitechapel Manor	HR		£100	24		T	D				yes		N/W		
Torquay	Table Restaurant	R		£70	20			L				yes		N/W		
Tuckenhay	Floyd's Inn (Sometimes)	IR	↑	£100	26		T	D				yes				
Whimple	Woodhayes Hotel	HR		£65	18					£125		yes				British
Winkleigh	Pophams	R		£30	10							yes				
Dorset																
Blandford Forum	La Belle Alliance	RR		£50	32	40		yes		£58						
Bournemouth	Ocean Palace	R		£45	150	60		All								Chinese

Location	Establishment	Cat	Star	Price	Private Seats	Rm	Crown	Open	Sun L	Sea Food	Room Price	Des	Good Cheese	O/S Wine	New World	Open Air	National Cooking
Bournemouth	Royal Bath Hotel	HR		£60	60			All	SL								
Bridport	Riverside Restaurant	R		£40	70			L		yes						yes	
Chedington	Chedington Court	HR		£65	25	22		D					yes	O/S	N/W		
Christchurch	Splinters Restaurant	R		£55	40	22											French
Dorchester	Mock Turtle	R		£55	50					yes							
Evershot	Summer Lodge	HR	*	£100	50	8	T	All	SL			Dsrt	yes	O/S	N/W	yes	
Gillingham	Stock Hill House	HR	*↑	£80	24	12	T	All				Dsrt	yes	O/S	N/W		
Maiden Newton	Le Petit Canard	R		£55	28										N/W		
Poole	Haven Hotel, Restaurant	HR		£55	150			All	SL								
Poole	Haven Hotel, La Roche Rest	R		£80	30		T										
Poole	Mansion House	HR		£65	100	40	T	L	SL				yes				
Powerstock	Three Horseshoes Inn	RR		£50	60	20		All	SL		£50						
Sturminster Newton	Plumber Manor	RR		£55	60	50		All	SL		£80						
Wareham	Priory Hotel	HR		£75	66	24		All	SL				yes		N/W	yes	
Weymouth	Perry's	R		£60	54			All		yes					N/W	yes	
Wimborne	Les Bouviers	R		£60	40	40		L							N/W		
Durham																	
Coatham Mundeville	Hall Garth Golf & C Club Hotel	HR		£60	60	12		L	SL								
Darlington	Sardis	R		£50	60								yes				Italian
Darlington	Victor's Restaurant	R		£55	30								yes		N/W		
Romaldkirk	Rose and Crown	IR		£65	24		T	L	SL		£74				N/W		
Essex																	
Broxted	Whitehall	HR		£80	60			All					Dsrt				
Coggeshall	White Hart Hotel	HR		£60	80	24	T	L	SL						O/S	N/W	Italian

Location	Restaurant	Type	Rating	Price	Seats	No.	T	Lic	SL	yes	£	Dsrt	yes	O/S	N/W	yes	Cuisine
Dedham	Fountain House & Dedham Hall	RR		£50	32	16		L	SL					O/S	N/W		
Dedham	Le Talbooth	R		£100	80	24		All	SL			Dsrt		O/S	N/W	yes	
Felsted	Rumbles Cottage	R		£55	50	22		L	SL			Dsrt	yes	O/S			
Great Dunmow	The Starr	RR		£75	50	36		All	SL				yes		N/W		
Harwich	Pier at Harwich	RR		£60	70	50		All		yes	£57						
Horndon-on-the-Hill	Hill House	RR		£50	32						£75						
Maldon	Francine's	R		£50	24						£63						
Wethersfield	Dicken's	R		£60	45	18					£54	Dsrt				yes	

Gloucestershire

Location	Restaurant	Type	Rating	Price	Seats	No.	T	Lic	SL	yes	£	Dsrt	yes	O/S	N/W	yes	Cuisine
Bibury	The Swan	HR		£100	65	12	T	All	SL				yes		N/W		
Birdlip	Kingshead House	R		£55	32			L	SL				yes	O/S	N/W	yes	
Charingworth	Charingworth Manor	HR		£80	48	36		All									
Cheltenham	Bonnets Bistro at Staithes	R		£50	30	10								O/S			
Cheltenham	Le Champignon Sauvage	R	*	£75	28		T	L	SL			Dsrt	yes	O/S	N/W		French
Cheltenham	Epicurean	R	**	£70	32	18	T	All	SL			Dsrt	yes		N/W		
Cheltenham	The Greenway	HR		£85	50	18	T	All	SL				yes	O/S			
Chipping Campden	Cotswold House	HR		£70	50	20	T	All	SL				yes	O/S	N/W		
Cirencester	Tatyan's	R		£45	60												Chinese
Corse Lawn	Corse Lawn House	HR		£75	50	35	T	All	SL			Dsrt	yes	O/S	N/W	yes	
Lower Slaughter	Lower Slaughter Manor	HR	↑	£80	26	16	T	All	SL			Dsrt	yes	O/S	N/W	yes	
Moreton-in-Marsh	Annie's	R		£60	30	10		L	SL				yes				
Moreton-in-Marsh	Marsh Goose	R		£65	60	15		L	SL			Dsrt	yes		N/W		
Northleach	Old Woolhouse	R	*	£90	18									O/S			
Northleach	Wickens	R		£55	36							Dsrt	yes				
Puckrup	Puckrup Hall	HR		£90	34							Dsrt	yes		N/W	yes	
Stow-on-the-Wold	Wyck Hill House	HR		£95	70	32		All	SL			Dsrt	yes	O/S	N/W		
Stroud	Oakes	R	*↑	£80	34		T	L				Dsrt	yes				British
Terbury	Calcot Manor	HR		£60	50	35	T	All				Dsrt	yes		N/W	yes	
Upper Slaughter	Lords of the Manor	HR		£90	60	60	T	All				Dsrt	yes			yes	

Location	Establishment	Cat	Star	Price	Seats	Private Rm	Crown	Open	Sun L	Sea Food	Room Price	Des	Good Cheese	O/S Wine	New World	Open Air	National Cooking
Greater Manchester																	
Bury	Normandie Hotel & Restaurant	HR	★	£90								Dsrt	yes	O/S			
Manchester	Gaylord	R		£50	50			All									Indian
Manchester	Market Restaurant	R		£55	90							Dsrt	yes				
Manchester	Penang Village	R		£45	42	24		All									S E Asian
Manchester	Quan Ju De	R		£60	60												Chinese
Manchester	Rajdoot	R		£40	120	48		D									Indian
Manchester	Siam Orchid	R		£60	67			All									Thai
Manchester	Sonarga	R		£60	55			D									Indian
Manchester	That Café	R		£45	64			L									
Manchester	Victoria & Albert Hotel	HR		£65	80	35		All	SL			Dsrt					
Manchester	Woodlands	R		£55	130	16		All								yes	
Manchester	Yang Sing	RR	★	£50	40			All									Chinese
Manchester Airport	Moss Nook	R		£80	140	200					£140★					yes	
Ramsbottom	Village Restaurant	R		£45	65	32	T	L	SL				yes	O/S	N/W		
West Didsbury	Lime Tree	R		£45	80	40		L	SL								
Hampshire																	
Basingstoke	Audleys Wood	HR		£66	66	40		All	SL				yes		N/W		
Basingstoke	Hee's	R		£40	80			D									Chinese
Botley	Cobbett's	R		£65	40	14		L									French
Brockenhurst	Le Poussin	R	★	£75	24								yes			yes	
Denmead	Barnard's	R		£45	30												
Dunbridge	Mill Arms Inn	R		£50	60	40		All	SL								
Eversley	New Mill Restaurant	R		£80	80	40	T	All	SL				yes	O/S	N/W		
Fareham	Solent Hotel	HR		£55	100	200		All	SL							yes	

Place	Name	Type	Price		Seats	Rooms	T			Price	Dsrt	yes	O/S	N/W	yes	Cuisine
Highclere	The Yew Tree	R	£50		50	20		All			Dsrt	yes			yes	
Hurstbourne Tarrant	Esseborne Manor	HR	£80		40			All	SL			yes			yes	
Lymington	Gordleton Mill	HR	£95	★	40	30		L	SL		Dsrt	yes	O/S	N/W	yes	
Lyndhurst	Parkhill Hotel	HR	£60		120	36		L				yes			yes	
Milford-on-Sea	Rocher's	R	£65		30			L									
New Alresford	Hunters	RR	£55		30	80		All	SL	£48	Dsrt	yes	O/S	N/W	yes	
New Milton	Chewton Glen	HR	£100	★	120	120	T	All	SL		Dsrt	yes	O/S	N/W	yes	
Romsey	Old Manor House	R	£90	★	42	22		L				yes		N/W	yes	
Rotherwick	Tylney Hall	HR	£95		100	100	T	All	SL			yes		N/W		
Southampton	Browns Brasserie	R	£70		26							yes				
Southampton	Kuti's	R	£45		74			All								Indian
Southsea	Bistro Montparnasse	R	£55		50	20						yes			yes	
Stuckton	Three Lions	R	£60		55			L				yes	O/S	N/W		
Wickham	Old House Hotel	HR	£70		40	14					Dsrt					French
Winchester	Old Chesil Rectory	R	£50		55	24										
Winchester	Wykeham Arms	IR	£55		72					£75		yes	O/S	N/W	yes	

Hereford & Worcester

Place	Name	Type	Price		Seats	Rooms	T			Price	Dsrt	yes	O/S	N/W	yes	Cuisine
Brimfield	Poppies Restaurant	RR	£75	↑	36	16		All		£60	Dsrt	yes			yes	
Broadway	Collin House	HR	£60		24			All	SL			yes			yes	
Broadway	Dormy House	HR	£90		85	180		L	SL					O/S	N/W		British
Broadway	Hunters Lodge	R	£65		40	20		All	SL			yes			yes	
Bromsgrove	Lygon Arms	HR	£80		120	96	T	All	SL		Dsrt	yes		N/W	yes	
Buckland	Grafton Manor	HR	£70		42	18		All	SL		Dsrt	yes				
Buckland	Buckland Manor	HR	£95		38		T	All	SL			yes	O/S	N/W	yes	French
Chaddesley Corbett	Brockencote Hall	HR	£80		50	28	T	All	SL			yes		N/W		
Evesham	Evesham Hotel	HR	£60		55	12		L	SL			yes			yes	
Evesham	Riverside Hotel	HR	£55		45			All	SL			yes				
Eyton	Marsh Country Hotel	HR	£55		24	24		All	SL						yes	
Harvington	The Mill at Harvington	HR	£60		40	14		All	SL							
Kington	Penrhos Court	RR	£65		70	20				£100						
Ledbury	Hope End	HR	£70		24			D				yes	O/S			

Location	Establishment	Cat	Star	Price	Seats	Private Rm	Crown Open	Open L	Sun L	Sea Food	Room Price	Des	Good Cheese	O/S Wine	New World	Open Air	National Cooking
Malvern	Anupam	R		£40	54			All									Indian
Malvern	The Cottage in the Wood	HR		£65	50	14		All	SL				yes	O/S	N/W	yes	
Malvern	Croque-en-Bouche	R	*	£90	24	6	T					Dsrt	yes	O/S	N/W		
Ross-on-Wye	Pheasants	RR		£70	22			L			£40		yes	O/S	N/W	yes	
Worcester	Brown's	R		£75	100								yes				

Hertfordshire

Location	Establishment	Cat	Star	Price	Seats	Private Rm	Crown Open	Open L	Sun L	Sea Food	Room Price	Des	Good Cheese	O/S Wine	New World	Open Air	National Cooking
Hadley Wood	West Lodge Park Hotel	HR		£65	75			All	SL			Dsrt	yes				
Melbourn	Pink Geranium	R	↑	£104	70	18		All	SL			Dsrt					
New Barnet	Mims Restaurant	R	↑	£75	40			All									
Thundridge	Hanbury Manor	HR		£125	40	8	T	L						O/S	N/W		

Humberside

Location	Establishment	Cat	Star	Price	Seats	Private Rm	Crown Open	Open L	Sun L	Sea Food	Room Price	Des	Good Cheese	O/S Wine	New World	Open Air	National Cooking
Hull	Ceruttis	R		£60	40	24							yes				
Walkington	Manor House	HR		£75	54	20							yes	O/S	N/W		
Winteringham	Winteringham Fields	RR	*	£90	36	10	T				£92	Dsrt	yes	O/S	N/W		

Isle of Wight

Location	Establishment	Cat	Star	Price	Seats	Private Rm	Crown Open	Open L	Sun L	Sea Food	Room Price	Des	Good Cheese	O/S Wine	New World	Open Air	National Cooking
Seaview	Seaview Hotel	HR		£50	32			L	SL	yes							
Shanklin Old Village	The Cottage	R		£60	32											yes	

Isles of Scilly

Location	Establishment	Cat	Star	Price	Seats	Private Rm	Crown Open	Open L	Sun L	Sea Food	Room Price	Des	Good Cheese	O/S Wine	New World	Open Air	National Cooking
St Martin's	St Martin's Hotel	HR		£55	60	10		D									
Tresco	Island Hotel	HR		£60	110	10		All						yes			yes

Kent

Location	Restaurant	Type	Price	Seats	Pvt	T	Cards	SL	Rooms	Dsrt	Other	N/W	Cuisine
Ashford	Eastwell Manor	R	£105	80	100	T	All		£110				
Billingshurst	The Gables	R	£50	45								N/W	
Boughton Monchelsea	Tanyard Hotel	HR	£60	30									
Canterbury	County Hotel	HR	£65	50	120	T	All				yes		
Canterbury	River Kwai	R	£40	70									Chinese
Edenbridge	Honours Mill Restaurant	R	£60	40			L						
Faversham	Read's	R	£75	40	18	T	All				yes	O/S N/W	
Folkestone	Paul's	R	£45	80							yes	yes	
Folkestone	La Tavernetta	R	£55	55	22								Italian
Herne Bay	L'Escargot	R	£45	40									French
Higham	The Knowle	R	£68	60	45		L	SL					
Maidstone	Mandarin Chef	R	£35	75	70		All						Chinese
Sevenoaks	Royal Oak	HR	£65	60	24		All						
Sissinghurst	Rankins	R	£65	30			L	SL					
St Margaret's	Wallett's Court	HR	£55	60	30						yes		
Tunbridge Wells	Cheevers	R	£60	32						Dsrt	yes		
Tunbridge Wells	Downstairs at Thackeray's	R	£45	34							yes		
Tunbridge Wells	Spa Hotel	HR	£60	90	180		All	SL		Dsrt	yes		
Tunbridge Wells	Thackeray's House	R	£90	40	40	T	L			Dsrt	yes	N/W	
Whitstable	Whitstable Oyster Fishery Co	R ★		67	30	T	All				yes		

Lancashire

Location	Restaurant	Type	Price	Seats	Pvt	T	Cards	SL	Rooms	Dsrt	Other	N/W	Cuisine
Blackpool	September Brasserie	R	£65	40							yes		
Broughton	Broughton Park	HR	£65	110		T	All	SL			yes	N/W	
Clitheroe	Browns Bistro	R	£55	65									
Cowan Bridge	Cobwebs	RR	£60	24									
Langho	Northcote Manor	HR ↑	£80	100	35	T	All	SL	£60	Dsrt	yes	N/W	
Longridge	Paul Heathcote's Restaurant	R **	£90	50	18	T	All	SL		Dsrt	yes	O/S N/W	
Lytham St Annes	Dalmeny Hotel	HR	£60	45							yes		
Thornton-le-Fylde	River House	RR	£75	40	12		L	SL	£100	Dsrt			French

Location	Establishment	Cat	Star	Price	Private Seats	Rm	Crown	Open	Sun L	Sea Food	Room Price	Des	Good Cheese	O/S Wine	New World	Open Air	National Cooking
Leicestershire																	
Hambleton	Hambleton Hall	HR	**	£110	80	20	T	All	SL			Dsrt	yes	O/S	N/W	yes	
Leicester	Curry Pot	R		£45	55	30		All									Indian
Leicester	Man Ho	R		£40	130	60		All									Chinese
Leicester	Rise of the Raj	R		£35	70	40		All									Indian
Oakham	Whipper-In Hotel	HR		£60	38	20		All	SL								
Quorn	Quorn Grange	HR		£60	50	30		All	SL								
Stapleford	Stapleford Park	HR		£75	70			All	SL				yes	O/S	N/W	yes	
Stretton	Ram Jam Inn	IR		£35	30	25		L			£57		yes			yes	
Uppingham	The Lake Isle	RR		£60	40	10		L	SL		£66		yes	O/S	N/W	yes	
Lincolnshire																	
Beckingham	Black Swan	R		£50	36	26		All	SL				yes			yes	
Great Gonerby	Harry's Place	R	★	£95	10		T						yes				
Lincoln	The Jew's House	R		£55	25							Dsrt					
Stamford	The George of Stamford	HR		£85	80	50	T	All					yes	O/S	N/W	yes	
Merseyside																	
Liverpool	Armadillo	R		£55	75												
Liverpool	La Grande Bouffe	R		£50	60	16											French
Middlesex																	
Hampton Wick	Le Petit Max	R		£50	35			All									French
Heathrow Airport	Heathrow Hilton, Zen Oriental	R		£60	60												Chinese

Town	Restaurant		Price	Seats		Service		Price					Cuisine
(North) Harrow	Percy's Restaurant	R	£70	80			yes						
Southall	Asian Tandoori Centre	R	£15	80		All							Indian
Twickenham	Hamiltons	R	£50	48	10	L SL							
Twickenham	McClements Restaurant	R	★	14	20								French
Twickenham	McClement's Bistro	R	£40	40	12	All					N/W	yes	

Norfolk

Town	Restaurant		Price	Seats		Service		Price					Cuisine
Cawston	Grey Gables	RR	£50	30	24	D		£54	Dsrt	yes	O/S N/W	yes	
Coltishall	Norfolk Place Restaurant	R	£65	30									
Diss	Weavers	R	£45	80	50								
Erpingham	The Ark	RR	£45	32	18	L				yes			
Great Yarmouth	Seafood Restaurant	R	£55	40									
Grimston	Congham Hall	HR	£85	50	18	T	yes	£90★		yes	N/W	yes	
Norwich	Adlard's	R	★	40		All SL	yes		Dsrt	yes	O/S N/W	yes	
Norwich	Brasted's	R	£60	22			yes						
Norwich	Greens Seafood Restaurant	R	£60	48									
Norwich	Marco's	R	£80	22						yes			Italian
Wymondham	Number Twenty Four	R	£45	75	60					yes			

Northamptonshire

Town	Restaurant		Price	Seats		Service		Price					Cuisine
Horton	French Partridge	R	£60	40									
Paulerspury	Vine House	RR	£55	45	12	L		£62		yes			
Roade	Roadhouse Restaurant	R	£56	45						yes			

Northumberland

Town	Restaurant		Price	Seats		Service		Price					Cuisine
Berwick-upon-Tweed	Funnywayt'mekalivin	R	£50	32	8					yes			
Wylam	Laburnum House	RR	£65	40		L		£50		yes			

Nottinghamshire

Location	Establishment	Cat	Star	Price	Private Seats	Rm	Crown	Open	Sun L	Sea Food	Room Price	Des	Good Cheese	O/S Wine World	New World	Open Air	National Cooking
Langar	Langar Hall	HR		£70	30	18							yes			yes	
Nether Langwith	Goff's Restaurant	RR		£60	45	28											
Newark	Gannets Café-Bistrot	R		£40	40			L			£50					yes	
Nottingham	Higoi	R		£50	35												Japanese
Nottingham	Loch Fyne Oyster Bar	R		£35	40					yes							
Nottingham	Man Ho	R		£40	270	126		All									Chinese
Nottingham	Noble House	R		£60	80			All									Chinese
Nottingham	Ocean City	R		£40	250			All									Chinese
Nottingham	Sonny's	R	↑	£60	80			All									
Plumtree	Perkins Bar & Bistro	R		£50	93	30						Dsrt	yes			yes	

Oxfordshire

Location	Establishment	Cat	Star	Price	Private Seats	Rm	Crown	Open	Sun L	Sea Food	Room Price	Des	Good Cheese	O/S Wine World	New World	Open Air	National Cooking
Burford	Lamb Inn	IR		£70	56			All			£80		yes				
Chadlington	The Manor	HR		£60	20		T	D	SL			Dsrt			N/W		
Charlbury	The Bull at Charlbury	R		£40	50			L									
Clanfield	The Plough at Clanfield	IR		£70	30	12		All			£85					yes	
Great Milton	Le Manoir aux Quat'Saisons	HR	***	£200	95	46	T	All				Dsrt	yes	O/S	N/W	yes	French
Moulsford-on-Thames	Beetle & Wedge	HR	★	£100	30	50		All	SL			Dsrt	yes			yes	
Moulsford-on-Thames	Beetle & Wedge, B'house Brass	RR	↑	£70	50			All	SL			Dsrt		O/S		yes	
Old Minster Lovell	Lovells at Windrush Farm	RR	↑	£80	18			All	SL		£145	Dsrt	yes				
Oxford	Al-Shami	R		£30	50			L									Lebanese
Oxford	Bath Place Hotel & Restaurant	RR		£80	30		T	L	SL		£100		yes		N/W	yes	
Oxford	Cherwell Boathouse	R		£45	50			L					yes	O/S	N/W	yes	
Oxford	Restaurant Elizabeth	R	↑	£75	40	40	T	All					yes	O/S			French
Oxford	15 North Parade	R		£70	55			L					yes				
Stonor	Stonor Arms	RR		£80	20	24	T	L	SL		£93		yes	O/S	N/W		

Location	Restaurant	Type	£			T	Meals	SL	Price/Dsrt		O/S N/W		Cuisine
Watlington	Well House	RR	£60	40	65		L			yes		yes	
Woodstock	Bear Hotel	HR	£60	75	60		All	SL	£66	yes	N/W		
Woodstock	Feathers Hotel	HR	£75	60	60		All	SL		yes	N/W		

Shropshire

Location	Restaurant	Type	£			T	Meals	SL	Price/Dsrt		O/S N/W		Cuisine
Dorrington	Country Friends	RR	£65	40					£98*	yes		yes	
Norton	Hundred House Hotel	IR	£65	60	30				£69 Dsrt	yes		yes	British
Worfield	Old Vicarage	HR	£72	45	16		All	SL	£69 Dsrt	yes	O/S N/W		British

Somerset

Location	Restaurant	Type	£			T	Meals	SL	Price/Dsrt		O/S N/W		Cuisine
Castle Cary	Bond's	HR	£55	20			D			yes		yes	
Dulverton	Ashwick House	HR	£60	30	15		All			yes		yes	
Glastonbury	No. 3 Restaurant & Hotel	RR	£75	20					£65	yes			
Porlock	Oaks Hotel	HR	£45	24			D			yes			
Shepton Mallet	Blostin's Restaurant	R	£50	30						yes			
Taunton	Castle Hotel	HR *↑	£80	60	28	T	All	SL	Dsrt	yes	O/S N/W		
Taunton	Porters Wine Bar	R	£40	50						yes			
Wells	Ritchers Restaurant	R	£55	14	18		All			yes		yes	
Williton	White House	RR	£65	26			D		£68	yes	O/S	yes	
Wiveliscombe	Langley House	HR	£65	16	20		D			yes	O/S		
Yeovil	Little Barwick House	RR	£55	40	20		D		£72	yes			

Staffordshire

Location	Restaurant	Type	£			T	Meals	SL	Price/Dsrt		O/S N/W		Cuisine
Penkridge	William Harding's House	R	£50	30	16		L	SL		yes		yes	
Stretton	Dovecliffe Hall	HR	£65	85	60		L	SL	£87	yes		yes	
Waterhouses	Old Beams	RR *↑	£80	50	20	T	L			yes		yes	

Suffolk

Location	Establishment	Cat	Star	Price	Seats	Private Rm	Crown	Open L	Sun L	Sea Food	Room Price	Des	Good Cheese	O/S Wine	New World	Open Air	National Cooking
Campsea Ashe	Old Rectory	RR		£50	45	30					£48				N/W		
Cavendish	Alfonso's	R		£60	30											yes	Italian
Fressingfield	Fox and Goose	R		£65	50			All	SL						N/W		
Hintlesham	Hintlesham Hall	HR		£90	120	30	T	All	SL						N/W		
Ixworth	Theobald's	R		£60	36			L					yes	O/S			
Lavenham	Great House	RR		£45	40			L	SL		£68		yes	O/S		yes	French
Lavenham	The Swan	HR		£75	70	40		All	SL				yes	O/S			British
Long Melford	Chimneys	R		£80	50			L									
Southwold	The Crown	IR		£50	22	22		All	SL				yes		N/W	yes	
Southwold	The Swan	HR		£65	60	40	T	All	SL		£63		yes	O/S	N/W	yes	British
Stonham	Mr Underhill's	R	★	£75	24							Dsrt	yes		N/W	yes	
Sudbury	Mabey's Brasserie	R		£55	50	35							yes		N/W	yes	

Surrey

Location	Establishment	Cat	Star	Price	Seats	Private Rm	Crown	Open L	Sun L	Sea Food	Room Price	Des	Good Cheese	O/S Wine	New World	Open Air	National Cooking
Camberley	Tithas	R		£30	65	16		All									Indian
Chobham	Quails Restaurant	R		£55	40	40		L	SL								
Claygate	Les Alouettes	R		£70	60	20	T	L	SL				yes		N/W		French
Cranleigh	La Barbe Encore	R		£55	60			L									
Dorking	Partners West Street	R		£75	45	30		L	SL				yes				
Esher	Good Earth	R		£55	85			All									Chinese
Farnham	Krug's	R		£55	80	40											Austrian
Grayshott	Woods Place	R		£55	36												Swedish
Guildford	Mandarin	R		£35	55			D									Chinese
Haslemere	Morel's	R	★	£90	50	15	T	L	SL			Dsrt	yes				French
Hersham	The Dining Room	R		£50	90	30		L	SL								
Horley	Langshott Manor	HR		£66	14	12		D									

Location	Restaurant		£	No.									Cuisine
Kew	Wine & Mousaka	R	£35	52								yes	Greek
Kingston-upon-Thames	Restaurant Gravier	R	£70	40				yes				yes	French
Reigate	La Barbe	R	£60	65									French
Reigate	The Dining Room	R	£65	50					Dsrt	yes			
Richmond	Burnt Chair	R	£55	31									
Richmond	Petersham Hotel	HR	£66	70		All	SL		Dsrt	yes			
Richmond	River Terrace	R	£35	36		All			Dsrt	yes		yes	
Ripley	Michels'	R *	£90	200	T	L							
Shere	Kinghams Restaurant	R	£55	50		L	SL					yes	French
Surbiton	Chez Max	R	£65	45									Chinese
Sutton	Heen's	R	£50	12		All							
Sutton	Partners Brasserie	R	£50	80						yes			French
Tadworth	Gemini Restaurant	R	£50	40		L	SL		Dsrt				Italian
Thornton Heath	Mamma Adele	R	£50	32									Italian
Weybridge	Casa Romana	R	£65	90		All	SL						

East Sussex

Location	Restaurant		£	No.									Cuisine
Battle	Netherfield Place	HR	£70	80	T	All			Dsrt	yes		yes	
Brightling	Jack Fuller's	R	£35	72		L						yes	
Brighton	Black Chapati	R	£45	30		L					N/W	yes	Indian
Brighton	Brighton Thistle Hotel	HR	£80	45	T	All				yes			French
Brighton	China Garden	R	£55	130		L	SL						Chinese
Brighton	Langan's Bistro	R	£70	42		L				yes			
Brighton	La Marinade	R	£60	36		L							
Brighton	Topps Hotel	HR	£50	24		D							
Eastbourne	Grand Hotel	HR	£70	50	T				Dsrt				
Hastings	Roser's	R *	£65	20							O/S N/W		
Herstmonceux	Sundial Restaurant	R	£90	40		L					O/S		
Hove	Quentin's	R	£50	20					Dsrt				
Jevington	Hungry Monk Restaurant	R	£60	46		All	SL						
Rye	Landgate Bistro	R	£60	40		All	SL		Dsrt		O/S N/W		
Uckfield	Horsted Place	HR	£95	36	T	All	SL		Dsrt			yes	

Location	Establishment	Cat	Star	Price	Private Seats	Private Rm	Crown	Open	Sun L	Sea Food	Room Price	Des	Good Cheese	O/S Wine	New World	Open Air	National Cooking
Wadhurst	Spindlewood	HR		£62	40	24		All		SL						yes	
Wych Cross	Ashdown Park Hotel	HR		£80	120	24	T	All	SL	SL				yes	O/S			

West Sussex

Location	Establishment	Cat	Star	Price	Private Seats	Private Rm	Crown	Open	Sun L	Sea Food	Room Price	Des	Good Cheese	O/S Wine	New World	Open Air	National Cooking
Amberley	Amberley Castle	HR		£110	36	32	T	All					Dsrt	yes				
Ashington	The Willows	R		£55	28			L					Dsrt					
Chichester	Comme Ca	R		£55	48			L	SL					yes			yes	French
Chichester	The Droveway	R		£60	40	8		L										
Chilgrove	White Horse Inn	R		£60	70	12								yes	O/S	N/W		
Climping	Bailiffscourt	HR		£80	80	40	T						Dsrt	yes				
Cuckfield	Murray's	R		£60	32	14								yes				
East Grinstead	Gravetye Manor	HR	★	£105	42	18	T	All	SL					yes	O/S	N/W		
Lower Beeding	Cisswood House	HR		£55	60	20							Dsrt					
Lower Beeding	South Lodge	HR		£100	40	30	T	All	SL					yes	O/S	N/W	yes	
Midhurst	Angel Hotel	IR		£60	50	80		All	SL		£65	Dsrt	yes	O/S		yes	
Pulborough	Stane Street Hollow	R		£60	32	24		All										
Storrington	Abingworth Hall	HR		£65	50	16	T	L						yes				
Storrington	Little Thakeham	HR		£90	30	24	T	L										
Storrington	Manleys	RR		£86	48	22	T	L	SL		£75	Dsrt			N/W		yes
Turners Hill	Old Forge	R		£55	24			L					yes				
Turners Hill	Alexander House	HR		£120	55	14	T	All							yes		

Tyne & Wear

Location	Establishment	Cat	Star	Price	Private Seats	Private Rm	Crown	Open	Sun L	Sea Food	Room Price	Des	Good Cheese	O/S Wine	New World	Open Air	National Cooking
East Boldon	Forsters	R		£65	28												
Newcastle-upon-Tyne	Blackgate Restaurant	R			43	12						Dsrt					British
Newcastle-upon-Tyne	Courtney's	R		£55	28	28							yes				

Town	Establishment		Price	Seats	Seats (2)	Cards	Cards	A/C	Dress	Smoke	N/W · O/S	Other	Cuisine
Newcastle-upon-Tyne	Fisherman's Lodge	R	£85	65	40			yes	Dsrt	yes		yes	
Newcastle-upon-Tyne	King Neptune	R	£45	120	65			yes	Dsrt	yes		yes	Chinese
Newcastle-upon-Tyne	21 Queen Street	R ★↑	£95	50					Dsrt	yes	N/W		
Seaton Burn	Horton Grange	RR	£80	30	8	M			£80 Dsrt	yes	N/W		

Warwickshire

Town	Establishment		Price	Seats	Seats (2)	Cards	Cards	A/C	Dress	Smoke	N/W · O/S	Other	Cuisine
Billesley	Billesley Manor	HR	£85	80	40		All	SL	Dsrt	yes	N/W	yes	
Hockley Heath	Nuthurst Grange	HR	£60	50	95		All			yes	N/W	yes	
Kenilworth	Restaurant Bosquet	R	£75	26									
Kenilworth	Simpson's Restaurant	R ★	£50	75	85								
Leamington Spa	Mallory Court	HR	£120	50	25	T	All	yes	Dsrt	yes	O/S N/W		
Leamington Spa	Regent Hotel	HR	£65	55	20			yes					
Stratford-upon-Avon	Liaison	R	£60	55		M	All	yes	Dsrt	yes			
Stratford-upon-Avon	The Opposition	R	£50	50								yes	

West Midlands

Town	Establishment		Price	Seats	Seats (2)	Cards	Cards	A/C	Dress	Smoke	N/W · O/S	Other	Cuisine
Birmingham	Adil Restaurant	R	£25	100	25		All						Indian
Birmingham	Chung Ying	R	£40	220			All						Chinese
Birmingham	Chung Ying Garden	R	£40	300	240		All						Chinese
Birmingham	Days of the Raj	R	£35	80	15		D						Indian
Birmingham	Henry's	R	£45	140	45								Chinese
Birmingham	Henry Wong	R	£45	140	40								Chinese
Birmingham	Hyatt Regency	HR	£80	80	200		All						
Birmingham	New Happy Gathering	R	£35	90	100		All						Chinese
Birmingham	Purple Rooms	R	£35	70	25		D						Indian
Birmingham	Rajdoot	R	£40	76			All				N/W		Indian
Birmingham	Royal Alfaisal	R	£25	120	50		D						Indian
Birmingham	Shimla Pinks	R	£50	140		M							Indian
Birmingham	Sloans	R	£60	66		T	All		Dsrt				
Birmingham	Swallow Hotel	HR	£96	55	20	T	All	SL		yes			

Location	Establishment	Cat	Star	Price	Seats	Private Rm	Crown	Open	Sun L	Sea Food	Room Price	Des	Good Cheese	O/S Wine	New World	Open Air	National Cooking
Birmingham	Swallow Hotel: Langtry's	R		£60	60								yes			yes	
Kinver	Berkley's Bistro	R		£55	35	40							yes			yes	
Stourbridge	Bon Appetit	R		£55	60	40						Dirt					
Sutton Coldfield	New Hall	HR		£95	60	15	T	All					yes	O/S	N/W	yes	

Wiltshire

Location	Establishment	Cat	Star	Price	Seats	Private Rm	Crown	Open	Sun L	Sea Food	Room Price	Des	Good Cheese	O/S Wine	New World	Open Air	National Cooking
Bradford-on-Avon	Woolley Grange	HR		£75	54	22		All	SL				yes				
Castle Combe	Manor House	HR		£95	75	30		All	SL				yes	O/S	N/W	yes	
Chiseldon	Chiseldon House	HR		£65	48	20		All					yes				
Colerne	Lucknam Park	HR		£90	85	28	T	All	SL				yes		N/W	yes	
Hinton	Hinton Grange	HR		£50	60	15		All	SL		£78		no			yes	
Lacock	At The Sign of The Angel	IR		£80	45	20		L	SL				yes				
Melksham	Toxique	R		£65	30	20		L					yes				
Purton	Pear Tree	HR		£65	50	50		All	SL				yes	O/S	N/W		British
Rowde	George & Dragon	R		£30	35								yes			yes	
Stanton St Quintin	Stanton Manor	HR		£50	30	30		All	SL								
Teffont Evias	Howard's House	HR		£75	34			All							N/W	yes	
Warminster	Bishopstrow House	HR		£80	65	22		All				Dsrt	yes	O/S	N/W	yes	

North Yorkshire

Location	Establishment	Cat	Star	Price	Seats	Private Rm	Crown	Open	Sun L	Sea Food	Room Price	Des	Good Cheese	O/S Wine	New World	Open Air	National Cooking
Bilbrough	Bilbrough Manor	HR		£65	70	20		All					yes			yes	
Harrogate	Café Fleur	R		£45	56			D								yes	French
Harrogate	Drum & Monkey	R		£45	50								yes				
Harrogate	Miller's, The Bistro	R	★	£60	40							Dsrt	yes				
Harrogate	Old Swan Hotel	HR		£70	30			All				Dsrt	yes			yes	
Harrogate	Tamin Level	R		£35	75	12											

Town	Restaurant	Class	Sym	£	Seats	Seats	Lic	SL	£2	Dsrt	yes	O/S	N/W	yes	Cuisine
Hetton	Angel Inn	R		£65	50	40	L			Dsrt					
Moulton	Black Bull	R		£55	100	36	L	SL		Dsrt				yes	
Reeth	Burgoyne Hotel	HR		£55	32	12	D	SL			yes				
Ripley	Boar's Head Hotel	HR		£70	38		All	SL				O/S	N/W		
Scarborough	Lanterna	R		£45	36										Italian
Staddlebridge	McCoy's	HR	★↑	£85	50	30				Dsrt	yes				
Stokesley	Chapters	HR		£40	36									yes	
Wath-in-Nidderdale	Sportsman's Arms	RR		£60	50	8	All				yes	O/S	N/W	yes	
York	Grange Hotel	HR		£60	65	70	All		£47		yes				
York	Melton's	R		£50	40	15	L			Dsrt	yes		N/W		
York	Middlethorpe Hall	HR		£100	60	50	All			Dsrt	yes		N/W		
York	19 Grape Lane	R		£75	34	22									

South Yorkshire

Town	Restaurant	Class	Sym	£	Seats	Seats	Lic	SL	£2	Dsrt	yes	O/S	N/W	yes	Cuisine
Barnsley	Armstrongs	R		£55	60	40				Dsrt	yes				
Barnsley	Restaurant Peano	R		£60	40						yes				
Chapeltown	Greenhead House	R		£75	34						yes				

West Yorkshire

Town	Restaurant	Class	Sym	£	Seats	Seats	Lic	SL	£2	Dsrt	yes	O/S	N/W	yes	Cuisine
Bradford	Nawaab	R		£30	120	30	All				yes				Indian
Bradford	Restaurant 19	RR	★	£70	36		T			Dsrt	yes				Indian
Guiseley	Prachee	R		£45	56		All				yes				
Haworth	Weavers	RR		£50	45		L		£70	Dsrt	yes		N/W		British
Ilkley	Box Tree	RR	★	£85	50	15	T		£68	Dsrt	yes				
Ilkley	Rombalds Hotel	HR		£65	32	24	All								
Leeds	Adriano Flying Pizza	R		£30	140		All							yes	Italian
Leeds	Bibi's Italian Restaurant	R		£50	160										
Leeds	Brasserie Forty Four	R	↑	£70	112	60	All								
Leeds	Darbar	R		£30	92								N/W	yes	Indian
Leeds	Dawat	R		£30	26										Indian

Location	Establishment	Cat	Star	Price	Private Seats	Rm	Crown	Open	Sun L	Sea Food	Room Price	Des	Good Cheese	O/S Wine	New World	Open Air	National Cooking
Leeds	Haley's Hotel	HR		£60	50	25		All									
Leeds	Leodis Brasserie	R		£80	169								yes				
Leeds	Maxi's Chinese Restaurant	R		£40	300			All									Chinese
Leeds	New Asia	R		£35	60			All									Chinese
Leeds	Olive Tree	R		£55	150	60		L									Greek
Leeds	Sang Sang	R		£50	90	16											Chinese
Leeds	Sous le Nez en Ville	R		£55	75	20									N/W		
Leeds	Thai Siam	R		£40	60			All									Thai
Linton	Wood Hall	HR		£85	60			All					yes			yes	
Wetherby	Sheba Tandoori Restaurant	R		£35	38	30		D									Indian

SCOTLAND

Please refer to the **How to Use This Guide** section (p18–19) at the front of the Guide for explanation of categories, pricing and star systems, crowns (Traditional or Modern), traditional Sunday Lunch, and Restaurants with Rooms (RR). See also wine and cheese awards feature (from p 41). * after a Room Price indicates that only half-board terms are offered.

Location	Establishment	Cat	Star	Price	Private Seats	Rm	Crown	Open	Sun L	Sea Food	Room Price	Des	Good Cheese	O/S Wine	New World	Open Air	National Cooking
Borders
Newtown St Boswells	Le Provencale	R		£40	40				All	SL							French
Peebles	Cringletie House	HR		£60	56	27											
Central
Aberfoyle	Braeval Old Mill	R	↑	£75	34			T	L	SL		Dsrt		O/S	N/W		
Dunblane	Cromlix House	HR		£90	32	40			All	SL			yes	O/S			French
Falkirk	Pierre's	R		£50	40												
Dumfries & Galloway
Auchencairn	Balcary Bay Hotel	HR		£60	50												
Auchencairn	Collin House	HR		£65				T									
Canonbie	Riverside Inn	IR		£55	24				D				yes			yes	
Newton Stewart	Kirroughtree Hotel	HR		£65	50	20		T	All	SL	£72	Dsrt	yes		N/W		
Portpatrick	Knockinaam Lodge	HR		£80	26			T	D								French

Location	Establishment	Cat	Star	Price	Private Seats	Rm	Crown	Open	Sun L	Sea Food	Room Price	Des	Good Cheese	O/S Wine	New World	Open Air	National Cooking
Fife																	
Anstruther	Cellar	R		£70	30									O/S	N/W		
Cupar	Ostlers Close	R		£60	26							Dsrt	yes				
Markinch	Balbirnie House	HR		£65	100	56		All	SL						N/W		
Peat Inn	The Peat Inn	RR	*↑	£85	48	24	T				£135		yes	O/S	N/W		
St Andrews	Grange Inn	R		£45	75	35											
Grampian																	
Aberdeen	Atlantis	R		£65	40			All	SL	yes							
Aberdeen	Courtyard on the Lane	R		£60	30				SL			Dsrt					
Aberdeen	Gerard's	R		£70	90	24											French
Aberdeen	The Marcliffe at Pitfodels	HR		£90	30	24	T										
Aberdeen	Silver Darling	R		£65	35					yes							
Ballater	Tullich Lodge	HR		£60	26		T	All	SL				yes				British
Banchory	Raemoir House	HR		£70	64	80		All	SL				yes				
Craigellachie	Craigellachie Hotel	HR		£70	40	25		All							N/W	yes	
Drybridge	Old Monastery Restaurant	R		£55	45												
Inverurie	Thainstone House Hotel	HR		£80	42	24	T	All	SL				yes				
Highland																	
Achiltibuie	Summer Isles	HR		£75	26			D					yes			yes	
Arisaig	Arisaig House	HR		£85	36			All					yes			yes	
Arisaig	Old Library Lodge & Restaurant	RR		£55	28			All			£59	Dsrt	yes			yes	
Colbost	Three Chimneys Restaurant	R		£60	30					yes		Dsrt	yes		N/W	yes	
Drumnadrochit	Polmaily House	HR		£45	40			D					yes				
Dulnain Bridge	Auchendean Lodge	HR		£55	20			D					yes				

Location	Restaurant	Class	Price	Seats	Pvt	Sym	Cards		Price 2	Dsrt	L	O/S N/W	D	Cuisine
Fort William	Crannog Seafood Restaurant	R	£50	70	20		All							
Fort William	The Factor's House	RR	£85	20		★	D		yes			O/S		
Fort William	Inverlochy Castle	HR	£100	40	14		All	T	£82	Dsrt	yes	N/W		
Garve	Inchbae Lodge	IR	£60	24			All							
Glenelg	Glenelg Inn	HR	£50	20			All				yes			
Inverness	Culloden House	HR	£80	50	35		All		£72	Dsrt	yes	O/S	yes	
Inverness	Dunain Park	HR	£65	36			D				yes		yes	
Kentallen of Appin	Ardsheal House	HR	£80	40			All				yes	N/W	yes	
Kingussie	The Cross	RR	£70	28			D	T	£150*		yes	N/W	yes	
Muir-of-Ord	Dower House	RR	£65	26			D	T	£90		yes	O/S N/W	yes	
Nairn	Clifton Hotel	HR	£60	40	12		All			Dsrt	yes	N/W		
Newtonmore	Ard-na-Coille Hotel	HR	£65	18	6		D				yes	O/S N/W		
Onich	Allt-Nan-Ros Hotel	HR	£55	45			All				yes	N/W		
Scarista	Scarista House	HR	£55	20	8		D				yes			
Sleat	Kinloch Lodge	HR	£75	30	12		D							
Spean Bridge	Old Station Restaurant	R	£35	30			All	T		Dsrt	yes	O/S N/W		
Ullapool	Altnaharrie Inn	HR	£120	18		***	D	T			yes			
Whitebridge	Knockie Lodge	HR	£70	22	12		D							

Lothian

Location	Restaurant	Class	Price	Seats	Pvt	Sym	Cards		Price 2	Dsrt	L	O/S N/W	D	Cuisine
Edinburgh	Alp-Horn	R	£45	66	28		All							Swiss
Edinburgh	The Atrium	R	£60	60		↑					yes			
Edinburgh	L'Auberge	R	£75	55		↑	All	M			yes	O/S		French
Edinburgh	The Balmoral, Bridges Brass	HR	£110	45			D	T		Dsrt				
Edinburgh	The Balmoral, Pompadour Room	R	£35	80			All	T			yes	N/W		
Edinburgh	Caledonian, Pompadour Room	R	£100	70			All	T						
Edinburgh	Caledonian, Carriages Rest	HR	£60	150			All	SL						
Edinburgh	Denzlers 121	R	£50	65			All				yes			Swiss
Edinburgh	Indian Cavalry Club	R	£45	80	40		All				yes			Indian
Edinburgh	Kalpna	R	£35	34										Indian
Edinburgh	Kelly's	R	£55	28	36									
Edinburgh	Martin's	R	£75	60	8						yes	O/S N/W		
Edinburgh	Ristorante Raffaelli	R	£45	60						Dsrt	yes			Italian

Location	Establishment	Cat	Star	Price	Private Seats	Rm	Crown	Open	Sun L	Sea Food	Room Price	Des	Good Cheese	O/S Wine	New World	Open Air	National Cooking
Edinburgh	Shamiana	R		£40	43			D									Indian
Edinburgh	Szechuan House	R		£30	150	25		D	SL								Chinese
Edinburgh	Ristorante Tinelli	R		£35	35												Italian
Edinburgh	Vintners Room	R		£55	60	36						Dsrt					
Gullane	Greywalls Hotel	HR		£80	50	20		All	SL						N/W		
Gullane	La Potinière	R	*	£75	30			L						O/S	N/W		
Kirknewton	Dalmahoy Golf&Country Club	HR		£70	120	120		All	SL						N/W		
Linlithgow	Champany Inn	R	*	£100	55	60	T					Dsrt	yes	O/S	N/W	yes	
Linlithgow	Champany Inn Chop & Ale House	R		£50	46			All					yes			yes	

Strathclyde

Location	Establishment	Cat	Star	Price	Private Seats	Rm	Crown	Open	Sun L	Sea Food	Room Price	Des	Good Cheese	O/S Wine	New World	Open Air	National Cooking
Alexandria	Cameron House	HR		£80	42		T	All	SL						N/W		
Ayr	Fouters Bistro	R		£40	38	36		D									
Ayr	The Stables	R		£30	52			L					yes			yes	
Bearsden	Fifty Five BC	R		£50	24			All					yes				
Cairndow	Loch Fyne Oyster Bar	R		£35	80			All		yes						yes	
Crinan	Crinan Hotel, Lock 16	HR	*	£95	20					yes			yes	O/S	N/W		
Crinan	Crinan Hotel, Westward Rest	R		£65	50			D					yes	O/S	N/W		
Cumbernauld	Westerwood Hotel	HR		£70	70	24	T	All	SL				yes		N/W		
Dunoon	Chatters	R		£50	30								yes			yes	
Eriska	Isle of Eriska	HR		£85	40		T	D				Dsrt	yes		N/W		
Fairlie	Fins Restaurant	R		£55	32			L		yes							
Glasgow	Amber	R		£40	70			All									Chinese
Glasgow	Ashoka West End	R		£30	60	36		D									Indian
Glasgow	Brasserie on West Regent Street	R		£45	100	55		D					yes				
Glasgow	Buttery	R		£75	50	8	T					Dsrt					
Glasgow	Café Gandolfi	R		£35	60			All									
Glasgow	D'Arcy's	R		£45	72			All									

Location	Restaurant	Cat	Price	Seats	No.	T	Cards	SL	Price2	Dsrt	—	yes	O/S N/W	yes	Cuisine
Glasgow	Glasgow Hilton, Camerons	HR	£95	60	12	T	D					yes	O/S N/W		
Glasgow	Loon Fung	R	£45	120	40		All								Chinese S E Asian
Glasgow	Mata Hari	R	£40	60	15										
Glasgow	One Devonshire Gardens	HR	£80	44	32	T	All	SL				yes	O/S N/W	yes	
Glasgow	La Parmigiana	R	£50	55											Italian
Glasgow	Puppet Theatre	R	£75	72	22		All	SL							
Glasgow	Ristorante Caprese	R	£35	60	25					Dsrt					Italian
Glasgow	Rogano	R	£75	55	16	T	D			yes		yes			
Glasgow	Two Fat Ladies	R	£55	30							yes				
Glasgow	Ubiquitous Chip	R	£75	140	30		All					yes	O/S N/W	yes	
Kilchrenan	Ardanaiseig	HR	£80	30		T	All	SL				yes			
Kilchrenan	Taychreggan Hotel	HR	£70	36			All					yes		yes	
Kilfinan	Kilfinan Hotel	IR	£70	22	24		All	SL	£72			yes		yes	
Kilmore	Glenfeochan House	HR	£60	10			D			Dsrt		yes			
Maybole	Ladyburn	HR	£60	25			D								
Oban	Knipoch Hotel	HR	£80	44	12	T	D					yes	O/S N/W		
Port Appin	Airds Hotel	HR	£80	36			All					yes	O/S N/W		
Tiroran	Tiroran House	HR	£70	20		T	D					yes	O/S		
Turnberry	Turnberry Hotel	HR	£90	180	110		All	SL				yes			

Tayside

Location	Restaurant	Cat	Price	Seats	No.	T	Cards	SL	Price2	Dsrt	—	yes	O/S N/W	yes	Cuisine
Aberfeldy	Farleyer House	HR	£75	24	30	T	D					yes			
Alyth	Drummacree House	RR	£55	30	12							yes			
Auchterarder	Auchterarder House	HR	£95	50	15	T	All	SL				yes	O/S N/W		
Auchterhouse	Old Mansion House	HR	£70	50	22	T	All	SL	£62				N/W		
Blairgowrie	Kinloch House	HR	£70	55	30	T	All					yes	O/S N/W		
Callander	Roman Camp Hotel	HR	£95	40	32		All							yes	
Dunkeld	Kinnaird	HR	£90	45			All			Dsrt		yes			
Glamis	Castleton House	HR	£50	28			All	SL							
Kinclaven by Stanley	Ballathie House	HR	£70	60	60		All	SL				yes			
Perth	Number Thirty Three	R	£55	42	60						yes		N/W		
Scone	Murrayshall House	HR	£60	60	30	T	All					yes			
St Fillans	Four Seasons Hotel	HR	£55	40	30		All	SL				yes		yes	

WALES

Please refer to the **How to Use This Guide** section (p18–19) at the front of the Guide for explanation of categories, pricing and star systems, crowns (Traditional or Modern), traditional Sunday Lunch, and Restaurants with Rooms (RR). See also wine and cheese awards feature (from p 41). ★ after a Room Price indicates that only half-board terms are offered.

Location	Establishment	Cat	Star Price	Private Seats	Rm	Crown	Open	Sun L	Sea Food	Room Price	Des	Good Cheese	O/S Wine	New World	Open Air	National Cooking
Clwyd																
Chirk	Starlings Castle	RR	£50	60	50		All			£55		yes				
Colwyn Bay	Café Nicoise	R	£45	32								yes				French
Llandrillo	Tyddyn Llan	HR	£60	70	44		All	SL				yes				
Northop	Soughton Hall	HR	£75	40	22	T	All					yes	O/S	N/W		
Dyfed																
Brechfa	Ty Mawr	RR	£50	35	24		D									
Penally	Penally Abbey	HR	£50	46	20		D			£68		yes				
Welsh Hook	Stone Hall	RR	£55	34	30		D			£63						
Mid Glamorgan																
Aberkenfig	New Garden	R	£35	160			D									Chinese
Coychurch	Coed-y-Mwstwr Hotel	HR	£75	50	24		All	SL				yes				

South Glamorgan

Location	Restaurant	Class	Price	Seats	Code		Other	Cuisine
Barry	Bunbury's	R	£50	32				
Cardiff	Armless Dragon	R	£50	45				
Cardiff	La Braserie	R	£40	50				
Cardiff	Champers	R	£40	75		D	yes	French
Cardiff	Le Monde	R	£40	70				British

West Glamorgan

Location	Restaurant	Class	Price	Seats	Rooms	Code	Dsrt	yes	O/S·N/W	yes	Cuisine
Gowerton	Cefn Goleu Park	HR	£60	48	20	T					
Mumbles	Norton House	HR	£65	36	16	L	SL				
Reynoldston	Fairyhill	HR	£55	70	16	D	Dsrt	yes		yes	
Swansea	Number One	R	£55	40		All	SL				

Gwent

Location	Restaurant	Class	Price	Seats	Seats2	Code	Dsrt/£	yes	O/S·N/W	yes	Cuisine
Abergavenny	Walnut Tree Inn	R	£77 *	46			Dsrt	yes	O/S N/W	yes	Italian
Chepstow	Leadon's Brasserie	R	£42	54							
Clydach	Drum & Monkey	R	£50	50	24	D All					
Trellech	Village Green	RR	£45	70	18	L	£45	yes		yes	
Whitebrook	Crown at Whitebrook	RR	£65	30	12	L	£80		N/W		

Gwynedd

Location	Restaurant	Class	Price	Seats	Code		Dsrt	yes	O/S·N/W	yes	Cuisine
Abersoch	Porth Tocyn Hotel	HR	£60	50	All			yes			
Capel Coch	Tre-Ysgawen Hall	HR	£75	64	T All	SL		yes	N/W	yes	
Llanberis	Y Bistro	R	£50	52	D			yes			
Llandudno	Bodysgallen Hall	HR	£85	80	T All	SL		yes	O/S N/W		British
Llandudno	St Tudno Hotel	HR	£65	55	All	SL		yes	O/S N/W		
Llansanffraid Glan Conwy	Old Rectory	HR	£70	16	T D		Dsrt	yes			

Location	Establishment	Cat	Star	Price	Private Seats Rm	Crown	Open	Sun L	Sea Food	Room Price	Des	Good Cheese	O/S Wine	New World	Open Air	National Cooking
Portmeirion	Hotel Portmeirion	HR		£65	100 35		All	SL					O/S	N/W		
Pwllheli	Plas Bodegroes	RR		£75	35 16	M	D					yes	O/S	N/W		
Talsarnau	Maes-y-Neuadd	HR		£70	50 12		All	SL		£140★	Dsrt	yes		N/W		British
Powys																
Eglwysfach	Ynyshir Hall	HR		£60	40 18		All					yes		N/W		
Lake Vyrnwy	Lake Vyrnwy Hotel	HR		£65	120 50							yes			yes	
Llangammarch Wells	Lake Country House Hotel	HR		£65	50		All	SL								
Llyswen	Llangoed Hall	HR		£105	46 22	T	All	SL				yes	O/S	N/W		

CHANNEL ISLANDS

Please refer to the **How to Use This Guide** section (p18–19) at the front of the Guide for explanation of categories, pricing and star systems, crowns (Traditional or Modern), traditional Sunday Lunch, and Restaurants with Rooms (RR). See also wine and cheese awards feature (from p 41). ★ after a Room Price indicates that only half-board terms are offered.

Location	Establishment	Cat	Star	Price	Private Seats	Rm	Crown	Open	Sun L	Sea Food	Room Price	Des	Good Cheese	O/S Wine	New World	Open Air	National Cooking
Alderney																	
Braye	First & Last	R		£30	75			All									
St Anne	Georgian House	R		£45	48	24		All	SL							yes	
St Anne	Inchalla Hotel	HR		£55	30			L	SL								
Guernsey																	
Castel	La Grande Mare Hotel	HR		£75	75	30		All	SL			Dsrt					
L'Eree	Taste of India	R		£35	35	20		All								yes	Indian
St Peter Port	Absolute End	R		£50	60					yes							
St Peter Port	Louisiana	R		£60	100			All	SL		yes						
St Peter Port	Le Nautique	R		£50	68	30								O/S	N/W		French
Herm																	
Herm	White House	HR		£40	118			All	SL								

Location	Establishment	Cat	Star	Price	Private Seats	Private Rm	Crown	Open	Sun L	Sea Food	Room Price	Des	Good Cheese	O/S Wine	World	New	Open Air	National Cooking
Jersey																		
Gorey	Jersey Pottery Garden Rest	R	↑	£60	300													
Rozel Bay	Chateau la Chaire	HR		£70	65			All									yes	
St Brelade	Hotel Chateau Valeuse	HR		£50	70			All					yes				yes	
St Brelade	Sea Crest	R		£70	60			All		yes							yes	Italian
St Helier	La Capannina	R		£60	130	18												
St Helier	De Vere Grand	HR		£75	250	21	T	L										
St Ouen	The Lobster Pot	RR		£65	90	45											yes	
St Saviour	Longueville Manor	HR		£90	65	65	T	All	SL		£70	Drt	yes				yes	
Sark																		
Sark	Aval Du Creux	HR		£55	40			All		yes							yes	
Sark	Dixcart Hotel	HR		£40	650			All	SL									
Sark	La Sablonnerie Hotel	HR		£55	40			All					yes				yes	
Sark	Stocks Hotel	HR		£50	60	8		All	SL								yes	
Isle of Man																		
Ballasalla	La Rosette	R		£75	45													
Ramsey	Harbour Bistro	R		£45	50			All					yes				yes	

NORTHERN IRELAND

Please refer to the **How to Use This Guide** section (p18–19) at the front of the Guide for explanation of categories, pricing and star systems, crowns (Traditional or Modern), traditional Sunday Lunch, and Restaurants with Rooms (RR). See also wine and cheese awards feature (from p 41). ★ after a Room Price indicates that only half-board terms are offered.

Location	Establishment	Cat	Star	Price	Private Seats	Rm	Crown	Open	Sun L	Sea Food	Room Price	Des	Good Cheese	O/S Wine	New World	Open Air	National Cooking
Co Antrim																	
Ballymena	Galgorm Manor	HR		£68	73	14	T	All	SL								
Belfast	Antica Roma	R		£65	160	70						Dsrt					Italian
Belfast	Bengal Brasserie	R		£35	46	50		D									Indian
Belfast	Manor House	R		£40	80	50		All									Chinese
Belfast	Roscoff	R	★	£75	70		M						yes	O/S			
Belfast	Speranza	R		£40	170												Italian
Belfast	Strand Restaurant	R		£35	80	25		All	SL								Italian
Belfast	Villa Italia	R		£45	110			D									Italian
Belfast	The Warehouse	R		£45	90	45											
Belfast	Welcome Restaurant	R		£40	80	30		D									Chinese
Carrickfergus	Wind-Rose Wine Bar	R		£0	85												
Portrush	Ramore	R	★	£55	80		M				yes	Dsrt	yes				
Co Down																	
Annalong	Glassdrumman Lodge	HR		£60	50	20		D									French
Helen's Bay	Deanes on the Square	R	←	£60	40			L					yes				
Holywood	Culloden Hotel	HR		£65	150	50		All	SL								
Holywood	Sullivans	R		£55	40							Dsrt					
Portaferry	Portaferry Hotel	HR		£65	80			All	SL	yes							

Co Londonderry

Location	Establishment	Cat	Star	Price	Private Seats	Rm	Crown	Open	Sun L	Sea Food	Room Price	Des	Good Cheese	O/S Wine	New World	Open Air	National Cooking
Garvagh	MacDuff's Rest, Blackheath Hse	RR	↑	£50	45	10		T	All			Dsrt	yes				
Londonderry	Beech Hill House Hotel	HR		£50	40	30			SL	yes	£60	Dsrt	yes				

REPUBLIC OF IRELAND

Please refer to the **How to Use This Guide** section (p18–19) at the front of the Guide for explanation of categories, pricing and star systems, crowns (Traditional or Modern), traditional Sunday Lunch, and Restaurants with Rooms (RR). See also wine and cheese awards feature (from p 41). ★ after a Room Price indicates that only half-board terms are offered.

Location	Establishment	Cat	Star	Price	Private Seats	Rm	Crown	Open	Sun L	Sea Food	Room Price	Des	Good Cheese	O/S Wine	New World	Open Air	National Cooking
Co Carlow																	
Leighlinbridge	Lord Bagenal Inn	R		£45	90	40		All	SL				yes	O/S			
Co Cavan																	
Blacklion	MacNean Bistro	R		£40	35			All	SL			Dsrt	yes				
Co Clare																	
Ballyvaughan	Gregans Castle	HR		£75	60	40							yes				
Bunratty	MacCloskey's	R		£70	60	22	T										
Newmarket-on-Fergus	Dromoland Castle	HR	↑	£115	90	60	T	All				Dsrt	yes	O/S			
Co Cork																	
Ahakista	Shiro	RR	★	£80	18	10		D			£36						Japanese
Ballydehob	Annie's Restaurant	R		£55	24												
Ballylickey	Larchwood House	RR		£60	20					yes	£36		yes				
Ballylickey	Seaview Hotel	HR		£55	45			All	SL	yes							

Location	Establishment	Cat	Star	Price	Seats	Private Rm	Crown	Open	Sun L	Sea Food	Room Price	Des	Good Cheese	O/S Wine	New World	Open Air	National Cooking
Baltimore	Chez Youen	R		£75	45	50		All		yes							
Carrigtwohill	Niblicks Restaurant	R		£38	100	70		L	SL							yes	
Castletownshend	Mary Ann's Bar & Restaurant	R	★	£50	50	14		L	SL							yes	
Cork	Arbutus Lodge	HR		£80	50	25	T					Dsrt		O/S	N/W		
Cork	Bully's	R		£25	40			All									
Cork	Clifford's	R	★	£70	45	50	M			yes		Dsrt	yes				
Cork	Crawford Gallery Café	R		£45	70	200							yes				
Cork	Flemings	RR		£55	50	36		All	SL		£55		yes			yes	
Cork	Isaacs	R		£35	90			D									
Cork	Ivory Tower Restaurant	R		£55	55												
Cork	Jacques	R		£55	36								yes				
Cork	Lovetts	R		£72	45	24	T			yes			yes		N/W		
Cork	Michael's Bistro	R		£45	27												
Cork	O'Keeffe's	R		£65	33								yes				
Dunworley	Dunworley Cottage	R		£60	50	20		All					yes				
Durrus	Blairs Cove House Restaurant	R		£60	59							Dsrt	yes				
Glandare	The Rectory	R		£65	80	40	T			yes		Dsrt	yes				
Goleen Harbour	Herons Cove Restaurant	RR		£35	30	24		All	SL	yes	£33	Dsrt	yes			yes	
Kanturk	Assolas Country House	HR	★	£65	25	20	T	D		yes		Dsrt	yes				
Kinsale	Blue Haven Hotel	HR	←	£60	45			D		yes			yes				
Kinsale	Chez Jean-Marc	R		£55	55	25				yes		Dsrt	yes				French
Kinsale	Man Friday	R		£55	80	35		D									
Kinsale	Max's Wine Bar	R		£40	40			All									
Mallow	Longueville House	HR	←	£65	45	20	T	All	SL				yes				
Midleton	Farm Gate	R		£50	60											yes	
Oysterhaven	The Oystercatcher	R		£65	30	20		D		yes			yes				
Shanagarry	Ballymaloe House	HR	★	£80	90	30		All	SL				yes				
Youghal	Aherne's Seafood Restaurant	RR		£60	60	20		All		yes	£100	Dsrt	yes			yes	

Co Donegal

County	Town	Restaurant		Price									Cuisine
Co Donegal	Bundoran	Le Chateaubrianne	R	£55	45	20	All	SL		yes			
	Dunkineely	Castle Murray House	HR	£55	45		All	yes		yes			
	Fahan	Restaurant St John's	R	£55	40	22	All	yes	Dsrt	yes			
	Greencastle	Kealy's Seafood Bar	R	£45	60	20	All	yes	Dsrt	yes			
	Rathmullan	Rathmullan House	HR	£60	60	20	All	yes	Dsrt	yes			
	Rossnowlagh	Smugglers Creek Inn	IR	£40	50	24	All	yes	£40	yes		yes	

Co Dublin

County	Town	Restaurant		Price									Cuisine
Co Dublin	Blackrock	Ayumi-Ya	R	£40	60	25				yes			Japanese
	Blackrock	Clarets	R	£70 ←	50								
	Dublin	Ayumi-Ya Japanese Steakhouse	R	£40	40								Japanese
	Dublin	Chapter One	R	£70	100	40	D	yes		yes		yes	Russian
	Dublin	Clarence Hotel	HR	£70	60		D	SL					
	Dublin	Commons Restaurant	R	£85	40	20	All	yes					
	Dublin	Cooke's Café	R	£65 ←→★	50	40	All			yes		yes	
	Dublin	Le Coq Hardi	R	£95	80	34				yes	O/S	yes	French
	Dublin	Dobbins Wine Bistro	R	£70	40	40		yes		yes			
	Dublin	L'Ecrivain	R	£70	60			yes		yes			French
	Dublin	Ernie's	R	£80	55				Dsrt	yes			
	Dublin	Les Frères Jacques	R	£80	60	40			Dsrt				French
	Dublin	Furama Chinese Restaurant	R	£75	90		All	yes	Dsrt				Chinese
	Dublin	George's Bistro & Piano Bar	R	£70	95	50							
	Dublin	Good World	R	£40	50	20	All	yes					Chinese
	Dublin	Grey Door	RR	£50	40	70			£99			yes	
	Dublin	Hibernian Hotel	HR	£55	55	25	All	SL		yes			French
	Dublin	Imperial Chinese Restaurant	R	£40	180	70	All						Chinese
	Dublin	Ivy Court	R	£55	80	70							
	Dublin	Kapriol	R	£65	30	26				yes		yes	Italian
	Dublin	Langkawi Malaysian Restaurant	R	£40	50					yes			S E Asian
	Dublin	Lobster Pot	R	£70	40	40		yes				yes	

Location	Establishment	Cat	Star	Price	Private Seats	Rm	Crown	Open	Sun L	Sea Food	Room Price	Des	Good Cheese	O/S Wine	New World	Open Air	National Cooking
Dublin	Locks	R		£85	47	30											French
Dublin	Le Mistral	R	★	£80	60	40						Dsrt					
Dublin	Oisins	R		£95	40					yes			yes				Russian
Dublin	Old Dublin Restaurant	R		£60	65	16		D					yes				
Dublin	101 Talbot	R		£32	90												
Dublin	Pasta Fresca	R		£30	85	25											Italian
Dublin	Patrick Guilbaud	R	★↑	£100	50	30	M			yes		Dsrt		O/S	N/W		French
Dublin	Pizzeria Italia	R		£25	18												Italian
Dublin	Il Primo	R		£45	44								yes				Italian
Dublin	Rajdoot	R		£48	92												Indian
Dublin	Roly's Bistro	R	↑	£50	120	65		All	SL				yes				
Dublin	Ryans of Parkgate Street	R		£55	32			All							N/W		
Dublin	Senor Sassi's	R		£58	65	30		D									
Dublin	Shalimar	R		£50	110	55		All									Indian
Dublin	La Stampa	R		£55	160	50							yes				
Dublin	Stephen's Hall Hotel	HR		£45	48								yes				
Dublin	Ta Se Mohogami Gaspipes	R		£45	40	40		All					yes			yes	
Dublin	The Westbury	HR	↑	£85	100			All	SL				yes				French
Dublin	Zen	R		£50	85	14	T			yes							Chinese
Dun Laoghaire	Restaurant Na Mara	R		£75	75	36				yes							
Howth	Adrian's	R		£50	46	15		All									
Howth	King Sitric	R		£70	70	22				yes			yes				French
Malahide	Bon Appetit	R		£80	55	20							yes	O/S			
Malahide	Eastern Tandoori	R		£40	64			D						O/S			Indian
Malahide	Roches Bistro	R		£55	35	36				yes			yes				French
Sandycove	Bistro Vino	R		£55	45												
Skerries	Red Bank Restaurant	R		£60	45	10		L		yes			yes				
Stillorgan	China-Sichuan Restaurant	R		£50	50			All									Chinese
Swords	Le Chateau	R		£55	60	20		All									French
Swords	Old Schoolhouse	R		£50	70	20						Dsrt	yes				

Co Galway

Aughrim	Aughrim Schoolhouse Restaurant	R	£45	50			L	SL			
Ballyconneely	Erriseask House	HR	£60	35	20		All			Dsrt	yes
Barna	Ty Ar Mor	R	£60	55	30		All			Dsrt	
Cashel	Cashel House	HR	£70	70	10		All				yes
Clifden	Ardagh Hotel	HR	£55	50		T	D		yes		
Clifden	Destry Rides Again	R	£40	32			All				
Clifden	O'Grady's Seafood Restaurant	RR	£50	50	12		All		yes		yes
Clifden	The Quay House	RR	£50	70	30						
Clifden	Rock Glen Manor	HR	£60	60	10				£36		
Galway	Casey's Westwood Restaurant	R	£60	120			All	SL	£50		yes
Galway	Malt House Restaurant	R	£50	55	16		D				
Leenane	Portfinn Lodge	RR	£55	36	40		D				
Letterfrack	Rosleague Manor	HR		60	10	T	All		£35		
Moycullen	Drimcong House Restaurant	R ←	£65	50	32	T	D			Dsrt	yes
Oughterard	Currarevagh House	HR	£50	28			All		yes		yes
Spiddal	Boluisce Seafood Bar	R	£45	60						Dsrt	
Tuam	Cre na Cille	R	£50	45	30						

Co Kerry

Ballyferriter	Tigh an Tobair: The Well House	R	£35	30							
Caherdaniel	Derrynane Hotel	HR	£45	100			All				yes
Caherdaniel	Loaves & Fishes	R	£55	32	12		All				yes
Cahirciveen	Brennan's Restaurant	R	£55	30			D	SL	yes	Dsrt	yes
Dingle	Beginish Restaurant	R	£55	52	18		All		yes	Dsrt	yes
Dingle	Doyle's Seafood Bar & T'house	RR	£50	50					yes		yes
Dingle	Half Door	R	£55	50	20		All		yes	Dsrt	yes
Dingle	Lord Baker's Bar & Restaurant	R	£60	85			All		yes		
Kenmare	d'Arcy's	RR	£70	40	25		D		£30		yes

Location	Establishment	Cat	Star	Price	Private Seats	Rm	Crown	Open	Sun L	Sea Food	Room Price	Des	Good Cheese	O/S Wine	New World	Open Air	National Cooking
Kenmare	The Horseshoe	R		£35	35	30		All	SL								
Kenmare	Packies	R		£45	35			All								yes	
Kenmare	Park Hotel Kenmare	HR	★	£90	80	30	T	All		yes		Dsrt	yes	O/S			
Kenmare	Sheen Falls Lodge	HR	★	£90	120	24	T	All		yes		Dsrt	yes	O/S			
Killarney	Aghadoe Heights Hotel	HR	←	£100	84	70	T	All	SL	yes					N/W	yes	
Killarney	Cahernane Hotel	HR		£65	90	14		D					yes	O/S	N/W	yes	
Killarney	Dingles Restaraunt	R		£45	45												
Killarney	Foley's Townhouse	RR		£80	95	25		All		yes	£70		yes	O/S	N/W		
Killarney	Gaby's Seafood Restaurant	R		£60	65					yes			yes	O/S	N/W		
Killarney	Strawberry Tree	R		£65	30	25							yes				
Killarney	West End House	R		£50	60	25											
Killorglin	Nick's Restaurant	R		£65	80	35		D		yes			yes	O/S	N/W		

Co Kildare

Location	Establishment	Cat	Star	Price	Private Seats	Rm	Crown	Open	Sun L	Sea Food	Room Price	Des	Good Cheese	O/S Wine	New World	Open Air	National Cooking
Athy	Tonlegee House	RR		£55	40					yes			yes				
Castledermot	Kilkea Castle	HR		£75	65	50	T	All	SL		£58	Dsrt	yes				
Maynooth	Moyglare Manor	HR		£75	80	35	T	All	SL					O/S			
Straffan	Barberstown Castle	HR		£65	55	44		All									
Straffan	Kildare Hotel	HR		£100	70		T	All									
Inistioge	The Motte	R		£60	24			D		yes		Dsrt	yes				
Kilkenny	Kilkenny Kitchen	R		£20	170	65		L					yes				
Kilkenny	Lacken House	RR		£60	35	20					£55		yes				
Thomastown	Mount Juliet Hotel	HR		£66	55	40	T	All					yes				

Co Laois

Location	Establishment	Cat	Star	Price	Private Seats	Rm	Crown	Open	Sun L	Sea Food	Room Price	Des	Good Cheese	O/S Wine	New World	Open Air	National Cooking
Mountrath	Roundwood House	HR		£60	26			All	SL			Dsrt					

Co Limerick

Adare	Adare Manor	HR	£85	↑	65	25	T	All	SL				yes	
Adare	Dunraven Arms	HR	£55		60	35		All	SL		Dsrt		yes	yes
Adare	Mustard Seed	R	£60	↑	50	30		L	SL	yes	Dsrt		yes	yes
Limerick	Castletroy Park Hotel	HR	£65		70								yes	yes
Limerick	Restaurant de La Fontaine	R	£60		40	45					Dsrt		yes	
Limerick	Quenelle's Restaurant	R	£55		35			L	SL					French

Co Longford

Moydow	The Vintage	R	£45					All	SL					yes

Co Louth

Ardee	The Gables	RR	£60		34			All	SL				yes	
Carlingford	Jordan's Bar & Restaurant	R	£55		34	16				£34			yes	

Co Mayo

Ballina	Mount Falcon Castle	HR	£50		28		T	D	SL		Dsrt		yes	
Cong	Ashford Castle, George V	HR	£110		135			All	SL	yes	Dsrt		yes	
Cong	Ashford Castle, Connaught Room	R	£100	★	40	40	T	D		yes	Dsrt		yes	
Newport	Newport House	HR	£70		39	35	T	D		yes	Dsrt		yes	O/S

Co Meath

Dunderry	Dunderry Lodge Restaurant	R	£75		40			L	SL		Dsrt			
Navan	Ardboyne Hotel	HR	£55		150	50		All	SL				yes	

Location	Establishment	Cat	Star	Price	Seats	Private Rm	Crown	Open	Sun L Food	Sea Food	Room Price	Des	Good Cheese	O/S Wine	New World	Open Air	National Cooking
Co Sligo																	
Boyle	Cromleach Lodge	HR	★	£75	50	20	T	D				Dsrt	yes				
Collooney	Glebe House	RR		£45				D		yes	£30		yes				
Riverstown	Coopershill House	HR		£50	14		T	D					yes				
Rosses Point	The Moorings	R		£45	90	45		All	SL	yes			yes				
Sligo	Truffles Restaurant	R		£25	38			D					yes				
Co Tiperary																	
Cashel	Chez Hans	R		£70	60					yes							
Co Waterford																	
Waterford	Dwyer's Restaurant	R		£55	30	10											
Waterford	Prendiville's Restaurant	RR		£60	50	20							yes				
Waterford	Waterford Castle	HR		£80	60	26	T	All			£46	Dsrt	yes				
Co Westmeath																	
Glasson	Glasson Village Restaurant	R		£50	55	12		L	SL	yes			yes				
Glasson	Wineport Restaurant	R		£40	45			All	SL			Dsrt					
Kinnegad	The Cottage	R		£25	30	26											
Mullingar	Crookedwood House	R		£55	35	25		L	SL				yes				

Co Wexford

Ballyhack	Neptune Restaurant	R	£50	45	30		All		yes				
Carne	Lobster Pot	R	£50	28	30		D		yes				
Ferrycarrig Bridge	Ferrycarrig Hotel	HR	£60	90			L	SL					
Foulksmills	Horetown House	R	£50	45	30		L	SL					
Gorey	Marlfield House	HR	£90	60	20	T	All	SL			yes		

Co Wicklow

Bray	Tree of Idleness	R	£65	50	50		D					O/S N/W	Greek
Dunlavin	Rathsallagh House	HR	£65	50	15		D				yes	O/S N/W	
Enniskerry	Curtlestown House	R	£50	45	25		L	SL			yes		
Enniskerry	Enniscree Lodge	HR	£60	40	10		All	SL			yes		
Greystones	The Hungry Monk	R	£55	40			All			£36 Dsrt	yes	O/S N/W	
Laragh	Mitchell's of Laragh	RR	£45	30	20		All	SL			yes		yes
Rathnew	Hunter's Hotel	HR	£55	54	20		All	SL		Dsrt			
Rathnew	Tinakilly House	HR	£75	50	40		All	SL					
Roundwood	Roundwood Inn	R	£60	45	32		L				yes	O/S	
Wicklow	Old Rectory	HR	£60	12			D						

Cellar of the Year Regional Winners

London
Downstairs at 190, SW7

A user-friendly, comfortable and sympathetically-priced list with something for everyone, although light in Beaujolais, in marked contrast to Alsace. Particularly well-chosen house selection, all available by the glass.

Home Counties
Hanbury Manor Thundridge

A predominantly under-aged list that is both comprehensive and carefully chosen. The list of ports is outstanding. Certain wines, ideally left a few more years, are highlighted as being drinkable by those who like their wines young. There are many more better suited to this practice that are not marked!

South of England
Röser's Hastings (St Leonards-on-Sea)

A catholic list with some serious, old vintages that need drinking, but prices encourage this. There are some real bargains among the classic clarets, an excellent range of Alsace wines and a super pudding selection.

West Country
Gidleigh Park Chagford

An eclectic list of quality throughout, with every area well represented, and offering an extensive range of vintages. The list has been assembled by a real enthusiast (Paul Henderson) with flair, and even includes a range of fine beers. Several reds are kept at cellar temperature (CT) and therefore need to be ordered well in advance of your meal, something the list doesn't tell you!

Midlands/Heart of England
See Cellar of the Year Winner page 51

East of England
Grey Gables Cawston

A list offering remarkable value with a surprising and enterprising width of choice. The helpful and informative notes even suggest you could bring your own bottle, subject to a modest corkage charge – though we cannot imagine that anyone would take up this offer, given what's available in the cellar.

North of England
Belfry Hotel Handforth

It is true that France hogs the list, but the rest of Europe and the New World are represented, though Bulgaria and Chile make only token appearances. The choice of some familiar wines perhaps reflects the restaurant's clientele, but for the most part the list has been carefully and knowledgeably compiled.

Scotland
Knipoch Hotel Oban

No tokenism here with areas such as Chile, Bulgaria, Hungary and even England having a good showing. An in-depth and well-priced list, which has not yet caught up with South Africa and is light in ports, but with an entry price of champagne at only £19.50 it is perhaps churlish to complain!

Wales
Bodysgallen Hall Llandudno

The wine list scores well with its house selection, cellarman's choice and pricing policy, but where's the merit in listing just New World wines by style, when the rest are presented in a more conventional and straightforward manner? Nevertheless, it's a super list, comprehensive without being biblical, with every wine carefully and well chosen.

Ireland
The Lord Bagenal Inn Leighlinbridge

The weighty wine list resembles a thesis with maps, notes on food, notes on wine, and notes on food *and* wine. It's highly personal, but then most of the best cellars are, with very knowledgeable tasting notes and comments by *le patron* James Kehoe. There's a fine balance between the new and the old, classics and lesser-known wines; a terrific and (equally important) a fairly-priced list.

Recommended by

EGON RONAY'S GUIDES

1995

YOUR GUARANTEE
OF
QUALITY AND INDEPENDENCE

- Establishment inspections are anonymous
- Inspections are undertaken by qualified Egon Ronay's Guides inspectors
- The Guides are completely independent in their editorial selection
- The Guides do not accept advertising, hospitality or payment from listed establishments

---

Hotels & Restaurants
Europe
Family Hotels & Restaurants
Oriental Restaurants
New Zealand & South Pacific

Pubs & Inns
Just a Bite
Paris
Ireland
Australia

Egon Ronay's Guides are available from all good bookshops or can be ordered from Leading Guides, 35 Tadema Road, London SW10 0PZ
Tel: 071-352 2485 / 352 0019   Fax: 071-376 5071

Photographic Round-up

Back by popular demand, a selection of photographs of the best hotels the length and breadth of the land.

London

The Berkeley SW1

Blakes Hotel SW7

Cannizaro House SW19

The Capital SW3

Churchill Inter-Continental Hotel W1

Claridge's W1

The Connaught W1

Hotel Conrad SW10

47 Park Street W1

Four Seasons Hotel W1

The Goring SW1

Grosvenor House W1

The Halcyon W11

The Halkin SW1

Hampshire Hotel WC2

Howard Hotel WC2

Hyatt Carlton Tower SW1

Hyde Park Hotel SW1

Hotel Inter-Continental London W1

The Lanesborough SW1

The Langham Hilton W1

May Fair Inter-Continental W1

Le Meridien W1

The Montcalm W1

The Park Lane Hotel W1

The Regent London NW1

The Ritz W1

The Savoy WC2

Sheraton Belgravia SW1

Sheraton Park Tower SW1

Whites Hotel W2

England

Amberley Amberley Castle

Aylesbury Hartwell House

Basingstoke Audleys Wood

Bath Bath Spa Hotel

Bath Priory Hotel

Bath Queensberry Hotel

Bath Royal Crescent Hotel

Bibury The Swan

Bilbrough Bilbrough Manor

Billesley Billesley Manor

Bournemouth Carlton Hotel

Bradford-on-Avon Woolley Grange

Brampton Farlam Hall

Bristol Swallow Royal Hotel

Broadway Lygon Arms

Castle Combe Manor House

Chaddesley Corbett Brockencote Hall

Chadlington The Manor

Chagford Gidleigh Park

Charingworth Charingworth Manor

Cheltenham The Greenway

Chester Chester Grosvenor

Chester Crabwall Manor

Colerne Lucknam Park

Dedham Maison Talbooth

East Grinstead Gravetye Manor

Eastbourne Grand Hotel

Freshford Homewood Park

Grasmere Michael's Nook

Great Milton Le Manoir aux Quat'Saisons

Grimston Congham Hall

Heathrow Radisson Edwardian Hotel

Hintlesham Hintlesham Hall

Hunstrete Hunstrete House

Leamington Spa Mallory Court

Linton Wood Hall

Longhorsley Linden Hall

Lower Beeding South Lodge

Lower Slaughter Lower Slaughter Manor

Maidenhead Fredrick's

Medmenham Danesfield House

Nantwich Rookery Hall

New Milton Chewton Glen

Nidd Nidd Hall

Oakham (Hambleton) Hambleton Hall

Oulton (Leeds) Oulton Hall Hotel

Puckrup Puckrup Hall

Rotherwick Tylney Hall

Sandiway Nunsmere Hall

Ston Easton Ston Easton Park

Storrington Little Thakeham

Stratford-upon-Avon Ettington Park

Sutton Coldfield New Hall

Taplow Cliveden

Taunton Castle Hotel

Tetbury Calcot Manor

Thornbury Thornbury Castle

Thundridge Hanbury Manor

Torquay Imperial Hotel

Turners Hill Alexander House

Uckfield Horsted Place

Ullswater Leeming House

Ullswater Sharrow Bay

Warminster Bishopstrow House

Whimple Woodhayes Hotel

Windsor Oakley Court

Wych Cross Ashdown Park Hotel

York Middlethorpe Hall

Scotland

Aberdeen The Marcliffe at Pitfodels

Alexandria Cameron House

Arisaig Arisaig House

Auchterarder Auchterarder House

Auchterarder Gleneagles Hotel

Dunblane Cromlix House

Dunkeld Kinnaird

Edinburgh The Balmoral

Edinburgh Caledonian Hotel

Fort William Inverlochy Castle

Glasgow One Devonshire Gardens

Gullane Greywalls Hotel

Inverurie Thainstone House Hotel

Kirknewton Dalmahoy Hotel, Golf & Country Club

Port Appin Airds Hotel

St Andrews St Andrews Old Course Hotel

Turnberry Turnberry Hotel

Wales

Capel Coch Tre-Ysgawen Hall

Llandudno Bodysgallen Hall

Llyswen Llangoed Hall

Northop Soughton Hall

Channel Islands

Castel La Grande Mare Hotel

St Saviour Longueville Manor

Republic of Ireland

Adare Adare Manor

Cashel Cashel House

Cong Ashford Castle

Dublin Davenport Hotel

Gorey Marlfield House

Kenmare Park Hotel Kenmare

Kenmare Sheen Falls Lodge

Maynooth Moyglare Manor

Newmarket-on-Fergus Dromoland Castle

Rathnew Tinakilly House

Straffan Kildare Hotel

Maps

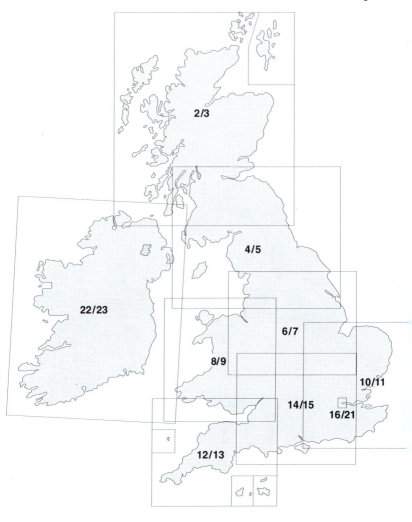

2/3

4/5

6/7

8/9

10/11

12/13

14/15

16/21

22/23

Motorways	● Restaurant
Primary Routes	☐ Hotel
Other Roads	⊡ Hotel and Restaurant
County Boundaries	

Designed and produced by
European Map Graphics Ltd. Finchampstead, Berks

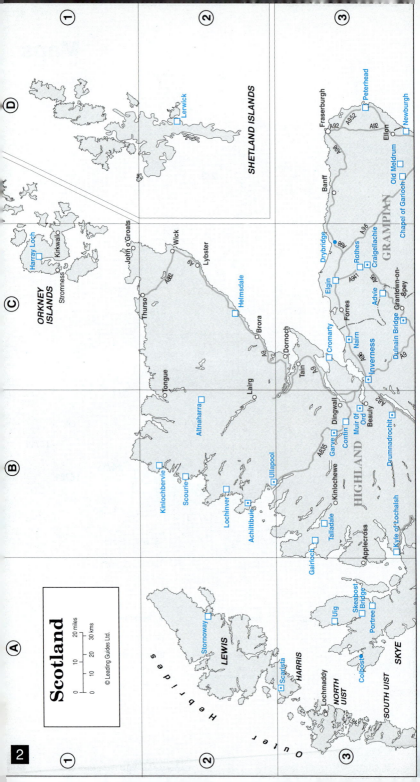

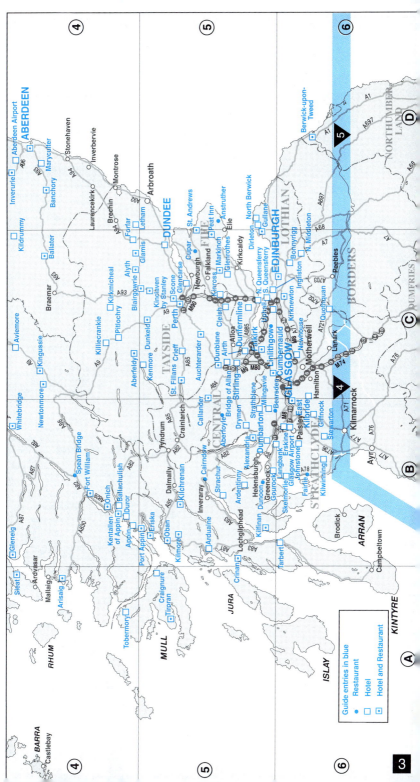

4

A

Helensburgh
Greenock

STRATHCLYDE

ARRAN

Ardrossan
Kilwinning
Irvine
Kilmarnock
Troon
Galston
Monkton
Prestwick
Ayr

Turnberry
Maybole

Girvan

Barrhill

Stranraer
Glenluce
Portpatrick
Wigtown

Port William

B

TAYSIDE

CENTRAL

GLASGOW
Falkirk

LOTHIAN

M8

M9

A811
A82

A726
A77
A71
M74

Lanark
Biggar

Abington

A74(M)
Cumnock
A76

Sanquhar
A75

New
Galloway
Dumfries
Castle
Douglas
Dalbeattie
Rockcliffe
Gatehouse
of Fleet
Auchencairn

Newton
Stewart

C

FIFE

EDINBURGH

M90
M9

Peebles
Galashiels
Tweedsmuir

A702
A703
A7
A68

3

Melrose
Dryburgh
Selkirk
Newtown
St. Boswells
Ettrickbridge

BORDERS

Hawick

Beattock
Moffat

Thornhill

DUMFRIES AND GALLOWAY

Eskdalemuir

Lockerbie
Langholm

Annan
A74 (M)
Gretna Green
Canonbie

Brampton
Crosby-on-Eden
Faugh
Wetheral

Carlisle

Silloth-
on-Solway
A596

3

Maryport
Cockermouth

Workington

Gosforth

Bassenthwaite
Lake
Bassenthwaite
Applethwaite
Braithwaite
Keswick
Buttermere
Borrowdale

Metmerby
Penrith

Ullswater

CUMBRIA

A6
M6

Langdale
Grasmere
Ambleside
Hawkshead
Coniston
Windermere
Troutbeck
Crook
Bowness-on-Windermere
Grizedale
Spark Bridge
Newby
Bridge
Ulverston
Grange-over-Sands
Barrow-in-Furness
Dalton-in
-Furness
Morecombe
Kendal
Witherslack
Cartmel
Crooklands
Cowan
Bridge
Kirkby
Lonsdale

6

4

ISLE OF MAN

Ramsey

Peel

Ballasalla
Douglas

LANCASHIRE

BLACKPOOL
M55
Preston
M6

Southport

Wigan

MERSEYSIDE

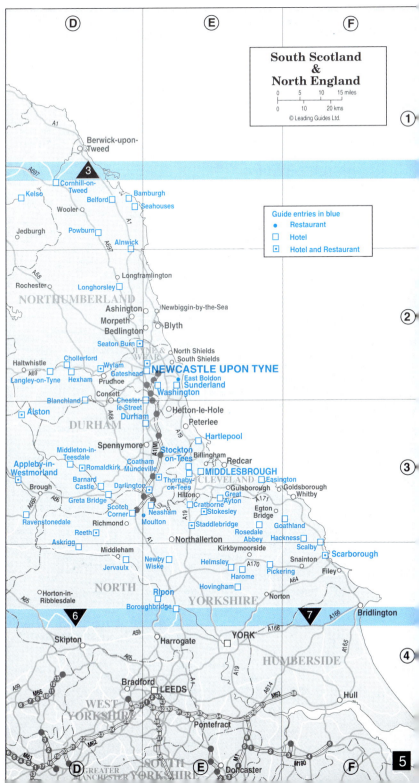

North & Heart of England

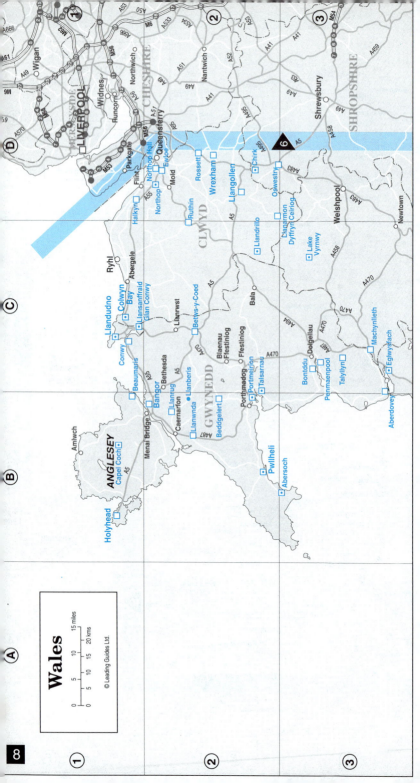

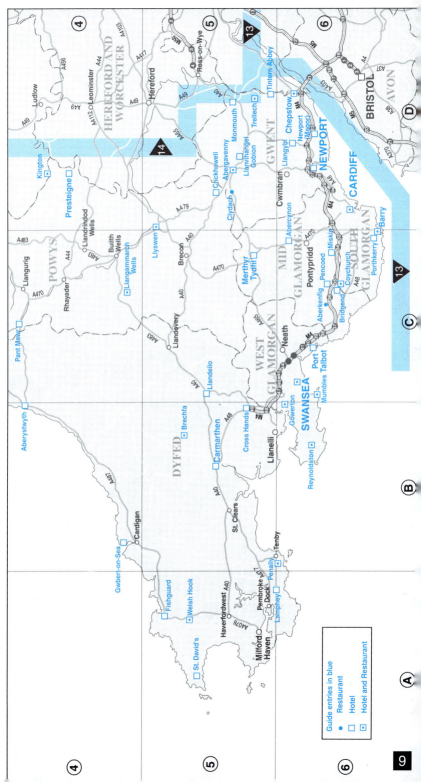

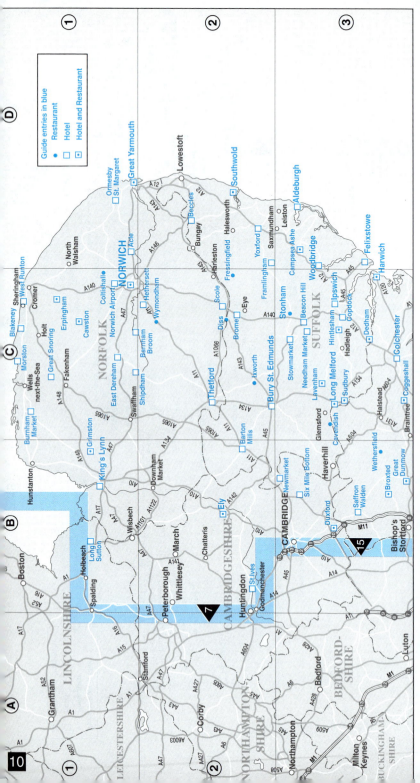

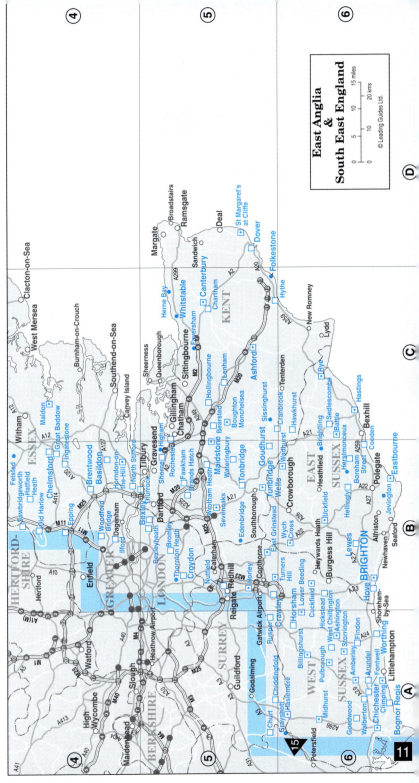

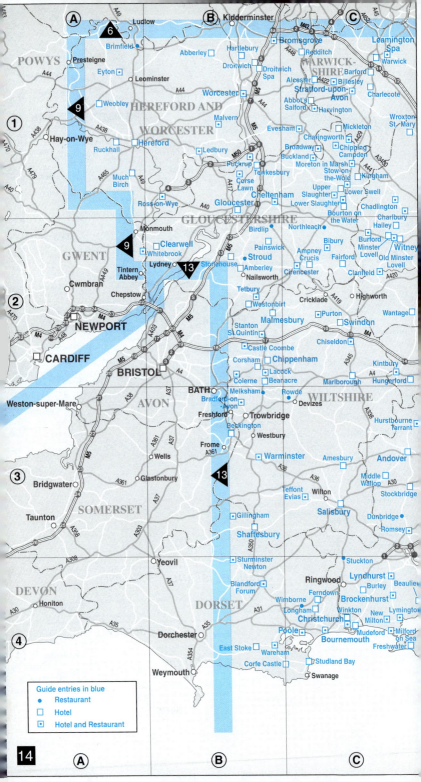

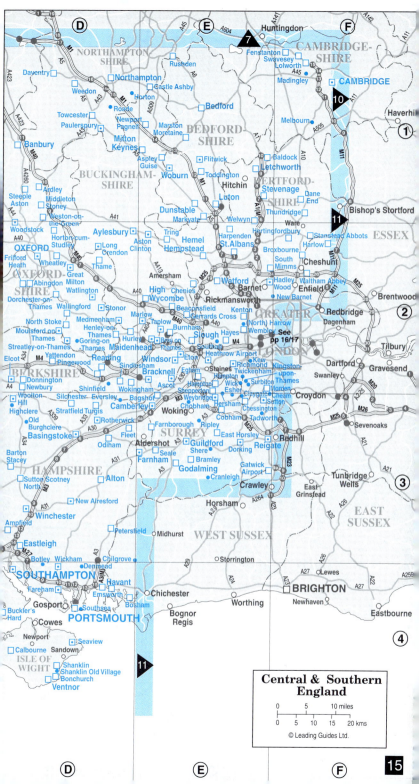

Central & Southern England

0   5   10 miles

0 5 10 15   20 kms

© Leading Guides Ltd.

15

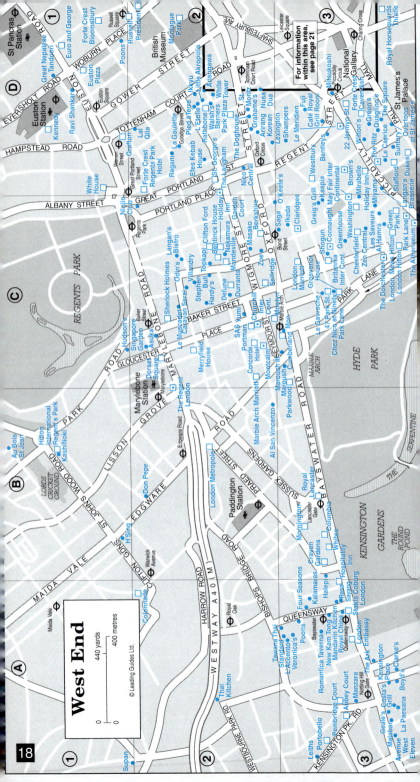

City of London

© Leading Guides Ltd.

0	220	440 yards
0	200	400 metres

Guide entries in blue
• Restaurant
□ Hotel
▣ Hotel and Restaurant

20

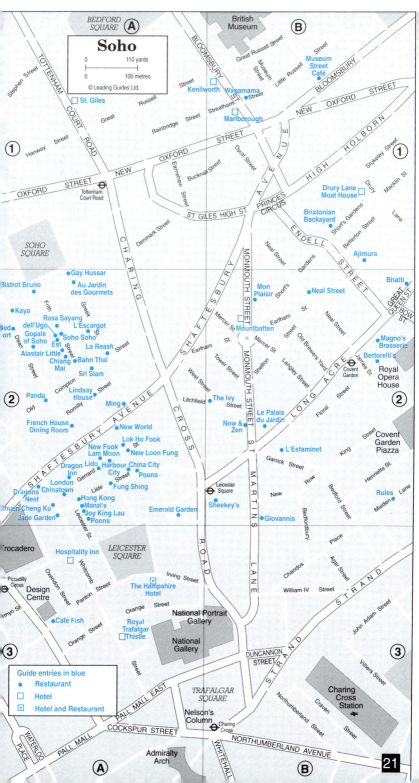

Soho

© Leading Guides Ltd.

0 — 110 yards
0 — 100 metres

Map labels:

BEDFORD SQUARE — A
British Museum — B

Great Russell Street
Museum Street Café
Kenilworth · Wagamama
Marlborough
Bainbridge Street
New Oxford Street
HIGH HOLBORN
Stukeley Street
Macklin Street
Drury Lane Moat House
Drury Lane
Brixtonian Backayard
Short's Gardens
Betterton Street
Ajimura
Endell Street

Stephen Street
TOTTENHAM COURT ROAD
St. Giles
Russell Street
Great Russell Street
Hanway Street
OXFORD STREET
NEW OXFORD STREET
Tottenham Court Road
St Giles High St.
Princes Circus

SOHO SQUARE
Denmark Street
Charing Cross Road

Gay Hussar
Bistrot Bruno
Au Jardin des Gourmets
Kaya
Rasa Sayang
dell'Ugo
Gopals of Soho
L'Escargot
Soho Soho
Est
La Reash
Alastair Little
Chiang Mai
Bahn Thai
Sri Siam
Panda
Lindsay House
Ming
French House Dining Room
New World
Lok Ho Fook
New Fook
Lam Moon
New Loon Fung
Dragon Inn
Lido
Harbour China City
London Chinatown
Poons
Fung Shing
Dragons Nest
Hong Kong
Chuen Cheng Ku
Manzi's
Joy King Lau
Jade Garden
Poons
Emerald Garden

Mon Plaisir
Neal Street
Mountbatten
Bhatti
GREAT QUEEN ST.
BOW ST.
Magno's Brasserie
Bertorelli's
Royal Opera House
Covent Garden Piazza
James St.
Covent Garden
The Ivy
Le Palais du Jardin
Now & Zen
L'Estaminet
Rules
Maiden Lane
Henrietta St.
Giovannis
Sheekey's
Leicester Square

SHAFTESBURY AVENUE
MONMOUTH STREET
MERCER ST.
LONG ACRE
CHARING CROSS ROAD
ST MARTINS LANE

Trocadero
Hospitality Inn
LEICESTER SQUARE
Piccadilly Circus
Design Centre
Café Fish
Royal Trafalgar Thistle
The Hampshire Hotel
National Portrait Gallery
National Gallery
Irving Street
Orange Street

STRAND
John Adam Street
Villiers Street
Charing Cross Station
Chandos
Agar Street
William IV Street
DUNCANNON STREET

TRAFALGAR SQUARE
Nelson's Column
Charing Cross
Admiralty Arch
COCKSPUR STREET
PALL MALL EAST
PALL MALL
WATERLOO PLACE
NORTHUMBERLAND AVENUE
WHITEHALL

Guide entries in blue

● Restaurant
□ Hotel
⊡ Hotel and Restaurant

21

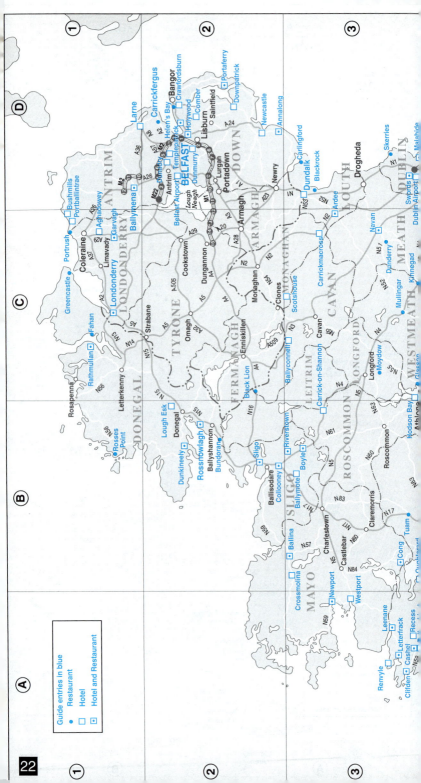

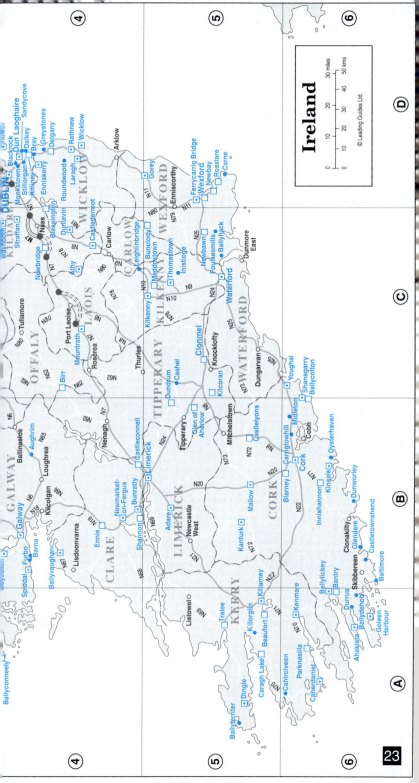

Index

READERS' NOMINATIONS

Cellnet Best of British Hospitality Awards 1996
in association with Egon Ronay's Guides

The Cellnet Best of British Hospitality Awards reward the very best that British tourism and leisure have to offer. They are judged by the Egon Ronay's Guides' team, Cellnet and industry experts. Now, for the first time, we are pleased to invite contributions and suggestions from you, our readers.

There are five categories of award:

Best Heritage Attraction

Best Leisure Attraction

Special Visitor Attraction For Innovation

Welcome to Overseas Visitors Award (given for high-quality facilities and provisions for overseas visitors)

Tourism Ambassador Award (given to an individual who has made a special contribution to British tourism)

If you would like to make a nomination for the Cellnet Best of British Hospitality Awards 1996, please use the form overleaf.

Please post to: **Egon Ronay's Guides, 35 Tadema Road, London SW10 0PZ**

Your Name

_____

Address

_____

_____

_____

_____

Telephone

_____

1366

Category	Name & address of suggested winner, plus reason for choice *(please give dates of visits, as appropriate)*

READERS' NOMINATIONS

Cellnet Best of British Hospitality Awards 1996
in association with Egon Ronay's Guides

The Cellnet Best of British Hospitality Awards reward the very best that British tourism and leisure have to offer. They are judged by the Egon Ronay's Guides' team, Cellnet and industry experts. Now, for the first time, we are pleased to invite contributions and suggestions from you, our readers.

There are five categories of award:

Best Heritage Attraction

Best Leisure Attraction

Special Visitor Attraction For Innovation

Welcome to Overseas Visitors Award (given for high-quality facilities and provisions for overseas visitors)

Tourism Ambassador Award (given to an individual who has made a special contribution to British tourism)

If you would like to make a nomination for the Cellnet Best of British Hospitality Awards 1996, please use the form overleaf.

Please post to: **Egon Ronay's Guides, 35 Tadema Road, London SW10 0PZ**

Your Name

_____

Address

_____

_____

_____

_____

Telephone

_____

1368

Category	Name & address of suggested winner, plus reason for choice *(please give dates of visits, as appropriate)*

READERS' COMMENTS

Please use this sheet, and the continuation overleaf, to recommend hotels or restaurants of **really outstanding quality** and to comment on existing entries.

Complaints about any of the Guide's entries will be treated seriously and passed on to our inspectorate, but we would like to remind you always to take up your complaint with the management at the time.

We regret that owing to the volume of readers' communications received each year, we will be unable to acknowledge all these forms, but they will certainly be seriously considered.

Please post to: **Egon Ronay's Guides, 35 Tadema Road, London SW10 0PZ**

Please use an up-to-date Guide. We publish annually. (H&R 1995)

Name and address of establishment	Your recommendation or complaint

Readers' Comments continued

Name and address of establishment	Your recommendation or complaint

Your Name (BLOCK LETTERS PLEASE)

Address

Telephone

READERS' COMMENTS

Please use this sheet, and the continuation overleaf, to recommend hotels or restaurants of **really outstanding quality** and to comment on existing entries.

Complaints about any of the Guide's entries will be treated seriously and passed on to our inspectorate, but we would like to remind you always to take up your complaint with the management at the time.

We regret that owing to the volume of readers' communications received each year, we will be unable to acknowledge all these forms, but they will certainly be seriously considered.

Please post to: **Egon Ronay's Guides, 35 Tadema Road, London SW10 0PZ**

Please use an up-to-date Guide. We publish annually. (H&R 1995)

Name and address of establishment	Your recommendation or complaint

1372

Readers' Comments continued

Name and address of establishment

Your recommendation or complaint

Your Name (BLOCK LETTERS PLEASE)

Address

Telephone

Special Purchase Offer: Reserve Your 1996 Guide Now!

Order a copy of *Egon Ronay's Heineken Guide 1995 Pubs & Inns*, published in November 1994 (£12.99 inc free p&p) and receive a **complimentary** copy of *Egon Ronay's Cellnet Guide 1996 Hotels & Restaurants* (worth £14.99 inc free p&p) when it is published in October 1995.

To take advantage of this special purchase offer please fill in the form below and return with payment of £12.99 per offer to:

Egon Ronay's Guides, Special Purchase Offer, 35 Tadema Road, London SW10 0PZ

▶ Please find enclosed cheque to the value of £......... made payable to **Leading Guides Ltd** or
▶ Please charge to my Access Mastercard / Visa / American Express account (delete as appropriate) the sum of £.........

Card Number: .... Expiry Date: ..../........

Name ....

Address ....

....

....

Post Code .... Daytime Tel No: ....

Delivery address (if different): ....

....

....

....

Offer Valid until 30th June 1995. Maximum order: two per household.

Orders will be despatched within 28 days of receipt or, if received in advance of publication, within 28 days of publication.

Recommended by

EGON RONAY'S GUIDES

1995

Hotels & Restaurants

Europe

Family Hotels & Restaurants

Oriental Restaurants

New Zealand & South Pacific

Pubs & Inns

Just a Bite

Paris

Ireland

Australia

Egon Ronay's Guides are available from all good bookshops or can be
ordered from Leading Guides, 35 Tadema Road, London SW10 0PZ
Tel: 071-352 2485 / 352 0019   Fax: 071-376 5071

Advertisers' Index

Acknowledgements

Egon Ronay's Guides would like to thank all those people who kindly supplied photographs for use in this book.

Thanks also to Peter Long for compiling the Gourmet Crossword, and to Mario Wyn-Jones for leading the Special Investigation: Cars Across the Channel.

STOP PRESS STOP PRESS STOP PRESS

Bob Payton

The sudden and tragic death of this larger-than-life character cannot pass without comment. His vibrant contribution to our catering industry is immense, not only through his fun and value-for-money restaurants, but also by his skilful marketing techniques in the promotion of his outlets, and, it must be said, but not unkindly, self-promotion. His proudest legacy is probably *Stapleford Park* (see page 730), an American's interpretation of a quintessential British country house.

Winchester   Hotel du Vin & Bistro
Tel 0962 841414   Fax 0962 842458
14 Southgate St Winchester Hampshire SO23 9EF

A Grade II listed Georgian town house, run by Robin Hutson (ex-Managing Director of *Chewton Glen*) and Gerard Basset (previously *sommelier extraordinaire* at the same hotel) was due to open as we went to press. The hotel will have a strong wine theme with rooms (£75 for a double with breakfast) sponsored by wine companies, and a 3-course dinner, including house wine, around £50 for two.

*   *   *

You can now catch Kevin Kennedy's cooking (previously at *Boulestin*) in less formal mode at **Bistro Bistrot, 140 Gloucester Road, SW7. Tel 071-373 5044.**

*   *   *

Robert Gutteridge (previously at *Belgo*) is currently cooking up a storm at the newly-opened **Alfred, 245 Shaftesbury Ave, London WC2. Tel 071-240 2566.**

*   *   *

Shaun Hill (ex *Gidleigh Park*, Chagford and our 1993 Chef of the Year) will shortly be opening at **The Merchant House, Corve Street, Ludlow, Shropshire SY8 1DU. Tel 0584 875438.** Shaun will be cooking in a similar style as before "without the fancy bits". A 20/25 cover restaurant charging around £30 a head.

*   *   *

Murdo MacSween (previously at *Oakley Court*, Windsor for many years) is now chef/director at **Boulter's Lock, Boulter's Island, Maidenhead, Berkshire SL6 8PE. Tel 0628 21291 Fax 0628 26048.**

*   *   *

Recently opened are Ken McCulloch's *Malmaison* hotels and informal brasseries in Edinburgh (25 rooms) and Glasgow (21 rooms). Standard rooms £70, suites £105 (+ Scottish breakfast @ £6 per person). Addresses: **1 Tower Place, Leith, Edinburgh EH6 7BD. Tel 031-555 6868 Fax 031-555 6999/278 West George Street, Glasgow G2 4LL. Tel 041-221 6400 Fax 041-221 6411.**

*   *   *

Shaw's, London SW7 (page 258) is now closed for Saturday lunch *but* open for Sunday lunch.

*   *   *

The Peasant, London EC1 (page 232) is not open for Sunday lunch."

*   *   *

Chef Stephen Morey has left Gravetye Manor, East Grinstead, for Woolley Grange, Bradford-on-Avon.

*   *   *

Price rises at **Forte Posthouse** hotels: between £2.50 and £6 per night.

*   *   *

Don't forget to try the Gourmet Crossword on page 95 – great prizes to be won!

Important Telephone Number Changes

The following UK area codes are changing from April 16th 1995. Each city will get a new area code and an additional digit in front of the existing six-digit local telephone number.

Leeds	0532 becomes 0113 2
Sheffield	0742 becomes 0114 2
Nottingham	0602 becomes 0115 9
Leicester	0533 becomes 0116 2
Bristol	0272 becomes 0117 9

In addition, all phone numbers commencing with 0 will now start 01.